1990

INTERNATIONAL TELEVISION & VIDEO ALMANAC

35th Edition

Editor: JANE KLAIN

British Editor: WILLIAM PAY

Canadian Editor: PATRICIA THOMPSON

Quigley Publishing Company, Inc.

159 West 53rd Street, New York, N.Y. 10019

•

(212) 247-3100

Foreword

In 1990 as the television and video industries continue to undergo vast changes, Quigley Publishing Company celebrates its 75th anniversary of publication under one continuous ownership and management. Completely revised and thoroughly updated annually, the International Television and Video Almanac, since 1955, and its companion volume, the International Motion Picture Almanac, since 1929, have served as indispensable reference tools to the industry, providing the hard data necessary to keep abreast of this constant flux and growth.

This 35th edition of the International Television and Video Almanac features expanded coverage throughout, including the addition of 200 new biographies of emergent filmmakers, actors, exhibitors and video and television executives to the nearly 5000 career profiles in the Who's Who. Also included is a 75th Anniversary history of Quigley Publishing Company.

I wish to thank the following friends and colleagues for generously sharing their expert knowledge: Alvin Marill, David Bartholomew, Roger Christiansen, Jim Tamulis, Larry Cohn, Ernest Cunningham, Mary Ann Grasso, Lloyd Ibert, Alan Barbour, Michael Schau, and most of all Stephen Klain. Thanks also to Robert McDonald, former Almanac editor Richard Gertner, Michelle Mart, George Groneman and Dick Rizzo for their invaluable assistance.

—JANE KLAIN

35th Edition
INTERNATIONAL
TELEVISION
& VIDEO
ALMANAC
For 1990
ISSN: 0539-0761
ISBN: 0-900610-43-3

PRINTED IN THE UNITED STATES OF AMERICA

Table of Contents

A Paramount Communications Company

ALPHABETICAL INDEX OF SUBJECTS

A

B

C

D

E

F

G

H

I

J

K

L

M

N

O

P

Q

R

S

T

U

V

W

X

Z

75TH anniversary

QP

EXHIBITORS HERALD

MOTOGRAPHY MOTION PICTURES

MOVING PICTURE WORLD

EXHIBITORS HERALD AND MOVING PICTURE WORLD

MERGERS MAKE GREATNESS

METRO-GOLDWYN-MAYER

MOTION PICTURE HERALD

Keeping the Faith

MOTION PICTURE DAILY

In 1915 a young drama editor of a Chicago newspaper covered the opening of D. W. Griffith's "The Birth of a Nation." Prior to that time Martin Quigley, along with most native-born Americans, considered motion pictures simply nickelodeon entertainment for the immigrant masses and not worthy of serious attention.

Griffith's epic, the first feature-length film Quigley had seen, changed all that. The young newspaperman dedicated the rest of his life to entertainment trade journalism and reference book publishing.

That same year Martin Quigley became editor of Exhibitors Herald, a weekly. Expansion was rapid with Quigley's company acquiring other early trade publications and merging them into the Herald. As a result the

FIRST MOTION PICTURE ALMANAC—1929

weekly's name was changed in 1928 to the Herald World and then in 1930 to Motion Picture Herald. In that same year Motion Picture Daily was established as the company moved its headquarters from Chicago to New York, becoming one of the first tenants of the new Radio City Music Hall building in Rockefeller Center.

MARTIN QUIGLEY

A major life-long interest of Martin Quigley was fulfilled in his creation in 1929 of the Motion Picture Almanac which he envisioned as an annual focusing on the WHO and WHAT of the entertainment world. His vision became a reality and Motion Picture Almanac has appeared every year since, making it the longest continually published reference book in the entertainment field. It has been extensively revised before each publication.

In 1956 the companion volume Television Almanac was established. In 1987 it was expanded to include the Home Video industry and the title was changed to Television & Video Almanac.

Martin Quigley was in frequent contact with all the pioneers of the film industry. When those who had created the industry and guided it for so many years decided to create a Foundation of the Motion Picture Pioneers, Martin Quigley was a prime mover. During World War II he was a member of the industry's War Activities Executive Committee which coordinated many aspects of the involvement of personnel and companies in the war effort.

As editor-in-chief and publisher Martin Quigley wrote articles from time to time, each of which attracted wide attention both within and outside the industry. He was in daily person-to-person contact with leading producers, major distribution executives and exhibitor leaders in his constant concern for the good reputation of the motion picture industry. At all times he was a champion of decent screen entertainment. He was the originator of the Motion Picture Production Code and the voluntary Motion Picture Production Code Administration. Often he was the liaison between film companies and the Catholic National Legion of Decency.

For a half century Motion Picture Herald was the major international publication of the American film trade. Subscribers were in more than 100 countries. Motion Picture Daily, for an equal period of time, was a prime organ of distribution and exhibition news on an up-to-the-minute basis. The Herald's Managers Round Table Department was sponsor for 40 years of the Quigley Showmanship Awards, the major recognition given theatre managers and independent exhibitors. The Herald's Merchandising Conferences for years promoted better understanding between distributors and leading theatre circuits as well as more effective film advertising and promotion. These Merchandising Conferences were directed by Martin Quigley, Jr.

For many years Quigley Publication's annual FAME was of great importance to the Hollywood community and the press as well as everywhere the status of screen, radio and television personalities was a major interest. Quigley established the annual poll of exhibitors to determine the Top Ten Money Making Stars. This highly regarded poll continues each year, now sponsored by the Motion Picture Almanac.

Economic conditions in the motion picture field in 1970-1972—when the major companies lost more money than in the decade of the Great Depression of the 1930s—forced a drastic curtailment of trade publications. In 1973 Quigley Publishing Company, Inc. suspended its periodicals and put its resources to work expanding and strengthening the Almanacs. In the years since both Almanacs have achieved international reputations as the authoritative source books on the Motion Picture, Television—and since 1987—the Home Video industries.

In the past decade and a half production of the Almanacs has gone through three different computer systems. The current editorial contents are substantially in excess of 20,000,000 characters with a third or more of them revised annually. Each edition builds on the past, all the way back to the periodicals founded 75 years ago. The 1990 editions of the Almanacs owe a great deal to the thousands of editions of Motion Picture Daily, Motion Picture Herald and other early Quigley Publications.

No over-view of the Company and the development of the Almanacs would be complete without credit being given to the earlier editors. The basic Almanac format and policy owe much to Terry Ramsaye, author of "A Million and One Nights," the classic history of the silent screen, and long-time editor of Motion Picture Herald. The subsequent editor, Charles S. Aaronson, carried on the Ramsaye tradition, until 1970. Beginning in 1970 and carrying on through 1987 Richard Gertner vastly improved and expanded the editorial contents. Under him the Almanac covers were changed to their present color coordinated combinations. The present editor, Jane Klain, took over in 1988; with Dick Gertner continuing as a consultant.

By the nature of the publishing industry many more men and women work on various stages of manufacture than on the editorial side. Hence many who played key roles in getting the Company's publications to our readers over these 75 years are unknown to us by name. Yet each of them, living or dead, well deserves a "Thank you" on this 75th Birthday.

MARTIN QUIGLEY, JR.

The Company may well be unique in the entertainment field in that it has had a father and son management over the entire span of three quarters of a century. The Company was founded a few years before the present head was born. Martin Quigley, Jr. joined as a cub reporter at the time his father had been president for 25 years. The younger Quigley served in various capacities: all editorial prior to his leave for four years of World War II; then editorial and management until his father's death in the 50th year with the Company he had founded. Since then Martin Quigley, Jr. has been president for the firm's third quarter of a century.

Looking only to developments in the entertainment field, the period from 1915 to 1990 has seen the following: the shift from shorts to feature length films; the move from silent to sound; black and white to full color; the birth and growth of radio; stereophonic sound and wide screen; magnetic recordings; records of a variety of types; black and white and then color television; satellite transmissions; video tapes; and, lasers. Surely more innovations are on the way!

Films, television and video are united in being different delivery systems bringing living images to the public in theatres and in homes. As in the beginning of screen entertainment, as in 1915, as now, the fundamental to success in any medium is subject matter deemed by the public worth seeing.

As the Company and its Almanacs look ahead to the decade of the 1990s and the 21st Century, all of us are challenged to serve a world wide readership by providing the best possible reference works for the motion picture, television and home video industries.

Martin Quigley, Jr.

The Year in Review

In the 1988–89 television season the share of the primetime audience dominated for so many years by the three major networks—ABC, CBS and NBC—fell three percentage points from the previous season to 61 percent—an all-time low since the A.C. Nielsen Company has been measuring the seasonal results from the early days of the industry.

In contrast the major cable channels—i.e., those covered under the basic monthly cable fee—rose from 20 to 24 percent in audience share control. Cable penetration, Nielsen said, increased seven percentage points over the previous year to 55.6 percent of households with television—a new all-time high. In other words, cable TV is now in more than 50 million of the estimated 90.4 million television households in the U.S.

An all-time low and an all-time high. Thus the battle is joined. What will the commercial networks do to combat the erosion caused by cable (though not exclusively—independent stations and videocassettes are other factors)? And what will the cable industry do to consolidate and increase its gains?

Primarily the network counter-attack strategy is four-pronged. One program calls for intensified efforts to increase advertising sales. A second calls for new and "innovative" promotional techniques to ensnare the viewing public. A third will be more vigorous attempts to share in the enormous profits to be had from syndication of successful network shows in the independent (as well as network affiliate) station market. The fourth scheme calls for better programming to win back former viewers as well as potential new ones.

The first of these strategies has already met with success. By the end of June, 1989, the three major networks had sold almost 90 percent of their primetime commercial time for the 1989–90 season. Commitments from advertisers—led by a revived interest from automobile manufacturers who increased their TV spending up to 85 percent over 1988–89—were close to $4 billion, up some $700 million from the previous season. Even the newcomer Fox Broadcasting Company tripled its advance sales to $300 million from $100 million the year before. All this means, of course, that the networks will earn more money in 1990 than had earlier been predicted by even the most optimistic industry analysts.

In the promotional department all three networks devised some new (for them) campaigns to spread the word to the public about their wares for 1989–90. Each arranged a tie-in—ranging from posters and buttons to contests and games with big money prizes—with a well-known retail giant. CBS joined with K-Mart; NBC with Sears; and ABC with Pizza Hut, along with a large-scale campaign in 5,000 theatres in the summer of 1989. Some critics thought these efforts to be acts of desperation that would not work too well and would hardly be worth the exorbitant costs. Time will tell whether they will be repeated in 1990.

As for the third strategy—the drive to cash in on the riches to be had from syndication—it is a complex one. Currently an FCC regulation bars the networks from sharing in the profits which go to the companies producing the TV shows (mostly subsidiaries of the major Hollywood studios) that go into syndication after network runs. (Sometimes, as with the current CBS program, "Murder, She Wrote", long-running shows are syndicated through old episodes while the show is still visible in new ones on network primetime.)

Efforts to get Washington to change the regulation favoring the production companies having been unsuccessful, the networks have adopted a new tactic. They are producing more and more of their own programs.

Of nine new series announced by CBS for 1989–90 two were produced by its own CBS

Entertainment. NBC's in-house production unit supplied two of five new series. Only ABC lagged in this area, although it planned to fill one primetime hour with an entry from its own news division.

Quotas set by the FCC for in-house production by the networks have limited them to five hours a week in primetime. This rule expires, however, in November, 1990, and is not expected to be extended—unless the studios can bring sufficient pressure to bear on Congress. Potentially, then, each network could produce all its primetime programming—thus shutting out the Hollywood studios entirely.

Concerning the fourth network campaign—better programming—that may well be the most difficult task of all. When the shows scheduled for the 1989–90 season were announced in the late spring of 1989, sighs of skepticism went up from many critics. Sitcoms based on families and their relationships again dominated all else.

NBC, in particular, stuck to the mixture as before. Still, well they might since that network finished first in 1988–89 (in the Nielsen rating report) for the fourth straight season. NBC's edge over second-place ABC was the second biggest lead in TV history. (In the 1955–56 season CBS's lead over NBC was slightly larger.) CBS, which had never finished third before the 1987–88 season, suffered the same fate for 1988–89.

In the final tally NBC averaged a 16 rating and a 26 share. (A rating point represents 1 percent of the nation's 90.4 million TV households; the share is the percentage tuned in of sets in use.) ABC averaged a 12.9 rating and 21 share and CBS a 12.6 rating and a 21 share.

NBC's five-year-old "The Cosby Show" finished first in the ratings for the 1988–89 season for the fourth year in a row, making it only the third series ever to hold first place for that long (the others were "Gunsmoke" and "All in the Family"). Finishing a close second was "Roseanne" (ABC), the highest-rated new show of the season. Others in the Top Ten were, in order: "A Different World" (NBC); "Cheers" (NBC); "The Golden Girls" (NBC); "60 Minutes" (CBS); "Who's the Boss?" (ABC); "Murder, She Wrote" (CBS); "Empty Nest" (NBC); and "Anything But Love" (ABC). For "60 Minutes" it was the 12th straight year it finished in the Top Ten. Highest-rated made-for-TV movie was "The Karen Carpenter Story" (CBS).

Two mini-series attracted widespread attention. CBS's eight-hour "Lonesome Dove" was the highest-rated of the season and, in fact, scored the biggest mini-series ratings triumph in five TV seasons. In contrast ABC's much-touted 29 and ½ hours-long "War and Remembrance" was a ratings disappointment to the network. Unlike CBS, which was estimated to have made over $30 million in advertising from "Lonesome Dove," NBC expected eventually to lose up to $40 million on "War and Remembrance." This would make the latter the biggest loss ever recorded by a network on a TV entertainment program. (ABC lost $65 million on the Winter Olympics in 1988.)

The fiasco of "War and Remembrance" stirred speculation that none of the networks would want to make many mini-series in the future, but that later proved not to be the case. Several were scheduled for the new 1989–90 season (including two to run six hours each).

Also noteworthy regarding 1988–89 programming was the resurgence in popularity of the theatrical movie. The highest rated feature film for the season was Paramount's "Beverly Hills Cop" (shown on ABC) which had already been seen on the network once before. The success of this and other theatrical films is credited to better scheduling and improved promotion by the networks.

While cable is viewed as the "enemy" by the Big Three, that is not the case with the new "fourth" network, Fox, which views cable instead as an "ally." This is because 80 percent of Fox's 126 stations are on the UHF dial instead of VHF. UHF's weaker signals are no problem for cable, which delivers all stations with equal force.

When it debuted in 1986, the Fox network was generally viewed as a dubious candidate for survival. In 1988–89, however, it made considerable strides in turning out shows that proved popular with the audience most coveted by advertisers: 18 to 49 year olds. For the 1989–90 season Fox expanded to a third night of primetime (Mondays) and expects to show a profit for the first time in this season.

Meanwhile, what's ahead for cable? In 1988–89 it continued to pose a stronger and stronger threat to the dominance of the Big Three. Advertising revenues again rose sharply and its other major source of income—subscriber fees—were likewise on the increase. (For recent statistics on other aspects of cable, see the section devoted to it in this book.)

Since so few areas in the U.S. remain unwired for cable, the industry's future plans call for signing up the households that have not yet subscribed. (Net growth of cable is now 10,000 homes a day and 300,000 a month.)

For all the rosy aspects of the cable picture, however, there are still some clouds on the horizon. Congressional critics have raised questions about its monopolistic tendencies and its ownership structure (many cable operators also own program supply firms), in addition to its now unregulated subscription rates and its bad reputation for consumer service.

Adding fuel to this adverse criticism in 1989 was the celebrated merger of Time, Inc. with Warner Communications. The former controls American Television and Communications, the nation's second-largest cable company, as well as HBO and Cinemax, two major cable movie channels. Warner, of course, is also a leading operator of cable TV systems and has a large television production operation.

From the videocassette industry there was good news and bad. The good: Rental revenues for 1989 were expected to increase by 10 percent to $5.6 billion, thus making total revenues for the year over $8.8 billion. The bad: sales of VCRs were expected to decline to about 10 million, which would be a decrease from the 11.2 million sold in 1988 and the 17.6 million of 1986. (For other statistics on the video industry, see that section in this book.)

The battle for the viewing audience continues apace, and so it will in the years to come.

Statistics

Television and Station Operations

GROWTH OF COMMERCIAL TELEVISION STATIONS

	1960	1965	1970	1975	1980	1985	1989
Total	515	569	677	706	734	883	1064
VHF	440	481	501	514	516	520	545
UHF	75	88	176	192	218	363	519

VIEWING HABITS

TELEVISION USAGE

Number of TV homes	90,400,000
Number of color TV homes	87,330,000
Homes with two or more sets	56,590,000
Home with VCR	58,400,000
Cable households	47,770,000
Pay cable households	26,100,000

	1950	1970	1988
Avg. Hours per Home, per Day	4 hrs. 35 min.	5 hrs. 56 min.	7 hrs. 3 min.

COLOR TELEVISION

	1960	1975	1989
Homes	340,000	48,500,000	87,330,000
Per Cent of TV Homes	0.7	70.8	96.6

Source: A. C. Nielsen

TELEVISION USAGE

A BREAKDOWN OF TELEVISION VIEWERS

Average TV Usage Per TV Household Per Day (Hours:Minutes)

Total U.S.	6:35
By Territory	
Northeast	6:08
East Central	6:52
West Central	6:30
South	6:59
Pacific	6:13
By Cable Status	
Any Cable	7:09
Pay Cable	7:55
Basic Cable	6:17
No Cable	5:50
By Household Size	
1 person	4:56
2 persons	6:03
3+ persons	7:48
4+ persons	8:20
By Household Income	
$30,000+	6:25
$40,000+	6:26
$50,000+	6:13
$60,000+	6:08
Other	
$40,000+ Income with children	7:19
$40,000+ Income and Head of House is Professional, Owner or Manager	5:38
$40,000+ Income and Head of House has 1+ Years of College	5:49

Source: Nielsen Television Index, "National Audience Demographics," August 1989. Copyright 1989, Nielsen Media Research.

TV EXPENDITURES

TOTAL ADVERTISING VOLUME (millions of dollars)

	1987	1988	% Change	% of Total
TELEVISION	$22,941	$24,490	+ 6.8	20.7
Newspapers	29,412	31,197	+ 6.1	26.4
Magazines	5,607	6,072	+ 8.3	5.1
Radio	7,206	7,798	+ 8.2	6.6
Cable	963	1,196	+24.2	1.0
Business Papers	2,458	2,610	+ 6.2	2.2
All Others	41,063	44,687	+ 8.8	38.0
Total Major Media	$109,650	$118,050	+ 7.7	100.0

Source: McCann-Erickson 5/89

NATIONAL ADVERTISING INVESTMENTS IN MAJOR MEDIA (millions of dollars)

	1987	1988	% Change	% of Total
TELEVISION	$16,108	$17,220	+ 6.9	53.4
Network	8,500	9,172	+ 7.9	28.4
Spot	6,846	7,147	+ 4.4	22.2
Nat'l Syndication	762	901	+18.2	2.8
Newspapers	3,494	3,586	+ 2.6	11.1
Magazines	5,607	6,072	+ 8.3	18.8
Radio (Network & Spot)	1,743	1,843	+ 5.7	5.7
Cable	760	940	+23.9	2.9
Business Papers	2,458	2,610	+ 6.2	8.1
Total Major Media	$30,170	$32,273	+ 7.0	100.0

Source: McCann-Erickson 5/89

LOCAL ADVERTISING INVESTMENTS IN MAJOR MEDIA (millions of dollars)

	1987	1988	% Change	% of Total
TELEVISION	$ 6,833	$ 7,270	+ 6.4	17.8
Newspapers	25,918	27,611	+ 6.5	67.6
Retail	15,227	15,840	+ 4.0	38.8
Classified	10,691	11,771	+10.1	28.8
Radio	5,463	5,955	+ 9.0	14.6
Total Major Media	$38,214	$40,836	+ 6.9	100.0

Source: McCann-Erickson 5/89

LEADING LOCAL TV CATEGORIES

add (000)

	1985	1986	1987	1988
1. Restaurants & Drive-Ins	$671,970.5	$744,800.0	$800,400.0	$804,000.0
2. Auto and Truck Dealers*	311,211.7	339,000.0	371,400.0	379,800.0
3. Food Stores & Supermarkets	259,028.5	302,900.0	346,300.0	339,000.0
4. Furniture Stores	186,999.9	194,600.0	218,700.0	237,900.0
5. Banks, Savings & Loans	195,283.9	209,800.0	202,200.0	191,400.0
6. Movies			177,000.0	186,000.0
7. Radio Stations & Cable TV	134,482.4	147,000.0	152,500.0	160,400.0
8. Department Stores	186,191.9	176,900.0	168,500.0	150,300.0
9. Appliance Stores	121,883.1	141,600.0	143,800.0	138,900.0

Source: BAR *Dealer Associations Not Included

LENGTH OF COMMERCIALS

Commercial Length	Non-Network 1985	1986	1987	1988
10 seconds	5.5%	4.9%	5.3%	.8%
15 seconds	1.3	3.5	2.6	5.2
20 seconds	0.1	0.1	0.1	0.1
30 seconds	88.0	86.3	86.7	84.2
45 seconds	0.6	0.4	0.2	0.2
60 seconds	2.7	2.9	2.9	3.5
90 sec. or more	1.8	1.9	2.1	2.0
	100%	100%	100%	100%

Commercial Length	Network 1985	1986	1987	1988
10 seconds	1.3%	0.5%	0.2%	0.22%
15 seconds	10.1	20.9	30.9	36.6
20 seconds	0.8	1.2	1.0	1.0
30 seconds	83.5	73.6	65.1	59.5
45 seconds	1.7	1.4	0.9	0.8
60 seconds	2.2	1.8	1.5	1.5
90 sec. or more	0.4	0.6	0.4	0.4
	100%	100%	100%	100%

Source: BAR

TELEVISION SET SALES (to dealers)

	Total	Color	Monochrome
1975	11,453,000	6,486,000	4,967,000
1980	17,239,000	10,954,000	6,285,000
1981	16,820,000	11,279,000	5,541,000
1982	17,248,000	11,483,000	5,765,000
1983	19,827,000	14,130,000	5,697,000
1984	21,187,000	16,278,000	4,909,000
1985	20,750,000	16,996,000	3,754,000
1986	22,163,000	18,204,000	3,959,000
1987	22,900,000	19,330,000	3,570,000
1988	22,796,000	20,216,000	2,580,000
1989 (est.)	23,200,000	20,700,000	2,500,000

Source: EIA, Domestic & Imports

	Total Sales to Dealers in Units (Thousands)	Total Factory Sales in in Dollars (Millions)	Average Value (Dollars per Unit)
COLOR TV RECEIVERS* (Excludes LCD and Projection Television)			
1986	18,204	6,026	331
1987	19,330	6,282	325
1988	20,216	6,570	325
1989 (est.)	20,400	6,630	325
1990 (est.)	20,900	6,813	326

**Includes monitors for consumer use.*

COLOR TV RECEIVERS WITH MTS (BUILT-IN STEREO CAPABILITY) (Included in Color TV Receivers Table)			
1986	3,116	1,680	540
1987	4,349	2,218	510
1988	5,090	2,545	500
1989 (est.)	6,000	3,000	500
1990 (est.)	6,900	3,415	495

LCD COLOR TELEVISION (Excluded from Color TV Receivers Table)			
1986 (est.)	70	14	200
1987 (est.)	100	21	210
1988 (est.)	150	30	200
1989 (est.)	200	40	200
1990 (est.)	250	50	200

MONOCHROME TV RECEIVERS* (Excludes LCD Television)			
1986	3,959	333	84
1987	3,570	296	83
1988	2,580	196	76
1989 (est.)	2,200	165	75
1990 (est.)	1,900	135	72

**Includes monitors (green, amber) for consumer use.*

PROJECTION TV (Excluded from TV Receivers Table).			
1986	304	529	1,740
1987	293	527	1,799
1988	302	529	1,750
1989 (est.)	305	534	1,750
1990 (est.)	315	550	1,750

CABLE TV OPERATING SYSTEMS AND SUBSCRIBERS

	1960	1965	1970	1975	1980	1985	1989
Operating Systems	640	1,325	2,490	3,366	4,048	6,600	9,010*
Subscribers (millions)	0.7	1.3	4.5	9.8	15.5	37.3	50.90
% of TV Homes	1.4%	2.4%	7.6%	14.3%	20.5%	43.7%	56.4%

Source: Television Digest & National Cable Television Association
*as of April, 1989

NIELSON TELEVISION INDEX TOP 75 PROGRAMS

Rank	Program	Telecast Date	Network	Duration (Minutes)	Average Audience (%)	Share	Average Audience (000)
1	M*A*S*H Special	Feb. 28, 1983	CBS	150	60.2	77	50,150
2	Dallas	Nov. 21, 1980	CBS	60	53.3	76	41,470
3	Roots Pt. VIII	Jan. 30, 1977	ABC	115	51.1	71	36,380
4	Super Bowl XVI Game	Jan. 24, 1982	CBS	213	49.1	73	40,020
5	Super Bowl XVII Game	Jan. 30, 1983	NBC	204	48.6	69	40,480
5	Super Bowl XX Game	Jan. 26, 1986	NBC	231	48.3	70	41,490
7	Gone With The Wind—Pt. 1 (Big Event—Pt. 1)	Nov. 7, 1976	NBC	179	47.7	65	33,960
8	Gone With The Wind—Pt. 2 (NBC Mon. Mov.)	Nov. 8, 1976	NBC	119	47.4	64	33,750
9	Super Bowl XII Game	Jan. 15, 1978	CBS	218	47.2	67	34,410
10	Super Bowl XIII Game	Jan. 21, 1979	NBC	230	47.1	74	35,090
11	Bob Hope Christmas Show	Jan. 15, 1970	NBC	90	46.6	64	27,260
12	Super Bowl XVIII Game	Jan. 22, 1984	CBS	218	46.4	71	38,800
12	Super Bowl XIX Game	Jan. 20, 1985	ABC	218	46.4	63	39,390
14	Super Bowl XIV Game	Jan. 20, 1980	CBS	178	46.3	67	35,330
15	ABC Theater (The Day After)	Nov. 20, 1983	ABC	144	46.0	62	38,550
16	Roots Pt. VI	Jan. 28, 1977	ABC	120	45.9	66	32,680
16	The Fugitive	Aug. 29, 1967	ABC	60	45.9	72	25,700
18	Super Bowl XXI	Jan. 25, 1987	CBS	206	45.8	66	40,030
19	Roots Pt. V	Jan. 27, 1977	ABC	60	45.7	71	32,540
20	Ed Sullivan	Feb. 9, 1964	CBS	60	45.3	60	23,240
21	Bob Hope Christmas Show	Jan. 14, 1971	NBC	90	45.0	61	27,050
22	Roots Pt. III	Jan. 25, 1977	ABC	60	44.8	68	31,900
23	Super Bowl XI	Jan. 9, 1977	NBC	204	44.4	73	31,610
23	Super Bowl XV	Jan. 25, 1981	NBC	220	44.4	63	34,540
25	Super Bowl VI	Jan. 16, 1972	CBS	170	44.2	74	27,450
26	Roots Pt. II	Jan. 24, 1977	ABC	120	44.1	62	31,400
27	Beverly Hillbillies	Jan. 8, 1964	CBS	30	44.0	65	22,570
28	Roots Pt. IV	Jan. 26, 1977	ABC	60	43.8	66	31,190
28	Ed Sullivan	Feb. 16, 1964	CBS	60	43.8	60	22,445
30	Super Bowl XXIII	Jan. 22, 1989	NBC	213	43.5	68	39,320
31	Academy Awards	Apr. 7, 1970	ABC	145	43.4	78	25,390
32	Thorn Birds Pt. III	Mar. 29, 1983	ABC	120	43.2	62	35,990
33	Thorn Birds Pt. IV	Mar. 30, 1983	ABC	180	43.1	62	35,900
34	CBS NFC Championship Game	Jan. 10, 1982	CBS	195	42.9	62	34,960
35	Beverly Hillbillies	Jan. 15, 1964	CBS	30	42.8	62	21,960
36	Super Bowl VII	Jan. 14, 1973	NBC	185	42.7	72	27,670
37	Thorn Birds Pt. II	Mar. 28, 1983	ABC	120	42.5	59	35,400
38	Super Bowl IX	Jan. 12, 1975	NBC	190	42.4	72	29,040
38	Beverly Hillbillies	Feb. 26, 1964	CBS	30	42.4	60	21,750
39	Super Bowl X	Jan. 18, 1976	CBS	200	42.3	78	29,440
40	Airport (Movie Special)	Nov. 11, 1973	ABC	170	42.3	63	28,000
40	Love Story (Sun. Night Mov.)	Oct. 1, 1972	ABC	120	42.3	62	27,410
40	Cinderella	Feb. 22, 1965	CBS	90	42.3	59	22,250
40	Roots Pt. VII	Jan. 29, 1977	ABC	60	42.3	65	30,120
45	Beverly Hillbillies	Mar. 25, 1964	CBS	30	42.2	59	21,650
46	Beverly Hillbillies	Feb. 5, 1964	CBS	30	42.0	61	21,550
47	Beverly Hillbillies	Jan. 29, 1964	CBS	30	41.9	62	21,490
47	Super Bowl XXII Game	Jan. 31, 1988	ABC	229	41.9	62	37,120
49	Miss America Pageant	Sept. 9, 1961	CBS	150	41.8	75	19,600
49	Beverly Hillbillies	Jan. 1, 1964	CBS	30	41.8	59	21,440
51	Wagon Train	Jan. 27, 1960	NBC	30	41.8	62	18,890
52	Super Bowl VIII	Jan. 13, 1974	CBS	160	41.6	73	27,540
52	Bonanza	Mar. 8, 1964	NBC	60	41.6	62	21,340
54	Beverly Hillbillies	Jan. 22, 1964	CBS	30	41.5	61	21,290
55	Gunsmoke	Apr. 2, 1960	CBS	30	41.4	69	18,710
55	Bonanza	Feb. 16, 1964	NBC	60	41.4	60	21,240
57	Gunsmoke	Mar. 5, 1960	CBS	30	41.3	66	18,670
57	Bill Cosby Show	Jan. 22, 1987	NBC	30	41.3	56	36,100
59	Academy Awards	Apr. 10, 1967	ABC	150	41.2	75	22,620
60	Bonanza	Feb. 9, 1964	NBC	60	41.0	58	21,030
60	Winds of War—Part 7	Feb. 13, 1983	ABC	177	41.0	56	34,150
62	Gunsmoke	Jan. 28, 1961	CBS	30	40.9	65	19,180
63	Bonanza	Mar. 28, 1965	NBC	60	40.8	63	21,460
63	Gunsmoke	Jan. 30, 1960	CBS	30	40.8	63	18,440
65	All In The Family	Jan. 8, 1972	CBS	30	40.7	62	25,270
65	Bonanza	Mar. 7, 1965	NBC	60	40.7	61	21,410
67	Gunsmoke	Mar. 26, 1960	CBS	30	40.6	66	18,350
67	Beverly Hillbillies	Feb. 20, 1963	CBS	30	40.6	59	20,220
69	Gunsmoke	Feb. 25, 1961	CBS	30	40.5	64	19,000
69	Beverly Hillbillies	May 1, 1963	CBS	30	40.5	62	20,170
69	Roots Pt. I	Jan. 23, 1977	ABC	120	40.5	61	28,840
69	Wagon Train	Feb. 10, 1960	NBC	30	40.5	61	18,310
69	Bonanza	Feb. 2, 1964	NBC	60	40.5	58	20,780
74	Gunsmoke	Dec. 17, 1960	CBS	30	40.4	68	18,260
75	Gunsmoke	May 7, 1960	CBS	30	40.4	67	18,260
75	Bonanza	Feb. 21, 1965	NBC	60	40.4	61	21,250

Source: 1989 Nielsen Media Research

Note: Average Audience % Rankings based on Reports—Jan. 30, 1960 through April 17, 1989. Above data represent sponsored programs, telecast on individual networks, i.e., no unsponsored or joint network telecasts are reflected in the above listings. Programs under 30 minutes scheduled duration are excluded.

Emmy Award Winners

ACADEMY OF TELEVISION ARTS AND SCIENCES

1988–89
TELEVISION ACADEMY AWARDS
Categories and Areas of Achievement
For the Emmy Award
FOR THE PERIOD
FROM July 1, 1988
THROUGH June 30, 1989

OUTSTANDING COMEDY SERIES
Cheers, James Burrows, Glen Charles, Les Charles (executive producers); Cheri Eichen, Bill Steinkellner (producers); Tim Berry Phoef Sutton (coproducers), NBC.

OUTSTANDING DRAMA SERIES
L.A. Law, Steven Bochco (executive producer); Rick Wallace (coexecutive producer); David E. Kelly (supervising producer); Scott Goldstein, Michele Gallery (producers); William M. Finkelstein, Judith Parker (coproducers); Philip M. Goldfarb, Alice West (coordinating producers), NBC.

OUTSTANDING MINISERIES
War and Remembrance, Dan Curtis (executive producer); Barbara Steele (producer), ABC.

OUTSTANDING VARIETY, MUSIC OR COMEDY PROGRAM
The Tracey Ullman Show, James L. Brooks, Heidi Perlman, Jerry Belson, Ken Estin, Sam Simon (executive producers); Richard Sakai, Ted Bessell (producers); Marc Flanagan (coproducer); Tracey Ullman (host), Fox.

OUTSTANDING DRAMA/COMEDY SPECIAL
Day One, (AT&T Presents), Aaron Spelling, E. Duke Vincent (executive producers); David W. Rintels (producer), CBS.
Roe Vs. Wade, Michael Manheim (executive producer); Gregory Hoblit (producer); Alison Cross (coproducer), NBC.

OUTSTANDING CLASSICAL PROGRAM/PERFORMING ARTS
Bernstein at 70! (Great Performances), Harry Kraut, Klaus Hallig (executive producers); Michael Bronson, Thomas P. Skinner (producers), PBS.

OUTSTANDING INFORMATIONAL SERIES
Nature, David Heeley (executive producer); Fred Kaufman (series producer), PBS.

OUTSTANDING INFORMATIONAL SPECIAL
Lillian Gish: The Actor's Life for Me (American Masters), Freida Lee Mock, Susan Lacy (executive producers); Terry Sanders (producer); William T. Cartwright (coproducer), PBS.

OUTSTANDING ANIMATED PROGRAM
Garfield: Babes and Bullets, Phil Roman (producer); Jim Davis (writer); Phil Roman (director); John Sparey, Bob Nesler (codirectors), CBS.

OUTSTANDING CHILDREN'S PROGRAM
Free To Be . . . A Family, Marlo Thomas, Christopher Cerf (executive producers, U.S.); Robert Dalrymple (producer, U.S.); Leonid Zolotarevsky (executive producer, USSR); Igor Menzelintsev (producer, USSR); Vern T. Calhoun (coproducer, ABC).

OUTSTANDING SPECIAL EVENTS PROGRAMMING
Cirque du Soleil ("The Magic Circus"), Helene Dufresne (producer), HBO.
The 11th Annual Kennedy Center Honors: A Celebration Of The Performing Arts, George Stevens Jr., Nick Vanoff (producers), CBS.
The 42nd Annual Tony Awards, Don Mischer (executive producer); David J. Goldberg (producer); Jeffrey Lane (co-producer), CBS.
The 17th Annual American Film Institute Life Achievement Award: A Salute to Gregory Peck, George Stevens, Jr. (producer); Jeffrey Lane (coproducer), NBC.

OUTSTANDING LEAD ACTOR IN A COMEDY SERIES
Richard Mulligan, "Empty Nest," NBC.

OUTSTANDING LEAD ACTOR IN A DRAMA SERIES
Carroll O'Connor, "In the Heat of the Night," NBC.

OUTSTANDING LEAD ACTOR IN A MINISERIES OR SPECIAL
James Woods, "My Name Is Bill W." (Hallmark Hall of Fame), ABC.

OUTSTANDING LEAD ACTRESS IN A COMEDY SERIES
Candice Bergen, "Murphy Brown," CBS.

OUTSTANDING LEAD ACTRESS IN A DRAMA SERIES
Dana Delaney, "China Beach," ABC.

OUTSTANDING LEAD ACTRESS IN A MINISERIES OR SPECIAL
Holly Hunter, "Roe vs. Wade," NBC.

OUTSTANDING SUPPORTING ACTOR IN A COMEDY SERIES
Woody Harrelson, "Cheers," NBC.

OUTSTANDING SUPPORTING ACTOR IN A DRAMA SERIES
Larry Drake, "L.A. Law," NBC.

OUTSTANDING SUPPORTING ACTOR IN A MINISERIES OR SPECIAL
Derek Jacobi, "The Tenth Man" (Hallmark Hall of Fame), CBS.

OUTSTANDING SUPPORTING ACTRESS IN A COMEDY SERIES
Rhea Perlman, "Cheers," NBC.

OUTSTANDING SUPPORTING ACTRESS IN A DRAMA SERIES
Melanie Mayron, "thirtysomething," ABC.

OUTSTANDING SUPPORTING ACTRESS IN A MINISERIES OR SPECIAL
Colleen Dewhurst, "Those She Left Behind," NBC.

OUTSTANDING GUEST ACTOR IN A COMEDY SERIES
Cleavon Little, "Dear John," ("Stand By Your Man"), NBC.

OUTSTANDING GUEST ACTOR IN A DRAMA SERIES
Joe Spano, "Midnight Caller," ("The Execution of John Saringo"), NBC.

OUTSTANDING GUEST ACTRESS IN A COMEDY SERIES
Colleen Dewhurst, "Murphy Brown" ("Mama Said"), CBS.

OUTSTANDING GUEST ACTRESS IN A DRAMA SERIES
Kay Lenz, "Midnight Caller" ("After It Happened . . ."), NBC.

OUTSTANDING INDIVIDUAL PERFORMANCE IN A VARIETY OR MUSIC PROGRAM
Linda Ronstadt, "Canciones de Mi Padre" ("Great Performances"), PBS.

OUTSTANDING WRITING IN A COMEDY SERIES
Diane English, "Murphy Brown" ("Respect") (Pilot), CBS.

OUTSTANDING WRITING IN A DRAMA SERIES
Joseph Dougherty, "thirtysomething" ("First Day/Last Day"), ABC.

OUTSTANDING WRITING IN A VARIETY OR MUSIC PROGRAM
Jim Downey (head writer); **John Bowman, A. Whitney Brown, Gregory Daniels, Tom Davis, Al Franken, Shannon Gaughan, Jack Handey, Phil Hartman, Lorne Michaels, Mike Myers, Conan O'Brien, Bob Odenkirk, Herb Sargent, Tom Schiller, Robert Smigel, Bonnie Turner, Terry Turner, Christine Zander** (writers); **George Meyer** (additional sketches), "Saturday Night Live," NBC.

OUTSTANDING WRITING IN A MINISERIES OR A SPECIAL
Abby Mann, Rubin Vote, Ron Hutchinson, "Murderers Among Us: The Simon Wiesenthal Story," HBO.

OUTSTANDING DIRECTING IN A COMEDY SERIES
Peter Baldwin, "The Wonder Years" ("Our Miss White"), ABC.

OUTSTANDING DIRECTING IN A DRAMA SERIES
Robert Altman, "Tanner'88" ("The Boiler Room"), HBO.

OUTSTANDING DIRECTING IN A VARIETY OR MUSIC PROGRAM
Jim Henson, "The Jim Henson Hour" ("Dog City"), NBC.

OUTSTANDING DIRECTING IN A MINISERIES OR A SPECIAL
Simon Wincer, "Lonesome Dove," CBS.

OUTSTANDING ACHIEVEMENT IN CHOREOGRAPHY
Walter Painter, "Disney/MGM Studios Theme Park Grand Opening," NBC.
Paula Abdul, "The Tracey Ullman Show" ("The Wave Girls," "D.U.I.," "The Cure," "Maggie In Peril, Pt. 1"), Fox.

OUTSTANDING SOUND EDITING FOR A SERIES
William Wistrom, (supervising sound and ADR editor); **James Wolvington, Mace Matiosian** (sound editors); **Wilson Dyer, Guy**

Tsujimoto; Gerry Sackman (supervising music editor), "Star Trek: The Next Generation" ("Q Who"), Syn.

OUTSTANDING SOUND EDITING FOR A MINISERIES OR A SPECIAL

David McMoyler (supervising sound editor); **Joseph Melody** (cosupervising sound editor); **Mark Steele, Rick Steele, Michael J. Wright, Gary Macheel, Stephen Grubbs, Mark Friedgen, Charles R. Beith, Scot A. Tinsley, Karla Caldwell, G. Michael Graham, George B. Bell** (sound editors); **Kristi Johns** (supervising ADR editor); **Tom Villano, Jamie Gelb** (supervising music editors), "Lonesome Dove" (Part 3—"The Plains), CBS.

OUTSTANDING CINEMATOGRAPHY FOR A SERIES

Roy H. Wagner, "Quantum Leap," (Pilot), NBC.

OUTSTANDING CINEMATOGRAPHY FOR A MINISERIES OR A SPECIAL

Gayne Rescher, "Shooter," NBC.

OUTSTANDING SOUND MIXING FOR A COMEDY SERIES OR A SPECIAL

Klaus Landsberg (production mixer); **Craig Porter, Alan Patapoff** (re-recording mixers), "Night Court" ("The Last Temptation of Mac"), NBC.

OUTSTANDING SOUND MIXING FOR A VARIETY OR MUSIC SERIES OR A SPECIAL

Robert Douglass (SFX mixer); **David E. Fluhr** (re-recording mixer); **Ed Greene** (production mixer); **Larry Brown** (music mixer), "Kenny, Dolly and Willie: Something Inside So Strong," NBC.

OUTSTANDING SOUND MIXING FOR A DRAMA SERIES

Chris Haire (re-recording mixer, dialog); **Doug Davey** (re-recording mixer, effects); **Richard Morrison** (re-recording mixer, music and Foley); **Alan Bernard** (sound mixer, production), "Star Trek: The Next Generation" ("Q Who"), Syn.

OUTSTANDING SOUND MIXING FOR A DRAMA MINISERIES OR A SPECIAL

Don Johnson (sound mixer); **James L. Aicholtz** (dialog mixer); **Michael Herbick** (music mixer); **Kevin O'Connell** (sound effects mixer), "Lonesome Dove" (Part 4—"The Return"), CBS.

OUTSTANDING LIGHTING DIRECTION (ELECTRONIC) IN A COMEDY SERIES

Mark Levin (lighting director), "Who's the Boss?" ("A Spirited Christmas"), ABC.

OUTSTANDING LIGHTING DIRECTION FOR A VARIETY/ MUSIC OR DRAMA SERIES, MINISERIES OR SPECIAL

Robert Andrew Dickinson (lighting director), "The Magic of David Copperfield XI: The Explosive Encounter," CBS.

OUTSTANDING EDITING FOR A SERIES (SINGLE CAMERA PRODUCTION)

Steven J. Rosenblum, "thirtysomething" ("First Day/Last Day"), ABC.

OUTSTANDING EDITING FOR A MINISERIES OR A SPECIAL (SINGLE CAMERA PRODUCTION)

Peter Zinner, John F. Burnett, "War and Remembrance" (Part 10), ABC.

OUTSTANDING EDITING FOR A SERIES (MULTI-CAMERA PRODUCTION)

Tucker Wiard "Murphy Brown" ("Respect" pilot), CBS.

OUTSTANDING EDITING FOR A MINISERIES OR A SPECIAL (MULTI-CAMERA PRODUCTION)

Mark D. West, "Dance in America: Gregory Hines Tap Dance in America" ("Great Performances"), PBS.

OUTSTANDING TECHNICAL DIRECTION/ELECTRONIC CAMERAWORK/VIDEO CONTROL FOR A SERIES

Robert G. Holmes (technical director); **Leigh V. Nicholson, John Repczynski, Jeffrey Wheat, Rocky Danielson,** camera operators; **Thomas G. Teimpidis**, senior video control, "Night Court" ("Yet Another Day in the Life"), NBC.

OUTSTANDING TECHNICAL DIRECTION/ELECTRONIC CAMERA/VIDEO CONTROL FOR A MINISERIES OR A SPECIAL

Ron Graft (technical director); **Richard G. Price, Kenneth Patterson, Greg Harms** (camera operators); **Mark Sanford** (senior video control), "The Meeting" ("American Playhouse"), PBS.

OUTSTANDING ACHIEVEMENT IN MAKEUP FOR A SERIES

Thomas R. Burman, Bari Dreiband-Burman (special makeup); **Carol Schwartz, Robin Lavigne** (makeup artists), "The Tracey Ullman Show" ("The Subway"), (Fox).

OUTSTANDING ACHIEVEMENT IN MAKEUP FOR A MINISERIES OR SPECIAL

Manlio Rocchetti (makeup supervisor); **Carla Palmer, Jean Black** (makeup artists), "Lonesome Dove" (Part 4—"The Return"), CBS.

OUTSTANDING ACHIEVEMENT IN HAIRSTYLING FOR A SERIES

Virginia Kearns, "Quantum Leap" ("Double Identity"), NBC.

OUTSTANDING ACHIEVEMENT IN HAIRSTYLING FOR A MINISERIES OR A SPECIAL

Betty Glasow (chief hairstylist); **Stevie Hall, Elaine Bowerbank** (hairstylists), "Jack the Ripper" (Part 1), CBS.

OUTSTANDING COSTUME DESIGN FOR A SERIES

Judy Evans, "Beauty and the Beast" ("The Outsiders"), CBS.

OUTSTANDING COSTUME DESIGN FOR A MINISERIES OR A SPECIAL

Van Broughton Ramsey, "Lonesome Dove" (Part 2—"On The Trail"), CBS.

OUTSTANDING COSTUME DESIGN FOR A VARIETY OR MUSIC PROGRAM

Daniel Orlandi "The Magic of David Copperfield XI: The Explosive Encounter," CBS.

OUTSTANDING ACHIEVEMENT IN COSTUMING FOR A SERIES

Patrick R. Norris (men's costumer); **Julie Glick** (women's costumer), "thirtysomething" ("We'll Meet Again"), ABC.

OUTSTANDING ACHIEVEMENT IN COSTUMING FOR MINISERIES OR SPECIAL:

Paula Kaatz (costume supervisor); **Andrea Weaver** (women's costumer, Los Angeles); **Janet Lawler** (women's costumer, Dallas); **Stephen Chudej**, men's costumer—"Pancho Barnes," CBS.

OUTSTANDING ART DIRECTION FOR A SERIES

James J. Agazzi, (production designer); **Bill Harp** (set decorator), "Moonlighting" ("A Womb with a View"), ABC.

OUTSTANDING ART DIRECTION FOR A VARIETY OR MUSIC PROGRAM

Bernie Yeszin (art director); **Portia Iversen** (set decorator), "The Tracey Ullman Show" ("All About Tammy Lee; Maggie in Peril—Part 2"), Fox.

OUTSTANDING ART DIRECTION FOR A MINISERIES OR SPECIAL

Jan Scott (production designer); **Jack Taylor** (art director); **Edward J. McDonald** (set director), "I'll Be Home for Christmas," NBC.

OUTSTANDING ACHIEVEMENT IN MUSIC COMPOSITION FOR A SERIES (DRAMATIC UNDERSCORE)

Joel Rosenbaum, "Falcon Crest" ("Dust to Dust"), CBS.

OUTSTANDING ACHIEVEMENT IN MUSIC COMPOSITION FOR A MINISERIES OR A SPECIAL (DRAMATIC UNDERSCORE)

Basil Poledouris, "Lonesome Dove" ("Part 4—The Return"), CBS.

OUTSTANDING ACHIEVEMENT IN MUSIC DIRECTION

Ian Fraser (music director); **Chris Boardman, J. Hill** (principal arrangers), "Christmas in Washington," NBC.

OUTSTANDING ACHIEVEMENT IN MUSIC AND LYRICS

Lee Holdridge (composer); **Melanie** (lyricist), "Beauty and the Beast" ("A Distant Shore"); song; "The First Time I Love Forever," CBS.

INDIVIDUAL ACHIEVEMENT—INFORMATIONAL PROGRAMMING—PERFORMING

Hal Holbrook, "Portrait of America: Alaska," TBS.

OUTSTANDING INDIVIDUAL ACHIEVEMENT—INFORMATIONAL PROGRAMMING—WRITING

John Heminway, "The Mind" ("Search for Mind"), PBS.

INDIVIDUAL ACHIEVEMENT—SPECIAL EVENTS PROGRAMMING—DIRECTING

Dwight Hemion, "The 11th Annual Kennedy Center Honors: A Celebration of the Performing Arts," CBS.

INDIVIDUAL ACHIEVEMENT—SPECIAL EVENTS PROGRAMMING—PERFORMANCE

Billy Crystal, "The 31st Annual Grammy Awards," CBS.

INDIVIDUAL ACHIEVEMENT—SPECIAL EVENTS PROGRAMMING—SOUND MIXING

Ed Greene (music production mixer); **Don Worsham** (dialog production mixer); **Carroll Pratt** (production mixer, audience reaction); **Paul Sandweiss** (production mixer, nomination categories), "The 31st Annual Grammy Awards," CBS.

INDIVIDUAL ACHIEVEMENT—SPECIAL EVENTS PROGRAMMING—WRITING

Jeffrey Lane, "The 42nd Annual Tony Awards," CBS.

INDIVIDUAL ACHIEVEMENT CLASSICAL MUSIC/DANCE PROGRAMMING—PERFORMANCE

Mikhail Baryshnikov, "Dance in America: Baryshnikov Dances Balanchine" ("Great Performances"), PBS.

OUTSTANDING SPECIAL VISUAL EFFECTS

Charles Stauffel, Martin Guttridge, Bill Schirmer (effects supervisors); **Bill Cruse, Simon Smith, Steve Anderson, Ed Williams** (miniature designers); **Egil Woxholt, Godfrey Godar** (directors of photography), "War and Remembrance," ABC.

CASTING FOR MINISERIES OR SPECIAL

Lynn Kressel, "Lonesome Dove," CBS.

GOVERNORS AWARD

Lucille Ball

1988–89
TELEVISION ACADEMY AWARDS
Categories and Areas of Achievement
For the Emmy Award for Daytime Programs
FOR THE PERIOD FROM March 6, 1988 THROUGH March 5, 1989

OUTSTANDING DRAMA SERIES
Santa Barbara, Jill Farren Phelps (executive producer); Steven Kent (senior supervising producer); Charlotte Savitz (supervising producer); Julie Hanan Carruthers and Leonard Friedlander (producers), NBC.

OUTSTANDING GAME-AUDIENCE PARTICIPATION SHOW
The $25,000 Pyramid, Bob Stewart (executive producer); Anne Marie Schmitt (supervising producer); Francine Bergman, David Michaels (producers), CBS.

OUTSTANDING CHILDREN'S SERIES
Newton's Apple, James Steinbach (executive producer); Lee Carey, Tacy Mangan (supervising producers); Richard Hudson, Elizabeth Schlick, Lynne Reeck, Leslie Kratz, Rita La Doux, Marie Domingo, Carrie Maloney (producers), PBS.

OUTSTANDING CHILDREN'S SPECIAL
Taking a Stand (ABC Afterschool Special), Frank Doelger (executive producer); Roberta Rowe (producer), ABC.

OUTSTANDING ANIMATED PROGRAM
The New Adventures of Winnie the Pooh, Karl Geurs (producer-director); Mark Zaslove (story editor-writer); Bruce Talkington and Carter Crocker (writers), ABC.

OUTSTANDING TALK/SERVICE SHOW
The Oprah Winfrey Show, Debra Di Maio (executive producer); Oprah Winfrey (supervising producer); Ellen Rakieten, Diane Hudson, Mary Kay Clinton, Angela Thame, Alice McGee (producers), Syn.

OUTSTANDING SPECIAL CLASS PROGRAM AREA
China: Walls and Bridges, Jimmy R. Allen and Richard T. McCartney (executive producers); Robert Thornton (supervising producer), ABC.
James Stewart's Wonderful Life, Mary Frances Shea (executive producer); Phil Delbourgo (supervising producer); Dan Gurskis (producer), Cinemax.

OUTSTANDING LEAD ACTRESS, DRAMA SERIES
Marcy Walker, "Santa Barbara," NBC.

OUTSTANDING LEAD ACTOR, DRAMA SERIES
David Canary, "All My Children," ABC.

OUTSTANDING SUPPORTING ACTRESS, DRAMA SERIES
Debbie Morgan, "All My Children," ABC.
Nancy Lee Grahn, "Santa Barbara," NBC.

OUTSTANDING SUPPORTING ACTOR, DRAMA SERIES
Justin Deas, "Santa Barbara," NBC.

OUTSTANDING JUVENILE FEMALE IN A DRAMA SERIES
Kimberly McCullough, "General Hospital," ABC.

OUTSTANDING JUVENILE MALE IN A DRAMA SERIES
Justin Gocke, "Santa Barbara," NBC.

OUTSTANDING PERFORMER IN A CHILDREN'S SERIES
Jim Varney, "Hey Vern, It's Ernest!" CBS.

OUTSTANDING PERFORMER IN A CHILDREN'S SPECIAL
Dana Barron, "No Means No" (CBS Schoolbreak Special), CBS.

OUTSTANDING GAME SHOW HOST
Alex Trebek, "Jeopardy!" Syn.

OUTSTANDING TALK/SERVICE SHOW HOST
Sally Jessy Raphael, "Sally Jessy Raphael," Syn.

OUTSTANDING DRAMA SERIES DIRECTING TEAM
Frank Pacelli, Heather Hill, Randy Robbins, Rudy Vejar (directors); **Betty Rothenberg, Kathryn Foster** (associate directors), "The Young and the Restless," CBS.

OUTSTANDING DIRECTING IN A GAME/AUDIENCE PARTICIPATION SHOW
Dick Schneider (director), "Jeopardy," Syn.

OUTSTANDING DIRECTING IN A TALK/SERVICE SHOW
Jim McPharlin (director), "The Oprah Winfrey Show," Syn.

OUTSTANDING DIRECTING IN A CHILDREN'S SERIES
Matthew Diamond (director), "Shining Time Station," PBS.
Ozzie Alfonso (director), "3-2-1 Contact!" PBS.

OUTSTANDING ACHIEVEMENT IN DIRECTING—SPECIAL CLASS
No award was given.

OUTSTANDING DRAMA SERIES WRITING TEAM
Charles Pratt Jr., Anne Howard Bailey (head writers); **Robert Guza Jr., Courtney Simon, Lynda Myles, Patrick Mulcahey, Gary Tomlin** (script writers); **Josh Griffith, Jane Atkins** (breakdown/script writers); **Don Harary** (breakdown writer), "Santa Barbara," NBC.

OUTSTANDING ACHIEVEMENT IN WRITING IN A CHILDREN'S SERIES
Normal Stiles (head writer); **Nancy Sans, Luis Santeiro, Cathi Rosenberg-Turow, Belinda Ward, Sonia Manzano, Jeff Moss, Sara Compton, Judy Freudberg, David Korr, John Weidman, Tony Geiss, Emily Perl Kingsley, Mark Saltzman, Jocelyn Stevenson, Christian Clark, Jon Stone** (writers), "Sesame Street," PBS.

OUTSTANDING ACHIEVEMENT IN WRITING IN A CHILDREN'S SPECIAL
Jeffrey Auerbach, (writer) "No Means No" (CBS Schoolbreak Special), CBS.

OUTSTANDING ACHIEVEMENT IN WRITING—SPECIAL CLASS
No award was given.

OUTSTANDING ACHIEVEMENT IN ART DIRECTION/SET DECORATION/SCENIC DESIGN
Anthony Sabatino, William H. Harris (production designers); **Phyllis Hofberg, Richard D. Bluhm** (art directors), "Fun House," Syn.

OUTSTANDING ACHIEVEMENT IN TECHNICAL DIRECTION/ELECTRONIC CAMERA/VIDEO CONTROL
Ray Angona (technical director); **Joseph Arvizu, Cesar Cabreira, Keeth Lawrence, Martin Wagner** (electronic cameras); Allen Latter (video control), "The Price Is Right," CBS.

OUTSTANDING ACHIEVEMENT IN CINEMATOGRAPHY
Ozzie Alfonso, Larry Engel, Howard Hall, Robert Leacock, Don Lenzer, Christophe Lanzenburg, Chuck Levey, Rick Malkamas, Dyanna Taylor, Jeri Sopanen, cinematographers "3-2-1 Contact!," PBS.

OUTSTANDING ACHIEVEMENT IN MUSIC DIRECTION AND COMPOSITION
Joe Raposo (music director-composer); **Jeff Moss, Christopher Cerf** (composers); **Dave Conner** (composer-arranger), "Sesame Street," PBS.

OUTSTANDING ACHIEVEMENT IN GRAPHICS AND TITLE DESIGN
Barbara Laszewski (animation designer); **Joel Anderson** (graphics artist), "Hey Vern, It's Ernest!" CBS.

OUTSTANDING ACHIEVEMENT IN MAKEUP
Paul Gebbia (makeup artist), "Encyclopedia," HBO.

OUTSTANDING ACHIEVEMENT IN HAIRSTYLING
Andre Walker (hairstylist), "The Oprah Winfrey Show," Syn.
Yolanda Toussieng, Jerry Masone (hairstylists), "Pee-wee's Playhouse" ("To Tell the Tooth"), CBS.

OUTSTANDING ACHIEVEMENT IN VIDEOTAPE EDITING
Charles Randazzo, Peter Moyer, David Pincus, Steve Percell (videotape editors), "Pee-wee's Playhouse" ("To Tell the Tooth"), CBS.

OUTSTANDING ACHIEVEMENT IN LIVE AND TAPE SOUND MIXING AND SOUND EFFECTS
Peter Miller, Rick Patterson (production mixers); **Pam Bartella, Paul D. Collins, Ferne Friedman, Ken Hahn, Grant Maxwell, John Purcell** (post-production mixers), "3-2-1 Contact!," PBS.

OUTSTANDING ACHIEVEMENT IN FILM EDITING
Harvey Greenstein, Sam Pollard, and Grace Tankersley (film editors), "3-2-1 Contact!," PBS.

OUTSTANDING ACHIEVEMENT IN FILM SOUND EDITING
Al Breitenbach (music editor); **Ron Fedele** (editor); **Steve Williams, Ken Burton** (sound effects editors), "Jim Henson's Muppet Babies," CBS.
Steve Michael (dialogue/ADR editor); **Peter Cole** (dialogue/music editor); **Steve Kirklys** (supervising sound effects editor); **Ken Dahlinger** (sound effects/ADR editor); **Greg Teall** (sound effects editor), "Pee-wee's Playhouse" ("To Tell the Tooth"), CBS.

OUTSTANDING ACHIEVEMENT IN FILM SOUND MIXING
Jeff Haboush, Greg Russell (sound mixers), "Jim Henson's Muppet Babies," CBS.

OUTSTANDING ACHIEVEMENT IN LIGHTING DIRECTION
Carl Gibson (lighting director), "Kids Incorporated," The Disney Channel.

OUTSTANDING ACHIEVEMENT IN COSTUME DESIGN
Calista Hendrickson (costume designer), "Encyclopedia," HBO.

OUTSTANDING ACHIEVEMENT IN ART DIRECTION/SET DECORATION/SCENIC DESIGN FOR A DRAMA SERIES
William Hulstrom, Norman Wadell (art directors); **Joseph**

Bevacqua, Andrea Joel, Eric Fischer (set decorators), "The Young and the Restless," CBS.

OUTSTANDING ACHIEVEMENT IN TECHNICAL DIRECTION/ELECTRONIC CAMERA/VIDEO CONTROL FOR A DRAMA SERIES

Chuck Guzzi (technical director); **Toby Brown, Ted Morales, Gordon Sweeney, Mike Glenn** (electronic cameras); **Roberto Bosio** (video control), "The Bold and the Beautiful," CBS.

OUTSTANDING ACHIEVEMENT IN MUSIC DIRECTION AND COMPOSITION FOR A DRAMA SERIES

Jez Davidson (music director-composer); **David Matthews** (music director); **David Kurtz, Jack Allocco** (composers), "The Young and the Restless," CBS.

OUTSTANDING ACHIEVEMENT IN MAKEUP FOR A DRAMA SERIES

Carlos Yeaggy, John Maldonado, Dawn Marando (makeup artists), "Santa Barbara," NBC.

OUTSTANDING ACHIEVEMENT IN HAIRSTYLING FOR A DRAMA SERIES

Janet Medford, Valerie Scott (hairstylists), "Santa Barbara," NBC.

OUTSTANDING ACHIEVEMENT IN VIDEOTAPE EDITING FOR A DRAMA SERIES

Dan Brumett, Marc Beruti (videotape editors), "The Young and the Restless," CBS.

OUTSTANDING ACHIEVEMENT IN LIVE AND TAPE SOUND MIXING AND SOUND EFFECTS FOR A DRAMA SERIES

Scott Millan, Tommy Persson (audio mixers); Donald Henderson, Rafael Valentin (postproduction mixers); **Maurice "Smokey" Westerfeld, Peter Romano** (sound effects), "The Young and the Restless," CBS.

OUTSTANDING ACHIEVEMENT IN LIGHTING DIRECTION FOR A DRAMA SERIES

Donna Larson, Alan Blacher, Dennis M. Size (lighting directors), "All My Children," ABC.

OUTSTANDING ACHIEVEMENT IN COSTUME DESIGN FOR A DRAMA SERIES

Margarita Delgado, Charles Schoomaker (costume designers), "Another World," NBC.

DIRECTORS GUILD OF AMERICA AWARDS 1948–49 TO 1988

(formerly Screen Directors Guild Awards)

1948–49: *Quarterly Awards* to FRED ZINNEMANN for The Search; HOWARD HAWKS for Red River; ANATOLE LITVAK for The Snake Pit; JOSEPH L. MANKIEWICZ for A Letter to Three Wives. *Annual Award* to JOSEPH L. MANKIEWICZ.

1949–50: *Quarterly Awards* to MARK ROBSON for The Champion; ALFRED L. WERKER for Lost Boundaries; ROBERT ROSSEN for All the King's Men; CAROL REED for The Third Man. *Annual Award* to ROBERT ROSSEN.

1950–1951: *Quarterly Awards* to BILLY WILDER for Sunset Boulevard; JOHN HUSTON for The Asphalt Jungle; JOSEPH L. MANKIEWICZ for All About Eve; VINCENTE MINNELLI for Father's Little Dividend. *Annual Award* to JOSEPH L. MANKIEWICZ for All About Eve.

1951: *May-July* to ALFRED HITCHCOCK for Strangers on a Train; *August–October* to GEORGE STEVENS for A Place in the Sun; *November–December* to VINCENTE MINNELLI for An American in Paris. *Annual Award* to GEORGE STEVENS for A Place in the Sun.

1952: *Quarterly Awards* to CHARLES CRICHTON for The Lavender Hill Mob; JOSEPH MANKIEWICZ for Five Fingers; FRED ZINNEMANN for High Noon; JOHN FORD for The Quiet Man. *Annual Award* to JOHN FORD.

1953: *Most Outstanding Directorial Achievement:* FRED ZINNEMANN for From Here to Eternity; *Outstanding Directorial Achievements:* CHARLES WALTERS for Lili; WILLIAM WYLER for Roman Holiday, GEORGE STEVENS for Shane, BILLY WILDER for Stalag 17. *Motion Picture Critic Award:* BOSLEY CROWTHER, New York *Times.*

1954: *Most Outstanding Directorial Achievement:* ELIA KAZAN for On The Waterfront; *Outstanding Directorial Achievement:* GEORGE SEATON for The Country Girl, ALFRED HITCHCOCK for Rear Window, BILLY WILDER for Sabrina, WILLIAM WELLMAN for The High and the Mighty; *Motion Picture Critic Award:* HAROLD V. COHEN, Pittsburgh *Post-Gazette*.

1955: *Most Outstanding Directorial Achievement:* DELBERT MANN for Marty: *Outstanding Directorial Achievement:* JOHN STURGES for Bad Day at Black Rock, JOHN FORD and MERVYN LEROY for Mister Roberts, ELIA KAZAN for East of Eden, JOSHUA LOGAN for Picnic. *Motion Picture Critic Award:* JOHN ROSENFIELD, Dallas *Morning Evening Star.*

1956: *Most Outstanding Directorial Achievement;* GEORGE STEVENS for Giant; *Outstanding Directorial Achievement:* MICHAEL ANDERSON for Around the World in 80 Days, WILLIAM WYLER for Friendly Persuasion, KING VIDOR for War and Peace, WALTER LANG for The King and I. *Motion Picture Critic Award:* FRANCIS J. CARMODY, Washington *News. D.W. Griffith Award:* KING VIDOR.

1957: *Outstanding Directorial Achievement:* DAVID LEAN for The Bridge On the River Kwai; JOSHUA LOGAN for Sayonara; SIDNEY LUMET for 12 Angry Men; MARK ROBSON for Peyton Place, and BILLY WILDER for Witness for the Prosecution. *Motion Picture Critic Award,* HOLLIS ALPERT and ARTHUR KNIGHT, critics for The Saturday Review.

1958: *Grand Award for Direction:* VINCENTE MINNELLI for Gigi; *D.W. Griffith Award for creative achievement in the film industry:* FRANK CAPRA; *Motion Picture Critic Award:* PHILIP K. SCHEUER, critic of the Los Angeles Times; *Special Award:* LOUELLA PARSONS; *Best Directed Non-English-Speaking Film;* RENE CLAIR for Gates of Paris (French); *Best Directed Television Film:* RICHARD BARE, for All Our Yesterdays, segment of the 77 Sunset Strip series.

1959: *Grand Award for Direction:* WILLIAM WYLER, Ben-Hur; *Most Outstanding Directorial Achievement:* Ben-Hur; *Motion Picture Critic Award:* JOHN E. FITZGERALD, entertainment editor of Our Sunday Visitor, a Sunday Supplement distributed by Catholic weeklies; *Guild's award for outstanding achievement in the television field:* THE UNTOUCHABLES (Part 1 and 2); *Director's Television Award:* PHIL KARLSON, The Untouchables.

1960: *Grand Award for Direction:* BILLY WILDER, The Apartment; *Motion Picture Critic Award:* PAUL BECKLEY, New York Herald Tribune; *Special Award of Honorary Membership:* Y. FRANK FREEMAN; *Television Director's Award:* GEORGE SCHAEFER, Macbeth; *Television Critic Award:* SHERWOOD KOHN, Louisville Times.

1961: *Directors Award:* ROBERT WISE, JEROME ROBBINS, West Side Story; *Critics Award:* JOHN BEAUFORT of the Christian Science Monitor.

1962: *Director's Awards:* DAVID LEAN, Lawrence of Arabia; *Television Director's Award:* DAVID FRIEDKIN, The Price of Tomatoes, Dick Powell Show; *Television Critic's Award:* DONALD KIRKLEY of The Baltimore Sun.

1963: *Film Director's Award:* TONY RICHARDSON, Tom Jones; *Outstanding Television Director's Award:* GEORGE SCHAEFER; *Motion Picture Critic's Award:* PAINE KNICKERBOCKER, San Francisco Chronicle; *Television Critic's Award:* ROBERT LOUIS SHAYON, Saturday Review.

1964: *Film Director's Award:* GEORGE CUKOR, My Fair Lady; *Television Director's Award:* LAMONT JOHNSON; *Motion Picture Critic's Award:* JAMES MEADE, The San Diego Union.

1965: *Film Director's Award:* ROBERT WISE, The Sound of Music; *Critics Award:* SAM LESNER, Chicago Daily News; *D.W. Griffith Award:* WILLIAM WYLER.

1966: *Film Director's Award:* FRED ZINNEMANN, A Man for All Seasons; *Television Director's Award:* ALEX SEGAL.

1967: *Film Director's Award:* MIKE NICHOLS, The Graduate; *Television Director's Award:* GEORGE SCHAEFER.

1968: *Film Director's Award:* ANTHONY HARVEY, The Lion in Winter; *Television Director's Award:* GEORGE SCHAEFER; *D.W. Griffith Award:* ALFRED HITCHCOCK.

1969: *Film Director's Award:* JOHN SCHLESINGER, Midnight Cowboy; *Television Director's Award:* FIELDER COOK, Teacher, Teacher. *D. W. Griffith Award:* FRED ZINNEMANN.

1970: *Film Director's Award:* FRANKLIN SCHAFFNER, Patton; *Television Director's Award:* LAMONT JOHNSON, My Sweet Charlie; *D. W. Griffith Award:* None Presented.

1971: *Film Director's Award:* WILLIAM FRIEDKIN, The French Connection; *Television Director's Award:* (Special) BUZZ KULICK, Brian's Song.

1972: *Film Director's Award:* FRANCIS FORD COPPOLA, The Godfather: *Television Director's Award:* LAMONT JOHNSON, That Certain Summer.

1973: *Film Director's Award:* GEORGE ROY HILL, The Sting: *Television Director's Award:* JOSEPH SARGENT, The Marcus Nelson Murders.

1974: *Film Director's Award:* FRANCIS FORD COPPOLA, The Godfather, Part II: *Television Director's Award:* JOHN KORTY, The Autobiography of Miss Jane Pitman.

1975: *Film Director's Award:* MILOS FORMAN, One Flew Over the Cuckoo's Nest; *Television Director's Award:* SAM O'STEEN, Queen of the Stardust Ballroom.

1976: *Film Director's Award:* JOHN G. AVILDSEN, Rocky; *Television Awards—Specials:* DANIEL PETRIE, Eleanor and Franklin: *Comedy Series:* ALAN ALDA, Dear Sigmond episode of M*A*S*H; *Dramatic Series:* GLENN JORDAN, Rites of Friendship; *Musical Variety:* TONY CHARMOLI, Shirley MacLaine's Gypsy in My Soul; *Documentary-News Special:* ARTHUR BLOOM, Democratic & Republican Conventions.

1977: *Film Director's Award:* WOODY ALLEN, Annie Hall; *Television Awards—Specials:* DANIEL PETRIE, Eleanor and Franklin—The White House Years; *Comedy Series:* PAUL BOGART, Edith's 50th Birthday episode of All in The Family; *Dramatic Series:* JOHN ERMAN, Show #2, Second Hour of Roots; *Musical Variety:* ART FISHER, Neil Diamond: Glad You're Here with Me Tonight; *News Specials/Sports:* RAY LOCKHART, A Day with President Carter; *Documentaries:* PERRY MILLER ADATO: Georgia O'Keeffe.

1978: *Film Director's Award:* MICHAEL CIMINO, The Deer Hunter; *Television Awards—Comedy Series:* PAUL BOGART, California, Here We Are, All in the Family; *Dramatic Series:* GENE REYNOLDS, Prisoner,

Lou Grant; *Musical/Variety:* MERRILL BROCKWAY, Choreography by Balanchine, Part 3; *News Specials/Sports:* DON MISCHER, The Kennedy Center Honors; *Documentaries:* JOHN KORTY, Who Are the Debolts?; *Specials:* MARVIN CHOMSKY, Holocaust.

1979: *Film Director's Award:* ROBERT BENTON, Kramer Vs. Kramer; *Television Awards—Comedy Series:* CHARLES S. DUBIN, Period of Adjustment episode of M*A*S*H; *Dramatic Series:* ROGER YOUNG, Cop segment of Lou Grant; *Musical/Variety:* TONY CHARMOLI, John Denver—The Muppets; *News Specials/Sports:* DON MISCHER, The Kennedy Center Honors; *Documentaries:* ALFRED R. KELMAN, The Magic Sense chapter of the Body Human; *Specials:* MICHAEL MANN, The Jericho Mile; *Commercials:* (directors judged by two or more examples of their work): ROBERT LIEBERMAN, Mary Ryan for McDonald's and Mary Lou for R.C. Cola.

1980: *Film Director's Award:* ROBERT REDFORD, Ordinary People; *Television Awards—Comedy Series:* NOAM PITLIK, Fog episode of Barney Miller; *Dramatic Series:* ROGER YOUNG, Lou episode of Lou Grant; *Musical/Variety:* DWIGHT HEMION, IBM Presents Baryshnikov on Broadway; *Actuality (recording live):* DON MISCHER, The Kennedy Center Honors; *Special:* JERRY LONDON, Shogun; *Documentaries:* (tie) PERRY MILLER ADATO, Picasso: A Painter's Diary; and ALFRED R. KELMAN, Body Beautiful segment of The Body Human.

1981: *Film Director's Award:* WARREN BEATTY, Reds; *Television Awards—Comedy Series:* ALAN ALDA, The Life You Save episode from M*A*S*H; *Dramatic Series:* ROBERT BUTLER, Hill Street Station episode from Hill Street Blues; *Musical/Variety:* EMILE ARDOLINO, The Spellbound Child (Dance in America, PBS); *Actuality (recording live):* STAN HARRIS, Command Performance at Ford's Theatre—The Stars Meet the President; *Special:* HERBERT WISE, Skokie; *Documentary:* ROBERT GUENETTE, Great Movie Stunts: Raiders of the Lost Ark; *Commercials:* RICK LEVINE, First Love and Papa spots for Pepsi Cola and Summer Colt for Kodak.

1982: *Film Director's Award:* SIR RICHARD ATTENBOROUGH, Gandhi; *Television Awards—Comedy Series:* ALAN ALDA, Where There's a Will, There's a War, episode from M*A*S*H; *Dramatic Series:* Personal Foul, episode from Hill Street Blues; *Musical/Variety:* DON MISCHER, Shirley MacLaine, Illusions (CBS); *Dramatic Special:* MARVIN J. CHOMSKY, Inside the Third Reich (ABC Circle Film); *Documentary:* PERRY MILLER ADATO, Carl Sandburg—Echoes and Silences (American Playhouse); *Commercials:* JOE PYTKA, Baseball, Basketball and Future Gallup.

1983: *Film Director's Award:* JAMES BROOKS, Terms of Endearment; *Robert B. Aldrich Service Award (honorary):* ROBERT WISE; *Television Awards—Comedy Series:* JAMES BURROWS, Showdown Part II (episode of Cheers); *Dramatic Series:* JEFF BLECKNER, Life in the Minors (episode of Hill St. Blues); *Musical/Variety:* DON MISCHER, Motown 25: Yesterday, Today, Forever (NBC); *Dramatic Special:* EDWARD ZWICK, Special Bulletin (NBC); *Documentary:* HARRY MOSES, Willie Loman Comes to China; *Commercials:* (tie) BOB BROOKS, Hallmark Cards and STU HAGMANN, IBC Home Computers and LDS; *Daytime Drama:* SHARRON MILLER, The Woman Who Willed a Miracle (ABC).

1984: *Film Director's Award:* MILOS FORMAN, Amadeus; *D.W. Griffith Award for Life Achievement:* BILLY WILDER; *Televison Awards—Comedy Series:* JAY SANDRICH, The Bill Cosby Show (pilot); *Dramatic Series:* THOMAS CARTER, The Rise and Fall of Paul The Wall (episode of Hill Street Blues); *Musical Variety:* DON MISCHER and TWYLA THARP, Baryshnikov by Tharp with American Ballet Theatre (PBS); *Dramatic Special:* DANIEL PETRIE, The Dollmaker (ABC); *Documentary:* ALFRED R. KELMAN, The Journey Within (The Body Human) (CBS); *Sports:* SANDY GROSSMAN, Super Bowl XVIII (CBS); *Daytime Drama:* JOAN DARLING, Mom's on Strike (chapter of After School Special, ABC); *Commercials:* STU HAGMANN, spots for McDonald's, Latter Day Saints, IBM.

1985: *Film Director's Award:* STEVEN SPIELBERG, The Color Purple; *D.W. Griffith Award for Life Achievement:* JOSEPH L. MANKIEWICZ; *Robfert B. Aldrich Award (honorary):* George Sidney; *Television Awards—Comedy Series:* JAY SANDRICH, Golden Girls (pilot); *Dramatic Series:* WILL MacKENZIE, My Fair David (episode of Moonlighting); *Musical Variety:* DON MISCHER, Motown Returns to the Apollo; *Dramatic Special:* JOHN ERMAN, An Early Frost; *Documentary:* HARRY RASKY, Homage to Chagall: The Colors of Love; *Sports:* ANDY J. KINDLE and DAVID MICHAELS, Tour De France; *Daytime Drama:* CRAIG SANDY TUNG, The Day the Senior Class Got Married; *Commercials:* EDWARD BIANCHI, spots for National Institute of Drug Abuse, Diet Pepsi, American Express, Bounce.

1986: *Film Director's Award:* OLIVER STONE, Platoon; *D.W. Griffith Award for Life Achievement:* ELIA KAZAN; *Frank Capra Award (to an assistant director or unit production manager for outstanding service to the industry):* HENRY E. "BUD" BRILL; *Television Awards—Comedy Series:* TERRY HUGHES, Golden Girls (Isn't It Romantic? episode); *Dramatic Series:* WILL MacKENZIE, Atomic Shakespeare (episode of Moonlighting); *Musical Variety:* WALTER C. MILLER, Liberty Weekend; *Dramatic Special:* LEE GRANT, Nobody's Child; *Documentary:* PERRY MILLER ADATO, Eugene O'Neill: A Glory of Ghosts; *Sports:* HARRY COYLE, Game 6 of the 1986 World Series; *Daytime Drama:* CATLIN ADAMS, Wanted: The Perfect Guy.

1987: *Film Director's Award:* BERNARDO BERTOLUCCI, The Last Emperor; *D.W. Griffith Award for Lifetime Achievement:* ROBERT E. WISE; Robert B. Aldrich Award (for work on behalf of the guild): SHELDON LEONARD; *Television Awards—Dramatic Special:* JUD TAYLOR, Foxfire. *Evening Series:* MARSHALL HERSKOVITZ, thirtysomething, pilot; *Comedy Series:* WILL MACKENZIE, My Name Is Alex (Family Ties); *Musical/Variety:* DWIGHT HEMION, Julie Andrews, Sound of Christmas; *Daytime Dramatic Show:* VICTORIA HOCHBERG, Just a Regular Kid: An AIDS Story (Afterschool Special); *Sports:* ROBERT A. FISHMAN, Syracuse-Indiana game (NCAA Basketball Championship); *Documentary:* ELENA MANNES, The Kingdom Divided (God and Politics); *Commercials:* RICK LEVINE, Pepsi Cola, Arnott's Biscuits and Dupont Commercials.

1988: *Film Director's Award:* BARRY LEVINSON, Rain Man; *Honorary Life Award:* SIDNEY LUMET; *Robert B. Aldrich Award (for work on behalf of the guild):* GILBERT CATES; *Special DGA Award:* U.S. Representative ROBERT J. MRAZEK (D-NY) who with SIDNEY R. YATES (D-IL) authored National Film Preservation Act of 1988.; *Television Awards—Dramatic Special:* LAMONT JOHNSON, Lincoln. *Evening Series:* MARSHALL HERSKOVITZ, thirtysomething, "Therapy" episode; *Comedy Series:* STEVE MINER, The Wonder Years, pilot; *Musical/Variety:* WALTER C. MILLER, 100th BIrthday Celebration (Irving Berlin); *Daytime Dramatic Show:* JESUS SALVADOR TREVINO, Gangs (CBS Schoolbreak special); *Sports:* HARRY COYLE, World Series between Los Angeles Dodgers and Oakland A's; *Documentary/Actuality:* MERRILL BROCKWAY, On the Move (Great Performances); *Commercials:* JAMES GARTNER, Journal (Church World Services), Interesting Friends (Major League Baseball), Braces & Glasses (L.D.S. Church).

GOLDEN GLOBE AWARDS 1989 (Television)

BEST TELEVISION SERIES—DRAMA: "thirtysomething," The Bedford Falls Co./MGM/UA Television; ABC.

BEST ACTRESS IN A SERIES—DRAMA: Jill Eikenberry, "L.A. Law"

BEST ACTOR IN A SERIES—DRAMA: Ron Perlman, "Beauty and the Beast"

BEST TELEVISION SERIES—MUSICAL OR COMEDY: "The Wonder Years," The Black/Marlens Co./New World Television; ABC.

BEST ACTRESS IN A SERIES—MUSICAL OR COMEDY: Candice Bergen, "Murphy Brown"

BEST ACTOR IN A SERIES—MUSICAL OR COMEDY: Michael J. Fox, "Family Ties," Judd Hirsch, "Dear John," Richard Mulligan, "Empty Nest"

BEST MINISERIES OR MOTION PICTURE MADE FOR TV: "War and Remembrance," Dan Curtis Prods.; ABC

BEST ACTRESS IN A MINISERIES OR A MOVIE MADE FOR TV: ANN JILLIAN, "The Ann Jillian Story"

BEST ACTOR IN A MINISERIES OR MOVIE MADE FOR TV: Michael Caine, "Jack the Ripper," Stacy Keach, "Hemingway"

BEST SUPPORTING ACTRESS IN A SERIES, MINISERIES, OR MOVIE MADE FOR TV: Katherine Helmond, "Who's the Boss?"

BEST SUPPORTING ACTOR IN A SERIES, MINISERIES, OR MOVIE MADE FOR TV: Barry Bostwick, "War and Remembrance," Sir John Gielgud, "War and Remembrance"

International Film Festivals and Markets

Listed alphabetically by country. Exact dates vary from year to year but months indicated are generally the same. Those marked with an asterisk are recognized by the International Federation of Film Producers Association, 33 Avenue Champs Elysées, 75008, Paris, France.

AUSTRALIA
*Sydney (June)
Melbourne (June)
*Adelaide (July)

AUSTRIA
*Vienna—Humor in Film (March)
Viennale (Vienna) (March)
Wels (Austrian) (October)

BELGIUM
Brussels—Belgian Festival and Market (January)
Antwerp (March)
Brussels DIDACTA Audiovisual (June)
Flanders (Ghent) (October)

BRAZIL
São Paolo (October)
Rio de Janeiro (November)

BULGARIA
Varna (June)

CANADA
Montreal World Film Festival (August)
Toronto (Festival of Festivals) (September)
Asian-American International (Vancouver) (September-October)
Stratford (September)
Ottawa (Animation) (October)
Montreal (new cinema) (October)
Vancouver (October)

COLOMBIA
Cartagena Film Festival (June)

CUBA
Havana (December)

CZECHOSLOVAKIA
Prague Television Festival (June)
*Karlovy Vary (July)
Brno Film and TV Market (October)

EAST GERMANY
Leipzig (November)

ENGLAND
Birmingham Film & Television (October-November)
London Film Festival (November-December)

FINLAND
Tampere Film Festival (February)

FRANCE
Cannes MIDEM Music Market (January)
Rheims Sport Films (March-April)
Cannes MIP-TV Video Market (April)
Beaune Historical Films (May)
*Cannes Film Festival (May)
Annecy (Animation) (May-June alternate years)
Grenoble Shorts (June-July)
Deauville (American Films) (September)
Riena (environmental) (September)
Noirmoutier (first films) (September)
Biarritz (Iberian, Latin American) (September)
Cannes VIDCOM (visual communications) (October)
Cherbourg (October)
Grenoble (Thrillers) (October)

GREECE
*Thessaloniki Film Festival (October)

HOLLAND
Rotterdam Film International (February)
Dutch Film Days & Film Market (September)
CineKid (Children's) (Amsterdam) (September)

HONG KONG
Hong Kong (March)

IRELAND
*Cork (September-October)

INDIA
New Delhi International Film Festival (January)

ISRAEL
Jerusalem (June-July)

ITALY

Bergamo at San Remo (March)
MIFED (film and TV market) at Milan (April)
Asolo (art and painting)
Alghero (June)
*Trieste (science fiction) (July)
Taormina Festival of Nations (July)
Venice Film Festival (September)
Sorrento (Canadian) (September)
Rimini (new cinema) (September)
Prix Italia (TV) at Florence (September)
MIFED TV Market at Milan (October)
Salerno (October)
Turin (youth films) (October)
Pordenone (silents) (October)
Lucca (animation) (October-November)
Porretta Temer (November)
Festival dei Popoli at Florence (December)

JAPAN

Tokyo-U.S. Film Festival (April)

MONTE CARLO

Monte Carlo TV Festival (February)

POLAND

*Cracow (shorts) (June)
Gdansk (September)
Katowice (scientific/technical) (November)

SCOTLAND

Edinburgh (August-September)

SPAIN

Gijón (children's) (June)
Cadiz (September)
*San Sebastian (September)
*Sitges (horror) (September-October)
Valencia (Mostra Cinema Mediterrani) (October)
*Valladolid (human values) (October)
*Barcelona (International) (October-November)

SWITZERLAND

Geneva Telecom (May)
Montreux TV Festival (May)
*Locarno (August)
Montreux (new form) (August)
Les Diablerets (Alpine) (September)
*Nyon (documentaries) (October)

TAIWAN

Taipei (Asian) (June)

UNITED STATES

Asian-American International Film Festival (touring)
U.S. Film Festival (Park City, Utah) (January)
*New York Animation Festival (January)
NATPE (Houston) (January)
Miami (February)
American Film Market (Los Angeles) (March)
*San Francisco International Film Festival (April)
AFI/L.A. International Film Festival (April)
National Assn. of Broadcasters (Las Vegas) (April)
Filmfest D.C. (Washington, D.C.) (April-May)
Seattle International (May-June)
Telluride (Colorado) (September)
Aspen (independent) (September)
Cinetex (Las Vegas) (film/TV mart) (September)
*New York Film Festival (September-October)
American Independent Feature Film Market (New York) (October)
Denver (October)
San Diego (October)
SMPTE (October, November)
Chicago (October)
Showeast (Atlantic City) (October)
International Film & TV (New York) (November)
Northwest Film & Video (Portland, OR) (November)
Hawaii (Honolulu) (December)

U.S.S.R.

*Tashkent (Afro-Asian) (May)
Teleforum (Moscow) (September)

WEST GERMANY

*Berlin (February)
*Oberhausen (shorts) (April)
Munich (Youth Prize—TV) (June)
Cologne Photokina (September-October)
Oberhausen Sports Festival (October)
Mannheim (October)
Hof (October)
Lubeck (Nordic films) (November)

YUGOSLAVIA

Belgrade Film Festival (February)
Belgrade (science and technology) (April)
*Zagreb (animation) (June)
Pula (national) (July)

Who's Who

In MOTION PICTURES and TELEVISION

A

AAMES, WILLIE: Actor. r.n. William Upton. b. California, July 15, 1960.
PICTURES: Hog Wild, Scavenger Hunt, Zapped!, Paradise, Cut and Run.
TELEVISION: Series: We'll Get By, Courtship of Eddie's Father, The Odd Couple, Swiss Family Robinson, Wait Til Your Father Gets Home, Eight Is Enough, Charles in Charge. Movies: Eight is Enough Reunion.

AARON, PAUL: Director. Broadway shows include Salvation, Paris Is Out, '70 Girls '70, Love Me Love My Children.
PICTURES: A Different Story, A Force of One, Deadly Force, Maxie.
TELEVISION: The Miracle Worker, Thin Ice, Maid in America, When She Says No, Save the Dog!, In Love and War.

AARON, ROY H.: Executive. b. April 8, 1929. e. UCLA, BA; USC, LLB. Attorney in L.A. law firm of Pacht, Ross, Warne, Bernhard & Sears. Joined Plitt Companies in 1978 as sr. v.p. & gen. counsel. In 1980 named pres. & chief operating officer of Plitt Theatres, Inc. and related Plitt companies.

ABARBANEL, SAM X.: Producer, Writer, Publicist. b. Jersey City, NJ, March 27, 1914. e. Cornell U., U. of Illinois, B.S. 1935. Newspaperman in Chicago before joining NY exploitation dept. of Republic, then to studio as asst. publicity director. W.W.II in Europe with 103rd Div. After war independent publicist and producer. Co-prod. Argyle Secrets, 1948. Co-wrote orig. s.p., co-produced U.A.'s Prehistoric Women, 1950. Exec. prod. U.A.'s Golden Mistress. In 1963 to Spain as associate prod. MGM's Gunfighters of Casa Grande, and Son of Gunfighter. Formed own co. in Spain, 1966. Produced Narco Men. Co-authored, prod. Last Day of War. Orig. & co-s.p. Avco's Summertime Killer, 1972.

ABELES, ARTHUR: Chairman, Filmarketeers, Ltd. b. 1914. Educated Duke U., Columbia U. 1939–41: general manager, West Indies, Warner. 1941. assistant general manager, Brazil, Universal. 1942–45: general manager, Uruguay, Warner. 1945–47: supervisor, Argentina, Chile, Uruguay, Paraguay, Warner. 1948–68: Managing director, Warner Bros. Pictures, Warner Theatre, Warner Bros. Production; Director Henderson Film Laboratories; Vice-pres., Warner Bros. Intl. in chg. of Europe, the Near East and North Africa. 1968–70; Managing director, Universal Pictures Ltd. Vice-president Universal International in charge of U.K., Continent and Middle East. 1970–77: Co-chairman, Cinema International Corporation. 1978: Co-chairman, A.M. Film Consultants Ltd. 1980: Chairman, Filmarketeers, Ltd.-Filmbond Group of Companies.

ABEND, SHELDON: Executive. b. New York, NY, June 13, 1929. Maritime Labor-Rel. Negotiator, 1954–56; chmn., Maritime Union, 1954–56; head, exec. dir. Authors' Research Co. rep. estates deceased authors, est. 1957. indep. literary negotiator, CC films, A.A.P., RKO General Inc., David O. Selznick, 1959–65; pres. American Play Co. Inc., Century Play Co. Inc., 1961–present; est. Million Dollar Movie Play Library, 1962; pres. Amer. Literary Consultants est. 1965; exec. v.p. Chantec Enterprises Inc. 1969–72. Marketing literary consultant for Damon Runyon Estate. Copyright analyst and literary rights negotiator, United Artists Corp. Founder and chmn., Guild for Author's Heirs, 1970–72, Literary negotiator and prod. consultant for Robert Fryer, 1972. Founder, Copyright Royalty Co. for Authors' Heirs, 1974; copyright consultant, Films, Inc. 1975; literary agent for Bway. play, Chicago, 1975. Owner of 53 classic RKO motion pictures for the non-theatrical markets, distributed by Films, Inc. Revived publishing of Damon Runyon stories in quality paperback in conjunction with Runyon-Winchell Cancer Fund. Published Cornell Woolrich mystery stories—all prod. by Alfred Hitchcock for TV & motion pictures, 1976. 1978, assoc. prod. of film, Why Would I Lie?; Originator of Million Dollar Movie Book Theatre and Million Dollar Movie Sound Track Co., 1980; assoc. prod. of Bdwy revival, Shanghai Gesture, 1981. Publ. 5 Cornell Woolrich books owned by S. Abend, 1982–83; Co-authored book, The Guardians; 1985, Romance of the Forties by Damon Runyon, 1986; 1985, founder and pres. American Concerts, Inc. and American Theatre Collections, Inc.; Pub. Into the Night by Cornell Woolrich. Packaged m.p. Bloodhounds of Broadway 1988; co-author s.p. Ultimate Demand.

ABRAHAM, F. MURRAY: Actor. b. Oct. 24, 1939. Attended U. of Texas, 1959–61; trained for stage at Herbert Berghof Studios with Uta Hagen. Stage debut in Los Angeles in The Wonderful Ice Cream Suit, 1965. New York debut in The Fantasticks, 1966.
THEATER: Antigone (NYSF, 1982), Uncle Vanya, The Golem (NYSF), Madwoman of Chaillot, Twelfth Night, Macbeth, A Midsummer's Night Dream.
PICTURES: Serpico (debut, 1964), The Sunshine Boys, All the President's Men, They Might Be Giants, The Ritz, Madman, The Big Fix, Scarface, Amadeus. (Acad. Award,-best actor), The Name of the Rose, Slipstream, The Favorite, Russicum, The Betrothed, Hard Rain, Personal Choice, Eye of the Widow.
TELEVISION: Love of Life, Kojak, Marco Polo, Sex and the Married Woman, How to Survive a Marriage, All in the Family, Dream West.

ABRAHAMS, GARY: Executive. e. U. of Arizona, B.A. In 1968 joined Paramount TV as asst. to v.p.; 1974–75, asst. to prod., The Movies; 1971–78, assoc. dir., Los Angeles Intl. Film Exposition (Filmex); 1978, joined Marble Arch Productions, as asst. to pres.; named dir. of corporate relations & merchandising, 1979; v.p., cable programming, Interscope Communications, 1982; assoc. dir., American Cinematheque, 1984–86; named pres., Great Entertainment Film Ventures, 1987; dir. of marketing, American Cinematheque, 1988–present.

ABRAHAMS, JIM: Producer, Writer, Director. b. Milwaukee, WI, May 10, 1944. e. U. of Wisconsin. Former private investigator. 1979, with friends David and Jerry Zucker, opened the Kentucky Fried Theatre in Madison, WI, a multimedia show specializing in live improvisational skits mixed with videotaped and film routines and sketches, with the threesome writing and appearing in most. Opened new theatre in Los Angeles in 1972 and developed large following.
PICTURES: The Kentucky Fried Movie (co-s.p. with Zuckers); Airplaine! (co-dir., co-exec. prod., co-s.p. with Zuckers); Top Secret! (co-dir., co-s.p.); Ruthless People (co-dir.), Big Business (dir.), The Naked Gun (exec. prod., co-s.p.), Cry Baby (exec. prod.).

ABRAHAMS, MORT: Producer. b. New York, NY. Dir. programming, prod., NTA, 1958–60; exec. prod. Cooga Mooga Prod. Inc., 1960–61. Producer: Target, The Corruptors 1961, Route 66, 1962–63; writer TV shows, 1963–64; prod., Kraft Suspense Theatre, 1965; prod., Man from U.N.C.L.E., 1965–66; exec. v.p., APJAC Prod. 1966. Assoc. prod.: Doctor Dolittle, Planet of the Apes, Goodbye, Mr. Chips; Prod.: Planet of the Apes; 1969, v.p. in chg. of prod., Rastar Prods.: 1971–74 exec. prod. American Film Theatre & v.p. Ely Landau Org. in chg. West Coast prod. Exec. prod.: Luther, Homecoming, Man in the Glass Booth; The Greek Tycoon, Hopscotch,; exec. in chg. prod.: The Chosen, Beatlemania; exec. prod.: The Deadly Game; Separate Tables, Mr. Halpern and Mr. Johnson; prod.: Arch of Triumph; exec. prod.: The Holcraft Covenant; prod., Seven Hours to Judgment.

ABRAMS, DIANNE: Executive. Held posts with San Diego division Los Angeles Times; asst. acct. exec. with Hubbert Advertising; press and publicity dept. of KNBC. 1982, joined Warner Bros. as asst. to Robert G. Friedman, v.p. worldwide pub.; 1987, named WB dir. of natl. promotion; 1988 joined VH-1 as segment prod. on Watch Bobby Rivers talk show;

named mgr., prog. & talent dev. April, 1989; named dir., talent relations for VH-1, Aug., 1989.

ABULADZE, TENGIZ: Director, Writer, b. Soviet Georgia, Jan. 31, 1924. e. studied directing in Tbilisi then in Moscow at the Higher State Institute of Cinematography.
PICTURES: Documentaries: Dmitry Arakishvili; Our Palace; The Georgian State Dancing Company; An Open Air Museum; Features: Magdan's Donkey; Someone Else's Children; Me, Grandma, Iliko and Hillarion; Prayer, A Necklace for My Beloved, The Wishing Tree; Repentance, Hadji Murat.

ACKERMAN, BETTYE: Actress. b. Cottageville, SC, Feb. 28, 1928. e. Columbia U., 1948–52. Taught dancing 1950–54.
PLAYS: No Count Boy, 1954; Tartuffe, Sophocles' Antigone, and Oedipus at Colonus, The Merchant of Venice.
PICTURES: Face of Fire, Rascal.
TELEVISION: Alcoa Premiere, Alfred Hitchcock Presents, Perry Mason, Breaking Point, Dr. Maggie Graham on Ben Casey series for five yrs., Hope-Chrysler Theatre, Bonanza, FBI Story, Mannix, Ironsides, Medical Center, regular on Bracken's World, Colombo, Sixth Sense, Heat of Anger, Return to Peyton Place, (6 months 1972) Rookies, Barnaby Jones, Police Story, Gunsmoke, Harry O, Streets of San Francisco, S.W.A.T., Petrocelli, Wonder Woman, Police Woman, Chips, 240-Robert, The Waltons, Dynasty, Falcon Crest, Me and Mom, Trapper John M.D. Movies: Companions in Nightmare, A Day for Thanksgiving on Walton's Mountain, Confessions of a Married Man.
RECORDS: Salome & School for Scandal.

ACKERMAN, HARRY S.: Executive. b. Albany, NY, Nov. 17, 1912. e. Dartmouth Coll. m. actress Elinor Donahue. Began as writer, actor, producer. Joined Young & Rubicam adv. agcy. 1936; became v.p. of program operations, 1946. Exec. prod. CBS, 1948. Dir. of network programs—Hollywood, 1948; v.p. in charge network radio programs, 1950; v.p. chg. network TV programs CBS-TV, Hollywood, 1951; exec. dir. spec. progs. CBS, 1956; formed independent co. 1957; v.p. and exec. prod. Screen Gems Inc., 1958–1973; pres. Harry Ackerman Prods.; Natl. pres., Academy TV Arts and Sciences, two terms; now pres., Harry Ackerman Prods.

ACKLAND, JOSS: Actor. b. London, England, Feb. 29, 1928. Member of Old Vic; toured U.S.S.R and U.S. with them. Spent time in Central Africa as a tea planter. Over 400 TV appearances.
PICTURES: Seven Days to Noon, Royal Flash, Crescendo, The House That Dripped Blood, Villain, England Made Me, The Black Windmill, Great Expectations, The Greek Tycoon, Someone Is Killing the Great Chefs of Europe, Saint Jack, The Apple, Rough Cut, Lady Jane, A Zed and Two Noughts, The Sicilian, White Mischief, To Kill a Priest, It Couldn't Happen Here, Lethal Weapon 2, To Forget Palermo.
TELEVISION: Queenie, Code Name: Kyril; Shadowlands, The Man Who Lived at the Ritz, A Quiet Conspiracy, The Justice Game.

ADAM, KEN: Art director, Prod. Designer. b. Berlin, Germany, Feb. 5, 1921. e. St. Pauls Sch., London; London U., student of architecture. 6 years war service as RAF pilot. Ent. m.p. ind. as draughtsman 1947 (This Was a Woman). Art dir.: The Devil's Pass, Soho Incident, Around the World in 80 Days, Trials of Oscar Wilde, Dr. No, Sodom and Gomorrah, Dr. Strangelove, Goldfinger, Thunderball, Ipcress File, You Only Live Twice, Funeral in Berlin, Chitty Chitty Bang Bang, Goodbye Mr. Chips, The Owl and the Pussycat, Diamonds Are Forever, Sleuth, The Last of Sheila, Barry Lyndon, (Acad. Award), Salon Kitty, 7% Solution, The Spy Who Loved Me, Moonraker, King David, Agnes of God, Pennies from Heaven, Crimes of the Heart, The Deceivers (prod. design), Dead-Bang.

ADAMS, BROOKE: Actress. b. New York, NY, Feb. 8, 1949. e. H.S. of Performing Arts; Inst. of American Ballet; Lee Strasberg. Made professional debut at age of six in Finian's Rainbow. Worked steadily in summer stock and TV until age 18. After hiatus resumed acting career.
THEATER: Split, Key Exchange, Linda Hur. Helps run small summer theater upstate NY.
PICTURES: The Lords of Flatbush, Car Wash, Shockwaves (Death Corps), Days of Heaven, Invasion of the Body Snatchers, Cuba, A Man, a Woman and a Bank, Utilities, The Dead Zone, Almost You, Key Exchange, Man on Fire.
TELEVISION: James Dean: Portrait of a Friend, The Last of the Belles, The Daughters of Joshua Cabe, Murder on Flight 502, The Bob Newhart Show, Police Woman, Lace, Special People, Lace II, The Lion of Africa, Bridesmaids. Specials: Paul Reiser: Out on a Whim. Series: O.K. Crackerby. Pilot: A Girl's life.

ADAMS, CATLIN: Actress. r.n. Barab. b. Los Angeles, CA, October 11, 1950. Began career as actress then studied directing at American Film Institute. Directorial debut: Wanted: The Perfect Guy (Emmy-winning ABC Afterschool Special). Also directed Little Shiny Shoes (short, written and prod. with Melanie Mayron).
THEATER: Safe House, Scandalous Memories, Dream of a Blacklisted Actor, The Candy Store.
PICTURES: As Actress: Katherine, Panic in Needle Park, The Jerk, The Jazz Singer. Director: Sticky Fingers (also co-s.p., co-prod.).
TELEVISION: How to Survive the 70's and Maybe Even Bump into a Little Happiness; She Loves Me, She Loves Me Not.

ADAMS, DON: Actor. b. New York, NY, April 13, 1926. Won Arthur Godfrey talent contest. Was nightclub impressionist before starting in TV.
PICTURE: The Nude Bomb.
TELEVISION: Bill Dana Show, Get Smart, The Partners, Hooray for Hollywood, Don Adams Screen Test, Three Times Daley, Inspector Gadget, Check It Out!, Get Smart Again!

ADAMS, EDIE: Actress, Singer. b. Kingston, PA, April 16, 1931. e. Juilliard Sch. of Music, Columbia Sch. of Drama.
STAGE: Wonderful Town, 1952–54; Lil Abner, 1956–57, Mame.
TELEVISION: The Chevy Show, 1958: Take a Good Look, 1960–61; Here's Edie, 1962–63; Movie: Ernie Kovacs' Between the Laughter, A Cry for Love, Fast Friends.
PICTURES: The Apartment, It's a Mad, Mad, Mad, Mad World, Call Me Bwana, Under the Yum, Yum Tree, Love With A Proper Stranger, Lover Come Back, The Best Man, Maid in Paris, The Honey Pot, Up in Smoke.

ADAMS, GERALD DRAYSON: Writer. b. Winnipeg, Manitoba. e. Oxford U. Export exec. 1925–30; literary agt. 1931–45. Member: Screen Writers' Guild.
PICTURES: (co-orig. screen story) Magnificent Rogue, (co-s.p.) Plunderers, (s.p.) Gallant Legion, (co-s.p.) Big Steal; collab. story, Dead Reckoning; orig. s.p.: Battle of Apache Pass, Son of Ali Baba, Flaming Feather, Flame of Araby; collab. s.p.: Lady from Texas, Steel Town, Untamed, Frontier; story, collab. s.p.: Duel at Silver Creek; st., s.p.: Princess of the Nile, Three Young Texans, Gambler from Natchez; story: Wings of the Hawk, Between Midnight and Dawn; st., adapt.: Taza Son of Cochise; collab. s.p. story: Gambler from Natchez, Chief Crazy Horse, s.p.: Golden Horde; adapt. s.p.: Prince Who Was a Thief; orig. s.p., Sea Hornet; s.p., Three Bad Sisters; orig., s.p.: Duel on the Mississippi; orig.: Black Sleep, s.p.: War Drums; story, collab. s.p.: Gun Brothers; story, Affair in Reno; story, s.p.: Frontier Rangers; story, s.p.: Gold, Glory & Custer; orig. story, collab. s.p.: Kissin Cousins. Orig. s.p.: Harem Scarem.
TELEVISION: Maverick, G.E. Theatre, Northwest Passage, Broken Arrow, Cheyenne, 77 Sunset Strip.

ADAMS, JULIE: Actress. r.n. Betty May Adams. b. Waterloo, LA, Oct. 17, 1928. e. jr. coll., Little Rock, AK. Coll. dramatic; m.p. debut in Red Hot and Blue; Star of Tomorrow, 1953.
PICTURES: Bright Victory; as Betty Adams in: The Dalton Gang, Marshal of Heldorado, West of the Brazos; Hollywood Story, Finders Keepers, Bend of the River, Treasure of Lost Canyon, Horizons West, Lawless Breed, Mississippi Gambler, The Creature From the Black Lagoon, Private War of Major Benson, Man from the Alamo, Wings of the Hawk, Tickle Me, The Last Movie, McQ, The Wild McCullochs, Killer Force, The Fifth Floor, Black Roses, Backtrack, One Under a Parasol.
TELEVISION: Go Ask Alice, Capitol.

ADAMS, MASON: Actor. b. NY, NY, Feb. 26, 1919. e. U. Wisconsin. B.A., 1940; M.A., 1941. Trained for stage at Neighborhood Playhouse. Began on radio in 1946, spending nearly two decades in title role of Pepper Young's Family. Broadway debut: Get Away Old Man (1943).
THEATER: Career Angel, Public Relations, Violet, Shadow of My Enemy, Inquest, The Sign in Sidney Brustein's Window, Tall Story, The Trial of the Catonsville Nine, Foxfire, Checking Out.
PICTURES: God Told Me To, Raggedy Ann and Andy, Northstar, The Final Conflict, F/X.
TELEVISION: Series: Lou Grant (1977–1982), Morningstar/Eveningstar. Pilot: Knight and Dave. Movies: The Deadliest Season, And Baby Makes Six, The Shining Season, Flamingo Road, The Revenge of the Stepford Wives, The Kid with the Broken Halo, Freedom to Speak, Solomon Northrup's Odyssey.

ADAMS, MAUD: Actress. r.n. Wikstrum. b. Lulea, Sweden, Feb. 12, 1945. Formerly a model. Film debut: as model in The Boys in the Band.
PICTURES: The Christian Licorice Store, U-Turn, Mahoney's Estate, The Man With the Golden Gun, Rollerball, Killer Force, The Merciless Man, Tattoo, Octopussy, Target Eagle, Jane and the Lost City, The Women's Club, A Man of Passion, The Favorite, Soda Cracker.
TELEVISION: Laura–Shades of Summer, The Hostage Tower, Playing for Time, Nairobi Affair. Series: Chicago Story, Emerald Point, N.A.S.

ADAMS, TONY: Producer. b. Dublin, Ireland, Feb. 15, 1953. Began career as asst. to dir. John Boorman and was associated with Burt Reynolds prior to joining Blake Edwards as a prod., 1973. Then president, Blake Edwards Entertainment; Pres., The Blake Edwards Company, 1988.
PICTURES: Assoc. Prod.: Return of the Pink Panther; The Pink Panther Strikes Again; Revenge of the Pink Panther; "10"; S.O.B.; Victor-Victoria; Trail of the Pink Panther; The Man Who Loved Women. Prod.: Micki & Maude, That's Life, A Fine Mess, Blind Date, Sunset, Skin Deep.
TELEVISION: Julie Andrews in Japan, Justin Case, Peter Gunn.

ADDISON, JOHN: Composer. b. West Chobham, Surrey, England, March 16, 1920. e. Wellington and Royal Coll. of Music. Entered m.p. ind. in 1948, Professor, Royal Coll. of Music.
PICTURES: Seven Days to Noon, The Man Between, The Maggie, Make Me An Offer, Privates Progress, Reach for the Sky, Lucky Jim, I Was Monty's Double, Carlton Brown of the Foreign Office, The Entertainer, The Honey Pot, Torn Curtain, A Fine Madness, I Was Happy Here, The Loved One, Guns at Batasi, The Uncle, Girl With Green Eyes, Tom Jones, The Loneliness of the Long Distance Runner, A Taste of Honey, The Charge of the Light Brigade, Smashing Time, Start the Revolution Without Me, Country Dance (in U.S., Brotherly Love), Forbush and the Penguins, Sleuth, Luther, Dead Cert, Ride a Wild Pony, Seven-Per-Cent Solution, Swashbuckler, Joseph Andrews, A Bridge Too Far, The Pilot, High Point, Strange Invaders, Grace Quigley, Code Name: Emerald.
BALLETS: Carte Blanche (at Sadlers Wells and Edinburgh Fest.), Cat's Cradle (Marquis de Cuevas, Paris, Monte Carlo).
PLAYS: The Entertainer, The Chairs, Luther, Midsummer Night's Dream, The Broken Heart, The Workhouse Donkey, Hamlet, Semi-Detached, The Seagull, Saint Joan of the Stockyards, Listen to the Mockingbird, Cranks (revue), Antony & Cleopatra, I Claudius, Twelfth Night, Bloomsbury, Antony and Cleopatra (LA Theatre Centre).
TELEVISION: Sambo and the Snow Mountains, Detective, Hamlet, The Search for Ulysses, Way of the World, Back of Beyond, Black Beauty, The Bastard, Deadly Price of Paradise, Love's Savage Fury, Like Normal People, The French Atlantic Affair, Mistress of Paradise, Eleanor First Lady of The World, Charles and Diana: A Royal Love Story, Mail Order Bride, Thirteen at Dinner, Dead Man's Folly, Mr. Boogedy, Something in Common, Firefighter, Amazing Stories, Bride of Boogedy, Strange Voices. Mini-series: Centennial, Pearl, Ellis Island, Beryl Markham: A Shadow on the Sun. Series: Nero Wolfe, Murder She Wrote.
STAGE MUSICALS: The Amazons, Popkiss.

ADELMAN, GARY: Executive. e. California State U., Long Beach State Coll. 1969, asst. dir. on feature, The Masterpiece; assoc. prod. on The Candy Snatchers. Produced first feature film, The Severed Arm, 1974. Assisted Winston Hock in development of 3-D process, 1975. 1976–82, pres. & COO of Monarch Prods. Post-prod. consultant for Jerry Gross Organization. 1983, founder and partial owner of New Image Releasing, Inc., new prod. & dist. co. Had post of secty./treas. 1987, named v.p., chg. prod., All-American Entertainment.

ADELMAN, JOSEPH A.: Executive. b. Winnipeg, Manitoba, Can., Dec. 27, 1933. e. NYU, B.A., 1954; Harvard Law Sch., J.D., 1957, graduated cum laude. Attorney, United Artists Corp., New York, 1958; named west coast counsel, Hollywood, 1964; named exec. asst. to the v.p. in charge of prod. 1968; named v.p., west coast business and legal affairs, 1972; appointed executive v.p., Association of Motion Pictures and Television Producers, 1977; appointed v.p. in chg. of business affairs, Paramount Pictures Corp., 1979; co-founder and exec. v.p. Kidpix, Inc. since 1984; founder and CEO of Kidpix Theaters Corp. since 1985; appointed senior v.p. for business/legal affairs, Color Systems Technology, Inc. 1986; named pres. of CST Entertainment, 1987. Admitted to NY, California and U.S. Supreme Court bars; member, Phi Beta Kappa; Alumni Achievement Award, NYU, 1982; American Bar Association; Los Angeles Copyright Society; Academy of Motion Picture Arts and Sciences; bd. of dirs., AMPTP, 1969–1979; National Assn. of Television Programming Executives.; bd. of trustees, Theatre Authority, 1970–79

ADELSON, GARY: Producer. b. 1954. e. UCLA (B.A.). Son of Merv Adelson. Joined Lorimar Prods. 1970 as prod. asst. on TV movie Helter Skelter. 1989: formed Adelson/Baumgarten Prods. with Craig Baumgarten.
TELEVISION: Helter Skelter (prod. asst.); Sybil (assoc. prod.); Eight Is Enough (prod.); The Blue Knight (prod.); Exec. prod.: Too Good To Be True, Our Family Business, Cass Malloy, John Steinbeck's The Winter of Our Discontent, Lace, Detective in the House, Lace II, Studio 5B (series.), Glitz.
PICTURE: The Last Starfighter (prod.), The Boy Who Could Fly, In The Mood, Tap, Seven Year Storm.

ADELSON, MERV: Producer. b. Los Angeles, CA, Oct. 23, 1929. e. UCLA. m. newscaster Barbara Walters. Pres., Markettown Builders Emporium, Las Vegas 1953–63; mgr. partner Paradise Dev. 1958–; pres. Realty Holdings 1962–; Bd. chmn., Lorimar Inc. 1969–86; chmn. bd. dirs. & CEO. Lorimar Telepictures 1986–.
PICTURES: Twilight's Last Gleaming, The Choirboys, Who Is Killing the Great Chefs of Europe?, Avalanche Express, The Big Red One.
TELEVISION: The Waltons, Eight Is Enough, Dallas, Kaz, The Waverly Wonders, Knots Landing, Sybil, A Man Called Intrepid, The Blue Knight, Helter-Skelter.

ADJANI, ISABELLE: Actress. b. Germany, June 27, 1955.
PICTURES: The Slap, The Story of Adele H., The Tenant, Faustine, Barocco, The Driver, Nosferatu—The Vampire, The Bronte Sisters, Quartet, Next Year If All Goes Well, One Deadly Summer, Subway, Ishtar, Possession, Camille Claudel, Henry & June.

ADLER, ALLEN: Executive Producer. b. New York, NY, 1946. e. Princeton U., B.A.; Harvard Business Sch., M.B.A. Started with Standard & Poor's Inter-Capital; then joined Alan Hirschfield at American Diversified Enterprises; next to Columbia Pictures 1973 as corporate officer. 1979, named sr. v.p., Columbia. 1981, teamed with Daniel Melnick in IndieProd Co.
PICTURE: Making Love.

ADRIAN, IRIS: Actress, r.n. Iris Adrian Hostetter. b. Los Angeles, CA, May 29, 1913. Dancer, on stage NY and abroad in Follies of 1931; m.p. debut in MGM two-reel color films.
PICTURES: Smart Woman, Out of the Storm, Paleface, Sky Dragon, There's a Girl in My Heart, Tough Assignment, Once a Thief, Always Leave Them Laughing, Stop That Cab, My Favorite Spy, Highway Magnet, Fast & The Furious, Crime Wave, Devil's Harbor, Carnival Rock, The Buccaneer, Blue Hawaii, The Errand Boy, Fate is the Hunter, That Darn Cat, The Odd Couple, The Love Bug, Freaky Friday.

AGAR, JOHN: Actor. b. Chicago, IL, Jan. 31, 1921. In service W.W.II. Film debut 1948: Fort Apache.
PICTURES: Adventure in Baltimore, I Married a Commu nist, Sands of Iwo Jima, She Wore a Yellow Ribbon, Breakthrough, Magic Carpet, Along the Great Divide, Woman of the North Country, Man of Conflict, Bait, Rocket Man, Shield for Murder, Golden Mistress, Revenge of the Creature, Hold Back Tomorrow, Tarantula, Star in the Dust, Joe Butterfly, St. Valentine's Day Massacre, Waco, Johnny Reno, Women of the Prehistoric Planet, Perfect Victims, Miracle Mile.

AGUTTER, JENNY: Actress. b. Taunton, England, 1952; e. Elmhurst Ballet Sch. m.p. debut East of Sudan, 1964. Emmy for best supporting actress, 1971; Variety Club of Grt. Britain Most Promising Artiste Award 1971; BAFTA best supporting actress award for Equus, 1976.
PICTURES: Ballerina, Gates of Paradise, Star!, I Start Counting, Walkabout, The Railway Children, War of Children, Logan's Run, The Eagle Has Landed, The Man in the Iron Mask, Equus, Dominique, Clayton & Catherine, The Riddle of the Sands, Sweet William, The Survivor, Amy, The American Werewolf, Secret Places, Dark Tower, King of the Wind, F.R.O.7.
PLAYS: School for Scandal, Rooted, Arms and the Man, The Ride Across Lake Constance, The Tempest, Spring Awakening, Hedda, Betrayal. Member, Royal Shakespeare Co.—King Lear, Arden of Taversham, The Body. Breaking the Silence, Shrew (Los Angeles), 1986.
TELEVISION: The Great Mr. Dickens, The Wild Duck, The Cherry Orchard, The Snow Goose, As Many as Are Here Present, A War of Children, The Man in the Iron Mask, A House in Regent Place, There's Love and Dove, Kiss Me and Die, A Legacy, The Waiting Room, Six Million Dollar Man, School Play, The Mayflower, Voyage of the Pilgrims, Beulah Land, Love's Labour's Lost, This Office Life, Magnum, The Two Ronnies, Silas Marner, The Twilight Zone, Murder She Wrote.

AIELLO, DANNY: Actor. b. June 20, 1933. On Broadway before entering films.
THEATER: Lampost Reunion, Wheelbarrow Closers, Knockout, The Floating Light Bulb, Hurlyburly, The House of Blue Leaves.
PICTURES: Blood Brothers, Fingers, Defiance, Hide in Plain Sight, Ft. Apache, the Bronx, Chu Chu and the Philly Flash, The Purple Rose of Cairo, Key Exchange, The Protector, Radio Days, Moonstruck, Man on Fire, The Pick-Up Artist, The January Man, Crack in the Mirror, Do the Right Thing, Russicum, Harlem Nights, Little Odessa, Jacob's Ladder.
TELEVISION: Family of Strangers (Emmy, 1981), Lady Blue, Daddy, Alone in the Neon Jungle.

AIMEE, ANOUK: Actress. r.n. Françoise Dreyfus. b. Paris France, April 27, 1934. Studied, Bauer-Therond dramatic school, Paris. Stage debut: 1946. La Maison Sous La Mer.
PICTURES: Les Amants De Verone, The Golden Salamander, Le Rideau Cramoisi, Nuit D'Orage, La Bergere et Le

Ramoneur (Cartoon), Mauvais Rencontres, Nina, Stresemann, Tous Peuvent Me Tuer, Pot Bouille, Modigliani of Montparnasse, Le Tete Contres Les Murs, Les Dragueurs, La Dolce Vita, Le Farceur, Lola, Les Amours de Paris L'Imprevu, 8½, Sodom and Gomorrah, La Fuga, A Man and a Woman, Un Soir, Un Train, The Appointment, The Model Shop, Justine, The Mandarins, Tragedy of a Ridiculous Man, Leap into the Void, A Man and A Woman: Twenty Years Later, The House of the Lord, Bethune: The Making of a Hero, Rabbit Face.

AKINS, CLAUDE: Actor. b. Nelson, GA, May 25, 1926. e. Northwestern U. Worked as salesman in Indiana before joining Barter Theatre for season. Came to New York; appeared in The Rose Tattoo. Spent several seasons with touring cos. Dinner Theater, Chicago, Houston, Jacksonville in Special Occasions, Goodbye Ghost, You Ought to Be in Pictures, Traveler in the Dark (L.A. Mark Taper Forum).
PICTURES: From Here to Eternity, The Caine Mutiny, Skyjacked, Flap, Devil's Brigade, Inherit the Wind, The Great Bank Robbery, Monster in the Closet, The Farm.
TELEVISION: Police Story, Cannon, McCloud, Marcus Welby, M.D., Mannix, The Streets of San Francisco, Movin' On, Sheriff Lobo and Nashville '99, Murder, She Wrote, Love Boat, Hotel. Series: The Misadventures of Sheriff Lobo. Mini-series: The Rhinemann Exchange, Dream West, Desperate Intruder, Celebrity. Movies: The Baron and the Kid, If It's Tuesday, It Still Must Be Belgium.

AKTER, MAHMOOD ALI KHAN: Producer, Distributor, Exhibitor: b. Hyderabad Deccan, India, April 12, 1926. Graduate of Arts. Formerly with Columbia Films of Pakistan Ltd., gen. mgr., Hussein & Co. controlling film dist. of United Artists Corp., Selznick Intl., London Films, Pathe Overseas. Participant foreign leaders prog. of Intl. Educational Exchange Service of U.S.A. State Dept.; mgr., Paramount Films of Pakistan, Ltd., 1959–64; mgr. dir., General Film Distributors, Lahore. Chmn., Motion Picture Importer's Group, Lahore, Mgr. dir., Pak Boor Corp.

ALBECK, ANDY: Executive. b. U.S.S.R., Sept. 25, 1921. Industry career began in 1939 with Columbia Pictures Intl. Corp. 1947, Central Motion Picture Exchange. 1949, Eagle Lion Classics, Inc. Joined UA in 1951 in intl. dept., functioning in the area of operations. After filling a number of key posts, named asst. treas. in 1970. In 1972 became v.p. of UA and its subsidiary, UA Broadcasting, Inc. 1973, appt. pres. of UA Broadcasting and in 1976 named sr. v.p.—operations. Named UA Corp. pres. & chief exec. officer in 1978. Retired, 1981.

ALBERGHETTI, ANNA MARIA: Singer, Actress. b. Pesaro, Italy, May 15, 1936; d. Daniele Alberghetti, cellist. Concert debut in 1948 in Pesaro, then toured Italy, Scandinavia, Spain; Am. debut Carnegie Hall, 1950, sang with NY Philharmonic Society, Phila. Symphony, on television. Screen debut in The Medium, 1950; Broadway stage debut: Carnival, 1962. (Tony Award for best actress).
PICTURES: Here Comes the Groom, Stars Are Singing, Last Command, 10,000 Bedrooms, Cinderfella.
TELEVISION: Toast of the Town, Cavalcade of Stars, Arthur Murray Show, Bob Hope, Eddie Fisher, Red Skelton, Dinah Shore, Desilu Playhouse, G.E. Theatre, Chevy Show, Dupont Show, Voice of Firestone, Colgate Hour, Climax, Loretta Young, Ford Jubilee, Perry Como.

ALBERT, EDDIE: Actor. r.n. Eddie Albert Heimberger. b. Rock Island, IL, April 22, 1908. e. U. of Minnesota. Radio NBC.
BROADWAY: Brother Rat, Say Darling, The Music Man, Room Service, The Boys from Syracuse, Seven Year Itch, Our Town, No Hard Feelings, Reuben Reuben, Miss Liberty, You Can't Take It With You.
PICTURES: Brother Rat, Four Wives, Angel from Texas, Dispatch from Reuter's, Rendezvous With Annie, Perfect Marriage, Smash-Up, The Story of a Woman, Time Out of Mind, Hit Parade of 1947, Dude Goes West, You Gotta Stay Happy, Fuller Brush Girl, You're in the Navy Now, Carrie, Meet Me After the Show, Actors and Sin, Roman Holiday, Girl Rush, I'll Cry Tomorrow, Oklahoma, Attack, Teahouse of the August Moon, Orders to Kill, Gun Runners, Roots of Heaven, The Young Doctors, The Longest Day, Captain Newman, The Heartbreak Kid, Miracle of the White Stallions, Seven Women, McQ, The Take, The Longest Yard, Escape to Witch Mountain, The Devil's Rain, Hustle, Birch Interval, Foolin' Around, Yesterday, The Concorde-Airport 79, The Border, Ladyfingers, How to Beat the High Cost of Living, Take This Job and Shove It, Yes, Giorgio, Bless 'em All, Dreamscape, Stitches, Head Office, Turnaround, The Big Picture, Brenda Starr, Accidents, Okavango.
TELEVISION: Green Acres, Switch!, The Yeagers, Benjamin Franklin, The Borrowers, Killer Bees, Nutcracker, Anything Goes, Crash, The Word, Evening in Byzantium, Pirates Key, Living in Paradise, Oklahoma Dolls, The Plan, Peter and Paul, The Fall Guy, Goliath Awaits, Concord, Beyond Witch Mountain, Rooster, Love Boat, Rhode Island Demon Murder, Coalfire, In Like Flynn, Dress Gray, Mercy or Murder?, Highway to Heaven, War and Remembrance, Falcon Crest, Murder She Wrote, thirtysomething.

ALBERT, EDWARD: Actor. b. Los Angeles, CA, Feb. 20, 1951. e. UCLA. Son of actor Eddie Albert and actress Margo. Was prod. asst. on Patton in Spain. Has appeared with father on radio and TV shows. Is photographer and has exhibited work in L.A.
PICTURES: Butterflies Are Free (debut), Forty Carats, Midway, The Domino Principle, The Greek Tycoon, When Time Ran Out, A Time To Die, Ellie, Getting Even, Distortions, The Underachievers, Fist Fighter, The Rescue, Mind Games.
TELEVISION: Falcon Crest, Beauty and the Beast. Movies: Killer Bees, Yellow Rose, The Last Convertible, Daddy Can't Read.

ALBRIGHT, LOLA: Actress. b. Akron, OH, July 20, 1925. e. Studied piano 12 years. Switchboard operator and stenographer NBC; stenographer with WHAM and bit player; photographers' model. Screen debut in The Pirate, 1948.
PICTURES: Easter Parade, Girl from Jones Beach, Tulsa, Champion, Good Humor Man, Bodyhold, When You're Smiling, Sierra Passage, Killer That Stalked New York, Arctic Flight, Silver Whip, Treasure of Ruby Hills, Magnificent Matador, Beauty on Parade, Tender Trap, A Cold Wind in August, Kid Galahad, Lord Love a Duck, Where Were You When the Lights Went Out?, The Impossible Years, The Money Jungle.
TELEVISION: Switch, The Eddie Capra Mysteries, Quincy, Airwolf.

ALCAINE, JOSE LUIS: Cinematographer. b. Tangier, Algeria, Dec. 26, 1938. e. Spanish Cinema Sch., Madrid. After graduation joined Madrid's Studio Moros doing commercials.
PICTURES: El Puente, El Sur, Taseo, Rustlers' Rhapsody, The Mad Monkey.

ALDA, ALAN: Actor, Writer, Director r.n. Alphonso D'Abruzzo b. New York, NY, Jan. 28, 1936. e. Fordham U., 1956 Son of actor Robert Alda. Studied at Cleveland Playhouse on Ford Foundation Grant; performed with Second City, then on TV in That Was The Week That Was. Has won 5 Emmys, 2 Writer Guild Awards, 3 Directors Guild Awards, 5 Golden Globes, 7 People's Choice Awards, Humanitas Award for Writing.
THEATER: Bdwy: The Owl and The Pussycat, Purlie Victorious, Fair Game For Lovers (Theatre World Award), The Apple Tree (Tony Award nom.).
PICTURES: Gone Are The Days, The Moonshine War, Jenny, The Mephisto Waltz, Paper Lion, To Kill a Clown, Same Time Next Year, California Suite, The Seduction of Joe Tynan (also s.p.), The Four Seasons (actor, dir., s.p.), Sweet Liberty (actor, dir., s.p.), A New Life (actor, dir., s.p.), Joint Venture.
TELEVISION: M*A*S*H (11 years), Isn't It Shocking?, Playmates, The Glass House, Kill Me If You Can, Free to Be You and Me, 6 Rms Riv Vu (actor, dir.); Created series We'll Get By and The Four Seasons.

ALDREDGE, THEONI V.: Costume designer. b. Salonika, Greece, Aug. 22, 1932. m. actor Tom Aldredge. e. American School, Athens; Goodman Theatre School, Chicago, 1949–52. Broadway: Timon of Athens, Two Gentlemen of Verona, A Chorus Line, Annie, 42nd Street, etc.
PICTURES: You're A Big Boy Now, No Way to Treat a Lady, Uptight, Last Summer, I Never Sang for My Father, Promise at Dawn, The Great Gatsby, Network, Semi-Tough, The Cheap Detective, The Fury, Eyes of Laura Mars, The Champ, The Rose, Rich and Famous, Middle Age Crazy, Annie, Ghostbusters, Racing With the Moon, Moonstruck.

ALEANDRO, NORMA: Actress. b. Argentina, 1941. Sister is actress Maria Vaner. As child, performed in parents, in theater troupe. In Argentina performed in every theatrical genre and epoch. Was also director. Has written published short stories (1986) and poems and screenplay for Argentinian film, Los Herederos. Was in exile in Uruguay (18 months) and Spain 1976–82 because of the military junta in Argentina. Before exile had made 12 films; after return in 1982 starred in theatre and 7 films.
THEATER: U.S.: About Love and Other Stories (one-woman show), toured South America, then at La Mama and later off-Bdwy at Public Theater (1986); The Senorita of Tacna (written for her by Mario Vargas-Llosa, 1987).
PICTURES: The Official Story (best actress award, Cannes Film Fest., 1986, shared with Cher); Gaby: A True Story (Acad. Award nom.); Cousins, Vital Signs.
TELEVISION: Movie: Dark Holiday.

ALEXANDER, JANE: Actress. b. Boston, MA, Oct. 28, 1939. r.n. Jane Quigley. m. director Edwin Sherrin. Mother of actor Jace Alexander. e. Sarah Lawrence Coll., U. of Edinburgh. Stage career includes appearances on Broadway, at Arena Stage, Washington, and Shakespeare Festival at Stamford, Conn.
THEATER: NY: The Great White Hope (Tony Award, 1969); Six Rms Riv Vu, Find Your Way Home, Hamlet, The Heiress,

First Monday in October, Losing Time, Monday After the Miracle, Old Times, Night of the Iguana, Approaching Zanzibar.

PICTURES: The Great White Hope, A Gunfight, The New Centurions, All the President's Men, Kramer vs. Kramer, Brubaker, The Betsy, Night Crossing, Testament, City Heat, Square Dance, Sweet Country, Glory, O'Keefe & Stieglitz.

TELEVISION: Welcome Home Johny Bristol, Miracle on 34th St., Death Be Not Proud, Circle of Children, Lovey, Eleanor and Franklin, Eleanor and Franklin: The White House Years, In the Custody of Strangers, Playing for Time (Emmy Award), When She Says No, Calamity Jane, Malice in Wonderland, Blood & Orchids, In Love and War, Open Admissions, A Friendship in Vienna, Daughter of the Streets. Special: Mountain View.

ALEXANDER, RALPH: Executive. Began career with Universal Pictures in sales, 1949; various sls. jobs with 20th Century Fox and Lorimar. 1981–82, v.p., theatrical foreign sls., Filmway Pictures; 1982–84, v.p., sls, for Latin America & Southeast Asia, Embassy Pictures Intl. 1984, exec. v.p., multimedia foreign sls. for Robert Meyers Intl. Nov., 1985, joined Dino De Laurentiis Corp. as intl. sls. dir. in chg. all foreign sls. theatrical and ancillary rights except tv. 1986, promoted to v.p., intl. sls., DEG; pres. marketing and sales, Kings Road Intl.—1989; joined Scotti Bros. Pictures as pres. intl. sales and marketing, 1989.

ALGAR, JAMES: Producer, Writer, Director. b. Modesto, CA, June 11, 1912. e. Stanford U., B.A., M.A. journalism. Entire career since 1934 with Walt Disney Prods. Wrote and co-produced Great Moments with Mr. Lincoln; New York World's Fair; Circarama, America the Beautiful, Circle Vision 1958 Brussels World's Fair, Disneyland, Hall of Presidents, Disney World, Florida. Shares in nine Oscars.

DOCUMENTARIES: war. health. True-Life Adventures: Seal Island, The Living Desert, Vanishing Prairie, The African Lion, Secrets of Life.

FEATURES: Animator: Snow White; Director: Fantasia, Bambi, Wind in the Willows, Ichabod & Mr. Toad, Ten Who Dared, The Incredible Journey, Gnome-Mobile, White Wilderness, Rascal, The Legend of Lobo, The Jungle Cat, Run, Cougar, Run.

TELEVISION: Producer: Run Light Buck, Run, The Not So Lonely Lighthouse Keeper, One Day on Beetle Rock, Wild Heart, Along the Oregon Trail, The Best Doggoned Dog in the World, One Day at Teton Marsh, Solomon, the Sea Turtle, Manado the Wolverine, Wild Geese Calling, Two Against the Arctic, Bayou Bay, Secrets of the Pond, Boy Who Talked to Badgers, Big Sky Man.

ALIN, MORRIS: Editor, Writer, Publicist, Lyricist. e. City Coll. of New York. Came into m.p. industry, auditor of Hunchback of Notre Dame, roadshow oper., 1924; asst. sls. prom. mgr. Universal, 1926–27; slsmn., Universal, 1927; assoc. editor. The Distributor, MGM publication, 1927; editor, 1928–33; writer, publicist, MGM Studio, 1933–34; writer, publicist, Hollywood, New York, 1935–38; rej. Universal. 1938, editor, Progress: (Univ. publication); Twice winner of award, International Competition on Industrial Journalism; Senior publicist and Progress editor, Universal, 1961–67; editor Enterprise Press, 1968; member, executive Enterprise Press 1973; American Guild of Authors and Composers, American Society of Composers, Authors and Publishers, National Academy of Popular Music, and Motion Picture Pioneers.

ALLAN, TED: b. Clifton, AZ. Comm. artist, actor SAG 1945, cameraman; photo training at Technicolor, Consolidated, MGM labs.; portrait photog., MGM, 20th-Century Fox, Selznick; created own film studio, 1952, prod. M.P. features, TV series, & pilots; Dir. of photog. 1956; 2 yr. contract Sinatra Enter.; 9 yrs. head CBS Cam. Dept. Hollywood; 3 yrs. 20th Cen. Fox, Pub-Stills & Featurettes for Von Ryan's Express, Fantastic Voyage, Sand Pebbles, Dr. Doolittle, The Detective, Lady in Cement, Tora, Tora, Tora. Featurettes for Universal: Seven Per Cent Solution, Hindenburg, Rollercoaster, Two Minute Warning, Gray Lady Down, The Promise, Dracula, Same Time Next Year.

ALLAND, WILLIAM: Producer. b. Delmar, DE, March 4, 1916. e. Baltimore. Acted in semi-professional groups; with Orson Welles' Mercury Theatre as actor, stage mgr.; asst. prod. Mercury Theatre radio series; actor, dialogue dir., Citizen Kane; act., Macbeth; U.S. Air Force, W.W.II; then radio writer; prod., Universal, 1952.

PICTURES: The Raiders, Flesh and Fury, Stand At Apache River, It Came From Outer Space, Creature From The Black Lagoon, Johnny Dark, This Island Earth, Dawn At Socorro, Four Guns To The Border, Chief Crazy Horse, Revenge Of The Creature, Tarantula, Creature Walks Among Us, Gun for a Coward, Land Unknown, Deadly Mantis, Mole People, Raw Wind in Eden, The Lady Takes a Flyer, As Young As We Are; The Party Crashers, Colossus of New York, The Space Children; Look In Any Window, The Lively Set, The Rare Breed, The Lawless Breed, Director: Look In Any Window.

ALLEN, COREY: Director, Actor. r.n. Alan Cohen. b. Cleveland, OH, June 29, 1934. e. UCLA, 1951–54; UCLA law sch. 1954–55. Actor turned dir. starred in Oscar-winning UCLA student film, appeared in 20 plays at Players Ring, Players Gallery and other L.A. theaters. Films as actor: Rebel Without a Cause (1955), Sweet Bird of Youth, Private Property, Party Girl, The Chapman Report; TV: Perry Mason, Alfred Hitchcock Presents. With partner John Herman Shaner, prod. Freeway Circuit Theatre. Led Actors Workshop with actor Guy Stockwell for 10 years.

PICTURES: Pinocchio, Thunder and Lightning, Avalanche.

TELEVISION: Director: This is the Life, Mannix, High Chaparral, Dr. Kildare, Streets of San Francisco, Ironside, Barnaby Jones, Police Woman, Rockford Files, Quincy, Dallas, Lou Grant, McClain's Law, Family Hovak, T.J. Hooker, Paper Chase: The Second Year, Hill Street Blues (Emmy), Sonny Spoons, Supercarrier, *Pilots*: Man Undercover, Stone, Capitol, Simon and Simon, Whiz Kids, Codename: Foxfire, Murder She Wrote, Star Trek: The Next Generation. Unsub. Movies: See the Man Run, Cry Rape!, Yesterday's Child, The Return of Frank Cannon, Man in the Santa Claus Suit, Brass, I-Man, Destination America, Beverly Hills Cowgirl Blues, The Last Fling, Ann Jillian Story.

ALLEN, DAYTON: Performer. b. New York, NY, Sept. 24, 1919. e. Mt. Vernon H.S. Motion picture road shows, 1936–40; disc jockey, WINS, N.Y., 1940–41; writer, vaudeville comedy bits, 1941–45; then radio comic, puppeteer and voices; TV since 1948; film commercials; shows include Oaky Doky, Bonny Maid Varieties, Howdy Doody, Jack Barry's Winky Dink, Abe Lincoln in Illinois, The Circle of Chalk, The Steve Allen Show.

ALLEN, DEBBIE: Actress, Choreographer. b. Houston, TX, Jan. 16, 1950. Sister of actress Phylicia Rashad. e. Howard U. Debut on television as one of the three women on NBC series 3 Girls 3 (1977).

THEATER: Ti-Jean and His Brothers (debut, 1972), Purlie, Raisin, Ain't Misbehavin', West Side Story (revival), Sweet Charity (revival, Tony Award, 1986), Carrie (choreographer).

PICTURES: The Fish That Saved Pittsburgh (1979), Fame, Ragtime, Jo Jo Dancer, Your Life is Calling.

TELEVISION: Series: The Jim Stafford Show (1975), Roots—The Next Generation, Ben Vereen—His Roots; Fame (series; 3 Emmys as choreographer, 1 nom. as actress), A Different World (prod., dir). Movies: The Greatest Thing That Almost Happened, Ebony, Ivory and Jade, Women of San Quentin, Celebrity. Specials: Loretta Lynn in Big Apple Country, Texaco Star Theater—Opening Night, The Kids from Fame, John Schneider's Christmas Holiday; A Tribute to Martin Luther King Jr.—A Celebration of Life, Motown Returns to the Apollo; The Debbie Allen Special (dir., chor.).

ALLEN, DEDE: Film editor. b. 1924. Once a messenger at Columbia Pictures, moved to editing dept., then to commercials and features.

PICTURES: Odds Against Tomorrow (1959), America, America, Bonnie and Clyde, Rachel Rachel, Alice's Restaurant, Little Big Man, Serpico, Dog Day Afternoon, Slapshot, The Wiz, Reds (also exec. prod.), Harry and Son, Mike's Murder, The Breakfast Club, Off Beat, The Milagro Beanfield War (co-ed.), Let It Ride (co-ed.).

ALLEN, IRWIN: Producer. b. New York, NY, June 12, e. Columbia U., City Coll. of New York, journalism & adv. ed. Hollywood; radio prod. dir., daily Hollywood program, 11 yrs.; radio & literary dir., own agency; then M.P. prod.

PICTURES: Double Dynamite, Girl in Every Port (co-prod.); Where Danger Lives (assoc., prod.); Dangerous Mission (prod.); The Animal World (prod.); The Story of Mankind (prod., dir., co-s.p.); Sea Around Us (prod., writer, director) (Academy Award); The Big Circus (prod., co-s.p.), The Lost World (prod., dir., co-s.p.), Voyage to the Bottom of the Sea (prod., dir., co-s.p.), Five Weeks in a Balloon (prod., dir., co-s.p.), The Poseidon Adventure (prod., dir. action sequences), The Towering Inferno (prod., dir. action sequences), The Swarm (prod., dir.); Beyond the Poseidon Adventure (prod., dir.); When Time Ran Out (prod.).

TELEVISION: Creator-prod., Voyage to the Bottom of the Sea, Lost in Space, Land of the Giant, The Time Tunnel, Adventures of the Queen, Swiss Family Robinson, Flood, Fire, The Return of Captain Nemo, Hanging by a Thread, Cave-In, Night the Bridge Fell Down, Memory of Eva Ryker. Producer: Code Red, Alice in Wonderland.

ALLEN, JAY PRESSON: Writer, Producer. b. Fort Worth, TX, March 3, 1922. m. prod. Lewis M. Allen. Playwright: Prime of Miss Jean Brodie, Forty Carats.

PICTURES: Marnie, Prime of Miss Jean Brodie, Travels with My Aunt, Cabaret, Funny Lady, Just Tell Me What You Want, It's My Turn (also exec. prod.), Prince of the City (s.p. & exec. prod.), Deathtrap (exec. prod.), Lord of the Flies.

TELEVISION: Family (creator), Clinic, Hothouse.

ALLEN, JOAN: Actress. b. Rochelle, IL, Aug. 20, 1956. Founding member of Steppenwolf Theatre Co., in Chicago where she performed in over 20 shows including A Lesson from Aloes,

Three Sisters, The Miss Firecracker Contest, Cloud 9, Balm in Gilead, Fifth of July. Off Broadway in The Marriage of Bette and Boo, And a Nightingale Sang (Clarence Derwent, Drama Desk, Outer Critics' Circle and Theatre World Awards). Broadway debut: Burn This (1987, Tony Award), The Heidi Chronicles.

PICTURES: Compromising Positions (debut, 1985), Manhunter, Peggy Sue Got Married, Tucker: The Man and His Dream, In Country.

TELEVISION: All My Sons.

ALLEN, KAREN: Actress. b. Carrollton, IL, Oct. 5, 1951. e. George Washington U., U. of Maryland. Auditioned for theatrical company in Washington, DC and won a role in Saint, touring with it for 7 months. Spent several years with Washington Theatre Laboratory Co. Moved to NY, acting in student films at NYU and studying acting with Lee Strasberg at Theatre Institute. Major film debut in National Lampoon's Animal House in 1978.

THEATER: Broadway debut: The Monday After the Miracle (Theatre World Award), Tennessee Williams: A Celebration (Williamstown Theatre, MA), Extremities, The Glass Menagerie, (Williamstown), The Miracle Worker.

PICTURES: Manhattan, The Wanderers, Cruising, A Small Circle of Friends, Raiders of the Lost Ark, Shoot the Moon, Split Image, Strange Invaders, Until September, Starman, The End of the Line, The Glass Menagerie, Animal Behavior, Scrooged, Secret Places of the Heart, Confidence, Exile.

TELEVISION: Circle of Children, Part II, East of Eden (1979), Alfred Hitchcock Presents (1986), Backfire.

ALLEN, LEWIS: Director. b. Shropshire, England, Dec. 25, 1905. e. Tettenhall Coll., Staffs, Eng. Exec. in chg. of N.Y. & London prod. for Gilbert Miller; actor & stage dir. N.Y. & England; dir. (N.Y.) Laburnum Grove, Amazing Doctor Clitterhouse, Ladies & Gentlemen; (London) The Women, studied m.p. prod. at Paramount 2 yrs.; appt. dir. with debut of The Uninvited 1943.

PICTURES: Our Hearts Were Young and Gay, The Unseen, Those Endearing Young Charms, The Perfect Marriage, The Imperfect Lady, Desert Fury, So Evil My Love, Sealed Verdict, Chicago Deadline, Valentino, Appointment with Danger, At Sword's Point, Suddenly, A Bullet For Joey, Illegal, Another Time Another Place, Whirlpool, Decision at Midnight.

ALLEN, LEWIS M.: Producer. b. Berryville, VA, 1922. m. writer-producer Jay Presson Allen.

PICTURES: The Connection, The Balcony, Lord of the Flies, Fahrenheit 451, Fortune and Men's Eyes, Never Cry Wolf, Swimming to Cambodia, 1918, End of the Line (co-prod.), Miss Firecracker (exec. prod.), Lord of the Flies (exec. prod., remake).

ALLEN, MEL: TV commentator b. Birmingham, AL, Feb. 14, 1913. e. U. of Alabama, A.B. 1932; U. Alabama Law Sch., LL.B. 1936. Started as sportscaster in Birmingham, while in law school; speech instructor in U. Ala. 1935–37; to N.Y. 1937, as staff announcer CBS to 1943; served in U.S. Army W.W.II in infantry until the war ended, then before discharge was transferred to work on NBC Army Hour; sportscasting throughout U.S., joined N.Y. Yankees, 1946, concurrently narrating many shorts incl. How to Make a Yankee, appearing on radio & video and in Babe Ruth Story; sports commentator Fox Movietonews; voted best sportscaster in Motion Picture Daily-Fame radio. TV polls; Monitor, NBC; NCAA TV College Football, NBC; World Series (1938–64), CBS-NBC; Rose Bowl (1951–62), NBC; Sports Broadcasters Hall Of Fame.

ALLEN, NANCY: Actress. b. New York, NY, June 24, 1950. e. H.S. Performing Arts, N.Y.

PICTURES: The Last Detail, Carrie, I Wanna Hold Your Hand, Home Movies, 1941, Dressed to Kill, Blow Out, Strange Invaders, The Buddy System, The Philadelphia Experiment, The Last Victim, Not for Publication, Terror in the Aisles, Robocop, Poltergeist III, Sweet Revenge, Out of the Dark, Limit Up.

TELEVISION: Movie: The Gladiator.

ALLEN, REX: Actor. b. Wilcox, AZ, Dec. 31, 1922. e. Wilcox H.S., 1939. Vaudeville & radio actor; WLS, Chicago, 5 yrs.; was rodeo star appearing in shows through U.S.

PICTURES: Arizona Cowboy, Hills of Oklahoma, Under Mexicali Stars, Thunder in God's Country, Rodeo King & the Senorita, I Dream of Jeannie, Last Musketeer, South Pacific Trail, Old Overland Trail, Down Laredo Way, Phantom Stallion, For the Love of Mike, Tomboy and the Champ; narr., Walt Disney.

TELEVISION: Perry Como Special; commercials, Wonderful World of Color (NBC) Frontier Doctor.

RECORDINGS: Crying in The Chapel, Don't Go Near the Indians, Warner Bros. Records. 1966 Radio Man of the Year; 1966 Cowboy Hall of Fame.

ALLEN, STEVE: Performer. b. New York, NY, Dec 26, 1921. m. actress Jayne Meadows. U.S. Army 1942; radio shows, Los Angeles; TV, N.Y., 1950; shows include: What's My Line, Steve Allen Show, Tonight, I've Got a Secret, Meeting of Minds, Laughback.

PICTURES: Down Memory Lane, Warning Shot, I'll Get By, Benny Goodman Story, College Confidential, Amazon Women on the Moon, Great Balls of Fire!

COMPOSER OR LYRICIST: This Could Be the Start of Something Big, Pretend You Don't See Her, South Rampart St. Parade, Picnic, Houseboat, On the Beach, Sleeping Beauty, Bell, Book and Candle, Gravy Waltz, Impossible, Score for Broadway musical Sophie, and TV musicals The Bachelor, and Alice in Wonderland.

AUTHOR: Fourteen For Tonight, Steve Allen's Bop Fables, The Funny Men, Wry On the Rocks, The Girls on the Tenth Floor, The Question Man, Mark It and Strike It, Not All of Your Laughter, Not All of Your Tears, Bigger Than a Breadbox, A Flash of Swallows, The Wake, Princess Snip-Snip and the Puppykittens, Curses, Schmock-Schmock!, Meeting of Minds, Ripoff, Meeting of Minds-Second Series, Rip-off, Explaining China, The Funny People, Talk Show Murders, Beloved Son: Story of the Jesus Cults, More Funny People, How To Make a Speech and How To Be Funny, Murder on the Glitter Box, The Passionate Non-smoker's Bill of Rights.

ALLEN, WOODY: Actor, Director, Writer. r.n. Allen Stewart Konigsberg. b. New York, NY, Dec. 1, 1935. e. student NYU, 1953; City Coll. NY, 1953. Began writing comedy at age 17, contributing to various magazines (Playboy, New Yorker) and top TV comedy shows incl. Sid Caesar (1957), Art Carney (1958–59), Herb Shriner (1953). Appeared in nightclubs since 1961 and as a jazz musician at Michael's Pub, NY. Special Award, Berlin Film Fest., 1975.

BOOKS: Getting Even, Without Feathers, Side Effects.

STAGE: Author of Play It Again, Sam; Don't Drink The Water, The Floating Lightbulb.

PICTURES: What's New Pussycat? (story, s.p., actor); Casino Royale (actor); What's Up Tiger Lily? (dubbed); *Director, screenplay and actor:* Take the Money and Run ; Bananas; Everything You Always Wanted to Know About Sex* But Were Afraid to Ask; Sleeper; Love and Death; The Front (actor only); Annie Hall; Interiors (dir., s.p. only); Manhattan ; Stardust Memories; A Midsummer Night's Sex Comedy; Zelig; Broadway Danny Rose ; The Purple Rose of Cairo (dir., s.p. only); Hannah and Her Sisters; Radio Days (dir., s.p. only); King Lear (actor only); September (dir., s.p. only); Another Woman (dir., s.p. only); New York Stories (dir., s.p., actor, Oedipus Wrecks segment).

ALLEY, KIRSTIE: Actress. b. Wichita, KS, Jan. 12, 1955. m. actor Parker Stevenson. e. KS State U., U. of Kansas.

PICTURES: One More Chance, Star Trek II—The Wrath of Khan; Blind Date; Champions; Runaways, Look Who's Talking, Loverboy, Madhouse.

TELEVISION: Series: Masquerade, Cheers. Movies: Tow Heads: Highway Honeys; A Midsummers Night's Dream, A Bunny's Tale; North and South.

ALLYSON, JUNE: Actress. r.n. Ella Geisman. b. Westchester, NY, Oct. 7, 1917. Started as chorus girl in school; m.p. debut in Best Foot Forward (1943). Voted one of ten best money-making stars in Motion Picture Herald-Fame poll, 1955.

BROADWAY: Best Foot Forward, 40 Carats, No No Nanette (national co.).

PICTURES: Girl Crazy, Thousands Cheer, Meet the People, Two Girls and a Sailor, Secret Heart, Reformer and Redhead, Right Cross, Too Young to Kiss, Girl in White, Battle Circus, Remains to be Seen, The Stratton Story, Little Women, Executive Suite, Glenn Miller Story, Woman's World, Strategic Air Command, The Strike, McConnell Story, You Can't Run Away From It, Opposite Sex, Interlude, My Man Godfrey, Stranger In My Arms, They Only Kill Their Masters, That's Entertainment!

TELEVISION': The June Allyson Show, Murder She Wrote, The Misfits of Science. Movies: See the Man Run, Three on a Date, The Kid With the Broken Halo, 20th Century Follies.

ALMENDROS, NESTOR: Cinematographer. b. Barcelona, Spain, Oct. 30, 1930. e. Havana U. (Ph.D.). Worked with numerous directors in Europe—notably Eric Rohmer and François Truffaut—before coming to U.S. Decorated Chevalier, Order of Arts and Letters, France (1976). Author: A Man With a Camera (1980).

PICTURES: La Collectionneuse, My Night at Maud's, Clare's Knee, Chloe in the Afternoon, Perceval, The Wild Child, The Man Who Loved Women, Two English Girls, The Story of Adele H., The Marquise of O, The Last Metro, Days of Heaven (Oscar, 1978), Goin' South, Madame Rosa, Kramer vs. Kramer, The Green Room, Love on the Run, The Valley, The Blue Lagoon, Still of the Night, Sophie's Choice, Improper Conduct (dir.), Heartburn, Places in the Heart, Nadine, Nobody Listened (co-prod., co-dir., with Jorge Ulla), New York Stories (Life Lessons).

ALMODÓVAR, PEDRO: Director, Writer. b. La Mancha, Spain, Sept. 25, 1951. Grew up in Calzada de Calatrava. At 17 moved to Madrid where worked 10 years for telephone co.

while writing comic strips and articles for underground newspapers and working as actor with independent theater co., Los Goliardos. Upon the end of Francoist repression in 1975, made Super-8 experimental films starring friends: Screw, Screw Me Tim. Wrote fiction, sang with rock band, published pornographic fotonovela (Todo Tuya), and created character of porn star, Patty Diphusa, whose fictionalized confessions he published under female pseudonym.
PICTURES: Pepi, Lucy, Bom, and Other Girls on the Heap (1980, cost $30,000), Labyrinth of Passion, What Have I Done to Deserve This? Dark Habits, Matador, Law of Desire, Women on the Verge of a Nervous Breakdown, Tie Me Up, Tie Me Down.

ALMOND, PAUL: Producer, Director, Writer. b. Montreal, Canada, April 26, 1931. e. McGill U., Balliol Coll., Oxford U. 1954–66 produced and directed over a hundred television dramas in Toronto, London, N.Y., and Hollywood; prod., dir., s.p., Isabel 1968, Act of the Heart; Etrog (dir.; best Canadian feature); Journey; Ups and Downs; Captive Hearts (dir.).

ALONSO, MARIA CONCHITA: Actress, Singer. b. Cuba, 1957. Family moved to Venezuela when she was five. 1971, named Miss Teenager of the World. 1975, Miss Venezuela. Appeared in four feature films and 10 soap operas before coming to U.S. Recorded several albums as singer, 3 gold albums.
PICTURES: Fear City, Moscow on the Hudson, Touch and Go, A Fine Mess, Extreme Prejudice, Colors, The Running Man, Vampire's Kiss.
TELEVISION: An American Cousin (RAI mini-series), Viva Miami!, The Night of the Super Sounds (host), One of the Boys (series).

ALONZO, JOHN A: Cinematographer, Director. b. Dallas, TX, 1934.
PICTURES: Bloody Mama; Vanishing Point; Chinatown; Harold and Maude; Lady Sings the Blues; Sounder; Pete 'n' Tillie; Conrack; Farewell, My Lovely; The Fortune; I Will . . . I Will . . . For Now; Once Is Not Enough; The Bad News Bears; Black Sunday; Beyond Reason; Casey's Shadow; Close Encounters of the Third Kind; Which Way Is Up?; The Cheap Detective; Norma Rae; Tom Horn; Back Roads; Zorro, The Gay Blade; Blue Thunder; Cross Creek; Scarface; Out of Control; Runaway; Terror in the Aisles; Jo Jo Dancer, Your Life Is Calling; Nothing in Common; 50 Years of Action, Overboard, Real Men, Physical Evidence.
TELEVISION: Champions, A Love Story; Belle Star (also dir.); Blinded By the Light (also dir.); The Kid From Nowhere (also dir.); Roots: The Gift.

ALTERMAN, JOSEPH GEORGE: Executive. b. New Haven, CT., Dec. 17, 1919. e. Wesleyan U., B.A., 1942; Inst. for Organization Management, Yale U. 1957–59. Exec. assist., SoundScriber Corp., 1945–48; district mgr., Industrial Luncheon Service, 1948–55; asst. secretary and admin. Secretary, Theatre Owners of America, 1955; Exec. dir. and vice pres., Natl. Assn. of Theatre Owners, 1966; Exec. v.p. COMPO., 1970. Retired Sept. 1988 from NATO. Consultant m.p. industry conventions and meetings.

ALTMAN, ROBERT: Director, Writer, Producer. b. Kansas City, MO, Feb. 20, 1925. e. U. of Missouri.
PICTURES: Debut: The James Dean Story, (1957, co-prod.); The Delinquents (dir.), Countdown (dir.), That Cold Day in the Park, M*A*S*H; s.p. and dir.; McCabe & Mrs. Miller, Brewster McCloud, Images, The Long Goodbye, Thieves Like Us, California Split, Nashville, Buffalo Bill and the Indians, The Late Show (prod.) Welcome to L.A. (prod.), Three Women (prod., dir., s.p.); A Wedding (prod., dir.); Remember My Name (prod.); Quintet (prod., dir.); A Perfect Couple (prod., dir.); Rich Kids (prod.); Health (prod., dir., s.p.), Popeye (dir.); Come Back to the Five & Dime, Jimmie Dean, Jimmie Dean (co-prod., dir.): Streamers (co-prod., dir.); Fool For Love (dir.), Beyond Therapy (dir., co-s.p.); Secret Honor (prod., dir.), Aria (sequence), O.C. and Stiggs.
THEATER: Come Back to the Five & Dime, Jimmy Dean, Jimmy Dean (dir. on Broadway, 1982).
TELEVISION: Wrote, prod. and dir.: Roaring Twenties, Bonanza, Bus Stop, Combat, Kraft Theatre, The Gallant Men (pilot), The Laundromat, Tanner '88 (dir., co-prod.) The Dumb Waiter, The Room, The Caine Mutiny Court-Martial (dir., co-prod.), Vincent and Theo (mini-series).

ALTON, JOHN: Cinematographer. b. Hungary, Oct. 5, 1901. Laboratory technician, MGM 1924; Paramount cameraman 1928; sent to Paris, France, chg. camera dept., 1931; installed studios for Lumiton & Sono Film (South America); writer, photographer & dir. many Spanish pictures; returned to U.S. 1937, cinematographer Hollywood; served in U.S. Signal Corps as Capt., W.W.II. Books include: Painting With Light, Photography and Lighting in General; received Sintonia Medal for best photography in Argentina, 1937. Academy Award best color photog. American in Paris ballet, 1951.
PICTURES: Witness to Murder, Big Combo, Catered Affair. Member: ASC, AMPAS.

ALVIN, JOHN: Actor. r.n. John Alvin Hoffstadt; b. Chicago, IL, Oct. 24, 1917. e. Pasadena Playhouse, CA. On radio Chicago & Detroit; on N.Y. stage Leaning on Letty, Life of the Party. Screen debut 1944 in Destination Tokyo. Under contract four years to Warner Bros., featured in 25 films.
PICTURES: Objective Burma, Destination Tokyo, San Antonio, Beast With Five Fingers, Night and Day, Cheyenne, Missing Women, Two Guys from Texas, Bold Frontiersman, Train to Alcatraz, Shanghai Chest, Carrie, April In Paris, Roughly Speaking, The Very Thought of You, Shadow of a Woman, Three Strangers, Romance on the High Seas, Torpedo Alley, Irma La Douce, Legend of Lylah Claire, Mr. Tibbs, Marnie, Inside Daisy Clover, They Shoot Horses, Don't They?, Somewhere in Time.
TELEVISION: Meet Millie, Burns and Allen, Death Valley Days, Asphalt Jungle, Climax, Dragnet, Jack Benny Show, My Three Sons, The Texan, Adventures in Paradise, Rawhide, Rifleman, Omnibus, Wells Fargo, Alfred Hitchcock, Mannix, I Spy, Legend of Lizzie Borden, All in the Family, McDuff, Lineup, My Favorite Husband, Family Affair, The Incredible Hulk, The Lucy Show, Ironside, Nightstalker, MASH, Lou Grant Show, Hart to Hart, Yellow Rose, Dennis the Menace (2 Hour Pilot), Murder She Wrote, Monster Squad, House of Evil, Aftermash, General Hospital, Starsky & Hutch, Policewoman, Amazing Stories, Capitol, Passions, The Quest, Visions/KCET, Rachel, Sweet Rachel, Swallows Came Back.

AMATEAU, ROD: Director. b. New York, NY, Dec. 20, 1927. Staff writer, CBS radio; stage mgr., Lux Radio Theatre; U.S. Army, 1941; junior writer, 20th Century-Fox; then test dir., second unit dir.
TELEVISION: Schlitz Playhouse of Stars, Four Star Playhouse, General Electric Theatre, Private Secretary, Dennis Day Show, Lassie, Ray Milland Show, Bob Cummings Show, dir. & prod. Burns & Allen Show, Dobie Gillis. Movies: Swimsuit (prod.).
PICTURES: The Statue, Where Does It Hurt?, The Wilby Conspiracy, Drive-In, Lovelines, Sunset (story), Garbage Pail Kids (s.p., prod., dir.), One Is Hawaii (dir.).

AMECHE, DON: Actor. b. Kenosha, WI, May 31, 1908. r.n. Dominick Amici. e. Columbia Coll., U. of Wisconsin. In stock; on radio (incl. Chase & Sanborn Hour, The Bickersons). 1938 appeared in Beauty (short at World's Fair); m.p. debut 1936. In television from 1951; on Broadway in Silk Stockings, (1955); Holiday For Lovers, Goldilocks, 13 Daughters, Henry Sweet Henry, Our Town.
PICTURES: Sins of Man, Ladies in Love, Ramona, You Can't Have Everything, Alexander's Ragtime Band, Midnight, Swanee River, Four Sons, The Story of Alexander Graham Bell, Lillian Russel, That Night in Rio, Kiss the Boys Goodbye, Heaven Can Wait, So Goes My Love, That's My Man, Sleep My Love, Slightly French, A Fever in the Blood, Ring Around the World, Picture Mommy Dead, Suppose They Gave a War & Nobody Came, The Boatniks, Trading Places, Cocoon, Harry and the Hendersons, Coming to America, Things Change (best actor award Venice Film Fest., 1988); Cocoon: The Return.
TELEVISION: International Showtime (host 1961–65), A Masterpiece of Murder, Pals, Mr. Smith, The Love Boat, Not in Front of the Kids (pilot), Detective in the House.

AMES, LEON: Actor. r.n. Leon Wycoff. b. Portland, IN, Jan. 20, 1903. Aviator; with Champlin Players, Lansford, PA, in stock and on stage; plays include: Tobacco Road, Male Animal, Land Is Bright; m.p. debut in Murders in the Rue Morgue, 1932; owner & vice-pres. Studio City Ford Co.
PICTURES: Meet Me in St. Louis, Thirty Seconds Over Tokyo, Yolanda and the Thief, Merton of the Movies, On an Island With You, Velvet Touch, Date With Judy, Battleground, Ambush, Big Hangover, Little Women, Dial 1119, Happy Years, Alias a Gentleman, Watch the Birdie, Cattle Drive, On Moonlight Bay, It's a Big Country, Angel Face, By the Light of the Silvery Moon, Let's Do It Again, Sabre Jet, Peyton Place, From the Terrace, Absent Minded Professor, Son of Flubber, Misadventures of Merlin Jones, The Monkey's Uncle, On a Clear Day You Can See Forever, Tora! Tora! Tora!, Testament, Peggy Sue Got Married.
TELEVISION: Life with Father, Father of the Bride, Mr. Ed, Bewitched, Frontier Judge, Maggie.

AMES, LOUIS B.: Executive. b. St. Louis, MO, Aug. 9, 1918. e. Washington U., St. Louis. m. Jetti Preminger. Began as music consultant and staff director of musical programs for NBC; music dir. 1948, WPIX; 1951 appt. program mgr., WPIX; assoc. prod., Today, NBC TV, 1954; feature editor Home, 1957; Adm.-prod. NBC Opera, 1958; dir. cultural prog. N.Y. World's Fair, 1960–63; dir. RCA Pavillion, N.Y. World's Fair, 1963–65; 1966 dir., Nighttime, TV; 1969, dir. of programming N.W. Ayer & Sons, Inc. 1973 Mgr. Station Services, Television Information Office. NYC.

AMIS, SUZY: Actress. b. Oklahoma City, OK, 1962. m. actor Sam Robards. At 16 was introduced on the Merv Griffin Show by Eileen Ford whose modeling agency she worked for, as "The

Face of the Eighties." After modeling and living in Europe, made film debut in Fandango (1985). Off-Broadway debut: Fresh Horses (Theatre World Award).
PICTURES: Fandango, The Big Town, Plain Clothes, Rocket Gibralter, Twister, Where the Heart Is.

AMOS, JOHN: Actor. b. Newark, NJ, Dec. 27, 1941. e. Colorado State U, Long Beach City Coll. Worked as professional football player, social worker (heading the Vera Institute of Justice in NY), and advertising copywriter before writing television comedy material (for the Leslie Uggams Show) and performing as stand-up comedian in Greenwich Village. Has also dir. theatre with Bahamian Rep. Co. Starred in L.A. in Norman, Is That You? and Master Harold...And the Boys, Split Second, The Emperor Jones, Broadway: Tough to Get Help. NYSF: Twelfth Night. Artistic dir. Keane-Brown Center Stage, NJ.
PICTURES: Vanishing Point (debut, 1971), The World's Greatest Athlete, Let's Do It Again, Touched By Love, The Beastmaster, Dance of the Dwarfs, American Flyers, Coming to America, Lock Up, Two Evil Eyes (The Black Cat).
TELEVISION: Series: Mary Tyler Moore, The Funny Side, Future Cop. Maude, Good Times, Hunter, South by Southwest. Movies: The President's Plane is Missing, Willa, Roots (mini-series), Bonanza-the Next Generation, Alcatraz—The Whole Shocking Story, Hang Tight, Willy Bill, Brother Tough, as well as guest appearances.

AMSTERDAM, MOREY: Producer, Writer, Composer, Musician, Actor. b. Chicago, IL, Dec. 14, 1914. e. U. of California, Berkeley. Boy soprano. Radio KPO, 1922; night club performer, Chicago, 1929; comedian, singer, musician. Rube Wolf Orchestra; comedian, Optimistic Doughnut Program, 1930; writer, vaudeville; comedian, writer, Al Pearce Gang, 1932; writer, MGM, 1937; co-writer, radio shows; m.p. Columbia, Universal; writer, performer, USO Shows, 1942–43; owner, performer, the Playgoers-club; v.p. American International Pictures.
TELEVISION: Stop Me If You've Heard This One, Broadway Open House, Morey Amsterdam Silver Swan Show, Dick Van Dyke Show. Exec. Prod.-Star, Can You Top This. Movies: Side By Side.
PICTURES: Don't Worry . . . We'll Think of a Title, Machine Gun Kelly, Murder, Inc.
SONGS: Rum and Coca Cola, Why Oh Why Did I Ever Leave Wyoming, Yak A Puk, etc.

ANDERSON, DAPHNE: Actress. b. London, England, April 27, 1922. e. Kensington H.S. Stage debut in pantomime chorus, 1937; screen debut in Trottle True, 1948.
PICTURES: Cloudburst, Beggar's Opera, Hobson's Choice, A Kid for Two Farthings, The Prince and the Showgirl, No Time for Tears, Snowball, Stork Talk, Captain Clegg, The Launching, I Want What I Want.
TELEVISION: Silas Marner (serial), Gideon's Way (serial), Dr. Finlay's Casebook, Happy Family, The Imposter, The Harry Worth Show, The Whitehall Worrier, The Suede Jacket, Casanova, Haunted Series, Thirty Minute Theatre, Justice Is a Woman, Paul Temple, Today, 2 Cars.

ANDERSON, GERRY: Hon. F.B.K.S., Producer, b. London, England, 1929. Ent. ind. 1946. Chmn./man. dir. Gerry Anderson Productions, Ltd. Over 320 pictures produced for TV worldwide. 1981 Co-founded Anderson Burr Pictures. 1982 prod. Terrahawks in association with London Weekend Television; second series, Terrahawks, 1984; Space Police pilot for series in assoc. with TVS, 1985–6; Dick Spanner stop motion series for Channel Four 1987. Entered commercials as a dir.: "Shoes" for Royal Bank of Scotland, and campaign for Tennent's Pilsner; 1989 retained by Moving Picture Co. as commercials dir.

ANDERSON, J. WAYNE: Executive. b. Clifton Forge, VA, Feb. 19, 1947. e. USA Signal School (1965–67); USN Service Schools (1967). USMC, 1965–69; opened 1st military 35mm m.p. theatre, DaNang, Vietnam, 1967–69; dist. mgr., R/C Theatres, 1971–75; v.p., 1976–83; pres. of opns., 1983–present; Bd. of dirs., Maryland Permanent Bank & Trust co., 1988-present.
MEMBER: Nat. Assn. of Theatre Owners technical advancement committee, 1981–present; Huntsman Condo bd. dir., 1979–83; pres., Huntsman, 1982–83; Bd. of directors, NATO, 1987–present.

ANDERSON, DAME JUDITH: Actress. b. Adelaide, Australia, Feb. 10, 1898. Stage debut (Sydney) in Royal Divorce, 1915; on New York stage & in stock 1918; toured 1920; m.p. debut in Blood Money. 1933. Entertained U.S. Armed Forces overseas, W.W.II; received Donaldson Award 1948, New York Critics Award 1948, American Academy of Arts & Sciences Award for Best Speech 1948. N.Y. stage, 1952, In the Summer House, 1953.
PLAYS: Dear Brutus, Cobra, Dove, Strange Interlude, Old Maid, Mourning Becomes Electra, Macbeth, Medea.
PICTURES: King's Row, Rebecca, Forty Little Mothers, Free & Easy, All Through the Night, The Edge of Darkness, Jane Eyre, Laura, Spector of the Rose, Diary of a Chambermaid, Strange Love of Martha Ivers, Red House, And Then There Were None, Tycoon, Pursued, The Furies, Salome, Don't Bother to Knock, The Ten Commandments, Come of Age, Cinderfella, Cat on a Hot Tin Roof, Macbeth, A Man Called Horse, Inn of the Damned, Star Trek III.
TELEVISION: Series: Santa Barbara (1984), Episodes: Telephone Times, 1956. Specials: Macbeth (Hallmark, 1954 & 1960), The Cradle Song, Caesar and Cleopatra, The Moon & the Sixpence, Elizabeth the Queen, The Borrowers. Movies: The File of Devlin, The Chinese Prime Minister.

ANDERSON, HARRY: Actor. b. Newport, RI, Oct. 14, 1952. m. actress-magician Leslie Pollack. Performed magic show prior to plays at Oregon Shakespeare Festival. Also opening act for Kenny Rogers, Debbie Reynolds and Roger Miller in Las Vegas. Owner of magic shop in Ashland OR. Received Stage Magician of Year Award, National Acad. of Magician Arts and Sciences.
PICTURES: The Escape Artist.
TELEVISION: Series: Night Court (Emmy nom.). Movies: Spies, Lies and Naked Thighs; The Absent-minded Professor. Guest: Cheers, The Tonight Show, David Letterman, Saturday Night Live, Wil Shriner. Specials: Comic Relief, Harry Anderson's Sideshow (also exec. prod., writer), Comic Relief II, The Best of Gleason, Magic with the Stars, Nell Carter: Never Too Old to Dream, Hello Sucker.

ANDERSON, KEVIN: Actor. b. Illinois, Jan. 13, 1960. e. Goodman School. Member of Chicago's Steppenwolf Theatre where he starred in Orphans. Moved with the play when it transferred to New York (1985) and later starred in the London production, as well as the film version.
THEATER: NY: Orphans, Brilliant Tracers, Orpheus Descending.
PICTURES: Risky Business, Pink Nights, A Walk on the Moon, Orphans, Miles from Home, In Country.

ANDERSON, LINDSAY: Director (cinema & theatre), Writer. b. Bangalore, India, April 17, 1923; e. Cheltenham Coll., Wadham Coll., Oxford (classical scholar). Ent. ind. 1948 as writer-director in charge industrial film prod., also contributing editor and co-founder (with Karel Reisz) independent film quarterly Sequence (1947–52). Wrote Making a Film 1951; About John Ford (1981). Principal doc. films: Meet the Pioneers, Dreamland (with Guy Brenton), Thursday's Children (collab. s.p. dir.) (Acad. Award, short subj. 1954), Three Installations, Pleasure Garden, Wakefield Express, Every Day Except Christmas (Venice Grand Prix, 1957), March to Aldermaston, The Singing Lesson (Documentary Studio, Warsaw). Founder mem. Free Cinema group. National Film Theatre 1956–9.Artistic director, Royal Court theatre 1969–70. Associate, 1970–76.
TELEVISION: Five episodes Robin Hood series, commercials, 1959–75. 1978 Dir. The Old Crowd. 1986 Free Cinema, Buston Keaton: A Hard Act to Follow (narrator); 1986–87: music videos for Carmel; 1988: movie masterclass My Darling Clementine, Glory, Glory (HBO).
PLAYS: The Long and the Short and the Tall, Billy Liar, The Fire Raisers, Diary of a Madman, Sergeant Musgrave's Dance, The Cherry Orchard, Inadmissible Evidence (at Contemporary Theatre, Warsaw), In Celebration, The Contractor, Home, The Changing Room, The Farm, Life Class, What the Butler Saw, The Sea Gull, The Bed Before Yesterday, The Kingfisher, Alice's Boys, Early Days, Hamlet, The Cherry Orchard, Playboy of the Western World, In Celebration (N.Y.), Hamlet (Washington, DC), Holiday, The March on Russia.
PICTURES: This Sporting Life, The White Bus; If...; O Lucky Man!, In Celebration, Britannia Hospital; If You Were There; The Whales of August.

ANDERSON, LONI: Actress. b. St. Paul, MN, Aug. 5. 1946. m. actor Burt Reynolds. e. U. of Minnesota. Taught school before acting.
TELEVISION: Series: WKRP in Cincinnati, Three on a Date, Christmas in Opryland, Easy Street, My Mother's Secret Life, Stranded, Shaun Cassidy Special, Bob Hope specials, etc. Movies: The Jayne Mansfield Story, Sizzle, A Letter to Three Wives, Necessity, A Whisper Kills, Leave Her to Heaven, Too Good to Be True, Sorry, Wrong Number.
PICTURES: Stroker Ace, All Dogs Go to Heaven (voice).

ANDERSON, MELISSA SUE: Actress. b. Berkeley, CA, Sept. 26, 1962. Took up acting at suggestion of a dancing teacher. Did series of commercials; guest role in episode of Brady Bunch; episode of Shaft. Gained fame as Mary Ingalls on Little House on the Prairie series (Emmy nom.).
PICTURE: Happy Birthday to Me, Chattanooga Choo Choo, Dead Men Don't Die.
TELEVISION: Very Good Friends, James at 15, The Loneliest Runner, The Survival of Dana, Which Mother Is Mine? (Emmy Award, 1980), First Affair, An Innocent Love, Midnight Offerings, Dark Mansions.

ANDERSON, MICHAEL: Director. b. London, England, 1920. e. France, Germany, Spain. Ent. m.p. industry as actor, 1936;

asst. dir., unit manager on such films as In Which We Serve, Pygmalion, French Without Tears; Army service 1942–46.
PICTURES: Private Angelo (co-dir., 1949), Waterfront, Hell Is Sold Out, Night Was Our Friend, Will Any Gentleman?, The Dam Busters, 1984, Around the World in 80 Days, Yangtse Incident (Battle Hell), Chase a Crooked Shadow, Shake Hands with the Devil, The Wreck of the Mary Deare, All the Fine Young Cannibals, The Naked Edge, Flight From Ashiya, Monsieur Cognac, Operation Crossbow, The Quiller Memorandum, Shoes of the Fisherman, Pope Joan, Dr. Savage, Conduct Unbecoming, Logan's Run, Orca, Dominique, The Martian Chronicles, Bells, Apple and Pair, Separate Vacations, Vengeance, Millenium, The Goldsmith's Shop, The Long Walk Home, So Help Me God! (exec. prod., dir.).

ANDERSON, MICHAEL, JR.: Actor. b. London, England, Aug. 6, 1943. Son of dir. Michael Anderson. Ent. films as child actor, 1954.
TELEVISION: Queen's Champion, Ivanhoe, The Monroes (series), Washington Behind Closed Doors (mini-series), The Martian Chronicles. Movies: The House That Would Not Die, In Search of America, The Family Rico, Coffee, Tea or Me? Shootout in a One-Dog Town, Evel Knievel, Making of a Male Model, The Million Dollar Face, Love Leads the Way.
PICTURES: Tiger Bay, The Moonraker, The Sundowners, Reach For Glory, In Search of the Castaways, Play It Cool, Greatest Story Ever Told, Dear Heart, Major Dundee, The Glory Days, The Sons of Katie Elder, The Last Movie, Logan's Run.

ANDERSON, RICHARD: Actor. b. Long Branch, NJ, Aug. 8, 1926. U.S. Army, W.W.II. Began acting career in summer theatre in Santa Barbara and Laguna Playhouse where spotted by MGM executives who signed him to six-yr. contract. Appeared in 26 films for MGM before leaving studio.
PICTURES: 12 O'Clock High, The People Against O'Hara,, The Story of Three Loves, Escape from Fort Bravo, Forbidden Planet, The Long Hot Summer, Compulsion, Scaramouche, Seconds, Paths of Glory, Tora! Tora! Tora!, Along Came a Spider, Macho Callahan, Doctors' Wives, Play It As It Lays, The Honkers, Stone.
TELEVISION: Ironside, The Big Valley, Mannix, My Friend Tony, The Mod Squad, Land of the Giants, The FBI, Gunsmoke. Series: Bus Stop, Perry Mason, Dan August, 12 O'Clock High, The Six Million Dollar Man, The Bionic Woman. Movies: Kane & Abel, The Return of the Six Million Dollar Man and the Bionic Woman, Pearl, Perry Mason Returns, Hoover vs. the Kennedys, Emminent Domain, Danger High, Stranger on My Land. The Bionic Showdown: The Six Million Dollar Man & The Bionic Woman (also co-prod.).

ANDERSON, RICHARD DEAN: Actor. b. Minneapolis, MN, Jan. 23, 1950. Planned to become professional hockey player. Became a street mime and jester. Performed with his own rock band, Ricky Dean and Dante.
PICTURES: Odd Jobs, Ordinary Heroes.
TELEVISION: Series: General Hospital (1976–81); Seven Brides for Seven Brothers; Emerald Point, N.A.S.; MacGyver.

ANDERSON, SYLVIA: Producer, Writer (Pinewood Studios). b. London, England. e. London U. Entered m.p. ind. 1960. First pub. novel, Love and Hisses. UK rep for Home Box Office of America.
TELEVISION: series created include: Thunderbirds, U.F.O.; Space 1999.

ANDERSON, WILLIAM H.: Producer; Member of Bd. of Dir. Walt Disney Productions. b. Utah, October 12, 1911. e. Compton Coll. Firestone Rubber Co.; Universal Credit Co.; Walt Disney Prods. 42 years.
PICTURES: Old Yeller, Swiss Family Robinson, Happiest Millionaire, The Computer Wore Tennis Shoes, Barefoot Executive, $1,000,000 Duck, Superdad, Strongest Man in the World, Apple Dumpling Gang, Treasure of Matecumbe, Shaggy D.A.
TELEVISION: Zorro Series 1958–59; 1959–60, Wonderful World of Disney: Zorro, Texas John Slaughter, Daniel Boone, The Swamp Fox, Pop Warner Football (1960–61), Johnny Shiloh, Mooncussers, 1962–63; Bristle Face, The Scarecrow of Romney Marsh (1963–64); The Legend of Young Dick Turpin (1965–66); Willie and the Yank (1966–67); A Boy Called Nuthin', The Young Loner (1967–68); The Wacky Zoo of Morgan City (1970–71); The Mystery of Dracula's Castle (1972–73); The Bull from the Sky, (co-prod.; 1975–76); Great Sleeping Bear Sled Dog Race, (co-prod. 1976–77).

ANDERSSON, BIBI: Actress. b. Stockholm, Sweden, Nov. 11, 1935. e. Royal Dramatic Theatre School.
PICTURES: (for director Ingmar Borgman) Smiles of a Summer Night (1955), The Seventh Seal, Wild Strawberries, Brink of Life, The Magician, The Devil's Eye, Not to Mention All These Women, Persona; other films: My Sister, My Love Le Vio A Passion, Black Palm Trees, Story of a Woman, Duel at Diablo, The Kremlin Letter, The Passion of Anna, I Never Promised You a Rose Garden, Quintet, The Concorde: Airport '79, Enemy of the People, Babette's Feast, Fordring sagare.
TELEVISION: Wallenberg—A Hero's Story.

ANDES, KEITH: Actor. b. Ocean City, NJ, July 12, 1920. e. Temple U., Oxford. U. Radio work; on Broadway in Winged Victory, Kiss Me Kate, Maggie, Wildcat.
PICTURES: Farmer's Daughter, Clash By Night, Blackbeard the Pirate, Split Second, Life at Stake, Second Greatest Sex, Away All Boats, Pillars of the Sky, Back from Eternity, Damn Citizen, Surrender, Hells Bloody Devils, And Justice for All.
TELEVISION: This Man Dawson, Glynis.

ANDRESS, URSULA: Actress. b. Berne, Switzerland, 1936. m.p. Hollywood, 1955.
PICTURES: Dr. No, Four For Texas, Fun in Acapulco, Toys For Christmas, She, Tenth Victim, What's New Pussycat?, Chinese Adventures in China, Casino Royale, The Southern Star, Perfect Friday, The Red Sun, Scaramouche, Clash of the Titans, Class Meeting.
TELEVISION: Peter the Great, Falcon Crest.

ANDREWS, ANTHONY: Actor. b. London, England, 1948.
PICTURES: Operation Daybreak, Under the Volcano, The Holcroft Covenant, The Second Victory, Hanna's War.
TELEVISION: A Beast With Two Backs, Romeo and Juliet, A War of Children, QB VII, Upstairs Downstairs, Danger UXB, Brideshead Revisited, Ivanhoe, The Scarlet Pimpernel, Sparkling Cyanide, A.D., Bluegrass, Suspicion, The Woman He Loved, Colombo Goes to the Guillotine.

ANDREWS, DANA: Actor, b. Collins, MS., Jan. 1, 1909. e. Sam Houston Coll., Pasadena Community Playhouse. Accountant with Gulf Refining Co., 1930; chief accountant Tobins, Inc., 1931; acted with Pasadena Playhouse 3 yrs.; m.p. debut in The Westerner 1939; Vice Pres. Screen Actor's Guild, 1962–63, Pres. 1964–66. Bway play, Two for the See-Saw.
PICTURES: The Best Years of Our Lives, Iron Curtain, My Foolish Heart, Forbidden Street, Laura, Edge of Doom, Where the Sidewalk Ends, Sealed Cargo, The Frogmen, I Want You, Assignment—Paris, Elephant Walk, Duel in the Jungle, Three Hours to Kill, Smoke Signal, Strange Lady in Town, While the City Sleeps, Comanche, Beyond a Reasonable Doubt, Spring Reunion, Night of the Demon, Zero Hour, Enchanted Island, The Fear Makers, The Crowded Sky, Madison Avenue, The Satan Bug, Crack in the World, In Harm's Way, Battle of the Bulge, Devil's Brigade, The Loved One, Innocent Bystander, The Last Tycoon, Airport, 1975, Born Again.
TELEVISION: Alas Babylon; G.E., The Playoff; Barbara Stanwyck; Dupont, Mutiny; 4 Star, Crazy Sunday; Checkmate, Alcoa, The Boy Who Wasn't Wanted; Twilight Zone, No Time Like The Past; Dick Powell, Last of the Big Spenders; Alcoa, The Town That Died, Bob Hope Chrysler, A Wind of Hurricane Force, One Small Step Forward (series), The Right Hand Man (Playhouse 90). Movies: Bright Promise, The Last Hurrah, Ike, Shadow in the Streets, The Failing of Raymond.
DINNER THEATRE: The Marriage-Go-Round; The Best of Friends, Angel Street, The Gang's All Here, Any Wednesday, A Man for All Seasons.

ANDREWS, JULIE: Actress, Singer. r.n. Julia Wells. b. Walton-on-Thames. England. Oct 1, 1935. m. dir. Blake Edwards. debut, Eng. Starlight Roof Revue; pantomime of Cinderella.
PLAYS: The Boy Friend, My Fair Lady, Camelot.
PICTURES: Mary Poppins (1964; Academy Award), The Americanization of Emily, The Sound of Music, Hawaii, Torn Curtain, Thoroughly Modern Millie, Star!, Darling Lili, The Tamarind Seed, "10," S.O.B, Victor/Victoria, The Man Who Loved Women, That's Life, Duet for One.
TELEVISION: High Tor, Julie and Carol at Carnegie Hall, The Andy Williams Show, The Julie Andrews Show, An Evening with Julie Andrews and Harry Belafonte, The World of Walt Disney, Julie and Carol at Lincoln Center, Julie Andrews Hour (series 1972–73), Julie on Sesame Street, Julie Andrews' Christmas Special; Julie and Dick in Covent Garden; Julie Andrews and Jackie Gleason Together, Julie Andrews—My Favorite Things, Julie Andrews—The Sound of Christmas, Julie and Carol: Together Again. Movies: The Laundromat, After the Laughter.
AUTHOR: Mandy, Last of the Really Great Whangdoodles (1973).

ANDRIEUX, ROGER: Director, writer. b. France, Aug. 24, 1940. Began in French theatre, went to UCLA, took his M.F.A., made several short subjects as well as his first feature film in English.
PICTURES: Mr. Brown (s.p., dir.); Bonjour Amour (co-s.p., dir.); La Petite Sirene (s.p., dir., prod.), Envoyez les violons. (dir., s.p.), Prisonnieres (prod.).

ANGERS, AVRIL: Actress, Comedienne, Singer. b. Liverpool, England, April 18. Stage debut at age of 14; screen debut in 1947 in Lucky Mascot.
PICTURES: Miss Pilgrim's Progress, Don't Blame the

Stork, Women Without Men, Green Man, Devils of Darkness, Be My Guest, Three Bites of the Apple, The Family Way, Two a Penny, The Best House in London, Staircase, There's a Girl in My Soup, Forbush and the Penguins, Gollocks, Confessions of a Driving Instructor, Dangerous Davies.

TELEVISION: How Do You View, Friends and Neighbors, Dear Dotty, Holiday Town, Charlie Fainsbarn Show, Arthur Askey Show, All Aboard, The Gold Hunter, Bob Monkhouse Show, Before The Fringe, Hudd, Coronation Street, Dick Emery Show, Dad's Army, Bright Boffins, The More We Are Together, The Millionairess, Liver Birds, Looks Familiar, No Appointment Necessary, The Songwriters, All Creatures Great and Small, Coronation Concert, Minder, Smuggler, Just Liz, Give Up a Clue, Are You Being Served, Trelawney of the Wells, Cat's Eye, C.A.B., Rude Health.

PLAYS: The Mating Game; Cockie; Murder at the Vicarage, Little Me, Norman, Is That You?, Blithe Spirit, Oklahoma!, Gigi, The Killing of Sister George, Cards on the Table, When We Are Married, Cinderella, Easy Virtue.

ANHALT, EDNA: Associate producer, Writer. b. New York, NY, April 10, 1914. e. Kathryn Gibbs Sch. 1932; U. doc. films; prod. mgr., Rockefeller Found. films. Academy Award, orig. story collab., Panic in the Streets.

PICTURES: (Orig. story, collab., assoc. prod., s.p.) Strange Voyage, Avalanche, Younger Brothers, Return of Frontiersman, Embraceable You, Sierra, The Sniper, My Six Convicts, Eight Iron Men, Member of the Wedding, Three Lives, The Big Kill, Not as a Stranger, Pride and the Passion, Girls, Girls, Girls, Decision at Delphi.

Member: Acad. of M.P. Arts & Sciences; S.W.G.

ANHALT, EDWARD: Writer. b. New York, NY. Academy Award. orig. story collab., Panic in the Streets.

PICTURES: The Young Savages, Becket (Acad. Award, s.p.), In Enemy Country, Boeing-Boeing, The Young Lions, Day of the Guns, Not As a Stranger, Madwoman of Chaillot, Member of the Wedding, Boston Strangler, Jeremiah Johnson, Q B VII (TV), Luther, Escape to Athena, Green Ice.

ANNAKIN, KENNETH: Director, Writer. b. Yorkshire, Eng., 1915.Worked with Experimental Theatre and as documentary filmmaker.

PICTURES: Across The Bridge, Swiss Family Robinson, Very Important Person, The Longest Day, The Fast Lady, The Informers, Those Magnificent Men in Their Flying Machines, Battle of the Bulge, The Long Duel, Monte Carlo or Bust, Call of the Wild, Paper Tiger, The Fifth Musketeer, Cheaper to Keep Her, The Pirate Movie, The New Adventures of Pippi Longstocking (dir., s.p., co-prod.), 'Tis the Season.

ANNAUD, JEAN-JACQUES: Writer, Director. b. Draveil, France, Oct. 1, 1943. Began career as film director in French army, making educational pictures. Also directed 500 commercials. Received 1989 cinema prize from French Acad. for career's work.

PICTURES: Black and White in Color (Acad. Award, Best Foreign Film, 1977); Coup de Tete (dir. only); Quest for Fire (dir. only; Cesar Award, best film & dir., 1982); The Name of the Rose (dir. only; Cesar Award, best foreign film, 1987), The Bear (dir., co-s.p.: Cesar Award, best dir., 1989).

ANN-MARGRET: Actress, singer. r.n. Ann-Margret Olsson. b. Valsjobyn, Sweden, April 28, 1941. m. Roger Smith, actor, dir., prod. e. grad., New Trier H.S., Winnetka, IL, attended Northwestern U. Radio shows, toured with band; worked with George Burns, Sahara, Las Vegas. TV debut, Jack Benny Show, April, 1961.

PICTURES: Pocketful of Miracles (debut, 1961), State Fair, Bye, Bye Birdie, Viva Las Vegas, Kitten With a Whip, The Pleasure Seekers, Bus Riley's Back in Town, Once A Thief, The Cincinnati Kid, The Swinger, Stagecoach, Murderer's Row, Made in Paris, The Tiger and the Pussycat, Criminal Affair, The Prophet, C. C. & Company, Carnal Knowledge, RPM, The Outside Man, The Train Robbers, Tommy, The Last Remake of Beau Geste, The Twist, Joseph Andrews, The Cheap Detective, Magic, The Villain, Middle Age Crazy, Lookin' to Get Out, I Ought To Be in Pictures, The Return of the Soldier, Twice in a Lifetime, 52 Pick-up, A Tiger's Tail, A New Life, Something More.

TELEVISION: Specials: Dames at Sea, When You're Smiling, Hollywood Movie Girls. Movies: Who Will Love My Children?, A Streetcar Named Desire, The Two Mrs. Grenvilles.

ANSARA, MICHAEL: Actor. b. Lowell, MA, April 15, 1922. e. Pasadena Playhouse. Served in U.S. Army; then summer stock, little theatre, road shows.

PICTURES: The Robe, Julius Caesar, Sign of the Pagan, Bengal Brigade, Soldiers Three, Only the Valiant, New Orleans Uncensored, Diane, Lone Ranger, Sol Madrid, Daring Game, The Bears and I, Mohammad, Messenger of God, The Manitou, Gas, Knights of the City.

TELEVISION: Broken Arrow, Law of the Plainsman, Westerner, Centennial, Guest: Simon and Simon, Gavilan, The Fantastic World of D.C. Collins, George Burns Comedy Week, Hunter, Hardcastle and McCormick, Buck Rogers in the 25th Century.

ANSPACH, SUSAN: Actress. b. New York, NY, Nov. 23, 1939. e. Catholic U., Washington, DC. After school returned to N.Y. and in 3 years had performed in 11 off-Broadway prods. Moved to Los Angeles and entered films.

PICTURES: Five Easy Pieces, The Landlord, Play It Again Sam, Blume in Love, The Big Fix, Running, The Devil and Max Devlin, Gas, Misunderstood, Blue Monkey, Into the Fire, Back to Back.

TELEVISION: Yellow Rose, Space. Series: The Slap Maxwell Story.

ANSPAUGH, DAVID: Director. b. Decatur, IN, Sept. 24, 1946. e. Indiana U., 1965–70; U. of Southern CA, 1974–76. School teacher, Aspen, CO 1970–74. Awards for Hill Street Blues: Emmy 1982–83; DGA 1982, Golden Globes, 1981–82.

PICTURES: Hoosiers, Fresh Horses, Hard Boiled.

TELEVISION: Hill St. Blues (assoc. prod. 1980–81; prod.-dir. 1981–82; prod.-dir. 1983–84, dir. 1985); St. Elsewhere (dir.), Miami Vice (dir.).

ANTHONY, TONY: Actor, Producer, Writer. b. Clarksburg, WV, Oct. 16, 1939. e. Carnegie Mellon.

PICTURES: Force of Impulse, Pity Me Not, The Wounds of Hunger, A Stranger in Town, The Stranger Returns, A Stranger in Japan, Come Together, Blindman, Pete Pearl and the Pole, Let's Talk About Men, Get Mean, The Boy Who Owned a Melephant, Treasure of the Four Crowns, Comin' at Ya.

ANTON, SUSAN: Actress. b. Oak Glen, CA, Oct. 12, 1951. e. Bernardino Coll. Voted Miss California 1969. Worked in night clubs and recorded country and western album, The First Time. Broadway debut: Hurlyburly (1985). Film debut, Golden Girl, 1979.

PICTURES: Spring Fever, Cannonball Run II, Options (cameo).

TELEVISION: The Cliffhangers, Presenting Susan Anton, Susan Anton—and 10,000 GIs, The Boy Who Loved Trolls, Placido Domingo's Steppin' Out With the Ladies, How to Be a Man.

ANTONIO, LOU: Actor, Writer, Director. b. Oklahoma City, OK, Jan. 23, 1934. e. U. of OK.

THEATER: Actor: The Girls of Summer, The Good Soup; The Garden of Sweets; Andorra; The Lady of the Camellias; The Ballad of the Sad Cafe, Ready When You Are, C.B.

PICTURES: The Strange One; Splendor in the Grass; America, America; Hawaii; Cool Hand Luke; The Phynx; Mission Batangas (s.p.); Micki and Maude (exec. prod.).

TELEVISION: Actor: Series: Snoop Sisters; Dog and Cat; Making It. Piece of Blue Sky, The Power and the Glory, Danny Thomas Hour, Partners in Crime, Sole Survivor, Where the Ladies Go, *Director*: Gentle Ben (and writer), Rich Man, Poor Man, Lannigan's Rabbi, The Young Rebels (and writer), Someone I Touched, The Girl in the Empty Grave, Something for Joey, The Critical List, Silent Victory—The Kitty O'Neil Story, Breaking Up Is Hard to Do, The Contender, We're Fighting Back, The Star Maker, Gage and Walker, The Steeler and the Pittsburgh Kid, Something So Right, A Good Sport, Threesome, Rearview Mirror, Face to Face, The Outside Woman, Dark Holiday (also exec. prod.).

ANTONIONI, MICHELANGELO: Director. b. Ferrara, Italy, Sept. 29, 1913. e. Bologna U. Film critic on local paper, then script writer and asst. director. First films as a director were documentaries, including: Gente del Po (1947), N.U., Roma-Montevideo, Oltre l'oblio, L'Amorosa menzogna, Superstizione, Bomarzo, . . . Chung Kuo.

PICTURES: Love Story, 1950; The Lady Without Camelias, Le Amiche (The Girl Friends), Il Grido, Love in a City, I Vinti, The Friend, The City, L'Avventura, The Night, The Eclipse, Three Faces of a Woman, The Red Desert, Blow-Up, Zabriskie Point, The Passenger, The Oberwald Mystery, Identification of a Woman, The Crew.

ANTONOWSKY, MARVIN: Executive. b. New York, NY, Jan. 31, 1929. e. City Coll. of New York, B.A., M.B.A. Joined Kenyon and Eckhart in 1957 for which was media research dir.; named marketing v.p. With Norman, Craig, & Kummel as v.p., mktg. services. 1965, became v.p. in chg. of media research and spot buying at J. Walter Thompson. In 1969 joined ABC-TV as v.p. in chg. research. Left to become v.p. in chg. of programming at NBC-TV. 1976, sr. v.p., Universal-TV. 1979, joined Columbia Pictures as pres., mktg. & research. Rejoined MCA/Universal Pictures as pres, mktg., Nov. 1983. Formed Marvin Antonowsky & Assoc. marketing consultancy firm, 1989.

ANTONY, SCOTT: Actor. b. Gosforth, Newcastle-upon-Tyne, England. e. Leeds U.; rec'd scholarship at Royal Acad. of Dramatic Art. Discovered there by Ken Russell who gave him lead role in Savage Messiah, 1972. Has done much TV work in Britain.

PICTURES: Savage Messiah, The Mutations, Dead Cert.

APFEL, EDWIN R.: Executive. b. New York, NY, Jan. 2, 1934. e. Franklin and Marshall Coll., B.A., 1955. copywriter and account executive, Donahue and Coe, 1955–60; adv. publicity dept., Metro-Goldwyn-Mayer, 1960–62; dir. of adv. and creative services, MGM, Verve Records, 1962–63; dir. of adv., Embassy Pictures 1963–65; Advertising Writer, Consultant, 1965.

APTED, MICHAEL: Director. b. Aylesbury, Eng., Feb. 10, 1941. e. Cambridge. Broke into show business at Granada TV in England in early 1960s as trainee, researcher, and finally director. By 1965 was producer-director for local programs and current affairs; then staff drama dir. for TV series, plays and serials. In late 1960s left Granada to freelance.
PICTURES: Triple Echo, Stardust, The Squeeze, Agatha, Coal Miner's Daughter, Continental Divide, Gorky Park, Firstborn, Kipperbang, 7 Up, 28 Up, Critical Condition, Gorillas in the Mist.
TELEVISION: Poor Girl, High Kampf, Highway Robbery, Kisses at 50, The Collection (Intl. Emmy Award 28-Up, (award winning documentary), Bring on the Night (doc. on Sting); Ptang Yang.

ARBEID, BEN: Producer. Films incl: The Barber of Stamford Hill, Children of the Damned, Private Potter, The Jokers, Hoffman; Murder Most Foul, Murder Ahoy, The ABC Murders, Assignment K, Before Winter Comes, The Hireling, (Grand Prix—Cannes), Mahmud Bridge, The Water Babies, Eagles Wing, Enigma, 1986–87: retained by Turner Broadcasting System Inc. as exec. prod. for The Fourth Season.

ARCAND, DENYS: Director. b. Deschambault, Canada, 1941. e. U. of Montreal, 1963. While still history student, co-prod. Seul ou avec D'Autres (1962). Joined National Film Board of Canada, where began making documentary shorts (Champlain, Les Montrealistes and La Route de l'ouest) forming a trilogy dealing with colonial Quebec. In 1970 socio-political doc. about Quebec textile workers, On Est a Coton, generated controversy resulting in the NFB banning film until 1976.
PICTURES: On Est au Coton, La Maudite Galette (1st feature, 1971), Rejeanne Padovani, Gina, Le Confort et L'Indifference (doc), Le Crime d'Ovide Plouffe, The Decline of the American Empire (Acad. Award nom.), Jesus of Montreal (jury prize, Cannes, 1989).
TELEVISION: Duplessis (s.p., 1977 series), Empire Inc. (series, dir.).

ARCHER, ANNE: Actress. b. August 25, 1947. Daughter of actress Marjorie Lord and actor John Archer. Married Terry Jastrow, TV network sports producer-director and pres. Jack Nicklaus Prods.
THEATER: A Coupla White Chicks Sitting Around Talking (off-Bdwy, 1981), Les Liaisons Dangereuses (Williamstown Fest., 1988).
PICTURES: The All-American Boy, Honkers, Cancel My Reservation, Trackdown, Lifeguard, Paradise Alley, Good Guys Wear Black, Hero at Large, Raise the Titanic, Green Ice, Waltz Across Texas, The Naked Face, Too Scared to Scream, The Check Is in the Mail, Fatal Attraction, Love at Large, Narrow Margin.
TELEVISION: Series: The Storefront Lawyers (1970), Bob and Carol and Ted and Alice, The Pirate (mini-series), Falcon Crest. Movies: The Blue Knight, The Mark of Zorro, Seventh Avenue, The Log of the Black Pearl, The Sky's No Limit, A Matter of Wife...and Death, The Dark Side of Innocence, A Different Affair, A Leap of Faith.

ARCHER, JOHN: Actor. r.n. Ralph Bowman, b. Osceola, NB, May 8, 1915. e. U. of Southern California. Won Jesse L. Lasky Gateway to Hollywood talent quest; m.p. debut in Flaming Frontiers 1938; on N.Y. stage also.
PICTURES: White Heat, After Nightfall, Destination Moon, Big Trees, Yank in Indo-China, Sound Off, Rodeo, Sea Tiger, The Stars Are Singing, Dragon's Gold, No Man's Woman, Emergency Hospital.

ARCHER, ROBERT V.: Executive. Joined Paramount Pictures in 1967 as adm. asst. to v.p. of facilities and TV prod. In 1975 named dir. of studio admin. 1977 promoted to dir. of studio operations and admin., responsible for prod. servicing and admin. depts. of studio.

ARCHERD, ARMY: Columnist, TV commentator. r.n. Armand Archerd, b. New York, NY, Jan. 13. e. UCLA, grad. '41, U.S. Naval Academy Post Graduate Sch., 1943. Started as usher at Criterion Theatre, N.Y., while in high school. After grad. UCLA, worked at Paramount studios before entering Navy, Lt., joined AP Hollywood bureau 1945, Herald-Express, Daily Variety as columnist, 1953. M.C. Hollywood premieres and Academy Awards. President, founder Hollywood Press Club, awards from Masquers, L.A. Press Club, Hollywood Foreign Press Club, and Newsman of the Year award from Publicists Guild, 1970; Movie Game. TV series; People's Choice, co-host.

ARDANT, FANNY: Actress. b. France. Raised in Monte Carlo. Majored in political science in college. Served a 5-year apprenticeship in the French theater acting in Polyeucte, Esther, The Mayor of Santiago, Electra and Tete d'Or. After TV debut in Les Dames de la Cote, went on to star in films by Truffaut who became her mentor.
PICTURES: Les Chiens, Les uns et les Autres, The Woman Next Door, Life is a Novel, Confidentially Yours, Benevenuta, Desire, Swann in Love, Love Unto Death, Les Enrages, L'Ete Prochain, Family Business, Melo, The Family, Three Sisters, Australia, Pleure pas My Love.

ARDEN, EVE: Actress. r.n. Eunice Quedens. b. Mill Valley, CA, 1912. Appeared with Alcazar stock co., Bandbox Repertory Theatre; Broadway debut in Ziegfeld Follies of 1936, also in Ziegfeld Follies of 1938, Autobiography: Three Phases of Eve, 1985.
PICTURES: Let's Face It, Night And Day, Cover Girl, Voice of the Turtle, Goodbye, My Fancy, We're Not Married, Our Miss Brooks, Anatomy of a Murder, Dark at the Top of the Stairs, Sergeant Deadhead, The Strongest Man in the World, Grease, Grease 2.
TELEVISION: Series: Our Miss Brooks, The Eve Arden Show, The Mothers-in-Law. Movies: A Very Special Person, The Dream Merchants, All My Darling Daughters, A Guide for the Married Woman, Faerie Tale Theatre (Cinderella).
STAGE: Mame, Hello Dolly, Butterflies Are Free.

ARDOLINO, EMILE: Producer, Director. b. New York, NY e. Queens Coll. Actor in touring co. of The Fantasticks. Filmed sequences for Oh, Calcutta. Began career as dir. and prod. of Dance in America and Live From Lincoln Center series for Public TV 1975–81 before feature film debut as dir. Dirty Dancing (1988).
PICTURES: He Makes Me Feel Like Dancin' (prod., dir., Acad. and Emmy Award-winning doc., Peabody, Christopher, Cine Golden Eagle Awards, 1983), Dirty Dancing (dir.), Chances Are (dir.)
TELEVISION: Dance in America (prod., dir. 28 progs. include. Nuryev and the Joffrey Ballet in Tribute to Nijinsky, Choreography By Balanchine IV (1979 Emmy), The Spellbound Child (DGA Award), Live From Lincoln Center (incl. New York City Ballet in Tribute to George Balanchine, Stravinsky and Balanchine: Genius Has a Birthday; The Saint of Bleeker Street), Baryshnikov at the White House, Mass by Leonard Bernstein, When Hell Freezes Over I'll Skate, Rumplestiltskin (Fairie Tale Theatre), Alice at the Palace, The Dance and The Railroad, A Midsummer Night's Dream, Good Morning Mr. Orwell, The Rise and Rise of Daniel Rocket (dir.).

ARKIN, ALAN: Actor, Director, b. New York, NY, March 26, 1934. e. Los Angeles City Coll., Los Angeles State Coll., Bennington (VT) Coll. Member folk singing group The Tarriers.
THEATER: off-Broadway, Second City, Man Out Loud, From the Second City; Broadway, Enter Laughing (Tony Award), Luv. Dir. Little Murders, White House Murders.
PICTURES: The Russians Are Coming, The Russians Are Coming, Wait Until Dark, The Heart Is a Lonely Hunter, Popi, Catch 22, Deadhead Miles, Last of the Red Hot Lovers, Freebie and the Bean, Rafferty and the Gold Dust Twins, Little Murders (also dir.), Hearts of the West, 7½ Per Cent Solution, The In-Laws (also exec. prod.), Simon, Chu Chu and the Philly Flash, The Return of Mr. Invisible, Joshua Then and Now, Bad Medicine, Big Trouble, Full Moon High, Coupe de Ville.
TELEVISION: The Defection of Simas Kurdirka, The Other Side of Hell, A Deadly Business, Escape from Sobibor, The Visit (Trying Times, dir.), Necessary Parties (also co-s.p.).

ARKOFF, SAMUEL Z.: Producer, Motion Picture executive. Chairman & president of the Samuel Z. Arkoff Company (formed 1980) and Arkoff Int'l Pictures (formed 1981). b. Fort Dodge, IA, June 12, 1918. e. U. of Colorado, U. of Iowa, Loyola U. Law Sch. m. Hilda Rusoff. U.S.A.F. cryptographer W.W.II. Co-founder American Releasing, 1954, and American International Pictures, 1955. Pres. and chmn. of bd. American International Pictures until 1979. Named with partner James H. Nicholson as Producers of the Year in 1963 by Allied States Association of Motion Picture Theatre Owners and in 1964 as Master Showmen of the Decade by the Theatre Owners of America. Also named Producers of the Year at the Show-A-Rama VIII, and in 1966 and 1967 voted among top ten producers in exhibitor ratings by the independent theatre owners. Named Commendatore of the Order of Merit by President of Republic of Italy, in Rome 1970. In 1971 he and Nicholson named Pioneers of the Year by the Foundation of the Motion Picture Pioneers, Inc. Since appointment in 1973, has served as intl. v.p. of Variety Clubs Intl. Vice pres., Permanent Charities Committee. Member of the bd. of Trustees of Loyola Marymount U., Los Angeles, in 1979. Honored by a retrospective on 25th anniversary of AIP at Museum of Modern Art, July–Sept., 1979.
PRODUCTION CREDITS: On more than 200 pictures including Amityville Horror, Dressed to Kill, How to Beat the High Cost of Living, The Earthling, Love at First Bite, Meteor, California Dreaming, Force Ten from Navarone, The House of Usher, Pit and the Pendulum, Tales of Terror, Master of The

World, Premature Burial, Panic in the Year Zero, The Raven, Beach Party, Haunted Palace, Comedy of Terrors, Bikini Beach, Masque of the Red Death, Muscle Beach Party, Pajama Party Tomb of Ligeia, Wild Angels, Devil's Angels, The Trip, Three in the Attic, Wild in the Streets, The Oblong Box, Scream and Scream Again, Murders in the Rue Morgue, Cry of the Banshee, Bloody Mama, Wuthering Heights, Dr. Phibes, Frogs, Blacula, Dillinger, Heavy Traffic, Hennessy, Cooley High, Food of the Gods, Futureworld, Great Scout and Cathouse Thursday, Land that Time Forgot, People that Time Forgot, At the Earth's Core, Island of Dr. Moreau, and A Winning Season.

ARKUSH, ALLAN: Director. b. New York, NY, Apr. 30, 1948. e. Franklin & Marshall, NYU. Film Sch. With New World Pictures as film editor, trailer editor. Co-directed Hollywood Boulevard and Death Sport and was 2nd unit dir. of Grand Theft Auto before directing on own.
PICTURES: Rock 'n' Roll High School; Heartbeeps; Get Crazy; Caddyshack II.
TELEVISION: Fame; rock videos; St. Elsewhere; L.A. Law; Bronx Zoo; Moonlighting (Emmy nom., 1987); Tattinger's. Pilots: The Bronx Zoo; Capital News; Summer.

ARLEDGE, ROONE: Executive. b. Forest Hills, NY, July 8, 1931. e. Columbia U. Entered industry with Dumont Network in 1952; joined U.S. Army, 1953, serving at Aberdeen Proving Ground in Maryland, where produced and directed radio programs. Joined NBC in 1954 where held various production positions. In 1960 went to ABC TV; 1964, named v.p. in chg. of ABC Sports. Created ABC's Wide World of Sports in April, 1961. Named pres. of ABC News in 1968; pres. of ABC News and Sports, 1977. Holds four George Foster Peabody Awards for sports reporting; 19 Emmy awards.

ARLING, ARTHUR E.: Cinematographer. b. Missouri, Sept. 2, 1906. e. N.Y. Inst. of Photography. Entered m.p. Fox studio 1927 as asst. cameraman, 2nd cameraman 1931; operative cameraman on Gone With the Wind which won the Academy Award for technicolor photography 1939. Lt. Comdr. U.S.N.R., W.W.II; received Academy Award as dir. of photography on The Yearling 1946. Member: Amer. Soc. of Cinematographers.
PICTURES: Homestretch, Captain from Castile, Mother Was a Freshman, You're My Everything, Wabash Avenue, My Blue Heaven, Call Me Mister, Belles on Their Toes, The Glass Slipper, Three for the Show, Love Me or Leave Me, I'll Cry Tomorrow, Ransom, Great American Pastime, Tammy & the Bachelor, Pay the Devil, Story of Ruth, Pillow Talk, Lover Come Back, Notorious Landlady, Boys Night Out, My Six Loves.

ARMOUR, REGINALD: Foreign distributor, Producer. b. Chicago, IL, Nov. 28, 1905. e. Edinburgh, Scotland. Exec. RCA Victor Co. to 1933; estab. exch. India, Burma, Ceylon RKO Radio; Far East gen. mgr.; European gen. mgr. (Paris) 1937; exec. asst. to pres. RKO 1941; asst. gen. mgr. RKO studios 1942; British & European rep. Walt Disney Prod. 1942; financial field (N.Y.) 1943; exec. v.p. Richard Condon, Inc. 1944; with overseas br. OWI 1945; foreign rep. Columbia Intl. Corp. (N.Y.) 1945–49; joined Republic Pictures Intl. Corp. 1949; apptd. v.p., 1950; supvr., Europe & Near East for Republic 1952, exec. v.p. Republic Pictures Intl. (Great Britain) and man. dlr. Republic Prod. (Gt. Brit.) Ltd.; exec. v.p. Republic Pictures Intl. Corp., 1955; pres., The Dorsey Corp., 1960; Vice chmn., The Dorsey Corp., 1964; pres., SOS Photo-Cine-Optics, Inc., 1965; pres. FB/Ceco of Calif. Inc., 1967; pres. Instant Protection Systems, Inc., 1971. Exec. v.p. and treas. The Quedo Corporation and International Producers Services, Inc. 1973; 1974, v.p. & treas. Dyna-Soar, Inc.; 1977, exec. v.p. & treas., Two Feathers Prods.; 1981, pres., Armour Enterprises, Inc.; 1985, pres., Group Media Prods., Inc.

ARMSTRONG, BESS: Actress. b. Baltimore, MD, Dec. 11, 1953. m. producer John Fiedler. e. Brown U.
PICTURES: The House of God, The Four Seasons, Jekyll and Hyde Together Again, High Road to China, Jaws 3-D, Nothing in Common, Second Sight, Mother, Mother.
TELEVISION: Series: On Our Own, All is Forgiven, This Girl For Hire (pilot). Movies: Getting Married, How to Pick Up Girls, Walking Through the Fire, 11th Victim, Barefoot in the Park (HBO), Lace.

ARMSTRONG, GILLIAN: Director. b. Melbourne, Australia, 1950. e. Swinburne Coll. Among 1st class in dirs. course at National Aust. Film & TV School, Sydney. Worked as art dir. on a number of films. Dir. numerous shorts (Storytime, Old Man and Dog, One Hundred a Day, etc.) and documentaries (A Time and a Place, Tassie Wood, etc.) before turning to features.
PICTURES: My Brilliant Career; Starstruck; Mrs. Soffel; High Tide; Bingo, Bridesmaids and Braces (prod., dir.).

ARMSTRONG, GORDON: Executive, b. East Orange, NJ, Nov. 26, 1937. e. Arizona State U., graduate studies at NYU. Entered ind. as newspaper contact for MGM (1960–63); with Allan, Foster, Ingersoll and Weber 1963–70 as acct. exec.; joined 20th Century-Fox in 1970 as nat. pub. dir. In 1975 appt. dir. of adv.-pub.-promo. for Dino De Laurentiis Corp. In 1978, became vice pres., worldwide marketing for the company; 1980, named v.p., adv.-pub.-prom., Universal Pictures; 1984, named exec. v.p., mktg. MCA Recreation.

ARNALL, ELLIS GIBBS: Lawyer, executive. b. Newnan, GA, March 20, 1907; e. Mercer U., U. of the South, A.B. 1928, D.C.L. 1947; U. of Georgia LL.B. 1931; Atlanta Law Sch., LL.D. 1941; Piedmont Coll., LL.D 1943; Bryant Coll., LL.D. 1948. Georgia state representative from Coweta County, 1936–38; asst. Attorney-General (Ga.) 1938–42; Attorney-General (Ga.) 1942–43; Governor of Ga. 1943–47; pres. Dixie Life Insurance Co.; pres., Columbus National Life Insurance Co. senior mem. law firm Arnall, Golden & Gregory; pres. Georgia State Jr. Chamber of Commerce 1939; trustee U. of South; author of The Shore Dimly Seen 1946. What The People Want 1948; member U.S. Natl. Com. on UNESCO; member U.S. delegation to 4th annual conference UNESCO, Paris, France, 1949. Member: SIMPP (Pres. 1948); 1952 on leave as dir. Office of Price Stabilization, Washington; back to SIMPP, Sept. 1952; pres. Ind. Film Prod. Export Corp., 1953; member bd. of dir., exec. com., U.S. Nat'l Comm. for UNESCO, 1964–65, trustee, Mercer U. 1964–68; chmn. bd. Coastal States Life Insurance Co., chmn. bd. National Association of Life Companies. Member Academy Motion Picture Arts & Sciences; vice chmn., Sun Life of America Group, Inc.

ARNAZ, JR., DESI: Actor, Singer, b. Jan. 19, 1953. Son of Lucille Ball and Desi Arnaz. Began appearing on I Love Lucy show on TV in infancy and on various Lucy shows since. Gained fame as rock singer and musician with the Dino, Desi and Billy group. Film debut in Red Sky at Morning in 1972.
PICTURES: Red Sky at Morning, Marco, Joyride, A Wedding, House of the Long Shadows.
TELEVISION: Flight to Holocaust, The Courage and the Passion, To Kill a Cop, How to Pick Up Girls, The Night the Bridge Fell Down, She Lives, Voyage of the Yes, The Love Boat, Fantasy Island, Wacked Out, Automan, Paul Reiser: Out on a Whim.

ARNAZ, LUCIE: Actress. b. Los Angeles, CA, July 17, 1951. Daughter of Lucille Ball and Desi Arnaz. m. actor Laurence Luckinbill. Broadway show: They're Playing Our Song; National touring companies: Whose Life is It Anyway?, My One and Only, Social Security. Nightclubs: Lucie Arnaz—Latin Roots, Irving Berlin in Concert—In Sicily.
PICTURES: Billy Jack Goes to Washington, The Jazz Singer, Second Thoughts.
TELEVISION: Here's Lucy, Who is the Black Dahlia, The Mating Season, The Washington Mistress, One More Try (pilot), The Lucie Arnaz Show, Who Gets the Friends?

ARNAUD, LEO: Composer, Arranger, Conductor. b. Lyons, France, July 24, 1904: e. Ormesson Music Acad., Ph.D. Faculty mem. & symph. cond., Ormesson Music Acad., 1922–27; mus. dir. & arr. in France & England, 1927–30; Fred Waring Orch., U.S., 1931–35; arr. vocal coach, comp., mus. dir., MGM, 1936–44; U.S. Armed Forces, 1945 dir. many orch. including; L.A. Concert Band, American Legion Band, Hollywood String Orch., Beverly Hills, Symph. Orch.; free-lance mus. dir., comp., arr. since 1945.
PICTURES: One Touch of Venus, Easter Parade, Date With Judy, Three Little Words, Lovely to Look At, Stars & Stripes Forever, Rose Marie, Seven Brides for Seven Brothers.

ARNELL, PETER: Producer. b. Bridgeport, CT. e. U. of Michigan, A.B. Pub. dir., prog., WJLS, Beckley, WV; m.c. & disc jockey, WPEN, Philadelphia; actor, announcer, N.Y.; creator of Rate Your Mate, Name's the Same; creator & prod. of Wheel of Fortune, Balance Your Budget, I'll Buy That, Take a Guess, What's in a Word? prod. Chance of Romance, Celebrity Talent Scouts, Face the Facts, Talent Scouts, Take My Word, Ernie Kovacs' Take a Good Look.

ARNESS, JAMES: Actor. b. Minneapolis, MN, May 26, 1923. e. Beloit Coll. Served in U.S. Army; worked in advertising, real estate; m.p. debut in The Farmer's Daughter (1947).
PICTURES: Battleground, Hell Gate, Man from Texas, People Against O'Hara, Iron Man, The Thing, Big Jim McLain, Horizon's West, Lone Hand, Island in the Sky, Veils of Bagdad, Hondo, Her Twelve Men, Them, Many Rivers to Cross, Flame of the Islands, Sea Chase.
TELEVISION: Gunsmoke (20 years), How the West Was Won, McLain's Law, The Alamo: 13 Days to Glory, Gunsmoke: Return to Dodge, Red River.

ARNOLD, DANNY: Writer, Actor. r.n. Arnold Rothman; b. New York, NY, Jan. 23, 1925. Appeared in summer stock, night clubs, vaudeville; entered m.p. ind. as sound effects ed., Columbia, 1944–46; then legit., night clubs, vaudeville, 1946–50. Appeared in m.p. Breakthrough, Inside the Walls of Folsom Prison, Sailor Beware, Jumping Jacks, Scared Stiff,

Stars Are Singing,; featured on Martin and Lewis TV show 2 yrs., and wrote their Comedy Hours to 1953.
PICTURES: The Caddy (co-s.p., story), Desert Sands (co-s.p.), Fort Yuma (story, s.p.), Rebel in Town (story, s.p.), Outside the Law (s.p.).
TELEVISION: Writer: Tennessee Ernie Ford Show. Prod., writer, dir: The Real McCoys (1961–62), Bewitched (1963–64), The Wackiest Ship in the Army (1964–65), That Girl (1967–1969), My World and Welcome to It (1969–70), Barney Miller.

ARNOLD, EDDY: Singer. b. Henderson, TN, May 15, 1918. Radio performer, Nashville, TN; recording star since 1946; records include That's How Much I Love You, Anytime; star of Eddy Arnold Show, ABC-TV.

ARNOLD, JACK: Producer, Director. b. New Haven, CT, Oct. 14, 1912. e. Ohio State U., Amer. Acad. of Dramatic Arts. Actor on Broadway, Brit. m.p.; U.S. Air force, 1942–45; prod. 25 documentary films for State Dept., Army & private industry including With These Hands; dir., 1952. Producer, Universal 1956.
PICTURES: The Mouse That Roared, Bachelor in Paradise, Global Affair, The Incredible Shrinking Man, It Came from Outer Space, The Creature from the Black Lagoon, Girls in the Night, Revenge of the Creature, The Tattered Dress, Glass Web, Man in the Shadow, Man from Bitter Ridge; dir. story; Tarantula, Red Sundown, Decision at Durango, Outside the Law, Pay the Devil, No Name on the Bullet, The Lady Takes a Flyer, The Lively Set, High School Confidential. dir., Black Eye, Swiss Conspiracy.

ARNOW, TED J.: Executive. b. Brooklyn, NY. e. St. Johns U., Washington and Lee U. Served as dir. of recreation for 262nd General Hospital in Panama. Veteran of over 50 yrs. in amusement industry. Is v.p. for adv., pub., & promo. for Loew's Theatres. Member: Motion Picture Pioneers, Variety Clubs, Will Rogers Hospital; former pres. of AMPA (Assoc. M.P. Advertisers).

ARQUETTE, ROSANNA: Actress. b. New York, NY, Aug. 10, 1959. Granddaughter of humorist Cliff Arquette (Charlie Weaver). Debut as teenage daughter on TV series Shirley (1979).
PICTURES: More American Graffiti, The World According to Garp, Off the Wall, S.O.B., Baby, It's You, The Aviator, Desperately Seeking Susan, After Hours, Silverado, Lies, 8 Million Ways To Die, Nobody's Fool, Amazon Women on the Moon, The Big Blue, New York Stories (Life Lessons), Black Rainbow, Fly Away Home, Wendy Cracked a Walnut.
TELEVISION: Movies: Having Babies II; The Dark Secret of Harvest Home; Zuma Beach; The Ordeal of Patty Heart; A Long Way Home; The Wall; The Executioner's Song; Johnny Belinda; One Cooks, the Other Doesn't; The Parade; Survival Guide; A Family Tree (PBS' Trying Times); Promised a Miracle. Specials: Mom and Dad Can't Hear Me.

ARTHUR, BEATRICE: Actress. r.n. Bernice Frankel. b. New York, NY, May 13, 1926. Franklin Inst. of Sciences & Art. Studied with Erwin Piscator at New School for Social Research; first stage role as Lysistrata; professional stage debut in Dog Beneath the Skin, 1947. Gas, Yerma, No Exit, Six Characters in Search of an Author. Stock appearances include Personal Appearance, Candlelight, Love or Money, The Voice of the Turtle.
THEATER: The Taming of the Shrew, (1948) The Owl and the Pussycat, The Threepenny Opera (1953 revival), The ShoeString Revue, What's the Rush?, Nature's Way, Ulysses in Nighttown, Gay Divorcee, Fiddler on the Roof, Mame (Tony Award), The Floating Light Bulb, Night of the 100 Stars.
PICTURES: That Kind of Woman, Lovers and Other Strangers, Mame.
TELEVISION: Debut: Once Upon a Time (1951), Numerous guest appearances; Series: Maude, On the Air, Amanda's Place, Golden Girls, All Star Gala at Ford's Theater (host), Jay Leno's Family Comedy Hour. Movies: My First Love.

ARTHUR, JEAN: Actress b. New York, NY, Oct. 17, 1908. On stage; minor roles. m.p. debut as lead in Warming Up, 1928.
PICTURES: Canary Murder Case, Mysterious Dr. Fu Manchu, Whirlpool, Mr. Deeds Goes to Town, You Can't Take It With You, Too Many Husbands, Talk of the Town, Lady Takes a Chance, Impatient Years, Foreign Affair, Shane.
N.Y. STAGE: Peter Pan, 1950.
TELEVISION: The Jean Arthur Show.

ARTHUR, KAREN: Director. b. Omaha, NB, Aug. 24, 1941. 1958–68: choreographer and musical comedy singer, dancer and actress. 1950–68: ballet dancer. 1968–75: actress, film, TV and theatre.
PICTURES: As director: Legacy (1975, International Film Critics Award, Best First Film, Josef Von Sternberg Award); The Mafu Cage; Lady Beware.
TELEVISION: Movies: Charleston, Return to Eden (mini-series), Victims for Victims (Christopher Award), A Bunny's Tale, The Rape of Richard Beck, Crossings (mini-series), Evil in Clear River (Christopher Award), Cracked Up, A Bridge to Silence, Orleans. Episodes: Rich Man, Poor Man, Emerald Point, Boone, Two Marriages, Hart to Hart, Remington Steele, Cagney & Lacey, (Emmy Award, best dir. dramatic episode, 1985).

ARTZ, BOB: Theatre executive. b. Spokane, WA, Aug 21, 1946 e., B.T.A. Pasadena Playhouse College of Theatre Arts. Began in 1968 as doorman; then asst. mgr to mgr. with National General Theatre Corporation. Joined Plitt Theatres in 1978 as dist. mgr and ad/pub. director, West Coast. Joined General Cinema Theatres in 1986 as reg. marketing mgr; Western region.
MEMBER: Variety Club, Life Member: Pasadena Playhouse Alumni & Assoc.

ASH, RENE: Producer. b. Brussels, Belgium, March 14, 1939; e. U. of Omaha. Member of the Publicists Guild since 1968; Eastern v.p. of Pub Guild 1973–1981; Author of The Film Editor in Motion Pictures & Television; employed with I.A.T.S.E. 1968–1979, prior to which was assoc. editor, Greater Amusements; various articles published in foreign film magazines; editor-in-chief, Backstage 1979–80; pres., Cinereal Pictures, 1984–85; exec. v.p., Eagle Films Corp., since 1985, pres. Eagle/Zalon Ent. since 1987.

ASHCROFT, DAME PEGGY: Actress. b. Croyden, England, Dec. 22, 1907. e. Woodford Sch, Croyden, Central Sch. of Dramatic Art. On stage since 1926. London debut One Day More, 1927. Broadway debut High Tor (1937). Has had a long, extensive stage career in classics with Old Vic, Royal Shakespeare Co., National Theater, and Royal Court Theater. Film debut The Thirty-Nine Steps, 1933.
RECENT THEATER: John Gabriel Borkman, Happy Days, Tribute to the Old Lady, Old World, Watch on the Rhine, Family Voices, All's Well that Ends Well (1981).
PICTURES: The Nun's Story, The Wandering Jew, Rhodes of Africa, Quiet Wedding, Secret Ceremony, Three into Two Won't Go, Sunday Bloody Sunday, Joseph Andrews, A Passage to India (Acad. Award, supp. actress, 1984, L.A. Film Critics Award), Madame Sousatzka, She's Been Away.
TELEVISION: The Shadow of Heroes, The Cherry Orchard, The Wars of Roses, Days in the Trees, Cream in My Coffee, Caught on a Train, The Jewel in the Crown.

ASHER, JANE: Actress. b. London, England, April 5, 1946.
PICTURES: Greengage Summer, The Girl in the Headlines, Masque of the Red Death, Alfie, Deep End, Henry the Eighth and His Six Wives, Runners, Dream Child, Paris By Night.
TELEVISION: Brideshead Revisited, Voyage 'Round My Father, East Lynne, The Mistress, Wish Me Luck.

ASHLEY, ELIZABETH: Actress. b. Aug. 30, 1939. e. Studied ballet LA State U 1957–58; grad. Neighborhood Playhouse, 1961. Author: Postcards From the Road.
THEATER: Take Her She's Mine (1960 Tony Award), The Highest Tree, Barefoot in the Park, Legend, Cat on a Hot Tin Roof (Bdwy revival), Agnes of God.
PICTURES: The Carpetbaggers, Ship of Fools, The Third Day, The Marriage of a Young Stockbroker, Paperback Hero, Golden Needles, Rancho DeLuxe, 92 in the Shade, Great Scout and Cathouse Thursday, Coma, Windows, Captured, Paternity, Split Image, Dragnet, Vampire's Kiss, A Man of Passion, Gypsy Angels, Dangerous Curves, Lost Memories.
TELEVISION: Stagecoach, Harpy, The Face of Fear, When Michael Calls, Second Chance, The Heist, Your Money or Your Wife, The Magician, One of My Wives is Missing, The War Between the Tates, Insight, Tom and Joann (pilot), A Fire in the Sky, Svengali, He's Fired, She's Hired; Warm Hearts Cold Feet, The Two Mrs. Grenvilles, Orleans (series), The Rope.

ASHLEY, JOHN: Actor, Producer. r.n. John Atchley. b. Kansas City, MO, Dec. 25, 1934. e. Oklahoma State U., B.A., 1956. Career started in Tulsa Little Theatre, 1956; screen debut, 1957, Dragstrip Girl; later: Motorcycle Gang, Suicide Battalion.
TV: Men of Annapolis, Sheriff of Cochise, Frontier Doctor; Matinee Theatre, Jefferson Drum, Something is Out There (co-exec. prod.), Prod: The A-Team, Werewolf.

ASHLEY, TED: Executive b. Brooklyn, NY, Aug. 3, 1922. e. City Coll. of New York. Sch. of Business Administration. 1937–39. With William Morris Agency, agent. 1939–46; formed Ted Ashley Associates, 1946; pres. Ashley Famous Agency, 1954; director and chairman of executive committee of Warner Communications Inc., 1967 to 1974; chairman of bd. and chief exec. officer, Warner Bros. 1969–75; chmn. & co-CEO, 1976–80; 1981, sr. consultant, Warner Communications; 1982–84, vice chmn. of bd., WC. Resigned 1988.

ASNER, EDWARD: Actor. b. Kansas City, KS, Nov. 15, 1929. e. U. of Chicago, where affiliated with campus acting group. Served two years with U.S. Army in France. Returned to Chicago to join Playwright's Theatre Club. Moved to N.Y.; Broadway debut in Face of a Hero. Appeared off-Broadway (Ivanov, Threepenny Opera, Legend of Lovers, The Tempest, Venice Preserved), in stock, and with NY Shakespeare

Festival (1960) and American Shakespeare Festival (1961). In 1961 moved to Hollywood to become active in films and TV. National pres. Screen Actors Guild (1981–85), With actress Timothy Blake founded Quince/Blake Productions. Winner of numerous humanitarian awards.

PICTURES: Kid Gallahad, The Slender Thread, The Satan Bug, The Venetian Affair, Eldorado, Peter Gunn, Change of Habit, Halls of Anger, They Call Me Mister Tibbs, Skin Game, Gus, Fort Apache—The Bronx, O'Hara's Wife, Daniel, Moon Over Parador (cameo).

TELEVISION: Series: Slattery's People, The Mary Tyler Moore Show (3 Emmy Awards), Lou Grant (2 Emmys), Off the Rack, The Bronx Zoo. Movies: The Doomsday Flight, Doug Selby, D.A., The House on Greenapple Road, The Old Man Who Cried Wolf, The Last Child, The Haunts of the Very Rich, Hey, I'm Alive, Twigs, Life and Assassination of the Kingfish, The Gathering, The Family Man, A Small Killing, A Case of Libel, Anatomy of an Illness, Vital Signs, Kate's Secret, The Christmas Star, Cracked. Mini-series: Rich Man, Poor Man (Emmy Award); Roots (Emmy Award), Tender Is the Night, A Friendship in Vienna, Not a Penny More, Not a Penny Less.

ASPEL, MICHAEL: Radio/TV Presenter. b. London, England. Entered industry 1957. Early career: BBC Radio as actor/presenter. BBC TV as announcer/newsreader. Presentations incl: Miss World, Crackerjack, Give Us A Clue, Family Favourites, Child's Play, ITV Telethon 1988, Aspel and Company, This Is Your Life.

ASSANTE, ARMAND: Actor. b. New York, NY, Oct. 4, 1949. e. American Acad. of Dramatic Arts. Appeared with regional theatre groups and off-Bdwy. On Broadway in Boccaccio, Comedians, Romeo and Juliet, Kingdoms; Yankees 3, Detroit 0.

PICTURES: Lords of Flatbush, Paradise Alley, Prophecy, Little Darlings, Love and Money, Private Benjamin, I, the Jury; Unfaithfully Yours, Belizaire the Cajun, The Penitent, Animal Behavior, Eternity, Q & A.

TELEVISION: Human Feelings, Lady of the House, The Pirate, Sophia Loren—Her Own Story, Why Me?, Evergreen, A Deadly Business, Stranger in My Bed, Hands of a Stranger, Jack the Ripper. Mini-Series: Napoleon and Josephine: A Love Story, Passion and Paradise.

ASSEYEV, TAMARA: Producer. e. Marymont College; UCLA (MA, theatre arts). Began career as asst. to Roger Corman, working on 8 films with him. In 1967 started to produce films independently. Then co-produced films with Alex Rose, starting with Drive-In. In 1966 at 24, became youngest member of Producers Guild of Amer. Member: Costume Council, LA City Museum; founding member LA Museum of Contemporary Art.

PICTURES: The Wild Racers, Paddy, The Arousers, The History of Atlantic Records, Co-produced with Ms. Rose: Drive-In, I Wanna Hold Your Hand, Big Wednesday, Norma Rae.

TELEVISION: Movies: Penalty Phase, After the Promise, A Shadow on the Sun (also actress), The Secret Life of Kathy McCormick, The Hijacking of the Achille Lauro (exec. prod.), Murder By Moonlight (exec. prod.).

ASTIN, JOHN: Actor. b. Baltimore, MD, March 30, 1930. e. Washington and Jefferson Coll., Washington Drama Sch., Johns Hopkins U., grad. B.A., U. of Minnesota Graduate School. First prof. job., Off-Broadway, Threepenny Opera; Broadway debut, Major Barbara; dir., co-prod., A Sleep of Prisoners, Phoenix Theatre; during 1955–59, did voices in cartoons, commercials.

TELEVISION: Series: I'm Dickens . . . He's Fenster; The Addams Family, The Pruitts of Southamption, Operation Petticoat, Mary. Special: Harry Anderson's Sideshow . Movies: Two on a Bench, Only with Married Men, Skyway to Death, The Dream Makers.

STAGE: The Cave Dwellers, Ulysses in Nighttown, Tall Story.

PICTURES: West Side Story, That Touch of Mink, Move Over Darling, The Wheeler Dealers, The Spirit is Willing, Prelude (prod., dir. short subj.) Candy, Viva, Max!, Bunny O'Hare, Get to Know Your Rabbit, Every Little Crook and Nanny, Freaky Friday, Teen Wolf Too, Return of the Killer Tomatoes, Night Life, National Lampoon's European Vacation.

ATHERTON, WILLIAM: Actor. b. New Haven, CT, June 30, 1947. While in high school became youngest member of Long Wharf Theatre Co. Given scholarship to Pasadena Playhouse; then switched to Carnegie Tech Sch. of Drama in 1965. Trained for stage with Aesthetic Realism Foundation, NY. In college years toured with USO prods in Europe and in stock and industrial shows. Came to NY. where first prof. job was in natl. co. of Little Murders.

PICTURES: The New Centurions, Class of '44, The Sugarland Express, The Day of the Locust, The Hindenburg, Looking for Mr. Goodbar, Ghostbusters, Real Genius, No Mercy, Die Hard.

THEATER: The House of Blue Leaves, The Basic Training of Pavlo Hummel, The Sign in Sidney Brustein's Window, Suggs, Rich and Famous, Passing Game, Happy New Year, The American Clock, Three Acts of Recognition, Caine Mutiny Court Martial.

TELEVISION: Centennial, Malibu, House of Mirth, Intrigue. Guest: The Equalizer.

ATKINS, CHRISTOPHER: Actor. b. Rye, NY, Feb. 21, 1961. e. Dennison U., Ohio. Early modelling jobs; theatrical film debut in The Blue Lagoon (1980).

PICTURES: The Pirate Movie, A Night in Heaven, Beaks, Mortuary Academy, Listen to Me, Fatal Charm.

TELEVISION: Movie: Raid on Short Creek. Series: Dallas.

ATTENBOROUGH, DAVID: Broadcaster. b. London, England, May 8, 1926; e. Wyggeston Sch., Leicester; Clare Coll., Cambridge. Early career, editor in educational publishing house, ent. BBC-TC Sept. 1952. Prod. Zoo Quest series, Travellers Tales, Adventure and other prog., travel, Eastward with Attenborough, The Tribal Eye, Life on Earth, exploration natural History and anthropology. Controller BBC-2, 1965–68; Dir. of Prog. BBC-TV, 1969–72.

ATTENBOROUGH, SIR RICHARD (SAMUEL), Kt 1976; CBE. 1967: Actor, Producer, Director. b. Cambridge, England, Aug. 29, 1923. m. 1945 Sheila Beryl Grant Sim. e. Wyggeston Grammar Sch., Leicester. Leverhulme Scholarship to Royal Acad. of Dramatic Art, 1941 (Bancroft Medal). First stage appearance Ah, Wilderness (Palmers Green, 1941). West End debut in Awake and Sing (1942), then The Little Foxes (Piccadilly Theatre, 1942). First film performance in In Which We Serve, 1942. Brighton Rock (Garrick Theatre 1943). Joined RAF 1943; seconded to RAF Film Unit, and appeared in Journey Together, 1944; demobilized, 1946. Returned to stage, 1949, in The Way Back (Home of the Brave), To Dorothy, A Son, Sweet Madness, The Mousetrap, 1952–54; Double Image, 1956–1957; The Rape of the Belt, 1957–1958, formed Allied Film Makers, 1959 formed Beaver Films with Bryan Forbes.

PICTURES:*Actor:* In Which We Serve (1942), School for Secrets, The Man Within (The Smugglers), Dancing With Crime, Brighton Rock (Young Scarface), London Belongs to Me (Dulcimer Street), The Guinea Pig, The Lost People, Boys in Brown, Morning Departure (Operation Disaster), Hell Is Sold Out, The Magic Box, Gift Horse (Glory at Sea), Father's Doing Fine, Eight O'Clock Walk, The Ship That Died of Shame, Private's Progress, The Baby and the Battleship, Brothers in Law, The Scamp, Dunkirk, The Man Upstairs, Sea of Sand, Danger Within, I'm All Right Jack, Jet Storm, SOS Pacific, The Angry Silence (also co-prod.), 1959; The League of Gentlemen, Only Two Can Play, All Night Long, The Dock Brief (Trial & Error), The Great Escape, Seance On a Wet Afternoon (also prod., best actor, San Sebastian Film Fest. and British Film Acad. 1964), The Third Secret, Guns at Batasi (Best Actor, British Film Acad.), The Flight of the Phoenix, The Sand Pebbles (Hollywood Golden Globe), Dr. Dolittle (Hollywood Golden Globe), The Bliss of Mrs Blossom, Only When I Larf, The Last Grenade, A Severed Head, David Copperfield, Loot, 10 Rillington Place, And Then There Were None, Rosebud, Brannigan, Conduct Unbecoming, The Chess Players, The Human Factor.

Producer: Whistle Down the Wind, 1961; The L-Shaped Room, 1962.

Producer & Director: Oh! What a Lovely War (16 Intl. Awards incl. Golden Globe and BAFTA UN Award), *Director:* Young Winston (Hollywood Golden Globe), A Bridge Too Far (Evening News Best Drama Award 1977), Magic, Gandhi (8 Oscars, 5 BAFTA Awards, 5 Hollywood Golden Globes, Dirs'. Guild of America Award for Outstanding Directorial Achievement 1982); A Chorus Line, Cry Freedom (Berlinale Kamera, 1987).

ATTERBURY, MALCOLM: Actor. b. Philadelphia, PA, Feb. 20, 1907, e. Hill Sch., PA. Radio editor, Phila. Ledger; prog. mgr., gen. mgr., performer, Phila. Ledger radio station, WHAT, 7 yrs.; concert, vaudeville, Schubert musicals, 7 yrs.; Tamarack Playhouse, 5 yrs.; owned, oper., Albany Playhouse, 6 yrs.; conducted thea. seminars, Skidmore, R.P.I., College of St. Rose.

TELEVISION: Hallmark Hall of Fame, Lux Video Thea., Playhouse 90, Studio One, G.E. Theatre, Cheyenne, Perry Mason, Gunsmoke, 77 Sunset Strip, Alfred Hitchcock Presents, Route 66, The Defenders, The Untouchables, Dr. Kildare, Profiles in Courage, Fugitive, FBI, Hazel, Bonanza, Voyage to the Bottom of the Sea, Judd.

PICTURES: Dragnet, Storm Center, Crime in the Streets, Reprisal, Crime of Passion, Toward the Unknown, No Time for Sergeants, Rio Bravo, North by Northwest, Wild River, From the Terrace, Summer and Smoke, Advise and Consent, The Birds, The Chase, Hawaii.

BROADWAY: One Flew Over the Cuckoo's Nest.

ATWATER, GLADYS: Writer. Has written many m.p. scripts; member of writing team with Robert Bren since 1939; v.p. Bremex, Inc., writings include: (collab. orig.) Man Who Found

Himself; (collab. orig. story) Argentine Nights, First Yank into Tokyo, In Old California; (collab. s.p.) Criminal Lawyer, Crashing Hollywood, The Marriage Business, Crime Ring; (collab. story) El Paso, Tag for Murder, Blood on the Shrine, Legacy in Nylons, Aztec Dagger, Female Menagerie. Collab. story, s.p., Overland Pacific; collab. story Naked Alibi, Treasure of Pancho Villa; TV: Lone Wolf in Mexico, Stolen Train, Casey Jones series, Winds of the Four Seasons, collab. s.p.; collab. s.p. orig. story The Hawaiians.

AUBERJONOIS, RENE: Actor. b. New York, NY, June 1, 1940. e. attended Carnegie Mellon U.

THEATER: A Cry of Players, Dark of the Moon, Beyond the Fringe, Charley's Aunt, Coco (Tony Award), Tricks, The Ruling Class, Twelfth Night, The Good Doctor, The New York Idea, Break a Leg, Every Good Boy Deserves Favor; Richard III, The Misanthrope, Flea in Her Ear, Big River, Metamorphosis.

PICTURES: MASH, Brewster McCloud, McCabe and Mrs. Miller, Pete 'n Tillie, Images, My Best Friend Is a Vampire, Hindenberg, King Kong, Eyes of Laura Mars, Where the Buffalo Roam, 3:15, Walker, Police Academy 5: Assignment Miami Beach, The Feud.

TELEVISION: Series: Benson. Movies: The Birdmen, Dark Street at Harvest Home, More Wild Wild West, The Rhineman Exchange, Smokey Mountain Christmas, The Christmas Star, Fire, Longarm.

AUBREY, JAMES T., JR.: Executive. b. La Salle, IL, Dec. 14, 1918. e. Princeton U., 1941. m. Phyllis Thaxter, U.S. Air Force, 1941–45; salesman, Street and Smith, Condé Nast Pub., 1946–47; account exec., KNX, Los Angeles, 1948; account exec., KNXT, 1951; sales mgr., then gen. mgr., KNXT and CTPN, 1952. Man. network prog., Hollywood CBS-TV, 1956; V.P. programs and talent, ABC-TV 1957; v.p. CBS. 1958; exec. v.p. CBS-TV, 1959; pres. CBS-TV, 1959. In 1969–73 MGM pres.; now indep. prod.

PICTURES: Futureworld (prod.), The Hunger, Hostage (co-exec. prod.).

AUDRAN, STEPHANE: Actress. b. France, 1938. Former wife of French star Jean-Louis Trintignant and director Claude Chabrol.

PICTURES: Les Cousins (debut under direction of Chabrol), The Champagne Murders, Les Biches, La Femme Infidele, The Beast Must Die, The Lady in the Car, Le Boucher, Without Apparent Motive, Dead Pigeon on Beethoven Street, The Discreet Charm of the Bourgeoisie, The Devil's Advocate, The Blackbird (American film debut), Silver Bears, Blood Relatives, Babette's Feast, Seasons of Pleasure, Faceless, Body-To-Body, Sons, Manika: The Girl Who Lived Twice, Love in C Minor, Poulet au Vinaigre.

TELEVISION: Mistral's Daughter, The Blood of Others, The Sun Also Rises, Poor Little Rich Girl: The Barbara Hutton Story, Champagne Charlie.

AUERBACH, NORBERT T.: Executive. b. Vienna, 1923. Educated in U.S. and served with U.S. Army Intelligence in Europe during W.W.II. Joined m.p. business in 1946 after grad. UCLA. (business admin.). First asst. dir. at Service Studios in CA. Moved to N.Y. to join domestic sales dept. of Film Classics. Joined Columbia Pictures in foreign dept. In 1950 assigned to Paris office, where remained for over decade, except for 18 mos. in Portugal as mgr. Returned to Paris in 1953 and filled number of exec. sls. positions for Columbia, ultimately rising to continental mgr. 1961, left Columbia to produce films in France. Resumed career in dist., as continental mgr at Paris office of United Artists. In 1966 returned to prod. to make The Thief of Paris. 1967, joined Seven Arts Prods. heading theatrical and TV sls. operations in Paris. When Seven Arts acquired Warner Bros., he became continental sls. mgr. for Warners in Paris. 1968, set up European prod. and dist. org. for CBS Cinema Center Films, operating from London. 1972, moved to L.A. as v.p., foreign mgr. for CCF. Returned to London in 1973 to be consultant in prod. and dist. Rejoined UA in 1977 as sls. mgr. for Europe and the Middle East. Named sr. v.p. & foreign mgr. in 1978. Named pres. & COO, Jan. 1981; pres., CEO, Feb. 1981. Co-pres., United Int'l Pictures, London, till 1982. In 1983 formed packaging and financing Co., Eliktra, Inc. 1982, acting pres. and chief exec. officer of Almi Distribution Corp. Now Almi consultant, Exec. v.p. American Screen Co.

AUGUST, BILLE: Director. b. Denmark, 1948. e. trained in advertising photography, Danish Film School, grad. 1971, cinematography. As cinematographer shot: Miesta ei voi raiskata (Men Can't Be Raped), Karleken, The Grass is Singing. Became dir. 1978 with short Kim G. and dramas for Danish TV.

PICTURES: Honnigmane, Zappa, Twist and Shout, Pelle the Conquerer (Acad. Award, 1988), The House of Spirits, Good Intentions.

AUMONT, JEAN PIERRE: Actor. b. Paris, France, 1909. e. Conservatoire of Drama. Roles French stage and films. In 1943 enlisted in Free French Army. Film debut, Jean de la Lune, 1932.

PICTURES: Assignment in Brittany, The Cross of Lorraine, Heartbeat, Siren of Atlantis, Affairs of a Rogue, Wicked City, Lili, Life Begins Tomorrow, Gay Adventure, Charge of the Lancers, Hilda Crane, Enemy General, The Devil at 4 O'Clock, Castle Keep, Cauldron of Blood, Cat and Mouse, Day for Night, The Happy Hooker, Mahogany, Catherine & Co., Blackout, Two Solitudes, Something Short of Paradise, Sweet Country, The Free Frenchman.

U.S. STAGE: Tovarich, Incident at Vichy, Hostile Witness, Carnival, Camino Real, Murderous Angels, A Talent for Murder.

TELEVISION: Sins, Windmills of the Gods.

AURELIUS, GEORGE M.: Executive. b. Grasston, MN, Sept. 16, 1911. e. U. of Minnesota. Ent. m.p. ind. 1927 as usher Finkelstein & Ruben, St. Paul; asst. mgr. 1929–30; to Warner Theatres, New York 1931; mgr. Moss' Broadway; Minnesota Amusement Co. 1932–41; city mgr. Publix-Rickards-Nace. Paramount-Nace Theatres, Tucson, Ariz. 1941–46; v.p. ABC Theas. of Arizona, Inc. 1949–67; pres. ABC North Central Theatres, Inc., 1967–72; v.p., ABC Intermountain Theatres, Inc., v.p. ABC Theatres of California, Inc. 1972–1974; Mgmt. Consulting and ShoWest Convention & Trade Show since 1975, named exec. dir., 1979. Retired 1985.

AUSTIN, JOHN: Producer. b. Australia, 1923; Asst. Dir. of Entertainment for American Red Cross, 1942–45; assoc. West Coast rep. of Rodgers & Hammerstein, 1945–47; with Ministry of Info., Gov't of India, 1947–48; prod. TV films in Europe, 1949; shows include Intrigue, International Rendezvous, International Affair; prod. film Lasca. Since 1954, representative of leading foreign newspapers in Hollywood as correspondent for the entertainment industry. 1974–77, west coast editor, Screen International. 1977–81, international editor, The Hollywood Reporter. President: Inter-Global FIlm Consultants. Since 1982, vice president, editor in chief, Film News-International for VPA, Inc. Consultant to foreign producers on U.S. marketing and advertising techniques.

AUSTIN, RAY: Director, Writer, Producer. b. London, England, Dec. 5, 1932. Has written, produced and directed many TV series, specials and movies.

TELEVISION: Director of series: Avengers, The Champions, Department S, Randall & Hopkirk, Ugliest Girl in Town, Journey into the Unknown, Magnum P.I., Simon and Simon, House Calls, Kings Crossing, Fall Guy, Lime Street, Spencer for Hire. Writer: Randall & Hopkirk, Department S. Producer-Director: The Perfumed Garden. Director: It's the Only Way to Go, Fun and Games, Space 1999, New Avengers, Hawaii Five-O, Sword of Justice, Webb, Barnaby Jones, Hardy Boys, Wonder Woman, Salvage, B.G. and the Bears, Hart to Hart, The Yeagers, Man Called Sloane, From Here to Eternity, Bad Cats, Westworld, Tales of the Gold Monkey (2-hr. pilot), The Return of the Man from U.N.C.L.E. Director-Writer: Black Beauty, Zany Adventures of Robin Hood, The Master, Hart to Hart (series), V, Air Wolf, Lime Street (pilot and episodes); Spenser for Hire (several episodes); Magnum P.I. (season premiere 2-hr. episode); Return of the Six Million Dollar Man (pilot); Our House (episodes), Dirty Dozen, Alfred Hitchcock Presents, A Fine Romance.

PICTURES: Virgin Witches, House of the Living Dead.

AUTANT-LARA, CLAUDE: Director. Began career as scenic designer for French films in early 1920s; then asst. dir. to Rene Clair. First solo venture experimental film, 1923; in Hollywood, 1930–32. dir. Parlor, Bedroom and Bath, Incomplete Athlete.

PICTURES: Devil in the Flesh, Seven Deadly Sins (seq.), Red Inn, Oh Amelia, Game of Love, Ciboulette, Red and the Black.

AUTEUIL, DANIEL: Actor. b. Algeria, Jan. 24, 1950. Parents were lyric opera singers in roving troupe. Lived in Avignon. Performed in Amer. prod. in Paris of Godspell. Then did musical comedy for 2 years.

PICTURES: L'Aggression/Sombres Vacanes, Attention Les Yeaux, La Nuit de Saint-Germain des Pres, Monsieuer Papa, L'Amour Viole, Les Heroes n'ont pas froid aux oreilles, A Nous Deux, Bete Mais Discipline, Les Sous-Doues, La Banquiere, Clara et les chic types, Men Prefer Fat Girls, Pour 100 briques t'as plus rien maintentant, Que les gros salaires levent le doigt!!!, L'Indic, P'tit Con, The Beast, L'Arbalete, Palace, L'Amour en Douce, Jean la Florette, Manon of the Springs, Romuald and Juliette, A Few Days With Me.

AUTRY, GENE: Actor. b. Tioga, TX, Sept. 29, 1907. Railroad telegrapher at Sapulpa, OK, 1925; became radio singer and recording artist (Columbia Records) 1928; screen debut 1934 at Mascot Pictures (later became Republic) as screen's first singing cowboy. Starred in 89 feature films and 91 half hour TV films. The Gene Autry Show, 1950–55. Formed Flying A Productions, produced Annie Oakley, The Range Rider, Buffalo Bill, Jr. and Adventures of Champion TV series. Wrote or co-wrote and recorded over two hundred songs, has 9 Gold Records, including all-time best seller, Rudolph the Red-Nosed Reindeer. Voted top money making Western star

1937–42, and in top Western stars 1936, 1946–54; first Western star to be in top ten money makers from 1938–42. Served in U.S.A.A.F. as flight officer, 1942–45; on USO tour overseas 3 mos.; immediately thereafter resumed radio career with former sponsor, the Wm. Wrigley Co., formed Gene Autry Productions, Inc., star of Madison Square Garden Rodeo first in 1940; composed & recorded song Here Comes Santa Claus; owner 4 radio stations, California Angels baseball team and chairman of the board of Gene Autry Western Heritage Museum.

AVALON, FRANKIE: Entertainer. r.n. Francis Thomas Avalone. b. Philadelphia, PA, Sept 18, 1940. e. South Philadelphia H.S. Trumpet prodigy age 9 yrs. Recording contract, Chancellor Records, Inc., 1957; Gold Record, Venus 1959; Gold Album, Swingin' on a Rainbow, 1959; Nightclubs.
TELEVISION: Ed Sullivan, Perry Como, Pat Boone, Arthur Murray, Dick Clark Shows, Milton Berle, Golden Circle Spectacular; Dinah Shore Show, Steve Allen Show, Easy Does It (series, 1976), Happy Days.
PICTURES: Guns of the Timberland, The Alamo, Voyage to the Bottom of the Sea, Sail a Crooked Ship, Panic in the Year Zero, Bikini Beach, Beach Blanket Bingo, Jet Set, I'll Take Sweden, Sgt. Deadhead, The Take, Grease, Back to the Beach.

AVEDON, DOE: Actress, b. Old Westbury, NY. Bookkeeper; then actress.
BROADWAY: Young and the Fair, My Name Is Aquilon.
PICTURES: High and the Mighty, Deep in My Heart, The Boss.
TELEVISION: Big Town.

AVERBACK, HY: Director. b. 1925. Theatrical dir. before turning to TV. Formerly actor and radio announcer on Jack Paar Show (1947), Let's Talk Hollywood, Bob Hope Show.
PICTURES: *As actor:* The Benny Goodman Story, Four Girls in Town, How to Succeed in Business . . . Without Really Trying. *Director:* Chamber of Horrors (also prod.); Where Were You When the Lights Went Out?, I Love You Alice B. Toklas, The Great Bank Robbery, Suppose They Gave a War & Nobody Came, Where the Boys Are—1984.
TELEVISION: *Actor:* Saturday Night Revue (1953–4), Meet Corliss Archer (also prod.), Tonight, Our Miss Brooks.- *Director:* The Brothers, The Real McCoys, Donna Reed Show, Tom Ewell Show (prod.), Mrs. G. Goes to College (prod., dir.), Bus Stop, Dick Powell Show, Ensign O'Toole, Burke's Law, Man From U.N.C.L.E., F Troop (exec. prod.), The Flying Nun, McMillan and Wife, Colombo, McCloud (also prod.), M*A*S*H, Friends, The New Maverick, Anna and the King, Needles and Pins, Movin' On, Look Out World, The Night Rider, A Guide for the Married Woman, The Girl, The Gold Watch, and Dynamite; She's in the Army Now, At Ease (also prod.), The Four Seasons.

AVILDSEN, JOHN G.: Director, Cinematographer, Editor. b. Chicago, IL. m. actress Tracy Brooks Swope. e. NYU. After service in Army made film with friend, Greenwich Village Story, then joined ad agency to write and produce film commercials. Entered m.p. industry as ass't cameraman on Below the Hill, followed with prod. mgr. job on Italian film made in U.S. Then made first theatrical short, Smiles. Asst. dir: Black Like Me; prod. mgr.: Mickey One, Una Moglie Americana; asst. dir.: Hurry Sundown. Produced, photographed & edited a short, Light, Sound, Diffuse. Returned to industry to make films for ad agencies before resuming theatrical career.
PICTURES: Turn on to Love (1st feature, dir., photo.), Out of It (assoc. prod., dir. of photog.), Sweet Dreams (aka Okay, Bill; dir., photo., editor), Guess What We Learned in School Today? (dir., photo., editor), Joe (dir., photo.), Cry Uncle (dir., photo., editor), The Stoolie (dir. photog.), Save the Tiger (dir.), W. W. and the Dixie Dancekings (dir.), Foreplay (dir. ed., photo.), Rocky (dir., Acad. Award, Best picture, dir., ed.), Slow Dancing in the Big City (dir., prod., editor, operator), The Formula (dir.), Neighbors (dir., supv. editor), Traveling Hopefully (documentary, dir.), A Night in Heaven (dir., editor, operator); The Karate Kid (dir., editor); Happy New Year (dir.); The Karate Kid: Part II (dir., editor); For Keeps (dir., editor), Lean On Me (dir., co-ed.), The Karate Kid Part III (dir., co-editor).
TELEVISION: From No House to Options House (2 On the Town, Emmy Award).

AVNET, JON: Producer, Director. b. Nov. 17, 1949. e. U. of PA, Sarah Lawrence Coll. Began career as director of off-Bdwy. prods. Produced and directed low-budget film, Confusion's Circle, which brought a directing fellowship at American Film Institute. Joined Weintraub/Heller Prods. as assoc. prod., where met Steve Tisch, with whom formed Tisch/Avnet Prods. Formed Avnet/Kerner Co., 1986.
PICTURES: Outlaw Blues (assoc. prod.), *Prod.:* Coast to Coast, Risky Business, Deal of the Century (exec. prod.), Less Than Zero, Men Don't Leave.
TELEVISION: No Other Love, Homeward Bound, Prime Suspect, Something So Right, Silence of the Heart, Calendar Girl Murders, Call to Glory (pilot and series), The Burning Bed, In Love and War (prod./exec. prod.), Between Two Women (prod., dir., co-s.p.), Side By Side (exec. prod.), My First Love (exec. prod.), Deceptions (exec. prod.), Breaking Point (prod.), O Do You Know the Muffin Man (exec. prod.).

AXEL, GABRIEL: Director. b. c. 1920. e. France, then studied acting at Danish National Conservatory. Returned to France where joined the Paris theater co. of Louis Jouvet as stagehand. Worked as actor in Copenhagen boulevard theater where made directing debut. Went on to dir. Danish TV, mostly classic plays.
PICTURES: The Red Mantle (1967), Danish Blue, Babette's Feast (Acad. Award, 1988), Christian (also s.p.).

AXELROD, GEORGE: Playwright, writer, prod., dir. b. New York, NY, June 9, 1922. Stage mgr., actor, summer stock, 1940–41; radio writer, 1941–52; writer, novels: Beggar's Choice, Blackmailer; co-writer, nightclub musical: All About Love, 1951.
BROADWAY: The Seven Year Itch, Will Success Spoil Rock Hunter?, Visit to a Small Planet, Once More with Feeling, Goodbye Charlie.
PICTURES: Phifft, The Seven Year Itch, Bus Stop, Breakfast at Tiffany's, The Manchurian Candidate, Paris When It Sizzles, How to Murder Your Wife, Lord Love a Duck, The Secret Life of an American Wife (prod., s.p.), Candy Barr.

AXELROD, JONATHAN: Writer. b. New York, NY, July 9, 1948. Stepson of writer George Axelrod. Started as on-set "gofer" before writing screenplays. 1978–80, v.p. primetime drama dev., ABC Entertainment; 1980–82, v.p. exec. dir. in chg. dev. ABC Ent.; 1983–85 exec. v.p., Columbia Pictures TV; 1985–87, pres. New World Pictures; 1987– , co-owner, Camden Artists.
PICTURES: The Dirty Movie, Every Little Crook and Nanny.

AYKROYD, DAN: Actor-Writer. b. Ottawa, Canada, July 1, 1952. m. actress Donna Dixon. Member of Toronto Co. of Second City Theater. Worked as mgr. Club 505, after-hours Toronto nightclub 1970–73. Performed and recorded with John Belushi as the Blues Brothers. Co-owner Hard Rock Cafe, NY.
TELEVISION: Coming Up Rosie (Canada), Saturday Night Live 1975–79 as writer and performer Steve Martin's Best Show Ever (actor, writer).
PICTURES: Love at First Sight, Mr. Mike's Mondo Video, 1941, The Blues Brothers (also co-s.p.), Neighbors, It Came From Hollywood, Doctor Detroit, Trading Places, Twilight Zone—The Movie, Ghostbusters (also co-s.p.), Nothing Lasts Forever, Indiana Jones and the Temple of Doom, Into the Night, Spies Like Us, Dragnet (also co-s.p.), The Couch Trip, The Great Outdoors, Caddyshack II, My Stepmother is an Alien, Ghostbusters II, (also co-s.p.), Loose Cannons, Driving Miss Daisy.

AYRES, GERALD: Producer, Writer. e. Yale U. where had four plays produced. Became Broadway play doctor and then joined Columbia Pictures as freelance reader. Named story editor; exec. asst. to v.p. Mike Frankovich; then v.p. in chg. creative affairs in Hollywood. Left in 1970 to become independent. Formed Acrobat Films.
PICTURES: Cisco Pike, The Last Detail, Rich and Famous (s.p. only), Foxes (also s.p.).

AYRES, LEW: Actor. b. Minneapolis, MN, Dec. 28, 1908. Toured Mexico with own orchestra; played with Henry Halstead's Orchestra; screen debut in The Sophomore, The Kiss, 1929; served as medical corpsman & asst. chaplain W.W.II.
PICTURES: All Quiet on the Western Front, Common Clay, East is West, Doorway to Hell, Okay America, State Fair, Dr. Kildare series; Hearts of Bondage (dir.), Dark Mirror, Unfaithful, Johnny Belinda, The Capture, New Mexico, No Escape, Donovan's Brain, The Carpetbaggers, Advise and Consent, Altars to the East (dir.-nar. star-prod.), Last Generation, 1971, Biscuit Eater, The Man, Battle for the Planet of the Apes, Damien-Omen II, Battlestar Galactica.
TELEVISION: Hawaii Five-O (pilot), Earth II, She Waits, The Man, The Biscuit Eater, The Stranger, The Questor Tapes, Heatwaves, Francis Gary Powers, The End of the World, Salem's Lot, Of Mice and Men, Under Siege.

AZNAVOUR, CHARLES: Singer, Songwriter, Actor. b. Paris, France, May 22, 1924. r.n. Shahnour Varenagh Aznavourian. Studied dance and drama as a child and was performing at the age of 10. Encouraged by Edith Piaf, became one of France's leading performers by the mid-1950s and an international concert star by the 1970s. Has also composed music for film.
PICTURES: Adieu Cherie (1947), C'est arrive a 36 Chandelles, Les Dragueurs, Shoot the Piano Player, Le testament d'Orphee, Le Passage du Rhin, Un taxi pour Tobrouk, Horace 62, Tempo di Roma, Les Quatres Verites, Le Rat'd Amerique, Pourquoi Paris?, Paris in August, Candy, The Adventurers, And Then There Were None, The Twist, Sky Riders, Ciao, Les Mees, The Tin Drum, The Magic Mountain, The Hatter's

Ghosts, What Makes David Run?, Edith and Marcel (lyrics), Long Live Life!, Mangeclous, Friend to Friend, Il Maestro, Double Game.

B

BABCOCK, DWIGHT V.: Writer. b. Ida Grove, IA, Feb. 19, 1909. e. Modesto Jr. Coll. Author short stories, novelist. First screenplay at Universal, 1943. 26 screen credits since at various studios. TV, freelance, includes 100 produced teleplays; co-author, Chautauqua.

BABENCO, HECTOR: Director. b. Buenos Aires, Argentina, Feb. 7, 1946. Early years spent in Mar del Plata. Left home at 17 and traveled throughout European capitals for 8 years working as a writer, house-painter, salesman, and, in Rome, as an extra at Cinecitta. Moved to Sao Paulo, Brazil where he made several short documentaries. First feature film, Rei Da Noite (1976).
PICTURES: Rei Da Noite, Lucio Flavio—Passageioro Da Agonia, Pixote (NY and LA Critics Awards, best foreign film), Kiss of the Spider Woman, Ironweed, Besame Mucho (prod. only).

BACALL, LAUREN: Actress. b. New York, NY, Sept. 16, 1924. e. American Acad. Dram. Arts. m. late Humphrey Bogart, actor. Fashion model; on stage, plays include: Johnny Two-by-Four, Franklin Street; m.p. debut in To Have and Have Not, 1944.
BROADWAY: Cactus Flower, Goodbye Charlie, Applause (Tony Award, best actress in musical), Woman of the Year, Sweet Bird of Youth (London).
PICTURES: Big Sleep, Confidential Agent, Dark Passage, Key Largo, Young Man with a Horn, Bright Leaf, How to Marry a Millionaire, Woman's World, Cobweb, Blood Alley, Written on the Wind, Designing Women, Flame over India, Shock Treatment, Gift of Love, Sex and the Single Girl, Harper, Murder on the Orient Express, The Shootist, Health, The Fan, Appointment with Death, Mr. North, Tree of Hands, The Actor.
TELEVISION: Petrified Forest, Applause, Perfect Gentlemen, Bacall on Bogart.

BACH, CATHERINE: Actress. b. Warren, Ohio, March 1, 1954.
PICTURES: The Midnight Man, Thunderbolt and Lightfoot, Hustle, Cannonball Run II, Tunnels, Music City Blues, Driving Force, Street Justice, Criminal Act.
TELEVISION: Series: The Dukes of Hazzard (1979–85), The Dukes (cartoon, voice), guest on many specials. Movies: Matt Helm, Strange New World, Murder in Peyton Place, White Water Rebels.

BACHARACH, BURT: Composer-Conductor-Arranger. b. Kansas City, MO, May 12, 1928. e. McGraw U., Mannes Sch. of Music, Music Acad. of the West. Studied with composers Darius Milhaud, Henry Cowell, and Bohuslav Martinu. Has conducted for Marlene Dietrich, Vic Damone. As a performer albums include: Burt Bacharach; Futures, Man! His Songs, Books: The Bacharach-David Song Book (1978).
THEATER: Promises, Promises (Tony Award, best score, 1969).
PICTURES: The Man Who Shot Liberty Valance, Wives and Lovers, Send Me No Flowers, A House Is Not a Home, Who's Been Sleeping in My Bed?, What's New Pussycat?, Casino Royale (Acad. Award), The April Fools, Promise Her Anything, Alfie (Oscar), Butch Cassidy and the Sundance Kid (Acad. Award, best song), Lost Horizon, Arthur, Baby Boom.
TELEVISION: Burt Bacharach Special.

BACK, LEON B.: Exhibitor. b. Philadelphia, PA, Oct. 23, 1912. e. Johns Hopkins U., B.E., 1932; U. of Baltimore, LL.B., 1933. Entered m.p. ind. as mgr. for Rome Theatres, Inc., Baltimore, Md., 1934; booker, ass't buyer, 1936; ass't to gen. mgr. 1939; U.S. Navy 1944–46; v.p., gen. mgr., Rome Theatres, 1946; Allied MPTO of Md. 1952–55; nat'l dir. Allied States, 1952–55; nat'l secy. 1954; Pres. NATO of Maryland 1969–80; Pres. USO Council, Greater Baltimore 1969–75; Chairman, board of trustees, Employees Benefit Trust for Health & Welfare Council of Central Maryland, 1970–79.

BACKE, JOHN DAVID: Executive. b. Akron, OH, July 5, 1932. e. Miami U., B.S., 1954; Xavier U., M.B.A., 1961. Various managerial positions in engineering, financing and marketing functions, Gen. Electric Co., 1957–66; v.p., dir. mktg. Silver Burdett Co., div. Gen. Learning Corp., 1969; pres., chief exec. officer, 1969–73; pres., CBS Pub. Group, 1973–76; v.p., dir., CBS, Inc., 1973–76; pres., chief exec. officer, mem., fin. comm., dir., 1976–80; now chmn., Tomorrow Entertainment, Inc., and chmn., The Backe Group., Inc.
PICTURES: A Killing Affair, Brenda Starr (exec. prod.).

BACON, KEVIN: Actor. b. Philadelphia, PA, July 8, 1958. m. actress Kyra Sedgwick. Studied at Manning St. Actor's Theatre. Apprentice at Circle-in-the-Square in N.Y. Bdwy. debut in Slab Boys with Sean Penn.
THEATER: Off-Bdwy debut: Getting Out, Album, Forty Deuce, (Obie Award), Poor Little Lambs, Flux, Slab Boys, Loot, Road.
PICTURES: National Lampoon's Animal House (1976), Friday the 13th, Hero at Large, Only When I Laugh, Diner, Footloose, Quicksilver, Rites of Summer, Planes, Trains & Automobiles, White Water Summer, Forty Deuce, She's Having A Baby, End of the Line, Criminal Law, The Big Picture, Beneath Perfection, Queens Logic, Tremors.
TELEVISION: Movies: The Gift, Enormous Changes at the Last Minute, The Demon Murder Case, Mr. Roberts, Lemon Sky. Series: Search for Tommorrow, Guiding Light.

BADHAM, JOHN: Director. b. Luton, Eng., Aug. 25, 1939, raised in Alabama. e. Yale U., B.A.; Yale Drama School, M.F.A. Landed first job at Universal Studio mailroom; later was Universal tour guide, a casting dir. and assoc. prod. to William Sackheim. Made film trailers and TV episodes. Twice nominated for Emmy Awards for TV movies.
PICTURES: The Bingo Long Travelling All-Stars and Motor Kings (debut 1976), Saturday Night Fever, Dracula, Whose Life Is It Anyway?, Blue Thunder, War Games, American Flyers, Short Circuit, Stakeout (also exec. prod.), Disorganized Crime (exec. prod.), Bird on a Wire, The Hard Way.
TELEVISION: Assoc. prod.: Night Gallery, Neon Ceiling. Director: The Law, Isn't It Shocking?, The Senator (also assoc. prod.), Reflections of Murder, The Impatient Heart, The Gun, The Godchild, Cuba and Claude (exec. prod.).

BAER, JOHN G.: Executive, Engineer. b. New York, NY, May 8, 1934. e. U. of Tennessee, Chattanooga, B.S., physics, 1955. Joined Bausch and Lomb, Inc. as optical and mechanical engineer, 1957–67; dir. of research and dev., 20th Century-Fox, N.Y., 1967–72; sales/engineering, Century Projector Corp., named pres. & chief exec. officer, Jan. 1, 1975.
MEMBER: Optical Society of America; Society of American Magicians; Intl. Brotherhood of Magicians; Magic Circle (London); 25–30 Club (honorary). Fellow of SMPTE and dir. Theatre Equip. Assn. Chm., PH-22 (motion picture) American Natl. Standards Institute. U.S. delegate to Intl. Standards Organization. Elected mayor West Windsor Township, NJ, 1977.

BAILEY, JOHN: Cinematographer. b. Missouri, August 10, 1942. m. film editor Carol Littleton. e. U. of Santa Clara, Loyola U., U.S.C., U. of Vienna. Lecturer, American Film Institute, 1982 and 84.
PICTURES: Premonition (1972); End of August; Legacy; The Mafu Cage; Boulevard Nights; American Gigolo; Ordinary People; Honky Tonk Freeway; Continental Divide; Cat People; That Championship Season; Without a Trace; The Big Chill; Racing With the Moon; The Pope of Greenwich Village; Mishima: A Life in Four Chapters; Silverado; Crossroads; Brighton Beach Memoirs; Light of Day; Swimming to Cambodia; Tough Guys Don't Dance; Vibes; The Accidental Tourist.
TELEVISION: Battered; City in Fear.

BAILEY, PEARL: Entertainer. b. Newport News, VA, March 29, 1918. m. drummer Louis Bellson, Jr. e. Philadelphia and Washington, DC. Career started when 15 years old, winner of amateur stage contest; toured mining towns of Pennsylvania as dancer; dancer and singer in vaudeville with Noble Sissle's band; many night club appearances and TV shows; screen debut 1947, Variety Girl.
THEATER: St. Louis Woman (Donaldson Award, best newcomer of 1946), Arms and the Girl, Bless You All, House of Flowers, Hello Dolly.
PICTURES: Carmen Jones, Isn't It Romantic, That Certain Feeling, St. Louis Blues, Porgy and Bess, All the Fine Young Cannibals, The Landlord, Last Generation, Norman, Is That You?, The Fox and the Hound (voice of Big Mama).
TELEVISION: Trauma Center, Silver Spoons, An American Portrait, Cindy Eller, The Pearl Bailey Show, Pearl Bailey and Carol Channing on Broadway, One More Time, Member of the Wedding (1982). Movie: Peter Gunn.

BAILEY, ROBIN: Actor. b. Hucknail (Nottingham), Eng., Oct. 5, 1919. e. Henry Mellish School, Nottingham.
STAGE: Barrets of Wimpole Street, Theatre Royal, Nottingham, 1938.
PICTURES: School for Secrets (1946), Private Angelo, Portrait of Clare, His Excellency, Gift Horse, Folly to Be Wise, Single Handed, Sailor of the King, The Young Lovers, For Better, For Worse, Catch Us If You Can, The Whisperers, Spy with a Cold Nose, You Only Live Twice, The Eliminator, Blind Terror, Down by the Riverside, Nightmare Rally, The Four Feathers, Jane and the Lost City.
TELEVISION: Olive Latimer's Husband, Seven Deadly Sins, The Power Game, Public Eye, Person to Person, Troubleshooters, Armchair Theatre, Split Level, The Newcomers, Discharge of Trooper Lusby, Brett, Owen M.D., Solidarity, General Hospital, Murder Must Advertise, Vienna 1900, Justice, The Pallisers, The Couch, Way of the World, Upstairs, Downstairs, Walk with Destiny, North and South, A Legacy, The Velvet Glove, Crown Court, Took and Co., The

Good Companions, Cupid's Darts, Sorry, I'm a Stranger Here Myself, Call My Bluff, Jane, Potter, Tales from a Long Room, Sharing Time, Bleak House, Charters and Caldicott, Looks Familiar, On Stage, Rumpole of the Bailey.

BAIO, SCOTT: Actor. b. New York, NY, Sept. 22, 1961. Started career at 9 doing commercials and voice-overs.
PICTURES: Bugsy Malone, Skatetown USA, Foxes, Zapped!, I Love New York.
TELEVISION: Luke Was There, Muggsy, Happy Days, The Boy Who Drank Too Much, Stoned, Joanie Loves Chachi, How to Be a Man. Series: Blansky's Beauties, Who's Watching the Kids?, We're Moving, Charles in Charge. Movies: Senior Trip, Alice in Wonderland, The Truth about Alex.

BAKER, BLANCHE: Actress. r.n. Blanche Garfein. b. New York, NY, Dec. 20, 1956. Daughter of actress Carroll Baker and dir. Jack Garfein. e. Wellesley, Coll., studied acting with Uta Hagen. Acting debut, White Marriage, Yale Repertory Co. (1978), Regional Theater. Bdwy. debut in Lolita (1981).
PICTURES: The Seduction of Joe Tynan (debut, 1978), French Postcards, Raw Deal, Cold Feet, Sixteen Candles, Bum Rap.
TELEVISION: The Holocaust (Emmy Award, supp. actress, 1978), Mary and Joseph, The Day the Bubble Burst, Romeo and Juliet, The Awakening of Candra.

BAKER, CARROLL: Actress. b. Johnstown, PA, May 28, 1931. e. schools there and St. Petersburg (FL) Junior Coll. Career started as dancer in nightclubs. Actors' Studio N.Y. Stage debut: Escapade. Then, All Summer Long. Autobiography: Baby Doll.
PICTURES: Easy to Love, Giant, Baby Doll, But Not for Me, The Miracle, Bridge to the Sun, Something Wild, How the West Was Won, The Carpetbaggers, Station Six Sahara, Sylvia, Cheyenne Autumn, Mister Moses, Harlow, The Sweet Body of Deborah, Paranoia, Andy Warhol's Bad, Watcher in the Woods, Ironweed, Star 80, Native Son, The Secret Diary of Sigmund Freud, Fatal Spell.
TELEVISION: Hitler's S.S.: Portrait in Evil, On Fire.

BAKER, DON: Theatre Executive. b. St. Louis, MO, Dec. 16, 1931. e. St. Louis U. V.P., adv.-prom., Loews Theatres, N.Y. Member NATO, bd. dir. & nat'l chmn. adv. comm., 1972–present; mem. bd. of dir., Will Rogers Memorial Fund, 1974; pub. chmn., Variety Clubs Intl. in Western Hemisphere; Commissioner, NJ Film & TV Development Commission.

BAKER, GEORGE: Actor, Writer. b. Varna, Bulgaria, April 1, 1931. e. Lancing College, Sussex. Stage debut Deal Repertory Theatre, 1946. Film debut The Intruder, 1953.
PICTURES: Dam Busters, Ship That Died of Shame, Woman for Joe, Extra Day, Feminine Touch, A Hill in Korea, No Time for Tears, These Dangerous Years, Tread Softly Stranger, Lancelot and Guinevere, Curse of the Fly, Mister Ten Per Cent, Goodbye Mr. Chips, Justine, The Executioners, On Her Majesty's Secret Service, A Warm December, The Fire Fighters, The Spy Who Loved Me, Thirty-nine Steps, A Nightingale Sang in Berkeley Square, Hopscotch, North Sea Hijack, For Queen and Country.
TELEVISION: Fan Show, Ron Raudell's programme 1956, Guinea Pig, Death of a Salesman, The Last Troubadour, The Square Ring, Nick of the River, Mary Stuart, Probation Officers, Far Away Music, It Happened Like This, Boule de Suif, Maigret, Zero One, Rupert Henzau, Miss Memory, Any Other Business, The Navigators, Common Ground, Alice, The Queen and Jackson, The Big Man Coughed and Died, Up and Down, Call My Bluff, The Baron, St. Patrick, Love Life, Seven Deadly Virtues, The Prisoner, The Sex Games, Z Cars, Paul Temple, Candida, Fenn Street, Man Outside, The Persuaders, Main Chance, Ministry of Fear, Voyage in the Dark, Dial M for Murder, Zodiac, The Survivors, I, Claudius, Print Out, Goodbye, Darling, Chinese Detective, Triangle, Minder, Hart to Hart, Goodbye Mr. Chips, Woman of Substance, The Bird Fancier, Robin of Sherwood, Time after Time, If Tomorrow Comes, Coast to Coast, Dead Head, The Canterville Ghost, Room at the Bottom, Ruth Rendell Mysteries, Journey's End.
WRITER: The Fatal Spring, Imaginary Friends, Going for Broke, The Marches of Wales, The Hopkins, Just a Hunch, Sister, Dear Sister.

BAKER, J. EDWIN: Executive. b. Detroit, MI, June 27, 1914. e. St. John's Coll. m. Marjorie R. Baker, actress. In 1935 produced Asylum of Horrors, stage show featuring the Frankenstein monster (in person), which played for over 40 years. Known professionally as Dr. Silkini. In 1960 organized Intl. Artists Pictures, of which he is pres., to produce films.
PICTURES: Phycoscope, Magic Land of Mother Goose, Santa Visits Mother Goose Land, Vampire's Coffin, Teenage Tramp, Aztec Mummy.

BAKER, JOE DON: Actor. b. Groesbeck, TX, Feb. 12, 1936. e. North Texas State Coll., B.B.A., 1958. Began career on N.Y. stage, in Marathon 33 and Blues for Mr. Charlie.
PICTURES: Cool Hand Luke (film debut), 1967. Guns of the Magnificent Seven, Adam at Six A.M., The Wild Rovers, Welcome Home, Soldier Boys, Junior Bonner, Walking Tall, Charley Varrick, The Outfit, Golden Needles, Mitchell, Framed, Wacko, The Natural, Fletch, Getting Even, The Living Daylights, The Killing Time, Leonard, Part 6, Criminal Law.
TELEVISION: Mongo's Back in Town, To Kill a Cop, That Certain Summer, Power (prod.), The Abduction of Karl Swenson. Series: Eisheid, In the Heat of the Night.

BAKER, ROBERT H.: Management consultant. b. Springfield, OH, Oct. 14, 1943. e. Kent State U.A., 1965 (broadcasting); Michigan State U. M.A. 1966 (TV/radio management). Disc jockey, newsman, anchor at various Ohio and Mich. AM and FM stations 1960–66. Storer Broadcasting Co.: local-regional acct. exec WSPD-TV, 1966–69; Storer TV Sales, national rep, 1969–72; WSPD-TV national sales mgr. 1972–74 and gen. sales mgr 1974–75. Owner-gen. mgr. WBIS-AM (Bristol, CT), 1975–76. Sales mgr KDKA-TV Pittsburgh 1976–79; Television Bureau of Advertising markting sales exec 1979– 81; v.p. local sales 1981–86; exec. v.p. operations 1986–88. President, Management Communications Consultants, Nashville, 1988–present. Mem.: National Speakers Assn. (and TN chap.) 1988–present.

BAKER, ROBERT S.: Producer. b. London, 1916. Entered industry 1937 as assistant director. 1939–46: Army Film Unit. Produced 50 films including Crossplot, Sea of Sand.
TELEVISION: Produced: The Saint (1962–69), Gideon's Way. Directed: The Treasure of Monte Cristo, Hellfire Club, The Siege of Sidney Street, Jack the Ripper. Producer: The Persuaders, 1976–78: Return of the Saint. Devised: Return to Treasure Island. Exec. prod.: The Saint in Manhattan.

BAKER, ROY: Producer, Director. b. London. e. Lycée Corneille, Rouen; City of London School. Ass't dir. with Gainsborough 1934–40; served in Army 1940–46.
PICTURES: Operation Disaster, Don't Bother to Knock, Inferno, One That Got Away, A Night to Remember, The Singer Not the Song, Flame in the Streets, Quartermass and the Pit, The Anniversary, Vampire Lovers, Dr. Jekyll and Mr. Hyde, Asylum (Paris Grand Prize), Seven Golden Vampires.
TELEVISION: The Human Jungle, The Saint, Gideon's Way, The Baron, The Avengers, The Champions, Department S., The Persuaders, Danger UXB, Minder.

BAKER, DR. WILLIAM F.: Executive. b. 1944. e. Case Western Reserve U., B.A., M.A., Ph.D. Began broadcasting career in Cleveland while still a student. Joined Scripps-Howard Broadcasting, 1971. Joined Group W as v.p. and general mgr., WJZ-TV, 1978; served as pres. and CEO, Group W Productions; pres. of Group W. Television, 1979; chmn., Group W Satellite Communications, 1981; 1983, carried Explorers Club flag to top of world, becoming one of few in history to visit both North and South Poles; April 1987, appointed pres. and CEO, WNET/Thirteen, N.Y. PBS station.

BAKSHI, RALPH: Animator, Writer, Director. b. Haifa, Palestine, Oct. 26, 1938. Began career at Terrytoons at age 21 as cell painter and animator, then dir. and creative dir. 1966, joined Paramount cartoon dept. Pres., Bakshi Prods. Created original "Deputy Dawg" and "Mighty Heroes."
PICTURES: Fritz the Cat, Heavy Traffic, Coonskin, Wizards (also prod.), The Lord of the Rings, Hey, Good Lookin', American Pop, Fire and Ice, Cannonball Run II (animator).
TELEVISION: Casper and Friends (dir.), creator of Mighty Mouse: The New Adventures, This Ain't Bebop (Amer. Playhouse, dir., s.p.).

BALA, JOHN: Executive. e. Yale U., Harvard U., UCLA Graduate Sch., management. Joined Rand Corp. to work in public-policy research for 4 years; then to 20th Fox as mgr. of financial analysis in corporate dev. dept. 1982–83, dir. of finance research for Times-Mirror Videotex Services. Dec. 1983, joined 20th-Fox as v.p. of worldwide mkt. research.

BALABAN, BOB: Actor. b. Chicago, IL, Aug. 16, 1945. Began working with Second City troupe while still in high school. Attended Colgate U. and NYU while appearing on Broadway in Plaza Suite.
PICTURES: Midnight Cowboy, Me Natalie, The Strawberry Statement, Catch 22, Making It, Day For Night, Bank Shot, Girlfriends, Close Encounters of the Third Kind, Report to the Commissioner, Altered States, Prince of the City, Absence of Malice, Whose Life Is It Anyway?, 2010, In Our Hands (doc.), End of the Line, Dead-Bang, Parents (dir. debut).
STAGE: You're a Good Man, Charlie Brown, The Inspector General, Who Wants to Be the Lone Ranger?, The Basic Training of Pavlo Hummel, The Children, The White House Murder Case, Some of My Best Friends, The Three Sisters, The Boys Next Door, Speed-the-Plow.
TELEVISION: Movies: Marriage: Year One. *Director:* Tales From the Darkside, Amazing Stories, Penn & Teller's Invisible Thread.

BALABAN, ELMER: President, H. & E. Balaban Corp., Chicago, IL. e. U. of Pennsylvania, 1931. With Paramount Publix 1931; Balaban & Katz, 1933; then H. & E. Balaban Corp. Pres., Plains Television; interest in WTVO, Rockford, IL; interest in WHNB, Hartford, Conn. and numerous cable-TV systems.

BALDWIN, ALEC: Actor. b. Amityville, NY, April 3, 1958. e. George Washington U., NYU. Trained at Lee Strasberg Theatre Inst. Started career in daytime TV on The Doctors while appearing on stage in A Midsummer Night's Dream. Moved to L.A. where cast in TV pilots, series and movies.
THEATER: Bdwy: The Wager, Summertree, A Life in the Theatre (Hartman), Study in Scarlet (Williamstown), Loot (Theatre World Award, 1986), Serious Money.
PICTURES: Forever Lulu (debut, 1986); She's Having a Baby; Beetlejuice, Married to the Mob, Cohen and Tate, Working Girl, Talk Radio, Next of Kin, Great Balls of Fire!, Miami Blues, The Hunt for Red October.
TELEVISION: Knots Landing (series), Movies: Dress Gray, The Alamo: 13 Days to Glory, Sweet Revenge.

BALIN, INA: Actress. b. Brooklyn, NY, Nov. 12, 1940. e. Forest Hills H.S.; parttime drama, psychology courses, NYU. Comm. model, salesgirl, receptionist. Prof. debut, Perry Como Show. Film debut, The Black Orchid. Toured Europe 1961. Int'l Star of Tomorrow. Hollywood Foreign Press Golden Globe Award, Theater World Award, Western Heritage Award (Natl. Cowboy Hall of Fame).
THEATER: Bdwy: Compulsion, Majority of One; Pre-Bdwy tryout: Garden in the Sea, Face to Face. Also 4 seasons summer stock and touring.
PICTURES: From the Terrace, The Young Doctors, The Comancheros, The Greatest Story Ever Told, The Patsy, Act of Reprisal, Run Like a Thief, The Desperate Mission, The Don is Dead, Charro!, The Projectionist, The Comeback Trail, Galyon.
TELEVISION: American Heritage, Stoney Burke, Adventures in Paradise, Kraft Theatre, The Lieutenant, Bonanza, The Loner, Voyage to the Bottom of the Sea, Run for Your Life, It Takes a Thief, Airwolf, Harry O, Ironsides, Murder She Wrote, and many others as well as guest on numerous talk shows. Movies: The Lonely Profession, Call to Danger (also pilot), The Police Story, The Immigrants, Panic on the 5:22, The Children of An Lac (also story, exec. prod.), Danger in Paradise, Hostage Flight.

BALLARD, CARROLL: Director. b. Los Angeles, Oct. 14, 1937. e. UCLA.
PICTURES: The Black Stallion; Never Cry Wolf; The Nutcracker.

BALLHAUS, MICHAEL: Cinematographer. b. Berlin, Germany, August 5, 1935.
PICTURES: Deine Zartlichkeiten, Two of Us, Whity, Beware of a Holy Whore, Tschetan, The Indian Boy, The Bitter Tears of Petra von Kant, Fox and his Friends, Mother Kusters Goes to Heaven, Summer Guests, Satan's Brew, I Only Want You To Love Me, Adolf and Marlene, Chinese Roulette, Bolweiser, Willie and the Chinese Cat, Women in New York, Despair, The Marriage of Maria Braun, Germany in Autumn, German Spring, The Uprising, Big and Little, Malou, Looping, Baby, It's You; Friends and Husbands, Dear Mr. Wonderful, Magic Mountain, Edith's Diary, Aus der Familie der Panzereschen, The Autograph, Heart Breakers, Old Enough, Reckless, After Hours, Under the Cherry Moon, The Color of Money, Sheer Madness, Baja Oklahoma, The House on Carroll Street, Broadcast News, The Last Temptation of Christ, Working Girl, Dirty Rotten Scoundrels, Good Fellas, The Fabulous Baker Boys.

BALSAM, MARTIN: Actor. b. New York, NY, Nov. 4, 1919. e. New School for Social Research. NY stage debut Ghost for Sale, 1941.
THEATER: Lamp at Midnight, The Wanhope Building, High Tor, A Sound of Hunting, Macbeth, Sundown Beach, The Closing Door, You Know I Can't Hear You When the Water's Running (Tony Award, 1967), Cold Storage (Obie Award).
PICTURES: On the Waterfront, (1954). Twelve Angry Men, Time Limit, Marjorie Morningstar, Al Capone, Middle of the Night, Psycho, Ada, Breakfast at Tiffany's, Cape Fear, Who's Been Sleeping in My Bed?, The Carpetbaggers, Youngblood Hawke, Seven Days in May, Harlow, The Bedford Incident, A Thousand Clowns (Academy Award), After the Fox, Hombre, 2001: A Space Odyssey, Trilogy, Catch 22, Little Big Man, Tora, Tora, Tora; The Anderson Tapes, The Stone Killer, Summer Wishes, Winter Dreams; The Taking of Pelham One Two Three, Murder on the Orient Express, Mitchell, All The President's Men, Two-Minute Warning, The Sentinel, Silver Bears, Cuba, The Goodbye People, St. Elmo's Fire, Death Wish, The Delta Force, Whatever It Takes, Private Investigations, Once Again.
TELEVISION: Actors Studio Theatre, US Steel Hour, Mr. Peepers, Alfred Hitchcock Presents, Arrest and Trial, Queenie, Archie Bunker's Place (series regular), Little Gloria, Happy at Last, Cold Storage, Space, Murder in Space, Raid on Entebbe, Grown Ups, Glitter, Kids Like These, The Child Saver.

BANCROFT, ANNE: Actress. r.n. Anna Maria Italiano; b. New York, NY, Sept. 17, 1931. m. director Mel Brooks. e. American Acad. of Dramatic Arts. Acting debut on TV, Studio One as Anne Marno; many TV shows.
THEATER: Two For the Seasaw (Tony Award, 1958), The Miracle Worker (Tony Award, 1960), Mother Courage, The Devils, A Cry of Players, Golda, Duet For One.
PICTURES: Don't Bother to Knock (debut, 1952), Tonight We Sing, Treasure of the Golden Condor, Kid from Left Field, Demetrius and the Gladiators, Gorilla at Large, The Raid, Life in the Balance, New York Confidential, The Naked Street, The Last Frontier, Walk the Proud Land, Nightfall, The Girl in the Black Stockings, Restless Breed, The Miracle Worker (Academy Award), The Pumpkin Eater, The Slender Thread, Seven Women, The Graduate, Young Winston, The Prisoner of Second Avenue, The Hindenburg, Lipstick, Silent Movie, The Turning Point, Fatso (also dir. & s.p.), The Elephant Man, To Be or Not to Be, Garbo Talks, Agnes of God, 'night Mother, 84 Charing Cross Road, Torch Song Trilogy, Bert Rigby, You're a Fool.
TELEVISION: Mini-series: Jesus of Nazareth; Marco Polo; Specials: I'm Getting Married; Annie and the Hoods; Annie: The Woman in the Life of a Man (dir., writer, star, Emmy Award, 1970).

BAND, ALBERT: Producer, Director. b. Paris, France, May 7, 1924. e. Lyceum Louis le Grand, won French-English Literature Prize 1938; entered film industry as cutter Pathe Lab.; prod. ass't to John Huston at MGM; first screen credit adaptation Red Badge of Courage novel; first direction, The Young Guns; formed Maxim Productions, Inc., Sept. 1956; prod. Recently formed Albert Band Intl. Prods., Inc.
PICTURES The Young Guns, (dir.), I Bury the Living, (prod., dir.). Face of Fire, (prod., dir.), The Avenger (dir.), Grand Canyon Massacre (dir.), The Tramplers (prod., dir.)The Hellbenders (prod.), A Minute to Pray, A Second to Die; Little Cigars, Dracula's Dog, She Came to the Valley, Metalstorm, The Destruction of Jared, Swordkill, Buy and Cell (exec. prod.), Troll, Terrorvision, Ghoulies II, Robojox.

BAND, CHARLES: Producer-Director. b. Los Angeles, CA, 1952. Son of Albert Band. Formed the Bandcompany, 1988.
PICTURES: Crash, End of the World, Laserblast, Tourist Trap, The Alchemist, Parasite, Metalstorm: The Destruction of Jared-Syn, Swordkill, Ghoulies, The Dungeonmaster, Future Cop, Re-Animator, I Eat Cannibals, Crawlspace, Troll, Eliminators, *Exec. Prod.:* Prison, Deadly Weapon, Ghoulies II, Buy and Cell, Catacombs, Arena, Pulse Pounders (prod.-dir.), Robojox, Ghost Town, The Pit and the Pendulum, Shadowzone, Puppet Master (also story), Meridian (dir.).

BANDY, MARY LEA: Director, Dept. of Film, Museum of Modern Art. b. Evanston, IL, June 16, 1943. e. Stanford U., B.A., 1965. Asst. editor, Harry Abrams and Museum of Modern Art. Administrator (1978–80) and since 1980 director, Dept. of Film, Museum of Modern Art. Editor of MOMA film publications incl.: Rediscovering French Film (1983). Member: Advisory Board, AFI's National Center for Preservation of Film and Video; Film Advisory Comm., American Federation of Arts; Advisory Comm. on Film, Japan Society; Advisory Comm. NY State Motion Picture and Television Advisory Board. Co-president, National Alliance of Media Arts Center, 1986–87, 1987–88. Bd. mem.: Intl. Film Seminars, Collective For Living Cinema, MacDowell Colony.

BANJERJEE, VICTOR: Actor. b. Calcutta, India. Was instrumental in forming the first Screen Extras Union in India, presently founding secretary. Won international recognition for A Passage to India (1985). Stage: Pirates of Penzance (at 5), An August Requiem (director, 1981), Desert Song, Godspell.
PICTURES: The Chess Players (debut). In India: Hullabaloo, Madhurban, Tanaya, Pratidan, Prarthana, Dui Prithri, Kalyug, Arohan, Jaipur Junction (German), A Passage to India, The Home and the World, Hard to Be a God.
TELEVISION: Dadah Is Death, Foreign Body.

BANNEN, IAN: Actor. b. Airdrie, Scotland, June 29, 1928. Early career Shakespeare Memorial Theatre (now RSC), Stratford-on-Avon. Film debut Battle Hell (1956).
STAGE: A View From the Bridge, The Iceman Cometh, Long Days Journey Into Night, Sergeant Musgrave's Dance. Royal Shakespeare Thea. Co. 1961–62. Toys in the Attic, Hamlet, As You Like It (with Vanessa Redgrave), Romeo and Juliet, Othello, The Blood Knot, Devil's Disciple, The Iceman Cometh, Hedda Gabler, Translations (Drama Critics Award, 1981); Riverside Mermaid Theatres, 1983; Moon for the Misbegotten (London, Boston, Broadway).
PICTURES: Private's Progress, Rotten to the Core, Miracle in Soho, The Third Key, Behind the Mask, A Tale of Two Cities, The French Mistress, Carlton-Browne of the F.O., Man in Cocked Hat, Macbeth, Station Six Sahara, Mister Moses, The Hill, Flight of the Phoenix, (nominated for AA), Sailor

From Gibraltar, Penelope, Too Late the Hero, The Deserter, Jane Eyre, Fright, The Offence (BAFTA nom.), The Macintosh Man, Bite the Bullet, Watcher in the Woods, Eye of the Needle, Night Crossing, Gandhi, Gorky Park, Defense of the Realm, Lamb, Hope and Glory (BAFTA nom.), The Courier, The Match, George's Island, Ghost Dad.

TELEVISION: Johnny Belinda, Jane Eyre, Jesus of Nazareth, Tinker, Tailor, Soldier, Spy, The Lady and the Highwayman; Fifteen Streets.

BANNER, BOB: Producer, Director. b. Ennis, TX, Aug. 15, 1921. e. Southern Methodist U., B.A., 1939–43; Northwestern U., M.A., 1946–48. U.S. Naval Reserve 1943–46; faculty, Northwestern U., 1948–50; staff dir., NBC-TV in Chicago, 1949–50; dir., Garroway at Large, 1949–50; prod. & dir., Fred Waring Show, 1950–53; dir. Omnibus. Metropolitan Opera Prod., 1953; Nothing But the Best (prod. dir.), 1953; Omnibus, 1953–54; Dave Garroway Show, 1953–54; (prod. dir); Dinah Shore Show, 1954–57; exec. prod. Garry Moore Show; exec. prod. Candid Camera TV show; exec. prod., Carnegie Hall Salutes Jack Benny; exec. prod., Julie & Carol at Carnegie Hall; exec. prod., Carol & Co., 1963; Jimmy Dean Show, 1963–66; Calamity Jane, Once Upon A Mattress, 1964; The Entertainers, 1965; Carol × 2, 1966; Kraft Summer Music Hall, 1966, Carol & Co., Ice Follies, Carol Burnett Show, Peggy Fleming at Madison Square Garden, 1967; John Davidson at Notre Dame, Here's Peggy Fleming; Peggy Fleming at Sun Valley, The American West of John Ford; Love! Love! Love!—Hallmark Hall of Fame; To Europe with Love.

PICTURES Mongo's Back in Town.

TELEVISION: Movies: Warning Shot, The Last Survivors, Journey From Darkness, My Sweet Charlie, Bud and Lou. Special: Peggy Fleming Visits the Soviet Union. Game Show: Almost Anything Goes. Specials: Perry Como's Lake Tahoe Holiday, Perry Como's Christmas In Mexico, Perry Como's Hawaiian Holiday, Perry Como's Spring In New Orleans. Daily Variety Series: Don Ho Show; Perry Como Las Vegas Style, Perry Como's Christmas in Austria, Jr. Almost Anything Goes, All-Star Anything Goes, Peggy Fleming and Holiday on Ice at Madison Square Garden; Julie Andrews, One Step Into Spring; Leapin' Lizards, It's Liberace; Perry Como's Easter By The Sea, Ford Motor Company's 75th Anniversary; Gift of Solid Gold; Specials starring Bob Hope, Julie Andrews, Andy Williams; Series: Solid Gold; Star Search; It's Showtime at the Apollo.

BAR, JACQUES JEAN LOUIS: Executive. Producer, Exhibitor. b. Chateauroux, France, Sept. 12, 1921. e. Lycées Lakanal and Saint Louis, France. Formed Cité-Films S.A., 1947; CIPRA in assoc. with MGM, 1961; S.C.B., Bourges, 8 cinemas; C.C.C., Cannes, 7 cinemas; S.C.M., Le Mans, 4 cinemas. Pres. Parafrance Production Intl.—Telecip (TV). Hollywood films: Bridge to the Sun, Scratch A Thief, Guns for San Sebastian. Prod. 57 films in France, Spain, Italy, Switzerland, Japan and Brazil 1948–89.

PICTURES: Where the Hot Wind Blows, Bridge to the Sun, Riffifi in Tokyo, A Very Private Affair, Swordsmen of Siena, Monkey in Winter, The Turfist, Any Number Can Win, The Day and the Hour, Joy House, Guns for San Sebastian, Last Known Address, The Homecoming.

BARBER, ARNOLD: Executive. b. London, England. Career in m.p. ind. started with RKO. Subsequently with AB-Pathe following war service until appointment with Warner-Pathe Dist. which led him through sales exec. positions until he headed company. Formed Sotia-Barber Distributors Ltd. in 1970. Now man. dir. Barber Intl. Films, Ltd.

BARBER, FRANCES: Actress. b. Wolverhampton, Eng., 1957. e. Bangor U.; grad. studies in theatre, Cardiff U. Stage experience with fringe theaters including improvisational troupe Hull Truck Theatre Company, Glasgow Citizens and Tricycle Theatre (Killburn) before joining Royal Shakespeare Co. (Camille, Hamlet).

PICTURES: The Missionary, A Zed and Two Noughts, White City, Castaway, Prick Up Your Ears, Sammy and Rosie Get Laid, We Think the World of You, The Grasscutter, Chamber à part.

TELEVISION: Clem, Jackie's Story, Home Sweet Home, Flame to the Phoenix, Reilly, Ace of Spies, Those Glory, Glory Days; Hard Feelings, Behaving Badly, The Nightmare Years.

BARBERA, JOSEPH R.: Executive. b. New York, NY. e. NYU, American Institute of Banking. After schooling joined Irving Trust Co. in N.Y.; started submitting cartoon drawings to leading magazines selling one to Collier's. Left banking to seek career in cartooning. Joined Van Buren Associates as sketch artist, later going to work in animation dept. of MGM Studios. At MGM met William Hanna, who became his lifelong business associate. Made first animated short together in 1940, starting the famous Tom & Jerry series which they produced for 20 years. Left MGM in 1957 to form Hanna-Barbera Productions to make cartoons for TV. Series have included Yogi Bear, Huckleberry Hound, The Flintstones and The Jetsons. Hanna-Barbera became a subsidiary of Taft Bdg. Co. in 1968 with both men operating studio under long-term agreements with Taft. Taft and the studio was sold to Great American Broadcasting, 1988. Barbera is pres. Company entered theatrical production with Hey There It's Yogi Bear, 1964. Then A Man Called Flintstone, Charlotte's Web, C.H.O.M.P.S., Heidi's Song.

BARBOUR, ALAN G.: Writer, Editor, Publisher. b. Oakland, CA, July 25, 1933. e. Rutgers U. m. Catherine Jean Callovini, actress, teacher, American Acad. of Dramatic Arts, American Mime Theatre. U.S. Army, worked as computer programmer. Formed Screen Facts Press in 1963, Screen Facts Magazine. Compiled, edited: The Serials of Republic, The Serials of Columbia, Great Serial Ads, The B Western, Serial Showcase, Hit the Saddle, The Wonderful World of B-Films, Days of Thrills and Adventure, Serial Quarterly, Serial Pictorial, Karloff—A Pictorial History, Errol Flynn—A Pictorial Biography, A Pictorial History of the Serial, A Thousand and One Delights, Cliffhanger, The Old-Time Radio Quiz Book. Direct Mktg. Div., RCA Records. Mgr., A & R, RCA Video Club.

BARBOUR, MALCOLM: Executive. b. London, England, May 3, 1934. e. Radley Coll., Oxford, England, Columbia Coll. At NBC was press info. asst., 1958–59; asst. magazine ed., 1959–62; assoc. mag. ed., 1962–64; sr. mag. ed., 1964–65; mgr. of magazine pub., National Broadcasting Co., 1965–67; pub. mgr., Buena Vista, 1967–68; Eastern story ed., Walt Disney Prod., 1968–69; dir. of adv. & pub. relations, Buena Vista, 1969. Partner, Producers Creative Services, 1976–79. President, The International Picture Show, 1980–81 (Tim Conway comedies The Billion Dollar Hobo and They Went That-A-Way & That-A-Way; Slayer. Distributor: Soldier of Orange, The Magic of Lassie, The Visitor, etc.). President, Barbour/Langley Productions, 1982–present. Producer, Geraldo Rivera specials: American Vice, Innocence Lost, Sons of Scarface, Murder: Live from Death Row, Satan Worship. Producer, Jack Anderson specials. Writer-Producer, Cocaine Blues. Co-screenplay, P.O.W. The Escape (Cannon Films). Executive producer, Cops (Fox).

BARDOT, BRIGITTE: Actress. b. Paris, France, Sept. 28, 1934. r.n. Camille Javal. e. Paris Conservatory. Model. Awarded French Legion of Honor, 1985. Active in the movement to preserve endangered animals. Auctioned her jewels and mementos from her film career, raising $500,000 to create an animal protection foundation, June 1987.

PICTURES Le Trou Normand, Un Acte D'Amour, Helen of Troy, Le Fils De Caroline Cherie, Les Grandes Maneuvres, Doctor at Sea, En Effeuillant La Marguerite, The Bride Is Much Too Beautiful, Moonlight Jewelers, La Femme et Le Pantin, Will You Dance With Me, Manina, La Fille Sans Voiles, Si Versailles M'Etait Conte, Trahi, Futures Vedettes, La Lumiere D'En Face, Une Sacre Gamine, And God Created Woman, Le Parisienne, En Cas De Malheur, Love Is My Profession, Babette Goes to War, La Verite Contempt, A Very Private Affair, Two Weeks in September, Viva Maria, Shalako, Spirits of the Dead, Les Femmes, Les Novices, Boulevard du rhum, Les petroleuses, Don Juan, L'Historie tres bonne et tres joyeuse de Colinot troussechemise.

BARE, RICHARD L.: Producer, Director. b. Turlock, CA. Dir. for Warner: Smart Girls Don't Talk, Flaxy Martin, This Side of the Law, House Across The Street, This Rebel Breed, Girl on the Run, Return of Frontiersman; SDG Best Dir. TV award, 1959; author, The Film Director (Macmillan), 1971.

TELEVISION: 77 Sunset Strip, Maverick, So This is Hollywood, The Islanders, Dangerous Robin, This Rebel Breed, Twilight Zone, Bus Stop, Adventures in Paradise, The Virginian, Kraft Theatre, Run For Your Life, Green Acres series, Farraday and Son, Westwind.

PICTURES: Wrote, directed and produced: Wicked, Wicked, Story of Chang & Eng, City of Shame, Sudden Target, Purple Moon.

BAREN, HARVEY M.: Executive. b. New York, NY, Nov. 25, 1931. e. State U. of New York. Served in U.S. Army, 1952–54; United Artists Corp., 1954–59 (contract dept., print dept., booker—N.Y. branch); asst. to general sls. mgr., Magna Pictures Corp., 1959–61; road show mgr., national sales coordinator, 20th Century-Fox, 1961–71; asst. general sales manager, Allied Artists Pictures, 1971–79; v.p., gen. sls. mgr., Nat'l. Screen Service, 1978–79; v.p., gen. sls. mgr., Cannon Pictures, 1979–80. 1980, pres. of Summit Feature Distributors; 1983, exec. V.P., dir., MGM/UA Classics; 1986, joined New Century/Vista as v.p., sls. admin.

BARENHOLTZ, BEN: Executive. b. Oct. 5, 1935. Whimsically describes ed. as Balcony U. Asst. manager: RKO Bushwick, Brooklyn, 1959–60. Manager: Village Theatre (Fillmore East), N.Y., 1966–68. Owner-operator: Elgin Cinema, 1968–72. President-owner: Libra Film Corp., 1982–84. 1984–present vice-president and partner: Circle Releasing (which launched and distributed The Family Game, Therese, Blood Simple and prod. Raising Arizona).

PICTURES: Miller's Crossing (exec. prod.).

BARI, LYNN: Actress. r.n. Marjorie Bitzer. b. Roanoke, VA, 1917. First Screen appearance as dancing girl in Dancing Lady (MGM). Became Fox contract player 1934.
PICTURES: Shock, Margie, Home Sweet Homicide, Nocturne, Amazing Mr. X, Kid from Cleveland, I'd Climb Highest Mountain, On the Loose, Sunny Side of the Street, Has Anybody Seen My Gal, I Dream of Jeanie, Francis Joins the WACs, AC Meet the Keystone Kops, Women of Pitcairn Island, Damn Citizen, Trauma.

BARISH, KEITH: Producer. b. Los Angeles, CA. Background in finance. 1984 formed partnership with Taft Broadcasting Co., Entertainment Div.
PICTURES: Exec. prod.: Endless Love, Sophie's Choice (prod.), Kiss Me Goodbye, Misunderstood, 9½ Weeks, Light of Day (prod.), The Running Man, The Monster Squad, Ironweed (prod.), The Serpent and the Rainbow, Her Alibi, Hand-Carved Coffins.
TELEVISION: A Streetcar Named Desire (exec. prod.).

BARKER, MICHAEL W.: Executive. b. Nurnberg, Germany, Jan. 9, 1954. e. U. of Texas at Austin, B.S. in intl. communications, 1976. Joined Films Inc. 1979–80, then MGM/UA 1980–83. Co-founder of Orion Classics, a div. of Orion Pictures Corp., v.p. sales and marketing, 1983–present. Member, bd. of dir. Independent Feature Project.

BARKER, ROBERT WILLIAM: TV host. b. Darrington, WA, Dec. 12. e. Springfield Central H.S., Drury Coll. News writer, announcer, disc jockey KTTS until 1949. News editor, staff announcer, Station WWPG; wife, Dorothy Jo. Emcee, Truth or Consequences, 1956. Pres. Bob Barker Prod., Inc., M.C. Miss USA Pageant, CBS-TV, since 1967, M.C. Miss Universe Pageant, CBS-TV since 1967, M.C. Rose Parade, since 1970. Prod.-M. C. Pillsbury Bakeoff, since 1970 CBS. Prod. Lucky Pair, syndicated, M.C. Price Is Right-CBS, 1972; Narrator, 500 Festival Parade, Indianapolis 1969–81.

BARKETT, STEVE: Actor, director, producer, film editor. b. Oklahoma City, OK, Jan. 1, 1950. Exhibited and scored over 52 feature length classic silent films 1966–1968 as dir. of two film series at the Okla. Art Ctr. and Science and Arts Fdn, prior to coming to LA in 1970. Toured in stage prod 1971–1972: Pajama Tops, Winnie the Pooh. Exec in several nontheatrical releasing cos, incl. Independent Film Associates. From 1968 to 1974 was active in film preservation and restoration work on early silent and sound films. Est. The Nautilus Film Co, 1978. Founded and operated Capt. Nemo's Video (1985–1987). Co-wrote and performed with Tricia Drake (Schiotis), 42 episodes of Capt. Nemo's Video Review for radio (1987).
PICTURES: Actor only: The Egyptians are Coming, Corpse Grinders, Dillinger, Night Caller, Cruise Missile, Beverly Hills Vampire, Sword of Vengeance. Prod, director, s.p., ed. only: Collecting, The Fisherman. S.P.: The Massacre, Essence of Evil; The Journey: Aftermath II and Judgment Day (co-s.p.), The Evil Night (co-s.p.). Ed. only: Hurricane Express. Spcl. Fx. only: Warlords. Actor, dir., s.p., prod. and ed: The Movie People; Cassavetes, The Aftermath, The Evil Night.

BARKIN, ELLEN: Actress. b. Bronx, NY, 1959. e. Hunter Coll.; Actors Studio.
THEATER: Irish Coffee (debut, Ensemble Studio Theatre), Shout Across the River, Killings on the Fast Lane, Tobacco Road, Extremities.
PICTURES: Diner, Daniel, Eddie and the Cruisers, Terminal Choice, Tender Mercies, The Adventures of Buckaroo Banzai, Harry and Son, Enormous Changes at the Last Minute, Desert Bloom, Down By Law, The Big Easy, Siesta, Made in Heaven (unbilled), Sea of Love, Johnny Handsome.
TELEVISION: Series: Search for Tomorrow. Movies: Kent State, We're Fighting Back, Act of Vengeance, Parole, Murder Inc., Terrible Joe Moran, Faerie Tale Theatre, Clinton and Nadine.

BARLOW, PHIL: Executive. Began career with National General Theatres in 1961 in Salt Lake City; later transferred to Los Angeles as Southern Calif. div. buyer. Worked as buyer for NGT and Syufy Theatres in San Francisco. Joined General Cinema Corp. in N.Y. as natl. coordinator of film. Served 10 years as v.p. with Edwards Theatre Circuit, being named sr. v.p. in January, 1985. Left to join Buena Vista Dist. Co. as v.p. & gen. sls. mgr. Promoted to senior v.p. & gen. sls. mgr., 1988.

BARNHOLTZ, BARRY: Executive. b. St. Louis, MO, Oct. 12, 1945. e. California State U., Northridge; U. of Southern California; UCLA; W.L.A.U. (studied law). Concert promotions in So. Calif. 1963–71; with Medallion TV as v.p. in chg. sls.; Barnholtz Organization, representing independent prod. cos. for feature films for cable; now sr. v.p. Vidmark, Inc.

BARON, MARK: Executive. Pub./mktg. career at Factors Etc., McFadden, Strauss & Irwin before joining Columbia Pictures as sr. exec. liaison to Coca-Cola Co., coordinating mktg. programs between parent co. and feature film div. Worked as dir. of pub./promo. on Annie and Gandhi. Left to go to Stone/Halinan Associates as exec. v.p., mktg./admin. 1985, formed own mktg./consulting firm specializing in independent film producers before joining Warner Bros. as v.p., pub., coordinating overall pub. & promo. efforts on specific WB film projects.

BARR, ANTHONY: Producer, Director, Actor. r.n. Morris Yaffe. b. St. Louis, MO, March 14, 1921. e. Washington U., B.S. 1942. Actor, asst. stage mgr., 1944–46; stage mgr., Katherine Dunham Dancers, 1946–47; teacher, actor, dir. in chg. Film Actors' Workshop, Professional Theatre Workshop, Hollywood; v.p. current prime time series, ABC-TV; v.p., current dramatic program production, CBS-TV; v.p., CBS Entertainment Prods.
BROADWAY: Jacobowsky and the Colonel, Winters' Tale, Embezzled Heaven.
PICTURES: Actor: People Against O'Hara, Border Incident, The Hollywood Story, The Mozart Story. Co-prod.: Dime with a Halo.
TELEVISION: Director: Art Linkletter's Houseparty, About Faces. Assoc. dir.: Climax, Shower of Stars. Prod.: Climax, Summer Studio One. Assoc. prod.: Climax, Playhouse 90, Pursuit, G.E. Theatre, The Law and Mr. Jones, Four-Star.
BOOK: Acting for the Camera, 1982.

BARR, ROSANNE: Actress. b. Salt Lake City, UT, Nov. 3, 1953. e. dropped out of high sch. to hitchike across country landing up in a Colorado artists' colony at 18. After marrying and raising 3 children, while working as a window dresser and part-time cocktail waitress in Denver, began performing in punk bars, biker bars and Unitarian Church coffee-house. Also prod. showcase for women performers, Take Back the Mike at U. of Boulder. 1983 won Denver Laff-Off. Moved to Los Angeles where performed at The Comedy Store, and showcased on TV special Funny and The Tonight Show. Autobiography: My Life as a Woman (1989).
PICTURE: She-Devil.
TELEVISION: Special: On Location: The Roseanne Barr Show (1987, 2 ACE awards). Series: Roseanne.

BARRAULT, MARIE-CHRISTINE: Actress. b. Paris, France, March 21, 1944.
PICTURES: My Night at Maud's; The Daydreamer; Lancelot of the Lake; The Aspern Papers; Les Intrus; La Famille Grossfeld; John Gluskstadt; Cousin Cousine; By the Tennis Courts; L'Etat Sauvage; Perceval; The Medusa Touch; Tout est a nous; Femme Entre Chien et Loup; Ma Cherie; Stardust Memories; Table for Five; Josephs Tochter; Eine Liebe in Deutschland; Les Mots Pour le Dire; Swann in Love; Grand Piano; Prisonnieres; Un Eté de orages.

BARRETT, JAMES LEE: Screenwriter, Producer. b. Charlotte, NC, Nov. 19, 1929. e. Anderson Jr. Coll., Furman U., Pennsylvania State U., Art Students League. U.S. Marine Corps.
PICTURES: The D.I. (Marine Corps Combat Correspondents Award), The Greatest Story Ever Told, The Truth About Spring, Shenandoah, The Green Berets, Bandolero, The Undefeated, tick ... tick ... tick, The Cheyenne Social Club, Fools' Parade, Something Big, Smokey and the Bandit, Wild Horse Hank.
STAGE: Shenandoah (Tony Award, best musical book, 1974–75; Theatre Club annual award).
TELEVISION: The Awakening Land, Parts I and II (Certificate of Commendation, American Women in Radio and Television), Stubby Pringles' Christmas (Humanitas nom.), The Day Christ Died, Belle Starr, Angel City, Mayflower: The Pilgrim Experience, You Are the Jury, Big Bad John, The Defiant Ones, Stagecoach (Wrangler Award, National Cowboy Hall of Fame), Vengeance, Poker Alice, April Morning, Jesse.
SERIES: Our House (creator).

BARRETT, RONA: News correspondent e. NYU (communications major). Created the column, Rona Barrett's Young Hollywood, which led to featured column in 1960 in Motion Picture Magazine and a nationally syndicated column distributed to 125 newspapers by the North American Newspaper Alliance. Turned to TV; initial appearances on ABC Owned Stations in 5 cities, providing two-minute reports for local newscasts. Resulted in Dateline Hollywood a network morning prog., co-hosted by Joanna Barnes. In 1969 created first daily syndicated TV news segment for Metromedia. 1975, became arts and entertainment editor for ABC's Good Morning America. 1980, joined NBC News. Publ. and exec. editor, newsletter, The Rona Barrett Report. 1985, pres., Rona Barrett Enterprises, Inc., sr. corresp., Entertainment Tonight; Mutual Radio Network. 1988: creator of original novels for television, for NBC prods.

BARRIE, BARBARA: Actress. b. Chicago, IL, May 23, 1931. e. U. of TX, B.F.A., 1953. Trained for stage at Herbert Berghof Studio. NY stage debut, The Wooden Dish (1955). Film debut, Giant (1956).
THEATER: The Crucible, American Shakespeare Fest., Stratford, CT 1958–59, The Beaux Stratagem, The Taming of the Shrew, Conversations in the Dark, All's Well That Ends Well, Happily Never After, Horseman, Pass By; Company,

The Selling of the President, The Prisoner of Second Avenue, The Killdeer, California Suite, Big and Little, Isn't It Romantic.
PICTURES: The Caretakers, One Potato, Two Potato (best actress, Cannes Film Fest, 1964), The Bell Jar, Breaking Away, Private Benjamin, Real Men, The Passage.
TELEVISION: Series: Diana (1973), Barney Miller (1975–76), Breaking Away, Tucker's Witch, Reggie, Double Trouble, Love of Life. Guest appearances: Ben Casey, The Fugitive, Dr. Kildare, Alfred Hitchcock Presents, The Defenders, Mary Tyler Moore Show, Lou Grant, Trapper John, M.D. Movies: To Be Young, Gifted and Black, 79 Park Avenue, Summer of My German Soldier, Roots, Part II, Tell Me My Name, To Race the Wind, Backstairs at the White House, Working, Barefoot in the Park, Two of a Kind, An American Romance, The Execution, Vital Signs, Winnie, My First Love. Special: What's Alan Watching?

BARRIE, GEORGE: Executive. b. Brooklyn, NY Feb. 9, 1918. e. NYU. Left school to embark on business career, beginning with soda fountain concessions in drugstores. Played in dance band and later became booker for bands. Turned to beauty products, forming co. Caryl Richards. In 1963 acquired Faberge, merging it with own firm. Entered leisure time field with records, books, films and TV.
PICTURES: A Touch of Class, Night Watch, Welcome to Arrow Beach, Book of Numbers, Hang-Up, Miracles Still Happen, Hugo the Hippo, Whiffs, Thieves.

BARRON, ARTHUR RAY: Executive. b. Mt. Lake, MN, July 12, 1934, e. San Diego State U. 1956–60, B.S. Accounting. Certified public acc't, Calif., 1960. Coopers & Lybrand, 1960–63; Desilu Productions, Inc., 1963–67; v.p. finance and administration, Paramount Television, 1967–70 v.p. Finance, Paramount Pictures Corp., 1970; sr. v.p. finance and admin., 1971; exec. v.p., finance & admin., 1974; exec. v.p. 1980; exec. v.p., Gulf & Western Industries, entertainment & communications group, 1983; promoted to pres., 1984–Feb., 1988. Retired.

BARRY, DONALD (Red): Actor, r.n. Donald Barry de Acosta; b. Houston, TX. e. Texas Sch. Mines. In 1936 in Night Waitress (RKO Radio), thereafter to 1939 in number of feature pictures, including The Woman I Love, Sinners in Paradise, The Crowd Roars. From 1939 in Westerns, attaining wide popularity as Republic Western star. Entertained troops overseas. Voted one of first ten Money-Making Western Stars in Motion Picture Herald-Fame Polls 1942, 1943, 1944.
PICTURES: Jesse James' Women, Untamed Heiress, Twinkle in God's Eye, I'll Cry Tomorrow, Seven Men From Now, Shalako, The Shakiest Gun in the West, Orca, The Swarm, Back Roads.

BARRY, GENE: Actor. r.n. Eugene Klass. b. New York, NY, June 14, 1921. e. New Utrecht H.S., Brooklyn. Appeared in little & summer theatre.
BROADWAY: Rosalinda, Catherine Was Great, Happy Is Larry, Bless You All, The Would-Be Gentleman, La Cage aux Folles.
PICTURES: Atomic City, Girls of Pleasure Island, War of the Worlds, Those Redheads from Seattle, Alaska Seas, Red Garters, Naked Alibi, Soldier of Fortune, Purple Mask, Houston Story, Back from Eternity, China Gato, 27th Day, Maroc 7.
TELEVISION: Bat Masterson, Burke's Law, The Name of the Game, The Adventurer. Movies: Prescription Murder, Aspen, A Cry for Love, Adventures of Nellie Bly, Paradise.

BARRY, JOHN: Composer, arranger, conductor. b. York, England, 1933. Artist and prod., CBS Records.
PICTURES: Beat Girl, Never Let Go, The Amorous Prawn, From Russia With Love, Seance on a Wet Afternoon, Zulu, Goldfinger, The Ipcress File, The Knack, King Rat, Born Free, Thunderball, The Chase, The Wrong Box, The Quiller Memorandum, The Whisperers, Deadfall, Petulia, You Only Live Twice, The Lion in Winter, Midnight Cowboy, The Appointment, The Tamarind Seed, The Dove, The Day of the Locust, Robin and Marian, King Kong, The Deep, The Betsy, Moonraker, The Black Hole, Hanover Street, Starcrash, Game of Death, Raise the Titanic, Somewhere in Time, Inside Moves, Touched By Love, Body Heat, The Legend of the Lone Ranger, Hammett, High Road to China, Octopussy, The Golden Seal, Frances, Mike's Murder, Until September, The Cotton Club, A View to a Kill, Jagged Edge, Out of Africa, Howard the Duck, Peggy Sue Got Married, The Living Daylights, Hearts of Fire, Masquerade, A Killing Affair.
TELEVISION: Elizabeth Taylor in London, Sophia Loren in Rome.

BARRYMORE, DREW: Actress. b. Los Angeles, CA, Feb. 22, 1975. Daughter of John Barrymore, Jr. At 11 months was in first commercial.
PICTURES: Altered States, E.T.: The Extra Terrestrial, Firestarter, Irreconcilable Differences, Cat's Eye, See You in the Morning, Far From Home.
TELEVISION: Suddenly Love, Bogey, Babes in Toyland, Disneyland's 30th Anniversary, Night of 100 Stars II, Con Sawyer and Hucklemary Finn, The Screaming Woman, Conspiracy of Love, 15 & Getting Straight.

BARRYMORE, JOHN BLYTH, JR.: Actor. b. Beverly Hills, CA, June 4, 1932. e. St. John's Military Acad., various public and private schools. p. late John Barrymore, Delores Costello. Debut in The Sundowners; many TV appearances.
PICTURES: High Lonesome, Big Night, Thunderbirds, While the City Sleeps, Shadow on the Window, War of the Zombies, Never Love a Stranger, The Night They Killed Rasputin, High School Confidential.

BART, PETER: Executive. e. Swarthmore Coll. and The London School of Economics. Eight years as corrp. for New York Times and wrote for such magazines as Harper's, The Atlantic, Saturday Review, etc. Joined Paramount Pictures in 1965. Named exec. ass't. to Robert Evans, exec. in charge of world-wide prod. Appointed v.p. prod. Resigned 1973 to develop and produce own films for Para. Appointed pres. Lorimar Films, 1978. Resigned, 1979, to be independent producer. 1983, joined MGM as sr. v.p., prod., m.p. div. Resigned, 1985, to be indep. prod. Novels: Author-Thy Kingdom Come (1983); Destinies (1979).
PICTURES: Islands in the Stream, Fun with Dick and Jane (prod.), Revenge of the Nerds (exec. prod.); Youngblood (prod.); Revenge of the Nerds II (prod.); Nobody's Children (prod., s.p.).

BARTEL, PAUL: Director, Writer, Actor. b. New York, NY, Aug. 6, 1938. e. UCLA, B.A. At 13 spent summer working at UPA Cartoons. Later at UCLA won acting and playwriting awards and prod. animated and doc. films. Awarded Fulbright schl. to study film dir. at Centro Sperimentale di Cinematografia in Rome where dir. short Progetti (presented Venice Fest., 1962). Then at Army Pictorial Center, L.I. City. Asst. dir. military training films and writer-dir. monthly news doc. series, Horizontos for U.S. Information Agency.
PICTURES: *Director*: The Secret Cinema (short), Naughty Nurse (short), Private Parts, Death Race 2000, Cannonball (also co-s.p.), Lust in the Dust. *Actor*: Hollywood Boulevard; Piranha, Rock 'n' Roll High School, Mr. Billion, Heart Like a Wheel, Into the Night, Heartbeeps, Amazon Women on the Moon, Baja Oklahoma, Mortuary Academy, Out of the Dark (exec. prod., actor). *Actor-Writer-Director*: Eating Raoul. Scenes From the Class Struggle in Beverly Hills. *Director-Writer*: Not for Publication.
TELEVISION: *Actor*: Alfred Hitchcock Presents, Fame, L.A. Law. *Director*: Amazing Stories (The Secret Cinema, Gershwin's Truck, also s.p., actor), The Hustler of Muscle Beach.

BARTHOLOMEW, FREDDIE: Actor. b. London, England, March 28, 1924. Stage debut 1927; m.p. debut U.S. in David Copperfield, 1935. Worked briefly as TV dir. before becoming a successful advertising exec. with Benton & Bowles in NY and prod. of As the World Turns in 1970s.
PICTURES: Anna Karenina, Lloyds of London, Little Lord Fauntleroy, Devil Is a Sissy, Lord Jeff, Captains Courageous, Kidnapped, Swiss Family Robinson, Naval Academy, Yank at Eton, Junior Army, The Town Went Wild, St. Benny the Dip.

BARTKOWIAK, ANDRZEJ: Cinematographer. b. Lodz, Poland, 1950. Attended Polish Film School. Moved to US in 1972, gaining experience in TV commercials and low-budget features. Protege of Sidney Lumet, for whom did several pictures.
PICTURES: Deadly Hero, Prince of the City, Deathtrap, The Verdict, Daniel, Terms of Endearment, Garbo Talks, Prizzi's Honor, The Morning After, Nuts, Twins, Q&A.

BARTLETT, HALL: Producer, Director, Writer. b. Kansas City, MO, Nov. 27, 1925. e. Yale U., B.A. 1942. U.S. Naval Reserve 1942–47; formed Hall Bartlett Productions, 1952; Author: The Rest of Our Lives.
PICTURES: prod. Navajo (winner of 27 nat'l awards & Festival of Brit. Award at Edinburgh); prod., s.p. Crazy-legs (winner of 9 nat'l awards, including Parents Mag. Gold Medal); prod., dir., s.p. Unchained (winner of Parents Mag. Gold Medal, Brotherhd. award of Nat'l Con. of Christians and Jews); prod., dir., s.p. Durango; prod. dir. s.p. Zero Hour, All the Young Men, Sol Madrid; photog., prod., Changes; prod. dir. Winner of the Sans Sebastian Festival, The Sandpit Generals, prod., dir., writer; winner of Grand Prize of VII International Film Festival of Moscow. Producer, director: Jonathan Livingston Seagull; Cleo Laine Special, Zubin Mehta Special; producer, director, The Children of Sanchez; prod., dir., s.p.: Comeback, Love Is Forever.

BARUCH, ANDRE: Announcer, Commentator. b. Paris, France. m. singer Bea Wain. e. Pratt Inst., Brooklyn; Columbia U.; Beaux Arts. Your Hit Parade (radio with Bea Wain). Commercials for L.A. Cellular, Belgian Waffles, Robinson's Western World Video, Lanvin Perfume. Fashion show commentator; sales conventions, M.C. Pres., Beand Products. (TV and radio.) Performed on over 7,000 radio and TV shows. Member, National Broadcasters Hall of Fame, Board of Pacific Pioneer Broadcasters.

BARUCH, RALPH M.: Executive. b. Paris, France, Aug. 5, 1923. e. The Sorbonne, Administrative aide, SESAC, Inc. 1944–48; account exec., DuMont Television Network, 1948–52; Eastern sales mgr., Consolidated Television Films, 1953–54; account exec., CBS Films, 1954; account supervisor, 1957; dir. intl. sales, 1959; v.p., CBS Enterprises, 1961–70; pres., Viacom Enterprises, 1971; pres., Viacom International, 1979; named chmn. & chief exec. officer, Viacom Intl.; pres., International Radio Television Society; chmn., Rewrite Committee (Communications Act), NCTA; former member of the bd. dirs. and former chmn., Pay Cable Committee, NCTA; chmn. NCTA Public Policy Planning Committee; gov. (NY), fellow of International Council of the National Academy of Television Arts Sciences.

BARWOOD, HAL: Writer, Producer, Director. e. U. of Southern California Sch. of Cinema. Has written scripts in collaboration with Matthew Robbins, Barwood branching out into producing with Corvette Summer in 1978 and directing with Warning Sign in 1985.

PICTURES: Screen plays, all with Robbins: The Sugarland Express, The Bingo Long Traveling All-Stars and Motor Kings, MacArthur, Corvette Summer (also prod.), Dragonslayer (also prod.), Warning Sign (also dir.).

BARYSHNIKOV, MIKHAIL: Dancer, Actor. b. Riga, Latvia, Jan. 27, 1948. Joined Kirov Ballet, Leningrad, 1969–74; defected to U.S. With American Ballet Theatre 1974–78; New York City Ballet Company 1978–79; named director of the American Ballet Theatre. Bdwy stage debut, Metamorphosis (1989).

PICTURES: The Turning Point, That's Dancing!, White Nights, Dancers.

TELEVISION: Baryshnikov at the White House, Bob Hope on the Road to China, Baryshnikov on Broadway, AFI Salute to Fred Astaire, Baryshnikov in Hollywood, AFI Salute to Gene Kelly, David Gordon's Made in USA, All Star Gala at Ford's Theater.

BASCH, BUDDY: Print Media Syndicater, Publicist, Producer. b. South Orange, NJ, June 28, 1922. e. Columbia U. Began career as youngest radio editor in U.S. at 15, since written for national mags, syndicates, wire services, and newspapers. Edited and published "Top Hit Club News"-7 years. Joined Donahue and Coe 1940 on m.p. accounts, U.S. Army in Europe 1942–45. 1945–67: own publicity and promotion office, working on m.p. company accounts and stars such as Burl Ives, Dinah Shore, Tony Martin, Danny Kaye, Peter Lorre, Tony Bennett, Gloria De Haven, McGuire Sisters, Rhonda Fleming, Sammy Davis, Jr., Anna Maria Alberghetti, Polly Bergen, Meyer Davis, The Beatles, Glenn Miller and Tommy Dorsey Orchestras. Produced many shows for radio, TV and stage in New York, Newark, Chicago, Hartford. Asst. to publisher, The Brooklyn Eagle 1962. 1966 formed Buddy Basch Feature Syndicate, covering assignments on show business, travel and general subjects for N.Y. Daily News, A.P., Travel/Holiday, Frontier Magazine, Kaleidoscope, True, United Features, Gannett Westchester-Rockland Newspapers, Bergen (NJ) Record, Argosy, N.A.N.A., Womens' New Service, Today Magazine, Christian Science Monitor, New York Post, Inflight Magazine, Deseret News, California Canadian, Diversion. Member: Friars Club since 1959. Chairman, VIP Reception and Security for Friars luncheons and dinners. Served as Chairman of Elections (6 times). Member of Admission Comm. and House Committee. Contributing ed. Friars Epistle.

BASINGER, KIM: Actress. b. Athens, GA, Dec. 8, 1953. e. Neighborhood Playhouse. Began career as a Breck shampoo model (as her mother had been) then as a Ford model in New York. Pursued singing career under the nom-de-chant, Chelsea.

PICTURES: Hard Candy, Never Say Never Again, Mother Lode, The Man Who Loved Women, The Natural, 9½ Weeks, Fool for Love, No Mercy, Blind Date, Nadine, My Stepmother is an Alien, Batman.

TELEVISION: Series: Six Million Dollar Man (1977); Dog and Cat (1977). Movies: From Here to Eternity, The Ghost of Flight 401, Katie: Portrait of a Centerfold, Killjoy.

BASS, SAUL: Director, Producer. b. New York, NY, May 8, 1920. e. Arts Students League. Pres., Saul Bass/Herb Yager & Assoc. Has directed short films, m.p. titles/prologues/epilogues, TV show openings, TV commercials. Directorial feature debut in 1974 with Phase IV.

PICTURES: (shorts), The Searching Eye, From Here to There, Why Man Creates (Academy Award); Notes on the Popular Arts (AA nomination), The Solar Film (AA nomination), Bass on Titles, Quest; *Titles* Carmen Jones, The Man With The Golden Arm, Anatomy of a Murder, Vertigo, Psycho, Around the World in 80 Days, West Side Story, That's Entertainment II, Broadcast News, Big.

BASSETT, LINDA: Actress. Extensive career in the English theatre.

THEATER: Began with Interplay Community Theatre Company. In 1977 joined Belgrade Theater-in-Education Company in Coventry as actress, writer, and director. 1982, joined Joint Stock Theatre Group for workshop production of Caryl Churchill's Fen (London and Public Theater, NY). Starred in Abel's Sister (London), The Cherry Orchard, Medea, Woyceck, The Bald Prima Donna and George Dandin with Leicester Haymarket Studio Season. Aunt Dan and Lemon (London and NY).

PICTURES: Debut as Gertrude Stein in Waiting for the Moon, Leave to Remain, Paris By Night.

TELEVISION: Traffik.

BATCHELOR, JOY: Director. b. Watford, England, May 12, 1914. e. grammar school & art school. Early career, illustrator & designer. Entered m.p. in 1935 & is connected with the production of over 500 cartoon films. Co-director, co-prod., collab. s.p., Animal Farm, first British full length color feature cartoon; dir. Dam the Delta, The Colombo Plan, The Commonwealth, Ruddigore, The Five, Wotdot, Contact, Ass and the Stick. Christmas Feast, Carry on Milkmaids.

BATEMAN, JASON: Actor. b. Rye, NY, Feb. 19, 1969. Brother of actress Justine Bateman. Son of prod.-theatrical mgr. Kent Bateman. Started career in commercials until cast in Little House on the Prairie at 12 (1981).

PICTURES: Teen Wolf Too (prod. by father), Sketches.

TELEVISION: Series: Little House on the Prairie, Silver Spoons, It's Your Move, Valerie, Valerie's Family, The Hogan Family. Movies: The Fantastic World of D.C. Collins, The Thanksgiving Promise, Robert Kennedy and His Times, Can You Feel Me Dancing, The Bates Motel, Crossing the Mob. Specials: Just a Little More Love, Candid Camera: Eat! Eat! Eat!

BATEMAN, JUSTINE: Actress, b. Rye, NY, 1966. Sister of actor Jason Bateman. Daughter of prod.-theatrical mgr. Kent Bateman.

PICTURES: Satisfaction.

TELEVISION: Tales from the Dark Side, One to Grow On, It's Your Move, Glitter. Series: Family Ties. Movies: Right to Kill?, Family Ties Vacation, Can You Feel Me Dancing?. Specials: First the Egg, Whatta Year . . . 1986, Fame, Fortune and Romance. Candid Camera: Eat! Eat! Eat!

BATES, ALAN: Actor. b. Allestree, Derbyshire, England, Feb. 17, 1934. e. member of Royal Acad. of Dramatic Art class with Albert Finney, Peter O'Toole and Tom Courtenay.

STAGE: On London and New York stage. Look Back in Anger, The Caretaker, Long Day's Journey Into Night, Poor Richard, In Celebration, Hamlet, Butley (Tony Award), The Taming of the Shrew, Life Class, Otherwise Engaged, The Seagull, Stage Struck, A Patriot for Me, One for the Road, Victoria Station, Dance of Death, Yonadab, Melon, Much Ado About Nothing, Ivanov.

PICTURES: The Entertainer, Whistle Down the Wind, A Kind of Loving, The Caretaker, Nothing But the Best, Zorba The Greek, Georgy Girl, King of Hearts, Three Sisters, Far from the Madding Crowd, The Fixer, Women in Love, Joe Egg, The Go Between, Impossible Object, Butley, In Celebration, Royal Flash, An Unmarried Woman, The Shout, Rose, Nijinsky, Quartet, The Return of the Soldier, The Wicked Lady, Duet for One, A Prayer for the Dying, We Think the World of You, Force Majeure, The Dog It Was That Died.

TELEVISION: The Thug, A Memory of Two Mondays, The Jukebox, The Square Ring, The Wind and the Rain, Look Back in Anger, Three on a Gasring, Duel for Love, A Hero for Our Time, Plaintiff & Defendant, Two Sundays, The Collection, The Mayor of Casterbridge, The Trespasser, Very Like a Whale, Voyage Round My Father, An Englishman Abroad, Separate Tables, Dr. Fischer of Geneva, One for the Road, Pack of Lies.

BATTY, PETER: Producer, Director, Writer. b. Sunderland, England, 1931. e. Bede Grammar Sch. and Queen's Coll., Oxford. Feature-writer both sides Atlantic 1954–58. Joined BBC TV 1958 dir. short films. Edited Tonight programme 1963–4. Exec. prod. ATV 1964–68. Awarded Grand Prix for doc. at 1965 Venice and Leipzig festivals. Official entries 1970 and 1971 San Francisco and Melbourne festivals. Nominated Intl. Emmy, 1986. Own company since 1968 prod. TV specials, series, commercials.

TELEVISION: The Quiet Revolution, The Big Freeze, The Katanga Affair, Sons of the Navvy Man, The Fall and Rise of the House of Krupp, The Road to Suez, The Suez Affair, Battle for the Desert, Vietnam Fly-In, The Plutocrats, The Aristocrats, Battle for Cassino, Battle for the Bulge, Birth of the Bomb, Search for the Super, Operation Barbarossa, Farouk: Last of the Pharaohs, Superspy, Spy Extraordinary, Sunderland's Pride and Passion, A Rothschild and His Red Gold, The World of Television, The Story of Wine, The Rise and Rise of Laura Ashley, The Gospel According to Saint Michael, Battle for Warsaw, Battle for Dien Bien Phu, Nuclear Nightmares. A Turn Up in A Million, Il Poverello, Swindle!, The Algerian War, Fonteyn and Nureyev: The Perfect Partnership, The Divided Union, Remembrance, The Sicilian Connection. Contributed 6 episodes to Emmy-winning World at War series.

BAUER, HARALD P.: Executive. b. Berlin, Germany, March 16, 1928 e. M.A. Pol. Sci./Int. Law. Joined Associated Press 1950, foreign correspondent; 1970, appointed regional mgr. Joined United Press International 1971 as regional mgr. (Southwest U.S.); 1974, appointed gen. mgr. for Unicom Economic News Service; 1978 appointed gen. exec. for Europe; 1981, appointed v.p. for news and information services and corporate development; 1983, joined United International Pictures as pres., Pay-TV Group; 1985, v.p. & gen. mgr., United Media, New York.

BAUER, STEVEN: Actor. b. Cuba, Dec. 2, 1956. r.n. Steve Echervarria. Moved with family to Miami at age 3. e. Miami Dade Jr. Coll. where studied acting. Breakthrough came with selection for role in Que Pasa U.S.A.? for Public TV. Signed by Columbia TV and moved to California.
PICTURES: Scarface, Thief of Hearts, Running Scared, The Beast, Wildfire, Gleaming the Cube, Bloody Murder!
TELEVISION: Series: The Rockford Files, Hill Street Blues. Movies: Doctors Private Lives, From Here to Eternity, One Day at a Time, She's in the Army Now, Nichols and Dymes, An Innocent Love, Sword of Gideon, Desperados: The "Kiki" Camorera Story (mini-series).

BAUM, MARTIN: Executive. b. New York, NY, March 2, 1924. President, ABC Pictures; previously partner Baum & Newborn Theatrical Agency; head of West Coast office General Artists Corp., head of m.p. dept., Ashley Famous Agency; President of Martin Baum Agency; sr. exec. v.p. Creative Management Associations; president Optimus Productions, Inc., producing Bring Me the Head of Alfredo Garcia, The Wilby Conspiracy, and The Killer Elite. Partners with Michael Ovitz, Ron Meyer, Rowland Perkins, Bill Haber in Creative Artists Agency, Inc.

BAUMGARTEN, CRAIG: Executive. b. Aug. 27, 1949. Partner in independent prod. co., New America Cinema. Joined Paramount Pictures as prod. exec.; named v.p., prod. In 1980 went to Keith Barish Prods., of which was pres. three years. In 1983 appt. exec. v.p. & exec. asst. to the pres. & CEO, Columbia Pictures. Resigned 1985; joined Lorimar Motion Pictures as pres. Joined 20th Century Fox m.p. div. as exec. v.p. of production Oct. 1987. Resigned. 1989 formed Adelson/Baumgarten Prods. with Gary Adelson.

BAXTER, BILLY: Executive. b. New York, NY, Feb. 8, 1926. e. Holy Cross, 1948. Mgr., Ambassador Brokerage Group, Albany, 1957–58; Bill Doll & Co., 1959–63; organ., prod., radio show, Earl Wilson Celebrity Column, 1962; prod. Broadway show, Mandingo, with Franchot Tone, 1962; dir. of promotion, spec. events, Rumrill Ad Agency, 1963–64; dir. of promotion, exploitation, Landau Co., 1964–65; dir. of adv. and pub., Rizzoli Co., 1965–66. Consultant on special events to the Philip Morris Corp. and American Express.
PICTURES: Coprod.: Love and Anarchy, Daughters-Daughters, Outrageous, One Man, Dawn of the Dead. Prod.: Diary of the Cannes Film Festival with Rex Reed, 1980. Prod.-dir. documentaries: Artists of the Old West, Remington & Russell, Buffalo Bill Cody (1988).

BAXTER, KEITH: Actor. b. Monmouthshire, Wales, April 29, 1933. e. Wales, entered Royal Acad. of Dramatic Art in 1951. 1952–55 in national service; returned to RADA. Did years of repertory work in Dublin, Croydon, Chichester, London's West End, and New York. Biggest stage hit in Sleuth, both London and N.Y. Later in Corpse (London, NY).
PICTURES: The Barretts of Wimpole Street, Peeping Tom, Chimes at Midnight, With Love in Mind, Ash Wednesday, Berlin Blues.
TELEVISION: For Tea on Sunday, Hold My Hand Soldier, Saint Joan.

BAXTER, STANLEY: Actor. b. Glasgow, Scotland, 1928. e. Hillhead H.S., Glasgow. Principal comedian in Howard & Wyndham pantomimes. Summer revues. Televised regularly on BBC-TV, and also frequent broadcaster. M.P. debut 1955 in Geordie.
STAGE: The Amorous Prawn, On the Brighter Side, Chase Me Comrade (Australia), Cinderella, What the Butler Saw, Phil The Fluter, Mother Goose Pantomime seasons 1970–74. Jack & The Beanstalk, Cinderella, Mother Goose, Aladdin, 1985–87.
PICTURES: Very Important Person, Crooks Anonymous, The Fast Lady, Father Came Too, Joey Boy.
TELEVISION: Baxter on (series) 1964; The Confidence Course, The World of Stanley Baxter, Stanley Baxter Show, Stanley Baxter Show, Time for Baxter, The Stanley Baxter Big Picture Show, The Stanley Baxter Moving Picture Show, Part III, Stanley Baxter's Christmas Box, Bing Crosby's Merrie Olde Christmas, Stanley Baxter's Greatest Hits, Baxter on Television, Stanley Baxter Series, The Stanley Baxter Hour, Children's Royal, Stanley Baxter's Christmas Hamper, Stanley Baxter's Picture Annual, 1986; Mr. Majeika (series, 1988–89).

BEAL, JOHN: Actor, r.n. J. Alexander Bliedung. b. Joplin, MO, Aug. 13, 1909. e. Wharton Sch., U. of Pennsylvania. On Broadway in Another Language, She Loves Me Not, Voice of the Turtle, Teahouse of the August Moon. Off Bdwy: Long Day's Journey into Night, Our Town. m.p. debut in Another Language, 1933; served in U.S.A.A.F., W.W.II.
PICTURES: Little Minister, Les Miserables, We Who Are About to Die, Man Who Found Himself, Arkansas Traveler, Cat and the Canary, Great Commandment, Doctors Don't Tell, Atlantic Convoy, Edge of Darkness, Stand By, All Networks; Key Witness, Madame X, Double Wedding, Beg, Borrow or Steal; Port of Seven Seas, Alimony, Song of Surrender, Chicago Deadline, My Six Convicts, Remains to Be Seen, The Vampire, The Sound and the Fury, That Night, Ten Who Dared, Amityville 3-D.

BEALS, JENNIFER: Actress. b. Chicago, IL, Dec. 19, 1963. Fashion model. Made film debut in small role in My Bodyguard, 1980.
PICTURES: Flashdance, The Bride, Vampire Kiss, Kid Gloves, Layover, Rider in the Dark, Split Decisions, The Lizard's Tale, Sons, Jackal's Run, A Reasonable Doubt.
TELEVISION: The Picture of Dorian Grey, Cinderella (Faerie Tale Theatre).

BEAN, ORSON: Actor. b. Burlington, VT, July 22, 1928. r.n. Dallas Burrows. Performed in nightclubs as comic and on Broadway (Never Too Late, Will Success Spoil Rock Hunter?, Subways Are for Sleeping, Roar of the Grease Paint, the Smell of the Crowd, Ilya Darling.) Author: Me and the Orgone. Founder, administrator, dir. 15th St. School, NY.
PICTURES: How to Be Very, Very Popular (debut, 1955), Anatomy of a Murder, Lola, Forty Deuce, Innerspace, Instant Karma.
TELEVISION: To Tell the Truth (reg. panelist).

BEATTY, NED: Actor. b. Lexington, KY, July 6, 1937. Worked at Barter Theatre in Virginia appearing in over 70 plays 1957–66 and with Arena Stage, Washington D.C. 1963–71. Broadway debut: The Great White Hope.
PICTURES: Deliverance (debut), The Thief Who Came to Dinner, The Life and Times of Judge Roy Bean, The Last American Hero, White Lightning, Nashville, W.W. and the Dixie Dance Kings, All the President's Men, The Big Bus, Micky and Nickey, Silver Streak, Exorcist II: The Heretic, Network, The Great Georgia Bank Hoax, Gray Lady Down, Superman, Alambrista!, 1941, Wise Blood, Promises in the Dark, American Success Company, Hopscotch, The Incredible Shrinking Woman, Superman II, The Toy, Touched, Stroker Ace, Back to School, The Big Easy, The Fourth Protocol, Switching Channels, Rolling Vengeance, The Trouble With Spies, The Passage, The Unholy, Midnight Crossing, Physical Evidence, Imagination, Purple People Eater, Tennessee Waltz, Big Bad John, Shadows in the Storm, Chattahoochee, Time Trackers, The Repossessed.
TELEVISION: Series: Szysznyk. Special: Our Town (1977). Movies: Footsteps, Dying Room Only, Marcus-Nelson Murders, The Execution of Private Slovik, The Deadly Tower, Attack on Terror, The FBI vs. the Ku Klux Klan, Tail Gunner Joe, Lucan, A Question of Love, Friendly Fire, All God's Children, Guyana Tragedy: The Story of Jim Jones, Splendor in the Grass, The Violation of Sarah McDavid, Pray TV, A Woman Called Golda, The Ballad of Gregorio Cortez, Kentucky Woman, The Last Days of Pompeii, Celebrity, Robert Kennedy and His Times, Murder She Wrote; Konrad (Wonderworks); Hostage Flight, Go Toward the Light.

BEATTY, ROBERT: Actor. b. Hamilton, Ont., Canada, Oct. 19, 1909. e. U. of Toronto. London stage debut: Idiot's Delight, 1938. On screen first in Suspected Persons, 1942.
PICTURES: San Demetrio London, It Happened One Sunday, Appointment with Crime, Odd Man Out, Green Fingers, Against the Wind, Another Shore, Portrait from Life, Her Favorite Husband, Captain Horatio Hornblower, Calling Bulldog Drummond, Magic Box, Wings of Danger, The Gentle Gunman, The Oracle, The Net (Project M.7), Man on the Tightrope, Broken Horseshoe, The Square Ring, Albert RN (Break to Freedom), Loves of Three Women, Out of the Clouds, Portrait of Alison (Postmark for Danger), Tarzan and the Lost Safari, Something of Value, Time Lock, The Shakedown, The Amorous Prawn, 2001: A Space Odyssey, Where Eagles Dare, Sitting Target, Pope Joan, The Pink Panther Strikes Again, Golden Rendezvous, Superman III, The Highlander, Superman IV, High Diamonds.
TELEVISION: Weekly Guide, Saturday Night Out, Dial 999 (series), The Human Jungle (series), Court Martial (series), Time Lock, Man at the Top, The Venturers, Thriller, Jesus of Nazareth, Blake's Seven, Park Ranger, The Martian Chronicles, Walk with Destiny, Suez, The Rose, Medallion, Tales of the Unexpected, Murder of a Moderate Man, Minder on the Orient Express, Breakthrough at Reykjavik.

BEATTY, WARREN: Actor., Producer, Director. r.n. Henry Warren Beaty. b. Richmond, VA, March 30, 1938. Brother of Shirley MacLaine. e. Northwestern U. Small roles on television; Compulsion, winter stock, North Jersey Playhouse; Broadway debut, A Loss of Roses.

PICTURES: Splendor in the Grass, The Roman Spring of Mrs. Stone, All Fall Down, Lilith, Mickey One, Promise Her Anything, Kaleidoscope, Bonnie and Clyde (prod., actor), The Only Game in Town, McCabe and Mrs. Miller, Dollars, The Parallax View, Shampoo (prod., co-author, actor), The Fortune, Heaven Can Wait (prod., co-dir., co-s.p., actor), Reds (actor, prod., dir., co-s.p.), Ishtar (prod., actor), Dick Tracy (prod., dir., actor).

TELEVISION: The Many Loves of Dobie Gillis (series reg. 1959–60); Alcoa Presents, One Step Beyond, Wagon Train.

BECK, ALEXANDER J.: Executive. b. Ung. Brod, Czechoslovakia, Nov. 5, 1926. e. Charles U., Prague, NYU. Owns 500 features and westerns for foreign distribution and library of 1400 shorts. Importer and exporter; Pres., chairman of bd. Alexander Beck Films, 1955; formed Albex Films and A.B. Enterprises, 1959; formed & pres., Beckman Film Corp., 1960; formed Alexander Beck Productions, 1964. In 1969 formed Screencom Int'l Corp., 1986, formed Beck Int'l Corp., 1987; formed Challenger Pictures Corp., 1988.

BECK, JACKSON: Actor-announcer-narrator. b. New York, NY. TV and radio commercials, children's records, comm. industrial films; Narrator.

BECK, JOHN: Actor. b. Chicago, IL. Jan. 28, 1943. Acted with midwestern theatre groups; in scores of TV series.

PICTURES: Three in the Attic (debut, 1968), Mrs. Pollifax, Spy; Lawman, Pat Garrett and Billy the Kid, Sleeper, Deadly Honeymoon, Rollerball, Paperback Hero, The Big Bus, Audrey Rose, The Other Side of Midnight, Deadly Illusion, From Father to Son.

TELEVISION: Guest star roles on Bonanza, Mannix, Hawaii Five-0, Love American Style; The Silent Gun, Lancer, Gunsmoke. Movies: Attack on Terror, The FBI vs the Ku Klux Klan; Wheels, What Really Happened to the Class of '65; The Time Machine; Greatest Heroes of the Bible; Time Express, Mind over Murder, Gridlock, Partners in Crime, Peyton Place: The Next Generation.

BECK, MICHAEL: Actor. b. Memphis, TN, Feb. 4, 1949. e. Millsap Coll. on football scholarship (quarterback). Became active in college theatre. In 1971 attended Central Sch. of Speech and Drama, London; studied 3 years, following which toured England with repertory companies for 2 years. Returned to U.S.; cast as lead in independent film, Madman (shot in Israel in 1977).

PICTURES: Madman; Blackout; The Warriors; Xanadu; Battletruck; Megaforce; Warriors of the 21st Century; The Golden Seal; Triumphs of a Man Called Horse.

TELEVISION: Holocaust; Mayflower: the Pilgrim's Adventure; Alcatraz: The Whole Shocking Story; Fly Away Home; The Last Ninja; Celebrity; Chiller; The Streets; Rearview Mirror. Series: Houston Knights.

BECK, MYER P.: Sales, prod. rep. b. Meriden, CT. e. NYU Sch. of Journalism. Newspaperman; publicist; publicity dir. United Artists; eastern mgr. Russell Birdwell Associates; formed own sls. prod. rep. office 1945, repr. Albert R. Broccoli; Jerome Hellman Productions, Stanley Kramer Pictures Corp.

BECKER, HAROLD: Director.

PICTURES: The Ragman's Daughter, The Onion Field, The Black Marble, Taps, Vision Quest, The Boost, Sea of Love.

BEDELIA, BONNIE: Actress. b. New York, NY, March 25, 1952. e. Hunter Coll.

THEATER: Enter Laughing, The Playroom, My Sweet Charlie.

PICTURES: The Gypsy Moths, They Shoot Horses Don't They?, Lovers and Other Strangers, The Big Fix, Heart Like a Wheel, The Boy Who Could Fly, Death of an Angel, Violets Are Blue, The Strange Vengeance of Rosalie, Die Hard, The Prince of Pennsylvania, Fat Man & Little Boy, Presumed Innocent.

TELEVISION: Hawkins on Murder, A Question of Love, Salem's Lot, Fighting Back, Alex: The Life of a Child, When the Time Comes, The New Land, No Means No, A Message to My Daughter, The Lady from Yesterday, Memorial Day.

BEERY, NOAH, JR.: Actor. b. New York, NY, Aug. 10, 1916. e. Urban and Harvard Mil. Acad. Son of Noah Beery, screen actor. Travelled with parents in stock company. Appeared as child in Mark of Zorro, 1920.

PICTURES: Father and Son, Road Back, Only Angels Have Wings, Doolins of Oklahoma, Davy Crockett, Indian Scout, Last Outpost, Savage Horde, Rocketship XM, Two Flags West, Tropic Zone, Cimarron Kid, Wagons West, Story of Will Rogers, Wings of the Hawk, War Arrow, The Yellow Tomahawk, Black Dakotas, White Feather, Jubal, Fastest Gun Alive, Journey to Shiloh, Heaven With A Gun, Walking Tall, The Spikes Gang, The Best Little Whorehouse in Texas.

TELEVISION: Yellow Rose.

BEGLEY, ED, JR.: Actor. b. Los Angeles, CA, Sept. 16, 1949. Son of late actor Ed Begley. Debut in a guest appearance on My Three Sons at 17.

PICTURES: Stay Hungry, Blue Collar, Citizens Band, The One and Only, Goin' South, Hardcore, Airport '79 The Concord, The In-Laws, Private Lessons, Buddy Buddy, Eating Raoul, An Officer and a Gentleman, Cat People, The Entity, Get Crazy, This Is Spinal Tap, Protocol, Streets of Fire, Transylvania 6-5000, The Accidental Tourist, Scenes From the Class Struggle in Beverly Hills, The Applegates, She-Devil.

TELEVISION: Series: Room 222, Roll Out, St. Elsewhere (1982– 88). Movies and specials: Amateur Night at the Dixie Bar and Grill, A Shining Season, Riker, Rascals and Robbers—The Secret Adventures of Tom Sawyer and Huck Finn, Tales of the Apple Dumpling Gang, Voyagers, Not Just Another Affair, Still the Beaver, An Uncommon Love, Insight/The Clearing House, Roman Holiday, Spies, Lies & Naked Thighs; Not a Penny More, Not a Penny Less.

BEICH, ALBERT: Writer. b. Bloomington, IL, June 25, 1919. e. McGill U. Radio writer.

PICTURES: You Can't Beat the Law, Girls in Chains, Gangs of the Waterfront, Gay Blades, Bridge Goes Wild, Key to the City, Yellow Cab Man, The Milkman, Lieutenant Wore Skirts.

BELAFONTE, HARRY: Actor, Singer, Producer. b. New York, NY, March 1, 1927. Trained for stage at the Actors Studio, New Sch. for Social Research and American Negro Theatre. Professional debut, Royal Roost nightclub, N.Y., Village Vanguard, 1950. Broadway debut: John Murray Anderson's Almanac, 1953. Recording, concert artist.

THEATER: Juno and the Paycock, John Murray Anderson's Almanac. (Tony Award, supp. actor, 1953), Three for Tonight, A Night With Belafonte, To Be Young, Gifted and Black (prod.), Asinamali (co-prod.).

PICTURES: Bright Road, Carmen Jones, Island in the Sun, Odds Against Tomorrow, The World, The Flesh and the Devil, The Angel Levine, Buck and the Preacher, Uptown Saturday Night (prod., actor), First Look, Beat Street (prod.).

BELAFONTE, SHARI: Actress. b. New York, NY, Sept. 22, 1954. Daughter of actor-singer Harry Belafonte. e. Carnegie-Mellon U., BFA, 1976. Worked as publicist's asst. at Hanna Barbera Prods. before becoming successful model (appearing on more than 200 magazine covers and in numerous TV commercials).

PICTURES: If You Could See What I Hear, Time Walker, Murder One, Murder Two.

TELEVISION: Series: Hotel (1983–88). Pilot: Velvet. Guest: Hart to Hart, Code Red, Trapper John, M.D., Different Strokes, The Love Boat, Matt Houston. Movies: The Night the City Screamed, The Midnight Hour, Kate's Secret. Host: Big Hex of Little Lulu, AM Los Angeles, Living the Dream: a Tribute to Dr. Martin Luther King, Jr.

BELFER, HAL B.: Executive producer, director, choreographer. b. Los Angeles, CA, Feb. 16. e. U. of Southern California (cinematography); U. of California (writing). Head of choreography dept. at 20th Century-Fox. Head of choreography dept. at Universal Studios. Dir. of entertainment, in Las Vegas, Riviera and Flamingo Hotels. Prod., musical shows for Mexico City, Aruba, Puerto Rico, Montreal, Las Vegas. Dir., TV commercials and industrials. H.R. Pufnstuf TV series. Theatricals: Over 150 features. Producer-director-choreographer, Premore, Inc. Develop TV specials and sitcom, tape and film. Exec. prod., Once Upon a Tour and Dora's World, Rose on Broadway, Secret Sleuth, Inn by the Side of the Road, Imagine That! Special staging "Tony The Pony" Series and prod., segment of What a Way to Run a Railroad; TV specials. Talent development programs, Universal Studios, 20th Century-Fox. Personal management and show packager; 1982, exec. prod., Enchanted Inn (TV Special), Cameo Music Hall I, Stage mgr.: Promises, Promises, A Chorus Line (Sahara Hotel, Las Vegas).

BEL GEDDES, BARBARA: Actress. r.n. Barbara Geddes Lewis. b. New York, NY, Oct 31, 1922. p. Norman Bel Geddes, scenic designer. Stage debut in Out of the Frying Pan; toured USO camps in Junior Miss, 1941; screen debut in The Long Night, 1946; Star of Tomorrow, 1949. On TV in Dallas. Author-illustrator children's books: I Like to Be Me (1963), So Do I (1972). Also designer of greeting cards for George Caspari Co.

THEATER: The Moon Is Blue, Cat on a Hot Tin Roof, Mary, Mary, Everything in the Garden, Finishing Touches.

PICTURES: I Remember Mama, Blood on the Moon, Caught, Panic in Streets, Fourteen Hours, Vertigo, The Five Pennies, Five Branded Women, By Love Possessed, Summertree, The Todd Killings.

TELEVISION: Live TV in 1950s: Robert Montgomery Presents, Schlitz Playhouse of the Stars, etc., several classic

Alfred Hitchcock Presents episodes including Lamb to the Slaughter; Our Town, Series: Dallas (1978–84; 1985–; Emmy, 1980).

BELL, TOM: Actor. b. Liverpool, England, 1932. Early career in repertory and on West End stage. First TV appearance in Promenade.
TELEVISION: No Trams to Lime Street, Love On the Dole, A Night Out, Cul de Sac, The Seekers, Long Distance Blue, The Virginian, The Rainbow.
PICTURES: Payroll (film debut, 1960), The Kitchen, H.M.S. Defiant, Prize of Arms, L-Shaped Room, Rebels Against the Light, Ballad in Blue, He Who Rides a Tiger, In Enemy Country, The Long Days Dying, Lock Up Your Daughters, Wish You Were Here, Resurrected, The Magic Toy Shop.

BELLAMY, EARL: Producer, Director. b. Minneapolis, MN, March 11, 1917. e. Los Angeles City Coll. Universal Studios. President, The Bellamy Productions Co.
PICTURES: Fluffy, Gun Point, Munsters Go Home, Sidewinder, Speedtrap.
TELEVISION: Bachelor Father, Wells Fargo, Lone Ranger, Alcoa Premiere, Arrest and Trial, The Virginian, The Crusaders, Schlitz Playhouse, Heinz, Rawhide, The Donna Reed Show, Andy Griffith Show, Wagon Train, Laramie, Laredo, I Spy, Mod Squad, Medical Center.

BELLAMY, RALPH: Actor. b. Chicago, IL, June 17, 1904. Stock and repertory, 1922–30; incl. own resident stock cos. Was v.p. Actors Equity 1949–52; pres. Actors Equity, 1952–64. Founding mem. Screen Actors Guild, 1933; Mem. The Players, on council, Lambs, 1952; Founder and bd. CA State Arts Comm. 1964–66. 1983 Acad. of Motion Picture Arts & Sciences achievement & humanitarian award. Autobiography: When the Smoke Hit the Fan (1979).
BROADWAY: Town Boy, Roadside, Tomorrow the World, State of the Union, Detective Story, Pretty Little Parlor (dir., co-prod.), Oh Men! Oh Women! Sunrise at Campobello (Tony Award).
PICTURES: The Secret Six (debut, 1931), Magnificent Lie, Surrender, West of Broadway, Air Mail, Almost Married, Disorderly Conduct, Forbidden, Rebecca of Sunnybrook Farm, Picture Snatcher, Spitfire, Hands Across the Table, Rendezvous at Midnight, The Man Who Lived Twice, The Awful Truth (Acad. Award), Counterfeit Lady, Boy Meets Girl, Carefree, Brother Orchid, Dance Girl Dance, Ellery Queen, Master Detective, Flight Angels, His Girl Friday, Meet the Wildcat, Public Deb No. 1, Queen of the Mob, Affectionately Yours, Dive Domber, Ellery Queen and the Murder Ring, The Wolf Man, The Ghost of Frankenstein, Great Impersonation, Lady on a Train, Guest in the House, Delightfully Dangerous, Court Martial of Billy Mitchell, Sunrise at Campobello, The Professionals, Rosemary's Baby, Oh, God!, Trading Places, Disorderlies, Amazon Women on the Moon, Coming to America, The Good Mother.
TELEVISION: live and film dramatic shows, voted many TV awards. Series: Man Against Crime (1949–53), The Eleventh Hour, The Survivors, The Most Deadly Game, Hunter. Mini-series: The Money-changers, Once An Eagle, Testimony of Two Men, Wheels, Space, The Winds of War, War and Remembrance. Movies: Wings of Fire, The Immortal, Something Evil, The Log of the Black Pearl, Search for the Gods, Adventures of the Queen, Murder on Flight 502, Return to Earth, The Boy in the Plastic Bubble, Nightmare in Badham County, McNaughton's Daughter, The Clone Master, The Millionaire, The Billion Dollar Threat, Condominium, Power, The Memory of Eva Ryker, Love Leads the Way, The Fourth Wise Man.

BELLFORT, JOSEPH: b. New York, NY. e. NYU, Brooklyn Law Sch. Joined RKO Service Corp., Feb., 1930; trans. to RKO Radio Pictures, legal dept., May 1942; joined RKO Fgn. dept., Oct., 1944, handled Far Eastern division, Dec. 1946; then asst. to European gen. mgr.; gen. European mgr., 1949–1958; gen. sales mgr. National Screen Service, 1959; home office supv., Europe & Near East, 20th Century-Fox, 1963; home office intl. mgr., 20th Century-Fox, 1966. Ass't v.p. and foreign mgr. 20th Cent.-Fox, 1967; vice president 20th Century-Fox, Intl. Corp. & Inter-America, Inc. 1968; named sr. v.p., 1975. Resigned from Fox, 1977, to become v.p., Motion Picture Export Assn. of America in New York. Retired 1983.

BELLOCCHIO, MARCO: Director, writer. b. Piacenza, Italy, Nov. 9, 1939. e. Milan (letters and philosophy); Centro Sperimentale di Cinematografia, Rome; School of Fine Arts, London 1959–63. Collaborated on Paola and Viva il primo maggio rosso.
PICTURES: Fists in the Pocket, China Is Near, Leap into the Void, In the Name of the Father, Strike the Monster on Page One (co-dir., co-s.p.), Vacations in Val Trebbia, The Eyes the Mouth, Henry IV, Sabbeth.

BELMONDO, JEAN-PAUL: Actor. b. Neuilly-sur-Seine, France, April 9, 1933. e. private drama school of Raymond Girard, and the Conservatoire d'Art Dramatique. Formed a theater group with Annie Girardot and Guy Bedos.
THEATRE: Jean Marais' production of Caesar and Cleopatra, Treasure Party. Oscar, 1958.
PICTURES: A Pied, A Cheval et En Voiture (By Foot, Horse and Car), Look Pretty and Shut Up, Drole de Dimanche, Les Tricheurs, Les Copains du Dimanche, Charlotte et Son Jules, A Double Tour, Breathless, Classe Tous Risques, Moderato Cantabile, La Francasie et l'Amour, Les Distractions, Mademoiselle Ange, La Novice, Two Women, La Viaccia, Une Femme Est une Femme, Leon Morin, Pretre, Les Amours Celebres, Un Singe en Hiver, Le Doulos, L'Aine des Ferchaux, La Mer A Boire, Banana Peel, That Man From Rio, Cent Mille Dollars au Soleil, Echappement Libre, La Chasse a l'Homme, Dieu a Choisi Paris, Weekend a Zuydcocte, Par Un Beau Matin d'Ete, Up to His Ears, Is Paris Burning?, The Thief of Paris, Tender Scoundrel, Pierrot le Fou, The Brain, Love Is a Funny Thing, Mississippi Mermaid, Borsalino, Inheritor, Stavisky, Fear Over the City, Itinerary of a Spoiled Child (also prod.).

BELSON, JERRY: Producer, Director, Writer. With Garry Marshall, writer of The Dick Van Dyke Show (Emmy), and prod. of The Odd Couple (Emmy). Together team wrote and prod. feature films: How Sweet It Is (1968) and The Grasshopper as well as co-authoring the Broadway play The Roast (1980).
PICTURES: Smile (s.p.); Fun With Dick and Jane (s.p.), Smokey and the Bandit II (s.p.), Student Bodies (exec. prod.), The End (s.p.); Surrender (dir., s.p.); For Keeps (prod.), Jekyll and Hyde Together Again (dir.) Always (co-s.p.).
TELEVISION: The Dick Van Dyke Show, The Odd Couple, The Tracey Ullmann Show (co-creator, co-exec. prod.).

BELUSHI, JAMES (Jim): Actor. b. Chicago, IL, June 15, 1954. e. DuPage Coll., Southern Illinois U. Brother, late John Belushi. Worked with Chicago's Second City Revue.
THEATER: Sexual Perversity in Chicago, Pirates of Penzance, True West.
PICTURES: Thief, Trading Places, The Man with One Red Shoe, Salvador, About Last Night, The Principal, Red Heat, Real Men, Who's Harry Crumb?, K-9, Homer and Eddie, King of the Mountain, Wedding Band (cameo), To Forget Palermo.
TELEVISION: Laverne and Shirley; Working Stiffs; Who's Watching the Kids?; The Joseph Jefferson Awards; The Best Legs in the 8th Grade; Saturday Night Live (series reg.) , Cinemax's Comedy Experiment's Birthday Boy (actor, prod., writer).

BENDHEIM, III, SAM: Executive. b. Richmond, VA, June 15, 1935. e. Washington & Lee U. Joined Neighborhood Theatre, Inc., 1958 as exec. trainee. Was dir. of adv. (1960–63); bd. member, ass't. treas. (1962); ass't to gen. mgr. (1963–67) v.p. (1967). Member: NATO of Virginia; former pres. & chmn., NATO of Virginia; bd., pres. advisory council, exec. comm., NATO; bd., Foundation of Motion Picture Pioneers; pres., SKS Enterprises, Inc. & Bendheim Booking & Buying Service. Regional head film buyer, Cineplex Odeon Corp., Richmond, VA. 1988, co-owner SKS Theatres.

BENDICK, ROBERT: Indep. documentary prod., dir. b. New York, NY, Feb. 8, 1917. e. NYU, White School Photography. U.S. Air Force, W.W.II. Documentary and still cameraman before joining CBS Television as cameraman and dir., 1940; rejoined CBS Television as dir. special events, 1946; promoted dir. news & special events; acting program dir. 1947; res. Oct. '51. Collab with Jeanne Bendick on Making the Movies, Electronics for Young People, Television Works Like This, Filming Works Like This, 1971; Prod. Peabody Award-winning U.N. show The U.N. in Action; v.p., Cinerama Prod., co-prod. This Is Cinerama; co-dir., Cinerama Holiday; prod. Dave Garroway Show Today, prod., Wide Wide World 1955–56, NBC prod. dir. C.V. Whitney Pict., June, 1956; Merian C. Cooper Ent., 1957; prod. NBC, 1958. Prod.; Garroway Today Show, Bob Hope 25 Yrs. of Life Show, 1961; Bell Telephone Threshold Science Series, Groucho Marx, Merrily We Roll Along, US Steel Opening New York World's Fair, 1964. Prod. First Look Series 1965 (Ohio St. Award); prod. & dir. American Sportsman, ABC; prod., pilot, Great American Dream Machine (NET) (Emmy Award, 1971 and 1972); 1975, Co-exec. prod., Dick Cavett—Feeling Good. pres. Bendick Assoc. Inc.,; prod. of education audio-visual systems, Bd. of Governors, N.Y. Academy of TV Arts and Sciences. 1976, co-author with Jeanne Bendick, TV Reporting. Consultant, Warner Qube Cable Co.; 1978, produced/directed, Fight for Food (PBS). Program consultant to Times-Mirror Cable Co., L.A. Produced segment ABC 20/20. Member awards committee, National TV Acad. Arts & Science.

BENEDEK, LASLO: Director. b. Budapest, Hungary, March 5, 1907. e. U. of Vienna; Psycho-Analytic Clinic. Writer & photographer while in coll.; cameraman Budapest; first asst. cameraman several studios; cameraman UFA & Terra; film cutter; cutter & asst. prod. to Joe Pasternak; to Paris as cutter, then Engl dial. on Antonia; writer (England) 2 yrs.; montage dir. MGM 1937; writer (Mexico); assoc. prod. (Hollywood) on musicals; contract dir. MGM; Stanley Kramer Co., Col.; 1976–80, chairman of Graduate Film Program, NYU. 1983, visiting professor, Annenberg Sch. of Communi-

cation, U. of Pennsylvania, 1984, Film & TV Academy, Munich, Germany. Production advisor, S. Carolina ETV.
STAGE: Belial, Twelfth Night.
PICTURES: Kissing Bandit, Port of New York, Death of a Salesman, Storm Over Tibet, The Wild One, Bengal Brigade; Sons, Mothers and a General, Affair in Havana, Moment of Danger, Recours en Grace, Namu, The Killer Whale, A Daring Game, The Night Visitor.
TELEVISION: 4 Star Playhouse, Dupont Theatre, Stage 7, Loretta Young Show, Telephone Time, Perry Mason, Naked City, Untouchables, Outer Limits, Alfred Hitchcock Hour.

BENEDICT, DIRK: Actor. r.n. Dirk Niewoehner. b. Helena, MT, March 1, 1945. e. Whitman Coll., Walla Walla, WA. Enrolled in John Fernald Academy of Dramatic Arts, Rochester, MI, after which had season with Seattle Repertory Theatre; also in summer stock at Ann Arbor, MI. Broadway debut, 1970, Abelard and Heloise. Film debut, Georgia, Georgia, 1972.
PICTURES: Ssssss, W, Battlestar Galactica, Scavenger Hunt, Ruckus, Underground Aces, Body Slam.
TELEVISION: Hawaii Five-O. Series: Chopper One, Battlestar Galactica, The A Team, Movie: Scruples. Movie: Trenchcoat in Paradise.

BENJAMIN, RICHARD: Actor, Director. b. New York, NY, May 22, 1939. m. actress Paula Prentiss. e. Northwestern U.
THEATER: Central Park productions of The Taming of the Shrew, As You Like It; toured in Tchin Tchin, A Thousand Clowns, Barefoot in the Park, The Odd Couple. Broadway debut in Star Spangled Girl, 1966, also in The Little Black Book, The Norman Conquests. Directed London productions of Barefoot in the Park, Packin' It In.
PICTURES: Goodbye, Columbus, Catch 22, Diary of a Mad Housewife, The Marriage of a Young Stockbroker, The Steagle, Portnoy's Complaint, The Last of Sheila, Westworld, The Sunshine Boys, House Calls, Love at First Bite, Scavenger Hunt, The Last Married Couple in America, How to Beat the High Cost of Living, First Family, *Director:* My Favorite Year, Racing with the Moon, City Heat, The Money Pit, Little Nikita, My Stepmother Is an Alien, Downtown.
TELEVISION: Series: He and She, (with Paula Prentiss, 1967). Special: Arthur Miller's Fame.

BENNETT, ALAN: Author, Actor. b. Leeds, England, May 9, 1934. e. Oxford U. With Jonathan Miller, Dudley Moore and Peter Cook co-authored and starred in satirical revue Beyond the Fringe in London (1961) and on Bdwy (special Tony Award, 1963).
THEATER: Forty Years On (actor, author), Getting On, Habeas Corpus (also actor), Intensive Care (also appeared), Our Winnie, A Woman Of No Importance, Rolling Home, Marks, Say Something Happened, An Englishman Abroad, Single Spies (also dir.).
PICTURES: A Private Function, Prick Up Your Ears.
TELEVISION: Famous Gossips, On the Margin (also actor), An Evening With, A Day Out, Sunset Across the Bay, A Little Outing, A Visit from Miss Prothero, Me—I'm Afraid of Virginia Wood, Doris and Doreen, The Old Crowd, Afternoon Off, An Office Story, All on the Sands, The Insurance Man, Talking Heads (6 TV monologues).

BENNETT, BRUCE: Actor. r.n. Herman Brix. b. Tacoma, WA, 1909; e. U. of Washington.
PICTURES: My Son Is Guilty, Lone Wolf Keeps a Date, Atlantic Convoy, Sabotage, Underground Agent, More the Merrier, Sahara, Man I Love, Stolen Life, Nora Prentiss, Cheyenne, Treasure of Sierra Madre, Dark Passage, Smart Girls Don't Talk, Second Face, Great Missouri Raid, Angels in the Outfield, Sudden Fear, Dream Wife, Dragonfly Squadron, Robbers Roost, Big Tipoff, Hidden Guns, Bottom of the Bottle, Strategic Air Command, Mildred Pierce, Danger Signal, Silver River, Younger Brothers, Task Force, Without Honor, Mystery Street, The Last Outpost, Three Violent People, The Outsider, etc.

BENNETT, CHARLES: Writer, Director. b. Shoreham, England. British Army. Contract, Universal, 1937; wrote for British Ministry of Information, W.W.II; dir. s.p. over 50 TV shows, including Cavalcade of America, Schlitz Playhouse, The Christophers, Four Star.
PLAYS: Blackmail, The Last Hour, Sensation, The Danger Line, Page From a Diary, The Return, After Midnight.
PICTURES: Blackmail, The 39 Steps, Secret Agent, The Man Who Knew Too Much (orig.), Sabotage, The Girl Was Young, Balalaika, The Young in Heart, Foreign Correspondent, Reap the Wild Wind, Joan of Paris, They Dare Not Love, The Story of Dr. Wassell, Unconquered, Ivy, Sign of the Ram, Kind Lady, The Green Glove, Dangerous Assignment, Madness of the Heart (dir.), The Big Circus, The Lost World, Voyage to the Bottom of the Sea, Five Weeks in a Balloon.

BENNETT, HARVE: Producer. r.n. Harve Fischman. b. Chicago, IL, Aug. 17, 1930. e. UCLA. Quiz Kids radio show, 5 yrs.; newspaper columnist, drama critic; freelance writer; Assoc. prod., CBS-TV; freelance TV writer; prod. of special events. CBS-TV; dir., Television film commercials; program exec., ABC, vice pres., programs west coast—ABC-TV
TELEVISION: Pres., Bennett-Katleman. Productions at Columbia Studios, prod.-writer, Mod Squad. Creator-writer, The Young Rebels, Screen Gems; exec. prod., Six Million Dollar Man, Bionic Woman, exec. prod. on American Girls series, From Here to Eternity, Salvage 1.Rich Man, Poor Man, Joined Paramount's Motion Picture Group, acting as exec. prod. & co-author of Star Trek II: The Wrath of Khan;
PICTURES: Exec. prod. & co-story: Star Trek II: The Wrath of Khan; Star Trek IV: The Voyage Home (prod., co-s.p.), Star Trek V: The Final Frontier (prod., co-story). prod. & author of Star Trek III: The Search for Spock. 1984, entered long-term deal with Para.

BENNETT, HYWEL: Actor, Director. b. Garnant, South Wales. Early career National Youth Theatre where he played many leading Shakespearean roles followed by extensive work in British theatre. 1971–81: directed numerous stage productions. Film debut, The Family Way. 1966.
PICTURES: Twisted Nerve, The Virgin Soldiers, The Buttercup Chain, Loot, Percy, Endless Night, Alice in Wonderland, Murder Elite, War Zone.
TELEVISION: Where The Buffalo Roam, Malice Aforethought, Tinker Tailor Soldier Spy, series, Artemis 81, Myself A Mandarin, Frankie and Johnnie, Check Point Chiswick, Twilight Zone, The Idiot, The Traveller, Death of a Teddy Bear, Three's One, Pennies From Heaven, Shelley (series), The Critic, The Consultant, Absent Friends, The Secret Agent.

BENNETT, JILL: Actress. b. Penang, Federated Malay States, Dec. 24, 1931. Stage debut at Stratford-on-Avon, 1948; screen debut 1952 in Moulin Rouge.
PICTURES: Hell Below Zero, The Criminal, Extra-Day, Lust For Life, The Skull, The Nanny, Charge of Light Brigade, Inadmissible Evidence, I Want What I Want, Quilp, Full Circle, For Your Eyes Only, Britannia Hospital, Lady Jane, Hawks.
TELEVISION: The Heiress, Trilby, Jealousy, A Midsummer Night's Dream, The Three Sisters, Glimpse of the Sea, Return to the Sea, The Book Bag (Somerset Maugham Series), It's Only Us, The Parachute, Hotel in Amsterdam, Speaking of Murder, Intent to Murder, Jill and Jack, Almost A Vision, Hello Lola, The Old Crowd, Orient Express (French TV), The Aerodrome, Poor Little Rich Girls (series), Country, Paradise Postponed, Worlds Beyond, Last Days of Summer.

BENNETT, JOAN: Actress. b. Palisades, NJ, Feb. 27, 1910. e. St. Margaret's Boarding School, Waterbury, CT; L'Ermitage, Versailles, France. Member of famous Bennett acting family; m. David Wilde, prod. On stage with father, Richard Bennett, in Jarnegan; m.p. debut in Bulldog Drummond, 1929 after small roles in The Valley of Decision, Power, The Divine Lady; vice-pres. & treas. Diana Prods. 1945. Author: The Bennett Playbill (1970, with Lois Kibbee).
PICTURES: Three Live Ghosts, Disraeli, The Mississippi Gambler, Puttin' on the Ritz, Crazy That Way, Moby Dick, Maybe It's Love, Scotland Yard, Doctors Wives, Hush Money, Many a Slip, She Wanted a Millionaire, Careless Lady, The Trial of Vivienne Ware, Week-ends Only, Wild Girl, Me and My Gal, Arizona to Broadway, Little Women, Pursuit of Happiness, Man Who Reclaimed His Head, Private Worlds, Mississippi, Two for Tonight, She Couldn't Take It, The Man Who Broke the Bank at Monte Carlo, Thirteen Hours By Air, Big Brown Eyes, Two in a Crowd, Wedding Present, Vogues of 1938, I Met My Love Again, The Texans, Artists and Models Abroad, Trade Winds, The Man in the Iron Mask, The Housekeeper's Daughter, Green Hill, The House Across the Bay, The Man I Married, The Son of Monte Cristo, Man Hunt, She Knew All the Answers, Wild Geese Chase, Confirm or Deny, Twin Beds, The Wife Takes a Flyer, Girl Trouble, Margin for Error, The Woman in the Window, Nob Hill, Scarlet Street, The Macomber Affair, The Woman on the Beach, Secret Beyond the Door, Hollow Triumph, Scar, Reckless Moment, For Heaven's Sake, Father of Bride, Father's Little Dividend, The Guy Who Came Back, Highway, Dragnet, We're No Angels, There's Always Tomorrow, Navy Wife, Desire in the Dust, House of Dark Shadows, Suspiria.
TELEVISION: Starred in Dark Shadows. Movies: Suddenly Love, A House Possessed, Divorce Wars.

BENSON, HUGH: Producer. Exec. Prod., Screen Gems, 1966; prod., Cinema Center Films, 1969–71; prod., MGM, 1972; appointed exec. prod., MGM Television, 1972. 1975 indep. prod. On staff Col.-TV, 1975, pilots and long form.
PICTURES: Nightmare Honeymoon (prod.), Logan's Run (assoc. prod.), Billy Jack Goes to Washington (prod.).
TELEVISION: Producer: Contract On Cherry St., Child Stealers, Goldie and the Boxer, A Fire in the Sky, Shadow Riders, Confessions of a Lady Cop, The Dream Merchants, Goldie and the Boxer Go to Hollywood, Goliath Awaits, The Blue and the Gray, Hart to Hart, Master of Ballantrae, Anna Karenina, The Other Lover, I Dream of Jeannie 15 Yrs. Later, Miracle of the Heart: A Boy's Town Story, Crazy Like a Fox, In the Heat of the Night (pilot and series).

BENSON, LEON: Producer, Director. b. Cincinnati, OH, Nov. 9. e. NYU, U. of Cincinnati. Advertising Dept. Paramount, 1938, head of Trailer Dept., 1940. U.S. Army Air Corps, 1942–46, Major. First head of TV Dept. L.A. office of J. Walter Thompson Co., 1946–51. Head of Story Dept. Ziv TV, 1951; prod. and dir. West Point, 1955–56; Sea Hunt, 1956–60; Ripcord, 1960–62. Prod.-Dir. Flipper TV series, 1963–64. Under contract, Universal, 1965–66, prod.-dir. episodes, Kraft Suspense Theatre, The Virginian, dir. episodes, Chrysler Theatre, Laredo. Prod. Tarzan TV series, 1966. Under contract, NBC Prods., 1967–70, as staff dir. Bonanza, High Chaparral. Prod. theatrical feature, Chosen Survivors, 1973. Also dir. Owen Marshall, Counsellor at Law, Mission Impossible, The Eleventh Hour, Ben Casey, Wild Wild West, Rat Patrol, The Lieutenant, Outer Limits, The Loner, Empire.

BENSON, ROBBY: Actor, Writer, Director. b. Dallas, TX, Jan. 21, 1956. m. actress Karla DeVito. Father, Jerry Segal, is writer and mother, Ann Benson, veteran of Dallas stage and nat'l summer stock. (Currently natl spokesperson for Merrill Lynch.). Appeared in commercials and summer stock at age five. First started on Bdwy at age 12 in Zelda. Dir. debut Crack in the Mirror (aka WhiteHot), (1988).

PICTURES: Jory, Jeremy, The Godfather—Part II, Ode to Billy Joe, Lucky Lady, One on One (co-s.p. with father, actor), The End, Ice Castles, Walk Proud, Die Laughing (also prod., co-s.p.), Tribute, The Chosen, Running Brave, Harry and Son, Rent-A-Cop, White Hot (dir., actor), Modern Love (prod., dir., s.p., actor).

TELEVISION: Search for Tomorrow, Death Be Not Proud, Our Town, The Death of Richie, Remember When, Virginia Hill, All the Kind Strangers, Two of a Kind, California Girls, Alfred Hitchcock Presents (1985).

STAGE: Zelda, The Rothschilds, The Pirates of Penzance.

BENTON, ROBERT: Writer, Director. b. Waxahachie, TX, 1932. e. U. of Texas, B.A. Was art director and later consulting ed. at Esquire Magazine where he met David Newman, a writer-editor, and formed writing partnership. Together wrote a monthly column for Mademoiselle (10 years). Benton made directorial debut with Bad Company, 1972.

PICTURES: With Newman wrote: Bonnie and Clyde, There Was a Crooked Man, What's Up, Doc? Bad Company (also directed, solo s.p.), The Late Show (written and directed solo), Superman (with Mario Puzo and Tom Mankiewicz), Money's Tight. As dir-writer: Kramer vs. Kramer (5 Oscars); Still of the Night; Places in the Heart, Nadine, The House on Carroll Street (co-exec. prod. only).

STAGE: It's a Bird . . It's a Plane . . . It's Superman (libretto), Oh! Calcutta (one sketch).

BERENGER, TOM: Actor. b. Chicago, IL, May 31, 1950. e. U. of Missouri (drama). Acted in regional theatres and off-off-Broadway. Plays include The Rose Tattoo, Electra, Streetcar Named Desire, End as a Man (Circle Rep.). Film debut in the Beyond the Door (1975).

PICTURES: Sentinel, Looking for Mr. Goodbar, In Praise of Older Women, Butch and Sundance: The Early Days, The Dogs of War, The Big Chill, Eddie and the Cruisers, Fear City, Firstborn, Rustler's Rhapsody, Platoon, Someone to Watch Over Me, Shoot to Kill, Betrayed, Last Rites, Major League, Love at Large, The Field.

TELEVISION: One Life to Live (series), Johnny We Hardly Knew Ye, Flesh and Blood, If Tomorrow Comes.

BERENSON, MARISA: Actress. b. New York, NY Feb. 15, 1947. Granddaughter of haute couture fashion designer Scaparelli. Former model.

PICTURES: Death in Venice; Cabaret; Barry Lyndon; Killer Fish; S.O.B.; The Secret Diary of Sigmund Freud; La Tete Dans Le Sac; L'Arbalete.

TELEVISION: Tourist; Playing for Time.

BERESFORD, BRUCE: Director, Writer. b. Sydney, Australia, 1949. e. U. of Sydney, B.A. 1962. Worked as teacher in London, 1961. Film editor, East Nigerian Film Unit, 1966; sect. and head of prod., British Film Inst. Production Board, 1966–71.

PICTURES: Director: The Adventures of Barry McKenzie, Barry McKenzie Holds His Own (also prod.), Don's Party, The Getting of Wisdom, Money Movers, Breaker Morant (also s.p.), The Club, Puberty Blues, Tender Mercies, King David, The Fringe Dwellers (also s.p.), Crimes of the Heart, Aria (sequence), Her Alibi, Driving Miss Daisy.

BERG, DICK: Writer, Producer. b. New York, NY. e. Lehigh U. 1942; Harvard Business Sch. 1943. Prior to 1960 writer for TV shows Playhouse 90 Studio One, Robert Montgomery Presents, Kraft Television Playhouse. 1961–69 prod., writer for Universal Studios; exec. prod. The Chrysler Theatre, Alcoa Premiere, Checkmate. Created and wrote Staccato (series). 1971–85: prod., writer of over 50 TV movies via his Stonehenge Prods. TV films won 15 Emmies, 23 nominations. Twice elected pres. National Acad. of Television Arts and Sciences.

PICTURES: Prod.: Counterpoint, House of Cards, Banning Shoot (also s.p.), Fresh Horses.

TELEVISION: Prod. &/or writer: Mini-series: A Rumor of War, The Martian Chronicles, The Word, Space, Wallenberg: A Hero's Story. Movies: Rape and Marriage: The Rideout Case, An Invasion of Privacy, Thief, Footsteps, Firehouse, American Geisha, Class of '63, Louis Armstrong, Chicago Style, Everybody's Baby: The Rescue of Jessica McClure (exec. prod.)

BERG, JEFF: Executive. b. Los Angeles, CA, May 26, 1947. e. U of California, Berkeley, B.A., 1969. V.P., head lit. div., Creative Mgt. Associates, Los Angeles, 1969–75; v.p., m.p. dept., International Creative Associates, 1975–80; pres., 1980–. Dir., Joseph Intl. Industries.

BERGEN, CANDICE: Actress. b. Beverly Hills, CA, May 9, 1946. m. dir. Louis Malle. Daughter of ventriloquist Edgar Bergen. e. U. of Pennsylvania. Modeled during college; freelance photojournalist. Autobiography: Knock Wood (1984).

PICTURES: The Group (debut, 1965), The Sand Pebbles, The Day the Fish Came Out, Live for Life, The Magus, The Adventurers, Getting Straight, Soldier Blue, Carnal Knowledge, The Hunting Party, T. R. Baskin, 11 Harrowhouse, Bite the Bullet, The Wind and the Lion, The Domino Principle, A Night Full of Rain, Oliver's Story, Starting Over, Rich and Famous, Gandhi, Stick.

TELEVISION: Hollywood Wives, Arthur the King, Murder: By Reason of Insanity, Mayflower Madam, Moving Day (Trying Times), Murphy Brown (series).

BERGEN, POLLY: Singer, Actress. r.n. Nellie Burgin b. Knoxville, TN, July 14, 1930. e. Compton Jr. Coll., CA. Prof. debut radio at 14; in light opera, summer stock; sang with orchestra and appeared in night clubs; Columbia recording star; on Bdwy stage, John Murray Anderson's Almanac, Champagne Complex, First Impressions. Bd. chmn. Polly Bergen Co.; chmn. Culinary Co., Inc.; co-chmn. Natl. Business Council for Equal Rights Amendment; Humanitarian Award: Asthmatic Research Inst. & Hosp., 1971; Outstanding Mother's Award, 1984.

PICTURES: At War With the Army, That's My Boy, The Stooge, Warpath, Half a Hero, Cry of the Hunted, Arena, Fast Company, Escape from Ft. Bravo, Cape Fear, The Caretakers, Move Over Darling, Kisses for My President, Making Mr. Right, Mother, Cry-Baby.

TELEVISION: Pepsi-Cola Playhouse (host 1954–55), To Tell the Truth (panelist), G.E. Theatre, Schlitz Playhouse, Playhouse 90, Studio One, Perry Como, Ed Sullivan Show, Polly Bergen Show, Bob Hope Show, Bell Telephone, Wonderful World of Entertainment, Dinah Shore Show, Dean Martin Show, Andy Williams Show, Red Skelton Show, Mike Douglas Show. Movies: The Helen Morgan Story (Emmy Award, best actress, 1958), Death Cruise, Murder on Flight 502, Telethon, How to Pick Up Girls, Born Beautiful, Velvet, The Winds of War, War and Remembrance, Addicted to His Love, She Was Marked For Murder, The Haunting of Sarah.

BERGER, HELMUT: Actor. b. Salzburg, 1942. e. Feldkirk College and U. of Perugia. First film, small role in Luchino Visconti's The Witches (Le Streghe) in 1966.

PICTURES: The Young Tigers, The Damned, Do You Know What Stalin Did To Women?, The Garden of the Finzi-Continis, Dorian Gray, A Butterfly with Bloody Wings, The Greedy Ones, The Strange Love Affair, Ludwig, Ash Wednesday, Conversation Piece, The Romantic Englishwoman, Orders to Kill, Madame Kitty, Merry-Go-Round, Code Name: Emerald, The Glass Heaven, Faceless, The Betrothed.

BERGER, RICHARD L.: Executive. b., Tarrytown, NY, Oct. 25, 1939. e. Cornell U., UCLA 1963, B.S. In 1964 joined acct. dept., 20th Century-Fox; promoted to exec. position in Fox-TV. Was dir. of programming, then v.p. of programs. Appt. asst. v.p. prod. 20th-Fox. Left in 1975 to join CBS-TV as v.p. dramatic development. Returned to 20th-Fox in 1977 as v.p., domestic prod., 20th Century-Fox Pictures. Joined Disney as pres. Walt Disney Pictures; resigned 1984. Named sr. v.p., United Artists Corp., promoted to pres.

BERGERAC, JACQUES: Actor. b. Biarritz, France, May 26, 1927. Career includes Five Minutes With Jacques Bergerac on radio; in the theatre, on tour in Once More with Feeling; on most major network TV shows.

PICTURES: Twist of Fate, The Time is Now, Strange Intruder, Come Away With Me, Les Girls, Gigi, Man and His Past, Thunder in the Sun, Hypnotic Eye, A Sunday in Summer, Fear No More, Achilles, A Global Affair, Taffy and the Jungle Hunter, The Emergency Operation, Lady Chaplin, The Last Party, One Plus One.

BERGMAN, ALAN: Songwriter. b. New York, NY, Sept. 11, 1925. e. U. of North Carolina, UCLA. m. Marilyn Bergman with whom collaborates.

PICTURES: In the Heat of the Night, The Thomas Crown Affair, Happy Ending, Gaily, Gaily, Pieces of Dreams, Sometimes a Great Notion, The Way We Were, A Star Is Born,

John and Mary, Life and Times of Judge Roy Bean, The One and Only, Same Time Next Year, And Justice for All, The Promise, A Change of Seasons, Yentl.
TELEVISION: Queen of the Stardust Ballroom, Hollow Image, Sybil, and themes for Maude, Good Times, Alice, Nancy Walker Show, etc.

BERGMAN, ANDREW: Writer, Director, Producer. b. Queens, NY, 1945. e. Harpur Coll., magna cum laude; U. of Wisconsin, Ph.D, history, 1970. Worked as publicist at United Artists. Author: We're in the Money, a study of Depression-era films, and the mysteries: The Big Kiss-Off of 1944 and Hollywood and Levine. Also wrote Broadway comedy, Social Security.
PICTURES: Writer: Blazing Saddles, Fletch, The In Laws, Oh God, You Devil, So Fine (also dir.) Chances Are (exec. prod. only), The Freshman (also dir.).

BERGMAN, INGMAR: Writer, Director. b. Uppsala, Sweden, July 14, 1918. e. Stockholm U. Directed university play prods.; wrote & dir. Death of Punch, 1940; first theatrical success, dir., Macbeth, 1940; writer-director, Svensk Film-industri, 1942-present; first s.p, Frenzy, 1943; first directorial assignment, Crisis, 1946; chief prod., Civic Malmo, 1956–60. Directed Swedish prod. Hamlet for stage at Brooklyn Acad. of Music, 1988.
PICTURES: Kris (1946) Det Regnar Pa Var Karlek, Skepp Till Indialand, Night is My Future, Port of Call, The Devil's Wanton, Three Strange Loves, Till Gladje, Summer Interlude (Illicit Interlude), High Tension, Bris (soap ads), Secrets of Women, Monika, The Naked Light, A Lesson in Love, Dreams, Smiles of a Summer Night, Sista Paret Ut, The Seventh Seal, Wild Strawberries, Brink of Life, The Magician, The Virgin Spring, The Devil's Eye, Through a Glass Darkly, Winter Light, The Silence, All These Women, Persona, Hour of the Wolf, Shame, The Passion of Anna, Cries and Whispers, Scenes from a Marriage, Face to Face, The Serpent's Egg, Autumn Sonata, Life of the Marionettes, Fanny and Alexander, After the Rehearsal.
AMERICAN TELEVISION: The Lie.

BERGMAN, MARILYN: Songwriter. b. New York, NY, Nov. 10, 1929. e. NYU. m. Alan Bergman with whom collaborates. See credits under his name.

BERKOFF, STEVEN: Actor, Director, Writer. b. London, Eng., 1937. e. studied drama in London and Paris. Founder of London Theatre Group. Author of plays, East, West, Greek Decadence, Sink the Belgrano, Kvetch (London, NY). Staged, adapted and toured with: Kafka's In the Penal Colony, The Trial and Metamorphosis; Agamemnon, The Fall of the House of Usher. Starred in Hamlet and Macbeth. NY theater: director: Kvetch (also writer, actor), Coriolanus, Metamorphosis (starring Baryshnikov). Also dir. Roman Polanski in Metamorphosis in Paris.
PICTURES: Actor: Barry Lyndon, A Clockwork Orange, Outlands, McVicar, Coming Out of the Ice, Octopussy, Rambo: First Blood II, Beverly Hills Cop, Revolution, Under the Cherry Moon, Absolute Beginners, Streets of Yesterday.
TELEVISION: Beloved Family, Knife Edge, War and Remembrance.

BERLE, MILTON: Actor. r.n. Milton Berlinger; b. New York, NY, July 12, 1908. e. Professional Children's Sch., N.Y. In vaudeville; on N.Y. stage (Ziegfeld Follies 1936, Life Begins at 8:40, etc.): nightclubs; concurrently on radio & screen. Author: Out of My Trunk (1945), Earthquake (1959), Milton Berle: An Autobiography (1974).
TELEVISION: Star of own NBC show; Texaco Star Theatre, 1948–54, Kraft Music Hall TV Show, 1958–59, Jackpot Bowling, 1960–61, Doyle Against the House, Dick Powell Show, Chrysler TV special, 1962, The Milton Berle Show, 1966. Movies: Side By Side.
PICTURES: Tall, Dark and Handsome, Sun Valley Serenade, Over My Dead Body, Margin for Error, Always Leave Them Laughing, Let's Make Love, It's a Mad, Mad, Mad, Mad World, The Happening, Who's Minding the Mint, Where Angels Go . . . Trouble Follows, Can Hieronymus Merkin Ever Forget Mercy Humppe and Find True Happiness?, Lepke, Broadway Danny Rose.

BERLIN, IRVING: Composer. r.n. Israel Baline; b. Russia, May 11, 1888. To New York, 1893. As youth, singing waiter in N.Y.; began writing songs. One of first successes, Alexander's Ragtime Band. Entered music pub.; member Waterson, Berlin & Snyder. W.W.I, sgt. inf. U.S. Army. Composer many indiv. and stage musical songs. In 1937 wrote songs for screen prod. Top Hat (RKO); in 1942 prod. stage musical This Is the Army for U.S. Army Emergency Relief Fund; in 1943 assoc. with Warner Bros. in prod. film version. Member: Lambs, Friars (N.Y.); pres. Irving Berlin Music Corp., music pub.
PICTURES: Follow the Fleet, On the Avenue, Carefree, Alexander's Ragtime Band, Second Fiddle, Holiday Inn, Blue Skies, Easter Parade, Annie Get Your Gun, Call Me Madam, White Christmas, There's No Business Like Show Business.

BERLINGER, WARREN: Actor, b. Brooklyn, NY, Aug. 31, 1937. e. Columbia U.
STAGE: Annie Get Your Gun, The Happy Time, Bernardine, Take A Giant Step, Anniversary Waltz, Roomful of Roses, Blue Denim, Come Blow Your Horn, How To Succeed in Business Without Really Trying, (London) Who's Happy Now?, California Suite (1977–78 tour).
PICTURES: Teenage Rebel, Three Brave Men, Blue Denim, Because They're Young, Platinum High School, The Wackiest Ship in the Army, All Hands on Deck, Billie, Spinout, Thunder Alley, Lepke, The Four Deuces, I Will . . . I Will . . . for Now, Harry and Walter Go to New York, The Shaggy D.A., The Magician of Dublin, The Cannonball Run, The World According to Garp, Take Two, Outlaw Force, Ten Little Indians.
TELEVISION: Secret Storm (serial), Alcoa, Goodyear, Armstrong, Matinee Theatre, Joey Bishop Show, The London Palladium, Kilroy, Billie, Bracken's World, The Funny Side, Touch of Grace, The Most Wanted Woman, The Other Woman, What Price Victory.

BERMAN, MONTY M.: Film and theatrical costumier. b. London, England, 1912. Personally costumed films and shows since 1931. Squad Leader RAF 1940–45; Bomber Command, M.B.E. Since war has costumed major films and shows and numerous TV prod.
PICTURES: Doctor Zhivago, Tom Jones, Longest Day, My Fair Lady, Oliver, Cromwell, Patton, Fiddler on the Roof, A Bridge Too Far, Julia, The Slipper and the Rose, A Little Night Music, Star Wars, Superman, James Bond Films, The Four Musketeers, Mommie Dearest, Raiders of the Lost Ark, Chariots of Fire, Superman II and III, Gandhi, Yentl, The Dresser, Indiana Jones and The Temple of Doom, Cotton Club, Out of Africa, The Living Daylights.

BERMAN, PANDRO S.: Producer. b. Pittsburgh, PA, March 28, 1905. Son of late Harry M. Berman, gen. mgr. Universal, FBO. Asst. dir. film ed., FBO; film & title ed. Columbia Studios; chief film ed. RKO, later asst. to William Le Baron & David Selznick; became prod. 1931 (RKO). A Champion of Champions Producer in Fame ratings. Joined MGM 1940.
PICTURES: What Price Hollywood, Symphony of Six Million, Bachelor Mother, The Gay Divorcee, Of Human Bondage, Morning Glory, Roberta, Alice Adams, Top Hat, Winterset, Stage Door, Vivacious Lady, Gunga Din, Hunchback of Notre Dame, Ziegfeld Girl, Honky Tonk, Seventh Cross, National Velvet, Dragon Seed, Portrait of Dorian Grey, Love Affair, Undercurrent, Sea of Grass, Three Musketeers, Madame Bovary, Father of the Bride, Father's Little Dividend, Prisoner of Zenda, Ivanhoe, All the Brothers Were Valiant, Knights of the Round Table, Long, Long Trailer, Blackboard Jungle, Bhowani Junction, Something of Value, Tea and Sympathy, Brothers Karamazov, Reluctant Debutante, Butterfield 8, Sweet Bird of Youth, The Prize, A Patch of Blue, Justine, Move.

BERMAN, STEVEN H: Executive. b. Middletown, OH, March 22, 1952. e. Ohio U., B.F.A. in playwriting, 1974; U. of Southern California, Annenberg Sch. of Communication studied management, 1977. m. Marcia Berman. Special research projects Paramount and ABC Television, 1977. Account exec., Gardner Advertising, 1978. Development exec., CBS Television, 1979–82. Dir. of comedy dev., CBS Television, 1982–84. Five years at CBS in series development, comedy and drama. Vice pres., dramatic dev., Columbia Pictures Television, 1984–85. Sr. v.p., Creative Affairs, Columbia Pictures Television, 1985–87. Exec. v.p., Columbia Television, div. of Columbia Entertainment Television, 1987–present.

BERNARD, MARVIN A.: Executive. b. New York, NY, Oct. 1, 1934. e. NYU. Lab technician to v.p. in charge of sales, Rapid Film Technique, Inc., 1949–63; developed technological advances in film rejuvenation and preservation, responsible for public underwriting; 1964–69; real estate sales & investments in Bahamas, then with Tishman Realty (commercial leasing div.); est. B-I-G Capital Properties; v.p. and operating head of International FilmTreat 1970–1973; authored Film Damaged Control Chart, a critical analysis of film care and repair—1971; founded Filmlife Inc. with latest chemical/mechanical and technical advancement in field of film rejuvenation and preservation. 1973–75 bd. chmn. and chief executive officer of Filmlife Inc., motion picture film rejuvenation, storage and distribution company. Feb. 1975 elected president in addition to remaining bd. chairman. 1979 consultant to National Archives of U.S. on m.p. preservation. 1981 dev. m.p. rejuvenation and preservation for 8mm and S8mm. 1986 introduced this technology to private home movie use before and after transfer to videotape. 1987, active mem. of awards comm. for tech. achievements, National Acad. TV Arts & Sciences. Recognition as leading authority and m.p. conservator from Intl. Communications Industries Assn. (ICIA), 1988.

BERNHARD, HARVEY: Producer. b. Seattle, WA, March 5, 1924. e. Stanford U. In real estate in Seattle, 1947–50; started live lounge entertainment at the Last Frontier Hotel, Las Vegas, 1950. Partner with Sandy Howard, 1958–60; v.p. in chg.

prod., David L. Wolper Prods., dividing time between TV and feature films, 1961–68; with MPC, v.p., chg. prod., 1968–70. Now pres. of Harvey Bernhard Ent., Inc.
PICTURES: The Mack (1973), The Omen, Damien—Omen II, The Final Conflict, The Beast Within, Ladyhawke (exec. prod.), Goonies (prod.), Lost Boys.

BERNHARD, SANDRA: Actress, Comedian, Singer. b. Flint, MI, June 6, 1955. Moved to Scottsdale, AZ at 10. Began career in Los Angeles 1974 as stand-up comedian while supporting herself as manicurist in Beverly Hills. Has written articles for Vanity Fair, Interview, Spin, recorded and written lyrics for debut album I'm Your Woman (1985) and starred in one-woman off-Bdwy show Without You, I'm Nothing (1988). Published collection of essays, short stories and memoirs, Confessions of a Pretty Lady (1988). Frequent guest on Late Night with David Letterman and Robin Byrd Show.
PICTURES: Cheech and Chong's Nice Dreams (debut, 1981), The King of Comedy, Sesame Street Presents: Follow that Bird, The Whoopee Boys, Casual Sex, Track 29, Without You, I'm Nothing.

BERNSEN, CORBIN: Actor. b. North Hollywood, CA, Sept. 7, 1954. m. actress Amanda Pays. Son of actress Jeanne Cooper. e. UCLA, B.A. theater arts; M.F.A playwriting. Teaching asst. at UCLA while working on playwriting degree. 1981 studied acting in NY while supporting self as carpenter and model (Winston cigarettes). Built own theater in loft.
PICTURES: King Kong, S.O.B., Hello Again, Bert Rigby, You're a Fool, Major League, Disorganized Crime.
TELEVISION: Series: Ryan's Hope, L.A. Law. Movie: Breaking Point.

BERNSTEIN, ARMYAN: Director-Writer.
PICTURES: Thank God It's Friday (s.p.); One From the Heart (co-s.p.); Windy City (dir. s.p.); American Date (dir.), Satisfaction (co-exec. prod.), Cross My Heart (dir., co-s.p.).

BERNSTEIN, BOB: Executive. Began public relations career 1952 at DuMont TV Network, followed by 2 yrs. as press agent for Liberace. With Billboard Magazine as review editor 3 yrs. Joined Westinghouse Bdg. Co. as p.r. director 1959. In 1963 named p.r. director for Triangle Publications, serving in various capacities to 1971. Joined Viacom Intl. as director of information services. In 1975 formed own co., March Five Inc., p.r. and promotion firm.

BERNSTEIN, ELMER: Composer, Conductor. b. New York, NY, April 4, 1922. Scholarship, Juilliard. e. Walden Sch., NYU., U.S. Army Air Force radio unit. After war 3 yrs. recitals, musical shows, United Nations radio dept; pres., Young Musicians Found.; 1st v.p. Academy of Motion Picture Arts & Sciences; co-chmn. music branch. Music dir. Valley Symphony. Recording artist, United Artists. More than 90 major films. Pres. of Composers & Lyricists Guild of America. Received ten Academy Award nominations and Oscar, 1967 for Thoroughly Modern Millie.
PICTURES: The Ten Commandments, Man With the Golden Arm, The Great Escape, To Kill a Mockingbird The Carpetbaggers, The Magnificent Seven, Birdman of Alcatraz, Walk on the Wild Side, Hallelujah Trail, The Reward, Seven Women, Cast A Giant Shadow, Hawaii, Thoroughly Modern Millie, True Grit, Cahill, U.S. Marshall, McQ., Gold, The Trial of Billy Jack, Report to the Commissioner, From Noon Till Three, Sarah, The Shootist, Blood Brothers, The Great Santini, Meatballs, Saturn 3, Airplane!, Going Ape, Stripes, An American Werewolf in London, Honky Tonk Freeway, The Chosen, Five Days One Summer, Airplane II: The Sequel, Spacehunter, Class, Trading Places, Bolero, Ghostbusters, Spies Like Us, Legal Eagles, Three Amigos, Amazing Grace and Chuck, Leonard Part 6, Da, Funny Farm, The Good Mother, Slipstream, My Left Foot.
TELEVISION: Specials: Hollywood: The Golden Years, The Race for Space: Parts I & II, D-Day, The Making of the President—1960 (won Emmy Award), Hollywood and the Stars, Voyage of the Brigantine Yankee, Crucification of Jesus, NBC Best Sellers Theme (1976). Series: Julia, Owen Marshall, Ellery Queen, Serpico, The Chisholms. Movies: Gulag, Guyana Tragedy.

BERNSTEIN, JACK B.: Executive. b. New York, NY, May 6, 1937. e. City U. of New York, B.A., sociology. U.S. Army-Europe, 1956–58; research bacteriologist, 1959–61. Entered industry in 1962 with S.I.B. Prods., Paramount, as v.p. gen. mgr.; 1964–66, v.p. gen. mgr. C.P.I. Prods, 1966–73 prod. mgr. asst. dir., free lance. 1973–1982, assoc. prod. exec. prod. at several studios. 1983–86, v.p. worldwide prod., Walt Disney Pictures; 1987, sr. v.p., worldwide prod., United Artists Pictures; Oct., 1988–present, sr. v.p. worldwide prod., MGM Pictures. Member: DGA, Friars, Academy of MP Arts & Sciences; Academy of TV Arts & Sciences.
PICTURES: Assoc. Prod.: The Other Side of Midnight, The Fury, Butch and Sundance, The Early Days, Six Pack, Unfaithfully Yours. Exec. Prod.: North Dallas Forty, Monsignore, The Beast Within.

BERNSTEIN, JAY: Producer, Personal manager. b. Oklahoma City, OK, June 7, 1937. e. Pomona Coll. 1963–76, pres. of Jay Bernstein Public Relations, representing over 600 clients. Formed Jay Bernstein Enterprises, acting as personal manager for Farrah Fawcett, Suzanne Somers, Kristy McNichol, Susan Hayward, Donald Sutherland, Bruce Boxleitner, Robert Conrad, Susan Saint James, Robert Blake, William Shatner, Linda Evans, Cicely Tyson, etc. Past pres., Bernstein-Thompson Entertainment Complex, entertainment and personal mgt. firm.
PICTURES: Exec. prod.: Sunburn, Nothing Personal.
TELEVISION: Exec. prod. Movies: The Return of Mike Hammer, Mickey Spillane's Margin for Murder; Wild, Wild, West, Revisited; More Wild, Wild West. Murder Me, Murder You, More Than Murder, The Diamond Trap. Series: Bring 'Em Back Alive, Mike Hammer, Houston Knights.

BERNSTEIN, BARON SIDNEY, Baron cr 1969 (Life Peer) of Leigh; Sidney Lewis Bernstein LLd; Chairman; Granada Group PLC from 1934–79. Pres. since 1979. (Granada Television, Granada Theatres, Granada TV Rental, Granada Motorway Services, Novello & Co). b. 30 Jan. 1899. A founder, Film Society, 1924. Films Adviser, Min. of Inf. 1940–45; Liaison, British Embassy, Washington 1942; Chief, Film Section SHAEF 1943–45. Lecturer on Film and International Affairs, NYU and Yale. Governor, Sevenoaks School. Member, Resources for Learning Committee, Nuffield Foundation, Member: Jerusalem Committee.

BERNSTEIN, WALTER: Director, Writer. b. New York, NY. Aug. 20, 1919. e. Dartmouth. Wrote for New Yorker Magazine; in W.W.II was roving correspondent for Yank Magazine. Returned to New Yorker after war. Wrote TV scripts; published book Keep Your Head Down (collection of articles).
PICTURES: Writer: Kiss the Blood Off My Hands (co-s.p.), That Kind of Woman, A Breath of Scandal (co-s.p.), Paris Blues, Heller in Pink Tights, The Magnificent Seven (uncredited), The Money Trap, Fail Safe, The Train, The Molly Maguires, The Front, The Betsy (co-s.p.), Semi-Tough, An Almost Perfect Affair, Yanks, Little Miss Marker (dir., debut), The House on Carroll Street (s.p.).

BERNSTEIN, WILLIAM: Executive. b. New York, NY, August 30, 1933. e. Yale Law Sch., LL.B., 1959; NYU, B.A., 1954. Exec. vice pres., Orion Pictures Corp. Asst. gen. counsel, then sr. v.p. United Artists 1959–78.

BERRI, CLAUDE: Actor, Director, Producer. b. Paris, July 1, 1934. r.n. Langmann. Began film career with short film Le Poulet, (prod. and dir.; won Acad. Award, short subject, 1966).
PICTURES: The Two of Us (dir.); Marry Me, Marry Me (dir., actor); Le Pistonne (dir.); Le Cinema de Papa (prod., dir.); Sex Shop (dir., s.p.); Male of the Century (dir., s.p., actor); The First Time (dir., s.p.); Tess (prod.); Inspecteur la Bavure (prod.); Je Vous Aime (prod., s.p.); Le Maitre d' Ecole (prod., dir., s.p.); A Quarter to Two Before Jesus Christ (prod.); L'Africain (prod.); Banzai (prod.); L'Homme Blesse (prod.); Garcon! Tchao Pantin (prod., s.p., dir.); Scemo Di Guerra; Jean la Florette (dir.); Manon of the Springs (dir.); The Bear (exec. prod.); The Door on the Left as You Leave the Elevator.

BERRY, JOHN: Director. b. New York, NY, 1917. Directed films in Hollywood mid and late '40s; went abroad during McCarthy era in U.S. where worked in French film industry. Later went to London to do stage work, acting as well as directing. Returned to U.S. to do stage work; returned to Hollywood to do TV.
PICTURES: Cross My Heart, From This Day Forward, Miss Susie Slagle's, Casbah, Tension, He Ran All the Way, Ça Va Barder, The Great Lover, Je Suis un Sentimental, Tamango, On Que Mambo, Claudine, Maya, The Bad News Bears Go to Japan, Thieves, Il y a maldonne, 'Round Midnight (actor only), A Man in Love (actor only).
TELEVISION: One Drink at a Time, Farewell Party, Mr. Broadway, Sister, Sister (also prod.); Angel on My Shoulder, Honeyboy.

BERRY, KEN: Actor. b. Moline, IL, Nov. 3.
PICTURES: Two for the Seesaw, Hello Down There, Herbie Rides Again, The Cat from Outer Space.
TELEVISION: The Reluctant Heroes, Wake Me When the War Is Over, Every Man Needs One (movie), Ken Berry Wow Show, Mayberry RFD, F. Troop, Mama's Family.

BERTINELLI, VALERIE: Actress. b. Wilmington, DE, April 23, 1960. Dramatic training at Tami Lynn Academy of Artists in California. Made early TV appearances in the series, Apple's Way, in commercials, and in public service announcements. Started own prod. company to acquire properties for self.
TELEVISION: Movies: Young Love, First Love; The Promise of Love, The Princess and the Cabbie, I Was a Mail Order Bride, The Seduction of Gina, Shattered Vows, Rockabye, Silent Witness, Ordinary Heroes, Pancho Barnes, Torn Apart. Specials: The Secret of Charles Dickens, The Magic of David Copperfield. Series: One Day at a Time. Mini-Series: I'll Take Manhattan.
PICTURE: Number One with a Bullet.

BERTOLUCCI, BERNARDO: Director, Writer, b. Parma, Italy, March 16, 1941. e. Rome U. Son of Attilio Bertolucci, poet and film critic. At age 20 worked as asst. dir. to Pier Paolo Pasolini on latter's first film, Accatone: in 1962 made debut film, The Grim Reaper, from script by Pasolini. 1962 published poetry book: In cerca del mistero. 1965–66: directed and wrote 3-part TV documentary: La vie del Petrolio for Ital. Oil co. in Iran. Collaborated on s.p. Ballata de un Milliardo, and Sergio Leone's Once Upon a Time in the West.
PICTURES: Before the Revolution, Partner, Love and Rage (one episode: Agony). The Spider's Strategem, The Conformist, Last Tango in Paris, 1900, Luna, Tragedy of a Ridiculous Man, The Last Emperor (Acad. Award, 1987), The Sheltering Sky.

BESMAN, MICHAEL: Executive. e. UCLA, B.A. in film studies. Gained first experience in m.p. industry as asst. to director Michael Wadleigh during post-production work on Wolfen. Served as asst. to prod. Aaron Russo in developing new projects, including Trading Places. 1983, joined Paramount Pictures as researcher for story dept. Named creative exec. with studio prod. dept. 1985, promoted to exec. dir., production, for Paramount M.P. Group.

BEST, BARBARA: Publicist. b. San Diego, CA, Dec. 2, 1921. e. U. of Southern California, AB, 1943. Pub., 20th Century-Fox, 1943–49; reporter, San Diego Journal, 1950 Stanley Kramer Co. 1950–53; own agency, Barbara Best & Associates, 1953–66; 1966 exec. v.p. Jay Bernstein Public rel.; Freeman and Best, 1967–74; Barbara Best Inc. publ. rel. 1975–85; Barbara Best Personal Management, current.

BEST, JAMES: Actor. b. Corydon, IN, July 26, 1926. Magazine model; on stage; in European roadshow cast of My Sister Eileen; served as M.P. with U.S.A.A.F., W.W.II; m.p. debut in Comanche Territory, 1949.
PICTURES: Winchester 73, Air Cadet, Cimarron Kid, Steel Town, Ma & Pa Kettle at the Fair, Francis Goes to West Point, Seminole, The President's Lady, City of Bad Men, Column South, Riders to the Stars, The Raid, Caine Mutiny, Return from the Sea, The Left-Handed Gun, They Rode West, Seven Angry Men, Come Next Spring, Baby, The Rack, Sounder, Ode to Billy Joe, The End, Hooper, Rolling Thunder.
RECENT TELEVISION: Hawkins, Savages, The Runaway, Barge, The Savage Bees, The Dukes of Hazzard (regular), Enos.

BETHUNE, ZINA: Actress, Dancer, Singer. b. New York, NY, 1950. Broadway: Most Happy Fella, National tours: Sweet Charity, Carnival, Oklahoma!, Damn Yankees, Member of the Wedding, The Owl and The Pussycat, Nutcracker. New York City Ballet (Balanchine), Zina Bethune & Company Dance Theatre, Bethune Ballet Theatre Danse.
PICTURES: Sunrise At Campobello, Who's That Knocking at My Door, The Boost.
TELEVISION: The Nurses, (series), Lancer, Cains Hundred, Naked City, Route 66, Little Women, Santa Barbara, Judy Garland Show, Jackie Gleason Show, Gunsmoke, Dr. Kildare, Emergency, Planet of The Apes, Police Story, Chips, Hardy Boys, The Gymnast, Nutcracker: Money, Madness, Murder, Heart Dancing.

BETTGER, LYLE: Actor b. Philadelphia, PA, Feb. 13, 1915. e. Haverford School, Philadelphia, American Acad. of Dramatic Art, N.Y. m. Mary Rolfe, actress. Started in summer stock; in road cos. of Brother Rat, Man Who Came to Dinner.
STAGE: John Loves Mary, Love Life, Eve of St. Mark.
PICTURES: No Man of Her Own, Union Station, First Legion, Greatest Show on Earth, Sea Chase, Gunfight at OK Corral, Johnny Reno, Nevada Smith, Return of The Gunfighter, The Hawaiians, Carnival Story, The Seven Minutes.
TELEVISION: Court of Last Resort, Grand Jury, Hawaii 5-0, Police Story.

BETUEL, JONATHAN: Director.
PICTURES: My Science Project; Tripwire.

BEVILLE, HUGH M., JR.: Executive; b. April 18, 1908. e. Syracuse U., NYU (MBA). To NBC 1930 statistician, chief statistician; Research mgr., dir., research; U.S. Army 1942–46; dir. of research and planning for NBC, v.p., planning and research, 1956; v.p., planning, 1964; consultant, 1968; professor Business Admin., Southampton Coll., 1968. Exec. dir., Broadcast Rating Council, 1971–82, author-consultant, contributing editor, TV/Radio Age, 1982–85. Author, Audience Ratings; Radio, Television, Cable, 1985, Elected member, Research Hall of Fame, 1986.

BEY, TURHAN: Actor. b. Vienna, Austria, March 30, 1920. Made U.S. m.p. debut in 1941.
PICTURES: Footsteps in the Dark, Burma Convoy, Bombay Clipper, Drums of the Congo, Destination Unknown, White Savage, Dragon Seed, Arabian Nights, Bowery to Broadway, Night in Paradise, Out of the Blue, Amazing Mr. X, Parole, Inc., Adventures of Casanova, Song of India, Prisoners of the Casbah, Stolen Identity.

BEYMER, RICHARD: Actor. r.n. George Richard Beymer, Jr., b. Avoca, IA, Feb. 21, 1939. e. N. Hollywood H.S., Actors Studio. Performer, KTLA, Sandy Dreams, Fantastic Studios, Inc., 1949, Playhouse 90.
PICTURES: Indiscretion of an American Wife, So Big, Johnny Tremaine, The Diary of Anne Frank, High Time, West Side Story, Bachelor Flat, Five Finger Exercise, Hemingway's Adventures of a Young Man, The Longest Day, The Stripper, Cross Country, Silent Night Deadly Night 3: Better Watch Out.

BIBAS, FRANK PERCY: Executive. b. New York, NY, 1917. e. Brown U., Columbia U. Capt., Army Air Corps, W.W.II. Entered m.p. ind. adv. dept., Donahue & Coe; later pub. dept. American Display, then to dist. dept., National Screen Service. In 1945 joined Casanave-Artlee Pictures Inc.; appt. v.p. in charge of sales 1946 (dist. Selznick reissues in U.S.); v.p. Casanave Pictures, Inc. & Sixteen M.M. Pictures Inc., from 1949 mgr. m.p. dept., McCann-Erickson ad agency; joined Roland Reed TV Inc., v.p., prod., 1955. Prod-dir. with Hal Roach Studios, 1957. 1961 to present N.Y.C. partner, Bibas-Redford Inc. Production Co. From 1986–, pres., Bibas Group Inc. and subsidiary, Spectrum Television Prod. (Miami, Fl). 1962 won Acad Award for Project Hope, documentary. Member: S.M.P.T.E., Acad. of TV Arts and Sciences, Directors Guild of America.

BICK, JERRY: Producer. b. New York, NY, April 26, 1927. e. Columbia U., Sorbonne. Taught English at U. of Georgia and was radio sports announcer in Savannah, GA, before entering film industry in pub. dept. of MGM, N.Y. Opened own literary agency in Hollywood after stint with MCA. Began career as producer in London; debut film, Michael Kohlhaas, 1969, made in Czechoslovakia. Oct. 1986–Jan. 1988, exec. v.p. worldwide prod., Heritage Entertainment.
PICTURES: The Long Goodbye, Thieves Like Us, Russian Roulette, Farewell My Lovely (exec. prod.), The Big Sleep, Against All Odds (exec. prod.), Swing Shift.

BIEHN, MICHAEL: Actor. b. Nebraska, 1957. At 18 years moved to Los Angeles and studied acting. First professional job in 1977 in TV pilot for Logan's Run.
PICTURES: Coach, Hog Wild, The Fan, The Lords of Discipline, The Terminator, Aliens, The Boarder, The Seventh Sign, Rampage, In a Shallow Grave, The Abyss.
TELEVISION: Pilots for James at Fifteen and The Runaways; several movies-of-the-week, ABC Afternoon Specials. Series: Police Story, Family. Movies: China Rose, Deadly Intentions.

BILBY, KENNETH W.: Executive. b. Salt Lake City, UT, Oct. 7, 1918. e. Columbia U., U. of Arizona, B.A. With N.Y. Herald-Tribune, 47–50; author, New Star in the Near East, 1950; pub. rel. rep. to RCA Victor, Camden, NJ, 1950–54; exec. v.p. National Broadcasting Co., N.Y., 1954–60; v.p. public affairs, RCA, 1960–62, exec. v.p., 1962–75; exec. v.p. corporate affairs, 1976–present.

BILIMORIA, N. M.: Distributor. b. Oct. 7, 1922, Partner in M. B. Bilimoria & Son, Bombay; dir. Dominion Films (P) Ltd. Bombay; Modern Films Private Ltd., Bombay; Partner, Bilimoria & Lalji, Calcutta; Distributors Combine, Bombay; Bilimoria & Chhotubhai, Delhi; Moti Talkies, Delhi; Agent: Union Carbide India Ltd., Calcutta and Union Carbide International Co., N.Y.

BILL, TONY: Actor, Producer. b. San Diego, CA, Aug. 23, 1940. e. Notre Dame U. Founded Bill/Phillips Prods. with Julia and Michael Phillips. 1971–73; Tony Bill Prods. 1973–, Acad. of M.P. Arts & Sciences, bd. of govs., bd of trustees, chmn. prods. branch.
PICTURES: Actor: Come Blow Your Horn (debut, 1963), Soldier in the Rain, Marriage on the Rocks, None But the Brave, You're a Big Boy Now, Ice Station Zebra, Never a Dull Moment, Castle Keep, Flap, Shampoo, Heartbeat, Pee Wee's Big Adventure, Less Than Zero. Co-producer: Deadhead Miles, Steelyard Blues, The Sting. Prod.: Hearts of the West, Harry and Walter Go to New York, Boulevard Nights (exec. prod.); Going in Style, The Little Dragons. Director: My Bodyguard, Six Weeks, Five Corners (also co-prod.), Crazy People.
TELEVISION: As actor: Pilot: Microcops. Special: Lee Oswald Assassin (BBC, 1966). Series: What Really Happened to the Class of '65? Movies: Haunts of the Very Rich, Having Babies II, Washington: Behind Closed Doors, Are We in the House Alone? The Initiation of Sarah, With This Ring, Portrait of an Escort, Freedom, Washington Mistress, Running Out, Alfred Hitchcock Presents (Night Caller, 1985). Director: Dirty Dancing (pilot).

BILLITTERI, SALVATORE: Executive. b. Belleville, NJ, March 21, 1921. e. Fordham U. U.S. Air Force, 1943–45; ent. m.p. ind., doorman in N.Y. theatre, 1939; theatre mgr., 1947; film slsman, Casolaro Film Distributing Co., 1947–51; co-owner many foreign films; film editor, I.F.E., 1951; head of editing, prod. dept., Titra Sound Corp., 1956; head of east coast production, American International Pictures, 1961; dir. Post

Prod., 1970; named v.p. 1974, sr. v.p. of Filmways Pictures, 1980; sr. v.p., post production, Orion Pictures Dist. Corp., 1982.

BILSON, BRUCE: Director. b. Brooklyn, NY, May 19, 1928. e. UCLA, BA, Theater Arts, 1950. m. actress Renne Jarrett. Father is prod. George Bilson, son is writer-dir. Danny Bilson. Asst. film ed. 1951–55; USAF photo unit 1952–53; asst. dir. 1955–65 including Andy Griffith Show, Route 66. Assoc. prod. The Baileys of Balboa. Dir. since 1965 of more than 335 TV shows. Emmy Award, Get Smart, DGA nom. The Odd Couple.
PICTURES: The North Avenue Irregulars, Chattanooga Choo Choo.
TELEVISION: Barney Miller, Get Smart, Hogan's Heroes, House Calls, Alice, Private Benjamin, Life With Lucy, Spenser: For Hire, Hotel, Dallas, Hawaii Five-O, Dynasty, The Fall Guy, Nightingales. Movies/pilots: The Dallas Cowboys Cheerleaders, BJ and the Bear, The Misadventures of Sheriff Lobo, Half Nelson, Finder of Lost Loves, The Girl Who Came Gift Wrapped, The Ghosts of Buxley Hall, The New Gidget, Barefoot in the Park, The Bad News Bears, The Odd Couple, Harper Valley PTA.

BINDER, STEVE: Producer, Director, Writer. b. Los Angeles, CA, Dec. 12. e. Univ. of Southern California. 1960–61 announcer in Austria and Germany with AFN, Europe. Prof. of Cinema, Univ. Southern CA. Mem.: DGA, Producers Guild of America, Writers Guild of America, NARAS, ATAS.
TELEVISION: Prod., Dir.: Steve Allen Show (1963–65, 1973); Elvis Presley Comeback Special; Barry Manilow Special (also writer, Emmy Award, 1977); Diana Ross in Central Park (dir., ACE Award), Diana Ross '81 (also writer); Ringling Bros & Barnum Bailey Circus (also writer), Pee-Wee's Playhouse (prod. only), Big Fun on Swing Street, Barry Manilow, Pee-Wee's Playhouse Christmas Special (prod.), Diana's World Tour and over 200 major TV prods.
PICTURES: Give 'Em Hell, Harry! (dir.)

BINNS, EDWARD: Actor. b. Pennsylvania, 1916. Broadway debut in Command Decision, 1947. Has since appeared in TV, theatre, m.p. and commercial voice-overs.
PICTURES: Fail-Safe, Twelve Angry Men, Compulsion, Patton, The Americanization of Emily, Judgment at Nuremburg, Lovin' Molly, Night Moves, Oliver's Story, Before God, After School.
TELEVISION: Kraft Theatre, Studio One, Danger, Brenner (series), The Defenders, The Nurses, It Takes a Thief (series).
STAGE: Detective Story, Caligula, The Caine Mutiny Court Martial, A Touch of the Poet.

BIONDI, JR. FRANK J.: Executive. b. Jan. 9, 1945. e. Princeton U.; Harvard U., MBA (1968). Various investment banking positions 1968–74; asst. treas. Children's TV Workshop 1974–78; v.p. programming HBO 1978–82; pres. HBO 1983, then chmn. & chief exec. off. 1984 joined Coca-Cola Co. as exec. v.p., entertainment business arm. Resigned 1987 to join Viacom International as pres. and CEO.

BIRMINGHAM, PAUL A.: Executive. b. Burbank, CA, Feb. 12, 1937. e. U. of California, U. of Southern California. Sr. v.p. studio operations and admin., Paramount Pictures.

BIRNEY, DAVID: Actor. b. Washington, DC, April 23, 1940. e. Dartmouth Coll., B.A., UCLA, M.A. Following college and the Army went to N.Y. where appeared in Lincoln Center prod. of Summertree. Appeared for two yrs. on TV daytime series, Love Is a Many Splendored Thing, doing other stage roles in same period.
THEATER: NY debut NY Shakespeare Fest; 3 seasons Lincoln Center Rep. Many NY and regional credits incl: Amadeus, Benefactors, Man and Superman, Hamlet, Richard II, III Major Barbara, Biko Inquest.
PICTURES: Caravan to Vaccares, Trial by Combat, Oh God, II, Goodbye, See You Monday, Prettykill, Nightfall.
TELEVISION: Series: St. Elsewhere, Glitter, Serpico, Bridget Loves Bernie (reg.), Beyond 2000 (host), Raising Kids (host), Mini-series: Seal Morning, Adam's Chronicles, Testimony of Two Men, Master of the Game, Valley of the Dolls, The Bible. Movies: The Deadly Game, Only With Married Men, OHMS The 5 of Me, Mom, The Wolfman & Me; High Rise, The Champions, Bronc, The Long Journey Home (also co-exec. prod.), Love and Betrayal, The Diaries of Adam and Eve (also exec. prod., s.p.). Specials: Missing: Have You Seen This Person? Drop Everything and Read, 15 and Getting Straight. Guest appearances in series & anthology shows.

BIRNEY, MEREDITH BAXTER: Actress. b. Los Angeles, CA, June 21, 1947. On stage in Guys and Dolls; Butterflies Are Free; Vanities; Country Wife; Talley's Folly.
PICTURES: Ben, Bittersweet Love, All the President's Men.
TELEVISION: Series: The Interns, Bridget Loves Bernie, Family, Family Ties. Movies: The Night That Panicked America, The Stranger Who Looks Like Me, The Imposter, The Two Lives of Carol Leitner, Take Your Best Shot, The Rape of Richard Beck, Kate's Secret, The Long Journey Home (and co-exec. prod.), Winnie: My Life in the Institution, She Knows Too Much. Mini-series: Beulah Land, Little Women, The Diaries of Adam and Eve.

BIROC, JOSEPH F.: Cinematographer. b. Union City, NJ, Feb. 12, 1900. e. Emerson H.S., Union City, NJ. At 18 worked at Paragon Studios film lab in Ft. Lee NJ. In 1920s became asst. cameraman and camera operator. During WW II, army capt. heading one of first crews to film liberation of Paris. 1989, Amer. Soc. of Cinematographers' Lifetime Achievement Award.
PICTURES: It's a Wonderful Life, Bwana Devil, Glass Wall, Tall Texan, Vice Squad, Donovan's Brain, Appointment in Honduras, Down Three Dark Streets, Lone Wolf, T-Men in Action, Man Behind the Badge, Dear Phoebe, Nightmare, Tension at Table Rock, Attack, Black Whip, Run of the Arrow, Ride Back, Garment Jungle, China Gate, Ice Palace, FBI Story, 13 Ghosts, Home Before Dark, Operation Eichmann, Devil at 4 O'clock, Gold of the Seven Saints, Reprieve, Opium Eaters, Hitler, Sail a Crooked Ship, Bye Bye Birdie, Toys in the Attic, Promises-Promises, Under the Yum-Yum Tree, Viva Las Vegas, Kitten With a Whip, Ride the Wild Surf, Renegade Posse, Gunfight at Commanche Pass, Hush . . . Hush, Sweet Charlotte, I Saw What You Did, Flight of the Phoenix, The Russians Are Coming, The Russians Are Coming, The Swinger, Warning Shot, Enter Laughing, Who Is Minding the Mint, Garden of Cucumbers, The Killing of Sister George, What Ever Happened to Aunt Alice?, Too Late the Hero, Mrs. Polifax Spy, Escape from the Planet of the Apes, The Organization, The Grissom Gang, Cahill, U.S. Marshall, The Longest Yard, The Towering Inferno (shared Acad. Award, 1974), Hustle, The Duchess and the Dirtwater Fox, The Choirboys, Beyond the Poseidon Adventure, Airplane!, Hammet, All the Marbles, Airplane II: The Sequel.
TELEVISION: The Honeymoon is Over (1951, one of 1st series prod. on film), Four Star Theatre, Readers Digest, Superman, Richard Diamond, Alcoa Theatre, Grindl, Solo, Ghost Breakers, Take Her She's Mine, Heaven Help Us, Hardy Boys, Brian's Song (Emmy Award, 1971), Gidget Gets Married, Ghost Story, Thursdays Game, Lonely Hearts, 555, Family Upside Down, S.S.T. Death Flight, Little Women, Scruples, The Gambler, A Death in California, A Winner Never Quits, Outrage.
TV PILOTS: Wonder Woman, Honky Tonk, The Moneychangers, Washington, D.C., Clone Master, Desperate Lives, Casablanca, Another Jerk, House Detective, Hell Town U.S.A., Flag, Time Out for Dad.

BISHOP, JULIE: Actress. b. Denver, CO, Aug. 30, 1917. e. Westlake, Kenwood, Schools for Girls. Former screen name Jacqueline Wells; m.p. debut 1941.
PICTURES: Nurse's Secret, International Squadron, Steel Against the Sky, Lady Gangster, Busses Roar, Cinderella Jones, Murder in the Music Hall, Idea Girl, Strange Conquest, Last of the Redmen, High Tide, Deputy Marshal, Threat, Sands of Iwo Jima, Westward the Women, Sabre Jet, High and the Mighty, Headline Hunters.

BISSET, JACQUELINE: Actress. b. Weybridge, England, September 13, 1944. e. French Lycée, London. After photographic modeling made film debut in The Knack, 1965.
PICTURES: Cul de Sac, Two For The Road, Casino Royale, The Sweet Ride, The Detective, Bullitt, The First Time, Secret World, Airport, The Grasshopper, The Mephisto Waltz, Believe in Me, The Life & Times of Judge Roy Bean, Stand Up and Be Counted, The Thief Who Came to Dinner, Day for Night, Murder on the Orient Express, End of the Game, The Spiral Staircase, St. Ives, Sunday Woman, The Deep, The Greek Tycoon, Secrets, Who Is Killing the Great Chefs of Europe?, When Time Ran Out, Rich and Famous, Inchon, Class, Under the Volcano, High Season, Scenes From the Class Struggle in Beverly Hills, La Maison de Jade, Wild Orchids.
TELEVISION: Forbidden, Choices, Anna Karenina, Napoleon and Josephine: A Love Story.

BIXBY, BILL: Actor. b. San Francisco, CA, Jan. 22, 1934. e. U. of California, Berkeley. Worked in indust. films. Gen. Motors, Chrysler.
TELEVISION: Dobie Gillis, Danny Thomas Show, Joey Bishop Show, Andy Griffith Show, My Favorite Martian, The Courtship of Eddie's Father, The Incredible Hulk, Goodbye Beantown, International Airport, J.J. Starbuck, Agatha Christie's Murder Is Easy, The Incredible Hulk Returns (also exec. prod.), The Trial of the Incredible Hulk (also exec. prod., dir.).
STAGE: Fantasticks (nat'l company), Under the Yum Yum Tree.
PICTURES: Lonely Are the Brave, Irma La Douce, Under the Yum Yum Tree, Ride Beyond Vengeance, This Way Out Please.

BLACK, ALEXANDER F.: Publicist. b. New Rochelle, NY, Dec. 27, 1918. e. Brown U., BA, 1940. Joined Universal 1941. U.S. Navy 1942–45, Lt. Sr. Grade. Rejoined Universal 1946 serving in various capacities in Foreign Department, becoming director of foreign publicity for Universal International Films, Inc. in 1967; 1974, named exec. in chg. intl. promotion for MCA-TV.

BLACK, KAREN: Actress. b. Park Ridge, IL, July 1, 1942. e. Northwestern U. Left school for NY to join the Hecscher House, appearing in several Shakespearean plays. In 1965 starred in Playroom, which ran only 1 month but won her NY Drama Critic nom. as best actress.
PICTURES: You're a Big Boy Now (debut, 1966), Hard Contact, Easy Rider, Five Easy Pieces, Drive, He Said, A Gunfight, Born To Win, Portnoy's Complaint, The Pyx, Rhinoceros, The Outfit, The Great Gatsby, Airport 1975, Law and Disorder, Day of the Locust, Nashville, Family Plot, Crime and Passion, Burnt Offerings, Capricorn One, Because He's My Friend, In Praise of Older Women, The Rip-off, Greed, Danny Travis, Chanel Solitaire, Come Back to the Five and Dime, Jimmie Dean, Jimmie Dean; Growing Pains, Martin's Day, Cut and Run, Invaders from Mars, It's Alive III, Hostage, After All These Years, The Invisible Kid, Eternal Evil, Homer and Eddie, Night Angel, Deadly Intent, Out of the Dark, Judgment, Miss Right, Dead Girls Don't Dance, Zapped Again.
STAGE: Happily Never After, Keep It in the Family.
TELEVISION: Mr. Horn, Power, Trilogy of Terror, The Strange Possession of Mrs. Oliver, Full Circle Again (Canadian TV).

BLACK, NOEL: Director. b. June 30, 1940. e. UCLA, B.A., 1959; M.A. 1964.
PICTURES: Skaterdater (short), Pretty Poison, Mirrors, A Man, a Woman, and a Bank, Private School, Mischief (s.p. only).
TELEVISION: I'm a Fool, The Golden Honeymoon, The Electric Grandmother, The Other Victim, Prime Suspect, Happy Endings, Quarterback Princess, Deadly Intentions (mini-series), Promises to Keep, A Time to Triumph, My Two Loves, The Doctors Wilde, Conspiracy of Love, The Town Bully, Meet the Munceys.

BLACK, STANLEY: Composer, conductor, musical director. Resident conductor, BBC, 1944–52. Musical director 105 feature films and Pathe Newsreel music: Music dir. Associated British Film Studios 1958–64. Guest conductor, Royal Philharmonic Orchestra and London Symphony. Orchestra; many overseas conducting engagements including (1977) Boston Pops and Winnipeg Symphony. Associated conductor Osaka Philharmonic Orchestra. Exclusive recording contract with Decca Record Co. since 1944.
PICTURES: Crossplot, The Long, The Short and The Tall, Rattle of a Simple Man, The Young Ones, Hell Is a City, Top Secret, Valentino.

BLACK, THEODORE R.: Attorney, b. New Jersey, Aug. 11, 1906. e. Harvard U., B.A., 1927, LL.B., 1930 (Sigma Alpha Mu fraternity). Formerly General Counsel, bd. member, Republic Pictures Corp. Member: Nat'l Panel of Arbitrators, American Arbit. Assn., Bd. N.Y. Ethical Culture Society.

BLACKMAN, HONOR: Actress. b. London, England. Stage debut. The Gleam 1946. Screen debut, Fame Is the Spur.
TELEVISION: African Patrol, The Witness, Four Just Men, Probation Officer series, Top Secret, Ghost Squad, Invisible Man, The Saint, The Avengers series.
PICTURES: Quartet, Daughter of Darkness, A Boy A Girl and a Bike, Diamond City, Conspirator, So Long at the Fair, Set a Murderer, Green Grow the Rushes, Come Die My Love, Rainbow Jacket, Outsiders, Delavine Affair, Three Musketeers, Breakaway, Homecoming, Suspended Alibi, Dangerous Drugs, A Night to Remember, The Square Peg, A Matter of Who, Present Laughter, The Recount, Serena, Jason & the Golden Fleece, Goldfinger, The Secret of My Success, Moment to Moment, Life at the Top, A Twist of Sand, Shalako, Struggle for Rome, Twinky, The Last Grenade, The Virgin and the Gypsy, Fright, Something Big, Out Damned Spot, Ragtime, Summer, Cat and the Canary.

BLADES, RUBEN: Actor, Composer, Singer, Writer. b. Panama City, Panama, July 16, 1948. e. U. of Panama (law and political science, 1974), Harvard U., L.L.M., 1985. Attorney, Banco Nacional de Panama, 1972–74. Legal advisor, Fania Records, Inc. 1975–78. Recorded award-winning albums (Buscando America, Escenas, Agua de Luna) for Elektra/Asylum Records. With his band Seis del Solar has toured U.S., Central America and Europe.
PICTURES: The Last Fight (debut, 1982), Crossover Dreams (also co-s.p.), When the Mountains Tremble, Beat Street, Critical Condition, The Milagro Beanfield War, Fatal Beauty, Oliver & Company (songs), Disorganized Crime, The Lemon Sisters, The Two Jakes, Love Supreme.
TELEVISION: Sesame Street. Movie: Dead Man Out.

BLAIN, GERARD: Actor, Director. b. Oct. 23, 1930, Paris. Began his professional career in 1943 as an extra in Marcel Carne's The Children of Paradise. Appeared on stage in Marcel Pagnol's Topaze (1944). Military service in a parachute regiment. In 1955 Julien Duvivier gave him his first major role in Voici le Temps des Assassins (Murder a la Carte). By 1969 had appeared in more than 30 stage and film roles before becoming a director and co-author.
PICTURES: Les Mistons (1957), Le Beau Serge, Les Cousins. In Italy: The Hunchback of Rome, L'Ora di Roma, I Defini, Run with the Devil, Young Husbands. In Germany: The American Friend, L'Enfant de l'Hiver. As director and author or co-author: Les Amis, Le Pelican (also actor), Un Enfant dans la Foule, Un Second Souffle, Le Rebelle, Portrait sur Michel Tournier, Pierre et Djemila.

BLAINE, VIVIAN: Actress. r.n. Vivian S. Stapleton. b. Newark, NJ, Nov. 21, 1924. e. South Side H.S., Newark. Singer with various bands in New Jersey 1937–39, thereafter nightclubs; 20th-Fox contract 1942. Personal appearance on British stage from 1947; created role of Adelaide in Guys and Dolls on Broadway, London and film; N.Y. stage in Hatful of Rain, Company. Member: Academy of M.P. Arts & Sciences, AFTRA, Equity, S.A.G., A.G.V.A.
PICTURES: He Married His Boss, Thru Different Eyes, It Happened in Flatbush, Girl Trouble, Jitterbugs, Greenwich Village, Something for the Boys, Nob Hill, State Fair, Doll Face, Three Little Girls in Blue, If I'm Lucky, Skirts Ahoy, Public Pigeon No. 1, Guys and Dolls, The Dark, Parasite, I'm Going to Be Famous.
TELEVISION: Mary Hartman, Mary Hartman; A Year at the Top; The Cracker Factory; Fast Friends; Katie—Portrait of a Centerfold; Amanda's; Murder She Wrote.

BLAIR, BETSY: Actress. r.n. Betsy Boger. b. New York, NY, Dec. 11, 1923. m. director Karel Reisz.
BROADWAY: Panama Hattie Beautiful People, Richard II, Face of a Hero, actress in little theatre groups.
PICTURES: A Double Life, Another Part of the Forest, Snake Pit, Kind Lady, Othello, Marty, Halliday Brand, A Delicate Balance, Betrayed.
TELEVISION: Appearances on U.S. Steel Hour, Ford Theatre, Philco, Kraft, Suspicion (PBS) thirtysomething. Movie: Marcus Welby, M.D.—A Holiday Affair.

BLAIR, JANET: Actress. b. Blair, PA, April 23, 1921. r.n. Martha Lafferty. With Hal Kemp's Orchestra; toured in South Pacific, 1950–52.
PICTURES: Three Girls About Town, Blondie Goes to College, Two Yanks in Trinidad, Burn Witch Burn, Broadway, My Sister Eileen, Something to Shout About, Once Upon a Time, Tars and Spars, Gallant Journey, Fabulous Dorseys, I Love Trouble, Black Arrow, Fuller Brush Man, Public Pigeon No. 1, Boys Night Out, The One and Only, Genuine, Original Family Band.
TELEVISION: Sid Caesar Show.

BLAIR, LARRY: Actor. r.n. Larry Bess. b. Newark, NJ, June 27, 1935; f. Herman Bess, N.Y.C. radio executive. e. public and private schools, Newark and Asbury Park, NJ. Began in showbusiness, age 13 as D.J. and actor in N.Y.C.; 1954–55, production assistant, WABC-TV, N.Y.C.; 1955–62, associate dir. and dir., WNEW-TV, N.Y.C.; 1962–71, D.J., newscaster with WFIL, Phila., WTIC, Hartford, WHN, WMCA, N.Y. 1971 to present, commercial spokesman, narrator and actor.

BLAIR, LINDA: Actress. b. St. Louis, MO, Jan. 22, 1959. Model and actress on TV commercials before going into films.
PICTURES: The Sporting Club, The Way We Live Now, The Exorcist, Airport '75, Sweet Hostage, Exorcist II: The Heretic, Hell Night, Chained Heat, Roller Boogie, Grotesque, SFX Retaliator, Silent Assassins, Night Patrol, Savage Streets, Savage Island, Night Force, Witchery, Aunt Millie's Will, The Chilling, Zapped Again, Bad Blood, W.B., Blue and the Bean, Moving Target, Up Your Alley, The Repossessed.
TELEVISION: Born Innocent, Sarah T.—Portrait of a Teenage Alcoholic, Victory at Entebbe, Sweet Hostage, Stranger in Our House.

BLAIR, STEWART D.: Executive. b. Scotland, 1950. e. U. of Glasgow, M.A., economics and political science. Worked in London office of Chase Manhattan Bank, moving to NY to join its teaching staff lecturing on corp. finance, 1972 and becoming youngest v.p. at 27. Joined Tele-Communications Inc. as dir. of finance and rose to sr. v.p., finance, working directly for chmn. John C. Malone, on acquisitions. When Tele-Communications acquired United Artists Communications Inc., named pres. and CEO of United Artists Communications, Inc. Following merger of U.A. Communications Inc. and United Cable Television Corp. into United Artists Entertainment Co., assumed position of vice chmn. and CEO.

BLAKE, DAVID M.: Producers' representative. b. Trincomalee, Ceylon, April 19, 1948. Ent. m.p. ind. 1968 British Lion Films, London. Lion Int'l. Films, O'Seas Division. Appointed 1970 U.S. representative. New York. British Lion Films, Shepperton Studios, Lion TV.

BLAKE, ROBERT: Actor. b. Nutley, NJ, Sept. 18, 1933. r.n. Michael Gubitosi. m. actress Sondra Kerry. Started as a child actor in

Our Gang comedies as Bobby Blake, also Little Beaver in Red Ryder series. Later was Hollywood stunt man in Rumble on the Docks and The Tijuana Story. First acting job was at the Gallery Theater in Hatful of Rain.

PICTURES: As child in: Andy Hardy's Double Life, The Horn Blows at Midnight, Treasure of Sierra Madre, Revolt in the Big House, The Purple Gang. As adult: Town Without Pity, PT-109, The Greatest Story Ever Told, The Connection, This Property Is Condemned, In Cold Blood, Tell Them Willie Boy Is Here, Corky, Electra-Glide in Blue, Busting, Second Hand Hearts, Coast to Coast.

TELEVISION: Baretta (Emmy Award, 1975), Blood Feud, Joe Dancer, Hell Town (also s.p.), The Heart of a Champion—The Ray Mancini Story.

BLAKELY, SUSAN: Actress. b. Germany, Sept. 7, 1950, where father was stationed in Army. Studied at U. of Texas. m. prod. Steve Jaffe. Became top magazine and TV commercial model in N.Y. Film debut in Savages, 1972.

PICTURES: The Lords of Flatbush, The Way We Were, The Towering Inferno, Report to the Commissioner, Shampoo, Capone, Dreamer, The Concorde—Airport '79, Over the Top, The Survivalist, My Mom's a Werewolf.

TELEVISION: Rich Man, Poor Man. Movies: Secrets, Make Me an Offer, A Cry For Love, The Bunker, The Oklahoma City Dolls, The Heart of a Champion, Will There Really Be A Morning?, International Airport, The Annihilator, The Ted Kennedy Jr. Story, Blood & Orchids, April Morning, Fatal Confession: A Father Dowling Mystery, Broken Angel, Hiroshima Maiden, Ladykillers, Sight Unseen. Special: Torn Between Two Fathers.

BLANCO, RICHARD M.: Executive, b. Brooklyn, NY. e. electrical engineering, Wentworth Institute. J.C., 1925–27; bus. admin., U. of California, 1939–40; U.S. Govt. Coll., 1942. Superv. Technicolor Corp., 1931–56; organ. and oper. Consumer Products, Kodachrome film process., Technicolor, 1956–62; dir. of MP Govt. and theatr. sales, N.Y. and Washington, DC, 1963–65; gen. mgr. of Technicolor Florida photo. operations at Kennedy Space Center., prod. document. and educ. films for NASA, 1965; VP of TV division, Technicolor Corp. of America; 1967 elected corporate v.p. Technicolor, Inc.; 1971 pres., Technicolor Graphic Services, Inc.; 1974, elected chmn. of bd. of Technicolor Graphic Services; 1977, elected to bd. of dirs. of Technicolor Inc.

BLANE, RALPH: Composer. b. Broken Arrow, OK, July 26, 1914. e. Northwestern U. Started as singer, then vocal arranger for Broadway shows; appeared on NBC radio. Formed partnership with Hugh Martin, wrote Best Foot Forward; m.p. composer since 1939.

PICTURES: Best Foot Forward, Meet Me in St. Louis, My Dream Is Yours, One Sunday Afternoon, My Blue Heaven, Friendly Island, Skirts Ahoy, French Line, Athena, Girl Rush, The Girl Most Likely, Who is Sylvia?, Ziegfeld Follies, Broadway Rhythm, Abbott and Costello in Hollywood, Easy to Wed.

TELEVISION: The Great Quillow. 1961; same in color for NBC, 1963.

BROADWAY: Three Wishes for Jamie, Tattered Tom, Something About Anne, Don't Flash Tonight.

BLANK, MYRON: Circuit executive. b. Des Moines, IA, Aug. 30, 1911. e. U. of Michigan. Son of A. H. Blank, circuit operator. On leaving coll. joined father in operating Tri-States and Central States circuits. On leave 1943–46 in U.S. Navy, officer in charge visual educ. Now pres. Central States Theatre Corp.; pres. TOA, 1955; chmn. bd. TOA Inc. 1956–57; exec. chmn. of NATO. Pres. of Greater Des Moines Comm.; treas., Iowa Methodist Medical Center; board, Iowa Des Moines Natl. Bank.; pres., Iowa Phoenix Corp., recipient of Brotherhood Award of National Conference of Christians & Jews; board, Simpson College; chmn., Blank Park Zoo.

BLATT, DANIEL: Producer. Independent producer since 1978; prior posts: resident counsel, ABC Pictures; exec. v.p. Palomar Pictures; partner with Edgar J. Scherick. Blatt-Singer Prods. Now Daniel H. Blatt Prods.

PICTURES: I Never Promised You a Rose Garden; The American Success Company; The Howling; Independence Day; Cujo; Restless, The Boost.

TELEVISION: Co-prod. with Robert Singer: The Children Nobody Wanted, Sadat, V—The Final Battle, Raid on Entebbe, Sacred Vows, A Winner Never Quits, Sworn to Silence.

BLATTNER, ROBERT: Executive. b. Dover, DE, March 5, 1952. e. Harvard Coll., B.A., 1974; Harvard Business Sch., M.B.A., 1976. 1980–81, dir. sls., Columbia Pictures Home Entertainment; 1981–82, promoted to v.p. & gen. mgr.; 1982–83, v.p., gen. mgr., RCA/Columbia Pictures Home Video; named pres., 1983. Appt. pres., MCA Home Video, 1989.

BLATTY, WILLIAM PETER: Writer, Producer. Novelist who wrote John Goldfarb, Please Come Home (filmed) and Twinkle, Twinkle, Killer Kane (prod., dir. also) before biggest success with The Exorcist, which became a 55-week best-selling book. He wrote s.p. and functioned as prod. on film version.

PICTURES: A Shot in the Dark (s.p.), What Did You Do in the War, Daddy? (s.p), The Great Bank Robbery, Darling Lili (co. s.p.), The Exorcist (prod., s.p.), The Ninth Configuration (prod. dir., s.p.), The Exorcist: 1990 (dir., s.p.).

BLAU, MARTIN: Executive. b. New York, NY, June 6, 1924. e. Ohio U., 1948. Employed on newspapers in OH, TX, WV. Pub. dept., Columbia Pictures, 1951; asst. pub. mgr. 1959; pub. mgr., Columbia Internat'l, 1961; admin. asst. to v.p. of adv. & pub. Columbia Pictures, 1966. Dir. adv. and publicity, Columbia Pictures International, 1970; v.p., 1971; sr. v.p., 1985. Retired, 1988.

BLAUSTEIN, JULIAN: Producer. b. New York, NY, May 30, 1913. e. Harvard U., 1933. Ent. m.p. ind. as reader for Universal 1935; asst. story ed. 1935–36; story ed. 1936–38; in chg. story dept. Music Corp. of America 1938–39; story ed. Paramount 1939–41; Signal Corps Photo. Center 1941–46; edit. supervisor of Selznick 1946–48; to 20th-Fox as prod. 1949; apptd. exec. prod. 20th Cent.-Fox, 1951–Dec. 1952. Independent 1955–75.

PICTURES: Broken Arrow, Mister 880, Half Angel, Just One More Chance, Take Care of My Little Girl, Day the Earth Stood Still, Outcasts of Poker Flat, Don't Bother to Knock, Desiree, The Racers, Storm Center, Cowboy, Bell, Book and Candle, The Wreck of the Mary Deare, Two Loves, The Four Horsemen of the Apocalypse, Khartoum, Three into Two Won't Go.

BLAY, ANDRE: Executive. In 1979, sold Magnetic Video to 20th Century Fox, named pres., CEO, 20th Century Fox Home Video; 1981, formed The Blay Corporation; 1982, joined with Norman Lear and Jerry Perenchio, founders of Embassy Communications, as chairman and CEO of Embassy Home Entertainment; 1986, when Embassy sold to Nelson Group, left to form Palisades Entertainment Group with Elliott Kastner.

PICTURES: Exec. Prod.: Prince of Darkness, They Live, Homeboy, The Blob, A Chorus of Disapproval.

BLECKNER, JEFF: Director. b. Brooklyn, NY, Aug. 12, 1943. e. Amherst College, BA., 1965; Yale Sch. of Drama, MFA 1968. Taught drama at Yale, also participated in the theater co. 1965–68. 1968–75 theater dir. NY Shakespeare Fest. Public Theatre (2 Drama Desk Awards, 1 Tony nom. for Sticks and Bones); Basic Training of Pavlo Hummel (Obie Award, 1971), The Unseen Hand (Obie Award). Began TV career directing The Guiding Light, 1975.

TELEVISION: Hill Street Blues (Emmy Award, DGA Award, 1983), Concealed Enemies (Emmy Award, 1984), Daddy, I'm Their Momma Now (Emmy nom.), Do You Remember Love (Christopher, Humanitas, Peabody Awards, Emmy nom.), Fresno, Terrorist on Trial, Brotherly Love, My Father, My Son; Favorite Son.

BLEES, ROBERT: Writer, Producer. e. Dartmouth, Phi Beta Kappa. Writer/photographer, Time and Life Magazines. Fiction: Cosmopolitan, etc. Exec. boards of Writers Guild, Producers Guild. Executive consultant, QM Prods.; BBC (England). Trustee, Motion Picture & TV Fund.

PICTURES: Magnificent Obsession, Autumn Leaves, The Glass Web, James Cain's Love's Lovely Counterfeit.

TELEVISION: Producer: Combat!, Bonanza, Bus Stop, Kraft Theater. Writer also: Alfred Hitchcock, Cannon, Barnaby Jones, Harry O, Columbo, co-creator: The New Gidget.

BLEIER, EDWARD: Executive. b. New York, NY, October 16, 1929. e. Syracuse U., 1951, C.U.N.Y., grad. courses. Reporter: Syracuse Herald Journal, Long Island Press 1947–50. Sportscaster: WNEW, N.Y.; WSYR, Syracuse, 1947–50. Prog. service mgr., DuMont Television Network, 1951; v.p., radio-television-film, Tex McCrary, Inc. 1958. American Broadcasting Company, 1952–57; 1959–68. v.p. in chg. pub. relations & planning (marketing, advertising, publicity), broadcast div.; v.p. in chg. of daytime programming & sales; vice pres./gen. sales mgr., ABC-TV Network. U.S. Army Psy. War School; Ex-chmn., TV Committee, NASL; ex-Trustee, NATAS; founder-director & ex-vice-chmn., International TV Council (NATAS); past-pres., IRTS; ATAS; AMPAS; guest lecturer at universities. Chmn., Steering comm., Aspen B'dcaster's Conference. 1969–present: Warner Bros. TV and Warner Bros. Inc.: Pres, pay-TV, animation & network features.

BLENDER, LEON PHILIP: Executive. b. Kansas City, MO, Feb. 15, 1920. e. Kansas State Coll., 1941. 20th Century-Fox Dist. Co., 1947–51; Kranz-Levin pictures, 1951–56. gen. sis. mgr. American International Film Dist. Corp., 1956–57; v.p. 1960; American Intl. Pictures, senior v.p., sales dist., later exec. v.p. sales and distribution; 1979, exec. v.p. sales & distribution, Film Ventures Intl.; 1983, exec. v.p., world-wide dist., Summa Vista Pictures.

BLIER, BERTRAND: Director. b. Paris, France, 1939. Son of late actor Bernard Blier. Served as asst. dir. to Georges Lautner, John Berry, Christian-Jaque, Denys de la Paatelliere and

Jean Delannoy for two years before dir. debut with Hitler Connais Pas.
PICTURES: Hitler Connais Pas (1963), Breakdown, Laisse Aller, C'Est une Valse (s.p. only), Going Places, Calmos, Get Out Your Handkerchiefs (Acad. Award, best foreign film, 1978), Buffet Froid, Beau-pere, My Best Friend's Girl, Notre Historie, Menage, Too Beautiful For You.

BLOCH, ROBERT: Writer. b. Chicago, IL, April 5, 1917. Novelist, short-story writer; 50 published books, incl. Psycho, Psycho II, The Night of the Ripper, Lori. Wrote radio series, Stay Tuned for Terror, adapting own stories; national pres., Mystery Writers of Amer., 1970–71; entered films, 1960.
PICTURES: The Couch, Cabinet of Caligari, Straitjacket, The Night-Walker, The Psychopath, The Deadly Bees, Torture Garden (co-s.p.), The House that Dripped Blood, Asylum. (Films adapted from published work): Psycho, The Skull.
TELEVISION: Features: The Cat Creature, The Dead Don't Die. Approx. 70 credits on Hitchcock, Thriller, Star Trek, Tales from the Dark Side, Monsters.

BLOCK, WILLARD: Executive. b. New York, NY, March 18, 1930.; e. Columbia Coll., Columbia U. Law Sch., 1952. Counter-Intelligence Corps., U.S. Army, 1952–54, account exec., Plus Marketing, Inc. 1954–55; joined sales staff, NBC Television Network, 1955–57; sales staff, CBS Enterprises, Inc., 1957; international sales mgr, 1960; dir., international sales, 1965; v.p., 1967; v.p., Viacom Enterprises, 1971; pres., 1972; v.p. MCA-TV, 1973; v.p., gen. mgr., Taft, H-B International, Inc.; pres. Willard Block, Ltd.; 1979, named pres., Viacom Enterprises; 1982–1989, pres. Viacom Worldwide Ltd. Currently consultant to Aaron Spelling Ent., Sumitomo Corp., Insight Telecast.

BLOOM, CLAIRE: Actress. b. London, England, Feb. 15, 1931. e. Badminton Sch. (U.K.). Stage debut at Playhouse, Oxford, Sept., 1947; Old Vic seasons, etc.; screen debut in Limelight, 1951. Author: Limelight and After.
PICTURES: Innocents in Paris, The Man Between, Richard III, Alexander the Great, The Brothers Karamazov, Look Back in Anger, The Royal Game, The Wonderful World of the Brothers Grimm, The Chapman Report, The Haunting, Alta Infidelita, Il Maestro di Vigevano, The Outrage, The Spy Who Came In From the Cold, Charley, The Illustrated Man, Three into Two Won't Go, A Severed Head, Red Sky at Morning, A Doll's House, Islands in the Stream, Clash of the Titans, Sammy and Rosie Get Laid.
TELEVISION: Misalliance, (Playhouse 90), Anna Karenina, Wuthering Heights, Ivanov, Wessex Tales, An Imaginative Woman, A Legacy, In Praise of Love, The Orestaia, Henry VIII, Brideshead Revisited, Hamlet, Cymbeline, King John, Ann and Debbie, Ellis Island, Separate Tables, Florence Nightingale, The Ghost Writer, Time and the Conways, Shadow Lands, Liberty, Promises to Keep, The Belle of Amherst, Hold the Dream, Anastasia, Queenie, Intimate Contact, Beryl Markham: A Shadow on the Sun, Oedipus the King, The Lady and the Highwayman.

BLOOM, VERNA: Actress. b. Lynn, MA, Aug. 7, 1939. e. Boston U. Studied drama at Uta Hagen-Herbert Berghof School. Performed with small theatre groups all over country; then started repertory theatre in Denver. Appeared on Broadway in Marat/Sade (played Charlotte Corday). Film debut, Medium Cool, 1969.
PICTURES: The Hired Hand, High Plains Drifter, Badge 373, National Lampoon's Animal House, After Hours, The Last Temptation of Christ.
TELEVISION: The Blue Knight, Contact on Cherry Street, Playing for Time, Rivlein—Bounty Hunter.

BLOOMER STEPHEN J.: Exhibitor. b. Belleville, IL, Nov. 12, 1947. e. Northern Illinois U., B.S. in education, 1969. Elementary school band director, 1969–75; insurance sales, New York Life Insurance Co., 1975–77; asst. mgr., New York Life, 1977–1979; joined BAC Theatres Jan., 1979 as warehouse mgr.; Nov. 1979, named gen. mgr.

BLOUNT, LISA: Actress. Auditioned for role as extra in film September 30, 1955 and was chosen as the female lead.
PICTURES: September 30, 1955, An Officer and a Gentleman, Cease Fire, Radioactive Dreams, What Waits Below, Cut and Run, Nightflyers, South of Reno, Stiffs, Prince of Darkness, Great Balls of Fire, Blind Fury.
TELEVISION: Pilot: Off Duty. Movies: Stormin' Home, Murder Me, Murder You, The Annihilator. Guest: Moonlighting, Magnum P.I., Starman, Hitchhiker.

BLUM, HARRY N.: Executive. b. Cleveland, OH, Oct. 3, 1932. e. U. of Michigan, B.B.A., LL.B. Was attorney in Ohio, toy & hobby industry executive, management consultant, and venture capital and investment manager before entering industry. Now heads The Blum Group, entertainment financing, packaging, production and international marketing co.
PICTURES: Executive Action (assoc. prod.); The Land That Time Forgot (assoc. prod.); At the Earth's Core (exec. prod.); Drive-In (assoc. prod.) Diamonds (exec. prod.); The Bluebird (assoc. prod.); Obsession (prod.); Skateboard (prod.); The Magician of Lublin (exec. prod.); Duran Duran—Arena (exec. prod.); The Actor (exec. prod.).

BLUM, MARK: Actor. b. Newark, NJ, May 14, 1950. Studied drama at U. of Minnesota and U. of Pennsylvania. Also studied acting with Andre Gregory, Aaron Frankel and Daniel Seltzer. Extensive Off-B'way work after debut in The Cherry Orchard (1976).
THEATER: Off-Broadway: The World of Sholem Aleichem, Brothers (New Brunswick, NJ), The Merchant (B'way), Say Goodnight, Gracie; Table Settings, Close Ties (Long Wharf), Key Exchange, Loving Reno, The Cherry Orchard (Long Wharf), Iago in Othello (Dallas), Messiah. At the Mark Taper Forum: An American Clock, Wild Oats, Moby Dick Rehearsed and An American Comedy, It's Only a Play (off-B'way), Little Footsteps, Cave Life, Gus and Al (Obie Award).
PICTURES: Desperately Seeking Susan, Just Between Friends, Crocodile Dundee, Blind Date, The Presidio, Worth Winning.
TELEVISION: Sweet Surrender, Miami Vice (guest), Capital News (series).

BLUMENSTOCK, SID: Ad. exec. New York, NY. Publicity dir. Warner Bros. Atlantic City theatres 1934–38; joined 20th Fox adv. dept. 1938; asst. exploitation mgr. 1944–49; advertising mgr. Paramount 1949; asst. nat'l dir. adv. pub., exploit, 1951–58; MPH Coord. 1959 Academy telecast; v.p. Embassy Pictures, 1959; v.p. Chas. Schlaifer Agency, Hollywood, October, 1959–62; v.p. Safranski Prod., Inc.; adv. dir., Embassy Pictures, 1964–67; Walter Reade Org., 1967–70 Levitt-Pickman Film Corp., adv. dir., 1971–72.

BLUMOFE, ROBERT F.: Producer. b. New York, NY. e. Columbia Coll., AB, Columbia U. Sch. of Law, JD. v.p., West Coast oper., U.A., 1953–66; independent prod., pres. RFB Enterprises, Inc; American Film Institute, director, AFI-West, Sept. 1, 1977–81. Now indep. prod.

BLUTH, DON: Animator, Director, Producer, Writer. e. Brigham Young U. Animator with Walt Disney Studios 1956 and 1971–79; animator with Filmation 1967; Co-founder and director with Gary Goldman and John Pomery, Don Bluth Productions, 1979–85; animator, Sullivan Studios, 1986–.
PICTURES: Animation director: Robin Hood, The Rescuers, Pete's Dragon, Xanadu, The Secret of Nimh (also prod., dir., s.p.), An American Tail (also co-prod., dir.), The Land Before Time, All Dogs Go to Heaven.
TELEVISION: Banjo the Woodpile Cat (prod., dir., story, music and lyrics).

BLYTH, ANN: Actress. b. Mt. Kisco, NY, Aug. 16, 1928. e. New Wayburn's Dramatic Sch. On radio in childhood; with San Carlos Opera Co. 3 years; Broadway debut in Watch on the Rhine; on tour.
PICTURES: Chip Off the Old Block, Merry Monahans, Brute Force, Swell Guy, Mr. Peabody and the Mermaid, Woman's Vengeance, Mildred Pierce, Free for All, Top o' the Morning, Our Very Own, Great Caruso, Katie Did It, Thunder on the Hill, I'll Never Forget You, Golden Horde, One Minute to Zero, World in His Arms, Sally and Saint Anne, All the Brothers Were Valiant, Rose Marie, The Student Prince, King's Thief, Kismet, Buster Keaton Story, Jazz Age, Slander, The Helen Morgan Story.

BOCHCO, STEVEN: Producer, Writer. b. New York, NY, Dec. 16, 1943. m. actress Barbara Bosson. e. Carnegie Tech, MFA. Won MCA fellowship in college, joined U-TV as apprentice. His shows typically feature several interwoven plots and characters, deal with social issues, and shift from comedy to drama within an episode.
PICTURES: The Counterfeit Killer (co-s.p.), Silent Running (co-s.p.).
TELEVISION: Writer and story ed.: Name of the Game; Columbo; McMillan and Wife; Delvecchio (writer-prod.); Paris (exec. prod.); Richie Brockelman (co-creator); Turnabout (writer); Invisible Man (writer); Vampire (writer); Hill St. Blues (creator, prod., writer; Emmy's 1981, 1982, 1983, 1984); Every Stray Dog and Kid (exec. prod.); Bay City Blues (exec. prod., writer, creator); L.A. Law, Hooperman.
AWARDS: 5 Emmys, Humanitas, NAACP Image Award, Writers Guild, George Foster Peabody, Edgar Allen Poe.

BOCHNER, HART: Actor. b. Toronto, Ontario, Oct. 3, 1956. Son of actor Lloyd Bochner. e. U. of. San Diego. Film debut, Islands in the Stream, 1975.
PICTURES: Breaking Away, Terror Train, Rich and Famous, Supergirl, The Wild Life, Making Mr. Right, Die Hard, Apartment Zero.
TELEVISION: Haywire, The Sun Also Rises, Having It All, East of Eden, War and Remembrance (mini-series), Fellow Traveller, Blood Sport.

BOCHNER, LLOYD: Actor. b. Canada, July 29, 1924. Father of actor Hart Bochner.
PICTURES: Drums of Africa, The Night Walker, Sylvia,

Tony Rome, Point Blank, The Detective, The Horse in the Gray Flannel Suit, Tiger by the Tail, Ulzana's Raid, The Man in the Glass Booth, Hot Touch, The Lonely Lady, Louisiana, Millenium.

TELEVISION: A Fire in the Sky, Greatest Heroes of the Bible, The Golden Gate Murders, Dynasty, Mazes & Monsters, Fantasy Island, Masquerade, The A-Team, Hotel, Crazy Like a Fox, A Mouse, a Mystery & Me.

BODE, RALF: Cinematographer. b. Berlin, Germany. Attended Yale where was actor with drama school and acquired degree in directing. Received on-job training teaching combat photography and making films for Army at Ft. Monmouth. First professional job in films was gaffer on Harry, followed by long association with director John G. Avildsen, for whom served as gaffer and lighting designer on Guess What We Learned in School Today, Joe, and Cry Uncle. Later dir. of photography for Avildsen on Inaugural Ball and as East Coast dir. phot. for Rocky.

PICTURES: Saturday Night Fever, Slow Dancing in the Big City, Rich Kids, Coal Miner's Daughter, Dressed to Kill, Raggedy Man, A Little Sex, Gorky Park, First Born, Violets Are Blue, Critical Condition, The Big Town, Bring on the Night, The Accused, Distant Thunder, Cousins, Uncle Buck.

TELEVISION: PBS Theatre in America, working as lighting designer and dir. of photo. Also many TV commercials.

BOEHM, SIDNEY: Writer. b. Philadelphia, PA, April 4, 1908. e. Lehigh U. 1935–29. m. Ellen Kasputis. Reporter, N.Y. Journal-American & I.N.S., 1930–45.

PICTURES: Union Station, Big Heat, Atomic City, Six Bridges To Cross, The Raid, Rogue Cop, The Savage, Violent Saturday, Hell on Frisco Bay, Tall Men, Bottom of the Bottle, Revolt of Mamie Stover, Woman Obsessed, Seven Thieves, Sylvia, Rough Night in Jericho.

BOETTICHER, BUDD: Producer, Director, Writer. r.n. Oscar Boetticher, Jr. b. Chicago, IL, July 29, 1916. e. Culver Military Acad., Ohio State U. bullfighter "Novillero"; then technical dir., Blood and Sand, 1941; asst. dir., Hal Roach studios and Columbia 1941–44; became feature director at Columbia in 1944; dir. Eagle Lion, 1946; dir., Universal; independ. prod., 1954. Autobiography: When, in Disgrace —

PICTURES: Behind Locked Doors, Assigned to Danger, Black Midnight, Killer Shark, Wolf Hunters, Bullfighter and the Lady, Cimarron Kid, Bronco Busters, Red Ball Express, Horizons West, City Beneath the Sea, Seminole, Man from the Alamo, Wings of the Hawk, East of Sumatra, Magnificent Matador, Killer Is Loose, Seven Men From Now, Decision at Sundown, The Tall T, Buchanan Rides Alone, Ride Lonesome Westbound, The Rise and Fall of Legs Diamond, Comanche Station, Arruza, A Time For Dying, My Kingdom For—. Orig. s.p.: Bullfighter and the Lady, Magnificient Matador, Two Mules for Sister Sara, A Time For Dying, My Kingdom For...A Horse for Mister Barnum.

BOGARDE, DIRK: Actor. b. Hampstead, London, March 28, 1921. r.n. Derek Van Den Bogaerd. e. Allen Glens Coll., Glasgow & University Coll., London. Started theatrical career with Amersham Repertory Co., then London stage; in Army in W.W.II; Top ten British star, 1953–54, 1956–64; number one British money-making star 1955, 1957, 1958, 1959; Variety Club Award—Best Performance 1961–64. Author of memoirs: A Postillion Struck by Lightning (1977), Snakes and Ladders (1978), An Orderly Man (1983).

THEATER: (U.K.) Power With Glory (1947), Point of Departure, The Shaughraun, The Vortex, Summertime, Jezebel.

PICTURES: Dancing With Crime (1947), Esther Waters, Quartet, Once a Jolly Swagman, Dear Mr. Prohack, Boys in Brown, The Blue Lamp, Five Angles on Murder, So Long at the Fair, Blackmailed, Woman in Question, Hunted (Stranger in Between), Penny Princess, The Gentle Gunman, Desperate Moment, They Who Dare, The Sleeping Tiger, Doctor in the House, For Better or Worse, The Sea Shall Not Have Them, Simba, Doctor at Sea, Cast a Dark Shadow, Doctor At Large, Spanish Gardener, Ill Met by Moonlight, Campbell's Kingdom, A Tale of Two Cities, The Wind Cannot Read, The Doctor's Dilemma, Libel, The Angel Wore Red, Song Without End, The Singer Not The Song, Victim, H.M.S. Defiant, The Password Is Courage, I Could Go on Singing, The Mind Benders, The Servant (British Academy Award, 1964), Hot Enough for June, Doctor Distress, The High Bright Sun, King and Country, Darling (Brit. Acad Award)., Modesty Blaise, Accident, Our Mother's House, Sebastion, The Fixer, Justine, Oh What a Lovely War, The Damned, Death in Venice, Le Serpent, The Night Porter, Permission to Kill, Providence, A Bridge Too Far, Despair.

TELEVISION: (U.S.) The Little Moon of Alban, Blithe Spirit, Upon This Rock, The Patricia Neal Story, May We Borrow Your Husband?, The Vision (U.K.).

BOGART, PAUL: Director. b. New York, NY, Nov. 21, 1919. Puppeteer-actor with Berkeley Marionettes 1946–48; TV stage mgr., assoc. dir. NBC 1950–52; numerous Emmy Awards, Christopher Awards.

PICTURES: Marlowe, Halls of Anger, Skin Game, Class of '44, Mr. Ricco, Oh, God! You Devil, Torch Song Trilogy, The Sparrow.

TELEVISION: U.S. Steel Hour, Kraft Theatre, Armstrong Circle Theatre, Goodyear Playhouse, Hallmark Hall of Fame 1953–60; The Defenders; All in the Family (1975–9). Specials: Ages of Man, Mark Twain Tonight, The Final War of Ollie Winter, Dear Friends, Secrets, The House Without a Christmas Tree, Look Homeward Angel, The Country Girl, Double Solitaire, The War Widow, The Thanksgiving Treasure, Tell Me Where It Hurts, The Adams Chronicles, Nutcracker: Money, Madness and Murder, Natica Jackson.

BOGDANOVICH, PETER: Director, Producer, Writer, Actor. b. Kingston, NY, July 30, 1939. e. Collegiate Sch., Stella Adler Theatre Sch., N.Y. 1954–58. Stage debut, Amer. Shakespeare Festival, N.Y. Shakespeare Festival, others, 1955–58. Off-Bway: dir.-co. prod. The Big Knife, 1959, Camino Real, Ten Little Indians, Rocket to the Moon, 1961, dir.-prod. Once in a Lifetime, 1964. Film critic and feature writer, Esquire, New York Times, Village Voice, Cahiers du Cinema, Los Angeles Times, 1958–85. Monographs for Museum of Modern Art Film Library on Orson Welles, Alfred Hitchcock, Howard Hawks, 1961–63. Books: John Ford, Fritz Lang in America, 1969; Allan Dwan—The Last Pioneer, 1971; Pieces of Time, 1973, enlarged 1985; The Killing of the Unicorn: Dorothy Stratten 1960–1980, 1984. Owner: Crescent Moon Prods. Inc., LA, 1986–present.

PICTURES: Second-unit dir.-writer, The Wild Angels, 1966. Dir.-prod.-writer-actor, Targets, 1968. The Last Picture Show (dir., s.p.), Directed by John Ford (dir., s.p.), What's Up Doc? (dir., prod., s.p), Paper Moon (dir., prod.), Daisy Miller (dir., prod.), At Long Last Love (dir., prod., s.p.), Nickelodeon (dir., s.p.), Saint Jack (dir, s.p., actor), They All Laughed (dir., s.p.), Mask (dir), Illegally Yours (prod., dir., co-s.p.), Friend to Friend, Texasville (prod., dir., co-s.p.).

TELEVISION: CBS This Morning (weekly commentary) 1987–.

AWARDS: N.Y. Film Critics' Award, best s.p., British Academy Award, best s.p. (The Last Picture Show) 1971; Writer's Guild of America Award, best s.p. (What's Up Doc?) 1972; Silver Shell, Mar del Plata, Spain (Paper Moon, 1973); Best Director, Brussels Festival (Daisy Miller) 1974; Pasinetti Award, Critics Prize, Venice Festival (Saint Jack) 1979.

BOGOSIAN, ERIC: Actor,. Writer. b. Woburn, MA 1953. e. studied 2 years at U. of Chicago, then Oberlin, theater degree, 1976. In high school, acted in plays written and dir. by Fred Zollo (now prod.) and Nick Paleologus (now MA congressman). Moved to NY and worked briefly as gofer at Chelea Westside Theater. Then joined downtown performance space, the Kichen, first acting in others pieces, then creating his own incl. character Ricky Paul, a stand-up comedian in punk clubs. Theater pieces include: The New World, Men Inside, Voices of America, FunHouse, Drinking in America (Drama Desk and Obie Awards), Talk Radio.

PICTURES: Special Effects, Talk Radio (also s.p.), Blue Smoke (also s.p.).

TELEVISION: Miami Vice, Twilight Zone, The Caine Mutiny Court Martial, Drinking in America.

BOHEM, ENDRE: Producer, Writer. b. Hungary. Exec. asst. to E. Mannix, MGM and Harry Cohn, Columbia. Prod. shorts series: Robert Benchly, Passing Parade, Nostradamus, What Do You Think, Crime Does Not Pay, Tell Tale Heart.

PICTURES: Alias Nick Beal, Bengazi, Blackmail, Boys of Paul Street (Foreign Film Oscar nom.), Cattle Empire, Desert Nights, House Of a Thousand Candles, Little Orphan Annie, Lord Jeff, Night Has a Thousand Eyes, Postal Inspector, The Redhead and the Cowboy, Street of Laredo, Television Spies, Thirst, Twin Stars, Two Wise Maids, Wonder of Women.

TELEVISION: Revlon Mirror, Ford Theatre, Rawhide.

BOLAN, JAMES: Actor. b. Sunderland, England. Ent. ind. 1960.

PICTURES: The Kitchen, A Kind of Loving, Loneliness of the Long Distance Runner, HMS Defiant, Murder Most Foul, In Celebration.

TELEVISION: Likely Lads, When The Boat Comes In, Only When I Laugh, The Beiderdecke Affair, Father Matthews Daughter, Room at the Bottom, Andy Capp.

BOLOGNA, JOSEPH: Actor, Writer. b. Brooklyn, NY., Dec. 30, 1938. e. Brown U. m. actress-writer Renee Taylor. Service in Marine Corps and on discharge joined ad agency, becoming director-producer of TV commercials. Collaborated with wife on short film, 2, shown at 1966 N.Y. Film Festival. Together they wrote Lovers and Other Strangers, Broadway play, in which both also acted. Wrote s.p. for film version. Both wrote and starred in Made for Each Other, and created and wrote TV series, Calucci's Dept.

PICTURES: Lovers and Other Strangers (co.-s.p.), Made for Each Other (co.-s.p., star). Actor: Cops and Robbers, Mixed Company, The Big Bus , Chapter Two, My Favorite Year, Blame It on Rio , The Woman in Red, Transylvania 6-5000, It Had to Be You (also, co-dir., co-s.p.), Coupe de Ville.

TELEVISION: Calucci's Dept. (co.-s.p.). Actor: Honor Thy Father (movie), Copacabana, Acts of Love and Other Comedies, Paradise, Torn Between Two Lovers, Chapter Two, A Time To Triumph. Series: Rags to Riches; Mini-Series: Sins, Not Quite Human.

BOLT, ROBERT: Writer, b. Sale, England, 1924. Ent. m.p. ind. 1961. m. actress Sarah Miles.
PICTURES: Lawrence of Arabia, Dr. Zhivago, A Man For All Seasons (play and film), Ryan's Daughter, Dir. own s.p. Lady Caroline Lamb, The Bounty.

BONANNO, LOUIE: Actor. b. Somerville, MA, Dec. 17, 1961. e. Bentley Coll., Waltham, MA, BS-economics, finance; AS accountancy, 1983. Moved to NY, 1983 to study at Amer. Acad. of Dramatic Arts. Toured U.S. 1985–86 as Dangermouse for MTV/Nickelodeon.
PICTURES: Sex Appeal (debut, 1986), Wimps, Student Affairs.
TELEVISION: Eisenhower & Lutz (series), 227, Tour of Duty, TV 101, Santa Barbara.

BOND, ANSON: Producer, Writer. b. Cleveland, OH, March 21, 1914. e. Yale Prep & pre-legal, Stuyvesant Sch., Warrenton, VA. p. Charles Anson Bond, founder, Bond Clothing Co. & Bond Stores, Inc. Washington corr., 30 Ohio newspapers, 1930–33; asst. to pres., C.W. Hord Co., N.Y. 1933–36; apprenticeship in m.p. prod. 1936–39; dir., prod., writer. U.S. armed forces, 1940–45; head pub. firm, Bond-Charteris, prod. radio program. The Saint; publ. Craig Rice Crime Digest & Movie Mystery Magazine.
PICTURES: The Judge, Not Wanted, Vicious Years, (co-prod.) Journey Into Light, Japanese War Bride, China Venture.

BOND, DEREK: Actor, Scriptwriter. b. Glasgow Scotland, Jan. 26, 1920. e. Haberdasher' Askes Sch., London. Stage debut in As Husbands Go, 1937; served in Grenadier Guards H.M. Forces 1939–46, awarded Military Cross; m.p. debut in Captive Heart, 1946; author of Unscheduled Stop, Two Young Samaritans, Ask Father Christmas, Packdrill, Double Strung, Order to Kill, The Riverdale Dam, Sentence Deferred, The Mavroletty Fund. Many TV appearances. Pres., British Actors Equity, 1984–86.
PICTURES: Nicholas Nickleby, Joanna Godden, Uncle Silas, Scott of the Antarctic, Marry Me, Poets Pub, Weaker Sex, Broken Journey, Christopher Columbus, Tony Draws a Horse, Quiet Woman, Hour of Thirteen, Distant Trumpet, Love's a Luxury, Trouble in Store, Svengali, High Terrace, Stormy Crossing, Rogues Yarn, Gideon's Day, The Hand, Saturday Night Out, Wonderful Life, Press For Time, When Eight Bells Toll, Intimate Reflections, Vanishing Army.

BONET, LISA: Actress. b. Los Angeles, CA, Nov. 16, 1967. First gained recognition on The Cosby Show as Denise Huxtable at the age of 15.
PICTURES: Angel Heart.
TELEVISION: Series: The Cosby Show, A Different World.

BONET, NAI: Actress, Producer. Worked in entertainment field since age of 13, including opera, films, TV, stage, night clubs and records.
PICTURES: Actress: The Soul Hustlers, The Seventh Veil, Fairy Tales, The Soul of Nigger Charlie, The Spy with the Cold Nose, John Goldfarb Please Come Home, etc. Wrote and starred in Nocturna and Hoodlums.
TELEVISION: Johnny Carson Show, Merv Griffin Show, Joe Franklin Show, Beverly Hillbillies, Tom Snyder Show.

BONO, SONNY: Singer, actor, director, writer. b. Detroit, MI, Feb. 16, 1935. r.n. Salvatore Bono. Started writing songs at age 16; entered record business with Specialty Records as apprentice prod. Became ass't. to Phil Spector, rock music prod. and did background singing. Recorded albums with former wife Cher, made two feature films and formed nightclub act with her. CBS comedy-variety series began as summer show in 1971 and made regular later that year. Elected Mayor, Palm Springs, CA 1988.
PICTURES: Good Times, Chastity (prod., s.p.), Escape to Athena, Airplane II: The Sequel, Special Delivery, Troll, Hairspray, Under the Boardwalk.
TELEVISION: Sonny & Cher Comedy Hour, Sonny Comedy Revue.

BOOKE, SORRELL: Actor. b. Buffalo, NY, Jan. 4, 1930. e. Columbia U. Joined summer stock company in Charleston, WV, and later in Provincetown, MA. After stint with armed forces returned to NY and off-Bdwy plays. Bdwy debut in The Sleeping Prince, followed by appearances in over 100 plays.
PICTURES: Special Delivery, What's Up Doc?, Freaky Friday, The Other Side of Midnight.
TELEVISION: Series: Route 66, Soap, What's Happening!, The Dukes of Hazzard, Alice, Newhart.

BOOKMAN, ROBERT: Executive. b. Los Angeles, CA. e. U. of California, Yale Law Sch. Motion picture literary agent, IFA 1972–74, ICM 1974–79. 1979 joined ABC Motion Pictures as v.p., worldwide production; 1984, Columbia Pictures, exec. v.p., world-wide prod. 1986, Creative Artists Agency, Inc. as motion picture literary and directors' agent.

BOONE, JR., ASHLEY A.: Executive. b. 1938. e. Brandeis U. Started career at United Artists in foreign adv./pub.; later with Cinema Center Films; adm. asst., Motown Records; assoc. prod. for Sidney Poitier's E & R Productions. Joined 20th-Fox in 1972 in sls. dept.; advanced to sr. sls. & mktg. positions in feature film operation. In 1979 appt. pres. of 20th-Fox Distribution & Marketing. Joined Ladd Co., v.p. in chg. dist. & mktg., 1983; Pres., Columbia Pictures Mktg. & Dist. Group, 1984. Resigned 1985 but remained special mkt. consultant. 1986, joined Lorimar Pictures as pres., mktg. & dist.

BOONE, PAT: Singer. b. Jacksonville, FL, June 1, 1934. e. David Lipscomb Coll., North Texas State Coll., grad. magna cum laude, Columbia U. Winner of Ted Mack's TV show; joined Arthur Godfrey TV show, 1955. m.p. debut in Bernadine. Most promising new male star, Motion Picture Daily-Fame Poll 1957. One of top ten moneymaking stars, M.P. Herald-Fame Poll, 1957.
AUTHOR: Twixt Twelve and Twenty, Between You & Me and the Gatepost, The Real Christmas.
RECORDINGS: Ain't That a Shame, I Almost Lost My Mind, Friendly Persuasion, Love Letters in the Sand, April Love, Tutti Frutti.
PICTURES: Bernadine, April Love, Mardi Gras, Journey to the Center of the Earth, All Hands on Deck, State Fair, The Main Attraction, The Yellow Canary, The Horror of It All, The Perils of Pauline, The Cross and the Switchblade.

BOORMAN, JOHN: Director, Producer. b. London, Eng., Jan. 18, 1933. Wrote film criticism at age of 17 for British publications incl. Manchester Guardian; founder TV Mag. Day By Day; served in National Service in Army; Broadcaster and BBC radio film critic 1950–54; film editor Independent Television News; prod. documentaries for Southern Television; joined BBC, headed BBC Documentary Film Unit 1960–64, indep. doc. about D.W. Griffith; chmn. Natl. Film Studios of Ireland 1975–85; governor Brit. Film Inst. 1985—.
PICTURES: Catch Us If You Can (a.k.a Having a Wild Weekend), Point Blank, Hell in the Pacific, Leo The Last (Directors Award, s.p. Cannes), Deliverance (prod., dir. Acad. Award noms.), Zardoz (prod., dir., s.p.), Exorcist II: The Heretic (prod., dir.), Excalibur (prod., dir., s.p.), The Emerald Forest (prod., dir.), Hope and Glory (prod., dir., s.p.; Acad. Award noms., U.S. National Critics Awards dir., s.p.; L.A. Critics Awards pic., s.p., dir.; U.K. Critics Awards pic.), Where the Heart Is (prod., dir., co-s.p.).
TELEVISION: Series: Citizen '63 (dir.), The Newcomers (dir.).

BOOTH, MARGARET: Film editor. b. Los Angeles, CA, 1898. Awarded honorary Oscar, 1977.
PICTURES: Why Men Leave Home, Husbands and Lovers, Bridge of San Luis Rey, New Moon, Susan Lenox, Strange Interlude, Smilin' Through, Romeo and Juliet, Barretts of Wimpole Street, Mutiny on the Bounty, Camille, etc. Supervising editor on Owl and the Pussycat, The Way We Were, Funny Lady, Murder by Death, The Goodbye Girl, California Suite, The Cheap Detective (also assoc. prod.), Chapter Two (also assoc. prod.); The Toy (assoc. prod.). Editor: Annie. Exec. Prod.: The Slugger's Wife.

BOOTH, SHIRLEY: Actress. b. New York, NY, Aug. 20, 1907. Joined Poli Stock Co., Hartford, CT, at 12; Broadway debut in Hell's Bells, 1925; on radio in Duffy's Tavern.
PLAYS: After Such Pleasures, 3 Men on a Horse, Philadelphia Story, My Sister Eileen, Tomorrow the World, Goodbye My Fancy, Come Back Little Sheba (Tony Award, 1950), A Tree Grows in Brooklyn, Time of the Cuckoo (Tony Award, 1953), The Desk Set, Look to the Lillies, Miss Isobel, Juno, Colettes Second String, The Glass Menagerie.
PICTURES: Come Back Little Sheba (debut, Acad. Award, best actress, 1952), About Mrs. Leslie, Hot Spell, The Matchmaker.
TELEVISION: Perle Mesta Story, Hazel (series, 1961–68; Emmy Awards, 1962 & 1963), A Touch of Grace, The Glass Menagerie.

BOOTHE, POWERS: Actor. b. Snyder, TX, 1949. e. Southern Methodist U. On Broadway in Lone Star.
TELEVISION: Skag, A Cry for Love, Guyana Tragedy–The Story of Jim Jones (Emmy Award), Philip Marlowe (series), Into the Homeland.
PICTURES: Cruising, Southern Comfort, A Breed Apart, The Emerald Forest, Extreme Prejudice, Stalingrad.

BORGE, VICTOR: Comedian, Pianist. b. Copenhagen, Denmark, Jan. 3, 1909. Child prodigy at age 8. Awarded scholarship to study in Berlin and Vienna. Later became humorous concert artist. Wrote and starred in musical plays and films in Denmark. Fled Nazis in 1940, came to America.
Appeared on Bing Crosby radio show. Concert and Nightclub tours. TV variety shows. One-man Broadway show

Comedy in Music. 1953, three-year run. Second edition in 1965. Third edition 1977. World tours. One-man TV shows. Guest conductor with major symphonies around the world. Recent recording, The Two Sides of Victor Borge. Author: My Favorite Comedies in Music. Awarded Medal of Honor by Statue of Liberty Centennial Comm. Knighted by 5 Scandinavian countries, honored by U.S. Congress and U.N. Created Thanks to Scandinavia Scholarship Fund.

BORGNINE, ERNEST: Actor. b. Hamden, CT, Jan. 24, 1918. e. Randall Sch. of Dramatic Art, Hartford, CT. Served in U.S. Navy; then little theatre work, stock companies; on Broadway in Harvey, Mrs. McThing; many TV appearances.
PICTURES: China Corsair (debut, 1951), The Mob, Whistle at Eaton Falls, From Here to Eternity, Demetruis & the Gladiators, Johnny Guitar, Vera Cruz, Bad Day at Black Rock, Marty (Acad. Award best actor 1955), Run for Cover, Violent Saturday, Last Command, Square Jungle, Catered Affair, Jubal, Best Things in Life are Free, Three Brave Men, Pay or Die, Go Naked in the World, Rabbit Trap, Summer of the Seventeenth Doll, Barabbas, Chuka, The Dirty Dozen, The Wild Bunch, The Adventurers, Suppose They Gave a War and Nobody Came?, A Bullet for Sandoval, Bunny O'Hare, Hannie Caulder, The Revengers, Legend of Lylah Clare, The Poseidon Adventure, The Emperor of the North, Law and Disorder, The Devil's Rain, Hustle, Shoot, The Greatest, Crossed Swords, Convoy, The Black Hole, When Time Ran Out, Escape from New York, Deadly Blessing, The Graduates of Malibu High, Codename: Wild Geese, Skeleton Coast, Spike of Bensonhurst, Silent Hero, Any Man's Death, Laser Mission, The Big Turnaround, Captain Henkel, Mortal Passions.
TELEVISION: Philco Playhouse, General Electric Theater, Wagon Train, Laramie, Zane Grey Theater, Alcoa Premiere, McHale's Navy, Blood Feud, Last Days of Pompeii, The Dirty Dozen: The Next Mission, The Dirty Dozen: The Deadly Mission, Treasure Island (Ital. TV), The Dirty Dozen: The Fatal Mission.

BORIS, ROBERT: Writer, Director. b. NY, NY, Oct. 12, 1945. Screenwriter before also turning to direction with Oxford Blues, 1984.
PICTURES: Electra Glide in Blue; Some Kind of Hero; Doctor Detroit; Oxford Blues (also dir.), Steele Justice (dir.); Buy and Cell (dir.).
TELEVISION: Birds of Prey; Blood Feud, Deadly Encounter, Izzy and Moe.

BORODINSKY, SAMUEL: Executive. b. Brooklyn, NY, Oct. 25, 1941. e. Industrial Sch. of Arts & Photography. Expert in film care and rejuvenation. Now exec. v.p., Filmtreat International Corp. Previously with Modern Film Corp. (technician) and Comprehensive Filmtreat, Inc. & International Filmtreat (service manager).

BOSCO, PHILIP: Actor. b. Jersey City, NJ, Sept. 26, 1930. e. Catholic U., Washington, DC, BA. drama, 1957. Studied for stage with James Marr, Josephine Callan and Leo Brady. Consummate stage actor (in over 100 plays, 61 in NY) whose career spans the classics (with NY Shakespeare Fest. and American Shakespeare Fest, CT.), 20 plays with Arena Stage 1957–60, to modern classics as a resident actor with Lincoln Center Rep. Co. in the 1960s, winning Tony and Drama Desk Awards for the farce Lend Me a Tenor, 1988.
THEATER: Auntie Mame (Bdwy debut, City Center revival, 1958), Measure for Measure, The Rape of the Belt (Tony nom.), Donnybrook, Richard III, The Alchemist, The East Wind, Galileo, Saint Joan, Tiger at the Gates, Cyrano de Bergerac, King Lear, The Miser, The Time of Your Life, Camino Real, Operation Sidewinder, Amphitryon, In the Matter of J. Robert Oppenheimer, The Good Woman of Setzuan, The Playboy of the Western World, An Enemy of the People, Antigone, Mary Stuart, The Crucible, Enemies, Mrs. Warren's Profession, Henry V, The Threepenny Opera, Streamers, Stages, The Biko Inquest, Whose Life Is It Anyway? A Month in the Country, Don Juan in Hell, Inadmissible Evidence, Ah! Wilderness, Come Back Little Sheba, Man and Superman, Major Barbara, The Caine Mutiny Court Martial, Heartbreak House, You Never Can Tell, A Man for All Seasons, Lend Me a Tenor.
PICTURES: Requiem for a Heavyweight, A Lovely Way to Die, The Pope of Greenwich Village, Walls of Glass, Heaven Help Us, Flanagan, Trading Places, The Money Pit, Children of a Lesser God, Three Men and a Baby, Suspect, The Luckiest Man in the World, Another Woman, Working Girl, Dream Team, Blue Steel.
TELEVISION: Prisoner of Zenda (1960), An Enemy of the People, A Nice Place to Visit. Guest: Nurses, Trials of O'Brien. Movies: Echoes in the Darkness, Second Effort, Internal Affairs.

BOSLEY, TOM: Actor. b. Chicago, IL, Oct. 1, 1927. e. DePaul U. Had roles on radio in Chicago and in stock productions before moving to New York. Appeared off-Broadway and on road before signed to play lead in Fiorello! for George Abbott on Broadway. First actor to win Tony, Drama Critics, ANTA and Newspaper Guild awards in one season for that role.
PICTURES: Love with the Proper Stranger, The World of Henry Orient, Divorce, American Style, Yours, Mine and Ours, The Secret War of Harry Frigg, Mixed Company, Gus, Million Dollar Mystery, Wicked Stepmother.
TELEVISION: Alice in Wonderland (1953), Arsenic and Old Lace, Focus, Naked City, The Right Man, The Nurses, Route 66, The Perry Como Show, The Rebels. Series: Debbie Reynolds Show, Sandy Duncan Show, Wait Til Your Father Gets Home, Happy Days, Murder She Wrote. Movies: The Girl Who Came Gift Wrapped, Death Cruise, The Night the Martians Landed, Love Boat. Specials: The Drunkard, Profiles in Courage, Testimony of Two Men, The Bastard, Fatal Confession: A Father Dowling Mystery, The Love Boat: A Valentine Voyage.

BOSTICK, ROBERT L.: b. Waynesboro, GA, Oct. 25, 1909. e. Georgia Inst. of Technology, M.E., eng., 1932. Started with National Theatre Supply, Atlanta, salesman, Memphis, 1933; br. mgr. 1937; br. mgr. Dallas, 1942; Vice Pres., Southern division mgr., 1952; retired 1968. Chief Barker Variety Club Tent 20, Memphis 1950–51. Since 1957, has served as International Rep., International Ambassador-at-Large, and International Vice Pres. for Variety Clubs International. Since 1968, owner & operator of theatres in Memphis and Charlotte areas.

BOSTWICK, BARRY: Actor. b. San Mateo, CA, Feb. 24, 1945. e. USIU Sch. of Performing Arts, San Diego, BFA in acting; NYU Grad. Sch. of the Arts. Made prof. stage debut while in coll. working with Walter Pidgeon in Take Her, She's Mine, Joined APA Phoenix Rep. Co. making his Bdwy debut in Cock-A-Doodle Dandy.
THEATER: Salvation, House of Leather, Soon, The Screens, Colette, Grease (created role of Danny Zuko, 1972), They Knew What They Wanted, The Robber Bridegroom (Tony Award), She Loves Me, L'Historie du Soldat.
PICTURES: The Rocky Horror Picture Show, Movie Movie, Megaforce.
TELEVISION: Series: Foul Play. Movies: Scruples, Moviola—The Silent Lovers, Summer Girl, An Uncommon Love, A Woman of Substance, You Can't Take It With You, Once Upon a Family, Red Flag, Working, Deceptions, Betrayed by Innocence, George Washington: The Forging of a Nation, I'll Take Manhattan, Body of Evidence, Addicted to His Love, Parent Trap III, Till We Meet Again. Mini-series: War and Remembrance.

BOSUSTOW, NICK: Producer. b. Los Angeles, CA, March 28, 1940. e. Menlo Coll., CA, administration. MCA, intl. sales, 1963. Pres., Stephen Bosustow Productions, 1967; pres., ASIFA-West; Academy Award '70 best short, Is It Always Right to Be Right?; 1973 Acad. Award nom., The Legend of John Henry. TV specials: The Incredible Book Escape, Misunderstood Monsters, A Tale of Four Wishes, Wrong Way Kid (Emmy, 1984); The Hayley Mills Story Book (series). 1973, pres., Bosustow Entertainment, Inc.

BOSUSTOW, TED: Producer, Director, Editor. b. Hollywood, CA, Feb 18, 1938. e. UCLA cinema in Westwood; La Sorbonne, Paris.
PICTURES: Beware of Thin Ice, Big Boys Don't Cry, Avati and the Mezzotint. Edited short, Is It Always Right to Be Right? (AA, 1971).
TELEVISION: About a Week (community affairs series; Emmy award).

BOSWALL, JEFFERY: Producer, Director, Writer. b. Brighton, Eng., 1931. e. Taunton House School, Montpelier Coll., Brighton. Started career as an ornithologist for the Royal Society for the Protection of Birds. Joined BBC in 1958 as radio producer, moving to TV 1964 making films in diverse locations (Ethiopia and Antarctica). Contributed to 50 films as wildlife cameraman. Co-founder of British Library of Wildlife Sounds. 1987: returned to RSPB, currently head of Film and Video Unit. Chairmanship BKSTS Intl Wildlife Filmmakers' Symposium.
TELEVISION: 18 films in the Private Lives series of which 4 (about the Kingfisher, Cuckoo, Starling and Jackass Penguin) won intl awards. Animal Olympians, Birds For All Seasons, Where the Parrots Speak Mandarin, Wildlife Safari to Ethiopia. Contributed to studio-based programs, behind the scenes and as presenter.
AUTHOR: Birds for All Seasons. Ed. Look and Private Lives. Contrib.: Times, Countryman, the Field, Wildlife and Countryside, BBC Wildlife, Scientific Film, Journal of the Society of Film and TV Arts, Image Technology. Has written for scientific journals and writes annual update for Encyclopedia Britannica on ornithology.

BOTTOMS, JOSEPH: Actor. b. Santa Barbara, CA, April 22, 1954. Brother of Sam and Timothy Bottoms. Did plays in jr. high school in Santa Barbara and then with community theatre. Made m.p. debut in The Dove, 1974.
PICTURES: Crime and Passion, King of the Mountain, Blind Date, Open House, Born to Race.

TELEVISION: Owen Marshall, Winesburg, Ohio, Side By Side: The True Story of the Osmond Family, I Married Wyatt Earp, The Sins of Dorian Gray, Celebrity, Time Bomb, Murder She Wrote; Braker, Island Sons, Cop Killer.

BOTTOMS, SAM: Actor. b. Santa Barbara, CA, Oct. 17, 1955. Brother of Timothy, Joseph and Ben Bottoms.
PICTURES: The Last Picture Show, Class of '44, Zandy's Bride, The Outlaw Josey Wales, Apocalypse Now, Up from the Depths, Bronco Billy, In 'n Out, Hunter's Blood, Gardens of Stone, Loner, Stranded, After School, Kill Crazy.
TELEVISION: Savages, Greatest Heroes of the Bible, East of Eden, Desperate Lives, Island Sons, Half Nelson, Cage Without a Key.

BOTTOMS, TIMOTHY: Actor. b. Santa Barbara, CA, Aug. 30, 1951. Brother of Joseph and Sam Bottoms. Early interest in acting; was member of S.B. Madrigal Society, touring Europe in 1967. Sang and danced in West Side Story local prod.
PICTURES: Johnny Got His Gun (debut), The Last Picture Show, Love and Pain, The Paper Chase, The White Dawn, The Crazy World of Julius Vrooder, Seven Men at Daybreak, A Small Town in Texas, Rollercoaster, The Other Side of the Mountain: Part II, Hurricane, First Hello, Hambone and Hillie, Invaders from Mars, The Drifter, Mio in the Land of Faraway, Return From the River Kwai, A Case of Law, Texasville, Istanbul.
TELEVISION: Look Homeward Angel, The Story of David, The Money Changers, Escape, A Shining Season, East of Eden, Island Sons.

BOUCHIER, CHILI: Actress. r.n. Dorothy Irene Boucher. b. Fulham, London, England, Sept. 12, 1909. m. Bluey Hill, Australian film director (d. 1986). British stage appearances include: Open Your Eyes, 1930; Lavender; Magnolia Street; Mother Goose; A Little Bit of Fluff; Rendezvous; Age of Consent; Tons of Money; The Mousetrap; Harvey; I Can't Imagine Tomorrow; Rookery Nook; French Dressing; Conduct Unbecoming; The Best of Dorothy Parker; Follies A Little Night Music (1987). Originally a model at Harrods, London. After her screen debut in 1927, she quickly became one of Britain's first international m.p. stars. Autobiography: For Dogs and Angels (1968).
PICTURES: A Woman in Pawn, Shooting Stars, Maria Marten, Dawn, Chick, You Know What Sailors Are, Warned Off, The Silver King, City of Play, Downstream, Enter the Queen, Call of the Sea, Kissing Cup's Race, Brown Sugar, Carnival, The Blue Danube, Ebb Tide, The King's Cup, Summer Lightning, Purse Strings, It's a Cop, To Be a Lady, The Office Wife, Death Drives Through, Royal Cavalcade, The Mad Hatters, Honours Easy, Lucky Days, Get Off My Foot, Mr. Cohen Takes a Walk, The Ghost Goes West, Faithful, Where's Sally?, Southern Roses, Gypsy, Mayfair Melody, The Minstrel Boy, Change for a Sovereign, The Dark Stairway, Mr. Satan, The Singing Cop, The Return of Carol Deane, Everything Happens to Me, The Mind of Mr. Reeder, My Wife's Family, Facing the Music, Murder in Reverse, The Laughing Lady, Mrs. Fitzherbert, The Case of Charles Peace, Old Mother Riley's New Venture, The Wallet, The Counterfeit Plan, The Boy and the Bridge, Dead Lucky.
TELEVISION: Yesterday's Witness, Looks Familiar, Saturday Night at the Pictures, Catch a Fallen Star.

BOUDOURIS, A: Executive. b. Toledo, OH, Jan. 31, 1918. e. U. of Toledo, 1945–47, USN, radio-radar, 1941–45; carrier pilot. Service, installation, projection equip., 1934–36; Strong Electric, 1936–41; Pres., Theatre Equip. Co., 1945–65; Theatre Operating Co., since 1947; pres. Eprad, Inc., 1949, bd. chmn., 1980. Member (ex-chmn.) of NATO'S Technical Advisory Comm., Pres. NATO of Ohio, NATO representative on American National Standards Committee; v.p., NATO; chmn, NATO Statistical Committee; Member, Projection Practices and Sound Comm. of SMPTE; NATO Representative Intl. Standards Org. (Geneva), Member National Electrical Code Comm. Panel #15. Recipient, SMPTE Fellowship Award, 1980.

BOULTING, ROY: Producer, Director. b. Bray, Buckinghamshire, England, Nov. 21, 1913. e. McGill U., Montreal. Capt., Brit. Army, W.W.II. Dir. Charter Film, Charter Film Prod. Ltd. London; dir. British Lion Films, Ltd., 1958. 1977, co-author with Leo Marks of play, Favourites, Danny Travis, 1978.
PICTURES: Inquest, Trunk Crime, Pastor Hall, Thunder Rock, Desert Victory, Burma Victory, Fame is the Spur, Brighton Rock, Guinea Pig, Seven Days to Noon, Lucky Jim, High Treason, Singlehanded (Sailor of the King), Seagulls Over Sorrento (Crest of the Wave), Josephine and Men, Private's Progress, Run for the Sun, Brothers in Law, Happy Is the Bride, Carlton-Browne of the F.O., I'm All Right Jack, The Risk, The French Mistress, Heavens Above!, Rotten to The Core, The Family Way, Twisted Nerve, There's a Girl in My Soup, Soft Beds, Hard Battles, The Last Word, Agatha Christie's The Moving Finger (BBC).

BOWER, DALLAS: Producer, Director. b. London, 1907. Ent. film prod. 1927; film ed., writer, dir., prod. with BBC-TV 1936. Prod. and dir. opening program of BBC Television service, 1936. Commissioned in Royal Corps of Signals, 1939; supvr. film prod., Ministry of Inf., Films Div., 1942; prod. official and commercial documentaries; author, Plan for Cinema, 1936.
PICTURES AND TELEVISION: Aida, Tristan & Isolde, Master Peter's Puppet Show, Cinderella, Julius Caesar, The Tempest, The Taming of the Shrew, The Silver Box, The Mock Emperor, The Emperor Jones, Rope, Path of Glory, Victory over Space, Henry V, Alice in Wonderland, The Second Mrs. Tanquery, Fire One, Doorway to Suspicion, Adventures of Sir Lancelot.

BOWIE, DAVID: Singer, Actor. b. Brixton, South London, England, Jan. 8, 1947. r.n. David Robert Jones. Broadway debut: The Elephant Man (1980).
PICTURES: Ziggy Stardust and the Spiders from Mars (1973, U.S. release 1983), The Man Who Fell to Earth, Just a Gigolo, The Hunger, The Cat People, Merry Christmas, Mr. Lawrence; Into the Night, Absolute Beginners (act., music), Labyrinth (act., music), The Last Temptation of Christ, Imagine—John Lennon.
TELEVISION: Christmas With Bing Crosby; The Midnight Special, Glass Spider Tour.

BOWSER, EILEEN: Curator, Film Archivist, Historian. b. Ohio, Jan. 1, 1928. e. Marietta Coll., B.A., 1950; U. of North Carolina, M.A., history of art, 1953. Joined Dept. of Film, Museum of Modern Art, 1954. Curator, Dept. of Film since 1976. Organized major exhib. of the films of D.W. Griffith, Carl-Theodor Dreyer, Art of the Twenties, recent acquisitions and touring shows. On exec. comm. of Federation Internationale des Archives du Film since 1969, v.p. FIAF 1977–85; pres. FIAF Documentation Commission 1972–81. Film Archives Advisory Comm. since 1971. Assoc. of Univ. Seminars on Cinema and Interdisciplinary Interpretation. Publications: The Movies, David Wark Griffith, Biograph Bulletins 1908–1912, Film Notes, D.W. Griffith, Carl Dreyer, Motion Picture Film (in Conservation in the Library), A Handbook for Film Archives. Has written numerous articles on film history.

BOX, BETTY, OBE: Producer. b. Beckenham, Kent, England, 1920. Assisted Sydney Box in prod. 200 propaganda films in W.W.II. Assoc. prod. Upturned Glass.
PRODUCTIONS: Dear Murderer, When the Bough Breaks, Miranda, Blind Goddess, Huggett Family series. It's Not Cricket, Marry Me, Don't Ever Leave Me, So Long At the Fair, The Clouded Yellow, Appointment With Venus (Island Rescue). Venetian Bird (The Assassin), A Day to Remember, Doctor in the House, Mad About Men, Doctor at Sea, The Iron Petticoat, Checkpoint, Doctor at Large, Campbell's Kingdom, A Tale of Two Cities, The Wind Cannot Read, The 39 Steps, Upstairs and Downstairs, Conspiracy of Hearts, Doctor in Love, No Love for Johnnie, No, My Darling Daughter, A Pair of Briefs, The Wild and the Willing, Doctor in Distress, Hot Enough for June (Agent 8¾), The High Bright Sun, (McGuire Go Home), Doctor in Clover, Deadlier Than the Male, Nobody Runs Forever, The High Commissioner, Some Girls Do, Doctor in Trouble, Percy, The Love Ban, Percy's Progress.

BOXLEITNER, BRUCE: Actor. b. Elgin, IL, May 12, 1950. After high school enrolled in Chicago's Goodman Theatre, staging productions and working with lighting and set design in addition to acting.
TELEVISION: Series: How the West Was Won, The Macahans, Bring 'Em Back Alive, Scarecrow and Mrs. King. Movies: Happily Ever After, Kenny Rogers as The Gambler, Kiss Me, Kill Me, Fly Away Home, Kenny Rogers as The Gambler: The Adventure Continues, Passion Flower, Angel in Green, The Last Convertible, Bare Essence, East of Eden, Kenny Rogers as the Gambler: The Legend Continues, Red River, The Town Bully, The Road Raiders, Till We Meet Again.
PICTURES: The Baltimore Bullet (debut 1980), Tron, The Crystal Eye, Breakaway.

BOYARS, ALBERT: Executive. b. New York, NY, Aug. 11: e. NYU. U.S. Navy, 1941–45. David O. Alber Assoc., 1945–51: Greater N.Y. Fund, Robert S. Taplinger Assoc., Michael Myerberg Prod., 1951–54: pub. rel. dir., Transfilm-Caravel Inc., and parent co. Buckeye Corp., 1954–63: director spec. projects in adv-pub-exploit. M-G-M, 1963–64; dir. of adv. & pub. Trans-Lux Corp., 1964, v.p. of adv. and pub. rel., Trans-Lux Multimedia Corp., 1976. Under his marketing aegis are the attractions The New York Experience, (in Rockefeller Center), and The Seaport Experience (at South Street Seaport, NY.).

BOYER, PHIL: TV Executive. b. Portland, OR, Dec. 13, 1940. e. Sacramento State U. Began broadcasting career as 12-year-old in Portland, establishing nation's first youth radio facility—a 5-watt facility in the basement of his home. At 16 began working at KPDQ, Portland; two years later joined KPTV, Portland, as announcer. In 1960 joined KEZI-TV, Eugene, OR, heading prod. and prog. depts. In 1965 named staff prod.-dir. for KCRA, TV, Sacramento, CA, becoming prod. mgr. in 1967 and prog. mgr. in 1969. In 1972 joined KNBC-TV, Los Angeles, as prog. dir. In 1974 named v.p., programming, of ABC Owned Television Stations; 1977, v.p.-gen. mgr., WLS-TV, Chicago; 1979, v.p.-gen. mgr. of WABC-TV, New York 1981; v.p., gen mgr., ABC-owned TV station div.; 1984, joined ABC Video Enterprises as v.p. intl. dev.; 1986 named sr. v.p., intl and prog. dev., CC/ABC Video Ent.

BOYETT, ROBERT LEE: Producer. e. Duke U., B.A.; Col. U., M.A., marketing. Began career in media and mkt. research at Grey Advertising, Inc. Was program development consultant for PBS. In 1973 joined ABC as dir. of prime time series TV, East Coast. In 1975 named ABC TV v.p. & asst. to v.p. programs for West Coast. In 1977 joined Paramount Pictures in newly created position of v.p., exec. asst. to pres. & chief operating officer. 1979, joined Miller-Milkis–Boyett Productions to produce for Paramount Television.
TELEVISION: Exec. prod.: Laverne and Shirley, Happy Days, Bosom Buddies, Mork and Mindy, Valerie, Perfect Strangers.

BOYLE, BARBARA D.: Executive. b. New York, NY, Aug. 11, 1935. e. U. of California, Berkeley, B.A., 1957; UCLA, J.D., 1960. Named to bar: California, 1961; New York, 1964; Supreme Court, 1964. Atty. in busn. affairs dept. & corp. asst. secty., American Intl. Pictures, Los Angeles, 1965–67; partner in entertainment law firm, Cohen & Boyle, L.A., 1967–74; exec. v.p. & gen. counsel, COO, New World Pictures, L.A., 1974–82. Sr. v.p. worldwide prod., Orion Pictures, L.A., 1982–86; exec. v.p., prod., RKO Pictures, L.A., 1986–87. President, Sovereign Pictures, L.A., 1988–present. Co-chmn. 1979–80, Entertainment Law Symposium Advisory Committee, UCLA Law Sch.
MEMBER: Academy of Motion Picture Arts & Sciences, Women in Film (pres., 1977–78, mem. of bd., chairperson 1981–84), Women Entertainment Lawyers Assn., California Bar Assn., N.Y. State Bar Assn., Beverly Hills Bar Assn., Hollywood Women's Political Committee, American Film Institute. Bd. mem.: Women Director's Workshop, Independent Feature Project/West, Los Angeles Women's Campaign Fund. Founding mem. UCLA Sch. of Law's Entertainment Advisory Council (& co-chairperson 1979 & 80).

BOYLE, PETER: Actor. b. Philadelphia, PA, Oct. 18, 1933. e. LaSalle Coll. Was monk in Christian Bros. order before leaving in early 60s to come to N.Y. Acted in off-Broadway shows and joined The Second City in Chicago. Also did TV commercials.
PICTURES: Joe (debut), T.R. Baskin, The Candidate, Steelyard Blues, Slither, The Friends of Eddie Coyle, Kid Blue, Crazy Joe, Young Frankenstein, Swashbuckler, F.I.S.T., Brinks' Job, Hardcore, Beyond the Poseidon Adventure, Where the Buffalo Roam, In God We Trust, Outland, Hammett, Yellowbeard, Johnny Dangerously, Turk 182, Surrender, Walker, Red Heat, The In Crowd, The Dream Team, Speed Zone, Men of Respect.
TELEVISION: Tail Gunner Joe, From Here to Eternity, Echoes in the Darkness, Disaster at Silo 7, Guts and Glory: The Rise and Fall of Oliver North, 27 Wagons Full of Cotton.

BRABOURNE, LORD JOHN: Producer. b. London, England, Nov. 9, 1924.
PRODUCTIONS: Harry Black, Sink the Bismarck, H.M.S. Defiant, Othello, The Mikado, Up the Junction, Romeo and Juliet, Dance of Death, Tales of Beatrix Potter, Murder on the Orient Express, Death On The Nile, Stories from a Flying Trunk, The Mirror Crack'd, Evil Under the Sun, A Passage to India, Little Dorrit.

BRACCO, LORRAINE: Actress. b. Brooklyn, NY, 1955. m. actor Harvey Keitel. At 16 began modelling for Wilhelmina Agency appearing in Mademoiselle, Seventeen, Teen magazine. Moved to Paris where modelling career continued and led to TV commercials. After making her film debut in Duo sur Canape became a disc jockey on Radio Luxembourg, Paris. 1983 produced a TV special on fashion and music. In Lincoln Center workshop performance of David Rabe's Goose and Tom Tom, 1986.
PICTURES: Cormorra, The Pick-up Artist, Someone to Watch Over Me, Talk Radio, Sing, The Dream Team, Sea of Love, On a Moonlit Night, The Good Fellas.

BRACKEN, EDDIE: Actor. b. New York, NY, Feb. 7, 1920. e. Prof. Children's Sch. for Actors, N.Y. m. Connie Nickerson, actress. Vaudeville & night club singer: stage debut in Lottery, 1930; m.p. debut in Life with Henry. 1940.
PLAYS: Lady Refuses, Iron Men, So Proudly We Hail, Brother Rat, What A Life, Too Many Girls, Seven Year Itch, Shinbone Alley, Teahouse of the August Moon, You Know I Can't Hear You When The Water's Running, The Odd Couple, Never Too Late, Sunshine Boys, Hotline to Heaven, Hello, Dolly, Damn Yankees, Sugar Babies, Show Boat.
PICTURES: Fleet's In, Happy Go Lucky, Sweater Girl, Star Spangled Rhythm, Young and Willing, Hail the Conquering Hero, Miracle of Morgan's Creek, Girl From Jones Beach, Summer Stock, Two Tickets to Broadway, About Face, We're Not Married, Slight Case of Larceny, National Lampoon's Vacation.
TELEVISION: Masquerade Party, Murder She Wrote, Blacke's Magic, Amazing Stories, Tales of the Dark Side.

BRADEN, WILLIAM: Executive, Producer. b. Alberta, Canada, 1939. e. Vancouver, B.C. Began career as stuntman in Hollywood, and has worked in all aspects of industry Worked for Elliott Kastner as prod. exec. and with Jeffrey Bloom, of Feature Films, Inc., as prod. and v.p. in chg. of prod. Also with Dunatai Corp., as head of film and TV prod. With Completion Bond Co. one yr. as prod. exec., Australia then with Filmaker Completion as pres. 4 years. Now indep. prod.
PICTURES: Pyramid (assoc. prod., prod. supv.), Russian Roulette (prod. exec.) 92 in the Shade (prod. exec.), Breakheart Pass (prod. exec.), Dogpound Shuffle (asst. dir.), Dublin Murders (supvr. re-edit); He Wants Her Back (prod.); Goldengirl (prod. exec.); Running Scared (prod.); Death Valley (asst. dir.); The Seduction (prod. exec.); Slapstick (prod. exec.).
TELEVISION: Requiem for a Planet (series, prod./creator); Specials: Nothing Great is Easy (exec. prod.); King of the Channel (exec. prod.); I Believe (prod.); If My People. . . (prod.). America: Life in the Family (dir./prod.) Also various Movies of the Week for networks and many industrial and doc. films.

BRADLEY, BILL: Performer, r.n. William M. Silbert. b. Detroit, MI, Jan. 1, 1921. e. U. of Detroit, Southern Methodist U. Disc jockey, m.c., many radio-TV shows, Detroit; panelist, Songs for Sale, 1952; emcee, Bill Silbert show, Let's Go Bowling, 1952–53; Bill Silbert Show. WMGM radio; announcer, Red Buttons Show; Philco Phonorama Time; m.c., National Radio Fan Club; Magazine of the Air, Mutual #1 disc jockey, Billboard Magazine, 1955; KLAC Hollywood, Bill Bradley Show; KTLA, Hollywood, m.c. Crime Story, Greet the People, Ad Lib, Hollywood Diary. gen. sales mgr., A.E. KLOS, Los Angeles.
PICTURES: Bundle of Joy, Thunderjets, The Alligator People, Young Jesse James, Lost Missile, Breakfast at Tiffany's, Return to Peyton Place, Looking for Love, Goonies.
TELEVISION: Bronco, 77 Sunset Strip, Hawaiian Eye, Sugarfoot, Combat, Adventures in Paradise, Police Station, Michael Shayne, Roaring 20's, The Outlaws, Breaking Point, The Fugitive, Bill Dana Show, My Living Doll, Joey Bishop Show, Ben Casey, Bing Crosby Show. Many commercials, Mannix, Wild Wild West, Name of the Game.
RADIO: WXYZ, WWJ, Detroit; WMGM, Mutual Network, NBC, NY; KLAC, KABC-FM, KLOS, L.A.

BRADLEY, ED: Newscaster. b. Philadelphia, Pa., June 22, 1941. e. Chayney State Coll, B.S. Worked way up through the ranks as local radio reporter in Philadelphia 1963–67 and NY 1967–71. Joined CBS News as stringer in Paris bureau, 1971; then Saigon bureau. Named CBS news correspondent, 1973. Became CBS News White House corr. and anchor of CBS Sunday Night News, 1976–81; principal corr. and anchor, CBS Reports, 1978–81; co-editor and reporter 60 Minutes since 1982.
TELEVISION: Special reports: What's Happened to Cambodia; The Boat People; The Boston Goes to China; Blacks in America—with all Deliberate Speed; Return of the CIA; Miami . . . The Trial That Sparked the Riot (Emmy); The Saudis; Too Little, Too Late (Emmy); Murder—Teenage Style (Emmy, 1981); In the Belly of the Beast (Emmy, 1982); Lena (Emmy, 1982).
AWARDS: Aside from numerous Emmys, has received Alfred I. duPont-Columbia University and Overseas Press Club Awards; George Foster Peabody and Ohio State Awards; and George Polk Award.

BRAEDEN, ERIC: Actor. b. Kiel, Germany. r.n. Hans Gudegast.
PICTURES: Colossus, The Forbin Project, The Law and Jake Wade, The Ultimate Thrill, Morituri, Escape from the Planet of the Apes, Lady Ice, A Hundred Rifles, Herbie Goes to Monte Carlo.
TELEVISION: The Young and the Restless (series).

BRAGA, SONIA: Actress. b. Maringa, Parana, Brazil, 1951. Began acting at 14 on live children's program on Brazilian TV, Gardin Encantado. Stage debut at 17 in Moliere's Jorge Dandin, then in Hair! Starred in many Brazilian soap operas including Gabriella, as well as a prod. of Sesame Street in Saõ Paulo.
PICTURES: The Main Road, A Moreninha, Captain Bandeira Vs. Dr. Moura Brasil, Mestica, The Indomitable Slave, The Couple, Dona Flor and Her Two Husbands, Gabriella, I Love You, A Lady in the Bus, Kiss of the Spider Woman, The Milagro Beanfield War, Moon Over Parador.
TELEVISION: The Man Who Broke 1000 Chains, The Bill Cosby Show.

BRANAGH, KENNETH: Actor, Director. b. Belfast, Northern Ireland, Dec. 10, 1960. Moved to Reading, England at 9. Went from drama school into West End hit Another Country. Left Royal Shakespeare Company to form his own Renaissance Theater Co. with actor David Parfitt for which he wrote a play Public Enemy, directed Twelfth Night and played Hamlet,

Benedick and Touchstone in a sold-out nationwide tour and London season.
PICTURES: High Season, A Month in the Country, Henry V (also dir. and adapt.).
TELEVISION: The Boy in the Bush, Billy, Maybury, To the Lighthouse, Coming Through, Ghosts, The Lady's Not For Burning, Fortunes of War (mini-series) Thompson (series).

BRAND, NEVILLE: Actor. b. Kewanee, IL, Aug. 13, 1921. e. high sch., Kewanee. U.S. Army, 10 yrs to 1946; studied acting in N.Y.: film debut in D.O.A. (1949).
PICTURES: Halls of Montezuma, Only the Valiant, The Mob, Flame of Araby, Stalag 17, Charge at Feather River, Man Crazy, Gun Fury, Riot in Cell Block 11, Long Gun, Prince Valiant, Return from the Sea, Fury at Gunsight Pass, The Prodigal, Return of Jack Slade, Bobby Ware Is Missing, Mohawk, Raw Edge, The Adventures of Huckleberry Finn, The Desperadoes, Three Guns for Texas, Birdman of Alcatraz, That Darn Cat, Scalawag, Cahill, U.S. Marshall, The Deadly Trackers, Psychic Killer, Evils of the Night.
TELEVISION: The Untouchables, Arroyo, Laredo, Captains and the Kings, The Eddie Capra Mysteries, Harper Valley, The Seekers, The Quest, The Barbary Coast.

BRANDAUER, KLAUS MARIA: Actor. b., Altaussee, Austria, June 22, 1944. m. film and TV dir.-screenwriter Karin Mueller. e. Acad. of Music and Dramatic Arts, Stuttgart, W. Germany. Was established in the German and Austrian theater before film debut.
PICTURES: The Salzburg Connection (1972), Mephisto (best actor, Cannes, 1981). Never Say Never Again, Colonel Redl, Out of Africa, The Lightship, Streets of Gold, The Death Ship, Burning Secret, Hanussen, Oskar Schindler—An Angel in Hell, Hitlerjunge Salomon, Das Spinnennetz (The Spider's Web) Seven Minutes (also dir.), The French Revolution, The Artisan (also dir.).
TELEVISION: Quo Vadis?

BRANDO, JOCELYN: Actress. b. San Francisco, CA, Nov. 18, 1919. Sister of actor Marlon Brando. e. Lake Forest Coll. m.p. debut in The Big Heat; on Broadway in Mr. Roberts, Desire Under the Elms, Golden State.
PICTURES: China Venture, Ten Wanted Men, Mommie Dearest.
TELEVISION: Dark Night of the Scarecrow, A Question of Love, Starflight—The Plane that Couldn't Land.

BRANDO, MARLON: Actor. b. Omaha, NB, April 3, 1924. Brother of actress Jocelyn Brando. e. Shattuck Military Acad., Faribault, MN. Studied Dramatic Workshop, NY; played stock Sayville, Long Island. Broadway debut: I Remember Mama, then Truckline Cafe, Candida, A Flag Is Born, A Streetcar Named Desire. One of top ten Money-Making Stars, M.P. Herald-Fame poll, 1954–55.
PICTURES: The Men, A Streetcar Named Desire, Viva Zapata, Julius Caesar, Wild One, On the Waterfront (Acad. Award, best actor, 1954), Guys and Dolls, Teahouse of the August Moon, Sayonara, The Young Lions, Mutiny on the Bounty, One-Eyed Jacks, The Ugly American, Bedtime Story, The Saboteur, Code Name, Morituri, The Fugitive Kind, The Chase, Appaloosa, The Countess From Hong Kong, Reflections in a Golden Eye, Night of the Following Day, Candy, Burn!, The Nightcomers, The Godfather (Acad. Award, best actor, 1972), Last Tango in Paris, The Missouri Breaks, Superman, The Formula, A Dry White Season, The Freshman, Jericho (also co-prod., s.p.).
TELEVISION: Roots: The Next Generations (Emmy Award, best supporting actor).

BRANDT, JANET: Actress. b. New York, NY. Acting debut at 6 years old with Yiddish Theater. Over 100 stage appearances in New York where she studied with Martha Graham and with Michael Chekov. Lectured on Shakespeare at the Strasberg Institute in L.A.
PICTURES: A Cold Wind in August, Kotch, Mad Adventures of Rabbi Jacob, Sheila Levine, Semi-Tough, Dialogue Director: Battle of the Bulge, El Cid, Phaedre, View from the Bridge, King of Kings, etc.
TELEVISION: The Super, Odd Couple, Mannix, Lou Grant, My First Love.

BRANDT, RICHARD PAUL: Executive. b. New York, NY, Dec. 6, 1927. e. Yale U., BS, Phi Beta Kappa. Chief exec. off. & chmn. Trans Lux Corp.; chmn., Brandt Theatres; dir., Presidential Realty Corp.; chmn. emeritus & trustee, American Film Institute; trustee, American Theatre Wing; member, Tony Awards Management Comm.; trustee, College of Santa Fe.

BRASLOFF, STANLEY H.: Producer, director. b. Philadelphia, PA, July 23, 1930. In U.S. Army was entertainment dir., Heidelberg military post, 1948–50; prod., dir. & acted for various little theatre & summer stock groups, 1950–60; created, wrote, co-prod., dir. & starred in Time For Teens, TV show (Chicago); formed VCS Pictures Ltd., prod. & dir. Two Girls for a Madman, 1967; formed SHB Productions, Inc., prod. Nightmare at Ghost Beach, 1968; wrote, co-prod. & dir. Toys Are Not for Children, 1971.

BRAUNSTEIN, GEORGE GREGORY: Producer. b. New York, NY, May 23, 1947. e. Culver Military Acad., U. of California, B.A., biology, chemistry, 1970. U. W.L.A. Law School, J.D. 1987. Father is Jacques Braunstein (Screen Televideo Prods. At War with the Army, Young Lions, etc.).
PICTURES: Train Ride to Hollywood, Fade to Black, Surf II, And God Created Woman, Out Cold, The Boyfriend School.

BRAVERMAN, CHARLES: Producer, Director. b. Los Angeles, CA, March 3, 1944. e. Los Angeles City Coll., U. of Southern California, B.A. m. Kendall Carly Browne, actress. Child actor, 1950–57. Two time Emmy winner.
TELEVISION: An American Time Capsule, The Smothers Brothers Racing Team Special, How to Stay Alive, David Hartman . . . Birth and Babies, Breathe a Sigh of Relief, The Television Newsman, Getting Married, The Making of a Live TV Show, Televisionland, Nixon: Checkers to Watergate, Braverman's Condensed Cream of Beatles, Two Cops, Peanuts to the Presidency: The Jimmy Carter Campaign; The Making of Beatlemania, Willie Nelson Plays Lake Tahoe, Tony Bennett Sings, What's Up, America?, The Big Laff Off, Engelbert at the MGM Grand, Oscar's First 50 Years, Frankie Valli Show, The Sixties, Showtime Looks at 1981, Roadshow, Kenny Rodger's America; St. Elsewhere; DTV (Disney Channel); Crazy Like a Fox; Dreams; The Richard Lewis Special; Prince of Bel Air, Brotherhood of Justice (both ABC movies); The Wizard; Heart of the City; Rags to Riches; The New Mike Hammer.
PICTURES: Dillinger, Soylent Green, Same Time Next Year (all montages, titles), Can't Stop the Music (titles), Hit and Run (prod./dir.).

BRAVERMAN, MILLICENT: Adv. agency president (Braverman-Mirisch Inc.). b. New York, NY. Syndicated radio Los Angeles commentator on books, literary critic, publishing specialist. B-M. Inc. founded 1963 to date. General advertising, print and broadcast media nationally.

BRAY, PAUL JR.: e. Rensselaer Polytechnic Inst. Experienced airline transport pilot and instrument flight instructor. Writer and director specializing in motion picture scripts and productions on all phases aviation, engineering and electronic from theoretical to practical industrial personnel training, and for Armed Forces and Vocational-Technical school instruction.

BRAZZI, ROSSANO: Actor. b. Bologna, Italy, 1916. e. U. of Florence. Started career on Italian stage; has appeared in numerous Italian pictures.
PICTURES: (U.S.) Little Women, Three Coins in the Fountain, Barefoot Contessa, Summertime, South Pacific, Light in the Piazza, The Battle of Villa Fiorita, Rome Adventure, Dark Purpose, The Christmas That Almost Wasn't, The Bobo, Woman Times Seven, Krakatoa, East of Java, The Adventurers, Psychout for Murder, The Great Waltz, The Final Conflict, Fear City, Michelanglo and Me.
TELEVISION: (U.S.) June Allyson Show, Run For Your Life, The Name of the Game, Hawaii Five-O, Fantasy Island, Charlie's Angels, Hart to Hart, The Survivors, Honeymoon With a Stranger, The Far Pavillions, Christopher Columbus.

BRECHER, IRVING: Writer. b. New York, NY, Jan. 17, 1914. Yonkers Herald reporter; network programs writer for Milton Berle, Willie Howard, Al Jolson, etc., m.p. writer since 1937.
PICTURES: (collab. s.p.) Shadow of the Thin Man, Best Foot Forward, Meet Me in St. Louis; (collab, adapt.) Summer Holiday: (s.p.), Go West, At the Circus, Du Barry Was a Lady, Yolanda and the Thief, Life of Riley, Somebody Loves Me, Cry for Happy, Bye Bye Birdie, Sail a Crooked Ship.
TELEVISION: The People's Choice, The Life of Riley.

BREGMAN, MARTIN: Producer, Writer. b. New York, NY, May 18, 1931. m. actress Cornelia Sharpe. e. Indiana U., NYU. Began career as business and personal mgr. to Barbra Streisand, Faye Dunaway, Candice Bergen, Al Pacino, etc. Chairman NY Advisory Council for Motion Pictures, Radio and TV (co-founder, 1974).
PICTURES: Serpico, Dog Day Afternoon, The Next Man, The Seduction of Joe Tynan, Simon, The Four Seasons, Eddie Macon's Run, Venom, Scarface, Sweet Liberty, Real Men, A New Life, Sea of Love, Nesting.
TELEVISION: Prod.: S*H*E (movie), The Four Seasons (series).

BREN, ROBERT J.: Producer, writer. b. Guanajuato, Mexico. Film writing debut with Looking for Trouble, 1934; in U.S. Signal Corps, W.W.II, also coordinator Inter-American Affairs as m.p. program office head, N.Y. & Washington, DC. Formed Bremex, indep. picture co., 1963.
PICTURES: This Marriage Business, Crime Ring, Parents on Trail, American Empire, Underground Agent, Charter Pilot, In Old California, Gay Senorita, Five Little Peppers and How They Grew, prod. First Yank into Tokyo, assoc. prod. El Paso, Overland Pacific; Naked Alibi, Treasure of Pancho Villa, The Great Sioux Uprising, Siege at Red River, Without Orders,

Maltrata (O.S., S.P., producer) for Bremex Corp., Mexico; Cajeme (O.S., S.P., producer) for Bremex, S.A., Mexico.
TELEVISION: Lone Wolf in Mexico, Stolen Train, Casey Jones series. collab. s.p., Winds of the Four Seasons; collab. s.p., orig. story, The Hawaiians, 1967. Wrote & collaborated on Blood On the Shrine, Legacy in Nylons, Aztec Dagger, Female Menagerie, Tag for Murder.

BRENNAN, EILEEN: Actress. b. Los Angeles, CA, Sept. 3, 1935. e. Georgetown U., American Acad. of Dramatic Arts, N.Y. Daughter of silent film actress Jean Manahan. Big break came with lead in off-Broadway musical, Little Mary Sunshine (Obie Award, 1960).
STAGE: The Miracle Worker (tour), Hello, Dolly! (Broadway), and revivals of The King and I, Guys and Dolls, Camelot, Bells Are Ringing, One-women revue, An Evening with Eileen Brennan.
PICTURES: Divorce, American Style, The Last Picture Show, Scarecrow, The Sting, Daisy Miller, At Long Last Love, Hustle, Murder by Death, The Cheap Detective, Private Benjamin, Clue, Rented Lips, Sticky Fingers, The New Adventures of Pippi Longstocking, It Had to Be You, Stella, Texasville.
TELEVISION: Series: Private Benjamin (Emmy Award), Off the Rack. Special: Working. Movies: The Blue Knight, Black Beauty, My Old Man, Playmates, When the Circus Comes to Town, Off Duty, Going to the Chapel.

BRENNER, JOSEPH: Executive. b. Brooklyn, NY, Oct. 27, 1918. e. Brooklyn Coll. Started as usher, 1935, becoming mgr., Rogers Theatre, 1936; salesman, Eagle Lion Films, 1946; Screen Guild Prods., 1948; sales mgr., Ellis Films, 1949; formed Joseph Brenner Associates, 1953.

BRESSON, ROBERT: Writer, director. b. France, Sept. 25, 1907.
PICTURES: Les Anges du Peche, Les Dames du Bois de Boulogne, Le Journal d'un Cure de Campagne, Pickpocket, The Trial of Joan of Arc, Au Hazard Balthasar, Mouchette, Une Femme Douce, Lancelot du Lac, Le Diable Probablement, De Weg Naar Bresson.

BREST, MARTIN: Director. b. Bronx, NY, 1951. e. NYU Sch. of Film. Made award-winning short subject, Hot Dogs for Gauguin. Accepted into fellowship program at American Film Institute, making first feature, Hot Tomorrows, as AFI project.
PICTURES: Going in Style, Beverly Hills Cop, Midnight Run (prod., dir.).

BRETT, JEREMY: Actor. b. Berkwell Grange, Warwickshire, Eng., Nov. 3, 1933. r.n. Jeremy Huggins. e. Eton, Central Sch. of Speech and Drama. London stage debut, Troilus and Cressida (Old Vic, 1956); NY stage debut, Richard II (1956).
THEATER: Selected London shows: Meet Me by Moonlight, Variations on a Theme, Mr. Fox of Venice, Marigold, The Edwardians, Johnny the Priest, The Kitchen, A Month in the Country, Macrune's Guevara, A Voyage Round My Father, Traveller Without Luggage, Design for Living. U.S.: With Old Vic in Amphytrion 38, Richard II, Macbeth, Romeo and Juliet, Troilus and Cressida, The Deputy, Robert and Elizabeth (L.A.), Dracula (L.A.), Aren't We All?
PICTURES: War and Peace, My Fair Lady, The Medusa Touch.
TELEVISION: Romeo and Juliet (1957), Macbeth, Florence Nightingale, Deceptions, Jennie, Katherine Mansfield, The Merry Widow, Rebecca, The Adventures of Sherlock Holmes (1985–86), Picture of Dorian Gray, Dinner with Family, The School for Scandal, Hart to Hart.

BREWER, ROY M.: b. Cairo, NB, Aug. 9, 1909. Was projectionist 1925; chief projectionist, Capitol Theatre, Grand Island, NB 1927–39; pres. Nebraska State Fed. of Labor 1933; active in Nebraska labor movement in this period; NRA labor compliance officer for Nebraska 1934–35; in chg. campaign hdqts. for U.S. Senator George W. Norris 1936; re-elected pres. Nebraska State Federation of Labor 1937; covered legislature for Federation 1939, 1941, 1943; chief, plant & community facilities service War Prod. Bd. Washington 1943–45; apptd. specl. intl. rep. LATSE 1945; then made intl. rep. in Hollywood, rep. Richard F. Walsh, LATSE pres.; exec. ass't Steve Broidy, Allied Artists president, October, 1953; mgr. of br. oper., 1955; apptd. admin. sls. asst. to Edward Morey, vice-pres., Allied Artists, 1962; mgr. prod. dev., 1965. Member: Hollywood AFL Film Council, M.P. Ind. Council, M.P. Alliance, Pres, Perm Char. Committee 1965 Studio mgr. and prod. rep. for West Coast.

BRIALY, JEAN-CLAUDE: Actor. b. Aumale, Algeria, March 30, 1933. e. Strasbourg U. (philosophy) also attended drama classes at Strasbourg Conservatoire. Made several short films with Jacques Rivette and Jean-Luc Godard. Popular actor in films of French New Wave directors.
PICTURES: Elena et les Hommes; Elevator to the Scaffold (1958); Les Cousins; Le Beau Serge; The 400 Blows; Tire au Flane; La Chambre Ardente; A Woman is a Woman; The Devil and Ten Commandments; La Ronde; Un Homme de Trop; Lamiel; King of Hearts; Le Rouge et le Noir; The Bride Wore Black; Claire's Knee; A Murder is a Murder; The Phantom of Liberty; Catherine et Cie; The Accuser; L'Annee Sainte; Robert and Robert; Eglantine; Les Violets Clos; L'oiseau Rare; Un Amour De Pluie; Bobo Jacco; L'oeil Du Maitre; La Banquiere; La Nuit de Varennes; Cap Canaille; Le Demon Dan L'Isle; Edith and Marcel; Sarah; Stella; The Crime; Papy Fait de la Resistance; Pinot, Simple Flic, Comedie dété.

BRIAN, DAVID: Actor. b. New York, NY, Aug. 5, 1914. e. City Coll. of New York. Doorman; chorus boy. Stage debut in New Moon.
STAGE: You Said It, Bittersweet, Princess Charming, Let 'Em Eat Cake, Crazy Quilt, Beat the Band, Candle in the Wind. By Jupiter and night club singer & dancer; in vaudeville; m.c. in South American night club; served as instructor in U.S. Coast Guard 1942–45.
PICTURES: Flamingo Road (debut, 1949), Intruder in the Dust, Beyond the Forest, Breakthrough, Damned Don't Cry, Inside Straight, Forth Worth, Inside Walls of Folsom Prison, This Woman is Dangerous, Springfield Rifle, Million Dollar Mermaid, Ambush at Tomahawk Gap, Perilous Journey, Dawn at Socorro, High and the Mighty, Timberjack, Fury at Gunsight Pass, The Rabbit Trap, The Seven Minutes.
TELEVISION: Mr. District Attorney, The Immortal.

BRICKMAN, MARSHALL: Writer, Director. b. Rio de Janeiro, Brazil, Aug. 25, 1941. e. U. of Wisconsin. Banjoist, singer, writer with folk groups The Tarriers and The Journeymen before starting to write for TV.
PICTURES: Writer (with Woody Allen): Sleeper; Annie Hall (Acad. Award, s.p., shared with Allen); Manhattan: Simon, Lovesick (dir., s.p.): The Manhattan Project (prod., dir., s.p.).
TELEVISION: Writer: Candid Camera 1966, The Tonight Show 1966–70. Specials: Johnny Carson's Repertory Co. in an Evening of Comedy (1969), Woody Allen Special; Prod.: Dick Cavett Show (1970—72, Emmy).

BRICKMAN, PAUL: Writer, Director. b. Chicago, IL. e. Claremont Men's Coll. Worked as camera asst., then story analyst at Paramount, Columbia, and Universal. Debut script: Citizen's Band (1977; also called Handle With Care). Debut as director with Risky Business (1983).
PICTURES: The Bad News Bears in Breaking Training (s.p.), Risky Business, (dir., s.p.), Deal of the Century (s.p.), That's Adequate (interviewee).

BRIDGES, ALAN: Director. b. England, Sept. 28, 1927.
PICTURES: An Act of Murder (1965), Invasion, Shelley, The Hireling, Out of Season, Summer Rain, The Return of the Soldier, The Shooting Party, Displaced Persons, Apt Pupil, Secret Places of the Heart, Fire Princess.
TELEVISION: The Father, Dial M For Murder, The Intrigue, The Ballade of Peckham Rye, The Initiation, Alarm Call: Z Cars, The Fontenay Murders, The Brothers Karamazov, The Idiot, Days to Come, Les Miserables, Born Victim, The Wild Duck, The Lie, Brief Encounter, Forget Me Not Lane, Double Echo, Saturday, Sunday Monday, Crown Matrimonial.

BRIDGES, BEAU: Actor. r.n. Lloyd Vernet Bridges III. b. Hollywood, CA, Dec. 19, 1941. e. UCLA, U. of Hawaii. f. Lloyd Bridges. After several feature film bit parts and numerous TV credits, made screen feature debut in The Incident (1967).
PICTURES: For Love of Ivy, Gaily, Gaily, The Landlord, Adam's Woman, The Christian Licorice Store, Hammersmith Is Out, Child's Play, Your Three Minutes Are Up, Lovin' Molly, The Other Side of the Mountain, Dragonfly, Swashbuckler, Two Minute Warning, Greased Lightning, Norma Rae, The Runner Stumbles, The Fifth Musketeer, Honky Tonk Freeway, Night Crossing, Heart Like a Wheel, Love Child, The Hotel New Hampshire, The Killing Time, The Wild Pair (also dir.), The Iron Triangle, Seven Hours to Judgement (also dir.), Signs of Life, The Fabulous Baker Boys, Daddy's Dyin', The Wizard.
TELEVISION: Ensign O'Toole, Sea Hunt, Ben Casey, Dr. Kildare, Mr. Novak, Combat, Eleventh Hour, Space, A Fighting Choice, Outrage, Cimarron Strip, The Kid from Nowhere, Dangerous Company, Witness for the Prosecution, Red Light Sting, Alice in Wonderland, Amazing Stories, The Thanksgiving Promise (also dir.), Three of a Kind, Everybody's Baby: The Rescue of Jessica McClure, Just Another Secret.

BRIDGES, JAMES: Actor, Writer, Director. b. Paris, AK, Feb 3, 1936. e. Arkansas Teachers Coll.; USC. Appeared as an actor in 50 TV shows and five feature films. Has written 16 plays and is published in New Theatre for Now, 18 hour Hitchcock Shows and one Great Adventure, Go Down Moses. Worked as writer on 14 features. As director, worked in New York, Edinburgh Festival, Mark Taper and Ahmanson in Los Angeles.
PICTURES: Limbo (s.p.), The Appaloosa (s.p.), Forbin Project (s.p.), The Baby Maker (dir., s.p.), The Paper Chase (dir., s.p.); September 30, 1955 (dir., s.p.); The China Syndrome (dir., co-s.p.); Urban Cowboy (co-s.p., dir.), Mike's Murder (dir., s.p.); Perfect (prod., dir., s.p.); Bright Lights, Big City (dir., co-s.p.), White Hunter, Black Heart (co-s.p. only).

BRIDGES, JEFF: Actor. b. Los Angeles, CA, Dec. 4, 1949. Made acting debut at eight in the TV series Sea Hunt starring his father, Lloyd Bridges. Studied acting at Herbert Berghof Studio, NY. Mil. service in Coast Guard reserves. Acad. Award nom.: The Last Picture Show (supp.); Thunderbolt and Lightfoot (supp.), Starman. Brother of actor-director Beau Bridges.
PICTURES: Halls of Anger (1969), The Yin and Yang of Mr. Go, The Last Picture Show, Bad Company, Fat City, The Iceman Cometh, The Last American Hero, Lolly-Madonna XXX, Thunderbolt and Lightfoot, Hearts of the West, Rancho Deluxe, King Kong, Stay Hungry, Somebody Killed Her Husband, The American Success Company, Winter Kills, Heaven's Gate, Kiss Me Goodbye, Cutter's Way (Cutter and Bone), Tron, Against All Odds, Starman, Jagged Edge, 8 Million Ways to Die, The Morning After, Nadine, Tucker, See You in the Morning, Cold Feet, The Fabulous Baker Boys, Texasville.
TELEVISION: Silent Night, Lonely Night; In Search of America; Faerie Tale Theatre (Rapunzel).

BRIDGES, LLOYD: Actor. b. San Leandro, CA, January 15, 1913. e. UCLA. Went into stock from college dramatics. Formed off-Bdwy theater, the Playroom Club. With wife taught drama at private sch. in Darien, CT when signed stock contract with Columbia. Bdwy. stage: Oh Men, Oh Women!, Cactus Flower, Man of La Mancha.
PICTURES: Miss Susie Slage's, Abilene Town, Canyon Passage, Ramrod, Trouble with Women, Hideout, Calamity Jane and Sam Bass, Trapped, Rocketship XM, Try and Get Me, Colt .45, Three Steps North, Whistle at Eaton Falls, Last of the Comanches, High Noon, Plymouth Adventure, Tall Texan, Kid from Left Field, City of Bad Men, Limping Man, Pride of the Blue Grass, Deadly Game, Apache Woman, Wichita, Wetbacks, The Rainmaker, Daring Game, The Goddess, The Happy Ending, The Fifth Musketeer, Airplane!, Airplane II, Weekend Warriors, The Wild Pair, Tucker: The Man and His Dream, Cousins, Winter People, Joe Versus the Volcano.
TELEVISION: Early work on Bigelow Theatre (1950), Kraft Suspense Theatre. Series: Police Story, Sea Hunt (1957–61), The Lloyd Bridges Show (1962–63), The Loner, San Francisco International Airport, Joe Forrester (1975–76); Movies: Tragedy in a Temporary Town, The Fortress, The People Next Door, Paper Dolls, Silent Night, Lonley Night, The Thanksgiving Promise, She Was Marked For Murder, Cross of Fire. Mini-series: Roots, Disaster on the Coastliner, East of Eden, Movieola, The Blue and the Gray, George Washington, Dress Gray, North & South Book II.

BRIGHT, RICHARD: Actor. b. Brooklyn, NY, June 11. e. trained for stage with Frank Corsaro, John Lehne and Paul Mann.
THEATER: The Balcony (1959), The Beard, The Salvation of St. Joan, Gogol, The Basic Training of Pavlo Hummel, Richard III, Kid Twist, Short Eyes as well as regional theater.
PICTURES: Odds Against Tomorrow, Lion's Love, Panic in Needle Park, The Getaway, Pat Garrett and Billy the Kid, The Godfather, The Godfather II, Rancho Deluxe, Marathon Man, Citizens Band, Looking For Mr. Goodbar, On the Yard, Hair, The Idolmaker, Vigilante, Once Upon a Time in America, Two of A Kind, Crackers, Crimewave, Cut and Run, Brighton Beach Memoirs, 52-Pick-up, Time Out.
TELEVISION: Lamp Unto My Feet, Armstrong Circle Theater, The Verdict Is Yours, Kraft Television Theatre, Studio One, Cagney and Lacey, Beacon Hill, Hill Street Blues, From These Roots. Movies: A Death of Innocence, The Connection, The Gun, Cops and Robin, Sizzle, There Must Be A Pony, Penalty Phase. Mini-series: From Here to Eternity, Skag.

BRIGHT, RICHARD S.: Executive. b. New Rochelle, NY, Feb. 28, 1936. e. Hotchkiss Sch., 1953–54; Wharton Sch. of Finance, U. of Pennsylvania, 1954–58. With U.S. Army Finance Corp., 1959–60. Was corporate exec. prior to founding in 1973 Persky-Bright Organization, private investment group to finance films. Now bd. chmn, Persky-Bright Productions, Inc.; adjunct professor at Columbia U. Sch. of Fine Arts.
PICTURES: Last Detail, Golden Voyage of Sinbad, For Pete's Sake, California Split, The Man Who Would Be King, Funny Lady, The Front, and Equus. Financing/production services for: Hard Times, Taxi Driver, Missouri Breaks, Bound for Glory, Sinbad and the Eye of the Tiger, Hair, Still of the Night. Executive Producer: Tribute.
TELEVISION: The President's Mistress (co-producer).
STAGE: A History of the American Film (1978); Album (Off-Broadway, co-prod.).

BRIGHTMAN, HOMER H.: Writer b. Port Townsend, WA. e. Washington State Nautical School-ship. Apprentice at 14, spent 10 years at sea as 2nd and 3rd officer; claims dept., Dollar Steamship Lines Shanghai, Hong Kong, Singapore: Academy Award for short Lend a Paw 1939; assoc. Walt Disney Prod. 13 years; created It's a Dog's Life, TV show; animated cartoon shorts for MGM, Walter Lantz, U.P.A.
PICTURES: Saludos Amigos, Three Caballeros, Make Mine Music, Fun and Fancy Free, Melody Time, Cinderella. Writer (collab.) TV shorts.

BRILLSTEIN, BERNIE: Producer, Talent Manager. b. New York, NY. 1931. e. NYU, B.S. advertising. Manager whose clients have incl. Lorne Michaels, John Belushi, Jim Henson and the Muppets. Chairman and chief exec. officer, Lorimar Film Entertainment. Founder, chmn., pres., The Brillstein Company.
PICTURES: Exec. prod.: The Blues Brothers, Up the Academy, Continental Divide, Neighbors, Doctor Detroit, Ghostbusters, Spies Like Us, Summer Rental, Armed and Dangerous, Dragnet, Ghostbusters II.
TELEVISION: Exec. prod.: Burns and Schreiber Comedy Hour, Buckshot, Open All Night, Show Business, Sitcom, Buffalo Bill, Jump, The Faculty, The Real Ghostbusters (exec. consultant), It's Gary Shandling's Show, The Days and Nights of Molly Dodd, The "Slap" Maxwell Show, The Boys (pilot).

BRIMLEY, WILFORD: Actor. b. Salt Lake City, UT, Sept. 27, 1934. Formerly a blacksmith, ranch hand and racehorse trainer, begain in films as an extra and stuntman. Original mem. L.A. Actors Theatre.
PICTURES: True Grit (1969), The Lawman, The Electric Horseman, Brubaker, The China Syndrome, Borderline, Death Valley, Absence of Malice, The Thing, Tender Mercies, Tough Enough, High Road to China, 10 to Midnight, Hotel New Hampshire, Harry and Son, The Stone Boy, The Natural, Country, Cocoon, Remo Williams: The Adventure Begins, End of the Line, Cocoon: The Return, Eternity.
TELEVISION: Movies: The Wild Wild West Revisited, Rodeo Girl, Amber Waves, Roughnecks, The Big Black Pill, Murder in Space, The Battle for Endor, Thompson's Last Run, Act of Vengeance, Joe Dancer, The Firm, Gore Vidal's Billy the Kid. Series: Our House.

BRINKLEY, DAVID: TV news correspondent. b. Wilmington, NC, July 10, 1920. e. U. of North Carolina, Vanderbilt U. Started writing for hometown newspaper. Joined United Press before entering Army, W.W.II. After discharge in 1943 joined NBC News in Washington as White House corr. Co-chmn. for many years with late Chet Huntley on NBC Nightly News. Then began David Brinkley's Journal. Moved to ABC to co-anchor nightly news, then to host This Week with David Brinkley.

BRISKIN, MORT: Producer, Writer. b. Oak Park, IL, 1919. e. U. of Southern California; attended Harvard and Northwestern law schools, being admitted to the bar at 20. Practiced law before entering m.p. industry in management with such stars as Mickey Rooney. Turned to production and also wrote screenplays for 16 of his 29 films. Created nine TV series and was prod. or exec. prod. of some 1,350 TV segments of which he wrote more than 300.
PICTURES: The River, The Magic Face, No Time for Flowers, The Second Woman, Quicksand, The Big Wheel, The Jackie Robinson Story, Ben, Willard, Walking Tall, Framed.
TELEVISION: Sheriff of Cochise, U.S. Marshal, The Texan, Grand Jury, The Walter Winchell File, Official Detective, Whirlybirds.

BRITTANY, MORGAN: Actress. r.n. Suzanne Cupito. b. Hollywood, CA, Dec. 5, 1951.
PICTURES: Marnie, Yours, Mine and Ours; The Birds, Gypsy, Gable and Lombard, Sundown, The Vampire in Retreat.
TELEVISION: Series: Dallas. Movies: Amazing Howard Hughes, Delta County U.S.A., Glitter, Going Home Again, The Dream Merchants, Moviola, The Scarlett O'Hara War, The Wild Women of Chastity Gulch, LBJ: The Early Years, Perry Mason: The Case of the Scandalous Scoundrel, Initiation of Sarah.

BRITTON, TONY: Actor, b. Birmingham, England, 1924. e. Thornbury Grammar Sch., Glos. Early career as clerk and in repertory; TV debut, 1952, The Six Proud Walkers (serial), m.p. debut, 1955 in Loser Takes All.
PLAYS: The Guv'nor, Romeo and Juliet, The Scarlet Pimpernel, The Other Man, The Dashing White Sergeant, Importance of Being Earnest, An Ideal Husband, School for Scandal, A Dream of Treason, That Lady, The Private Lives of Edward Whiteley, Affairs of State, The Night of The Ball, Gigi, The Seagull, Henry IV Part 1, Kill Two Birds, Cactus Flower, A Woman of No Importance, The Boston Story, Lady Frederick, My Fair Lady, Move Over Mrs. Markham, No No Nanette, Dame of Sark, The Chairman, Murder Among Friends, The Seven Year Itch, St. Joan, The Tempest, King Lear, A Man for All Seasons.
PICTURES: Birthday Present, Behind the Mask, Operation Amsterdam, The Heart of a Man, The Rough and the Smooth, The Risk, The Horsemasters, Stork Talk, The Break, There's a Girl in My Soup, Forbush and The Penguins, Sunday Bloody Sunday, Night Watch, The Day of the Jackal.
TELEVISION: The Man Who Understood Women, Ooh La

La, Call My Bluff, The Nearly Man. Friends and Brothers. Series: Melissa, Father Dear Father, Robins Nest, Don't Wait Up.

BROADNAX, DAVID: Producer, Writer, Actor. b. Columbus, GA, Dec. 16.
PICTURES: The Landlord (act.), Come Back Charleston Blue (act.), Sharpies (prod., co-s.p., act.), Zombie Island Massacre (prod., act., original story).
TELEVISION: As the World Turns, Another World, Edge of Night, Love Is a Many Splendored Thing, Search for Tomorrow, Saturday Night Live.

BROCCOLI, ALBERT: Producer. b. New York, NY, April 5, 1909. e. City Coll. of New York. Agriculturist in early years; entered m.p. ind. as asst. director, 20th Century-Fox, 1938. Worked with theatrical agent Charles Feldman 1948–51; producer, Warwick Films 1951–60; prod, Eon Prods., Ltd. since 1961. Thalberg Award, 1982.
PRODUCTIONS: Red Beret (Paratrooper), Hell Below Zero, Black Knight, Prize of Gold, Cockleshell Heroes, Safari, Zarak, April in Portugal, Pickup Alley, Fire Down Below, Arrivederci Roma, Interpol, How to Murder a Rich Uncle, Odongo, High Flight, No Time to Die, The Man Inside, Idle on Parade, Adamson of Africa, Bandit of Zhobe, Jazz Boat, Killers of Killimanjaro, In the Nick, Let's Get Married, The Trials of Oscar Wilde, Johnny Nobody, Carolina, Dr. No, Call Me Bwana, From Russia with Love, Goldfinger, Thunderball, You Only Live Twice, Chitty Chitty Bang Bang, On Her Majesty's Secret Service, Diamonds Are Forever, Live and Let Die, The Man with the Golden Gun, The Spy Who Loved Me, Moonraker, For Your Eyes Only, Octopussy, A View to a Kill, The Living Daylights, Licence to Kill.

BROCKMAN, JOHN J.: Executive. Vice pres. and gen. mgr. Microband Wireless Cable of New York, Inc. b. Sheboygan, WI, July 12, 1946. e. U. of Wisconsin, B.S., 1969; Bowling Green State U., M.S., 1971. Graduate asst., Bowling Green State U., 1969–70. 1972–75: system mgr. for Teltron Cable TV of The Milwaukee Journal Co. 1975–77: gen. mgr. for Lynchburg Cablevision and American Cablevision of Amer. Television & Communications Corp., Englewood, CO. 1977–78: gen. mgr. for Citizens Cable Communications, Inc., Ft. Wayne, IN. 1978–83: mid-east. and mid-central region mgr., Cox Cable Communications, Inc., Norfolk, VA and Ft. Wayne, IN. 1984–86: corp. v.p., corporate operating comm. member, pres. of operating cable co., Adams-Russell Co., Inc., Waltham, MA. 1986: consultant to Arthur D. Little, Inc., Cambridge, MA. 1974–75: co-chmn., technical comm., Wisc. Cable Communications Assn. 1975–76: advisor comm., Cable TV Curriculum, Indiana Vocational and Technical Coll. 1980: annual grad. school alumni lecturer, Today's Operating Communications Media, Bowling Green State U. 1981–82: founding comm. member and moderator for Great Lakes Cable Exposition. 1978–83: v.p. and dir., Illinois-Indiana Cable Assn.

BROCKMAN, MICHAEL: Executive. b. Brooklyn, NY, Nov. 19, 1938. e. Ithaca Coll. Became ABC v.p., daytime programming, ABC Entertainment, 1974; later v.p., tape prod. operations and admin. Left to become v.p., daytime programs, NBC Entertainment, 1977–1980. Became v.p. programs, Lorimar Prods. 1980–82; v.p. daytime and children's prog. CBS Entertainment, 1982–86. Added Late Night to title 1986. Returned to ABC 1989 as pres., daytime, children's & late night entertainment.

BRODERICK, MATTHEW: Actor. b. New York, NY, Aug. 21, 1962. Son of late actor James Broderick and writer-dir. Patricia Broderick. Acted in a workshop prod. of Horton Foote's Valentine's Day with his father (1979). Theatrical film debut in Max Dugan Returns, 1983.
STAGE: Torch Song Trilogy, Brighton Beach Memoirs (Tony Award), Biloxi Blues.
PICTURES: War Games, Ladyhawke, 1918, On Valentine's Day, Ferris Bueller's Day Off, Project X, Biloxi Blues, Torch Song Trilogy, Family Business, Lay This Laurel, The Freshman, Glory.
TELEVISION: Master Harold . . . and the Boys.

BRODKIN, HERBERT: Producer. b. New York, NY, Nov. 9, 1912. e. U. of Mich., B.A.; Yale Drama Sch., M.F.A. (directing and design.) Army major, served as film dir. for Signal Corps, directing 40 films on military subjects, then transferred to Special Services to launch legit. play prog. for U.S.O. and Army, supervising prod. of 300 plays in 2 years. Worked in summer stock and rep. as designer and in Hollywood as scenery designer. Designed Bdwy plays and operas for City Center and Theater Guild. After Army, designed scenery at Buck's County Playhouse and Westport Country Playhouse, also prod. manager and director. Began as scenic designer for CBS. Charlie Wild, Private Detective, first TV show as prod. and designer. Has prod. nearly 600 shows for TV. 1960 formed Titus Productions, Inc., prod. and COO.
PICTURES: Sebastian, The People Next Door.
TELEVISION: Series: ABC Album (1951), The TV Hour, The Motorola TV Hour, Center Stage, The Elgin Hour, The Alcoa Hour, Goodyear Playhouse, Studio One, Playhouse 90 (21 shows, won 2 Emmys), Brenner, The Defenders (1961–65, 3 Emmys and other awards), The Nurses, Espionage, For the People, Coronet Blue, The Doctors and Nurses, Shane. Specials, pilots, movies: The Happeners (pilot), One Eyed Jacks are Wild (pilot), Dear Friends, The People Next Door (3 Emmys), Lights Out (pilot), Crawlspace, RX For the Defense, Pueblo (Golden Hugo Award, Chicago Film Fest., Peabody Award and 5 Emmys), F. Scott Fitzgerald and the Last of the Belles (Silver Phoenix, Atlanta Film Fest.), The Missiles of October (Golden Hugo, Chicago Film Fest), Land of Hope, F. Scott Fitzgerald in Hollywood, The Four of Us, The Deadliest Season, Siege, Holocaust (mini-series, winner of 40 awards, including San Francisco Film Fest, Peabody and 8 Emmys), The Last Tenant, Hollow Image, Death Penalty, Dr. Franken, The Henderson Monster, F.D.R. The Last Year, King Crab, Skokie, My Body, My Child; Benny's Place, The Firm, Ghost Dancing, Sakharov (ACE Awards), Doubletake, Murrow, Welcome Home, Bobby; Johnny Bull, Night of Courage, Mandela, Stones For Ibarra, Internal Affairs.

BRODNEY, OSCAR: Writer, Producer. b. Boston, MA, 1905. e. Boston U., LL.B., 1927; Harvard, LL.M., 1928. Atty., MA Bar, 1928–35.
PICTURES: She Wrote the Book, If You Knew Susie, Are You With It?, For the Love of Mary, Mexican Hayride, Arctic Manhunt, Yes Sir, That's My Baby, Double Crossbones, Gal Who Took the West, South Sea Sinner, Comanche Territory, Harvey; story, Frenchie, Francis Goes to the Races, Little Egypt, Francis Covers the Big Town, Willie and Joe Back at the Front, Scarlet Angel, Francis Goes to West Point, Walking My Baby Back Home, Sign of the Pagan, Glenn Miller Story, Black Shield of Falworth, Captain Lightfoot, The Spoilers, Purple Mask, Lady Godiva, Day of Fury, Star in the Dust, Tammy and the Bachelor, When Hell Broke Loose, Bobkins, Tammy Tell Me True, The Right Approach, All Hands on Deck, Tammy and the Doctor, The Brass Bottle, I'd Rather Be Rich.

BRODSHAUG, MELVIN: Producer. b. Davenport, ND, May 22, 1900. e. North Dakota State U., B.S., 1923; Litt.D. 1958; U. of Chicago, M.A. 1927; Columbia U., Ph.D. 1931. Supt. of Schools, Arnegard, ND 1923–28; research assoc. Erpi Classroom Films 1930; apptd. dir. research Encyclopedia Britannica Films Inc., apptd. vice-pres. 1945, in chg. of product development; apptd. member bd. dir. 1951, Dean of Boston U. Sch. of Public Relations & Communications, 1954–62,dir., Boston U. film library, 1962–65. Prof. and consultant, Norfolk State Coll., VA, 1965–70; independent educational film producer 1970.

BRODSKY, JACK: Producer. b. Brooklyn, NY, July 3, 1932. e. George Washington H.S. Writer for N.Y. Times; joined 20th-Fox publicity in N.Y. in 1956. Left in 1961 to head national ad-pub for Filmways. Joined Rastar Productions to work on Funny Girl; later named v.p. in charge of prod. In 1976 named v.p. in chg. film prod. prom., Rogers & Cowan; 1978, Columbia Pictures v.p., adv., pub., promo.; 1979, named exec. v.p. of Michael Douglas' Big Stick Productions; 1983; joined 20th-Fox as exec. v.p., worldwide adv., pub., exploit. Resigned 1985 to resume career as producer.
PICTURES: Little Murders, Everything You Always Wanted To Know About Sex (exec. prod.), Summer Wishes, Winter Dreams, Jewel of the Nile, Dancers (co-exec. prod., actor).
AUTHOR: The Cleopatra Papers, with Nat Weiss.

BROKAW, NORMAN R.: Executive. b. New York, NY, April 21, 1927. Joined William Morris Agency as trainee, in 1943, junior agent, 1948; sr. agent, company exec. in m.p. and TV, 1951; 1974, v.p., William Morris Agency, World Wide all areas. 1981, named exec. v.p. & mem. of bd., William Morris Agency, worldwide; 1986, named co-chmn. of bd., WMA, worldwide. 1989, named pres. & CEO, William Morris Inc. worldwide. Member Acad. of TV Arts & Sciences, Academy M.P. Arts & Sciences. Member bd. of dir. of Cedars-Sinai Medical Center, Los Angeles; pres., The Betty Ford Cancer Center. Clients include former President and Mrs. Gerald R. Ford, Bill Cosby, Gen. Alexander Haig, Priscilla Presley, and Andy Griffith.

BROKAW, TOM: TV Host, Anchorman. b. Yankton, S.D., Feb. 6, 1940, e. U. of South Dakota. Newscaster, weatherman, staff announcer KTIV, Sioux City, IA, 1960–62. Joined KMTV, NBC affiliate in Omaha, in 1962; 1965, joined WSB-TV, Atlanta. Worked in L.A. bureau of NBC News, anchored local news shows for KNBC, NBC station (1966–73). In 1973 named NBC News' White House correspondent; was anchor of NBC Saturday Night News. Named host of Today show in August, 1976. In 1982 co-anchor, NBC Nightly News. Special: Conversation with Mikhail S. Gorbachev.

BROLIN, JAMES: Actor. b. Los Angeles, CA, July 18, 1940. e. UCLA. Debut in Bus Stop (TV series); named most promising actor of 1970 by Fame and Photoplay magazines.
PICTURES: Take Her She's Mine, Goodbye, Charlie; Von Ryan's Express, Morituri, Our Man Flint, The Boston Stran-

gler, Skyjacked, Westworld, Gable and Lombard, The Car, Capricorn One, The Amityville Horror, The Gringos, Bad Jim, Stainless Steel.
TELEVISION: The Monroes, Marcus Welby, M.D., (Emmy award), Short Walk to Daylight, Class of '63, Hotel, Beverly Hills Cowgirl Blues, Hold the Dream, Intimate Encounters, Deep Dark Secrets, Voice of the Heart, Finish Line.

BROMHEAD, DAVID M.: Executive. b. Teaneck, NJ, Jan. 7, 1960. e. Leighton Park Sch., Reading, England, 1973–78. Overseas sls. exec., Rank Film Dist., 1980; joined New World Pictures, 1984, dir. intl. dist.; named dir., TV dist., 1986.

BRON, ELEANOR: Actress. b. Stanmore, Middlesex, Eng., 1934. Started career in Establishment Club, London, and on American tour. Leading lady on British TV show Not So Much a Programme, More a Way of Life.
PICTURES: Help, Alfie, Two for the Road, Bedazzled, Women in Love, The Millstone, Little Dorrit.
THEATRE: The Doctor's Dilemma, Howard's End, The Prime of Miss Jean Brodie.
TELEVISION: (U.S.) The Day Christ Died; The Attic: The Hiding of Anne Frank, Intrigue, Changing Step.

BRONDFIELD, JEROME: Writer. b. Cleveland, OH, Dec. 9, 1913. e. Ohio State U., 1936. Reporter, ed. on Columbus Dispatch, Associated Press, story ed., script head, RKO Pathe, Oct., 1944; writer, dir. & supvr. of many doc. shorts incl. This Is America series; TV writer; short story writer; collab. s.p., Below the Sahara; s.p. Louisiana Territory; doc. film writer; Author, Woody Hayes, The 100-Yard War, Knute Rockne, The Man and the Legend.

BRONSON, CHARLES: Actor. b. Ehrenfeld, PA, Nov. 3, 1920. r.n. Charles Buchinsky. m. Jill Ireland, actress. Worked as a coal miner. Studied at Pasadena Playhouse.
PICTURES: Red Skies of Montana, Pat and Mike, House of Wax, Drumbeat, Vera Cruz, Jubel, Lonely Are the Brave, Machine Gun Kelly, Never So Few, A Thunder of Drums, The Magnificent Seven, The Great Escape, The Sandpiper, The Battle of the Bulge, Pancho Villa, The Dirty Dozen, This Property Is Condemned, Once Upon a Time in the West, Goodbye, Friend, Rider in the Rain, You Can't Win Em All, Someone Behind the Door, Red Sun, Chato's Land, The Mechanic, The Valachi Papers, The Stone Killer, Mr. Majestyk, Death Wish, Breakout, Hard Times, Breakheart Pass, From Noon Till Three, St. Ives, The White Buffalo, Telefon, Borderline, Caboblanco, Death Hunt, Death Wish II, The Evil That Men Do, Death Wish 3, Murphy's Law, Assassination, Death Wish IV, Kinjite.
TELEVISION: Star of own series Meet McGraw, Man With a Camera, Travels of Jamie McPheeters. Guest on Philco Playhouse (Adventure in Java), Medic, A Bell for Adano, Gunsmoke, Have Gun Will Travel, The FBI, The Fugitive, The Virginian. Movies: Act of Vengeance, Raid on Entebbe.

BRONSTON, SAMUEL: Producer. b. Bessarabia, Russia, March 26, 1908. e. Sorbonne, Paris. Film distributor, Paris; prod. exec. Columbia Studios, Hollywood; Martin Eden, City Without Men, Producer, Columbia Pictures; resigned to form Samuel Bronston Pict., Inc.; exec. prod. Jack London, A Walk in the Sun. color documentaries produced first time in Vatican; prod. John Paul Jones 1959; Received U.S. Navy Meritorious Pub. Serv. Citation; pres. Samuel Bronston Productions; 1960 prod. King of Kings, El Cid; 1962, 55 Days at Peking; 1963. The Fall of the Roman Empire; prod. Circus World, 1964, Condor Award, Society for Pan American Culture—for El Cid, 1962 (award shared with Stanford U.), The Hollywood Foreign Press Association Golden Globe for the achievement of his outstanding production of El Cid, 1962, Italian Order of Merit with Medal of Commendatore. Grand Cross of Merit by the Equestrian Order of the Knights of the Holy Sepulchre (the highest honor of the Catholic Church), the Encomienda of the Order of the Great Cross of Isabel la Catolica. President Samuel Bronston Studios, Madrid, Spain.

BROOK, PETER: Director. b. London, England, March 21, 1925. e. Magdalen Coll., Oxford. Gained fame as stage director before doing films. (Man and Superman, Marat/Sade, A Midsummer Night's Dream, etc.)
PICTURES: The Beggar's Opera, Moderato Cantabile, Lord of the Flies, Marat/Sade, Tell Me Lies, King Lear, Meetings with Remarkable Men, The Tragedy of Carmen, The Mahabharata.

BROOKE, PETER R.: Writer. b. Berlin, Germany, April 12, 1929. e. Germany, Switzerland, England. With Warner Bros., 1944–46, mail room, pub. dept., then asst. casting dir.; contract writer, Robert Riskin Prod., Paramount; then free lance; radio writer many shows; TV writer for Teevee Prod., Celebrity Playhouse, Science Fiction Theatre; staff writer, Universal Pictures; left Universal to join Excelsior under new banner of Warbrook Inc. as writer-producer.
PICTURES: Basketball Fix, Sweet Violence orig., Outside the Law.
TELEVISION: Sea Hunt, 77 Sunset Strip, Sugar Foot, The Fugitive, Six Million Dollar Man.

BROOKS, ALBERT: Director, Writer, Actor. r.n. Einstein. b. Los Angeles, CA, July 22, 1947. e. Carnegie Tech. Son of late comedian Harry Einstein (Parkyakarkus); brother, Bob Einstein. Sports writer KMPC, L.A. 1962–63. Recordings: Comedy Minus One, A Star is Bought (Grammy nom.).
PICTURES: Taxi Driver (act. only); Real Life (dir., s.p., actor); Private Benjamin (act. only); Modern Romance (dir., s.p., actor); Twilight Zone—The Movie (act. only); Unfaithfully Yours (act. only); Lost in America; Broadcast News (actor).
TELEVISION: Gold-diggers of 1969 (actor); Hot Wheels (voices). Specials: Milton Berle's Mad Mad Mad World of Comedy, General Electric's All-Star Anniversary, Saturday Night Live (prod., dir., short films 1975–76). The Associates (theme song).

BROOKS, DICK: Executive, b. New York, NY. e. U. of Georgia. Reporter, Atlanta (GA) Journal; sports ed. Gainesville Times; correspondent, Pacific Stars & Stripes; entered m.p. industry as staff writer, 20th Century-Fox pub. dept; nat'l pub. dir, Seven Arts Productions, Paramount pub. mgr.; nat'l pub. dir. 20th Century-Fox; adv-pub. dir, Rastar Prods; Warner Bros. pub. dir; formed Dick Brooks Unlimited, Beverly Hills entertainment p.r. company 1980. Formed Bay Entertainment, prod. company, 1988.

BROOKS, JAMES L.: Director, Producer, Writer. b. North Bergen, NJ, May 9, 1940. e. NYU. Copyboy for CBS News, N.Y.; promoted to newswriter. 1965 moved to L.A. to work for David Wolper's documentary prod. co. 1969 conceived idea for series, Room 222; formed partnership with fellow writer Allan Burns. Together they created Mary Tyler Moore Show in 1970. 1977, established prod. co. on Paramount lot with other writers, producing and creating the series, The Associates and Taxi.
PICTURES: Modern Romance (actor only); Starting Over (s.p., co-prod.); Terms of Endearment (dir., prod., s.p.) (Academy Award, best film, dir., s.p., 1984); Broadcast News (dir., prod., s.p.); Big (co-prod.); Say Anything (exec. prod.), The War of the Roses (prod.).
TELEVISION: Thursday's Game (writer, prod., 1971); Rhoda (writer, prod.); The New Lorenzo Music Show, 1976 (writer); Lou Grant, 1977 (co-exec. prod.); Co-creator, and/or exec. prod: Taxi, Cindy, The Associates, Cheers, Tracey Ullman Show.

BROOKS, JOSEPH: Producer, Director, Writer, Composer, Conductor. Well-known for composing music for TV commercials before turning to producing, directing, writing and scoring theatrical feature, You Light Up My Life, in 1977. Winner of 21 Clio Awards (made by adv. industry); created music for 100 commercials. Has also composed for theatrical films.
PICTURES: Scores: The Garden of the Finzi-Continis, Marjoe, Jeremy, The Lords of Flatbush. Produced, directed, wrote, and composed, arranged and conducted music for You Light Up My Life. Produced, directed, wrote starred in and composed music for If Ever I See You Again.

BROOKS, MEL: Writer, Director, Actor. b. Brooklyn, NY, June 28, 1926. r.n. Kaminsky. m. actress Anne Bancroft. e. VA Military Inst. 1944. U.S. Army combat engineer 1944–46. As child did impressions and was amateur drummer and pianist. First appearance as actor in Golden Boy in Red Bank, NJ. Was also director and social dir. of Grossingers in the Catskills. Became writer for Sid Caesar on TV's Broadway Review and Your Show of Shows, writing for latter for decade. Teamed with Carl Reiner for comedy record album, 2000 Year Old Man and The 2000 and 13 Year Old Man. Founded Brooksfilms Ltd., 1980.
PICTURES: The Critic (short, dir., s.p., narrator, Acad Award, 1964), The Producers (Acad. Award, s.p.), The Twelve Chairs, Blazing Saddles, Young Frankenstein, Silent Movie, High Anxiety (prod., dir., s.p.). History of the World—Part 1 (prod., dir., s.p., actor, composer), To Be or Not To Be (prod., actor), Spaceballs (prod., dir., co-s.p., actor).
PICTURES AS EXEC. PROD.: The Elephant Man, The Doctor and the Devils, The Fly, 84 Charing Cross Road, Solarbabies.
TELEVISION: Get Smart (co-creator, writer), When Things Were Rotten (creator, prod.), The Nutt House (prod.).
STAGE: New Faces of 1952 (sketches), Shinbone Alley (book), All-American (book for musical).

BROOKS, RICHARD: Writer, Director. b. Philadelphia, PA, May 18, 1912. e. Temple U. Radio writer, narrator and commentator, NBC. Author of several short stories. Novels, Brick Fox Hole, Boiling Point, The Producer.
PICTURES: Swell Guy, Brute Force, To the Victor, Crossfire, Key Largo, Mystery Street, Storm Warning, Deadline U.S.A., Battle Circus, Take the High Ground, Flame and the Flesh, Last Time I Saw Paris, Blackboard Jungle, Last Hunt, Catered Affair, Something of Value, The Brothers Karamazov, Cat on a Hot Tin Roof, Elmer Gantry (Acad. Award s.p. 1961), Sweet Bird of Youth, Lord Jim, The Professionals, In Cold

Blood, The Happy Ending, Dollars, Bite the Bullet, Looking for Mr. Goodbar, Wrong Is Right (also prod.), Fever Pitch (also prod.), Saxo (actor only), Shocker (actor only).

BROSNAN, PIERCE: Actor. b. Ireland, May 16, 1953. Left County Meath, Ireland for London at 11. Worked as commercial illustrator, then joined experimental theater workshop and studied at the Drama Center. On London stage (Wait Until Dark, The Red Devil Battery Sign, etc.)
PICTURES: The Mirror Crack'd, The Long Good Friday, Nomads, The Fourth Protocol, The Deceivers, Taffin.
TELEVISION: Remington Steele (series), Murphy's Stroke, The Manions of America, Nancy Astor, Noble House, Around the World in 80 Days, The Heist.

BROUGH, WALTER: Producer, Writer. b. Phila. PA, Dec. 19, 1935. e. La Salle U., UCLA. Began career with Stage Society Theatre, LA. Currently CEO, Orb Enterprises.
PICTURES: Gabriella, A New Life, No Place to Hide, Run Wild, Run Free, The Desperadoes, Funeral for an Assassin (also prod.), On a Dead Man's Chest (also prod.), Jed and Sonny (also prod.).
TELEVISION: Doctor Kildare The Fugitive, Branded, Name of the Game, Mannix, Mission Impossible, The Magician, Man From Atlantis, Lucas, Police Story, Wildside, Heart of the City (also prod.), Spencer for Hire (also co-prod.), Law & Harry McGraw, New Mission Impossible (also co-prod.).

BROUGHTON, BRUCE: Composer. b. Los Angeles, CA , March 8, 1945. e. U. of Southern California, B.M., 1967. Music supvr., CBS-TV, 1967–77. Since then has been freelance composer for TV and films. Member: Academy of TV Arts & Sciences; Society of Composers & Lyricists, Academy of Motion Picture Arts & Sciences. Nominated 11 times for Emmy; won in 1981 for Buck Rogers, in 1983 for Dallas and in 1984 for Dallas and The First Olympics. Nom. in 1986 for Oscar for Silverado and Grammy for Young Sherlock Holmes.
PICTURES: The Prodigal, The Ice Pirates, Silverado, Young Sherlock Holmes, Sweet Liberty, The Boy Who Could Fly, Square Dance, Harry and the Hendersons, Monster Squad, Big Shots, Cross My Heart, The Rescue, The Presidio, Last Rites, Moonwalker, Jacknife.
TELEVISION: Series: Hawaii Five-0, Gunsmoke, Quincy, How the West Was Won, Logan's Run, The Oregon Trail, Buck Rogers, Dallas. Movies: The Paradise Connection, Desperate Voyage, The Return of Frank Cannon, Desperate Lives, Killjoy, One Shoe Makes It Murder, The Master of Ballantrae, MADD, The Candy Lightner Story, Cowboy, A Thanksgiving Promise. Mini-Series: The Blue and the Gray, The First Olympics–Athens: 1896, George Washington II.

BROUMAS, JOHN G.: Executive. b. Youngstown, OH, Oct. 12, 1917. e. Youngstown. Usher, Altoona Publix Theatres, 1933, usher to asst. mgr., Warner Thea. 1934–39; mgr. Grand 1939–40; mgr. Orpheum 1940–41. W.W.II active, Officer Chemical Corps, past commander 453rd Chem. Grp. (Reserve); Life member Reserve Officers Assoc.; Gen. mgr. Pitts & Roth Theatres 1946–54; President, Broumas Theatres; V.P. NATO, 1969; bd. of dir. of NATO of Va., Md., D.C.; pres., Broumas Theatre Service 1954–82; bd. chmn., Showcase Theatres 1965–82; mem. bd., Foundation of Religious Action (FRASCO). Mem. Nat'l Immigration Comm. Founder of John G. Broumas Scholarship for Drama at Youngstown State Univ.; past pres. & bd. chmn. Maryland Theatre Owners; v.p. & bd. of dir.—Virginia Theatre Owners bd. of dir. NATO of D.C.; pres. B.C. Theatres; Sponsor of Andre G. Broumas Memorial Award—West Point; sponsor, Broumas Scholastic and Athletic Scholarship for AHEPA Wash. D.C. area; director, McLean Bank McLean, Va. 1972–86; honorary mem., West Point Class 1954; Past dir. and mem. Motion Picture Pioneers; Advisory Council: Will Rogers Memorial Hospital; Washington, D.C. Variety Club, Tent #11, bd. of gov. 1959, 1st asst. chief. barker, 1964 & 71, Chief barker 1965-66, 1972, and 1978-79, and bd. chmn., 1980; Life Patron, Variety Clubs Int'l, 1978 Life Liner, Variety Clubs Intl.; AHEPA Humanitarian Award, 1981; Dept. of Army, Patriotic Civilian Service Medal, 1982; WOMPI "good guy" award, 1974; Gold Medal for distinguished service to m.p. industry, 1978; bd. chmn., Tantallon Country Club, Oxon Hill, MD.; Chm. bd., McLean Bank; 1983–86; chmn. bd & pres. Madison Natl. Bank of VA. 1986–present; chmn. exec. comm., Mad. Natl. Bank of VA; dir. James Madison LT. Wash. D.C. 1987: order of St. Andrew; 1988 Bd. trustee, Leukemia Soc. of Amer.; 1989 bd. dir. Natl. Fdn. Coll., Football Hall of Fame (appreciation award Wash., D.C. 1989).

BROWN, BLAIR: Actress. b. Washington, DC, 1948. e. National Theatre Sch. of Canada.
THEATER: The Threepenny Opera (NY Shakespeare Fest), Comedy of Errors. Acted with Old Globe, San Diego, Stratford, Ont. Shakespeare Fest., Guthrie Theatre MN, Arena Stage, Wash.
PICTURES: Paper Chase, The Choirboys, One-Trick Pony, Altered States, Continental Divide, Flash of Green. Stealing Home, Strapless.
TELEVISION: Series: The Days and Nights of Molly Dodd. Mini-series: Captains and the Kings, James Michener's Space, Arthur Hailey's Wheels. Movies: The 3,000 Mile Chase, The Quinns, Eleanor and Franklin: The White House Years, And I Alone Survived, The Child Stealer, The Bad Seed, Kennedy, Hands of a Stranger. Specials: School for Scandal, The Skin of Your Teeth.

BROWN, BRYAN: Actor. b. Australia, June 23, 1947. Began acting professionally in Sydney. Worked in repertory theatres in England with the National Theatre of Great Britain. Returned to Australia to work in films while continuing stage work with Theatre Australia. Theatrical film debut, Love Letters from Teralba Road, 1977.
PICTURES: The Irishman, Weekend of Shadows, Newsfront, Third Person Plural, Money Movers, Palm Beach, Cathy's Child, The Odd Angry Shot, Breaker Morant, Blood Money, Stir, Winter of Our Dreams, Far East, F/X, Tai-Pan, The Good Wife, Cocktail, Gorillas in the Mist, Shall We Dance, Confidence (also prod.), Blood Oath.
TELEVISION: Mini-series: Against the Wind, A Town Like Alice, The Thorn Birds. Movie: The Shiralee (Aust.).

BROWN, DAVID: Executive, Producer. b. New York, NY, July 28, 1916. m. writer-editor Helen Gurley Brown. e. Stanford U., A.B., 1936; Columbia U. Sch. of Journalism, M.S., 1937. Apprentice reporter, copy-editing, San Francisco News & Wall Street Journal, 1936; night ed. asst. drama critic, Fairchild Publications, N.Y., 1937–39; edit. dir. Milk Research Council, N.Y., 1939–40; assoc. ed., Street & Smith Publ., N.Y., 1940–43; assoc. ed., exec. ed., then ed.-in-chief, Liberty Mag., N.Y., 1943–49; edit. dir., nat'l education campaign, Amer. Medical Assn., 1949; assoc. ed., man. ed., Cosmopolitan Mag., N.Y., 1949–52; contrib. stories & articles to many nat'l mags.; man. ed., story dept., 20th-Fox, L.A., Jan., 1952; story ed. & head of scenario dept., May, 1953–56; appt'd. member of exec. staff of Darryl F. Zanuck, 1956; mem. of exec. staff, 20th-Fox studios, and exec. studio story editor, 1956–1960; Prod. 20th-Fox Studios, Sept. 1960–62; Editorial v.p. New American Library of World Literature, Inc., 1963–64; exec. story opers., 20th Century-Fox, 1964–67; vp. dir. of story operations, 1967; exec. v.p., creative operations and mem. bd. of dir., 1969–71. Exec. v.p., mem. bd. of directors Warner Bros., 1971–1972; partner and director, The Zanuck/Brown Co., 1972–1988. Pres., Manhattan Project Ltd., 1988–; mem., bd. of trustees, American Film Institute, 1972–80.
PICTURES: The Sugarland Express, The Black Windmill, Sssssss, The Eiger Sanction, The Sting, MacArthur, Jaws, Jaws 2, Willie Dynamite, The Girl from Petrovka, The Island, Neighbors, The Verdict, Cocoon, Target, Cocoon: The Return, Driving Miss Daisy.

BROWN, GEORG SANFORD: Actor, Director. b. Havana, Cuba, June 24, 1943. m. actress Tyne Daly. Acted on stage with the New York Shakespeare Fest., NY, in the 1960s. Gained fame as one of the rookie cops in the 1970s TV series The Rookies before turning to TV directing.
THEATER: All's Well That Ends Well; Measure for Measure; Macbeth; Murderous Angels; Hamlet; Detective Story.
PICTURES: The Comedians; Dayton's Devils; Bullitt; Colossus; The Forbin Project; The Man; God Bless You, Uncle Sam.
TELEVISION: The Rookies (series); Barefoot in Athens; The Young Lawyers; Next Time, My Love; Dawn: Portrait of a Teenage Runaway; Roots; Roots: The Next Generations; The Night the City Screamed; Grambling's White Tiger (dir.); The Greatest American Hero (dir.); Cagney and Lacey (dir. Emmy, best dir., 1986); The Kid With the Broken Halo; In Defense of Kids; The Jesse Owens Story. Dir. of episodes: Charlie's Angels; Starsky and Hutch; Dynasty; Hill Street Blues.

BROWN, HAROLD: Executive. Pres., International Picture Show Co. since Dec., 1980. Previously pres., American International TV; v.p. & bd. mbr., American International Pictures (now Filmways).

BROWN, HENRY: Executive. b. New York, NY, Feb. 18, 1899. e. City Coll. of New York, 1920; Columbia U. 1923. Pres., Lakewood Amusement Corp.; pres., Atlas TV Corp.; pres. Capt. Zero Prods., Inc.

BROWN, HIMAN: M.P. Producer, Director, b. New York, NY, July 21, 1910. e. City Coll. of New York, St. Lawrence U. Radio & TV package prod. since 1927 include: Inner Sanctum, Thin Man, Bulldog Drummond, Dick Tracy, Terry and the Pirates, Joyce Jordan MD, Grand Central Station, CBS Radio Mystery Theatre, pres. Production Center, Inc.
PICTURES: That Night, Violators, The Stars Salute, The Price of Silence, The Road Ahead.

BROWN, HOWARD C.: Executive. b. Newport, NH, Aug. 15, 1901. e. Boston U. Assoc. with Technicolor Motion Picture Corp., Before org. Colorart Pictures, 1926. Merged with Synchrotone Pictures & Kennedy Pictures, 1929, forming Colorart Synchrotone Corp. In 1930 org. Brown-Nagel Productions. Since 1933 has produced numerous shorts. Sales mgr., Cinecolor, 1936–37; pres. Howard C. Brown Co. 1937–1938. Sales mgr., Trimble Laboratories, Inc. 1947; formed

Howard C. Brown Productions 1948, to release for United Artists. Prod. Kangaroo Kid; prod. Mating Urge, inter-nations, documentary; 1969, Film Exporter.

BROWN, JIM: Actor. b. St. Simons Island, GA, Feb. 17, 1936. e. Manhasset H.S., Syracuse U. For nine years played football with Cleveland Browns; in 1964 won Hickock Belt as Professional Athlete of the year; founder, Black Economic Union.
PICTURES: Rio Conchos, The Dirty Dozen, Ice Station Zebra, The Split, Riot, Dark Of The Sun, 100 Rifles, Kenner, Tick . . . Tick . . . Tick, The Grasshopper, Slaughter, Slaughter's Big Rip-Off, I Escaped from Devil's Island, The Slams, Three the Hard Way, Take a Hard Ride, The Running Man, L.A. Heat, Rock House.

BROWN, WILLIAM: Executive. b. Ayr, Scotland, June 24, 1929. e. Ayr Acad., U. of Edinburgh, where graduated Bachelor of Commerce, 1950. Served to Lieutenant, Royal Artillery, 1950–52. Sales mgr. for Scotland Television Ltd. in London, 1958 to 1961, sales dir. 1961 to 1963. Deputy mng. dir. of Scottish Television Ltd. at Glasgow 1963–66, mng. dir. in 1966. Deputy chmn. and mng.-dir. of STV from 1974. Director, independent TV Publications, London, 1968. On bd. of dir. for Scottish National Orchestra, 1973. Member of Independent TV Companies Association, and chmn. of same 1978–80. Holds C.B.E. honor from British royalty.

BROWN, WILLIAM H., JR.: Director, concert mgr., Juilliard Sch. of Music, 1946; TV prod., Young and Rubicam, 1948; dir., Life with Father, Climax, CBS-TV, 1954, Studio One 1955; prod. Paramount Television, 1958; Exec. prod., Shirley Temple Show, NBC, 1960; TV prod., Norman, Craig and Kummel, 1962; Compton, 1963; Post-Keyes-Gardner, 1965; Freelance, 1967.

BROWN, WILLET HENRY: Executive. Assist. gen. mgr., Don Lee, Inc., 1932–33; exec. v.p. Don Lee Broadcasting System, Hollywood, 1933–48; Pres., Thomas S. Lee Enterprises, 1947–50; v.p., dir. Don Lee Broadcasting System, div. RKO Teleradio Pictures, Inc. 1950–58; pres. Don Lee Broadcasting System, 1949–58; consultant, R.K.O. General Inc.; pres. Don Lee, Inc; pres. Laurie Leasing Corp.; pres. Pacific States Invest. Corp.; 1948, pres. Don Lee Motor Corp., pres. Hillcrest Motor Company: Operating: KXOA-AM 1978–; & KXOA- FM 1970, Sacramento, CA and KKSF-FM, San Francisco, CA. 1987–; Owner-Pres., KGB Inc, KGB-AM and KGB-FM, San Diego, CA, 1962; sr. partner, Brown Bdcstng. Co., operating KYNO FM & AM, Fresno, CA, 1984–; And KKAT-FM, Salt Lake City, UT 1985–; sr. partner, Keys Mountain Co., 1987–; Holder of TV patent.

BROWNE, CORAL: Actress. b. Melbourne, Australia, July 23, 1913. Wife of actor Vincent Price. Theatre includes Mated, The Golden Gander, Death Asks a Verdict, The Man Who Came to Dinner, The Rehearsal, Lady Windermere's Fan, What the Butler Saw, The Waltz of the Toreadors, etc.
PICTURES: The Amateur Gentlemen, Pygmalion, The Prime Minister, Quartet, Madeleine, All at Sea, Rooney, The Ruling Class, The Killing of Sister George, The Drowning Pool, American Dreamer, Dreamchild.
TELEVISION: Eleanor: First Lady of the World, Time Express, An Englishman Abroad.

BROWNE, ROSCOE LEE: Actor, Director, Writer. b. Woodbury, NJ, 1925. e. Lincoln U., PA; postgraduate studies in comparative literature and French at Middlebury Coll., VT, Columbia U., N.Y. Taught French and lit. at Lincoln U. until 1952. National sales rep. for Schenley Import Corp. 1946–56; United States' intl. track star and a member of ten A.A.U. teams. Twice American champion in the 1000-yard indoor competition, twice all-American and, in 1951 in Paris, ran the fastest 800 meters in the world for that year. Professional acting debut, 1956, in Julius Caesar at the NY Shakespeare Fest.; published poet and short story writer. Trustee: Millay Colony Arts, NY; Los Angeles Free Public Theatre.
NY STAGE: The Ballad of the Sad Cafe, The Cool World, General Seeger, Tiger, Tiger Burning Bright!, The Old Glory A Hand Is on the Gate (dir., actor), My One and Only, Off-Broadway—The Connection, The Blacks, Aria da Capo, Benito Cereno (Obie Award), Joe Turner's Come and Gone (L.A.).
PICTURES: The Comedians, Uptight, The Liberation of L. B. Jones, The Cowboys, World's Greatest Athlete, The Big Ripoff, Superfly T.N.T., Topaz, Uptown Saturday Night, Logan's Run, Twilight's Last Gleaming, The Fifth Door, Legal Eagles, Oliver & Company.
TELEVISION: Space, King, Dr. Scorpion.

BROWNING, KIRK: TV Director; b. New York, NY, March 28, 1921. e. Brooks School, Andover, MA, Avon Old Farms, Avon, CT., and Cornell U. 1940, reporter for News-Tribune in Waco, TX; with American Field Service, 1942–45; adv. copywriter for Franklin Spier, 1945–48; became floor mgr. NBC-TV 1949; app't asst. dir. NBC-TV Opera Theatre in 1951 directing NBC Opera Theatre, TV Recital Hall, and Toscanini Simulcasts.
TELEVISION: Trial of Mary Lincoln; Jascha Heifetz Special; Harry and Lena; NBC Opera Theatre; Producers Showcase; Evening with Toscanini; Bell Telephone; The Flood; Beauty and the Beast; Lizzie Borden; World of Carl Sandburg; La Gioconda (Emmy, 1980); Big Blonde; Working; Ian McKellan Acting Shakespeare; Fifth of July; Alice in Wonderland; Live From the Met—Centennial.

BROWNLOW, KEVIN: Film historian, Writer, Director, Film Editor. b. Crowborough, Eng., June 2, 1938. e. University College Sch. Asst. ed./editor, World Wide Pictures, London, 1955–61; film editor, Samaritan Films, 1961–65; film editor, Woodfall Films, 1965–68. Director Thames Television 1980–present.
BOOKS: How It Happened Here (1968); The Parade's Gone By...; Adventures with D.W. Griffith (editor); The War, the West and the Wilderness (1979); Hollywood: The Pioneers (1980); Napoleon: Abel Gance's Classic Film (1983).
PICTURES: It Happened Here (dir. with Andrew Mollo) 1964; Charge of the Light Brigade (editor); Winstanley (with Andrew Mollo); Napoleon (restoration of 1927 film, re-released 1980).
TELEVISION: All with David Gill: Hollywood (dir., s.p.); Unknown Chaplin (dir.), Buster Keaton: A Hard Act to Follow. Movie: Charm of Dynamite (dir., ed.).

BRUBAKER, JAMES D.: Producer. b. Hollywood, CA, March 30, 1937. e. Eagle Rock H.S. Transportation coordinator 15 years before becoming unit prod. mgr., 1978–84. Then assoc. prod., exec. prod. & prod.
PICTURES: Assoc. Prod.: True Confessions, Rocky III, Rhinestone. Exec. Prod.: The Right Stuff, Beer, Rocky IV, Cobra, Over the Top. Prod.: Rambo III. Prod. mgr.: K-9.

BRUCE, BRENDA: Actress. b. Manchester, England, 1922. e. privately. London stage debut, 1066 And All That; On screen 1944; Millions Like Us; TV Best Actress Award 1962.
PICTURES: Night Boat to Dublin, I See a Dark Stranger, They Came to a City, Carnival, Piccadilly Incident, While the Sun Shines, When the Bough Breaks, My Brother's Keeper, Don't Ever Leave Me, The Final Test, Law and Disorder, Behind the Mask, Peeping Tom, Nightmare, The Uncle.
BROADWAY: Gently Does It (1953), This Year Next Year, Happy Days, Woman in a Dressing Gown, Victor Eh!, Merry Wives of Windsor, The Revenger's Tragedy, Little Murders, Winter's Tale, Pericles, Twelfth Night, Hamlet.
TELEVISION: Mary Britton series, Nearer to Heaven, Wrong Side of the Park, The Lodger, The Monkey and the Mohawk, Love Story, A Piece of Resistance, Give the Clown His Supper, Knock on Any Door, The Browning Version, Death of a Teddy Bear, Softly, Softly, The Girl, Happy, Family at War, Budgie.

BRUCKHEIMER, JERRY: Producer. b. Detroit, MI. e. U. of Arizona. Was adv. agency exec. in TV commercials before becoming producer of films. 1983, formed Don Simpson/Jerry Bruckheimer Prods. with Don Simpson and entered into deal with Paramount Pictures to produce.
PICTURES: Assoc. Prod.: Culpepper Cattle Company, Rafferty and the Gold Dust Twins. Producer: Farewell My Lovely, March or Die, Defiance, American Gigolo, Thief, Cat People (exec. prod.), Young Doctors in Love, Flashdance, Thief of Hearts, Beverly Hills Cop, Top Gun, Beverly Hills Cop II, Daytona.

BRUNING, RICHARD R.: Executive. b. Kansas City, MO. e. Yale U., Harvard Business Sch. Asst. treas. Transamerica Corp., parent corp. of United Artists, from 1972. In 1979 named treas. of UA. 1980, named v.p. and treas. of UA Corp.

BRYAN, DORA: Actress. b. Southport, Lancashire, Eng., Feb. 7, 1924. e. Council Sch. Stage debut 1935. Screen debut The Fallen Idol, 1948.
PICTURES: No Room at the Inn, Once Upon a Dream, Blue Lamp, Cure for Love, Now Barabas, The Ringer, Women of Twilight, The Quiet Woman, The Intruder, You Know What Sailors Are, Mad About Men, See How They Run, Cockleshell Heroes, Child in the House, Green Man, Carry on Sergeant, Operation Bullshine, Desert Mice, The Night We Got the Bird, A Taste of Honey, Two a Penny, Apartment Zero.
TELEVISION: According to Dora (1968), Both Ends Meet.

BRYON, KATHLEEN: Actress. b. London, England, Jan. 11, 1922. e. London U., Old Vic. co. student, 1942. Screen debut in Young Mr. Pitt, 1943.
PICTURES: Silver Fleet, Black Narcissus, Matter of Life and Death, Small Back Room, Madness of the Heart, Reluctant Widow, Prelude to Fame, Scarlet Thread, Tom Brown's Schooldays, Four Days, Hell Is Sold Out, I'll Never Forget You, Gambler and the Lady, Young Bess, Night of the Silvery Moon, Profile, Secret Venture, Hand in Hand, Night of the Eagle, Hammerhead, Wolfshead, Private Road, Twins of Evil, Craze, Abdication, One of Our Dinosaurs Is Missing, The Elephant Man, From a Far Country.
TELEVISION: The Lonely World of Harry Braintree, All My Own Work, Emergency Ward 10, Probation Officer, Design for Murder, Sergeant Cork, Oxbridge 2000, The Navigators, The Worker; Hereward the Wake, Breaking Point, Vendetta, Play

To Win, Who Is Sylvia, Portrait of a Lady, Callan, You're Wrecking My Marriage, Take Three Girls, The Confession of Mariona Evans, Paul Temple, The Worker, The Moonstone, The Challengers, The Golden Bowl, The Edwardians, The New Life, Menace, The Rivals of Sherlock Holmes, The Brontes, On Call, Edward VII, Sutherland's Law, Crown Court, Anne of Avonlea, Heidi, Notorious Woman, General Hospital, North & South, Angelo, Within these Walls, Jubilee, Z Cars, Tales from the Supernatural, Secret Army, An Englishman's Castle, The Professionals, Forty Weeks, Emmerdale Farm, Blake Seven, The Minders, Together, Hedda Gabler, Nancy Astor, God Speed Co-operation, Take Three Women, Reilly.

BUCHHOLZ, HORST: Actor. b. Berlin, Germany, Dec. 4, 1933. e. high school. In radio and stage plays. Film debut. Marianne (French), 1955.
PICTURES: Himmel Ohne Sterne (No Star in the Sky), Robinson Must Not Die, Mon Petit, The Confessions of Felix Krull, Tiger Bay, Fanny, One, Two, Three, Nine Hours to Rama, The Empty Canvas, The Great Waltz, Cervantes, Sahara, Code Name: Emerald, And the Violins Stopped Playing.
TELEVISION: Raid on Entebbe, Crossings.

BUCK, JULES: Producer. b. St. Louis, MO, July 30, 1917. Asst. to prod., The Killers; assoc. prod., Brute Force, Naked City, We Were Strangers; prod., Love Nest, Fixed Bayonets, Treasure of the Golden Condor, O.S.S., TV series; prod., The Day They Robbed the Bank of England, Great Catherine; formed Keep Films with Peter O'Toole. Co-prod., Under Milkwood. Prod., The Ruling Class. Exec. Prod., Man Friday. Prod., The Great Scout and Cathouse Thursday.
TELEVISION: (U.S.) Berlin Tunnel, The French Atlantic Affair, Raid on Entebbe, The Savage Bees.

BUCKLEY, BETTY: Actress. b. Fort Worth, TX, July 3, 1947. e. Texas Christian U., BA. Studied acting with Stella Adler. NY Stage debut: 1776 (1969); London debut: Promises Promises. Made film debut as the gym teacher in Carrie (1976) and starred as the mother in the Bdwy musical Carrie (1988).
THEATER: Johnny Pott, What's a Nice Country Like You Doing in a State Like This?, Pippin, I'm Getting My Act Together and Taking It on the Road, Cats (Tony Award, supp. actress, 1983), The Mystery of Edwin Drood, Carrie.
PICTURES: Carrie, Tender Mercies, Frantic, Another Woman.
TELEVISION: Series: Eight is Enough (1977–81); Movies: The Devil's Work, The Ordeal of Bill Carney, Bobby and Sarah, Salute to Lady Liberty, The Three Wishes of Billy Grier, Evergreen, Babycakes.

BUCKLEY, DONALD: Executive. b. New York, NY, June 28, 1955. e. C.W. Post Coll, NY, Sch. of Visual Arts. Ad. mgr., United Artists Theatres, 1975–78; acct. exec., Grey Advertising, 1978–80. Joined Warner Bros. in 1980 as NY adv. mgr.; 1986, promoted to east. dir. of adv./promo. for WB; 1988, named eastern dir. of adv. and publicity.

BUCKNER, ROBERT H.: Producer, Writer. b. Crewe, VA, May 28, 1906. e. U. of Virginia., U. of Edinburgh, Scotland. Newspaper corresp. New York World. 1926–27 in England: instructor, Belgian Mil. Acad. 1927–28: with Alfred A. Knopf, Inc., Doubleday, Doran, N.Y., pub., 1928–33; corresp. in Russia, Scandinavia, 1933–35; contrib. fiction, Amer. & Brit. mags., 1926–36. Author & collab. many s.p. A Champion of Champion Producer in Fame ratings.
PICTURES: Gold Is Where You Find It, Jezebel, Dodge City, Virginia City, Knute Rockne, Santa Fe Trial, Dive Bomber, Yankee Doodle Dandy, Desert Song. Gentleman Jim (prod.), Mission to Moscow, Desert Song, The Gang's All Here, Cheyenne, Life with Father. Rogue's Regiment (prod.), Sword in the Desert, Free For All, Deported, Bright Victory, The Man Behind the Gun, Safari.

BUJOLD, GENEVIEVE: Actress. b. Montreal, Canada, July 1, 1942. e. Montreal Conservatory of Drama. Worked in a Montreal cinema as an usher; American TV debut: St. Joan.
STAGE: The Barber of Seville, A Midsummer Night's Dream, A House . . . A Day.
PICTURES: La Guerre est Finie, La Fleur de L'Age, Entre La Mer et L'eau Douce, Final Assignment, King of Hearts, The Thief, Isabel, Anne of the Thousand Days, The Act of the Heart, The Journey, Earthquake, Alex and the Gypsy, Kamouraska, Obsession, Swashbuckler, Another Man, Another Chance, Coma, Murder by Decree, The Last Flight of Noah's Ark, Monsignore, Tightrope, Choose Me, Trouble in Mind, The Suspect, The Moderns, Dead Ringers, Secret Places of the Heart.
TELEVISION: Antony and Cleopatra, Mistress of Paradise, Red Earth, White Earth.

BURKE, ALFRED, Actor. b. London, England, 1918. Ent. films 1954.
PICTURES: The Angry Silence, Moment of Danger, The Man Inside, The Man Upstairs, No Time To Die, Law and Disorder, Yangtse Incident, Interpol, Bitter Victory.
TELEVISION: The Crucible, Mock Auction, Parole, No Gun, No Guilt, The Big Knife, Parnell, The Strong Are Lonely, Home of the Brave, The Birthday Party, The Watching Eye, Public Eye series.

BURKE, PAUL: Actor. b. New Orleans, LA, July 21, 1926. e. prep schools, New Orleans, Pasadena Playhouse.
TELEVISION: Five Fingers, Harbor Master, Noah's Ark, Naked City, Playhouse 90, Studio One, Medic, Frontier, Men in Space, Man and the Challenge, Target, M-Squad, Black Saddle, Philip Marlowe, Martin Kane, Line Up, Dragnet, Man Without a Gun, Tightrope, Panic, Highway Patrol, Men of Annapolis, Flight, Naked City, 12 O'Clock High, Magnum P.I., Dynasty, Hotel, T.J. Hooker, The Seduction of Gina, Finder of Lost Loves, Murder She Wrote.
PICTURES: Once You Kiss a Stranger, Daddy's Gone A-Hunting, Valley of the Dolls.

BURKS, J. COOPER: Executive. b. Pilot Point, TX, April 26, 1919. e. Oklahoma City U., Oklahoma City Law Sch., American Inst. of Banking (special finance courses), U.S. Navy Schools at Wesleyan Coll., Middletown, CT, U. of North Carolina, Chapel Hill,, Virginia Polytechnic Inst., Blacksburg, Virginia Military. Commander USNR-Ret. W.W.II PT boats, North Atlantic then as Naval Aviator—latter part W.W.II and Korean War. Prior to theatre business, was in banking & construction. Formed present co. March, 1970. Now pres. & chmn. of bd., AATI (American Automated Theatres, Inc.) in Oklahoma City. Military Affairs Committee, Chamber of Commerce, Life Member-Navy League.

BURNETT, CAROL: Actress, Comedienne, Singer. b. San Antonio, TX, April 26, 1933; Jody and Louise (Creighton) Burnett. e. Hollywood H.S., UCLA. children: Carrie Louise (actress), Judy Ann, Erin Kate Hamilton. Introduced comedy song, I Made a Fool of Myself Over John Foster Dulles, 1957; regular performer Garry Moore TV show, 1959–62; appeared several CBS-TV spls., 1962–63. Recipient outstanding commedienne award Am. Guild Variety Artists, 5 times; 5 Emmy awards for outstanding variety performance, Acad. TV Arts and Scis., TV Guide award for outstanding female performer 1961, 62, 63; Peabody Award, 1963; Golden Globe award for outstanding comedienne of year, Fgn. Press Assn.; Woman of Year award Acad. TV Arts and Scis. Voted one of the world's 20 most admired women in 1977 Gallup Poll. First Annual National Television Critics Award for Outstanding Performance, 1977. Inducted Acad. of Television Arts and Sciences Hall of Fame, 1985.
THEATER: Once Upon a Mattress (debut, 1959); Fade Out-Fade In (1964). Regional: Plaza Suite (1970); I Do, I Do; Same Time, Next Year (1977).
PICTURES: Who's Been Sleeping in My Bed? (1963); Pete 'n Tillie, The Front Page, A Wedding (Best Actress, San Sebastian Film Fest.); Health; The Four Seasons; Chu Chu and the Philly Flash; Annie.
TELEVISION: The Garry Moore Show 1959–62; Julie & Carol at Carnegie Hall (1963); Carol & Company; Calamity Jane; Once Upon a Mattress; Carol + 2; The Carol Burnett Show (1966–77, now in syndication as Carol Burnett and Friends.); Julie & Carol at Lincoln Center; 6 Rms Riv Vu; Twigs; Sills & Burnett at the Met; Dolly & Carol in Nashville; The Grass Is Always Greener Over the Septic Tank; Friendly Fire; The Tenth Month; Life of the Party: The Story of Beatrice; Between Friends; The Laundromat; Burnett Discovers Domingo; Hostage.

BURNS, GEORGE: Actor. r.n. Nathan Birnbaum; b. New York, NY, Jan. 20, 1896. In vaudeville as singer in children's quartet, later as roller skater, then comedian; formed team Burns & (Gracie) Allen, 1925; m. partner 1926. Team many years on Keith and Orpheum vaudeville circuits, then on screen in Paramount short subjects, on radio in England; in 1930 began long career Amer. radio. Feature picture debut 1932 in The Big Broadcast. Books: How to Live to Be 100: or More!: The Ultimate Diet, Sex and Exercise Book; Dr. Burns' Prescription for Happiness; Dear George: Advice and Answers from America's Leading Expert on Everything from A to Z; Gracie.
PICTURES: International House, College Humor, Six of a Kind, We're Not Dressing, Love in Bloom, College Swing, College Holiday, A Damsel in Distress, Honolulu, Two Girls and A Sailor, The Sunshine Boys (Acad. Award, supp. actor 1975), Oh, God, Just You and Me, Kid, Oh, God! Book II, Oh, God! You Devil, 18 Again.
TELEVISION: Co-star Burns & Allen show, CBS-TV. Movies: Two of a Kind; Grandpa, Will You Run With Me?; Wendy and Me; Disney's Magic in the Magic Kingdom (host); and numerous specials.

BURNS, RALPH: Musical conductor, Composer. b. Newton, MA, June 29, 1922.
PICTURES: Lenny, Cabaret (AA), Lucky Lady, New York, New York, Movie, Movie, All That Jazz (AA), Urban Cowboy, Jinxed, Annie, My Favorite Year, Star 80, Perfect, Kiss Me

Goodbye, National Lampoon's Vacation,; After the Promise, Bert Rigby, You're a Fool.
TELEVISION: Baryshnikov on Broadway, Liza and Goldie Special (both Emmy awards), Ernie Kovacs—Between the Laughter, Sweet Bird of Youth.

BURR, RAYMOND: Actor. b. New Westminster, B.C., Canada, May 21, 1917. e. Stanford U., U. of California, Columbia U., U. of Chungking. Forestry svce.: appeared on stage in many countries in Night Must Fall, Mandarin, Crazy with the Heat, Duke in Darkness; dir., Pasadena Community Playhouse, 1943; on radio. Formed Royal Blue Ltd, TV prod. co. with business partner Robert Benevides, 1988.
PICTURES: Pitfall, Raw Deal, Key to the City, His Kind of Woman, Place in the Sun, New Mexico, Meet Danny Wilson, Mara Maru, Horizons West, Blue Gardenia, Fort Algiers, Casanova's Big Night, Gorilla at Large, Khyber Patrol, Rear Window, Passion, They Were So Young, You're Never Too Young, A Man Alone, Count Three and Pray, Please Murder Me, Godzilla King of the Monsters, Great Day in the Morning, Secret of Treasure Mountain, Cry in the Night, P.J., Airplane II: The Sequel.
TELEVISION: Perry Mason (series, 1957–66); Ironside (series, 1967–75); Kingston: Confidential, 79 Park Ave., Centennial, 1978. Movies: Perry Mason Returns; Perry Mason Movies: The Case of the Murdered Madam, The Avenging Ace, The Case of the Lady in the Lake, The Case of the Scandalous Scoundrel, Trial By Jury, The Case of the Lethal Lesson.

BURRILL, TIMOTHY: Producer, Executive. b. North Wales, 1931. e. Eton Coll., Sorbonne U. Paris. Grenadier Guards 2 yrs, then London Shipping Co. Ent. m.p. ind. as resident prod. mgr. Samaritan Films working on shorts, commercials, documentaries, 1954. Ass't. dir. on feature films: The Criminal, The Valiant Years (TV series), On The Fiddle, Reach for Glory, War Lover, Prod. mgr: The Cracksman, Night Must Fall, Lord Jim, Yellow Rolls Royce, The Heroes, Of Telemark, Resident prod. with World Film Services. 1970 prod. two films on pop music for Anglo-EMI. 1972 first prod. administrator National Film School in U.K. 1974 Post prod. administrator The Three Musketeers. Prod. TV Special The Canterville Ghost; assoc. prod, That Lucky Touch; UK Administrator, The Prince and the Pauper; North American Prod. controller, Superman 1; 1974–1983 council member of BAFTA; mng. dir., Allied Stars (Breaking Glass, Chariots of Fire); 1979–80 V. chmn. Film BAFTA; 1980–1983 chmn. BAFTA; 1981 Gov. National Film School, executive BFTPA mem. Cinematograph Films Council. 1982 Gov National Theatre; 1987, chmn., Film Asset Developments, Formed Burrill Prods.
PICTURES: Prod.: Privlege, Oedipus the King, A Severed Head, three Sisters, Macbeth (assoc. prod.), Alpha Beta, Tess (co-prod.), Pirates of Penzance (co-prod.), Supergirl, The Fourth Protocol, To Kill a Priest (co-prod.), Return of the Musketeers, Valmont.

BURROWS, JAMES: Director. b. Los Angeles, CA, Dec. 30, 1940. e. Oberlin, B.A.; Yale, M.F.A. Son of late Abe Burrows, composer, writer, director. Directed off-Bdwy.
PICTURE: Partners.
TELEVISION: Series: Mary Tyler Moore; Bob Newhart; Laverne and Shirley; Rhoda; Phyllis; Fay; Taxi; Lou Grant; Cheers; Dear John. Movies: More Than Friends; Like Father Like Daughter; Goodbye Doesn't Mean Forever; In the Lion's Den.

BURROWS, JOHN, H.: Producer. b. Brooklyn, NY, September 4, 1924. e. Yale U., NYU Law with interruption for service. U.S. Navy, W.W.II, lieut., son of George D. Burrows, vice-president Allied Artists, started film career as salesman for AA later joining studio; asst. prod. Lindsley Parsons Productions.

BURROWS, ROBERTA: Executive. e. Brandeis U; Academia, Florence, Italy. Career includes freelance writing and post as dir. of pub. for Howard Stein Enterprises and with Rogers & Cowan and Billings Associates. Joined Warner Bros. as sr. publicist 1979; named dir. east coast publicity, 1986. Resigned 1989 to dev. novelty products.

BURRUD, BILL: Executive. b. Los Angeles, CA, Jan. 12, 1925. e. U. of Southern California, B.S.; Harvard Business Sch. Ent. ind. as child actor; U.S. Navy, W.W. II; formed Bill Burrud Prods., 1954.
TELEVISION: Animal World, World of the Sea, Safari to Adventure, Challenging Sea, Secret World of Reptiles, Vanishing Africa, The Great American Wilderness, Predators of the Sea, Creatures of the Amazon, The Amazing Apes, The Amazing World, Animals Are the Funniest People.

BURSTYN, ELLEN: Actress. b. Detroit, MI, Dec. 7, 1932. r.n. Edna Rae Gilhooley. Majored in art; was fashion model in Texas at 18. Moved to Montreal as dancer; then N.Y. to do TV commercials (under the name of Ellen McRae), appearing for a year on the Jackie Gleason show (1956–57). In 1957 turned to dramatics and won lead in Bdwy show, Fair Game. Then went to Hollywood to do TV and films. Returned to N.Y. to study acting with Lee Strasberg; worked in TV serial, The Doctors. Co-artistic dir. of Actor's Studio. 1982–8. Pres. Actors Equity Assn. 1982–85. On 2 panels of Natl. Endowment of the Arts and Theatre Advisory Council (NY).
THEATER: Same Time, Next Year (Tony Award, 1975); 84 Charing Cross Road, Shirley Valentine.
PICTURES: For Those Who Think Young, Goodbye, Charlie, Pit Stop, Tropic of Cancer, Alex in Wonderland, The Last Picture Show, The King of Marvin Gardens, The Exorcist, Harry and Tonto, Alice Doesn't Live Here Anymore (Acad. Award), Providence, A Dream of Passion, Same Time Next Year, Resurrection, Silence of the North, The Ambassador, Twice in a Lifetime, Dear America: Letters Home From Vietnam (reader), Hanna's War.
TELEVISION: Surviving, Act of Vengeance, Into Thin Air, Thursday's Game; The People vs. Jean Harris; Something in Common, Pack of Lies. Series: The Iron Horse, The Doctors, The Ellen Burstyn Show.

BURTON, BERNARD: Producer. Started as film ed.; prod. "Vagabond Lady" 1935.
PICTURES: She Gets Her Man, Fighting Youth, Invisible Ray, Showboat, When Love is Young, One Hundred Men and a Girl, You're a Sweetheart, Midnight Intruder, Little Tough Guy, Three Smart Girls Grow Up, Spring Parade, Moonlight in Havana, Get Help to Love, Gentleman Joe Palooka, Fighting Mad, Smart Woman, Underworld Story, Cry Danger, The Highwayman, Triple Cross, Beast from 20,000 Fathoms.

BURTON, KATE: Actress. b. Geneva, Switzerland, Sept. 10, 1957. e. Yale Drama Sch. D. of late Richard Burton. m. director Michael Ritchie. Worked at Yale Repertory Theatre, Hartford, Stage Co., the Hartman, Williamstown, Berkshire Theatre festivals. Theatrical film debut: Big Trouble in Little China, 1986.
THEATER: Present Laughter (debut, 1982, Theatre World Award), Alice in Wonderland, Winners, The Accrington Pals, Doonesbury, The Playboy of the Western World, Wild Honey, Measure For Measure.
TELEVISION: Ellis Island, Evergreen, Alice in Wonderland, Uncle Tom's Cabin.

BURTON, LEVAR: Actor. b. Landstuhl, Germany, Feb. 16, 1957. e. U. of Southern California. Signed to play role of Kunta Kinte in TV mini-series, Roots, while still in school. Has hosted Public TV children's shows, Rebop, and The Reading Rainbow.
PICTURES: Looking for Mr. Goodbar, The Hunter.
TELEVISION: Roots; Almos' A Man; Billy: Portrait of a Street Kid; Battered; Guyana: the Story of Jim Jones; The Ron LeFlore Story; Dummy; The Jesse Owens Story; A Special Friendship; Star Trek: The Next Generation; Roots: The Gift.

BURTON, TIM: Director. b. 1960. Cartoonist since grade school in suburban Burbank. Won Disney fellowship to study animation at California Institute of the Arts. At 20 went to Burbank to work as apprentice animator on Disney lot where made Vincent, 6-minute animated short on his own which was released commercially in 1982 and won several film fest. awards. Also made Frankenweenie, 29 minute live-action film.
PICTURES: Pee-wee's Big Adventure, Beetlejuice, Batman.
TELEVISION: Aladdin (Faerie Tale Theatre).

BUSCH, H. DONALD: Exhibitor. b. Philadelphia, PA, Sept. 21, 1935. e. U. of Pennsylvania, physics, math, 1956; law school, 1959. 1960 to 1987 practiced law, anti-trust & entertainment. 1984, named pres., Budco Theatres, Inc. 1975–1987, pres., Busch, Grafman & Von Dreusche, P.C. 1987, pres. & CEO, AMC Philadelphia, Inc.
MEMBER: Former posts: Suburban General Hospital (dir.); Rainbow Fund (dir.); NATO (dir.); NATO of Pennsylvania (pres.); Society Hill Synagogue (dir.); Philadelphia All-Star Forum (dir.); Montgomery County Bar Assn. (dir.); Dir. & pres., Abington, PA school board (1974–77); dir., Sports Legends, Inc. (1972–84).

BUSCH, NIVEN: Writer. b. New York, NY, April 26, 1903. e. Princeton U. p. Briton Niven Busch, former v.p., Lewis J. Selznick Enterprises; Exec. prod., Samuel Goldwyn Productions. Assoc. ed. Time mag., 1923–31; assoc. ed. & contrib. New Yorker, 1927–31; numerous articles, many national magazines. Regents professor, U. of California, 1971–78. Special lectures on film. Regents professor, U. of California, Irvine, 1971–75. San Diego, 1974; Lecturer Berkeley, 1977. Lecturer, Princeton U., 1985, Ferris Teaching Fellow, Princeton U., 1986.
AUTHOR: Books: Twenty One Americans, Carrington Incident, Duel in the Sun, They Dream of Home, Day of the Conquerors, The Furies, The Hate Merchant, The Actor, California Street, The San Franciscans, The Gentlemen from California, The Takeover, No Place for a Hero, Continent's Edge.
PICTURES: The Crowd Roars, In Old Chicago, The

Westerner, The Postman Always Rings Twice, Duel in the Sun, Till the End of Time, Pursued, Moss Rose; prod., The Capture, Distant Drums, Man from the Alamo, Moonlighter, Treasure of Pancho Villa, Moss Rose, He Was Her Man, The Angels Wash Their Face, Big Shakedown, Little Miss Pinkerton.

BUSEY, GARY: Actor, Musician. b. Goose Creek, TX, June 29, 1944. e. Coffeyville Jr. Coll. A.B., 1963; attended Kansas State Coll, OK State U. Played drums with the Rubber Band 1963–70. Also drummer with Leon Russell, Kris Kristofferson, Willie Nelson as Teddy Jack Eddy.
PICTURES: Angels Hard as They Come, Dirty Little Billy, The Magnificent Seven Ride, The Last American Hero, Lolly Madonna, Hex, Thunderbolt and Lightfoot, Gumball Rally, Alex and the Gypsy, A Star Is Born, Straight Time, Big Wednesday, The Buddy Holly Story, Foolin' Around, Carny, Barbarosa, D.C. Cab, The Bear, Silver Bullet, Insignificance, Let's Get Harry, Hider in the House, Howling at the Moon, Neon Empire, Eye of the Tiger, Lethal Weapon, Act of Piracy, Bulletproof, Home Grown.
TELEVISION: High Chaparel (debut, 1970). Series: The Texas Wheelers (1974–75). Movies: Bloodsport, The Execution of Private Slovik, The Law, A Dangerous Life (mini-series).

BUSFIELD, TIMOTHY: Actor. b. Lansing, MI, June 12, 1957. e. East Tennessee State U; Actor's Theatre of Louisville (as apprentice and resident). Founded Fantasy Theatre in Sacramento, 1986, a professional acting co., which performs in Northern CA schools, providing workshops on playwriting for children and sponsors annual Young Playwrights contest.
THEATER: Richard II, Young Playwrights Festival (Circle Rep.), A Tale Told, Getting Out (European tour), Green Mountain Guilds Children Theatre, Mass Appeal, The Tempest.
PICTURES: Stripes, Revenge of the Nerds, Revenge of the Nerds II, Field of Dreams.
TELEVISION: Series: thirtysomething (2 Emmy noms.), Trapper John, M.D., Reggie. Guest: Family Ties, Matlock, Paper Chase, Love American Style, After M.A.S.H.

BUTTERFIELD, ELIZABETH: Production manager. b. London, England. e. London. Extensive theatrical experience as stage manager for The Old Vic Company (Michael Benthall, Tyrone Guthrie) and Donald Wolfit Company. Emigrated to Canada in 1957. Television includes: Quentin Durgens M.P. and Whiteoaks of Jaina for C.B.C., Seaway, Ind.
PICTURES: A Fan's Notes, (1971), Sunday in the Country, It Seemed Like a Good Idea at the Time, Find the Lady, Running, Middle Age Crazy, Torment.

BUTTOLPH, DAVID: Music director. b. New York, NY, Aug. 3, 1902.
PICTURES: Phantom of Rue Morgue, Secret of the Incas, Bounty Hunter, Long John Silver, Jump into Hell, Target Zero, Lone Ranger, Steel Jungle, Santiago, Burning Hills, Cry in the Night.

BUTTONS, RED: Performer. r.n. Aaron Chwatt; b. New York, NY, Feb. 5, 1919. Singer at the age of 13; comic, Minsky's. U.S. Army, 1943; in Army and film version of Winged Victory.
TELEVISION: Many TV appearances; star of Red Buttons Show CBS-TV, 1953; Best Comedian award 1953; NBC-TV, 1954; Alice in Wonderland, The Dream Merchants, Leave 'Em Laughing, Louis Armstrong—Chicago Style; Knots Landing (series); Reunion at Fairborough.
THEATER: Vickie, Wine, Women and Song; Barefoot Boy With Cheek, Hold It.
PICTURES: Winged Victory (1944, debut), 13 Rue Madeleine, The Big Circus, Sayonara (Acad. Award, supp. actor, 1957), Imitation General, Hatari!, One, Two, Three, The Longest Day, Five Weeks in a Balloon, Harlow, Up From the Beach, Your Cheatin' Heart, Stagecoach, They Shoot Horses Don't They, Who Killed Mary What's 'er Name?, The Poseidon Adventure, Gable and Lombard, Viva, Knievel!, Movie Movie, When Time Ran Out, 18 Again, Into Thin Air.

BUTTS, R. DALE: Composer. b. Lamasco, KY, March 12, 1910. e. Louisville Conservatory of Music. Started in vaudeville at 16, later playing, arranging for dance bands; staff arranger, pianist, radio stations; to Republic Pictures, 1944.
PICTURES: The Plunderers, Too Late for Tears, House by the River, Sea Hornet, The Outcast, Geraldine, Shanghai Story, Hell's Outpost, Santa Fe Passage, Fighting Chance, No Man's Woman, Headline Hunter's, Lay That Rifle Down, Double Jeopardy, City of Shadows, Terror at Midnight, Stranger at My Door, Dakota Incident.

BUXBAUM, JAMES M.: Executive, Producer, Writer. b. Jamaica, NY, March 8. e. Harvard U., B.A., 1949; Columbia Law Sch., LL.B., 1955; spec. studies, The Hague Acad., Netherlands, 1953. Story ed. ZIV, Ivan Tors' Sea Hunt series, then assoc. prod., ZIV-CBS, Ivan Tors' Aquanauts series, story ed., 1957–60. Attorney, Wm. Morris Agency, 1962–63. Joined Ivan Tors Films, Inc. as v.p., prod. and wrote many episodes of Flipper series, 1964; exec. v.p. Ivan Tors Miami Studios, 1967–69; exec. v.p. Ivan Tors Films, Inc. 1968–69. Gen. mgr. Amer. Film Institute Center, Beverly Hills, 1969. Member: State Bar of CA, Amer. Bar Assoc. Exec. in charge of prod. for Island of the Lost.

BUZZI, RUTH: Actress. b. Wequetequock, CT, July 24, 1939. e. Pasadena Playhouse. Launched TV career on Garry Moore Show as comedy partner of Dom DeLuise. Created character Gladys Ormphby with Artie Johnson on TV's Laugh-In plus over 150 other characters.
PICTURES: Nightfalls, The Being, The Trouble with Hello, Record City, Freaky Friday, The Apple Dumpling Gang Rides Again, The North Avenue Irregulars, The Villian, Surf Two, Skatetown USA, Chu Chu and the Philly Flash, The Bad Guys, Dixie Lanes, Up Your Alley, The Dozen Say Bye Bye, My Mom's a Werewolf, Aunt Millie's Will, Wishful Thinking.
TELEVISION: Lead on 7 TV series including: Rowan & Martin's Laugh-In; The Steve Allen Comedy Hour; The Donny & Marie Show and Carol Burnett's The Entertainers; semi-regular on 12 other series including Flip, Tony Orlando & Dawn, That Girl, The Dean Martin Variety Hour; guest on 75 TV series and specials including Medical Center, Trapper John M.D., Love Boat. Eight cartoon voice-over series and over 150 on-camera commercials.
STAGE: Sweet Charity (Broadway), 4 off-Broadway shows incl. A Man's A Man, Little Mary Sunshine, 18 musical revues and Las Vegas club act.
AWARDS: 4 Grammy nominations; Golden Globe winner, AGVA Variety Artist of the Year, 1977, Rhode Island Hall of Fame, Presidential commendation for outstanding artist in the field of entertainment, 1980.

BYGRAVES, MAX: Comedian, actor. b. London, England, October 16, 1922. e. St. Joseph's R.C. School, Rotherhithe. After RAF service, touring revues and London stage, M.P. debut 1949 in Skimpy in The Navy. TV debut in 1953, with own show. Autobiography, I Wanna Tell You A Story, pub. 1976. Received O.B.E., New Year's Honours 1983.
TELEVISION: Roamin' Holiday series.
PICTURES: Tom Brown's Schooldays, Charlie Moon, A Cry from the Streets, Boobikins, Spare the Rod.
NOVEL: The Milkman's on His Way, pub. 1977.

BYRD, CARUTH C.: Production executive. b. Dallas, TX, March 25, 1942. Multi-millionaire businessman, chmn. of Caruth C. Byrd Enterprises, Inc., who entered entertainment industry forming Communications Network Inc. in 1972, producer of TV commercials. Was principal investor in film Santee (1972) and in 1973 formed Caruth C. Byrd Prods. to make theatrical features. 1983, chrm., Lone Star Pictures.
PICTURES: Allan and Murph the Surf, The Monkeys of Bandapur (both exec. prod.).

BYRD, JOHN: Writer, Director, Producer. Entered m.p. industry 1934 via scenario dept. Rock Studios, Elstree; visited Hollywood to study requirements of U.S. market, 1939; 1940–45 B.B.C. War Correspondent, 1945–46 Riverside Studios, 1947–8 British National Studios. 1949 formed own org. prod. bus. TV films. Prod. films in South Africa, Uganda, Kenya, Portugal and Mexico.
PICTURES: Murder in Reverse, World Owes Me a Living, Waltz Time, Filmed Durgapur Steelworks project, India; Steel Strides Ahead, Concerning Colour, Design for Tall Building, Jungle to Steel Town, Steelworks in Action; Dryer Felt Loom, Bridging the Highways; Built from Top; Building with Steel and Plastics; The Desert Will Yield; Long Sea Outfall, One Steelworks, One Contract, Highweld Process: Go-Con Process, Mechanical Handling. Undersea Tunnel to Hong Kong: Contract 1306—Zambia, Bridge Across the Avon; filming for British Steel Corp. Murder in Reverse, World Owes Me a Living, Waltz Time. Anchor Project for British Steel. Filming in Mexico AHMSA Steelworks project. More Steel for Mexico; 1978, Filming in South Africa; Filming in France & Spain; Filming Construction of Humber Bridge; 1983–84, New Zealand on steel development project. 1984, Better Coal for Kellingly; 1985, SCAW Metals Project; 1986, SAPPI Paper Mill Project; 1987, More Steel for New Zealand (doc.).

BYRNE, DAVID: Actor, Singer, Director. b. Dumbarton, Scotland, May 14, 1952. Moved to Baltimore at 7. e. Rhode Island Sch. of Design studying photography, performance and video, and Maryland Inst. Coll. of Art 1971–72. Prod. and dir. music videos. Awarded MTV's Video Vanguard Award, 1985. Best known as the lead singer and chief songwriter of Talking Heads. Composed and performed original score for choreographer Twyla Tharp's The Catherine Wheel (Bdwy). Wrote music for Robert Wilson's The Knee Plays.
PICTURES: Stop Making Sense (conceived and stars in concert film), True Stories (director, s.p., narrator), The Last Emperor (music, Acad. Award), Married to the Mob (music), Heavy Petting.
CONTRIBUTED MUSIC: Times Square, The Animals' Film, King of Comedy, America is Waiting, Revenge of the Nerds, Down and Out in Beverly Hills, Dead End Kids, Cross My Heart.

TELEVISION: A Family Tree (Trying Times), Alive From Off-Center (also composed theme), Survival Guides; Rolling Stone Magazine's 20 Years of Rock and Roll.

BYRNE, GABRIEL: Actor. b. Dublin, Ireland, 1950. e. University Coll., Ireland. Worked as archaeologist. Then became a Spanish teacher at girls' school. Participated in amateur theater before acting with Ireland's Focus Theatre, an experimental rep. co. and joining Dublin's Abbey Theatre Co. Cast in long-running TV series the Riordans. Also worked with National Theater in London.
PICTURES: On a Paving Stone Mounted, The Outsider, Excalibur, Wagner, Hanna K, Defence of the Realm, Gothic, Lionheart, Siesta, Julia and Julia, Hello Again, A Soldier's Tale, The Courier, Diamond Skulls, Miller's Crossing.
TELEVISION: Series: The Riordan's, Branken, Movies: Mussolini, Christopher Columbus.

BYRNES, EDD: Actor. b. New York, NY, July 30, 1933. e. Harren H.S. Prof. debut, Joe E. Brown's Circus Show; appeared on stage in Tea and Sympathy, Picnic, Golden Boy.
PICTURES: Up Periscope, Marjorie Morningstar, Yellowstone Kelly, The Secret Invasion, Wicked, Wicked, Star Wars, Grease, Stardust, Mankillers, Troup Beverly Hills..
TELEVISION: Has appeared in over 300 TV shows incl.: Matinee Theatre, Crossroads, Jim Bowie, Wire Service, Navy Log, Oh Susanna!, 77 Sunset Strip (series), Throb, Rags to Riches.

BYRON, WARD: TV Producer, Writer, Director. b. New York, NY, June 2, 1910. e. New York. Orchestra leader, 1929–32; radio prod., writer, 1932–39. Ent. TV as asst. to prog. dir. of ABC; writer & producer of Paul Whiteman show in 1950; The Ameche-Langford Show; app'td exec. prod. of ABC-TV in 1950. Exec. prod., Canadian TV Young & Rubicam, 1955–57. Freelance writer prod., TV Specials & film series, v.p. gen, mgr. Trans-Nat'l Communications O'way Recording Studios; 1970, v.p. & sec. International Coproductions, motion picture distributors. Named pres. in 1979. Currently lecturing on early radio and TV.

BYRUM, JOHN: Writer, Director. b. Winnetka, IL, March 14, 1947. e. New York U. Film School. First job as "go-fer" on industrial films and cutting dailies for underground filmmakers. Went to England where wrote 1st s.p., Comeback. From 1970–73 was in N.Y. writing and re-writing scripts for low-budget films.
PICTURES: Mahogany (s.p.), Inserts (s.p., dir.) Harry and Walter Go to New York (story, s.p.), Heart Beat (dir, s.p.), Sphinx (s.p.), Scandalous (co.-s.p.), The Razor's Edge (co-s.p., dir.), The Whoopee Boys (dir.), The War at Home (dir., s.p.).
TELEVISION: Alfred Hitchcock Presents (1985).

C

CAAN, JAMES: Actor. b. Bronx, NY, March 26, 1940. e. Hofstra U. Studied with Sanford Meisner at the Neighborhood Playhouse. Appeared off-Broadway in La Ronde, 1961. Also on Broadway in Mandingo; Blood, Sweat and Stanley Poole.
PICTURES: Lady in a Cage, The Glory Guys, Red Line 7000, Eldorado, Games, Journey to Shiloh, Submarine X-1, Rain People, Rabbit, Run, The Godfather, Slither, Cinderella Liberty, Freebie and the Bean, T.R. Baskin, The Gambler, Godfather II, Funny Lady, Rollerball, The Killer Elite, Harry and Walter Go To New York, Silent Movie, A Bridge Too Far, Another Man, Another Chance, Comes a Horseman, Chapter Two, Hide in Plain Sight (also dir.), Thief, Kiss Me Goodbye, Gardens of Stone, Alien Nation, Nowhere Man, Dad.
TELEVISION: Much series work (Naked City, Route 66, Wagon Train, Ben Casey, Alfred Hitchcock Presents, etc.) 1962–69; Brian's Song (Emmy nom., 1971).

CACOYANNIS, MICHAEL: Producer, Director, Writer. b. Cyprus, June 11, 1922. Studied law in London, admitted to bar at age 21. Became a producer of BBC's wartime Greek programs while attending dramatic school. After acting on the stage in England, left in 1952 for Greece, where he made his first film, Windfall in Athens, with his own original script. While directing Greek classical plays, he continued making films.
PICTURES: Stella, The Girl in Black, A Matter of Dignity, Our Last Spring, The Wastrel, Electra, Zorba the Greek, The Day the Fish Came Out, The Trojan Women, Sweet Country, Zoe.

CAESAR, IRVING: Author, Composer, Publisher. b. New York, NY, July 4, 1895. e. City Coll. of New York. Abroad with Henry Ford on Peace Ship, W.W.I; songwriter since then, songs with George Gershwin, Sigmund Romberg, Vincent Youmans, Rudolph Friml and others, songwriter for stage, screen and radio, including Swanee, Tea for Two, Sometimes I'm Happy, I Want to Be Happy, Lady Play Your Mandolin, Songs of Safety, Songs of Friendship, Songs of Health and Pledge of Allegiance to the Flag.

CAESAR, SID: Performer. b. Yonkers, NY, Sept. 8, 1922. Musician. Joined Coast Guard in 1942. Appeared in Tars and Spars. voted best comedian (tied) in M.P. Daily's TV poll, 1951. Best Comedian, 1952; Best Comedy Team (with Imogene Coca), 1953; 5 Emmy Awards 1957; Sylvania Award, 1958. Formed Shelbrick Corp., TV, 1959; Bway Play: Little Me, 1962–64; Sid Caesar and Company (1989; off Bdwy, then Bdwy). Author: Where Have I Been? (autobiography, 1982).
PICTURES: It's a Mad, Mad, Mad, Mad World, The Spirit is Willing, The Busy Body, Guide for the Married Man, Ten from Your Show of Shows, Airport 1975, Silent Movie, Fire Sale, Grease, The Cheap Detective, Grease II, History of the World—Part I, Over the Brooklyn Bridge, Cannonball Run III, The Emperor's New Clothes.
TELEVISION: Signed for Broadway Revue by Max Liebman, 1949. Star of Your Show of Shows on NBC-TV 1950–54; star of Caesar's Hour, 1954–1957; Sid Caesar Invites You, 1958; As Caesar Sees It, 1962; The Sid Caesar Show, 1963–64.Movies: Found Money, Love Is Never Silent, Alice in Wonderland, Freedom Fighter, Side By Side.

CAGE, NICOLAS: Actor. b. Long Beach, CA, Jan. 7, 1964. r.n. Nicholas Coppola. Nephew of Francis Ford Coppola. First starring role in Valley Girl (1983).
PICTURES: Rumble Fish, Racing with the Moon, The Cotton Club, Birdy, The Boy in Blue, Raising Arizona, Peggy Sue Got Married, Moonstruck, Vampire's Kiss, Killing Time, The Short Cut, Queens Logic, Wild of Heart, Wings of the Apache.

CAHN, SAMMY: Lyricist, Producer. b. New York, NY, June 18, 1913. e. Seward Park H.S. Org. dance band with Saul Chaplin; collab. song writer for shows. m.p. 30 Acad. Award nominations, Four Oscars for Three Coins in Fountain, All the Way, High Hopes, and Call Me Irresponsible! Only TV Emmy ever given a song, Love & Marriage from the TV award winning Our Town. 1972, inducted into Songwriters' Hall of Fame.
BDWY. MUSICALS: High Button Shoes, Skyscraper, Walking Happy many songs.
PICTURES: Anchors Aweigh, Three Coins in Fountain, Romance on High Seas, Some Came Running, Robin & Seven Hoods, The Tender Trap, Pocketful of Miracles, Thoroughly Modern Millie.

CAIN, SUGAR: Actress. r.n. Constance McCain. b. Jerome, AZ, March 13. e. U. of Washington, B.A., radio-drama; Colorado Woman's Coll., A.A., journalism; Columbia U., grad TV. MP. Reg. on radio serials. Hopalong Cassidy, Clyde Beatty Show, Night club act, Mexico; appeared TV, Hollywood & N.Y. Plays include: nat. tours, Pajama Tops, In One Bed, Idiots Delight, Streetcar Named Desire, The Rainmaker, Dead End, Druid Circle.
PICTURES: Breakstone Affair, Life with Edmer, I've Been Here Before, Monster from 20,000 Fathoms, Dalton Women, I Shot Billy the Kid, Hostile Country, Dalton Gang, Africa Screams; Sporting Club, Apple Man, Klute, Panic in Needle Park, The French Connection, Effect of Gamma Rays, Summer Wishes, Winter Dreams; Dir.-writer, m.p. short, Rama.

CAINE, MICHAEL: Actor. r.n. Maurice Micklewhite. b. London, England, March 14, 1933. Asst. stage mgr. Westminster Rep. (Sussex, UK 1953); Lowestoft Rep. 1953–55. London stage: The Room, The Dumbwaiter, Next Time I'll Sing For You (1963). Author: Michael Caine's Moving Picture Show or Not Many People Know This is the Movies.
TELEVISION: Series: Rickles (1975). In more than 100 British teleplays 1957–63 incl. The Compartment, The Playmates, Hobson's Choice, Funny Noises with Their Mouths, The Way with Reggie, Luck of the Draw, Hamlet, The Other Man; Jack the Ripper, Jekyll and Hyde.
PICTURES: A Hill in Korea, How to Murder A Rich Uncle, Two Headed Spy, Foxhole in Cairo, Zulu, Ipcress File, Alfie, The Wrong Box, Gambit, Funeral in Berlin, Hurry Sundown, Billion Dollar Brain, Woman Times Seven, Deadfall, The Magus, Play Dirty, Italian Job, The Battle of Britain, Too Late the Hero, The Last Valley, Get Carter, Kidnapped, Zee and Company, Pulp, Sleuth, The Black Windmill, The Destructors, The Wilby Conspiracy, Peepers, The Romantic Englishwoman, The Man Who Would Be King, Harry and Walter Go to New York, The Eagle Has Landed, A Bridge Too Far, The Silver Bears, The Swarm, Ashanti, California Suite, Beyond the Poseidon Adventure, The Island, Dressed to Kill, The Hand, Victory, Deathtrap, The Jigsaw Man, Educating Rita, Beyond the Limit, Blame It on Rio, Water. The Holcroft Covenant, Hannah and Her Sisters (Acad. Award, supp. actor 1987), Sweet Liberty, Half Moon Street, Mona Lisa, The Whistle Blower, Surrender, The Fourth Protocol (also exec. prod.), Jaws—The Revenge, Without a Clue, Dirty Rotten Scoundrels, A Shock to the System, Bullseye!

CALHOUN, RORY: Actor. r.n. Francis Timothy. McCown. b. Los Angeles, CA, Aug. 8, 1922. e. Santa Cruz H.S. Worked as logger, miner, cowpuncher, firefighter; m.p. debut in Something for the Boys, 1944.

PICTURES: Sunday Dinner for a Soldier, Nob Hill, Great John L, Red House, Adventure Island, That Hagen Girl, Sand, Massacre River, Ticket to Tomahawk, County Fair, I'd Climb the Highest Mountain, Rogue River, Meet Me After the Show, With a Song in My Heart, Way of a Gaucho, The Silver Whip, Powder River, How to Marry a Millionaire, River of No Return, Yellow Tomahawk, Bullet Is Waiting, Dawn at Socorro, Four Guns to the Border, The Looters, Ain't Misbehavin', Shotgun, The Domino Kid, Treasure of Pancho Villa, The Spoilers, Red Sundown, Raw Edge, Flight to Hongkong, Utah Blaine, Big Caper, Adventures of Marco Polo, Colossus of Rhodes, Gun Hawk, Young and the Brave, Face in the Rain, Call Me Bwana, Black Spur, Lady of the Nile, Night of the Lepus, Won Ton Ton, Father Keno Story, Revenge of Bigfoot, Motel Hell, Angel, Rollerblade Warriors, Hell Comes to Frogtown, Avenging Angel, Big Jim, Fists of Steel, One By One.

TELEVISION: The Road Ahead, Day Is Done, Bet the Wild Queen, Zane Grey Theater, The Texan, U.S. Camera (series 1957–60); Killer Instinct, Lands End, The Blue and the Gray, Capitol, Champion, The Rebels, Hart to Hart, Police Woman, Movin' On, Alias Smith & Jones.

CALLAN, MICHAEL: Actor, singer, dancer. b. Philadelphia, PA, 1935. Singer, dancer, Philadelphia nightclubs; to New York in musicals, including The Boy Friend and West Side Story; dancer Copacabana; in short-run plays, Las Vegas: That Certain Girl.

PICTURES: They Came to Cordura, (debut) The Flying Fontaines, Because They're Young, Pepe, Mysterious Island, Gidget Goes Hawaiian, 13 West Street, Bon Voyage, The Interns, The Victors, The "New" Interns, Cat Ballou, Frasier, The Sensuous Lion, Lepke, The Photographer, The Cat and The Canary (1977), Record City; The Donner Party, Freeway.

TELEVISION: Guest on major dramatic TV shows and Occasional Wife (series, star). Movies: Blind Ambition, Scruples.

CALLEY, JOHN: Executive. b. New Jersey, 1930. Dir. of night time programming, dir. programming sales, NBC, 1951–57; prod. exec. and TV prod. Henry Jaffe Enterprises, 1957; v.p. in charge of Radio and Television, Ted Bates Advertising Agency, 1958; joined Filmways, Inc., 1960; exec. v.p. and prod. to 1969; exec. v.p. chg. world-wide prod. Warner Bros.; Pres., W.B. from Jan. 6, 1975; vice chmn. bd., 1977. Now consultant.

PICTURES: Wheeler Dealer, The Americanization of Emily, Topkapi, The Cincinnati Kid, Loved One, Don't Make Waves, Ice Station Zebra, Catch-22.

CALLOW, EVERETT C.: Publicist. b. Perth Amboy, NJ. e. St. John's Coll. On ed. staff N.Y. World; service staff chief Paramount Thea., N.Y., 1926; mgr. Keith & Albee Theas., Phila., 1928; mgr. Stanley Theatre, Phila., 1929–31; dist. theatre mgr. various dists. in NJ, PA & DE; apptd. dir. of adv. & publicity Warner Bros., Phila. zone, 1939; winner Quigley Silver Award, 1940; Lt. Col. U.S.M.C., 1943; returned to Warner post after war; 1950–51, internat'l dir. adv., pub., Cinerama, Feb., 1954. Member: American Legion Variety Post 713 (past commdr.); Military Order of Foreign Wars of U.S.; Adv. pub. dir., National Screen Service, 1965; VP in charge of adv. and pub. sales. TV, Foreign; pres. United Screen Arts, Inc. 1966; worldwide dist. and adv. and production. Presently consultant.

CALLOW, SIMON: Actor, Writer, Director. b. London, June 15, 1949. e. Queens, U. of Belfast, The Drama Centre. Originated role of Mozart in London premiere of Amadeus and Burgess/Chubb in Single Spies. Author: Being an Actor; Charles Laughton: A Difficult Actor.

THEATER: London: Plumber's Progress, The Doctor's Dilemma, Soul of the White Ant, Blood Sports, The Resistible Rise of Arturo Ui, Amadeus, Restoration, The Beastly Beatitudes of Balthazar B, Titus Andronicus (Bristol Old Vic), Faust. Shakespear's Sonnets. Director: The Infernal Machine (also translator), Jaques and His Master (also trans.), Single Spies, Shirley Valentine (London, NY).

PICTURES: Amadeus, A Room With a View, The Good Father, Maurice, Manifesto, For a Night of Love, Mr. and Mrs. Bridge.

TELEVISION: Man of Destiny, La Ronde, All the World's a Stage, Wings of Song, The Dybbuk, Instant Enlightenment, Chance of a Lifetime (series), David Copperfield, Honour, Profit and Pleasure, Old Flames.

CALVET, CORINNE: Actress. r.n. Corinne Dibos. b. Paris, France, April 30, 1925. e. U. of Paris School of Fine Arts; Comedie Francaise. French stage and radio. Screen debut in France; La Part de L'Ombre, Nous Ne Sommes Pas Maries, Petrus. American screen debut: Rope of Sand. Author: Has Corinne Been a Good Little Girl?

PICTURES: When Willie Comes Marching Home, My Friend Irma Goes West, Quebec, On the Riviera, Peking Express, Thunder in the East, Sailor Beware, What Price Glory?, Powder River, Flight to Tangier, The Far Country, So This Is Paris, Mail Order Bride, Apache Uprising, Bluebeard's Ten Honeymoons, Adventures of a Young Man, Pound, Side Roads.

CAMERON, JAMES: Director, Writer. b. Kapuskasing, Ontario, Aug. 16, 1954. e. CA State U. (physics). Supported himself as truck driver while writing screen plays. First film work was with Roger Corman's New World Pictures as miniature set builder, process projection supervisor and art dir. on Battle of the Stars.

PICTURES: Pirhana II—The Spawning (dir., co-s.p.), The Terminator (dir.), Rambo: First Blood Part II (co-s.p.); Aliens (dir.), Alien Nation (s.p.), The Abyss (dir., s.p.).

CAMERON, JOANNA: Actress, director. r.n. Patricia Cameron. b. Aspen, CO, Sept. 20. e. U. of California, Sorbonne, Pasadena Playhouse, 1968. Guinness Record: Most network programmed TV commercials. Prod., dir.: El Camino Real (doc. 1987).

PICTURES: How To Commit Marriage (debut), P.S., I Love You, Pretty Maids All in a Row.

TELEVISION: Features: The All-American Beauty Contest, It Couldn't Happen to a Nicer Guy, High Risk. Other: The Survivors, Love American Style, Daniel Boone, Mission Impossible, The Partners, Search, Medical Center, Isis (series), Name of the Game, The Bold Ones, Marcus Welby, Petrocelli, Columbo, Switch, Bob Hope Special, Bob Hope 25th NBC Anniversary Special, Westwind, MacMillian, Spiderman, Swan Song, Johnny Carson, numerous commercials. Director: Various commercials, CBS Preview Special, closed circuit program host U.S.N., all TV equipped ships—actress and dir. Razor Sharp (prod., dir.), 1982.

CAMERON, KIRK: Actor. b. Canoga Park, CA, 1971. Started doing TV commercials at age 9. Appeared in TV movies, series episodes, and Two Marriages (short-lived series).

PICTURES: Like Father, Like Son, Listen to Me.

TELEVISION: Series: Two Marriages, Growning Pains. Movie: Goliath Awaits. Special: Ice Capades with Kirk Cameron.

CAMP, COLLEEN: Actress. b. San Francisco, 1953. Performing since age of three. Spent 2 years as a bird trainer before being noticed by an agent and cast on TV. TV debut on The Dean Martin Show; feature film debut, Battle for the Planet of the Apes (1973). Assoc. prod. on Martha Coolidge's film The City Girl.

PICTURES: Smile, Funny Lady, Apocalypse Now, They All Laughed, The Seduction, Smokey and the Bandit III, Valley Girl, The Joy of Sex, Rosebud Beach Hotel, Police Academy II, D.A.R.Y.L., Clue, Doin' Time, Illegally Yours, Track 29, Walk Like a Man, Strike It Rich, Wicked Stepmother.

TELEVISION: Magnum P.I., Dukes of Hazzard, WKRP in Cincinnati, Dallas, Addicted to His Love.

CAMP, JOE: Producer, Director, Writer. b. St. Louis, MO, Apr. 20, 1939. e. U. of Mississippi, B.B.A. Acct. exec. McCann-Erickson Advt., Houston 1961–62; owner Joe Camp Real Estate 1962–64; acct. exec. Norsworthy-Mercer, Dallas 1964–69; dir. TV commercials; founder and pres. Mulberry Square Prods.

PICTURES: Benji, Hawmps, For the Love of Benji, The Double McGuffin, Oh Heavenly Dog, Benji the Hunted.

TELEVISION: The Phenomenon of Benji, Benji's Very Own Christmas Story, Benji at Work, Benji at Marineland.

CAMPAGNOLA, GINO: Executive. Joined Paramount Pictures in 1975; held various sales positions, including v.p., sls. admin. In 1980 named v.p., asst. gen. sls. mgr.; now sr. v.p.

CAMPANELLA, TOM: Executive. Joined Paramount Pictures 1968 as asst. business mgr.; later worked for corporate div. and Motion Picture Group. Named exec. dir., nat'l adv. 1979, made v.p., nat'l adv. 1982, appt. sr. v.p., adv., for M.P. Group. of Paramount, 1984.

CAMPBELL, GLEN: Actor, Singer. b. Delight, AK, April 22, 1936. After forming local band became guitarist in Hollywood; records won two Grammy awards, 1967.

PICTURES: True Grit, Norwood.

TELEVISION: The Smothers Brothers Comedy Hour, The Glen Campbell Goodtime Hour, many specials.

CAMPBELL, ROBERT MAURICE: Producer, Director. b. Detroit, MI, Feb. 16, 1922. e. Michigan Conservatory of Music, Detroit Inst. of Musical Arts, American Theatre Wing. Featured player. assoc. dir., Detroit stage prod.; numerous radio appearances; pub. relations, U.S. Coast Guard, W.W.II; since 1946 dir., off-Broadway show; dir.-prod., Springer Pictures, Inc.; TV show: All-Star News; exec., Visual Transcriptions, Inc.; prod. Jazz Dance (Robert J. Flaherty Award, Edinburgh Film Festival Merit Award); co-author, prod. designer, See No Evil.

CAMPBELL, WILLIAM: Actor. b. Newark, NJ. e. Feagin Sch. of Drama. Appeared in summer stock. Broadway plays; m.p. debut in The Breaking Point (1950).

PICTURES: People Against O'Hara, Holiday for Sinners, Battle Circus, Code Two, Big Leaguer, Escape from Fort Bravo, High and the Mighty, Man Without a Star, Cell 2455 Death Row, Battle Cry, Running Wild, Backlash, Pretty Maids All in a Row, Black Gunn.
TELEVISION: The Heat: When You Lie Down With Dogs (pilot).

CANBY, VINCENT: Journalist, Critic. b. Chicago, IL, July 27, 1924. e. Dartmouth Coll. Navy officer during W.W.II. Worked on newspapers in Paris and Chicago. Joined Quigley Publications in 1951 in editorial posts on Motion Picture Herald. Reporter for Weekly Variety 1959–1965. Joined New York Times film news staff, 1965; named film critic, 1969. Author: Living Quarters (1975); End of the War (play, 1978); Unnatural Scenery (1979); After All (play, 1981); The Old Flag (1984).

CANDY, JOHN: Actor, Writer. b. Toronto, Ont., Oct. 31, 1950. Began acting in 11th grade and continued while studying journalism at Centennial Community College, Toronto. First professional job as member of children's theatre group; performed in satirical review, Creeps. Had roles in several low-budget Canadian films before joining Chicago's Second City Theatre in 1972 for two years. Returned to Toronto to join Second City group there, which evolved into SCTV television series. Contributed as both performer and writer (1975–83), earning two Emmy Awards (writing) when show picked up by NBC.
PICTURES: The Class of '44, Tunnelvision, The Clown Murders, Faceoff, 1941, Lost and Found, The Blues Brothers, Heavy Metal, Stripes, National Lampoon's Vacation, Going Berserk, Splash, Brewster's Millions, Volunteers, Summer Rental, Armed and Dangerous, The Little Shop of Horrors, Spaceballs, Planes, Trains & Automobiles; The Great Outdoors, Hot to Trot, Who's Harry Crumb? (also exec. prod.), Speed Zone, Uncle Buck.
TELEVISION: Comic Relief, The Last Polka, Young Comedians, Super Bowl 1989.

CANFIELD, ALYCE: Writer. b. Los Angeles, CA. e. U. of California. Magazine writer; author Mervyn LeRoy book It Takes More Than Talent; in collab. with Howard Duff original story for Models, Inc.; story Journey Into Fire, Assignment for Murder; s.p. for latter in collab. with Jerry Jerome; creator, exec. prod. Ziv TV series, Underground, USA.

CANNELL, STEPHEN J.: Writer, Producer. b. Los Angeles, CA, Feb. 5, 1942. e. U. of Oregon, B.A., 1964. After coll. worked at father's decorating firm for 4 years while writing scripts in evening. Sold 1st script for Adam 12, 1966. Asked to serve as head writer at Universal Studios. Chief exec. officer, Stephen J. Cannell Prods. TV prod. co. he formed 1979. Also formed The Cannell Studios, parent co. 1986. Natl. chmn., Orton Dyslexia Society. Received Mystery Writers award 1975; Emmy Awards. 1979, 1980, 1981. 4 Writers Guild Awards. Film acting debut: Identity Crisis (1989).
TELEVISION: Created or co-created over 20 series, has written more than 200 episodes and prod. or exec. prod. over 500 episodes. The Rockford Files (creator, writer, prod.), The Jordan Chance, The Duke, Stone, 10 Speed and Brownshoe, Nightside, Midnight Offerings, The Greatest American Hero, The Quest, Prod.: The A-Team, Hardcastle and McCormick, The Rousters, Riptide, Brothers-in-Law, Creator, prod.: Baa, Baa Black Sheep, Richie Brockelman, Hunter, Wise Guy, 21 Jump Street, J.J. Starbuck, Sonny Spoon, Sirens (co-exec. prod.), Unsub (exec. prod., s.p. pilot), Booker (exec. prod.), Top of the Hill (exec. prod.).

CANNON, DYAN: Actress. r.n. Samille Diane Friesen. b. Tacoma, WA, Jan. 4, 1937. e. U. of Washington. Studied with Sanford Meisner. Modelled.
TELEVISION: Playhouse 90, Movies: Diane's Adventure, The Virginia Hill Story, Lady of the House, Master of the Game, Arthur the King, Jenny's War, Rock 'n' Roll Mom.
BROADWAY: The Fun Couple, Ninety-Day Mistress.
ROAD TOUR: How to Succeed in Business Without Really Trying.
PICTURES: Bob and Carol and Ted and Alice (Academy Award nom.), Doctors' Wives, The Anderson Tapes; The Love Machine, The Burglars, Such Good Friends, Shamus, The Last of Sheila, Child Under a Leaf, Heaven Can Wait, Revenge of the Pink Panther, Coast To Coast, Honeysuckle Rose, Deathtrap, Caddyshack II, One Point of View (also dir., s.p.).

CANNON, JUDY: Actress. b. Santa Fe, NM, June 16, 1938. e. Santa Monica City Coll., 1957. Teenage Adrian model, 1954–56; toured as band singer, Orlo Wagner Orchestra, 1957; appeared in: The Little Hut, Girls of Summer, Made in Japan, Los Angeles Little Theatre, 1959–61; midwest musical comedy tour group, 1962; m.p. debut, Lullaby, 1963; Critics Choice, '63; A Comedy Tale of Fanny Hill, 1964.
TELEVISION: Smothers Bros. Comedy Hour, Man From U.N.C.L.E., Chrysler Theatre, Run for Your Life, The Road West, My Three Sons, Death Valley Days.
PICTURES: More (1970).

CANNON, WILLIAM: Writer, Producer, Director. b. Toledo, OH, Feb. 11, 1937. e. Columbia Coll., B.A., 1959, M.B.A., 1962. Dir. Off-Broadway, Death of a Salesman, Pirates of Penzance, 1960. Wrote, prod., dir., Square Root of Zero, Locarno and San Francisco Film Festivals, 1963–65; Distrib., Doran Enterprises, Ltd.; author, Skidoo, (Par-Otto Preminger), 1968, Brewster McCloud, HEX, Knots Landing, Heaven on Earth, Author, Novel, The Veteran, 1974; Publisher, Highlife and Movie Digest, 1978; The Good Guys, 1987. Co-inventor: Cardz (TM), 1988.

CANOVA, DIANA: Actress. b. West Palm Beach, FL, June 1, 1952. Daughter of actress Judy Canova and musician Filberto Rivero. NY theater: They're Playing Our Song (1981). People's Choice award, favorite female performer, 1981.
PICTURE: The First Nudie Musical.
TELEVISION: Ozzie's Girls (debut); Happy Days; Love Boat; Fantasy Island; Hotel; Chico and the Man; Barney Miller; Soap (series); I'm a Big Girl Now (series); Throb (series). Movies: Peking Encounter; Night Partners; With This Ring; Death of Ocean View Park.

CANTON, ARTHUR H.: Motion Picture Producer. b. New York, NY. e. NYU, Columbia U. Capt. USAF. Pres., Canton-Weiner Films, indep. foreign films importers, 1947; Van Gogh (Acad. Award, short, 1949); MGM Pictures, eastern div. publicity mgr., executive liaison, advertising-publicity, Independent Productions; public relations executive, v.p.; pres., Blowitz, Thomas & Canton Inc., 1964; pres., Arthur H. Canton Co. Inc.; prod. exec., Warner Bros., 1968–70; advertising-publicity v.p., Columbia Pictures, 1971; exec. v.p. of advertising and publicity, Billy Jack Productions, 1974–76. Co-founder of Blowitz & Canton Co. Inc., 1976, chmn of bd. Now pres. of Arthur H. Canton Co. Member Academy of Motion Picture Arts and Sciences, Film Information Council.

CANTON, MARK: Executive. b. New York, NY, June 19, 1949. e. UCLA, 1978. v.p., m.p. dev., MGM; 1979, exec. v.p., JP Organization; 1980, v.p. prod., Warner Bros.; named sr. v.p., 1983 and pres. worldwide theatrical prod. div., 1985.

CAPRA, FRANK: Producer, Director. b. Palermo, Italy, May 18, 1897. e. Manual Arts H.S., California Inst. of Technology, B.Sc., 1918. dir., The Strong Man, Long Pants, Platinum Blonde, American Madness, Bitter Tea of General Yen, Lady for a Day, Broadway Bill, It Happened One Night, Mr. Deeds Goes to Town, You Can't Take It With You, Lost Horizon, Mr. Smith Goes to Washington, Meet John Doe, Arsenic and Old Lace, It's a Wonderful Life, State of the Union, Riding High, Here Comes the Groom, A Hole in the Head, Pocketful of Miracles; prod., dir., Why We Fight Series, U.S. Army; pres. Academy of Motion Picture Arts and Sciences, 1935–39; pres., Directors Guild of America, 1938–40, 1959. 1964 Prod. & Dir. Rendezvous in Space. 1952–56, produced and directed four educational science films: Our Mr. Sun, Hemo The Magnificent, Strange Case of Cosmic Rays and Unchained Goddess.

CAPRA, FRANK, JR: Executive. Son of famed director Frank Capra. Served in various creative capacities on TV series (Zane Grey Theatre, Gunsmoke, The Rifleman, etc.). Associate producer on theatrical films (Planet of the Apes, Play It Again Sam, Marooned, etc.). Joined Avco Embassy Pictures,1981, as v.p., worldwide production. In July, 1981, became pres. of A-E. Resigned May, 1982 to become indep. producer. Now with Pinehurst Industry Studios, NC.
PICTURES: Producer: Born Again, The Black Marble, An Eye for an Eye, Vice Squad, Firestarter, Marie. Exec. prod.: Death Before Dishonor.

CAPSHAW, KATE: Actress. b. Ft. Worth, TX, 1953; e. U. of Missouri. Taught school before moving to New York to try acting. Success came on TV before theatrical debut in A Little Sex, 1981.
PICTURES: Indiana Jones and the Temple of Doom, Best Defense, Dreamscape, Windy City, Power, SpaceCamp, Black Rain, Love at Large, Home Grown.
TELEVISION: The Quick and the Dead, The Edge of Night, Missing Children: A Mother's Story, Her Secret Life, Internal Affairs.

CAPUCINE: Actress. r.n. Germaine Lefebvre. b. Toulon, France, January 6, 1935. e. attended schools at Saumur, France, B.A. Photographer's model, Paris. Came to N.Y. to model. Signed contract, Famous Artists.
PICTURES: debut, Song Without End, North To Alaska, Walk On the Wild Side, The Pink Panther, The Lion, The 7th Dawn, What's New Pussycat?, The Honey Pot, The Queens, Fraulein Doktor, Fellini's Satyricon, Red Sun, Jaguar Lives, Arabian Adventure, Trail of the Pink Panther, The Curse of the Pink Panther, Story of a Woman.
TELEVISION: Sins.

CAPUTO, GEORGE: Executive. b. Genoa, Italy, Oct. 24, 1916. e. Lycée de Nice, France, 1930; Sorbonne, Paris, 1934. Partner, gen. mgr., Caputo & Co., Colombia, S.A.; pres., Master Films Dist., Inc., 1950; pres., Fiesta Tele-Cinema, S.A.; pres.

International Sound Studios Inc.; pres., Fall River Investments S.A.; acquired Latin America and South America rights in perpetuity to full RKO package feature films library, 1961.

CARA, IRENE: Singer, Actress. b. New York, NY, March 18, 1959. Off-Broadway shows include The Me Nobody Knows, Lotta. On Broadway in Maggie Flynn, Ain't Misbehavin', Via Galactica.
PICTURES: Aaron Loves Angela, Sparkle, Fame, D.C. Cab, City Heat, Certain Fury, Killing 'em Softly, Paradiso, Maximum Security.
TELEVISION: Roots—The Next Generation, Guyana Tragedy, For Us the Living, Tribute to Martin Luther King, Jr.

CARDIFF, JACK: Cinematographer, Director. b. Yarmouth, Eng., Sept. 18, 1914. Early career as child actor, later *cinematographer* on Stairway to Heaven, Black Narcissus, The Red Shoes, Scott of the Antarctic, Black Rose, Under Capricorn, Pandora and the Flying Dutchman, The African Queen, Magic Box, The Brave One, War and Peace, The Vikings, Ride A Wild Pony, The Prince and The Pauper, Behind the Iron Mask, Death on the Nile, Avalanche Express, The Fifth Musketeer, A Man, a Woman and a Bank; The Awakening, The Dogs of War, Ghost Story, The Wicked Lady, Scandalous, Conan the Destroyer, Cat's Eye, Rambo: First Blood II, Blue Velvet, Tai-Pan, Million Dollar Mystery; directorial debut 1958.
PICTURES: as director: Intent to Kill, Beyond This Place, Scent of Mystery, Sons and Lovers, Fanny, My Geisha, The Lion, The Long Ships, Young Cassidy, The Liquidator, Dark of the Sun, The Girl on the Motorcycle, Penny Gold, The Mutations, Wild Pony.
TELEVISION: As cinematographer: The Far Pavillions, The Last Days of Pompeii.

CARDINALE, CLAUDIA: Actress. b. Italy, April 15, 1939.
PICTURES: Persons Unknown, 1958; Upstairs and Downstairs, Il Bell' Antonio, Rocco and His Brothers, Cartouche, The Leopard, Eight and a Half, The Pink Panther, Circus World, Of A Thousand Delights, Blindfold, Last Command, The Professionals, Don't Make Waves, The Queens, Day of the Owl, The Hell With Heroes, Once Upon a Time in the West, A Fine Pair, The Red Tent, Conversation Piece, Escape to Athena, The Salamander, Immortal Bachelor, History, Torrents of Spring, The French Revolution, Hiver '54, L'abbe Pierre.
TELEVISION: Princess Daisy, Jesus of Nazareth.

CAREY, HARRY JR.: Actor. b. Saugus, CA, May 16, 1921. e. Newhall, CA, public school, Black Fox Military Acad., Hollywood. m. Marilyn Fix. Summer stock, Skowhegan, ME., with father; page boy, NBC, New York; U.S. Navy 1941–46; Screen debut: Pursued, then Red River, Moonrise.
PICTURES: Three Godfathers, She Wore a Yellow Ribbon, Wagonmaster, Rio Grande, Copper Canyon, Warpath, Wild Blue Yonder, Monkey Business, San Antone, Island in the Sky, Gentlemen Prefer Blondes, Beneath the 12-Mile Reef, Silver Lode, The Outcast, Long Gray Line, Mister Roberts, House of Bamboo, Great Locomotive Chase, The Undefeated Big Jake, Something Big, One More Train To Rob, The Long Riders, Endangered Species, Mask, The Whales of August, Cherry 2000, Illegally Yours, Breaking In, Big Jim.
TELEVISION: Black Beauty, The Shadow Riders, Wild Times, Once Upon a Texas Train.

CAREY, MACDONALD: Actor. b. Sioux City, IA, March 15, 1913. e. Phillips Exeter Acad., U. of Wisconsin, U. of Iowa. On stage (stock); in radio serials. On Broadway in Anniversary Waltz; m.p. debut in 1942.
PICTURES: Dr. Broadway, Take a Letter Darling, Wake Island, Suddenly It's Spring, Variety Girl, Dream Girl, Hazzard, Streets of Laredo, Song of Surrender, South Sea Sinner, Copper Canyon, Great Missouri Raid, Mystery Submarine, Excuse My Dust, Meet Me After the Show, Let's Make It Legal, Cave of the Outlaws, My Wife's Best Friend, Count the Hours, Outlaw Territory, Fire Over Africa, Stranger At My Door, Tammy and the Doctor, Broken Sabre, End of the World, American Gigolo, It's Alive III.
TELEVISION: Days of our Lives (since 1965), Roots, Miracle on 34th Street, The Rebels.

CAREY, PHIL: Actor. b. Hackensack, NJ, July 15, 1925. e. Mohawk U., U. of Miami. U.S. Marines; New England stock; m.p. debut in Operation Pacific. TV: Laredo.
PICTURES: Inside the Walls of Folsom Prison, This Woman Is Dangerous, Springfield Rifle, Calamity Jane, Gun Fury, The Nebraskan, Massacre Canyon, Outlaw Stallion, They Rode West, Pushover, The Long Gray Line, Wyoming Renegades, Mister Roberts, Count Three and Pray, Three Stripes in the Sun, The Time Traveler, Once You Kiss a Stranger, Three Guns for Texas, The Seven Minutes.

CARISCH, GEORGE: Exhibitor. b. Minneapolis, MN, Dec. 12, 1935. e. Hamline U., B.S.; U. of Minnesota, B.E.E. Chmn., Carisch Theatres, Inc.

CARLINO, LEWIS JOHN: Writer. b. New York, NY, Jan. 1, 1932. e. U. of Southern California. Early interest in theatre, specializing in writing 1-act plays. Winner of Obie award (off-Broadway play). Won Rockefeller Grant for Theatre, the Int'l. Playwriting Competition from British Drama League, Huntington Hartford Fellowship.
PICTURES: Seconds, The Brotherhood, The Fox (co-s.p.), The Mechanic, The Sailor Who Fell From Grace With the Sea, (s.p., dir.), I Never Promised You a Rose Garden (co-s.p.), The Great Santini (s.p., dir.), Resurrection (s.p.), Class (dir.), Haunted Summer (s.p.).
PLAYS: Cages, Telemachus Clay, The Exercise, Double Talk, Objective Case, Used Car for Sale, Junk Yard.
TELEVISION: Honor Thy Father, In Search of America, Where Have All the People Gone?

CARLISLE, ROBERT: Producer. b. Los Angeles, CA, Sept. 19, 1906. Cutter, Metro; Universal; John Stahl; Columbia; film ed. in chf. Columbia; prod. short subjects with Jerry Fairbanks including: Popular Science, Unusual Occupations, Speaking of Animals (two Academy of M.P. Arts & Sciences awards); prod. industrials for Dupont, Union Pacific RR; trophy at Italy's Cortina Sports Film Festival for ski film, 1957; prod. and dir. films on world affairs for Dept. of Defense; prod. Wondsel, Carlisle & Dunphy, Inc., 1957.

CARLTON, RICHARD: Executive. b. New York, NY, Feb. 9, 1919. e. Columbia U., Pace Inst. Columbia Pictures 1935–41; U.S. Army 1941–45; National Screen Serv. 1945–51; Sterling Television 1951–54; U.M. & M. TV Corp. 1955; v.p. in charge of sales, Trans-Lux Television Corp., 1956; exec. v.p., Television Affiliates Corp., 1961; exec. v.p. Trans-Lux Television Corp.; v.p. Entertainment Div. Trans-Lux Corp., 1966. Pres., Schnur Appel, TV, Inc. 1970; Deputy Director, American Film Institute, 1973. Pres., Carlton Communications Corporation, 1982; exec. dir., International Council, National Academy of Television Arts and Sciences, 1983.

CARMEN, JEAN: See Jean Carmen Dillow.

CARMICHAEL, IAN: Actor. b. Hull, England, June 18, 1920. e. Scarborough Coll., Bromsgrove Sch. Stage debut: R.U.R. 1939. Bdwy debut: Boeing-Boeing (1965). One of the top ten British money making stars Motion Picture Herald—Fame Poll 1957, 1958.
TELEVISION: New Faces, Twice Upon a Time, Passing Show, Tell Her The Truth, Lady Luck, Give My Regards to Leicester Square, Jill Darling, Don't Look Now, Regency Room, Globe Revue, Off the Record, Here and Now, The Girl at the Next Table, Gilt and Gingerbread, The Importance of Being Earnest, Simon and Laura, 90 Years On, The World of Wooster (series), The Last of the Big Spenders, The Coward Revue, Odd Man In, Bachelor Father, Lord Peter Wimsey, Alma Mater, Comedy Tonight, Song by Song, Country Calendar, Down at the Hydro.
PICTURES: Bond Street, Trottie True, Mr. Prohack, Time Gentlemen Please, Meet Mr. Lucifer, Betrayed, Colditz Story, Storm Over the Nile, Simon and Laura, Private's Progress, Brothers in Law, Lucky Jim, Happy Is the Bride, The Big Money, Right, Left and Center, I'm Alright Jack, School for Scoundrels, Light Up the Sky, Double Bunk, The Big Money, The Amorous Prawn, Hide and Seek, Heavens Above, The Case of the 44's, Smashing Time, The Magnificent Seven, Deadly Sins, From Beyond the Grave, The Lady Vanishes, Diamond Skulls.

CARNEY, ART: Performer. b. Mt. Vernon, NY, Nov. 4, 1918. Many radio shows. U.S. Army, 1944–45; played Ed Norton on Jackie Gleason's Honeymooners.
TELEVISION: Studio One, Kraft, Omnibus, Chevy Show, Playhouse 90, Dupont Show of the Month—Harvey, Sid Caesar Show, Alfred Hitchcock Presents—Safety for the Witness, Art Carney Meets Peter and the Wolf, Playhouse 90—Fabulous Irishman, Charley's Aunt, Velvet Alley, Art Carney Meets the Sorcerer's Apprentice, The Sid Caesar-Art Carney Show, Our Town, Very Important People, Man in the Dog Suit, Call Me Back, Batman, Carol Burnett Show, Jonathan Winters Show, The Cavanaughs. Movies: The Night They Saved Christmas, A Doctor's Story, Terrible Joe Moran, Izzy and Moe, Faerie Tale Theater (The Emperor's New Clothes), Blue Yonder.
PICTURES: Harry and Tonto, W. W. and the Dixie Dancekings, Won Ton Ton, The Late Show, Take This Job and Shove It, Better Late Than Never, Firestarter, The Naked Face, Sunburn, Going in Style, Defiance, Roadie, Night Friend.
STAGE: The Rope Dancers. Broadway: Take Her She's Mine, The Odd Couple , Lovers, The Prisoner of Second Avenue.

CARNEY, FRED: Producer, Director. b. Brooklyn, NY, June 10, 1914. e. Mt. Vernon H.S., 1932. Actor on Broadway & summer stock; prod. mgr. for radio show, Truth or Consequences; asst. to prod.-dir of Kraft TV Theatre, 3 yrs.; dir., Kraft, Pond's Show; creator-prod., Medical Horizons; dir., Lux Video Theatre; prod. commercials at Cunningham & Walsh. Assoc. Prod. Everybody's Talking for ABC-TV. Ass't. Exec. Dir., Hollywood

Chpt., Nat'l Acad. TV; Assoc. prod. 40th Acad. Award show, ABC-TV Arts & Sciences.

CARON, LESLIE: Dancer, Actress. b. Paris, France, July 1, 1931. e. Convent of Assumption, Paris; Nat'l Conservatory of Dance, Paris 1947–50; Ballet de Paris 1954; joined Ballet des Champs Elysees.
THEATER: Orvet, Ondine, 13 Rue de l'Amour The Rehearsal, Women's Games, On Your Toes, One For the Tango.
PICTURES: An American in Paris (1950), Man with a Cloak, Glory Alley, Story of Three Loves, Lili, Glass Slipper, Daddy Long Legs, Gaby, Gigi, The Doctor's Dilemma, The Man Who Understood Women, The Subterraneans, Fanny, Guns of Darkness, The L Shaped Room, Father Goose, Promise Her Anything, A Very Special Favor, Is Paris Burning, Head of the Family, The Beginners, Madron, Chandler, Purple Night, Valentino, The Man Who Loved Women, Golden Girl, Contract, Unapproachable, Warriors and Prisoners, Courage Mountain.
TELEVISION: Master of the Game, Love Boat, Tales of the Unexpected, Carola, QB VII, Falcon Crest (series), The Man Who Lived at the Ritz, The Sealed Train.

CARPENTER, CARLETON: Actor. b. Bennington, VT, July 10, 1926 e. Bennington H.S., Northwestern U. (summer scholarship). Began career with magic act, clubs, camps, hospitals, New Eng.; then toured with carnival; first N.Y. stage appearance in Bright Boy. Appeared nightclubs; radio; as model magazines. TV debut, Campus HoopLa show. Screen debut Lost Boundaries (also wrote song for film, I Wouldn't Mind). Member: SAG, AFTRA, AEA, ASCAP, Dramatists Guild, Mystery Writers of Amer. (ex.-treas., bd. mem.).
NY STAGE: Career Angel, Three To Make Ready, The Magic Touch, The Big People, Out of Dust, John Murray Anderson's Almanac, Hotel Paradiso, Boys in the Band, Dylan, Hello Dolly!, Light Up the Sky, Murder at Rutherford House, Rocky Road, Apollo of Bellac, Sweet Adaline.
PICTURES: Summer Stock, Father of the Bride, Three Little Words, Two Weeks With Love, Whistle at Eaton Falls, Fearless Fagan, Sky Full of Moon, Vengeance Valley, Up Periscope, Take the High Ground, Some of My Best Friends Are. . ., The Prowler, Simon, Byline, That's Entertainment, Cauliflower Cupids.
TELEVISION: Over 6,000 shows (live and filmed) since 1945.

CARPENTER, JOHN: Director, Writer. b. Carthage, NY, Jan. 16, 1948. e. U. of Southern California. At U.S.C. became involved in film short, Resurrection of Bronco Billy, which won Oscar as best live-action short of 1970. Also at U.S.C. began directing what ultimately became Dark Star, science fiction film that launched his career.
PICTURES: Assault on Precinct 13, Halloween (also music), Eyes of Laura Mars (s.p. only), The Fog (also music), Escape from New York (also music); The Thing (dir.); Christine (dir., music); Starman (dir.); The Philadelphia Experiment (exec. prod.); Big Trouble in Little China (dir., music), Prince of Darkness (dir., music, and as Martin Quatermass, music), They Live (dir., music).
TELEVISION: Elvis, Someone is Watching Me (also s.p.), Zuma Beach (s.p.).

CARPENTER, ROBERT L.: Executive. b. Memphis, TN, March 20, 1927. Joined Universal Pictures in 1949 as booker in Memphis exchange; promoted to salesman there in 1952 and branch mgr. in 1958. In 1963 named Los Angeles branch mgr. In Dec. 1971 moved to New York to become asst. to general sales mgr. Named gen. sls. mgr. 1972, replacing Henry H. Martin when latter became pres. of Universal. Left in 1982 to become consultant and producer's rep. 1984, joined Cannon Releasing Corp. as east. div. mgr. Left in 1989 to become consultant and producers rep.

CARR, ALLAN: Producer, Personal Manager. b. Highland Park, IL, 1939. e. Lake Forest College, Northwestern U. First venture in show business as one of creators of Playboy Penthouse TV series in Chicago which subsequently inspired the Playboy Clubs for Hugh Hefner. Asst. to Nicholas Ray on King of Kings shot in Madrid. Became talent scout, launching Marlo Thomas in West Coast premiere of Sunday in New York. As personal manager guided careers of Ann-Margret, Peter Sellers, Tony Curtis, Marvin Hamlisch, Paul Anka, Herb Alpert and Melina Mercouri. Special marketing of The Deer Hunter, Tommy, The Natural.
PICTURES: Producer: The First Time, C.C. and Company, Grease (co-prod. and adapt.), Can't Stop the Music (co-prod. co. s.p.), Grease 2 (co-prod.), Where the Boys Are, Cloak and Dagger, Survive.

CARR, JOHN: Executive Producer, Director, Writer. b. West Virginia, Jan. 19, 1930. Now pres. of Pan-American Pictures Corp.
PICTURES: Sanitarium, Gretta (dir.); The Dark Side of Love, The Rebel's Mistresses, The Runaways, The Talisman (s.p.).

CARR, MARTIN: Producer, Director, Writer. b. New York, NY, Jan 20, 1932. e. Williams Coll. Worked for all three networks.
TELEVISION: PBS Smithsonian World (exec. prod.). For CBS prod., wrote and dir. CBS Reports: Hunger in America, The Search for Ulysses, Gauguin in Tahiti, Five Faces of Tokyo, Dublin Through Different Eyes. For NBC prod., wrote and dir. NBC White Paper: Migrant, NBC White Paper: This Child Is Rated X. Also directed drama, dance, music, opera specials and daytime serial for CBS-TV. ABC Close-Up. The Culture Thieves. PRS Global Paper: Waging Peace, ABC News 20/20; NBC, The Human Animal.
AWARDS: Winner of 5 Emmys; 3 Peabody awards; 2 DuPont Col. Journalism awards; Robert F. Kennedy award; Sidney Hillman award; Writers Guild Award.

CARR, THOMAS: Director. b. Philadelphia, PA, July 4, 1907. On screen at 2½ yrs. for Lubin Co., Phil.; starred in Little Britches at 5 yrs., actor on stage, radio & screen until 1937; then became dialogue clerk, Republic Studios, advancing to script; asst. assoc. prod; assoc. prod. 1944; dir. 1945. Retired 1970.
PICTURES: Include many westerns, Bobby Ware is Missing, Superman (serial), Dino, Three For Jamie Dawn.
TELEVISION: Superman; Rawhide; Trackdown; Wanted, Dead or Alive; Richard Diamond; 4 Star Theatre; Bonanza; Wild Bill Hickock; Laramie; Honey West; Stagecoach West; Shenandoah; Daniel Boone; Guns of Will Sonnet.

CARRADINE, DAVID: Actor. b. Hollywood, CA, Dec. 8, 1936. e. San Francisco State U. Son of late actor John Carradine. Brother of actors Keith and Robert Carradine. Began career in local repertory; first TV on Armstrong Circle Theatre and East Side, West Side; later TV includes Shane series and Kung Fu; N.Y. stage in The Deputy, Royal Hunt of The Sun.
PICTURES: Taggart, Bus Riley's Back in Town, Too Many Thieves, The Violent Ones, Heaven With a Gun, Young Billy Young, The Good Guys and the Bad Guys, Gallery of Horrors, The McMasters, Macho Callahan, A Gunfight, McCabe & Mrs. Miller, Boxcar Bertha, Death Race 2000, Bound for Glory, The Serpent's Egg, Gray Lady Down, Deathsport, Circle of Iron, The Long Riders, Cloud Dancer, The Winged Serpent, Safari 3000, Lone Wolf McQuade, Americana, Kain of Dark Planet, P.O.W. The Escape, Armed Response, Wheels of Terror, Warlords, Crime Zone, Night Children; Wizard of the Lost Age 2, Sundown, Future Force, The Vampire in Retreat, Caddo Lake, Run For Your Life, Bird on a Wire, Crime of Crimes, Ministry of Vengeance, Nowhere to Run.
TELEVISION: Movies: Jealousy, The Bad Seed, Kung Fu: The Movie, Six Against the Rock, The Cover Girl & the Cop, I Saw What You Did. Mini-series: North & South; Book II.

CARRADINE, KEITH: Actor. b. San Mateo, CA, Aug. 8, 1949. e. Colorado State U. Father of actress Martha Plimpton. Son of late actor John Carradine, brother of David and Robert. First break in rock opera Hair. Screen debut in A Gunfight, 1971. Composer: I'm Easy (Nashville, Academy Award Best Song, 1975). Theater: Foxfire, 1982.
PICTURES: McCabe and Mrs. Miller, Hex, Emperor of the North, Thieves Like Us, Antoine et Sebastien, Run Joe Run, Idaho Transfer, Nashville, You and Me, Lumiere, Welcome to L.A., The Duellists, Pretty Baby, Sgt. Pepper's Lonely Heart Club Band, Old Boyfriends, An Almost Perfect Affair, The Long Riders, Southern Comfort, Maria's Lovers, Choose Me, Trouble in Mind, The Moderns, The Investigation, Street of No Return, Cold Feet, Dr. Grassler.
TELEVISION: A Rumor of War, Chiefs, Scorned and Swindled, A Winner Never Quits, Murder Ordained; Eye on the Sparrow, Stones for Ibarra, My Father, My Son; The Revenge of Al Capone, Backfire, Confessional.

CARRADINE, ROBERT: Actor. b. Hollywood, CA, March 24, 1954. Son of Late actor John Carradine; brother of Keith and David Carradine.
PICTURES: The Cowboys, Mean Streets, Aloha Bobby and Rose, Jackson County Jail, The Pom Pom Girls, Cannonball, Massacre at Central High, Joyride, Orca, Blackout, Coming Home, The Long Riders, The Big Red One, Heartaches, Wavelength, Just the Way You Are, Number One with a Bullet, Revenge of the Nerds, Revenge of the Nerds II, Buy and Cell, All's Fair, Rude Awakening.
TELEVISION: Movies: Footsteps, Rolling Man, Go Ask Alice, The Hatfields and the McCoys, The Survival of Dana, The Sun Also Rises, Monte Carlo, The Liberators, As Is, I Saw What You Did; Alfred Hitchcock Presents (1985); Disney's Totally Minnie, The Hitchiker.

CARRERA, BARBARA: Actress. Fashion model before film debut in The Master Gunfighter, 1976.
PICTURES: Embryo, The Island of Dr. Moreau, When Time Ran Out, Condorman, I the Jury, Lone Wolf McQuade, Never Say Never Again, Wild Geese II, The Underachievers, Loverboy, The Favorite, Wicked Stepmother.
TELEVISION: Centennial, Matt Houston, Masada, Emma: Queen of the South Seas.

CARRERAS, SIR JAMES K.C.V.O. M.B.E.: Chairman Hammer Film Productions Ltd. 1949–1980. President, Variety Clubs Int'l. 1961–63; 22 years: past chairman; vice chairman, Royal Naval Film Corporation; Friends of the Duke of Edinburgh's Award Scheme; Mem. of board, Services Kinema Corp. 12 years; president, London Federation of Boys' Clubs 5 years; trustee of the council, Cinema and Television Benevolent Fund. Chairman of the Cinema Veteran, 1982–83.

CARROLL, CARROLL: Writer, Producer, b. New York, NY, April 11, 1902. m.p. critic, feature writer, N.Y. Sunday World; freelance writer, nat'l mags: radio writer, J. Walter Thompson, N.Y. 1932–36; West Coast, 1936–46; v.p., writer, prod., Ward Wheelock Co., West Coast, 1946–53. CBS, NBC, JWT, East Coast 1957–67. Now based in Hollywood.
SHOWS INCLUDE: (radio) Bing Crosby, Al Jolson, Rudy Vallee, Eddie Cantor, Burns & Allen, Joe Penner, Kraft Music Hall, Edgar Bergen, Frank Sinatra, Bob Crosby, Corliss Archer, Double or Nothing. Club 15; (TV) head writer, Bob Crosby Show; CBS-TV creative staff, 1953–55; General Electric Hour; Young & Rubicam TV, 1955; NBC-TV creative staff, 1956–57; ed. dept., J. Walter Thompson Co., 1957–67. Writer, prod., Chase & Sanborn 100th Anniv. Radio Show with Edgar Bergen, 1964; C & S 101. Anniv. Show with Fred Allen, 1965; 1966 NBC 40th Anniv. Show. Freelance writer and adv. consultant, 1967–77. Book Reviewer for Variety and Columnist, And Now a Word from. . . in Variety, 1967–84.
AUTHOR: None of Your Business or My Life with J. Walter Thompson, 1970. My Life With. . . 1978. Co-author with Henny Youngman: Take My Wife . . . Please! Editoral consultant Liberace. Editorial consultant Mike Douglas: My Story, Co-author with Ed McMahon, Here's Ed. Co-author with Bob Hope: I Never Left Home, So This is Peace. Author, Carroll's First Book of Proverbs, or Life Is a Fortune Cookie.

CARROLL, DIAHANN: Actress, Singer. b. New York, NY, July 17, 1935. m. singer Vic Damone. On Broadway in House of Flowers, No Strings, Agnes of God. Film debut in Carmen Jones, 1954.
PICTURES: Porgy and Bess, Goodbye Again, Paris Blues, Hurry Sundown, The Split, Claudine.
TELEVISION: Series: Julia, Dynasty. Movies: I Know Why the Caged Bird Sings, Sister Sister; Roots, The Next Generation, From the Dead of Night. many specials.

CARROLL, GORDON: Producer. b. Baltimore, MD, Feb. 2, 1928. e. Princeton U. Advtg. exec., Foote, Cone & Belding, 1954–58; Ent. industry, Seven Arts Prods., 1958–61; v.p., Staff Prod., Jalem Prods., 1966–1969; Independent Producer to present.
PICTURES: How to Murder Your Wife, Luv, Cool Hand Luke, The April Fools, Pat Garrett and Billy the Kid, Alien, Blue Thunder, The Best of Times, Aliens, Red Heat.

CARROLL, PAT: Performer. b. Shreveport, LA, May 5, 1927. e. Immaculate Heart Coll., L.A, Catholic U., Washington, DC. Joined U.S. Army in capacity of Civilian Actress Technician. Night club entertainer in N.Y., 1950.
TELEVISION: Red Buttons, George Gobel, Jimmy Durante and Mickey Rooney; Caesar's Hour, (Emmy, 1956), Masquerade Party (panelist); Keep Talking (regular); Busting Loose (series); The Ted Knight Show (series); She's the Sheriff (series); Cinderella; Gertrude Stein.
STAGE: Catch a Star (debut, 1955); Gertrude Stein, Gertrude Stein (Drama Desk, Outer Critics Circle, Grammy Awards); Dancing in the End Zone.
PICTURES: With Six You Get Eggroll, The Brothers O'Toole, The Last Resort.

CARSON, JEANNIE: Actress. b. Yorkshire, England. Amer. Citizen, 1966. In musicals Ace of Clubs, Love from Judy; Ent. motion pictures in 1954 in As Long as They're Happy; Alligator Named Daisy, Mad Little Island. 1979: founded Hyde Park Festival Theatre with husband William Biff McGuire. Has taught music and drama at U. of Washington.
THEATER: U.S.: The Sound of Music, Blood Red Roses, Finian's Rainbow (revival). Also extensive work with the Seattle Repertory Theatre as actress, and dir. with Seattle Bathhouse Theatre.
TELEVISION: Best Foot Forward, Little Women, Berkeley Square, The Rivals, Frank Sinatra Show. Series: Hey Jeannie and Jeannie Carson Show.

CARSON, JOHNNY: Comedian. b. Corning, IA, Oct. 23, 1925. e. U. of Nebraska, B.A. 1949. U.S. Navy service during WWII; announcer with station KFAB, Lincoln, Neb.; WOW radio-TV, Omaha, 1948; announcer, KNXT, Los Angeles, 1950; then program, Carson's Cellar (1951); quiz-master, Earn Your Vacation, 1954; head writer for Red Skelton Show; star of Johnny Carson Show, CBS-TV; Who Do You Trust, ABC-TV; The Tonight Show Starring Johnny Carson, NBC-TV since 1962. President Carson Productions. Author: Happiness Is a Dry Martini (1965).

CARTER, DIXIE: Actress. b. McLemoresville, TN, May 25, 1939. m. actor Hal Holbrook. e. U. of Tennessee, Knoxville, Rhodes Coll.; Memphis, Memphis State U. Off-Bdwy debut, A Winter's Tale with NY Shakespeare Fest (1963). London debut, Buried Inside Extra (1983). Lincoln Center musicals: The King & I, Carousel, The Merry Widow.
THEATER: Pal Joey (1976 revival), Jesse and the Bandit Queen, Fathers and Sons, Taken in Marriage, A Coupla White Chicks Sitting Around Talking, Buried Inside Extra, Sextet.
PICTURE: Going Berserk.
TELEVISION: The Edge of Night. Series: On Our Own, Filthy Rich, Out of the Blue, Different Strokes, Designing Women. Movies: The Killing of Randy Webster, OHMS.

CARTER, HELENA BONHAM: Actress. b. England, May 26, 1966. Great granddaughter of Liberal Prime Minister Lord Asquith. e. Westminster. Appeared on BBC in A Pattern of Roses; seen by director Trevor Nunn who cast her in Lady Jane, 1986, theatrical film debut.
PICTURES: Lady Jane, A Room with a View, Maurice, Francesco, The Mask, Getting It Right.
TELEVISION: Miami Vice. Movies: A Hazard of Hearts, The Vision (U.K.).

CARTER, JACK: Actor, r.n., Jack Chakrin. b. New York, NY, June 24, 1923. e. Brooklyn Coll., Feagin Sch. of Dramatic Arts. Worked as comm. artist for adv. agencies. Debut Broadway in Call Me Mister, 1947; starred in TV Jack Carter Show. Seen on most major variety, dram. programs, incl. Ed Sullivan Show. Emmy nom. 1962 for Dr. Kildare seg. Played most major nightclubs. On Broadway in Top Banana, Mr. Wonderful.
PICTURES: The Horizontal Lieutenant, Viva Las Vegas, The Extraordinary Seaman, The Resurrection of Zachary Wheeler, Red Nights, Sexpot, Deadly Embrace, Caged Fury, Princess of Darkness.

CARTER, LYNDA: Actress. b. Phoenix, AZ, July 24. e. Arizona State U. Wrote songs and sang professionally in Arizona from age of 15; later toured for 4 yrs. with rock n' roll band. Won beauty contests in Ariz. and became Miss World-USA in 1973. Dramatic training with Stella Adler and Charles Conrad.
TELEVISION: The New Adventures of Wonder Woman; 5 variety specials; Movies: Baby Brokers; Last Song; Hotline; Rita Hayworth, Love Goddess; Stillwatch (also exec. prod.). Mickey Spillane's Mike Hammer: Murder Takes All.

CARTER, MAURICE: Art director, Designer. b. London, England, 1913. Grad. of the Royal Society of Art Masters. Early career as interior decoration designer. Ent. m.p. ind. 1934/5 Islington Studios, became art dir. 1938. Involved in development back projection. Has art dir. or designed over eighty features include Man in Grey, Becket, The Battle of Britain, Anne of the Thousand Days, Innocent Bystanders, The Land that Time Forgot, At the Earth's Core, The People that Time Forgot, The Great Train Robbery. Specializes in period subject and special effect. Three times nominated for American Academy awards and twice for British Film Academy awards. Founder of Guild of Film Art Directors.

CARTER, NELL: Actress. b. Birmingham, AL, Sept. 13, 1948.
THEATER: Hair, Dude, Don't Bother Me, I Can't Cope, Jesus Christ Superstar, Ain't Misbehavin' (Tony Award), Ain't Misbehavin' (1988 revival).
TELEVISION: Baryshnikov on Broadway; The Big Show; Lobo; An NBC Family Christmas; Ain't Misbehavin' (Emmy Award); Gimme a Break (series); Christmas in Washington; Nell Carter, Never Too Old To Dream, Morton's By the Bay (pilot).
PICTURES: Hair; Quartet; Back Roads; Modern Problems.

CARTLIDGE, WILLIAM: Director, Producer. b. England. Ent. m.p. ind. 1959. Early career in stills dept., Elstree Studios. Later worked as an asst. dir. on The Young Ones, Summer Holiday, The Punch & Judy Man, The Naked Edge. As 1st asst. dir. pictures included Born Free, Alfie, You Only Live Twice, The Adventurers, Young Winston, Friends. As assoc. prod., Paul and Michelle, Seven Nights in Japan, The Spy Who Loved Me, Moonraker. Prod.: Educating Rita, Not Quite Paradise, Consuming Passions, Dealers.

CARTWRIGHT, VERONICA: Actress. b. Bristol, Eng., 1949. m. writer-dir. Richard Compton. Sister of actress Angela Cartwright. Began career as a child actress on TV series Daniel Boone, 1964–66. Stage: The Hands of Its Enemies, (Mark Taper Forum, LA 1984), The Triplet Connection (off-Bdwy).
PICTURES: In Love and War, The Children's Hour, The Birds, One Man's Way, Spencer's Mountain, Inserts, Goin' South, Invasion of the Body Snatchers, Alien, Nightmares, The Right Stuff, My Man Adam, Flight of the Navigator, Wisdom, The Witches of Eastwick, Valentino's Return.
TELEVISION: Leave It to Beaver, Twilight Zone, Mini-series, Robert Kennedy and His Times. Movies: Guyana Tragedy—the Story of Jim Jones, The Big Black Pill, Prime Suspect, Intimate Encounters, Desperate for Love. Specials: Who Has Seen the Wind, Bernice Bobs Her Hair, Tell Me Not the Mournful Numbers (Emmy Award), Joe Dancer.

CARVER, STEVE: Director. b. Brooklyn, NY, April 5, 1945. e. U. of Buffalo; Washington U., MFA. Directing, writing fellow, Film Institute Center for Advanced Studies, 1970. (Writer, dir. films Patent and the Tell-Tale Heart). Teacher of filmmaking art and photo. Florissant Valley Col., MO 1966–68. News photographer, UPI. Instructor, film and photography, Metropolitan Ed. Council in the Arts; St. Louis Mayor's Council on the Arts, Give a Damn (dir., prod.); asst. dir. Johnny Got His Gun; writer, editor with New World Pictures. Member: Sierra Club, National Rifle Assn.

PICTURES: Arena, Big Bad Mama, Capone, Drum, Fast Charlie, The Moonbeam Rider, Steel, An Eye for an Eye, Lone Wolf McQuade (also prod.), Oceans of Fire, Jocks (also co-s.p.), Bulletproof (also co-s.p.), River of Death.

CARVEY, DANA: Actor. b. San Carlos, CA, 1955. e. San Francisco State Coll. As teenager created comic characters which later led to work as a stand-up comedian in local San Francisco comedy clubs. TV debut as Mickey Rooney's grandson on series, One of the Boys, 1982. Best known for the Church Lady character from his three seasons as performer-sketch writer on Saturday Night Live.

PICTURES: Racing With the Moon, Tough Guys, Opportunity Knocks.

TELEVISION: Series: One of the Boys, Blue Thunder, Saturday Night Live.

CASS, PEGGY: Actress. b. Boston, MA, May 21, 1924. On Broadway in Burlesque, Bernardine, Auntie Mame, Don't Drink the Water, Front Page, Last of the Red Hot Lovers.

PICTURES: The Marrying Kind, Auntie Mame, Gidget Goes Hawaiian, The Age of Consent, Paddy.

TELEVISION: Major Dad (series), The Hathaways, Garry Moore Show, To Tell the Truth, Women in Prison.

CASSEL, ALVIN I.: Executive. b. New York , NY, July 26. e. U. of Michigan, B.A., 1938. Capt. in U.S. Army European Theatre, 1941–45. Surveyed Central Africa for MGM, 1946–50, then assumed duties as asst. mgr. for MGM South Africa. Continued with MGM in West Indies, 1950–51 and Philippines, 1951–57. In 1957 joined Universal as mgr./supvr. for Southeast Asia; back to MGM in 1963 as supvr. S.E. Asia; 1967, with CBS Films as Far East supvr. In 1972 established Cassel Films to secure theatrical films for foreign distributors, principally in Far East, 1979, consultant for Toho-Towa co. of Japan and other Far East distributors.

CASSEL, JEAN-PIERRE: Actor. b. Paris, France, Oct. 27, 1932. Began as dancer, attracting attention of Gene Kelly in Left Bank nightspot, who gave him film work. Appeared in plays before becoming established as leading French screen star.

PICTURES: Games of Love, The Gay Deceiver, Five Day Lover, The Vanishing Corporal, The Male Companion, A Woman Passed By, Is Paris Burning?, Those Magnificent Men in Their Flying Machines, The Killing Game, Oh! What a Lovely War, The Bear and The Doll, The Rupture, The Boat on the Grass, Baxter!, The Discreet Charm of the Bourgeoisie, The Three Musketeers, Le Mouton Enrage, Murder on the Orient Express, Who Is Killing the Great Chefs of Europe?, Chouans! Grandeson, From Hell to Victory, Les Ville des Silence, The Green Jacket, Ehrengard, The Trout, Viva la Sociale! Franches de Vie, Mangeclous, The Return of the Musketeers.

TELEVISION: Casanova (U.S.).

CASSEL, SEYMOUR: Actor. b. Detroit, MI, Jan. 22, 1935. As a boy travelled with a troupe of burlesque performers including his mother. After high school appeared in summer stock in Michigan. Studied acting at American Theatre Wing and Actor's Studio. After joining a workshop taught by John Cassavetes, began a long creative association with the director-actor. Broadway: The World of Suzy Wong, The Disenchanted.

PICTURES: Murder Inc., Too Late Blues, Shadows, Juke Box Racket, Coogan's Bluff, The Revolutionary, Faces, Minnie and Moskowitz, Black Oak Conspiracy, Death Game, The Killing of a Chinese Bookie, Scott Joplin, Opening Night, The Last Tycoon, Valentino, California Dreaming, Convoy, Ravagers, Sunburn, King of the Mountain, The Mountain Men, I'm Almost Not Crazy...John Cassavetes—The Man and His Work (doc.), Love Streams, Eye of the Tiger, Tin Men, Johnny Be Good, Plain Clothes, Track 29, Wicked Stepmother, Dick Tracy.

TELEVISION: The Killers, Beverly Hills Madame, Blood Feud, Angel on My Shoulder, I Want to Live.

CASSIDY, DAVID: Actor. b. April 12, 1950. Son of late Jack Cassidy; brother of Shaun and Patrick.

THEATER: Bdwy: Fig Leaves (1968), Joseph and the Amazing Technicolor Dreamcoat; London: Time.

PICTURE: Instant Karma, Spirit of '76.

TELEVISION: The Partridge Family (series), Man Undercover, The Night the City Screamed, Alfred Hitchcock Presents.

CASSIDY, JOANNA: Actress. b. Camden, NJ, Aug. 2, 1944. e. Syracuse U.

PICTURES: Bullitt, The Fools, The Laughing Policeman, The Outfit, Bank Shot, The Stepford Wives, Stay Hungry, Prime Time, The Late Show, Night Child, Stunts, The Glove, Our Winning Season, Night Games, Blade Runner, Club Paradise, The Fourth Protocol, Who Framed Roger Rabbit?, Under Fire, 1969, The Package.

TELEVISION: Series: Shields and Yarnell, The Roller Girls. 240–Robert, Family Tree, Buffalo Bill. Movies: Reunion, The Children of Times Square, Pleasures, The Devlin Connection, Invitation to Hell, Codename: Foxfire, Hollywood Wives, A Father's Revenge, Nightmare at Bitter Creek. Special: Roger Rabbit and the Secrets of Toontown (host). Pilot: Second Stage.

CASSIDY, SHAUN: Actor, Singer, Composer. b. Los Angeles, CA, Sept. 27, 1958. One of 3 sons of Shirley Jones and late Jack Cassidy. e. Beverly Hills H.S. Began recording in 1976 and toured Europe and Australia, appearing on numerous TV shows. Has had several hit records.

TELEVISION: Hardy Boys Mysteries, Matlock. Movies: Once Upon a Texas Train, Roots: The Gift. Numerous specials.

PICTURES: Born of Water (debut for Amer. Film Inst.).

CASTLE, NICK: Writer, Director. b. Los Angeles, CA, Sept. 21, 1947. e. Santa Monica Coll., U. of Southern California film sch. Son of late film and TV choreographer Nick Castle Sr. Appeared as child in films Anything Goes, Artists and Models. Worked with John Carpenter and other USC students on Acad. Award-winning short, The Resurrection of Bronco Billy.

PICTURES: Kiss Me, Kill Me; (dir. only); Skatedown USA (s.p. only); Tag: The Assassination Game; Escape from New York (s.p. only); The Last Starfighter (dir. only); The Boy Who Could Fly (dir. only), Tap.

CASTLE, WALTER H.: Cinematographer. b. Santa Ana, CA, May 19, 1905. Engaged continuously in photographic work for 27 years with Fox Films Corp. and 20th Century-Fox Film Corp., as director of photography; Walt Disney Prod., TV, Hardy Boys, American Dairy Story, Spin, Mickey Mouse Club, Our Friend the Atom, Saga of Andy Burnett; spec. effects for Trapeze.

CATES, GILBERT: Director, Producer. b. New York, NY, June 6, 1934. e. Syracuse U. Began TV career as guide at NBC studios in N.Y., working way up to prod. and dir. of game shows (Camouflage, Haggis Baggis, Mother's Day, etc.). Created Hootenanny and packaged and directed many TV specials. Pres. Directors Guild of America 1983–87. Awarded DGA's Robert B. Aldrich award 1989.

PICTURES: The Painting (short), Rings Around the World, I Never Sang for My Father, Summer Wishes, Winter Dreams (dir. only); One Summer Love, (prod.-dir.); The Promise, The Last Married Couple in America, Oh, God!—Book II, Boardwalk.

TELEVISION: International Showtime (1963–65 exec. prod.-dir.), Electric Showcase Specials (dir.-prod.), To All My Friends on Shore (dir.-prod.), The Affair (dir.), After the Fall (dir.-prod.), Johnny, We Hardly Knew Ye, (prod.-dir.), The Kid from Nowhere (prod.); Country Gold (dir.); Hobson's Choice (dir.); Burning Rage (dir.); Consenting Adult (dir.), Fatal Judgement, My First Love (dir) Backfire, O Do You Know the Muffin Man (dir.)

STAGE: Director: Tricks of the Trade, Voices, The Price (Long Wharf Theatre). Producer: Solitaire/Double Solitaire, The Chinese and Mr. Fish, I Never Sang for My Father, You Know I Can't Hear You When the Water's Running.

CATES, JOSEPH: Producer, Director. b. 1924. e. NYU. Brother of Gilbert Cates. Father of actress Phoebe Cates. One of first producers and dirs. of live TV with Look Upon a Star, 1947. Prod., Jackie Gleason Cavalcade of Stars, game shows, ($64,000 Question, $64,000 Challenge, Stop the Music, Haggis Baggis), NBC Spectaculars (1955–60), High Button Shoes, The Bachelor, Accent on Love, Gene Kelly, Ethel Merman, Victor Borge, Yves Montand shows.

THEATER: Prod. on B'way: What Makes Sammy Run?, Joe Egg, Spoon River Anthology, Gantry, Her First Roman.

PICTURES: Director: Who Killed Teddy Bear, The Fat Spy, Girl of the Night.

TELEVISION: Series: International Showtime (Don Ameche Circuses). Prod.-dir. of spectaculars and special programs, 1955–1988: Johnny Cash, David Copperfield, Steve Martin; Emmy Awards as prod: Anne Bancroft: The Woman in the Life of Man, Jack Lemmon and Fred Astaire, S'marvelous, S'wonderful, S'Gershwin, Annual Ford Theater Salutes to the President, Country Music Awards Show, Miss Teen Age America, Junior Miss pageants. Movies: Prod.: The Quick and the Dead, The Last Days of Frank and Jessie James, The Cradle Will Fall, Special People.

CATES, PHOEBE: Actress. b. New York, NY, 1964. Daughter of prod-dir. Joseph Cates. Dance prodigy and fashion model

before launching acting career in Paradise. Studied with Actors Circle theatre group. NY stage debut The Nest of the Wood Grouse (1984).
PICTURES: Paradise, Fast Times at Ridgemont High, Private School, Gremlins, Bright Lights, Big City; Shag, Date With an Angel, Heart of Dixie, Gremlins II.
TELEVISION: Series: Mr. and Mrs. Dracula. Movies: Baby Sister, Lace, Lace II.

CATTRALL, KIM: Actress. b. Liverpool, Eng., Aug. 21, 1956. e. American Acad. of Dramatic Arts, N.Y. Started stage career in Canada's Off-Bdwy. in Vancouver and Toronto; later performed in L.A. in A View from the Bridge, Agnes of God, Three Sisters, etc. On Bdwy in Wild Honey.
PICTURES: Rosebud (debut 1975), The Other Side of the Mountain—Part II, Tribute, Ticket to Heaven, Porky's, Police Academy, Turk 182, City Limits, Hold-Up, Big Trouble in Little China, Mannequin, Masquerade, Midnight Crossing, Palais Royale, For Better or For Worse, The Return of the Musketeers, Brown Bread Sandwiches.
TELEVISION: The Bastard, The Night Rider, The Rebels, Scruples, The Gossip Columnist, Sins of the Past.

CAULFIELD, JOAN: Actress. b. Orange, NJ, June 1, 1922. e. Columbia U. Harry Conover model 1942–43; on stage 1943–44; screen debut in Miss Susie Slagle's, 1945. Appt. v.p. in chg. TV programming, Donnelly Telecommunications.
PICTURES: Dear Ruth, Variety Girl, Unsuspected, Sainted Sisters, Larceny, The Pretty Girl, Blue Skies, Lady Said No, The Rains of Ranchipur, Buckskin.
TELEVISION: Sally, My Favorite Husband, The Magician (series); Murder She Wrote.

CAULFIELD, MAXWELL: Actor. b. Glasgow, Scotland, Nov. 23, 1959. m. actress Juliet Mills. First worked as a dancer at a London nightclub. After coming to NY in 1978, ran the concession stand at the Truck and Warehouse Theatre. Won a Theatre World Award for Class Enemy.
THEATER: Entertaining Mr. Sloane, Salonika.
PICTURES: Grease 2, Electric Dreams, The Boys Next Door, Sundown, Mind Games, No Cause For Alarm.
TELEVISION: The Colbys (series); Orleans (series); The Parade, Till We Meet Again.

CAVANAUGH, ANDREW: Executive. Held positions with Norton Simon, Inc. and Equitable Life Insurance Co. before joining Paramount Pictures in 1984 as v.p., human resources. 1985, appt. sr. v.p., administration, mng. personnel depts. on both coasts. Also oversees corp. admin. function for Paramount.

CAVANI, LILIANA: Director. b near Modena, in Emilia, Italy, January 12, 1937. e. U. of Bologna, diploma in classic literature, 1960; Ph.D. in linguistics. In 1960 took courses at Centro Sperimentale di Cinematografia in Rome where made short films Incontro Notturno and L'Evento. 1961 winner of RAI sponsored contest and started working for the new second Italian TV channel, 1962–66 directing progs. of serious political and social nature incl. History of 3rd Reich, Women in the Resistance, Age of Stalin, Philippe Petain—Trial at Vichy (Golden Lion Venice Fest.), Jesus My Brother, Day of Peace, Francis of Assisi. Has also directed operas Wozzeck, Iphigenia in Tauris and Medea on stage.
PICTURES: Galileo, I Cannibali, L'Ospite, Milarepa, Night Porter, Beyond Good and Evil, The Skin, Oltre la Porta, The Berlin Affair, Francesco.

CAVETT, DICK: Actor, Writer. b. Kearny, NE, Nov. 19, 1937. e. Yale U. Acted in TV dramas and Army training films. Was writer for Jack Paar and his successors on the Tonight Show. Also wrote comedy for Merv Griffin, Jerry Lewis, Johnny Carson. In 1967 began performing own comedy material in night clubs. On TV starred in Where It's At (special on ABC Stage 67) and What's In (special). Began daytime series for ABC-TV in 1968, three-weekly series summer of 1969. The Dick Cavett Show. 1989: The Dick Cavett Show (CNBC). Author: Cavett (with Christopher Porter) 1974.
THEATRE: Otherwise Engaged, Into the Woods.
PICTURES: Beetlejuice, Before God, Cameo: Moon Over Parador, After School.

CAZENOVE, CHRISTOPHER: Actor. b. Winchester, Eng., Dec. 17, 1945. m. Angharad Rees. e. Eton, Oxford U., trained at Bristol Old Vic Theatre School. West End theater includes Hamlet (1969), The Lionel Touch, My Darling Daisy, The Winslow Boy, Joking Apart, In Praise of Rattigan, The Life and Poetry of T.S. Eliot. Bdwy. debut: Goodbye Fidel (1980).
PICTURES: There's a Girl in My Soup (1970), Royal Flash, East of Elephant Rock, The Girl in Blue Velvet, Zulu Dawn, Eye of the Needle, From a Far Country, Heat and Dust, Until September, Mata Hari, The Fantastist, Hold My Hand I'm Dying.
TELEVISION: Series: The Regiment, The Duchess of Duke Street. Dynasty, A Fine Romance. Specials/movies: The Rivals of Sherlock Holmes (1971), Affairs of the Heart, Jennie: Lady Randolph Churchill, The Darkwater Hall Mystery, Ladykillers—A Smile Is Sometimes Worth a Million, The Red Signal, Lou Grant, The Letter, Jenny's War, Lace 2, Kane and Abel, Windmills of the Gods, Shades of Love, Souvenir, The Lady and the Highwayman, Tears in the Rain.

CELENTINO, LUCIANO: Producer, Director, Writer. b. Naples, Italy, 1940. e. Rome, Paris, London. Ent. ind. 1959. Wrote, prod., dir. many plays incl: Infamita di Questa Terra, Black Destiny, Honour, Stranger's Heart, Youth's Sin, Wanda Lontano Amore. Stage musicals such as Songs...Dots...And Fantasies, Night Club's Appointment, Filumena, Serenada, Mamma. Since 1964 film critic of Il Meridionale Italiano. From 1962 co-writer and first asst. director to Luigi Capuano and Vittoria De Sica. 1972: formed own company, Anglo-Fortunato Films. Co-wrote, prod., dir. Blood Money. Dir. Bandito (in Italy). Wrote and dir. Toujours, Parole, Jackpot.

CELLAN-JONES, JAMES: Director. b. Swansea, Wales, July 13, 1931. e. St. John's Coll., Cambridge. Best known for his adaptations of classic novels for the BBC and PBS (shown on Masterpiece Theatre), he has been called "master of the mini-series."
PICTURES: The Nelson Affair.
TELEVISION: The Scarlet and the Black, The Forsythe Saga, Portrait of a Lady, The Way We Live Now, Solo, The Roads to Freedom, Eyeless In Gaza, The Golden Bowl, Jennie, Caesar and Cleopatra, The Adams Chronicles, The Day Christ Died, The Ambassadors, Unity Mitford, Oxbridge Blues, Sleeps Six (also prod.), The Comedy of Errors, Fortunes of War, You Never Can Tell, Arms and the Man.

CHABROL, CLAUDE: Director. b. Paris, France, June 24, 1930. A founding director of the French New Wave. Has starred his former wife Stephane Audran in numerous films.
PICTURES: Le Beau Serge, The Cousins, Leda, Les Bonnes Femmes, Les Godelureaux, The Third Lover, Seven Capital Sins, Ophelia, Landru, Le Tigre Aime la Chair Fraiche, Marie-Chantal Contre le Docteur Kah, Le Tigre Se Parfume a la Dunamite, Paris vu par . . . Chabrol, La Ligne de Demarcation, The Champagne Murders, The Route to Corinth, Les Biches, Le Femme Infidele, This Man Must Die, Le Boucher, La Rapture, Ten Days' Wonder, Just Before Nightfall, Dr. Popaul, Les Noces Rouges, Nada, The Blood of Others (TV in U.S.), The Horse of Pride, Alouette, je te plumera; Poulet au Vinaigre (dir., s.p.), Clichy Days, The Lark (actor only), Women's Business (dir. co.-s.p.).

CHAFFEY, DON: Director. b. Hastings, England, 1917. Trained as artist; secured work in art dept. of Gainsborough Studios in early 40s. Eventually moved to Gaumont British International where directed first film, a documentary on dog-fish.
PICTURES: Time Is My Enemy, The Girl in the Picture, The Flesh is Weak, A Question of Adultery, The Man Upstairs, Danger Within, Dentist in the Chair, Greyfriars Bobby, Nearly a Nasty Accident, A Matter of Who, The Prince and the Pauper, Jason and the Argonauts, A Jolly Bad Fellow, One Million Years B.C., The Viking Queen, A Twist of Sand, Creature the World Forgot, The Three Lives of Thomasina, The Horse Without a Head, Ride a Wild Pony.

CHAIKIN, WILLIAM E.: Executive. b. Cleveland, OH, April 7, 1919. e. Ohio State U., B.S., journalism, M.S., political science. Was newspaper reporter and columnist Ohio, Indiana and Florida before joining 20th-Fox pub. dept. in 1945. And in pub. depts. of Republic and Eagle Lion Films. Later pres., Chaikin-Perret, p.r. firm. Became v.p. and treas. of Standard Capital, investment banking firm, where financed and supervised prod. of over 60 films. In 1963 named pres. and bd. chmn. of Charter Title Insurance Co. in Los Angeles. Mem: Board of Mariners Savings and Loan, bd. of Mariners Financial Corp., financial holding co. diversified building firm; 1968–74 v.p. in chg. of West Coast operations of Avco Embassy Pictures Corp. and asst. to James R. Kerr, pres. of Avco Corp., July 1974–80, pres. of Avco Embassy Pictures Corp.

CHAKERES, MICHAEL H.: Executive b. Ohio. e. Wittenberg U. Pres. and chmn. of bd. of Chakeres Theatres of Ohio and Kentucky. U.S. Army AF 1942–45. Bd. of Dir.: National NATO, NATO of Ohio, Will Rogers Hospital, Motion Picture Pioneers, Society National Bank, Wittenberg U., Community Hosp. board, Springfield Foundation board. Member: Variety Club, Masons, Scottish Rite, I.O.O.F. Order of AHEPA, Ohio Heart Ass'n., Rotary Club, City of Hope, University Club.

CHAKIRIS, GEORGE: Actor. b. Norwood, OH, Sept. 16, 1934. Entered m.p. industry as a dancer in There's No Business Like Show Business, White Christmas and Brigadoon; academy award for West Side Story. Starred in Diamond Head, The Young Girls of Rochefort, The Big Cube, Why Not Stay for Breakfast?, Pale Blood.
TELEVISION: Fantasy Island, Chips, Matt Houston, Scarecrow and Mrs. King, Hell Town, Dallas.

CHAMBERLAIN, RICHARD: Actor. b. Los Angeles, CA, March 31, 1935. Studied voice, LA Conservatory of Music 1958; acting with Jeff Corey. Founding mem. City of Angels, LA Theater Company. TV series: pilot: Paradise Kid. Became TV star in

Dr. Kildare series, 1961–66. Film debut in 1962, A Thunder of Drums. Founded prod. co. Cham Enterprises.
THEATER: Breakfast at Tiffany's, Night of the Iguana, Fathers & Sons, Blithe Spirit.
PICTURES: Secret of Purple Reef, Twilight of Honor, Joy in the Morning, Petulia, The Madwoman of Chaillot, Julius Caesar, The Music Lovers, Lady Caroline Lamb, The Three Musketeers, The Towering Inferno, The Four Musketeers, The Slipper and the Rose, The Last Wave, The Swarm, Murder by Phone, King Solomon's Mines, Alan Quartermain and the Lost City of Gold, The Return of the Musketeers.
TELEVISION: Hamlet (1970), Portrait of a Lady (BBC); Movies: The Woman I Love, F. Scott Fitzgerald and the Last of the Belles, The Lady's Not For Burning, The Man in the Iron Mask, The Count of Monte Cristo, Cook and Perry: The Race to the Pole, Wallenberg: A Hero's Story, Casanova. Mini-Series: Centennial, Shogun, The Thorn Birds, Dream West, The Bourne Identity. *Series:* Dr. Kildare, Island Son (also co-exec. prod.).

CHAMBERS, EVERETT: Producer, Writer, Director. b. Montrose, CA; Aug. 19, 1926. e. New School For Social Research, Dramatic Workshop, N.Y. Entered industry as actor; worked with Fred Coe as casting dir. and dir., NBC, 1952–57; prod., dir. Run Across the River. Author: Producing TV Movies.
PICTURES: The Kiss (1958, dir., nom. best short film, Acad. Awards), The Lollipop Cover (prod., writer, dir., best film and actor awards, Chicago Film Fest.).
TELEVISION: Producer: Series: Johnny Staccato (also writer), Target the Corrupters, The Dick Powell Theatre, The Lloyd Bridges Show (also writer); Peyton Place, Columbo, Future Cop, Lucan (also writer). Movies: Beverly Hills Madam, A Matter of Sex (exec. prod.) Partners in Crime, Airwolf (also writer), Timeslip (exec. prod., writer). (1985 Christopher Award, A.W.R.T. Award), Will There Really Be a Morning?, Berlin Tunnel 21 (sprv. prod.), Night Slaves (also writer), Moon of the Wolf, Trouble Comes to Town, Great American Beauty Contest, Can Ellen Be Saved? (also writer), Jigsaw John, Street Killing, Nero Wolfe, Twin Detectives (also writer), The Girl Most Likely to. . ., Sacrifice the Queen. Co-writer: Movies: The Perfect Town for Murder, Last Chance (pilot).

CHAMPION, JOHN C.: Director, Producer, Writer. b. Denver, CO, Oct. 13, 1923. e. Stanford U., Wittenberg Coll. p. Lee R. Champion, Supreme Court judge. Col. Entered m.p. in Fiesta; did some radio work; in stock at MGM briefly; co-pilot Western Air Lines, Inc., 1943; served in U.S. Army Air Force, air transport command pilot 1943–45; public relations officer AAF; writer & prod. for Allied Artists; v.p. prod. Commander Films Corp.: press. Champion Pictures, Inc.; prod., MGM, Warner, Para., Universal, Member: SAG, SWG, SIMPP, SPG; TV Academy, Prod. Writer, Mirisch-U.A.; prod. TV Laramie series; created McHales Navy; author, novel, The Hawks of Noon, 1965; National Cowboy, Hall of Fame Award, 1976.
PICTURES: Panhandle, Stampede, Hellgate, Dragonfly Squadron, Shotgun, Zero Hour, The Texican, Attack on the Iron Coast, Submarine X-1, The Last Escape, Brother of the Wind, Mustang Country (dir-prod-writer).

CHAMPION, MARGE: Dancer, Actress. b. Los Angeles, CA, Sept. 2, 1923. e. Los Angeles public schools. p. Ernest Belcher, ballet master. Made debut with former husband Gower Champion as dancing team, played many nightclubs; m.p. Debut in Mr. Music; then signed by MGM; Fame Star of Tomorrow, 1952.
STAGE: In Blossom Time, Student Prince for Los Angeles Civic Opera; Dark of the Moon. Beggar's Holiday in N.Y. in 3 for Tonight, (Broadway 1955); toured, Invitation to A March, 1962. Director: Stepping Out, Lute Song (Berkshire Theatre Fest, 1989).
PICTURES: Show Boat, Lovely to Look At, Everything I Have Is Yours, Give a Girl a Break, Three for the Show, Jupiter's Darling, The Swimmer, The Party, The Cockeyed Cowboys of Calico County, Whose Life Is It Anyway? (choreographer).
TELEVISION: GE Theatre, Chevy Show, Telephone Hour, Ed Sullivan, Shower of Stars, Marge & Gower Champion Show. Movie: Queen of the Stardust Ballroom (Emmy Award, choreography 1975).

CHANCELLOR, JOHN: TV Anchorman, News Reporter. b. Chicago, IL, 1927. e. U. of Illinois. Following military service joined Chicago Sun-Times (1948) and after two years moved to NBC News as Midwest corr. In 1948 assigned to Vienna bureau. Subsequently reported from London; was chief of Moscow bureau before appt. as host of Today program for one year (1961). Left NBC 1965–67 to become dir. of Voice of America. In recent yrs. anchorman for special coverage of moon landings, political conventions, inaugurations etc. Anchorman, NBC Nightly News, 1970–82. Now sr. commentator, NBC News, delivering news commentaries on NBC Nightly News.

CHANNING, CAROL: Actress. b. Seattle, WA, Jan. 31, 1923. e. Bennington Coll. Long career on Broadway and road; most notably in Gentlemen Prefer Blondes, Lend an Ear, and Hello Dolly! (Tony Award), Lorelei, Legends (on tour with Mary Martin).
PICTURES: First Traveling Saleslady, Thoroughly Modern Millie, Skidoo.
TELEVISION: Svengali and the Blonde, Three Men on a Horse, Crescendo; many guest appearances.

CHANNING, STOCKARD: Actress. r.n. Susan Stockard. b. New York, NY, Feb. 13, 1944. e. Radcliffe Coll., B.A., 1965. With Theater Co. of Boston, experimental drama company, 1967. Has performed in some 25 plays winning 2 Tony nominations and a Tony Award for Joe Egg (best actress, 1985).
THEATER: Two Gentlemen of Verona, No Hard Feelings, Vanities (Mark Taper Forum, LA), The Rink, Joe Egg.
PICTURES: Comforts of Home (1970), The Fortune, The Big Bus, Sweet Revenge, Grease, The Cheap Detective, The Fish That Saved Pittsburgh, Without a Trace, Heartburn, The Men's Club, A Time of Destiny, Staying Together, The Applegates.
TELEVISION: Silent Victory: The Kitty O'Neil Story, The Girl Most Likely To, Stockard Channing Show (series, 1979–80), Not My Kid, The Room Upstairs, Echoes in the Darkness.

CHAPIN, DOUG: Producer. Began career as actor; then switched to film production, making debut with When a Stranger Calls, 1979.
PICTURES: Pandemonium, American Dreamer.
TELEVISION: Movies: Belle Starr, Missing Pieces, Second Sight.

CHAPLIN, CHARLES S.: Executive. b. Toronto, Ont., Canada, June 24, 1911. Studied law. Entered m.p. ind. 1930 as office boy with United Artists; then office mgr. booker, St. John, N.B., 1933; br. mgr. 1935; to Montreal in same capacity, 1941; named Canadian gen. mgr., June 11, 1945; resigned 1962. Vice-pres. Canadian sls. mgr., Seven Arts Prod., 1962; chief exec. off., v.p., dir. TV sls., Europe-Africa, Middle East-Socialist countries, 1968–70; v.p., WB-Seven Arts, 1970–72; exec. v.p. intl. film dist., NTA (Canada) Ltd., Toronto Intl. Film Studios, 1972–80; pres., Charles Chaplin Enterprises, specializing in theatrical and TV sls. and prod. Pres.: B'nai Brith-, Toronto Bd. of Trade, various charitable org., many trade assns., past pres. Canadian M.P. Dist. Assn., Chmn. m.p. section Com. Chest, chmn. publ. rel. comm. & past-chmn., M.P. Industry Council; Natl. Board Council Christians & Jews, U. of Haifa, etc.

CHAPLIN, GERALDINE: Actress. b. Santa Monica, CA, July 3, 1944. e. Royal Ballet School, London. Daughter of Charles Chaplin. Starred in over 20 European productions, including seven with Spanish filmmaker, Carlos Saura.
PICTURES: Doctor Zhivago, Stranger in the House, I Killed Rasputin, The Hawaiians, Zero Population Growth, Innocent Bystanders, The Three Musketeers, The Four Musketeers, Nashville, Buffalo Bill and the Indians, Welcome to L.A., Cria, Roseland, Remember My Name, A Wedding, The Mirror Crack'd, Voyage en Douce, Bolero, L'Amour Par Terre, The Moderns, White Mischief, The Return of the Musketeers, I Want to Go Home.
TELEVISION: The Corsican Brothers, My Cousin Rachel.

CHAPLIN, SAUL: Musical director, Producer. b. Brooklyn, NY, Feb. 19, 1912. e. NYU, 1929–34. Wrote vaudeville material, 1933–36; songwriter Vitaphone Corp.; other, 1934–40; Columbia, 1940–48; MGM, from 1948; songs include: Bei Mir Bist Du Schoen, Shoe Shine Boy, Anniversary Song.
PICTURES: Acad. Award, collab. best scoring of mus., American in Paris, 1951, 7 Brides for 7 Brothers, 1954; West Side Story, 1961; mus. dir., Lovely to Look At, Give A Girl a Break, Kiss Me Kate, Jupiter's Darling; mus. supv. Interrupted Melody, High Society; assoc. prod. Les Girls; music assoc. prod. Merry Andrew; assoc. prod. Can Can, West Side Story, The Sound of Music; prod. Star, assoc. prod., The Man of La Mancha; co-prod. That's Entertainment, Part Two.

CHAPMAN, MICHAEL: Cinematographer. b. New York, NY, Nov. 21, 1935. m. writer-dir. Amy Jones. Early career in N.Y. area working on documentaries before becoming camera operator for cinematographer Gordon Willis on The Godfather, Klute, End of the Road, The Landlord. Also camera operator Jaws.
PICTURES: The Last Detail, White Dawn, Taxi Driver, The Front, The Next Man, Fingers, The Last Waltz, Invasion of the Body Snatchers, Hard Core, The Wanderers, Raging Bull, Dead Men Don't Wear Plaid, Personal Best, The Man With Two Brains, All the Right Moves (dir.); The Clan of the Cave Bear (dir.); Shoot to Kill, Scrooged, Ghostbusters II.
TELEVISION: Death Be Not Proud, King, Gotham. Dir.: The Annihilator (pilot).

CHARI, V.K.N.: Public relations counsel, Publicity advisor. b. Salem, 1913. Till 1956 publicity & pub. relations officer, Gemini Studios, Madras. Presently film publicity adviser to film studios and film producers. Editor: Advertiser's Vademecum, Indian Advertising Year Book, An Economic Guide to India, The Languages of India. Refer-india, etc. Hon. Genl.

Secretary. The Indian Council of Public Affairs, Madras. Journalist & news correspondent, B44 First mainroad Sastrinagar, Madras 20.

CHARISSE, CYD: Dancer, Actress. r.n. Tula Ellice Finklea. b. Amarillo, TX, March 8, 1923. e. Hollywood Prof. Sch. m. Tony Martin, singer. Toured U.S. & Europe with Ballet Russe; screen debut in Something to Shout About, 1943. Named Star of Tomorrow 1948.
PICTURES: Mission to Moscow, Three Wise Fools, Till the Clouds Roll By, On an Island with you, Words and Music, Kissing Bandit, Tension, East Side, West Side, Mark of the Renegade, Wild North, Singin' in the Rain, Sombrero, Band Wagon, Easy to Love, Brigadoon, Deep in My Heart, It's Always Fair Weather, Meet Me in Las Vegas, Silk Stockings, Black Tights, Two Weeks in Another Town, The Silencers, Maroc 7.
TELEVISION: Movie: Portrait of an Escort, Swimsuit, Cinderalla Summer; many specials.

CHARLES, MARIA: Actress. b. London, England, Sept. 22, 1929. Trained at Royal Acad. of Dramatic Art. London Stage Debut 1946 in Pick Up Girl. Subseq.
STAGE (London): Women of Twilight, The Boy Friend, Divorce Me, Darling!, Enter A Free Man, They Don't Grow on Trees, Winnie the Pooh, Jack the Ripper, The Matchmaker, Measure for Measure, Annie (1979–80), Fiddler on the Roof, Steaming, Peer Gynt, The Lower Depths, When We Are Married, Follies. Dir.: Owl and the Pussycat.
PICTURES: Folly To Be Wise, The Deadly Affair, Eye of the Devil, Great Expectations, The Return of the Pink Panther, Cuba, Victor/Victoria.
TELEVISION: The Likes of 'Er, The Moon and the Yellow River, Down Our Street, Easter Passion, Nicholas Nickleby, The Voice of the Turtle, The Fourth Wall, The Good Old Days, Turn Out the Lights, Angel Pavement, The Ugliest Girl in Town, Other Peoples Houses, Rogues Gallery, The Prince and the Pauper, Crown Court, Bar Mitzvah Boy, Secret Army, Agony, Never the Twain, La Ronde, Shine of Harvey Moon, Sheppey, La Ronde, Brideshead Revisited.

CHARLESON, IAN: Actor. b. Edinburgh, Scotland, Aug. 11, 1949. e. Edinburgh U.; trained for stage at London Acad. of Music and Dramatic Art. On London stage: Cat on a Hot Tin Roof, 1988.
PICTURES: Jubilee, Chariots of Fire, Gandhi, Ascendancy, Greystoke, Opera.
TELEVISION: Rock Follies, Churchill's People, The Paradise Run, Antony and Cleopatra, Something's Got to Give, Master of the Game, A Month in the Country, The Devil's Lieutenant, Code Name: Kyril, Oxbridge Blues.

CHARTERIS, LESLIE: Writer, Producer. b. Singapore, 1907; e. Cambridge U. Novelist; creator The Saint, protagonist of mystery novels and series of pictures based on them prod. by RKO from 1938 and by Julian Lesser from 1952.

CHARTOFF, ROBERT: Producer. b. New York, NY., Aug. 26, 1933. e. Union College, A.B.; Columbia U., LL.B. Met Irwin Winkler through mutual client at William Morris Agency (N.M.) and established Chartoff-Winkler Prods. Currently pres., Chartoff Prods., Inc.
PICTURES: Double Trouble, Point Blank, The Split, They Shoot Horses Don't They?, The Strawberry Statement, Leo The Last, Believe in Me, The Gang That Couldn't Shoot Straight, The New Centurions, Up the Sandbox, The Mechanic, Busting, The Gambler, SPYs, Breakout, Nickelodeon, New York, New York, Valentino, Rocky, Comes a Horseman, Uncle Joe Shannon, Rocky II, Raging Bull, True Confessions, Rocky III, The Right Stuff, Rocky IV, Beer, The Return of the Musketeers, Rocky V.

CHASE, BRANDON: Producer, Director. President MPA Feature Films, Inc.; newscaster-news director NBC-TV 1952–57. Executive director Mardi Gras Productions, Inc. and member of Board of Directors. Now pres., Group I Films, Ltd., and V.I. Prods., Ltd.
PICTURES: The Dead One, The Sinner and the Slave Girl, Bourbon Street Shadows, Verdict Homicide, Face of Fire, Four for the Morgue, Mission To Hell, The Wanton, Harlow, Girl In Trouble, Threesome, Wild Cargo, Alice in Wonderland, The Models, The Four Of Us, Against All Odds, The Giant Spider Invasion, House of 1,000 Pleasures, The Rogue, Eyes of Dr. Chaney, Alligator, Crash!, Take All of Me, The Psychic, UFOs Are Real, The Actresses, The Sword and the Sorcerer.
TELEVISION: Wild Cargo (series prod.-dir.); This Strange and Wondrous World (prod.-dir.), Linda Evans: Secrets to Stay Young Forever.

CHASE, CHEVY: Actor. r.n. Cornelius Crane. b. New York, NY, Oct. 8, 1944. e. Bard Coll.; B.A. Studied audio research at CCS Institute. Worked as writer for Mad Magazine 1969. Teamed with Kenny Shapiro and Lane Sarasohn while still in school to collaborate on material for underground TV, which ultimately became off-off-Broadway show and later movie called Groove Tube. Co-wrote and starred in Saturday Night Live on TV, winning 2 Emmys as continuing single performance by a supporting actor and as writer for show. Wrote Paul Simon Special 1977 (Emmy Award).
PICTURES: Foul Play (debut 1978), Oh, Heavenly Dog, Caddyshack, Seems Like Old Times, Under the Rainbow, Modern Problems, National Lampoon's Vacation, Deal of the Century, Fletch, National Lampoon's European Vacation, Spies Like Us, Follow That Bird, Three Amigos, The Couch Trip, Funny Farm, Caddyshack II, Fletch Lives, National Lampoon's Christmas Vacation.

CHASE, STANLEY: Producer. b. Brooklyn, NY, May 3. e. NYU, B.A.; Columbia U, postgraduate. m. actress/artist Dorothy Rice. Began career as assoc. prod. of TV show Star Time; story dept., CBS-TV; then produced plays Off-Broadway and on Broadway, winner Tony and Obie awards for The Threepenny Opera. Joined ABC-TV as dir. in chg. programming; exec. consultant, Metromedia Producers Org.; prod. & exec. Alan Landsburg Productions. Formed Stanley Chase Productions, Inc. in 1975, which heads as pres.
PICTURES: The Hell with Heroes, Colossus: The Forbin Project; High-Ballin' (exec. prod.); Fish Hawk (exec. prod.); The Guardian (HBO); Mack the Knife.
TELEVISION: Inside Danny Baker (pilot); Al Capp special (prod., writer); Happily Ever After (pilot; prod., writer); Bob Hope Presents the Chrysler Theatre series; Jigsaw (pilot); Fear on Trial (Emmy nomination); Courage of Kavik (exec. prod.); An American Christmas Carol, Grace Kelly.
STAGE: Producer of following Bdwy. plays: The Threepenny Opera, The Potting Shed, The Cave Dwellers, A Moon for the Misbegotten, European Tour: Free and Easy.

CHASMAN, DAVID: Executive. b. New York, NY, Sept. 28, 1925. e. Sch. of Industrial Art, 1940–43; Academie De La Grande-Chaumiere, 1949–50. Monroe Greenthal Co., Inc. 1950–53; Grey Advertising Agency, Inc., 1953–60. Freelance consultant to industry 1950–60; worked on pictures for UA, 20th-Fox, Columbia, Samuel Goldwyn, City Film; Adv. mgr. United Artists, 1960; exec. dir. adv., United Artists, 1962; exec. production, United Artists, London, 1964; v.p. in prod. United Artists, 1969; v.p. of west coast operations, U.A. 1970; Senior v.p. in charge of prod., U.A. 1972; president, Convivium Productions Inc., 1974. Joined Columbia 1977, named exec. v.p. worldwide theatrical prod. 1979. Joined MGM 1980; named exec. v.p.-worldwide theatrical prod.
PICTURES: Exec. prod.: Brighton Beach Memoirs, The Secret of My Success.

CHATELAIN, DIDIER: Production executive. b. Paris, France, Jan. 24. e. Paris and Polytechnic, London. Degree in Business Administration, Marketing & Advertising. Entered industry in 1970 joining Herman Cohen Productions in London and Hollywood, starting with the advertising & promotion of Crooks and Coronets, Trog, Today We Kill . . . Tomorrow We Die!, The Strangers Gundown, Assistant Producer, Craze, Now v.p., Cobra Media, Inc.

CHAUDHRI, AMIN QAMAR: Director, Cinematographer, Editor. b. Punjab, India, April 18, 1942. e. Hampstead Polytechnic, London, City U. of New York. Pres., Filmart Enterprises Ltd. & Filmart Int'l Ltd., Pres./CEO, Continental Film Group Ltd.
PICTURES: Director: Kashish, Sweet Vengeance, Khajuraho, Eternal, Urvasi, Konarak, Black Rodeo, The Land of Buddha. Producer: Night Visitors. Producer/Director: Once Again, An Unremarkable Life, Tiger Warsaw, The Last Day of School.
CINEMATOGRAPHY: Right On, Sweet Vengeance, The Hopefuls, The Wicked Die Slow, The Love Statute, Who Says I Can't Ride a Rainbow, Black Rodeo, Medium Is the Message, Death of a Dunbar Girl, Kashish, Deadly Vengeance, The Last Day of School.
TELEVISION: Reflections of India (prod.-dir.).

CHER: Singer, Actress. r.n. Cherilyn Sarkisian. b. El Centro, CA, May 20, 1946. Began singing as backup singer for Crystals and Ronettes then, with then husband Sonny Bono in 1965; first hit record I Got You Babe, sold 3 million. Made two films and then debuted nightclub musical-comedy act in 1969. CBS comedy-variety series started as summer show in 1971; became regular following December. NY stage debut: Come Back to the Five and Dime, Jimmy Dean, Jimmy Dean (1982).
PICTURES: Good Times, Chastity, Come Back to the Five and Dime, Jimmy Dean, Jimmy Dean, Silkwood, Mask, The Witches of Eastwick, Suspect, Moonstruck (Acad. Award, 1987), Mermaid.
TELEVISION: Sonny & Cher Comedy Hour (1971–74), Cher; The Sonny and Cher Show (1976–77).

CHEREN, ROBERT M.: Executive. b. Winthrop, MA, June 12, 1947. e. Graham Coll., 1967. 1968, joined 20th Century Fox sales dept. in Boston; 1969, named branch mgr. 1975, transferred by Fox to Los Angeles as dist. mgr.; 1976, promoted to west. div. mgr. 1979, to Columbia Pictures as west, div. mgr.; 1981, joined Filmways (later Orion Pictures) as v.p. & gen. sls. mgr. 1984, named Orion exec. v.p., then pres., Orion Pictures Dist. Corp.

MEMBER: Academy of Motion Picture Arts & Sciences, Variety Club New York, Variety Club Tent 25 So. Calif.; Foundation of Motion Picture Pioneers.

CHERMAK, CY: Producer, Writer. b. Bayonne, NJ, Sept. 20, 1929. e. Brooklyn Coll., Ithaca Coll.
TELEVISION: Writer, prod., exec. prod.: Ironsides, The Virginian, The New Doctors, Amy Prentiss, Night Stalkers, Barbary Coast, CHIPS. Movie: Murder at the World Series (prod., s.p.).

CHERTOK, HARVEY: Executive. b. New York, NY, Oct. 29, 1932. e. NYU, grad. school, bus. admin. Merchandising mgr., National Telefilm Assocs., Jan. 1956–Aug. 1959; supv., adv., United Artists Associated, Aug. 1959–March 1961; dir., adv., sls. prom., publicity, Seven Arts Associated Corp., 1961–1968; prod., 7 Surprizes, 1964; 1968 TV v.p. advertising-publicity, Warner-7 Arts, co.-prod., The Great Charlie Chan (Golden Press) 1968; pres. The Children's Movie of the Month, Inc., 1969–71; marketing consultant, United Artists Television, 1972–73; v.p.-special-projects, The American Film Theatre, Inc. 1973–75; v.p. adv., sls. pro., pub. for Time-Life Television, 1975; named v.p., adv./promo, Time Life-TV, 1978–81. Formed Quartel Int'l. to dist. foreign TV rights.
PICTURES: The Impossible Spy (exec. prod.).

CHERTOK, JACK: Producer. b. Atlanta, GA, July 13, 1906. Began career as script clerk, MGM; later asst. cameraman, asst. dir., head of music dept., short subjects prod. (including Crime Does Not Pay, Robert Benchley, Pete Smith series.) Feature prod. MGM 1939–42 (The Penalty, Joe Smith, American, Kid Glove Killer, The Omaha Trail, Eyes in the Night, etc.). In 1942, apptd. Hollywood prod. chief, Co-Ord. Inter-Amer. Affairs, serving concurrently with regular studio work. Left MGM 1942 and prod. for Warner Bros. to late 1944; pres.: Produced The Corn is Green and Northern Pursuit for Warner Bros. Pres. Jack Chertok TV, Inc.
TELEVISION: Prod.: My Favorite Martian, Lone Ranger, Sky King, Cavalcade, Private Secretary, My Living Doll, Western Marshal, The Lawless Years.

CHESTER, HALE: Producer. b. Brooklyn, NY, March 6, 1921. On N.Y. stage; film debut in Crime School 1937, followed by Little Tough Guy series. Juvenile Court; personal appearance tour of U.S. and Canada 1941–44; entered m.p. production 1944, doing a series of musical shorts. Member: IMPPA. Prod. Joe Palooka series begin with Joe Palooka Champ, 1946, released via Monogram, Smart Woman; v.p. in chge. prod., Mutual Films Corp., 1951.
PICTURES: Joe Palooka in The Squared Circle, Underworld Story, The Highwayman, Triple Cross, Models, Beast from 20,000 Fathoms, Crashout, Bold and The Brave, The Weapon, The Haunted, School for Scoundrels, Two-Headed Spy, His and Hers, Hide and Seek, The Comedy Man, The Double Man, The Secret War of Harry Frigg.

CHETWYND, LIONEL: Executive, Writer, Director. b. London, England, 1940. m. actress Gloria Carlin. Emigrated to Canada, 1948. e. Sir George Williams U., Montreal, BA, economics; BCL-McGill U., Montreal. Graduate Work-Law—Trinity Coll. Oxford. Admitted to bar–Province of Quebec, 1968. C.B.C.—TV-Public Affairs and Talks, 1961–1965. CTV network 1965–67. Controller commercial TV and film rights, Expo '67. Freelance writer and consultant 1961–68. Asst. man. dir. Columbia Pictures (U.K.) Ltd. London 1968–72. Asst. man. dir. Columbia-Warner UK, 1971. Story and book for musical Maybe That's Your Problem, 1971–1973. Then Bleeding Great Orchids (staged London, and Off-Bdwy). Also wrote The American 1776, official U.S. Bi-centennial film and We the People/200 Constitutional Foundation. Former mem. of NYU grad. film sch. faculty, lecturer on screenwriting at Frederick Douglass Ctr. Harlem. Mem of Canadian Bar Assc. Served on bd. of gov., Commission on Battered Children, and the Little League.
PICTURES: The Apprenticeship of Duddy Kravitz (s.p.; Acad. Award nom.), Morning Comes (dir., s.p.), Two Solitudes (prod., dir., s.p., Grand Award Salonika), Quintet (s.p.), The Hanoi Hilton (dir., s.p.), Redline, (dir., s.p.).
TELEVISION: Johnny We Hardly Knew Ye (prod., s.p.; George Washington Honor Medal, Freedom Fdn.), It Happened One Christmas (s.p.), Goldenrod (prod., s.p.), A Whale for the Killing (s.p.), Miracle on Ice (s.p.; Christopher Award), Escape From Iran: The Canadian Caper (s.p.), Sadat (s.p.; NAACP Image Award), Children in the Crossfire (s.p.), To Heal a Nation (writer, exec. prod.), Evil in Clear River (exec. prod.; Christopher Award), So Proudly We Hail (dir., s.p.), The Godfather Wars (s.p.).

CHIKADA, TADASHI: Executive. b. Japan, Nov. 20, 1919. e. Tokyo Foreign Language U. 1940–6 with Showa Tsusho in Japan and China; 1947–50 Izumi Sangyo, transferring to Nihon Eiga Shizai (Japan Movie Equipment Co.) which later became Toshiba Photo Phone Co.; appt. director and gen. mgr. of Trade Div. in 1972, and in 1974 director in charge of trade.

CHILDS, RICHARD B. (REG): Executive. b. Oakland CA, March 14, 1937. e. Stanford U., 1964. President and Chief Operating Officer, Nelson Entertainment.

CHIN, ELIZABETH MAE: Executive. b. New York, NY, Nov. 2, 1938. e. City Coll. of New York, Business Administration, 1960. Internal Auditor 1960; International trade and entrepreneur of intl. dairy franchise 1968. Entered m.p. industry in 1974 as agent for independent film distribution in theatrical and TV. Presently, exec. of Far East Enterprises, and Emcee World Associates, Inc. and Bergen Intl. Corp.

CHINICH, JESSE: Executive. b. Hoboken, NJ, Dec. 17, 1921. e. NYU Law School, LLB, 1938. Lawyer with Hovell, Clarkson and Klupt, 1938–41; Capt., Air Force Intelligence, Pacific Theatre, 1941–46; joined Paramount Theatres as film buyer, 1946–51; circuit supervisor, Rugoff & Becker, NYC, 1951–53; western div. sales mgr., Buena Vista Film Dist., Co., 1953–61; Ass't gen. sales mgr. co-ordinator Cinema V Dist.; ass't sales mgr., Allied Artists; sales executive, special projects, Warner Bros. Dist. Corp. Now Publisher of weekly newsletters.

CHINICH, MICHAEL: Producer. b. New York, NY. e. Boston U. Began career as casting agent in N.Y.; moved to L.A. to join MCA-Universal Pictures as executive in casting. Named head of feature film casting; then prod. v.p. Began association with director John Hughes at Universal, later joining him at Paramount.
PICTURES: *Casting dir.:* Dog Day Afternoon, Coal Miner's Daughter, Animal House, Melvin and Howard, The Blues Brothers, Midnight Run, Twins, Lisa. *Exec. Prod.:* Pretty in Pink, Ferris Bueller's Day Off, Some Kind of Wonderful, Planes, Trains and Automobiles (co-exec. prod.).

CHOMSKY, MARVIN J.: Director. b. Bronx, NY, May 23, 1929. e. Syracuse U., B.S.; Stanford U., M.A. Started in theatre business at early age as art dir. with such TV credits as U.S. Steel Hour, Playhouse 90, Studio One, etc. Later worked with Herbert Brodkin who advanced him to assoc. prod. with such TV shows as The Doctors and The Nurses. Brought to Hollywood in 1965 as assoc. prod. for Talent Associates, producing series of TV pilots. Art dir.: The Bubble.
PICTURES: Evel Knievel, Murph the Surf, Mackintosh and T.J., Good Luck Miss Wycoff, Tank.
TELEVISION: The Wild, Wild West, Gunsmoke, Star Trek, Then Came Bronson. Movies: Assault on the Wayne, Mongo's Back in Town, Family Flight, Fireball Forward, The F.B.I. Story, The F.B.I. vs. Alvin Karpis, Mrs. Sundance, Brinks: The Great Train Robbery, Law and Order, Holocaust (Emmy Award), Victory at Entebbe, Roots, Attica (Emmy), Inside the Third Reich (Emmy), My Body, My Child; The Narobi Affair, Robert Kennedy: His Life and Times, Evita (also prod.), Peter the Great (also prod.), The Deliberate Stranger (also prod.), Anastasia, Billionaire Boys Club (sprv. prod., dir.), Angel in Green (dir.), I'll Be Home for Christmas (also prod.), Brotherhood of the Rose (also prod.).

CHONG, RAE DAWN: Actress. b. Vancouver, 1962. Daughter of director-comedian Tommy Chong. Debut at 12 in The Whiz Kid of Riverton (TV).
PICTURES: Quest for Fire, The Corsican Brothers, Beat Street, Fear City, American Flyer, Choose Me, Commando, The Color Purple, Soul Man, The Squeeze, The Principal, City Limits, Walking After Midnight, Loon, Far Out Man, Amazon.
TELEVISION: Badge of the Assassin.

CHONG, TOMMY: Singer, Actor, Writer, Director. b. Edmonton, Alta., May 24, 1938. Was guitar player with various Canadian rhythm and blues combinations, teamed with Richard Marin (Cheech) in improvisational group. Has made comedy recordings.
PICTURES: Cheech and Chong's Up in Smoke, Cheech and Chong's Next Movie, Cheech and Chong's Nice Dreams, Things Are Tough All Over, It Came from Hollywood, Still Smokin', The Corsican Brothers (also dir., s.p.), After Hours, Far Out Man (also dir., s.p.).
TELEVISION: Trial and Error (co-exec. prod.).

CHOOLUCK, LEON: Producer, Director. b. New York, NY, March 19, 1920. e. City Coll. of New York, 1938. Production, distribution, editing with Consolidated Film Industries Ft. Lee 1936–40; staff sergeant, Army Pictorial Service as news photographer 1941–45; Indep. as asst. dir. and prod. mgr. 1946–56; prod. for Regal Films (Col) Clover Prods. (Col.) Hugo Haas Prods. (Col). and Orbit Pro., (Fox) 1957–58; dir. Highway Patrol, 1958. Various occupations on stage 1947–58; prod. mgr., Captain Sinbad, Daystar Prods., Stoney Burke (series), prod. mgr., assoc. prod., Daystar Prods., 1962–63 The Outer Limits, Lockup (dir.), prod. supv., Encyclopedia Britannica Films, in Spain, 1964; prod. supv., U.S. Pictures, Battle of the Bulge; loc. mgr., Three F Prods., assoc. prod. I Spy, TV Series, 1965–67. Vice Pres. Fouad Said Cinemobile Systems, 1969–70; ABC Pictures 1970–71 (Grissom Gang, Kotch).
PICTURES: Hell on Devil's Island, Plunder Road, Murder

by Contract, City of Fear (prod.), The Fearmakers, Day of the Outlaw, Bramble Bush, Rise and Fall of Legs Diamond (assoc. prod.), Studs Lonigan, Three Blondes in His Life (dir.), El Cid, Midas Run (assoc. prod.), Payday; Three the Hard Way, Take a Hard Ride, Apocalypse Now, Loving Couples. Wonders of China for Disney Circlevision Epcot (supv.).

TELEVISION: Prod. supv. 1974–76; Specials: Strange Homecoming, James Mitchener's Dynasty, Judge Horton and the Scottsboro Boys, Pearl, A Rumor of War, Murder in Texas, Love Boat, Dynasty, Breakdown (Alfred Hitchcock), On Wings of Eagles, Square Dance.

CHOW, RAYMOND: Producer. b. Hong Kong, 1927. e. St. John's U., Shanghai. Worked as journalist for Hong Kong Standard; then joined the U.S. Information Agency, establishing its Chinese radio station which broadcast to the Chinese mainland. In late 1950s joined Shaw Brothers as head of their publicity operations. In next 12 years became right-hand man of Run Run Shaw and head of production. In 1971 formed The Golden Harvest Group to produce Chinese-language films in Hong Kong. Two kung-fu films featuring Bruce Lee put Harvest into int'l market. Started English-language films in 1977, beginning with The Amsterdam Kill and The Boys in Company C.

FILMS: Lassiter, Cannonball Run II, The Reincarnation of Golden Lotus.

CHRISTIAN, LINDA: Actress. r.n. Blanca Rosa Welter. b. Tampico, Mexico, Nov. 13, 1924. e. Mexico, Venezuela, Palestine, South Africa, Holland, Italy; attended medical school in Palestine. Worked for British Censorship Bureau in Palestine; asst. to plastic surgeon; screen debut in Holiday in Mexico (1946).

PICTURES: Green Dolphin Street, Tarzan and the Mermaids, The Happy Time, Battle Zone, Slave of Babylon, Athena, Thunderstorm, The VIPs.

CHRISTIANSEN, ROBERT W.: Producer. b. Porterville, CA. e. Bakersfield Coll. Spent 3 years in Marine Corps. Worked on Hollywood Reporter in circulation and advertising. Joined Cinema Center Films; prod. asst. on Monte Walsh and Hail Hero. Co-produced first feature in 1970, Adam at Six A.M., with Rick Rosenberg, with whom co-produced all credits listed.

PICTURES: Adam at Six A.M., Hide in Plain Sight.

TELEVISION: Features: Suddenly Single, The Glass House, Gargoyles, A Brand New Life, The Man Who Could Talk to Kids, The Autobiography of Miss Jane Pittman, I Love You . . . Goodbye, Queen of the Stardust Ballroom, Born Innocent, A Death in Canaan, Strangers, Robert Kennedy and His Times, Kids Don't Tell, As Summers Die, Gore Vidal's Lincoln, Red Earth, White Earth, The Heist.

CHRISTIE, HOWARD J: Producer. b. San Francisco, CA, Sept. 16, 1912. e. U. of California, Berkeley. Entered m.p. ind. following graduation from coll. in 1934, as actor; asst. dir. 1936–40; assoc. prod., 1942–44, Deanna Durbin pictures. Member: Screen Directors Guild, Screen Producers Guild, Delta Tau Delta, vice pres., Reeve M.C.A. Inc., 1961.

PICTURES: Lady on a Train, Because of Him I'll Be Yours, Abbott & Costello Meet the Invisible Man, Golden Horde, Comin' Round the Mountain, Lost in Alaska, Against All Flags, Yankee Buccaneer, Seminole, Lone Hand, Abbott and Costello Go to Mars, Abbott and Costello Meet Dr. Jekyll and Mr. Hyde, Back to God's Country, Yankee Pasha, Abbott and Costello Meet Keystone Kops, Smoke Signal, The Looters, Purple Mask, Abbott and Costello Meet the Mummy, Price of Fear, Congi Crossing, Showdown at Abilene, Toy Tiger, Away All Boats, I've Lived Before, Wagon Train, The Raiders, Sword of Ali Baba, Senes, Laredo, Ride to Hangman's Tree, Journey to Shiloh, Nobody's Perfect, A Man Called Gannon.

TELEVISION: The Virginian.

CHRISTIE, JULIE: Actress. b. Chukua, Assam, India, July 14, 1941. e. year in France followed by drama school in England. TV debut in A for Andromeda. Birmingham Rep.; Royal Shakespeare Co.; East European and American tour. NY stage, Uncle Vanya.

PICTURES: Crooks Anonymous (1962), Fast Lady, Billy Liar, Young Cassidy, Darling (Academy Award, 1965), Dr. Zhivago, Farenheit 451, Far from the Madding Crowd, Petulia, In Search of Gregory, The Go-Between, McCabe and Mrs. Miller, Don't Look Now, Shampoo, The Demon Seed, Heaven Can Wait, Memories of a Survivor, The Return of the Soldier, Golddiggers, Heat and Dust, Power, Miss Mary, La Memoire tatourée., Fools of Fortune.

TELEVISION: Debut: A is for Andromedia (UK series, 1962); Fathers and Sons (Italian TV), Dadah Is Death (Amer. TV debut, 1988).

CHRISTINE, VIRGINIA: Actress. b. Stanton, IA, March 5, 1920. e. UCLA. Has appeared in more than 400 motion pictures and television productions.

PICTURES: Mission to Moscow, Counter Attack, The Killers, Cover Up, The Men, Cyrano De Bergerac, Cobweb, High Noon, Not as a Stranger, Spirit of St. Louis, Three Brave Men, Judgment At Nuremberg, The Prize, Four For Texas, Edge of Darkness, The Mummy's Curse, Girls of the Big House, Murder is My Business, The Wife of Monte Cristo, Dragnet, Flaming Star, Cattle King, A Rage to Live, Guess Who's Coming to Dinner, Hail Hero, Daughter of the Mind.

TELEVISION: Dragnet, Abbot & Costello, Dangerous Assignment, Racket Squad, Superman, Schlitz Playhouse, Four Star Playhouse, The Whistler, Code 3, Ford Theatre, You Are There, Stage 7, Passport to Danger, Soldier of Fortune, Heinz Show, Anthology, Four Star Playhouse, Cavalcade of America, Alfred Hitchcock Presents, Father Knows Best, Crusader, Kellogg, Front Row Center, The Twisted Road, Matinee, Private Secretary, Fort Laramie, Big Town, Science Fiction, Frontier Detective, Lone Ranger, Jim Bowie, Wire Service, Whirlybirds, Gunsmoke, Las Vegas Story, Trackdown, The Thin Man, San Francisco Beat, Stranger In Town, T Men, Casey Jones, Climax, Mickey Spillane, The Millionaire, Behind Closed Doors, Target, Peter Gunn, Zane Grey Theatre, Wyatt Earp, Secret Mission, The Donna Reed Show, Wanted Dead Or Alive, Buckskin, Loretta Young Show, Starperformance, Rescue 8, Steve Canyon, State Trooper, Twilight Zone, General Electric Theatre, How to Marry A Millionaire, Rifle Man, June Allyson Show, Rawhide, M Squad, Coronado 9, Man From Black Hawk, Grand Jury, Riverboat, 77 Sunset Strip, Happy, The Thriller, Lawless Years, The Untouchables, Death Valley Days, Verdict Is Yours, Deputy, Perry Mason, Wagon Train, Mr. Ed, Maverick, The Shirley Temple Show, Asphalt Jungle, Harrigan and Son, Tales of Wells Fargo, Bronco, Line of Duty, The New Breed, Going My Way, Stoney Burke, Bonanza, The Eleventh Hour, Ben Casey, The Virginian, The Fugitive, Day in Court, Hazel, Singing Nun, Billy the Kid, The Big Valley, The FBI, Laredo, A Man Called Shenandoah, Jericho, Judd for the Defense, The Invaders, Lancer, Nanny and the Professor.

STAGE: Hedda Gabler, Mary, Queen of Scots, Miss Julie, Desdemona.

CHRISTOPHER, DENNIS: Actor. b. Philadelphia, PA, Dec. 2, 1955. e. Temple U. NY stage debut, Yentl the Yeshiva Boy (1974). Other NY theater: Dr. Needle and the Infectious Laughter Epidemic, The Little Foxes, Brothers. Regional theater.

PICTURES: The Young Graduates (1971), Blood and Lace (1971), Fellini's Roma, Salome, Three Women, September 30, 1955, A Wedding, California Dreaming, The Last Word, Breaking Away, Fade to Black, Chariots of Fire, Don't Cry, It's Only Thunder, The Falling, Flight of the Spruce Goose, Jake Speed, Friends, A Sinful Life.

TELEVISION: Cagney & Lacey; Moonlighting; Trapper John M.D.; Jack and the Beanstalk (Faerie Tale Theatre); Tales of the Unexpected; Berenice Bobs Her Hair.

CHRISTOPHER, JORDAN: Actor, Musician. b. Youngstown, OH. Oct. 23, 1941. e. Kent State U. Led rock 'n' roll group, The Wild Ones. Broadway debut, Black Comedy, 1967.

PICTURES: Return of the Seven, The Fat Spy, The Tree, Pigeons, Brainstorm, Star 80.

CHUNG, CONNIE: TV News Anchor. r.n. Constance Yu-Hwa Chung. m. reporter Maury Povitch. b. Washington, D.C., Aug. 20, 1946. e. U. of Maryland, B.A.Entered field 1969 as copy editor, writer then on-camera reporter for WTTG-TV, Washington; 1971, named Washington corr., CBS; 1976, anchor KNXT, Los Angeles; 1983, anchor, NBC News at Sunrise; Summer Sunday USA; Summer Showcase; anchor, NBC Saturday Evening News and news specials; 1989 moved to CBS as anchor, Sunday Night Evening News; host, Saturday Night with Connie Chung, 1989. Received Emmy Award for Shot in Hollywood (1987).

CILENTO, DIANE: Actress. b. Queensland, Australia, April 2, 1934. e. Toowoomba. Went to New York and finished schooling and then American Acad. of Dramatic Art. First theatre job at 16; toured U.S. with Barter Co.; returned to London and joined Royal Acad. of Dramatic Art; several small parts and later repertory at Manchester's Library Theatre.

PICTURES: Wings of Danger (debut, 1952), The Angel Who Pawned Her Harp, Passing Stranger, Passage Home, Woman for Joe, Admirable Crichton, Truth About Women, Stop Me Before I Kill!, I Thank a Fool, Jet Storm, The Full Treatment, The Naked Edge, Tom Jones, Rattle of a Simple Man, The Agony and the Ecstacy, The Breaking Point, Once Upon A Tractor , Hombre, Negatives, Zero Population Growth, The Boy Who Had Everything, The Wicker Man, Hitler: The Last Ten Days.

THEATRE: London stage: Tiger at the Gates, The Third Secret, The Four Seasons, The Bonne Soup, Heartbreak House. (NY), the Big Knife, Orpheus, Altona, Castle in Sweden, Naked, Marys, I've Seen You Cut Lemons.

TELEVISION: La Belle France (series), Court Martial, Blackmail, Dial M for Murder, Rogues Gallery, Rain, Lysistrata, The Kiss of Blood, For the Term of His Natural Life.

CIMINO, MICHAEL: Writer, Director. b. New York, NY, 1943. e. Yale U. BFA, MFA (painting). Dir. docs., industrial films and TV commercials, 1963–71. Protege of Clint Eastwood, who signed him to do s.p. for Magnum Force and then to write and direct Thunderbolt and Lightfoot, in both of which Eastwood starred.

PICTURES: Silent Running (s.p.), The Deer Hunter (Academy Award, best dir., best film 1978.), Heaven's Gate, Year of the Dragon, The Sicilian (dir., prod.), The Desperate Hours.

CIPES, ARIANNE ULMER: Executive. b. New York, NY, July 25; e. Royal Acad. of Dramatic Art, London, U. of London. Daughter of film director Edgar G. Ulmer. Actress, then production and dubbing, Paris; CDC, Rome; Titra, New York; 1975–77, v.p., Best International Films (international film distributor), Los Angeles; 1977 co-founder and sr. v.p./sales & services of Producers Sales Organization, 1981, named exec. v.p., American Film Marketing Assn. 1982, founded AUC Films, consulting and intl. and domestic sales-producers rep.

CIPES, JAY H.: Executive. b. New York, NY, Dec. 14. e. Cornell U. 1960–66, independent producer-packager-distributor European features for U.S. TV sales; 1967, producer, 20th Century-Fox TV; 1970, producer, Four Star TV; 1971, marketing exec. Technicolor, Inc.; 1973, v.p., marketing, Technicolor, Inc.; 1979 sr. v.p., director worldwide marketing, Technicolor, Inc. Professional Film Division.

CLARK, BOB: Director. b. New Orleans, LA, Aug. 5, 1941. e. Hillsdale Coll.

PICTURES: The Emperor's New Clothes, Children Shouldn't Play with Dead Things (as Benjamin Clark), Dead of Night, Black Christmas, Breaking Point, Murder by Decree, Tribute, Porky's (also prod., s.p.), Porky's II—The Next Day (also prod., s.p.), A Christmas Story (also prod., s.p.), Rhinestone, Turk 182, Loose Cannons, (dir., co.-s.p.), Over My Dead Body (dir.).

CLARK, CANDY: Actress. b. Norman, OK, June 20, 1947. Was successful model in N.Y. before landing role in Fat City, 1972. Off-Broadway debut 1981: A Couple of White Chicks Sitting Around Talking.

PICTURES: Fat City, American Graffiti, The Man Who Fell To Earth, Citizens Band, The Big Sleep, When You Comin' Back, Red Ryder, More American Graffiti, National Lampoon Goes to the Movies, Blue Thunder, Amityville 3-D, Hambone and Hillie, Cat's Eye, At Close Range, The Blob, Blind Curve, Original Intent.

TELEVISION: Amateur Night at the Dixie Bar and Grill, Johnny Belinda, Popeye Doyle, James Dean, Where the Ladies Go, Rodeo Girl.

CLARK, DANE: Actor. b. New York, NY, Feb. 18, 1915. e. Cornell U., Johns Hopkins U. In radio series 2 yrs.; on N.Y. stage (Of Mice and Men, Dead End, etc.).

PICTURES: Glass Key, Sunday Punch, Pride of the Yankees, Tennessee Johnson, Action in the North Atlantic, Destination Tokyo, Very Thought of You, Hollywood Canteen, God Is My Co-Pilot, Her Kind of Man, That Way With Women, Deep Valley, Embraceable You, Moonrise, Whiplash, Without Honor, Backfire, Barricade, Never Trust a Gambler, Fort Defiance, Highly Dangerous, Gambler and the Lady, Go Man Go, Blackout, Paid to Kill, Thunder Pass, Port of Hell, Toughest Man Alive, Last Rites.

TELEVISION: No Exit, The Closing Door, Wire Service, Bold Venture (series), The French Atlantic Affair, Police Story.

CLARK, DICK: Performer; Chairman, CEO, Dick Clark Prods., Inc. b. Mt. Vernon, NY, Nov. 30, 1929. e. Syracuse U. graduated 1951, summer announcer WRUN, Utica 1949, staff announcer WOLF, Syracuse 1950. After grad. 1951, took regular job with WOLF. Rejoined WRUN, Utica, then joined WKTV, Utica. Announcer WFIL Philadelphia 1952. Author: Your Happiest Years, 1959; Rock, Roll & Remember, 1976; To Goof or Not to Goof, 1963; Dick Clark's Easygoing Guide to Good Grooming, 1986; The History of American Bandstand, 1986. Formed Dick Clark Productions 1956, TV and motion picture production with in-person concert division, marketing and communications div., cable TV programing dept., compact disc label, home video and radio division. Host and producer of two weekly radio programs: Countdown American and Rock Roll & Remember. Founder and principal owner of United Stations Radio Network. Winner of 5 Emmys. Took company public in January, 1987 (NASDAQ: DCPI), serves as chmn. & CEO.

TELEVISION: *Host* of American Bandstand *(ABC-TV nationwide)*, the Dick Clark Beechnut Show, Dick Clark's World of Talent, The Object Is, Missing Links, Record Years, Years of Rock. $25,000 Pyramid, $100,000 Pyramid. *Producer:* Where The Action Is, Swinging Country, Happening, Get It Together, Shebang, Record Years, Years of Rock. *Executive Producer:* American Music Awards, Academy of Country Music Awards, Dick Clark's New Year's Rockin' Eve, Golden Globe Awards, Soap Opera Awards, Superstars and Their Moms; *TV series:* American Bandstand, TV's Bloopers & Practical Jokes, Puttin' on the Hits, Puttin' on the Kids, Dick Clark's Nitetime, Inside America, In Person From the Palace, Getting in Touch, Live! Dick Clark Presents! *TV movies:* Elvis, Man in the Santa Claus Suit, Murder in Texas, Reaching for the Stars, The Demon Murder Case, The Woman Who Willed a Miracle, Birth of the Beatles, Copacabana, Promised a Miracle, The Town Bully, Liberace. *TV specials:* Live Aid—An All-Star Concert for African Relief, Farm Aid III, TV Censored Bloopers, American Bandstand's 33⅓ Celebration, America Picks the #1 Songs, You Are the Jury, Thanks for Caring, Supermodel of the World, Freedom Festival '89.

PICTURES: Because They're Young, The Dark, The Young Doctors, Psychout, The Savage Seven, Killers Three, Remo Williams: The Adventure Begins, Backtrack.

CLARK, DUNCAN C.: Executive. b. July, 1952, Sutton, Surrey, England. Entered industry in 1972. Appointed dir. of publicity and advertising, CIC, Jan. 1979, taking up similar post in 1981 for United Artists. On formation of U.I.P. in 1982, appt. dir., pub. and advertising, and deputy man. dir., July 1983. Feb., 1987 appt. v.p. advertising and pub., Columbia Pictures International (NY). In Aug. 1987, senior v.p. international marketing for Columbia (Burbank); appt. sr. v.p., Columbia Tri-Star Film Distributors, Inc., (NY).

CLARK, GREYDON: Producer, Director, Writer. b. Niles, MI, Feb. 7, 1943. e. Western Michigan U., B.A., theatre arts, 1963. Heads own company, World Amusement Corp., Sherman Oaks, CA.

PICTURES: Writer: Satan's Sadists, Psychic Killer. Dir.-writer: Mothers, Fathers, and Lovers, Bad Bunch. Prod.-writer-dir.: Satan's Cheerleaders, Hi-Riders, Angel's Brigade, Without Warning, Joysticks (prod., dir), Uninvited (dir.), Skinheads (prods., dir., co-s.p.).

CLARK, HILARY J.: Executive. e. U. of Southern California, B.A., 1976. Began industry career 1978 as ad-pub admin. in co-op adv. dept., Buena Vista Dist. Co. Promoted to mgr. of natl. field pub & promo. Acted as unit publicist on numerous films (Explorers, Sylvester, Swing Shift, Crossroads, etc.) before returning to BV 1986 as natl. pub. dir. for Walt Disney Pictures.

CLARK, JOHN L.: Executive. b. Owenton, KY, Sept. 13, 1907. e. U. of Tennessee. Talent scout, Brunswick Phono. Co.; mgr., WLW, Cincinnati; formed Transamerican Broad. & Tele. Corp. with Warner Bros.; prod. 50 TV films, 1941–44; created & prod. many radio & TV programs; pres. & sole owner, Transamerican.

CLARK, KENNETH: Journalist, Executive. b. Dekalb, IL, Aug. 1, 1899. e. U. of Illinois. Washington & foreign corresp. United Press, Internatl. News Service, Universal Service. Joined M.P. Prod. & Dist. Amer., 1936. Leave of absence 1942 to join U.S. Army; Maj., Lt. Col. and Col.; Returned to MPAA, Nov., 1945; v.p., 1953; exec. v.p., MPAA, 1962; v.p., MPEAA, 1953, Retired, 1984.

CLARK, PETULA: Actress, Vocalist. b. Ewell, Surrey, England, Nov. 15, 1932. On British stage in Sound of Music. Winner of two Grammy Awards, 1964, 1965.

PICTURES: The Huggets, Dance Hall, White Corridors, The Card, Made In Heaven, Gay Dog, Runaway Bus, That Man Opposite, Finian's Rainbow, Goodbye Mr. Chips.

CLARK, SUSAN: Actress. r.n. Nora Golding. b. Canada, March 8. Trained at Royal Acad. of Dramatic Art, London and Stella Adler Academy. Made m.p. debut in Banning, 1967.

PICTURES: Banning, Coogan's Bluff, Madigan, Colossus: The Forbin Project, Tell Them Willie Boy Is Here, Skullduggery, Skin Game, Valdez Is Coming, Showdown, The Midnight Man, Night Moves, Airport 1975, The Apple Dumpling Gang, The North Avenue Irregulars, Murder by Decree, City on Fire, Promises in the Dark, Porky's, Nobody's Perfekt. Producer: Jimmy B and Andre, Word of Honor.

TELEVISION: Webster (series); The Astronaut, Amelia Earhart, Babe, The Choice, Jimmy B and Andre, Maid in America (prod.), Something For a Lonely Man, Hedda Gabler, Double Solitaire.

CLAYBURGH, JILL: Actress. b. New York, NY, April 30, 1944. m. playwright David Rabe. e. Sarah Lawrence Coll. 1966. Former member of Charles Playhouse, Boston.

THEATER: The Nest (off-Broadway), The Rothschilds, Jumpers, Pippin, In the Boom Boom Room, Design For Living.

PICTURES: The Wedding Party, Portnoy's Complaint, The Thief Who Came to Dinner, Terminal Man, Gable and Lombard, Silver Streak, Semi-Tough, An Unmarried Woman, Starting Over, Luna, It's My Turn, First Monday in October, I'm Dancing as Fast as I Can, Hannah K, Where Are The Children?, Shy People.

TELEVISION: Search For Tomorrow, Miles To Go, Hustling, Griffin and Phoenix, Who Gets the Friends?, Unspeakable Acts.

CLAYTON, JACK: Producer, Director. b. 1921. Ent. m.p. 1935 as asst. dir. for London Films, Fox, Warner. Served H.M. Forces 1940–46; Naples is a Battlefield (dir., co-cine., s.p., 1944); prod. man. Ideal Husband; assoc. prod.: Queen of Spades,

Flesh and Blood, Moulin Rouge, Beat the Devil, The Good Die Young, I Am a Camera.

PICTURES: Bespoke Overcoat (prod., dir. Oscar best short, 1956; Venice Festival prize-winning film); prod.: Sailors Beware, Dry Rot, Three Men in a Boat. *Director:* Room at the Top, (BAFTA award best film 1958), The Innocents, The Pumpkin Eater, Our Mother's House (also prod.), The Great Gatsby, Something Wicked This Way Comes, The Lonely Passion of Judith Hearne.

CLEESE, JOHN: Actor. b. Weston-Super-Mare, England, Oct. 27, 1939. e. Clifton Coll., Cambridge U. Member Monty Python's Flying Circus. Co-author (with psychiatrist Robin Skynner), Families and How to Survive Them.

PICTURES: Interlude, The Best House in London, The Rise and Rise of Michael Rimmer, And Now for Something Completely Different (also co-s.p.), Monty Python and the Holy Grail (also co-s.p.), The Life of Brian (also co-s.p.), The Great Muppet Caper, Time Bandits, Privates on Parade, Monty Python's The Meaning of Life, Yellowbeard, Silverado, Clockwise, The Secret Policeman's Third Ball, A Fish Called Wanda (also exec. prod., co-s.p.), The Big Picture (cameo), Erik the Viking.

TELEVISION: Taming of the Shrew. Series: Monty Python's Flying Circus, Fawlty Towers.

CLEMENS, BRIAN: Writer, Producer, Director. b. Croydon, England, 1931. Early career in advertising then wrote BBC TV play. Later TV filmed series as writer, script editor and features. Script editor "Danger Man"; Won Edgar Allen Poe Award for Best TV Thriller of 1962 (Scene of the Crime for U.S. Steel Hour). Various plays for Armchair Theatre; ATV Drama 70; Love Story. Winner two Edgar Allen Poe Awards, Cinema Fantastique Award for best s.p.

PICTURES: The Tell-Tale Heart, Station Six-Sahara, The Peking Medallion, And Soon The Darkness, The Major, When The Wind Blows, See No Evil, Dr. Jekyll and Sister Hyde, Golden Voyage of Sinbad, Watcher in the Woods, Stiff.

TELEVISION: Wrote and prod.: The Avengers (2 Emmy nom., Best Production, 1967 & 1968), The New Avengers, The Professionals, Escapade (in U.S. for Quinn Martin).

CLIFFORD, GRAEME: Director.

PICTURES: Frances, Burke & Wills, Gleaming the Cube.

TELEVISION: The Boy Who Left Home, Little Red Riding Hood (Faerie Tale Theatre), The Turn of the Screw.

CLORE, LEON: Producer. Co-prod.: Conquest of Everest, Virgin Island, Every Day Except Christmas (Grand Prix Venice), Apaches. Executive Producer: Time Without Pity. Producer: Sunday by the Sea. (Grand Prix Venice), Bow Bells, We Are the Lambeth Boys (Grand Prix Tours), Dispute (British Film Academy Award), I Want to Go to School, All Neat in Black Stockings, Morgan—A Suitable Case For Treatment, The French Lieutenant's Woman.

CLORK, HARRY: Writer. r.n. Clarke; b. Galveston, TX. e. St. Paul's Academy, Garden City, NY. Was husband of late Nora Bayes, writer of her stage material; author several stage plays (Smiling Faces, The Milky Way, See My Lawyer) (collab., filmed in 1936 by Paramount); adapt. many plays for Shubert stage enterprises; radio writer. From 1935 writer many s.p. & adapt.

PICTURES: Thrill of Brazil, Mighty McGurk, Sainted Sisters, Painting the Clouds with Sunshine, Tea for Two, Ma and Pa Kettle at Waikiki, The Prisoner.

TELEVISION: Beulah, Life of Riley.

CLOSE, GLENN: Actress. b. Greenwich, CT., Mar. 19, 1947. e. Coll. of William and Mary. Began performing with a repertory group Fingernails, then toured country with folk-singing groups. Professional debut at Phoenix Theatre, New York, in season of plays including Love for Love, The Member of the Wedding, Rules of the Game. Also accomplished musical performer (lyric soprano).

THEATER: The Crucifer of Blood (1978), The Singular Life of Albert Nobbs (Obie Award), Rex, Barnum, The Real Thing (Tony Award, 1984), Benefactors, Wine Untouched, Uncommon Women and Others.

PICTURES: The World According to Garp (debut), The Big Chill, The Natural, The Stone Boy, Greystoke: The Legend of Tarzan, Lord of the Apes (dubbed voice), Jagged Edge, Maxie, Fatal Attraction, Light Years (voice), Dangerous Liaisons, Immediate Family, Orders, Reversal of Fortune, The White Crow.

TELEVISION: Movies: The Orphan Train, Too Far To Go, Something About Amelia, Stones for Ibarra.

CLOVER, DAVID: Actor. b. November 10.

TELEVISION: Policewoman, Police Story, McLaren's Raiders; Kate McShane; One Day At A Time; Delphi Bureau; On The Rocks; The Dick Cavett Special.

CLUG, A. STEPHEN: Executive. b. New York, NY, Apr. 2, 1929. e. Colgate U., Columbia Law Sch. Was special agent, U.S. Army Counter Intelligence Corps, Far East Command, 1951–54. Started with industry as branch mgr., Paramount Films of Indonesia, 1954; mgr. dir., Paramount Films of India, Ltd., supervising India, Burma, Pakistan, Persian Gulf, 1955–57; Far East supvr. for special handling, The Ten Commandments, 1957–8; co-ordinator worldwide program theatrical re-releases, Paramount Intl., 1958–9; mgr., dir., Paramount Films of Brasil, 1959–65; v.p. & exec. prod., Gold Dolphin Prods., Inc., N.Y., 1965–69; gen. mgr. & supvr. Central America/Caribbean areas, MGM Intl. Inc., Panama, 1969–71; gen. mgr., MGM Puerto Rico/supvr. Caribbean area/MGM Cinemas, 1971–3; dir. sls. & asst. continental supvr. for Europe, UK, Middle East, MGM Intl., Inc. 1973–79; v.p./sls. mgr., MGM Intl., headquartered in Paris, 79–82; joined MPEAA as v.p. and regional rep. for Far East and Australia, headquartered in Singapore, 1982.

COATES, ANNE V.: Film editor, Producer. b. Reigate, Surrey, Eng. e. Bartrum Gables Coll. m. late dir. Douglas Hickox. Worked as nurse at East Grinstead Plastic Surgery Hospital.

PICTURES: Pickwick Papers, Grand National Night, Forbidden Cargo, To Paris With Love, Mongongo, The Truth About Women, The Horse's Mouth, Tunes of Glory, Don't Bother to Knock, Lawrence of Arabia (Acad. Award nom. & ACE nom.), Becket (Acad. Award and ACE nom.), Young Cassidy, Those Magnificent Men in Their Flying Machines (co-ed.), Hotel Paridiso, Great Catherine, The Bofors Guns, The Adventurers, Friends, The Public Eye, The Nelson Affair, 11 Harrow House, Murder on the Orient Express (BAFTA nom.), Man Friday, Aces High, The Eagle Has Landed, The Medusa Touch (prod. & sprv. ed.), The Legacy, Catholics, The Elephant Man (Acad. Award nom., BAFTA nom.), The Bushido Blade, Ragtime (co-ed.), The Pirates of Penzance, Greystoke: The Legend of Tarzan, Lord of the Apes; Lady Jane, Raw Deal, Masters of the Universe, Farewell to the King (co-ed.), Listen to Me, I Love You to Death.

COBE, SANDY: Executive, Producer, Distributor. b. New York, NY, Nov. 30, 1928. e. Tulane U., B.A., fine arts. U.S. Army W.W.II & Korea, combat photographer; produced 11 features for Artmark Pictures, N.Y. General Studios, exec. v.p., distribution; First Cinema Releasing Corp., pres. Formed Sandy Cobe Productions, Inc., producer, packager, European features for U.S. theatrical & television. 1974 pres., Intercontinental Releasing Corporation, domestic and foreign distribution of theatrical features; 1989, named chmn. of bd. and CEO.

MEMBER: Dir. of bd., American Film Marketing Assn., Dir. of bd., Scitech Corp. USA, 14 year mem., Academy of Television Arts and Sciences, 32nd degree Mason, Shriner, Variety Club Int'l. Special commendations from: Mayor of Los Angeles, California State Senate, City and County of L.A., California Assembly and Senate, and Governor of CA.

PICTURES: Terror on Tour (prod.), Access Code (exec. prod.), A.R.C.A. D.E. (prod.), Terminal Entry (exec. prod.), Open House (prod.).

COBE, SHARYON REIS: Executive, Producer. b. Honolulu, HI, e. U. of Hawaii, Loyola Marymount U. Dancer Fitzgerald, & Sample, N.Y. United Air Lines, N.Y.; v.p., story editor, Gotham Publishing N.Y.; v.p., distribution-foreign sales, World Wide Film Distributors, L.A.; pres. and chief operating officer, Intercontinental Releasing Corp., L.A.

MEMBER: Women in Show Business, Ladies of Variety (tent 25), Women in Film.

PICTURES: Terror on Tour (prod. co-ordinator), Home Sweet Home (prod. mgr.), To All a Good Night (assoc. prod.), Access Code (co-prod.), Terminal Entry (prod.), Open House (exec. in chg. of prod.).

COBLENZ, WALTER: Producer.

PICTURES: The Candidate, All the President's Men, The Onion Field, The Legend of the Lone Ranger, Strange Invaders, Sister Sister, 18 Again!, For Keeps.

COBURN, JAMES: Actor. b. Laurel, NB, Aug. 31, 1928. e. Los Angeles City Coll., where he studied drama. Served in U.S. Army. First acting role in coast production of Billy Budd. Later to New York, where he worked on TV commercials, then in teleplays on Studio One, GE Theatre, Robert Montgomery Presents. Summer stock in Detroit before returning to Hollywood. First film, 1959, was Ride Lonesome.

PICTURES: Foes of the Fugitive, The Magnificent Seven, Hell Is for Heroes, The Great Escape, Charade, The Americanization of Emily, The Loved One, Major Dundee, A High Wind in Jamaica, Our Man Flint, What Did You Do in the War, Daddy?, Dead Heat on a Merry-Go-Round, In Like Flint, Waterhole No. 3, Candy, Hard Contract, The Last of the Mobile Hot Shots, The Carey Treatment, The Honkers, Duck, You Sucker, The Last of Sheila, Harry in Your Pocket, A Reason to Live, A Reason to Die, The Internecine Project, Bite the Bullet, Hard Times, Sky Riders, The Last Hard Men, Midway, Cross of Iron, Firepower, The Big Bullet, Loving Couples, Looker, Martin's Day, Death of a Soldier, Walking After Midnight, Train to Heaven.

TELEVISION: Draw!, Sins of the Fathers, Malibu, The Dain Curse, Valley of the Dolls, Pinocchio (Faerie Tale Theater).

COCA, IMOGENE: Actress. b. Philadelphia, PA, Nov. 18, 1908. p. the late Joe Coca, orchestra leader, and Sadie Brady, vaudevillian. At 11, debut tap dancer in New York vaudeville; solo dancer Broadway musicals; as comedienne, in New Faces of 1934; with former husband, Bob Burton, in Straw Hat Revue in 1939, and others through 1942. New York night clubs, Cafe Society and Le Ruban Bleu, Palmer House, Chicago; Park Plaza, St. Louis, and at Tamiment resort. Seen on early experimental TV telecasts in 1939.1949 to TV via Broadway Revue, co-starring with Sid Caesar. Emmy Award, 1951. Returned to Broadway in Musical On the Twentieth Century.
PICTURES: Under the Yum Yum Tree, Rabbit Test, National Lampoon's Vacation, Nothing Lasts Forever, Buy and Cell, Papa Was a Preacher.
TELEVISION: Buzzy Wuzzy (host, 1948), Admiral Broadway Revue (1949), Your Show of Shows (1950–54). Imogene Coca Show (1954, 1955), Sid Caesar Invites You (1958), Glinda (series); It's About Time (series); Ruggles of Red Gap (special); Moonlighting. Movies: Alice in Wonderland, Return of the Beverly Hillbillies.

COCCHI, JOHN: Writer, Critic. b. Brooklyn, NY, June 19, 1939. e. Fort Hamilton H.S., 1957; Brooklyn College, A.A.S., 1961. U.S. Army, 1963–65. Puritan Film Labs, manager,1967–9. Independent-International Pictures, biographer-researcher, 1969. Boxoffice Magazine, critic, reporter, columnist, 1970–79. Co-author: The American Movies Reference Book (Prentice-Hall). Contributor: Screen Facts, Film Fan Monthly, Films in Review. Actor in: The Diabolical Dr. Ongo, Thick as Thieves, Captain Celluloid VS. the Film Pirates. Worked on dubbing: Dirtymouth, 1970. Author many books incl., The Westerns, a Movie Quiz Book, Second Feature (A History of the 'B' Movie), A Pictorial Treasury of the "B" Film. Now free lance writer, researcher, agent. Recent credits: researcher for American Movie Classics; contributor to books, 500 Best American Films, 500 Best British and Foreign-Language Films. Consultant to Killiam Shows, Prof. Richard Brown, Photofest, Star Magazine.

COEN, ETHAN: Producer, Writer. b. St. Louis Park, MN, 1958. e. Princeton U. Co-wrote s.p. with brother, Joel, XYZ Murders (renamed Crime Wave).
PICTURES: Blood Simple (prod., co-s.p., co-edited under pseudonym Roderick James); Raising Arizona (prod., co-s.p.), Miller's Crossing (prod., co-s.p.).

COEN, GUIDO: Producer, Executive. In 1959 Became production exec. Twickenham Studios, 1963 Appt. a dir. there, then producer and executive prod. series pictures for Fortress Films and Kenilworth Films.
PICTURES: One Jump Ahead, Golden Link, The Hornet's Nest, Behind the Headlines, Murder Reported, There's Always a Thursday, Date with Disaster, The End of the Line, The Man Without a Body, Woman Eater, Kill Her Gently, Naked Fury, Operation Cupid, Strictly Confidential, Dangerous Afternoon, Jungle Street, Strongroom, Penthouse, Baby Love, One Brief Summer, Burke and Hare, Au Pair Girls, Intimate Games.

COEN, JOEL: Director, Writer. b. St. Louis Park, MN, 1955. e. Simon's Rock College, MA; studied film at NYU. Was asst. editor on Fear No Evil and Evil Dead and worked with rock video crews. Co-wrote with brother, Ethan, s.p. for XYZ Murders (renamed Crime Wave.)
PICTURES: Blood Simple (dir., co-s.p., co-editor with brother, Ethan under pseudonym Roderick James), Raising Arizona (dir., co-s.p.), Miller's Crossing (dir., co-s.p.).

COHEN, CHARLES: Executive. b. Brooklyn, NY, Sept. 15, 1912. e. Brooklyn Coll. Pub. dept., MGM, 1931; U-I, 1948–50; 20th-Fox, 1950; assoc. adv. mgr.; eastern asst. adv. & pub. mgr. Allied Artists, 1955; home off. pub. mgr. Warner Bros., 1957. Eastern adv. mgr. 1958; eastern adv., pub. mgr., 1960; Exec. asst. to adv. pub. director, 1960; expl. dir., Embassy Pictures, 1961; nat. adv. & pub. dir., Cinema V Dist., 1964; adv. & pub. dir., Sigma III, 1968; adv., pub. mgr., The Cannon Group, 1970, v.p., adv.-pub. rel. 1971; adv.-pub. dir., U.A. Eastern Theatres, 1973–77 (retired). Since 1978, has served as volunteer writer for Variety Clubs International magazine, the Barker, and in the creation of institutional fund-raising ad campaigns for V.C.I. Co-author with Morton Sunshine of This Is Variety, a brochure tracing the origins, development and accomplishments of Variety Clubs around the world.

COHEN, ELLIS A.: Producer, Writer. b. Baltimore, MD, Sept. 15, 1945. e. Baltimore Jr. Coll., A.A. 1977, Prod., Henry Jaffe Enterprises, Inc., 1963, talent coordinator, Cerebral Palsy Telethon, WBAL-TV, Baltimore; 1964, p.r. asst. Campbell-Ewald Adv. Agency, L.A.; 1966, and mgr., Hochschild Kohn Dept. Stores, Baltimore; 1968–69, asst. dir., p.r. entertainment, talent booking for Club Venus Night Club, Baltimore; 1968, created-edited The Forum Oracle, national entertainment mag. 1969–72, dir., p.r., Jewish Community Center of Baltimore; 1970, leave of absence to work as corr. in Israel, Denmark & London; 1972, dir., p.r.& adv., The Camera Mart, NY; 1972–74 creator & editor-in-chief, TV/New York Magazine, nationwide TV mag.; 1974–76 dir., worldwide pub./adv., William Morris Agency, Producer, New York Area Emmy Awards Telecast (1973 & 1974), WOR-TV (prod.), chmn., exec. prod. of TV Academy Celebrity drop-in luncheon series; 1972, talent coordinator Bob Hope's Celebrity Flood Relief Telethon. Executive producer, 1976 Democratic National Convention Gala. 1978, Account Exec., Solters & Roskin P.R. L.A. 1978 director of TV Network Boxing Events, Don King Productions, Inc., N.Y. 1980, pres. Ellis A. Cohen Prods. Since 1983, pres., Hennessey Entertainment, Ltd.
MEMBER: Writers Guild of America, Producers Guild of America, Friars Club, Amer. Newspaper Guild, Intl. Press Corp., Israeli Press Corp., National Academy of TV Arts & Sciences, Academy of Television Arts & Sciences, Screen Actors Guild. Mayor Beame's Committee in the Public Interest for N.Y.C.;
TELEVISION: Aunt Mary (prod.-story); New York Area Emmy Awards, (prod. 1973 and 1974). First Steps (prod.), Love Mary (prod.).

COHEN, IRWIN R.: Exhibition Executive. b. Baltimore, MD, Sept. 4, 1924. e. U. of Baltimore, (LLB) 1948, admitted to Maryland and U.S. Bar same year. Active limited practice. R/C Theatres outgrowth of family business started in 1932. One of founders of Key Federal Bank, chairman of board Loan Comm., director and member of exec. comm. Pres. NATO of Virginia 1976–78, chairman 1978–80. Director, member of exec. comm., and chairman of finance comm. National NATO. Member of Motion Picture Pioneers, and various other orgs.

COHEN, LARRY: Writer, Director. b. Chicago, IL, April 20, 1947. e. U. of Wisconsin.
PICTURES: Carrie (s.p.), God Told Me To (s.p.), The American Success Company (s.p.), The Jury (s.p.), The Winger Serpent (prod., dir., s.p.), Special Effects (dir., s.p.), Perfect Strangers (dir., s.p.), Full Moon High (prod., dir., s.p.), It's Alive III (dir., s.p.), Deadly Illusion (co-dir., s.p.), Best Seller (s.p.), Maniac Cop (prod., s.p.). Wicked Stepmother (exec. prod., dir., s.p.), Friend to Friend (prod.), Into Thin Air (dir., s.p.), Fever of the Hunt (s.p.), The Man Who Loved Hitchcock (dir., s.p.).

COHEN, MILTON E.: Distributor. b. Chicago, IL. e. U. of Illinois. Entered motion picture industry as salesman. United Artists, Chicago, 1925–29; Columbia, Chicago, 1929–31; salesman, Detroit, 1931–38; sales mgr., RKO, Detroit, 1938; branch mgr., 1943; Eastern-Central dist. mgr., 1946; Eastern sales mgr., Eagle Lion Classics, 1948; genl. sales mgr., 1951; western & southern sales mgr., United Artist, 1951; eastern & southern sales mgr., 1952; sprv., sales, Around The World In 80 Days, 1958; Eastern Canadian sales mgr., 1959; natl. dir., Roadshow Sales, 1961; retired. United Artists, 1969; exec. v.p. in charge of theatrical distrib. for Trans Globe Films, Inc., 1971.

COHEN, ROB: Producer, Director. b. Cornwall-on-the-Hudson, NY, March 12, 1949. e. Harvard U. BA. Formerly exec. v.p. in chg of m.p. and TV for Motown. Started as dir. of m.p. for TV at 20th Century-Fox. Joined Motown at age of 24 to produce films. Headed own production co. 1985, appt. pres., Keith Barish Prods.
PICTURES: Mahogany, Bingo Long and the Traveling All-Stars, Scott Joplin, Almost Summer, Thank God It's Friday, The Wiz, A Small Circle of Friends (dir.), Scandalous (dir., co-s.p.), The Razor's Edge (prod.), The Legend of Billie Jean (prod.), Light of Day (co-prod.), The Witches of Eastwick (co-exec. prod.), The Monster Squad (co-exec. prod.); Ironweed (co-exec. prod.); The Running Man (co-exec. prod.); The Serpent and the Rainbow, The Hard Way (prod.)., Disorganized Crime (exec. prod.), The Hard Way (prod.).
TELEVISION: Miami Vice (dir.), Cuba and Claude (exec. prod.).

COHEN, ROBERT B.: Executive. e. George Washington U., B.A., Southern Texas Sch. of Law. 1980–84. Atty. for Greenberg, Glusker, Fields, Clamans and Machtinger (L.A.). Was asst. gen. counsel for Columbia Pictures. Joined Paramount 1985 as sr. atty. for M.P. Group. to oversee legal functions for assigned feature films; 1988 named v.p. in charge of legal affairs, Motion Picture Group of Paramount.

COHN, ROBERT: Producer. b. Avon, NJ, Sept. 6, 1920. e. U. of Michigan, B.A., 1941. p. Jack Cohn. Joined Columbia as asst. dir. In W.W.II, as Signal Corps film cutter. Air Corps Training Lab. unit mgr., combat aerial m.p. camera man with 13th A.A.F. Awarded: DFC, Air Medal & 3 clusters, Purple Heart. Assoc. prod. Lone Wolf In London, 1947; prod. Adventures in Silverado, 1948, all Col. Headed Robert Cohn prod. unit at Columbia, pres. International Cinema Guild. Columbia European prod.: exec. Columbia Studios. Hollywood: formed Robert Cohn Prod.
PICTURES: Black Eagle, Rusty Leads the Way, Palomino, Kazan, Killer That Stalked New York, The Barefoot Mailman, Mission Over Korea, The Interns, The New Interns, The Young Americans.

COLBERT, CLAUDETTE: Actress: r.n. Lily Chauchoin. b. Paris, Sept. 13, 1903. e. public schools, Paris, New York; Art Students League, N.Y. On N.Y. stage (debut, Wild Wescotts; following Marionette Man, We've Got to Have Money, Cat Came Back, Kiss in a Taxi, Ghost Train, The Barker, Dynamo, etc.). First screen role in Love O' Mike (silent); Academy Award best actress, 1934 (It Happened One Night); voted one of ten top Money Making Stars in Fame Poll, 1935, '36, '47.

PICTURES: The Hole in the Wall, The Lady Lies, The Big Pond, Young Man of Manhattan, Manslaughter, Honor Among Lovers, The Smiling Lieutenant, Secrets of a Secretary, His Woman, The Wiser Woman, Misleading Lady, The Man From Yesterday, The Phantom President, The Sign of the Cross, Tonight is Ours, I Cover the Waterfront, Three Cornered Moon, The Torch Singer, Four Frightened People, It Happened One Night, Cleopatra, Imitation of Life, The Gilded Lily, Private Worlds, She Married Her Boss, The Bride Comes Home, Under Two Flags, Maid of Salem, I Met Him in Paris, Tovarich, Bluebeard's Eighth Wife, Zaza, Midnight, It's a Wonderful World, Drums Along the Mohawk, Boom Town, Arise My Love, Skylark, Remember the Day, The Palm Beach Story, No Time for Love, Practically Yours, Since You Went Away, So Proudly We Hail, Guest Wife, Tomorrow Is Forever, The Egg and I, Sleep My Love, Family Honeymoon, Bride for Sale, Three Came Home, The Secret Fury, Thunder on the Hill, Let's Make It Legal, Outpost in Malaya, Daughters of Destiny, Texas Lady, Parrish.

BROADWAY: Marriage Go Round, Irregular Verb to Love, The Kingfisher, Aren't We All?

TELEVISION: The Two Mrs. Grenvilles.

COLBY, RONALD: Producer, Director, Writer. b. New York, NY. e. Hofstra U., NYU. Began career as playwright at Cafe La Mama and Caffe Cino; performed in off-Bdwy shows; spent year as actor-writer in residence at Pittsburgh Playhouse. Served as dialogue coach and asst. to Francis Coppola; was v.p. of Zoetrope Studios. Directed several documentaries and short films.

PICTURES: Rain People (prod.), Hammett (prod.), Some Kind of Wonderful (exec. prod.), She's Having a Baby (exec. prod.).

TELEVISION: Margaret Bourke-White (co-prod.)

COLE, GARY: Actor. b. Park Ridge, IL, Sept. 20. e. Illinois State, theater major. Dropped out of coll. after 3 years and moved to Chicago where he tended bar, painted houses and worked with Steppenwolf Theatre group. In 1979 helped to form Remains Theatre, left in 1986 to become ensemble member of Steppenwolf.

TELEVISION: Series: Midnight Caller. Movies: Heart of Steel, Fatal Vision, Vital Signs, Those She Left Behind. Miniseries: Echoes in the Darkness.

COLE, GEORGE: Actor. b. London, Eng., Apr. 22, 1925. e. secondary sch. Surrey. Stage debut in White Horse Inn, 1939; m.p. debut in Cottage to Let, 1941.

PICTURES: Henry V, Quartet, My Brother's Keeper, Laughter in Paradise, Scrooge, Lady Godiva Rides Again, Who Goes There (Passionate Sentry), Morning Departure (Operation Disaster), Top Secret (Mr. Potts Goes to Moscow), Happy Family, Will Any Gentleman, Apes of the Rock, The Intruder, Happy Ever After (Tonight's the Night), Our Girl Friday (Adventures of Sadie), Belles of St. Trinian's, Prize of Gold, Where There's a Will, Constant Husband, Quentin Durward, The Weapon, It's a Wonderful Life, Green Man, Bridal Path, Too Many Crooks, Blue Murder at St. Trinians, Don't Panic Chaps, Dr. Syn, One Way Pendulum, Legend of Young Dick Turpin, The Great St. Trinian's Train Robbery, Cleopatra, The Green Shoes, Vampire Lovers, Fright, The Bluebird.

TELEVISION: Life of Bliss, A Man of Our Times, Don't Forget To Write, The Good Life, Minder.

COLE, SIDNEY: Producer, Director, Writer. b. London, England, 1908. e. Westminster City Sch., London U., B.Sc. Began at Stoll Studios 1930; then various feature and documentary studios. Dir. Roads Across Britain. Spanish ABC. Behind the Spanish Lines. Ed. Gaslight. Mr. Pimpernel Smith, San Demetrio, London, Nine Men, etc.; tech. adviser First of the Few; writer and assoc. prod. They Came to a City, Return of the Vikings; assoc. prod Dead of Night, Loves of Joanna Godden, Against the Wind, Scott of the Antarctic, The Magnet, Man in the White Suit, Train of Events (co-dir.); Operation Swallow (Eng. adapt.); The Angel Who Pawned Her Harp (writer-prod.); s.p., North Sea Bus. Assoc. prod. Escapade; prod. Sword of Sherwood Forest; prod. s.p. The Kitchen; prod. We Are The Engineers, One in Five.

TELEVISION: prod. Adventures of Robin Hood, The Buccaneers, Sword of Freedom, The Four Just Men, Danger Man (Secret Agent), Man in a Suitcase, Adventures of Black Beauty, Dick Turpin, Smuggler, Adventurer.

COLEMAN, DABNEY: Actor. b. Austin, TX, Jan. 3, 1932. e. VA Military Inst. 1949–51; U. Texas 1951–57; Neighborhood Playhouse School Theater 1958–60.

PICTURES: This Property Is Condemned, The Slender Thread, The Scalphunters, The Other Side of the Mountain, The Black Streetfighter, Rolling Thunder, Viva Knievel, North Dallas Forty, Nothing Personal, How To Beat the High Cost of Living, Melvin and Howard, Nine to Five, On Golden Pond, Modern Problems, Young Doctors in Love, The Muppets Take Manhattan, Tootsie, WarGames, Cloak and Dagger, The Man with One Red Shoe, Dragnet, Hot to Trot, The Applegates, Where the Heart Is, Short Time.

TELEVISION: Movies: Apple Pie, When She Was Bad, Murrow, Guilty of Innocence, Sworn To Silence (Emmy Award), Plaza Suite, Baby M, Maybe Baby. Mini-Series: Fresno. Series: Mary Hartman, Mary Hartman, Forever Fernwood, Buffalo Bill, The Slap Maxwell Story.

COLEMAN, GARY: Actor. b. Zion, IL, Feb. 8, 1968. Gained fame as star of TV's Diff'rent Strokes.

TELEVISION: The Little Rascals, America 2-Night, Good Times, The Jeffersons, Diff'rent Strokes, Lucy Moves to NBC, The Big Show, etc. Movies: The Kid from Left Field, Scout's Honor, Playing with Fire, The Kid With the Broken Halo; The Kid with the 200 I.Q.

PICTURES: On the Right Track, Jimmy the Kid.

COLEMAN, NANCY: Actress. b. Everett, WA, Dec. 30, 1917. e. U. of Washington. In radio serials; on New York stage (with Gertrude Lawrence, in Theatre Guild productions), Desperate Hours, 1955; American Theatre Guild Rep. Co. tour of Europe and So. America. m.p. debut, 1941.

PICTURES: Kings Row, Dangerously They Live, Gay Sisters, Desperate Journey, Edge of Darkness, In Our Time, Devotion, Violence, Mourning Becomes Electra, That Man from Tangier, Slaves.

TELEVISION: Valiant Lady, Producers Showcase, Kraft Theatre, Silver Theatre, Adams Chronicles.

COLEMAN, THOMAS J.: Executive. b. Connecticut, Apr. 13, 1950. e. Boston U. Pres., Twalzo Music Corp., 1972–73; v.p., natl. sls. mgr., United Intl. Pictures, 1973–74; founded Atlantic Releasing Corp., 1974; Atlantic Television, Inc., 1981. All Atlantic corps. consolidated into Atlantic Entertainment Group, 1986. Co. has distributed over 100 films and produced 30 features and TV movies. Sold Atlantic, March, 1989. Formed Independent Entertainment Group, named chmn.

PICTURES: Producer or Exec. Prod.: Valley Girl, Alphabet City, Roadhouse, Night of the Comet, Starchaser, Teen Wolf, Extremities, The Men's Club, Modern Girls, Nutcracker, Teen Wolf Too (exec. prod.); Cop (exec. prod.); Patty Hearst (exec. prod.), 1969 (exec. prod.).

COLER, JOEL H.: Executive. b. Bronx, NY, 1931. e. Syracuse U., B.A., journalism. Worked as adv. asst. NBC; acct. exec. Grey advertising. Joined 20th Century-Fox 1964 as adv. coordinator Fox Intl.; 1967, named intl. adv./pub. mgr. 1974, named v.p. dir., intl. adv./pub.

COLIN, MARGARET: Actress. b. Brooklyn, NY. e. left Hofstra U. to pursue acting career in Manhattan where she was cast in daytime TV series The Edge of Night.

PICTURES: Pretty in Pink, Something Wild, Like Father, Like Son; Three Men and a Baby, True Believer, Martians Go Home.

TELEVISION: Series: The Edge of Night, As the World Turns, Foley Square. Movies: Warm Hearts, Cold Feet, The Return of Sherlock Holmes, The Traveling Man.

COLLERAN, BILL: Producer, Director. b. April 16. Story department 20th Century-Fox 1945–46; Director Louis de Rochemont 1946–50; stage mgr. NBC 1951; assoc. dir. The Hit Parade 1952–53; Dir. The Hit Parade, various TV specs. 1954–56; Dir. Cinerama Windjammer 1956; TV Specs. Bing Crosby, Frank Sinatra, Debbie Reynolds 1957–60; various TV specs. 1960–65, Exec. Prod. Judy Garland Show, Dean Martin Show, 1965–66; Dir. Richard Burton's "Hamlet" film, Prod. "Popendipity" ABC-TV spec. various other TV specs. 1967–70; 1971–77 Various TV specials and series; 1978–83, prod., dir., writer for Hill-Eubanks Group and Little Joey, Inc.; 1984–86, dir. music video for Simba; developing film and TV projects for own production co.

COLLIN, REGINALD: Producer, Director. Trained at the Old Vic Theatre School as actor. Directed in repertory, also pantomimes and summer shows. Entered TV 1958. Producer ITV's First Arts Programme Tempo, Callan, Mystery And Imagination, Special Branch, Napoleon And Love. Producer/director two Armchair Cinemas, also documentary on the Royal Shakespeare Theatre. 1976: Vice-Chmn of the British Acad. of Film and Television Arts. Chmn of the Awards Committee. Dir. of BAFTA 1977–87. Fellow of the RTS.

COLLINS, JOAN: Actress. b. London, Eng., May 23, 1933. e. Francis Holland Sch., London. Made stage debut in A Doll's House, Arts Theatre 1946. Screen debut in I Believe in You, 1952. TV appearances include Dynasty series, 1981-89. Autobiography: Past Imperfect (1978). Author: Katy, A Fight For Life, Joan Collins Beauty Book, Spare Time. Received Emmy and Golden Globe Awards.

PICTURES: I Believe in You, Judgment Deferred, Decameron Nights, Cosh Boy, The Square Ring, Turn the Key

Softly, Our Girl Friday (Adventures of Sadie), The Good Die Young, Land of the Pharaohs, Virgin Queen, Girl in the Red Velvet Swing, Opposite Sex, Sea Wife, Island in the Sun, Wayward Bus, Stopover Tokyo, The Bravados, Rally Round the Flag Boys, Seven Thieves, Esther and the King, Warning Shot, Can Hieronymus Merkin Ever Forget Mercy Humpe and Find True Happiness?, The Executioner, Tales from the Crypt, The Bawdy Adventures of Tom Jones, Empire of the Ants, The Big Sleep, Sunburn, The Stud, The Bitch.

TELEVISION: Movies: The Cartier Affair, The Making of a Male Model, Her Life as a Man, Paper Dolls, The Wild Women of Chastity Gulch, Hansel and Gretel (Faerie Tale Theater). Mini-Series: Sins, Monte Carlo (also exec. prod.).

COLLINS, PAULINE: Actress. b. Exmouth, Devon, Eng., Sept. 3, 1940. m. actor John Alderton (Thomas on Upstairs, Downstairs). e. Central School of Speech and Drama. Stage debut A Gazelle in Park Lane (Windsor, 1962). Best known to US audiences as Sarah in Upstairs, Downstairs.

THEATER: Passion Flower Hotel (London debut, 1965), The Erpingham Camp, The Happy Apple, The Importance of Being Earnest, The Night I Chased the Women with an Eel, Come as You Are, Judies, Engaged, Confusions, Romantic Comedy, Woman in Mind, Shirley Valentine (in London won Olivier Award as best actress, in NY won Tony, Drama Desk and Outer Critics Circle Awards.)

PICTURE: Shirley Valentine.

TELEVISION: Series: Upstairs, Downstairs; Thomas and Sarah, Forever Green, No—Honestly (all with husband), Tales of the Unexpected, Knockback, Tropical Moon Over Dorking.

COLLINS, STEPHEN: Actor. b. Des Moines, IA, Oct. 1, 1947. Appeared off-Bdwy. in several Joseph Papp productions before Bdwy. debut in The Ritz. Also on Bdwy. in Moonchildren, Anatol.

PICTURES: All the President's Men, Between the Lines, The Promise, Star Trek, Fedora, Loving Couples, Brewster's Millions, Jumpin' Jack Flash, Choke Canyon, The Big Picture, Stella.

TELEVISION: Tales of the Gold Monkey, Chiefs, Dark Mirror, Threesome, Hold the Dream, Inside the Third Reich, The Two Mrs. Grenvilles, Weekend War, Tattinger's (series, revamped as Nick & Hillary).

COLT, MARSHALL: Actor. b. New Orleans, LA, Oct. 26. e. Tulane U. B.S. Physics. Did naval tour in Southeast Asia during Vietnam War. Acted in local stage productions in San Francisco (Hotel Universe, Who's Afraid of Virginia Woolf?, Zoo Story, etc.).

PICTURES: Bimbo (short), North Dallas Forty, Those Lips, Those Eyes, Jagged Edge, Flowers in the Attic, Illegally Yours, Deceptions.

TELEVISION: Series: Family, Paper Chase, Streets of San Francisco, Barnaby Jones, McClain's Law, Lottery! Movies: Colorado C-1, Sharon: Portrait of a Mistress, Once an Eagle, To Heal a Nation, Mercy or Murder, Guilty of Innocence.

COLTRANE, ROBBIE: Actor. b. Rutherglen, Scotland, 1950. Ent. ind. 1974. Early career at Traverse Theatre, Edinburgh. Work included John Byrn's Slab Boys Trilogy.

TELEVISION: Kick Up The Eighties, Alfresco, Laugh I Nearly Paid My Licence Fee, Comic Strip Presents Five Go Mad in Dorset, Beat Generation, Susie, Gino and Bullshitters, Tutti Frutti, Danny, the Champion of the World, The Miners Strike.

PICTURES: Subway Riders, Ghost Dance, Krull, Caravaggio, Defence of the Realm, Chinese Boxes, Supergrass, Mona Lisa, Fruit Machine, Bert Rigby You're a Fool, Let It Ride, Henry V, Nuns on the Run.

COLUMBUS, CHRIS: Director, Writer: b. Spangler, PA, 1959. Grew up in Ohio. Started making short super 8 films in high school, studied screenwriting at New York U. Film Sch., graduated 1980. Sold first s.p., Jocks, while at college. Wrote for and developed TV cartoon series, Galaxy High School.

PICTURES: writer: Reckless, Gremlins, The Goonies, Young Sherlock Holmes; worked on third Indiana Jones s.p., Little Nemo in Slumberland (animated film). Directing debut: Adventures in Babysitting (1987), Heartbreak Hotel (dir., s.p.).

TELEVISION: Amazing Stories, Twilight Zone, Alfred Hitchcock Presents.

COLVILLE, JOHN: Producer, Director. Started in theatre. Worked in all departments before becoming Film Editor on Features, Documentaries, and Television Series for both BBC/ITV. Extensive experience in Greece, Singapore, Spain, Switzerland—now establishing new Unit, Studios, and Producing films in Nigeria.

COMDEN, BETTY: Writer. b. Brooklyn, NY, May 3, 1919. e. New York U., B.S. Nightclub performer and writer with The Revuers, 1939–44. NY City Mayor's Award Art and Culture, 1978. Named to Songwriters Hall of Fame, 1980. NYU Alumnae Assn.'s Woman of Achievement award, 1987.

THEATER: With Adolph Green: writer book, sketches & lyrics for Bway. shows. On the Town (book, lyrics, actress, 1944), Billion Dollar Baby (bk., Lyrics), Bonanza Bound! (bk., lyrics), Two on the Aisle (sketches and lyrics), Wonderful Town (lyrics, Tony Award, 1953), Peter Pan (lyrics), Bells Are Ringing (bk., lyrics), Say, Darling (lyrics), A Party With Comden and Green (bk., lyrics, star; 1959 and 1977); Do Re Mi (lyrics), Subways Are For Sleeping (bk., lyrics), Fade Out-Fade In (bk., lyrics), Leonard Bernstein's Theatre Songs; Hallelujah, Baby (lyrics, Tony Award, 1968); Applause (book, Tony Award); Lorelei (revision to book); By Bernstein (book and some lyrics); On the Twentieth Century (2 Tony Awards, book and lyrics); A Doll's Life (bk., lyrics). Actress only: Isn't It Romantic.

PICTURES: Writer with Adolph Green: Good News, On the Town, Barkleys of Broadway, Singin' in the Rain, Band Wagon, It's Always Fair Weather, What a Way to Go, Bells Are Ringing, Auntie Mame. Films made from their stage musicals: On the Town, Bells Are Ringing. Actress only: Greenwich Village, Garbo Talks, Slaves of New York, The Teddy Bear Habit.

COMO, PERRY: Singer. b. Canonsburg, PA, May 18, 1912. e. Canonsburg local schools. p. Pietro and Lucille Travaglini Como. Barber at 15; joined Carlone Band, then Ted Weems in 1936; CBS sustaining show; played many night clubs, records for RCA Victor. Screen debut, Something for the Boys (1944). Best Male vocalist M.P. Daily, TV poll, 1952–55; radio poll, 1954. Best Male vocalist M.P. Daily, TV Poll, 1956: best TV performer M.P.D.—Fame poll 1957. Interfaith Award, 1953; Emmy, Peabody, Christopher Awards, 1955–56. Knight Commander and Lady Com. (Mrs. Como) of Equestrian Order of Holy Sepulchre of Jerusalem; personality of the yr., Variety Club, 1956.

PICTURES: Doll Face, If I'm Lucky, Words and Music.

TELEVISION: Perry Como show, NBC-TV. Perry Como Kraft Music Hall, NBC-TV; numerous annual holiday specials.

COMPTON, JOYCE: Actress. b. Lexington, KY. e. Tulsa U. Screendebut in Ankles Preferred.

PICTURES: The Awful Truth, Spring Madness, Sky Murder, Turnabout, A Southern Yankee, If I Had a Million, Christmas in Connecticut, Artists and Models Abroad, Rustlers of Red Dog, The White Parade, Wild Party, Three Sisters, Grand Canyon, Jet Pilot, The Persuader, Girl in the Woods.

CONAWAY, JEFF: Actor. b. New York, NY, Oct. 5, 1950. Started in show business at the age of 10 when he appeared in Bdwy. production, All the Way Home. Later toured in Critics Choice before turning to fashion modeling. Toured with musical group, 3½, as lead singer and guitarist. Entered theatre arts program at NYU. Film debut at 19 in Jennifer on My Mind.

THEATER: Grease, The News.

PICTURES: The Eagle Has Landed, Pete's Dragon, I Never Promised You a Rose Garden, Grease, The Patriot, Elvira: Mistress of the Dark, Cover Girl, Ghostwriter!, The Banker, Tale of Two Sisters, The Sleeping Car.

TELEVISION: From Sea to Shining Sea (1974), Joe Forrester, The Mary Tyler Moore Show, Happy Days, Movin' On, Barnaby Jones, Kojak, Wizards and Warrior, Mickey Spillane's Mike Hammer, Taxi (regular), Benengers. Movies: Having Babies, Delta County, U.S.A., Breaking Up Is Hard to Do, For the Love of It, Nashville Grab, The Making of a Male Model, Bay Coven, The Dirty Dozen: The Fatal Mission.

CONDE, RITA: Actress. b. Cuba. r.n. Elizabeth Eleanor Conde Griffiths. Now American citizen. In numerous films and on TV in Hollywood and starred in Mexican film, El Ahijado de la Muerte.

PICTURES: Ride the Pink Horse, Two Roaming Champs, No Sad Songs for Me, Topaz, Change of Habit, Barquero, World's Greatest Lover, Love at First Bite.

TELEVISION: I Love Lucy, Zorro, I Spy, Thriller, Night Gallery, Ironside, Chico and the Man, Days of Our Lives, Capitol.

CONDON, CHRIS J.: Producer, Director, Motion Equipment Designer. b. Chicago, IL, Dec. 7, 1922. e. Davidson Inst., U. of Southern California. U.S. Air Force 1943–46. Founded Century Precision Optics, 1948. Designed Athenar telephoto lenses, Century Super wide-angle lenses and Duplikins. Co-founded StereoVision International, Inc. 1969 specializing in films produced in new 3-D process. Member SMPTE. Lecturer and consultant on motion picture optics and 3-D motion picture technology.

FILMS PRODUCED: The Wild Ride, The Surfer, Girls, Airline, The New Dimensions.

CONN, ROBERT A.: Executive. b. Philadelphia, PA, Jan. 16, 1926. e. Lehigh U. 1944; U. of Pennsylvania, 1948. 1st Lt. Army Security Agency, 1944–46, 1951–52; furniture dist., Philadelphia, 1948–51; band & act. dept., MCA, 1952–53; dir. of adv. & prom. Official Films N.Y. 1954; head of Official Films Philadelphia sales office serving PA, Baltimore, Washington, Cleveland and Detroit, 1956. Eastern Reg. Sls. Mgr. Flamingo Films, 1957; acct. exec. Dunnan and Jeffrey, Inc., 1961; v.p., Dunnan and Jeffrey, 1962; pres., adv. mgr., Suburban

Knitwear Co., 1963; exec. v.p. Rogal Travel Service, 1964–68. 1968–78, pres. RAC Travel, Inc., Jenkintown, PA. and pres. Royal Palm Travel, Inc. Palm Beach, Florida, 1978; Rosenbluth Travel Service, 1979; v.p., natl. retail mktg., E.F. Hutton & Co. (N.Y.), 1983.

CONNELLY, PAUL V.: Executive. b. Boston, MA, June 11, 1923. e. Boston Coll., MA, 1951, B.S.B.A., 1949; Fordham U., 1951–54; Asst. professor of Economics, Manhattan Coll., 1950–54; treas., America Corp. (formerly Chesapeake Industries), 1957–59; treas., dir., Pathe-America Dist. Co. Inc., Sutton Pictures Co.; v.p., dir., Pathe Labs., Inc.; pres., dir., Pathe-Deluxe of Canada, Ltd. 1959–65; pres. International Business Relations, 1965–67; v.p., treas., dir. Movielab, Inc., 1968; v.p.—finance, Tele-Tape Corp., 1970.

CONNER, CHARLES M.: Writer, Producer, Director. b. Covington, IN, April 19, 1925. e. U. of Wisconsin. Active in designing and creating pressbooks for theatrical m.p. producers and distributors, plus theatrical m.p. still photography, locations and studio sets. Now heads Charles M. Conner Film & Video Cassette Distribution & Marketing. Member: Writers Guild of America, West, both screen & TV branches. Winner, 1965–66 regional Emmy award, Guns Are for Killing.
CREDITS: Guns Are for Killing, Fulfillment, Something Worth Remembering, Albuquerque Lawman, The Protector, Bay of Pigs, Richest Man in the World, Tiger, Thru These Eyes, The Sound of Christmas Around the World, House of Sin, The Female Art of Man Hunting, Surfside Six, Far Out West, The Bunny Snatch, Listen, Girl Hunters, America's Greatness, Meet the Under World, Introduction, Christmas Tree, The Wounded Are Dangerous, Gorilla.

CONNERY, SEAN: Actor. b. Edinburgh, Scotland, Aug. 25, 1930. r.n. Thomas Connery. Worked as a lifeguard and a model before landing role in chorus of London prod. of South Pacific, 1953.
Prod. dir., The Bowler and the Bonnet (film doc.), I've Seen You Cut Lemons (London stage). Director of Tantallon Films Ltd. (First production: Something Like the Truth).
PICTURES: No Road Back (1955), Time Lock, Hell Drivers, Action of the Tiger, Another Time, Another Place; Darby O'Gill and the Little People, Tarzan's Greatest Adventure, Frightened City, On the Fiddle, The Longest Day, Dr. No, From Russia With Love, Marnie, Woman of Straw, Goldfinger, The Hill, Thunderball, A Fine Madness, You Only Live Twice, Shalako, The Molly Maguires, The Red Tent, The Anderson Tapes, Diamonds Are Forever, The Offence, Zardoz, Ransom, Murder on the Orient Express, The Terrorists, The Wind and The Lion, The Man Who Would Be King, Robin and Marian, The Next Man, A Bridge Too Far, The Great Train Robbery, Meteor, Cuba, Outland, Time Bandits, Wrong Is Right, Five Days One Summer, Never Say Never Again, Highlander, The Name of the Rose, The Untouchables (Acad. Award, 1987), The Presidio, Indiana Jones and the Last Crusade, Family Business, Russia House.
TELEVISION: Requiem for a Heavyweight, Anna Christie, Boy with the Meataxe, Women in Love, The Crucible, Riders to the Sea, Colombe, Adventure Story, Anna Karenina, Macbeth (Canadian TV).

CONNOR, KENNETH: Actor. b. London, England. Ent. m.p. industry 1949 in The Lady Killers.
TELEVISION: Ted Ray Show, Show Called Fred, Charlie Farnabarn's Show, Alfred Marks Time, As You Like It, Dickie Valentine Show, Black and White Minstrel, Anne Shelton, Hi Summer, Don't Say a Word (series), Room at the Bottom, On the Houses, Frankie Howard Reveals All, Allo Allo, Hi de Hi, That's My Boy.
PICTURES: Carry on Sergeant, Carry on Nurse, Carry on Constable, Watch Your Stern, Carry on Regardless, Nearly a Nasty Accident, What a Carve Up, Call Me a Cab, Carry on Cleo, Captain Nemo, Carry On Up The Jungle, Carry On Matron, Carry On Abroad, Carry on England, Carry On Emanuelle.

CONNORS, CHUCK: Actor. r.n. Kevin Joseph Connors. b. Brooklyn, NY, April 10, 1921. e. Adelphi Acad., Seton Hall Coll., U.S. Army 3 yrs., then prof. baseball player with Brooklyn Dodgers, 1949; Chicago Cubs 1951. On stage in Chicago 1971–79 in My Three Angels, Mary, Mary.
PICTURES: Pat and Mike, Code Two, Trouble Along the Way, South Sea Women, Dragonfly Squadron, Naked Alibi, Human Jungle, Target Zero, Three Stripes in the Sun, Good Morning Miss Dove, Hold Back the Night, Hot Rod Girl, Tomahawk Trail, Walk the Dark Street, Designing Woman, Hired Gun, Lady Takes a Flier, Old Yeller, Death in Small Doses, The Big Country, Geronimo, Kill Them All and Come Back Alive, Move Over Darling, Ride Beyond Vengeance, Capt. Nemo and the Underwater City, Proud, Damned and Dead, Profane Comedy, The Deserter, Support Your Local Gunfighter, Pancho Villa, Embassy, The Mad Bomber, Soylent Green, 99 and 44/100% Dead, The Sea Wolf, The Tourist Trap, Virus, The Women of Jeremias, Day of the Assassin, Red Alert West, Mortuary, Balboa, Valley Girls, Target Eagle, Airplane II: The Sequel, Kelsey and Son, The Butterfly Revolution, Summer Camp Nightmare, Terror Squad, Mania, Hell's Hero, Trained to Kill, Mania, Skinheads, Jump, Taxi Killers.
TELEVISION: Series: The Rifleman (1958–63), Arrest and Trial, Branded (1964–65), Police Story (1972–75, pilot and episodes), Stone (1979), Werewolf (1987). Movies: Cowboy in Africa, Set the Town on Fire, The Profane Comedy, Birdman of Beckstadt, Banjo Hackett, Roots (mini-series), Nightmare in Batham County, The Night They Took Miss Beautiful, Standing Tall, The Texans, Walking Tall, Great Mysteries of Hollywood, The Capture of Grizzly Adams, Celebrity Daredevils, Lone Star, The Yellow Rose, The American Cowboy, Steel Collar Man (pilot), Spenser for Hire (pilot), Once Upon a Texas Train, Paradise, The Hunters. Guest: Six Million Dollar Man, Fantasy Island, Best of the West, Love Boat, Murder She Wrote.

CONNORS, MIKE: Actor. r.n. Krekor Ohanian. b. Fresno, CA, Aug. 15, 1925. e. UCLA. Film debut in Sudden Fear (1952).
PICTURES: Sky Commando, Day of Triumph, Flesh and Spur, Seed of Violence, Harlow, Good Neighbor Sam, Where Love Has Gone, Avalanche Express, Too Scared to Scream, Fist Fighter, Friend to Friend.
TELEVISION: Tightrope, Mannix (Golden Globe award). Movies: Casino, High Midnight, Revenge for a Rape. Mini-series: War and Remembrance.

CONRAD, ROBERT: Actor, Singer. r.n. Conrad Robert Falk; b. Chicago, IL, March 1, 1935. e. public schools, Northwestern U. Prof. debut, nightclub singer. Formed Robert Conrad Productions, 1966. Later, A Shane Productions.
TELEVISION: Lawman, Maverick, 77 Sunset Strip. Series: Hawaiian Eye, Wild Wild West, Baa, Baa, Black Sheep, A Man Called Sloane (series), Centennial (mini-series). Movies: Wild Wild West Revisited, More Wild Wild West, Breaking Up Is Hard To Do, Will: G. Gordon Liddy, Confessions of a Married Man, Hard Knox, Two Fathers' Justice, Assassin, Charley Hannah, The Fifth Missile, One Police Plaza, High Mountain Rangers (also dir., co-story), Glory Days (also dir.), Jesse Hawkes (also dir.).
PICTURES: Thundering Jets, Palm Springs Weekend, Young Dillinger, Murph the Surf, Sudden Death, The Women in Red, Wrong Is Right, Moving Violations, Uncommon Courage.

CONRAD, WILLIAM: Actor, Producer, Director. b. Louisville, KY, Sept. 27, 1920. e. Fullerton Coll. Announcer-writer-director for L.A. radio station KMPC before becoming WWII fighter pilot in 1943; returned to radio drama as original Matt Dillon of Gunsmoke series.
PICTURES: The Killers, (debut 1946), 30, Body and Soul, Sorry, Wrong Number, East Side, West Side, The Naked Jungle; producer for Warner Bros.: Two on a Guillotine, Brainstorm, An American Dream, A Covenant with Death, First to Fight, The Cool Ones, The Assignment.
TELEVISION: This Man Dawson, Klondike (prod. and dir.), 77 Sunset Strip (prod.), True (dir. 35 episodes). Actor: The Brotherhood of the Bell, The D.A., Conspiracy to Kill, O'Hara, U.S. Treasury; Cannon (series), Vengeance: The Story of Tony Cimo, Jake and the Fatman (series).

CONROY, THOMAS: Executive. r.n. Coleman Thomas Conroy. b. Camden, NJ, Nov. 3, 1924. e. Yale U. Hd. prof. camera dept., Bell and Howell Inc., New York, 1951; hd. camera dept., Cinerama Inc., 1952–55; National Theatres Inc., 1955; hd. camera dept., Cinemiracle; v.p. prod., prod. supv., Cinerama, Inc. 1960. Developed Cinerama single-lens system; v.p., production, Shannon Prod., Inc., 1967.
PICTURES: This Is Cinerama, Cinerama Holiday, Seven Wonders of the World, Windjammer, The Wonderful World of the Brothers Grimm, How the West Was Won, The Best of Cinerama, The Golden Head.

CONTE, JOHN: Actor, Singer. b. Palmer, MA.. e. Lincoln H.S., Los Angeles. Actor, Pasadena Playhouse; radio anncr., m.c.; Armed Forces, W.W.II. Pres. KMIR-TV, Channel 36, Desert Empire Television Corp., Palm Springs.
THEATRE: On Broadway in Windy City, Allegro, Carousel, Arms and the Girl.
TELEVISION: John Conte's Little Show (1950–52), Max Liebman Spectaculars and dramatic shows, host and star of NBC Matinee Theatre; (1955–58). TV Hour of Stars; Mantovani Welcomes You.
PICTURES: Debut in Man With the Golden Arm, The Carpetbaggers.

CONTI, BILL: Composer. b. Providence, RI, April 13, 1942. Studied piano at age 7, forming first band at age 15. e. Louisiana State U., Juilliard School of Music. Toured Italy with jazz trio where scored first film, Candidate for a Killing. Returned to U.S. to be music supvr. on Blume in Love for Paul Mazursky.
PICTURES: Harry and Tonto; Next Stop, Greenwich Village; Rocky, Handle With Care, Slow Dancing in the Big City, An Unmarried Woman, F.I.S.T., The Big Fix, Paradise Alley, Uncle Joe Shannon, Rocky II, A Man, A Woman, and A Bank;

Goldengirl, The Seduction of Joe Tynan, The Formula, Gloria, Private Benjamin, Carbon Copy, Victory, For Your Eyes Only, I The Jury, Rocky III, Neighbors, Split Image, Bad Boys, That Championship Season, Unfaithfully Yours, The Right Stuff (Acad. Award, Best Score), Mass Appeal, The Karate Kid, The Bear, Big Trouble, Gotcha, Beer, Nomads, F/X, The Karate Kid II, A Prayer for the Dying, Masters of the Universe, Baby Boom, Broadcast News, For Keeps, A Night in the Life of Jimmy Reardon, Betrayed, Cohen and Tate, Big Blue, Lean On Me, The Karate Kid Part III, Lock Up.

TELEVISION: Kill Me If You Can, Stark, North and South, Napoleon and Josephine, Murderers Among Us: The Simon Wiesenthal Story. Series themes: Cagney and Lacy, Dynasty, Falcon Crest, The Colbys, Kenya, Heartbeat, Lifestyles of the Rich and Famous, Emerald Point N.A.S., Dolphin Cove.

CONTI, TOM: Actor. b. Paisley, Scotland, Nov. 22, 1941. Trained at Royal Scottish Academy of Music, Glasgow. Did repertory work in Scotland before London stage debut appearing with Paul Scofield in Savages, 1973.

THEATER: London: They're Playing Our Song, Romantic Comedy, Two Into One, Italian Straw Hat. Director: Before the Party, The Housekeeper. NY: Whose Life Is It Anyway? (Tony Award, 1980), Last Licks (dir.).

PICTURES: Galileo (debut, 1975), The Duellists, The Haunting of Julia (Full Circle), Merry Christmas, Mr. Lawrence; Reuben, Reuben; American Dreamer, Miracles, Saving Grace, Beyond Therapy, Gospel According to Vic, Two Brothers Running, That Summer of White Roses, Shirley Valentine.

TELEVISION: Mother of Men (1959), The Glittering Prizes, Madame Bovery, Treats, The Norman Conquests, The Wall, Nazi Hunter, The Quick and the Dead, Roman Holiday, The Dumb Waiter, Faerie Tale Theater, Fatal Judgement, Blade on the Feather.

CONVERSE, FRANK: Actor. b. St. Louis, MO, May 22, 1938. e. Carnegie Tech. Early training on stage in New York. Active in repertory theatres. Two seasons with Amer. Shakespeare Fest.

PICTURES: Hurry Sundown, Hour of the Gun, Everybody Wins.

TELEVISION: Mod Squad, Medical Center, The Bold Ones, Series: N.Y.P.D., Coronet Blue, The Guest Room, Movin' On, Dolphin Cove. Movies: The Widowing of Mrs. Holyrod, The Rowdyman, Shadow of a Gunman, Tattered Web, Dr. Cook's Garden, Anne of Green Gables—The Sequel; Alone in the Neon Jungle.

STAGE: The Seagull, Death of a Salesman, Night of the Iguana, A Man for All Seasons, The House of Blue Leaves, First One Asleep Whistle, Arturo Ui, A Streetcar Named Desire (1988 revival).

CONVY, BERT: Actor. b. St. Louis, MO, July 23, 1934. e. UCLA. Was professional baseball player before turning to acting. On Broadway in The Matchmaker, Billy Barnes Revue, Cabaret, Nine.

PICTURES: Gunman's Walk, Susan Slade, Act One, Semi-Tough, Jennifer, Hero at Large, The Cannonball Run.

TELEVISION: Dallas Cowboys Cheerleaders, Ebony, Ivory and Jade, Man in the Santa Claus Suit, Valley of the Dolls. Host on game show, Tattletales, Love Thy Neighbor, Win, Lose or Draw.

CONWAY, GARY: Actor. r.n. Gareth Carmody. b. Boston, MA, 1939. e. U. of California at L.A. As college senior was chosen for title role in Teen-Age Frankenstein. After graduating served in military at Ford Ord, CA. In 1960 began contract with Warner Bros., doing bits for films and TV. Has also appeared on stage. Has given several one-man shows as painter.

PICTURES: Young Guns of Texas, Once Is Not Enough, The Farmer (also prod.), American Ninja (also s.p.), Over The Top (s.p.), American Ninja III: Blood Hunt (story).

TELEVISION: Burke's Law, Land of the Giants (series).

CONWAY, KEVIN: Actor. b. New York, NY, May 29, 1942.

THEATER: One Flew Over the Cuckoo's Nest, When You Comin' Back Red Ryder? (Obie and Drama Desk Awards), Of Mice and Men, Moonchildren, Life Class, Saved, The Elephant Man, Other Places, King John (NYSF), Other People's Money (Outer Critics Circle Award, best actor, 1989). Dir.: Mecca, Short Eyes (revival), One Act Play Fest. (Lincoln Center), Milk Train Doesn't Stop Here Anymore (revival), The Elephant Man (tour).

PICTURES: Slaughterhouse Five, Shamus, Believe in Me, Portnoy's Complaint, F.I.S.T., Paradise Alley, The Fun House, Flashpoint, Homeboy, The Sun and the Moon (dir., prod.), Funny Farm.

TELEVISION: Series: All My Children. Movies: Rage of Angels, Johnny We Hardly Knew You, The Deadliest Season, The Scarlet Letter, The Lathe of Heaven, Attack on Fear, Something About Amelia, Jesse, The Elephant Man.

CONWAY, TIM: Actor. b. Willoughby, OH, Dec. 15, 1933. e. Bowling Green State U. After 2 yrs. Army service joined KWY-TV in Cleveland as writer-director and occasional performer. Comedienne Rose Marie discovered him and arranged audition for the Steve Allen Show on which he became regular. In 1962 signed for McHale's Navy, series. Also has done night club appearances.

PICTURES: McHale's Navy, The World's Greatest Athlete, The Apple Dumpling Gang, Gus, The Shaggy D.A., Cannonball Run II, The Longshot (also s.p.), Cyclone.

TELEVISION: The Steve Allen Show, The Garry Moore Show, McHale's Navy, guest appearances on Hollywood Palace and shows starring Carol Burnett, Red Skelton, Danny Kaye, Dean Martin, Cher, Doris Day, The Tim Conway Show, The Longshot, Plaza Suite, many specials.

CONWAY, SHIRL: Actress. r.n., Shirl Conway Larson; b. Franklinville, NY, June 13, 1916. e. U. of Michigan, 1934–38. Singer, comedian, nightclubs.

PLAYS: Gentlemen Prefer Blondes, Plain and Fancy.

TELEVISION: The Doctors and The Nurses.

COOK, ELISHA, JR.: Actor. b. San Francisco, CA, Dec. 26, 1907. e. St. Albans, Chicago boarding school. Joined Frank Bacon in Lightnin' at the age of 14.

THEATRE: Appeared with Ethel Barrymore in Kingdom of God, Henry, Behave, Many a Slip, Three Cornered Moon, Coquette (London). Played in vaudeville and summer stock companies. Chrysalis, Ah, Wilderness (Theatre Guild).

PICTURES: Two in a Crowd (signed by Paramount, 1936), Pigskin Parade, The Maltese Falcon, Up in Arms, Casanova Brown, Cinderella Jones, Dillinger, The Big Sleep, The Long Night, Don't Bother to Knock, I the Jury, Shane, Thunder Over the Plains, Drum Beat, Outlaw's Daughter, Timberjack, Indian Fighter, The Killing, Voodoo Island, Rosemary's Baby, Welcome to Hard Times, Blacula, The Great Northfield, Minnesota Raid, Emperor of the North, Electra-Glide in Blue, The Outfit, The Black Bird, The Champ, Carny, Hammett.

TELEVISION: Chicago Story, Terror at Alcatraz, Bring 'em Back Alive, It Came Upon a Midnight Clear, The Man Who Broke 1000 Chains.

COOK, FIELDER: Producer, Director. b. Atlanta, GA, Mar. 9, 1923. e. Washington & Lee U., B.A., 1947; U. of Birmingham, Eng., post grad., 1948. Doctor of Fine Arts (Hon) (1973) (W & L). USNR, 1944; 7th Amphibious Force, 1944–45, J. Walter Thompson Co., 1947–56.

TELEVISION Films/Specials: Family Reunion; Gauguin, The Savage; John Updike's Too Far to Go; Maya Angelou's I Know Why the Caged Bird Sings; My Luke And I—The Lou Gehrig Love Story; Judge Horton & The Scottsboro Boys; Beacon Hill (series); Miles To Go Before I Sleep: This Is the West That Was; Miracle on 34th Street; The Homecoming (pilot, The Waltons); The Hands of Carmac Joyce; Sam Hill; Beauty and the Beast; Teacher, Teacher; The Rivalry; Valley Forge; The Price; Harvey; Goodbye, Raggedy-Ann (also exec.-prod.) Brigadoon (also prod.); Will There Ever Be a Morning?; Why Me?, Evergreen, A Special Friendship, Saul Bellow's Seize the Day, Third and Oak: The Pool Hall.

PICTURES: Patterns, Home Is the Hero, A Big Hand for the Little Lady, How to Save a Marriage and Ruin Your Life, Prudence and the Pill, Eagle in a Cage, From the Mixed Up Files of Mrs. Basil E. Frankweiler.

PLAYS: A Cook For Mr. General, Maneuvers.

AWARDS: Various for (after 1956): Patterns, Project Immortality; Big Deal in Laredo; Teacher, Teacher; Ben Casey Pilot; The Price; Brigadoon; Judge Horton and the Scottsboro Boys; The Homecoming, Too Far to Go, Seize the Day.

COOK, KWENAM DAVID: Executive. b. Seoul, Korea, Mar. 16, 1922. e. Waseda U., Tokyo, Japan. ROK national assemblyman (Congress) 1959–61. Pres. Korean Gymnastic Assoc. 1967–70. Chairman: Century Co., Ltd., Seoul, producers, distributors, exhibitors, and importers of films. Honorary consul general for Peru.

COOK, PETER: Actor, Writer. b. Torquay, Devonshire, Eng., Nov. 17, 1937. e. Cambridge U. Owner-producer of The Establishment Theatre Co. 1962–. Director, Private Eye magazine. With Cambridge classmates Dudley Moore, Alan Bennett and Jonathan Miller co-wrote and starred in Beyond the Fringe (London 1959, Broadway 1964). With Dudley Moore in revue Good Evening (Tony Award, 1974). Books with Dudley Moore: Dud and Pete, The Dagenham Dialogues. Contributor to satirical periodicals.

PICTURES: The Wrong Box, Bedazzled (also co-s.p.), A Dandy in Aspic, The Bed Sitting Room, Monte Carlo or Bust, Pleasure at Her Majesty's, The Hound of the Baskervilles, Derek and Clive, The Secret Policeman's Other Ball (co-s.p. only), Yellowbeard, The Haunted (prod. only), Supergirl, Without a Clue, Getting It Right.

TELEVISION: On the Braden Beat, Royal Variety Performance, Eamonn Andrews Show, The Rise and Rise of Michael Rimmer, The New London Palladium Show, Alice in Wonderland. Series: own show with Dudley Moore, Not Only But Also (also s.p.), Soho, Two's Company (U.S.), The Last Resort.

COOK, RICHARD: Executive. Began career 1971 as Disneyland sls. rep.; promoted 1974 to mgr. of sls. Moved to studio in 1977 as mgr., pay TV and non-theatrical releases. 1980, named asst. domestic sls. mgr., for Buena Vista; 1981 promoted to v.p. & asst. gen. sls. mgr.; 1984, promoted to v.p. & gen. sls. mgr., B.V.; 1985, appt. sr. v.p., domestic distribution. 1988: appt. pres. Buena Vista Distribution.

COOKE, SIR ALISTAIR: Journalist, Broadcaster. b. Eng., Nov. 20, 1908. e. Jesus Coll., Cambridge U.; Yale U.; Harvard U. Film crit. of BBC 1934–37. London corr. NBC 1936–37. BBC commentator in U.S. since 1937. Chief Amer. corr., Manchester Guardian, 1948–72; English narrator, The March of Time, 1938–39; v.o. narrator, Sorrowful Jones, 1948; narrator, Three Faces of Eve, 1957; narrator, Hitler, 1973; Peabody award winner for International reporting, 1952, 1973–83; author, Douglas Fairbanks, Garbo & The Night Watchmen. A Generation on Trial, One Man's America, Christmas Eve, The Vintage Mencken, etc.; m.c. Omnibus, TV show, 1952–61; m.c. prod. U.N.'s International Zone (Emmy Award, 1958); m.c., Masterpiece Theatre since 1971. Writer & narrator, America: A Personal History of The United States, TV series BBC, NBC, PBS, for which won 5 Emmy Awards, 1973; Franklin Medal, Royal Society of Arts, 1973; Knighted, KBE, 1973.

BOOKS: America, 1973; Six Men, 1977; Talk About America, 1968; The Americans, 1979; Above London, 1980; Masterpieces, 1981; The Patient Has the Floor, 1986, America Observed, 1988.

COOLIDGE, MARTHA: Director, Writer, Producer. b. New Haven, CT, 1946. e. Rhode Island Sch. of Design, School of Visual Arts, and Columbia U., NYU Inst. of Film and TV grad. sch. m. producer Michael Backes. Dir. short films while in school. Worked on commercials and political doc. film crews. Prod., dir. and writer of docs. which have won festival awards, including Passing Quietly Through; David: Off and On (American Film Fest.), Old Fashioned Woman (CINE Golden Eagle Award). 1968 wrote and prod. daily children's TV show Magic Tom in Canada. Made student film Mondo Linoleum (co-star and dir.). First feature film Not a Pretty Picture (won Blue Ribbon Award, Amer. Film Fest.) Helped start assn. of Indep. Video and Filmmakers, Inc. As an AFI/Academy Intern worked with Robert Wise on his film Audrey Rose, 1976. Wrote orig. story that was filmed as the The Omega Connection. Directed short film Bimbo.

PICTURES: The City Girl, Valley Girl, National Lampoon's Joy of Sex, Glory Days, Real Genius, Plain Clothes, The Friendly, That's Adequate (interviewee), Rope Dancing.

TELEVISION: The Twilight Zone; Sledge Hammer (pilot); House and Home (pilot), Roughhouse. Movie: Trenchcoat in Paradise.

COONEY, JOAN GANZ: Executive, Producer. b. Phoenix, AZ, Nov. 30, 1929. e. U. of Arizona. After working as a reporter in Phoenix, moved to NY in 1953 where she wrote soap-opera summaries at NBC. Then was publicist for U.S. Steel Hour. Became producer of live weekly political TV show Court of Reason (Emmy Award) and documentaries (Poverty, Anti-Poverty and the Poor) before founding Children's Television Workshop and Sesame Street in 1969. Currently exec. dir. CTW.

COOPER, BEN: Actor. b. Hartford, CT, Sept. 30, 1933. e. Columbia U. On stage in Life with Father, (1942); numerous radio, TV appearances (500 shows), first show May 1945.

PICTURES: Woman They Almost Lynched, A Perilous Journey, Sea of Lost Ships, Flight Nurse, Fortune Hunter, Johnny Guitar, Hell's Outpost, Eternal Sea, Last Command, Fighting Chance, Headline Hunters, Rose Tattoo, Rebel in Town, Chartroose Caboose, Red Tomahawk, The Fastest Gun Alive, One More Train to Rob, Support Your Local Gunfighter, Arizona Raiders, Gunfight at Comanche Creek, Outlaws Son.

COOPER, HAL: Director, Performer. b. New York, NY, Feb. 22, 1923. e. U. of Michigan. m. Marta Salcido; child actor in various radio prog. since 1932; featured Bob Emery's Rainbow House, Mutual, 1936–46; asst. dir. Dock St. Theatre, Charleston, SC, 1946–48.

TELEVISION: Your Sch. Reporter, TV Baby Sitter, The Magic Cottage (writer, prod.,) dir., Valiant Lady, Search for Tomorrow, Portia Faces Life; dir., assoc. prod. Kitty Foyle; prod. dir. Indictment; assoc. prod. dir. The Happy Time; prod. dir. For Better or Worse; dir., The Clear Horizon; Assoc., prod., dir., Surprise Package; dir., Dick Van Dyke Show; prod., dir., The Art Linkletter Show, The Object Is. Dir.: Death Valley Days, I Dream of Jeannie, That Girl, I Spy, Hazel, Gidget, Gilligan's Island, NYPD, Mayberry, Courtship of Eddie's Father, My World and Welcome to It, The Odd Couple, Mary Tyler Moore, All in the Family. Exec. prod., dir. Maude, Phyl and Mikky, Love, Sidney, Gimme a Break, Empty Nest, Dear John.

COOPER, JACKIE: Actor, Director, Producer. b. Los Angeles, CA, Sept. 15, 1922. Began theatrical career at age of 3 as m.p. actor; was member of Our Gang comedies. First starring role in 1930 in Skippy. Worked at every major studio, always with star billing. At 20 enlisted in Navy. After three-yr. tour of duty went to N.Y. to work in live TV. Appeared on Broadway stage in Mr. Roberts and on natl. tour and in London. Directed as well as acted in live and filmed TV. Served as v.p. in chg. of TV prod., for Screen Gems, 1964-69, when resigned to return to acting, directing, producing.

PICTURES: Actor—Movietone Follies, Sunny Side Up, Skippy, Sooky, The Champ, When a Fellow Needs a Friend, Lumpy, Lost, The Bowery, Treasure Island, O'Shaughnessy's Boy, The Devil Is a Sissy, Gangster's Boy, Seventeen, Gallant Sons, Her First Beau, Syncopation, Stork Bites Man, Kilroy Was Here, Everything's Ducky, The Love Machine, Chosen Survivors, Superman, Superman II, Surrender. Director: Stand Up and Be Counted.

TELEVISION: People's Choice (directed 71 segments; also starred), Hennesey (dir. 91 segments; also starred) 1975 series: Mobile Two (star). Movies: The Last Detail; Perfect Gentlemen; Having Babies; Rainbow; White Mama (dir.); Leave 'Em Laughing (dir.); Rosie (also prod.); (dir.), Glitter; The Night They Saved Christmas (dir.), Izzy and Moe (dir.).

COOPER, SHELDON: Executive. e. Indiana U. Joined WGN Television, 1950 holding various positions in prod. including floor mgr., dir., prod.; 1961, named mgr. prod.; 1961 became exec. prod. for station; 1964, named asst. prog. mgr.; 1965, mgr. of dept.; 1966, v.p. prog. dev. with WGN Continental Productions Co.; elected to bd. of dir., Continental Broadcasting Co. and appointed station mgr., WGN TV, April 1974.; 1975, named v.p. and gen. mrg., WGN Continental Broadcasting.; 1977, dir., broadcasting; 1979, pres. and gen. mgr., WGN Television; 1982, chief exec. of newly formed Tribune Entertainment Co. and dir. of Tribune Co. Syndicate, Inc., 1982–present. One of founders of Operation Prime Time, consortium of independent stations. Awarded Emmys: 1960 as television's "man of the year behind the cameras" and 1964 for continuing excellence as writer, prod., executive, WGN TV. Chmn., Assoc. of Independent TV Stations, Inc. (INTV), 1980 and 1981; National v.p., Muscular Dystrophy Assoc.; 1980, on bd. National Assoc. of TV Prog. Executives (NATPE); first v.p., Chicago chap. Acad. of TV Arts and Sciences; v.p., trustee of national chap.

COOPERMAN, ALVIN: Producer. b. Brooklyn, NY. Started career with Lee & J. J. Shubert, 1939–51; color team, dev. color TV for FCC approval, 1953; prod. first color TV shows with mobile unit, 1954; developed & prod. first Wide Wide World, June 1955; mgr. program sls., NBC Network, 1955; exec. prod. Producers Showcase, Dodsworth, Rosalinda, 1956; prod. Jack and the Beanstalk, Festival of Music, 1957; dir. prog. NBC-TV, Apr. 1957; joined HJ Enterprises as prod. NBC-TV, The Shirley Temple Storybook, 1957; exec. prod. Screen Gems, 1958; prod. Du Pont Show, 1959; exec. prod. Roncom Prod. 1960; Prod., Untouchables, 1961–63; exec. dir., Shubert Thea. Ent. 1963; v.p., special programs, NBC, 1967–68; exec. v.p., Madison Square Garden Center, 1968–72; President, Madison Square Garden Center, Inc.; Founder, Madison Sq. Garden Prods. and Network. Chairman of the Board, Athena Communications Corporation. Pres., NY Television Academy, 1987–89.

TELEVISION: Producer: Romeo and Juliet, (Emmy nominee); Pele's Last Game; The Fourth King; Amahl and the Night Visitors; Live from Studio 8H—A Tribute to Toscanini, (Emmy Award); Live from Studio 8H—An Evening with Jerome Robbins and the New York City Ballet, (Emmy Award); Live from Studio 8H—Caruso Remembered; Ain't Misbehavin', (Emmy nominee, NAACP Image Award, Best TV Show of the Year); Pope John Paul II; My Two Loves, Safe Passage; Family Album, U.S.A. (26 half hours).

COPPOLA, CARMINE: Composer. b. New York, NY, June 11, 1910. Father of director Francis Coppola and actress Talia Shire. Studied flute and composition at Juilliard and Manhattan School of Music. Orchestra musician and arranger at Radio City Music Hall in the 1930s. First flutist, Detroit Symphony. Conductor of orchestra of Broadway shows: Kismet, Once Upon a Mattress, 110 in the Shade, La Plume de ma Tante, Stop the World, I Want to Get Off; The Great Waltz. Played first flute with NBC Symphony Orchestra under Toscanini.

PICTURES: The Godfather; The Godfather, Part II (Academy Award); Apocalypse Now; The Black Stallion; Napoleon; Gardens of Stone, Blood Red, Tucker: The Man and His Dream (additional music), New York Stories (music, actor).

TELEVISION: The People, Rip Van Winkle (Showtime).

COPPOLA, FRANCIS FORD: Writer, Producer, Director. b. Detroit, MI, April 7, 1939. Son of composer Carmine Coppola. Brother of actress Talia Shire. e. Hofstra U, B.A., 1958; UCLA, 1958–68, M.F.A., cinema. While at UCLA was hired as asst. to Roger Corman as dialogue dir., sound man and assoc. prod. 1969; est. American Zoetrope, (later Zoetrope Studios), a prod. center in San Francisco. Publisher, City (magazine, 1975–6).

PICTURES: The Playgirls and the Bellboy (co-dir., co-s.p., 1962); Tonight For Sure (prod., dir.); The Premature Burial (asst. dir.); The Terror (assoc. prod., co-dir.); Dementia 13 (dir., s.p.); Is Paris Burning? (co-s.p.); This Property is Condemned (co-s.p.), You're a Big Boy Now (dir., s.p.); Reflections in a Golden Eye (s.p.); Finian's Rainbow (dir.); The Rain People (dir., s.p.); Patton (co-s.p., Acad. Award); THX 1138 (exec. prod.); The Godfather (dir., co-s.p., prod., Acad. Award, best picture and s.p.); American Graffiti (exec. prod.); The Conversation (prod., dir., s.p.); The Godfather Part II (co-s.p., dir.; Acad. Award, s.p., dir., picture); The Great Gatsby (s.p.); Apocalypse Now (prod., dir., co-s.p.); The Black Stallion (exec. prod.); One From the Heart (prod., dir., co-s.p.); Hammett (exec. prod.); The Outsiders (prod., dir., s.p.); The Escape Artist (prod.); The Black Stallion Returns (prod.); Rumble Fish (prod., dir., s.p.); The Cotton Club, (dir., co-s.p.); Mishima (prod.); Peggy Sue Got Married (dir.); Gardens of Stone (dir.); Tough Guys Don't Dance (exec. prod.); Lionheart (exec. prod.), Tucker: The Man and His Dream (dir.); New York Stories (Life Without Zoe, dir., co-s.p.).

TELEVISION: The People; Rip Van Winkle (Faerie Tale Theatre). Series: The Outsiders (exec. prod.).

CORD, ALEX: Actor. r.n. Alexander Viespi. b. Floral Park, NY, May 3, 1933. Early career in rodeo; left to become actor. Studied at Shakespeare Academy (Stratford, Conn.) and Actor's Studio (N.Y.). Spent two yrs. in summer stock; in 1961 went on tour with Stratford Shakespeare Co. Made m.p. debut in Synanon, 1965. Author of novel Sandsong.

PICTURES: Stagecoach, The Scorpio Letters, The Prodigal Gun, The Brotherhood, Stiletto, The Dead Are Alive, Chosen Survivors, Sidewinder One, Grayeagle, Uninvited.

TELEVISION: Airwolf (series), Hunter's Man; Genesis II, Beggerman Thief, The Girl Who Saved America, The Dirty Dozen: The Fatal Mission.

CORDAY, BARBARA: Executive. b. New York, NY, Oct. 15, 1944. m. Barney Rosenzweig, TV producer. Began career as publicist in N.Y. and L.A. Turned to writing for TV; named v.p., ABC-TV, in chg. of comedy series development. 1982–84, headed own production co. in association with Columbia Pictures TV; June, 1984–1987 pres., Columbia Pictures TV. Aug., 1988: appointed CBS Entertainment, exec. v.p. primetime programs. Member: Caucus of Writers, Producers & Directors; Hollywood Women's Coalition.

TELEVISION: Writer: American Dream (pilot); and co-creator, Cagney and Lacey (series).

COREY, JEFF: Actor. b. New York, NY, Aug. 10, 1914. e. Feogin Sch. of Dram. Art. On stage in Leslie Howard prod. of Hamlet, 1936; Life and Death of an American, 1938, In the Matter of J. Robert Oppenheimer and Hamlet-Mark Taper Forum, L.A. King Lear, Beverly Music Center '73.

PICTURES: All That Money Can Buy, Syncopation, The Killers, Ramrod, Joan of Arc, Roughshod, Black Shadows, Bagdad, Outriders, The Devil and Daniel Webster, My Friend Flicka, Canyon City, Singing Guns, Seconds, In Cold Blood, Golden Bullet, Boston Strangler, True Grit, Butch Cassidy and The Sundance Kid, Beneath the Planet of the Apes, Getting Straight, Little Big Man, They Call Me Mister Tibbs, Clear and Present Danger, High Flying Lowe, Catlow, Something Evil, Premonition, Shine, Rooster, Oh, God!, Butch and Sundance: The Early Days, Up River, Conan the Destroyer, Cognac, Messenger of Death, The Judas Project, Rooster.

TELEVISION: The Untouchables, The Beachcomber, The Balcony, Yellow Canary, Lady in a Cage, Outer Limits, Channing, The Doctors and the Nurses, Perry Mason, Gomer Pyle, Wild, Wild West, Run for Your Life, Bonanza, Iron Horse, Judd for Defense, Garrisons Gorillas, Gunsmoke, Hawaii Five O, Star Trek, dir. The Psychiatrist, Night Gallery, Alias Smith and Jones, Sixth Sense, Hawkins, Owen Marshall, Police Story, Bob Newhart Show, Six Million Dollar Man, Doctors Hospital, Starsky and Hutch, Land of the Free (film), Kojak, McCloud, Captains Courageous (Bell Tel. Hr.), Bionic Woman, Barney Miller, One Day at a Time, The Pirate, Lou Grant, The Powers of Jonathan Starr, Cry for the Strangers, Today's FBI, Knots Landing, Archie Bunker's Place, Faerie Tale Theatre, Night Court, Helltown (series), Morning Star/Evening Star (series), New Love American Style, Starman, The A Team, A Deadly Silence (movie).

CORMAN, GENE: Producer. r.n. Eugene H. Corman. b. Detroit, MI, Sept. 24, 1927. e. Stanford U. Went to work for MCA as agent 1950-57; left to produce his first feature film, Hot Car Girl. Partner with brother Roger in Corman Company and New World Distributors. Vice pres. 20th Century Fox Television, 1983-87; exec. v.p. worldwide production, 21st Century Film Corp.

PICTURES: Attack of the Giant Leaches, Not of This Earth, Blood and Steel, Valley of the Redwoods, Purple Reef, Beast from Haunted Cave, Cat Burglar, The Intruder, Tobruk, You Can't Win Em All, Cool Breeze, Hit Man, The Slams, Von Richthofen and Brown, I Escaped from Devil's Island, Secret Invasion, Vigilante Force, F.I.S.T. (exec. prod.), The Big Red One, If You Could See What I Hear, Paradise, A Man Called Sarge.

TELEVISION: What's In It For Harry, A Woman Called Golda (won Emmy and Christopher Awards as prod.), Mary and Joseph, a Love Story.

CORMAN, ROGER WILLIAM: Executive, Director, Producer, Writer, Distributor. b. Detroit, MI, April 5, 1926. e. Stanford U. 1947; Oxford U., England 1950. U.S. Navy 1944; 20th Century-Fox, production dept., 1948, story analyst 1948–49; Literary agent, 1951–52; story, s.p., assoc. prod. Highway Dragnet. Formed Roger Corman Prod. and Filmgroup. Prod. over 200 feature films and dir. over 60 of them. Formed production-releasing company, org., New World Pictures, Inc., 1970. Formed prod. co., New Horizons, 1984; distribution co., Concorde, 1985.

PICTURES: Five Guns West (1953), House of Usher, Little Shop of Horrors, Pit and the Pendulum, The Intruder, Masque of the Red Death, Tomb of Ligeia, The Secret Invasion, The Wild Angels, The Trip, Bloody Mama, Von Richtofen and Brown, Gasss, St. Valentine's Day Massacre, Box Car Bertha, Big Bad Mama, Death Race 2000, Eat My Dust, Capone, Jackson County Jail, Fighting Mad, Thunder & Lightning, Grand Theft Auto, I Never Promised You A Rose Garden, Deathsport, Avalanche, Battle Beyond the Stars, St. Jack, Love Letters, Smokey Bites the Dust, Galaxy of Terror, Slumber Party Massacre Part II (prod.), Death Stalker, Barbarian Queen, Munchies, Stripped To Kill, Big Bad Mama II (prod.), Sweet Revenge (co-exec. prod.), The Drifter (exec. prod.), Daddy's Boys (prod.), Singles (exec. prod.), Crime Zone (exec. prod.), Watcher (exec. prod.), The Lawless Land (exec. prod.), Stripped to Kill 2 (exec. prod.), The Terror Within (prod.), Lords of the Deep (prod.), Two to Tango (prod.), Time Trackers (prod.), Heros Stand Alone (prod.), Bloodfist (prod.), Silk 2 (prod.), Edgar Allan Poe's The Masque of Red Death (prod.), Roger Corman's Frankenstein Unbound (prod., dir., s.p.), Hollywood Boulevard II (exec. prod.), Rock and Roll High School Forever (exec. prod.).

CORNELL, JOHN: Producer, Director, Writer. b. Kalgoorlie, Western Australia, 1941. m. actress Delvene Delancy. Grew up Bunbury. e. studied pharmacy for two years in Perth. Won internship at Western Australian Newspapers at 19, becoming columnist then London editor at 26. As Melbourne prod. of TV show, A Current Affair, discovered bridge rigger Paul Hogan. Put him on show, became his manager and formed JP Productions with him in 1972. Prod. and appeared on The Paul Hogan Show. Formed movie co. with Hogan, Rimfire Films.

PICTURES: Crocodile Dundee (prod., co-s.p.); Crocodile Dundee II (prod., dir., editor).

CORNFELD, STUART: Producer. b. Los Angeles, CA. e. U. of California, Berkeley. Entered America Film Institute's Center for Advanced Film Studies as producing fellow, 1975. Joined Brooksfilm as asst. to Mel Brooks on High Anxiety. Assoc. prod., History of the World Part I.

PICTURES: Fatso (1980), The Elephant Man, (exec. prod.), National Lampoon's European Vacation (co-prod.), Girls Just Want to Have Fun (exec. prod.), The Fly, Moving, The Fly II (exec. prod.), Hider in the House (co-prod.).

CORNFIELD, HUBERT: Director, Writer, Producer. b. Istanbul, Turkey. e. U. of Pennsylvania. Actors' Studio, 1952–54. Story analyst Allied Artists 1954. Directed first picture 1955. Has lived in Paris since 1964.

PICTURES: Sudden Danger, Lure of the Swamp, Plunder Road, The Third Voice, Pressure Point, The Night of the Following Day.

CORRI, ADRIENNE: Actress. r.n. Adrienne Riccoboni. b. Glasgow, Scotland, Nov. 13, 1933. Ent. Royal Acad. of Dramatic Art at 13; parts in several stage plays including The Human Touch; m.p. debut in The River. Numerous TV appearances.

PICTURES: Quo Vadis, The River, The Kidnappers, Devil Girl From Mars, Lease of Life, Make Me An Offer, Feminine Touch, The Big Chance, Corridors of Blood, Doctor of Seven Dials, The Rough and the Smooth, Hellfire Club, The Tell-Tale Heart, A Study in Terror, Bunny Lake is Missing, Dynamite Jack, Doctor Zhivago, Epilogue to Capricorn, A Clockwork Orange, Rosebud, Vampire Circus, Madhouse.

CORT, BUD: Actor. r.n. Walter Edward Cox. b. New Rochelle, NY, March 29, 1950. e. NYU. School of the Arts. Stage debut in Wise Child, Bdwy. Theatrical film debut in M•A•S•H, 1970. Television debut in The Doctors.

PICTURES: Brewster McCloud, Harold and Maude, Why Shoot the Teacher?, The Secret Diary of Sigmund Freud, Invaders from Mars, Burnin' Love, Maria's Lovers, The Chocolate War, Out of the Dark.

TELEVISION: Brave New World, Bernice Bobs Her Hair, Faerie Tale Theatre, The Hitchhiker: Made for Each Other (HBO), The Bates Motel.

CORT, ROBERT W.: Executive. e. U. of Pennsylvania (Phi Beta Kappa). Moved into feature prod. after having worked primarily in marketing/advertising. Joined Columbia Pictures as v.p., 1976; elevated to v.p., adv./pub./promo. Named exec. v.p. of mktg. for 20th-Fox, 1980. Moved into feature prod. as senior v.p., 1981. In 1983 named exec. v.p., prod., 20th-Fox Prods. 1984, joined Interscope Communications as pres., entertainment division.
PICTURES: Co.-prod.: Critical Condition, Outrageous Fortune, Revenge of the Nerds II, Three Men and a Baby, The Seventh Sign, Cocktail, Bill & Ted's Excellent Adventure, Renegades (exec. prod.), Blind Fury (exec. prod.), An Innocent Man, Bird on a Wire.

CORTESE, VALENTINA: Actress. b. Milan, Italy, Jan. 1, 1925. Started career at 15 in Orizzonte di pinto while studying at Rome Acad. of Dramatic Art. Screen debut: La Cens Delle Beffe, 1941; brought to Hollywood by 20th Century-Fox, following picture, A Yank in Rome; experience on dramatic stage in variety of roles inc. Shakespeare, O'Neill, Shaw.
PICTURES: Cagliostro, Glass Mountain, House on Telegraph Hill, Lulu, Barabbas, The Visit, Brother Sun, Sister Moon; Thieves' Highway, Les Miserables, Secret People, Barefoot Contessa, Shadow of the Eagle, Magic Fire, The Legend of Lylah Clare, Juliet of the Spirits, Day for Night, When Time Ran Out, The Adventures of Baron Munchausen.

CORTEZ, STANLEY: Dir. Photography. b. New York, NY, 1908. e. NYU. br. Ricardo Cortez, actor. Began working with portrait photographers (Steichen, Pirie MacDonald, Bachrach, etc.), N.Y. Entered film indust. with Paramount Pictures; to Hollywood as camera asst. and later second cameraman, various studios; pioneer in use of montage; Signal Corps W.W.II, Yalta, Quebec, etc. Received Film Critics of Amer. award for work on Magnificent Ambersons. Under personal contract to David O. Selznick, Orson Welles, Walter Wanger, David Wolper. Contributor, Encyclopedia Britannica.
PICTURES: Man on the Eiffel Tower, Shark River (A.A. nominee), Bad Lands of Dakota, Magnificent Ambersons, Eagle Squadron, Powers Girl, Since You Went Away (A.A. nominee) Smash Up, Flesh and Fantasy, Captain Kidd, Secret Beyond the Door, Fort Defiance, Riders to the Stars, Black Tuesday, Night of the Hunter, Man from Del Rio, Three Faces of Eve, Top Secret Affair, Angry Red Planet, Dionosaurus, Back Street, Shock Corridor, Nightmare in the Sun, The Naked Kiss, The Candidate, Blue, The Bridge of Remagen, The Date, Another Man, Another Chance. Special sequences on Damien, Omen II, Day the World Ended, Le Bon Vivant.

CORWIN, BRUCE CONRAD: Exhibitor. b. June 11, 1940, Los Angeles, CA. e. Wesleyan U. Pres., Metropolitan Theatres Corp.; chmn., Will Rogers Hospital area ind. campaigns; pres., Variety Boys Club; Board of Trustees American Film Institute; Board of Trustees U.C.L.A. Foundation; pres., Variety Club Tent 25; Pres., L.A. Children's Museum.

CORWIN, NORMAN: Writer, Producer, Director. b. Boston, MA, May 3, 1910. Sports ed. Greenfield, Mass. Daily Recorder, 1926–29; radio ed., news commentator, Springfield Republican & Daily News, 1929–36; prog. dir., CBS, 1938. Bok Medal "for distinguished services to radio," 1942; Peabody Medal, 1942; awarded grant by Amer. Acad. of Arts & Letters, 1942; Page One Award, 1944; Distinguished Merit Award, Nat'l Conf. of Christians & Jews, 1945; Unity Award, Interracial Film & Radio Guild, 1945; Wendell Willkie One World Flight Award, 1946; Met. Opera Award for modern opera in collab. Bernard Rogers, 1946; first award, Res. Comm. of U.N., 1950; Radio & TV first award, Nat'l Conf. of Christians & Jews, 1951; Honor Medal of Freedom Foundation for TV show, Between Americans, 1951; ent., Radio Hall of Fame, 1962. Hon. doctorate Columbia Col. of Comms., 1967; Valentine Davies Award, WGA, 1972; P.E.N. Award, 1986; author of Thirteen by Corwin, More by Corwin, Untitled & Other Plays; The Plot to Overthrow Christmas, Dog in the Sky, Overkill and Megalove, Prayer for the 70s, Holes in a Stained Glass Window, Trivializing America; lectured at various colleges; taught courses UCLA, U.of Southern California, San Diego State U., regents lecturer, U.of California at Santa Barbara; Chairman, Creative Writing, U.S.C.-Isomata; U. of Alberta, U.S.C., Witswatersrand U., Rand Afrikaans U., So. Africa, Cantatas, The Golden Door, 55; Yes Speak Out Yes (commissioned by U.N., 1968). Faculty, U.S.C. Sch. of Journalism, 1980–. Industry Achievement Award, Broadcast Promotion Assn. 1984; Stasheff lecturer, Univ. Michigan, 1984; sect'y., M.P. Academy Foundation, 1985.
STAGE PLAYS: The Rivalry, The World of Carl Sandburg, The Hyphen, Overkill and Megalove, Cervantes. Together Tonight: Jefferson, Hamilton and Burr.
PICTURES: Once Upon a Time, Blue Veil, The Grand Design, Scandal in Scourie, Lust for Life, The Story of Ruth.
TELEVISION: Inside the Movie Kingdom, The FDR series, The Plot to Overthrow Christmas, Norman Corwin Presents, The Court Martial of General Yamashita, Network at 50 (CBS). Writer-host Academy Leaders (PBS).
Chmn. Doc. Award Com., Motion Picture Acad. 1965–86; elected to bd. of gov., 1980; first v.p., 1988–89; Chmn., writers' exec. comm., M.P. Academy; co-chmn. scholarship com., m.p. Academy; mem.: Film Advisory Bd.; L.A. County Museum; Norman Corwin Presents series; bd. of trustees, Advisory Board, Filmex; bd. of dirs., WGA. Secretary, Academy Fdn. mem. bd. of dirs., Intl. Documentary Assoc.

COSBY, BILL: Actor, Comedian. b. Philadelphia, PA, July 12, 1938. e. Temple U., U. of Mass., Ed.D. Served in United States Navy Medical Corps. Started as night club entertainer. Has appeared on TV variety shows, in numerous one-nighters across the country, and concert tours. Books: Fatherhood, Time Flies.
TELEVISION: Emmy Award 1966, 1967, 1968: Best Actor in Dramatic Series—I Spy; Emmy Award, 1969; The First Bill Cosby Special, I Spy, The Bill Cosby Special, The Second Bill Cosby Special, The Bill Cosby Show, Fat Albert, Fat Albert and the Cosby Kids, The Cosby Show; A Different World (exec. prod. only).
COMEDY ALBUMS: Bill Cosby Is A Very Funny Fellow . . . Right!; I Started Out As a Child; Why Is There Air?; Wonderfulness; Revenge; To Russell, My Brother, Whom I Slept With; 200 MPH; It's True, It's True; 8:15, 12:15.
SINGING ALBUMS: Silverthroat, Hooray for the Salvation Army Band. Grammy Award, 1964, 1965, 1966, 1967, 1969: Best Comedy Album.
RADIO: The Bill Cosby Radio Program.
PICTURES: Man and Boy, Uptown Saturday Night, Let's Do It Again, Mother, Jugs and Speed, A Piece of the Action, California Suite, The Devil and Max Devlin, Bill Cosby Himself, Leonard: Part VI (also co-prod., and story), Ghost Dad.

COSELL, HOWARD: Sports Commentator. r.n. Howard Cohen. b. Winston-Salem, NC, March 25, 1920. e. NYU, 1940. Served with U.S. Army Transportation Corp. during WW II. Studied law and practiced 1946–56. Broadcasting career began in 1953 when hired to host program on which N.Y. area Little Leaguers were introduced to baseball stars. In 1956 ABC hired him for ten five-minute sports shows on weekends. He dropped legal work to concentrate on sports reporting. Has had wide variety of roles in TV: host of Sports Focus, commentator on ABC Monday Night Football, Monday Night Baseball, Sports Beat, and various sports specials. Has hosted the Howard Cosell Sports Magazine for 4 yrs. and hosts 14 shows each week on American Contemporary Radio Network. Has guested as himself on Laugh-In, Dean Martin Show, The Odd Couple and on numerous prime-time TV shows. Founder, Legend Prods. Columnist, Daily News 1986–; Faculty mem. Brown U. 1986–.
PICTURES: Bananas, Sleeper, The World's Greatest Athlete, Two Minute Warning, Broadway Danny Rose.

COSMATOS, GEORGE PAN: Director, Producer, Writer. b. Jan. 4, 1941. e. London U. Asst. dir., Exodus and Zorba the Greek.
PICTURES: Restless (co.-prod., s.p., dir.); Massacre in Rome (co-s.p., dir.); The Cassandra Crossing (co.-s.p., dir.); Escape to Athena (co-s.p., dir.); Of Unknown Origin (dir.); Rambo: First Blood Part II (dir.), Cobra (dir.), Leviathan (dir.).

COSTA-GAVRAS, CONSTANTIN: Director. r.n. Konstaninos Gavras. b. Athens, Greece, 1933. French citizen. e. Studied at the Sorbonne; Hautes Etudes Cinematographique, (IDHEC). Was leading ballet dancer in Greece before the age of 20. Worked as second, then first assistant to Marcel Ophuls, Rene Clair, Rene Clement and Jacques Demy.
PICTURES: The Sleeping Car Murders (dir., s.p.), Un Homme De Trop (won prize at the Moscow Fest., 1966), Z (dir., co-s.p., Acad. Award, Best Foreign Lang. Film), L'Aveu (The Confession), State of Siege, Special Section, Clair de Femme, Missing (also co-s.p., Acad. Award, s.p.; Palm d'Or, Cannes Fest.), Hannah K. (also co.-s.p.), Family Business (also s.p.), Betrayed, Music Box.

COSTNER, KEVIN: Actor. b. Los Angeles, CA, Jan. 18, 1955. e. CA. State U, Fullerton majored in marketing. Acted with South Coast Actors' Co-op, community theater gp. while at coll. After grad. took marketing job which lasted 30 days. Early film work in low budget exploitation film, Sizzle Beach. Then one line as Luther Adler in Frances. 1989, set up own prod. co. TIG Prods. at Raleigh Studios.
PICTURES: Shadows Run Black (debut, 1981), Sizzle Beach, U.S.A., Night Shift, Testament, Stacy's Knights, Table for Five, Silverado, Fandango, American Flyers, The Untouchables, No Way Out, Bull Durham, Field of Dreams, The Gunrunner, Revenge (also exec. prod.), Chasing Dreams (cameo, filmed 1981), Dances with Wolves (also dir., prod.).

COTTEN, JOSEPH: Actor. b. Petersburg, VA, 1905. m. actress Patricia Medina. In stock and on NY stage, 1930–40, incl. Accent on Youth, Philadelphia Story; also Orson Welles' Federal Theatre's productions and Mercury Theatre of the Air. Autobiography: Vanity Will Get You Nowhere (1988).
STAGE: Sabrina Fair, Once More With Feeling, Prescription: Murder, Calculated Risk.

TELEVISION: narrator, Hollywood and the Stars; Alfred Hitchcock Presents; On Trial; Desilu Playhouse; Movies: Aspen; The Lindbergh Kidnapping Case; Cutter's Trail; Casino, The Screaming Woman.
PICTURES: Citizen Kane, Lydia, Magnificent Ambersons, Journey Into Fear, Shadow of a Doubt, Hers to Hold, Temptation, The Last Sunset, Two Flags West, September Affair, Walk Softly, Stranger, Half Angel, Peking Express, Man With a Cloak, The Untamed Frontier, The Steel Trap, Niagara, Blueprint for Murder, Special Delivery, Bottom of the Bottle, Killer Is Loose, Halliday Brand, From the Earth to the Moon, The Angel Wore Red, The Great Sioux Massacre, The Oscar, The Hellbenders, The Tramplers, The Money Trap, They Also Killed, The White Comanche, Petulia, The Grasshopper, The Abominable Dr. Phibes, Soylent Green, A Delicate Balance, Twilight's Last Gleaming, Airport '77, Caravans, Heaven's Gate.

COURTENAY, TOM: Actor. b. Hull, England, Feb. 25, 1937 e. University Coll., London, Royal Acad. of Dramatic Art, 1960–61; Old Vic. Ent. TV 1961 in Private Potter and the Lads; I Heard the Owl Call My Name (U.S.).
STAGE: Billy Liar, Andorra, Hamlet, She Stoops to Conquer, Otherwise Engaged (N.Y. debut), The Dresser.
PICTURES: Loneliness of the Long Distance Runner, Private Potter, Billy Liar, King and Country, Operation Crossbow, King Rat, Dr. Zhivago, Night of the Generals, The Day the Fish Came Out, A Dandy in Aspic, Otley, One Day in the Life of Ivan Denisovich, Catch Me a Spy, The Dresser, Happy New Year, Leonard: Part VI.
TELEVISION: Series: The Lads; Ghosts; Private Potter; Movies: I Heard the Owl Call My Name, Jesus of Nazareth, Absent Friends, Chekhov in Yalta.

COURTLAND, JEROME: Actor-Producer-Director. b. Knoxville, TN, Dec. 27, 1926. Began career in 40s as actor, then turned to directing and producing.
PICTURES: Actor: Kiss and Tell, Man from Colorado, Battleground, The Barefoot Mailman, The Bamboo Prison, Tonka, Black Spurs. Director: Run, Cougar, Run, Diamond on Wheels. Producer: Escape to Witch Mountain, Ride a Wild Pony, Return from Witch Mountain, Pete's Dragon.
TELEVISION: Actor: The Saga of Andy Burnett, Tonka. Director: Hog Wild (also co-prod.), Harness Fever. Director: Knots Landing, Dynasty, Hotel, Love Boat, Fantasy Island.

COUSTEAU, JACQUES-YVES, CAPTAIN: Producer. b. St. Andre de Cubzac, Gironde, 1910. e. French Naval Acad. Trained as Navy flier, switched to Gunnery office and started diving experiments. 1943 with Emile Gagnan conceived and released Aqua-Lung, first regulated compressed air breathing device for deep sea diving. After WWII org. Experimental Diving Unit, performed oceanographic research. 1951 perfected first underwater camera equipment for TV. Founded environmental org. The Cousteau Society 1974. Awarded Chevalier de la Legion d Honneur for work in Resistance. Member National Acad. of Sciences.
PICTURES: 20 short documentaries 1942–56; The Silent World (Acad. Award, 1957; Grand Prize Cannes, 1956); The Golden Fish (Acad. Award, short subject, 1959), World Without Sun (Acad. Award, 1965), Voyage to the Edge of the World.
TELEVISION: Nearly 70 TV films on his series: The World of Jacques-Yves Cousteau; The Undersea World of Jacques Cousteau; (including 8 Emmy's) Oasis in Space; The Cousteau Series; The Cousteau Odyssey series; Amazon series, Rediscovery of the World series, Sharks of Treasure Island (exec. prod.).

COUTARD, RAOUL: Cinematographer. b. Paris, France, 1924. Spent 4 years in Vietnam working for French Military Info. Service, later a civilian photographer for Time and Paris-Match. During WWII worked in photo labs. After war returned to France and formed prod. co. making documentaries. Joined Jean-Luc Godard as his cinematographer on Breathless (1960). His use of hand-held camera and natural light established him as a seminal cameraman of the French New Wave, working with Godard, Truffaut and later with Costa Gavras. Director: Hoa Binh (1971).
PICTURES: Breathless, Shoot the Piano Player, Lola, Jules and Jim, Bay of Angels, Les Carabiniers, Alphaville, The Soft Skin, Pierrot le Fou, La 317 eme Section, Weekend, Sailor From Gibralter, The Bride Wore Black, Z, The Confession, Le Crabe Tambour, Passion, First Name: Carmen, Dangerous Moves, Salt on the Skin, La Garce, Max My Love, Burning Beds, Let Sleeping Cops Lie, Bethune: The Making of a Hero.

COWAN, THEODORE: Executive. b. Letchworth, Eng. e. Parmiters Sch. Entered m.p. ind., J. Arthur Rank Productions, pub. div., asst. dir. pub. & adv., 1960. Formed own pr. & publ. Co., 1962.

COWAN, WARREN J.: Publicist. b. New York, NY, Mar. 13. e. Townsend Harris H.S., UCLA, graduated 1941. Entered public relations, 1941, with Alan Gordon & Associates; three yrs. Air Force; joined Henry C. Rogers office in 1945; became partner, 1949, and changed name to Rogers & Cowan, Public Relations; Advisor, Rogers & Cowan, Inc., 1960; pres., Rogers & Cowan, Inc., 1964; named bd. chmn., 1983. Active in various entertainment industry, civic and philanthropic orgs., including current post as national communications chmn. for the United Way of America. On advisory bd. of the National Association of Film Commissioners; serves on the Second Decade Council of the American Film Institute. On bd. L.A. County High School for the Arts.

COX, ALEX: Director. b. Liverpool, Eng., Dec. 15, 1954. Studied law at Oxford U. where he dir. and acted in plays for school drama society. Studied film prod. Bristol U. Received Fulbright Scholarship to study at UCLA film school, 1981.
PICTURES: Repo Man, Sid and Nancy, Straight to Hell, Walker (dir., co-editor).

COX, COURTENEY: Actress. b. Birmingham, AL, June 15, 1964. Left AL to pursue modelling career in NY. Dir. Brian DePalma selected her to be the young woman who jumps out of audience and dances with Bruce Springsteen in his music video Dancing in the Dark. This break led to featured role in short-lived TV series Misfits of Science (1985–86).
PICTURES: Masters of the Universe, Down Twisted, Cocoon: The Return.
TELEVISION: Series: Misfits of Science, Family Ties. Movie: I'll Be Home for Christmas, Till We Meet Again.

COX, RONNY: Actor. b. Cloudcroft, NM, Aug. 23, 1938. e. Eastern New Mexico U.
PICTURES: The Happiness Cage, Deliverance, Hugo the Hippo, Gray Lady Down, Harper Valley PTA, The Onion Field, Taps, Beverly Hills Cop, Vision Quest, Steel Justice, Beverly Hills Cop II, Robocop, One Man Force, Total Recall.
TELEVISION: Series: Apple's Way, St. Elsewhere. Movies: Transplant, When Hell Was in Session, Fugitive Family, Alcatraz—The Whole Shocking Story, Two of a Kind, The Jesse Owens Story, The Abduction of Kari Swenson, Baby Girl Scott, The FBI Murders, Bloody Friday, Roughhouse, Favorite Son, In the Line of Duty: The FBI Murders, The Comeback, When We Were Young.

COYOTE, PETER: Actor. r.n. Peter Cohon. b. 1942. Studied with San Francisco Actors Workshop. Theatre includes The Minstrel Show (dir.), Olive Pits (also co-writer), The Red Snake, True West, The Abduction of Kari Swenson, Baby Girl Scott.
PICTURES: Die Laughing, Tell Me a Riddle, The Pursuit of D.B. Cooper, Southern Comfort, E.T.: The Extra Terrestrial, Endangered Species, Timerider, Cross Creek, Stranger's Kiss, Slayground, Heartbreakers, The Legend of Billie Jean, Troupers, Jagged Edge, Outrageous Fortune, Stacking, A Man in Love, Baja Oklahoma, Out (released on Video), Heart of Midnight.
TELEVISION: Movies: Alcatraz: The Whole Story, Isabel's Choice, The People vs. Jean Harris, In the Child's Best Interest, Up and Coming, Golden Gate, Scorned and Swindled, The Blue Yonder, Child's Cry, Time Flyer, Sworn to Silence, Echoes in the Darkness, Unconquered. Act of Will.

CRAIG, MICHAEL: Actor. b. India, 1929. At 16 joined Merchant Navy. 1949 returned to England and made stage debut in repertory. M.P. debut as crowd artist 1950.
PICTURES: Malta Story, The Love Lottery, Passage Home, The Black Tent, Yield to the Night, Eye-Witness, House of Secrets, High Tide At Noon, Sea of Sand, Sapphire, Upstairs and Downstairs, The Angry Silence, Cone of Silence, Doctor In Love, The Mysterious Island, Payroll, No My Darling Daughter, A Pair of Briefs; A Life for Ruth, The Iron Maiden, Captive City, Summer Flight, Of a Thousand Delights, Life at the Top, Modesty Blaise, Star, a Town Called Hell, Ride a Wild Pony, The Irishman, Turkey Shoot, The Timeless Land, Appointment with Death.

CRAIN, JEANNE: Actress. b. Barstow, CA, May 25, 1925. Model; crowned Miss Long Beach of 1941: Camera Girl of 1942.
PICTURES: Home in Indiana, In the Meantime Darling, Winged Victory, State Fair, Leave Her to Heaven, Margie, Centennial Summer, You Were Meant for Me, Apartment for Peggy, Letter to Three Wives, Pinky, Cheaper by the Dozen, Take Care of My Little Girl, People Will Talk, Model and the Marriage Broker, Belles on Their Toes, O. Henry's Full House, City of Bad Men, Dangerous Crossing, Vicki, Duel in the Jungle, Man Without a Star, Second Greatest Sex, Gentlemen Marry Brunettes, Fastest Gun Alive, Tattered Dress, The Joker, Guns of the Timberland, Skyjacked.

CRAMER, DOUGLAS S.: Executive. b. Aug. 22, 1931. e. Northwestern U., Sorbonne, U. of Cincinnati, B.A.; Columbia U.M.F.A. m. Joyce Haber, columnist. Taught at Carnegie Inst. of Tech., 1954–55; Production asst. Radio City Music Hall 1950–51; MGM Script Dept. 1952; Manag. Dir. Cincinnati Summer Playhouse 1953–54. TV supvr. Procter and Gamble 1956–59; Broadcast supvr. Ogilvy, Benson and Mather, Adv. 1959–62; v.p. program dev. ABC-TV 1962–66; v.p. program

dev. 20 Cent.-Fox TV 1966; Exec. v.p. in chg. of production, Paramount Television, 1968–71; exec. v.p. Aaron Spelling Prods. 1976–; Pres. Douglas S. Cramer Foundation.
PLAYS: Call of Duty, Love is a Smoke, Whose Baby Are You.
TELEVISION: Exec. prod.: Bridget Loves Bernie, OB VII, Dawn: Portrait of a Runaway, Co-exec. prod.: Love Boat (1977–86), Vegas (1978–81), Wonder Woman, Dynasty, Matt Houston, Hotel, Colbys, Crossings, Nightingales. Movie: The Love Boat: The Valentine Voyage.

CRAVEN, GEMMA: Actress. b. Dublin, Ireland, June 1, 1950. e. Loretto Coll. Studied acting at Bush Davies School. London stage debut, Fiddler on the Roof (1970). Considerable work in musical theater throughout England and Ireland.
THEATER: London: Audrey, Trelawny of the Wells, Dandy Dick, They're Playing Our Song, Song and Dance, Loot, A Chorus of Disapproval.
PICTURES: Kingdom of Gifts; Why Not Stay for Breakfast; The Slipper and the Rose; Wagner.
TELEVISION: Pennies From Heaven; Must Wear Tights; She Loves Me; Song by Song by Noel Coward; Song by Song by Alan Jay Lerner; East Lynne; Robin of Sherwood; Treasure Hunt; Gemma Girls and Gershwin.

CRAVEN, WESLEY: Director. b. Cleveland, OH, Aug. 2, 1949. e. Wheaton Coll., B.A.; Johns Hopkins, M.A. (philosophy). Worked as humanities prof. and synch-up asst. to dir. Sean Cunningham before initial film work on Together (asst. prod., 1971), It Happened in Hollywood (editor), You've Got to Walk It Like You Talk It or You Lose the Beat (ed.).
PICTURES: The Last House on the Left (also ed.), The Hills Have Eyes (also ed.), Deadly Blessing; Swamp Thing, The Hills Have Eyes Part II, A Nightmare on Elm Street, Deadly Friend, A Nightmare on Elm Street III: Dream Warriors (exec. prod.), The Serpent and the Rainbow, Shocker (exec. prod., dir., s.p.).
TELEVISION: Series: Twilight Zone (1985, 7 episodes: Word Play, A Little Peace and Quiet, Shatterday, Chameleon, Dealer's Choice, The Road Less Traveled, Pilgrim Soul). The People Next Door (exec. prod.). Movies: A Stranger in Our House, Invitation to Hell, Chiller, Casebusters.

CRAWFORD, MICHAEL: O.B.E. Actor. b. Salisbury, England, Jan. 19, 1942. Early career as boy actor in children's films, as a boy soprano in Benjamin Britten's Let's Make an Opera and on radio. Later star of TV's Not So Much a Programme, More a Way of Life. Solo album: Michael Crawford: Songs from the Stage and Screen (1988).
STAGE: Come Blow Your Horn, Traveling Light, The Anniversary, White Lies and Black Comedy (N.Y.), No Sex Please We're British, Billy, Same Time Next Year, Flowers for Algernon, Barnum, The Phantom of the Opera (London-Laurence Olivier Award; and New York; Tony, Drama Desk, Drama League and Outer Circle Critics Awards, 1988).
PICTURES: Soap Box Derby (1950), Blow Your Own Trumpet, Two Left Feet, The War Lover, Two Living, One Dead; The Knack...And How to Get It, A Funny Thing Happened on the Way to the Forum, The Jokers, How I Won the War, Hello, Dolly!, The Games, Hello and Goodbye, The Adventures of Alice in Wonderland, Condorman.
TELEVISION: Still Life, Destiny, Byron, Move After Checkmate, Three Barrelled Shotgun, Home Sweet Honeycomb, Some Mothers Do 'ave 'em, Chalk and Cheese, BBC Play for Today, Private View, Barnum.

CRENNA, RICHARD: Actor. b. Los Angeles, CA, Nov. 30, 1927. e. Belmont H.S., U. of Southern California.
RADIO: Boy Scout Jamboree, A Date With Judy, The Hardy Family, The Great Gildersleeve, Burns & Allen, Our Miss Brooks.
TELEVISION: Our Miss Brooks, The Real McCoys, Slattery's People, All's Fair. Movies: Passions, A Case of Deadly Force, The Day the Bubble Burst, Centennial, The Rape of Richard Beck, Doubletake, The Price of Passion, Police Story: The Freeway Killings, Plaza Suite, Kids Like These, On Wings of Eagles, Internal Affairs, Blood Brothers: The Case of the Hillside Stranglers, Montana.
PICTURES: Pride of St. Louis, It Grows on Trees, Red Skies Over Montana, John Goldfarb, Please Come Home; Wait Until Dark, The Sand Pebbles, Star, Marooned, The Deserter, Doctor's Wives, Red Sky at Morning, A Man Called Noon, Catlow, Dirty Money, Death Ship, First Blood, Body Heat, Table for Five, The Flamingo Kid, Rambo: First Blood Part II, Summer Rental, Rambo III, Leviathan.

CRICHTON, CHARLES: Director. b. Wallasey, Aug. 6, 1910. e. Oundle & Oxford. Collab. dir. Dead of Night.
PICTURES: Painted Boats, Hue and Cry, Against the Wind, Another Shore, Dance Hall, Lavender Hill Mob, Hunted (Stranger in Between), Titfield Thunderbolt, The Love Lottery, Divided Heart, Man in the Sky, Floods of Fear, Battle of the Sexes, The Third Secret, He Who Rides a Tiger, A Fish Called Wanda.
TELEVISION: The Wild Duck, Danger Man, The Avengers, Man in a Suitcase, The Strange Report, Shirley's World, Black Beauty, The Protectors, Space 1999, Return of the Saint, Dick Turpin 1 & 2 Series, Smuggler, Video Arts Shorts.

CRICHTON, MICHAEL: Writer, Director. b. Chicago, IL, Oct. 23, 1942. e. Entered Harvard Medical School in 1965; while there completed first novel, Easy God, under pseudonym, John Lange. Has written 15 books under four different names, including A Case of Need (filmed as The Carey Treatment) and The Andromeda Strain (first book to appear under his own name). Recent books: Travels. Did post-graduate work at Salk Institute in La Jolla 1969–70. Also wrote novels Dealing and The Terminal Man, both filmed. Recipient Edgar award, Mystery Writers Amer. 1968, 1980. Named medical writer of year, Assn. of Amer. Med. Writers, 1970.
PICTURES: Westworld (dir., s.p.), Coma (dir., s.p.), The Great Train Robbery (dir., s.p.), Looker (dir., s.p.)., Runaway (dir., s.p.), Physical Evidence (dir.).
TELEVISION: Pursuit (Movie of Week), dir.; script by Robert Dozier based on Crichton's book, Binary.

CRIST, JUDITH: Journalist, Critic. b. New York, NY, May 22, 1922. e. Hunter College, Columbia U. School of Journalism. Joined New York Herald Tribune, serving as reporter, arts editor, assoc. drama critic, film critic. Continued as film critic for New York World Journal Tribune, NBC-TV Today Show, New York Magazine, New York Post, Saturday Review, TV Guide, WWOR-TV. Now regular film critic for Coming Attractions. Teaches at Col. Grad. School of Journalism.
AUTHOR: The Private Eye, The Cowboy and the Very Naked Girl; Judith Crist's TV Guide to the Movies; Take 22: Moviemakers on Moviemaking.

CRISTALDI, FRANCO: Producer. b. Turin, Italy, Oct. 3, 1924. Owner, prod. Vides Cinematografica; President of Italian Producer's Union.
PICTURES: White Nights, The Strawman, The Challenge, Big Deal On Madonna Street, Kapo, The Dauphins, Salvatore Giuliano, The Assassin, Divorce Italian Style, The Organizer, Bebo's Girl, Seduced and Abandoned, Time of Indifference, Sandra, A Rose for Every-One, China Is Near, A Quiet Couple, The Red Tent, New Paradise Cinema.
TELEVISION: Marco Polo.

CRITCHFIELD, EDWARD: Producer. B. Cleveland, OH, Jan. 9, 1919. e. Glenville H.S., 1937. Gen. insurance broker; real estate mortgage financing; motion picture financier, Delta Diamond Productions; then joined Bernfield Publications Inc., as vice-pres.; assoc. prod. Terrified.

CRON, JOHN B.: Executive. b. Mt. Vernon, NY, June 11, 1923. e. Princeton U.: Exec. v.p,, Robert Lawrence Productions; managing dir., Screen Gems (Europe); sales dir., N.B.C. Film Division; v.p., sales dir. SIB Productions.

CRONENBERG, DAVID: Writer, Director. b. Toronto, Ont., May 15, 1943. e. U. of Toronto. In college produced two short movies on 16mm. 1971, to Europe on a Canadian Council grant where shot in 1975 his first feature, Shivers (aka They Came From Within).
PICTURES: They Came From Within, Rabid, Fast Company (both dir. only), The Brood, Scanners, Videodrome, The Dead Zone, Dead Ringers (dir., co-prod., co-s.p.), Nightbreed (actor only), The Naked Lunch.

CRONKITE, WALTER: Correspondent. b. St. Joseph, MO, Nov. 4, 1916. e. U. of Texas. Reporter and editor Scripps-Howard News Service, TX; radio reporter; U.P. correspondent. WW II corres. Germany, N. Africa, France, Belgium. Joined CBS as Washington news correspondent, 1950; anchorman and mng. editor, CBS Evening News, 1962–81; special correspondent, CBS News, 1981–present. Many TV shows including You Are There, Twentieth Century, Eyewitness to History: CBS Reports: 21st Century, Walter Cronkite's Universe. Past nat'l pres. & mem. bd. Trustees, Acad. TV Arts & Sciences. Mng. editor of CBS Evening News 1963–81; Special corres., Children of Apartheid, Walter Cronkite at Large.

CRONYN, HUME: Actor, Writer, Director. b. London, Ont., Canada, July 18, 1911. m. Jessica Tandy, actress. e. Ridley Coll., McGill U., Amer. Acad. of Dramatic Art; m.p. acting debut in Shadow of a Doubt.
STAGE: (Actor N.Y. plays) High Tor, Escape This Night, Three Men on a Horse, Boy Meets Girl, Three Sisters, Mr. Big, The Survivors; plays Now I Lay Me Down to Sleep (dir.), Hilda Crane (dir.), The Fourposter (dir.); Madam Will You Walk; The Honeys, A Day by the Sea; The Man in the Dog Suit; The Egghead (dir.); Triple Play (dir. and toured with wife); Big Fish, Little Fish (also in London); The Miser; The Three Sisters; Hamlet; The Physicists; Slow Dance on The Killing Ground (prod.); Appeared at the White House; Hear America Speaking; Richard III; Revival The Miser; A Delicate Balance (1966 and tour, 1967); The Miser; Hadrian VII (tour); Caine Mutiny Court Martial; Promenade All; Krapp's Last Tape, Happy Days, Act Without Words; Coward In Two Keys, Concert recital Many Faces Of Love; Noel Coward in Two Keys (National tour), Merchant of Venice and A Midsummer Night's Dream, at (Stratford Festival Theatre); Canada; The

Gin Game (with Miss Tandy; Long Wharf Thea., New Haven, Bdwy, 1977, co-prod. with Mike Nichols; also toured U.S., Toronto, London, U.S.S.R., 1978–79). Foxfire (co-author, actor, at Stratford, Ont., 1980, Minneapolis, 1981 and N.Y., 1982–83); Traveler in the Dark (Amer. Repertory Theatre, Cambridge, MA), Foxfire (Ahmanson, LA 1985–86), The Petition (NY 1986).

PICTURES: Cross of Lorraine, Lifeboat, Seventh Cross, Main Street, After Dark, The Sailor Takes a Wife, A Letter for Evie, The Green Years, Brute Force, Bride Goes Wild, Postman Always Rings Twice, Top o' the Morning, People Will Talk, Crowded Paradise, Sunrise at Campobello, Cleopatra, Gaily, Gaily, The Arrangement, There Was a Crooked Man, Conrack, Parallax View, Honky Tonk Freeway, Rollover, Garp, Impulse, Brewster's Millions, Cocoon, Batteries Not Included, Cocoon: The Return.

TELEVISION: The Marriage, and other network dramatic shows, 1957. The Dollmaker (Co-author), Foxfire (star and co-author), Day One, Age-old Friends.

CROSBY, BOB: Band leader, Actor. r.n. George Robert C. b. Spokane, WA, Aug. 23, 1913. Brother of late singer-actor Bing Crosby. e. Gonzaga U. Began as singer; later featured vocalist Jimmie & Tommy Dorsey band. Org. own band (Bobcats); appeared with orch. on screen in Let's Make Music, 1940.

PICTURES: Sis Hopkins, Reveille with Beverly, Thousands Cheer, Presenting Lily Mars, See Here Private Hargrove; Meet Miss Bobby Socks, Kansas City Kitty, My Gal Loves Music, Pardon My Rhythm, Singing Sheriff, Two Tickets to Broadway.

TELEVISION: Bob Crosby Show.

CROSBY, CATHY LEE: Actress. b. Los Angeles, CA, Dec. 2. e. Grad. of U. of Southern California. Studied with Lee Strasberg. Theatrical film debut in The Laughing Policeman (1973).

STAGE: Downside Risk, Almost Perfect (Off-Bdwy debut), Jellyroll Shoes, They Shoot Horses, Don't They? (wrote, dir. starred in 1st theatrical adapt. Hollywood Amer. Legion), Zoot Suit—The Real Story (writer, dir., actress, adapt., Beverly Hills).

PICTURES: Call Me by My Rightful Name, Trackdown, The Dark, Coach, Training Camp (s.p.), San Sebastian (s.p.).

TELEVISION: Movies: Wonder Woman, Keefer, Kingston Confidential, Mommy's Little Girl (s.p.), 5th & Philly (s.p.). Series: That's Incredible, Specials: A Spectacular Evening in Egypt, Battle of the Network Stars, Circus of the Stars, Bob Hope Specials. Mini-series: World War III, Intimate Strangers, Roughnecks.

CROSBY, KATHRYN: Actress. r.n. Kathryn Grandstaff. b. Houston, TX, Nov. 25, 1933. e. U. of Texas, UCLA. m. late actor-singer Bing Crosby.

PICTURES: Forever Female, Rear Window, Living It Up, Arrowhead, Casanova's Big Night, Unchained, Cell 2455 Death Row, Tight Spot, Five Against the House, Reprisal, Guns of Fort Petticoat, Phenix City Story, Wild Party, Mister Cory, Night the World Exploded, Brothers Rico, Operation Mad Ball, The Big Circus.

TELEVISION: Bob Hope Chrysler Theatre, Bing Crosby Christmas Specials, Suspense Theatre, Ben Casey, The Kathryn Crosby Show KPIX-TV, San Francisco.

CROSS, BEN: Actor. r.n. Bernard Cross. b. London, England, Dec. 16, 1947. e. Royal Acad. of Dramatic Art. Worked as stagehand, prop-master, and master carpenter with Welsh Natl. Opera and as set builder, Wimbledon Theatre.

THEATER: The Importance of Being Earnest (Lancaster, debut, 1972), I Love My Wife, Privates on Parade, Chicago, Lydie Breeze (NY debut, 1982), Caine Mutiny Court Martial.

PICTURES: A Bridge Too Far (debut, 1977), Chariots of Fire, The Assisi Underground, The Unholy, The Goldsmith's Shop, Paperhouse, The House of the Lord, Eye of the Widow.

TELEVISION: Melancholy Hussar of the German Legion (1973, BBC), The Flame Trees of Thika, The Citadel, The Far Pavilions, Coming Out of the Ice, Arthur Hailey's Strong Medicine, Steal the Sky, Pursuit, Twist of Fate.

CROUSE, LINDSAY: Actress. b. New York, NY, May 12, 1948. m. playwright-dir. David Mamet. Daughter of playwright Russel Crouse. e. Radcliffe. Began career as modern and jazz dancer; is also flutist and pianist.

THEATER: Was member of Circle Repertory Co. NY. The Shawl, The Cherry Orchard, Foursome, Present Laughter (Kennedy Center), Long Day's Journey Into Night, Hamlet (Circle Rep.), Twelfth Night (Circle Rep.), Reunion (Obie Award), Serenading Louie.

PICTURES: All the President's Men, Slap Shot, Between the Lines, The Verdict, Daniel, Iceman, Places in the Heart, House of Games, Communion: A True Story.

TELEVISION: Eleanor and Franklin, The Tenth Level, Lemon Sky. Pilot: American Nuclear.

CROWTHER, LESLIE: Actor, Comedian. b. Nottingham, England. Ent. TV ind. 1960. Early career incl: Hi Summer revue, Crackerjack, Black and White Minstrel Show. Stage: Let Sleeping Wives Lie, and Pantomine. 1971–72. Own TV series (LWT). 1978–82 Hi Summer series (LWT). Starred in Bud 'n Ches (stage). Since 1985 presented The Price is Right (Central TV).

CRUEA, EDMOND D.: Executive. b. Jersey City, NJ, June 3. Joined Grand National Pictures, L.A., 1935; Monogram Pictures, 1938–41, L.A. & Seattle; U.S. Army Signal Corps, 1942–46; Monogram Pictures, Seattle, 1946–48; branch mgr., 1948–49; branch mgr. and district mgr. Allied Artists, 1950–65 (Seattle, Portland, San Francisco, and Los Angeles); v.p.-gen. sls. mgr., Allied Artists 1965–71; dir. distribution, Abkco Films div. of Abkco Industries, Inc., 1971–73; pres. of Royal Dist. Corp., 1974; pres., Esco Film Corp., 1975; joined Film Ventures Intl. in 1976 as exec. v.p., succeeding to pres. and chief operating officer in 1976. Resigned 1977 to form Fil-Mark Inc. Co-founded New Image Releasing, Inc., 1982, as pres. & CEO 1985, v.p. theatrical, Cinetel Films; 1987 theatrical dist. consultant, Sony Pictures (NY) and Shining Armour Commun (London).

CRUISE, TOM: Actor. b. Syracuse, NY, 1962. m. actress Mimi Rogers. Acted in high school plays; secured role in dinner theatre version of Godspell. First film role in Endless Love (1981).

PICTURES: Taps, Losin' It, The Outsiders, Risky Business, All the Right Moves, Legend, Top Gun, The Color of Money, Cocktail, Rain Man, Born on the 4th of July, Daytona.

TELEVISION: Amazing Stories.

CRYER, JON: Actor. b. 1965. Son of actor David Cryer and songwriter-actress Gretchen Cryer. On Bdwy. stage in Brighton Beach Memoirs. Film debut: No Small Affair (1984).

PICTURES: Pretty in Pink, O.C. and Stiggs, Superman IV, Morgan Stewart, Hiding Out, Dudes, Penn and Teller Get Killed.

TELEVISION: The Famous Teddy Z (series).

CRYSTAL, BILLY: Actor. b. Long Island, NY, Mar. 14, 1947. e. Marshall U., NYU. Father, Jack, produced jazz concerts; family owned Commodore jazz record label. Worked with Alumni Theatre Group at Nassau Community College. Later teamed with two friends (billed as 3's Company) and toured coffee houses and colleges. Became stand-up comedian on own, appearing on TV.

PICTURES: Rabbit Test, Spinal Tap, Running Scared, The Princess Bride, Throw Mama From the Train, Memories of Me (actor, co-prod., co-s.p.), When Harry Met Sally.

TELEVISION: Tonight Show, Dinah, Mike Douglas Show, That Was the Year That Was, All in the Family, Love Boat. Series: Soap, Saturday Night Live. Special: On Location: Billy Crystal Midnight Train to Moscow (also exec. prod., co-writer). Movies: Death Flight, Breaking Up Is Hard to Do.

CULBERG, PAUL S.: Executive. b. Chicago, IL, June 14, 1942. Began career in record industry, holding positions with Elektra Records & Wherehouse Record; 1977–80; v.p. sls. mktg., Cream Records.; 1980–82, dir. sls. Paramount Home Video; 1982, v.p. sls. mktg., Media Home Entertainment; 1984 to present, pres., New World Video.

CULLEN, BILL: Performer. b. Pittsburgh, PA, Feb. 18, 1920; U. of Pittsburgh, B.A. Asst. disc jockey; announcer, KDKA, Pittsburgh; sportscaster; staff announcer. CBS radio, 1943; then m.c., panel member; shows include; m.c. Three on a Match, To Tell the Truth, Winning Streak, 25,000 Pyramid; Love Experts.

CULLEN, JAMES V.: Executive. b. San Francisco, CA, Dec. 29, 1938. e. City Coll. of San Francisco. Sales mgr., M.P.I. Toys, Los Angeles, 1963–65; entered film industry 1965 with 20th-Fox in S.F. exchange as ass't. field man; Named Southwest ad-pub. mgr. for Fox 1966 and Western Division ad-pub mgr. 1968. Appointed Fox director of exploitation 1971; then nat'l. dir. field adv. & pro.; Joined Sandy Howard Prods., v.p. creative affairs, 1974. Produced The Devils' Rain, 1975.

CULP, ROBERT: Actor, Writer, Director. b. Berkeley, CA, Aug. 16, 1930. e. Stockton, College of the Pacific, Washington U., San Francisco State; to N.Y. to study with Herbert Berghof. Starred in off-Bway prod. He Who Gets Slapped. Best Actor of the Year in an off-Bway Play; motion picture debut, 1962; P.T. 109; television guest appearances in Rawhide, Wagon Train, Bob Hope Presents the Chrysler Theatre; wrote and acted in Rifleman, Cain's Hundred, The Dick Powell Show.

BROADWAY: The Prescott Proposals, A Clearing in the Woods.

TELEVISION: Series: Trackdown, I Spy (also wrote pilot and 7 shows), The Greatest American Hero (also wrote 2 shows). Movies: The Hanged Man, Sammy, The Way Out Seal; The Raiders, See How They Run, From Sea to Shining Sea, Ingmar Bergman's The Lie, Root's: The Next Generation, Women in White, Mrs. Columbo, The Dream Merchants, The Night the City Screamed, Killjoy, The Calendar Girl Murders, Brothers-in-Law, The Blue Lightning, The Gladiator,

Thou Shalt Not Kill, Her Life as a Man, No Man's Land, The Key to Rebecca, Flood, Combat High, A Cry for Help, The Achille Lauro.
PICTURES: PT 109, The Raiders, Sunday in New York, Rhino, The Hanged Man, Bob & Carol & Ted & Alice, The Grove, A Name For Evil, Hannie Caulder, Hickey and Boggs (also dir. and s.p. uncredited), Castaway Cowboy, Sky Riders, Breaking Point, Great Scout and Cathouse Thursday, Flood,Golden Girl, Turk 182, Big Bad Mama II, Silent Night Deadly Night 3: Better Watch Out.

CUMMINGS, BOB: Actor, Director. b. Joplin, MO, June 9, 1910. Godson of Orville Wright. e. Drury Coll., Carnegie Inst. of Tech., American Acad. of Dramatic Arts: on dram. & musical stage, also radio. Has toured Dinner Theater Circuit since 1973 and established new attendance records in 16 theaters playing Never Too Late, Marriage Go Round, No Hard Feelings, Harvey, Fun and Games.
TELEVISION: Series: My Hero, Bob Cummings Show. Special: Twelve Angry Men (Emmy, 1954) The Great American Beauty Contest.
PICTURES: Three Smart Girls Grow Up, Spring Parade, Saboteur, Heaven Only Knows, So Red the Rose, Kings Row, Flesh and Fantasy, Princess O'Rourke, You Came Along, Reign of Terror, The Accused, Free for All, Tell It to the Judge, Paid in Full, Petty Girl, For Heaven's Sake, Barefoot Mailman, The Lost Moment, Free and Easy, First Time, Marry Me Again, Lucky Me, Dial M for Murder, How to Be Very Very Popular, My Geisha, Beach Party, The Carpetbaggers, What A Way to Go, Stage Coach, Promise Her Anything, Gidget Grows Up.

CUMMINGS, CONSTANCE: C.B.E. Actress. b. Seattle, WA, May 15, 1910. p. D.V. Halverstadt, attorney, and Kate Cummings, concert soprano; m. Benn Levy, English playwright. Was chorus girl in The Little Show and also appeared in June Moon. Broadway debut: Treasure Girl, 1928; London debut: Sour Grapes, 1934. Film debut: Movie Crazy 1932. Joined National Theatre Co. 1971.
THEATER: Recent work: A Long Day's Journey into Night (with Laurence Olivier), The Cherry Orchard, Wings (Tony, Obie Awards 1979), The Chalk Garden.
PICTURES: Behind the Mask, Washington Merry-Go-Round, Broadway Through a Keyhole, Remember Last Night?, Channel Crossing, Glamour, Doomed Cargo, Busman's Honeymoon, This England, The Outsider, The Foreman Went to France, Somewhere in France, Blithe Spirit, Into the Blue, The Scream, John and Julie, The Intimate Stranger, Battle of the Sexes, A Boy 10 Feet Tall.
TELEVISION: Touch of the Sun, Clutterbuck, The Last Tycoon, Ruth, Late Summer, Long Day's Journey Into Night, Wings, Agatha Christie's Dead Man's Folly.

CUMMINGS, SANDY: Executive. r.n. Sanford Cummings. b. Oct. 31, 1913. e. U. of Southern California. Child actor; Broadway. Summer stock, 1935; asst. prod., Paramount; assist. to Walter Wanger, 1936; started Hollywood office of Benton & Bowles, 1937; major, army, 1939–46; Head American Forces Network, Germany; prod. Columbia, 1946; ABC Coordinator, Walt Disney Studios, 1954; manager, TV Net Programs, Western Div. ABC, 1957; dir. TV Net Prog., 1958; V.P. & Dir. of pgms., Western Div., 1958–62; prod. specials, STV, 1964; prod., 20th Fox Television, 1965–66; NBC Broadcast Standards; 1969 mgr., live night-time and special programs, NBC.

CUMMINS, PEGGY: Actress. b. Prestatyn, North Wales, 1925. e. Alexandra Sch., Dublin, Gate Theatre, Dublin. Starred in Let's Pretend on London Stage 1938. In 1942; Salute John Citizen; Welcome Mr. Washington; On London Stage in Junior Miss, Alice in Wonderland, Peter Pan. From 1946 Hollywood, starred in Late George Apley. Returned to Eng. 1950.
PICTURES: Made Dr. O'Dowd, Moss Rose, Green Grass of Wyoming, Escape, That Dangerous Age, Gun Crazy, My Daughter Joy, Who Goes There (Passionate Sentry), Street Corner (Both Sides of the Law), Meet Mr. Lucifer, Always a Bride, Love Lottery, To Dorothy a Son, Cash on Delivery, March Hare, Carry on Admiral, Night of the Demon, Hell Drivers, The Captain's Table, Your Money or Your Wife, Dentist in the Chair, In the Doghouse.
TELEVISION: The Human Jungle, Looks Familiar.

CUNNINGHAM, SEAN S.: Producer, Director. b. New York, NY, Dec. 31 1941. e. Franklin & Marshall, B.A.; Stanford U., M.F.A. Worked briefly as actor, moving into stage-managing. Became producer of Mineola Theatre (Long Island, NY) and took several productions to Broadway. Formed Sean S. Cunningham Films, Ltd., 1971. Produced commercials, industrial film, documentaries, features.
PICTURES: Together (prod.-dir.); Last House on the Left (prod.); The Case of the Full Moon Murders (prod.); Here Come the Tigers (prod.-dir.); Kick (prod.-dir.); Friday the 13th (prod.-dir.); A Stranger Is Watching (prod.-dir.); Spring Break (prod.-dir.); The New Kids (prod., dir.); House (prod.); House II (prod.), A Taste of Hemlock (dir.), House III (prod.), Deepstar Six (prod., dir.), The Horror Show (prod.).

CURTIN, JANE: Actress. b. Cambridge, MA, Sept. 6, 1947. e. Northeastern U. On stage in Proposition, Last of the Red Hot Lovers, Candida. Author, actress off-Bdwy musical revue Pretzel 1974–75.
PICTURES: Mr. Mike's Mondo Video, How to Beat the High Cost of Living, O.C. and Stiggs.
TELEVISION: Series: Saturday Night Live 1974–79; Kate & Allie. Movies: What Really Happened to the Class of '65, Divorce Wars—A Love Story, Candida, Suspicion, Maybe Baby.

CURTIS, DAN: Producer, Director. b. Bridgeport, CT, Aug. 12, 1928. e. U. of Bridgeport, Syracuse U., B.A. Was sales exec. for NBC and MCA before forming own company, Dan Curtis Productions, which he now heads. Producer/owner of CBS Golf Classic (1963–73).
PICTURES: House of Dark Shadows (prod., dir.), Night of Dark Shadows (prod.-dir.), Burnt Offerings (prod., dir., co-s.p.).
TELEVISION: Producer: Dark Shadows (ABC serial, 1966–71). Movies: The Night Stalker, Frankenstein, The Picture of Dorian Gray. Producer-Director of movies: The Night Strangler, The Norliss Tapes, The Turn of the Screw, Dracula, The Scream of the Wolf, Purvis, The Winds of War, War and Remembrance (also co-s.p.). Director: The Last Ride of the Dalton Gang, The Long Days of Summer, I Think I'm Having a Baby, Mrs. R's Daughter.

CURTIS, JAMIE LEE: Actress. b. Los Angeles, CA, Nov. 22, 1958. m. actor, dir. Christopher Guest. Daughter of Janet Leigh and Tony Curtis.
PICTURES: Halloween, The Fog, Terror Train, Halloween II, Road Games, Prom Night, Love Letters, Trading Places, The Adventures of Buckaroo Banzai: Across the 8th Dimension, Grandview, USA, Perfect, 8 Million Ways to Die, Amazing Grace and Chuck, A Man in Love, Dominick and Eugene, A Fish Called Wanda, Blue Steel.
TELEVISION: Callahan (pilot), She's in the Army Now (pilot), Tall Tales (Annie Oakley). Series: Operation Petticoat (1977–78), Anything But Love. Movies: Death of a Centerfold: The Dorothy Stratten Story, Money on the Side, As Summers Die.

CURTIS, KEN: Actor. b. Lamar, CO, July 2, 1916. e. Colorado Coll. Success as songwriter for college prod. steered him to musical career in Hollywood. Sang with several groups, including Sons of the Pioneers, Tommy Dorsey Orchestra, Shep Fields band. In infantry and anti-aircraft unit in W.W.II. Signed by Columbia Pictures for series of westerns with "Big Boy" Williams in 1945.
PICTURES: The Searchers, The Alamo, The Quiet Man, Cheyenne Autumn, How the West Was Won, The Killer Shrews, The Giant Gila Monster, My Dog, Buddy.
TELEVISION: Ripcord, Perry Mason, Rawhide, Have Gun, Will Travel, Gunsmoke (joined later series as Festus Haggen in 1963), The Yellow Rose (series); Gunsmoke: Return to Dodge, Once Upon a Texas Train.

CURTIS, TONY: Actor. r.n. Bernard Schwartz. b. New York, NY, June 3, 1925. e. Seward Park H.S. In U.S. Navy, amateur dramatics, N.Y., started Empire Players Theatre, Newark, NJ, with Dramatic Workshop, Cherry Lane Theatre, Jr. Drama workshop of Walt Whitman School; first prod. work with Stanley Woolf Players; m.p. debut in Criss-Cross; signed with U-I. Star of Tomorrow, 1953.
PICTURES: City Across the River, Johnny Stool Pigeon, Francis, Sierra, I Was a Shoplifter, Winchester 73, Kansas Raiders, Prince Who Was a Thief, Flesh and Fury, Son of Ali Baba, No Room for the Groom, Houdini, All American, Forbidden, Beachhead, Johnny Dark, Black Shield of Falworth, 6 Bridges to Cross, So This Is Paris, Purple Mask, Square Jungle, Rawhide Years, Trapeze, Mister Cory, Midnight Story, Sweet Smell of Success, Some Like It Hot, Spartacus, Operation Petticoat, Who Was That Lady?, The Rat Race, The Defiant Ones, Perfect Furlough, The Great Impostor, The Outsider, Taras Bulba, 40 Pounds of Trouble, Paris When It Sizzles, The List of Adrian Messenger, Captain Newman, M.D., Wild and Wonderful, Sex and the Single Girl, Goodbye, Charlie, The Great Race, Boeing-Boeing, Arrivederci, Baby!, Not with My Wife, You Don't!, Don't Make Waves, On My Way to the Crusades I Met a Girl Who—; The Boston Strangler, Those Daring Young Men in Their Jaunty Jalopies, Suppose They Gave a War and Nobody Came, You Can't Win 'Em All, Lepke, The Last Tycoon, The Manitou, Bad News Bears Go to Japan, The Mirror Crack'd, Insignificance, The Last of Philip Banter, Welcome to Germany, Midnight, Lobster Man From Mars, The High-Flying Mermaid.
TELEVISION: Series: The Persuaders, Vegas, Movies: The Second Girl on the Right, The Count of Monte Cristo, Moviola: The Scarlett O'Hara War, Harry's Back, Mafia Princess, Murder in Three Acts, Portrait of a Showgirl.

CUSACK, CYRIL: Actor. b. Durban, South Africa, Nov. 26, 1910. e. Newbridge, Co. Kildare; University Coll., Dublin, Eire. LL.D (Honoris Causa-National U. of Ireland); D. Litt (Hon. Causa-

Dublin U.); Litt. D. (Hon. Causa-New U. of Ulster). Stage debut: Candida, Abbey Theatre, 1932. Screen debut: Odd Man Out, 1945.
PICTURES: Esther Waters, Escape, The Blue Lagoon, Once a Jolly Swagman, All Over the Town, Small Back Room, The Elusive Pimpernel, Soldiers Three, Blue Veil, Secret of Convict Lake, Gone to Earth (Wild Heart), Saadia, Passage Home, Man in the Road, Man Who Never Was, March Hare, Jacqueline, Spanish Gardener, Ill Met by Moonlight, Rising of the Moon, Miracle in Soho, Shake Hands with the Devil, Floods of Fear, Gideon's Day, A Terrible Beauty, Johnny Nobody, The Waltz of the Toreadors, I Thank a Fool, 80,000 Suspects, Passport to Oblivion, The Spy Who Came In from The Cold, Fahrenheit 451, Taming of the Shrew, I Was Happy Here, Oedipus Rex, Galileo, King Lear, Country Dance, David Copperfield, Harold and Maude, Sacco and Vanzetti, La La Polizia Ringrazia, The Day of the Jackal, Juggernaut, Homecoming, Galileo, Tristan and Iseult, True Confessions, Little Dorrit, My Left Foot.
TELEVISION: The Dummy, The Moon and Sixpence, What Every Woman Knows, The Enchanted, The Power and The Glory, The Chairs, Don Juan in Hell, The Lotus Eater, Krapp's Last Tape, Murder in the Cathedral, Six Characters in Search of An Author, The Big Toe, Workhouse Ward, In the Train, Purgatory, The Moon in the Yellow River, Passage to India, Deirdre, The Tower, Dial M for Murder, St. Francis, The Physicists, Trial of Marshal Petain, In the Bosom of the Country, Uncle Vanya, A Time of Wolves and Tigers, Them, Clochemerle, The Golden Bowl, The Reunion, I Stand Well With All Parties, Catholics, Crystal & Fox, Jesus of Nazareth, The Plough and The Stars, You Never Can Tell, Accidental Death, Oedipus the King (Theban plays), The Hitchhiker, Menace Unseen, The Small Assassin, Glenroe, The Tenth Man, Danny, The Champion of the World.

CUSACK, JOAN: Actress. b. Evanston, IL, 1963. Sister of actor John Cusack. e. U. of Wisconsin, Madison. Studied acting at Piven Theatre Workshop, Evanston, IL. While in coll. joined The Ark, local improvisational comedy group. Joined Saturday Night Live as regular for 1985–86 season.
THEATER: Road, Brilliant Tracers, Cymbeline.
PICTURES: My Bodyguard (debut, 1980), Class, Sixteen Candles, Grandview U.S.A., Cutting Loose, The Allnighter, Broadcast News, Stars and Bars, Married to the Mob, Say Anything, Working Girl, Heart of Midnight, Men Don't Leave, Fatman and Little Boy.

CUSACK, JOHN: Actor. b. June 28, 1966. Brother of actress Joan Cusack. Member of Piven Theatre Workshop, IL. 10 years beginning when 8.
PICTURES: Class (debut, 1983), Sixteen Candles, Grandview, U.S.A.; The Sure Thing, Journey of Natty Gann, Better Off Dead, Stand By Me, One Crazy Summer, Hot Pursuit, Eight Men Out, Tapeheads, Say Anything, Dog Fight, Fatman and Little Boy, The Grifters.

CUSHING, PETER: O.B.E.: Actor. b. Kenley, Surrey, Eng., May 26, 1913. e. Purley Secondary Sch. Stage debut with Worthington Repertory Co. Daily Mail TV award actor, 1953–54; Guild of TV award, 1955; News Chronicle T.V. Top Ten award, 1956.
TELEVISION: Asmodee, Anastasia, 1984, Gaslight, Home at Seven, Tovarich, Beau Brummell, Epitaph for a Spy, Pride and Prejudice, The Moment of Truth, Uncle Harry, Eden End, Rookery Nook, The Creature, The Browning Version, Winslow Boy, Peace With Terror, Julius Caesar (Cassius), Monica. The Plan, Caves of Steel, Sherlock Holmes (series), Morecambe & Wise Show, Wild-life Spectacular, The Zoo Gang, Orson Welles Great Mysteries, Space 1999, The New Avengers, The Great Houdini, A Land Looking West, A Tale of Two Cities; The Vordal Blade, Tales of the Unexpected, Helen and Teacher, A One-way Ticket to Hollywood.
PICTURES: Vigil in the Night, Moulin Rouge, Hamlet, Black Knight, End of the Affair, Alexander the Great, Magic Fire, Time Without Pity, Curse of Frankenstein, Abominable Snowman, Dracula, John Paul Jones, The Hound of the Baskervilles, Violent Playground, The Mummy, Suspect, The Flesh and the Friends, The Revenge of Frankenstein, Cone of Silence, Bride of Dracula, Sword of Sherwood Forest, The Naked Edge, Cash on Demand, The Devil's Agent, Captain Clegg, Fury at Smuggler's Bay, Hell-Fire Club, The Man Who Finally Died, The Evil of Frankenstein, The Gorgon, Dr. Terror's House of Horrors, She, The Skull, Dr. Who and Daleks, The Frighten Bed Island, Daleks Invade Earth, Frankenstein Created Woman, Torture Garden, Some May Live, The Night of the Big Heat, Corruption, Death's Head Moth, Frankenstein Must Be Destroyed, Doctors Wear Scarlet, The Vampire Lovers, Scream and Scream Again, House That Dripped Blood, I Monster, Twins of Evil, Tales from the Crypt, Dracula Today, Fear in the Night, Horror Express, The Creeping Flesh, Asylum, Nothing But the Night, Bride of Fengriffen, Frankenstein and the Monster from Hell, The Satanic Rites of Dracula, The Revenge of Dr. Death, From Beyond the Grave, The Beast Must Die, Dracula and the Legend of the Seven Golden Vampires, Shatter, Tender Dracula, The Ghoul, Legend of the Werewolf, The Devil's People, Death Corps, Trial by Combat, At The Earth's Core, Star Wars, Battleflag, The Uncanny, Hitler's Son, Touch of the Sun, Arabian Adventure, Black Jack, House of the Long Shadows, Sword of the Valiant, Top Secret!, Biggles.

D

D'ARBANVILLE, PATTI: Actress. b. New York, NY, 1951. Grew up in Greenwich Village. Landed first job as baby in Ivory Soap commercials. In early teens worked as disc jockey where discovered by Andy Warhol and cast in small role in film Flesh. Moved to Paris at 15 where she became successful model and was featured in book Scavullo on Beauty. Made film debut in Gerard Brach's 1969 film La Maison. Fluent in French, worked in French films until 1973 when moved to Los Angeles. Won Dramalogue Award for John Patrick Shanley's Italian-American Reconciliation (L.A., 1987).
PICTURES: La Maison, La Saigne, The Crazy American Girl, Rancho DeLuxe, Big Wednesday, The Main Event, Time After Time, The Fifth Floor, Hog Wild, Modern Problems, The Boys Next Door, Real Genius, Call Me, The Accused, Fresh Horses, Wired.
TELEVISION: Crime Story, R.E.L.A.X., Tough Cookies, Charlie's Angels, Once an Eagle, Captra, Barnaby Jones, Miami Vice, Murder She Wrote, Movie: Crossing the Mob.

DAFOE, WILLEM: Actor. b. Appleton, WI, July 22, 1955. Worked with experimental group Theatre X on the road before coming to New York. Built sets and debuted with the Wooster Group at the Performing Garage playing (literally) a chicken heart in Spalding Gray's Nayatt School. Current member of the Wooster Group.
PICTURES: The Loveless (1983, debut, as a biker-poet), The Hunger, Streets of Fire, Roadhouse 66, To Live and Die in L.A., Platoon (nom. for an Oscar as best supp. actor), Off Limits, The Last Temptation of Christ, Mississippi Burning, Born on the Fourth of July, Triumph of the Spirit, Wild at Heart.

DAHL, ARLENE: Actress, Writer, Designer. b. Minneapolis, MN, Aug. 11, 1928. e. MN Business Coll.; U. of Minnesota, summers 1941–44; Minneapolis. Coll. of Music. m. Marc A. Rosen. Mother of actor Lorenzo Lamas. At age 8, played heroine of children's adventure serials on radio. Internationally syndicated beauty columnist, Chgo. Tribune-N.Y. News Syndicate, 1951–71; Pres. Arlene Dahl Enterprises, (1951–75), Sleepwear Designer, A.N. Saab & Co., 1952–57; Natl. Beauty Advisor, Sears Roebuck & Co., 1970–75; v.p. Kenyon & Eckhart Advg. Co., pres., Women's World Div., Kenyon-Eckhart, 1967–72; Fashion Consultant, O.M.A. 1975–78, Int'l. Director of S.M.E.I., 1973–76, Designer, Vogue Patterns 1978–85. Pres., Dahlia Parfums Inc., 1975, pres., Dahlia Prods., 1978–81: pres. Dahlmark Prods. 1981–. Publs: Always Ask a Man, 1965, Your Beautyscope, 1969, Secrets of Hair Care, 1971, Your Beautyscope 1977–78. Profl. Assns. include: Screen Actors Guild, Actors Equity, Am. Fedn. of TV & Radio Artists, Intl. Platform, Inc., Acad. of Motion Picture Arts and Sciences. Honrs. include: 8 Motion Picture Laurel Awards, 1948–63; Hds. of Fame Award, 1971, Woman of the Year, N.Y. Adv. Council, 1969. Mother of the Year, 1979; Coup de Chapeau, Deauville Film Fest 1983.
THEATER: Broadway: Mr. Strauss Goes to Boston (debut, 1946), Cyrano de Bergerac; Applause; major US tours include: Questionable Ladies, The King and I, One Touch of Venus, I Married an Angel, Mame, Pal Joey, Bell Book and Candle, The Camel Bell, Life With Father, A Little Night Music, Lilliom, Marriage Go Round, Blythe Spirit.
PICTURES: My Wild Irish Rose (debut, 1947), The Bride Goes Wild, A Southern Yankee, Ambush, The Black Book, Three Little Words, Desert Legion, Here Come the Girls, Sangaree, The Diamond Queen, Bengal Brigade, Slightly Scarlet, Woman's World, Journey to the Center of the Earth, Kisses for My President, Jamaica Run, Caribbean, Gold, The Landraiders, A Place to Hide.
TELEVISION: Arlene Dahl's Beauty Spot, 1965; Hostess, Model of the Year Show, 1969, Arlene Dahl's Starscope, 1980, Arlene Dahl's Lovescopes, 1982, One Life to Live (1981–84), Night of One Hundred Stars, Happy Birthday, Hollywood, Who Killed Max Thorn?

DALE, JIM: Actor. b. Rothwell, Northants, England, Aug. 15, 1935. Debut as solo comedian at the Savoy, 1951. Joined National Theatre Co. in 1969 playing in Love's Labour's Lost, The Merchant of Venice, The National Health, etc. Toured Europe. U.S. theater: Mark Taper Forum: Comedians, Privates on Parade. NY Theater: Taming of the Shrew, Scapino, Barnum (Tony and Drama Desk Award), Joe Egg, Me and My Girl, Privates on Parade. Has written songs and music for films: Twinky, Shalako, Joseph Andrews, Georgy Girl.
PICTURES: Raising the Wind, Carry on Spying, Carry On Cleo, The Big Job, Carry On Cowboy, Carry on Screaming,

Lock Up Your Daughters, The National Health, Digby, Joseph Andrews, Pete's Dragon, The Unidentified Flying Oddball, Scandalous.

DALEY, ROBERT: Producer. Began career in pictures at Universal International and TV at Desilu.
PICTURES: Dirty Harry, Magnum Force (both exec. prod.), Thunderbolt and Lightfoot, The Enforcer, The Gauntlet, Every Which Way But Loose, Escape from Alcatraz (exec. prod.), Any Which Way You Can (exec. prod.), Bronco Billy (exec. prod.), Stick (exec. prod.).
TELEVISION: The Untouchables, Ben Casey, The FBI, 12 O'Clock High, The Invaders, etc.

DALSIMER, SUSAN: Executive. Editor for E.P. Dutton before joining Lorimar Prods., as v.p. of east coast development. Left to become consultant for original programming at Home Box Office. 1987, named v.p., creative affairs, east coast, for Warner Bros.

DALTON, TIMOTHY: Actor. b. Colwyn Bay, Wales, March 21, 1946.
THEATER: Antony and Cleopatra, The Taming of the Shrew, Little Malcolm and His Struggle Against the Eunuchs, A Game Called Arthur, King Lear, Love's Labour's Lost, Henry IV, Henry V, Romeo and Juliet, The Vortex, The Romans, A Touch of the Poet.
PICTURES: The Lion in Winter, Cromwell, The Voyeur, Wuthering Heights, Mary Queen of Scots, Permission to Kill, Sextette, Agatha, Flash Gordon, Chanel Solitaire, The Doctor and the Devils, The Living Daylights, Brenda Starr, Hawks, Licence to Kill
TELEVISION: Mistral's Daughter, Sins, The Master of Ballantrae, Florence Nightingale, Candida, Five Finger Exercise, Jane Eyre, Centennial.

DALTREY, ROGER: Singer, Actor. b. London, England, March 1, 1944. Lead vocalist with The Who.
PICTURES: Woodstock, Tommy, Lisztomania, The Legacy, The Kids Are Alright, McVicar (also prod.), Pop Pirate, The Beggar's Opera, The Teddy Bear Habit, Father Jim.

DALY, JIM: Executive Director, Rank Organisation plc. b. 1938. Managing director of Film and Television Services division which includes: Pinewood Film Studios, Rank Film Laboratories, Rank Film Distributors, Rank Advertising Films, Rank Theatres, Rank Video Services, Rank Video Services America. Appt. exec. dir., Rank Org. 1982.

DALY, JOHN: Executive. b. London, England, 1937. After working in journalism joined Royal Navy. On leaving Service after three years, trained as underwriter with an Assurance Company. In 1966 became David Hemmings manager and in 1967 formed the Hemdale Company with Hemmings (who later sold interest) Chmn. Hemdale Holdings Ltd.
PICTURES: Images, Sunburn (co-prod., co-s.p.), High Risk, Going Ape, Deadly Force, Carbon Copy, Yellowbeard, Falcon and the Snowman, Terminator, Salvador, Rivers Edge, At Close Range, Hoosiers, Platoon, Best Seller, Shag (exec. prod.), Vampire's Kiss (exec. prod.), Miracle Mile (prod.), Criminal Law (co-exec. prod.), War Party (prod.), The Boost, Out Cold (exec. prod.), Staying Together (exec. prod.).

DALY, ROBERT A.: Executive. b. New York, NY, Dec. 8, 1936. e. Brooklyn Coll., Hunter Coll. Joined CBS-TV in 1955; dir. of program acct.; dir. of research and cost planning; dir. of business affairs. Later named v.p., business affairs, NY; exec. v.p. of network on April, 1976. Named president, CBS Entertainment, Oct. 1977. In Oct. 1979 became responsible for CBS Theatrical Films as well as the TV operation. In 1980, appointed co-chmn. and co-chief exec. officer of Warner Bros. Sole title holder since Jan., 1982.

DALY, TIMOTHY: Actor. b. New York, NY, March 1, 1956. m. actress Amy Van Nostrand. Son of late actor James Daly, brother of actress Tyne Daly. e. Bennington Coll., B.A. Acted in summer stock while in college. Moved to NY where had own rock and roll band. Has performed in cabaret at Williamstown Theater Festival.
THEATER: Fables for Friends, Oliver, Oliver, Mass Appeal, Bus Stop, Coastal Disturbances (Theatre World Award).
PICTURES: Diner, Made in Heaven, Love or Money, Spellbinder.
TELEVISION: The Rise and Rise of Daniel Rocket. Mini-series: I'll Take Manhattan. Series: Ryan's Four, Almost Grown. Movies: Mirrors.

DALY, TYNE: Actress. r.n. Ellen Tyne Daly. b. Madison, WI, Feb. 21, 1946. Daughter of late actor James Daly and actress Hope Newell, sister of actor Timothy Daly. m. actor-dir. Georg Stanford Brown. On stage in The Butter and Egg Man (1966), That Summer, That Fall, Come Back Little Sheba (L.A., 1987), Gypsy.
PICTURES: John and Mary, Angel Unchained, Play It As It Lays, The Enforcer, Telefon, Speedtrap, Zoot Suit, The Aviator, Movers & Shakers.
TELEVISION: Series: Cagney and Lacey (Emmy Awards). Movies: A Howling in the Woods, Heat of Anger, The Man Who Could Talk to Kids, Larry, The Entertainer, Better Late Than Never, Intimate Strangers, The Women's Room, A Matter of Life or Death, Your Place or Mine, Kids Like These.

DAMON, MARK: Executive. b. Chicago, IL, April 22, 1933. e. UCLA, B.A. literature, M.A. business administration. Actor: 1958 under contract to 20th Century Fox, 1960 winner Golden Globe Award—Newcomer of the Year; early career includes The Fall of The House of Usher, The Longest Day; 1961 moved to Italy, stayed 16 years appearing in leading roles in 50 films; 1974 head of foreign dept. for PAC, a leading film distributor in Italy; 1976 returned to the U.S. as exec. prod. of The Choirboys and in charge of its foreign distribution; 1977 founder and pres. of Producers Sales Organization, intl. distribution org. 1987: formed Vision Int'l.
PICTURES: The Arena (prod.), Exec. prod. or co-exec. prod.: The Choirboys, The Neverending Story, Das Boot, 9-1/2 Weeks (prod.), Short Circuit, Lost Boys, High Spirits, Bat 21 (co-prod.), Adventure 1, Dark Angel, Wild Orchid (prod.).

DAMONE, VIC: Singer, Actor. r.n. Vito Farinola. b. Brooklyn, NY, June 12, 1928. m. actress-singer Diahann Carroll. e. Lafayette H.S., Brooklyn. Winner Arthur Godfrey talent show, 1945; then night clubs, radio, theatres, hotels. Film debut in Rich, Young and Pretty (1951); U.S. Army, 1951–53.
PICTURES: The Strip, Athena, Deep in My Heart, Hit the Deck, Kismet, Hell to Eternity.
TELEVISION: Vic Damone Show, 1958. Lively Ones, 1962.

DAMSKI, MEL: Director. b. New York, NY, July 21, 1946. e. Colgate U., AFI. Worked as reporter, journalism professor. USC Cinema instructor.
PICTURES: Yellowbeard, Mischief, Happy Together.
TELEVISION: M*A*S*H, Lou Grant, Dolphin Cove. Movies: Long Journey Back, The Child Stealer, Word of Honor, The Legend of Walks Far Woman, American Dream, For Ladies Only, Making the Grade, An Invasion of Privacy, Badge of the Assassin, A Winner Never Quits, Attack on Fear, Hero in the Family, Murder by the Book, Hope Division, The Three Kings, Everybody's Baby: The Rescue of Jessica McClure.

DANA, BILL: Actor, Writer. b. Quincy, MA, 1924. In night clubs and on TV.
PICTURES: The Right Stuff (actor), Busy Body (actor), The Nude Bomb (writer, actor).
TELEVISION: The Steve Allen Show (performer, head writer, 1961), The Bill Dana Jose Jimenez Show (star, writer), Ed Sullivan Show (performer), Spike Jones Show (prod., writer, performer), Milton Berle Show (prod., writer, performer), All in the Family (writer). Actor: Facts of Life, Too Close for Comfort, Golden Girls, Zorro and Son, Hollywood Palace, St. Elsewhere.

DANCE, CHARLES: b. Worcestershire, Eng., Oct. 10, 1946. e. Plymouth Coll. Art., Leicester Coll. of Art (graphic design degree). After first working as a West End theatre stagehand, made acting debut in 1970 in a touring company of It's a Two-Foot-Six-Inches-above-the Ground World. Worked in provincial repertory theaters. Joined the Royal Shakespeare Company 1975–80: Hamlet, Richard III, As You Like It. Lead in Henry V (1975, N.Y.), and Coriolanus (1979, Paris).
THEATER: revival of Irma La Douce (West End), Turning Over (London's Bush Theatre).
PICTURES: For Your Eyes Only, Plenty, The Golden Child, Good Morning, Babylon; White Mischief, The Hidden City, Pascali's Island, Secret Places of the Heart.
TELEVISION: The Jewel in the Crown, Out On a Limb, BBC's The Secret Servant, Rainy Day Woman, Out of the Shadows, First Born, Phantom of the Opera (mini-series).

D'ANGELO, BEVERLY: Actress. b. Columbia, OH, 1954. Studied visual arts and was exchange student in Italy before working as cartoonist for Hanna-Barbera Studios in Hollywood. Toured Canada's coffeehouse circuit as singer and appeared with rock band called Elephant. Joined Charlotte Town Festival Company. Bdwy. debut in rock musical, Rockabye Hamlet.
PICTURES: The Sentinel (debut 1977). Annie Hall, First Love, Every Which Way But Loose, Hair, Coal Miner's Daughter, National Lampoon's Vacation, Finders Keepers, Paternity, National Lampoon's European Vacation, Big Trouble, Aria, Maid to Order, In the Mood, Trading Hearts, High Spirits, National Lampoon's Christmas Vacation, Daddy's Dyin'.
TELEVISION: Captains and the Kings, A Streetcar Named Desire, Doubletake, Sleeping Beauty (Faerie Tale Theater), Slow Burn, Hands of a Stranger.

DANGERFIELD, RODNEY: Actor, Comedian. b. Babylon, NY, 1921. Performer in nightclubs as Jack Roy 1941–51. Businessman 1951–63. Comedian 1963–present. Founder Dangerfields Nightclub 1969.
PICTURES: The Projectionist, Caddyshack, Easy Money (also co. s.p.), Back to School, Moving, The Scout.

DANIEL, SEAN: Executive. b. Aug. 15, 1951. e. California Inst. of Arts film school. BFA, 1973. Was journalist for Village Voice before starting m.p. career as documentary filmmaker and asst. dir. for New World Pictures. In 1976 joined Universal Pictures as prod. exec.; 1979, named v.p., then pres., production. Resigned March, 1989 to become pres., The Geffen Co., film div.

DANIELEWSKI, TAD: Director-Writer. b. Poland. Studied Royal Acad. of Dramatic Art, London; Ohio U.; State U. of Iowa. At Johns Hopkins Univ. won national award for research in prod. and dir. methods for TV. Prod. and dir. various dramatic shows on CBS, ABC & NBC networks. Emmy Award for Africa (special). Professor & assoc. chair, UCLA film & theatre school.
STAGE: Artistic dir. NY Repertory Theatre; dir. Man with a Load of Mischief (London), A Desert Incident (Bdwy.), Brouhaha (off-Bdwy.), Hamlet, Death of a Salesman, Travesties, Born Yesterday.
PICTURES: Imperial Woman (co-s.p.), No Exit (dir.), The Guide (dir., s.p.), Spain (dir., s.p.), Copernicus (dir., s.p. of English ver.).
TELEVISION: Omnibus, Wide Wide World, Eddie Fisher Show, Matinee Theatre, Robert Montgomery Presents, etc.

DANIELS, HAROLD: Director, Producer, Writer, b. Buffalo, NY. e. Carnegie Tech. Drama Dept. B.A., U. of Pittsburgh, PHG. Joined MGM in 1940, directed shorts and won award from M.P. Council; joined David Selznick as director, 1943–45; produced, directed and wrote Prince of Peace, won spec. award for dir.
STAGE: Director in Pittsburgh for Prof. Stage Guild Co., N.Y., Rhode Island and Boston Repertoire. Directed over 50 plays.
PICTURES: Woman from Tangier, Sword of Venus, Port Sinister, Roadblock, Daughter of the West Classics, Terror in the Haunted House, Date with Death, My World Dies Screaming, Bayou, Poor White Trash, Ten Girls Ago; directed, Night of the Beast, House of Black Death, Annabelle Lee, Moonfire. Pigmy, 1971.
TELEVISION: directed over 200 half-hour and hour films including My Hero, Readers Digest, Fury, Colt 45, Ellery Queen, Jim Backus Theatre, G.E. Theatre, etc. Wrote many original screenplays for both films and TV. The Phantom, On Guard, Death Valley Days, Hannibal Cobb.

DANIELS, JEFF: Actor. b. Georgia. 1955. e. Central Michigan U. Apprentice with Circle Repertory Theatre, New York.
THEATRE: Brontosaurus, Short-Changed Review, The Farm, Fifth of July, Johnny Got His Gun (Obie Award), Lemon Sky, The Three Sisters, The Golden Age.
PICTURES: Ragtime (debut), Terms of Endearment, The Purple Rose of Cairo, Marie, Something Wild, Heartburn, Radio Days, The House on Carroll Street, Sweet Hearts Dance, Checking Out, Love Hurts.
TELEVISION: Movies: A Rumor of War, Invasion of Privacy, Fifth of July, The Caine Mutiny Court Martial, The Visit (Trying Times), Homeless. Breaking Away (pilot), Hawaii 5-0.

DANIELS, PAUL: TV performer, magician. b. South Bank, England, 1938. Early career starring in British and overseas theatres. 1983, Magician Of The Year Award by Hollywood's Academy of Magical Arts. 1985, his BBC TV special awarded Golden Rose of Montreux trophy. Presenter of Every Second Counts and Paul Daniels Magic Show. Devised children's TV series, Wizbit and radio series Dealing With Daniels.

DANIELS, WILLIAM: Actor. b. Brooklyn, NY, Mar 31, 1927. m. actress Bonnie Bartlett. e. Northwestern U. Traveled around NY area as part of The Daniels Family song and dance troupe. Appeared with family on experimental TV in 1941. Stage debut in Life with Father. Brought to national attention in A Thousand Clowns in original Bdwy. play and film version.
PICTURES: The Graduate, Marlowe, 1776, The Parallax View, Two for the Road, Black Sunday, Oh God, Sunburn, The Blue Lagoon, Blind Date, Her Alibi.
TELEVISION: East Side/West Side; For the People; Toma, The Rockford Files. Movies: Rehearsal for a Murder; Drop Out Father; A Case of Rape, Blind Ambition, The Little Match Girl. Series: Captain Nice, The Nancy Walker Show, Freebie and the Bean, Knight Rider, St. Elsewhere (Emmy Awards, Best Actor 1985, 1986). Mini-series: The Adams Chronicles.
STAGE: The Zoo Story, On a Clear Day You Can See Forever, 1776, Dear Me, The Sky Is Falling, A Little Night Music.

DANNER, BLYTHE: Actress. b. Philadelphia, PA, Feb. 3, 1943. e. Bard Coll. m. writer-producer Bruce Paltrow. Appeared in repertory cos. in U.S. before Lincoln Center (N.Y.) productions of Cyrano de Bergerac, Summertree, and The Miser (Theatre World Award for last).
THEATER: Butterflies Are Free (Tony Award, 1971), Major Barbara, Twelfth Night, The Seagull, Ring Around The Moon, Betrayal, Blithe Spirit, A Streetcar Named Desire, Much Ado About Nothing.
PICTURES: 1776, To Kill a Clown, Lovin' Molly, Hearts of the West, Futureworld, The Great Santini, Man, Woman and Child, Brighton Beach Memoirs, Another Woman, Mr. and Mrs. Bridge.
TELEVISION: Dr. Cook's Garden, To Confuse the Angel, George M, To Be Young, Gifted and Black, The Scarecrow, F. Scott Fitzgerald and The Last of the Belles; A Love Affair: Eleanor and Lou Gehrig, Too Far to Go: Eccentricities of a Nightingale; Inside the Third Reich, In Defense of Kids, Helen Keller: The Miracle Continues; Guilty Conscience, Dead Air. Series: Adam's Rib, Tattingers (revamped as Nick & Hillary).

DANO, ROYAL: Actor. b. New York, NY, Nov. 16, 1922. On Broadway stage (Finian's Rainbow, That's the Ticket, Metropole, Mrs. Gibbins Boys, Three Wishes for Jaime, She Stoops to Conquer) before entering films.
PICTURES: Undercover Girl, Under the Gun, The Red Badge of Courage, Bend of the River, Johnny Guitar, The Far Country, The Trouble With Harry, Tribute to a Bad Man, Santiago, Moby Dick, Tension at Table Rock, Crime of Passion, Trooper Hook, All Mine to Give, Man in the Shadow, Saddle the Wind, Never Steal Anything Small, These Thousand Hills, Hound Dog Man, Huckleberry Finn, Cimarron, King of Kings, Welcome to Hard Times, If He Hollers Let Him Go, The Undefeated, The Great Northfield Minnesota Raid, The Culpepper Cattle Company, Ace Eli and Rodger of the Skies, Electra Glide in Blue, Big Bad Mama, Death of a Gunfighter, The Outlaw Josey Wales, The Killer Inside Me, In Search of the Historic Jesus, Take This Job and Shove It, Hammett, Something Wicked This Way Comes, The Right Stuff, Red-Headed Stranger, Killer Klowns From Outer Space, Ghoulies II, Martians!!!
TELEVISION: Movies: Backtrack, Simon Run, Moon of the Wolf, Huckleberry Finn, Manhunter, Murder at Peyton Place, Donner Pass, Strangers, Death Valley Days, Planet of the Apes, Heroes of the Bible, From Here to Eternity, Once Upon a Texas Train.

DANSON, TED: Actor. b. Flagstaff, AZ, Dec. 29, 1947. e. Kent Sch., Stanford U., Carnegie-Mellon U, 1972. Studied at Actors Inst. with Dan Fauci. New York stage debut, The Real Inspector Hound, 1972; 1978, mgr. and teacher, Actors Inst., L.A. Film debut in The Onion Field, 1979. Television debut, The Doctors. Founded Amer. Oceans Campaign; bd. mem. Futures for Children.
PICTURES: The Onion Field, Body Heat, Creepshow, Little Treasure, A Fine Mess, Just Between Friends, Three Men and a Baby, Cousins, The Hard Way, Dad.
TELEVISION: Series: Somerset, Cheers. Movies: The Women's Room, The Good Witch at Laurel Canyon, Cowboy, Something about Amelia, Quarterback Princess, When the Bough Breaks (also prod.), We Are the Children.

DANTE, JOE: Director. b. Morristown, NJ. Managing editor for Film Bulletin before going to Hollywood to work in advertising, creating campaigns for many films. Became protege of Roger Corman, co-directing Hollywood Boulevard. Edited Grand Theft Auto.
PICTURES: Piranha (dir., co-editor), Rock n' Roll High School (co-s.p. only), Grand Theft Auto (editor, only), The Howling (also co-editor), Twilight Zone—The Movie (segment), Gremlins, Explorers, Innerspace, Amazon Women on the Moon (co-dir.), The 'Burbs, Gremlins II, Monoliths.

DANTON, RAY: Actor. b. New York, NY, Sept. 19, 1931. e. Horace Mann Sch., Carnegie Tech. m. Julie Adams. Radio actor on many programs; summer stock; London prod. of Mr. Roberts; U.S. Army, 1951–53; then TV actor numerous programs. Became dir. in 1976 with Psychic Killer (also co-s.p.).
PICTURES: Chief Crazy Horse, The Looters, The Spoilers, I'll Cry Tomorrow, Outside the Law, The Night Runner, Onionhead, Too Much Too Soon, Ice Palace, Legs Diamond, Tarawa Beachhead, Majority of One, The George Raft Story, Fever In The Blood, Portrait of a Mobster, The Chapman Report, The Longest Day, Sandokan, FBI Code 98, New York Calling Superdrago.
TELEVISION: Vietnam Story Home (dir.).

D'ANTONI, PHILIP. Producer. Director. b. New York, NY, Feb. 19, 1929. e. Fordham U., business administration. Joined CBS in mailroom, advanced into prod., sales development, prog. analysis, mkt. rsrch. Became indep. radio-TV repr. in 1954 for two years; then joined Mutual Broadcasting as sales manager; later, exec. v.p. Resigned in 1962 to form own prod. co. Made theatrical film debut with Bullitt as producer; directing debut with The Seven Ups. Heads Phil D'Antoni Prods.
PICTURES: Producer: Bullitt, The French Connection (Academy Award). Prod.-Dir.: The Seven Ups.
TELEVISION: Movin' On (series, 1969), Elizabeth Taylor in London, Sophia Loren in Rome, Melina Mercouri in Greece, Jack Jones Special, This Proud Land, and two movies: Mr. Inside/Mr. Outside, The Connection.

DANZ, FREDRIC A.: Executive. b. Seattle, WA, Feb. 28, 1918. Is chairman of Sterling Recreation Organization Co., Seattle; member, Foundation of M.P. Pioneers; v.p., Variety Club Intl.

DANZA, TONY: Actor. b. Brooklyn, NY, Apr. 21, 1951. e. U. of Dubuque, IA on a wrestling scholarship. After grad. professional boxer before tested for role in TV pilot (Fast Lane Blues) which he won. Back to New York and fighting until called to coast to appear as Tony Banta in Taxi series.
PICTURES: Hollywood Knights, Going Ape, Cannonball Run II, She's Out of Control.
TELEVISION: Series: Taxi, Who's the Boss. Movies: Doing Life (also exec. prod.), Single Bars, Single Women; Freedom Fighters (also co-exec. prod.).

DARBY, KIM: Actress. r.n. Derby Zerby. b. Hollywood, CA, July 8, 1948. e. Swanson's Ranch Sch., Van Nuys H.S. Studied at the Desilu Workshop in Hollywood. Professional debut on the Mr. Novak TV series.
TELEVISION: Eleventh Hour, Gunsmoke, Flesh and Blood (special); Enola Gay; Embassy; The People; Rich Man, Poor Man.
PICTURES: Bus Riley's Back in Town, True Grit, Generation, Norwood, The Strawberry Statement, The Grissom Gang, The One and Only, Better Off Dead, Teen Wolf Too.

DARK, JOHN: Producer. Films include, as associate: Light Up the Sky, Lost Innocence, The 7th Dawn, Casino Royale. Production exec., Paramount Pictures. Exec. producer: Half a Sixpence, There's a Girl in My Soup, Shirley Valentine. Produced: Wind of Change, Bachelor of Arts, Land That Time Forgot, At the Earth's Core, People That Time Forgot, Warlords of Atlantis, Arabian Adventure, Slayground.

DARLEY, DICK: Director, Producer network TV series and specials. Over 180 TV film shows; over 1,370 TV live/tape shows. Numerous pilots and commercials. Credits in U.S. and 27 foreign countries include drama, musical-variety, comedy, sports and documentary.

DARNBOROUGH, ANTONY: Producer, Director. b. London, Eng., ent. m.p. ind. 1944.
PICTURES: Seventh Veil, Years Between, Daybreak, Girl in a Million, Upturned Glass, When the Bough Breaks, Dear Murderer, The Calendar, My Brother's Keeper, The Girl in the Painting, Helter Skelter, Once Upon a Dream, Traveller's Joy, Boys in Brown, The Astonished Heart, So Long at the Fair, Quartet, Trio, Highly Dangerous, Encore, The Net (Project M. 7), Personal Affair, To Paris with Love, Baby and the Battleship.
TELEVISION: Also made many TV and documentary films for own co. and in assoc. with NSS.

DARREN, JAMES: Actor. b. Philadelphia, PA, June 8, 1936. Studied with Stella Adler group. Film debut: Rumble on the Docks (1956).
PICTURES: The Brothers Rico, Guns of Navarone, Gidget Goes Hawaiian, The Lively Set, 633 Squadron, Venus in Furs.
TELEVISION: T.J. Hooker, Fantasy Island, One Day at a Time.

DARRIEUX, DANIELLE: Actress. b. Bordeaux, France, May 1, 1917. e. Lycée LaTour, Conservatoire de Musique.
PICTURES: La Crise Est Finis, Mayerling, Club des Femmes, Abus de Confiance, Counsel for Romance, Mademoiselle Ma Mere, Katia, Orders from Tokyo, Oh Amelia, Rage of Paris, Rich Young and Pretty, 5 Fingers, La Ronde, Le Plaisir, Earrings of Madame De, Alexander the Great, Adorable Creatures, A Friend of the Family, Loss of Innocence, Scene of the Crime, A Few Days With Me.
THEATRE: Coco, The Ambassador (Bdwy).

DARTIGUE, JOHN: Executive. b. Port-au-Prince, Haiti, Sept. 12, 1940. e. Brandeis U., B.A., 1961; Columbia U., M.A., 1965. United Artists: named director of worldwide pub. in 1975; appointed executive assistant to the senior vice president for advertising and publicity in 1977; named v.p. adv.-pub., 1978. Joined Warner Bros. in 1978 as project executive. Named sr. exec. asst. to the exec. v.p. of worldwide adv./pub., Jan., 1980, v.p., publicity, July 1980.

DARTNALL, GARY: Executive. b. Whitchurch, Eng., May 9, 1937. e. Kings Coll., Taunton. Overseas Div., Associated British Pathe; Eur. rep., 1958–60; Middle & Far East rep., Lion International Films; Amer. rep., 1962; pres., Lion International Inc., 1963; Amer. rep., Alliance International Films Distributors, Ltd., and London Independent Producers, Ltd.; pres., Alliance International Films Corp. & Dartnall Films Ltd., 1966; managing dir., Overseas Division, Walter Reade Organization, 1969. pres., EMI Film Distributors, Inc., 1971; vice chairman, EMI Television Programs, Inc., 1976; pres., EMI Videograms, Inc., 1979; pres., VHD Programs, Inc. & VHD Disc Mfg. Co., 1980; chmn. & chief exec. officer, Thorn EMI Films, Ltd., & Thorn EMI Video, 1983. Also pres. & CEO, Thorn EMI Films, Inc.; chmn., Thorn EMI Cinemas; CEO, Thorm EMI Screen Entertainment Ltd. 1987: Acquired Southbrook Intl. Television and formed Palladium Inc., chairman and chief exec. officer.

Da SILVA, RAUL: Creative consultant, Writer, Director, Producer, b. New York, NY, June 12, 1933. e. Adelphi U., B.A. 1958, elected to Acad. of Distinction, Adelphi Alumni Assoc. 1978. Specializes in unusual conceptualization and plotting rework, stressing classic artistry and production values. Corporate AV dir., exec. prod. adv. agencies; indep. writer, producer, dir., univ. lecturer (creative aspects of film prod. writing).
PUBLICATIONS: Making Money in Film & Video (1986); The World of Animation (Kodak, 1979); The Business of Filmmaking (Kodak, 1978); SOUND, Magnetic Recording for Motion Pictures (Kodak, 1977). Wrote articles for Millimeter, American Cinematographer, Back Stage and many other trades.
PICTURES: Fear No Evil (creative consultant).
TELEVISION: Nat Hurst, M.D.; The Strangest Voyage (dir., prod.), Standing Tall (script consultant). Video: The Rime of the Ancient Mariner.
AWARDS: 1984 Writer's Digest screenwriting award and numerous as dir.-prod. for films; six in 1975–76 for Coleridge and his masterpiece, The Ancient Mariner with Sir Michael Redgrave. First place, annual Soc. for Technical Communications competition, 1980, for The World of Animation. Numerous for informational films.

DA SILVA, RAY: Director and designer of animated films, Animator, Illustrator, Character designer. b. New York, NY, July 13, 1934. e. School of Visual Arts, N.Y., also instructor there. Specializes in animation direction, character design. Numerous national and international TV spots for the advertising industry.
PICTURES: Raggedy Ann & Andy; Heavy Metal.
TELEVISION: The Strangest Voyage, Noah's Animals, The Little Brown Burro, Ichabod Crane.

DASSIN, JULES: Director. b. Middletown, CT, Dec. 18, 1911. m. actress Melina Mercouri. Actor on dramatic stage several years; radio writer. Joined MGM, 1940, as dir. short subjects; later dir. features.
PICTURES: Canterville Ghost, Brute Force, Naked City, Thieves' Highway, Night and the City, Rififi, He Who Must Die, The Law, Never on Sunday, Topkapi, Phaedra, 10:30 p.m. Summer, Promise at Dawn, Uptight, The Rehearsal, A Dream of Passion, Circle of Two.
PLAYS: Ilya, Darling, 1967.

DAVEE, LAWRENCE W.: Engineer. b. Foxcroft, ME, March 28, 1900. e. U. of Maine., B.S., elec. eng. Research eng. Bell Telephone Lab.; Fox Case Corp.; studio mgr. Fox Hearst Corp.; Bronx Studio. Elec. Research Prods., Inc.; Century Projector Corp., N.Y.; engineer & sales mgr.; pres. 1959. Member: 25–30 Club (Honorary). Lifemember, N.Y. State Projectionists.

DAVENPORT, NIGEL: Actor. b. Cambridge, England, May 23, 1928. e. Trinity Coll., Oxford. Began acting after stint in British military at 18 years. First 10 years of professional career in theatre. Majority of screen work in British films in 1960s and 70s.
PICTURES: Peeping Tom, In the Cool of the Day, A High Wind in Jamaica, Where the Spies Are, The Third Secret, Life at the Top, A Man for All Seasons, Sebastian, Sinful Davey, Play Dirty, Virgin Soldiers, Royal Hunt of the Sun, No Blade of Grass, Villain, Mary, Queen of Scots; Island of Dr. Moreau, Zulu Dawn, Nighthawks, Chariots of Fire, Greystoke, Without a Clue, Caravaggio.
TELEVISION: A Christmas Carol (1984), Dracula, The Picture of Dorian Gray, The Ordeal of Dr. Mudd, Masada.

DAVID, PIERRE: Executive. Producer. b. Montreal, Canada. e. U. of Montreal. Joined radio sta. CJMS 1966 as pub. relns. & spec. events dir. 1969, while running Mutual Broadcasting Network of Canada's live entertainment div., created new film dist. co. Mutual Films. 1972 added prod. unit and as prod. or exec. prod. prod. and dist. 19 French-lang. Canadian films. With filmmaker Roger Corman est. Mutual Pictures of Canada, Ltd to dist. films in English Canada; 1978 teamed Mutual Films with Victor Solnicki and Claude Heroux to prod. Eng.-lang. m.p. Pioneered 3-picture concept for Canadian m.p. investors. Moved to L.A. 1983 where became pres., Film Packages Intl. where prod. exec. on Platoon, Hot Pursuit. Then joined Larry Thompson Org. as partner involved in dev. and/or prod. of m.p., Jan., 1987, named chmn. of bd. and chief exec. officer, Image Org., Inc. intl. dist. co. formed by David, Malofilm Group, Nelvana Ent. and New Star Ent; April, 1989 with Rene Malo acquired shares of New Star and Nelvana giving them 92% owership of Image. Also pres. Lance Entertainment, prod. co.
PICTURES: Prod.: The Brood; Hog Wild; Scanners; Dirty Tricks; Gas; The Funny Farm, Visiting Hours; Videodrome, Going Berserk; Of Unknown Origin; Covergirl; Breaking All the Rules; For Those I Loved, My Demon Lover (Exec. prod.), PIN (exec. prod.), Blind-Fear (co-prod.), Internal Affairs (exec. prod.), Scanners II, The New Order..

DAVID, SAUL: Producer. b. Springfield, MA., June 27, 1921. e. Classical H.S., Springfield; Rhode Island Sch. of Design.

Started in radio, newspaper work and as editorial director for Bantam Books. Worked for Columbia Pictures, 1960–62; Warner Bros., 1962–63; 20th Century-Fox, 1963–67, and Universal, 1968–69; Executive story editor at MGM, 1972. Author: The Industry.
PICTURES: Von Ryan's Express, Our Man Flint, Fantastic Voyage, In Like Flint, Skullduggery, Logan's Run, Ravagers (exec. prod.).

DAVIDSON, JOHN: Actor, Singer. b. Pittsburgh, PA, Dec. 13, 1941. e. Denison U. In numerous school stage prods. before coming to N.Y. in 1964 to co-star with Bert Lahr in Bdwy. show, Foxy. Signed as regular on The Entertainers with Carol Burnett.
PICTURES: The Happiest Millionaire, The One and Only Genuine Original Family Band, The Concorde—Airport '79, The Squeeze.
TELEVISION: The Fantasticks, USA, The FBI, The Interns, Owen Marshall, Kraft Summer Music Hall (own variety series), The Tonight Show, The Girl with Something Extra, The John Davidson Talk Show (1980), Host, That's Incredible, New Hollywood Squares, Time Machine (game show), Incredible Sunday.

DAVIDSON, MARTIN: Director. b. New York, NY, Nov. 7, 1939. Acted in and directed off-Bdwy. plays, wrote material for Sid Caesar, worked as agent with N.Y. offices of Int'l. Famous Artists.
PICTURES: The Lords of Flatbush, Almost Summer, Hero at Large, Eddie and the Cruisers, Heart of Dixie (also exec. prod.).
TELEVISION: Series: Family Honor, Call to Glory. Movies: Long Gone.

DAVIES, WILLIAM C.: Director. b. Auburn, NY, June 17, 1932, e. Auburn Community Coll., Sch. of Radio Technique. Radio & TV announcer & narrator, then cameraman & editor. Formed Virgo Productions, 1965.
PICTURES: Legend of Horror, Orgy of the Dead, The Seekers, Day the Adults Died, Pink Garter Gang, Night at the Feast, Laughter in Hell, The Crimson Cult, Submarine X-1.

DAVIS, ARTHUR: Executive. b. New York, NY, Dec. 28, 1927. e. NYU. Began as exhibitor in U.S.; founded Arthur Davis Organization in Tokyo, Japan, in 1963, representing European and American films for sales to Japanese TV and motion picture industry. 1979, released two documentaries, Brutes and Savages, The Art of Killing.

DAVIS, BRAD: Actor. b. Florida, Nov. 6, 1949. Won music talent contest at 17; moved to Atlanta and acted in theatre before settling in New York, N.Y. stage debut in Crystal and Fox; did several off-Bdwy. plays. Appeared in TV soap opera, How to Survive a Marriage, for 10 months.
THEATER: The Elusive Angel, Entertaining Mr. Sloane, The Normal Heart.
PICTURES: Midnight Express, A Small Circle of Friends, Chariots of Fire, Querelle, Heart, Cold Steel, Rosalie Goes Shopping.
TELEVISION: Walt Whitman, Sybil, Roots, A Rumor of War, The Greatest Man in the World, Chiefs, Robert Kennedy and His Times, Vengeance: The Story of Tony Cimo, Blood Ties, When the Time Comes, The Caine Mutiny Court Martial, Unspeakable Acts, The Rope.

DAVIS, CARL: Composer. b. Brooklyn, NY, Oct. 28, 1936. e. Queens Coll., Bard Coll. and New England Coll. of Music. Worked as pianist with Robert Shaw Chorale and wrote music for revue Diversions (1958) and Twists (London), Moved to England 1961 writing incidental music for Joan Littlewood's Theatre Workshop Co., Royal Shakespeare Co. and National Theatre. Other theater music includes Jonathan Miller's Tempest, Forty Years On, and the musical The Vaccies. Best known for composing new scores for silent classics (Napolean, The Crowd, Greed, Intolerance, etc.) for screenings at which he conducts and for Thames TV The Silents series. Also conductor with London Philharmonic Orch.
PICTURES: The Bofors Gun, Up Pompeii, Rentadick, Man Friday, The Sailor's Return, Birth of the Beatles, The French Lieutenant's Woman, Praying Mantis, The Aerodrome, Champions, Weather in the Streets, George Stevens: a Filmmaker's Journey, King David, The Rainbow, Scandal, Girl in the Swing.
TELEVISION: That Was the Week That Was, Hollywood, the Pioneers, World at War, Mayor of Casterbridge, Lorna Doone, Unknown Chaplin. Buster Keaton—A Hard Act to Follow, Treasure Island.

DAVIS, COLIN: Executive. Held executive positions in Canada in adv., bdcst., & p.r. with several companies, including Procter & Gamble, Young & Rubicam. Joined MCA TV Canada as v.p. & gen. mgr., 1977. Named dir. intl. sls., 1978. In 1986 appt. pres., MCA TV Int'l.

DAVIS, FRANK I.: Executive. b. Poolesville, MD, Feb. 18, 1919. e. U. of Maryland, A.B., 1941; Harvard Law School, LL.B., 1948. Law firm, Donovan, Leisure, Newton, Lombard and Irvine, 1948–50; v.p., gen. counsel, Vanguard Films, 1951; v.p., gen. counsel, Selznick Releasing Org., 1951–53; pres., The Selznick Company, 1953–55; v.p., Famous Artists Corp., 1956–62; v.p. George Stevens Productions Inc., 1962–65; exec. prod., The Greatest Story Ever Told; v.p. in charge of m.p. affairs, Seven Arts, 1966; exec. in chg. talent and exec. asst. to v.p. in chg. prod., MGM, 1967; dir. m.p. business affairs, MGM, 1970; v.p., business affairs, MGM, 1972; sr. v.p., motion picture business affairs, MGM/UA, 1983, exec. v.p., business affairs, MGM Pictures, 1986–88; sr. exec. v.p., business affairs, Pathe Entertainment Inc., 1989.

DAVIS, GEENA: Actress. b. Wareham, MA, 1959. m. actor Jeff Goldblum. e. Boston U. Acted with Mount Washington Repertory Theatre Co., NH. Model before debut in Tootsie, 1982.
PICTURES: Tootsie, Fletch, Transylvania 6-5000, The Fly, Beetlejuice, The Accidental Tourist, Earth Girls Are Easy, Quick Change, The Grifters.
TELEVISION: Series: Buffalo Bill, Sara. Special: The Hit List.

DAVIS, GEORGE W.: Art director, b. Kokomo, IN, Apr. 17, 1914. e. U. of Southern California.
PICTURES: The Robe, The Diary of Anne Frank, Love Is A Many Splendored Thing, All About Eve, David and Bathsheba, Americanization of Emily, Unsinkable Molly Brown, Funny Face, Cimarron, Period of Adjustment, Mutiny on the Bounty, Twilight of Honor, How the West Was Won, Patch of Blue, The Wonderful World of the Brothers Grimm, Mr. Buddwing, The Shoes of the Fisherman, etc. Including 200 feature films and 2000 TV segments.

DAVIS, JORDAN P.: Executive. b. New York, NY, Oct. 29, 1933. e. Lehigh U., 1954; Columbia U. Law Sch., 1958. Attorney for five years. Director of Business Affairs, ABC TV Network, 1963–67. NBC TV Network 1967–69. Director of Talent and Program Admin. v.p. Warner Bros. Television, 1969–72. Executive, The Sy Fischer Company, 1972–73. Executive in charge of production, Four D. Productions, Inc.; The Mimus Corp., The Triseme Corporation, 1973–82. Pres., Jorlee Ltd., 1982–present.

DAVIS, JUDY: Actress. b. Australia. m. actor Colin Friels. Left convent school as teenager to become a singer in a rock band. Studied at West Australia Inst. of Technology and National Inst. of Dramatic Art, Sydney. Worked with theatre companies in Adelaide and Sydney and at Royal Court Theatre, London. Los Angeles stage debut Hapgood. Theatrical film debut in My Brilliant Career, 1979.
PICTURES: Hoodwink, Heatwave, Winter of Our Dreams, The Final Option, A Passage to India, Kangaroo, High Tide, Georgia, Impromtu.
TELEVISION: Rocket to the Moon, A Woman Called Golda.

DAVIS, LUTHER.: Writer, Producer. b. New York, Aug. 29, 1921. Collab. book B'way musical Kismet (Tony Award), collab. s.p.; author, prod., Lady In A Cage. Prod. and wrote book for Bdwy musical, Timbuktu!, 1978–79. Wrote book for Bdwy musical The Grand, 1989. Co-prod., Eden Court and Not About Heroes (off-Bdwy. plays, 1985 and 1986).
PICTURES: Solo s.p., The Hucksters, B.F.'s Daughter, Black Hand, A Lion Is in the Streets, The Gift of Love, Holiday for Lovers, The Wonders of Aladdin; Across 110th St., Lady in a Cage (also prod.).
TELEVISION: Wrote, prod., Kraft Suspense Theatre and many pilots for series (Run for Your Life, Combat, The Silent Force, Eastside, Westside, etc.). Wrote, prod. Arsenic and Old Lace (TV special). Prod.: The People Trap (TV special). Wrote teleplays for MOW's Daughter of the Mind, The Old Man Who Cried Wolf, Colombo.

DAVIS, MAC: Singer, Songwriter, Actor. b. Lubbock, TX, Jan 21, 1942. e. Emory U., Georgia State Coll. Employed as ditch digger, service station attendant, laborer, probation officer and record company salesman before gaining fame as entertainer-singer in 1969. Recording artist and composer of many popular songs.
PICTURES: North Dallas Forty, Cheaper to Keep Her, The Sting II.
TELEVISION: Brothers-In-Law, What Price Victory?

DAVIS, MARTIN S.: Executive. b. New York, NY, Feb. 5, 1927. e. City Coll. of New York, NYU. U.S. Army, 1943–46; joined Samuel Goldwyn Prod., Inc., 1944; with pub. dept. Allied Artists, 1955; Paramount Pictures, 1958. as dir. sales and marketing then dir. adv., pub. expl. 1960; v.p. in chg. of home office and asst. to pres.; 1963; exec. v.p., 1966; exec. comm. & bd. of dir. Member of Bd., Gulf & Western, 1967, named sr. v.p. 1969; elected Exec. v.p. and mem. exec. comm. Gulf & Western, 1974; elected CEO and chmn. of bd. and chmn. exec. comm. 1983. Member: bd. trustees, Economic Club of NY and Fordham U; bd. of advisors, John Jay Coll. of Criminal Justice; chmn,. NYC chap, Natl. Multiple Sclerosis

Society and serves on bd. Natl. Ms; bd. of trustees Carnegie Hall. (Gulf & Western renamed Paramount Pictures Communications 1989).

DAVIS, OSSIE: Actor, Writer, Director. b. Cogdell, GA, Dec. 18, 1917. e. Howard U., Washington, DC. m. actress Ruby Dee. Studied acting in N.Y. with Rose McLendon Players, leading to Broadway debut in 1946 in Jeb. For 11 years thereafter was one of best-known black actors on Broadway stage (Anna Lucasta, Jamaica, The Green Pastures, Wisteria Tree, A Raisin in the Sun, I'm Not Rappaport.) Wrote and starred in Purlie Victorious, repeating role for film version. Directed and appeared with Ms. Dee in her musical Take It From the Top. Co-hosted Ossie Davis and Ruby Dee Story Hour on radio (3 years). Published plays: Purlie Victorious, Langston, Escape to Freedom, Curtain Call, Mr. Aldredge, Sir.
PICTURES: Actor: The Joe Louis Story, Fourteen Hours, Shock Treatment, No Way Out, The Cardinal, The Hill, Man Called Adam, The Scalphunters, Sam Whiskey, Let's Do It Again, Harry and Son, Avenging Angel, School Daze, Do the Right Thing, Love Supreme. Director: Cotton Comes to Harlem, Black Girl, Gordon's War, Countdown at Kusini (also star).
TELEVISION: Author: East Side/West Side, The Eleventh Hour. Acted in many top dramatic series (Name of the Game, Night Gallery, Bonanza, etc.), Martin Luther King: The Dream and the Drum; Co-host and co-prod.: With Ossie and Ruby; Today is Ours (writer, dir.), Movies: All God's Children, Roots: The Next Generations, King, Teacher, Teacher. Series: B.L. Stryker.

DAVIS, PETER: Author, Filmmaker. b. Santa Monica, CA, Jan. 2, 1937. e. Harvard Coll., 1953–57. Parents were screenwriter Frank Davis, and novelist-screenwriter Tess Slesinger. Writer-interviewer, Sextant Prods., FDR Series, 1964–65. Host, The Comers, PBS 1964–65. Author: Hometown (1982), Where Is Nicaragua? (1987), articles for Esquire, NY Times Mag., The Nation, NY Woman, TV Guide.
PICTURES: Hearts and Minds (prod., dir.; Acad. Award, best documentary, 1975; Prix Sadoul, 1974).
TELEVISION: Writer-prod.: Hunger in America (assoc. prod., Writers Guild of America Award, 1968); The Heritage of Slavery; The Battle of East St. Louis, (Saturday Review Award, 1970; 2 Emmy nom.); The Selling of the Pentagon (Writers Guild, Emmy, Peabody, George Polk, Ohio State, Sat. Review Awards, 1971); 60 Minutes (segment prod.); Middletown (series, prod., Dupont Citation, Emmy noms. 1983); The Rise and Fall of the Borscht Belt.

DAVIS, ROGER H.: Attorney. b. Chicago, IL, June 19, 1923. e. U. of California, Berkeley, 1951, A.B., LL.B. Private law practice, partner, Loeb and Loeb, Los Angeles, 1951–61; atty., William Morris Agency, head of west coast legal, literary and M.P. depts., exec./admin., asst. sec. WMA, Inc., 1969–present, made v.p., 1974. exec. v.p. & bd. member, 1980. Also chmn. bd.'s exec. comm.

DAVIS, SAMMI: Actress. b. Kidderminster, Worcestershire, Eng., 1965. Convent-educated before taking drama course. Performed in stage prods. with local drama society in Midlands, then Birmingham Rep. and Big Brum Theatre Co. Plays include The Home Front, The Apple Club, Nine Days, Databased, Choosey Susie. London stage debut: A Collier's Friday.
PICTURES: Mona Lisa, Lionheart, Hope and Glory, A Prayer for the Dying, Consuming Passions, The Lair of the White Worm, The Rainbow.
TELEVISION: Auf Wiedersehn Pet, The Day After the Fair.

DAVIS, SAMMY, JR.: Entertainer. b. New York, NY, Dec. 8, 1925. Father: Sammy Davis, Sr., entertainer. Professional debut at age 2, Gibson Theatre, in act with father and uncle, Will Mastin; singer, dancer, comedian, vocal and acting impressions; song writer; recording artist; starred on Bdwy in Mr. Wonderful, and Golden Boy; other stage incl. Stop the World, I Want to Get Off, Salute to Selma, Two Friends: Sammy and Company. Autobiographies: Yes, I Can (1966); Why Me? (1989).
PICTURES: Rufus Jones For President (as child dancer), Season's Greetings, Anna Lucasta, Porgy and Bess, Ocean's 11, Sergeants 3, Robin and the Seven Hoods, Pepe, Salt and Pepper, A Man Called Adam, Sweet Charity, One More Time, The Cannonball Run, Cannonball Run II, Moon Over Parador, Tap.
TELEVISION: The Pigeon, The Trackers (also prod.). Guest: All in the Family and all major variety and talk shows. Host: Sammy Davis Jr. Show.

DAVISON, BRUCE: Actor. b. Philadelphia, PA, 1946. e. Pennsylvania State U., NYU. debut, Lincoln Center Repertory.
THEATER: The Front Page (Long Wharf), Streamers (Westwood Playhouse, LA Critics Award), King Lear (Lincoln Center), The Elephant Man, Richard III (NY Shakespeare Fest.), The Glass Menagerie, The Caine Mutiny Court Martial (Ahmanson), The Normal Heart (Las Palmas Theatre), Downside (Long Wharf).
PICTURES: Last Summer, The Strawberry Statement, Willard, Been Down So Long It Looks Like Up To Me, The Jerusalem File, Ulzana's Raid, Mame, Mother, Jugs, and Speed, Short Eyes, Brass Target, French Quarter, High Risk, A Texas Legend, Lies, Crimes of Passion, Spies Like Us, The Ladies Club, Wheels of Terror, Misfit Brigade.
TELEVISION: Taming of the Shrew. Movies: Deadman's Curve, Summer of My German Soldier, Alfred Hitchcock Presents (1985), Mind Over Murder, The Gathering, Tomorrow's Child, Ghost Dancing, Poor Little Rich Girl: The Barbara Hutton Story; Amazing Stories, Hunter (series).

DAVISON, DALE: Executive. b. North Hollywood, CA, March 21, 1955. e. U.C.L.A., B.A., 1978. Entered the motion picture industry in 1973 working for Pacific Theatres. Employed with Great Western Theatres 1974–77 as manager, dir. of concessions, and asst. vice pres. Partner with Great Western Theatres, 1978–1984. Founder and CEO, CinemaCal Enterprises, Inc., 1985–present.

DAVISON, JON: Producer. b. Haddonfield, NJ, July 21, 1949. e. NYU Film School. Taught film history there one summer and ran NYU Cinema two years. 1972, joined New World Pictures as natl. dir. of publ./adv.; 1977, named in charge of prod.; 1980, became indep. prod.
PICTURES: Hollywood Boulevard, Grand Theft Auto, Piranha, Airplane!, White Dog, Twilight Zone—The Movie (episode), Top Secret! RoboCop, RoboCop II.

DAWBER, PAM: Actress, Singer. b. Detroit, MI, Oct. 18, 1954. m. actor Mark Harmon. e. Farmington H.S., Oakland Community Coll. In 1971 worked as model and did commercials. First professional performance as singer in Sweet Adeleine at Goodspeed Opera House, East Haddam, CT.
STAGE: Regional: My Fair Lady, The Pirates of Penzance, The Music Man, She Loves Me.
PICTURE: A Wedding (1978).
TELEVISION: Series: Mork and Mindy, My Sister Sam. Movies: The Girl, the Gold Watch and Everything; Remembrance of Love, Through Naked Eyes, Last of the Great Survivors, American Geisha, This Wife For Hire; Quiet Victory: The Charlie Wedemeyer story, O Do You Know the Muffin Man. Specials: Kennedy Center Honors, Salute to Andy Gibb, Night of the 100 Stars, 3rd Annual TV Guide Special.

DAY, DORIS: Singer, Actress. r.n. Doris Kappelhoff. b. Cincinnati, OH, Apr. 3, 1924. e. dancing, singing. Toured as dancer; radio and band singer; screen debut in Romance on the High Seas, 1948. Voted one of Top Ten Money-Making Stars in Motion Picture Herald-Fame poll, 1951–52. Best female vocalist. M. P. Daily radio poll, 1952.
PICTURES: Young Man With a Horn, Tea for Two, Storm Warning, West Point Story, Lullaby of Broadway, On Moonlight Bay, I'll See You in My Dreams, Starlift, Winning Team, April in Paris, By the Light of the Silvery Moon, Calamity Jane, Lucky Me, Young at Heart, Love Me or Leave Me, Man Who Knew Too Much, Julie, Pajama Game, Teacher's Pet, Pillow Talk, Please Don't Eat the Daisies, Midnight Lace, Lover, Come Back, That Touch of Mink, Jumbo, Thrill of It All, Move Over, Darling, Do Not Disturb, Send Me No Flowers, Glass Bottom Boat, Caprice, The Ballad of Josie, Where Were You When the Lights Went Out, With Six You Get Eggrolls, Sleeping Dogs.
TELEVISION: The Doris Day Show (1968–73); Cable show: Doris Day and Friends (1985–86).

DAY, LARAINE: Actress. r.n. Laraine Johnson. b. Roosevelt, UT, Oct. 13, 1917. In school dramatics; with Players Guild, Long Beach, Calif.; toured in church prod. Conflict; Professionally on stage in Lost Horizon, The Women, Time of the Cuckoo, Angel Street; m.p. debut in Border G-Men 1938.
PICTURES: Story of Dr. Wassell, Those Endearing Young Charms, Locket, Tycoon, My Son, My Son, Foreign Correspondent, Woman on Pier 13, Without Honor, High and the Mighty, Mr. Lucky, Toy Tiger, Three for Jamie Dawn, The Third Voice, Yank on the Burma Road, The Bad Man, Fingers at the Window, Bride By Mistake, My Dear Secretary.
TELEVISION: Climax, Playhouse 90, Alfred Hitchcock, Wagon Train, Let Freedom Ring, Name of the Game, FBI, Sixth Sense, Medical Center, Murder on Flight #504 (movie), Fantasy Island, Love Boat, Lou Grant, Airwolf, Hotel, Murder She Wrote.

DAY, ROBERT: Director. b. England, Sept. 11, 1922. Started as cinematographer before turning to direction.
PICTURES: Director: The Green Man, Grip of the Stranger; First Man into Space; Corridors of Blood; Bobbikins; Two-Way Stretch; The Rebel; Operation Snatch; Tarzan's Three Challenges; She; Tarzan and the Valley of Gold; Tarzan and the Green River; Logan's Run; The Man with Bogart's Face.
TELEVISION: Pilots include: Banion, Kodiak; Dan August; Sunshine, Switch, Kingston, Dallas. Movies include: Ritual of Evil; The House of Greenapple Road; In Broad Daylight; Having Babies; The Grass Is Always Greener over the Septic

Tank; Peter and Paul; Running Out; Scruples; Cook and Peary—The Race to the Pole; Hollywood Wives; The Lady from Yesterday; Diary of a Perfect Murder; Celebration; Family, Higher Ground.

DAY-LEWIS, DANIEL: Actor. b. London, England, 1958. Son of late C. Day-Lewis, poet laureate of Eng., and actress Jill Balcon. Grandson of late Sir Malcolm Balcon who prod. Hitchcock's Brit. films. e. Bristol Old Vic. Theatre School. First professional job at 12 as ruffian scratching cars with broken bottle in film, Sunday Bloody Sunday. Then acted with Bristol Old Vic and Royal Shakespeare Co. Appeared in West End in, among others, Another Country, Hamlet (Natl Theater, 1989).
PICTURES: Gandhi, The Bounty, A Room With a View, My Beautiful Laundrette, The Unbearable Lightness of Being, Stars and Bars, Nanou, Eversmile, New Jersey, My Left Foot.
TELEVISION: A Frost in May, How Many Miles to Babylon?, My Brother Jonathan, The Insurance Man.

DAYTON, LYMAN D.: Producer. b. Salt Lake City, UT. Aug. 17, 1941. e. Brigham Young U.. m. Elizabeth Doty Dayton. After college worked in film lab at MGM, 1967–68; joined Screen Gems and General DeLuxe, 1968–69; became indep. prod. 1969. Heads Doty-Dayton Productions.
PICTURES: Where the Red Fern Grows, Seven Alone, Against A Crooked Sky, Pony Express Rider, Baker's Hawk, Young Rivals, Powder Keg.

DEAN, EDDIE: Actor. r.n. Edgar D. Glosup. b. Posey, TX. 1930–33 in radio throughout middle west; 1934 National Barn Dance, Station WLS; 1935 on CBS & NBC with same program. Featured male singer on TV KTLA Western Varieties 1944–55. Came to Hollywood in 1936; since then has starred in many westerns. Featured performer in western series for PRC in 1945. Voted one of the ten best money making Western Stars in Motion Picture Herald-Fame Poll 1936–47; recording artists, personal appearances, rodeos, fairs, etc.; 1966 V.P. Academy of Country & Western Music; 1967–68 on Bd. of Dir. of Academy of Western Music, Calif. Winner, Pioneer Award of Academy of Country Music, 1978. In 1983 named ACM v.p.; also v.p. in 1985. Recorded video cassette 1986, A Tribute to Eddie Dean.

DEAN, JIMMY: Performer. b. Plainview, TX, Aug. 10, 1928. Joined armed forces, 1946–49; first appeared in various clubs in Wash., 1949; then app. on Town and Country Jamboree; toured Caribbean and Europe with his troupe.
SONGS: Composer: Big Bad John, Little Black Book, I.O.U. to a Sleeping Beauty.
PICTURE: Big Bad John.
TELEVISION: Sunday Night at the Palladium (London), The Jimmy Dean Show.

DEAN, MERRILL C.: Executive. b. May 24, 1941. e. UCLA, M.B.A., bus. admin. 1967–68, involved with Walt Disney Productions, 11 yrs. starting in m.p. distribution internationally with Buena Vista Intl., concentrating on Latin America. Later involved with worldwide publications and gen. mgr. of direct mktg. Was v.p. & gen. mgr. Walt Disney Records Music Division, four years. 1978–82, pres. of Televisa Intl. Distribution Corp., whose activities are principally involved with dist. of films to the Hispanic mkt. in U.S. & Puerto Rico. Now pres. InterFilm, Inc., Los Angeles, and Azimuth Communications Corp.

DEAN, MORTON: Television Newsman. b. Fall River, MA, Aug. 22, 1935. e. Emerson Coll. News dir., N.Y. Herald Tribune Net, 1957; corr. WBZ, 1960, corr. WCBS-TV, 1964; anchor, WCBW-TV News, 1967; corr., CBS News, 1967; anchor, CBS Sunday Night News, 1975; anchor, Sunday edition CBS Evening News, 1976; co-anchor, Independent Network News, 1985.

DEARDEN, JAMES: Writer, Director, b. London, Eng. Sept. 14, 1949. Son of late British director Basil Dearden. e. New Coll., Oxford U. Entered film industry in 1967 as production runner. After editing commercials and documentaries, and working as asst. dir., wrote, prod. and dir. first short film, The Contraption (Silver Bear Award, 1978 Berlin Film Fest.). 1978, began dir. commercials and made short, Panic (Cert. of Merit, 1980 Chicago Film Fest.). 1979, made 45-min film Diversion, which became basis for Fatal Attraction (Gold Plaque, best short drama, 1980 Chicago Film Fest.).
PICTURES: Fatal Attraction (s.p.); Pascali's Island (dir., s.p.).
TELEVISION: The Cold Room (dir., s.p., Special Jury Prize, dir., 1985 Fest. Intl. d'Avoriaz du Film Fantastique).

DE BELDER, GUIDO: Actor, Author, Screenwriter. b. Tienen, Belgium, Mar. 14, 1939.
PICTURES: Mirliton, Obsessie, Spielgelvan Het Geluk, Mireille Dans La Vie Des Autres, Exit Seven, Ten Years After, Chock, Slachtvee, Deterugtocht, Mama Dracula, Traverses Traversees, Une Femme en Fuite, The Afterman.
TELEVISION: De Machinist (serial in 3 parts), Portrait of Guido De Belder (documentary).

DE BROCA, PHILIPPE: Director. b. 1933.
PICTURES: Les Jeux de l'Amour, L'Amant, de Cinq Jours, Cartouche, That Man from Rio, Un Monsieur de Compagnie, Tribulations, Chinoise en Chine, King of Hearts, Devil by the Tail, Give Her the Moon, Chere Louise, Le Magnifique, Dear Inspector (and s.p.), The Skirt Chaser, Someone's Stolen the Thigh of Jupiter, The African, Louisiana (TV in U.S.), The Gypsy, Chouans! (dir., co-s.p.), Scheherazade..

DE CAESAR, GABRIEL: Producer. b. New York, NY, Nov. 15, 1928. e. Los Angeles City College, 1952. Dir.-mgr. Little Theatre, L.A. Group, 3 yrs.; actor, 6 years; acting member Catholic Coll. Thea., Santa Monica Thea. Group, Pilgrimage Play Thea. Group, 3 yrs., producer: Three Wishes for Jamie, Bullfight; assoc. prod., asst. prod., Viscount Films, Inc. 1957–59; dir., N.A.B.E.T.; acted: Unexpected, TV series; producer, TV pilots, 1958; asst. prod., pictures; Tank Battalian, Speed Crazy; pres., exec. prod. Marqhis Productions, Inc., 1959; assoc. prod., Why Must I Die?

DE CAMP, ROSEMARY: Actress. b. Prescott AZ, 1913.
TELEVISION: Robert Cummings Show, That Girl, Life of Riley (with Jackie Gleason); Death Valley Days; Partridge Family; Love American Style, Police Story, Rockford Files, Days of Our Lives, Misadventures of Sheriff Lobo, Love Boat, Blind Ambition, B.J. & the Bear.
PICTURES: Cheers for Miss Bishop, Hold Back the Dawn, Jungle Book, Yankee Doodle Dandy, Eyes in the Night, Pride of the Marines, Look for the Silver Lining, Story of Seabiscuit, Big Hangover, Scandal Sheet, On Moonlight Bay, Treasure of Los Canyon, By the Light of the Silvery Moon, Main Street to Broadway, So This Is Love, Many Rivers to Cross, Strategic Air Command, Saturday the 14th.

DE CAPRIO, AL: Producer-director. e. Brooklyn Tech., NYU. Started as radio engineer, cameraman, tech. dir., prod. & dir. CBS; dir. Sgt. Bilko, Car 54 Where Are You?, Musical specials for ABC, CBS, NBC; v.p. exec. prod. dir., MPO Videotronics, Pres. World Wide Videotape.

DE CARLO, YVONNE: Actress. b. Vancouver, B.C., Sept. 1, 1926. e. Vancouver School of Drama, Fanchon & Marco, Hollywood. Specialty dancing at Florentine Gardens, Earl Carroll's; m.p. debut in This Gun for Hire, 1942. One-woman club act and 7-person club act. Autobiography, Yvonne (1987).
PICTURES: Harvard Here I Come, Youth on Parade, Road to Morocco, Story of Dr. Wassell, Salome, Where She Danced; Frontier Gal, Brute Force, Song of Scheherazade, Black Bart, Casbah, River Lady, Criss Cross, Gal Who Took the West, Calamity Jane and Sam Bass, Buccaneer's Girl, Tomahawk, Hotel Sahara, Silver City, Scarlet Angel, San Francisco Story, Hurricane Smith, Sombrero, Sea Devils, Fort Algiers, Border River, Captain's Paradise, Passion, Tonight's the Night, Shotgun, Magic Fire, Flame of the Islands, Ten Commandments, Raw Edge, Death of a Scoundrel, Band of Angels, Timbuktu, Law of the Lawless, Munster Go Home, Hostile Guns, The Power, McClintock, Play Dead, Satan's Cheerleaders, Guyana Cult of the Damned, The Man With Bogart's Face, Liar's Moon, American Gothic, Cellar Dweller.
BROADWAY STAGE: Follies.
TELEVISION: The Munsters (series), The Mark of Zorro, A Masterpiece of Murder. Guest: Bonanza, Man From U.N.C.L.E., Murder, She Wrote, Hollywood Sign (special), Johnny Carson, Merv Griffin, Steve Allen, David Frost, Perry Como.

DE CORDOVA, FREDERICK: Director. b. New York, NY, Oct. 27, 1910. e. Northwestern U., B.S. 1931. Gen. stage dir. Shubert enterprises, N.Y., 1938–41; same for Alfred Bloomingdale Prods., N.Y., and prod. Louisville (Ky.) Amphitheatre 1942–43; m.p. dir. Author: Johnny Came Lately, 1988.
PICTURES: (dial. dir.) San Antonio, Janie, Between Two Worlds; (dir.) Too Young to Know, Her Kind of Man, That Way with Women, Always Together, Wallflower, For the Love of Mary, Countess of Monte Cristo, Illegal Entry, Girl Who Took the West, Buccaneer's Girl, Peggy, Desert Hawk, Bedtime for Bonzo, Katie Did It, Little Egypt, Finders Keepers, Here Come the Nelsons, Yankee Buccaneer, Bonzo Goes to College, Column South.
TELEVISION: prod., dir. Burns and Allen, 1955–56; prod., December Bride, 1954–55; prod. and dir., Mr. Adams and Eve, prod. dir. December Bride; prod. dir. George Gobel Show; prod. dir., Jack Benny Program, 1960–63; dir., program planning, Screen Gems, 1964; prod. dir., Smothers Bros. Show, 1965–66; 1965 dir. I'll Take Sweden and Frankie & Johnny; 1966–70 dir. My Three Sons; 1971–present, prod., Tonight Show.

DE CUIR, JOHN: Art Director-Production Designer. b. San Francisco, CA. 1918. Universal 1938–49; Mark Hellinger Prods., 1946. 20th Fox 1949. Nominated for Acad. Award 11 times.
PICTURES: The Naked City, Snows of Kilimanjaro, My Cousin Rachel, Call Me Madam, Three Coins in the Fountain, There's No Business Like Show Business, Daddy Long Legs, The King and I (A.A., Art Dir.), Island in the Sun, South

Pacific, The Big Fisherman, A Certain Smile, Cleopatra (A.,A.: Prod. Des.), The Agony and the Ecstasy, The Honey Pot, Zefferelli's Taming of The Shrew, Dr. Faustus, Hello, Dolly! (A.A.: Prod. Des.), On A Clear Day You Can See Forever, The Great White Hope, Once Is Not Enough, That's Entertainment, Too!, The Other Side of Midnight, Ziegfeld: The Man and His Women, Love and Bullets, Charlie, Raise the Titanic, (prod. design), Monsignor, Ghostbusters, (prod. design), Jo Jo Dancer, Legal Eagles.

DeCUIR, JR., JOHN F.: Art Director, Production Designer. b. Burbank, CA, Aug. 4, 1941. e. U. of Southern California, bachelor of architecture, 1965. Son of John F. De Cuir, Sr. 1966–68, U.S. Coast Guard (holds commission with rank of Lt. Commander, USCGR). 1968–72, project designer, Walt Disney World, Walt Disney Prods. 1972–74, dir. of design, Six Flags Corp. 1974–9, project designer, EPCOT, Walt Disney Prods. 1980–86, pres., John F. De Cuir, Jr. Design Consultants, Inc.; 1987-pres., Cinematix Inc.
PICTURES: Illustrator: Cleopatra, The Honey Pot. Design Concepts: The Agony and the Ecstasy. Art Director: Raise the Titanic, Dead Men Don't Wear Plaid, Monsignor (also special effects consultant), Ghostbusters. Producer: Jazz Club, The Baltimore Clipper, The Building Puzzle. Production Designer: Fright Night, Top Gun, Apt Pupil, Eliva, Mistress of the Dark, Turner & Hooch.
TELEVISION: Art Director: Frank Sinatra Special—Old Blue Eyes Is Back, Annual Academy Awards Presentation 1971, Double Agent. Production Design: Double Switch, Earth * Star Voyager.

DEE, RUBY: Actress. b. Cleveland, OH, Oct. 27. e. Hunter Coll. m. actor-dir.-writer Ossie Davis. Worked as apprentice at Amer. Negro Theatre, 1941–44, studied at Actor's Workshop. Stage appearances include Jeb, Anna Lucasta, The World of Sholom Aleichem, A Raisin in the Sun, Purlie Victorious, Wedding Band, Boseman and Lena, Hamlet, Checkmates.
PICTURES: Jackie Robinson Story, Tall Target, Go Man Go, Take a Giant Step, St. Louis Blues, A Raisin in the Sun, Purlie Victorious, The Balcony, Uptight, Buck and the Preacher, Countdown at Kusini, Do the Right Thing.
TELEVISION: Actor's Choice, Seven Times Monday, Go Down Moses, It's Good to Be Alive, Twin-Bit Gardens, Roots: The Next Generation, I Know Why The Caged Bird Sings, Wedding Band, To Be Young, Gifted and Black, The Atlanta Child Murders, Long Day's Journey into Night, Go Tell it on the Mountain, Windmills of the Gods, Gore Vidal's Lincoln. Series: With Ossie and Ruby.

DEE, SANDRA: Actress. b. Bayonne, NJ, April 23, 1942. Modeled, Harry Conover and Huntington Hartford Agencies, N.Y., 1954–56; signed long term exclusive contract, U-I, 1957.
PICTURES: Until They Sail, The Restless Years, Stranger in My Arms, The Reluctant Debutante, Gidget, The Wild and the Innocent, Imitation of Life, Summer Place, Portrait in Black, Romanoff and Juliet, Come September, Tammy Tell Me True, If a Man Answers, Tammy and the Doctor, Take Her, She's Mine, I'd Rather Be Rich, That Funny Feeling, Doctor You've Got to Be Kidding!, Rosie, The Dunwich Horror.

DEELEY, MICHAEL: Producer. b. London, Eng. August 6, 1932. Ent. m.p. ind. 1951 and TV, 1967, as alt. dir. Harlech Television Ltd. Film editor, 1951–58. MCA-TV 1958–61, later with Woodfall as prod. and assoc. prod. Assoc. prod. The Knack, The White Bus, Ride of the Valkyrie. Great Western Investments Ltd.; 1972; Great Western Festivals Ltd.; 1973, man. dir. British Lion Films Ltd. 1975, purchased BLF, Ltd. Appt. Jnt. man. dir. EMI Films Ltd., 1977; pres., EMI Films, 1978, Member Film Industry Interim Action Committee, 1977–82; Deputy Chairman, British Screen Advisory Council, 1985. Appt. Chief Executive Officer, Consolidated Television Production & Distribution Inc., 1984.
PICTURES: Prod. One Way Pendulum, Robbery, The Italian Job, Long Days Dying (exec. prod.), Where's Jack, Sleep Is Lovely, Murphy's War, The Great Western Express, Unbecoming, The Man Who Fell to Earth, Convoy, The Deer Hunter (Acad. Award), Blade Runner, A Gathering of Old Men (exec. prod.).

De HAVILLAND, OLIVIA: Actress b. Tokyo, Japan, July 1, 1916. Sister of actress Joan Fontaine. e. California schools and Notre Dame Convent, Belmont. Acting debut, Max Reinhardt's stage prod., A Midsummer Night's Dream; film debut in m.p. version, 1935; won Academy Award as best actress for To Each His Own, 1946, and The Heiress, 1949; N.Y. Film Critics award twice, 1948–49; Women's Natl. Press Club Award, 1949; Look award, best perf. 3 times, 1941-48-49. Autobiography: Every Frenchman Has One (1960).
PICTURES: Alibi Ike, Captain Blood, The Irish in Us, Anthony Adverse, The Charge of the Light Brigade, Call It a Day, The Great Garrick, It's Love I'm After, The Adventures of Robin Hood, Four's a Crowd, Gold Is Where You Find It, Hard to Get, Dodge City, Gone With the Wind, The Private Lives of Elizabeth and Essex Raffles, Wings of the Navy, My Love Came Back, Santa Fe Trail, Hold Back the Dawn, Strawberry Blonde, In This Our Life, The Male Animal, They Died With Their Boots On, Princess O'Rourke, Government Girl, Dark Mirror, Devotion, To Each His Own, The Well Groomed Bride, Snake Pit, The Heiress, My Cousin Rachel, Not as a Stranger, Ambassador's Daughter, Proud Rebel, Libel, Light in the Piazza, Hush . . . Hush, Sweet Charlotte, Lady in a Cage, The Adventurers, Pope Joan, Airport '77, Behind the Iron Mask, The Swarm.
STAGE: Romeo and Juliet, 1951; U.S. tour Candida, 1951–52, N.Y., 1952; A Gift of Time, Bdwy. 1962.
TELEVISION: Noon Wine (Stage 67). Mini-series: Roots: The Next Generation, North & South Book II. Movies: Anastasia, Agatha Christie's Murder is Easy, The Royal Romance of Charles and Diana, The Screaming Woman, Anastasia: the Mystery of Anna, The Woman He Loved.

DEIN, EDWARD: Director, Writer. b. Chicago, IL.
PICTURES: Dir., s.p. Shack Out on 101, Seven Guns to Sin, Curse of the Undead, Calypso Joe, I Trust My Wife, Hard Yellow, Come Die My Love (Spain), The Naked Sword (Mexico), Gaby (Brazil); story s.p. The Fighting Guardsman, Calling Dr. Death, The Gallant Blade, Leopard Man, All This and More, 13 French Street, Hang Me High; dir., prod., wrote, Capito, in Italy.
TELEVISION: Lawless Years, Hawaiian Eye, Bronco, Philip Marlowe, Not for Hire, Wild, Wild West series.

De LANE LEA, JACQUES: Executive. b. Nice, France, 1931. m. filmmaker Agnes Varda. Early career as prod. shorts, second features; later prod. sup. features. Ent. m.p. ind. 1952, prod. own films. Became man. dir. De Lane Lea Ltd., after death his father 1964. Also dir. Delmore Film Productions Ltd., Mole-Richardson (England) Ltd., Humphries Holdings, Ltd., Int'l Library Service Ltd., CTS Ltd. Pres., dir. gen., SIS (1982), Paris. Director, Video-London Sound Studios, Ltd.

DELANNOY, JEAN: Director. b. Noisy-le-Sec, France, Jan. 12, 1908. e. Université de Paris, Lycée Montaigne, Lycée Louis le Grand, La Sorbonne; actor, 1927–29; film edit., 1929–37; dir., 1937–52.
PICTURES: Black Diamond, The Eternal Return, Symphonie Pastorale, The Chips Are Down, Souvenir, The Secret of Mayerling, Savage Triangle, Moment of Truth, Daughter of Destiny, The Bed, Action Man, La Peau de Torpedo, Pas folle la guêpe, Bernadette.

De LAURENTIIS, DINO: Producer, Executive. b. Torre Annunziata, Italy, Aug. 8, 1919. Took part in Rome Experimental Film Center; dir., prod. chmn. of the bd. and CEO, De Laurentiis Entertainment Group Inc.; founded in 1984 the DEG Film Studios in Wilmington, NC. Resigned 1988.
PICTURES: L'amore Canta, Il Bandito, La Figlia del Capitano, Riso Amaro, La Lupa, Anna, Ulysses, Mambo, La Strada, Gold of Naples, War and Peace, Nights of Cabiria, The Tempest, La Grande Guerra, Five Branded Women, Barabbas, The Bible, Operation Paradise, The Witches, The Stranger, Diabolik, Anzio, Barbarella, Waterloo, Valachi Papers, Stone Killers, Serpico, Death Wish, Casanova, Mandingo, Three Days of the Condor, Drum, Face to Face, Buffalo Bill and the Indians, King Kong, The Shootist, Orca, White Buffalo, Serpent's Egg, King of the Gypsies, The Brink's Job, Hurricane, Flash Gordon, Halloween II, Ragtime, Conan the Barbarian, Fighting Back, Amityville II: The Possession, Halloween III, The Dead Zone, Amityville 3-D, Firestarter, The Bounty, Conan the Destroyer, Stephen King's Cat's Eye, Red Sonja, Year of the Dragon, Marie, Silver Bullett, Raw Deal, Maximum Overdrive, Tai-Pan, Blue Velvet, The Bedroom Window, Crimes of the Heart, King Kong Lives, Million Dollar Mystery, Weeds, The Desperato Hours.

De LAURENTIIS, RAFFAELLA: Producer. Daughter of Dino De Laurentiis. Began career as prod. asst. on father's film Hurricane.Independent producer.
PICTURES: Beyond the Reef, Conan the Barbarian, Conan the Destroyer, Dune, Tai-Pan, Prancer.

De La VARRE, ANDRE, JR.: Producer, Director. b. Vienna, Austria, Oct. 26, 1934. Prod. Grand Tour travelogues; producer of promotion films for KLM, Swissair, tourist offices, recent productions: Bicentennial films for state of Virginia, city of Charleston, NY state; winner, Atlanta Film Festival, Sunset Travel Film Festival; Burton Holmes Travelogue subjects; V-P-R Educational Films; producer, director, lecturer, narrator.

DEL BELSO, RICHARD: Marketing Executive. e. NYU, 1965. Began career in adv./research dept. at Benton & Bowles Advertising, NY. Served as research dept. group head for Kenyon and Eckhart; group head for Grudin/Appell/Haley Research Co. (now known as A/H/F/ Marketing Research, Inc.). Two years as assoc. dir. of mktg., research for Grey Advertising (N.Y.). Joined MCA/Universal in 1976 as assoc. dir., mktg. research. In 1980 named v.p. & dir. of mktg. research for Warner Bros; became worldwide v.p. of mktg. research, 1984.

DELERUE, GEORGES: Composer, Conductor. b. Roubaix, France, 1924. Studied with Busser and Milhaud at Paris Cons. Was conductor for RTF (Radio-TV Français).

PICTURES: Hiroshima Mon Amour (1958), Jeux de L'Amour, Shoot the Piano Player, Jules and Jim, The Soft Skin, The Pumpkin Eater, Viva Maria, A Man for All Seasons, King of Hearts, The 25th Hour, Interlude, Women in Love, The Conformist, The Horsemen, The Day of the Jackal, The Day of the Dolphin, The Slap, Julia, Tender Cop, Dear Inspector, Get Out Your Handkerchiefs, A Little Romance (Acad. Award, 1979), Love on the Run, Day for Night, True Confessions, The Woman Next Door, Rich and Famous, A Little Sex, Partners, Richard's Things, The Last Metro, Broken English, The Escape Artist, Man, Woman and Child, The Black Stallion Returns, Confidentially Yours, Exposed, One Deadly Summer, Silkwood, The Vultures, Mesmerized, Agnes of God, Family Council, Maxie, Salvador, Crimes of the Heart, The Pick-Up Artist, Platoon, The Lonely Passion of Judith Hearne, Paris By Night, The House on Carroll Street, Biloxi Blues, A Summer Story, Chouans!, Memories of Me, Heartbreak Hotel, Twins, Beaches, Her Alibi, Casanova (restored 1927 film), Der Aten (The Spirit).

TELEVISION: Le Chandelier, Photo Souvenir, A Smile for the Crocodile, Our World (Emmy, 1968), Easter Island, The Nile, Borgia, Deadly Intentions, Aurora, Arch of Triumph, Amos, Silence of the Heart, Sword of Gideon, The Execution.

DELFONT, LORD BERNARD: Chairman, First Leisure Corporation PLC. b. Tokmak, Russia, September 5, 1909. Brother of Lord Lew Grade. e. London, England. Dir. more than 30 companies incl. Delfont Productions. Ent. theatrical management 1941. Since presented over 250 shows in London; pantomimes in provinces and seaside shows; presented annual Royal Variety Performance. Controls Prince of Wales Theatre in London's West End. 1969: Chief Barker (Pres.) Variety Club of Great Britain; Companion of the Grand Order of Water Rats, President of Entertainment. Artistes' Benevolent Fund, member of Saints and Sinners organisation.

DELMAINE, BARRY: Writer, Director. b. London. Began motion picture career as extra. Later roles in comedies; then asst. dir. for Gloria Swanson prod. in England. From 1936–39 wrote sketches, lyrics London stage musicals; radio scripts. In 1939 apptd. chief scenarist Gaumont-British Instructional. In 1941 dir. films for Brit. Ministry of Information; 1942–43 scenarist, Brit. War Office mi. training films. In 1944 author & dir. Here We Come Gathering, J. Arthur Rank experimental film for child audiences. In 1946 joined Film Producers Guild, writer, dir.; 1949–50, dir. Concord Productions, Ltd., freelance writer films, radio, TV; s.p. Heir Conditioned; dir. ind. films, Concord Prod. Ltd., ass't dir. Advance Films; The Great Game, Les Parent Terrible (Eng. version), Is Your Honeymoon Really Necessary? Unit dir. Don't Blame the Stork; Unit dir., loc. mgr. Douglas Fairbanks Ltd.; prod. mgr. 1955; prod. mgr. Chase a Crooked Shadow, Ice Cold in Alex, Jetstream; prod. sup. The Night We Dropped a Clanger. Prod. Sup., Nothing Barred; prod. mgr., The Hellions; prod. The Golden Rabbit; prog. sup., Man of The World, Sentimental Agent, assoc. prod., Danger Man (secret agent) series. Assoc. prod., Man in the Suitcase series; Assoc. prod., Strange Report series; assoc. prod. Mr. Jerico feature. TV series: assoc. prod. The Firechasers; prod. Shirley's World; assoc. prod. The Adventurers. Assoc. prod., Three For All. Currently: Freelance Writer and Prod. Consultant.

DELON, ALAIN: Actor. b. Sceaux, France, Nov. 8, 1935. Discovered by Yves Allegret. Served in French Navy as a Marine. Worked as cafe waiter, heavy-load carrier.

PICTURES: When a Woman Gets Involved, Be Beautiful, and Keep Quiet, Plein Soleil and Quelle Joie de Vivre, Rocco and His Brothers, L'Eclipse, The Leopard, The Big Crab, The Black Tulip, The Felines, The Yellow Rolls Royce, The Killers of San Francisco, The Centurions, Is Paris Burning?, Texas, Here We Come, The Adventurers, Extraordinary Stories, Le Samourai, Diaboliquement Votre, The Motorcycle, Goodbye Friend, The Swimming Pool, Jeff, The Sicilian Clan, Borsalino, Red Sun, Assassination of Trotsky, Scorpio, Dirty Money, Mr. Klein, The Concorde-Airport '79, Swann in Love, Separate Rooms, Cop's Honor, The Passage, Let Sleeping Cops Lie (also prod., co-s.p.), Nouvelle Vague.

Del ROSSI, PAUL R.: Executive. b. Winchester, MA, Oct. 19, 1942. e. Harvard Coll, 1964; Harvard Business Sch., 1967. Sr. v.p., The Boston Co., 1977–1980; sr. consultant, Arthur D. Little, Inc.; presently pres., General Cinema Theatres.

De LUISE, DOM: Comedian, Actor. b. Brooklyn, NY, Aug. 1, 1933. e. Tufts Coll. Spent two seasons with Cleveland Playhouse. Launched TV career on The Garry Moore Show with character, Dominick the Great, a bumbling magician.

PICTURES: Fail Safe, The Busybody, The Glass Bottom Boat, 12 Chairs, Who Is Harry Kellerman?, Every Little Crook and Nanny, The Adventures of Sherlock Holmes' Smarter Brother, Silent Movie, The World's Greatest Lover, The End, The Cheap Detective, The Last Married Couple in America, Fatso, Hot Stuff (dir.), Wholly Moses, Smokey and the Bandit II, History of the World—Part I, The Cannonball Run, The Best Little Whorehouse in Texas, Cannonball Run II, Johnny Dangerously, Haunted Honeymoon, My African Adventure, A Taxi Driver in New York, Going Bananas, Oliver & Company (voice), All Doges Go To Heaven (voice), Loose Cannons, Benito (also co-s.p.).

TELEVISION: The Entertainers, The Dean Martin Summer Show, Dom DeLuise Variety Show, The Barrum-Bump Show, The Dean Martin Show, The Tonight Show, Lotsa Luck. Movie: Happy (also exec. prod.).

STAGE: The Student Gypsy, Last of the Red Hot Lovers, Here's Love.

del VALLE, JOHN: Publicist. b. San Francisco, CA, Mar. 23, 1904. e. U. of California. Adv., edit. staff various newspapers including asst. drama ed. S.F. Call-Bulletin, L.A. Mirror; adv.-publicity dir. San Francisco Fox Theatre 1933–36; publicist, Paramount Studio, 1936–42; dir. pub., adv. Arnold Prod. 1946; Chaplin Studios, 1947; Nat Holt Prod., 1948–52; Editor, TV Family mag., N.Y., 1952–53; adv. pub. dir. Century Films, 1954; pub. rel. Academy M.P. Arts & Sciences, 1965; publicist, various U.A. indep. film prod., 1955–56; unit publicist, Para., 1956; TC-F 1957–62, Para., 1962–63; Universal 1964–65; Mirisch Corp.—UA Filming, Hawaii, 1965; pub. rel. and editor, Atomics Int'l div. North American Rockwell, 1966–71; present, freelance writer. NY Times Op. Ed. (1985), Gourmet Mag. (1989), others.

DEMBY, EMANUEL H.: Producer, Writer. b. New York, NY, Dec. 12, 1919. e. City Coll. of New York, New School, Chung Ang U., Ph.D. Pioneered new programs for radio, 1936–47; story dept., Universal Pictures, 1937; writer, Gangbusters, Crime of the Week, Thrill of the Week (NBC, CBS); TV shows; What's Playing, 1950–52; Hollywood to Broadway, How To Be a Cowboy; The Shadow; prod., theatrical features, filmed commercials; pub. rel. consultant. Author: My Forty Year Fight for Korea; Indonesia; King of the Hill; Hot Tip on Wall St.; prod. Cavalcade of Music (TV); The World in Space (TV, theatrical); The Edge of Violence (stage); Man Into Space; Year III-Space Age (TV); The Communications Gap, The Creative Consumer, (P.R. films). Book: Who's Alienated, Youth or Society? Research Consultant, NBC TV News; consultant, Radio Advertising Bureau, Smash, Crash, Pow! (feature).

DEMME, JONATHAN: Director, Writer, Producer. b. Rockville Centre, NY, 1944. e. U. of Florida. First job in industry as usher; was film critic for college paper, The Florida Alligator and the Coral Gable Times. Did publicity work for United Artists, Avco Embassy; sold films for Pathe Contemporary Films; wrote for trade paper, Film Daily, 1966–68. Moved to England in 1969; musical co-ordinator on Irving Allen's EyeWitness in 1970. In 1972 co-prod and co-wrote first film, Angels, Hard As They Come.

PICTURES: Hot Box (prod., co-s.p.); Caged Heat (dir, s.p.); Crazy Mama (dir., s.p.); Fighting Mad (dir., s.p.), Citizen's Band (aka Handle With Care, dir.), Last Embrace (dir.), Melvin and Howard (dir.), Swing Shift (dir.), Stop Making Sense (dir.), Something Wild (co-prod., dir.), Swimming to Cambodia (dir.), Married to the Mob (dir.), The Cannibal Island, Miami Blues.

TELEVISION: Who Am I This Time (dir.), (PBS); Accumation with Talking plus Water Motor (doc. on choreographer Trisha Brown); Survival Guides; numerous music videos (for UB40, Chrissie Hynde, Sun City Video of Artists United Against Apartheid); A Family Tree (Trying Times series, PBS); Haiti: Dreams of Democracy.

VIDEO: Suzanne Vega's Solitude Standing.

De MORNAY, REBECCA: Actress. b. California, 1961. Spent childhood in Europe, graduating from high school in Austria. Returned to America, enrolling at Lee Strasberg's Los Angeles Institute; apprenticed at Zoetrope Studios.

THEATER: Born Yesterday (Pasadena Playhouse).

PICTURES: One from the Heart, Risky Business, Testament, The Slugger's Wife, Runaway Train, The Trip to Bountiful, Beauty and the Beast, And God Created Woman, Feds, Dealers.

TELEVISION: The Murders in the Rue Morgue.

DEMPSEY, PATRICK: Actor. b. Lewiston, ME, 1966. In high school became State downhill skiing champion. Juggling, magic and puppetry led to performances before Elks clubs and community org. Cast by Maine Acting Co. in On Golden Pond. In 1983 acted in Torch Song Trilogy in San Francisco and toured in Brighton Beach Memoirs.

PICTURES: Heaven Help Us, Meatballs III, In the Mood, Can't Buy Me Love, In a Shallow Grave, Happy Together, Some Girls, Iron Will, Loverboy, Coupe de Ville.

TELEVISION: A Fighting Choice (debut), Fast Times at Ridgemont High (series).

DEMY, JACQUES: Director, Writer. b. Pont-Chateau, France, 1931. m. filmmaker Agnes Varda. After completing studies in art and film, worked as asst. to Paul Grimault and Georges Rouquier. Made shorts before dir. first feature Lola (1961).

PICTURES: Lola, Seven Capital Sins, Bay of Angels, The Umbrellas of Cherbourg (Golden Palm Award, Cannes, 1964), The Young Girls of Rochefort (also music), Model Shop, Donkey-Skin, The Pied Piper, The Slightly Pregnant Man,

Lady Oscar, A Room in Town, Parkway, Three Seats for the 26th (dir., s.p.).

DENBAUM, DREW: Director, Screenwriter. b. New York, NY, Dec. 12, 1949. e. The Lawrenceville Sch., 1967; Yale U., 1971; NYU Grad. Institute of Film & TV, 1973–75, asst. to visiting directors Frank Perry and Gilbert Cates.
PICTURES: Writer-Director: Nickel Mountain; Lovesick (dramatic short); The Last Straw (dramatic short based on play by Charles Dizenzo).
AWARDS: First Prize, 20th Century Fox Screenwriting Competition (Caught In the Act); Silver Medal, Chicago Film Festival (Lovesick); Academy Award Finalist (Lovesick); Leo Jaffe Producer's Award (NYU Grad. Inst. of Film & TV); Saybrook Fellows Prize (Yale Univ.); American Legion Award (1964). Lovesick and The Last Straw featured in Cineprobe Series, New York Museum of Modern Art.

DENCH, JUDI, O.B.E.: Actress. b. York, England, 1934. Studied for stage at Central Sch. of Speech and Drama. Theatre debut Old Vic, 1961. Recent Theatre: Cymbeline, Juno and the Paycock, A Kind of Alaska, Importance of Being Earnest, Pack of Lies, Mr. and Mrs. Nobody, Antony and Cleopatra. *Director:* Much Ado About Nothing, Look Back in Anger.
TELEVISION: Major Barbara, Pink String and Sealing Wax, Talking to a Stranger, The Funambulists, Age of Kings, Jackanory, Hilda Lessways, Luther, Neighbours, Parade's End, Marching Song, On Approval, Days to Come, Emilie, The Comedy of Errors, Macbeth (both RSC productions), Langrishe Go Down, On Giant's Shoulders, Love in a Cold Climate, Village Wooing, A Fine Romance (series), The Cherry Orchard, Going Gently, Saigon, Year of the Cat, Ghosts, Behaving Badly.
PICTURES: He Who Rides a Tiger, Study in Terror, Four in the Morning, A Midsummer Night's Dream (RSC Production), The Third Secret, Dead Cert, Wetherby, A Room With a View, 84 Charing Cross Road, A Handful of Dust, Henry V.

DENEAU, SIDNEY, G.: Sales executive. Head film buyer Fabian Theatres; U.S. Army 1942–46; gen. mgr. Schine Theatres 1947; v.p., gen. sales mgr., Selznick Releasing Orgn., 1949; 1956; v.p. asst. gen. sls. mgr., Para. Film Dist., 1958; exec. v.p., Rugoff Theatres, 1964. Resigned, September, 1969 to engage in own theatre consultant business.

DENEUVE, CATHERINE: Actress. r.n. Catherine Dorleac. b. Paris, France, Oct. 22, 1943. Sister was the late Françoise Dorleac.
PICTURES: Les Petits Chats (1956), Les Collegiennes, The Doors Slam, Vice and Virtue, Satan Leads the Dance, Umbrellas of Cherbourg, (received the French Film Academy's best actress award); Repulsion, Le Chant du Monde, La Vie de Chateau, Les Creatures, The Young Girls of Rochefort, Belle de Jour, Benjamin, Manon 70, Mayerling, La Chamade, April Fools, Mississippi Mermaid, Tristana, It Only Happens to Others, Dirty Money, Hustle, Lovers Like Us, Act of Agression, March or Die, La Grande Bourgeoise, The Last Metro, A Second Chance, Reporters, The Hunger, Fort Saganne, Scene of the Crime, FM—Frequency Murder, Drole d'endroit Pour Une Rencontre, Helmut Newton: Frames From the Edge (doc.).

DENHAM, MAURICE: Actor. b. Beckenham, Kent, England, Dec. 23, 1909. e. Tonbridge Sch. Started theatrical career with repertory com. 1934. Served in W.W.II. Played in numerous plays, films & radio shows.
PICTURES: Blanche Fury, London Belongs To Me, It's Not Cricket, Traveller's Joy, Landfall, Spider and the Fly, No Highway in the Sky, The Net, Time Bomb, Street Corner (Both Sides of the Law), Million Pound Note (Man With a Million), Eight O'Clock Walk, Purple Plain, Simon and Laura, 23 Paces to Baker Street, Checkpoint, Carrington V.C. (Court Martial), Doctor at Sea, Night of the Demon, Man With a Dog, Barnacle Bill, The Captain's Table, Our Man in Havana, Sink the Bismark, Two-Way Stretch, Greengage Summer, Invasion, Quartette, The Mark, HMS Defiant.
RECENT PICTURES: The Very Edge, Paranoiac, The Set Up, Penang, The King's Breakfast, Downfall, Hysteria, The Uncle, Operation Crossbow, Legend of Dick Turpin, The Alphabet Murders, The Night Callers, The Nanny, Those Magnificent Men in Their Flying Machines, Heroes of Telemark, After the Fox, The Torture Garden, The Long Duel, The Eliminator, Danger Route, Attack on the Iron Coast, The Best House in London, Negatives, The Midas Run, Some Girls Do, The Touch of Love, The Virgin and the Gypsy, Bloody Sunday, Countess Dracula, Nicholas and Alexandra, The Day of the Jackal, Luther, Shout at the Devil, Julia, The Recluse, From a Far Country, Mr. Love, The Chain, Monsignor Quixote, Murder on the Orient Express, 84 Charing Cross Road.
TELEVISION: Uncle Harry, Day of the Monkey, Miss Mabel, Angel Pavement, The Paraguayan Harp, The Wild Bird, Soldier Soldier, Changing Values, Maigret, The Assassins, Saturday Spectacular, Vanishing Act, A Chance in Life, Virtue, Somerset Maugham, Three of a Kind, Sapper, Pig in the Middle, Their Obedient Servants, Long Past Glory, Devil in The Wind, Any Other Business, The Retired Colourman, Sherlock Holmes (series), Blackmail, Knock on Any Door, Danger Man, Dr. Finley's Casebook, How to Get Rid of Your Husband, Talking to a Stranger, A Slight Ache, From Chekhov with Love, Home Sweet Honeycomb, St. Joan, Julius Caesar, Golden Days, Marshall Petain, The Lotus Eaters, Fall of Eagles, Carnforth Practice. The Unofficial Rose, Omnibus, Balzac, Loves Labour Lost, Angels, Huggy Bear, The Portrait, The Crumbles Murder, A Chink In The Wall, Porridge, For God's Sake, Bosch, Marie Curie, Upchat Line, Secret Army, My Son, My Son, Edward and Mrs. Simpson, Gate of Eden, Potting Shed, Double Dealer, Minder, Agatha Christie Hour, Chinese Detective, The Old Men at the Zoo, The Hope and the Glory, Luther, Love Song, Mr. Palfrey, The Black Tower, Boon, Rumpole, All Passions Spent, Trial of Klaus Barbie, Miss Marple, Tears in the Rain, Behaving Badly, Seeing in the Dark.

DE NIRO, ROBERT: Actor. b. New York, NY, Aug. 17, 1943. Studied acting with Stella Adler and Lee Strasberg.
THEATER: One Night Stand of a Noisy Passenger (off-Bdwy); Cuba and His Teddy Bear (Public Theater and Bdwy., 1986).
PICTURES: Greetings (1968); Sam's Song, The Wedding Party, Jennifer on My Mind, Bloody Mama, Hi, Mom, Born to Win, The Gang That Couldn't Shoot Straight, Bang the Drum Slowly, Mean Streets, Godfather II (Academy Award, best supporting actor, 1974), Taxi Driver, 1900, The Last Tycoon, New York, New York, The Deer Hunter, Raging Bull (Academy Award, 1980), True Confessions, The King of Comedy, Once Upon a Time in America, Falling in Love, Brazil, The Mission, Angel Heart, The Untouchables, Midnight Run, Dear America: Letters Home From Vietnam (reader), Jacknife, Stanley and Iris, We're No Angels, Good Fellas, Awakenings.

DENISON, MICHAEL: C.B.E., Actor. b. Doncaster, York, Eng., Nov. 1, 1915. e. Harrow, Magdalen Coll., Oxford and Webber Douglas Sch. m. Dulcie Gray, actress. Served overseas, Capt. Intelligence Corps, 1940–46. On stage first, 1938, Charlie's Aunt. Screen debut 1940, Tilly of Bloomsbury.
THEATRE: 50 London plays including Ever Since Paradise, Rain on the Just, Queen Elizabeth Slept Here, Fourposter, Dragon's Mouth, Bad Samaritan; Shakespeare Season Stratford-on-Avon; Edinburgh Festival. Meet Me By Moonlight, Let Them Eat Cake, Candida, Heartbreak House, My Fair Lady (Australia), Where Angels Fear to Tread, Hostile Witness, An Ideal Husband, On Approval, Happy Family, No. 10, Out of the Question, Trio, The Wild Duck, The Clandestine Marriage, The Dragon Variation, At the End of the Day, The Sack Race, Peter Pan, The Black Mikado, The First Mrs. Fraser, The Earl and the Pussycat, Robert and Elizabeth, The Cabinet Minister, Old Vic Season: Twelfth Night, Lady's Not for Burning, Ivanov, Bedroom Farce, The Kingfisher, Relatively Speaking, Coat of Varnish, Capt. Brassbound's Conversion, School for Scandal, Song at Twilight, See How They Run, The Tempest, Ring Round the Moon, The Apple Cart, Court in the Act, You Never Can Tell, The Chalk Garden.
PICTURES: Hungry Hill, My Brother Jonathan, The Blind Goddess, The Glass Mountain, Landfall, The Franchise Affair, Angels One Five, Tall Headlines, Importance of Being Earnest, There Was a Young Lady, Contraband Spain, The Truth About Women, Faces in the Dark.
TELEVISION: Boyd QC Series, Funeral Games, Unexpectedly Vacant, Tale of Piccadilly, The Twelve Pound Look, The Provincial Lady, Subject: This Is Your Life, Bedroom Farce, Private Schultz, Blood Money, The Critic, Scorpion, Cold Warrior, Good Behavior.

DENNEHY, BRIAN: Actor. b. Bridgeport, CT, 1939. e. Columbia U. In Marine Corps five years, including Vietnam. After discharge in 1965 studied with acting coaches in N.Y., while working at part time jobs as a salesman, bartender, truck driver. Cast by Michael Ritchie in Semi-Tough, 1977.
THEATER: Streamers, Galileo (Goodman Theatre), The Cherry Orchard.
PICTURES: Looking for Mr. Goodbar, Foul Play, F.I.S.T., 10, Butch and Sundance: The Early Days, Little Miss Marker, Split Image, First Blood, Never Cry Wolf, Gorky Park, Finders Keepers, River Rat, Cocoon, Silverado, The Check Is in the Mail, F/X, Twice in a Lifetime, Legal Eagles, Best Seller, The Belly of an Architect, Return to Snowy River, Part II, Cocoon II: The Return, Miles From Home, Indigo, The Artisan, Street Legal, Presumed Innocent.
TELEVISION: Movies: It Happened at Lake Wood Manor (1977), Johnny We Hardly Knew Ye, Pearl, Real American Hero, A Death in Canaan, Ruby and Oswald, The Jericho Mile, Dummy, Silent Victory: The Kitty O'Neil Story, A Rumor of War, The Seduction of Miss Leona, Skokie, Fly Away Home, I Take These Men, Off Sides, Blood Feud, The Last Place on Earth, Evergreen, Acceptable Risks, Private Sessions, The Lion of Africa, A Father's Revenge, Day One, Perfect Witness, Pride and Extreme Prejudice. Series: Big Shamus, Little Shamus, Star of the Family, Cagney and Lacey, Hunter, Tall Tales (Annie Oakley).

DENNIS, SANDY: Actress. b. Hastings, NB, April 27, 1937. m. Gerry Mulligan. Joined the Lincoln Community Theatre group. Made her professional acting debut in summer stock at London, NH. Studied with Herbert Berghof, N.Y. Understudy for N.Y. prod. Dark at the Top of the Stairs. Broadway debut in Burning Bright (1960).
THEATER: Face of A Hero; The Complaisant Lover; A Thousand Clowns (Tony Award, best sup. actress, 1963); Any Wednesday (Tony Award, 1964); Daphne in Cottage D; How the Other Half Loves; Let Me Hear You Smile; Absurd Person Singular; Same Time, Next Year; Come Back to the 5 & Dime, Jimmy Dean, Jimmy Dean; Buried Inside Extra.
PICTURES: Who's Afraid of Virginia Woolf? (Acad. Award, best supporting actress), Up the Down Staircase, Sweet November, The Fox, Thank You All Very Much, That Cold Day in the Park, The Out-of-Towners, Nasty Habits, The Four Seasons; Another Woman, Parents, 976-EVIL.
TELEVISION: The Execution, Perfect Gentlemen, Something Evil, Alfred Hitchcock Presents (1985).

DE NORMAND, GEORGE: Actor, Director. b. New York, NY, Sept. 22. Actor many westerns & TV series; dir., TV series, Man of Tomorrow. Member: SAG, SEG, NSTP.

DENVER, BOB: Actor. b. New Rochelle, NY, 1935.
PICTURES: Take Her She's Mine, For Those Who Think Young, Who's Minding the Mint? The Sweet Ride, Do You Know the One About the Travelling Saleslady?
TELEVISION: Dobie Gillis, Gilligan's Island, Dusty's Trail, The Castaways on Gilligan's Island; Bring Me the Head of Dobie Gillis.

DENVER, JOHN: Singer, Actor. r.n. Henry John Deutschendorf. b. Roswell, NM, Dec. 31, 1943. Records, concerts, nightclubs.
PICTURES: Oh, God!, America Censored.
TELEVISION: An Evening with John Denver (Emmy, 1975), Rocky Mountain Christmas, John Denver and the Muppets, Rocky Mountain Holiday, Salute to Lady Liberty, Jacques Costeau—The First 75 Years, Julie Andrews . . . The Sound of Christmas. Movies: The Christmas Gift, Foxfire, Higher Ground (co-exec. prod., co-music, actor), John Denver's Christmas in Aspen.

DE PALMA, BRIAN: Director, Writer. b. Newark, NJ, Sept. 11, 1940. e. Columbia U.,B.A.; Sarah Lawrence, M.A. While in college made series of shorts, including Wotan's Wake, winner of Rosenthal Foundation Award for best film made by American under 25. Also judged most popular film of Midwest Film Festival (1963); later shown at San Francisco Film Festival. Dir.: The Responsive Eye (doc., 1966).
PICTURES: Murder a La Mod, Greetings (also ed.), The Wedding Party (also co-s.p., prod., ed.), Hi Mom, Dionysus in '69 (also co-prod., co-cine., co-ed.), Get To Know Your Rabbit, Sisters (also co-s.p.), Phantom of the Paradise (also co-s.p.), Obsession (also co-s.p.), Carrie, The Fury, Home Movies (dir., s.p. and co-prod.), Dressed to Kill (also s.p.), Blow Out (also s.p.), Scarface, Body Double (prod., dir., s.p.), Wiseguys (dir.), The Untouchables (dir.), Casualties of War, The Bonfire of the Vanities.

DEPARDIEU, GERARD: Actor. b. Chateauroux, France, Dec. 27, 1948. Studied acting at Theatre National Populaire in Paris. Made film debut at 16 in short by Roger Leenhardt (Le Beatnik et Le Minet). Acted in feature film by Agnes Varda (uncompleted).
PICTURES: Going Places, Stavisky, 1900, Vincent François, Paul and the Others; Maitresse, The Last Woman, Barocco, Le Camion, Get Out Your Handkerchiefs, Loulou, The Last Metro, Mon Oncle d'Amerique, The Woman Next Door, La Chevre, The Return of Martin Guerre, The Moon in the Gutter, Les Comperes, Fort Saganne, Police, One Woman or Two, Menage, Jean de Florette, Under Satan's Sun, Traffic Jam, Five Days in June, I Want to Go Home, A Strange Place for an Encounter, Camille Claudel, Troup Belle Pour Toi, Deux, Green Card, Cyrano de Bergerac.

DEPEW, RICHARD H.: Executive. b. New York, NY, Jan. 16, 1925. e. Princeton U. U.S. Navy; American Broadcasting Co., 1947; television director, 1950; assistant, Eastern TV network program director, 1953; mgr. of TV network program oper., 1954–57; Cunningham & Walsh; Radio & TV acct. supv. & programming coordinator, 1961–65 v.p. & dir. of TV programming; 1965 Broadcast supr., Ogilvy and Mather; 1967, v.p. dir. TV programing Fuller & Smith & Ross. V.P. Media and Programming 1969, FSR.; 1973, Director of Corporate Underwriting Department WNET/13, Educational Broadcasting Corp. 1977 Management Supervisor, J. Walter Thompson, N.Y.; 1978, v.p., Account Director, 1980, Marsteller, Inc., mgt. supvr., v.p., corporate adv., Doremus & Co., 1983; exec. v.p., Knox Minisk & Harwood, Stowe, VT.

DEPP, JOHNNY: Actor. b. Kentucky, 1964. Raised in Miramar, FL. At 13 started own rock group and has since been in 15 different groups. Played lead guitar with band The Kids, with whom he moved to L.A. in 1983. With no prior acting experience made film debut in A Nightmare on Elm Street.
PICTURES: A Nightmare on Elm Street, Private Resort, Platoon, Cry Baby.
TELEVISION: Series: 21 Jump Street.

DEREK, BO: Actress. r.n. Cathleen Collins. b. Torrance, CA., Nov. 20, 1956. Discovered by John Derek, actor turned filmmaker. Now married to him. Film debut in Orca (1977).
PICTURES: 10, Once Upon A Time, Change of Seasons, Tarzan, the Ape Man (also prod.), Bolero (also prod.), Ghosts Can't Do It (also prod.).

DEREK, JOHN: Actor, Producer, Director. b. Hollywood, CA, August 12, 1926. Acting debut in 1945 in I'll Be Seeing You; appeared in numerous films throughout 1950s. In 1963, Nightmare in the Sun (debut as prod., dir., cinematographer), followed by Once Before I Die, 1965.
PICTURES: Actor: Knock on Any Door, All the King's Men, Mask of the Avenger, Scandal Sheet, Mission Over Korea, The Adventures of Hajji Baba, Prince of Players, Run for Cover, The Leather Saint, The Ten Commandments, Omar Khayyam, Prisoner of the Volga, Exodus. Prod., dir., s.p., cinematography: A Boy . . . a Girl, Childish Things, Once Upon a Time, Tarzan, The Ape Man (dir., cinematography), Bolero (dir., s.p., cinematography), Ghosts Can't Do It (dir., cinematography).

DERN, BRUCE: Actor. b. Chicago, IL, June 4, 1936. e. U. of Pennsylvania. Studied acting with Gordon Phillips, member, Actor's Studio, 1959 after N.Y. debut in Shadow of a Gunman. Broadway: Sweet Bird of Youth, Orpheus Descending.
PICTURES: The Trip, The Wild Angels, Hush, Hush, Sweet Charlotte, Support Your Local Sheriff, Thumb-tripping, Drive, He Said; They Shoot Horses, Don't They?; The Cowboys, Silent Running, The King of Marvin Gardens, The Laughing Policeman, The Great Gatsby, Smile, Posse, Family Plot, Won Ton Ton, Black Sunday, Coming Home, The Driver, Middle Age Crazy, Tattoo, That Championship Season, On the Edge, The Big Town, World Gone Wild, 1969, The 'Burbs.
TELEVISION: Space, Toughlove, Roses Are for the Rich, Uncle Tom's Cabin, Trenchcoat in Paradise.

DERN, LAURA: Actress. b. Los Angeles, CA, 1966. Daughter of actors Diane Ladd and Bruce Dern. Was an extra in several of her father's films and her mother's Alice Doesn't Live Here Anymore. Film debut at age 11 in Foxes (1980).
PICTURES: Teachers, Mask, Smooth Talk, Blue Velvet, Haunted Summer, Wild of Heart.
TELEVISION: Happy Endings, Three Wishes of Bill Greer.

DE SANTIS, GIUSEPPE: Director. b. Italy, 1917. Film publicist; asst. dir.
PICTURES: Tragic Hunt, Bitter Rice, Under the Olive Tree, Rome 11 O'Clock, A Husband for Anna Zaccheo, Days of Love.

DE SANTIS, GREGORY JOSEPH: Producer, Writer, Director. b. Los Angeles, CA, July 12, 1947. e. U.S.C., Canaan Coll, Franklin Pierce Coll, Durham U., Hatfield Coll. 1970–74 owned commercial prod. co.: wrote, prod., dir. radio and TV commercials; 1972–74 owned marketing firm; 1974– present pres. of prod. placement co. that phased into prod. of TV documentary Volleyball: A Sport Come of Age. Cameo performance in Moon Rise (1974). Pres. & CEO The Beverly Hills Org. and Beverly Hills Productions Ltd.
PICTURES: Prod.: Diary of a Surfing Film, The Companion, Die Sister Die, Our Musical (also writer), Zioux (s.p. only), Car Trouble, Pass the Buck (also dir., s.p.), Beverly Hills (s.p.).
TELEVISION: California Day (co-prod.), The Bell (prod.).

DE SCHAAP, PHILIP: Former Dutch correspondent, Quigley Publications, N.Y. b. Amsterdam, Holland, May 26, 1911. Entered m.p. ind. 1934 as publicity mgr., MGM br. office, Amsterdam; in 1936 corresp. for Quigley Publications. Also in 1937 exploitation mgr., RKO Radio Pictures, Amsterdam; to Paris 1938 as spec. publicity repr. in Paris and Brussels, RKO: in 1939 org. own co. for exploitation and publicity; nonactive 1940–45; on Oct. 1, 1945 estab. Phidesa Publiciteitsbureau voor de Filmbranche.

DESCHANEL, CALEB: Cinematographer, Director. b. Philadelphia, PA, Sept. 21, 1941. m. actress Mary Jo Deschanel. e. Johns Hopkins U., U. of Southern California Film Sch. Studied at Amer. Film Inst., interned under Gordon Willis then started making commercials, short subjects, docs.
PICTURES: *Cinematographer:* More American Graffiti, Being There, The Black Stallion, Apocalypse Now (2nd unit photog.), The Right Stuff, Let's Spend the Night Together (co-cinematographer), The Black Stallion Returns (add. photog. only), The Natural, The Slugger's Wife. *Director:* The Escape Artist, Crusoe.

DE TITTA ARTHUR A.: Newsreel editor. b. North Bergen, NJ, July 9, 1904. Began work 1916 in employ newspaper in Union City, NJ; joined Fox Film Corp., N.Y. office & lab. staff; later became asst. & second cameraman, performing in that capacity numerous pictures Fox and other producers. (The Mountain Woman, When Knighthood Was in Flower, The

Royale Girl, East Side, West Side, Untamed, etc.). In 1928 joined Movietonnews, Inc.; Wash. (D.C.) suprv. to 1938; asst. Europ. supvr. to 1940; Pacific Coast supvr. to 1943. Commis. Lt. USNR, assigned to M.P. Sect., 1943; ret. 1944. Appt. news ed. Movietonews; west coast superv., 1951–63; pub. rel., prod., documentaries; West Coast Bureau mgr. for foreign editions of Movietone News, now retired.

DE TOTH, ANDRE: Writer, Director, Producer. b. Hungary. Dir.-writer European films, 1931–39; U.S. assoc. Alexander Korda prod., 1940; dir. Columbia, 1943; assoc. David Selznick, 1943; assoc. Hunt Stromberg-UA, 1944–45; staff dir., Enterprise 1946–47; dir., 20th-Fox, 1948–49; collab. story, The Gunfighter; dir., Columbia & Warner Bros., 1951; contract dir., Warner Bros., 1952; U.A. Columbia, W.B., 1953–55; Palladiums U.A., Denmark, 1956; Col. U.A. 1957; Columbia, 1960; assoc., Sam Spiegel, Horizon Pictures, Columbia, 1962; Harry Saltzman, Lowndes Prod., U.A. 1966–68; National General, 1969–70.
PICTURES: Passport to Suez, None Shall Escape, Since You Went Away, Pitfall, Springfield Rifle, Thunder Over the Plains, House of Wax, Bounty Hunter, Tanganyika, Indian Fighter, Monkey on My Back, Two Headed Spy, Man on a String, Morgan, The Pirate, The Mongols, Gold for the Caesars, Billion Dollar Brain, Play Dirty, El Condor, The Dangerous Game.

DEUTCH, HOWARD: Director. b. New York, NY. e. Ohio State U. Son of music publisher Murray Deutch. Spent almost 10 yrs. working in various film media, including music videos and film trailer advertising, before feature directorial debut with Pretty in Pink, 1986.
PICTURES: Some Kind of Wonderful, The Great Outdoors.

DEUTCHMAN, IRA J.: Executive. b. Cherry Point, NC, Mar. 24, 1953. e. Northwestern U., B.S., majoring in film. Began career with Cinema 5, Ltd. serving, 1975–79, as non-theatrical sls. mgr.; dir. theatrical adv./pub./dir. acquisitions. Joined United Artists Classics, 1981 as dir. of adv./pub. 1982, left to become one of the founding partners in Cinecom Intl. Films, where headed mktg./dist. div. from inception. Resigned, Jan. 1989. Adjunct prof. Columbia U. film dept. Serves on board of Independent Feature Project-West and Collective for Living Cinema. On advisory bds. U.S. Film Festival and the Sundance Institute.
PICTURES: Miles From Home (co-exec. prod.), Scenes from the Class Struggle in Beverly Hills (exec. prod.).

DEUTSCH, ARMAND S.: Producer. b. Chicago, IL, Jan. 25, 1913. e. U. of Chicago, 1935, B.A. Producer, MGM.
PICTURES: Ambush, Right Cross, Magnificent Yankee, Three Guys Named Mike, Kind Lady, Girl in White, Carbine Williams, Girl who Had Everything, Green Fire, Slander.

DEUTSCH, DAVID: Producer, Writer. b. Birmingham, England, January 10, 1926. e. in Birmingham and Queen Mary Coll., London U. Ent. m.p. ind. apprentice at Gainsborough Pictures, Ltd., 1949; asst. Sydney Box, 1954; J. Arthur Rank asst. to prod. 1955 Lost. Anglo Amalgamated Film Dist. Ltd., as exec. in chrg. prod., 1960.
PICTURES: Assoc. prod. High Tide at Noon, The One That Got Away, Floods of Fear; prod. Blind Date; Play It Cool, 1962, Nothing But the Best, Catch Us If You Can, Interlude, Lock Up Your Daughter, A Day in the Death of Joe Egg; Co-prod. The Day of the Jackal; s.p., The Blue Train, The Jacaranda Tree; Prod. Shakespeare Lives; prod. The Chain; prod. The Verger, Mr. Knowall and The Colonel's Lady.

DEUTSCH, HELEN: Writer. b. New York, NY. e. Barnard Coll., B.A. Author: The Provincetown. Wrote book of Broadway musical, Carnival, 1961.
PICTURES: Seventh Cross, National Velvet, King Solomon's Mines, Golden Earrings, Kim, Plymouth Adventure, Lili, The Glass Slipper, I'll Cry Tomorrow, Forever Darling.
TELEVISION: Jack and the Beanstalk, NBC Gen. Motors 50th Anniv. Show, 1957.

DEUTSCH, STEPHEN: Producer. b. Los Angeles, CA, June 30, 1946. e. UCLA, B.A.; Loyola Law Sch., 1974. Son of late S. Sylvan Simon. Stepson of Armand Deutsch. Private law practice before joining Rastar 1976 as asst. to Ray Stark; 1977, sr. v.p., Rastar; prod. head for SLM Inc. Film Co. entered independent prod. 1978.
PICTURES: Somewhere in Time; All the Right Moves, Russkies (co-exec. prod.), She's Out of Control, Bill & Ted's Excellent Adventure (exec. prod.), Lucky Stiff.

DEVANE, WILLIAM: Actor. b. New York, NY, Sept. 5, 1939. Appeared in some 15 productions with N.Y. Shakespeare Festival and Bdwy off-Bdwy. shows before heading for California and films and TV.
PICTURES: Bad News Bears in Breaking Training, Rolling Thunder, Marathon Man, Yanks, Honky Tonk Freeway, Testament, Vital Signs.
TELEVISION: The Big Easy, Jane Doe, The Missiles of October, Fear on Trial, From Here to Eternity (series), Knots Landing (series), Timestalker, With Intent to Kill, Black Beauty, Heavenly Curse, Chips, The War Dog.

DE VITO, DANNY: Actor. b. Asbury Park, NJ, Nov. 17, 1944. m. actress Rhea Perlman. e. Oratory Prep Sch. Studied at American Acad. of Dramatic Arts. Wilfred Acad. of Hair and Beauty Culture. At 18 worked as hair dresser for 1 yr. at his sister's shop. NY stage in The Man With a Flower in His Mouth (debut, 1969), Prod. short films: The Sound Sleeper (1973), Minestore (1975). Down the Morning Line, The Line of Least Existence, The Shrinking Bride, Call Me Charlie, Comedy of Errors, Merry Wives of Windsor (NYSF). Three By Pirandello. Performance in One Flew Over the Cuckoo's Nest led to casting in the film version.
PICTURES: Deadly Hero (small bit, 1976), Lady Liberty, Scalawag, Hurry Up or I'll be 30, One Flew Over the Cuckoo's Nest, Car Wash, The Van, The World's Greatest Lover, Goin' South, Goin' Ape, Terms of Endearment, Romancing the Stone, Johnny Dangerously, Head Office, Jewel of the Nile, Wiseguys, Ruthless People, Tin Men, Throw Momma from the Train (also dir.), Twins, War of the Roses (dir., actor).
TELEVISION: Series: Taxi (also dir.); Mary (dir. only); Movies: Valentine, The Rating Game (dir.); All the Kids Do It (Afterschool Special), A Very Special Christmas Party, Two Daddies? (voice).

DEWHURST, COLLEEN: Actress. b. Montreal, Canada, June 3, 1926. e. Downer Coll., Milwaukee; Acad. of Dramatic Art; student of Harold Clurman and Joseph Anthony. Theater debut: The Royal Family (1946). Gained fame as stage actress.
THEATER: Desire Under the Elms, Tamberlain the Great, Camille, The Eagle Has Two Heads, The Country Wife, All The Way Home, Great Day in the Morning, Ballad of the Sad Cafe, Taming of the Shrew, Hello and Goodbye, Good Woman of Setzuan, More Stately Mansions, Children of Darkness, All Over, Moon For the Misbegotten, Mourning Becomes Elecktra, An Almost Perfect Person, The Queen and the Rebels, Dance of Death, You Can't Take It With You, Who's Afraid of Virginia Woolf? (revival), Ah! Wilderness, Long Day's Journey into Night.
PICTURES: The Nun's Story, A Fine Madness, McQ, The Cowboys, The Last Run, Annie Hall, Ice Castles, When a Stranger Calls, Tribute, The Dead Zone, The Boy Who Could Fly, Obsessed, Bed and Breakfast, Termini Station.
TELEVISION: The Price, The Crucible, The Hands of Cormac Joyce, Jacob and Joseph, Studs Lonigan, The Kitty O'Neill Story, And Baby Makes Six, The Blue and the Gray, The Glitter Dome, You Can't Take It With You, A.D., Between Two Women (Emmy Award), Johnny Bull, Sword of Gideon, Anne of Green Gables—the Sequel: Anne of Avonlea, Jane of Lantern Hill, The March of the Living, Those She Left Behind.

DE WITT, JOYCE: Actress. b. Wheeling, WV, April 23. e. Ball State U., B.A., theatre; UCLA, MFA in acting. Classically trained, worked in theater since 13 as actress and dir. Has staged and/or starred in numerous musical revues.
TELEVISION: Series: Three's Company. Guest: musical specials, children's specials, telethon co-host and series incl. Baretta, The Tony Randall Show, Most Wanted, Risko, Finder of Lost Loves. Movie: With This Ring.

DEY, SUSAN: Actress. b. Pekin, IL, Dec. 10, 1952. Signed as magazine teen model at age 15. Made professional TV debut at 17, appearing in The Partridge Family, 1970–74.
TELEVISION: Series: Barnaby Jones, Hawaii Five-0, Switch, Loves Me, Loves Me Not, L.A. Law. Movies: Cage Without a Key, Terror on the Beach, Mary Jane Harper Cried Last Night, Little Women, The Comeback Kid, The Gift of Life, Sunset Limousine, Echo Park, Angel in Green, A Place at the Table, Love Me Perfect.
PICTURES: Skyjacked, First Love, Looker, Echo Park, That's Adequate.

DE YOUNG, CLIFF: Actor. b. Inglewood, CA, Feb. 12, 1947. e. California State Coll., Illinois State U. On stage in Hair, Sticks and Bones, Two By South, The Three Sisters, The Orphan.
PICTURES: Harry and Tonto, Blue Collar, Pilgrimage. Shock Treatment, Independence Day, The Hunger, Reckless, Protocol, Secret Admirer, F/X, Flight of the Navigator, Bulldance, Rude Awakening, Fear, Pulse, Flashback.
TELEVISION: Sunshine, Sticks and Bones, Centennial, The Lindbergh Kidnapping Case, Scared Straight, Invasion of Privacy, Captains and the Kings, The Seeding of Sarah Burns, The Night that Panicked America, This Girl for Hire, The Awakening of Candra, Master of the Game, Deadly Intentions, King, Sunshine Christmas, Robert Kennedy and His Times, Fun and Games.

DIAMANT, LINCOLN: Executive. Biographer, Historian. b. New York, NY, Jan. 25, 1923. e. Columbia Coll., A.B. cum laude 1943. Cofounder, Columbia U. radio station. WKCR-FM; served in Wash. as prod., Blue Network (NBC), then in NY as CBS newswriter; 1949 joined World Pub. Co. as adv. and promo. dir.; 1952 worked in creative/TV dept. McCann-Erickson, Grey then Ogilvy & Mather ad agencies (winning 6 Clio Awards). Prod. Lend Us Your Ears (broadcast series); founder, pres., Spots Alive, Inc., broadcast adv. consultants, 1969; Author, The Broadcast Communications Dictionary, Anatomy of a Television Commercial, Television's Classic Commercials, biography of Bernard Romans, Chaining the Hudson, Stamping Our History. Contrib., to Effective Advertising, to Messages and Meaning; New Routes to English; columnist Back Stage. Member, Broadcast Pioneers, Acad. TV Arts & Sciences; v.p. Broadcast Advertising Producer's Society of America. Adjunct faculty member, Pace U., Hofstra U. Fellow, Royal Society of Arts. President, Teatown Lake Reservation. Named U.S. Interior Dept.'s National Natural Landmark Patron for Hook Mt. and Nyack Beach State Park.

DIAMOND, BERNARD: Theatre Executive. b. Chicago, IL, Jan. 24, 1918. e. U. of Indiana, U. of Minnesota. Except for military service was with Schine Theatre chain from 1940 to 1963, working up from ass't. mng., booker, buyer, dir. of personnel to gen. mgr. Then joined Loews Theatres; last position, exec. v.p. Retired, 1985.

DIAMOND, NEIL: Singer, Songwriter. b. Brooklyn, NY, Jan. 24, 1941. Many concert tours.
PICTURES: Jonathan Livingston Seagull (music), Every Which Way But Loose (music), The Last Waltz (actor), The Jazz Singer (actor, music).

DICKERSON, ERNEST: Cinematographer. b. Newark, NJ, 1952. e. Howard U., architecture, NYU, grad. film school. First job, filming surgical procedures for Howard U. medical school. At NYU film school shot classmate Spike Lee's student films Sarah, and Joe's Bed Stuy Barbershop: We Cut Heads. Also shot Nike commercial and several music videos including Bruce Springsteen's Born in the U.S.A., Patti LaBelle's Stir It Up and Miles Davis' Tutu; and Branford Marsalis' Royal Garden Blues directed by Spike Lee.
PICTURES: Brother From Another Planet, She's Gotta Have It (also cameo), Krush Groove, School Daze, Raw, Laser Man, Do the Right Thing.

DICKINSON, ANGIE: Actress. r.n. Angeline Brown. b. Kulm, ND, Sept. 30, 1931. e. Immaculate Heart Coll., Glendale Coll., secretarial course. Beauty contest winner.
PICTURES: Lucky Me (small part, 1954), Man With the Gun, The Return of Jack Slade, Tennessee's Partner, The Black Whip, Hidden Guns, Tension at Table Rock, China Gate, Gun the Man Down, Shoot Out at Medicine Bend, Cry Terror, I Married a Woman, Sins of Rachel Cade, Rio Bravo, Bramble Bush, Ocean's 11, A Fever in the Blood, Jessica, Rome Adventure, Capt. Newman, M.D., The Killers, The Art of Love, Cast a Giant Shadow, The Chase, The Last Challenge, Point Blank, Sam Whiskey, Some Kind of Nut, Young Billy Young, Pretty Maids All in a Row, The Resurrection of Zachary Wheeler, The Outside Man, Big, Bad Mama, The Angry Man, Klondike Feaver, Dressed to Kill, Charlie Chan and the Curse of the Dragon Queen, Death Hunt, Big Bad Mama II.
TELEVISION: The Jimmy Durante Show (debut, 1956), Movies: The Love War, Thief, See the Man Run, Pray for the Wildcats, A Sensitive, Passionate Man; Overboard, The Suicide's Wife, One Shoe Makes It Murder, Jealousy, Hollywood Wives, A Touch of Scandal, Pearl, Stillwatch, Police Story, The Freeway Killings, Once Upon A Texas Train. Series: Mickey Spillane's Mike Hammer, Men into Space, Police Woman, Cassie & Co.

DIEHL, WALTER F.: Executive. b. Revere, MA, April 13, 1907. e. Northeastern U., Boston Catholic Labor Guild Sch. Became projectionist in Boston in 1927 and member of Boston Moving Picture Machine Operators Local 182 in 1933. After several years of service on the exec. board became business agent in 1946 and held that post until 1953, when he resigned to accept an appointment as an International Rep., handling assignments throughout New Eng until 1957, when was appointed assistant international president. In 1952 made a member of the Minimum Wage Commission for the amusement industry in the state of Massachusetts. Also served several years on the exec. board of the Boston Central Labor Union and as Labor Rep. on the Suffolk County March of Dimes. Elected IATSE pres. March, 1974., currently International Pres. emeritus, IATSE.

DIETRICH, MARLENE: Actress. r.n. Maria Magdalene von Losch. b. Berlin, Germany, Dec. 27, 1901. e. pvt. sch., Weimar; Musical Acad., Berlin. m. Rudolph Sieber; d. Maria Riva, actress. Stage training, Max Reinhardt's Sch. of Drama; debut in Viennese version of play, Broadway; then mus. com. Film debut Der Mensch am Wege (1923). With Army overseas (USO) 1942–45.
PICTURES: In Germany: Blue Angel; in Hollywood: Morocco, Dishonored, Blonde Venus, Shanghai Express, Scarlet Empress, Song of Songs, The Devil is a Woman, Desire, Angel, Garden of Allah, Knight Without Armour, Destry Rides Again, Seven Sinners, Flame of New Orleans, Manpower, The Lady is Willing, Pittsburgh, The Spoilers, Follow the Boys, Kismet, Golden Earrings, Martin Roumagnac (French), Foreign Affair, Stage Fright, No Highway in the Sky, Rancho Notorious, The Monte Carlo Story, Around the World in 80 Days, Witness for the Prosecution, Touch of Evil, Judgment at Nuremberg, Paris When it Sizzles, Just a Gigolo.

DILLER, BARRY: Executive. b. San Francisco, CA, Feb. 2, 1942. Joined ABC in April, 1966, as asst. to v.p. in chg. programming. In 1968, made exec. asst. to v.p. in chg. programming and dir. of feature films. In 1969, named v.p., feature films and program dev., east coast. In 1971, made v.p., Feature Films and Circle Entertainment, a unit of ABC Entertainment, responsible for selecting, producing and scheduling The Tuesday Movie of the Week, The Wednesday Movie of the Week, and Circle Film original features for airing on ABC-TV, as well as for acquisition and scheduling of theatrical features for telecasting on ABC Sunday Night Movie and ABC Monday Night Movie. In 1973, named v.p. in chg. of prime time TV for ABC Entertainment. In 1974 joined Paramount Pictures as bd. chmn. and chief exec. officer. 1983, named pres. of Gulf & Western Entertainment and Communications Group, while retaining Paramount titles. Resigned from Paramount in 1984 to join 20th Century-Fox as bd. chmn. and chief. exec. officer. Named chmn. & CEO of Fox, Inc. (comprising 20th Fox Film Corp., Fox TV Stations & Fox Bdcstg. Co.), Oct., 1985. Named to bd., News Corp. Ltd., June, 1987.

DILLER, PHYLLIS: Comedienne. b. Lima, OH, July 17, 1917. e. Sherwood Music Sch., 1935–37; Bluffton Coll., OH, 1938–39.
THEATER: Hello, Dolly! (Bdwy), Nunsense (San Francisco)
PICTURES: Boy, Did I Get a Wrong Number!, Mad Monster Party, Eight on the Lam, Did You Hear the One About the Traveling Saleslady, The Private Navy of Sergeant O'Farrell, The Adding Machine, Motel: The Great American Tradition, Tips, Dr. Hackenstein, Friend to Friend.
TELEVISION: Series: The Phyllis Diller Show, ABC 1966–67; The Beautiful Phyllis Diller Show, 1968. Guest spots on major shows here and abroad.
BOOKS: Phyllis Diller's Housekeeping Hints, 1968, Phyllis Diller's Marriage Manual, Phyllis Diller's The Complete Mother, The Joys of Aging and How to Avoid Them.
RECORDS: Verve and Columbia
CONCERTS: A dozen annual piano concerts with symphony orchestras.

DILLMAN, BRADFORD: Actor. b. San Francisco, CA, April 14, 1930. m. actress-model Suzy Parker. e. Yale U., 1951.
THEATER: The Scarecrow (1953), Third Person, Long Day's Journey into Night (premiere), The Fun Couple.
PICTURES: A Certain Smile, In Love and War, Compulsion, Crack in the Mirror, Circle of Deception, Sanctuary, Francis of Assisi, A Rage to Live, Sergeant Ryker, Bridge at Remagen, Jigsaw, Suppose They Gave a War and Nobody Came, Mastermind, Brother John, The Mephisto Waltz, Helicopter Spies, Escape from the Planet of the Apes, The Way We Were, The Iceman Cometh, Chosen Survivors, 99 and 44/100% Dead, Gold, Bug, One Away, The Enforcer, Amsterdam Kill, The Lincoln Conspiracy, The Swarm, Love and Bullets, Piranha, Guyana-Crime of the Century, Running Scared, Sudden Impact, Treasure of the Amazon, Man Outside, Lords of the Deep, Heroes Stand Alone.
TELEVISION: Movies: The Legend of Walks Far Woman, Covenant, Adventures of the Queen, Fear No Evil, Jennifer-A Woman's Story, The Memory of Eva Ryker, Revenge.

DILLON, KEVIN: Actor. b. Mamaroneck, NY, 1965. Younger brother of actor Matt Dillon. Stage work includes Dark at the Top of the Stairs, The Indian Wants the Bronx.
PICTURES: Heaven Help Us (debut, 1985), Platoon, Dear America: Letters Home from Vietnam, Remote Control, The Rescue, The Blob, War Party.

DILLON, MATT: Actor. b. New Rochelle, NY, Feb. 18, 1964. Discovered at age 14 in junior high school by casting dir who cast him in Over the Edge, 1978. Theater debut: Boys of Winter.
PICTURES: Little Darlings, My Bodyguard, Liar's Moon, Tex, The Outsiders, Rumble Fish, The Flamingo Kid, Target, Rebel, Native Son, The Big Town, Kansas, Bloodhounds of Broadway, Drugstore Cowboy, The Crew.

DILLON, MELINDA: Actress. b. Hope, AR, Oct. 13, 1939. Launched career an Broadway in original prod. of Who's Afraid of Virginia Woolf? Screen debut with bit in The April Fools, 1969.
PICTURES: Bound for Glory, Slap Shot, Close Encounters of the Third Kind, F.I.S.T., Absence of Malice, A Christmas Story, The Songwriter, Harry and the Hendersons, Spontaneous Combustion, Staying Together, Capt. America.
TELEVISION: Guest: Twilight Zone, The Jeffersons, Good Morning America, The Today Show, Dick Cavett Show, Dinah Shore Show. Specials: Merv Griffin Special, Paul Sills Story Theatre, The Paul Sand Show. Movies: Hellenger's Law, Critical List, Point of Departure, Enigma, Mississippi, Sara, Space, The Shadow Box, Fallen Angel, Right of Way,

Transplant, Shattered Innocence, Shattered Dreams, Nightbreaker.

DILLOW, JEAN CARMEN: Producer, Writer, Actress, Director. In private life is Jean, Countess de l'Eau. At age 5 on stage, screen as last of the Wampas Baby Stars. Film work in Eng., Germany, Switzerland, Mexico, Italy. Play writing with George S. Kaufman; screenplay-writing with Andrew Solt. Wrote and prod. with John Croydon. Wrote prod., dir., starred in TV feature The Pawn. Stage: There Is No Other Prince but Aly (London), Stage Door, The Man Who Came to Dinner, What a Life. Scripts: Spirit-Doll, The Resurrection. Starred in series of westerns for Republic, Monogram First National, Universal. Sang and danced in musicals and nightclubs. 1979, non-fiction books on phenomena: Do You Hear the Voices? and The Kidnapping of Aldo Moro. 1983 book Western Bullets are Blank, Mommy Angel, Dear Mr. Trump; screenplay The Shoe of the Ghost; teleplays: Jikoku-ten, The Ghost of Palazzo Palladio, Give the Highest Award to Mommy Angel; The House in Athens. 1986, prod., dir., co-starred in film with Rossano Brazzi. Co-starred and prod. with late son Guy. See Carmen Prods. under Corporations.

DIMMOCK, PETER: C.V.O., O.B.E. Vice President-Managing Director, ABC Sports Worldwide Enterprises Ltd. & ABC Sports Intl., Inc., Director Screensport. b. Dec. 6, 1920. e. Dulwich Coll. & in France. R.A.F. pilot & staff officer during war. TV as prod. commentator BBC Outside Broadcasts Dept., 1946. Prod. more than 500 TV relays including telecast from Windsor Castle of King George VI's funeral, 1952. Coronation telecast Westminster Abbey; State Opening Parliament. Commentator, introduced BBC-TV weekly Sportsview, 1954–64. Head of BBC-TV Outside Broadcasts 1954–72. Head of BBC Enterprises 1973, v.p. ABC Cos., Inc., 1977. Fellow Royal TV Society.

DI PIETRA, ROSEMARY: Executive. Joined Paramount Pictures in 1976, rising through ranks to become director-corporate administration. 1985, promoted to exec. dir.-corporate administration.

DISHY, BOB: Actor. b. Brooklyn, NY. e. Syracuse U.
THEATER: Damn Yankees, From A to Z, Second City, Flora the Red Menace, By Jupiter, Something Different, The Goodbye People, The Good Doctor, The Creation of the World and Other Business, An American Millionaire, Sly Fox, Murder at Howard Johnsons, Grown Ups, Cafe Crown.
PICTURES: Tiger Makes Out, Lovers and Other Strangers, The Big Bus, The Last Married Couple in America, First Family, Author! Author!, Brighton Beach Memoirs.
TELEVISION: That Was the Week That Was, (1964–65), Story Theatre (dir.), The Cafeteria, The Comedy Zone.

DISNEY, ROY E.: Producer, Director. Writer, Cameraman, Film editor. b. Los Angeles, CA, Jan. 10, 1930. e. Pomona Coll., CA. 1951 started as page, NBC-TV. Asst. film editor Dragnet TV series. 1952–78, Walt Disney Prods., Burbank, Calif., various capacities; vice chmn. of the board, The Walt Disney Co.; bd. chmn., Shamrock Holdings, Inc., bd. dir., Walt Disney.
PICTURES: Perri, Mysteries of the Deep, Pacific High, Cheetch (exec. prod.).
TELEVISION: Walt Disney's Wonderful World of Color; The Hound That Thought He Was A Raccoon, Sancho, The Homing Steer, The Silver Fox and Sam Davenport, Wonders of the Water World, Legend of Two Gypsy Dogs, Adventure in Wildwood Heart. Also, The Postponed Wedding, (Zorro series), (Wonder World of Color); An Otter in the Family, My Family is a Menagerie, Legend of El Blanco, Pancho, The Fastest Paw in the West, The Owl That Didn't Give A Hoot, Varda the Peregrine Falcon, Cristobalito, The Calypso Colt, Three Without Fear, Hamade and the Pirates, Chango, Guardian of the Mayan Treasure, Nosey, the Sweetest Skunk in the World, Mustang!, Call It Courage, Ringo, the Refugee Raccoon, Shokee, the Everglades Panther, Deacon, the High-Noon Dog, Wise One, Whale's Tooth, Track of African Bongo, Dorsey, the Mail-Carrying Dog.

DIXON, BARBARA: Executive. b. Pasadena CA. e. U. of Southern California. Served as staff member of Senate Judiciary Committee and was deputy dir. of legislation for Sen. Birch Bayh, 1974–79. Left to become dir. of Office of Government & Public Affairs of Natl. Transportation Safety Board. Named v.p., Fratelli Group, p.r. firm in Washington; took leave of absence in 1984 to serve as deputy press secty. to Democratic V.P. candidate, Geraldine Ferraro. In 1985 joined Motion Picture Assn. of America as v.p. for public affairs.

DIXON, DONNA: Actress. b. Alexandria, VA, July 20, 1957. m. actor, writer Dan Aykroyd. e. Studied anthropology and medicine, Mary Washington U. Left to become a model, both on magazine covers and in TV commercials (Vitalis, Max Factor, Gillette). TV debut on comedy series Bosom Buddies.
PICTURES: Dr. Detroit; Twilight Zone—The Movie; Spies Like Us; The Couch Trip; It Had To Be You; Speed Zone, Lucky Stiff.
TELEVISION: Series: Berengers. Movies: Mickey Spillane's Margin for Murder, No Man's Land, Beverly Hills Madam. Specials: Women Who Rate a "10," The Shape of Things, The Rodney Dangerfield Show: I Can't Take it No More.

DIXON, WHEELER WINSTON: Educator, Writer, Filmmaker. b. New Brunswick, NJ, March 12, 1950. e. Rutgers U. In 1960s asst. writer for Time/Life publications; also writer for Interview magazine. 1976, directed TV commercials in NY. Two years with TVTV, Los Angeles, as post-prod. suprv.; produced programming for Theta Cable there. 1978, formed Deliniator Films, Inc., serving as exec. prod./dir. 1982, consultant to Vestron Industries, acquiring classic feature films. Since 1984 has directed film prod. program at Univ. of Nebraska, where holds rank of tenured assoc. prof. 1988, made chair, Film Studies prog.; received Rockefeller Foundation grant. Author: The 'B' Directors, 1985; The Cinematic Vision of F. Scott Fitzgerald, 1986; PRC: A History of Producer's Releasing Corp., 1986; books on Freddie Francis, Terence Fisher, Reginald Le Borg, 1989.

DMYTRYK, EDWARD: Director. b. Grand Forks, B.C., Canada, Sept. 4, 1908. Entered employ Paramount 1923, working as messenger after school. Film editor 1930–1939; dir. from 1939. One of the "Hollywood Ten" who was held in contempt by the House UnAmerican Activities Comm. 1947. The only one to recant. Autobiography: It's a Hell of a Life But Not a Bad Living (1979).
PICTURES: The Hawk, Television Spy, Emergency Squad, Golden Gloves, Mystery Sea Raider, Her First Romance, The Devil Commands, Under Age, Sweethearts of the Campus, Blonde From Singapore, Confessions of Boston Blackie, Secrets of the Lone Wolf, Counter Espionage, Seven Miles from Alcatraz, Hilter's Children, The Falcon Strikes Back, Behind the Rising Sun, Captive Wild Woman Tender Comrade, Murder My Sweet, Back to Bataan, Cornered Crossfire (Acad. Award nom.), So Well Remembered, Till the End of Time, Obsession, Give Us This Day, Mutiny, The Sniper, Eight Iron Men, The Juggler, The Caine Mutiny, Broken Lance, End of the Affair, Left Hand of God, Soldier of Fortune, The Mountain (also prod.), Raintree County, The Young Lions, Warlock, The Blue Angel, The Reluctant Saint (It.), A Walk on the Wild Side, The Carpetbaggers, Where Love Has Gone, Mirage, Alvarez Kelly, Shalako, Anzio, Bluebeard, The Human Factor, He is My Brother.

DODD, WILFRID E.: Executive, b. Hamburg, Germany, March 19, 1923. e. Institut Fisher, Montreux, Switzerland; Downside Coll., Bath, England; Royal Military Coll., Sandhurst, England. In the '50s formed the Canadian Investing Banking firm: Oswald Drinkwater & Graham Ltd., Vice Pres. and partner. Pres. Allied Artists International Corp., 1964. President of Allied Artists Productions, Inc., 1969. Formed Cinepix Inc., Canadian dist. firm, 1963.

DOLGEN, JONATHAN L.: Executive. e. Cornell U., NYU Sch. of Law. Began career with Wall Street law firm, Fried, Frank, Harris, Shriver & Jacobson. In 1976 joined Columbia Pictures Industries as asst. gen. counsel and deputy gen. counsel. 1979, named sr. v.p. in chg. of worldwide business affairs; 1980, named exec. v.p. Joined Columbia m.p. div., 1981; named pres. of Columbia Pay-Cable & Home Entertainment Group. Also pres. Columbia Pictures domestic operations, overseeing Music Group. 1985, joined 20th-Fox in newly created position of sr. exec. v.p. for telecommunications.

DOLLINGER, IRVING: Exhibitor. Columbia Amusement Co. b. New York, NY, Sept. 20, 1905. e. U. of Pennsylvania. Stanley-Fabian mgr., 1926. Then with Warner Theatres in New Jersey. Owner and operator of theatre since 1929. Past pres. Allied Theat. Owners of N.J. Pres., Assoc. Theats. of N.J., booking org. 1938–44; v.p. & buyer, Independent Theatre Service Eastern regional v.p. Allied States Assoc., 1949–54; treas., Nat'l Allied, 1955–56; partner, Triangle Theatre Service, 1957; chief barker, N.Y. Tent 35, Variety Club, 1966.

DOMINGUEZ, MARINE: Filmmaker. b. El Paso, TX, Oct. 6, 1952. e. Western New Mexico U., 1970–72; Michigan State U., 1972–74; U. of San Francisco, B.P.A., 1980. Educational counselor and director for non-profit community service org., assisting Hispanic youth with admission into academic or technical progs. and univs. Taught photography and Spanish to adults in recreational prog. Since 1982 has developed Hearts on Fire, fictional film about the prod. of the 1954 labor film Salt of the Earth. Produces television progs. and industrial videos. President, Saldeterre Productions, Inc.

DONAHUE, PHIL: Television Personality. b. Cleveland, OH, Dec. 21, 1935. e. Notre Dame, BBA. m. actress Marlo Thomas. Worked as check sorter, Albuquerque Natl. Bank, 1957, then as announcer at KYW-TV & AM, Cleveland; news dir. WABJ radio, Adrian, MI; morning newscaster WHIO-TV. Interviews with Jimmy Hoffa and Billy Sol Estes picked up nationally by CBS. Host of Conversation Piece, phone-in talk show. Debuted The Phil Donahue Show, daytime talk show in

Dayton, Ohio, 1967. Syndicated 2 years later. Moved to Chicago, 1974. Host, Donahue, now in 165 outlets in U.S. In 1979 a mini-version of show became 3-times-a-week segment on NBC's Today Show. Winner of several Emmys. Books: Donahue: My Own Story (1980), The Human Animal (1985).

DONAHUE, TROY: Actor. r.n. Merle Johnson, Jr. b. New York, NY, Jan. 27, 1937. e. Bayport H.S., N.Y. Military Acad. Directed, wrote, acted in school plays. Columbia U., Journalism. Summer stock, Bucks County Playhouse, Sayville Playhouse; contract, Warner Brothers, 1959.
PICTURES: Tarnished Angels (1957), Man Afraid, This Happy Feeling, The Perfect Furlough, Imitation of Life, A Summer Place, The Crowded Sky, Parrish, Susan Slade, Palm Springs Weekend, Rome Adventure, A Distant Trumpet, My Blood Runs Cold, Rocket to the Moon, Come Spy With Me, Sweet Savior, Godfather, Part II, Tin Man, Grandview, U.S.A., Low Blow, Cyclone, Deadly Prey, American Revenge, Back to the Beach, Dr. Alien (aka I Was a Teenage Sex Mutant), Sexpot, Hard Rock Nightmare, Bad Blood, John Travis, Solar Survivor, The Chilling, The Housewarming, Deadly Spy Games, Assault of the Party Nerds, Deadly Diamonds, Deadly Embrace.
TELEVISION: Series: Hawaiian Eye (1959–60), Surfside 6. Guest: Matt Houston, Malibu.

DONALDSON, ROGER: Director. b. Ballarat, Australia, Nov. 15, 1945. Emigrated to New Zealand at 19. Established still photography business; then began making documentaries. Directed Winners and Losers, a series of short dramas for NZ-TV. First theatrical feature, Sleeping Dogs.
PICTURES: Smash Palace (also s.p.), The Bounty, Marie, No Way Out, Cocktail, Cadillac Man.

DONEN, STANLEY: Producer, Director. b. Columbia, SC, April 13, 1924. e. U. of South Carolina. Former dancer who co-dir. classic Amer. musicals with Gene Kelly.
PICTURES: Royal Wedding; Singin' in the Rain; It's Always Fair Weather, Deep in My Heart, Seven Brides for Seven Brothers, On the Town, Funny Face, Pajama Game, Kiss Them for Me, Indiscreet, Damn Yankees, Once More with Feeling, Surprise Package, The Grass Is Greener, Charade, Arabesque, Two for the Road, Bedazzled, Staircase, The Little Prince, Lucky Lady, Movie, Movie, Saturn 3 (prod., dir.), Blame It on Rio (prod., dir.).

DONIGER, WALTER: Writer, Director, Producer. b. New York NY. e. Valley Forge Military Academy, Duke U., Harvard U. Graduate Business Sch. Entered m.p. business as writer later writer-prod-dir. Wrote documentaries in Army Air Forces M.P. Unit in W.W.II. WGA award nominee and other awards.
PICTURES: Rope of Sand; Desperate Search, Cease Fire, Safe At Home, House of Women, Duffy of San Quentin, Along the Great Divide, Tokyo Joe, Alaska Seas, Steel Cage, Steel Jungle, Hold Back the Night, Guns of Fort Petticoat, Unwed Mother, Jive Junction (dir., prod., s.p.), The Brotherhood.
TELEVISION: Movies: Kentucky Woman, Mad Bull, The Outlaws. Over 600 episodes on 50 different series including: Delvecchio, Mad Bull, Switch, Moving On, Baa, Baa, Blacksheep, McCloud, The Man and the City, Sarge, Owen Marshall, Peyton Place (200 episodes), Mr. Novak, The Greatest Show on Earth, Travels of Jaimie McPheeters, Outlaws, Hong Kong, Checkmate, Bat Masterson, The Web, Bold Venture, Tombstone Territory, Maverick, Rough Riders, Captain Grief, Lockup, Dick Powell, The Survivors, Bracken's World, Bold Ones, Kung Fu, Barnaby Jones, Marcus Welby, Lucas Tanner.

DONLAN, YOLANDE: Actress, b. Jersey City, NJ. e. Immaculate Heart Convent, Hollywood, CA. English stage debut in Born Yesterday at the Garrick Theatre (London) 1947; screen debut in Miss Pilgrim's Progress 1950. Autobiography: Shake the Stars Down, 1976, Third Time Lucky (U.S., 1977).
PICTURES: To Dorothy a Son, The Body Said No, Traveller's Joy, Mr. Drake's Duck, Penny Princess, They Can't Hang Me, Expresso Bongo, Jigsaw, 80,000 Suspects, The Adventurers, Seven Nights in Japan.
TELEVISION: I Thought They Died Years Ago.

DONNELLY, DONAL: Actor. b. Bradford, Eng. July 6, 1931. Studied for theatre at the Dublin Gate Theatre. Broadway debut: Philadelphia, Here I Come (1966). Other NY theater includes: Joe Egg, Sleuth (NY and U.S. tour), The Elephant Man, The Faith-Healer, The Chalk Garden, My Astonishing Self, Big Maggie, Execution of Justice.
PICTURES: Rising of the Moon (1957); Gideon's Day; Shake Hands With the Devil; Young Cassidy; The Knack; Up Jumped a Swagman; The Mind of Mr. Soames; Waterloo; The Dead.
TELEVISION: Juno and the Paycock (BBC, 1958); Home Is the Hero, The Venetian Twins; The Plough and the Stars; Playboy of the Western World; Sergeant Musgrave's Dance; Yes-Honestly (series).

DONNELLY, RALPH E.: Executive. b. Lynbrook, NY, Jan. 20, 1932. e. Bellmore, NY public school; W. C. Mepham H.S., 1949. Worked for Variety (publication) as writer, 1950; Long Island Press as daily columnist, 1951; joined Associated Independent Theatres, 1953, as gen. mgr.; later film buyer; in 1973 left to become independent buyer and booker for Creative Films; film buyer and v.p., RKO/Stanley Warner Theatres, 1976–79; v.p. & gen. mgr. for Cinema 5 Ltd. circuit, N.Y., 1980–87; now exec. v.p. City Cinemas, N.Y.

DONNENFELD, BERNARD: Executive. b. New York, NY, Oct. 28, 1926. e. NYU, LL.B. Admitted to New York, California Bar. Spvsr., corp. affrs., legal dept., Paramount Pictures Corp., New York, 1957–61; exec. asst., asst. secy. corp., Hollywood Studio, 1961–64; asst. to pres., asst. secy. corp., New York, 1964–65; assoc. hd. stud. activities, asst. secy. corp., Hollywood Studio, 1965, v.p. in chg. worldwide prod. admin., Paramount, 1965–69. Pres. The Filmakers Group, 1970.

DONNER, CLIVE: Director. b. London, Eng., Jan 21, 1926. Ent. m.p. ind. 1942. Asst. film ed. Denhem Studios, 1942. Dir. London stage: The Formation Dancers, The Front Room Boys, Kennedy's Children (also NY), Film ed.: A Christmas Carol (1951), The Card (The Promoter), Genevieve, Man With a Million, The Purple Rain, I Am a Camera.
PICTURES: Director: The Secret Place, Heart of a Child, Marriage of Convenience, Some People, The Caretaker, Nothing But the Best, The Sinister Man, What's New Pussy Cat, Luv, Here We Go Round the Mulberry Bush, Alfred the Great, Marriage of Convenience, Vampira, Spectre, Rogue Male, Three Hostages, She Fell Among Thieves, The Nude Bomb, Charlie Chan and the Curse of the Dragon Queen, Stealing Heaven.
TELEVISION: Danger Man, Documentaries: Sir Francis Drake, Mighty and Mystical, British Institutions, Tempo. Movies: Spectre, The Thief of Baghdad, Oliver Twist, The Scarlet Pimpernel, Arthur the King, To Catch a King, A Christmas Carol, Dead Man's Folly, Babes in Toyland, Not a Penny More, Not a Penny Less.

DONNER, RICHARD: Director. b. New York, NY, 1939. Began career as actor off-Bdwy. Worked with director Martin Ritt on TV production of Maugham's Of Human Bondage. Moved to California 1958, directing commercials, industrial films and documentaries. First TV drama: Wanted: Dead or Alive.
PICTURES: X-15, Salt and Pepper, Twinky, The Omen, Superman, Inside Moves, The Final Conflict, The Toy (exec. prod.), Ladyhawke (prod.-dir.), Goonies (co-prod., dir.), Lethal Weapon (co-prod., dir.), Scrooged (co-prod., dir.), Lethal Weapon 2 (prod., dir.).
TELEVISION: Episodes of Have Gun Will Travel; Perry Mason; Cannon; Get Smart; The Fugitive; Kojak; Bronk; Lucas Tanner. Movies: Portrait of a Teen-Age Alcoholic; Senior Year; A Shadow in the Streets, Tales From the Crypt (exec. prod., dir. Dig That Cat . . . He's Real Gone).

DONOVAN, ARLENE: Producer. b. Kentucky. e. Stratford Coll., VA. Worked in publishing before entering industry as asst. to late dir. Robert Rosen on Cocoa Beach, uncompleted at his death. Worked as story editor, Columbia Pictures. 1969–82, literary head of m.p. dept. for ICM; involved in book publishing as well as stage and screen projects. Debut as film producer, Still of the Night, 1982.
PICTURES: Places in the Heart, Nadine, The House on Carroll Street (co-exec. prod.).

DONOVAN, HENRY B.: Executive, Producer. b. Boston, MA. Entered m.p. ind. for RKO Pathe Studios, property master, special effects dir., unit mgr., asst. dir., prod. mgr.; worked on over 310 pictures; Harry Sherman, Hopalong Cassidy features. 10 yrs., U.S. Army Signal Corps, as head of dept. of California studios prod. training m.p.; pres.: Telemount Pictures, Inc. Prod., dir., writer Cowboy G Men (TV series). Wrote novel, Corkscrewed, Live Television.
PICTURES: Hopalong Cassidy Features, Gone with the Wind, Becky Sharp, dir. Our Flag; Magic Lady (live-action TV show); Magic Lady (13 one-reel features), others. Prod. writer, Cowboy G Men (39 films).
TELEVISION: programming, financing, distribution. Global Scope; International TV; Dist., Financing, programming; sls. consultant, Internat'l TV & motion pictures. Cable TV & distribution & program development, collector of movie memorabilia; DBS TV programming & financing: production software. Worldwide TV consultant.

DOOHAN, JAMES: Actor. b. Vancouver, B.C., Mar. 3, 1920. W.W.II capt. in Royal Canadian Artillery. 1946 won scholarship to Neighborhood Playhouse in N.Y. and taught there later. 1953, returned to Canada to live in Toronto, becoming engaged in acting career on radio, TV and in film. Then to Hollywood and chief fame as Chief Engineer Scott in TV series, Star Trek.
PICTURES: The Wheeler Dealers, The Satan Bug, Bus Riley's Back in Town, Fellowship;, Star Trek—The Motion Picture, Star Trek II: The Wrath of Khan, Star Trek III: The Search for Spock, Star Trek IV: The Voyage Home.
TELEVISION: Hazel, Bonanza, The Virginia, Gunsmoke,

Peyton Place, The Fugitive, Marcus Welby MD, Ben Casey, Bewitched, Fantasy Island, etc.

DOOLEY, PAUL: Actor. b. Parkersburg, WV, Feb. 22, 1928. Began career on N.Y. stage in Threepenny Opera. Later member of Second City. Bdwy. credits include The Odd Couple, Adaptation/Next, The White House Murder Case, Hold Me, etc. Co-creator and writer for The Electric Company on PBS. Owns co. called All Over Creation, which produces original industrial films and shows and has created over 1,000 radio commercials.
PICTURES: What's So Bad About Feeling Good?, Slap Shot, Gravy Train, Death Wish, The Out-of-Towners, A Wedding, A Perfect Couple, Rich Kids, Breaking Away, Popeye, Paternity, Endangered Species, Kiss Me Goodbye, Health, Strange Brew, Going Berserk, 16 Candles, Little Shop of Horrors, O.C. and Stiggs, Big Trouble, Monster in the Closet, Last Rites, Flashback.
TELEVISION: Faerie Tale Theater, The Firm, The Murder of Mary Phagan, Lip Service, Guts and Glory: The Rise and Fall of Oliver North. Series: Coming of Age.

DORAN, LINDSAY: Executive. b. Los Angeles, CA. e. U. of California at Santa Cruz. Moved to London where was contributing author to The Oxford Companion to Film and the World Encyclopedia of Film. Returned to U.S. to write and produce documentaries and children's programs for Pennsylvania public affairs station WPSX-TV. Career in m.p. industry began in story dept. at Embassy Pictures which she joined in 1979; 1982 promoted to dir. of development; then v.p., creative affairs. 1985, joined Paramount Pictures as v.p., production, for M.P. Group. 1987, promoted to senior v.p., production.

DORFMAN, IRVIN S.: Executive. b. New York, NY, Sept. 3, 1924. e. Yale U., B.A., 1945. Following three years in U.S. Navy, joined Dorfman Associates, press rep. organ. handling film, and TV personalities. Handled pub. and promotion for more than 100 B'way shows and worked for 20th Cen.-Fox and U.A. Also produced off-B'way The Lion in Love. Top ranking amateur tennis star, 1950; pres., Surrogate Releasing and Dandrea Releasing.

DORTORT, DAVID: Executive Producer. b. New York, NY, Oct. 23, 1916. e. City Coll. of New York. Served U.S. Army, 1943–46. Novelist and short story writer, 1943–49. Also TV writer. Now pres. of Xanadu Prods., Aurora Enterprises, Inc., and Bonanza Ventures, Inc. & Pres. TV branch, WGA, West, 1954–55; TV-radio branch, 1955–57; v.p. PGA, 1967; pres. 1968. Chairman of The Caucus for Producers, Writers and Directors, 1973–75. Pres., PGA, 1980–81; campaign director, Permanent Charities Comm., 1980–81; chmn., Interguild Council 1980–81.
AUTHOR: Novels include Burial of the Fruit and The Post of Honor.
PICTURES: The Lusty Men, Reprisal, The Big Land, Cry in the Night, Clash by Night, Going Bananas (exec. prod.).
TELEVISION: Creator and exec. prod., Bonanza; High Chaparral, The Chisholms, Hunter's Moon. Producer: The Restless Gun, The Cowboys. Creator, story and exec. prod. Bonanza: The Next Generation.

DOUGHERTY, MARION: Executive. Gained fame as casting director. Acted as co-executive producer on Smile, 1975. In 1977 named v.p. in chg. talent for Paramount Pictures. In 1979 joined Warner Bros. v.p. in chg. talent to work with production dept. and producers and directors.
CASTING: A Little Romance (co-casting), Urban Cowboy (co-), Honky Tonk Freeway, Reds, Fire-Fox Honkytonk Man, The World According to Garp, Sudden Impact, The Man With Two Brains (co-), The Killing Fields (co-), Swing Shift, The Little Drummer Girl.

DOUGLAS, GORDON: Director, b. New York, NY, Dec. 15, 1907. Actor. Hal Roach stock company; writer; collab. Topper series, Housekeeper's Daughter; dir., 30 Our Gang shorts.
PICTURES: Saps at Sea, Broadway Limited, Devil with Hitler, First Yank into Tokyo, San Quentin, If You Knew Suzie, Black Arrow, Walk a Crooked Mile, Doolins of Oklahoma, Mr. Soft Touch, The Nevadan, Between Midnight and Dawn, Kiss Tomorrow Goodbye, Great Missouri Raid, Only the Valient, I Was a Communist for the FBI, Come Fill the Cup, Mara Maru, Iron Mistress, She's Back on Broadway, So This Is Love, The Charge at Feather River, Them, Young at Heart, McConnell Story, Sincerely Yours, Santiago, The Big Land, Bombers B-52, Fort Dobbs, Yellowstone Kelly, Rachel Cade, Gold of 7 Saints, Follow That Dream, Call Me Bwana, Rio Conchos, Robin and the Seven Hoods, Sylvia, Harlow, Stagecoach, Way Way Out, In Like Flint, Chuka, Tony Rome, The Detective, Lady in Cement, Barquero, They Call Me Mr. Tibbs, Slaughter's Big Rip Off.
TELEVISION: Nevada Smith.

DOUGLAS, KIRK: Actor, Producer, Director. r.n. Issur Danielovitch (changed to Demsky). b. Amsterdam, NY, Dec. 9, 1918. m. Anne Buydens, pres. of Bryna Prod. Co. Father of Michael, Joel, Peter, Eric. e. St. Lawrence U, B.A. Stage debut in New York: Spring Again. U.S. Navy during W.W.II; resumed stage work. Did radio soap operas. Signed by Hal B. Wallis. Screen debut: The Strange Love of Martha Ivers. Autobiography: The Ragman's Son (1988).
AWARDS: Recipient of U.S. Presidential Medal of Freedom, 1981. Three Academy Award nominations: Champion, The Bad and the Beautiful, Lust for Life. N.Y. Critics Award, Best Actor for Lust for Life. Cecil B. DeMille Award–1968. Cited in Congressional Record three times: on discrimination (1977), on good will ambassador work (1964), testimony on abuse of elderly (1985). Received Jefferson Award in 1983 for public service by a private citizen. Made Goodwill Ambassador to U.S. State Dept. and U.S.I.A, 1963. 1979: Commander in the Order of Arts and Letters, Chevalier de la Legion d'Honneur, 1985. American Cinema Award, 1987. Golden Kamera Award (Germany 1988). Career achievement award, National Board of Review, 1989.
THEATER: Spring Again, Three Sisters, Kiss and Tell, Trio, The Wind is Ninetry, Star in the Window, Man Bites Dog, One Flew Over the Cuckoo's Nest, The Boys of Autumn.
TELEVISION: Mousey, 1974; The Money Changers, Draw! (HBO), Victory at Entebbe, Holocaust 2000, Remembrance of Love, Amos, Queenie, Inherit the Wind.
PICTURES: Out of the Past, I Walk Alone, Mourning Becomes Electra, The Walls of Jericho, My Dear Secretary, Letter to Three Wives, Champion, Young Man with a Horn, The Glass Menagerie, The Big Carnival (a.k.a. Ace in the Hole), Along the Great Divide, Detective Story, The Big Trees, The Big Sky, Bad and the Beautiful, Story of Three Loves, The Juggler, Act of Love, Ulysses, Man Without a Star, 20,000 Leagues Under the Sea, The Racers, The Indian Fighter, Lust for Life, Top Secret Affair, Gunfight at the OK Corral, Paths of Glory, The Vikings, Last Train from Gun Hill, The Devil's Disciple, Strangers When We Meet, Spartacus, The Last Sunset, Town Without Pity, Lonely Are the Brave, Two Weeks in Another Town, The Hook, List of Adrian Messenger, For Love or Money, Seven Days in May, In Harm's Way, Cast a Giant Shadow, Is Paris Burning?, The Way West, The War Wagon, The Heroes of Telemark, A Lovely Way to Die, The Brotherhood, The Arrangement, There Was a Crooked Man, A Gunfight, The Light at the Edge of the World, Catch Me a Spy, Master Touch, The Chosen, The Fury, The Villain, Saturn III, Home Movies, The Final Countdown, The Man from Snowy River, Eddie Macon's Run, Tough Guys. Producer: The Indian Fighter, The Vikings, Spartacus, Lonely Are the Brave, List of Adrian Messenger, Seven Days in May, The Brotherhood, Summertree, (prod.) Scalawag; (prod., dir., act.) Once Is Not Enough, Posse (prod., dir., act.).

DOUGLAS, MICHAEL: Actor, Producer. b. New Brunswick, NJ, Sept 25, 1944. f. Kirk Douglas. e. Black Fox Military Acad., Choate, U. of California. Worked as asst. director on Lonely Are The Brave, Heroes of Telemark, Cast a Giant Shadow; after TV debut in The Experiment, appeared off-Broadway in City Scene, Pinkville; m.p. debut in Hail Hero (1969).
PICTURES: Adam at 6 A.M., Summertree, Napoleon and Samantha, Coma, China Syndrome (also prod.). Co-prod., One Flew Over the Cuckoo's Nest; Running (actor). It's My Turn (actor). Star Chamber (actor). Romancing the Stone (prod., actor), Starman (exec. prod.); A Chorus Line (actor); Jewel of the Nile (prod., actor); Fatal Attraction; Wall Street (Acad. Award, 1987); Black Rain; The Tender (co-exec. prod.), The War of the Roses.
TELEVISION: The FBI, Medical Center, When Michael Calls, Streets of San Francisco (series).

DOUGLAS, MIKE: TV host, Commentator. r.n. Michael Delaney Dowd, Jr. b. Chicago, IL, Aug. 11, 1925. Started career singing with bands in and around Chicago. 1950–54 featured singer with Kay Kyser's band. In 1953 became host of WGN-TV's Hi Ladies in Chicago; also featured on WMAQ-TV, NBC, Chicago, as singer and host. Moved to Hollywood in late '50s, working as piano bar singer. In 1961 hired as host for new show on station KYW-TV in Cleveland, owned by Westinghouse Bdg. Co., featuring celebrity guests. This became the Mike Douglas Show which was later nationally syndicated and moved base of operations to Philadelphia, then Los Angeles. Ran 21 years til Mid-1982. Books: The Mike Douglas Cookbook (1969), Mike Douglas My Story (1978).

DOUGLAS, VALERIE: Executive. b. Hollywood, CA, Dec. 3. e. UCLA, journalism. Uncle was actor Elmo Lincoln (first Tarzan). 1945–46, publicist, Vic Shapiro Public Relations; 1946–49, sub-agent, Manning O'Conner Agency; 1949–51, TV coordinator, Bing Crosby Enterprises, Fireside Theatre Series; 1951–52, publicist, RKO Studios; 1952–59, personal mgr., Richard Burton, v.p. & dir. Denham Films, Ltd., London; 1959–61, pub. coordinator, Hecht-Lancaster-Hill; 1961–64, dir. of pub. relations, IPAR Productions, France; 1964–67, v.p., Illustra Films, West Coast branch; 1967–75, asst. dir. pub., United Artists Corp., West Coast; 1975–78, exec. v.p., Guttman & Pam Public Relations; 1978, formed Suvarie, Inc., m.p. representation, of which is pres. 1978–84, personal mgr, the late actor Richard Burton.

DOURIF, BRAD: Actor. b. Huntington, WV, Mar. 18, 1950. Stage actor, three years with Circle Repertory Co., NY (When You Comin Back, Red Ryder?), before films and TV.
PICTURES: Split, W. W. and the Dixie Dancekings, One Flew Over the Cuckoo's Nest (Acad. Award nom., Golden Globe, British Oscar), Group Portrait with Lady, Eyes of Laura Mars, Wise Blood, Heaven's Gate, Ragtime, Dune, Impure Thoughts, Blue Velvet, Fatal Beauty, Sonny Boy, Child's Play, Mississippi Burning, Medium Rare, The Exorcist: 1990, Spontaneous Combustion.
TELEVISION: Guest: Miami Vice, The Hitchhiker, Spencer for Hire, Tales of the Unexpected. Movies: Mound Builders, The Gardener's Son, Sgt. Matlovitch vs. the U.S. Air Force, Studs Lonigan, Guyana Tragedy—The Story of Jim Jones, I Desire: The Story of a Female Vampire, Vengeance: The Story of Tony Cimo, Rage of Angels: The Story Continues.

DOWN, LESLEY-ANNE: Actress. b. London, England, March 17, 1954. At age of 10 modeled for TV and film commercials, leading to roles in features. Stage debut at 14 in All the Right Noises.
PICTURES: Pope Joan, Scalawag, Brannigan, The Pink Panther Strikes Again, The Betsy, A Little Night Music, The Great Train Robbery, Hanover Street, Sphinx, Rough Cut, Nomads, Scenes from the Goldmine.
TELEVISION: Series: Upstairs, Downstairs; Heartbreak House, North & South Books I and II, Shivers (pilot). Movies: The One and Only Phyllis Dixey, The Last Days of Pompeii, Arch of Triumph, Indiscreet, Lady Killers, Night Walk.
STAGE: Great Expectations, Hamlet, etc.

DOWNEY, ROBERT, JR.: Actor. b. New York, NY, April 4, 1965. Son of indep. filmmaker Robert Downey. Film debut in his father's Pound (1970), then Greaser's Palace and Up the Academy. Later appeared in father's films This is America The Movie, Not the Country (a.k.a. America) and Rented Lips. Was a cast regular on Saturday Night Live, 1985–86. Named Rolling Stone's Hottest Actor for 1988.
PICTURES: Baby, Its You; Back to School, Firstborn, Tuff Turf, Weird Science, To Live & Die in L.A., America, Less Than Zero; The Pick-Up Artist; Johnny B. Good, Rented Lips, True Believer, 1969, Chances Are, That's Adequate, Three of Hearts, Air America.
TELEVISION: Mussolini: The Untold Story.

DOWNS, HUGH: Broadcaster. b. Akron, OH, Feb. 14, 1921. e. Bluffton Coll., 1938. Wayne U., 1941. Col. U., N.Y., 1955; Supervisor of Science Programming, NBC's Science Dept. one yr.; science consultant for Westinghouse Labs., Ford Foundation, etc.; chm. of bd., Raylin Prods., Inc. Today, Chairman, U.S. Committee for UNICEF. Chm., National Space Institute.
TELEVISION: Hawkins Falls, Kukla, Fran & Ollie, Short Story Playhouse, American Inventory, Home, Sid Caesar Show, Tonight (Jack Paar Show), Concentration, Today. Host: ABC-TV 20/20 Program, Host: Over-Easy, PBS Network.
RADIO: NBC's Monitor.

DOYLE, KEVIN: Executive. b. Sydney, Australia, June 21, 1933. e. N. Sydney Tech. HS., Aust. Jr. exec., asst. adv. & pub. div., 20th Century-Fox, Aust., 1947–59; adv. & pub. dir., Columbia Pictures Aust., 1960–66; international ad/pub. mgr.; Columbia Pictures Int'l, N.Y. 1966; intl. pub./promo. mgr., 1980; 1987, Columbia Int'l. rep., Coca-Cola promotions/mktg. sub-committee; int'l pub./promo. mgr. Columbia Tri-Star Film Distributors Inc., 1988.

DRABINSKY, GARTH: Executive. b. Toronto, Canada, 1948. e. U. of Toronto, LL.B., 1973. Called to Ontario Bar, 1975. Former publisher, Canadian Film Digest, Co-founder, Pan-Canadian Film Distributors. Co-founder Cineplex Odeon Corp. 1979, m.p. exhibitor and distributor in Canada and U.S.; Opened first Cineplex in Toronto's Eaton Centre, 1979. Entered U.S. exhibition, acquiring regional theatre chains in 1985. Chmn, CEO and pres., Cineplex Odeon Corp., theatre circuit in Canada and U.S. Dir., CFMT-TV, Toronto.
PICTURES: Co-prods. with Joel B. Michaels: The Silent Partner, The Changeling; Tribute; The Amateur; Losin' It.
MEMBER, bd. of govs., Baycrest Centre for Geriatric Care (Toronto); bd. of dirs. of Mount Sinai Hospital (Toronto); bd. of trustees, Sundance Institute (Utah); bd. of trustees, American Museum of the Moving Image (NY); advisory bd., Centre for Research in Neurodegenerative Diseases at the U. of Toronto; bd. of dirs. of: the Toronto Film Fest.; The Actors Studio Inc., NY; the American Cinematheque, L.A.; trustee, The American Film Institute, L.A.; American Film Institute's Second Decade Council, L.A.; Acad. of M.P. Arts and Sciences.
AWARDS: Variety Club of Greater Washington, D.C.'s Heart of Variety Award, June 1989; B'nai B'rith Intl. Distinguished Achievement Award, May 1989; Honorary Fellowship, from the Ryerson Polytechnical Inst. of Toronto, 1987; named "The Renaissance Man of Film" by the Montreal World Film Fest., 1987; Lifetime Achievement Award, Canada CA Chamber of Commerce, 1987; Canadian Film & TV Assoc.'s Chetwynd Award for Entrepreneurial Achievement, 1987; Amer. Marketing Assoc.'s Award for Marketing Excellence, 1986; Air Canada Award for Outstanding Contribution to the Business of Filmmaking in Canada, 1987; ShoWest's award as The Industry's Consummate Showman, 1988; Canada's 1987 Vanier Award.

DRAGOTI, STAN: Director. b. New York, NY, Oct. 4, 1932. e. Cooper Union and Sch. of Visual Arts. 1959 hired as sketch at ad agency, promoted to sr. art dir., later TV dept. and art dir. of Young & Rubicam. Studied acting HB Studios. Directed Clio awarding-winning TV commercials (including I Love New York campaign).
PICTURES: Dirty Little Billy (1972), Love at First Bite, Mr. Mom, The Man with One Red Shoe, She's Out of Control, Love at Second Bite: Dracula Goes to Hollywood (prod.).

DRAI, VICTOR: Producer. b. Casablanca, Morocco, July 25, 1947. e. Lycée de Port Lyautey, 1957–63. In real estate in Los Angeles 1976–82; clothing designer/mfg. in Paris, France, 1969–76. Began producing features in 1984, The Woman in Red.
PICTURES: The Man with One Red Shoe, The Bride, Weekend at Bernie's.

DRAKE, CHARLES: Actor. r.n. Charles Ruppert; b. New York, NY, Oct. 2, 1914. e. Nicholas Coll., 1937. With Electric Boat Co., Groton, CT; adv. salesman; in little theatres; in m.p. as an actor.
PICTURES: I Wanted Wings, Man Who Came to Dinner, Now, Voyager, Air Force, Mr. Skefflington, Whistle Stop, Pretender, You Came Along, Tender Years, Bowie Knife, Comanche Territory, Air Cadet, Winchester '73, Harvey, Little Egypt, You Never Can Tell, Treasure of Lost Canyon, Red Ball Express, Bonzo Goes to College, Gunsmoke, Lone Hand, It Came from Outer Space, War Arrow, Glenn Miller Story, Tobor the Great, Four Guns to the Border, Female on the Beach, All That Heaven Allows, Price of Fear, The Arrangement.

DRAKLICH, NICK: Executive. b. Bakersfield, CA, Oct. 16, 1926. e. Fresno State Coll., Stanford U., Claremont Graduate Sch. Sr. v.p.—home entertainment for Republic Pictures Corp.

DRAZEN, LORI: Executive. Began career as asst. to dir. of adv. for Orion Pictures; creative dept. mgr., Kenyon & Eckhardt; gen. mgr., Seiniger Advertising; joined Warner Bros. 1985 as v.p., world-wide adv. & pub. services.

DREIFUSS, ARTHUR: Producer, Director, Writer. b. Frankfurt on Main, Germany, March 25, 1908. e. U. of Frankfurt on Main, Conservatory of Music, Columbia U. Choreographer, producer; many U. lectures; legit. producer: Allure, Baby Pompadour; producer many night club shows; associate producer Fanchon & Marco, Hollywood; dir. over 50 features and 53 TV shows for Columbia, RKO, Universal, Allied Artists, other majors; director Paul Muni debut Screen Gems-Ford Theatre, TV 1953; executive producer New Age Productions, 1970 to 1972; executive producer The Peter Hurkos Show, CBS; writer Owl Hill; Dolls behind Walls, 1973, director, Wildlife in Crisis, Viacom TV series 1975. Assoc. prod. Chennault China Tiger (Genson Prods.), 1978; assoc. video editor Creative Editing, Inc., 1979; dir. literary dept, Georg Michaud Agency, 1979–86; dir., literary dept., Schoeman Agency. 1987; dir. literary dept. William Carroll Agency, 1988.
PICTURES: prod.-dir.: features Secret File and Assignment Abroad, 1956; dir.: The Last Blitzkrieg; Life Begins at Seventeen; Juke Box Rhythm; writer-dir.: Brendan Behan's The Quare Fellow; dir.: Riot on Sunset Strip; The Love-Ins; For Singles Only; The Young Runaways; A Time to Sing; assoc. prod.: Angel, Angel, Down We Go.

DREXLER, ELIAS J.: Executive. b. New York, NY, Dec. 24, 1911. e. Columbia U., Columbia Law Sch., LL.B., 1936. Special agent. Div. of Investigations, U.S. Dept. of Interior, 1937–40; dir., Preclusive operations, 1940–45; dir., Surplus Property Div., Foreign Economic Admin; exec., National Screen Service, 1945–56; general counsel and nat. sales mgr. AGFA-Gavaert; 1956–65; nat. sales mgr. and exclusive U.S. and Mexican dist. of motion picture products manufactured by Fuji Photo Film Co., Ltd., Tokyo, Japan, 1965–present.

DREYFUSS, RICHARD: Actor. b. Brooklyn, NY, Oct. 29, 1947. e. Beverly Hills H.S.; San Fernando Valley State Coll. 1965– 67. Prof. career began at Gallery Theatre (L.A.) in In Mama's House. Has also acted off-Bdwy. and on Bdwy.
PICTURES: Hello Down There, The Young Runaways, Dillenger, American Graffiti, The Apprenticeship of Duddy Kravitz, Jaws, Inserts, Close Encounters of the Third Kind, The Goodbye Girl (Acad. Award), The Big Fix (also co-prod.) The Competition, Whose Life Is It Anyway?, The Buddy System, Down and Out in Beverly Hills, Stand by Me, Tin Men, Stakeout, Nuts, Moon Over Parador, Let It Ride, Rosencrantz and Guildenstern are Dead, Always, Once Again Postcards From the Edge.
TELEVISION: The Big Valley, Room 222, Judd for the Defense, Mod Squad, The Bold Ones, Funny, You Don't Look 200 (host, co-prod., co-writer).

STAGE: Journey to the Day, Incident at Vichy, People Need People, Enemy, Enemy, Line, Whose Little Boy Are You, But Seriously, Major Barbara, The Time of Your Life, The Hands of Its Enemy (Mark Taper Forum, L.A.).

DROMGOOLE, PATRICK: Film director, Stage prod., Executive. b. Iqueque, Chile, Aug. 30, 1930; e. Dulwich Coll., University Coll., Oxford. Joined BBC Radio as dir. 1954, later directing TV plays for BBC and ABC, incl. Armchair Theatre, Frontier, Dracula, Mystery Imagination. Joined HTV as West Country Programme Controller, 1968; dir. award-winning dramas; Thick as Thieves, Machinegunner. Developed Company's drama output and promoted policy of international pre-sales with such dramas as Jamaica Inn, Separate Tables, Catholics, Kidnapped, Robin of Sherwood, Arch of Triumph, Mr. Halpern and Mr. Johnson, Jenny's War, Codename Kyril, Wall of Tyranny, Strange Interlude, The Woman He Loved, Grand Larceny, Maigret. Made Fellow of RTS, 1978; chief exec. HTV Group since 1988. Fellow of RSA, 1989.

THEATER: Director: incl. first plays of Charles Wood, Joe Orton, David Halliwell, Colin Welland; Peter O'Toole in Man and Superman.

PICTURES: Two Vale South, Hidden Face, Dead Man's Chest, Anthony Purdy Esq., Point of Dissent, The Actors, King of the Wind (exec. prod.).

TELEVISION: Outpost (sprv. exec. prod.).

DRU, JOANNE: Actress. r.n. Joanne La Cock; b. Logan, WV, Jan. 31, 1923. Sister of Peter Marshall. John Robert Powers model: on stage as showgirl in Hold on to Your Hats; a Samba Siren at Ritz Carlton & Paramount; with theatrical group under Batami Schneider. Hollywood: m.p. debut in Abie's Irish Rose, 1946.

PICTURES: Red River, She Wore a Yellow Ribbon, All the King's Men, Wagonmaster, Vengeance Valley, 711 Ocean Drive, Mr. Belvedere Rings the Bell, Siege at Red River, Outlaw Territory, Southwest Passage, Three Ring Circus, Day of Triumph, Hell on Frisco Bay, Sincerely Yours, The Warriors, Thunder Bay, My Pal Gus, Pride of St. Louis, September Storm, Light in the Forest, Forbidden, Return of the Texan, Duffy of San Quentin, Supersnoopers.

TELEVISION: Guestward Ho (series).

DRURY, JAMES: Actor. b. New York, NY, 1934. e. New York U. Acting debut at age 8 in biblical play for children at Greenwich Settlement Playhouse. Performed on stage while youngster. Signed by MGM in 1955, working one day in each of seven movies that year, including Blackboard Jungle. Then got two-year contract at 20th-Fox. Gained fame as hero of TV series, The Virginian, which had nine-year run.

PICTURES: Love Me Tender, Bernardine.

TELEVISION: Series: The Virginian (1962–71), Firehouse, The Devil and Miss Sarah (movie).

DUBAND, WAYNE: Executive. Joined Warner Bros. 1969 as mgr. trainee in Australia. 1973, transferred to South Africa as mgr. dir.; 1977 gen. mgr. of CIC/Warner Bros. joint venture, also managing the CIC theatre operation there. 1980, named exec. asst. to Myron D. Karlin, pres. WB Intl., in Burbank. 1981, mgr. dir. of Warner/Columbia joint venture in France. 1985, appt. v.p. of sls. for WB Intl. division. 1987, appt. senior v.p. for Warner Bros. Intl. division.

DUBBINS, DON: Actor. b. Brooklyn, NY, June 28, 1929. Appeared in national company of Mr. Roberts, also Tea and Sympathy. Many television shows including Ed Sullivan Show.

PICTURES: From Here to Eternity, Caine Mutiny, Tribute to a Bad Man, These Wilder Years, The D.I., Gunfight in Abilene, The Illustrated Man, The Prize.

DUBE, JACKSON E.: Executive. b. New York, NY. e. U of North Carolina. m. Pat Lavelle, actress. USAF 1942–45 Radar-Gunner, AAF, Italy. Writer: Television and Sponsor Magazine 1947–48; reviews of recorded music. 1947–51, Consol Film Inds. Penthouse Prods. Dist: E. sales mgr. Atlas Tel. Corp, 1951–54; vp & gen. mgr., Craftsman Film Greatest Fights of the Century 1954; vp, Conquest Prods. CBS Net. Docus. 1954–57. TV and radio dir. Cote Fischer & Rogow Adv., 1957–59; exec vp, Bon Ami Film; dist: UA Feats. abroad 1959–63; prod's rep. Le Vien Prods—Finest Hours King's Story; E. sls. mgr. Desilu, 1964–67; exec vp, UCC Films; dist. RKO feature library abroad, 1969–70; pres. JED Prns. Corp Dist. London Films, Rank children's features, 1967–88. Consultant: New Century Ent., Windsor Pdns., Turner Program Services, 1985–88.

DUBENS, STANLEY: Writer, Producer. b. London, England, 1920. e. St. Paul's Sch. s. of Harry Dubens. Royal Corps Signals 1939–1945. From 1946, agent and theatrical productions. Ent. film production 1963. 1975 formed with Roger Moss, The Original Electric Picture Company, making commercials, doc., video, AV presentations.

THEATRE: prod. incl. Sweet and Low, And No Birds Sing, The Train for Venice, The Man Who Let It Rain, The Hands of Eurydice, I Want to See Mioussov, Sign Here Please.

PICTURES: Operation Snatch, Live Now Pay Later, The World Ten Times Over, Modesty Blaise, Marble Heroes, Matchgirls, Archie's Caper.

DUBS, ARTHUR R.: Executive, Producer, Director, Writer, President and Owner of Pacific International Enterprises, b. Medford, OR, Feb. 26, 1930. e. Southern Oregon State Coll. Founded Pacific International Enterprises, 1969.

PICTURES: Producer-Director: American Wilderness, Vanishing Wilderness, Wonder of It All. Exec. Prod.: Challenge to Be Free. Prod.: Adventures of the Wilderness Family, Wilderness Family Part 2 (also s.p.), Mountain Family Robinson (also s.p.), Across the Great Divide, Sacred Ground, Mystery Mansion, Dream Chasers (also co-dir.). Co-Prod.: Windwalker.

DUDELHEIM, HANS R.: Producer, Director, Editor. Began film career in Germany after W.W.II. Hired by U.S. Army Signal Corps as photographer, being sent to Far East Command. Came to New York, where joined ABC-TV as film editor. Beginning with hard news, moved to documentaries, editing many films. In 1981 established Cinema Arts Associates, Inc. as film society; 1966 expanded into indep. m.p. prod. co., of which he is pres.

DUDELSON, STANLEY E.: Executive. b. Cleveland, OH, July 12, 1924. Regnl. sales mgr., Hygo-Unity; natl. sales mgr. Screen Gems; producer's rep., Selma Ent., Italian Intl. Uni-Export Films of Rome, AIP; first vice pres., American Intl. Television, Inc. Joined New Line Dist. Corp., pres., New Line Intl. Releasing. Co-exec. prod. Nightmare on Elm Street. Left 1985 to be pres. & chief exec., Inter-pictures Releasing Corp.

DUFF, HOWARD: Actor. Bremerton, WA, Nov. 24, 1917. e. Repertory Playhouse, Seattle. With KOMO radio station 1935; served with U.S. Army 1941–5; entered m.p. 1947. Radio's original Sam Spade.

PICTURES: Brute Force (debut, 1947), Naked City, All My Sons, Calamity Jane and Sam Bass, Illegal Entry, Johnny Stoolpigeon, Red Canyon, Woman in Hiding, Shakedown, Lady From Texas, Models Inc., Steel Town, Spaceways, Roar of the Crowd, Jennifer, Tanganyika, Private Hell 36, Women's Prison, Yellow Mountain, Flame of the Islands, Broken Star, Sierra Stranger, Blackjack Ketchum Desperado, While the City Sleeps, Boy's Night Out, Syria Against Babylon, Panic in the City, The Late Show, A Wedding, Kramer vs. Kramer, Double Negative, Oh, God! Book II, Monster in the Closet, No Way Out.

TELEVISION: Series: Mr. Adams and Eve, Dante, Felony Squad; Flamingo Road; Knots Landing; Guest: Detective in the House. Hotel; Murder She Wrote; Movies: The D.A.: Murder One, The Heist, Flamingo Road, Snatched, In the Glitter Palace, Ski Lift to Death, The Dream Merchants, The Wild Women of Chastity Gultch, East of Eden, This Girl for Hire, Love on the Run, Roses Are for the Rich. Mini-series: War and Remembrance.

DUFFY, JAMES E.: Executive. b. Decatur, IL, April 2, 1926. e. Beloit Coll. Radio announcer, then reporter; joined publicity dept., ABC in 1949; named director of adv. & promo., then account exec. for Central division of ABC Radio Network; director of sales ABC Radio, 1957; central division account exec., ABC Television Network, 1955; natl. director of Sales, ABC Radio central division, 1960; vice president, ABC Radio Network, 1961; exec. v.p. & natl. director of sales, 1962; vice president in charge of sales, ABC Television Network, 1963; president, ABC Television Network, 1970–85; pres., communications, 1985–86; v.p. Capital Cities/ABC, Inc.; pres., communications, ABC Network & Bdgst. Divisions.

DUFFY, PATRICK: Actor. b. Townsend, MT, March 17, 1949. e. U. of Washington. Became actor-in-residence in state of Washington, where performed with various statefunded groups. Acted off-Bdwy. Taught mime and movement classes in summer camp in Seattle. Moved to L.A. and began TV acting career.

TELEVISION: Specials: The Last of Mrs. Lincoln; George Burns Comedy Week; Alice in Wonderland, Freedom Festival '89 (host). Movies: The Stranger Who Looks Like Me, Hurricane, 14 Going on 30, Leave Her to Heaven, Unholy Matrimony. Series: Man from Atlantis (star), Switch (guest), Dallas (star).

DUIGAN, JOHN: Writer, Director. b. Australia. e. Melbourne U., philosophy, M.A. Taught for several years at Melbourne U. and Latrobe U. before entering films. Made experimental short, The Firm Man (1974).

PICTURES: The Trespassers, Mouth to Mouth, Dimboola (d., only), Winter of Our Dreams, Far East, The Year My Voice Broke (dir., s.p.), Romero (dir.).

DUKAKIS, OLYMPIA: Actress. b. Lowell, MA, June 20, 1931. m. actor Louis Zorich. e. Boston U., B.A., M.F.A. Founding mem. of The Charles Playhouse, Boston, establishing summer theatre 1957–60. Taught acting at NYU 1967–70 as instructor, 1974–83 as master teacher, and at Yale U. 1976. With husband conceived and guided artistic dev. of Whole Theatre Monclair, NJ, since 1977; producing artistic dir. Has adapted plays for her co. and dir. theater there, at Williamstown Theatre Fest. and Delaware Summer Fest. Appeared in more than 100 plays on Bdwy, Off-Bdwy and in regional and summer theater.

THEATER: Who's Who in Hell, The Aspern Papers, Night of the Iguana, The Breaking Wall, Curse of the Starving Class, Snow Orchid, The Marriage of Bette and Boo (Obie Award), Social Security.

PICTURES: Lilith, Made for Each Other, Deathwish, Twice a Man, The Idolmaker, Rich Kids, The Wanderers, National Lampoon Goes to the Movies, Flanagan, Moonstruck (Acad. Award, supp. actress, 1987), Working Girl, Daddy's Home, Steel Magnolias, Dad, In the Spirit.

TELEVISION: The Rehearsal, Sisters, Nicky's World, Search for Tomorrow; FDR—The Last Days, One of the Boys, King of America.

DUKE, PATTY: Actress. r.n. Anna Marie Duke. b. New York, NY, Dec. 14, 1946. e. Quintano Sch. for Young Professionals. Pres. Screen Actors Guild, 1985–88. Author: Surviving Sexual Assault (1983), Call Me Anna (1987).

THEATRE: The Miracle Worker, Isle of Children.

PICTURES: I'll Cry Tomorrow (debut as extra 1955), The 4-D Man, The Goddess, Happy Anniversary, The Miracle Worker (Acad. Award, best supp. actress, 1963), Valley of the Dolls, Billie, My Sweet Charlie, Me, Natalie, The Swarm, The Hitch Hikers.

TELEVISION: Series regular: The Brighter Day (1957), Patty Duke Show (1963–66); It Takes Two (1982–83); Hail to the Chief (1985). Episodes: Armstrong Circle Theatre (1955), The SS Andrea Doria, U.S. Steel Hour (1959), All's Fair (1982); Movies: The Prince and the Pauper, Wuthering Heights, Swiss Family Robinson, Meet Me in St. Louis, The Power and the Glory, My Sweet Charlie, The Miracle Worker (Emmy Award, 1979), Before and After, The Baby Sitter, The Women's Room, Something So Right, Perry Mason: The Avenging Ace, A Time of Triumph, Fatal Dosage, See You in the Morning, Fatal Judgment, Everybody's Baby: The Rescue of Jessica McClure, Amityville: The Evil Escapes. Mini-series: Captains and the Kings; George Washington. Host: Fatal Passions.

DUKES, DAVID: Actor. b. San Francisco, CA, June 6, 1945. On Bdwy. in Don Juan, The Visit, Holiday, School for Wives, Dracula, Travesties, Frankenstein, Bent, Amadeus, M. Butterfly.

PICTURES: The Wild Party, A Little Romance, The First Deadly Sin, Only When I Laugh, Without a Trace, The Men's Club, Catch the Heat, Date With an Angel, Deadly Intent, See You in the Morning, Rawhead Rex.

TELEVISION: Beacon Hill (series), 79 Park Avenue, Family, Some Kind of Miracle, The Triangle Factory Fire Scandal, Mayflower—the Pilgrim Adventure, Margaret Sanger–Portrait of a Rebel, George Washington, Sentimental Journey, Space, Kane and Abel, Strange Interlude, The Winds of War, War and Remembrance.

DULLEA, KEIR: Actor. b. Cleveland, OH, May 30, 1936. e. San Francisco State Coll., Sanford Meisner's Neighborhood Playhouse. Worked as ice cream vendor, carpenter with a construction co. Acted as resident juvenile at the Totem Pole Playhouse in PA. N.Y. theatre debut in the revue Sticks and Stones, 1956; appeared in stock co. prods. at the Berkshire Playhouse and Philadelphia's Hedgerow Theatre, 1959, off-Broadway debut in Season of Choice, 1969.

THEATER: Dr. Cooks Garden, Butterflies Are Free, Cat on a Hot Tin Roof, P.S. Your Cat is Dead.

TELEVISION: All Summer Long, Law and Order, Legend of the Golden Gun.

PICTURES: The Hoodlum Priest, David and Lisa (Best Actor Award, San Francisco Int'l Film Festival), The Thin Red Line, Mail Order Bride, The Naked Hours, Madame X, Bunny Lake Is Missing, The Fox, 2001: A Space Odyssey, de Sade, Pope Joan, Paul and Michelle, The Paperback Hero, Silent Night, Evil Night, Leopard in the Snow, Brainwave, 2010, Devil in the Brain, Black Christmas, Welcome to Blood City, Full Circle.

DUNAWAY, FAYE: Actress. b. Bascom, FL, Jan. 14, 1941. e. Texas, Arkansas, Utah, Germany, U. of Florida. Awarded a Fulbright scholarship in theatre. Boston U. of Fine Applied Arts. Appeared on N.Y. stage in: A Man for All Seasons, After the Fall (with Lincoln Center Repertory Co., three years), Hogan's Goat.

PICTURES: The Happening, Bonnie and Clyde, Hurry Sundown, The Thomas Crown Affair, The Extraordinary Seaman, A Place for Lovers, The Arrangement, Puzzle of a Downfall Child, Little Big Man, Doc, Oklahoma Crude, The Three Musketeers, Chinatown, The Towering Inferno, The Four Musketeers, Three Days of the Condor, Network (Acad. Award, 1976), Voyage of the Damned, Eyes of Laura Mars, The Champ, The First Deadly Sin, Mommie Dearest, The Wicked Lady, Ordeal by Innocence, Supergirl, Barfly, Midnight Crossing, Burning Secret, Circe and Bravo, The Match. Helmut Newton: Frames From the Edge (doc.), The Handmaid's Tale, Wait Until Spring, Bandini, On a Moonlit Night.

TELEVISION: Portrait: The Woman I Love, The Disappearance of Aimee, Evita, Ellis Island, 13 at Dinner, Beverly Hills Madam, The Country Girl, Christopher Columbus, Casanova, The Raspberry Ripple, Cold Sassy Tree.

DUNCAN, LINDSAY: Actress. Stage actress with National Theatre, Royal Shakespeare Company.

THEATRE: Plenty, The Provok'd Wife, The Prince of Homburg, Top Girls, Progress, The Merry Wives of Windsor, Les Liaisons Dangereuses (RSC, West End, Broadway).

PICTURES: Loose Connections, Samson & Delilah, Prick Up Your Ears, Muck and Brass, Manifesto, The Reflecting Skin.

TELEVISION: Reilly, Ace of Spies, Dead Head (serial), Traffik.

DUNCAN, SANDY: Actress. b. Henderson, TX, Feb. 20, 1946. m. singer-dancer Don Correia. e. Len Morris Coll.

THEATER: The Music Man (NY debut, 1965); The Boyfriend, Ceremony of Innocence, Your Own Thing, Canterbury Tales, Peter Pan, My One and Only.

PICTURES: $1,000,000 Duck, Star Spangled Girl, The Cat from Outer Space.

TELEVISION: Funny Face (1971), The Sandy Duncan Show, Roots, Valerie's Family (later called Hogan Family).

DUNING, GEORGE: Composer, Conductor, Arranger. b. Richmond, IN, Feb. 25, 1908. e. Cincinnati Conservatory of Music, U. of Cincinnati. Musical director; music scores for many m.p. including: Jolson Sings Again, Eddy Duchin Story, From Here to Eternity, Picnic, World of Susie Wong, Devil at 4 O'Clock, Toys in the Attic, Any Wednesday, The Man with Bogart's Face. TV: No Time for Sergeants, Wendy and Me, The Farmer's Daughter, Big Valley, The Long Hot Summer, The Second Hundred Years, Star Trek, Mannix, Then Came Bronson; music dir. Aaron Spelling Prods., 1970–71, Bobby Sherman Show, Movies of the Week. Board of Directors, ASCAP.

DUNLAP, RICHARD D.: Producer, Director. b. Pomona, CA, Jan. 30, 1923. e. Yale U., B.A., 1944; M.F.A., 1948. U.S. Navy 1943–46; Instructor, English dept., Yale U., 1947–48; Prod.-dir., Kraft TV Theatre, 3 years; Dir, Assoc. Prod., Omnibus, 3 seasons; Dir., 25 half-hr. Dramatic Film Shows. Frank Sinatra Specials, Prod.-Dir., 11 Academy Award Shows, 4 Emmy Award Shows. Artistic dir. Berkshire Theatre Festival.

DUNNE, DOMINICK: Producer. Writer. Father of actor-prod. Griffin Dunne. Began career as stage manager at NBC-TV; then produced shows for CBS Studio One. Later exec. prod. at 20th-Fox TV, v.p. at Four Star. Novels: The Winner, The Two Mrs. Grenvilles.

PICTURES: Boys in the Band (exec. prod.), The Panic in Needle Park, Play It as It Lays, Ash Wednesday.

DUNNE, GRIFFIN: Actor, Producer. b. New York, NY, June 8, 1955. Son of prod.-writer Dominick Dunne. Formed Double Play Prods. with Amy Robinson. Studied at Neighborhood Playhouse and with Uta Hagen. On Stage in Album, Marie and Bruce, Coming Attractions, Hotel Play.

PICTURES: Actor: Head Over Heels (also prod.); American Werewolf in London; The Fan; Almost You; Johnny Dangerously; After Hours (also co-prod.), Who's That Girl, Amazon Women on the Moon, Big Blue, Me and Him, Perugia. Producer only: Baby It's You, Running on Empty.

TELEVISION: The Wall, Lip Service.

DUNNE, IRENE: Actress. b. Louisville, KY, Dec. 20, 1904. e. Loretta Acad. in St. Louis, MO; Chicago Coll. of Music, D.M., 1945; N.Y. One child, Mary Frances. Screen debut Leathernecking 1930. Kennedy Center Honors (1986).

THEATRE: Stage prods. include Sweetheart Time, The City Chap, Show Boat.

PICTURES: Cimarron, The Great Lover, Consolation Marriage, Bachelor Apartment, Back Street, Symphony of Six Million, Thirteen Women, No Other Women, The Secret of Madame Blanche, Silver Cord, Ann Vickers, If I Were Free, This Man of Mine, Stingaree, The Age of Innocence, Sweet Adeline, Roberta, Magnificent Obsession, Showboat, Theodora Goes Wild, The Awful Truth, Hide Wide and Handsome, Joy of Living, Love Affair, Invitation to Happiness, My Favorite Wife, Penny Serenade, Unfinished Business, Lady in a Jam, A Guy Named Joe, The White Cliffs of Dover, Together Again, Over 21, Anna and the King of Siam, Life with Father, I Remember Mama, Never A Dull Moment, The Mudlark, It Grows on Trees.

TELEVISION: Schlitz Playhouse (host).

DUNNE, PHILIP: Writer, Producer, Director. b. New York, NY, Feb. 11, 1908. p. Finley P. and Margaret Abbott Dunne. e. Harvard U. m. Amanda Duff.

PICTURES: How Green Was My Valley, Stanley and Livingstone, The Rains Came, Johnnie Apollo, Son of Fury, Suez, Lancer Spy, The Last of the Mohicans, The Count of Monte Cristo, The Late George Apley, Forever Amber, The Ghost and Mrs. Muir, Escape, Luck of the Irish, Pinky, David and Bathsheba, Anne of the Indies, Lydia Bailey, Way of a Gaucho, Demetrius and the Gladiators, The Egyptian, Prince

of Players, View from Pompey's Head, Hilda Crane, Three Brave Men, Ten North Frederick, In Love and War, Blue Denim, Wild In The Country, Lisa, Blindfold, The Agony and the Ecstasy.
PUBLICATIONS: Mr. Dooley Remembers, Atlantic-Little Brown. Take Two (McGraw Hill, 1980).

DUNNING, JOHN: Film editor. b. Los Angeles, CA, May 5, 1916. e. UCLA, A.B., 1939. With MGM since 1935; U.S. Armed Forces, 1942–45. Post prod. supv., MGM, Inc.
PICTURES: Cass Timberlane, Homecoming, Julia Misbehaves, Battleground, Show Boat, Julius Caesar, Take the High Ground, Rhapsody, Last Time I Saw Paris, Tender Trap, Interrupted Melody, The Swan, Brothers Karamozov, Raintree County, Cimarron, Ben-Hur (Acad. Award).

DUNNOCK, MILDRED: Actress. b. Baltimore, MD, Jan. 25, 1906. e. Goucher Co., Baltimore. Teacher, Brearly Sch., N.Y.; acted in summer stock.
THEATRE: B'way debut: Life Begins; since in Corn Is Green; Richard III, Vicki, Lute Song, Another Part of the Forest, Death of a Salesman, Cat on a Hot Tin Roof, The Chinese, Colette.
PICTURES: Corn Is Green, Kiss of Death, I Want You, Death of a Salesman, Viva Zapata, Girl in White, The Jazz Singer, Bad for Each Other, Hansel & Gretel (voice), Children of Fortune, Trouble with Harry, Love Me Tender, Baby Doll, The Nun's Story, Story on Page One, Farewell Eugene, Butterfield 8, Sweet Bird of Youth, Seven Women, Barefoot in the Park, Whatever Happened to Aunt Alice?, Dragonfly, The Pick-Up Artist.
TELEVISION: The Power and the Glory, Death of a Salesman.

DURNING, CHARLES: Actor. b. Highland Falls, NY, Feb. 28, 1933. Many stage credits on Broadway (That Championship Season, The Happiness Cage, etc.).
PICTURES: Harry and Walter Go to New York, Twilight's Last Gleaming, The Choirboys, Breakheart Pass, The Hindenburg, Enemy of the People, The Sting, Dog Day Afternoon, The Fury, The Greek Tycoon, Tilt, The Muppet Movie, North Dallas Forty, Starting Over, When a Stranger Calls, The Final Countdown, True Confessions, Sharky's Machine, Tootsie, The Best Little Whorehouse in Texas, To Be or Not to Be, Two of a Kind, Stick, Mass Appeal, The Man with One Red Shoe, Big Trouble, Stand Alone, Happy New Year, Tough Guys, Where the River Runs Black, The Rosary Murders, A Tiger's Tail, Cop, Far North, Ballerina, Brenda Starr, Etolie, Cat Chaser, No Cause For Alarm.
TELEVISION: Captains and the Kings, The Rivalry, The Dancing Bear, The Cop and the Kid (1975 series), Queen of the Stardust Ballroom, Studs Lonigan, Working, Mr. Roberts, Side by Side (pilot), P.O.P. (pilot), Eye to Eye, Death of a Salesman, Kenny Rogers as The Gambler III—The Legend Continues, The Man Who Broke 1000 Chains, Case Closed, Unholy Matrimony. It Nearly Wasn't Christmas, Dinner at Eight.

DURSTON, DAVID E.: Writer, Director. b. Newcastle, PA, Sept. 10, 1925. e. Evanston Township H.S. Served as TV-radio director, Lynn Baker Adv. Agency, 1952–57; assoc. producer, Your Hit Parade, 1957–58. Acting credits include Winged Victory (B'way, film), Young Man's Fancy (B'way); Radio includes The Woolworth Hour (prod.), CBS Workshop (writer).
PICTURES: Felicia, Love Statue, Reflections, Blue Sextet (also edited), I Drink Your Blood, Stigma, Molokai, Savages Apprentice.
TELEVISION: as writer: Tales of Tomorrow, Navy Log, Hart to Hart, Ladies Man, The New Adventures of Flipper (story editor), Tournament of Roses Parade (exec. prod., 1954 & 55).

DURWOOD, RICHARD M.: Executive. b. Kansas City, MO, Aug. 18, 1929. e. Brown U., A.B. Pres. Crown Cinema Corp. Member: Motion Picture Assn. of Kansas City (pres.); United Motion Pictures Assn. (pres. 1972–73); Young NATO (chmn., 1968–69); Past Chief Barker, Tent #8; Past mem., exec. comm., National NATO.

DURWOOD, STANLEY H.: Chairman of the Board, American Multi-Cinema, Inc. b. 1920; e. Harvard Coll., B.S. (football, wrestling). Air Force navigator 3 years. Member: Harvard Club of Kansas City; Harvard Club of New York. On board of United Missouri Bankshares.

DUSSAULT, NANCY: Actress. b. Pensacola, FL, Jun. 30, 1936. e. Northwestern U. On Bdwy. in Street Scene, The Mikado, The Cradle Will Rock, Do Re Mi, Sound of Music, Carousel, Fiorello, The Gershwin Years, Into the Woods.
PICTURE: The In-Laws.
TELEVISION: The Beggars Opera, Good Morning America (hostess). Series: The New Dick Van Dyke Show, Too Close for Comfort, The Ted Knight Show.

DUTFIELD, RAY: Executive. Early career as chief accountant in Hawker Siddeley Group. Ent. m.p. ind. 1957, as exec. accountant with Rank Film Laboratories, gen. man., 1967; Appt. to board of dir., 1969; Appt. man. dir., 1970. Appt. man. dir., Rank Leisure Services, 1976 and vice-chmn., Rank Film Laboratories. 1979 January appt. chmn. and chief executive officer, Technicolor Limited, Fellow Member of Inst. Chartered Accounts, SMPTE, BKSTS, Member Institute of Directors, Institute of Marketing.

DUVALL, ROBERT: Actor. b. San Diego, CA, Jan. 5, 1931. e. Principia College, IL. Studied at the Neighborhood Playhouse, NY.
THEATER: A View From the Bridge (Obie Award, 1965); Wait Until Dark; American Buffalo.
PICTURES: To Kill a Mockingbird, Captain Newman, M.D., Nightmare in the Sun, The Chase, Countdown, The Detective, Bullitt, True Grit, The Rain People, M*A*S*H, The Revolutionary, THX-1138, Lawman, The Godfather, Tomorrow, The Great Northfield, Minn. Raid, Joe Kidd, Lady Ice, Badge 373, The Outfit, The Conversation, Godfather, Part II, Break-out, The Killer Elite, The Seven Percent Solution, Network, We're Not the Jet Set (dir., co-prod. only), The Eagle Has Landed, The Greatest, The Betsy, Invasion of the Body Snatchers, Apocalypse Now, The Great Santini, True Confessions, The Pursuit of D.B. Cooper, Tender Mercies (Acad. Award, 1984; also co-prod.); Angelo, My Love (dir., s.p. only), The Stone Boy, The Natural, Belzaire the Cajun, The Lightship, Let's Get Harry, Hotel Colonial, Colors, Convicts, Roots in a Parched Ground, The Handmaid's Tale, A Show of Force.
TELEVISION: The Outer Limits; Guilty or Not Guilty; Movies: Fame is the Name of the Game, Ike; Lonesome Dove.

DUVALL, SHELLEY: Actress, Producer. b. Houston, TX, 1949. Founded Think Entertainment, TV prod. co.
PICTURES: Brewster McCloud, McCabe and Mrs. Miller, Thieves Like Us, Nashville, Buffalo Bill and the Indians, Three Women (best actress, Cannes Fest., 1977), Annie Hall, The Shining, Popeye, Time Bandits, Roxanne.
TELEVISION: Bernice Bobs Her Hair, Lily, Twilight Zone. Producer: Faerie Tale Theatre, Tall Tales and Legends. Exec. prod.: Nightmare Classics (Turn of the Screw), Dinner at Eight.

DYER, TONY: Actor. b. Feb. 8, 1919. e. U. of Missouri, Alvine Sch. of Theatre. Acting debut: Cotton Blossom Showboat and Arthur Casey-Mary Hart Repertoire.
PICTURES: To Please A Lady, Children of An Loc, Apocalypse Now, Up from the Lower Depths, Bushido Blade.
TELEVISION: Shogun.

DYSART, RICHARD A.: b. Brighton, MA. e. Emerson Coll., Actor. On Bdwy. in The Quare Fellow, Our Town, Epitaph for George Dillon, Six Characters in Search of an Author, A Man for All Seasons, The Little Foxes, A Place without Doors, That Championship Season, Another Part of the Forest.
PICTURES: Petulia; The Lost Man; The Sporting Club; The Hospital; The Terminal Man; The Crazy World of Julius Vrooder; The Day of the Locust; The Hindenberg; Prophecy; Meteor; Being There; An Enemy of the People; The Thing; The Falcon and the Snowman; Mask; Warning Signs; Pale Rider; Wall Street.
TELEVISION: Movies: The Autobiography of Miss Jane Pittman; Blood and Orchids; First You Cry; Bogie; The Ordeal of Dr. Mudd; Churchill and the Generals; People Vs. Jean Harris; A Bitter Harvest; The Last Days of General Patton; The Seal; Missing Children—A Mother's Story; Concealed Enemies; Malice in Wonderland, Day One. War and Remembrance (mini-series). Series: L.A. Law. Special: Jay Leno's Family Comedy Hour; Moving Target.

DZUNDZA, GEORGE: Actor. b. Rosenheim, Germany, 1945. Spent part of childhood in displaced-persons camps before he was moved to Amsterdam in 1949. Came to NY in 1956 where he attended St. John's U. as speech and theater major.
THEATER: King Lear (NY Shakespeare Fest., debut, 1973), That Championship Season (tour, 1973), Mert and Phil, The Ritz, Legend, A Prayer for My Daughter.
PICTURES: The Happy Hooker (1975), Honky Tonk Freeway, The Deer Hunter, Streamers, Best Defense, No Mercy, No Way Out, The Beast, Impulse, Honor Bound.
TELEVISION: Guest: Starsky and Hutch, The Waltons. Series: Open All Night. Movies: The Execution of Raymond Graham, The Rape of Richard Beck, Brotherly Love, Salem's Lot, Police Plaza, The Lost Honor of Kathryn Beck, Implied Force, The Face of Rape, We're a Family Again, The Ryan White Story, Terror on Highway 91.

E

EASTWOOD, CLINT: Actor, Producer, Director. b. San Francisco, CA, May 31, 1930; e. Oakland Technical H.S., Los Angeles City Coll. Worked as a lumberjack in Oregon before being drafted into the Army, Special Services 1950–54. Then contract player at Universal Studios. Starred in TV series

Rawhide, 1958–65. Formed Malpaso Productions, 1969. Made a Chevalier des Lettres by French gov., 1985. Mayor, Carmel, CA 1986–88.
PICTURES: Revenge of the Creature (debut, 1955), Francis in the Navy, Lady Godiva, Tarantula, Never Say Goodbye, The First Traveling Saleslady, Star in the Dust, Escapade in Japan, Ambush at Cimarron Pass, Lafayette Escadrille, A Fistful of Dollars, For a Few Dollars More, The Witches, The Good The Bad and The Ugly, Hang 'Em High, Coogan's Bluff, Where Eagles Dare, The Witches (Le Streghe), Paint Your Wagon, Kelly's Heroes, Two Mules For Sister Sara, Beguiled, Play Misty For Me (dir. and star); Dirty Harry, Joe Kidd, Breezy (dir. only); High Plains Drifter, (also dir.), Magnum Force, Thunderbolt & Lightfoot; The Eiger Sanction (also dir.), The Outlaw Josey Wales (also dir.), The Enforcer, The Gauntlet (also dir.), Every Which Way But Loose, Escape from Alcatraz, Bronco Billy (dir., star), Any Which Way You Can, Firefox (prod., dir., star), Honky Tonk Man (prod., dir., star), Sudden Impact (prod., dir., star), Tightrope (also prod.), City Heat, Pale Rider (prod., dir., star), Heartbreak Ridge (prod., dir., star); The Dead Pool (prod., star), Bird (dir. only), Thelonius Monk: Straight, No Chaser (exec. prod. only), Pink Cadillac, White Hunter, Black Heart (prod., dir., actor).
TELEVISION: Series: Rawhide. Specials: Fame, Fortune and Romance, Happy Birthday Hollywood. Dir.: Amazing Stories.

EBERTS, JAKE: Producer, Financier. r.n. John Eberts. b. Montreal, Canada, July 10, 1941. President Goldcrest. 1983 joined Embassy Pictures; 1985 founded Allied Filmmakers.
PICTURES: Chariots of Fire, Another Country, Local Hero, The Dresser, Cal, The Emerald Forest, Gandhi, The Name of the Rose, Cry Freedom, White Mischief, The Adventures of Baron Munchausen (exec. prod.).

EBSEN, BUDDY: Actor. r.n. Christian Ebsen, Jr. b. Belleville, IL, April 2, 1908. e. U. of Florida, Rollins Coll. Won first Broadway role as dancer in Ziegfeld's Whoopee in 1928. Sister, Vilma, became dancing partner and they played nightclubs and did road tours. Went to Hollywood and appeared in many musicals as single. Later became dramatic actor and appeared on TV.
PICTURES: Broadway Melody of 1936, Captain January, Banjo on My Knee, Four Girls in White, My Lucky Star, Thunder in God's Country, Red Garters, Davy Crockett, Attack, Breakfast at Tiffany's, Mail Order Bride, The One and Only Original Family Band.
TELEVISION: Hawaii Five-O, Gunsmoke. Series: Davy Crockett, Northwest Passage, The Beverly Hillbillies, Barnaby Jones, Matt Houston. Movies: Stone Fox, Fire on the Mountain, The Bastard, Tom Sawyer.
STAGE: Take Her, She's Mine, Our Town.

EBY, GEORGE W.: Executive. b. Pittsburgh, PA, Jan. 2, 1914. e. Carnegie Tech., Pennsylvania State U., B.A. 1934. pres., Ice Capades, Inc., 1963–78, chmn., Jan. 1, 1979; Int. Chief Barker Variety Clubs, 1958–60. Retired, 1983.

ECCLES, TED: Executive. Began career with Modern Film Effects developing special effects & title sequences for feature films. At Paramount Pictures for year as admin., west coast audio visual services. Joined Walt Disney Pictures 1985 as dir. of creative film svcs.

ECKERT, JOHN M.: Producer, Production Executive. b. Chatham, Ontario, Canada, e. Ryerson Polytechnical Inst., 1968–71 (film major). 12 features as unit prod. mgr. or asst. dir. Member: DGA, DGC.
PICTURES: Power Play (assoc. prod.), Running (co-prod.), Middle Age Crazy (co-prod.), Dead Zone (unit prod. mgr.), Cats Eye (exec. in charge of prod.), Silver Bullet (assoc. prod.), Home Is Where the Heart Is (prod.), Millenium (suprv. prod.).
TELEVISION: Terry Fox Story (assoc. prod.), Special People (prod., Christopher Award), Danger Bay (series supv. prod., 1985–87).

EDDINGTON, PAUL: C.B.E., 1987. Actor. b. London, Eng., June 18, 1927. Since 1944 extensive career on stage. Ent. TV ind. 1955. Numerous television plays and series incl: Quartet, Blithe Spirit, Outside Edge, Murder at the Vicarage, The Adventures of Robin Hood, Fall of Eagles, The Rivals of Sherlock Holmes, Danger Man, The Prisoner, The Avengers, Van der Valk, Frontier, Special Branch, The Good Life, Yes, Minister, Yes, Prime Minister.
PICTURES: The Man Who Was Nobody, Jet Storm, The Devil's Brigade, Baxter.

EDELE, DURAND (BUD) J.: Executive. e. St. Louis U., Washington U. Reportorial staff, St. Louis Globe Democrat, 1934–35; booking dept., Paramount, 1935; booker & salesman, Warner Bros., 1936–41; branch & dist. mgr., Film Classics, 1946; branch mgr., United Artists, 1952–60; managed various divisions, United Artists, 1960–63; gen. sales mgr., v.p., Avco Embassy Pictures Corp., 1964, gen. sales mgr., Venture Dist. Inc., 1976; Consultant, RCMC 1976–78.

EDEN, BARBARA: Actress. b. Tucson, AZ, Aug. 23, 1934. e. San Francisco Conservatory of Music. Pres. Mi-Bar Productions. Dir. Security National Bank of Chicago.
PICTURES: Back from Eternity, Twelve Hours to Kill, Flaming Star, Voyage to the Bottom of the Sea, Five Weeks in a Balloon, The Wonderful World of the Brothers Grimm, The Brass Bottle, Seven Faces of Dr. Lao, Harper Valley PTA.
TELEVISION: Series: How to Marry a Millionaire, I Dream of Jeannie, A Brand New Life.Movies: The Feminist and the Fuzz, Guess Who's Sleeping in My Bed, The Stranger Within, Let's Switch, How to Break Up a Happy Divorce, A Howling in the Woods, I Dream of Jeannie: 15 Years Later, The Stepford Children, The Secret Life of Kathy McCormick (also co-prod.), Your Mother Wears Combat Boots.

EDWARDS, ANTHONY: Actor. b. Santa Barbara, CA, July 19, 1962. Grandfather designed Walt Disney Studios in the 1930s and worked for Cecil B. De Mille as conceptual artist. Acted in 30 plays from age 12 to 17. At 16 worked professionally in TV commercials. 1980 attended Royal Acad. of Arts, London. and studied drama at USC. Film debut: Fast Times at Ridgemont High (1982).
PICTURES: Heart Like a Wheel, Revenge of the Nerds, The Sure Thing, Gotcha, Top Gun, Summer Heat, Mr. North, Miracle Mile, Hawks, How I Got Into College, Downtown.
TELEVISION: Series: It Takes Two. Movies: The Killing of Randy Webster, High School, U.S.A., The Bill Johnson Story.

EDWARDS, BLAKE: Writer, Director, Producer. r.n. William Blake McEdwards. b. Tulsa, OK, July 26, 1922. m. actress Julie Andrews. e. Beverly Hills H.S. Coast Guard during war. Film acting debut, Ten Gentlemen from West Point (1942).
RADIO: Johnny Dollar, Line-up; writer-creator: Richard Diamond.
PICTURES: Writer: Panhandle, Stampede, Sound Off, Bring Your Smile Along, All Ashore, Cruisin' Down the River, Rainbow Round My Shoulder, He Laughed Last, Drive a Crooked Road, My Sister Eileen, Mr. Cory, This Happy Feeling, The Perfect Furlough, Operation Mad Ball, Notorious Landlady. Director: Operation Petticoat, High Time, Breakfast at Tiffany's, Experiment in Terror, Days of Wine and Roses, Soldier in the Rain, The Pink Panther, Shot in the Dark, The Great Race, What Did You Do in the War, Daddy, Gunn, Darling Lili, The Party, The Wild Rovers, Carey Treatment, The Tamarind Seed (dir., s.p.) The Return of the Pink Panther (prod., dir., co-s.p.), The Pink Panther Strikes Again (prod., dir., co-s.p.), Revenge of the Pink Panther (prod., dir., co-s.p.); "10" (co-prod., dir., s.p.). S.O.B. (co-prod., dir., Victor/Victoria (co-prod., dir., s.p.); Trail of the Pink Panther (co-prod., dir., co-s.p.); The Man Who Loved Women (prod., dir., co-s.p.); Micki and Maude (dir.); A Fine Mess (dir., s.p.), That's Life (dir., co-s.p.); Blind Date (dir.); Sunset (dir., s.p.); Skin Deep (dir., s.p.), Switch.
TELEVISION: City Detective (prod., 1953), The Dick Powell Show (dir.), creator: Dante's Inferno, Peter Gunn, Mr. Lucky, Justin Case (exec. prod., dir., writer), Peter Gunn (exec. prod., dir., writer). Specials: Julie! (prod., dir.), Julie on Sesame St. (exec. prod.), Julie and Dick in Covent Garden (dir.).

EDWARDS, DOUGLAS: News Correspondent. b. Ada, OK, July 14, 1917. Became radio reporter in Troy, AL, at 15 yrs. e. U. of Alabama, Emory U., U. of Georgia. News reporter for WAGF, Dothan, AL; asst. news editor for Atlanta Journal and its station, WSB. Transferred to WXYZ, Detroit, returning to WSB as asst. news editor 2 yrs. later. Joined CBS Radio News staff, 1942, appearing on Report to the Nation, and The World Today. Chief of CBS News Paris Bureau. First major newsman to make transition to TV, 1947. Anchorman on CBS Afternoon News and Douglas Edwards with the News for 15 years on CBS-TV. CBS Mid-Day News with Douglas Edwards. Retired from CBS, 1988.

EDWARDS, JAMES H.: Executive. President, Storey Theatres, Inc. b. Cedartown, GA, Aug. 14, 1927. e. Georgia State. U.S. Navy, 1948–50. With Ga. Theatre Co., 1950–1952; Storey Theatres, 1952–present. Formerly pres. & chmn., NATO of Ga; formerly pres., Variety Club of Atlanta. Former dir. at large, Nat'l. NATO. Director, numerous theatre cos.

EDWARDS, RALPH: Producer, Emcee. b. Merino, CO, June 13, 1913. e. U. of California, Berkeley. Began career in radio in 1929 as writer-actor-producer-announcer at station KROW, Oakland. Later joined CBS & NBC Radio in New York as announcer. 1940, originated, produced and emceed Truth or Consequences for both radio & TV. Also has produced and hosted This Is Your Life, The Ralph Edwards Show, Name That Tune, Cross Wits, The People's Court, This Is Your Life (special edition, 1987).

EDWARDS, VINCE: Actor. b. New York, NY, July 9, 1928. e. Ohio State U., U. of Hawaii, American Acad. of Dramatic Arts. N.Y. stage. High Button Shoes.
TELEVISION: Series: Ben Casey. Guest: Studio One, Phil-

co, Kraft, The Untouchables, General Electric Theatre, Hitchcock, The Deputy. Movies: Firehouse, The Rhinemann Exchange, The Dirty Dozen: The Deadly Mission, The Return of Ben Casey.

PICTURES: Sailor Beware, Hiawatha, Rogue Cop, Night Holds Terror, Serenade, The Killing, Hit and Run, The Scavengers, The Three Faces of Eve, City of Fear, Murder by Contract, The Victors, Devil's Brigade, The Desperados, Las Vegas, Los Angeles, The Seduction, Space Raiders, Deal of the Century, Cellar Dweller, The Gumshoe Kid.

EGGAR, SAMANTHA: Actress. b. London, Eng., March 5, 1939. e. student Webber-Douglas Dramatic Sch., London; Slade Sch. of Art.

PICTURES: The Wild and the Willing, Dr. Crippen, Doctor in Distress, Psyche 59, The Collector, Walk Don't Run, Return From the Ashes, Doctor Dolittle, The Molly Maguires, The Lady in the Car, Walking Stick, The Grove, Light at the Edge of the World, 7% Solution, Demonoid, Why Shoot the Teacher, Blood City, The Uncanny, Curtains, Loner, The Exterminator, The Brood.

TELEVISION: Anna and the King (series), Man of Destiny, Double Indemnity, All The Kind Strangers, The Killer Who Wouldn't Die, Ziegfeld: the Man and His Women, The Hope Diamond, Columbo, Baretta, The Hemingway Play, Love Story, Kojak, McMillan & Wife, Streets of San Francisco, Starsky and Hutch, Love Among Thieves, Hart to Hart, Murder She Wrote, Finder of Lost Loves, George Burns Comedy Week, Lucas Tanner, Hotel, Fantasy Island, Magnum, Stingray, Tales of the Unexpected, Heartbeat, Davy Crockett: Rainbow in the Thunder, Family Love Boat, Terror in the Aisles, 1st & Ten, Outlaws.

EHRLICH, ROSEANNE: Executive. e. Sarah Lawrence Coll., B.A., English literature. Entered m.p. industry as freelance reader for Warner Bros., Avco Embassy and Robert Stigwood Org. 1977–80, East Coast story editor for Lorimar Productions. 1981, joined Paramount Pictures as dir. of literary affairs. 1985, promoted to v.p., prod., East Coast for M.P. Group.

EICHHORN, LISA: Actress. b. Reading, PA, 1952. e. Queen's U. Kingston, Canada and Eng. for literature studies at Oxford. Studied at Royal Acad. of Dramatic Art. Made film debut in Yanks (1979).

THEATER: The Hasty Heart (debut, L.A.), The Common Pursuit.

PICTURES: The Europeans, Why Would I Lie?, Cutter and Bone, Weather in the Streets, Wild Rose; Opposing Force, Moon 44.

TELEVISION: Series: All My Children (1987), Movies: The Wall, Blind Justice, Wings of the Dove, East Lynne, Murder in Three Acts.

EIKENBERRY, JILL: Actress. b. New Haven, CT, Jan. 21, 1947. e. Yale U. Drama Sch. m. actor Michael Tucker.

THEATER: Broadway: All Over Town, Watch on the Rhine, Onward Victoria, Summer Brave, Moonchildren. Off-Bdwy: Lemon Sky, Life Under Water, Uncommon Women and Others, Porch, The Primary English Class.

PICTURES: Between the Lines, The End of the World in Our Usual Bed in a Night Full of Rain, An Unmarried Woman, Butch and Sundance: The Early Days, Rich Kids, Hide in Plain Sight, Arthur, Grace Quigley, The Manhattan Project.

TELEVISION: The Deadliest Season, Orphan Train, Swan Song, Uncommon Women and Others, Sessions, Kane & Abel, Assault and Matrimony, Family Sins, A Stoning in Fulham Country, My Boyfriend's Back, The Diane Martin Story. Series: L.A. Law, The Best of Families (PBS). Special: Destined to Live (prod., host), A Family Again.

EILBACHER, LISA: Actress. b. May 5, Saudi Arabia. Moved to California at age 7; acted on TV as child.

PICTURES: War Between Men and Women (1972), Run for the Rose (aka Thoroughbred), On the Right Track, An Officer and a Gentleman, Ten to Midnight, Beverly Hills Cop, Deadly Intent, Leviathan, Never Say Die.

TELEVISION: Series: Wagon Train, Laredo, My Three Sons, Gunsmoke, Combat, Ryan's Four. Series: The Texas Wheelers, The Hardy Boys Mysteries, Ryan's Four, Me and Mom. Movies: Bad Ronald, The Patty Hearst Story, Love for Rent, To Race the Wind, This House Possessed, Monte Carlo, Deadly Deception. Mini-Series: Wheels, The Winds of War.

EISNER, MICHAEL D.: Executive. b. Mt. Kisco, NY, March 7, 1942. e. Denison U., B.A. Started career with programming dept. of CBS TV network. Joined ABC in 1966 as mgr. talent and specials. Dec., 1968 became dir. of program dev.—east coast. In March, 1971 named v.p., daytime programming, ABC-TV. In June, 1975 made v.p., prog. planning and dev. In May, 1976 named sr. v.p., prime time production and dev., ABC Entertainment. In Nov., 1976, left ABC to join Paramount Pictures as pres. & chief operating officer. 1984, joined Walt Disney Prods. as chmn. & CEO.

EKBERG, ANITA: Actress. b. Malmö, Sweden, Sept. 29, 1931. Started career as a model.

PICTURES: Man in the Vault, Blood Alley, Artists and Models, War and Peace, Back from Eternity, Zarak, Pickup Alley, Sheba and the Gladiator, Sign of the Gladiator, La Dolce Vita, Boccaccio '70, The Alphabet Murder, The Cobra, Fellini's Clowns, Federico Fellini's Intervista.

EKLAND, BRITT: Actress. b. Stockholm, Sweden, Sept. 29, 1942.

TELEVISION: England: A Cold Peace. U.S.A.: Trials of O'Brien, McCloud, Six Million Dollar Man.

PICTURES: After the Fox, Double Man, Bobo, Night They Raided Minsky's, At Any Price, Stiletto, Cannibals, Tintomara, Percy, Carter, Night, Endless Night, Baxter, Asylum, Wicker Man, Ultimate Thrill, Man With Golden Gun, Royal Flash, Slavers, King Solomon's Treasure, Fraternity Vacation, Moon in Scorpio, Scandal, Beverly Hills Vamp.

ELAM, JACK: Actor. b. Miami, AZ, Nov. 13, 1916. e. Santa Monica Jr. Coll., Modesto Jr. Coll. Worked in Los Angeles as bookkeeper and theatre mgr.; served in Navy in W.W.II. Introduction to show business was as bookkeeper for Sam Goldwyn. Later worked as controller for other film producers. Given first acting job by producer George Templeton in 1948; has since appeared in over 100 films.

PICTURES: Wild Weed (debut, 1949), Rawhide, Kansas City Confidential, The Moonlighter, Vera Cruz, Moonfleet, Kiss Me Deadly, Gunfight at OK Corral, Baby Face Nelson, Edge of Eternity, The Comancheros, The Rare Breed, The Way West, Firecreek, Once Upon a Time in the West, Support Your Local Sheriff, Rio Lobo, Support Your Local Gunfighter, Dirty Dingus Magee, The Cannonball Run, Cannonball Run II, Big Bad John.

TELEVISION: The Texas Wheelers, The Dakotas, Temple Huston, Gunsmoke. Series: The Texas Wheelers, Struck by Lightning, Easy Street. Movies: Black Beauty, Once Upon a Texas Train, Where The Hell's that Gold!!!?.

ELEFANTE, TOM: Executive. Began career as usher at Loews Riviera in Coral Gables, FL; progressed through ranks to asst. mgr., mgr. & Florida division mgr. 1972, joined Wometco Theatres as gen. mgr. 1975, returned to Loews Theatres as southeast div. mgr.; 1979, named natl. dir. of concessions, moving to h.o. in New York. 1987, appt. sr. v.p. & gen. mgr., Loews. Served as pres. and chmn. of NATO of Florida.

ELFAND, MARTIN: Executive. b. Los Angeles, CA, 1937. Was talent agent for ten years with top agencies; joined Artists Entertainment Complex in 1972. First film project as producer: Kansas City Bomber, first venture of AEC, of which he was sr. v.p. In 1977 joined Warner Bros. as production chief. 1980.

PICTURES: Prod.: Dog Day Afternoon, It's My Turn, An Officer and a Gentleman, King David, Clara's Heart. Exec. prod.: Her Alibi.

ELG, TAINA: Actress, Dancer. b. Helsinki, Finland, March 9, 1931. e. Helsinki, Sadler's Wells Ballet. Toured with Marquis de Cuevas Ballet; m.p. debut in The Prodigal.

PICTURES: The Prodigal, Diane, Gaby, Les Girls, Watusi, Imitation General, The 39 Steps.

ELIAS, HAL: Executive. b. Brooklyn, NY, Dec. 23. Publicity dir., State Theatre, Denver; western exploitation mgr., MGM; adv. dept., pub. dept., MGM, Culver City studios; Head, MGM cartoon studio (Tom and Jerry); UPA Pictures, Inc., vice-pres. studio mgr.: Hollywood Museum; bd. dir., Academy of Motion Picture Arts & Sciences, 35 years; treasurer, AMPAS 1976–1979. Academy Oscar, 1979, for dedicated and distinguished service to AMPAS.

ELIZONDO, HECTOR: Actor. b. New York, NY, Dec. 22, 1936. m. actress Carolee Campbell. Studied with Ballet Arts Co. of Carnegie Hall and Actors Studio. Many stage credits in N.Y. and Boston.

STAGE: Island in Infinity, Madonna of the Orchard, Drums in the Night, The Prisoner of Second Avenue, Dance of Death, Steambath (Obie Award), The Great White Hope, Medal of Honor Rag, Sly Fox.

PICTURES: Pocket Money, Born to Win, Deadhead Miles, Stand Up and Be Counted, One Across, Two Down, The Taking of Pelham One Two Three, Report to the Commissioner, American Gigolo, The Flamingo Kid, Young Doctors in Love, Nothing in Common, Leviathan, Chains of Gold.

TELEVISION: Debut: The Wendie Barrie Show (1947), The Impatient Heart, Kojack, the Jackie Gleason Show, All in the Family. Series: Popi (1976); A.K.A. Pablo (also dir.), Freebie and the Bean; Foley Sq. Movies: Casablanca, Medal of Honor Rag, The Dain Curse, Courage, Honeyboy, Out of the Darkness, Death on a Day Pass, Natica Jackson, Addicted to His Love, Your Mother Wears Combat Boots.

ELKINS, HILLARD: Producer. b. New York, NY, Oct. 18, 1929. e. NYU, B.A., 1951. Exec., William Morris Agy., 1949–51; exec. v.p., Gen. Artists Corp., 1952–53; pres., Hillard Elkins Mgmt.,

1953–60; Elkins Prods. Intl. Corp., N.Y., 1960–71; Elkins Prods. Ltd., 1972–; Hillard Elkins Entertainment Corp., 1974–; Media Mix Prods., Inc., 1979–82.

Member: Academy of Motion Picture Arts & Sciences, Acad. of TV Arts & Sciences, Dramatists Guild, League of New York Theatres, American Fed. of TV & Radio Artists.

PICTURES: Alice's Restaurant; A New Leaf; Oh, Calcutta!; A Doll's House; Richard Pryor Live in Concert; Sellers on Sellers.

THEATRE: Come On Strong; Golden Boy; Oh, Calcutta!; The Rothschilds; A Doll's House; An Evening with Richard Nixon; Sizwe Banzi Is Dead, etc.

TELEVISION: The Importance of Being Earnest; The Deadly Game, Princess Daisy. The Meeting (exec. prod.).

ELKINS, SAUL: Producer. b. New York, NY, June 22, 1907. e. City Coll. of New York, B.S., 1927. Radio writer, dir., prod. 1930–2; dir., prod. stock co. touring Latin America 1932–4; writer Fox Films, 20th Century-Fox; writer RKO, Columbia 1937–42; writer, dial-dir., dir. Warner Bros. 1943–7; prod. Warner Bros. since 1947. Member: AMPAS, Screen Writer's Guild. Exec. prod., Comprenetics, Inc. Dir., Pioneer Prods., 1982.

PICTURES: Younger Brothers, One Last Fling, Homicide, House Across the Street, Flaxy Martin, Barricade, Return of the Frontiersmen, This Side of the Law, Colt 45, Sugarfoot, Raton Pass, The Big Punch, Smart Girls Don't Talk, Embraceable You.

ELLIOTT, DENHOLM: C.B.E. Actor. b. London, Eng., May 31, 1922; e. Malvern Coll. Screen debut in Dear Mr. Proback, 1948; NY stage: Write Me A Murder, The Seagull, 1964.

PICTURES: The Sound Barrier, The Holly and the Ivy, The Ringer, The Cruel Sea, Heart of the Matter, They Who Dare, Man Who Loved Redheads, Lease of Life, Night My Number Came Up, Pacific Destiny, Scent of Mystery, Nothing But the Best, Station Six Sahara, King Rat, You Must Be Joking, The High Bright Sun, Alfie, Here We Go Round The Mulberry Bush, The Night They Raided Minskys, The Seagull, Too Late the Hero, The Rise and Rise of Michael Rimmer, A Doll's House, The Apprenticeship of Duddy Kravitz, Robin & Marian, To The Devil A Daughter, Russian Roulette, Voyage of the Damned, The Boys from Brazil, St. Jacques, Zulu Dawn, A Game for Vultures, Cuba, Illusions, Saint Jack, Bad Timing, Sunday Lovers, Marco Polo, Brimstone and Treacle, The Missionary, The Wicked Lady, Trading Places, The Razors Edge, A Private Function, A Room with a View, Defense of the Realm, Whoopee Boys, Maurice, September, Stealing Home, Return from the River Kwai, Indiana Jones and the Last Crusade, Killing Dad.

TELEVISION: Bleak House, Marco Polo, Camille, Hotel du Lac, Mrs. Delafield Wants To Marry, A Child's Christmas in Wales, Noble House, Code Name: Kyril, The Bourne Identity, Keys to Freedom.

ELLIOTT, LANG: Producer, Director. b. Los Angeles, CA, Oct. 18, 1949. Given first job in films by his uncle, the late actor William Elliott (known as Wild Bill Elliott). Worked as actor from early years; employed by, among others the McGowan Brothers. Turned to film production; co-founded distribution co., The International Picture Show Co., serving as exec. v.p. in chg. of financing, production & distribution. Under banner of TriStar Pictures, Inc. also finances productions. 1982, formed Lang Elliott Productions, Inc.

PICTURES: Prod: Ride the Hot Wind, Where Time Began, The Farmer, The Billion Dollar Hobo, They Went That-a-Way & That-a-Way, The Prize Fighter. Prod.-dir. The Private Eyes, Cage.

TELEVISION: Experiment in Love (prod.), Boys Will Be Boys (writer).

ELLIOTT, RICHARD B.: Executive. b. San Francisco, CA, Oct. 20, 1952. e. Stanford U., M.B.A., 1983; U. of California, B.S., 1974. Worked for Price Waterhouse & Co. in Brussels, Belgium, as sr. tax acct., 1976–78; Touche Ross & Co. in Brussels, tax spvr., 1978–81; mgr. planning & special projects, Pay Cable and Home Entertainment Group of Columbia Pictures, 1983; dir. opns., Pay Cable & Home Entertainment Group, 1984; v.p., sls. planning, Marketing and Distribution Group, 1985.

ELLIOTT, SAM: Actor. b. Sacramento, CA, Aug. 9, 1944; m. actress Katharine Ross. e. U. of Oregon.

PICTURES: Debut as card player in Butch Cassidy and the Sundance Kid, The Games, Frogs, Molly and Lawless John, Lifeguard, The Legacy, Mask, Fatal Beauty, Shakedown, Road House, Prancer.

TELEVISION: Movies: The Challenge, Assault on the Wayne, The Blue Knight, I Will Fight No More Forever, The Sacketts, Shadow Riders, A Death in California. The Blue Lightning, Houston: The Legend of Texas, The Quick and the Dead. Series: Mission: Impossible (1970–71), Once an Eagle, Aspen, The Yellow Rose.

ELLSWORTH, JAMES: Producer. b. Deltaville, VA, March 12, 1927. e. UCLA, 1949. Pro. baseball player.

TELEVISION SERIES: Champions of Sports.

PICTURES: Naked Fury, Marine, Life Story of Lt. General Lewis B. (Chesty) Fuller, Door to Door Maniac (Five Minutes to Live).

ELWES, CARY: Actor. b. London, England, Oct. 26, 1962. e. Harrow. Studied for stage with Julie Bovasso at Sarah Lawrence, Bronxville, NY.

PICTURES: Another Country, (debut 1984), Oxford Blues, The Bride, Lady Jane, The Princess Bride, Glory.

ENDERS, ROBERT: Producer, Writer. Began in television, being responsible for 64 hrs. of live programming weekly for industry and govt. as pres. of Robert J. Enders, Inc. In 1961 turned to theatrical prod. and writing. 1973: formed Bowden Prods. with partner Glenda Jackson. Made countless award-winning documentaries for govt. and industry including Dept. of Defense, U.S. Air Force, Civil Defense, Ford Motor Co.

PICTURES: A Thunder of Drums (prod.), The Maltese Bippy (prod.), How Do I Love Thee (prod.), Rowan and Martin at the Movies, Zig Zag (story), Voices (prod., s.p.), The Maids, (also s.p.), Hedda (prod.), Out of Season (exec. prod.), Conduct Unbecoming (s.p. and prod.), Nasty Habits (prod., s.p.), Stevie (prod., dir.), How to Score a Movie (dir., prod., s.p.), Seeing the Unseen (doc.), The Visit.

TELEVISION: The Best of the Post (prod. of series), Ben Franklin, High Noon (prod., special), Co-prod. of Acad. Award Show, 1968, The Princess and the Goblin (dir., writer, prod.), They Went That-Away (prod.), Strange Interlude (exec. prod., writer).

ENGEL, CHARLES F.: Executive. b. Los Angeles, CA, Aug. 30, 1937. e. Michigan State U., UCLA. Son of writer-producer Samuel G. Engel. Pgm. devel., ABC-TV, 1964–68; v.p. Univ.-TV, 1972; sr. v.p., 1977; exec. v.p., 1980; pres., MCA Pay-TV New Programming, 1981. ACE Award, 1988 for outstanding contribution to cable; v.p. Universal TV, exec. in chg. ABC Mystery Movie, 1989.

TELEVISION: Run a Crooked Mile (exec. prod.), Road Raiders (prod.), ABC Mystery Movie (exec. in chg. of prod.).

ENGELBERG, MORT: Producer. b. Memphis, TN. e. U. of Illinois, U. of Missouri. Taught journalism; worked as reporter for UPI, AP. Worked for US government, including USIA, Peace Corps., Office of Economic Opportunity; President's Task Force on War on Poverty. Left gov. service in 1967 to become film unit publicist, working on three films in Europe: Dirty Dozen, Far From the Madding Crowd, The Comedians. Returned to U.S.; appt. pub. mgr. for United Artists. Sent to Hollywood as asst. to Herb Jaffe, UA head of west coast prod., which post he assumed when Jaffe left. Left to join indep. prod., Ray Stark.

PICTURES: Smokey and the Bandit, Hot Stuff, The Villain, The Hunter, Smokey and the Bandit II, Smokey and the Bandit III, Nobody's Perfekt, The Heavenly Kid, The Big Easy, Maid to Order, Dudes, Three For the Road, Russkies, Pass the Ammo, Trading Hearts, Fright Night Part 2, Rented Lips, Remote Control.

ENGLANDER, MORRIS: Executive. e. Wharton Sch., U. of Pennsylvania. With General Cinema Corp. circuit before joining RKO Century Warner Theatres 1984 as exec. v.p., develp.; later co-vice chmn. of circuit. 1986, sr. real estate advisor, American Multi-Cinema. 1988: v.p. real estate Hoyts Cinema Corp.

ENGLUND, GEORGE H.: Producer, Director. b. Washington, DC, June 22, 1926. Producer, Paramount, Pennebaker Prods.; prod., MGM; prod.-dir., Universal.

PICTURES: The World the Flesh and the Devil, The Ugly American, Signpost to Murder, Snow Job.

TELEVISION: The Vegas Strip War (exec. prod., dir., s.p.), A Christmas to Remember, Dixie: Changing Habits; Terrorist on Trial: The United States vs. Salim Ajami (exec. prod.).

ENGLUND, KEN: Writer. b. Chicago, IL, May 6, 1914. e. Lane Tech., Chicago. Started career as magazine writer; then vaudeville routines, comedy radio shows. Bdwy revues and musicals. Twice elec. pres. screen branch Writers Guild of America, West, then pres. of WGAW. Member national council.

TELEVISION SHOWS: Jackie Gleason Show, Dear Phoebe, Ray Milland Show, Loretta Young Show, several spectaculars. Prod.-writer CBS-TV staff 1957; Sonja Henie Spect. London, 1958; 20th Fox and Warner Bros. TV Films, My Three Sons; sev. teleplays, Bewitched, 1965, That Girl!, Dr. Joyce Brothers (head writer for series).

PICTURES: Big Broadcast of 1938, Artists and Models Abroad, Good Girls Go to Paris, Slightly Honorable, Doctor Takes a Wife, No No Nanette, This Thing Called Love, There's That Woman Again, Nothing But the Truth, Springtime in the Rockies, Sweet Rosie O'Grady, Here Comes the Waves, Secret Life of Walter Mitty, Androcles and the Lion, Good Sam, A Millionaire for Christy, The Caddy, Never Wave at a WAC, Vagabond King, The Wicked Dreams of Paula Schultz, Surviving the Savage Sea.

AUTHOR: Tour D'Amour, Larks in a Casserole; Co-author (with George Marshall) The Ghost in Emily's Trunk.

EPSTEIN, JULIUS J: Screenwriter. b. New York, NY, Aug. 22, 1909. e. Pennsylvania State U. Worked as publicist before going to Hollywood where began writing. Had long collaboration with twin brother, Philip G. Epstein. Under contract with Warner Bros. over 17 years.
PICTURES: Casablanca (AA), Arsenic and Old Lace, The Man Who Came to Dinner, Four Daughters, Saturday's Children, Mr. Skeffington, My Foolish Heart, Pete n' Tillie, Reuben, Reuben (and co-prod.).

EPSTEIN, MEL: Producer. b. Dayton, OH, Mar. 25, 1910; e. Ohio State U. Adv. & edit. depts. on newspapers; entered m.p. ind. as player in 1931; then asst. dir., unit prod. mgr., second unit & shorts dir.; U.S. Army Signal Corps (1st Lt.); apptd Para. prod., 1946. Now retired.
PICTURES: Whispering Smith, Hazard, Copper Canyon, Dear Brat, Branded, The Savage, Alaska Seas, Secret of the Incas.
TELEVISION: Broken Arrow, Men into Space, The Islanders, Asphalt Jungle, Rawhide, Long Hot Summer, The Monroes, Custer, Lancer (pilot), unit mgr. Lancer (series), Medical Center (series).

ERDMAN, RICHARD: Actor, Director. b. Enid, OK, June 1, 1925. e. Hollywood H.S.
PICTURES: Actor: Janie, Objective Burma, Time of Your Life, Four Days Leave, The Men, Cry Danger, Jumping Jacks, Happy Time, The Stooge, Stalag 17, The Power and the Prize, Saddle the Wind, Namu, The Killer Whale. Director: Bleep, The Brothers O'Toole.
TELEVISION: Ray Bolger Show, Perry Mason, Police Story, Tab Hunter Show, Alice, Bionic Woman, One Day at a Time, Playhouse of Stars, Twilight Zone, The Lucy Show, Lou Grant. Movie: Jesse. Director: The Dick Van Dyke Show, Mooch (special).

ERICSON, JOHN: Actor. b. Dusseldorf, Germany, Sept. 25, 1926. e. American Acad. of Dramatic Arts. Appeared in summer stock; m.p. debut, Teresa, 1951, then Stalag 17 on Broadway.
PICTURES: Rhapsody, Student Prince, Green Fire, Bad Day at Black Rock, Return of Jack Slade, Pretty Boy Floyd, Bedknobs and Broomsticks.
TELEVISION: Honey West.

ERLICHT, LEWIS H.: Executive. b. New York, NY. e. Long Island U. Began career with ABC in 1962 with Television Spot Sales. Promoted to mgr. of research for spot sales in 1965 became sls. mgr., gen. sls. mgr. of WABC-TV, New York, from 1969 to 1974. Named v.p., gen. mgr. of WLS-TV, Chicago, in 1975. Moved to ABC Entertainment in 1977; named v.p., gen. mgr., in 1978; v.p., asst. to pres. in 1979. In 1980 made sr. v.p. & asst. to pres.; 1981, sr. v.p., prime time. Promoted to pres. of ABC Entertainment in June, 1983.

ERMAN, JOHN: Director. b. Chicago, IL, Aug. 3, 1935. e. U. of California. Debut as TV director, Stoney Burke, 1962.
TELEVISION: Green Eyes, Alexander the Other Side of Dawn, Child of Glass, Just Me and You, My Old Man, Roots: The Next Generation, Family, Moviola, The Letter, Eleanor First Lady of the World, Who Will Love My Children?, The Atlanta Child Murders, A Streetcar Named Desire, An Early Frost (also prod.); The Two Mrs. Grenvilles (also spvr. prod.), When the Time Comes, The Attic: The Hiding of Anne Frank (sprv. prod.-dir.), David (also spvr. prod.).
PICTURES: Making It, Ace Eli and Rodger of the Skies, Stella.

ESBIN, JERRY: Executive. b. Brooklyn, NY, 1931. Started in mailroom at Columbia at 17 and worked for co. nearly 25 years. Then joined American Multi Cinema. Joined Paramount Pictures in 1975 as mgr. of branch operations; later named v.p., asst. sls. mgr. In 1980 named v.p., gen. sls. mgr. 1981, sr. v.p., domestic sls. & mktg. 1981, joined United Artists as sr. v.p., mktg. & dist.; 1982, named pres., MGM/UA m.p. dist. & mktg. div; 1983, sr. v.p., domestic dist., Tri-Star Pictures; 1985, promoted to exec. v.p.; 1989, joined Loews Theaters as sr. exec. v.p. and chief oper. officer, also in 1989 named pres. as well as chief operating officer, Loews Theater Management Corp.

ESMOND, CARL: Actor. b. Vienna, Austria, June 14, 1906. e. U. of Vienna. On stage Vienna, Berlin, London (Shakespeare, Shaw, German modern classics). Originated part of Prince Albert in Victoria Regina (London). On screen in Brit. prod. incl. Blossom Time, Even Song, Invitation to the Waltz. To U.S. in 1938. Guest star on many live and filmed TV shows.
PICTURES: Dawn Patrol, First Comes Courage, Address Unknown, Margin for Error, Master Race, Ministry of Fear, Story of Dr. Wassell. The Catman of Paris, Smash-up, Story of a Woman, Slave Girl, Walk a Crooked Mile, The Navy Comes Through, Sundown, Lover Come Back, This Love of Ours, Without Love, Mystery Submarine, The World in His Arms, Agent for H.A.R.M., Morituri.

ESSENFELD, BARRY: Executive. b. Bronx, NY, Feb. 16, 1936. e. De Witt Clinton H.S., NYU Acct., American Broadcasting Company, 1957–62; division controller, International Paper Co., 1962–67; group controller & division exec., New England Industries, 1968–70; Controller & asst. secty., Allied Artists Pictures Corp., 1970–73; named asst. treas. & dir. admin., Sept. 1973; gen. sls. mgr. 1979. Allied Artists Industries, v.p., finance, 1980–.

ESSERT, GARY: Executive. b. Oakland, CA, Oct. 15, 1938. e. UCLA. Entered entertainment field through m.p. exhibition; managed theatres in San Francisco and L.A.; has created advertising art campaigns for major studios and main titles for feature films. Tech. designer for professional motion picture presentation installations; coordinated and supervised design and planning of U.C.L.A. Motion Picture Center—Melnitz Hall (1964–67). Technical coordinator for the American Film Institute's Center for Advanced Film Studies (1968–70). Co-owned and operated a multi-media dance/concert hall in Hollywood known as The Kaleidoscope. Produced The Movies, a two-part, four-hour compilation doc. on the history of American motion pictures, 1975. Founder (1971) and CEO for 13 years of the Los Angeles International Film Exposition (Filmex). Founder (1984) and current artistic dir., American Cinematheque in Hollywood.

ESSEX, DAVID: Actor, Singer, Composer. b. Plaistow, London, Eng. July 23, 1947. e. Shipman Sch., Custom House. Started as a singer-drummer in East London band. 1967: Joined touring Repertory Co. in The Fantasticks, Oh, Kay, etc. 1970: West End debut in Ten Years Hard, 1972: Jesus Christ in Godspell, Che in Evita; Lord Byron in Childe Byron, 1983/4: Fletcher Christian in own musical Mutiny! on album and stage. International recording artist. Variety Club of Great Britain show business personality of 1978. Many gold & silver disc intl. awards.
TELEVISION: Top of the Pops, Own Specials, The River (also composed music), BBC series. Appearances on TV: France, Japan, Germany, Spain, Denmark, Australia. U.S.: Merv Griffin, Johnny Carson, Dinah Shore, American Bandstand, Midnight Special, Grammy Awards, Salute To The Beatles, Don Kirshner's Rock Concert, A.M. America, Phil Everly in Session, Paul Ryan Show.
PICTURES: Assault, All Coppers Are. . ., That'll Be the Day, Stardust, Silver Dream Racer (also wrote score).

ESSEX, HARRY J.: Writer. b. New York, NY, Nov. 29, 1915. e. St. John's U., Brooklyn, B.A. With Dept. Welfare. Wrote orig. story, Man Made Monster, for Universal. During W.W.II in U.S. Army Signal Corps; scenarist, training films on combat methods, censorship.
PICTURES: Boston Blackie and the Law (orig. s.p.), Dangerous Business, Desperate Bodyguard, He Walked by Night, Dragnet, Killer That Stalked New York, Wyoming Mail, The Fat Man, Undercover Girl, Las Vegas Story, Models, Inc., Kansas City Confidential, The 49th Man, It Came From Outer Space; I the Jury (dir., s.p.); Creature from the Black Lagoon; collab. s.p., story, Southwest Passage; adapt., Devil's Canyon; Mad at the World (dir., s.p.); Teen-age Crime Wave (collab. s.p.); Raw Edge; Lonely Man (story, s.p.); collab.: Sons of Katie Elder, Man and Boy; s.p. & dir. Octman, s.p., dir., prod. The Cremators, The Amigos (story and s.p.). Collaboration with Oscar Saul; Chrysalis, in collaboration with Ray Bradbury.
TELEVISION: Untouchables, The Racers, Alcoa Hour, Westinghouse, Desilu; story consultant and head writer: Target, The Corruptors, The Dick Powell Show, Bewitched, I Dream of Jeannie, Kraft Suspense Theatre, Hostage Flight.
NOVELIST: I Put My Right Foot In (Little Brown); Man and Boy, (Dell), 1971, Marina (Playboy Press), 1981.
PLAYS: Something for Nothing, Stronger Than Brass, Neighborhood Affair, One for the Dame, Fatty, Twilight, When the Bough Breaks, Dark Passion, Casa D'Amor.

ESTEVEZ, EMILIO: Actor. b. 1963. Oldest son of actor Martin Sheen; brother of actor Charlie Sheen.
PICTURES: Tex, The Outsiders, Repo Man, The Breakfast Club, That Was Then This is Now, (also s.p.), St. Elmo's Fire, Never on Tuesday, Wisdom (also s.p., dir.), Stakeout, Young Guns. Men at Work (also dir., s.p.), National Lampoon's Family Dies (exec. prod.).
TELEVISION: Movies: In the Custody of Strangers. Nightbreaker.

ESTRADA, ERIK: Actor. r.n. Enrique Estrada. m. actress Peggy Rowe. b. New York, NY, Mar. 16, 1949. Began professional career in Mayor John Lindsay's Cultural Program, performing in public parks. Joined American Musical Dramatic Acad. for training. Feature film debut in The Cross and the Switchblade (1970).
PICTURES: The New Centurions, Airport '75, Midway, Trackdown, Where Is Parsifal?, Lightblast, The Repentant, Hour of the Assassin, The Lost Idol, A Show of Force, Night of the Wilding, Silver Circle, Vengeance in Little Saigon.
TELEVISION: Series: CHiPS, guest roles on Hawaii Five-0, Six Million Dollar Man, Police Woman, Kojak, Medical Center,

Hunter, Alfred Hitchcock Presents (1988). Movies: Fire!, Honeyboy, Grandpa, Will You Run With Me?, The Dirty Dozen: The Fatal Mission, She Knows Too Much.

ESZTERHAS, JOE: Writer. Author of novel Charlie Simpson's Apocalypse (nom. National Book Award, 1974).
PICTURES: F.I.S.T., Flashdance, Jagged Edge, Big Shots, Betrayed, Checking Out, Music Box (also co-exec. prod.)

ETKES, RAPHAEL: Executive. b. Paris, France, May 6, 1930. Joined MCA in 1961; named v.p. of Universal Pictures in 1973. Appt. v.p. of MCA, Inc. in 1978; named sr. v.p., Universal Pictures, 1979; 1980, named prs. chief exec. off., AIP; 1981, joined United Artists as sr. v.p.—Worldwide Prod; 1983–85, pres., production, Embassy Pictures. Resigned April 1985.

ETTINGER, EDWIN D.: Publicist. b. New York, NY, 1921. Entered m.p. ind. as office boy, MGM; pub. rel. and publ. for industrial, comm. clients, 1946–52; joined Ettinger Co., pub. rel., 1952; pub. rel. dir., Disneyland Inc., 1955; marketing dir., Disneyland, 1955–65; v.p., M.C.A. Enterprises, Inc., 1955.

ETTLINGER, JOHN A.: Producer, Director, Distributor. b. Chicago, IL, Oct. 14, 1924. e. Peddie Inst., Cheshire Acad. Signal Corps Photog. Center, 1942–45; with Paramount Theatres Corp., 1945–47; dir., KTLA, Paramount TV Prod., Inc., Los Angeles, 1948–50; radio-TV dir., Nat. C. Goldstone Agency, 1950–53; pres. Medallion TV Enterprises, Inc.; TV prod., View the Clue, Greenwich Village, High Road to Danger, Sur Demande, Star Route, Las Vegas Fights, Celebrity Billiards; Pres., KUDO-FM, Las Vegas.

EVANS, ANDREW C.: Executive. Joined Paramount Pictures 1977 as dir. of financial reporting. Named v.p., corporate controller, 1980; sr. v.p., 1984. Same year named exec. v.p., finance, for Motion Picture Group of co. 1985, promoted to sr. v.p., finance.

EVANS, BARRY: Actor, Director. b. Guildford, England, 1943. Trained Central School. Repertory: Barrow, Nottingham, Chester, Royal Court, Nat. Theatre, Hampstead Th. Club, Chips with Everything, London and B'way. Young Vic. Theatre Clwyd Mold.
TELEVISION: Redcap, Undermined, The Baron, The Class, Armchair Theatre, Love Story, Doctor in the House, Doctor at Large, Short Story, Crossroads, Mind Your Language, Dick Emery Show.
PICTURES: The White Bus, Here We Go 'Round the Mulberry Bush, Alfred the Great, Die Screaming, Marriane, The Adventures of a Taxi-Driver, Under the Doctor.

EVANS, GENE: Actor. b. Holbrook, AR, July 11, 1924. e. Colton H.S. Started career in summer stock, Penthouse Theatre, Altadena, CA. Screen debut: Under Colorado Skies, 1947.
PICTURES: Crisscross, Larceny, Berlin Express, Assigned to Danger, Mother Was a Freshman, Sugarfoot, Armored Car Robbery, Steel Helmet, I Was an American Spy, Force of Arms, Jet Pilot, Fixed Bayonets, Mutiny, Park Row, Thunderbirds, Donovan's Brain, Golden Blade, Hell and High Water, Long Wait, Cattle Queen of Montana, Wyoming Renegades, Crashout, Helen Morgan Story, Bravados, Sad Sack, The Hangman, Operation Petticoat, Support Your Local Sheriff, War Wagon, Nevada Smith, Young and Wild, Ballad of Cable Hogue, There Was a Crooked Man, Support Your Local Gunfighter, Camper John, Walking Tall, People Toys, Pat Garrett and Billy the Kid, Magic of Lassie, Blame It on the Night.
TELEVISION: Matt Helm (series), Spencer's Pilots (series); Kate Bliss & Ticker Tape Kid, Fire, The Sacketts, Shadow Riders, Travis McGee, The Alamo: 13 Days to Glory, Once Upon a Texas Train.

EVANS, LINDA: Actress. b. Hartford, CT, Nov. 18, 1942. e. Hollywood H.S., L.A. TV commercials led to contract with MGM and film debut in Twilight of Honor, 1963.
PICTURES: The Klansman, Avalanche Express, Tom Horn.
TELEVISION: Series: The Big Valley, The Hunter, The Love Boat, Dynasty. Movies: Nowhere to Run, Standing Tall, Gambler II, The Alice Marble Story (also prod.). Mini-Series: Bare Essence, North & South Book II, The Last Frontier.

EVANS, RAY: Songwriter. b. Salamanca, NY, Feb. 4, 1915. e. Wharton Sch. of U. of Pennsylvania. Musician on cruise ships, radio writer spec. material. Hellzapoppin', Sons o' Fun. Member: exec. bd. Songwriters Guild of America, Dramatists Guild, West Coast advisory bd. ASCAP., bd., Myasthenia Gravis Fdn. CA chap., Songwriters Hall of Fame, Motion Picture Acad.
SONGS: To Each His Own, Golden Earrings, Buttons and Bows (Academy Award, 1948), Mona Lisa (Academy Award, 1950), Whatever Will Be Will Be (Academy Award, 1956), A Thousand Violins, I'll Always Love You, Dreamsville, Love Song from Houseboat, Tammy, Silver Bells, Dear Heart, Angel, Never Let Me Go, Almost in Your Arms, As I Love You, In the Arms of Love, Wish Me a Rainbow.
PICTURES: Paleface, Sorrowful Jones, Fancy Pants, My Friend Irma, Aaron Slick From Pumpkin' Crick, Son of the Paleface, My Friend Irma Goes West, The Night of Grizzly, Saddle the Wind, Isn't It Romantic, Capt. Carey U.S.A., Off Limits, Here Come the Girls, Red Garters, Man Who Knew Too Much, Stars Are Singing, Tammy, Houseboat, Blue Angel, A Private's Affair, All Hands on Deck, Dear Heart, The Third Day, What Did You Do in the War Daddy?, This Property Is Condemned.
BROADWAY MUSICALS: Oh Captain! Let It Ride!, Sugar Babies.
TELEVISION THEMES: Bonanza, Mr. Ed, Mr. Lucky, To Rome With Love.

EVANS, ROBERT: Producer. b. New York, NY, June 29, 1930. Radio actor at age 11; went on to appear in more than 300 radio prog. (incl. Let's Pretend, Archie Andrews, The Aldrich Family, Gangbusters) on major networks. Also appeared on early TV. At 20 joined brother, Charles, and Joseph Picone, as partner in women's clothing firm of Evan-Picone, Inc., 1952–67. In 1957 signed by Universal to play Irving Thalberg in The Man of a Thousand Faces after recommendation by Norma Shearer, Thalberg's widow. Guest columnist NY Journal American, 1958. Independent prod. at 20th Century-Fox. August, 1966–76, joined Paramount Pictures as head of prod., then exec. v.p. worldwide prod. (supervising Barefoot in the Park, Rosemary's Baby, Barbarella, Goodbye, Columbus, Love Story, The Godfather I & II, The Great Gatsby, etc.). Resigned to become indep. prod. again; with exclusive contract with Paramount.
PICTURES: Actor: The Sun Also Rises, The Fiend Who Walked the West, The Best of Everything. Independent Producer: Chinatown, Marathon Man, Black Sunday, Players, Urban Cowboy, Popeye, The Cotton Club, The Two Jakes.
TELEVISION: Actor: Elizabeth and Essex (1947), Young Widow Brown, The Right to Happiness; Prod.: Get High on Yourself.

EVERETT, CHAD: Actor. r.n. Ray Canton. b. South Bend, IN, June 11, 1936. e. Wayne State U., Detroit. Signed by William T. Orr, head of TV prod. for Warner Bros. to 3-year contract. Appeared in many TV series as well as films. Next became contract player at MGM.
PICTURES: Claudelle Inglish, The Chapman Report, The Singing Nun, The Last Challenge, Made in Paris, Johnny Tiger, Return of the Gunfighter, The Impossible Years, Airplane II: The Sequel, Fever Pitch, The Jigsaw, Murders, Heroes Stand Alone.
TELEVISION: Series: The Dakotas (1963), Medical Center (1969–76), Centennial, Hagen, The Rousters. Guest: Hawaiian Eye, 77 Sunset Strip, Surfside Six, Lawman, Bronco, The Lieutenant, Redigo, Route 66, Ironside.

EVERETT, RUPERT: Actor. b. Norfolk, England, 1959. e. Ampleforth Central School for Speech & Drama. Apprenticed with Glasgow's Citizen's Theatre. Originated role of Guy Bennett in Another Country on London stage in 1982 and made feature film debut in screen version in 1984.
PICTURES: Real Life, Dance with a Stranger, Duet for One, Chronicle of a Death Foretold, The Right Hand Man, Hearts of Fire, Haunted Summer, The Gold-Rimmed Glasses, Jigsaw, The Comfort of Strangers.
TELEVISION: Arthur, the King, The Far Pavilions, Princess Daisy.

EVERSON, WILLIAM K.: Writer. b. Yeovil, Eng., April 8, 1929. Pub. dir., Renown Pictures Corp., Ltd., London, 1944; film critic; m.p. journalist; in armed forces, 1947–49; thea. mgr., pub. & booking consultant, Monseigneur News Theatres, London, 1949; pub. dir., Allied Artists Inc. Corp., 1951; prod., writer Paul Killiam Dorg., 1956. Writer-editor-researcher on TV series Movie Museum and Silents Please, also on TV specials and theatrical features Hollywood the Golden Years, The Valentino Legend, The Love Goddesses and The Great Director. Lecturer, archival consultant, American Film Institute representative. Film History instructor at NYU, The New School and Sch. of Visual Arts, all in NY. Also, Harvard U.
AUTHOR: Several books on movie history, including The Western, The Bad Guys, The American Movie, The Films of Laurel & Hardy, The Art of W. C. Fields, Hal Roach. The Detective in Film, Classics of the Horror Film, Claudette Colbert.

EWELL, TOM: Actor. r.n. Yewell Tompkins. b. Owensboro, KY, April 29, 1909. e. U. of Wisconsin. Active in coll. dramatics; salesman at Macy's. NY stage debut: They Shall Not Die, 1934; thereafter many unsuccessful plays. U.S. Navy 1942–46.
THEATRE: Returned to stage in John Loves Mary; Small Wonder; on road in Stage Door, Tobacco Road, Roberta, Key Largo; on Broadway in Seven-Year Itch, Tunnel of Love, Thurber Carnival (and in London), Patate (in Paris).
PICTURES: Adam's Rib, Mr. Music, A Life of Her Own, American Guerilla in the Philippines, Up Front, Finders Keepers, Lost in Alaska, Willie & Joe Back at the Front, Seven-Year Itch, Lieutenant Wore Skirts, Girl Can't Help It, Tender Is the Night, State Fair, Suppose They Gave A War

and Nobody Came?, To Find a Man, They Only Kill Their Masters, The Great Gatsby, Easy Money.

TELEVISION: The Tom Ewell Show; Baretta (series); Promise Him Anything; The Return of Mod Squad; Terror at Alcatraz.

F

FABRAY, NANETTE: Actress. b. San Diego, CA, Oct. 27, 1920. e. Los Angeles City Coll. d. Raoul Fabares and Lillian (McGovern) Fabares. m. Ranald MacDougall 1957, deceased 1973. First prof. stage appearance at age of three in vaudeville as Baby Nan. Leading lady in Charlie Chan radio series. Member of the cast, radio, Showboat. 1938, won two-year scholarship to Max Reinhardt school in Hollywood, and starred in his CA productions of The Miracle, Six Characters in Search of an Author, and Servant With Two Masters.

PICTURES: Elizabeth and Essex, A Child is Born, The Happy Ending, Cockeyed Cowboys, The Bandwagon, That's Entertainment II, Magic Carpet, Amy, Personal Exemptions.

TELEVISION: Own TV Series, Yes, Yes Nanette 1961–62. Two years on Caesar's Hour. One Day at a Time (series); George M!; High Button Shoes; Alice Through the Looking Glass; many specials.

BROADWAY SHOWS: Meet the People, By Jupiter, Jackpot, My Dear Public, Let's Face It, Bloomer Girl, Arms and the Girl, High Button Shoes, Make a Wish, Love Life, Mr. President, No Hard Feelings, Yes-Yes-Yes Nanette! (one-woman show by Danny Daniels). .

AWARDS: Two Donaldson Awards for High Button Shoes and Love Life; Three Emmy Awards for Caesar's Hour as best comedienne, 1955, 1956, best supporting actress 1955; Woman of the Year, 1955, Radio and TV Editors of America; Hollywood Women's Press Club, 1960; Honorary Mayor of Pacific Palisades 1967–68; One of Ten Best Dressed Women in America, Fashion Academy Award, 1950. President's Distinguished Service Award, 1970; Eleanor Roosevelt Humanitarian Award; Public Service Award; Amer. Acad. of Otolaryngology, 1977; Woman of the Year, CA Museum, Science and Industry 1975; Award of Merit, Amer. Heart Assoc. 1975; Screen Actors Guild Humanitarian Award, 1986.

FABRIZI, ALDO: Actor. b. Rome, Italy, 1905. Stage actor to 1942.

PICTURES: Go Ahead, Passengers, Square of Rome, Open City, My Son, the Professor, To Live in Peace, Christmas at Camp 119, Emigrants, Welcome, Reverend, First Communion (Father's Dilemma), Flowers of St. Francis, Mishappy Family, Thieves and Cops, Times Gone By, Lucky Five, Too Young for Love, Voice of Silence, Lucky Five, The Angel Wore Red, Three Bites of the Apple, Those Were the Days, We All Loved Each Other So Much.

FADIMAN, CLIFTON: Writer, Performer. b. Brooklyn, NY, May 15, 1904. e. Columbia U. Contributor to magazines since 1924. Asst. ed. Simon & Schuster, 1927–29, ed. 1929–35. Book ed. The New Yorker, 1933–43. Mc. on Information Please radio program 1938–48; TV, 1952; edit. com., Book of the Month Club, since 1944; Mc. This Is Show Business, TV; author, Party of One; Any Number Can Play; Enter Conversing; The Lifetime Reading Plan; editor, American Treasury, 50 years; m.c., Conversation, 1954; m.c., Quiz Kids, 1956; Metropolitan Opera Roving Reporter, 1955–60; m.c., Alumni Fun, 1964; bd. of editors, Encyclopaedia Britannica; Advisory Board, CRICKET: The Magazine for Children, Co-author, The Joys of Wine, 1975. Co-author, The Wine Buyers Guide, 1977; Co-author, Empty Pages: A Search for Writing Competence in School and Society, 1979; editor, World Treasury of Children's Literature, 1984–85; commentator, First Edition, 1983–84; editor, Little, Brown Book of Anecdotes, 1985; editor, The World of the Short Story, 1986. 3rd ed. Lifetime Reading Plan, 1988; assoc. ed., Great Books of the Western World, 1988–.

FAIMAN, PETER: Director. b. Australia. Entered entertainment business through TV, involved early in production-direction of major variety series in Australia. Assoc. prod.-dir. of over 20 programs for The Paul Hogan Show and two Hogan specials filmed in England (1983). Developed Australia's most popular and longest-running national variety program, The Don Lane Show. Responsible for creative development of the TV Week Logie Awards on the Nine Network. For 4 years headed Special Projects Division of the Nine Network Australia. Resigned to establish own prod. co., Peter Faiman Prods. Pty Ltd. 1984. Made m.p. theatrical film debut as director of Crocodile Dundee.

FAIN, SAMMY: Composer. b. New York, NY, June 17, 1902. e. public and high schools. Self taught on piano. Commenced career in Tin Pan Alley as teenage staff pianist-composer for leading music publishers, then in vaudeville. Recording contract at Harmony Records (Columbia); featured solo performer on many New York radio stations. Joined ASCAP, 1926. Wrote first song hit, Let A Smile Be Your Umbrella. Lyrics by Irving Kahal, 1927.

STAGE: Scores for Hellzapoppin', Son's of Fun, George White's Scandals, Ed Wynn's Boys & Girls Together, Flahooley, Christine & others.

PICTURES: Scores & Songs—Big Pond, Young Man of Manhattan, Footlight Parade, Sweet Music, Harold Teen, New Faces of '37, Geo. White's Scandals, Call Me Mister, Alice in Wonderland, Peter Pan, Jazz Singer, Weekend at the Waldorf, Anchors Aweigh, Imitation of Life, Mardi Gras, Calamity Jane, April Love, Marjorie Morningstar, A Certain Smile, Love Is a Many Splendored Thing, Tender Is the Night, Made in Paris, The Stepmother and many others.

SONGS: Let a Smile Be Your Umbrella, Wedding Bells Are Breaking Up That Old Gang of Mine, When I Take My Sugar to Tea, You Brought a New Kind of Love to Me, Was That the Human Thing to Do, By A Waterfall, Are You Having Any Fun, I'm Late, I Can Dream Can't I, That Old Feeling, I'll Be Seeing You, Dear Hearts and Gentle People, April Love, A Certain Smile, A Very Precious Love, Tender Is the Night, Secret Love, Love Is a Many Splendored Thing, many others.

CITATIONS: Oscar awards for Secret Love and Love is a Many Splendored Thing, plus eight Acad. Oscar nominations: International awards—Diploma Di Benemerenza most coveted honor by the Hall of Artists in Nice, France, and Augasto Messinesse Gold Award from Messina, Italy. Also two Laurel Awards. Elected to Songwriters' Hall of Fame.

FAIRBANKS, SIR DOUGLAS, JR.: O.B.E. Actor, Producer, Business executive. b. New York, NY, Dec. 9, 1909. e. Pasadena (CA) Polytech. Sch.; Harvard Mil. Acad., Los Angeles; Bovee and Collegiate Sch., N.Y.; also Paris, London. Son of late Douglas Fairbanks; stepson of Mary Pickford. Began as screen actor 1922 in Stephen Steps Out; thereafter in more than 75 pictures. Stage from 1927 in U.S. Since sound in both British & U.S. prods.; formed own co. 1935, prod. & starring, The Amateur Gentleman, etc.; U.S. Navy, 1941; Appt. special envoy to South Amer. by Pres. Roosevelt. Helped org. British War Relief and was natl. chmn. CARE. Commander Awarded U.S. Silver Star Combat Legion of Merit; K.B.E. (first Amer. film star knighted by British King, 1946), D.S.C., Legion of Honor, Distinguished Service Cross, Croix de Guerre, etc. 1949. Entered TV film prod., 1952. Autobiography: The Salad Days (1988).

THEATER: U.K. (Young Woodley, Saturday's Children, etc.); 1934 in Manchester, England (The Winding Journey), London (Moonlight in Silver), 1968–77 My Fair Lady, The Secretary Bird, Present Laughter (U.S.), The Pleasure of His Company (U.S., U.K., Ireland, Australia and Hong Kong), Out on a Limb, Sleuth (U.S.).

PICTURES: (since sound): Dawn Patrol, Little Caesar, Outward Bound, Union Depot, Captured, Catherine the Great, Accused, The Prisoner of Zenda, Having Wonderful Time, Gunga Din, Morning Glory, Angels Over Broadway, The Corsican Brothers, The Exile, Sinbad the Sailor, That Lady in Ermine, Joy of Living, Fighting O'Flynn, State Secret; Another Man's Poison (prod.), Chase Crooked Shadow, Ghost Story, Old Explorers.

TELEVISION: prod. Douglas Fairbanks Presents, The Rheingold Theatre; Guest: B.L. Stryker. Movie: The Restless Heart.

FAIRBANKS, JERRY: Executive Producer. b. San Francisco, CA, Nov. 1, 1904. Cameraman, 1924–29; prod., shorts, Universal, 1929–34; prod., Popular Science, Unusual Occupations, Speaking of Animals Series, Para., 1935–49; Winner two Acad. Awards; set up film div., NBC, 1948; formed, NBC Newsreel, 1949; devel. Zoomar Lens and Multicam System; formed Jerry Fairbanks Prods., 1950.

TELEVISION: Public Prosecutor (first film series for TV); other series: Silver Theatre, Front Page Detective, Jackson and Jill, Hollywood Theatre, Crusader Rabbit.

PICTURES: The Last Wilderness, Down Liberty Road, With This Ring, Counterattack, Collision Course, Land of the Sea, Brink of Disaster, The Legend of Amaluk, North of the Yukon, Damage Report, The Boundless Seas.

FAIRCHILD, MORGAN: Actress. b. Dallas, TX, Feb. 3, 1950. e. Southern Methodist U.

PICTURES: Bullet for Pretty Boy, The Seduction, Red-Headed Stranger, Campus Man, Sleeping Beauty, Midnight Cop, Phantom of the Mall.

TELEVISION: Series: Search for Tomorrow, Murder in Music City, The Memory of Eva Ryker, Flamingo Road (series), Magnum P.I. (series), Honeyboy, Falcon Crest (series), The Dream Merchants, The Initiation of Sara, The Zany Adventures of Robin Hood, Time Bomb, North and South Book II, Paper Dolls, 79 Park Avenue, Deadly Illusion, Street of Dreams, The Haunting of Sarah.

FAIRCHILD, WILLIAM: Director, Screenwriter, Playwright, Novelist. b. Cornwall, England, 1918. e. Royal Naval Coll., Dartmouth. Early career Royal Navy.

PICTURES: Screenplays: Morning Departure, Outcast of the Islands, The Gift Horse, The Net, Newspaper Story, Malta

Story, The Seekers, Passage Home, Value For Money, Star!, Embassy, The Darwin Adventure, Invitation to the Wedding, Dir.: John and Julie, The Extra Day, The Horsemasters, The Silent Enemy.
TELEVISION PLAYS: The Man with the Gun, No Man's Land, The Signal, Four Just Men, Some Other Love, Cunningham 5101, The Break, The Zoo Gang, Lady with a Past.
STAGE: Sound of Murder, Breaking Point, Poor Horace, The Pay-Off, The Flight of the Bumble B.
BOOKS: A Matter of Duty, The Swiss Arrangement, Astrology for Dogs, Astrology for Cats, Catsigns (U.S.), The Poppy Factory, No Man's Land (U.S.).

FALK, PETER: Actor. b. New York, NY, Sept. 16, 1927. e. New Sch. for Social Research, B.A., 1951; Syracuse U. M.F.A. Studied with Eva Le Galliene and Sanford Meisner. Worked as efficiency expert for Budget Bureau State of CT.
THEATRE: Off-Broadway: Don Juan (debut, 1956), The Iceman Cometh, Comic Strip, Purple Dust, Bonds of Interest, The Lady's Not for Burning, Diary of a Scoundrel. On Broadway: Saint Joan, The Passion of Josef D., The Prisoner of Second Avenue. Light Up the Sky (L.A.), Glengarry Glen Ross (tour).
TELEVISION: Studio One, Kraft Theatre, Alcoa Theatre, N.T.A. Play of the Week, Armstrong Circle Theatre, Omnibus, Robert Montgomery Presents, Brenner, Deadline, Kraft Mystery Theatre, Rendezvous, Sunday Showcase, The Untouchables, The Sacco—Vanzetti Story, Dick Powell Show (The Price of Tomatoes, Emmy Award, 1962), Danny Kaye Show, Edie Adams Show, Bob Hope Chrysler Hour, Series: The Trials of O'Brien, Columbo (series, 1971–77, Emmy Awards 1972, 1975, 1976), Columbo (1989, also co-exec. prod.) Movies: A Step Out of Line, Griffen and Phoenix: A Love Story. Specials: The Million Dollar Incident Brigadoon, A Hatful of Rain, Clue: Movies, Murder and Mystery.
PICTURES: Wind Across the Everglades, The Bloody Brood, Pretty Boy Floyd, The Secret of the Purple Reef, Murder, Inc., Pocketful of Miracles, The Pressure Point, The Balcony, Robin and the Seven Hoods, Mad, Mad, Mad World, Italiani Brava Gente, The Great Race, Penelope, Luv, Castle Keep, Anzio, Husbands, Machine Gun McCann, A Woman Under the Influence, Mikey and Nicky, Murder by Death, The Cheap Detective, Brinks' Job, Opening Night, The In-Laws, The Great Muppet Caper, All the Marbles, Big Trouble, Happy New Year, The Princess Bride, Vibes, Wings of Desire, Cookie, In the Spirit. Aunt Julia and the Scriptwriter.

FANTOZZI TONY: Theatrical Agent. b. New Britain, CT, May 1, 1933. William Morris Agency.

FARBER, BART: Executive. Joined United Artists Corp. in early 1960s when UA acquired ZIV TV Programs. Served as v.p. United Artists Television and United Artists Broadcasting. In 1971 named v.p. in charge of legal affairs of the cos. In January 1978, named sr. v.p.—TV, video and special markets; indep. consultant, TV, Pay TV, home video. 1982, joined Cable Health Network as v.p., legal & business affairs; 1984, v.p., business & legal affairs, Lifetime Network; 1986, independent communications consultant.

FARENTINO, JAMES: b. Brooklyn, NY, Feb. 24, 1938. e. American Acad. of Dramatic Arts.
THEATRE: Broadway: Night of the Iguana. A Streetcar Named Desire (revival, 1973).
TELEVISION: Naked City, daytime soap operas, Laredo, Route 66, The Alfred Hitchcock Hour, Ben Casey, Twelve O'Clock High, Death of a Salesman, Sins, That Secret Sunday; Something So Right; The Cradle Will Fall; License to Kill; Blue Thunder; A Summer to Remember; Family Sins; The Red Spider; Who Gets the Friends? Pilot: American Nuclear.
PICTURES: The Pad (And How to Use It) (Golden Globe Award, 1966), The Ride of Hangman's Tree, Banning, Rosie!, The Story of a Woman, The Final Countdown, Dead and Buried, Her Alibi.

FARGO, JAMES: Director. b. Republic, WA, Aug. 14, 1938. e. U. of Washington (B.A.).
PICTURES: The Enforcer; Caravans; Every Which Way But Loose; Forced Vengeance; Born to Race; Voyage of the Rock Aliens; Riding the Edge (also actor).
TELEVISION: Tales of the Gold Monkey; Gus Brown and Midnight Brewster; The Last Electric Knight.

FARNSWORTH, RICHARD: Actor. b. Los Angeles, CA, Sept. 1, 1920. Active as stuntman for 40 years before turning to acting.
PICTURES: Comes a Horseman, Tom Horn, Resurrection, Ruckus, The Legend of the Lone Ranger, The Grey Fox, The Natural, Into the Night, Sylvester.
TELEVISION: Anne of Green Gables, Chase, Ghost Dancing, Wild Horses, Travis McGee, Red Earth, White Earth, Good Old Boy.

FARR, FELICIA: Actress. b. Westchester, NY, Oct. 4, 1932. e. Pennsylvania State Coll. m. Jack Lemmon. Stage debut: Picnic (Players Ring Theatre).
PICTURES: Timetable, Jubal, Reprisal, First Texan, Last Wagon, 3:10 to Yuma, Hell Bent for Leather, Kiss Me Stupid, Kotch, Charley Varrick, That's Life!

FARR, JAMIE: Actor. r.n. Jameel Joseph Farah. b. Toledo, OH, July 1, 1934. e. Columbia Coll. Trained for stage at Pasadena Playhouse. Film debut in Blackboard Jungle, 1955. Comedy entertainer, 1975. Gained fame as Klinger in TV series, M*A*S*H.
PICTURES: Cannonball Run, Murder Can Hurt You, Return of the Rebels, Cannonball Run II, Scrooged, Speed Zone, Curse II: the Bite.
TELEVISION: Dear Phoebe, The Red Skelton Show, The Dick Van Dyke Show, The Danny Kaye Show, Chicago Teddy Bears, M*A*S*H (series reg.), After M*A*S*H (also dir. of both M*A*S*H series), The Love Boat, For Love or Money, The New Love American Style, Murder She Wrote. Movie: Run Till You Fall.

FARRELL, CHARLES: Actor. b. Onset Bay, MA, Aug. 9, 1900. e. Boston U. Entered m.p. ind. in silent films teamed with the late actress Janet Gaynor. U.S. Navy, 1942–45; mayor of Palm Springs in 1947 and 1952.
PICTURES: The Ten Commandments, Wings of Youth, Old Ironsides, Seventh Heaven, Street Angel, Lucky Star, Sunny Side Up, High Society Blues, Liliom, Tess of the Storm Country, Wild Girl, Big Shakedown, Change of Heart, Fighting Youth, Moonlight Sonata, Just Around the Corner, Tailspin, The Deadly Game.
TELEVISION: My Little Margie; The Charles Farrell Show.

FARRELL, HENRY: Author of novels and screenplays
SCREENPLAYS: Whatever Happened to Baby Jane? Hush . . . Hush, Sweet Charlotte, and What's the Matter with Helen?
TELEVISION: How Awful About Allan, The House That Would Not Die.

FARREN, JACK: Producer, Writer. b. New York, NY. e. NYU, B.A. Theatre: prod., Take a Giant Step, Lorenzo 1967, Robert Anderson's You Know I Can't Hear You When the Water's Running; 1968, The Education of Hyman Kaplan.
PICTURES: Silent Night, Lonely Night; Fuzz.
TELEVISION: Goodson-Todman Productions; NBC, CBS. Movie: Fatal Judgment (exec. prod.).

FARROW, MIA: Actress. b. Los Angeles, CA, Feb. 9. 1945. d. of actress Maureen O'Sullivan and late dir. John Farrow. e. Marymount, Los Angeles, Cygnet House, London. Screen debut: Guns at Batasi (1964).
PICTURES: Guns at Batasi, A Dandy in Aspic, Rosemary's Baby, John and Mary, Secret Ceremony, See No Evil, The Public Eye, The Great Gatsby, Full Circle, A Wedding, Death on the Nile, Hurricane, A Midsummer Night's Sex Comedy, Zelig, Broadway Danny Rose, Supergirl, The Purple Rose of Cairo, Hannah and Her Sisters, Radio Days, September, Another Woman, New York Stories (Oedipus Wrecks).
TELEVISION: Peyton Place (series), Johnny Belinda.
THEATRE: Debut: Importance of Being Earnest (Madison Ave. Playhouse, NY, 1963); Royal Shakespeare Co. (Twelfth Night, A Midsummer Night's Dream, Ivanov, Three Sisters, The Seagull, A Doll's House), Mary Rose (London). B'way debut: Romantic Comedy (1979).

FASS, M. MONROE: Theatre Broker. b. New York, NY, Feb. 26, 1901. e. City Coll. of New York, M.E., engineering. Firm: Fass & Wolper. Entered real estate business in 1925, making first deal with Marcus Loew for land on which Paradise Theatre, Bronx, NY, was built. Thereafter made theatre deals (sale or lease of land or building) in most major cities in the U.S. and in major shopping centers. Member: Real Estate Board of N.Y.: Natl. Institute of Real Estate Brokers, Natl. Assoc. of Real Estate Board; Amer. Society of Real Estate Appraisers, Natl. Assoc. of Theatre Owners.

FAWCETT, FARRAH: Actress. b. Corpus Christi, TX, Feb. 2, 1947. e. U. of Texas. Picked as one of the ten most beautiful girls while a freshman; went to Hollywood and signed by Screen Gems. Did films, TV shows, and made over 100 TV commercials. Off B'way debut: Extremities (1983).
PICTURES: Love Is a Funny Thing, Myra Breckinridge, Logan's Run, Somebody Killed Her Husband, Sunburn, Saturn III, Cannonball Run, Extremities, See You in the Morning, Candy Barr.
TELEVISION: Owen Marshall, Counselor at Law, The Six Million Dollar Man, Rockford Files, Charlie's Angels (regular). Movies: The Girl Who Came Gift-Wrapped, Murder on Flight 502, Murder in Texas, The Feminist and the Fuzz, The Burning Bed, Red Light Sting, Between Two Women, Beate Klarsfeld, Nazi Hunter; Poor Little Rich Girl: The Barbara Hutton Story, Margaret Bourke-White, Small Sacrifices.

FAY, PATRICK J.: Director, Producer. b. June 7. e. Carnegie Tech. Dumont TV Network, 10 years. Director of over 100 Army training films.

TELEVISION: Bishop Sheen, Broadway to Hollywood, Manhattan Spotlight, Life is Worth Living, Front Row Center, Ilona Massey Show, Alec Templeton Show, Maggi McNellis Show, Key to Missing Persons, Kids and Company; co-prod., dir., Confession; dir., TV film series, Confession; dir. IBM Industrials, IBM World Trade, Europe Industrial, The Big Picture.

AUTHOR: Melba, The Toast of Pithole, The Last Family Portrait in Oil, Coal Oil Johnny, French Kate, No Pardon in Heaven, An Ill Wind, Tighten Your G-String.

FILMS: Director for RCA, General Electric H.G. Peters Company, Bransby Films.

FEHR, RUDI: Executive. b. Berlin, Germany, 1911. m. Maris Wrixon, actress. Started career with Tobis-Klangfilm, Berlin. Joined Warner Bros. editorial department, 1936. Became producer, 1952; promoted to executive, 1956; Post Production Exec. Warner Bros.; WB title changed to dir. of editorial & post-prod. operations. Now retired; is consultant to industry.

PICTURES: Editor: Invisible Enemies, Honeymoon for Three, Desperate Journey, Watch on the Rhine, The Conspirators, Humoresque, Possessed, Key Largo, The Inspector General, House of Wax, Dial M for Murder. Co-edited One From the Heart. Nominated for Oscar as co-editor of Prizzi's Honor.

FEINBERG, MILTON: Executive. b. Milwaukee, WI. e. U. of Minnesota, School of Bus. Admin. Salesman, 20th Century-Fox, Des Moines, 1942–44; branch mgr., National Screen Service, Des Moines, 1945–57; branch mgr., in Chicago, superv. Chicago, Milwaukee, Des Moines exchange territories, National Screen Service, 1958–65; gen. sales mgr., NSS, 1966; v.p. & gen. sls. mgr. 1967; May, 1974, sr. v.p., N.S.S.

FEINSTEIN, ALAN: Actor. b. New York, NY, Sept. 8, 1941.

TELEVISION: Series: Edge of Night, Love Of Life, Search for Tomorrow. Movies: Alexander: The Other Side of Dawn, The Users, Visions, The Runaways, The Two Worlds of Jenny Logan, Masada, The Wedding, On Fire, Jigsaw John, Berrengers.

PICTURE: Looking for Mr. Goodbar.

STAGE: Malcolm, Zelda, A View from the Bridge, As Is, A Streetcar Named Desire.

FEITSHANS, BUZZ: Executive. Worked for 10 years at American-International as supvr. of prod., jobs including film editing and supervision of editing and dubbing. Bowed as producer on Dillinger (1973). In 1975 formed A-Team Productions with John Milius.

PICTURES: Producer: Big Wednesday, Hardcore, 1941, Extreme Prejudice (exec. prod.). Conan the Barbarian, First Blood, Uncommon Valor, Rambo II, Red Dawn, Rambo III, Total Recall.

FELD, FRITZ: Actor. b. Berlin, Germany, Oct. 15, 1900. e. U. of Berlin; Max Reinhardt Sch. of Drama, Berlin. Actor, prod. asst. dir. for Reinhardt in Berlin 7 yrs.; on screen 1918 in The Golem, UFA. Since found variously assoc. U.S. m.p. prod., as writer, director, actor: has appeared in more than 410 pictures. 1971; nat'l bd. dir., Screen Actors Guild. 1968 chairman of the American National Theatre Comm., Southern California Chapter. 1976 chairman Hollywood Museum Project committee—Screen Actors Guild, 20th Century-Fox Film corp. staged A Tribute to Fritz Feld—60 Years in the Movies and the Los Angeles City named a theater in Brentwood the Fritz Feld Community Theatre. In April 1979, elected honorary Mayor of Brentwood by the Chamber of Commerce.

TELEVISION: Dangerous Assignment, Racket Squad, Mr. & Mrs. North, Jimmy Durante Show, Jack Paar, Thin Man, Chevy Show, Red Skelton, Milton Berle, Colonel Flack, Accused, Peter Gunn, General Electric Thea., Kraft Music Hall, Danny Thomas, Bachelor Father, Adventures in Paradise, Follow the Sun, The Donna Reed Show, Valentine Day, No Time for Sergeants, The Farmer's Daughter, The Bing Crosby Show, Batman, Lost in Space, The Man From U.N.C.L.E., Laredo, Please Don't Eat the Daisies, Girl From U.N.C.L.E., The Smothers Bros., The Wild, Wild, West, Bewitched, Donald O'Connor Show, The Beverly Hillbillies, Land of the Giants, Arnie, Love, American Style, The Merv Griffin Show, The New Bill Cosby Show, The Julie Andrews Hour, Fire House, The Odd Couple, The Night Couple, The Night Stalker, Only with Married Men, The Mike Douglas Show, The Tonight Show, Tabitha, The Hardy Boys, Flying High, Over Easy, Hizzonner, General Hospital, Heidi, Supertrain, Love, Sidney, No Soap, Radio, Magnum P.I., Simon & Simon, Amazing Stories, George Burns Comedy Week, Shell Game, Last of the Great Survivors, Get Smart, Again; B-Men (pilot).

STAGE: The Miracle, Once More With Feeling, Would Be Gentleman, Midsummer Night's Dream, Arsenic and Old Lace, You Can't Take It With You.

PICTURES: Wives and Lovers, Promises, Promises, Who's Minding the Store?, Four for Texas, The Patsy, Harlow, Made in Paris, Three on a Couch, Way . . . Way Out, The Comic, Hello, Dolly!, The Computer Wore Tennis Shoes, The Phynx, Which Way to the Front? Herbie Rides Again, The Strongest Man in the World, Hoyt Axton's Country Western Rock 'Roll Show, The Sunshine Boys, Won Ton Ton, the Dog Who Saved Hollywood, Broadway Rose, Silent Movie, Pennsylvania Lynch, Freaky Friday, The World's Greatest Lover, Herbie Goes Bananas, History of the World, All the Marbles, A Fine Mess, Barfly, Homer & Eddy.

FELDMAN, COREY: Actor. b. Reseda, CA, July 16, 1971. Has been performing since the age of 3 in over 100 commercials, television (Love Boat, Father Murphy, Foul Play, Mork and Mindy, Eight Is Enough, Alice, Gloria) and films.

PICTURES: Time and Again, Born Again, The Fox and the Hound (voice); Friday the 13th—The Final Chapter; Friday the 13th—A New Beginning; The Goonies; Gremlins; Stand by Me; Lost Boys; License to Drive; The 'Burbs; Dream a Little Dream.

TELEVISION: Series: The Bad News Bears (1979–80); Madame's Place. Movies: Kid with a Broken Halo, Open All Night, Out of the Blue, When the Whistle Blows, I'm a Big Girl Now, Specials: 15 & Getting Straight. How to Eat Like a Child.

FELDMAN, EDWARD S.: Producer. b. New York, NY, Sept. 5, 1929. e. Michigan State U. Trade press contact, newspaper and mag. contact, 20th Century Fox, 1950; dir. info. services, Dover Air Force Base. 1954–56; publicity coordinator, The World of Suzie Wong, Para., 1959; joined Embassy, dir. of publicity, 1969; vice pres. in chg., adv. & pub, Seven Arts Prods., 1962; v.p. exec. asst. to head prod. Warner-7 Arts Prods., 1967, pres., m.p. dept., Filmways, 1970; Formed Edward S. Feldman Co., 1978; later F/M Entertainment with Charles Meeker.

PICTURES: What's the Matter With Helen? (exec. prod.), Fuzz (exec. prod.), Save the Tiger, The Other Side of the Mountain (prod.),Two-Minute Warning (prod.), The Last Married Couple in America (co-prod.); Six Pack (co. exec. prod.); The Sender (prod.), Hot Dog. . .The Movie!; Witness, Explorers, The Golden Child, The Hitcher (exec. prod.), Near Dark (exec. prod.), Wired (prod.), Green Card.

TELEVISION: Exec. Prod.: Valentine, 300 Miles for Stephanie, Charles and Diana: A Royal Love Story, 21 Hours at Munich, King, Not in Front of the Children, Obsessed with a Married Woman.

FELDMAN, PHIL: Producer. b. Boston, MA. Jan. 22, 1922. e. Harvard U., 1943; Georgetown U., 1946; Harvard Business Sch., 1947; Harvard Law Sch., 1949. First Lieutenant, U.S. Army, 1943–46. Owner, Wholesale and retail dry goods firm, 1946–49. Law practice, 1950–51. Legal counsel Famous Artists Corp. 1951–53. Assoc. Dir. of Business Affairs CBS, 1953; Dir. of Business Affairs CBS, 1954–57. V.P. Talent & Contract Properties CBS, 1957–60. Exec. v.p. Broadcast Management, 1960–62. Head Business Relations 20th-Century Fox, 1962. V.P. 7 Arts Assoc. Corp. 1962–66 Pres., Phil Feldman Prods., Inc., 1967. Pres., First Artists, 1969; 1980, joined Rastar Films as exec. v.p.

PICTURES: You're a Big Boy Now, The Wild Bunch, The Ballad of Cable Hogue, Blue Thunder (exec. prod.).

FELL, NORMAN: Actor. b. Philadelphia, PA, March 24, 1924. e. Temple U. Studied acting with Stella Adler. Member, Actors Studio. Professional debut at Circle-in-the-Square Theatre in N.Y. in Bonds of Interest. Summer Stock; appearances on TV; moved to Hollywood in 1958 to begin theatrical film career.

PICTURES: The Graduate, Pork Chop Hill, Oceans 11, Rat Race, Inherit the Wind, Bullitt, If It's Tuesday, This Must Be Belgium, Catch 22, The End, C.H.U.D.II: Bud the Chud.

TELEVISION: Over 150 live plays from NY and some 200 shows filmed in Hollywood. Series: Joe and Mabel, 87th Precinct, Dan August, Needles and Pins, Three's Company, The Ropers, Teachers Only. Guest: Matt Houston, Crazy Like a Fox, Simon and Simon. The Boys (pilot). Mini-Series: Rich Man, Poor Man, Roots: The Next Generations. Movies: The Jessie Owens Story.

FELLINI, FEDERICO: Director. b. Rimini, Italy. Jan. 8, 1920. m. actress Giulietta Masina. e. U. Rome. Journalist 1937–39; writer of radio dramas 1939–42, also cartoonist, caricaturist; then m.p. writer, actor, s.p., dir.

PICTURES: Writer: Open City, Paisan, Ways of Love, Senza Pieta; director: Variety Lights, The White Sheik, I Vitelloni, The Matrimonial Agency (Love in the City), Il Bidone, The Wastrels, La Strada (Acad. Award, best foreign film, 1954); The Swindlers, La Dolce Vita, Boccaccio '70, "8½"(Acad. Award, foreign film), The Nights of Cabiria (Acad. Award, foreign film, 1957); Juliet of the Spirits, Spirits of the Dead, Fellini Satyricon, The Clowns, Fellini's Roma, Amarcord (Acad. Award, foreign film, 1975); Casanova, Orchestra Rehearsal, City of Women, And The Ship Sails On, Ginger and Fred, Federico Fellini's Intervista, The Voices From the Moon.

FELLMAN, DANIEL R.: Executive. b. Cleveland, OH, March 14, 1943. e. Rider Coll., B.S., 1964. Joined Paramount N.Y. 1964; later sales mgr. Washington DC, Dallas. Next branch mgr.

Cleveland; then Chicago. In 1969 joined Loews Theatres as film buyer. In 1971 joined Cinema National Theatres, division of Carrols Development Corp., as v.p./chief film buyer. In 1973 named v.p./dir., Cinema National Theatres. 1977, pres., American Theatre Mgt. Joined Warner Bros. in 1978 as eastern sales mgr. 1979 named v.p./ass't. gen. sales mgr. 1982, v.p., sls. mgr., WB. 1985, named v.p. & gen. sls. mgr.; sr. v.p., gen sales mgr., 1987. President Variety Club Tent 35, 1977–78. 1986, board mem. and chmn., Will Rogers Fund raising; member of board 1987 Will Rogers, bd. member and v.p. Motion Picture Pioneers; bd. member Streisand Center for Performing Arts.

FELLMAN, NAT D.: Executive. b. New York, NY, Feb. 19, 1910. Started as office boy, Warner Bros. Pictures, 1928; transferred to Warner Bros. Theatres, asst. to chief booker; handled pool, partnership operations; head buyer, booker for Ohio zone, 1941; asst. to chief film buyer in New York, 1943; apptd. chief film buyer, 1952; exec. asst. to v.p. and gen. mgr., Stanley Warner Theatres, 1955; asst. gen. mgr., Stanley Warner Theatres, 1962; acting gen. mgr., Stanley Warner Theatres, July, 1964; Stanley Warner Theatres, v.p. and gen. mgr., 1965; v.p., NGC Theatre Corp. and division mgr. Fox Eastern Theatres, 1968; v.p. National General Corp., and pres., National General Theatres, 1969; 1974, formed Exhibitor Relations Co., operations consultant; sold it and retired in 1982. Served as vice pres., Variety Clubs International and NATO, Chrm., presidents' advisory comm. Currently on bd. of dir., Motion Picture Pioneers and Will Rogers Inst.

FENADY, ANDREW J.: Producer, Writer. b. Toledo, OH, Oct. 4, 1928. e. U. of Toledo, 1946–50. Radio-prod.-actor-writer. Novels: The Man With Bogart's Face, The Secret of Sam Marlow, The Claws of the Eagle, The Summer of Jack London.

PICTURES: Stakeout on Dope Street, The Young Captives, Ride Beyond Vengeance, Chisum, Terror in the Wax Museum, Arnold, The Man with Bogart's Face.

TELEVISION: series: Confidential File, The Rebel, Branded, Hondo. Movies: The Woman Hunter, Voyage of the Yes, The Stranger, The Hanged Man, Black Noon, Sky Heist, Mayday 40,000 Ft., The Hostage Heart, Mask of Alexander, Masterpiece of Murder, Who Is Julia?, The Old Dick.

FENNELLY, VINCENT M.: Producer. b. Brooklyn, July 6, 1920. e. Holy Cross, 1938–42. U.S. Navy, 1942–46; salesman, Monogram, Des Moines, 1947; entered prod. field, 1949; indep. prod. for Monogram, 1950; Ent. TV field, 1957; prod. Transwestern Films, Inc., Frontier Pictures, Silvermine Productions Co., Allied Artists; Malcolm Enterprises, Hilgarde Enter.

PICTURES: Kansas Territory, Wagons West, Fargo, Marksman, Star of Texas, Topeka, Texas Bad Man, Bitter Creek, The Desperado, Seven Angry Men, Dial Red O, Bobby Ware Is Missing, At Gunpoint, Crime in the Streets, Last of the Badmen.

TELEVISION: Four Star Films, Alcoa-Goodyear, Trackdown, Wanted Dead or Alive, David Niven Show, Richard Diamond, Stagecoach West, The Dick Powell Theatre, Target, The Corruptors, Rawhide; A Man Called Shenandoah.

FENNEMAN, GEORGE: M.C., Announcer. b. Peking, China, Nov. 10, 1919. e. San Francisco State U.

CREDITS: Groucho Marx Show, You Bet Your Life, M.C. Host: Surprise Package, Funny Funny Films, Talk About Pictures, On Campus, Donny & Marie, Spokesman for Home Savings of America/Savings of America.

FERRAZZA, CARL J.: Executive. b. Cleveland, OH, Aug. 29, 1920. e. Catholic U. of America, Washington, DC. Started career 1945: as asst. mgr. & mgr. for Loews Theatres. 1952, joined Cincinnati Theatre Co., first as mgr. for Keith's Theatre, Cincinnati, and after prom. dir. for circuit. 1963, field rep. for United Artists, covering midwest. 1968, UA prom. mgr., N.Y. 1975–83, dir. of field activities, MGM/UA; 1984, joined Orion Pictures Distributing Corp. as v.p. promotional and field activities.

FERRER, JOSE: Producer, Director, Actor. b. Santurce, Puerto Rico, Jan. 8, 1909. e. Princeton U. Director and actor, New York stage, prior to screen career. Won Academy Award as best actor for Cyrano de Bergerac, 1950.

THEATER: Let's Face It, Othello, Strange Fruit (prod., dir.), Stalag 17 (prod., dir.), Twentieth Century (1951), The Chase (prod., dir.), The Shrike (prod., dir., actor), Richard III, My Three Angels (dir.), The Dazzling Hour, The Girl Who Came to Supper, Man of La Mancha.

PICTURES: Joan of Arc, Whirlpool, Crisis, Cyrano de Bergerac, Anything Can Happen, Moulin Rouge, Miss Sadie Thompson, Caine Mutiny, Deep in My Heart, The Shrike (also dir.), Cockleshell Heroes (also dir.), Great Man (also dir., s.p.), I Accuse (also dir.), The High Cost of Living (dir. only), Return to Peyton Place (dir. only), State Fair (dir. only), Lawrence of Arabia, Nine Hours to Rama, Stop Train 349 From Berlin, The Greatest Story Ever Told, Ship of Fools, Enter Laughing, Cervantes, Orders to Kill, The Big Bus, Voyage of the Damned, The Sentinel, Crash, The Private Files of J. Edgar Hoover, Dracula's Dog, The Swarm, Fedora, The Fifth Musketeer, The Big Brawl, A Midsummer Night's Sex Comedy, To Be or Not to Be, The Evil That Men Do, Dune, Old Explorers.

TELEVISION: What Makes Sammy Run?, The Aquarians, Cross Current, The Missing Are Deadly, The Marcus-Nelson Murders, Orders to Kill, The French-Atlantic Affair, The Art of Crime, Truman at Potsdam, The Rhinemann Exchange, Gideon's Trumpet, The Dream Merchants, This Girl for Hire, Hitler's SS: Portrait in Evil, Samson and Delilah, Blood and Orchids, Newhart (series), Strange Interlude, Mother's Day, The Rope.

FERRER, MEL: Producer, Director, Actor. b. Elberon, NJ, Aug. 25, 1917. e. Princeton U. During coll. and early career spent summers at Cape Cod Playhouse, Dennis, MA; then writer in Mexico, authored juvenile book, Tito's Hats; later ed. Stephen Daye Press, VT. Left publishing upon reaching leading-man status at Dennis; on Bdwy as dancer in You'll Never Know, Everywhere I Roam; others. Kind Lady, Cue For Passion; then to radio, serving apprenticeship in small towns; prod.-dir., NBC: dir. Land of the Free, The Hit Parade, and Hildegarde program. Entered m.p. ind., 1945, when signed by Columbia, dial. dir.: The Girl of the Limberlost; later, returned to Broadway, leading role, Strange Fruit; signed by David Selznick as producer-actor, on loan to John Ford as prod. asst. on The Fugitive; then to RKO for Vendetta. Stage: Ondine on Bway., 1954. The Best Man (L.A., 1987).

THEATER: Kind Lady, Cue for Passion, Strange Fruit, Ondine, The Best Man (L.A., 1987).

PICTURES: Lost Boundaries, Born to Be Bad, Vendetta (dir. only), The Secret Fury (dir. only), The Brave Bulls, Rancho Notorious, Scaramouche, Lili, Knights of the Round Table, Saada, War and Peace, The Sun Also Rises, Paris Does Strange Things, The Vintage, Fraulein, The World, The Flesh, and the Devil, Green Mansions, Blood and Roses, Devil and the 10 Commandments, The Longest Day, Fall of the Roman Empire, Hands of Orlac, Sex and the Single Girl, El Greco; (also prod.), Every Day is a Holiday (dir.), Wait Until Dark, (prod. only), A Time For Loving (prod.), Embassy (prod. only), "W." (prod., only), Brannigan, The Tempter, Lili Marleen, The Visitor, The Fifth Floor, Robocop, Mad Dog Anderson.

TELEVISION: Series: Behind the Screen, Falcon Crest. Movies: One Shoe Makes It Murder, Seduced, Outrages, Dream West, Peter the Great.

FETZER, JOHN E.: Executive. b. Decatur, IN, March 25, 1901. e. Purdue U., U. of Michigan, A.B., Andrews U. Hon LL.D., Western Michigan U. 1958. Chairman, owner Fetzer Broadcasting Co., Kalamazoo, MI; chmn., Detroit Baseball Club; pres., owner Fetzer Communications, Inc., Kalamazoo; chairman, dir., Cornhusker TV Corp.; Mem., former bd. dir., Amer. Nat'l Bank and Trust Co., former mem. Bd. of Trustees, Kalamazoo Coll. Radio research Europe, 1925; asst. dir., U.S. Censorship in charge of radio. 1944–46; served as war corr. in ETO, 1945; spl. assignment radio, TV, newspaper mission to Europe and Middle East, 1952. chmn., TV code review bd., NARTB, 1952–55. Pres., Pro Am Sports System, 1983; Member, bd., Domino's Pizza, 1983. Fellow, Royal Society of Arts, London; mem., Acad. of Polit. Science. Clubs: Park, Kalamazoo Country, Kalamazoo; Radio and Television Execs. Soc. (Assoc.); Broadcast Pioneers, N.Y.

FIEDLER, JOHN: Executive. Launched m.p. career in 1975 working in commercials and industrial and ed. films. Joined Technicolor as sr. exec. in prod. svcs. in mktg. Joined Rastar 1980 as v.p., prod. dev. and asst. to Guy McElwaine, pres. & CEO. Joined Paramount as v.p. in prod.; then to Tri-Star Pictures in same post. Resigned to join Columbia Pictures as exec. v.p., worldwide prod., 1984, then pres. of prod. 1986. 1987, left to become independent prod. 1989 named pres. of prod., Rastar IndieProd.

PICTURES: The Beast, Aunt Julia and the Scriptwriter (prod.).

FIELD, DAVID M.: Executive. b. Kansas City, MO. e. Princeton U. Worked as reporter on city desk at Hartford (CT) Courant. In 1968 with NBC News in N.Y. and Washington, DC. Entered film school at U. of Southern California (L.A.) after which joined Columbia Pictures as west coast story editor. In 1973 went to ABC-TV Network as mgr., movies of the week. 1975, moved to 20th-Fox as v.p., creative affairs. Joined United Artists in 1978; named sr. v.p.—west coast production. Left in 1980 to become 20th-Fox exec. v.p. in chg. of worldwide production 1983, resigned to enter independent production deal with 20th-Fox, Consultant, Tri-Star Pictures. Wrote and produced Amazing Grace and Chuck, 1987.

FIELD, SALLY: Actress. b. Pasadena, CA, Nov. 6, 1946. m. prod. Alan Greisman. Daughter of Paramount contract actress Maggie Field Mahoney. Stepdaughter of actor Jock Mahoney. e. Actor's Studio 1973–75. Acting classes at Columbia studios. Picked over 150 finalists to star as lead in TV series, Gidget, 1965, followed by The Flying Nun, 1967–68. Theatrical film debut in The Way West, 1967.

PICTURES: Stay Hungry, Smokey and the Bandit, Heroes,

The End, Hooper, Norma Rae (Oscar), Beyond the Poseidon Adventure, Smokey and the Bandit II, Back Roads, Absence of Malice, Kiss Me Goodbye, Places in the Heart (Oscar), Murphy's Romance (also exec. prod.), Surrender, Punchline, Steel Magnolias.
TELEVISION: Series: Gidget, The Flying Nun, Alias Smith and Jones, The Girl With Something Extra. Maybe I'll Come Home in the Spring, Marriage Year One, Home for the Holidays, Bridges, Sybil (Emmy Award, 1977).

FIELD, SHIRLEY ANNE: Actress. b. London, 1938. Ent. films after repertory experience 1955. Under contract to Ealing-M.G.M. 1958.
THEATRE: The Lily White Boys, Kennedy's Children, Fire Wait Until Dark, The Life and Death of Marilyn Monroe, How the Other Half Loves.
PICTURES: Saturday Night and Sunday Morning, The Man in the Moon, War Lover, Lunch Hour, Kings of the Sun, Doctor in Clover, Alfie, Hell Is Empty, The Entertainer, The Damned, My Beautiful Laundrette, The Rachel Papers.
TELEVISION: Risking It, Buccaneer, U.S. Santa Barbara.

FIELD, TED: Producer. e. U. of Chicago, Pomona Coll. Started career as one of owners of Field Enterprises of Chicago; transferred to west coast, concentrating on real estate. Founded Interscope Communications, diversified co., which develops and produces theatrical films, TV series and movies-of-the-week.
PICTURES: Revenge of the Nerds, Turk 182, Critical Condition, Outrageous Fortune, Three Men and a Baby, The Seventh Sign, Cocktail, Bill & Ted's Excellent Adventure (exec. prod.), Renegades (exec. prod), Innocent Man, Bird on a Wire.
TELEVISION: The Father Clements Story (co-exec. prod.). Everybody's Baby: The Rescue of Jessica McClure (co-exec. prod.).

FIELDS, ALAN: Executive. Spent five years with Madison Square Garden before joining Paramount Pictures. Career there included various positions: v.p. for pay-TV and Home Video TV. Spent two years at studio lot in L.A. as part of network TV organization. 1981, named bd. director for Paramount Pictures (U.K.) in London, serving as liaison to United Intl. Pictures and Cinema Intl. Corp., serving on operating committees of both. 1985, appt. v.p., Entertainment & Communications Group of Gulf & Western Industries, Inc., parent co. of Paramount; C.O.O., exec. v.p. Madison Square Garden Corp.

FIELDS, FREDDIE: Executive. b. Ferndale, NY, July 12, 1923. Vice-pres., member of bd. of directors, MCA-TV, MCA Canada Ltd., MCA Corp.; mem., Pres. Club, Wash., D.C.; pres., Freddie Fields Associates Ltd., 1960; Founder pres., chief exec. officer Creative Management Assoc. Ltd. Agency, Chicago, Las Vegas, Miami, Paris, Los Angeles, N.Y., London, Rome, 1961. Was exclusive agent of Henry Fonda, Phil Silvers, Judy Garland, Paul Newman, Peter Sellers, Barbra Streisand, Steve McQueen, Woody Allen, Robert Redford, Ryan O'Neal, Liza Minnelli and others. In 1975 sold interest in CMA (now International Creative Mgt.) but continued as consultant. Produced for Paramount Pictures. 1977: Looking for Mr. Goodbar. American Gigolo, Citizen's Band; Victory. In 1983 named pres. and COO, MGM Film Co. Resigned 1985 to become independent producer for MGM/UA. Fever Pitch. Poltergeist II, Crimes of the Heart, Millenium, Glory.

FINCH, JON: Actor. b. England, 1942. Came to acting via backstage activities, working for five years as company manager and director.
PICTURES: Vampire Lovers; Horror of Frankenstein; Sunday, Bloody Sunday; Macbeth; L'affaire Martine Desclos; Frenzy; Lady Caroline Lamb; The Final Programme; Diagnosis Murder; Une Femme Fidele; The Man of the Green Cross; Battleflag; El Mister; Death on the Nile; La Sabina; Gary Cooper Which Art in Heaven; Breaking Glass; Power Play; Doktor Faustus; Giro City; Plaza Real; Streets of Yesterday. The Voice; Beautiful in the Kingdom. Mirror, Mirror.
TELEVISION: (U.S.) The Martian Chronicles, Peter and Paul, The Rainbow, Unexplained Laughter.

FINE, HARRY: Producer. e. St. Andrew's Coll. and Dublin U.
FILMS: Up The Junction, The Liquidator, The Penthouse, Long Days Dying, Vampire Lovers, Fright, Twins of Evil, Too Far to Go, Quadrophenia, McVicar, Journey to a Safe Place.
TELEVISION FILM SERIES: Sir Francis Drake, Man of The World, The Sentimental Agent.

FINESHRIBER, WILLIAM H., JR.: Executive. b. Davenport, IA, Nov. 4, 1909. e. Princeton U., B.A., 1931. Pub., CBS, 1931–34; mgr. Carnegie Hall, N.Y., 1934–37; script writer, dir., music comm., dir. of music dept., CBS, 1937–40; dir. of short wave programs, CBS, 1940–43; gen. mgr. CBS program dept. 1943–49; v.p. in charge of programs MBS, 1949–51; exec. v.p. & dir., MBS, 1951–53; v.p. & gen. mgr. of networks, NBC, 1953–54; v.p. in charge of Radio Network, NBC, 1955; v.p. Television Programs of America, 1956; director International operations, Screen Gems, 1957; v.p., Motion Picture Assoc. of America and Motion Picture Export Assoc. of America, 1960; bd. of dir., NARTB: exec. comm., bd. of dir., R.A.B; v.p. Radio Pioneers.

FINKELMAN, KEN: Director.
PICTURES: Airplane II: The Sequel; Head Office.

FINKELSTEIN, HERMAN: Attorney, b. Torrington, CT, Jan. 9, 1903. e. Clark U., A.B.; Yale Law School, LL.B., member of CT, PA & NY, U.S. Sup. Ct. bar; honorary L.L.D., New England Coll. of Law. Director, ASCAP Nathan Burkan Memorial Competition; Mem.; American Law Institute; State Dept. Panel on intl. Copyright; U.S. National Commission for UNESCO 1957–62; Consultant to U.S. Delegation, Inter-Amer. Conf. of Copyright Exports, Wash., D.C., 1946; Mem. U.S. Delegation, Intergovernmental Conference on Universal Copyright Convention Geneva, 1952, Berne Convention-Stockholm Revision Conf. 1967, Paris Revision Conf. 1971, Communication Satellite Conf. 1973, past pres., Copyright Soc. U.S.A., past pres., Exec. Bureau, CISAC: past pres., SCRIBES.
AUTHOR: Numerous articles on copyright.

FINLAY, FRANK: Actor. b. Farnworth, Eng., Aug. 6, 1926. e. Studied acting at RADA. Appeared with Guildford Repertory Theatre Co. 1957. London stage debut: The Queen and the Welshman, 1957. Broadway debut, Epitaph for George Dillon, 1958. Extensive stage career, especially with the Royal Court, Chichester Fest., and National Theatre includes: Sergeant Musgrave's Dance; Chicken Soup with Barley; Roots; Platonov; Chips with Everything; Saint Joan; Hamlet; Othello (Iago to Olivier's Othello), Saturday, Sunday, Monday; Plunder; Watch It Come Down; Weapons of Happiness; Tribute to a Lady; Filumena (and N.Y.), Amadeus; Mutiny.
PICTURES: The Longest Day (1962); The Loneliness of the Long Distance Runner; Agent 8 3/4; Doctor in the Wilderness; Private Potter; The Comedy Man; Underworld Informers; A Study in Terror; Othello; The Jokers; The Shoes of the Fisherman; Inspector Clouseau; The Deadly Bees; Robbery; I'll Never Forget What's 'is Name; Twisted Nerve; Cromwell; The Molly Maguires; Assault; Gumshoe; Shaft in Africa; The Three Musketeers; The Four Musketeers; The Wild Geese; Murder by Decree; Enigma; The Ploughman's Lunch; 1919; Return of the Soldier; Lifeforce; The Return of the Musketeers, King of the Wind.
TELEVISION: The Adventures of Don Quixote; The Thief of Baghad; Casanova; Julius Caesar; Les Miserables; This Happy Breed; The Lie; The Death of Adolph Hitler; Voltaire; The Merchant of Venice; 84 Charing Cross Road, Saturday, Sunday, Monday; Count Dracula; Aspects of Love; Sakharov; A Christmas Carol; Arch of Triumph.

FINNEY, ALBERT: Actor. b. Salford, England, May 9, 1936. Studied for stage at Royal Acad. Dramatic Art making his West End debut 1958 in The Party, Pres. of Stage Golf Society in Great Britain.
THEATER: Appeared at Stratford-on-Avon 1959 playing title role in Coriolanus, etc. 1960; on West End stage in The Lily White Boys and Billy Liar, Luther (NY, National Theatre), Much Ado About Nothing, Armstrong's Last Goodnight, Love for Love, Miss Julie, Black Comedy, A Flea in Her Ear; Joe Egg (NY), Alpha Beta, Krapp's Last Tape, Cromwell, Chez Nous, Hamlet, Tamburlaine, Uncle Vanya, Present Laughter. National Theatre: The Country Wife, The Cherry Orchard, Macbeth, The Biko Inquest, Sergeant Musgrave's Dance (also dir.), Orphans, Another Time.
PICTURES: The Entertainer, Saturday Night and Sunday Morning, Tom Jones, Night Must Fall, Two for the Road, Charlie Bubbles (also dir.), The Picasso Summer, Scrooge, Gumshoe, Alpha Beta, Murder on the Orient Express, The Duellists, Wolfen, Looker, Loophole, Looker, Shoot the Moon, Annie, The Dresser, Under the Volcano, Orphans, Miller's Crossing.
TELEVISION: The Claverdon Road Job, The Miser, Pope John Paul II, Endless Game.

FINNEY, EDWARD: Producer. b. New York, NY, April 18, 1913. e. City Coll. of New York. Began as engineer, Western Electric. Then property man, Johnny Hines, C.C. Burr comedies. To MGM as press sheet ed.; sales promotion mgr., Pathe; asst. adv. dir. UA; story ed. and adv. dir., Mon-Rep., prod. & adv. dir., Grand Natl.; then prod. Monogram, many westerns. In 1941 org. Edward Finney Prod. Discovered Tex Ritter and made his first 40 features. Prod. & dir. Silver Stallion, Code of the Redman, Queen of the Amazons, etc. Clubs: Masquers. ex. pres. Catholic Press Council, Board Member Permanent Charities, M.P. Acad. of Arts and Sciences Dramatic Guild; pres., Indep. M.P. Prod. Assn. Film chmn. Catholic Press Council.
PICTURES: Corregidor, Golden Stallion, Call of the Forest, Hi Diddle Diddle, Primitive Passion, Mormon Battalion, This Is Pippin (TV); Seven Wonders, Baron Munchausen, Enchanted Years, Buffalo Bill in Tomahawk Territory, Slash of the Knife, Gun Girls, Journey to Freedom, London After Dark, Dark Road, Halfway to Hell, The Prairie, Secret Tower, Barrels

Away, Things That Make America Great (TV); Spring Affair, Dragons Across Asia, The Madcaps, The Happy Clown, The Great Dogtown Robbery.
TELEVISION: Pilots for Law and the People and the Circle Kids.

FIRTH, COLIN: Actor. b. Grayshott, Hampshire, Eng., Sept. 10, 1960. On stage in Doctor's Dilemma, Another Country.
PICTURES: Another Country, Dutch Girls, 1919, A Month in the Country, Apartment Zero, Valmont, Wings of Fame.
TELEVISION: Series: Lost Empires. Movies: Camille, Tumbletown.

FIRTH, PETER: Actor. b. Bradford, Yorkshire, Oct. 27, 1953. Appeared in local TV children's show where casting director spotted him and got him role in series, The Flaxton Boys. Moved to London and worked in TV, first in children's show, later on dramas for BBC. Breakthrough role in Equus at National Theatre, 1973 which he repeated in film.
PICTURES: Brother Sun and Sister Moon, Daniel and Maria, Diamonds on Wheels, Joseph Andrews, Aces High, Equus, When You Comin' Back Red Ryder, Tess, Lifeforce, Letter to Brezhnev, Trouble in Paradise, A State of Emergency, Born of Fire, The Tree of Hands, Prisoner of Rio, Burndown.
STAGE: Equus, Romeo and Juliet, Spring Awakening.
TELEVISION: Series: The Flaxon Boys, Home and Away, Country Matters. Movies and specials: Here Comes the Doubledeckers, Castlehaven, The Sullen Sisters, The Simple LIfe, The Magistrate, The Protectors, Black Beauty, Arthur, Her Majesty's Pleasure, the Picture of Dorian Gray, Lady of the Camillias, The Flip Side of Domenic Hide, Blood Royal, Northanger Abbey, The Way, The Truth: the Video.

FISCHOFF, RICHARD: Executive. 1977, joined Stanley Jaffe Productions as v.p. where he was assoc. prod. for Kramer vs Kramer and was involved in dev. and prod of Taps and Without a Trace; 1982, v.p. prod., Paramount where he supervised Jaffe-Lansing prods., Racing with the Moon, and Nate and Hays; 1984–86, pres., Carson Prods., assisted in dev. of The Big Chill; 1986–87, production pres., Jaffe-Lansing Prods., involved in prod. of Fatal Attraction and with dev. co.'s initial foray into TV; Nov. 1987, named sr. v.p. prod., Tri-Star Pictures.
PICTURES: Kramer vs. Kramer (assoc. prod.); Desert Bloom (exec. prod.).
TELEVISION: Mistress (exec. prod.).

FISHBURNE, LARRY: Actor. b. 1963. Made feature film debut at 12 as star of Cornbread, Earl and Me (1975).
PICTURES: Fast Break, Willie and Phil, Apocalypse Now, Death Wish II, Rumble Fish, The Cotton Club, The Band of the Hand, The Color Purple, Quicksilver, Gardens of Stone, Red Heat, School Daze, King of New York, Nightmare on Elm Street III.
TELEVISION: M*A*S*H, Trapper John, M.D., Spenser: For Hire, Pee-wee's Playhouse, Father Clements (movie). One Life to Live (series).

FISHER, AL: Executive. b. Brooklyn, NY. Entered m.p. industry as office boy, Fox Metropolitan Theatres; U.S. Army Provost Marshal General's Office, 1942–46; Universal Pictures, mgr., Park Avenue Theatre, N.Y. & Copley Plaza Theatre, Boston, 1946; Eagle Lion Film Co., mgr., Red Shoe's Bijou Theatre, N.Y., 1947; Stanley Kramer Prods., exploitation, Cyrano de Bergerac, 1951; press agent, 1951; prod., Bway show, Daphine, 1952; joined United Artists Corporation, 1952, named dir. of exploitation; now freelancing as producer's repr.

FISHER, CARRIE: b. Beverly Hills, CA, Oct. 21, 1956. e. London Central Sch. of Speech & Drama. Daughter of Debbie Reynolds and Eddie Fisher. On Broadway in the chorus of revival of Irene (1972) and Censored Scenes from King Kong. Author: Postcards From the Edge (1988).
PICTURES: Shampoo, Star Wars, Mr. Mike's Mondo Video, The Empire Strikes Back, The Blues Brothers, Under the Rainbow, Return of the Jedi, Garbo Talks, The Man with One Red Shoe, Hannah and Her Sisters, Appointment with Death, The Time Guardian, Amazon Women on the Moon, Loverboy, The 'Burbs, She's Back, When Harry Met Sally, Postcards From the Edge (s.p.).
TELEVISION: Laverne and Shirley (series); Come Back Little Sheba (1977), Leave Yesterday Behind, Classic Creatures: Return of the Jedi, Frankenstein, Tumblina (Faerie Tale Theater), Sunday Drive, George Burns Comedy Week, Paul Reiser: Out On a Whim, Two Daddies? (voice).

FISHER, EDDIE: Singer. b. Philadelphia, PA, Aug. 10, 1928. Band, nightclub, hotel singer; discovered by Eddie Cantor, 1949; U.S. Army, 1951–53; many hit records include; Wish You Were Here, Lady of Spain; radio & TV shows, NBC.
PICTURES: Bundle of Joy, Butterfield 8, Nothing Lasts Forever.

FISHER, LUCY: Executive. b. Oct. 2, 1949. e. Harvard U., B.A. Exec. chg. creative affairs, MGM; v.p., creative affairs, 20th Century Fox; v.p., prod., Fox. 1980, head of prod., Zoetrope Studios; 1980–82, v.p., sr. prod. exec., Warner Bros.; 1983, sr. v.p. prod., WB.

FISK, JACK: Director. b. Ipava, IL, Dec. 19, 1934. e. Cooper Union. m. actress Sissy Spacek. Career in films as designer turning to direction with Heart Beat (1980).
PICTURES: Director: Raggedy Man, Violets Are Blue, Daddy's Dyin'.

FISZ, BENJAMIN: Producer. b. Warsaw, Poland, Nov. 4, 1922. Formed in assoc. Golden Era Films, 1954. Later Aqua Films Ltd., 1957 as ind. prod. for Rank Org. and formed S. Benjamin Fisz Prod. Ltd., 1963 formed Benton Film Prod. Ltd. in assoc. with Anthony Mann. 1967 Spitfire Prods. with Harry Saltzman. 1969 Benmar Prods. Incorporated into Scotia Investments Ltd. Formed Scotia Intl. under name group for dist. Dir., Scotia-Barber. 1970: Created studios complex, Spain Esterdios, Madrid. 1972: Formed Scotia Int. (Film Sales.) Jointly formed Scotia Deutschland and International Film Theatre Ltd. For Intl. Films Theatre Ltd. with Kenneth Rive. Formed Sintel Intl. Ltd. for worldwide dist., 1976. Formed London Leisure Centre and acquired Wembley Stadium Complex, 1983.
PICTURES: Capri, The Secret, Child in the House, Hell Drivers, Sea Fury, On the Fiddle, The Heroes of Telemark, The Battle of Britain, A Town Called Bastard, Aces High, A Nightingale Sang in Berkeley Square, Jigsaw Man. Exec. in chg. prod.: Captain Apache, Bad Man's River, Pancho Villa, Royal Hunt of the Sun, Horror Express, Psychomania.

FITELSON, H. WILLIAM: Attorney, counsel to Fitelson, Lasky and Aslan, law firm, New York, specializing in the field of communications (publishing, motion pictures, theatre, television, radio); b. New York, NY, Jan. 21, 1905. e. Columbia U. (extension), New York Law School. Newspaper and editorial work, librarian and tutor New York Law School, Story Department Tiffany-Stahl Productions 1929, counsel Tiffany-Stahl Productions 1929–32, United States counsel to British and foreign motion picture and theatrical producers, counsel to The Theatre Guild and numerous members motion picture industry, theatre industry, newspaper and publishing, television and radio interests, managing director Theatre Guild Television and radio divisions, including U.S. Steel Hour. Non-legal consultant on communications projects to Allen & Co., and Columbia Pictures Industries.

FITZGERALD, GERALDINE: Actress. b. Dublin, Eire, Nov. 24, 1914. e. Dublin Art Sch. On stage Gate Theat., Dublin; then in number of Brit. screen prod. including Turn of the Tide, Mill on the Floss. On N.Y. stage in Heartbreak House. In U.S. screen prod. from 1939 Wuthering Heights. Founded Everyman Street Theatre with Brother Jonathan Ringkamp.
PICTURES: (U.S.) include Dark Victory, Till We Meet Again, Flight from Destiny, Gay Sisters, Ladies Courageous, Watch on the Rhine, Wilson, The Strange Affair of Uncle Harry, Three Strangers, Nobody Lives Forever, So Evil My Love, Obsessed, Ten North Frederick, The Pawnbroker, Rachel, Rachel, Believe in Me, The Last American Hero, Harry and Tonto, Echoes of a Summer, Arthur, Easy Money, Pope of Greenwich Village, Poltergeist II, Arthur 2: On the Rocks.
STAGE: Sons and Soldiers, Portrait in Black, The Doctor's Dilemma, King Lear, Hide and Seek, A Long Day's Journey Into Night, (1971), Ah, Wilderness, The Shadow Box, A Touch of the Poet, Songs of the Streets (one woman show), Mass Appeal (dir. only), The Lunch Girls (dir.).
TELEVISION: The Best of Everything, Dixie: Changing Habits, Kennedy, Street Songs, Do You Remember Love, Circle of Violence, Night of Courage.

FLAKS, STEPHEN: Executive. b. New York, NY, Jan. 1, 1941. e. City Coll. of New York, B.B.A. Early career as an investment banker & stock broker for various companies, including First Hanover, First Devonshire, 1962–69. Founded Flaks-Zaslow in 1969. Entered motion picture industry in 1974 in capacity of production financing. Established VideoVision, Inc., in 1978.
PICTURES: The Understudy: Graveyard Shift II (prod.).

FLATTERY, THOMAS L.: Executive-Lawyer b. Detroit, MI, Nov. 14, 1922. e. U.S. Military Acad., West Point, B.S., 1944–47; UCLA, J.D., 1952–55; U. of Southern California, LL.M. 1955–65. Gen'l counsel and asst. sec'y, McCulloch Corp., CA, 1957–64; sec'y and corporate counsel, Technicolor, Inc., 1964–70; Vice President, Secretary & General Counsel, Amcord, Inc. (formerly American Cement Corporation) 1970–72; Vice President, Secretary & General Counsel, Schick Incorporated, 1972–75; counsel asst. secretary, C.F. Braun & Co., 1975–76; sr. vice pres., secretary & general counsel PCC Technical Industries, Inc. 1976–86; V.P. & gen counsel and asst. secretary, G & H Technology, Inc., 1986–present.

FLAXMAN, JOHN P.: Producer. b. New York, NY, March 3, 1934. e. Dartmouth U., B.A. 1956. 1st Lt. U.S. Army, 1956–58. Ent. m.p. industry in executive training program, Columbia Pictures Corp., 1958–63; exec. story consultant, Profiles in Courage, 1964–65; head of Eastern Literary Dept., Universal

Pictures, 1965; writer's agent, William Morris Agency, 1966; partner with Harold Prince in Media Productions, Inc. 1967; prod. m.p. Something for Everyone. Founded Flaxman Film Corp., 1975 Prod. Jacob Two-Two Meets the Hooded Fang, 1976. President-Tricorn Productions 1977; pres. Filmworks Capital Corp., 1979–83; Becker/Flaxman & Associates, 1979–83; pres., Cine Communications, 1983–present. Producer Off-Broadway, Yours, Anne (1985).
TELEVISION: The Caine Mutiny Court-Martial (prod.).

FLEISCHER, RICHARD O.: Director. b. Brooklyn, NY, Dec. 8, 1916. e. Brown U., B.A.; Yale U., M.F.A. Stage dir.; joined RKO Pathe 1942.
PICTURES: Flicker Flashbacks (writer, prod.), This Is America (dir., writer), Design for Death (co-prod.), Child of Divorce, Banjo, So This Is New York, Bodyguard, Follow Me Quietly, The Clay Pigeon, Narrow Margin, The Happy Time, Arena, 20,000 Leagues Under the Sea, Violent Saturday, Girl in the Red Velvet Swing, Bandido, Between Heaven and Hell, The Vikings, These Thousand Hills, Compulsion, Crack in the Mirror, The Big Gamble, Barabbas, Fantastic Voyage, Doctor Dolittle, Boston Strangler, Tora! Tora! Tora!, Ten Rillington Place, The Last Run, See No Evil, The New Centurions, Soylent Green, The Don Is Dead, The Spikes Gang, Mister Majestyk, Mandingo, The Incredible Sarah, Crossed Swords, Ashanti, The Jazz Singer, Tough Enough, Amityville 3-D, Conan the Destroyer, Red Sonja, Million Dollar Mystery.

FLEMING, JANET BLAIR: Executive. b. Ottawa, Canada, November 29, 1944. e. Carlton U., Ottawa, Canada, B.A. Secretary to Canada's Federal Minister of Transport 1967–72; 1973–77, asst. to Sandy Howard—business affairs; 1977, co-founder and v.p./sales & admin. of Producers Sales Organization; 1981, named sr. v.p., admin.; 1982, sr. v.p., acquisitions; 1983, exec. v.p., Skouras Pictures; 1985 promoted to pres., intl. div.; 1987–88 mgr. Lift Haven Inn, Sun Valley, ID; 1989, owner, Premiere Properties (prop. management, Sun Valley, ID).

FLEMING, RHONDA: Actress. r.n. Marilyn Louis. b. Los Angeles, CA, Aug. 10, 1923. e. Beverly Hills H.S. p. Harold and Effie Graham Louis, Screen debut: Spellbound (1945). L.A. Civic Light Opera in Kismet revival, 1976. Broadway debut, 1973: The Women (revival).
PICTURES: Spiral Staircase, Adventure Island, Out of the Past; singing debut: A Connecticut Yankee in King Arthur's Court, The Last Outpost, Cry Danger, The Redhead and the Cowboy, The Great Lover, Crosswinds, Little Egypt, Hong Kong, Golden Hawk, Tropic Zone, Pony Express, Serpent of the Nile, Inferno, Those Redheads from Seattle, Jivaro, Yankee Pasha, Tennessee's Partner, While the City Sleeps, Killer Is Loose, Slightly Scarlet, Odongo, Queen of Babylon, Gunfight at the OK Corral, Buster Keaton Story, Gun Glory, Home Before Dark, Alias Jesse James, The Big Circus, The Crowded Sky, Instant Love, The American Wife, Won Ton Ton, The Dog Who Saved Hollywood, The Nude Bomb.
TELEVISION: Guest: Wagon Train, Police Woman, Love Boat, McMillian and Wife. Movie: The Last Hours Before Morning.

FLEMYNG, ROBERT: Actor. b. Liverpool, England, Jan. 3, 1912. e. Halleybury Coll. Stage debut: Rope, 1931. Screen debut; Head Over Heels, 1937.
PICTURES: Bond Street, The Guinea Pig, The Conspirators, The Blue Lamp, Blackmailed, The Magic Box, The Holly and the Ivy, Cast a Dark Shadow, Man Who Never Was, Funny Face, Let's Be Happy, Wisdom's Way, Blind Date, A Touch of Larceny, Radtus (Italian), The King's Breakfast, The Deadly Affair, The Spy with the Cold Nose, The Quiller Memorandum, Deathhead Avenger, Oh! What a Lovely War, Battle of Britain, Cause for Alarm, Young Winston, The Darwin Adventure, Travels with My Aunt, Golden Rendezvous, The Medusa Touch, The Four Feathers, The Thirty-Nine Steps, Paris By Night.
TELEVISION: appearances in England, U.S. inc.: Rainy Day, Playhouse 90, Wuthering Heights, Browning Version, After the Party, Boyd Q.C., They Made History, Somerset Maugham Show, Woman in White, The Datchet Diamonds, Probation Officer, Family Solicitor (series), Man of the World, Zero One, Compact, (serial), Day by the Sea, The Living Room, Hawks and Doves, Vanity Fair, The Inside Man, The Doctor's Dilemma, The Persuaders, Major Lavender, Public Eye, Florence Nightingale, Edward VIII, Spy Trap, The Venturers' Loyalties, The Avengers, Crown Court, Enemy at the Door, Rebecca, Edward and Mrs. Simpson, The Ladykiller, Professionals, Fame Is the Spur, Crown Court, Spider's Webb, Executive Suite, Small World.

FLETCHER, LOUISE: Actress. b. Birmingham, AL, 1934. e. U. of North Carolina, B.A. Came to Hollywood at age 21; studied with Jeff Corey. Worked on TV shows (including Playhouse 90, Maverick). Gave up career to be a mother for 10 yrs.; returned to work in 1973.
PICTURES: Thieves Like Us, Russian Roulette, One Flew Over the Cuckoo's Nest (Acad. Award, 1975), Exorcist II: The Heretic, The Cheap Detective, Natural Enemies, The Magician of Lublin, The Lucky Star, The Lady in Red, Strange Behavior, Mamma Dracula, Dead Kids Talk to Me, Once Upon a Time in America, Brainstorm, Strange Invaders, Firestarter, Overnight Sensation, Invaders from Mars, The Boy Who Could Fly, Nobody's Fool, Flowers in the Attic, Two Moon Junction, Blue Steel, Shadow Zone, Best of the Best.
TELEVISION: Thou Shalt Not Commit Adultery, Can Ellen Be Saved: A Summer to Remember, Island, Second Serve, J. Edgar Hoover, The Karen Carpenter Story, Final Notice.

FLEXER, DAVID: Executive. b. Mt. Pleasant, TN, June 29, 1909. e. Wallace U. School, 1926; Vanderbilt U., 1930. m. Eleanor Handmacher, concert pianist. Was adv. rep. on national magazines, 1930–32; joined United Artists 1932–33; entered exhib. 1933, head of Flexer Theatres, operating in Tenn. and Miss.; The Albany Corp.; Theatre Real Estate Corp.; v.p. Impossible pictures, Inc., producers of cartoons currently distrib. by Republic; constructed first drive-in theatres in Minneapolis, and St. Louis, 1947; pres., Flexer Theatres of Tenn., Inc., Flexer Theatres of Miss., Inc., The Albany Corp. Pres., Inflight Motion Pictures.

FLINN, JOHN C.: Publicist. b. Yonkers, NY, May 4, 1917. e. U. of California. p. late John C. Flinn, pioneer m.p. executive. In pub. dept. David O. Selznick, 1936–39; unit publicist, then head planter, Warner, 1936–46; joined Monogram as asst. to nat'l adv. & pub. head & pub. mgr. Aug. 5, 1946; apptd. nat'l dir. of pub. & adv. of Allied Artists Pictures Corp., March, 1951, appt'd studio dir. adv. & pub., Columbia, March, 1959; v.p., Jim Mahoney & Associates (pub. rel. firm) in 1971. Joined MGM West Coast publicity department as publicity coordinator, January, 1973; Rejoined Columbia Pictures in Feb., 1974 as studio pub. dir.; 1979, promoted to dir. industry relations. Joined MGM/UA pub. staff, 1988 to work on m.p. academy campaign for Moonstruck. Engaged by Paramount 19888–89 to assist in Acad. Award campaigns.

FLOREA, JOHN: Producer-Director. b. Alliance, OH, May 28, 1916. Served as photo journalist with Life magazine, 1940–50; assoc. editor Colliers magazine, 1950–53. Prod.-dir. with David Gerber 1979–84.
TELEVISION: Dir. several episodes: Sea Hunt series, 1957–60; Bonanza, Outlaws, Outpost (pilot), The Virginian, Honey West, Daktari, Gentle Ben, Cowboy in Africa, High Chapparal, Destry Rides Again, Not For Hire, Ironside, Highway Patrol, Target, Everglades, (also prod.), CHIPS, MacGyver. Prod.-dir. of film Islands of the Lost. With Ivon Tors Films. Nominated as one of the Top 10 directors in America by DGA for 1968 Mission Impossible episode. Dir. several Ironside episodes. Doc: Kammikazi, Attack Hawaiian Hospitality, Million Dollar Question, Marineland, Brink of Disaster. (Valley Freedom Award), Dangerous Report, (for CIA), The Runaways (Emmy Award).
PICTURES: A Time to Every Purpose, The Astral Factor, The Invisible Strangler, Hot Child in the City.

FLYNN, JOHN: Director-Writer. b. Chicago IL. e. George Washington U, Stanford, UCLA, B.A. (Eng.). Worked in mailroom at MCA then with p.r. firm. Began career as trainee script supvr. for dir. Robert Wise on West Side Story. Soon working as ass't. dir. on MGM-TV shows. Made dir. debut with The Sergeant, 1969.
PICTURES: The Jerusalem File (dir.), The Outfit (s.p., dir.), Rolling Thunder (dir.), Defiance (dir.), Touched (dir.), Best Seller (dir.), Lock Up (dir.).
TELEVISION: Marilyn—The Untold Story (dir.).

FOCH, NINA: Actress. b. Leyden, Holland, April 20, 1924; daughter of Consuelo Flowerton, actress, & Dirk Foch, symphony orch. conductor. Many stage, radio, television appearances. Adjunct Prof., U. of Southern California, 1966–67; 1978–80, Adjunct professor, USC Cinema-TV grad. sch. 1986–; sr. faculty, American Film Inst,, 1974–77; Board of Governors, Hollywood Acad. of Television Arts & Sciences, 1976–77; Exec. Comm. Foreign Language Film Award, Acad. of Motion Picture Arts & Sciences, 1970–. Co-chmn., exec. comm. Foreign Language Film Award 1983–.
PICTURES: Nine Girls, Song to Remember, My Name is Julia Ross, An American in Paris, Scaramouche, Young Man in Hurry, Undercover Man, Sombrero, Fast Company, Executive Suite, Four Guns to the Border, Ten Commandments, Illegal, You're Never Too Young, Cry of the Werewolf, Escape in the Fog, I Love A Mystery, Johnny Allegro, Johnny O'Clock, Prison Ship, Return of the Vampire, Shadows In The Night, The Dark Past, The Guilt of Janet Ames, Three Brave Men, Spartacus, Cash McCall, Such Good Friends, Salty, Mahogany, Jennifer, Rich and Famous, Dixie Lanes, Skin Deep.
TELEVISION: Guest star, most major series, talk shows, specials and TV movies. Series: Shadow Chasers. Movie: Outback Bound. Mini-series: War and Remembrance.

FOGARTY, JACK V.: Executive, Producer, Writer. b. Los Angeles, CA. e. UCLA. Management, MGM, 1960–62; exec. prod. mgr., Cinerama, Inc., 1962–64; assoc. prod., The Best of Cinerama, 1963; est. own p.r. firm, 1965; pres., AstroScope, Inc., 1969–74.

TELEVISION: (writer) The Rookies, S.W.A.T., Charlie's Angels, Most Wanted, Barnaby Jones, A Man Called Sloane, Trapper John, T.J. Hooker, Crazy Like a Fox, The Equalizer, Jake and the Fatman. Story editor, Charlie's Angels; exec. story consultant: Most Wanted, A Man Called Sloane, Sheriff Lobo, T.J. Hooker. Producer: T.J. Hooker. Co-prod.: Jessie.

FOGELSON, ANDREW: Executive. b. New Rochelle, NY, August 5, 1942. e. Union Coll., 1960–64. First entered m.p. industry in 1968 with Warner Bros., starting as copywriter and soon made exec. asst. to v.p. of adv.-pub. In 1973 appt. v.p., marketing services. Joined Columbia Pictures in Dec. 1973, as v.p. in chg. world-wide adv.-pub. In 1977 went to Warner Bros. as exec. v.p. in chg. worldwide adv.-pub. 1979 left to become pres. of Rastar Prods. Resigned 1981 to become indep. prod. under Summa Entertainment Group banner. Formed AFA co., a marketing co., 1988.
PICTURES: Wrong Is Right (exec. prod.); Blue Thunder (exec. prod.); Spring Break (exec. prod.); Just One of the Guys (prod.).

FOLSEY, GEORGE, JR: Producer, Editor. b. Los Angeles, CA, Jan. 17, 1939. Son of late cinematographer George Folsey Sr. e. Pomona Coll., B.A., 1961.
PICTURES: Editor: Glass Houses (1973), Bone, Hammer, Black Caesar, Schlock, Trader Horn, Bucktown, J.D.'s Revenge, Norman . . . Is That You?, Tracks, The Chicken Chronicles, The Kentucky Fried Movie, Sourdough, National Lampoon's Animal House, Freedom Road, The Great Santini, The Blues Brothers (also assoc. prod.), Producer: An American Werewolf in London, Twilight Zone—The Movie (assoc. prod.); Trading Places (exec. prod. & 2nd unit dir.), Into the Night (co-prod.), Three Amigos, Coming to America (co-prod., co-editor).
VIDEO: Michael Jackson's Thriller (co-prod., editor).

FONDA, BRIDGET: Actress. b. 1964. Daughter of actor-director Peter Fonda. Grew up in Los Angeles and Montana. e. NYU theater prog. Starred in grad. student film PPT. Workshop stage performances include Confession and Pastels.
PICTURES: Aria (Tristan and Isolode sequence), You Can't Hurry Love, Shag, Scandal, Strapless, Frankenstein Unbound.
TELEVISION: Jacob Have I Loved (Wonderworks).

FONDA, JANE: Actress. b. New York, NY, Dec. 21, 1937. e. Emma Willard Sch., Troy, NY. active in dramatics, Vassar. Father, late actor Henry Fonda. Sister of actor-dir. Peter Fonda. Appeared with father summer stock production, The Country Girl, Omaha, NB. Studied painting, languages, Paris. Art Students League, N.Y. Appeared in The Male Animal, Dennis, MA. Modeled, appeared on covers, Esquire, Vogue, The Ladies Home Journal, Glamour, and McCall's, 1959.
PICTURES: Tall Story (debut), Walk on the Wild Side, The Chapman Report, Period of Adjustment, In the Cool of The Day, Sunday in New York, The Love Cage, La Ronde, Cat Ballou, The Chase, La Curee, Any Wednesday, The Game Is Over, Hurry Sundown, Barefoot in the Park, Barbarella, Spirits of the Dead, They Shoot Horses, Don't They? (Acad. Award nom.), Klute (Acad. Award, 1970), Steelyard Blues, F.T.A. (also prod.), Tout va Bien, A Doll's House, The Bluebird, Fun with Dick and Jane, Julia, Coming Home (Acad. Award, 1978), Comes a Horseman, California Suite, The China Syndrome, The Electric Horseman, Nine To Five, Roll-Over, On Golden Pond, Agnes of God, The Morning After, Stanley and Iris, Old Gringo, Women on the Verge of a Nervous Breakdown.
STAGE: There Was A Little Girl, Invitation to a March, The Fun Couple, Strange Interlude.
TELEVISION: Lily—Sold Out, 9 to 5 (exec. prod.), Tell Them I'm a Mermaid, The Doll Maker (Emmy, 1984).

FONDA, PETER: Actor, Director. b. Feb. 23, 1940. e. studied at U. of Omaha. Son of late actor Henry Fonda. Brother of Jane Fonda and father of actress Bridget Fonda.
PICTURES: Tammy and the Doctor, The Victors, Lilith, The Young Lovers, The Trip, The Wild Angels, Easy Rider (also writer, co-prod.), Idaho Transfer (dir.), The Last Movie, The Hired Hand (also dir.), Two People, Dirty Mary Crazy Larry, Open Season, Two People (also dir.), Race with the Devil, 92 In the Shade, Killer Force, Fighting Mad, Futureworld, Outlaw Blues, High Ballin!, Wanda Nevada (also dir.), Split Image, Smokey and the Bandit II, Certain Fury, Dance of the Dwarfs, Mercenary Fighters, Jungle Heat, Diajobu My Friend, Peppermint Frieden, Spasm, The Rose Garden.
TELEVISION: A Reason to Live, The Hostage Tower, A Time of Indifference, Sound, Certain Honorable Men.

FONTAINE, JOAN: Actress. b. Tokyo, Oct. 22, 1917. e. American School in Japan. Sister of Olivia de Havilland, actress. On B'way in Tea and Sympathy (1954); won Academy Award best performance, 1941, for Suspicion. Acad. Award nom. for Rebecca and The Constant Nymph. Author: No Bed of Roses (1978).
PICTURES: No More Ladies (debut, 1935), Quality Street, You Can't Beat Love, Music for Madame, Maid's Night Out, A Damsel in Distress, Blonde Cheat, The Man Who Found Himself, The Duke of West-Point, Sky Giant, Gunga Din, Man of Conquest, The Women, Rebecca, Suspicion, This Above All, The Constant Nymph, Jane Eyre, Frenchman's Creek, Affairs of Susan, From This Day Forward, Ivy, The Emperor Waltz, Kiss the Blood Off My Hands, You Gotta Stay Happy, Letter from an Unknown Woman, Born to Be Bad, Something to Live For, Darling How Could You?, September Affair, Ivanhoe, Decameron Nights, Flight to Tangier, The Bigamist, Casanova's Big Night, Serenade, Beyond a Reasonable Doubt, Island in the Sun, Until They Sail, A Certain Smile, Tender Is the Night, Voyage to the Bottom of the Sea, The Devil's Own, Bare Essence.
TELEVISION: Numerous guest appearances during the 1950s and 1960s, Crossings, Dark Mansions, Cannon, The Users.

FOOTE, HORTON: Writer. b. Wharton, TX, March 14, 1916. Actor before becoming playwright. Plays include Only the Heart, The Chase, Trip to Bountiful, Traveling Lady, etc.
PICTURES: Storm Fear, To Kill a Mockingbird (Oscar, 1962); Baby, The Rain Must Fall; Hurry Sundown, Tomorrow, Tender Mercies (Oscar, 1983); 1918; The Trip to Bountiful, On Valentine's Day, Convicts, Roots; in a Parched Ground.
TELEVISION: Only the Heart, Ludie Brooks, The Travelers, The Old Beginning, Trip to Bountiful, Young Lady of Property, Death of the Old Man, Flight, The Night of the Storm, The Roads to Home, Drugstore: Sunday Night, Member of the Family, Traveling Lady, Old Man, Tomorrow, The Shape of the River, The Displaced Person, Barn Burning, Habitation with Dragon, Dividing the Estate.

FORBES, BRYAN: Actor, Writer, Producer, Director. m. actress Nanette Newman. Former head of prod., man. dir., Associated British Prods. (EMI). b. Stratford (London), July 22, 1926. Stage debut, The Corn Is Green (London), 1942; screen debut, The Small Back Room, 1948.
THEATER: Director: Macbeth, Killing Jessica, The Living Room.
PICTURES: All Over the Town, The Wooden Horse, Dear Mr. Prohack, Appointment in London, Sea Devils, Wheel of Fate, Million Pound Note (Man with a Million), An Inspector Calls, Colditz Story, Passage Home, The Quartermas Experiment, Now and Forever, The Last Man to Nang, the Extra Day, It's Great to be Young, Satellite in the Sky, Quartermass 11, Cockleshell Heroes, Black Tent, House of Secrets, Baby and the Battleship, I Was Monty's Double, A Piece of Cake, Yesterday's Enemy, The League of Gentlemen, The Guns of Navarone, A Shot in The Dark, Man in the Moon, Whistle Down the Wind, League of Gentlemen, Only Two Can Play, The L-Shaped Room, Of Human Bondage, Station Six Sahara, Seance on a Wet Afternoon, King Rat, The Wrong Box, The Whisperers, Deadfall, The Madwoman of Chaillot, The Go-Between (executive producer), The Railway Children (exec. prod.) Tales of Beatrix Potter (exec. prod.) The Raging Moon (U.S. title, Long Ago Tomorrow), Goodbye Norma Jean and Other Things, The Stepford Wives (dir.), The Slipper and The Rose, International Velvet, Sunday Lovers, Jessie, Hopscotch (s.p.), Better Late Than Never (s.p./dir.) The Naked Face (s.p./dir.), Life of Henry Ford (s.p.), The Endless Game (dir., s.p.).
TELEVISION: I Caught Acting Like the Measles (produced/directed), The Breadwinner, French Without Tears, Johnnie Was a Hero, The Gift, The Road, The Heiress. Theatre: Flarepath, Fighters Calling, Gathering Storm, September Tide, The Holly and the Ivy, Tobias and the Angel, A Touch of Fear, Three Way Switch, December Flower, First Among Equals, Sister Ruth.
PUBLICATIONS: Truth Lies Sleeping (short stories) 1951; Distant Laughter (novel) 1972; Notes For a Life (Autobiog.) 1973/4. The Slipper and the Rose (book of Film) 1975/6. Ned's Girl, 1977, International Velvet 1978 (novel); Familiar Strangers (novel), 1979 (U.S. title, Stranger), That Despicable Race, 1980. the Rewrite Man 1983 (novel), The Endless Game (novel) 1986, A Song at Twilight (novel) 1989.

FORBES, DAVID: Executive. b. Omaha, NE, Nov. 9, 1945. e. U. of Nebraska. Began career with MGM in 1968 as field man in Detroit; later named asst. natl. field coordinator at studio. director, Metrovision, 1973. Director special projects for 20th-Fox, 1974; made natl. dir. marketing services, 1976. In 1977 left to join Rastar Prods. as marketing dir. Named v.p. & asst. to pres., Columbia Pictures, 1980; 1982, joined Almi Distributing Corp. as vice chmn. Joined MGM/UA, 1987. Pres. MGM/UA Distribution and pres. worldwide marketing, MGM Film Group; 1989 UA Film Group pres. marketing and dist.

FORD, GLENN: Actor. r.n. Gwylin Ford; b. Quebec, Canada, May 1, 1916. On stage in western co. Children's Hour 1935; on Broadway in: Broom for a Brlde, Soliloquy; served in U.S. Marine Corps 1942–45; m.p. debut in Heaven with a Barbed Wire Fence 1940.
PICTURES: Men Without Souls, Lady in Question, So Ends Our Night, Desperadoes, Stolen Life, Gilda, Framed, Mating of Millie, Return of October, Loves of Carmen, Mr. Soft Touch, Man from Colorado, Undercover Man, Lust for Gold,

Doctor and the Girl, Flying Missile, The Redhead and the Cowboy, Follow the Sun, The Secret of Convict Lake, Green Glove, Young Man with Ideas, Affair in Trinidad, Man from the Alamo, Terror on a Train, Plunder of the Sun, Big Heat, Appointment in Honduras, Human Desire, The Americano, Violent Men, Blackboard Jungle, Interrupted Melody, Trial, Ransom, Fastest Gun Alive, Jubal, Teahouse of the August Moon, Don't Go Near the Water, Cowboy, The Sheepman, Imitation General, Torpedo Run, It Started with a Kiss, The Gazebo, Cimarron, Cry for Happy, The Four Horsemen of The Apocalypse, Experiment in Terror, Love Is a Ball, The Courtship of Eddie's Father, The Rounders, The Money Trap, Fate Is the Hunter, Dear Heart, The Last Challenge, Heaven with a Gun, Smith!, The Day of the Evil Gun, A Time for Killing, Midway, Superman, Happy Birthday to Me, Casablanca Express.

TELEVISION: Series: Cade's County; The Family Holvak; Movies: Once Upon an Eagle; Brotherhood of the Bell; Beggarman, Thief; Evening in Byzantium.

FORD, HARRISON: Actor. b. Chicago, IL, July 13, 1942. e. Ripon Coll. After acting in L.A. and films for 5 years, undertook carpentry work including building Sergio Mendes' recording studio. Returned to acting and won notice in American Graffiti.

PICTURES: Dead Heat on a Merry-Go-Round, Luv, Getting Straight, The Long Ride Home, Journey to Shiloh, Zabriskie Point, The Conversation, American Graffiti, Star Wars, Heroes, Force 10 from Navarone, Hanover Street, Apocalypse Now, The Frisco Kid, The Empire Strikes Back, Raiders of the Lost Ark, Blade Runner, Return of the Jedi, Indiana Jones and the Temple of Doom, Witness, The Mosquito Coast, Frantic, Working Girl, Indiana Jones and the Last Crusade, Presumed Innocent.

TELEVISION: Dynasty, Trial of Lt. Calley, The Possessed.

FORD, TENNESSEE ERNIE: Singer. r.n. Ernest J. Ford. b. Bristol, TN, Feb. 13, 1919. Radio anncr., 1939–41; U.S. Air Force, 1942–45; radio anncr., San Bernardino, CA; hillbilly disc jockey, Pasadena; Capital Recording Star. Medal of Freedom recipient 1984.

TELEVISION: own TV shows, NBC; guest appearances on I Love Lucy, Red Skelton Show, Perry Como Show, George Gobel Show; own show, Tennessee Ford Show, ABC.

RECORDS: 16 Tons, many others.

FORD, TONY: Executive. b. New York, NY, August 6, 1925. e. St. Johns U. In U.S. Navy W.W.II; in life insurance business, 1946–48. Agent with MCA 1949–53. TV indep. prod., specials for Timex, Ringling Bros. Circus, Pontiac Victor Borge. Re-entered agency business, General Artists Corp., v.p., TV dept. Headed own agency, Tony Ford Mgt., Inc., which was acquired by William Morris Agency. Headed creative services division WMA representing producers, directors, writers specializing in the packaging of TV series and specials, left Morris Agency Jan. 1, 1977 to re-open Tony Ford Productions; 1979, named v.p. Metromedia Producers Corp.; 1984, named exec. v.p. Gaylord Television Prods.

FOREMAN, JOHN: Producer. b. Idaho Falls, ID. Cofounder of CMA Agency. Resigned Jan., 1968, to form production co. with Paul Newman: Newman-Foreman Company.

PICTURES: Winning, Butch Cassidy and the Sundance Kid, WUSA (co-prod.), Puzzle of a Downfall Child, They Might Be Giants, Sometimes a Great Notion, The Life and Times of Judge Roy Bean, Pocket Money, The Effect of Gamma Rays on Man-in-the-Moon Marigolds (exec. prod.), The Mackintosh Man, The Man Who Would Be King, Bobby Deerfield, The Great Train Robbery, Brainstorm, Eureka, The Ice Pirates, Prizzi's Honor, Millennium (exec. prod.).

FORMAN, SIR DENIS, O.B.E., M.A.: Executive. b. Moffat, Dumfriesshire, Scot., Oct. 13, 1917. e. Loretto Sch., Musselburgh, Pembroke Coll., Cambridge. Served in Argyll & Sutherland Highlanders, W.W.II. Entered film business May, 1946, production staff Central Office of Information, 1947; Chief Production Officer C.O.I. 1948; appointed dir. of the British Film Inst., 1949; joined Granada Television Ltd., 1955. Jnt. Mng. Dir., 1965 chmn., British Film Inst., Bd. of Gov., 1971–73. Chmn. Granada T.V. 1975–1987. Chmn. Novello & Co. 1972. Fellow, British Acad. Film & TV Arts, 1976. Dep. chrm. Granada Group, 1986.

FORMAN, MILOS: Director. b. Czechoslovakia, Feb. 18, 1932. Trained as writer at Czech Film Sch. and as director at Laterna Magika. Won Int'l. attention with first film Black Peter, 1963. Emigrated to U.S. after collapse of Dubcek govt. in Czechoslovakia.

PICTURES: Peter and Pavla (Czech Film Critics Award, 1963; Grand Prix Locarno, 1964.). The Loves of a Blonde, Firemen's Ball, Taking Off, Visions of Eight (segment), One Flew Over the Cuckoo's Nest (Acad. Award, best dir. 1975), Hair, Ragtime, Amadeus (Acad. Award, best dir., 1984), Valmont (dir., co-s.p.), New Year's Day (actor only).

FORREST, FREDERIC: Actor. b. Waxahachie, TX, Dec. 23, 1936. e. Texas Christian U., U. of Oklahoma, B.A. Studied with Sanford Meisner and Lee Strasberg. Began career off-off Bdwy at Caffe Cino in The Madness of Lady Bright then off-Bdwy in Futz, Massachusetts Trust and Tom Paine, all with La Mama Troupe under direction of Tom O'Horgan. Moved to Hollywood in 1970. Film debut in When the Legends Die, 1972.

PICTURES: The Conversation, The Don Is Dead, The Dion Brothers, The Gravy Train, Permission to Kill, The Missouri Breaks, It Lives Again, Apocalypse Now, The Rose, One from the Heart, Hammett, Valley Girl, The Stone Boy, Where Are the Children? Season of Dreams, Tucker: The Man and His Dream, Valentino Returns, Music Box, Cat Chaser, The Two Jakes.

TELEVISION: Movies: Larry, Calamity Jane, Right to Kill?, The Deliberate Stranger, Quo Vadis, Little Girl Lost, Saigon, Year of the Cat (U.K.); Best Kept Secrets, Who Will Love My Children? A Shadow on the Sun, Margaret Bourke-White.

FORREST, STEVE: Actor. b. Huntsville, TX, Sept. 29, 1924. r.n. William Forrest Andrews. Brother of Dana Andrews. e. UCLA, 1950. Acted at La Jolla Playhouse; appeared on radio, TV; m.p. debut in Geisha Girl.

PICTURES: Bad and the Beautiful, Battle Circus, The Clown, Band Wagon, Dream Wife, So Big, Take the High Ground, Phantom of the Rue Morgue, Prisoner of War, Rogue Cop, Bedeviled, It Happened to Jane, Heller in Pink Tights, Five Branded Women, Flaming Star, The Second Time Around, Rascal, The Wild Country, The Late Liz, North Dallas Forty, Mommie Dearest, Sahara, Spies Like Us, Amazon Women on the Moon.

TELEVISION: Movies: The Hatfields and the McCoys, Wanted: The Sundance Women, The Last of the Mohicans, Testimony of Two Men, Maneaters are Loose, Hollywood Wives; Gunsmoke, Return to Dodge, Dallas. Series: The Baron, S.W.A.T., Hotel, Dallas.

FORSTATER, MARK: Producer. b. Philadelphia, PA, 1943. e. City Coll. of New York, Temple U. In 1967 moved to England; studied at U. of Manchester and London Intl. Film School. First job in industry with Anglia TV on program, Survival. Began producing in 1970 with British Film Institute. Set up Chippenham Films to make documentaries. Moved into features in 1974 with Monty Python and the Holy Grail.

PICTURES: The Odd Job, Marigolds in August, The Grass Is Singing, Xtro, Paint It Black, Wherever She Is, The Wolves of Willoughby Chase, Death of a Schoolboy, Streets of Yesterday, Wherever You Are (exec. prod.). Shorts: The Glitterball, Wish You Were Here.

TELEVISION: The Cold Room, Forbidden.

FORSTER, ROBERT: Actor. b. Rochester, NY, July 13, 1941. e. Heidelberg Coll., Alfred U., Rochester U., B.S.

THEATRE: Mrs. Dally, 1965. Summer tour, A Streetcar Named Desire, 1967.

PICTURES: Reflections in a Golden Eye, Medium Cool, Justine, Journey Through Rosebud, The Don is Dead, The Black Hole, Alligator, Vigilante, Walking the Edge, Committed, Counterforce. Princess of Darkness, The Banker.

TELEVISION: Judd for the Defense, Banyon, Once a Hero, Jesse Hawkes, Mick & Frankie (pilot).

FORSYTH, BILL: Director. Writer. b. Glasgow, Scotland, 1947. At 16 joined film co. For next 10 years made industrial films, then documentaries. Joined Glasgow Youth Theater.

PICTURES: Director-Writer: That Sinking Feeling (also prod.), Gregory's Girl, Local Hero, Comfort and Joy, Housekeeping, Breaking In, Rebecca's Daughters.

TELEVISION: Andrina.

FORSYTHE, JOHN: Actor. b. Penn's Grove, NJ, Jan. 29, 1918.

STAGE: Mr. Roberts, All My Sons, Yellow Jack, Teahouse of the August Moon, and others.

TELEVISION: Started in 1947; appeared on Studio One, Kraft Theatre, Robert Montgomery Presents, and others. Series: Bachelor Father; To Rome with Love; Dynasty. Movies: The Mysterious Two, On Fire.

PICTURES: Captive City, It Happens Every Thursday, The Glass Web, Escape from Fort Bravo, Trouble with Harry, Ambassador's Daughter, Everything But the Truth, Kitten with a Whip, Madame X, In Cold Blood, The Happy Ending, Topaz, And Justice for All, Scrooged.

FORTE, FABIAN: Singer, Actor. b. Philadelphia, PA, Feb. 6, 1943. e. South Philadelphia H.S. At 14, signed contract with Chancellor Records. Studied with Carlo Menotti.

RECORDS: Turn Me Loose, Tiger, I'm a Man, Hound Dog Man, The Fabulous Fabian (gold album).

PICTURES: Hound Dog Man, High Time, North To Alaska, Love in a Goldfish Bowl, Mr. Hobbs Takes a Vacation, Ride the Wild Surf, Dear Brigette, Longest Day, 10 Little Indians, Fireball 500, Thunder Alley, Five Weeks in a Balloon, Devil's Eight, The Longest Day, A Bullet for Pretty Boy, Little Laura and Big John.

FOSSEY, BRIGITTE: Actress. b. Tourcoing, France, 1947. After a remarkable debut at the age of 5 in Rene Clement's Forbidden Games (1952) returned to school, studying philosophy and translating. Rediscovered by director Jean-Gabriel Albicocco and cast in Le Grand Meaulnes (1967).
PICTURES: Forbidden Games, The Happy Road, Le Grand Meaulnes, Adieu l'Ami, M Comme Matheiu, Making It, The Blue Country, The Man Who Loved Women, The Good and the Bad, The Swiss Affair, Quintet, Mais ou et donc Orincar, The Triple Death of the Third Character, A Bad Son, The Party, Chanel Solitaire, A Bite of Living, Imperativ, The Party-2, Enigma, Au nom de tous les Meins, Scarlet Fever, A Strange Passion, A Case of Irresponsibility, The Future of Emily, The False Confidences, Cinema Paradiso.

FOSTER, CHRISTINE: Executive. r.n. Mary Christine Foster. b. Los Angeles, CA, March 19, 1943. e. Immaculate Heart Coll, B.A. 1967. UCLA MJ, 1968. Teacher while member of Immaculate Heart Community, 1962–65. Teacher, Pacific U., Tokyo, 1968; dir., research and dev. Metromedia Producers Corp., 1968–71; dir., dev. and prod. services, The Wolper Org. 1971–76; manager, film progs. NBC Television Network 1976–77; v.p. movies for TV & mini-series, Columbia Pictures TV, 1977–81; v.p. series programs, Columbia Pictures TV 1981; v.p. prog. dev., Group W. Prods. 1981–87; v.p. television, The Agency, 1988. Member: exec. comm. Humanitas Awards, 1986– ; L.A. Sr. v.p. The Agency, 1989–; Roman Catholic Archiodean Communications Comm., 1986–; Immaculate Heart H.S. bd of trustees, 1981–88; Women in Film, bd of dirs., 1977–78; Teacher UCLA Extension, 1987. University lecturer.

FOSTER, DAVID: Producer. b. New York, NY, Nov. 25, 1929. e. Dorsey H.S., U. of Southern California Sch. of Journalism. U.S. Army, 1952–54; entered public relations field in 1952 with Rogers, Cowan & Brenner; Jim Mahoney, 1956; Allen, Foster, Ingersoll & Weber, 1958; left field in 1968 to enter independent m.p. production. Partner in Turman-Foster Co.
PICTURES: Co-produced (with Mitchell Brower) McCabe and Mrs. Miller, The Getaway; co-produced (with Lawrence Turman), The Nickel Ride (exec. prod.), The Drowning Pool, The Legacy, Tribute (exec. prod.), Caveman, The Thing, Second Thoughts, Mass Appeal, The Mean Season (prod.), Short Circuit; Running Scared (co-prod.); Full Moon in Blue Water; Short Circuit II; Gleaming the Cube.
TELEVISION: Jesse (co-exec. prod), Between Two Brothers, Surrogate Mother.

FOSTER, JODIE: Actress. r.n. Alicia Christian Foster. b. Los Angeles, CA, Nov. 19, 1962. e. Yale U. Acting debut on Mayberry, R.F.D. TV series (1969). Followed with many TV appearances, from series to movies of the week.
PICTURES: Napoleon and Samantha (1972), Menace of the Mountain, One Little Indian, Tom Sawyer, Kansas City Bomber, Alice Doesn't Live Here Anymore, Taxi Driver, Echoes of a Summer, Bugsy Malone, Freaky Friday, The Little Girl Who Lives Down the Lane, Candleshoe, Foxes, Carny, The Hotel New Hampshire, Five Corners, Siesta, The Accused (Acad. Award, 1988), Stealing Home, Backtrack.
TELEVISION: Series: The Courtship of Eddie's Father (regular), My Three Sons (regular), Paper Moon (regular), The Secret Life of T.K. Dearing. Movies: Smile, Jenny, You're Dead, Rookie of the Year, The Blood of Others.

FOSTER, JULIA: Actress. b. Lewes, Sussex, England, 1944. First acted with the Brighton Repertory Company, then two years with the Worthing, Harrogate and Richmond companies. 1956, TV debut as Ann Carson in Emergency Ward 10.
PICTURES: Term of Trial, The Loneliness of the Long Distance Runner, The Small World of Sammy Lee, The System, The Bargee, One Way Pendulum, Alfie, Half A Sixpence.
TELEVISION: A Cosy Little Arrangement, The Planemakers, Love Story, Taxi, Consequences, They Throw It at You, Crime and Punishment, The Image.
STAGE: No. 1 tour of The Country Wife; 1969, What the Butler Saw.

FOSTER KEMP, CECIL R.: M.B.E. Associate Producer, Production Supervisor. b. Shanghai. e. Brighton Coll.
PICTURES: Paris Holiday, Interpol, Tarzan and the Lost Safari, Around the World in Eighty Days, Front Page Story, Appointment in London, South of Algiers, Under Capricorn, Scott of the Antarctic, Untamed, John Paul Jones, King of Kings, Offbeat, El Cid, Fifty Five Days at Peking, The Fall of the Roman Empire, William The Conqueror, Girl on the Motorcycle, Arthur! Arthur!, I Saw Him Die, Ferdinand and Isabella, Wild Violets.

FOSTER, MAURICE DAVID: Producer-Writer. e. St. Paul's. Ent. m.p. ind. 1943 as asst. to gen. man. and prod. sup. Easling Studios. From 1950–61, prod. sup. and dir. Film Finances, 1961–63, dir. and gen. man. MGM British Studios.
PICTURES: The Jokers, Assignment K, The Osterman Weekend.

FOSTER, MEG: Actress. b. May 10, 1948. e. N.Y. Neighborhood Playhouse.
PICTURES: Adam at 6 A.M., Promise Her Anything, A Different Story, Once in Paris, Carny, Ticket to Heaven, The Emerald Forest, The Wind, Blind Fury, They Live, Levianthan, Relentless, Tripwire.
TELEVISION: Movies: The Death of Me Yet, Sunshine, Things In This Season, James Dean, Washington: Behind Closed Doors, Sunshine Christmas, Desperate Intruder, Desperate; Series guest: Here Comes the Brides, Mod Squad, Men at Law, Hawaii Five-O, Cagney and Lacey, Murder She Wrote, Miami Vice.

FOWLER, HARRY: Actor. b. Lambeth Walk, London, 1926. Stage debut, Nothing Up My Sleeve (London) 1950; Screen debut, 1941.
PICTURES: Demi-Paradise, Don't Take It to Heart, Champaigne Charlie, Painted Boats, Hue and Cry, Now Barabbas, The Dark Man, She Shall Have Murder, The Scarlet Thread, High Treason, The Last Page, I Believe in You, Pickwick Papers, Top of the Form, Angels One Five, Conflict of Wings (Fuss Over Feathers), A Day to Remember, Blue Peter, Home and Away, Booby Trap, Town on Trial, Lucky Jim, Birthday Present, Idle on Parade, Don't Panic Chaps, Heart of a Man, Crooks Anonymous, The Longest Day, Lawrence of Arabia, Flight from Singapore, The Golliwog, Ladies Who Do, Clash By Night, The Nanny, Life at the Top, Start the Revolution Without Me, The Prince and The Pauper, Fanny Hill, Chicago Joe and the Showgirl.
TELEVISION: Stalingrad, I Remember the Battle, Gideon's Way, That's for Me, Our Man at St. Mark's, Dixon of Dock Green, Dr. Finlay's Case Book, I Was There, Cruffs Dog Show, The Londoners, Jackanory, Get This, Movie Quiz, Get This series, Going a Bundle, Ask a Silly Answer, London Scene, Flockton Flyer, Sun Trap, The Little World of Don Camillo, World's End, Minder, Dead Ernest, Morecambe Wise Show, Gossip, Entertainment Express, Fresh Fields, Supergram, A Roller Next Year, Harry's Kingdom, Body Contact, Davro's Sketch Pad.

FOWLEY, DOUGLAS: Actor. b. New York, NY, May 30, 1911. e. St. Francis Xavier's Mil. Acad., N.Y. In stock; operated dramatic sch. N.Y.; on screen in bit parts. From 1934 in regular roles.
PICTURES: Battleground, Just This Once, This Woman Is Dangerous, Singin' in the Rain, Man Behind the Gun, Slight Case of Larceny, Naked Jungle, Casanova's Big Night, Lone Gun, The High and the Mighty, Three Ring Circus, Texas Lady, Broken Star, Girl Rush, Bandido, Nightmare in the Sun, The North Avenue Irregulars, From Noon Till Three, The White Buffalo.
TELEVISION: The Moneychangers, Starsky and Hutch, Sunshine Christmas, Oregon Trail. Series: The Life and Legend of Wyatt Earp, Pistols and Petticoats, Gunsmoke.

FOX, EDWARD: Actor. b. England, April 13, 1937. Comes from theatrical family; father was agent for leading London actors; brother of actor James Fox.
PICTURES: The Mind Benders, The Long Duel, Morgan, The Naked Runner, The Jokers, I'll Never Forget What's 'is Name, The Battle of Britain, Oh! What a Lovely War, Skullduggery, The Breaking of Bumbo, The Day of The Jackal, A Doll's House, Galileo, The Squeeze, A Bridge Too Far, The Duellists, The Big Sleep, Force 10 from Navarone, The Mirror Crack'd, Gandhi, The Dresser, The Bounty, Wild Geese II, Return From the River Kwai.
TELEVISION: Edward and Mrs. Simpson, A Hazard of Hearts; Anastasia: The Mystery of Anna; Shaka Zulu.

FOX, JAMES: Actor. b. London, England, May 19, 1939. Brother of actor Edward Fox. Ent. films as child actor in 1950 as William Fox in The Magnet and The Miniver Story. Left acting in 1973 to lead religious life. Returned to films 1982.
TELEVISION: The Door, Espionage, Love Is Old, Love Is New, Nancy Astor, Country, New World, Beryl Markham: A Shadow on the Sun, Sun Child, She's Been Away (BBC).
PICTURES: The Loneliness of the Long-Distance Runner, Tamahine, The Servant, Those Magnificent Men in Their Flying Machines, King Rat, The Chase, Thoroughly Modern Millie, Arabella, Duffy, Loves of Isadora, Performance, Anna Pavlova, Runners, A Passage to India, Absolute Beginners, The Whistle Blower, Comrades, High Season, The Mighty Quinn, Farewell to the King, The Boys in the Island, She's Been Away.

FOX, MICHAEL J.: Actor. b. Edmonton, Canada, June 9, 1961. m. actress Tracy Pollan.
PICTURES: Midnight Madness, The Class of 1984, Back to the Future, Teen Wolf, Light of Day, The Secret of My Success, Bright Lights, Big City, Dear America: Letters Home From Vietnam (reader), Casualties of War, The Hard Way.
TELEVISION: Palmerstown, U.S.A.; Trapper John, M.D.; Teachers Only; Time Travel: Fact, Fiction and Fantasy; Leo and Me; Letters from Frank; Family Ties (series, 2 Emmy Awards); High School USA, Poison Ivy.

FOX, RICHARD: Executive. Joined Warner Bros. Intl. as mgt. trainee in October 1975, working in Australia and Japan. 1977, named gen. mgr. of Columbia-Warner Dist., New Zealand. Served as gen. mgr. of WB in Tokyo, 1978–1981. Joined WB in L.A. as exec. asst. to Myron D. Karlin, pres. of WB Intl., 1981; appt. v.p., sls. 1982; 1983, promoted to exec. v.p. of intl. arm; 1985, named pres. of WB Intl., assuming post vacated by Karlin.

FOX, RICHARD A.: Executive. b. Buffalo, NY, Jan 5, 1929. e. U. of Buffalo, 1950. Chmn., Fox Theatres Management Corp. Pres., Nat'l NATO 1984–86; chmn., Nat'l NATO 1986–1988.

FOXWELL, IVAN: Producer. b. Feb. 22, 1914, London, Eng. Entered m.p. ind. 1933 as technician with British & Dominions Film Corp., subsequently with Paramount British & London Films; Assoc. with Curtis Bernhardt in Paris 1937 becoming producer & collaborating on story, s.p. of Carefour, Le Train pur Venise, Sarajevo, others. In W.W.II with BEF and AEF 1939–46. Returned to British films 1947 as producer, co-author screen adapt., No Room at the Inn; prod., collab. s.p., Guilt Is My Shadow; prod., Twenty-Four Hours of a Woman's Life; co-author s.p. and prod. The Intruder, The Colditz Story (TV series adapt. 1972), Manuela, A Touch of Larceny, Tiara Tahiti, The Quiller Memorandum; s.p. and prod. Decline and Fall. Director, Foxwell Film Prods. Ltd.

FOXWORTH, ROBERT: Actor. b. Houston, TX, Nov. 1, 1941. e. Mellon U. Began acting at age 10 at Houston Alley Theatre and stayed with stage part-time while completing formal education. Returned to theatre on full-time basis after graduation from Mellon. Made TV debut in Sadbird, 1969.
TELEVISION: The Storefront Lawyers (series), Mrs. Sundance, Hogan's Goat, Falcon Crest (series), The Return of the Desperado, Double Standard, Face to Face.
PICTURES: Treasure of Matecumbe (debut), The Astral Factor, Airport '77, Damien-Omen II, The Black Marble, Invisible Strangler, Personal Choice.
STAGE: P.S., Your Cat Is Dead.

FOXX, REDD: Actor, Performer. r.n. John Elroy Sanford. b. St. Louis, MO, Dec. 9, 1922. Began career by running away from home to join a washboard band at age 13; Member of amateur music group Bon-Bons 1939–41. First nightclub appearances as a single, then with Slappy White 1947–51; 50 record albums in last 17 years.
TELEVISION: Sanford and Son (series); The Redd Foxx Comedy Hour 1977; Ghost of a Chance (movie).
PICTURE: Cotton Comes to Harlem; Norman, Is That You?, Harlem Nights.

FRAKER, WILLIAM A.: Cinematographer-Director. b. Los Angeles, CA, 1923. Graduate, U. of Southern California Film Sch. Worked as operator with Conrad Hall; moved to TV before feature films.
PICTURES: Cinematographer: Games, The Fox, President's Analyst, Fade In, Rosemary's Baby, Bullitt, Paint Your Wagon, Dusty and Sweets McGee, Day of the Dolphin, Rancho Deluxe, The Killer Inside Me, Aloha, Bobby and Rose, Gator, Close Encounters of the Third Kind, Looking for Mr. Goodbar, Heaven Can Wait, Old Boyfriends, 1941, Divine Madness, The Legend of the Lone Ranger, Sharky's Machino, The Best Little Whorehouse in Texas, WarGames, Irreconcilable Differences, Murphy's Romance, Fever Pitch, Murphy's Romance, SpaceCamp, Burglar, Baby Boom, Chances Are, An Innocent Man. Director: Monte Walsh, Reflection of Fear, Legend of the Lone Ranger.
TELEVISION: Stony Burke, Outer Limits, Ozzie and Harriet, Daktari, B.L. Stryker: The Dancer's Touch (dir.).

FRANCIOSA, ANTHONY: Actor. b. New York, NY, Oct. 25, 1928. e. high school there. Erwin Piscator's Dramatic Workshop (4-year scholarship). First stage part in YWCA play; joined Off-Broadway stage group; stock at Lake Tahoe, CA, Chicago and Boston.
THEATRE: Broadway: stage in End as a Man, The Wedding Breakfast, A Hatful of Rain.
PICTURES: A Face in the Crowd, This Could Be The Night, A Hatful of Rain, Wild Is The Wind, The Long Hot Summer, The Naked Maja, Career, Story On Page One, Go Naked in the World, Period of Adjustment, The Swinger, Fathom, A Man Called Gannon, The Sweet Ride, Rio Conchos, In Enemy Country, Across 110th Street, The Drowning Pool, Firepower, Death Wish II, Julie Darling, Ghost in the Noonday Sun, Death Is in Fashion, Tenebrae, Help Me to Dream, The Cricket, Senelith, The World is Full of Married Men, A Texas Legend, Backstreet Strays, Death House, Ghostwriter!, Brothers in Arms.
TELEVISION: Series: Valentine's Day, The Name of the Game, Search, Matt Helm, Finder of Lost Loves. Movies: Stagecoach, Earth II, The Black Widow, Till Death Do Us Part, The Deadly Hunt, Side Show. Mini-series: Aspen, Wheels. Guest: Kraft Theatre, Philco Playhouse, Danger, Naked City, Arrest & Trial, Playhouse 90, etc.

FRANCIS, ANNE: Actress b. Ossining, NY, Sept. 16, 1932. Child model; radio TV shows as child & adult; on B'way in Lady in the Dark.
PICTURES: Summer Holiday, So Young So Bad, Whistle at Eaton Falls, Lydia Bailey, Elopement, Dream Boat, Lion Is in the Streets, Rocket Man, Susan Slept Here, Rogue Cop, Bad Day at Black Rock, Battle Cry, Blackboard Jungle, Scarlet Coat, Forbidden Planet, The Rack, Great American Pastime, Don't Go Near the Water, Crowded Sky, Girl of the Night, Satan Bug, Brainstorm, Hook, Line, and Sinker, More Dead Than Alive, The Impasse, The Love God, Funny Girl, Born Again, The High Fashion Murders.
TELEVISION: Honey West (series), O'Malley; Riptide; Partners in Crime; Crazy Like a Fox; Jake and the Fatman; Twilight Zone; Dallas; Finder of Lost Loves. Movies: Rona Jaffe's Mazes and Monsters; Poor Little Rich Girl: The Barbara Hutton Story, Laguna Heat, My First Love.

FRANCIS, ARLENE: Actress. r.n. Arlene Francis Kazanjian; b. Boston, MA, 1908. e. Convent of Mount St. Vincent Acad., Riverdale, NY, Finch Finishing Sch., Theatre Guild Sch., NY. m. Martin Gabel, late actor. Author: That Certain Something (1960); Arlene Francis—A Memoir (1978).
STAGE: The Women (1937), Horse Eats Hat (Mercury Theater), Danton's Death, All That Glitters, Doughgirls, The Overtons, Once More With Feeling, Tchin-Tchin, Beekman Place, Mrs. Dally, Dinner at Eight, Kind Sir, Lion in Winter, Pal Joey, Who Killed Santa Claus?, Gigi, Social Security.
TELEVISION: Soldier Parade 1949–55; Blind Date, Regular panelist What's My Line; Home, Arlene Francis Show; Talent Patrol, etc.
RADIO: Arlene Francis Show, Emphasis, Monitor, Luncheon at Sardis.
PICTURES: Stage Door Canteen, All My Sons, One, Two, Three, The Thrill of It All, Fedora.

FRANCIS, CONNIE: Singer. r.n. Constance Franconero. b. Newark, NJ, Dec. 12, 1938. Appeared, Star Time when 12 years old; won Arthur Godfrey's Talent Scout Show, 12 years old. Autobiography: Who's Sorry Now (1984).
GOLD RECORDS: Who's Sorry Now, My Happiness. Numerous vocalist awards: All Major TV shows.
PICTURES: Where the Boys Are, Follow the Boys, Looking For Love.

FRANCIS, FREDDIE: Producer, Director, Cameraman. b. London, 1917. Joined Gaumont British Studios as apprentice to stills photographer; then clapper boy at B.I.P. Studios, Elstree; camera asst. at British Dominion. After W.W.II returned to Shepperton Studios to work for Korda and with Powell and Pressburger as cameraman.
PICTURES: Director: Two and Two Make Six, Paranoiac, Vengeance, Evil of Frankenstein, Nightmare, Hysteria, Dr. Terror's House of Horrors, The Skull, Traitor's Gate, The Psychopath, The Deadly Bees, They Came from Beyond Space, Torture Garden, Mumsy and Nanny and Sonny and Girly, Dracula Has Risen from the Grave, Girly, Trog, Tales from the Crypt, The Creeping Flesh, Countdown, Tales That Witness Madness, The Ghoul, Legend of The Werewolf, The Doctor and the Devils, Dark Tower. Cameraman: Moby Dick (second unit photo., special effects), Room at the Top, Saturday Night and Sunday Morning, Sons and Lovers (Oscar), The Innocents, The Elephant Man, The French Lieutenant's Woman, Dune, Code Name: Emerald, Clara's Heart, Her Alibi, Brenda Starr, Glory.

FRANCIS, KEVIN: Producer, Executive. b. London, England, 1949. 1967–70, production mgr., assoc. producer. 1970–72, produced It's Life, Passport, Trouble with Canada. 1972 founder, Tyburn Productions Limited; 1973, produced Persecution; 1974, produced The Ghoul and Legend of the Werewolf; 1975, founder, Tyburn Productions Inc.; 1976, prod. Film Techniques Educ. Course for BFI. Since 1977 exec. prod., Master of the Shell, The Masks of Death, Courier, Murder Elite, The Abbot's Cry, A One-Way Ticket to Hollywood, The Moorgate Legacy.

FRANCISCUS, JAMES: Actor. b. Clayton, MO, Jan. 31, 1934. e. Taft Prep, Yale U.
PICTURES: Four Boys and a Gun, I Passed for White, The Outsiders, The Miracle of the White Stallions, Youngblood Hawke, The Valley of Gwangi, Marooned, Beneath the Planet of the Apes, The Cat O' Nine Tails, Hell Boats, The Amazing Dobermans, Puzzle, Good Guys Wear Black, The Greek Tycoon, Greed, Concorde, City on Fire, When Time Ran Out, Butterfly.
TELEVISION: Naked City, Mr. Novak, Longstreet (TV film feature). Movies: The 500 Pound Jerk, The Pirate, The Dream Makers, Jacqueline Bouvier Kennedy.

FRANK, EDMOND: Executive. b. New York, NY, Feb. 11, 1945. e. American U., B.A., Washington Coll. of Law, J.D. Admitted to Fla. Bar 1971. Vice-pres. and gen. counsel, World Film. pres., South Florida Entertainment Counsel Guild.

FRANKEL, DANIEL: Executive. b. New York, NY, Aug. 21, 1903. e. U. of Michigan, U. of Berlin, Germany. Gen. mgr., Films Erka, Paris, 1925–30. Ran Theatre des Champs Elysees, 1928–29. Produced two French pictures. Returned to New York and joined Pathe 1930; dir. foreign dept., later of all sales to 1941; resigned to engage in prod. unit org. Vice-pres. & exec. dir., Four Continents Films, 1945; with U.A. in Europe 1953–56; ret. U.S. & org., pres., Zenith Int'l Film Corp., 1956, distr., Lovers, 400 Blows, Hiroshima, Mon Amour, etc. Governor IFIDA.

FRANKENHEIMER, JOHN: Director. b. Malba, NY, Feb. 19, 1930. e. Williams Coll. Actor, dir., summer stock; radio-TV actor, dir., Washington, DC; then joined CBS network. Theater: The Midnight Sun (dir., 1959).
TELEVISION: I Remember Mama, You Are There, Danger, Climax (Emmy Award), Studio One, Playhouse 90, Du Pont Show of the Month; Ford Startime, Sunday Showcase; The Comedian, For Whom the Bell Tolls, The Days of Wine and Roses, Old Man, The Turn of the Screw, The Browning Version, The Rainmaker (1982).
PICTURES: The Young Stranger, The Young Savages, Birdman of Alcatraz, All Fall Down, The Manchurian Candidate, Seven Days in May, The Train, Seconds, Grand Prix, The Extraordinary Seaman, The Fixer, The Gypsy Moths, I Walk the Line, The Horsemen, The Impossible Object, The Iceman Cometh, 99 and 44/100% Dead, French Connection II, Black Sunday, Prophecy, The Challenge, The Holcroft Covenant, 52 Pick-Up, Dead-Bang, The Fourth War.

FRANKLIN, BONNIE: Actress. b. Santa Monica, CA, Jan. 6, 1944. e. UCLA. On Bdwy. in Dames at Sea, Your Own Thing, Applause. Off-Bdwy in Frankie and Johnny in the Claire de Lune.
TELEVISION: Series: One Day at a Time. Movies: Breaking Up Is Hard to Do, A Guide for the Married Woman, Portrait of a Rebel: Margaret Sanger, Your Place or Mine, Sister Margaret and Saturday Night Ladies, Shalom Sesame.

FRANKLIN, MICHAEL HAROLD: Executive. b. Los Angeles, CA, Dec. 25, 1923. e. U. of California, A.B., U. of Southern California, LL.B. Admitted to CA bar, 1951; pvt. practice in L.A. 1951–52; atty. CBS, 1952–54; atty. Paramount Pictures, 1954–58; exec. dir. Writers Guild Am. West, Inc. 1958–78; national exec. dir., Directors Guild of America 1978–. Mem. Am. Civil Liberties Union, Los Angeles Copyright Soc., Order of Coif.

FRANKLIN, PAMELA: Actress. b. Tokyo, Japan, Feb. 4, 1950. Attended Elmshurst Ballet Sch., Camberley, Surrey.
PICTURES: The Innocents, The Lion, Flipper's New Adventure, The Prime of Miss Jean Brodie, The Night of the Following Day, And Soon the Darkness, The Legend of Hell House, Food of the Gods.

FRANKLIN, RICHARD: Director. b. Melbourne, Australia, July 15, 1948.
PICTURES: The True Story of Eskimo Nell; Fantasm; Patrick (also co-prod.); The Blue Lagoon (co-prod. only); Road Games (also prod.); Psycho II; Cloak and Dagger; Into the Night (act. only).
TELEVISION: Beauty and the Beast (pilot), A Fine Romance.

FRANKLIN, ROBERT A.: Executive. b. New York, NY, April 15. e. U. of Miami, B.B.A., 1958; Columbia Pacific U., M.B.A., 1979; Ph.D., 1980 majoring in marketing. Before entering film industry worked with House of Seagram (1959–64); Canada Dry Corp. (1964–66); J. M. Mathes Adv. (1966–67). In 1967 joined 20th Century-Fox as dir. of mkt. planning. Formed RP Marketing Intl. (entertainment consulting firm) in 1976 and World Research Systems (computer software marketer). In 1981 joined MPAA; 1983, named v.p., administration and information services. In 1986, named v.p. worldwide market research. Chmn., MPAA research comm.; member, AMA and ESOMAR.

FRANKOVICH, M. J.: Executive. b. Bisbee, AZ, Sept. 29, 1910. e. UCLA, B.A. Ent. Radio 1934 as producer, commentator; began writing screenplays for Universal, 1938; Republic Pictures, 1940–49 (except for period war service U.S. Army); to Europe 1949 to make Fugitive Lady, Lucky Nick Kane, Thief of Venice etc.; England 1952. prod., Decameron Nights, Malaga, Footsteps in the Fog, Joe Macbeth; apptd. man. dir. Columbia Pictures Corp. Ltd., in U.K. and Eire Aug. 1955; elected vice-pres., Columbia Pictures International Corp., Dec. 1955; head Col. Pictures Int. Prod., 1958; vice-pres., Col. Pics. Corp., 1959. Appt. Chmn., Columbia Pics. Corp. Ltd., 1959. Variety Club Crew Member; chief barker, Tent 36 Variety Club, 1957. dir., BLC Films; chmn., Screen Gems Ltd.; first v.p. chge. world prod., Columbia; resigned July, 1967 to return to independent production. Long Term Deal, 1969, rel. through Columbia. Won Jean Hersholt Humanitarian Award, 1984.
PICTURES: Bob & Carol & Ted & Alice, Marooned, Cactus Flower, The Looking Glass War, Doctors' Wives, There's A Girl in My Soup, The Love Machine, Dollars, Butterflies Are Free, Stand Up and Be Counted, 40 Carats, Report to the Commissioner, From Noon Till Three, The Shootist.

FRANZ, ARTHUR: Actor. b. Perth Amboy, NJ, Feb. 29, 1920. e. Blue Ridge Coll., MD. U.S. Air Force. Radio, TV shows.
THEATRE: Streetcar Named Desire, Second Threshold.
PICTURES: Jungle Patrol, Roseanna McCoy, Red Light, Doctor and the Girl, Sands of Iwo Jima, Strictly Dishonorable, Submarine Command, Member of the Wedding, Flight Nurse, Bad for Each Other, Eddie Cantor Story, Caine Mutiny, Steel Cage, Battle Taxi, New Orleans Uncensored, Bobby Ware Is Missing, Atomic Submarine, The Human Factor, That Championship Season.

FRAWLEY, JAMES: Director. b. Houston, TX, 1937. Studied drama at Carnegie Tech. and Actors Studio, where later taught and ran the directors unit. Was charter member of comedy group, The Premise; has acted in plays on and off Bdwy. Won Emmy Award for Monkees series, where staged two musical numbers a week for two seasons.
PICTURES: Kid Blue, The Big Bus, The Muppet Movie, Fraternity Vacation.
TELEVISION: Columbo, Delancy Street, Capra, Cagney and Lacey, Assault and Matrimony, Spies, Lies and Naked Thighs.

FRAZIER, CLIFF: Director, Actor. b. Detroit, MI, Aug. 27, 1934. e. Wayne State U., Harold Clurman. Exec. dir., The Community Film Workshop Council; was co-founder & artistic dir.: Stable Theatre, Detroit, 1960–63; Concept East Theatre, Detroit, 1962–64; co-produced and acted in Study in Color, 1964–65; assoc. dir., Theatre of Latin America, Inc., N.Y., 1968; dir. of drama, Mobilization for Youth, N.Y., 1966–68; East Coast dir. of rsch., Brooks Foundation, Santa Barbara, 1966–68.
TELEVISION: Today, Tell It Like It Is, NYPD. The Nurses, The Negro Experimental Theatre, Othello.
THEATRE: Stage repertories: Washington Theatre Club, Irish Hills Rep., Will-O-Way Playhouse.
Co-author, Discovery in Drama and book critic, Catholic Reporter, 1969.

FRAZIER, SHEILA E.: Actress. b. Bronx, NY, Nov. 13, 1948. e. Englewood, NJ. Was exec. sect'y. and high-fashion model. Steered to acting career by friend Richard Roundtree. Studied drama with N.Y. Negro Ensemble Co. and New Federal Theatre, N.Y.
PICTURES: Super Fly (debut), Superfly T.N.T., The Super Cops, California Suite, What Does It Take?, Three the Hard Way, The Hitter, I'm Gonna Git You Sucker.

FREARS, STEPHEN: Director. b. Leicester, Eng., June 20, 1941. e. Cambridge, B.A in law. Joined Royal Court Theatre, working with Lindsay Anderson on plays. Later asst. dir. on Morgan: A Suitable Case for Treatment; Charlie Bubbles, and Anderson's films: If . . . and O Lucky Man! Worked afterwards mostly in TV, directing and producing.
PICTURES: Gumshoe (also co-s.p.) (dir. debut 1971), Bloody Kids, The Hit, My Beautiful Laundrette, Prick Up Your Ears, Sammy and Rosie Get Laid, Dangerous Liaisons, The Grifters.
TELEVISION: A Day Out (1971); England Their England; Match of the Day; Sunset Across the Bay; Three Men in a Boat; Daft as a Brush; Playthings; Early Struggles; Last Summer; 18 Months to Balcomb Street; A Visit from Miss Protheroe; Abel's Will; Cold Harbour; series of six Alan Bennett plays; Long Distance Information; Going Gently; Loving Walter; Saigon, Year of the Cat; December Flower.

FREDERIC, MARC: Producer. b. New York, NY, Apr. 25, 1916. e. Washington & Lee U. Capt. U.S. Air Force. Prod., dist. Little Theatre, 1948, 104 episodes. First to make deal through AFTRA for kinescope release of live shows for dist. Tales of Tomorrow series. Org., Marc Frederic Prods., Inc.
PICTURES: Giant of the Unknown, She Demon, Missile to the Moon, Frankenstein's Daughter, Girl in Room 13, Career Girl, Festival Girl.

FREDERICKSON, H. GRAY, JR.: Producer. b. Oklahoma City, OK, July 31, 1937. e. U. of Lausanne, Switzerland, 1958–59; U. of Oklahoma. B.A., 1960. m. Victoria Schmidlapp. Worked one yr. with Panero, Weidlinger & Salvatori Engineering Co., Rome Italy. In 1979 named v.p. of feature films, Lorimar Films.
PICTURES: Candy, Inspector Sterling, Gospel 70, An Italian in America, The Man Who Wouldn't Die, The Good, the Bad and the Ugly, Intrigue in Suez, How to Learn to Love Women, God's Own Country, Wedding March, An American Wife, Natika, Echo in the Village, Little Fauss and Big Halsey, Making It, The Godfather, The Godfather, Part II, Hit (exec. prod.), Apocalypse Now (co.-prod.), One From the Heart, The Outsiders, UHF.
TELEVISION: Producer: The Return of Mickey Spillane's Mike Hammer, Houston Nights.

FREEDMAN, JERROLD: Director, Writer.
PICTURES: Kansas City Bomber, Borderline.
TELEVISION: Writer: A Cold Night's Death, Blood Sport,

The Last Angry Man, Betrayal, Some Kind of Miracle, Legs. Director: The Streets of L.A., The Boy Who Drank Too Much, Victims, The Seduction of Gina, Best Kept Secrets, Seduced, Family Sins, Unholy Matrimony, The Comback, Night Walk.

FREEMAN, AL, JR.: Actor. b. San Antonio, TX, March 21, 1934. e. LA City Coll.
THEATER: The Long Dream (1960), Kicks and Co., Tiger Tiger Burning Bright, Trumpets of the Lord, Blues for Mister Charlie, Conversation at Midnight, Look to the Lilies, Are You Now or Have You Ever Been?, The Poison Tree.
PICTURES: Torpedo Run, Dutchman, Finian's Rainbow, Castle Keep, The Lost Man, The Detective, A Fable (also dir.), Seven Hours to Judgement.
TELEVISION: My Sweet Charlie, Roots, King, One Life to Live (Emmy, 1979).

FREEMAN, EVERETT: Writer. b. New York, NY, 1912. Contrib. Sat. Eve. Post. From 1942 writer for screen.
PICTURES: George Washington Slept Here, Princess and the Pirate, It Happened on Fifth Ave., Secret Life of Walter Mitty, Too Young to Kiss, Lady Takes a Sailor, Jim Thorpe—All American, Pretty Baby, Million Dollar Mermaid, Destination Gobi, Kelly and Me, My Man Godfrey, Marjorie Morningstar, Sunday in New York, The Glass Bottom Boat, Where Were You When the Lights Went Out?, The Maltese Bippy, How Do I Love Thee.
TELEVISION: Prod. Bachelor Father series.

FREEMAN, JOEL: Producer. b. Newark, NJ, June 12, 1922. e. Upsala Coll. Began career at MGM studios in 1941. In Air Force Mot. Pic. Unit 1942–46. Became assist. dir. at RKO in 1946. In 1948 returned to MGM as asst. dir.; later assoc. prod. In 1956 entered indep. field as prod. supv. on various features and TV series. In 1960 to Warner Bros., assoc. producing Sunrise at Campobello, The Music Man and Act One. After such films as Camelot and Finian's Rainbow, became studio exec. at Warners. Presently senior v.p. prod., New Century Entertainment Corp.
PICTURES: Producer: The Heart Is a Lonely Hunter, Shaft, Trouble Man, Love at First Bite, Octagon, The Kindred.

FREEMAN, MORGAN: Actor. b. Memphis, TN, June 1, 1937. e. LA C Coll. Served in Air Force 1955–59 before studying acting. Broadway debut in Hello Dolly! with Pearl Bailey. Took over lead role in Purlie. Became known nationally when he created Easy Reader on TV's The Electric Company (1971–76).
THEATER: The Nigger Lovers (1967), Hello Dolly!, Scuba Duba, Purlie, Cockfight, The Last Street Play, The Mighty Gents (Drama Desk, Clarence Derwent Awards), Coriolanus (Obie Award), Julius Caesar, Mother Courage, Buck, Driving Miss Daisy (Obie Award), The Gospel at Colonus (Obie Award).
PICTURES: Who Says I Can't Ride a Rainbow! (1972), Brubaker, Eyewitness, Harry and Son, Teachers, Marie, That was then...This Is Now, Street Smart (NY, LA Film Critics Award, National Board of Review, supp. actor awards, 1987), Clean and Sober, Lean on Me, Johnny Handsome, Glory, Driving Miss Daisy.
TELEVISION: Movies: Hollow Image, Attica, The Marva Collins Story, The Atlanta Child Murder, Resting Place, Flight For Life, Roll of Thunder, Hear My Cry, Charlie Smith and the Fritter Tree, Clinton and Nadine.

FRELENG, FRIZ: Writer-Producer. b. Kansas City, MO, Aug. 21, 1906. Animator, Walt Disney Studio, 1928–29; Charles Mintz Studio, 1929–30, prod.-dir., Warner Bros., 1930–63. Formed partnership with David DePatie in 1963. Five Academy Awards, 3 Emmy Awards.
CARTOON FILMS: Bugs Bunny series, Daffy Duck, Sylvester, Yosemite Sam, Porky Pig, Tweetie Pie, Speedy Gonzales, Halloween Is Grinch Night, Pink Panther in Olympinks, Dr. Seuss' Pontoffel Pock. Recent compilations: The Looney, Looney Bugs Bunny Movie, Bugs Bunny's 3rd Movie: 1001 Rabbit Tales. Numerous series of television shows.

FRENKE, EUGENE: Producer. b. Russia, Jan. 1, 1907. m. Anna Sten.
PICTURES: Life Returns, Two Who Dared, Three Russians Girls, Let's Live a Little, Lady in Iron Mask, Miss Robin Crusoe, Heaven Knows, Mr. Allison, Barbarian and the Geisha, The Last Sunset, Royal Hunt of the Sun.

FRESCO, ROBERT M.: Writer. b. Burbank, CA, Oct. 18, 1928. e. Los Angeles City Coll. Newspaperman. Los Angeles, 1946–47; U.S. Army, 1948–49; staff writer, Hakim Prod., 1950–51; various screenplays, 1951–56.
PICTURES: Tarantula, They Came to Destroy the Earth, Monolith.
TELEVISION: Scripts for Science Fiction Theatre, Highway Patrol.

FRIED, MAX: Executive. b. New York City, 1910. e. James Madison H.S. Started with Warner Bros., 1927; 1940, buyer & booker for Century Theatres; 1950, exec. dir. & buyer, J.J. Theatres; 1957, buyer & booker for Seymour Florin Enterprises. Now pres. Maxi Cinema Enterprises; (consultant on m.p. industry); adv. & sls. rep. for Motion Picture Almanac and Television & Video Almanac; exec. dir., Motion Picture Bookers club. (also former pres.).
MEMBER: Variety Club Children's Charity; natl. chmn., William Rogers Memorial Fund's Academy Award Sweepstakes' Drive; past. pres., cinema-radio-tv unit, B'nai B'rith.

FRIEDBERG, A. ALAN: Executive. b. New York, NY, Apr. 13, 1932. e. Columbia Coll., B.A. 1952; Harvard Law School 1955. President, Sack Theatres, Boston; sr. v.p. and chief operating officer, Loews Theatres; 1988, exec. consultant Columbia Pictures Entertainment, exhibition business. Past pres. and chmn. of bd. NATO. NATO bd. mbr.

FRIEDKIN, JOHN: Executive. b. New York, NY, Dec. 9, 1926. Entered industry in New York as publicist for Columbia Pictures; spent eight years at Young & Rubicam adv. agency. Formed Sumner & Friedkin with Gabe Sumner as partner; left to join Rogers & Cowan, where named v.p. In 1967 resigned to join 20th-Fox, moving to California in 1972 when home offices were transferred. Appointed Fox v.p. worldwide publ. & promo. In 1979 joined Warner Bros. as v.p.—adv. pub. for intl. div; 1988, joined Odyssey Distributors Ltd. as sr. v.p., intl. marketing.

FRIEDKIN, WILLIAM: Director. b. Chicago, IL, 1939. Joined WGN-TV, 1957, worked for National Education TV, did TV documentaries before feature films. Dir. Bdwy play Duet for One.
PICTURES: Good Times, The Night They Raided Minsky's, The Birthday Party, The Boys in the Band, The French Connection. (Academy Award, best picture, dir. 1971), The Exorcist (10 Acad. Award nominations), Sorcerer (prod.-dir.), The Brink's Job, Cruising (dir.-s.p.), Deal of the Century, To Live and Die in L.A. (dir., co-s.p.), Rampage (dir., s.p.).
TELEVISION: C.A.T. Squad (dir., exec. prod.).

FRIEDMAN, ARNOLD J.: Executive b. New York, NY. Entered m.p. industry as exploiteer for Columbia Pictures Corp. 1957–60; advng dept. United Artists Corp. 1960–62; adv. mgr., Embassy Pictures Corp. and later director of adv., publ., prom. for Embassy Pictures Television, 1962–67; pres. Arnold Friedman's Company, 1967–70; dir. of ad./pub./promo for Metromedia Producers Corp., 1970–72; creative dir., ITC, 1973–76; vice pres. of theatrical & TV adv./pub./promo. for Cinema Shares International. Ltd., 1976–79; pres., Arcady Communications, 1980–present.

FRIEDMAN, DAVID F.: Executive. b. Birmingham, AL, Dec. 24, 1923. e. Cornell U. With U.S. Army Signal Corps, 1944–46. With Paramount Pictures as booker office manager 1946–50; circus press agent, 1950–51; Para. publ. agent, 1952–55; partner, Modern Film Distributors, 1956–60; partner, Sonney Amusement, 1960–64. Formed Entertainment Ventures, Inc. in 1965, of which he is pres. Produced a total of 59 features between 1958 and 1988.

FRIEDMAN, JOSEPH: Executive. b. New York, NY. e. City Coll. of New York, 1940–42, NYU, 1946–47. U.S. Navy 3 yrs. Asst. to nat'l dir. field exploitation, Warner Bros. Pictures, 1946–58; nat'l exploitation mgr., Paramount Pictures, 1958–60; exec. asst. to dir. of adv., publicity & exploitation, Para., 1961; dir. adv. & pub., Paramount 1964; a v.p., Para., 1966; v.p. in charge of Marketing, 1968; v.p., adv., and p.r., Avco Embassy Pictures, 1969; v.p., p.r. American Film Theatre, 1973; v.p., adv. and p.r., ITC, motion picture div., 1976, pres., Joseph Friedman Marketing and Advertising, Inc., 1977. Exec. dir. New Jersey M.P. & T.V. Commission, 1978; v.p. worldwide adv./pub./promo., Edie & Ely Landau, Inc., 1980; exec. dir., New Jersey Motion Picture & Television Commission, 1981.

FRIEDMAN, ROBERT L.: Executive. b. Bronx, NY, March 1, 1930. e. DeWitt Clinton H.S. Started as radio announcer and disc jockey with Armed Forces Radio Service in Europe and U.S. v.p., marketing, United Artists Corp.; pres. domestic distribution, Columbia Pictures. 1984, named pres., AMC Int'l., subsidiary of AMC Entertainment.
MEMBER: M.P. Associates Foundation, Phila., pres. 2 yrs.; Variety Club (on board) M.P. Pioneers; (on board) area chmn. and N.Y. participation in Will Rogers Hospital Foundation, American Film Inst., Academy of M.P. Arts & Sciences.

FRIEDMAN, SEYMOUR MARK: Director. b. Detroit, MI, Aug. 17, 1917. e. Magdalene Coll., Cambridge, B.S. 1936; St. Mary's Hospital Medical Sch., London. Entered m.p. ind. as asst. film ed. 1937; 2nd asst. dir. 1938; 1st asst. dir. 1939, on budget pictures; entered U.S. Army 1942; returned to ind. 1946; dir. Columbia Pictures 1947. Vice president & executive production for Columbia Pictures Television, division of Columbia Pictures Industries, 1955.
MEMBER: Screen Directors Guild.
PICTURES: To the Ends of the Earth, Rusty's Birthday, Prison Warden, Her First Romance, Rookie Fireman, Son of Dr. Jekyll, Loan Shark, Flame of Calcutta, I'll Get You, Saint's

Girl Friday, Khyber Patrol, African Manhunt, Secret of Treasure Mountain.

FRIEDMAN, STEPHEN: Writer, Producer. b. March 15, 1937. e. U. of Pennsylvania, Harvard Law School. Worked as lawyer for Columbia Pictures (1960–63) and Ashley-Famous Agency. 1963–67: Paramount Pictures. Formed and heads Kings Road Productions.
PICTURES: Producer: The Last Picture Show, Lovin' Molly (also s.p.), Slap Shot, Bloodbrothers, Fast Break, Hero at Large, Little Darlings, Eye of the Needle, All of Me, Creator, Enemy Mine.

FRIENDLY, FRED W.: Producer, Journalist, Writer, Educator. r.n. Fred Wachenheimer. b. New York, NY, October 30, 1915. e. Cheshire Acad., Nichols Junior Coll. U.S. Army, Information and Education Section 1941–45. Editor and correspondent for China, Burma and India for CBI Roundup 1941–45. President, CBS News 1964–66: Edward R. Murrow Professor of Broadcast Journalism, Columbia U., 1966–present; advisor on TV, Ford Foundation, 1966–; member: Mayor's Task Force on CATV and Telecommunications, NYC, 1968; teacher and director: Television Workshop, Columbia U. Sch. of Journalism.
RADIO: Producer-writer-narrator, Foodprints in the Sand of Time, 1938; co-prod. Hear It Now, 1951.
BOOKS: See It Now (1955); Due to Circumstances Beyond Our Control (1967); The Good Guys, the Bad Guys and the First Amendment: Free Speech vs. Fairness in Broadcasting (1976), Minnesota Rag: The Dramatic Story of the Landmark Supreme Court Case that Gave New Meaning to Freedom of the Press (1981); The Constitution: That Delicate Balance (1984); The Presidency and the Constitution (1987).
AWARDS: Ten George Foster Peabody Awards; DeWitt Carter Reddick Award, 1980; See It Now (35 major awards incl. Overseas Press Club, Page One Award, New York Newspaper Guild, National Headliners Club Award, 1954); CBS Reports (40 major awards). Honorary L.H.D. degrees: U. of Rhode Island, Grinnell U., Iowa U. Military: Legion of Merit medal, Soldier's Medal for heroism, 4 Battle Stars.

FRIES, CHARLES W.: Executive. b. Cincinnati, OH, Sept. 30, 1928. e. Ohio State U., B.S. Exec.-prod., Ziv Television; v.p., prod., Screen Gems; v.p., prod., Columbia Pictures; exec. v.p., prod. and exec. prod., Metromedia Prod. Corp., 1970–74; pres., exec. prod., Alpine Prods. and Charles Fries Prods. 1974–83; chmn. & pres., Fries Entertainment, 1984. Nat'l. treas., TV Academy; pres., Alliance TV Film Producers; exec. comm., MPPA. Chmn., Caucus of Producers, Writers and Directors, board of governors and exec. comm. of Academy of TV Arts and Sciences. Bd. governors, secretary & chmn., TV committee, American Film Institute.
PICTURES: Exec. Prod.: Flowers in the Attic; Troup Beverly Hills.
TELEVISION: Movies: Toughlove; The Right of the People; Intimate Strangers; Bitter Harvest; A Rumor of War; Blood Vows: The Story of a Mafia Wife; The Alamo: 3 Days to Glory; Intimate Betrayal; Two Women; Drop Out Mother; LBJ: The White House Years; The Crucible; The Rose Kennedy Story; It's Howdy Doody Time: A 40 Year Celebration; Crash Course; Supercarrier; Bridge to Silence; The Case of the Hillside Stranglers.

FRISCH, LARRY: Producer, Director, Writer. b. Indianapolis, IN, Dec. 27, 1929. e. U. of Southern California, 1947–49, Columbia U, 1951–54. Prof. child actor, Radio 1944–47; writer/dir. with Caravel Films, N.Y., 1950; Assist. dir., Exodus, El Cid (Spain); Prod., Dir.; Writer, Tel Aviv Taxi, 1956 (Israel), Pillar of Fire 1962 (Israel), Casablan, 1963 (Greece).
TELEVISION: Dir., Story of a Teenage Drug Addict, Power of Pot Roast, Beyond Three Doors, Destination Vietnam, Bus to Sinai (NBC-TV), Biafra Eye-Witness (UPI-TV); Metromedia TV News, overseas correspondent 1969–71; prod., Miracle of Survival (TV special), An American Family In China, 1971.

FRONTIERE, DOMINIC: Executive, Composer. b. New Haven, CT, June 17, 1931. e. Yale School of Music. Studied composing, arranging and conducting; concert accordionist, World's Champion Accordionist, 1943; An Hour with Dominic Frontiere, WNHC-TV, New Haven, 3 years, 1947; exec. vice-pres., musical dir., Daystar Prods. Composer or arranger over 75 films.
PICTURES: Giant, Gentlemen Prefer Blondes, Let's Make Love, High Noon, Meet Me in Las Vegas, 10,000 Bedrooms, Hit the Deck; composer-conductor; Marriage-Go-Round, The Right Approach, One Foot in Hell, Hero's Island, Hang 'Em High, Popi, Barquero, Chisum, A for Alpha, Cancel My Reservation, Hammersmith is Out, Freebie and the Bean, Brannigan, The Gumball Rally, Cleopatra Jones and the Casino of Gold, The Stunt Man, Modern Problems, The Aviator.
TELEVISION: Composer-conductor: The New Breed, Stoney Burke, Bankamericard commercials (Venice Film Festival Award Best Use of Original Classical Music for filmed TV commercials), Outerlimits, Branded, Iron Horse, Rat Patrol, Flying Nun, The Invaders, Name of the Game, That Girl, Twelve O'Clock High, Zig Zag, The Young Rebel, The Immortal, Jean C. Killy, Fugitive, The Love War. Movies: Washington Behind Closed Doors.

FROST, LINDA SMITH: Executive. Vice pres. marketing, Media Home Entertainment. b. Louisville, KY, March 13, 1956. e. Wellesley College. Dir. of marketing, South Coast Plaza. dir. of marketing Rouse Company. dir. special events and marketing, Broadway Dept. Stores. V.P. marketing Media Home Entertainment.

FRUCHTMAN, MILTON A.: Producer, Director. b. New York, NY, e. Columbia U. B.S.; Columbia U., M.S. Worked for Columbia and independent producers in various production capacities, set up first worldwide TV network, Eichmann Trial. Received numerous Peabody, Emmy, and Gabriel awards, Gold Hugo Awards (Chicago Film and TV Festival), Martin Luther King Festival Award, DGA Award.
TELEVISION: High Adventure Series, Every Man's Dream, ABC, Verdict for Tomorrow (Peabody Award, 1962), Assignment Southeast Asia, It Happened in Naples; Son of Sulan, The Secret of Michaelangelo, Every Man's Dream (Peabody), Dance Theatre of Harlem, Those Who Sing Together, The Makebelievers.

FRYE, WILLIAM: Producer. Was agency exec. before beginning prod. career as associate prod. of Four Star Playhouse in assoc. with late Dick Powell, David Niven and Charles Boyer. Later joined Revue Prods., which became Universal TV; he produced General Electric Theatre and other series. Has produced many Movie of the Week entries for ABC-TV.
PICTURES: The Trouble with Angels, Where Angels Go, Trouble Follows, Airport 1975, Airport 1977, Raise the Titanic, Apt Pupil.

FUCHS, LEO L.: Independent producer. b. Vienna, June 14, 1929. Moved to U.S., 1939. e. Vienna and New York. U.S. Army cameraman 1951–53; int'l. mag. photographer until entered motion pictures as producer with Universal in Hollywood in 1961.
PICTURES: Gambit, A Fine Pair; Jo (French version of The Gazebo), Sunday Lovers, Just the Way You Are.

FUCHS, MICHAEL: Executive. b. New York, NY, March 9, 1946. e. Union Coll., NYU Law School (J.D. degree). Show business lawyer before joining Home Box Office in 1976, developing original and sports programming. Named chmn. and CEO of HBO in 1984 till present.

FUEST, ROBERT: Director. b. London, 1927. Early career as painter, graphic designer. Ent. TV industry as designer with ABC-TV, 1958. 1962: directing doc., commercials. 1966: Wrote and dir. Just Like a Woman, 1967–68; dir. 7 episodes of The Avengers, 1969: wrote and directed 6 episodes of The Optimists.
PICTURES: And Soon the Darkness, Wuthering Heights, Doctor Phibes, Doctor Phibes Rides Again (also .p.); The Final Programme (also s.p., design), The Devil's Rain, The Geller Effect (s.p. only), The New Avengers, The Gold Bug, Revenge of the Stepford Wives, The Big Stuffed Dog, Mystery on Fire Island, Aphrodite, Worlds Beyond, Cat's Eyes.

FULLER, SAMUEL: Director, Writer, Producer. b. New York, NY, 1911. m. actress Christa Lang. Copy boy, N.Y. Journal; reporter, rewrite man, N.Y. Graphic, N.Y Journal, San Diego Sun; journeyman reported many papers. Author of novel The Dark Page; many orig. s.p.; in U.S. Army, 16th Inf. 1st U.S. Inf. Div. 1942–45.
PICTURES: I Shot Jesse James, Baron of Arizona (s.p., dir.); The Steel Helmet (prod., dir.); Fixed Bayonets (dir.); Park Row (s.p., dir., prod.); Pickup On South Street (s.p., dir.); Hell and High Water, House of Bamboo (s.p., dir.); Run of the Arrow, China Gate, Forty Guns, Verboten, The Crimson Kimono, Underworld U.S.A., Merril's Marauders (prod. dir., s.p.), (collab. s.p., dir.); Shock Corridor (s.p., dir., prod.); The Naked Kiss (s.p. prod., dir.); Dead Pigeon on Beethoven Street (s.p. dir.); The Big Red One (s.p. dir.); White Dog, Thieves After Dark, (co-s.p., dir.), Return to Salem's Lot (actor only); Street of No Return (dir., s.p., actor), Helsinki Napoli, Tini Kling (dir., s.p.), All Night Long (actor only), Sons (actor only).
AUTHOR: Novel, Crown of India. Novel; 144 Piccadilly Street; Dead Pigeon on Beethoven Street; The Rifle; The Big Red One, The Dark Page, La Grande Melee (Battle Royal), Pecos Bill and the Soho Kid, Once Upon Samuel Fuller (Stories of America-interview bk.).

FUNT, ALLEN: Producer, Performer. b. New York , NY, Sept. 16, 1914. Best known as producer and creator of Candid Camera series which originated on radio in 1947 as Candid Microphone which inspired theatrical film shorts. TV version began in 1948 as Candid Mike, changed in 1949 to Candid Camera which played off and on until 1960 when became regular series on CBS, lasting until 1967. Revived briefly in early '70s and again in mid '80s in new format; then syndicated as The New Candid Camera. Candid Camera Christmas Special, 1987, Candid Camera: Eat! Eat! Eat!, Candid Camera on

Wheels. Produced and starred in film, What Do You Say to a Naked Lady?

FURIE, SIDNEY J.: Director, Writer, Producer. b. Toronto, Canada, Feb. 28, 1933. Ent. TV and films 1954. Canadian features include: Dangerous Age, A Cool Sound from Hell. Also dir. many Hudson Bay TV series. To England 1960. Films since include Dr. Blood's Coffin, During One Night, Brewster's Millions, The Young Ones, The Boys. 1961 appt. exec. dir. Galaworldfilm Productions, Ltd.
PICTURES: The Leather Boys, Wonderful Life, The Ipcress File, The Appaloosa, The Naked Runner, The Lawyer, Little Fauss and Big Halsy, Lady Sings the Blues, Hit!, Sheila Levine, Gable and Lombard, The Boys in Company C, The Entity, Purple Hearts (prod., dir., s.p.), Iron Eagle, Superman IV: The Quest For Peace, Iron Eagle II (dir., co-s.p.).

FURNESS, BETTY: Actress, TV Correspondent. b. New York, NY, Jan. 3, 1916. Stage and screen actress in the '40s; TV commercial spokeswoman for Westinghouse in '50s, leading consumer advocate in '70s. Host on both local TV and radio shows in New York (Dimension in a Woman's World, At Your Beck and Call, Ask Betty Furness, etc.). Named President Johnson's asst. for consumer affairs in 1967. 1970, chmn, exec. dir. of New York state's consumer protection board. Commissioner NY City Dept. of Consumer Affairs. Joined WNBC-TV in 1974 as consumer reporter and weekly contributor to Today Show. 1988: Betty's Attic.
PICTURES: Professional Sweetheart, Emergency Call, Lucky Devils, Beggars in Ermine, Keeper of the Bees, Magnificent Obsession, Swing Time, The President's Mystery, Mama Steps Out, North of Shanghai.

FURST, AUSTIN O.: Executive. e. Lehigh U., B.S. in economics/marketing. Began career in marketing dept., Proctor and Gamble; 1972 joined Time Inc. as dir., new subscription sales for Time magazine; later joined Time Inc.'s new magazine dev. staff for People magazine; named circulation mgr., People magazine, 1974; 1975 named pres., Time Inc.'s Computer Television Inc., a pay-per-view hotel operation and was responsible for successful turnaround and sale of co.; 1976, vice pres., programming, Home Box Office; named exec. v.p. HBO, 1979; appointed pres. and CEO, Time-Life Films, Inc., 1980; 1981 established Vestron after acquiring home video rights to Time/Life Video Library; chmn. and CEO, Vestron, Inc.

FURST, RENEE: Publicist. President, Renee Furst Advertising and Public Relations. b. New York, NY, Oct. 23. e. New School, Columbia U. m. Peter Furst, journalist. Adv. acct. exec. for Cinema 5 Theatres at Diener Hauser. 1974–89: has done p.r. on such films as Missing, Napoleon, The Gods Must Be Crazy, Fanny and Alexander, Cousin Cousine, Official Story, Barfly, Mephisto, Madame Rosa, Blood Simple, Breaker Morant. Worked on adv. and p.r. for Astor Pictures on classics such as La Dolce Vita, Last Year at Marienbad, Rocco and His Brothers.

G

GABOR, ZSA ZSA: Actress. r.n. Sari Gabor. b. Hungary, Feb. 6, 1918. e. Budapest, Lausanne, Switzerland. Stage debut in Europe. Author: Zsa Zsa's Complete Guide to Men (1969); How to Get a Man, How to Keep a Man and How to Get Rid of a Man (1971).
PICTURES: Lovely to Look At, We're Not Married, The Story of Three Loves, Lili, Moulin Rouge, Three Ring Circus, Death of a Scoundrel, Girl in the Kremlin, For the First Time, Boys' Night Out, Picture Mommy Dead, Jack of Diamonds, Won Ton Ton, the Dog Who Saved Hollywood.

GAFFNEY, ROBERT: Producer. Director. b. New York, NY, Oct. 8, 1931. e. Iona Coll., 1949–51. Staff, Louis de Rochemont; prod., Rooftops of New York, in assoc. with Robert Associates, prod. staff, Cinerama Holiday, Man on a String; camera technical consultant, Cinemiracle prod., Windjam-McCarty, 1960; prod. industrial films, Seneca Prods., Prod., Light Fantastic; prod., Troublemaker; assoc. prod., Harvey Middleman Fireman; dir., Frankenstein Meets the Space Monster.

GALANTE, M. CHRISTINA: Executive. b. Tucson, AZ, Aug. 30, 1942. e. U. of Arizona, New Sch. for Social Research, N.Y. Started career as child model in 1948. Entered film career as stunt double in 1955 working in dozens of major films made in Arizona, 1962–66, feature vocalist with big bands for USO tours and major night clubs. 1967–70, spokeswoman and actress in TV commercials and feature films. 1970–74, television commercials producer. 1974–77, film coordinator for mayor's office, City of New York, coordinating and supervising all m.p. and television filming in City. 1977 named special consultant to California Motion Picture Council. 1980, named to Council by Governor Edmund G. Brown and elected its chairman. 1980, named to Los Angeles Film Commission by Mayor Tom Bradley, currently on executive board. 1981–82, special consultant for m.p. & TV development for city of Los Angeles. Currently creative services director, Rogers and Cowan (public relations).

GALE, BOB: Writer, Producer. b. St. Louis, MO, 1951. e. U. of Southern California Sch. of Cinema. Joined with friend Robert Zemeckis to write screenplays, starting with episode for TV series, McCloud. Also co-wrote story for The Nightstalker series. Turned to feature films, co-writing with Zemeckis script for I Wanna Hold Your Hand, on which Gale also acted as associate producer.
PICTURES: 1941 (s.p.); Used Cars (prod., co-s.p.); Back to the Future (co.-prod., s.p.); Back to the Future 2 (prod., s.p.).

GALE, GEORGE: Executive, e. Sorbonne U., Paris, France. Feature editor, Budapest Ed., U.S. Army Pictorial Service. Feature and TV editor MGM, Hal Roach, Disney Studios; prod. and prod. exec. Ivan Tors; American National Enterprises, Inc. Producer and director. Supervised the production of over 30 features for television syndication and numerous theatrical and TV features. Member ACE and Academy of Motion Picture Arts and Sciences. Formed George Gale Productions, Inc. in 1976.

GALLIGAN, ZACH: Actor. b. New York, NY, Feb. 14, 1964. e. Columbia U.
PICTURES: Gremlins, Nothing Lasts Forever, Waxwork, Rebel Waves, Mortal Passions, Rising Storm, Gremlins II.
TELEVISION: Prisoner Without a Name, Cell Without a Number; Crossings, Surviving, The Return of Hickey, The Beginning of the Firm.

GALLOP, RICHARD C.: Executive. e. Harvard Law Sch. Now managing dir., Allen & Co., Inc. Previously, pres. & chief operating officer, Columbia Pictures Industries (appt. 1983); also chmn. of m.p. div., Columbia Pictures. Previously exec. v.p-finance, law and admin. of Columbia (since 1982); also served as gen. counsel, 1981–83. Joined Columbia as sr. v.p. & gen. counsel, 1981. Began career in 1963 as associate of law firm, Milbank Tweed Hadley & McCloy, New York; named partner, 1970. 1979, partner of Washington, DC law firm, Caplin & Drysdale, specializing in corporate and financial matters. In that capacity served as outside corporate legal counsel to Columbia two yrs. Member: finance committee, Williams Coll.; board of trustees, Marymount Coll.

GAMBON, MICHAEL: Actor. b. Dublin, Ireland, 1940. Ent. Ind. 1966. Early experience in theatre. 1985–87 Acting at National Theatre and London's West End. 1988: in Harold Pinter's Mountain Language.
PICTURES: The Beast Must Die, Turtle Diary, Paris By Night, The Rachel Papers, A Dry White Season, The Cook, the Thief, His Wife and Her Lover.
TELEVISION: Uncle Vanya, Ghosts, Oscar Wilde, The Holy Experiment, Absurd Person Singular, The Singing Detective, (serial).

GANIS, SIDNEY M.: Publicist. b. New York, NY, Jan. 8, 1940. e. Brooklyn Coll. Staff writer, newspaper and wire service contact, 20th Century-Fox 1961–62; radio, TV contact and special projects, Columbia Pictures 1963–64. Joined Seven Arts Prod. 1965 as publicity mgr.; 1967, appt. prod. publicity mgr. Warner-7 Arts, Ass't prod., There Was a Crooked Man, 1969. Studio publicity dir., Cinema Center Films, 1970. Director of Ad-Pub for Mame, Warner Bros., 1973; Director of Advertising, Warner Bros., 1974; named WB v.p., worldwide adv. & pub., 1977; 1979, sr. v.p., Lucasfilm, Ltd.; 1982 Emmy winner, exec. prod., best documentary, The Making of Raiders of the Lost Ark. 1986, joined Paramount Pictures as pres., worldwide mktg; 1988, named pres., Paramount Motion Picture Group. 1986, elected to board of dir. University Art Museum, Berkeley, CA.

GANZ, BRUNO: Actor. b. Zurich, Switzerland, March 22, 1941.
THEATER: Member of the Berlin Theater troupe, Schaubuhne. Hamlet (1967), Dans La Jungle Des Villes, Torquato Tasso, La Chevauchee Sur Le Lac de Constance, Peer Gynt, Hamlet (1984).
PICTURES: Der Sanfte Lauf (1967), Sommergaste (1975), The Marquise of O, Lumiere, The Wild Duck, The American Friend, The Lefthanded Woman, The Boys from Brazil, Black and White Like Day and Night, Knife in the Head, Nosferatu the Vampyre, Return of a Good Friend, 5% Risk, An Italian Woman, Polenta, La Provinciale, La Dame Aux Camelias, Der Erfinder, Etwas Wird Sichtbar, Circle of Deceit, Hande Hoch, Logik Der Gerfuhls, War and Peace, In the White City, System Ohne Schatten, Der Pendler, Wings of Desire, Bankomatt, Strapless.
TELEVISION: Father and Son (Italian TV).

GANZ, TONY: Producer. b. New York, NY. e. studied film at Harvard U. Produced documentaries for PBS in N.Y. Moved to L.A. 1973 where in charge of dev., Charles Fries Productions. Then joined Ron Howard Productions 1980. Left to form own prod. co. with Deborah Blum.
PICTURES: Gung Ho, Clean and Sober, Vibes.
TELEVISION: Series: American Dream Machine, Maxi-

mum Security (exec. prod.). Movies: Bitter Harvest, Into Thin Air.

GARBO, GRETA: Actress. r.n. Greta Gustafson. b. Stockholm, Sept. 18, 1906. e. Stockholm. Stage career as a dancer in Sweden. Hollywood screen career started 1926 with Torrent. Voted one of the Ten Best Money-Making Stars in Motion Picture Herald-Fame Poll 1932. Spec. Academy Award, 1954.
PICTURES: Peter the Tramp (1922), The Atonement of Gösta Berling, Joyless Street, The Torrent, The Temptress, Flesh and the Devil, Love, Divine Woman, Mysterious Lady, Single Standard, Wild Orchids, Woman of Affairs, Kiss, Anna Christie, Susan Lennox, Her Fall and Rise, Romance, Inspiration, Mata Hari, Grand Hotel, As You Desire Me, Queen Christina, Anna Karenina, Camille, Conquest, Ninotchka, Two-Faced Woman.

GARCIA, ANDY: Actor. b. Havana, Cuba, 1956. e. Florida International U, Miami. Family moved to Miami Beach in 1961. Spent several years acting with regional theaters in Florida.
PICTURES: Blue Skies Again (debut, 1983), The Mean Season, 8 Million Ways to Die, The Untouchables, Stand and Deliver, American Roulette, The Sixth Family, Black Rain, Internal Affairs, A Show of Force.
TELEVISION: Hill Street Blues, Brothers, Foley Square, Clinton and Nadine.

GARDENIA, VINCENT: Actor. r.n. Vincent Scognamiglio. b. Naples, Italy, Jan. 7, 1922. f. was actor and singer who brought Vincent to U.S. at age 2, formed theatrical co. in which Vincent took part. U.S. Army, W.W.II, and after landed first English-speaking role in summer stock prod. of Burlesque. Trained at Italian Theater, NY. Made off-Bdwy. debut in The Man with the Golden Arm; first Bdwy. role in The Visit, 1958, with the Lunts. Film debut: Murder, Inc. (1960).
STAGE: Shoe Shine (1927 Brooklyn); The Man With the Golden Arm; The Visit; The Cold Wind and the Warm; Rashomon; The Power of Darkness; Only in America; Machinal, The Wall, Gallows Humor, Daughter of Silence; Endgame; Seidman and Son; Little Murders; Passing Through from Exotic Places, The Prisoner of Second Avenue (Tony Award, 1972); California Suite; God's Favorite; Sly Fox, Buried Inside Extra, Glengary Glen Ross; I'm Not Rappaport.
PICTURES: Cop Haters, Cold Turkey, Little Murders, Hickey and Boggs, Bang the Drum Slowly, Luciano, The Manchu Eagle, Death Wish, The Front Page, Heaven Can Wait, Firepower, Home Movies, The Last Flight of Noah's Ark, Movers and Shakers, Little Shop of Horrors, Moonstruck, Freedom Fighter, Skin Deep, Cavalli Si Nasce.
TELEVISION: All in the Family, (series) Breaking Away, Age-Old Friends.

GARDINER, PETER R.: Executive. Independent still photographer and industrial filmmaker before joining Paramount, 1973, in feature post-prod. 1979, joined Warner Bros. as asst. dir., corporate services. 1987, promoted to v.p., opns., WB corporate film-video services.

GARDNER, ARTHUR: Producer, b. Marinette, WI. Entered m.p. ind. as actor, in orig. cast All Quiet on the Western Front, 1929. Juvenile leads in: Waterfront, Heart of the North, Assassin of Youth, Religious Racketeer; production asst. dir. King Bros. 1941, then asst. prod. U.S. Air Force 1st Motion Picture Unit, 1943–45. Formed Levy-Gardner-Laven Prods. with Jules Levy, Arnold Laven, 1951.
PICTURES: (Asst. dir.) Paper Bullets, I Killed That Man, Rubber Racketeers, Klondike Fury, I Escaped From the Gestapo, Suspense; (Asst. prod.) Gangster, Dude Goes West, Badmen of Tombstone, Gun Crazy, Mutiny, Southside 1-1000; Prod.: Without Warning, Vice Squad, Down Three Dark Streets, Return of Dracula, The Flame Barrier, The Vampire, The Monster that Challenged the World, Geronimo, The Glory Guys, Clambake, Scalphunters, Sam Whiskey, Underground, McKenzie Break, The Honkers, Hunting Party, Kansas City Bomber, White Lightning, McQ, Brannigan, Gator, Safari 3000.
TELEVISION: Rifleman, Robert Taylor's Detectives, Law of the Plainsman, The Big Valley.
MEMBER: Producers Guild of America, Directors Guild of America, Screen Actors Guild, Actors Equity, Writers Guild of Amer., West.

GARDNER, AVA: Actress. b. Smithfield, NC, Dec. 24, 1922. e. Atlantic Christian Coll.
PICTURES: We Were Dancing, Joe Smith, American, Lost Angel, Three Men in White, Maisie Goes to Reno, Whistle Stop, The Killers, The Hucksters, Singapore, One Touch of Venus, The Bribe, Great Sinner, East Side, West Side, Show Boat, Pandora and the Flying Dutchman, Lone Star, Snows of Kilimanjaro, Ride Vaquero, Mogambo, Knights of the Round Table, Barefoot Contessa, Bhowani Junction, Little Hut, The Naked Maja, On the Beach, The Fair Bride, 55 Days at Peking, Night of the Iguana, The Bible, Mayerling, Life and Times of Judge Roy Bean, The Devil's Widow, Earthquake, The Bluebird, Permission to Kill, The Cassandra Crossing, The Sentinel, City on Fire, Priest of Love, Regina.

TELEVISION: Harem, The Long Hot Summer, Falcon Crest (series).

GARFIELD, WARREN: Writer, Publicist, b. Nov. 18, 1936. e. UCLA, Loyola of Los Angeles Sch. of Law. Story analyst, assistant to dir., Hecht-Hill-Lancaster, 1948–58; casting dir. assist., assist. film editor, Columbia Pictures, films, featurettes, trailers, TV spots, Paramount Pictures, 1966–68; creative film services, Walt Disney Productions, 1968–present. Member: Academy of Motion Picture, Arts & Sciences.
CREDITS: A Stranger in Town (wrote s.p.), Cat Ballou, Wild and Wonderful, Flight From Ashiya, Taras Bulba (as assist. to Harold Hecht); The High Chaparral (wrote, TV).

GARFINKLE, LOUIS: Writer, Director, Producer. b. Seattle, WA, February 11, 1928. e. U. of California, U. of Washington, U. of Southern California. Writer KOMO, Seattle, 1945; Executive Research, Inc., 1948; Writer, educ. doc. screenplays, Emerson Films, EBF. 1948–50; s.p. You Can Beat the A-Bomb (RKO), 1950; Writer-dir. training films, info. films, Signal Photo, 1950–53; Copy, Weinberg Adv., 1953; Head of Doc. Research in TV, U. of California, Berkeley, 1954–55; staff, Sheilah Graham Show, 1955; formed Maxim Prod. Inc. with Albert Band, 1956; story and s.p. The Young Guns.
PICTURES: I Bury the Living (story, s.p, co-prod.), (Killer on the Wall); Face of Fire (s.p. and co-prod.), A Minute to Pray A Second to Die (story, s.p. and co-producer); The Love Doctors (story, s.p. and director); Beautiful People (s.p. (collab.); The Models (story & s.p. (collab.); The Doberman Gang (co-s.p.); Little Cigars (story & co-s.p.); The Deer Hunter (story collab.)
TELEVISION: Writer, 712 teleplays for Day in Court, Morning Court, Accused for Selmur—ABC-TV, 1959–66; Co-writer-creator Direct Line pilot, Selmur; Story and t.p. June Allyson Show, Threat of Evil; s.p. in collab. The Hellbenders; story and t.p. Death Valley Days, Crullers At Sundown; story, Death Valley Days, Captain Dick Mine; head writer, No. 3 Peanut Place (pilot).

GARFUNKEL, ART: Actor, Singer, Composer. b. New York, NY, Nov. 5, 1942. e. Columbia Coll. Began singing at age 4. Long partnership with Paul Simon began in grade school at 13 in Queens, NY; first big success in 1965 with hit single, Sound of Silence. Partnership dissolved in 1970. Film debut in Catch 22 (1969). Winner of 4 Grammy Awards.
PICTURES: Carnal Knowledge, Bad Timing/A Sensual Obsession, Good to Go.

GARLAND, BEVERLY: Actress. b. Santa Cruz, CA, Oct. 17, 1930. e. Glendale Coll., 1945–47.
TELEVISION: starred, Decoy, Bing Crosby; Twilight Zone, Dr. Kildare, Medic, (Emmy Nomination, 1954); My Three Sons; Scarecrow and Mrs. King, Magnum P.I., Remington Steele. Movies: This Gun for Hire.
PICTURES: The Mad Room, Where the Red Fern Grows, Airport, 1975, Roller Boogie, It's My Turn, Death Falls.

GARNER, JAMES: Actor. b. Norman, OK, April 7, 1928. e. high school there. Then joined Merchant Marine, U.S. Army ser. in Korean War. Prod. Paul Gregory suggested acting career. Studied drama at N.Y. Berghof School. Toured with road companies; Warner Bros. studio contract followed with screen debut in Toward the Unknown (1956).
PICTURES: Shoot-out at Medicine Bend, Darby's Rangers, Sayonara, Up Periscope, Cash McCall, The Children's Hour, The Great Escape. Thrill of It All, Move Over Darling, The Americanization of Emily, 36 Hours, The Art of Love, Mister Buddwing, Duel at Diablo, Grand Prix, Hour of the Gun, Support Your Local Sheriff, Marlowe, Support Your Local Gunfighter, Skin Game, They Only Kill Their Masters, One Little Indian, Hawaiian Cowboy, Health, The Fan, Victor/Victoria, Tank, Murphy's Romance, Sunset.
TELEVISION: Cheyenne, Maverick, Rockford Files. Movies: The Long Summer of George Adams, The Glitter Dome, Heartsounds, Promise (also exec. prod.), Obsessive Love, My Name is Bill W. (also exec. prod.). Mini-Series: Space.

GARR, TERI: Actress. b. Lakewood, OH, 1949. Began career as dancer, performing S.F. Ballet at 13. Later appeared with L.S. Ballet and in original road show co. of West Side Story. Did commercials; appeared in film Head written by a fellow acting student, Jack Nicholson. Career boosted by appearance on TV as semi-regular on The Sonny and Cher Show.
PICTURES: The Conversation, Young Frankenstein, Won Ton Ton, The Dog Who Saved Hollywood, Oh, God!, Close Encounters of the Third Kind, Mr. Mike's Mondo Video, The Black Stallion, One from the Heart, The Sting II, Tootsie, The Black Stallion Returns, Mr. Mom, Firstborn, Lies, Miracles, After Hours, Full Moon in Blue Water, Out Cold, Let It Ride, Waiting for the Light, Short Time.
TELEVISION: Series regular: The Ken Berry "Wow" Show, (1972), Burns and Schreiber Comedy Hour, Girl With Something Extra, The Sonny and Cher Comedy Hour, The Sonny Comedy Revue. Movies: Law and Order, Prime Suspect; The Tale of the Frog Prince (Faerie Tale Theatre); Winter of Our

Discontent, To Catch a King, Intimate Strangers, Pack of Lies, Drive, She Said (Trying Times), Paul Reiser: Out on a Whim. Mini-Series: Fresno.

GARRETT, BETTY: Singer, Actress. b. St. Joseph, MO, May 23, 1919. e. scholarships; Annie Wright Seminary, Tacoma, WA, Neighborhood Playhouse, N.Y. Sang in night clubs, hotels, Broadway shows (1942–46); won Donaldson award for best musical comedy performance of 1946 for Call Me Mister; Spoon River Anthology. A Girl Could Get Lucky, Meet Me in St. Louis (1989). Motion Picture Herald, Star of Tomorrow, 1949. Starred in one woman autobiographical show, No Dogs or Actors Allowed (Pasadena Playhouse, 1989).
PICTURES: The Big City, (debut, 1947), Words and Music, Take Me Out to the Ball Game, Neptune's Daughter, On the Town, My Sister Eileen, Shadow on the Window.
TELEVISION: Series: Laverne and Shirley, All in the Family. Guest: Love Boat, Black's Magic, Somerset Gardens, Murder She Wrote, Movies: All the Way Home, Who's Happy Now.

GARRETT, LAWRENCE G. JR.: Executive. b. San Francisco, Nov. 5, 1942. e. U. of California; Thunderbird Graduate Sch. 1967, joined Columbia Pictures Intl., Panama, Mexico; 1969, Paramount Pictures, mgr., Venezuela; 1973, MCA-TV asst. mgr., Mexico; 1973–76, Shearson Hayden Stone Institutional investment; 1977, United Artists, Argentina, Austral-Asia mgr. dir.; 1980, Avco Embassy, sls. supvr. Latin American-Far East; 1981, head intl. sls., Shapiro Entertainment; 1982, head intl. sls., Goldfarb Distributors; 1983–86, dir./intl. sls. & acquisitions, Arista Films; 1987, v.p. intl. theatrical & video sls., ITC Entertainment.

GARSON, GREER: Actress. b. County Down, Northern Ireland, 1912. e. London U., B.A. cum laude; post grad. studies, Grenoble U. France. After early career in art research and editing for Encyclopaedia Britannica and market research with Lever's Intl. Advertising Service became actress with Birmingham Rep. Co. starring in 13 West End prods. before lured to Hollywood by MGM, 1938. Screen debut 1939 in Goodbye, Mr. Chips. Academy Award best performance by actress, 1942 (Mrs. Miniver, MGM). Voted one of the ten best Money-Making Stars in Motion Picture Herald-Fame Poll 1942–46 inclusive. Photoplay Mag. Gold Medal 1944–45 and top British Award 1942, 1943, 1944. Numerous other awards incl. L.A. Times Woman of the Year, Woman of the World Award from Intl. Orphans, Inc. 1987 Gov. Award for contrib. to arts NM, 1988 USA Film Fest. Master Screen Artist. Active in civic and benevolent activities. With late husband Col. E.E. (Buddy) Fogelson, awarded Dept. of Interior's citation for environmental preservation efforts. Founded Fogelson Museum NM 1987.
THEATER: Stage debut Birmingham (England) Rep. theat. 1932 in Street Scene; London debut 1935 in Golden Arrow opposite Laurence Olivier; continued London stage to 1938 (Vintage Wine, Mademoiselle, Accent on Youth, Page from a Diary, Old Music, etc.).
PICTURES: Pride and Prejudice, Blossoms in the Dust, When Ladies Meet, Mrs. Miniver, Random Harvest, Mme. Curie, Mrs. Parkington, Valley of Decision, Adventure, Desire Me, Julia Misbehaves, That Forsythe Woman, The Miniver Story, The Law and the Lady, Scandal at Scourie, Julius Caesar, Her Twelve Men, Strange Lady in Town, Sunrise at Campobello, The Singing Nun, The Happiest Millionaire.
TELEVISION: Crown Matrimonial, My Father Gave Me America, Little Women, Holiday Tribute to Radio City, Perry Como's Christmas in New Mexico, A Gift of Music (host). Bicentennial Tribute to Los Angeles.

GARTNER, MICHAEL G.: Executive. b. 1938. e. Carleton Coll., Northfield, MN; NYU Sch. of Law. Began newspaper career at 15 with The Des Moines Register in Iowa. Became the paper's editor, later pres., COO and editorial chmn. of the parent Des Moines Register and Tribune Co. Worked for 14 years at the Wall Street Journal in various positions. Served as editor of Gannett-owned Louisville Courier-Journal and Louisville Times, and owner of the Daily Tribune of Ames, IA. Appointed president of NBC News, August 1988.

GASSMAN, VITTORIO: Actor. b. Genoa, Italy, Sept. 1, 1922. e. Acad. of Dramatic Art, Rome. Stage actor, 1943; m.p. debut, 1946.
PICTURES: Daniele Cortis, Mysterious Rider, Bitter Rice, Lure of Sila, The Outlaws, Anna, Streets of Sorrow; to U.S., Cry of the Hunted, Sombrero, The Glass Wall, Rhapsody, Girls Marked Danger, Mambo, War and Peace, World's Most Beautiful Woman, Tempest, The Love Specialist, The Great War, Let's Talk About Women, Il Successo, The Tiger, Woman Times Seven, Ghosts—Italian Style, Scent of a Woman, Viva Italia!, A Wedding, Quintet, Immortal Bachelor, The Nude Bomb, Sharky's Machine, Tempest, I Picari, The Family, The Uncle, The House of the Lord, The Hateful Dead, To Forget Palermo, Los Alegres Picaro, Scheherzade.

GATWARD, JAMES: Executive. b. London, England. Ent. Ind. 1957. Early career as freelance drama prod. dir. in Canada, USA, UK (with ITV & BBC). Prod. dir. various intern. co-productions in UK, Ceylond, Australia, Germany. Currently chief executive and Dep. chmn. TVS Television Ltd., chmn. Telso Communications Ltd., dir. of ITN, Channel Four, Super Channel, Oracle Teletext.

GAVIN, JOHN: Actor. b. Los Angeles, CA, April 8, 1932. m. actress Constance Towers. e. St. John's Military Acad., Villanova Prep at Ojai, Stanford Univ., Naval service: air intelligence officer in Korean War. Broadway stage debut: Seesaw, 1973. 1961–73 public service experience as spec. advisor to Secretary Gen. of OAS, performed gp. task work for Dept. of State and Exec. Office of the President. Pres. Screen Actors Guild, 1971–73. Named U.S. Ambassador to Mexico, 1981–86. Joined UNIVISA Communications Gp. as pres. satellite communications. Consultant to Dept. of State and serves on many boards.
PICTURES: A Time to Love and a Time to Die, Imitation of Life, Spartacus, A Breath of Scandal, Romanoff and Juliet, Tammy, Tell Me True, Back Street, Thoroughly Modern Millie, Mad Woman of Chaillot, Psycho, Midnight Lace.

GAY, JOHN: Writer. b. Whittier, CA, April 1, 1924. e. LA City Coll.
PICTURES: Run Silent, Run Deep; Separate Tables; The Happy Thieves; Four Horsemen; The Courtship of Eddie's Father; The Hallelujah Trail; The Last Safari; The Power; No Way to Treat a Lady; Soldier Blue; Sometimes a Great Notion; Hennessey; A Matter of Time.
TELEVISION: Amazing Howard Hughes; Kill Me If You Can; Captains Courageous; Red Badge of Courage; All My Darling Daughters; Les Miserables; Transplant; A Private Battle; A Tale of Two Cities; The Bunker; Berlin Tunnel 21; Stand By Your Man; Dial "M" For Murder; The Long Summer of George Adams; A Piano for Mrs. Cimino; The Hunchback of Notre Dame; Ivanhoe; Witness for the Prosecution; Samson and Delilah; Fatal Vision; Doubletake, Uncle Tom's Cabin, Outlaw, Six Against the Rock, Around the World in 80 Days, Blind Faith, And The Band Played On, Giant.

GAYNOR, MITZI: Actress. r.n. Francisca Mitzi Von Gerber. b. Chicago, IL, Sept. 4, 1931. e. Powers Professional H.S., Hollywood. Studied ballet since age four; was in L.A. Light Opera prod. Roberta. Stage: Anything Goes (natl. co., 1989).
OPERA: Fortune Teller, Song of Norway, Louisiana Purchase, Naughty Marietta, The Great Waltz.
PICTURES: My Blue Heaven, Take Care of My Little Girl, Golden Girl, The I Don't Care Girl, We're Not Married, Bloodhounds of Broadway, There's No Business Like Show Business, Anything Goes, Three Young Texans, Down Among the Sheltering Palms, Birds and the Bees, The Joker, Les Girls, South Pacific, Surprise Package, Happy Anniversary, For Love or Money.

GAZZARA, BEN: Actor. b. New York, NY, Aug. 28, 1930. e. Studied at CCNY 1947–48. Won scholarship to study with Erwin Piscator; joined Actor's Studio, where students improvised a play, End as a Man, which then was performed on Broadway with him in lead. Screen debut (1957) in film version of that play retitled The Strange One.
PICTURES: Anatomy of a Murder, Joy of Laughter, The Passionate Thief, The Young Doctors, Convicts Four, Conquered City, A Rage to Live, The Bridge at Remagen, Husbands, Capone, High Velocity, Killing of a Chinese Bookie, Voyage of the Damned, Bloodline, They All Laughed, Inchon, Tales of Ordinary Madness, Road House, Quicker Than the Eye, Don Bosco, Silent Memory.
TELEVISION: Arrest and Trial, Run for Your Life. Movies: A Question of Honor; An Early Frost, A Letter to Three Wives, Police Story: The Freeway Killings, Downpayment on Murder.
THEATER: Jezebel's Husband, End as a Man, Cat on a Hot Tin Roof, A Hatful of Rain, The Night Circus, Epitaph for George Dillon, Two for the Seesaw, Strange Interlude, Traveler Without Luggage, Hughie, Who's Afraid of Virginia Woolf.

GEARY, ANTHONY: Actor. b. Coalville, UT, May 29, 1947. e. U. of Vermont.
TELEVISION: Series: Bright Promise, General Hospital (1978–83); Guest: The Young and the Restless, Osmond Family Holiday Special, General Hospital, Movies: Intimate Agony, Sins of the Past, The Imposter, Kicks, Perry Mason: The Case of the Murdered Madam, O Do You Know the Muffin Man?
PICTURES: Blood Sabbath (debut, 1969), Johnny Got His Gun, The Amazing Capt. Nemo, Private Investigations, Disorderlies, Penitentiary III, You Can't Hurry Love, Pass the Ammo, Dangerous Love, It Takes Two, UHF, Sorority Kills, Night Life, Rock House.

GEBHARDT, FRED: Producer, Writer, Exhibitor. b. Vienna, Austria, Mar. 16, 1925. e. Schotten Gymnasium, Vienna, UCLA, 1939. Usher Boyd Theatre, Bethlehem, PA; Mgr., Rivoli Thea. L.A., 1944; 18 yrs. mgr. many theatres. Fox West Coast, then Fine Arts Theatre. Writer, prod.: 12 To the Moon, The Phantom Planet; prod., Assignment Outer Space, Operation

M; s.p., All But Glory, The Starmaker, Shed No Blood, Fortress in Heaven, Eternal Woman.
BOOKS: Mental Disarmament, All But Glory, Starmaker, Shed No Blood, The Last of the Templars.
Pres., Four Crown Prods., Inc.; recipient of Medal of Americanism, D.A.R., 1963; Honorary Lifetime Member, P.T.A., Young Man of The Year Award, 1956, 24 Showmanship Awards; Mem. Acad. M.P. Arts and Sciences, Ind. M.P. Prod. Assoc.

GEE, CHARLOTTE: Executive. Served for 6 years as adv.-pub. mgr. for Village Roadshow Corp., Warner Bros. Australian dist. Left to join Apogee (special effects co.) as v.p., mktg. 1986, joined WB as dir. project pub. 1987, named WB v.p., pub.

GEESON, JUDY: Actress. b. Arundel, Sussex, England, Sept. 10, 1948. e. Corona Stage Sch. Began professional career on British TV, 1960.
PICTURES: To Sir with Love, Circus of Blood, Here We Go Round the Mulberry Bush, Hammerhead, Three into Two Won't Go, Two Gentlemen Sharing, The Executioner, 10 Rillington Place, Brannigan, The Eagle Has Landed, Carry On England, It's Not the Size That Counts, Horror Planet, Dominique (made 1977).
TELEVISION: Dance of Death, Lady Windermere's Fan, Room with a View, The Skin Game, Star Maidens, Poldark, She, The Coronation, Murder She Wrote, Movie: The Secret Life of Kathy McCormick.
THEATRE: Othello, Titus Andronicus, Two Gentlemen of Verona, Section Nine, An Ideal Husband.

GEFFEN, DAVID: Executive, Producer. b. Brooklyn, NY, Feb. 21, 1943. Began in mailroom of William Morris Agency before becoming agent there and later at Ashley Famous. With Elliott Roberts founded own talent management co. for musicians. Founded Asylum Records, 1970. Pres. then chmn. Elektra-Asylum Records 1973–76. Sold co. to Warner Communications for whom he headed film prod. unit. Vice-chmn. Warner Bros. Pictures, 1975; exec. asst. to chmn., Warner Communications, 1977; Member music faculty Yale U., 1978. Formed Geffen Records 1980 and Geffen Film Co. Producer of Broadway shows Master Harold . . . and the Boys, Cats, Good, Dreamgirls, Social Security, Chess.
PICTURES: Personal Best, Risky Business, Lost in America, Little Shop of Horrors, Beetlejuice (exec. prod.).

GELBART, LARRY: Writer. b. Chicago, IL, Feb. 25, 1925. Began at 16 writing material for Danny Thomas on Fanny Brice Show. Followed by Duffy's Tavern, shaping routines for Eddie Cantor, Bob Hope, Jack Paar. Was one of Sid Caesar's stable of comedy writers on Show of Shows.
THEATER: The Conquering Hero, A Funny Thing Happened on the Way to the Forum (with Burt Shevlove); Sly Fox, Mastergate, City of Angels.
PICTURES: The Notorious Landlady, The Wrong Box, Not With My Wife You Don't, Oh, God!, Movie. Movie; Neighbors, Tootsie (co-s.p.), Blame It on Rio (exec. prod., co.-s.p.).
TELEVISION: M*A*S*H (Emmy, 1974, also co-prod.), United States, Karen.

GELFAN, GREGORY: Executive. Was entertainment atty. with two firms before joining Paramount Pictures in 1983 as dir. of business affairs. 1985, named v.p., business affairs, for M.P. Group of Paramount; 1989 promoted to sr. v.p. in chg. of business affairs.

GELLER, BRIAN L.: Executive. b. New York, NY, Feb. 3, 1948. e. Queens Coll. Entered industry with Columbia Pictures as sls. trainee in 1966, leaving in 1968 to go with American Intl. Pictures as asst. branch mgr. In 1969 joined Cinemation Industries as eastern div. sls. mgr.; 1978, left to become gen. sls. mr. of NMD Film Distributing Co. 1982, named dir. of dist., Mature Pictures Corp. 1983, gen. sls. mgr., Export Pix.; with Cinema Group as east. sls. mgr.; joined Scotti Brothers Pictures as national sales, mgr.
Member: Motion Picture Bookers Club of N.Y.; Variety Tent 35, Motion Picture Pioneers.

GENDECE, BRIAN K.: Producer, Executive. b. St. Louis, MO. e. Drury Coll., Springfield, MO. 1981–85, Director of Business Affairs, Weinstein/Skyfield Productions and Skyfield Management. 1986–87, dir. of business affairs,Cannon Films; 1987–88, dir. creative affairs, Cannon Films; 1989 pres., Sheer Entertainment.
PICTURES: Runaway Train, Salsa, Rope Dancin'.
STAGE: Jack Klugman as Lyndon.
VIDEO: Bad Habits, Shape Up with Arnold, Laura Branigan's Your Love.

GEORGE, GEORGE LOUIS: Director. b. Moscow, Russia, July 31, 1907. e. U. of Paris, law. Began as cutter, later asst. dir., French prods. To Hollywood 1935 as corresp. French pubs. Re-entered prod. 1939 as asst. dir. & prod. French version of The Four Hundred Million; in similar capacity numerous French versions of Hollywood prods. thereafter. In 1942 asst. prod. Our Russian Front. Became assoc. Natl. Film Board of Canada in prod. war information films; also dir. The Labor Front for World in Action series. In 1944 dir. University Town for Co-ord. Inter-Amer. Affairs; 1946–49 dir. 16 films for Signal Corps Photo. Center, Astoria, L.I., incl. Acad. Award winner Toward Independence. In 1949 dir. in TV, also Women of Tomorrow, WB. 1950, dir. in Israel for Palestine Films; dir., prod., TV & documentary films, 1950–55; exec. secr., Screen Directors International Guild, 1956–63; admin., SDIG Trust Fund, 1963–67; member, Natl. Bd., Directors Guild of America 1966–69; member Eastern Directors Council, DGA 1966–89; pres. Film & TV Book Club, Inc. 1967–69. Currently freelancing.

GEORGE, GEORGE W.: Writer, Producer. b. New York, NY, Feb. 8, 1920. e. Williams Coll. U.S. Navy, 1941–44; screenwriter since 1948. President, Jenso Enterprises, dev. theatrical and m.p. projects.
PICTURES: *Writer:* Bodyguard, The Nevadan, Woman on Pier 13, Peggy Mystery Submarine, Red Mountain Experiment, Alcatraz, Fight Town, Smoke Signal, Desert Sands, Uranium Boom, Halliday Brand, Doc, The James Dean Story, The Two Little Bears, *Prod.:* The James Dean Story, A Matter of Innocence, Twisted Nerve, Hello-Goodbye, Night Watch, Rich Kids, My Dinner with Andre.
STAGE: *Prod.:* Dylan, Any Wednesday, Ben Franklin in Paris, The Great Indoors, Happily Never After, Night Watch, Via Galactica, Bedroom Farce.
TELEVISION: Climax, Screen Gems, Loretta Young Show, The Rifleman, Peter Gunn, The Real McCoys, Adventures in Paradise, Hong Kong, Follow the Sun.

GEORGE, LOUIS: Executive. Pres. & chief executive officer, Arista Films, Inc. b. Karavas, Kyrenia, Cyprus, June 7, 1935. e. Kyrenia Business Acad., Cyprus (honored 1951). Emigrated to U.S. in 1952. After brief stint in Foreign Exchange Dept. of City National Bank, New York, served in U.S. Army, 1953–55. Entered industry in 1956 as theatre manager with Loew's Theatres in N.Y. metro area, managing Metropolitan, Triboro, New Rochelle, between 1958–66. In 1966 joined MGM as dir. of intl. theatre dept. In 1969 promoted to dir. of world-wide non-theatrical sales. From 1972 to 1974 served as regional dir. of MGM Far East operations. In 1974 left MGM to establish Arista Films, Inc., an indep. prod./dist. co. Also v.p., American Film Marketing Assn.
PICTURES: Slaughterhouse Rock, Buying Time, Violent Zone (exec. prod.).

GEORGE, SUSAN: Actress, Producer. b. Surrey, England, 1950. m. actor-prod. Simon MacCorkindale. e. Corona Acad. m.p. debut Million Dollar Brain, 1965.
PICTURES: The Sorcerers, Up the Junction, The Strange Affair, The Looking Glass War, All Neat in Black Stockings, Twinky, Spring and Port Wine, Eye Witness, Die Screaming Marianne, Fright, Straw Dogs, Sonny and I, Dr. Jekyll and Mr. Hyde, Dirty Mary Crazy Larry, Mandingo, Out of Season, A Small Town in Texas, Tiger Shark, Tomorrow Never Comes, Venom, A Texas Legend, House Where Evil Dwells, Jigsaw Man, The White Stallion, Stealing Heaven (exec. prod.), That Summer of White Roses (also exec. prod.).
TELEVISION: Swallows and Amazons, Adam's Apple, Weaver's Green, Compensation Alice, The Right Attitude, Dracula, Lamb to the Slaughter, Royal Jelly, Masquerade, Czechmate, Hotel, Blacke's Magic, Jack the Ripper.

GERALD, HELEN: Actress. b. New York, NY, Aug. 13. e. U. of Southern California, 1948. Stage: Italian Teatro D'Arte, Les Miserables, The Civil Death, Feudalism.
PICTURES: The Gay Cavalier, The Trap, Tarzan and the Leopard Woman, Cigarette Girl, Meet Miss Bobby Socks, G.I. War Brides, Gentleman's Agreement, A Bell for Adano, Tomorrow Is Forever, Janie, Grand Prix, The Sandpiper, Make Mine Mink, Best of Everything.
TELEVISION: Robert Montgomery Presents, Frontiers of Faith, Valiant Lady, Kraft Theatre, Gangbusters, Adventures of The Falcon, Schlitz Playhouse of Stars, This Is the Answer, Man from U.N.C.L.E., Run for Your Life, Perry Mason.

GERARD, GIL: Actor. b. Little Rock, AK, Jan. 23, 1940. e. Arkansas State Teachers Coll. Appeared in over 400 TV commercials. On stage in I Do! I Do!
PICTURES: Some of My Best Friends Are (1971), Man on a Swing, Hooch (also co-prod.), Airport '77, Buck Rogers in the 25th Century.
TELEVISION: Series: The Doctors, Buck Rogers in the 25th Century, Sidekicks. Movies: Washington Mistress, Not Just Another Affair, Help Wanted: Male, Hear No Evil, Johnny Blue (pilot), For Love or Money, Stormin' Home, International Airport.

GERARD, LILLIAN: Publicist, Writer. Publicity, Rialto Theatre, 1936; publicity-adv. Filmarte Theatre, 1938, Gerard Associates, 1938–47; V.P. and managing dir. of Paris Theatre, 1948–62; publicity-adv. dir., Rugoff Theatres, 1962. Film consultant to Times Films, Lopert Films, Landau Co., 1962–65. Exec. secy. to the National Soc. of Film Critics, 1966–68. Adjunct

Professor, Film, 1968–70, Columbia U., Sch. of the Arts, Special Projects Co-Ordinator, Museum of Modern Art, 1968–80. Contributor to American Film. Published by American Film Inst. Now associated with Philip Gerard in Gerard Associates.

GERARD, PHILIP R.: Executive. b. New York, NY, Aug. 23, 1913. e. City Coll. of New York, B.B.A. 1935; Columbia U.. Publicity dir. Mayer-Burstyn 1936–39; Gerard Associates, 1939–41; in public relations U.S. War Dept. 1942–44; with MGM 1944–48; with Universal Pictures since 1948; Eastern pub. mgr., 1950–59; Eastern ad. and pub. dir., Dec. 1959; N.Y. Production Exec., 1968–76. As of Jan. 1, 1977 formed Gerard Associates, film consultants on marketing, production and acquisitions. N.Y.C. Advisory Council of CSS/RSVP (Retired Seniors Volunteer Program); Community Service Society. Member: Visitor's Day Comm., New York Hospital.

GERBER, DAVID: Executive. b. Brooklyn, NY. e. U. of the Pacific. m actress Laraine Stephens. Joined Batten, Barton, Durstine and Osborn ad agency in N.Y. as TV supvr. Left to become sr. v.p. of TV at General Artists Corp. In Jan., 1956, named v.p. in chg. sales at 20th-Fox TV where sold and packaged over 50 prime-time series and specials. Entered indep. prod. with The Ghost and Mrs. Muir, followed by Nanny and the Professor. In 1970 was exec. prod. of The Double Deckers, children's series made in England. In 1971 was exec. prod. of Cade's County (CBS). In 1972 he joined Columbia Pictures Television as an indep. prod., 1974 was named exec. v.p. worldwide prod. for CPT. 1976 returned to indep. prod. 1985, joined MGM/UA TV broadcasting group in chg. world-wide prod. 1986 named president, MGM/UA Television. Nov., 1988, appt. chmn and CEO, MGM/UA Television Prods. group.
TELEVISION: exec. prod.: Cade's County, Police Story (Emmy, best dramatic series), Police Woman, The Lindbergh Kidnapping Case, Joe Forrester, The Quest and Gibbsville, To Kill a Cop, Power, Medical Story, Born Free, Beulah Land, The Night the City Screamed, Follow the North Star.

GERBER, MICHAEL H.: Executive. b. New York, NY, Feb. 6, 1944. e. St. Johns U., B.A., 1969; St. Johns U. School of Law, J.D., 1969. Atty, for Screen Gems, 1969–71; asst. secy. & asst. to gen. counsel, Columbia Pictures Industries, 1971–74; corporate counsel and secretary, Allied Artists Pictures, 1974, v.p. Corporate affairs, Allied Artists, 1978; v.p., business affairs, Viacom Intl.

GERE, RICHARD: Actor. b. Philadelphia, PA, Aug. 29, 1949. e. U. of Massachusetts. Started acting in college; later joined Provincetown Playhouse and Seattle Repertory Theatre. Composed music for productions of these groups. Appeared on Broadway in Grease, Soon, Habeas Corpus, Bent, A Midsummer Night's Dream (Lincoln Center); and in London in Taming of the Shrew with Young Vic. Off-Bdwy in Killer's Head.
PICTURES: Report to the Commissioner, Baby Blue Marine, Looking for Mr. Goodbar, Days of Heaven, Bloodbrothers, Yanks, American Gigolo, An Officer and a Gentleman, Breathless, Beyond the Limits, The Cotton Club, King David, Power, No Mercy, Miles From Home, Internal Affairs.
TELEVISION: Kojak, Strike Force (movie), D.H.P. (pilot).

GERETY, T. MICHAEL: Executive. b. Rockville Center, NY, Oct. 30, 1942. U.S., Navy, 1961–64. Started industry career in Chicago with MGM as regional adv/pub. repr.; transferred to Atlanta in same capacity, 1966 and then to Dallas, 1967–70. Joined Durwood Theatres in Dallas in 1971 as div. operations mgr. In 1972 returned to MGM as south west div. dir. adv./pub. in Dallas. Moved to MGM Studios in 1973 as asst. natl. adv. coordinator. In 1974 joined American International as dir. of cooperative adv./exploit. In 1976 named exec. dir. of adv./pub. for AIP. In 1980 joined the Milton I. Moritz Co., film marketing firm, as v.p. In 1981, named v.p., Market Relay Systems, a mktg./communications co. 1982–83, pres., The Newslink Corp. (videotext news service). Joined Hanson & Schwam p.r., 1985. Member: Academy of MP. Arts & Sciences.

GERTZ, IRVING: Composer, Musical director. b. Providence, RI, May 19, 1915. e. Providence Coll. of Music, 1934–37. Assoc. with Providence Symph. Orch., comp. choral works for Catholic Choral Soc.; music dept., Columbia, 1939–41; U.S. Army, 1941–46; then comp. arranger, mus. dir. for many cos. incl. Columbia, U-I, NBC, 20th Century Fox.
PICTURES: Bandits of Corsica, Gun Belt, Long Wait, The Fiercest Heart, First Travelling Saleslady, Fluffy, Nobody's Perfect, Marines, Let's Go! It Came from Outer Space, The Man from Bitter Ridge, Posse from Hell, The Creature Walks Among Us, The Incredible Shrinking Man, Hell Bent for Leather, Seven Ways from Sundown, Francis Joins the WACS, Raw Edge, East of Sumatra, A Day of Fury, To Hell and Back, Cult of the Cobra, Plunder Road, Top Gun, Tombstone Express, The Alligator People, Khyber Patrol, The Wizard of Baghdad.
Record album (Dot Records) Leaves of Grass; published works for mixed voices; Fluffy, feature, Universal. Marines, Let's Go! feature, 20th Century Fox Serenata for String Quartet, Divertimento for String Orchestra, Tableau for Orchestra.
TELEVISION: Orig. theme & scores: America, The Golden Voyage, Across the Seven Seas, The Legend of Jesse James, Daniel Boone, Voyage to the Bottom of the Sea, Peyton Place, Land of the Giants, Lancer, Medical Center, Boutade for Wood-Wind Quartet, Salute to All Nations, A Village Fair, Liberty! Liberte! (for symphony orchestra).

GERTZ, JAMI: Actress. Won a nationwide talent search competition headed by Normal Lear to cast TV comedy series Square Pegs. Following series studied at NYU drama school. Los Angeles theater includes Out of Gas on Lovers' Leap and Come Back Little Sheba. Also appeared in the Julian Lennon music video Stick Around.
PICTURES: Endless Love (debut, 1981), Alphabet City, Mischief, Sixteen Candles, Crossroads, Quicksilver, Solarbabies, The Lost Boys, Less Than Zero, Renegades, Listen to Me, Silence Like Glass, The Boyfriend School.

GETTY, ESTELLE: Actress. b. New York, NY, July 25, 1923. e. attended New School for Social Research. Trained for stage with Gerald Russak and at Herbert Berghof Studios. Worked as comedienne on Borscht Belt circuit and as actress with Yiddish theatre. Founder Fresh Meadows Community theater. Also worked as acting teacher and coach and secretary. Author, If I Knew What I Know Now . . . So What? (1988).
THEATER: The Divorce of Judy and Jane (off-Bdwy debut, 1971), Widows and Children First, Table Settings, Demolition of Hannah Fay, Never Too Old, A Box of Tears, Hidden Corners, I Don't Know Why I'm Screaming, Under the Bridge There's a Lonely Place, Light Up the Sky, Pocketful of Posies, Fits and Starts, Torch Song Trilogy (off-Bdwy, Bdwy and tour, Drama Desk nom., 1982, Helen Hayes Award, best supp. performer in a touring show).
PICTURES: Tootsie, The Chosen, Mask, Protocol, Mannequin.
TELEVISION: Series: The Golden Girls (Golden Globe Award). Movies: No Man's Land, Victims for Victims: the Teresa Saldana Story, Copacabana. Guest: Cagney and Lacey, Nurse, Baker's Dozen, One of the Boys, Fantasy Island.

GETTY, J. RONALD: Producer. b. Berlin, Germany, Dec. 19, 1929. e. Zurich U., Heidelberg U., U. of Southern California. Prior to entering m.p. industry was oil executive, Tidewater Oil Co., mgn. dir. Veedol GmbH, 1955; Getty Oil, Hamburg, 1954–61; pres. & chmn. of bd., Veedol Petroleum Int'l, Switzerland, 1961–69; dir., Huiles Veedol France, 1961–69. President & Chmn. of bd., Getty Picture Corp.; pres. & chmn., Getty Labs, Inc.; dir., Home Theatre Network.
PICTURES: Flare Up, Zeppelin, Shelia.

GETZ, DON: Executive. b. Chicago, IL. March 28, 1920, Early career in radio until 1952. 1952: Ent. dist. with GBD Int. Releasing handling US and foreign dist. for Mr. Hulot's Holiday, Jour de Fete, Diabolique, Holiday for Henrietta, Ali Baba. 1957: formed Getz-Buck Productions and prod. number of films in UK and France. 1961: formed Playpont Films Ltd., for prod. and dist. of TV and theatrical films in UK and Continent. 1963: formed Artxo Films with Artie Shaw to dist. imported films in the USA. 1964: joined Official Films Inc. as vice-pres. Int. 1968: consultant to Humphries Group. 1971: reactivated Playpont Films as sales agent for foreign producers handling The Great Catherine, Foxtrot, Caligula, One Away, Disappearance, The Illusionist, The Pointsman, Turkish Delight, The Lift, Chain Reaction, Year of the Quiet Sun, Shadow of Victory, Istanbul, Iris, Good Hope, One Month Later, Great Rock 'n Roll Swindle.

GIANNINI, GIANCARLO: Actor. b. Spezia, Italy, Aug. 1, 1942. Acquired degree in electronics but immediately after school enrolled at Acad. for Drama in Rome. Cast by Franco Zeffirelli as Romeo at age of 20. Subsequently appeared in a play also directed by Zeffirelli, Two Plus Two No Longer Make Four, written by Lina Wertmuller.
PICTURES: Love and Anarchy, The Seduction of Mimi, Swept Away by an Unusual Destiny in the Blue Sea of August, Seven Beauties . . . That's What They Call Him, How Funny Can Sex Be?, A Night Full of Rain, The Innocent, Buone Notizie (also prod.), Revenge, Travels with Anita, Lili Marleen, Lovers and Liars, La Vita e Bella, Picone Sent Me, Immortal Bachelor, American Dreamer, Fever Pitch, Saving Grace, New York Stories (Life Without Zoe), I Picari, The Uncle, Snack Bar Budapest, Oh King, Blood Red, Brown Bread Sandwiches, Killing Time, Short Cut.
TELEVISION: Sins.

GIBBS, DAVID: Executive. b. 1944. Ent. motion picture industry 1961, Kodak research, worked as a photographer for Kodak 1963–66. Lectured at Harrow College of Technology and Kodak Photographic School until 1972. Left Kodak, 1975, after three years as a market specialist to join Filmatic Laboratories. Appt. asst. man. director, 1977, becoming chmn. and man. director, 1989. Member of RTS, SMPTE and

IVCA. Past Chmn. BISFA, currently President of the British Kinematograph, Sound and Television Society.

GIBBS, MARLA: Actress. b. Chicago, IL, June 14, 1931. e. Cortez Peters Business School, Chicago. Worked as receptionist, switchboard operator, travel consultant (1963–74) before co-starring as Florence Johnston on the Jeffersons (1974–85). Formed Marla Gibbs Enterprises, Los Angeles, 1978. Member of CA State Assembly, 1980. Image Award NAACP, 1979–83.
TELEVISION: Series: The Jeffersons, Florence, 227. Movies: You Can't Take It With You, Tell Me Where It Hurts, The Moneychanger, Nobody's Child.
PICTURES: Black Belt Jones, Sweet Jesus, Preacher Man.

GIBSON, HENRY: Actor. b. Germantown, PA, Sept. 21, 1935. e. Catholic U. of America. Appeared as child actor with stock companies, 1943–57; Bdwy. debut in My Mother, My Father and Me, 1962.
PICTURES: The Nutty Professor, Kiss Me Stupid, Charlotte's Web, The Long Goodbye, Nashville (best supp. actor, Nat'l Soc. Film Critics, 1975), The Last Remake of Beau Geste, Kentucky Fried Movie, The Incredible Shrinking Woman, The Blue Brothers, Tulips, Health, A Perfect Couple, Monster in the Closet, Brenda Starr, Inner Space, Switching Channels, The 'Burbs, Night Visitor.
TELEVISION: Laugh-In co-star (1968–72). Movies: Every Girl Should Have One, Escape from Bogen County, The Night They Took Miss Beautiful, Evil Roy Slade, Amateur Night at the Dixie Bar & Grill, For the Love of It, Jailhouse Grab, Long Gone, Slow Burn, Around the World in 80 Days.

GIBSON, MEL: Actor. b. Peekskill, NY, Jan. 3, 1956. Emigrated in 1968 to Australia with family. Attended Nat'l Inst. of Dramatic Art in Sydney; in 2nd yr. was cast in his first film, Summer City (1977). Graduated from NIDA, 1977. Joined South Australian Theatre Co. in 1978, appearing in Oedipus, Henry IV, Cedoona. Other plays include Romeo and Juliet, No Names No Pack Drill, On Our Selection, Waiting for Godot, Death of a Salesman.
PICTURES: Summer City, Mad Max, Tim, Attack Force Z, Gallipoli, The Road Warrior (Mad Max II), The Year of Living Dangerously, The Bounty, The River, Mrs. Soffel, Mad Max Beyond Thunderdome, Lethal Weapon, Tequila Sunrise, Lethal Weapon 2, Bird on a Wire, Hamlet, Air America.
TELEVISION: Series: The Sullivans, The Oracle (Aust.) Special: The Ultimate Stuntman: A Tribute to Dar Robinson. Guest host: Saturday Night Live.

GIELGUD, SIR JOHN: Actor. b. London, England, Apr. 14, 1904. e. Westminster Sch., Lady Benson's Sch. (dram.), London; Royal Acad. of Dramatic Art. Knighted, 1953. Autobiography: Early Stages (1983).
THEATRE: Began stage career in Shakespearean roles; on London stage also in the Constant Nymph, The Good Companions, Dear Octopus, The Importance of Being Earnest, Dear Brutus, etc., various Shakespearean seasons, London & N.Y. 1988: The Best of Friends.
PICTURES: Insult (Brit. film debut, 1932); later (Brit.) films The Good Companions, Secret Agent, The Prime Minister, Other films: Julius Caesar, Richard III, Around the World in 80 Days, Barretts of Wimpole Street, Becket, The Loved One, Chimes at Midnight, St. Joan, Sebastian, The Assignment, Charge of the Light Brigade, The Shoes of the Fisherman, Oh, What a Lovely War, Eagle in a Cage, Lost Horizon, 11 Harrowhouse, Gold, Murder on the Orient Express, Providence, Portrait of the Artists as a Young Man, Joseph Andrews, Murder by Decree, The Human Factor, The Elephant Man, The Formula, Sphinx, Lion of the Desert, Arthur, Chariots of Fire, Priest of Love, Gandhi, The Wicked Lady, Scandalous, Wagner, Appointment with Death, Whistle Blower; Bluebeard, Bluebeard; Arthur 2 on the Rocks, Getting It Right, Loser Takes All.
TELEVISION: A Day by the Sea, The Browning Version (U.S.), The Rehearsal, Great Acting, Ages of Man, Mayfly and the Frog, Cherry Orchard, Ivanov, From Chekhov With Love, St. Joan, Good King Charles' Golden Days, Conversation at Night, Hassan, Deliver Us from Evil, Heartbreak House, Brideshead Revisited, The Canterville Ghost; The Hunchback of Notre Dame; Inside the Third Reich; Marco Polo; The Scarlet and the Black; The Master of Ballantrae; The Far Pavillions; Camille; Romance on the Orient Express; Funny, You Don't Look 200, Oedipus the King, A Man For All Seasons, War and Remembrance. Special: John Gielgud: An Actor's Life.

GIGLIOTTI, DONNA: Executive. b. Utica, NY, Nov. 30, 1954. e. Sarah Lawrence Coll., A.B., 1976. Assistant to dir. Martin Scorsese, 1978–80; v.p., acquisitions, United Artists Classics 1980–82; co-founder, Orion Classics and v.p., acquisitions 1983–present. Knighted Chevalier des Arts et Lettres of the French Republic, 1987.

GIL, DAVID: Producer. b. Tel Aviv, Israel, Jan. 24, 1930. e. U. of Jerusalem. m. Joan Andre. After commission in Israeli Army worked for Israeli Embassy, Paris, 1950–52; Israeli Film ind., 1953–55; prod. educational films, 1955–61; headed Gilart Productions, 1962–68; foreign sales dir., Commonwealth United, 1968; prod. Guess What We Learned in School Today, Joe, A Journey Through Rosebud, A Change in the Wind, Gas Pump Girls.

GILBERT, ARTHUR N.: Producer. b. Detroit, MI, Oct. 17, 1920. Lt., U.S.M.C., 1941–45. e. U. of Chicago, 1946. Special Agent, FBI, 1946–53; world sales dir., Gen. Motors, Cadillac Div., 1953–59; investments in mot. pictures and hotel chains, 1959–64; exec. prod., Mondo Hollywood, 1965; exec. prod. Jeannie-Wife Child, 1966; assoc. prod., The Golden Breed, 1967; commissioned rank of Colonel U.S.M.C., 1968; 1970–80, exec. prod. Jaguar Pictures Corp; Columbia, 1981–86; Indi Pic. Corp. Also account exec. and v.p. Pacific Western Tours.
PICTURES: The Glory Stompers, Fire Grass, Cycle Savages, Bigfoot, Incredible Transplant, Balance of Evil.

GILBERT, BRUCE: Producer. b. Los Angeles, CA, March 28, 1947. e. U. of California. Pursued film interests at Berkeley's Pacific Film Archive; in summer involved in production in film dept. of San Francisco State U. Founded progressive pre-school in Bay Area. Became story editor in feature film division of Cine-Artists; involved in several projects, including Aloha, Bobby and Rose. Partnered with Jane Fonda and IPC Films, Inc. President, American Filmworks, 1980–
PICTURES: Coming Home (assoc. prod.); The China Syndrome (exec. prod.); Nine to Five (prod.); On Golden Pond (prod.); Rollover (prod.); The Morning After (prod.); Another World (dir.).
TELEVISION: Nine to Five (series-exec. prod.); The Dollmaker (movie-exec. prod.).

GILBERT, LEWIS: Producer, Writer, Director, Former Actor. b. London, England, Mar. 6, 1920. In RAF, W.W.II. Screen debut, 1932; asst. dir. (1930–39) with London Films, Assoc. British, Mayflower, RKO-Radio; from 1939–44 attached U.S. Air Corps Film Unit (asst. dir., Target for Today). In 1944 joined G.B.I. as writer and dir. In 1948, Gainsborough Pictures as writer, dir., 1949; Argyle Prod. 1950; under contract Nettlefold Films, Ltd. as dir.
PICTURES: Under One Roof, I Want to Get Married, Haunting Melody, Director: The Little Ballerina, Marry Me (s.p. only), Once a Sinner, Scarlet Thread, There Is Another Sun, Time Gentlemen Please, Emergency Call, Cosh Boy, Johnny on the Run, Albert R.N., The Good Die Young, The Sea Shall Not Have Them, Reach for the Sky, Cast a Dark Shadow, The Admirable Crichton, Carve Her Name with Pride, A Cry from the Street, Ferry to Hong Kong, Sink the Bismarck, Light Up the Sky, The Greengage Summer, H.M.S. Defiant, The Patriots, Spare the Rod, Alfie, The Seventh Dawn, You Only Live Twice, The Adventurers, Friends, Paul & Michelle, Operation Daybreak, Seven Nights in Japan, The Spy Who Loved Me, Moonraker, Educating Rita, Not Quite Paradise, Shirley Valentine (also prod.).

GILBERT, MELISSA: Actress. b. Los Angeles, May 8, 1964. m. actor Bo Brinkman. Made debut at age of 3 in TV commercial. Comes from show business family: father, late comedian Paul Gilbert; mother, former dancer-actress Barbara Crane. NY Off-Bdwy debut A Shayna Madel (1987).
TELEVISION: Gunsmoke, Emergency, Tenafly, The Hanna-Barbera Happy Hour, Christmas Miracle in Caufield U.S.A., Love Boat, Little House on the Prairie (regular). Movies: The Miracle Worker, Splendor in the Grass, Choices of the Heart, Choices, Penalty Phase, Family Secrets, Killer Instincts.
PICTURE: Sylvester (debut), Ice House.

GILER, DAVID: Producer, Writer, Director. b. New York, NY. Son of Bernie Giler, screen and TV writer. Began writing in teens; first work an episode for ABC series, The Gallant Men. Feature film career began as writer on Myra Breckenridge (1970).
PICTURES: Writer: The Parallax View, Fun with Dick and Jane, The Blackbird (also dir.), Southern Comfort (also prod.), Alien (prod. only), Rustlers' Rhapsody (prod. only), Let It Ride (prod. only).
TELEVISION: Writer: The Kraft Theatre, Burke's Law, The Man from U.N.C.L.E., The Girl from U.N.C.L.E., Tales From the Crypt (exec. prod.).

GILFORD, JACK: Actor. r.n. Jacob Gellman. b. New York, NY, July 25, 1907. m. actress-producer Madeline Lee. Made first stage appearances in amateur night performances as stand-up comic at Cafe Society Downtown 1939, and Cafe Society Uptown, 1946. Wrote own material, specializing in imitations. Author 170 Years of Show Business, with wife and Zero and Kate Mostel. 1987: returned to cabaret act at the Ballroom, NY.
THEATER: (Selected NY credits): Frank Fay Vaudeville (debut, 1939); Meet the People, They Should Have Stood in Bed, Count Me In; Meet the People; Alive and Kicking; The Live Wire; Die Fledermaus (Met. Opera); The World of Sholom Aleichem; The Passion of Gross; Once Over Lightly (revue); The Diary of Anne Frank; Romanoff and Juliet; Drink

to Me Only; Look After Lulu; Once Upon a Mattress; The Tenth Man; A Funny Thing Happened on the Way to the Forum; Cabaret; Three Men on a Horse; No, No Nanette; Sly Fox; The Supporting Cast; The World of Sholom Aleichem (1982); Of Thee I Sing; Let Them Eat Cake (Brooklyn Acad. of Music).

PICTURES: Hey, Rookie (debut, 1944); The Reckless Age; Main Street to Broadway; Mister Budwing; A Funny Thing Happened on the Way to the Forum; Enter Laughing; Who's Minding the Mint; The Incident; Harry and Walter Go to New York; Catch-22; They Might Be Giants; Save the Tiger; Cheaper to Keep Her; Wholly Moses; Cave Man; Cocoon; Arthur 2 On the Rocks; Cocoon II: The Return; The Island on Bird Street.

TELEVISION: The Arrow Show (1948); Paul Sand in Friends and Lovers; Apple Pie (1974–75); The Defenders; All in the Family; Rhoda; Soap; Taxi; Trapper John M.D., Tattingers. Specials: The World of Sholom Aleichem; Once Upon a Mattress; Of Thee I Sing; The Cowboy and the Tiger; the Very Special Jack Gilford Special; Anna to the Infinite Power; Twigs. Movies: Seventh Avenue; Hostage Flight; Goldie and the Bower Go to Hollywood.

GILLASPY, RICHARD M.: Producer, Director. b. St. Louis, MO, Dec. 10, 1927. Joined NBC in New York as exec. trainee, 1947; headed Marine Corps Radio, 1952–54; rejoined NBC-TV as stage mgr., became prod. dir.; won Emmy Award, 1960, for Nixon-Khrushchev debate; pres., Seven League Productions, 1961–63, owner, Radio Station WIII, Homestead, Fla., 1963–67; freelance prod.-dir., 1967–70; v.p. of Ivan Tors Studios, N. Miami, 1970–72; pres. RMG Productions, 1972.

GILLIAM, TERRY: Writer, Director, Actor, Animator. b. Minneapolis, MN, Nov. 22, 1940. e. Occidental Coll. Freelance writer and illustrator for various magazines and ad agencies before moving to London. Member, Monty Python's Flying Circus (1969–76).

PICTURES: And Now for Something Completely Different (animator), Monty Python and the Holy Grail (co-dir.), Jabberwocky (dir.); Life of Brian (also s.p.), Time Bandits (prod., dir., co-s.p.), Monty Python's The Meaning of Life (s.p., act.), Brazil (s.p., dir.), The Adventures of Baron Munchausen (dir., co-s.p.).

GILLIAT, LESLIE: Producer. b. New Malden, England, 1917. e. Epsom Coll. Ent. m.p. ind. 1935.

PICTURES: Only Two Can Play, The Amorous Prawn, Joey Boy, The Great St. Trinians Train Robbery, A Dandy in Aspic, The Virgin Soldiers, The Buttercup Chain, Endless Night, Priest of Love (prod. supvr.), The Zany Adventures of Robin Hood (assoc. prod.).

GILLIN, DONALD T.: Executive. b. Council Bluffs, IA, June 17, 1914; e. U. of Minnesota., bus. adm., 1929–32. Sls., Warner Bros., 1932–39; W.W.II; home office sup., Warner Bros., 1946–48; sls. exec., Universal, 1948–50; v.p., gen. sls. mgr., mgr., Sol Lesser, 1950–59; establ., Donald T. Gillin Inc., producers' rep., 1960. Muchnic-Gillin Internat'l, Inc., 1961; Producers' Representatives, Inc., 1967.

GILLIS, ANNE: Actress. r.n. Alma Mable O'Connor. b. Little Rock, AK, Feb. 12, 1927. Screen debut 1936 in The Garden of Allah; thereafter in number child roles.

PICTURES: King of Hockey, Off to the Races, The Californian, The Adventures of Tom Sawyer, Peck's Bad Boy with the Circus, Little Orphan Annie, Edison the Man, All This and Heaven Too, Janie; A Wave, a Wac, a Marine; The Cheaters, Gay Blades, Big Town After Dark, 2001: A Space Odyssey.

GILMORE, WILLIAM S.: Producer. b. Los Angeles, CA, March 10, 1934. e. U. of California at Berkeley. Started career as film cutter before becoming asst. dir. and prod. mgr. at Universal Studios, where worked on 20 feature films. Headed prod. for Mirisch Co. in Europe; then to Zanuck/Brown Co. as exec. in chg. prod. Produced several TV movies for EMI-TV. Sr. v.p./prod. of Filmways Pictures, supervising literary development, prod. and post-prod.

PICTURES: Swashbuckler (assoc. prod.), The Last Remake of Beau Geste, Rock n' Roll Hotel, Tough Enough, Deadly Blessing, Defiance, Against All Odds, Return of the Living Dead Part II, Midnight Run.

TELEVISION: Just You and Me, One in a Million—The Ron Leflore Story, The Legend of Walks Far Woman, S.O.S. Titanic, Another Woman's Child.

GILROY, FRANK: Writer, Director. b. New York, NY, Oct. 13, 1925. e. Dartmouth; postgrad. Yale School of Drama. TV writer: Playhouse 90, US Steel Hour, Omnibus, Kraft Theatre, Lux Video Theater, Studio One. Bdwy. playwright; won Pulitzer Prize & Tony for The Subject Was Roses, 1965. Other plays: Who'll Save the Plowboy?; The Only Game in Town; Present Tense; The Housekeeper; Last Licks. Novels: Private (with Ruth Gilroy); Little Ego; From Noon to 3.

PICTURES: Writer: The Fastest Gun Alive; The Subject Was Roses; The Gallant Hours; The Only Game in Town; Desperate Characters (also dir., prod.); From Noon Till Three (also dir.); Once in Paris (also dir.); The Gig (also dir.), The Luckiest Man in the World (also dir.).

TELEVISION: Dir.: Nero Wolfe, Turning Point of Jim Maloy.

GIMBEL, ROGER: Producer. b. March 11, 1925. e. Yale. Began television prod. career as copy and creative chief of RCA Victor TV, then became assoc. prod. of the Tonight Show for NBC; named head of prog. dev. of NBC daytime programming; then prod. of the 90-minute NBC Tonight Specials, including The Jack Paar Show and the Ernie Kovacs Show. Became prod. and co-packager of the Glen Campbell Goodtime Hour for CBS, 1969; v.p. in chg. of prod. for Tomorrow Entertainment, 1971. Formed his own prod. co., Roger Gimbel's Tomorrow Enterprises, Inc., 1975; prod. Minstrel Man. Became U.S. pres. of EMI-TV, 1976. Received special personal Emmy as exec. prod. of War of the Children, 1975. Produced 33 movies for TV under the EMI banner and won 18 Emmys. In January, 1984, EMI-TV became The Peregrine Producers Group, Inc., of which he was pres. & COO. 1987, spun off Roger Gimbel Prods. as an independent film co; 1988–89, president-exec. prod., Carolco/Gimbel Productions, Inc.

TELEVISION: The Autobiography of Miss Jane Pittman, Born Innocent, Birds of Prey, Brand New Life, Gargoyles, Glass House, In This House of Brede, I Heard the Owl Call My Name, I Love You, Good-Bye, Larry, Miles to Go, Queen of the Stardust Ballroom, Tell Me Where It Hurts, Things in Their Season, War of the Children (Emmy award, Outstanding Single Program, Drama or Comedy), Aurora, Rockabye, Blackout, Apology, Montana.

GINGOLD, DAN: Freelance Executive Producer, Producer, Director. Credits include all types live and film prod. Specialist in Special Events and Documentary. Awards include Emmy, Ohio State U., DuPont/Columbia U., Ed Murrow, Assoc. Press, San Francisco State, Cine Golden Eagle, NY Int'l. Film Fest. Asst prof., School of Journalism, U. of Southern California.

GINNA, ROBERT EMMETT, JR.: Producer, Writer. b. New York, NY, Dec. 3, 1925. e. U. of Rochester, Harvard U., M.A. In U.S. Navy, W.W.II. Journalist for Life, Scientific American, Horizon, 1950–55; 1958–61, contributor to many magazines. Staff writer, producer, director NBC-TV, 1955–58; v.p., Sextant, Inc., dir., Sextant Films Ltd., 1961–64; Founded Windward Productions, Inc., Windward Film Productions, Ltd., 1965. Active in publishing 1974–82; sr. ed. People; ed. in chief, Little Brown; asst. mging., Life. Resumed pres., Windward Prods, Inc., 1982; publishing consultant.

PICTURES: Young Cassidy (co-prod.); The Last Challenge (co-s.p.); Before Winter Comes (prod.); Brotherly Love (prod.).

GINSBERG, SIDNEY: Executive. b. New York, NY, Oct. 26, 1920. e. City Coll. of New York, 1938. Entered m.p. ind., as asst. mgr., Loew's Theatres; joined Trans-Lux 1943, as thea. mgr.; film booker; helped form Trans-Lux Distributing Corp., 1956; asst. to pres., Trans-Lux Dist. Corp.; asst. vice-pres., Trans-Lux Picture, Distributing and TV Corp., 1961, V.P. Trans-Lux Dist. Corp., 1967, V.P. in charge of worldwide sales, 1969. Haven International Pictures, Inc., Haven Int'l 1970; IFIDA gov., 1970, v.p. sales, Scotia International Films, Inc., 1971; exec. v.p., Scotia American Prods; 1977, pres., Rob-Rich Films Inc.; 1979, exec. v.p., A Major Studio, Inc.; 1980, exec. v.p., The Health and Entertainment Corp. of America; 1982, sr. acct. rep., 3M-Photogard; 1984, pres., Rob-Rich Films.

GINSBURG, LEWIS S.: Distributor, Importer, Prod. b. New York, NY, May 16, 1914. e. City Coll. of New York, 1931–32. Columbia U., 1932–33. Ent. film industry, tabulating dept., United Artists, Sept. 1932; sls. contract dept. 1933; asst. to eastern district mgr., 1938; slsmn., New Haven exch., 1939. Army, 1943. Ret. to U.S., then formed first buying & booking service in Connecticut, 1945–55; in chg., New England Screen Guild Exchanges, 1955; TV film distr., 1955; Formed & org. International Film Assoc., Vid-EX Film Distr. Corp., 1961. Prod., TV half-hour series; vice-pres. in chg., dist., Desilu Film Dist. C., 1962; organized Carl Releasing Co., 1963; Walter Reade-Sterling Inc., 1964–65; formed L.G. Films Corp.; contract and playdate mgr., 20th Fox, 1965–68. Cinerama Releasing Corp. Adm. Ass't to sales mgr., 1968–69; 20th Cent.-Fox. Nat'l sales coordinator, 1969–present. 1970, 20th Century-Fox, Asst. to the Sales Mgr. 1971, Transnational Pictures Corp., v.p. in chg. of dist., pres., Stellar IV Film Corp., 1972.

GIRARDOT, ANNIE: Actress. b. France, Oct. 25, 1931. Studied nursing. Studied acting at the Paris Conservatory, made her acting debut with the Comedie Française. Has acted on the French stage and in reviews in the Latin Quarter.

PICTURES: Rocco and His Brothers, The Organizer, Les Galoises Bleues, Live For Life, Trois Chambres A Manhattan (Best Actress Award at the Venice Film Festival), Story of a Woman, Love Is a Funny Thing, The Slap, No Time for

Breakfast, Traffic Jam, Five Days in June, Prisonniers, Comedie D'Amour.

GISH, LILLIAN: Actress. b. Springfield, OH, Oct. 14, 1899. r.n. Lillian de Guiche. Sister of Dorothy Gish, actress. At 5 appeared in In Convict's Stripes, at Rising Sun, OH; following year danced in Sarah Bernhardt prod. in N.Y. In 1913 appeared with Mary Pickford in A Good Little Devil, N.Y. Began screen career 1912 with Biograph, beginning assn. with D. W. Griffith, dir., for whom she made 40 films including The Birth of a Nation, Intolerance, Hearts of the World, The Great Love, Broken Blossoms, Way Down East and Orphans of the Storm. One of the first women to dir. film (Remodeling Her Husband, 1920), and one of first actors to gain artistic control of projects (La Boheme, The Scarlet Letter). Continued in films: White Sister, Romola, The Wind, La Boheme, Scarlet Letter. From 1930 on N.Y. stage in number orig. prods. & classics 1969–71, One woman int'l concert tour, Lillian Gish and the Movies. Received honorary Oscar, 1971. International touring with illustrated lecture on the art of film and TV, 1974. Lecture tour on Queen Elizabeth 2, 1975. Campaigned for film preservation and lobbied for D. W. Griffith commemorative stamp. Honoree Kennedy Center Honors, 1982; 1983, AFI Life Achievement Award, Commander of Arts & Letters from French govt.

THEATER: Uncle Vanya, Camille, 9 Pine Street, Within the Gates, Hamlet, Star Wagon, Old Maid, Dear Octopus, Life With Father, Mr. Sycamore, The Marquise, Legend of Leonora, Crime and Punishment, Miss Mable, Curious Savage, A Passage to India, Too True to be Good; Romeo and Juliet, Stratford Shakespeare Theatre, 1965. The Trip to Bountiful (Theatre Guild 1954); Chalk Garden, The Family Reunion; in Berlin, Ger., Portrait of a Madonna, Wreck of the 5:25, Uncle Vanya, 1973. All The Way Home, Anya, 1965; I Never Sang for My Father, A Musical Jubilee (1976).

PICTURES: One Romantic Night, His Double Life, Commandos Strike at Dawn, Duel in the Sun, Miss Susie Slagle's, Portrait of Jennie, Follow Me Boys!, Night of the Hunter, The Cobweb, The Unforgiven, Orders to Kill; Warning Shot, The Comedians, A Wedding (her 100th film), Hambone and Hillie, Sweet Liberty, The Whales of August.

TELEVISION: I Mrs. Bibbs, Sound and the Fury, Ladies in Retirement, Detour, The Joyous Season, The Trip to Bountiful, Grandma Moses, The Quality of Mercy, The Corner Drugstore, Day Lincoln Was Shot, Mornings at Seven, The Grass Harp, Grandma T.N.T., Mr. Novak, Alfred Hitchcock Hour, Breaking Point, The Spiral Staircase, Arsenic and Old Lace, A Gift of Music, Kennedy Center Honors (1982), AFI Salute to Lillian Gish, The Silent Years (hostess). Movies: Twin Detectives; Thin Ice; Hobson's Choice.

AUTHOR: The Movies, Mr. Griffith and Me (Prentice-Hall), 1969; Dorothy and Lillian Gish (1973), An Actor's Life For Me (1987).

GLASER, PAUL MICHAEL: Actor. b. Cambridge, MA, March 25, 1943. e. Tulane U., Boston U., M.A. Did five seasons in summer stock before starting career in New York, making stage debut in Rockabye Hamlet in 1968. Appeared in numerous off-Bdwy. plays and got early TV training as regular in daytime series, Love of Life and Love Is a Many Splendored Thing.

PICTURES: Fiddler on the Roof, Butterflies Are Free. Director: Band of the Hand, The Running Man, Blue Lightning.

TELEVISION: Kojak, Toma, The Streets of San Francisco, The Rockford Files, The Sixth Sense, The Waltons. Movies: Trapped Beneath the Sea, The Great Houdini, Princess Daisy, Jealousy, Attack on Fear, Single Bars Single Women, Amazons (dir.). Series: Starsky and Hutch.

GLASER, SIDNEY: Exec. adv., Producer. b. New York, NY, July 12, 1912. e. City Coll. of New York, b. Eng., 1936; NYU, m. Eng., 1942. Office boy, adv. dept., Metro-Goldwyn-Mayer, 1929; prod. asst. 1934; prod. mgr., 1957; adv. prod. mgr., 1972; gen. adv. exec.

GLAZER, WILLIAM: Executive b. Cambridge, MA. e. State U. of New York, Entered m.p. ind. with Ralph Snider Theatres 1967–69; General Cinema Corp. 1969–71; Loews Theatres 1971–73; Joined Sack Theatres 1973 as Dist. mgr.; 1974 Exec. Asst. to Pres.; 1976 Gen. Mgr.; 1980 V.P. Gen. Mgr.; 1982 Exec. V.P. Member of SMPTE; NATO (Bd of Dir); Theatre Owners of New England Bd of Dir, also pres.; 1982–1985.

GLAZIER, SIDNEY: Producer. b. Philadelphia, PA, May 29, 1918. Managed movie and legitimate theatres in Pennsylvania and Ohio. Air Force captain during W.W.II. Became v.p. of Washington Federal Savings and Loan Bank in Miami. Org. and became exec. dir. of Eleanor Roosevelt Cancer Foundation. Prod. network TV public service programs. First m.p. The Eleanor Roosevelt Story won Academy Award, 1966. Pres. of U-M Film Distributors, 1969.

PICTURES: The Producers, Take the Money and Run, The Gamblers, Quackser Fortune Has a Cousin in the Bronx, The 12 Chairs, Glen and Wanda, The Night Visitor, The Only Way.

GLEASON, LARRY: Executive. b. Boston, MA, Apr. 30, 1938. e. Boston Coll., M.A., 1960. Held various positions, western div., mgr., General Cinema Corp.; 1963–73; gen. mgr., Gulf States Theatres, New Orleans, 1984–85; pres., Mann Theatres, 1974–85; joined DeLaurentiis Entertainment Group as pres., mktg./dist., Dec., 1985. Named sr. v.p., Paramount Pictures Corp, theatrical exhibition group, Jan. 1989.

GLEN, JOHN: Director. b. Sunbury on Thames, Eng., May 15, 1932. Entered industry in 1947. Second unit dir. The Spy Who Loved Me, Wild Geese, Moonraker (also editor). Editor: The Sea Wolves.

PICTURES: For Your Eyes Only, Octopussy, A View to a Kill, The Living Daylights, Licence to Kill.

GLENN, CHARLES OWEN: Executive. b. Binghamton, NY, March 27, 1938. e. Syracuse U., B.A., U. of Pennsylvania. Capt., U.S. Army, 1961–63. Asst. to dir. of adv., 20th Cent. Fox, 1966–67; asst. adv. mgr., Paramount, 1967–68; acct. spvsr. & exec., MGM record & m.p. div., 1968–69; nat'l adv. mgr., Paramount, 1969–70; nat'l. dir. of adv., Paramount, 1970–71; v.p. adv.-pub.-prom., 1971–73; v.p. marketing, 1974; v.p. prod. mktg., 1975; joined American Intl. Pictures as v.p. in chg. of adv./creative affairs, 1979. 1980, when Filmways took AIP over he was named their v.p. in chg. worldwide adv./pub./promo.; joined MCA/Universal in 1982 as exec. v.p., adv.-promo.; 1984, appt. Orion Pictures adv.-pub.-promo. exec. v.p.; 1987, appt. Orion mktg. exec. v.p.

MEMBER: Exec. comm. public relations branch, Academy of M.P. Arts & Sciences. Holder of NATO mktg. exec. of year (1983) award, Variety Club, Motion Picture Pioneers.

GLENN, SCOTT: Actor. b. Pittsburgh, PA, Jan. 26, 1942. e. William & Mary Coll. Worked as U.S. Marine, newspaper reporter before going to New York to study drama. Off-Bdwy. productions included Fortune in Men's Eyes, Long Day's Journey into Night. On Bdwy in Burn This. Member of Actors Studio. Film debut in The Baby Maker, 1970.

PICTURES: Nashville, Apocalypse Now, Urban Cowboy, Personal Best, The Challenge, The Right Stuff, The Keep, The River, Wild Geese II, Silverado, Verne Miller, Man on Fire, Off Limits, Two Telegrams, Miss Firecracker, The Hunt for Red October, Home Grown.

TELEVISION: As Summers Die, Countdown to Looking Glass, Intrigue, The Outside Woman.

GLESS, SHARON: Actress. b. Los Angeles, CA, May 31, 1943.

TELEVISION: Mini-series: Centennial. Movies: The Longest Night; All My Darling Daughters; My Darling Daughters' Anniversary; The Immigrants; The Scream of Eagles; The Last Convertible; Hardhat and Legs; The Kids Who Knew Too Much; Moviola; The Miracle of Kathy Miller; Palms; Hobson's Choice; The Sky's the Limit; Letting Go, The Outside Woman. Series: Marcus Welby, M.D., Faraday and Co., Switch, Turnabout, House Calls, Cagney and Lacey (1982–, 2 Emmys).

PICTURE: The Star Chamber.

GLICK, HYMAN J.: Executive. b. Russia, Dec. 15, 1904. e. NYU, B.C.S., 1926. C.P.A. (N.Y.); with public accounting firm, N.Y., 1923–29; own public accounting business, 1929–32. Became assoc. m.p. ind. as member comptrollers' com., repr. Republic; 1932–36, tax & financial counsel Mascot Pictures Corp. Joined Republic 1936 as comptroller; apptd. asst. secy.-asst. treas. Jan., 1945. Retired, 1985.

Member: B'nai Brith Lodge 1325; State Soc. of Certified Public Accountants, Am. Inst. of Accountants. Resigned Republic, 1959; CPA (Calif.), member, Calif. Soc. of CPA; Own Accounting and Tax Practice.

GLICK, PHYLLIS: Executive. b. New York, NY. e. Queens Coll. of C.U.N.Y. Began career with Otto-Windsor Associates, as casting director; left to be independent. 1979, joined ABC-TV as mgr. of comedy series development; promoted 1980 to director, involved with all comedy series developed for network. 1985, joined Paramount Pictures as exec. dir., production, for M.P. Group.

GLICKMAN, JOEL: Producer. b. Los Angeles, CA, July 29, 1930. e. UCLA (film dep't.). Was actor and director for L.A. little theatre groups and writer-director for industrial films. Early TV work on series, documentaries and commercials. Directed videotaping of off-Broadway shows. Was production assoc. on film, Wedding and Babies, 1958. Was assoc. prod. and prod. mgr. on films (Terror in the City, The Balcony, All the Way Home, For Love of Ivy, Hamlet (Richard Burton, assoc. director), Dion Brothers, Last Summer, The Best of Times, Hanoi Hilton, The Telephone) and TV (East Side, West Side, Mr. Broadway), N.Y.P.D., Love Song of Barney Kempinski, Among the Paths To Eden. Member, D.G.A. Has own co.: Selznick/Glickman Productions.

PICTURES: Brother John, Buck and the Preacher, Trial of the Catonsville Nine (exec. prod.).

TELEVISION: Night Terror, Angel on Horseback, Kennedy-Hoffa War (called Blood Feud for OPT), Hoover vs. the Kennedys (mini-series), Psychic Crimebusters (special).

GLOBUS, YORAM: Producer. b. Israel, Came to U.S. 1979. Has co-produced many films with cousin and former partner Menahem Golan. Sr. exec. v.p., Cannon Group; Pres. and CEO Cannon ENtertainment and Cannon Films; 1989 named chmn. and C.E.O Cannon Entertainment and officer of Cannon Group Inc.; then co-pres. Pathe Communications Corp. and chmn. and C.E.O. Pathe Intl.
PICTURES: All as producer or exec. prod. with Menahem Golan: Sallah; Trunk to Cairo; My Margo; What's Good for the Goose; Escape to the Sun; I Love You, Rosa; The House on Chelouch Street; The Four Deuces; Kazablan; Diamonds; God's Gun; Kid Vengeance, Operation Thunderbolt, The Uranium Conspiracy, Savage Weekend, The Magician of Lublin, The Apple, The Happy Hooker Goes to Hollywood, Dr. Heckyl and Mr. Hype, The Godsend, New Year's Evil, Schizoid, Seed of Innocence, Body and Soul, Death Wish II, Enter the Ninja, Hospital Massacre, The Last American Virgin, Championship Season, Treasure of Four Crowns, 10 to Midnight, Nana, I'm Almost Not Crazy...John Cassavetes: The Man and His Work, The House of Long Shadows, Revenge of the Ninja, Hercules, The Wicked Lady, Sahara, The Ambassador, Bolero, Exterminator 2, The Naked Face, Missing in Action, Hot Resort, Love Streams, Breakin', Grace Quigley, Making the Grade, Ninja III—The Domination, Breakin' 2: Electric Boogaloo, Lifeforce, Over the Brooklyn Bridge, The Delta Force, The Assisi Underground, Hot Chili, The Berlin Affair, Missing in Action 2—The Beginning, Rappin', Thunder Alley, American Ninja, Mata Hari, Death Wish 3, King Solomon's Mines, Runaway Train, Fool for Love, Invasion U.S.A., Maria's Lovers, Murphy's Law, The Naked Cage, P.O.W.: The Escape, The Texas Chainsaw Massacre, Part 2, Invaders from Mars, 52 Pick-Up, Link, Firewalker, Dumb Dicks, The Nutcracker: The Motion Picture, Avenging Force, Hashigaon Hagadol, Journey to the Center of the Earth, Prom Queen, Salome, Otello, Cobra, America 3000, American Ninja 2: The Confrontation, Allan Quartermain and the Lost City of Gold, Assassination, Beauty and the Beast, Down Twisted, Duet for One, The Emperor's New Clothes, The Hanoi Hilton, The Barbarians, Dutch Treat, Masters of the Universe, Number One with a Bullet, Rumpelstiltskin, Street Smart, UnderCover, The Assault, Hansel and Gretel, Going Bananas, Snow White, Sleeping Beauty, Tough Guys Don't Dance, Shy People, Dancers, Red Riding Hood, King Lear, Braddock: Missing in Action III, Too Much, Die Papierene Brucke, Field of Honor, Barfly (exec. prod.), Surrender (exec. prod.), Death Wish 4: The Crackdown (exec. prod.), Gor (exec. prod.), Business as Usual (exec. prod.), Over the Top, Superman IV: The Quest for Peace, *prod.:* Delta Force, Operation Crackdown, Manifesto, Stranglehold, Delta Force II, Cyborg, Step By Step. *exec. prod.:* The Kitchen Toto, Doin' Time on Planet Earth, Kickboxer,Kinjite, A Man Called Sarge, The Rose Garden, The Secret of the Ice Cave.

GLOVER, CRISPIN: Actor. b. New York, NY 1964. e. Mirman School. Trained for stage with Dan Mason and Peggy Feury. Stage debut, as Friedrich Von Trapp, The Sound of Music, Los Angeles, 1977. Wrote books, Rat Catching (1987), Concrete Inspection (1988).
PICTURES: My Tutor (debut, 1982), The Orkly Kid, Friday the 13th—The Final Chapter, Teachers, Racing with the Moon, Back to the Future, River's Edge, At Close Range, Wild at Heart.
TELEVISION: Movie: High School U.S.A.

GLOVER, DANNY: Actor. b. San Francisco, CA, 1947. e. San Francisco State U. Trained at Black Actors Workshop of American Conservatory Theatre. Appeared in many stage productions (Island, Macbeth, Sizwe Banzi Is Dead, etc.). On N.Y. stage in Suicide in B Flat, The Blood Knot, Master Harold . . . and the Boys (Theatre World Award).
PICTURES: Chu Chu and the Philly Flash, Iceman, Escape from Alcatraz, Witness, Places in the Heart, The Color Purple, Silverado, Lethal Weapon, Out (video); Bat-21, Lethal Weapon 2, To Sleep with Anger (also exec. prod.).
TELEVISION: Hill Street Blues, Many Mansions, Chiefs, Face of Rage, Mandela, A Place at the Table, Lonesome Dove, A Raisin in the Sun, Dead Man Out.

GLOVER, JOHN: Actor. b. Salisbury, MD, Aug. 7, 1944. e. Towson State Coll., Baltimore. On regional theatre circuit; in plays off-Bdwy. (A Scent of Flowers, Subject to Fits, The House of Blue Leaves, The Selling of the President). With APA Phoenix Co. in Great God Brown (Drama Desk Award), The Visit, Don Juan, Chermin de Fer, Holiday. Other NY stage: The Importance of Being Earnest, Hamlet, Frankenstein, Whodunnit, Digby.
PICTURES: Julia, Annie Hall, Somebody Killed Her Husband, Shamus, Last Embrace, Success, Melvin and Howard, The Mountain Men, The Incredible Shrinking Woman, A Little Sex, The Evil That Men Do, White Nights, 52 Pick-Up, Life on the Edge, Masquerade, A Killing Affair, The Chocolate War, Rocket Gibraltar, Scrooged, Monoliths, Gremlins II.
TELEVISION: A Rage of Angels, George Washington, Ernie Kovacs—Between the Laughter, An Early Frost, Apology, Moving Target, Hot Paint, Nutcracker: Money, Madness, and Murder, Paul Reiser: Out on a Whim, David, The Traveling Man, Twist of Fate, Breaking Point.

GLYNN, CARLIN: Actress. b. Feb. 19, 1940. m. actor-writer Peter Masterson, mother of actress Mary Stuart Masterson. e. Sophie Newcomb College, 1957–58. Studied acting with Stella Adler, Wynn Handman and Lee Strasberg in NY. Debut, Gigi, Alley Theatre, Houston, TX 1959. NY stage debut Waltz of The Toreadors, 1960. On stage in The Best Little Whorehouse in Texas (Tony Award and Eleanora Duse Award), Winterplay, Alterations.
PICTURES: Three Days of the Condor, Continental Divide, Sixteen Candles, Night Game.

GOATMAN, ALAN H.: Consultant. Entered m.p. industry 1934. Officer of the Venerable Order of St. John of Jerusalem. Fellow Society of Company and Commercial Accountants. Memb. Brit. Computer Soc. Fellow Brit. Inst. Management; member Inst. Data Processing; Management Dir. British Film & TV Producers Assoc.; Exec. mem., AGICOA, Geneva. Pres., AGICOA Services, S.A. Brussels, Freeman of the City of London.

GODARD, JEAN-LUC: Writer, Director. b. Paris, France, Dec. 3, 1930. e. Lycee Buffon, Paris. Journalist, film critic Cahiers du Cinema. Acted in and financed experimental film Quadrille by Jacques Rivette, 1951. 1954: dir. first short, Operation Beton. 1956, was film editor. 1957: worked in publicity dept. 20th Century Fox.
PICTURES: Breathless (feature debut, 1960), Le Petit Soldat, A Woman is a Woman, My Life to Live, Les Carabiniers, Contempt, Band of Outsiders, The Married Woman, Alphaville, Pierrot le Fou, Masculine-Feminine, Two or Three Things I Know About Her, La Chinoise, Weekend, Sympathy for the Devil, Le Gai Savoir, Tout a Bien (co-dir.), Numero Deux, Every Man For Himself, First Name Carmen, Hail Mary, Aria, King Lear, Keep Up Your Right (dir., edit, s.p., actor), Nouvelle Vague.

GODBOLD, GEOFF: Executive. b. London, England, 1935. Ent. ind. 1959. Specialized in supply of location requirements for film and TV prods. Formed Prop Workshops Ltd., co-promoted Television Recordings Ltd. Man. dir. Facilities (Screen & Television) Ltd. Dir. TV Recordings, Investments, Ltd.; Centrepoint Screen Prod. Ltd.; Tape Commercials, Ltd. Council Mem. Film and TV Contractors Assoc. Dir. Lancair Export Services Ltd.; 1968 Freelance production buyer, Screen Gems and Tigon. 1969. Feature Prod. Rep. Film Div. N.A.T.T.K.E. Man. Dir. Setpieces Ltd. Film & TV Prop. Hire. 1984: Carlton Communication. 1985: mng. dir., Set Pieces Ltd.
PICTURES: Dubious Patriot, Every Home Should Have One, Melody, Up Pompeii. Morocco location, Young Winston. The Asphyx, Our Miss Fred, Death of a Snow Queen, Man in the Iron Mask. TV: The Professionals.

GODDARD, PAULETTE: Actress. r.n. Marion Levy. b. Great Neck, NY, June 3, 1911. On N.Y. stage as a Ziegfeld girl at 14, then in Rio Rita; then member of Hal Roach Studios stock co. Became a Goldwyn girl in Hollywood. In 1936 opposite her then husband Charles Chaplin in Modern Times.
PICTURES: The Girl Habit (1931), The Mouthpiece, The Kid From Spain, Modern Times, The Young in Heart, The Women, The Cat and the Canary, The Ghostbreakers, Northwest Mounted Police, The Great Dictator, Second Chorus, Hold Back the Dawn, Reap the Wild Wind, Star Spangled Rhythm, I Love a Soldier, So Proudly We Hail, Standing Room Only, Duffy's Tavern, Kitty, The Diary of a Chambermaid, Unconquered, An Ideal Husband, Hazard, On Our Merry Way, Bride of Vengeance, Anna Lucasta, Babes in Bagdad, Vice Squad, Paris Model, Sins of Jezebel, Charge of the Lancers, Unholy Four, Time of Indifference.
TELEVISION: Female Instincts, The Snoop Sisters.

GODMILOW, JILL: Director, Producer, Editor.
PICTURES: Antonia: Portrait of a Woman (co-directed with Judy Collins) received Academy Award nomination and won Independent N.Y. Film Critics Award for Best Documentary, 1975; Nevelson In Process, Odyssey, (created with Susan Fanshel); The Popovich Brothers (co-dir., co-prod.); The Vigil (co-directed with Chiquita and Andre Gregory): At Nienadowka with Grotowskski, Far from Poland; Waiting for the Moon.

GODUNOV, ALEXANDER: Dancer, Actor. b. Ujno-Sakalin, Soviet Union, Nov. 28, 1949. e. Riga Music Sch. 1958–67; trained for dance at Riga Choreography Sch. and for stage at Stella Adler Acting Sch. Dancer with Moiseyev's Ballet Co. 1958–66; principal dancer Bolshoi Dance Co. 1967–79; American Ballet Theatre, NY 1979–82.
PICTURES: Witness (debut, 1985), The Money Pit, Die Hard.
TELEVISION: Godunov: The World to Dance In (1983).

GODWIN, FRANK: Producer, Writer, Director.
PICTURES: Woman in a Dressing Gown, No Trees in the Street, Operation Bullshine, Don't Bother to Knock, The Small World of Sammy Lee, Danny the Dragon, Headline Hunters, Demons of the Mind, The Boy with Two Heads, The Firefighters, Sky Pirates, Sammy's Super T-Shirt, Electric Eskimo, The Boy Who Never Was, Break Out, Terry on the Fence.

GOEBEL, LAWRENCE A. JR.: Executive. b. Shreveport, LA, May 29, 1950. e. Marquette U., 1968–74; U. of Southern California. Cinema Dept. Graduate Sch. (1973–75). Began career as sports editor, Marquette Tribune, 1972; dir. of special events ticket sales—L.A. Sharks World Hockey Assn., 1973; freelance filmmaker, 1974–75. Now v.p., intl. & ancillary sls. for Film Ventures International.
MEMBER: American Film Marketing Assn's market advisory committee and fact book committee; 1986; Film Ventures' rep. for AFMA, 1983–86; film industry juror for L.A. Film Teacher's regional film festival, 1978–82.

GOLAN, MENAHEM: Producer, Director, Writer. b. Israel, 1929. e. NYU. Studied theater dir. at Old Vic Theatre London, m.p. prod. at City Coll, NY. Co-founder and prod. with cousin Yoram Globus, Golan-Globus Prods., Israel, then L.A., 1962. Later Noah Films, Israel, 1963, Ameri-Euro Pictures Corp, before buying controlling share in Cannon Films, 1979. Sr. exec. v.p., Cannon Group; chmn. of bd., Cannon Entertainment and Cannon Films. 1988, dir. and sr. exec. v.p. Cannon Group, chmn. and head of creative affairs, Cannon Entertainment when it became div. of Giancarlo Parretti's Pathe Communications Corp. Resigned March, 1989 to form 21st Century Film Corp as chmn. and CEO.
PICTURES: Director/co-writer: Kasablan, Diamonds, Entebbe (Operation Thunderbolt), Teyve and His Seven Daughters, What's Good for the Goose? Lepke, The Magician of Lublin, The Goodsend, Happy Hooker Goes to Hollywood, Enter the Ninja. Producer-Writer-Director: The Threepenny Opera, Hanna's War. Producer-Director: The Uranium Conspiracy, Delta Force, Over the Brooklyn Bridge, Over the Top. Producer/Exec. prod.: Sallah, Runaway Train, Sallah, Fool For Love, Maria's Lovers, Cobra, Evil Angels, I Love You Rosa, Body and Soul, also: Deathwish II, The Last American Virgin, That Championship Season, House of Long Shadows, Revenge of the Ninja, Hercules, The Movie Tales (12 children's fairy tales films), The Wicked Lady, Cobra, Barfly (exec. prod.), Breakin', Missing in Action, Dancers (prod.), Surrender (exec. prod.), Death Wish 4: The Crackdown (exec. prod.), King Lear (prod.), Too Much (prod.), Powaqquatsi (exec. prod.), Mercenary Fighters (prod.), Doin' Time on Planet Earth (prod.), Manifesto (prod.), Kinjite (exec. prod.), Messenger of Death (exec. prod.), Alien From L.A. (prod.), Hero and the Terror (exec. prod.), Haunted Summer (exec. prod.), A Cry in the Dark (exec. prod.), Delta Force—Operation Crackdown (prod.), A Man Called Sarge (exec. prod.), Stranglehold: Delta Force II (prod.), Cyborg (prod.), The Rose Garden (exec. prod.), Rope Dancing (exec. prod.).

GOLD, ERNEST: Composer, Conductor. b. Vienna, Austria, July 13, 1921. e. State Acad. for Music and Performing Arts, Austria 1937–38; private study, 1939–49 in U.S. Worked as song writer 1939–42 and taught in private schools, 1942. Composed 1st score for Columbia Pictures, 1945. Musical dir., Santa Barbara Symphony, 1958–59. Taught at UCLA, 1973 and 1983–84 (adult ed.). Gold record for soundtrack of Exodus, 1968.. Acad. Award nom., On the Beach (1959), It's a Mad, Mad, Mad, Mad World (song and score 1963), The Secret of Santa Vittoria (1968). Won Acad. Award for Exodus (1961). Received star on Walk of Fame on Hollywood Blvd., 1975. Elected to bd. of govs., Acad. of Motion Picture Arts and Sciences, 1984.
PICTURES: include: Girl of the Limberlost, The Falcon's Alibi, Too Much Too Soon, On the Beach, Exodus, Inherit the Wind, Judgment at Nuremberg, A Child Is Waiting, Pressure Point, It's a Mad, Mad, Mad, Mad World, Ship of Fools, The Secret of Santa Vittoria, Cross of Iron, The McCullochs, Fun With Dick and Jane, Good Luck Miss Wyckoff, The Runner Stumbles, Tom Horn, Safari 3000, Lost in America.
TELEVISION: Small Miracle, Betrayal.

GOLD, MELVIN: Executive. b. Chicago, IL, Sept. 3, 1909. In 1930 joined MGM, Chicago, as asst. office mgr. To Reinheimer Circuit 1932 to operate theatres Hammond, IN; in 1940 org. own advertising agency, Sales, Inc., mgr.; mgr. Vogue Theatre, Hollywood, CA, 1943. Joined National Screen Service 1943 as editor Mister Showman; Feb., 1945 named director of advt. and publicity; assumed east coast film prod. and TV, Sept., 1948 to May, 1954. Formed Mel Gold Productions, Inc., June 1954. Partner Melmon Productions; Melvin L. Gold Enterprises, 1958; pres., Mesal Prods., Inc., 1961; wrote s.p., Not For Love, 1961; pres., Associated Motion Picture Advertisers, 1963–66; gen. sls. mgr., National Screen Service, 1963. Pres., Melvin L. Gold Enterprises, Inc. 1966. Pres. Manhattan Sound Studios 1967, v.p. in chg. m.p. div., National Showmanship Services, 1968; 1971, Pres. East Side Productions; Pres. Melvin L. Gold Enterprises. Motion picture consultant, Philip Morris, Inc., 1976–present. Operations director, Benson & Hedges 100, Film classics, 1976–79. Wrote s.p., The Sheriff Is a Lady, 1979.
Member Publicity Club of N.Y.; Associated Motion Picture Advertisers; founded National Television Film Council in 1948, elected Honorary Lifetime President, 1955.

GOLDBERG, BERNARD: Executive. b. Bronx, NY, Aug. 25, 1932. e. Queens Coll., B.A. Co-owner, Golden Theatre Mgt. Corp.; named vice pres. 1973.

GOLDBERG, FRED: Publicist. b. New York, NY, Aug. 26, 1921. e. Pace Coll., School of Marketing and Advertising. Expl., Paramount, 1946; asst. expl. mgr., trade paper contact, syndicate contact, N.Y. newspaper contact promotion mgr., 1946–52; ass't publ. mgr., RKO, 1952,; national publ. mgr.; IFE, 1953; v.p. Norton and Condon, pub., 1953; returned to IFE Sept., 1954, as nat'l pub. mgr.; head of N.Y. office, Arthur Jacobs, then Blowitz-Maskel, 1956; exec. asst. to dir. pub., adv., United Artists Corp., 1958; exec. dir., adv., pub., exploitation, United Artists Corp., 1961; named vice pres., 1962, senior vice president, 1972, sr. v.p., dir. of marketing, 1977. Left in 1978 to be consultant with Piener, Hauser & Bates Agency. In 1979 joined Columbia Pictures as sr. v.p. in chg. adv./pub. Left in 1981 to form new company.

GOLDBERG, LEONARD: Executive. b. Brooklyn, NY, Jan. 24, 1934. e. Wharton Sch., U. of Pennsylvania. Began career in ABC-TV research dept.; moved to NBC-TV research div.; 1961 joined Batten, Barton, Durstine & Osborn ad agency in chg. of daytime TV shows and overall bdcst. coordinator. In 1963 rejoined ABC-TV as mgr. of program devel. In 1966 named VP in chg of network TV programming. Resigned in 1969 to join Screen Gems as VP in chg. of prod. Left for partnership with Aaron Spelling in Spelling/Goldberg Prods.; later produced TV and theatrical films under own banner, Mandy Prods. 1981: co-prod. All Night Long. 1983: WarGames. 1984: Space Camp; 1986, named pres., COO, 20th Century Fox. Resigned, 1989.
TELEVISION: The Rookies (1972–76), Starsky and Hutch, Charlie's Angels, Family, Hart to Hart, T.J. Hooker, Paper Dolls, The Cavanaughs. Movies: Brian's Song, Little Ladies of the Night, The Legend of Valentino, The Boy in the Plastic Bubble, Something About Amelia, Alex: The Life of a Child.

GOLDBERG, WHOOPI: Actress. b. New York, NY, Nov. 13, 1949. e. Sch. for the Performing Arts. Began performing at age 8 in N.Y. with children's program at Hudson Guild and Helena Rubenstein Children's Theatre. Moved to San Diego, CA, 1974, and help found San Diego Rep. Theatre appearing in Mother Courage, Getting Out. Member: Spontaneous Combustion (improv. group). Joined Blake St. Hawkeyes Theatre in Berkeley, partnering with David Schein. Went solo to create The Spook Show, working in San Francisco and later touring U.S. & Europe. 1983 performance caught attention of Mike Nichols which led to Bdwy. show based on it and directed by him. Founding member of Comic Relief benefits. Theatrical film debut in The Color Purple (1985) (Image Award, NAACP, Golden Globe).
THEATER: small roles in B'way prods. of Pippin, Hair, Jesus Christ Superstar. 1988: toured in Living on the Edge of Chaos.
PICTURES: Jumpin' Jack Flash, Burglar, Fatal Beauty, The Telephone, Homer and Eddie, Clara's Heart, Beverly Hills Brats, 'Tis the Season, The Long Walk Home.
TELEVISION: Whoopi Goldberg Direct From Broadway, Comic Relief, Comic Relief II, Carol, Carl, Whoopi and Robin, Moonlighting (Emmy nom., 1985), Scared Straight: 10 Years Later, Funny, You Don't Look 200, Comedy Tonight (host), Star Trek: The Next Generation (series), My Past is My Own (Schoolbreak Special), Free to Be . . . a Family, The Debbie Allen Special. Movies: Kiss Shot.

GOLDBLUM, JEFF: Actor. b. Pittsburgh, PA, Oct. 22, 1952. m. actress Geena Davis. Studied at Sanford Meisner's Neighborhood Playhouse in New York. On Bdwy. in Two Gentleman of Verona, The Moony Shapiro Songbook. Off-Bdwy: El Grande de Coca Cola, City Sugar, Our Last Night.
PICTURES: Death Wish (debut), California Split, Nashville, Next Stop, Greenwich Village, St. Ives, Special Delivery, Annie Hall, The Sentinal, Between the Lines, Remember My Name, Thank God, It's Friday, Escape to Athena, Invasion of the Body Snatchers, Threshold, The Big Chill, The Right Stuff, The Adventures of Buckaroo Banzai, Into the Night, Silverado, Transylvania 6-5000, The Fly, Beyond Therapy, Vibes, Earth Girls Are Easy, The Tall Guy, The Mad Monkey.
TELEVISION: Movies: The Legend of Sleepy Hollow, Rehearsal for Murder, Ernie Kovacs: Between the Laughter, The Double Helix (BBC). Series: Tenspeed and Brownshoe.

GOLDEN, HERBERT L.: b. Philadelphia, PA, Feb. 12. e. Temple U., 1936, B.S. Reporter, rewrite man. asst. city ed., Philadelphia Record, 1933–38; joined Variety, 1938; on leave of absence, 1942–43, when asst. to John Hay Whitney and

Francis Alstock, directors, M.P. Division, Coordinator of Inter-American Affairs (U.S.); commissioned in U.S. Navy, 1943, served on destroyer to 1946; then returned to Variety. m.p. ed. Consultant on motion pictures, Good Housekeeping magazine McGraw-Hill Publications, American Yearbook. Ent. Ind. Div. Bankers Trust Co., N.Y., 1952; named v.p. 1954–56; treas., Children's Asthma Research Institute, 1956; v.p. & mem. of bd. United Artists Corp., 1958; member of board, MPAA, 1959; pres., Lexington Int., Inc. investments, 1962; mem. bd., chmn. exec. com., Perfect Photo Inc., 1962; 1965 sect. & mem. bd. Century Broadcasting Group; chmn. G & G Thea. Corp.; pres. Diversifax Corp., 1966; consult. Pathe Lab, 1967; Mem. bd. Childhood Prod. Inc., 1967. Member bd. Music Makers Group, Inc., 1962. Mem. bd. Cinecom Corp., 1968; pres., Vere/Swiss Corp., 1977; mem. bd., Coral Reef Publications, Inc., 1977. Returned to Bankers Trust, 1979, to head its Media Group (service to film and TV industries).

GOLDEN, JEROME B.: Executive, Attorney. b. New York, NY, Nov. 26, 1917. e. St. Lawrence U., LL.B., 1942. Member legal dept., Paramount Pictures, Inc., 1942–50; United Paramount Theatres, Inc., 1950–53; American Broadcasting Companies, Inc., 1953; secy., ABC, 1958–86; vice-pres., ABC, 1959–86. Consultant.

GOLDENSON, LEONARD H.: Executive. b. Scottsdale, PA, December 7, 1905. e. Harvard Coll., B.A., Harvard Law School, LL.B. Practiced law, New York; counsel in reorg. Paramount theats. in New England, 1933–37; in 1937 apptd. asst. to vice-pres. Paramount in charge theat. operations; became head of theat. operations, 1938; elected pres. Paramount Theat. Service Corp., vice-pres. Paramount Pictures, Inc., 1938; dir. Paramount Pictures, 1942 (also pres. various Paramount theat. subsids., see Paramount circuits in Theatre Circuits section). Pres., chief exec. off. and director United Paramount Theatres, Inc., 1950, and of American Broadcasting-Paramount Theatres, Inc., 1953, result of merger of ABC and United Paramount Theatres, Inc.; name changed to American Broadcasting Companies, Inc. 1965; Chairman of the Board and Chief Executive Officer; of American Broadcasting Companies, Inc. since January 17, 1972; mem., board chmn. of United Cerebral Palsy Assns.; trustee, John F. Kennedy Center for the Performing Arts; dir., Daughters of Jacob Geriatric Center; mem., International Radio and Television Society; Founder Member of Hollywood Museum; Trustee of Children's Cancer Research Foundation of the Children's Medical Center, Boston, MA; Director of Allied Stores Corporation; Trustee of Highway Users Federation for Safety and Mobility; Member of National Academy of Television Arts and Sciences; Member of Uptown Advisory Committee of Bankers Trust Company; Graduate Director of The Advertising Council, Inc.; Associate Trustee and Member of Advisory Council for the Performing Arts of University of Pennsylvania; Member of Broadcast Pioneers; Member of Inter Lochen Arts Academy-National Advisory Board; Member of Motion Picture Pioneers; Member of National Citizens' Advisory Committee on Vocational Rehabilitation; Member of United Negro College Fund-National Corporations Committee; Director of World Rehabilitation Fund, Inc.

GOLDFARB, HOWARD GERALD: Executive. b. New York, NY, Sept. 19, 1941. e. Wharton Sch. of Business. Exec. trainee, Columbia Pictures, 1962–64; mgr. dir., United Artists Corp., in Panama/Central America, 1964–69; v.p. & foreign mgr., Cannon Releasing Corp., 1970–72; pres., H.G. Entertainment Ltd. & Salt Water Releasing Co., Inc., 1972–75; dir. dist., C.I.C. (cassettes co.), 1976; v.p., dir. intl. opns., National Telefilm Associates, 1976–78; dir. intl. sls., Dino de Laurentiis Corp., 1978–79; pres., Goldfarb Distributors, 1979–1980, distributing films for independent producers worldwide.
PICTURES: Producer: The Unseen, Venus in 3-D, Mission Kills, Car Trouble, On the Fringe.

GOLDIN, BERNARD: Executive. Began career with Universal Pictures as branch mgr. in number of territories. Named Philadelphia mgr. for United Artists; 1977–81, Midwestern div. mgr. for Columbia Pictures. Returned to UA, 1981, as v.p. & asst. gen. sls. mgr.

GOLDING, DAVID: Executive. b. New York, NY, Oct. 20, 1915. e. U. of Wisconsin, B.A. Now operating public relations consultancy in London, David Golding and Associates Ltd. Formerly Universal advertising and publicity representative in UK. During war, mg. ed. Mediterranean edition, The Stars and Stripes. Also pub. dir. Samuel Goldwyn, 20th-Fox, Hecht-Hill-Lancaster, Otto Preminger.

GOLDMAN, BO: Writer. b. New York, NY, Sept. 10, 1932. e. Princeton U., B.A., 1953. Wrote lyrics for Bdwy musical of Pride and Prejudice called First Impressions (1959). Assoc. prod. Playhouse 90 1958–60; writer-prod., NET Playhouse 1970–71; Theater in America 1972–74.
PICTURES: One Flew Over the Cuckoo's Nest (Acad. Award, 1975), Murder on the Bridge, The Rose, Melvin and Howard (Acad. Award, s.p., 1980), Shoot the Moon, Little Nikita, Swing Shift.

GOLDMAN, EDMUND: Executive-Producer. b. Shanghai, China, Nov. 12, 1906. e. in Shanghai and San Francisco. Entered ind. as asst. mgr., for Universal in Shanghai, 1935–36; named mgr. Columbia Pictures' Philippine office, 1937. In 1951 named Far East. supvr. for Columbia, headquartering in Tokyo. From 1953 to present indep. m.p. dist., specializing in foreign marketing, representing indep. producers and distributors. Now v.p., Quixote Prods.
PICTURES: Surrender Hell (prod.), The Quick and the Dead (exec. prod.).

GOLDMAN, JANE: Executive. e. Barnard Coll., New York U. School of Law. Represented Warner Bros. in special assignments while in general law practice; joined Warner Communications Inc. in N.Y. as full-time attorney, counselling dist. div. in copyright and anti-trust matters. 1985, named v.p., gen. counsel for WB Dist. Corp., at Warner Studio.

GOLDMAN, MARVIN: Executive. b. New York, NY. e. Fordham U., U. of Miami. Served in U.S. Navy in WWII, leaving with rank of Lt. commander. In 1947 went to Washington, D.C. to work for K-B Theatres; purchased the chain of five theatres. Circuit now operates 52 theatres in the DC, Maryland, Virginia area. (Partnership now includes son, Ronald.) Goldman also involved with son in indep. film prod. co., which has completed 6 features and planning more. Active in theatre organizations for many years; named pres. of National NATO in 1976. Former pres. of Metropolitan, Washington, DC area chapter of NATO and now bd. chmn. Past chief barker of Variety Club of Washington. Named exhibitor of year by IFIDA in 1966. With son operated European Classics, distributing imported films in U.S. & Canada.

GOLDMAN, MICHAEL F.: Executive. b. Manila, Philippines, Sept. 28, 1939. e. UCLA, B.S. in acct., 1962. C.P.A. certificate issued June, 1972. In 1962 incorporated Manson International, which was sold in 1986. Incorporated Quixote Prods., 1979. Also owner and sole proprietor Taurus Film co. of Hollywood, founded 1964. Co-founder and first chief financial officer of American Film Marketing Association, sponsor of First American Film Market in Los Angeles in 1981; v.p. of AFMA 1982 and 1983 and President AFMA 1984 and 1985. AFMA bd. mbr., 1981–87, 1988–89; Co-founder, Cinema Consultants Group, 1988. Produced feature, Jessi's Girls in 1975.

GOLDMAN, SHEPARD: Writer, Producer. Pres., Scaramouche Productions. b. Brooklyn, NY; e. Hofstra U, NYU: Comedy/dramas. Varied genres; novels and songs made into films.
PICTURES: An Unfinished Victory, Our Tender Hearts, Queens, Salsa (co-s.p.), Spiderman, The Merry Wives of Beverly Hills, The China.
STAGE: The Last Salt of Summer.
TELEVISION: Chumbles Story Hour; Sensations.
AWARDS: Gold Medal–best adaptation, 15th Houston Int'l Film Festival; Gold Medal–best original comedy, 17th Houston Int'l Film Festival.

GOLDMAN, WILLIAM: Writer. b. Chicago, IL, 1931. e. Oberlin College, B.A., Columbia U., M.A. Novels include The Temple of Gold; Your Turn to Curtsy, My Turn to Bow; Soldier in the Rain (filmed); Boys and Girls Together; The Thing of It Is; No Way to Treat a Lady (filmed), Father's Day; The Season; The Princess Bride (filmed), Marathon Man (filmed), Magic (filmed), Tinsel, Control, The Silent Gondoliers, The Color of Light.
PICTURES: Harper, Butch Cassidy and the Sundance Kid (Acad. Award, screenplay), The Great Waldo Pepper, Marathon Man (based on own book), All the President's Men, A Bridge Too Far, Magic (based on own book), Heat (based on own book), The Princess Bride (s.p., based on his novel).

GOLDSMITH, JERRY: Composer. b. Los Angeles, CA, Feb. 10, 1929. e. Los Angeles City Coll. Studied piano with Jacob Gimpel and music composition, harmony, theory with Mario Castelnuovo-Tedesco. With CBS radio first with own show (Romance) and then moved on to others (Suspense). Began scoring for TV, including Climax, Playhouse 90, Studio One, Gunsmoke, etc.
PICTURES INCLUDE: Black Patch (debut), Lonely Are the Brave, Freud (AA nom.), The Stripper, The Prize, Seven Days in May, Lilies of the Field, In Harm's Way, Von Ryan's Express, Our Man Flint, A Patch of Blue (AA nom.), The Blue Max, Seconds, Stagecoach, The Sand Pebbles (AA nom.), In Like Flint, Planet of the Apes (AA nom.), The Ballad of Cable Hogue, Tora! Tora! Tora!, Patton (AA nom.), The Wild Rovers, The Other, Papillon (AA nom.), The Reincarnation of Peter Proud, Chinatown (AA nom.), Logan's Run, The Wind and the Lion (AA nom.), The Omen (Acad. Award), Islands in the Stream, MacArthur, Coma, The Great Train Robbery, Damian: Omen II, The Boys From Brazil (AA nom.), Alien, Star Trek—The Motion Picture (AA nom.), The Final Conflict, Outland, Raggedy Man, Mrs. Brisby: The Secret of Nimh, Poltergeist (AA nom.), First Blood, Under Fire, Twilight Zone—The Movie, Psycho II, Under Fire (AA nom.), Gremlins, Legend (European ver.), Explorers, Rambo: First

Blood II, Poltergeist II: The Other Side, Hoosiers (AA nom.), Extreme Prejudice, Innerspace, Lionheart, Rent-a-Cop, Rambo III, Criminal Law, The 'Burbs, Leviathan, Star Trek V: The Final Frontier.

GOLDSMITH, MARTIN M.: Writer. b. New York, NY, Nov. 6, 1913. Bush pilot.
AUTHOR: Novels include: Double Jeopardy, Detour, Shadows at Noon, Miraculous Fish of Domingo Gonzales.
PICTURES: Detour, Blind Spot, Narrow Margin, Mission Over Korea, Overland Pacific, Hell's Island.

GOLDSTEIN, MILTON: Executive. b. New York, NY, Aug. 1, 1926. e. NYU, 1949. In exec. capac., Paramount; foreign sales coord., The Ten Commandments, Psycho; v.p. foreign sales, Samuel Bronston org.; asst. to Pres., Paramount Int'l, special prods., 1964; Foreign sales mgr., 1966; v.p., world wide sales, 1967, Cinerama; Sr. v.p. Cinema Center Films, 1969; pres., Cinema Center Films, 1971; v.p. Theatrical Mktg. & Sales, Metromedia Producers Corp., 1973; in March, 1974, formed Boasberg-Goldstein, Inc., consultants in prod. and dist. of m.p.; 1975, named exec. vice pres., Avco Embassy Pictures; 1978, named exec. v.p. & chief operating officer, Melvin Simon Prods. 1980, named pres.; 1985, pres. Milt Goldstein Enterprises, Inc.

GOLDSTONE, JAMES: Director. b. Los Angeles, CA. June 8, 1931. e. Dartmouth Coll., B.A., Bennington Coll., M.A. Film editor from 1950. Writer, story editor from 1957.
TELEVISION: From 1958, including pilots of Star Trek, Ironside, The Senator, etc., A Clear and Present Danger (Emmy nomination); Eric (Virgin Islands Int'l. Film Festival Gold Medal); Journey from Darkness (Christopher Award); Studs Lonigan (miniseries 1978), Kent State, (Emmy, best direction, special), Things in Their Season, Calamity Jane; The Sun Also Rises; Dreams of Gold; Earthstar Voyager.
PICTURES: Jigsaw, Man Called Gannon, Winning, Brother John, Red Sky at Morning, The Gang That Couldn't Shoot Straight, They Only Kill Their Masters, Swashbuckler, Rollercoaster, When Time Ran Out.

GOLDSTONE, RICHARD: Producer. b. New York, NY, July 14, 1912. e. UCLA, B.A., 1933. Capt., Army Air Forces, office of Motion Picture Services, W.W.II. Adv. exec. Entered m.p. ind. 1934 as writer, MGM; in 1935 asst. head short subjects dept.; in 1939 assoc. prod. short subjects; apptd. prod. mgr., MGM short subjects dept., co-holder 3 Academy Awards short subjects, 1942. Prod. The Set-Up, (Int'l Critics Grand Prix, Cannes, 1949), v.p. Dudley Pict. Corp.; v.p., Goldcoast Productions, Inc.
PICTURES: The Outriders, Yellow Cab Man, Dial 1119, Inside Straight, The Tall Target, Talk About a Stranger, Devil Makes Three, Terror on the Train, Tabor the Great, The Big Search, East of Kilimanjaro, South Seas Adventures; No Man Is an Island, Rage, The Sergeant, The Babymaker.
TELEVISION: Prod. Adventures in Paradise, Combat, Peyton Place, We Ask, Why Not? (doc.)

GOLDWURM, JEAN: Executive. b. Bucharest, Rumania, Feb. 21, 1893. e. U. of Vienna. pres. Times Film Corp. officer French Legion of Honor; commander Italian Order of Merit, Commander French Order of Arts and Letters.

GOLDWYN, SAMUEL, JR.: Producer, Director. b. Los Angeles, CA, Sept. 7, 1926. e. U. of Virginia. U.S. Army, 1944; following war writer, assoc. prod., J. Arthur Rank Org.; prod. Gathering Storm on London stage; returned to U.S., 1948; assoc. prod., Universal; recalled to Army service, 1951; prod., dir., Army documentary films including Alliance for Peace (Edinburgh Film Festival prize); prod. TV shows, Adventure series for CBS, 1952–53; prod. TV series, The Unexpected, 1954; pres., The Samuel Goldwyn Company.
PICTURES: Prod.: Man With the Gun, The Sharkfighters, The Proud Rebel, The Adventures of Huckleberry Finn, The Young Lovers, Cotton Comes to Harlem, Come Back Charleston Blue, The Golden Seal, Mystic Pizza (exec. prod.), Stella.
TELEVISION: The Academy Awards, 1987; April Morning (co-exec. prod.); Acad. Awards, 1988 (prod.).

GOLIGER, NANCY: Executive. Began career in entertainment industry at Bill Gold Adv. & B.G. Charles. Joined Warner Bros. as natl. adv. mgr.; promoted to dir., creative adv. With Universal as dir. adv.; PolyGram Pictures, v.p., domestic & foreign adv./pub.; Seiniger Advertising, exec. v.p. & gen. mgr. 1985, joined Paramount Pictures as sr. v.p., prod./mktg. for M.P. Group.

GONZALEZ-GONZALEZ, PEDRO: Actor. b. Aguilares, TX, May 24, 1925. Comedian in San Antonio Mexican theatres.
PICTURES: Wing of the Hawk, Ring of Fear, Ricochet Romance, High and the Mighty, Strange Lady in Town, Bengazi, I Died a Thousand Times, Bottom of the Bottle, Gun the Man Down, Wetbacks, The Love Bug, Hellfighters, Support Your Local Gunfighter.
TELEVISION: O'Henry Stories, Felix, the Fourth, Hostile Guns.

GOOD, CHARLES E.: Executive. b. 1922. Joined Buena Vista in 1957 in Chicago office; progressed from salesman to branch mgr. and then district mgr. Later moved to Burbank as domestic sales mgr. in 1975; 1978, named v.p. & general sales mgr.; 1980, appointed pres., BV Distribution Co. Resigned presidency 1984; became BV consultant until retirement, April, 1987.

GOODMAN, DAVID Z.: Writer. e. Queens Coll., Yale School of Drama.
PICTURES: Straw Dogs, Lovers and Other Strangers, Farewell, My Lovely, Logan's Run, The Eyes of Laura Mars, Man, Woman and Child (co.-s.p.).

GOODMAN, GENE: Executive. Joined United Artists as salesman in 1954; promoted to branch mgr., Atlanta (1958–61). Served successively as branch mgr., New Orleans (1961–68); southern regional mgr. (1968–70); and southern div. mgr., (1970–78), New Orleans. Moved to N.Y. in 1978 to become asst. gen. sls. mgr. Promoted to v.p. & gen. sls. mgr. in 1980. Later in year named sr. v.p. for domestic sls.

GOODMAN, JOHN: Actor. b. St. Louis, MO, June 20, 1952. e. Southwest Missouri State U. Moved to NY in 1975 where he appeared off-off Broadway and in commercials. On Broadway in Big River.
PICTURES: Eddie Macon's Run (1983, debut), The Survivors, Revenge of the Nerds, C.H.U.D., Maria's Lovers, Sweet Dreams, The Big Easy, True Stories, Blind Date, Raisin' Arizona, The Wrong Guys, Burglar, Punchline, Everybody's All American, Sea of Love, Stella, Always.
TELEVISION: Heart of Steel, The Face of Rape, The Mystery of Moro Castle, Chiefs (mini-series), Roseanne (series).

GOODMAN, JULIAN: Executive. b. Glasgow, KY, May 1, 1922. e. Western Kentucky U., B.A.; George Washington U., B.A. Office mgr., Comb. Prod. & Resources, 1943–45. History at NBC: news writer, WRC, NBC owned station in Washington, DC, 1945; Washington ed., News of the World, NBC Radio network; mgr. of news and special events, NBC-TV, 1951; dir. of news and public affairs, NBC News Div., 1959; v.p., NBC News, 1961; exec. v.p., 1965; sr. exec. v.p., Operations, Jan. 1, 1966; pres., NBC, April 1, 1966. Mem. bd. of dirs., NBC, 1966; chief executive officer, Jan. 1, 1970; elected director or RCA Corporation, Jan. 1, 1972; chmn., chief exec. off., NBC, April, 1, 1974; chmn., Jan. 5, 1977.

GOODMAN, MORT: Advertising, Public Relations Executive. b. Cleveland, OH, Oct. 17, 1910. e. Western Reserve U. With sports dept. Cleveland News 1928–29 joined pub. dept. Warner Bros. theatres (Ohio), 1930; transferred to Hollywood as pub. dir. for Pacific Coast zone, 1937; pub. dir. Republic Studios, 1946; res. 1952, apptd. v.p. Stodel Adv. Agcy., formed Mort Goodman Adv., 1953; formed Goodman Org., advertising agency, pub. rel., 1955. Currently pres., Goodman Nemoy and Partners, adv.-p.r. firm started 1977. In 1980 became adv. & p.r. consultant for m.p. industry.

GOODRICH, ROBERT EMMETT: Executive. b. Grand Rapids, MI, June 27, 1940. e. U. of Michigan, B.A., 1962; J.D., 1964; NYU. LL.M, 1966. Pres. & Secty., Goodrich Theaters, Inc. 1967–present, developed circuit from father's one theater to 40 screens at 7 locations in seven Mich. communities. Owns and operates AM/FM radio stations: Lansing & Muskegon, MI, Davenport, IA.
MEMBER: NATO; Will Rogers Inst. advisory comm; bd., Mich. Millers Mutual Insurance Co.; State of Mich. Bar Assn.

GOODSON, MARK: TV Producer; b. Sacramento, CA, Jan. 24, 1918; s. Abraham Ellis and Fannie (Gross) G.; U. of California, A.B., 1937. Announcer, newscaster, dir. Radio Sta. KFRC, San Francisco, 1938–41; radio announcer, dir., N.Y. 1941–43; producer—Appointment with Life, ABC, 1943; dir. Portia Faces Life, Young & Rubicam, advt. agy., 1944; radio dir. U.S. Treasury War Bond Drive, 1944–45; formed Goodson-Todman Prodns., 1946, originated radio shows Winner Take All, 1946, Stop the Music, 1947, Hit the Jackpot, 1947–49. Creator of TV game programs What's My Line, It's News To Me, The Name's the Same, I've Got a Secret, Two for the Money, To Tell the Truth, The Price Is Right, Password, Match Game, Family Feud, and others; TV film series, The Web, The Rebel, Richard Boone Theater, Branded. 1st v.p. Capitol City Pub. Co.; v.p. New Eng. Newspapers, Inc.; dir. City Center Music and Drama, Board American Film Institute; trustee, Museum of Broadcasting. Recipient nat. television award Great Britain, 1951; Emmy award Acad. TV Arts and Scis., 1951, 52; Sylvania award. Pres. N.Y. Acad. TV Arts and Sci. 1957–58. Phi Beta Kappa.

GOODWIN, RICHARD: Producer. b. Bombay, India, Sept. 13, 1934. e. Rugby. Entered film world by chance: while waiting to go to Cambridge U. took temporary job as tea boy at studio which led to 20-year-long association with producer Lord Brabourne.
PICTURES: Prod. Mgr.: The Sheriff of Fractured Jaw, Carve Her Name with Pride, The Grass Is Greener, Sink the

Bismarck, HMS Defiant. Prod.: The Tales of Beatrix Potter. Co-Prod.: Murder on the Orient Express, Death on the Nile, The Mirror Crack'd, Evil Under the Sun, A Passage to India, Little Dorrit.

GOODWIN, RONALD: Composer, Arranger, Conductor. b. Plymouth, Eng., 1930. Early career: arranger for BBC dance orchestra; mus. dir., Parlophone Records; orchestra leader for radio, TV and records. Fut. m.p. ind., 1958. Many major film scores. Guest cond. R.P.O., B.S.O., Toronto Symph. Orch. New Zealand Symphony Orch., Sydney Symphony Orch. Scottish National Orch., BBC Scottish Symphony Orch., BBC Welsh Symphony Orch., BBC Radio Orch., BBC Concert Orch., London Philharmonic Orch., Gothenberg Symphony Orch., Norwegian Opera Orch. & Chorus, Halle Orchestra, Singapore Symphony Orch., Australian Pops Orch.

PICTURES: Whirlpool, I'm All Right Jack, The Trials of Oscar Wilde, Johnny Nobody, Village of the Damned, Murder She Said, Follow the Boys, Murder at the Gallop, Children of the Damned, 633 Squadron, Murder Most Foul, Murder Ahoy, Operation Crossbow, The ABC Murders, Of Human Bondage, Those Magnificent Men in Their Flying Machines, The Trap, Mrs. Brown, You've Got a Lovely Daughter; Submarine X-1, Decline and Fall, Where Eagles Dare, Monte Carlo or Bust, Battle of Britain, The Executioner, The Selfish Giant, Frenzy, Diamonds on Wheels, The Little Mermaid, The Happy Prince, One of Our Dinosaurs Is Missing, Escape From the Dark, Born to Run, Beauty and the Beast, Candleshoe, Force Ten from Navarone, Spaceman and King Arthur, Clash of Loyalties, Valhalla.

GORDON, ALEX: Producer. b. London, Eng., Sept. 8, 1922. e. Canford Coll., Dorset, 1939. Writer, m.p. fan magazines, 1939–41; British Army, 1942–45; pub. dir. Renown Pictures Corp., 1946–47; P.R. and pub. rep. for Gene Autry, 1948–53; v.p. and prod. Golden State Productions, 1954–58; prod. Alex Gordon Prods., 1958–66; producer Twentieth Century-Fox Television, 1967–76; film archivist/preservationist, 1976–84; v.p., Gene Autry's Flying A Pictures, 1985.

PICTURES: Lawless Rider, Bride of the Monster, Apache Woman, Day the World Ended, Oklahoma Woman, Girls in Prison, The She-Creature, Runaway Daughters, Shake Rattle and Rock, Flesh and the Spur, Voodoo Woman, Dragstrip Girl, Motorcycle Gang, Jet Attack, Submarine Seahawk, Atomic Submarine, The Underwater City, The Bounty Killer, Requiem for a Gunfighter.

TELEVISION: Movie of the Year, Golden Century, Great Moments in Motion Pictures.

GORDON, BERT I.: Producer, Director, Writer. b. Kenosha, WI; U. of Wisconsin.

PICTURES: Beginning of the End, The Amazing Colossal Man, The Fantastic Puppet People, The Cyclops, The Spider, Tormented, Boy and The Pirates, The Magic Sword, Village of the Giants, Picture Mommy Dead, How to Succeed With the Opposite Sex, Necromancy, Geronimo, The Mad Bomber, The Police Connection, The Food of the Gods, The Coming, The Big Bet, Malediction.

GORDON, BRUCE: Executive. b. Sidney, Australia, Feb. 4, 1929. Began career in Australian entertainment industry 1952 with Tivoli Circuit, live theatre chain; acted as advance man, front-of-house mgr., adv. dir.; promoted to busn. mgr., 1958. Named Tivoli membr. bd. of management, 1960–62. Joined Desilu Studios in 1962, developing Far East territories; promoted 1968 when Paramount acquired Desilu to mng. dir. Para. Far East opns. Named to bd. of TV Corp., 1969, operator of Channel 9 TV stns. & co.'s theatres in Sydney, Melbourne. Dir. on bd. of Academy Investments, operator of Perth theatre chain; responsible for building Perth Entertainment Centre. Named pres., Paramount TV Intl. Services, Ltd., 1974, in New York office. Based in Bermuda since 1985.

GORDON, CHARLES: Executive, Producer. b. Belzoni, MS. Began career as a talent agent with William Morris Agency. Left to write and develop television programming creating and producing 5 pilots and 3 series. Left TV to enter motion picture production in partnership with brother Lawrence Gordon. President and chief operating officer, The Gordon Company.

PICTURES: Exec. prod.: Die Hard, Leviathan. Co-prod.: Night of the Creeps, The Wrong Guys, Field of Dreams, K-9, Lock Up.

TELEVISION: Writer-creator: When the Whistle Blows. Exec. prod.: The Renegades. Exec. prod.-creator: Just Our Luck, Our Family Honor.

GORDON, GALE: Actor. r.n. Charles T. Aldrich, Jr. b. New York, NY, Feb. 2, 1906. Son of vaudeville performer Charles Aldrich and actress Gloria Gordon. Was radio performer in 1930s (Received award from Radio Hall of Fame). Stage debut in The Dancers; m.p. debut in The Pilgrimage Play, 1929.

PICTURES: Rally Round the Flag Boys, All in a Night's Work, Don't Give Up the Ship, Visit to a Small Planet, All Hands on Deck, Speedway, The 'Burbs.

TELEVISION: Series: My Favorite Husband, Our Miss Brooks, The Brothers, Dennis The Menace, The Lucy Show, Here's Lucy, Life With Lucy.

GORDON, JACK: Executive. b. Brooklyn, NY, Mar. 13, 1929. e. UCLA. Father is Mack Gordon, songwriter. Started in industry as TV production asst. in 1949. Served in U.S. Infantry, Korea, 1951–52. Joined MGM in 1953; named dir. of non-theatrical div., 1956; v.p., MGM Intl., 1972. Appointed exec. v.p., MGM, Intl. 1979; sr. v.p., MGM/UA International Motion Pictures Distribution, 1981; pres., 1983.

GORDON, LAWRENCE: Producer, Executive. b. Belzoni, MS, March 25, 1936. e. Tulane U. (business admin.). Assist. to prod. Aaron Spelling at Four Star Television, 1964. Writer and assoc. prod. on several Spelling shows. 1965, joined ABC-TV as head of west coast talent dev; 1966, TV and motion pictures exec. with Bob Banner Associates; 1968 joined AIP as v.p. in charge of project dev.; 1971 named v.p., Screen Gems (TV div. of Columbia Pictures) where he helped dev. Brian's Song and QB VII. Returned to AIP as v.p. worldwide prod. Formed Lawrence Gordon Prods. at Columbia Pictures; 1984–86, pres. and COO 20th Century Fox. Currently indep. prod. with 20th Century Fox. Producer of Bdwy. musical Smile.

PICTURES: Dillinger (1973), Hard Times, Rolling Thunder, The Driver, The End, Hooper, The Warriors, Xanadu, Paternity, Jekyll and Hyde, Together Again, 48 Hours, Streets of Fire, Brewster's Millions, Lucas, Jumpin' Jack Flash, Predator, The Couch Trip, The Wrong Guys, Die Hard, Field of Dreams, Lock Up, Family Business. Leviathan (exec. prod.), K-9

TELEVISION: (Co-creator and co-exec. prod.) Dog and Cat, Matt Houston, Renegades, Just Our Luck, Our Family Honor.

GORDON, MICHAEL: Director. b. Baltimore, MD, Sept. 6, 1909. e. Johns Hopkins U., B.A.; Yale, M.F.A. Stage experience as technician, stage mgr., actor, stage dir. (Stevedore, Home of the Brave, Anna Christie, One Bright Day). Member Group Theater 1935–40. m.p. debut: dial. dir. Columbia on over 20 films; dir. in 1942. Professor of Theater Arts, UCLA.

PICTURES: Boston Blackie Goes Hollywood, Underground Agent, One Dangerous Night, The Crime Doctor, The Web, Another Part of the Forest, An Act of Murder, The Lady Gambles, Woman in Hiding, Cyrano de Bergerac, I Can Get It for You Wholesale, The Secret of Convict Lake, Any Way the Wind Blows, Pillow Talk, Portrait in Black, Boy's Night Out, For Love or Money, Move Over Darling, Texas Across the River, A Very Special Favor, The Impossible Years, How Do I Love Thee?

OTHER PLAYS: Deadfall, The Lovers, Tender Trap, Male Animal, His & Hers, Champagne Complex, Home of the Brave, etc.

GORDON, RICHARD: Producer. b. London, Eng., Dec. 31, 1925. e. U. of London, 1943. Served in Brit. Royal Navy, 1944–46; ed. & writer on fan magazines & repr. independent American cos. 1946, with publicity dept. Assoc. Brit. Pathe 1947; org. export-import business for independent, British and American product; formed Gordon Films, Inc., 1949; formed Amalgamated prod., 1956; formed Grenadier Films, Ltd. 1971.

PICTURES: The Counterfeit Plan, The Haunted Strangler, Fiend Without a Face, The Secret Man, First Man into Space, Corridors of Blood, Devil Doll, Curse of Simba, The Projected Man, Naked Evil, Island of Terror; Tales of the Bizarre, Tower of Evil, Horror Hospital, The Cat and the Canary, Inseminoid.

GORDY, BERRY: Executive. b. Nov. 28, 1929. Was working on auto assembly line in Detroit when decided to launch record co., Motown. In 1961 wrote song, Shop Around; recording by Smokey Robinson made it his first million dollar record. Expanded into music publishing, personal mgt., recording studios, film and TV, also backing stage shows. Former bd. chmn., Motown Industries. Chmn. The Gordy Co. Received Business Achievement Award, Interracial Council for Business Opportunity, 1967; Whitney M. Young Jr. Award, L.A. Urban League, 1980; Inducted into Rock and Roll Hall of Fame, 1988.

PICTURES: Lady Sings the Blues (prod.), Bingo Long Traveling All-Stars and Motor Kings (exec. prod.), Mahogany (dir.), Almost Summer, The Last Dragon (exec. prod.).

GORING, MARIUS: Actor. b. Newport, Isle of Wight, 1912. e. Cambridge U., Universities of Frankfurt-on-Main, Munich, Vienna, Paris. Early career with Old Vic; stage debut 1927, Jean Sterling Rackinlay's Children's Matinees. 1940–46 served with H. M. Forces and Foreign Office.

PICTURES: Rembrandt, Dead Men Tell No Tales, Flying 55, Consider Your Verdict, Spy in Black, Pastor Hall, The Case of the Frightened Lady, The Big Blockade, The Night Raider, Lilli Marlene, Stairway to Heaven, Night Boat to Dublin, Take My Life, Red Shoes, Mr. Perrin and Mr. Traill, Odette, Pandora and the Flying Dutchman, Circle of Danger, Highly Dangerous, So Little Time, The Man Who Watched Trains Go By, Rough Shoot, The Barefoot Contessa, Break in the Circle, Quentin Durward, Ill Met by Moonlight, The Moonraker, Family Doctor, Angry Hills, Whirlpool, Treasure of

St. Teresa, Monty's Double, Beyond the Curtain, Desert Mice, The Inspector, Girl on a Motorcycle, Subterfuge.
TELEVISION: Numerous appearances, Sleeping Dog, Man in a Suitcase, Scarlet Pimpernel, The Expert.

GOROG, LASZLO: Writer. b. Hungary, Sept. 30, 1903. e. U. of Sciences, Budapest. Playwright, short story writer, asst. editor, Budapest, 1928–39.
PICTURES: Tales of Manhattan, The Affairs of Susan, She Wouldn't Say Yes, The Land Unknown, Mole People.
TELEVISION: 4 Star, Dupont, The Roaring Twenties, 77 Sunset Strip, Maverick, etc.

GORTNER, MARJOE: Actor, Producer. b. Long Beach, CA, Jan. 14, 1944. Was child evangelist, whose career as such was basis for documentary film, Marjoe (AA). Acted in films and TV; turned producer in 1978 for When You Comin' Back, Red Ryder.
PICTURES: Bobbie Joe and the Outlaw, The Food of the Gods, Viva Knievel, Sidewinder One, Earthquake, When You Comin' Back, Red Ryder, Mausoleum, Hellhole, American Ninja III: Blood Hunt.
TELEVISION: Films: The Marcus-Nelson Murders, The Gun and the Pulpit, Pray for the Wildcats. Guest appearances on Police Story, Mayday: 40,000 Feet. Series: Falcon Crest.

GOSSET, LOUIS, JR.: Actor. b. Brooklyn, NY, May 27, 1936. e. NYU, B.S. Basketball player with NY Knicks. Also nightclub singer during 1960s. On stage in Take a Giant Step (1953), The Desk Set, Lost in the Stars, A Raisin in the Sun, Golden Boy, The Blacks, Blood Knot, The Zulu and the Zayda, My Sweet Charlie, Carry Me Back to Morningside Heights, Murderous Angels (L.A. Critics Award).
PICTURES: A Raisin in the Sun (debut, 1961), The Bushbaby, The Landlord, Skin Game, Travels With My Aunt, The Laughing Policeman, The White Dawn, River Niger, J.D.'s Revenge, Choirboys, The Deep, It Rained All Night the Day I Left, Private Benjamin, An Officer and a Gentleman (Oscar), Jaws 3-D, Finders Keepers, Enemy Mine, Iron Eagle, Firewalker, The Principal, Iron Eagle II: Battle Beyond the Flag, The Punisher.
TELEVISION: Series: Gideon Oliver. Movies: Companions in Nightmare, It's Good to Be Alive, Sidekicks, Delancey Street, The Crisis Within, Don't Look Back, Roots (Emmy), Little Ladies of the Night, To Kill a Cop, The Critical List, Backstairs at the White House, This Man Stands Alone, Sadat, The Guardian, A Gathering of Old Men, The Father Clements Story, Roots: The Gift. Series: The Power of Matthew Star, The Lazarus Syndrome, The Young Rebels. Specials: Welcome Home, A Triple Play; Sam Found Out.

GOTTESMAN, STUART: Executive. Started career in mailroom of Warner Bros., 1972; later named promo. asst. to southwestern regional fieldman; promoted to that post which held for 10 years. 1987, named WB dir. field activities.

GOTTLIEB, CARL: Writer, Director, Actor. b. March 18, 1938. e. Syracuse U., B.S., 1960.
PICTURES: Actor: Maryjane (1968), M.A.S.H., Up the Sandbox, Cannonball, The Jerk, The Sting II, Johnny Dangerous. The Committee, Into the Night. Director: The Absent-Minded Waiter (short), Co-Writer: Jaws; Which Way Is Up?; Jaws II; The Jerk (also act.); Caveman (also dir.); Doctor Detroit; Jaws 3-D. Actor: The Committee, Into the Night, Amazon Women on the Moon (co-dir.).
TELEVISION: Writer: Smothers Bros. Comedy Hour (Emmy); The Odd Couple; Flip Wilson; Bob Newhart Show; The Super; Crisis at Sun Valley, The Deadly Triangle, Paul Reiser: Out on a Whim.

GOTTLIEB, STAN: Actor, Film Distributor. b. New York, NY, April 22, 1917. e. NYU, Columbia U. Has acted in films, theatrical, stage and TV since 1970. Gen. mgr. for Impact Films, Inc. 1966–72. Gen. Mgr., Mammoth Films (1973–76).
PICTURES: Actor: Putney Swope, You Gotta Walk It Like You Talk It, The Owl and the Pussycat, Pound, The Anderson Tapes, Cold Turkey, Slaughterhouse Five, Black Fantasy, Greaser's Place, Compliments to the World.
TELEVISION: Actor: Sticks & Bones, Hot l Baltimore, The Jeffersons.
STAGE: Steambath.

GOUGH, MICHAEL: Actor. b. Malaya, Nov. 23, 1917. e. Rose Hill Sch., in Kent, England, and at Durham School. Studied at Old Vic School in London; first stage appearance in 1936 at Old Vic Theatre. N.Y. stage debut 1937 in Love of Women. London debut in 1938 in The Zeal of Thy House. M.P. debut in 1948 in Blanche Fury; since in over 50 films.
PICTURES: Anna Karenina, The Man in the White Suit, Rob Roy, The Sword and the Rose, Richard III, Reach for the Sky, Horror of Dracula, The Horse's Mouth, Konga, Mr. Topaze, The Phantom of the Opera, The Skull, Walk with Love and Death, Berserk, Women in Love, Julius Caesar, Trog, The Go-Between, Henry VIII and His Six Wives, Savage Messiah, The Legend of Hell House, The Boys from Brazil, The Dresser, Top Secret!, Caravaggio, The Fourth Protocol, Out of Africa, The Serpent and the Rainbow, Batman, Strapless, Blackeyes.
TELEVISION: Mini-series: The Search for the Nile, QB VII, Shoulder to Shoulder, The Citadel. Smiley's People, Brideshead Revisited, Mistral's Daughter, Lace II, Inside the Third Reich, To the Lighthouse, The Citadel, Suez, Vincent the Dutchman, Heart Attack Hotel, Oxford Blues.

GOULD, ELLIOTT: Actor. (Producer). r.n. Elliott Goldstein. b. Brooklyn, NY, August 29, 1938. e. Professional Children's Sch., NY 1955. Vaudeville: appeared at Palace Theater, 1950. Broadway debut in Rumple (1957).
STAGE: Say Darling, Irma La Douce, I Can Get It for You Wholesale, On the Town (London), Fantasticks (tour), Drat the Cat, Little Murders, Luv (tour), A Way of Life, The Guys in the Truck, Hit the Deck (Jones Beach).
TELEVISION: Specials: Once Upon A Mattress, Come Blow Your Horn, Jack and the Beanstalk (Faerie Tale Theater), Prime Time, Electric Company, Saturday Night Live, (Emmy; 6 times), Out to Lunch, Casey at the Bat (Tall Tales & Legends), Guest: Twilight Zone, George Burns Comedy Week, Paul Reiser: Out on a Whim. Movies: Vanishing Act, The Rules of Marriage, Conspiracy: The Trial of the Chicago 8. Series: E/R, Together We Stand.
PICTURES: Quick, Let's Get Married (debut, 1965), The Night They Raided Minsky's, Bob & Carol & Ted & Alice, M*A*S*H, Getting Straight, Move, Little Murders (also prod.), The Touch, I Love My Wife, The Long Goodbye, Busting, S*P*Y*S!, California Split, Who?, Nashville, (guest), Whiffs, I Will . . . I Will . . . For Now, Harry and Walter Go to New York, Mean Johnny Barrows, A Bridge Too Far, Capricorn One, Matilda, Escape to Athena, The Last Flight of Noah's Ark, The Muppet Movie, The Lady Vanishes, Falling in Love Again, The Devil and Max Devlin, Dirty Tricks, The Bums, The Naked Face, The Silent Partner, Over the Brooklyn Bridge, Inside Out, The Muppets Take Manhattan, My First 40 Years, The Telephone, Lethal Obsession (Der Joker), The Big Picture, Dangerous Love, Story of a Woman, Night Visitor, The Wounded King, The Lemon Sisters, Judgment, Dead Men Don't Die, Strawanser.

GOULD, HAROLD: Actor. b. Schenectady, NY, Dec. 10, 1923. e. Cornell U., MA., Ph.D. Instructor of theatre and speech, 1953–56; asst. prof. drama and speech, 1956–60. Acted with Ashland, OR Shakespeare Fest. in 1950s and Mark Taper Forum (The Miser, Once in a Lifetime). Won Obie Award for Off-Bdwy debut in The Increased Difficulty of Concentration, 1969.
THEATER: The House of Blue Leaves, Fools, Grown Ups.
PICTURES: Two for the Seesaw, The Couch, Harper, Inside Daisy Clover, Marnie, An American Dream, The Arrangement, The Lawyer, Mrs. Pollifax: Spy, Where Does It Hurt?, The Sting, The Front Page, Love and Death, The Big Bus, Silent Movie, The One and Only, Seems Like Old Times, Playing for Keeps, Romero.
TELEVISION: Series: Rhoda, Soap, Tickets Please (pilot). Movies: To Catch a Star, Feather and Father Gang, Park Place, Foot in the Door, Moviola, Washington Behind Closed Doors, Aunt Mary, Better Late Than Never, King Crab, Have I Got a Christmas for You, Man in the Santa Claus Suit, I Never Sang For My Father, Tales from the Hollywood Hills: The Closed Set, Get Smart, Again!.

GOULD, JOSEPH: Executive. b. New York, NY, Jan. 30, 1915. e. NYU, B.A., 1935; Columbia U., Pulitzer School of Journalism, M.S., 1936. Adv. dept., United Artists, 1939–46; W.W.II service, 1944–46: Office Strategic Services (London), Office of Military Govt. for Germany (US), Berlin; Universal, 1947–48; asst. adv. mgr. 20th Century-Fox. 1949–52; adv. consultant, Joseph Burstyn. Louis De Rochemont Assoc., I.F.E. Releasing Corp. 1953–55; adv. mgr. United Artists, 1955–60; adv. mgr. Paramount Pictures, 1960–62; David Singer Associates, 1962–64; partner, Konheim Gould & Ackerman, 1968–74; principal, Joseph Gould Associates, 1974–77; creative services director, WIXT-TV, Syracuse, 1978–82; Joseph Gould Associates, Falls Church, VA, 1982–84; Center for Defense Information, Public Affairs, director, Washington, DC, 1984–.

GOULET, ROBERT: Singer, Actor. b. Lawrence, MA., Nov. 26, 1933. e. school, Edmonton; scholarship, Royal Conservatory of Music. Sang in choirs, appeared with numerous orchestras; disk jockey, CKUA, Edmonton; pub. rel., The Merrick Co.
STAGE: Camelot, The Happy Time, numerous tours.
TELEVISION: The Ed Sullivan Show, Garry Moore, The Enchanted Nutcracker, Omnibus, The Broadway of Lerner and Loewe, Rainbow of Stars, Judy Garland Show, Bob Hope Show, The Bell Telephone Hour; England: Granada—TV special, Jack Benny; Dean Martin; Andy Williams; Jack Paar; Red Skelton; Hollywood Palace; Patty Duke Show, Star of Robert Goulet Show, Blue Light (series), Brigadoon, Carousel, Kiss Me Kate, Fantasy Island, Matt Houston, Glitter.
PICTURES: Honeymoon Hotel, I'd Rather Be Rich, I Deal in Danger, Underground, Atlantic City, Beetlejuice, Scrooged.

RECORDS: Always You, Two of Us, Sincerely Yours, The Wonderful World of Love, Robert Goulet in Person, This Christmas I Spend With You, Manhattan Tower, Without You, My Love Forgive Me, Travelling On, Robert Goulet on Tour, Robert Goulet on Broadway, Robert Goulet on Broadway II, Camelot, Happy Time.

GOWDY, CURT: Sportscaster. b. Green River, WY, 1919. Basketball star at U. of Wyoming. All-Conference member; graduated U. of Wyoming. 1942. Officer in U.S. Air Force WWII, then became sportscaster. Voted Sportscaster of the Year, 1967, Nat'l Assn. of Sportswriters Broadcasters. Best Sportscaster, Fame, 1967. Did play-by-play telecasts for 16 World Series, 7 Super Bowls, 12 Rose Bowls, 8 Orange Bowls, 18 NCAA Final 4 college basketball championships. In 1970 was the first individual from the field of sports to receive the George Foster Peabody Award. Hosted the American Sportsman outdoor TV show on ABC for 20 years. (Received 8 Emmy Awards). Inducted into the Sportscasters Hall of Fame in 1981, the Fishing Hall of Fame in 1982, and the Baseball Hall of Fame in 1984.

GRADE, LORD LEW: Executive. r.n. Louis Winogradsky. b. Tokmak, Russia, Dec. 25, 1906. Brother of Lord Bernard Delfont. Came to Eng. 1912. Was first a music hall dancer until 1934 when he became an agent with Joe Collins, founding Collins and Grade Co. Joint managing dir. Lew & Leslie Grade Ltd. theatrical agency until 1955; Chmn. & mng. dir., ITC Entertainment Ltd. 1958–82; chmn. & chief exec., Associated Communications Corp. Ltd., 1973–82; pres. ATV Network Ltd., 1977–82; chmn., Stoll Moss Theatres Ltd., 1969–82; chmn. & chief exec., Embassy Communications International Ltd., 1982–85; chmn. & chief exec., The Grade Co. 1985–; Gov., Royal Shakespeare Theatre, Fellow BAFTA, 1979, KCSS 1979. Autobiography: Still Dancing (1988).
NY THEATER: Prod.: Merrily We Roll Along, Starlight Express.

GRADE, MICHAEL: Executive. b. London, England, 1943. Entered industry 1966. Early career as newspaper columnist, became an executive at London Weekend Television then Embassy Television in Hollywood. Joined BBC Television, 1983 as controller of BBC 1 and director of Programmes (TV), 1986. Joined Channel 4 as chief executive, 1988.

GRADUS, BEN: Producer, Director, Writer. b. New York, NY. e. Brooklyn Coll. Is principal in Directors Group Motion Pictures, Inc. Positions held include v.p. Filmways, Inc.; prod.-dir. for Screen Gems. Specialist in educational and doc. films; also has done feature, children's comedy TV shows and series, Decision: The Conflicts of Harry S. Truman. Author, Directing the Television Commercial. Nominee for Emmy, Grammy.
CREDITS: Dawn over Ecuador, Gentlemen of the Jury, To Save Your Life, Lifewatch Six, Ford Around the World, Art Heritage, A Girl from Puerto Rico, Span of Life, Crowded Paradise.

GRAF, BILLY: Executive. b. 1945. Entered industry 1965. Was asst. dir.; unit/location mgr./production mgr. for American, British and European companies. Now line producer, production mgr., asst. director.
PICTURES: Alfie, A Man for All Seasons, Billion Dollar Brain, Scrooge, Run Wild Run Free, The Best House in London, Chitty Chitty Bang Bang, Galaxina, Khartoum, You Only Live Twice, Women in Love, Song of Norway, Prudence and the Pill, Hammerhead, Underground Aces, Purple Rain, Teen Wolf, Housesitter, The Spoiler.
TELEVISION: Secret Agent, The Saint, "Q" Branch, Private Eye Public Ear, The Avengers, Department "S," The Dave Cash Radio Show.

GRAF, WILLIAM N.: Executive. b. New York, NY, Oct. 11, 1912. Entered industry in 1934. 1937–42, exec. secty./asst. to Mark Hellinger at Warner Bros. & 20th-Fox. 1942–45, writer of armed forces training films. 1946–50, exec. secty./asst. to Harry Cohn, pres., Columbia Pictures; 1951, prod. asst. to Jack Fier, prod. head, Columbia. 1952–65, Amer. repr. for British productions, Columbia Pictures; 1965–66, exec. asst. to J. J. Frankovich, Columbia Pictures, London; 1965–66, v.p., Columbia Pictures Intl., London; 1969–70, indep. prod., Cinema Center Films; 1980, v.p. in chg. of prod., Legion Films, Inc., Beverly Hills; 1984, pres., Billy Graf Prods. 1984, 1st v.p., Interguild Federal Credit Union, Writers, Dirs, Prods, & Cameramen; 1988, appt. bd. of dirs., Permanent Charities Comm.; 1987, exec. comm., Foreign Films Acad. of M.P. Arts & Sciences. Also comm. mem., Short and Feature Documentaries.
PICTURES: (Producer): The Red Beret, A Man for All Seasons, Sinful Davey, The African Elephant.

GRAFF, RICHARD B.: Executive. b. Milwaukee, WI, Nov. 9. e. U. of Illinois. Served U.S. Air Force; Universal Pictures 1946 to 1964 in Chicago, Detroit, Chicago and NY home office as asst. to genl. sales mgr.; 1964 joined National General in Los Angeles. In 1967 became v.p. and general sales mgr. of National General Pictures, formed and operated company. 1968, exec. v.p. in charge of world-wide sales and marketing. 1968 made v.p. of parent company; v.p. general sales mgr. AIP in 1971; 1975, pres. Cine Artists Pictures; 1977, pres. The Richard Graff Company Inc; 1983, pres. of domestic distribution, MGM/UA. 1987, pres., worldwide distribution, Weintraub Entertainment Group.

GRANET, BERT: Producer, Writer. b. New York, NY, July 10, 1910. e. Yale U. Sch. of Fine Arts (47 workshop). From 1936 author s.p. orig. & adapt. numerous pictures. Exec. prod.: Universal, 1967–69, CBS, Desilu Studios.
PICTURES: Quick Money, The Affairs of Annabel, Mr. Doodle Kicks Off, Laddie, A Girl a Guy and a Gob, My Favorite Wife, Bride by Mistake, Sing Your Way Home, Those Endearing Young Charms, The Locket, Do You Love Me?, The Marrying Kind, Berlin Express, The Torch, Scarface, Mob.
TELEVISION: Desilu (1957–61), Twilight Zone, The Untouchables (pilot), Scarface Mob; Loretta Young Show (1955–56), Walter Winchell File 1956–57, Lucille Ball-Desi Arnaz Show 1957–60, Westinghouse Desilu Playhouse, The Great Adventure.

GRANGER, FARLEY: Actor. b. San Jose, CA, July 1, 1925. e. Hollywood. School prior to m.p. career; screen debut in North Star 1943; in U.S. Armed Forces 1944–46. Joined Eva Le Gallienne's National Rep. Co. in 1960s (The Sea Gull).
PICTURES: The Purple Heart, They Live by Night, Rope, Enchantment, Roseanna McCoy, Side Street, Our Very Own, Edge of Doom, Strangers on a Train, Behave Yourself, I Want You, O. Henry's Full House, Hans Christian Andersen, Story of Three Loves, Small Town Girl, Summer Hurricane, Brass Ring, Naked Street, Girl in the Red Velvet Swing, Arrow Smith, The Heiress, The Prisoner of Zenda, Senso, The Serpent, A Man Called Noon, Those Days in the Sun, The Chief of Homicide, The Painter and the Red Head, Call Me Trinity, The Syndicate, Arnold, A Crime for a Crime, The Imagemaker.
TELEVISION: Playhouse of Stars, U.S. Steel Hour, Producer's Showcase, Climax, Ford Theatre, Playhouse 90, 20th Century Fox Hour, Robert Montgomery Presents, Arthur Murray Dance Party, Wagon Train, Masquerade Party, Kojak, 6 Million Dollar Man, Ellery Queen, 9 Lives of Jenny Dolan, Widow, One Life to Live, As the World Turns.

GRANGER, STEWART: Actor. r.n. James Stewart. b. May 6, 1913. e. medicine; Webber-Douglas Sch. of Acting, London. In Brit. Army, W.W.II. On stage from 1935, Hull Repertory theat.; Birmingham Repertory; Malvern Festivals (1936–37); Old Vic Co. Film debut. A Southern Maid (1933). Voted one of Brit. top ten money-making stars in M.P. Herald-Fame Poll, 1943, 1944, 1945, 1946, 1947, 1949.
PICTURES: In Great Britain: So This Is London, Convoy, Secret Mission, Thursday's Child, Man in Grey, The Lamp Still Burns, Fanny by Gaslight, Love Story, Waterloo-Road, Madonna of the Seven Moons, Caesar and Cleopatra, Caravan, Magic Bow, Captain Boycott, Blanche Fury, Saraband for Dead Lovers, Woman Hater, Adam and Evalyn. In U.S.: King Solomon's Mines, Soldiers Three, Light Touch, Wild North, Scaramouche, Prisoner of Zenda, Salome, Young Bess, All the Brothers Were Valiant, Beau Brummell, Green Fire, Moonfleet, Footsteps in the Fog, Bhowani Junction, Last Hunt, The Little Hut, Gun Glory, The Whole Truth, Harry Black, North to Alaska, Sodom and Gomorrah, Swordsman of Siena, Last Patrol, The Secret Invasion, The Last Safari, The Trygon Factor, The Wild Geese, Hell Hunters.
TELEVISION: The Hound of the Baskervilles, Crossings, A Hazard of Hearts, Royal Romance of Charles and Diana.

GRANT, HUGH: Actor. b. London. e. New Coll., Oxford U. Acted with OUDS before landing role in Oxford Film Foundation's Privileged (1982) that began career. Acted at Nottingham Playhouse and formed revue group, The Jockeys of Norfolk.
PICTURES: Maurice (debut, 1987), The Lair of the White Worm, The Dawning, Remando al Viento.
TELEVISION: The Last Place on Earth (mini-series); The Demon Lover; The Detective; Handel: Honour, Profit and Pleasure; Ladies in Charge, The Lady and the Highwayman, Champagne Charlie, Till We Meet Again.

GRANT, LEE: Actress. r.n. Lyova Rosenthal. b. New York, NY, Oct. 31, 1931. m. producer Joseph Feury. At 4 was member of Metropolitan Opera Company; played princess in L'Orocolo. Member of the American Ballet at 11. e. Juilliard Sch. of Music, studied voice, violin and dance. At 18 with road co. Oklahoma as understudy. Acting debut: Joy to the World.
THEATRE: acted in a series of one-acters at ANTA with Henry Fonda. The Detective Story (won Critics Circle Award 1949), Lo and Behold, A Hole in the Head, Wedding Breakfast; road co. Two for the Seesaw, The Captains and the Kings; toured with Electra, Silk Stockings, St. Joan, Arms and the Man, The Maids (Obie Award), Prisoner of Second Avenue.
TELEVISION: Studio One, The Kraft Theatre, Slattery's People, The Fugitive, Ben Casey, The Nurses, The Defenders, East Side/West Side, Peyton Place (Emmy Award,

Best Supporting Player, 1966), One Day at a Time, Fay (series), Bob Hope Show (Emmy nom.). Movies: The Love Song of Bernard Kempenski, BBC's The Respectful Prostitute, The Neon Ceiling (Emmy Award), The Spell, Thou Shalt Not Kill, Bare Essence, Plaza Suite, Will There Really Be A Morning?, Mussolini—The Untold Story (mini-series) Director: Nobody's Child, Shape of Things, When Women Kill, A Matter of Sex, Down and Out in America, The Hijacking of the Achille Lauro, Homeless (dir.).

PICTURES: The Detective Story, Terror in the Streets, Affair of the Skin, The Balcony, Divorce American Style, Valley of the Dolls, In the Heat of the Night, Buona Sera, Mrs. Campbell, The Big Bounce, Marooned, The Landlord, There Was a Crooked Man, Plaza Suite, Portnoy's Complaint, Shampoo (Acad. Award, supp. actress, 1975), Voyage of the Damned, Airport '77, When You Comin' Back, Red Ryder, Charlie Chan and the Curse of the Dragon Queen, Teachers, The Big Town. Dir.: Tell Me a Riddle, Willmar Eight, Staying Together.

GRANT, RICHARD E.: Actor. b. Mbabane, Swaziland, May 5, 1957. e. Cape Town U., South Africa (combined English and drama course). Co-founded multi-racial Troupe Theatre Company with fellow former students and members of Athol Fugard and Yvonne Bryceland's Space Theatre, acting in and directing contemporary and classic plays. Moved to London 1982 where performed in fringe and rep. theater. Nominated most promising newcomer in Plays and Players, 1981 for Tramway Road.

PICTURES: Withnail and I, Hidden City, Warlock, How to Get Ahead in Advertising, Mountains of the Moon, Killing Dad.

TELEVISION: Series: Sweet Sixteen. Movies: Honest, Decent and True, Lizzie's Pictures, Codename Kyril, Thieves in the Night, Here Is the News.

GRASGREEN, MARTIN: Executive. b. New York, NY, July 1, 1925. Entered m.p. ind. Jan., 1944, Columbia Pictures h.o. in contract dept. Promoted to travelling auditor April, 1946. Appt. office mgr. Omaha branch Dec., 1948; salesman Omaha, Dec., 1950. Transferred to Indianapolis, 1952, as city salesman; transferred to Cleveland as sales mgr., 1953. Left Columbia in 1960 to become 20th-Fox branch mgr. in Cleveland. Transferred to Philadelphia in 1965 as branch mgr.; transferred to N.Y. in 1967 as Eastern dist. mgr. Resigned in 1970 to form Paragon Pictures, prod.-dist. co. In Jan., 1975, formed Lanira Corp., representing producers for U.S. sales and dist. of films in U.S. Retired to Sanibor, FL.

GRASSHOFF, ALEX: Director. e. UCLA. 3 Acad. Award nominations for feature documentaries; Really Big Family; Journey to the Outer Limits; Young Americans (Acad. Award, 1968).

PICTURES: A Billion For Boris, J.D. and the Salt Flat Kid, The Last Dinosaur, The Jailbreakers.

TELEVISION: Series: The Rockford Files, Toma, Chips, Night Stalker, Barbary Coast, Movin' On. Specials: The Wave (Emmy), Future Shock (honored 1973 Cannes Film Fest.), Frank Sinatra, Family and Friends.

GRASSO, MARY ANN: Executive. b. Rome, NY, Nov. 3, 1952. e. U. of Calif., Riverside, B.A. art history, 1973; U. of Oregon, Eugene, Master of Library Science, 1984. Dir., Warner Research Collection, 1975–85; mgr., CBS-TV, docu-drama, 1985–88; exec. dir. National Association of Theater Owners, 1988–present. Member: Acad. Motion Picture Arts & Sciences, Acad. TV Arts and Sciences, Women in Film, American Society of Association Executives.

GRAVES, PETER: Actor. b. London, Oct. 21, 1911. e. Harrow. With Knight, Frank & Rutley, then Lloyds prior to theat. career. First stage appearance 1934 in Charles B. Cochran's Streamline.

THEATRE: Novello musicals at Drury Lane; repertory at Windsor, Old Chelsea, The Merry Widow, The Sound of Music, Private Lives. Recent: The Reluctant Peer, The Last of Mrs. Cheyney, Dear Charles, An Ideal Husband (S. Africa), A Boston Story (tour), His, Hers, and Theirs, The Great Waltz, No Sex Please We're British.

PICTURES: Mrs. Fitzherbert, Spring in Park Lane, Maytime in Mayfair, Lady With a Lamp, Encore, Derby Day (Four Against Fate), Lilacs in the Spring (Let's Make Up), Admirable Crichton, Alfie, The Wrong Box, The Jokers, I'll Never Forget What's Is Name, How I Won the War, Assassination Bureau, The Adventurers, The Slipper and the Rose.

TELEVISION: Those Wonderful Snows, Chelsea at 9, One O'Clock Show, Lunch Box, 2 Cars, Dickie Henderson Show, Ivor Novello Series, East Lynne, Ninety Years On, The Sleeping Doe, The Frobisher Game, The Jazz Age series, Kate series, Crown Court, Softly, Softly, 10 from the 20s, Quiller, Duchess of Duke Street, Looks Familiar, Bulman, Shades of Darkness, God Knows Where's Port Talbot, Campaign, The Woman He Loved, Shadow on the Sun.

GRAVES, PETER: Actor. r.n. Peter Aurness. b. Minneapolis, MN, March 18, 1926. e. U. of Minnesota. Brother, James Arness. Played with bands, radio announcer, while at school; U.S. Air Force 2 yrs.; summer stock appearances; m.p. debut in Rogue River (1950).

PICTURES: Fort Defiance, Stalag 17, East of Sumatra, Beneath the 12-Mile Reef, The Raid, Black Tuesday, Wichita, Long Gray Line, Night of the Hunter, Naked Street, Fort Yuma, Court Martial of Billy Mitchell, The Ballad of Josie, Sergeant Ryker, The Five Man Army, Sidecar Racers, Airplane!, Airplane II: The Sequel.

TELEVISION: Series: Fury, (1955–58), Mission Impossible, (1967–73), New Mission: Impossible (1988–90). Movies: Winds of War, If It's Tuesday, It Still Must Be Belgium, War and Remembrance (mini-series). Host/narrator: Discover! The World of Science (1985–90); Biography (1987– 90).

GRAVES: RUPERT: Actor. Before film debut worked as a clown with the Delta travelling circus in England.

THEATER: Sufficient Carbohydrates, Amadeus.

PICTURES: A Room with a View, Maurice, A Handful of Dust.

TELEVISION: British: Vice Versa (1980–81); A Life of Puccini; Fortunes of War.

GRAY, COLEEN: Actress. r.n. Doris Jensen. b. Staplehurst, NB, Oct. 23, 1922. e. Hamline U., B.A. summa cum laude, 1943, Actor's Lab. m. Fritz Zeiser. Member: Nat'l Collegiate Players, Kappa Phi, a capella choir, little theatres, 1943–44; screen debut State Fair, 1945.

PICTURES: Kiss of Death, Nightmare Alley, Fury at Furnace Creek, Red River, Sleeping City, Riding High, Father Is a Bachelor, Models Inc., Kansas City Confidential, Sabre Jet, Arrow in the Dust, The Fake, The Vanquished, Las Vegas Shakedown, Twinkle in God's Eye, Tennessee's Partner, The Killing, Wild Dakotas, Death of a Scoundrel, Frontier Gambler, Black Whip, Star in the Dust, The Vampires, Hell's Five Hours, Copper Sky, Johnny Rocco, The Leech Woman, The Phantom Planet, Town Tamer, P.J., The Late Liz, Cry from the Mountain.

TELEVISION: Days of Our Lives, (1966–67). Family Affair, Ironside, Bonanza, Judd for the Defense, Name of the Game, Bright Promise, The FBI, The Bold Ones, World Premiere, Mannix, Sixth Sense, McCloud, The Best Place to Be, Tales from the Dark Side.

GRAY, DULCIE: C.B.E. Actress b. Malaya, Nov. 20, 1919. e. Webber Douglas Sch. London Stage debut 1939, Aberdeen, Hay Fever, Author: Love Affair (play), 18 detective novels, book of short stories. 8 radio plays; co-author with husband Michael Denison, An Actor and His World; Butterflies on My Mind, The Glanville Women, Anna Starr; Mirror Image.

STAGE: 40 West End plays including Little Foxes, Brighton Rock, Dear Ruth, Rain on the Just, Candida, An Ideal Husband, Where Angels Fear to Tread, Heartbreak House, On Approval, Happy Family, No. 10, Out of the Question, Village Wooing, Wild Duck, At The End of the Day, The Pay Off, A Murder Has Been Announced, Bedroom Farce, A Coat of Varnish, School for Scandal, The Living Room.

PICTURES: Two Thousand Women, A Man About the House, Mine Own Executioner, My Brother Jonathan, The Glass Mountain, They Were Sisters Wanted for Murder, The Franchise Affair, Angels One Five, There Was a Young Lady, A Man Could Get Killed, The Trail of the Pink Panther, The Curse of the Pink Panther.

TELEVISION: Milestones, The Will, Crime Passionel, Art and Opportunity, Fish in the Family, The Governess, What the Public Wants, Lesson in Love, The Happy McBaines, Winter Cruise, The Letter, Tribute to Maugham, Virtue, Beautiful Forever, East Lynne, Unexpectedly Vacant, The Importance of Being Earnest, This Is Your Life, Crown Court, Making Faces, Read All About It, The Voysey Inheritance, Life After Death, The Pink Pearl, Britain in the Thirties, Rumpole (The Old Boy Net.), Cold Warrior, Hook, Line and Sinker, Howard's Way, Three Up and Two Down.

GRAY, GORDON: Broadcast Management Consultant. b. Albert Lea, MN, Nov. 16, 1905. e. U. of Missouri. Entered broadcasting ind. 1932, v.p., gen. mgr., WOR, WOR TV; pres. WKTV, Utica, N.Y., KAUZ, Wichita Falls, Tex. Founded Central N.Y. Cable, Utica, N.Y. Chmn., Board of Governors, WFTV, Orlando, Fla. and management consultant, presently.

GRAY, SPALDING: Performance artist, Actor, Writer. b. Barrington, RI, 1941. Began career as actor in 1965 at Alley Theater, Housten, then off-Bdwy in Tom Paine at LaMama Co. In 1969 joined the Wooster Group, experimental performance group. Has written and performed autobiographical monologues (Three Places in Rhode Island, Sex and Death to the Age 14, Swimming to Cambodia) throughout U.S, Europe and Australia. Has taught theater workshops for adults and children and is recipient of Guggenheim fellowship. Artist in resident Mark Taper Forum, 1986–87. Bdwy debut: Our Town (1988).

PICTURES: Actor: The Killing Fields, Swimming to Cambodia, True Stories, Stars and Bars, Clara's Heart, Beaches, Heavy Petting.

TELEVISION: Terrors of Pleasure (HBO Special). Movie: The Image.

GRAYSON, KATHRYN: Actress. r.n. Zelma Hedrick. b. Winston-Salem, NC, Feb. 9, 1923. e. St. Louis schools. Singer. Screen debut; Andy Hardy's Private Secretary, 1940. Achieved stardom in Anchors Aweigh, 1945.
PICTURES: The Vanishing Virginian, Rio Rita, Seven Sweethearts,Thousands Cheer; Ziegfeld Follies of 1946, Two Sisters from Boston, Showboat, That Midnight Kiss, Grounds for Marriage, The Toast of New Orleans, The Kissing Bandit, Lovely to Look At, Desert Song, So This Is Love, Kiss Me Kate, Vagabond King.
TELEVISION: GE Theatre (Emmy nomination), 1960; Die Fledermaus, ABC, 1966; Murder, She Wrote.
STAGE: Debut in N.Y. and tour, Camelot, 1963; Rosalinda, Merry Widow, Kiss Me Kate, Showboat (N.Y. and U.S. tour).

GRAZER, BRIAN: Producer. b. Los Angeles, CA, July 12, 1953. e. U. of Southern California. Started as legal intern at Warner Bros.; later script reader (for Brut/Faberge) & talent agent. Joined Edgar J. Scherick-Daniel Blatt Co.; then with Ron Howard as partner in Imagine Films Entertainment.
PICTURES: Night Shift; Splash; Real Genius, Like Father, Like Son (prod.), Parenthood, Opportunity Knocks (exec. prod.).
TELEVISION: Zuna Beach; Thou Shalt Not Commit Adultery, O'Hara (exec. prod.).

GREEN, ADOLPH: Writer, Actor. b. New York, NY, Dec. 2, 1915. m. actress-singer Phyllis Newman. Began career in the cabaret act The Revuers with partner Betty Comden and Judy Holliday (1944).
THEATER: Wrote book, sketches and/or lyrics for many Broadway shows including: On the Town (also actor), Billion Dollar Baby, Bonanza Bound! (also actor), Two on the Aisle, Wonderful Town (Tony Award, lyrics), Peter Pan (Mary Martin); Say Darling; Bells are Ringing; A Party with Comden and Green (1959 & 1977); Do Re Mi; Subways Are For Sleeping; Fade Out, Fade In; Halleuljah, Baby (Tony Awards, lyrics & best musical), Applause (Tony Award, book), Lorelei or Gentlemen Still Prefer Blondes (new lyrics), By Bernstein (book), On the Twentieth Century (Tony Awards, best book & lyrics, 1978), A Doll's Life.
PICTURES: Writer With Betty Comden: Good News, On the Town, Barkleys of Broadway, Take Me Out to the Ball Game, Singin' in the Rain, Bandwagon, It's Always Fair Weather, Auntie Mame; What a Way to Go, all in collab. with Betty Comden. As actor: Greenwich Village, Simon, My Favorite Year, Lily in Love, Garbo Talks, I Want to Go Home.

GREEN, GUY: Director. b. Somerset, Eng. 1913. Joined Film Advertising Co. as projectionist & camera asst. 1933; camera asst., Elstree Studios (BIP) 1935; started as camera operator on films including One of Our Aircraft Is Missing, In Which We Serve, This Happy Breed. 1944: Director of Photography; Dir of Allied Film Makers Ltd.
PICTURES: Dir. of Photography: The Way Ahead, Great Expectations (Acad. Award), Oliver Twist, Captain Horatio Hornblower, I Am A Camera, River Beat, Tears For Simon, House of Secrets, Sea of Sand, The Angry Silence, The Mark, Light In The Piazza, Diamond Head, A Patch of Blue (also writer), Pretty Polly, A Matter of Innocence, The Magus, A Walk in the Spring Rain, Luther, Once Is Not Enough, The Devil's Advocate, The Outlander.
TELEVISION: (U.S.) Incredible Journey of Dr. Meg Laurel; Isabel's Choice; Jennifer: A Woman's Story; Arthur Hailey's Strong Medicine.

GREEN, JOSEPH: Executive. b. Warsaw, Poland, Apr. 23, 1905. e. high school, prep school. Industry, legitimate theatre prod. Foreign film dist. since 1933; headed Green Film Co., Warsaw, Poland; head of Sphinx Film Dist. Co., N.Y., until 1940. co-owner, Art Theatre Circuit, N.Y., 1940–52; pres., Globe Dist. Co. of Foreign Films; formed President Films, Inc., 1954, now Globe Pictures, Inc. Beginning in 1979 a renaissance of Joseph Green's Yiddish film Classics produced in Poland in pre-W.W.II days, including Yiddle with He's Fiddle, Abriele der Mamen, Der Purinspieler, Mamele.

GREEN, JOSEPH. Executive, Producer, Director. b. Baltimore, MD, Jan. 28, 1938. e. U. of Maryland, B.A. Since 1970 has headed own distribution co. Joseph Green Pictures and released its library of 150 features to theatres, TV and cable.
PICTURES: The Brain that Wouldn't Die (dir., s.p.), The Perils of P.K. (assoc. prod., dir.), Psychedelic Generation (prod., dir.).

GREEN, MALCOLM C.: Theatre Executive. b. Boston, MA, Mar. 1, 1925. e. Harvard Coll. Began career as asst. mgr., Translux Theatre, Boston & Revere Theatre, Revere, MA. Treas., Interstate Theatres, 1959–64. Film Buyer, Interstate, 1959–72. Formed Theatre Management Services in 1972 with H. Rifkin and P. Lowe and Cinema Centers Corp. with Rifkin and Lowe families in 1973. Treas., Cinema Center, & pres., Theatre Mgmt. Services. Cinema Center grew to 116 theatres in 6 Northeast states, sold to Hoyts Cinemas Corp., 1986. Now sr. v.p., Hoyts Cinemas Corp. 1986–89.
Pres., Theatre Owners of New England, 1964–65; chmn bd., 1965–69; treas., 1970–84. Pres., NATO, 1986–89, Chmn Bd, 1988–89. Dir., Natl. Assoc. Theatre Owners. Chmn., NATO of New York State. Director, Vision Foundation.

GREEN, MICHAEL L.: Executive-chmn., Entertainment Film Distributors Ltd., chmn., Entertainment in Video Ltd., chmn., Michael Green Enterprises Ltd., mng. dir., Blackwater Film Productions Ltd.

GREEN, NATHANIEL CHARLES: Executive (retired). b. Spokane, WA. Feb. 16, 1903. e. Pleasant Prairie Sch. until 14 yrs. old. Ent. banking bus., Spokane & Eastern Trust Co., until 1921; came to CA, became associated Bank of America. Br. bank mgr., 26 yrs. of age, youngest in the U.S. at the time; became vice-pres., 1941; Jan. 1960 became v.p., and sr. pub rel. officer between bank and m.p. and TV industry.

GREENE, CLARENCE: Producer, Writer. b. New York, NY, 1918. e. St. John's U., L.L.B. Author of play Need a Lawyer. Formed Greene-Rouse prods. with Russell Rouse; Acad. Oscar co-orig. story Pillow Talk. Acad. award nom. co-orig. s.p. The Well. Two Writers Guild nominations. Writers Guild award outstanding teleplay, One Day in the Life of Ivan Denisovitch. Co-prod., writer TV series Tightrope.
PICTURES: Prod., collab. s.p. The Town Went Wild, D.O.A., The Well, The Thief, Wicked Woman, New York Confidential, A House Is Not a Home, The Oscar. Prod.: Unidentified Flying Objects, The Gun Runners, Fastest Gun Alive, Thunder in the Sun, The Caper of the Golden Bulls. D.O.A. (story, 1988).

GREENE, DAVID: Director, Writer. b. Manchester, Eng., Feb. 22, 1921. Early career as actor. To U.S. with Shakespeare company early 1950's; remained to direct TV in Canada, New York and Hollywood.
TELEVISION: The Defenders. Emmy Awds. The People Next Door, Rich Man, Poor Man, Roots, Friendly Fire, The Trial of Lee Harvey Oswald, Friendly Fire (Emmy Award), A Vacation in Hell, The Choice, World War III, Rehearsal For Murder, Take Your Best Shot, Ghost Dancing, Prototype, Sweet Revenge, The Guardian, Fatal Vision, Guilty Conscience, Murder Among Friends, This Child Is Mine, Triplecross, Vanishing Act, Miles to Go, Circle of Violence, The Betty Ford Story, After the Promise; Inherit the Wind, Liberace: Behind the Music, Red Earth, White Earth; The Penthouse (dir., exec. prod.), Small Sacrifices.
PICTURES: The Shuttered Room, Sebastian, The Strange Affair, I Start Counting, Madame Sin, Godspell, Count of Monte Cristo, Gray Lady Down, Hard Country (prod., dir.).

GREENE, ELLEN: Actress, Singer. b. Brooklyn, NY, Feb. 22. e. Ryder Coll. After coll. joined musical road show. Appeared in cabaret act at The Brothers & the Sisters Club and Reno Sweeney's, NY. Off-Bdwy debut, Rachel Lily Rosenbloom. Bdwy in the The Little Prince and The Aviator. With NY Shakespeare Fest. in In the Boom Boom Room, The Sorrows of Steven, The Threepenny Opera (Tony nom.). Film debut Next Stop, Greenwich Village (1976). Off Bdwy. co-starred in musical Little Shop of Horrors 1982, repeated role in film.
PICTURES: Next Stop, Greenwich Village; I'm Dancing As Fast as I Can; Little Shop of Horrors; Me and Him; Talk Radio.
TELEVISION: Rock Follies, Glory, Glory. Pilot: Road Show.

GREENFIELD, LEO: Executive, b. New York, NY, April 25, 1916. e. St. John's U, Coll. of Arts & Sciences. v.p., gen. sales mgr. Buena Vista, 1962; Columbia road show sales mgr. 1966; v.p.-gen. sales mgr., Cinerama Rel. Corp. 1966; pres.-gen. sales mgr., Warners, 1969; sr. v.p. worldwide distribution, MGM 1975; v.p. distribution & marketing, Marble Arch Productions, 1978; exec. v.p. Associated Film Distribution, 1979; pres., distribution, F/M, 1986; pres., dist., Kings Road Entertainment, 1987; pres., Greenlee Assoc., 1988.

GREENHUT, ROBERT: Producer. b. New York, NY. Began career as prod. assistant on Arthur Hiller's The Tiger Makes Out, 1967. Worked in prod. capacities with NY based filmmakers Woody Allen, Milos Forman, Bob Fosse, Sidney Lumet and Alan J. Pakula. Received crystal apple from city of NY and Eastman Kodak for lifetime achievement.
PICTURES: Annie Hall, Interiors, Hair (assoc. prod.), Manhattan (exec. prod.), Stardust Memories, Arthur (also 1st asst. dir.), The King of Comedy (exec. prod.), A Midsummer Night's Sex Comedy, Zelig, Broadway Danny Rose, The Purple Rose of Cairo, Hannah and Her Sisters, Heartburn, Radio Days, September, Another Woman, New York Stories.

GREENWALD, ROBERT: Director, Producer, Teacher. b. New York, NY, Aug. 8, 1945. e. Antioch Coll., New School for Social Research. Teaches film and theatre at NYU, New Lincoln, New School. Formed Robert Greenwald Prods.
PICTURES: Xanadu (dir.), Sweethearts Dance (exec. prod., dir.).
TELEVISION: Prod: The Desperate Miles, 21 Hours at Munich, Delta Country USA, Escape From Bogen County, Getting Married, Portrait of a Stripper, Miracle on Ice, The Texas Rangers, The First Time; Exec. prod.: A Deadly

Silence. Director: Sharon: Portrait of a Mistress, A Deadly Silence. In the Custody of Strangers, Burning Bed; Katie: Portrait of a Centerfold. Flatbed Annie and Sweetpie, Lady Truckers and Shattered Spirits (also exec. prod.).
STAGE: A Sense of Humor, I Have a Dream, Me and Bessie.

GREENWOOD, JACK: Producer. b. 1919.
PICTURES: Horrors of the Black Museum, Concrete Jungle, Invasion, Act of Murder, We Shall See, Face of A Stranger, Scotland Yard, The Scales of Justice 1967–68.
TELEVISION: Edgar Wallace series, Avengers series, From a Bird's Eye View, TV series with Sheldon Leonard 1969. Prod. exec. with ATV Network (ITC) since 1970.

GREER, JANE: Actress. b. Washington, DC, Sept. 9, 1924. Orchestra singer; photograph as WAC on Life Magazine cover won screen debut in Pan-Americana 1945.
PICTURES: They Won't Believe Me, Out of the Past, Station West, Big Steal, You're in the Navy Now, The Company She Keeps, You For Me, Prisoner of Zenda, Desperate Search, The Clown, Down Among the Sheltering Palms, Run for the Sun, Man of a Thousand Faces, Where Love Has Gone, Billie, The Outfit, Against All Odds, Just Between Friends, Immediate Family.

GREGORY, JOHN R.: Executive, Producer, Writer. b. Brooklyn, NY, Nov. 19, 1918. e. Grover Cleveland H.S., 1935, New Inst. of M.P. & Telev., 1952; Sls., adv. dept. Fotoshop, Inc., N.Y., 1938–42; Spec. Serv., Photo. instructor, chief projectionist, supv., war dept. theatres, U.S. Army, 1942–46; sls. mgr., J. L. Galef & Son, N.Y.; 1948–49, gen. mgr., Camera Corner Co.; 1949–58, pres.; City Film Center, Inc., 1957; exec. v.p., Talent Guild of New York, 1958; pres., Teleview Prods., Inc., 1961; executive producer, City Film Productions, 1970. Executive post-production supervisor, Jerry Liotta Films, 1977.
AUTHOR: many articles in nat'l publications dealing with m.p. practices and techniques; tech. editor, Better Movie-Making magazine, 1962; editor, pub., National Directory of Movie-Making Information, 1963; assoc. ed., Photographic Product News, 1964; contrib. editor, U.S. Camera. M.P. columnist, contributing ed. Travel and Camera magazine, 1969; Advisory panelist, Photo-methods (N.Y.), 1975. Consultant, Photographic Guidance Council, 1957, assoc. Society of M.P. & Television-Engineers, 1952.

GREIST, KIM: Actress. b. Stamford, CT, May 12, 1958. e. New Sch. for Social Research. Film debut C.H.U.D., 1984.
THEATER: Second Prize: Two Months in Leningrad, Twelfth Night (NY Shakespeare Fest.).
PICTURES: Brazil, Manhunter, Throw Momma from the Train, Punchline, Why Me?, Manhunter.
TELEVISION: Miami Vice, Tales From the Darkside.

GRESHLER, ABNER J.: Producer. b. New York, NY. e. Fordham U., St. John's U. Sch. of Law. Prior to entering m.p. ind., prod. shows for resort hotels; mgd., booked artists for vaudeville, hotels, cafes. Now pres., York Pictures Corp.; Abner J. Greshler Prod., Inc. Executive prod. At War with the Army, 1951; Hundred Hour Hunt, Yesterday and Today, 1953; Johnny and the Gaucho, 1955; prog. consultant, NBC; coord. of prog. development dept., NTA; pres., R.G. Prod., Ltd. Pres. Damond Artists Ltd.; dir. Yesterday and Today, The Fugitive, Odd Couple; v.p., Astron Prod Ltd.

GREY, JENNIFER: Actress. Daughter of actor Joel Grey.
PICTURES: Reckless, The Cotton Club, Reckless, Red Dawn, American Flyers, Ferris Bueller's Day Off, Dirty Dancing, Bloodhounds of Broadway.
TELEVISION: Murder in Mississippi.

GREY, JOEL: Actor, Singer. b. Cleveland, OH, April 11, 1932. Son of performer Mickey Katz; father of actress Jennifer Grey. e. Alexander Hamilton H.S., L.A. Acting debut at 9 years in On Borrowed Time at Cleveland Playhouse. Extensive nightclub appearances before returning to theatre and TV.
PICTURES: About Face, Calypso Heat Wave, Come September, Cabaret (Acad. Award, supp. actor, 1972), Man on a Swing, Buffalo Bill and the Indians, 7 Percent Solution, Remo Williams.
TELEVISION: Maverick, December Bride, Ironside, Night Gallery, Jack and the Beanstalk (special), The Burt Bacharach Show, The Tom Jones Show, The Englebert Humperdinck Show, George M! (special), The Carol Burnett Show, The Julie Andrews Hour, Queenie (mini-series).
STAGE: Come Blow Your Horn, Stop the World—I Want to Get Off, Half a Sixpence, Harry, Noon and Night, Littlest Revue, Cabaret (Tony Award), George M!, Goodtime Charley, The Grand Tour, Cabaret (1987, Bdwy revival).

GREY, VIRGINIA: Actress. b. Los Angeles, CA, March 22, 1923. Screen career started 1935 with She Gets Her Man.
PICTURES: Who Killed Doc Robbin, Bullfighter and the Lady, Highway 301, Slaughter Trail, Desert Pursuit, Perilous Journey, Forty-Niners, Target Earth, Eternal Sea, Last Command, Rose Tattoo, All That Heaven Allows, Tammy Tell Me True, Bachelor In Paradise, Back Street, Madame X, Rosie, Airport.

GRIEM, HELMUT: Actor. b. Hamburg, Germany, 1940; e. Hamburg U.
PICTURES: The Damned, The Mackenzie Break, Cabaret, Ludwig, Voyage of the Damned, Sergeant Steiner, Breakthrough, The Glass Cell, Berlin Alexanderplatz, La Passante, The Second Victory.
TELEVISION: Peter the Great.

GRIFFIN, MERV: Executive, Singer, M.C. b. San Mateo, CA, July 6, 1925. e. U. of San Francisco, Stanford U. The Merv Griffin Show, KFRC-Radio, 1945–48; vocalist, Freddy Martin's orch., 1948–52; Contract Warner Bros., 1952–54. co-starred, So This Is Love, The Boy From Oklahoma; toured Niteclubs, 1954–55; Prod. Finian's Rainbow, City Center, N.Y., 1955.
TELEVISION: Vocalist, The Freddy Martin Show, Morning Show, and Robt. Q. Lewis Show, 1956; M.C., Look Up and Live, Going Places, 1957, Merv. Griffin Show, 1958, Play Your Hunch, 1960; M.C., Keep Talking, 1960; Merv. Griffin Show, 1962; Word for Word, 1963; Merv. Griffin Show, Westinghouse Broadcasting, 1965–86; Secrets Women Never Share (exec. prod., host, 1987). Chairman, Merv Griffin Prods.

GRIFFITH, ANDY: Actor. b. Mount Airy, NC, June 1, 1926. e. U. of North Carolina. Began career as standup comedian, recording artist.
THEATRE: Broadway: No Time for Sergeants, Destry Rides Again.
TELEVISION: Series: The Andy Griffith Show, Andy of Mayberry, No Time for Sergeants, The Headmaster, Matlock. Movies: Go Ask Alice, Salvage I, Murder in Coweta County, The Demon Murder Case, Fatal Vision, Crime of Innocence, Diary of a Perfect Murder, Return to Mayberry, Under the Influence.
PICTURES: A Face in the Crowd, No Time for Sergeants, Onionhead, The Second Time Around, Angel in My Pocket, Hearts of the West, Rustler's Rhapsody.

GRIFFITH, MELANIE: Actress. b. New York, NY, Aug. 9, 1957. m. actor Don Johnson. Daughter of actress Tippi Hedren. Moved to Los Angeles at 4. e. Catholic academies until Hollywood Prof. Sch., 1981. Did some modeling before being cast in Night Moves at 16. Studied acting with Stella Adler. Debut in Israeli film, The Garden (1975).
PICTURES: Night Moves, The Drowning Pool, Smile, One on One, Roar, Roar, Joyride, Underground Aces, Fear City, Body Double, Something Wild, Cherry 2000, The Milagro Beanfield War, Stormy Monday, Working Girl (Acad. Award nom.), In the Spirit, The Grifters.
TELEVISION: Series: Carter Country, Mini-series: Once an Eagle, Movies: Daddy, I Don't Like This, Steel Cowboy, The Star Marker, Pilots: She's in the Army Now, Golden Gate, Guest: Alfred Hitchcock Presents.

GRILLO, BASIL F.: Executive. b. Angel's Camp, CA, Oct. 8, 1910. e. U. of California, Berkeley, A.B. Certified public accountant, exec. vice-pres., dir., Bing Crosby Ent., Inc., 1948–57; bus. mgr., Bing Crosby, 1945; co-organizer, dir., 3rd pres., & treas., Alliance of T.V. Film Producers, 1950–54; exec. prod., BCE, Inc., shows incl. Fireside Thea., Rebound, Royal Playhouse, The Chimps; dir., KCOP, Inc., 1957–60; dir. KFOX, Inc., 1958–62; pres., dir., Bing Crosby Prods., 1955–72; dir., Seven Leagues Ent., Inc., 1958; dir. Electrovision Prods., 1970, chief exec. off., Bing Crosby Enterprises.

GRIMALDI, ALBERTO: Producer. b. Naples, 1927. Studied law, serving as counsel to Italian film companies, before turning to production with Italian westerns starring Clint Eastwood and Lee Van Cleef. Is pres. of P.E.A. (Produzioni Europee Associate, S.A.S.).
PICTURES: For a Few Dollars More, The Good, the Bad and the Ugly, Three Steps in Delerium, Satyricon, Burn!, The Decameron, The Canterbury Tales, 1001 Nights, Salo, or the 100 Days of Sodom, Bawdy Tales, Man of La Mancha, Last Tango in Paris, Avanti, Fellini's Casanova, 1900, The True Story of General Custer.

GRIMES, GARY: Actor. b. San Francisco, CA, 1955. Family moved to L.A. when he was nine. Made film debut at 15 in Summer of '42, 1971. Voted Star of Tomorrow in QP poll, 1971.
PICTURES: The Culpepper Cattle Company, Cahill, United States Marshall, Class of '44, The Spikes Gang, Gus.

GRIMES, TAMMY: Actress. b. Lynn, MA, Jan. 30, 1934. Mother of actress Amanda Plummer. e. Stephens Coll. Member of staff Westport Playhouse, CT 1954.
THEATER: Look After Lulu (1959); Littlest Revue, Stratford (Ont.) Shakespeare Fest., Bus Stop, Cradle Will Rock, Unsinkable Molly Brown (Tony Award), High Spirits, Finian's Rainbow, Only Game in Town, Private Lives (Tony Award), California Suite, 42nd Street, Tartuffe, A Month in the Country, The Importance of Being Earnest, Mademoiselle

Columbe, Tammy Grimes: A Concert in Words and Music, Orpheus Descending.
PICTURES: Three Bites of an Apple, Play It as It Lays, Somebody Killed Her Husband, The Runner Stumbles, Can't Stop the Music, America, Mr. North, No Big Deal, Slaves of New York.
TELEVISION: Omnibus, Hollywood Sings, Hour of Great Mysteries, Four Poster, St. Elsewhere, Last Unicorn, The Tammy Grimes Show. Movies: The Other Man, The Horror at 37,000 Feet, The Borrowers, You Can't Go Home Again.

GRISSMER, JOHN: Executive, Producer, Director. b. Houston, TX, Aug. 28, 1933. e. Xavier U., B.S., 1955; Catholic U., M.F.A., dramatic writing, 1959. Taught drama courses, directed student productions at U. of Connecticut & American U., Washington, DC. Produced and co-wrote House That Cried Murder, 1973; co-produced, wrote and directed Scalpel; directed Nightmare at Shadow Woods. Partner in P.J. Productions Co. & Producer's Marketing Group, Ltd.

GRIZZARD, GEORGE: Actor. b. Roanoke Rapids, NC, April 1, 1928. e. U. of North Carolina, B.A., 1949. Has been member of Arena Stage, Washington, D.C., APA repertory company and Tyrone Guthrie resident company in Minneapolis.
THEATER: The Desperate Hours. (Bdwy debut, 1955), The Happiest Millionaire, The Disenchanted, Face of a Hero, Big Fish, Little Fish, Who's Afraid of Virginia Woolf?, The Glass Menagerie, You Know I Can't Hear You When the Water's Running, The Gingham Dog, Inquest, The Country Girl, The Creation of the World and Other Business, Crown Matrimonial, The Royal Family, California Suite, Man and Superman, Another Antiqone.
PICTURES: From the Terrace, Seems Like Old Times, Advise and Consent, Warning Shot, Happy Birthday, Wanda June, Comes a Horseman, Firepower, Wrong Is Right, Bachelor Party.
TELEVISION: Mini-series: The Adams Chronicles. Movies: The Strangler Within, Indict & Convict, Attack on Terror: The FBI vs. the Ku Klux Klan, The Lives of Jenny Dolan, Attica, Not In Front of the Children, The Deliberate Stranger, Underseige, That Secret Sunday, Robert Kennedy and His Times, The Shadey Hill Kidnapping, International Airport, Embassy, Oldest Living Graduate, Perry Mason: The Case of the Scandalous Scoundrel, David, Caroline?

GRODIN, CHARLES: Actor, Director. b. Pittsburgh, PA, April 21, 1935. e. U. of Miami. After time with Pittsburgh Playhouse studied acting with Uta Hagen and Lee Strasberg; began directing career in New York 1965 as asst. to Gene Saks. Has appeared in some 75 plays all over country. Has also written scripts produced plays.
THEATER: Tchin-Tchin (Bdwy debut, 1962); Absence of a Cello; Same Time, Next Year; It's a Glorious Day . . . And All That (dir., co-author); Lovers and Other Strangers (dir.), Thieves (prod., dir.); Unexpected Guests (prod.,dir.).
PICTURES: Actor: Sex and the College Girl (1964), Rosemary's Baby, Catch-22, The Heartbreak Kid, 11 Harrowhouse, King Kong, Thieves, Heaven Can Wait, Real Life, Sunburn, It's My Turn, Seems Like Old Times, The Incredible Shrinking Woman, Great Muppet Caper, The Lonely Guy, The Woman in Red, Movers and Shakers (also co-prod., s.p.), Last Resort, Ishtar, The Couch Trip, You Can't Hurry Love, Midnight Run.
TELEVISION: Candid Camera (writer, dir.); Simon and Garfunkel Special (writer, dir.); Acts of Love and Other Comedies (dir.); Paradise (prod., dir.); Fresno (actor); Grown Ups (actor).

GROSBARD, ULU: Director. b. Antwerp, Belgium. Jan. 9, 1929. e. U. of Chicago, B.A. 1950, M.A. 1952. Trained at Yale Sch. of Drama 1952–53. Asst. dir. to Eliza Kazan Splendor in the Grass, 1961; asst. dir.: West Side Story, The Hustler, The Miracle Worker. Unit mgr.: The Pawnbroker.
THEATER: The Days and Nights of Beebee Fenstermaker, The Subject Was Roses, A View From the Bridge, The Investigation, That Summer—That Fall, The Price, American Buffalo, The Woods, The Wake of Jamie Foster.
PICTURES: The Subject Was Roses, Who Is Harry Kellerman?, Straight Time, True Confessions, Falling in Love.

GROSS, KENNETH H.: Executive. e. New School for Social Research, U. of London. Conducted film seminars at New School and active in several indep. film projects. Published film criticism in various journals and magazines. Joined ABC Entertainment Oct. 1971. Named supvr. of feature films for ABC-TV. Appt. mgr. of feature films, Jan. 1974. Promoted in Nov, 1975 to program executive, ABC Entertainment Prime Time/West Coast. Moved to L.A. offices, Nov. 1975, promoted to exec. producer, movies for TV, ABC Ent. 1976; 1978, with literary agency F.C.A. as partner in Los Angeles; 1979 producer for Lorimar; then with Intl. Creative Mgt; 1982, formed own literary talent agency, The Literary Group; 1985, merged agency with Robinson-Weintraub & Assoc. to become Robinson-Weintraub-Gross & Assoc.

GROSS, MARY: Actress. b. Chicago, IL, March 25, 1953. Sister of actor Michael Gross. e. Loyola U. Is also student of the harp. In 1980 discovered by John Belushi who saw her perform as resident member of Chicago's Second City comedy troupe, where she won Chicago's Joseph Jefferson Award as best actress for the revue, Well, I'm Off to the Thirty Years War. First came to national attention as regular on Saturday Night Live, 1981–85.
PICTURES: Club Paradise, Couch Trip, Casual Sex, Big Business, Feds, Troop Beverly Hills.
TELEVISION: Series: Saturday Night Live, The People Next Door. Specials: Comic Relief I, The Second City 25th Anniversary Reunion.

GROSS, MICHAEL: Actor. b. Chicago, IL, June 21, 1947. m. casting dir. Elza Bergeron. Brother of actress-comedienne Mary Gross. e. U. Illinois, B.A., Yale School of Drama, M.F.A. Worked NY Shakespeare Fest. (Sganarelle, An Evening of Moliere Farces, Othello). Off-Bdwy in Endgame, Put Them All Together, Geniuses, Territorial Rites. Broadway: Bent, The Philadelphia Story.
PICTURES: Just Tell Me What You Want, Big Business.
TELEVISION: Series: Family Ties, Movies: FDR: The Last Years, A Girl Named Sooner, Dream House, Little Gloria Happy at Last, Cook and Peary—The Race to the Pole, Summer Fantasies, Family Ties Vacation, A Letter to Three Wives, Bloody Friday, Right to Die, In the Defense of Duty: The FBI Murders, Quiet Victory: The Charlie Wedemeyer Story.

GROSSBERG, JACK: Producer, Executive. b. Brooklyn, NY, June 5, 1927. Member: Academy of Motion Picture Arts & Sciences. New York Friars Club, Producers Guild of America, Directors Guild of America.
PICTURES: Requiem For A Heavyweight, Pretty Poison, The Producers, Don't Drink the Water, Take the Money and Run, Bananas, Everything You Always Wanted To Know About Sex, Sleeper, A Delicate Balance, Luther, Rhinoceros, Leadbelly, King Kong, The Betsy, Fast Break, A Stranger is Watching, Brainstorm, Strange Brew, Touch and Go, The Experts, Little Monsters.

GROSSMAN, ERNIE: Executive. b. New York, NY, Sept. 19, 1924. Still dept., pressbook edit., asst. field mgr., Warner Bros., 1940–58; Studio publicist, 1958–60; exploitation, promo. mgr. field dept., 1960–64; nat'l mgr., pub., exploit., promo.; 1964–67 exec. co-ord. advt., pub. & promo., Warner-7 Arts, 1967; WB nat'l supv. ad.-pub., 1970. exec. assist. to Richard Lederer, 1971–72; 1973 nat'l dir. of Pub. & Promotion, Warner Bros. Inc.; 1977, natl. dir. of adv.-pub.; 1980–85, natl. dir. promo. 1987, named south-west special events dir.

GRUEN, ROBERT: Executive. b. New York, NY, Apr. 2, 1913, e. Carnegie Mellon U., B.A. Stage designer, 1934–35; designer, 20th-Fox, 1936; prod. exec., National Screen Service Corp., 1936; head, Robert Gruen Associates, ind. design org., 1940; nat. pres. Industrial Designers Inst., 1954–55; dir. and v.p., National Screen Service Corp. since 1951; senior v.p. 1975–78; dir., NSS Corp., Continental Lithograph and NSS, Ltd., 1978–85.

GRUENBERG, JERRY: Executive. b. Minneapolis, MN, June 7, 1927, e. U. of Minnesota. United Artists, Minneapolis, 1952; m.p. exhibitor CEO Wisconsin Theatres, 1952–67; v.p. Sigma III Corp. 1965–67. division mgr., 20th Century-Fox, 1967–71; senior v.p., general sales mgr., Allied Artists Pictures, 1971–79. Pres., Blossom Pictures, Inc. 1979–present. Member of Variety Club, Friars Club. Director of Will Rogers Memorial Fund.

GRUENBERG, LEONARD S.: Executive. b. Minneapolis, MN, Sept. 10, 1913, e. U. of Minnesota. Began as salesman Republic Pictures, Minneapolis, 1935; with RKO in same capacity, 1936; promoted to city sales mgr., St. Louis, 1937, then branch mgr., Salt Lake City, 1941; later that year apptd. Rocky Mt. Dist. Mgr. (hqts., Denver, CO); 1946 Metropolitan, div. mgr., v.p. NTA, v.p. Cinemiracle Prods.; Pres., Chmn. of bd., Sigma III Corp., 1962. Chmn. of bd., Filmways, 1967. Chmn. of bd. Gamma III Dist. Co. & Chmn of bd. and Pres. Great Owl Corp., 1976. Member Variety Club, Sigma Alpha Mu Fraternity; Lieut. Civil Air Patrol, Lieut. Comdr., U.S.N.R.

GRUSIN, DAVID: Composer, Conductor, Performer. b. Littleton, CO, 1934. Directed music for the Andy Williams Show on TV for 7 yrs in the 1960s, where met Norman Lear and Bud Yorkin, producers of the series, who signed him to score their first feature film, Divorce, American Style (1967).
PICTURES: The Graduate, Winning, The Heart Is a Lonely Hunter, Tell Them Willie Boy Is Here, The Front, Murder by Death, The Yakuza, Three Days of the Condor, Bobby Deerfield, The Goodbye Girl, Heaven Can Wait, And Justice for All, The Champ, The Electric Horseman, My Bodyguard, Absence of Malice, On Golden Pond, Reds, Author! Author!, Tootsie, Scandalous, Racing with the Moon, The Pope of Greenwich Village, The Little Drummer Girl, Falling in Love,

Goonies, The Milagro Beanfield War (Acad. Award, 1988), Clara's Heart, Tequila Sunrise, A Dry White Season.
TELEVISION: Movies: Deadly Dream; Prescription: Murder; Scorpio Letters; Eric; The Family Rico; The Death Squad; themes to many series.

GUARDINO, HARRY: Actor. b. Brooklyn, NY, Dec. 23. 1925, e. Haaren H.S.
STAGE: Bdwy: End as a Man, A Hatful of Rain, Anyone Can Whistle, One More River, Natural Affection, The Rose Tattoo (revival), Seven Descents of Myrtle, Woman of the Year.
TELEVISION: Studio One, Playhouse 90, The Alcoa Theatre, Naked City, Dr. Kildare, The Untouchables, The Dick Powell Show, The Reporter (series), The New Perry Mason. Movies: Contract on Cherry Street, Police Story, Sophisticated Gentry, The Last Child, Evening in Byzantium.
PICTURES: Pork Chop Hill, The Five Pennies, Houseboat, The Pigeon That Took Rome, Treasure of San Grennaro, Madigan, Lovers and Other Strangers, Red Sky at Morning, Dirty Harry, They Only Kill Their Masters, St. Ives, The Enforcer, Rollercoaster, Matilda, Any Which Way You Can.

GUBER, PETER: Producer. b. 1942. e. Syracuse U., B.A.; U. at Florence (Italy), S.S.P.; NYU Grad. Sch. Business Admin, MBA; Sch. of Law, J.D., L.L.M. Recruited by Columbia Pictures as exec. asst. in 1968 while pursuing M.B.A. at NYU. Graduate Sch. of Business Adm. With Col. seven yrs. in key prod. exec. capacities, serving last three as exec. v.p. in chg. of worldwide prod. Formed own company, Peter Guber's Filmworks, which in 1976 was merged with his Casablanca Records to become Casablanca Record and Filmworks where he was co-owner & chmn. bd. 1980 formed Polygram Pictures bringing in Jon Peters as partner. May 1980 formed Boardwalk with Neil Bogart and Jon Peters, retaining connection with Polygram of which he was 50% owner; 1981 Boardwalk partnership dissolved; 1983 sold Polygram and formed Guber-Peters. 1988 merged co. with Burt Sugarman's Barris Industries to form Guber-Peters-Barris Entertainment Co. Co-chmn. & man. dir. 1989 took full control of co. with Sugarman's exit and addition of Australia's Frank Lowy as new partner. Awards: Producer of Year, NATO, 1979; NYU Albert Gallatin Fellowship; Syracuse U Ardent Award. Visiting prof., & chmn. producer's dept., UCLA Sch. of Theatre Arts. Member of NY, CA and Wash. DC Bars. Books: Inside the Deep, Above the Title.
PICTURES: The Deep (first under own banner), Midnight Express (6 Golden Globes, 2 Oscars), Co Prod. with Jon Peters: An American Werewolf in London, Missing, Flashdance (exec. prod.), D.C. Cab (exec. prod.), Endless Love, Vision Quest (exec. prod.), The Legend of Billie Jean, Head Office, Clan of the Cave Bear, Six Weeks (exec. prod.), The Pursuit of D.C. Cab (exec. prod.), Clue (exec. prod.), The Color Purple (exec. prod.), The Witches of Eastwick; Innerspace (exec. prod.), Who's That Girl (exec. prod.); Gorillas in the Mist (exec. prod.); Caddyshack II, Rain Man (exec. prod, 4 Golden Globes, 4 Oscars), Batman, The Bonfires of the Vanities, Setup, Johnny Handsome, Contact, The Bright Shining Lie.
TELEVISION: Mysteries of the Sea (doc. Emmy Award), Exec. prod.: Television and the Presidency, Double Platinum, Dreams (series), Movies: Stand By Your Man, The Toughest Man in the World (exec. prod.), Bay Coven, Oceanquest, Brotherhood of Justice, Nightmare at Bitter Creek, Finish Line.

GUEST, CHRISTOPHER: Actor, Writer, Composer. m. actress Jamie Leigh Curtis. b. New York, NY, Feb. 5, 1948. Wrote the musical score and acted in National Lampoon's Lemmings off-Bdwy. On Bdwy in Room Service, Moonchildren. Cast member Saturday Night Live 1984–85.
PICTURES: Actor: Girlfriends, The Last Word, The Long Riders, The Missing Link, The Fortune, Death Wish, The Hot Rock, Heartbeeps, This is Spinal Tap, Little Shop of Horrors, The Princess Bride, Beyond Therapy, The Big Picture (also dir. co-s.p. and story).
TELEVISION: The TV Show, The Chevy Chase Special (also writer); The Billion Dollar Bubble; Lily Tomlin (also writer, Emmy Award, 1976), A Nice Place to Visit (writer only), A Piano for Mrs. Cimino, The Million Dollar Infield, Haywire, Blind Ambition.

GUEST, LANCE: Actor. b. Saratoga, CA, July 21, 1960. e. UCLA.
PICTURES: I Ought To Be in Pictures, Halloween II, The Last Starfighter, Jaws—The Revenge, The Wizard of Loneliness.
TELEVISION: Lou Grant, St. Elsewhere. Movies: Between Two Loves, Why Us?, Please Don't Hit Me Mom, Confessions of a Married Man, One Too Many, My Father My Rival, The Roommate, Favorite Son.

GUEST, VAL: Writer, Director, Producer. b. London, England. e. England and America. Journalist with Hollywood Reporter, Zit's Los Angeles Examiner and Walter Winchell.
PICTURES: Murder at the Windmill, Miss Pilgrim's Progress, The Body Said No, Mr. Drake's Duck, Happy Go Lovely, Another Man's Poison, Penny Princess, The Runaway Bus, Life With the Lyons, Dance Little Lady, Men of Sherwood Forest, Lyons in Paris, Break in the Circle, It's A Great Life, Quatermass Experiment, They Can't Hang Me, The Weapon, The Abominable Snowman, Carry on Admiral, It's a Wonderful World, Camp on Blood Island, Up the Creek, Further Up the Creek, Life Is a Circus, Yesterday's Enemy, Expresso Bongo, Hell Is a City, Full Treatment, The Day the Earth Caught Fire, Jigsaw, 80,000 Suspects, The Beauty Jungle, Where the Spies Are, Casino Royale, Assignment K, When Dinosaurs Ruled the Earth, Tomorrow, The Persuaders, Au Pair Girls, The Adventurer, Confessions of a Window Cleaner, Killer Force, Diamond Mercenaries, The Boys in Blue.
TELEVISION: Space 1999, The Shillingbury Blowers, The Band Played On, Sherlock Holmes & Dr. Watson, Shillingbury Tales, Dangerous Davies, The Last Detective, In Possession, Mark of the Devil, Child's Play, Scent of Fear.

GUILLAUME, ROBERT: Actor. b. St. Louis, MO, Nov. 30. e. St. Louis U., Washington U. Scholarship for musical fest. in Aspen, CO. Then apprenticed with Karamu Theatre when performed in operas and musicals. acting career debut in Carousel. Has appeared in many Bdwy. plays and musicals include Fly Blackbird, Kwamina, Guys and Dolls, Purlie, Jacques Brel is Alive and Well and Living in Paris.
TELEVISION: Dinah, Mel and Susan Together, Rich Little's Washington Follies, Jim Nabors, All in the Family, Sanford and Son, The Jeffersons, Marcus Welby, M.D., Soap, (series), Benson, (series, two Emmy Awards), Purlie, North and South (mini-series), Penthouse, Fire and Rain, The Kid From Left Field, John Grin's Christmas, The Kid with the Broken Halo, The Kid with the 100 I.Q. (also exec. prod.); Perry mason: The Case of the Scandalous Scoundrel, The Robert Guillaume Show. Living the Dream: A Tribute to Dr. Martin Luther King Jr. (host), The Debbie Allen Special.
PICTURES: Seems Like Old Times, Dusted, Lean On Me, Wanted Dead or Alive.

GUILLERMIN, JOHN: Director. b. London, England, Nov. 11, 1925. e. City of London Sch., Cambridge U. RAF pilot prior to entering film industry.
PICTURES: The Waltz of the Torreadors, Guns at Batasi, Rapture, The Blue Max, House of Cards, The Bridge of Remagen, El Condor, Skyjacked, Shaft in Africa, The Towering Inferno, King Kong, Death on the Nile, Mr. Patman, Sheena, King Kong Lives, The Favorite.
TELEVISION: The Tracker.

GUINNESS, SIR ALEC: Actor. b. London, Eng., April 2, 1914; e. Pembroke Lodge, Southbourne & Roborough Sch., Eastbourne. Created C.B.E. 1955; Knighted 1959. Stage debut: London, 1934. Theatre appearances in London, New York & Continent. Special AA, 1979, for services to film.
THEATER: includes: Libel! (walk-on debut, 1934), Hamlet, with Old Vic Co. (1936–37), with John Gielgud's Co. (1937–38), Great Expectations (own adapt.), Cousin Murial, The Tempest, Thunder Rock, Flare Path (NY), The Brothers Karamozov, Vicious Circle, The Cocktail Party (NY), The Prisoner, Hotel Paradiso, Ross, Exit the King, Dylan (NY), A Voyage Round My Father, Habeas Corpus, Yahoo, The Old Country, The Merchant of Venice (1983), A Walk in the Woods.
PICTURES: Great Expectations, Oliver Twist, Kind Hearts & Coronets, Run For Your Money, Last Holiday, The Mudlark, Lavender Hill Mob (Acad. nom.), The Man in the White Suit, The Card (The Promoter), Malta Story, Captain's Paradise, Father Brown (The Detective), To Paris with Love, The Prisoner, The Ladykillers, The Swan, The Bridge on the River Kwai (Academy Award 1957, best actor); The Horse's Mouth (Academy nom. for s.p.), The Scapegoat, Our Man in Havana, Tunes of Glory, A Majority of One, H.M.S. Defiant, Lawrence of Arabia, Dr. Zhivago, The Comedians, Cromwell, Scrooge, Brother Sun and Sister Moon, Hitler: The Last Ten Days, Murder by Death, Star Wars (Acad. nom.), The Empire Strikes Back, Return of the Jedi, Lovesick, A Passage to India, Little Dorrit, A Handful of Dust.
TELEVISION: The Wicked Scheme of Jebel Deeks (National Acad. nom.), Twelfth Night, Conversation at Night, Solo, E.E. Cummings, Little Gidding, The Gift of Friendship, Caesar and Cleopatra, Little Lord Fauntleroy, Tinker, Tailor, Soldier, Spy (7-part series), Smiley's People (mini-series), Edwin, Monsignor Quixote.

GULAGER, CLU: Actor. b. Holdenville, OK, Nov. 16, 1928. Father, John Gulager, cowboy entertainer. e. Baylor U. Starred at school in original play, A Different Drummer, where spotted by prod. of TV's Omnibus; invited to New York to recreate role on TV.
PICTURES: The Killers, The Last Picture Show, Winning, Company of Killers, McQ, The Other Side of Midnight, A Force of One, Touched by Love, The Initiation, Into the Night, Prime Risk, The Return of the Living Dead, Hunter's Blood, The Hidden, Tapeheads, Uninvited, I'm Gonna Git You Sucka, Teen Vamp.

TELEVISION: The Virginian, San Francisco International, Glass House, Ski Lift to Death, Space, Living Proof: The Hank Williams Jr. Story, Bridge Across Time, King, Once an Eagle, North and South II, Space.

GUMBEL, BRYANT: Announcer, News Show Host. b. Chicago, IL, Sept. 29, 1948. e. Bates Coll. Started as writer for Black Sports Magazine, NY, 1971; sportscaster, then sports dir., KNBC, Los Angeles. Sports host NBC Sports NY 1975–82. Now co-host on Today Show, New York (Emmy Awards, 1976, 1977).
TELEVISION: Super Bowl games, Games People Play, Different as Night and Day.

GUMPERT, JON: Executive. e. Cornell U. Law Sch. Sr. v.p., business affairs, MGM/UA Entertainment; pres., World Film Services, Inc., indep. prod. co. in N.Y. 1985, named v.p., business affairs, Warner Bros; 1989 sr. v.p. Vista Films.

GUNN, MOSES: Actor. b. St. Louis, MO, Oct. 2, 1929. e. Tennessee State U. Taught speech and drama at Grambling Coll. Came to N.Y. and first cast in off-Bdwy. prod. of Genet's The Blacks. Later joined Negro Ensemble Company.
PICTURES: WUSA, The Great White Hope, The Wild Rovers, Shaft, Shaft's Big Score, Eagle in a Cake, Hot Rock, The Iceman Cometh, Amazing Grace, Rollerball, Aaron Loves Angela, Ragtime, Amityville II: The Possession, Firestarter, Heartbreak Ridge, Leonard Part 6, The Luckiest Man in the World, Dixie Lanes.
STAGE: In White America, Day of Absence, Song of the Lusitanian Bogey, Summer of the 17th Doll, Daddy Goodness, Harvest, Titus Andronicus, Measure for Measure, Romeo and Juliet, The Tempest, As You Like It, Macbeth, Othello, A Hand Is on the Gate, Sty of the Blind Pig, The Poison Tree, First Breeze of Summer, King John.
TELEVISION: Mr. Carter's Army, The Borgia Stick, Of Mice and Men, Haunts of the Very Rich, Hawaii Five-O, The FBI, Kung Fu; If You Give a Dance, You Gotta Pay the Band; The Cowboys, Roots, First Breeze of Summer, The Women of Brewster Place.

GUNSBERG, SHELDON: Executive. b. Jersey City, NJ, Aug. 10, 1920. e. St. Peters Coll., New Jersey State Normal, NYU. With Night of Stars, Madison Sq. Garden, 1942; for. pub., 20th-Fox 1942; United Artists, 1945–47; Universal, roadshows. Rank product, asst. adv., pub. dir., 1947–54; v. pres., Walter Reade Theatres; exec. v.p. & dir., Walter Reade Org. 1962; Made chief operating officer, 1971; president, and Chief Executive Officer, 1973; chmn. & CEO, 1984.

GUNZBURG, M.L.: President, Natural Vision Corporation. b. Denver, CO. e. UCLA, Columbia U. Newspaper man, columnist, Los Angeles Times, New York Times; radio writer, screenwriter many m.p. cos.
Developed 3-D process, Natural Vision; contract Polaroid Corp. for 3-D, 1953.

GURIAN, PAUL R.: Executive. b. New Haven, CT, Oct. 18, 1946. e. Lake Forest Coll., U. of Vienna, NYU. Started producing films in 1971 with Cats and Dogs, a dramatic short which won prizes at Chicago Int. Film Fest and Edinburgh Fest. In 1977 formed Gurian Entertainment Corp., to acquire film properties for production.
PICTURES: The Garden Party (PBS program), Profile Ricardo Alegria (short), Bernice Bobs Her Hair (shown at 1977 N.Y. Film Festival); Cutter and Bone; Peggy Sue Got Married, The Seventh Sign (exec. prod.).

GUTTENBERG, STEVE: Actor. b. Brooklyn, NY, Aug. 24, 1958. e. Sch. of Performing Arts, N.Y. Off-Bdwy. in The Lion in Winter; studied under John Houseman at Juilliard; classes with Lee Strasberg and Uta Hagen. Moved to West Coast in 1976; landed first TV role in movie, Something for Joey. Theatrical film debut in The Chicken Chronicles (1977).
PICTURES: Rollercoaster, The Boys from Brazil, Players, Can't Stop the Music, Diner, The Man Who Wasn't There, Police Academy, Police Academy 2, Cocoon, Bad Medicine, Police Academy 3, Short Circuit, The Bedroom Window, Police Academy 4: Citizens on Patrol (also prod. assoc.), Three Men and a Baby, Surrender, Amazon Women on the Moon, High Spirits, Cocoon II: The Return, The Boyfriend School.
TELEVISION: Police Story, Doc, Series: Billy, No Soap, Radio, Movies: To Race the Wind, Miracle on Ice, The Day After, Gangs (co-prod.). Specials: Pecos Bill: King of the Cowboys.

GWYNNE, FRED: Actor. b. New York, NY, July 10, 1926. e. Harvard U. Copywriter J. Walter Thompson 1955–60. On stage in Mrs. McThing, Irma La Douce, Twelfth Night, Texas Trilogy, The Lincoln Mask, Cat on a Hot Tin Roof, Winter's Tale, Arsenic and Old Lace.
PICTURES: On the Waterfront, Munster Go Home, Luna, Simon, So Fine, The Cotton Club, Off Beat, Water, The Boy Who Could Fly, Ironweed, Fatal Attraction, Disorganized Crime, Pet Sematary.
TELEVISION: Series: Car 54, Where Are You? (1961–63); The Munsters (1964–66); Specials: Harvey, The Hasty Heart, Arsenic and Old Lace, The Lesson, Dames at Sea. Movies: Captains Courageous, Vanishing Act, The Christmas Star, Murder by the Book. Mini-Series: Kane & Abel.

H

HAAS, LUKAS: Kindergarten school principal told casting dir. about him which resulted in film debut at 4 in Testament. NY stage debut in Mike Nichols' Lincoln Center production of Waiting for Godot (1988).
PICTURES: Testament, The Doctor (AFI Film), Witness, Solarbabies, Lady in White, The Wizard of Loneliness, See You in the Morning, Music Box, Convicts, Roots in a Parched Ground.
TELEVISION: Guest: Amazing Stories (Ghost Train), Twilight Zone. Movies: A Place at the Table, Shattered Spirits, Love Thy Neighbor, My Dissident Mom, The Ryan White Story.

HABEEB, TONY G.: Executive. b. San Francisco, CA, Oct. 26, 1927. e. San Francisco City Coll., 1945–47, U. of California, 1947–49, Lincoln U. Law Sch., LL.B, 1949–53. TV Editor, San Francisco Chronicle, 1949–54; Information Specialist, U.S. Army, 1954–56; managing editor; Torrance Press, 1956–57; CBS-TV Network Press information Division, 1957–61; ass't. dir. promo. and pub., Screen Gems, 1961–63; dir. promo. and pub., Screen Gems, 1963–67; worldwide dir. advertising, pub. and promo., Paramount Television; 1967–70. v.p., adv. and publicity, Metromedia Producers Corp. 1970–74. v.p. adv. and publicity, Irwin Allen Productions, 1974–81, pres., Publicist Guild of America; 1982 dir., pub-ad., Warner Bros.-TV. 1987: sr. v.p. publicity and promotion New Century/Vista Film Co. 1988: sr. v.p. promotion and marketing Fries Entertainment.

HABER, JOYCE: Writer, syndicated Hollywood columnist. r.n. Mrs. Joyce Haber Cramer. b. New York, NY, Dec. 28, 1932. e. Brearley Sch., N.Y., class of 1948; Bryn Mawr Coll., 1949–50, cum laude list; Barnard Coll., B.A., 1953.
Researcher, Time magazine, 1953–63; Hollywood Reporter, L.A. Bureau Time, 1963–66; Columnist, Los Angeles Times, 1966–75; contributing editor, Los Angeles Magazine, 1977–80.
Published Caroline's Doll Book, illus. by R. Taylor, 1962. freelance writing: Esquire, Herald Tribune's New York Magazine, Harper's Bazaar, New York Magazine, Town and Country. Published The Users, a novel, 1976.

HACK, SHELLEY: Actress. b. CT, July 6. e. Smith Coll. and U. of Sydney, Australia. Made modeling debut at 14 on cover of Glamour Magazine. Gained fame as Revlon's Charlie Girl on TV commercials.
PICTURES: Annie Hall, If Ever I See You Again, The King of Comedy, Troll, Blind Fear.
TELEVISION: Series: Charlie's Angels, Cutter to Houston, Jack and Mike, Movies: Death Car, Trackdown, Found Money, Single Bars Single Women, Bridesmaids.

HACKER, CHARLES R.: Executive. b. Milwaukee, WI, Oct. 8. e. U. of Wisconsin. Thea. mgr., Fox Wisc. Amuse. Corp., 1940; served in U.S.A.F., 1943–45; rejoined Fox Wisconsin Amusement Corp.; joined Standard Theatres Management Corp. 1947, on special assignments; apptd. district mgr. of Milwaukee & Waukesha theatres 1948; joined Radio City Music Hall Corp. as administrative asst. July, 1948; mgr. of oper., 1952; asst. to the pres., Feb. 1957; v.p., Radio City Music Hall Corp., 1964; appointed executive vice president and chief operating officer, February 1, 1973. Pres., Landmark Pictures, May, 1979. Elected treas. Will Rogers Memorial Fund, 1978. Award: Quigley Silver Grand Award for Showmanship, 1947. Member: U.S. Small Business Admin. Region 1, Hartford Advisory Council since 1983.

HACKETT, BUDDY: Actor, Comedian. b. Brooklyn, NY, Aug. 31, 1924. Prof. debut, borscht circuit.
TELEVISION: Stanley series, Bud and Lou (movie).
THEATRE: Bdwy: Call Mr. Mister, Lunatics and Lovers, I Had a Ball.
PICTURES: Walking My Baby Back Home, God's Little Acre, All Hands on Deck, The Music Man, The Wonderful World of Brothers Grimm, Everything's Ducky, It's a Mad, Mad, Mad, Mad World, Golden Head, Muscle Beach Party, The Love Bug, Friend to Friend.

HACKFORD, TAYLOR: Director. b. Dec. 3, 1944. e. USC, B.A. (international relations). Was Peace Corps volunteer in Bolivia 1968–69. Began career with KCET in Los Angeles 1970–71. As prod.-dir. won Oscar for short, Teenage Father, 1978. Theatrical film debut as director with The Idolmaker (1980). Formed New Visions Inc. which merged with New Century Entertainment 1988 to become New Century/New Visions.
PICTURES: The Idolmaker, An Officer and a Gentleman, Against All Odds (also co.-prod.), White Nights (also co-

prod.), La Bamba (co-prod. only), Chuck Berry: Hail! Hail! Rock 'n Roll (dir.); Everyone's All-American (dir., co-prod.), Rooftops (exec. prod.), Confidence (exec. prod.).

HACKMAN, GENE: Actor. b. San Bernardino, CA, Jan. 30, 1930. First major broadway role in Any Wednesday. Other stage productions include: Poor Richard, Children from Their Games, A Rainy Day in Newark, The Natural Look. Formed own production co., Chelly Ltd.
TELEVISION: CBS Playhouse's My Father, My Mother, The F.B.I., The Invaders, The Iron Horse.
PICTURES: Mad Dog Coll (1960), Lilith, Hawaii, A Covenant With Death, Bonnie and Clyde (Acad. Award nom. for best supporting actor), First to Fight, Out by the Country Club, Riot, The Split, The Gypsy Moths, Downhill Racer, Marooned, I Never Sang for My Father, Doctor's Wives, The Hunting Party, Cisco Pike, The French Connection (Acad. Award best actor, 1971), Prime Cut, The Poseidon Adventure, Scarecrow, The Conversation, Zandy's Bride, Young Frankenstein, Night Moves, Bite the Bullet, French Connection II, Lucky Lady, The Domino Principle, A Bridge Too Far, March or Die, Superman, All Night Long, Superman II., Reds, Eureka, Under Fire, Uncommon Valor, Misunderstood, Power, Target, Twice in a Lifetime, Hoosiers, No Way Out, Superman IV, Another Woman, Full Moon in Blue Water, Mississippi Burning, Bat-21, Split Decisions, Loose Cannons, The Package, Narrow Margin, Postcards From the Edge.

HADLOCK, CHANNING M.: Marketing. TV Executive. b. Mason City, IA. e. Duke U., U. of North Carolina. Newspaperman, Durham, NC Herald, war corr., Yank; NBC, Hollywood; television prod.-writer, Cunningham & Walsh Adv.; v.p. account supr. Chirug & Cairns Adv.; v.p. Marketing Innovations; dir. mktg. Paramount Pictures; mktg. svcs, Ogilvy & Mather; mktg, Time Life Books.

HAGERTY, JULIE: Actress. b. Cincinnati, OH, June 15, 1955. Studied drama for six years before leaving for NY where studied with William Hickey and at Juilliard Sch. of Drama. Also worked as Eileen Ford model. Made acting debut in her brother Michael's theatre group in Greenwich Village called the Production Company. Film debut in Airplane!, 1980.
THEATER: The Front Page (Lincoln Center), The House of Blue Leaves (Theatre World Award, 1986), Wild Life, Born Yesterday (Phil. Drama Guild).
PICTURES: A Midsummer Night's Sex Comedy, Airplane II: The Sequel, Goodbye New York, Lost in America, Bad Medicine, Beyond Therapy, Aria, Bloodhounds of Broadway, Rude Awakening.
TELEVISION: The Visit (Trying Times). House of Blue Leaves, Necessary Parties, Movies: The Day the Women Got Even.

HAGGAR, PAUL: Executive. Veteran of over 30 yrs. with Paramount Pictures, working way up from studio mail room to become apprentice editor in 1953; promoted to asst. editor 1955; music editor, 1957. In 1968 named head of post-prod. for all films made by Paramount. 1985, named sr. v.p., post-prod. for Studio Group.

HAGGARD, PIERS: Director. b. Scotland, 1939. e. U. of Edinburgh. Son of actor Stephen Haggard; great grandnephew of author Rider Haggard. Began career in theatre in 1960 as asst. to artistic dir. at London's Royal Court. Named director at Glasgow Citizens' Theatre. 1963–65 worked with the National Theatre, where co-directed Hobson's Choice and The Dutch Courtesan. Has directed many plays and series for TV.
PICTURE: Blood on Satan's Claw. Venom, The Fiendish Plot of Dr. Fu Manchu, A Summer Story.
TELEVISION: Pennies from Heaven, Quatermass, A Triple Play: Sam Found Out, The Fulfillment of Mary Gray, Back Home.

HAGMAN, LARRY: Actor. b. Fort Worth, TX, Sept. 21, 1931. e. Bard Coll. Son of actress Mary Martin. First stage experience with Margo Jones Theatre in the Round in Dallas. Appeared in N.Y. in Taming of the Shrew; one year with London production of South Pacific. 1952–56 was in London with US Air Force where produced and directed show for servicemen. Returned to N.Y. for plays on and off Bdwy. (God and Kate Murphy, The Nervous Set, The Warm Peninsula, The Beauty Part). Starred in daytime serial, Edge of Night, for over 2 years.
PICTURES: Fail Safe, Ensign Pulver and the Captain, The Group, In Harm's Way, Beware!, The Blob, The Cavern, Stardust, 3 in the Cellar, Mother, Jugs and Speed, Harry and Tonto, The Eagle Has Landed, Superman, S.O.B.
TELEVISION: Series: The Edge of Night, I Dream of Jeannie, The Good Life, Here We Go Again, Dallas. Movies: The President's Mistress, Last of the Good Guys, Battered, Deadly Encounter.

HAHN, HELENE: Executive. b. New York, NY. e. Loyola U. Instructor of entertainment law at Loyola. Attorney for ABC before joining Paramount in 1977 in studio legal dept. 1979, moved to business affairs; promoted to dir. 1980, v.p., 1981; sr. v.p., 1983. Left in 1985 to join Walt Disney Pictures as sr. v.p., business & legal affairs for m.p. division. 1987, promoted to exec. v.p., Walt Disney Studios.

HAIM, COREY: Actor. b. Toronto, Canada, Dec. 23, 1972. Performed in TV commercials at 10; signed as regular on children's show, The Edison Twins. Theatrical m.p. debut, Firstborn (1984).
PICTURES: Secret Admirer, Silver Bullet, Lucas, Murphy's Romance, Lost Boys, License to Drive, Dream a Little Dream, Watchers.
TELEVISION: A Time to Live; Roomies (series).

HAIMOVITZ, JULES: Executive. b. New York, NY, 1951. e. Brooklyn Coll., B.A., M.A., theoretical mathematics. Worked at ABC-TV in operations and audience research before joining Viacom International for 11 years finally as pres. of Viacom Networks Group with responsibility for Showtime/The Movie Channel, MTV and other pay TV networks. Sept. 1987, named pres. and COO, Aaron Spelling Productions, Inc.

HALAS, JOHN: Director. b. Budapest, Apr. 16, 1912. e. Hungary, Paris. Entered m.p. ind. 1928; prod. over 500 documentary, educational shorts & cartoons, including Masters of Animation (series 13 TV programs).
PICTURES: Animal Farm, The Owl and the Pussycat (3-D), History of the Cinema, Animal, Vegetable and Mineral, The Candlemaker; anim. seq., The First 99, The Energy Picture, Habatales, A Christmas Visitor, Hamilton Cartoon series, Automania 2000, Is There Intelligent Life on Earth, Midsummer Nightmare, Hoffnung Cartoon Series, Dodo, The Kid from Outer Space (series), Ruddigore, The Question, Children and Cars, Parkinson's Law, Tomfoolery Show, Max and Moritz series, Ten for Survival, Autobahn, Dilemma, Players, Botticelli—A New Vision, Toulouse-Lautrec, Leonardo da Vinci, The Light of the World.

HALE, ALAN: Actor. b. Los Angeles, CA, 1918. Son of late Alan Hale, actor.
PICTURES: Short Grass, The Gunfighter, West Point Story, At Sword's Point, Wait Till the Sun Shines Nellie, Big Trees, Lady in the Iron Mask, Springfield Rifle, Man Behind the Gun, Capt. John Smith and Pocahontas, Iron Glove, Silver Lode, Rogue Cop, Young at Heart, Many Rivers to Cross, Destroy, A Man Alone, Sea Chase, Indian Fighter, Killer Is Loose, Up Periscope, Advance to the Rear, Hang 'Em High, The True Story of Jesse James, Hambone and Hillie.
TELEVISION: The Lucy Show, Hazel, Wagon Train, Cheyenne, Maverick, Route 66, Jack Benny Show, Biff Baker, U.S.A. (series), Casey Jones (series), Gilligan's Island (series), The Law and Harry McGraw.

HALE, BARBARA: Actress. b. DeKalb, IL, April 18, 1922. m. actor Bill Williams. Mother of actor William Katt. e. Chicago Acad. of Fine Arts. Beauty contest winner, Little Theatre actress. Screen debut, 1943: Higher and Higher. Della Street on TV's Perry Mason series (1956-66; Emmy 1959).
PICTURES: Belle of the Yukon, Goin' to Town, Boy with Green Hair, Window, Jolson Sings Again, And Baby Makes Three, Emergency Wedding, Jackpot, Lorna Doone, First Time, Last of the Comanches, Seminole, Lone Hand, Lion Is in the Streets, Unchained, Far Horizons, Houston Story, Buckskin, Airport.
TELEVISION: Perry Mason Returns (1985) and other Perry Mason's: The Case of the Murdered Madam; The Avenging Ace, The Case of the Lady in the Lake, The Case of the Scandalous Scoundrel, The Case of the Lethal Lesson.

HALEY, JR., JACK: Executive. b. Los Angeles, CA, Oct. 25, 1933. e. Loyola U. Son of late actor Jack Haley. 1959–67 Wolper Prods., 1967–73. sr. v.p. at Wolper before joining MGM. Named dir. of creative affairs. Left in 1974, to join 20th Century-Fox as pres. of TV div. and v.p., TV for 20th-Fox Film Corp. Winner of 2 Peabody Awards, best prod. at Int'l. TV Festival at Monte Carlo and 3 Silver Lion Awards at Venice Film Festival. Won Emmy for best dir. in music or variety shows for Movin' On with Nancy. Directed M.P. Academy Awards Show in 1970; prod. it in 1974 and 1979. Left Fox 1976 to be indep. prod.
PICTURES: Norwood, The Love Machine, That's Entertainment (prod, dir., s.p.), Better Late Than Never (prod.), That's Dancing.
TELEVISION: The Incredible World of James Bond, The Legend of Marilyn Monroe, The Supremes, The Hidden World, Movin' with Nancy (Emmy, dir., 1968), With Love Sophia, Monte Carlo, Life Goes to War: Hollywood and the Homefront; Heroes of Rock n' Roll (exec. prod.), 51st Academy Awards (Emmy, 1979), Hollywood, the Golden Years (with David Wolper), Ripley's Believe It or Not, The Night They Saved Christmas, Cary Grant: A Celebration (exec. prod.).

HALL, ANTHONY MICHAEL: Actor. b. New York, NY, 1968.
PICTURES: Six Pack, National Lampoon's Vacation, Six

teen Candles, The Breakfast Club, Weird Science, Out of Bounds, Johnny Be Good, Upworld.
TELEVISION: Rascals and Robbers: The Secret Adventures of Tom Sawyer and Huck Finn.

HALL, ARSENIO: Actor. Comedian. b. Cleveland, OH. Feb. 12, 1958. e. Kent State U. Became interested in magic at 7, which later led to own local TV special, The Magic of Christmas. Switched from advertising career to stand-up comedy, 1979. Discovered at Chicago nightclub by singer Nancy Wilson.
PICTURES: Amazon Women on the Moon (debut, 1987), Coming to America, Harlem Nights.
TELEVISION: The 1/2 Hour Comedy Hour (1983, co- host), Thicke of the Night (regular), Solid Gold, The Late Show (host), The Arsenio Hall Show.

HALL, CONRAD: Cinematographer. b. Tahiti, 1926. Worked as camera operator with Robert Surtees, Ted McCord, Ernest Haller; moved to TV as director of photography before feature films.
PICTURES: Wild Seed, The Sabateur—Code Name Morituri, Harper, The Professionals, Rogue's Gallery, Incubus, Divorce, American Style, In Cold Blood, Cool Hand Luke, Hell in the Pacific, Butch Cassidy and the Sundance Kid, Tell Them Willie Boy Is Here, The Happy Ending, Fat City, Electra-Glide in Blue, The Day of the Locust, Smile, Marathon Man, Black Widow, Tequila Sunrise.
TELEVISION: It Happened One Christmas.

HALL, HUNTZ (HENRY): Actor. b. Boston, MA, 1920. In 1937 appeared in stage and screen production Dead End.
PICTURES: Crime School, Angels with Dirty Faces, They Made Me a Criminal, Hell's Kitchen, Muggs Rides Again, Live Wires, A Walk in the Sun, Jinx Money, Smuggler's Cove, Fighting Fools, Blues Busters, Bowery Battalion, Ghost Chasers, Crazy Over Horses, Let's Go Navy, Here Come the Marines, Hold That Line, Feudin' Fools, No Holds Barred, Private Eyes, Paris Playboys, Bowery Boys Meet the Monsters, Clipped Wings, Jungle Gents, Bowery to Bagdad, High Society, Spy Chasers, Jail Busters, Dig That Uranium, Up in Smoke, Second Fiddle to a Steel Guitar, Gentle Giant, Cyclone.
TELEVISION: The Teddy Bears (series).

HALMI, ROBERT SR.: Producer: b. Budapest, Hungary, Jan 22, 1924. Originally writer-photographer under contract to Life Magazine.
PICTURES:: Documentaries for U.N. Features include: Hugo the Hippo; Visit to a Chief's Son; One and Only; Brady's Escape, Cheetah, Mr. and Mrs. Bridge.
TELEVISION: Bold Journey (dir.-cin.); American Sportsman; The Oriental Sportsman; The Flying Doctor; The Outdoorsman; Julius Boros Series; Rexford; Who Needs Elephants; Calloway's Climb; Oberndorf Revisited; True Position; Wilson's Reward; Nurse; Buckley Sails; A Private Battle; My Old Man; Mr. Griffin and Me; When the Circus Came to Town; Best of Friends; Bush Doctor; Peking Encounter; Svengali; China Rose; Cook and Peary—The Race to the Pole; Terrible Joe Moran; Nairobi Affair; The Night They Saved Christmas, Spies, Lies and Naked Thighs; exec. prod.: The Prize Pulitzer, Paradise, Bridesmaids, Face to Face, Margaret Bourke-White, Incident at Lincoln Bluff.

HALPERN, NATHAN L.: Executive. b. Sioux City, IA, Oct. 22, 1914. e. U. of Southern California, B.A. 1936; Harvard Law Sch., L.L.B. 1939. With general counsel's office, U.S. Securities & Exchange commission, 1939–41; exec. asst. to dir., Civilian Supply, U.S. War Prod. Board, 1941–43; naval officer, Psychological Warfare Div., Supreme Headquarters, Allied Expeditionary Force, 1943–45; exec. asst. to dir., U.S. Information Service, Paris, 1945; asst. to pres., Columbia Broadcasting System, 1945–49; 1949–present; pres., TNT Communications, Inc.

HAMADY, RON: Producer. b. Flint, MI, June 16, 1947. e. U. of California, B.A. 1971, co-founder of The Crystal Jukebox, record productions, music management and music publishing co. Produced 12 hit albums for Decca Records of England and London Records, U.S. Entered m.p. industry in 1975–76, producing Train Ride to Hollywood for Taylor-Laughlin dist. Co.
PICTURES: Fade to Black, Surf II, And God Created Woman (1987), Out Cold, The Boyfriend School.

HAMEL, VERONICA: Actress. b. Philadelphia, PA, Nov. 20, 1943. e. Temple U. Moved to NY and began a modelling career with Eileen Ford Agency. Off B'way debut: The Big Knife. Acted in dinner theater prods. Moved to L.A. 1975.
PICTURES: Cannonball, Beyond the Poseidon Adventure, When Time Ran Out, A New Life, The Package.
TELEVISION: Ski Lift, 79 Park Avenue, The Gathering, The Gathering II, Valley of the Dolls, Sessions, Kane and Abel, Twist of Fate. Series: Hill Street Blues (5 Emmys).

HAMILL, MARK: Actor. b. Oakland, CA, Sept. 25, 1952. Started in TV, including General Hospital (serial) and the Texas Wheelers (series). Film debut in Star Wars (1977). Bdwy debut: The Elephant Man. Then in The Nerd.
PICTURES: Star Wars, Corvette Summer, The Big Red One, The Empire Strikes Back, The Night the Lights Went Out in Georgia, Return of the Jedi, Slipstream.
TELEVISION: Eric Mallory: Circumstantial Evidence, Delancy Street; The Crisis Within; The City; Sarah T: Portrait of A Teenage Alcoholic; The F.B.I.; Owen Marshall; Room 222; The Partridge Family.

HAMILL, PETE: Journalist, Writer. b. Brooklyn, NY, June 24, 1935. Worked as ad designer, NBC page boy and sheet metal worker before joining staff of New York Post. In 1962 won Mike Berger Award of Columbia U. Graduate Sch. of Journalism for N.Y.'s worst slum. Received citation from Newspaper Reporters' Assn. for series on N.Y. Police Dept. Made s.p. writing debut with Doc, 1971.
PICTURES: Doc, Death at an Early Age, Badge 373, Report from Engine Co. 82, The Neon Empire.
TELEVISION: Laguna Heat, Adaptations of novels Flesh and Blood, The Gift.
BOOKS: A Killing for Christ (novel), Irrational Ravings (collection of N.Y. Post columns), The Seventeenth Christmas (novel), The Invisible City: A NY Sketchbook.

HAMILTON, GEORGE: Actor. b. Memphis, TN, Aug. 12, 1939. e. grammar, Hawthorne, CA; military sch., Gulfport, MS, N.Y. Hackley Prep Sch., FL, Palm Beach H.S. Won Best Actor Award for the state of Florida, high sch. contest.
TELEVISION: Rin Tin Tin, The Donna Reed Show, The Veil, Roots, Two Fathers' Justice, Monte Carlo, Poker Alice. Series: Spies.
PICTURES: Crime and Punishment, USA (debut), Home from the Hill, All The Fine Young Cannibals, Angel Baby, Where the Boys Are, By Love Possessed, A Thunder of Drums, Light in the Piazza, Two Weeks in Another Town, The Victors, Your Cheatin' Heart, Viva Maria, That Man George, Doctor, You've Got to Be Kidding!, The Long Ride Home, Jack of Diamonds, A Time for Killing, The Power, Evel Knievel, The Man Who Loved Cat Dancing, Once Is Not Enough, Love at First Bite (also exec. prod.), Zorro, the Gay Blade (also co-prod.), Love at Second Bite: Dracula Goes to Hollywood, The Experts.

HAMILTON, GUY: Director. b. Paris, Sept. 1922. Ent. m.p. industry 1939 as apprentice at Victorine Studio, Nice; Royal Navy, 1940–45, in England asst. dir., Fallen Idol, Third Man, Outcast of the Islands, African Queen.
PICTURES: The Ringer, The Intruder, An Inspector Calls, Colditz Story, Manuela, The Devil's Disciple, A Touch of Larceny, The Best of Enemies, The Party's Over, Man in the Middle, Goldfinger, Funeral in Berlin, Battle of Britain, Diamonds Are Forever, Live and Let Die, The Man with the Golden Gun, Force Ten from Navarone, The Mirror Crack'd, Evil Under the Sun, Remo Williams.

HAMLIN, HARRY: Actor. b. Pasadena, CA, Oct. 30, 1951. e. U. of California, Yale U., 1974 in theatre, psychology. Awarded IT&T Fulbright Grant, 1977. Joined American Conservatory Theatre, San Francisco, for two years' study before joining McCarter Theatre, Princeton (Hamlet, Faustus in Hell.) Bdwy debut Awake and Sing! (1984). Screen debut in Movie, Movie, 1979.
PICTURES: King of the Mountain, Clash of the Titans, Making Love, Blue Skies Again.
TELEVISION: Mini-series: Studs Lonigan, Master of the Game, Space, Laguna Heat, Favorite Son. Series: L.A. Law.

HAMLISCH, MARVIN: Composer. b. New York, NY, June 2, 1944. e. Juilliard. Accompanist and straight man on tour with Groucho Marx 1974–75; debut as concert pianist 1975 with Minn. Orch. Scores of Broadway shows: A Chorus Line (Tony Award); They're Playing Our Song, Smile. Winner 4 Grammy Awards.
PICTURES: The Swimmer (1968); Take the Money and Run; Bananas; Save the Tiger, Kotch; The Way We Were (Oscars for original score and song), The Sting (Oscar for adaptation), Same Time, Next Year; Ice Castles; Chapter Two; Seems Like Old Times; The Spy Who Loved Me, Starting Over, Ordinary People, The Fan, Sophies' Choice, I Ought to Be in Pictures, Romantic Comedy, D.A.R.Y.L., Three Men and a Baby, Little Nikita, The January Man, The Experts.
TELEVISION: Good Morning, America (theme); The Entertainer (also prod.); A Streetcar Named Desire; The Two Mrs. Grenvilles.

HAMMOND, PETER: Actor, Writer, Director. b. London, Eng., Nov. 15, 1923. e. Harrow Sch. of Art. Stage debut: Landslide, Westminster Theatre. Screen debut: Holiday Camp.
PICTURES: The Huggetts, Helter Skelter, Fools Rush In, The Reluctant Widow, Fly Away Peter, The Adventurers, Operation Disaster, Come Back, Peter, Little Lambs Eat Ivy, Its Never Too Late, The Unknown, Morning Departure, Confession, dir.: Spring and Port Wine.
TELEVISION: William Tell, Robin Hood, The Buccaneers series. 1959–61. writ., dir. TV plays. Dir.: Avengers, 4

Armchair Theatres, Theatre 625, BBC classic serials Count of Monte Cristo, Three Musketeers, Hereward the Wake, Treasure Island, Lord Raingo, Cold Comfort Farm, The White Rabbit, Out of the Unknown, Follyfoot; Lukes Kingdom, Time to Think, Franklin's Farm, Sea Song, Shades of Greene, Our Mutual Friend, The House that Jack Built, The King of the Castle, The Black Knight, Kilvert's Diary, Turgenev's Liza, Wuthering Heights, Funnyman, Little World of Don Camillo, Rumpole of the Bailey, Bring on the Girls, Hallelujah Mary Plum, Aubrey Beardsley, The Happy Autumn Fields, The Combination, Tales of the Unexpected, The Glory Hole, The Hard Word, Shades of Darkness—The Maze, The Blue Dress.

HAMNER, EARL: Producer, Writer. b. Schuyler, VA, July 10, 1923. e. U. of Richmond 1940–43, Northwestern U.; U of Cincinnati, Coll. Conservatory of Music, B.F.A., 1958. With WLW, Cincinnati, as radio writer-producer; joined NBC 1949 as writer; (The Georgia Gibbs Show, The Helen O'Connell Show). 1960, freelance 1961–71; writer, prod. Lorimar Prods. 1971–86; writer prod. Taft Ent. 1986–; Pres. Amanda Prods.
PICTURES: Palm Springs Weekend, Spencer's Mountain, Chitty, Chitty Bang Bang, The Tamarind Seed, Charlotte's Web (adaptor), Where the Lilies Bloom.
TELEVISION: Exec. prod.: Series: The Waltons (creator, co-prod., narrator), Apple's Way (creator), The Young Pioneers (creator); Joshua's World, Falcon Crest; Boone (also creator), Morning Star/Evening Star (also narrator), Movies: The Homecoming: A Christmas Story (s.p. only), You Can't Get There From Here (s.p. only), A Wedding on Walton's Mountain; Mother's Day on Walton's Mountain, A Day of Thanks on Walton's Mountain (exec. prod. actor), The Gift of Love—A Christmas Story (exec. prod., s.p.).

HAMPSHIRE, SUSAN: Actress. b. London, Eng., May 12, 1941.
STAGE: Expresso Bongo, Follow That Girl, Fairy Tales of New York, Ginger Man, Past Imperfect, She Stoops to Conquer, On Approval, The Sleeping Prince, A Doll's House, Taming of the Shrew, Peter Pan, Romeo & Jeanette, As You Like It, Miss Julie, The Circle, Arms and the Man, Man and Superman, Tribades, An Audience Called Edward, The Crucifer of Blood, Night and Day, The Revolt, House Guest, Blithe Spirit, Married Love.
TELEVISION: Andromeda, The Forsyte Saga, Vanity Fair, Katy, The First Churchills; An Ideal Husband, The Lady Is a Liar, The Improbable Mr. Clayville, musical version of Dr. Jekyll and Mr. Hyde, The Pallisers, Barchester Chronicles, Leaving, Leaving II, Going to Pot I, II, and III.
PICTURES: The Three Lives of Thomasina, Night Must Fall, Wonderful Life, Paris Au Mois d'Aout, The Fighting Prince of Donegal, The Trygon Factor, Monte Carlo or Bust, Rogan, David Copperfield, A Room in Paris, Living Free, Time for Loving, Malpertius, Baffled, Neither the Sea nor the Sand, Roses and Green Peppers, David the King, Bang.

HANCOCK, JOHN: Director. b. Kansas City, MO, Feb. 12, 1939. e. Harvard. Was musician and theatre director before turning to films. Dir. play A Man's a Man, NY 1962. Artistic dir. San Francisco Actors Workshop 1965–66. Nominated for AA for short, Sticky My Fingers, Fleet My Feet.
PICTURES: Let's Scare Jessica to Death, Bang the Drum Slowly, Baby Blue Marine, California Dreaming, Weeds (also co-s.p.), Steal the Sky, Why Me? Prancer.
TELEVISION: The Twilight Zone (1986).

HAND, BETHLYN J.: Executive. b. Alton, IL. e. U. of Texas. Entered motion picture industry in 1966 as administrative assistant to president of Motion Picture Association of America, Inc. In 1975 became associate director of advertising administration of MPAA. In 1976 became director of advertising administration; in 1979 became; v.p.—west coast activities, board of directors, Los Angeles. S.P.C.A. 1981, appointed by Governor to Calif. Motion Picture Council 1983, elected vice chmn., California Motion Picture Council.

HANDEL, LEO A.: Producer. b. Vienna. Dir. audience research, MGM, 1942–51; organized Meteor Prod., 1951; organized Leo A. Handel Prod., for TV films, 1953; author, Hollywood Looks at Its Audience, also TV plays; pres., Handel Film Corp. Exec. prod. & v.p., Four Crown Prods., Inc. Prod.-writer-dir., feature film, The Case of Patty Smith, 1961; book, A Dog Named Duke, 1965.
TELEVISION: prod. TV series including Everyday Adventures, Magic of the Atom. exec. prod., Phantom Planet, 1961; Americana Series, 1963; Specials, Age of the Atom; Sweden-Vikings Now Style, Benjamin Franklin, The Mexican American Heritage and Destiny, The American Indian, Police Dog, Art in America (10 half-hour films), Stress-Distress, Computer and You, Thailand, The Philippines, Germ Wars, Measuring Things, Safety for Seniors, The Dropouts; Singapore—Crossroad of the Orient, Black American Odyssey, Puerto Rico—Progress in the Caribbean, Nuclear Power Production (1988).

HANKS, TOM: Actor. b. Concord, CA, July 9, 1956. m. actress Rita Wilson. Traveled around Northern CA. with family before settling in Oakland, CA. e. Chabot Jr. Coll. California State U. Began career with Great Lakes Shakespeare Festival, Cleveland (3 seasons) and NY's Riverside Theater (Taming of the Shrew).
PICTURES: He Knows You're Alone, Splash, Bachelor Party, The Man with One Red Shoe, Volunteers, The Money Pit, Nothing in Common, Every Time We Say Goodbye, Dragnet, Big, Punchline, The 'Burbs, Turner and Hooch, Joe Versus the Volcano.
TELEVISION: The Love Boat, Bosom Buddies (series), Taxi, Happy Days, Family Ties. Movie: Rona Jaffe's Mazes and Monsters; Saturday Night Live (host).

HANNA, WILLIAM: Executive. b. Melrose, NM, July 14, 1911. e. Compton Coll. Studied engineering and journalism. Joined firm in CA as structural engineer; turned to cartooning with Leon Schlessinger's company in Hollywood. In 1937 hired by MGM as director and story man in cartoon dept. There met Joseph R. Barbera and created famous cartoon series Tom & Jerry, continuing to produce it from 1938 to 1957. Left MGM in 1957 to form Hanna-Barbera Productions to make cartoons for TV. Series have included Yogi Bear, Huckleberry Hound, The Flintstones, The Jetsons. Hanna-Barbera became a subsidiary of Taft Broadcasting Co. in 1968 with both men operating studio under long-term agreements with Taft (which became Great American Broadcasting, 1987). Hanna is sr. v.p. of Hanna-Barbera Productions. Company entered theatrical production with Loopy De Loop in 1960, Hey There It's Yogi Bear, Man Called Flintstone, Charlotte's Web, C.H.O.M.P.S., Heidi's Song.

HANNAH, DARYL: Actress. b. Chicago, IL, 1960. Niece of cinematographer Haskell Wexler. e. UCLA. Studied ballet with Maria Tallchief. Studied with Stella Adler.
PICTURES: The Fury (debut, 1978), The Final Terror, Hard Country, Blade Runner, Summer Lovers, Splash, The Pope of Greenwich Village, Reckless, Clan of the Cave Bear, Legal Eagles, Roxanne, Wall Street, High Spirits, Steel Magnolias, Crazy People.
TELEVISION: Paper Dolls.

HANNEMANN, WALTER A.: Film editor. b. Atlanta, GA, May 2, 1914. e. U. of Southern California, 1935. Editorial training, RKO 1936–40; edit. supvr., Universal, 1941–42; consultant 1970–75 national educational media. Bd. of Govs., TV Academy (2 terms, 1960 & 1970); bd. of govs., Acad of M.P. Arts and Sciences. 1983–86.
PICTURES: Interval, The Revengers, Dream of Kings, Guns of the Magnificent Seven, East of Java, Pay or Die, Al Capone, (Amer. Cinema Editor's Award, 1959), Hell's Five Hours, Armoured Command, Only the Valiant, Time of Your Life, Kiss Tomorrow Goodbye, Blood on the Sun, Guest in the House, Texas Masquerade, Cannon for Cardoba, El Condor, Maurie, Lost in the Stars, Mad Mad Movie Making, Big Mo, Two Minute Warning, (Oscar nominee) The Peter Hill Puzzle, Smokey and the Bandit, Other Side of the Mountain—Part II, The Visitor, The Villain, Return of Maxwell Smart, Charlie Chan and the Curse of the Dragon Woman.
TELEVISION: Death Valley Days, Reader's Digest, Rosemary Clooney Show, The New Breed, The Fugitive, Twelve O'Clock High, The Invaders, Hawaii Five-O, Streets of San Francisco, Cannon, Barnaby Jones, Caribe. Movies: The Man Who Broke a 1000 Chains, Intimate Strangers, The Abduction of Saint Anne.

HANSEN, PETER: Actor. b. Oakland, CA, Dec. 5, 1921. e. Cranbrook Acad. of Arts, Bloomfield Hills, MI; U. of Michigan, 1940–41. p. Sydney and Lee Hansen. Studied acting at Pasadena Playhouse, CA, 1946, following war service as marine fighter pilot. Campagne, Arsenic and Old Lace, This Happy Breed; m.p. debut in Branded (1950).
PICTURES: Molly, Something to Live For, When Worlds Collide, Passage West, Darling How Could You, The Savage, Violent Men, Proud and Profane, Harlow.
TELEVISION: Matinee Theatre; New Dir. KCOP-TV: Day in Court; General Hospital (series, since 1965; Emmy supp., 1975).

HARBACH, WILLIAM O.: Producer. b. Yonkers, NY, Oct. 12, 1919, e. Brown U. p. Otto Harbach, lyricist, author. U.S. Coast Guard, 1940–45; actor, MGM, 1945–47; broadcast co-ordinator. NBC, 1947–49; stage mgr., 1949–50; dir., NBC, 1950–53; prod., Tonight, 1954; prod. Steve Allen Show, 1960–61 prod., dir., Bing Crosby shows; prod., Milton Berle Special, 1962; prod., Hollywood Palace Shows, 1963–69.; co-produced Julie Andrews Show, 1972–73. Emmy for Shirley MacLaine's Gypsy in My Soul, 1976; Bob Hope Special, 1981 and 1982.

HARBERT, TED: Executive. b. New York, NY, June 15, 1955. e. Boston U., B.S. magna cum laude, 1977, degree in bdcst. & film. Started career as producer in news dept. WHDH Radio in Boston, 1976. Joined ABC in 1977 as feature film coordinator for ABC Entertainment. Named spvr., feature film and late-night program planning, 1979. Named asst. to v.p., program planning & scheduling, 1979. Named dir., program planning-scheduling, 1981. V.P., program planning & scheduling, 1983. Promoted to newly created position of v.p., motion pictures, ABC Entertainment, 1986; given title v.p. motion pictures and scheduling, 1987; v.p. primetime ABC Entertainment, 1988.

HARDIMAN, JAMES W.: Publicist. b. Brighton, England 1926. Director advtg. & pub., Rank Organisation of Canada & Odeon Canada, 1947–56. Asst. dir. ad & pub, National Theatres, 1956–58. Dir. radio & TV promotion, Walt Disney, 1959–60. Dir. pub, Screen Gems Hollywood, 1960–64. Dir. press infmtn, CBS TV Network, Hollywood, 1964–67. Studio dir. promtn. & pub, Screen Gems, Hollywood, 1967–70. VP Yuni public rels, Tokyo and v.p. and resident director, Sijohn o Enterprises, Japan, 1970–75. Dir. pub, (entertainment) Rogers & Cowan, Beverly Hills, 1975–77. President, Suhosky & Hardiman Public Rels, 1977 to date. 1968 named Hollywood Showman of the Year by the Publicists Guild.

HARE, DAVID: Director, Writer. b. Sussex, England, 1947. e. Lancing Coll., Jesus Coll., Cambridge. After leaving univ. in 1968 formed Portable Theatre Company, experimental touring group. Hired by Royal Court Theater as literary manager, 1969. 1970, first full-length play, Slag, prod. at Hampstead Theatre Club. Resident dramatist, Royal Court (1970–71), and Nottingham Playhouse (1973). West End debut, Knuckle.
THEATER: Slag, Brassneck, Knuckle, Fanshen, Teeth 'n' Smiles, Plenty, A Map of the World, Pravda, Secret Rapture (London, NY, Also dir.).
PICTURES: Plenty (writer); Wetherby (dir., s.p.); Paris by Night (dir., s.p.), Strapless (dir., s.p.).
TELEVISION: Licking Hitler (1979, dir., s.p.); Dreams of Leaving; Saigon: Year of the Cat, Knuckle.

HAREWOOD, DORIAN: Actor. b. Dayton, OH, Aug. 6. m. actress Ann McCurry. e. U. of Cincinnati.
THEATER: Jesus Christ Superstar (road co.), Two Gentlemen of Verona, Miss Moffat, Streamers, Over Here, Don't Call Back, The Mighty Gents.
PICTURES: Foster & Laurie, Gray Lady Down, Looker, Tank, Against All Odds, The Falcon and the Snowman, Full Metal Jacket.
TELEVISION: Panic in Echo Park, Siege, Roots—The Next Generations, An American Christmas Carol, High Ice, Beulah Land (mini-series), Strike Force, The Ambush Murders; I, Desire; Trauma Center, The Jesse Owens Story, Dirty Work, Guilty of Innocence, Amerika, Hope Division, God Bless the Child, Kiss Shot, Half 'n' Half (pilot).

HARGREAVES, JOHN: Executive. Joined Gainsborough Pictures 1945. Transferred to Denham Studios 1946 and later Pinewood Studios. Joined Allied Film Makers 1960, then Salamander Film Productions as Bryan Forbes' financial controller and asst. prod. 1965. Joined EMI Film Prods. Ltd. as asst. man. dir. and prod. controller May 1969–May 1972. Produced Don Quixote (with Rudolf Nureyev, in Australia), 1973. Asst. prod. The Slipper and The Rose 1975, man. dir; Cinderella Promotions Ltd, 1978: assoc. prod., International Velvet. Orion repr., 1979, The Awakening; post prod. exec., Fiendish Plot of Dr. Fu Manchu, 1980; Orion rep. for Excalibur, 1981; MGM rep., Year of Living Dangerously, Australia, 1982. 1983, U.K. production executive for Completion Bond Company, Inc.

HARMON, MARK: Actor. b. Burbank, CA, Sept. 2, 1951. Son of actress Elyse Knox and football star Tom Harmon. m. actress Pam Dawber.
PICTURES: Beyond the Poseidon Adventure; Comes a Horseman; Summer School, The Presidio, Stealing Home, Two Too Many, Cold Heaven.
TELEVISION: Series: Sam, Laverne & Shirley, Nancy Drew, Police Story, Adam-12, 240-Robert, St. Elsewhere (regular), Moonlighting. Movies: Eleanor and Franklin: The White House Years, Little Moe, Getting Married, The Deliberate Stranger, Prince of Bel Air, Sweet Bird of Youth.

HARMON, TOM: Performer. b. Rensselaer, IN, Sept. 28, 1919. e. U. of Michigan, B.S., 1941. m. Elyse Knox, actress. All American football player, 1939–40; 1940 Heisman Trophy Winner. U.S. Air Corps, 1941–46; sports dir., WJR, Detroit, 1941; KFI, Los Angeles, 1947; broadcaster, many football, baseball games; sports dir., Columbia Pacific Radio Network, 1948–61; Tom Harmon Sports Show (ABC) 1961–70; Golden West Broadcasters (Channel 5, Hollywood), 1970; 1974—Hughes Television Network—sports dir.; 1976—Editor-Publisher—Tom Harmon's Football Today. (weekly national football paper).

HARNELL, STEWART D.: Executive. b. New York, NY, Aug. 18, 1938. e. U. of Miami, UCLA, New School for Social Research. Entertainer with Youth Parade in Coral Gables, FL, 1948–55, performing for handicapped children, Variety Club, etc. Singer, dancer, musician. Had own bands, Teen Aces & Rhythm Rascals, 1950–56; performed on Cactus Jim TV show and Wood & Ivory, 1953–54, WTVJ, Miami. Catskills, Sand Lake, NY, 1954–55. Joined National Screen Service as exec. trainee in 1960 in Chicago; worked as booker & salesman. Transferred to N.Y. home office, 1963; worked in special trailer production. Promoted to asst. gen. sls. mgr., 1964–66; New Orleans branch mgr., 1966–67; Atlanta division mgr., 1967–70. Formed own independent distribution co., 1970–77 Harnell Independent Productions. Resumed post as gen. sls. mgr. of NSS, New York, 1977–78; resigned to become pres. of Cinema Concepts Theatre Service, Atlanta, in 1978 to present. Chief barker of Variety Club of Atlanta, Tent 21, 1972, 1976, 1979, 1988, 1989. In 1986 formed Cinema Concepts Communications, film-video animation studio in Atlanta.

HARPER, JESSICA: Actress. b. Chicago, IL, Oct. 10, 1949. m. prod. exec. Thomas E. Rothman. e. Sarah Lawrence Coll. Understudied on Broadway for Hair for one year. Appeared in summer stock and off-Bdwy shows. (Richard Farina: Long Time Coming, Longtime Gone, Doctor Selavy's Magic Theatre.) Theatrical film debut in Phantom of the Paradise (1974).
PICTURES: Taking Off, Inserts, Love and Death, Stardust Memories, The Evictors, Suspiria, Shock Treatment, Pennies from Heaven, My Favorite Year, The Imagemaker, Once Again, The Blue Iguana, Big Man on Campus.
TELEVISION: Series: Little Women. Mini-series: Studs Lonigan. Movies: Aspen, When Dreams Come True, Special: The Garden Party.

HARPER, JOE: Theatre Executive. b. Dallas, TX, Aug. 11, 1941. e. El Centro Coll., Dallas; Georgia. State U. Was in public relations, N.Y., 1961–65 when joined Academy Theatres, Dallas. In 1968–69, with American Multi-Cinema, Dallas. In 1969 joined R. C. Cobb Theatre, Atlanta. Now v.p. in chg. booking, buying, Member: Democratic Executive Committee, Officer Ruritan International. Active in Scouting and Little League sports.

HARPER, TESS: Actress. b. Mammoth Springs, AR. e. Southwest Missouri State Coll., Springfield. Worked in Houston, then Dallas in children's theater, dinner theater, and commercials.
PICTURES: Tender Mercies (debut, 1982); Amityville 3-D; Silkwood; Flashpoint; Crimes of the Heart (Acad. Award nom.); Ishtar; Criminal Law; Her Alibi, Home Grown, Daddy's Dyin'.
TELEVISION: Chiefs (mini-series); Celebrity; Kentucky Woman; A Summer to Remember; Promises to Keep; Far North; Little Girl Lost; Unconquered.

HARPER, VALERIE: Actress. b. Aug. 22, 1940. Suffern, NY. e. Hunter Coll, New Sch. for Social Research. Started as dancer in stage shows at Radio City Music Hall. First professional acting in summer stock in Conn.; actress with Second City Chicago 1964–69; Appeared on Bdwy. in Take Me Along, Wildcat, Subways Are for Sleeping, Something Different, Story Theatre, Metamorphoses. Won 3 Emmys for best performance in supporting role in comedy for portrayal of Rhoda on The Mary Tyler Moore Show.
PICTURES: Freebie and the Bean, Chapter Two, The Last Married Couple in America, Blame It on Rio.
TELEVISION: Series: The Mary Tyler Show, Rhoda, Valerie. Movie: The Execution, Fun and Games, The Shadow Box, The Day the Loving Stopped, Strange Voices, Drop Out Mother, The People Across the Lake.

HARPER, WILLIAM A.: Producer, b. Port Jervis, NY, Sept. 3, 1915. e. U. of Southern California, B.S., 1936. Founder member Delta Kappa Alpha fraternity (cinematography), U.S.C.; started in m.p. ind. in pub.; later asst. dir., prod. mgr., director; In W.W.II Major, USMC. Organized Marine Corps Photo Service, then in chg. Marine Corps Photo activities Pacific Ocean Areas. End of war organized Reliance Film Co., Inc., eng. in prod., dist., early TV prod. Recalled active duty for Korean War, headed USMC Photo Service. Co-prod. with Navy (Adm. John Ford) feat. documentary, This is Korea; govt. liaison with March of Time, Crusade in Pacific and with NBC U.S. Navy Victory at Sea; prod. dir., writer, Loucks & Norling Studios, 1952; free lance writer-director 1953–55; with Fred Feldkamp Prods. 1955–56; in Europe 1956–58. Assoc. prod. The Silken Affair (RKO) 1956; Producer, The Stranding in Holland 1957; prod. advisor The Last Blitzkreig (Col.), Europe, (1958); producer, The Stone, 1962; Managing Director, St. James Productions Ltd., (England) and Pres. American-European Entertainments, Inc. (Paris).

HARRINGTON, CURTIS: Director, Writer. b. Los Angeles, CA, Sept. 17, 1928. e. U. of Southern California, B.A. Exec. asst. to Jerry Wald, 1955–61 Associate producer at 20th Cent. Fox.
PICTURES: Hound Dog Man, Return to Peyton Place, The Stripper, Night Tide, Queen of Blood, What's the Matter with Helen? Gingerbread House, The Killing Kind, Games, Who Slew Auntie Roo?.
TELEVISION: Series: Hotel, Dynasty, Tales of the Unexpected, Logan's Run, Twilight Zone (1986). Movies: The Cat Creature, The Dead Can't Die, How Awful About Alan, Killer Bees, Devil Dog.

HARRINGTON, PAT: Actor. b. New York, NY, Aug. 13, 1929. e. Fordham U. Served USAF as 1st Lt., 1952–54. Time sales

man for NBC, 1954–58. Some 150 TV appearances on Jack Paar, Steve Allen and Danny Thomas TV shows, 1958–61; nightclub appearances, 1960–63. TV and films, 1963 to present. Television series include: Mr. Deeds Goes to Town, Owen Marshall, and One Day at a Time.
PICTURES: The Wheeler Dealers, Move Over Darling, Easy Come, Easy Go, The President's Analyst, 2000 Years Later, The Candidate.

HARRIS, BARBARA: Actress. b. Evanston, IL, July 25, 1935. e. Wright Junior Coll., Chicago; Goodman Sch. of the Theatre; U. of Chicago. Joined acting troup, The Compass. Founding member, Second City Players, 1960. Came to N.Y. where first role was in Oh, Dad, Poor Dad, Mamma's Hung You in the Closet and I'm Feeling So Sad, repeating in m.p.
THEATER: Mother Courage and Her Children, Dynamite Tonight, On a Clear Day You Can See Forever, The Apple Tree (Tony Award), Mahogany.
PICTURES: A Thousand Clowns, Plaza Suite, Who Is Harry Kellerman?, The War Between Men and Women, Mixed Company, Nashville, Freaky Friday, Family Plot, Movie Movie, The North Avenue Irregulars, The Seduction of Joe Tynan, Peggy Sue Got Married, Nice Girls Don't Explode, Dirty Rotten Scoundrels.
TELEVISION: The Return of Ben Casey.

HARRIS, BURTT: Producer, Actor. Began career as actor; later worked with Elia Kazan as prod. asst. and asst. dir. on America America, Splendor in the Grass, and The Arrangement. Worked as second unit dir. and asst. dir. on many films as well as producer and actor.
PICTURES: Associate Producer: Little Murders, The Wiz, Cruising, Gilda Live. Executive Producer: The Verdict, Just Tell Me What You Want. See No Evil, Hear No Evil, Family Business. Producer: Prince of the City, Daniel, Deathtrap, Garbo Talks, The Glass Menagerie, Q & A. Co-Producer: D.A.R.Y.L. Actor: Splendor in the Grass, Fail Safe, The Taking of Pelham 1–2–3, The Wanderers, The Verdict, Daniel, Garbo Talks, D.A.R.Y.L., Running on Empty.

HARRIS, ED: Actor. b. Tenafly, NJ, Nov. 28, 1950. m. actress Amy Madigan. Played football 2 years at Columbia U. prior to enrolling in acting classes at OK State U. Summer stock. Grad. CA Institute of the Arts, B.F.A, 1975. Worked in West Coast Theater.
THEATER: Fool For Love (off-Bdwy debut, Obie Award), Precious Sons.
PICTURES: Coma, Borderline, Knightriders, Dream On, Creepshow, The Right Stuff, Under Fire, Swing Shift, Places in the Heart, Alamo Bay, A Flash of Green, Sweet Dreams, Code Name: Emerald, The Suspect, Walker, To Kill a Priest, Jackknife, The Abyss, State of Grace.
TELEVISION: Movies: The Amazing Howard Hughes, The Seekers, The Last Innocent Man, Pilot: The Aliens Are Coming.

HARRIS, JAMES B.: Producer, Director, Writer. b. New York, NY, Aug. 3, 1928. e. Juilliard Sch. U.S. film export, 1947; Realart Pictures, 1948; formed Flamingo Films, 1949; formed Harris-Kubrick Productions, 1954. Producer of The Killing, Paths of Glory, Lolita; formed James B. Harris Prods., Inc., 1963; prod., dir., The Bedford Incident, 1965; Some Call It Loving, (prod., dir., s.p.), Telefon, prod.; Fast-Walking, (prod., dir., s.p.); Cop (prod., dir., s.p.).

HARRIS, JULIE: Designer. b. London, England. e. Chelsea Arts Sch. Entered industry in 1945 designing for Gainsborough Studios. First film, Holiday Camp.
PICTURES: Greengage Summer, Naked Edge, The War Lover, Fast Lady, Chalk Garden, Psyche 59, A Hard Day's Night, Darling, Help, The Wrong Box, Casino Royale, Deadfall, Prudence and the Pill, Decline and Fall, Goodbye Mr. Chips, Sherlock Holmes, Follow Me!, Live and Let Die, Rollerball, Slipper and The Rose, Dracula.
TELEVISION: Laura (with Lee Radziwill), Candleshoe, The Sailor's Return, Lost and Found, The Kingfisher, Arch of Triumph, Sign of Four, Hound of the Baskervilles, A Hazard of Hearts.

HARRIS, JULIE: Actress. b. Grosse Pointe, MI, Dec. 2, 1925. e. Yale Drama Sch. m.p. debut in Member of the Wedding (1952).
THEATER: Sundown Beach, Playboy of the Western World, Macbeth, Young and the Fair, Magnolia Alley, Monserrat, Member of the Wedding, I Am a Camera, Colombe, The Lark; A Shot in the Dark; Marathon 33; Ready When You Are, C.B.; Break a Leg; Skyscraper; Voices; And Miss Reardon Drinks a Little; The Last of Mrs. Lincoln (Tony Award); In Praise of Love; The Belle of Amherst; Driving Miss Daisy (Natl. co.).
PICTURES: East of Eden, I Am a Camera, The Trouble with Women, The Haunting, Harper, Reflection in a Golden Eye, The Poacher's Daughter, You're a Big Boy Now, The Split, The People Next Door, The Hiding Place, The Moving Target, Voyage of the Damned, The Bell Jar, Gorillas in the Mist.
TELEVISION: Little Moon of Alban, Johnny Belinda, A Doll's House, Ethan Frome, The Good Fairy, The Lark, He Who Gets Slapped, The Heiress, Victoria Regina, Pygmalion, Anastasia, The Holy Terror, The Power and The Glory, The Woman He Loved, Leave Her to Heaven, Too Good To Be True, The Christmas Wife. Series: Thicker Than Water, Knot's Landing.

HARRIS, JULIUS: Actor.
PICTURES: Nothing But a Man, Live and Let Die, The Taking of Pelham 1-2-3, Looking for Mr. Goodbar, Hell Up In Harlem, Let's Do It Again, The Fox, Superfly, Salty, Islands in the Stream, Shaft's Big Score, Alambrista, First Family, My Chauffeur, A Gathering of Old Men, Berserk, The Enchanted.
THEATER: on B'way and in National tour of No Place To Be Somebody.
TELEVISION: To Kill a Cop; Blue and The Gray; Victory at Entebbe; Rich Man, Poor Man.

HARRIS, PHIL: Orchestra leader. b. Linton, IN, June 24, 1906. m. Alice Faye, actress. In 1933: with orchestra in Melody Cruise. In 1936: Vitaphone short prod. In 1937: Turn Off the Moon. In 1939: Man About Town. In 1940: Buck Benny Rides Again, Dreaming Out Loud.
PICTURES: I Love a Bandleader, Wabash Avenue, Wild Blue Yonder, Starlift, High and the Mighty, Anything Goes, Good-Bye My Lady, The Aristocrats (voice of Scat Cat). Co-starred with Alice Faye in weekly radio show; many TV appearances.

HARRIS, RICHARD: Actor. b. Limerick, Ireland, Oct. 1, 1930. Attended London Acad. of Music and Dramatic Arts. Prod.-dir. Winter Journey 1956. Prof. acting debut in Joan Littlewood's prod. of The Quare Fellow, Royal Stratford, 1956.
THEATER: London: A View from the Bridge; Man, Beast and Virtue; The Ginger Man. (U.S.): Camelot.
PICTURES: Alive and Kicking, Shake Hands With the Devil, The Wreck of the Mary Deare, A Terrible Beauty, The Long, The Short and The Tall, Guns of Navarone, Mutiny on the Bounty, This Sporting Life, The Red Desert (Italy), Major Dundee, The Heroes of Telemark, The Bible, Hawaii, Camelot, The Molly Maguires, A Man Called Horse, Cromwell, Bloomfield (actor & dir.), Man in the Wilderness, The Snow Goose, The Deadly Trackers, Gulliver, 99 and 44/100% Dead, Juggernaut, Echoes of a Summer, Robin and Marian, Return of the Man Called Horse, The Cassandra Crossing, Orca, Golden Rendezvous, The Wild Geese, The Ravagers, The Number, Game for Vultures, High Point, Your Ticket Is No Longer Valid, Martin's Day, Mack the Knife, King of the Wind, Outlaws, A Knight in NY, The Field.
TELEVISION: Camelot. Movie: Maigret, The Return.

HARRIS, ROBERT: Executive. Sr. v.p., Universal TV, with responsibility of supervising Universal programming on CBS network. In 1981 named pres. of Universal TV. Pres. MCA, Television Group.

HARRIS, ROBERT A: Archivist, Producer. b. New York, NY, Dec. 27, 1945. e. NYU, Sch. of Commerce and Sch. of Arts, 1968. Worked as exec. trainee with 7 Arts assoc., NY while in school, 1960–68; worked in corp. communications, Pepsico, 1970–71; formed Center for Instructional Resources, SUNY Purchase, 1971–73; organized Images Film Archive, dist. of classic theatrical and non theat. films, 1974; pres., Images Video and Film Archive, 1985; formed Davnor Prods. with partner Jim Painten, president 1986–present; formed The Film Preserve, Ltd. pres. 1989–.
PICTURES: 1975–80: restored Abel Gance films Beethoven, J'Accuse, Lucetia Borgia; 1974–79: worked with Kevin Brownlow to complete restoration of Abel Gance's Napoleon. Partnered with Francis Coppola/Zoetrope Studios to present Napoleon at Radio City Music, Jan. 1981 and worldwide tour; 1986–89: reconstruction and restoration of David Lean's Lawrence of Arabia for Columbia Pictures, released Feb., 1989.

HARRIS, ROSEMARY: Actress. b. Ashby, Suffolk, Sept. 19, 1930. e. India and England. Early career, nursing; studied Royal Acad. of Dramatic Art, 1951–52. Screen debut in Beau Brummell (1954).
PLAYS: Climate of Eden (NY debut 1952), Seven Year Itch, Confidential Clerk (Paris Festival), and with Bristol Old Vic in The Crucible, Much Ado About Nothing, Merchant of Venice; also in The Tale of Two Cities, Dial M for Murder, etc. On stage, at Old Vic, 1955–56; U.S. tour, 1956–57; U.S. stage, 1958–63. Chichester Festivals 1962 and 63; Nat'l Theatre 1963–64; You Can't Take It With You, 1965; The Lion in Winter (Tony Award, 1966), 1967, APA Repertory Co., Heartbreak House, The Royal Family, The New York Idea (Obie Award), A Pack of Lies, Hay Fever.
TELEVISION: Cradle of Willow (debut, 1951); Othello, The Prince and the Pauper, Twelfth Night; Wuthering Heights, Notorious Woman, (Emmy, 1976), Blithe Spirit, Holocaust, Profiles in Courage, To the Lighthouse, Strange Interlude, Tales From the Hollywood Hills: The Old Reliable.
PICTURES: Beau Brummell, The Shiralee, A Flea in Her

Ear, Camelot, The Boys from Brazil, The Ploughman's Lunch, Crossing Delancey.

HARRIS, TIMOTHY: Writer, (Producer). b. Los Angeles, CA, July 21, 1946. e. Charterhouse, 1963–65; Peterhouse Coll., Cambridge, 1966–69, M.A. Honors Degree, Eng. lit. Author of novels, Knonski/McSmash, Kyd For Hire, Goodnight and Goodbye; author of novelizations, Steelyard Blues, Hit, Heatwave, American Gigolo.

PICTURES: Co-writer with Herschel Weingrod: Cheaper to Keep Her, Trading Places (BAFTA nom., orig. s.p.; NAACP Image Awards, best m.p. 1983), Brewster's Millions, My Stepmother is an Alien, Paint It Black, Twins (People's Choice Award, best comedy, 1988).

TELEVISION: Street of Dreams (based on his novel Goodnight and Goodbye; also exec. prod.).

HARRISON, GEORGE: Singer, Composer, Producer. b. Liverpool, England, Feb. 25, 1943. Member, The Beatles. Winner of 2 Grammys on own in addition to Beatles' group awards.

PICTURES: Appeared with Beatles in A Hard Day's Night, Help, Let It Be. As individual. Score: Let It Be. Exec. Prod.: Life of Brian; Time Bandits; Monty Python Live at the Hollywood Bowl; The Missionary; Privates on Parade; Scrubbers; Bullshot; A Private Function; Water; Mona Lisa; Shanghai Surprise, Withnail and I, Five Corners, Bellman and True, The Lonely Passion of Judith Hearne, Track 29, The Raggedy Rawney, How to Get Ahead in Advertising, Powwow Highway, Checking Out, Cold Dog Soup, Nuns on the Run.

HARRISON, GREGORY: Actor. b. Avalon, Catalina Island, CA, May 31, 1950. Started acting in school plays; then joined Army. Studied at Estelle Harman Actors Workshop; later with Lee Strasberg and Stella Adler. Film debut in Jim, the World's Greatest (1976). Formed Catalian Productions with Franklin Levy.

THEATER: Picnic, The Hasty Heart, Journey's End.

PICTURES: Fraternity Row, Razorback, North Shore.

TELEVISION: Series: Logan's Run, M*A*S*H, Barnaby Jones, Trapper John, Falcon Crest, The Gregory Harrison Show (pilot). Movies: The Gathering, Enola Gay, Trilogy in Terror, The Best Place To Be, The Women's Room, For Ladies Only, The Fighter, Seduced, Oceans of Fire, Hot Paint (co-exec. prod., star), Red River (co-exec. prod., actor). Mini-series: Centennial, Fresno.

HARRISON, JOAN: Writer, producer. b. Guildford, Surrey, England, 1911. e. U. Sorbonne; Oxford U., B.A. Began screen career in England as asst. & writer with Alfred Hitchcock, dir. To U.S. 1939 to write s.p. Rebecca.

PICTURES: Foreign Correspondent, Suspicion, Saboteur, Phantom Lady (prod.); Dark Waters, The Strange Affair of Uncle Harry, Ride a Pink Horse, Circle of Danger, Eye Witness.

Prod. Alfred Hitchcock Presents, TV.

HARRISON, SIR REX: Actor. b. Derry House, Huyton, Lancashire, Eng., Mar. 5, 1908. In the RAF W.W.II. Stage debut 1924 in Thirty Minutes in a Street, Liverpool Repertory Theatre, England; later on British tour (Charley's Aunt, Alibi, etc.) London debut 1930 in Getting George Married. NY debut Sweet Aloes (1936). Voted one of top ten British money-making stars in Motion Picture Herald-Fame Poll, 1945–46. Top ten world box office star, 1966.

THEATER: London, repertory, tour. New York stage: Anne of a Thousand Days (Tony Award, 1949), Henry VIII; Cocktail Party (London); Bell, Book and Candle, (NY); Venus Observed, Love of 4 Colonels, (NY): Bell, Book and Candle, (London). My Fair Lady, 1956–57 (NY) (Tony Award), (1958–59, London); The Fighting Cock, 1959–60; Platonov (London), August for The People. Both Seasons at Royal Court Theatre (London). In Praise of Love (spec. Tony Award, 1969); Heartbreak House, Aren't We All?, The Circle.

PICTURES: Began screen career, 1929. Men Are Not Gods, Storm in a Teacup, School for Husbands, Over the Moon, The Citadel, Ten Days in Paris, Sidewalks of London, Night Train, Major Barbara, Blithe Spirit. *To Hollywood, 1946.* I Live in Grosvenor Square, The Rake's Progress, Anna and the King of Siam, The Ghost and Mrs. Muir, Foxes of Harrow, Escape, Unfaithfully Yours, The Long Dark Hall, The Four Poster, King Richard & the Crusaders, Constant Husband, The Reluctant Debutante, Midnight Lace, Once a Thief, Cleopatra (Acad. Award nom.), My Fair Lady (Acad. Award, NY Film Critics Award, Golden Globe 1965), The Yellow Rolls-Royce, The Agony and the Ecstasy, The Honey Pot, Dr. Doolittle, A Flea in her Ear, Staircase, The Prince and the Pauper, Crossed Swords, Ashanti, The Fifth Muskateer, A Time to Die.

TELEVISION: Anastasia, The Mystery of Anna.

HARROLD, KATHRYN: Actress. b. Tazewell, VA, 1950. e. Mills Coll. Studied acting at Neighborhood Playhouse in N.Y., also with Uta Hagen. Appeared in Off-Off-Bdwy. plays for year; then joined experimental theatre group, Section Ten, touring East, performing and teaching at Connecticut Coll. and NYU. Cast in TV daytime serial, The Doctors.

PICTURES: Nightwing (debut), The Hunter, Modern Romance, The Pursuit of D.B. Cooper, Yes, Gorgio. The Sender, Into the Night, Raw Deal.

TELEVISION: Movies: Son-Rise, a Miracle of Love, Vampire, Bogie, An Uncommon Love, Women in White, Man Against the Mob, Dead Solid Perfect, Capital News. Series: Starsky and Hutch, Bronx Zoo.

HARRYHAUSEN, RAY: Producer, Writer, Special Effects Expert. b. Los Angeles, CA. e. Los Angeles City Coll. While at coll. made 16mm animated film, Evolution, which got him job as model animator for George Pal's Puppetoons in early '40s. Served in U.S. Signal Corps; then made series of filmed fairy tales with animated puppets for schools and churches. In 1946 worked on Mighty Joe Young as ass't. to Willis O'Brien. Designed and created special visual effects for The Beast from 20,000 Fathoms; then began evolving own model animation system called Dynarama. In 1952 joined forces with prod. Charles H. Schneer, using new process for first time in It Came from Beneath the Sea. Subsequently made many films with Schneer in Dynarama.

PICTURES: Twenty Million Miles to Earth, The Three Worlds of Gulliver, Jason and the Argonauts, the First Men in the Moon, One Million Years B.C., The Valley of Gwangi, The Golden Voyage of Sinbad, Sinbad and the Eye of the Tiger, Clash of the Titans (co. prod., special effects).

HART, HARVEY: Director. b. Canada, Mar. 19, 1928. Began career on TV in native country then went to Hollywood.

PICTURES: Dark Intruder, Bus Riley's Back in Town, Sullivan's Empire, The Sweet Ride, Fortune and Men's Eyes, The Pyx, Aliens Are Coming, The High Country, Utilities.

TELEVISION: East of Eden, This Is Kate Bennett, Maserati and the Brain, Born Beautiful, Master of the Game (co-dir.), Reckless Disregard, Beverly Hills Madam, Stone Fox, Passion and Paradise (mini-series).

HARTFORD, K.: Executive, b. New York, NY, July 5, 1922. Graduate U. of Cincinnati, Los Angeles City Coll. Active in film financing, co-production, packaging. Executive of Hartford Industries, Latin American Development & Investment Co., Western International. Has offices in 8 countries.

HARTLEY, MARIETTE: Actress. b. New York, NY, June 21, 1940. Student Carnegie Tech. Inst. 1956–57; studied with Eva Le Gallienne. Appeared with Shakespeare Festival, Stratford 1957–60. Co-host Today Show, 1980. Co-host on CBS Morning Show, 1987. Returned to stage in King John (NYSF in Central Park), 1989.

PICTURES: Ride the High Country, Marooned, Skyjacked, Marnie, Improper Channels, O'Hara's Wife, 1969.

TELEVISION: Peyton Place, Stone, The Incredible Hulk, Second Time Around, The Hero, Good Night Beantown. Movies: Earth II, Sandcastles, Genesis II, Killer Who Wouldn't Die, Last Hurrah, Silence of the Heart, My Two Loves, Passion and Paradise (mini-series).

HARTMAN, DAVID: Actor. b. Pawtucket, RI, May 19, 1935. e. Duke U., 1956. Was 2nd Lt. in Air Force; entered American Acad. of Dramatic Arts, N.Y. Appeared in off-Bdwy. musicals and summer stock; toured with Belafonte singers. Bdwy. debut in Hello, Dolly!

PICTURES: The Ballad of Josie, Nobody's Perfekt, Ice Station Zebra, The Island at tho Top of the World.

TELEVISION: World Premiere: I Love a Mystery. Series: The Virginian, The Bold Ones, Lucas Tanner, Berth and Babies (prod.). Host ABC's Good Morning, America, The Shooters (writer, exec. prod.; narrator), David Hartman—The Future Is Now (also exec. prod.; writer).

HARTZ, JIM: TV Newsman, Panelist. b. Feb. 3, 1940, Tulsa, OK. Pre-med student at U. of Tulsa, where worked in spare time as reporter for radio station KRMG. In 1963 left studies for career as newsman and joined KOTV in Tulsa. In 1964 moved to NBC News in New York, acting as reporter and anchorman. In 1974 became co-host of Today Show, joined Barbara Walters.

HARVEY, ANTHONY: Director. b. London, Eng., June 3, 1931. Royal Acad. of Dramatic Art. Two yrs. as actor. Ent. m.p. ind. 1949 with Crown Film Unit.

PICTURES: *As actor or editor:* Private's Progress, Brothers-in-Law, Man in the Cocked Hat, Carlton Brown of the F.O., I'm Alright Jack, The Angry Silence, The Millionairess, Lolita, The L-Shaped Room, Dr. Strangelove, Spy Who Came In From the Cold, The Whisperers, *Director:* Dutchman; The Lion in Winter, They Might Be Giants, Eagles' Wing, Players, The Abdication, Richard's Things, The Ultimate Solution of Grace Quigley.

TELEVISION: The Disappearance of Aimee, The Missiles of October, Svengali, The Patricia Neal Story, The Glass Menagerie.

HARWOOD, RONALD: Writer. b. Cape Town, South Africa, 1934. e. Royal Acad. of Dramatic Art. Gave up acting to become dresser for actor-mgr. Donald Wolfit (later basis for his play and film The Dresser.)

THEATER: The Dresser, Another Time.
TELEVISION: The Barber of Stamford Hill, Private Potter, Take a Fellow Like Me, The Lads, Convalescence, Guests of Honor, The Guests. Adapted several of the Tales of the Unexpected, Mandela, Breakthrough at Rykjavik.
PICTURES: Barber of Stamford Hill, Private Potter (written with Casper Wrede), subsequently High Wind in Jamaica, Eye Witness, One Day in the Life of Ivan Denisovich, Operation Daybreak, The Dresser, The Doctor and the Devils.

HASSANEIN, RICHARD C.: Executive. b. New York, NY, Aug. 13, 1951; e. Staunton Military Acad., 1966–70; American U., 1970–74. Booker/real estate dept. opns., United Artists Theater Circuit, 1974–77; joined United Film Distribution Co., 1977; named pres. 1978. Resigned as pres. Feb. 1988. Currently pres. of Myriad Enterprises, NY.

HASSANEIN, SALAH M.: Executive. b. Suez, Egypt, May 31, 1921. e. British Sch., Alexandria, Egypt. Nat'l Bank of Egypt, Cairo, 1939–42. Asst. division mgr. Middle East, 20th-Fox, Cairo, Egypt, 1942–44: U.S. armed forces, 1945–47; usher, asst. mgr., Rivoli Theatre, N.Y., 1947–48. Film buyer, booker, oper. v.p. U.A. Eastern Theas., 1948–59; pres. 1960; exec. v.p. U.A. Communications, Inc. 1960; v.p. United Artists Cable News Corp.; pres. Todd-AO Corp., 1963. Exec. v.p., Todd-AO Corp., 1987. President, Warner Bros. International Theaters, 1988.
PICTURES: Exec. prod.: Knightriders; Creepshow; Hello Again; Love or Money.

HASSELHOFF, DAVID: Actor. b. Baltimore, MD, July 17, 1952.
PICTURES: Starcrash, Witchery, W.B., Blue and the Bean.
TELEVISION: The Young and the Restless, Knight Rider (series). Movies: Griffin and Phoenix, Semi Tough, After Hours—Getting to Know Us, The Cartier Affair, Bridge Across Time, Perry Mason: The Case of the Lady in the Lake, Baywatch: Panic at Malibu Pier.

HASTINGS, DON: Performer; b. Brooklyn, NY, Apr. 1, 1934. e. Professional Children's Sch. On Bdwy in Life With Father, I Remember Mama, Summer and Smoke, etc.; on various radio shows, Video Ranger on Capt. Video 1949–55; The Edge of Night, 1956–60; As the World Turns since 1960. Author of scripts for As the World Turns, The Guiding Light.

HATFIELD, BOBBY: Performer. b. Beaver Dam, WI, Aug. 10, 1940. e. Long Beach State Coll. Member, Righteous Bros. recording group.
TELEVISION: Shindig, The Danny Kaye Show, Ed Sullivan Show.
PICTURES: Beach Ball, Swingin' Summer.

HATFIELD, HURD: Actor. b. New York, NY, 1918. e. Morristown prep, Horace Mann H.S., Riverdale Acad., Columbia U., Chekhov Drama Sch., Devonshire, Eng. On dramatic stage, Lower Depths, Twelfth Night, Cricket on the Hearth, King Lear, then screen debut Dragon Seed, The Picture of Dorian Gray, 1943–44. N.Y. stage 1952, Venus Observed.
PICTURES: The Diary of a Chambermaid, The Beginning or the End, The Unsuspected, The Checkered Coat, Joan of Arc, Chinatown at Midnight, Destination Murder, Tarzan and Slave Girl, Left-Handed Gun, King of Kings, El Cid, Mickey One, The Boston Strangler, Harlow, Von Richtofen and Brown, King David, Crimes of the Heart, Her Alibi.
TELEVISION: Thief, The Norliss Tapes, The Word, You Can't Go Home Again.

HATFIELD, TED: Executive. b. Wilton Junction, IA, Aug. 26, 1936. e. Hot Springs, AR. U.S. Army-NCO Academy, 1954. 1949–67 ABC Paramount Theatres, advanced from usher to district mgr. 1967–70 MGM asst. exploitation dir.; 1970–83, MGM national advertising coordinator; 1983–87, MGM/UA v.p., field operations. 1987–present, MGM/UA v.p., exhibitor relations.
MEMBER: Motion Picture Pioneers; Western LA Council, Boy Scout Commissioner; Culver City Chamber of Commerce, past v.p./presidents award; Jaycees, Past State v.p.; Advertising Federation, past state pres., Culver City Commissioner.

HAUER, RUTGER: Actor. b. Breukelen, Netherlands, Jan. 23, 1944. Stage actor in Amsterdam for six years. Motion picture debut in Turkish Delight, 1975.
PICTURES: The Wilby Conspiracy, Keetje Tippl'e, Max Havelaar, Soldier of Orange, Pastorale 1943, Femme Entre Chien et Loup, Mysteries, Nighthawks, Blade Runner, Chanel Solitaire, Eureka, The Osterman Weekend, A Breed Apart, Ladyhawke, Flesh and Blood, The Hitcher, Wanted: Dead or Alive; Bloodhounds of Broadway, Blind Fury, The Legend of the Holy Drinker, Salute of the Juggler, Ocean Point, On a Moonlit Night.
TELEVISION: Escape from Sobibor, Inside The Third Reich.

HAUSMAN, MICHAEL: Producer. Former stockbroker and still photographer. Entered film industry as assoc. prod. and prod. mgr. on The Heartbreak Kid and Taking Off. Worked as head of prod. for Robert Stigwood on Saturday Night Fever.
PICTURES: I Never Promised You A Rose Garden; Alambrista!; Heartland; Rich Kids; One-Trick Pony; Ragtime (exec. prod., 1st asst. dir.); The Ballad of Gregorio Cortez; Silkwood; Amadeus (exec. prod.); Places in the Heart (exec. prod.); Desert Bloom; Flight of the Spruce Goose; No Mercy; House of Games; Things Change; Valmont, Homicide, State of Grace.
TELEVISION: Lip Service (exec. prod.).

HAVERS, NIGEL: Actor. b. London, Eng., Nov. 6, 1949. e. Leicester U., trained for stage at Arts Educational Trust. Father Sir Michael Havers, is Attorney General of Britain. As child played Billy Owen on British radio series, Mrs. Dale's Diary. Records voice overs and books for the blind.
THEATER: Conduct Unbecoming, Richard II, Man and Superman (RSC), Family Voices, Season's Greetings, The Importance of Being Earnest.
PICTURES: Pope Joan (debut, 1972), Full Circle, Who is Killing the Great Chefs of Europe?, Chariots of Fire, A Passage to India, Burke and Wills, The Whistle Blower, Empire of the Sun, Farewell to the King, Cliche Days.
TELEVISION: Series: A Horseman Riding By, Don't Wait Up. Mini-series: The Glittering Prizes, Nicholas Nickleby, Pennies From Heaven, Winston Churchill: The Wilderness Years, Nancy Astor, The Little Princess, Death of the Heart, Naked Under Capricorn. Movies: The Charmer, Private War of Lucina Smith. Guest: Thriller, Star Quality: Noel Coward Stories (Bon Voyage), A Question of Guilt, Aspects of Love, Upstairs Downstairs, Edward VII.

HAVOC, JUNE: Actress. r.n. Hovick. b. Seattle, WA, 1916. Sister of late Gypsy Rose Lee, actress. Made film bow when two in Hal Roach prod. Danced with Anna Pavlova troupe, then entered vaudeville in own act. Later, joined Municipal Opera Company, St. Louis, and appeared in Shubert shows. Musical comedy debut: Forbidden Melody (1936). To Hollywood, 1942. Author: Early Havoc (1959), More Havoc (1980).
PICTURES: Hello Frisco, Hello, No Time for Love, Sweet and Low Down, Brewster's Millions, Intrigue, Gentleman's Agreement; Red, Hot and Blue; Chicago Deadline, Once a Thief, Follow the Sun, Lady Possessed, Can't Stop the Music.
PLAYS: Pal Joey, Sadie Thompson, Mexican Hayride, Dunnigan's Daughter, Dream Girl, Affairs of State, The Skin of Our Teeth, A Midsummer Night's Dream (Stratford, CT. American Shakespeare Fest., 1958), Tour for U.S. Dept. of St., 1961; wrote Marathon 33. The Ryan Girl, The Infernal Machine, The Beaux Strategem, A Warm Peninsula, Dinner at Eight, Habeas Corpus. An Unexpected Evening with June Havoc (one woman show, London 1985). Toured England in The Gift, 1987.
TELEVISION: Anna Christie, The Bear, Cakes and Ale, Daisy Mayme, The Untouchables; co-owner, Willy, MacMillan & Wife, The Paper Chase, Murder She Wrote. Series: More Havoc (1964–65).

HAWN, GOLDIE: Actress. b. Washington, DC, November 21, 1945. Was a professional dancer (performed in Can-Can at the N.Y. World's Fair, 1964), and made TV debut dancing on an Andy Griffith Special; TV acting debut Good Morning World followed by Laugh-In. Screen debut: Cactus Flower (1969).
PICTURES: There's A Girl In My Soup, Dollars, Butterflies Are Free, The Sugarland Express, The Girl from Petrovaka, Shampoo, The Duchess and the Dirtwater Fox, Foul Play, Private Benjamin (also prod.), Seems Like Old Times, Best Friends, Swing Shift, Protocol (also exec. prod.); Wildcats; Overboard, Bird on a Wire.

HAWTHORNE, NIGEL: Actor. b. Coventry, England, 1929. Extensive career on stage. Ent. TV ind. 1953. Films, 1957.
TELEVISION: Mapp and Lucia, The Knowledge, The Miser, The Critic, Barchester Chronicles, Marie Curie, Edward and Mrs. Simpson, Yes, Minister, Yes, Prime Minister (series). The Shawl, Relatively Speaking.
PICTURES: Gandhi, Firefox, King of the Wind, The Chain, A Handful of Time.

HAYES, HELEN: Actress, r.n. Helen H. Brown. b. Washington, DC, Oct. 10, 1901. e. Sacred Heart Convent, Wash. Wife of the late writer, Charles MacArthur. Started film career in 1931. Dubbed "The First Lady of the American Stage."
PLAYS: What Every Woman Knows, Coquette, Petticoat Influence, The Good Fairy, Mary of Scotland, Victoria Regina, Harriet, Happy Birthday, Wisteria Trees, Mrs. McThing, Skin of Our Teeth, Glass Menagerie, The Show Off, Front Page (revivals).
PICTURES: Arrowsmith, The White Sister, Another Language, Night Flight, A Farewell to Arms, The Sin of Madelon Claudet (Academy Award 1931–32), My Son, John, Main Street to Broadway, Anastasia, Airport (AA, 1970), Herbie Rides Again, One of Our Dinosaurs Is Missing, Candleshoe.
TELEVISION: Twelve Pound Look, Mary of Scotland, Dear Brutus, Skin of Our Teeth, Christmas Tie, Drugstore on a

Sunday Afternoon, Omnibus, A Caribbean Mystery, Murder with Mirrors.

HAYES, JOHN MICHAEL: Writer. b. Worcester, MA, May 11, 1919. e. U. of Massachusetts, 1941.
PICTURES: Red Ball Express, Thunder Bay, Torch Song, War Arrow, Rear Window, To Catch a Thief, Trouble with Harry, It's A Dog's Life, Man Who Knew Too Much, The Matchmaker, Peyton Place, But Not for Me, Butterfield 8, The Children's Hour, Where Love Has Gone, The Chalk Garden, Judith, Nevada Smith.
TELEVISION: Pancho Barnes.

HAYES, PETER LIND: Actor: b. San Francisco, CA, June 25, 1915. m. Mary Healy. Was radio singer, actor, vaudeville, night clubs. Producer, Grace Hayes Lodge Review: on TV show with Mary Healy.
PICTURES: Million Dollar Legs, All Women Have Secrets, These Glamour Girls, Seventeen, Dancing on a Dime, Playmates, Seven Days Leave, 5000 Fingers of Dr. T, Once You Kiss a Stranger.

HAYNES, TIGER: Actor. b. St. Croix, V.I., Dec. 13, 1914. Organized singing group The Three Flames, whose hit record Open the Door, Richard led to a vaudeville career, 39 weeks on radio and nightclub and TV dates.
THEATER: introduced in New Faces of 1956, Finian's Rainbow, Kiss Me Kate (City Center revival), Fade Out-Fade In, Two Gentlemen of Verona, The Great White Hope (National Company), The Wiz (Tin Woodsman), A Broadway Musical, Comin' Uptown, My One and Only. Off-Bdwy: Bags, Louis, Taking My Turn.
PICTURES: Times Square, Moscow on the Hudson, All that Jazz, Trading Places, Ratboy, The Mosquito Coast, The Long Lost Friend, Enemy Territory, A Gathering of Old Men, Dead Bang.
TELEVISION: In the Heat of the Night, The Cosby Show, On the 5:48, Benny's Place.

HAYS, ROBERT: Actor. b. Bethesda, MD, July 24, 1947. e. Grossmont Coll., San Diego State U. Left school to join Old Globe Theatre, San Francisco for five years.
PICTURES: Airplane, Take This Job and Shove It!, Some Summer Day, Airplane II: The Sequel, Utilities, Trenchcoat, Touched, Scandalous, Cat's Eye, For Better or Worse.
TELEVISION: Love Boat, Harry O, Laverne and Shirley, Most Wanted, Wonder Woman, Series: Angie, Starman, FM. Movies: Young Pioneers, Young Pioneers' Christmas, Delta County U.S.A., The Initiation of Sarah, The Girl, The Gold Watch and Everything, California Gold Rush, The Fall of the House of Usher, The Day the Bubble Burst, Murder by the Book. Mini-series: Will Rogers: Champion of the People.

HAZEN, JOSEPH H.: Attorney b. Kingston, NY, May 23, 1898. e. George Washington U. Law Sch. Formerly assoc. as member of firm, Thomas and Friedman. In 1939 member ind. com. in discussions with Commerce Dept. Member com. which negotiated consent decree. Member ind. Committee of Six, lawyers to study and reorganize ind. activities. Mem. War Activities Committee. In 1944 resigned as v.p. and dir., Warner Bros. to join Hal Wallis Prods. as pres., 1944–48; pres. Wallis-Hazen, Inc., Tillco. dissolved, June 1953; photoplay prod., Hal B. Wallis, Paramount Pictures Corp., since 1953. Dir. USO Camps, Inc., M.P.A.A.

HEADLY, GLENNE: Actress. b. New London, CT, March 13, 1955. m. actor John Malkovich. e. High Sch. of Performing Arts. Studied at HB Studios then American Coll. of Switzerland. In Chicago joined St. Nicholas New Works Ensemble. Won 3 Joseph Jefferson awards for work with Steppenwolf Ensemble in Say Goodnight Gracie, Miss Firecracker Contest, Balm in Gilead, Coyote Ugly, Loose Ends. Directed Canadian Gothic. Film debut: Fandango, 1985.
THEATER: Balm in Gilead, Arms and the Man, Extremities, The Philanthropist.
PICTURES: Fandango (debut, 1985), Nadine, Making Mr. Right, Eleni, Purple Rose of Texas, Stars and Bars, Dirty Rotten Scoundrels, Paperhouse, Dick Tracy.

HEALY, JOHN T.: Executive. e. Brooklyn Coll. Taught economics and was associated with Lehigh Valley Industries and General Food Corp. before joining ABC, Inc. in 1970 as assoc. dir. of corp. planning. Named dir. of planning and develop. June, 1972. Elected v.p., planning and admin. of ABC Leisure Group, March, 1974; elected vice pres. of corporate planning, Feb., 1976.

HEARD, JOHN: Actor. b. Mar. 7, 1946. Married, actress Margot Kidder. Career began at Organic Theatre, starring in Chicago & N.Y. productions of Warp. Other stage roles include Streamers, G.R. Point, Othello, The Glass Menagerie.
PICTURES: Between the Lines, On the Yard, Head Over Heels, Heartbeat, Cutter and Bone, Cat People, Violated, Heaven Help Us, Lies, After Hours, The Trip to Bountiful, The Telephone, The Milagro Beanfield War, The Seventh Sign, Big, Betrayed, Beaches, The Package, One Point of View, Mindwalk.

TELEVISION: The Scarlet Letter, Tender Is the Night, Out on a Limb, Necessity, Cross of Fire.

HEATHERTON, JOEY: Actress. b. Rockville Centre, NY, Sept. 14, 1944. Daughter of singer & TV's "Merry Mailman" Ray Heatherton.
PICTURES: Twilight of Honor, Where Love Has Gone, My Blood Runs Cold, Bluebeard, The Happy Hooker Goes to Washington.
TELEVISION: Dean Martin Presents The Golddiggers, Joey and Dad.

HECKART, EILEEN: Actress. b. Columbia, OH, Mar. 29, 1919. e. Ohio State U., American Theatre Wing. m. Jack Yankee.
THEATER: Voice of the Turtle, Brighten the Corner, They Knew What They Wanted, Hilda Crane, Picnic, The Bad Seed, A View From the Bridge, Family Affair, Pal Joey, Invitation to a March, Everybody Loves Opal, Dark at the Top of the Stairs, And Things That Go Bump in the Night, You Know I Can't Hear You When the Water's Running, Too True to Be Good, Barefoot in the Park, Butterflies Are Free, Veronica's Room, The Effect of Gamma Rays on Man in the Moon Marigolds, Eleemosynary.
PICTURES: Miracle in the Rain (debut), Somebody Up There Likes Me, The Bad Seed, Bus Stop, Hot Spell, Heller in Pink Tights, My Six Loves, Up the Down Staircase, No Way to Treat a Lady, Butterflies Are Free (Acad. Award), Zandy's Bride, The Hiding Place, Burnt Offerings, Heartbreak Ridge.
TELEVISION: Kraft, Suspense, Philco Playhouse, The Web, Mary Tyler Moore, Annie McGuire.
AWARDS: Daniel Blum and Outer Circle (Picnic), Foreign Press, and Donaldson, Oscar nom. and Film Daily Citation, (Bad Seed), TV Sylvania for the Haven, Variety Poll of N.Y. and Drama Critics (Dark at The Top of the Stairs); Emmy, (Save Me a Place at Forest Lawn).

HECKERLING, AMY: Director. b. New York, NY, May 7, 1954. m. writer-dir. Neal Israel. e. Art & Design H.S., NYU, (film and TV), American Film Institute. Made shorts (Modern Times, High Finance, Getting It Over With), before turning to features.
PICTURES: Fast Times at Ridgemont High, Johnny Dangerously, National Lampoon's European Vacation, Permanent Record, Look Who's Talking.
TELEVISION: Twilight Zone (1986), Fast Times at Ridgemont High (series).

HEDLUND, DENNIS: Executive. b. Hedley, TX, Sept. 3, 1946. e. U. of Texas, Austin, B.A., business admin., 1968. Captain U.S. Marine Corps, 1966–70. 1970–74, newscaster and disc jockey, KGNC, Amarillo, TX; KOMA, Oklahoma City, OK; WTIX, New Orleans, LA; WFLA, Tampa, FL; 1974–77, national sales mgr., Ampex Corp., NY; 1977–80, vice pres., Allied Artists Video Corp., NY; 1980–present, founder and president, Kultur Video.

HEFFNER, RICHARD: Executive. b. Aug. 5, 1925. e. Columbia U. Instrumental in acquisition of Channel 13 (WNET) as New York's educational tv station; served as its first general manager. Previously had produced and moderated Man of the Year, The Open Mind, etc. for commercial TV. Served as dir. of public affairs programs for WNBC-TV in N.Y. Was also dir. of special projects for CBS TV Network and editorial consultant to CBS, Inc. Editorial Board. Was radio newsman for ABC. Exec. editor of From The Editor's Desk on WPIX-TV in New York. Taught history at U. of California at Berkeley, Sarah Lawrence Coll., Columbia U. and New School for Social Research, N.Y. Served as American specialist in communications for U.S. Dept. of State in Japan, Soviet Union, Germany, Yugoslavia, Israel, etc. Prof. of Communications and Public Policy at Rutgers U. In July, 1974 appt. chmn. of classification and rating admin. rating board.

HEFFRON, RICHARD T.: Director. b. Chicago, Oct. 6, 1930.
PICTURES: Fillmore, Newman's Law, Trackdown, Futureworld, Outlaw Blues, I, the Jury, The French Revolution.
TELEVISION: The Morning After, Dick Van Dyke Special, I Will Fight No More Forever, Toma (pilot), Rockford Files (pilot), North and South (mini-series). Movies: The California Kid, Young Joe Kennedy, A Rumor of War, A Whale for the Killing, The Mystic Warrior, V: The Final Battle, Anatomy of an Illness, Convicted: A Mother's Story, Guilty of Innocence, Samaritan, Napoleon and Josephine: A Love Story, Broken Angel, Pancho Barnes.

HEIDER, FREDERICK: Producer. b. Milwaukee, WI, April 9, 1917. e. Notre Dame U., Goodman Theatre, Chicago. Actor in Globe Theatre, Orson Welles' Mercury Theatre.
TELEVISION & RADIO: Chesterfield Supper Club, Sammy Kaye's So You Want to Lead a Band, Frankie Carle Show, Jo Stafford Show, prod., writer, Paul Whiteman Goodyear Revue, Billy Daniels Show, Martha Wright Show, Earl Wrightson Show, Club Seven, Mindy Carson Show; prod., ABC, Ted Mack Family Hour, Dr. I.Q., Miss America Pageant, Bishop Sheen's Life Is Worth Living, Voice of Firestone, Music for a Summer Night. Music for a Spring Night, The Bell Telephone

Hour. Publisher, Television Quarterly, National Academy of Television Arts and Sciences. Currently columnist, The Desert Sun, Palm Springs, CA.

HELD, DAVID: Executive. Entered industry as atty. in United Artists' legal dept. 1976, joined Paramount as sr. atty. in legal dept.; transferred to business affairs 1977; promoted to v.p., business affairs, 1979. Left for sabbatical 1983; re-entered industry with Samuel Goldwyn Co. as v.p., business affairs. 1984, returned to Paramount as sr. v.p. in chg. business affairs.

HELLER, FRANKLIN: Producer, Director. b. Dover, NJ. e. Carnegie Inst. of Technology, B.A., 1934. Actor, 1934–36; stage mgr., Sam Harris-Max Gordon Prods., 1936–44; exec. prod., USO shows N.Y., 1944–45; prod. & dir., Paramount, 1945–47; dir., summer stock, 1947–48; prod. & dir., CBS TV, 1949–54; exec., prod. and dir. Goodson-Todman Prods., 1954–69; exec. prod. Protocol Prods., 1969–72 Literary Representative 1972. Dirs. Guild of America, Nat'l bd. 1965–77; Treas. 1965–69; Sec. 1970–73; Chr. Publications 1966–76.
TELEVISION SHOWS: What's My Line?, Beat the Clock, The Front Page, The Web, Danger, To Tell the Truth, I've Got a Secret.

HELLER, PAUL M.: Producer. b. New York, NY, Sept. 25, 1927. e. Hunter Coll., Drexel Inst. of Technology. President, Intrepid Productions. Studied engineering until entry into U.S. Army as member of security agency, special branch of signal corps. Left Army and went into fine arts and theatre. Worked as set designer (Westport, East Hampton, Palm Beach) and in live TV and then on theatrical films. Involved with the NY Experience and South Street Venture. Debut as film producer, David and Lisa, 1963. From 1964 to 1969 was president of MPO Pictures Inc. Joined Warner Bros. as prod. exec., 1970. In 1972 founded Sequoia Pictures, Inc. with Fred Weintraub. Pres. of Paul Heller Prods. Inc. formed in 1978.
PICTURES: David and Lisa, The Eavesdropper, Secret Ceremony, Enter the Dragon, Truck Turner, Golden Needles, Dirty Knight's Work, Outlaw Blues, The Pack, The Promise, Pygmalion (cable), First Monday in October, Withnail and I, My Left Foot (exec. prod.).

HELLMAN, JEROME: Producer. b. New York, NY, Sept. 4, 1928. e. NYU. Joined ad dept. of New York Times then went to William Morris Agency as apprentice. Made asst. in TV dept. Worked as agent for Jaffe Agency. After hiatus in Europe joined Ashley-Steiner Agency (later IFA) where clients included Franklin Schaffner, Sidney Lumet, George Roy Hill, John Frankenheimer. Functioned as TV prod., including Kaiser Aluminum Hour. Left to form own agency, Ziegler, Hellman and Ross. Switched to feature prod. with The World of Henry Orient in 1964.
PICTURES: A Fine Madness, Midnight Cowboy (AA), The Day of the Locust, Coming Home, Promises in the Dark (also dir.), The Mosquito Coast.

HELMOND, KATHERINE: Actress. b. Galveston, TX, July 5, 1934. Initial stage work with Houston Playhouse and Margo Jones Theatre, Dallas. Joined APA Theatre, NY, and Trinity Square Rep. Co., RI, Hartford Stage, CT and Phoenix Rep. NY. In 1950s opened summer stock theatre in the Catskills. Taught acting at American Musical and Dramatic Acad., Brown U. and Carnegie-Mellon U. 1983, accepted into AFI's Directing Workshop for Women. Directed Bankrupt.
THEATER: The Great God Brown, House of Blue Leaves (Clarence Derwent, NY and LA Drama Critics Awards, 1972).
PICTURES: The Hindenberg; Baby Blue Marine; Family Plot; Time Bandits; Brazil; Shadey; Lady in White; The Lies of Muenchhausen.
TELEVISION: Series: Soap; Who's The Boss? (also dir); Benson (dir. only). Movies: The Autobiography of Miss Jane Pittman; The Legend of Lizzie Borden; Wanted: The Sundance Woman; Diary of a Teenage Hitchhiker; Honeymoon Hotel; Rosie: The Rosemary Clooney Story; World War III; Meeting of the Minds.

HEMINGWAY, MARGAUX: Actress. b. Portland, OR, Feb. 1955. Granddaughter of writer Ernest Hemingway. Model. Sister of Mariel Hemingway.
PICTURES: Lipstick, Killer Fish, A Fistful of Chopsticks, Over the Brooklyn Bridge, Porta Mi La Luna.

HEMINGWAY, MARIEL: Actress. b. Nov. 22, 1961. Granddaughter of writer Ernest Hemingway. Sister of Margaux Hemingway, model and actress.
PICTURES: Lipstick (debut, 1976), Manhattan, Personal Best, Star 80, The Mean Season, Creator, Sunset, The Suicide Club (also co-prod.), Love in C Minor.
TELEVISION: I Want to Keep My Baby, Amerika, Steal the Sky.

HEMMINGS, DAVID: Actor, Director. b. Guildford, England, 1941. Early career in opera. Ent. m.p. ind. 1956. Former co-partner in Hemdale Company.
THEATER: Dylan Thomas in Adventures in the Skin Trade, Jeeves.
TELEVISION: Auto Stop, The Big Toe, Out of the Unknown, Beverly Hills Cowgirl Blues, In the Heat of the Night (dir.), Clouds of Glory, Davy Crockett: Rainbow in the Thunder (also dir.). Director only: Hardball, Magnum PI, A-Team, Airwolf, Murder She Wrote, Quantum Leap, The Turn of the Screw.
PICTURES: Some People, Two Left Feet, The System, The Eye of the Devil, Blow Up, Camelot, Charge of the Light Brigade, Only When I Larf, Barbarella, The Best House in London, Alfred the Great, The Walking Stick, Fragment of Fear, Unman Wittering and Zigo, Voices, Juggernaut, Crossed Swords. Running Scared (director), The 14, Quilp, Profundo Rosso, Islands in the Stream, The Squeeze, Murder by Decree, Man, Woman, and Child, Prisoners (also exec. prod.), Coup D'Grat (also prod.), The Rainbow.

HENDERSON, SKITCH: Music director. r.n. Lyle Henderson. b. Birmingham, England, Dec. 7, 1918. e. U. of California.
TELEVISION: Steve Allen Show, Tonight Show.

HENDRICKS, BILL L.: Owner/Director, Bill Hendricks Films; writer, prod. dir. of documentaries & shorts and TV commercials. b. Grand Prairie, TX, May 3. e. St. John's Coll. Formerly Warner Bros. Studio publicity director; special asst. to Jack Warner; and director WB Cartoon Studios. Winner first Quigley Grand Award; mgr., Friendship Train & Merci Train. Author: Encyclopedia of Exploitation with Howard Waugh; Showmanship in Advertising with Montgomery Orr; writer, prod., A Force in Readiness, (Academy Award). The John Glenn Story (Oscar nomination), The FBI, Seapower, The Land We Love, A Free People, Top Story, A World of Pleasure, Red Nightmare, Star Spangled Revue, This is Eucom, An American Legend, Scenes to Remember, Freedom and You, Jobs, Wonderful World of Warner, Global Marine; Football Safety; An American Partnership, Free Enterprise, Today's Demand, Tomorrow's Challenge, That's Us in the USA, A Special Day. As ASCAP lyricist, songs include Wintersong; Vaya Con Dios, Amigo; March of the Americans; Paris Je T'aime; Hollywood!; Toys For Tots Parade; Merry Christmas!; Happy Song; On With the Show; Ho! To the West; Wait For Me. Colonel, USMCR (Ret); Founder Marine Corps Toys For Tots program.

HENKIN, HOWARD, H.: Executive writer, Producer, Director. b. New York, NY, Sept. 13, 1926. e. U. of Delaware, 1944. U.S. Army, 1944–46, TV dept., Newell Emmett Agency, 1947–48; gen. mgr., TelePrompter, 1950–54; eastern sales mgr., Shamus Culhane Prod. 1955–57; Academy Pictures 1957–58; pres. HFH Productions, 1958; pres., Henkin Prods. Inc. & Henkin-Faillace Prods. Inc., 1962–68; ch. of bd., Trio Prods., Inc., 1968–80; author of The Dot System.

HENNER, MARILU: Actress. b. Chicago, IL, Apr. 6, 1952. e. U. of Chicago. Studied singing and dancing, appearing in musicals in Chicago and on Broadway in Over Here and Pal Joey. Gained fame as Elaine in TV series, Taxi.
PICTURES: Between the Lines, Blood Brothers, Hammett, The Man Who Loved Women, Cannonball Run II, Johnny Dangerously, Perfect, Rustler's Rhapsody, Chains of Gold, Honeymoon.
TELEVISION: Movies: Dream House, Stark, Love with a Perfect Stranger, Ladykillers.

HENNING, LINDA KAYE: Actress, Singer. b. Toluca Lake, CA, Sept. 16, 1944. Daughter of prod. Paul Henning. e. Cal State Northridge, UCLA.
STAGE: Gypsy, Applause, Damn Yankees, I Do, I Do, Pajama Game, Sugar, Wonderful Town, Fiddler on the Roof, Sound of Music, Vanities, Born Yesterday, Mary, Mary, Bus Stop, etc.
PICTURES: Bye Bye Birdie.
TELEVISION: Series: Petticoat Junction, Happy Days, Mork & Mindy, Double Trouble, Barnaby Jones, The New Gidget, Hunter. Pilots: Kudzu, The Circle, Family. Movies: The Dog Days of Arthur Kane, The Return of the Beverly Hillbillies, Gift of Terror.

HENNING, PAUL: TV Producer, Writer. b. Independence, MO, Sept. 16, 1911. e. Kansas City Sch. of Law, grad. 1932. Radio singer and disc jockey. Also acted, ran sound effects, sang, wrote scripts. To Chicago 1937–38, to write Fibber McGee and Molly. m. Don Quinn. To Hollywood as writer for Rudy Vallee, 1939. Wrote scripts for Burns and Allen 10 years, including transition radio to TV. In 1953 wrote, produced live and film shows for Dennis Day. Created, wrote, produced Bob Cummings Show, 1954–59. Wrote Beverly Hillbillies, 1962–71. Created, prod. wrote Petticoat Junction. Exec. prod. Green Acres series. Wrote motion pictures, Lover Come Back, Bedtime Story, Co-writer, Dirty Rotten Scoundrels.

HENREID, PAUL: Actor, Director, Producer. b. Trieste, now Italy (then Austria), 1908. e. Maria Theresianishe Acad. Inst. Graphic Arts, Vienna. Son of Carl Alphons Hernried Knight of Wasel-Waldingau. With book pub. taking night courses at Konservatorium, dramatic arts Acad. in Vienna. In Max Reinhardt's Vienna Theat., then in many Austrian plays and films. London: on dramatic stage including Jersey Lily and Victoria Regina, Don Juan in Hell 1972–73 on U.S. and

Canadian tour. Arrived in N.Y. 1940 for stage play Flight to the West. In U.S. film Night Train. In 1980 awarded Austrian Cross of Honor, 1st Class, for Science and Arts. 1980: Received The American Classic Screen Award from National Film Society. 1983: Texas Film Society Award for Artistic Achievement. 1984: Legend Silver Screen Award. 1986, Malteser Ehren Ritter (Maltes Honor-Knight), 1988: Golden Star of Honor for meritorious deeds about the land Vienna. Autobiography, Ladies Man (1984, with Julius Fast).

PICTURES: Goodbye Mr. Chips, An Englishman's Home, Nighttrain to Munich, Joan of Paris, Now Voyager, Casablanca, Of Human Bondage, The Spanish Main, In Our Time, Devotion, Deception, Between Two Worlds, The Spanish Main, Conspirators, Song of Love, Rope of Sand, Last of the Buccaneers, Pardon My French, So Young—So Bad, Stolen Face, Man in Hiding, Cabaret, Pirates of Tripoli; For Men Only (also prod., dir.), Acapulco (also prod.); Hollow Triumph (also prod.), Ten Thousand Bedrooms (also prod.); Holiday for Lovers, Never So Few, The Four Horsemen of The Apocalypse, The Great Spy Mission, Meet Me in Las Vegas. dir.: Live Fast Die Young, Take Five From Five, Deadringer, Blues For Lovers. Girls on the Loose, Actor: The Madwoman of Chaillot, Operation Crossbow, Colors of Love, Exorcist II: The Heretic, Pardon My French (co-prod., star).

TELEVISION: Dir. of TV films for Revue Productions, Warner, Desilu, 4-Star, CBS, Screen Gems, Universal, 20th Century-Fox Studios, Series: Dir.: Bracken's World, The Man and the City. Film: Any Number Can Kill and many other films and series as actor and director.

HENRY, BUCK: Actor, Writer. b. New York, NY, 1930. r.n. Henry Zuckerman. e. Dartmouth Coll. Acted in Life with Father, (tour, 1948), Fortress of Glass, Circle in the Square; Bernardine, Bdwy; 1952–54, U.S. Army; No Time for Sergeants, (Nat'l. Co.), The Premise, improvis. theatre, off-Bdwy; TV's The Steve Allen Show, writer, performer; That Was the Week That Was, writer, performer.

TELEVISION: Garry Moore Show; Steve Allen Show; Get Smart, co-creator with Mel Brooks, story editor; producer of Captain Nice series, Alfred Hitchcock Presents (1985, actor and s.p.), Falcon Crest (series).

PICTURES: The Troublemaker; The Graduate (s.p.), Catch 22 (s.p. & actor); Taking Off, Candy (s.p.), The Owl and the Pussycat (s.p.), What's Up, Doc?, The Day of the Dolphin (s.p.), The Man Who Fell to Earth, Heaven Can Wait (actor, co-dir., co-s.p.), Old Boyfriends, Gloria, First Family (s.p., dir., act.), Protocol (s.p.), Aria (actor), Rude Awakening (actor).

HENRY, JUSTIN: Actor. b. Rye, NY, May 25, 1971. Debut at 8 in Kramer vs. Kramer, 1979.

PICTURES: Sixteen Candles, Martin's Day, Sweet Hearts Dance.

TELEVISION: Tiger Town.

HENSLEY, PAMELA: Actress. b. Los Angeles, CA, Oct. 3, 1950. Game show model on The New Treasure Hunt at age 18. Under contract to Universal Studios for seven years, appearing in TV series and movies.

PICTURES: Buck Rogers, Rollerball, Doc Savage, Double Exposure.

TELEVISION: Movies: Any Member Can Kill, Mrs. R., Kingston, Confidential. Series: Marcus Welby, M.D., Kingston: Confidential, Buck Rogers in the 25th Century. 240 Robert, Matt Houston. Guest: Toma, Banacek, The Six Million Dollar Man, Switch.

HENSON, JIM: Producer, Director, Writer. b. Greenville, MS, Sept. 24, 1936. e. U. of Maryland. Early TV work with Washington station, appearing with puppets he built called The Muppets. Did commercials in Washington area, followed by bookings on Today, Tonight shows and Ed Sullivan Show. Followed with Sesame Street, The Muppet Show, Fraggle Rock, The Storyteller, The Jim Henson Hour, The Ghost of Faffner Hall and series of TV specials he produced and/or directed. Heads own production company, Jim Henson Productions (sold to the Walt Disney Co., 1989). First theatrical feature: The Muppet Movie, 1979.

PICTURES: The Great Muppet Caper (dir.), The Dark Crystal (co-prod., co-dir.), The Muppets Take Manhattan, Labyrinth (dir.), The Witches (exec. prod.).

AWARDS: NATAS/ATAS, Emmy Award, George Foster Peabody Award.

HENSON, LISA: Executive. e. Harvard U. Joined Warner Bros., 1983, as exec. asst. to head of prod. 1985, named dir. of creative affairs. 1985, promoted to v.p., prod.

HEPBURN, AUDREY: Actress. b. Brussels, May 4, 1929. Appeared on London stage; screen debut in Laughter in Paradise (1951); on B'way in Gigi, Ondine; named Star of Tomorrow, 1954.

PICTURES: One Wild Oat, Young Wives' Tales, Lavender Hill Mob, Secret People, Roman Holiday (Academy Award, best actress, 1953), Sabrina, War and Peace, Funny Face, Love in the Afternoon, Green Mansions, The Nun's Story, The Unforgiven, Breakfast at Tiffany's, Paris When It Sizzles, Charade, My Fair Lady, Two for the Road, Wait Until Dark, Robin and Marian, Bloodline, They All Laughed, Always.

TELEVISION: Producers Showcase, Mayerling, 1957; Love Among Thieves, 1986.

HEPBURN, KATHARINE: Actress. b. Hartford, CT, Nov. 8, 1909. On stage in Death Takes a Holiday, Warrior's Husband, The Lake, The Philadelphia Story, As You Like It, Millionairess. Film debut A Bill of Divorcement (1932); then Christopher Strong and won Academy Award same year for Morning Glory. Returned to stage in Merchant of Venice, Taming of the Shrew, Measure for Measure, Coco, A Matter of Gravity, West Side Waltz. Author: The Making of the African Queen, 1987.

PICTURES: A Bill of Divorcement, Christopher Strong, Morning Glory, (Acad. Award, 1932). Little Women, Spitfire, The Little Minister, Break of Hearts, Alice Adams, Sylvia Scarlett, Mary of Scotland, A Woman Rebels, Quality Street, Stage Door, Bringing Up Baby, Holiday, The Philadelphia Story, Woman of the Year, Keeper of the Flame, Stage Door Canteen, Dragon Seed, Without Love, Undercurrent, The Sea of Grass, Song of Love, State of the Union, Adam's Rib, The African Queen, Pat and Mike, Summertime, Iron Petticoat, The Rainmaker, Desk Set, Suddenly Last Summer, Long Day's Journey Into Night, Guess Who's Coming to Dinner (Acad. Award), The Lion in Winter (Acad. Award), The Madwoman of Chaillot, The Trojan Women, A Delicate Balance, Rooster Cogburn, Olly, Olly, Oxen Free, On Golden Pond (Acad. Award), Grace Quigley.

TELEVISION: The Glass Menagerie, Love Among the Ruins (Emmy Award), The Corn Is Green, Mrs. Delafield Wants To Marry, Laura Lansing Slept Here.

HEPPEL, ALAN: Executive. e. Harvard U., B.A., Yale U., Stanford Law Sch. With Haldeman and Peckerman as associate, practicing entertainment law. 1985, joined Paramount Pictures as atty. for M.P. Group. Member, California Bar Assn.

HERALD, PETER: Executive. e. UCLA, B.A. US Gov't. film officer in Germany 4 years. In charge of continental European prod. operation, Walt Disney Prods., 6 years. Supervisory prod. manager, Columbia Pictures, 3 years.

PICTURES: assoc. prod.: Almost Angels, Magnificent Rebel, Miracle of the White Stallions, Waltz King, Emil and the Detectives, The Young Loner; prod. supr.: There Was a Crooked Man, Soldier Blue; co-prod., Outrageous Fortune, Ballerina, National Lampoon's Class Reunion, Doctor Detroit, D. C. Cab; assoc. prod.; The Great Waltz, Assignment: Vienna, Crazy World of Julius Vrooder, Foul Play, Nightwing. Also: W. W. and the Dixie Dancekings, Mandingo, W. C. Fields and Me, Alex and the Gypsy, Silver Streak, Fire Sale, Star Wars.

HERB, THOMAS: Executive. Joined Warner Bros. Intl. 1981 as trainee; 1981–82 in Australia, also as trainee, before moving to Brazil as asst. gen. mgr., 1982–84. Returned to Burbank 1984 as asst. dir. of sls. 1985, named dir. of sls. for WBI.

HERDER, W. ED: Producer. b. New York, NY. U. of Miami, B.B.A. Pres. and chmn. of bd., Worldfilm Corp. Financial investor in many m.p. and TV prods.

PICTURES: Without Each Other, Force of Impulse, Black Cobra, Shoot, Never Too Young to Rock, The Siberian Move, The Gang, Intercept, Scenes from a Murder.

TELEVISION: The World of Brigitte Bardot, The Goldie Hawn Special, The Rolling Stones in Concert, The Janis Joplin Special, The Young Rebels, Hollywood: The Magic Kingdom.

HERMAN, NORMAN: Producer, Director. b. Newark, NJ, Feb. 10, 1924. e. Rutgers U., NYU. Was accountant in California; in 1955 switched to film ind., joining American Int'l Pictures. Headed AIP prod. dept. 4 years, incl. prod., post-prod., labor negotiations, supervising story dept., etc. Now pres. of Zide-Herman Co., Inc.

PICTURES: Prod. except as noted: Sierra Stranger, Tokyo After Dark (also dir.), Hot Rod Girl, Hot Rod Rumble, Crime Beneath Seas, Look in any Window, Mondy Teeno (also dir. co-s.p.), Glory Stompers, Three in the Attic, Bloody Mama, Pretty Boy Floyd, Dunwich, Three in the Cellar, Angel Unchained, Bunny O'Hare, Psych-Out, Killers Three, Frogs, Blacula, Legend of Hell House, Dirty Mary Crazy Larry.

TELEVISION: Writer: Robert Taylor Detectives, Iron Horse, Invaders, Adam 12, Lancer. Director-Producer: Hannibal Cobb, You Are the Judge.

HERMAN, PEE-WEE: Actor, Writer. r.n. Paul Rubenfeld. Professional name Paul Reubens. b. Peekskill, NY, July, 1952. Raised in Sarasota, FL. e. Boston U., California Inst. of the Arts (1982). As Paul Reubens, appeared as Pinocchio on Faerie Tale Theatre. Pee-wee character made debut, 1978 at Groundlings, improvisational theater, Los Angeles followed by The Pee-wee Herman Show, a live show which gave 5 months of sold-out performances at the L.A. rock club, Roxy and was later taped for HBO special. Guest appearances on Late Night With David Letterman, The Gong Show and The Dating Game before film debut in Pee-wee's Big Adventure.

PICTURES: Pee-wee's Big Adventure (also co-s.p.); Big Top Pee-Wee (also co-s.p., co-prod.).
TELEVISION: Pinocchio (as Paul Reubens, Faerie Tale Theatre), Pee-wee's Playhouse (creator, co-dir., co-writer; 6 Emmys), Pee wee's Playhouse Christmas Special (star, exec. prod., co-dir. co-writer).

HERMAN, PINKY: Journalist, Songwriter. b. New York, NY, Dec. 23, 1905. e. NYU. Song writer; member, ASCAP. Counsel member, S.P.A.; writer, M.P. News, 1930; 1934; charter member, Songwriters Protective Assoc.; writer, M.P. Daily, 1935–43; columnist, Radio Daily, 1943–50; TV columnist for M.P. Daily. Retired, 1973. Councilman; The Lambs. Exec. prod., Lambs Club Productions (1960–69). Former TV editor, Quigley Publications.
SONGS: (collab.) Face the Sun, All Around the Town, Boom Ta Ra Ra, It Must Be LUV, Piano Teacher Song, Manhattan Merry Go Round, Lucky, I'm Still in Love With You, Havin' A Wonderful Time, Where Can You Be, Seven Days a Week, Texas Lullaby, Lighthouse in the Harbor, I'm Cuckoo Over Your, It's a Coincidence, If I Had a Million Dollars, Masquerade of Love, Mademoiselle Hortensia, Come Back to Me My Love, Someday When Shadows Fall, Myrtle the Turtle & Flip the Frog, Good-Lookin' It's Good Lookin' at You, Carib Gold, What Makes the Rainbow, Right Across de Ribber, Shadows in the Moonlight, Bible My Mother Left to Me, Poor Little Doll, Little Bit O'Ryhthm in the Best of Us, Lovely Lady, When a Girl's in Love, Never Leave A Lady When She Loves You, Without You, That's The Way to Live, It's Time to Sing, Acapulco (By The Sea), Heart to Heart, This is Your Day (Bride & Groom), My Baby Said Yes, Yes, Yes, It's a Wonderful Feeling, I'd Like to Kiss Susie Again, Face the Sun, If You're Mine (Say You're Mine), The Boss of Santa Claus, The Declaration of Independence, We're Americans All, Right Around the Corner from My House, My Fav'rite Initials Are U.S.A.

HEROUX, CLAUDE: Producer. b. Montreal, Canada, Jan. 26, 1942. e. U. of Montreal. 1979, prod. v.p., Film Plan Intl., Montreal.
PICTURES: Valerie; L'Initiation; L'Amour Humain; Je t'aime; Echoes of a Summer; Jacques Brel Is Alive and Well and Living in Paris; Breaking Point; Born for Hell; Hog Wild; City of Fire; Dirty Tricks; Gas; Visiting Hours; Videodrome; The Funny Farm; Going Berserk; Of Unknown Origin; Covergirl.
TELEVISION: The Park is Mine, Popeye Doyle.

HERRMANN, EDWARD: Actor. b. Washington, DC, July 31, 1943. e. Bucknell U. Postgrad. Fulbright scholar, London Acad. Music and Dramatic Art 1968–69. Acted with Dallas Theater Center 4 years.
THEATER: The Basic Training of Pavlo Hummel, Moonchildren, Mrs. Warren's Profession (Tony Award, supp. actor), Journey's End, The Beach House, The Philadelphia Story, Plenty, Tom and Viv, Julius Caesar, Not About Heroes, A Walk in the Woods (London).
PICTURES: Lady Liberty, The Paper Chase, The Day of the Dolphin, The Great Gatsby, The Great Waldo Pepper, The Betsy, The North Avenue Irregulars, Brass Target, Take Down, Harry's War, Reds, Death Valley, A Little Sex, Annie, Mrs. Soffel, Compromising Positions: The Man With One Red Shoe, The Purple Rose of Cairo, The Lost Boys, Overboard, Big Business.
TELEVISION: MASH, Series: Beacon Hill, Movies: Eleanor and Franklin, Eleanor and Franklin: The White House Years, The Lou Gehrig Story, Portrait of a Stripper, Freedom Road, Valley Forge, Sorrows of Gin, The Private History of The Campaign That Failed, Murrow, Dear Liar, The Gift of Life, Concealed Enemies, The Return of Hickey, The Beginning of the Firm.

HERSHEY, BARBARA: Actress. r.n. Barbara Herzstein. b. Los Angeles, CA, Feb. 5, 1948. e. Hollywood H.S. Briefly in the mid-1970s acted under the name Barbara Seagull. Screen debut in With Six You Get Eggroll, 1968.
PICTURES: Last Summer, Heaven With a Gun, The Liberation of Lord Byron Jones, The Baby Maker, The Pursuit of Happiness, Boxcar Bertha, Dealing, Angela—Love Comes Quietly, Vrooder's Hooch, Diamonds, The Last Hard Men, Dirty Knights' Work, The Stunt Man, Choice of Weapons, Take This Job and Shove It, The Entity, The Right Stuff, The Natural, Hannah and Her Sisters, Hoosiers, Tin Men, Shy People (best actress award, Cannes 1987), A World Apart (best actress award, Cannes, 1988), The Last Temptation of Christ, Beaches, Defenseless, Aunt Julia and The Scriptwriter.
TELEVISION: Gidget, The Monroes (series), The Farmer's Daughter, Run for Your Life, The Invaders, Daniel Boone, CBS Playhouse, Chrysler Theatre, Kung Fu, Alfred Hitchcock Presents (1985). Movies: From Here to Eternity, My Wicked, Wicked Ways, Passion Flower, In the Glitter Palace, Just a Little Inconvenience, Sunshine Christmas, Angel on My Shoulder, A Man Called Intrepid.

HERSKOVITZ, ARTHUR M.: Executive. b. Mukden, China. Nov. 28, 1920. e. City Coll. of New York, 1939. Joined RKO, scenario dept., 1939. U.S. Army, 1942–46; appt. mgr., RKO Radio Pictures of Peru, 1955; RKO Pict. Peru, 1958; Warner Bros., Peru, 1958–64; MGM, Panama, 1965–67; MGM rep. in Japan, 1968; Far East supvr., 1970; Joined National General Pictures, 1973 as foreign sls. mgr. In 1974 appt. dir. of sls., JAD Films Int'l.; named v.p., 1978; pres., 1979.

HERSKOVITZ, MARSHALL: Producer, Director, Writer. b. Philadelphia, PA, Feb. 23, 1952. e. Brandeis U., BA, 1973; American Film Inst., MFA. 1975. Worked as freelance writer, dir., and prod. on several TV shows. Received Humanitas Award, 1983 and Writers Guild award, 1984.
TELEVISION: Family (writer, dir.), White Shadow (writer), Special Bulletin (prod., writer, 2 Emmys for writing and dramatic special), thirtysomething (exec. prod., co-writer, dir; 2 Emmy awards for writing and dramatic series, 1988; Also Humanitas Award and Directors Guild Award, 1988).

HERTZ, WILLIAM: Executive. b. Wishek, ND, Dec. 5, 1923. e. U. of Minnesota. Began theatre career in 1939 with Minnesota Amusement in Minneapolis; 1946 joined Fox West Coast Theatres; theatre mgr., booking dept.; 1965 appointed Los Angeles first-run district mgr.; promoted to Pacific Coast Division Mgr., National General Corp., 1967; v.p. Southern Pacific Div. Mgr., National General Theatres, Inc. 1971. Now with Mann Theatres as dir. of marketing, public relations, and labor relations.

HERZOG, WERNER: Producer, Director. r.n. Werner Stipetic. b. Sachrang, Germany, September 5, 1942. e. U. of Munich, Duquesne U., Pittsburgh. Wrote first s.p. 1957; 1961 worked nights in steel factory to raise money for films; 1966, worked for U.S. National Aeronautics and Space Admin.
PICTURES: Signs of Life, Even Dwarfs Started Small, Fata Morgana, The Land of Silence and Darkness; Aguirre—Wrath of God, The Great Ecstasy of the Sculptor Steiner, Every Man for Himself and God Against All, Soufriere, Heart of Glass, Stroszek, Kaspar Hauser, Nosferatu, Woyzeck (also s.p.), Fitzcarraldo, Where the Green Ants Dream, Slave Coast (dir., s.p.).

HESSEMAN, HOWARD: Actor. b. Salem, OR, Feb. 27, 1940. Started with the San Francisco group, The Committee and worked as a disc jockey in San Francisco in the late 1960s.
PICTURES: Petulia, Billy Jack, Steelyard Blues, Shampoo, The Sunshine Boys, Jackson County Jail, The Big Bus, The Other Side of Midnight, Silent Movie, Honky Tonk Freeway, Private Lessons, Loose Shoes, Doctor Detroit, Spinal Tap, Police Academy 2—Their First Assignment, Heat, Amazon Women on the Moon.
TELEVISION: Series: Mary Hartman, Mary Hartman, Fernwood 2night, WKRP in Cincinnati, One Day at a Time, Head of the Class. Movies: Hustling, The Amazing Howard Hughes, The Ghost on Flight 401; The Great American Traffic Jam, Loretta Lynn—The Lady The Legend, Victims, One Shoe Makes It Murder, How To Be a Man, The Diamond Trap.

HESSLER, GORDON: Producer, Director. b. Berlin, Germany, 1930. e. Reading U., England. Dir., vice pres., Fordel Films, Inc., 1950–58; dir., St. John's Story (Edinborough Film Festival), March of Medicine Series, Dr. Albert Lasker Award; story edit., Alfred Hitchcock Presents 1960–62; assoc. prod., dir., Alfred Hitchcock Hour, 1962; prod., Alfred Hitchcock Hour; prod., dir., Universal TV 1964–66.
PICTURES: The Woman Who Wouldn't Die, The Last Shot You Hear, The Oblong Box, Scream and Scream Again, Cry of the Banshee, Murders of the Rue Morgue, Sinbad's Golden Voyage, Medusa, Embassy, Puzzle, Pray for Death, Rage of Honour, The Misfit Brigade, The Girl in a Swing (also s.p.), Out on Bail.
TELEVISION: Alfred Hitchcock Presents, 1960–62; Alfred Hitchcock Hour, 1962–65; Run For Your Life, Convoy, Bob Hope Chrysler Show, 1964–66; ABC Suspense Movies of the Week, ABC Movies of the Week, 1973. Lucas Tanner, Night Stalker, Amy Prentiss, Switch; Kung Fu, Sara, Hawaii Five-O; Blue Knight; Wonder Woman, Master, Chips, Tales of the Unexpected, Equilizer.
Pilots: Tender Warriors.

HESTON, CHARLTON: Actor. b. Evanston, IL, Oct. 4, 1924. e. Northwestern U. Sch. of Speech. Radio, stage, TV experience. Following coll. served 8 yrs. 11th Air Force, Aleutians. After war, co-acted (leads) and dir. with wife, Thomas Wolfe Memorial Theatre, Asheville, NC in State of the Union, Glass Menagerie; member, Katharine Cornell's Co., during first year on Broadway; Anthony and Cleopatra, other Bway. plays, Leaf and Bough, Cockadoodle Doo; Studio One (TV): Macbeth, Taming of the Shrew, Of Human Bondage, Julius Caesar; 1988: The Caine Mutiny Court-Martial (director, in China). Pres. Screen Actors Guild 1966-71; Member, Natl. Council on the Arts, 1967-72; Trustee: Los Angeles Center Theater Group, American Film Inst. 1971-, chmn. 1981-; Received Jean Hersholt Humanitarian award from Amer. Acad. M.P. Arts and Sciences, 1978.

RECENT THEATER: A Man for All Seasons, The Caine Mutiny.
PICTURES: Dark City, Greatest Show on Earth, The Savage, Ruby Gentry, President's Lady, Pony Express, Arrowhead, Bad for Each Other, Naked Jungle, Secret of the Incas, Far Horizons, Lucy Gallant, Private War of Major Benson, Ten Commandments, The Maverick, Ben Hur (Acad. Award, 1959), Wreck of the Mary Deare, El Cid, The Pigeon That Took Rome, 55 Days at Peking, Major Dundee, The Agony and the Ecstasy, The War Lord, The Greatest Story Ever Told, Khartoum, The Battle Horns, Planet of the Apes, Beneath the Planet of the Apes, The Omega Man, Antony and Cleopatra (star & dir.), Skyjacked, Soylent Green, The Three Musketeers, Airport 1975, Earthquake, The Four Musketeers, The Last Hard Men, Midway, Two Minute Warning, The Prince and the Pauper (Crossed Swords), Gray Lady Down, The Awakening, Mother Lode (also dir.), Drums of Fire.
TELEVISION: Chiefs, The Nairobi Affair, The Colbys, The Proud Men, A Man For All Seasons (also dir.), Original Sin, Treasure Island.

HETZEL, RALPH D.: Executive. b. Corvallis, OR, August 18, 1912. e. Pennsylvania State U., A.B., 1933; U. of London, 1935–36. Private secy. to Gov. Pinchot of PA, 1933–35; did research & study, 1936–39; exec. secty. natl. hdqts., CIO, 1937–40; economic dir., 1938–40; in service, 1942–45. Consultant on labor, Natl. Selective Service hdqts., 1942; manpower consultant War Prod. Bd., 1942–43; dept. vice chmn., manpower requirements, W.P.B., 1943–45; acting vice-chmn., 1945; dir. Office of Labor Requirements, Civilian Prod. Admin., 1945–46; asst. to Secy. of Commerce, U.S. Dept. of Comm., 1946–48; asst. to secty. & dir. Office of Program Planning, 1948–51; asst. admin., Economic Stabilization Agency, 1951; exec. v.p. Motion Picture Association, MP Export Assn., 1951–71, Past president, International Federation of Film Producers Assns.; member of Board of Trustees, California Institute of the Arts and of Pennsylvania State U.; member of Film Advisory Committee of Museum of Modern Art, and of Advisory Council of Edward R. Murrow Center of Public Diplomacy at Tufts U. Dean, Coll. of Fine and Professional Arts, Professor of Art, Kent State U., 1971–76; provost and vice president, academic affairs, California Inst. of the Arts 1976–80; faculty member, 1976–.

HEYMAN, JOHN: Producer. b. England, 1933. e. Oxford U. Started with British TV, creating writing and producing entertainment and documentary programs; expanded into field of personal management, forming International Artists, largest independent p.r. agency in Europe. 1963, formed World Film Services, Ltd. to produce, package and finance films. 1973, formed Genesis Project, educational film co. whose first venture was to translate the Bible onto film.
PICTURES: Privilege, Boom!, Secret Ceremony, Twinky, Bloomfield, The Go-Between, Daniel, Beyond the Limit, The Dresser, A Passage to India (co-prod.), Martin's Day, Steaming, D.A.R.Y.L.

HEYWOOD, ANNE: Actress. b. England, 1931. m. late producer Raymond Stross. Family tree dates back to Shakespearean actor Thomas Heywood (1570-1641). e. scholarship London Acad. of Dramatic Art and Music. Joined Highbury Theater Players and Birmingham Rep. Starred as Peter Pan, Shakespeare Memorial Theatre, Stratford on Avon.
PICTURES: Checkpoint, Doctor at Largo, Dangerous Exile, The Depraved, Violent Playground, Floods of Fear, Heart of a Man, Upstairs and Downstairs, A Terrible Beauty, Carthage in Flames, Petticoat Pirates, Stork Talk, Over My Dead Body, The Very Edge, 90 Degrees in the Shade, The Fox, A Run on Gold, The Most Dangerous Man in the World, The Nun of Monza, I Want What I Want, and Presumed Dead.
TELEVISION: The Equalizer.

HICKMAN, DARRYL: Actor. b. Hollywood, CA, July 28, 1930. Started screen career 1938 with The Starmaker. Was with CBS as exec. prod., daytime programming. Returned to acting with Network in 1977.
PICTURES: Grapes of Wrath, Young People, Jackass Mail, Northwest Rangers, Keeper of the Flame, And Now Tomorrow, Salty O'Rourke, Captain Eddie, Kiss and Tell, Leave Her to Heaven, Black Gold, Happy Years, Submarine Command, Destination Gobi, Island in the Sky, Sea of Lost Ships, Southwest Passage, The Human Comedy, Men of Boys Town, Fighting Father Dunn, Tea and Sympathy, Network, Looker, Sharky's Machine.

HICKS, CATHERINE: Actress. b. New York NY, raised in Scottsdale, AZ, Aug. 6, 1951. e. St. Mary's Notre Dame; Cornell U. (2 year classical acting prog.). On Bdwy. in Tribute, Present Laughter.
PICTURES: Death Valley, Better Late Than Never, Garbo Talks, The Razor's Edge, Fever Pitch, Star Trek IV: The Voyage Home; Peggy Sue Got Married, Like Father, Like Son; Souvenir, Child's Play, She's Out of Control, Cognac.
TELEVISION: Series: Tucker's Witch, Ryan's Hope. Movies: The Bad News Bears, Marilyn—the Untold Story, Valley of the Dolls 1981, Happy Endings, Laguna Heat, To Race the Wind.

HIFT, FRED: Executive. b. Vienna, Nov. 27, 1924. e. Vienna, London, Chicago. Early career reporter Chicago Sun and radio work with CBS News, New York. 1946 joined Boxoffice magazine; 1947 Quigley Publications; 1950 Variety. 1960 began career as publicist on Exodus. 1961 dir. pub., The Longest Day for Darryl Zanuck. 1962 joined Fox in Paris as ad-pub. dir. for Europe. 1964 became dir. European prod. pub. with headquarters London. Formed own pub., p.r. co., Fred Hift Associates, 1970. 1979, joined Columbia Pictures as dir. of eastern ad-pub operations in N.Y.; 1980, to United Artists as intl. adv./pub. v.p. Left to establish Fred Hift Associates, intl. mktg. consultant in New York. 1983, joined Almi Pictures as v.p., mktg. 1985, reactivated F.H.A.

HILL, ARTHUR: Actor. b. Saskatchewan, Canada, Aug. 1, 1922. e. U. of British Columbia. Moved to England in 1948, spending ten years in varied stage & screen pursuits; starred on Broadway in The Matchmaker, Home of the Brave, The Male Animal, Look Homeward Angel, All the Way Home, Who's Afraid of Virginia Woolf? (Tony Award), later in More Stately Mansions; film debut in Miss Pilgrim's Progress; other British work includes The Body Said No, Raising A Riot, The Deep Blue Sea.
PICTURES: The Young Doctors, The Ugly American, In the Cool of the Day, Moment to Moment, Harper, Petulia, Don't Let the Angels Fall, The Chairman, The Pursuit of Happiness, Rabbit Run, The Andromeda Strain, The Killer Elite, Future World, A Bridge Too Far, A Little Romance, The Champ, Dirty Tricks, Making Love, The Amateur, One Magic Christmas.
TELEVISION: Owen Marshall, Counselor-At-Law (series). Movies: The Other Man, Vanished, Ordeal, Death Be Not Proud, Judge Horton and the Scottsboro Boys, Tell Me My Name, The Ordeal of Dr. Mudd, The Revenge of the Stepford Wives, Angel Dusted, Murder in Space, Churchill and the Generals, The Guardian.

HILL, BENJAMIN (BENNY): TV performer. b. Southampton, England, Jan. 21, 1925. TV debut 1952; since many TV appearances including Showcase, Benny Hill Show; Midsummer Night's Dream, 1964; winner Daily Mail Award TV personality of the year 1954; m.p. debut, Who Done It, 1955; Light Up the Sky, 1960; Those Magnificent Men in Their Flying Machines, 1965; Chitty Chitty Bang Bang.

HILL, BERNARD: Actor: b. Manchester, Eng., December 17, 1944. Joined amateur dramatic society in Manchester then studied drama at Manchester Art Coll. Joined Liverpool Everyman rep. co. West End debut as John Lennon in John, Paul, George, Ringo . . . and Burt. Also in Normal Service, Shortlist, Twelfth Night, Macbeth.
PICTURES: The Bounty, Gandhi, The Chain, Restless Natives, No Surrender, Bellman and True, Drowning by Numbers, Shirley Valentine, Mountains of the Moon.
TELEVISION: I Claudius, Squaring the Circle, John Lennon: A Journey in the Life, New World, St. Luke's Gospel, Boys from the Blackstuff, Burston Rebellion.

HILL, DEBRA: Producer. b. Haddonfield, NJ. Started in film business with Adventure Films helping make documentaries in Africa, the Caribbean, etc. Career on feature films started with work as script supvr., asst. dir. and 2nd unit dir. of 13 pictures. Producer's debut with Halloween, 1980, for which also co-wrote script with director John Carpenter.
PICTURES: Halloween (also co-s.p.), The Fog (and co-s.p.), Escape from New York, Halloween II (and co-s.p.), Halloween III: Season of the Witch, The Dead Zone, Head Office, Adventures in Babysitting, Big Top Pee Wee, Heartbreak Hotel, Gross Anatomy.
TELEVISION: Adventures in Babysitting (pilot, exec. prod.).

HILL, GEORGE ROY: Director. b. Minneapolis, MN, Dec. 20, 1921. e. Yale U., Trinity Coll., Dublin. Started as actor, Irish theatres and U.S. Margaret Webster's Shakespeare Repertory Co., also off-Bdwy and in film Walk East on Beacon. Served as Marine pilot in W.W.II and Korean War. Wrote TV play, My Brother's Keeper, for Kraft Theatre, later rose to director with show. TV assignments as writer-dir. included A Night to Remember, The Helen Morgan Story, Judgment at Nuremberg, Child of Our Time. Directed first Broadway play in 1957, Look Homeward Angel, followed by The Gang's All Here, Greenwillow. Period of Adjustment, Moon on a Rainbow Shawl (also prod.), Henry, Sweet, Henry.
PICTURES: Period of Adjustment (1962), Toys in the Attic, The World of Henry Orient, Hawaii, Thoroughly Modern Millie, Butch Cassidy and the Sundance Kid, Slaughterhouse Five, The Sting, The Great Waldo Pepper (also prod., s.p.), Slap Shot, A Little Romance, The World According to Garp (also prod.), The Little Drummer Girl, Funny Farm.

HILL, JAMES: Producer, Director, Writer. b. Yorkshire, England. Ent. ind. 1938. Early career as asst. dir. and asst. editor. Wrote and dir. many documentaries incl. Giuseppina (Oscar), The Home-Made Car, several children's features. Dir. The

Kitchen, Born Free, The Dock Brief, Lunch Hour, Black Beauty, The Belstone Fox, A Study in Terror, Cuba Si (TV series), A Sunday in September, The Saint TV series, The Avengers, The Wild and the Free, Worzel Gummidge (TV series.) Prod. dir. The Young Visitors (Channel 4).

HILL, TERENCE: Actor. r.n. Mario Girotti. b. Venice, March, 1941. First attracted attention as actor in Visconti's The Leopard, 1963. Gained fame in European-made westerns. Formed Paloma Films.
PICTURES: God Forgives, I Don't, Boot Hill, Ace High, Barbagia, Anger of the Wind, They Call Me Trinity, Trinity Is Still My Name, My Name Is Nobody, Mr. Billion, March or Die; Don Camillo (dir., actor), Renegade Luke (also exec. prod.).

HILL, WALTER: Director, Writer, Producer. b. Long Beach, CA, Jan. 10, 1942.
PICTURES: Writer: Hickey & Boggs, The Getaway, The Thief Who Came to Dinner, The Mackintosh Man, The Drowning Pool. Writer-Director: Hard Times, The Driver, The Warriors, The Long Riders, Southern Comfort, 48 Hrs., Streets of Fire, Alien (co-prod.), Brewster's Millions (dir.), Crossroads (dir.), Blue City (co-prod., co-s.p.), Extreme Prejudice (dir.), Aliens (co-prod, co.-s.p.), Red Heat (dir., co.-prod., co-s.p.), Johnny Handsome.
TELEVISION: Tales From the Crypt. (exec. prod., dir., s.p. The Man Who Was Death).

HILLER, ARTHUR: Director. b. Edmonton, Alberta, Can., Nov. 22, 1923. e. U. of Alberta, U. of Toronto, U. of British Columbia.
TELEVISION: Matinee Theatre, Playhouse 90, Climax, Alfred Hitchcock Presents, Gunsmoke, Ben Casey, Rte. 66, Naked City, The Dick Powell Show.
PICTURES: The Careless Years, Americanization of Emily, Tobruk, The Tiger Makes Out, Popi, The Out-of-Towners, Love Story, Plaza Suite, The Hospital, Man of La Mancha, The Man in the Glass Booth, W. C. Fields and Me, Silver Streak, Nightwing, The In-Laws (also co-prod.), Author, Author; Making Love, Romantic Comedy, Lonely Guy (also prod.), Teachers, Outrageous Fortune, See No Evil, Hear No Evil.

HILLER, DAME WENDY: D.B.E., 1975, O.B.E., 1971, Hon. LLD, Manchester, 1984. Actress. b. Bramhall, Cheshire, Eng., Aug. 15, 1912. e. Winceby House Sch., Bexhill. On stage 1930, Manchester Repertory Theatre, England; then on British tour. London debut 1935 in Love On the Dole; to N.Y., same role 1936. m.p. debut in Lancashire Luck, 1937.
PLAYS: First Gentleman, Cradle Song, Tess of the D'Urbervilles, Heiress, Ann Veronica, Waters of the Moon, Night of the Ball, Old Vic Theatre, Wings of the Dove, Sacred Flame, Battle of Shrivings, Crown Matrimonial, John Gabriel Borkman, Waters of the Moon (revival), Aspern Papers (revival), The Importance of Being Earnest, Driving Miss Daisy.
PICTURES: Lancashire Luck (debut, 1937), Pygmalion, Major Barbara, I Know Where I'm Going, Outcast of the Islands, Single Handed (Sailor of the King), Something of Value, Uncle George, Separate Tables, (Acad. Award, 1959) Sons and Lovers, Toys in the Attic, Man For All Seasons, Murder on the Orient Express, Voyage of The Damned, The Cat and the Canary, The Elephant Man, Country, Making Love, The Lonely Passion of Judith Hearne.
TELEVISION: The Curse of King Tut's Tomb, David Copperfield, Witness for the Prosecution, Anne of the Green Gables—The Sequel, Peer Gynt, The Kingfisher, All Passion Spent, A Taste for Death, Ending Up.

HILLMAN, WILLIAM BRYON: Writer, Director, Producer. b. Chicago, IL, Feb. 3. e. Oklahoma Military Acad., UCLA. Head of production at Intro-Media Productions; Fairchild Entertainment; Spectro Productions; Double Eagle Entertainment Corp; Excellent Films Inc.; Creative consultant for The Hit 'Em Corp. Presently head of SpectroMedia Entertainment.
PICTURES: Strangers (dir., s.p., co-prod.), Back on the Street (dir., s.p., co-prod.), Loner (dir., s.p., co-prod.), Fast & Furious (dir., s.p.), The Master (dir., s.p.), Lovelines (s.p.), Double Exposure (dir., s.p., co-prod.), The Passage (dir. s.p.), Campus (dir., s.p.), The Photographer (dir., prod., s.p.), The Man From Clover Grove (dir., s.p., co-prod.), Thetus (dir., s.p.), The Trail Ride (dir., s.p., co-prod.), Betta Betta (dir., s.p., prod.).
TELEVISION: Working Together (pilot s.p.), Disco-Theque Pilot (dir., s.p.), Everything Will Be Alright (s.p.), Money (dir., s.p.), RIPA (CBS movie, s.p.).
NOVELS: Silent Changes, The Combination, The Liar, Additives The Perfect Crime, Why Me, The Loner.

HILLERMAN, JOHN: Actor. b. Denison, TX, Dec. 20, 1932. e. U. of Texas. While in U.S. Air Force joined community theatre group and went to New York after completing military service. Studied at American Theatre Wing, leading to summer stock and off-Bdwy.
PICTURES: The Last Picture Show, What's Up Doc?, Paper Moon, At Long Last Love, Lawman, Blazing Saddles, The Day of the Locust, Chinatown, Up the Creek.
TELEVISION: Series: Ellery Queen, The Betty White Show, Magnum P.I. (Emmy Award). Movies: The Law, Kill Me If You Can, A Guide for the Married Woman, Betrayal, Marathon, Battles, Little Gloria . . . Happy at Last, Assault and Matrimony, Street of Dreams, Around the World in 80 Days.

HINES, GREGORY: Actor-Dancer. b. NY, Feb. 14, 1946. Early career as junior member of family dancing act starting at age 2. Nightclub debut at 5 as Hines Kids with brother Maurice (later renamed Hines Brothers as teenagers) and joined by father as Hines, Hines and Dad. Bdwy debut at 8 in The Girl in Pink Tights. Continued dancing with brother until 1973. Formed and performed with jazz-rock band, Severance. Solo album, Gregory Hines (1988).
THEATER: The Last Mistral Show (closed out of town), Eubie (Tony nom.), Comin' Uptown, Sophisticated Ladies, Twelfth Night.
PICTURES: History of the World—Part I, Deal of the Century, The Cotton Club, White Nights, Running Scared, Off Limits, Tap.
TELEVISION: The Tonight Show, Motown Returns to the Apollo, Saturday Night Live.

HINGLE, PAT: Actor. b. Miami, FL, July 19, 1924. e. U. of Texas, 1949. Studied at Herbert Berghof Studio, American Theatre Wing, Actor's Studio.
THEATRE: End as a Man (N.Y. debut, 1953), The Rainmaker, Festival, Cat on a Hot Tin Roof, Girls of Summer, Dark at the Top of the Stairs, J.B., The Deadly Game, Macbeth and Troilus and Cresida (with American Shakespeare Festival, Stratford, CT), Strange Interlude, Blues for Mr. Charlie, A Girl Could Get Lucky, The Glass Menagerie, The Odd Couple, Johnny No-Trump, The Price, Child's Play, The Selling of the President, That Championship Season, The Lady from the Sea, A Life, Thomas Edison: Reflections of a Genius (one man show).
RADIO: Voice of America.
PICTURES: On the Waterfront, The Strange One, No Down Payment, Splendor in the Grass, All the Way Home, The Ugly American, Sol Madrid, Hang 'em High, Jigsaw, Norwood, Bloody Mama, WUSA, Corporal Crocker, The Carey Treatment, One Little Indian, The Super Cops, The Gauntlet, When You Comin' Back, Red Ryder, Norma Rae, Sudden Impact, Running Brave, Going Berserk, The Falcon and the Snowman, Brewster's Millions, Baby Boom, The Land Before Time (voice), Batman.
TELEVISION: Gunsmoke, MASH, Blue Skies, (series), Stone, Matlock, Twilight Zone, The Untouchables, Trapper John M.D., Murder She Wrote. Movies: The Lady from Yesterday, LBJ: The Early Years, If Tomorrow Comes, Elvis, The Last Angry Man, Sunshine Christmas, Of Mice and Men, Stranger on My Land, The Town Bully, War and Remembrance. Everybody's Baby: The Rescue of Jessica McClure, The Kennedy's of Massachusetts.

HINKLE, ROBERT: Actor, Producer, Director. b. Brownfield, TX, July 25, 1930. e. Brownfield H.S. Joined Rodeo Cowboys Association, 1950 and rodeoed professionally until 1953 when began acting career in Outlaw Treasure. Pres. Hinkle Pictures, Inc.
PICTURES: Giant, All the Fine Young Cannibals, Hud, The First Texan, Dakota Incident, Gun the Man Down, The Oklahoman, First Traveling Saleslady, No Place to Land, Under Fire, Speed Crazy, The Gunfight at Dodge City, Broken Land, Law in Silver City, *Producer-director:* Ole Rex (award for Family Entertainment), Born Hunter, Trauma, Something Can Be Done, Mr. Chat, Stuntman, Hud, Jumping Frog Jubilee, Mr. Chat-Mexico Safari, Trail Ride, Virginia City Cent., Texas Today, Texas Long Horns, Kentucky Thoroughbred Racing, Country Music, Guns of a Stranger, Old Rex.
TELEVISION: Test Pilot, Dial 111, Juvenile Squad, X13 Vertijet, Cellist Extraordinary, Sunday Challenge.

HIRD, THORA: Actress. b. Morecambe, Lancashire, Eng., May 28, 1914. e. The Nelson Sch., Morecambe.
PICTURES: (Screen debut, 1940) The Black Sheep of Whitehall; Street Corner, Turn the Key Softly, Personal Affair, The Great Game, Storks Don't Talk, Shop Soiled, For Better or Worse; Love Match, One Good Turn, Quatermass Experiment, Simon and Laura, Lost, Sailor Beware, Home and Away, Good Companions, The Entertainer, A Kind of Loving, Term of Trial, Bitter Harvest, Rattle of a Simple Man, Some Will, Some Won't, The Nightcomers, Consuming Passions.
TELEVISION: The Winslow Boy, The Bachelor, What Happens to Love, The Witching Hour, So Many Children, The Queen Came By, Albert Hope, All Things Bright and Beautiful, Say Nothing, Meet the Wife, Who's a Good Boy Then? I AM! Dixon of Dock Green, Romeo and Juliet, The First Lady, Ours Is a Nice House, The Foxtrot, Seasons, She Stoops to Conquer, Villa Maroc, When We Are Married, In Loving Memory, Flesh and Blood, Your Songs of Praise Choice, Hallelujah, Happiness, That's the Main Thing, Intensive Care, In Loving Memory, Praise Be, Last of the Summer Wine, The Fall.

HIRSCH, JUDD: Actor. b. New York, NY, March 15, 1935. e. City Coll. of New York. Studied physics but turned to acting; first acting job in 1962 performing with stock co. in Colorado. Returned to N.Y. to work on stage and since has also done films and TV. Won Emmy as best actor in a comedy 1981 and 1983 for Taxi.

THEATER: Barefoot in the Park; Scuba Duba; Mystery Play; Hot L Baltimore; King of the United States; Knock, Knock; Chapter Two; Talley's Folly (Obie Award), I'm Not Rappaport (Tony Award).

PICTURES: King of the Gypsies, Serpico, Ordinary People, Without a Trace, The Goodbye People, Teachers, Running on Empty.

TELEVISION: Series: Delvecchio, Taxi (1978-83), Detective in the House, Dear John (series),. Movies: Fear on Trial, Valentino, The Law, The Keegans, Brotherly Love, First Steps, The Last Resort, The Halloween That Almost Wasn't, The Great Escape: The Untold Story.

HIRSCHFIELD, ALAN J.: Executive. b. Oklahoma City, OK; Oct. 10, 1935. e. U. of Oklahoma, B.A.; Harvard Business School, M.B.A. Film Corp. V.P., Allen & Co., 1959–66; Financial v.p. & dir. Warner/7 Arts, 1967–68; v.p. & dir., American Diversified Enterprises, 1969–73; pres. & chief exec. officer, Columbia Pictures Industries, 1973–78; consultant, Warner Communications, 1979, 1980–85, chmn. and chief exec. officer, 20th Century-Fox. Current: Investments.

Vice Chairman and trustee: Cancer Research Institute. Director: American Film Institute. Stendig Corp., Jackson Hole Land Trust, Motown Records.

HIRSHAN, LEONARD: Theatrical Agent. b. New York, NY, Dec. 27, 1927. e. NYU. Joined William Morris Agency as agent trainee, New York, 1951. Agent legit theatre & TV dept. 1952–54. Sr. exec. agent M.P. dept., California office, 1955; sr. v.p., 1983; head of m.p. dept., west coast, 1986; named exec. v.p. and mem. bd. of dir., William Morris Agency, 1989; mem. bd. of dir., Center Theater Group, 1988.

HIRT, AL: Musician. b. New Orleans, LA, Nov. 7, 1922. e. Cincinnati Conservatory of Music. Military service four years. Played with Tommy and Jimmy Dorsey bands, Ray McKinley and Horace Heidt; appeared, Dunes Hotel, Harrah's Club, Basin Street East, Cloisters, Palmer House, Eden Roc Hotel, Greek Theatre. European tour concerts. Inaugural Ball, President John F. Kennedy, Jan. 1961.

TELEVISION: Dinah Shore Show, Jack Paar Show, Ed Sullivan, NBC Special Home For the Holidays, Bell Telephone Hour Rainbow of Stars, Andy Williams Show, Tonight Show, Today Show, Perry Como Show, Lively Ones, Jerry Lewis Show.

PICTURES: World By Night, Rome Adventure.

RECORDINGS: RCA: The Greatest Horn in the World, Al—He's the King—Hirt, Horn-A-Plenty, Al Hirt at the Mardi Gras, Trumpet & Strings, Our Man in New Orleans, Honey in the Horn, Beauty and the Beard, Pop Goes the Trumpet, Boston Pops.

HITZIG, RUPERT: Producer. e. Harvard. At CBS as doc. writer-producer-director; later moved into dramas and comedy. Alan King's partner in King-Hitzig Prods.

TELEVISION: Much Ado About Nothing; The Wonderful World of Jonathan Winters; Playboy After Dark; How to Pick Up Girls; Return to Earth, Saturday Night Live, television series and numerous specials.

PICTURES: Electra Glide in Blue; Happy Birthday, Gemini; Cattle Annie and Little Britches; Jaws 3-D; Wolfen (also 2nd unit dir.); The Last Dragon, The Squeeze, Night Visitor (dir.), Backstreet Strays (dir).

HOBERMAN, DAVID: Executive. Started career as prod. exec. with TAT Communications for five years. 1982–85, worked as m.p. agent with Writers and Artists Agency and later at Ziegler Associates and ICM. 1985, named v.p. of prod. for Walt Disney Pictures based at studio. 1987, promoted to sr. v.p., prod. 1988, named president, production.

HOBIN, BILL: TV Producer, Director. r.n. Charles W. Hobin; b. Evanston, IL, Nov. 12, 1923. e. U. of Southern California. Prod. mgr., Coronet Instructional Films, Glenview, IL; dir., Garroway at Large, Wayne King Show from Chic., 1949–51; dir., Assignment Manhunt; Nothing But the Best; Les Paul and Mary Ford; Your Show of Shows, 1951–54; assoc. prod.-dir., Max Liebman Presents (Spectaculars), prod. dir. Fred Waring Show, Andy Williams Show, Pat Boone, Timex All-Star Jazz Show. dir. Your Hit Parade. Prod.-dir. The Golden Circle, 1959; The Bell Telephone Hour, 1959–60; The American Cowboy; Sing Along with Mitch, 1960–63; dir., Judy Garland Show; prod., dir., Victor Borge at Carnegie Hall; dir., m.p. Chrysler Show-Go-Round, N.Y. World's Fair. Dir.: Meredith Willson Special; Jack Jones on the Move Special; Red Skelton Hour, 1964–68; prod.; Red Skelton Hour, 1968–70; prod. and dir. The Bill Cosby Special I, 1968; prod., dir., The Tim Conway Comedy Hour; prod., dir. The CBS Newcomers series; dir. An Evening With My Three Sons special, prod., dir. Michel Legrand Special; prod., dir. Fred Astaire special; director, Maude; director, A Touch of Grace; prod.-dir.: Dinah, Won't You Please Come Home!; Bobby Goldsboro Show (syn); Your Hit Parade; prod.-dir. Flip Wilson Special, Dionne Warwick Special, Wayne Newton Special, all 1975; 1976—dir., Welcome (Back), Kotter, Prod.-dir., Monty Hall's Variety Special. Dir., Bert Convy Show; dir., George Burns Special; McLean Stevenson Show; dir., Three's Company. Producer-director Bob Hope Specials, (1978–79); director Celebrity Challenge of the Sexes, 1979; director, Steve Allen Special; director, No Soap Radio, 1982.

HOCK, MORT: Executive. b. New York, NY, June 24, 1929. Blaine-Thompson Agency; A. E. Warner Bros., 1948; David Merrick B'way Prod., 1958; asst. adv. mgr., Paramount Pictures Corp., 1960; adv. mgr., United Artists Corp., 1962; dir. adv., United Artists Corp., July 1964; adv. dir., Para., 1965; v.p. advertising and public relations, Paramount Pict. Corp., 1968–71; v.p., marketing, Rastar Prods., 1971; exec. v.p., Charles Schlaifer & Co., 1974; sr. v.p. entertainment div., DDB Needham Worldwide, 1983.

HODGE, PATRICIA: Actress. b. Cleethorpes, Lincolnshire, England, Sept. 29, 1946. Studied at London Acad. of Music and Dramatic Arts.

THEATER: Rookery Nook, Popkiss, Two Gentlemen of Verona, Pippin, The Mitford Girls.

PICTURES: The Elephant Man, Betrayal, Sunset, Falcon's Malteser. Thieves in the Night, Heat of the Day, Just Ask For Diamond.

TELEVISION: The Naked Civil Servant, Rumpole of the Baily, Edward and Mrs. Simpson, Holding the Fort, Jemima Shore Investigates, Hay Fever, Hotel Du Lac, The Life and Loves of a She-Devil, Exclusive Yarns, Let's Face the Music of. . ., Inspector Morse.

HOFFMAN, DUSTIN: b. Los Angeles, CA, Aug. 8, 1937. m. Lisa Hoffman. e. Los Angeles Conservatory of Music, Santa Monica Coll., Pasadena Playhouse, 1958. Worked as an attendant at a psychiatric institution, a demonstrator in Macy's toy dept., and a waiter. First stage role in Yes Is for a Very Young Man, at Sarah Lawrence Coll. Acted in summer stock, television and dir. at community theatre. Broadway and Off Broadway plays include: Harry, Noon and Night (1964, American Place Theatre); Journey of the Fifth Horse (APT, Obie Award); Eh? (Vernon Rice & Theatre World Award); Jimmy Shine. A View from the Bridge (Asst. Dir.) (1974): All Over Town (Dir.), 1984, Death of a Salesman (Drama Desk Award), The Merchant of Venice (London).

TELEVISION: Journey of the Fifth Horse, The Star Wagons, Death of a Salesman (Emmy Award).

PICTURES: The Tiger Makes Out (debut, 1967), Madigan's Millions, The Graduate (Acad. Award nom.); Midnight Cowboy (Acad. Award nom.); John and Mary, Little Big Man, Who Is Harry Kellerman?, Straw Dogs; Alfredo, Alfredo; Papillon, Lenny (Acad. Award nom), All the President's Men, Marathon Man, Straight Time, Agatha, Kramer vs. Kramer (Acad. Award), Tootsie, Ishtar, Rain Man (Acad, Award), Family Business.

HOFFMAN, JOSEPH: Writer. b. New York, NY, Feb. 20, 1909. e. UCLA. Newspaperman, screen writer, magazine writer. TV prod. Now TV and screen freelance writer.

PICTURES: China Sky, Don't Trust Your Husband, Gung-Ho, And Baby Makes Three, Weekend with Father, Duel at Silver Creek, At Sword's Point, Has Anybody Seen My Gal?, Against All Flags, No Room for the Groom, Lone Hand, Yankee Pasha, Rails into Laramie, Tall Man Riding, Chicago Syndicate, Live a Little, How to Make Love and Like It, Sex and the Single Girl.

TELEVISION: Producer: Ford Theatre, Colt 45. Writer: Leave It to Beaver, My Three Sons, The Virginian, Love American Style, etc.

HOGAN, PAUL: Actor, Writer. b. Australia, 1942. Worked as rigger before gaining fame on Australian TV as host of nightly current affairs show (A Current Affair) and The Paul Hogan Show. Shows now syndicated in 26 countries. In U.S. gained attention with commercials for Australian Tourist Commission. 1985, starred in dramatic role on Australian TV in series, Anzacs. Made m.p. theatrical debut in Crocodile Dundee, 1986, Crocodile Dundee II (actor, exec. prod., co-s.p.).

TELEVISION: Anzacs: The War Down Under.

HOGARTH, JOHN M.: Executive. b. Hampstead, London, England, 1931. Man. Dir. Hobo Film Enterprises Ltd.

HOLBROOK, HAL: Actor. b. Cleveland, OH, Feb. 17, 1925. m. actress Dixie Carter. e. Denison U., 1948. Summer stock 1947–53. Gained fame and several awards for performance as Mark Twain on stage in Mark Twain Tonight over a period of years throughout the country.

THEATER: American Shakespeare Fest., Lincoln Center Repertory, The Glass Menagerie, The Apple Tree, I Never Sang For My Father, Man of La Mancha, Does a Tiger Wear a Necktie?, Lake of the Woods, Buried Inside Extra, The Country Girl.

PICTURES: The Group, Wild in the Streets, The People Next Door, The Great White Hope, They Only Kill Their

Masters, Magnum Force, The Girl from Petrovka. All the President's Men, Midway, Rituals, Julia, Capricorn One, Natural Enemies, The Fog, Creepshow, Star Chamber, Wall Street, The Unholy, Fletch Lives.

TELEVISION: Series: The Senator (Emmy), Designing Women. Movies & Specials: The Whole World is Watching, A Clear and Present Danger, Mark Twain Tonight, Travis Logan, Suddenly Single, Goodbye Raggedy Ann, That Certain Summer, The Pueblo, Sandburg's Lincoln (Emmy Award), Our Town, The Awakening Land, When Hell Was in Session, Off the Minnesota Strip, The Killing of Randy Webster, Celebrity, George Washington, Under Siege, Behind Enemy Lines, Dress Gray, North and South Book II, The Fortunate Pilgrim, Plaza Suite, Designing Women (series), Emma, Queen of the South Seas, Day One, Rockport Christmas, Portrait of America (series, 4 annual ACE Awards).

HOLDRIDGE, LEE: Composer. b. Port-au-Prince, Haiti, March 3, 1944. e. Manhattan School of Music. Music arranger for Neil Diamond, 1969–73, with whom he collaborated on the score for Jonathan Livingston Seagull. Wrote score for Bdwy musical Into the Light (1986). With Alan Relph wrote score for the Joffrey Ballet's Trinity.

PICTURES: Winterhawk, Forever Young, Forever Free; Goin' Home; Mustang Country; The Other Side of the Mountain-Part 2; The Pack; Moment By Moment; Oliver's Story; French Postcards; Tilt; American Pop; The Beastmaster; Mr. Mom; Micki and Maude; Splash; Sylvester; 16 Days of Glory; Transylvania 6-5000; The Men's Club, Big Business, Old Gringo.

TELEVISION: Themes: McCloud; Hec Ramsey; Moonlighting; Beauty and the Beast. Movies: East of Eden; Fly Away Home; The Day the Loving Stopped; For Ladies Only; Skyward Christmas; The Sharks; Thou Shalt Not Kill; This is Kate Bennett; In Love With an Older Woman; Running Out; Thursday's Child; Wizards and Warriors; The Mississippi; Legs; I Want to Live; He's Fired, She's Hired; Letting Go; My Africa; Fatal Judgment; Higher Ground (with John Denver), The Tenth Man, I'll Take Manhattan.

HOLLENDER, ALFRED L.: Advertising executive. b. Chicago, IL. e. U. of Illinois. Was associated with Radio Stations WIND-WJJD, Chicago as continuity ed., program dir. & asst. to pres.; entered military service in 1943; exec. v.p. & partner of Louis G. Cowan, Inc., exec. v.p. and dir. radio-TV dept., Grey Adv. Agency; pres., Grey Int'l.

HOLLIMAN, EARL: Actor. b. Delhi, LA, Sept. 11, 1928. e. U. of Southern California, Pasadena Playhouse. Pres., Actors and Others for Animals. Golden Globe winner.

STAGE: Camino Real (Mark Taper Forum), A Streetcar Named Desire (Ahmanson).

PICTURES: Scared Stiff, Girls of Pleasure Island, Destination Gobi, East of Sumatra, Devil's Canyon, Tennessee Champ, Bridge at Toko-Ri, Broken Lance, Big Combo, I Died a Thousand Times, Forbidden Planet, Giant, Burning Hills, The Rainmaker, Gunfight at the OK Corral, Trooper Hook, Don't Go Near the Water, Hot Spell, The Trap, Last Train From Gun Hill, Visit to a Small Planet, Armored Command, Summer and Smoke, The Sons of Katie Elder, A Covenant with Death, The Power, Anzio, The Biscuit Eater, Sharky's Machine.

TELEVISION: Series: Hotel de Paree (1959—60); Wide Country (1962–63); Police Woman (1974–78). Movies: Tribes, Cannon, The Desperate Mission, I Love You. . .Goodbye, Trapped, Cry Panic, Alexander: The Other Side of Down, The Solitary Man; Where the Ladies Go, The Country Gold, The Thorn Birds; Gunsmoke: Return to Dodge, American Harvest.

HOLLOWAY, STERLING: Actor. b. Cedartown, GA, 1905. e. Georgia Military Acad., Atlanta, American Acad. of Dramatic Art. On screen from 1927.

THEATRE: N.Y. Plays include: Shepherd of the Hills, The Failures, Garrick Gaieties (4 editions), Donna Magana; vaude.; night clubs; radio; U.S. armed forces, 1943.

PICTURES: Casey at the Bat, Elmer the Great, Gold Diggers of 1933, Gift of Gab, Down to Their Last Yacht, Maid of Salem, Varsity Show, Remember the Night, Cheers for Miss Bishop, The Lady Is Willing, Twilight in Rio Grande, The Adventures of Huckleberry Finn, Walk in the Sun, Death Valley, Beautiful Blonde from Bashful Bend, Her Wonderful Lie, Alice in Wonderland, Life Begins at Forty, Live a Little, Love a Little, Winnie the Pooh (voice), The Jungle Book (voice), The Aristocats (voice), Won Ton Ton, The Dog Who Saved Hollywood, Thunder and Lightning,

TELEVISION: The Life of Reilly, Willy, The Baileys of Balboa.

HOLM, CELESTE: Actress. b. New York, NY, Apr. 29, 1919. e. Univ. Sch. for Girls, Chicago, Francis W. Parker, Chicago, Lyceé Victor Durui (Paris), U. of Chicago, UCLA. p. Theodor Holm and Jean Parke Holm. m. actor Wesley Addy.

THEATRE: On Bdwy incl. Time of Your Life, 8 O'Clock Tuesday, Return of the Vagabond, Papa Is All, The Damask Cheek, Oklahoma!, Bloomer Girl, Affairs of State, Anna Christie, The King and I, Third Best Sport, Invitation to a March, A Month in the Country; Theatre-in-Concert for the U.S. State Department in 8 countries May–July 1966. Habeas Corpus (Bdwy), The Utter Glory of Morrissey Hall.

PICTURES: The Little Girls in Blue, Gentlemen's Agreement (Acad. Award, 1947), Come to the Stable (acad. nom.), All About Eve (Acad. nom.), Snake Pit, Road House, Chicken Every Sunday, Everybody Does It, Champagne for Caesar, Tender Trap, High Society, Bachelor Flat, Doctor, You've Got To Be Kidding, Tom Sawyer, Bittersweet Love, Three Men and a Baby.

TELEVISION: A Clearing in the Wood, Play of the Week, Cinderella, Love Boat, Backstairs at the White House, Midnight Lace, The Shady Hill Kidnapping, Trapper John, M.D., This Girl for Hire, Murder by the Book, Magnum P.I., Polly. Pilot: Road Show.

RADIO: People at the U.N., Theatre Guild on the Air, Mystery Theatre.

HOLM, IAN: C.B.E. Actor. b. Ilford, Essex, England, Sept. 12, 1931. r.n. Ian Cuthbert. e. Royal Acad. of Dramatic Art. On British stage—Love Affair, Titus Andronicus, Henry IV, Ondine, Becket, The Homecoming, The Seat, etc.—before entering films.

PICTURES: The Bofors Gun, A Midsummer Night's Dream, The Fixer, A Severed Head, Nicholas and Alexandra, Mary Queen of Scots, Young Winston, The Homecoming, Juggernaut, Shout at the Devil, Alien, Chariots of Fire, Time Bandits, Return of the Soldier, Brazil, Dreamchild, Dance With a Stranger, Greystoke: The Legend of Tarzan, Langerhouse, Wetherby, Another Woman, Henry V.

TELEVISION: Les Miserables, S.O.S. Titanic, Napoleon, We, the Accused, All Quiet on the Western Front, Holocaust, Man in the Iron Mask, Jesus of Nazareth, Game, Set and Match.

HOMEIER, SKIP: Actor. r.n. George Vincent Homeier. b. Chicago, IL, Oct. 5, 1930. e. UCLA. Started in radio, 1936–43; on B'way stage, Tomorrow the World, 1943–44.

PICTURES: Tomorrow the World, Boy's Ranch, Mickey, Arthur Takes Over, The Big Cat, The Gunfighter, Halls of Montezuma, The Black Widow, Cry Vengeance, Dakota Incident, The Captives, No Road Back, Decision at Durango, Showdown.

TELEVISION: Playhouse 90, Alcoa Hour, Kraft Theatre, Studio 1, Armstrong Circle Theatre, Alfred Hitchcock, The Wild Wild West Revisited.

HONG, WILSON S.: Cinematographer. b. Butte, MT, Dec. 18, 1934. e. Montana State U., Brooks Inst. of Photography. 1965, Freelance photographer for national magazine and worldwide newspaper syndication; 1966, Photographic Director of U.S Forest Service Fire & Research Division; 1967, first cameraman on various documentaries, industrials, commercials, sports specials.

PICTURES: Bigfoot, Operation North Slope, John Wayne's No Substitute for Victory', The Hellcats, Dear Dead Delilah, Zodiac Killer, Velvet Vampire, Mrs. McGrudy, The Day the Adults Died, Sundown in Watts, Parallax View, 1776, Don't Go West, Drum, White Buffalo, MacArthur, An Enemy of the People, Sergeant Pepper's Lonely Hearts Club Band, Mulefeathers, Winter Kills, Mission to Glory, The Unfinished, They Only Kill Their Masters, The Fearless Five.

TELEVISION: Snowmobile Grand Prix, Indianapolis International Drag Races, The Great Outdoors (23 episodes), Thank you America (spec.), The Unser Story, Gun Hawks (pilot), Keep it Up (pilot), Where are they Now? (pilot), Hunting and Fishing the North American Continent (spec.), The Blue Knight, A Dream for Christmas, The Toy Game, Moose (pilot), The Jerry Show, Apple's Way, The Moneychangers, Young Maverick, Rudi Gernreich/Future, Ours, Max Factor and Pepsi-Cola commercials, The Groovy Seven (pilot).

HOOKS, KEVIN: Actor. b. Philadelphia, PA, Sept. 19, 1958. Son of actor-director Robert Hooks.

PICTURES: Sounder; Aaron Loves Angela; A Hero Ain't Nothin' But a Sandwich; Take Down.

TELEVISION: Just an Old Sweet Song; The Greatest Thing That Almost Happened; Friendly Fire; Backstairs at the White House; White Shadow; Can You Hear the Laughter?—The Story of Freddie Prinze; For Members Only; Roots: The Gift (dir.). Special: Home Sweet Homeless (dir.).

HOOKS, ROBERT: Actor, Director, Producer. b. Father of actor Kevin Hooks. b. Washington, D.C., April 18, 1937. Co-founder and exec. dir. Negro Ensemble Co. NY 1968–present. Founder DC Black Theatre, Washington, D.C. 1973–77. Co-star of TV series; NYPD, 1967–69.

THEATER: Tiger, Tiger Burning Bright (Bdwy. debut, 1962); Ballad for Bimshire; The Blacks; The Dutchman; Henry V; Happy Ending; Day of Absence; Where's Daddy?; Hallelujah, Baby?; Kongi's Harvest; A Soldier's Play (Mark Taper Forum, LA). Co-prod.: with Gerald S. Krone: Song of the Lusitanian Bogey, Daddy Goodness, Ceremonies in Dark Old Men, Day of Absence; The Sty of the Blind Pig; The River Niger; The First Breeze of Summer.

PICTURES: Hurry Sundown, The Last of the Mobile Hotshots; Trouble Man; Aaron Loves Angela; Airport '77; Fast-Walking; Star Trek III: The Search For Spock.
TELEVISION: Pilots: The Cliff Dweller; Two for the Money; Down Home. Movies: Carter's Army; Vanished; The Cable Car Murder; Crosscurrent; Trapped; Ceremonies in Dark Old Men; Just an Old Sweet Song; The Killer Who Wouldn't Die; The Courage and the Passion; To Kill A Cop; A Woman Called Moses; Hollow Image; Madame X; The Oklahoma City Dolls; The Sophisticated Gents; Cassie and Co.; Starflight—The Plane that Couldn't Land; Feel the Heat; Sister, Sister; The Execution.

HOOPER, TOBE: Director. b. Austin, Texas, 1943. Began film career making documentary and industrial films and commercials in Texas. Was asst. dir. of U. of Texas film program, continuing filmmaking while working with students. First feature film: Eggshells.
PICTURES: Eaten Alive, The Texas Chainsaw Massacre, Funhouse, Poltergeist, Lifeforce, Invaders from Mars, The Texas Chainsaw Massacre Part 2, Spontaneous Combustion.
TELEVISION: Salem's Lot, Amazing Stories, A Nightmare on Elm Street-Freddy's Nightmare: The Series. (No More Mr. Nice Guy-1st episode), Equalizer (No Place Like Home).

HOPE, BOB: Actor. b. Eltham, England, May 29, 1903. Started in vaudeville; plays include: Roberta, Ziegfeld Follies, Red, Hot & Blue; author, They Got Me Covered, I Never Left Home, So This Is Peace. Voted one of ten best Money-Making Stars in M.P. Herald-Fame Poll, 1941–47, 49–53. On radio and TV with numerous specials U.S.O shows and guest appearances. Emmy Governors Award, 1984.
PICTURES: Big Broadcast of 1938, College Swing, Give Me a Sailor, Thanks for the Memory, Never Say Die, Some Like It Hot, Cat and Canary, Road to Singapore, Ghost Breakers, Road to Zanzibar, Caught in the Draft, Louisiana Purchase, My Favorite Blonde, Road to Morocco, Nothing But the Truth, They Got Me Covered, Star Spangled Rhythm, Let's Face It, Road to Utopia, Princess and Pirate, Monsieur Beaucaire, My Favorite Brunette, Where There's Life, Road to Rio, Paleface, Sorrowful Jones, Great Lover, Fancy Pants, Lemon Drop Kid, My Favorite Spy, Son of Paleface, Road to Bali, Off Limits, Here Come the Girls, Casanova's Big Night, Seven Little Foys, That Certain Feeling, Iron Petticoat, Beau James, Paris Holiday, Alias Jesse James, Facts of Life, Bachelor in Paradise, Road to Hong Kong, Call Me Bwana, A Global Affair, I'll Take Sweden, Boy Did I Get a Wrong Number, Eight on the Lam, The Private Navy of Sgt. O'Farrell, How to Commit Marriage, Cancel My Reservation.

HOPE, HARRY: Producer, Director, Writer. b. May 26, 1926. e. UCLA, Etudes Universitaires Internationales, Ph.D. Entered m.p. industry as special effects man, Republic Studios, 1944; associate producer Star Productions; formed Blue Bird Film Co. Has since produced, directed and written 33 feature films, including Like the Gull, 1967, which won creative classical film award as Asian Film Festival. Founded Western International and directed First Leisure Corp. as exec. v.p. until 1972. From then until present, pres. of Harry Hope Production. Among recent film credits: Smokey and the Judge, Sunset Cove, Doomsday Machine, Death Dimension, Thunderfist, Tarzana, The Mad Butcher, Death Blow, Pop's Oasis.

HOPKINS, ANTHONY: Actor. b. Port Talbot, South Wales, Dec. 31, 1937. Trained at Royal Acad. of Dramatic Art; Cardiff Coll. Drama. Joined National Theatre, gaining fame on stage in England, then TV and films.
THEATER: Julius Caesar (debut, 1964), Juno and the Paycock, A Flea in Her Ear, The Dance of Death, Three Sisters, As You Like It, The Architect and the Emperor of Assyria, Equus (London and NY). Pravda, King Lear, Anthony and Cleopatra, M. Butterfly.
PICTURES: White Bus, Lion in Winter, Hamlet, The Looking Glass War, When Eight Bells Toll, Young Winston, The Girl from Petrovka, Juggernaut, A Doll's House, Audrey Rose, A Bridge Too Far, International Velvet, Magic, Change of Seasons, The Elephant Man, The Bounty, 84 Charing Cross Road, The Good Father, A Chorus of Disapproval.
TELEVISION: QB VII, War and Peace, The Lindbergh Kidnapping Case (Emmy Award, 1976), All Creatures Great and Small, The Bunker (Emmy Award), Peter and Paul, A Married Man, Hollywood Wives, Guilty Conscience, Arch of Triumph, The Dawning, The Tenth Man, Across the Lake, Heartland, Great Expectations.

HOPKINS, BO: Actor. b. Greenwood, SC, Feb. 2, 1942. Studied with Uta Hagen in N.Y. then with Desilu Playhouse training school in Hollywood. Parts in several prods. for that group won him an agent, an audition with director Sam Peckinpah and his first role in latter's The Wild Bunch.
PICTURES: Monte Walsh, The Culpepper Cattle Co., The Moonshine War, White Lightning, The Getaway, The Man Who Loved Cat Dancing, American Graffiti, The Nickel Ride, The Day of the Locust, Posse, The Killer Elite, A Small Town in Texas, More American Graffiti, The Fifth Floor, Sweet Sixteen, Night Shadows, Trapper Country, War, The Bounty Hunter, The Stalker, Nightmare at Noon, The Tenth Man, Big Bad John.
TELEVISION: Series: Doc Elliott, Aspen, The Rockford Files, Dynasty. Movies: A Smoky Mountain Christmas, Beggerman Thief, Down the Long Hills, Last Ride of the Dalton Gang, Casino.

HOPPER, DENNIS: Actor. b. Dodge City, KS, May 17, 1936. e. San Diego, CA, public schools. Author: Out of the Sixties (1988), book of his photographs.
TELEVISION: Medic, Loretta Young Show, Stark.
PICTURES: Jagged Edge, Rebel Without a Cause; I Died a Thousand Deaths, Giant, The Steel Jungle, The Story of Mankind, Gunfight at OK Corral, From Hell to Texas, The Young Land, Key Witness, Night Tide, Tarzan and Jane Regained Sort Of, The Sons of Katie Elder, Queen of Blood, Cool Hand Luke, Glory Stompers, The Trip, Hang 'Em High, Cool Hand Luke, True Grit, The American Dreamer, Kid Blue, The Sky is Falling, James Dean-The First American Teenager, Mad Dog Morgan, Tracks, Easy Rider (dir., s.p., actor), The Last Movie, Hex, The American Friend, Apocalypse Now, King of the Mountain, White Star, Human Highway, Reborn, Out of the Blue (also dir.), Rumble Fish, The Osterman Weekend, Slagskampen, My Science Project, The Texas Chainsaw Massacre Part 2, Blue Velvet, Hoosiers, Black Widow, River's Edge, Straight to Hell, Colors (dir. only), The Pick Up Artist, O.C. and Stiggs, Riders of the Storm, Backtrack (also dir.), Chattachoochee, Flashback, Blood Red.

HORDERN, SIR MICHAEL: Actor. b. Berkhampstead, Eng. Oct. 3, 1911. e. Brighton Col. Early career in business before stage appearance, 1937. M.P. debut The Girl in the News, 1939. TV debut 1946. 1939–45 Naval Service. Knighted 1983.
PICTURES: School for Secrets, Passport to Pimlico, The Astonished Heart, Trio, A Christmas Carol, Tom Brown's School Days, The Heart of the Matter, The Constant Husband, The Night My Number Came Up, Alexander the Great, The Black Prince, Storm Over The Nile, Pacific Destiny, The Baby and the Battleship, The Spanish Gardener, No Time for Tears, Windom's Way, Monty's Double, Girls at Sea, Moment of Danger, Sink the Bismarck, Man in the Moon, El Cid, Cleopatra, V.I.P.s, Dr. Syn, The Yellow Rolls Royce, Ghengis Khan, The Spy Who Came in From the Cold, Khartoum, Cast a Giant Shadow, A Funny Thing Happened on the Way to the Forum, Taming of the Shrew, The Jokers, How I Won the War, I'll Never Forget What's 'is Name, Prudence and the Pill, The Bed-sitting Room, Where Eagles Dare, Anne of the Thousand Days, Futtocks End, Some Will, Some Won't, Up Pompeii, The Possession of Joel Delaney (U.S.), Pied Piper, Blood Will Have Blood, England Made Me, Girl Stroke Boy, Alice's Adventures in Wonderland, Theatre of Blood, The Mackintosh Man, Quilp, Barry Lyndon (narrator), The Slipper and the Rose, Joseph Andrews, The Medusa Touch, Wildcats of St. Trinians, Gandhi, Ivano, Oliver Twist, The Missionary, Yellowbeard, Robin Hood, Trouble at the Royal Rose, Young Sherlock Holmes (voice of older Watson), Lady Jane, Comrades, Labyrinth (voice), The Trouble With Spies, Diamond Skulls, Ending Up.
TELEVISION: Doctor's Dilemma, The Great Adventure, The Witness, The Indifferent Shepherd, Dock Brief, Mr. Kettle and Mrs. Moon, Guinea Pig, The Gathering Dusk, Farewell My City, Flowering Cherry, I Have Been Here Before, Without the Grail, The Outstation, The Square, Any Other Business, The Stone Dance, The Quails, A Waltz on the Water, August for the People, Land of My Dreams, Condemned to Acquittal, Nelson, The Browning Version, Whistle and I'll Come to You, The Man Who Murdered in Public, A Crack in the Ice, Sir Jocelyn the Minister Would Like a Word, Six Dates with Barker, Don Juan in Hell, Tartoffe, Tall Stories, The Magistrate, Edward VII, King Lear, Cakes and Ale, Chester Mystery Cycle, Paddington Bear (story teller), The Saints Go Marching In, Mrs. Bixby and the Colonel's Coat, Romeo and Juliet, The Tempest, All's Well That Ends Well, You're Alright: How Am I?, King Lear, Rod and Line, Cymbeline, Trelawney of the Wells, Paradise Postponed,The Secret Garden, Suspicion, Danny, the Champion of the World.

HORN, ALAN: Executive. b. New York, NY, Feb. 28, 1943. e. Union Coll., Harvard Business Sch. 1972, joined Tandem Prods., 1972; named v.p., business affairs, and of sister co., T.A.T. Communications, 1973; 1977, exec. v.p. & COO; pres., 1978. In 1983 named pres. Embassy Communications. 1986 joined 20th Century Fox as pres. COO. Left Fox Sept. 1986. Co-founded Castle Rock Entertainment 1987.

HORNE, LENA: Vocalist, Actress. b. Brooklyn, NY, June 30, 1917. Radio with Noble Sissle, Charlie Barnet, other bands. Floor shows at Cotton Club, Cafe Society, Little Troc, etc. Started screen career 1942. Autobiographies: In Person (1950), Lena (1965) Recipient Kennedy Center Honors for Lifetime contribution to the Arts, 1984. Spingarn Award, NAACP, 1983; Paul Robeson Award, Actors Equity Assn., 1985.
THEATRE: Blackbirds, Dance With Your Gods, Jamaica, Pal Joey (L.A. Music Center), Lena Horne: The Lady and Her Music (Tony Award).

PICTURES: Duke is the Tops, Panama Hattie, Cabin in the Sky, Stormy Weather, I Dood It, Thousands Cheer, Broadway Rhythm, Swing Fever, Two Girls and a Sailor, Ziegfeld Follies, Till the Clouds Roll By, Words and Music, Duchess of Idaho, Meet Me in Las Vegas, Death of a Gunfighter, The Wiz.
TELEVISION: Guest: Music '55, Perry Como Show, Here's to the Ladies, The Cosby Show. Specials: The Lena Horne Show (1959), The Frank Sinatra Timex Show, Lena in Concert, Harry and Lena, Lena Horne: The Lady and Her Music.

HORNER, HARRY: Art director, Director. b. Holic, Czechoslovakia, July 24, 1910. e. U. of Vienna, Dept. of Architecture, 1928–33; Acad. of the Theatre, Vienna, 1930–32, Max Reinhardt's Seminary. Joined Max Reinhardt Thea. Co., Vienna and Salzburg Festivals; to U.S. as asst. to Reinhardt on pageant, The Eternal Road. Stage designer, N.Y. theatre 10 yrs. (Lady in the Dark, Family Portrait, others). First m.p. as prod. designer, 1938, Our Town (co-credit, Wm. Cameron Menzies). later Little Foxes, Stage Door Canteen. Army service, 1942–45; designed Winged Victory for Air Force. In 1949, won Acad. award black and white art dir., The Heiress.
PICTURES: *Designer:* Born Yesterday, Separate Tables, They Shoot Horses, Don't They? (Acad. nom.), The Hustler; (Acad. award). exec. prod., dir., Enterprise Films of Can., Anglo Ent. Films, London; co-prod., Fahrenheit 451, 1966, They Shoot Horses, Don't They? (Acad. nom.), Who Is Harry Kellerman?, Up the Sandbox, He Ran All the Way, Androcles and the Lion, Outrage. *Films Directed:* Beware My Lovely, Red Planet Mars, Vicki, New Faces, Life in the Balance, Step Down to Terror, Lonesome Gun, Wild Party Man From Del Rio, Winner of 2 acad. awards, 6 acad. nominations for Art Dir. 1975: The Black Bird, Harry and Walter Go to New York, Audrey Rose, The Driver, Moment by Moment, The Jazz Singer.
TELEVISION: Omnibus, Cavalcade, Reader's Digest, Author's Playhouse, Four Star Theatre, Gunsmoke, Revue Productions, Dupont Theatre. Since 1959 prod., dir., TV series, The Royal Canadian Mounted Police.
OPERA: designer & director at San Francisco Opera, Metropolitan Opera, N.Y., Vancouver Festivals, Hollywood Bowl. Operas designed & directed: David, Joan at the Seake, Magic Flute. Amer. Premiere of New Opera, Midsummer Night's Dream. Designed Idiots Delight, Ahmanson Theatre, 1970, winner, L.A. Drama Critics Award, best stage design. Designed Time of the Cuckoo, Ahmanson Theatre 1974.

HORSLEY, LEE: Actor. b. Muleshoe, TX, May 15, 1955. e. U. of No. Colorado. On stage in Mack and Mabel, West Side Story, Sound of Music, Oklahoma!, Forty Carats.
PICTURE: The Sword and the Sorcerer.
TELEVISION: Series: Nero Wolfe, Matt Houston, Paradise. Mini-series: Crossing, North and South Book II. Movies: The Wild Women of Chastity Gulch, Infidelity, When Dreams Come True, Thirteen at Dinner.

HORTON, ROBERT: Actor. b. Los Angeles, CA, July 29, 1924. e. U. of Miami, UCLA U.S. Coast Guard; many legit. plays; many radio & TV appearances; co-star, Wagon Train; screen debut in A Walk in the Sun. Star of Broadway musical 110 in the Shade.
PICTURES: The Tanks Are Coming, Return of the Texan, Pony Soldier, Apache War Smoke, Bright Road, The Story of Three Loves, Code Two, Arena, Prisoner of War, Men of the Fighting Lady, The Green Slime, The Dangerous Days of Kiowa Jones, The Spy Killer, Foreign Exchange.
TELEVISION: Kings Row (series), Wagon Train (series), As the World Turns (series), Red River, The Man Called Shennandoah (series), Alfred Hitchcock Presents, Suspense.

HORWITZ, SOL: Executive. b. Chicago, IL, April 2, 1920. e. U. of Chicago. U.S. Navy, 1942–45. Film booker and buyer for Balaban and Katz and Allied Theatres of Illinois, in Chicago before moving to New York where served in same capacity for Walter Reade Org., Cinema 5, Loews, Inc. In sls. divisions of EDP Films, Screenvision, and Castle Hill Prods. Now project administrator for Short Film Showcase and v.p. development, Angelika Films.

HOSKINS, BOB: Actor. b. England, Oct. 26, 1942. Porter and steeplejack before becoming actor at 25. Veteran of Royal Shakespeare Co. Appeared with Britain's National Theatre (Man Is Man, King Lear, Guys and Dolls, etc.)
PICTURES: National Health, Royal Flash, Inserts, Zulu Dawn, The Wall, The Long Good Friday, Beyond the Limit, Lassiter, The Cotton Club, Brazil, Sweet Liberty, Mona Lisa, A Prayer for the Dying, The Lonely Passion of Judith Hearne, Who Framed Roger Rabbit?, The Secret Policeman's Third Ball (voice of the Secret Policeman), The Raggedy Rawney (dir., debut; actor and co-s.p.), Heart Condition, That All Men Should Be Brothers.
TELEVISION: Villians on the High Road (debut, 1972), New Scotland Yard, On the Move, Rock Follies, In the Looking Glass, Napoleon, Flickers (serial), Pennies from Heaven, Othello, Mussolini, The Dunera Boys.

HOUGH, JOHN: Director. b. London, Eng., Nov. 21, 1941. Worked in British film prod. in various capacities; impressed execs. at EMI-MGM Studios, Elstree, London, so was given chance to direct The Avengers series for TV. Began theatrical films with Sudden Terror for prod. Irving Allen, 1971.
PICTURES: Twins of Evil, Treasure Island, The Legend of Hell House, Dirty Mary Crazy Larry, Escape to Witch Mountain, Return to Witch Mountain, Brass Target, Watcher in the Woods, Biggles—Adventures in Time, Howling IV—The Original Nightmare.
TELEVISION: A Hazard of Hearts (dir., co-prod.), The Lady and the Highwayman (prod., dir.).

HOWARD, CY: Producer, Director. b. Milwaukee, WI, Sept. 27, 1915. e. U. of Minnesota, U. of Wisconsin. Entered radio Station KTRH, Houston, TX as writer, prod., actor; served 1 yr. Army Air Corps; to WBBM, Chicago, as writer, prod., actor, 1942; to Jack Benny's radio writing staff; actor, Storm Operation (stage), 1943; to ABC as writer, comedian on What's New program; to NBC where orig. wrote Palmolive Party; radio writer for Milton Berle, Danny Thomas, Bert Lahr, Jerry Lewis; orig. My Friend Irma, Life with Luigi, radio and TV shows; to Hal B. Wallis Prod. as writer and assoc. prod. My Friend Irma; exec. prod., Desilu Studios, created and produced Harrigan and Son, Westward Ho, Fair Exchange, My Friend Irma Goes West (films), That's My Boy; writer, Marriage on the Rocks; co-writer: Won Ton Ton, The Dog Who Saved Hollywood; director, Lovers and Other Strangers and Every Little Crook and Nanny.

HOWARD, CYRIL: C.B.E. Managing Director of Rank's Pinewood Studios, England. Formerly Secretary and general manager of the studios. Joined Rank Organisation 1941.

HOWARD, KEN: Actor. b. El Centro, CA, March 28, 1944. e. Yale Drama Sch. Left studies to do walk-on in Bdwy. musical, Promises, Promises. Starred as Thomas Jefferson in 1776 on Bdwy. (Theatre World Award) and in film version.
PICTURES: Tell Me That You Love Me, Junie Moon (debut), Such Good Friends, 1776, Second Thoughts.
TELEVISION: Series: Manhunter, Bonanza, Medical Center, Adam's Rib, The White Shadow, It's Not Easy. Movies: The Trial of George Armstrong Custer, He's Not Your Son, Rage of Angels: The Story Continues, Strange Interlude, The Man in the Brown Suit.
STAGE: Promises, Promises; Child's Play, Seesaw, 1600 Pennsylvania Avenue, The Norman Conquests, Equus, Rumors.

HOWARD, ROBERT T.: Executive. b. Red Bank, NJ, June 18, 1927. e. U. of Virginia, Columbia U., N.Y. Began prof. career as NBC page, joining guest relations staff in N.Y., 1947. Moved up to NBC TV research dept., where worked in program testing and audience measurement. Became head of research for NBC Radio Spot Sales in 1953; 1955, promoted to acct. exec. in same dept. Joined TV Spot Sales in 1959 and named natl. sales mgr. of WNBC-TV, New York in 1963 named gen. mgr. of KNBC, Los Angeles. Elected v.p. of NBC a month later. Returned to N.Y and named pres. of NBC TV Network 1974. Elected to NBC bd. and named exec. v.p.; 1977, v.p. & gen. mgr. WNBC TV, New York; 1980, pres. & chmn. Citicom Communications Co.

HOWARD, RON: Actor, Director, Producer. b. Duncan, OK, March 1, 1954. e. U. of Southern California. Acting debut at age of two with parents, Rance and Jean Howard, in The Seven Year Itch at Baltimore's Hilltop Theatre. Two years later travelled to Vienna for his first film, The Journey. Many TV appearances over years. Is brother of Clint Howard, also former child actor.
PICTURES: Actor: Frontier Woman, The Journey, Wild Country, Five Minutes to Live, The Music Man, Courtship of Eddie's Father, A Village of the Giants, Happy Mother's Day . . . Love, George, American Graffiti, The Spikes Gang, The Shootist, More American Graffiti. Director: Grand Auto Theft (dir., debut, 1974); also co-s.p. and actor), Night Shift, Splash, Cocoon, Gung Ho (also exec. prod.), Willow, Vibes (co-exec. prod.), Clean and Sober (exec. prod.), Parenthood.
TELEVISION: Series: Andy Griffith Show, Happy Days. Guest: Red Skelton Hour, Playhouse 90, Dennis, the Menace, Many Loves of Dobie Gillis, Five Fingers, Twilight Zone, Dinah Shore Show, The Fugitive, Dr. Kildare, Big Valley, I Spy, Danny Kaye Show, Gomer Pyle, USMC, The Monroes, The FBI, Judd for the Defense, Daniel Boone, Lancer, Land of the Giants, Gentle Ben, Gunsmoke, Disney TV films (A Boy Called Nuthin', Smoke), No Man's Land (co-exec. prod), Huckleberry Finn, Act of Love, Bitter Harvest. Director: Cotton Candy, Through the Magic Pyramid, Skyward.

HOWARD, SANDY: Producer. b. Aug. 1, 1927. e. Florida So. Coll. Ent. m.p. ind. 1946.
PICTURES: Perils of the Deep, One Step to Hell, Jack of Diamonds, Tarzan and the Trappers, A Man Called Horse, Man in the Wilderness, Together Brothers, Neptune Factor, The Devil's Rain, Sky Riders, The Last Castle, Embryo, Magna I—Beyond the Barrier Reef, The Battle, Island of Dr.

Moreau, City on Fire, Death Ship (exec. prod.), Avenging Angel, The Boys Next Door, Street Justice (exec. prod.), Nightstick, Dark Tower (exec. prod.), Truk Lagoon (exec. prod.).
TELEVISION: Over 50 TV series.

HOWELL, C. THOMAS: Actor. b. Dec. 7, 1966. Former junior rodeo circuit champion.
PICTURES: E.T.: The Extra Terrestrial, The Outsiders, Tank, Grandview U.S.A., Red Dawn, Secret Admirer, The Hitcher, Soul Man, A Tiger's Tale, Far Out Man, Young Toscanini, The Return of the Musketeers, Sketches, Side Out.
TELEVISION: Series: Little People (only 4 yrs. old), Two Marriages, Into the Homeland.

HOWELLS, URSULA: Actress. b. Sept. 17, 1922. e. St. Paul's Sch., London. Stage debut, 1939, at Dundee Repertory with Bird in Hand followed by several plays inc. Springtime for Henry in N.Y., 1951; m.p. debut in Flesh and Blood, 1950; TV debut in Case of the Frightened Lady for BBC, 1948.
TELEVISION: Many appearances including The Small Back Room, A Woman Comes Home, For Services Rendered, Mine Own Executioner, The Cocktail Party.
PICTURES: The Oracle (Horse's Mouth), Track the Man Down, They Can't Hang Me, Keep It Clean, Long Arm (Third Key), Death and The Sky Above, Mumsy, Nanny, Sonny, and Girly, Crossplot.

HOWERD, FRANKIE: Performer. b. York, Eng. March 6, 1921. e. Shooters Hill, London, Sch. Stage debut, Sheffield Empire, 1946. Film: Runaway Bus; BBC radio & TV appearances include Tons of Money, Frankie Howerd Show, Howerd Crowd. Autobiography: On My Way I Lost It (1977).
PICTURES: The Runaway Bus, Jumping for Joy, An Alligator Named Daisy, The Ladykillers, A Touch of the Sun, Further Up the Creek, Cool Mikado, Fast Lady, Watch It Sailor, The Mouse on the Moon, The Great St. Trinian's Train Robbery, Carry On Doctor, Up Pompei, Up the Chastity Belt, Up the Front, The House in Nightmare Park, Sgt. Pepper's Lonely Hearts Club Band.
TELEVISION: BBC series. Comedy Playhouse, Frankie Howerd Show, Up The Convicts—Series (4) (Australia 1975), The Frankie Howerd Show—Series (13) (Canada 1976), Up Pompeii. TV-Video: HMS Pinafore, Trial by Jury.
STAGE: Old Vic Midsummer Night's Dream, A Funny Thing Happened on the Way to the Forum, Way Out in Piccadilly, Wind in the Sassafras Trees, Die Fledermaus.

HUDDLESTON, DAVID: Actor, Producer. b. Vinton, VA, Sept. 17, 1930. e. American Acad. of Dramatic Arts. On stage in A Man for All Seasons, Front Page, Everybody Loves Opal, Ten Little Indians, Silk Stockings, Fanny, Guys and Dolls, The Music Man, Desert Song, Mame. Broadway: The First; Death of a Salesman.
PICTURES: All the Way Home, A Lovely Way to Die, Slaves, Norwood, Rio Lobo, Fools Parade, Country Blue, Bad Company, Blazing Saddles, McQ, Capricorn I, World's Greatest Lover, Gorp, Smokey and the Bandit II, Santa Claus: The Movie; Frantic.
TELEVISION: Series: Hizzoner, Tenafly, Petrocelli. Movies: The Priest Killer, The Homecoming, Brian's Song, How the West Was Won, Winner Take All, Heatwave, The Oregon Trail, Sherlock Holmes in New York, Kate Bliss and the Ticker Tape Kid, Finnegan Begin Again, Family Reunion, Spot Marks the X, The Tracker, Margaret Bourke-White.

HUDSON, HUGH: Producer, Director. b. England. e. Eton. Began career as head of casting dept. with ad agency in London; left for Paris to work as editor for small film co. Returned to London to form Cammell-Hudson-Brownjohn Film Co., production house., turning out award-winning documentaries (Tortoise and Hare, Fangio). 1970, joined with Ridley Scott to make TV commercials. 1975, formed Hudson Films to produce. Debut as director of theatrical features with Chariots of Fire, 1981.
PICTURES: Chariots of Fire (dir.), Greystoke: The Legend of Tarzan, Lord of the Apes (prod., dir.), Revolution (dir.), Lost Angels. (dir.), Josephine (dir.).

HUGGINS, ROY: Writer, Director. b. Litelle, WA, July 18, 1914. e. U. of California 1935–39; U. of California Graduate School, 1939–41. m. Adele Mara, actress. Spec. rep., U.S. Civil Service Comm., 1941–43; industrial eng., 1943–46; writer 3 novels and many stories for Sat. Eve. Post; pres., Public Arts, Inc., 1968. V.P., 20th Century-Fox TV, 1961.
PICTURES: I Love Trouble, Too Late for Tears, Lady Gambles; story, Fuller Brush Man, Good Humor Man; adap., Woman in Hiding; collab., s.p., Sealed Cargo; s.p., dir., Hangman's Knot; collab. s.p., Gun Fury, Three Hours to Kill; s.p., Pushover; prod. A Fever in the Blood.
TELEVISION: Prod. Warner Bros. Presents Cheyenne series, anthologies, 1955–56; Conflict (series); produced pilots of Colt .45, 77 Sunset Strip, Maverick, prod. Maverick, 1957–58; won Emmy Award 1958. Created, The Fugitive, 1962; v.p., MCA Revue, 1963; exec.-prod. Run for Your Life, 1965; exec. prod., The Outsiders, The Bold Ones, Alias Smith and Jones, Toma, 1968–74. ABC Movie of Week, Pretty Boy Floyd. 1974: Co-creator of The Rockford Files pilot and series for NBC; 1975: Co-creator of City of Angels, Captains and the Kings, (exec. prod.): Aspen (exec. prod.): Wheels, (exec. prod.), The Last Convertible.

HUGHES, BARNARD: Actor. b. Bedford Hills, NY, July 16, 1915. Winner of Emmy for role as Judge in Lou Grant series (1978) and Tony Award for Da (1978).
PICTURES: Midnight Cowboy, Oh, God!, Where's Poppa, The Hospital, Rage, Sisters, Cold Turkey, Pursuit of Happiness, Deadhead Miles, Tron, Best Friends, Maxie, Where Are the Children?, Da, Joe Versus the Volcano.
TELEVISION: Series: Doc, Mr. Merlin, The Cavanaughs. Movies: Guilty or Innocent, The Sam Sheppard Murder Case, See How She Runs, The Caryl Chessman Story, Tell Me My Name, Look Homeward, Angel, Father Brown: Detective, Nova, Homeward Bound, The Sky's No Limit, A Caribbean Mystery, Night of Courage, A Hobo's Christmas, Day One, Home Fires Burning, Guts and Glory: The Rise and Fall of Oliver North.

HUGHES, JOHN: Writer, Director, Producer. Editor of National Lampoon before writing film scripts of National Lampoon's Class Reunion (1982); National Lampoon's Vacation and Mr. Mom (both in 1983). Co-wrote Nate and Hayes. Made directorial debut with Sixteen Candles in 1984 which also wrote. In 1985 entered into deal with Paramount Pictures to write, direct and produce films with his own production unit, The John Hughes Co.
PICTURES: The Breakfast Club (s.p., dir.); Weird Science (s.p., dir.); Pretty in Pink (s.p., dir., prod.); Planes, Trains & Automobiles (s.p., dir., prod.), She's Having a Baby (prod., dir., s.p.); The Great Outdoors (s.p., exec. prod.), Uncle Buck (dir, prod., s.p.), National Lampoon's Christmas Vacation (prod., s.p.).

HUGHES, KATHLEEN: Actress. r.n. Betty von Gerkan; b. Hollywood, CA, Nov. 14, 1928. e. Los Angeles City Coll., UCLA. m. Stanley Rubin, producer, mother of 4, Michael played Baby Matthew on Peyton Place. Studied drama; under contract, 20th-Fox, 1948–51; starred in Seven Year Itch 1954, La Jolla Playhouse; signed by UI, 1952.
PICTURES: Road House, Mother is a Freshman, Mr. Belvedere Goes to College, Take Care of My Little Girl, I'll See You in My Dreams, Thy Neighbor's Wife, For Men Only (The Tall Lie), Sally and Saint Anne, Golden Blade, It Came From Outer Space, Dawn at Socorro, Glass Web, Cult of the Cobra, Three Bad Sisters, Promise Her Anything, The President's Analyst, The Take, Pete and Tillie, Revenge.
TELEVISION: Bob Cummings Show, Hitchcock, 77 Sunset Strip, G.E. Theatre, Bachelor Father, The Tall Man, Dante, Tightrope, Markham, I Dream of Jeannie, Peyton Place, Gomer Pyle, Kismet, Ghost and Mrs. Muir, Bracken's World, The Survivors, Julia, Here's Lucy, To Rome with Love, The Interns, The Man and the City, Mission Impossible, The Bold Ones, Lucas Tanner, Marcus Welby, Barnaby Jones, Medical Center, M.A.S.H., General Hospital, Quincy, Finder of Lost Loves, The Young and the Restless. Movies: Babe, Forbidden Love, The Spell, Portrait of an Escort, Capitol, Mirror, Mirror, And Your Name is Jonah.

HUGHES, KEN: Writer, Director. b. Liverpool, Eng., 1922. Ent. ind. as sound engineer with BBC, 1940; Doc. films, Army training films. Novels: High Wray, The Long Echo. Scripts: The Matarese Circle, Tussy is Me, The Queen's Own, Rats.
PICTURES: Joe Macbeth, Confession, The Trials of Oscar Wilde, The Small World of Sammy Lee, Arrivederci Baby, Casino Royale, Chitty Chitty Bang Bang, Cromwell, Internecine Project, Sextette.
TELEVISION: Eddie (Emmy Award), Sammy (Brit. Acad. Award). Serials: Solo for Canary, Enemy of the State. Series: Lenin 1917 (The Fall of Eagles), The Haunting, The Voice, Oil Strike North, Colditz, Churchill.
AWARDS: Golden Globe, Emmy, British TV Acad. Award (Script Writer of Year), Avorias Festival Merit Award, British Writer's Guild Award, British Critics Award (best serial).

HUKE, BOB, B.S.C.: Cinematographer. Ent. m.p. ind. 1937, Asst. cameraman Pygmalion, French Without Tears, etc.; 1939–44 Royal Navy. 1945–9 camera operator Great Expectations, Uncle Silas, Seven Days to Noon and others. 1950–56 Brazil. Contract dir. of photo. for Cia Cinematographica Vera Cruz, 1957–59 dir. own company, Zenith, 1960. dir. photo, 3 Dinah Shore Shows, Spain, Paris, Copenhagen. NBC 1961. Dir. photo. Reach For Glory, The War Lover, The Very Edge, 1962; The Brain, 8 Danny Thomas Shows in Europe. 1963 Sandres of the River. 1964, Ballad in Blue, License to Share. TV & cinema commercials, 1955. 1966, 2nd Unit You Only Live Twice; 1968, 2nd Unit, Battle of Britain, 1969; dir. photo, The Virgin and the Gypsy. 1971; Under Milk Wood.

HULCE, THOMAS: Actor. b. White Water, WI, Dec. 6, 1953. e. NC School of the Arts. Understudied and then co-starred in

Equus on Broadway. Directorial stage debut Sleep Around Town. Film debut September 30, 1955 (1977).
THEATER: Memory of Two Mondays; Julius Caesar; Candida; The Sea Gull; The Rise and Rise of Daniel Rocket.
PICTURES: National Lampoon's Animal House; Those Lips, Those Eyes; Amadeus; Echo Park; Dominick and Eugene; Shadowman; Parenthood, Black Rainbow.
TELEVISION: Emily, Emily; The Rise and Rise of Daniel Rocket, Murder in Mississippi.

HUNNICUT, GAYLE: Actress. b. Fort Worth, TX, February 6, 1943. e. UCLA, B.A., with honors, theater arts & English major. Early career, community theatres in Los Angeles. Ent. m.p. ind. 1967.
PICTURES: Eye of the Cat, Marlowe, Fragment of Fear, The Freelance, Voices, Running Scared, New Face in Hell, Scorpio, L'Homme Sans Visage, The Spiral Staircase, The Sell Out, Tony Siatta, Once in Paris, One Take Two, Fantomas, Return of the Man from U.N.C.L.E, Privilege, Sherlock Holmes, Target, Dream Lover, Turnaround, Silence Like Glass.
TELEVISION: Man and Boy, The Golden Bowl, The Ripening Seed, Fall of Eagles, The Switch, Humboldts Gift, The Life and Death of Dylan Thomas, Return of the Saint, Martian Chronicles, A Man Called Intrepid, Kiss Inc., Love Boat—The Mallory Quest, The Lady Killers, Philip Marlowe, The Quest, Fantasy Island, Taxi, Savage in the Orient, The First Olympics: Athens 1896, Dream West, Strong Medicine, Dallas, The Saint.
THEATER: The Ride Across Lake Constance, Twelfth Night, The Tempest, Dog Days, The Admirable Crichton, A Woman of No Importance, Hedda Gabler, Peter Pan, Macbeth, Uncle Vanya, The Philadelphia Story, Miss Firecracker Contest, Exit The King, The Doctor's Dilemma, So Long on Lonely Street, The Big Knife.

HUNT, LINDA: Actress. b. Morristown, NJ, Apr. 2, 1945. e. Interlochen Arts Acad., MI, and Chicago's Goodman Theatre & Sch. of Drama.
PICTURES: Popeye, The Year of Living Dangerously (Acad. Award, supp. actress, 1985), Dune, The Bostonians, Silverado, Eleni, Waiting for the Moon, She-Devil.
THEATRE: Long Wharf Theatre, New Haven: (Hamlet, The Rose Tattoo, Ah, Wilderness); Mother Courage, End of the World (Tony nom.), A Metamorphosis in Miniature (Obie Award), Top Girls (Obie Award), Aunt Dan and Lemon, The Cherry Orchard.
TELEVISION: The Room Upstairs, The Room.

HUNT, MARSHA: Actress. b. Chicago, IL, Oct. 17, 1917. Screen debut 1935.
BROADWAY PLAYS: Joy to the World, Devils Disciple, Legend of Sarah, Borned in Texas, Tunnel of Love, The Paisley Convertible.
PICTURES: Virginia Judge, College Holiday, Easy to Take, Blossoms in the Dust, Panama Hattie, Joe Smith American, These Glamour Girls, Winter Carnival, Irene, Pride and Prejudice, Flight Command, The Affairs of Martha, Kid Glove Killer, Seven Sweethearts, Cheers for Miss Bishop, Trial of Mary Dugan, Thousands Cheer, The Human Comedy, None Shall Escape, Lost Angel, Cry Havoc, Bride by Mistake, Music for Millions, Valley of Decision, A Letter for Evie, Smash-Up, Carnegie Hall, Raw Deal, Take One False Step, Actors and Sin, Happy Time, No Place To Hide, Bombers B-52, Blue Denim, Johnny Got His Gun.
TELEVISION: Philco, Studio One, Ford Theatre, Show of Shows, G.E. Theatre, Climax, Hitchcock, Peck's Bad Girl Series, The Defenders, Twilight Zone, Cains Hundred, Gunsmoke, The Breaking Point, Outer Limits, Profiles in Courage, Ben Casey, Accidental Family, Run For Your Life, My Three Sons, The Outsiders, Name of the Game, Univ.'s 120, Ironside, Marcus Welby, M.D., Police Story, The Young Lawyers, Harry-O, The Mississippi, Hot Pursuit, Shadow Chaser, Matlock, Murder She Wrote, Star Trek: The Next Generation.

HUNT, PETER: Director, Editor. b. London, Eng., March 11, 1928. e. Romford, England and Rome, Italy, London Sch. of Music. Actor English Rep. Entered film as camera asst. Documentary, later asst film editor documentary, then asst editor features. London Films then editor—credits incl. Hill in Korea, Admirable Crichton, Cry From the Streets, Greengage Summer (Loss of Innocence in U.S.), Ferry To Hong Kong, H.M.S. Defiant (Damn the Defiant in U.S.), Supervising editor/2nd Unit Director, Dr. No, Call Me Bwana, From Russia With Love, Goldfinger, Ipcress File, Thunderball, You Only Live Twice; associate producer, Chitty Chitty Bang Bang; director, On Her Majesty's Secret Service, Gullivers Travels (Live & Animation) Gold, Shout at the Devil, Death Hunt; Wild Geese II, Hyper Sapien, Assassination.
TELEVISION: Director: The Persuaders, Shirley's World, The Pencil, Smart Alec Kill (Philip Marlowe), The Beasts in the Streets, Last Days of Pompeii.

HUNT, PETER H.: Director. b. Pasadena, CA, Dec. 16, 1938. e. Hotchkiss, Yale U., Yale Drama Sch. m. actress Barbette Tweed. Director for Williamston Theatre since 1957. Lighting designer on Bdwy. (1963–69)
PICTURES: 1776; Give 'Em Hell, Harry; Bully, Adventures of Huckleberry Finn.
TELEVISION: Huckleberry Finn (mini-series), It Came Upon the Midnight Clear, The Parade, Life on the Mississippi, A Private History of a Campaign That Failed, A New Start, Skeezer, Mysterious Stranger. Pilots: Adam's Rib, Hello Mother Goodbye, Ivan the Terrible, Quark, Mixed Nuts, Flying High, Wilder and Wilder, Rendezvous Hotel, The Main Event, Nuts and Bolts, The Good Witch of Laurel Canyon, Masquerade, Stir Crazy, Charley Hannah, The Wizard of Elm Street, Travelling Man, My Africa.
CABLE: Sherlock Holmes, Bus Stop.
STAGE: 1776 (London & Bdwy.), Georgy (Bdwy.), Scratch (Bdwy.), Goodtime Charley (Bdwy.), Give 'Em Hell Harry, Magnificent Yankee (Kennedy Center). Tours: Bully, Three Penny Opera, Sherlock Holmes, Bus Stop.
AWARDS: Tony, Ace, Peabody (twice), N.Y. Drama Critics, London Drama Critics, Edgar Allan Poe, Christopher.

HUNT, WILLIE: Executive Producer. b. Van Nuys, CA, Oct. 1, 1941. e. Utah State U., B.A., 1963. m. writer Tim Considine. Started in industry as secretary at Warner Bros., 1965; named exec. secty. to Ted Ashley, WB, 1969; story analyst, WB, 1974; story editor, WB, 1975; named West Coast story editor for WB, 1978; joined MGM in 1979 as v.p., motion picture development. Moved to United Artists as v.p.-prod., 1982. In 1983 sr., v.p. of prod. at Rastar Prods.; 1984, indep. prod., Tri-Star Pictures; 1986, sr. v.p., Freddie Fields Prods. 1988: Loverboy (co-prod.)

HUNTER, HOLLY: Actress. b. Conyers, GA. March 20, 1958. e. studied acting Carnegie Mellon. Appeared Off-Broadway in Battery (1981) and Weekend Near Madison. Appeared in four Beth Henley plays: The Miss Firecracker Contest (Off-B'way), as a replacement in Crimes of the Heart (B'way) The Wake of Jamey Foster (B'way) and Lucky Spot (Williamstown Theater Festival). Also A Lie of the Mind (L.A.). Film debut: The Burning (1981).
PICTURES: The Burning (debut, 1981), Swing Shift, The End of the Line, Raising Arizona, Broadcast News, Animal Behavior, Miss Firecracker, Always, Once Again.
TELEVISION: Fame (pilot). Movie: Svengali, An Uncommon Love, With Intent to Kill, A Gathering of Old Men, Roe vs. Wade, (Emmy Award).

HUNTER, KIM: Actress. r.n. Janet Cole; b. Detroit, MI, Nov. 12, 1922. e. public schools. d. Donald and Grace Mabel (Lind) Cole. Student acting with Carmine Lantaff Camine, 1938–40, Actors Studio; First stage appearance, 1939; played in stock, 1940–42; Broadway debut in A Streetcar Named Desire, 1947; frequent appearances summer stock and repertory theater, 1940–; appeared Am. Shakespeare Festival, Stratford, CT, 1961. Autobiography-cookbook: Loose in the Kitchen (1975).
STAGE: Two Blind Mice (tour), 1950; Darkness at Noon, 1951; The Chase; They Knew What They Wanted (tour); The Children's Hour (revival); The Tender Trap; Write Me a Murder; Weekend; The Penny Wars; And Miss Reardon Drinks a Little (tour); The Glass Menagerie (Atlanta), The Women; In Praise of Love (tour); The Lion in Winter (NJ); The Cherry Orchard; The Chalk Garden (PA); Elizabeth the Queen (Buffalo); Semmelweiss (Buffalo); The Belle of Amherst (NJ); The Little Foxes (MA); To Grandmother's House We Go, 1987; Another Part of the Forest (Seattle); When We Dead Awaken; Ghosts (Garden City and Tarrytown, NY), 1982; Territorial Rites; Death of a Salesman (Stratford, Ont.); Cat on a Hot Tin Roof; Life With Father (Coconut Grove, FL); Sabrina Fair (BTF, MA); Faulkner's Bicycle (Yale Rep., and N.Y.); Antique Pink (U. of Michigan, Theatre); The Belle of Amherst (NH); Painting Churches (Stamford, CT & E. Carolina U. Theatre, NC); A Delicate Balance (BTF, MA); Jokers (Goodspeed, CT); Remembrance (Boston, MA); Man and Superman (NY); The Gin Game (Lancaster, PA), A Murder of Crows.
PICTURES: Film debut in The Seventh Victim, 1943; Tender Comrade; When Strangers Marry (re-released as Betrayed); You Came Along; A Canterbury Tale; Stairway to Heaven; A Streetcar Named Desire; Anything Can Happen; Deadline: U.S.A.; Bermuda Affair; The Young Stranger; Money, Women and Guns; Lilith; Planet of the Apes; The Swimmer; Beneath the Planet of the Apes; Escape from the Planet of the Apes; Dark August; The Kindred.
TELEVISION: Made TV debut on Actors Studio Program, 1948; numerous TV appearances include: Requiem for a Heavyweight; The Comedian, (both on Playhouse 90); Give Us Barabbas; Love, American Style; Columbo; Cannon; Night Gallery; Mission Impossible; The Magician, 1972–73; Marcus Welby; Hec Ramsey; Griff; Police Story; Ironside; Medical Center; Bad Ronald; Born Innocent; Once an Eagle; Baretta; Gibbsville; Hunter; The Oregon Trail; Project: U.F.O.; Stubby Pringle's Christmas; Backstairs at the White House; Specter on the Bridge; Edge of Night; F.D.R.'s Last Year;

Skokie; Scene of the Crime; Private Sessions; Three Sovereigns for Sarah; Hot Pursuit; Martin Luther King, Jr.: The Dream and the Drum; Drop-out Mother, Cross of Fire.
RECORDED: From Morning 'Til Night (and a Bag Full of Poems), RCA Victor, 1961; Come, Woo Me—Unified Audio Classic, 1964.
AWARDS: Recipient Donaldson Award for best supporting actress in A Streetcar Named Desire, 1948, also on Variety N.Y. Critics Poll, 1948, for film version, 1952; winner Acad. Award, LOOK award, Hollywood Fgn. Corrs. Golden Globe award; Emmy nominations for Baretta, 1977, Edge of Night, 1980; Carbonnell award for Big Mama in Cat on a Hot Tin Roof, So. Fla., 1984.

HUNTER, ROSS: Producer. r.n. Martin Fuss. b. Cleveland, OH, May 6, 1926. e. Western Reserve U., M.A. School teacher, 1938–43; actor, Columbia Pictures, 1944–46; returned to school teaching; stage prod. & dir.; m.p. dialogue dir.; assoc. prod. U-I, 1950–51; prod., U-I, 1951. Moved production Co. from Universal to Columbia, 1971. Moved to Paramount, 1974.
PICTURES: As actor: Louisiana Hayride, Ever Since Venus, Bandit of Sherwood Forest, Groom Wore Spurs. As producer: Take Me to Town, All I Desire, Tumbleweed, Taza Son of Cochise, Magnificent Obsession, Naked Alibi, Yellow Mountain, Captain Lightfoot, One Desire, The Spoilers, All That Heaven Allows, There's Always Tomorrow, Battle Hymn, Tammy and the Bachelor, Interlude, My Man Godfrey, The Wonderful Years, Stranger in My Arms, Imitation of Life, Pillow Talk, Portrait in Black, Midnight Lace, Back Street, Flower Drum Song, Tammy and the Doctor, The Thrill of It All, The Chalk Garden, I'd Rather Be Rich, The Art of Love, Madame X, The Pad, Thoroughly Modern Millie, Rosie, Airport, Lost Horizon.
TELEVISION: Lives of Jenny Dolan, The Moneychangers, The Best Place to Be, Sid and Nancy, A Family Upside Down, Suddenly Love.

HUNTER, TAB: Actor. b. New York, NY, July 11, 1931. U.S. Coast Guard; odd jobs. Entered industry in 1948.
PICTURES: The Lawless, Island of Desire, Gun Belt, Steel Lady, Return to Treasure Island, Track of the Cat, Battle Cry, Sea Chase, Burning Hills, Girl He Left Behind, Lafayette Escadrille, Gunman's Walk, Damn Yankees, That Kind of Woman, Pleasure of His Company, The Golden Arrow, War Gods of the Deep, Ride the Wild Surf, Hostile Guns, Life and Times of Judge Roy Bean, Grease 2, Lust in the Dust (also prod.), Cameron's Closet, Grotesque, Out of the Dark.

HUNTER, TIM: Director.
PICTURES: Over the Edge (co-s.p.), Tex, Sylvester, River's Edge, Paint It Black, Robocop II.

HUNTLEY, RAYMOND: Actor. b. Birmingham, England, Apr. 23, 1904. On stage from 1922 repertory, tour; London debut in Back to Methuselah, 1924; N.Y. debut in Venetian Glass Nephew, 1931; m.p. debut 1934; many TV appearances.
PICTURES: Rembrandt, Knight Without Armour, Night Train to Munich, They Came to a City, Pimpernel Smith, Freedom Radio, Way Ahead, I See a Dark Stranger, School for Secrets, Broken Journey, So Evil My Love, Mr. Perrin and Mr. Traill, It's Hard to Be Good, Passport to Pimlico, Trio, I'll Never Forget You, The Last Page, Laxdale Hall, Meet Mr. Lucifer, Mr. Denning Drives North, Hobson's Choice, Orders Are Orders, Constant Husband, Geordie, The Prisoner, Doctor at Sea, Dam Busters, Teckman Mystery, Green Man, Brothers in Law, Room at the Top, Carlton-Browne of the F.O., Suspect, A French Mistress, Pure Hell of St. Trinians, Only Two Can Play, Waltz of the Toreadors, Crooks Anonymous, On the Beat, Carry On Nurse, The Great St. Trinian's Train Robbery, Hostile Witness, The Gaunt Woman, Arthur! Arthur!, Young Winston, That's Your Funeral, Symptoms.
TELEVISION: Upstairs, Downstairs (Lord Jeffrey, the Family Solicitor).

HUPPERT, ISABELLE: Actress. b. Paris, France, March 16, 1955. e. Conservatoire National d'Art Dramatique.
PICTURES: Faustine et le Bel Ete, Cesar and Rosalie, Going Places, Rosebud, The Rape of Innocence, The Lacemaker, Violette (Cannes, best actress award, 1977), The Bronte Sisters, Loulou, Heaven's Gate, The True Story of Camille, Wings of the Dove, Deep Water, The Trout, Cactus, Signed Charlotte, The Bedroom Window, The Possessed, Milan Noir.

HURD, GALE ANNE: Producer. b. Los Angeles, CA, Oct. 25, 1955. e. Stanford U., Phi Beta Kappa, 1977. Joined New World Pictures in 1977 as exec. asst. to pres. Roger Corman, then named dir. of advertising and pub. and moved into prod. management capacities on several New World films. Left in 1982 to form own co., Pacific Western Productions. Honored by NATO with special merit award for Aliens. Served as juror, U.S. Film Fest., Utah, 1988 and for 1989 Focus Student Film Awards. Member, Hollywood Women's Political Committee. The Amer. Film Inst. created Gale Anne Hurd production grants for Institute's Directing Workshop for Women.
PICTURES: Smokey Bites the Dust (co-prod. with Roger Corman, 1981), The Terminator (Grand Prix, Avoriaz Film Fest., France), Aliens (Huga Award; 7 Acad. Award nom., winning best sound effects editing and best visual effects), Alien Nation (Saturn nom.), The Abyss, Downtown (exec. prod.), Tremors (exec. prod.).

HURLOCK, ROGER W.: Pres. Hurlock Cine-World. b. Cambridge, MD, May 30, 1912. e. Baltimore City Coll. Ent. m.p. ind. as publicist, Hippodrome Theatre, Balt.; asst. mgr., Lessor-operator Imperial and Majestic Theatres, Balt., 1931–35; real estate, bldg., farming, Maryland and Alaska, 1936–58; elected bd. mem., Allied Artists, 1958; asst. to pres., 1961–63; chmn. budget comm., 1963; chmn. policy comm., 1964; c.p. exec. comm. member, 1964; v.p., chf. operating officer 1965; chmn. exec. comm., 1966; pres., 1967. pres., Hurlock Cine-World, 1969.

HURT, JOHN: Actor. b. Shirebrook, Derbyshire, Jan. 22, 1940. e. St. Martin's Sch. for Art, London. Debut in British film, The Wild and the Willing (1962).
PICTURES: A Man for All Seasons, Before Winter Comes, Sinful Davey, In Search of Gregory, 10 Rillington Place, Forbush and the Penguins, East of Elephant Rock, Disappearance, Spectre, Pied Piper of Hamelin, The Ghoul, Little Malcolm, The Shout, Midnight Express, Alien, Heaven's Gate, The Elephant Man, Partners, Night Crossing, The Osterman Weekend, Champions, The Hit, From the Hip, Aria, White Mischief, Jake Speed, Slaves of New York, Little Sweetheart, The Bengali Night, Scandal, Frankenstein Unbound, The Field.
TELEVISION: Playboy of the Western World, A Tragedy of Two Ambitions, Green Julia, Nijinsky, Shades of Green, Ten from the Twenties, The Peddler, The Naked Civil Servant, I, Claudius, Crime and Punishment, The Storyteller (series host), Deadline, The Jim Henson Hour.
STAGE: The Dwarfs, Little Malcolm and His Struggle Against the Eunuchs, Man and Superman, Belcher's Luck, Ride a Cock Horse, The Caretaker, Romeo and Juliet, Ruffian on the Streets, The Dumb Waiter, Travesties, The Arrest, The Seagull.

HURT, MARY BETH: Actress. b. Marshalltown, IA, Sept. 26, 1948. m. writer-director Paul Schrader. e. U. of Iowa, NYU Sch. of Arts. Stage debut in 1973 with N.Y. Shakespeare Fest. (More Than You Deserve, Pericles, The Cherry Orchard).
THEATER: As You Like It (Central Park), 2 seasons with Phoenix Theater, Love For Love, Tralawny of the Wells, Secret Service, Boy Meets Girl, Father's Day, Crimes of the Heart, The Misanthrope, Benefactors, The Nest of the Wood Grouse, The Day Room.
PICTURES: Interiors, Head Over Heels, Change of Seasons, The World According to Garp, D.A.R.Y.L., Compromising Positions, Slaves of New York, Parents, Defenseless.
TELEVISION: Secret Service (NET Theatre), Kojak, Baby Girl Scott (movie), The Five Forty Eight, Nick & Hillary (series).

HURT, WILLIAM: Actor. b. Washington, DC, Mar. 20, 1950. Lived as child in South Pacific when father was dir. of Trust Territories for U.S. State Dept. e. Tufts as theology major, switched to drama in jr. year, Juilliard. Oregon Shakespearean Fest. Leading actor with New York's Circle Repertory Company since 1976, appearing in The Fifth of July, My Life, Ulysses in Traction, The Runner Stumbles, Hamlet, Childe Byron. Also appeared with the New York Shakespeare Festival—Henry V (1976) and Midsummer's Night's Dream (1982), and in Hurlyburly off-Bdwy and on Bdwy.
PICTURES: Altered States (debut), Eyewitness, Body Heat, The Big Chill, Gorky Park, Kiss of the Spider Woman (Academy Award), Children of a Lesser God, Broadcast News, A Time of Destiny, The Accidental Tourist, I Love You to Death, The Plastic Nightmare.
TELEVISION: Verna: USO Girl, Best of Families, All The Way Home.

HUSSEIN, WARIS: Director. b. Lucknow, UP India, Dec. 9, 1938.
TELEVISION: Sleeping Dog, Death of a Teddy Bear, Toggle, Spoiled, Days In the Trees, A Passage to India, Girls in Uniform, St. Joan, A Casual Affair, Divorce His, Divorce Hers, Shoulder to Shoulder, Georges Sand, Chips With Everything, The Glittering Prizes, Love Letters on Blue Paper, Sarah Bernhardt, Blind Love, Romance, Daphne Laureola, Waiting for Sheila, Armchair Thriller, Edward and Mrs. Simpson, Death Penalty, And Baby Makes Six, The Henderson Monster, Baby Comes Home, Callie and Son, Coming Out of the Ice, Little Gloria: Happy at Last, Princess Daisy, Winter of Our Discontent, Arch of Triumph, Copacabana, Surviving, When the Bough Breaks, Intimate Contact, Downpayment on Murder, Onassis: The Richest Man in the World, Killer Instinct, Those She Left Behind.
PICTURES: A Touch of Love, Quackser Fortune, Melody, The Possession of Joel Delaney, Henry VIII and His Six Wives, The Shell Seekers.

HUSTON, ANJELICA: Actress. b. CA, 1952. Daughter of late writer-dir.-actor, John Huston. Granddaughter of actor Walter Huston. Raised in St. Clerans, Ireland.
PICTURES: Sinful Davey, A Walk with Love and Death, The Last Tycoon, The Postman Always Rings Twice, Swashbuckler, This is Spinal Tap, The Ice Pirates, Prizzi's Honor (Acad. Award, supp. actress, 1985), Gardens of Stone, Captain Eo, The Dead, Mr. North, A Handful of Dust, The Witches, Enemies, A Love Story.
TELEVISION: The Cowboy and the Ballerina (movie), Faerie Tale Theatre, A Rose for Miss Emily, Lonesome Dove.

HUSTON, DANNY: Director. b. Rome, Italy, May 14, 1962. Youngest son of director-actor John Huston and actress Zoe Sallis. Brother of actress Anjelica and screenwriter Tony Huston. e. Overseas School, Rome; Intl branch of Milfield School in Exeter, London Film School. A constant visitor to his father's sets throughout the world, he began working on his father's films, beginning in Cuernavaca, Mexico as second-unit dir. on Under the Volcano. Directed TV doc. on Peru and on making of Santa Claus: The Movie; and TV features Bigfoot and Mr. Corbett's Ghost. Feature film debut, Mr. North (1988).

HUSTON, VIRGINIA: Actress. b. Omaha, NB, Apr. 24, 1925. Did radio and stage work while in school; acted at Omaha Community playhouse; started in m.p. with RKO 1945.
PICTURES: Nocturne, Out of the Past, Tarzan's Peril, The Highwayman, Racket, Flight to Mars, Night Stage to Galveston, Sudden Fear, Knock on Wood.

HUTTE, ROBERT E.: Exhibitor, b. Escanaba, MI, Oct. 22, 1917. e. Wisc. Inst. of Technology 1937. Mgr. insp. lab. Iowa Ord. Plant 1940–42, Army Artil. 1942, Entered business as exhibitor in Southern Iowa 1943, Owned & managed theatres in Southern Iowa 1943–68. Elected board of directors, Allied Theatre Owners of Iowa, Nebraska & Missouri 1948, 50, 52. Democratic candidate Iowa State Auditor 1960; Pres. Insurance Advisors, Des Moines, IA 1962–68; pres Leisure Homes, Nursing Homes 1966–67; pres., Leisure Homes of Texas 1968–69; pres. Wodon & Romar Prods., Austin, TX 1970–75. Real estate broker & pres Leisure Mor, theatres in West TX 1976–; elected board of dir. National Independent Theatre Exhibitors 1979; Pres. Southwestern Indep. Theatre Exhibitors Assn. of TX, OK, AR, LA & NM; 1979 elected pres. Natl. Independent Theatre Exhibitors Assn. 1980–.

HUTTON, BETTY: Actress. b. Battle Creek, MI, Feb. 26, 1921. Made screen debut in 1942.
PICTURES: The Fleet's In, Star Spangled Rhythm, Happy Go Lucky, Miracle of Morgan's Creek, Incendiary Blonde, And the Angels Sing, Here Come the Waves, Duffys Tavern, The Stork Club, Perils of Pauline, Annie Get Your Gun, Let's Dance, The Greatest Show on Earth, Somebody Loves Me, Spring Reunion.
TELEVISION: Goldie (series).

HUTTON, BRIAN, G.: Director. b. New York, NY, 1935.
PICTURES: The Wild Seed, The Pad, Sol Madrid, Where Eagles Dare, Kelly's Heroes, X, Y, and Zee, Night Watch, The First Deadly Sin, High Road to China, Hostile Takeover.
TELEVISION: Someone is Watching Me, Institute For Revenge.

HUTTON, LAUREN: Actress. r.n. Mary Hutton. b. Charleston, SC, Nov. 17, 1943. e. U. of South Florida, Sophie Newcombe Coll. As model featured on more covers than any other American. Stage: Extremities.
PICTURES: Paper Lion (debut, 1968), Little Fauss and Big Halsey, The Wine and the Music, Rocco Papaleo, The Gambler, Gator, Welcome to L.A., Viva Knievel, A Wedding, American Gigolo, Paternity, Zorro, the Gay Blade, Tout Feu, Tout Flamme, Hecate, Lassiter, Perfect, Once Bitten, Flagrante Desir, From Here to Maternity, Malone, Blue Blood, Bulldance, Run For Your Life, Fear.
TELEVISION: A New Kind of Love, A Spectacular Evening in Paris, Someone is Watching Me, The Rhinemann Exchange, Starflight One, The Cradle Will Fall, The Snow Queen, Scandal Sheet, Sins, The Return of Mike Hammer, Time Stalker, Monte Carlo, Perfect People. Series: Paper Dolls, Falcon Crest.

HUTTON, ROBERT: Actor. r.n. R. Winne. b. Kingston, NY, June 11, 1920. e. Blair Acad., NJ. In summer stock prior to screen career, 1943.
PICTURES: Destination Tokyo, Janie, Roughly Speaking, Hollywood Canteen, Too Young to Know, Love and Learn, Always Together, Steel Helmet, New Mexico, Racket, Slaughter Trail, Casanova's Big Night, Cinderella; co-prod., dir., star, The Slime People; asso. prod., Now It Can Be Told. The Vulture, You Only Live Twice, They Came From Beyond Space, Torture Garden, Tales from the Crypt.

HUTTON, TIMOTHY: Actor. b. Malibu, CA, Aug. 16, 1960. Father, late actor Jim Hutton. m. actress Debra Winger. In high school plays; toured with father in Harvey during vacation. NY stage debut, Orpheus Descending (1984). Directed Cars video, Drive (1984). Film debut in Ordinary People, 1980.
TELEVISION: Movies: Zuma Beach, Best Place To Be, Baby Makes Six, Sultan and the Rock Star, Young Love, First Love, Friendly Fire, Father Figure, A Long Way Home, We're a Family Again, Amazing Stories (dir. only).
PICTURES: Ordinary People (Acad. Award, supp. actor, 1980), Taps, Daniel, Iceman, The Falcon and The Snowman, Turk 182, Made in Heaven, A Time of Destiny, Everybody's All American, Torrents of Spring, Q&A.

HUYCK, WILLARD: Writer, Director. e. U. of Southern California. Went to work as reader for Larry Gordon, executive at American-International Pictures; named Gordon's asst., working on scene rewrites for AIP films. First screen credit on The Devil's Eight as co-writer with John Milius, also U.S.C. graduate. Left AIP to write original scripts, with Gloria Katz. Both signed by Francis Ford Coppola to write and direct films for his America Zoetrope but projects never materialized. Co-wrote American Graffiti with Katz (1973) and Lucky Lady (1975). Huyck made directorial debut in 1979 with French Postcards, co-written with Katz, who also produced.
PICTURES: French Postcards (dir., co-s.p.), Indiana Jones and the Temple of Doom (co.-s.p.); Best Defense (dir., co.-s.p.); Howard the Duck (dir., co.-s.p.).
TELEVISION: A Father's Homecoming (co-exec. prod., co-s.p.), American River (co-exec. prod., co-s.p.).

HYAMS, JOSEPH: Advertising & Publicity Executive. b. New York, NY, Sept. 21, 1926. e. NYU Ent. industry, 1947. Various publicity posts, 20th Century-Fox, Columbia Pictures, 1947–55; eastern pub. mgr., Figaro Prods., 1955–56; West Coast pub. mgr., Hecht-Hill-Lancaster, 1955–58; pub. adv. dir., Batjac Prods. 1959–60 national adv. & pub. dir., Warner Bros., Seven Arts, 1960. v.p., world-wide pub., Warner Bros., Inc., 1970–1987; appointed sr. v.p., special projects, Dec., 1987.

HYAMS, PETER: Director, Writer. b. New York, NY, July 26, 1943. e. Hunter Coll., Syracuse U. Joined CBS news staff N.Y. and made anchor man. Filmed documentary on Vietnam in 1966. Left CBS in 1970 and joined Paramount in Hollywood as writer. Hired by ABC to direct TV features.
PICTURES: Busting (s.p., dir.), Our Time (dir.), Peeper, Telefon (co-s.p.), Capricorn One (s.p., dir.), Hanover Street (dir., s.p)., The Hunter (co-s.p.), Outland (dir., s.p.), Star Chamber (s.p., dir.), 2010 (prod., dir., s.p.), Running Scared (exec. prod., dir.), The Monster Squad (co-exec. prod.), The Presidio (dir., cinematographer), Narrow Margin (dir., s.p.).
TELEVISION: The Rolling Man, Goodnight My Love (both s.p., dir.).

HYDE, JOHN W.: Executive. b. Jackson, MI. e. NYU, B.A. 1963. Joined ABC upon graduation from N.Y.U. 1963 hired by MCA-Universal as exec. assist. to then v.p. Ned Tanen becoming assoc. prod. on several MCA features. Also wrote, produced and directed musical shorts for MCA Records. 1969 joined Filmways, Inc. as v.p. and exec. asst. to then-pres. Richard R. St. Johns. 1972 formed own company, Acmelab, Ltd., multi-faceted special effects, commercial and post-production facility, which included Cinefex, Videoconversion and Acme Film Laboratories. 1976 Hyde sold Acmelab to produce The Ravagers for Columbia Pictures. During production of that film, Hyde rejoined Richard St. Johns as v.p. of the Morison Film Group, a Guinness co.; 1977 became v.p. in charge of production for all Morison films; 1981, named pres. of MFG.
TELEVISION: The Andy Williams Show, The Lloyd Thaxton Show.
PICTURES: Games, Midnight Patient, Skullduggery, The Ravagers, Death Hunt, Rituals, The Uncanny, Silent Flute (Circle of Iron), Matilda, The Wanders, Nightwing, The Mountain Men, The Final Countdown, A Change of Seasons, Dead and Buried, American Pop, Venom, Fire and Ice, UHF.

HYDE, TOMMY: Executive. r.n. Thomas L. b. Meridian, MS, June 29, 1916. e. Lakeland H.S., grad., 1935. Worked E.J. Sparks Theatres, 1932–41. Florida State Theatres, 1941–42. U.S. Navy, 1942–46. Florida State Theatres, 1946–47; city mgr. (Tallahassee). Talgar Theatres, 1947–58; v.p. and gen. mgr. Kent Theatres, 1958–86; vice-pres. Motion Picture Films, Inc.; pres., NATO of Florida, 1961–62; chmn. bd. 1963–70; 1987–89, theatre consultant.

HYER, MARTHA: Actress. b. Fort Worth, TX, Aug. 10, 1924. e. Northwestern U., Pasadena Playhouse.
PICTURES: Thunder Mountain, Indian Summer, Roughshod, Velvet Touch, The Lawless, Outcast of Black Mesa, Salt Lake Raiders, Frisco Tornado, Abbott and Costello Go to Mars, Scarlet Spear, So Big, Sabrina, Kiss of Fire, Paris Follies of 1956, Francis in the Navy, Red Sundown, Showdown at Abilene, Kelly and Me, Battle Hymn, Mister Cory, My Man Godfrey, Paris Holiday, Once Upon a Horse, Houseboat, Some Came Running, Big Fisherman, Best of Everything, Ice Palace, Desire in the Dust, The Right Approach, The Last Time I Saw Archie, Girl Named Tamiko, Man from the Diner's Club, Wives and Lovers, Pyro, The Carpetbaggers, First Men in the Moon, Blood on the Arrow, Bikini Beach, Sons of Katie

Elder, The Chase, Night of the Grizzly, Picture Mommy Dead, The Happening, Some May Live, House of a Thousand Dolls, Once You Kiss a Stranger, Crossplot.

HYSON, KEVIN: Executive. b. Duxford, U.K., Jan. 7, 1951. e. Kings' School, Ely, U.K. 1960–1969. Joined Universal Pictures Ltd., London, 1969 in print and technical dept. Joined Cinema International Corp. London, 1970; gen. mgr., Cinema International Corp., Dominican Republic, 1974–76; gen. mgr., Cinema International Corp., Panama and Central America, 1976–79; mng. dir., CIC/Warner, South Africa, 1979–81; v.p., YK Cinema International Corp., Japan, 1981–83. Joined Columbia Pictures International, 1983; v.p., Latin America and Pacific for Columbia Pictures Int'l, 1984; v.p., advertising and publicity, 1985; exec. v.p., theatrical distribution and marketing, Columbia Pictures Int'l., 1986. Joined Walt Disney Pictures as v.p. int'l marketing, 1988; appt. sr. v.p., theatrical distribution and marketing, Buena Vista Intl., 1989.

I

IANNUCCI, SALVATORE J.: Executive. b. Brooklyn, NY, Sept. 24, 1927. e. NYU, B.A., 1949; Harvard Law School, J.D., 1952. 2 yrs. legal departments RCA and American Broadcasting Companies, Inc.; 14 yrs. with CBS Television Network: asst. dir. of bus. affairs, dir. of bus. affairs, v.p. of bus. affairs; 2 yrs. v.p. admin. National General Corp.; 2½ yrs. pres. of Capital Records; 4½ yrs. Corp. v.p. and dir. of Entertainment Div. of Playboy Enterprises, Inc.; 4 yrs. partner with Jones, Day, Reavis & Pogue in Los Angeles office, handling entertainment legal work; Pres., Filmways Entertainment, and sr. v.p., Filmways, Inc.; exec. v.p., Embassy Communications; COO, Aaron Spelling Prods.; sr. partner Bushkin, Gaims, Gaines, & Jonas; now pres. and chief operating officer, Brad Marks International.

IBBETSON, ARTHUR: Cinematographer. b. England, Sept. 8, 1922.

PICTURES: The Horse's Mouth, The Angry Silence, The League of Gentlemen, Tunes of Glory, Whistle Down the Wind, Nine Hours to Rama, I Could Go on Singing, The Chalk Garden, A Countess from Hong Kong, Inspector Clouseau, Where Eagles Dare, The Walking Stick, Anne of the Thousand Days, The Railway Children, Willy Wonka and the Chocolate Factory, A Doll's House, 11 Harrow House, A Little Night Music, The Medusa Touch, The Prisoner of Zenda, Hopscotch, Nothing Personal (co-cin.), The Bounty, Santa Claus: The Movie.

TELEVISION: Frankenstein: the True Story, Little Lord Fauntleroy (Emmy), Brief Encounter, Babes in Toyland, Witness for the Prosecution, Master of the Game.

IBERT, LLOYD: Executive. Began career as mgng. editor, Independent Film Journal. 1973, joined Paramount Pictures pub. dept.; named sr. publicist. 1985, appointed dir., natl. pub. for M.P. Group.

IDLE, ERIC: Actor, Writer. b. South Shields, Durham, Eng., March 29, 1943. e. Pembroke Coll., Cambridge, 1962–65. Pres. Cambridge's Footlights appearing at Edinbourgh Fest. 1963–64. Member Monty Python's Flying Circus appearing on BBC, 1969– 74.

STAGE: Oh What a Lovely War, Monty Python Live at the Hollywood Bowl, 1970; Monty Python Live (NY, 1976), The Mikado (English Natl. Opera, 1986). Author: Pass the Butler, 1982.

BOOKS: Hello Sailor, The Rutland Dirty Weekend Book, as well as co-author of Monty Python books: Monty Python's Big Red Book, The Brand New Monty Python Book, Monty Python and the Holy Grail, The Complete Works of Shakespeare and Monty Python.

PICTURES: And Now for Something Completely Different, Monty Python and the Holy Grail, Monty Python's Life of Brian, Yellowbeard, Monty Python Live at the Hollywood Bowl, Pirates of Penzance (s.p. only), The Secret Policeman's Other Ball, Monty Python's The Meaning of Life, National Lampoon's European Vacation, The Adventures of Baron Munchausen, Nuns on the Run.

TELEVISION: Isadora (debut, 1965), The Frost Report (writer), Do Not Adjust Your Set, Monty Python's Flying Circus, Rutland Weekend Television (series), The Rutles, Faerie Tale Theater (The Frog Prince, dir., writer ACE Award, 1982), Saturday Night Live, The Mikado, Around the World in 80 Days, Nearly Departed (series).

IGER, ROBERT: Executive. b. 1951. Joined ABC in 1974 as studio supervisor. In 1976 moved to ABC Sports where in 1985 was named v.p. in charge of program planning and dev. as well as scheduling and rights acquisitions for all ABC Sports properties. In 1987, named v.p. programming for ABC Sports and mgr. & dir. for ABC's Wide World of Sports; 1988, appt. exec. v.p., ABC Network Group. April, 1989 named pres., ABC Entertainment.

IMAMURA, SHOHEI: Director, Producer. b. Tokyo, Japan, Sept. 15, 1926. e. Waseda U. Joined Shochiku Ofuna Studio 1951 asst. dir., transferred Nikkatsu in 1954 as asst. dir., director Stolen Desire 1958 then 4 more films before refusing to work on any film distasteful to him; and wrote play later made into film directed by him in 1968; later turned to documentaries and from 1976 onward as independent; Ballad of Narayamá awarded Golden Palm Prize, Cannes Festival, 1983.

PICTURES: Stolen Carnal Desire, Big Brother, Hogs and Warships, Insect Woman, God's Profound Desire, Human Evaporation, Postwar Japan, Vengeance Is Mine, Swing Along, Black Rain (dir., s.p.).

IMI, TONY: Cinematographer. b. London, March 27, 1937. Ent. ind. 1959. Has worked primarily in England and Germany.

PICTURES: The Raging Moon, Dulcima, The Slipper and the Rose, International Velvet, Brass Target, Ffolkes, The Sea Wolves, Night Crossing, Nate and Hayes, Not Quite Jerusalem, Enemy Mine, Empire State, American Roulette, Buster, Options, Wired.

TELEVISION: Queenie, The Return of Sherlock Holmes, Oceans of Fire, The Last Days of Frank and Jesse James, Reunion at Fairborough, A Christmas Carol, Sakharov, Princess Daisy, John Paul II, Little Gloria-Happy at Last, Inside the Third Reich, Dreams Don't Die, For Ladies Only, Nicholas Nickleby, A Tale of Two Cities, Babycakes.

IMMERMAN, WILLIAM J.: Producer. b. Dec. 29, 1937. Joined 20th Century-Fox in 1972 as v.p., business affairs. Promoted 1975 to sr. v.p., administration and worldwide business affairs of the Feature Film Division. Previously was with American International Pictures for 7 yrs. as v.p. business affairs & assoc. counsel. From 1963–65 was deputy dist. atty. for Los Angeles County. Was founder of and bd. chmn. of Cinema Group, Inc. 1979–82. Presently vice-chmn., Cannon Productions, Inc. Special consultant to office of pres., Pathe Communications Corp. and "of counsel" to law firm of Barash and Hill. Exec. prod., Highpoint, Southern Comfort, Hysterical, Mind Games, Take this Job and Shove It. Prod.: Primal Rage, Nightmare Beach.

INGALLS, DON: Producer, Writer. b. Humboldt, NB, July 29, e. George Washington U., 1948. Columnist, Washington Post; producer-writer, ATV England and Australia; writer-prod., Have Gun Will Travel, also prod. for TV: The Travels of Jamie McPheeters, The Virginian, Honey West, Serpico, Kingston: Confidential. Exec. story consultant The Sixth Sense; prod.: Fantasy Island, T.J. Hooker.

WRITER: Gunsmoke, Have Gun Will Travel, The Bold Ones, Marcus Welby M.D., Mod Squad, Star Trek, Honey West, Bonanza, The Sixth Sense, Then Came Bronson, Police Story, World Premier Movie, Shamus, Flood, Capt. America, The Initiation of Sarah, Blood Sport, and others.

FEATURE FILMS: Airport-1975, Who's Got the Body?

INGELS, MARTY: Actor. Former Comedian, Executive. b. Brooklyn, NY, Mar. 9, 1936. m actress-singer Shirley Jones. U.S. Infantry 1954–58. Ent. show business representing Army, Name That Tune. Stage: Sketchbook revue, Las Vegas. Pres., Celebrity Brokerage, packaging celebrity events and endorsements. Active in community affairs and charity funding.

TELEVISION: Phil Silvers Show, Steve Allen, Jack Paar, Playboy Penthouse, Bell Telephone Hour, Manhunt, Ann Sothorn Show, Peter Loves Mary, The Detectives, Joey Bishop Show, Hennessey, Dick Van Dyke Show, I'm Dickens . . . He's Fenster (series), Burke's Law, Hollywood Palace, Family.

PICTURES: Ladies Man, Armored Command, Horizontal Lieutenant, Busy Body, Wild and Wonderful, Guide for a Married Woman, If It's Tuesday It Must be Belgium, For Singles Only, Instant Karma.

INGSTER, BORIS: Writer, Director. b. 1913. In 1935; collaborated on adaptation, The Last Days of Pompeii, RKO. In 1936: Dancing Pirate, RKO. In 1937: collaborated on screen play Thin Ice, 20th-Fox. In 1938: Happy Landing.

PICTURES: Judge Steps Out, Southside 1–1000; Something for the Birds, Abdullah's Harem, California-story, Cloak & Dagger, The Amazing Mrs. Holliday.

TELEVISION: Wagon Train, The Alaskans, The Roaring 20's, Travels of Jaimie McPheeters, The Man From U.N.C.L.E.

INSDORF, ANNETTE: Film professor, critic, translator, and television host. b. Paris, France, July 27, 1950. e. 1963–68 studied voice, Juilliard Sch. of Music and performed as singer; Queens Coll. (summa cum laude), B.A. 1972; Yale U., M.A., 1973; Yale U., Ph.D., 1975. 1973: soloist in Leonard Bernstein's Mass (European premiere in Vienna and BBC/WNET TV). 1975–87: professor of film, Yale U. Author of François Truffaut (1979); Indelible Shadows: Film and the Holocaust (1983, updated 1989). Since 1979: frequent contributor to NY Times (Arts and Leisure), Los Angeles Times, San Francisco Chronicle, Elle, and Premiere. Named Chevalier dans l'ordre des arts et lettres by French Ministry of Culture, 1986. Since

1987, dir. of Undergrad. Film Studies, Columbia U., and prof. Graduate Film Div. 1987: exec.-prod. Shoeshine (short film written and dir. by Tom Abrams, nom. for Oscar). 1989: exec. prod., Abrams' Performance Pieces (named best fiction short, Cannes Fest). 1981–84: host for TeleFrance Cine-club (natl. cable TV prog.) Host for Years of Darkness (PBS, 1983). Host for Holocaust film series (WNYC, 1985). Moderator-translator since 1979 for seminars and directors Telluride Film Festival; trans. for Truffaut, AFI Retrospective (Wash. and L.A.) 1979; since 1979 trans. for Polish dirs. NY Film Fest.; since 1984 trans. Cannes Film Fest. Since 1981 coordinated and hosted lecture series at 92nd St. Y (NY) including Holocaust on Film, Critics on Criticism, Screenwriters on Screenwriting.

IRELAND, JILL: Actress. b. London, England, April 24, 1936. m. actor Charles Bronson. Began career in music halls of England at age of 12; went on to sing, dance and entertain at London's Palladium, in cabarets and a tour of the continent in ballet. Began acting in West End repertory; then signed to major film studio contract at 16 by J. Arthur Rank. Screen debut as ballet dancer in Oh, Rosalinda, first of 16 feature films for Rank. Author: Life Wish, Lifeline.
PICTURES: There's Always a Thursday, Three Men in a Boat, Hell Drivers, Robbery Under Arms, Carry On, Nurse, The Desperate Man, Girl of the Latin Quarter, So Young, So Evil, The Battleaxe, Raising the Wind, Roommates, Twice Round the Daffodils, Jungle Street Girls, The Karate Killers, Villa Rides, Rider on the Rain, Cold Sweat, The Family, Someone Behind the Door, The Mechanic, The Valdez Horses, The Valachi Papers, Breakout, Hard Times, Breakheart Pass, From Noon Till Three, Love and Bullets, Death Wish II, The Evil That Men Do (co-prod. only), Murphy's Law (co-prod. only), Assassination, Caught.
TELEVISION: Shane (series), The Man from U.N.C.L.E., Ben Casey, Night Gallery, Daniel Boone, Mannix, Star Trek (series). Movie: The Girl, the Gold Watch and Everything.

IRELAND, JOHN: Actor. b. Vancouver, B.C., Jan. 30, 1916. Prof. debut at Abbey Theatre, Dublin. To Hollywood, 1945 and has appeared in over 200 films.
THEATRE: On N.Y. stage: Macbeth, Moon Is Down, Native Son, Counter Attack, Robert W. Service (one-man show), Dublin Theatre Fest., Oxford Playhouse, The Pleasure of His Company (Toronto, 1985).
PICTURES: A Walk in the Sun, Wake Up and Dream, My Darling Clementine, Red River, The Gangsters, Roughshod, All The King's Men (Acad. Award nom.), Return of Jesse James, Vengeance Valley, Red Mountain, Basketball Fix, Bushwackers, Hurricane Smith, 49th Man, Combat Squad, Southwest Passage, Security Risk, Steel Cage, Outlaw Territory, Fast and Furious, Good Die Young, Queen Bee, Gunfight at OK Corral, Party Girl, Spartacus, The Ceremony, The Fall of the Roman Empire, Faces in the Dark, I Saw What You Did, Fort Utah, Once Upon a Time in the West, The Adventurers, The Dirty Heroes, Madam Kitty, Escape to the Sun, The Incubus, Messenger of Death, Farewell, My Lovely, Martin's Day, Sundown, Final Curtain.
TELEVISION: Crossbar (CBC), The Last Tycoon, The Cheaters (UK, series), Take Over, Marilyn: The Real Story, A Little Late Lamented, Cassie & Co., Bonanza: The Next Generation; Perry Mason: The Case of the Lady in the Lake.

IRETON, KIKUKO MONICA: Managing Editor. Movie/TV Marketing; Tokyo, Japan. b. May 22, 1929. e. Seijo Gaguen, Tokyo. Daughter of late Shoichiro Kobayashi, manager of Bank of Japan in New York (1937–41) and later director. Co-founder with husband (Glenn F. Ireton) of Far East Film News in 1953, renamed Movie Marketing in 1961, Movie/TV Marketing in 1966.

IRONS, JEREMY: Actor. b. Isle of Wight, Sept. 19, 1948. m. actress Sinead Cusack. e. Sherbourne Sch., Dorset. Stage career began at Marlowe Theatre, Canterbury, where he was student asst. stage manager. Accepted at Bristol Old Vic Theatre Sch. for two-yr. course; then joined Bristol Old Vic Co. In London played in Godspell, Much Ado About Nothing, The Caretaker, Taming of the Shrew, Wild Oats, Rear Column, An Audience Called Edouard, etc. N.Y. stage debut, The Real Thing (Tony Award, 1984).
PICTURES: Nijinsky, The French Lieutenant's Woman, Moonlighting, Betrayal, The Wild Duck, Swann in Love, The Mission, Dead Ringers, A Chorus of Disapproval, Australia, Reversal of Fortune.
TELEVISION: The Pallisers, Notorious Woman, Love for Lydia, Langrishe Go Down, Brideshead Revisited, Danny, the Champion of the World.

IRVIN, JOHN: Director. b. England, May 7, 1940. In cutting rooms at Rank Organisation before making first film—documentary Gala Day on grant from British Film Inst. Other documentaries before turning to features.
PICTURES: Dogs of War, Ghost Story, Champions, Turtle Diary, Raw Deal, Hamburger Hill, Next of Kin.
TELEVISION: Hard Times, Tinker Tailor Soldier Spy.

IRVINE, RICHARD H: Executive. b. 1942. e. U. of Southern California. Early career in marketing positions with Time-Life & Campbell Soup Co.; dir. of mktg., Disneyland; suprv. worldwide non-theatrical dist. for Walt Disney Prods. Pres. & CEO of Straight Arrow Publishing; v.p.-mktg. for Trans American Video, Inc. Served as exec. v.p. & COO of Talent Payments, Inc., Production Payments, Inc. & Central Casting Corp., all subsidiaries of IDC Services, Inc., of which he was also corp. sr. v.p.–west coast, 1976–78. In 1978 joined in formation of Aurora Pictures, of which is pres. & CEO.
PICTURES: Exec. Prod.: Why Would I Lie?, The Secret of NIMH, Eddie and the Cruisers, Heart Like a Wheel, East of the Sun, West of the Moon.

IRVING, AMY: Actress. b. Palo Alto, CA, Sept. 10, 1953. e. American Conservatory Theatre, London Acad. of Dramatic Art. Daughter of late Jules Irving and actress Priscilla Pointer.
THEATER: NY: Amadeus, Heartbreak House, Road to Mecca.
PICTURES: Carrie, The Fury, Honeysuckle Rose, The Competition, Voices, Yentl, Micki and Maude, Rumpelstiltskin, Crossing Delancey, Show of Force.
TELEVISION: Movies: James Dean, Dynasty, Panache, Once an Eagle, Anastasia, The Mystery of Anna. Special: Turn of the Screw.

IRWIN, CHRISTOPHER: Producer, Executive, b. England 1948. e. U. of Sussex, Eng., B.A., social studies. From 1967 to 1969 worked as freelance producer-presenter for BBC Radio Brighton. Was with the Federal Trust (the institute concerned with European affairs) 1969 to 1975, during which time worked for the Secretariat of the North Atlantic Assembly. Joined the BBC's External Services as talks producer in 1975, moving in 1977 to the BBC's central Secretariat. From 1977 to 1978 was seconded to the International Institute for Strategic Studies. In 1978 went to Scotland as Secretary, BBC Scotland, and was closely associated with early stages of Radio Scotland. Member of BBC's Future Policy Group, the "think tank" of the Corporation. Appointed Head of Radio Scotland May 1980.

ISAACS, CHERYL BOONE: Executive. Entered m.p. industry 1977 as staff publicist for Columbia Pictures. Worked five years after that for Mel Simon Prods., named v.p. Left to become dir. of adv./pub. for The Ladd Co. 1984, named dir., pub. & promo., West Coast, for Paramount Pictures. Currently vice pres., publicity, Paramount Pictures since 1986.

ISAACS, PHIL: Executive. b. New York, NY, May 22, 1922. e. City Coll. of New York. In U.S. Navy, 1943–46. Joined Paramount Pictures in 1946 as bookers asst., N.Y. exch. Branch mgr. in Washington; then mgr. Rocky Mt. div. In 1966 was Eastern-Southern sls. mgr.; 1967 joined Cinema Center Films as v.p. domestic dist. In 1972 named v.p., marketing, for Tomorrow Entertainment; Joined Avco-Embassy 1975 as v.p., gen. sls. mgr., named exec. v.p., 1977. 1978 joined General Cinema Corp. as v.p. 1980 v.p., gen. sls. mgr., Orion Pictures. 1983, formed Phil Isaacs Co; 1988, v.p., general sales mgr., TWE Theatrical; 1989, appointed pres.

ISRAEL, NEAL: Writer, Director. m. director Amy Heckerling.
PICTURES: Tunnelvision (exec. prod., s.p.); Cracking Up (s.p.); Americathon (dir., s.p.); Police Academy (s.p.); Bachelor Party (dir., s.p.); Moving Violations (dir., s.p.); Real Genius (s.p.); It's Alive III (s.p.); Buy and Cell (co-s.p.), Sketches, Spurting Blood (exec. prod., s.p.).
TELEVISION: Lola Falana Special (s.p.); Mac Davis Show; Ringo; Marie (prod.); Twilight Theatre (writer, prod.), The Cover Girl and the Cop (dir.).

ITAMI, JUZO: Director, Actor. b. Kyoto, Japan, 1933. m. actress Nobuko Miyamoto. Son of Mansaku Itami, pioneering Japanese film director. After successful stint as commercial artist, became an actor as well as essayist (Listen, Women, a collection of his work). Directing debut The Funeral (1984).
PICTURES: Actor: 55 Days at Peking, Lord Jim, I Am a Cat, The Makioka Sisters, The Family Game. Director: The Funeral (5 Japanese Acad. Awards), Tampopo, A Taxing Woman (8 Japanese Acad. Awards), A Taxing Woman's Return (dir., s.p.), Sweet Home (exec. prod. only).

IVANEK, ZELJKO: Actor. b. Ljubljana, Yugoslavia, Aug. 15, 1957. Came to U.S. with family in 1960 and returned to homeland before settling in Palo Alto, CA, in 1967. Studied at Yale, majoring in theatre studies: graduated in 1978. Also graduate of London Acad. of Music and Dramatic Arts. Regular member of Williamstown Theatre Festival, appearing in Hay Fever, Charley's Aunt, Front Page. Bdwy. debut in The Survivor.
THEATER: Brighton Beach Memoirs, Loot, Master Harold . . . and the Boys (Yale Rep. premiere prod.). Off Bdwy: Cloud 9, A Map of the World, The Cherry Orchard.
PICTURES: Tex, The Sender, The Soldier, Mass Appeal, Rachel River.
TELEVISION: The Sun Also Rises, All My Sons, Echoes in the Darkness.

IVERS, IRVING N.: Executive. b. Montreal, Canada, Feb. 23, 1939. e. Sir George Williams U. Worked for 10 years in radio and TV in variety of executive capacities in station management before entering film business. Joined Columbia Pictures in 1973, serving as director of mktg. and dir. of adv. 1973–77; named Canadian sls. mgr. 1977–78; v.p. of adv./pub. 1978–80. In 1980 joined 20th Century-Fox as sr. v.p. of adv./pub./promo.; exec. v.p., worldwide adv., pub., promo. 1980–83; pres., worldwide mkt., MGM/UA/Entertainment Co., 1983–86. In 1986 to Warner Bros. as v.p., intl. adv./pub.

IVES, BURL: Ballad singer, Actor. r.n. Burl Icle Ivanhoe b. Hunt Township, IL, June 14, 1909. e. Teacher's Coll., Charleston, IL. Professional football player, itinerant worker, radio singer, specializing ballads.
STAGE: On Bdwy in Cat on a Hot Tin Roof.
PICTURES: Smoky, Green Grass of Wyoming, Station West, So Dear to My Heart, Sierra, East of Eden, The Big Country (Acad. Award, supp., 1958), Cat on a Hot Tin Roof, Day of the Outlaw, Our Man in Havana, Robin and the Seven Hoods, Just You and Me, Kid, Earthbound, Two Moon Junction.
TELEVISION: Rudolph the Red-Nosed Reindeer (narrator), Frosty the Snowman (narrator), Poor Little Rich Girl, Captains and the Kings, Roots, The Ewok Adventure.

IVEY, JUDITH: Actress. b. El Paso, TX, Sept. 4, 1951. m. prod.-cable TV exec., Tim Braine. e. Illinois State U. Acted with the Goodman Theatre, Chicago and in approx. 60 commercials. Stage debut in The Sea in Chicago, 1974.
STAGE: Bedroom Farce, The Goodbye People, Oh, Coward!, Design for Living, Piaf, Romeo and Juliet, Pastorale, Two Small Bodies, Steaming (Tony and Drama Desk Awards), Second Lady (off-Bdwy work she helped develop), Hurlyburly (Tony and Drama Desk Awards), Precious Sons (Drama Desk nom.), Blithe Spirit, Mrs. Dally Has a Lover.
PICTURES: Harry and Son (debut, 1974), The Lonely Guy, The Woman in Red, Compromising Positions, Brighton Beach Memoirs, Hello Again, Sister, Sister, Miles from Home, Love Hurts, In Country, Delores (short), Everybody Wins.
TELEVISION: The Shady Hill Kidnapping, Dixie: Changing Habits, We Are the Children, The Long Hot Summer, Jesse and the Bandit Queen.

IVORY, JAMES: Director. b. Berkeley, CA, June 7, 1928. e. U. of Oregon, B.F.A., 1951; U. of Southern California, M.A. (cinema) 1956. First film Venice: Theme and Variations (doc. made as M.A. thesis, 1957). American director who first gained his reputation making films in India (The Sword and the Flute, The Delhi Way, Adventures of a Brown Man in Search of Civilization). Formed Merchant-Ivory Productions with prod. Ismail Merchant and long-time script writer Ruth Prawer Jhabvala.
PICTURES: The Householder, Shakespeare Wallah (also co-s.p.), The Guru (also co-s.p.), Bombay Talkie (also co-s.p.), Savages (also co-s.p.), The Wild Party, Autobiography of a Princess, Roseland, Hullabaloo Over Georgie & Bonnie's Pictures, The Europeans (also prod. and cameo), Jane Austen in Manhattan, Quartet (also co-s.p.), Heat and Dust, The Bostonians, A Room with a View, Maurice (also co-s.p.), Slaves of New York, Mr. and Mrs. Bridge.
TELEVISION: The Five Forty Eight (dir.), Noon Wine (exec. prod.).

J

JACKSON, ANNE: Actress. b. Allegheny, PA, Sept. 3, 1926. e. Neighborhood Playhouse, Actors Studio. Married to actor Eli Wallach. Stage debut in The Cherry Orchard, 1944. Autobiography: Early Stages.
THEATER: Major Barbara, Middle of the Night, Typists and the Tiger, LUV. Waltz of the Toredors, Twice Around the Park, Summer and Smoke, Nest of the Woodgrouse, Marco Polo Sings a Solo, The Mad Woman of Chaillot, Cafe Crown.
PICTURES: So Young, So Bad (debut, 1950), The Secret Life of an American Wife, Zig Zag, Lovers and Other Strangers, Dirty Dingus Magee, The Shining.
TELEVISION: Out on a Limb (movie); Everything's Relative (series), 84 Charing Cross Road, Golda, Private Battles, Baby M.

JACKSON, BRIAN: Actor, Film/Stage Producer. b. Bolton, England, 1931. Early career in photography then numerous stage performances incl. Old Vic, Royal Shakespeare. Ent. film/TV industry 1958. Formed Quintus Plays, 1965; formed Brian Jackson Productions 1966; formed Hampden Gurney Studios Ltd. 1970. Co-produced The Others 1967; presented The Button, 1969; co-produced the documentary film Village in Mayfair, 1970; 1971: Formed Brian Jackson Films Ltd.; produced Yesterday, The Red Deer; 1972: produced The Story of Tutankhamen.
TELEVISION: Moon Fleet, Private Investigator, Life of Lord Lister, Z Cars, Vendetta, Sherlock Holmes, Mr. Rose, Hardy Heating International, Nearest & Dearest, The Persuaders, The Paradise Makers, The New Avengers, Smugglers Bay, The Tomorrow People, Secret Army, Last Visitor for Hugh Peters, Six Men of Dorset, Commercials: featured as the man from Delmonte for 5 years.
PICTURES: Incident in Karandi, Carry On Sergeant, Gorgo, Jack the Ripper, Taste of Fear, Heroes of Telemark, Only the Lonely, The Deadly Females, The Revenge of the Pink Panther, Deceptions.
STAGE: Mame, Drury Lane, Fallen Angels, In Praise of Love.

JACKSON, FREDA: Actress. B. Nottingham, Eng., Dec. 29, 1909. e. U. Coll., Nottingham. Stage debut 1933, Northampton Repertory Theatre; London debut 1936, Old Vic; screen debut in A Canterbury Tale, 1942.
PICTURES: Henry V, Beware of Pity, Great Expectations, No Room at the Inn, Flesh and Blood, Women of Twilight, The Good Die Young, The Crowded Day, The Enchanted Doll, Bhowani Junction, Last Man to Hang, The Flesh Is Weak, Brides of Dracula, Greyfriar's Bobbie, Shadow of the Cat, Attempt to Kill, West Eleven, Monster of Terror, The Third Secret, Gwangi, Tom Jones, Clash of the Titans.
TELEVISION: Macadam and Eve, Sorry Wrong Number, Trial of Marie Lafarge, Release, Colombe, Maigret in Montmartre, Sergeant Musgrave's Dance, Dr. Finlay's Casebook, Sunset, Knock On Any Door, The Spies, Adam Adamant, Midland Profile, Owen Md., The Kilvert Diaries, She Fell Among Thieves, Randall and Hopkirk, The Old Curiosity Shop, Blake's Seven.

JACKSON, GLENDA: Actress. b. Birkenhead, England, May 9, 1936. Stage debut: Separate Tales (Worthing, Eng. 1957). Ent. m.p. ind. 1955.
THEATER: (Eng.): All Kinds of Men, Hammersmith, The Idiot, Alfie. Joined Royal Shakespeare Co in experimental Theatre of Cruelty season. Marat Sade (London, N.Y.), Three Sisters, The Maids, Hedda Gabler, The White Devil, Rose, Strange Interlude (N.Y.), Macbeth (N.Y.).
PICTURES: Marat-Sade, Negatives, Women in Love (Acad. Award, 1970), The Music Lovers, Sunday, Bloody Sunday, Mary Queen of Scots, Triple Echo, The Nelson Affair, A Touch of Class (Acad. Award, 1973), The Maids, The Tempter, The Romantic Englishwoman, Hedda, Sarah, Nasty Habits, House Calls, Stevie, The Class of Miss McMichael, Lost and Found, Health, Hopscotch, Giro City, The Return of the Soldier, Turtle Diary, Beyond Therapy, Business as Usual, Salome's Last Dance, The Rainbow, The Visit.
TELEVISION: The Patricia Neal Story, Queen Elizabeth, Sakharov, Strange Interlude.

JACKSON, GORDON: Actor. b. Glasgow, Scotland, Dec. 19, 1923. e. Glasgow. On radio since 1939; screen debut in Foreman Went to France, 1940. Best known as Hudson on Upstairs, Downstairs.
PICTURES: Nine Men, San Demetrio, Millions Like Us, Pink String and Sealing Wax, Captive Heart, Against the Wind, Eureka Stockade, Whiskey Galore, Floodtide, Stop Press Girl, Bitter Springs, Happy Go Lovely, The Lady with the Lamp, Meet Mr. Lucifer, Malta Story, Castle in the Air, Quartermass Experiment, Pacific Destiny, Baby and the Battleship, Sailor Beware, Seven Waves Away (Abandon Ship), As Long as You're Happy, Hell Drivers, Rockets Galore, Bridal Path, Yesterday's Enemy, Blind Date, Cone of Silence, Tunes of Glory, Greyfriar's Bobbie, Mutiny on the Bounty, The Great Escape, The Long Ships, Those Magnificent Men in Their Flying Machines, The Great Spy Mission, The Ipcress File, Cast a Giant Shadow, Fighting Prince of Donegal, Night of the Generals, Triple Cross, The Eliminator, Prime of Miss Jean Brodie, Run Wild, Run Free, Hamlet, Scrooge, Kidnapped, Madame Sin, Russian Roulette, Spectre, Golden Rendezvous, Medusa Touch, Last Giraffe, Shooting Party, The Masks of Death, Whistle Blower, Gunpower.
TELEVISION: Numerous TV appearances incl: Upstairs, Downstairs, The Professionals, A Town Like Alice, Hart to Hart, My Brother Tom, Shaka Zulu, Noble House, The Lady and the Highwayman, The Winslow Boy.

JACKSON, JOHN HENRY: Executive. b. New York, NY, April 27, 1916. e. Holy Cross Acad., 1930; Professional Children's Sch., 1934; Georgia Tech, 1936. Performed as vaudeville artist touring Europe, 1928–29; Fair dates and indoor circus, 1929–34; Billy Rosie's Jumbo, 1935; Texas Centennial, 1936; George Abbott's Too Many Girls, 1938. Joined Radio City Music Hall, 1943 with Glee Club; stage manager, 1944–51; director of stage operations, 1958; v.p., 1970; prod., 1971; pres., Tri-Marquee Productions, Ltd., 1979. Retired 1980. Produced p.r. events W.R. Grace Co. 1980–86.

JACKSON, KATE: Actress. b. Birmingham, AL, Oct. 29, 1949. e. U. of Mississippi, Birmingham Southern U. Did summer stock before going to N.Y. to enter American Acad. of Dramatic Arts, appearing in Night Must Fall, The Constant Wife, Little Moon of Alban, etc. Worked as model and became tour guide at NBC. First role on TV in Dark Shadows (series).

PICTURES: Thunder and Lightning, Dirty Tricks, Making Love, Loverboy.
TELEVISION: The Jimmy Stewart Show (pilot). Movies: Killer Bees, The Shrine of Lorna Love, The Jenny Storm Homicide, Listen to Your Heart, Topper, Thin Ice. Series: Charlie's Angels, Scarecrow and Mrs. King, Baby Boom.

JACKSON, MICHAEL: Singer, Composer. b. Aug. 29, 1958. Musical recording artist with family group known as Jackson 5: all brothers, Jackie, Tito, Marlon, Randy and Michael. Sister is singer Janet Jackson.
PICTURE: The Wiz, Moonwalker (also exec. prod., story).
TELEVISION: Motown on Showtime: Michael Jackson.

JACOBI, DEREK: Actor. b. London, England, Oct. 22, 1938. e. Cambridge. On stage in Pericles, The Hollow Crown, Hobson's Choice, The Suicide, Breaking the Code (London, NY).
PICTURES: Day of the Jackal, Blue Blood, The Odessa File, The Medusa Touch, The Human Factor, Enigma, Little Dorrit, Henry V.
TELEVISION: She Stoops to Conquer, Man of Straw, The Pallisers, I, Claudius, Philby, Burgess and MacLean, Hamlet. Movies: Othello, Three Sisters, Interlude, Charlotte, The Man Who Went Up in Smoke, The Hunchback of Notre Dame, Inside the Third Reich, The Secret Garden, The Tenth Man. Series: Minder, Tales of the Unexpected, Mr. Pye.

JACOBS, BARRY: Executive. b. London, England, 1924. Ent. m.p. ind. 1938. Served in RAF 1943–46. Circuit rep. Warner Bros. 1938–59. Overseas sales rep. independent producers 1960–62. Formed Eagle Films Ltd. dist. organization UK 1962. Entered prod. 1969. Exec. prod. The Wife Swappers, Groupie Girl, Bread, Naughty, The Love Box, Sex and The Other Woman, On the Game, Eskimo Nell. Formed Elephant Entertainment Ltd. & Elephant Video Ltd., 1986.

JACOBS, JOHN: Executive. b. New York, NY. e. Syracuse U.'s Newhouse Communications Sch. Full-service agency background, including 13 years with Grey Advertising agency, where handled Warner Bros. & Warner Home Video accts. Supvr. media on RCA, ABC-TV, Murdoch Publishing, Radio City Musical Hall, etc. Named v.p. & group media dir. for Grey. 1986, left to join Warner Bros. as v.p., media.

JACOBY, FRANK DAVID: Director, Producer. b. New York, NY, July 15, 1925. e. Hunter Coll., Brooklyn Coll. m. Doris Storm, producer/director educational films, actress. 1949–52: NBC network TV director; 1952–56: B.B.D.O., Biow Co., TV producer/director; 1956–58 Metropolitan Educational TV Association, Director of Production; 1958–65: United Nation, film producer/director; 1965 to present: President, Jacoby/Storm Productions, Inc., Westport, Conn., documentary, industrial, educational films and filmstrips. Clients include Xerox Corp., Random House, Publ., Lippincott Co., IBM, Heublein, G.E., and Pitney Bowes. Winner, Sherwood Award, Peabody Award. Member, Director's Guild of America; winner, Int'l TV & Film Festival, National Educational Film Festival, American Film Festival.

JACOBY, JOSEPH: Producer, Director, Writer. b. Brooklyn, NY, 1942. e. NYU. Sch. of Arts and Sciences, majoring in m.p. As undergraduate worked part-time as prod. asst. on daytime network TV shows and as puppeteer for Bunin Puppets. In 1963 joined Bill Baird Marionettes as full-time puppeteer, working also on Baird film commercials. Made feature m.p. debut as prod.-dir of Shame, Shame, 1968.
PICTURES: Hurry Up, or I'll Be 30, The Great Georgia Bank Hoax (co.-prod., dir., s.p.).

JACOBY, SCOTT: Actor. b. Chicago, IL, Nov. 19, 1956.
PICTURES: The Little Girl Who Lives Down the Lane, Midnight Auto Supply, Our Winning Season, To Die For.
TELEVISION: Movies: No Place to Run, That Certain Summer, (Emmy Award, supp. 1973), The Man Who Could Talk to Kids, Bad Ronald, Smash-Up on Interstate 5, 79 Park Avenue, No Other Love, The Diary of Anne Frank.

JACON, BERNARD: Executive. b. Louisiana. Manager, promotion, Small & Strausberg Theatres, New York; buyer & gen. mgr., Mantell Theatres N.Y., gen. mgr. & assoc., Rockaway Beach Theatres, Universal Pictures, home office & field, br. operations & sales. Mgr., sales & dist. (Continental Films) Superfilms Distribution Corp., New York 1946–49; vice-pres. in chg. of sales & dist., Lux Film Distributing Corp., N.Y., 1949–52; v.p. sales, dist. IFE Releasing, 1952–55; org. nat'l distrib. co., Jacon Film Distributors, Inc., as pres., 1956; nat'l consultant to independent distributors, producers & exhibitors, member of the Pioneers & Variety; 1979, formed Bernie Jacon, Inc., natl. co-ordinator for producers and distributors.

JACQUEMIN, ROBERT: Executive. Began career as media buyer; later in station representation as v.p. of regional sls. for Telerep, Inc. Entered syndication as pres. of Television Marketing Services, St. Louis. Joined Paramount Domestic Television and Video Programming as midwest div. mgr. in St. Louis; later sr. v.p., sls. in N.Y. 1981, named exec. v.p., sls. & mktg. 1985, joined Walt Disney Pictures as sr. v.p., domestic TV dist., a new syndication div. formed by the co.; promoted to president, Oct. 1988.

JACQUES, ROBERT C.: Film editor. b. Cincinnati, OH, Feb. 24, 1919. e. U. of Michigan, U. of Southern California. Asst. film ed., RKO Radio 1939–42; film ed., Pathe News, 1942–44; chief film ed., NBC Television, 1944–48; prod. chief, Ziv TV film dept. 1948–51; free lance m.p. film ed., 1951–52; supervising film ed., prod. mgr., American Film Prod., 1952–53; prod. supvr., ed., Telenews and Screen Gems 1953; film ed., RKO Radio, 1953–55; supervising film ed., George Blake Enterprises, 1955–57; v.p. Peter Elgar Productions 1957–60; supv. film editor, Transfilm-Caravel Inc. 1960–62; v.p. in chg. of completion, Filmex, Inc., 1962. V.P. in charge of completion, Filmex Inc. 1962–69. Free lance film editor, May–Nov. 1969. V.P. of own co., Double Image Inc., film and videotape editorial service, Nov. 1969–1983. Freelance post-prod. consultant, 1983. Retired 1983.

JAECKEL, RICHARD HANLEY: Actor. b. Long Beach, NY, Oct. 10, 1926. e. Hollywood H.S., 1943. Performed odd jobs upon graduation, with plans toward entering Merchant Marine when of age; worked as delivery boy in mail room, 20th Century-Fox; Film debut Guadalcanal Diary (1943).
PICTURES: The Gunfighter, Sea Hornet, Hoodlum Empire, My Son John, Come Back Little Sheba, Big Leaguer, Sea of Lost Ships, Shanghai Story, Violent Men, Apache Ambush, Sands of Iwo Jima, Fragile Fox, 3:10 to Yuma, The Gallant Hours, The Dirty Dozen, Sometimes a Great Notion, Ulzanas Raid, Pat Garrett and Billy the Kid, The Outfit, Chosen Survivors, The Drowning Pool, Part II—Walking Tall, Chisum, Twilights Last Gleaming, All the Marbles, Starman, Stranglehold: Delta Force II, Ghetto Blasters.
TELEVISION: U.S. Steel Hour, Elgin Hour, Goodyear Playhouse, Kraft, Producer's Showcase, The Petrified Forest. Movies: The Red Pony, Born Innocent, Firehouse, The Last Day Reward, Dirty Dozen: The Next Mission, Baywatch: Panic at Malibu Pier. Series: Spenser for Hire, Supercarrier.

JAFFE, HERB: Executive, Producer. b. New York, NY. e. Brooklyn Coll., Columbia U. Press agent; then talent agent, MCA personal appearance div.; sales exec., MCA-TV, Ltd., syndic. film div.; eastern sales mgr., Motion Pictures for Television; joined Official Films as v.p., sales mgr.; Herb Jaffe Assoc. 1957; sold Herb Jaffe Assoc. to Ashley-Steiner-Famous Artists, Inc.; v.p. in prod., United Artists, 1965; v.p. of West Coast Operations, 1966. 1970, was v.p. charge of World-Wide prod, 1973 entered field of independent motion picture production. Was pres., TVO Productions, Inc. Presently indep. producer.
PICTURES: The Wind and the Lion, Demon Seed, Who'll Stop the Rain, Time After Time, Those Lips, Those Eyes, Motel Hell, Jinxed, The Lords of Discipline, Little Treasure, Fright Night, The Gate, 3 for the Road, Maid to Order, Nightflyers, Pass the Ammo, Dudes, Fright Night Part Two, Trading Hearts (co-prod.), Remote Control.

JAFFE, LEO: Executive. b. April 23, 1909. e. NYU. Started at Columbia, 1930; v.p., Columbia Pictures, January, 1954; 1st v.p., treas., member of board, 1956; v.p. & treas., 1958; exec. v.p., Columbia Pictures, 1962; Pres. Columbia Pictures, 1968; pres., Columbia Pictures Industries, Inc, 1970, president & chief executive officer, Columbia Pictures Industries, Inc., Chairman of board of directors to Aug., 1978. Currently chmn. emeritus. Industry honors: Motion Picture Pioneer of the Year, 1972; Acad. of Motion Picture Arts and Sciences Jean Hersholt Humanitarian Award, 1979; NATO Award-Knight of Malta.

JAFFE, STANLEY R.: Producer. b. New Rochelle, NY, July, 31, 1940. Graduate of U. of Pennsylvania Wharton Sch. of Finance. Joined Seven Arts Associates, 1962; named exec. ass't to president, 1964; later, head of East Coast TV programming. Produced Goodbye, Columbus, in 1968 for Paramount; then joined that company as exec. v.p., 1969. Produced A New Leaf, 1969. Named pres. of Paramount in 1970; resigned 1971 to form own prod. unit. Joined Columbia as exec. v.p. of global prod. in 1976, but resigned to be independent producer.
PICTURES: A New Leaf, Bad Company (1972); Man on the Swing, Bad News Bears. Kramer vs. Kramer; Taps; Without a Trace (prod.-dir.). *Co-prod.* with Sherry Lansing: Racing with the Moon, Firstborn, Fatal Attraction, The Accused, Black Rain.

JAFFE, STEVEN-CHARLES: Producer. b. 1954. e. U. of Southern California, cinema. Worked on production in Holland and Switzerland; served as prod. asst. on The Wind and the Lion in Spain. Assoc. prod. on Demon Seed (written by brother Robert); served as location mgr. on Who'll Stop the Rain; assoc. prod. on Time After Time. Full producer on Those Lips, Those Eyes, Motel Hell (also co-s.p.), The Fly II.

JAFFEY, HERBERT: Executive. b. Somerville, NJ. Cap't. U.S. Army, pressbook writer, 20th Century-Fox; theatre management, Loew's; field exploitation, United Artists, Ad. pub. dir.

20th Century-Fox Int and Inter-Amer. Corp.; dir., adv. & publicity, Rugoff Theatres; Independent Film Prod.; Paramount foreign advertising & publicity mgr., screenplay writer.

JAGGER, DEAN: Actor. b. Lima, OH, Nov. 7, 1903. e. Wabash Coll., Crawfordsville, IN. On N.Y. stage, stock, vaudeville. Screen debut 1929 in Woman from Hell. Academy Award supp. role 1949 for 12 O'Clock High.
PICTURES: College Rhythm, Home on the Range, Car 99, Woman Trap, 13 Hours by Air, Woman in Distress, Escape by Night, Brigham Young, Western Union, Valley of the Sun, I Escaped from the Gestapo, North Star, Alaska, When Strangers Marry, Pursued, Driftwood, Dark City, Rawhide, Warpath, Denver and Rio Grande, My Son John, It Grows on Trees, The Robe, Executive Suite, Private Hell 36, White Christmas, Bad Day at Black Rock, The Eternal Sea, On the Threshold of Space, It's a Dog's Life, Red Sundown, Great Man, Three Brave Men, The Nun's Story, Cash McCall, Elmer Gantry, Parrish, Jumbo, Stay Away Joe, Firecreek, Smith, The Kremlin Letter, Vanishing Point, Tiger by the Tail, Evil Town.
TELEVISION: Glass House, Mr. Novak (series), Brotherhood of the Bell, The Lie, Gideon's Trumpet, Haywire.

JAGGER, MICK: Singer, Composer, Actor. b. Dartford, Kent, England, July 26, 1943. Lead singer with Rolling Stones.
PICTURES: Performance, Ned Kelly, Gimme Shelter, Sympathy for the Devil, Ladies and Gentlemen, The Rolling Stones, The London Rock 'n' Roll Show, Let's Spend the Night Together.

JAGGS, STEVE: Executive. b. London, England. Ent. motion picture industry, 1964. Gained experience in the film production and laboratory areas with Colour Film Service and Universal Laboratories. Joined Agfa-Gevaert Ltd., Motion Picture Division, 1976. Appt. sales manager, 1979; divisional manager, 1989.

JAGLOM, HENRY: Director, Writer, Editor. b. New York, NY, Jan. 26, 1943. Studied acting, writing and directing at U. of Pennsylvania and with Actors Studio. Did off-Bdwy. shows; went to West Coast where appeared in TV series (Gidget, The Flying Nun, etc.). Started shooting documentary film in Israel during Six Day War; turned it into 3-hr. silent film. Hired to edit asst. Easy Rider by producer Bert Schneider. Acted in Psych Out, Drive, He Said and Last Movie. Wrote and dir. first feature, A Safe Place, in 1971.
PICTURES: A Safe Place; Tracks; Sitting Ducks; Can She Bake a Cherry Pie?; Always; Someone to Love; New Year's Day (dir., s.p., actor); Eating.

JALBERT, JOE JAY: Executive. e. U. of Washington. Was ski captain in school and began film career as technical director on Downhill Racer, 1969, also cinematographer and double for Robert Redford. 1970, produced Impressions of Utah, documentary, with Redford. Won Emmy for cinematography on TV's Peggy Fleming Special. In 1970 formed Jalbert Productions, Inc., to make feature films, TV sports, specials, commercials, etc. Co. has produced official films at Innsbruck Winter Olympics (1976), Lake Placid (1980), Sarajevo (1984).

JAMES, CLIFTON: Actor. b. Portland, OR, May 29, 1925. e. U. of Oregon. Studied at Actors Studio. Made numerous appearances on stage and TV, as well as theatrical films.
PICTURES: On The Waterfront, The New Centurions, Live and Let Die, The Last Detail, Bank Shot, Juggernaut, The Man with the Golden Gun, Rancho DeLuxe, The Untouchables, Eight Men Out, The High Flying Mermaid.

JAMES, DENNIS: Performer. b. Jersey City, NJ, Aug. 24, 1917. e. St. Peter's Coll., Jersey City. TV personality for over 30 years. Formerly M.C., actor, sports commentator in Radio; award winning sports commentator for wrestling, 25 TV first to credit; currently pres., Dennis James Prod.
TELEVISION: Chance of a Lifetime, High Finance, First Impressions, What's My Line?, PDQ, Your All-American College Show; host New Price Is Right, Nightime; Host, Name That Tune, Daytime.

JAMES, POLLY: Writer. b. Ancon, Canal Zone. e. Smith Coll. Newspaper work, Panama; with trade mag., N.Y.; screenwriter since 1942.
PICTURES: Mrs. Parkington, The Raiders, Redhead from Wyoming, Quantrill's Raiders.
TELEVISION: Several shows.

JAMESON, JERRY: Director. b. Hollywood, CA. Started as editorial asst; then editor and supv. editor for Danny Thomas Prods. Turned to directing.
PICTURES: Dirt Gang, The Bat People, Brute Core, Airport '77, Raise the Titanic.
TELEVISION: Movies: Heatwave!, The Elevator, Hurricane, Terror on the 40th Floor, The Secret Night Caller, The Deadly Tower, The Lives of Jenny Dolan, The Call of the Wild, The Invasion of Johnson County, Superdome, A Fire in the Sky, High Noon—Part II, The Return of Will Kane, The Red Spider, Terror on Highway 91.

JANKOWSKI, GENE F.: Executive. b. Buffalo, NY, May 21, 1934. e. Canisius Coll., B.S., Michigan State U., M.A. in radio, TV and film. Joined CBS radio network sls, 1961 as acct. exec.; eastern sls. mgr., 1966; moved to CBS-TV as acct. exec. 1969; gen. sls. mgr. WCBS-TV, 1970; dir. sls, 1971; v.p. sls., CBS-TV Stations Divisions, 1973; v.p., finance & planning, 1974; v.p., controller, CBS Inc. 1976; v.p. adm., 1977; exec. v.p. CBS/Broadcast Group, 1977; pres., CBS/Broadcast Group, 1977; chmn. CBS/Broadcast Group, 1988–89; chmn. Jankowski Communications System, Inc. Aug., 1989–. Member: Pres., Intl. Council of National Acad. of Television Arts & Sciences; chmn. & trustee Amer. Film Institute; trustee, Catholic U. of Amer.; director, Georgetown U.; bd. of gov. American Red Cross; vice chmn., business comm. Metropolitan Museum of Art.
AWARDS: Received Distinguished Communications Medal from South Baptist Radio & Television Commission; honorary Doctorate of Humanities, Michigan State U.; Humanitarian Award, National Conference of Christians and Jews.

JANNI, JOSEPH: Producer. b. Milan, Italy, May 21, 1916. e. Milan U., Rome Film Sch. Entered m.p. industry 1941. Assistant producer. Founded Vic Films Ltd.
PICTURES: The Glass Mountain, White Corridors, Something Money Can't Buy, Romeo and Juliet (co-prod.), A Town Like Alice (prod.); The Captain's Table, Savage Innocents, A Kind of Loving, Billy Liar, Darling, Modesty Blaise, Far from the Madding Crowd, Poor Cow, In Search of Gregory, Sunday, Bloody Sunday, Made, Yanks (co-prod.).

JARMAN, CLAUDE, JR.: Actor. b. Nashville, TN, Sept. 27, 1934. e. MGM Sch. Film debut in The Yearling, 1946.
PICTURES: High Barbaree, Sun Comes Up, Intruder in the Dust, Roughshod, Outriders, Inside Straight, Rio Grande, Hangman's Knot, Fair Wind to Java, Great Locomotive Chase.
TELEVISION: Centennial.

JARMUSCH, JIM: Director, Writer, Composer, Actor. b. Akron, OH, 1953. e. attended Columbia U., went to Paris in senior year. NYU Film Sch., studied with Nicholas Ray and became his teaching asst. Appeared as an actor in Red Italy and Fraulein Berlin. Composed scores for The State of Things and Reverse Angle. Directorial debut Permanent Vacation (also prod., s.p., music, ed. 1980). Wrote and directed New World using 30 minutes of leftover, unused film from another director. (Won International Critics Prize, Rotterdam Film Festival.) Expanded it into Stranger Than Paradise.
PICTURES: Stranger Than Paradise (also s.p., ed., Best Film Award, National Society of Film; Golden Leopard, Locarno Film Festival; Camera d'Or best new director, Cannes), Down by Law, All Night Long (actor only), Mystery Train (dir., s.p.).

JARRE, MAURICE: Composer. b. Lyon, France, 1924. Studied at Paris Cons. Was orchestra conductor for Jean Louis Barrault's theatre company four years. In 1951 joined Jean Vilar's nat'l theatre co., composing for plays by Shakespeare, Moliere, O'Neill, Eliot, and Victor Hugo. Musical dir., French National Theatre for 12 years before starting to compose film scores in 1952. Also written ballets (Masques de Femmes, Facheuse Rencontre, The Murdered Poet, Maldroros) and served as cond. with Royal Phil. Orch, London, Japan Phil. Orch, Osaka Symph. Orch., Quebec Symp. Orch.
PICTURES: Hotel des Invalides, La Tete contre les Murs, Eyes Without a Face, Crack in the Mirror, Sundays and Cybele, The Longest Day, Lawrence of Arabia (AA, 1962), The Collector, Is Paris Burning?, Weekend at Dunkirk, Dr. Zhivago (AA, 1965), Night of the Generals, The Professionals, Grand Prix, Five Card Stud, Isadora, The Damned, Ash Wednesday, The Life and Times of Judge Roy Bean, The Mackintosh Man, The Effect of Gamma Rays on Man-in-the-Moon Marigolds, Island at the Top of the World, Mandingo, Posse, Winter Kills, The Magician of Lublin, Resurrection, The American Success Company, The Black Marble, Taps, Firefox, Young Doctors in Love, Don't Cry, It's Only Thunder; The Year of Living Dangerously, Dreamscape, A Passage to India, Top Secret!, Witness, Mad Max Beyond Thunderdome, Solarbabies, The Mosquito Coast, Tai-Pan, No Way Out, Julia and Julia, Fatal Attraction, Gaby—A True Story, Moon Over Parador, Gorillas in the Mist, Wildfire, Distant Thunder, The Palanquin of Tears, Chances Are, Dead Poets Society.

JARRICO, PAUL. Writer, Producer. b. Los Angeles, CA, Jan. 12, 1915.
PICTURES: Salt of the Earth, Tom, Dick and Harry (Academy nomination), Thousands Cheer, Song of Russia, The Search, The White Tower, Not Wanted, The Girl Most Likely, Messenger of Death (s.p.).
TELEVISION: Call to Glory, Fortune Dane, Seaway, The Defenders.

JARROTT, CHARLES: Director. b. London, England, June 16, 1927. Son of British businessman and former singer-dancer at Gaiety Theatre. Joined British Navy; wartime service in Far East. After military service turned to theatre as asst. stage mgr. with Arts Council touring co. In 1949 joined Nottingham Repertory Theatre as stage dir. and juvenile acting lead. In 1953 joined new co. formed to tour Canada; was leading man and became resident leading actor for Ottawa Theatre. In 1955 moved to Toronto and made TV acting debut opposite Katharine Blake whom he later wed. 1957 dir. debut in TV for Canadian Bdcstg. Co. Became CBC resident dir. Moved to London to direct for Armchair Theatre for ABC-TV. Then became freelance dir., doing stage work, films, TV.

PICTURES: Anne of the Thousand Days, Mary, Queen of Scots, Lost Horizon, The Dove, The Littlest Horse Thieves, The Other Side of Midnight, The Last Flight of Noah's Ark, Condorman, The Amateur, The Boy in Blue.

TELEVISION: The Hot Potato Boys, Roll On, Bloomin' Death, Girl in a Birdcage, The Picture of Dorian Gray, Rain, The Rose Affair, Roman Gesture, Silent Song, The Male of the Species, The Young Elizabeth, A Case of Libel, Dr. Jekyll and Mr. Hyde, A Married Man, Poor Little Rich Girl: The Barbara Hutton Story; The Woman He Loved, Till We Meet Again (mini-series).

STAGE: The Duel, Galileo, The Basement, Tea Party, The Dutchman, etc.

JASON, RICK: Actor. b. New York, NY, May 21, 1926. e. American Acad. of Dramatic Arts.

THEATRE: Broadway debut: Now I Lay Me Down To Sleep (Theatre World Award).

PICTURES: Sombrero, Saracen Blade, This Is My Love, Lieutenant Wore Skirts, Wayward Bus, Illegally Yours. and approx. 35 others.

TELEVISION: The Case of the Dangerous Robin, Combat (series), Around the World in 80 Days. and approx. 200 others.

JAY, LESLIE: Executive. b. New York, NY, May 12. e. Fordham U., B.A., 1977. Entered industry in 1969 as publicist with Bob Perilla Associates. 1970, pub. asst. on Such Good Friends, 1976–present, with Penthouse Films Intl., Ltd., asst. to producers on Caligula; then world-wide project coordinator on Caligula. Director of pub. & promo. for Omni: The New Frontier for Omni Productions Intl., Ltd. Director of p.r. for Penthouse Int'l., Ltd; 1984, v.p. & dir. public relations, Penthouse.

JAYSTON, MICHAEL: Actor. b. Nottingham, England, Oct. 28, 1935. Member of Old Vic theatre Co. & Bristol Old Vic.

PICTURES: Cromwell, The Nelson Affair, Nicholas and Alexandra, A Midsummer Night's Dream, The Public Eye.

TELEVISION: She Fell Among Thieves, Tinker, Tailor, Soldier, Spy.

JEFFEE, SAUL: Executive. b. Elizabeth, NJ, March 30, 1918. Established Movielab, Inc., 1936, pres., bd. chmn., & chief exec. officer. Also chmn. & CEO, Movielab Video, Inc.; chmn. & pres. 619 West 54th St. Corp.; chmn. & pres., MLH Realty Corp.; chmn. & pres., Film Recoupment Corp.; Life Fellow, SMPTE, Treas.; Pres. & chmn., Movielab Theatre Service; Pres. Assoc. of Cinema Labs, 1963; American Tech. Rep. & Deleg. in the U.S.-U.S.S.R. Cult. Exch. 1965; Trustee, UJA Federation of Jewish Philanthropies, Chmn. Enter. & Commu. Div., U.J.A., 1967–68; Life member, Motion Picture Pioneers, Friars, City Athletic Club; Author of Narcotics—An American Plan, chmn. Bd. of Trustees, Lorge School, 1968–81; Pres. & Chmn., Movielab-Hollywood, Inc., vice chmn., Film Society of Lincoln Center, Patron, Lincoln Center for The Performing Arts, life member, chmn., Life Patron Program, Variety Clubs International, holder of 16 patents, Professional Motion Picture Equipment, Trustee, Federation of Jewish Philanthropies; Trustee, Will Rogers Memorial Fund; Mason (Shriner, 32 deg); Life Member, The Jewish Chautagui Society. Member, National Advisory Committee for the Handicapped Boy Scouts of Amer.; Advisory Board, Cinema Lodge No. 6000 B'nai B'rith. Academy of Motion Picture Arts & Sciences; Mayor of N.Y.C. Advisory Council on Motion Pictures. Member, Natl. Academy of TV Arts & Sciences, Film Acquisition Comm., U.S.I.A.; Member, Int'l. Radio & TV Society.

JEFFREYS, ANNE: Actress. b. Goldsboro, NC, Jan. 26, 1923. m. actor Robert Sterling. Named by Theatre Arts Magazine as "one of the 10 outstanding beauties of the stage." Trained for operatic career. Sang with NY's Municipal Opera Co. while supplementing income as a Powers model. Appeared as Tess Trueheart in Dick Tracy features.

PICTURES: I Married an Angel, Step Lively, Dillinger, Sing Your Way Home, Trail Street, Riffraff, Return of the Bad Men, Boys' Night Out.

THEATER: On Bway. in Street Scene, Kiss Me Kate, Romance, Three Wishes for Jamie, Kismet.

TELEVISION: Series: Topper, Love That Jill, Bright Promise, Delphi Bureau, General Hospital, Finder of Lost Loves; appearances on Falcon Crest, Hotel, Murder She Wrote.

STOCK: Camelot, King & I, Kismet, Song of Norway, Bells Are Ringing, Marriage Go Round, No Sex Please, We're British, Take Me Along, Carousel, Anniversary Waltz, Do I Hear a Waltz, Ninotchka, Pal Joey, Name of the Game, Destry Rides Again, The Merry Widow, Bitter Sweet, Desert Song, High Button Shoes, Sound of Music.

JEFFRIES, LIONEL: Actor. b. Forest Hill, London, England, 1926. Ent. m.p. ind. 1952.

THEATER: Hello, My Fair Lady, See How They Run, Two Into One, Pygmalion (U.S.).

PICTURES: The Nun's Story, Two-Way Stretch, The Trials of Oscar Wilde, Fanny, The Notorious Landlady, The Wrong Arm of the Law, First Men in the Moon, Call Me Bwana, The Truth About Spring, You Must Be Joking, The Crimson Blade, Arrivederci Baby, Spy with the Cold Nose, Journey to the Moon, Camelot, Chitty Chitty Bang Bang, Eye Witness, The Prisoner of Zenda, Railway Children, (dir., s.p.), Gingerbread House, Baxter, (dir.), The Amazing Mr. Blunden, (dir., s.p.), The Water Babies, A Chorus of Disapproval, Ending Up.

TELEVISION: Father Charlie, Tom, Dick, and Harriet, Cream in My Coffee, Minder, Danny, the Champion of the World.

JENKINS, CHARLES: Animation producer. b. Yorkshire, England, 1941. Ent. m.p. ind. 1957. Joined T.V.C. as gen. ass't 1958. Animated and prod. various prods. Joined Dick Williams, pioneered use of Oxberry Camera for animation, 1966. Esta. Trickfilm Ltd., prod. optical effects for Yellow Submarine, 1967.

JENKINS, DAN: Public Relations Executive. b. Montclair, NJ, Dec. 5, 1916. e. U. of Virginia. 1938. U.S. Army, 1940–45; major, infantry. P.R. officer, Hq. Eighth Army. Mng. ed., Motion Picture Magazine, 1946–48; editor, Tele-Views Magazine, 1949–50; TV editor, columnist, Hollywood Reporter, 1950–53; Hollywood bureau chief, TV Guide, 1953–63; v.p., exec. dir. TV dept., Rogers, Cowan & Brenner, Inc., 1963–71. Formed Dan Jenkins Public Relations, Inc. 1971. Joined Charles A. Pomerantz Public Relations, Ltd. as v.p., 1975, while retaining own firm. Sr. associate, Porter, Novelli, Assocs., 1981. Mem. bd. trustees, Natl. Academy of TV Arts & Sciences; bd. gov., Hollywood chapter, Natl. Academy of TV Arts & Sciences, 1967–71. Rejoined Rogers & Cowan, 1983, v.p., TV dept. Retired, 1988.

JENKINS, GEORGE: Art dir. b. Baltimore, MD, Nov. 19, 1908. e. U. of Pennsylvania. Hollywood-New York art dir. since 1946; TV pictures for Four Star Playhouse and revue productions; NBC-TV opera, Carmen; color dir., CBS-TV, 1954; NBC color spec. Annie Get Your Gun, 1957; TV music with Mary Martin, 1959. Professor, Motion Picture Design, UCLA, 1985–88.

STAGE: Mexican Hayride, I Remember Mama, Dark of the Moon, Lost in the Stars, Bell, Book and Candle, Bad Seed, Happiest Millionaire, Two for the Seesaw, Ice Capades, Jones Beach spec., Song of Norway, Paradise Island, Around the World in 80 Days, Mardi Gras, Miracle Worker, Critics Choice, A Thousand Clowns, Jennie, Generation, Wait Until Dark, Only Game in Town, Night Watch, Sly Fox.

PICTURES: Best Years of Our Lives, Secret Life of Walter Mitty, Miracle Worker, Mickey One, Up the Down Staircase, Wait Until Dark, Subject Was Roses, Klute, 1776, Paper Chase, Parallax View, Night Moves, Funny Lady, All the President's Men (Acad. Award), Comes a Horseman, China Syndrome, Starting Over, The Postman Always Rings Twice, Rollover, Sophie's Choice, Orphans, See You in the Morning, Presumed Innocent.

TELEVISION: The Dollmaker.

JENNINGS, PETER. TV News Anchor. b. Toronto, Canada, July 29, 1938. Son of Canadian broadcaster Charles Jennings. e. Carleton U.; Rider Coll. Worked as a bank teller and late night radio host in Canada. Started career as host of Club Thirteen, a Canadian American Bandstand-like dance prog., then as a newsman on CFJR (radio), Ottawa; then with CJOH-TV and CBS before becoming co-anchor of first national news program on Canadian commercial network, CTV. Joined ABC in 1964 as NY corr.; 1965, anchor, Peter Jennings with the News; 1968, natl. corr., ABC News; 1969, overseas assignments; 1975, Washington corr. and anchor for AM America; 1977, chief foreign corr.; 1978, foreign desk anchor, World News Tonight; 1983, anchor, sr. editor, World News Tonight.

JENS, SALOME: Actress. b. Milwaukee, WI, May 8, 1935. e. Northwestern U. Member Actors Studio. On stage in The Disenchanted, Far Country, Night Life, Winter's Tale, Mary Stuart, Antony and Cleopatra, After the Fall, Moon For the Misbegotten, The Balcony.

PICTURES: Angel Baby, The Fool Killer, Seconds, Me, Natalie, Cloud Dancer, Harry's War, Just Between Friends.

TELEVISION: Movies: In the Glitter Palace, Sharon: Portrait of a Mistress, From Here to Eternity, The Golden Moment: An Olympic Love Story, A Killer in the Family, Playing with Fire, Uncommon Valor, Mary Hartman, Mary Hartman, Falcon Crest (series).

JEPHCOTT, SAMUEL C.: Executive. b. 1944, Southampton, England. e. Arts Educational Sch., London. Entered industry as child actor The Grove Family BBC TV, 1956. Eight years in advertising producing TV commercials. Emigrated to Toronto, Canada in 1968. Exec. secty., Directors Guild of Canada, 1969–72. Film prod. management, 1972–75. Joined Compass Film Sales Ltd., 1975–77. Joined Nielsen-Ferns Intl. Ltd. in chg. of distribution and prod., 1977–81. Mgr. distribution, CBC Enterprises, 1982–84. Mako Films, 1985–87. Currently president, Canadian Film & TV Assn., pres., Cyclops Communications Corp.

PICTURES: The Hard Part Begins (prod. mgr.); Sunday In The Country (2nd a.d.); Me (prod. mgr.); Lions For Breakfast (prod. mgr.), It Seemed Like a Good Idea at the Time, (2nd A.D.); Love at First Sight, (prod. accountant); Find the Lady (stills); The New Avengers, TV, (prod. mgr.); The Wars (prod. supvr.); (TV) The Last Frontier (TV prod.).

JERGENS, ADELE: Actress. b. Brooklyn, NY, Nov. 28, 1922. Began career in musical shows during summer vacation at 15; won contest, New York's World Fair, as model; appeared on New York stage; night clubs, U.S. and abroad.

PICTURES: Edge of Doom, Side Street, Abbott and Costello Meet the Invisible Man, Sugarfoot, Try and Get Me, Show Boat, Somebody Loves Me, Aaron Slick from Punkin' Crick, Overland Pacific, Miami Story, Fireman Save My Child, Big Chase, Strange Lady in Town, The Cobweb, Girls in Prison, The Lonesome Trail.

JESSEL, IAN: Executive. b. London, England, 1939. e. Oxford. Joined Rank Organisation in 1962 as graduate trainee and became responsible for acquisition of indep. product. Formed Target International Pictures in 1968. In 1970 joined World Film Sales becoming man. dir. 1972. World Film Sales merged with ITC in 1974. Elected to board 1975. Appointed dir. Classic Cinemas and ITC Film Distributors (UK), 1979. Appt. man. dir. ITC Films Int., 1980. Joined CBS Theatrical Films, Sept. 1981, as vice-pres. int. distribution, now based in Los Angeles.

JEWISON, NORMAN P.: Producer, Director. b. Toronto, Canada, July 21, 1926. e. Malvern Collegiate Inst., Toronto, 1940–44; Stage and TV actor 1950–52. Director, Canadian Broadcasting Corp 1953–58. Victoria Coll., U. of Toronto, 1946–50, B.A. Awarded 1988 Acad. of Canadian Cinema and Television Special Achievement Award.

TELEVISION: Exec. prod. of 8 Judy Garland shows; prod.-dir., Judy Garland specials, The Andy Williams Show (dir., Specials: Tonight with Harry Belafonte, The Broadway of Lerner and Loewe.).

PICTURES: *Director:* 40 Pounds of Trouble, The Thrill of It All, Send Me No Flowers, Art of Love, The Cincinnati Kid, The Russians Are Coming, The Russians Are Coming, In The Heat of the Night (also prod.), The Thomas Crown Affair (also prod.), Gaily, Gaily, (also prod.), The Landlord (prod. only). *Prod.-Director:* Fiddler on the Roof, Jesus Christ Superstar; Billy Two Hats (prod. only); Rollerball, F.I.S.T.; And Justice for All; Best Friends; Iceman (prod. only), A Soldier's Story; Agnes of God; Moonstruck; The January Man (prod. only), In Country.

JHABVALA, RUTH PRAWER: Writer. b. Cologne, Germany, May 7, 1927. Emigrated with her family to England, 1939. e. Hendon County Sch., Queen Mary Coll., London U. (degree in English). m. architect C.S.H. Jhabvala, 1951 and moved to Delhi. Novels published in England: 1955–60: To Whom She Will, Esmond in India, The Nature of Passion, The Householder; Get Ready for Battle; Heat and Dust, In Search of Love and Beauty, Three Continents. Has written most of the screenplays for the films of Ismail Merchant and James Ivory.

PICTURES: The Householder (1963, wrote s.p. based on her novel), Shakespeare Wallah (with Ivory), The Guru (with Ivory), Bombay Talkie (with Ivory), Autobiography of a Princess, Roseland, Hullabaloo Over Georgie and Bonnie's Pictures, (TV), The Europeans (with Ivory), Jane Austen in Manhattan, Quartet (with Ivory), Heat and Dust (based on her own novel), The Bostonians, A Room with a View; Madame Sousatzka (co.-s.p.), Mr. and Mrs. Bridge.

JILLIAN, ANN: Actress. b. Cambridge, MA, Jan. 29, 1951. Began career at age 10 in Disney's Babes in Toyland; in film version of Gypsy at age 12. Broadway debut in musical, Sugar Babies, 1979. Formed own company: 9-J Productions, developing TV movies and series.

PICTURES: Babes in Toyland, Gypsy, Mr. Mom.

TELEVISION: Series: Hazel, It's a Living, Jennifer Slept Here. Many appearances on series (Love Boat, Fantasy Island, Twilight Zone, Ben Casey). Mini-series: Ellis Island (Emmy nom.), Alice in Wonderland, Malibu. Movies: Mae West (Emmy nom.), Death Ride to Osaka, Killer in the Mirror, Convicted: A Mother's Story, Perry Mason: The Case of the Murdered Madam, The Ann Jillian Story (Golden Globe Award; Emmy nom.), Original Sin, First Impressions, Throwaway Wives.

JOFFE, CHARLES H.: Executive. b. Brooklyn, NY, July 16, 1929. e. Syracuse U. Joined with Jack Rollins to set up management-production org., clients including Woody Allen, Ted Bessell, Billy Crystal, David Letterman, Tom Poston, Robin Williams.

PICTURES: Produced: Don't Drink the Water, Take the Money and Run, Everything You Always Wanted to Know About Sex but Were Afraid To Ask, Love and Death, Annie Hall, House of God, Arthur. Exec. prod.: Play It Again Sam, Bananas, Sleeper, Arthur, Manhattan, Interiors, Stardust Memories, A Midsummer Nights' Sex Comedy, Zelig, Broadway Danny Rose, The Purple Rose of Cairo, Hannah and Her Sisters, Radio Days, September, Another Woman, New York Stories (Oedipus Wrecks).

TELEVISION: Woody Allen specials. Star of the Family, Good Time Harry.

JOFFE, EDWARD: Producer, Director, Writer. Worked in m.p., theatre, commercial radio and as journalist before ent. TV ind. in Britain 1957 as writer/prod with ATV. Has prod. & dir. over 4000 progs. 1959–61 staff prod. Granada TV, 1962, dir., Traitor's Gate & Traveling Light for Robt Stigwood, prod. dir., numerous series for Grampian TV; 1967, dir. film The Price of a Record—Emmy finalist, Special Mention Salerno Film Fest shown in over 70 countries; 1967—8 films, Columba's Folk & So Many Partings ITV entries in Golden Harp Fest.; 1968, prod., dir. Tony Hancock's Last Series in Aust. prod. dir. Up At The Cross; prod. dir. ind. film, Will Ye No' Come Back Again; dir., This Is . . . Tom Jones; prod. dir., The Golden Shot; 1971, senior production lecturer, Thomson TV College; dir., films for U.S. for London Television Service; Evening Standard Commercials for Thames TV. Co. prod. dir.,ind. film Sound Scene, 1972–8, Contract prod. dir. Thames TV various series: Magpie, Today, Opportunity Knocks. The David Nixon Show, Seven Ages of Man, Problems, Finding Out; 1980; production consultant, CBC-tv, 1978–82, prod. dir. series Writers' Workshop, About Books; 1978, film, Places & Things (British Academy Award nom.) film, Who Do You Think You Are? (British Academy Award nom., ITV's Japan Prize entry, Special Jury Award San Francisco Intl. Film Fest), 1981, Film Images, (British Academy Award nom.); Gold Plaque Chicago Intl. Film Fest.); The Protectors (medal winner Intl. Film & TV Festival, N.Y.). 1982–86: Film Rainbow Coloured Disco Dancer. 1988: The Buzz. Various Series: Taste of China, Jobs Ltd. Spin-Offs.

JOFFE, ROLAND: Director. b. London, Eng., Nov. 17, 1945. e. Manchester U., England. Worked in British theatre with the Young Vic, the National Theatre and the Old Vic. 1973 became youngest director at National Theatre. 1978, moved into directing TV for Granada TV, then Thames and B.B.C. before feature debut in 1984 with The Killing Fields.

TELEVISION: Documentaries: Rope, Anne, No, Mama No. Plays: The Spongers, Tis Pity She's a Whore, The Legion Hall Bombing, United Kingdom (also co-wrote). Series: The Stars Look Down.

PICTURES: The Killing Fields (best film award, Cannes, 1986), The Mission, Fat Man and Little Boy (also co-s.p.), Made in Bangkok (prod. only).

JOHNS, GLYNIS: Actress. b. Durban, South Africa, Oct. 5, 1923. e. in England. Daughter of Mervyn Johns, actor, and Alys Steele, pianist. On London stage from 1935 (Buckie's Bears, The Children's Hour, A Kiss for Cinderella, Quiet Week-End; Gertie, N.Y. stage, 1952; Major Barbara, N.Y., 1956–57.) On screen 1936: South Riding. Voted one of top ten British Money-making stars in Motion Picture Herald-Pathe poll, 1951–54.

STAGE: N.Y. 1964, Too Good to Be True, London, 1967: The King's Mare; 1970, Come as You Are. 1971–2 Tour of Britain, Canada and U.S. in The Marquise, A Little Night Music, NY 1973 (Tony Award); Cause Celebre (London, 1977); Harold and Maude (Canada, 1977); Hay Fever (U.K. tour, 1978); The Boy Friend (Toronto, 1984); the Circle (NY 1989).

PICTURES: Murder in Family, Prison Without Bars, Mr. Brigg's Family, 49th Parallel, Adventures of Tartu, Half-Way House, Perfect Strangers, This Man Is Mine, Frieda, An Ideal Husband, Miranda, Third Time, Lucky Mr. Proback, The Great Manhunt, Flesh and Blood, No Highway in the Sky, Appointment With Venus (Island Rescue), Encore, The Card (The Promoter), The Sword and the Rose, Rob Roy, Personal Affair, The Weak and the Wicked, The Seekers (Land of Fury), The Beachcomber, Mad About Men, Court Jester, Josephine and Men, Loser Takes All, Day They Gave Babies Away, Another Time Another Place, Shake Hands with the Devil, The Sundowners, The Spider's Web, The Chapman Report, Mary Poppins, Dear Brigette, Don't Just Stand There, Lock Up Your Daughters, Zelly and Me, Nuckie.

TELEVISION: Series: Glynis, Coming of Age. Episodes of: Dr. Kildare, Roaring Twenties, Naked City, The Defenders, Danny Kaye Show. Also: Noel Coward's Star Quality, Mrs. Amworth, All You Need Is Love, Across a Crowded Room, Little Gloria, . . . Happy at Last, Skagg.

JOHNSON, ARTE: Actor. b. Chicago, IL, Jan. 20, 1934. Gained fame on Rowan and Martin's Laugh-In.

PICTURES: Miracle in the Rain, The Subterraneans, The

Third Day, The President's Analyst, Love at First Bite, A Night at the Magic Castle, Tax Season.
TELEVISION: Alice in Wonderland, Bud and Lou, Condominium.

JOHNSON, BEN: Actor. b. Pawhuska, OK, June 13, 1918, Stunt rider & performer in rodeos, touring country; did stunt work in War Party; m.p. debut in Mighty Joe Young.
PICTURES: Three Godfathers, She Wore a Yellow Ribbon, Wagonmaster, Rio Grande, Wild Stallion, Fort Defiance, Shane, Rebel in Town, The Wild Bunch, The Undefeated, Chisum, The Last Picture Show, (Academy Award, best supporting actor, 1971), Junior Bonner, The Getaway, Dillinger, The Train Robbers, Kid Blue, The Sugarland Express, Bite The Bullet, Hustle, The Town That Dreaded Sundown, The Greatest, Grayeagle, The Swarm, The Hunter, Terror Train, Tex, Champions, Let's Get Harry, Dark Before Dawn, Cherry 2000, Back to Back, Home Grown.
TELEVISION: Blood Sport, Dream West, Locusts, The Shadow Riders, Red Pony, The Sacketts, Wild Horses, Wild Times, Stranger on My Land.

JOHNSON, DON: Actor. b. Flatt Creek, MO, Dec. 15, 1950. m. actress Melanie Griffith. Worked at ATC, San Francisco. On stage there in Your Own Thing in L.A. in Fortune and Men's Eyes. Recording: Heartbeat (1986).
PICTURES: The Magic Garden of Stanley Sweetheart (debut, 1970), The Harrad Experiment, A Boy and His Dog, Zachariah, Return to Macon County, Soggy Bottom, USA, Cease Fire, Sweet Hearts Dance, Dead-Bang, Centrifuge.
TELEVISION: Miami Vice (series). Mini-series: The Rebels, From Here to Eternity—The War Years, Beulah Land, The Long Hot Summer. Movies: First You Cry, Ski Lift to Death, Katie: Portrait of a Centerfold, Revenge of the Stepford Wives, Amateur Night at the Dixie Bar and Grill, Elvis and the Beauty Queen, The Two Lives of Carol Letner. Special: Don Johnson's Heartbeat (music video, also exec. prod.).

JOHNSON, G. GRIFFITH: Executive. b. New York, NY, Aug. 15, 1912. e. Harvard U., 1934, A.M. 1936, Ph.D. 1938. U.S. Treasury Dept. 1936–39; Dept. of Comm., 1939–40; O.P.A. & predecessor agencies, 1940–46; consulting economist, 1946–47; dir., Econ. Stab. Div., Nat'l. Security Resources Bd., 1948–49; chief econ., U.S. Bur. of Budget, 1949–50; econ. advisor to Econ. Stab. Admin. 1950–52; Exec. v.p. MPEAA, 1965, MPAA, 1971; Asst. Sec'y of State for Economic Affairs, 1962–65; v.p. MPAA, 1953–62; Author of several books & articles.

JOHNSON, J. BOND: Producer, Executive. b. Fort Worth, TX, June 18, 1926. e. Texas Wesleyan Coll., B.S., 1947; Texas Christian U., M.Ed., 1948; Southern Methodist U., B.D., 1952; U. of Southern California, Ph.D., 1967. Army Air Forces, W.W.II; public information officer, captain, U.S. Marine Corps. Korean War. Formerly member Marine Corps Reserve, Motion Picture Production Unit, Hollywood. Now Colonel, U.S. Army Reserve. Newspaper reporter, Fort Worth Star-Telegram, 1942–48; pres., West Coast News Service, 1960; pres., exec. prod., Bonjo Prods., Inc., 1960, President, chief executive officer, Cine-Media International, 1975 managing partner, Capra-Johnson Productions, Ltd., 1978.
PICTURES: Sands of Iwo Jima, Retreat Hell, Flying Leathernecks; photographed aerial portions, Jamboree 53, Norfleet, Devil at My Heels, Kingdom of the Spiders, Ordeal at Donner Pass, Place of the Dawn, Lies I Told Myself, Backstretch, Airs Above The Ground, The Jerusalem Concert, The Berkshire Terror, The Seventh Gate.
TELEVISION: Series: Creator, story consultant, tech. advisor, Whirlpool. Exec. producer, creator: On The Go (TV News-Sports), Coasties, Desert Rangers. Producer: Fandango.

JOHNSON, LAMONT: Director, Producer, Actor. b. Stockton, CA, Sept. 30, 1922. e. UCLA.
TELEVISION: The Defenders, Profiles in Courage, Twilight Zone, That Certain Summer, My Sweet Charlie, The Execution of Pvt. Slovik, Fear on Trial, Ernie Kovacs: Between the Laughter, Wallenberg: A Hero's Story (co-prod., dir.), Unnatural Causes, Gore Vidal's Lincoln, The Kennedys of Massachusetts.
PLAYS: The Egg, Yes is For a Very Young Man; dir., two operas, L.A. Philharmonic, 1964; founder, dir., UCLA Professional Theatre Group.
PICTURES: Thin Ice, Covenant With Death, McKenzie Break, A Gunfight, The Groundstar Conspiracy, You'll Like My Mother, The Last American Hero, Lipstick, One on One, Somebody Killed Her Husband, Sunny Side, Foxes, Cattle Annie and Little Britches, Spacehunter.

JOHNSON, LAURIE: Music Composer, Director. b. 1927. Studied Royal Coll. of Music.
STAGE: Lock Up Your Daughters, Pieces of Eight, The Four Musketeers.
PICTURES: Good Companions, Moonraker, Girls at Sea, Operation Bullshine, Tiger Bay, I Aim at the Stars, Spare The Road, What a Whopper, Bitter Harvest, Seige of the Saxons, Dr. Strangelove, The First Men in the Moon, Beauty Jungle, East of Sudan, Hot Millions, And Soon the Darkness, Mister Jerico, Cause for Alarm, The Beltstone Fox, Hedda, It Lives Again.
TELEVISION: All Things Bright and Beautiful, The Lady and the Highwayman (exec. prod., music).

JOHNSON, RICHARD: Actor. b. Essex, England, July 30, 1927. Studied at Royal Acad. of Dramatic Art. First stage appearance Opera House, Manchester, then with John Gielgud's repertory season, 1944. Served in Royal Navy 1945–48. Subsequent stage appearances incl. The Madwoman of Chaillot, The Lark. Visited Moscow with Peter Brook's production of Hamlet. Royal Shakespeare Thea.: Stratford, London, 1957–62. Royal Shakespeare Co. 1972–73. National Theatre, 1976–77. Founded United British Artists, 1983.
PICTURES: The Haunting, 80,000 Suspects, Moll Flanders, Operation Crossbow, Khartoum, La Strega in Amore, Deadlier than the Male, The Rover, Danger Route, Twist of Sand, Oedipus the King, Trajan's Column, Lady Hamilton, Some Girls Do, Julius Caesar, The Deserters, The Beloved, Hennessy, Aces High, The Four Feathers, Turtle Diary. Producer: Turtle Diary, Castaway, The Lonely Passion of Judith Hearne.
TELEVISION: (U.S.): The Flame is Love, Haywire, The Four Feathers, Portrait of a Rebel: Margaret Sanger, A Man For All Seasons.

JOHNSON, RUSSELL: Actor. b. Ashley, PA, 1924. e. Girard Coll, Actors Laboratory, L.A. W.W.II, Army Air Corps.
PICTURES: A Town of the 80's, Stand at Apache Landing, A Distant Trumpet, Ma & Pa Kettle at Waikiki, Rogue Cop, Loan Shark, Seminole, Tumbleweed, Blue Movies, It Came From Outer Space, Many Rivers to Cross, Law and Order, Black Tuesday, For Men Only, The Greatest Story Ever Told, MacArthur.
TELEVISION: Black Saddle (series), Mobile One (series), The Great Adventure (narrator), Jane Powell Show, Climax, You Are There, Rawhide, Twilight Zone, Gilligan's Island (series), Vanished, Harry Truman Biography, Truman vs. MacArthur.

JOHNSON, VAN: Actor. b. Newport, RI, Aug. 25, 1916. Began in vaudeville; then on N.Y. stage New Faces of 1937, Eight Men of Manhattan, Too Many Girls, Pal Joey. Film debut in Too Many Girls (1940). Voted one of the top ten Money Making Stars in Motion Picture Herald-Fame Poll 1945–46. Stage includes The Music Man (London), La Cage aux Folles (NY) and numerous tours.
PICTURES: Murder in Big House, War Against Mrs. Hadley, Dr. Gillespie's New Assistant, Pilot No. 5, Dr. Gillespies's Criminal Case, Guy Named Joe, Three Men in White, Two Girls and a Sailor, Thirty Seconds Over Tokyo, Ziegfeld Follies, Between Two Women, Thrill of Romance, Week-End at the Waldorf, Romance of Rosy Ridge, Bride Goes Wild, State of the Union, Command Decision, In the Good Old Summertime, Scene of the Crime, Battleground, Big Hangover, Three Guys Named Mike, Grounds for Marriage, Go For Broke, Too Young to Kiss, It's a Big Country, Invitation, When in Rome, Washington Story, Plymouth Adventure, Confidentially Connie, Remains to Be Seen, Easy to Love, Caine Mutiny, Siege at Red River, Men of the Fighting Lady, Brigadoon, Last Time I Saw Paris, End of the Affair, Bottom of the Bottle, Miracle in the Rain, 23 Paces to Baker Street, Slander, Kelly and Me, The Lost Blitzkreig, Beyond This Place, Subway in the Sky, Web of Evidence, Enemy General, Wives and Lovers, Where Angels Go . . . Trouble Follows, Eagles Over London, The Purple Rose of Cairo, Killer Crocodile, Taxi Killer.
TELEVISION: Black Beauty; Pied Piper of Hamelin; Rich Man, Poor Man; Call Her Mom; Doomsday Flight; San Francisco International Superdome; Murder She Wrote.

JOHNSTON, MARGARET: Actress. e. Sydney U., Australia. London stage debut: Murder Without Crime. Screen debut: Rake's Progress, 1945.
TELEVISION: Always Juliet, Taming of the Shrew, Man with a Load of Mischief, Light of Heart, Autumn Crocus, Androcles and the Lion, Sulky Five, Windmill Near a Frontier, The Shrike, The Out of Towners, Looking for Garrow, The Typewriter, The Glass Menagerie, That's Where the Town's Going, The Vortex.
PICTURES: A Man about the House, Portrait of Clare, The Magic Box, Knave of Hearts, Touch and Go, Night of the Eagle, The Nose on My Face, Life at the Top, Schizo, Mr. Sebastian.
THEATRE: Ring of Truth, The Masterpiece, Lady Macbeth, Merchant of Venice, Measure for Measure, Othello.

JOHNSTONE, DAVID: b. Kilmarnock, Scotland, July 4, 1926. o. Ayr Acad. Journalist: Ayrshire Post; Glasgow Herald. Night News Editor, Scottish Daily Mail; Scottish Correspondent, News Chronicle. Joined Scottish Television May, 1958 as News Editor. Later producer, director. Originated daily magazine, Here and Now. Producer ITV World Cup (part) 1976.

Head of News, Current Affairs, Documentaries and Sport. Assistant controller of programmes; controller (now director) of programmes, 1977.

JOLLEY, STAN: Producer, Director, Production Designer, Art Director. b. New York, NY, May 17, 1926. e. U. of Southern California, col. of architecture. Son of actor I. Stanford Jolley. In Navy in W.W.II. Has acted in capacities listed for many feature films and TV series. Nominated for AA, Witness.
PICTURES: Producer and Production Designer: Knife For the Ladies. Assoc. Producer and Prod. Designer, The Good Guys and the Bad Guys; assoc. prod. & prod. designer, Jessie; Director: Today's FBI, Macgyver; 2nd Unit director, Superman. Production Designer: The Good Mother, Witness, Taps, Caddyshack, Cattle Annie and Little Britches, Americathon (also second unit director), Swarm, Drum, Framed, Dion Brothers, Mixed Company, Walking Tall, Terror in the Wax Museum, Night of the Lepus (also second unit director), War Between Men and Women, Law Man, The Phynx. Art Director: Young Billy Young, Ride Beyond Vengeance, Broken Saber, The Restless Ones, Mail Order Bride, Toby Tyler, Nine Lives of Elfego Baca. Assoc. producer & prod. designer & 2nd unit director, Happily Ever After.
TELEVISION FEATURES: 2nd Unit Director and Production Designer: Swiss Family Robinson, Adventures of the Queen, Woman Hunter, Production Designer: Abduction of Carrie Swenson, Eagle One, No Man's Land, Last of the Great Survivors, Like Normal People, Rescue From Gilligan's Island, Flood, Voyage of the Yes, The Stranger, Punch & Jody, City Beneath the Sea, Women of San Quentin, Mini-series: Howard, the Amazing Mr. Hughes.
TELEVISION SERIES: Art Director: Walt Disney Presents, Pete and Gladys, Gunsmoke, Mr. Ed., Branded, Voyage to the Bottom of the Sea, Land of the Giants, O'Hara, etc. Production Designer: Walking Tall, Today's F.B.I., For Love and Honor, Macgyver. Pilots: 8, including Get Smart. Docudrama: Under Fire. Cartoon: Disney's Donald in Mathmagic Land.

JONES, AMY HOLDEN: Director, Writer. b. Philadelphia, PA, Sept. 17, 1953. m. cinematographer, Michael Chapman. e. Wellesley Coll., B.A., 1974; film and photography courses, Massachusetts Inst. of Technology. Winner, first place, Washington National Student Film Festival, 1973.
PICTURES: Editor: Hollywood Boulevard (debut, 1976), American Boy, Corvette Summer, Second Hand Hearts; Director: Slumber Party Massacre, Love Letters (dir., s.p.), Mystic Pizza (s.p. only), Maid to Order (dir., co-s.p.), It Had to Be Steve (dir., co-s.p.).

JONES, CHUCK: Prod., Dir., Writer, Animator. b. Spokane, WA, Sept. 21, 1912. e. Chouinard Art Inst. Dir., Warner Bros. Animation until 1962 where he created and directed Roadrunner & Coyote, Pepe le Pew; directed and helped create Bugs Bunny, Porky Pig, Daffy Duck etc. Created Snafu character, U.S. Armed Service. Co-prod., wrote, dir., Bugs Bunny Show, ABC-TV. Headed MGM Animation Dept. dir. How the Grinch Stole Christmas, Horton Hears a Who, The Dot and the Line, Pogo, The Phantom Tollbooth. Lecturer and teacher at many universities. Currently independent, Chuck Jones Enterprises, Producer, Director, Writer (for ABC-TV) The Cricket in Times Square; A Very Merry Cricket; Yankee Doodle Cricket and (for CBS-TV) Rudyard Kipling's Rikki-Tikki-Tavi; The White Seal; Mowgli's Brothers, Saint-Saens' The Carnival of the Animals, Ogden Nash lyrics, with Daffy Duck & Bugs Bunny; A Connecticut Rabbit in King Arthur's Court, based on Mark Twain's original story, with Bugs Bunny, Daffy Duck, Porky Pig, Elmer Fudd, etc., two specials featuring Raggedy Ann and Andy in The Great Santa Claus Caper and The Pumpkin Who Couldn't Smile; plus a feature compilation of past work: Chuck Jones' Bugs Bunny/Road Runner Movie. Most recently: Daffy Duck's Thanks-for-Giving Special and Bugs Bunny's Bustin' Out All Over.
AWARDS: Recipient Academy Award for best animated cartoons for Scenti-Mental Reasons, 1950, The Dot and The Line, 1965; best documentary short subject for So Much for So Little, 1950. Honored with retrospectives at Deauville Film Festival, 1978, British Film Inst., 1979. N.Y. Film Festival, 1982; Telluride Film Festival, 1976. N.Y. Museum of Modern Art, 1985, 25 gallery exhibition of cartoon art and unique art, 1983–84–85. Cartoon and other art displayed in gallery exhibitions throughout U.S., 1983–84. Honored at Cambridge Film Festival, 1985; received Great Director Award, U.S.A. Film Festival, 1986; received best animation award from National Society of Cartoonists, 1986, 1987 & 1988; appeared for Children's Hospital Telethon New Orleans, 1985–88; Children's Hospital Benefit St. Louis, 1985; Lecturer Emeritus, U. of California, San Diego, 1986; Children's book William the Backwards Skunk, 1986 by Crown Publ. Autobiography WW Norton Publishers, lifetime Achievement Awards from Zagreb Film Festival (1988), Chicago Film Festival (1987), Houston Film Fest. (1988).

JONES, CHUCK: Public Relations Executive. b. Detroit, MI, Dec. 6. e. Michigan State U., B.A., advertising. U.S. Marine Corps 1964–66. Staff writer, Pacific Stars & Stripes, Tokyo, Japan and DaNang, Vietnam. Contributing editor, Leatherneck Magazine, Naval Aviation News, Navy Times. Entered motion picture industry 1969. Critic/writer Motion Picture Daily, 1969. Publicist, Harold Rand & Co., Public Relations, 1970–71. Publicist, American International Pictures, 1971. Radio/TV, newspaper, magazine & syndicate contact, United Artists Corp., 1972–73. Established Chuck Jones Public Relations in 1973 and has been pres. since then. Had stint as eastern adv./pub. dir., Embassy Pictures, 1981–82.

JONES, CLARK R.: Producer, Director. b. Clearfield, PA, April 10, 1920. e. Northwestern U.
TELEVISION SHOWS: The Tony Awards, Peter Pan, Sleeping Beauty Ballet, Ford 50th Anniversary Show, Caesar's Hour, Your Hit Parade, Jack and the Beanstalk; Romeo & Juliet, Perry Como, Bell Telephone Hour, Carol Burnett series; Carol Channing and Pearl Bailey on Broadway, Tony Awards, 6 Rms Riv Vu, Twigs, CBS 50th Anniversary, Emmies, Miss U.S.A., Miss Universe.

JONES, DAVID: Director, Producer. b. Poole, Eng., Feb. 19, 1934. e. Christ's Coll., Cambridge U., B.A., 1954, M.A., 1957. Immigrated to U.S. in 1979. Artistic controller, then assoc. dir., Royal Shakespeare Co., 1964–75; artistic dir, RSC at Aldwych Theatre 1975–78; artistic dir, Brooklyn Acad. of Music Theatre Co., NY 1979–81; prof. Yale Sch. of Drama, 1981.
THEATER: Sweet Agonistes (debut, 1961); U.S.: Summerfolk, Loves Labour's Lost.
PICTURES: Betrayal, Jacknife.
TELEVISION: Prod.: Monitor 1958–64 (BBC series); Play of the Month (prod.); dir.: Shakespeare series, BBC 1982–83; prod. The Beaux' Stratagem, Langarishe Go Down; Ice Age, Dir.: The Christmas Wife.

JONES, DEAN: Actor. b. Morgan County, AL, Jan. 25, 1936. e. Asbury Coll., Wilmore, KY. Prof. debut as blues singer, New Orleans; U.S. Navy, 1953.
STAGE: There Was a Little Girl, Company, Into the Light.
PICTURES: Handle with Care, Never So Few, Under the Yum-Yum Tree, The New Interns, That Darn Cat, Two on a Guillotine, The Ugly Daschshund, Monkeys, Go Home, Blackbeard's Ghost, The Love Bug, The $1,000,000 Duck, Snowball Express, Mr. Super Invisible, The Shaggy D.A., Herbie Goes to Monte Carlo, Born Again, Friend to Friend.
TELEVISION: Series: Ensign O'Toole, The Teddy Bears.

JONES, GEMMA: Actress. b. London, Eng., Dec. 4, 1942. e. Royal Acad. of Dramatic Art.
THEATER: Baal; Alfie; The Cavern; The Pastime of M Robert; Portrait of a Queen; Next of Kin; The Marriage of Figaro; And A Nightingale; Breaking the Silence.
PICTURES: The Devils; Paperhouse; On the Black Hill.
TELEVISION: The Lie; The Way of the World; The Merchant of Venice; The Duchess of Duke Street (series), The Jim Henson Hour.

JONES, GRACE: Singer, Actress. b. Spanishtown, Jamaica, May 19, 1952. e. Syracuse U. Modelled and appeared in several Italian pictures before career as singer.
PICTURES: Conan the Destroyer, A View to a Kill, Siesta.

JONES, GRIFFITH: Actor. b. London, England, 1910. e. University College, London; Royal Acad. of Dramatic Art (gold medal 1932). In H.M. Forces, W.W.II. Stage debut, London, 1930, in Carpet Slippers; N.Y. debut 1935 in Escape Me Never. Many stage successes. In many Brit. pictures from 1932.
PICTURES: Escape Me Never, The Faithful Heart, Catherine the Great, The Mill on the Floss, A Yank at Oxford, Four Just Men, Atlantic Ferry, This Was Paris, The Day Will Dawn, Uncensored, Henry V. Rake's Progress, Wicked Lady, They Made Me a Fugitive, Good Time Girl, Miranda, Look Before You Love, Once Upon a Dream, Honeymoon Deferred, Star of My Night, Scarlet Web, The Sea Shall Not Have Them, Face in the Night, Wanted on Voyage, The High Wall, Hidden Homicide, Strangler's Web, Decline and Fall.
PLAYS: The Moonraker, Quadrille, Alice Thro' the Looking Glass, Love Machine, Dead on Nine, The Entertainer, Expresso, The Sound of Murder, Treasure Island, Two Accounts Rendered, The Cavern, The Doctor's Dilemma, Jockey Club Stakes. 1973, Nottingham P'House, 1974 Crucible, Sheffield. Member of Royal Shakespeare Co. 1975–80, 1981–86.
TELEVISION: The Breaking Point, The Ware Case, When in Rome, A Moment in the Sun, Hell Hath No Fury, Margret, No Hiding Place, The Collection, By Invitation Only, A Woman of No Importance, Freedom in September, Blythe Spirit, Treasure Island, The Three Sisters, Emergency Ward, Vendetta, The Cabinet Papers, Man in a Suitcase, Boy Meets Girl, Troubleshooters, Strange Report, Avengers, Inside Man, A Matter of Principle, Doom Watch, Warm Feet, Warm Heart, Paul Temple, The Persuaders, The Lotus Eaters, The Black Arrow, Arrow, Spy Trap, Crown Court, Fallen Eagles, The Apple Cart, Comedy of Errors, Macbeth, The Three Sisters, Nicholas Nickleby.

JONES, HENRY: Actor. b. Philadelphia, PA, Aug. 1, 1912. e. St. Joseph's Coll. On stage in Hamlet, Henry IV, Time of Your Life, My Sister Eileen, The Solid Gold Cadillac, Bad Seed, Sunrise at Campobello (Tony Award, 1958), Advise and Consent.
PICTURES: This is the Army, Lady Says No, Taxi, The Bad Seed, The Girl He Left Behind, The Girl Can't Help It, Will Success Spoil Rock Hunter?, 3:10 to Yuma, Vertigo, Cash McCall, The Bramble Bush, Never Too Late, The Champagne Murders, Stay Away Joe, Project X, Support Your Local Sheriff, Rascal, Angel in My Pocket, Butch Cassidy and the Sundance Kid, Rabbit Run, Dirty Dingus Magee, Skin Game, Napoleon and Samantha, Tom Sawyer, Pete 'n' Tillie, The Outfit, Nine to Five, Death Trap, Balboa, Caddo Lake, Nowhere to Run.
TELEVISION: Series: Honestly, Celeste! (1954), Channing, Lost in Space, The Girl With Something Extra, We'll Get By. Phyllis, Kate Loves a Mystery, B.J. and the Bear, Gun Shy, Code Name: Foxfire, Falcon Crest. I Married Dora. Movies: The Crucible, Something for a Lonely Man, The Movie Murderer, Love, Hate, Love, Who is the Black Dahlia?, Tall Gunner Joe, California Gold Rush, The Leftovers.

JONES, JAMES EARL: Actor. b. Arkabutla, MS, Jan. 17, 1931. e. U. of Michigan. Son of actor Robert Earl Jones. Awarded Hon. Doctor of Fine Arts (Yale, Princeton); Medal for Spoken Language (Amer. Acad. and Inst. of Arts and Letter; Hon. Doctor of Humane Letters (Columbia Coll. & U. of Mich.).
THEATER: The Cool World, Othello, Paul Robeson, Les Blancs, The Great White Hope (Tony Award, 1969), The Iceman Cometh, Of Mice and Men, A Lesson from Aloes, Master Harold . . . and the Boys, Fences (Tony Award, 1986).
PICTURES: Dr. Strangelove, The Comedians, The End of the Road, The Great White Hope, The Man, Claudine, The Swashbuckler, The Bingo Long Travelling All-Stars and Motor Kings, The Greatest, The Last Remake of Beau Geste, A Piece of the Action, The Bushido Blade, Conan the Barbarian, Soul Man, Alan Quartermain and the Lost City of Gold, Gardens of Stone, My Little Girl, Matewan, Coming to America, Three Fugitives, Field of Dreams, Convicts, Best of the Best, The Hunt for Red October, Into Thin Air.
TELEVISION: Movies: The UFO Incident, Jesus of Nazareth, The Greatest Thing That Almost Happened, Roots: The Next Generations, Guyana Tragedy—The Story of Jim Jones, Golden Moment: An Olympic Love Story, Philby, Burgess and MacLean, The Atlanta Child Murders, The Vegas Strip War, King Lear, Soldier Boy, Mathnet, Bailey's Bridge, Third and Oak: The Pool Hall.

JONES, JEFFREY: Actor. b. Buffalo, NY, Sept. 28. e. Lawrence U., Wisconsin. While pre-med student, performed in 1967 prod. of Hobson's Choice and was invited by Sir Tyrone Guthrie to join Guthrie Theatre in Minneapolis. After short time in South America, studied on full scholarship at London Acad. of Music and Dramatic Arts before joining Stratford Theater in Ontario. 1973–74 worked with Vancouver touring children's theater co. Playhouse Holiday. Move to N.Y. where performed on stage.
THEATER: The Elephant Man (Bdwy debut), Trelawney of the Wells, Secret Service, Boy Meets Girl, Cloud Nine, Comedy of Errors, The Tempest.
PICTURES: The Revolutionary, Underground (debut, 1976), A Wedding, The Soldier, Easy Money, Amadeus, Transylvania 6-5000, Ferris Bueller's Day Off, Howard the Duck, The Hanoi Hilton, Beetlejuice, Without a Clue, Who Is Harry Crumb?, Valmont, The Hunt for Red October, Enid is Sleeping.
TELEVISION: Mini-series: George Washington: The Forging of a Nation. Movies: Kenny Rogers as "The Gambler" III—The Legend Continues, Fresno. Guest: Amazing Stories, Twilight Zone, Remington Steele, The People Next Door (series).

JONES, JENNIFER: Actress. r.n. Phyllis Isley. b. Tulsa, OK, Mar. 21, 1919. e. Northwestern U., American Acad. of Dramatic Arts. Daughter of Phil R., Flora Mae (Suber) Isley, exhib. m. industrialist Norton Simon. Toured with parents stock company as child; in summer stock in East; little theat. East & West. Began screen career (as Phyllis Isley) in several Republic Westerns, first major role The Song of Bernadette (Acad. Award, 1943). Pres., Norton Simon Museum.
PICTURES: Since You Went Away, Love Letters, Duel in the Sun, Cluny Brown, Portrait of Jennie, We Were Strangers, Madame Bovary, Carrie, Wild Heart, Ruby Gentry, Indiscretion of an American Wife, Beat the Devil, Love Is a Many-Splendored Thing, Good Morning Miss Dove, Man in the Gray Flannel Suit, Barretts of Wimpole Street, Farewell to Arms, Tender Is the Night, The Idol, Angel, Down We Go, The Towering Inferno.

JONES, KATHY: Executive. Began career as acct. exec. for m.p. clients, Stan Levinson assoc., Dallas. Joined Paramount Pictures in 1977 as sr. publicist in field marketing then exec. dir., field mktg. Left to join Time-Life Films as v.p., domestic mktg., for m.p. div. Returned to Paramount 1981 as v.p., domestic pub. & promo. 1984, appt. sr. v.p., domestic pub. & promo. for Motion Picture Group, Paramount. Formed m.p. consultancy with Buffy Shutt. 1989, appt. exec. v.p., marketing, Columbia Pictures.

JONES, QUINCY: Composer, Arranger, Producer. b. Chicago, IL, March 14, 1933. e. Seattle U., Berlee Sch. Music, Boston Conservatory, Trumpeter and arranger for Lionel Hampton's orch. 1950–53, played with Dizzy Gillespie, Count Basie and arranged for orchs. singers-Ray Anthony, Count Basie, Sarah Vaughn, Peggy Lee, Lesley Gore Also music dir. Bachlay Disques, Paris and led own orch. for European tours, concerts, TV and recordings, 1960; music dir. Mercury Records 1961; v.p. 1964 before scoring films.
PICTURES: In the Heat of the Night, In Cold Blood, (Acad. Award nom.), The Pawnbroker, Mirage, The Slender Thread, Made in Paris, Walk, Don't Run, Banning, The Deadly Affair, Enter Laughing, A Dandy in Aspic, The Counterfeit Killer, For Love of Ivy, The Split, Bob & Carol & Ted & Alice, The Lost Man, Cactus Flower, John and Mary, The Last of the Mobile Hotshots, The Out-of-Towners, They Call Me Mister Tibbs, Brother John, Dollars, The Anderson Tapes, The Hot Rock, The New Centurions, The Getaway, The Color Purple (also co-prod.), Stalingrad (exec. prod.).
TELEVISION: Roots (Emmy, 1977).

JONES, SAM J.: Actor. b. Chicago, IL, Aug. 12, 1954.
PICTURES: "10," Flash Gordon, My Chauffeur, Silent Assassins, White Fire, One Man Force, Under the Gun, Driving Forces.
TELEVISION: Stunts Unlimited, Code Red (series), No Man's Land, The Highwayman.

JONES, SHIRLEY: Actress. b. Smithton, PA, March 31, 1934. m. actor-prod. Marty Ingels. Former Miss Pittsburgh. Natl. chair, Leukemia Foundation.
THEATRE: Appeared with Pittsburgh Civic Light Opera in Lady in the Dark, Call Me Madam. Broadway: South Pacific, Me and Juliet, Maggie Flynn.
PICTURES: Oklahoma, Carousel, Bobbikins, April Love, Never Steal Anything Small, Elmer Gantry (Acad. Award, supp., 1960), Pepe, Two Rode Together, The Music Man, A Ticklish Affair, The Secret of My Success, Fluffy, The Happy Ending, The Cheyanne Social Club, Beyond the Posiedon Adventure, Tank.
TELEVISION: Movies: Silent Night, Lonely Night, The Girls of Huntington House, The Family Nobody Wanted, Winner Take All, Yesterday's Child, Who'll Save the Children, A Last Cry For Help, Children of An Lac, Intimates: A Love Story, There Were Times Dear, Widow. Series: The Partridge Family, Shirley, The Slap Maxwell Story.

JONES, TERRY: Writer, Actor. b. Wales, 1942. Worked with various rep. groups before joining BBC script dept. Member of Monty Python's Flying Circus.
PICTURES: And Now for Something Completely Different; Monty Python and the Holy Grail (and co-dir.); Monty Python's Life of Brian (also dir.); Monty Python's The Meaning of Life (dir., music), Labyrinth (s.p.), Erik the Viking (actor, dir., s.p.).
TELEVISION: Late Night Lineup; The Late Show; A Series of Birds; Do Not Adjust Your Set; The Complete and Utter History of Britain; Monty Python's Flying Circus, Secrets.

JONES, TOMMY LEE: Actor. b. San Saba, TX, Sept. 15, 1946. Worked in oil fields; studied acting at Harvard, where earned a degree in English. Broadway debut in A Patriot for Me; appeared in Four in a Garden, Ulysses in Nighttown, Fortune and Men's Eyes. Film debut in Love Story, 1970.
PICTURES: Eliza's Horoscope, Jackson County Jail, Rolling Thunder, The Betsy, Eyes of Laura Mars, Coal Miner's Daughter, Back Roads, Nate and Hayes, River Rat, Black Moon Rising, The Big Town, Stormy Monday, The Package.
TELEVISION: The Amazing Howard Hughes, The Executioner's Song (Emmy), The Rainmaker, Cat on a Hot Tin Roof, Broken Vows, The Park is Mine; Yuri Nosenko: KGB; Gotham, Stranger on My Land; April Morning, Lonesome Dove.

JORDAN, GLENN: Producer, Director. b. San Antonio, TX, April 5, 1936. e. Harvard, B.A.; Yale Drama Sch. Directed plays off-Bdwy. and on tour.
PICTURES: Director: Only When I Laugh; The Buddy System; Mass Appeal.
TELEVISION: *Director:* Hogan's Goat; Paradise Lost; Benjamin Franklin (Emmy); Family; In the Matter of Karen Ann Quinlan; Sunshine Christmas; Delta County; The Women's Room (also prod.); Lois Gibbs and the Love Canal; Heartsounds, Eccentricities of a Nightingale, Dress Grey, Promise, Echoes in the Darkness (prod., dir.), Jesse (prod., dir.), Home Fires Burning (prod. dir.).

JORDAN, HENRIETTA: Executive. b. New York, NY, Feb. 26. Ent. m.p. ind. as ass't to exec. v.p., UPA Pictures, 1950; v.p. in charge of sales, Format Prods, Inc. v.p. and assoc. prod., 1962–71. Assoc. prod. Levitow-Hanson Films, Inc., 1972–74;

Producer, Image West, Ltd., 1975–84; dir. sls., Cause & EFX, 1984–85; dir. sls., Modern Videofilm Graphics, 1986–88; Personal Communications, Hank Jordan Enterprises, 1988–.

JORDAN, NEIL: Director, Writer. b. Sligo, Ireland, Feb. 25, 1950. e. University Coll, Dublin, B.A., 1972. Entered industry when hired by John Boorman as script consultant on Excalibur. Also made doc. on making of that film. Novels: The Past, Night in Tunisia, Dream of a Beast.
PICTURES: Dir.-s.p.: Traveller (writer only), Angel, The Company of Wolves, Mona Lisa, High Spirits, The Courier (co-exec. prod. only), We're No Angels.
TELEVISION: Mr. Solomon Wept (BBC), RTE (Ireland), Seduction, Tree, Miracles and Miss Langan.

JORDAN, RICHARD: Actor. b. New York, NY, July 19, 1938. e. Harvard U.
PICTURES: Ready for the People, Valdez is Coming, Lawman, Chato's Land, Trial of the Catonsville Nine, Kamouraska, The Friends of Eddie Coyle, Rooster Cogburn, The Yakuza, Logan's Run, One Night Stand, Old Boyfriends, Interiors, Raise the Titanic, A Flash of Green (also prod.), Dune, The Mean Season, The Secret of My Success, The Men's Club, Solarbabies, Romero.
TELEVISION: Mini-series: Captains and the Kings, The French Atlantic Affair. Movies: The Defection of Simas Kudirka, Les Miserables, The Bunker, Washington Mistress, The Murder of Mary Phagan.

JOSEPH, KENNETH. Executive. b. New York, NY, July 15, 1922. e. Syracuse U. Entered industry as announcer and program director of various N.Y. radio stations, including WNYC, 1946–53; exec. in various capacities of United Artists Television and predecessor companies, 1953–68; exec. v.p., syndication, Four Star Entertainment Corp., 1968–70; exec. v.p., world-wide syndication, Metromedia Producers Corp., 1970 to present.

JOSEPHSON, ERLAND: Actor, Director, Writer. b. Stockholm, Sweden, June 15, 1923. Acted in over 100 plays in Sweden. Joined Sweden's Royal Dramatic Theatre in 1956 replacing Ingmar Bergman as head of the theater, 1966–76. Closely associated with Bergman, with whom he staged plays in his late teens. Co-authored s.p. The Pleasure Garden and Now About These Women. Also has pub. poetry, six novels, and scripts for stage, screen and radio. American stage debut: The Cherry Orchard, 1988.
PICTURES: It Rains on Our Love, To Joy, Brink of Life, The Magician; Hour of the Wolf; The Passion of Anna; Cries and Whispers; Scenes from a Marriage; Face to Face; Beyond Good and Evil; I'm Afraid; Autumn Sonata; To Forget Venice; One and One (also dir.); The Marmalade Revolution (also dir., s.p.); Montenegro; Sezona Mira u Parizu; Fanny and Alexander; Bella Donna; Nostalgia; House of the Yellow Carpet; After the Rehearsal; Angela's War; Behind the Shutters; A Case of Irresponsibility; Dirty Story; Amarosa; The Flying Devils; Garibaldi, The General; The Last Mazurka, The Sacrifice; Saving Grace; Unbearable Lightness of Being; Hanussen.

JOSEPHSON, MARVIN: Executive. b. New York, NY, June 5, 1935. e. Long Island U. Started with Liebling-Wood Agency as agent; later with Music Corp. of America, General Artists Corp., Agency for the Performing Arts.

JOSEPHSON, MARVIN: Executive. b. Atlantic City, NJ, March 6, 1927. e. Cornell U., B.A., 1949; L.L.B. NYU, 1952. Lawyer at CBS Television 1952–55; founded Broadcast Management Inc. which became Josephson International Inc. in 1955. Josephson International Inc. is the parent co. of International Creative Management, Inc. and ICM Artists Ltd.

JOSIAH, JR., WALTER J.: Executive. b. New York, NY. e. Fordham U., B.S.:SS, 1955–58: Harvard Law School, LL.B., 1962. U.S. Air Force, 1955–58, First Lt. and Pilot. Associate, Simpson Thacher & Bartlett, 1962–67. Legal staff, Paramount Pictures, 1967–69. Asst. resident counsel, 1969; chief resident counsel, 1970 and v.p. & chief resident counsel, 1971–82. ex.-v.p. & general counsel, Motion Picture Association of America, Inc., 1983.
Professional Associations: Chmn., Committee 307, Authors Rights, 1981–82, Patent, Trademark & Copyright Law Section of the American Bar Assn.; Association of the Bar of the City of NY (Committee on Copyright and Literary Property, 1976–79, 1982–85, chmn. 1986–89): Copyright Society of the U.S.A.—Member of the Board of Trustees commencing June, 1981; v.p., from June 1988; member, Motion Picture Academy of Arts and Sciences; Copyright Office Advisory Committee, 1981–82; National Sculpture Society—advisor to the president; Advisory Board, Publication: Communications and the Law; Member, President's Club Executive Committee and Annual Fund Council, Fordham U.

JOURDAN, LOUIS: Actor, r.n. Louis Gendre. b. Marseille, France, June 19, 1921. Stage actor prior to m.p. On radio as regular on Connie Boswell Presents, 1944. On Bdwy in The Immoralist, Tonight in Samarkand, On a Clear Day You Can See Forever (Boston, previews), 13 Rue de l'Amour.
PICTURES: Le Corsaire (debut, 1940), Her First Affair, La Boheme, L'Arlesienne, La Belle, Adventure, Felicie Nanteuil, The Paradine Case, Letter from an Unkown Woman, No Minor Vices, Madame Bovary, Bird of Paradise, Anne of the Indies, The Happy Time, Three Coins in the Fountain, Decameron Nights, The Swan, Julie, The Bride is Much Too Beautiful, Dangerous Exiles, Gigi, The Best of Everything, Can-Can, Leviathan, Streets of Montmartre, Story of the Count of Monte Cristo, Mathias Sandorf, VIP's, Made in Paris, A Flea in Her Ear, To Commit a Murder, Silver Bears, Double Deal, Octopussy, The Return of the Swamp Thing, Counterforce.
TELEVISION: Series: Paris Precinct (1954–55), Host: Romance Theatre. Mini-series: The French Atlantic Affair, Dracula. Movies: Run a Crooked Mile, Fear No Evil, Ritual of Evil, The Great American Beauty Contest, The Count of Monte Cristo, The Man in the Iron Mask, The First Olympics-Athens, Beverly Hills Madam. Guest: Ford Theatre, The FBI, Name of the Game, Charlie's Angels.

JOY, ROBERT: Actor. b. Montreal, Canada, Aug. 17, 1951. e. Newfoundland U. Rhodes Scholar. Acted in regional and off-Broadway theatre. Off-Bdwy debut The Diary of Anne Frank (1978). Has composed music for stage, radio and film. On board of Canadian Center for Advanced Film Studies.
THEATER: NY Shakespeare Fest. (Found a Peanut, Lenny and the Heartbreakers; The Death of von Richtofen); Life and Limb; Fables for Friends; Welcome to the Moon; What I Did Last Summer; Lydie Breeze; Romeo and Juliet (La Jolla Playhouse, Drama-Logue Award); Hay Fever (Bdwy debut); Big River (premiere); The Nerd.
PICTURES: Atlantic City, Ragtime, Threshold, Ticket to Heaven, Terminal Choice, Amityville 3-D, Desperately Seeking Susan, Joshua Then and Now, Adventure of Faustus Bidgood (also co-prod. music), Big Shots, The Suicide Club, She's Back!, Millenium.
TELEVISION: One Life to Live, The Equalizer, Moonlighting, The Prodigious Hickey, The Return of Hickey, The Beginning of the Firm.

JUDD, EDWARD: Actor. b. Shanghai, 1934. e. Far East. Stage; The Long and the Short and the Tall, The Tinker. Numerous TV appearances.
PICTURES: The Day the Earth Caught Fire, Stolen Hours, The World Ten Times Over, Mystery Submarine, The Long Ships, First Men on the Moon, Strange Bedfellows, Invasion, Island of Terror, The Vengeance of Shee, Shakedown, The Kitchen Toto.

JULIA, RAUL: Actor. b. San Juan, PR, Mar. 9, 1940. e. U. of Puerto Rico; studied for theatre with Wynn Handman. New York stage debut in La Vida Es Sueño, 1964. Film debut in Panic in Needle Park, 1971.
THEATER: The Marriage Proposal (1966); Macduff in Macbeth (first assgn. with NY Shakespeare Fest., 1966); The Ox Cart; Titus Andronicus; No Exit; The Memorandum; Your Own Thing; The Cuban Thing (Bdwy debut); Paradise Gardens East; Conercio Was Here to Stay; City Way; The Castro Complex; Pinkville; Two Gentlemen of Verona; Hamlet (Delacorte Theater); As You Like It; King Lear; The Robber Bridegroom, Via Galactica; Where's Charley; Threepenny Opera (Lincoln Center); Dracula; The Taming of the Shrew; Betrayal; Othello; Nine; The Tempest; Design for Living; Arms and the Man.
PICTURES: The Organization Man, Been Down So Long It Looks Like Up to Me, Panic in Needle Park, Gumball Rally, The Eyes of Laura Mars, Strong Medicine, Tempest, The Escape Artist, One from the Heart, Compromising Positions, Kiss of the Spider Woman, The Morning After, La Gran Fiesta, The Penitent, Moon Over Parador, Trading Hearts, Tequila Sunrise, Tango Bar, Romero, Mack the Knife, Frankenstein Unbound, Presumed Innocent.
TELEVISION: Sesame Street (recurring role), King Lear, The National Health, McCloud, Love of Life, Aces Up. Movies: Death Scream, Florida Straits, Mussolini: The Untold Story, Onassis: The Richest Man in the World.

JUNKIN, RAYMOND: Executive. b. New York, NY, Nov. 4, 1918. e. U. of Alabama, U. of Pennsylvania. Air Force, W.W.II. Eastern sls. mgr., Robert H. Clark Co., southwestern sls. mgr., then ass't to president; v.p., director of sales, Official Films, Inc., 1951–58; self-employed as a film and program consultant, 1959–60; pres. Program Sales Inc.; gen. sls. mgr., Programs For Television, Inc., since 1961; v.p. & gen. mgr., Screen Gems (Canada), Ltd.; v.p. Domestic Sales Mgr. Screen Gems Internat'l; 1967 gen. sls. mgr., Trans-Lux TV Corp., v.p. & gen. sls. mgr., 1968 to date. CTV Television Network Ltd.

JURADO, KATY: Actress. r.n. Maria Christina Jurado Garcia. b. Guadalajara, Mexico, 1927. Numerous Mexican films. Also m.p. columnist for Mexican publications; American m.p. debut in Bullfighter and the Lady (1951).
PICTURES: High Noon, San Antone, Arrowhead, Broken Lance, The Racers, Trial, Trapeze, Man from Del Rio, The

Badlanders, One Eyed Jacks, Barabbas, A Covenant with Death, Pat Garrett and Billy the Kid, Under the Volcano.
TELEVISION: Lady Blues.

JUROW, MARTIN: Producer. b. New York, NY. Dec. 14, 1911. e. William and Mary, Harvard Law Sch. Associated with MCA, William Morris, pres., Famous Artists; prod., G & E Productions; co-prod. with Richard Shepherd Jurow-Shepherd Productions.
PICTURES: The Hanging Tree, The Fugitive Kind, Love in a Goldfish Bowl, Breakfast at Tiffany's, The Great Race, Soldier in the Rain, Terms of Endearment, Sylvester, Pink Panther, Papa Was a Preacher, Waltz Across Texas.

JUSTIN, GEORGE: Executive. Assoc. prod. for Marathon Man and On the Waterfront; prod. exec. on The Goddess and Twelve Angry Men. V.p. & exec. prod. mgr. at Paramount Pictures; four years; left to join Columbia as prod. exec, where was assoc. prod. for The Deep and Prod. exec. on The Eyes of Laura Mars. In April, 1979 joined Orion Pictures; named exec. prod. mgr. Promoted to v.p./exec. prod. mgr. in April, 1980.
PICTURES: Middle of the Night (prod.), Tiger Makes Out (prod.), Rollover (exec. prod.); No Small Affair (exec. prod.)

K

KAEL, PAULINE: Critic. b. June 19, 1919, Sonoma County, CA. e. U. of California, Berkeley, 1936–40, majoring in philosophy. Managed two art theaters in CA for which she wrote program notes. Broadcast weekly about films on Pacifica network. Made experimental shorts. Has written on films for many magazines. Since 1968 movie critic for The New Yorker.
AUTHOR: I Lost it at the Movies, Kiss Kiss Bang Bang, Going Steady, The Citizen Kane Book, Deeper into Movies, Reeling, When the Lights Go Down, 5001 Nights at the Movies, Taking It All In, State of the Art, Hooked.
AWARDS: Guggenheim Fellow, 1964; George Polk Memorial Award for Criticism, 1970; The National Book Award, 1974, for Deeper into Movies; Front Page Award for best magazine column in 1974 from Newswomen's Club of N.Y and for distinguished journalism, 1983.

KAGAN, JEREMY: Director, Writer. b. Mt. Vernon, NY, Dec. 14, 1945. e. Harvard; NYU, MFA; student Amer. Film Inst. 1971. Film animator, 1968; multi-media show designer White House Conf. on Youth and Ed.
PICTURES: Heroes, The Big Fix, The Chosen, (1st prize, Montreal World Film Fest, 1981), The Sting II, The Journey of Natty Gann, (Gold Prize, Moscow Film Fest., 1987), Big Man on Campus.
TELEVISION: Columbo, The Bold Ones, Unwed Father, Judge Dee, My Dad Lives in a Downtown Hotel, Katherine (also s.p.), Scott Joplin, Courage, Conspiracy: The Trial of the Chicago 8 (also s.p., ACE Award, 1988).

KAHN, JUDITH: Executive. Background in mktg., including graphic design, adv./promo. Creative dir. at Intralink Film Graphic Design; art dir. for Seiniger & Associates. 1983, returned to New York as consultant to corporate clients, including cable, TV, and m.p. accts. 1985, joined Paramount Pictures as v.p., creative svcs. of M.P. Group.

KAHN, MADELINE: Actress, Singer. b. Boston, MA., Sept. 29. e. Hofstra U. Broadway bow in New Faces of '68. Trained as opera singer and appeared in La Boheme, Showboat, Two by Two, Candide.
PICTURES: What's Up Doc? (debut), Paper Moon, From the Mixed-Up Files of Mrs. Basil E. Frankweiler, Blazing Saddles, At Long Last Love, Young Frankenstein, The Adventures of Sherlock Holmes' Smarter Brother, Won Ton Ton, High Anxiety, The Cheap Detective, Simon, Happy Birthday, Gemini, Wholly Moses, First Family, History of the World—Part I, Yellowbeard, City Heat, Clue, Benito.
THEATER: Promenade, Two by Two, In the Boom Boom Room, On the Twentieth Century.
TELEVISION: Oh Madeline! (series), Mr. President (series); The Perfect Guy (afterschool special), Celebrating Gershwin: The Jazz Age.

KAHN, MILTON: Publicist. b. Brooklyn, NY, May 3, 1934. e. Syracuse U., Ohio U., B.S.J. 1957. Formed Milton Kahn Associates, Inc. in 1958. Represented: Gregory Peck, Joan Crawford, Steve Allen, Glenn Ford, Herb Alpert, Roger Corman, Robert Aldrich, Larry Cohen, Arthur Hiller, Chuck Norris, Michael Landon, Dean Hargrove, Bill Conti, etc. and New World Pictures (1970–83), Avco-Embassy, Vista Films.

KAHN, RICHARD: Executive. b. New Rochelle. NY, Aug. 29, 1929. e. Wharton Sch. of Finance and Commerce, U. of Pennsylvania, B.S., 1951; U.S. Navy, 3 yrs.; joined Buchanan & Co., 1954; ent. m.p. ind., pressbook writer, Columbia Pictures, 1955; exploitation mgr., 1958; natl. coord. adv. and pub., 1963; natl. dir. of adv., pub. and exploitation, 1968; v.p., 1969; 1974 v.p. in chg. of special marketing projects; 1975; moved to MGM as v.p. in chg. of worldwide advertising, publicity and exploitation; 1978, named sr. v.p. in chg. worldwide mktg. & pres., MGM Intl. 1980, elected bd. of govs, Academy of M.P. Arts & Sciences. 1982, named exec. v.p. of adv., pub., promo. for MGM/UA; 1983, formed the Richard Kahn Co., dist. & mktg. consultancy. Faculty mem. Peter Stark m.p. producing prog., USC Sch. of Cinema & TV. Exec. chmn, Film Industry Council. 1982 elected sect. Acad. of Motion Picture Arts & Sciences; elected pres. 1988.

KALB, MARVIN: TV news reporter. e. City Coll. of New York; Harvard, M.A., 1953, Russian Language Sch., Middlebury Coll. Worked for U.S. State Dept., American Embassy, Moscow; CBS News, 1957; writer, reporter-researcher. Where We Stand: reporter-assignment editor; Moscow Bureau Chief, 1960–63; first dip. corres., Washington Bureau, 1963. Chief diplomatic corr. CBS News and NBC News, moderator Meet the Press; Teacher and lecturer; first dir. Joan Shorenstein Barone Center on the Press, Politics and Public Policy at John F. Kennedy Sch. of Govt. of Harvard U., since June, 1987. Host of PBS series, Candidates '88.
BOOKS: Eastern Exposure, Kissinger, Dragon in the Kremlin, Roots of Involvement, The U.S. in Asia, 1784–1971, Candidates '88 (with Hendrik Hertzberg).

KALISH, EDDIE: Executive. Reporter/reviewer, Variety, 1959–64; sr. publicist, Paramount Pictures, 1964–65; adv./pub./promo dir., Ken Greengras Personal Management, 1965–66; pub. dir., Harold Rand & Co., 1966–67; independent publicist overseas, 1967–75; rejoined Paramount Pictures in 1975 as dir. of intl. mktg.; later named v.p.; 1978, named v.p., worldwide pub. & promo. In 1979 appt. senior v.p., worldwide mktg. In 1980 joined United Artists as v.p.—domestic mktg.; sr. v.p., adv., pub., promo, for MGM/UA 1981–82; became sr. v.p., worldwide mkt., PSO, 1982–1986. Now pres., Kalish/Davidson Marketing, Inc.

KALSER, KONSTANTIN: Executive, b. Munich, Germany, Sept. 4, 1920. e. Switzerland, UCLA. Color photographer, newsreel cameraman, founded Marathon International Prods., Inc., pres., executive producer; Crashing the Water Barrier, 1956 (Acad. Award); Give and Take (Venice Award), The Carmakers, Chris Award. Director, The One for the Road, 1973 Gold Award, Intl. Film & Festival of N.Y. Director, We Did It! 1978 Gold Medal Intl. Film & TV Festival of N.Y.; Production Executive, The Unknown War 1978 Grand Award, Intl. Film & TV Festival of N.Y. 1984, For Years To Come! (dir., s.p.), winner of CINE Golden Eagle.

KAMBER, BERNARD M.: Executive. e. U. of Pennsylvania. New England exploitation rep. U.A. 1940; Army service 1941–43; dir. special events dept. U.A., 1943; asst. to Gradwell L. Sears, nat'l distrib. chmn. 6th War Loan Drive; dir. pub. 7th War Loan Drive, 1943–47; dir. pub. & prom. Eagle Lion Classics, 1951; org. Kamber Org., pub. rel. rep. for ind. prod. v.p. sales, adv. pub. Ivan Tors Prod. Greene-Rouse Prods.; June 1953; exec. asst. Hecht-Hill-Lancaster, chg. of N.Y. off., 1957; v.p. Hecht-Hill-Lancaster Companies, 1958; formed Cinex Distr. Corp., 1962; Pres. Cinex and Posfilm, Inc.; 1967 v.p. in chg. sls. Du Art Film Lab. Inc; 1975 joined Technicolor, Inc.

KAMEY, PAUL: b. New York, NY, Aug. 25, 1912. Worked on newspapers including NY Journal American. Ent. m.p. industry 1938; worked for MGM and 20th Century Fox; during ware, writer, Office of War information; joined Universal, 1949; eastern pub. mgr., Universal Pictures. 1968. Freelance publicist.

KANANACK, ARTHUR: Executive. e. Cornell U., Cornell Law School. Started in industry in business affairs dept., ABC-TV, New York. Moved to London 1963 with Horizon Pictures; 1966 with Creative Management Associates (now ICM); returned to N.Y. 1968 to join UMC Pictures as exec v.p.; then business affairs dept. of 20th Century Fox. 1971–79, v.p., Warner Bros of business affairs intl., London. 1979–82, V.P., business affairs, WB-TV Distribution. 1982, joined ITC Productions as exec. v.p. 1985, named pres., ITC Entertainment. 1987, named president, Viacom Enterprises.

KANE, CAROL: Actress. b. Cleveland, OH, June 18, 1952. e. Professional Children's Sch., NY. Began professional acting career at age 14, touring, then on Bdwy, in The Prime of Miss Jean Brodie. Other stage credits include, The Tempest, The Effect of Gamma Rays on Man-in-the-Moon Marigolds, Are You Now or Have You Ever Been? Arturo Ui, The Enchanted, The Tempest, Macbeth, Tales of the Vienna Woods, Frankie and Johnny in the Claire de Lune.
PICTURES: Carnal Knowledge, Desperate Characters, Wedding in White, The Last Detail, Hester Street, Dog Day Afternoon, Harry and Walter Go to New York, Annie Hall, Valentino, The World's Greatest Lover, The Muppet Movie, The Mafu Cage, Sabina, When a Stranger Calls, Pandemonium, Norman Loves Rose, Can She Bake a Cherry Pie? Over the Brooklyn Bridge, Racing with the Moon, The Secret

Diary of Sigmund Freud, Transylvania 6-5000, Jumpin' Jack Flash, Ishtar, The Princess Bride, Sticky Fingers, License to Drive, The Lemon Sisters, Flashback, Benito.
TELEVISION: Many Mansions, Series: Taxi (Emmy Award), All is Forgiven. Movies: An Invasion of Privacy, Burning Rage, Drop Out Mother. Specials: Faerie Tale Theatre, Paul Reiser: Out on a Whim.

KANE, JOHN: Publicity Manager. b. New York, NY. e. Rutgers, B.A.; NYU, M.A. Publicist, Solters & Roskin, 1976–80. Unit publicist: Fame, Tender Mercies, Prince of the City, 1980– 82. 1982–present, Home Box Office, unit publicist, manager.

KANE, STANLEY D.: Judge. b. Minneapolis, MN, Dec. 21, 1907. e. U. of Minnesota, B.A. (magna cum laude), 1930;, M.A., 1931; Minnesota Coll. of Law, LL.B., 1940. Instructor, U. of Minnesota, 1930–33. Exec. sec. Allied Theatre Owners of the Northwest, 1933–37; city attorney, Golden Valley, MN, 1940–63; City Atty., Champlin, MN, 1955–60; on faculty, Minnesota Coll. of Law, 1940–44; trial attorney & trial examiner, National Labor Relations Board, Minneapolis, New Orleans, N.Y., 1943–46; special, gen. counsel, Puerto Rico Labor Relations Bd., 1946; exec. vice-pres. & gen. counsel, North Central Allied Independent Theatre Owners, 1946–63; recording sec. Allied States Assn., 1947 to 1956; Dist. Court Judge, Hennepin County, 1963; elected to 6-yr. term, 1964; re-elected, 1970; serving full-time as sr. judge since 1978.

KANEW, JEFF: Director.
PICTURES: Black Rodeo; Natural Enemies; Eddie Macon's Run; Revenge of the Nerds; Gotcha; Tough Guys, Troup Beverly Hills.
TELEVISION: Alfred Hitchcock Presents (1985).

KANIN, FAY: Writer. b. New York, NY. e. Elmira Coll., U. of Southern California, 1937. m. Michael Kanin, writer. Contrib. fiction to mags.; Writers Guild of Amer. pres. 1971–73; Acad. Motion Picture Arts & Sciences 1983–88. also bd. mem. of latter. Co-chair, National Center for Film and Video Preservation; Bd. of trustees, Amer. Film Institute.
PICTURES: Blondie for Victory, Sunday Punch, My Pal Gus, Rhapsody, The Opposite Sex, Teacher's Pet, Swordsman of Siena, The Right Approach.
BROADWAY: Goodbye My Fancy, His and Hers, Rashomon, The Gay Life, Grind (1985).
TELEVISION: Heat of Anger, 1972; Tell Me Where It Hurts, 1974 (Emmy Award), Hustling, Friendly Fire (also co-prod., Emmy Award, San Francisco Film Fest. Award, Peabody Award), Heartsounds (Peabody Award).

KANIN, GARSON: Director, Writer. b. Rochester, NY, Nov. 24, 1912. e. American Acad. of Dramatic Arts. m. the late actress Ruth Gordon. Musician, actor, appearing in Spring Song, Little Ol' Boy, and others. Prod. assist. George Abbott on Three Men on a Horse, Brother Rat, Room Service; dir. Hitch Your Wagon, Too Many Heroes, Broadway plays; In June, 1937, Samuel Goldwyn's prod. staff, 1938, joined RKO, prod.-dir. contract. In 1942: prod. for U.S. Office of Emergency Management. Joined armed forces, W.W.II; co-dir. True Glory. 1989, received Writers Guild Valentine Davies Award with brother Michael. Pres., Authors League of America.
PICTURES: A Double Life, Adam's Rib, Born Yesterday, Marrying Kind, Pat and Mike, It Should Happen to You, Next Time I Marry, Man to Remember, Great Man Votes, Bachelor Mother, My Favorite Wife, They Knew What They Wanted, Tom, Dick and Harry, From This Day Forward, The Girl Can't Help It, The Rat Race, High Time, The Right Approach, Where It's At, Some Kind of a Nut, Woman of the Year, The More the Merrier.
THEATRE: Born Yesterday, The Smile of the World, The Rat Race, The Live Wire, A Gift of Time, Do Re Mi, Come on Strong, The Amazing Adele, The Good Soup, Dreyfus in Rehearsal. (writer and/or dir.) Dir.: The Rugged Path; Years Ago; How I Wonder; The Leading Lady; The Diary of Anne Frank; Into Thin Air; Small War on Murray Hill; Hole in the Head; Sunday in New York; Funny Girl; I Was Dancing; A Very Rich Woman; We Have Always Lived in the Castle; Idiot's Delight; Ho! Ho! Ho!, Happy Ending, Peccadillo.
BOOKS: Remembering Mr. Maugham, Cast of Characters, Tracy and Hepburn; Hollywood; Blow Up a Storm; The Rat Race; A Thousand Summers; One Hell of an Actor; It Takes a Long Time to Become Young; Moviola, Smash, Together Again!, Cordelia.
TELEVISION: Hardhat and Legs (movie); Mr. Broadway (series, 1964).

KANIN, MICHAEL: Writer. b. Rochester, NY, Feb. 1, 1910. m. Fay Mitchell Kanin. Member SWG, officer; WGA, AMPAS. Commercial artist, musician, N.Y. prior to m.p. career; contrib. fiction mags.; s.p. Panama Lady, They Made Her a Spy, 1939. 1989, received Writers Guild Valentine Davies Award with brother Garson.
PICTURES: Anne of Windy Poplars, Woman of the Year, Sunday Punch, The Cross of Lorraine, Centennial Summer Honeymoon, A Double Life, My Pal Gus, When I Grow Up (also dir.), Rhapsody, The Opposite Sex, Teacher's Pet, The Right Approach, The Swordsman of Siena, The Outrage, How to Commit Marriage.
BROADWAY: Goodbye My Fancy, Seidman and Son, His and Hers, Rashomon, The Gay Life.

KANTER, HAL: Writer, Director, Producer. b. Savannah, GA, Dec. 18, 1918. On Bdwy. contributor to Hellzapoppin. Then began writing radio dramas before mil. service, WW II. Served as combat corresp. Armed Forces Radio; writer, Paramount, 1951–54; dir., RKO, 1956; Received Writers Guild Paddy Chayefsky Laurel Award, 1989. Writer, Danny Kaye Show, Amos 'n Andy, Bing Crosby Show, Jack Paar; Beulah; Ed Wynn TV Show, 1949; creator, writer, prod., stager, George Gobel Show; Prod., dir., writer, Kraft Music Hall, 1958–59; exec. prod., TCF-TV; Valentine's Day; writer, prod. dir. Chrysler Theatre 1966–67. Creator W.D.P., Julia, NBC, 1968–71; creator W.D.P., Jimmy Stewart, 1971. W.P. Many TV specials. 1975–76 exec. prod. All In The Family. Sup. Prod. Chico & The Man, 1976–77; exec. prod., WB-TV; 1978; prod./writer, Lucille Ball Prod., 1979–80; dir./writer, ABC TV Movies, 1980; Walt Disney Prods., 1981; Savannah Prods., 1982–86. Writer, AFI Life Achievement Awards: Henry Fonda, Alfred Hitchcock; writer, 21 Annual Academy Awards; prod./writer, You Can't Take It With You (TV series, 1987–88).
PICTURES: My Favorite Spy, Off Limits, Road to Bali, Casanova's Big Night, About Mrs. Leslie, Money from Home, Artists and Models, Mardi Gras, Rose Tattoo, I Married a Woman, Loving You, Once Upon a Horse, Blue Hawaii, Pocketful of Miracles, Bachelor in Paradise, Move Over, Darling, Dear Brigitte, etc.

KANTER, JAY: Executive. b. Dec. 12, 1926. Entered industry with MCA, Inc., where was v.p. Left after more than 20 yrs. to become indep. prod., then pres. of First Artists Production Co., Ltd. In 1975 joined 20th-Fox as v.p. prod.; 1976, named sr. v.p., worldwide prod. Named v.p., The Ladd Co., 1979. Joined MGM/UA Entertainment Co. as pres., worldwide prod., Motion Picture Division, 1984. In 1985, named pres., worldwide prod., UA Corp.; then pres., production MGM Pictures Inc.; 1989, named chmn. of prod. of Pathé Entertainment Co.

KANTOR, IGO: Producer, Film Editor. b. Vienna, Austria, Aug. 18, 1930. e. UCLA, A.A. 1950; B.S., 1952; M.S., 1954. Foreign corres., Portugal magazine, FLAMA, 1949–57, music supvr., Screen Gems, Columbia 1954–63; post-prod. supvr., film ed., features, TV; assoc. prod., 1963–64; prod., exec., International Entertainment Corp., 1965. pres., Synchrofilm, Inc., post-production co. and Duque Films, Inc., production co. 1968–74. 1975—present, produced and edited films. 1982, pres., Laurelwood Prods; 1988, pres. Major Arts Corp.
PICTURES: Bye Bye Birdie, Under the Yum Yum Tree, Gidget Goes to Rome, A House Is Not a Home, Pattern for Murder, Willy. Co.-prod., editor: Assault on Agathon; co-prod, FTA; assoc., prod., editor, Dixie Dynamite; prod., editor, music supvr., Kingdom of the Spiders; assoc. prod., The Dark; prod. supvr., Good Luck Miss Wyckoff; prod., Hardly Working; Kill and Kill Again; Mutant, Shaker Run, Act of Piracy; So Help Me God! (co-prod.).
TELEVISION: From Hawaii with Love (1984); The Grand Tour; It's a Wonderful World (prod.-dir.); Nosotros Golden Eagle Awards (prod.), United We Stand (pre-Olympic special).

KAPLAN, BORIS: Executive. b. New York, NY, Sept. 23, 1897. e. City Coll. of New York. m. General mgr. of Selwyn Theatrical Enterprises, 1925–32. Prod. Plays for legitimate stage, Broadway; joined Paramount Pictures Corp., 1933; head of eastern casting and talent dept., Paramount 1936–62; independent casting dir.; m.p. consultant.

KAPLAN, GABRIEL: Actor, Comedian. b. Brooklyn, NY, March 31, 1945. After high school worked as bellboy at Lakewood, NJ hotel, spending free time studying comedians doing routines. Put together a comedy act, landing engagements in small clubs and coffee houses all over U.S. Made several appearances on Tonight Show, Merv Griffin Show, Mike Douglas Show, etc. Has played Las Vegas clubs.
TELEVISION: Welcome Back, Kotter (series), Gabriel Kaplan Presents the Future Stars, Love Boat, Lewis and Clark.
PICTURES: Fast Break, Tulips, Nobody's Perfect.

KAPLAN, JONATHAN: Director, Writer. b. Paris, Nov. 25, 1947. e. U. of Chicago, B.A.; NYU, M.F.A. Member of tech. staff Fillmore East, NY 1969–71. New World Pictures' Roger Corman post-grad. sch. of filmmaking, Hollywood, 1971–73. As actor on Bdwy in Dark at the Top of the Stairs, Happy Anniversary. In film: Rumplestiltskin.
PICTURES: Night Call Nurses; Student Teachers; The Slams; Truck Turner; White Line Fever (dir., co-s.p.); Mr. Billion; Over the Edge; The Accused (dir.), Heart Like a Wheel; Project X; Immediate Family.
TELEVISION: The 11th Victim; The Hustler of Muscle Beach; The Gentleman Bandit; Girls of the White Orchid.

KAPOOR, SHASHI: Actor. b. Calcutta, India, 1938. Son of late Prithviraj Kapoor, Indian film and stage actor. As child worked in Prithvi Theatre and in brother, Raj's films. Toured with father's co. at 18 and joined the Kendals' Shakespeareana Co. in India. Starred in over 200 Indian films as well as several Merchant-Ivory Prods.

PICTURES: Pretty Polly, Siddhartha, The Householder, Bombay Talkie, Shakespeare Wallah, Heat and Dust, USTAV (Festival of Love, also prod.), The New Delhi Times, Sammy and Rosie Get Laid, The Deceivers, Nomads, Ajuba.

KARDISH, LAURENCE: Curator, Dept. of Film, Museum of Modern Art. b. Ottawa, Ontario, Canada, Jan. 5, 1945. e. Carlton U. Ottawa, Canada, 1966, Honors B.A. in philosophy; Columbia U., Sch. of the Arts, 1968, M.F.A. in film, radio, and television. 1965–66: Canadian Film Inst., programmer for National Film Theatre, Ottawa; researched a history of Canadian filmmaking. 1965: founded first film society in Canada to exhibit Amer. avant-garde films (Carleton U. Cine Club); directed summer seminar on film, Carleton U., 1966. 1966–68: New American Cinema Group, Inc., NY, worked for the Film-Makers' Distribution Center. 1968: joined Dept. of Film, MOMA; made curator 1984. Since 1968 involved with Cineprobe prog., since 1972 participated in selection of films for New Directors/New Films series; dir. exhibitions of surveys of national cinemas (Senegal, Scandinavia, French-speaking Canada) and retrospectives of indep. Amer. filmmakers (includ. Rudolph Burkhardt, Stan Brakhage, Shirley Clarke), The Lubitsch Touch, Columbia Pictures, Warner Bros., MGM, Universal, RKO, and directors. 1980: toured Europe with prog. of indep. Amer. films. Author of: Reel Plastic Magic (1972); as well as essays and monographs–Mark Rappaport and the Scenic Route; Senegal: 15 Years of an African Cinema; New Cinema from Iceland; Of Light and Texture: Andrew Noren and James Herbert; Michael Balcon and the Idea of a National Cinema; Intl. Avant-Garde: Scattered Pieces; Berlin and Film. Directed feature film Slow Run (1968). On jury for Channel 13's Indep. Focus series and on Board of Advisors, Collective for Living Cinema, NY. 1982–82: bd. of dirs. of National Alliance of Media Arts Centers; 1987–89: on Jerome Foundation panel. 1986 on Camera d'Or jury, Cannes Film Fest.

KARINA, ANNA: Actress. b. Copenhagen, Denmark, 1940. r.n. Hanna Karin Bayer. Had appeared in Danish shorts before going to Paris at 17 and working in commercials. Gained international renown in the 7 films she made with former husband Jean-Luc Godard.

PICTURES: Celo From Five to Seven, Three Fables of Love, My Life to Live, A Woman is a Woman, Sweet and Sour, Circle of Love, She'll Have to Go, Le Petit Soldat, Band of Outsiders, Pierrot le Fou, Alphaville, Made in U.S.A., The Stranger, La Religieuse, The Oldest Profession, The Magus, Before Winter Comes, Laughter in the Dark, Justine, Rendevous a Bray, Willie and the Chinese Cat, Vivre Ensemble (also dir.), Story of a Mother, L'Ami de Vincent, Ave Maria.

KARLIN, FRED: Composer, Conductor. b. Chicago, IL, June 16, 1936. e. Amherst Coll., B.A. Composer and arranger for Benny Goodman and Harry James' Orchestras. Won Academy Award for Best Song for For All We Know (from Lovers and Other Strangers) and Emmy for original music in The Autobiography of Jane Pittman. Adapted Huddie Ledbetter melodies for film Leadbelly. Co-author (with Rayburn Wright) or On the Track: A Guide to Contemporary Film Scoring (Schirmer).

PICTURES: Up the Down Staircase, Yours, Mine and Ours, The Sterile Cuckoo (including music for song, Come Saturday Morning), Westworld, Futureworld, Lovers and Other Strangers, Vasectomy: A Delicate Matter, Gravy Train, Mixed Company, Leadbelly, Loving Couples.

TELEVISION: More than 85 movies, including The Autobiography of Miss Jane Pittman, The Awakening Land, The Plutonium Incident, Minstrel Man, Sophia Loren—Her Own Story, Fighting Back, Mom, The Wolfman, and Me; Calamity Jane, Ike: the War Years, Inside the Third Reich, Hollywood—The Gift of Laughter, Not in Front of the Children, Dream West, Hostage Flight, A Place to Call Home, Robert Kennedy and His Times, Dadah is Death, Bridge to Silence.

KARLIN, MYRON D.: Executive. b. Revere, MA, Sept. 21, 1918. e. UCLA. Joined m.p. business in 1946 as gen. mgr. for MGM in Ecuador. Two yrs. later assigned same spot for MGM in Venezuela. In 1952–53 was gen. sales mgr. for MGM in Germany, after which managing dir. in Argentina, returning to Germany as mgr. dir. in 1956. Named mgn. dir. for United Artists in Italy. 1960–68 was pres. of Brunswick Int'l., while also serving as advisor to World Health Organization and UNESCO. In 1969 was European mgr. for MGM and mgn. dir. in Italy. Joined Warner Bros. Int'l. in May, 1970 as v.p. of European dist. In March, 1972 appt. v.p. in chg. of int'l. operations for WB; 1977, appt. pres., WB Intl. & exec. v.p., Warner Bros., Inc; 1985, named exec. v.p., intl. affairs, WB, Inc. Now pres. & COO, Motion Picture Export Assn.

KARRAS, ALEX: Actor. b. Gary, IN, July 15, 1935. e. Univ. of Iowa. As football player with Iowa State U., picked for All Amer. team. Received Outland Trophy, 1957. Former professional football player with Detroit Lions, 1958–62, and 1964–71. Sportswriter, Detroit Free Press, 1972–73. Also worked as prof. wrestler, salesman, steel worker and banquet lecturer. Autobiographies: Even Big Guys Cry (with Herb Gluck, 1977), Alex Karras: My Life in Football, Television and Movies (1979).

PICTURES: Paper Lion (as himself), Blazing Saddles, FM, Win Place or Steal, The Great Lester Boggs, Another Day at the Races, Jacob Two-Two Meets the Hooded Fang, When Time Ran Out, Nobody's Perfekt, Porky's, Victor, Victoria, Against All Odds.

TELEVISION: Commentator: and host: Monday Night Football. Mini-series: Centennial. Movies: Hardcase, The 500-Pound Jerk, Babe, Mulligan's Stew, Mad Bull, Jimmy B. & Andre, Alcatraz: The Whole Shocking Story, Word of Honor (also exec. prod.), Maid in America. Series: Webster.

KARTOZIAN, WILLIAM F.: Executive. b. San Francisco, CA, July 27, 1938. e. Stanford U., 1960; Harvard Law Sch., 1963. Deputy Attorney General State of CA, 1963–64; assoc. in law firm of Lillick, McHose, Wheat, Adams & Charles, San Francisco, 1964–65; corp. counsel and dir., Natl. Convenience Stores, Houston, 1965–67; v.p. and corp. counsel, United Artists Theatre Circuit, 1967–75; owner, Festival Enterprises, Inc., 1970–86; chmn. San Francisco Theatre Employers Assoc., 1973–76; Theatre Assoc. of CA, Inc., dir. 1972–86, v.p. 1974–75, pres. 1975–79, chmn. of bd. 1979–81; member, State of CA Industrial Welfare Comm. Amusement and Recreation Industries Wage Board, 1975–76; National Assoc. of Theatre Owners: dir. 1976–86, v.p. 1980–86, president 1988–present. Owner, Regency Enterprises, Inc., 1986–present; chmn. of bd., Lakeside Inn & Casino, Stateline, NV 1985–present.

Member: Stanford U. Alumni Assoc. dir. 1968–72, pres. 1971–72; dir. Stanford U. Athletic Board 1987–present; chmn. bd. of trustees, James T. Watkins IV Fund 1973–79; dir. Frontier Village, Inc. 1972–73; dir., Stanford Daily Publishing Corp. 1974–78; Variety Club Blind Babies Fdn.: trustee 1979–present, v.p. 1980–82, pres. 1982–85; member: CA and TX bar assocs., American Judicature Society, Commonwealth Club of CA, Blackhawk Country Club.

KASDAN, LAWRENCE: Writer, Director. b. West Virginia, Jan. 14, 1949. e. U. of Michigan. Clio award-winning advertising copywriter, Detroit and LA before becoming screen writer. Became director with Body Heat (1981).

PICTURES: The Empire Strikes Back (co-s.p.); Raiders of the Lost Ark (s.p.); Continental Divide (s.p.); Return of the Jedi (co-s.p.); Body Heat (dir., s.p.); The Big Chill (co-exec. prod., dir., co-s.p.); Silverado (prod., dir., co-s.p.), Cross My Heart (prod.), The Accidental Tourist (dir., co-prod., co-s.p.), Immediate Family (exec. prod.), I Love You to Death (dir.).

KASLOFF, STEVE: Executive. b. New York, NY, Nov. 13, 1952. e. Pratt Institute, 1974, cum laude. Writer/supvr., Young & Rubicam, 1974–76; writer/sprv., Ally & Gargano, 1976; writer/supvr., Marsteller Inc., 1976–79; writer/creative supvr., Scali, McCabe, Sloves, 1979–82. hired as youngest v.p., Columbia Pictures, 1982; promoted to sr. v.p., creative dir., Columbia, 1983.

AWARDS: Winner of numerous Clio Awards when at ad agencies and over 100 other awards & medals for creative work (trailers, TV commercials, radio commercials, posters, etc.) on such films as Body Double, Tootsie, Karate Kid, Ghostbusters, Soldier's Story, Agnes of God, etc. Has directed stage production (Wait Until Dark), and commercials & special teaser trailers. Now working on screenplay.

KASSAR, MARIO: Executive, Producer.

At age of 18 formed own foreign distribution co. Kassar Films International, specializing in sale, dist. and exhibition of films in Asia and Europe. In 1976 became partners with Andrew Vajna who had own dist. co., forming Carolco. First prod. First Blood, followed by Rambo: First Blood Part II.

PICTURES: Exec. Prod.: Angel Heart, Extreme Prejudice, Rambo III, Red Heat, Deepstar Six, Iron Eagle II, Johnny Handsome, Air America, Total Recall.

KASTNER, ELLIOTT: Producer. b. New York, NY, Jan. 7, 1933. e. U. of Miami, Columbia U. Was agent then v.p. with MCA, before becoming indep. prod., financing and personally producing 50 feature films in 25 yrs. Based in London.

PICTURES: Harper, Kaleidoscope, Sweet November, Laughter in the Dark, Where Eagles Dare, When Eight Bells Toll, X, Y, Zee, The Nightcomers, Fear Is the Key, The Long Goodbye, Cops and Robbers, Jeremy, 11 Harrowhouse, Rancho Deluxe, 92 in the Shade (exec. prod.); First Deadly Sin (co-exec. prod.); The Missouri Breaks (co-prod.), Equus (co-prod.), The Big Sleep (co-prod.); Ffolkes (prod.); Death Valley (prod.); Man, Woman, and Child (prod.); Garbo Talks (co-prod.); Oxford Blues (co-prod.); Angel Heart (co-prod.); The Big Picture (co-exec. prod.); Jack's Back (exec. prod.); The Blob; Likewise; White of the Eye; Zombie High; Never on Tuesday; Homeboy; A Chorus of Disapproval (exec. prod.), Jericho (exec. prod.).

KATLEMAN, HARRIS L.: Executive. b. Omaha, NB, Aug. 19, 1928. e. UCLA, B.A. in admin., 1949. Joined MCA in 1949; in 1952 transferred to N.Y. as head of TV Packaging Dept. Left to join Goodson-Todman Prods. in 1955, where named v.p., 1956; exec. v.p., 1958; sr. exec. v.p., 1968. Was directly responsible for all film prod. in L.A., including such shows as The Rebel, Branded, The Richard Boone Show (Emmy nominations, Fame Award of Year), and Don Rickles Show, on which was exec. prod. Joined Metro-Goldwyn-Mayer in 1972 as v.p. of MGM-TV; promoted following year to pres., MGM-TV and sr. v.p. of MGM, Inc. Resigned as pres., MGM-TV September, 1977. Formed Bennett/Katleman Productions under contract to Columbia Pictures. Exec. prod.: From Here to Eternity, Salvage 1; 1980, named bd. chmn. 20th-Fox Television.

KATSELAS, MILTON: Director. b. Pittsburgh, PA, Feb. 22, 1933. e. drama dept., Carnegie Inst. of Technology (now Carnegie Mellon U.). Has directed more than 30 stage prods., including in New York, The Rose Tattoo and Camino Real (both revivals), The Zoo Story, Butterflies Are Free, Private Lives.
PICTURES: Butterflies Are Free (debut), 40 Carats, Report to the Commissioner, When You Comin' Back, Red Ryder.
TELEVISION: The Rules of Marriage.

KATT, WILLIAM: Actor. b. Los Angeles, CA, 1955. Son of Barbara Hale and Bill Williams. e. Orange Coast Coll. Majored in music, playing piano and guitar. Acted with South Coast Repertory Theatre, later working in production at the Ahmanson and Mark Taper Theatres in L.A. Film debut in Carrie (1976).
PICTURES: Carrie, First Love, Big Wednesday, Butch and Sundance: The Early Days, Baby, Rising Storm, House, White Ghost, Wedding Band.
TELEVISION: The Greatest American Hero (series); Perry Mason Returns and 8 Perry Mason follow-ups (Murdered Madam; Avenging Ace; The Case of the Scandalous Scoundrel; The Case of the Lady in the Lake); Top of the Hill (series); The Rainmaker, Swim Suit.

KATZ, GLORIA: Producer, Writer. e. UCLA. Film Sch. Joined Universal Pictures as editor, cutting educational films. Later joined forces with Willard Huyck, whom she had met at U.C.L.A. Pair signed by Francis Ford Coppola to write and direct for his newly created company, American Zoetrope. Projects didn't materialize but Katz and Huyck teamed to write script for America Graffiti for director George Lucas. Wrote Lucky Lady, 1975 together. Katz made debut as producer with French Postcards in 1979 which co-wrote with Huyck, who directed.
PICTURES: Indiana Jones and the Temple of Doom (co.-s.p.); The Best Defense (prod., co.-s.p.); Howard the Duck (prod., co.-s.p.).
TELEVISION: A Father's Homecoming (co-prod., co-s.p.).

KATZ, MARTY: Executive. b. Landsburg, West Germany, Sept. 2, 1947. e. UCLA, U. of Maryland. Served in Vietnam War as U.S. Army first lt.; awarded Bronze Star as combat pictorial unit director. 1971, dir. of film prod., ABC Circle Films; 1976, exec. v.p., prod., Quinn Martin Prods; 1978–80, producer and consultant, Paramount Pictures' 1981–85, independent producer (Lost in America, Heart Like a Wheel). 1985, joined Walt Disney Prods. as sr. v.p., motion picture & TV prod. Named exec. v.p. motion picture and TV production, 1988.

KATZ, NORMAN B.: Executive. b. Scranton, PA, Aug. 23, 1919. e. Columbia U. In U.S. Army 1941–46 as intelligence officer, airborne forces. Entered m.p. industry in 1947 with Discina Films, Paris, France, as prod. asst. Named exec. asst. to head of prod. in 1948. In 1950 named v.p. Discina Int'l. Films and in 1952 exec. v.p. In 1954 joined Associated Artists Prods. as foreign mgr.; named dir. of foreign operation in 1958. In 1959 became dir. of foreign operations for United Artists Associated. 1961 joined Seven Arts Associated Corp. of v.p. in chg. of foreign operations; named exec. v.p., Seven Arts Prods. Int'l. in 1964. Named exec. v.p. Warner Bros.—Seven Arts Int'l. in 1967. In 1969 appt. exec. v.p. and chief exec. off. Warner Bros. International and bd. mem. of Warner Bros. Inc. In 1974 named sr. v.p. int'l. div. of American Film Theatre. Pres. of Cinema Arts Associated Corp. 1979, exec. v.p. and bd. member, American Communications Industries and pres., chief exec. off. of ACI subsidiary, American Cinema; 1983, pres., The NORKAT Co., Also, bd. chmn., CEO, American Film Mktg. Assoc., 1985–87; chmn. Amer. Film Export Assn. 1988–89.

KATZENBERG, JEFFREY: Executive. b. 1950. Entered motion picture industry in 1975 as asst. to Paramount Pictures chmn. and CEO Barry Diller in NY. In 1977, became exec. dir. of mktg.; later same year moved to west coast as v.p. of programming for Paramount TV. Promoted to v.p., feature production for Paramount Pictures 1978; 2 years later assumed role of sr. v.p. prod. of m.p. div; 1982, pres. of prod., m.p. and TV, Paramount Pictures. Left to join The Walt Disney Company, 1984; chairman of The Walt Disney Studios since 1984.

KATZKA, GABRIEL: Producer. b. New York, NY, Jan. 25, 1931. e. Kenyon Coll. Bdwy. prods. include Pal Joey, Hamlet, The Little Foxes, Anna Christie, The Comedians, etc.
PICTURES: Marlowe; Kelly's Heroes; Soldier Blue; The Parallax View; The Taking of Pelham 1-2-3; The Heartbreak Kid; Sleuth; A Bridge Too Far; Who'll Stop the Rain; Meteor; Butch and Sundance—The Early Days; The Beast Within; The Lords of Discipline; The Falcon and the Snowman.
TELEVISION: Kavik—The Wolf Dog; Isabel's Choice; Ellis Island.

KAUFMAN, HAL: Creative director, TV Writer, Producer. b. New York, NY, Dec. 16, 1924; e. U. of Texas, 1943–44; U. of Michigan, 1944–47. Started career as petroleum geologist, Western Geophysical Co., 1947–48; TV writer-prod-dir., KDYL-TV, Salt Lake City, 1948–49; prog. dir., WLAV-TV, Grand Rapids, 1949–51; prod. mgr., WOOD-TV, Grand Rapids, 1951–54; TV writer-prod., Leo Burnett Company, Chicago, 1954–56; TV writer-prod., Gordon Best Company, Chicago, 1957–58; sr. writer, TV/Radio creative dept., Needham, Louis & Brorby, Inc., 1959; vice-pres., asst. copy dir., Needham, Louis & Brorby, Inc., 1962; dir., TV, Radio prod., Needham, Louis & Brorby, Inc., 1963; dir., broadcast design, production, Needham, Louis & Brorby, Inc., 1964; assoc. creat. dir., asst. Exec. v.p., Needham, Harper & Steers, Inc., 1965; Creat. dir. L.A., 1966; Sr. v.p. and mem. bd. of dir., 1966. 1969, creative & marketing consultant in Beverly Hills. 1970 Exec. v.p., principle, Kaufman, Lansky Inc., Beverly Hills and San Diego; editor and publisher Z Magazine; program dir., Z Channel, Theta Cable TV. 1979, sr. v.p./adv. & p.r. & asst. to pres. & bd. chmn., World Airways, Inc. 1982–v.p., Creative director, Admarketing, Inc., Los Angeles. 1985, mktg. & adv. consultant copy dir., Teleflora, Inc.; pres. Hal Kaufman Inc., mktg. & adv. consultant. Member, Directors Guild of America, SAG, AFTRA. 1974.

KAUFMAN, J. L. (Les): Publicist. b. Chicago, IL, June 3: e. Morgan Park (IL) Military Acad. Police reporter, City News Bureau, Chicago. In 1926 adv. dept., Balaban & Katz Theats. In 1929 pub. Paramount Public Theats. To Columbia, 1933 asst. exploit, dir. In 1938 adv. & pub. dir., Fanchon & Marco Serv. Corp., St. Louis. Adv.-pub. dir., Republic Studios, 1944–46; Nat'l. adv. pub. dir., International Pictures Corp. In 1947 named studio pub. dir., Universal-International; sales prom. counsel, Kaiser-Frazer Corp., 1950; v.p. in chge. West Coast, Ettinger Co., 1950; v.p. Grant Adv. Inc., Hollywood, Detroit, 1952–55; v.p., adv. dir., UPA Pictures, Inc., 1956; P.R. dir., Fedderson Productions & Lawrence Welk, 1957–83; My Three Sons, Hollywood Palladium, 1961, Family Affair, To Rome with Love. The Smith Family; pres., Hollywood Press Club, 1964–65, 1967–68. Bd. governors—NATVAS, Hollywood chapter. Director/promotion, Nederlander Companies, 1983.

KAUFMAN, LEONARD B.: Producer, Writer, Director. b. Newark, NJ, Aug. 31, 1927. e. NYU. In W.W.II served with Army Special Services writing and directing camp shows. Nat'l magazine writer, 1945–48; radio writer, including Errol Flynn Show, 1948–50; radio and TV writer, 1950–52. Headed own public relations firm: Kaufman, Schwartz, and Associates, 1952–64. Joined Ivan Tors Films as writer-prod., 1964. Films Corp., 1958.
PICTURES: Clarence, the Cross-eyed Lion, Birds Do It, Story.
TELEVISION: Daktari, Ivan Tors' Jambo, O'Hara, U.S. Treasury (pilot feature and series). Producer: Hawaii-Five O, The New Sea Hunt, Scruples (mini-series), The Hawaiian (pilot), Writer: Knightrider, Dukes of Hazzard, Hawaii-Five O, Wet Heat (pilot), Hawaiian Heat, Island Sons (movie).

KAUFMAN, PHILIP: Writer, Director. b. Chicago, IL, Oct. 23, 1936. e. U. of Chicago, Harvard Law Sch. Was teacher in Italy and Greece before turning to film medium.
PICTURES: *Director-co-writer:* Goldstein (co-dir., co-prod. only), Fearless Frank, The Great Northfield, Minnesota Raid, The White Dawn (dir. only), Invasion of the Body Snatchers (dir. only), The Wanderers, The Right Stuff (dir., s.p.); The Unbearable Lightness of Being, Henry & June (prod., dir., co-s.p.).

KAUFMAN, VICTOR: Executive. b. New York, NY, June 21, 1943. e. Queens Coll.; NYU Sch. of Law, J.D., 1967. Taught criminal law at UCLA before joining Wall St. law firm, Simpson Thacher & Bartlett. Joined Columbia Pictures as asst. general counsel, 1974. Named chief counsel, 1975; then made vice chmn. Columbia Pictures. Later exec. v.p. Columbia Pictures Industries and vice chmn. Columbia Pictures motion picture div. when conceived a new studio as a joint venture between Coca-Cola, Time Inc.'s Home Box Office and CBS, Inc. forming Tri-Star Pictures. Named chmn. and CEO Tri-Star, 1983. When Columbia Pictures and Tri-Star merged in late 1987, became pres. and CEO of new entity, Columbia Pictures Entertainment. In June 1988, dropped title of chmn. of Tri-Star.

KAUFMANN, CHRISTINE: Actress. b. Lansdorf, Graz, Austria, Jan. 11, 1945. e. school in Munich, Germany. Film debut as a dancer. Salto Mortale at 7 yrs of age.
PICTURES: Rosenrosli (Little Rosie), Schweigende Engel (Silent Angel), Maedchen in Uniform, Winter Vacation, The Last Days of Pompeii, Red Lips, Town Without Pity, Taras Bulba (first American-made film), Murder in the Rue Morgue, Bagdad Cafe, Der Geschichtenerzahler.

KAVANAGH, DECLAN M.: Executive. b. Hollywood, CA, Oct. 29, 1956. e. California State U., B.A., acct. & mktg.; U. of Southern California, M.B.A. Co-producer of original Jane Fonda Workout, 1981; founded Video Associates (formerly Video Odyssey), 1981; co-producer home video, Everyday with Richard Simmons, 1982; organized first home video dist. deal with V.C.I. and Media Home Entertainment, 1983; founded Active Home Video, 1984; produced Bruce Jenner Winning Workout, 1984; sold Active Home Video, 1985. Now v.p. mktg. & sls., Video Associates, Inc.

KAVNER, JULIE: Actress. b. Los Angeles, Sept. 7, 1951. e. San Diego State U. Professional debut as Brenda Morgenstern on TV's Rhoda, 1974–78.
TELEVISION: Movies: The Girl Who Couldn't Lose (Afternoon Playbreak), No Other Love, The Revenge of the Stepford Wives, Katherine, A Fine Romance (pilot). Also on Lou Grant, Petrocelli, Taxi, The Tracey Ullman Show (series).
PICTURES: Bad Medicine, National Lampoon Goes to the Movies, Hannah and Her Sisters, Radio Days, Surrender, New York Stories (Oedipus Wrecks).
STAGE: Particular Friendships (Off-B'way.), Two for the Seesaw (Burt Reynolds' dinner theater, FL), It Had to Be You (Canada).

KAY, GILBERT LEE: Director, Writer. b. Chicago, IL, June 28. e. Los Angeles City Coll. Was asst. dir. at various studios from 1942–53; started directing on own in 1954. Formed Pearly Gate Productions, London.
PICTURES: Three Bad Sisters, The Tower, Ocean's 11 (s.p.), Comeback, (s.p.), Take Five (s.p.), Fame! (s.p.), Anything for Money (s.p.), The Wrong Mrs. Wright, Now It Can Be Told (s.p.), It Happened in Lisbon (s.p.), The Secret Door, A Harvest of Evil (s.p., dir.), Sometimes I Love You (s.p.), White Comanche, Ragan, Devil May Care, Maybe September (s.p.), Recent screenplays: The Oedipus Vendetta, The Lotus Affair, Candle in the Wind, Royal Flush.
TELEVISION: Directed: Treasury Men in Action, Man Behind the Badge, Reader's Digest, Passport to Danger, Hollywood Profile, Highway Patrol, Arabian Nights, Telephone Time, Silent Service, The Grey Ghost, Man with a Camera, Adventures in Paradise, Shotgun Slade, Perry Mason, Follow the Sun, Frontier Circus. Wrote: The Uncivil Engineer, 8:46 to Southampton.
PLAYS: Directed: Two Faced Coin, Some Call It Love, French Without Tears, Burlesque, London by Night, The Man from Madrid, Paris, With Love. Wrote and Directed: West End, Please Omit Flowers, The Girl from Soho.

KAY, GORDON: Producer. b. Montreal, Canada, Sept. 6, 1916; e. Williams Coll., M.A. Asst. prod. Republic 1946, assoc. prod., 1947. apptd. secy.-treas.; exec. asst. to head of prod. at Republic, Feb., 1951; prod., Univ. 1955; pres. Gordon Kay & Assoc., 1958.
PICTURES: Wild Frontier, Bandits of Dark Canyon, Oklahoma Badlands, Bold Frontiersman, He Rides Tall, Fluffy, Taggart, Gunpoint, Beardless Warriors.

KAYAMA, YUZO: Actor. b. April 11, 1937. e. law school, Keio U. Debut Toho Studio 1959 in Man Against Man.
PICTURES: Westward Desperado, Man from the East, Blood in the Sea, Three Dolls series, Bull of Ginza, Tsubaki Sanjuro.

KAYLOR, ROBERT: Director.
PICTURES: Derby; Carny.

KAZAN, ELIA: Director. b. Constantinople, Turkey, Sept. 7, 1909. e. Williams Coll., Yale Dramatic Sch. With Group Theatre as apprentice & stage mgr.; on stage, 1934–41; plays include: Waiting for Lefty, Golden Boy, Gentle People, Five-Alarm, Lilliom; m.p. acting debut in City For Conquest, 1941. m.p. dir., 1944; Acad. Award best direction, 1947, for Gentleman's Agreement, 1954; for On the Waterfront. Author novels, The Arrangement, 1967, The Assassins, The Understudy, 1974; Acts of Love, 1978; The Anatolian, 1982; A Life (autobiography), 1988.
THEATER: Director: Skin of Our Teeth (Critics Award best direction). All My Sons, Streetcar Named Desire, Death of a Salesman, Cat on a Hot Tin Roof; (co-dir., prod.), One Touch of Venus, Harriet, Jocobowsky and the Colonel, Tea and Sympathy, Dark at the Top of the Stairs, J.B., Sweet Bird of Youth; Lincoln Center Repertory Theatre; (co-dir., prod.), After The Fall, But For Whom Charlie.
PICTURES: A Tree Grows in Brooklyn, Boomerang, Sea of Grass, Gentleman's Agreement, Panic in the Streets, Pinky, Streetcar Named Desire, Viva Zapata, Man on a Tightrope, On the Waterfront (Acad. Award, 1954), East of Eden, Baby Doll, Face in the Crowd, Wild River, Splendor in the Grass, America, America, The Arrangement, The Visitors, The Last Tycoon.

KAZAN, LAINIE: Singer, Actress. b. New York, NY, May 15, 1942. e. Hofstra U. On stage and performed in niteries.
PICTURES: Romance of a Horse Thief, Lady in Cement, Dayton's Devils, One from the Heart, My Favorite Year, Lust in the Dust, The Delta Force, The Adventures of Natty Gann, Harry and the Hendersons, Beaches, Medium Rare, Friend to Friend, Eternity.
TELEVISION: A Cry for Love, Sunset Limousine, The Jerk Too, Obsessive Love, Family Business (pilot), The Lainie Kazan Show, Paper Chase, Karen's Song, St. Elsewhere, Hotel, Johnny Carson Show, Dean Martin, Merv Griffin, Joan Rivers, Amazing Stories, Pat Sajak Show, The Famous Teddy Z (series).

KAZANJIAN, HOWARD G.: Producer. b. Pasadena, CA, July 26, 1943. e. U. of Southern California Film Sch.; DGA Training Program.
PICTURES: Asst. Dir.: Camelot; Finian's Rainbow; The Wild Bunch; The Arrangement; The Front Page; The Hindenberg; Family Plot. Assoc. Prod.: Rollercoaster. Producer: More American Graffiti; Raiders of the Lost Ark; The Making of Raiders of the Lost Ark (exec. prod.); Return of the Jedi.

KAZURINSKY, TIM: Actor, Writer. b. Johnstown, PA, March 3, 1950. Raised in Australia. Worked as copywriter for Chicago ad agency. Took acting class at Second City and quit job to become actor and head writer for Second City Comedy Troupe. Co-starred with John Candy in CTV/NBC's series Big City Comedy, 1980. Actor, Chicago City Limits NY.Joined cast of Saturday Night Live as writer-actor 1981–84.
PICTURES: Actor: My Bodyguard, Somewhere in Time, Continental Divide, Neighbors, Police Academy II: Their First Assignment, Police Academy III: Back in Training, About Last Night (also co-s.p.), Police Academy IV: Citizens on Patrol, For Keeps (s.p. only), Road to Ruin (also s.p.), Hot to Trot, Wedding Band.
TELEVISION: Movie: This Wife for Hire, Dinner at Eight.

KEACH, STACY: Actor, Director, Producer. b. Savannah, GA, June 2, 1942. Began professional acting career in Joseph Papp's 1964 prod. of Hamlet in Central Park. Has won three Obie Awards, Vernon Rice Drama Desk Award for Macbird, Drama Desk Award, Tony Nomination for Indians.
PICTURES: The Heart Is a Lonely Hunter, End of the Road, The Traveling Executioner, Brewster McCloud, Doc, Judge Roy Bean, The New Centurions, Fat City, The Killer Inside Me, Conduct Unbecoming, Luther, Street People, The Squeeze, Gray Lady Down, The Ninth Configuration, Longriders, (also exec. prod., co-s.p.), Road Games, Butterfly, Up in Smoke, Nice Dreams, That Championship Season, The Lover.
TELEVISION: Caribe, The Blue and the Gray, Princess Daisy, Murder Me, Murder You, More Than Murder, Wait Until Dark, Mistral's Daughter, Mickey Spillane's Mike Hammer (series), Hemingway. Mickey Spillane's Mike Hammer: Murder Takes All, The Forgotten. Director: Incident at Vichy, Six Characters in Search of an Author.
STAGE: Long Day's Journey into Night, Macbird, Indians, Hamlet, Deathtrap, Hughie, Barnum, Cyrano de Bergerac, Peer Gynt, Henry IV Parts I & II, Idiot's Delight.

KEACH, SR., STACY: Executive. b. Chicago, IL, May 29, 1914. Father of actors, Stacy and James. e. Northwestern U., B.S. & M.A. Was instructor in theatre arts at Northwestern and Armstrong Coll. and dir. at Pasadena Playhouse before entering industry. For 4½ yrs. was under contract at Universal Pictures; 3 yrs. at RKO; had own prod. on NBC, CBS. In 1946 began producing and directing industrial stage presentations for Union Oil Co. and from then on became full-time prod. of m.p. and stage industrial shows. In 1946 formed Stacy Keach Productions, of which he is pres. In addition to directing, producing and writing he occasionally appears as actor in films. Played Clarence Birds Eye on TV commercials as well as other commercials. Presently spokesman for National Liberty Life Insurance.

KEATON, DIANE: Actress. b. Santa Ana, CA, Jan. 5, 1946. e. Santa Ana Coll. Appeared in summer stock and studied at Neighborhood Playhouse in N.Y. Made prof. debut in Bdwy. prod. of Hair (1968); then co-starred with Woody Allen in Play It Again, Sam, repeating role for film version. Off-B'way: The Primary English Class. Author: photography books: Reservations (co-ed.), Still Life.
PICTURES: Lovers and Other Strangers, The Godfather, Play It Again, Sam, Sleeper, The Godfather, Part II, Love and Death, I Will . . . I Will . . . for Now, Harry and Walter Go to New York, Annie Hall (Acad. Award, 1977), Looking for Mr. Goodbar, Interiors, Manhattan, Reds, Shoot the Moon, The Little Drummer Girl, Mrs. Soffel, Crimes of the Heart, Radio Days, Baby Boom, The Good Mother, The Lemon Sisters (also prod.), Running Mates.

DIRECTOR: What Does Dorrie Want? (short, 1982), Heaven.

KEATON, MICHAEL: Actor. r.n. Michael Douglas. b. Coraopolis, PA, Sept. 5, 1951. Speech major, Kent State U. 2 years. Drove cab and ice-cream truck while performing in local coffeehouses. Became mem. of improvisational troup Jerry Vale. Moved to L.A. where honed craft at Comedy Store and Second City Improv. Workshops as stand-up comic.
PICTURES: Night Shift, Mr. Mom, Johnny Dangerously, Touch and Go, Gung Ho, The Squeeze, Beetlejuice, Clean and Sober, The Dream Team, Batman.
TELEVISION: Series: All's Fair, The Mary Tyler Moore Comedy Hour, Working Stiffs, Report to Murphy. Movie: Roosevelt and Truman.

KEEL, HOWARD: Actor. r.n. Harold Keel. b. Gillespie, IL, April 13, 1919. e. high school, Fallbrook, CA. Began career following George Walker scholarship award for singing, L.A.; appeared in plays, Pasadena Auditorium, concerts; won awards, Mississippi Valley and Chicago Musical Festivals. Stage debut: Carousel, 1945; principal role (Oklahoma). Screen debut, The Small Voice, London, 1948.
PICTURES: Annie Get Your Gun, Pagan Love Song, Three Guys Named Mike, Show Boat, Texas Carnival, Callaway Went Thataway, Lovely to Look At, Desperate Search, Ride Vaquero, Fast Company, Kiss Me Kate, Calamity Jane, Rose Marie, Seven Brides for Seven Brothers, Deep in My Heart, Jupiter's Darling, Kismet, Floods of Fear, Big Fisherman, Armored Command, Arizona Bushwackers.
PLAYS: Saratoga, No Strings, The Ambassador, Man of La Mancha.
TELEVISION: Dallas (series).

KEESHAN, BOB: Performer. b. Lynbrook, NY, June 27, 1927. e. Fordham U. As network page boy became assistant to Howdy Doody's Bob Smith and originated role of Clarabelle the Clown; created children's programs Time for Fun, 1953; Tinker's Workshop, 1954; Captain Kangaroo, 1955–present; Mister Mayor, 1965.

KEITEL, HARVEY: Actor. b. Brooklyn, NY, 1941. m. actress Lorraine Bracco. Served in U.S. Marine Corps. Over 10 yrs. experience in summer stock repertory and little theatre after study at Actors Studio with Lee Strasberg and Frank Corsaro. Starred in Martin Scorsese's film student film prod. of Who's That Knocking at My Door?; Has since become repertory member of Scorsese films.
THEATER: Death of a Salesman, Hurlyburly.
PICTURES: Who's That Knocking at My Door?, Street Scenes, Mean Streets, Alice Doesn't Live Here Anymore, Taxi Driver, Mother, Jugs and Speed, Buffalo Bill and the Indians, Welcome to L.A., The Duellists, Fingers, Blue Collar, Bad Timing, The Border, Exposed, Falling in Love, Off Beat, Wise Guys, The Men's Club, The Investigation, Blindside, The Pick-Up Artist, The January Man, Dear Gorbachev, The Last Temptation of Christ, In From the Cold, The Two Jakes, Two Evil Eyes (The Black Cat).
TELEVISION: This Ain't Bebop (Amer. Playhouse).

KEITH, BRIAN: Actor. b. Bayonne, NJ, Nov. 14, 1921. p. Robert Keith, actor. U.S. Marines, 1942–45; worked in stock co., radio shows, comm. films for TV; on B'way in Mr. Roberts, Darkness at Noon; m.p. debut in Arrowhead (1953).
PICTURES: Jivaro, Alaska Seas, Bamboo Prison, Violent Men, Tight Spot, Five Against the House, Storm Center, Run of the Arrow, Nightfall, Sierra Baron, Those Calloways, The Raiders, The Young Philadelphians, Dino, A Tiger Walks, The Parent Trap, The Hallelujah Trail, Rare Breed, Nevada Smith, Reflections in a Golden Eye, Krakatoa, East of Java, Gaily, Gaily, Suppose They Gave a War and Nobody Came, McKenzie Break, Scandalous John, Something Big, The Yakuza, The Wind and the Lion, Nickelodeon, Hooper, Meteor, Charlie Chan and the Curse of the Dragon Queen, Sharkey's Machine, Death Before Dishonor, Young Guns, Welcome Home.
TELEVISION: Numerous dramas on Studio One, Suspense, Philco Playhouse. Series: Archer Family Affair, The Little People, The Westerner, Hardcastle and McCormick, Heartlands. Movies: Centennial, The Chisholms, 13 Days at the Alamo, Perry Mason: The Case of the Lethal Lesson.

KEITH, DAVID: Actor. b. Knoxville, TN, May 8, 1954. e. U. of Tennessee, B.A., speech and theater. Appearance at Goodspeed Opera House in musical led to role in CBS sitcom pilot, Co-Ed Fever. Followed by first film role in The Rose (1979).
PICTURES: Actor: The Great Santini, Brubaker, Back Roads, Take This Job and Shove It, An Officer and a Gentleman, Independence Day, Lords of Discipline, Firestarter, White of the Eye, The Curse (dir.), The Further Adventures of Tennessee Buck (dir., actor), Heartbreak Hotel, The Two Jakes.
TELEVISION: Are You in the House Alone?, Friendly Fire, Gulag, Mini-series: Golden Moment—An Olympic Love Story, If Tomorrow Comes, Guts and Glory: The Rise and Fall of Oliver North.

KEITH, PENELOPE: O.B.E. Actress. b. Sutton, Surrey, Eng., 1939. London stage debut, The Wars of the Roses (RSC, 1964). Extensive theater work including The Norman Conquests, Donkey's Years, The Apple Cart, Hobson's Choice, Captain Brassbound's Conversion, Hay Fever. Film debut, Think Dirty, 1970.
PICTURES: Take a Girl Like You, Penny Gold, Priest of Love.
TELEVISION: Series: Kate, The Good Life, To the Manor Born, Executive Stress; Movies: Private Lives, The Norman Conquests, Donkey's Years.

KELLER, MARTHE: Actress. b. Basel, Switzerland, 1946. e. Stanislavsky Sch. Munich. Joined a Heidelberg repertory group and Schiller Rep. in Berlin. Started acting in France and attracted attention of U.S. directors after appearing in Claude Lelouch's And Now My Love. Has acted in over 50 plays in French, German, Eng. & Italian.
PICTURES: Funeral in Berlin, The Devil by the Tail, Give Her the Moon, Old Maid, Elle Court, Le Chute d'un corps, And Now My Love, Down the Ancient Staircase, Marathon Man, Black Sunday, Bobby Deerfield, Fedora, The Formula, The Amateur, Wagner, Femmes de Personne, Joan Luiu: But One Day in the Country, I Come on Monday Dark Eyes, Rouge Basier, The Artisan.
TELEVISION: The Charthouse of Parma, The Nightmare Years.

KELLERMAN, SALLY: Actress. b. Long Beach, CA, June 2, 1936. m. Jonathan Krane. e. Hollywood H.S. Studied acting in N.Y. at the Actors Studio and in Hollywood with Jeff Corey. Film debut Reform School Girls (1959).
TELEVISION: Mannix, It Takes a Thief, Chrysler Theatre, Centennial, Dempsey, Secret Weapons, September Gun, Faerie Tale Theatre, Dr. Paradise.
PICTURES: The Boston Strangler, The April Fools, M*A*S*H, Brewster McCloud, Last of the Red Hot Lovers, Lost Horizon, Slither, Rafferty and the Gold Dust Twins, The Big Bus, Welcome to L.A., A Little Romance, Foxes, Loving Couples, The Serial, Moving Violations, Back to School, That's Life!, Meatballs III, Three For the Road, Someone to Love, You Can't Hurry Love, Boris and Natasha, (also assoc. prod.), Boardwalk, All's Fair, The Secret of the Ice Cave.

KELLEY, DeFOREST: Actor. b. Atlanta, GA, Jan. 20, 1920.
PICTURES: Fear in the Night, Canon City, The Men, House of Bamboo, Man in the Gray Flannel Suit, Tension at Table Rock, Gunfight at the O.K. Corral, Raintree County, The Law and Jake Wade, Warlock, Where Love Has Gone, Marriage on the Rocks, Star Trek—The Motion Picture, Star Trek II—The Wrath of Khan, Star Trek III: The Search for Spock, Star Trek IV: The Voyage Home, Star Trek V: The Final Frontier.
TELEVISION: Star Trek (series).

KELLEY PATRICK: Executive. Joined MCA in 1950 as agent; with them for 20 years; named v.p. in chg. of talent for Universal's theatrical and TV project in 1964. Left MCA in 1970 to form First Artists with star partners Barbra Streisand, Sidney Poitier, Paul Newman (later joined by Steve McQueen and Dustin Hoffman). Resigned 1975 as F.A. bd. chmn. to head Pan Arts Corp., prod. co. of which George Roy Hill is bd. chmn.
PICTURES: A Little Romance (exec. prod.), The Little Drummer Girl (exec. prod.), The World According to Garp (exec. prod.), Funny Farm (exec. prod.), Deadly Friend (exec. prod.).

KELLOGG, PHILIP M.: Executive. b. March 17, 1912, Provo, WA. e. UCLA. Special feature writer for Hearst papers and magazines, 1933–34; MGM story dept., production dept., Irving Thalberg unit, 1934–35; Warner Bros. Film editor, 1935–41; Berg-Allenberg Agency, 1941–50; U.S. Naval Reserve officer, 1941–46; William Morris Agency, 1950–present, co-head of m.p. dept., dir. WMA, Ltd., London.

KELLY, GABRIELLE: Producer. b. Ireland. e. U. of Sussex. Moved to U.S. in 1975, working at the New York Review of Books before going into independent film production. Has worked with producers Jay Presson Allen, Burtt Harris and director Sidney Lumet, optioning, developing and producing projects. Co-producer of D.A.R.Y.L.

KELLY, GENE: Actor, Director. b. Pittsburgh, PA, Aug. 23, 1912. e. Pennsylvania State U., U. of Pittsburgh. Bricklayer, concrete mixer, soda clerk, dance instructor before going on stage, in N.Y. prods. (Leave It to Me, One for the Money, The Time of Your Life, Pal Joey). On screen 1942 in For Me and My Gal; Special Academy Award for advancing dance films, 1951.
THEATER: Director: Flower Drum Song.
PICTURES: Pilot No. 5, Du Barry Was a Lady, As Thousands Cheer, The Cross of Lorraine, Christmas Holiday, Anchors Aweigh, Cover Girl, Ziegfeld Follies, The Pirate, Three Musketeers, Words and Music, Take Me Out to the Ball

Game, Black Hand, On the Town (also co-dir.), An American in Paris, Summer Stock, Singin' in the Rain (also co-dir.), It's A Big Country, Devil Makes Three, Love is Better Than Ever, Brigadoon, Crest of the Wave, Deep in My Heart, Invitation to the Dance (also dir.), It's Always Fair Weather, The Happy Road (also prod., dir.), Les Girls, Marjorie Morningstar, The Tunnel of Love (dir. only), Inherit the Wind, Let's Make Love (cameo), Gigot (dir. only), What a Way to Go, A Guide for the Married Man (dir. only), The Young Girls of Rochefort, Hello, Dolly! (dir. only), The Cheyenne Social Club (prod., dir. only), 40 Carats, That's Entertainment, That's Entertainment, Part Two, Viva, Knievel!, Xanadu, That's Dancing.

TELEVISION: Jack and the Beanstalk, Going My Way (series), The Gene Kelly Show, Woman of the Year (dir. only), many specials.

KELLY, JIM: Actor. b. Paris, KY. e. U. of Louisville. Studied karate at univ., winning trophies and int'l. middleweight championship. Opened school for karate in L.A. Did modelling and TV commercials. Was technical advisor for fight scenes on Melinda and played role in it.

PICTURES: Enter the Dragon (debut), Black Belt Jones, Three the Hard Way.

KELLY, NANCY: Actress. b. Lowell, MA, March 25, 1921. e. Immaculate Conception Acad., N.Y.; St. Lawrence Acad., L.I.; Bentley Sch. for Girls. In number of pictures as child, and on stage in Susan and God (N.Y. prod. 1937). Returned to screen in Submarine Patrol (1938).

PICTURES: Tailspin, Jesse James, Stanley and Livingstone, Tornado, Tailspin, Frontier Marshal, He Married His Wife, One Night in the Tropics, To the Shores of Tripoli, Tarzan's Desert Mystery, Women in Bondage, Gamblers Choice, Show Business, Double Exposure, Song of the Sarong, Woman Who Came Back, Murder in the Music Hall, Crowded Paradise, The Bad Seed.

STAGE: The Big Knife, Season in the Sun, 1950–51; Bad Seed, 1954–55 (Tony Award); The Gingerbread Lady (Nat'l tour); Remote Asylum.

TELEVISION: The Imposter (debut 1974); Medical Center.

KELSEY, LINDA: Actress. b. Minneapolis, MN, July 28, 1946. e. U. of Michigan, B.A.

TELEVISION: Lou Grant (series, 1977–82), The Picture of Dorian Gray, Something for Joey; Eleanor and Franklin, The Last of Mrs. Lincoln, A Perfect Match, Attack on Fear, His Mistress. Special: Home Sweet Homeless.

KEMENY, JOHN: Producer. b. Budapest, Hungary. Producer for National Film Board of Canada, 1957–69. Formed International Cinemedia Center, Ltd. in 1969 in Montreal, as partner.

PICTURES: The Apprenticeship of Duddy Kravitz, White Line Fever, Shadow of the Hawk, Ice Castles, Bay Boy, The Wraith, Quest for Fire (co-prod.), Nowhere to Hide (exec. prod.), Iron Eagle II.

TELEVISION: Murderers Among Us: The Simon Wiesenthal Story (co-prod.).

KEMP, JEREMY: Actor. b. Chesterfield, England, Feb. 3, 1935. e. Abbottsholme Sch., Central Sch. of Speech and Drama. Service with Gordon Highlanders. Early career on stage incl. Old Vic Theatre Company, 1959–61. Recent theatre: Celebration, Incident at Vichy, Spoiled, The Caretaker. National Theatre, 1979–80.

TELEVISION: Z Cars, The Lovers of Florence, The Last Reunion, Colditz, Brassneck, Rhinemann Exchange, Lisa, Goodbye, Henry VIII, St. Joan, The Winter's Tale, Unity, The Contract, Winds of War, Sadat, King Lear, Sherlock Holmes, George Washington, Peter the Great, War and Remembrance, Slip-Up.

PICTURES: Cast a Giant Shadow, Operation Crossbow, The Blue Max, Assignment K, Twist of Sand, Strange Affair, Darling Lilli, The Games, The Saltzburg Connection, The Blockhouse, The Bellstone Fox, 7% Solution, A Bridge Too Far, East of Elephant Rock, Caravans, The Prisoner of Zenda, The Return of the Soldier, Top Secret!, Uncommon Valour, When the Whales Came.

KEMP, MATTY: Producer, Director, Writer. b. Rockville Center, NY. e. St. Paul's School, Hemstead, NY. Entered as actor-writer 1926 Universal Pictures: variously employed by Mack Sennett, Fox, Paramount, RKO: prod. Authors' Guild show for radio and musical shorts. Served in U.S. Army 1942–45 in Signal Corps Pictorial, Information Education, and Training film branch. Prod. dir. for series of musical shorts Universal 1945; formed Cameo Productions (CA) 1946: formed Masque Productions with Gene Raymond 1948.

PICTURES: (prod., dir.) Linda Be Good, Million Dollar Weekend. (story) The French Line: (writer, prod., dir.) Pan American Showtime 13 half hour musical TV series. (prod., dir.) Meet the Family series (3) with Arthur Lake. (prod., dir.), Adventurous Hobby series (story, prod., dir.), The Birth of a Legend, documentary on Mary Pickford & Douglas Fairbanks. (Story, co-producer) America's Sweetheart, feature TV documentary. Managing dir., prod. executive, Mary Pickford Co.

KEMPER, VICTOR J.: Cinematographer. b. Newark, NJ, April 14, 1927. e. Seton Hall, B.S. Engineer Channel 13, Newark 1949–54; Tech. supervisor EUE Screen Gems NY 1954–56; v.p. engineering General TV Network. Pres. VJK Prods.

PICTURES: Husbands, The Magic Garden of Stanley Sweetheart, They Might Be Giants, Who is Harry Kellerman?, The Hospital, The Candidate, Last of the Red Hot Lovers, Shamus, The Friends of Eddie Coyle, Gordon's War, The Hideaways, The Gambler, The Reincarnation of Peter Proud, Dog Day Afternoon, Stay Hungry, The Last Tycoon, Mikey and Nicky, Slapshot, Audrey Rose, Oh God!, The One and Only, Coma, Eyes of Laura Mars, Magic, Night of the Juggler, And Justice for All, The Jerk, The Final Countdown, Xanadu, The Four Seasons, Chu Chu and the Philly Flash, Partner, Author! Author! National Lampoon's Vacation, Mr. Mom, The Lonely Guy, Cloak and Dagger, Secret Admirer, Pee Wee's Big Adventure, Clue, Bobo, Hot to Trot, Cohen and Tate, See No Evil, Hear Evil, Crazy People.

KEMP-WELCH, JOAN: Freelance, TV Director, Producer, Actress. b. Wimbleton, Eng., 1906. First appearance on stage 1927. Subsequently many stage parts and stage directorial assignments. First appeared in films 1938. Films included 60 Glorious Years, They Flew Alone, The Citadel, Busman's Honeymoon. Over 200 repertory and touring productions. West End theatre prods. include: Dead on Nine, Vicious Circle, Our Town, Desire Under the Elms. Since 1954 TV dir. Received TV Oscar for Light Entert., 1958. Desmond Davis Award for services to TV 1963. Silver Dove Monte Carlo Award, 1961 for Electra. The Lover, awarded Prix Italia 1963 (drama). Many other productions, incl. musicals, ballet, dramas, series, outside broadcasts. Dear Octupus, The Birthday Party, The Collection, View from the Bridge, Electra, 3 Sisters, A Midsummer Nights Dream, Dangerous Corner. Upstairs, Downstairs; prod. Armchair Theatre, 1973–74. 1974–75. French Without Tears, Wait Till Dark, The Price, Cranford Musical. The Other Side of the Swamp, TV. Romeo and Juliet. 1977 in S. Africa. Deep Blue Sea, The Kingfisher, The Monkey Walk in Vienna, The Circle, Hay Fever. TV Hay Fever (London), It Happened in Harrods, A Man and His Wife, You Can't Take It With You (South Africa), Home, Cause Celebre, Your Place or Mine, TV. The Piano, Shades of Brown, Winter Journey, I Am Who I Am, TV Lady Killers. In S. Africa: The Elocution of Benjamin Franklin, Pitlochry. Gaslight & The Unvarnished Truth (S. Africa), Happy Birthday in Vienna, Murder at the Vicarage, Revival. Other Side of the Swamp, (Vienna). Dangerous Corner. Arsenic and Old Lace, The Killing of Sister George. 1983 (in Australia) On the Razzle, Romeo and Juliet. Tales from Chekhov (New York). Shades of Brown, (Adelco Award) On Golden Pond, The Voices; Sleuth (Vienna); An Inspector Calls in Cincinnati, USA; West Side Waltz, The Glass Menagerie (Frankfurt), The Amorous Prawn, Outside Edge; Catherine of Sienna; The Mousetrap; The Secret Garden. Blithe Spirit (Vienna), Death Trap (Frankfurt), Deep Blue Sea (vienna), 1989 Wait Till Dark (Frankfurt).

KENNEDY, ARTHUR: Actor. b. Worcester, MA, February 17, 1914. e. Carnegie Inst. of Technology. m. Mary Cheffey, prof. Has worked for George M. Cohan; Guthrie McClintic, Marc Connelly and others well known to theatregoers. Film debut: City for Conquest (1940).

PICTURES: They Died with Their Boots On, High Sierra, Strange Alibi, Knockout, Highway West, Air Force, Devotion, Boomerang, The Window, Champion, Chicago Deadline, The Glass Menagerie, Red Mountain, Bright Victory, Bend of the River, Rancho Notorious, Girl in White, Lusty Men, Man from Laramie, Trial, Naked Dawn, Desperate Hours, Crashout, Rawhide Years, Peyton Place, Some Came Running, Claudelle Inglish, Adventures of a Young Man, Barabbas, Lawrence of Arabia, Italiano Brava Gentle, Stay Away Joe, A Minute to Pray, a Second to Die, Hail Hero, Shark, My Old Man's Place, The Sentinel; Signs of Life.

TELEVISION: Many appearances between 1954–69. Movies: Murderer, Death of Innocence, Crawlspace, The President's Plane is Missing, Nakia.

KENNEDY, BURT: Director. b. Muskegon, MI, Sept. 3, 1922. U.S. Army 1942–46; awarded Silver Star, Bronze Star and Purple Heart with Oak Leaf Cluster. Began as writer of TV and film scripts, and was writer, producer and director of Combat series and many TV and theatrical westerns.

PICTURES: The Canadians, Mail Order Bride (dir., prod., s.p.), The Rounders, The Money Trap, Return of the Seven, The War Wagon, Welcome to Hard Times, Support Your Local Sheriff, The Good Guys and the Bad Guys, Young Billy Young, The Devil's Backbone, Dirty Dingus Magee, Support Your Local Gunfighter, Hannie Caulder, The Train Robbers (also s.p.), The Killer Inside Me, Wolf Lake, The Trouble with Spies (prod., dir., s.p.), Big Bad John (dir.).

TELEVISION: Series: Combat (prod., dir.,) The Rounders (prod), How the West Was Won (dir.), The Yellow Rose, Simon & Simon, Magnum P.I., Movies: The Rhinemann Exchange, More Wild Wild West, The Honor Guard, Kate Bliss and the Ticker Tape Kid, The Concrete Cowboys. The

Alamo-Thirteen Days to Glory, Shootout in a One Dog Town, All the Kind Strangers, Down the Long Hills, Sidekicks, Once Upon a Texas Train, Where the Hell's that Gold!!! (dir., prod., s.p.).

KENNEDY, GEORGE: Actor. b. New York, NY, Feb. 18, 1925. f. orchestra leader at N.Y. Proctor Theatre, m. dancer with Le Ballet Classique in vaudeville. At 2 acted in touring co. of Bringing Up Father. At 7, disc jockey with his own radio show for children. Joined W.W.II Army at 17, earned two Bronze Stars and combat and service ribbons. In Army 16 years, became Capt. and Armed Forces Radio and TV officer. 1957, opened first Army Information Office, N.Y. Served as technical advisor to Phil Silvers's Sergeant Bilko TV series. Began acting in 1959 when discharged from Army.
TELEVISION: Sugarfoot, Cheyenne, Series: Blue Knight (series), Sarge, Dallas. Movies: Jesse Owens Story, Liberty, Cry in the Wilderness, International Airport, Kenny Rogers as the Gambler III, The Gunfighters, Backstairs at the White House, What Price Victory.
PICTURES: Little Shepard of Kingdom Come, Lonely Are the Brave, Strait Jacket, The Silent Witness, Island of the Blue Dolphins, The Man from the Diners Club, Little Shepherd of Kingdom Come, Mirage, See How They Run, McHale's Navy, Charade, In Harm's Way, The Sons of Katie Elder, Shenandoah, Hush . . . Hush Sweet Charlotte, The Dirty Dozen, Hurry Sundown, Cool Hand Luke (Acad. Award Best Supporting Actor), The Ballad of Josie, Jolly Pink Jungle, Bandolero!, The Boston Strangler, Guns of the Magnificent Seven, Gaily, Gaily, The Good Guys and the Bad Guys, Airport, . . . tick . . . tick . . . tick, Zig Zag, Dirty Dingus Magee, Fool's Parade, Lost Horizon, Cahill, Thunderbolt and Lightfoot, Airport 1975, Earthquake, The Human Factor, Airport '77, Death on the Nile, Brass Target, The Concorde—Airport 79, Death Ship, The Delta Force, Creepshow 2, Born to Race, Demon Warp, Counterforce, Nightmare at Noon, Private Roads, Uninvited, The Terror Within, The Naked Gun, Esmeralda Bay, Ministry of Vengeance.

KENNEDY, KATHLEEN: Producer. e. San Diego State U. Early TV experience on KCST, San Diego, working as camera operator, video editor, floor director and news production coordinator. Produced talk show, You're On. Left to enter m.p. industry as prod. asst. on Steven Spielberg's 1941.
PICTURES: Raiders of the Lost Ark (prod. assoc.); Poltergeist (assoc. prod.); E.T.: The Extra-Terrestrial (prod.); Twilight Zone: The Movie (co-assoc. prod.), Indiana Jones and the Temple of Doom (assoc. prod.); *Exec. prod. with Frank Marshall:* Gremlins; Goonies; Back to the Future; The Color Purple (prod.); Young Sherlock Holmes (co-prod.); An American Tail; Innerspace, Empire of the Sun; Batteries Not Included; Who Framed Roger Rabbit?, The Land Before Time, Indiana Jones and the Last Crusade, (prod. exec.), Dad, Always (prod.), Joe Versus the Volcano (exec. prod.), Gremlins II (exec. prod.).
TELEVISION: Steven Spielberg's Amazing Stories (supervising prod.), You're On (prod.), Roger Rabbit & the Secrets of Toontown (exec. prod.).

KENNEY, H. WESLEY: Producer, Director, stage, TV, film. b. Dayton, OH, Jan. 3, 1926. grad. Carnegie Inst. of Technology. Six-time Emmy winner; 1974–75 dir., All in the Family; exec. prod. Days of Our Lives; 1979–81, dir., Ladies Man, Filthy Rich, 1981. Exec. prod. Young and Restless, 1981–86; now exec. prod., General Hospital.

KENT, JEAN: Actress. b. London, England, June 29, 1921. e. Marist Coll., Peekham, London; p. prof. Fields & Norrie. First stage appearance at 3 and at 10 played in parents' act; chorus girl at Windmill Theatre, London, 1935; 2 yrs. repertory; Screen debut: It's That Man Again, 1941.
PICTURES: Trottle True, Her Favorite Husband, The Reluctant Widow, The Woman in Question, The Browning Version, Big Frame, Before I Wake, Shadow of Fear, Prince and the Showgirl, Bon Jour Tristesse, Grip of the Strangler, Beyond This Place, Please Turn Over, Bluebeard's Ten Honeymoons, Shout at the Devil.
TELEVISION: A Call on the Widow, The Lovebird, The Morning Star, November Voyage, Love Her to Death, The Lion and the Mouse, The Web, Sir Francis Drake series, Yvette, Emergency Ward 10, County Policy, Coach 7, Smile on the Face of the Tiger, No Hiding Place, Kipling, This Man Craig, The Killers, Vanity Fair, A Night with Mrs. Da Tanka, United serial. The Family of Fred, After Dark, Thicker than Water series, The Young Doctors, Brother and Sister, Up Pompei, Steptoe and Son, Doctor at Large, Family at War, K is for Killing, Night School, Tycoon series, Crossroads (series), Lyttons Diary.

KENT, JOHN B.: Theatre executive, Attorney. b. Jacksonville, FL, Sept. 5, 1939. e. Yale U., U. of Florida, Law Sch., NYU grad. sch. of law (L.L.M. in taxation, 1964). Partner in Kent, Ridge & Crawford, P.A.; Pres. & dir, Kent Investments, Inc. (1977 to present); dir. and off. Kent Theatres, Inc. and affiliated corps (1961 to present); v.p. and gen. counsel, (1970 to present). Was pres. 1967–70 when resigned to devote full time to law practice. NATO dir. (1972) and Presidents' Advisory Cabinet, (1979 to present) v.p. NATO of Fla., 1968–72, dir; 1973 to present. Member of Rotary Club of Jacksonville, Fla. Bar Ass'n., American Bar Ass'n., American Judicature Society.

KENYON, CURTIS: Writer.
TV PLAYS: Cavalcade of America, Fireside Theatre, Schlitz Playhouse, U.S. Steel Hour, 20th Century-Fox Hour.
PICTURES: Woman Who Dared, Lloyds of London, Wake Up and Live, Love and Hisses, She Knew All the Answers, Twin Beds, Seven Days' Leave, Thanks for Everything, Princess and the Pirate, Bathing Beauty, Fabulous Dorseys, Tulsa, Two Flags West.

KERASOTES, GEORGE G.: Exhibitor. Springfield, IL. e. U. of Illinois, 1929–33; Lincoln Coll. of Law 1935–37. Past pres. Theatre Owners of Illinois. Past pres. Kerasotes Theatres, 1935–85. Past pres., Theatre Owners of America, 1959–60. Chmn. of board of TOA 1960–62; chmn. ACE Toll TV com.; bd. mem. NATO; treas., bd. of dir., mem. exec. comm., chmn. insurance comm. chmn., George Kerasotes Corp., GKC Theatres. Director St. Anthony's Hellenic Church—Hellenic Golf Classic. Director, Will Rogers Hospitals; Director, Pioneers.

KERKORIAN, KIRK: Executive. b. Fresno, CA, June 6, 1917. e. Los Angeles public schools. Served as capt., transport command, RAF, 1942–44. Commercial air line pilot from 1940; founder Los Angeles Air Service (later Trans Intl. Airlines Corp.), 1948; Intl. Leisure Corp., 1968; controlling stockholder, Western Airlines, 1970; chief exec. officer, MGM, Inc., 1973–74; chmn. exec. com., vice-chmn. bd., 1974–1978. Stepped down from exec. positions while retaining financial interest in MGM/UA.

KERR, DEBORAH: Actress. b. Helensburgh, Scotland, Sept. 30, 1921; e. Phyllis Smale Ballet Sch. m. Anthony Bartley. On stage 1939 in repertory. Began Brit. screen career 1940 in Major Barbara; voted "Star of Tomorrow" Motion Picture Herald-Fame Poll, 1942. Voted one of top ten British money-making stars in Motion Picture Herald-Fame Poll, 1947. Bdwy debut in Tea and Sympathy, 1953.
PICTURES: Major Barbara, Love on the Dole, Hatler's Castle, The Day Will Dawn, The Avengers, Perfect Strangers, Colonel Blimp, Black Narcissus, The Hucksters, If Winter Comes, Edward My Son, Please Believe Me, King Solomon's Mines, Quo Vadis, Thunder in the East, Prisoner of Zenda, Dream Wife, Julius Caesar, Young Bess, From Here to Eternity, End of the Affair, King and I, Proud and Profane, Tea and Sympathy, Heaven Knows Mr. Alison, Affair to Remember, Count Your Blessings, Beloved Infidel, Sundowners, The Grass Is Greener, The Innocents, The Naked Edge, The Chalk Garden, Night of the Iguana, Marriage On the Rocks, Casino Royale, Eye of the Devil, The Gypsy Moths, The Arrangement, The Assam Garden.
TELEVISION: A Woman of Substance, Reunion at Fairborough, Hold the Dream, Witness for the Prosecution.

KERR, FRASER: Actor. b. Glasgow, Scotland, 1931. Early career in repertory. Tours of Canada and America. Ent. TV 1956. Series incl. Emergency Ward 10, Dixon of Deck Green, Murder Bag. Many Shakespeare plays. Radio: BBC Drama Rep. Co., 39 Steps, The Ringer, The Bible, What Every Woman Knows.
STAGE & TELEVISION: Night Must Fall, Never a Cross Word, The Inside Man, On the Buses, Dr. Finlay's Casebook, Wicked Woman, Madelaine July, Doctor in the House, Counterstrike, Waggoner's Walk, Juno and the Paycock, Aquarius, Ev, Upstairs and Downstairs, Cover to Cover, Janine, Robert the Bruce, Caliph of Bagdad, Watch it, Sailor!, The Fosters, Weekend World, Doctor at Sea, Dads Army, Algernon Blackwood, Waiting for Sheila, Weekend Show, Mind Your Language, Yes, Minister, Dick Emery Show, Bottle Boys, The Hard Man.
PICTURES: What a Whopper, Carry on Regardless, Way of McEagle, Thomasina, Theatre of Death, Tom, Dick and Harriet, Granny Gets the Point, Nothing but the Night, The Lord of the Rings, Kidnapped, The Derelict, Bloomfield, Ace of Diamonds, Andy Robson, It's a Deal!, Howard's Way, One Step Beyond.
RECORD PRODUCER: Tales of Shakespeare Series, The Casket Letters of Mary Queen of Scots.

KERR, JOHN: Actor. b. New York, NY, Nov. 15, 1931. p. Geoffrey Kerr, actor, and June Walker, actress. e. Harvard U., B.A., Columbia U., M.A. Actor in summer stock, TV; on Broadway in Bernardine, Tea and Sympathy, All Summer Long.
PICTURES: The Cobweb, Gaby, Tea and Sympathy, The Vintage, South Pacific, Girl of the Night, Pit and the Pendulum, Seven Women from Hell.
TELEVISION: Peyton Place (series), Washington: Behind Closed Doors, Incident on a Dark Street.

KERSHNER, IRVIN: Director. b. Philadelphia, PA, April 29, 1923. e. Tyler Sch. of Fine Arts of Temple U., 1946; Art Center Sch., U. of Southern California. Designer, photography, adv., docu-

mentary, architectural; doc. filmmaker, U.S.I.S., Middle East, 1950–52; dir., cameraman, TV doc., Confidential File, 1953–55; dir.-prod.-writer, Ophite Prod.
PICTURES: Stakeout on Dope Street, Young Captives, Hoodlum Priest, The Luck of Ginger Coffey, A Fine Madness, The Flim Flam Man, Loving, Up the Sandbox, S*P*Y*s, Return of a Man Called Horse, Raid on Entebbe. (TV in U.S.), Eyes of Laura Mars, The Empire Strikes Back, Never Say Never Again, Wildfire (exec. prod.), Orders, The White Crow.
TELEVISION: The Rebel, Naked City, numerous pilots and other nat'l. shows. Movie: The Traveling Man.

KEYES, EVELYN: Actress. b. Port Arthur, TX, 1925. e. high school. Began career as a dancer in night clubs. Autobiography: Scarlett O'Hara's Younger Sister (1977).
PICTURES: The Buccaneer, Union Pacific, Gone with the Wind, A Thousand and One Nights, The Jolson Story, Mating of Millie, Johnny O'Clock, Enchantment, Mr. Soft Touch, The Prowler, The Killer That Stalked New York, Smuggler's Island, The Iron Man, One Big Affair, Shoot First, 99 River Street, Hell's Half Acre, Top of the World, Seven Year Itch, Around the World in 80 Days, Wicked Stepmother.
TELEVISION: Murder She Wrote.

KEYLOUN, MARK: Actor. b. Dec. 20, 1960. e. Georgetown U. Worked in New York theatre.
PICTURES: Those Lips, Those Eyes, Sudden Impact, Forty-Deuce, Mike's Murder.
TELEVISION: Evergreen, War Stories: The Mine.

KIDDER, MARGOT: Actress. b. Yellowknife, Canada, Oct. 17, 1948.
PICTURES: Gaily, Gaily, Black Christmas, Quackser Fortune Has a Cousin in the Bronx, Sisters, The Great Waldo Pepper, 92 in the Shade, The Reincarnation of Peter Proud, Superman, Mr. Mike's Mondo Video, The Amityville Horror, Willy and Phil, Superman II, Heartaches, Shoot the Sun Down, Some Kind of Hero, Little Treasure, Superman III, Keeping Track, Superman IV: The Quest for Peace, Miss Right, Mob Story, White Room.
TELEVISION: Series: Nicholas (1971–72), Shell Game. Movies: Suddenly Single, The Bounty Man, Honky Tonk, Louisiana, The Glitter Dome, Bus Stop, Picking Up the Pieces, Vanishing Act, Hoax, Body of Evidence.

KIEL, RICHARD: Actor. b. Detroit, MI, Sept. 13, 1939.
PICTURES: The Human Duplicators, Skidoo, The Longest Yard, The Spy Who Loved Me, Force 10 from Navarone, They Went Thataway and Thataway, Flash and the Firecat, Moonraker, So Fine, Cannonball Run II, Pale Rider.

KILEY, RICHARD: Actor. b. Chicago, IL, Mar. 31, 1922. e. Loyola U. Started prof. career radio, Jack Armstrong, All American Boy.
STAGE: Streetcar Named Desire (touring co.), Misalliance, Kismet, Time Limit, Redhead (Tony Award), No Strings, Man of LaMancha (Tony Award), Her First Roman, The Incomparable Max, Voices, Absurd Person Singular, All My Sons.
PICTURES: The Mob, The Sniper, Eight Iron Men, Pick-Up on South Street, Blackboard Jungle, Phenix City Story, Spanish Affair, Pendulum, The Little Prince, Endless Love, Looking for Mr. Goodbar, Howard the Duck.
TELEVISION: Mini-series: The Thorn Birds, George Washington, Murder Once Removed, Friendly Persuasion, The Macahans, Angel on My Shoulder, Isabel's Choice, Pray TV, The Bad Seed, A.D., Do You Remember Love, If Tomorrow Comes, A Year in the Life (series), My First Love, The Final Days.

KILLIAM, PAUL: Producer, Performer. b. Mass., Sept. 12, 1916. e. Harvard U. News supervisor, WOR-Mutual; prod.-performer TV Hometown. Matinee in N.Y. units for CBS-TV Morning Show, NBC-TV Home Show; ind. prod. cartoons, shorts, comedies: prod. film series, Paul Killiam Show, Movie Museum, Silents Please.

KILMER, VAL: Actor. b. Los Angeles, CA, Dec. 31, 1959. m. actress Joanne Whalley. e. Hollywood's Professional's Sch., Juilliard, NY. NY stage: Electra and Orestes. Co-wrote and starred in How It All Began (later presented at Public Theatre), Henry IV, Part One, and As You Like It (Gutherie, MN). Broadway debut, Slab Boys. Also: Hamlet (Colorado Shakespeare Fest.).
PICTURES: Top Secret! (debut, 1984), Real Genius, Top Gun, Willow, Kill Me Again.
TELEVISION: The Murders in the Rue Morgue, Gore Vidal's Billy the Kid.

KIMBLEY, DENNIS: Business Manager, Motion Picture, AV Television, Sales, Kodak Limited., in U.K. Early career in Kodak Testing Dept. responsible for quality control motion picture films. Joined Marketing Division 1966. Chairman BKSTS FILM 75 and FILM 79 Conference Committee. President BKSTS 1976–78. Governor, London International Film School, 1983.

KING, ALAN: Actor, Producer. b. New York, NY, Dec. 26, 1927. Stars semi-annually at Sands Hotel, Las Vegas. Author, Anybody Who Owns His Own Home Deserves It, Help I'm a Prisoner in a Chinese Bakery.
TELEVISION: The Tonight Show, Kraft Music Hall, Comedy is King. Prod-star NBC-TV specials. Host and guest star, Tonight Show. Seventh Avenue (mini-series), On Location: An Evening with Alan King at Carnegie Hall.
STAGE: The Impossible Years, The Investigation, Dinner at Eight, The Lion in Winter, Something Different.
PICTURES: Bye Bye Braverman, Anderson Tapes, Just Tell Me What You Want, Author! Author! Producer: Happy Birthday, Gemini, Cattle Annie and Little Britches (co-prod.), Lovesick, Cat's Eye, Wolfen (exec. prod.), Memories of Me (actor, co-prod.), Enemies, a Love Story.

KING, ANDREA: Actress, r.n. Georgette Barry; b. Paris, France, Feb. 7, 1915. e. Edgewood H.S., Greenwich, CT. m. N.H. Willis, attorney. Started career on N.Y. stage, following high school; in Growing Pains & Fly Away Home, Boy Meets Girl, Angel Street (Boston); Life with Father (Chicago); signed by Warner, 1943. Screen debut: The Very Thought of You.
PICTURES: My Wild Irish Rose, Ride the Pink Horse, Mr. Peabody and the Mermaid, Song of Surrender, Southside 1-10001, Dial 1119, Lemon Drop Kid, Mark of the Renegade, World in His Arms, Red Planet Mars, Daddy's Gone A-Hunting.
TELEVISION: Prescription Murder.

KING, HERMAN: Producer. b. Chicago, IL. Was engaged in vending machine business; mfr. Hollywood Talkitone Soundie Projectors; org. prod. co., King Bros. Prod. (with bros. Maurice and Franklin), 1941.
PICTURES: When Strangers Marry, Dillinger, Suspense, The Gangster, The Dude Goes West, Badman of Tombstone, Gun Crazy, Southside 1-1000, Drums in the Deep South, Mutiny, The Ring, Carnival Story, The Brave One, Gorgo, Captain Sinbad, Maya, Return of The Gunfighter, Heaven with a Gun.
TELEVISION: Maya series, King International Corp.

KING, PERRY: Actor. b. Alliance, OH, Apr. 30, 1948. e. Yale. Studied with John Houseman at Juilliard.
PICTURES: The Possession of Joel Delaney (debut), Slaughterhouse-Five, Big Truck, Poor Clare, The Lords of Flatbush, Mandingo, The Wild Party, Lipstick, Andy Warhol's Bad, The Choirboys, A Different Story, The Clarivoyant.
TELEVISION: Medical Center, Hawaii Five-O, Apple's Way, Cannon, I'll Take Manhattan, Riptide (series), The Last Convertible, Captain and the Kings, The Cracker Factory, Stranded, Perfect People, Shakedown on Sunset Strip, The Man Who Lived at the Ritz, Half 'n' Half (pilot), Disaster at Silo 7, The Prize Pulitzer.

KING, PETER: Executive. b. London, England, 1928. e. Marlborough Coll., Oxford U. Bd., Shipman & King Cinemas Ltd., 1956; borough councillor, 1959–61; chmn., London & Home counties branch, CEA, 1962–63; pres., CEA, 1964; dir. film ind. Defense Organization dir., Grade Org. 1966–68; man. dir. Shipman & King Cinemas Ltd., 1959–68. Ch. man. dir. Paramount Pictures (U.K.) Ltd. Britain, 1968–70. Man., dir., EMI Cinemas and Leisure Ltd., 1970–74. Chairman: King Publications Ltd.; Publisher: Screen International.

KING, STEPHEN: Writer. b. 1940. Best-selling novelist specializing in thrillers many of which have been adapted to film by others (Carrie, Salem's Lot, The Shining, The Dead Zone, Christine, Cujo, Firestarter, Cat's Eye). Stand By Me (The Body), The Running Man, Night Shift Collection (The Woman in the Room & The Boogey Man), Apt Pupil. TV adaptation: It.
PICTURES: Creepshow (s.p., actor), Silver Bullet (s.p.), Maximum Overdrive (s.p., actor, dir.), Creepshow II (s.p., actor), Children of the Corn (s.p.), Pet Sematary (s.p.).

KINGMAN, DONG: Fine Artist. b. Oakland, CA, Mar. 31, 1911. e. Hong Kong 1916–1920. 1928, mem. motion picture co., Hong Kong branch; 1935; began to exhibit as fine artist in San Francisco; promotional, advertising or main title artwork for following films: World of Suzie Wong, Flower Drum Song, 55 Days of Peking, Circus World, King Rat, The Desperados, The Sand Pebbles, Lost Horizon-1973. 1966–7, created 12 paintings for Universal Studio Tour for posters and promotion; 1968, cover painting for souvenir program for Ringling Bros.-Barnum and Bailey Circus; treasurer for Living Artist Production since 1954; Exec. V.P. 22nd-Century Films, Inc. since 1968, Prod. & dir. short, Hongkong Dong. Also short subject film Dong Kingman, filmed and directed by James Wong Howe.

KINGSLEY, BEN: Actor. b. Yorkshire, England, Dec. 31, 1943. Started career with Salford Players, amateur co. in Manchester. Turned pro in 1966 and appeared on London stage at a Chichester Festival Theatre. 1967, joined Royal Shakespeare Co., where starred in A Midsummer Night's Dream, Tempest, Measure for Measure, Merry Wives of Windsor, Volpone, Cherry Orchard, Hamlet, Othello, Judgement, Kean. (NY).

Played Squeers in Nicholas Nickleby in 1980 in London. Film debut in Fear is the Key (1972).
PICTURES: Gandhi (Acad. Award, 1982), Betrayal, Turtle Diary, Harem, Slipstream, Testimony, Pascali's Island, Without a Clue, The Secret of the Sahara, The 5th Monkey.
TELEVISION: Silas Marner, Kean, Oxbridge Blues, Camille, The Train, Sahara Secret, Murderers Among Us: The Simon Wiesenthal Story, Testimony, Sealed Train.

KINGSLEY, DOROTHY: Writer. (Mrs. William W. Durney). b. New York, NY, Oct. 14, 1909. e. Detroit Arts and Crafts Acad. Radio writer for Bob Hope, 1938; Edgar Bergen, 1939–43.
PICTURES: Date With Judy, Neptune's Daughter, Two Weeks with Love, Angels in the Outfield, Texas Carnival, It's a Big Country, When in Rome, Small Town Girl, Dangerous When Wet, Kiss Me Kate, Seven Brides for Seven Brothers, Jupiter's Darling, Don't Go Near the Water, Pal Joey, Green Mansions, Can-Can, Pepe, Half a Sixpence, Valley of the Dolls.
TELEVISION: Created series, Bracken's World.

KINGSLEY, WALTER: Executive. b New York, NY, Oct. 20, 1923. e. Phillips Acad., Andover; Amherst Coll., B.A., 1947. Charter member Big Brothers of Los Angeles. WCOP, Boston, 1948–50; Ziv Television Programs, Inc., 1950–58; President, Independent Television Corp., 1958–62. Member bd. dir Big Brothers of Amer.; pres. Kingsley Co., 1962–66; exec. v.p. Wolper Prods. Metromedia Prods. Corp., 1966–72; faculty, Inter-Racial Council of Business Opportunity, N.Y.; 1972–82, pres., Kingsley Company, Commercial Real Estate; 1982–present, special consultant, American Film Inst.; bd. mem.: Big Brothers/Big Sisters of America; Big Brothers of Greater Los Angeles.

KINOSHITA, KEISUKE: Director. b. Japan, 1912. Entered Shochiku studio as film processor and progressed to director.
PICTURES: Twenty-four Eyes, Sun and Rose, Wild Chrysanthemum, A Japanese Tragedy, Times of Joy and Sorrow, Snow Flurry, Candle in the Wind, Carmen's Pure Love.

KINOY, ERNEST: Writer. Started career in radio writing sci. fic. programs (X Minus One, Dimension X). Wrote for nearly all early dramatic shows, including Studio One, Philco Playhouse, Playhouse 90.
PICTURES: Brother John, Buck and the Preacher, Leadbelly, White Water Summer (co-s.p.).
TELEVISION: The Defenders, Naked City, Dr. Kildare, Jacob and Joseph (special), David, the King (special), Roots I & II, Victory at Entebbe, Skokie, Murrow, The President's Plane is Missing, Stones for Ibarra, Gore Vidal's Lincoln, The Fatal Shore.

KINSKI, KLAUS: Actor. b. Poland, 1928. r.n. Nicolaus Nakszynski. Drafted into German army at 16; became British prisoner. After release began acting career in postwar German theatre. Since early 1950s has made nearly 170 films throughout Europe. Autobiography: All I Need is Love (1989).
PICTURES: Cold Blooded Beast, Pleasure Girls, The Bloody Hands of the Law, Doctor Zhivago, For a Few Dollars More, Aguirre: The Wrath of God, Woyzeck, Nosferatu, the Vampyre, Love and Money (American debut), The Soldier, The Little Drummer Girl, Codename: Wild Geese, Cobra Verde, Paganini (dir., s.p., actor), Nosferatu in Venice, The Great Hunter, Magdalene.
TELEVISION: Beauty and the Beast (Faerie Tale Theatre), The Hitchhiker, Timestalkers.

KINSKI, NASTASSJA: Actress. r.n. Nastassja Nakszynski. b. Berlin, Germany, Jan. 24, 1960. m. prod and talent agent, Ibrahim Moussa. Daughter of actor Klaus Kinski.
PICTURE: Falsche Bewegung (1975), To the Devil a Daughter, Passion Flower Hotel, Stay as You Are, Tess, Cat People, For Your Love Only, One From the Heart, Exposed, The Moon in the Gutter, Unfaithfully Yours, The Hotel New Hampshire, Maria's Lovers, Paris, Texas, Revolution, Symphony of Love, Harem, Malady of Love, Silent Night, Torrents of Spring, On a Moonlit Night, Magdalene, The Secret.

KIRK (BUSH), PHYLLIS: Actress. b. Syracuse, NY, Sept. 18, 1930. Perfume repr. model, Conover Agcy.; B'way play debut in My Name Is Aquilon; actress, summer stock; screen debut in Our Very Own; B'way production of Point of No Return. Worked as interviewer-host on all three major networks Executive with ICPR and Stone Associates. Joined CBS News in Los Angeles, 1978; 1988 named v.p. media relations Stone/Hallinan Associates.
TELEVISION: The Thin Man.
PICTURES: A Life of Her Own, Two Weeks with Love, Mrs. O'Malley and Mr. Malone, Three Guys Named Mike, About Face, Iron Mistress, Thunder over the Plains, House of Wax, Crime Wave, River Beat, Canyon Crossroads, City After Midnight.

KIRKLAND, SALLY: Actress. b. NY, NY, Oct. 31, 1944. e. Actors Studio, studied acting with Uta Hagen and Lee Strasberg. Achieved notoriety in the 1960s for on-stage nudity (Sweet Eros, Futz), for work in experimental off-off Bdwy theater and as part of Andy Warhol's inner circle. Appeared as featured actress in over 25 films and countless avant-garde shows, before winning acclaim (and Acad. Award nom.) as the star of Anna (1987). 1983 founded Sally Kirkland Acting Workshop, a traveling transcendental meditation, yoga and theatrical seminar. Formed Artists Alliance Prods. with Mark and David Buntzman, 1988.
THEATER: The Love Nest, Futz, Tom Paine, Sweet Eros, Witness, One Night Stand of a Noisy Passenger, The Justice Box, Where Has Tommy Flowers Gone?, In the Boom Boom Room (L.A., Drama-Logue's best actress award, 1981), Largo Desolato.
PICTURES: The Thirteen Most Beautiful Woman (1964), Blue, Futz!, Coming Apart, Going Home, The Sting, The Young Nurses, The Way We Were, Cinderella Liberty, Candy Stripe Nurses, Big Bad Mama, Bite the Bullet, Crazy Mama, Breakheart Pass, A Star is Born, Pipe Dreams, Hometown U.S.A., Private Benjamin, The Incredible Shrinking Woman, Human Highway, Love Letters, Fatal Games, Talking Walls, Anna, Melanie Rose, Crack in the Mirror, Paint It Black, Cold Feet, High Stakes, Best of the Best, Bullseye.
TELEVISION: Willow B—Women in Prison, Georgia Peaches, Summer, Falcon Crest (series).

KIRKPATRICK, DAVID: Executive. e. California Inst. of Arts. Wrote screenplay, The Great Texas Dynamite Chase, produced by New World Pictures. Joined Paramount Pictures 1979 as analyst in story dept; left to head Sidney Beckerman's production co. at United Artists. Returned to Paramount 1982 as exec. dir. of production. 1984, promoted to v.p., prod., Paramount. 1985, named exec. v.p., prod. Named pres. mp. div., Weintraub Entertainment Group, 1987, resigned, 1989.

KIRKWOOD, GENE: Producer. Company: Kanter-Kirkwood Entertainment.
PICTURES: Rocky ((Acad. Award, picture, 1976), New York, New York (assoc. prod.); Comes a Horseman; Uncle Joe Shannon; The Idolmaker; A Night in Heaven; Gorky Park; The Keep; The Pope of Greenwich Village; Legs Diamond; Ironweed, UHF (co-prod.).

KITT, EARTHA: Actress, Singer. b. Columbia, SC, Jan. 26, 1928. Professional career started as dancer in Katherine Dunham group; toured U.S., Mexico & Europe with group, then opened night club in Paris; in Orson Welles stage prod. of Faust for European tour; N.Y. night clubs; stage in U.S., New Faces of 1952; at Macambo Hollywood, 1953; author, Thursday's Child; A Tart Is not a Sweet; Alone with Me.
PICTURES: Accused, New Faces of 1952, The Mark of the Hawk, St. Louis Blues, Anna Lucasta; St. of Devil's Island, Synanon, Up the Chastity Belt, All By Myself (doc.); Dragonard, Erik of the Viking, Living Doll.
TELEVISION: Played Catwoman on Batman Series.

KLAIN, JANE: Editor, Writer. b. New York, NY, Jan. 5. m. exec.-writer Stephen Klain. e. NYU, B.A., M.A. (film and theater). Reporter and film reviewer, Motion Picture Daily and Motion Picture Herald and asst. editor, Motion Picture Almanac and Television Almanac, Quigley Publishing Co.; asst. credit mgr., Seabury Press; assoc. ed., film and theater reviewer, Where Magazine, 1974–76; Video editor, Television & Video Almanac, 1986; assoc. editor, Motion Picture Almanac and Television and Video Almanac, 1987; editor, 1988. Also theater and film reviewer, Good Times, 1985–.

KLAIN, STEPHEN: Executive, Journalist. b. New York, NY, August 12. m. Jane Klain. e. St. Julian's Sch., Portugal; Bedford Sch., Bedford, Eng.; NYU (B.A., M.A.). Entered industry as reporter-reviewer, Motion Picture Daily & Motion Picture Herald, 1971; man. ed., M.P. & T.V. Almanacs, ed., Fame, 1973; Independent Film Journal, managing ed., 1973–76; joined Variety as reporter-reviewer, 1977; motion picture dept. editor, 1982–84; joined Tri-Star Pictures, 1984, as asst. to exec. v.p. dist. & mktg; named v.p., intl. mktg., 1986; joined Columbia Tri-Star Film Distributors Inc. as v.p., intl. mktg., 1988.

KLEES, ROBERT E.: Executive. b. New York, NY, Feb. 21, 1927. e. Duke U., 1947–51; U. of California Graduate Sch. of Management, 1973–75. U.S. Navy, 1944–46; Union Carbide Corp., 1951–57; director of communications, Beckman Instruments, Inc., 1957–69; co-founder and v.p. mktg., International Biophysics Corp., 1969–73; sr. v.p., mktg., Deluxe Laboratories, Inc., div. of 20th Century-Fox Film Corp, 1975–83; marketing consultant to businesses based in Third World nations, 1983–present. Member: Navy League of U.S., U.S. Naval Institute, Sons of American Revolution.

KLEIN, ALLEN: Producer. b. Dec. 18, 1931. Pres. ABKCO Films, a division of ABKCO Music & Records, Inc.
PICTURES: Force of Impulse, Pity Me Not, Mrs. Brown, You've Got A Lovely Daughter, Stranger in Town, The Stranger Returns, The Silent Stranger, Pete, Pearl & The Pole, The Grand Bouffe, Come Together, Let It Be, The Holy Mountain, El Topo, The Concert for Bangladesh, The Greek Tycoon, Personal Best, Blind Man, It Had to Be You, Sympathy for the Devil, Charlie Is My Darling.

KLEIN, HAROLD J.: Executive. b. New York, NY, e. U. of West Virginia, New York Law Sch. Reviewer, sales staff. Showman's Trade Review; booker, Brandt Theatres; booker, later vice-pres., gen. mgr., JJ Theatres, 1941–59; account exec., exec. v.p., dir. of world-wide sales, ABC Films, Inc., N.Y., Pres., Klein Film Assn.; exec. v.p., Plitt Theatres, Inc. to Nov., 1985; now pres., H.J.K. Film Associates, also acting consultant to P.E.G. (Plitt Entertainment Gp.).

KLEIN, MALCOLM C.: Executive. b. Los Angeles, CA, Nov. 22, 1927. e. UCLA, grad., 1948; U. of Denver. Prod. dir. management, KLAC-TV (KCOP), L.A., 1948–52; acct. exec., KABC-TV, 1952–56; asst. gen. sales mgr., KABC-TV, 1956–59; exec. vice-pres. gen. mgr., NTA Broadcasting, N.Y., 1959; v.p., gen. mgr., RKO-General-KHJ-TV, 1960; joined National General Corp. 1968, vice-pres. Creative Services and Marketing. Pres. National General Television Productions, Inc., Pres. NGC Broadcasting Corp.; 1971, pres. Filmways TV Presentations; 1972, pres. Malcolm C. Klein & Assoc. mgmt. & mktg. consultants; 1973 gen'l. exec. Sterling Recreation Organization & Gen'l Mgr. Broadcast Division; pres., American Song Festival 1976; Exec. v.p., Telease Inc. & American Subscription Television; 1981, sr. v.p., mng. dir., STAR-TV (subscription TV); 1982, sr. v.p., InterAmerican Satellite TV Network. 1983: Pres. Malcolm C. Klein & Assoc., management consultant.

KLEIN, PAUL L.: Television Executive. b. Brooklyn, NY, Nov. 6, 1928. e. Brooklyn Coll. Veteran of U.S. Army Air Corps. Research analyst with Biow Co., ad agency, 1953–54; research manager for Doyle Dane Bernbach ad agency, 1955–60. Started with NBC in 1961 as supervisor, ratings, and rose to position of v.p., audience measurement in October, 1965. In August, 1970, left NBC to found Computer Television Inc., first independent pay-per-view TV co. in world. Time, Inc. bought his interest in CTI. Returned to NBC in March, 1976. as v.p., network mktg. & planning; then named v.p., programs. Appointed exec. v.p., programs, NBC-TV, November, 1977. Became independent 1978.

KLEINER, HARRY: Writer, Producer. b. Philadelphia, PA, 1916. e. Temple U., B.S.; Yale U., M.F.A.
PICTURES: Screenplay: Miss Sadie Thompson, Salome, Carmen Jones, Garment Jungle (also prod.), Fantastic Voyage, Bullitt (co-s.p.), Le Mans, Extreme Prejudice, Red Heat (co-s.p.).
TELEVISION: Writer: Rosenberg Trial.

KLEISER, RANDAL: Director, Producer. b. July 20, 1946. e. U. of Southern California.
PICTURES: Grease, The Blue Lagoon, Grandview, U.S.A., Summer Lovers, Flight of the Navigator, North Shore (exec. prod.), Big Top Pee Wee, Getting it Right (dir., prod.).
TELEVISION: Movies: All Together Now, Dawn: Portrait of a Teenage Runaway, The Boy in the Plastic Bubble, The Gathering. Series: Marcus Welby, M.D., The Rookies, Starsky and Hutch, Family.

KLINE, FRED W.: Publicist. b. Oakland, CA, May 17, 1918. e. U. of California, Berkeley. M.P. pub. rel. since 1934; pres. The Fred Kline Agency; pres. Kline Communications Corporation; Owner, Fred Kline Agency, Inc.; Kline Communications Corp.; Fred W. Kline Prod., Inc.; Capitol News Service, Sacramento; L.A. News Bureau; Capitol Radio News Service, Inc.; Commissioner, Motion Picture Council, State of California; Commissioner, Los Angeles County Fire Commission.

KLINE, KEVIN: Actor. b. St. Louis, MO, Oct. 24, 1947. m. actress Phoebe Cates. e. Indiana U. Studied at Juilliard Theater Center (1968–72), and became founding member of John Houseman's The Acting Company, touring in classics, including The School for Scandal, She Stoops to Conquer, The Three Sisters, and modern works. Bdwy. debut in musical, The Robber Bridegroom (1977).
THEATER: Understudied Raul Julia in Lincoln Center's The Threepenny Opera, On the Twentieth Century (Tony Award), Loose Ends, The Pirates of Penzance (Tony Award), Richard III, Henry IV (Central Park), Arms and the Man, Hamlet, Much Ado About Nothing.
PICTURES: Sophie's Choice (debut, 1982), The Pirates of Penzance, The Big Chill, Silverado, Violets Are Blue, A Fish Called Wanda (Acad. Award, supp. 1988), The January Man, I Love You to Death.
TELEVISION: Search For Tomorrow (1976–77), The Time of Your Life.

KLINGER, HENRY: Eastern story editor, 20th Century-Fox Film Corp. b. New York, NY, Mar. 15, 1908. e. City Coll. of New York, B.A.: NYU, B.B.A. Assoc. ed., Chatterbox, nat'l mag., 1931–33; pres. Booklovers' Guild, 1930–33; freelance story dept. work, RKO, Cosmopolitan & Fox Films, 1931–33; story dept., pub. contract, Fox, 1934; asst. story ed., 20th-Fox, 1936; acting story ed., 1941; assoc. story ed., 1942; story ed., 1956; exec. story ed., 1964; exec. aide, 1971–73. Lecturer, Author.

KLINGER, TONY: Producer/Writer. Chairman, Sr. V.P., Avton Films International Inc. b. London, 1950. Ent. m.p. industry, 1966.
PICTURES: The Kids are Alright, Extremes, The Butterfly Ball, The Festival Gamer, Rock of Ages, Promo Man, The Assassinator (exec. prod.), Retribution (exec. prod.), Zombie Cop (prod.).

KLUGMAN, JACK: Actor. b. Philadelphia, PA, April 27, 1922. e. Carnegie Tech. After several menial jobs appeared on Broadway in Saint Joan, Stevedore; later understudied in Mister Roberts, taking over the doctor role; recent stage work includes Gypsy, The Odd Couple (on tour and stock), I'm Not Rappaport.
PICTURES: Timetable, Twelve Angry Men, Cry Terror, The Scarface Mob, Days of Wine and Roses, I Could Go on Singing, The Yellow Canary, Act One, Hail Mafia, The Detective, The Split, Goodbye Columbus, Who Says I Can't Ride a Rainbow?, Two Minute Warning.
TELEVISION: The Defenders (Emmy Award for role in Blacklist segment), The FBI, Ben Casey, 90 Bristol Court, The Odd Couple (Emmy, 1971 and 1973), Quincy, M.E.; You, Again?, Around the World in 80 Days, The Odd Couple One More Time.

KNIGHT, ARTHUR: Critic, Educator. b. Philadelphia, PA, Sept. 3, 1916. e. City Coll. of New York, B.A., 1940. Asst. curator Museum of Modern Art Film Library, 1939–49; film consultant CBS-color television, Omnibus, Odyssey, Seven Lively Arts, etc; film courses at C.C.N.Y., New Sch. for Social Research, Hunter Coll.; contributor to Encyclopedia Britannica, Collier's Encyclopedia, etc.; author: The Liveliest Art, The Hollywood Style; film critic, Hollywood Reporter; formerly Saturday Review; prof. U. of Southern California Sch. of Cinema/TV.

KNIGHT, SHIRLEY: Actress. b. Goessell, KA, July 5, 1936. e. Lake Forest Coll., D.F.A., 1978.
PICTURES: Five Gates to Hell (debut), Ice Palace, The Dark at the Top of the Stairs, (Acad. Award nom.) The Couch, Sweet Bird of Youth (Acad. Award nom.), House of Women, Flight from Ashiya, The Group, Dutchman (Best Actress, Venice Film Fest.), Petulia, The Counterfeit Killer, The Rain People, Juggernaut, Beyond the Poseidon Adventure, Endless Love, The Sender, Prisoners.
TELEVISION: 21 Hours at Munich, Friendly Persuasion, Playing For Time, Return to Earth, Billionaire Boys Club.

KNOPF, DAVID A. Producer's Representative. b. Boston, MA, Feb. 9, 1942. e. U. of Wisconsin. m. Jane Gibbons. vice-pres., Knopf/Polier Representation. 1964 started in Universal Studios mailroom, moved up to publicity department. Began career in exhibition 1968 as film buyer, National General Theatres. Head film buyer for S. Cal, UA Theatres and General Cinema before joining Warner Bros. as sales exec. in Boston. Returned to Los Angeles as S. Cal. film buyer for Mann theatres. Started Knopf/Polier, 1979.

KNOTTS, DON: Actor. b. Morgantown, WV, July 21, 1924. e. U. of West Virginia, U. of Arizona. Drafted into U.S. Army where became part of show called Stars and Grapes, teamed with comedian Mickey Shaughnessy. After schooling resumed, was offered teaching fellowship but went to New York to try acting instead. Appeared on radio and TV, leading to role in No Time for Sergeants on Bdwy.; appeared in film version.
PICTURES: It's a Mad, Mad, Mad, Mad World, The Incredible Mr. Limpet, The Shakiest Gun in the West, The Apple Dumpling Gang, Herbie Goes to Monte Carlo, The Apple Dumpling Gang Rides Again, Cannonball Run II.
TELEVISION: Garry Moore Show, Steve Allen Show, Andy Griffith Show (played Barney Fife), The Don Knotts Show, Three's Company, Return to Mayberry.

KNOWLES, PATRIC: Actor. r.n. Reginald Lawrence Knowles; b. Horsforth, Yorkshire, England, Nov. 11, 1911. Joined Abby Repertory Theatre, 1930; Oxford Playhouse Repertory, 1932–33. Film debut (Ireland) in Irish Hearts, 1934; on London stage in By Appointment; U.S. m.p. debut in Charge of the Light Brigade, 1936; served in Canadian RAF & as civilian instructor USAF, W.W.II.
PICTURES: Honours Easy, Mister Hobo, Two's Company, Give Me Your Heart, It's Love I'm After, Expensive Husbands, Adventures of Robin Hood, How Green Was My Valley, Forever and a Day, Of Human Bondage, Bride Wore Boots, Ivy, Kitty, Monsieur Beaucaire, Dream Girl, Big Steal, Quebec, Three Came Home, Mutiny, Tarzan's Savage Fury, Jamaica Run, Flame of Calcutta, World Ransom, Khyber Patrol, No Man's Woman, Band of Angels, Auntie Mame, The Way West, In Enemy Country, The Devil's Brigade, Chisum, The Man, Terror in the Wax Museum, Arnold.

KNOX, ALEXANDER: Actor. b. Strathroy, Ont., Jan. 16, 1907. e. Western Ontario U. Author, novels: Bride of Quietness, Night of the White Bear, The Enemy I Kill, Raider's Moon, The Kidnapped Surgeon; plays, Old Master, The Closing Door, Red On White.
TELEVISION: Potsdam, Tinker Tailor Soldier Spy, Suez, Churchill And The Generals, Helen and Teacher, Empire, Darwin, Oppenheimer, The Last Place on Earth, Lovejoy.
STAGE: (N.Y.) Romeo and Juliet, The Three Sisters,

Jupiter Laughs, Jason, The Closing Door; (London) King of Nowhere, Geneva, In Good King Charles' Golden Days, The Jealous God, Winter Journey, Henry VIII, Return to Tyassi, Burnt Flower Bed, When We Dead Awaken.

PICTURES: The Sea Wolf, This Above All, Commandos Strike at Dawn, None Shall Escape, Over 21, Wilson, Sign of the Ram, Judge Steps Out, Sister Kenny, I'd Climb the Highest Mountain, Saturday's Hero, Sleeping Tiger, Divided Heart, Crack in the Mirror, The Viking, The Night My Number Came Up, Reach for the Sky, High Tide at Noon, Davy, Operation Amsterdam, The Longest Day, Wreck of the Mary Deare, Man in the Middle, Woman of Straw, Mr. Moses, Accident, Villa Rides, Shalako, Skullduggery, Puppet on a Chain, Khartoum, Nicholas and Alexandra, Gorky Park, Joshua Then and Now.

KNOX, GORDON: Producer. b. Greenville, TX. e. U. of Missouri. In addition to making documentary films for several years has been employed by Warner Bros., and Walter Wanger Prods. Joined Princeton Film Center in 1940; Pres. SKS Prod. Inc., Santa Fe, NM Pres., PAC Productions, Inc., Princeton, NJ.

KOBAYASHI, MASAKI: Director. b. Japan, Feb. 4, 1916. e. Waseda U. Joined Shochiku 1941 as asst. Director. Army. Rejoined Shochiku 1946.

PICTURES: No Greater Love, Road to Eternity, A Soldier's Prayer, Black River, Room with Thick Walls, Somewhere Beneath Wide Sky, Fountainhead, I'll Buy You, The Human Condition, The Inheritance.

KOCH, HOWARD: Writer. b. New York, NY, Dec. 12, 1902. e. St. Stephen's Coll., 1922, B.A.; Columbia Law Sch., 1925. LL.B. Hon. degree Doctor of Human Letters, Bard Coll., 1972. Playwright (Give Us This Day, In Time to Come, Straitjacket). Began screen career collab. s.p. The Sea Hawk. Radio: wrote War of the Worlds play for Orson Welles' broadcast. book: The Panic Broadcast (Little, Brown & Co.); Academy Award best s.p. (Casablanca). As Time Goes By, Memoirs of a Writer in Hollywood, New York and Europe published by Harcourt, Brace and Jovanovich.

PICTURES: The Letter, Shining Victory, In This Our Life, Casablanca, Mission to Moscow, Letter From an Unknown Woman, The Thirteenth Letter, The War Lover, The Fox, Loss of Innocence, No Sad Songs for Me, Sergeant York, Three Strangers.

KOCH, HOWARD W.: Producer, Director. b. New York, NY, Apr. 11, 1916. Runner on Wall St. Began film career in Universal's contracts and playdate dept. in NY; asst. cutter, 20th-Fox; asst. dir., 20th-Fox, Eagle Lion, MGM; 2nd unit dir., freelance; In 1953, joined Aubrey Schenck Prod. forming Bel Air Prods., made films for U.A.; 1961–64, prod. Frank Sinatra Enterprises; v.p., chg. prod., Paramount Pictures Corp., 1964–66, Past pres. of the Academy of Motion Picture Arts and Sciences, 1977–79. On June 11, 1977, elected to the National Board of Directors Guild of America for two year term. 1980 honored by NATO as prod. of year. 1985 Silver Medallion Award of Honor, Motion Picture Television Fund. Produced eight Academy Award shows, 1972–1983. Has had a 24 year relationship with Paramount as exec., prod., and dir.

TELEVISION: Director, Miami Undercover, The Untouchables, Maverick, Cheyenne, Hawaiian Eye. Movies: The Pirate (prod.); Hollywood Wives (1985 mini-series), Crossings (1986 mini-series). Specials: Ol' Blue Eyes Is Back (prod.); Oscar's Best Actors (prod., dir.); Oscar's Best Movies (prod., dir.); Who Loves Ya Baby (prod.); On the Road with Bing (prod., dir.); The Stars Salute the Olympics (prod.).

PICTURES: Executive Producer: Come Blow Your Horn; Sergeant's Three; Manchurian Candidate; X-15; Robin and the Seven Hoods; None But The Brave; The President's Analyst; For Those Who Think Young; Dragonslayer. Producer: War Paint; Beachhead; Yellow Tomahawk; Desert Sands; Fort Yuma; Quincannon; Frontier Scout; Ghost Town; Broken Star; Crimes Against Joe; Three Bad Sisters; Emergency Hospital; Rebel in Town; The Black Sheep; Pharaoh's Curse; Tomahawk Train; Revolt at Fort Laramie; War Drums; Voodoo Island; Hellbound; The Dalton Girls; The Odd Couple; On a Clear Day You Can See Forever; Plaza Suite; Star Spangled Girl; Last of the Red Hot Lovers; Jacqueline Susann's Once Is Not Enough; Some Kind of Hero; Airplane II: The Sequel; Collision Course. A Howard W. Koch Production: A New Leaf, Airplane!; Producer/Director: Badge 373. Director: Jungle Heat; Shield for Murder; Big House USA; Fort Bowie; Violent Road; Untamed Youth; Born Reckless; Frankenstein 1970; Andy Hardy Comes Home; The Last Mile; Girl in Black Stockings.

KOCH, HOWARD W., JR.: Producer. b. Los Angeles, CA, Dec. 14, 1945. Was asst. dir. and in other industry posts before turning to production. Pres. & chief exec. off., Rastar (Peggy Sue Got Married, The Secret of My Success, Nothing in Common, Violets Are Blue, Amazing Chuck and Grace prod. under presidency); 1987, set up own prod. co. at De Laurentiis Entertainment Group. Oct. 1987: named president of the De Laurentiis Entertainment Group, Resigned April 1988 to produce independently.

PICTURES: Heaven Can Wait, The Other Side of Midnight, The Frisco Kid (exec. prod.); Co-prod./prod.: The Idolmaker, Gorky Park, Honky Tonk Freeway, The Keep, A Night in Heaven, The Pope of Greenwich Village, Rooftops, The Long Walk Home.

KOCH, JOANNE: Executive Director, The Film Society of Lincoln Center. b. NY, NY, Oct. 7, 1929. e. Goddard College, B.A. political science, 1950. Dept. of Film, Museum of Modern Art, as circulation asst., film researcher, motion picture stills archivist, 1950. Early 1960s, technical dir., film dept. MOMA, supervised the implementation of MOMA's film preservation program. 1967, asst. to publisher of Grove Press, active in preparation of Grove's case in I Am Curious Yellow censorship trial. Joined film div., Grove, first in distribution then as tech. dir. and prod. coord. 1971 joined Film Society of Lincoln Center as prog. dir. of Movies-in-the-Parks. June, 1971 made admin. dir. Exec. dir. of N.Y. Film Festival, Film Comment magazine, Movies-in-the-Park, Film-in-Education, New Directors/New Films and annual Film Society Tribute.

KOENEKAMP, FRED J.: Cinematographer. b. Los Angeles, CA, Nov. 11, 1922. Member of American Society of Cinematographers.

PICTURES: Beyond the Valley of the Dolls, Billy Jack, Embryo, The Other Side of Midnight, The Champ, Amityville Horror, Love and Bullets, First Family, The Domino Principle, Towering Inferno (Acad. Award), The Hunter, When Time Ran Out, First Monday in October, Carbon Copy, Yes, Giorgio, Two of a Kind, Wrong is Right, Adventures of Buckarroo Banzai, Across the 8th Dimension, Mismatch, Listen to Me, Welcome Home.

TELEVISION: Nearly 30 TV movies including Disaster on the Coastline, Tales of the Gold Monkey, Money on the Side, Return of the Man from U.N.C.L.E., Summer Girl, Whiz Kids, Flight 90—Disaster on the Potomac, Obsessive Love, City Killer, Las Vegas Strip, A Touch of Scandal, Not My Kid, Hard Time on Planet Earth (pilot).

KOENIG, WALTER: Actor, Writer, Director , Producer. b. Chicago, IL, Sept. 14. e. Grinnell Coll. (IA), U. of California. Performed in summer stock; after college enrolled at Neighborhood Playhouse, N.Y.; first acting job in TV's Day in Court. Books: Chekov's Enterprise, Buck Alice and the Actor Robot.

PICTURES: The Deadly Honeymoon, Star Trek—The Motion Picture, Star Trek II: The Wrath of Khan, Star Trek III: The Search for Spock, Star Trek IV: the Voyage Home, Star Trek V: the Final Frontier, Moontrap.

TELEVISION: Actor: Colombo, Medical Center, Ironside, Mannix, Alfred Hitchcock Presents, Mr. Novak, Ben Casey, The Untouchables, Combat. Films: The Questor Tapes, Goodbye Raggedy Ann. Writer: Family, The Class of '65, The Powers of Matthew Starr.

KOHN, HOWARD EDWARD., II: Executive. b. McKeesport, PA. National dir. of adv., publicity, roadshow dept., United Artists; indep. prod., Hidden Fear, 1957; pres. Lioni-Warren-Kohn, Inc., 1958; national roadshow dir., Columbia Pictures, Porgy and Bess, 1959; World wide co-ordinator, national co-ordinator adv. & pub. for El Cid, June 1961; named world wide co-ordinator adv., pub. all Samuel Bronston Productions, April 1962; pres., Starpower Inc., 1968; exec. v.p., Avanti Films, 1970; v.p. Avariac Prods., 1971; pres., Blossom Films, 1973. Elected member of ASCAP, 1975. Pres., Avanti Associates, 1976. Pres. Channel Television Prods., Inc., 1985; pres. Search Television Prods. 1988.

KOHNER, PANCHO: Producer. b. Los Angeles, CA, Jan. 7, 1939. e. U. of Southern California, U. of Mexico, Sorbonne.

PICTURES: The Bridge in the Jungle (also dir-s.p.); The Lie; Mr. Sycamore; St. Ives; The White Buffalo; Love and Bullets; Why Would I Lie?; 10 to Midnight; The Evil That Men Do; Murphy's Law; Assassination; Death Wish IV; Kinjite.

KOHNER, SUSAN: Actress, b. Los Angeles, CA. Nov. 11, 1936. m. designer John Weitz. Mother, Lupita Tovar, was one of Mexico's leading film actresses. Father was talent rep. Paul Kohner. e. U. of California, 1954–55. Received Acad. Award nom. for Imitation of Life 1959, and Golden Globe Awards, 1959 and 1960. Currently does a weekly broadcast on In Touch Network for the Blind, and is on bd. of associates, Juilliard Sch. NY.

STAGE: Love Me Little, He Who Gets Slapped, A Quiet Place, Rose Tatoo, Bus Stop, St. Joan, Sunday in New York, Take Her She's Mine, Pullman Car, Hiawatha, as well as summer stock.

PICTURES: To Hell and Back, The Last Wagon, Trooper Hook, Dino, Imitation of Life, The Big Fisherman, The Gene Krupa Story, All the Fine Young Cannibals, By Love Possessed, Freud.

TELEVISION: Alcoa Hour, Schlitz Playhouse, Four Star Theatre, Matinee Theatre, Climax, Suspicion, Playhouse 90, Route 66, Dick Powell Theatre.

KONCHALOVSKY, ANDREI: (also known as Mikhalov-Konchalovski) Director. b. Moscow, Soviet Union, 1937. Great grandfather: painter Sourikov; grandfather: painter Konchalovski; father is a writer; mother poet Natalia Konchalovskaia; brother is director Nikita Mikhalkov. e. as pianist Moscow Conservatoire, 1947–57; State Film Sch. (VGIK) under Mikhail Romm (1964). Worked as scriptwriter during 1960s especially with Andrei Tarkovsky. 1962: asst. to Tarkovsky on Ivan's Childhood. 1980: moved to US.

PICTURES: The Boy and the Pigeon (1961, short film, dir.); The Steamroller and the Violin (s.p.); Andrey Rublev (s.p.); The First Teacher (dir., s.p.); The Story of Asya Klyachina, Who Loved But Did Not Marry (dir., s.p.); A Nest of Gentlefolk (dir., s.p.); Tashkent City of Bread (s.p.); The Song of Manshuk (s.p.); Uncle Vanya (dir.); The End of Chieftain (s.p.); Romance for Lovers (dir.); Siberiade (Jury prize, Cannes, 1979); Split Cherry Tree (short for U.S., cable TV, 1982); Duet for One; Shy People (dir., story, co-s.p.), Homer and Eddie, Setup.

KONIGSBERG, FRANK: Executive. b. Kew Gardens, NY, March 10, 1933. e. Yale, Yale Law Sch. Worked as lawyer at CBS for six years; moved to NBC 1960–65 in legal dept. as dir. prog. and talent administration. Left to package TV special for Artists Agency Rep. (later AFA) in Los Angeles. being sr. v.p. of West Coast office seven years. Executive producer of many TV series, pilots, variety specials and made-for-TV movies. Formed own Konigsberg Company. Theatrical film debut as prod., Joy of Sex (1984).

TELEVISION: Movies (all exec. prod.): Pearl, Ellis Island, Bing Crosby: His Life and Legend, Dummy, Before and After, Guyana Tragedy, A Christmas Without Snow, The Pride of Jesse Hallam, Hard Case, Divorce Wars, Coming Out of the Ice, Onassis: The Richest Man in the World (exec. prod.), Where the Hell's That Gold!!!, Senior Prom, Babycakes. Series (all exec. prod.): It's Not Easy, Breaking Away, Dorothy.

KONTOS, SPERO L.: Thea. Equip. Dealer. b. Chicago, IL, Dec. 17, 1922. e. Illinois Inst. of Technology, B.S. B.M., eng.; UCLA. Ent. Ind. as Chicago exhib., 1937; thea. mgmt. until 1942. U.S. Army, 1942–46; sis. eng., Abbott Theatre Equip. Co., 1946–48; sis. mgr., 1948–51; gen. mgr. 1951–54; sis. mgr. John P. Filbert Co. Inc., 1954–59; hd. Century 70/35 mm. projector program, 1959–60; Filbert Co., v.p. chg. sis. & eng., 1960–64; pres., 1964; pres. Theatre Equipment Dealers Assoc., 1965–67; bd. chmn., TEDA, 1967–69; chief barker, L.A. Variety, 1971–72; pres., Megaron Corp., 1973, Academy of Motion Picture Arts & Sciences, 1975.

KOPELSON, ARNOLD: Producer, Packager, Financier, Distributor. b. New York, NY, Feb. 14, 1935. e. New York Law Sch., J.D., 1959; NYU, B.S. Has executive-produced, produced, packaged, developed or distributed over 100 films. Handled intl. dist. of Twice in a Lifetime Salvador, Warlock, Triumph of the Spirit and prod. Platoon. Chmn. Arnold Kopelson Prods., Co-chmn. Inter-Ocean Film Sales, Ltd.

PICTURES: Foolin' Around (prod.), The Legacy (exec. prod.), Lost and Found (exec. prod.), Night of the Juggler (exec. prod.), Dirty Tricks, Final Assignment (exec. prod.), Platoon (prod., Acad. Award, best picture, 1986), Warlock (exec. prod.), Triumph of the Spirit (prod.).

KORBAN, BERNARD: Executive. b. New York, NY, Nov. 28, 1923; e. RCA Inst. of Technology, NYU. U.S. Army 1942–46; 1951–58, public relations and promotions for Davega Stores; 1959–62, exploitation fieldman for Universal Pictures; 1962–66, supvr. of fieldmen and exploitation activities; 1966–68, exec. in chg. field activities; exec. assist. to v.p., adv. pub. and promotion; 1972 dir. of exploitation, National General Pictures; 1973, dir. of marketing, promotion and worldwide dist. for Brut Prods; 1974, dir. of mkt., Avco Embassy Pictures, 1975, v.p., of advertising/publicity/promotion, Cine Artists Pictures Corp.; advertising/publicity, United Artists Corp. West Coast ad. mgr.; then UA v.p., West Coast adv.; v.p. West Coast adv./promo., MGM/UA; 1983, v.p., gen. mgr., AC&R/DHB & BESS, San Diego.

KORMAN, HARVEY: Actor, Director. b. Chicago, IL, Feb. 15, 1927. e. Wright Junior Coll. Began dramatic studies at Chicago's Goodman Sch. of Drama at the Arts Inst. Acted in small roles in Broadway plays and did TV commercials until break came as comedian for Danny Kaye Show on TV. Staged comedy sketches for Steve Allen variety series in 1967. Became Carol Burnett's leading man on her show 1967 to 1978. Directed two episodes of The New Dick Van Dyke Show.

PICTURES: Actor: Three Bites of an Apple, Lord Love a Duck, Last of the Secret Agents, The April Fools, Blazing Saddles, Huckleberry Finn, High Anxiety, Americathon, First Family, History of the World–Part I, Trail of the Pink Panther, Curse of the Pink Panther, The Longshot, Munchies.

TELEVISION: The Danny Kaye Show, Carol Burnett Show, Crash Course. Series: The Nutt House.

KORMAN, LEWIS J.: Executive. b. 1945. Partner, Kaye, Scholer, Fierman, Hays & Handler 1978; founding partner, Gelberg & Abrams where pioneered dev. of public limited partnerships, Delphi Partners, to help finance Columbia Pictures' and Tri-Star Pictures' films. 1985, became pres. of PSO-Delphi (which incl. Producers Sales Organization. Left PSO/Delphi in 1986 and became consultant to Tri-Star involved in negotiations that led to acquisition of Loews Theatre Corp. that year. Joined Tri-Star, 1987, as sr. exec. v.p. In 1988 appt. to additional post of chief operating officer and named dir. of Columbia Pictures Entertainment Inc.; 1989 also became chmn, Motion Picture Group.

KORTY, JOHN: Director, Producer, Writer, Cameraman, Animator. b. Lafayette, IN, June 22, 1936. e. Antioch Coll., B.A., 1959. President, Korty Films, Inc., Mill Valley, CA.

INDEPENDENT FEATURES: Crazy Quilt, (1964); Funnyman; Riverrun.

THEATRICAL FEATURES: Alex and the Gypsy; Oliver's Story; Twice Upon a Time.

TELEVISION FEATURES: The Autobiography of Miss Jane Pittman, (1974 Emmy, DGA Award); Farewell to Manzanar, 1976 (Humanitas, Christopher Awards); Forever (1977); A Christmas Without Snow (1980), A Deadly Business (1986); Resting Place (1986), Baby Girl Scott; Eye on the Sparrow, Winnie. DOCUMENTARIES: Who Are the DeBolts?, (Oscar, Emmy, DGA Award); Can't It Be Anyone Else?; Stepping Out: The DeBolts Grow Up, The Ewok Adventure.

SHORT FILMS: The Language of Faces (AFSC, 1961); Imogen Cunningham, Photographer (AFI grant, 1970); The Music School. ANIMATION: Breaking the Habit, (Oscar nominee); Various children's films; Segments for Sesame Street and The Electric Company.

KOSCINA, SYLVA: Actress. b. Yugoslavia, Aug. 22, 1933. Grew up in Italy; as model placed under contract for films by Carlo Ponti.

PICTURES: The Railroad Man (debut), Juliet of the Spirits, Deadlier Than the Male, The Hornet's Nest, Casanova & Co., Sunday Lovers.

KOTCHEFF, WILLIAM THEODORE (Ted): Director. b. Toronto, Canada, 1931. Ent. TV ind. 1952. After five years with Canadian Broadcasting Corp. joined ABC-TV in London, 1957.

PLAYS: Of Mice and Men, Desperate Hours, The Human Voice, Edna the Inebriate Woman, Signalman's Apprentice, Lights Out, Rx for the Defence.

LONDON STAGE: Progress the Park, Play with a Tiger, Luv, Maggie May, The Au Pair Man, Have You Any Dirty Washing, Mother Dear?

PICTURES: Tiara Tahiti (debut, 1963), Life at the Top, Two Gentlemen Sharing, Outback, Billy Two Hats, The Apprenticeship of Duddy Kravitz, Fun with Dick and Jane, Who Is Killing The Great Chefs of Europe?, North Dallas Forty (also co-s.p.), First Blood, Split Image (also prod.), Uncommon Valor (also exec. prod.), Joshua Then and Now, Switching Channels, Winter People, Weekend at Bernies.

KOTTO, YAPHET: Actor. b. New York, NY, Nov. 15, 1937. Has many stage credits, including starring roles on Broadway in The Great White Hope, The Zulu and the Zayda. Off-Bdwy.: Blood Knot, Black Monday, In White America, A Good Place To Raise a Boy.

PICTURES: The Limit (star, prod.), Nothing But a Man, The Liberation of L. B. Jones, Live and Let Die, Across 110th Street, Truck Turner, Bone, Report to the Commissioner, Sharks' Treasure, Hey Good Lookin', Friday Foster, Night Chase, Drum, Monkey Hustle, Blue Collar, Alien, Brubaker, Fighting Back, Star Chamber, Eye of the Tiger, Prettykill, The Running Man, Midnight Run, Nightmare of the Devil (prod., dir., actor), Terminal Entry, Jigsaw, A Whisper to a Scream, Tripwire, Black Snow, Ministry of Vengeance.

TELEVISION: Movies: Raid on Entebbe, Rage, Playing With Fire, The Park Is Mine, Women of San Quentin, Badge of the Assassin, Harem, Desperado, Alfred Hitchcock Presents (1985), Perry Mason: The Case of the Scandalous Scoundrel.

KOVACS, LASZLO: Cinematographer. b. Hungary, May 14, 1933. Came to U.S. 1957; naturalized 1963. e. Acad. Drama and M.P. Arts, Budapest, MA 1956.

PICTURES: Hell's Angels on Wheels, The Savage Seven, Targets, Easy Rider, That Cold Day in the Park, Getting Straight, Alex in Wonderland, The Last Movie, Marriage of a Young Stockbroker, The King of Marvin Gardens, Pocket Money, What's Up, Doc?, Paper Moon, Huckleberry Finn, For Pete's Sake, Freebie and the Bean, Shampoo, At Long Last Love, Baby Blue Marine, Close Encounters of the Third Kind, Harry and Walter Go to New York, New York, New York, F.I.S.T., The Last Waltz, Paradise Alley, Butch and Sundance: The Early Days, The Runner Stumbles, Heart Beat, Inside Moves, The Legend of the Lone Ranger, Frances, The Toy, Crackers, Ghostbusters, Mask, Legal Eagles, Little Nikita, Say Anything, Friend to Friend.

KOZLOWSKI, LINDA: Actress. Began professional acting career soon after graduating from Juilliard Sch., N.Y., 1981. Stage debut in How It All Began at the Public Theatre. In regional theatre appeared in Requiem, Translations, Make and Break, as well as on Broadway and on tour with Dustin Hoffman in Death of a Salesman and the TV adaptation.

PICTURES: Crocodile Dundee, Crocodile Dundee II, Helena.
TELEVISION: Favorite Son.

KRABBE, JEROEN: Actor. b. Amsterdam, The Netherlands, Dec. 5, 1944. Trained for stage at De Toneelschool, Acad. of Dramatic Art, Amsterdam, 1965. Also studied at Acad. of Fine Arts, grad. 1981. Founded touring theater co. in the Netherlands and translated plays into Dutch. Also costume designer. As a painter, work has been widely exhibited. Author: The Economy Cookbook. Dir. debut, new stage adaptation of The Diary of Anne Frank, 1985 in Amsterdam.
PICTURES: Soldier of Orange (debut, 1979), A Flight of Rainbirds, Spetters, The Fourth Man, Turtle Diary, Jumpin' Jack Flash, No Mercy, The Living Daylights, Shadow of Victory, A World Apart, Crossing Delancey, Shadowman, Scandal, The Punisher, Melancholia.
TELEVISION: Danton's Death (debut, 1966), William of Orange, World War Three. Movies: One for the Dance, Family of Spies, After the War.

KRAMER, JEROME: Executive, Producer, Director. b. Los Angeles, CA, 1945. e. U. of Southern California Law Sch., 1971. Joined Braverman Productions, Inc. 1971; named exec. v.p. Co-producer with Charles Braverman of network specials (21 Years of A.I.P., Horror Hall of Fame), show titles (Rhoda, Cher) corporate and promotional films for Xerox, Petersen Publishing, etc. Producer and director of various television commercials (for Chevrolet, United Artists Records, Gulf Oil), educational films for United States Information Agency, special films and montages.

KRAMER, LARRY: Writer, Producer. b. Bridgeport, CT, 1935. e. Yale U., B.A. 1957. Ent. m.p. ind. 1958. Story edit. Columbia Pictures, N.Y. London 1960–65. Asst. to David Picker and Herb Jaffe, UA, 1965. Assoc. prod. and additional dialogue Here We Go Round the Mulberry Bush, 1968. Writ. prod. Women in Love (Acad. Award nom., 1969). Lost Horizon, 1971 (s.p.). Novel: Faggots (1978). Theater: The Normal Heart. (NY Shakespeare Festival and throughout the world), Just Say No. Cofounder: Gay Men's Health Crisis, Inc. (community AIDS org.).

KRAMER, SIDNEY: Sales executive. b. New York, NY. e. New York Law Sch., LL.B., City Coll. of New York. Gen. sales mgr., RKO Pathe, June 1953; dir. and v.p. Cellofilm Corp. 1941–56; foreign sales mgr., RKO Radio, 1954–59; v.p. Cinemiracle Intl. 1960–61; v.p. T.P.E.A., 1960–61; foreign sls. mgr., Cinerama, Inc., 1962–65; Exec. Commonwealth Theatres, Puerto Rico, Inc., 1965–68; Exec. v.p. Cobian Jr. Enterprises Inc. 1968. M.P. consultant-exhibition, dist., foreign and Caribbean area, Oct., 1968–70. Pres. Coqui Internat'l. Inc.; 1970–80; vice. pres. of UAPR, Inc., Puerto Rico, U.A. Communications, Inc. 1981–present, consultant in Florida, UA Theatres.

KRAMER, STANLEY E.: Executive producer, Director. b. New York, NY, Sept. 29, 1913; e. NYU, B.Sc., 1933. Entered m.p. ind. via back lot jobs; with MGM research dept.; film cutter 3 yrs.; film ed.; m.p. & radio writer; served in U.S Signal Corps, 1st Lt.
PICTURES: Champion, Home of the Brave, The Men, Cyrano de Bergerac, Death of a Salesman, High Noon, My Six Convicts, The Sniper, The Four Poster, The Happy Time, Eight Iron Men, 5,000 Fingers of Dr. T, Wild One, The Juggler, Caine Mutiny, Not as a Stranger, Pride and the Passion; prod. dir., The Defiant Ones, On the Beach, Inherit the Wind, Judgment at Nuremberg; prod., dir., It's a Mad, Mad, Mad, Mad World, Invitation to a Gunfighter, prod., Ship of Fools, Prod. Dir. Guess Who's Coming to Dinner, The Secret of Santa Vittoria, R.P.M.*, Bless the Beasts and Children, Oklahoma Crude, The Domino Principle, The Runner Stumbles (prod., dir.), Polonaise (prod., dir.).
TELEVISION: Guess Who's Coming to Dinner? (pilot).

KRANE, JONATHAN: Executive. b. 1952. m. actress Sally Kellerman. e. St. Johns Coll. grad. with honors, 1972; Yale Law Sch., 1976. Joined Blake Edwards Entertainment in 1981, becoming pres. Formed talent management co. Management Company Entertainment Group representing clients such as John Travolta, Sally Kellerman, Kathryn Harrold, Sandra Bernhard, Howie Mandel, Drew Barrymore, others. Began producing vehicles for clients and transformed co. into production, distribution, management and finance co. Chairman and chief exec. officer, Management Company Entertainment Group (MCEG).
PICTURES: Exec. prod./prod.: Boardwalk, Honeymoon, Fly Away Home, The Man Who Loved Women, Micki & Maude, A Fine Mess, That's Life, The Chocolate War, The Experts, Fatal Charm, Boris and Natasha, Look Who's Talking, Chud II: Bud the Chud, Convicts, Cold Heaven, With You I'm Nothing (prod.).
TELEVISION: Prod.: Howie Mandel Life at Carnegie Hall, Howie Mandel: The North American Watusi Tour.

KRANTZ, STEVE: Executive. b. New York, NY, May 20, 1923. m. novelist Judith Krantz. e. Columbia U., B.A. Dir. progs., NBC, New York, 1953; dir. prog. dev., Screen Gems, N.Y., 1955; v.p., gen. mgr. Screen Gems, Canada, 1958; dir. int. sls., 1960; formed Krantz Films, Inc. 1964.
TELEVISION': Steve Allen Show, Kate Smith Show, Hazel, Dennis the Menace, Winston Churchill—The Valiant Years, Telefilms, Marvel Super Heroes, Rocket Robin Hood, Animated Films. Mini-series: Princess Daisy, Sins, Mistral's Daughter, I'll Take Manhattan. Movie: Dadah is Death (exec. prod.), Till We Meet Again.
PICTURES: Fritz the Cat, Heavy Traffic (prod.), Cooley High, Ruby, Which Way Is Up?

KREIMAN, ROBERT T.: Executive. b. Kenosha, WI, Sept. 16, 1924. Served W.W.II Capt Army Corps of Engineers-ETO. e. Stanford U., 1943; U. of Wisconsin, 1942—1946–49. Dir., sales training, mgr., audio visual sales, Bell & Howell Co., 1949–58; V.P., Argus Cameras, Inc., 1958–61; V.P., gen. mgr., Commercial & Educ. Div., Technicolor 1961–69, v.p. gen. mgr., The Suburban Companies; 1969–71: pres. and chief exec. officer, Deluxe General, Inc. pres. and director of Movietonews, Inc. Bd. chmn. Keith Cole Photograph, Inc. 1972–78. bd. chmn., pres. and chief exec. officer, Pace International Corp., 1969 to present. past pres. of U.C.L.A. Executive Program Ass'n. Fellow SMPTE, Member M.P. Academy; TV Academy; assoc. mem., American Society of Cinematographers.

KRESS, HAROLD F.: Director, Film editor. b. Pittsburgh, PA, June 26, 1913. e. UCLA. Film ed., Command Decision, Madame Curie, Mrs. Miniver, The Yearling; crime shorts; 5-reel Army documentary short, Ward Care for Psychotic Patients. Member: Acad. of M.P. Arts and Sciences, Screen Directors Guild, Film Editors Guild.
PICTURES: Painted Hills, No Questions Asked, Apache War Smoke, Ride Vaquero, Saadia, Rose Marie, Valley of the Kings, The Cobweb, The Prodigal, I'll Cry Tomorrow, Teahouse of the August Moon, Silk Stockings, Until They Sail, Merry Andrew, Imitation General, The World, the Flesh and the Devil, Count Your Blessings, Home from the Hills, The Greatest Story Ever Told, Walk Don't Run, Alvarez Kelly, Academy Award for film editing on How the West Was Won.
FILM EDITOR: Poseidon Adventure, The Iceman Cometh, 99 and 44/100% Dead, The Towering Inferno.

KREUGER, KURT: Actor. b. St. Moritz, Switzerland, July 23, 1917. e. U. of Lausanne, U. of London. Came to U.S. 1937, partner in travel bureau: acted in Wharf Theat. group. Cape Cod, 1939; Broadway debut in Candle in the Wind with Helen Hayes, 1941.
PICTURES: Mademoiselle Fifi, Hotel Berlin, Paris Underground, Dark Corner, Unfaithfully Yours, Fear, The St. Valentine's Day Massacre, What Did You Do in the War Daddy?

KRIEGE, ALICE: Actress. b. Upington, South Africa, June 28, 1954. Moved to London at 22 and studied at School of Speech and Drama. Professional debut on British TV: The Happy Autumn Fields. In London prod. of Forever Yours, Maylou. West End debut, Arms and the Man, 1981. Two seasons with Royal Shakespeare Co. at Stratford and London (The Tempest, King Lear, The Taming of the Shrew, Cyrano de Bergerac.)
PICTURES: Chariots of Fire, Ghost Story, King David, Barfly, Baja Oklahoma, See You in the Morning, Haunted Summer, S.P.O.O.K.S.
TELEVISION: Wallenberg: A Hero's Story, Dream West, A Tale of Two Cities, Ellis Island, Second Serve, Max and Helen: A Remarkable Love Story.

KRIER, JOHN N.: Executive. b. Rock Island, IL. e. Augustana Coll. Joined A. H. Blank Theatres, Grad. Publix Theatres Manager Training Sch., 1930: managed theatres in Illinois, Iowa, Nebraska; joined Intermountain Theatres, Salt Lake City, 1937: appointed Purchasing Head, 1946: buyer-booker, 1952: v.p., gen. mgr., 1955: appt. v.p. gen mgr. ABC Theas., Arizona, 1968: appt. v.p. gen'l mgr. director Film Buying ABC Theatres of California & ABC Intermountain Theatres, Feb. 1972. Became consultant ABC Southern Theatres, 1974. Joined Exhibitors Relations Inc. as partner, 1978. Elected pres., 1982. Became owner, 1988.

KRIM, ARTHUR B.: Attorney. b. New York, NY, 1910. e. Columbia U., B.A., 1930; J.D. 1932; L.L.D (hon.) 1982. 1932 became member law firm Philips, Nizer, Benjamin, Krim & Ballon; sr. partner 1935–78; of counsel 1978–. Pres. Eagle Lion films 1946–49. N.Y. elected pres. United Artists Feb. 20, 1951; chairman of bd., 1969 to January 1978; Chmn. of Board, Orion Pictures Company, March, 1978–.
Special cons. to Pres. U.S. 1968–69; mem. President's Gen. Adv. Com. Arms Control 1977–80; chmn. Democratic Nalt. Finance Comm. 1966–68. Bd. of dirs: Weizmann Inst. Science, 1948–; UN Association 1961–; Lyndon Baines Johnson Foundation 1969–; John F. Kennedy Foundation 1964–; chmn. Arms Control Assn. 1985–; chmn. bd. trustee Columbia U. 1977–82, chmn. emeritus 1982–. Received Jean Hersholt Humanitarian Award from Acad. M.P. Arts & Sciences 1975.

KRISEL, GARY: Executive. b. California. Senior vice-president, Network Television, Walt Disney Pictures; 1989 appt. exec. v.p. animation, Walt Disney Television.

KRISTOFFERSON, KRIS: Actor, Singer. b. Brownsville, TX, June 22, 1936. e. Pomona Coll., Oxford U. (Rhodes Scholar). Joined U.S. Army briefly and taught English literature at West Point. Started writing songs (country music) and hits have included Me and Bobby McGee, Why Me, Lord, Sunday Mornin' Comin' Down, etc. Film debut in Cisco Pike, 1971. Continues to make records, do concert tours and appear in films.

PICTURES: Cisco Pike, Pat Garrett and Billy the Kid, Blume in Love, Bring Me the Head of Alfredo Garcia, Alice Doesn't Live Here Anymore, Vigilante Force, The Sailor Who Fell from Grace with the Sea, A Star Is Born, Semi-Tough, Convoy, Heaven's Gate, Roll-Over, Songwriter, Flashpoint, Trouble in Mind, Big Top Pee-wee, Millenium, Welcome Home, Helena, Ryder, Sandino, Original Intent.

TELEVISION: Freedom Road, The Lost Honor of Kathryn Beck, Blood and Orchids, Stagecoach, The Last Days of Frank and Jesse James, Amerika, The Tracker.

KRONICK, WILLIAM: Writer, Director. b. Amsterdam, NY. e. Columbia Coll., A.B. U.S. Navy photography; wrote, dir. featurette, A Bowl of Cherries.

TV DOCS: Wrote, dir., prod.: The Ultimate Stuntman: a Tribute to Dar Robinson, To the Ends of the Earth, Mysteries of the Great Pyramid; George Plimpton Specials; National Geographic, Ripley's Believe It or Not, The World's Greatest Stunts (dir., writer). Prod.: In Search of . . . Series.

PICTURES: Nights in White Satin (s.p.); Horowitz in Dublin (dir., s.p.); Flash Gordon and King Kong (2nd unit dir.); The 500 Pound Jerk (dir., TV movie).

KROST, BARRY: Producer. Partner with Doug Chapin and Mel Simon in The Movie Company, a film, TV, and theatrical production co. Also pres., BKM Management, involved in managing stars. Credits are as exec. prod.

PICTURES: When a Stranger Calls, Uforia, Pandemonium, American Dreamer.

TELEVISION: Movies: Second Sight, Missing Pieces, The Rules of Marriage, When the Circus Comes to Town, Belle Starr, Rearview Mirror.

KRUEGER, RONALD P.: Executive. b. St. Louis, MO, Oct. 19, 1940. e. Westminister Coll., 1961. Began working in theatres as a teenager. Assumed presidency Wehrenberg Theatres, 1962.

MEMBER: NATO and regional v.p.; American Film Inst.; Second Decade, advisory bd. mbr., Salvation Army; Motion Picture Pioneers; Demolay Legion of Honor.

KRUGER, HARDY: Actor. b. Berlin, Germany, April 12, 1928. Ent. m.p. ind. 1943; on stage since 1945.

PICTURES: The One That Got Away, Bachelor of Hearts. German version of The Moon Is Blue (U.A.), The Rest Is Silence (German film of Hamlet), Blind Date (Britain). Has also starred in twenty-four German films. Filming in France and Germany. 1961–62: Films include: Taxi Pour Tobrouk (France), Hatari (Paramount, Hollywood), Les Dimanches de Ville d'Avray (France), Le Gros Coup (France), Les Pianos Mecaniques (France), Le Chant du Monde (France), Flight of the Phoenix (Hollywood), The Defector (U.S.), La Grande Sauterelle, Le Franciscain de Bourge (France), The Battle of the Neretva, The Red Tent, The Nun of Monza, The Secret of Santa Vittoria, Night Hair Child, Death of a Stranger (Israel), Le Solitaire (France), Barry Lyndon (England), Paper Tiger (England/Germany), Potato Fritz (Germany), A Bridge Too Far (England/U.S.), L'Autopsie d'un Monstre (France), The Wild Geese (England); Wrong Is Right (U.S.).

TELEVISION: War and Remembrance.

KRUGER, JEFFREY S.: Producer, Concert impresario, Record and music publisher, Film distribution executive. b. April 19, 1931, London, England. Chmn., of the Kruger Organisation (Concert Promotions) Ltd., Bulldog Records, Ember Records, Kruger Leisure Organisation Ltd., Visual and Audio Leisure Co. Ltd. Produced feature films Rock You Sinners; Sweet Beat; The Amorous Sex. Distributor of Jack Nicolson's The Shooting, Love Child, Dial Rat For Terror, Starcrash; Kill the Shogun; Red Light In the Whitehouse; Enforcer from Death Row; A Whale of A Tale, Vengeance of the Barbarians, From Nashville with Music, Togetherness, Forbidden Love, Search for the Evil One, Gallery of Horrors, Grave of the Vampire, Tomb of the Undead, Sex and the Lonely Woman, House of Terror, Smoke in the Wind, Ten Fingers of Steel, Psychopath, Choppers, Deadwood 76, Good Time Outlaws, Ground Zero, Journey to the Centre of Time, and others. Produced (in association with B.B.C.-TV): 20 musical specials starring Glen Campbell, Marvin Gaye, Jacksons, Charley Pride, George Burns, Charlie Rich, Anne Murray, Helen Reddy, Dionne Warwick, Blood Sweat and Tears, War, David Soul, Frankie Laine, Jerry Lee Lewis, others. Concert presentations include Julio Iglesias, Placido Domingo, etc., Anne Murray, George Burns. Music publ. through Songs For Today. Own record prod. and dist. via Bulldog Records and Visual and Audio Leisure Co. Ltd. Director The Kruger Organisation (Concerts) Ltd. Songs For Today Ltd. Ember Enterprises Inc. Visual and Audio Leisure Co. Ltd. Hillbrow Productions Ltd. Recipient, certificate of merit from city of Beverly Hills & commendation from city of Los Angeles.

KUBRICK, STANLEY: Producer, Director, Writer. b. New York, NY, July 26, 1928. e. Taft H.S. Staff photog., Look magazine; writer, prod., dir., documentaries including Day of the Fight, Flying Padre; Received Luchino Visconti Award, Italy for contribution to cinema, 1988.

PICTURES: prod., dir., s.p., Fear and Desire, Killer's Kiss; dir., s.p., The Killing; writer-dir., Paths of Glory; dir. Spartacus; prod. dir., Lolita; prod. dir., writer, Dr. Strangelove; prod. dir., writer, 2001; A Space Odyssey; A Clockwork Orange; Barry Lyndon; The Shining; Full Metal Jacket (dir., co-prod., co-s.p.).

KUHN, THOMAS G.: Executive. b. Chicago, IL, Nov. 10, 1935. e. Northwestern U., 1957; U. of Southern California, M.B.A., 1966. Singer on Roulette Records, 1958–59. KNBC-TV sales 1960–62; NBC business affairs, 1962–64; NBC mgr. live night time progs., 1965–67; dir. live night time progs., 1968–69. Warner Bros. TV, v.p. program dev. 1970; v.p. TV prod., 1971; exec. prod., Alice; exec. prod., The Awakening Land; exec. v.p. for Alan Landsburg Prods.; exec. prod., Torn Between Two Lovers; exec. prod., The Jayne Mansfield Story; Long Way Home. Staff, v.p., west coast, for RCA Selectavision Video Discs, 1980; division v.p., 1981. Pres., RCA Video Prods., 1984; pres., Lightyear Ent., 1987. Exec. prod.: Aria, The Return of the Swamp Thing, Heaven, The Lemon Sisters.

KULIK, SEYMOUR (BUZZ): Producer, Director. b. New York, NY, 1923. Joined CBS-TV as prod.-dir., 1956; 1964: v.p. chg. West Coast Prods., Bob Banner Associates Inc., 1965; 1967 Prod-Dir. with Paramount Studios.

TELEVISION: Lux Video, Kraft; dir.: You Are There, Climax, Playhouse 90, Defenders, Dr. Kildare, Twilight Zone, Dick Powell Playhouse, Kentucky Jones (exec. prod.). Movies: Brian's Song, Women of Valor, Her Secret Life, Babe, Ziegfield: The Man and His Woman, Vanished, The Lindbergh Kidnapping Case, Her Secret Life, From Here to Eternity, Insight/Decision to Love; Kane and Abel, George Washington (supr. prod.–dir.), Rage of Angels, Too Young the Hero, Around the World in 80 Days.

PICTURES: Warning Shot, The Riot, Shamus, Villa Rides, The Hunter, Pursuit.

KUNO, MOTOJI: Sr. Managing Director. Tokyo Shibaure Electric Co., Ltd. (Toshiba), Tokyo, Japan. Graduated Law Dept., Tokyo Imperial U. Mar., 1923. Became Toshiba auditor June, 1941; dir. June, 1942; sr. managing dir. Nov., 1948, perm. auditor Apr. 1949; dir. Fem., 1950; exec. dir. May, 1952; sr. managing dir. May, 1958.

KURALT, CHARLES: TV News Correspondent. b. Wilmington, NC, Sept. 10, 1934. e. U. of North Carolina. Reporter-columnist for Charlotte News until joining CBS News as writer in 1957. Promoted to news assignment desk in 1958. Became first host of CBS News series, Eyewitness, in 1960. Named CBS News chief Latin American correspondent (based in Rio de Janeiro) in 1961 Appt. CBS News chief west coast correspondent in 1963; transferred to New York, 1964. Has worked on CBS Reports, CBS News Specials, and On the Road series for CBS Evening News. Now host of CBS News Sunday Morning. Author: To the Top of the World (1968), Dateline America (1979), On the Road with Charles Kuralt (1985).

KUREISHI, HANIF: Writer. b. South London, Eng., Dec. 1956. e. King's Coll. (philosophy). At 18, first play presented at Royal Court Theatre where he ushered before becoming writer in residence. Early in career, wrote pornography as Antonia French. Stage and TV plays include: The Mother Country, Outskirts, Borderline and adaptations (Mother Courage). The Rainbow Sign, With Your Tongue Down My Throat (novella) and short stories have been pub. Anglo-Pakistani writer's first s.p. My Beautiful Laundrette earned Acad. Award nom., 1986 and began creative relationship with dir. Stephen Frears.

PICTURES: My Beautiful Laundrette, Sammy and Rosie Get Laid.

KURI, EMILE: Set decorator. b. Mexico City, Mex., June 11, 1907. e. Chaminade Coll., 1924–27. Interior decorator Be Hennesey Art Studio, 1929–32; then set decorator property dept. dir.

PICTURES: I'll Be Seeing You, Silver Queen, Spellbound, Duel in the Sun, Paradine Case, The Heiress (Academy Award, 1949), A Place in the Sun, Carrie, Shane, The Actress, Executive Suite, 20,000 Leagues Under the Sea (Academy Award, 1954); in charge of interior exterior decorations Disneyland. Several Golden Chair Awards (L.A. Furniture Mart). Mem.: Nat'l Acad. of TV Arts and Sciences, American Institute of Interior Designers, Bd. of Gov. Acad. of M.P. Arts and Sciences (1959–69). Honorary Sir Knights of Royal Rosarians, State of Oregon (1970), Decorating Consultant, Disney World, Fla.

KURI, JOHN A.: Producer, Writer. b. 1945. Son of set designer and Disneyland co-designer, Emile Kuri. At 16 worked at Disneyland in ride operations and construction maintenance until joining set dressing crew at Disney Studios, 1969. 1971, became set decorator there 1973, became art dir.; 1975 exec. asst. to prod. Irwin Allen. Formed own co., 1976. Wrote and dir. doc. on city of Las Vegas. 1986 formed own Canadian co.
PICTURES: Captive Hearts (prod., co.s.p. 2nd unit dir., co-lyrics.) Art dir./ set decorator: Apple Dumpling Gang, Leadbelly, Report to the Commissioner, Hawaiian Cowboy, Superdad, Mad Mad Movie Makers.
TELEVISION: Through the Magic Pyramid (assoc. prod.), Skyward (prod., 2nd unit dir.), Skyward Christmas (prod., 2nd unit dir.), Airwolf (dir.); O'Hara (co-creator, series). Art dir.: The Plutonium Incident, Scared Straight Another Story, Young Love First Love, Marriage is Alive and Well, Little Shots, The Red Pony (and set decorator, Emmy nom., 1973).

KURODA, TOYOJI: Executive. b. Tokyo. April 29, 1920. e. Waseda U. Joined Motion Picture Producers Association 1945; appointed inspectorate Board of Trade in export film division 1948. On occasion of founding of Association for Diffusion Japanese Films Abroad (UniJapan Film) became manager.

KUROSAWA, AKIRA: Director, Writer. b. Japan. March 23, 1910. e. Attended Tokyo Acad. of Fine Arts, 1928. Asst. dir. to Kajiro Yamamoto, Photo-Chemical Laboratories (PCL Studios, later renamed Toho Films), 1936–43. Became dir., 1943. Founded Kurosawa Prods., 1960; Dir. Yonki Kai Prods., 1971. Autobiography: Something Like An Autobiography (1982).
PICTURES: Sanshiro Sugata, The Most Beautiful, Zoku Sugato Sanshiro, Those Who Tread on The Tiger's Tail, No Regrets for Our Youth, Those Make Tomorrow, One Wonderful Sunday, The Quiet Duel, Scandal, Stray Dog, Rashomon, The Seven Samurai, The Drunken Angel, The Lower Depths, The Idiot, Ikiru, I Live in Fear, The Hidden Fortress (also prod.), Throne of Blood, Yojimbo, High and Low, Red Beard, The Bad Sleep Well, Sanjuro, Dodes'kaden (also prod.), Dersu Uzala, Kagemusha, Ran, Runaway Train (orig. s.p. only), Such Dreams I Have Dreamed.

KURTIS, BILL: News Correspondent, Anchor. b. Pensacola, FL, Sept. 21, 1940. e. U. of Kansas, Washington U. Sch. of Law, Topeka. Member, American Bar Assn. Career in broadcast journalism began at WIBW Radio in Topeka. Joined CBS News as reporter-producer at Los Angeles bureau in 1970; named CBS news correspondent in 1971. Joined WBBM-TV, Chicago, in 1973 as co-anchor of news broadcasts. In 1982 returned to CBS News as correspondent and co-anchor of CBS Morning News. Left in 1985 to return to Chicago.

KURTZ, GARY: Producer, Director. b. Los Angeles, CA, July 27, 1940. e. U. of Southern California Cinema Sch. Began prof. career during college. Has worked as cameraman, soundman, editor, prod. supervisor and asst. dir. on documentaries and features. Worked on many low budget features for Roger Corman including: The Terror, Beach Ball, Track of the Vampire, Planet of Blood, The Shooting, Ride in the Whirlwind. Drafted into Marines. Spent 2 yrs. in Photo Field as cameraman, editor and still photo.
PICTURES: The Hostage (prod. spvr., ed.), Two-Lane Blacktop (line prod.), Chandler (line prod.), American Graffiti (co.-prod.); Star Wars (prod.), The Empire Strikes Back (prod.); The Dark Crystal (prod., 2nd unit dir.), Return to Oz (exec. prod.), Slipstream (prod.), Feathers (dir., exec. prod.).

KURTZ, SWOOSIE: Actress. b. Omaha, NB, Sept. 6, 1944. e. Studied at U. Southern Calif., Acad. of Music and Dramatic Art, Eng. Regional theatre 1966–70.
THEATER: Who's Afraid of Virginia Woolf? (with Mike Nichols and Elaine May), The Effect of Gamma Rays on Man-in-the Moon Marigolds, Enter a Free Man, Life Class, Children and the Middle Ages, Summer, Fifth of July (Tony Award), House of Blue Leaves (Tony and Obie Awards), Uncommon Women and Others.
PICTURES: Slap Shot, First Love, Oliver's Story, The World According to Garp, Against All Odds, Wildcats, True Stories, Vice Versa, Bright Lights, Big City, Baja Oklahoma, Dangerous Liaisons, Stanley and Iris, A Shock to the System.
TELEVISION: Uncommon Women, Marriage Is Alive and Well, Mating Season, Love Sidney, The Fifth of July, A Caribbean Mystery, Guilty Conscience, A Time to Live, House of Blue Leaves, The Visit (Trying Times), The Image.

KURYS, DIANE: Director. b. France. 1970 joined Jean-Louis Barrault's theatre group, acted for 8 years on stage, television and film. Adapted and translated staged plays. 1977, wrote screenplay for Dibolo Menthe (Peppermint Soda) which she also directed and co-prod. Film won Prix Louis Deluc, Best Picture. Co-prod. Alexandre Arcady's Coup de Sirocco and Le Grand Pardon.
PICTURES: Peppermint Soda (dir., co-prod., s.p.), Cocktail Molotov (s.p., dir.); Entre Nous (s.p., dir.); A Man in Love (s.p., dir.), La-Baule-les-Pins.

KUTNER, MARTIN: Executive. Joined Paramount Pictures in 1971 as eastern div. mgr.; has held various positions in sls. dept. Named v.p., gen. sls. mgr.; in 1980 appt. sr. v.p., domestic distribution; 1983, exec. v.p., distribution; 1984, exec. v.p., intl. mkt. & dist.

KWIT, NATHANIEL TROY, JR.: Executive. b. New York, NY, May 29, 1941. e. Cornell U., B.A.; NYU, M.B.A. 1964–68, American Broadcasting Co., Inc., exec. asst. to pres. of ABC Films. 1968–71, National Screen Service Corp., New York branch mgr., asst. genl. sls. mgr. 1971, founder, CEO Audience Marketing, Inc., later acquired by Viacom International as operating subsidiary. 1974 named v.p. marketing services, Warner Bros., Inc. 1979, named v.p. in charge video and special markets division, United Artists Corp.; 1981, named sr. v.p. in chg. UA television, video, special market div. Following acquisition of UA Corp. by MGM in 1981 promoted to pres., dist. & mktg. for MGM/UA Entertainment Co. 1983, pres. & CEO, United Satellite Communications, direct broadcast TV co. formed with Prudential Insurance Co. backing.

KYO, MACHIKO: Actress. b. Osaka, Japan, 1924. e. Osaka. Dancer in Osaka and Tokyo music halls; entered films 1948 with Daiei Studio; has appeared in numerous Japanese films.
PICTURES: Rashomon, Gate of Hell, Golden Demon, Story of Shunkin, Tales of Genji, Street of Shame, Teahouse of the August Moon, Ugetsu.

L

LACHMAN, ED: Cinematographer. b. 1948. Son of a Morristown, NJ movie theater owner. e. Ohio U., BFA. Filmed documentaries Ornette: Made in America, Strippers, Huie's Sermon. Assisted Sven Nykvist on King of the Gypsies, Hurricane; Vittorio Storaro on Luna; Robby Muller on The American Friend and They All Laughed. Co-director of photography on Werner Herzog's La Soufriere and Stroszek and Wim Wenders' Lightning Over Water and A Tokyo Story.
PICTURES: Scalpel, Union City, Say Amen, Somebody, Little Wars, Split Cherry Tree, Strippers, The Little Sister, Insignificance (American sequences) Desperately Seeking Susan, True Stories, Making Mr. Right, Hail, Hail Rock and Roll, A Gathering of Old Men, Less Than Zero, Backtrack, El Dia Que Me Quieras.
TELEVISION: Get Your Kicks on Route 66 (dir., cinematography, American Playhouse.)

LADD, JR., ALAN: Executive. b. Los Angeles, CA, Oct. 22, 1937. Son of late actor Alan Ladd. Motion picture agent, Creative Management Associates, 1963–69. M.p. producer, 1969–73; produced 9 films in 4 yrs. Joined 20th Century-Fox in 1973 in chg. of creative affairs in feature div. Promoted to v.p., production, 1974. In 1975 named sr. v.p. for worldwide prod.; 1976, promoted to pres. of 20th Century-Fox Pictures. Resigned & formed The Ladd Co., 1979. In 1985 appt. pres. & COO, MGM/UA Entertainment Film Corp; appointed chairman of board, CEO Metro-Goldwyn-Mayer Pictures Inc., 1986; resigned Sept., 1988; 1989 named co-chmn. Pathe Communications Corp. and co-chmn., CEO, Pathe Entertainment.
PICTURES: Prod.: Walking Stick, A Severed Head, Tam-Lin, Villian, Zee and Co., Exec. prod.: Fear is the Key, Nightcomers, Visa Versa.

LADD, CHERYL: Actress. r.n. Cheryl Stoppelmoor. b. Huron, S.D., July 2, 1951. Joined professional Music Shop Band while in elementary school; toured with group ending up in Los Angeles. Cast as voice of Melody character in animated Josie and the Pussycats. Studied acting with Milton Katselas. Did TV commercials, small parts in TV, Film debut 1976 in Jamaica Reef (aka Evil in the Deep, unreleased).
TELEVISION: Series: The Ken Berry "Wow" Show, Charlie's Angels. Specials: Ben Vereen . . . His Roots, General Electric's All-Star Anniversary, John Denver and the Ladies. Guest: Police Woman, Happy Days, Switch, etc. Had 3 specials. Movies: Satan's School for Girls, When She Was Bad, Grace Kelly Story, Romance on the Orient Express, A Death in California, Crossings, Deadly Care, Bluegrass, Kentucky Woman, The Fulfillment of Mary Gray.
PICTURE: Purple Hearts, Now and Forever, Millennium, Lisa.

LADD, DAVID ALAN: Actor, Producer. b. Los Angeles, CA, Feb. 5, 1947. Son of late actor Alan Ladd. On stage in The Glass Menagerie and Alpha Beta.
PICTURES: The Lone Ranger, The Big Land, The Proud Rebel, Raymie, Misty, R.P.M., Dog of Flanders, Catlow,

Deathline, Jamaica Reef, Day of the Locusts, Klansman, Wild Geese. Producer: The Serpent and the Rainbow.
TELEVISION: Zane Gray Theatre, Wagon Train, Playhouse 90, Pursuit, Ben Casey, Gunsmoke, Love American Style, Kojak, Emergency, Tom Sawyer, Producer: When She Was Bad, ABC Variety specials.

LADD, DIANE: Actress. b. Meridian, MS, Nov. 29, 1939. Mother of actress Laura Dern. e. St. Aloysius Acad.; trained for stage with Frank Corsaro in N.Y. Worked as model and as Copacabana nightclub dancer. At 18 in touring co. of Hatful of Rain. NY debut: Orpheus Descending. Film debut in Wild Angels, 1966.
THEATER: Carry Me Back to Morningside Heights, One Night Stands of a Noisy Passenger. The Wall, The Goddess, The Fantastiks, Women Speak, Texas Trilogy; Lu Ann Hampton Laverty.
PICTURES: Wild Angels, The Reivers, Macho Calahan, W.U.S.A., White Lightning, Alice Doesn't Live Here Anymore, Chinatown, Embryo, All Night Long, Something Wicked This Way Comes, Black Widow, Plain Clothes, S.P.O.O.K.S., National Lampoon's Christmas Vacation.
TELEVISION: Alice (series), Rose and Eddie, Addie and the King of Hearts, Willa, Black Beauty, The Secret Storm, Love Boat, Crime of Innocence, Celebration Family, Bluegrass.

LAFFERTY, PERRY: Executive. b. Davenport, IA, Oct. 3, 1920. e. Yale U. With CBS-TV as v.p., programs, Hollywood, 1965–76. Joined Filmways as exec. prod. In 1979 named sr. v.p., programs and talent, west coast, for NBC Entertainment. 1985, resigned. Now indep. producer.
TELEVISION: Maybe Baby (exec. prod.).

LAFONT, BERNADETTE: Actress. b. Oct. 28, Nimes, France. Made her debut in 1957 in Truffaut's first film Les Mistons. Has worked with such international directors as Chabrol, Szabo, Eustache.
PICTURES: Le Beau Serge, Leda, Male Hunt, Les Bonnes Femmes, The Thief of Paris, Such a Gorgeous Kid Like Me, The Mother and the Whore, Zig-Zag, Violette, Like a Turtle on Its Back, Il Ladrone (The Thief), Waiting for the Moon, The Seasons of Pleasure, Prisonnieres.

LAHTI, CHRISTINE: Actress. b. Birmingham, MI, April 4, 1950. m. dir., Thomas Schlamme. e. U. of Michigan. Trained for stage at Herbert Berghof Studios with Uta Hagen. TV commercials. As a mime, performed with Edinburgh Scotland's Travis Theatre. N.Y. stage debut in The Woods, 1978. Film debut in And Justice for All, 1980.
THEATER: The Zinger, Hooter (Playwrights Horizon), Loose Ends, Division St., The Woods, Scenes and Revelations, Present Laughter, The Lucky Spot, Summer and Smoke (LA), The Heidi Chronicles.
PICTURES: Whose Life Is It, Anyway?, Swing Shift, Just Between Friends, Housekeeping, Stacking, Running on Empty, Miss Firecracker (cameo).
TELEVISION: Love Lives On, Single Bars, Single Women, The Last Tenant, The Executioner's Song, Homeless.

LAI, FRANCIS: Composer. b. France, April 26, 1933.
PICTURES: A Man and a Woman, Mayerling, House of Cards, Rider on the Rain, Love Story (Oscar), Le Petit Matin, Another Man, Another Chance, Wanted: Babysitter, Bilitis, The Good and the Bad, Widow's Nest, Cat and Mouse, The Body of My Enemy, Emmanuelle 2; The Forbidden Room, International Velvet, Oliver's Story (Oscar), Passion Flower Hotel, Robert and Robert, The Small Timers, By the Blood Brothers, Beyond the Reef, Bolero, A Second Chance, Edith and Marcel, My New Partner, Marie, A Man and a Woman: 20 Years Later, Bernadette, Itinerary of a Spoiled Child., Der Aten (The Spirit).
TELEVISION: The Berlin Affair, The Sex Symbol, Sins.

LAMARR, HEDY: Actress. r.n. Hedwig Kiesler. b. Vienna, 1915. At 15 starred in Ecstasy (awarded top Italian film-prize). Autobiography, Ecstasy and Me (1966).
PICTURES: Algiers, I Take This Woman, Lady of the Tropics, Boom Town, Comrade X, Come Live with Me, Ziegfeld Girl; H. M. Pulham, Esq.; Tortilla Flat, Crossroads, White Cargo, Heavenly Body, Conspirators, Strange Woman, Samson and Delilah, A Lady Without a Passport, Dishonored Lady, Experiment Perilous, Let's Live a Little, Copper Canyon, My Favorite Spy, Story of Mankind, The Female Animal.

LAMAS, LORENZO: Actor. b. Los Angeles, CA, Jan. 20, 1958. e. Santa Monica City Coll. Son of the late Fernando Lamas and Arlene Dahl. Studied at Tony Barr's Film Actors Workshop (Burbank Studios).
PICTURES: Grease, Tilt, Take Down, Body Rock, Snake-eater's Revenge.
TELEVISION: Series: The Love Boat, Switch, Sword of Justice, California Fever, Secrets of Midland Heights, Falcon Crest. Movie: Detour.

LAMBERT, CHRISTOPHER: (also CHRISTOPHE) Actor. b. New York , NY, 1958; reared in Geneva. Parents French. Studied at Natl Conservatory of Dramatic Art, Paris. Won role in small French film, Le Bar du Telephone.
PICTURES: La Dame de Coeur, Legitime Violence, Greystoke: The Legend of Tarzan, Lord of the Apes, Subway, Highlander, The Sicilian, Priceless Beauty, To Kill a Priest, After the Rain, Why Me?, Highlander's 2020, Priceless Beauty.

LAMBERT, MARY: Director. b. Arkansas. e. attended U. of Denver, Rhode Island Sch. of Design where began making short films. Worked in variety of prod. jobs before moving to Los Angeles and directing TV commercials and music videos (includ. Madonna's Material Girl, Like a Virgin, Like a Prayer, others for Sting, Janet Jackson and Mick Jagger).
PICTURES: Siesta, Pet Sematary.

LAMBERT, VERITY: Producer. b. London, England. Ent. TV 1961; prod. Dr. Who, Adam Adamant Lives, Detective, Somerset Maugham (all BBC series). Since 1971: Shoulder to Shoulder (series), Budgie, Between The Wars. 1974: Appt. controller of Drama, Thames Television. 1979: Chief exec. Euston Films. 1983: Director of Production Thorn EMI Films Ltd. Relinquished her position as controller of Drama Thames Television and retaining pos. as chief exec., Euston Films. Became indep. prod. developing projects for film and TV incl. BBC.
PICTURES: Exec. prod.: American Roulette, A Cry in the Dark.
TELEVISION: May to December, Mrs. Love, Sleepers.

LAMOUR, DOROTHY: Actress. b. New Orleans, LA, Dec. 10, 1914. e. Spence's Business Sch. Miss New Orleans 1931; sang on radio programs; screen debut in Jungle Princess 1938.
PICTURES: Spawn of the North, St. Louis Blues, Man About Town, Disputed Passage, Johnny Apollo, Typhoon, Road to Singapore, Caught in the Draft, Star Spangled Rhythm, Road to Utopia, Practically Yours, Medal for Benny, Duffy's Tavern, My Favorite Brunette, Road to Rio, Wild Harvest, Miracle Can Happen, Lulu Belle, Girl from Manhattan, Lucky Stiff, Slightly French, Manhandled, The Greatest Show on Earth, Road to Bali, Road to Hong Kong, Donovan's Reef, The Phynx, Creepshow 2.
TELEVISION: Death at Love House (movie), Murder, She Wrote.

LANCASTER, BURT: Actor. b. New York, NY, Nov. 2, 1913. e. NYU. Performed as acrobat with Ringling Bros., in carnivals and vaudeville as part of Lang and Cravat, acrobatic team with Nick Cravat, 1932–39. Floor walker, dept. store salesman Chicago, 1939–42. Also fireman and engineer in meat packing plant. Served in U.S. Army Special Service in Italy & N. Africa, W.W.II; NY stage debut: A Sound of Hunting (1945); screen debut in The Killers, 1946. Formed Hecht-Lancaster Orgn. in partnership with Harold Hecht; 1954–57 became Hecht-Hill-Lancaster (with James Hill).
PICTURES: Desert Fury, I Walk Alone, Brute Force, Variety Girl, Sorry Wrong Number, Kiss the Blood Off My Hands, Criss Cross, All My Sons, Rope of Sand, Mister 880, Flame and the Arrow, Vengeance Valley, Ten Tall Men, Jim Thorpe—All American, Crimson Pirate, Come Back Little Sheba, South Sea Woman, From Here to Eternity, His Majesty O'Keefe, Three Sailors and a Girl, Apache, Vera Cruz, The Kentuckian (also dir.), Rose Tattoo, Trapeze, The Rainmaker, Gunfight at the OK Corral, Sweet Smell of Success, Run Silent, Run Deep, Separate Tables, The Devil's Disciple, The Unforgiven, Elmer Gantry (Acad. Award), The Young Savages, Judgment at Nuremberg, Birdman of Alcatraz, The Leopard, A Child is Waiting, The List of Adrian Messengers, Seven Days in May, Hallelujah Trail, The Train, The Professionals, The Swimmer, The Scalphunters, The Gypsy Moths, Castlekeep, Airport, King: A Filmed Record . . . Montgomery to Memphis, Valdez Is Coming, Lawman, Ulzana's Raid, Scorpio, Executive Action, The Midnight Man (prod., dir., co-s.p. & star), Conversation Piece, Buffalo Bill and the Indians, The Cassandra Crossing, Twilight's Last Gleaming, The Island of Dr. Moreau, 1900, Go Tell the Spartans, Cattle Annie and Little Britches, Zulu Dawn, Atlantic City, Local Hero, The Osterman Weekend, Little Treasure, Tough Guys, The Suspect, Rocket Gibraltar, The Goldsmith's Shop, Field of Dreams.
TELEVISION: Moses, Victory at Entebbe, Marco Polo, Scandal Sheet, On Wings of Eagles, Barnum, Scandal Sheet, Control, Legacy of the Hollywood Blacklist (narrator), Fathers and Sons (Ital. TV), Phantom of the Opera (mini-series).

LANDAU, ELY A.: Executive. b. New York, NY, Jan. 20, 1920. Formed National Telefilm Associates, Inc., 1954; org. NTA Film Network, 1956; pres., chmn. of bd., National Telefilm Associates, Inc., 1957; resigned, 1961; formed Ely Landau Company, Inc., 1963; dist. The Servant, King and Country, Umbrellas of Cherbourg; prod. Long Day's Journey into Night, The Fool Killer, The Pawnbroker, A Face of War, The Madwoman of Chaillot. Prod. King—A Filmed Record—Montgomery to Memphis, 1968; organized, directed one-night simultaneous charity showing 633 theatres U.S., 1970; 1972 Formed American Film Theatre, and the Ely Landau

Organization, Inc. 1972–74 produced Iceman Cometh, Rhinoceros, The Homecoming, A Delicate Balance, Luther, Lost in the Stars, Butley, Galileo, In Celebration, The Man in the Glass Booth. Also prod.: The Greek Tycoon; Hopscotch; The Chosen; Beatlemania—The Movie; The Deadly Game; Separate Tables; Mr. Halpern and Mr. Johnson; The Holcroft Covenant.
THEATER: Off-B'way: The Chosen (co-prod.) (1987).

LANDAU, MARTIN: Actor. b. New York, NY, June 20, 1931. e. Pratt Inst., Art Students League, Cartoon and staff artist on N.Y. Daily News; studied 3 yrs. at Actors Studio.
PICTURES: Pork Chop Hill, North by Northwest, Gazebo, Stagecoach to Dancer's Rock, Cleopatra, The Hallelujah Trail, The Greatest Story Ever Told, Decision at Midnight, Alien Attack, Nevada Smith, They Call Me Mister Tibbs, Operation Snafu, A Town Called Hell, Black Gunn, Welcome Home Johnny Bristol, Mission: Impossible vs. the Mob, Dark Shadows in an Empty Room, Meteor, The Savage Report, Death of Ocean View Park, Destination Moonbase Alpha, The Fall of the House of Usher, Without Warning, Trial By Terror, Cosmic Princess, Journey Through the Black Sun, Beauty and the Beast, The Last Word, The Return, Alone in the Dark, Access Code, Treasure Island, Run if You Can, W.A.R., Sweet Revenge, Cyclone, Real Bullets, Empire State, Delta Fever, Kung Fu: The Movie, Tucker: The Man and His Dream (Acad. Award nom.), Paint It Black, The Neon Empire.
TELEVISION: Series: Mission Impossible (1966–68), Space 1999. Movie: Max and Helen: A Remarkable Love Story. Numerous guest appearances.
STAGE: Middle of the Night, Uncle Vanya, Stalag 17, Wedding Breakfast, First Love, The Goat Song.

LANDAU, RICHARD H.: Writer. b. New York, NY, Feb. 21, 1914. e. U. of Arizona, Yale U. With Small-Landau agency handling writers and stories; shorts dept. writer MGM 1939; writer for RKO Radio since 1942; wrote documentaries and training films for U.S. Army.
PICTURES: Gun in His Hand, Strange Confession, Challenge in the Night, Back to Bataan, Little Iodine, Christmas Eve, Crooked Way, Johnny One Eye, Roadblock, Lost Continent, F.B.I. Girl, Stolen Face, Bad Blonde, Spaceways, Sins of Jezebel, Blackout, Deadly Game, A Race for Life, Pearl of the South Pacific, Creeping Unknown.

LANDERS, HAL: Producer. b. Chicago, IL, June 26, 1928. Company: The Hal Landers Co.
PICTURES: Joy Ride; Damnation Alley; Gypsy Moths; Monte Walsh; The Hot Rock; Bank Shot; Death Wish; Death Wish II (exec. prod.).

LANDES, MICHAEL: Executive. b. Bronx, NY, Feb. 4, 1939. e. Fairleigh Dickinson, B.A., 1961; Rutgers, J.D., 1964; NYU, L.L.M., 1965. 20 years of corporate law and financing experience as partner in law firm of Hahn and Hessen. Co-chairman of The Landes Group (L.P.). Formed The Almi Group, 1978. Formed Almi Pictures, 1982. In July 1986, Almi sold its 97-screen RKO Warner Century Warner Theatre chain to Cineplex Odeon. Nov. 1986, Almi purchased Video Shack chain. May 1987, RKO Warner Video acquired Salt Lake City-based Adventureland Video (franchise network). March 1988, RKO Warner Video purchased Super Video chain. May 1988, became chairman, Damon Creations, Inc. which merged with Enro Holding Corp. and Enro Shirt Co. into Damon Creations. Member: Young Presidents' Organization (YPO); Metropolitan President's Org. (MPO), World Business Council (WBC). exec. comm., Association for a Better New York; trustee, Citizens Budget Commission; trustee, Motion Picture Pioneers; member, Academy of Motion Picture Arts and Sciences.

LANDIS, JOHN: Director. b. Chicago, IL, Aug. 3, 1950.
PICTURES: Schlock (stuntman, dir., writer), Kentucky Fried Movie, National Lampoon's Animal House, The Blues Brothers (also co-s.p.), An American Werewolf in London (also s.p.), Trading Places, Twilight Zone—The Movie (prod., dir., s.p. also), Into the Night, Spies Like Us, Three Amigos (dir.), Amazon Women on the Moon (co-dir., co-exec. prod.), Coming to America (dir.).

LANDON, MICHAEL: Actor, Writer, Director. r.n. Eugene Maurice Orowitz. b. Forest Hills, NY, Oct. 31, 1936. e. U. of Southern California. Was athlete before signed by Warner Bros. to attend acting school. Roles in films and TV followed; big break came with Bonanza.
TELEVISION: Actor: Restless Gun, Bonanza, Little House on the Prairie; Highway To Heaven. Guest appearances on Variety Shows. Writer-Director: Love Came Laughing (Love Story series). Director: Roy Campanella Story. Producer: Little House on the Prairie, Highway to Heaven.

LANDRES, PAUL: Director. b. New York, NY, Aug. 21, 1912. e. UCLA. Started as asst. film editor at Universal 1931. Editor 1937 to 1949 of many feature films. Director of feature films and TV since 1949. Under directorial contract to Warner Bros. 1961–62. Director of 22 feature films for theatrical release.
PICTURES: Oregon Passage, A Modern Marriage, Mark of the Vampire, Navy Bound, The Curse of Dracula, Miracle of the Hills, 54 Washington Street and Son of a Gunfighter made in Spain for MGM release.
TELEVISION: 91 hour films and over 300 half hour shows including among many others, multiple episodes of Bonanza, Daktari, The Rifleman, 77 Sunset Strip, Maverick Hawaiian Eye, The Plainsman, Readers Digest, Topper, Wyatt Earp, Blondie, etc.

LANDSBURG, ALAN: Executive, Producer. b. New York, NY, May 10, 1933. e. NYU. Producer for NBC News Dept., 1951–59; producer-writer, CBS, 1959–60; exec. prod., Wolper Productions/Metromedia Producers Corp., 1961–70; chairman, The Alan Landsburg Company, 1970–present. Co-exec. prod.: Jaws 3-D, Porky's II: The Next Day.
TELEVISION: *Exec. prod.:* Biography, National Geographic Specials (1965–70): The Undersea World of Jacques Cousteau; In Search of. . ., That's Incredible. Movies: Adam, Fear on Trial, Parent Trap II, Adam: His Song Continues, The George McKenna Story, Long Gone, Strange Voices, Bluegrass, A Place at the Table, Too Young the Hero, A Stoning in Fulham County, High Risk, Destined to Live, Quiet Victory: The Charlie Wedemeyer Story, The Ryan White Story, Unspeakable Acts (prod., s.p.).

LANE, DIANE: Actress. b. New York, NY, Jan., 1965. Acted in stage classics (Medea, Electra, As You Like It) at La Mama Experimental Theatre Club, NY. Debut in A Little Romance, 1979.
PICTURES: Watcher in the Woods, Touched by Love, National Lampoon Goes to the Movies, Cattle Annie and Little Britches, Six Pack, Ladies and Gentlemen: The Fabulous Stains, Streets of Fire, The Outsiders, Rumble Fish, The Cotton Club, The Big Town, Lady Beware, Priceless Beauty, After the Rain, Vital Signs.
STAGE: The Cherry Orchard, Agamemmon, Runaways.
TELEVISION: Child Bride of Short Creek, Summer, Miss All-American Beauty, Lonesome Dove.

LANG, CHARLES: Cinematographer. b. Bluff, UT, March 27, 1902. e. Lincoln H.S., Los Angeles; U. of Southern California. Entered m.p. ind. with Paramount Film Laboratory, then asst. cameraman; dir. of photography, Paramount, 1929–52; then freelance.
PICTURES: A Farewell to Arms (Academy Award for best photography, 1933), The Uninvited, Ghost and Mrs. Muir, A Foreign Affair, September Affair, Ace in the Hole, Sudden Fear, Sabrina, Queen Bee, Man from Laramie, The Rainmaker, Some Like It Hot, The Magnificent Seven, Facts of Life, One-Eyed Jacks, Summer and Smoke, Charade, Father Goose, Wait Until Dark, Inside Daisy Clover, Hotel, Flim Flam Man, The Stalking Moon, Cactus Flower, Bob & Carol & Ted & Alice, The Love Machine, Doctors' Wives, Butterflies Are Free.

LANG, DAVID: Writer. b. New York, NY, Nov. 30, 1913. Was in Merchant Marine three years. Joined Charles Mintz Studio (Columbia) as cartoonist. Moved to MGM cartoon dept. 1938–40. Radio writer, Calling All Cars, KNX, Los Angeles, 1941. Contract writer at MGM, 1941–43. Yank on the Burma Road, Gambler's Choice, Hired Gun, North West Mounted Police, Midnight Manhunt, People Are Funny, Caged Fury, One Exciting Night, Flaxy Martin, Smart Money, Chain of Circumstance, Ambush at Tomahawk, The Nebraskan, Black Horse Canyon for U.I. Also Screaming Eagles, Hellcats of the Navy, Buckskin Lady, Queen of Burlesque.
TELEVISION: Cheyenne, 87th Precinct, Ford Theatre, Gallant Men, Westinghouse Theatre, Adventures in Paradise, Bonanza, Trackdown, Wanted Dead or Alive, Rifleman, Rawhide, Have Gun Will Travel. At least two hundred credits in above series. Novelist. Oedipus Burning.

LANG, JENNINGS: Executive. b. New York, NY, May 28, 1915. e. St. John's U. Law Sch. m. actress-singer Monica Lewis. Went into law practice in 1937 with Seligsburg and Lewis, m.p. law specialists. 1938 to Hollywood as 2nd asst. dir. at Grand National Studios. Opened own office as actor's agent; first client, comedian Hugh Herbert. In 1940 joined Jaffe Agency; made partner and v.p. in 1942. Was pres. from 1948 to May, 1950, when resigned to join MCA. Worked in all phases of MCA operations; in 1952 made v.p. of MCA TV Ltd., and bd. mem. Involved with prod. and sales of TV prods. from inception of Revue (now Universal City Studios) in 1950. Organized Revue's New Projects Dept., creator and exec. in chg. of prog. dev. Involved with creation and sales of such series as Wagon Train, The Robert Cummings Show, Bachelor Father, Wells Fargo, Mike Hammer. Supvr. of Universal's World Premiere films. Made exec. prod. at MCA (Universal) for motion pictures.
PICTURES: exec. prod.: Winning, They Might Be Giants, Puzzle of a Downfall Child, Coogan's Bluff, The Beguiled, Act of the Heart, Tell Them Willie Boy Is Here, Play Misty for Me, Pete 'n Tillie, High Plains Drifter, Slaughterhouse Five, Charley Varrick, Breezy, The Great Waldo Pepper, Airport '75,

Earthquake, Joe Kidd, The Great Northfield Minnesota Raid, The Eiger Sanction, Airport 1977, The Front Page, The Hindenburg. Producer: Swashbuckler, Roller Coaster, House Calls, Nunzio, Airport '79—The Concorde, Little Miss Marker, The Nude Bomb, The Sting II, Stick.

LANG, OTTO: Producer, Director, Four Academy Award nominations for Cinemascope Specials, Twentieth Century-Fox Film Corp. Saga of Western Man; ABC-TV Specials—The Legend of Cortez; Beethoven: Ordeal and Triumph.
TELEVISION: Man from U.N.C.L.E.; Daktari; Iron Horse; Cheyenne; Dick Powell Show; Zane Gray Theatre; Ann Sothern Show; Rifleman; Bat Masterson; Seahunt; The Deputy; Surfside 6; Hawaiian Eye. Prod. Twentieth Century Fox Hour. Dir. Man and the Challenge; Aquanauts; World of Giants. Dir. feature for Cinerama: Search for Paradise, Lancer, Felony Squad.
PICTURES: Prod., Call Northside 777; Five Fingers; White Witch Doctor. Specialist for foreign locations. Many segments for This World of Ours; Wide, Wide World. 1969. Assoc. prod: Tora! Tora! Tora!

LANGAN, GLENN: Actor. b. Denver, CO, July 8, 1917. e. Wheatridge H.S. Started career as asst. mgr. Elitch Gardens, Denver; traveled to N.Y., worked at odd jobs, until walk-on part in play, Swing Your Lady; signed by Hollywood after appearance in A Kiss for Cinderella, oppos. Luise Rainer.
PICTURES: Riding High, Four Jills in a Jeep, Something for the Boys, Margie, Homestretch, Forever Amber, Iroquois Trail, Treasure of Monte Cristo, Rapture, Hangman's Knot, One Girl's Confession, 99 River Street, Big Chase, Mutiny in Outer Space, Chisum.

LANGE, HOPE: Actress. r.n. Hope Elise Ross Lange; b. Redding Ridge, CT, Nov. 28, 1936. e. Reed Coll., Portland, OR; Barmore Jr. Coll., N.Y. Parents: John Lange, musician (Arr. music for stage shows, including Show Boat); Minnette Buddecke Lange, actress. Prof. stage debut at age 12 in The Patriots on Broadway; then in The Hot Corner. Film debut: Bus Stop (1956).
PICTURES: Jesse James, Peyton Place, The Young Lions, In Love and War, Wild in the Country, The Best of Everything, A Pocketful of Miracles, How the West Was Won, Love Is a Ball, Jigsaw, Death Wish, I Am the Cheese, The Prodigal, A Nightmare on Elm Street: Part 2, Blue Velvet.
TELEVISION: Series: The Ghost and Mrs. Muir, The New Dick Van Dyke Show. Pilot: Knight and Dave. Movies: That Certain Summer, I Love You—Goodbye, Beulah Land, The Day Christ Died, Crowhaven Farm, A Family Tree (Trying Times), The Henry Ford Story: Man and the Machine (mini-series).

LANGE, JESSICA: Actress. b. Cloquet, MN, Apr. 20, 1949. e. U. of Minnesota. Left to study mime 2 years under Etienne Decroux in Paris. Dancer, Opera Comique, Paris; model with Wilhelmina agy, NY. Worked in experimental theatre in New York. Theatrical film debut in King Kong (1976).
PICTURES: All That Jazz, How to Beat the High Cost of Living, The Postman Always Rings Twice, Frances, Tootsie (Acad. Award, supp., 1982), Country (also co-prod.), Sweet Dreams, Crimes of the Heart, Far North, Everybody's All American, Men Don't Leave, Music Box.
TELEVISION: Cat on a Hot Tin Roof.

LANGELLA, FRANK: Actor. b. Bayonne, NJ, Jan. 1, 1940. Studied acting at Syracuse U., later in regional repertory, summer stock, and on and off Bdwy. B'way debut: Seascape (1977, Tony Award). Film debut in The Twelve Chairs (1970).
THEATER: member Lincoln Ctr. Rep. co. 1963, Off B'way debut: The Immoralist (1963), Benito Cereno, The Old Glory (Obie Award), Good Day (Obie Award), The White Devil (Obie Award), Long Day's Journey Into Night, Yerma, The Devils, Dracula, A Cry of Players, Cyrano de Bergerac, other classics, The Tooth of the Crime, Ring Around the Moon, Passion, Design for Living, Sherlock's Last Case, Les Liaisons Dangereuses (Ahmanson, L.A.).
PICTURES: Diary of a Mad Housewife, The Deadly Trap, The Wrath of God, Dracula, Those Lips, Those Eyes, Sphinx, The Men's Club, And God Created Woman.
TELEVISION: Benito Cereno (1965), The Good Day, The Mark of Zorro, The Ambassador, The Sea Gull, The Amer. Woman: Portrait in Courage, Eccentricities of a Nightingale, Sherlock Holmes, Liberty.

LANGFORD, FRANCES: Singer, Actress. b. Lakeland, FL, April 4, 1913. e. Southern Coll. Stage experience in vaudeville, nightclubs, national radio programs. In 1935: collab. on lyrics and appeared in Every Night at Eight, Collegiate Broadway Melody of 1936, Palm Springs, Born to Dance, The Hit Parade, Hollywood Hotel, Dreaming Out Loud, Too Many Girls, The Hit Parade of 1941, All-American Coed, Swing It Soldier, Mississippi Gambler, Yankee Doodle Dandy, This Is the Army, Career Girl, The Girl Rush, Dixie Jamboree, Radio Stars on Parade, People Are Funny, Deputy Marshall, Purple Heart Diary, Glenn Miller Story; TV appearances with Don Ameche.

LANGNER, PHILIP: Producer, b. New York, NY, Aug. 24, 1926. e. Yale U. President of The Theatre Guild and Theatre Guild Films, Inc. Producer the Westport Country Playhouse 1947–53. Joined The Theatre Guild 1954. Produced 28 plays on Broadway at the Theatre Guild including the Matchmaker, Bells Are Ringing, The Tunnel of Love, Sunrise at Campobello, A Majority of One, The Unsinkable Molly Brown, A Passage to India, Seidman and Son, The Royal Hunt of the Sun, The Homecoming, Absurd Person Singular and Golda.
FILMS: Producer of The Pawnbroker, Slaves and Born to Win. Associate Prod., Judgment at Nuremberg, and A Child Is Waiting.

LANSBURY, ANGELA: Actress. b. London, England, Oct. 16, 1925. Sister of Bruce and Edgar Lansbury. e. South Hampstead Sch. for Girls, England; Acad. of Music, London; Feagin Dramatic Sch., N.Y. p. Moyna Macgill, actress; also rel. to Robert B. Mantell, actor, Rt. Hon. George Lansbury, gov't. official. Screen debut in Gaslight, 1943, which won Hollywood Foreign Correspondents' Assoc. award. Exercise and lifestyle video: Positive Moves, 1988.
PICTURES: Gaslight, National Velvet, Picture of Dorian Gray, Harvey Girls, Hoodlum Saint, Till the Clouds Roll By, Tenth Avenue Angel, If Winter Comes, State of the Union, Three Musketeers, Red Danube, Samson and Delilah, Kind Lady, Mutiny, Remains to Be Seen, Key, Man, Purple Mask, A Lawless Street, A Life at Stake, Court Jester, Please Murder Me, The Long Hot Summer, The Reluctant Debutante, The Summer of the 17th Doll, Season of Passion, Dark at the Top of the Stairs, A Breath of Scandal, All Fall Down, Hawaii, In the Cool of the Day, The Manchurian Candidate, The World of Henry Orient, Mr. Buddwing, Dear Heart, The Greatest Story Ever Told, Harlow, The Amorous Adventures of Moll Flanders, Something for Everyone, Bedknobs and Broomsticks, Death on the Nile, The Mirror Crack'd, The Pirates of Penzance, The Shell Seekers.
BROADWAY: Hotel Paradiso (NY debut, 1957), A Taste of Honey, Anyone Can Whistle, Mame, Dear World, Gypsy, The King and I, Sweeney Todd, Mame (1983 revival).
TELEVISION: The Lady Vanishes, Sweeney Todd, Little Gloria...Happy at Last, Lace, The First Olympic Race, The Gift of Love; Rage of Angels: The Story Continues; Shootdown, Wings of the Water. Series: Murder She Wrote.

LANSBURY, BRUCE: Executive. b. London, England, Jan. 12, 1930. Brother of Angela and twin Edgar. e. UCLA. m. actress Moyna Macgill. Writer, prod. KABC-TV, Los Angeles, 1957–59; joined CBS-TV, 1959, was ass't. dir., program dev., Hollywood, director for daytime and nighttime programs, producer of Great Adventure series; and v.p., programs, New York; 1964–66, indep. prod., Broadway stage; 1966–69 producer, Wild Wild West, CBS series; 1969–72, prod. Mission: Impossible, Paramount Movies of Week; now v.p., creative affairs, Paramount TV.
TELEVISION: Wings of the Water (exec. prod.).

LANSBURY, EDGAR: Producer, Designer. b. London, England, Jan. 12, 1930. e. UCLA. Brother of Angela and Bruce Lansbury. Started career as scenic designer and art director. 1955–60, art dir., CBS; 1962–63, exec. art dir. prod. for WNDT-TV, educational sta.; On Bdwy. produced such shows as The Subject Was Roses, Promenade, Waiting for Godot, Long Day's Journey into Night, Gypsy, The Night That Made America Famous, American Buffalo, etc.
PICTURES: Producer: The Subject Was Roses, Godspell, The Wild Party, Squirm, Blue Sunshine, He Knows You're Alone, The Clairvoyant.
TELEVISION: The Defenders (art. dir.); Summer Girl (exec. prod.), etc., Wings of the Water (exec. prod.)

LANSING, SHERRY: Executive. b. Chicago, IL, July 31, 1944. e. Northwestern U. Taught math, English and drama in L.A. city high schools, 1966–69. Acted in films (Loving, Rio Lobo) and numerous TV shows. Story editor for Wagner Intl. Prod. Co., 1972–74. Talent Associates, in chg. West Coast development (all projects), 1974–75. Appt. MGM story editor, 1975. In 1977 named MGM v.p. of creative affairs, Nov., 1977, appointed vice pres., production, at Columbia Pictures. January, 1980, appointed pres., Twentieth Century-Fox Productions. Resigned 1982 to form new production co. with Stanley R. Jaffee: Jaffee—Lansing Prods.
PICTURES: Co-prod.: Racing with the Moon, Firstborn, Fatal Attraction, The Accused, Black Rain.
TELEVISION: When the Time Comes (exec. prod.), Mistress.

LANTZ, WALTER: Animated cartoon producer. b. New Rochelle NY, April 27, 1900. Producer and creator of Woody Woodpecker, Andy Panda, Chilly Willy. Started with Gregory La Cava, 1916 with Katzenjammer Kids, Happy Hooligan and Krazy Kat. Joined J. R. Bray in 1922, producing Col. Heeza Liar, Dinky Doodle. Started with Universal Pictures in 1928. Produced first Technicolor cartoon for Paul Whiteman's King of Jazz. Produced Oswald Rabbit. Created Woody Woodpecker in 1941. Produced the first Woody Woodpecker TV show in 1957. Toured the Pacific War Zone on a handshake tour for the USO, with wife Gracie, the voice of Woody Woodpecker. Has been awarded the Golden Globe Award, the ASIFA Award, and in 1979 the Oscar for achievement in the field of animation. Now producing the Woody Woodpecker TV show. 1986, awarded a star on Hollywood Walk of Fame.

LARDNER, RING W., JR.: Writer. b. Chicago, IL, Aug. 19, 1915. p. writer-humorist Ring W. and Ellis A. e. Phillips Andover Acad, Princeton U. Was reporter on New York Daily Mirror. Publ. writer, Selznick International. Shared orig. screenplay Academy Award with Michael Kanin for Woman of the Year, 1942. 1947, mem. of "Hollywood 10" Wrote and conceived 5 TV series under pseudonyms while blacklisted. M*A*S*H (Acad. Award, s.p. based on material from another medium, 1970). 1989, received Writers Guild Laurel Award. Author of novels: The Ecstacy of Owen Muir, All For Love, and memoir, The Lardners" My Family Remembered. Also collab. on Bdwy musical Foxy.
PICTURES: The Cross of Lorraine, Tomorrow the World, Forever Amber, Forbidden Street, Four Days Leave, Cloak and Dagger, The Cincinnati Kid, M*A*S*H, The Greatest.

LARKIN, JAMES J.: Executive. b. Brooklyn, NY, Nov. 2, 1925. e. Columbia U., 1947–52. U.S. Air Force, 1943–46; BOAC rep. to entertainment ind., 1948–60; pres., Transportation Counselors Inc., 1960–62; pres., Larkin Associates, Inc., 1962–65; exec. Radio N.Y. Worldwide, 1965–68, V.P. Grolier Educational Corp., 1968–69; V.P. Visual Informational Systems, 1969–73. Pres., Business Television Services, Inc., 1973; exec. prod., Madhouse Brigade, 1977–79; prod.-writer, All Those Beautiful Girls, 1979–80.

LARROQUETTE, JOHN: Actor. b. New Orleans, LA., Nov. 25, 1947. Disc jockey on FM radio during 1960s and early 70s. Acted on L.A. stage from 1973 (The Crucible, Enter Laughing, Endgame). Prof. debut, TV series Doctor's Hospital, 1976–78. Was narrator for film Texas Chainsaw Massacre.
PICTURES: Altered States; Heart Beat; Green Ice; Stripes; Cat People; Hysterical; Twilight Zone—the Movie; Choose Me; Meatballs, Part II; Star Trek III: The Search for Spock; Summer Rental; Blind Date; Second Sight, Madhouse
TELEVISION: Series: Doctor's Hospital; Baa Baa Black Sheep; Night Court (Emmy, 1985–88). Movie: Hot Paint.

LARSON, BOB: Producer. e. UCLA. First job while in high school as prod. asst. on Sol Lesser's The Red House (1947). Worked way up after schooling thru film ranks; prod. mgr., Forty Pounds of Trouble, Freud, etc., for Universal Pictures. Joined Bryna Prods. as exec. in chg. prod. (Spartacus, The Vikings). Assoc. prod., asst. dir. for Clint Eastwood on Play Misty for Me. Rejoined Universal for decade; then went to David Wolper Prods. Became independent, producing TV pilot, Strange New World, at Warner Bros.; two films at Universal: Now partner with director Michael Apted, collaborating on Coal Miner's Daughter, Continental Divide, Bring on the Night, 28 Up, River Rat, Critical Condition, Fletch Lives.

LASSALLY, WALTER: Cinematographer. b. Berlin, Germany, 1926. Entered indust. as clapper-boy at Riverside Studios. During 1950s allied himself with Britain's Free Cinema filmmakers working for Lindsay Anderson, Gavin Lambert, Tony Richardson and Karel Reisz.
PICTURES: A Girl in Black (1956), Beat Girl, A Taste of Honey, Electra, The Loneliness of the Long Distance Runner, Tom Jones, Zorba the Greek (Acad. Award, 1965), Joanna, Savages, The Wild Party, Something for Everyone, Pleasantville, Shenanigans, Woman Across the Way, Hullabaloo Over George and Bonnie's Pictures, Something Short of Paradise, The Blood of Hussain, Angels of Iron, Memoirs of a Survivor, Too Far to Go, Heat and Dust, Private School, The Bostonians, Adventures of Huckleberry Finn, The Deceivers, Kamilla's Friend.
TELEVISION: Mrs. Delafield Wants to Marry, My Africa.

LASSER, LOUISE: Actress. b. New York, NY, April 11, 1941. e. Brandeis U., New School for Social Research. Appeared on stage before theatrical film debut in 1965 with What's New, Pussycat?
THEATER: I Can Get It For You Wholesale; The Third Ear; Henry, Sweet, Henry; Lime Green/Khaki Blue, The Chinese.
PICTURES: What's Up, Tiger Lily?, Take the Money and Run, Bananas, Everything You Always Wanted to Know About Sex, Such Good Friends, Slither, In God We Trust, Stardust Memories, Crimewave, Sing, Nightmare at Shadow Woods, Surrender, Sing, Rude Awakening.
TELEVISION: Masquerade, Mary Hartman, Mary Hartman (series); Movies: The Lie, Isn't It Shocking?, Just Me and You (also s.p.), For Ladies Only, Coffee, Tea or Me?.

LASZLO, ANDREW: Cinematographer. b. Hungary, Jan. 12, 1926.
PICTURES: One Potato, Two Potato, You're a Big Boy Now, The Night They Raided Minskys, Popi, Teacher, Teacher, The Out of Towners, Lovers and Other Strangers, The Owl and the Pussycat, Jennifer on Mind, To Find a Man, Class of 44, Countdown at Kussini, Thieves, Angela, Somebody Killed Her Husband, The Warriors, Shogun, The Funhouse, Southern Comfort, I, the Jury, First Blood, Love is Forever, Streets of Fire, Thief of Hearts, Remo Williams: The Adventure Begins, Poltergeist II, Innerspace, Star Trek V: The Final Frontier, Ghost Dad.
TELEVISION: Documentaries: High Adventure with Lowell Thomas, The Twentieth Century. Series: The Phil Silvers Show, Joe and Mabel, Mama, Brenner, Naked City, The Nurses, Doctors and Nurses, Coronet Blue. Specials: New York, New York, The Beatles at Shea Stadium, Ed Sullivan specials. Movies and feature pilots: The Happeners, The Cliffdwellers, Daphne, Teacher, Teacher, Blue Water Gold, The Man Without a Country, The Unwanted, Spanner's Key, Thin Ice, Lover is Forever. Mini-series: Washington Behind Closed Doors, The Dain Curse, Top of the Hill, Shogun, and numerous commercials.

LATHROP, PHILIP: Cinematographer. b. Oct. 22, 1916.
PICTURES: Experiment in Terror, Days of Wine and Roses, The Pink Panther, Lonely Are the Brave, Soldier in the Rain, Thirty Six Hours, The Americanization of Emily, The Cincinnati Kid, Never Too Late, What Did You Do in the War Daddy? The Happening, The Russians Are Coming, Point Blank, Finian's Rainbow, I Love You Alice B. Toklas, The Illustrated Man, The Gypsy Moths, Rabbit Run, The Hawaiians, The Traveling Executioner, They Shoot Horses Don't They?, The Wild Rovers, The Thief Who Came to Dinner, Mame, The Prisoner of Second Avenue, Earthquake, Airport '75, The Blackbird, Hard Times, Killer Elite, The Swashbuckler, Airport 1977, The Driver, A Different Story, Moment By Moment, Foolin' Around, The Concorde—Airport '79, Little Miss Marker, Loving Couples, A Change of Seasons, All Night Long, Jekyll and Hyde Together Again, National Lampoon's Class Reunion, Deadly Friend.
TELEVISION: Captains Courageous, Celebrity, Malice in Wonderland (Emmy Award), Picking Up the Pieces, Love on the Run, Christmas Snow (Emmy Award, 1987), Little Girl Lost.

LATSIS, PETER C.: Publicist. b. Chicago, IL, Mar. 9, 1919. e. Wright Jr. Coll., Chicago. Newspaper reporter, Chicago Herald-American, 1942–45; Army, 1943; joined Fox West Coast Theatres, Los Angeles, in theatre operations 1945; adv.-pub. dept. 1946; asst. dir. adv.-pub. 1955; press rep. National Theatres, 1958; press relations dir., National General Corp., 1963; home office special field pub. repr., American International Pictures, 1973; Filmways Pictures, 1980–82; Recipient of Publicists Guild's Robert Yeager Award, 1983.

LATTANZI, MATT: Actor. m. actress-singer Olivia Newton-John.
PICTURES: Xanadu (1980), Rich and Famous, Grease 2, My Tutor, That's Life!, Blueberry Hill, Blue Suede Shoes, Call Backs, Catch Me If You Can, Diving In.

LATTUADA, ALBERTO: Director. b. Milan, Italy, 1914. Son of Felice Lattuada, musician, opera composer, and writer of scores of many of son's films. Studied architecture; founded the periodical Cominare. Later founded Italian Film Library, of which he is still pres. Also, pres., Cinema D'Essay, First screen work as scriptwriter and asst. dir. of two films, 1940.
PICTURES: Mill on the Po, Anna, The Overcoat, La Lupa, Love in the City, White Sister, Flesh Will Surrender, Without Pity, The She Wolf, Tempest, The Unexpected, Mafioso, The Mandrake, Matchless, The Betrayal, The Steppe, Oh, Serafina, Stay as You Are.

LAUGHLIN, TOM: Actor, Producer, Director, Writer. b. Minneapolis, MN, 1938. e. U. of Indiana, U. of Minnesota where had athletic scholarships. m. actress Delores Taylor. Travelled around world, studying in Italy with Dr. Maria Montessori. Established, ran a Montessori school in Santa Monica for several yrs. Worked his way to Hollywood, where acted in bit parts until stardom came in Born Losers in 1967. Produced and starred in Billy Jack and The Trial of Billy Jack, also writing s.p. with wife under pseudonym Frank Christina. Heads own prod. co., Billy Jack Enterprises.
PICTURES: South Pacific, Tea and Sympathy, Gidget, Born Losers, Billy Jack, The Trial of Billy Jack, The Master Gunfighter, Billy Jack Goes to Washington.

LAURENTS, ARTHUR: Writer, Director. b. New York, NY, July 14, 1918. e. Cornell U., B.A., 1937. First professional writing as radio script writer in 1939. In Army 1941–45.
STAGE PLAYS: Author: Home of the Brave, The Bird Cage, The Time of the Cuckoo, A Clearing in the Woods, Invitation to a March, West Side Story, Gypsy, Hallelujah, Baby!, The Enclave. Director: Invitation to a March, I Can Get It for You Wholesale, La Cage aux Folles (Tony Award). Author-Director: Anyone Can Whistle, Do I Hear a Waltz?, Gypsy (revival).
SCREENPLAYS: The Snake Pit, Rope, Caught, Anna Lucasta, Anastasia, Bonjour Tristese, The Way We Were (from his own novel), The Turning Point (also co-prod.).

LAURIE, PIPER: Actress. r.n. Rosetta Jacobs. b. Detroit, MI, Jan. 22, 1932. e. Los Angeles H.S. Acted in school plays, signed by U.I. in 1949; m.p. debut in Louisa (1950); Broadway, The Glass Menagerie (revival).

PICTURES: The Milkman, Francis Goes to the Races, Prince Who Was a Thief, Son of Ali Baba, Has Anybody Seen My Gal, No Room for the Groom, Mississippi Gambler, Golden Blade, Dangerous Mission, Johnny Dark, Dawn at Socorro, Smoke Signal, Ain't Misbehavin', Until They Sail, The Hustler, Carrie, Ruby, Return to Oz, Tim, Children of a Lesser God, Distortions, Appointment with Death, Tiger Warsaw, Dream a Little Dream, Mother, Mother.

TELEVISION: The Days of Wine and Roses, Rainbow, Thorn Birds, Love Mary, Tender Is the Night, Promise (Emmy Award), Go Toward the Light.

LAUTER, ED: Actor. b. Long Beach, NY, Oct. 30, 1940.

PICTURES: The Last American Hero, Executive Action, Lolly Madonna, The Longest Yard, The French Connection II, Breakheart Pass, Family Plot, King Kong, Magic, Death Hunt, Timerider, Lassiter, Cujo, Finders Keepers, Death Wish 3, Youngblood, Raw Deal, Chief Zabu, Gleaming the Cube, Judgment, Tennessee Waltz.

TELEVISION: Movies: Class of '63, The Migrants, The Godchild, Satan's Triangle, A Shadow in the Streets, Last Hours Before Morning, The Clone Master, The Jericho Mile, Undercover with the KKK, The Boy Who Drank Too Much, Guyana Tragedy—The Story of Jim Jones, Alcatraz—The Whole Shocking Story, The Last Days of Patton, The Thanksgiving Promise.

LAVEN, ARNOLD: Director, Producer. Chicago, IL.

PICTURES: Without Warning, Vice Squad, Down Three Dark Streets, The Rack, Slaughter on Tenth Ave., Anna Lucasta, The Glory Guys, Rough Night in Jericho, Sam Whiskey.

TELEVISION: Part creator and director TV pilots: The Rifleman, Robert Taylor's Detectives, The Plainsmen. Many TV films.

LAVIN, LINDA: Actress. b. Portland, ME, Oct. 15, 1937. e. Coll. of William & Mary. First professional job in chorus of Camden County (N.J.) Music Circus. Worked in plays both off and on Broadway before turning to TV, where guest-starred on such series as Family, Rhoda, Phyllis and Harry O.

THEATER: Oh Kay! (Off-Bdwy debut, 1960); A Family Affair, Revues: (Wet Paint, The Game Is Up); The Mad Show, member acting co., Eugene O'Neil Playwright's Unit, 1968; It's a Bird, It's a Plane...It's Superman, Something Different, Little Murders, Cop Out, The Last of the Red Hot Lovers, Story Theatre, Dynamite Tonight, Broadway Bound (Tony Award).

PICTURES: See You in the Morning, I Want to Go Home.

TELEVISION: Series: Barney Miller, Alice. TV movies: A Place to Call Home, Lena: My Hundred Children.

LAW, JOHN PHILLIP: Actor. b. Hollywood, CA, Sept. 7, 1937. e. U. of Hawaii. Trained at Repertory Theatre of Lincoln Center under Elia Kazan. Has made more than fifty films in more than 20 countries worldwide.

PICTURES: The Russians Are Coming, The Russians Are Coming, The Hawaiians, Barbarella, Von Richtofen and Brown, The Last Movie, The Sergeant, The Love Machine, The Golden Voyage of Sinbad, The Cassandra Crossing, Tarzan, the Ape Man, Night Train to Terror, American Commandos, Moon in Scorpio, A Case of Honor, Combat Force (Striker), Space Mutiny, Outlaw, Alienator.

TELEVISION: The Young and the Restless.

LAW, LINDSAY: Producer. e. NYU School of the Arts. Producer of specials for Warner Bros. Television, head of drama for WNET/New York and prod. for Theatre in America before becoming exec. prod. of American Playhouse. Advisory Board of Independent Feature Project/West, U.S. Film Festival, AFI Television Comm.

PICTURES: *Exec. prod.:* On Valentine's Day; Smooth Talk; Native Son; In a Shallow Grave; Stand and Deliver; The Thin Blue Line; El Norte; The Wizard of Loneliness; Signs of Life; Bloodhounds of Broadway, Big Time; Eat a Bowl of Tea; Gold Mountain; Longtime Companions.

TELEVISION: Prod.: The Girls in Their Summer Dresses; The Time of Your Life; You Can't Take It With You; The Good Doctor; The Most Happy Fella; The Eccentricities of a Nightingale; Cyrano de Bergerac (assoc. prod.); Prod. for American Playhouse: Working; For Colored Girls Who Have Considered Suicide/When the Rainbow Is Enuf; Private Contentment; *Exec. prod.:* Concealed Enemies; Land of Little Rain; Ask Me Again, The Diaries of Adam and Eve; A Walk in the Woods.

LAWRENCE, BARBARA: Actress. b. Carnegie, OK, Feb. 24, 1930. e. UCLA. Mother Berenice Lawrence. Child model; successful screen try-out, 1944; screen debut in Billy Rose Diamond Horse Shoe (1945).

PICTURES: Margie, Captain from Castile, You Were Meant for Me, Give My Regards to Broadway, Street with No Name, Unfaithfully Yours, Letter to Three Wives, Mother Is a Freshman, Thieves Highway, Two Tickets to Broadway, Here Come the Nelsons, The Star, Arena, Paris Model, Her 12 Men, Oklahoma, Man with a Gun, Pay the Devil, Joe Dakota.

LAWRENCE, MARC: Actor. r.n. Max Goldsmith. b. New York, NY, Feb. 17, 1914. e. City Coll. of New York. On stage in Sour Mountain, Waiting for Lefty, Golden Boy, View From the Bridge.

PICTURES: White Woman, Little Big Shot, Dr. Socrates, Road Gang, San Quentin, I Am the Law, While New York Sleeps, Dillinger, Flame of Barbary Coast, Club Havana, Don't Fence Me In, The Virginian, Life with Blondie, Yankee Fakir, Captain from Castile, I Walk Alone, Calamity Jane and Sam Bass, The Asphalt Jungle, Hurricane Island, My Favorite Spy, Girls Marked Danger, Helen of Troy, Custer of the West, Nightmare in the Sun, Krakatoa East of Java, Marathon Man, A Piece of the Action, Foul Play, Goin' Coconuts, Hot Stuff, Supersnooper, Dog and Cat, Night Train to Terror, The Big Easy.

LAWRENCE, STEVE: Actor. b. New York, NY, July 8, 1935. m. singer Eydie Gorme. Singer in nightclubs and on TV.

PICTURES: Stand Up and Be Counted, The Blues Brothers, The Lonely Guy.

TELEVISION: Steve and Eydie Celebrate Irving Berlin, many specials: Police Story, Murder, She Wrote, Alice in Wonderland (mini-series).

LAWRENCE, VICKI: Actress. b. Inglewood, CA, March 26, 1949. Singer and recording artist appearing with Young Americans group for several years. Gained fame on The Carol Burnett Show as comedienne (1967–78). 1982: TV series, Mama's Family.

TELEVISION: Movie: Having Babies.

LAWSON, SARAH: Actress. b. London, Eng., Aug. 6, 1928. e. Heron's Ghyll Sch., Sussex. Stage debut in Everyman (Edinburgh Festival) 1947; screen debut in The Browning Version, 1953; TV debut in Face to Face, 1949.

PICTURES: Street Corner, You Know What Sailors Are, Blue Peter, It's Never Too Late, Links of Justice, Three Crooked Men, Man with a Dog, Night Without Pity, The World Ten Times Over; The Stud, The Dawning (prod.).

TELEVISION: Face to Face, River Line, Whole Truth, Lady From the Sea, Mrs. Moonlight, Silver Card, An Ideal Husband, Love and Money, Rendezvous, Invisible Man, Saber Buccaneers, White Hunter, Flying Doctor, On the Night of the Murder, Haven in Sunset, The Odd Man, Zero 1 series, The Innocent Ceremony, Department S, The Marrying Kind, The Expert, The Persuaders, Trial, Starcast, The Midsummer of Colonel Blossum, Callen, Crimes of Passion, Full House, Father Brown, Within These Walls Series, The Standard, The Purple Twilight, The Professionals, Bergerac, Cuffy, Lovejoy.

LAZARUS, PAUL N.: Executive. b. Brooklyn, NY, March 31, 1913. e. Cornell U., B.A., 1933. In U.S. Army, W.W.II. Entered m.p. ind. 1933 as gen. asst., press book dept., Warner Bros.; pres., AMPA, 1939–40. Joined Buchanan & Co., 1942 as m.p. account exec. To United Artists 1943 as dir. adv. & pub. Named asst. to pres., July 1948; joined Columbia exec. staff, New York, Aug. 1950; elected v.p. Columbia, Jan., 1954–62; exec. vice-pres. Samuel Bronston Prods., 1962–64; v.p., chg. Motion Pictures, Subscription Television Inc., 1964; exec. officer and partner, Landau Releasing Organization, 1964–65, exec. v.p., member bd. of dir., Nat'l Screen Serv. Corp., 1965–75. Lecturer and consultant, Film Studies Dept., U. of California at Santa Barbara. 1975 to present. Consultant to Kenya Film Corp., Nairobi, 1983. Director, Santa Barbara Intl. Film Festival, 1986–87. Chief of Staff, Santa Barbara Writers' Conference, 1976–.

LAZARUS, PAUL N. III: Executive. b. New York, NY, May 25, 1938. e. Williams Coll., BA.; Yale Law Sch, L.L.B. Third generation film exec. Began career with Palomar Pictures Int'l. as exec. v.p.; joined ABC Pictures Corp. as v.p. in chg. of creative affairs. Mng. dir., CRM Productions, maker of educational films; v.p. for motion pictures. Marble Arch Productions; 1983, v.p. in chg. of prod., Home Box Office.

PICTURES: Prod.: Extreme Close-Up, Westworld, Futureworld, Capricorn One, Hanover Street, Barbarosa.

LAZARUS, THEODORE R.: Executive. b. Brooklyn, NY, Aug. 5, 1919. e. Yale U., B.A., 1940. Adv. mgr., Eagle Lion Classics, 1951; adv., sales prom. mgr., WMGM, New York, 1951; then with Donahue and Coe adv. agency; secy., treas., George Blake Enterprises, TV film prod. firm, 1955; v.p. Gommi-TV, 1956; Charles Schlaifer and Co., Inc., 1957; adv. mgr., Paramount Pictures Corp., 1964; pres., Cinema Lodge, B'nai B'rith, 1968–71. Member, bd. of directors, NY chapter, Variety, The Children's Charity.

LEACHMAN, CLORIS: Actress. b. Des Moines, IA, April 30, 1930. e. Northwestern U. Broadway stage, television, motion pictures.

TELEVISION: Series: Lassie, Mary Tyler Moore Show (Emmy Award), Phyllis (Emmy and Golden Globe Awards), The Facts of Life, The Nutt House. Movies: A Brand New Life, The Migrants, Twigs, Ernie Kovacs: Between the Laughter,

Deadly Intentions, Love Is Never Silent, Wedding Bell Blues.
PICTURES: Kiss Me Deadly, Butch Cassidy and the Sundance Kid, The Steagle, The Last Picture Show, (Acad. award, best supporting actress, 1971), W.U.S.A., Dillinger, Daisy Miller, Young Frankenstein, Crazy Mama, High Anxiety, Charlie and the Angel, The North Avenue Irregulars, Scavenger Hunt, Herbie Goes Bananas, History of the World—Part I, Shadow Play, Walk Like a Man, Hansel and Gretel, Going to the Chapel, Love Hurts, Prancer, Texasville.

LEACOCK, PHILIP: Producer, Director. b. London, England, Oct. 8, 1917. Moved from British film industry to American films and TV.
PICTURES: The Brave Don't Cry, Appointment in London, The Kidnappers, Escapade, The Spanish Gardener, High Tide at Noon, Innocent Sinners, The Rabbit Trap, Let No Man Write My Epitaph, Hand in Hand, Take a Giant Step, Reach for Glory, West Street, The War Lover, Tamahine, Adam's Woman.
TELEVISION: Movies: The Birdmen, When Michael Calls, The Daughters of Joshua Cabe, Baffled, The Great Man's Whiskers, Dying Room Only, Key West, Killer on Board, Wild and Wooly, Three Sovereigns for Sarah. Series: Gunsmoke, Cimarron Strip, Hawaii 5-O.

LEAN, SIR DAVID: Director, Writer, Producer. b. Croydon, England, Mar. 25, 1908. e. Leighton Park. Entered m.p. ind. in 1919 as tea boy, later clapper boy, cutter, camera asst. Gaumont Sound News and Movietone News; asst. dir. & ed.; co-dir. 1942; dir. Founded Cineguild (prod. co. with Noel Coward and Ronald Neame, 1944. Knighted in 1984.
PICTURES: Pygmalion (editor), Invaders (editor) Major Barbara (editor, co.-dir.), The Invaders (aka the 49th Parallel, editor). One of Our Aircraft Is Missing (editor), In Which We Serve (co-dir.), *Director:* This Happy Breed (and co-s.p.), Blithe Spirit (also co-s.p.), Brief Encounter (also co-s.p.), Great Expectations (also co-s.p.), The Passionate Friends (also co-s.p.), Oliver Twist (also co-s.p.), Escape Me Never (co-dir.), Madeleine, One Woman's Story. Breaking The Sound Barrier (also prod.), Hobson's Choice (also prod., co-s.p.), Summertime (also co-s.p.), The Bridge on the River Kwai (Academy Award 1957, best direction), Lawrence of Arabia (Academy Award), Dr. Zhivago, Ryan's Daughter, A Passage to India (also s.p. and editor).

LEAR, NORMAN: Producer, Director, Writer. b. New Haven, CT, July 27, 1922. e. Emerson Coll. In public relations 1945–49. Began in TV as co-writer of weekly one-hour variety show, The Ford Star Revue in 1950. Followed as writer for Dean Martin and Jerry Lewis on the Colgate Comedy Hour and for the Martha Raye and George Gobel TV shows. With partner, Bud Yorkin, created and produced such specials as Another Evening with Fred Astaire, Henry Fonda and the Family, An Evening with Carol Channing, and The Many Sides of Don Rickles. In 1965 their company, Tandem Productions, also produced the original Andy Williams Show. Moved into motion pictures in 1963, writing and producing Come Blow Your Horn. Formed Act III Communications, 1987.
PICTURES: Never Too Late (prod.), Divorce-American Style (prod., s.p.), The Night They Raided Minsky's (co.-prod., co-s.p.), Start the Revolution Without Me (exec.-prod.), Cold Turkey, (s.p., prod., dir.), The Princess Bride (exec. prod.), Breaking In (exec. prod.).
TELEVISION: Creator-dir.: TV Guide Award Show (1962), Henry Fonda and the Family (1963), Andy Williams Specials, Robert Young and the Family. Exec. prod. and creator or developer: All in the Family, Maude, Good Times, Sanford and Son, The Jeffersons, Mary Hartman, Mary Hartman, One Day at a Time, All's Fair, A Year at the Top, All that Glitters, Fernwood 2 Night, The Baxters, Palmerstown, I Love Liberty, Heartsounds.

LEARNED, MICHAEL: Actress. b. Washington, DC, Apr. 9, 1939. Studied ballet and dramatics in school. Many stage credits include Under Milkwood, The Three Sisters, A God Slept Here, etc.; resident performances with Shakespeare festivals in Canada, Stratford, CT, and San Diego, CA. Gained fame on hit TV series, The Waltons, as the mother, Olivia.
PICTURES: Touched by Love, Power.
TELEVISION: Gunsmoke, Police Story, Movies: It Couldn't Happen to a Nicer Guy, Hurricane, Widow, Little Mo, Off the Minnesota Strip, A Christmas Without Snow, Mother's Day on Walton Mountain, The Paradde. A Deadly Business, Mercy or Murder?, All My Sons, Picnic, Roots: The Gift. Series: The Waltons (Emmy Award, 1973, 1974, 1976); Nurse (Emmy, 1982), Hothouse, Living Dolls.

LEAUD, JEAN-PIERRE: Actor. b. Paris, France, 1944. Parents were screenwriter Pierre Leaud and actress Jacqueline Pierreux. At 14 chosen to play Antoine Doinel in Truffaut's The 400 Blows and subsequent autobiographical films Love at 20, Stolen Kisses, Bed and Board, Love on the Run. Also closely identified with major films by Jean-Luc Godard.
PICTURES: The 400 Blows, The Testament of Orpheus, Love at Twenty, Masculine-Feminine, Made in USA, Le Depart, La Chinoise, Weekend, Stolen Kisses, Le Gai Savoir, Pigsty, The Oldest Profession, Bed and Board, Last Tango in Paris, Day for Night, Lola's Lolos, Love on the Run, Rebelote, Detective, Just a Movie, Seen by...20 Years After, Treasure Island, The Grandeur and Decadence of a Small-Time Filmmaker, With All Hands, Time to Aim, Jane B, par Agnes V.; 36 Fillete, La Femme de Paille (The Straw Woman), The Color of the Wind, Femme de Papier, Bunker Palace Hotel.

LEDER, HERBERT JAY: Writer, Director, Producer, b. New York, NY, Aug. 15, 1922. e. B.A., Ph.D. Play Doctor on Broadway; Director TV dept., Benton and Bowles Adv. chg. all T.V. & Film production, 13 yrs.; Features: writer, Fiend Without a Face; writer-director co-prod., Pretty Boy Floyd; writer-director, co-producer, Nine Miles to Noon; writer, Aquarius Mission, Love Keeps No Score of Wrongs; writer, prod-dir., The Frozen Dead, It; Mia, writer-dir., Candyman, writer-director; writer, The Winners, The Way It Is, The Cool Crazies. Sponsored Films: Child Molester, Bank Robber, Shoplifter, Untouchables.

LEDERER, RICHARD: Executive. b. New York, NY, Sept. 22, 1916. e. U. of Virginia, B.S., 1938. Freelance writer, 1939–41; U.S. Army. Cryptanalyst, Signal Intell. Serv 1941–45; Adv. copywriter, Columbia Pictures, 1946–50; Adv. copywriter, Warner Bros., 1950–53; copy chief, Warner Bros., 1950–53; copy chief, Warner Bros., 1953–57; Asst. Nat'l Adv. mgr., Warner Bros. studios, 1957–59; Prod., theatrical, TV. Warner Bros. studios, 1959–60; Dir. of adv., publicity, Warner Bros. Pictures, 1960; v.p. Warner Bros. Pictures, 1963. V.P. production, Warner Bros. Studio, 1969–70; indep. prod. to May, 1971, when returned to WB as adv.-pub., v.p. Independent producer. 1980: Hollywood Knights. Joined Orion Pictures as v.p., adv. Resigned, 1984.

LEE, ANNA: Actress. M.B.E., 1983. r.n. Joan Boniface Winnifrith. b. Jan. 2, Kent, England. e. Central School of Speech Training and Dramatic Art, Royal Albert Hall. With London Repertory Theatre; toured in the Constant Nymph and Jane Eyre. In 1930s known as Britain's Glamour Girl. 1939 came to US to star in My Life With Caroline. Entertained troops with U.S.O. during WWII. 1950 moved to N.Y. to appear in live TV.
PICTURES: British: The Camels Are Coming, Non Stop New York, King Solomon's Mines, You're in the Army Now, Passing of the Third Floor Back, Return to Yesterday, Young Man's Fancy, The Four Just Men. Hollywood: My Life With Caroline, Flying Tigers, How Green Was My Valley, This Earth is Mine, Flesh and Fantasy, Bedlam, Fort Apache, Horse Soldiers, Gideon of Scotland Yard, The Last Hurrah, Commandoes Strike at Dawn, Hangmen Also Die, Seven Women, The Sound of Music, In Like Flint.
TELEVISION: Guest star on all major television shows from 1950 to 1977. Eleanor and Franklin, The Night Rider, The Beasts are Loose, Scruples, General Hospital (continuing role as Lila Quartermaine, 1978–present).

LEE, BONNI: Executive. Prod. exec. at MGM/UA, 1982; joined Warner Bros. as v.p.—creative affairs, 1984; v.p., production, 1986.

LEE, CHRISTOPHER: Actor. b. London, England, May 27, 1922. e. Wellington Coll. Served RAF 1940–46. Ent. m.p. ind. 1947. Founder and owner, Charlemagne Prods., Ltd. 1972. Autobiography: Tall, Dark and Gruesome (1977).
PICTURES: Corridor of Mirrors (debut, 1947), One Night With You, A Song for Tomorrow, Scott of the Antarctic, Capt. Horatio Hornblower, The Crimson Pirate, Hamlet, Moulin Rouge, Cockleshell Heroes, Storm Over the Nile, Moby Dick, River Plate, Truth About Women, Tale of Two Cities, Curse of Frankenstein, Dracula, Man Who Could Cheat Death, The Mummy, Too Hot to Handle, Beat Girl, City of the Dead, Two Faces of Dr. Jekyll, The Terror of the Tongs, The Hands of Orlac, Taste of Fear, The Devil's Daffodil, Pirates of Blood River, Devil's Agent, Red Orchid, Valley of Fear, Katharsis, Faust '63, The Virgin of Nuremberg, The Whip and the Body, Carmilla, The Devil Ship Pirates, The Gorgon, The Sign of Satan, The House of Blood, The Dunwich Horror, Dr. Terror's House of Horrors, She, The Skull, The Mask of Fu Manchu, Dracula, Prince of Darkness, Rasputin, Theatre of Death, Circus of Fear, The Brides of Fu Manchu, Five Golden Dragons, Diabolica, Vengeance of Fu Manchu, Night of the Big Heat, The Pendulum, The Face of Eve, The Devil Rides Out, The Blood of Fu Manchu, The Crimson Altar, Dracula Has Risen from the Grave, The Oblong Box, De Sade 70, Scream and Scream Again, The Magic Christian, Julius Caesar, One More Time, Count Dracula, Bloody Judge, Taste the Blood of Dracula, Private Lives of Sherlock Holmes, El Umbragolo, Scars of Dracula, House That Dripped Blood, I Monster, Hannie Caulder, Dracula 72, Horror Express, Creeping Flesh, Death Line, Nothing but the Night, The Wicker Man, Poor Devil, Dark Places, Dracula Is Dead?, Eulalie Quitte les champs, The Three Musketeers, Earthbound, Man with the Golden Gun, The Four Musketeers, Killer Force, Diagnosis—Murder, Whispering Death, The Keeper, To the Devil a Daughter, Pere et Fils, Airport 77, Alien Encounter, The End of the World, Return from Witch Mountain, Caravans, The Silent Flute, The Passage, The Pirates, Jaguar Lives, Arabian Adventure, An Eye for an Eye, House of Long

Shadows, Howling II, The Far Pavilions, The Return of Captain Invincible, Roadtrip, Dark Mission, Olympus Force, Murder Story, Mio In the Land of Faraway, The Girl, The Return of the Musketeers, For Better, For Worse, The French Revolution, Murder Story.

TELEVISION: The Disputation, Metier du Seigneur, Movies: Poor Devil, Harold Robbins' The Pirate, Captain America II, Once a Spy, Charles and Diana: A Royal Love Story, Far Pavilions, Shaka Zulu, Goliath Awaits, Massarati and the Brain, Around the World in 80 Days, Treasure Island.

LEE, JOHN: Actor. b. Launceston, Tasmania, Australia, March 31, 1928. Early career on Australian stage and radio. Ent. m.p. ind. in England 1957.

PICTURES: Dunkirk, Cat Girl, Silent Enemy, Flying Scot, Gypsy and The Gentleman, Under Ten Flags, The Liar, Seven Keys, The Secret Partner, Dr. Crippen, Stitch in Time, Go Kart Go, Space Flight.

TELEVISION: Adventures of the Sea Hawk, International Detective, Rendezvous, Flying Doctor, Danger Man, Shadow Squad, Man and Superman, A Man Involved, Aren't We All, Probation Officer, Ladies of the Corridor, Golden Girl, After the Crash, The Net, Emergency Ward 10, Zero One, Sapper Series, Dr. Fancy, The Shifting Heart, Sergeant Cork, Dr. Who, The Materialists, The July Plot.

LEE, MICHELE: Actress. b. Los Angeles, CA, June 24, 1942. On Broadway in How to Succeed in Business Without Really Trying, Seesaw.

PICTURES: How To Succeed in Business Without Really Trying, The Love Bug, The Comic.

TELEVISION: Knots Landing (series), The Tim Conway Show. Movies: Bud and Lou, Dark Victory, Letter to Three Wives.

LEE, PEGGY: Singer, Actress. r.n. Norma Egstrom; b. Jamestown, ND, May 26, 1920. Began career as night club vocalist in Fargo & radio singer, WDAY, then with Sev Olsen, bandleader, Minneapolis, Will Osborne; Benny Goodman; collab. (with Dave Barbour) popular songs, Manana, It's a Good Day, What More Can a Woman Do? Leading song stylist-composer. TV & records; screen debut in Mr. Music (Bing Crosby) (1950); singer on Bing Crosby program, many TV specials.

PICTURES: Jazz Singer, Pete Kelly's Blues, Lady and the Tramp (actress, song collab.).

LEE, SPIKE: Director, Writer, Actor. b. Atlanta, GA, 1956. r.n. Shelton Jackson Lee. Son of jazz bass musician, composer Bill Lee. e. Morehouse Coll B.A.(Mass communications), NYU Film Sch. Completed 2 student features and hour-long thesis: Joe Bed Stuy Barbershop: We Cut Heads which won student Acad. Award from Acad. M.P. Arts & Sciences. Wrote, prod., dir., co-starred in indep. feature, She's Gotta Have It, budgeted at $175,000, won L.A. Film Critics Award, best new dir., 1986.

PICTURES: She's Gotta Have It (dir., prod., s.p., actor). School Daze (dir., prod., s.p., actor). Do the Right Thing (prod., dir., s.p., actor), Love Supreme.

TELEVISION: Guest: The Debbie Allen Special.

LEEDS, MARTIN N.: Film-TV Executive. b. New York, NY, Apr. 6, 1916. e. NYU, B.S., 1936; J.D., 1938. Admitted N.Y. Bar, 1938, Calif. Bar, 1948; dir. indsl. relations Wabash Appliance Corp., 1943–44 indsl. bus. relations cons. Davis & Gilbert. 1944–45; dir. indsl. relations Flying Tiger Lines, 1947; dir. bus. affairs CBS. TV div., 1947–53; exec. v.p. Desilu Productions, Inc., 1953–60; v.p. Motion Picture Center Studios, Inc.: mem. Industry comm. War Manpower Comm., 1943; chmn. Com. to form Television Code of Ethics: U.S. Army 1941. Mem. Los Angeles Bar Assn., Century City Bar Assn.; exec. v.p. in chg. of West Coast oper. & member of bd. of dir. Talent Associates—Paramount Ltd., Hollywood, 1962; TV production consultant; exec. v.p., Electronovision Prods. Inc., 1964; TV prod. & MP prod. consultant, 1965. Pres., chief exec. officer member of bd., Beverly Hills Studios, Inc., 1969, sr. v.p., American Film Theatre, 1973; 1975, motion picture and TV attorney & consultant.

LEENHOUTS, LEWIS GRANT: Executive. b. Los Angeles, CA. m. Edith Hargrave. 1934–38 variously stunt man, unit manager, cutter & asst. dir., Collab. orig. story No More Women, wrote orig. Heroes at Leisure. In 1939 wrote training films, U.S. Officer of Education; 1940–41 assoc. prod., writer, dir., Caravel Films Inc.; 1942–45 head of planning and production U.S. Navy Training Film & Motion Picture branch, Navy Dept.; 1946–47 gen. mgr. in charge of prod., National Educational Films, Inc. Later coordinator-producer, Industry Film Project, Motion Picture Assoc.; prod. California's Golden Beginning, Paramount assoc. chief and head of prod., International M.P. Div., U.S. Dept. of State, 1950–51; exec. v.p., Cinerama, Inc., 1952–53; planning and prod. head, Ford Foundation Fund for Adult Education, 1954, v.p., prod. head Cinerama, Inc., 1955–60. Ind. producer; prod. consultant Macbeth, Compass Prods. and Grand Prize Films, London; pres., Leehouts Prods., Inc., 1961; prod., 20th Century Fox, Movietone Digest, Children's Digest, 1963; Prod. Consultant, Cascade Pics. of Calif., 1964–65; 1967, dir. prod., Breakfast at the Capitol; prod., New Sounds in Africa; prod. head, Eddie Albert, Inc., 1971.

LEEWOOD, JACK: Producer. b. New York, NY. May 20, 1913. e. Upsala Coll., Newark U., NYU. 1926–31 with Gottesman-Stern circuit as usher, asst. and relief mgr.; 1931–43 Stanley-Warner, mgr. of Ritz, Capitol and Hollywood theatres 1943–47. Joined Warner Bros. field forces in Denver-Salt Lake; Seattle-Portland, 1947–48. Dir. pub. & adv. Screen Guild Prod.; 1948–52 Lippert Productions; prod. exec.; 1953–56 Allied Artists; 1957–62 prod. 20th Cent. Fox; 1965–68 prod., Universal; 1976–78. Affiliated Theatre S.F. & HTN.; 1978–83. Hamner Prod.

PICTURES: Holiday Rhythm, Gunfire, Hi-Jacked, Roaring City, Danger Zone, Lost Continent, F.B.I. Girl, Pier 23, Train to Tombstone, I Shot Billy the Kid, Bandit Queen, Motor Patrol, Savage Drums, Three Desperate Men, Border Rangers, Western Pacific Agent, Thundering Jets, Lone Texan, Little Savage, Alligator People, 13 Fighting Men, Young Jesse James, Swingin' Along, We'll Bury You, 20,000 Eyes, Thunder Island, The Plainsman, Longest 100 Miles, Escape to Mindanao, Dallas Cowboys Cheerleaders, When Hell Was in Session, Fugitive Family, Dallas Cowboys Cheerleaders II, Million Dollar Face, Portrait of a Showgirl, Margin For Murder, Anatomy of an Illness, Malibu.

LEFFERTS, GEORGE: Producer, Writer, Director. b. Paterson, NJ. Dir., numerous award-winning TV series, films, exec. prod.-Time-Life films 1977–78; prod./writer, Movie of the Week (NBC) 1977–78. Biog: Who's Who in America, Who's Who in the World. 1975 Emmy Award Benjamin Franklin Specials (CBS). Exec. prod., Bing Crosby Productions, prod., NBC 10 yrs, Independent.

TELEVISION: 1969 Emmy Award, prod. Hallmark Hall of Fame Teacher Teacher; 1963 Emmy Award, wrote, prod., directed Purex Specials for Women; 1965 Producer's Guild Award, exec. prod. Breaking Point series. 1987, writer, Our Group; 1988 Emmy Award, writer, Never Say Goodbye; 1989 the Jean Seberg Story. Other shows: The Bill Cosby Show, Studio One, Kraft Theatre, Chrysler Theatre, Sinatra Show, Lights Out, Alcoa, The Harness (Movie of the Week), The Bold Ones.

PICTURES: The Stake, Mean Dog Blues, The Living End, The Boat, The Teenager.

BROADWAY: The Boat, 1968, Hey Everybody, 1970.

LEFKO, MORRIS E.: b. March 30, 1907. Entered m.p. ind. as poster clerk; booker, salesman, br. mgr., Indianapolis, RKO, June 1941; br. mgr., Pittsburgh, July 1944; East Central dist. mgr., July, 1948; appt. sales exec. of Ten Commandments Unit. Para. Film Dist. Corp., N.Y., 1956; v.p. in chg. sls., Michael Todd Co., 1958. Joined MGM, Inc., July 1960 sls. mgr., of road shows, Ben-Hur, King of Kings, Mutiny on the Bounty; vice pres., gen. sales mgr., MGM, 1963. Exec. consultant to Pres., Cinema 5 Ltd., Jan. 1970. v.p., Network Cinema Corp., 1972; American Film Theatre, Ely Landau Co., Nov., 1972; v.p., sls. mgr. Brut Prods., 1976.

LE GALLIENNE, EVA: Actress, Producer. b. London, England, Jan. 11, 1899. Stage career began in 1914. Founded Civic Repertory Theatre in 1926, starring in and directing such classics as Hedda Gabler, Romeo and Juliet, Alice in Wonderland, Camille, The Cherry Orchard. Also co-founder of American Repertory Theatre; 1946; toured with National Repertory Theatre. Won special Tony Award, 1964.

TELEVISION: Alice in Wonderland, The Corn Is Green, The Bridge of San Luis Rey, Mary Stuart, The Royal Family (Emmy award, 1977).

PICTURES: Prince of Players, The Devil's Disciple, Resurrection.

LEGRAND, MICHEL JEAN: Composer, Conductor. b. France, 1931. Son of well-known arranger, composer and pianist, Raymond Legrand. At 11 Michel, a child prodigy, entered Paris Cons. and graduated nine years later with top honors in composition and as solo pianist. In late fifties turned to composing for films and has composed, orchestrated and conducted scores of more than 50 films.

PICTURES: Lola, Eva, Vivre Sa Vie, La Baie des Anges, The Umbrellas of Cherbourg, Banda a Part, Un Femme Mariee, Les Demoiselles de Rochefort, Ice Station Zebra, The Thomas Crown Affair, Pieces of Dreams, The Happy Ending, Wuthering Heights, The Go-Between, Summer of '42, Picasso Summer, The Nelson Affair, Breezy, The Three Musketeers, Sheila Levine, Gable and Lombard, Ode to Billy Joe, The Savage, The Other Side of Midnight, The Fabulous Adventures of the Legendary Baron Munchausen, The Roads of the South, The Hunter, The Mountain Men, Atlantic City, Falling in Love Again, Melvin and Howard, Best Friends, A Love in Germany, Never Say Never Again, Yentl, Hell Train, Micki and Maude, Secret Places, Spirale, Parking, Switching Channels, Three Seats for the 26th Cinq jours en juin (dir. debut, s.p., music).

TELEVISION: Brian's Song, The Jesse Owens Story, A

Woman Called Golda, As Summers Die, Crossings, Sins, Promises to Keep.

LEHMAN, ERNEST: Writer, Producer, Director. b. NY, NY. e. City Coll. of New York. Began career as financial editor and free-lance short story and novelette writer. First pub. books, The Comedian, The Sweet Smell of Success. First hardcover novel, The French Atlantic Affair followed by Farewell Performance, and first non-fiction book, Screening Sickness. 1988: Acad. Awards show (co-writer).
PICTURES: Inside Story, The King and I, Executive Suite, Sabrina, Sweet Smell of Success, (based on own novelette). Somebody Up There Likes Me, North by Northwest, From the Terrace, West Side Story, The Prize, The Sound of Music. Became a prod.-wr. for first time with Who's Afraid of Virginia Woolf? Hello Dolly! (prod.-s.p.), Portnoy's Complaint (prod., dir., s.p.), Family Plot (s.p.), Black Sunday (co.-s.p.).

LEHMAN, GLADYS: Writer, Scenarios identified with such Reginald Denny pictures as Out All Night, Clear the Deck, On Your Toes and Companionate Trouble; joined Columbia in 1929.
SCRIPTS: The Little Accident, A Lady Surrenders, The Cat Creeps, Many a Slip, Seed, Strictly Dishonorable, Back Street, Embarrassing Moments, Nice Women, Good Girls Go to Paris, Blondie, Two Girls and a Sailor, Thrill of a Romance, Her Highness and the Bellboy, This Time for Keeps, collab. s.p. Luxury Liner, Golden Girl.

LEIBMAN, RON: Actor. b. New York, NY, Oct. 11, 1937. m. actress Jessica Walter. e. Ohio Wesleyan U. Joined Actor's Studio in N.Y.; first professional appearance in summer theatre production of A View from the Bridge.
STAGE: The Premise, Dear Me, The Sky is Falling, We Bombed in New Haven, Cop Out, Room Service, I Oughta Be in Pictures, Rumors.
PICTURES: Where's Poppa (debut), The Hot Rock, Slaughterhouse Five, Your Three Minutes Are Up, Super Cops, Law and Disorder, Won Ton Ton, Norma Rae, Up the Academy, Zorro, the Gay Blade, Romantic Comedy, Phar Lap, Rhinestone, Door to Door, Seven Hours to Judgement.
TELEVISION: Kaz (series). Movies: A Question of Guilt, Many Happy Returns, Christmas Eve, Rivkin—Bounty Hunter, Terrorist on Trial: The United States vs. Salim Ajami.

LEIBOWITZ, SAM: Executive. b. New York, NY, Feb. 12, 1913. Service mgr., Reel Photos, 1931–34; svg. mgr., Consolidated Film Ind., 1935; Apco Photo Co., Inc., treas., 1936–62; Apco-Apeda Photo Co., Inc., 1962–present, pres. & chief operating officer.

LEIDER, GERALD J.: Producer, Executive. b. Camden, NJ, May 28, 1931. e. Syracuse U., 1953; Bristol U., Eng., 1954, Fulbright Fellowship in drama. m. Susan Trustman. 1955 joined MCA, Inc., N.Y.; 1956–59 theatre producer in N.Y., London; Shinbone Alley, Garden District, and Sir John Gielgud's Ages of Man. 1960–61; director of special programs, CBS/TV; 1961–62, dir. of program sales, CBS-TV; 1962–69, vice pres., television operation, Ashley Famous Agency, Inc. Sept. 1969–Dec. 1974, pres. Warner Bros. Television, Burbank. Jan. 1975–Dec. 1976, exec. vice pres. foreign production Warner Bros. Pictures, Rome. Jan. 1977–1982, independent producer under Jerry Leider Productions; 1982–87, pres., ITC Prods., Inc. Named pres. and CEO, ITC Entertainment Group, 1987–present.
PICTURES: Wild Horse Hank, The Jazz Singer (1980), Trenchcoat.
TELEVISION: And I Alone Survived, Willa, The Hostage Tower, The Scarlet and the Black, Secrets of a Married Man, The Haunting Passion, Letting Go, A Time to Live, The Girl Who Spelled Freedom, Unnatural Causes, Poor Little Rich Girl.

LEIGH, JANET: Actress. r.n. Jeanette Helen Morrison; mother of actress Jamie Leigh Curtis. b. Merced, CA, July 6, 1927. e. Coll. of Pacific, music. Screen debut in Romance of Rosy Ridge, 1947, Autobiography: There Really Was a Hollywood. (1984).
PICTURES: If Winter Comes, Hills of Home, Words and Music, Act of Violence, Little Women, That Forsyte Woman, Red Danube, Doctor and the Girl, Holiday Affair, It's a Big Country, Two Tickets to Broadway, Strictly Dishonorable, Angels in the Outfield, Just This Once, Naked Spur, Confidentially Connie, Houdini, Walking My Baby Back Home, Prince Valiant, Living It Up, Black Shield of Falworth, Rogue Cop, My Sister Eileen, Pete Kelly's Blues, Safari, The Vikings, The Perfect Furlough, Psycho, The Manchurian Candidate, Bye, Bye, Birdie, Wives and Lovers, Kid Rodello, Grand Slam, Hello Down There, One Is a Lonely Number, Night of the Lepus, Boardwalk, The Fog.
TELEVISION: Honeymoon With a Stranger; Mirror, Mirror; Telethon; Murder at the World Series; Murder, She Wrote.

LEIGH, JENNIFER JASON: Actress. b. Los Angeles, CA, 1958. Daughter of late actor Vic Morrow and TV writer Barbara Turner. Theatrical film debut in Wrong Is Right (1982). Won L.A. Valley Coll. best actress award for The Shadow Box on stage (1979).
PICTURES: Fast Times at Ridgemont High, Eyes of a Stranger, Easy Money, Grandview U.S.A., The Hitcher, Flesh and Blood, Sister, Sister; The Men's Club, The Big Picture, Heart of Midnight, The Last Exit to Brooklyn, Miami Blues.
TELEVISION: Movies: The Best Little Girl in the World, The Killing of Randy Webster, Angel City.

LEIGH, SUZANNA: Actress. b. England, 1945. Studied at the Arts Educational Sch. and Webber Douglas Sch. Film debut in Oscar Wilde (1961). 1964: TV series made in France, Three Stars. 1965–66: Under contract to Hal Wallis and Paramount, TV film series in West Indies, One On An Island. 1969: TV play, The Plastic People. 1970.
PICTURES: Bomb in High Street; To Love a Vampire; Boeing Boeing; Paradise Hawaiian Style; The Deadly Bees; Deadlier Than the Male; The Lost Continent; Subterfuge; Beware My Brethren; Son of Dracula.
TELEVISION: The Persuaders.

LEITCH, DONOVAN: Actor. Son of folksinger Donovan. Brother of actress Ione Skye. Acted in jr. high sch. musical then had bit part in PBS. show K.I.D.S.
PICTURES: And God Created Women (1987), The Blob, The In Crowd, Glory, The Cutting Class

LELAND, DAVID: Director, Writer, Actor. b. Cambridge, Eng., April 20, 1947. Began as actor at Nottingham Playhouse. Then joined newly formed company at Royal Court Theatre, London. Also appeared in films Time Bandits, The Missionary, and his own Personal Services and on TV in The Jewel in the Crown. As stage director specialized in complete seasons of new works at the Crucible in Sheffield as well as several premieres. Wrote play Psy-Warriors.
PICTURES: Mona Lisa (co-s.p.), Personal Services (s.p.), Wish You Were Here (dir., s.p.), Checking Out (dir.).
TELEVISION: Wrote Birth of a Nation, Flying Into the Wind, Rhino, Made in Britain, Beloved Enemy, Ligmalion.

LELOUCH, CLAUDE: Director, Cinematographer. b. Paris, France, Oct. 30, 1937. Began m.p. career with short subjects, 1956; French military service, motion picture department, 1957–60; formed Films 13, 1960; publicity Films and Scopitones, 1961–62.
PICTURES: Le Propre de L'homme (Man's Own), L'amour avec des Si (Love With Ifs), Une fille et des Fusils (Guns and a Girl), To Be a Crook, A Man and A Woman, Live for Life, Challenge in the Snow, Far From Vietnam, A Man I Like, Life, Love, and Death, Love Is a Funny Thing (dir., photog., s.p.); The Crook (dir., photog., s.p.), Simon the Swiss, Adventure Is Adventure (prod., dir., s.p.). Smic, Smac, Smoc, La Bonne Annee, And Now My Love, Seven Suspects For Murder, Another Man, Another Chance, Edith and Marcel (prod., s.p.); A Man and a Woman: 20 Years Later, Bandits, Itinerary of a Spoiled Child (prod., dir., s.p.).

LEMASTERS, KIM: Executive. e. U.C.L.A., B.A., 1971. Joined CBS in July, 1979 as director, dramatic program dev. Named vice pres., dramatic program dev., 1979; vice pres., comedy program dev., 1980; vice pres., program dev., Nov. 1981; and vice pres. program dev. and production, 1982. Left CBS to serve as vice pres., motion picture production for Walt Disney Productions 1984–85; returned to CBS, 1985 as vice pres., mini-series, CBS Entertainment; appointed vice pres., programs, 1986. Named president, CBS Entertainment, 1987.

LE MAT, PAUL: Actor. b. New Jersey. Studied with Milton Katselas, Herbert Berghof Studio, A.C.T., San Francisco, Mitchel Ryan-Actor's Studio.
PICTURES: American Graffiti, Citizen's Band, Melvin and Howard, Death Valley, Jimmy the Kid, Strange Invaders, The Hanoi Hilton, Private Investigations, More American Graffiti, P.K. and the Kid, Veiled Threats, Puppet Master, Easy Wheels.
TELEVISION: Movies: Firehouse, The Night They Saved Christmas, The Burning Bed, Long Time Gone, Secret Witness. Mini-Series: On Wings of Eagles, Into the Homeland.

LEMLEIN, NEAL C.: Executive. e. Tulane U., NYU. Began career at Young & Rubicam in N.Y.; later joined Doyle Dane Bernbach, Inc., where named sr. acct. exec. assigned to 20th-Fox feature films account and CBS-TV Entertainment Division. In March, 1980, joined Universal Pictures as dir. of mktg.; 1986, v.p., mktg., 20th Century Fox.

LEMMON, JACK: Actor. b. Boston, MA. Feb. 8, 1925. m. actress Felicia Farr. e. Harvard U. Stage debut as a child; radio actor on soap operas; stock companies; U.S. Navy, W.W.II; many TV shows.
THEATER: Broadway: Room Service (debut, 1953); Face of a Hero (1960), Tribute (1978), Long Day's Journey into Night (1986). Regional: Idiot's Delight (1970, L.A.), Juno and the Paycock (1975, L.A.), Tribute (1979, Denver and L.A.), A Sense of Humor (Denver, L.A., S.F., 1983–84); Long Day's

Journey into Night (Durham, NC, Washington, DC, London, Israel), Veterans Day (London, 1989).
PICTURES: It Should Happen to You, (debut, 1953), Three for the Show, Phfft, My Sister Eileen, Mr. Roberts (Acad. Award, supp. actor, 1955), You Can't Run Away from It, Fire Down Below, Operation Mad Ball, Bell Book and Candle, It Happened to Jane, Some Like It Hot, The Apartment, The Wackiest Ship in the Army, Notorious Landlady, Days of Wine and Roses, Irma La Douce, Under the Yum Yum Tree, Good Neighbor Sam, How to Murder Your Wife, The Great Race, The Fortune Cookie, Luv, The Odd Couple, The April Fools, The Out of Towners. Debut as director: Kotch, 1971, Save the Tiger (Acad. Award, Best Actor), The War Between Men and Women, Avanti, The Prisoner of Second Avenue, The Front Page, Alex and the Gypsy, Airport '77, The China Syndrome (Cannes fest. award, best actor, 1979), Tribute, Buddy, Buddy, Missing (Cannes award, best actor 1982), Mass Appeal, Macaroni, That's Life, Dad.
TELEVISION: Series: That Wonderful Guy (1949–50), Toni Twin Time (host), Ad Libbers, Heaven For Betsy (1952); Soap Operas: The Brighter Day, Road of Life; numerous dramatic shows (Studio One, Playhouse 90 etc.); Specials: Wonderful, 's Marvelous, 's Gershwin (Emmy Award 1972), The Entertainer, Long Day's Journey into Night, The Murder of Mary Phagan.

LENO, JAY: Comedian, Actor. r.n. James Leno. b. New Rochelle, NY, April 28, 1950. e. Emerson College, B.A. speech therapy, 1973. Raised in Andover, MA. Worked as Rolls Royce auto mechanic and deliveryman while seeking work as stand-up comedian. Performed in comedy clubs throughout the U.S. and as opening act for Perry Como, Johnny Mathis, John Denver and Tom Jones. Guest on numerous talk shows and specials.
PICTURES: Silver Bears, Fun With Dick and Jane, American Hot Wax, Americathon, Collision Course.
TELEVISION: Series: The Marilyn McCoo & Billy Davis Jr. Show (1977). Permanent guest host, The Tonight Show, 1987–. Specials: Jay Leno and the American Dream (also prod.), The Jay Leno Show, Our Planet Tonight, Jay Leno's Family Comedy Hour.

LENZ, KAY: Actress. b. Los Angeles, CA, March 4, 1953.
PICTURES: American Graffiti, Breezy, White Line Fever, The Great Scout and Cathouse Thursday, Moving Violations, The Passage, Fast Walking, Stripped to Kill, House, Death Wish IV, Headhunter, Honor, Physical Evidence, Fear.
TELEVISION: Movies: The Weekend Nun, Lisa, Bright and Dark, A Summer Without Boys, Unwed Father, The Underground Man, The FBI Story: The FBI Versus Alvin Karpis, Journey from Darkness, Rich Man, Poor Man, The Initiation of Sarah, The Seeding of Sarah Burns, Sanctuary of Fear, The Hustler of Muscle Beach, Murder by Night. Guest: Midnight Caller.

LEON, SOL: Executive. b. New York, NY, July 2, 1913. e. NYU, City Coll. of New York, Brooklyn Law Sch., B.B.L., master of law. Sr. v.p., William Morris Agency, L.A.

LEONARD, SHELDON: Actor. r.n. Sheldon Leonard Bershad. b. New York, NY, Feb. 22, 1907. e. Syracuse U., B.A. Theatre mgr., Publix; N.Y. stage, 10 yrs.; sec., Directors Guild of America. 3 Emmy awards, Sylvania award, 4 TV Director of the Year nominations by D.G.A.
PICTURES: Another Thin Man, Tall, Dark and Handsome, Tortilla Flat, Rise and Shine, Lucky Jordan, Somewhere in the Night, Her Kind of Man, It's a Wonderful Life, The Gansters, If You Knew Susie, Sinbad the Sailor, My Dream Is Yours, Take One False Step, Iroquois Trail, Here Come the Nelsons, Young Man with Ideas, Stop You're Killing Me, Diamond Queen, Money from Home, Guys and Dolls; dir. Real McCoys, Pocketful of Miracles.
TELEVISION: dir. Make Room for Daddy, 1953–56: Damon Runyon, G.E. Theatre, Electric Theatre, Jewelers' Showcase, Jimmy Durante Show; prod.-dir. Danny Thomas Show; package & exec. prod., Andy Griffith Show, Dick Van Dyke Show; exec. prod., Gomer Pyle, U.S.M.C., I Spy, My World and Welcome To It. In 1975 starred in Big Eddie (series), 1977, exec. prod. and co-star in Top Secret.

LEONE, ALFRED: Producer, b. Nov. 30, 1926. In entertainment industry since 1958. Assistant producer for Braken Productions and Hallmark Productions. In 1968 formed Europa-America in Rome, Italy. 1974, formed Leone Intl. SPA in Rome. In 1978 opened offices in Beverly Hills. Produced and distributed over 35 films, among them: Vengeance, Four Times That Night, Baron Blood, Lisa And The Devil, House of Exorcism, Love by Appointment, Gold of the Amazon Women, The Snake.

L'EPINE-SMITH, ERIC: Producer, Director, Writer. m. Brenda Cameron. Stage as actor, prod. playwright, formed own co. Aldwitch Films; joined Wieland's Agency; apptd. dir. of co.; casting dir. Warner Bros. 1st Natl.; assoc. prod. Edward Dryhurst Productions, then prod. Now artists' mgr., L'Epine-Smith, Ltd and Carney Associates.
PICTURES: Down on the Farm, Pitchfork and Powder-Puff, Making a Man of Him, House of Silence, Five Pound Man, Coming of Age, While I Live, Noose, Prod.: Romantic Age, Come Die My Love.

LERNER, JOSEPH: Producer, Director, Writer. m. Geraldine Lerner, film ed. radio stage mgr. & actor on Broadway; with RKO, Columbia and Republic as dir., dial. dir., writer, 2nd unit dir., test dir., dir.-writer & head of special productions U.S. Army Signal Corps Photographic Center; writer of commercial and educational films 1946–47; vice-pres. in chg. of prod. Visual Arts Productions 1947; vice-pres. in chg. prod. Laurel Films 1949; prod.-dir., TV Gangbusters series, Grand Tour series; Girl on the Run, com. ind. films, Three Musketeers series TV, dir.-prod, 1961; Director, producer, writer, many TV commercials, documentaries 1967–73. President, The Place for Film Making, Inc.; pres., Astracor Associates Ltd. in production: The Ditch Digger's Daughter, The Little Hat, The Mapmakers, Trip the Light Fantastic. Also lecturer and instructor at NYU, Wm. Patterson Coll., Broward Community Coll. (FL), College at Boca Raton.
CREDITS: (writer-dir.) Fight Never Ends; (prod.-writer) Kings of the Olympics, Olympics Cavalcade; (prod.-dir.-writer) United Nations Case Book (for CBS-TV), C-Man; (prod.-dir.) Guilty Bystander, Mr. Universe, writer, director co-producer, The Dark of Day, Polish and/or rewrite. Many others in U.S. and abroad.

LESLIE, ALEEN: Writer. b. Pittsburgh, PA, Feb. 5, 1908. e. Ohio State U. Contributor to magazines; columnist Pittsburgh Press; orig. & wrote radio series A Date with Judy 1941–50. Bdwy play Slightly Married, 1943; wrote, prod. Date with Judy, TV series; author, The Scent of the Roses, The Windfall.
PICTURES: Doctor Takes a Wife, Affectionately Yours, Henry Aldrich Plays Cupid, Stork Pays Off, Henry Aldrich Gets Glamour, It Comes Up Love, Rosie the Riveter, Father Was a Fullback, Father Is a Bachelor.

LESLIE, JOAN: Actress. Star of Tomorrow, 1946. r.n. Joan Brodell; b. Detroit, MI, January 26, 1925. p. Agnes and John Brodell. e. St. Benedicts, Detroit; Our Lady of Lourdes, Toronto; St. Mary's Montreal; Immaculate Heart. H.S., L.A. Now on bd. of dir., St. Anne's Maternity Home, Damon Runyon Foundation.
PICTURES: The Sky's the Limit, This Is the Army, Yankee Doodle Dandy, Thank Your Lucky Stars, Rhapsody in Blue, Cinderella Jones, Hollywood Canteen, Where Do We Go From Here?, Too Young to Know, Repeat Performance, Northwest Stampede, Born To Be Bad, Skipper Surprised His Wife, Man in the Saddle, Hellgate, Flight Nurse, Jubilee Trail, Revolt of Mamie Stover.
TELEVISION: Ford Theatre, G.E. Theatre, Queen for a Day, Simon and Simon, Murder, She Wrote. Movies: Charley Hannah, The Keegans, Various commercials.

LESTER, MARK: Actor. b. Oxford, England, 1958. Ent. m.p. ind. 1963.
PICTURES: Allez France, Our Mother's House, 1967; Oliver; Run Wild, Run Free; The Boy Who Stole the Elephant, Eye Witness, SWALK (Melody), Black Beauty, Whoever Slew Auntie Roo?, Redneck, Crossed Swords.
TELEVISION: Special for Disney in Hollywood. 1970: American series for Krofft Television Productions, Scalawag, 1972; Graduation Trip; Danza Alla Porto Gli Olmi (Italian Entry Berlin '75), Seen Dimly Before Dawn.
STAGE: The Murder Game; The Prince and the Pauper 1976.

LESTER, MARK LESLIE: Director. b. Cleveland, OH, Nov. 26, 1946. e. U. of California, Northridge, B.A.
PICTURES: Steel Arena; Truck Stop Women; The Way He Was; Bobbi Jo and the Outlaw; Stunts; Roller Boogie; The Class of 1984; The Funhouse (exec. prod. only); Firestarter; Commando; Armed and Dangerous; Class of 1999.
TELEVISION: Gold of the Amazon Women.

LESTER, RICHARD: Director, Composer. b. Philadelphia, PA, Jan. 19, 1932. Early career: dir. and mus. dir. TV, CBS, Phila., CBC-TV, Toronto. Ent. m.p. ind. 1957. TV: dir. TV Goon Shows. Composed (with Reg. Owen) Sea War Series. Films: composed and dir., Running, Jumping and Standing Still.
PICTURES: It's Trad, Dad, Mouse on the Moon, Hard Day's Night, The Knack, Help! A Funny Thing Happened on the Way to the Forum, How I Won the War, Petulia, The Bedsitting Room, The Three Musketeers, Juggernaut, The Four Musketeers, Royal Flash, Robin & Marian, The Ritz, Butch and Sundance: The Early Days, Superman (prod. only), Cuba, Superman II, Superman III, Finders Keepers (also exec. prod.), The Return of the Musketeers.

LESTZ, EARL: Executive. Affiliated for 18 years with Federal Department Stores, of which was sr. v.p. of operations for its Bullock's chain before joining Paramount Pictures in April, 1983, as sr. v.p. of studio operations. 1985, named pres., operations for Paramount Studio Group.

LETTER, LOUIS N.: Executive, b. New York, NY, August, 1937. e. Brooklyn Coll., business administration. v.p. and dir. of operations, Century Theatres, New Hyde Park, N.Y. Exec. v.p., RKO Century Warner Theatres, New York.

LETTERMAN, DAVID: Writer, Actor. b. Indianapolis, IN, Apr. 12, 1947. e. Ball State U. Began career as weatherman and talk show host on Indianapolis TV before going to Hollywood.
TELEVISION: Writer: Good Times, Paul Lynde Comedy Hour, John Denver Special, Bob Hope Special. Actor: Mary, Good Friends, Tonight Show (guest host from 1978), Late Night with David Letterman Show, An NBC Family Christmas.

LE VIEN, JACK: Producer, Director. b. New York, NY, 1918. Film ed., reporter, Pathe News; military service, 1941–46; news ed., gen. mgr., v.p., Pathe News; chmn, American Newsreel Assoc., 1956–59; dir. of prod., Hearst Metrotone News; prod. in assoc., ABC-TV, The Valiant Years; exec. prod., Black Fox; prod. The Finest Hours, A King's Story; chmn., exec. prod., Le Vien Films Ltd.; prod.; Other World of Winston Churchill, The Gathering Storm, Walk With Destiny, The Amazing Voyage of Daffodil and Daisy, The Queens Drum Horse, Where the Lotus Fell, Churchill and the Generals, The Glittering Crowd, A Question of Choice.

LEVIN, ALAN M.: Executive. b. New York, NY, 1943. e. Brooklyn Coll., Brooklyn Law Sch. In law practice before joining CBS News Business Affairs dept. in 1969 as asst. dir.; 1970, talent and program negotiator for network business affairs; 1971, assoc. dir. business affairs; 1974, dir. talent and program contracts; 1975, dir., talent and program negotiations; 1976, v.p., business affairs, CBS, New York; 1977, v.p. business affairs CBS Entertainment. April 1978, v.p. and asst. to pres.; then v.p., business affairs. In 1980 named to business affairs and admin.; 1982, exec. v.p.; 1984, head of CBS Productions.

LEVIN, IRVING H.: Executive. b. Chicago, IL., Sept. 8, 1921. e. grad., U. of Illinois. U.S. Air Force, 1943–45; entered m.p. ind. as partner of Kranz-Levin Pictures and Realart Pictures of Calif. Inc.; indep. exch. in 1948; formed Mutual Prod, 1952; pres., Filmakers Releasing Org., 1953; secy., Filmakers Prod., Inc., 1952; pres. AB-PT Pictures Corp., 1956; pres., exec. prod., Oakhurst Television Prod., Inc., Sindee Prod., Inc.; pres., exec. prod. Atlas Enterprises, Inc.; pres., prod. Atlantic Pictures, 1959; exec. vice-pres., mem. of bd. of dir., National General Corp. (formerly NTT) 1961 and Pres. National General Prod. Inc. 1966 & Pictures Corp. 1967. Pres. and chief operating officer, NGC. In 1975 formed Levin-Schulman Prods. 1983, pres., Royal Theatres, Hawaii.

LEVIN, ROBERT B.: Executive. b. Chicago, IL. e. U. of Illinois. Operated own adv. firm for five years. 1982, named sr. v.p., Needham Harper World Wide Advertising Agency, Chicago. 1985, joined Walt Disney Pictures as sr. v.p., mktg. 1988: Named pres. Buena Vista Pictures marketing.

LEVINSON, ART: Producer. Began film career as office boy at Universal Studios where he entered training program and rapidly rose from asst. director to production manager on Harry and Tonto. Assoc. prod.: Breaking Away, Mr. Mom, Teachers.
PICTURES: My Favorite Year, Racing with the Moon, The Money Pit, Mannequin, Little Nikita, My Stepmother Is an Alien (exec. prod.).
TELEVISION: Billionaire Boys Club (assoc. prod.).

LEVINSON, BARRY: Director, Writer. b. Baltimore, MD, June 2, 1932. m. actress-screenwriter Valerie Curtin. e. American U. Wrote and acted in tv comedy show in L.A., leading to work on network tv. Wrote and performed on The Carol Burnett Show. Worked on film scripts with Mel Brooks (Silent Movie, High Anxiety) and co-wrote scripts with Valerie Curtin: And Justice for All, Inside Moves, Best Friends, Unfaithfully Yours. Appeared in films Silent Movie, High Anxiety, History of the World, Part I. Partner, Savan-Levinson-Parker Talent Agency, 1959–.
PICTURES: *Prod.:* First Love, The Internecine Project, Who? (aka, The Man in the Steel Mask), *Director-co-writer:* Diner, The Natural, Young Sherlock Holmes, Tin Men, Good Morning Vietnam, Rain Man (Acad. Awards, best dir., 1988).
TELEVISION: Tim Conway Comedy Hour (writer), The Marty Feldman Comedy Machine, The Carol Burnett Show (writer, Emmy, 1974, 75). Catholics (s.p.), Harry (exec. prod.,), Stopwatch: 30 Minutes of Investigative Ticking (exec. prod.), Diner (pilot, exec. prod., dir.) Movies: Displaced Persons (prod.), Suspicion (prod., co-s.p.).

LEVINSON, NORM: Executive. b. New Haven, CT. Started theatre business as usher for Loew's Theatres, 1940. U.S. Army, 1943–46. Returned Loew's Theatres managerial positions New Haven and Hartford, CT. MGM press representative, Minneapolis, Jacksonville, Atlanta, Dallas. General Manager, Trans-Texas Theatres, Dallas. President, Academy Theatres, Inc., Dallas. Promoted Championship Boxing, Dallas and Johannesburg, South Africa. Executive Vice President, Cobb Theatres, Birmingham, Alabama; v.p., world-wide mktg., Artists Releasing Corp., Encino, CA.; head film buyer, Chakeres Theatres, Ohio & Kentucky.

LEVITT, RUBY REBECCA: Set decorator. b. Corinth, NY, Sept. 10, 1907. e. Pratt Inst., Brooklyn. Buyer, interior decorator, department stores; store mgr.; set decorator, Universal, since 1944.
Staff Decorator for television commercials, Filmways of California, Inc. Staff of Filmways of Calif., 1966. Universal Studios, 1968.
PICTURES: Letter from an Unknown Woman, Magnificent Obsession, The Shrike, Six Bridges to Cross, Private War of Major Benson, This Earth Is Mine, Pillow Talk, 40 Pounds of Trouble, For the Love of Money, Sound of Music, Willie Boy, The Scavengers, Colossus, Change of Habit, Andromeda Strain, Vanished, Happy Birthday, Wanda June, The Other, Freebie and the Bean, The Manchu Eagle, Chinatown, Once Is Not Enough, Let's Do It Again, Harry and Walter Go to New York, A Star Is Born, New York-New York, Looking for Mr. Goodbar, The One the Only, Matilda, Promises in the Dark, The Jazz Singer.
TELEVISION: Mr. Ed, Addams Family, Double Life of Henry Phyffe, Movies of the Week, ABC, Banyon TV Series, Genesis II, Name of the Game, Love Story, Having Babies, Return Engagement.

LEVY, BERNARD: Executive. b. Boca Raton, FL. e. Brooklyn Law Sch., L.L.B. Legal staff of Superintendent of Insurance of the state of New York in the rehabilitation and liquidation of guaranteed title and mortgage companies, 1934–36; private practice of law, 1936–46; legal staff, Paramount Pictures, Inc., 1946–50; legal staff, United Paramount Theatres, 1950–51; exec. asst. to Edward L. Hyman, vice-pres., American Broadcasting Companies, Inc., in chg. of theatre administration, north, 1951–62; apptd. exec. liaison officer for southern motion picture theatres, ABC, Inc., 1962–64; exec. liaison officer, m.p. theas., ABC, Inc., 1965–72; vice pres., ABC Theatre Division, 1973. Retired, 1976.

LEVY, BUD: Executive. b. Jackson Heights, NY, April 3, 1928. e. NYU. Member: Variety Clubs Int'l., M.P. Pioneers, President's Advisory Board-NATO; director: NATO, TOP, CATO. Elected pres., Trans-Lux Corp., 1980. Pres. Trans Lux Theatres, (a subsidiary of Cinamerica Theatres). Will Rogers Memorial Fund, Chmn., Cara Committee for NATO; chmn. ShowEast; v.p. NATO; dir. Motion Picture Pioneers.

LEVY, DAVID: Executive. b. Philadelphia, PA, Jan. 2. e. Wharton Sch., U. of Pennsylvania, B.S. in Eco., M.B.A., As v.p. & assoc. dir., Young & Rubicam. Inc., 1938–59, acquisitions for clients include: People's Choice, Wagon Train, Four Star Playhouse, What's My Line, Father Knows Best, Goodyear Playhouse, Life of Riley, Gunsmoke. Was v.p. in chg. of network TV progs. & talent, NBC, 1959–61. Acquisitions for network include: Sing-a-Long With Mitch, Peter Pan, Bonanza, Dr. Kildare, Bob Newhart Show, Dick Powell Show, Saturday Night at the Movies, Hazel, Klondike. Created: Bat Masterson, The Addams Family, Americans, Outlaws, Pruitts of Southampton, Sarge, Hollywood Screen Test, Face the Music. Developed: Double Life of Henry Phyffe, Name That Tune, You Asked for It. Novels: The Chameleons, The Gods of Foxcroft, Network Jungle, as well as numerous TV plays and short stories.

LEVY, EUGENE: Actor, Writer. b. Hamilton, Canada, Dec. 17, 1946. e. McMaster U. Acted with coll. ensemble theater. Film debut in Ivan Reitman's Cannibal Girls, 1970, before joining Toronto's Second City troupe which eventually led to his work as writer-performer on Second City Television's various programs (Second City TV, SCTV Network 90, SCTV Network) 1977–83. Canadian theater: Godspell (1971), The Owl and the Pussycat, Love Times Four.
PICTURES: Cannibal Girls, Running, Strange Brew, Heavy Metal, Going Berserk, National Lampoon's Vacation, Splash, Armed and Dangerous, The Canadian Conspiracy, Club Paradise, Speed Zone.

LEVY, HERMAN M.: Attorney. Hamden, CT. b. New Haven, CT, Sept. 27, 1904. e. Yale, B.A., 1927, Yale Law Sch., LL.B., 1929; Phi Beta Kappa, was in legal dept. RCA Photophone; newspaper reporter; admitted to Connecticut bar, 1929. In 1939 elected exec. secy. of MPTO of Connecticut. In 1943: Elected general counsel MPTOA. Elected gen. counsel, Theatre Owners of America, 1947–63. Pres., New Haven County Bar Assn., 1964; legislative agent, Conn. Assn. of Theatre Owners. Retired as legislative agent, 1981.
AUTHOR: More Sinned Against . . . Natl. Bd. of Review Magazine, 1941. Proving the Death of a Non-Resident Alien, Conn. Bar Journal, 1950; Need for a System of Arbitration M.P. Ind., Arbitration Journal, 1950; reprint of Industry Case Digest, 20th Century-Fox vs. Boehm in the Journal (Screen Producers Guild); Book Review of Antitrust in the Motion Picture Industry, by Michael Conant (Univ. of Calif. Law Review).

LEVY, JULES V.: Producer. b. Los Angeles, CA, Feb. 12, 1923. e. U. of Southern California. Property dept., W.B., 1941; First motion picture unit, Army Air Force, Culver City, CA.
PICTURES: The Vampire, Return of Dracula, Vice Squad,

Without Warning, Down Three Dark Streets, Geronimo, Glory Guys, Clambake, Scalphunters, Sam Whiskey, Underground, McKenzie Break, The Hunting Party, The Honkers, McQ, Brannigan, White Lightning, Gator, Kansas City Bomber, Safari 3000.
TELEVISION: Rifleman, Robert Taylor's Detectives, Law of the Plainsman, The Big Valley.

LEVY, MICHAEL: Executive. b. Brooklyn, NY. e. Brown U. Started in industry in editorial dept. of trade-paper Variety; held posts in New York with ABC Motion Pictures and with Diener/Hauser/Bates Advertising. Worked for Lawrence Gordon Productions as exec. asst. to Gordon and as story editor. Joined 20th Century Fox in January, 1985, as dir. of creative affairs for studio. 1986, named v.p., production, m.p. div., Fox; appointed sr. v.p. production, 20th Century Fox, 1988; named pres., Silver Pictures, 1989.

LEVY, MIKE: Executive. b. England, 1931. Served RAF 1949–52. Joined Technicolor Ltd., 1953, diverse tech. assignments incl. technical control spvr. & plant supt. 1970, feature film sls. mgr. 1978, joined Rank Film Laboratories as int'l. sls. mgr. & adv. exec. 1981, sls. & mktg. controller. 1986, appt. mem. of board and sls. dir.

LEVY, NORMAN: Executive. b. Bronx, NY, Jan. 3, 1935. e. City Coll. of New York. In 1957 joined Universal Pictures, holding various sales positions; 1967, went to National General Pictures, ultimately being named v.p. and exec. asst. to pres.; 1974, Columbia Pictures, v.p., gen. sls. mgr. In 1975 named Columbia exec. v.p. in chg. of domestic sls.; 1977, exec. v.p., mktg; 1978. pres., Columbia Pictures Domestic Distribution. In 1980 joined 20th-Fox as pres. of Entertainment Group; 1981, vice-chmn., 20th Century-Fox Film Corp. Resigned 1984 to become mktg./dist. consultant. 1986, joined New Century Productions as head of domestic production. Now head of New Century/Vista.

LEWELLEN, A. WAYNE: Executive. b. Feb. 16, 1944. e. U. of Texas. Joined Paramount Pictures 1973 as brch. mgr., Dallas-Oklahoma City territory; named South. dist. mgr.; 1978, South. div. mgr. July, 1984, named v.p., domestic dist., South. div.; 1985, appt. exec. v.p., gen. sls. mgr. (New York). 1986, named pres., domestic dist.

LEWINE, ROBERT F.: Executive. b. New York, NY, Apr. 16, 1913. e. Swarthmore Coll. Worked for restaurant chain, in real estate; U.S. Navy, 1942; creative staff, Cine-Television Studios, Inc.; v.p. in charge of oper., 1946; formed own co., 1947, for prod. of TV comm., industrial m.p.; also eastern rep., Dudley Films; radio-TV dir., Hirshon-Garfield, Inc., 1953; eastern prog. dir., ABC, 1953; dir., ABC-TV network prog. dept., 1954; v.p. in charge of programming and talent ABC-TV network, 1956; v.p., NBC, prog. dept. chg. nighttime programming, 1957; v.p. network programs, 1958; v.p. Figaro, Inc., 1958; v.p. programs, CBS Films, 1959; v.p. programs, Hollywood CBS Television Network, Apr., 1962; officer Acad. TV Arts & Sciences from 1954, Exec. comm., dir., Acad. TV Arts & Sciences. Pres., N.Y. Chapter 1959; nat'l. pres., 1961; nat'l. trustee, 1961–63; National pres., Academy TV Arts & Sciences, 1961–63; first vice pres., dir., Academy TV Arts & Sciences Foundation; pres., 1964; exec. v.p., Creative Management Associates Ltd.; v.p., Warner Bros., TV Pres. Nat'l Acad. of Television Arts and Sciences; trustee, Columbia College, L.A., Calif.; trustee, American Women in Radio and Television Foundation. 1977-NBC Television Network, exec. prod. dir.; chmn. PAW Society (Preservation of Animal Wildlife); Member Int'l Advisory Council, Population Institute; Chmn. of the bd., Riverside Broadcasting Company. Since 1978 guest lecturer at UCLA and U. of Southern California.

LEWIS, ARTHUR: Producer, Director, Writer. b. New York, NY, Sept. 15, 1916. e. U. of Southern California, Yale U. Began career as writer and assoc. prod. on the Jones Family TV series. Five years in U.S. Army; returned to screenwriting before producing Three Wishes for Jamie on Broadway and producing and directing Guys and Dolls in London's West End. In mid-60s produced plays with Bernard Delfont at Shaftesbury Theatre in London.
PICTURES: Producer: Loot, Baxter, The Killer Elite, Brass Target.
TELEVISION: Brenner, The Asphalt Jungle (prod. writer).

LEWIS, EDWARD: Producer. Began entertainment career as script writer, then co-produced The Admiral Was a Lady and teamed with Marion Parsonnet to bring the Faye Emerson Show to TV. Subsequently prod. first Schlitz Playhouse and China Smith series. Was v.p. of Kirk Douglas' indep. prod. co., where was assoc. prod. and writer-prod. Collaborated with John Frankenheimer on 8 films.
PICTURES: Lizzie (assoc. prod.), The Careless Years (prod., s.p.), Spartacus, The Last Sunset, Lonely Are the Brave, The List of Adrian Messenger, Seconds, Grand Prix, The Fixer (exec. prod.), The Gypsy Moths (exec.), I Walk the Line (exec.), The Horsemen, The Iceman Cometh (exec.), Rhinoceros, Lost in the Stars, Missing (co-prod.), Crackers, The River, Executive Action, Brothers (prod., s.p.).
TELEVISION: Islai: The Last of His Tribe (exec. prod.), The Thorn Birds (exec. prod.).

LEWIS, EMMANUEL: Actor. b. Brooklyn, NY, March 9, 1971. Began in TV commercials and has done TV and radio voice-overs. Singer and dancer and, following personal appearance tours in Japan, became recording star there. Theatrical debut in A Midsummer Night's Dream at N.Y. Shakespeare Festival (1982).
TELEVISION: Tonight Show, The Phil Donahue Show, Webster (series). Movie: Lost in London.

LEWIS, HAROLD G: Executive. b. New York, NY, Sept. 18, 1938. e. Union Coll., 1960, electrical engineer. Joined ATA Trading Corp. in 1960 and has been pres. since 1977. Producer of feature animation. Importer and exporter for theatrical and TV features, documentaries, series, classics. Pres., ATA Trading Corp., and Favorite TV, Inc.

LEWIS, JERRY: Actor. r.n. Joseph Levitch. b. Newark, NJ, Mar. 16, 1926. e. Irvington H.S. Parents Danny and Rae Lewis, prof. entertainers. Debut at 5 at a NY Borscht Circuit hotel singing "Brother Can You Spare a Dime?" Worked as a drugstore lunch counter counterman, an usher at Loew's State in NY and a shipping clerk in a hat factory whle perfecting comedy routines. 1946 formed comedy-team with Dean Martin (singer, straight man) at 500 Club, Atlantic City, NJ; appeared Latin Casino, Phila., then other nightclubs, on NBC television; played many m.p. theatres; signed by Hal Wallis; team m.p. debut in My Friend Irma 1949. Partnership with Martin lasted 10 years, during which they made 16 films. 1959, signed contract between Paramount Pictures and Jerry Lewis Prods. for $10 million plus 60% of profits for 14 films over next 7 years. Partnership dissolved 1965. Voted Most Promising Male Star in Television in m.p. Daily's 2nd annual TV poll, 1950. Voted (as team) one of top ten money making stars in m.p. Herald-Fame poll, 1951, 1953–54–57. Number 1, 1952; best comedy team in m.p. Daily's 16th annual radio poll, 1951, 1952, 1953; 1956 formed Jerry Lewis Prods. Inc., functioning as prod., dir., writer & star. Full professor USC, taught grad. film dir. Book: The Total Filmmaker (1971) based on classroom lectures. National Chairman Muscular Dystrophy Association 39 years and bd. member. Autobiography: Jerry Lewis In Person (1982).
PICTURES: My Friend Irma Goes West, At War with the Army, That's My Boy, The Caddy, Sailor Beware, Jumping Jacks, Scared Stiff, The Stooge, Money from Home, Living It Up, Three Ring Circus, You're Never Too Young, Artists and Models, Pardners, Hollywood or Bust, Delicate Delinquent, Sad Sack, Rock-A-Bye Baby, Geisha Boy, Don't Give Up the Ship, Visit to a Small Planet, Cinderfella, Bellboy, The Ladies Man, The Errand Boy, It's Only Money, The Nutty Professor, Who's Minding the Store?, The Patsy, The Disorderly Orderly, Boeing-Boeing, The Family Jewels, Three on a Couch, (dir. prod., star), Way . . . Way Out, The Big Mouth, (prod., s.p., star), Don't Lower the Bridge Raise the River, (prod., s.p., star), Hook Line and Sinker, Which Way to the Front?, (prod., dir., star), One More Time, (dir.), The Day the Clown Cried (also dir., co.-s.p.), Hardly Working (star, dir., co-s.p.), King of Comedy, Smorgasbord (also dir.), To Catch a Cop, How Did You Get In?, Cookie.
TELEVISION: Fight for Life (movie). Guest: Wiseguy (5 episodes).
RECORDS: Rock-A-Bye Your Baby.
AWARDS: AFL-CIO Murray-Green Award for Community Services, 1971; 1976 US Senate resolution of appreciation for fight against muscular dystrophy; NAPTE Award of the Year for humanitarian efforts, 1978; Amer. Institute for Public Service's Jefferson Award; Touchdown Club of Washington, D.C. Awarded Hubert H. Humphry Humanitarian Award, 1980; Boston U Sch of Law's N. Neal Pike Prize for Service to the Handicapped, 1984; Inducted into French Legion of Honor and made Commander in the Order of Arts and Letters France, 1984; Dept. of Defense Medal for Distinguished Public Service, 1985; Doctor of Humane Letters, Mercy Coll., Westchester, NY, 1987.

LEWIS, JOSEPH H.: Director. b. New York, NY, Apr. 6, 1907. e. DeWitt Clinton H.S. Camera boy, MGM; then asst. film ed. in chge. film ed., Republic; dir. in chge. 2nd units; dir. Universal; U.S. Signal Corps., WW II; dir. RKO, Columbia, W.B.
PICTURES: My Name is Julia Ross, So Dark the Night, Jolson Story, The Swordsman, Return of October, Undercover Man, Gun Crazy, Lady Without Passport, Retreat Hell!, Desperate Search, Cry of the Hunted, Big Combo, A Lawless Street.
TELEVISION: Rifleman series, Barbara Stanwyck Show: The Big Valley.

LEWIS, MICHAEL J.: Composer. b. Wales, 1939. First film score 1968, The Mad Woman of Chaillot, won Ivor Novello Award for best film score. 1973: first Broadway musical, Cyrano, Grammy Nomination '74, Caesar and Cleopatra (T.V. '76); The Lion, the Witch, and the Wardrobe (Emmy, 1979).

PICTURES: The Man Who Haunted Himself, Julius Caesar. Upon This Rock, Unman, Wittering and Zigo, Running Scared, Baxter, Theatre of Blood, 11 Harrowhouse, 92 in the Shade, Russian Roulette, The Stick-Up, The Medusa Touch, The Legacy, The Passage, The Unseen, ffolkes, Sphinx, Yes, Giorgio, The Hound of the Baskervilles, On the Third Day, The Naked Face.

LEWIS, MONICA: Singer, Actress. b. Chicago, IL, May 5, 1925. e. Hunter Coll., N.Y. p. Leon Lewis, concert pianist, former medical dir. CBS; Jessica Lewis, child star with Nazimova; member Ben Greet's Shakespearean players, sang leading roles. Chicago Opera Co.; later vocal teacher. Started career as radio singer, own show, WMCA, N.Y.; on Beat the Band, 1946; co-star Chesterfield program; sang leading role, Girl Crazy, Ford Sunday Evening Hour, Own program, Monica Makes Music; co-star Revere Camera show. Among first ten female singers in country on recording polls. Vocalist: Stork Club, Astor Roof, Copacabana, Persian Room.
PICTURES: Inside Straight, Excuse My Dust, The Strip, Everything I Have Is Yours, Affair With a Stranger, Charlie Varrick, Earthquake, Roller Coaster, Airport '77, Nunzio, Concorde-Airport '79.

LIBERMAN, FRANK P.: Publicist, b. New York, NY, May 29, 1917. e. Cheshire Acad., CT, 1934; Lafayette Coll., Easton, PA, B.A. 1938. m. Patricia Harris, casting dir. Worked as copy boy, N.Y. Daily News, 1938–39. Began career as publicist at Warner Bros., home office as messenger, 1939, promoted to press-books dept., transferred to Warner's Chicago office as field exploitation man. U.S. Signal Corps, 1941, public relations officer, Army Pictorial Service, on temporary duty with War Dept., Bureau of Public Relations in Pentagon. Discharged as Capt., 1946. Rejoined Warner Bros. on coast 2 years, 1947, est. own public relations office, 1949. Owner, Frank Liberman and Associates, Inc.

LIBERTINI, RICHARD: Actor. b. Cambridge, MA, May 21. Original member of Second City troupe in Chicago. With MacIntyre Dixon appeared as the Stewed Prunes in cabaret performances.
THEATER: With Stewed Prunes: Three by Three (1961), Plays for Bleecker Street, The Cat's Pajamas, The Mad Show (also co-writer). Solo: The White House Murder Case, Don't Drink the Water, Paul Sill's Story Theatre, Ovid's Metamorphoses, The Primary English Class.
PICTURES: The Night They Raided Minsky's, Don't Drink the Water, Catch-22, The Out-of-Towners, Lovers and Other Strangers, Lady Liberty, Fire Sale, Days of Heaven, The In-Laws, Popeye, Sharkey's Machine, Soup for One, Best Friends, Deal of the Century, Going Berserk, Unfaithfully Yours, Big Trouble, All of Me, Fletch, Family Man.
TELEVISION: Series: The Melba Moore-Clifton Davis Show, Soap, George Burns Comedy Week, Family Man. Pilots: Calling Dr. Storm, M.D., Fair Game. Movies: Three on a Date. Specials: Let's Celebrate, The Fourth Wise Man, Fame (Hallmark Hall of Fame), The Trial of Bernhard Goetz.

LICCARDI, VINCENT G.: Executive. b. Brooklyn, NY. Started as messenger at Universal Pictures, asst. adv. mgr. on Around the World in 80 Days, asst. to exec. coord. of sales & Adv. on Spartacus; National Dir. of Adv. & Publ., Continental; Nat. Dir. Adv. & Publ., Braintree Prod., adv. pub. mgr. Allied Artists, ad. mgr. Paramount, National Dir. Adv.-Pub., UMC Pictures, Screenwriter, Playboy to Priest, The Rivals, The Rivals-Part II, The Greatest Disaster of All Time, The Lady on the 9:40, All That Heaven Allows, All Mine to Love, Twice Over, Lightly!, Mr. Jim.

LIDER, EDWARD W. Executive. b. New Bedford, MA, March 13, 1922. e. Dartmouth, Harvard Law Sch. Served as attorney-at-law, 1948–50. President & treasurer, Fall River Theatres Corp. & Nathan Yamins Enterprises, 1950 to present; member of bd., Theatre Owners of New England; past pres., Theatre Owners of New England; past member of bd. & past treas., Allied States Assoc. of M.P. Exhibitors; general manager of Sonny & Eddy's Theatres in Boston: Exeter St., Academy, Harvard Square, Central Square, Allston C1nema-C2nema and Galeria Theatres.

LIEBERFARB, WARREN: Executive. e. Wharton Sch. of Commerce and Finance, U. of Pennsylvania, B.S., economics; U. of Michigan, M.B.A. Started career in industry at Paramount Pictures as dir. of mktg. and exec. asst. to Stanley Jaffe, then pres. Later joined 20th-Fox as v.p.—special market dist. (cable, pay-TV, non-theatrical). Joined Warner Bros. as v.p., exec. asst. to Ted Ashley, bd. chmn.; later named v.p., intl. adv.-pub. In 1979 joined Lorimar as v.p., of Lorimar Productions, Inc., the parent company, based in New York, Promoted to sr. v.p. 1982, named v.p. mktg., Warner Home Video; named pres., 1985.

LIEBERMAN, ROBERT: Director.
PICTURE: Table for Five.
TELEVISION: Movies: Fighting Back—The Story of Rocky Blier; Will—G. Gordon Liddy.

LIEBERSON, SANFORD: Producer. b. Los Angeles, CA, 1936. 1979, named pres. of 20th-Fox Productions, which company he joined in 1977 as v.p.—European production. Previously an independent producer forming Goodtimes VPS, (Performance, Bugsy Malone, Jabberwocky, etc.). Prior to that exec. in chg. of European operations of Creative Management Associates. In 1980 named int'l. v.p. for Ladd Co., based in London. Supervising prod. chief, Goldcrest Film & TV (Outland, Blade Runner.) Returned to indep. prod. 1985. 1989 appt. head of Pathé Entertainment's European prod. office.
PICTURES: Prod.: Rita, Sue and Bob, Stars and Bars, The Mighty Quinn.

LIGHTMAN, M. A.: Exhibitor. b. Nashville, TN, Apr. 21, 1915. e. Southwestern U., Vanderbilt U., 1936, B.A. Bd. chmn. Malco Theatres, Inc., Memphis, Tenn.

LINDBLOM, GUNNEL: Actress, Director. b. Gothenburg, Sweden, 1931. Discovered by Ingmar Bergman while studying at drama school of Gothenburg Municipal Theatre (1950–53); she moved to Malmo, where he was director of the local Municipal Theatre. Under Bergman's direction she played in Easter, Peer Gynt, Faust, etc. between 1954–59. Later appeared in many Bergman films. Since 1968 has been on staff of Stockholm's Royal Dramatic Theatre, assisting Bergman and then beginning to direct on her own. Made film debut as director with Summer Paradise in 1977.
PICTURES: Actress: The Seventh Seal, Wild Strawberries, The Virgin Spring, Winter Light, The Silence, Rapture, Loving Couples. Director: Summer Paradise, Sally and Freedom, Summer Nights on Planet Earth.

LINDEN, HAL: Actor. b. Bronx, NY, March 20, 1931. e. City Coll. of New York. Began career as saxophone player and singer, playing with bands of Sammy Kaye, Bobby Sherwood, etc. Drafted and performed in revues for Special Services. After discharge enrolled at N.Y.'s American Theatre Wing; appeared on Bdwy. in Bells Are Ringing, replacing Sydney Chaplin.
THEATRE: On a Clear Day, Wildcat, Something More, Subways Are for Sleeping, Ilya Darling, The Apple Tree, Wildcat, The Education of HYMAN KAPLAN, Three Men on a Horse, Pajama Game, The Rothschilds (Tony Award), I'm Not Rappaport.
TELEVISION: Host on ABC series, Animals Animals Animals; Barney Miller (series), I Do! I Do!, The Best of Everything. Movies: Father Figure; My Wicked, Wicked Ways; The Other Woman; How to Break Up a Happy Divorce, Dream Breakers.
PICTURES: When You Comin' Back Red Ryder?, A New Life.

LINDFORS, VIVECA: Actress. b. Uppsala, Sweden, Dec. 29, 1920. e. Royal Dramatic Sch., Stockholm. Stage debut in Ann-Scofi Hedvig school prod. Screen debut in The Crazy Family, 1941; reached stardom in If I Should Marry the Minister. U.S. screen debut in Night Unto Night.
PICTURES: Adventures of Don Juan, Dark City, Flying Missile, Gypsy Fury, No Sad Songs For Me, Journey into Light, Four in a Jeep, The Raiders, No Time for Flowers, Run for Cover, Captain Dreyfus, Coming Apart, Puzzle of a Downfall Child, The Way We Were, Welcome to L.A., Girl Friends, A Wedding, Voices, The Hand, Creepshow, The Sure Thing, Rachel River, Going Undercover, Misplaced, Forced March.
TELEVISION: A Doctor's Story, Passions, The Three Wishes of Billy Grier; Playing for Time; Inside the Third Reich; Marilyn: The Untold Story; Secret Weapons; The Ann Jillian Story.

LINDNER, TERRELL M.: Executive. b. Dromana, Australia. Aug. 10, 1915. Entered m.p. ind. in pub. dep. Columbia Pictures, Melbourne, Australia, 1942. Columbia, mgr. Western Australia, Dec. 1946. gen. mgr. Columbia, New Zealand, 1948. United Artists home office rep. for India, Burma, Pakistan, Ceylon, 1952. apptd. United Artists dist. supvr. for Southeast Asia. hdqts. Bombay. Dec. 1953. Rank overseas. 1957. Opened West Indies offices. man. dir. Rank Filmes do Brasil, 1958. man. dir. Filmcenter Internacional Ltda., Brazil, (successors Rank) 1970.

LINDSAY, ROBERT: Actor. b. Ilkeston, Derbyshire, Eng., Dec. 12, 1949. e. Royal Acad. of Dramatic Art. With Manchester's Royal Exchange Theatre Co. (Hamlet, The Cherry Orchard, The Lower Depths). Also in Godspell, The Three Musketeers, Me and My Girl, (London—Olivier Award, NY—Tony and Drama Desk Awards, 1987).
PICTURES: That'll Be the Day (debut, 1974), Bert Rigby, You're a Fool; Loser Takes All; Rosencrantz and Guildenstern Are Dead.
TELEVISION: Series: Citizen Smith, Give Us A Break. Mini-series: Confessional. Special: King Lear.

LINK, WILLIAM: Writer, Producer. b. Philadelphia, PA, Dec. 15, 1933. e. U. of Pennsylvania, B.S., 1956. With partner, late Richard Levinson, wrote and created numerous TV series and movies, specializing in detective-mystery genre. Books: Fineman, Stay Tuned: An Inside Look at the Making of Prime-Time Television.

PICTURES: The Hindenberg, Rollercoaster.

TELEVISION: Series writer-creator: Mannix, Ellery Queen, Tenafly, Columbo (Emmy, 1972), Murder She Wrote (exec. prod.), Gideon Oliver (exec. prod.). Movies, writer-prod.: That Certain Summer, My Sweet Charlie (Emmy, 1970), Two on a Bench, The Judge and Jake Wyler, Savage (exec. prod., s.p.), The Execution of Private Slovik, The Gun, A Cry for Help (prod. only), The Storyteller, Murder by Natural Causes, Stone, Crisis at Central High, Rehearsal For Murder (also exec. prod.), Take Your Best Shot, Prototype (also exec. prod.), The Guardian (also exec. prod.), Guilty Conscience (also exec. prod.), Vanishing Act (also exec. prod.).

LINKLETTER, ART: Emcee, Producer. b. Moose Jaw, Saskatchewan, Canada, July 17, 1912. e. San Diego State Coll. Radio prg. mgr., San Diego Exposition, 1935; radio pgm. mgr. S.F. World's Fair, 1937–39; freelance radio ann. and m.c. 1939–42; m.c. People are Funny since 1942. Starred Inside Beverly Hills, NBC-TV, 1955; exec. prod. host, NBC-TV spec. Salute to Baseball, 1956; host, Art Linkletter's Secret World of Kids, NBC-TV's Ford Startime, 1959; 1969 House Party series became the Linkletter Show.

Author of: The Secret World of Kids, 1959, Kids Say the Darndest Things, 1957, Linkletter Down Under, 1969, Yes, You Can, 1979; Old Age is Not For Sissies, 1988.

PICTURES: People Are Funny, Champagne Caesar.

LINSON, ART: Producer, Director. b. Chicago, IL. e. UCLA; LLD. UCLA, 1967. Was rock music manager with record prod. Lou Adler and ran own record co., Spin Dizzy records before turning to film production. Debuted as director also with Where the Buffalo Roam.

PICTURES: Rafferty and the Gold Dust Twins, (co.-prod.), Car Wash, American Hot Wax (also co-s.p.), Melvin and Howard, Singles, Fast Times at Ridgemont High (co-prod.), Where the Buffalo Roam, (dir.), The Wild Life (dir.), The Untouchables (prod. only), Scrooged (co-prod.), We're No Angels, Casualties of War (prod.).

LIPPERT, ROBERT J., JR.: Producer, Director, Film editor. b. Alameda, CA, Feb. 28, 1928. e. St Mary's Coll., 1946; all conference football 1947. Film editor of 65 motion pictures. Produced and directed nine pictures for Lippert Pictures and 20th Century Fox. Present position is president, for Lippert Theatres headquartered in Pebble Beach, CA.

LIPSTONE, HOWARD H.; Executive, Producer. b. Chicago, IL, Apr. 28, 1928. e. UCLA, U. of Southern California. Ass't to gen. mgr. at KLTA, 1950–55; program dir. at KABC-TV, 1955–65; exec. ass't to pres. at Selmur Prods., ABC subsidiary, 1965–69. Ivan Tors Films & Studios as exec. v.p., 1969–70; pres.; pres., Alan Landsburg Prods., 1970–1985; The Landsburg Co., 1985 to present. Co-exec. prod.: The Outer Space Connection, The Bermuda Triangle, Mysteries, The White Lions, Jaws 3-D.

TELEVISION: exec. in charge of prod.: The Savage Bees, Ruby and Oswald, The Triangle Factory Fire Scandal, Strange Voices, A Place at the Table.

LIPTON, DAVID A.: Executive. b. Chicago, IL, Nov. 6, 1906. U.S. Army, W.W.II. Entered m.p. ind. 1921 as office boy, Balaban & Katz, Chicago; in 1922 joined pub. dept.; in 1929 transf. Detroit; in 1930 joined Famous Players Canadian Corp., org. pub. dept.; ret'd to Chicago office 1931; res. 1933 to become publ. dir. for Sally Rand. In 1937 joined CBS, N.Y. as press relations counsel. Named publ. dir. Universal N.Y., 1938; later to West Coast as studio publ. dir. In 1941 to N.Y. as dir. adv. publ. & exploit., Columbia; returned to Universal as exec. coordinator of adv. & promotion, 1946; nat'l dir. adv. pub., Jan. 1949; elected v.p. in chge. adv. pub.; 1974, MCA Discovision, Inc., public relations director; 1979, Retired.

LISI, VIRNA: Actress. b. Ancona, Italy, Nov. 8, 1937.

PICTURES: How To Murder Your Wife, Casanova 70, Not with My Wife You Don't, Assault on a Queen, The Lady and the General, Arabella, Better a Widow, Ernesto, I Love N.Y., I Ragazzi di Via Panisperna, Merry Christmas, Happy New Year, Miss Right.

TELEVISION: (U.S.) Christopher Columbus.

LISTER, MOIRA: Actress. b. Capetown, South Africa, b. Aug. 6, 1923. e. Holy Family Convent, Johannesburg. Stage debut at 6 yrs. of age in Vikings of Heligoland; screen debut in Shipbuilders, 1943. Numerous TV appearances.

PICTURES: Love Story, Wanted for Murder, Don Chicago, Uneasy Terms, So Evil My Love, Another Shore, Once a Jolly Swagman, Run for Your Money, Pool of London, White Corridors, Something Money Can't Buy, Cruel Sea, Grand National Night, Limping Man, Trouble in Store, John and Julie, Deep Blue Sea, Seven Waves Away, The Yellow Rolls Royce, Joey Boy, Double Man, Stranger in the House, The Choice, Ten Little Indians.

LITHGOW, JOHN: Actor. b. Rochester, NY, Oct. 19, 1945. Father was prod. of Shakespeare Fests. in midwest. e. Harvard. Fulbright fellowship to study at London Acad. of Music and Dramatic Art. Acted and directed in London with Royal Shakespeare Co. and Royal Court Theatre.

THEATER: The Changing Room (Tony Award, supp. 1973), My Fat Friend, The Comedians, A Memory of Two Mondays, Anna Christie, Once in a Lifetime, Requiem for a Heavyweight, Beyond Therapy, Kaufman at Large, The Front Page, M Butterfly.

PICTURES: Obsession, Rich Kids, Dealing, Blow Out, All That Jazz, The World According to Garp, Twilight Zone—The Movie, The Adventures of Buckaroo Banzai, Terms of Endearment, Footloose, 2010, Santa Claus: The Movie, The Manhattan Project, Harry and the Hendersons, Out Cold, Distant Thunder, Memphis Belle.

TELEVISION: Amazing Stories (Emmy Award, 1987), Movies: The Day After, The Glitter Dome, Resting Place, Baby Girl Scott, Mesmerized, The Traveling Man.

LITTLE, CLEAVON: Actor. b. Chickasha, OK, June 1, 1939. e. San Diego Coll., B.A. 1965. Amer. Acad. of Dramatic Art, 1965–67.

THEATER: Macbeth, Scuba Duba, Hamlet, Jimmy Shine, Someone's Comin' Hungry, Purlie (Tony Award, 1970), All Over Town, The Poison Tree, I'm Not Rappaport.

PICTURES: What's So Bad About Feeling Good, Cotton Comes to Harlem, John and Mary, Vanishing Point, Blazing Saddles, FM, Greased Lightning, Scavenger Hunt, High Risk, Jimmy the Kid, Surf II, Toy Soldiers, Gig, Once Bitten, Fletch Lives.

TELEVISION: Series: The David Frost Revue (1971–73), Temperature's Rising, Tickets Please (pilot). Movies: Don't Look Back, The Day the Earth Moved, Homecoming, Denmark Vesey's Rebellion, Now We're Cookin', Gore Vidal's Lincoln.

LITTLE, RICH: Actor. b. Ottawa, Canada, Nov. 26, 1938. Impersonator in night clubs. On screen in Dirty Tricks.

TELEVISION: Rich Little's Christmas Carol, Rich Little's Washington Follies, You Asked for It, Parade of Stars, The Christmas Raccoons, Rich Little and Friends in New Orleans, etc.

LITTMAN, LYNNE: Director, Producer. b. New York, NY, June 26, 1941. e. Sarah Lawrence. B.A., 1962; Student the Sorbonne 1960–61. Wife of director Taylor Hackford. Researcher for CBS News 1965; assoc. prod. Natl. Educational TV 1966–69; dir. NIMH film series on drug abuse UCLA Media Center 1970; prod., dir. documentary films, news and pub. affairs series KCET Community TV, So. Calif. 1971–77; dir. WNET Indep. Filmmakers Series 1979; exec. v.p., movies-for-TV, ABC, 1979–80. Received Ford Fdn. Grant 1978 and numerous awards.

PICTURES: In the Matter of Kenneth (doc.); Wanted-Operadoras (doc.); Till Death Do Us Part (doc.); Number Our Days (doc. short; Acad Award 1977); Testament (co-prod., dir.).

TELEVISION: Co-prod., dir.: Rick Nelson: It's All Right Now, In Her Own Time.

LITTO, GEORGE: Executive. b. Philadelphia, PA, Dec. 9, 1930. e. Temple U. Joined William Morris Agency in New York and then became indep. literary agent. Opened own office in Hollywood, 1962. Packaged film and TV productions, including six films for Robert Altman. Hawaii Five-O for TV prior to entering indep. prod.; 1981–82, chmn. bd. & CEO, Filmways; 1983–85 indep. prod. 20th Century Fox.

PICTURES: Thieves Like Us (exec. prod.), Drive-In (exec. prod.), Obsession (prod.), Over the Edge (prod.), Dressed To Kill (prod.). Blow Out (prod.), Kansas (prod.), Night Game (prod.).

LITVINOFF, SI: Producer, Executive. b. New York, NY, April 5, 1929. e. Adelphi Coll., A.B.; NYU Sch. of Law, LL.B. Theatrical lawyer, personal and business manager in New York until 1967 when left firm of Barovick, Konecky & Litvinoff to produce plays and films. June, 1987: sr. v.p. for production and dev., Hawkeye Entertainment, Inc..

STAGE: Leonard Bernstein's Theatre Songs, Cry of the Raindrop, Girl of the Golden West, Little Malcolm and His Struggle Against the Eunuchs, I and Albert (London).

PICTURES: The Queen, All the Right Noises, Walkabout, A Clockwork Orange (exec. prod.), Glastonbury Fayre (exec. in chg. prod.); The Man Who Fell to Earth (exec. prod.)

TELEVISION: Exec. prod.: 15th Annual Saturn Awards, Doobie Brothers Retrospective 1989.

LIVINGSTON, JAY: Composer, Lyricist. b. McDonald, PA, March 28, 1915; e. U. of Pennsylvania, 1937, UCLA, 1964–65. Army, W.W.II. Accompanist and arranger for various NBC singers and singing groups 1940–42, N.Y.; author music and special material for Olsen & Johnson, including various editions of Hellzapoppin', and Sons O'Fun: began composing picture songs, 1944. Under contract to Paramount, 1945–55; then freelance. Composed songs for over 100 films. Writer of songs and special material for Bob Hope, 1965–present. Collab. music and lyrics for Bdwy show Oh Captain! 1958; Let It Ride, 1961. Two songs for Sugar Babies, 1980.

SONG HITS: G'bye Now, Stuff Like That There, To Each His Own, Golden Earrings, Silver Bells, Buttons and Bows (Acad. Award, 1949), Mona Lisa (Acad. Award, 1951), Que Sera Sera (Acad. Award, 1957), Tammy (Acad. nom.), Almost In Your Arms (Acad. nom.), Bonanza (TV Theme), Mister Ed (TV Theme), Dear Heart, (Acad. nom.), Wish Me a Rainbow, In the Arms of Love, Never Let Me Go, As I Love You, All the Time, Maybe September.

PICTURES: The Paleface, Fancy Pants, The Lemon-Drop Kid, Houseboat, Tammy and the Bachelor, The Man Who Knew Too Much, Dear Heart, Here Comes the Groom, My Friend Irma, The Night of the Grizzly, This Property Is Condemned, The Oscar, Never Too Late, Harlow, What Did You Do in the War Daddy?, Wait Until Dark, Red Garters, Sorrowful Jones.

LIVINGSTONE, PERCY: C.B.E. Pres. Society of Film Distributors, Ltd., pres. Cinema and Television Benevolent Fund.

LLOYD, CHRISTOPHER: Actor. b. Stamford, CT, Oct. 22, 1938. Studied at Neighborhood Playhouse, NY. Starred off-Bdwy. in Kaspar, winning Drama Desk and Obie Awards, 1973. Feature film debut in One Flew Over the Cuckoo's Nest, 1975.

PICTURES: Butch and Sundance: The Early Days, The Onion Field, The Black Marble, The Legend of the Lone Ranger, Mr. Mom, To Be or Not to Be, Star Trek III: The Search for Spock, Adventures of Buckaroo Banzai, Back to the Future, Clue, Who Framed Roger Rabbit?, Track 29, Walk Like a Man, Eight Men Out, The Dream Team, Why Me?

TELEVISION: Taxi (series), Best of the West (series), The Dictator (series), Tales From Hollywood Hills: Pat Hobby—Teamed With Genius.

LLOYD, EMILY: Actress. b. North London, Eng., 1971. Father is a stage actor, mother worked as Harold Pinter's secretary. Father's agent recommended that she audition for screenwriter David Leland's directorial debut Wish You Were Here when she was 15.

PICTURES: Wish You Were Here, Cookie, In Country, Chicago Joe and the Showgirl.

LLOYD, EUAN: Producer. b. Rugby, Warwick, England, Dec. 6, 1923. e. Rugby. Entered m.p. ind. in 1939 as theatre manager, then pub. dir.; dir. of Publ. Rank, 1946; joined Associated British-Pathe, Ltd. in same capacity; 1952 asst. to prod., Warwick Film Prod. Ltd. v.p. Highroad Productions, 1962–64. Rep. Europe Goldwyn's Porgy & Bess 1959.

PICTURES: April in Portugal, Heart of Variety, Invitation to Monte Carlo, The Secret Ways, Genghis Khan, Poppy Is Also a Flower, Murderer's Row, Shalako, Catlow, The Man Called Noon, Paper Tiger, The Wild Geese, The Sea Wolves, Who Dares Wins, Wild Geese II, The Final Option, Centrifuge.

LLOYD, NORMAN: Producer. b. Jersey City, NJ, Nov. 8, 1914. e. NYU, 1932. Acted on Bdwy in: Noah, Liberty Jones, Everywhere I Roam, 1935–44; in various stock companies. Founder with Orson Welles and John Houseman of Mercury Theatre, NY.

PICTURES: *Actor:* Saboteur, Spellbound, The Southerner, A Walk in the Sun, A Letter for Evie, The Unseen, Within These Walls, Green Years, Limelight. Prod. asst. on Arch of Triumph and The Red Pony, 1946, Young Widow, No Minor Vices, The Black Book, Scene of the Crime, Calamity Jane and Sam Bass, Buccaneer's Girl, The Flame and the Arrow, He Ran All the Way, The Light Touch, Audrey Rose, FM, King Cobra, The Nude Bomb, Dead Poets Society. Producer: Up Above the World.

STAGE: The Cocktail Party, The Lady's Not for Burning, Madame Will You Walk, The Golden Apple.

TELEVISION: Assoc. prod. The Alfred Hitchcock Show, 1957 and exec. prod. 1963. *Prod.-Dir.:* The Alfred Hitchcock Hour, The Name of the Game, Hollywood Television Theater, Tales of the Unexpected. *Actor:* St. Elsewhere (series). Movies: *Prod.-Dir.:* The Smugglers, Companions in Nightmare, What's a Nice Girl Like You (prod.), The Bravos (prod.), Amityville: The Evil Escapes.

LOBELL, MICHAEL: Producer. b. New York, NY, May 7, 1941. e. Michigan State U. on athletic baseball scholarship. Worked briefly in garment indust. Formed Lobell/Bergman Prods. with Andrew Bergman.

PICTURES: Dreamer; Windows; So Fine; The Journey of Natty Gann, Chances Are, The Freshman.

LO BIANCO, TONY: Actor. b. New York, NY. Oct. 19, 1936. Performed on N.Y. stage as well as in films and TV. Former artistic dir. Triangle Theatre, NY. Won Obie Award for performance in Yanks 3, Detroit 0, Top of the Seventh. Also acted on stage in The Office, The Rose Tattoo, The View From the Bridge, The Royal Hunt of the Sun.

PICTURES: Valentine, The French Connection, The Honeymoon Killers, The 7-Ups, McGee and the Lady, Separate Ways, F.I.S.T., Bloodbrothers, Blood Ties, City Heat, La Romana. Dir.: Too Scared to Scream.

TELEVISION: The Story of Joseph and Jacob, Hidden Faces, Legend of Black Hand, Lady Blue, Marco Polo, Welcome Home Bobby, Blood Ties, Madigan; A Last Cry for Help; Mr. Inside, Mr. Outside; Marciano; Another Woman's Child; The Last Tenant; Goldenrod; Shadow in the Streets; Eugene O'Neill's A Glory of Ghosts, Police Story: The Freeway Killings, The Ann Jillian Story, Body of Evidence, Hizzoner (Emmy Award), Off Duty, Truck One (pilot). Director: Police Story, Kaz, Cliffhangers.

LOCKE, SONDRA: Actress. b. Shelbyville, TN, May 28, 1947. Film debut in The Heart Is a Lonely Hunter, 1968.

PICTURES: Run, Shadow, Run; The Second Coming of Suzanne, Willard, A Reflection of Fear, The Outlaw—Josey Wales, The Gauntlet, Every Which Way But Loose, Bronco Billy, Any Which Way You Can, Sudden Impact. Debut as director: Ratboy, 1987 (also star), Impulse (dir.).

TELEVISION: Rosie: The Rosemary Clooney Story; Friendships; Secrets and Lies; Amazing Stories.

LOCKHART, JUNE: Actress. b. New York, NY, June 25, 1925. p. actors, Gene and Kathleen Lockhart. Bdwy debut For Love or Money, 1947. On TV in Lassie series.

PICTURES: A Christmas Carol (1938), All This and Heaven Too, Sergeant York, Miss Annie Rooney, Meet Me in St. Louis, Son of Lassie, White Cliffs of Dover, Keep Your Powder Dry, Bury Me Dead, T-Men, It's a Joke, Son, Time Limit, Troll, Rented Lips, The Big Picture.

TELEVISION: Lost in Space, Petticoat Junction, General Hospital, Perfect People, A Whisper Kills.

LOCKWOOD, GARY: Actor. r.n. John Gary Yusolfsky. b. Van Nuys, CA, Feb. 21, 1937. Began in Hollywood as stuntman.

PICTURES: Tall Story, Splendor in the Grass, Wild in the Country, The Magic Sword, It Happened at the World's Fair, Firecreek, 2001: A Space Odyssey, They Came to Rob Las Vegas, Model Shop, The Body, R.P.M., Stand Up and Be Counted, The Wild Pair.

LOCKWOOD, ROGER: Executive. b. Middletown, CT, June 7, 1936. e. Ohio Wesleyan U. Sports writer for Akron Beacon Journal, 1960–62. On executive staff of Lockwood & Gordon Theatres; exec. v.p. SBC Theatres, 1969–73. In 1974 asst. to exec. v.p., General Cinema Corp. In 1975 formed Lockwood/Friedman Theatres, buying-booking and exhibition organization. Pres., Theatre Owners of New England, 1971–72; pres., Young NATO 1965–67; bd. of dir. NATO, 1962–1968. Board of dir. Tone, 1968–present; pres., Jimmy Fund, present; 1979–80, Variety Club of New England, pres. Director, Dana-Farber Cancer Institute, 1983–present.

LOGGIA, ROBERT: Actor. b. New York, NY, Jan. 3, 1930. e. U. of Missouri, B.A. journalism, 1951. Studied with Stella Adler at Actors Studio. Broadway debut, The Man with the Golden Arm, 1955. Film debut, Somebody Up There Likes Me, 1956.

THEATER: Toys in the Attic, The Three Sisters, In the Boom Boom Room, Wedding Band.

PICTURES: The Greatest Story Ever Told, Cop Hater, Cattle King, The Garment Jungle, Che, First Love, Speed Trap, Revenge of the Pink Panther, The Sea Gypsies, The Ninth Configuration, An Officer and a Gentleman, S.O.B., Trail of the Pink Panther, Curse of the Pink Panther, Psycho II, Scarface, Jagged Edge, Prizzi's Honor, Armed and Dangerous, Hot Pursuit, The Believers, That's Life, Over the Top, Big, Oliver & Company (voice), Relentless, S.P.O.O.K.S., White Hot, Triumph of the Spirit, Opportunity Knocks.

TELEVISION: Series: T.H.E. Cat, 1966–67; Emerald Point N.A.S., Mancuso. Play of the Week: Miss Julie; Movies: The Nine Lives of Elfego Baca (1958), No Other Love, Casino, A Woman Called Golda, A Touch of Scandal, Intrigue, Favorite Son, The O'Connors, Dream Breakers.

LOLLOBRIGIDA, GINA: Actress. b. Subiaco, Italy, July 14, 1927. e. Acad. of Fine Arts, Rome. Film debut (Italy) L'aguila nera, 1946.

PICTURES: Pagliacci, The City Defends Itself, The White Line, Fanfan the Tulip, Times Gone By, Beat the Devil, Crossed Swords, The Great Game, Beauties of the Night, Wayward Wife, Bread Love and Dreams, Bread Love and Jealousy, Young Caruso, World's Most Beautiful Woman, Trapeze, Hunchback of Notre Dame, Solomon and Sheba, Never So Few, Go Naked in the World, Come September, Imperial Venus, Woman of Straw, That Splendid November, Hotel Paradisio, Buona Sera, Mrs. Campbell, Bad Man's River, King, Queen, Knave, The Lonely Woman, Bambole, Plucked.

TELEVISION: Deceptions, Falcon Crest (series).

LOM, HERBERT: Actor. r.n. Herbert Charles Angelo Kuchacevich ze Schluderpacheru. b. Prague, 1917. e. Prague U. Stage training London Embassy, Old Vic—Sadlers Wells and Westminster Schools. British film debut (Mein Kampf—My Crimes) (1941); on TV, The Human Jungle Series.

PICTURES: Tomorrow We Live, Secret Mission, Young Mr.

Pitt, Dark Tower, Cage of Gold, Whispering Smith vs. Scotland Yard, Two on the Tiles, Mr. Denning Drives North, Hell Is Sold Out, Gaunt Stranger, Rough Shoot, The Net, The Love Lottery, Star of India, Beautiful Stranger, The Ladykillers, War and Peace Action, Fire Down Below, Hell's Drives, Chase a Crooked Shadow, Passport to Shame, Roots of Heaven, The Big Fisherman, North-West Frontier, I Aim at the Stars, Spartacus, Mysterious Island, Mr. Topaz, The Frightened City, El Cid, Tiara Tahiti, The Phantom of the Opera, Horse Without a Head, A Shot in the Dark, Uncle Tom's Cabin, Return from the Ashes, Gambit, The Assignment, Three Faces of Eve, Villa Rides, Doppelganger, Mr. Jericho, Dorian, Mark of the Devil, Count Dracula, Murders in the Rue Morgue, Dark Places, Death in Persepolis, Return of the Pink Panther, The Pink Panther Strikes Again, Charleston, Revenge of the Pink Panther, The Man with Bogarts' Face, Hopscotch, The Acts of Peter and Paul, The Trail of the Pink Panther, The Curse of the Pink Panther, Memed, My Hawk, Dead Zone, King Solomon's Mines, Whoops Apocalypse, Coast of Skeletons, Master of Dragonard Hill, Going Bananas, Skeleton Coast, Ten Little Indians, River of Death, The Masque of the Red Death, The Crystal Eye.

LOMBARDO, GOFFREDO: Executive. b. Naples, Italy, May 13, 1920. President Titanus Films.
PICTURES: Rocco and His Brothers, Sodom and Gomorrah, The Leopard, Four Days of Naples.

LOMITA, SOLOMON: Executive. b. New York, NY, April 23, 1937. Started industry career with United Artists Corp. as follows: adm., intl. dept., 1962; asst., intl. sales, same year. 1963, asst. intl. print mgr.; 1965, intl., print mgr. In 1973 appt. dir. of film services. 1981, v.p., film services. In 1985 named v.p., post-prod., Orion Pictures; in March, 1989 promoted to sr. v.p.

LONDON, BARRY: Executive. Joined Paramount Pictures 1971 in L.A. branch office as booker; later salesman. 1973, sls. mgr., Kansas City-St. Louis; 1974, branch mgr. Transferred to San Francisco, first as branch mgr.; later as district mgr. 1977, eastern div. mgr. in Washington, DC, 1978–81, western div. mgr. In March, 1981, named v.p., gen. sls. mgr. June, 1983, advanced to sr. v.p., domestic distribution. 1984, named pres., domestic div., for Motion Picture Group of Paramount; 1985, named president, marketing and domestic distribution; 1988, named pres. Motion Picture Group.

LONDON, JERRY: Director. b. Los Angeles, CA, Jan 21, 1937. Apprentice film editor, Desilu Prods., 1955; film ed., Daniel Boone, 1962; staged plays in local theater workshops; editor, assoc. prod., then dir. Hogan's Heroes. Formed Jerry London Prods., 1984.
PICTURES: Rent-a-Cop (feature debut, 1987).
TELEVISION: Series: Mary Tyler Moore Show, Love American Style, The Bob Newhart Show, Marcus Welby, M.D., Kojak, The Six Million Dollar Man, Police Story, Rockford Files. Mini-series: Wheels, Shogun (DGA, best dir., specials award), Chiefs (also sprv. prod.), Ellis Island (also sprv. prod.), If Tomorrow Comes, A Long Way From Home. Movies: Swan Song, Women in White, Evening in Byzantium, Father Figure, The Chicago Story, The Ordeal of Bill Carney (also prod.), The Gift of Life (also prod.), The Scarlet and the Black, Arthur Hailey's Hotel (also prod.), With Intent to Kill (exec. prod.), Manhunt For Claude Dallas, Family Sins, Macgruder and Loud (also prod.), Dadah Is Death (prod., dir.), Kiss Shot (exec. prod., dir.), The Haunting of Sarah (exec. prod., dir.).

LONDON, JULIE: Singer, Actress. r.n. Julie Peck. b. Santa Rosa, CA, Sept. 26, 1926. Launched as actress by agent Sue Carol (wife of Alan Ladd) who arranged screen test, followed by contract for 6 films. As singer has appeared in nightclubs and recorded.
PICTURES: The Red House, The Fat Man, The Great Man, Saddle the Wind, Man of the West, The Third Voice.
TELEVISION: Perry Como Show, Steve Allen Show, Ed Sullivan Show, Emergency (series).

LONDON, MILTON H.: Executive. b. Detroit, MI, Jan. 12, 1916. e. U. of Michigan, B.A., 1937. Wayne U. Law Sch., 1938. U.S. Army 1943–46. Invented Ticograph system of positive admissions control for theatres, 1950; pres. Theatre Control Corp., 1950–62; secy-treas. Co-op. Theas. of Michigan Inc., 1956–63; exec. comm., Council of M.P. Organizations, 1957–66; dir. M.P. Investors, 1960–67; exec. dir. Allied States Assoc. of M.P. Exhib., 1961–66; exec. dir. National Assoc. of Theatre Owners, 1966–69 pres., NATO of Michigan, 1954–74; Mich. State Fire Safety Bd., Chief Barker, Variety Club of Detroit, Tent No. 5. 1975–76; Life Patron and Lifeliner, Variety Clubs International; trustee, Variety Club Charity for Children; chmn., Variety Club Myoelectric Center; dir., Motion Picture Pioneers; advisory comm., Will Rogers Inst.; trustee, Detroit Inst. for Children; pres., Metropolitan Adv. Co.; Intl. ambassador, Variety Clubs Int'l.

LONG, ROBERT A.: Executive. b. McCune, KS, Oct. 31, 1931. e. U. of Kansas, 1957. Mng. partner, K.C., Arthur Andersen & Co., 1970–80; now exec. v.p., Commonwealth Theatres, Inc.
MEMBER: Past. pres., Civic Council of Greater Kansas City; past pres., Chamber of Commerce Greater Kansas City; Heart of America Council of Boy Scouts; United Way; bd. mbr., Rockhurst Coll., U. of Missouri at Kansas City, city trustees; Advisory Council, U. of Kansas, school of business & medicine; bd. trustees, Endowment Assoc. of U. of Kansas. Named Mr. Kansas City, 1981.

LONG, SHELLEY: Actress. b. Ft. Wayne, IN, Aug. 23, 1949. e. Northwestern U.
PICTURES: A Small Circle of Friends, Caveman, Night Shift, Losin' It, Irreconcilable Differences, The Money Pit, Outrageous Fortune, Hello Again, Troup Beverly Hills, The Boyfriend School.
TELEVISION: Cheers (series), The Cracker Factory, Princess and the Cabbie, Promise of Love.

LONGSTREET, STEPHEN: Writer, Painter. b. New York, NY, April 18, 1907; e. Rutgers U.; Parsons Coll.; Rand Sch., London, B.A. Humorist, cartoonist (New Yorker, Collier's, etc.) 1930–37; ed. Free World Theat., radio plays; ed. film critic, Saturday Review of Literature, 1940, U.S. at War, Time 1942–43; writer for screen from 1942. On staff UCLA. Elected pres. Los Angeles Art Assoc. 1970. 1974: appointed Prof. English Dep., U. of Southern California. Modern Writing Course. Writers Guild, Comm. of Public Relations. Film and book critic for Readers' Syndicate since 1970. Professor performing arts dept. U. of Southern California since 1973, where in 1979, presented 12 great silent films, The Art & Entertainment of Silent Films. Rutgers U., lecturer, 1986, on Griffith, Hawks, Hitchcock, Ford, Welles. L.A. Art Assoc. lecture series 1988 The Dreams That Swallowed the World: The Hollywood Scene 1940–88. Art show Movie Faces.
WRITINGS: Decade, The Golden Touch, The Gay Sisters, Last Man Around the World, Chico Goes to the Wars, Pedlocks, Lion at Morning, Promoters, Boy in the Model T, Sometimes I Wonder, Wind at My Back, The Young Men of Paris, The Wilder Shore, War Cries on Horseback, Yoshiwara, Geishas and Courtesans, Canvas Falcons, Men and Planes of World War I, We All Went to Paris. New publications in 1973: Chicago 1860–1919, (show business & society), Divorcing (a novel); The General (novel, 1974), All Star Cast, 1977; The Queen Bees (1979), Our Father's House (1985), Storyville to Harlem (Jazz 1988); Dictionary of Jazz, (1989); Dreams that Swallowed the World (The Movies, 1989).
STAGE: High Button Shoes (book, revived in Jerome Robbins' Broadway, 1989).
PICTURES: The Gay Sisters, Golden Touch, Stallion Road, Jolson Story, Silver River, Helen Morgan Story, First Traveling Saleslady, Untamed Youth, Duel in the Sun, Greatest Show on Earth, Streets of Montmarte, The Crime, Uncle Harry, Rider on a Dead Horse, The Imposter.
TELEVISION: Casey Jones (series), Clipper Ship, Man Called X, m.c. author of The Sea; m.c. Press & Clergy, 1960–63; Viewpoint; series Boy in the Model T, Young Man From Boston, 1967, Blue and the Grey. Appeared on Early Hollywood.

LONSDALE, PAMELA: Producer and Executive Producer for Children's drama, Thames TV for 15 years. Now freelance. Prod. short feature film, Exploits at West Poley (for CFTF), Prod.: News at Twelve (Central TV comedy series). Currently exec. prod. for E.B.U.'s world drama exchange for 2 years. Winner British Acad. Award for Rainbow, 1975.

LOOS, MARY: Writer. b. San Diego, CA, May 6, 1914. e. Stanford U., 1933. Actress m.p.; in public relations field N.Y. 1938; jewelry designer for Paul Flato; author of novel Return in the Vineyard, 1945. secy. Voyager Films, Inc., literary exec. M. J. Frankovich Prod. Novel: The Beggars Are Coming, 1974, Belinda, 1976; The Barstow Legend, 1978; A Pride of Lovers, 1981.
PICTURES: Rose Marie, Maytime, Crusades, Cleopatra, Mr. Belvedere Goes to College, Mother Was a Freshman, Ticket to Tomahawk, When Willie Comes Marching Home, Father Was a Fullback, I'll Get By, Meet Me After the Show, Let's Do It Again, The French Line, Gentlemen Marry Brunettes, Over-Exposed, Woman's World.

LORD, JACK: Actor, Writer, Artist, Director, Producer. b. New York, NY, Dec. 30, 1930. e. NYU. (Chancellor Chase scholarship), B.S., Fine Arts, 1954. Studied at Sanford Meisner Neighborhood Playhouse and with Lee Strasberg at the Actors Studio. Artist, represented in various museums incl. Metropolitan Museum of Art, Museum of Modern Art, Brooklyn Museum, in NY, Bibliotheque National, Paris; British Museum; Fogg Museum, Harvard U. St. Gaudens Plaque for Fine Arts; On Bway in Traveling Lady (Theatre World Award, 1959), Cat on a Hot Tin Roof. Fame Award, new male star, 1963, Named to Cowboy Fall of Fame, 1963. mem. of Directors Guild of America. Recent Awards: St. Gauden's Artist Award, 1948; G. Washington Honor Medal from Freedom Foundation at Valley Forge, 1984; Veterans Admin., Administrator's Award, 1980; Salute to Hospitalized Veterans, Tripler Army Medical Center, 1985; East-West Center Distinguished Service Award, 1981.

Author: Jack Lord's Hawaii. . . A Trip Through the Last Eden, 1971. Pres., Lord and Lady Enterprises, Inc.

PICTURES: The Court Martial of Billy Mitchell, Williamsburg—The Story of a Patriot, Tip On a Dead Jockey, God's Little Acre, Man of the West, The Hangman, True Story of Lyman Stuart, Walk Like a Dragon, Doctor No, Doomsday Flight, Ride to Hangman's Tree, Counterfeit Killer.

TELEVISION: Debut: Series: Man Against Crime, Omnibus Constitution, Stoney Burke (star, 1963), Hawaii Five-O (star, 1968–79), creator of Tramp Ship, McAdoo, Yankee Trader, The Hunter TV series. Guest: Playhouse 90, Goodyear Playhouse, Studio One, U.S. Steel. Have Gun Will Travel (pilot), Untouchables, Naked City, Rawhide, Bonanza, The Americans, Route 66, Gunsmoke, Stagecoach West, Dr. Kildare, Greatest Show on Earth, Combat, Chrysler Theatre, 12 O'Clock High, The Loner, Laredo, The FBI, The Invaders, The Fugitive, The Virginian, Man from U.N.C.L.E., High Chaparral, Ironside. Director: Death with Father, How to Steal a Masterpiece; Honor Is an Unmarked Grave, The Bells Toll at Noon, Top of the World, Why Won't Linda Die, Who Says Cops Don't Cry; episodes of Hawaii Five-O. Creator, director, and exec. producer of M Station: Hawaii (2-hr special for TV), 1979.

LORD, ROSEMARY: Actress, Writer. b. May 16, Taunton, Somerset, England. Now living in Hollywood.

PICTURES: Actress: The Whisperers, The Watchers, Touch of Class, Duchess and the Dirtwater Fox, Frances.

TELEVISION: Monty Python, Sherlock Holmes, Spyder's Web, Days of Our Lives.

LOREN, SOPHIA: Actress. b. Rome, Italy, Sept. 20, 1934. e. Naples. In films since 1950. m. producer Carlo Ponti. Autobiography: Sophia: Living and Loving (with A.E. Hotchner, 1979).

PICTURES: Africa Beneath the Seas, Village of the Bells, Good People's Sunday, Neapolitan Carousel, Day in the District Court, Pilgrim of Love, Aida, Two Nights with Cleopatra, Our Times, Attila, Scourge of God, Too Bad She's Bad, Pride and the Passion, Gold of Naples, Boy on a Dolphin, Scandal in Lorrinto, Miller's Beautiful Wife, Desire Under the Elms, Houseboat, The Black Ordeal, That Kind of Woman, Heller With a Gun, Anatomy of Love, Breath of Scandal, Heller in Pink Tights, Bay of Naples, Two Women (Acad. Award, 1961), El Cid, Boccaccio 70, Il Coltello nello Piaga, French, The Fall of the Roman Empire, The Great Spy Mission, Lady L, Marriage Italian Style, Judith, Arabesque, The Countess from Hong Kong, Happily Ever After, More than a Miracle, Ghosts—Italian Style, Sunflower, The Priest's Wife, Lady Liberty, White Sister, Man of La Mancha, The Voyage, The Verdict, The Cassandra Crossing, A Special Day, Angela, Brass Target, Firepower, Saturday, Sunday and Monday.

TELEVISION: Movies: Brief Encounter, Sophia Loren—Her Own Story; Softly, Softly, Rivals of Sherlock Holmes, Fantasy Island, Aurora, Courage, Mario Puzo's The Fortunate Pilgrim.

LORING, LYNN E.: Executive. b. July 14, 1947. e. Barnard Coll., NY, sociology. Began career as a 6 year old TV soap opera actress, continued acting until joining Aaron Spelling Prods. 1980–85 where she dev. film Mr. Mom. Also prod. TV movie, The Best Little Girl in the World. Joined MGM/UA Communications as a TV programming and prod. exec. 1985; 1989 named pres. MGM/UA Television Productions, Inc., TV development and prod.

LOUIS, JEAN: Designer. b. Paris, France, Oct. 5, 1907. Head designer, Hattie Carnegie, 7 yrs., before accepting post as Chief Designer Columbia Pictures. Later Universal Studios. Free lance in m.p. & TV. Pres. Jean-Louis, Inc.

LOUISE, TINA: Actress. b. New York, NY, Feb. 11. e. Miami U., N.Y. Neighborhood Playhouse, Actors Studio, Bdwy.

STAGE: Two's Company, The Fifth Season, John Murray Anderson's Almanac, Li'l Abner, Fade Out, Fade In.

PICTURES: God's Little Acre, Day of the Outlaw, For Those Who Think Young, The Wrecking Crew, The Good Guys and the Bad Guys, How to Commit Marriage, The Happy Ending, The Stepford Wives, Mean Dog Blues, Dog Day, Hell Riders, Evil in the Night, O.C. and the Stiggs, Dixie Lanes, The Pool.

TELEVISION: Gilligan's Island (series), Rituals (series), Mannix, Ironside, Kung Fu, Police Story, Kojak. Movies: Friendship, Secrets and Lies; Advice to the Lovelorn; The Day the Women Got Even, The Woman Who Cried Murder; SST Death Flight; Look What's Happened to Rosemary's Babies; Nightmare in Badham County.

LOVITZ, JON: Actor, Comedian. b. Tarzana, CA, July 21, 1957. e. U. of California at Irvine. Studied acting at Film Actors Workshop. Took classes at the Groundlings, L.A. comedy improvisation studio, 1982. Performed with Groundling's Sunday Company, before joining main company in Chick Hazzard: Olympic Trials. Developed comedy character of pathological liar here which later performed when became regular member of Saturday Night Live in 1985.

PICTURES: The Last Resort, Ratboy, Brave Little Toaster, Jumpin' Jack Flash, Three Amigos, Big, My Stepmother Is an Alien.

TELEVISION: The Paper Chase. Series: Foley Square, Saturday Night Live.

LOWE, PHILIP L.: Executive. b. Brookline, MA, Apr. 17, 1917. e. Harvard. Army 1943–46. Checker, Loew's 1937–39; treasurer, Theatre Candy Co., 1941–58; Pres., ITT Sheraton Corp., 1969–70; Principal, Philip L. Lowe and Assoc.

LOWE, PHILIP M.: Executive. b. 1944. e. Deerfield Acad., Harvard Coll., cum laude in psychology, 1966; Columbia Business Sch., 1968. Work experience includes major marketing positions at General Foods, Gillette, Gray Advertising, and Estee Lauder Cosmetics before co-founding Cinema Centers Corp. and Theatre Management Services in Boston. Pres. of Lowe Group of Companies (cable television, broadcasting, hotels, real estate and management consulting). Past pres. and chmn. of the bd; National Association of Concessionaires (NAC); past director, National Association of Theater Owners (NATO). Past professor of marketing, Bentley Coll., Waltham, MA.; Contributing Editor; The Movie Business Book, Prentice-Hall, Inc. 1983.

LOWE, ROB: Actor. b. Charlottesville, VA, Mar. 17, 1964. Appeared in Go Go's music video, Turn to You.

PICTURES: The Outsiders (debut, 1983), Class, The Hotel New Hampshire, Oxford Blues, St. Elmo's Fire, About Last Night . . ., Youngblood, Square Dance, Illegally Yours, Masquerade, Bad Influence.

TELEVISION: Series: A New Kind of Family. Movies: Thursday's Child, Home is Where the Heart Is. Specials: A Matter of Time, Schoolboy Father.

LOWRY, DICK: Director. b. Oklahoma City, OK. e. U. of Oklahoma. Commercial photographer before being accepted by AFI.

PICTURES: The Drought (short); Smokey and the Bandit—Part 3.

TELEVISION: Jayne Mansfield Story; Kenny Rogers as the Gambler; The Pigs V. the Freaks; Angel Dusted; Coward of the County; A Few Days in Weasel Creek; Missing Children—A Mother's Story; Living Proof; The Secret Adventures of Tom Sawyer and Huck Finn; Kenny Rogers as the Gambler—the Adventure Continues (also prod.); Wet Gold; The Toughest Man in the World; Murder with Mirrors, American Harvest, Kenny Rogers as The Gambler III (co-exec. prod., dir.); Dream West (mini-series); Case Closed; In the Line of Duty: the FBI Murders, Unconquered (prod., dir.), Howard Beach: Making the Case For Murder.

LOWRY, HUNT: Producer. b. Oklahoma City, OK, Aug. 21, 1954. e. Rollins Coll., & Wake Forest. Abandoned plans to study medicine to enter film-making industry; first job for New World Pictures where he met Jon Davison, with whom was later to co-produce. Next made TV commercials as prod. asst. and then producer. Left to go freelance as commercials producer. 1980, appt. assoc. prod. to Davison on Airplane!

PICTURES: Humanoids from the Deep, Top Secret!, Get Crazy, Baja Oklahoma (exec. prod.), Wildfire (co-prod.), Hard Boiled.

TELEVISION: Rascals and Robbers: The Secret Adventures of Tom Sawyer and Huckleberry Finn.

LOY, MYRNA: Actress. r.n. Myrna Williams; b. Helena MT, Aug. 2, 1905. e. Westlake Sch. for Girls. Appeared in stage presentations, Grauman's Chinese theatre, then Hollywood. Film debut Pretty Ladies, 1925; thereafter in more than 100 pictures, variously starred, co-starred & featured. Voted one of the ten best Money-Making Stars in Motion Picture Herald-Fame Poll, 1937, 38. Organizer Hollywood Film com. U.S. Natl Comm. for UNESCO, 1948; mem. eomm, 1950–54; asst. head welfare activities ARC, NY 1941–45; mem. Amer. Assn. UN, Natl Comm. Against Discrimination in Housing. Recipient Kennedy Center Honor, 1988.

STAGE: Marriage-Go-Round, There Must Be a Pony, Good Housekeeping, Barefoot in the Park, Dear Love, The Women, Don Juan in Hell, Relatively Speaking.

PICTURES: The Jazz Singer, The Desert Song, Last of the Duanes, Body and Soul, A Connecticut Yankee, Hush Money, Transatlantic, Arrowsmith, Vanity Fair, Love Me Tonight, The Mask of Fu Manchu, Animal Kingdom, Topaze, The Barbarian, The Prizefighter and the Lady, When Ladies Meet, Penthouse, Night Flight, Men in White, Manhattan Melodrama, The Thin Man, Evelyn Prentice, Wife Versus Secretary, The Great Ziegfeld, To Harry With Love, Libeled Lady, After the Thin Man, Test Pilot, The Rains Came, Another Thin Man, Third Finger, Left Hand; Shadow of the Thin Man, The Thin Man Goes Home, Best Years of Our Lives, The Bachelor and the Bobby Soxer, The Song of the Thin Man, Mr. Blandings Builds His Dream House, Red Pony, If This Be Sin, Cheaper by the Dozen, My Daughter Joy, Belles on Their Toes, Ambassador's Daughter, Lonely Hearts, From the Terrace, Midnight Lace, The April Fools, Airport 1975, The End, Just Tell Me What You Want.

TELEVISION: Meet Me in St. Louis, Minerva, George

Gobel, Perry Como, Happy Birthday—June Allyson Show, Family Affair, The Virginians, Movies: Death Takes a Holiday (1970), Do Not Spindle or Mutilate, The Couple Takes a Wife, Ironside, The Elevator, It Happened at Lakewood Manor, Summer Solstice.

LUBCKE, HARRY R.: Registered Patent Agent. b. Alameda, CA, Aug. 25, 1905. e. U. of California, B.S., 1929. Holds numerous U.S. and foreign patents on television. In 1931: station W6XAO went on air on what is now television Channel No. 2 to become first station of kind in nation. New Mt. Lee studios built at cost of $250,000 in 1941, housing then largest TV stage 100x60x30 ft. Pioneered present television standard of 525 line (Aug., 1940). In 1942, television programs to promote war bond sale. 1942–46 dir. war research for which certificates of commendation were received from Army & Navy.
MEMBER: Pres., Acad. TV Arts & Sciences, 1949. Dir. TV Don Lee Broadcasting System to Dec. 31, 1950; cons. TV engineer, 1951; registered patent agent, 1952. Life Fellow, 1951, IEEE, AAAS, SMPTE, 1967. Board of Governors, Patent Law Association of Los Angeles, 1974. Life Member National Academy of Television Arts & Sciences, member engineering Emmy Awards Committee. Member Blue Ribbon panel Emmy Awards Committee; 1978; Diamond Circle, of Pacific Pioneer Broadcasters, 1980; American Bar Assn., 1982.

LUBIN, ARTHUR: Director. b. Los Angeles, CA. Since 1935 has directed numerous pictures, including John Wayne's first four films at Universal: Hell on Ice, California Straight Ahead, Adventure's End, I Covered the War.
PICTURES: Buck Privates in the Navy, Hold That Ghost, Keep 'em Flying, Ride 'em Cowboy, Eagle Squadron, Phantom of the Opera, White Savage, Ali Baba and the Forty Thieves, Delightfully Dangerous, Francis, Queen for a Day, Francis Goes to the Races, Rhubarb, Francis Covers the Big Town, Francis Goes to West Point, It Grows on Trees, South Sea Woman, Star of India, Lady Godiva, Francis in the Navy, Footsteps in the Fog, First Traveling Saleslady, Escapade in Japan, The Thief of Baghdad, The Incredible Mr. Limpett, Rain for a Dusty Summer, Night in Paradise, The Spider Woman Strikes Back, New Orleans, Impact, Queen for a Day, Star of India, Hold On!
TELEVISION: Maverick (Henry Fonda episodes), 77 Sunset Strip, Bonanza, the entire Mister Ed series (prod.-dir.).

LUCAS, GEORGE: Producer, Director, Writer. b. Modesto, CA, 1944. e. U. of Southern California, cinema. Made short film called THX-1138 and won National Student Film Festival Grand Prize, 1967. Signed contract with WB. Ass't. to Francis Ford Coppola on The Rain People, during which Lucas made 2-hr. documentary on filming of that feature.
PICTURES: THX-1138 (dir., co-s.p.), American Graffiti (dir., co-s.p.), Star Wars (dir., s.p.); More American Graffiti (exec. prod.); The Empire Strikes Back (exec. prod.); Raiders of the Lost Ark (co-exec. prod., co-story). Return of the Jedi (exec. prod., co-s.p., story); Indiana Jones and the Temple of Doom (exec. prod., story); Labyrinth (exec. prod.); Howard the Duck (exec. prod.); Willow (exec. prod., story); Tucker: The Man and His Dream (exec. prod.), The Land Before Time (co-exec. prod.); Indiana Jones and the Last Crusade (co-exec. prod., co-story).
TELEVISION: The Ewok Adventure (exec. prod.); Ewoks: the Battle for Endor (exec. prod.).

LUCCHESI, GARY: Executive. b. San Francisco, CA, 1955. Entered industry as a trainee with the William Morris Agency, 1977. Joined Tri-Star, 1983, as vice pres. of production, became sr. vice pres., 1985. Joined Paramount Pictures as exec. vice pres., April 1987; appointed head of motion picture production division, Dec. 1987.

LUCKINBILL, LAURENCE: Actor. b. Fort Smith, AZ, Nov. 21, 1934. m. actress Lucie Arnaz. e. U. of Arizona, Catholic U. of America. On Bdwy. in A Man for All Seasons, Arms and the Man, The Boys in the Band, Alpha Beta, The Shadow Box.
PICTURES: The Boys in the Band, Such Good Friends, The Money, The Promise, Not for Publication, Cocktail, Messenger of Death, Star Trek V: The Final Frontier.
TELEVISION: Movies: The Delphi Bureau, Death Sentence, Panic on the 5:22, Winner Take All, The Lindbergh Kidnapping Case, Ike, Lyndon Johnson (one-man show), Voices and Visions (narrator), To Heal a Nation.

LUDDY, TOM: Producer. e. U. of California at Berkeley where he operated student film societies and rep. cinemas. Entered industry via Brandon Films. 1972, prog. dir. and curator of Pacific Film Archives. 1979, joined Zoetrope Studios as dir. of special projects where dev. and supervised revival of Gance's Napoleon and Our Hitler—A Film From Germany. Coordinated Koyaanisqatsi, Every Man For Himself, Passion. A founder, Telluride Film Fest. Served on selection comm., N.Y. and San Francisco Film Fest.
PICTURES: Mishima (co-prod.); Tough Guys Don't Dance (co-exec. prod.); Barfly, King Lear (assoc. prod.), Manifesto (exec. prod.), Wait Until Spring Bandini.

LUDWIG, IRVING H.: Executive. b. Nov. 3. Rivoli Theatre, N.Y., mgr., theatre oper., Rugoff and Becker, 1938–39; opened first modern art type theatre, Greenwich Village, 1940. With Walt Disney Prod. in charge of theatre oper. on Fantasia, 1940–41; buyer-booker, Rugoff and Becker, 1942–45; film sales admin., Walt Disney Prod. home office, 1945–53; v.p. and domestic sales mgr., Buena Vista Dist. Co., 1953; pres. gen. sales mgr., 1959–80.
MEMBER: Bd. of dir., Will Rogers Memorial Fund, Foundation of M.P. Pioneers; M.P. Bookers of NY; Academy of M.P. Arts & Sciences.

LUEDTKE, KURT: Writer. b. Grand Rapids, MI, Sept. 29, 1938. e. Brown U., B.A., 1961. Reporter Grand Rapids Press 1961—62. Miami Herald, 1963–65; Detroit Free Press (reporter, asst. photography dir., asst. mgr. ed., asst. exec. ed., exec. ed. 1965–78.).
PICTURES: Absence of Malice, Out of Africa (Acad. Award, 1985), Walls.

LUFKIN, DAN W.: Executive. Chairman of Exec. Comm., Columbia Pictures Industries (appt. July, 1978). Co-founder of Donaldson, Lufkin & Jenrette Securities Corp., investment banking and brokerage firm. Served as first commissioner of Dept. of Environmental Protection for state of Connecticut. Joined Columbia board in November, 1977.

LUKE, KEYE: Actor, Artist. b. Canton, China, 1904. e. Franklin H.S., Seattle. Formerly artist for Fox West Coast Theats. & RKO Studios; also technical advisor on Chinese films. Screen debut as actor in Painted Veil, 1935.
STAGE: Flower Drum Song (3 yr).
PICTURES: The Great McGinty, Charlie Chan series, Oil for the Lamps of China, King of Burlesque, The Good Earth, International Settlement, Sued for Libel, Disputed Passage, Dragon Seed, Three Men in White, Between Two Women, First Yank in Tokyo, Tokyo Rose, Sleep My Love, Hell's Half Acre, World for Ransom, Bamboo Prison, Love Is a Many Splendored Thing, 80 Days Around the World, Their Greatest Glory, Battle Hell, Fair Winds to Java, Nobody's Perfect, Project X, The Chairman, The Hawaiians, Noon Sunday, Won Ton Ton, Amsterdam Kill, Just You and Me, Kid, They Call Me Bruce, Gremlins, A Fine Mess, Dead Heat, The Mighty Quinn.
TELEVISION: Gunsmoke, Danger, December Bride, Crusader, Wireservice, Crossroads, Soldiers of Fortune, My Little Margie, Annie Oakley, Ray Milland Show, Medic, Citizen Chang, Climax, Jerry Lewis, Trackdown, Perry Mason Show, The Littlest Hobo, This Is the Life, Smothers Bros., I Spy, FBI, Wackiest Ship in Army, Mickey Rooney Show, Johnny Quest, Kentucky Jones, Never Too Young, Bob Hope Chrysler Show, Family Affair, Big Valley, Dragnet, It Takes a Thief, Star-Trek, Adventures of Huck Finn, The Outsider, Scooby Doo, Paris 7000, Johnny Carson Show, Marcus Welby, M.D., Adam 12, Hawaii 5-O, Dinah Shore Show, The Lucy Show, Anna and the King of Siam (series), Kung Fu (series), Amazing Chan and Chan Clan, Follow The Sun, Target, The Corrupters, Fair Exchange, Cannon, Cat Creature, Love American Style, Judgment—Trial of Yamashita, Judge Dee, Khan, Harry O, M*A*S*H, Quincy, How the West Was Won, Meeting of Minds, Vegas, Battle of the Planets, The Yee Family, Might Man and Yukk, Rickety Racket, Tang Face, Charlie's Angels, Reach for the Sun, Fly Away Home, Brothers, Adventures of Goldie Gold, Spider Man, Unit Four, Remington Steele, Magnum P.I., Falcon Crest, Voyagers, The A-Team, Mike Hammer, Cocaine and Blue Eyes, Miami Vice, Street Hawk, Trapper John, Blade in Hong Kong, Mr. T, Night Court, T. J. Hooker, Crazy Like a Fox, Kung Fu, Golden Girls, Down to Earth, General Hospital, Sidekicks, Downtown, Friday the 13th, MacGyver, The Judge, 9 to 5, Beauty and the Beast, Family Medical Center, Hollywood Chronicles.

LUKE, PETER: Playwright, Director. b. England, Aug. 12, 1919. Author of plays for TV: Small Fish Are Sweet, 1958; Pigs Ear with Flowers, 1960; Roll on Bloomin' Death, 1961; A Man on Her Back (with William Sansom), 1965; Devil a Monk Won't Be, 1966. wrote and directed films for BBC-TV: Anach 'Cuan (about the late Sean O Riada) 1967; Black Sound—Deep Song (about Federico Garcia Lorca) 1968; Author of Stage play, Hadrian VII, first produced at Birmingham Rep in 1967 and has been staged around the world. Stage Play, Bloomsbury. Author of autobiography, Sisyphus & Reilly, publ., 1972, Prod. Phoenix Theatre 1974.

LUMET, SIDNEY: Director. b. Philadelphia, PA, June 15, 1924. e. Professional Children's Sch.; Columbia U. Child actor in plays: Dead End, George Washington Slept Here, My Heart's in the Highlands. U.S. Armed Forces, W.W.II, 1942–46; dir. summer stock, 1947–49; taught acting, H.S. of Prof. Arts. Assoc. dir. CBS, 1950, dir. 1951.
PICTURES: 12 Angry Men, Stage Struck, That Kind of Woman, The Fugitive Kind, A View From the Bridge, A Long Day's Journey into Night, Fail Safe, The Pawnbroker, The Hill,

The Group, The Deadly Affair (also prod.), Bye Bye Braverman, The Sea Gull (also prod.), King: A Filmed Record. . .Montgomery to Memphis (prod., dir.), The Appointment, Last of the Mobile Hot-Shots, The Anderson Tapes, Child's Play, The Offence, Lovin' Molly, Serpico, Murder on the Orient Express, Dog Day Afternoon, Network, Equus, The Wiz, Just Tell Me What You Want (also co-prod.), Prince of the City (also co-s.p.), Deathtrap, The Verdict, Daniel (also co-exec. prod.), Garbo Talks, Power, The Morning After, Running on Empty, Family Business, Q & A. (dir., s.p.).

TELEVISION: Mama, Danger, You Are There, Omnibus, Best of Broadway, Alcoa, Goodyear Playhouse, Kraft Television Theatre (Mooney's Kid Don't Cry, The Last of My Gold Watches, This Property is Condemned), Playhouse 90, Play of the Week (The Dybbuk, Rashomon, The Iceman Cometh—Emmy), Specials: The Sacco and Vanzetti Story, John Brown's Raid, Cry Vengeance.

LUNDGREN, DOLPH: Actor. b. Stockholm, Sweden, 1959. e. Washington State U., won Fulbright to Massachusetts Inst. of Technology, Royal Inst. of Technology, Stockholm, M.A. Was doorman at Limelight disco in NY while studying acting. Kickboxing champion. Made workout video, Maximum Potential.

PICTURES: A View to a Kill, Rocky IV, Masters of the Universe, Red Scorpion, The Punisher, Dark Angel.

LUPINO, IDA: Actress, Director. b. London, England, Feb. 4, 1918. e. Royal Acad. of Dramatic Art, London. Daughter of Stanley Lupino, English stage and screen comedian. Brit. m.p. debut in Her First Affair, 1932; in U.S. m.p. 1934; ent. independent prod., becoming one of the first major women director-screenwriters beginning with Not Wanted (also writer, prod.). Also maintained acting career at same time.

PICTURES: Money for Speed, High Finance, The Ghost Camera, I Lived with You, Prince of Arcadia, Search for Beauty, Come on Marines, Peter Ibbetson, Anything Goes, Yours for the Asking, The Gay Desperado, Sea Devils, Let's Get Married, Artists and Models, The Adventures of Sherlock Holmes, The Light That Failed, High Sierra, Ladies in Retirement, Moontide, The Hard Way, Devotion, Man I Love, Escape Me Never, Deep Valley, Road House, Lust for Gold, Not Wanted, Never Fear (dir.), Outrage (also dir., s.p.), Hard Fast & Beautiful (dir.), On Dangerous Ground, Beware My Lovely, The Hitch-Hiker (dir., s.p.), Jennifer (dir., s.p.), The Bigamist (dir.), Private Hell 36 (s.p.), Women's Prison, Big Knife, While the City Sleeps, Trouble With Angels (dir.), Junior Bonner, The Devil's Rain, The Food of the Gods.

TELEVISION: Mr. Adams and Eve (series), No. 5 Checked Out, The Trial of Mary Surrat, Honey West, Virginian, I Love a Mystery, Sam Benedict, Untouchables, G. E. Theater, Have Gun Will Travel, Thriller, Mr. Novak, Hong Kong, The Rogues, Chrysler Theatre, Kraft Theatre, Gilligan's Island, The Ghost and Mrs. Muir, The Bill Cosby Show, To Catch a Thief, Mod Squad, Family Affair.

LURASCHI, LUIGI G.: Exec. b. London, Jan 7, 1906. e. U. of Zurich. Long Island Studio, Paramount, 1929; home officer mgr. For. dept. hd, For. & dom. Censorship; Hollywood to 1960. Asst. Prod., Dino De Laurentiis Prod. 1960–65; asst. to pres. for prod. activities, Paramount, 1965. 1967 continental prod. exec. Paramount-Rome. Now v.p., intl.

LYDON, JAMES: Actor. b. Harrington Park, NJ, May 30, 1923; e. St. Johns Mil. Sch. On N.Y. stage in Prologue to Glory, Sing Out the News. On screen 1939, Back Door to Heaven.

PICTURES: Thoroughbreds, Naval Academy, Henry Aldrich series, Twice Blessed, Life With Father, Out of the Storm, Joan of Arc, Miss Mink of 1949, Tucson, Gasoline Alley, Island in the Sky, The Desperado, Battle Stations, My Blood Runs Cold (assoc. prod.), Brainstorm, An American Dream, A Covenant With Death, First to Fight, The Cool Ones, Chubasco, Countdown, Assignment to Kill, The Learning Tree, Scandalous John, Vigilante Force.

TELEVISION: Frontier Circus (assoc. prod.), Wagon Train, Alfred Hitchcock Hour, McHale's Navy, 77 Sunset Strip, Mr. Roberts. Series: So This Is Hollywood, The First Hundred Years, Love That Jill.

LYLES, A. C.: Producer. b. Jacksonville, FL. May 17, 1918. e. Andrew Jackson H.S. Paramount Publix's Florida Theatre, 1928; interviewed Hollywood celebrities, Jacksonville Journal, 1932; mail boy, Paramount Studios, Hollywood, 1937; publicity dept., 1938; hd. of adv., publ. dept., Pine-Thomas unit at Paramount, 1940; assoc. prod., The Mountain; prod., Short Cut to Hell; assoc. prod., Rawhide (TV series). President, A. C. Lyles Productions, Inc. (Paramount Pictures).

PICTURES: Raymie, The Young and the Brave, Law of the Lawless, Stage to Thunder Rock, Young Fury, Black Spurs, Hostile Guns, Arizona Bushwackers, Town Tamer, Apache Uprising, Johnny Reno, Waco, Red Tomahawk, Fort Utah, Buckskin, Rogue's Gallery, Night of the Lepus, The Last Day, Flight to Holocaust.

TELEVISION: A Christmas for Boomer, Here's Boomer (series), Dear Mr. President, Conversations With the Presidents.

LYNCH, DAVID: Director, Writer. b. Missoula, Montana, Jan. 20, 1946. e. Pennsylvania Acad. of Fine Arts, where received an independent filmmaker grant from America Film Institute. Made 16mm film, The Grandmother. Accepted by Center for Advanced Film Studies in Los Angeles, 1970. Wrote and directed Eraserhead (with partial AFI financing) which became cult movie.

PICTURES: Eraserhead (dir., s.p.), The Elephant Man, Dune, Blue Velvet (s.p., dir.), Zelly and Me (actor only), Wild of Heart (dir., s.p.).

TELEVISION: Northwest Passage (dir., exec. prod., s.p.).

LYNCH, PAUL M.: Director. b. Nov. 6, 1946.

PICTURES: Hard Part Begins; Blood and Guts; Prom Night; Hummungus; Cross Country; Flying, Blindside.

TELEVISION: Series: Voyagers, Blacke's Magic, Murder She Wrote, Twilight Zone (1987), Moonlighting, Movies: Cameo By Night, Going to the Chapel, She Knows Too Much.

LYNCH, RICHARD: Actor. b. Feb. 12, 1942. Made Bdwy. debut in The Devils, both on and off Bdwy. Also in Live Like Pigs, The Orphan, The Basic Training of Pavlo Hummel, The Lady From the Sea, Arthuro-U, Lion in Winter. Film debut in Scarecrow (1973).

PICTURES: The Premonition, Steel, The Formula, The 7-Ups, The Sword and the Sorcerer, Invasion U.S.A., The Delta Fox, Savage Dawn, Cut and Run, Night Force, Little Nikita, Bad Dreams, Melanie Rose, Spirit, Aftershock, High Stakes, Return to Justice, One Man Force.

TELEVISION: Vampire, Alcatraz—The Whole Shocking Story, The Last Ninja, Sizzle, Good Against Evil.

LYNDON, VICTOR: Producer, Writer. b. London. Ent. m.p. ind. as asst. dir., Gainsborough Pictures, 1946–56; prod. mgr., 26 feature pictures; since 1957 prod., assoc. prod., pictures for Columbia, United Artists, M-G-M, Paramount, British Lion. 1984: novel, Bermuda Blue.

PICTURES: as prod. mgr. The African Queen, Albert R.N., The Admirable Crichton, As assoc. prod., Dr. Strangelove, Darling, 2001 A Space Odyssey. As prod., Spare The Rod, Station Six—Sahara, The Optimists.

LYNE, ADRIAN: Director.

PICTURES: Foxes; Flashdance; 9½ Weeks; Fatal Attraction; Jacob's Ladder.

LYNLEY, CAROL: Actress. b. New York, NY, Feb. 13, 1942.

PICTURES: The Light in the Forest, Holiday for Lovers, Blue Denim, Return to Peyton Place, The Last Sunset, The Stripper, The Cardinal, The Pleasure Seekers, Bunny Lake Is Missing, The Maltese Bippy, Norwood, The Poseidon Adventure, Harlow, The Cat and the Canary, The Shape of Things to Come, Dark Tower, Blackout.

TELEVISION: Movies: Shadow on the Land, The Smugglers, The Immortal, Weekend of Terror, The Cable Car Murder, The Night Stalker, The Elevator, Death Stalk, Willow B, Women in Prison, Flood, Fantasy Island, Having Babies II, Cops and Robin, The Beasts Are on the Streets.

LYNN, ANN: Actress. b. London, England, 1934. Ent. films and TV, 1958.

PICTURES: Naked Fury, Piccadilly Third Stop, The Wind of Change, Strongroom, Flame in the Streets, Black Torment, Four in the Morning, Baby Love, Hitler—The Last Days.

TELEVISION: After The Show, All Summer Long, Trump Card, Man at the Top, The Expert, Hine, The Intruders, Too Far, King Lear, The Zoo Gang. Movies: The Uncle, Morning Tide, Shot In the Dark, Estuary, Who Pays the Ferryman, The Professionals, Zeticula, Westway. The Perfect House, Minder, To the Sound of Guns, Crown Court, Just Good Friends, Starting Out, Paradise Park. Series: The Cheaters, The Other Side of the Underneath.

LYNN, JEFFREY: Actor. r.n. Ragnar Godfrey Lind. b. Auburn, MA, Feb. 16, 1909: e. Bates Coll. m.p. debut in 1938.

PICTURES: Four Daughters, Yes My Darling Daughter, Daughters Courageous, Espionage Agent, Roaring Twenties, Four Wives, Child Is Born, Fighting 69th, It all Came True, All This and Heaven, Too; My Love Came Back, Four Mothers, Million Dollar Baby, Law of the Tropics, Body Disappears, For the Love of Mary, Black Bart, Letter to Three Wives, Strange Bargain, Home Town Story, Up Front, Captain China, Lost Lagoon, Butterfield 8, Tony Rome.

BROADWAY: (Revival) Dinner at Eight.

LYON, EARLE: Producer, Executive. b. Waterloo, IA, April 9, 1923. e. UCLA. Entered m.p. industry 1947. Independent prod. 1954–55 and 1958–59; 20th Century-Fox prod., 1956–57; at Columbia, 1959–60; Universal, 1960–63; developed new TV projects with Bob Banner Assoc., 1963; v.p. and gen. mgr. United Pictures Corp.

PICTURES: Silent Raiders, The Lonesome Trail, The Silver Star, Stagecoach Fury, The Quiet Gun, The Rawhide Trail, The Rebel Set, The Destructors, Cyborg 2087, Dimension 5, Destination Inner Space, Haunting at Castle Montego, The Ten Billion Dollar Caper, Panic in the City. TV: Tales of Wells Fargo.

LYON, FRANCIS D. "PETE": Director. b. Bowbells, ND, July 29, 1905. e. Hollywood H.S., UCLA. WWII: writer, prod., dir., OWI; assoc. with training, exploitation and information films. Maj. U.S. Army Signal Corps.
PICTURES: *As film editor:* Shape of Things to Come (parts), Knight Without Armour, Rembrandt, Intermezzo, Adam Had Four Sons, The Great Profile, Four Sons, Daytime Wife, Body and Soul (Acad. Award), He Ran All the Way. *As director:* Crazylegs, The Bob Mathias Story (Christopher Award), Walt Disney's The Great Locomotive Chase, Cult of the Cobra, The Oklahoman, Gunsight Ridge, Bailout at 43,000, Escort West, parts of Cinerama South Seas Adventure, The Young and the Brave, Destination Inner Space, The Destructors, The Money Jungle, The Girl Who Knew Too Much. *Producer:* Tiger by the Tail.
TELEVISION: Laramie, Perry Mason, Zane Grey Theatre, Bus Stop, M. Squad, Wells Fargo, Kraft Suspense Theatre, Death Valley Days, Follow the Sun, etc.

LYON, SUE: Actress. b. Davenport, IA, July 10, 1946. e. Hollywood Prof. Sch.
PICTURES: Lolita, Seven Women, Night of the Iguana, The Flim Flam Man, Evel Knievel, Crash, End of the World, Astral Factor.

LYONS, STUART: Producer. b. Manchester, England, Dec. 27, 1928. e. Manchester U. Ent. m.p. ind. 1955. Asst. dir. TV series 1955–56. Casting dir. Associated British, 1956/60. Freelance cast. dir., 1960/63. Joined 20th Century-Fox Productions as cast. dir., 1963. Appt. director 20th Century-Fox Productions Ltd., 1967, man. dir. 1968. 1971: left Fox on closure Europe prod. Joined Hemdale Group as head of production, May, 1972. Left Hemdale Aug. 1973 to resume indep. prod.
PICTURES: As casting director: Over thirty films including Those Magnificent Men in Their Flying Machines, Cleopatra, The Long Ships, Guns at Batasi, High Wind in Jamaica, Rapture, The Blue Max. As indep. producer: The Slipper and the Rose, Meetings with Remarkable Men, Danses Sacrees, Turnaround. As prod. consultant: Eleni.

M

MAC ARTHUR JAMES: Actor. b. Los Angeles, CA, Dec. 8, 1937. e. Harvard. p. Helen Hayes, Charles MacArthur. Stage debut, summer stock; The Corn Is Green, 1945; Life with Father, 1953.
PICTURES: The Young Stranger, The Light in the Forest, The Third Man on the Mountain, Kidnapped, Swiss Family Robinson, The Interns, Spencer's Mountain, The Love-Ins, Cry of Battle, Angry Breed.
TELEVISION: Strike a Blow, Hawaii Five-0 (series).

MACCHIO, RALPH: Actor. b. Long Island, NY, Nov. 4, 1962. Started with TV commercials; first theatrical film role in Up the Academy (1980). On Broadway in Cuba and His Teddy Bear, 1986.
PICTURES: Up the Academy, The Karate Kid, Teachers, Crossroads, The Karate Kid: Part II, Distant Thunder, The Karate Kid Part III.
TELEVISION: Eight is Enough (series, 1980–81); Movies: Journey to Survival, Dangerous Company, The Three Wishes of Billy Grier.

MAC CORKINDALE, SIMON: Actor, Producer. b. England, Feb. 2, 1952. m. actress Susan George. On stage in Dark Lady of the Sonnets, Pygmalion, French Without Tears, etc.
PICTURES: Death on the Nile, Riddle of the Sands, Quatermass Conclusion, Caboblanco, The Sword and the Sorcerer, Jaws 3-D, Sincerely Violet, Stealing Heaven (prod.), That Summer of White Roses (prod., co-s.p.).
TELEVISION: I Claudius, Romeo and Juliet, Jesus of Nazareth, Manimal, Twist of Fate, Obsessive Love, Falcon Crest (series). Mini-series: Pursuit.

MAC DONALD, PHILIP: Writer. b. Scotland; e. St. Paul's Sch. London. Novelist, playwright. Began screen career 1933.
PICTURES: Sahara, Action in Arabia, The Body Snatcher, Strangers in the Night, Dangerous Intruder, Man Who Cheated Himself, Circle of Danger, Mask of the Avenger, Ring of Fear, Tobor the Great.

MAC GRAW, ALI: Actress. b. Pound Ridge, NY, Apr. 1, 1938. e. Wellesley Coll. Editorial asst. Harper's Bazaar Mag.; asst. to photographer Melvin Sokolsky. Was top fashion model.
PICTURES: Lovely Way to Die (debut, 1968). Goodbye Columbus, Love Story, The Getaway, Convoy Players, Just Tell Me What You Want.
TELEVISION: The Winds of War, China Rose, Falcon Crest (series).

MACKERRAS, SIR (ALAN) CHARLES (MACLAURIN): Kt 1979; CBE 1974; Chief Conductor, Sydney Symphony Orchestra, Australian Broadcasting Commission, from 1982–85; frequent guest conductor, Vienna State Opera, Geneva and Zurich Opera, Royal Opera House Covent Garden, English National Opera, San Francisco Opera; b. Nov. 17, 1925; s. of late Alan Patrick and Catherine Mackerras, Sydney, Australia; m. 1947, Helena Judith (Née Wilkins); e. Sydney Grammar Sch. Principal oboist, Sydney Symphony Orchestra, 1943–46; staff conductor, Sadler's Wells Opera, 1949–53; principal conductor BBC Concert Orchestra, 1954–56; freelance conductor with most British and many continental orchestras, concert tours U.S.S.R., S. Africa, N. America, 1957–66; conductor, Hamburg State Opera, 1966–69; musical dir., Sadler's Wells Opera, later ENO, 1970–77; chief guest conductor, BBC SO, 1976–79; frequent radio and TV broadcasts; many commercial recordings, notably Handel series for DGG and Janáček operas for Decca; appearances at many intl. festivals and opera houses. Evening Standard Award for Opera, 1977; Janáček Medal, 1978; Gramophone Record of the Year Award, 1978, 1980 and 1983. Grammy Award for best opera recording 1981 The House of the Dead by Janáček. Prix Fondation Jacques Ibert and the Stereo Review's Records of the Year Award 1983 and 1985 for Cunning Little Vixen by Janáček Publications: ballet arrangements of Pineapple Poll and of Lady and the Fool; articles in Opera Magazine, Music and Musicians and other musical jls. Musical dir., Welsh National Opera, from 1987.

MAC LACHLAN, KYLE: Actor. b. 1960. Acted in high school and college, then in summer stock. Cast as lead in Dune by director David Lynch in a nationwide search.
PICTURES: The Hidden, Dune, Blue Velvet, The Boyfriend School.

MAC LAINE, SHIRLEY: Actress. b. Richmond, VA, April 24, 1934. Sister of actor-prod. Warren Beatty. e. Washington and Lee H.S., Arlington, VA. Dancer, singer; signed by Hal Wallis; film debut in Trouble with Harry (1955). Producer of film documentary on China, The Other Half of The Sky. Star of video: Relaxing Within.
PICTURES: Artists and Models, Around the World in 80 Days, Hot Spell, The Matchmaker, The Sheepman, Some Came Running, Ask Any Girl, Career, Can-Can, The Apartment, All in a Night's Work, Two Loves, My Geisha, The Children's Hour, Two for the Seesaw, Irma La Duce, What A Way To Go, John Goldfarb Please Come Home, The Yellow Rolls Royce, Gambit, Woman Times Seven, The Bliss of Mrs. Blossom, Sweet Charity, Two Mules for Sister Sara, Desperate Characters, The Possession of Joel Delaney, The Turning Point, Being There, Loving Couples, Change of Seasons, Terms of Endearment (Acad. Award, 1983), Cannonball Run II, Madame Sousatzka, Steel Magnolias, Waiting for the Light, Postcards From the Edge.
TELEVISION: Shirley's World, Specials. Mini-Series: Out on a Limb (also co-s.p.).
AUTHOR: Don't Fall off the Mountain, You Can Get There from Here, Out on a Limb, Dancing in the Light, It's All In the Playing. Editor: McGovern: The Man and His Beliefs (1972), Going Within.

MACLEOD, GAVIN: Actor. b. Mt. Kisco, NY, Feb. 28, 1931. e. Ithaca Coll.
PICTURES: I Want to Live, Compulsion, Operation Petticoat, McHale's Navy, The Sand Pebbles, Deathwatch, The Party, Kelly's Heroes.
TELEVISION: Hogan's Heroes (series), Mary Tyler Moore Show, The Love Boat. Movies: The Intruders, Only with Married Men, Ransom for Alice, Murder Can Hurt You, Scruples, Student Exchange, The Love Boat: The Valentine Voyage.

MAC MAHON, ALINE: Actress. b. McKeesport, PA, May 3, 1899. e. Erasmus Hall, Barnard Coll. stage experience; Once in a Lifetime, Candida, Yurma (Lincoln Center). Screen debut 1931 in Five Star Final.
PICTURES: The Mouthpiece, One Way Passage (1931), Life Begins, Once in a Lifetime, Gold Diggers of 1933, Heroes For Sale, World Changes, Babbitt, Side Streets, Kind Lady, I Live My Life, Ah Wilderness, When You're in Love, Back Door to Heaven, Out of the Fog, The Lady Is Willing, Dragon Seed, Guest in the House, Mighty McGurk, The Search, Roseanna McCoy, Flame and the Arrow, Eddie Cantor Story, Man From Laramie, Cimarron, I Could Go On Singing, All the Way Home.

MAC MURRAY, FRED: Actor. b. Kankakee, IL, Aug. 30, 1908. e. Carroll Coll., WI. Sang and played in orchestra to earn tuition. To Hollywood with band; worked as screen extra; to N.Y. with comedy stage band, then joined Three's a Crowd revue; vaudeville circuits, nightclubs. Film debut, Girls Gone Wild (1929).
PICTURES: Friends of Mr. Sweeney, Grand Old Girl, Car 99, Gilded Lily, Alice Adams, Hands Across the Table, Bride Comes Home, Trail of the Lonesome Pine, 13 Hours By Air, The Princess Comes Across, The Texas Rangers, Maid of Salem, Champagne Waltz, Swing High, Swing Low; Exclusive, True Confession, Men with Wings, Coconut Grove, Sing You Sinners, Cafe Society, Invitation to Happiness, Honey-

moon in Bali, Little Old New York, Remember the Night, Too Many Husbands, Rangers of Fortune, Virginia, One Night in Lisbon, New York Town, Dive Bomber, The Lady Is Willing, Take a Letter Darling, The Forest Rangers, Star Spangled Rhythm, Flight for Freedom, Above Suspicion, No Time For Love, Standing Room Only, Double Indemnity, Murder He Says, Practically Yours, Where Do We Go From Here?, Captain Eddie, Smoky, Pardon My Past, Suddenly It's Spring, Egg and I, Singapore, A Miracle Can Happen, Miracle of the Bells, Don't Trust Your Husband, Family Honeymoon, Father Was a Fullback, Borderline, Never a Dull Moment, Callaway Went Thataway, Millionaire for Christy, Fair Wind to Java, The Moonlighter, Caine Mutiny, Pushover, Woman's World, Far Horizons, There's Always Tomorrow, At Gunpoint, Rains of Ranchipur, Gun For a Coward, Quantez, Good Day for a Hanging, The Shaggy Dog, Face of a Fugitive, The Oregon Trail, The Apartment, The Absent Minded Professor, Bon Voyage, Son of Flubber, Kisses for My President, Follow Me Boys, The Happiest Millionaire, Charlie and the Angel, The Swarm.

TELEVISION: My Three Sons (1960–72), The Chadwick Family. Movie: Beyond the Bermuda Triangle.

MAC NAUGHTON, ROBERT: Actor. b. New York, NY, Dec. 19, 1966. Entered entertainment industry in 1979. Member Circle Rep. Co., N.Y.

TELEVISION: Angel City, Big Bend Country, The Electric Grandmother, Hear My Cry.

PICTURES: E.T.: The Extra-Terrestrial, I Am the Cheese.

STAGE: Critic's Choice, A Thousand Clowns, Camelot, The Diviners, The Adventures of Huckleberry Finn, Henry V, Tobacco Road, Master Harold . . . and the Boys, Tomorrow's Monday, Talley and Son.

MAC NICOL PETER: Actor. b. Dallas, TX, 1954. m. film prod. Marsue Cumming. e. U. of Minnesota. Screen debut, Dragonslayer, 1981.

THEATER: NY Shakespeare Fest. Public Theater: Found a Peanut, Rum and Coke, Twelfth Night, Richard II. Regional theatre includes Guthrie, Alaska Rep., Long Wharf, Dallas Theatre Center, Trinity Rep. (Providence, RI); Execution of Justice, Crimes of the Heart (B'way debut), The Nerd, Romeo and Juliet, Fakebook.

PICTURES: Sophie's Choice, Heat, Ghostbusters II, American Blue Note.

TELEVISION: Johnny Bull, Faerie Tale Theatre, Molly Dodd, Walt Whitman (narrator).

MAC RAE, JEAN: Actress. b. Montreal, Quebec, Mar. 24, 1930. Worked for National Film Bd. of Canada, Canadian Bdcst. Corp., and repertory theatre in Canada; U.S. studios, including MGM, 20th-Fox, Columbia, and Paramount; as TV studios at Desilu and 20th-Fox.

MADDEN, BILL: Executive. b. New York, NY, March 1, 1915. e. Boston U. Joined Metro-Goldwyn-Mayer as office boy, 1930; student salesman, 1938; asst. Eastern div. sales mgr., 1939; U.S. Navy, 1942–46; Boston sales rep., M.G.M., 1947–53; Philadelphia branch mgr., 1954–59; Midwest div. sales mgr., 1960–68; roadshow sales mgr., 1969; v.p., general sales mgr., 1969–74, M.G.M.; corp., v.p. & gen. sls. mgr., MGM, 1974; retired from MGM, 1975; 1976-present, exec. consultant to motion picture industry; lecturer and instructor at UCLA. Member: Academy M.P. Arts & Sciences, Motion Picture Associates, American Film Institute. Motion Picture Pioneers.

MADDEN, DAVID: Executive. e. Harvard U., 1976; UCLA, M.A., 1978. Joined 20th Century-Fox in Nov., 1978 as story analyst. Named story editor, 1980; exec. story editor, 1982. Appt. v.p., creative affairs for 20th-Fox Prods., 1983; v.p., prod., 20th Century-Fox Prods; 1980, v.p., production, Paramount Pictures.

PICTURES: Renegades (prod.), Blind Fury (exec. prod.).

MADIGAN, AMY: Actress. b. Chicago, IL, 1957. m. actor Ed Harris. For 10 years traveled country performing in bars and clubs with band. Then studied at Lee Strasberg Inst., L.A.

PICTURES: Love Child, Streets of Fire, Places in the Heart, Alamo Bay, Twice in a Lifetime, Nowhere To Hide, The Prince of Pennsylvania, Field of Dreams, Uncle Buck.

TELEVISION: The Laundromat, The Day After, The Ambush Murders, Travis McGee, Victims, Crazy Times, Roe vs. Wade.

MADISON, GUY: Actor. r.n. Robert Moseley. b. Bakersfield, CA, Jan. 19, 1922. e. Bakersfield Jr. Coll. U.S. Navy; m.p. debut in Since You Went Away, 1944; Wild Bill Hickok radio and TV shows, Star of Tomorrow, 1954.

PICTURES: Till the End of Time, Honeymoon, Texas, Brooklyn and Heaven, Massacre River, Drums in the Deep South, Red Snow, Charge at Feather River, The Command, The Hard Man, Five Against the House, Beast of Hollow Mountain, Last Frontier, On the Threshold of Space, Hilda Crane, Bullwhip, Gunmen of The Rio Grande, Sandokan Fights Back, Sandokan Against the Leopard of Sarawak, Mystery of Thug Island, Shatterhand, Payment in Blood. 1960–75 starred in 45 foreign films; Pacific Connection, Cross Bow, River River.

TELEVISION: Red River.

MADONNA: Singer, Actress. r.n. Madonna Louise Veronica Ciccone. b. Pontiac, MI, 1961. e. U. of Michigan. Gained fame as rock & recording star before film debut in Desperately Seeking Susan, 1985. NY stage debut: Speed-the-Plow, 1988.

PICTURES: Shanghai Surprise, Who's That Girl?, Bloodhounds of Broadway, Dick Tracy.

MADSEN, VIRGINIA: Actress. b. Winnetka, IL, 1963. Mother is Emmy-winning Chicago filmmaker, brother is actor Michael Madsen. Studied with Chicago acting coach Ted Liss. Prof. debut, PBS, A Matter of Principle.

PICTURES: Class (debut, 1983), Dune, Electric Dreams, Creator, Fire With Fire, Modern Girl, Zombie High, Slam Dance, Mr. North, Hot to Trot, Heart of Dixie.

TELEVISION: The Hitchhiker. Movies: Mussolini: The Untold Story; The Hearst and Davies Affair, Long Gone, Gotham, Third Degree Burn.

MAGNOLI, ALBERT: Director, Writer.

PICTURES: Jazz (dir. only); Purple Rain; American Anthem (dir. only).

MAGNUSON, ANN: Actress, Writer, Performance Artist. b. Charleston, WV, 1956. e. Denison U. Intern at Ensemble Studio Theatre when she came to NY in 1978. Ran Club 57, an East Village club, 1979. Has performed in East Village clubs, downtown art spaces & on college campuses since 1980 and at Whitney Museum, Soguestu Hall (Tokyo), Walker Art Ctr. (Minn.), Lincoln Center, Serious Fun Festival. Also performs with band Bongwater (Shimmy Disc Records).

PICTURES: The Hunger, Desperately Seeking Susan, Making Mr. Right, A Night in the Life of Jimmy Reardon, Sleepwalk, Mondo New York, Tequila Sunrise, Checking Out, Heavy Petting, Love at Large.

TELVISION: Night Flight, Made for TV, Alive from Off Center (co-host), Vandemonium, Table at Ciro's (Tales From the Hollywood Hills), Anything but Love.

MAHARIS, GEORGE: Actor. b. Sept. 1, 1928.

PICTURES: Exodus, Sylvia, Quick Before It Melts, The Satan Bug, Covenant with Death, The Happening, The Desperadoes, Sword and the Sorcerer, Last Day of the War, The Land Grabbers.

TELEVISION: Naked City. Series: Route 66, Most Deadly Game. Movies: Escape to Mindanao, The Monk, The Victim, Murder on Flight 502, Rich Man, Poor Man, Look What's Happened to Rosemary's Baby, SST-Death Flight, Return to Fantasy Island, Crash, A Small Rebellion.

MAHONEY, JOCK: Actor. r.n. Jacques O'Mahoney. b. Chicago, IL, Feb. 7, 1919. Stepfather of Sally Field. e. U. of Iowa. Fighter pilot instructor, U.S.M.C.; enter m.p. ind. as stuntman; then started in westerns; TV show, Range Rider, many appearances on Loretta Young Show. Personal appearances; 1974–present, Gallant Charger Prods., advertising mgr.

PICTURES: Away All Boats, Day of Fury, Showdown at Abilene, Battle Hymn, I've Lived Before, Land Unknown, Joe Dakota, Money, Women and Guns, Moro Witch Doctor, Walls of Hell, Tarzan Goes to India, Tarzan's Three Challenges. Serials: Son of the Guardsman, Cody of Pony Express, Roar of Iron Horse; Speak of Brothers, Glory Stompers, Spirits of the Wild.

TELEVISION: Range Riders (series), Yancy Derringer (series), The Fall Guy, Simon and Simon.

MAHONEY, JOHN: Actor. b. Manchester, Eng., 1940. Mem. of Stratford Children's Theatre from age 10–13. Moved to U.S. at 19, taught Eng. at Western Illinois U. Then freelance ed. of medical manuscripts; assoc. ed., Quality Review Bulletin. At 35 quit medical book editing to become an actor. Studied acting, Chicago's St. Nicholas Theatre. Prof. debut, The Water Engine, 1977. Joined Steppenwolf Theatre Co., 1979. (The Hothouse, Taking Steps, Death of a Salesman).

THEATER: Orphans (Theatre World Award), The House of Blue Leaves (Tony and Clarence Derwent Awards).

PICTURES: Mission Hill, Code of Silence, The Manhattan Project, Streets of Gold, Tin Men, Suspect, Moonstruck, Frantic, Eight Men Out, Betrayed, Say Anything, Love Hurts.

TELEVISION: The Killing Floor, Chicago Story. Movies: First Steps, Listen to Your Heart, Series: Lady Blue, Dance of the Phoenix, First Steps, Trapped in Silence, Favorite Son, The Image, Dinner at Eight. . Special: The House of Blue Leaves.

MAIBAUM, RICHARD: Writer, Producer, b. New York, NY, May 26, 1909. e. NYU, U. of Iowa, B.A., M.A., Phi Beta Kappa. Plays on Broadway: The Tree, Birthright, Sweet Mystery of Life, See My Lawyer (1939), Member, Shakespearean Repertory Theatre in New York as player, 1933, From 1935 to 1942 worked on screenplays in Hollywood: MGM (They Gave Him a Gun, Stablemates, etc.); Columbia (Amazing Mr. Williams); Paramount (I Wanted Wings); 20th-Fox (Ten Gentlemen from

West Point). Army, 1942–46, dir. Combat Film Div., final rank Lt. Col. To Para. prod.-writer, 1946, free lance, 1953; collab. s.p., Paratrooper; adapt., Hell Below Zero; writer of Teleplays; exec. prod. MGM-TV, 1958–60.
PICTURES: wrote-produced O.S.S., Song of Surrender; collab. & prod. The Great Gatsby. Prod.: Sainted Sisters, The Big Clock, Bride of Vengeance, Dear Wife, No Man of Her Own, Capt. Carey, U.S.A.; *Writer:* Ransom, Cockleshell Heroes, Bigger Than Life, Zarak, Tank Force, Killers of Kilimanjaro, The Day They Robbed the Bank of England, Battle at Bloody Beach, Dr. No, From Russia with Love, Goldfinger, Thunderball, Chitty, Chitty, Bang Bang, On Her Majesty's Secret Service, Diamonds Are Forever, The Man with the Golden Gun, The Spy Who Loved Me, For Your Eyes Only, Octopussy, A View to a Kill, The Living Daylights, Licence to Kill (co-s.p.).
TELEVISION: Jarrett (prod., s.p.), Combat, Wagon Train.

MAIN, DAVID: Writer, Producer. b. Essex, Eng., 1929. Extensive television experience in Britain producing and directing for A.T.V., Granada, A.B.C. and B.B.C. Emigrated to Canada in 1960. Directed Moment of Truth for N.B.C., and Quentin Durgens M.P. for C.B.C., Famous Jury Trials for 20th Century Fox. In 1977–78 directed King of Kensington, Le Club, A Gift to Last for CBC. President of Velvet Screen Plays Ltd. a subsidiary of Quadrant Films Ltd.
PICTURES: Sunday in the Country, 1973 (story & co-writer), and It Seemed Like a Good Idea at the Time (co-writer); Find the Lady (story, co-writer, co-producer); Double Negative (co-prod.); Nothing Personal (co-prod.).

MAJORS, LEE: Actor. b. Wyandotte, MI, April 23, 1939. Star athlete in high school; turned down offer from St. Louis Cardinals in final year at Eastern Kentucky State Coll. to pursue acting career. In L.A. got job as playground supervisor for park dept. while studying acting at MGM Studio.
PICTURES: Will Penny (debut), The Liberation of L. B. Jones, Agency, Norsemen, Scrooged, Keaton's Cop.
TELEVISION: The Big Valley, The Man From Shiloh, The Six Million Dollar Man (series), The Fall Guy (series). Pilot: Road Show (also exec. prod.). Movies: The Ballad of Andy Crocker, Weekend of Terror, The Gary Francis Powers Story, The Cowboy and the Ballerina, A Rocky Mountain Christmas, The Return of the Six Million Dollar Man and the Bionic Woman, Danger Down Under (exec. prod., actor), The Bionic Showdown: the Six Million Dollar Man and the Bionic Woman.

MAKEPEACE, CHRIS: Actor. b. Montreal, Canada, April 22, 1964. e. Jarvis Collegiate Institute. Trained for stage at Second City Workshop.
PICTURES: Meatballs (debut, 1979), My Bodyguard, The Last Chase, The Terry Fox Story, The Oasis, The Falcon and the Snowman, Hanauma Bay, Vamps, Aloha Summer.
TELEVISION: The Mysterious Stranger, Mazes and Monsters, The Undergrads. Series: Going Great (host, 1982–84), Why On Earth?

MALDEN, KARL: Actor. r.n. Mladen Sekulovich. b. Gary, IN, Mar. 22, 1914. e. Art Inst. of Chicago 1933–36; Goodman Theatre Sch. Elected pres., Acad. of Motion Picture Arts & Sciences, 1989.
BWAY PLAYS: Golden Boy, Key Largo, Flight to West, Missouri Legend, Uncle Harry, Counterattack, Truckline Cafe, All My Sons, Streetcar Named Desire, Desperate Hours, Desire Under the Elms, The Egghead.
PICTURES: They Knew What They Wanted (debut, 1940), Winged Victory, 13 Rue Madeleine, Boomerang, The Kiss of Death, The Gunfighter, Where the Sidewalk Ends, Hall of Montezuma, Streetcar Named Desire, (Acad. Award best supp. actor, 1951), The Sellout, Diplomatic Courier, Operation Secret, Ruby Gentry, I Confess, Take the High Ground, Phantom of the Rue Morgue, On the Waterfront, Baby Doll, Bombers B-52, Desperate Hours, Fear Strikes Out, The Hanging Tree, One Eyed Jacks, Parrish, Pollyanna, Time Limit (dir.), The Birdman of Alcatraz, Gypsy, How the West Was Won, Come Fly With Me, Cheyanne Autumn, Dead Ringer, The Cincinnati Kid, Nevada Smith, The Silencers, Murderer's Row, The Adventures of Bull Whip Griffin, Billion Dollar Brain, Hot Millions, Blue Hotel, Patton, Cat O'Nine Tails, Wild Rovers, Summertime Killer, Beyond the Poseidon Adventure, Meteor, The Sting II, Twilight Time, Billy Galvin, Nuts.
TELEVISION: Series: Streets of San Francisco, Skag, Movies: Captains Courageous, Word of Honor, With Intent to Kill, Alice in Wonderland, Fatal Vision (Emmy Award); My Father, My Son, The Hijacking of the Achille Lauro.

MALICK, TERENCE: Producer, Writer, Director. b. Waco, Texas, Nov. 30, 1943. e. Harvard U. Attended Oxford U. on Rhodes scholarship. Worked for Newsweek, Life and The New Yorker; lectured in philosophy at M.I.T. Studied at American Film Inst. in Beverly Hills and made short funded by AFI.
PICTURES: Pocket Money (co-s.p. only), The Gravy Train (co-s.p. under pseudonym David Whitney), Deadhead Miles (co-s.p.), Badlands (prod., dir., s.p.), Days of Heaven (s.p., dir.).

MALIN, AMIR JACOB: Executive. b. Tel-Aviv, Israel, Mar. 22, 1954. e. Brandeis U., 1972–76; Boston U. Sch. of Law, 1976–79. Staff atty., WGBH-TV, Boston, 1979–81; now pres. and co-CEO, Cinecom Entertainment Group, Inc. Films acquired and distributed include Come Back to the Five and Dime, Jimmy Dean, Jimmy Dean; Metropolis; The Brother from Another Planet; Stop Making Sense; Coca-Cola Kid; A Room with a View; Swimming to Cambodia; Matewan; A Man in Love; Maurice, Miles From Home.
PICTURES: Exec. prod.: Swimming to Cambodia, Matewan, Miles From Home, Scenes from the Class Struggle in Beverly Hills, The Handmaid's Tale, Aunt Julia and the Scriptwriter.

MALKOVICH, JOHN: Actor, Producer, Director. b. Benton, IL, Dec. 9, 1953. m. actress Glenne Headley. e. Illinois State U. Founding member Steppenwolf Ensemble in Chicago with group of college friends 1976. Starred in Say Goodnight, Gracie and True West (Obie Award) which then was brought to New York. NY Stage work includes Death of Salesman on Bdwy. and TV with Dustin Hoffman. Director: Balm in Gilead, Arms and the Man, The Caretaker. Actor: Burn This.
PICTURES: The Killing Fields (debut), Places in the Heart, Eleni, Making Mr. Right, The Glass Menagerie, Empire of the Sun, Miles From Home, Dangerous Liaisons, The Accidental Tourist (co-exec. prod.), Queens Logic, The Sheltering Sky.
TELEVISION: Death of a Salesman, Rocket to the Moon, American Dream, Word of Honor.

MALLE, LOUIS: Director, Producer. b. Thumeries, France, Oct. 30, 1932. m. actress Candice Bergen. e. Sorbonne (Pol. Science). Studied filmmaking at Institut des Hautes Etudes Cinematographiques 1951–53. Started in film industry as assistant to Robert Bresson and cameraman to oceanographer Jacques Cousteau, 1954–55 then corres. for French TV in Algeria, Vietnam and Thailand 1962–64. Began career somewhat ahead of most young French directors referred to as the Nouvelle Vougue (New Wave). Became internationally known with Les Amants (The Lovers) in 1958. Has also acted in films (A Very Private Affair, A Very Curious Girl).
PICTURES: The World of Silence (co-dir. with J. Y. Cousteau, Acad. Award), A Man Escaped (asst. to Bresson); Elevator to the Gallows (also exec. prod.) Mon Oncle (cinematographer only), The Lovers (also exec. prod.), *Director & Prod.:* Zazie in the Metro, A Very Private Affair (dir. only), Vive Le Tour (doc.), The Fire Within (dir. only), Bon Baisers de Bangkok (doc.), Viva Maria, The Thief of Paris, William Wilson, In Spirits of the Dead (dir. only), Calcutta (doc.), Phantom India (doc.), Murmur of the Heart (dir. only), Humain, Trop Humain (doc.), Place de la Republique, Lacombe, Lucien, Black Moon, Pretty Baby, *Director:* Atlantic City, My Dinner with Andre, Crackers, Alamo Bay (also prod.), Au Revoir Les Enfants (winner Golden Lion, Venice Film Fest., 1987), Milou in May.
TELEVISION: Documentaries: God's Country, And the Pursuit of Happiness.

MALLERS, ANTHONY: Theatre Owner. b. Portland, IN, Oct. 4, 1933. e. Indiana U., B.S., business admin. Entered industry in 1957. Now pres. of Mallers Theatres, headquartered in Muncie, Ind.

MALMUTH, BRUCE: Director. b. Brooklyn, NY, Feb. 4, 1937. e. City Coll. of New York, Brooklyn Coll. Grad. studies in film, Columbia U. and U. of Southern California. Acted in and dir. college productions. Moved to California and obtained job as page at NBC. In Army assigned to special services as director; reassigned to New York. Upon release began 10-year Clio-winning career as dir. of TV commercials. Debut as director of features with Nighthawks, 1981. Founder, Los Angeles Aspiring Actors and Directors Workshop.
PICTURES: Nighthawks, The Man Who Wasn't There, Where Are the Children?, Seven Year Storm.
TELEVISION: Baseballs or Switchblades? (prod., writer, dir., Emmy Award-winning doc.), A Boy's Dream, Twilight Zone (Emmy), Beauty and the Beast (Heartbreak winner, Emmy).

MALONE, DOROTHY: Actress. b. Chicago, IL, Jan. 30, 1925. e. Southern Methodist U. Screen debut in The Big Sleep, 1946.
PICTURES: Young at Heart, Battle Cry, Pillars of the Sky, Written on the Wind (Acad. Award, best supporting actress, 1956), Man of a Thousand Faces, The Last Voyage, The Last Sunset, Beach Party, Abduction, Golden Rendezvous, Winter Kills, The Day Time Ended.
TELEVISION: Dick Powell Theatre, Dr. Kildare, Bob Hope Show, Jack Benny Show, The Untouchables, The Greatest Show On Earth, Peyton Place (series), Peyton Place: The Next Generation (movie).

MAMET, DAVID: Writer. b. Chicago, IL, Nov. 30, 1947. e. Goddard Coll. m. Lindsay Crouse. Artist-in-residence, Goddard Coll. 1971–73. Artistic dir. St. Nicholas Theatre Co., Chicago, 1973–75. Co-founder Dinglefest Theatre; assoc. artistic dir., Goodman Theatre, Chicago. Plays include Lakefront, The Woods, American Buffalo, Sexual Perversity in Chicago,

Duck Variations, The Long Canoe, Edmond, A Life in the Theatre, The Water Engine, Prairie du Chien, Glengarry Glen Ross (Pulitzer Prize 1984 & 4 Tony Awards), Speed-the-Plow, Sketches of War (benefit for homeless Veterans).

PICTURES: The Postman Always Rings Twice, The Verdict, The Untouchables, House of Games (also dir.), Things Change (dir., co-s.p), We're No Angels, Homicide (dir.), Glengarry Glen Ross.

TELEVISION: L.A. Law, Lip Service (exec. prod.).

MANASSE, GEORGE: Producer. b. Florence, Italy, Jan. 1, 1938. e. U. of North Carolina.

PICTURES: *Line Prod.:* Who Killed Mary What's 'er Name? Squirm, Blue Sunshine, He Knows You're Alone. *Prod. Mgr.:* Greetings, Fury on Wheels, Tribute, Porky II, The Next Day, Neighbors, Death Wish III, Torch Song Trilogy.

TELEVISION: *Line Prod.:* Series: American Playwright's Theatre (Arts & Ent.) The Saint in Manhattan (pilot), Movie: The Killing Floor, Vengeance: The Story of Tony Cimo. *Prod. Mgr.:* Series: Saint Elsewhere, Annie McGuire. Movies: Sanctuary of Fear, Mr. Griffith and Me, Peking Encounter, When the Circus Came to Town, Murder, Inc. Muggable Mary, Running Out, Dropout Father, He's Hired, She's Fired, Intimate Strangers, Drop Out Mother, Vengeance: The Story of Tony Cimo, The Saint in Manhattan, The Diamond Trap, The Prize Pulitzer. Mini-series: John and Koko.

MANBY, C. R.: Executive. b. Battle Creek, MI, Feb. 24, 1920. e. Hillsdale Coll., MI, A.B., 1942; Harvard Grad. Sch. of Bus. Admin., 1953. v.p., RKO General Inc., 1955–58; pres. Show Corp. of Amer., 1958–75; pres., RKO Pictures, 1978–84; chmn., 1985–86. Retired.

MANCIA, ADRIENNE: Curator, Dept. of Film, Museum of Modern Art. b. New York, NY. e. U. of Wisconsin. B.A.; Columbia U., M.A. Worked in film distribution industry in New York prior to joining Dept. of Film, Museum of Modern Art, 1964; responsible for film exhibition since 1965. In 1977, appointed curator. Restructured Museums' Auditorium Exhibition Prog., creating a balance between classic cinema and contemporary work. Initiated innovative programs such as Cineprobe and What's Happening? Served on numerous int'l film juries. Co-founder New Directors/New Films. Chevalier de l'ordre des arts et des lettres (Republic of France, 1985). Ufficiale dell Ordine al Meritor della Republica Italiana, 1988.

MANCINI, HENRY: Composer. b., Cleveland, OH, April 16, 1924. Arranged music for the Glenn Miller Story, The Benny Goodman Story, then began composing scores.

PICTURES: Touch of Evil, High Time, Breakfast at Tiffany's (AA, 1961), Bachelor in Paradise, Hatari, The Pink Panther, Charade, A Shot in the Dark, Dear Heart, What Did You Do in the War, Daddy?, Two for the Road, Visions of Eight, Oklahoma Crude, 99 44/100% Dead, The White Dawn, The Girl from Petrovka, The Great Waldo Pepper, W. C. Fields and Me, The Pink Panther Strikes Again, Silver Streak, Revenge of the Pink Panther, Who Is Killing the Great Chefs of Europe?, Prisoner of Zenda, Nightwing, "10," Little Miss Marker, Change of Seasons, Back Roads, S.O.B., Mommie Dearest, Victor, Victoria, Whose Little Girl Are You?, Trail of the Pink Panther, Curse of the Pink Panther, The Man Who Loved Women, Harry and Son, Life Force, Santa Claus: The Movie, That's Life!, Blind Date, The Glass Menagerie, Without a Clue, Physical Evidence, Mother, Mother.

TELEVISION: Peter Gunn, Mr. Lucky, Newhart (theme), The Moneychangers, The Shadow Box, Thorn Birds, Blue Knights, Best Place to Be, Justin Case, Peter Gunn (1989).

MANCUSO, FRANK G.: Executive. b. Buffalo, NY, July 25, 1933. e. State U. of New York. Film buyer and operations supvr. for Basil Enterprises, theatre circuit, from 1958 to 1962. Joined Paramount as booker in Buffalo branch, 1962. Named sls. repr. for branch in 1964 and branch mgr. in 1967. In 1970 appt. v.p./gen. sls. mgr., Paramount Pictures Canada, Ltd., becoming pres. in 1972. In 1976 relocated with Paramount in U.S. as western div. mgr. in L.A. In Jan., 1977, appt. gen. sls. mgr. of N.Y., office; two months later promoted to v.p.—domestic distribution; 1979, named exec. v.p., distribution & mktg. In 1983 made pres. of entire Paramount Motion Picture Group. 1984, appointed chmn. and chief exec. officer, Paramount Pictures. Motion Picture Pioneers Man of the Year, 1987.

MEMBER OF BOARD: Acad. of M.P. Arts and Sciences, M.P. Association of America, Will Rogers Memorial Fund, Variety Clubs Intl., Sundance Institute, Amer. Film Institute, Museum of Broadcasting, Motion Picture Pioneers.

MANCUSO, FRANK, JR.: Producer. b. Buffalo, NY, Oct. 9, 1958. Son of Frank G. Mancuso. e. Upsala Coll. Began with industry at age 14, booking short subjects in Canadian theatres. Worked in gross receipts dept. in Paramount corporate offices in New York and later with paralegal div. Initial prod. work as location asst. for Urban Cowboy in Houston, TX. Served as assoc. prod. of Friday the 13th Part II and prod. of Friday the 13th Part III in 3-D.

PICTURES: Off the Wall, The Man Who Wasn't There, April Fool's Day, Friday the 13th, Part IV: The Final Chapter; Friday the 13th—A New Beginning (exec. prod.), Friday the 13th, Part VII (exec. prod.); Back to the Beach; Permanent Record, Internal Affairs.

TELEVISION: Friday the 13th: The Series (exec. prod.).

MANDEL, LORING: Writer. b. Chicago, IL, May 5, 1928. e. U. of Wisconsin, B.S. 1949. Long career writing scripts for TV, dating back to 1955 when penned Shakedown Cruise. Governor, Natl. Acad. of TV Arts & Sciences 1964–68; Pres. Writers Guild of America East 1975–77; Natl. chmn. 1977–79.

PICTURES: Countdown, Promises in the Dark, The Little Drummer Girl, etc.

TELEVISION: Do Not Go Gentle Into that Good Night (Emmy, 1967), Breaking Up, Project Immortality (Sylvania Award, 1959), A House His Own, Trial of Chaplain Jensen, Bailey's Bridge (also exec. prod.).

MANDEL, ROBERT: Director.

PICTURES: Night at O'Rears; Independence Day; F/X; Touch and Go, Big Shots.

TELEVISION: Hard Time on Planet Earth.

MANDELL, ABE: Executive. b. Oct. 4, 1922. e. U. of Cincinnati. Entered broadcasting as actor on Cincinnati radio station prior to W.W.II. Served U.S. Army in Southwest Pacific, 1942–45. Formed indep. motion picture distribution co. in the Far East. Company, which became the largest indep. motion picture dist. in the Far East, also operated and owned motion picture theaters throughout the Phillipines and Indonesia, 1946–56; network-regional sales exec., Ziv Television, 1956–58; dir. foreign operations, Independent Television Corporation, 1958; v.p.-foreign oper., 1960; v.p.-sales and adm., 1961; exec. v.p., 1962; pres. 1965. 1976 corporate name changed from Independent Television Corp. to ITC Entertainment, Inc. President to 1983 of ITC Entertainment, with Robert Mandell heads New Frontier Prods.

MANES, FRITZ: Producer. TV ad exec. and stuntman before becoming exec. prod. on films for Clint Eastwood.

PICTURES: in various capacities: The Outlaw Josey Wales, The Enforcer. Assoc. prod.: The Gauntlet, Every Which Way But Loose, Escape From Alcatraz, Bronco Billy. Prod.: Any Which Way You Can (also 2nd asst. dir.), Firefox (exec. prod.), Honky Tonk Man (exec. prod.), Tightrope (prod.), Sudden Impact (exec. prod.), City Heat (prod.), Pale Rider (exec. prod.), Ratboy (exec. prod.), Heartbreak Ridge (exec. prod., prod. mgr.).

MANGANO, SILVANA: Actress. b. Rome, Italy. Apr. 23, 1930. e. Dance Acad. of Jia Ruskaja. Model to 1949; Named Miss Rome. Film debut in L'Elisir D'Amore (1946).

PICTURES: Bitter Rice, Lure of Sila, Musolino, The Brigand; Anna, Ulysses, Mambo, Gold of Naples, This Angry Age, Tempest, The Sea Wall, Five Branded Women, La Grande Guerra, Crimen, Una Vita Difficlie, Il Giudizio Universale, Barabbas, Teorema, Le Streghe, Oedipus Rex, Medea, Death in Venice, Decameron, Ludwig, Conversation Piece, Dune, Dark Eyes.

MANKIEWICZ, DON M.: Writer. b. Berlin, Germany, Jan. 20, 1922. p. Herman J. Mankiewicz. e. Columbia, B.A., 1942; Columbia Law Sch. Served in U.S. Army, 1942–46; reporter, New Yorker magazine, 1946–48; author of novels See How They Run, Trial, It Only Hurts a Minute; magazine articles, short stories. President, Producers Guild of America (1987).

TELEVISION: Studio One, On Trial, One Step Beyond, Playhouse 90, Profiles in Courage. Exec. story consultant: Hart to Hart, Simon & Simon, Crazy Like a Fox, Adderly.

PICTURES: Trial, I Want to Live.

TV PILOTS: Ironside, Marcus Welby, M.D., Sarge; Lanigan's Rabbi (collab.); Rosetti and Ryan (collab.)

MANKIEWICZ, JOSEPH L.: Writer, Director. b. Wilkes-Barre, PA, Feb. 11, 1909. e. Columbia U. Asst. corr. in Berlin, Chicago Tribune; Ufa studio, translating subtitles into Eng. for release in Eng. & U.S.; returned to U.S. 1929 to join brother, Herman, on Paramount writing staff; MGM, 1933; Fox, 1943–51; dir., La Boheme, Metropolitan Opera House, 1953. Founding member & secretary Screen Writers Guild 1933. President Dir. Guild of Amer., 1950.Academy Awards: 1949, Letter to Three Wives, best s.p., dir.; 1950, All About Eve, best s.p., dir. D.W. Griffith Award for Lifetime Achievement, Directors Guild of Amer., 1986; Golfen Lion Award, lifetime achievement, Venice Film Fest. 1987.

PICTURES: Skippy, Million Dollar Legs, If I Had a Million, Alice in Wonderland, Fury, Gorgeous Hussy, Mannequin, Three Comrades, Shopworn Angel, Philadelphia Story, Woman of the Year, Keys of the Kingdom, Dragonwyck, Somewhere in the Night, No Way Out, Late George Apley, Ghost and Mrs. Muir, House of Strangers, Letter to Three Wives, All About Eve, People Will Talk, 5 Fingers, Julius Caesar, Barefoot Contessa, Guys and Dolls, Quiet American, Suddenly Last Summer, The Honey Pot, There Was a Crooked Man, Sleuth.

MANKIEWICZ, TOM: Writer. b. Los Angeles, CA, June 1, 1942. Specializes in adventure/suspense films.
PICTURES: The Sweet Ride (debut), Diamonds Are Forever, Live and Let Die, The Man with the Golden Gun, Mother, Jugs and Speed (also prod.), The Cassandra Crossing, The Eagle Has Landed, Superman (creative consultant), Superman II (creative consultant), Ladyhawke, Hot Pursuit (exec. prod.). Dragnet (also dir.).
TELEVISION: Hart to Hart (s.p., dir.).

MANKOWITZ, WOLF: Author, Playwright, Producer, Impresario. b. London, 1924. Journalist. Ent. m.p. in 1952. Musical play based his story Expresso Bongo. Musical play, Make Me An Offer; Belle; Pickwick; Passion Flower Hotel.
PICTURES: Make Me An Offer, Kid For Two Farthings, The Bespoke Overcoat, Trapeze, Expresso Bongo, The Millionairess, The Long and Short and Tall, The Day The Earth Caught Fire, Where the Spies Are, Assassination Bureau, Bloomfield: Black Beauty, Treasure Island, The Hireling, Almonds and Raisins.
TELEVISION: The Killing Stones, A Cure for Tin Ear, The Battersea Miracle, Series: Conflict, Dickens of London.

MANN, ABBY: Writer. b. Philadelphia, PA, 1927. e. NYU. First gained fame on TV writing for Robert Montgomery Theatre, Playhouse 90, Studio One, Alcoa, Goodyear Theatre. Acad. Award for film adaptation of own teleplay Judgment at Nuremberg into theatrical film.
PICTURES: Judgment at Nuremberg, A Child Is Waiting, The Condemned of Altona, Ship of Fools, The Detective, Report to the Commissioner, War and Love.
TELEVISION: Medical Center, Kojak (creator), The Marcus-Nelson Murders, The Atlanta Child Murders, King, War and Love, Skag, Murderers Among Us, The Simon Wiesenthal Story (co-s.p., co-exec. prod.; Emmy Award).

MANN, DANIEL: Director. b. New York, NY, Aug. 8, 1912. e. Erasmus Hall, Brooklyn; Professional Children's Sch. Started as musician in resort hotels; then in Canada, on road; U.S. Army, W.W.II; then received scholarship to Neighborhood Playhouse, N.Y.; dir. teaching, TV dir.
BROADWAY: Come Back Little Sheba, Rose Tattoo, Streetcar Named Desire (City Center prod.), Paint Your Wagon.
PICTURES: Come Back Little Sheba, About Mrs. Leslie, Rose Tattoo, I'll Cry Tomorrow, Teahouse of the August Moon, Hot Spell, Last Angry Man, Mountain Road, Butterfield 8, Ada, Judith; A Dream of Kings, Who's Got the Action?, Who's Been Sleeping in My Bed?, For Love of Ivy, Willard, The Revengers, Maurie, Interval, Lost in the Stars, Matilda.
TELEVISION: Playing for Time, The Day the Loving Stopped, The Man Who Broke 1000 Chains.

MANN, DELBERT: Director, Producer. b. Lawrence, KS, Jan. 30, 1920. e. Vanderbilt U., Yale U. U.S. Air Force, 1942–45; stage mgr., summer stock, dir. Columbia, S.C. Town Theatre, 1947–49; asst. dir., NBC-TV, 1949; dir., NBC-TV, 1949–55. Past pres. Directors Guild of America.
STAGE: A Quiet Place, Speaking of Murder, Zelda, opera: Wuthering Heights; New York City Center.
PICTURES: Marty (Academy Award, best director, 1955), Bachelor Party, Desire Under the Elms, Separate Tables, Middle of the Night, The Dark at the Top of the Stairs, The Outsider, Lover Come Back, That Touch of Mink, A Gathering of Eagles, Dear Heart, Quick Before It Melts, Mister Buddwing, Fitzwilly, The Pink Jungle, Kidnapped, Birch Interval, Night Crossing.
TELEVISION: Philco-Goodyear TV Playhouse, Producer's Showcase, Omnibus, Playwrights '56, Playhouse 90, Ford Star Jubilee, Lights Out, Mary Kay and Johnny, The Little Show, Masterpiece Theatre, Ford Startime. Movies: Specials: Heidi, David Copperfield, Jane Eyre. The Man Without a Country, A Girl Named Sooner, Breaking Up, Tell Me My Name, Home to Stay, All Quiet on the Western Front, To Find My Son, All the Way Home, The Member of the Wedding, Bronte, The Gift of Love, Love Leads the Way, A Death in California, The Last Days of Patton, The Ted Kennedy, Jr. Story, April Morning (co-prod., dir.).

MANN, MICHAEL: Producer, Director, Writer. b. Chicago, IL. e. U. of Wisconsin, London Film Sch. 1965–72, directed commercials and documentaries in England, including Insurrection for NBC in Paris during the 1968 riots. Directed short film, Jaunpuri, winner of Jury Prize at Cannes Film Festival. Returned to U.S. in 1972 to direct documentary, 18 Days Down the Line. Wrote for prime-time TV (episodes of Starsky and Hutch, Police Story, Vegas).
PICTURES: Thief (exec. prod., s.p., dir.), The Keep (s.p. dir.), Manhunter.
TELEVISION: The Jericho Mile (s.p., dir.). (DGA, 1980 best director award). Miami Vice (exec. prod.), Crime Story (exec. prod.).

MANNE, S. ANTHONY: Executive. b. New York, NY, July 19, 1940. e. Wharton Sch., U. of Pennsylvania, B.S., economics. Joined Columbia Pictures 1963; international dept. 1964; asst. mgr., Brazil, 1968; mgr., Brazil, 1972–76. Joined JAD Films, 1976; United Artists, v.p., Latin American supervisor, 1980; Columbia Pictures Intl., v.p., continental mgr., 1981; appointed sr. v.p., sales manager, 1984; exec. v.p., Tri-Star Intl, 1987; appointed exec. v.p., foreign mgr. Columbia Tri-Star Film Distributors, 1988.

MANNIX, DAVID K.: Executive. b. Brooklyn, NY, 1952. e. Fordham U., B.S.; Pepperdine U., M.B.A. Joined Paramount Pictures in 1973 as supervisor, TV accounting; 1976, Mgr. financial analysis; 1978, asst. studio controller; 1979, director, production operations; 1981, executive director, studio operations; 1984, promoted to v.p. 1988; promoted to sr. v.p. studio operations.

MANOFF, DINAH: Actress. b. New York, NY, January 25, 1958. e. CalArts. Daughter of actress-director Lee Grant and late writer Arnold Manoff. Prof. debut PBS prod. The Great Cherub Knitwear Strike. Guest starred on Welcome Back, Kotter.
THEATER: I Ought to Be in Pictures (Tony Award, Theatre World Award, 1980), Gifted Children, Leader of the Pack, Alfred and Victoria: A Life (L.A. Theatre Center), Kingdom of Earth (TheatreWest).
PICTURES: Grease (debut, 1977), Ordinary People, I Ought to Be in Pictures, Child's Play, Staying Together, Bloodhounds of Broadway.
TELEVISION: Series: Soap (1978–79); Empty Nest. Movies; Raid on Entebee, High Terror, The Possessed, For Ladies Only, A Matter of Sex, The Seduction of Gina, Celebrity, Flight #90, Classified Love, Crossing the Mob, Backfire.

MANSON, ARTHUR: Executive. b. Brooklyn, NY, Feb. 21, 1928. e. City Coll. of New York, grad. Inst. Film Technique, 1945; editor, American Traveler, U.S. Army, 1946; Advance agent, co. mgr., Henry V, U.S., 1948–50; producer's publ. rep., Stanley Kramer Distributing Corp., Samuel Goldwyn Productions, Lopert Films, dir. of adv. and publ., MGM Pictures of Canada, Ltd., 1952–53; publ. and adv. rep., Cinerama Corp., 1953–58; worldwide ad-pub Cinerama (wide screen process) 1958–60; adv. mgr., Columbia Pictures, 1961–62; nat'l dir. of adv., publ., Dino De Laurentiis, 1962–64; exec. asst. to v.p. chg. adv. & pub., 20th Century-Fox, 1964–67; v.p. chg, adv. & pub. Cinerama. Inc., and Cinerama Releasing Corp.; 1967–74; exec. v.p., sales & marketing, BCP, service of Cox Broadcasting Corp., 1974–75; v.p. chg. worldwide adv.-pub. Warner Bros., 1976. In 1977 formed own company, Cinemax Mkt. & Dist. Corp. and is pres.

MANTEGNA, JOE: Actor. b. Chicago, IL, Nov. 13, 1947. e. Morton Jr. Coll., Goodman Sch. of Drama, 1967–69. Member: The Organic Theatre Company, Chicago (The Wonderful Ice Cream Suit, Cops, and 2 European tours with ensemble). Later mem. of Goodman Theater where he began long creative assoc. with playwright-dir. David Mamet (A Life in the Theatre, The Disappearance of the Jews). In national co. of Hair, Godspell, Lenny. Broadway debut: Working.
THEATER: Bleacher Bums (also conceived and co-author), Leonardo (L.A., co-author), Glengarry Glen Ross (Tony Award), Speed-the-Plow.
PICTURES: Towing, Second Thoughts, Compromising Positions, The Money Pit, Off Beat, Three Amigos, Critical Condition, House of Games, Weeds, Suspect, Things Change (Venice Film Fest., best actor award, 1988), Wait Until Spring, Bandini, Queens Logic.
TELEVISION: Soap, The Comedy Zone, Open All Night, Bleacher Bums (Emmy).

MANULIS, MARTIN: Producer, Director. b. New York, NY, May 30, 1915. e. Columbia U., B.A. 1935. Head of prod. John C. Wilson, 1941–49; mgr. dir., Westport Country Playhouse, 1945–50; dir. Bdwy plays; staff prod. & dir. CBS-TV, 1951–58; head prod. 20th-Fox Television. Now pres. Martin Manulis Prods. Ltd. 1987, artistic dir., Ahmanson Theatre, L.A.
BROADWAY: (and on tour): Private Lives, Made in Heaven, The Philadelphia Story, Pride's Crossing, Laura, The Men We Marry, The Hasty Heart, The Show Off.
TELEVISION: Suspense, Studio One, Climax, Best of Broadway, Playhouse 90. Mini-Series: Chiefs, Space, The Day Christ Died.
PICTURES: Days of Wine and Roses, The Out-of-Towners, Luv, Duffy.

MARA, ADELE: Actress. r.n. Adelaida Delgado; b. Dearborn, MI, April 28, 1923. m. Roy Huggins. Singer, dancer with Xavier Cugat orchestra; TV: Wheels (1978).
PICTURES: Shut My Big Mouth, Blondie Goes to College, Alias Boston Blackie, You Were Never Lovelier, Riders of the Northwest Mounted, Magnificent Rogue, Passkey to Danger, Traffic in Crime, Exposed, The Trespasser, Blackmail, Campus Honeymoon, Sands of Iwo Jima, Sea Hornet, Count The Hours, Wake of the Red Witch, Back from Eternity, Curse of the Faceless Man, The Big Circus.

MARAIS, JEAN: Actor. b. Cherbourg, France, Dec. 11, 1913. e. Coll. St. Germain, Lycée Janson de Sailly, Lycée Condorcet. Painter; photog; stage actor; French Air Army; m.p. debut in Pavillon Brule.
PICTURES: Carmen, Eternal Return, Beauty and the Beast, Ruy Blas, Les Parents Terribles, Secret of Mayerling, Souvenir, Orpheus, Eagle with Two Heads, Inside a Girl's Dormitory, Royal Affairs in Versailles, Paris Does Strange Things, Le Capitan, Le Bossu, La Princesse de Cleves, Le Capitaine Fracasse, Honorable Stanilleu, Agent Secret, Patute, Fantomas, Le Gentleman de Cocody.

MARANS, MARDI: Executive. e. U. of California. Worked in L.A. office of Doyle Dane Bernbach ad agency. Joined Warner Bros. in March, 1975, as asst. to media director. In 1979 appt. v.p. and director of media for WB, responsible for worldwide planning and placement of all film advertising. 1986, exec. v.p., worldwide mktg., Paramount Pictures.

MARCH, DONALD: Production Executive. b. New York, NY, July 26, 1942. Held sr. programming positions with ABC-TV network and Robert Stigwood Org. before joining CBS in 1977 as director, special projects, motion pictures for TV and mini-series. Later promoted to v.p., motion pictures for TV. Left CBS to serve as pres. of Filmways' theatrical div. in early 1979; later that year rejoined CBS as v.p., theatrical films, with responsibility for selection, dev. and prod. of pictures for theatrical release. 1984, sr. v.p., HBO Premiere Films. Independent prod., 1987 with ITC.
TELEVISION: Billionaire Boys Club (exec. prod.), Clinton and Nadine (prod.), David (prod.).

MARCHAND, NANCY: Actress. b. Buffalo, NY, June 19, 1928. m. actor-dir. Paul Sparer. e. Carnegie Tech. Stage debut The Late George Apley (In ME, 1946), Bdwy debut Taming of the Shrew (1951). Also in The Balcony (Obie Award, 1960), Morning's at Seven, Sister Mary, Ignatius Explains It All to You, Taken in Marriage, The Plough and the Stars, Awake and Sing, The Cocktail Party. Was an original mem of APA-Phoenix Theater. Film debut, Bachelor Party (1957).
PICTURES: Ladybug, Ladybug, Me, Natalie, Tell Me That You Love Me, Junie Moon, The Hospital, The Bostonians, From the Hip, The Naked Gun.
TELEVISION: Little Women (1951), numerous live prods. (incl. Marty), Series: Lou Grant, Beacon Hill, Adams Chronicles, Love of Life, Search for Tomorrow. Movies: Some Kind of Miracle, Willa, The Golden Moment—An Olympic Love Story, Sparkling Cyanide. Mini-Series: North and South Book II.

MARCUS, LOUIS: Producer, Director, Writer. b. Cork, Ireland, 1936. e. National U. of Ireland, B.A., 1959. Based in Dublin since 1959, where has made nearly 30 theatrical documentary films. Produces and directs for Louis Marcus Documentary Film Production of Dublin and Louis Marcus Films Ltd. of London. In 1964 appt. by Irish govt. as bd. mem. of Dublin's Abbey Theatre. In 1972 appt. by govt. as mem. of Cultural Relations Comm. of Dept. of Foreign Affairs. Elected mem. of Academy of M.P. Arts & Sciences (short subject branch) 1974.
PICTURES: Fleadh Cheoil, Horse Laughs, Woes of Golf, Children at Work, Conquest of Light.
AUTHOR: The Irish Film Industry (1968).

MARENSTEIN, HAROLD: exec. b. New York, NY, e. City Coll. of New York, 1937. Shipping, picture checking service, Warner Bros., 1935–45; Booking, Loew's Inc., 1945–48; Booking, contracts, Selznick Rel. Org., 1948–51; contracts, Paramount, 1951–52; asst. sls. gr., International Rel. Org., 1952; asst. sls. mgr., Janus Films, 1961–64; sls. exec., Rizzoli Films, 1965; 1967, nat'l. sales dir., Continental Dist.; gen. sales mgr., Cinemation Industries, 1968. v.p.-sales, dir., Cinemation Industries, 1971; 1976, gen. sls. mgr., General National Films; 1980, gen. sls. mgr., Lima Productions. Now retired.

MARGOLIN, JANET: Actress. b. New York, NY, 1943. e. N.Y.H.S. of Performing Arts. While playing in Bdwy. show, Daughter of Silence, discovered by dir. Frank Perry and hired for lead in his David and Lisa (1963).
PICTURES: The Greatest Story Ever Told, Bus Riley's Back in Town, Morituri, Nevada Smith, Enter Laughing, Buona Sera, Mrs. Campbell, Take the Money and Run, Annie Hall, Last Embrace, Distant Thunder, Ghostbusters II.
TELEVISION: Planet Earth, The Last Child, Lanigan's Rabbi, The Triangle Factory Fire Scandal, Plutonium Incident, Murder in Peyton Place.

MARGULIES, STAN: Producer. b. New York, NY, Dec. 14, 1920. e. De Witt Clinton H.S., NYU, B.S., June, 1940. Army Air Force, May, 1942; pub. rels. Air Force and the Infantry, wrote service magazines, newspapers including Yank; spec. feature writer & asst. Sunday editor, Salt Lake City Tribune; publicist, RKO Studios, Hollywood, March, 1947; continued publicity work at CBS-Radio, 20th Century-Fox, Walt Disney Productions. Bryna Films, 1955; became vice-pres., 1958; also served exec. prod., TV series, Tales of the Vikings; prod. aide. Spartacus.
PICTURES: 40 Pounds of Trouble, Those Magnificent Men in Their Flying Machines, Don't Just Stand There, The Pink Jungle, If It's Tuesday, This Must Be Belgium, I Love My Wife, Willy Wonka and the Chocolate Factory, One Is a Lonely Number, Visions of Eight.
TELEVISION: The Morning After, I Will Fight No More Forever, Collision Course, Roots, Roots: The Next Generation, Moviola, Murder Is Easy, The Thorn Birds, A Caribbean Mystery, Sparkling Cyanide, A Killer in the Family, The Mystic Warrior, A Bunny's Tale, Out on a Limb, Broken Angel.

MARILL, ALVIN H.: Executive Editor. b. Brockton, MA, Jan. 10, 1934. e. Boston U., 1955. Director music programming, writer/prod., WNAC, Boston 1961–65; dir. music prog., WRFM, NY 1966– 67; publicity writer, RCA Records 1967–72; sr. writer/editor, RCA Direct Marketing 1972–80; partner, TLK Direct Marketing 1977–80; mgr., A & R Administration, RCA Direct Marketing 1980–83; Exec. editor, CBS TV (1984–88); editor, Carol Publ. Group (1988–); Television editor, Films in Review 1973–84; Author: Samuel Goldwyn Presents; Robert Mitchum on the Screen; The Films of Anthony Quinn; The Films of Sidney Poitier; Katharine Hepburn: A Pictorial Study; Boris Karloff—A Pictorial Biography; Errol Flynn—A Pictorial Biography; Movies Made for Television 1964—89. Co-author: The Cinema of Edward G. Robinson; The Films of Tyrone Power. Editor: Moe Howard & The 3 Stooges. Assoc. editor: Leonard Maltin's TV Movies; Writer/researcher: The Great Singers (record/tape collections). Jury member: 1983 Locarno Film Fest.

MARIN, RICHARD (CHEECH): Actor, Writer. b. Los Angeles, CA, July 13, 1946. e. California State U, B.S. Teamed with Tommy Chong in improvisational group, City Works (Vancouver). Their comedy recordings include Sleeping Beauty, Cheech and Chong Big Bama, Los Cochinos, The Wedding Album (Grammy Award), Get Out of My Room.
PICTURES: Cheech and Chong's Up in Smoke, Cheech and Chong's Next Movie, Cheech and Chong's Nice Dreams, Things Are Tough All Over, It Came from Hollywood, Still Smokin', Yellowbeard, Cheech and Chong's The Corsican Brothers, After Hours, Echo Park, Born in East L.A. (also s.p., dir.), Fatal Beauty, Oliver & Company (voice), Ghostbusters II, Rude Awakening.
TELEVISION: Get Out of My Room (also dir., songs), Charlie Barnett—Terms of Enrollment.

MARK, LAURENCE M.: Producer, Executive. b. New York, NY. e. Wesleyan U., B.A.; & NYU, M.A. Started career as trainee and publicist for United Artists; also asst. to producer on Lenny, Smile, etc. Joined Paramount Pictures as mktg./prod. liaison dir. and then exec. dir., pub. for m.p. division in New York. Named v.p., prod./mktg. at Paramount Studio; 1980, v.p., west coast mktg.; 1982 promoted to post as v.p., prod. 1984, joined 20th Century-Fox as exec. v.p., prod.; 1986, established Laurence Mark Productions at Fox.
PICTURES: Black Widow (exec. prod.); Working Girl (exec. prod.); My Stepmother is an Alien (exec. prod.); Cookie (prod.).
TELEVISION: Sweet Bird of Youth (exec. prod.).

MARKHAM, MONTE: Actor. b. Manatee, FL, June 21, 1938. e. U. of Georgia. Military service in Coast Guard after which joined resident theatre co. at Stephens College, MO, where also taught acting. Joined Actor's Workshop Theatre, San Francisco, for three years. Made TV debut in Mission: Impossible episode.
PICTURES: One Is a Lonely Number, Hour of the Gun, Guns of the Magnificent Seven, Midway, Airport '77, Ginger in the Morning, Jake Speed, Hot Pursuit, Defense Play (also dir.), Judgment Day.
TELEVISION: Series: The Second Hundred Years, Mr. Deeds Goes to Town, The New Perry Mason, Baywatch. Movies: Visions, The Astronaut, Death Takes a Holiday, Baywatch: Panic at Malibu Pier, Hustling.
BROADWAY: Irene, Same Time Next Year.

MARKLE, FLETCHER: Writer, Director, Producer. b. Canada, March 27, 1921. Writer, dir., prod. Canadian Broadcasting Co. & BBC, London, 1942–46; prod., dir. Studio One series, CBS, 1947–48; Ford Theatre, CBS, 1948–49; writer, ed. & narrator The Robot Bomb, prize-winning doc. short, 1941; first m.p. dir. Jigsaw, 1949; thereafter Night into Morning, The Man with a Cloak; prod. Studio One series, CBS, 1952–53; prod., dir., Life with Father, CBS-TV, 1953–55; Front Row Center, 1955. Contributing dir. and/or prod. to various TV film series: Mystery Theatre, Panic, No Warning, Colgate Theatre, Lux Playhouse, M Squad, Buckskin, Rendezvous, Tales of the Vikings, Thriller, Hong Kong, 1956–61. Dir. Father of the Bride, 1961; dir. m.p., The Incredible Journey, 1962; Telescope series, CBC-TV, 1963–72. Head of TV Drama, Canadian Broadcasting Corp. 1970–73, Exec. prod., CBC-TV features and writer in residence. University of Toronto, 1974–75.

MARKLE, PETER: Director.
PICTURES: The Personals; Hot Dog; Youngblood, Bat-21.
TELEVISION: Nightbreaker, Breaking Point.

MARKOWITZ, ROBERT: Director. Mostly on TV before theatrical debut with Voices, 1979.
TELEVISION: Children of the Night, Phantom of the Opera, The Deadliest Season, Song of Myself, With All Deliberate Speed, The 34th Star, The Storyteller, Kojak: The Belarus File, My Mother's Secret Life, Pray TV, A Long Way Home, Alex: The Life of a Child, Adam: His Story Continues, Life or Death in the Emergency Room, The Wall, A Dangerous Life (mini-series).

MARKS, ALFRED: O.B.E. Actor-Comedian. b. London, 1921. TV, own series, Alfred Marks Time with wife, comedienne Paddie O'Neil.
PICTURES: Desert Mice, There Was a Crooked Man, Weekend with Lulu, The Frightened City, She'll Have to Go, Scream and Scream Again, Our Miss Fred, Valentino, Sleeps Six.
TELEVISION: Blanding's Castle, Hobson's Choice, Paris 1900, The Memorandum.

MARKS, ARTHUR: Producer, Director, Writer, Film Executive. b. Los Angeles, CA, Aug. 2, 1927. At 19 began work at MGM Studios as production messenger. Became asst. dir. in 1950, youngest dir. member of Directors Guild of Amer., 1957. President and board member of Arthur Prod., Inc.
PICTURES: Togetherness (prod., dir., s.p.), Class of '74 (dir., s.p.), Bonnie's Kids (dir., s.p.), Roommates (dir., s.p.), Detroit 9000 (prod., dir.), The Centerfold Girls (prod., dir.), A Woman For All Men (dir.), Wonder Woman (exec. prod.), The Candy Snatchers (exec. prod.), Bucktown (dir.), Friday Foster (prod., dir.) J.D.'s Revenge (prod.-dir.), Monkey Hustle (prod., dir.). Writer: Empress of the China Seas; Gold Stars; Mean Intentions; Hot Times.
TELEVISION: Prod. of Perry Mason series, 1961–66; dir. of over 100 Perry Mason episodes; writer-dir. of numerous TV shows including I Spy, Mannix, Starsky & Hutch, Dukes of Hazzard.

MARKS, RICHARD E.: Executive. e. UCLA; UCLA Sch. of Law. 1978–82, v.p., legal & business affairs for Ziegler/Diskant Literary Agency. Appt. pres., Major Business Brokers. Joined Paramount Pictures 1984 as sr. atty. for Network TV Div., as project atty. for Family Ties & Cheers. 1985, named sr. atty. for M.P. Group for The Golden Child, Beverly Hills Cop II, etc.; 1987 joined Weintraub Entertainment Group as v.p. business affairs, m.p. div.

MARKSON, BEN: Writer. b. Creston, IA, Aug. 6. Army Capt., W.W.II. Reporter, feature writer columnist, playwright (Is My Face Red?). Joined Warners, 1932 as writer; since author orig. s.p. dial., adapt., collab., many pictures. Writes many TV plays.
PICTURES: Here Comes the Navy, Woman-Wise, Danger, Love at Work, Is My Face Red?, Brides Are Like That, Half-Naked Truth, Lady Killer, That I May Live, White Cockatoo, Goodbye Again, Great Mr. Nobody, The Beautiful Cheat, A Close Call for Boston Blackie, Prison Ship, The Falcon in San Francisco, Mr. District Attorney, It Happened on Fifth Ave., Edge of Eternity, With My Face to the Enemy.

MARLOWE, LOUIS J.: Producer, Director. r.n. L. J. Goetten. b. St. Cloud, MN, Jan. 4. e. Hollywood H.S., U. of Southern California. Prop man, asst. dir., unit mgr., dr. special effects, shorts, second units Warner Bros., freelance dir. comedy series; Director features both theatrical and TV programs.
PICTURES: On the Air, Always Tomorrow, Handing It Back, Tradition, One Above All, Just a Boy.

MARSH, JEAN: Actress, Writer. b. London, Eng., July 1, 1934. NY stage debut Much Ado About Nothing, 1959. As a child appeared in films: Tales of Hoffman; as principal dancer in Where's Charley. Co-creator, co-author and starred as Rose, Upstairs, Downstairs.
THEATER: Broadway: Travesties, The Importance of Being Earnest, Too True to Be Good, My Fat Friend, Whose Life Is It Anyway?, Blithe Spirit.
PICTURES: Cleopatra, The Limbo Line, Frenzy, Dark Places, The Eagle Has Landed, The Changeling, Return to Oz, Willow.
TELEVISION: Series: Upstairs, Downstairs (Emmy Award 1972, 1974, 1975), Nine to Five, The Grover Monster, A State Dinner with Queen Elizabeth II, Mad About the Boy: Noel Coward—A Celebration, Habeas Corpus, Uncle Vanya, Twelfth Night, Pygmalion, On the Rocks Theatre, The Corsican Brothers, Master of the Game, Danny, the Champion of the World, Act of Will.

MARSHALL, ALAN: Producer. b. London, Eng., Aug. 12, 1938. Co-founder Alan Parker Film Company, 1970. Formerly film editor. Received Michael Balcon Award, British Acad., Outstanding Contribution to Cinema, 1985.
PICTURES: Bugsy Malone, Midnight Express, Fame, Shoot the Moon, Pink Floyd: The Wall, Another Country (Cannes Film Fest, best artistic contribution award, 1984), Birdy (Special Jury Award, Cannes Film Fest., 1985), Angel Heart, Homeboy.
TELEVISION: No Hard Feelings, Our Cissy, Footsteps.

MARSHALL, E. G.: Actor. r.n. Everett G. Marshall. b. Minnesota, June 18, 1910. Acting debut with Oxford Players, 1933. Numerous TV appearances on all networks; film debut in House on 92nd St. (1945).
BROADWAY: Jason, Jacobowsky and the Colonel, Skin of Our Teeth, Iceman Cometh, Woman Bites Dog, The Survivors, The Gambler, The Crucible, The Little Foxes.
PICTURES: 13 Rue Madeleine, Call Northside 77, Caine Mutiny, Pushover, Bamboo Prison, Broken Lance, Silver Chalice, Left Hand of God, Scarlet Hour, 12 Angry Men, Bachelor Party, Town Without Pity, The Chase, Tora, Tora, Tora, The Bridge at Remagen, The Pursuit of Happiness, Interiors, Superman II, Creepshow, Power, My Chauffeur, La Gran Fiesta, National Lampoon's Christmas Vacation., Two Evil Eyes (The Black Cat).
TELEVISION: The Defenders, The Bold Ones. Movies: The Winter of Our Discontent, Under Siege, At Mother's Request, Emma, Queen of the South Seas, The Hijacking of the Achille Lauro.

MARSHALL, FRANK: Producer. Worked on first feature film in 1967 while still a student at UCLA. Protege of Peter Bogdanovich, working on his production crew and serving as assoc. prod. on Paper Moon, Daisy Miller, Nickelodeon, etc. Line producer on Orson Welles' The Other Side of the Wind (unreleased) and Martin Scorsese's The Last Waltz. Worked with Walter Hill on The Driver (assoc. prod.) and The Warriors (exec. prod.). Began collaboration with Steven Spielberg as prod. for Raiders of the Lost Ark.
PICTURES: Raiders of the Lost Ark (prod.), Poltergeist (prod.); E.T.: The Extra-Terrestrial (prod. supvr.); Twilight Zone—The Movie (exec. prod.); Indiana Jones and the Temple of Doom (exec. prod.); Fandango (exec. prod.); Gremlins (exec. prod.); Goonies (exec. prod.); Back to the Future (exec. prod.); The Color Purple (prod.); Young Sherlock Holmes (exec. prod.), An American Tail (co-exec. prod.); Innerspace (co-exec. prod.), The Money Pit (prod.), The Land Before Time (exec. prod.), Empire of the Sun (prod.), Who Framed Roger Rabbit? (prod.); Indiana Jones and the Last Crusade (exec. prod.), Always (prod.), Dad (exec. prod.), Back to the Future II. (exec. prod.), Joe Versus the Volcano (exec. prod.), Gremlins II (exec. prod.).
TELEVISION: Roger Rabbit and the Secrets of Toontown (exec. prod.).

MARSHALL, GARRY: Producer, Director, Writer. b. New York, NY, Nov. 13, 1934. Brother of Penny Marshall. e. Northwestern U. Copy boy and reporter for N.Y. Daily News while writing comedy material for Phil Foster, Joey Bishop. Was drummer in his own jazz band and successful stand-up comedian and playwright. Turned Neil Simon's play The Odd Couple into long running TV series (1970). Partner with Jerry Belson many years. Wrote Bdwy play, The Roost (with Belson, 1980).
PICTURES: Writer-Producer: How Sweet It Is, The Grasshopper. Director: Young Doctors in Love (also exec. prod.), The Flamingo Kid (also s.p.), Nothing in Common, Overboard (dir. only), Beaches. 3000 (dir. only). Acted in Psych-Out, Lost in America.
TELEVISION: Writer for Jack Paar Show, Joey Bishop Show, Danny Thomas Show, Lucy, Dick Van Dyke Show, I Spy. Dir.-writer: Hey, Landlord, The Odd Couple, The Little People (Brian Keith Show). Creator and exec. prod.: Happy Days, Laverne and Shirley, Blansky's Beauties, Who's Watching the Kids? Mork and Mindy, Angie, Joanie Loves Chachi.

MARSHALL, LARRY: Comedian, Actor, Writer, Songwriter. b. Clarkston, Scotland. Trained Rutherglen repertory theatre. Own daily lunchtime television show for eight years. Appeared in many major television drama series; and light entertainment show; own evening shows; comedy and panel games. Since 1973 written, produced and starred in summer show, Jamie's Scottish Night Out running to 1987.

MARSHALL, PENNY: Actress, Director. b. New York, NY, Oct. 15, 1942. Daughter of industrial filmmaker and Laverne and Shirley prod., Tony Marscharelli, and sister of prod.-dir. Garry Marshall. Dropped out of U. of New Mexico to teach dancing. Acted in summer stock and competed on The Original Amateur Hour before going to Hollywood to make TV debut in The Danny Thomas Hour (1967–68). Debut as theatrical director 1986: Jumpin' Jack Flash.
PICTURES: How Sweet It Is, The Savage Seven, The Grasshopper, 1941, Movers and Shakers, Jumping Jack Flash (dir.), Big (dir.), Awakening (dir.).
TELEVISION: Danny Thomas Hour. Series: The Odd Couple (1971–75), Friends and Lovers (1974–75), Laverne and Shirley (1976–83). Pilot: Evil Roy Slade. Guest: The Super, Bob Newhart Show, Happy Days, Saturday Night Live, Comedy Zone, Chico and the Man. Movies: The Feminist and the Fuzz, The Couple Takes a Wife, The Crooked Hearts, Love Thy Neighbor, Let's Switch, More Than Friends, Chal-

lenge of a Lifetime. Specials: Lily for President. *Director:* Laverne and Shirley, Working Shifts, Tracey Ullman Show.

MARSHALL, PETER: Actor, TV Show Host. r.n. Pierre La Cock. b. Clarksburg, WV, March 30. Brother of actress Joanne Dru. Began career as NBC page in N.Y. Teamed with the late Tommy Noonan in comedy act for nightclubs, guesting on Ed Sullivan Show and other variety shows. In 1950 made Las Vegas stage debut and since has been headliner there and in Reno and Lake Tahoe. New York stage, in Bdwy musical Skyscraper. On London stage in H.M.S. Pinafore; Bye, Bye Birdie. In La Cage aux Folles (national company and Bdwy), 42nd St. (Atlantic City).

PICTURES: Ensign Pulver, The Cavern, Americathon, Annie.

TELEVISION: Two of the Most (local N.Y. show), The Hollywood Squares (host), many guest appearances.

MARSHALL, ZENA: Actress. b. Kenya, Africa, 1926. e. France, finishing school in Ascot, Eng. Made her stage debut in repertory. Many TV appearance U.S. and England including Bob Hope show, Harpers W.I., Ghost Squad.

PICTURES: Caesar and Cleopatra (debut, 1945), Good Time Girl, Miranda, Sleeping Car to Trieste, Marry Me, Dark Interval, Blind Man's Bluff, Love's a Luxury, Deadly Nightshade, My Wife's Family, Bermuda Affair, Let's Be Happy, Dr. No, The Guilty Party, Those Magnificent Men in Their Flying Machines, The Terrornauts.

TELEVISION: International Detective, Invisible Man, Dial 999, Danger Man, Sir Francis Drake, Man of the World, Human Jungle, Sentimental Agent, Court Martial.

MARTEL, GENE: Producer, director. b. New York, NY, June 19, 1916. e. City Coll. of New York , U. of Alabama, Sorbonne, Paris. Newspaperman, New York and Birmingham, AL; dancer, actor, choreographer, director Broadway; prod. dir., many documentaries; films for State Dept., others; dir. for Paramount Pictures. Joined Princess Pictures 1952 to make films in Europe; formed own co., Martel Productions Inc., 1954.

PICTURES: Check-mate, Double-barrelled Miracle, The Lie, Double Profile, Sergeant and the Spy, Black Forest, Eight Witnesses, Fire One, Phantom Caravan, Doorway to Suspicion, Diplomatic Passport, Immediate Disaster.

MARTENS, RALPH R.: Executive b. New York, NY. e. State U. of New York at Albany. USMC-USMCR 1962–present, 1970–73 Tampax Inc. 1973–79 Pannell Kerr Forster and Co., CPA's 1979–84, asst. treas. Motion Picture Association of America, MPEAA, AMPECA, AFRAM FILMS, 1984 Treas., MPAA, MPEAA, AMPECA and AFRAM. In 1988, named vice president.

MARTIN, DEAN: Actor. r.n. Dino Crocetti. b. Steubenville, OH, June 7, 1917. e. Steubenville H.S. Was amateur prizefighter; worked at odd jobs, mill hand, gasoline attendant, prior to acting career. Joined Jerry Lewis, comedian at 500 Club, Atlantic City, NJ, as straight man-singer, 1946; played many theatres, night clubs until 1956. Team film debut: My Friend Irma (1949). Voted (with Jerry Lewis) one of the top ten Money-Making Stars in Motion Picture Herald-Fame poll, 1951, 1953–55; Number One, 1952.

PICTURES: My Friend Irma Goes West, At War with the Army, That's My Boy, The Stooge, Sailor Beware, Jumping Jacks, The Caddy, Scared Stiff, Money from Home, Living It Up, Three Ring Circus, You're Never Too Young, Artists and Models, Pardners, Hollywood or Bust, 10,000 Bedrooms, The Young Lions, Some Came Running, Rio Bravo, Career, Who Was That Lady?, Bells Are Ringing, Ocean's 11, Ada, Sergeants 3, Who's Got the Action?, Toys in the Attic, Who's That Sleeping in My Bed, Robin and the Seven Hoods, Kiss Me Stupid, Sons of Katie Elder, Rough Night in Jericho, How to Save a Marriage, Airport, The Ambushers, The Wrecking Crew, Something Big, Showdown, Mr. Ricco, The Cannonball Run, Cannonball Run II.

TELEVISION: Club Oasis, Dean Martin Show. Golden Globe Award.

MARTIN, DEWEY: Actor. b. Katemcy, TX, Dec. 8, 1923. e. U. of Georgia. U.S. Navy, W.W.II; actor, little theatres & stock; film debut in Knock on Any Door (1949).

PICTURES: Kansas Raiders, The Thing, Big Sky, Tennessee Champ, Prisoner of War, Men of the Fighting Lady, Land of the Pharaohs, Desperate Hours, Proud and Profane, 10,000 Bedrooms, Battle Ground, The Longest Day, Savage Sam, Seven Alone.

TELEVISION: Live: G.E. Theatre, U.S. Steel, Playhouse 90, Playwrights 56; Daniel Boone (mini-series), Doc Holliday (series), Wheeler and Murdoch, Outer Limits, Twilight Zone.

MARTIN, EDWIN DENNIS: Executive. b. Columbus, GA, Jan. 30, 1920. e. U. of Georgia, B.S., 1940. Past pres., Martin Theatre Cos.; past pres. TOA, International. Retired.

MARTIN, MARY: Actress. b. Wetherford, TX, Dec. 1, 1914. e. Ward-Belmont Sch., Nashville, TN. Mother of actor Larry Hagman. m.p. debut in 1939. Received Special Tony Award, 1948. Autobiography: My Heart Belongs (1976).

STAGE: Lute Song, Leave It to Me, One Touch of Venus, South Pacific, Annie Get Your Gun, Kind Sir, Peter Pan (Tony Award, 1955), Jennie, Sound of Music (Tony Award, 1960), I Do I Do, Do You Turn Somersaults?, Legends (road tour with Carol Channing).

PICTURES: Great Victor Herbert (debut, 1939), Rhythm on the River, Love Thy Neighbor, Kiss the Boys Goodbye, New York Town, Birth of the Blues, Star Spangled Rhythm, True to Life, Happy Go Lucky, Night and Day, Main Street to Broadway.

TELEVISION: Ford anniversary show, Rodgers & Hammerstein Cavalcade show. Peter Pan (Emmy, 1955), Valentine, Together with Music (with Noel Coward), Over Easy (series host).

MARTIN, MILLICENT: Actress, Singer. b. Romford, Eng., June 8, 1934. Toured U.S. in The Boy Friend, 1954–57.

STAGE: Expresso Bongo, The Crooked Mile, Our Man Crichton, Tonight at 8, The Beggars Opera, Puss 'n Boots, The Card, Absurd Person Singular, Aladdin, Side by Side by Sondheim, King of Hearts, Move Over Mrs. Markham, Noises Off, One Into Two, 42nd Street (N.Y. & L.A.), Follies.

TELEVISION: International Detective Series, Millie, That Was the Week That Was, Harry Moorings; own series, Mainly Millicent, Kiss Me Kate; 1966 own series, Millicent TV; London Palladium Color Show, USA, Danny Kaye, Piccadilly London; From a Bird's Eye View (own series); Tom Jones show, Englebert Humperdinck show, Downtown with Michael Nouri, LA Law, Max Headroom, Newhart.

PICTURES: The Horsemaster, The Girl on the Boat, Nothing But the Best, Alfie, Stop the World I Want To Get Off.

MARTIN, PAMELA SUE: Actress. b. Westport, CT, Jan. 15, 1953. Did modelling and TV commercials before entering films.

PICTURES: To Find a Man, The Poseidon Adventure, Buster and Billie, Our Time, The Lady in Red, Torchlight (also assoc. prod. & s.p.).

TELEVISION: Series: Nancy Drew Mysteries, Hardy Boy Mysteries, Dynasty. Pilots: The Gun and the Pulpit, Human Feelings. Movies: The Girls from Huntington House, Arthur Hailey's Strong Medicine. Angel on My Shoulder, Bay Coven.

MARTIN, STEVE: Actor. b. Waco, TX, Aug., 1945. m. actress Victoria Tennant. e. Long Beach Coll., UCLA. Writer for various TV comedy shows (Smothers Brothers, Sonny & Cher, etc.). Broadway debut Waiting For Godot, (with Robin Williams), 1988.

PICTURES: The Kids Are Alright, The Muppet Movie, The Jerk (also co-s.p.), Pennies from Heaven, Dead Men Don't Wear Plaid (also co.-s.p.), The Man with Two Brains (also co-s.p.), Lonely Guy, All of Me, Little Shop of Horrors, Three Amigos (also co-s.p. & exec. prod.); Roxanne (also exec. prod., s.p.); Planes, Trains & Automobiles, Dirty Rotten Scoundrels, Parenthood.

TELEVISION: Steve Martin—A Wild and Crazy Guy, Steve Allen Comedy Hours, Comedy Is Not Pretty, Saturday Night Live, Smothers Brothers Comedy Hour 20th Reunion.

MARTIN, TONY: Singer, Musician, Actor. b. Oakland, CA, Dec. 25, 1913. r.n. Alvin Morris. e. Oakland H.S., St. Mary's Coll. m. Cyd Charisse, actress-dancer. Sang, played saxophone & clarinet in high school band, engaged by nearby theatres for vaudeville; with Five Red Peppers, jazz group at 14 yrs.; two yrs. later with band, Palace Hotel, San Francisco; radio debut Walter Winchell program, 1932; joined Tom Gerund's band, World's Fair Chicago, 1933; played night clubs. First starring radio show, Tune Up Time (singer & emcee); on Burns and Allen program; own show for Texaco, Carnation Contented Hour.

RECORDINGS: Begin the Beguine, Intermezzo, The Last Time I Saw Paris, I'll See You in My Dreams, Domino, September Song, For Every Man There's a Woman.

PICTURES: Sing Baby Sing, Follow The Fleet, You Can't Have Everything; Ali Baba Goes To Town, Music in My Heart, Ziegfield Girl, The Big Store, Till The Clouds Roll By, Cabash, Two Tickets to Broadway, Here Come the Girls, Easy to Love, Deep in My Heart, Hit the Deck, Quincannon Frontier Scout, Let's Be Happy.

MARTON, ANDREW: Director. b. Budapest, Hungary, Jan. 26, 1904. Vita Film, Vienna, 1922; to Hollywood, with Ernst Lubitsch, 1923; started directing in Berlin, then in London, Wolf's Clothing, Secret of Stamboul, School for Husbands; in Hollywood, Little Bit of Heaven, Gentle Annie, Gallant Bess.

PICTURES: King Solomon's Mines, Wild North, Storm Over Tibet, Devil Makes Three, Gypsy Colt, Prisoner of War, Men of the Fighting Lady, Green Fire, Underwater Warrior, Cinerama Seven Wonders of the World, It Happened in Athens, The Longest Day, The Thin Red Line, Crack in the World, Clarence the Crosseyed Lion, Around the World Under the Sea, Birds Do It, Africa-Texas Style, Mohammed, Messenger of God.

TELEVISION: Man and the Challenge, Daktari, Cowboy in Africa, The Sea Hunt.

MARX, SAMUEL: Writer, Producer. b. New York, NY, Jan. 26, 1902.
PICTURES: Lassie Come Home, This Man's Navy, My Brother Talks to Horses, The Beginning or End, A Lady Without Passport, Grounds for Marriage, Kiss of Fire, Ain't Misbehavin', Waterloo, Rome, The Ravine.

MASEFIELD, JOSEPH R.: Executive, Producer, Director, Writer. b. New York, NY, June 20, 1933. e. American Acad. of Dramatic Arts, 1950. Writer-performer, club work (as Steve Parker). Later, actor in stock; formed EEF Film Productions, 1956; prod. A Story Like Two (short), A City Eats (doc.). In m.p. as unit mgr., asst. dir. and prod. mgr. Later writer and film editor: Montage (Time-Life); Ages of Man (IBM); Festival of Two Worlds (Bell Telephone Hour) and special, The New Face of Israel. Asst. dir., prod. mgr., Mitgebracht Aus New York (German TV), The Devils Doubloon, (feature); Writer-director, Citizen Smith, feature documentary. Co-director and assoc. prod. Hear My Song, (Cavalier Films), 1969 producer The Spy. 1969, vice pres. in charge of prod. PCI, Inc. Pub. rel. director, The Max Steiner Music Society; pres., Joseph R. Masefield & Associates. In 1974, formed Majer Prods. with Steve Jerro.
PICTURES: A New Life, The Vanquished, Trio, Living Planet, The Burning Man.

MASINA, GIULIETTA: Actress. b. Giorgio di Piano, Italy, Feb. 22, 1921. m. director Federico Fellini. e. U. of Rome. Was a school teacher before acting on stage and on radio in Rome. Met Fellini when he asked her to audition for radio soap opera, 1942. Film debut: Rossallini's Paisan, 1946.
PICTURES: Without Pity, Variety Lights, The White Sheik, Behind Closed Shutters, The Greatest Love, La Strada, Forbidden Women, The Swindlers, Nights of Cabiria, Fortunella, Juliet of the Spirits, Non Stuzzicate la Zanazara, The Madwoman of Chaillot, Ginger and Fred.

MASLANSKY, PAUL: Producer, Director, Writer. b. New York, NY, Nov. 23, 1933. Trumpet player on NY club circuit. Worked in Kansas City at AM radio station selling ad time and working for band. Studied filmmaking at Cinemateque Français where made a documentary (Letter from Paris) which won Cannes Festival award. Asst. dir. on Counterfeit Traitor; followed by prod. mgr. on several films in Europe, 1959–72 incl. The Running Man and Jason and the Argonauts. Wrote and produced Gothic horror films, including Castle of the Living Dead. Covered Israeli war in 1967 with CBS film group; spent year in Russia on The Red Tent, followed by The Blue Bird. Filmed Big Truck and Poor Claire in Israel; Miracles Still Happen in Brazil.
PICTURES: Damnation Alley (co-prod.), When You Comin' Back, Red Ryder (co-prod.), Hot Stuff, The Villain, Scavenger Hunt, Police Academy 2 (assoc. prod.), Circle of Iron (co-prod.), Love Child (prod.), Return to Oz, Police Academy 3, Police Academy 4, Police Academy 5: Assignment Miami Beach, For Better or Worse (exec. prod.), Police Academy 6: City Under Siege (prod.), The Lost (exec. prod.), Ski Patrol (exec. prod.), Mysterious Island (exec. prod.), The Russia House (co-prod.).
TELEVISION: The Gun and the Pulpit, King.

MASON, JACKIE: Comedian. Actor. b. Sheboygan, WI, June 9, 1931. Was a rabbi and later a restaurant owner before becoming stand-up comedian.
THEATER: Enter Solly Gold (1965), A Teaspoon Every Four Hours (Amer. National Theatre & Academy Theatre), Sex-a-Poppin (revue, prod. only), The World According to Me! (one-man show, special Tony Award, 1987).
PICTURES: Operation Delilah (debut, 1966), The Stoolie (also prod.), The Jerk, The History of the World, Part I, The Perils of P.K., Caddyshack II.
TELEVISION: Steve Allen, Ed Sullivan, Jack Paar, Garry Moore, Perry Como and Merv Griffin Shows. Evening at the Improv, Late Night with David Letterman. Movies: The Best of Times. Specials: Jack Paar is Alive and Well!, The World According to Me!

MASON, JOHN DUDLEY: Executive. b. Ashland, KY, Oct 29, 1949. e. Amherst Coll., B.A., cum laude, 1971; Claremont Graduate Sch. and University Center, M.A., 1973; Amos Tuck Sch. of Business Administration, Dartmouth Coll., M.B.A., 1978. Program officer, National Endowment for the Humanities, 1972–76; analyst (1978–79), asst. mgr. (1979–80), mgr. (1980) strategic planning, Consolidated Rail Corp.; Consultant, Frito-Lay, Division, PepsiCo (1980–82); mgr, corporate planning, The Dun & Bradstreet Corp. (1982–86); finance director, anti-piracy, Motion Picture Association of America, Inc. (1986–present). Chairman, Finance Comm. and mem., bd. of dir. Association de Gestion Int'l. Collective des Oeuvres Audiovisuelles (AGICOA) 1987–88. Director, Instituto Venezolano de Representacion Cinematografica (INVERECI), Caracas, Venezuela (1988–present). Director: Foundation for the Protection of Film & Video Works (FVWP), Taipei, Taiwan (1987–present).

MASON, KENNETH M.: Executive. b. Rochester, NY; Sept. 21, 1917. e. Washington and Jefferson Coll.; U. of Rochester, graduate work; Dr. of Laws (H), Washington & Jefferson Coll., 1989. Began career with Eastman Kodak Co. in Kodak Park cine processing dept. in 1935; transferred following year to film dev. dept., Kodak Research Lab. Returned to coll. in 1938, 1939 returned to Kodak same dept. Later joined film planning dept., remaining there until entering U.S. Navy in 1943. Returned to Kodak in 1946 as staff engineer in Kodak Office motion picture film dept. In 1950 appt. mgr. of Midwest Division, of M.P. Film Dept.; became gen. mgr., Midwest Division, m.p. products sales dept. in 1963; named sls. mgr. of NYC region in 1965; appt. regional sls. mgr., Pacific Southern Region, Hollywood, in 1970; 1974 appt. mgr., product programs and research, Motion Picture and Audiovisual Markets Division, Kodak Office; 1974 named gen. mgr. of that division. Elected asst. v.p. of co. on March 28, 1974, v.p., Dec. 11, 1978. Retired Oct. 1, 1982. Former chmn., Inter-Society Committee for the Enhancement of Theatrical Presentation.
MEMBER: Trustee emeritus, Board of Trustees of Washington and Jefferson Coll. (and former chmn); past pres. of Society of Motion Picture & Television Engineers and honorary member; honorary fellow of British Kinematograph Sound & Television Society; mem. of University Film & Video Assn., Motion Picture Academy, American Society of Cinematographers, Variety Club. Board of dir.: Will Rogers Institute, Allied Film & Video, Univ. Film & Video Fdn.

MASON, MARSHA: Actress. b. St. Louis. April 3, e. Webster Coll. Came to N.Y. to continue dramatic studies and embark on theatre career. Member of American Conservatory Theatre, San Francisco.
THEATER: The Deer Park, Cactus Flower, The Indian Wants the Bronx, Happy Birthday, Wanda June, Private Lives, You Can't Take It With You, Cyrano de Bergerac, A Dolls House.
PICTURES: Blume in Love (debut), Cinderella Liberty, Audrey Rose, The Goodbye Girl, The Cheap Detective, Promises in the Dark, Chapter Two, Only When I Laugh, Max Dugan Returns, Heartbreak Ridge, Stella.
TELEVISION: Love of Life (series), Brewsie and Willie, Cyrano de Bergerac, Surviving, Trapped in Silence, The Image, Dinner at Eight. Dir.: Little Miss Perfect.

MASON, PAMELA: Actress, Writer. b. Westgate. England. Mar. 10, 1918. Stage debut, 1936, The Luck of the Devil, London; also playwright (in collab. James Mason, Flying Blind, Made in Heaven), Author novels This Little Hand, A Lady Possessed, The Blinds Are Down, Ignoramus, Began Brit. screen career 1938, I Met a Murderer (rig. story & s.p.; cast); also in They Were Sisters, 1944. In 1946 (s.p. & cast) The Upturned Glass; (acted) Pandora and the Flying Dutchman; acted, collab. s.p. Lady Possessed, Syndicated TV, Pamela Mason Show, author Marriage Is the First Step Toward Divorce. syndicated TV The Weaker Sex?; author, The Female Pleasure Hunt; lectures at women's clubs countrywide. Columnist for Movieline Magazine.

MASSEN, OSA: Actress. b. Denmark, Copenhagen. Jan. 13, 1916.
PICTURES: Honeymoon in Bali, Honeymoon for Three, A Woman's Face, Accent on Love, You'll Never Get Rich, The Devil Pays Off, Ireland, Strange Journey, Night Unto Night, Deadline at Dawn, Gentleman Misbehaves, Rocketship XM.

MASSEY, ANNA: Actress. b. Sussex, England, Aug. 11, 1937. Daughter of Raymond Massey. Sister of Daniel Massey. On London stage in The Reluctant Debutante (debut, 1958), The Prime of Jean Brodie, Slag, The Importance of Being Earnest, Spoiled, Doctor's Delimma, School for Scandal, With National Theatre, 1989.
PICTURES: Peeping Tom, Bunny Lake Is Missing, The Looking Glass War, David Copperfield, Frenzy, A Little Romance, Sweet William, Another Country, The Chain, Five Days One Summer, Foreign Body, Mountains of the Moon, La Couleur du Vent, The Tall Guy, Killing Dad.
TELEVISION: A Doll's House, Remember the Germans, Wicked Woman, The Corn Is Green, Sakharov, Hotel Du Lac (BAFTA Award), A Hazard of Hearts, Around the World in 80 Days, Tears in the Rain.

MASSEY, DANIEL: Actor. b. London, Eng., Oct. 10, 1933. e. Eaton and King's Colleges. e. Cambridge U. Son of Raymond Massey. Brother of Anna Massey. Active on stage and TV. On Broadway in She Loves Me, Gigi.
PICTURES: In Which We Serve (1942), Girls at Sea, Upstairs and Downstairs, The Queen's Guard, Go to Blazes, The Entertainer, Operation Bullshine, Moll Flanders, The Jokers, Star!, Fragment of Fear, Mary, Queen of Scots, The Vault of Horror, The Incredible Sarah, The Devil's Advocate, Warlords of Atlantis, Bad Timing, Victory, Scandal.
TELEVISION: Aren't We All (debut, 1958). Series: The Roads to Freedom. Mini-series: The Golden Bowl. Movies: Love with a Perfect Stranger, Intimate Contact.

MASSIE, PAUL: Actor. b. Ontario, Canada. July 7, 1932. Early career on Canadian stage. Attended Central Sch., London, 1952, later jnd. Scottish National Children's Theatre. Entered m.p. ind. 1954 in Orders to Kill.
PICTURES: High Tide at Noon, Sapphire, Libel, The Two Faces of Dr. Jekyll, The Rebel, The Pot Carriers, Raising the Wind.
STAGE: Cat On a Hot Tin Roof.
TELEVISION: The Mark of the Warrior, The Last of the Brave, Ring Around the Moon, Secret Mission and Her Romeo.

MASTERS, BEN: Actor. b. Corvallis, OR, May 6, 1947.
THEATER: The Cherry Orchard, Waltz of the Toreadors, Plenty, Captain Brassbound's Conversion, The Boys in the Band, Eden Court, What the Butler Saw, The White Whore and the Bit Player, Key Exchange.
PICTURES: Mandingo (1975), All That Jazz, Key Exchange, Dream Lover, Making Mr. Right.
TELEVISION: Barnaby Jones, Kojack. Movies: Celebrity, Class of '65, Riviera, The Shadow Box, Nightstalker, The Deliberate Stranger, Street of Dreams, Heart Beat.

MASTERSON, MARY STUART: Actress. b. New York, NY, 1967. Daughter of writer-director-actor Peter Masterson and actress Carlin Glynn. e. NYU. Made film debut at age 8 in The Stepford Wives (1975). Spent summer at Stage Door Manor in Catskills; two summers at Sundance Inst. Studied acting with Estelle Parsons. Off-Bdwy debut The Lucky Spot (Manhattan Theatre Club) followed by Lily Daly.
PICTURES: Heaven Help Us, At Close Range, Some Kind of Wonderful, Gardens of Stone, My Little Girl, Mr. North, Chances Are, Bloodhounds of Broadway, Immediate Family.
TELEVISION: Love Lives On.

MASTERSON, PETER: Actor, Writer, Director. r.n. Carlos Bee Masterson, Jr. b. Houston, TX, June 1, 1934. m. actress Carlin Glynn. Father of actress Mary Stuart Masterson. e. Rice U., Houston, BA. 1957. NY stage debut, Call Me By My Rightful Name, 1961. Film debut Ambush Bay, 1965.
THEATER: Marathon '33, Blues for Mr. Charlie, The Trial of Lee Harvey Oswald, The Great White Hope, That Championship Season, The Poison Tree, The Best Little Whorehouse in Texas (co-author, dir.), The Last of the Knucklemen (dir.).
PICTURES: Counterpoint, In the Heat of the Night, Tomorrow, The Exorcist, Man on a Swing, The Stepford Wives, The Best Little Whorehouse in Texas (s.p. only), *Director:* The Trip to Bountiful, Full Moon in Blue Water, Palisades Park, Convicts, Night Game.
TELEVISION: Camera Three, Pueblo; The Quinns; A Question of Guilt.

MASTORAKIS, NICO: Writer, Director, Producer. b. Athens, Greece, 1941. Writer of novels and screenplays, including Fire Below Zero, and Keepers of the Secret (co-author). Pres. Omega Entertainment Ltd. since Jan. 1978.
PICTURES: Writer/dir./prod.: The Time Traveller, Blind Date, Sky High, The Zero Boys, The Wind, Terminal Exposure, Nightmare at Noon, Glitch, Ninja Academy. Prod.: The Greek Tycoon, Red Tide, Grandmother's House, Darkroom, Bloodstone (prod., co-s.p.), Hired to Kill.

MASTRANTONIO, MARY ELIZABETH: Actress. b. Oak Park, IL, Nov. 17, 1958. e. U. of Illinois 1976–78 where trained for opera. Worked as singer & dancer for summer at Opryland Theme Park in Nashville. Came to NY as understudy and vacation replacement as Maria in West Side Story revival. NY stage appearances, Copperfield (1981), Oh Brother, Amadeus, Sunday in the Park With George (Playwright's Horizons), The Human Comedy, Henry V, Figaro, Measure For Measure, The Knife, Twelfth Night.
PICTURES: Scarface (debut, 1983), The Color of Money, Slam Dance, The January Man, The Abyss, Fools of Fortune.
TELEVISION: Mussolini: The Untold Story.

MASTROIANNI, MARCELLO: Actor. b. Fontana Liri, Italy, Sept. 28, 1924. e. U. of Rome theatrical company. Draftsman in Rome, 1940–43. WWII, drew military maps until captured by Nazis and escaped. Theatrical debut in Rome in Angelica, 1948. Film debut in I Mizrabili (1948). Formed indep. prod. co., Master Films, 1966.
PLAYS: Death of a Salesman, Streetcar Named Desire, Ciao Rudy.
PICTURES: Too Bad She's Bad, A Dog's Life, Three Girls from Rome, The Miller's Beautiful Wife, Fever to Live, The Ladykillers of Rome, Love a La Carte, Days of Love, White Nights, Big Deal on Madonna Street, Divorce Italian Style, La Notte, A Very Private Affair, Bell Antonio, Where the Hot Wind Blows, La Dolce Vita, The Organizer, 8½, Yesterday, Today and Tomorrow, Marriage Italian Style, Casanova '70, The 10th Victim, The Poppy Is Also a Flower, Shoot Loud, Louder . . . I Don't Understand, The Stranger, A Place for Lovers, Leo the Last, Diamonds for Breakfast, Sunflower, Jealousy Italian Style, The Priest's Wife, What?, The Grande Bouffe, Massacre in Rome, Down the Ancient Stairs, The Sunday Woman, A Special Day, Stay as You Are, Blood Feud, City of Women, Gabriella, La Nuit de Varennes, Macaroni, Ginger and Fred, Federico Fellini's Intervista, Dark Eyes, Miss Arizona, Traffic Jam, The Two Lives of Martia Pascal, Splendor.

MATALON, DAVID A.: b. Israel. Executive. Sr. exec. v.p. and theatrical mgr. of Columbia Pictures International before joining Tri-Star Pictures in 1983 as exec. v.p. with responsibility for worldwide marketing and distribution. 1985, named Pres; 1989, named exec. v.p. of Columbia Pictures Entertainment Inc.

MATHESON, TIM: Actor. b. Los Angeles, CA, Dec. 31, 1947. e. California State U. Debut on TV at age 12 in My Three Sons. At 19 contract player for Universal, regular on Bonanza. 1985, turned to direction: St. Elsewhere episode and music videos. Set up own productions co. at Burbank Studios 1985, acted off-Bdwy. in True West. With partner Daniel Grodnick bought out National Lampoon founder Matty Simons, becoming exec. officer and chmn 1989.
PICTURES: Divorce American Style, Yours, Mine and Ours, How to Commit Marriage, Magnum Force, Almost Summer, National Lampoon's Animal House, Dreamer, The Apple Dumpling Gang Rides Again, 1941, A Little Sex, To Be or Not To Be, Up the Creek, Impulse, Fletch, Blind Fury (also co-prod.), Speed Zone.
TELEVISION: Movies: Owen Marshall, Counselor-at-Law, Lock, Stock and Barrel, Hitched, Remember When, The Last Day, The Runaway Barge, The Quest, Bus Stop, Classmates, Mary White, Obsessed with a Married Woman, Blind Justice, Warm Hearts Cold Feet, Bay Coven, Just in Time (co-exec. prod., actor), The Littlest Victims, Series: Nikki & Alexander.

MATHEWS, CAROLE: Actress. b. Montgomery, IL, Sept. 13. e. Aurora, IL H.S. Started as night club, radio entertainer; to Hollywood, 1944.
PICTURES: Massacre River, Great Gatsby, Special Agent, Meet Me At the Fair, Swamp Woman, Port of Heil, Shark River, Treasure of Ruby Hills, Requirement for a Redhead, Look In Any Window, Thirteen Men, Female Fiend, Tender Is the Night, End of the Road.
TELEVISION: Steel Hour, Kraft Theatre, Lux Video, Hitchcock Presents, Studio One, Californians, Texan, 77 Sunset Strip, Perry Mason, Four Star Theatre, M-Squad, Death Valley Days, Guestward Ho, Two Faces West, Johnny Midnight, Pete & Gladys, 87th Precinct, Ben Casey.

MATLACK, JACK D.: Theatre executive, Publicist. b. Manton, CA, Feb. 22, 1914. e. Chico (CA) State Teachers Coll. Entered m.p. ind. as doorman Criterion, Medford, OR; then mgr. dir.; joined J.J. Parker Theatres, Portland, OR, 1943; as exec. asst. to pres. and adv. dir. eight theatres; now pres. Jack Matlack Promotions. Portland, OR, N.W.P.R. for studios; well known showman, winner 20 exploit. awards including Grand (Silver) Quigley Award, 1943; Quigley War Showmanship Award, 1942–44; numerous Quigley Pub. citations; cited by U.S. govt. for outstanding contrib. to W.W.II effort; active as civic worker; on bd. Portland, OR C. of C., Kiwanis, Portland City Planning Comm., Oregon Advertising Club; named First Citizen of Portland, 1944. Secretary/treasurer and co- founder, American Advertising Museum, Portland.

MATLIN, MARLEE: Actress. b. Morton Grove, IL, Aug. 24, 1965. e. John Hershey H.S., Chicago, public school with special education program for deaf. e. William Rainey Harper Coll., majoring in criminal justice. Performed at Children's Theatre of the Deaf in Des Plaines at age 8, playing many leading roles. As adult appeared in only one stage show. Theatrical film debut in Children of a Lesser God, 1986 (Acad. Award).
PICTURES: Children of a Lesser God, Walker, Fox, A Reasonable Doubt.
TELEVISION: Bridge to Silence.

MATTHAU, CHARLES: Director. b. New York, NY 1965. Son of actor Walter Matthau. e. U. of Southern California Film School. While at USC wrote and dir. The Duck Film, a silent comedy short (Golden Seal Award, London Amateur Film Fest. and C.I.N.E. Eagle Award.) Also dir. short, I Was a Teenage Fundraiser. Served in various capacities from gofer to assoc. prod. on father's films. President, The Matthau Company organized 1980.
PICTURES: Doin' Time on Planet Earth. (nom. Saturn Award, best dir., Acad. of Science Fiction.)

MATTHAU, WALTER: Actor. b. New York, NY, Oct. 1, 1920. Served in Air Force W.W.II. Studied journalism at Columbia U. and acting at New Sch. for Social Research's dramatic workshop, 1946, then acted in summer stock. First Broadway role, 1948, in Anne of a Thousand Days.
THEATRE: Will Success Spoil Rock Hunter?, The Odd Couple.
PICTURES: A Face in the Crowd, The Kentuckian, Slaughter on Tenth Avenue, Indian Fighter, No Power on Earth, Middle of the Street, Onion Head, Voice in the Mirror, King Creole, Lonely Are the Brave, Strangers When We Meet, Who's Got the Action, The Gangster Story, Charade, Goodbye Charlie, Mirage, The Fortune Cookie, A Guide for the

Married Man, The Odd Couple, Candy, Cactus Flower, Hello Dolly, A New Leaf, Plaza Suite, Pete n' Tillie, Charley Varrick, The Laughing Policeman, The Taking of Pelham One, Two, Three, The Front Page, The Sunshine Boys, The Bad News Bears, Casey's Shadow, House Calls, California Suite, Little Miss Marker (also exec. prod.), Hopscotch, First Monday in October, Buddy, Buddy, I Ought To Be in Pictures, The Survivors, Movers and Shakers, Pirates, The Couch Trip, Il Piccolo Diavolo.

TELEVISION: Many appearances 1952–65 on Philco-Goodyear Playhouse, Studio One, Playhouse 90, Kraft Theatre, Awake and Sing, Inight, Muni. Series: Tallahassee 7000 (1961). Movie: Incident at Lincoln Bluff.

MATURE, VICTOR: Actor. b. Louisville, KY, Jan. 29, 1916. TV retail store; trainee, Pasadena Theatre, Playbox Theatre; on Bdwy in Lady in the Dark; U.S. Coast Guard, W.W.II.

PICTURES: Housekeeper's Daughter, One Million B.C., Captain Caution, No No Nanette, I Wake Up Screaming, Shanghai Gesture, Song of the Islands, My Gal Sal, Footlight Serenade, Seven Days Leave, My Darling Clementine, Moss Rose, Kiss of Death, Cry of the City, Red Hot and Blue, Fury at Furnace Creek, Easy Living, Samson and Delilah, Wabash Avenue, Stella, Gambling House, Las Vegas Story, Androcles and the Lion, Million Dollar Mermaid, Something for the Birds, Glory Brigade, Affair with a Stranger, The Robe, Veils of Bagdad, Dangerous Mission, Betrayed, Demetrius & the Gladiators, The Egyptian, Chief Crazy Horse, Violent Saturday, Last Frontier, Safari, Zarak Pickup Alley, Tank Roce, The Bandit of Zhobe, Escort Wst., Big Circus, Timbuktu, Hannibal The Tartars, After the Fox, Every Little Crook and Nanny, Won Ton Ton, the Dog That Saved Hollywood, Firepower, The Screamer.

TELEVISION: Samson and Delilah.

MAURA, CARMEN: Actress. b. Madrid, Spain, 1946. Daughter of ophthalmologist faced family disapproval and custody battle when she became an actress. After working as cabaret entertainer, translator (has degree in French), and occasional voiceover dubber, met aspiring director Pedro Almodovar when they were cast in stage prod. of Sartre's Dirty Hands and starred in all his films to date.

PICTURES: Pepi, Luci, Bom . . . And a Whole Lot of Other Girls (1980), Dark Habits, What Have I Done to Deserve This? Matador, Law of Desire, Women on the Verge of a Nervous Breakdown, Baton Rouge.

MAUREY, NICOLE: Actress. b. France, 1925. Studied dancing; French films include Blondine, Pamela, Le Cavalier Noir; stage appearances in France; U.S. film debut in Little Boy Lost (1953).

PICTURES: Secret of the Incas, Bold and the Brave, House of the Seven Hawks, Day of the Triffids, The Very Edge, Gloria, Chanel Solitaire.

MAXWELL, RONALD F.: Writer, Director. b. Jan. 5, 1947. e. NYU Coll. of Arts & Sciences; NYU Sch. of the Arts, Inst. of Film & Television Graduate Sch., M.F.M., 1970. Producer-Director for PBS Theater-in-America.

PICTURES: The Guest, Little Darlings (dir.); The Night the Lights Went Out in Georgia (dir.); Kidco (dir.); The Killer Angels (prod., dir., co-s.p.).

TELEVISION: Sea Marks (prod., dir.); Verna: USO Girl (prod., dir.), Parent Trap II (dir.).

MAY, ELAINE: Actress, Screenwriter. b. Philadelphia, PA, April 21, 1932. Mother of actress Jeannie Berlin. Father was prod.-dir. Jack Berlin whose travelling theater she acted with from age 6 to 10. Repertory theatre in Chicago, 1954; comedy team with Mike Nichols, 1955. Appeared with improvisational theater group, The Compass, Chicago. Co-starred in An Evening with Mike Nichols and Elaine May.

PICTURES: Luv, Enter Laughing; A New Leaf (writer, dir., star); The Heartbreak Kid (dir.); Mikey and Nicky (dir., s.p.); Heaven Can Wait (co-s.p.); California Suite (actress); Ishtar (s.p., dir.), In the Spirit (actress).

TELEVISION: Jack Paar, Omnibus, Dinah Shore Show, Perry Como, Laugh Lines (panelist, 1959).

MAYEHOFF, EDDIE: Comedian. b. Baltimore, MD, July 7, 1914. e. Yale Sch. of Music. Adv. salesman, 1932; dance band leader, 6 yrs.; on radio with Norman Corwin; own show, Eddie Mayehoff on the Town; night clubs; Bdwy shows.

THEATRE: Let Freedom Sing, Early to Bed, Rhapsody, Billy Rose's Concert Varieties, Season in the Sun, Visit to a Small Planet.

TELEVISION: Adventures of Fenimore J. Mayehoff.

PICTURES: That's My Boy, The Stooge, Off Limits, Artists and Models, How to Murder Your Wife, Luv.

MAYER, BEN: Executive. b. Nov. 22, 1925. e. Manchester All Saints Sch. of Art, England; Royal Coll. of Art. President, Ben Mayer Design, Inc.

MAYER, GERALD: Producer, Director. b. Montreal, Canada; p. both deceased: Jerry G., mgr. MGM studio, and Rheba G Mayer (later Mrs. Hal Elias). e. Stanford U., journalism; corr. for San Francisco Examiner; pres. Sigma Delta Chi, prof. journalism soc. Navy lieut. amphibious forces, W.W.II. Entered m.p. ind. in prod. dept. MGM studios; first dir. assignment Dial 1119 (1950).

PICTURES: Inside Straight, Sellout, Holiday for Sinners, Bright Road (Christopher Award for direction), The Marauders, African Drumbeat, and The Man Inside (Canadian).

TELEVISION: Canadian Broadcasting Corp. (prod./dir., TV drama), prod. The Swiss Family Robinson (British-Canadian-West German TV series). Director for U.S. TV: One Last Ride (mini-series), Airwolf, Night Heat, Lou Grant, Eight Is Enough, Quincy, Logan's Run, Mannix, Mission Impossible, Police Surgeon, Cimarron Strip, Peyton Place, Judd for the Defense, Bonanza, The Fugitive, Chrysler Thea., Ben Casey, Slattery's People, Profiles in Courage, The Defenders, Gunsmoke, etc.

MAYER, MICHAEL F.: Attorney, Executive. b. White Plains, NY, Sept. 8, 1917. e. Harvard Coll., B.S., 1939; Yale Law Sch., L.L.B., 1942. Armed Forces 1942–46, Air Medal (1945); vice-pres. Kingsley International Pictures Corp., 1954–62. Exec. Dir. and general counsel, Independent Film Importers and Distributors of America Inc. (IFIDA), 1959–67. Special Counsel, French Society of Authors, Composers and Publishers, 1961–72; British Performing Rights Society, 1962–67. Author: Foreign Films on American Screens (1966); Divorce and Annulment (1967); What You Should Know About Libel and Slander (1968); Rights of Privacy (1972); The Film Industries (1973)—revised ed. pub. in 1978). Lecturer on motion picture problems at NYU, Stanford U., U. of Pennsylvania, Dartmouth Coll., State U. of New York, Albany. Teacher of courses on Business Problems in Film, New School (1971–82). Secty. of Film Society of Lincoln Center, Inc. (1972–88).

MAYER, ROGER LAURANCE: Executive. b. New York, NY, Apr. 21, 1926. e. Yale U., B.A. 1948; Yale Law Sch., L.L.B. and J.D. 1951. In 1952 was practicing attorney; joined Columbia Pictures that year as atty. and named general studio exec., 1957. Left in 1961 to join MGM Studio as asst. gen. mgr. Since with MGM as follows: v.p., operations, 1964; v.p., administration, 1975–84. Also exec. v.p., MGM Laboratories, 1974–83. Named pres., MGM Laboratories and sr. v.p., studio admin.; MGM Entertainment Co. 1983–86; joined Turner Entertainment Co. as pres. and chief operating officer 1986–present.

MEMBER: Los Angeles County Bar Assn., Calif. Bar Assn., Los Angeles Copyright Society, Acad. of Motion Picture Arts & Sciences. Trustee, Motion Picture & TV Relief Fund and asst. v.p., Permanent Charities Fund.

MAYER, SEYMOUR R.: Executive. b. New York, NY, July 30, 1912. e. N.Y. schools. Div. mgr., Loew's in-town theatres, 1933; Armed Forces, W.W.II, as Major in charge of overseas m.p. service; with Loew's International: 1946, 1st v.p.; MGM Int'l.: 1963–69; pres., MGM Int'l.; worldwide sales, 1970; pres., MSD Int'l. worldwide sales.

MAYES, WENDELL: Writer. b. Hayti, MO, July 21, 1919. e. Johns Hopkins U., Columbia U. Military service in Pacific, W.W.II. Began career as actor legit theatre, turned to writing for television. Gained television recognition before moving to Hollywood as motion picture writer.

PICTURES: Spirit of St. Louis, The Way to the Gold, Enemy Below, The Hunters, From Hell to Texas, The Hanging Tree, Anatomy of a Murder, Advise And Consent, In Harm's Way, Von Ryan's Express, Hotel, The Stalking Moon, The Poseidon Adventure, The Revengers, Bank Shot, Death Wish, Love and Bullets, Charlie, Go Tell the Spartans, Monsignor.

MAYO, VIRGINIA: Actress. r.n. Virginia Jones. b. St. Louis, MO, Nov. 30, 1920. e. St. Louis dramatic school. With Billy Rose's Diamond Horseshoe; then N.Y. stage, Banjo Eyes.

PICTURES: Kid from Brooklyn, Best Years of Our Lives, Secret Life of Walter Mitty, Out of the Blue, Smart Girls Don't Talk, The Girl from Jones Beach, Flaxy Martin, Colorado Territory, Always Leave Them Laughing, Flame and the Arrow, West Point Story, Along the Great Divide, Captain Horatio Hornblower, Painting the Clouds with Sunshine, Starlift, She's Working Her Way Through College, Iron Mistress, She's Back on Broadway, South Sea Woman, Devil's Canyon, King Richard & the Crusaders, Silver Chalice, Pearl of the South Pacific, Great Day in the Morning, Proud Ones, Congo Crossing, Big Land, Young Fury, Fort Utah, Castle of Evil, Won Ton Ton, The Dog Who Saved Hollywood, French Quarter.

MAYRON, MELANIE: Actress. b. Philadelphia, PA, Oct. 20, 1952. e. American Academy of Dramatic Arts, 1972. Debut Godspell (tour), NY stage debut: The Goodbye People, 1979. Gethsemane Springs, (Mark Taper Forum, 1976), Crossing Delancey, (1986, Jewish Rep. Theatre, NY). With Catlin Adams, co-prod., co-wrote short, Little Shiny Shoes.

PICTURES: Harry and Tonto (1974), The Great Smokey Roadblock, You Light Up My Life, Car Wash, Gable and Lombard, The Last of the Cowboys, Girl Friends (Best actress award, Locarno Film Festival) Heartbeeps, Missing,

The Boss' Wife, Sticky Fingers (actress, co-s.p., co-prod. with Catlin Adams), Checking Out.
TELEVISION: Playing For Time, Will There Really Be a Morning?, Hustling, The Best Little Girl in the World, Lily Tomlin, Sold Out, Wallenberg: A Hero's Story, Rhoda, thirtysomething (Emmy, 1989).

MAYSLES, ALBERT: Director, Cinematographer. b. Boston, MA, 1926. e. Boston U, M.A. Taught psychology there for 3 years. With late brother David (1933–87) pioneered in "direct cinema" documentary filmmaking, using hand-held cameras to capture slices of daily life, synchronous sound, no narration, and establishing rapport with the subject. Entered indust. photographing Primary with D.A. Pennebaker, Richard Leacock and John Drew, 1960. Formed Maysles Production Co., 1962, making commercials and corp. films.
PICTURES: Showman (1962), Salesman, What's Happening! The Beatles in the U.S.A., Meet Marlon Brando, Gimme Shelter, Christo's Valley Curtain, Grey Gardens, Running Fence, Vladimir Horowitz: The Last Romantic, Ozawa, Islands, Horowitz Plays Mozart, The Umbrellas, Heart, Fellow Passengers.
TELEVISION: Sports Illustrated: The Making of the Swimsuit Issue (co-dir.).

MAZURKI, MIKE: Actor. b. Ukrainian descent; Tarnopal, Austria, Dec. 25, 1909. e. Manhattan Coll., N.Y., B.A., 1930. Toured United States and Canada as heavyweight wrestler. Screen debut 1941 in Shanghai Gesture.
PICTURES: I Walk Alone, Unconquered, Nightmare Alley, Relentless, Neptune's Daughter, Come to the Stable, Rope of Sand, Samson and Delilah, Light Touch, Criminal Lawyer, Ten Tall Men, My Favorite Spy, The Egyptian, New Orleans Uncensored, New York Confidential, Blood Alley, Kismet, Davy Crockett, King of the Wild Frontier, Comanche, Around the World in 80 Days, It's a Mad, Mad, Mad, Mad World, Four for Texas, Cheyenne Autumn, 7 Women, Bullwhip Griffin, Challenge to Be Free, The Magic of Lassie, The Man with Bogart's Face, Doing Time.
TELEVISION: Series: It's About Time, Chicago Teddy Bears.

MAZURSKY, PAUL: Producer, Director, Writer, Actor. b. Brooklyn, NY, April 25, 1930. e. Brooklyn Coll. Started acting in 1951 Off-Bdwy (Hello Out There, The Seagull, Major Barbara, Death of a Salesman, He Who Gets Slapped), TV and films (Fear and Desire, 1951, Blackboard Jungle, Deathwatch). Was nightclub comic 1954–1960 and directed plays. Began association with Larry Tucker by producing, directing, writing and performing in Second City, semi-improvisational revue. For four years they wrote the Danny Kaye TV show and created and wrote the Monkees series. First theatrical film I Love You, Alice B. Toklas, 1969, which he wrote with Tucker and both men acted as exec. prod.
PICTURES: Prod.-Dir.-Co-Writer: Bob and Carol and Ted and Alice, (dir., co-s.p.), Alex in Wonderland (dir., co-s.p., actor), Blume in Love (also actor), Harry and Tonto; Next Stop, Greenwich Village; An Unmarried Woman; Willie and Phil (also actor); Tempest; Moscow on the Hudson (also actor); Down and Out in Beverly Hills (also actor), Moon Over Parador (also actor), Enemies, A Love Story, A Star is Born (actor only).
PICTURES: *As actor only:* A Star is Born, A Man, a Woman and a Bank, Into the Night, Scenes From the Class Struggle in Beverly Hills.

McBRIDE, JIM: Writer, Director. b. New York, NY, Sept. 16, 1941. m. costume designer Tracy Tynan. Began in underground film scene in New York. First film: David Holzman's Diary, 1967, which won grand prize at Mannheim and Pesaro Film Festivals.
PICTURES: My Girlfriend's Wedding (actor, s.p., dir.), Glen and Randa (s.p., dir.), Pictures for Life's Other Side (dir.), Hot Times (dir., s.p., actor), Last Embrace (actor only), Breathless (co.-s.p., dir.); The Big Easy (dir.), Great Balls of Fire (dir., co-s.p.).

McCALL, JOAN: Writer, Actress. b. Grahn, KY. e. Berea Coll. Starred on Broadway in Barefoot in the Park, The Star Spangled Girl, A Race of Hairy Men, and road companies of Barefoot in the Park, Star Spangled Girl, and Don't Drink the Water, Los Angeles co. of Jimmy Shine.
PICTURES: Grizzly, Act of Vengeance, The Devil Times Five. Screenwriter: The Predator, Between Two Worlds, Fly Away Home. Staff writer for The Days of Our Lives, Another World, As the World Turns, under the pen name Joan Pommer; Search for Tomorrow, Capitol, Santa Barbara, Divorce Court.

McCALLUM, DAVID: Actor. b. Scotland, Sept. 19, 1933. Early career in rep. theatres and dir. plays for Army. Ent. m.p. Ind. 1953.
PICTURES: The Secret Place, Hell Drivers, Robbery Under Arms, Violent Playground, A Night to Remember, The Long and the Short and the Tall, Billy Budd, Freud, The Great Escape, The Greatest Story Ever Told, To Trap a Spy, Three Bites of the Apple, Sol Madrid, Mosquito Squadron, Watcher in the Woods, The Wind, The Haunting of Maurella.
TELEVISION: The Man From U.N.C.L.E. (series), The Invisible Man (series), Hitchcock, Murder She Wrote, Mother Love. Movies: Teacher, Teacher; Hauser's Memory; Colditz (BBC series 1972–74); Frankenstein: The True Story; Behind Enemy Lines; Freedom Fighters; She Waits; The Man Who Lived at the Ritz.

McCALLUM, JOHN: Actor, Producer, Director. b. Brisbane, Australia, CBE. Mar. 14, 1918. e. Royal Acad. of Dramatic Art. Served in Australian Imperial Forces, W.W.II. Appeared in repertory with Old Vic & Stratford-on-Avon. On stage, 1937 in Judgment Day, Australian tour, 1955–56; on screen first 1944, Australia is Like This. Asst. man. dir. J. C. Williamson Theatres, Ltd., Australia, 1958; man. dir., 1960–66. Resigned chmn. Williamson-Powell Int. Films, 1965; chmn. Fauna Prod.; dir.: Relatively Speaking; Plaza Suite, My Fair Lady (Australia). Prod. TV Series, Skippy, Barrier Reef, Boney, Shannons Mob; London Stage Constant Wife. 1974 Comedy Theatre, Melbourne. 1976 Chichester Fest. 1976–77 The Circle. Exec. prod. Bailey's Bird, TV series. The Chalk Garden. The Kingfisher (tour, Far and Middle East), 1988, Hayfever, The Royal Baccarat Scandal Chichester Fest.
PICTURES: A Son Is Born, Joe Goes Back, Root of All Evil, The Loves of Joanna Godden, It Always Rains on Sunday, Miranda, The Calendar, A Boy, a Girl and a Bike, Traveler's Joy, The Woman in Question, Valley of the Eagles, Lady Godiva Rides Again, Derby Day (Four Against Fate), Trent's Last Case, The Long Memory, Melba, Devil on Horseback, Trouble in the Glen, Smiley (in Australia), Safe Harbour, Nickel Queen (dir.); The Z Men (prod.); The Highest Honor (exec. prod.).

McCAMBRIDGE, MERCEDES: Actress. b. Joliet, IL, March 17, 1918. e. Mundelein Coll., Chicago, B.A. Did some radio work while in college; opposite Orson Welles two seasons, on Ford Theatre, other air shows; New York stage in: Hope for the Best, (1945); Place of Our Own, Twilight Bar, Woman Bites Dog, The Young and Fair; left latter play for Hollywood. Screen debut: All the King's Men (Academy Award for best supporting actress, 1950); own radio show, 1952. Member: National Inst. Alcohol Abuse and Alcoholism, Washington.
PICTURES: Lightning Strikes Twice, Inside Straight, The Scarf, Johnny Guitar, Giant, A Farewell to Arms, Suddenly Last Summer, Cimarron, Angel Baby, Last Generation, Jigsaw, 99 Women, Thieves, The Concorde—Airport '79.
AUTHOR: The Two of Us.
TELEVISION: Numerous appearances, Who is the Black Dahlia?

McCARTHY, ANDREW: Actor. b. Westfield, NJ, 1962. e. NYU. Studied acting at Circle-in-the-Square; on Broadway in The Boys of Winter; Off Bdwy: Bodies, Rest and Motion; Life Under Water; Neptune's Hips, Mariens Hammer. Class Film debut, 1984.
PICTURES: Heaven Help Us, St. Elmo's Fire, Pretty in Pink, Manequin, Waiting for the Moon, Less Than Zero, Fresh Horses, Kansas, Weekend at Bernies, Clichy Days.

McCARTHY, KEVIN: Actor. b. Seattle, WA, Feb. 15, 1914. Brother of author Mary McCarthy. e. U. of Minnesota. Acted in sch. plays, stock; B'way debut in Abe Lincoln in Illinois. In U.S. Army; On London stage in Death of a Salesman (1949–50). m.p. debut: Death of A Salesman.
BROADWAY THEATER: Flight to West, Winged Victory, Truckline Cafe, Joan of Lorraine, Death of a Salesman, Anna Christie, Red Roses For Me, Love's Labour's Lost, Advise and Consent, The Day The Money Stopped, Two For the Seesaw, Cactus Flower, Alone Together, The Three Sisters, Happy Birthday Wanda June.
PICTURES: Drive a Crooked Road, Gambler from Natchez, Stranger on Horseback, Annapolis Story, Nightmare, Invasion of the Body Snatchers, A Big Hand for the Little Lady, Hotel, Kansas City Bomber, Buffalo Bill and the Indians, Hero at Large, Those Lips, Those Eyes, Innerspace, Dark Tower, Hostage, Love or Money, Twilight Zone—The Movie, U.H.F., Fast Food, The Sleeping Car.
TELEVISION: Active on TV since 1949. Pilot: Second Stage. Movies: The Making of a Male Model, Deadly Intentions, The Midnight Hour, A Masterpiece of Murder, Poor Little Rich Girl: The Barbara Hutton Story; The Long Journey Home; Once Upon a Texas Train; In the Heat of the Night, Channel 99. Mini-series: Passion and Paradise. Series: The Colbys, The Survivors, Flamingo Road, Amanda's Second Start.

McCARTNEY PAUL: Singer, Musician. b. Liverpool, England, June 18, 1942. As member of The Beatles co-starred in A Hard Day's Night, Help!, and Let It Be. Wrote songs for several films on own, including Live and Let Die (title), Oh Heavenly Dog. Formed group Wings for tours and recordings. Wrote script and music and acted in Give My Regards to Broad Street, cameo in Eat the Rich.

McCLANAHAN, RUE: Actress. b. Healdton, OK, Feb. 21, 1934. e.

U. of Tulsa. On Bdwy. in Sticks and Bones, Jimmy Shine, California Suite. Obie Award for Who's Happy Now? (1970).
PICTURES: They Might Be Giants, The People Next Door, The Pursuit of Happiness, Modern Love.
TELEVISION: Series: Maude, Mama's Family, Golden Girls (Emmy Award, 1987). Movies: Topper, Rainbow; The Great American Traffic Jam; Word of Honor; The Day the Bubble Burst, The Little Match Girl; Liberace; The Man in the Brown Suit; Take My Daughters, Please; The Wickedest Witch, Let Me Hear You Whisper.

McCLORY, SEAN: Actor. b. Dublin, Ireland, March 8, 1924. e. Jesuit Coll., U. of Galway. With Gaelic Theatre, Galway; Abbey Theatre. Dublin. Brought to U.S., in 1946 under contract to RKO Pictures. Prod. and dir. numerous plays, member of the Directors Guild of America and author of drama, Moment of Truth.
PLAYS: Shining Hour, Juno and the Paycock, Anna Christie, Escape to Autumn, King of Friday's Men, Lady's Not for Burning, Billy Budd, Dial M for Murder, The Winslow Boy, Shadow of a Gunman, Saint Joan.
PICTURES: Film debut: Dick Tracy vs. Cueball, Roughshod, Beyond Glory, Daughter of Rosie O'Grady, Storm Warning, Lorna Doone, What Price Glory, The Quiet Man, Diane, Island in the Sky, Ring of Fear, Them, Long Grey Line, Cheyenne Autumn, Plunder of the Sun Bay, Anne of the Indies, I Cover the Underworld, Botany Man in the Attic, Guns of Fort Petticoat, Kings Thief, Moonfleet, Bandolero, Day of the Wolves, Valley of the Dragons, Follow Me Boys, Rogues March, The Gnomobile, Well of the Saints, In Search of the Historical Jesus, Roller Boogie, My Chauffeur, The Dead.
TELEVISION: Matinee Theatre, Climax, Lost in Space, My Three Sons, Suspense, The Untouchables, Hitchcock, Thriller, Beverly Hillbillies, Bonanza, Gunsmoke, Mannix, Little House on the Prairie, Perry Mason, S.W.A.T., The New Daughters of Joshua Cabe, The Captains And the Kings, Once an Eagle, Fish, Columbo, How the West Was Won, Fantasy Island, Battlestar Galactica, Trapper John, Blue Knight. Falcon Crest, Simon and Simon, Murder She Wrote, Young Houdini. Series: The Californians (also dir.), Kate McShane; Bring 'Em Back Alive, Guest in continuing role: General Hospital.

McCLURE, DOUG: Actor. b. Glendale, CA, May 11, 1935. e. UCLA.
PICTURES: Because They're Young, The Unforgiven, Shenandoah, Beau Geste, The King's Pirate, Nobody's Perfect, The Land That Time Forgot, At the Earth's Core, The House Where Evil Dwells, Warlords of Atlantis, Humanoids from the Deep, Cannonball Run II, 52 Pick-Up, Omega Syndrome, Nightside, Tapeheads, Prime Suspect, Dark Before Dawn.
TELEVISION: Movies: The Longest Hundred Miles, Terror in the Sky, The Birdmen, The Death of Me Yet, Playmates, The Judge and Jake Wyler, Shirts/Skins, Death Race, Satan's Triangle, Roots, SST-Death Flight, Search, Wild and Woolly, The Rebels, Checkmate, Men From Shiloh, Barbary Coast, Out of This World. Series: Overland Trail, The Virginian.

McCOWEN, ALEC: Actor. b. Tunbridge Wells, England, May 26, 1925. e. Royal Acad. of Dramatic Art. On stage in London in Ivanhoe, The Mask and the Face, Hadrian the Seventh, etc. On Bdwy. in Antony and Cleopatra, No Laughing Matter, After the Rain, The Assam Garden, etc.
PICTURES: The Cruel Sea, Time Without Pity, A Midsummer Night's Dream, The Loneliness of the Long Distance Runner, The Agony and the Ecstasy, The Devil's Own, The Hawaiians, Frenzy, Travels with My Aunt, Stevie, Hanover Street, Never Say Never Again, The Young Visitors, The Assam Garden, Personal Services, Cry Freedom, Henry V.

McCREA, JOEL: Actor. b. Los Angeles, CA, Nov. 5, 1905. e. Pomona Coll. Husband of Frances Dee, actress. Stage experience: amateur dramatics and community plays taking male lead in The Patsy, Laff That Off and The Little Journey. In many pictures since 1932.
PICTURES: 1940, He Married His Wife, Primrose Path, Foreign Correspondent, Reaching for the Sun, Sullivan's Travels, The Great Man's Lady, The Palm Beach Story, The More the Merrier, Virginian, Ramrod, Four Faces West, South of St. Louis, Outriders, Colorado, Territory, Stars in My Crown, Saddle Tramp, Cattle Drive, San Francisco Story, Lone Hand, Shoot First, Border River, Black Horse Canyon, Stranger on Horseback, Wichita, First Texan, The Oklahoman, Trooper Hook, Fort Massacre, The Gunfight at Dodge City, Ride the High Country, Mustang Country, George Stevens: A Filmmaker's Journey.

McDORMAND, FRANCES: Actress. b. Illinois, 1958. Daughter of a Disciples of Christ preacher traveled Bible Belt with family, settling in PA at 8. e. Yale Drama School. Regional theater includes Twelfth Night, Mrs. Warren's Profession, The Three Sisters, All My Sons. Two seasons with O'Neill Playwrights Conference.
THEATER: Awake and Sing, Painting Churches, On the Verge, A Streetcar Named Desire (Tony nom.).
PICTURES: Blood Simple, Raising Arizona, Mississippi Burning (Acad. award nom.), Chattahoochee, Dark Man.
TELEVISION: Twilight Zone, Spenser: For Hire, Hill St. Blues. Series: Leg Work.

McDOWALL, BETTY: Actress. b. Sydney, Australia. e. Mt. Bernard Convent, N. Sydney. Early career radio, stage in Australia; ent. BBC TV, 1952; since in West End plays, many TV and radio plays and films.
STAGE: Age of Consent, Ghost Train, The Kidders, The Dark Halo, Period of Adjustment, Rule of Three, Signpost to Murder, Hippolytus, The Winslow Boy, Woman in a Dressing Gown, As Long as It's Warm, Caprice—in a Pink Palazzo, Sweet Bird of Youth, There Was an Old Woman, What the Butler Saw, Two Dozen Red Roses, A Boston Story, The Man Most Likely To. . ., Sleeping Partner.
TELEVISION: Mid-Level and Glorification of Al Toolum, The Black Judge, Phone Call for Matthew Quade, Thunder on the Snowy, Shadow of Guilt, Traveling Lady, Torment, Biography, Notes for a Love Song, Esther's Altar, The Corridor People, The Braden Beat, The Douglas Fairbanks, Ivanhoe, The Foreign Legion, Fabian of the Yard, Four Just Men, Flying Doctor, No Hiding Place, Z' Cars, Days of Vengeance, Flower of Evil, Outbreak of Murder, Call Me Sam, The Prisoner, Public Eye, The Forgotten Door, All Out for Kangaroo Valley, Barry Humphries Scandals, Castle Haven, Albert and Victoria, Follyfoot, The Man Who Came to Dinner, Anne of Avoniea, Little Lord Fauntleroy, The Bass Player and the Blond (4 plays), The Gingerbread Lady. Series: Boyd Q.C.
PICTURES: First lead in England, Timelock, She Didn't Say No, Jack the Ripper, The Shiralee, Jackpot, Dead Lucky, Spare the Rod, Golliwog, Echo of Diana, First Men in the Moon, Ballad in Blue, The Liquidators, Willy Wagtails by Moonlight, The Omen.
RADIO: Anna Christie, The Little Foxes, Another Part of the Forest, The Archers.

McDOWALL, RODDY: Actor. b. London, England, Sept. 17, 1928. e. St. Joseph's, London. First appeared in Murder in the Family at age of 8. Later, You Will Remember, The Outsider, Just William, Hey, Hey, U.S.A., This England, all made in England. In 1940 signed by 20th Century-Fox. Star of Tomorrow, 1944. Named Screen Actors Guild representative on National Film Preservation Bd., 1989.
PICTURES: Man Hunt, How Green Was My Valley, Confirm or Deny, Son of Fury, On the Sunny Side, The Pied Piper, My Friend Flicka, Lassie Come Home, White Cliffs of Dover, Macbeth, Act, assoc. prod., Rocky, Kidnapped, Big Timber, Tuna Clipper, Black Midnight, Killer Shark, Steel Fist, The Subterraneans, Midnight Lace, Cleopatra, The Longest Day, The Greatest Story Ever Told, Shock Treatment, That Darn Cat, The Loved Ones, The Third Day, Daisy Clover, Bullwhip Griffin, Lord Love A Duck, The Defector, It, The Cool Ones, Planet of the Apes, Hello, Down There, Midas Run, Escape from the Planet of the Apes, Conquest of the Planet of the Apes. Directorial Debut, The Devil's Widow, 1971. Actor: The Legend of Hellhouse, The Poseidon Adventure, Arnold, Funny Lady, The Cat from Outer Space, Scavenger Hunt, Charlie Chan and the Curse of the Dragon Queen, Evil Under the Sun, Class of 1984, Fright Night, Dead of Winter, Overboard (also exec. prod.), The Big Picture, Destroyer, Fright Night Part 2, Cutting Class.
THEATRE: On B'way in Misalliance, Escapade, Doctor's Dilemma, No Time for Sergeants, Good as Gold, Compulsion, Handful of Fire, Look After Lulu, The Fighting Cock, 1959–60, Camelot, 1960–61, The Astrakhan Coat, 1966.
TELEVISION: Stratford Shakespeare Festival, 1955. Camilla (Nightmare Classics) Movies: This Girl for Hire, The Zany Adventures of Robin Hood, Hollywood Wives, Alice in Wonderland, Mae West, The Rhinemann Exchange, The Thief of Baghdad, Miracle on 34th Street, Around the World in 80 Days.

McDOWELL, MALCOLM: Actor. b. Leeds, England, June 13, 1943. Married actress Mary Steenburgen. Was spearholder for the Royal Shakespeare Co. in season of 1965–66 when turned to TV and then to films. NY stage: Look Back in Anger (also on video); In Celebration. Made debut in small role in Poor Cow, 1967.
PICTURES: If. . ., Figures in a Landscape, The Raging Moon, A Clockwork Orange, O Lucky Man!, Royal Flash, Aces High, Voyage of the Damned, Caligula, The Passage, Time after Time, Cat People, Britannia Hospital, Blue Thunder, Cross Creek, Get Crazy, The Caller, Sunset, Buy and Cell, The Big Picture, The Hateful Dead, Moon 44, Double Game, Il Maestro, Class of 1999.
TELEVISION: Arthur the King, Gulag, Monte Carlo, Faerie Tale Theatre (Little Red Riding Hood).

McELWAINE, GUY: Executive. b. Culver City, CA, June 29, 1936. Started career in pub. dept. of MGM, 1955; 1959, joined m.p. div. of Rogers and Cowen. 1964, formed own public relations firm; then joined CMA. Left to become sr. exec. v.p. in chg. worldwide m.p. production, Warner Bros., 1975. In 1977 became sr. exec. v.p. in chg. worldwide m.p. activities and pres. of intl. film mktg. at Intl. Creative Management (ICM), formerly CMA. 1981, named pres. and chief exec. officer Rastar Films. Left in 1982 to become pres., Columbia Pictures; given additional title of chief exec. officer, 1983. In 1985 named chmn. and on board of Columbia Pictures Industries. Resigned, 1986. Joined Weintraub Entertainment Group as exec. v.p. and chmn., m.p. div. 1987–89; returned to Intl. Creative Management, Aug. 1989.

McEVEETY, BERNARD: Director. Comes from film family; father was pioneer as unit mgr. at New York's Edison Studios; brothers Vincent, also a dir., and Joseph, writer are at Disney Studios. Bernard's career began in 1953 at Paramount where was asst. dir. for 6 yrs. Earned full dir. responsibility on The Rebel, TV series.

PICTURES: Napoleon and Samantha, One Little Indian, The Bears and I.

TELEVISION: Numerous episodes on Bonanza, Gunsmoke, Combat and Cimarron Strip (also prod.), Centennial, Roughnecks, The Machans.

McEVEETY, VINCENT: Director. Joined Hal Roach Studios in 1954 as second asst. dir. Then to Republic for The Last Command. First Disney assignments: Davy Crockett shows and Mickey Mouse Club. Moved to Desilu as first asst. dir. on The Untouchables; made assoc. prod. with option to direct. Did segments of many series, including 34 Gunsmoke episodes. First theatrical film: Firecreek, 1968.

PICTURES: $1,000,000 Duck, The Biscuit Eater, Charley and the Angel, Superdad, The Strongest Man in the World, Gus, Treasure of Matecumbe, Herbie Goes to Monte Carlo, Apple Dumpling Gang Rides Again, Herbie Goes Bananas.

TELEVISION: Blood Sport, Wonder Woman, High Flying Spy, Ask Max, Gunsmoke: Return to Dodge.

McGAVIN, DARREN: Actor. b. San Joaquin Valley, CA, May 7, 1922. e. Coll. of the Pacific.

PLAYS: Death of a Salesman, My Three Angels, The Rainmaker, The Lovers, Dinner at Eight (revival), The Night Hank Williams Died.

PICTURES: Summertime, The Man with the Golden Arm, Court Martial of Billy Mitchell, Beau James, Delicate Delinquent, The Great Sioux Massacre, Bullet for a Badman, Mission Mars, Airport 77, A Christmas Story, The Natural, Turk 182, From the Hip, Dead Heat. Directorial debut: Happy Mother's Day . . . Love, George, 1973.

TELEVISION: Series: Mike Hammer, The Outsider, The Night Stalker. Movies: My Wicked Wicked Ways, The Rookies, Tribes, Something Evil, The Users, Inherit the Wind, The Diamond Trap, Around the World in 80 Days. Special: Unclaimed Fortunes (host).

McGILLIS, KELLY: Actress. b. Newport Beach, CA, 1958. e. Juilliard. Stage: The Merchant of Venice (Washington, D.C., 1988).

PICTURES: Reuben, Reuben, Witness, Top Gun, Made in Heaven, Promised Land, The House on Carroll Street, The Accused, Winter People, Lie Down With Lions, Cat Chaser, Before and After Death.

TELEVISION: Sweet Revenge.

McGOOHAN, PATRICK: Actor. b. New York, Mar. 19, 1928. Early career in repertory in Britain. London stage 1954 in Serious Charge; 1955 Orson Welles' Moby Dick. Ent. films 1955. On Broadway in Pack of Lies (1987).

PICTURES: Passage Home, High Tide at Noon, Hell Drivers, The Gypsy and the Gentleman, Nor the Moon by Night, Two Living, One Dead, All Night Long, The Quare Fellow, Thomasina, Dr. Syn, Ice Station Zebra, The Moonshine War, Brass Target, Scanners, Baby, Kings and Desperate Men.

TELEVISION: Series: Danger Man; (also directed episodes); Secret Agent, The Prisoner. Movies: Jamaica Inn; Of Pure Blood, Man in the Iron Mask.

McGOVERN, ELIZABETH: Actress. b. Evanston, IL, July 18, 1961. Acted in high school in California; studied at American Conservatory Theatre, San Francisco and Juilliard Sch. of Dramatic Art. Film debut in Ordinary People, 1980.

THEATER: NY: To Be Young, Gifted and Black (1981, debut), My Sister in This House (Theatre World, Obie Awards), Painting Churches, The Hitch-Hiker, A Map of the World, Aunt Dan and Lemon (L.A.), Two Gentlemen of Verona, A Midsummer Night's Dream (NY Shakespeare Fest.).

PICTURES: Ragtime, Lovesick, Racing with the Moon, Once Upon a Time in America, The Bedroom Window, Native Son, She's Having a Baby, Johnny Handsome, The Handmaid's Tale, A Shock to the System.

McGRATH, THOMAS J.: Producer. b. New York, NY. e. Washington Square Coll. of NYU, B.A., 1956; NYU Sch. of Law, LL.B., 1960. Has practiced law in N.Y. from 1960 to date. Became indep. prod. with Deadly Hero in 1976; Author, Carryover Basis Under The 1976 Tax Reform Act, published in 1977.

McGREGOR, CHARLES: Executive. b. Jersey City, NJ, April 1, 1927. e. NYU. 1958–1969, co-founder, pres. and chief exec. officer, Banner Films, Inc. (World Wide TV Distribution), 1955–58, salesman and div. mgr., Flamingo Films (domestic TV Dist.). 1953–55; Professional mgr. ABC Music Publishing. 1951–53: Prod. and partner Telco Prods. and GM Productions (prods. of network and local shows). 1969–77: exec. v.p. in chg. of w-w dist., WB-TV; 1977: pres. WB-TV Distribution.

McGUIRE, DON: Writer, Director. b. Chicago, IL, Feb. 28, 1919. U.S. Army, 4 yrs.; press agent, Chicago and Hollywood; newsman, Hearst papers, Chicago; then actor, writer.

PICTURES: Double Deal, Dial 1119, Meet Danny Wilson, Willie and Joe in Back at the Front, Walking My Baby Back Home, Three Ring Circus, Bad Day at Black Rock, Artists and Models, Johnny Concho, Delicate Delinquent, Suppose They Gave a War and Nobody Came, Tootsie, Hear Me Good.

TELEVISION: Writer, dir., co-prod., Henessey (series); creator, series Not for Hire; creator, writer, prod. series, Don't Call Me Charlie, From Here to Eternity, Berlin Air Lift.

AUTHOR: Novels, The Day Television Died, 1600 Floogle Street, The Hell with Walter Cronkite.

McGUIRE, DOROTHY: Actress. b. Omaha, NB, June 14, 1919. e. Ladywood convent, Indianapolis; Pine Manor, Wellesley, MA.

STAGE: Our Town, My Dear Children, Swinging the Dream, Claudia, Legend of Lovers, Winesberg, Ohio, Night of the Iguana (1976), Cause Celebre; Another Part of the Forest; I Never Sang for My Father.

PICTURES: Claudia, A Tree Grows in Brooklyn, The Enchanted Cottage, Spiral Staircase, Claudia and David, Gentleman's Agreement, Mister 880, Callaway Went Thataway, I Want You, Make Haste to Live, Invitation, 3 Coins in the Fountain, Trial, Friendly Persuasion, Old Yeller, The Swiss Family Robinson, This Earth Is Mine, Remarkable Mr. Pennypacker, Dark at the Top of the Stairs, A Summer Place, Susan Slade, The Greatest Story Ever Told, Flight of the Doves.

TELEVISION: She Waits, Another Part of the Forest, The Runaways, The Philadelphia Story, Rich Man, Poor Man, Little Women, American Geisha, Ghost Dancing, The Incredible Journey of Dr. Meg Laurel, I Never Sang for My Father. Guest on: Love Boat, The Young & Restless, Highway to Heaven, Between Darkness and Dawn, Amos, Fantasy Island, St. Elsewhere. Movie: Caroline?

McHATTIE, STEPHEN: Actor. b. Antigonish, Nova Scotia, Canada, Feb. 3, e. Acadia U. Trained for stage at American Acad. of Dramatic Arts.

THEATER (NY): The American Dream (debut, 1968), Pictures in the Hallway, Twelfth Night, Mourning Becomes Electra, The Iceman Cometh, Alive and Well in Argentina, The Winter Dancers, Casualties, The Three Sisters, The Misanthrope, Heartbreak House, Mensch Meier, Haven.

PICTURES: Von Richthofen and Brown (debut, 1970), The People Next Door, The Ultimate Warrior, Moving Violation, Tomorrow Never Comes, Death Valley, Best Revenge, Belizaire the Cajun, Salvation!, Call Me, Sticky Fingers.

TELEVISION: Series: Highcliffe Manor, Mariah. Mini-series: Cenennial. Movies: Search for the Gods, James Dean, Look What's Happened to Rosemary's Baby, Mary and Joseph: A Story of Faith, Roughnecks.

McHUGH, JAMES: Agent, Manager. b. Boston, MA, Oct. 21, 1915. e. Holy Cross Coll. Joined MCA 1939. U.S. Army Signal Corps, 1944–46. MCA-British and European, 1945–50. Post grad. studies, Boston Coll. Formed James McHugh, Talent Agency 1953. Pres., Artists Mgr. Corp., pres., Turquoise Prod., Inc., v.p. Selective Activity.

McINTIRE, JOHN: Actor. b. Spokane, WA, June 27, 1907. e. local schools. m. Jeanette Nolan, actress. Radio announcer, actor teamed with wife.

PICTURES: Asphalt Jungle, Francis, Saddle Tramp, Winchester '73, Ambush, Scene of the Crime, You're in the Navy Now, Under the Gun, Raging Tide, Westward the Women, World in His Arms, Glory Alley, Sally & St. Anne, Horizons West, Lawless Breed, Mississippi Gambler, The President's Lady, Lion Is In the Street, War Arrow, Apache, Four Guns to the Border, Yellow Mountain, Far Country, Stranger on Horseback, Scarlet Coat, Phenix City Story, Backlash, The Spoilers, The Kentuckian, World in My Corner, Away All Boats, The Tin Star, Who Was That Lady, Flaming Star, Two Rode Together, Summer and Smoke, Herbie Rides Again, Honkytonk Man, Cloak and Dagger, Turner and Hooch.

TELEVISION: Series: Wagon Train, Naked City, The Virginian. Movie: Dream Breaker.

McKEE, LONETTE: Actress. b. Detroit, MI, 1954. Started career as singer at age of 14 on dance show, Swingin' Time. TV debut at 16 in The Wacky World of Jonathan Winters. Bdwy debut as Mrs. Jackie Robinson in The First, then in Bdwy revival of Showboat and off Bdwy in one woman show, Lady Day At Emerson's Bar and Grill.

PICTURES: Sparkle (debut, 1976), Which Way Is Up?,

PICTURES: *Prod.*:Straw Dogs, That's Entertainment! (exec. prod.); That's Entertainment, Two!; All That Jazz (exec. prod.); Altered States (exec. prod.); First Family, Making Love, Unfaithfully Yours (exec. prod.), Footloose (exec. prod.), Quicksilver; Roxanne, Punchline (co-prod.), Mountains of the Moon, Total Recall, Air America.
TELEVISION: Death of a Salesman (prod., Emmy Award), The Ages of Man (prod., Emmy Award, 1966); exec. prod. with David Susskind: East Side/West Side, N.Y.P.D., Get Smart, Chain Letter (pilot, exec. prod.). Movie: Get Smart Again! (exec. prod.).

MELNICK, SAUL: Executive. With a background in the video industry at CBS Video Enterprises, Pacifica Manufacturing Co. and Arista Records, joined MGM/UA Home Video in 1982 as national sales manager, rising to sales v.p. in 1983, and v.p. sales and marketing in 1984. Joined Tri-Star as pres. of home video unit, 1987; June 1988, appointed exec. v.p. Loews Theater Management.

MELNIKER, BENJAMIN: Motion Picture Producer, Attorney; b. Bayonne, NJ. e. Brooklyn Coll.; LL.B., Fordham Law Sch. Loew's Theatres usher, private law practice employed Legal Department Metro-Goldwyn-Mayer, vice president and general counsel, 1954–69, executive vice president, 1968–70, resigned from MGM December 1971; also member MGM bd. dir. and mem. MGM exec. com.; Adjunct associate professor, New York Law Sch., 1976–77; prod. & exec. prod. motion pictures, 1974–86; former motion picture chmn. Anti-Defamation League, B'nai B'rith; Mem. Am., N.Y. State bar assns., Bar Assn. City N.Y., Acad. of Motion Picture Arts and Scis.
PICTURES: Mitchell, Shoot, Winter Kills, Swamp Thing, Batman (exec. prod.), The Return of the Swamp Thing (prod.).
TELEVISION: Three Sovereigns for Sarah, Television's Greatest Bets.

MENGERS, SUE: Talent Agent. b. Bronx, NY, Sept. 2, 1938. Started as receptionist, secretary with Music Corp. of America in New York. In 1963 became agent in small partnership. Two years later joined Creative Management Associates and went to Hollywood. With Intl. Creative Mgt. (co. formed by merger of CMA and Marvin Josephson Associates). Clients have included Barbra Streisand, Gene Hackman, Ryan O'Neal, Tatum O'Neal, Ali MacGraw, Cybill Shepherd, Peter Bogdanovich, Sidney Lumet, Arthur Penn, Nick Nolte, Robin Williams, Roman Polanski, Michael Caine. 1988, appointed sr. v.p. worldwide head of motion picture and m.p. literary division, William Morris Agency.

MENGES, CHRIS: Cinematographer, Director. b. Kingston, Eng., Sept. 15, 1940.
PICTURES: Cinematographer: If. . ., The Empire Strikes Back (second unit), Local Hero, Comfort and Joy, The Killing Fields (Acad. Award, 1984), Marie, The Mission (Acad. Award, 1986), Singing the Blues in Red, Shy People, High Season, A World Apart (dir. debut, 1988), White Fang (dir.).
TELEVISION: World in Action, Opium Warlords, Opium Trail, East 103rd Street, etc.

MERCHANT, ISMAIL: Producer, Director. b. Bombay, India, Dec. 25, 1936. e. St. Xavier's Coll., Bombay; NYU, M.A. business admin. Formed Merchant Ivory Prods., 1961 with James Ivory. First film, The Creation of Women (theatrical short, 1961, nom. for Acad. Award). Published cookbook, Ismail Merchant's Indian Cuisine; and book Hullabaloo in Old Jeypore: The Making of "The Deceivers" (1989).
PICTURES: *Producer:* The Householder, Shakespeare Wallah, The Guru, Bombay Talkie, Savages, Autobiography of a Princess, The Wild Party, Roseland, Hullabaloo Over Georgie and Bonnie's Pictures, The Europeans, Jane Austen in Manhattan, Quartet, Heat and Dust, The Bostonians, A Room With a View, Maurice, My Little Girl (exec. prod.), The Deceivers, Slaves of New York, The Perfect Murder (exec. prod.), Mr. and Mrs. Bridge.
TELEVISION: Director: Mahatma and the Mad Boy, Courtesans of Bombay.

MERCHANT, LAWRENCE H., JR.: Producer. b. Cambridge, MA. e. Boston Latin Sch.; Hebron Acad., ME; Columbia U.; NYU. Pres., Educational Book Div., Prentice-Hall; pres., Pillsbury Productions; prod. exec., TV-Today, Home, Tonight, Milton Berle, Show of Shows, Hallmark Hall of Fame, Eye Witness, R. Montgomery Presents, Wide, Wide World, Walter Winchell; TV advisor, Gen. Dwight D. Eisenhower; prod. CBS films; pres., Kachina Productions.
PICTURES: Hands of Dr. Maniacal, Back Track, Present Tense of Love.

MERCOURI, MELINA: Actress, b. Athens, Oct. 18, 1925. m. dir.-prod. Jules Dassin. Schooling and training in Athens, fluent in French, German and English. Stage debut on Athens stage in avant-garde work; early stage career in Paris. Also made vocal recordings. Mem. of Greek Parliament for Port of Piraeus, 1977–present; Minister of Culture and Sciences for Greek Gov't. 1981–85; Minister of Culture, Youth and Sports, 1985–present.
PLAYS: Mourning Becomes Electra, La Nuit de Samaracande, Les Compagnons de la Marjolaine, Il Etait une Gare, Le Moulin de la Galette; to Greece 1954, in Stella. Also: A Streetcar Named Desire, Helen or the Joy of Living, The Queen of Clubs, The Seven Year Itch, Sweet Bird of Youth, Ilya Darling (Bdwy).
PICTURES: Stella, He Who Must Die, The Gypsy and the Gentleman, The Law, Never on Sunday, Phaedra, The Victors, Topkapi, 10:30 P.M. Summer, A Man Could Get Killed, Gaily, Gaily, Promise at Dawn, Earthquake, Once Is Not Enough, Nasty Habits, Maya and Brenda, A Dream of Passion.

MEREDITH, BURGESS: Actor. b. Cleveland, OH, Nov. 16, 1909. e. Amherst Coll., M.A. (hon.). m. Kaja Sundsten. Capt. U.S. Army Air Corps, W.W.II. On stage, 1929, Civic Repertory Co., N.Y.
STAGE PLAYS: Little Ol' Boy, She Loves Me Not, The Star Wagon, Winterset, High Tor, Remarkable Mr. Pennypacker, etc.
PICTURES: Began screen career 1936 in Winterset. Idiot's Delight, Of Mice and Men, Second Chorus, That Uncertain Feeling, Tom, Dick and Harry, Street of Chance, Miracles Can Happen, Story of G.I. Joe, Diary of a Chambermaid, Magnificent Doll, Mine Own Executioner, Man on the Eiffel Tower, Gay Adventure, Joe Butterfly, Advise and Consent, Hurry Sundown, Fortune Garden, Stay Away Joe, McKenna's Gold, Hard Contract, There Was a Crooked Man, The Clay Pigeon, Such Good Friends, Golden Needles, The Day of the Locust, 92 in the Shade, The Hindenburg, Burnt Offerings, Rocky, The Sentinel, The Manitou, Foul Play, Magic, The Great Georgia Bank Hoax, Golden Rendezvous, Rocky II, When Time Ran Out, Clash of the Titans, True Confessions, Rocky III, Santa Claus: The Movie, King Lear, Full Moon in Blue Water.
TELEVISION: Movies: The Last Hurrah, Johnny We Hardly Knew Ye, Tail Gunner Joe, Probe, Outrage!, Wet Gold.

MERRICK, DAVID: Producer. r.n. David Margulois. b. Hong Kong, Nov. 27, 1912. e. Washington U.; St. Louis U. L.L.B. Famed Broadway stage impresario with long record of hits, including Fanny, The Matchmaker, Look Back in Anger, The Entertainer, Jamaica, World of Suzie Wong, La Plume de Ma Tante, Epitaph for George Dillon, Destry Rides Again, Gypsy, Take Me Along, Irma La Douce, A Taste of Honey, Becket, Do Re Mi, Carnival, Sunday in New York, Ross, Subways Are For Sleeping, I Can Get It for You Wholesale, Stop the World. . .I Want to Get Off, Tchin Tchin, Oliver!, Luther, 110 in the Shade, Arturo Ui, Hello Dolly!, Oh, What a Lovely War, Pickwick, The Roar of the Greasepaint . . ., Inadmissible Evidence, Cactus Flower, Marat/Sade, Philadelphia Here I Come, Don't Drink the Water, I Do! I Do!, How Now Dow Jones, The Happy Time, Rosencrantz and Guildenstern are Dead (Tony Award), 40 Carats, Promises, Promises, Play It Again Sam, Child's Play, Four in a Garden, A Midsummer Night's Dream, Sugar, Out Cry, Mack and Mabel, Travesties, Very Good Eddie, Private Lives, 42nd Street.
PICTURES: Child's Play (debut), The Great Gatsby, Semi-Tough, Rough Cut.

MERRILL, DINA: Actress. r.n. Nedenia Hutton; b. New York, NY, Dec. 9, 1928. Fashion model, 1944–46. Acting debut: Here Today, Mrs. January and Mr. X, Newport (1945). Co-owner Pavilion, m.p. and TV prod. co.
PLAYS: Regional theatre: My Sister Eileen, Major Barbara, Misalliance, Loved, Surprise. Off-Broadway: Importance of Being Earnest, Smile of the Cardboard Man, Suddenly Last Summer. Broadway: Angel Street, On Your Toes.
PICTURES: Desk Set (debut), Don't Give Up the Ship, Brass Ring, Catch Me If You Can, Operation Petticoat, The Sundowners, Butterfield 8, Running Wild, Twenty Plus Two, The Courtship of Eddie's Father, Young Savages, I'll Take Sweden, The Greatest, A Wedding, Just Tell Me What You Want, Do Me a Favor—Don't Vote For My Mom, Caddyshack II, The Meal, Twisted, Fear.
TELEVISION: debut, Kate Smith Show 1956; Four Star Theatre, Playwrights '56, Climax!, Playhouse 90, Westinghouse Presents, The Investigators, Checkmate, The Rogues, Bob Hope Presents, To Tell the Truth, Hotel, Hawaii Five-O Hot Pursuit. Movies: Roots: The Next Generations, Seven in Darkness, The Letters, Family Flight, The Tenth Month, Sunshine Patriot, Repeat Performance.

MERRILL, GARY: Actor. b. Hartford, CT, Aug. 2, 1915. e. Loomis Prep. Sch., Bowdoin Coll., Trinity Coll. Stage career started in 1937, minor role, stage play, The Eternal Road; toured Brother Rat co.; then, Morning Star, See My Lawyer; on air in Young Dr. Malone, Helen Hayes Theatre, Theatre Guild, Gangbusters, Superman; army service 1941–45; upon disch. to stage in Born Yesterday, At War With the Army. Screen debut: Slattery's Hurricane (1949).
PICTURES: Twelve O'Clock High, Where the Sidewalk Ends, All About Eve, The Frogmen, Decision Before Dawn,

Another Man's Poison, Phone Call From a Stranger, Girl in White, Night Without Sleep, Blueprint for Murder, Black Dakotas, Human Jungle, Pleasure of His Company, The Woman Who Wouldn't Die, Clambake, The Incident, The Last Challenge, The Power, Huckleberry Finn, Thieves.
TELEVISION: The Mask, Justice, Dr. Kildare.

MERSON, MARC: Producer. b. New York, NY, Sept. 9, 1931. e. Swarthmore Coll. Entered Navy in 1953; assigned as publicist to Admiral's Staff of Sixth Fleet Command in the Mediterranean. Upon discharge joined trade paper Show Business as feature editor. Joined CBS-TV as asst. to casting director. Left after 3 yrs. to work for Ely Landau as casting dir., packager and sometime producer of The Play of the Week on TV. Returned to CBS for 3-yr. stint doing specials and live programs. Left to organize Brownstone Productions as indep. prod. Now partner with Alan Alda in Helix Productions to package and produce TV shows.
PICTURES: The Heart Is a Lonely Hunter, People Soup (short), Leadbelly.
TELEVISION: Stage 67, Androcles and the Lion, Dummler and Son (pilot), The David Frost Revue (synd. series), We'll Get By.

MESSICK, DON: Actor. b. Buffalo, NY, Sept. 7, 1926. e. Ramsay Streett, Sch. of Acting, Baltimore; American Theatre Wing, NY. Began performing as ventriloquist at age 13 in rural Maryland. Own radio show at 15 in Salisbury, MD (WBOC) for two years, writing and portraying all the characters in a one-man weekly comedy show. Worked in Hanna-Barbera cartoons since company began in 1958, voicing Ruff in their first series on NBC, 1959. Voiced Boo Boo Bear and Ranger Smith on Yogi Bear Show, Astro of The Jetsons. Voices: Scooby Doo and Scrappy Doo on Scooby Doo series; Papa Smurf and Azrael on Smurfs. Has done numerous national commercials.

MESTRES, RICARDO: Executive. b. New York, NY, 1958. e. Harvard U. Gained filmmaking experience during summers as prod. asst. on TV features. Joined Paramount Pictures as creative exec. 1981. Promoted to exec. dir. of production, 1982 and to v.p., prod. in 1984. Named v.p. of prod., Walt Disney Pictures, 1985. Promoted to sr. v.p., prod.,1986. Named president, production, Touchstone Pictures, 1988. In 1989, appt. pres., Hollywood Pictures, a new m.p. company created by The Walt Disney Company.

METZGER, RADLEY: Producer, Director, Writer. b. 1930. Worked as asst. dir. also distributor of Swedish film I, A Woman before making own films.
PICTURES: Dark Odyssey (p.d., s.p.); Passionate Sunday, The Dirty Girls, The Alley Cats, Carmen, Baby (p.d,); Therese and Isabelle (p., d.); Camille 2000 (p.,d.); The Lickerish Quartet (p., d.); Score (p.d.); Little Mother (p., d.); Naked Came the Stranger (d.); The Image (d.), The Opening of Misty Beethoven; The Cat and the Canary; The Princess and the Call Girl.

METZLER, JIM: Actor. b. Oneonda, NY. e. Dartmouth Coll.
PICTURES: Four Friends, Tex, Hot to Trot, Sundown, The Vampire in Retreat, 976–EVIL.
TELEVISION: North and South, North and South Book II, On Wings of Eagles, Do You Remember Love, Princess Daisy, Christmas Star, Murder By Night.

MEYER, BARRY M: Executive. With ABC-TV in legal and business affairs depts. before joining Warner Bros. TV in 1971 as dir. of business affairs. 1972, named v.p. of business affairs for Warner TV arm; promoted to exec. v.p. of div. 1978. 1984, named exec. v.p. of Warner Bros., Inc.

MEYER, NICHOLAS: Director, Writer. b. Dec. 24, 1945. e. U. of Iowa. Was unit publicist for Love Story, 1969. Story ed. Warner Bros. 1970–71. Author: The Seven-Per-Cent Solution, Target Practice, The West End Horror, Confession of a Homing Pigeon.
PICTURES: The Seven-Per-Cent Solution (s.p.), Time After Time (s.p., dir.), Star Trek II: The Wrath of Khan (dir.), The Deceivers (dir.).
TELEVISION: Judge Dee (s.p.), The Night That Panicked America (s.p.); The Day After (dir.).

MEYER, RUSS: Producer, Director. b. Oakland, CA, March 21, 1922. In 1942 joined Army Signal Corps, learned m.p. photography and shot combat newsreels. Worked as photographer for Playboy Magazine Partner in RM Films Intl. Inc.
PICTURES: The Immoral Mr. Teas, Eve and the Handyman, Motor Psycho, Fanny Hill, Mondo Topless, Finders Keepers, Lovers Weepers, Goodmorning and Goodbye, Vixen, Beyond the Valley of the Dolls, The Seven Minutes, and Sweet Suzy, Beneath the Valley of the Dolls, Cherry Harry and Raquel, The Breast of Russ Meyer, Ultra Vixens, Amazon Women on the Moon (actor).

MEYERS, ROBERT: Executive. b. Mount Vernon, NY, Oct. 3, 1934. e. NYU. Entered m.p. industry as exec. trainee in domestic div. of Columbia Pictures, 1956. Sales and adv. 1956–60; transferred to sales dept. Columbia Pictures International, N.Y., posts there included supervisor of intl. roadshows and exec. ass't. to continental mgr. Joined National General Pictures as v.p.-foreign sales, 1969. Created JAD Films International Inc. in Feb. 1974 for independent selling and packaging of films around the world. September, 1977, joined Lorimar Productions Inc. as sr. v.p. of Lorimar Distribution Intl. Became pres. in April, 1978. Joined Filmways Pictures in 1980, named pres. & COO. Pres. of American Film Mktg. Assn.; 1982, formed new co., R.M. Films International. Rejoined Lorimar 1985. as pres., Lorimar Motion Pictures, intl. distribution. Nov., 1988 joined Orion as pres., Orion Pictures Intl.

MICHAELS, JOEL B.: Producer. b. Buffalo, NY, Oct. 24, 1938. Studied acting with Stella Adler. Many co-prods. with Garth Drabinsky, Cineplex Corp.
PICTURES: The Peace Killers; Your Three Minutes Are Up (prod. spvr.); Student Teachers (prod. spvr.); The Prisoners (assoc. prod.); Lepke (assoc. prod.); The Four Deuces (asso. prod.); Bittersweet Love; The Silent Partner; The Changeling; Tribute; The Amateur; Losin' It (exec. prod.); The Philadelphia Experiment.

MICHAELS, LORNE: Writer, Producer. b. Toronto, Canada, Nov. 17, 1944. r.n. Lorne Lipowitz. e. U. of Toronto, 1966. President, Broadway Video, since 1979.
TELEVISION: Rowan and Martin's Laugh-In (writer, 1968–69); CBC comedy specials (writer, prod., 1969–72); Lily Tomlin Specials (writer, prod., 1972–75, 2 Emmy Awards); Perry Como (writer, prod., 1974); Flip Wilson (writer, prod.); Saturday Night Live (creator, prod., writer 1975–80, 3 Emmys); Beach Boys (writer, prod.); Paul Simon (writer, prod., Emmy Award, 1978); The Rutles: All You Need Is Cash (writer, prod.); Steve Martin's Best Show Ever (prod.); Simon and Garfunkel: The Concert in Central Park (exec. prod.); The Coneheads (exec. prod.); The New Show (prod.); Emmy Awards, (prod., 1988); Coca-Cola Presents Live: The Hard Rock; On Location: Kids in the Hall (exec. prod.).
PICTURES: Gilda Live (prod., writer); Nothing Lasts Forever (prod.); Three Amigos (prod.).

MICHAELS, RICHARD: Director. b. Brooklyn, NY, Feb. 15, 1936. e. Cornell U. Script supervisor 1955–64 and associate producer before starting directing career in 1968 with Bewitched (54 episodes), of which was also assoc. prod.
TELEVISION: Series: episodes of Love, American Style, The Odd Couple, Delvecchio, Ellery Queen, Room 222. Movies: Once an Eagle (mini-series), Charlie Cobb, Having Babies II, Leave Yesterday Behind, My Husband Is Missing, . . .And Your Name Is Jonah (winner, Christopher Award), Once Upon a Family, The Plutonium Incident, Scared Straight, Another Story (winner, Scott Newman Drug Abuse Prevention Award), Homeward Bound (winner, Banff Intl. TV Festival Special Jury Award & Christopher Award), Berlin Tunnel 21, The Children Nobody Wanted, One Cooks, The Other Doesn't, Sadat (mini-series), Jessie (pilot), Silence of the Heart, Heart of a Champion: The Ray Mancini Story, Rockabye, Kay O'Brien (pilot), I'll Take Manhattan (mini-series); Leg Work (pilot), Red River (movie), Indiscreet, Love and Betrayal.
PICTURE: Blue Skies Again.

MICHEL, WERNER: Executive. e. U. of Berlin, U. of Paris, Ph.D. Radio writer, dir., co-author two Broadway revues, 1938, 1940; dir. French feature films; dir. Broadcast Div., Voice of America, 1942–46; prod., dir., CBS, 1946–48; asst. prog. dir., CBS, 1948–50; dir. of Kenyon and Eckhart TV dept., 1950–52; prod., DuMont TV network, 1952–55; dir., Electronicam TV-Film Prod., 1955–56; prod., Benton and Bowles; Procter and Gamble, 1956–57; v.p. & dir. TV-radio dept., Reach, McClinton Advertising, Inc., 1957–62; consultant, TV Programming & Comm'l-Prod., N. W. Ayer & Son, Inc.; v.p., dir., TV dept., SSCB Advertising, 1963, pgm. exec., ABC-TV Hollywood, 1975; director, dramatic programs, 1976; sr. v.p., creative affairs, MGM-TV, 1977; exec. v.p., Wrather Entertainment Intl., 1979; sr. v.p., creative affairs, MGM-TV, 1980–82; COO, Guber-Peters TV, 1982–84; sr. v.p., corporate TV dept., Kenyon & Eckhart, & NY, 1984–86; sr. v.p. TV dept. Bozell, Inc. NY, 1986–.

MICHELET, MICHEL: Composer. b. Kiev, Russia, June 27, 1899. Prof., Kiev & Vienna Conserv. Composed concert compositions, ballets, stage music; ent. m.p. industry, composed scores 105 films, in France, Italy and Germany; to U.S. 1941; author many concert compositions. Recent works incl. Requiem, Oratorio, 7 Visions of Judea (1989). Member: French Soc. of Composers (SACEM).
PICTURES: Voice in the Wind (AA nom.), Hairy Ape (AA nom.), Music for Millions, The Chase, Lured, Siren of Atlantis, Man on the Eiffel Tower, Once a Thief, Tarzan's Peril, Fort Algiers, Un Missionaire, Le Secret de Soeur Angele, Petersburger, Nachte, Challenge (Tribute to Modern Art). Also did scores for many U.S. Information Service documentaries; arr. of Russian music Anastasia; Afrodife (score); The January (orig. songs & arr. of Russian music).

MICHELL, KEITH: Actor. b. Adelaide, Australia, Dec. 1, 1926. Early career as art teacher, radio actor; toured Australia with Stratford Shakespearean Co. 1952–53; Stratford Memorial Theatre 1954–55, Old Vic Theatre 1956–57. Irma la Douce, Chichester, Art of Seduction, The First 400 Years, Robert & Elizabeth, Kain, The King's Mare, 1969: Man of La Mancha (London, N.Y.): Abelard & Heloise (London); (NY and LA), Hamlet, (London). Artistic Director, Chichester Festival Theatre. Toured Australia with Chichester Festival Co., London: Crucifer of Blood, (London): On the Twentieth Century, (Melbourne Theatre Co.): Pete McGynty, (London): Captain Beaky Christmas Show. (Chichester): On the Rocks (Brisbane): The Tempest, (UK tour 1983): Amadeus (San Francisco). 1984–85: La Cage aux Folles (USA and Australia), Portraits, The Bacarat Scandal (Chicester, 1988).
TELEVISION: Pygmalion, Act of Violence, Mayerling Affair, Tiger at the Gates, Traveller Without Luggage, Guardian Angel, Wuthering Heights, The Bergonzi Hands, Ring Round The Moon, Spread of the Eagle, The Shifting Heart, Loyalties, Soldier in Love, Hallmark Hall of Fame, series; Kain, The Ideal Husband, The Six Wives of Henry VIII (series). Keith Michell at various London theatres, Dear Love. Selections from Keith Michell in Concert at Chichester, Captain Beaky & his Band, Captain Beaky, Volume 2, The Gondoliers, The Pirates of Penzance, Ruddigore, My Brother Tom (series, 1986), Capt. James Cook (series, 1987).
PICTURES: True as a Turtle, Dangerous Exile, Gypsy and the Gentleman, The Hellfire Club, All Night Long, Seven Seas to Calais, Prudence and the Pill, House of Cards, Henry VIII and his Six Wives, Moments, The Deceivers.

MIDLER, BETTE: Actress, Singer. b. Honolulu, HI, Dec. 1, 1945. e. U. of Hawaii. Appeared on Bdwy. in Fiddler on the Roof; Salvation, 1970; Tommy, Seattle Opera Co., 1971. Gained fame as singer-comic in nightclubs and cabarets. Has toured extensively with own stage shows: Divine Miss M, Clams on the Half-Shell. Author: The Saga of Baby Divine, 1983. Special Tony Award, 1973.
PICTURES: Hawaii (debut, 1965), The Rose, Divine Madness, Jinxed, Down and Out in Beverly Hills, Ruthless People, Outrageous Fortune, Big Business, Oliver & Company (voice), Beaches (also prod.), Stella.
TELEVISION: Ol' Red Hair is Back (Emmy Award, 1978); Bette Midler's Mondo Beyondo.

MIFUNE, TOSHIRO: Actor. b. Tsingtao, China, April 1, 1920. e. Japanese schools. Served five years Japanese army. Joined Toho Studio 1946.
PICTURES: Snow Trail, Drunken Angel, Eagle of Pacific, Seven Samurai, I Live in Fear, Legend of Musashi, Throne of Blood, Riksha Man, Three Treasures, Last Gunfight, I Bombed Pearl Harbor, Rose in Mud, Rashomon, Yojimbo, Animus Trujano (Mexican), Kiska, Red Beard, High and Low, Judo Sag, The Lost World of Sinbad, Hell in the Pacific, Paper Tiger, Midway, Winter Kills, 1941, The Challenge, Inchon, The Bushido Blade, Princess from the Moon, The Death of a Master.
TELEVISION: (U.S.) Shogun.

MIGDEN, CHESTER L.: Executive. b. New York, NY, May 21, 1921; e. City Coll. of New York, B.A., 1941, Columbia U., LL,B, 1947. Member New York Bar. Attorney for National Labor Relations Board 1947–51. Currently exec. dir., Assn. of Talent Agents. Was exec of Screen Actors Guild 1952–81; nat'l. exec. secty., 1973–81.

MIKELL, GEORGE: Actor. b. Lithuania. In Australia 1950–56 acting with Old Vic Co. Ent. films 1955. TV 1957. To England 1957; since appeared in numerous film and TV prod.
TELEVISION: Counsel at Law, Six Eyes on a Stranger, The Mask of a Clown, Green Grows the Grass, Opportunity Taken, OSS Series, Espinage, The Danger Man, Strange Report, The Survivors, The Adventurer, Colditz, The Hanged Man, Quiller, Martin Hartwell, Flambards, Sweeney, The Secret Army, Sherlock Holmes, When the Boat Comes In, Brack Report, Bergerac, The Brief, Glass Babies (Australia), Hannay.
PICTURES: The Guns of Navarone, The Password Is Courage, The Great Escape, Deadline for Diamonds, Where The Spies Are, The Spy Who Came in From the Cold, I Predoni Del Sahara, Sabina, The Double Man, Attack on the Iron Coast, Zeppelin, Young Winston, Scorpio, The Tamarind Seed, Sweeney Two, The Sea Wolves, Escape to Victory, Emerald, Kommissar Zufall (Germany).
STAGE: Five Finger Exercise, Altona, The Millionairess, Love from a Stranger, Portrait of a Queen, Farewell, Judas, Flare Path.

MIKHALKOV, NIKITA: Director, Writer. b. Moscow, Soviet Union, Oct. 21, 1945. His great grandfather was the painter Sourikov; his grandfather, painter Konchalovski; his father, Sergei Mikhalhov is a writer and chmn. of USSR Writers Union. His mother is poet Natalia Konchalovskaia; brother is director Andrei Mikhalkov-Konchalovski. e. Theater School of Varkhtangok, and High School for Cinema. Directed first short film 1968: I'm Coming Home. Directed short film for graduation: A Quiet Day at the End of the War. Debut as actor in I'm Wandering Through Moscow (1964). Acted in more than 25 films including: The Call, A Nest of Noblemen, Song to Manchuk, The Red Tent, Siberiad.
PICTURES: Dir. and co-s.p.: At Home Among Strangers (1974), Ours Among Ours, The Slave of Love, Unfinished Work for Pianola (also actor), Five Evenings, Oblomov, Relatives (also actor), Without Witness, Dark Eyes, The Barber of Siberia.

MILCHIN, ARNON: Producer. b. Israel. Began producing and financing films in Israel. Also producer of stage plays incl. Ipi Tombi, It's So Nice to be Civilized, and Amadeus in Paris starring Roman Polanski.
PICTURES: Black Joy, The Medusa Touch, Dizengoff, The King of Comedy, Brazil, Once Upon a Time in America, Stripper, Legend, Man on Fire, Big Man on Campus, Who's Harry Crumb? Family Business.
TELEVISION: Masada.

MILES, CHRISTOPHER: Director. b. England, April 19, 1939. Brother of actress Sarah Miles.
PICTURES: Up Jumped a Swagman; The Virgin and the Gypsy; Time for Loving; The Maids; That Lucky Touch; Priest of Love (also prod.), Murder in Mesopotamia.

MILES, SARAH: Actress. b. Sept. 9, 1941. m. writer Robert Bolt. e. Royal Acad. of Dramatic Art. Film debut, Term of Trial (1963).
PICTURES: The Servant, The Ceremony, Six-Sided Triangle, Those Magnificent Men In Their Flying Machines, Blowup, Ryan's Daughter, Lady Caroline Lamb, The Man Who Loved Cat Dancing, The Sailor Who Fell from Grace with the Sea, The Big Sleep, Venom, Ordeal by Innocence, Steaming, Hope and Glory, White Mischief.
THEATRE: Vivat! Vivat Regina!
TELEVISION: James Michener's Dynasty; Great Expectations; Harem, Queenie.

MILES, VERA: Actress. b. Boise City, OK, Aug. 23, 1930. e. public schools, Pratt and Wichita, KS.
TELEVISION: Climax, Pepsi Cola Playhouse, Schlitz Playhouse, Ford Theatre. Movie: International Airport, Rough Necks, Baffled, McNaughton's Daughter, State Fair, Runaway, The Underground Man, The Strange and Deadly Occurrence, Smash-up on Interstate 5, Judge Horton and the Scottsboro Boys, Helen Keller—The Miracle Continues, Travis McGee, The Hijacking of the Achille Lauro.
PICTURES: For Men Only, Rose Bowl Story, Charge at Feather River, Pride of the Blue Grass, Wichita, The Searchers, 23 Paces to Baker Street, Autumn Leaves, Wrong Man, Beau James, Web of Evidence, FBI Story, Touch of Larceny, Five Branded Women, Psycho, The Spirit Is Willing, Gentle Giant, Sergeant Ryker, Kona Coast, It Takes All Kinds, Hellfighters, The Wild Country, One Little Indian, Psycho II, Brainwaves, Starcrossed.

MILGRAM, HENRY: Theatre Executive. b. Philadelphia, PA, April 20, 1926. e. U. of Pennsylvania, Wharton Sch. In industry 42 years; now exec. v.p. Milgram Theatres. Variety Club Board member for past 25 years, past president and chairman of the board of Variety Club of Phila.; presently Variety Club Intl. v.p. Board member. Hahnemann University, trustee.

MILIUS, JOHN: Writer, Director. b. St. Louis, MO. April 11, 1944. e. Los Angeles City Coll., U. of Southern California (cinema course). While at latter won National Student Film Festival Award. Started career as ass't. to Lawrence Gordon at AIP. Began writing screenplays, then became director with Dillinger (1973).
PICTURES: Devil's 8 (s.p.), Evil Knievel (s.p.), The Life and Times of Judge Roy Bean, Jeremiah Johnson (co-s.p.), Dillinger (s.p.-dir.), Magnum Force (co.-s.p.), The Wind and the Lion (s.p., dir.), Big Wednesday (dir. co.-s.p.); Apocalypse Now (s.p.); Hardcore (exec. prod.), Used Cars (co-exec. prod.), 1941 (exec. prod., co.-s.p.); Conan the Barbarian (dir., co.-s.p.); Uncommon Valor (co-prod.), Red Dawn (dir., co-s.p.), Extreme Prejudice (story), Farewell to the King (dir., s.p.).

MILKIS, EDWARD: Producer: b. Los Angeles, CA, July 16, 1931. e. U. of Southern California. Began career as asst. editor, ABC-TV, 1952; Disney, 1954; MGM, 1957; editor, MGM, 1960–65; assoc. prod., Star Trek, 1966–69; exec. in chg. post-prod., Paramount, 1969–72; formed Miller-Milkis Prods., 1972; Miller-Milkis-Boyett, 1979. Now heads Edward K. Milkis Prods.
PICTURES: Silver Streak; Foul Play; The Best Little Whorehouse in Texas.
TELEVISION: Petrocelli; Bosom Buddies (exec. prod.); Happy Days; Laverne and Shirley; Feel the Heat.

MILLAR, STUART: Producer, Director. b. New York, NY, 1929. e. Stanford U.; Sorbonne, Paris. Ent. industry working for Motion Picture Branch, State Dept., Germany. documentaries, Army Signal Corps, Long Island, Germany; journalist, International News Service, San Francisco; assoc. prod.-dir.,

The Desperate Hours; assoc. prod.-dir., Friendly Persuasion.
PICTURES: The Young Stranger; Stage Struck; Birdman of Alcatraz. I Could Go On Singing, The Young Doctors, Stolen Hours, The Best Man, Paper Lion, Little Big Man, When The Legends Die, Rooster Cogburn, Shoot the Moon (co-exec. prod.).
TELEVISION: Vital Signs, Killer Instinct (prod.), Dream Breaker (prod., dir., co-s.p.), Lady in a Corner (co-exec. prod.).

MILLER, ANN: Actress. r.n. Lucille Ann Collier; b. Houston, TX, Apr. 12, 1923. e. Albert Sidney Johnson H.S., Houston; Lawler Prof. Sch., Hollywood. Studied dance as child; played West Coast vaudeville theatres, Screen debut: New Faces of 1937. Autobiography, Miller's High Life (1974).
STAGE: George White's Scandals, (1940), Mame, (1969), Sugar Babies.
PICTURES: Life of the Party, Stage Door, New Faces of 1937, Radio City Revels, Having a Wonderful Time, Room Service, You Can't Take It with You, Too Many Girls, Time Out for Rhythm, Priorities on Parade, Reveille with Beverly, Jam Session, Eve Knew Her Apples, Thrill of Brazil, Easter Parade, The Kissing Bandit, On the Town, Watch the Birdie, Texas Carnival, Two Tickets to Broadway, Lovely To Look At, Small Town Girl, Kiss Me Kate, Deep in My Heart, Hit the Deck, Opposite Sex, Great American Pastime.

MILLER, ARTHUR: Writer. b. New York, NY, Oct. 17, 1915. e. U. of Michigan. Plays include Situation Normal; All My Sons, Death of a Salesman (Pulitzer Prize, 1949), The Crucible (Tony Award), A View from the Bridge, After the Fall, Incident at Vichy, The Price, Up From Paradise, Situation Normal, The American Clock. Novel: Focus. Autobiography: Timebends (1987).
PICTURES: Film versions of plays: All My Sons, Death of a Salesman, The Crucible, A View From the Bridge, The Misfits (orig. s.p.), Everybody Wins (orig. s.p.).
TELEVISION: Death of a Salesman, Fame, After The Fall, Playing for Time.

MILLER, BARRY: Actor. b. Los Angeles, CA, Feb. 6, 1958. New York stage debut, My Mother, My Father and Me, 1980. Film debut, Saturday Night Fever, 1977.
THEATER: Forty Deuce, The Tempest, Biloxi Blues (Tony and Drama Desk Awards, 1985).
PICTURES: Voices, Fame, The Chosen, The Journey of Natty Gann, Peggy Sue Got Married, The Last Temptation of Christ.
TELEVISION: The Roommate, Joe and Sons, Szysznyk, The Bill Cosby Show.

MILLER, CHERYL: Actress. b. Sherman Oaks, CA, Feb. 4, 1943. e. UCLA, Los Angeles Conservatory of Music.
PICTURES: First film, Casanova Brown, age 19 days. Appeared in over 100 films as child, more recently in the Monkey's Uncle, Clarence the Cross-Eyed Lion, The Initiation, The Man from Clover Grove, Doctor Death.
TELEVISION: Perry Mason, Bachelor Father, Flipper and as co-star in Daktari, Donna Reed, Leave It to Beaver, Farmer's Daughter, Wonderful World of Color, Dobie Gillis, Bright Promise, Love American Style, Emergency, Cades County.

MILLER, DAVID: Director. b. Paterson, NJ, Nov. 28, 1909. U.S. Army, W.W.II. Film ed. 1930, Columbia; Walter Futter prods. In 1933 short subjects ed. MGM; then dir. short subjects. Dir. features 1941.
PICTURES: Billy the Kid, Sunday Punch, Flying Tigers, Love Happy, Top O the Morning, Our Very Own, Saturday's Hero, Sudden Fear, Twist of Fate, Diane, Opposite Sex, The Story of Esther Costello, Happy Anniversary, Midnight Lace, Backstreet, Lonely Are the Brave, Captain Newman, MD, Hammerhead, Hail Hero, Executive Action, Bittersweet Love.
TELEVISION: Best Place to Be, Goldie and The Boxer, Love for Rent.

MILLER, DICK (RICHARD): Actor, Writer. b. New York, NY, Dec. 25, 1928. e. City Coll. of New York, Columbia U. Grad. NYU. Theater Sch. of Dramatic Arts. Commercial artist, psychologist (Bellevue Mental Hygiene Clinic, Queens General Hosp. Psychiatric dept.) Served in U.S. Navy, W.W.II. Boxing champ, U.S. Navy. Semi-pro football. Broadway stage, radio disc jockey, The Dick Miller Show, WMCA, WOR-TV. Over 500 live shows. Did first live night talk show with Bobby Sherwood, Midnight Snack, CBS, 1950. Wrote, produced and directed radio and TV shows in NY in early 1950s. Wrote screenplays; T.N.T. Jackson, Which Way to the Front, Four Rode Out and others. Has appeared on all major TV series and Fame (3 years).
PICTURES: Has appeared in over 100 features, including: Not of This Earth, Thunder Over Hawaii, Rock All Night, Sorority Girl, The Terror, Bucket of Blood, Little Shop of Horrors, Targets, War of the Satellites, The Long Ride Home, St. Valentine's Day Massacre, Capone, Executive Action, White Line Fever, Cannonball, Mr. Billion, New York, New York, Gremlins, Explorers, Inner Space, After Hours, Terminator, The 'Burbs, Monolith, Gremlins II.

MILLER, (DR.) GEORGE: Director. b. Chinchilla, Queensland, Australia, 1945. Practiced medicine in Sydney; quit to work on films with Byron Kennedy, who became longtime partner until his death in 1983. Early work: Violence in the Cinema Part One (short, dir., s.p.), Frieze—An Underground Film (doc., editor only), Devil in Evening Dress (doc., dir., s.p.). First worldwide success with Mad Max.
PICTURES: Mad Max (dir., s.p.), Chain Reaction (assoc. prod. only), The Road Warrior, Twilight Zone—The Movie (segment), Mad Max Beyond Thunderdome, The Witches of Eastwick, Dead Calm (prod. only).
TELEVISION: Five Mile Creek, The Cowra Breakout.

MILLER, GEORGE: Director. b. Australia.
PICTURES: In Search of Anna (asst. dir.), The Man from Snowy River, The Aviator, The Return of the Man from Snowy River, The Never Ending Story II.
TELEVISION: Cash and Company, Against the Wind, The Last Outlaw, The Dismissal, All the Rivers Run, Bodyline (also s.p.).

MILLER, JAMES R.: Executive. Began m.p. industry career in 1971 in legal dept. of United Artists (N.Y.). Left to go with Paramount Pictures in legal dept.; then moved to Columbia in 1977 as sr. counsel; later assoc. gen. counsel. In 1979 named Warner Bros. v.p.—studio business affairs; 1984, v.p. chg. world-wide business affairs; 1987, sr. v.p.

MILLER, JP: Writer. b. San Antonio, TX, Dec. 18, 1919. e. Rice U., 1937–41; Yale Drama Sch., 1946–47. U.S. Navy, Lieut., 1941–46; pub. poetry, short stories.
ORIGINAL DRAMAS: Philco TV Playhouse: Hide and Seek, Old Tasslefoot, The Rabbit Trap, The Pardon-me Boy; Playhouse 90, Days of Wine and Roses, CBS Playhouse, The People Next Door (Emmy Award, 1969), The Unwanted, The Lindbergh Kidnapping Case, Helter Skelter, Gauguin the Savage, I Know My First Name is Steven (co-s.p.).
PICTURES: The Rabbit Trap, (story, s.p.) Days of Wine and Roses (story s.p.) The Young Savages (co-author, s.p.) Behold A Pale Horse, (s.p.) The People Next Door (story, s.p.).
NOVELS: The Race for Home, Liv, The Skook.

MILLER, JASON: Writer, Actor. b. Scranton, PA, April 22, 1939. Entered regional playwriting contest during high school in Scranton, PA and since has moved back and forth between acting and writing. Wrote That Championship Season, winner of N.Y. Drama Critics Best Play award, 1972, Tony Award, 1973, and Pulitzer Prize for Drama.
PICTURES: The Exorcist (actor), That Championship Season (s.p.), The Nickel Ride (actor), A Home of our Own (actor), A Love Story (s.p.); *Actor:* Monsignor, Light of Day, The Ninth Configuration, The Exorcist: 1990.
TELEVISION: Actor: Deadly Care, Dain Curse, F. Scott Fitzgerald in Hollywood, Best Little Girl in the World, Vampire, A Home of Our Own, Henderson Monster, Marilyn: The Untold Story, Night Heat, Deadly Care.

MILLER, MAX B.: Executive. Father, Max Otto Miller, producer silent features and shorts. e. Los Angeles Valley Coll., UCLA, Sherwood Oaks Coll. Writer of articles on cinema for American Cinematographer and other publications. Owns and manages Fotos Intl., entertainment photo agency with offices in 46 countries. Recipient of Golden Globe Award in 1976 for Youthquake, documentary feature. Also director of Films International (prod., Shoot Los Angeles) and pres. of MBM Prod., Inc. Active member of Hollywood Foreign Press Assn. (from 1974–82 bd member; twice chmn.), Independent Feature Project, Acad. of TV Arts & Sciences, L.A. Int'l, Film Exhibition.

MILLER, PENELOPE ANN: Actress. b. Los Angeles, CA, Jan. 13, 1964. Daughter of actor-filmmaker Mark Miller and journalist Bea Miller. e. studied acting with Herbert Berghof.
THEATER: The People From Work (1984), Biloxi Blues (Bdwy and L.A.), Moonchildren, Our Town.
PICTURES: Adventures in Babysitting (1987, debut), Biloxi Blues, Big Top Pee-Wee, Miles From Home, Dead-Bang, The Freshman Downtown.
TELEVISION: The Guiding Light, As the World Turns, The Popcorn Kid (series), Tales From the Darkside, Miami Vice, St. Elsewhere, Family Ties, The Facts of Life, Tales From the Hollywood Hills: The Closed Set, Our Town.

MILLER, ROBERT ELLIS: Director. b. New York, NY, July 18, 1932. Worked on Broadway and TV before feature film debut with Any Wednesday (1966).
PICTURES: Sweet November, The Heart Is a Lonely Hunter, The Buttercup Chain, Big Truck and Poor Claire, The Girl from Petrovka, The Baltimore Bullet, Reuben, Reuben, Hawks, Brenda Starr, Bed and Breakfast.
TELEVISION: The Voice of Charlie Pont, And James Was a Very Small Snail, The Other Lover, Madame X, Just an Old

Sweet Song, Her Life as a Man, Ishi, Last of His Tribe; Intimate Strangers.

MILLER, RONALD W.: Producer. b. Los Angeles, CA, April 17, 1933. e. U. of Southern California. Football player with Los Angeles Rams. Two years U.S. Army. 1957 joined Walt Disney Productions as 2nd asst. dir. Old Yeller. Assoc. prod. TV series Walt Disney Presents; assoc. or co-prod. additional 37 episodes Disney TV. Exec. prod. Walt Disney's Wonderful World of Color. Assisted Walt Disney, Pageant Direct 1960 U.S. Olympics. By 1968, v.p., exec. prod. mem. bd. of dir. Walt Disney Productions. 1980, named pres. & chief operating off.; 1983, pres. & chief executive off., Disney Productions. Resigned in 1984.
PICTURES: Bon Voyage, Summer Magic, Son of Flubber, Moon Pilot, The Misadventures of Merlin Jones, A Tiger Walks, The Monkey's Uncle, That Darn Cat, Robin Crusoe, U.S.N., Monkey's Go Home, Prod. of: Never a Dull Moment, The Boatniks, The Wild Country, No Deposit, No Return, Treasure of Matecumbe, Freaky Friday, The Littlest Horse Thieves, Herbie Goes to Monte Carlo, Pete's Dragon, Candleshoe, Return from Witch Mountain, Cat from Outer Space, The North Avenue Irregulars, Herbie Goes Bananas, The Black Hole, Midnight Madness, Watcher in the Woods, The Last Flight of Noah's Ark. Exec. prod.: Condorman; The Devil and Max Devlin, Tex, Never Cry Wolf, Night Crossing, Tron.

MILLER, WINSTON: Writer. b. St. Louis, MO, June 22, 1910. e. Princeton U. In 1935 entered m.p. ind.
PICTURES: Good Morning, Judge, Song of Texas, Home in Indiana, One Body Too Many, They Made Me a Killer, Double Exposure, My Darling Clementine, Relentless, Station West, Last Outpost, Rocky Mountain, Hong Kong, Blazing Forest, Carson City, The Vanquished, Boy from Oklahoma, Jivaro, Bounty Hunter, Run for Cover, Far Horizons, Lucy Gallant, Tension at Table Rock, April Love, A Private's Affair, Hound Dog Man, Escapade In Japan, Mardi Gras.

MILLS, DONNA: Actress. b. Chicago, IL, Dec. 11, 1944. e. U. of Illinois. Left school to pursue career in theatre, beginning as dancer with stage companies around Chicago and touring. In NY became regular on soap opera, The Secret Storm. On Bdwy in Don't Drink the Water.
TELEVISION: Series: Love Is a Many Splendored Thing, Lancer, Dan August, The Good Life, Knots Landing. Movies: Waikiki, Doctor's Private Lives, Superdome, The Hunted Lady, Woman on the Run, Fire!, The Bait, Outback Bound, The Lady Forgets. Mini-Series: Hanging by a Thread, Bare Essence, Intimate Encounters.
PICTURES: The Incident, Play Misty for Me.

MILLS, HAYLEY: Actress. b. London, Eng., April 18, 1946. Daughter of actor John Mills. e. Elmhurst Boarding Sch., Surrey. m.p. debut Tiger Bay 1959 with father; signed Disney contract 1960.
PICTURES: Pollyanna, The Parent Trap, Whistle Down the Wind, The Castaways, Summer Magic, The Chalk Garden, The Moonspinners, The Truth About Spring, Sky West and Crooked, Trouble with Angels, The Family Way, Pretty Polly, A Matter of Innocence, Twisted Nerve, Take a Girl Like You, Deadly Strangers, Silhouettes, What Changed Charley Farthing, The Diamond Hunters, That Darn Cat, Forbush and the Penguins, Endless Night, Appointment with Death.
TELEVISION: The Flame Trees of Thika, Parent Trap II, IV, V, Amazing Stories, Illusion of Life, Good Morning Miss Bliss (series), Murder She Wrote, Back Home.

MILLS, SIR JOHN: Actor, Producer. b. Suffolk, England, February 22, 1908, m. Mary Hayley Bell. Father of actresses Hayley and Juliet. Previously clerk. Film actor since 1933. One of top ten money-making Brit. stars in Motion Picture Herald-Fame Poll, 1945, 1947, 1949–50, 1954, 1956–58. Oscar for Ryan's Daughter. Recipient special award 1988, British Academy of Film and Television Arts.
PICTURES: We Dive at Dawn, The Young Mr. Pitt, In Which We Serve, This Happy Breed, Blue for Waterloo, Cottage To Let, Way to the Stars, Waterloo Road, Great Expectations, So Well Remembered, October Man, Scott of the Antarctic, Operation Disaster, Mr. Denning Drives North, Gentle Gunman, Long Memory, Hobson's Choice, End of the Affair, Colditz Story, Above Us the Waves, Escapade, It's Great to be Young, Around the World in 80 Days, War and Peace, Baby and the Battleship, Town on Trial, Monty's Double, Dunkirk, Summer of the 17th Doll, Tiger Bay, Swiss Family Robinson, Tunes of Glory, The Singer Not the Song, Flame In the Streets, Tiara Tahiti, The Valiant, The Chalk Garden, The Truth about Spring, The Great Spy Mission, King Rat, The Wrong Box, Sky West and Crooked (dir.), The Family Way, Cowboy in Africa, Chukka, A Black Veil For Lisa, Oh! What a Lovely War, Run Wild, Run Free, Ryan's Daughter, Adam's Woman, Dulcima, Oklahoma Crude, Young Winston, Lady Caroline Lamb, The Human Factor, Trial By Combat, The Big Sleep, 39 Steps, Gandhi, Sahara, Who's That Girl.
STAGE: Good Companions, 1975; Great Expectations, 1976; Separate Tables, 1977; Goodbye, Mr. Chips, 1982; Little Lies, 1983; Little Lies (Toronto, 1984), The Petition, Pygmalion.
TELEVISION: Masks of Death, Murder with Mirrors, Woman of Substance, Hold the Dream, Edge of the Wind, When the Wind Blows, Around the World in 80 Days, The Lady and the Highwayman, The True Story of Spit MacPhee, A Tale of Two Cities, Ending Up.

MILLS, JULIET: Actress. b. London, England, Nov. 21, 1941. m. actor, Maxwell Caulfield. Daughter of John Mills. Made stage debut at 14 in Alice Through the Looking Glass.
PICTURES: So Well Remembered, The History of Mr. Polly, No, My Darling Daughter, Twice Around the Daffodils, Nurse on Wheels, Carry on Jack, The Rare Breed, Wings of War, Oh, What a Lovely War!, The Challengers, Avanti!, Beyond the Door, The Second Power, The Last Melodrama.
TELEVISION: Nanny and the Professor (series); Movies: Wings of Fire, The Challengers, Letters from Three Lovers, QB VII, Once an Eagle, Alexander: The Other Side of Dawn, The Cracker Factory.

MILNER, JACK: Executive Producer. b. Jersey City, NJ, Nov. 2, 1910. e. Roosevelt H.S., L.A., CA. M.P. industry 1927. Worked many phases from laboratory-camera-editorial dept. to financing and co-producing feature pictures; formed Milner Bros. Productions with brother Dan Milner, 1955; prod. Phantom from 10,000 Leagues, From Hell It Came, Jail Break, etc.
TELEVISION: prod. My Dog Sheppy, From Here to Now, Come as You Are.

MILNER, MARTIN: Actor. b. Detroit, MI, Dec. 28, 1931. e. U. of Southern California. Debut in Life with Father, 1947; U.S. Army 1952–54, directed 20 training films.
PICTURES: Sands of Iwo Jima, The Halls of Montezuma, Operation Pacific, The Captive City, Battle Zone, Mr. Roberts, Pete Kelly's Blues, On the Threshold of Space, Gunfight at the O.K. Corral, Sweet Smell of Success, Marjorie Morningstar, Too Much, Too Soon, Compulsion, 13 Ghosts, Valley of the Dolls.
TELEVISION: Series: The Stu Erwin Show (1954–55), The Life of Riley, Route 66 (1960–64), Adam-12 (1968–75), Swiss Family Robinson (1975–76). Movies: Black Beauty, The Last Convertible, Flood, Hurricane, The Seekers, Little Mo.

MILO, GEORGE: Set Decorator, r.n. George Milo Vescia. b. New York, NY, Dec. 19, 1909. e. high school, art schools. Landscape, seascape, still life painter, portrait sculptor; set decorator since 1937.
TELEVISION: Republic Studios, Revue Studios; Dangerous Assignment, Stories of the Century, Thriller, Alfred Hitchcock, Checkmate, General Electric.
PICTURES: Wake of the Red Witch, Fair Wind to Java, Borderline, Jubilee Trail, Make Haste to Live, Eternal Sea, Last Command, Come Next Spring, Psycho, Judgement at Nuremberg, The Last Cowboy, That Touch of Mink, The Birds.

MIMIEUX, YVETTE: Actress. b. Los Angeles, CA, Jan. 8, 1944. e. Vine Street Sch., Le Conte Jr. H.S., Los Angeles, Los Ninos Heroes de Chapultepec, Mexico City, Hollywood H.S., CA. Appeared with a theatrical group, Theatre Events; Sympn. Concert: Persephone, Oakland Orchestra, 1965, N.Y. Philharmonic, Lincoln Center, L.A. Philharmonic, Hollywood Bowl.
PICTURES: Time Machine (debut), Where the Boys Are, The Four Horsemen of the Apocalypse, Light in the Piazza, The Wonderful World of the Brothers Grimm, Diamond Head, Toys In the Attic, Joy In The Morning, Reward, Monkeys Go Home, Dark of the Sun, Caper of the Golden Bulls, Picasso Summer, Three in the Attic, Skyjacked, The Neptune Factor, Jackson County Jail, The Black Hole, Mystique.
TELEVISION: Tyger Tyger, 1964. 1970: series, Most Deadly Game, Berrengers. Movies: Death Takes A Holiday, Black Noon, Obsessive Love.
STAGE: I Am a Camera, 1963; Owl and the Pussycat, 1966.
CONCERTS: Persephone—Houston Symphony, London Royal Philharmonic.

MINER, STEVE: Director. b. Chicago, IL, June 18, 1951. Began career as prod. asst. on Last House on the Left (1970). Launched a NY-based editorial service, and dir., Prod., edited sport, educational and indust. films.
PICTURES: Here Come the Tigers! (co-prod.), Manny's Orphans (co-prod., s.p.), Friday the 13th (assoc. prod.), Friday the 13th Part 2 (dir. debut, also prod.); Friday the 13th Part 3; Soul Man, House, Warlock (also prod.).
TELEVISION: The Wonder Years (sprv. prod., dir., DGA Award for pilot), B-Men (pilot).

MINNELLI, LIZA: Actress, Singer. b. Los Angeles, CA, Mar. 12, 1946. p. actress-singer Judy Garland & Vincente Minnelli. m. sculptor Mark Gero. e. attended sch. in CA, Switzerland, and the Sorbonne. Left to tour as lead in The Diary of Anne Frank Anne, The Fantastiks, Carnival and the Pajama Game. In concert with mother, London Palladium 1964. In concert

Carnegie Hall, 1979. Film debut as child with mother in In the Good Old Summertime (1949).

THEATER: Best Foot Forward (off-Bdwy debut, 1963), Flora, The Red Menace (Tony award), Chicago, The Act (Tony Award). Also won Special Tony Award, 1973 for Liza at the Winter Garden. The Rink (Tony nom., 1984).

PICTURES: Charlie Bubbles, The Sterile Cuckoo (Acad. award nom.), Tell Me That You Love Me, Junie Moon, Cabaret (Acad. Award, 1972), That's Entertainment!, Lucky Lady, Silent Movie, A Matter of Time, New York, New York, Arthur, Rent a Cop, Arthur On The Rocks.

TELEVISION: Liza, Liza with a Z (Emmy Award). Liza at the Winter Garden, Goldie and Liza Together, Baryshnikov on Broadway, Faerie Tale Theater. Movie: A Time to Live, Special: A Triple Play: Sam Found Out.

MINSKY, HOWARD G.: Writer, Producer, Sales and Distribution Exec. Paramount-Twentieth Century-Fox. Agency Exec. Wm. Morris Pres. Cinema Consultants. Prod.: Love Story. 1970.

MIOU MIOU: Actress r.n. Sylvette Hery. b. Paris, France, Feb. 22, 1950. Worked as child with mother unloading fruits and vegetables at Les Halles market. First job as apprentice in upholstery workshop. In 1968 helped created Montparnasse cafe-theatre, Cafe de la Gare with comedian Coluche. Returned to stage in Marguerite Duras' La Musica, 1985.

PICTURES: La cavale (debut, 1971), Themroc, Quelques messieurs trop tranquilles, elle court, la banlieue, Les granges brulees, The Adventures of Rabbi Jacob, Going Places, La grand trouille, Lily aime-moi, The Genius, No Problem!, Victory March, F comme Fairbanks, Jonah Who Will Be 25 in the Year 2000, Al piacere di rivederla, Dites-lui que je l'aime, Les routes du Sud, L'ingorgo una storia imposibile, Au revoir...a lundi, Le Derobade, La femme flic, Est-ce raisonnable?, La guerule du loup, Josepha, Guy De Maupassant, Entre Nous, Attention, une femme peut en chacher une autre!, Canicule, Flight of the Phoenix, Blanche et Marie, Menage, Les portes tournates, La lectrice, Milou in May.

MIRISCH, DAVID: Executive. b. Gettysburg, PA, July 24, 1935. e. Ripon Coll. United Artists Corp., 1960–63; former exec. with Braverman-Mirisch adv. public rel. firm.

MIRISCH, MARVIN E.: Executive. b. New York, NY, March 19, 1918. e. City Coll. of New York, B.A., 1940. Print dept., contract dept., asst. booker, N.Y. exch.; head booker, Grand National Pictures, Inc., 1936–40; officer, gen. mgr. vending concession operation 800 theatres, Midwest, Theatres Candy Co., Inc., Milwaukee, Wisc., 1941–52; exec., corporate officer in chg., indep. producer negotiations, other management functions, Allied Artists Pictures, Inc., 1953–57; Chmn. of Bd., chief exec. officer in chg. of all business affairs, admin. & financing, distr. liaison, The Mirisch Company, Inc., 1957 to present. Member of Board of Governors and former vice-president of Academy of Motion Pictures Arts & Sciences. Member Motion Pictures Pioneers. Past president of Academy of MPAS Foundation.

PICTURES: Exec. prod.: Dracula, Romantic Comedy.

MIRISCH, WALTER: Producer. b. New York, NY, Nov. 8, 1921. e. U. of Wisconsin, B.A., 1942; Harvard Grad. Sch. of Business Admin., 1943. In m.p. indust. with Skouras Theatres Corp., 1938–40; Oriental Theatre Corp., 1940–42. 1945 with Monogram, A.A.: apptd. exec. prod. Allied Artists, July, 1951; pres. and exec. head of prod. The Mirisch Corporation 1969; 1960–61 pres. Screen Prod. Guild; 1962, mem. bd. dir., MPAA; bd. Gvnrs., Academy of Motion Pictures Arts and Sciences, 1964; 1967, pres., Center Thea. Group of L.A.; bd. dir., Wisconsin Alum. Assn.; bd. of dir. Cedars-Sinai Medical Center, Bd. of Advisors, California State U.—Northridge, Board of Governors, Acad. of Motion Picture Arts & Sciences—1972. President, Permanent Charities Committee 1962–63; President, Acad. of Motion Picture Arts & Sciences—1973–77.

PICTURES: By Love Possessed, Two for the Seesaw, Toys in the Attic, Hawaii, Fitzwilly, In the Heat of the Night, They Call Me Mister Tibbs, The Organization, Mr. Majestyk, Midway, Gray Lady Down, Same Time, Next Year, Prisoner of Zenda, Dracula, Romantic Comedy.

MIRREN, HELEN: Actress. b. England, 1946. On stage in various Shakespearean roles as well as The Silver Tassle, Enemies, The Sea Gull, Faith Healer, etc.

PICTURES: Age of Consent, Savage Messiah, O! Lucky Man, Hamlet, Caligula, The Long Good Friday, The Fiendish Plot of Dr. Fu Manchu, Excalibur, Cal, 2010, White Nights, The Mosquito Coast, Pascali's Island, When the Whales Came, Bethune: The Making of a Hero, The Cook, The Thief, His Wife and Her Lover, Red King, White Knight, The Comfort of Strangers.

TELEVISION: Miss Julie, The Applecart, The Little Minister, A Midsummer Night's Dream, Cause Celebre.

MISCHER, DON: Producer, Director. b. San Antonio, TX, March 5, 1941. e. U. of Texas, B.A. 1963, M.A. 1965. Prod.-dir. of specials starring Goldie Hawn, Shirley MacLaine, Barry Manilow, Cheryl Ladd, John Denver, Mikhail Baryshnikov. Directed The Kennedy Center Honors annually, Motown 25: Yesterday, Today, Forever (DGA & Emmy Award, 1982), The Great American Dream Machine; Donahue and Kids (Emmy, 1981), Ain't Misbehavin', Making Television Dance with Twyla Tharp, Shirley MacLaine...Illusions, An Evening with Robin Williams, Marlo Thomas Special; Goldie and Liza Together, Famous Lives, Happy Birthday Bob, Motown Returns to the Apollo (prod. also), AFI Salute to Gene Kelly. Founded Don Mischer Productions, 1978.

MR. T: Actor. r.n. Lawrence Tureaud. b. Chicago, IL, May 21, 1953. Professional bodyguard when hired by Sylvester Stallone in 1980 to play prizefighter in Rocky III.

TELEVISION: The A Team (series); T & T (series), The Toughest Man in the World (movie).

PICTURES: Rocky III, D.C. Cab.

MITCHELL, ANDREW: Producer. b. Giffnock, Scotland, 1925. e. Fettes Coll., Edinburgh. Early career, banking; Associated British Picture Corporation, Elstree Studios; gen. mgr., Elstree Distributors, 1961; dir., Kenwood Films Ltd., 1963; assoc. prod., Hand in Hand, The Young Ones, Summer Holiday, French Dressing, Wonderful Life. 1965; Prod.: Up Jumped a Swagman. Asst. to mgr. dir., Assoc. British Prods., Ltd. Prod. con. Associated British Productions Ltd. 1969–70: Film Finances, Mng. dir., Leslie Grade Film Ltd, 1973. Mng. Dir. Cannon, Elstree Studios. 1977 Prod. Are You Being Served? 1988, Mng. dir., Goldcrest Elstree Studios.

MITCHELL, CAMERON: Actor. b. Dallastown, PA, Nov. 4, 1918. e. Theatre Sch., N.Y.; New York Theatre Guild, 1938–40. On stage with Lunt & Fontanne, Taming of the Shrew. Radio announcer, sportscaster before joining U.S. Army Air Forces 1942–44. Star of Tomorrow, 1954.

PICTURES: Mighty McGurk, High Barbaree, Cass Timberlane, Leather Gloves, The Sellout, Death of a Salesman, Japanese War Bride, Flight to Mars, Man in the Saddle, Outcasts of Poker Flat, Okinawa, Les Miserables, Pony Soldier, Powder River, Man on a Tightrope, How to Marry a Millionaire, Hell & High Water, Gorilla at Large, Garden of Evil, Desiree, Strange Lady in Town, Love Me Or Leave Me, House of Bamboo, Tall Men, View from Pompey's Head, Carousel, Monkey on My Back, Face of Fire, Inside The Mafia, The Unstoppable Man, The Last of the Vikings, Three Came to Kill, Blood and Black Lace, Ride in the Whirlwind, Hombre, Island of the Doomed, Nightmare in Wax, Buck and the Preacher, Slaughter, The Midnight Man, The Klansman, Viva, Knievel!, The Swarm, Night Train to Terror, Low Blow, Night Force, Deadly Prey, Trapped, Rage to Kill, Terror in Beverly Hills, Final Curtain, Space Mutiny, Code Name Vengeance, Action U.S.A., Easy Kill.

TELEVISION: Series: High Chapparal, Swiss Family Robinson. Movies: Andersonville Trial, The Bastard, Black Beauty, How the West Was Won, Partners in Crime, Wild Times.

MITCHUM, JIM: Actor. b. Los Angeles, CA, May 8, 1941. m. actress Wendy Wagner. Son of Robert Mitchum. e. Univ. H.S., L.A. Went directly from school to Hollywood Professional Sch. On-job prof. training at Barter Theatre in Virginia.

PICTURES: Thunder Road (debut), The Last Time I Saw Archie, The Victors, Ambush Bay, Tramplers, In Harm's Way, Invisible Six, Moonrunners, Beat Generation, Ride the Wild Surf, Trackdown, Mercenary Fighters.

MITCHUM, ROBERT: Actor. b. Bridgeport, CT, Aug. 6, 1917. Odd jobs; to California; joined Long Beach Players Guild; appeared in Hopalong Cassidy series with William Boyd; in Westerns 8 yrs. RKO. Biography: It Sure Beats Working (1975, by Mike Tomkies).

PICTURES: Hoppy Serves a Writ (debut, 1943), The Leather Burners, Border Patrol, Follow the Band, Colt Comrades, The Human Comedy, We've Never Been Licked, Beyond the Last Frontier, Bar 20, Doughboys in Ireland, Corvette K-225, Aerial Gunner, The Lone Star Trail, False Colors, The Dancing Masters, Riders of the Deadline, Cry Havoc, Gung Ho, Johnny Doesn't Live Here Anymore, When Strangers Marry, The Girl Rush, Thirty Seconds Over Tokyo, Nevada, West of the Pecos; *(All made 1943–44) Gained recognition*: Story of G.I. Joe, Undercurrent, Pursued Locket, Til' the End of Time, Desire Me, Crossfire, Out of the Past, Rachel and the Stranger, Blood on the Moon, Red Pony, Big Steal, His Kind of Woman, Where Danger Lives, Her Forbidden Past, Macao, Racket, One Minute to Zero, Lost Men, Angel Face, White Witch Doctor, Second Chance, She Couldn't Say No, River of No Return, Track of the Cat, Night of the Hunter, Not as a Stranger, Man with the Gun, Foreign Intrigue, Bandido, Heaven Knows Mr. Allison, Fire Down Below, Wonderful Country, Home from the Hill, Sundowners, The Last Time I Saw Archie, Cape Fear, The Longest Day, List of Adrian Messenger, Two for the Seesaw, Rampage, Mr. Moses, El Dorado, Anzio, Villa Rides, Five Card Stud, Secret Ceremony, Young Billy Young, Good Guys and the Bad Guys, Ryan's Daughter, Going Home, Wrath of God, Friends of Eddie Coyle, The Yakuza, Farewell My Lovely, Midway, The

Last Tycoon, Amsterdam Kill, The Big Sleep, Matilda, That Championship Season, Maria's Lovers, The Ambassador, Mr. North, Scrooged, The Old Dick.
TELEVISION: Mini Series: The Winds of War, North and South, War and Remembrance; Movies: A Killer in the Family, The Hearst and Davies Affair, Reunion at Fairborough, Promises to Keep, Thompson's Lost Run, Brotherhood of the Rose. Series: Family Man.

MOCIUK, YAR W.: Executive. b. Ukraine, Jan. 26, 1927. e. City Coll. of New York; World U.; Peoples U. of Americas, Puerto Rico. Expert in field of m.p. care and repair; holds U.S. patent for method and apparatus for treating m.p. film. Has also been film producer and director. Founder and pres. of CM Films Service, Inc. until 1973. Now chmn. of bd. and pres. of Filmtreat International Corp. Member: M.P. & TV Engineers; Univ. Film Assn. Pres., Ukrainian Cinema Assn. of America.

MODINE, MATTHEW: Actor. b. Loma Linda, CA, March 22, 1959. Studied with Stella Adler.
PICTURES: Baby It's You, Private School, Streamers, Hotel New Hampshire, VisionQuest, Mrs. Soffel, Birdy, Full Metal Jacket, Orphans, Married to the Mob, The Match, Gross Anatomy, Memphis Belle.
TELEVISION: Eugene O'Neill: Journey Into Greatness, Texas, Amy and the Angel.

MOFFAT, DONALD: Actor. b. Plymouth, England, Dec. 26, 1930. Studied acting Royal Academy of Dramatic Art, 1952–54. London stage debut Macbeth, 1954. On stage with Old Vic before Broadway debut in Under Milkwood, 1957. Worked with APA-Phoenix Theatre Co. and as actor and dir. of numerous regional productions.
THEATER: The Bald Soprano; Jack; Ivanov; Much Ado About Nothing; The Tumbler; Duel of Angels; A Passage to India; The Affair; The Taming of the Shrew; The Caretaker; Man and Superman; War and Peace; You Can't Take It With You; Rich You Are . . . If You Think You Are; School for Scandal; The Wild Duch; The Cherry Orchard; Cock-A-Doodle Dandy; Hamlet; Chemin de Fer; Father's Day; Painting Churches; Play Memory; Passion Play; The Iceman Cometh.
PICTURES: Pursuit of the Graf Spee (debut, 1957); Rachel, Rachel; The Trial of the Catonsville Nine; R.P.M.; Great Northfield Minnesota Raid; Showdown; Terminal Man; Earthquake; On the Nickel; Strangers; Health; Promises in the Dark; Popeye; License to Kill; The Land of No Return; The Thing; Monster in the Closet; The Right Stuff; Alamo Bay; The Best of Times; The Unbearable Lightness of Being; Far North.
TELEVISION: Guest: Camera Three (1958); You Can't Have Everything (U.S. Steel Hour); Murder, She Wrote; Dallas. Series: The New Land (1974); Logan's Run. Movies: Eleanor and Franklin; Sergeant Matlovich vs. the U.S. Air Force; Forget-Me-Not Lane; Tartuffe; Who Will Love My Children; Jacqueline Bouvier Kennedy; A Gift of Love; Necessary Parties.

MOGER, ART: Publicity executive, Author. b. Boston, MA, April 4. e. Boston U. Coll. of Journalism, B.S. Cartoonist & caricaturist, stage & screen attractions; feature writer. nat. mag.; script writer, guest appearances with Fred Allen, and many radio, TV shows (Mike Douglas Show, Merv Griffin); creator cartoon strip Seymour Shoze, dealing with m.p. and comic strip, Groucho, based on Groucho Marx: orig., About Faces, puzzle series; in 1937 syndicated cartoon series; pressbook cartoonist; handled personal appearances of celebrities. Pub. exec., Warner Bros. & other m.p. cos. Holds record for My Favorite Jokes in Parade Magazine (8 consecutive times). First honorary trustee of Nat'l. Broadcasters Hall of Fame; member Sigma Delta Chi, professional journalism society. Kentucky Colonel and Admiral. Pres., Advertising Enterprises, Boston; exec., Amuse-A-Menu Co.; dorArt Enterprises; pres. and originator Tub Thumpers of Amer. Charter member, Nat'l. Hall of Humor.
AUTHOR: You'll Dial Laughing, Pros and Cons, Some of My Best Friends Are People, The Complete Pun Book, Hello! My Real Name Is. . . , The Best Book of Puns.

MOGER, STANLEY H.: Executive. Pres., SFM Entertainment, Exec. Vice Pres., SFM Media Corp. b. Boston, MA, Nov. 13, 1936. e. Colby Coll., Waterville, ME, B.A., 1958. Announcer/TV personality/WVDA and WORL (Boston) 1953–54; WGHM (Skowhegan) 1955–56; WTWO-TV (Bangor) 1955; WMHB (Waterville) 1956–57; WTVL (Waterville) 1957–58; unit pub. dir., Jaguar Prods., 1958–59; US Army reserve, 1958–64, with calls to active duty in 1958–59 and 1961–62; account exec., NBC Films/California National Productions, Chicago; 1959–60, asst. sales mgr., Midwest, RCA/NBC Medical Radio System; acct. exec. Hollingbery Co., Chicago, 1960–63; and NY 1963–66; acct. exec., Storer TV Sales, 1966–69; co-founded SFM, Sept. 29, 1969. In 1978, named pres., SFM Entertainment which was responsible for the revival of Walt Disney's Mickey Mouse Club, The Adventures of Rin-Tin-Tin; Mobil Showcase Network; SFM Holiday Network. Exec. prod.: Television-Annual 1978–79: Your New Day with Vidal Sassoon, The Origins Game; Believe You Can and You Can (from Disneyland), Walt Disney Presents Sport Goofy (series); The World of Tomorrow. March of Time . . . on the March (England), Sports Pros and Cons, Unclaimed Fortunes.
PROPERTIES: SFM Holiday Network, SFM Documentary Network, Car Care Central, Your New Day with Vidal Sassoon, March of Time series, Co-Packager Superstars; Adventures of the Wilderness Family; Across the Great Divide; Mysteries from Beyond Earth; To the Ends of the Earth; Challenge To Be Free; Wonder of It All; Great American Cowboy; Deal; Dayan; Sports Illustrated; General Foods Golden Showcase Network–Shock Trauma; 1983 official film of the America's Cup Challenge: Countdown to the Cup; Pinocchio in Outer Space; Rudyard Kipling's Jungle Book; The Heisman Trophy Annual Award Specials; Walt Disney World's Very Merry Xmas Parade; The Indomitable Teddy Roosevelt; Crusade in the Pacific; Rosepetal Place; Hugga-Bunch; Jayce and the Wheeled Warriors; Time Travel: Fact, Fiction and Fantasy; Zoobilee Zoo; Photon; Just the Facts (Dragnet special); Willie Nelson's Summer Picnic; Crusade in Europe; King Kong: The Living Legend; SFM Children's Theatre; Ghost Dance; Sea World's All-Star, Lonestar Celebration; George Stevens: A Filmmaker's Journey; Gorillas in the Mist Special; Tappin'; Care Bears (series); Crystal Light National Aerobics Championships (1986 & 87); U.S. Man of the Year Pageant; The Digital Discovery (series); The Infinite Voyage, Sea World's Miracle Babies & Friends; Think Fast (racing series), So Power Passes; Pillar of Fire; The Centennial of the Eiffel Tower; Biography of Cary Grant; In Our Image; Command Performance at Ford's Theatre.

MOLINA, ALFRED: Actor. b. London, Eng. e. Guildhall Sch. of Music and Drama. Stand-up comic for street theatre group. Joined Royal Shakespeare Co., 1977 (Frozen Assets, The Steve Biko Inquest, Dingo, Bandits, Taming of the Shrew, Happy End), Also in Serious Money, Speed-the Plow. Plays and Players' Most Promising New Actor Award for Accidental Death of an Anarchist.
PICTURES: Raiders of the Lost Ark, Meantime, Ladyhawke, Letter to Brezhnev, Prick up Your Ears, Manifesto, Twice Upon a Time.
TELEVISION: The Losers, Anyone for Dennis, Joni Jones, Number One, City Hospital, Russian Roulette, Cats' Eyes, Blat, Casualty, Virtuoso, Apocolyptic Butterflies.

MOLINARO, EDOUARD: Director. b. Bordeaux, France, May 13, 1928. Made amateur films at university and launched professional career via award-winning technical shorts. First feature film, Le Dos au Mur, 1957.
PICTURES: Girls for the Summer, A Ravishing Idiot, Gentle Art of Seduction, La Cage aux Folles (also Part II), Sunday Lovers, Just the Way You Are, The Door on the Left as You Leave the Elevator.

MONASH, PAUL: Producer, Writer. b. New York, NY, June 14, 1917. e. U. of Wisconsin, Columbia U. Was in U.S. Army Signal Corps and Merchant Marine; newspaper reporter; high school teacher; and civilian employee of U.S. gov't. in Europe. Wrote two novels: How Brave We Live, The Ambassadors. Entered industry writing TV scripts for Playhouse 90, Studio One, Theatre Guild of the Air, Climax, etc. Authored two-part teleplay which launched The Untouchables. In 1958 won Emmy award for The Lonely Wizard, dramatization of life of German-born electrical inventor Charles Steinmetz. Made m.p. debut as exec. prod. of Butch Cassidy and the Sundance Kid, 1969.
PICTURES: Slaughterhouse-Five (prod.), The Friends of Eddie Coyle (prod., s.p.), The Front Page (prod.), Carrie (prod.), Big Trouble in Little China (prod.).
TELEVISION: Child Bride of Short Creek, The Day the Loving Stopped; Trial of Chaplain Jensen.

MONICELLI, MARIO: Director. b. Rome, Italy, May 15, 1915. Ent. m.p. industry in production; later co-authored, collab., comedies. Dir.: Big Deal on Madonna Street, The Great War, Tears of Joy, Boccaccio '70, The Organizer, Casanova, Girl With a Pistol, Amici Mie, Viva Italia!, Travels With Anita, Lovers and Liars (also, s.p.), Il Marchese de Grillo (also s.p.), Amici, Miei, Atto (All My Friends 2, also s.p.), Bertoldo, Bertoldino, E Cacasenna (also, s.p.), The Two Lives of Mattia Pascal, I Picari (dir., co-s.p.).

MONKHOUSE, BOB: TV-radio-cabaret Comedian, Comedy writer. b. Beckenham, Kent, June 1, 1928. e. Dulwich Coll. Debut 1948 while serving in RAF, own radio comedy series 1949–83 (winters), own TV series, BBC 1952–56, ITV 1956–83; BBC (ongoing). Several West End revues, Boys from Syracuse; Come Blow Your Horn; The Gulls; others. Films include: Carry On, Sergeant; Weekend with Lulu; Dentist in the Chair; She'll Have to Go; Bliss of Mrs. Blossom; others. Major cabaret attraction U.K., Australia, Hong Kong. British star of numerous TV series including: What's My Line?; Who Do You Trust?; Mad Movies; Quick on the Draw; Bob Monkhouse Comedy Hour; The Golden Shot (8 years); Celebrity Squares (4 yrs); I'm Bob, He's Dickie! (1978–81); Family Fortunes (1979–83); Bob Monkhouse Tonight (1983–ongoing). Regular dramatic guest spots ITV & BBC-TV, was under exclusive contract to BBC till 1986 for Tonight Show and new game shows.

MONKS, JOHN, JR.: Writer, Actor, Producer, Director. b. Brooklyn, NY. e. Virginia Military Inst., A.B. Actor, stock, B'way, radio, m.p. U.S. Marines, 1942; commissioned Major, 1945. Playwright Co-author Brother Rat.
PICTURES: Brother Rat, Co-author, Brother Rat and a Baby, Strike Up the Band, The House on 92nd Street, 13 Rue Madeleine, Wild Harvest, Dial 1119., The West Point Story, People Against O'Hara. Where's Charley. So This Is Love, Knock on Any Door, No Man Is an Island.
TELEVISION: Climax: The Gioconda Smile, A Box of Chocolates; 20th Century-Fox Hour: Miracle on 34th St.; Gen. Electric Theatre: Emily; CBS Special: High Tor; SWAT; Creator serial: Paradise Bay.

MONROE, CHAUNCEY: Actor, Writer, Prod., Dir., Stuntman, Singer. b. Gatlinburg, TN, July 7, 1950. e. Sonia Moore Studio of the Theater, NY; Amer. Stanislavski Inst., 1969–70; De Mille On Camera Workshop, CA 1983–85. At age 10, professional portrait painter. Film debut A Walk in the Spring Rain. At 17 worked for Roy Acuff and formed own country five-piece group, The Highlanders. Worked off-Bdwy., in film (as actor, singer, stuntman) and TV as well as MTV rock videos with Weird Al Yankovitch, Kim Carnes, etc. Formed Chauncey Monroe Productions, Extraordinaire, Ltd.
PICTURES: Batteries Not Included, Ten to Midnight, The Exterminator, Girls Just Wanna Have Fun, The Naked Cage, Smorgasbord, Star 80, Throwback.
TELEVISION: The Equalizer, Saturday Night Live, Search for Tomorrow, As the World Turns, Another World, Romance Theater, Divorce Court, General Hospital, Cagney and Lacey. Movies: The Day After, Copacabana.

MONTAGNE, EDWARD J.: Producer, Director. b. Brooklyn, NY. e. Loyola U., of Notre Dame. RKO Pathe, 1942; U.S. Army, 1942–46; prod. many cos. after army.
PICTURES: Tattooed Stranger, The Man with My Face, McHale's Navy, McHale's Navy Joins the Air Force, P.J., The Reluctant Astronaut.
TELEVISION: Man Against Crime, Cavalier Theatre, The Vaughn Monroe Show, The Hunter, I Spy, McHale's Navy; exec. prod. of film-CBS-N.Y., Phil Silvers Show. Prod. & head of programming, Wm. Esty Adv. Co., 1950; Program consultant, William Esty Co.; v.p. Universal TV prod. & dir.: 5 Don Knotts features; prod.: Andy Griffith, Angel in My Pocket, Ellery Queen, A Very Missing Person, Short Walk to Daylight, Hurricane, Terror on the 40th Floor, Francis Gary Powers, Million Dollar Ripoff, Crash of Flight 401, High Noon—Part 2, Harper Valley PTA.

MONTALBAN, RICARDO: Actor. b. Mexico City, Mex., Nov. 25, 1920. Appeared in Mexican pictures 1941–45; to U.S. On Bdwy in Her Cardboard Lover with Tallulah Bankhead. Later in Jamaica, The King and I, Don Juan in Hell. Autobiography: Reflections: A Life in Two Worlds (1980).
PICTURES: Fiesta, On an Island With You, Kissing Bandit, Neptune's Daughter, Battleground, Mystery Street, Right Cross, Two Weeks with Love, Across the Wide Missouri, Mark of Renegade, My Man and I, Sombrero, Border Incident, Latin Lovers, Saracen Blade, Life in The Balance, Sayonara, Hemingway's Adventures of a Young Man, The Reluctant Saint, Love Is a Ball, Sol Madrid, Blue, Sweet Charity, Conquest of the Planet of the Apes, The Train Robbers, Joe Panther, Won, Ton, Ton, the Dog Who Saved Hollywood, Star Trek II: The Wrath of Khan, Cannonball Run II, The Naked Gun.
TELEVISION: Series: Fantasy Island, The Colbys. Movies: How the West Was Won, Part II (emmy Award), The Pigeon, The Aquarian, Fireball Foreward, The Mark of Zorro, McNaughton's Daughter, Return to Fantasy Island.

MONTAND, YVES: Actor, Singer. r.n. Yvo Livi. b. Monsumano, Italy, Oct. 13, 1921. m. the late actress Simone Signoret. Worked as a truck loader, waiter in dockside bar, and barber. Performed in Marseilles as singer in clubs and music halls.
PICTURES: Etoile Sans Lumiere, Les Portes de La Nuit, L'Idole, Souvenir Perdus, Wages of Fear, Nostri Tempi, Mar, Napoleon, Les Heros Sont Fatigues, Marguerite de la Nuit, Uomini e Lupi, The Crucible, La Lunga Strada, Un Denomme Squarcio, Le Pere et L'enfant, Where the Hot Wind Blows, Let's Make Love, Sanctuary, My Geisha, Goodbye Again, The Sleeping Car Murders, La Guerre est Finie, Is Paris Burning?, Grand Prix, Live for Life, One Night. . . A Train, The Devil By the Tail, Mr. Freedom, Le Cercle rouge, Z, On a Clear Day You Can See Forever, The Confession, La Folie des grandeurs, Cesar and Rosalie, Tout va bien, State of Siege, Python. 357, The Savage Vincent, Francois, Paul and the Others, Womanlight, The Case Against Ferro, Choice of Arms, Jean de Florette, Manon of the Springs, Three Seats for the 26th.

MONTGOMERY, ELIZABETH: Actress. b. Los Angeles, CA, April 15, 1933. e. Amer. Acad. of Dramatic Arts. Daughter of the late actor Robert Montgomery. Bdwy debut: Late Love.
PICTURES: The Court Martial of Billy Mitchell, Johnny Cool, Who's Been Sleeping in My Bed?
TELEVISION: Series: Bewitched. Movies: The Victim, Mrs. Sundance, A Case of Rape, The Legend of Lizzie Borden, Dark Victory, A Killing Affair, The Awakening Land, Jennifer: A Woman's Story, Missing Pieces, Second Sight: A Love Story, Amos, Between Darkness and Dawn, Face to Face.

MONTGOMERY, GEORGE: Actor. r.n. George Montgomery Letz; b. Brady, MT, Aug. 29, 1916. e. U. of Montana. Armed Services, W.W.II.
PICTURES: Cisco Kid and the Lady (1939), Star Dust, Young People, Charter Pilot, Jennie, Cowboy and the Blonde, Accent on Love, Riders of the Purple Sage, Last of the Duanes, Cadet Girl, Roxie Hart, Ten Gentlemen from West Point, Orchestra Wives, China Girl, Brasher Doubloon, Three Little Girls in Blue, Lulu Belle, Belle Starr's Daughter, Girl From Manhattan, Sword of Monte Cristo, Texas Rangers, Indian Uprising, Cripple Creek, Pathfinder, Jack McCall Desperado, Fort Ti, Gun Belt, Battle of Rogue River, Lone Gun, Masterson of Kansas, Seminole Uprising, Robbers' Roost, Too Many Crooks, Stallion Trail, The Steel Claw, Watusi, Samar, Hallucination Generation, Hostile Guns, Ransom in Blood.

MONTY PYTHON: Group of six British comedians who performed on Monty Python's Flying Circus for BBC-TV during the '60s and '70s. They include Graham Chapman, John Cleese, Terry Gilliam, Eric Idle, Terry Jones, and Michael Palin. (See individual biographies.)
PICTURES: And Now for Something Completely Different, Monty Python and the Holy Grail, The Life of Brian, Monty Python at the Hollywood Bowl, Monty Python's The Meaning of Life.

MOONJEAN, HANK: Producer, Director. Began as asst. dir. at MGM. Later turned to producing.
PICTURES: *Assoc. Prod.:* The Great Gatsby, WUSA, The Secret Life of An American Wife, Child's Play, Welcome to Hard Times, The Singing Nun. *Exec. Prod.:* The Fortune, The End. *Producer:* Hooper, Smokey and the Bandit II, The Incredible Shrinking Woman, Paternity, Sharky's Machine, Stroker Ace, Dangerous Liaisons, Beauty and the Beast, Stealing Home.

MOORE, CONSTANCE: Actress. b. Sioux City, IA, Jan. 18, 1922. Sang on radio; Lockheed prog., 2 yrs; Jurgen's Show, 2 yrs. Screen debut 1938. TV shows, nightclubs. N.Y. Stage: The Boys from Syracuse, By Jupiter.
PICTURES: Prison Break, A Letter of Introduction, I Wanted Wings, Take A Letter Darling, Show Business, Delightfully Dangerous, Earl Carroll Sketchbook, In Old Sacramento, Hit Parade of 1947, Spree.

MOORE, DEMI: Actress. b. Roswell, NM, Nov. 11, 1962. r.n. Demi Guynes. m. actor Bruce Willis. Since age 16 worked as model. Appeared on TV series Kaz, Vegas. Off B'way debut: The Early Girl, 1987.
PICTURES: Choices (debut, 1981), Parasite, Young Doctors in Love, Blame It on Rio, No Small Affair, St. Elmo's Fire, One Crazy Summer, Wisdom, About Last Night, Wisdom, The Seventh Sign, Rapid Fire, We're No Angels, Ghost.
TELEVISION: General Hospital, Bedrooms.

MOORE, DICKIE: Actor. b. Los Angeles, CA, Sept. 12, 1925. m. actress Jane Powell. Began picture career when only 11 months old, appearing with John Barrymore in The Beloved Rogue. Appeared in numerous radio, television and stage prods. in NY and L.A. and over 100 films. Co-author and star, RKO short subject, The Boy and the Eagle (nom. Acad. Award). Author: Opportunities in Acting, Twinkle Twinkle Little Star (But Don't Have Sex or Take the Car), 1984. Now public relations executive.
PICTURES: Oliver Twist, Peter Ibbetson, Sergeant York, Heaven Can Wait, Dangerous Years, Out of the Past, Eight Iron Men, Member of the Wedding.

MOORE, DUDLEY: Actor, Writer, Musician. b. England, April 19, 1935. e. Oxford, graduating in 1958. Toured British Isles with jazz group before joining Peter Cook, Jonathan Miller and Alan Bennett to put on revue, Beyond the Fringe, which was a hit in U.K. and N.Y. Appeared later with Peter Cook on Bdwy. in Good Evening. Composed film scores: 30 is a Dangerous Age, Cynthia; Inadmissible Evidence, The Staircase, Six Weeks.
PICTURES: Monte Carlo or Bust, The Wrong Box, 30 is a Dangerous Age, Cynthia; Alice in Wonderland, Those Daring Young Men in Their Jaunty Jalopies, The Bed Sitting Room, Bedazzled, The Hound of the Baskervilles, Foul Play, "10", Wholly Moses, Arthur, Six Weeks, Lovesick, Romantic Comedy, Unfaithfully Yours, Best Defense, Micki and Maude, Santa Claus—The Movie; Like Father, Like Son; Arthur 2 On the Rocks (actor, exec. prod.), Crazy People, The Adventures of Milo and Otis (narrator).

MOORE, ELLIS: Consultant. b. New York, NY, May 12, 1924. e. Washington and Lee U., 1941–43. Newspaperman in AK, TN, 1946–52. Joined NBC 1952; mgr. of bus. pub., 1953; dir., press dept., 1954; dir., press & publicity, Dec. 22, 1959; vice-pres., 1961; pub. rel. dept., Standard Oil Co. (N.J.), 1963–66; v.p. press relations, ABC-TV Network, 1966–68; v.p. public relations ABC-TV Network, 1968–70; v.p. public relations, ABC, 1970, v.p. public relations, ABC, Inc., 1972; v.p. corporate relations, ABC, Inc., 1979; v.p., public affairs, ABC, Inc., 1982–85. P.R. consultant, 1985.

MOORE, GARRY: Performer. r.n. Thomas Garrison Morfit; b. Baltimore, MD, Jan. 31, 1915. Continuity writer, WBAL; announcer, sports commentator, KWK, St. Louis; comedian, writer, Club Matinee show, Chicago; Everything Goes, N.Y.; teamed with Jimmy Durante on radio to 1947; m.c., Take It or Leave It, Breakfast in Hollywood. Elected to TV Academy Hall of Fame.

TELEVISION: Star of Garry Moore Show, I've Got A Secret. Best TV daytime show: Fame Poll, 1958; To Tell The Truth (Best Primetime Variety Show, Emmy Award, 1963; Peabody Award, 1970.)

MOORE, KIERON: Actor. b. Skibereen, Co. Cork, Eire, 1925. e. St. Mary's Coll., Dublin. Stage debut, 1945 in Desert Rats; appeared in Red Roses For Me. Film debut 1947 in A Man About the House.

PICTURES: Anna Karenina, Mine Own Executioner, Ten Tall Men, David and Bathsheba, Saints and Sinners, Naked Heart, Honeymoon Deferred, Man Trap (Man in Hiding), Conflict of Wings (Fuss Over Feathers), Green Scarf, Blue Peter, Satellite in the Sky, Three Sundays to Live, The Key, The Angry Hills, The Day They Robbed the Bank of England, League of Gentlemen, The Siege of Sidney Street, Faces of Evil, Lion of Sparta, Steel Bayonet, I Thank a Fool, Double Twist, The Day of the Triffids, The Thin Red Line, The Main Attraction, Crack in the World, Son of a Gunfighter, Never Love a Savage, Run Like a Thief, Custer of the West, Ryan International, The Dolmetch Story, Zoo Gang, The Progress of Peoples, The Parched Land.

MOORE, MARY TYLER: Actress. b. Brooklyn. NY, Dec. 29, 1936. Began as professional dancer and got first break as teenager in commercials (notably the elf in Hotpoint appliance ads); then small roles in series Bachelor Father, Steve Canyon (1958) and finally as the switchboard oper. in Richard Diamond (though only her legs were seen). Broadway debut: Breakfast at Tiffany's, also Whose Life Is It, Anyway? (special Tony, 1980), Sweet Sue. Chairman of Bd., MTM Enterprises, Inc, which founded with then husband Grant Tinker.

TELEVISION: Bachelor Father, Steve Canyon, 77 Sunset Strip, Hawaiian Eye, Bachelor Father; Series: Richard Diamond, Private Eye (1959), The Dick Van Dyke Show (1961–66, 2 Emmy awards); The Mary Tyler Moore Show (1970–77, 3 Emmys), The Mary Tyler Moore Hour (1979), Mary (1985–86), Annie McGuire. Movies: Love American Style, Run a Crooked Mile, First You Cry, Heartsounds, Finnegan Begin Again; Gore Vidal's Lincoln. Special: How to Survive the 70s, How to Raise a Drugfree Child.

PICTURES: X-15, Thoroughly Modern Millie, Don't Just Stand There, What's So Bad About Feeling Good, Change of Habit, Ordinary People, Six Weeks, Just Between Friends.

MOORE, ROGER: Actor, Director. b. London, England, Oct. 14, 1927. e. art school, London; Royal Acad. of Dramatic Art.

PLAYS: Mr. Roberts, I Capture the Castle, Little Hut, others.

BROADWAY: A Pin to See the Peepshow.

TELEVISION: Maverick, The Alaskans, Ivanhoe, The Saint, The Persuaders, Sherlock Holmes in New York.

PICTURES: Last Time I Saw Paris, Interrupted Melody, King's Thief, Diane, The Miracle, Gold of the Seven Saints, Rachel Cade, Rape of the Sabines, No Mans Land, Crossplot, The Man Who Haunted Himself, Live and Let Die, Gold, The Man with the Golden Gun, That Lucky Touch, Street People, Shout at the Devil, The Spy Who Loved Me, The Wild Geese, Escape To Athena, Moonraker, ffolkes, The Sea Wolves, Sunday Lovers, For Your Eyes Only, The Cannonball Run, Octopussy, The Curse of the Pink Panther, The Naked Face, A View to a Kill, The Magic Snowman (voice), Bullseye!, Bed and Breakfast.

MOORE, TERRY: Actress. r.n. Helen Koford; b. Los Angeles, CA, Jan. 1, 1932. mother Luella Bickmore, actress. Photographer's model as a child; on radio; with Pasadena Playhouse 1940; in m.p. 1933. Star of Tomorrow: 1958. Formed Moore/Rivers Productions, 1988 with partner-manager Jerry Rivers.

PICTURES: Gaslight, Son of Lassie, Sweet and Low Down, Shadowed, Devil on Wheels, Return of October, Mighty Joe Young, He's a Cockeyed Wonder, Gambling House, Two of a Kind, Sunny Side of the Street, Man on a Tightrope, Beneath the 12-mile Reef, King of the Khyber Rifles, Daddy Long Legs, Shack Out on 101, Postmark for Danger, Come Back Little Sheba, Bernardine, Why Must I Die?, Platinum High School, A Private's Affair, Cast a Long Shadow, City of Fear, Black Spurs, Town Tamer, Waco, A Man Called Dagger, Death Dimension, Hellhole, Beverly Hills Brats.

MOORE, THOMAS W.: Executive. e. U. of Missouri. Naval aviator, USNR, 1940–45. Adv. dept., Star, Meridian, MS; v.p., adv. mgr., Forest Lawn Memorial Park; account exec., CBS-TV Film Sales, Los Angeles; gen. sales mgr., CBS-TV Film Sales, 1956; v.p. in chg. programming & talent, 1958; pres., ABC-TV Network, 1962; chmn. bd., Ticketron, 1968; pres., Tomorrow Entertainment, Inc. 1971; chmn., 1981.

MORANIS, RICK: Actor, Writer. b. Toronto, Canada. Began career as part-time radio engineer while still in high school. Hosted own comedy show on radio then performed in Toronto cabarets and nightclubs and on TV. Joined satarical TV series SCTV during its 3rd season on CBC, for which he won Emmy for writing when broadcast in U.S. Created characters of the McKenzie Brothers with Dave Thomas and won Grammy nom. for McKenzie Brothers album. With Thomas co-wrote, co-directed and starred in film debut Strange Brew, 1983.

PICTURES: Strange Brew, Streets of Fire, Club Paradise, Head Office, Brewster's Millions, The Wild Life, Ghostbusters, Spaceballs, Little Shop of Horrors, Ghostbusters II, Honey, I Shrunk the Kids, Parenthood.

MOREAU, JEANNE: Actress. b. Paris, France, Jan. 23, 1928. e. Nat'l Conservatory of Dramatic Art. Stage debut with Comedie Française, acting there until 1952 when she joined the Theatre Nationale Populaire. Directorial debut: La Lumière (film), 1976.

PLAYS: A Month in the Country, La Machine Infernale, Pygmalion, Cat on a Hot Tin Roof.

PICTURES: The She-wolves, Elevator to the Scaffold, The Lovers, Le Dialogue Des Carmelites, Les Liaisons Dangereuses, Moderato Cantabile, La Notte, Jules and Jim, A Woman Is a Woman, Eva, The Trial, Bay of Angels, The Victors, Le Feu Follet, Diary of a Chambermaid, The Yellow Rolls-Royce, The Train, Mata Hari, Viva Maria, Mademoiselle, Chimes at Midnight, Sailor From Gibraltar, The Bride Wore Black, The Immortal Story, Great Catherine, Monte Walsh, Alex in Wonderland, The Little Theatre of Jean Renoir, The Last Tycoon, French Provincial, La Lumière (actress, dir., s.p.), Mr. Klein, The Adolescent (dir., s.p. only), Plein Sud, Querelle, The Trout, Nikita.

MORENO, FRANK: Executive. Distribution executive for First Artists and v.p. of dist. & world-wide mktg. for New World Pictures, before setting up own company, The Frank Moreno Co. In January, 1984, joined Almi Pictures as pres. & CEO. 1987, formed own dist. co., MC Releasing.

MORENO, RITA: Actress. r.n. Rosa Dolores Alvario. b. Humacao, Puerto Rico, Dec. 11, 1931. Spanish dancer since childhood; night club entertainer; m.p. debut in So Young, So Bad (1950). Has won Oscar, Tony and Grammy Awards.

THEATER: debut Skydrift (1945), Sign in Sidney Brustein's Window, Gantry, Last of the Red Hot Lovers, The National Health (Long Wharf, CT), The Ritz (Tony Award, supp., 1975), Wally's Cafe.

PICTURES: Pagan Love Song, Toast of New Orleans, Singin' in the Rain, The Ring, Cattle Town, Latin Lovers, Jivaro, Yellow Tomahawk, Garden of Evil, Untamed, Seven Cities of Gold, Lieutenant Wore Skirts, King and I, This Rebel Breed, Summer and Smoke, The Little Sister, Cry of Battle, West Side Story (Acad. Award, supporting actress, 1961), The Night of the Following Day, Marlowe, Popi, Carnal Knowledge, The Ritz, Happy Birthday, Gemini, The Four Seasons.

TELEVISION: Nine to Five, Eva Peron, Anatomy of a Seduction, The Electric Company (series), The Muppet Show (Emmy, 1977), The Rockford Files (Emmy, 1978), Picture of a Showgirl, Tales From the Hollywood Hills: The Golden Land. Series: B.L. Stryker.

MORGAN, ANDRE: Producer. b. Morocco, 1952. e. U. of Kansas. Golden Harvest Films 1972–84, Producer. Exec. v.p., Golden Communications 1976–84. Formed Ruddy-Morgan Productions with Albert S. Ruddy, 1984.

PICTURES: Enter the Dragon, The Amsterdam Kill, The Boys in Company C, Cannonball Run II, High Road to China, Lassiter, Farewell to the King, Speed Zone, Impulse.

MORGAN, DENNIS: Actor. r.n. Stanley Morner; b. Prentice, WI, Dec. 10, 1910. e. Carroll Coll. Started with State Lake Theat., Chicago. Toured midwest in Faust, sang in Empire Room of Palmer House, Chicago, appeared on NBC programs and sang lead in Xerxes. Screen debut, 1936. Star of Tomorrow (1941).

PICTURES: Susy, The Fighting 69th, Three Cheers for the Irish, My Wild Irish Rose, Two Guys from Milwaukee, Two Guys from Texas, Cheyenne, Perfect Strangers, To the Victor, One Sunday Afternoon, Raton Pass, Pretty Baby, Painting the Clouds with Sunshine, This Woman Is Dangerous, Cattle Town, Gun That Won the West, Pearl of the South Pacific, Uranium Boom, Won Ton Ton, The Dog Who Saved Hollywood.

TELEVISION: Beacon Street (series).

MORGAN, HARRY: Actor. r.n. Harry Bratsburg; b. Detroit, MI, Apr. 10, 1915. e. U. of Chicago. Screen debut 1942.
TELEVISION: Series: December Bride, Pete and Gladys, M*A*S*H, Dragnet, After M*A*S*H, You Can't Take It With You, 14 Going on 30 (movie).
PLAYS: Gentle People, My Heart's in the Highlands, Thunder Rock, Night Music, Night Before Christmas.
PICTURES: To the Shores of Tripoli, Loves of Edgar Allen Poe, Orchestra Wives, Dragonwyck, Appointment with Danger, The Highwayman, When I Grow Up, The Well, Blue Veil, Bend of the River, Scandal Sheet, My Six Convicts, Boots Malone, High Noon, What Price Glory, Stop You're Killing Me, Arena, Torch Song, Glenn Miller Story, About Mrs. Leslie, Forty-Niners, Far Country, Not As a Stranger, Backlash, Strategic Air Command, Support Your Local Sheriff, Charlie and the Angels, Snowball Express, The Apple Dumpling Gang, The Greatest, The Shootist, Cat from Outer Space, The Apple Dumpling Gang Rides Again, Dragnet.

MORGAN, MICHELE: Actress. r.n. Simone Roussel; b. Paris, France, Feb. 29, 1920. e. Dieppe, dramatic school, Paris. Decided on acting career at 15 yrs., won role at 17 opposite Charles Boyer in Gribouille (later filmed as The Lady in Question, Hollywood). Made several pictures abroad; to U.S. 1940. First Amer. film Joan of Paris, 1942.
PICTURES: Higher and Higher, Passage to Marseilles, The Chase, Symphonie Pastorale, Fallen Idol, Fabiola, 7 Deadly Sins, Moment of Truth, Daughters of Destiny, Naked Heart, Proud and the Beautiful, Grand Maneuver, Marguerite de la Nuit, The Mirror Has Two Faces, Landru, Oasis, Lost Command, Benjamin, Cat and Mouse, Seven Steps to Murder, Robert et Robert.

MORGAN, TERENCE: Actor. b. London, Eng., Dec. 8, 1921. e. Ewell Castle, Surrey, Royal Acad. of Dramatic Art. Stage debut: There Shall Be No Night, London 1943; m.p. debut: Hamlet, 1948.
PICTURES: Capt. Horatio Hornblower, Encore, Mandy, It Started in Paradise, Steel Key, Street Corner, Turn the Key Softly, Always a Bride, Forbidden Cargo, Dance Little Lady, Femina, Svengali, They Can't Hang Me, March Hare, It's a Wonderful World, The Scamp, Tread Softly Stranger, The Shakedown, Picadilly Third Stop, The Curse of the Mummy's Tomb, The Penthouse, Hide and Seek, The Lifetaker.
TELEVISION: Crime Passionnel, Twelfth Night, The Bridesman's Danger, In Writing, Nothing to Declare, Perchance to Dream, More Than Robbery (serial), Now Barabbas, Women in Love, Sir Francis Drake (series of 26), Memoirs of a Chaise Lounge, No Place Like Earth, The Persuaders, King and Castle.

MORIARTY, MICHAEL: Actor. b. Detroit, MI, April 5, 1941. e. Dartmouth. Studied at London Acad. of Music and Dramatic Arts. Appeared with New York Shakespeare Festival, Charles Street Playhouse (Boston), Alley Theatre (Houston) and Tyrone Guthrie Theatre (Minneapolis). Broadway debut in The Trial of the Catonsville Nine.
THEATER: Find Your Way Home (Tony Award, 1974), Richard III, Long Day's Journey Into Night, Henry V, GR Point, Whose Life Is It Anyway (Kennedy Center), The Ballad of Dexter Creed, Uncle Vanya, Caine Mutiny Court Martial.
PICTURES: Glory Boy (debut), Hickey and Boggs, Shoot It, Bang the Drum Slowly, The Last Detail, Report to the Commissioner, Who'll Stop the Rain, Shoot It Black, Shoot It Blue, Too Far To Go, The Winged Serpent, Pale Rider, The Stuff, Troll, The Hanoi Hilton, It's Alive III., Dark Tower, The Secret of the Ice Cave.
TELEVISION: The Glass Menagerie (Emmy Award), Girls of Summer, The Deadliest Season, Holocaust, Windmills of the Gods, Frank Nitti: The Enforcer, Tailspin:Behind the Korean Airline Tragedy.

MORIN, ROBERT B.: Executive. b. New York, NY, Nov. 24. e. Harvard Coll. Merch, Mgr., ad agency. AAP sls., 1955; AAP mgr. program sls., 1956; eastern sls. mgr., MGM-TV, 1957; sls. mgr., Lopert-UA, 1959; v.p., Allied Artists TV; formed Scandia Films, pres., 1965; joined RKO, 1966, in chg. foreign operations; 1968, pres. Lin Medallion Pict. Corp.; 1970–73, Talent Associates; 1973–76, exec. v.p., Heritage Eng.; 1976–78, v.p., MGM TV; 1978–80, pres. Lorimar Syndication; 1980, exec. v.p., 20th Century Fox; 1985, pres., New Century Telecommunications; Dec., 1988, named chmn. & CEO of CST Entertainment.

MORITA, NORIYUKI "PAT": Entertainer, Actor. b. CA, 1930. Began show business career as opening act in nightclubs for such stars as Ella Fitzgerald, Johnny Mathis, Diana Ross and the Supremes, Glen Campbell, etc. Worked in saloons, coffee houses, and dinner theatres before becoming headliner in Las Vegas showrooms, Playboy Clubs, Carnegie Hall, etc. Guest on most TV talk and variety shows and regular on many series: M*A*S*H, Love Boat, Magnum, P.I.
PICTURES: Thoroughly Modern Millie, Midway, Savannah Smiles, Jimmy the Kid, The Karate Kid, The Karate Kid: Part II, Captive Hearts, Collision Course, The Karate Kid, Part III.
TELEVISION: Series: Happy Days, O'Hara, The Karate Kid (voice for animated series). Movies: The Vegas Strip War, Farewell to Manzanar, Amos.

MORITZ, MILTON I: Executive. b. Pittsburgh, PA, Apr. 27, 1933. e. Woodbury Coll., grad. 1955. Owned, operated theatres in L.A., 1953–55; U.S. Navy 1955–57; American International Pictures asst. gen. sls. mgr., 1957; nat'l. dir. of adv. and publ. 1958; v.p. and bd. mem. of American International Pictures, 1967; 1975, named sr. v.p.; in 1980 formed own co., The Milton I. Moritz Co., Inc., Inc., mktg. & dist. consultant. 1987, joined Pacific Theatres as v.p. in chg. of adv., p.r. & promotions. Pres. of Variety Club of Southern California Tent 25, 1975–76.

MORLEY, ROBERT: Actor, writer. b. Wiltshire, England, May 26, 1908. e. Royal Acad. of Dramatic Art, London. U.S. Air Force, 1943; prod., assoc. prod., Captain Gallant, Arsen, Chicot, Forbidden Cargo; TV Series: Captain Gallant; Scene of the Crime; TV Advisor, Telepictures of Morroco, Telerama, Ltd., Eng., 1954–59; helped org., Alliance of TV Film Producers; prod., Telerama, Inc., Georgetown Films, Inc., 1960; prod., dir., TV film series closeup, Telefilm, Inc. Presently president, Creative Assoc., Inc. and co-prod. with Helen Ainsworth; exec. prod. with Leon Fromkess, The Long Corridor.
PLAYS: Brit. stage debut London 1929 in Treasure Island, also tour and repertory; N.Y. debut 1938 in Oscar Wilde; other appearances include Great Romancer, Pygmalion; 1948, Edward My Son, co-author, lead London and B'way stage; author several plays (Short Story, Goodness, How Sad, Staff Dance).
PICTURES: Marie Antoinette, You Will Remember, Major Barbara, Big Blockade, This Was Paris, Foreman Went to France, Young Mr. Pitt, I Live in Grosvenor Square, Outcast of the Islands, African Queen, Edward My Son, Curtain Up, The Final Test, Melba, Gilbert and Sullivan, Beat the Devil, Beau Brummell, Rainbow Jacket, Good Die Young, Quentin Durward, Loser Takes All, Six Months Grace, Full Treatment, Hippo Dancing, Around the World in 80 Days, Sheriff of Fractured Jaw, The Journey, The Doctor's Dilemma, Battle of the Sexes, Libel, Oscar Wilde, Go To Blazes, The Young Ones, Nine Hours to Rama, Murder at the Gallop, Topkapi, Amanda, Take Her She's Mine, Genghis Khan, Hot Enough for June, The Alphabet Murders, Sinful Davey, Hot Millions, Some Girls Do, The Trygon Factor, Song of Norway, The Blue Bird, Who Is Killing the Great Chefs of Europe?, Scavenger Hunt, The Human Factor, The Great Muppet Caper, The Wind, The Trouble With Spies, Little Dorrit.
TELEVISION: Call My Bluff (series), Charge!, The Lady and the Highwayman, War and Remembrance, Around the World in 80 Days.

MORRICONE, ENNIO: Composer, Arranger. b. Rome, Nov. 10, 1928. Studied with Goffredo Petrassi at the Acad. of Santa Cecilia in Rome. Began career composing chamber music and symphonies as well as music for radio, TV and theater. Wrote for popular performers incl. Gianni Morandi. Early film scores for light comedies. Gained reknown for assoc. with Ital. westerns of Sergio Leone (under name of Dan Davio).
PICTURES: IL Federal (1961, debut), A Fistful of Dollars, The Good the Bad and the Ugly, El Greco, Fists in the Pocket, Battle of Algiers, Matcheless, Theorem, Once Upon a Time in the West, Investigation of a Citizen, Fraulein Doktor, Burn, The Bird with the Crystal Plumage, Cat O'Nine Tails, The Red Tent, Four Flies in Grey Velvet, The Decameron, The Black Belly of the Tarantula, Bluebeard, The Serpent, Blood in the Streets, Eye of the Cat, The Human Factor, Murder on the Bridge, Sunday Woman, The Inheritance, Partner, Orca, The Heretic, Exorcist II, 1900, La Cage aux Folles, Days of Heaven; Bloodline; Stay as You Are, The Humanoid, The Meadow, A Time to Die, Travels With Anita, When You Comin' Back Red Ryder?, Almost Human, La Cage aux Folles II, The Island, Tragedy of a Ridiculous Man; Windows; Butterfly, So Fine; White Dog, Copkiller, Nana, The Thing; Treasure of the Four Crowns, Sahara, Once Upon a Time in America, Thieves After Dark, The Cage, La Cage aux Folles III, The Forester's Sons, The Red Sonja, Repentier, The Mission, The Venetian Woman, The Untouchables, Quartiere (Neighborhood), Rampage, Frantic, A Time of Destiny, Cinema Paradiso, Casualties of War.
TELEVISION: (U.S.): Marco Polo, Moses—The Lawgiver, Scarlet and the Black, C.A.T. Squad, The Endless Game, Octopus 4.

MORRIS, HOWARD: Actor. b. New York, NY, Sept. 4, 1919. e. NYU. U.S. Army, 4 yrs.; dir., Who's Minding the Mint, Don't Drink the Water, End of the Line.
BROADWAY: Hamlet, Call Me Mister, John Loves Mary, Gentlemen Prefer Blondes.
TELEVISION: Your Show of Shows, Caesar's Hour.

MORRIS, JOHN: Composer, Conductor, Arranger. b. Elizabeth, NJ, e. student Juilliard; Sch. Music 1946–48, U. of Washington. 1947, New Sch. Social Research 1946–49. Member: ASCAP, Acad. of M.P. Arts & Sciences, American Federation of Artists.
STAGE: Composer: Broadway: My Mother, My Father and

Me, Doll's House, Camino Real, A Time For Singing (musical), Take One Step, Young Andy Jackson, 15 other Shakespeare plays for NY Shakespeare Fest. & Amer. Shakespeare Fest, Stratford CT. Musical supervisor, conductor, arranger: Mack and Mabel, Much Ado About Nothing, Bells Are Ringing; Off-Bdwy: Hair.

RECORDS: Wildcat, All-American, Bells Are Ringing, First Impressions, Bye Bye Birdie, Kwamina, Baker Street, Rodgers and Hart, George Gershwin Vols. 1 & 2, Jerome Kern, Lyrics of Ira Gershwin, Cole Porter, others.

PICTURES: The Producers, The Twelve Chairs, The Gambler, Blazing Saddles (Acad. Award nom.), The Bank Shot, Young Frankenstein, Sherlock Holmes' Smarter Brother, Silent Movie, The Last Remake of Beau Geste, The In-Laws, The World's Greatest Lover, In God We Trust, High Anxiety, The Elephant Man (Acad. Award nom.), Table for Five, History of the World, Part One, Yellowbeard, The Doctor and the Devils, Clue, To Be or Not to Be, The Woman in Red, Johnny Dangerously, Haunted Honeymoon, Dirty Dancing, Spaceballs, Ironweed, The Wash.

TELEVISION: Composer: Fresno, Katherine Anne Porter, Ghost Dancing, The Firm, The Mating Season, Splendor in the Grass, The Electric Grandmother, The Scarlet Letter, Georgia O'Keeffe, The Adams Chronicles, The Franken Project, The Tap Dance Kid (Emmy, 1986), Make Believe Marriage, The Desperate Hours, The Skirts of Happy Chance, Infancy and Childhood, The Fig Tree, The Little Match Girl, Favorite Son. *Themes:* ABC After School Special, Making Things Grow, The French Chef, Coach. Musical sprv., conductor, arranger Specials: Anne Bancroft Special #1 (Emmy Award), 'S Lemmon, 'S Gershwin, 'S Wonderful (Emmy Award), Hallmark Christmas specials.

MORRIS, OSWALD: Cinematographer. b. London, Eng., 1915. Left school at 16 to work for two years as camera dept. helper at studios. Was lensman for cameraman Ronald Neame who gave Morris first job as cameraman; in 1949 when Neame directed The Golden Salamander he made Morris dir. of photography.

PICTURES: The Golden Salamander, The Card, The Man Who Never Was, Mister Moses, Moulin Rouge, Beat the Devil, Moby Dick, Heaven Knows, Mr. Allison, The Roots of Heaven, Reflections in a Golden Eye, The Mackintosh Man, Oliver!, Scrooge, The Pumpkin Eater, The Hill, The Spy Who Came in from the Cold, A Farewell to Arms, The Key, The Guns of Navarone, Lolita, Term of Trial, Fiddler on the Roof (Acad. Award), Sleuth, Goodbye, Mr. Chips; Lady Caroline Lamb; The Mackintosh Man; The Odessa File, The Man Who Would Be King, Seven Per Cent Solution, Just Tell Me What You Want; Equus, The Wiz; The Great Muppet Caper, The Dark Crystal.

TELEVISION: Dracula (1974).

MORRIS, RICHARD: Director, Writer. b. San Francisco, CA, May 14, 1924. e. Burlingame H.S., 1939–42; Chouinard Art Inst., 1946–47; Neighborhood Playhouse, 1947–48. U.S. Army special services, writing shows, Victory Bond; Universal-Int., talent dept., writing directing skits, writing music for acting class and Korean War entertainment troups; s.p. Take Me to Town, Finders Keepers.

AUTHOR, STAGE: The Unsinkable Molly Brown.

PICTURES: If a Man Answers, Thoroughly Modern Millie, Change of Habit.

TELEVISION: Wrote & dir. teleplays, Loretta Young Show, wrote & dir. The Pearl (Loretta Young Show), wrote teleplays, Private Secretary, Ford Theatre, Kraft Television Theatre, dir., The Wild Swans (Shirley Temple Show-Christopher Award).

MORRIS, WILLIAM, JR.: Consultant, retired president, William Morris Agency, Inc. b. New York, NY, Oct. 22, 1899.

MORRISSEY, PAUL: Writer, Director. b. New York, NY, 1939. e. Fordham U. Service in Army. Was involved in indep. film prod. prior to joining Andy Warhol for whom he produced such films as Chelsea Girls, Four Stars, Bike Boy, Nude Restaurant, Lonesome Cowboys, Blue Movie, L'Amour, Women in Revolt.

PICTURES: Flesh, Trash, Heat, Flesh Fur, Frankenstein, Blood For Dracula, Forty Deuce, Madame Wang's, Mixed Blood, Throwback, Beethoven's Nephew (dir., co-s.p.), Spike of Bensonhurst (dir., s.p.).

MORRISON, JR., HENRY T.: Executive. b. Mt. Pleasant, NY, Dec. 21, 1939. e. U. of Minnesota, B.A., 1963;, IMEDE, Switzerland, PED, 1971; Yale U. Divinity Sch., M.A., 1980. Episcopal priest 1983 to present. Positions in banking and marketing before entering m.p. industry 1972. 1976–85, independent financial consultant to industry. 1985, pres. & CEO, Mill City Entertainment, Minneapolis. 1987, pres. & CEO, Crocus Entertainment, Inc. MN. as well as Mill City Entertainment.

PICTURES: Dangerous Relations (assoc. prod.); Mitchell (assoc. prod.); The Devil's Men (exec. prod.) Author: Intercept, s.p., based on his own novel.

MORROW, JEFF: Actor. b. New York, NY, Jan. 13, 1917. e. Pratt Inst. Starred 2 years as radio's Dick Tracy, star of TV series Union Pacific, U.S. Steel, Wagon Train, etc.

BROADWAY: Cornell's Romeo and Juliet, St. Joan; Billy Budd. Starred in Lace On Her Petticoat, Three Wishes For Jamie. In Los Angeles Lincoln in Norman Corwin's Lincoln-Douglas Debates.

PICTURES: The Robe, Tanganyika, Sign of the Pagan, Captain Lightfoot, This Island Earth, Story of Ruth, Dino Risi's Giovane Normale (Italy) Hour of Decision (England).

MORSE, ROBERT: Actor. b. Newton, MA, May 18, 1931. Served U.S. Navy. Studied with American Theatre Wing, New York, where he had small role in film The Proud and the Profane, 1956. Following radio work, appeared on Broadway stage in The Matchmaker, 1956.

BROADWAY: Say, Darling, Take Me Along, How to Succeed in Business Without Really Trying (Tony Award, 1962), Sugar, So Long 174th Street.

PICTURES: The Matchmaker, Honeymoon Hotel, Quick Before It Melts, The Loved One, Oh Dad Poor Dad, How to Succeed in Business Without Really Trying, Guide for the Married Man, The Boatniks, Hunk, The Emperor's New Clothes.

TELEVISION: That's Life (series), The Stingiest Man in Town, Kennedy Center Tonight—Broadway to Washington, Masquerade, The Calendar Girl Murders.

MORTON, ARTHUR: Composer, Arranger. b. Duluth, MN, Aug. 8, 1908. e. U. of Minnesota, 1929. Composer for various film cos. including Universal, RKO, United Artists; with Columbia since 1948.

PICTURES: Night Life of the Gods, Princess O'Hara, Riding on Air, Fit for a King, Turnabout, Walking Hills, The Nevadan, Rogues of Sherwood Forest, Father is a Bachelor, Never Trust a Gambler, Harlem Globetrotters, Big Heat, Pushover, He Laughed Last.

ORCH. ARRANGEMENTS: Laura, Smokey, From Here to Eternity, Jolson Story, Salome, Phfft, No Sad Songs For Me, Born Yesterday, Long Gray Line, Man from Laramine, My Sister Eileen, Queen Bee, Picnic, Jubal, Autumn Leaves, Johnny Concho, Harder They Fall, 3:10 to Yuma, Full of Life, Garment Jungle, They Came to Cordura, Strangers When We Meet, Touch of Mink, Critics Choice, Diamond Head, Toys in the Attic, Man from the Diners' Club, Von Ryan's Express, The Saboteur, Code Name—Morituri, In Harm's Way, What a Way to Go, The New Interns, Rio Conchos, Dear Briggitte, Our Man Flint, Planet of the Apes, Flim Flam Man, Justine, Patton, Tora Tora Tora, Mephisto Waltz, Ballad of Cable Hogue, Traveling Executioner, Escape From the Planet of the Apes, Cold Turkey, Wild Rovers, The Other, Ace Eli, One Little Indian, The Don is Dead, Papillon, Chinatown, Breakout, The Wind and the Lion, Logan's Run, The Omen, Islands in the Stream, Passover Plot, Twilight's Last Gleaming, Damnation Alley, MacArthur, Capricorn One, Coma, The Swarm, Omen II (Damien), Boys from Brazil, Magic, Superman, Alien, Players, Meteor, Star Trek, Inchon, Masada, The Final Conflict, Outland, Raggedy Man, Night Crossing, Poltergeist, The Secret of NIMH, First Blood, Psycho II, Twilight Zone, Under Fire, The Lonely Guy, Gremlins, Supergirl, Rambo: First Blood Part II, Explorers, King Solomon's Mines, Link, Poltergist II, Hoosiers, Lionheart, Extreme Prejudice, Innerspace, Rent a Cop, Rambo III, Warlock, The 'Burbs, Leviathan, Star Trek V: The Final Frontier.

TELEVISION: Black Saddle, Laramie, Bus Stop, Follow the Sun, My Three Sons, Peyton Place, Medical Center, Daniel Boone, Lancers, National Geographic, Say Goodbye, How to Stay Alive, Hooray For Hollywood, The Waltons, Apple's Way, Medical Story.

MOSES, CHARLES ALEXANDER: Executive, Writer, Producer. b. Chicago, CA, March 1, 1923. e. Aeronautical U., Northwestern U., Englewood Eve. Jr. Coll., Antioch U. Pub. rel. dir., Goldblatt Bros. dept. store chain, Chicago; field adv-promo exec., United Artists, unit publicist for over 30 films, exec., Screen Gems; European adv-pub superv., Paris, United Artists; adv-pub dir., Bel Air Prod., V.P. adv-pub dir., Associates & Aldrich Co., adv-pub dir., Sinatra Enterprises, assoc. studio pub. dir., Universal Studios, adv-pub rep., Universal Studios from Paris for Europe, exec-in-chg New York domestic & foreign adv-pub dept., Universal, adv-pub superv., Orion Pictures Co. Own firm, Charles A. Moses Co., adv-marketing-pub. rel., acc'ts included United Artists, Columbia Picts., 20th Century-Fox, UA-TV, Brut Prod., Michael Klinger Ltd., ITT, Cinecom, Cinemation Industries, Hemdale Leisure Corp., Faberge, Stein & Day Publishers; Information, Inc., Automated Learning, Darrell Waters Ltd., Ebefilms, Phoenix Films, Valley Cable TV, Jensen Farley Picts., Taft Internat'l Picts, auto shows, TV shows, art galleries, events, guilds, Cinevent Prod., Dimitri Tiomkin, Dale Wasserman, American Internat'l Picts., Filmways. Orig, stories, Frankenstein 1970 (Allied Artists), Store (Brut Prod.); Prod., Radio Free Europe, Munich, Goldblatt radio, TV shows (WGN); Writer-prod-dir., documentaries, Carson Prod., Mason City; Screenplays, Abigail, The Callers; Musical book, Daddy. Past pres., The Publicists Guild of America (IATSE, Local 818).

MOSES, GILBERT: Director. b. Cleveland, OH, Aug. 20, 1942. Staff mem. Free Press, Jackson, MS 1963–64; editor, 1964; co-founder artistic dir. Free Southern Theatre; member Second City, Chicago, 1967. New York Stage director; m.p. debut Willie Dynamite (also score and lyrics), 1973; The Fish That Saved Pittsburgh, 1979.
STAGE: Ain't Supposed to Die a Natural Death, Slave Ship, The Taking of Miss Janie (Obie Award), 1600 Pennsylvania Avenue.
TELEVISION: Roots, A Fight for Jenny, The Greatest Thing That Almost Happened. Runaway (Wonderworks).

MOSLEY, ROGER E.: Actor. b. Los Angeles, CA. Planned career in broadcasting but turned to acting, first appearing in small roles on TV in: Night Gallery, Baretta, Kojak, Cannon, Switch. Film debut in The New Centurions (1972).
PICTURES: Stay Hungry, The Greatest, Semi-Tough, Leadbelly.
TELEVISION: Series: Switch, Magnum P.I. Movies: I Know Why the Caged Bird Sings, The Jericho Mile, Attica, etc.

MOSS, ARNOLD: Actor, Director. b. New York, NY, Jan. 28, 1910. e. City Coll. of New York, B.A. (Phi Beta Kappa); Columbia U., M.A.; NYU, Ph.D.. Teacher, B'klyn Coll. 1932–39; visiting prof., U. of Connecticut, 1973–74; Pace U., 1975; Coll. of William and Mary, 1976; Purdue U., 1977. Neighborhood Playhouse Sch. of the Theatre, 1974–76; U. of Wyoming, 1985; Theatre, film opera & TV actor-director.
PICTURES: Temptation, Loves of Carmen, Reign of Terror, Border Incident, Kim, Mask of the Avenger, My Favorite Spy, Viva Zapata, Salome, Casanova's Big Night, Bengal Brigade, Hell's Island, Jump into Hell, The 27th Day, The Fool Killer, Caper of the Golden Bulls, Gambit.
TELEVISION: Star Trek, Bonanza, Alfred Hitchcock, Hallmark Hall of Fame, many others. Actor-writer, CBS Radio Mystery Theater (over 500 programs as actor, over 60 as writer).

MOSS, CHARLES B., JR.: Theatre Executive, Producer. b. New York, NY, Aug. 29, 1944. e. U. of Pennsylvania, B.A., 1966; Boston U. Sch. of Law, LL.B., 1969. Was asst. prof. of law at Boston U., 1969–70. Entered ind. as v.p. of B.S. Moss Enterprises, 1970; now pres. Has produced three films: Let's Scare Jessica to Death, Stigma, Diary of the Dead.

MOSS, FRANK L.: Writer, Producer. b. New York, NY. e. Duke U., Columbia U. Reporter, drama & film critic, N.Y.: U.S. Army Air Force, 1942–46, Instructor, UCLA, 1985–86 on advanced screenplay writing. 1987–88 private tutoring on screenplay and TV writing.
PLAYS: author: Glamour Girl, Call To Arms, (collab), So Goes the Nation, (collab), Some People's Children, American Pastoral, City on a Hill.
PICTURES: The Unvanquished, Whiphand, Caribbean, Sangaree, Papago Wells, The Half Breed, Sweetheart of Sigma Chi. MILITARY: 22 Air Force Training Films; 17 documentaries.
TV PILOTS: Outer Limits, Grand Jury, The Texan.
TV SCRIPTS: Telephone Hour, Four Star Playhouse, Winston Churchill's Valiant Years, Route 66, Wagon Train, Laramie, Wild Wild West, The Texan, G.E. Theater, Wire Service, U.S. Marshall, M-Squad, Stoney Burke, Tales of the Texas Rangers, T.V. Reader's Digest, Sheriff of Cochise, Whirlybirds, Line-Up, Wyatt Earp, Rin Tin Tin, Walter Winchell File, Daniel Boone, Man Who Never Was, Felony Squad, Richard Diamond, Lassie, Like the Rich People, Hired Mother, Shenandoah, Counterspy, White Hunter.
PROD-STORY ED: Screen Televideo, Sovereign Prod., Wire Service, T.V. Reader's Digest, Wyatt Earp.

MOSS, IRWIN: Executive. e. Syracuse U., Harvard Law Sch. Member NY State Bar. Began industry career as director of package negotiations for CBS-TV; 1970–80, exec. v.p. & natl. head of business affairs for I.C.M.; 1978–80, sr. v.p., NBC Entertainment; 1980, pres., Marble Arch TV. 1982, joined Paramount Pictures as sr. v.p. for motion picture div. 1984, exec. v.p., L. Taffner Ltd.

MOSTEL, JOSH: Actor. b. Dec. 21, 1946. Son of late Zero Mostel. m. producer Peggy Rajski. e. Brandeis U., B.A. 1970. Part of The Proposition, a Boston improvisational comedy group. Stage debut The Homecoming (Provincetown Playhouse, MA). Film debut Going Home, 1971.
STAGE: Unlikely Heroes, The Proposition, An American Millionaire, A Texas Trilogy, Gemini, Ferocious Kisses (dir.), Men in the Kitchen (Long Wharf, New Haven.), The Dog Play, The Boys Next Door, Love As We Know It (dir.).
PICTURES: Jesus Christ Superstar, Harry and Tonto, Sophie's Choice, Compromising Positions, Almost You, Star 80, Windy City, The Money Pit, Radio Days, Matewan, Wall Street, Heavy Petting, Animal Behavior.
TELEVISION: Seventh Avenue, Delta House, At Ease, The Boy Who Loved Trolls (PBS). Co-wrote Media Probes: The Language Show; Murphy's Law (series).

MOUND, FRED: Executive. b. St. Louis, MO, April 10, 1932. e. St. Louis U., Quincy Coll. 1946–52, assoc. with father, Charles Mound, at Park Theatre in Valley Park, Mo.; 1952–53, Universal Pictures (St. Louis); 1953, booker, UA, St. Louis; 1955 promoted to salesman in Kansas City; 1957, salesman, St. Louis; 1962, Indianapolis branch mgr. In 1967 named UA regional mgr., Dallas and in 1970 became S.W. Div. mgr; 1976–77, asst. gen. sls. mgr. for Southern, N.W. and S.W. Division operating out of Dallas. In June, 1977 appt. v.p., asst. gen. sls. mgr. of UA; Nov. 1978, appt. v.p. gen sls. mgr. for A.F.D. Pictures in Los Angeles; April, 1981, v.p. asst. gen. sls. mgr. for Universal Pictures; Jan., 1984, sr. v.p., gen. sls. mgr., Universal Pictures Distribution; named exec. v.p. Sept., 1988.

MOUNT, THOM: Executive. b. Durham, NC, May 26, 1948. e. Bard Coll.; CA Institute of the Arts, MFA. Started career with Roger Corman and as asst. to prod., Danny Selznick at MGM. Moved to Universal under prod. exec. Ned Tanen. At 26, named pres. and head of prod. at Universal. During 8-year tenure was responsible for dev. and prod. of more than 140 films (including Smokey and the Bandit, Animal House, Coal Miner's Daughter and Missing.).
PICTURES: Pirates (exec. prod.), Can't Buy Me Love, Frantic, Bull Durham (co-prod.); Stealing Home, Tequila Sunrise, Roger Corman's Frankenstein Unbound.
TELEVISION: Son of the Morning Star, Open Admissions.

MOYERS, BILL: TV Correspondent. b. Hugo, OK, June 5, 1934. e. U. of Texas; Southwestern Baptist Theological Sem. Asst. to Lyndon B. Johnson, 1959–60, 1961–63; assoc. dir., Peace Corps, 1961–63; spec. asst. to Pres. Johnson, 1963–67 and press secty. 1965–67. Editor and chief corr., CBS Reports. Bill Moyers Journal on PBS. Specials: Facing Evil.

MUDD, ROGER: Newscaster. b. Washington, DC, Feb. 9, 1928. e. Washington & Lee U., U. of North Carolina. Reporter for Richmond News-Leader, 1953; news. dr., WRNL, 1954; WTOP, Washington, 1956; joined CBS News 1961 as Congressional corr. 1977, Natl. Aff. corr.; 1978, corr., CBS Reports; 1980–87: NBC News as chief Washington corr., chief political corr., co-anchor; 1987 joined The MacNeil/Lehrer News Hour as special correspondent; essayist, and chief congressional corr.

MUHL, EDWARD E.: Executive, Producer. b. Richmond, IN, Feb. 17, 1907. Gen. mgr., Universal 1948–53; v.p., C.E.O. studio 1953–68. Consultant, Alcor Prods., Dallas, 1985–87. Co-author, consultant, s.p., Soldier: The Other Side of Glory, 1987.

MUIR, E. ROGER: Producer. b. Canada, Dec. 16, 1918. e. U. of Minnesota. Partner Minn. Advertising Services Co.; Photographer, Great Northern Railway; motion picture producer Army Signal corps; NBC TV producer, Howdy Doody, exec. producer, Concentration. Now pres. Nicholson-Muir Prods, TV program packager, U.S. Spin-Off, Pay Cards, Canada Pay Cards, Headline Hunters, Definition, Celebrity Dominoes; co-creator Newlywed Game, exec. prod. I Am Joe's Heart, I Am Joe's Lung, I Am Joe's Spine, I Am Joe's Stomach, The New Howdy Doody Show, Supermates, Second Honeymoon, Groaner, Generation Jury, Shopping Game, Guess What, I Am Joe's Kidney, I Am Joe's Liver, It's Howdy Doody Time: A 40 Year Celebration.

MULDAUR, DIANA: Actress. b. New York, NY, Aug. 19, 1938. e. Sweet Briar Coll. Began on New York stage the turned to films and TV, appearing on numerous major network shows.
PICTURES: The Swimmer, Number One, The Lawyer, One More Train to Rob, The Other, Chosen Survivors, Beyond Reason, McQ.
TELEVISION: Series: Born Free, The Tony Randall Show, Hizzoner, McCloud, The Survivors, Star Trek: The Next Generation, A Year in the Life. Movies: Murder in Three Acts, Black Beauty, Call to Danger, The Miracle Worker, The Return of McCloud.

MULGREW, KATE: Actress. b. Dubuque, IA, April 29, 1955. e. NYU. Stage work includes stints with American Shakespeare Festival, O'Neill Festival and at Hartman Theatre, Stamford. Film debut: Lovespell (1978).
PICTURES: Jennifer, Tristan and Isolt, A Stranger Is Watching, Throw Momma from the Train.
TELEVISION: Ryan's Hope (1975–77), The Word, Jennifer, A Woman's Story, Mrs. Colombo, Kate Loves a Mystery, A Time for Miracles, The Manions of America, Mother Seaton, Roses Are for the Rich, Heat Beat, Roots: The Gift., Heartbeat (Paradise Lost).

MULHOLLAND, ROBERT E.: Executive. b. 1934. e. Northwestern U. Joined NBC News as newswriter in Chicago in 1962. In 1964 made midwestern field producer for Huntley-Brinkley Report. In 1964 moved to London as European producer for NBC News; 1967, named Washington producer of Huntley-Brinkley Report. Transferred to L.A. in 1967 to be director of news, west coast. Named exec. prod. of NBC Nightly News. In 1973 appt. v.p., NBC news.; 1974 exec. v.p. of NBC News.

In 1977 appt. pres. of NBC Television Network; also elected to board of directors. Resigned, 1984.

MULL, MARTIN: Actor. b. Chicago, IL, Aug. 18, 1943. e. Rhode Island Sch. of Design. Started as humorist, making recordings for Warner Bros., Capricorn, ABC Records, etc. Theatrical m.p. debut, FM, 1978.
PICTURES: My Bodyguard, Serial, Take This Job and Shove It, Private School, Growing Pains, Flicks, Mr. Mom, Clue, O.C. and Stiggs, Home is Where the Hart Is, Rented Lips (actor, s.p., exec. prod.), Cutting Class, Ski Patrol, Far Out Man, Think Big.
TELEVISION: Mary Hartman Mary Hartman, Fernwood 2-Night, America 2-Night, Domestic Life, numerous talk shows, etc. Wrote produced and starred in The History of White People in America for HBO, Candid Camera Christmas Special (1987), Portrait of a White Marriage.

MULLER, PETER: Executive, Producer, Attorney. b. Teplitz-Sanov, Czechoslovakia, March 4, 1947. e. NYU, NYU Law Sch. Served as entertainment editor, Ambience and Women's Life magazines. Former CEO, Producers Releasing Corp., Pres. of PRC's entertainment div. Consultant to German TV show Am Laifen Band. Has worked with French and Eng. communication cos. Co-organizer; album and video of theater artists to fight world hunger, Broadway Feeds the World. Pres. and founder of The Muller Entertainment Group, Inc. Member: bd. of dirs. NYU Alumni Assoc., NYU's nominating comm.; American Bar Assoc.; ABA Forum on the Entertainment and Sports Industries; and ABA Forum on Patent, Trademark, Copyright Law; NY State Bar Assoc.; Volunteer Lawyers for the Arts.

MULLER, ROBBY: Cinematographer. b. Netherlands, April 4, 1940. e. Dutch Film Sch. Asst. cameraman in Holland before moving to Germany where he shot 9 films for Wim Wenders.
PICTURES: Kings of the Roads, Alice of the Cities, Saint Jack, Honeysuckle Rose, They All Laughed, Body Rock, Repo Man, Paris, Texas, The Longshot, To Live and Die in L.A., Down By Law, Tricheurs, Barfly, Il Piccolo Diavolo, Mystery Train, Till the End of the World.

MULLIGAN, RICHARD: Actor. b. New York, NY, Nov. 13, 1932. On stage in All the Way Home, Never Too Late, Thieves, etc.
PICTURES: The Mixed Up Files of Mrs. Basil E. Frankweiler, Irish Whiskey Rebellion, One Potato, Two Potato, The Group, the Big Bus, Little Big Man, Scavenger Hunt, S.O.B., Trail of the Pink Panther, Meatballs Part II, Teachers, Micki and Maude, Doin' Time, The Heavenly Kid, A Fine Mess, Quicksilver, Oliver & Company (voice).
TELEVISION: Having Babies, Poker Alice, Series: The Hero, Diana, Soap (Emmy Award, 1980), Reggie, Empty Nest (Emmy Award).

MULLIGAN, ROBERT: Director. b. Bronx, NY. Aug. 23, 1925. e. Fordham U., A.B. With CBS-TV, asst. supv. in radio oper.; prod. asst. on Supense, TV; then asst. dir. & dir.: TV Playhouse, NBC, Alcoa-Goodyear, Studio One, Playhouse 90, Hallmark Hall of Fame and dir. teleplays by Paddy Chayefsky, Tad Mosel and Robert Alan Aurther. In mid-1950s formed partnership with Alan J. Pakula.
PICTURES: Fear Strikes Out (1957), The Rat Race, The Great Imposter, Come September, To Kill a Mockingbird, The Spiral Road, Love with the Proper Stranger, Baby the Rain Must Fall, Inside Daisy Clover, Up the Down Staircase, Pursuit of Happiness, Summer of '42, The Other, The Nickel Ride, Blood Brothers, Same Time Next Year, Kiss Me Goodbye (also prod.), Clara's Heart.
TELEVISION: The Moon and the Sixpence, Billy Budd, Ah Wilderness, A Tale of Two Cities, The Bridge of San Luis Rey.

MURDOCH, RUPERT: Executive. b. Australia, March 11, 1931. Son of Sir Keith Murdoch, head of The Melbourne Herald and leading figure in Australian journalism. e. Oxford U., England. Spent two years on Fleet St. before returning home to take over family paper, The Adelaide News. Acquired more Australian papers and in 1969 expanded to Britain, buying The News of the World. Moved to U.S. in 1973, buying San Antonio Express and News. Conglomerate in 1985 included New York Post, New York Magazine, The Star, The Times of London, The Boston Herald, The Chicago Sun-Times along with TV stations, book publishing companies, airline, oil and gas companies, etc. 1985, made deal to buy 20th Century-Fox Film Corp. from owner Martin Davis. Sold the NY Post, 1988 to conform with FCC regulations. Purchased Triangle Publications 1988 (including TV Guide).

MURPHY, BEN: Actor. b. Jonesboro, AR, March 6, 1942. e. U. of Illinois. Degree in drama from Pasadena Playhouse. Acted in campus productions and toured in summer stock. Film debut with small role in The Graduate, 1967.
PICTURES: The Thousand Plane Raid, Yours, Mine and Ours, Sidecar Racer.
TELEVISION: Series: The Name of the Game, Alias Smith and Jones, Griff, Gemini Man, The Chisholms, Lottery!, Berrengers, The Dirty Dozen. Movies: Wild Bill Hickock, Bridger, Heat Wave, Runaway, This Is the West That Was, Hospital Fire, The Cradle Will Fall. Mini-Series: The Winds of War.

MURPHY, EDDIE: b. Hempstead, NY, Apr. 3, 1961. e. Roosevelt High Sch. Wrote and performed own comedy routines at youth centers and local bars at age 15. Worked on comedy club circuit; at 19 joined TV's Saturday Night Live, 1980–84. 1982, became writer for SNL as well as performer. Recordings: Eddie Murphy, Eddie Murphy: Comedian; How Could It Be? Quigley Poll, voted Top-Money Making Star, 1988.
PICTURES: 48 Hrs. (debut, 1982), Trading Places, The Best Defense, Beverly Hills Cop, The Golden Child, Beverly Hills Cop II, Eddie Murphy Raw, Coming to America (also story), Harlem Nights (exec. prod., dir., s.p., actor).
TELEVISION: Special: What's Alan Watching? (actor, exec. prod.). Pilot: Coming to America (exec. prod.).

MURPHY, GEORGE: Actor, Former U.S. Senator. b. New Haven, CT, July 4, 1902. e. Yale U. Toolmaker for Ford Co., miner, real estate agent, nightclub dancer, actor. On stage from 1927 (Good News, Of Thee I Sing, Roberta, etc.). Screen debut 1934 in Kid Millions. Member: Screen Actors Guild (former pres.); Nat'l. Com. WAC. Spcl. Academy Award (1951) "for interpreting m.p. ind. correctly to country at large," 1940; chmn., Hollywood Coordinating Com.; bd. mem., USO Inc.; v.p., Acad. of M.P. Arts & Sciences; div. of pub. rel., MGM, 1954–58; bd. mem. & past pres., Screen Actors Guild; bd. mem., M.P. Relief Fund. Joined Desilu Productions as v.p. in chg. public affairs, 1959; v.p., bd. of dir., Technicolor Corp. 1953, a year after last film, became chmn. Republican National Convention; Elected U.S. Senator, California, 1964–70. Autobiography: Say, Didn't You Used to Be George Murphy? (1970).
PICTURES: I'll Love You Always, You're a Sweetheart, London by Night, Broadway Melody of 1938, Risky Business, Two Girls on Broadway, A Girl, a Guy and a Gob, Tom, Dick and Harry, Ringside Maisie, Mayor of 44th Street, For Me and My Gal, Powers Girl, This Is the Army, Broadway Rhythm, Show Business, Step Lively, Having a Wonderful Crime, Up Goes Maisie, Arnelo Affair, Cynthia, Tenth Avenue Angel, Big City, Battleground, Border Incident, No Questions Asked, Talk About a Stranger, It's a Big Country, Walk East on Beacon, Jamboree (Boy Scout film), This Is the Army, Broadway Melody.

MURPHY, JOHN F.: Theatre Executive. b. Brooklyn, NY, Mar. 25, 1905. e. City Coll. of New York. Entire career with Loew's Theatres; started over 45 yrs. ago as asst. mgr. Hillside & Valencia Theatres, Jamaica, NY; apptd. gen. mgr. in chg. of out-of-town Theatres, 1942–54; v.p., Loew's Theatres, Aug., 1954; dir., Loew's Theatres, Oct., 1956; exec. v.p., Loew's Theatre, 1959; ret. July 1963; continues on bd. as advisor and director emeritus.

MURPHY, MICHAEL: Actor. b. Los Angeles, CA, May 5, 1938. e. U. of Arizona. Taught English and Drama in L.A. city school system, 1962–64. N.Y. stage debut as director of Rat's Nest, 1978–.
PICTURES: The Legend of Lylah Clare, The Arrangement, Brewster McCloud, MASH, McCabe and Mrs. Miller, What's Up Doc?, Nashville, An Unmarried Woman, The Front, Manhattan, The Year of Living Dangerously, Strange Behavior, Cloak and Dagger, Salvador, Shocker.
TELEVISION: Saints and Sinners, Ben Casey, Dr. Kildare, Bonanza, Combat, Autobiography of Miss Jane Pittman, John Cheever's Oh Youth and Beauty, Two Marriages, Tanner '88: The Caine Mutiny Court-Martial, Tailspin: Behind the Korean Airlines Tragedy.

MURPHY, RICHARD: Writer, Director. b. Boston, MA, 1912. e. Williams Coll. Entered m.p. Ind. 1937 Capt. U.S. Army Sig. Corps. SWPA, 1942–45. Contract writer, 20th Century-Fox, 1945–54 Writer-Prod., 20th-Fox, 1964–72; pres. Cinecom World Ent. Ltd., 1974.
PICTURES: Boomerang, Deep Waters, Cry of the City, Panic in the Streets, You're in the Navy Now, Les Miserables, Desert Rats, Broken Lance, Three Stripes in the Sun, Wackiest Ship in the Army, Compulsion, Last Angry Man, The Kidnapping of the President (s.p.).
TELEVISION: Our Man Higgins, creator, TV series, The Felony Squad.

MURRAY, BARBARA: Actress. b. London, England, Sept. 27, 1929. Stage debut in Variety, 1946; screen debut in Badger's Green, 1948. Various TV appearances.
PICTURES: Passport to Pimlico, Don't Ever Leave Me, Boys in Brown, Poets Pub, Tony Draws a Horse, Dark Man, Frightened Man, Mystery Junction, Another Man's Poison, Hot Ice, Street Corner (Both Sides of the Law), Meet Mr. Lucifer, Doctor at Large, Campbell's Kingdom, A Cry from the Streets, Girls in Arms.

MURRAY, BILL: Actor. b. Wilmette, IL, Sept. 21, 1950. e. attended Regis Coll. Was pre-med student; left to join brother, Brian Doyle-Murray, in Second City, the Chicago improvisational

troupe. Appeared with brother on radio in National Radio Hour Lampoon Show, and in off-Bdwy. revue, National Lampoon Show. Also on radio provided voice of Johnny Storm, the Human Torch, on Marvel Comics' Fantastic Four. Hired by ABC for Saturday Night Live; then by NBC.
PICTURES: Jungle Burger (debut, 1975), Meatballs, Mr. Mike's Mondo Video, Where the Buffalo Roam, Loose Shoes (aka Coming Attractions), Caddyshack, Stripes, Tootsie, Ghostbusters, The Razor's Edge (also co-s.p.), Nothing Lasts Forever, Little Shop of Horrors, Scrooged, Ghostbusters II, Quick Change (also co-prod., dir.).
TELEVISION: Series: Saturday Night Live (1977–80 also writer; Emmy-as writer 1977), Pilot: The TV TV Show (1977). Movies: All You Need Is Cash, Things We Did Last Summer. Specials: It's Not Easy Being Me—The Rodney Dangerfield Show, Steve Martin's Best Show Ever, Second City—25 Years in Revue.

MURRAY, DON: Actor, Director, Writer. b. Hollywood, CA, July 31, 1929. Mother was a Ziegeld Girl, father was dance dir. for Fox Studio.
PLAYS: Broadway: Insect Comedy, Rose Tattoo, The Skin of Our Teeth, The Hot Corner, Smith (a musical), The Norman Conquests; Same Time, Next Year. National tours: California Suite, Chicago.
PICTURES: Bus Stop, Bachelor Party, Hatful of Rain, From Hell to Texas, The Hoodlum Priest (also prod., writer), Advise and Consent, Baby the Rain Must Fall, Sweet Love, Bitter, The Cross and the Switchblade (dir., s.p. only), Conquest of the Planet of the Apes, One Man's Way, The Plainsman, Escape from East Berlin, Shake Hands with the Devil, From Hell to Texas, Confessions of Tom Harris (also prod., s.p.), Call Me by My Rightful Name (also prod., co-s.p.), The Borgia Stick, Deadly Hero, Damien (dir., s.p. only), Endless Love, Radioactive Dreams, Peggy Sue Got Married, Scorpion, Made in Heaven, Ghosts Don't Do It.
TELEVISION: Series: The Outcasts, Knots Landing, Brand New Life. Movies: The Sex Symbol, Rainbow, License to Kill, A Touch of Scandal, Something in Common, Stillwatch, The Stepford Children, The Borgia Stick, Return of the Rebels, The Boy Who Drank Too Much. Quarterback Princess, For I Have Loved Strangers, Hasty Heart, Billy Budd, Winterset, Alas Babylon, Mistress, My Dad Isn't Crazy, Is He?

MURRAY, JAN: Performer. b. New York City, NY, 1917. Performed in nightclubs, vaudeville, Bdwy, radio, TV, films. Was m.c., Songs for Sale, and Sing It Again, CBS-TV; TV guest star many programs; on Dollar a Second; Jan Murray Time; Treasure Hunt.
PLAYS: A Funny Thing Happened on the Way to the Forum.
PICTURES: Who Killed Teddy Bear?

MUSANTE, TONY: Actor. b. Bridgeport, CT, June 30. e. Oberlin Coll. B.A. Directed local theatre, then appeared off-Broadway, in regional theater, and on Dupont Show of the Month (Ride With Terror).
THEATER: Bdwy: The Lady From Dubuque; P.S., Your Cat Is Dead; 27 Wagons Full of Cotton and Memory of Two Mondays; (Off-bdwy): Grand Magic; Cassatt; A Gun Play; Benito Cereno; L'Histoire du Soldat; Match-Play; The Zoo Story; The Pinter Plays (The Collection); Kiss Mama; The Balcony, Frankie and Johnny in the Claire de Lune. Regional: The Big Knife, A Streetcar Named Desire, The Taming of the Shrew, Widows, The Archbishop's Ceiling, Dancing in the Endzone, Two Brothers, Souvenir. APA Shakespeare Rep., others.
PICTURES: Once a Thief, The Incident, The Detective, The Mercenary, One Night at Dinner, The Bird with the Crystal Plumage, The Grissom Gang, The Last Run, Anonymous Venetian, Collector's Item, The Repenter, The Pisciotta Case, Goodbye and Amen, Break Up, Nocturne, The Pope of Greenwich Village.
TELEVISION: Chrysler Theatre, Alfred Hitchcock Hour, N.Y.P.D., The Fugitive, Trials of O'Brien, Police Story, Medical Story, Toma (series); Movies: Rearview Mirror, The Court Martial of Lt. William Calley, Desperate Miles, The Quality of Mercy, Nowhere to Hide, My Husband is Missing, The Story of Esther, High Ice, Last Waltz on a Tightrope, Weekend (Amer. Playhouse). Mini-series: Nutcracker: Money, Madness & Murder; Breaking Up Is Hard To Do; the Legend of the Black Hand, Devil's Hill, Appointment in Trieste.

MUSTO, MICHAEL J.: Producer, Writer. b. New York, NY. e. S. Niagara U. Apprentice for J. J. Shubert. Comedy Workshop, N.Y. W-Co. Hellzapoppin, Wrote, Prod. Dir. Burlesque shows and stage revues. Prod. Industrial Films, Commercials, Operas, Fund Raising Shows. Prod. Films: The Glass House, Phenomena 7-7, Down Tin Pan Alley, Single Room Furnished, Educated Heart, Agnes, Spring Fancy, The Atheist, Man Who Cried Wolf, Several Robert Montgomery Presents, Hallmark Hall of Fame, TV Specials, The Bold Ones, Strange Is the Wind. Wrote: Due-Bill Marriage, Spring Fancy, Who's On First, Pratt's Fall, Charlie Daniels Band, Special Break, Heads-Feed Cats, Seymour, Granada, Seppi and His Brothers, Amato and the Yenta, The Cliffdwellers, Other. Owner. Empire Films and Cinema City Studios, dinner theatres.

MUTSU, IAN YONOSUKE: Producer, Distributor. b. London, England, Jan. 14, 1907. e. U. of Birmingham, England. Journalist 1931–48. Daily Express, UPI, etc.; Japan repr. MGM-Hearst Metrotone News, U.S. Newsreel Pool, later Telenews, UPI-Movietone News, ITN London; 1952 pres. International Motion Picture Co. for news coverage, documentaries, custom films for worldwide clients; 1966 agent BBC TV sales, Modern Talking Picture Service NYC; 1973 founded Mutsu Inc. (Canada). Productions include numerous documentaries on Japan, Japanese background films for overseas clients.

MYERS, JULIAN F.: Public Relations. b. Detroit, MI, Feb. 22, 1918. e. Wayne U., 1935–37, U. of Southern California, 1937–39. Distribution, Loew's Detroit, 1941–42; asst. story editor, idea man, Columbia, 1942–46; publicist, 20th Century-Fox, 1948–62; public relations, Julian F. Myers, Inc., 1962; pres., Myers Studios, Inc., 1966; pres., New Horizons Broadcasting Corp., 1968–69; sr. publicist American Intl. Pictures, 1970–80. Executive Board Hollywood Press Club; member Variety Clubs; Academy of Motion Pictures Arts & Sciences; Board of Governors Film Industry Workshops, Inc. 1977, western vice-pres., The Publicists Guild; Recipient of Publicists Guild's Robert Yeager Award; 1979, re-elected western v.p., Publicists Guild. First male member Hollywood Women's Press Club. Co-founder HANDS (Hollywood Answering Needs of Disaster Survivors). Member, M.P. Pioneers. Winner, 1980 Publicists Guild Les Mason Award. Instructor in publicity, UCLA, 1979 to present. Filmways Pictures, pub. dept., 1980–81. Exec. v.p., worldwide m.p. and TV pub./mktg., Hanson & Schwam Public Relations 1981 to present.

MYERS, PETER S.: Executive. b. Toronto, Ont., Canada, May 13, 1923. e. U. of Toronto. Toronto br. mgr., 20th Century-Fox, 1948; man. dir. Canada, 1951; gen. sales mgr. in chg. of dom. distribution, 1968; v.p., 1969; named snr. v.p.; domestic dist., 1979; snr. v.p., 20th-Fox Entertainment, 1980; pres., 20th-Fox Classics, 1983; pres., Hemdale Releasing Corp. and PSM Entertainment Inc., 1985; pres. & CEO, Four Seasons Entertainment, 1989.

MYERS, STANLEY: Composer. Since 1966 has composed scores for over 60 British, American, German and French films including:
PICTURES: Kaleidoscope (1966), Ulysses, No Way to Treat a Lady, Lady, Michael Kohlhaas, Otley, Two Gentlemen Sharing, Take a Girl Like You, Tropic of Cancer, The Walking Stick, Long Ago Tomorrow, A Severed Head, Tam Lin, King, Queen, Knave; Sitting Target, Summer Lightning, X,Y, Zee; The Blockhouse, The Apprenticeship of Duddy Kravitz, Caravan to Vaccares, Little Malcolm, The Wilby Conspiracy, The Coup de Grace, The Class of Miss MacMichael, The Deerhunter, The Greek Tycoon, The Martian Chronicles, A Portrait of the Artist as a Young Man, The Secret Policeman's Other Ball, Yesterday's Hero, Watcher in the Woods, Absolution, The Incubus, Lady Chatterly's Lover, Eureka, Moonlighting, Blind Date, Beyond the Limit, The Next One, Success is the Best Revenge, The Chain, Dreamchild, Insignificance, The Lightship, The Wind, Castaway, My Beautiful Laundrette, Prick Up Your Ears, Wish You Were Here, The Second Victory, Baja Oklahoma, Taffin, Track 29, Stars and Bars, Trading Hearts, Sammy and Rosie Get Laid, Torrents of Spring, Scenes From the Class Struggle in Beverly Hills.
TELEVISION: Series (U.K.): Widows (parts 1 & 2), Nancy Astor, Diana. Series (U.S.): The Martian Chronicles, Florence Nightingale. Movies: Strong Medicine, Smart Money, Monte Carlo.

MYERSON, BERNARD: Executive. b. New York, NY, March 25, 1918. Entered m.p. ind. with Fabian Theatres, 1938–63; last position as exec. v.p.; joined Loew's Theatres as v.p., 1963; exec. v.p. and board member, Loew's Corp.; pres. Loew's Theatres, 1971. Chmn. & pres., Loews Theatre Management Corp., 1985. Vice chmn. & mem. of Executive Committee Greater N.Y. Chapter, National Foundation of March of Dimes; Honorary chmn. & bd. mem., Will Rogers Memorial Fund; Mem. exec. comm., bd., National Assn. Theatre Owners; bd. mem., Motion Picture Pioneers. v.p., Variety Intl.; mem., finance comm., Friars; Board of Directors Burke Rehabilitation Center; mem. N.Y.S. Governor's Council on M.P. & T.V. Development; mem. M.P. & T.V. Com. USIA.

N

NABORS, JIM: Actor. b. Sylacauga, AL, June 12, 1932. Developed a second career as a singer. Between 1966–72 had 12 albums on best selling charts.
PICTURES: The Best Little Whorehouse in Texas, Stroker Ace, Cannonball Run II, etc.
TELEVISION: Series: Andy Griffith Show, Gomer Pyle

USMC, The Jim Nabors Show, etc. Movie: Return to Mayberry.

NADEL, ARTHUR: Producer, Director, Writer. b. New York, NY, April 25. Film editor for Paramount, 20th Century-Fox, Walt Disney, U.S. Air Force m.p. div., United Artists; superv. editor, McCann-Erickson; prod., dir., writer, Universal; v.p., Levy-Gardner-Laven. Currently exec. v.p. creative affairs, Filmation Studios, Co-chair, Documentary Comm. of Acad. of Motion Picture Arts and Sciences; Governor of Television Academy.
PICTURES: Clambake, Lola, Underground, No Trumpets, No Drum.
TELEVISION: The Rifleman, The Plainsman, Great Adventure, Arrest and Trial, Kraft Theatre, The Virginian, Big Valley, Daniel Boone, Cowboy in Africa, Bonanza, Delphi Bureau, Banyon, Streets of San Francisco; NBC Specials, Welcome Home (Emmy Winner); This Year in Jerusalem, Vortex in Oatmeal, The Chase; Crime Without Punishment (Emmy Award); Shazam, The Secrets of Isis, Bravestarr, He-Man; She-Ra, Bravo Bugzburg.

NADER, GEORGE: Actor. b. Pasadena, CA, Oct. 19, 1921. e. Occidental Coll., B.A.; Pasadena Playhouse, B.T.A. Served in U.S. Navy. Many TV appearances, film debut in Monsoon (1953). First novel, Chrome, (Putnam).
PICTURES: Carnival Story, Miss Robin Crusoe, Sins of Jezebel, Fours Guns to the Border, Six Bridges to Cross, Lady Godiva, Second Greatest Sex, Away All Boats, Congo Crossing, Unguarded Moment, Four Girls in Town, Man Afraid, Joe Butterfly, Nowhere to Go, The Secret Mark of D'Artagnan, The Great Space Adventure, Zigzag, The Human Duplicators, Sumuru, House of a Thousand Dolls, Alarm on 83rd Street, Murder at Midnight, Count-Down for Manhattan, Dynamite in Green Silk, The Check and Icy Smile, The Murder Club From Bklyn, Death in a Red Jaguar, End Station of the Damned, Bullets on Broadway, Beyond Atlantis.
TELEVISION: Letter to Loretta, Fireside Theatre, Chevron Theatre, Ellery Queen, Man and the Challenge, Shannon.

NAIFY, MARSHALL: Executive. b. Sacramento, CA, March 23, 1920. e. U. of Southern California. U.S.A.F. Chmn. exec. comm. & bd. chmn., United Artists Communications, Inc.; pres., Magna Pictures Corp.

NAIFY, ROBERT: Executive. b. Sacramento, CA. e. Attended Stanford U. Worked for United California Theatres since 1946 in various capacities: theatre manager, purchasing agent, film buyer, general manager and president. 1963 became exec. vice president, United Artists Communications; and in 1971 became president and CEO until 1987. Currently president Todd-AO Corporation.

NAIR, MIA: Director, Producer. b. Bhubaneswar, India, 1957. e. Irish Catholic Missionary School in India, Delhi U., Harvard U. A course in documentary filmmaking at Harvard led to directing 4 non-fiction films includ. India Cabaret (1985) and Children of Desired Sex. Feature debut as producer-director, Salaam Bombay! in 1988 won Camera d'Or for best first feature, and Prix du Publique at Cannes Fest. as well as Acad. Award nomination for best foreign film.

NAKAMURA, MOTOHIKO: Executive. b. Tokyo, Japan, Aug. 10, 1929. e. U. of California at Berkeley, U. of Pennsylvania, Tokyo U. Joined Fuji Film Co., Ltd. in Tokyo, 1953; assigned to Japan Camera Center, New York, 1956–67; North American rep. for Fuji Photo Film Co., Ltd., 1957–63; assistant export sales mgr., Fuji Photo Co., Ltd. in charge of international marketing of all products, 1964–71; exec. v.p., resident mgr., Fuji Photo Film U.S.A., Inc.

NALLE, BILLY: Theatre concert organist, popular field, ASCAP Composer. b. Fort Myers, FL; graduate, The Juilliard Sch. Over 5000 major TV shows from New York; now artist-in-residence, Wichita Theatre Organ, Inc. Reader's Digest, Telarc & WTO Records Artist. Public Relations: Billy Nalle Music, Wichita.

NAMATH, JOE: Actor. b. Beaver Falls, PA, May 31, 1943. e. U. of Alabama. Former professional football star. Film debut in Norwood (1970).
PICTURES: C.C. & Co., The Last Rebel, Avalanche Express.
TELEVISION: The Waverly Wonders (series), Marriage Is Alive and Well, All American Pie, Kate and Allie.

NARDINO, GARY: Executive. b. Garfield, NJ, Aug. 26, 1935. e. Seton Hall U. Awarded honorary degree of Doctor of Laws. Entered industry in 1959 as agent, representing Lorimar Prods. and Talent Associates, among others. Named sr. v.p. of ICM's New York TV dept; then v.p. of William Morris Agency, heading N.Y. TV dept. Pres. of Paramount TV Production Division, 1977–83. Pres., of Gary Nardino Prods., Inc., formed 1983, to dev. and produce theatrical features and TV programming; 1988, named chmn. & CEO, Orion Television Entertainment.
PICTURES: Star Trek III: the Search for Spock (exec. prod.); Fire with Fire (prod.).
TELEVISION: Exec. prod.: Brothers, At Your Service, Joanna.

NARIZZANO, SILVIO: Producer, Director. b. Montreal, Canada, Feb. 8, 1927. e. U. of Bishop's, Lennoxville, Quebec, B.A. Was active as actor-director in Canadian theatre before going to England for TV and theatrical film work.
PICTURES: Director: Under Ten Flags (co-dir.), Die! Die! My Darling!, Georgy Girl, Blue, The Man Who Had Power Over Women, Loot, Redneck, The Sky Is Falling, Why Shoot the Teacher?, The Class of Miss MacMichael, Choices, Double Play. Producer: Negatives, Fadeout, Redneck.
TELEVISION: Come Back Little Sheba, Staying On, Young Shoulders, Miss Marple (series).

NASH, N. RICHARD: Writer. r.n. Nusbaum, b. Philadelphia, PA, June 8, 1913.
BROADWAY: Second Best Bed, The Young and Fair, See the Jaguar, The Rainmaker, Girls of Summer, Handful of Fire, Wildcat, 110 in the Shade, The Happy Time, Echoes, Wildfire, The Torch, Magic, The Bluebird of Happiness, Breaking the Til, Come As You Are.
PICTURES: Nora Prentiss, The Vicious Years, The Rainmaker, Porgy and Bess, Sainted Sisters, Dear Wife, Welcome Stranger, Dragonfly.
TV: Many TV plays for Television Playhouse, U.S. Steel, General Electric.
NOVELS: Cry Macho; East Wind, Rain; The Last Magic; Aphrodite's Cave; Radiance; Behold the Man.

NATWICK, MILDRED: Actress. b. Baltimore, Md, June 19, 1908. e. Bryn Mawr Sch., Baltimore, Bennett Sch., Millbrook. Prof. stage debut in Carry Nation, 1932; London debut in Day I Forget.
PLAYS: Wind and the Rain, Distaff Side, End of Summer, Love from a Stranger, Candida, Missouri Legend, Stars in Your Eyes, Grass Harp, Blithe Spirit, (Barter Theatre award), Waltz of the Toreadors (nominated for Tony), The Firstborn, The Good Soup, Critic's Choice, Barefoot in the Park, Our Town, Landscape, 70, Girls 70, (nominated for Tony), Bedroom Farce.
PICTURES: Long Voyage Home, Enchanted Cottage, Yolanda and the Thief, Late George Apley, Woman's Vengeance, Three Godfathers, Kissing Bandit, She Wore a Yellow Ribbon, Cheaper by the Dozen, Quiet Man, Against All Flags, Trouble with Harry, Court Jester, Teenage Rebel, Tammy and the Bachelor, Barefoot in the Park (nominated for Oscar), If It's Tuesday This Must Be Belgium, Trilogy, The Maltese Bippy, Daisy Miller, At Long Last Love, Kiss Me Goodbye, Dangerous Liaisons.
TELEVISION: Blithe Spirit (nominated for Emmy), House Without a Xmas Tree, Thanksgiving Treasure, Money to Burn, The Snoop Sisters (Emmy award), The Easter Promise, Little Women, McMillan and Wife, Hawaii Five-O, Love Boat, You Can't Take It With You, Alice—Made in America, Deadly Deception.

NAUGHTON, DAVID: Actor, Singer. b. Hartford, CT, Feb. 13, 1951. Brother of actor James Naughton. e. U. of Pennsylvania, B.A. Studied at London Acad. of Music and Dramatic Arts. Numerous TV commercials, including music for Dr. Pepper. On Bdwy. in Hamlet, Da, Poor Little Lambs.
PICTURES: Midnight Madness; An American Werewolf in London; Separate Ways; Hog Dog—The Movie; Not for Publication, The Boy in Blue, Separate Vacations, Kidnapped, Ti Presento un' Amica. Quite By Chance, The Sleeping Car.
TELEVISION: Series: Making It; I, Desire; At Ease; Getting Physical; My Sister Sam; Movies: Goddess of Love. Guest: Twilight Zone, Murder She Wrote.

NAUGHTON, JAMES: Actor. b. Middletown, CT, Dec. 6, 1945. Brother of actor David Naughton. e. Brown U., A.B., 1967; Yale U., M.F.A., drama, 1970.
THEATER: I Love My Wife (Bdwy debut, 1977), Long Day's Journey Into Night (Theatre World, Drama Desk and New York Critics Circle Award, 1971), Whose Life Is It, Anyway?, Who's Afraid of Virginia Woolf? (Long Wharf), The Glass Menagerie (Long Wharf).
PICTURES: The Paper Chase (debut, 1972), Second Wind, A Stranger is Watching, Cat's Eye, The Glass Menagerie, The Good Mother.
TELEVISION: Look Homeward, Angel (1972); Series: Faraday and Company (1973–74); Planet of the Apes, Making the Grade; Trauma Center; Raising Miranda. Movies: F. Scott Fitzgerald and the Last of the Belles; The Last 36 Hours of Dr. Durant; The Bunker; My Body, My Child; Parole; The Last of the Great Survivors; Between Darkness and the Dawn; Sin of Innocence.

NEAL, PATRICIA: Actress. b. Packard, KY, Jan. 20, 1926. e. Northwestern U. Doctor's asst., cashier, hostess, model, jewelry store clerk. In summer stock; Broadway debut in Another Part of the Forest, 1947, (winning the Tony, Donaldson & Drama Critic Awards), also in Children's Hour. Autobiography: As I Am (with Richard DeNeut, 1988).

TELEVISION: The Bastard, The Homecoming, All Quiet on the Western Front (Emmy Award), Tail Gunner Joe, Love Leads the Way, Eric, Carolyn?

PICTURES: John Loves Mary (debut 1948), The Fountainhead, Hasty Heart, Bright Leaf, Three Secrets, Breaking Point, Raton Pass, Operation Pacific, Day the Earth Stood Still, Weekend With Father, Diplomatic Courier, Washington Story, Something for the Birds, Face in the Crowd, Hud (Academy Award, 1963), Psych 59, In Harms Way, The Subject Was Roses (Acad. Award nom.), The Night Digger, Baxter!, Happy Mother's Day . . . Love, George, The Passage, Ghost Story, An Unremarkable Life.

NEAME, RONALD: Cinematographer, Producer, Director. b. Hendon, Eng. April 23, 1911. e. U. Coll. Sch., London. p. Elwin Neame, London photog., & Ivy Close, m.p. actress. Entered m.p. ind. 1928; asst. cameraman on first full-length Brit. sound Blackmail, dir. by Alfred Hitchcock, 1929; became chief cameraman & lighting expert, 1934; in 1945 joint assoc. prod., Noel Coward Prods.

PICTURES: Cinematographer: Girls Will Be Boys (co-c), Happy (co-c), Elizabeth of England, Honours Easy (co-c), Invitation to the Waltz (co-c), Joy Ride, Music Hath Charms, The Crimes of Stephen Hawke, The Improper Dutchess, A Star Fell From Heaven, Against the Tide, Brief Ecstasy, Feather Your Nest, Keep Fit, Weekend Millionaire, Gaunt Stranger, The Phantom Strikes, The Crime of Peter Frame, Dangerous Secrets, I See Ice (co-c), Penny Paradise, Who Goes Next? Cheers Boys Cheer, Sweeney Todd: The Demon Barber of Fleet Street, Let's Be Famous, Trouble Brewing, The Ware Case, It's In the Air (co-c), Let George Do It, Return to Yesterday, Saloon Bar, Four Just Men, Major Barbara, A Yank in the R.A.F. (Brit. flying sequence), One of Our Aircraft is Missing, In Which We Serve, This Happy Breed, Blithe Spirit, Brief Encounter, Great Expectations (also co-s.p.), Oliver Twist (also co-s.p.), A Young Man's Fancy, Passionate Friends, Take My Life.

PICTURES: Director: Golden Salamander (also co-s.p.), Magic Box, The Card (The Promoter), Million Pound Note (Man With a Million), Man Who Never Was, Seventh Sin, Windom's Way, A Man Could Get Killed, Prudence and the Pill (co-dir.), The Horse's Mouth, Tunes of Glory, Escape from Zahrain, I Could Go on Singing, The Chalk Garden, Mister Moses, Gambit, The Prime of Miss Jean Brodie, Scrooge, The Poseidon Adventure, The Odessa File, Meteor, Hopscotch, First Monday in October, Foreign Body, The Magic Balloon.

NEEDHAM, HAL: Director, Writer. b. Memphis, TN, March 6, 1931. e. Student public schools. Served with Paratroopers U.S. Army 1951–54. Founder Stunts Unlimited, Los Angeles, 1956; stuntman Stunts Unltd. 1956–68; dir. and stunt coordinator second unit, 1968–86; dir., writer, 1976–present. Chmn. of bd., Camera Platforms International, Inc. 1986. Owner Budweiser Rocket Car (fastest car in the world). Member Screen Actors Guild, AFTRA.

PICTURES: Dir. and writer: Smokey and the Bandit (dir. debut), Hooper, The Villain, Smokey and the Bandit II, The Cannonball Run, Megaforce, Stroker Ace, Cannonball Run II, Rad, Body Slam, S.E.A.L.S.

TELEVISION: Hal Needham's Wild World of Stunts (syndicated series he wrote, directed and starred in): Directed Death Car on the Freeway (movie); Stunts Unlimited (pilot).

NEESON, LIAM: Actor. b. Ballymena, Northern Ireland, 1952. Was driving a fork lift truck for a brewery when he joined the Lyric Player's Theatre in Belfast. Made prof. debut in The Risen (1976) and stayed with rep. co. 2 years. Moved to Dublin as freelance actor before joining the Abbey Theatre. Stage includes The Informer (Dublin Theatre Fest.), Translations (National Theatre, London). Film debut: Excalibur (1981).

PICTURES: Krull, The Bounty, Lamb, The Innocent, Duet For One, The Mission, A Prayer for the Dying, Suspect, Satisfaction, The Dead Pool, The Good Mother, High Spirits, The Big Man, Dark Man, Next of Kin, The Big Man.

TELEVISION: Merlin and the Sword, Across the Water (BBC), Ellis Island, A Woman of Substance, Sweet As You Are.

NEFF, HILDEGARDE: Actress, author. r.n. Hildegard Knef. b. Ulm, Germany, Dec. 28, 1925. e. Art Acad., Berlin. Film cartoonist for UFA, Berlin; on Berlin stage after war; appeared in German films: Murderers Are Among Us, Between Yesterday and Tomorrow, Film Without Title, The Sinner. On B'way in: Silk Stockings. U.S. m.p. debut in Decision Before Dawn. Author of best-selling autobiography, The Gift Horse, 1971.

PICTURES: Diplomatic Courier, Night Without Sleep, Snows of Kilimanjaro, Holiday for Henrietta, Man Between, Svengali, The Girl From Hamburg, Subway in the Sky, And So to Bed, Mozambique, The Lost Continent, Witchery.

NEGULESCO, JEAN: Director. b. Craiova, Rumania , Feb. 29, 1900. e. Liceul Carol U., Rumania. Stage dir., artist, painter, Came to U.S. in 1927. Memoirs: Things I Did and Things I Think I Did (1983).

PICTURES: The Mask of Dimitrios, The Conspirators, Nobody Lives Forever, Three Strangers, Humoresque, Deep Valley, Johnny Belinda, Road House, Forbidden Street, Three Came Home, Under My Skin, Mudlark, Take Care of My Little Girl, The Full House, Phone Call From a Stranger, Lydia Bailey, Lure of the Wilderness, Titanic, Scandal at Scourie, How to Marry a Millionaire, The Rains of Ranchipur, Woman's World, Three Coins in the Fountain, Daddy Long Legs, Boy on a Dolphin, The Gift of Love, A Certain Smile, Count Your Blessings, The Best of Everything, Jessica, The Pleasure Seekers, Hello, Goodbye.

NEILL, SAM: Actor. b. New Zealand, 1948. e. U. of Canterbury. In repertory before joining N.Z. National Film Unit, acting and directing documentaries and shorts.

PICTURES: Landfall, Ashes, Sleeping Dogs, The Journalist, My Brilliant Career, Just Out of Reach, Attack Force Z, The Final Conflict, Possession, Enigma, The Country Girls, Robbery Under Arms, Plenty, For Love Alone, The Good Wife, A Cry in the Dark, Dead Calm, The French Revolution, The Hunt for Red October.

TELEVISION: The Sullivans, Young Ramsay, Lucinda Brayford, Mini-series: Kane and Abel, Reilly Ace of Spies, Amerika. Movies: From a Far Country, Pope John Paul II, Ivanhoe, The Blood of Others, Arthur Hailey's Strong Medicine, Leap of Faith.

NELLIGAN, KATE: Actress. b. London, England, March 16, 1951. On stage in Barefoot in the Park, A Streetcar Named Desire, Playboy of the Western World, Private Lives, Plenty, Serious Money, Spoils of War.

PICTURES: The Romantic Englishwoman, Dracula, Mr. Patman, Eye of the Needle, Without a Trace, The Mystery of Henry Moore, Eleni, White Room.

TELEVISION: The Onedin Line, The Lady of the Camelias, Therese Raquin, Count of Monte Cristo, Victims, Kojak: The Price of Justice, Love and Hate: The Story of Colin and Joann Thatcher.

NELSON, BARRY: Actor. r.n. Robert Neilson. b. Oakland, CA, 1923. e. U. of California. London stage: No Time for Sergeants, 1957.

PICTURES: A Guy Named Joe, Winged Victory, Man with My Face, First Traveling Saleslady, Mary, Mary, The Borgia Stick, Airport, Pete 'n Tillie, The Shining.

BROADWAY: Light Up the Sky, Rat Race, Moon Is Blue, Mary, Mary, Cactus Flower, Everything in the Garden, Seascape, The Norman Conquests, The Act, 42nd Street.

TELEVISION: series: The Hunter, My Favorite Husband, Washington: Behind Closed Doors, Climb an Angry Mountain, Seven In Darkness, Murder She Wrote.

NELSON, CRAIG T.: Actor. b. Spokane, WA, April 4, 1946. Began career as writer/performer on Lohman and Barkley Show in Los Angeles. Teamed with Barry Levinson as a comedy writer. Wrote for Tim Conway Show, Alan King TV special; guest appearances on talk shows and Mary Tyler Moore Show. Produced series of 52 half-hour films on American artists, American Still. Returned to L.A. in 1978 and acting career. Film debut in And Justice for All, 1979.

PICTURES: The Formula, Where the Buffalo Roam, Private Benjamin, Poltergeist, The Osterman Weekend, Silkwood, All the Right Moves, The Killing Fields, Poltergeist II, Red Riding Hood, Rachel River, Action Jackson, Me and Him, Troup Beverly Hills, Turner & Hooch.

TELEVISION: Wonder Woman, Charlie's Angels, Series: Coach. Movies: How the West Was Won, Diary of a Teenage Hitchhiker, Alex: The Life of a Child, The Ted Kennedy Jr. Story, Call to Glory, Murderers Among Us: The Simon Wiesenthal Story, Desperados: the "Kiki" Camarera Story.

NELSON, DAVID: Actor. b. New York, NY, Oct. 24, 1936. e. Hollywood H.S., U. of Southern California. Son of Ozzie Nelson, Harriet Hilliard, brother of late Rick Nelson.

PICTURES: Here Comes the Nelsons, Peyton Place, The Remarkable Mr. Pennypacker, Day of the Outlaw, The Big Circus, "30," The Big Show, No Drums, No Bugles, The Wheel, The Sinners. Director: A Rare Breed, The Last Plane Out.

TELEVISION: Adventures of Ozzie and Harriet; dir.: Easy To Be Free (special), OK Crackerby series.

NELSON, GENE: Dancer, actor, director, choreographer. r.n. Gene Berg. b. Seattle, WA, March 24, 1920. e. Santa Monica, CA H.S. Began dancing and ice skating in school; joined Sonja Henie Hollywood Ice Revue, featured in It Happens on Ice, Center Theatre, NY; played in This Is the Army, W.W.II; after discharge. To Hollywood for I Wonder Who's Kissing Her Now; joined Hollywood group prod. stage musical, Lend an Ear; to Warner for Daughter of Rosie O'Grady (1950).

PICTURES: Apartment For Peggy, Gentlemen's Agreement, Tea for Two, Starlift, West Point Story, Lullaby of Broadway, Painting the Clouds With Sunshine, She's Working Her Way Through College, She's Back on Broadway, Three Sailors and a Girl, Crime Wave, So This Is Paris, Oklahoma, The Way Out, Atomic Man, 20,000 Eyes, The Purple Hills, Thunder Island. Director: The Hand of Death, Hootenany

Hoot, The Cool Ones (also s.p.), Your Cheatin' Heart, Kissin' Cousins, Harum Scarum.
TELEVISION: Director: Mod Squad, I Dream of Jeannie, FBI, 12 O'Clock High, Hawaii Five-O, Farmer's Daughter, Donna Reed Show, Burke's Law, Felony Squad, Laredo, The Rifleman, The Wackiest Ship, Iron Horse, FBI, The Rookies, Quincy, Operation Petticoat. Movies: Wake Me When the War is Over, The Letters.
BROADWAY: Follies, 1971; Music, Music, 1974, Good News.

NELSON, HARRIET: Singer, actress. r.n. Harriet Hilliard. b. Des Moines, IA, July 18, 1914, e. H.S., Kansas City. m. Ozzie Nelson. Appeared in dramatic & musical roles in shows; singer with Ozzie Nelson band; on radio shows: Believe It or Not, Seeing Stars, Red Skelton, Adventures of Ozzie & Harriet. Appeared in film: Here Come the Nelsons.
TELEVISION: Adventures of Ozzie and Harriet, (1952–66).
STAGE: Marriage-Go-Round; rec.: Ozzie and Harriet.
PLAYS: Impossible Years, State Fair.

NELSON, JUDD: Actor. b. Portland, ME, 1959. e. Haverford/Bryn Mawr Coll. Studied acting at Stella Adler Conservatory. Theatrical m.p. debut in Fandango, 1984.
PICTURES: Fandango, Making the Grade, The Breakfast Club, St. Elmo's Fire, Blue City, From the Hip, The Dark Backward, Relentless.
TELEVISION: Moonlighting, Billionaire Boys Club.

NELSON, LORI: Actress. r.n. Dixie Kay Nelson; b. Santa Fe, NM, Aug. 15, 1933. e. H.S., L.A. Child actress; photographer's model; film debut in Ma and Pa Kettle at the Fair (1952).
PICTURES: Bend of the River, Francis Goes to West Point, All I Desire, All-American, Walking My Baby Back Home, Tumbleweed, Underwater, Destry, Revenge of the Creature, I Died a Thousand Times, Sincerely Yours, Mohawk, Day the World Ended, Pardners, Hot Rod Girl, Ma and Pa Kettle at Waikiki, Gambling Man, Untamed Youth.
TELEVISION: How to Marry a Millionaire (series), Wagon Train, Laramie, Bachelor Father, The Texan, Wanted Dead or Alive, Sam Spade, G.E. Theatre, Riverboat, Sugarfoot, The Young and the Restless, etc.

NELSON, WILLIE: Composer, Singer, Actor. b. Abbott, TX, April 30, 1933. Worked as salesman, announcer, host of country music shows on local Texas stations; bass player with Ray Price's band. Started writing songs in the 60s; performing in the 70s. Film debut in Electric Horseman, 1979.
PICTURES: Honeysuckle Rose, Thief, Barbarosa, Songwriter, Red-Headed Stranger (also prod.), Baja Oklahoma, Walking After Midnight.
TELEVISION: Movies: The Last Days of Frank and Jesse James, Stagecoach, Coming Out of the Ice, Once Upon a Texas Train, Willie Nelson, Texas Style (star, prod.), Where That Hell's the Gold!!?

NERO, FRANCO: Actor. r.n. Franceso Sparanero. b. Parma, Italy, 1941.
PICTURES: The Bible—The Beginning (debut, 1966), Django, Camelot, The Hired Killer, The Wild, Wild Planet, The Brute and the Beast, The Day of the Owl, Sardinia, Mafia, Vendetta, Companeros, Detective Belli, The Mercenary, A Quiet Place in the Country, Tristana, The Virgin and the Gypsy, Battle of the Neretva, Confessions of a Police Captain, The Vacation, Pope Joan, Deaf Smith and Johnny Ears, The Last Days of Mussolini, Force Ten From Navarone, The Roses of the Danzig, Mimi, The Man With Bogart's Face, Enter the Ninja, Mexico in Flames, Querelle, Kamikaze '89, The Salamander, Wagner, Victory March, The Day of the Cobra, Ten Days That Shook the World, Der Falke, The Repenter, The Forester's Sons, Garibaldi, the General; The Girl, Sweet Country.
TELEVISION: Mini-series: The Last Days of Pompeii. Movies: The Legend of Valentino, 21 Hours at Munich, The Pirate.

NETTER, DOUGLAS: Executive, Producer. b. Seattle, WA, 1955–57, gen. mgr. Todd A.O.; 1958–60, Sam Goldwyn Productions; 1961–67, Formed own co. representing producers; 1968–69, Jalem Productions; 1969–75, exec. v.p. MGM; 1976, prod., Mr. Ricco. 1977, American co-prod., The Wild Geese.
TELEVISION: prod., Louis L'Amour's The Sacketts, (mini-series). exec. prod., The Buffalo Soldiers (pilot); prod., Wild Times, (mini-series); exec. prod. Roughnecks, (mini-series); exec. prod. Cherokee Trail; exec. prod., Five Mile Creek (Australian based TV series for Disney Channel); prod., Captain Power and the Soldiers of the Future (pilot); exec. prod., Captain Power and the Soldiers of the Future (syn. series); exec. prod., Stealth F22 (film for Lockheed Aeronautical Systems); exec. prod.: Babylon 5 (syn. series).

NETTLETON, LOIS: Actress. b. Oak Park, IL. e. Studied at Goodman Theatre, Chicago and Actors Studio. Replaced Kim Hunter in Darkness at Noon on Broadway. Emmy Award: Performer Best Daytime Drama Spec., The American Woman: Portraits in Courage (1977). Also Emmy: Religious Program, Insight (1983).
PLAYS: Cat on a Hot Tin Roof, Silent Night, Lonely Night, God and Kate Murphy, The Wayward Stork, The Rainmaker, A Streetcar Named Desire.
PICTURES: Period of Adjustment, Come Fly with Me, Mail Order Bride, Valley of Mystery, Bamboo Saucer, The Good Guys and the Bad Guys, Dirty Dingus Magee, The Sidelong Glances of a Pigeon Kicker, The Honkers, Echoes of a Summer, Butterfly, Deadly Blessing, The Best Little Whorehouse in Texas.
TELEVISION: Brass, No Hiding Place, Medical Center, Barnaby Jones, Alfred Hitchcock, Series: Accidental Family (1967–68), All That Glitters, In the Heat of the Night. Movies: The Woman in White, The Light That Failed, Centennial, Any Second Now, Washington: Behind Closed Doors, Women in Chains, You Can't Take It With You (series).

NEWBERY, CHARLES BRUCE: Executive. b. Melbourne, Australia. e. All Saints Grammar Sch., Melbourne; Melbourne U. Entered m.p. ind. with Hoyt's Theatres, Ltd., Melbourne, 1929; publ. mgr., Fox Studios, Eng., 1934; controller, Fox Newsreel Theatres, 1935; man. dir., Fox Films, India, 1937; Supvr., India, China, Malaya, Fox Films, 1940; Film advisor, Government of India, 1941; estab. film studios & Newsreel for Government of India. suprv. Far East & Australia Republic, 1945; supvr. Middle, Near & Far East. Republic, 1947; supvr. Eng. & Europe, Republic, 1948; estab. Republic Productions Great Britain, 1952; v.p. bd. mem. dir. of sales, Republic, U.S.A., 1953; pres., Charles Newbery Assoc., Newbery-Warden Associates, London, 1960; mgr. dir., Santor Film Prods., Americon Prods, Inc., 1964; sr. v.p., bd. mem., administration, In-Flight Motion Pictures Inc., v.p., Intransit Motion Pictures, Inc., 1965. Sr. v.p. sales and marketing 1967, pres. & CEO, May 1973; vice chmn. bd., Inflight, June, 1979; Dir. of Mktg., Life Services Co., of America June, 1979 chmn. bd., Inflight and sls.—Europe, East and Africa, 1980. Bd. mem./consultant to Inflight, 1985.
PICTURES: Deadlier Than the Male, Catch Me if You Can, Kiss Her Goodbye.

NEWBROOK, PETER: Producer, Director of photography. Entered m.p. ind. Warner Bros. Studios, Teddington. Chmn. Titan Int'l. Productions, Ltd. Esquire Records Ltd. & Esquire Music Co. Past Pres., British Society of Cinematographers.
PICTURES: After working on such pictures as The Sound Barrier, The Captain's Paradise, Hobson's Choice, Summer Madness, The Deep Blue Sea, Anastasia, The Bridge on the River Kwai; became dir. photog.: Lawrence of Arabia (2nd unit), 1961; In The Cool of the Day, That Kind of Girl, 1962; The Yellow Teddybears, Saturday Night Out, The Black Torment, Prod. and photog; Gonks Go Beat, prod. and photog; The Sandwich Man, Press For Time, Corruption, The Smashing Bird I Used to Know, Bloodsuckers, She'll Follow You Anywhere, Crucible of Terror, The Asphyx, The Wonderful World of Greece, Bosom Friends, Where's Your Sense of Humor?, Last of the Midnight Gardeners.
TELEVISION: Tales of the Unexpected, Coronation Street, Emmerdale Farm.

NEWCOM, JAMES E.: Associate producer. b. Indianapolis, IN, Aug. 29, 1907. e. U. of California. Reader, MGM, 1926, then in stocks and bonds with E. F. Hutton; then actor and film editing dept., MGM, 1930; film ed. 1933; asst. prod., 1952. Now retired.
PICTURES: Gone With the Wind, Rebecca, Since You Went Away, Annie Get Your Gun, Trial, Somebody Up There Likes Me, Wings of Eagles, Until They Sail, Farewell to Arms, The Inn of the Sixth Happiness; Revue Television; Paramount Studios. Nine Hours to Rama, The Impossible Years, editor: Tora Tora Tora.

NEWELL, MIKE: Director. b. 1942.
PICTURES: The Awakening, Bad Blood, Dance With a Stranger, Amazing Grace and Chuck, Soursweet.
TELEVISION: Series: Budgie, Eleventh Hour. Movies: Big Soft Nelly, Mrs. House, The Man in the Iron Mask, The Gift of Friendship, Blood Feud.

NEWHART, BOB: Actor, Comedian. b. Chicago, IL, Sept. 5, 1929. e. Loyola U. In Army 2 yrs., then law school; left to become copywriter and accountant. Acted with theatrical stock co. in Oak Park; hired for TV man-in-street show in Chicago. Recorded comedy album for Warner Bros. Record Co., The Button Down Mind of Bob Newhart, which was big hit. Followed by two more successful albums. Did series of nightclub engagements and then acquired own TV variety series in 1961. Frequently appears in Las Vegas and headlines college concerts. Has guested on most major TV variety and comedy series.
PICTURES: Cool Millions, Catch 22, Cold Turkey, First Family.
TELEVISION: The Bob Newhart Show (series), Thursday's Game (movie), Newhart (series).

NEWLAND, JOHN: Director, Actor. b. Cincinnati, OH, Nov. 23, 1917. Began as a singer-dancer in vaudeville and on Bdwy; many TV appearances, especially as host of One Step Beyond. Actor, dir., Robert Montgomery Show, My Lover, My Son. Turned to full-time dir. and prod. in the 1960's.
PICTURES: Bulldog Drummond, That Night, The Violators, The Spy With My Face, Hush-a-Bye Murder, Purgatory.
TELEVISION: Producer: A Sensitive, Passionate Man; Overboard; Angel City; The Five of Me; Timestalker; The Next Step Beyond, The Suicide's Wife, Arch of Triumph, Too Good to be True.

NEWLEY, ANTHONY: Actor, Writer, Composer, Singer. b. Hackney, Eng., Sept. 24, 1931.
PICTURES: Oliver Twist, Cockleshell Heroes, Battle of the River Plate, Port Afrique, Fire Down Below, Good Companions, X the Unknown, High Flight, No Time to Die, The Man Inside, The Bandit, The Lady Is a Square, Idle on Parade, Killers of Kilimanjaro, Let's Get Married, Jazz Boat, In the Nick, The Small World of Sammy Lee, Dr. Dolittle; Can Hieronymus Merkin Ever Forget Mercy Humppee and Find True Happiness?, Sweet November, Quilp (star, music) Willie Wonka and the Chocolate Factory (score); Summer Tree (dir.), Boris and Natasha.
TELEVISION: Sammy, Sunday Night Palladium, The Strange World of Gurney Slade (series), Saturday Spectaculars, The Johnny Darling Show, Hollywood Squares, Merv Griffin Show, The Tonight Show, Anthony Newley Special (London), Blade in Hong Kong (movie), Limited Partners, Fame, Magnum P.I., Alfred Hitchcock Theatre, Murder She Wrote, Alice in Wonderland, Simon & Simon.
PLAYS: West End stage; Stop The World—I Want to Get Off. N.Y. stage: Roar of the Greasepaint (wrote, composed with Leslie Bricusse), Good Old Bad Old Days, Chaplin.
AWARDS: Male Singer of the Year Award, Las Vegas, 1972; Elected to Songwriters Hall of Fame, 1989. Gold records for composing Goldfinger, Candy Man, What Kind of Fool Am I.

NEWMAN, ALFRED S.: Executive. b. Brooklyn, NY, Nov. 16, 1940. e. NYU. Public relations work for Equitable Life Insurance, Trans World Airlines prior to joining Columbia Pictures in 1968 as writer in publicity dept.; named New York publicity mgr., 1970; national publicity mgr., 1972; joined MGM as East adv't-pub. dir., 1972; named director of adv't, pub. and promotion, 1974; named v.p., worldwide adv., pub., promo., 1978; v.p., pub./promo., MGM/UA, 1981. With 20th Century-Fox as v.p. adv./pub./promo. for TV & corporate, 1984–85; joined Rogers & Cowan as sr. v.p. & head of corporate entertainment, 1985; named exec. v.p., 1987; Oct. 1988 named pres. and CEO. Sterling Entertainment Co. and exec. v.p. worldwide marketing of parent co. MCEG. Left in 1989.

NEWMAN, DAVID: Writer. b. New York, NY, Feb. 4, 1937. e. U. of Michigan, M.S., 1959. Was writer-editor at Esquire Magazine where he met Robert Benton, an art director, and formed writing partnership. All early credits co-written with Benton; later ones with Leslie Newman and others.
PICTURES: Bonnie and Clyde, There Was a Crooked Man, Floreana, What's Up, Doc?, Money's Tight, Bad Company, The Crazy American Girl, Superman (co-s.p.), Superman II (co-s.p.), Jinxed (co-s.p.), Superman III (co-s.p.), Sheena (co-s.p.), Still of the Night, Santa Claus—The Movie, Moonwalker.
STAGE: It's a Bird . . . It's a Plane . . . It's Superman (libretto), Oh! Calcutta (one sketch).

NEWMAN, EDWIN: News Correspondent. b. New York, NY, Jan. 25, 1919. Joined NBC News in 1952, based in N.Y. since 1961. Reports news on NBC-TV and often assigned to anchor instant specials. Has been substitute host on Today, appeared on Meet the Press and has reported NBC News documentaries. Host of interview series, Speaking Freely, on WNBC-TV, N.Y.; Television (PBS series, host).

NEWMAN, JOSEPH M.: Producer, Director, Writer. b. Logan, UT, Aug. 7, 1909. Started as office boy MGM, 1925; jobs in production dept. to 1931; asst. to George Hill, Ernst Lubitsch, etc., 1931–37; asstd. in organization of MGM British studios 1937; dir. short subjects 1938; dir. Crime Does Not Pay series 1938–42; Major in U.S. Army Signal Corps 1942–46; dir. 32 Army Pictorial Service Pictures. Member: AMPAS, SDG Masons.
PICTURES: Northwest Rangers, Abandoned, Jungle Patrol, Great Dan Pitch, 711 Ocean Drive, Lucky Nick Cain, Guy Who Came Back, Love Nest, Red Skies of Montana, Outcasts of Poker Flat, Pony Soldier, Dangerous Crossing, Human Jungle, Kiss of Fire, This Island Earth, Flight to Hong Kong, Fort Massacre, Big Circus, Tarzan The Ape Man, King of the Roaring Twenties, Twenty Plus Two, The George Raft Story, Thunder of Drums.

NEWMAN, MARTIN H.: Executive. b. Brooklyn, NY, Nov. 16, 1913; e. NYU, 1934. Certified Public Accountant (N.Y.); Century Theatres, 1936–1974, exec. v.p. 1966–1974; National Association of Theatre Owners, 1975–1977; exec. dir., Will Rogers Memorial Fund, 1977–present.

NEWMAN, NANETTE: Actress, Writer. b. Northampton, Eng., 1934. m. to prod.-dir.-writer Bryan Forbes. Ent. films in 1946 and TV in 1951. Author: God Bless Love, That Dog, Reflections, The Root Children, Amy Rainbow, Pigalev, Archie, Christmas Cookbook, Summer Cookbook, Small Beginnings, Bad Baby, Entertaining with Nanette Newman and Her Daughters, Charlie the Noisy Caterpillar, Sharing.
TELEVISION: The Glorious Days, The Wedding Veil, Broken Honeymoon, At Home, Trial by Candlelight, Diary of Samuel Pepys, Faces in the Dark, Balzac (BBC), Fun Food Factory, TV series, Stay with Me Till Morning, Let There Be Love (series), West Country Tales, Jessie, Late Expectations.
FILMS: The Personal Affair, The League of Gentlemen, The Rebel, Twice Around the Daffodils, The L-Shaped Room, Wrong Arm of the Law, Of Human Bondage, Seance on a Wet Afternoon, The Wrong Box, The Whisperers, Deadfall, The Madwoman of Chaillot, The Raging Moon, (U.S. title: Long Ago Tomorrow), The Stepford Wives, It's A 2′2″ Above the Ground World (The Love Ban), Man at the Top, International Velvet, The Endless Game.

NEWMAN, PAUL: Actor, Director. b. Cleveland, OH, Jan. 26, 1925. m. actress Joanne Woodward. e. Kenyon Coll., Yale Sch. of Drama, The Actors Studio. Summer stock; on Broadway in Picnic, The Desperate Hours, Sweet Bird of Youth, Baby Want a Kiss. Formed First Artists Prod. Co. Ltd. 1969 with Sidney Poitier, Steve McQueen and Barbra Streisand.
TELEVISION: Philco, U.S. Steel, Playhouse 90. Dir.: The Shadow Box.
PICTURES: The Silver Chalice, The Rack, Somebody Up There Likes Me, Until They Sail, The Helen Morgan Story, The Long, Hot Summer, Cat on a Hot Tin Roof, The Left-Handed Gun, Rally Around the Flag Boys, The Young Philadelphians, Exodus, The Hustler, Paris Blues, Sweet Bird of Youth, Adventures of a Young Man, Hud, A New Kind of Love, The Prize, The Outrage, What a Way to Go, Lady L., Torn Curtain, Harper, Hombre, Cool Hand Luke, The Secret War of Harry Frigg, Winning, Butch Cassidy and the Sundance Kid. Rachel, Rachel (dir.), Sometimes A Great Notion (dir., actor), Pocket Money, Life & Times of Judge Roy Bean, The Effect of Gamma Rays (dir.), The Mackintosh Man, The Sting, The Towering Inferno, The Drowning Pool, Buffalo Bill and the Indians, Slap Shot, Quintet, When Time Ran Out, Fort Apache, The Bronx, Absence of Malice, The Verdict, Harry and Son (co-s.p., actor, dir., co-prod.), The Color of Money (Acad. Award), The Glass Menagerie (dir. only), Fat Man & Little Boy, Mr. and Mrs. Bridge.

NEWMAN, SYDNEY.: O. C. (F.R.S.A.), Chief Creative Consultant for Canadian Film Development Corp. b. Toronto, Canada. Studied painting, drawing, commercial art at Central Techn. Sch. To Hollywood in 1938. Joined National Film Board of Canada under John Grierson. Prod. over 300 shorts. Later became exec. prod. all Canadian government cinema films, 1947–52; Canadian Broadcasting Corp., 1952, as dir. outside broadcasts, features and documentaries. Later became drama sup. and prod. Canadian Television Theatre. Joined ABC-TV in England, 1958. as sup. of drama and prod. of Armchair Theatre: Head of Drama Group, TV, BBC, 1963. Commissioned and prod. first TV plays by Arthur Hailey, Harold Pinter, Alun Owen, Angus Wilson, Peter Lake. Fellow Society of Film & TV Arts, 1968; Prod. Associated British Pictures. SFTA award 1968; Zeta award, Writers Guild, Gt. Btn., 1970. 1970: Special advisor, ch. dir., Broadcast Programmes branch, Canadian Radio & TV Commission, Ottawa. Aug., 1970: Appt. Canadian Govt. Film Commissioner and chmn., National Film Board of Canada; Trustee, National Arts Centre, Ottawa; bd. mem., Canadian Broadcasting Corporation, Canadian Film Development Corp., Canadian Picture Pioneers Special Award. Special Advisor on Film to the Secretary of State for Canada, 1975–77; pres., Sydney Newman Enterprises. 1981: Made Officer of the Order of Canada.

NEWMAN, WALTER BROWN: Writer. b. 1920.
PICTURES: Ace in the Hole (co-s.p.), Underwater, The Man with the Golden Arm (co-s.p.), The True Story of Jesse James, Crime and Punishment, USA, The Interns (co-s.p.), Cat Ballou (co-s.p.), Bloodbrothers, The Champ.

NEWTON-JOHN, OLIVIA: Actress, Singer. b. Cambridge, Eng. Sept. 26, 1948. m. actor Matt Lattanzi. Brought up in Melbourne, Australia, where won first talent contest at 15, with prize trip to England. Stayed there 2 yrs. performing as part of duo with Australian girl singer, Pat Carroll (Farrar), in cabarets and on TV. Started recording; several hit records. Became a regular guest on TV series, It's Cliff Richard. Gained world-wide prominence as singer, winning several Grammys and other music awards. 1983 opened Koala Blue, U.S. Clothing Stores featuring Australian style clothes and goods.
PICTURES: Grease, Xanadu, Two of a Kind.
TELEVISION: Olivia Newton-John—Let's Get Physical, Standing Room Only—Olivia Newton-John, Olivia Newton-John in Australia.

NEY, RICHARD: Actor, Writer, Producer, Financier. b. New York, NY, 1917. e. Columbia U., B.A. Acted in RCA TV demonstration, New York World's Fair; on stage in Life with Father. On screen 1942 in Mrs. Miniver. In armed services, W.W.II. Many TV shows. Financial advisor consultant, Richard Ney and Associates; financial advisor, lecturer; author, The Wall Street Jungle.
PICTURES: War Against Mrs. Hadley, Late George Apley, Ivy, Joan of Arc, The Fan, Secret of St. Ives, Lovable Cheat, Babes in Bagdad, Miss Italia, Sergeant and The Spy, The Premature Burial.

NIBLEY, SLOAN: Writer. b. Oregon; e. U. of Utah, UCLA. m. Linda Stirling, actress. Three yrs. U.S. Navy; employed as writer at major studios; contributor to mags.; wrote many western pictures incl.: Carson City, Springfield Rifle; prod., and writer many TV shows on film and live TV for Ralph Edwards.

NICHOLS, MIKE: Actor, Director. b. Berlin, Germany, Nov. 6, 1931. m. news correspondent Diane Sawyer. e. U. of Chicago. Compass Players, teamed with Elaine May; night clubs.
STAGE: Barefoot in the Park (Tony Award), The Knack, Luv (Tony Award), The Odd Couple, The Apple Tree, The Little Foxes, Plaza Suite (Tony Award), Uncle Vanya, The Prisoner of 2nd Avenue (Tony Award), Streamers, Comedians, The Gin Game, Drinks Before Dinner. Annie (prod. only), The Real Thing (Tony Award), Hurlyburly, Social Security.
PICTURES: Who's Afraid of Virginia Woolf, The Graduate (Acad. Award), Catch 22, Carnal Knowledge, The Day of the Dolphin, The Fortune, Gilda Live, Silkwood (also co-prod.), Heartburn, Biloxi Blues, Working Girl, Postcards From the Edge.
TELEVISION: Broadway, An Evening with Mike Nichols and Elaine May. Exec. prod.: Family, The Thorns.

NICHOLSON, JACK: Producer, Director, Actor, Writer. b. Neptune, NJ, April 22, 1936. Began career in cartoon department of MGM. Made acting debut in Hollywood stage production of Tea and Sympathy. Made directing debut with Drive, He Said (1971).
PICTURES: *Producer:* Ride the Whirlwind, The Shooting, Head, Drive, He Said. *Actor:* The Shooting, Psych Out, Hell's Angels on Wheels, Little Shop of Horrors, The Raven, Ride the Whirlwind, Flight to Fury, Ensign Pulver, Too Young To Live, Studs Lonigan, Cry Baby Killer, Easy Rider, Five Easy Pieces, Carnal Knowledge, A Safe Place, (Writing credits) The Trip, Head, Flight to Fury, Ride the Whirlwind, Drive, He Said, The Last Detail, 1973, Chinatown, Tommy, The Passenger, The Fortune, One Flew Over the Cuckoo's Nest (Acad. Award), The Missouri Breaks, The Last Tycoon, Goin' South (also dir.), The Shining, The Postman Always Rings Twice, The Border, Reds, Terms of Endearment (Acad. Award, supp. actor), Prizzi's Honor, Heartburn, The Witches of Eastwick, Broadcast News, Ironweed, Batman, The Two Jakes (also dir.).

NICKELL, PAUL: Director. e. Morehead, KY, State Teachers Coll., U. of North Carolina. English instructor, North Carolina State Coll.; then cameraman, asst. dir., dir. WPTZ, Philadelphia; dir. CBS-TV 1948.
TELEVISION: Studio One, Best of Broadway, Climax, Playhouse 90.

NICKSAY, DAVID: Executive., Producer. e. Mass., Hampshire Coll. Entered industry thru Directors Guild of America's training program, apprenticing on Rich Man Poor Man and rising to second asst. dir. on Oh, God. Producer of many TV projects and theatrical films with Edgar Scherick prod. co. 1986, joined Paramount Pictures as v.p., prod., for M.P. Group. Assoc. prod., prod. mgr.: I'm Dancing as Fast as I Can. Became sr. v.p., prod. Paramount, M.P. Group, 1987; resigned 1989 to become pres. and head of prod. at Morgan Creek Prods. Mem. of bd.
PICTURES: Prod.: Mrs. Soffel, Lucas Sprv. prod.: Big Top Pee-Wee, Summer School, Coming to America, The Untouchables, Scrooged, Star Trek V: The Final Frontier, Major League, Were No Angels, Harlem Nights, The Two Jakes.
TELEVISION: Call to Glory (pilot), Little Gloria Happy at Last, etc.

NICOL, ALEX: Actor, Director. b. Ossining, NY, Jan. 20, 1919; e. Fagin Sch. of Dramatic Arts, Actor's Studio. U.S. Cavalry.
THEATRE: Forward the Heart, Sundown Beach, Hamlet, Richard II, South Pacific, Mr. Roberts, Cat on a Hot Tin Roof.
PICTURES: Sleeping City, Target Unknown, Air Cadet, Raging Tide, Meet Danny Wilson, Red Ball Express, Because of You, Tomahawk, Redhead From Wyoming, Lone Hand, Law and Order, Champ for a Day, Black Glove, Heat Wave, About Mrs. Leslie, Dawn at Socorro, Strategic Air Command, Man from Laramie, Great Day in the Morning, Sincerely Yours, Five Branded Women, Via Margutta, Under 10 Flags, Gunfighters at Casa Grande, Sleeping Skull (dir.), Then There Were Three (dir.), The Brutal Land, Bloody Mama, Homer, The Gilded Cage, Point of Terror (dir.), Hells Black Night, Screaming Skull (dir.).

NIELSEN, LESLIE: Actor. b. Regina, Sask., Canada, Feb. 11, 1926. e. Victoria H.S., Edmonton. Disc jockey, announcer for Canadian radio station; studied at Lorne Greene's Acad. of Radio Arts, Toronto and at Neighborhood Playhouse; N.Y. radio actor summer stock. Toured country in one-man show, Darrow, 1979.
TELEVISION: Studio One, Kraft, Philco Playhouse, Robert Montgomery Presents, Pulitzer Prize Playhouse, Suspense, Danger, Justice, Man Behind the Badge, Death of a Salesman, Series: The New Breed, Peyton Place, The Protectors, Bracken's World, Police Squad. Home is Where the Heart Is. Guest: Swamp Fox, Ben Casey, Wild Wild West, The Virginian, The Loner, Blade in Hong Kong, Movies: Fatal Confession: A Father Dowling Mystery. Mini-series: Backstairs at the White House.
PICTURES: Vagabond King, Forbidden Planet, Ransom!, Opposite Sex, Hot Summer Night, Tammy and the Bachelor, Night Train To Paris, Harlow, Dark Intruder, Beau Geste, Gunfight in Abilene, The Reluctant Astronaut, Counterpoint, Rosie, Dayton's Devils, How to Commit Marriage, Change of Mind, The Resurrection of Zachary Wheeler, The Poseidon Adventure, Viva, Knievel!, City on Fire, Airplane!, Wrong Is Right, Creepshow, The Patriot, Police Squad—The Movie, Wall Street, Nightstick, Nuts, The Naked Gun, Dangerous Curves, The Repossessed.

NIMOY, LEONARD: Actor, director. b. Boston, MA, Mar. 26, 1931. Along with active career in films, TV and stage, has been writer and photographer. Author of three books on photography and poetry, as well as autobiography, I Am Not Spock. Has also been speaker on college lecture circuit.
PICTURES: Queen for a Day, Rhubarb, The Balcony, Catlow, Invasion of the Body Snatchers, Star Trek—The Movie, Star Trek II; The Wrath of Khan, Star Trek III: The Search for Spock (also dir.), Star Trek IV: The Voyage Home (also. dir.), Three Men and a Baby (dir. only), The Good Mother (dir. only), Star Trek V: The Final Frontier.
TELEVISION: Series: Star Trek, Mission: Impossible, In Search Of . . . (host); . Movie: The Sun Also Rises, Marco Polo, A Woman Called Golda, Baffled.
STAGE: Equus, Sherlock Holmes, Vincent (one-man show).

NIVEN, DAVID, JR.: Executive. b. London, England, Dec. 15, 1942. Joined William Morris Agency in Beverly Hills in 1963. Transferred same yr. to New York; in next five yrs. worked for agency's European offices in Rome, Madrid and London. In 1968 joined Columbia Pictures' U.K. office as a prod. exec.; 1972, named mg. dir. of Paramount Pictures in U.K. In 1976 became indep. prod., forming partnership with Jack Wiener.
PICTURES: The Eagle Has Landed, Escape to Athena, Monsignor, That's Dancing!
TELEVISION: The Night They Saved Christmas (exec. prod., s.p.), Cary Grant: A Celebration.

NIX, WILLIAM PATTERSON: Executive. b. Philadelphia, PA, April 10, 1948. e. Georgetown U., A.B., 1970; Antioch, M.A., 1971; Hofstra U. Sch. of Law, J.D., 1976; NYU Sch. of Law, LL.M., 1979. Sr. v.p. of both the Motion Picture Association of America and Motion Picture Export Assoc. of America. Chmn. of MPAA committee on copyright and literary property matters, and worldwide director of film industry's anti-piracy programs. Member, Acad. of M.P. Arts & Sciences.

NIXON, AGNES: Writer, Producer. b. Nashville, TN, Dec. 10, 1927. e. Northwestern Sch. of Speech, Catholic U. Landed 1st job writing radio serial dialogue (Woman in White, 1948–51), three days after graduating from college. Became a freelance writer for TV dramatic series Studio One, Philco Playhouse, Robert Montgomery Presents, Somerset Maugham Theatre, Armstrong Circle Theatre, Hallmark Hall of Fame, My True Story, Cameo Theatre. Then wrote for daytime series Search For Tomorrow, As The World Turns, Guiding Light and Another World before creating her first soap opera. As creator-producer: One Life to Live, All My Children, Loving. Also evening mini-series The Manions of America. Credited with bringing social issues (Vietnam War, abortion, drug addiction, child abuse, AIDS) to daytime TV. Guest writer, the New York Times 1968–72, and TV Guide. Appeared on Good Morning America and other interview and news programs. Trustee, Television Conference Inst., 1979–82. Received National Acad. of Television Arts & Sciences' Trustee Award, 1981; Junior Diabetic Assn. Super Achiever Award, 1982; Communicator Award for American Women in Radio and Television, 1984.

NIXON, CYNTHIA: Actress. b. NY, NY, April 9, 1966. e. Barnard Coll. Started stage career at 12. Broadway: Hurlyburly, The Real Thing, The Heidi Chronicles. Off-Broadway: Moonchildren, Romeo and Juliet.
PICTURES: Little Darlings (1980), Tatoo, Prince of the City, I Am the Cheese, Amadeus, The Manhattan Project, Let It Ride.
TELEVISION: Guest: The Equalizer, Gideon Oliver, Tanner '88. Movies/specials: The Fifth of July, The Murder of Mary Phagan.

NIZER, LOUIS: Author, Attorney. b. London, Eng., Feb. 6, 1902. e. Columbia Coll., B.A., 1922; Columbia U. Law Sch., LL.B., 1924. Recipient of Columbia U. Curtis Oratorical Prize two times. Sr. partner of law firm, Phillips, Nizer, Benjamin, Krim & Ballon & special counsel to the Motion Picture Assn. of America. Writer of numerous books and articles in leading periodicals and newspapers; lecturer on legal subjects at many universities and bar associations. Also painter and writer of musical compositions.
BOOKS: Reflections without Mirrors, The Implosion Conspiracy, The Jury Returns, My Life in Court, What to Do With Germany, Thinking on Your Feet, Between You and Me, New Courts of Industry, Legal Essays. Excerpt from My Life in Court adapted to Bdwy. play, A Case of Libel, and also for TV movie. Chapter of The Jury Returns adapted for TV movie.

NOBLE, PETER: Writer, Producer, Actor, TV personality. b. London, Eng., June 18; e. Hugh Myddelton Sch., Latymer Sch. Author several books on m.p. ind.; writer & conducts movie radio prog. for B.B.C. & Luxembourg (Film Time, Movie-Go-Round, Peter Noble's Picture Parade). Formed Peter Noble Productions, 1953; Acted in many pictures; Ed. Screen International since 1975. Editor Screen International Film & TV Yearbook since 1974. London Columnist, Hollywood Reporter, 1967–75.
PICTURES: Production assoc., Runaway Bus; asst. prod., To Dorothy a Son; co-prod., s.p. Fun at St. Fanny's; s.p.; Three Girls in Paris; assoc. prod., Lost; s.p., Captain Banner; prod., Strange Inheritance.
AUTHOR: Editor, British Film Year Book; author of biographies of Bette Davis, Erich Von Stroheim, Ivor Novello, Orson Welles. Author books, I Know That Face, The Negro in Films. Wrote screen plays, The King of Soho, Love in the Limelight, The Story of Ivor Novello.
TELEVISION: Find the Link, Other Screen, Film Fanfare, Movie Memories, Yakity Yak, Startime, Thank Your Lucky Stars, Juke Box, Jury, Simon Dee Show, Star Parade, Who's Whose, Movie Magazine, The Big Noise, The Name Game, Line Up, Tea Break, Today. Prod. consult. On The Braden Beat, The Frost Program, Dee Time. 1969–70 Prod. Cons. Simon Dee Show. Appeared on Anything You Can Do Looks Familiar, Password; prod. consultant Movie Quiz (series). Appears frequently on Today TV series, Two's Company, Looks Familiar. Prod. con. Musical Time Machine BBC2 series, Talking about films on radio, including BBC Star Sound, Radio Luxembourg, Film Focus, Newsnight, Looks Familiar Nationwide, Hotel TV Network, The Time of Your Life, Channel 4 News, Nationwide. TV series: Show Business, This Is Britain. TV appearances: Looks Familiar, Electric Picture Show, Gossip, Entertainment Tonight (USA), This Is Britain (TV cable series; Cannes Film Festival (Premiere TV Cable), The Colour Supplement (series); Good Afternoon New York (WOR weekly show U.S.); Loose Ends (BBC); The Golden Gong (TV film). 1988–89: Elstree—The British Hollywood; Saturday Night at the Movies (series), News of the Arts.

NOIRET, PHILIPPE: Actor. b. France, Oct. 1, 1930. e. Centre Dramatique de l'Ouest. Company mem. Theatre National Populaire 1951–63, and worked as nightclub entertainer before film debut in Agnes Varda's short, La Pointe Court. Bdwy debut Lorenzaccio (1958). Has played character roles in numerous international films.
PICTURES: Zazie dans le Metro, (1960), The Billionaire, Crime Does Not Pay, Therese Desqueyroux, None But the Lonely Spy, Death Where Is Thy Victory?, Les Copains, Lady L, La Vie de Chateau, Tender Scoundrel, The Night of the Generals, Woman Times Seven, The Assassination Bureau, Mr. Freedom, Justine, Topaz, Clemarbard, Give Her the Moon, A Room in Paris, Murphy's War, A Time for Loving, Five-Leaf Clover, The Assassination, Sweet Deception, Poil de Carotte, The French Conspiracy, The Serpent, The Day of the Jackel, La Grande Bouffe, Let Joy Reign Supreme, The Old Gun, The Judge and the Assassin, A Woman at Her Window, Dear Inspector, Due Pezzi di Pane, Who Is Killing the Great Chefs of Europe?, Death Watch, Street of the Crane's Foot, A Week's Vacation, Heads or Tails, Three Brothers, Kill Birgitt Haas, Coup de Torchon, L'Etoile Du Nord, Amici, Miei, Atto 2, L'Africain, A Friend of Vincents, Le Grand Carnival, Fort Saganne, Les Ripoux, Souvenirs, Next Summer, The Gold-Rimmed Glasses, No Downing Allowed, My New Partner, 'Round Midnight, Let's Hope It's a Girl, The 4th Power, The Thrill of Genius, The Secret Wife, Twist Again in Moscow, Masks, The Family Chouans!, IL Frullo del Passero, Young Toscanini, The Return of the Musketeers, Moments of Love, Cinema Paradiso, Life and Nothing But, To Forget Palermo.

NOLTE, C. ELMER, JR.: Executive v.p. b. Baltimore, Md., Oct. 19, 1905. Managing dir., F. H. Durkee Enterprises, Baltimore. Pres., NATO of Md., 1955–56; treas., 1957–59; pres., 1952–66, 67–69. Now v.p. & gen. mgr.

NOLTE, NICK: Actor. b. Omaha, NB, Feb. 8, 1941. Attended 5 colleges in 4 yrs. on football scholarships, including Pasadena City Coll. and Phoenix City Coll. Joined Actors Inner Circle at Phoenix and appeared in Orpheus Descending, After the Fall, Requiem For a Nun. Did stock in Colorado. In 1968 joined Old Log Theatre in Minneapolis and after 3 yrs. left for New York, appearing at Cafe La Mama. Went to L.A. and did several TV series before big break in mini-series Rich Man, Poor Man as Tom Jordache.
PICTURES: Return to Macon County Line, The Deep, Who'll Stop the Rain, North Dallas Forty, Heart Beat, Cannery Row, 48 Hrs., Under Fire, Teachers, Grace Quigley, Down and Out in Beverly Hills, Extreme Prejudice, Weeds, Three Fugitives, Farewell to the King, New York Stories (Life Lessons), Everybody Wins, Q&A.
TELEVISION: Guest: Medical Center, Gunsmoke. Mini-series: Rich Man, Poor Man. Movies: Winter Kill (pilot), The California Kid, Death Sentence, Adams of Eagle Lek, The Treasure Chest Murder, The Runaways, Barge.

NORMAN, BARRY: Writer/presenter. b. London. Early career as show business editor London Daily Mail; humorous columnist The Guardian. Entered TV as writer, presenter FILM 72–81 and 83–88. 1982: presenter Omnibus. Writer/host: The Hollywood Greats and Talking Pictures. Radio work incl.: Going Places, The News Quiz, Breakaway, The Chip Shop. Books incl.: The Hollywood Greats, Movie Greats, Film Greats (all non-fiction). Seven novels incl.: A Series of Defeats, Have a Nice Day and Sticky Wicket.

NORRIS, CHARLES GLENN: Executive. b. Taylorsville, NC, Nov. 24, 1906; e. Nat'l U. Law Sch., Washington, DC. Asst. poster clerk, Fox Film Co., 1928; booker, Wash., D.C., 1934; ad-sales mgr., Aug., 1935; salesman, Phila.; Wash., July, 1937; Baltimore, July, 1944; br. mgr., Wash., Jan. 1946; dist. mgr., July, 1946; br. mgr., Wash., Apr., 1948; Atlantic div. mgr., Wash., Jan., 1952; eastern sales mgr., April, 1954; central Canadian sales mgr., April, 1956; asst. gen. sales mgr., April, 1959; gen. sls. mgr., 1960–69; exec. capacity in distribution, 20th Century-Fox, The Glenoris Corp.
MEMBER: Variety Club, English Speaking Union, M.P. Pioneers.

NORRIS, CHUCK: Actor. r.n. Carlos Ray. b. Ryan, OK, 1939. World middleweight karate champion 1968–74. Owner of karate schools. Film debut in The Wrecking Crew (1968).
PICTURES: Return of the Dragon, The Student Teachers, Breaker! Breaker!, Good Guys Wear Black, Game of Death, A Force of One, The Octagon, An Eye for an Eye, Slaughter in San Francisco, Silent Rage, Forced Vengeance, Lone Wolf McQuade, Missing in Action, Missing in Action 2, Code of Silence, Invasion U.S.A. (also s.p.), Delta Force, Firewalker, Braddock: Missing in Action III (also co-s.p.), Hero and the Terror, America's Red Army, Stranglehold: Delta Force II.
TELEVISION: Chuck Norris's Karate Kommandos (animated series, voice), The Ultimate Stuntman: A Tribute to Dar Robinson (host).

NORTH, ALEX: Composer. b. Chester, PA, Dec. 4, 1910; e. Curtis Inst., 1928–29; Juilliard Sch. of Music, 1932–34. Composer for ballet, radio, TV, theatre; U.S. Army, 1942–46; Guggenheim Fellowship, 1947–48; comp., 40 documentary films, 1937–50; composed Revue for Clarinet & Orch. for Benny Goodman, 1947. Member ASCAP; Dramatists Guild.
PICTURES: A Streetcar Named Desire, Death of a Salesman, Viva Zapata, Les Miserables, Pony Soldier, Member of the Wedding, Go Man Go, Desiree, Unchained, The Racers, Man with the Gun, Rose Tattoo, I'll Cry Tomorrow, Cleopatra (Composers and Lyricists Award, best film score, 1964), Shoes of the Fisherman (Golden Globe Award; best film score 1968), The Children's Hour, The Misfits, Cheyenne Autumn, Spartacus, The Rainmaker, The Agony and the Ecstacy, Who's Afraid of Virginia Woolf?, A Dream of Kings, Willard, Pocketmoney, Rebel Jesus, Once Upon a Scoundrel, Lost in the Stars, (musical director) Journey Into Fear, Shanks, Bite the Bullet, Somebody Killed Her Husband, Wise Blood, Carny, Dragonslayer, Under the Volcano, Prizzi's Honor, The Penitent, The Dead, Good Morning Vietnam. 15 Acad. Awards nominations.
TELEVISION: Rich Man, Poor Man; Death of a Salesman; The Word; Sister, Sister.
AWARDS: Honorary Oscar, 1986; ASCAP Golden Soundtrack Award, 1986; Society for Preservation of Film Music Award, 1986; American Society of Music Arrangers & Composers Golden Score Award, 1986.

NORTH, EDMUND H.: Writer. b. New York, NY, e. Stanford U. U.S. Army Signal Corps, five yrs., W.W.II, sep. as major.
PICTURES: One Night of Love, I Dream Too Much, Dishonored Lady, Flamingo Road, Young Man with a Horn, In a Lonely Place. collab. Only the Valiant; s.p. Day the Earth Stood Still, Outcasts of Poker Flat; collab. s.p., Destry, Far Horizons, Proud Ones; s.p. Cowboy; screen story and s.p., Sink the Bismarck!; collab. s.p., H.M.S. Defiant; collab. story and s.p. Patton; story and collab. s.p. Meteor.
TELEVISION: Fireball Foreward, Murdock's Gang.

NORTH, SHEREE: Actress. r.n. Dawn Bethel. b. Los Angeles, CA, Jan. 17, 1933. e. Hollywood H.S. Amateur dancer with USO at 11; prof. debut at 13; many TV appearances; on Broadway in Hazel Flagg, I Can Get It For You Wholesale.
PICTURES: Excuse My Dust, Living It Up, How To Be Very Very Popular, Lieutenant Wore Skirts, Best Things in Life Are Free, No Down Payment, Way to the Gold, In Love and War, Mardi Gras, Destination Inner Space, Madigan, The Gypsy Moths, The Trouble with Girls, Lawman, Charley Varick, The Outfit, Breakout, The Shootist, Telefon, Rabbit Test, Only Once in a Lifetime, Maniac Cop, Cold Dog Soup.
TELEVISION: Series: Big Eddie, Women in White, I'm a Big Girl Now, Bay City Blues, Guest: Archie Bunker's Place. Movies: The Seekers, Scorned and Swindled; Marilyn: The Untold Story; Legs; Vanished.

NOSSECK, NOEL: Producer, Director. b. Los Angeles, CA, 1943. Began as editor with David Wolper Prods; made documentaries; turned to features.
PICTURES: Best Friends (dir. only), Youngblood (prod. only), Dreamer; King of the Mountain.
TELEVISION: Movies: Return of the Rebels; The First Time; Night Partners; Summer Fantasies. Different Affair; Stark: A Mirror Image; Roman Holiday, Full Exposure: the Sex Tapes Scandal. Pilots: Aaron's Way; Half 'n Half, Fair Game.

NOURI, MICHAEL: Actor. b. Washington, DC, Dec. 9, 1945. e. Avon Old Farms, Rollins Coll., Emerson Coll. Studied for theatre with Larry Moss and Lee Strasberg. New York stage debut in Forty Carats, 1969. Film debut in Goodbye Columbus, 1969.
PICTURES: Flashdance, The Imagemaker, The Hidden, Chamelleon, No Cause For Alarm.
TELEVISION: Series: Beacon Hill, Downtown. Movies: The Gangster Chronicles, Contract on Cherry Street, Between Two Women, Rage of Angels: The Story Continues, Bay City Blues, Quiet Victory: the Charlie Wedemeyer Story.

NOVAK, KIM: Actress. r.n. Marilyn Novak. b. Feb, 13, 1933. e. Wright Junior Coll., Los Angeles City Coll. Started as model, named World's Favorite Actress, Brussels World Fair; film debut in The French Line (1953).
PICTURES: Pushover, Phfft, Five Against the House, Picnic, Man with the Golden Arm, Eddy Duchin Story, Jeanne Eagles, Pal Joey, Middle of the Night, Bell, Book and Candle, Vertigo, Pepe, Strangers When We Meet, The Notorious Landlady, Boys' Night Out, Of Human Bondage, Kiss Me, Stupid, The Amorous Adventures of Moll Flanders, The Legend of Lylah Clare, The Great Bank Robbery, Tales That Witness Madness, The White Buffalo, The Mirror Crack'd, The Children.
TELEVISION: Falcon Crest (series), Alfred Hitchcock Presents (1985), Malibu, Santa's Triangle, Third Girl From the Left.

NOVELLO, DON: Writer, Comedian, Producer. b. Ashtabula, OH, Jan. 1, 1943. e. U. of Dayton, B.A., 1964. Best known as Father Guido Sarducci on Saturday Night Live. Was advertising copy writer before writing and performing on The Smothers Brothers Comedy Hour (1975). Writer for Van Dyke and Company, and writer-performer on Saturday Night Live 1978–80. Producer: SCTV Comedy Network (1982) and performer-writer on Broadway in Gilda Radner—Live From New York (1979) as well as filmed version (Gilda Live!). Recordings: Live at St. Douglas Convent, Breakfast in Heaven. Author: The Laszlo Letters: The Amazing Real-Life Actual Correspondence of Lazlo Toth, American!
PICTURES: Head Office, Tucker: The Man and His Dream, New York Stories (Life Without Zoe).
TELEVISION: Cable specials: Fr. Guido Sarducci Goes to College, The Vatican Inquirer—The Pope Tour.

NOYCE, PHILIP: Director. b. Griffith New South Wales, Australia, 1950. Began making films at school and university. 1980 became part-time mgr., Sydney Filmmaker's Co-operative and in 1973 was selected for Sydney Film School year-long training prog. which resulted in 60-minute film Backroads.
PICTURES: Better to Reign in Hell (short, 1968), Good Afternoon (doc.), Caravan Park (short), Castor and Pollux (doc.), God Knows Why But It Works (doc.), Backroads, Newsfront, Heatwave, The Umbrella Man, Dead Calm.

NUREYEV, RUDOLF: Dancer, Actor. b. Russia, Mar. 17, 1938. e. Leningrad Ballet Sch. Mem. Kirov Ballet 1955–61. Asked for and granted political asylum in 1961 in Paris while performing with Kirov Ballet. Joined Marquis de Cuevas Ballet Co., 1961. Artistic dir. Paris Opera Ballet, 1983–. Has appeared as guest artist with 25 major cos. incl. ABT, Australian Ballet, Deutsche Opera Ballet, Dutch Natl. ballet, Natl. Ballet of Canada, etc. Received Capezio Dance Award, 1987.
PICTURES: An Evening with the Royal Ballet, Swan Lake, Romeo and Juliet, The Sleeping Beauty, Don Quixote, Valentino, Exposed.
TELEVISION: Julie Andrews Invitation to the Dance with Rudolf Nureyev.

NYKVIST, SVEN: Cinematographer. b. Moheda, Sweden, Dec. 3, 1922. e. Stockholm Photog. Sch. Asst. cameraman 1941–44. Became internationally known through photographing most of Ingmar Bergman's pictures.
PICTURES: Sawdust and Tinsel, The Virgin Spring, Winter Light, Karin Mansdotter, The Silence, Loving Couples, Persona, Hour of the Wolf, Cries and Whispers (AA), The Dove, Black Moon, Scenes from a Marriage, The Magic Flute, Face to Face, One Day in the Life of Ivan Denisovich, The Tenant, The Serpents' Egg, Pretty Baby, Autumn Sonata, King of the Gypsies, Hurricane, Starting Over, Willie and Phil, From the Life of the Marionettes, The Postman Always Rings Twice, Cannery Row, Fanny and Alexander (Acad. Award), Swann in Love, The Tragedy of Carmen, After the Rehearsal, Agnes of God, Dream Lover, The Sacrifice, The Unbearable Lightness of Being, Katinka, Another Woman, New York Stories (Oedipus Wrecks).
TELEVISION: Nobody's Child.

O

O'BRIAN, HUGH: Actor. r.n. Hugh J. Krampe. b. Rochester, NY, Apr. 19, 1930; U. of Cincinnati, UCLA. U.S. Marine Corps. Actor, stock cos.; actor with many m.p. cos. Pres. H.O.B. Inc. Bev. Hills, 1956. Founder, chmn. and C.E.O.: Hugh O'Brian Youth Foundation; Nat'l Chmn., Cystic Fibrosis Research Foundation 1969–74; Co-founder and pres. Thalians 1956–57; Founder Hugh O'Brian Annual Acting Awards at UCLA.
PICTURES: Young Lovers, Never Fear, Vengeance Valley, Little Big Horn, On the Loose, The Cimarron Kid, Red Ball Express, Sally and Saint Anne, The Raiders, The Lawless Breed, Meet Me at the Fair, Seminole, Man from the Alamo, Back to God's Country, Saskatchewan, Fireman Save My Child, Drums Across the River, Broken Lance, There's No Business Like Show Business, White Feather, The Fiend Who Won the West, Twinkle in God's Eye, Brass Legend, Rope Law, Come Fly with Me, Love Has Many Faces, In Harm's Way, Ten Little Indians, Ambush Bay, Cowboy in Africa, Harpy, Killer Force, The Shootist, Game of Death, Doing Time on Planet Earth, Twins.
TELEVISION: Series: Wyatt Earp; Search, Probe; Specials: Dial M for Murder; A Punt, A Pass and A Prayer; It's a Man's World. Movies: Wild Women, Tomorrow is Now, Space in the Age of Aquarius, Murder on Flight 502, Fantasy Island, Cruise Into Terror, Paradise.
THEATER: Bdwy Plays: Destry Rides Again, First Love, Guys and Dolls. National co. of Cactus Flower.

O'BRIEN, LIAM: Writer. b. New York, NY, March, 1913. e. Fordham U., Manhattan Coll., A.B., 1935. Author B'way play Remarkable Mr. Pennypacker, 1953.
PICTURES: Chain Lightning, Redhead and the Cowboy, Of Men and Music, Diplomatic Courier, Here Comes the Groom, The Stars Are Singing, Young at Heart.

O'BRIEN, MARGARET: Actress. r.n. Angela Maxine O'Brien. Los Angeles, CA, Jan. 15, 1938. Screen debut at 4 in Babes on Broadway (1941). Acad. Award best child actress, 1944. Voted one of ten best money-making stars in Motion Picture Herald-Fame Poll 1945–46.
PICTURES: Journey for Margaret, Dr. Gillespie's Criminal Case, Lost Angel, Thousands Cheer, Madame Curie, Jane Eyre, The Canterville Ghost, Meet Me in St. Louis, Music for Millions, Our Vines Have Tender Grapes, Bad Bascomb, Three Wise Fools, Unfinished Dance, Tenth Avenue Angel, The Secret Garden, Big City, Little Women, Her First Romance, Glory, Heller in Pink Tights, Anabelle Lee, Diabolic Wedding, Amy.
TELEVISION: Guest: Marcus Welby (1972), Death in Space, Split Second to an Epitaph, Testimony of Two Men.

O'BRIEN, VIRGINIA: Actress. b. Los Angeles, CA, Apr. 18, 1919. Singer, comedienne with a distinctive dead-pan delivery. On stage in Meet the People. Screen debut 1940 in Hullabaloo; now retired.
PICTURES: The Big Store, Lady Be Good, Ringside Maisie, Ship Ahoy, Panama Hattie, DuBarry Was a Lady, Thousands Cheer, Meet the People, Two Girls and a Sailor, The Harvey Girls, Ziegfeld Follies, Till Clouds Roll By, The Showoff, Merton of the Movies.

O'CONNELL, JACK: Producer, Director, Writer, Lyricist. b. Boston, MA. After Germany in W.W.II got B.A. Princeton U., M.B.A. Harvard U. Business Sch. After being copy group head at McCann-Erickson advertising and doing 500 TV commercials entered feature films working with Fellini on La Dolce Vita, then asst. director to Antonioni on L'Avventura, then writer-producer-director Greenwich Village Story, Revolution, Christa (aka Swedish Flygirls), Up the Girls Means Three Cheers for Them All, Our 20th Century Revolution. Features have been invited by critics to represent U.S. at Cannes, Locarno, Berlin and Venice Film Festivals.

O'CONNOR, CARROLL: Actor. b. New York, NY, Aug. 2, 1925. e. University Coll., Dublin; U. of Montana. Three years with Dublin's Gate Theatre, then N.Y. where stage credits include Ulysses in Nighttown, Playboy of the Western World, The Big Knife; m.p. debut in Fever in the Blood, 1960.
PICTURES: Lad Had a Dog, By Love Possessed, Lonely Are the Brave, Cleopatra, In Harm's Way, What Did You Do in the War, Daddy?, Hawaii, Not With My Wife You Don't, Warning Shot, Waterhole No. 3, The Devil's Brigade, For Love of Ivy, Kelley's Heroes, Doctors' Wives, Death of a Gunfighter, Law and Disorder.
TELEVISION: US Steel Hour, Armstrong Circle Theatre, Kraft Theatre, All in the Family (Emmy, Golden Globe awards), Of Thee I Sing, In the Heat of the Night (series). Movies: The Last Hurrah, The Sacco and Vanzetti Story, Brass, Convicted, The Father Clements Story.
AUTHOR: Ladies of Hanover Tower (play); Little Anjie Always, The Great Robinson (screenplays).

O'CONNOR, DONALD: Actor. Star of Tomorrow, 1943. b. Chicago, IL, Aug. 28, 1925. In vaudeville with family and Sons o' Fun (Syracuse, N.Y.) before screen debut 1938 in Sing You Sinners; in number other pictures 1938–39 (Sons of the Legion; Tom Sawyer, Detective, Beau Geste, On Your Toes, etc.); in vaudeville 1940–41, then resumed screen career with What's Cookin'?, 1942. Entered armed services, 1943.
PICTURES: Private Buckaroo, Give Out, Sisters, When Johnny Comes Marching Home, It Comes Up Love, Mr. Big, Top Man, Patrick the Great, Follow the Boys, The Merry Monahans, Bowery to Broadway, This Is the Life, Something in the Wind, Are You With It? Feudin', Fussin' and a-Fightin'. Yes Sir, That's My Baby, Francis series, Curtain Call at Cactus Creek, The Milkman, Double Crossbones, Singin' in the Rain, I Love Melvin, Call Me Madam, Walking My Baby Back Home, There's No Business Like Show Business, Anything Goes, Buster Keaton Story, Cry for Happy, That Funny Feeling, That's Entertainment, Ragtime, A Mouse, A Mystery and Me.
TELEVISION: Colgate Comedy Hour, 1953–54. Voted best TV performer, M.P. Daily poll, 1953, The Donald O'Connor Show.

O'CONNOR, GLYNNIS: Actress. b. New York, NY, Nov. 19, 1955. Daughter of prod. Daniel O'Connor and actress Lenka Peterson. e. State U., NY at Purchase. Stage includes Domestic Issues (Circle Rep., NY, 1983) and The Taming of the Shrew (Great Lakes Shakespeare Fest.)
PICTURES: Jeremy (debut, 1973), Baby Blue Marine, Ode to Billy Joe, Kid Vengeance, California Dreaming, Those Lips, Those Eyes, Night Crossing, Melanie, Johnny Dangerously.
TELEVISION: Series: Sons and Daughters. Mini-series: Black Beauty. Movies: The Chisholms, Someone I Touched, All Together Now, The Boy in the Plastic Bubble, Little Mo, My Kidnapper, My Love, The Fighter, Love Leads the Way, Why Me?, Sins of the Father, The Deliberate Stranger, To Heal a Nation.

O'CONNOR, PAT: Director. b. Ardmore, Ireland. After working in London at odd jobs (putting corks in wine bottles, paving roads), came to U.S. e. UCLA, B.A. Studied film and TV at Ryerson Institute in Toronto. 1970, trainee prod., dir. with Radio Telefis Eireann. 1970–78 prod. and dir. over 45 TV features and current affairs documentaries. (The Four Roads, The Shankhill, Kiltyclogher, One of Ourselves, Night in Ginitia). A Ballroom of Romance won British Acad. Award (1981).
PICTURES: Cal, (1984), A Month in the Country, Stars and Bars, The January Man, Fools of Fortune.

OFFENHAUSER, WILLIAM H., JR.: Executive, Engineer; b. Brooklyn, NY, May 8, 1904. e. Columbia U. RCA, 1929–32; inventor MGM squeezetrack, 1929; contractor, Army Sig. Corps, 1933–34; sales eng., J. A. Maurer, Inc., 1936–39; mgr., Precisions Films Labs., N.Y., v.p., mem. of bd., J. A. Maurer, 1939–43; project eng., Johns Hopkins U., 1942–43; consultant, Sig. Corps. Photo Center, 1944–45; consultant, film in color TV, CBS, 1946–47, 1949–51; research project, Cornell U. Med. Coll., 1947–49, consultant, Telenews Prod., 1951–52; v.p., Andre Debrie of America, Inc., 1953; ind. consultant, films & TV, 1954. 1960–61, (Photo Staff) M.I.T. Lincoln Laboratory, Lexington, MA. Author, 16mm Sound Motion Pictures—A Manual; co-author, Microrecording-Industrial and Library Microfilming; ind. consultant, Films, TV, biological Acoustics and Biophysics; 1968, pres. Radio Club of America; 1969–73 Bd. Dir. Radio Club of America.

O'HARA, GERRY: Director. b. Boston-Lincs., England 1924. e. St. Mary's Catholic Sch., Boston. Junior Reporter Boston Guardian. Entered industry in 1942 with documentaries and propaganda subjects. Dir. debut 1963 That Kind of Girl.
PICTURES: Game for Three Lovers; Pleasure Girls (wrote & dir.); Maroc 7; Love in Amsterdam; All the Right Noises (orig. screenplay & dir.); Leopard in the Snow; The Bitch; Fanny Hill; Ten Little Indians (s.p.); Havoc in Chase County (s.p.), Phantom of the Opera (co-s.p.).
TELEVISION: The Avengers; Man in a Suitcase, Journey into the Unknown, The Professionals (story editor, writer); Special Squad (story consultant); Cats Eyes (exec. story editor), Operation Julie (s.p., mini-series).

O'HARA, MAUREEN: Actress. r.n., Maureen FitzSimons. b. Dublin. Aug. 17, 1921. Abbey Sch. of Acting. Won numerous prizes for elocution. Under contract to Erich Pommer-Charles Laughton. Co-starred, Abbey & Repertory Theatre: U.S. film debut in Jamaica Inn (1939).
PICTURES: Hunchback of Notre Dame, A Bill of Divorcement, Dance, Girls, Dance, They Met in Argentina; How Green Was My Valley, To the Shores of Tripoli, Ten Gentlemen from West Point, The Black Swan, The Fallen Sparrow, Buffalo Bill, The Spanish Main, Do You Love Me?, Miracle on 34th Street, Foxes of Harrow, The Homestretch, Sitting Pretty, Woman's Secret, Forbidden Street, Sentimental Journey, Sinbad the Sailor, Father Was a Fullback, Comanche Territory, Tripoli, Bagdad, Rio Grande, At Sword's Point, Kangaroo, Flame of Araby, Quiet Man, Against All Flags, Redhead from Wyoming, War Arrow, Fire over Africa, Magnificent Matador, Lady Godiva, Long Gray Line, Everything But the Truth, Wings of Eagles, The Deadly Companions, Our Man in Havana, Mr. Hobbs Takes a Vacation, McLintock, Spencer's Mountain, The Parent Trap, The Rare Breed, The Battle of Villa Fiorita, How Do I Love Thee, Big Jake.
TELEVISION: The Red Pony, Mrs. Miniver, Scarlet Pimpernel, Spellbound, High Button Shoes, Who's Afraid of Mother Goose.

O'HERLIHY, DAN: Actor. b. Wexford, Ireland, May 1, 1919. e. National U. of Ireland (Bachelor of Architecture). Actor with Abbey Theatre, Dublin Gate, Longford Prod.; announcer on Radio Eireann; on Broadway in The Ivy Green. Extensive TV from 1952. Nom. Acad. Award, Best Actor, 1954.
PICTURES: Odd Man Out, Hungry Hill, Kidnapped, Larceny, Macbeth, The Iroquois Trail, The Blue Veil, The Desert Fox, The Highwayman, Soldiers Three, At Swords Point, Invasion U.S.A., Operation Secret, Actors and Sin, Sword of Venus, Adventures of Robinson Crusoe, Black Shield of Falworth, Bengal Brigade, The Purple Mask, Imitation of Life, Virgin Queen, City After Midnight, Home Before Dark, The Young Land, The Night Fighters, One Foot in Hell, King of the Roaring 20s, The Cabinet of Dr. Caligari, Fail Safe, The Big Cube, Waterloo, Last Starfighter, 100 Rifles, The Carey Treatment, The Tamarind Seed, MacArthur, Halloween III: The Season of the Witch, Robocop, The Dead.
TELEVISION: Series: The Travels of Jamie McPheeters (1953–54), The Long Hot Summer, Hunter's Moon, The Whiz Kids, Man Called Sloane. Mini-series: QB VII, Jennie: Lady Randolph Churchill, Nancy Astor. Movies: The People, Deadly Game, Woman on the Run, Good Against Evil. BBC: Colditz, The Secret Servant, Artemis 81. Guest: The Equalizer, L.A. Law, Murder She Wrote.

OHLMEYER, DONALD W. JR.: Executive, Producer, Director. b. New Orleans, LA, Feb. 3, 1945. e. U. of Notre Dame, B.A. (Communications), 1967. Producer and director at both ABC and NBC. Formed Ohlmeyer Communications Company, 1982 (diversified prod. and dist. of entertainment and sports prog.). Assoc. dir., ABC Sports, NY 1967–70; director, ABC Sports, 1971–72 (dir. 1972 Olympic Games); prod.: ABC Sports, NY 1972–77 (prod. and dir. 1976 Winter and Summer Olympics; prod. ABC's Monday Night Football, 1972–76); exec. prod.: NBC Sports, NY 1977–82 (exec. prod., 1980 Olympics, The World Series, The Super Bowl). Special Bulletin (exec. prod.), John Denver's Christmas in Aspen (exec. prod.). Chmn. and CEO, Ohlmeyer Communications Co., LA, 1982–present. Recipient of 11 Emmy Awards, Humanitas Prize, Award for Excellence, National Film Board. Member, Directors Guild of America.

O'HORGAN, TOM: Director. e. DePaul U. At age 12 wrote opera, Doom on the Earth. Is also musician, singer, actor. Responsible for developing many revolutionary off-off Bdwy. artistic innovations in such productions as The Maids, Tom Paine, Futz.
PICTURES: Futz, Rhinoceros.
STAGE: Broadway: Hair, Lenny, Jesus Christ, Superstar, Inner City, Dude.

OHTANI, HIROSHI: Executive. b. Tokyo, Nov. 2, 1910. e. Kobe Commercial C. 1935; entered Shochiku Co., Ltd., 1936; exec. dir. 1937; man. dir. 1944; dir. Taisho-kan Theatre Co., Ltd. 1948; dir. Chuei Co., Ltd. 1953; man. dir. 1953; aud. Schochiku Co., 1954; pres. 1960–62; pres., Chugai motion picture chain. 1962.

O'KEEFE, MICHAEL: Actor. b. Larchmont, NY, April 24, 1955. e. NYU. Amer. Acad of Dramatic Arts. Co-founder, Colonnades Theatre Lab, NY. On Bdwy. stage in Streamers, Mass Appeal and Fifth of July. Off-Bdwy: Killdeer (NYSF), Moliere in Spite of Himself, Christmas on Mars, Short Eyes.
PICTURES: Gray Lady Down, The Great Santini, Caddyshack, Split Image, Nate and Hayes, Finders Keepers, The Slugger's Wife, The Whoopee Boys, Ironweed, Fear.

TELEVISION: Friendly Persuasion, Panache, A Rumor of War, The Lindbergh Kidnapping Case. The Dark Secret of Harvest Home, The Oaths, Unholy Matrimony, Bridge to Silence, Disaster at Silo 7.

OKON, TED: Producer, Director. b. New Kensington, PA, Oct. 27, 1929. e. U. of Pittsburgh, B.A., 1949. Started career as radio announcer, disk jockey; John Harris Enterprises, theatres and Ice Capades, 1 year; prod. dir., WDTV-TV, Pittsburgh, formed Togo Productions prod. live and film TV shows: Reach, Yates and Matoon. TV-radio dir. 1956; TV-radio pro. dir. Reach McClinton & Co., 1957. sr. v.p. pro. TV comm. Benton and Bowles Adv. 1958–63; Exec. TV prog. dir. art., Ogilvy, Benson & Mather Adv. 1963–65; v.p. prog. dir. Van Praag Prod.; Exec. prod. Girl Game, TV show, 1966; Pres. Rough & Ready, 1966–69; Pres. prod-dir. Tape 16, Teletronics 1969–70; Pres. 1970's Productions; Exec. prod. Women's Clubhouse, TV show, Pres., exec. prod., Pennysaver Productions, Inc., TV programming syndication. Exec. prod. The Pennysaver Place, Dance Party '76, $50,000 Crossword, Sho-Biz-Quizz, Polka Party, Salsa Time, Northstage Theatre Restaurant. Founded OK-Tape, video tape reloading operation.

OLDMAN, GARY: Actor. b. New Cross, South London, Eng., March 21, 1958. Won scholarship to Rose Bruford Drama College, (B.A. Theatre Arts) after studying with Greenwich Young People's Theatre. Acted with Theatre Royal, York and joined touring theatre co. Then in 1980 appeared with Glasgow Citizens Theatre in Massacre at Paris, Chinchilla, Desperado Corner, A Waste of Time (also touring Europe and South America). London stage: Minnesota Moon, Summit Conference, Rat in the Skull, Women Beware Women, The War Plays, Real Dreams, The Desert Air, Serious Money (Royal Shakespeare Co.), The People Wedding (won Time Out's Fringe Award, best newcomer 1985–86; British Theatre Assc. Drama Mag. Award, Best Actor 1985).
PICTURES: Sid and Nancy, Prick Up Your Ears, Track 29, Criminal Law, We Think The World of You, Chattahoochee, State of Grace, Exile, Before and After Death.
TELEVISION: Remembrance; Meantime; Morgan's Boy; Honest, Decent and True; Rat in the Skull.

OLEMBERT, THEODORA: Producer, Writer. Doctor of Law Criminology of Paris U. Entered films through documentaries on child delinquency. Worked during the war as assistant to Prof. René Cassin on Franco/British cultural relations including films. Afterwards joined Jean Benoit-Lévy, chief of the United Nations Film Section. Formed Triangle Films Ltd. for international coproductions; associated with l'Editon Française Cinématographique (Paris).
PRODUCED: Leonardo da Vinci, G. B. Shaw, Chopin, Teiva, The Sixth Day of Creation, Salvador Dali, Is Venice Sinking?, Edith Piaf and Corsica. Co-produced: Midnight Episode, Van Gogh, Moliere, Mont St. Michel and Chinese Theatre. Preparing further films for international releases.

OLMI, ERMANNO: Director. b. Bergamo, Italy, July 24, 1931. e. Accademia d'Arte Drammatica, Milan. Worked as a clerk for an electric company Edisonvolta 1949–52, until 1952 when he began directing theatrical and cinematic activities sponsored by co. 1952–61, directed or supervised over 40 short 16mm and 35mm documentary films. 1959 first feature film, semi-doc. Time Stood Still. With other friends and Tullio Kezich formed prod. co. 22 December S.P.A., 1961. Helped found Hypothesis Cinema, a sch. for aspiring dirs. and technicians.
PICTURES: The Sound of Trumpets, The Fiances, A Man Named John, One Fine Day, The Scavengers, (TV), During the Summer, The Circumstance, The Tree of the Wood Clogs (Palm d'or, Cannes, 1978), Camminacammina.

OLMOS, EDWARD JAMES: Actor. b. East Los Angeles, CA, February 24, 1947. e. East Los Angeles Coll., CA State U. Started as rock singer with group Eddie James and the Pacific Ocean. By the early 1970s acted in small roles on Kojak and Hawaii Five-O. 1978 starred in Luis Valdez's musical drama Zoot Suit at Mark Taper Forum (L.A. Drama Critics Circle Award, 1978). On Bdwy (Theatre World Award, Tony nom.), and in subsequent film. Formed YOY Productions with director Robert Young.
PICTURES: El Alambrista, Aloha Bobby and Rose, Virus, Wolfen, Zoot Suit, Blade Runner, The Ballad of Gregorio Cortez (also assoc. prod., composer and musical adaptor), Saving Grace, Stand and Deliver (also co-prod.), Triumph of the Spirit.
TELEVISION: Evening in Byzantium, 300 Miles for Stephanie, Seguin, Y.E.S. Inc., Miami Vice (series, Emmy, supporting actor, 1985). Mini-series: Mario Puzo's The Fortunate Pilgrim.

O'LOUGHLIN, GERALD STUART: Actor. b. New York, NY, Dec. 23, 1921. e. Blair Acad., Lafayette Coll., U. of Rochester, Neighborhood Playhouse. U.S. Marine, W.W.II.
THEATRE: Broadway: Streetcar, Shadow of a Gunman, Dark at the Top of the Stairs, A Touch of the Poet, Cook for Mr. General, One Flew over the Cuckoo's Nest, Calculated Risk, Lovers and Strangers. Off Broadway: Who'll Save the Plowboy (Obie Award), Harry, Noon and Night, Machinal.
PICTURES: Lovers and Lollypops, Cop Hater, Hatful of Rain, Ensign Pulver, A Fine Madness, In Cold Blood, The Valachi Papers, Desperate Characters, The Organization, Twilight's Last Gleaming, Frances, Quicksilver, Crimes of Passion, Ice Station Zebra, City Heat.
TELEVISION: Guest: Alcoa Premiere, Armstrong Circle Theatre, Philco-Goodyear, Danger, Suspense, The Defenders, For the People, Ben Casey, Dr. Kildare, 12 O'Clock High, Going My Way, Naked City, Quincey (3 times), Gunsmoke, FBI, Green Hornet, The Senator, Medical Center, Ironsides, Mission Impossible Mannix, Judd For The Defense, Hawaii 5 O, Cades County, Cannon, Room 222, Trapper John, Fame, Matt Houston, Too Close for Comfort, Riptide, Murder She Wrote, Highway to Heaven, Dirty Dancing. *Movies:* Murder At The Series, Something For Joey, Wheels, Blind Ambition, Women In White, Wilson's Reward, Matter of Death & Life, Perry Mason (2 hr. revival: Notorious Nun), Child's Cry (aka: Who'll Hear The Child Cry), Crash (of Flight 401), Roots II, Detour. *Series:* Men At Law (aka Storefront Lawyers), The Rookies, Our House, Auto Man.

OLSON, DALE C: Executive. b. Fargo, ND, Feb. 20, 1934. e. Portland State Coll., OR. Owner, Dale C. Olson & Associates; formerly sn. v.p. & pres., m.p. div., Rogers & Cowan public relations. Journalist on Oregonian newspaper, West Coast editor, Boxoffice Magazine, 1958–1960; critic and reporter, Daily Variety, 1960–1966; director of publicity, Mirisch Corporation, 1966–1968; Rogers & Cowan, 1968–1985. Past pres., Hollywood Press Club, awarded Bob Yaeger and Les Mason award by Publicists Guild; v.p. Diamond Circle, City of Hope; delegate for U.S. to Manila International Film Festival.

OLSON, NANCY: Actress. b. Milwaukee, WI, July 14, 1929. e. U. of Wisconsin, UCLA. No prof. experience prior to films.
PICTURES: Union Station, Canadian Pacific, Sunset Boulevard, Mr. Music, Submarine Command, Force of Arms, So Big, Boy from Oklahoma, Battle Cry, Pollyanna, The Absent-Minded Professor, Smith!, Airport 1975, Making Love.
TELEVISION: Paper Dolls.

O'NEAL, FREDERICK: Actor, Director, Lecturer. b. Brooksville, MS, Aug. 27, 1905. e. public schools, Brooksville, St. Louis, MO, New Theatre Sch., American Theatre Wing, NYC. Acted primarily on stage. Pres. Emeritus Actors Equity and of Associated Actors and Artists of America. Named to Black Filmmakers Hall of Fame, 1975.
PICTURES: Pinky, No Way Out, Something of Value, Anna Lucasta, Take a Giant Step, Free White and Twenty One.
TELEVISION: Car 54, Where Are You? (series, 1961–62).

O'NEAL, PATRICK: Actor. b. Ocala, FL, Sept. 26, 1927. e. U. of Florida; Neighborhood Playhouse. In stock cos. before N.Y. TV, 1951. Has appeared in over 300 television shows (live and film).
PICTURES: The Mad Magician, The Black Shield of Falworth, From the Terrace, A Matter of Morals, The Cardinal, In Harm's Way, King Rat, Chamber of Horrors, A Fine Madness, Alvarez Kelly, Matchless, The Assignment, Where Were You When the Lights Went Out?, The Secret Life of an American Wife, Castle Keep, Stiletto, Corky, The Way We Were, The Stepford Wives, The Kremlin Letter, King Rat, Like Father, Like Son, New York Stories (Life Lessons), Q & A.
TELEVISION: The Moneychangers, The Last Hurrah, Perry Mason Returns, To Kill a Cop. Series: Dick and the Duchess, Emerald Point NAS, Diagnosis: Unknown, Kaz, War Chronicles (mini-series), Maigret.

O'NEAL, RON: Actor. b. Utica, NY, Sept. 1, 1937. e. Ohio State U. Spent 8 yrs. at Karamu House in Cleveland (inter-racial theatre) from 1957 to 1966, acting in 40 plays. 1967–68 spent in N.Y. teaching acting in Harlem. Appeared in all-black revue 1968, The Best of Broadway, then in summer stock. Acted off-Bdwy in American Pastorale and The Mummer's Play. 1970 joined the Public Theatre. Break came with No Place To Be Somebody, which won him Obie, the Clarence Derwent, the Drama Desk and the Theatre World Awards.
PICTURES: Move, The Organization, Super Fly, Super Fly TNT, The Master Gunfighter, Brothers, A Force of One, When a Stranger Calls, The Final Countdown, St. Helens, Red Dawn, Mercenary Fighters, Trained to Kill, Hero and the Terror.
TELEVISION: Series: Bring 'em Back Alive, The Equalizer. Movies: North and South, As Summers Die, Brave New World, Freedom Road, Sophisticated Gents, Guyana Tragedy: The Story of Jim Jones, Playing with Fire, North Beach and Rawhide, As Summers Die. The Equalizer (series), A Triple Play; Sam Found Out.
STAGE: Tiny Alice, The Dream of Monkey Mountain.

O'NEAL, RYAN: Actor. r.n. Patrick Ryan O'Neal. b. Los Angeles, CA, April 20, 1941. Parents, screenwriter-novelist, Charles O'Neal, and actress Patricia Callaghan. Father of actress Tatum O'Neal. Boxer, L.A. Golden Gloves, 1956 & 57. Began as stand-in, then stunt man, then actor in Tales of the Vikings

series, in Germany, 1959; freelanced in Hollywood; Screen Gems Pilots, Donny Dru, Our Man Higgins.
PICTURES: The Big Bounce, The Games, Love Story, The Main Event, Wild Rovers, What's Up Doc, Paper Moon, The Thief Who Came to Dinner, Barry Lyndon, Nickelodeon, A Bridge Too Far, The Driver, Oliver's Story, The Main Event, Green Ice, Partners, So Fine, Irreconcilable Differences, Fever Pitch, Tough Guys Don't Dance, Chances Are.
TELEVISION: Series: Empire (1962–63), Peyton Place (1964–69). Movie: Love, Hate, Love; Small Sacrifices. Special Liza Minnelli: Triple Play.

O'NEAL, TATUM: Actress. b. Los Angeles, CA, Nov. 5, 1963. Daughter of Ryan O'Neal and Joanna Moore. Won Acad. Award, 1973 for debut performance in Paper Moon.
PICTURES: Paper Moon, The Bad News Bears, Nickelodeon, International Velvet, Little Darlings, Circle of Two, Prisoners, Certain Fury.
TELEVISION: 15 and Getting Straight.

O'NEIL, THOMAS F.: Executive. b. Kansas City, MO, Apr. 18, 1915. e. Holy Cross Coll., 1933–37. Employed by General Tire and Rubber Co., 1937–41; U.S. Coast Guard, 1941–46; v.p., dir., Yankee Network, Boston, 1948–51; pres. chmn. of bd. RKO General, Inc., since 1952. Arranged purchase RKO Radio by General Teleradio, Inc. from Howard Hughes, July, 1955; chairman of the Board, RKO General, Inc., dir., General Tire & Rubber Co.

O'NEILL, JENNIFER: Actress. b. Rio de Janeiro, Brazil, Feb. 20, 1949. Model before entering films. Spokeswoman: CoverGirl cosmetics. Pres., Point of View Productions and Management.
PICTURES: Rio Lobo (debut, 1970), Summer of '42, Such Good Friends, The Carey Treatment, Glass Houses, Lady Ice, The Reincarnation of Peter Proud, Whiffs, Caravans, Innocent, A Force of One, The Psychic, Scanners, Cloud Dancer, Steel, Committed, I Love N.Y.
TELEVISION: Series: Bare Essence, Cover Up; Movies: Love's Savage Fury, Chase, The Red Spider, The Other Victim, Glory Days, Full Exposure: the Sex Tapes Scandal. Mini-series: A.D.

ONTKEAN, MICHAEL: Actor. b. Canada, Jan. 24, 1950. e. U. of New Hampshire. Son of Leonard and Muriel Cooper Ontkean, actors. Acting debut at 4 with father's rep. theater. Child actor with Stratford Shakespeare Fest., CBC and Natl Film Bd. Attended coll. 2 years on hockey scholarship. Theater: Public Theatre, NY, Willamstown Theatre Fest., Mark Taper Lab, The Kitchen, Soho.
PICTURES: The Peace Killers, Pick Up on 101, Necromancy, Hot Summer Weekend, Slap Shot, Voices, Willie and Phil, Making Love, Just the Way You Are, Street Justice, Maid to Order, Clara's Heart, The Allnighter, Bye Bye Blues, Street Justice.
TELEVISION: The Rookies (series). Movies: The Blood of Others, Kids Don't Tell, The Right of the People, Man From the South, Summer.

OPATOSHU, DAVID: Actor. b. New York, NY, Jan. 30, 1918. e. Morris H.S. U.S. Army, 1942–46; played character roles, The Group Theatre at 21; appeared on Broadway.
THEATRE: Me and Molly, Once More With Feeling, Silk Stockings, The Reclining Figure, The Wall, Bravo Giovanni, Does a Tiger Wear a Neck-Tie?
PICTURES: Cimmarron, Naked City, The Brothers Karamazov, Exodus, Act of Mercy, Best of Enemies, Enter Laughing, Romance of a Horse Thief, The Fixer, Public Enemy No. 1, The Light Ahead, Forty Days of Musa Dagh.
TELEVISION: Movies: Conspiracy of Terror, Masada, Raid on Entebbe, Under Siege, Francis Gary Powers, The Smugglers, Conspiracy "Chicago 8.".

OPHULS, MARCEL: Director, Writer. b. Frankfurt-am-Main, Germany, Nov. 1, 1927. r.n. Marcel Oppenheimer. Son of German director Max Ophuls. e. Occidental Coll., U. of California, Berkeley, Sorbonne (philosophy). Family moved to France, 1932, then to Hollywood, 1941. Military service with Occupation forces in Japan, 1946; performed with theater unit, Tokyo. 1951 began working in French film industry as asst. dir., using name Marcel Wall. 1956–59, radio and TV story ed., West Germany. Later worked for French TV as reporter and dir. news mag. features. 1968 doc. dir. for German TV. 1975–78 staff prod. CBS News, then ABC News.
PICTURES AND DOCUMENTARIES: Asst. dir.: Moulin Rouge (1953); Act of Love; Marianne de ma jeunesse, Lola Montes (dir. by Max Ophuls); Director and writer: Matisse; Love at 20 (German sketch); Banana Peel, (co-s.p.); Fire at Will (co-s.p.); Munich, or Peace in Our Time (TV); The Sorrow and the Pity (Awards include: Prix de Dinard, National Society of Film Critics, New York Film Critics.) Clavigo; The Harvest of My Lai (TV); America Revisited (TV); Two Whole Days (TV); A Sense of Loss; The Memory of Justice; Hotel Terminus—the Life and Times of Klaus Barbie (Awards include: Intl. Jury Prize, Cannes; Peace prize, Berlin; Special Acad. Award, best documentary, 1989).

OPOTOWSKY, STAN: Executive. e. Tulane U. Served in U.S. Marine Corps as combat corr. and later joined United Press, working in New Orleans, Denver, and New York. Published own weekly newspaper in Mississippi before returning to N.Y. to join New York Post as mgr. editor and traveling natl. corr. Is also cinematographer and film editor. Joined ABC News as TV assignment editor; named asst. assignment mgr. In 1974 named dir. of operations for ABC News TV Documentaries. In 1975 named dir. of TV News Coverage, ABC News.
AUTHOR: TV: The Big Picture, The Longs of Louisiana, The Kennedy Government, Men Behind Bars.

OPPENHEIMER, GEORGE: Writer. b. New York, NY, Feb. 7, 1900; e. Williams Coll., 1916–20; Harvard, 1921. Alfred A. Knopf, publishers, 1921–25; co-founder, Viking Press, 1925–33; W.W.II, 1942–45; playwright; short stories; radio.
PICTURES: Rendezvous, We Went to College, Libeled Lady, Day at the Races, Married Before Breakfast, Adventures of Don Juan, Anything Can Happen, Tonight We Sing, Decameron Nights.
TELEVISION: 30 Topper episodes.

ORBACH, JERRY: Actor. b. Bronx, NY, Oct. 20, 1935. e. U. of Illinois, Northwestern U. Trained for stage with Herbert Berghof and Lee Strasberg. N.Y. stage debut in Threepenny Opera, 1955.
THEATER: The Fantasticks (original cast, 1960); Carnival; The Cradle Will Rock; Guys and Dolls; Scuba Duba; Promises, Promises; 6 Rms Riv Vu, Chicago, 42nd Street.
PICTURES: Please Come Home, The Gang That Couldn't Shoot Straight, A Fan's Notes, Sentinel, Prince of the City, Brewster's Millions, F/X, The Imagemaker, Dirty Dancing, Someone to Watch Over Me, Last Exit to Brooklyn, I Love N.Y., Upworld, California Casanova.
TELEVISION: Shari Lewis Show, Jack Paar, Bob Hope Presents, Love American Style, Out on a Limb, Dream West, Love Among Thieves, Murder She Wrote, The Law and Harry McGraw (series).

OREAR, RICHARD: Executive. b. Kansas City, MO, June 11, 1911. e. Findlay Engineering Coll. Exhibitor since 1931 in various capacities. 1947, named to board of Commonwealth Theatres; 1955, exec. v.p.; 1959, bd. chmn.

ORKIN, AD: Executive. b. Jackson, MS, Dec. 7, 1922. e. U. of Mississippi. With Trans World Airlines as flt. eng. 1945–50. Previously co-owner of Orkin Amusements in Jackson. Now owner, Pike Triple Cinema in Troy area. Operates Orkin Badge Co. & Orkin Equipment Co.

O'ROURKE, JOHN J.: Executive. b. New York, NY, July 3, 1922. e. City Coll. of New York, 1950. Entered the industry 1939 Music Hall/New York. 20th Century Fox Film Corp. 1941–59, asst. to dir. of exploitation, MGM, 1960–62; asst. exploitation mgr. Astor Pictures 1962–63; exploitation mgr. 1963–67; National dir. of exploitation Avco Embassy Pictures, 1967; national coordinator roadshows, United Artists, 1968; asst. roadshow mgr. Universal Pictures. 1969 joined Cinemation Industries as dir. advertising, publicity and exploitation. 1974, v.p., Harry K. McWilliams Assoc. Advertising, 1977, vice pres., Benjamin Philip Associates, Inc., Advertising.

ORR, WILLIAM T.: Executive. b. New York, NY, Sept. 27, 1917. e. Coburn Sch., Rumsey Hall, Philips Exeter Acad. Impersonator, Meet the People, revue. Contract, Warner Bros. Joined U.S. Air Force, 1942. Assigned production duties. Air Force's first motion picture unit, 1945. Joined Warner Bros. staff, 1946. Entertained, various night clubs and acting on Broadway stage, New York. Returned to Warner Bros., 1947 as exec. talent dept. and shortly named asst. to Steve Trilling, exec. asst. to Mr. Warner. Chg., studio's TV opers., 1955 as exec. prod. vice-pres., Warner Bros. Pictures, Inc., Nov. 29, 1957–62; vice-pres. in chg. of prod. both features and television, March 1961 to March 1962; vice pres. in chg. of television production, 1962–63; prod., Sex and the Single Girl; asst. to pres., exec. prod., TV div., J. L. Warner, 1963–65; formed Wm. T. Orr Co., 1966, for prods. of M.P.s and TV films.
PICTURES: My Love Came Back, Thieves Fall Out, Navy Blues and Three Sons O'Guns, The Mortal Storm, The Big Street, Unholy Partners, Wicked, Wicked (exec. prod.).

OSBORNE, JOHN: Dramatist. b. London, England, Dec. 12, 1929.
AUTHOR: Plays include 1956: Look Back in Anger. 1957: Epitaph for George Dillon. 1958: The Entertainer. 1959: The World of Paul Slickey. 1961: Luther. 1963: Plays for England. 1964: Inadmissible Evidence, A Patriot for Me, A Bond Honoured, Time Present, The Hotel in Amsterdam, West of Suez, Hedda Gabler (adaptn.).
PICTURES: Films of his plays include Look Back in Anger, The Entertainer. Film scripts: Tom Jones (Oscar, 1964), The Charge of the Light Brigade, Moll Flanders, Tomorrow Never Comes.
TELEVISION: The Right Prospectus, Very Like A Whale, A Subject of Scandal and Concern, The Gift of Friendship; Jack and Jill; You're Not Watching Me, Mummy; Try a Little Tenderness.

O'SHEA, MILO: Actor. b. Dublin, Ireland, June 2, 1926. Member of Dublin Gate Theatre Co., 1944. before screen career. On Bdwy. in Staircase, Dear World, The Comedians, A Touch of the Poet, Waiting For Godot (Brooklyn Acad. of Music). Mass Appeal, My Fair Lady, Corpse!
PICTURES: You Can't Beat the Irish (1952), This Other Eden, Mrs. Gibbons' Boys, Carry on Cabby, Never Put it in Writing, Ulysses, Romeo and Juliet, Barbarella, The Adding Machine, The Angel Levine, Paddy, Sacco and Vanzetti, Loot, Digby, The Biggest Dog in the World, Theatre of Blood, It's Not the Size that Counts, Arabian Adventure, The Verdict, The Purple Rose of Cairo, The Dream Team, Opportunity Knocks.
TELEVISION: QB VII, Two By Forsythe, Peter Lundy and the Medicine Hat Stallion, Portrait of a Rebel: Margaret Sanger, And No One Could Save Her, A Times for Miracles, Broken Vows, Angel in Green.

OSHIMA, NAGISA: Director, Writer. b. Kyoto, Japan, March 31, 1932. e. U. of Kyoto (law), 1954. Joined Shochiku Ofuna Studios in 1954 as asst. dir.; 1956 wrote film criticism and became editor-in-chief of film revue Eiga hihyo; 1959 promoted to director. 1962–65 worked exclusively in TV; 1962–64 made documentaries in Korea and Vietnam; 1975 formed Oshima Prods. 1976, his book of Realm of the Senses seized by police. With editor, prosecuted for obscenity, acquitted. Pres. of Directors Guild of Japan, 1980–present.
PICTURES: A Town of Love and Hope (1959); Cruel Story of Youth, The Sun's Burial; Night and Fog in Japan; The Catch, The Rebel; A Child's First Adventure; The Pleasures of the Flesh; Violence at Noon; Ban on Ninja; Death By Hanging; He Died After the War; The Ceremony; Dear Summer Sister; In the Realm of the Senses; Phantom Love; Empire of Passion; Merry Christmas, Mr. Lawrence (also s.p.); Max Mon Amour; Cruel Story of Youth.

OSMOND, DONNY: Recording artist. b. Ogden, UT, Dec. 9, 1957. Was fifth member of family to become professional singer. (Four brothers, Alan, Wayne, Merrill and Jay, were original members of Osmond Bros., who originally sang barbershop quartet.) Made debut at 4 on Andy Williams Show. Has had 12 gold albums. Was co-host with sister of Donny & Marie on TV. Prod./dir. with own film and video co.
PICTURES: Goin' Cocoanuts (with Marie).
TELEVISION: Wild Women of Chastity Gulch.

OSMOND, MARIE: Singer, TV Host. b. Ogden, UT, Oct. 13, 1959. Began career at age of 7 while touring with her brothers. Her first album, Paper Roses, became a gold one. Appeared as co-host with brother Donny on TV's Donny & Marie.
TELEVISION: Gift of Love, I Married Wyatt Earp, Side By Side.

O'STEEN, SAM: Editor, Director. b. Nov. 6, 1923. Entered m.p. industry 1956 as asst. to editor George Tomassini on The Wrong Man. Became full editor in 1963 on Youngblood Hawke. Directorial debut with TV film A Brand New Life, 1972.
PICTURES: Editor: Kisses for My President; Robin and the 7 Hoods; Youngblood Hawke; Marriage on the Rocks; None But the Brave; Who's Afraid of Virginia Woolf?; Cool Hand Luke; The Graduate; Rosemary's Baby; The Sterile Cuckoo (supr. ed.); Catch-22; Carnal Knowledge; Portnoy's Complaint; Day of the Dolphin; Chinatown; Straight Time; Sparkle (dir); Hurricane; Amityville II: The Possession, Silkwood; Heartburn; Nadine; Biloxi Blues; Frantic; Working Girl; A Dry White Season (co-ed.).
TELEVISION: Director: A Brand New Life; I Love You, Goodbye; Queen of the Stardust Ballroom (DGA Award); High Risk; Look What's Happened to Rosemary's Baby; The Best Little Girl in the World; Kids Don't Talk.

O'SULLIVAN, KEVIN P.: Executive. b. New York, NY, April 13, 1928. e. Queens Coll., Flushing, NY. Associated with television 40 yrs., initially as a talent; later as businessman. Won first prize in Arthur Godfrey Talent Scouts competition in 1948. 1950–55 professional singer, actor on TV, in theatre, night clubs. 1955–57 on radio-TV promotion staff, Ronson Corp. 1958–61 salesman, Television Programs of America. 1961–67 director of program services, Harrington, Righter and Parsons. In 1967 joined ABC Films, domestic sales div. as v.p. & gen. sales mgr. In Jan., 1969 named v.p., gen. mgr., ABC Films, Inc.; in April same yr. named pres. In July 1970 made pres., ABC Int'l. TV, while retaining position as pres., ABC Films. In April, 1973 became pres., chief operating officer, Worldvision Enterprises, Inc., co. formed to succeed ABC Films when FCC stopped networks from TV program dist. Elected chmn. & chief exec. officer Worldvision, 1982. Named pres., Great American Broadcasting Group, 1987. Resigned, 1988.

O'SULLIVAN, MAUREEN: Actress. b. Boyle, Eire, May 17, 1911; mother of actress Mia Farrow. e. convents in Dublin, London; finishing sch., Paris. Film debut: Song O' My Heart (1930). On many TV shows.
PICTURES: A Connecticut Yankee, The Big Shot, MGM Tarzan series, Tugboat Annie, The Barretts of Wimpole Street, The Thin Man, David Copperfield, Anna Karenina, Cardinal Richelieu, The Voice of Bugle Ann, The Devil Doll, A Day at the Races, Big Clock, Bonzo Goes to College, Pride and Prejudice, All I Desire, Mission Over Korea, Duffy of San Quentin, Steel Cage, The Tall T, Never Too Late, Hannah and Her Sisters, Peggy Sue Got Married, Stranded.
STAGE: Never Too Late, The Front Page, 1971; No Sex Please, We're British, 1973, Mornings at Seven.
TELEVISION: The Crooked Hearts, The Great Houdinis, Good Old Boy (Wonderworks).

O'TOOLE, ANNETTE: Actress. b. Houston, TX, April 1, 1953. e. UCLA.
PICTURES: Smile, One on One, King of the Gypsies, Foolin' Around, Cat People, 48 Hours, Superman III, Cross My Heart, Love at Large.
TELEVISION: Movies: The Girl Most Likely To. . ., The Entertainer, The War Between the Tates, Love For Rent, Stand By Your Man, Copacabana, Arthur Hailey's Strong Medicine, Broken Vows, The Kennedys of Massachusetts. Specials: Vanities, Best Legs in the Eighth Grade, Secret World of the Very Young, Guts and Glory: the Rise and Fall of Oliver North.

O'TOOLE, PETER: Actor. b. Ireland, Aug. 2, 1932. Studied at Royal Acad. of Dramatic Art. Early career with Bristol Old Vic. London Stage in The Long, the Short and the Tall. 1960, with the Stratford-on-Avon Company. Ent. films 1959 in Kidnapped. Partner with Jules Buck, Keep Films, Ltd.
PICTURES: The Savage Innocents, The Day They Robbed the Bank of England, Lawrence of Arabia, Becket, Lord Jim, What's New Pussycat, How to Steal a Million, The Night of the Generals, The Bible, Great Catherine, The Lion in Winter, Goodbye Mr. Chips, Brotherly Love, Murphy's War, Under Milk Wood, The Ruling Class, Man of La Mancha, Rosebud, Man Friday, Foxtrot, Caligula, The Stunt Man, My Favorite Year, Supergirl, Creator, Club Paradise, The Last Emperor, High Spirits, On a Moonlit Night, Helena, Wings of Fame, The Pit and the Pendulum.
TELEVISION: Movies: Svengali, Kim, Pygmalion; Strumpet City (serial), Masada (mini-series), Pied Piper.

O'TOOLE, STANLEY: Producer. Earliest experience with production costs; worked on Cleopatra, Singer, Not the Song, No Love for Johnny, Victim, etc. In 1966 named chief cost acct. for Paramount in U.K.; 1967, promoted to prod. exec. Worked on Downhill Racer, Running Scared, etc. Produced The Last of Sheila in 1972; 1974–75 was in Prague working on Operation Daybreak. Produced The Seven-Per-Cent Solution. Formed own Martinat Co. and produced The Squeeze, The Boys from Brazil, Nijinsky, Sphinx, Outland, Enemy Mine, Lionheart, The Last Emperor, Quigley Down Under.

OTWELL, RONNIE RAY: Theatre Executive. b. Carrollton, GA, Aug. 13, 1929. e. Georgia Inst. of Technology. Entered industry as mgr., Bremen Theatre (GA), 1950; dir. pub., adv., Martin Theatres, Columbus (GA), 1950–63; v.p., dir. Martin Theatres of Ga., Inc., 1963, Martin Theatres of Ala., Inc., 1963; dir. Martin Theatres of Columbus, 1963; sr. v.p., Martin Theatres Companies, 1971. Member: NATO, GA, NATO, Columbus C of C; Columbus Mus. Arts & Crafts; Assn. U.S. Army.

OWEN, ALUN: Writer. b. Liverpool, Eng., Nov. 25, 1925.
STAGE: A Little Winter Love, Maggie May, Progress to the Park, The Rough and Ready Lot, There'll Be Some Changes Made, Norma (Mixed Doubles), Shelter, Fashion of Your Time, The Ladies, Lucia.
TELEVISION: The Ruffian, No Trams to Lime Street, After the Funeral, Lena O My Lena (for ITV's Armchair Theatre); The Rose Affair (two awards, 1961), Ways of Love, You Can't Win 'Em All, A Hard Knock, Dare to be a Daniel, The Stag, The Strain, A Local Boy, Ruth, Funny, Pal, Giants and Ogres, The Piano Player, The Web Flight, Buttons, Lucky, Left. Ronnie Barker and Forget-me-not series, Lady of the Lake, The Look, Passing Through, The Runner, Sea Link, Kisch-Kisch, Colleagues, Francis.
PICTURES: The Criminal, A Hard Day's Night, Minding the Shop, Park People, You'll Be the Death of Me, McNeil, Cornelius, Emlyn, Caribbean Idyll, Ned Kelly, No Trams to Lime Street.

OWEN, BILL: Actor. r.n. Bill Rowbotham. b. Acton, Eng., Mar. 14, 1914. Screen debut in Way to the Stars (1945). Numerous TV appearances.
PICTURES: School for Secrets, Daybreak, Dancing With Crime, Easy Money, When the Bough Breaks, My Brother's Keeper, Martha, Parlor Trick, The Roundabout, Trottie True, Once a Jolly Swagman, A Day to Remember, You See What I Mean, Square Ring, Rainbow Jacket, Ship That Died of Shame, Not so Dusty, Davy, Carve Her Name with Pride, Carry on Sergeant, Carry on Nurse, Night Apart, Shakedown, Hell Fire Club, Carry on Regardless, Carry on Cabby!, Secret of Blood Island, Georgy Girl, Headline Hunters, O Lucky

Man!, Kadoyng, In Celebration, When The Screaming Stopped, Comeback, Laughter House.
TELEVISION: Last of the Summer Wine (1974–89 series).

OWENSBY, EARL: Producer, Actor. b. North Carolina, 1935. Set up his own studio in Shelby, NC. Built new studio in Gaffney, SC, 1985.
PICTURES: Challenge, Dark Sunday, Buckstone County Prison, Frank Challenge—Manhunter, Death Driver, Wolfman, Seabo, Day of Judgment, Living Legend, Lady Grey, Rottweiler, Last Game, Hyperspace, Hit the Road Running, Rutherford County Line.

OXENBERG, CATHERINE: Actress. b. NY, NY, Sept. 21, 1961. Daughter of the exiled Princess Elizabeth of Yugoslavia, raised among intl. jet set with Richard Burton acting as her tutor. Modeled before making TV debut in The Royal Romance of Charles and Diana (1983).
PICTURES: The Lair of the White Worm, The Return of the Musketeers.
TELEVISION: Dynasty (series), Movies: Roman Holiday, Swimsuit, Trenchcoat in Paradise.

OZ, FRANK: Puppeteer, Director. b. Herford, Eng., May 25, 1944. r.n. Frank Oznowicz. Gained fame as creator and performer of various characters on Sesame Street and the Muppet Show (Fozzie Bear, Miss Piggy, Animal, The Swedish Chef, Cookie Monster, Grover and Burt) 1976–81, winning Emmy Awards 1974, 1976, 1978. Feature film directorial debut The Dark Crystal. Vice president Wenson Associates.
PICTURES: The Blues Brothers; The Empire Strikes Back; The Muppet Movie; The Great Muppet Caper (also prod.); American Werewolf in London; The Dark Crystal (also dir.); Return of the Jedi; The Muppets Take Manhattan (also dir. and s.p.); Little Shop of Horrors (dir.); Dirty Rotten Scoundrels (dir.).
TELEVISION: Sesame Street, The Muppet Show, Big Bird in China; various variety shows.

P

PAAR, JACK: Actor. b. Canton, OH, May 1, 1918. Radio announcer in Cleveland, Buffalo; served in U.S. Armed Forces, W.W.II; entertained in Pacific zone with 28th Special Service Div. On radio with own show; First host of The Tonight Show, various specials.
TELEVISION: Up to Paar, 1952; Bank on the Stars, 1953; Jack Paar Show, The Morning Show, The Tonight Show (retitled The Jack Paar Show (1958–62), The Jack Paar Program, 1962–5; Stage 67; ABC Late Night, 1973; Jack Paar Tonight, Jack Paar is Alive and Well (prod., 1987), He Kids You Not.
PICTURES: Variety Time (debut, 1948), Walk Softly Stranger, Footlight Varieties, Love Nest, Down Among the Sheltering Palms.
BOOKS: I Kid You Not (1960), My Sabre is Bent, Three on a Toothbrush, P.S. Jack Paar (1983).

PACINO, AL: Actor. b. New York, NY, Apr. 25, 1940. e. High Sch. for the Performing Arts, NY; Actors Studio, 1966; HB Studios, NY. Gained attention as stage actor initially at Charles Playhouse, Boston (Why Is a Crooked Letter, The Peace Creeps, Arturo, Ui.) Artistic dir. (with Ellen Burstyn, Actors Studio, 1982–84.
STAGE: The Indian Wants the Bronx (Obie award), Does a Tiger Wear A Necktie? (Tony Award), The Local Stigmatic, Camino Real, The Connection, Hello Out There, Tiger at the Gates, The Basic Training of Pavlo Hummel (Tony Award), Richard III, American Buffalo, Julius Caesar.
PICTURES: Me Natalie (debut, 1969), Panic in Needle Park, The Godfather, Scarecrow, Serpico, The Godfather II, Dog Day Afternoon, Bobby Deerfield, And Justice for All, Cruising, Author! Author!, Scarface, Revolution, Sea of Love, Glengarry Glen Ross.

PAGE, ANTHONY: Director. b. Bangalore, India, Sept. 21, 1935. e. Oxford. Stage work includes Inadmissible Evidence, Waiting for Godot, A Patriot for Me, Look Back in Anger, Uncle Vanya, Cowardice, etc.
PICTURES: Inadmissible Evidence, Alpha Beta, I Never Promised You a Rose Garden, Absolution, The Lady Vanishes.
TELEVISION: Pueblo, The Missiles of October, The Parachute, FDR—The Last Year, The Patricia Neal Story, Bill, Johnny Belinda, Grace Kelly, Bill—On His Own, Forbidden, Monte Carlo, Second Serve, Pack of Lies, The Nightmare Years.

PAGE, PATTI: Performer, recording artist. r.n. Clara Ann Fowler. b. Claremore, OK, 1927. e. U. of Tulsa. Staff performer, radio stat. KTUL, Tulsa; Top recording star of the 1950s and 60s (The Tennessee Waltz, How Much is That Doggie in the Window, etc.). Appeared on CBS radio show; star Patti Page Show, TV film series, The Big Record; author, Once Upon a Dream.
PICTURES: Elmer Gantry, Dondi, Boys Night Out.

PAGET, DEBRA: Actress. r.n. Debralee Griffin. b. Denver, CO, Aug. 19, 1933; e. drama & dancing privately. Stage debut in Marry Wives of Windsor, 1946; in Jeanne D'Arc little theatre prod.; m.p.; debut in Cry of the City, 1948.
PICTURES: House of Strangers, Broken Arrow, Fourteen Hours, Bird of Paradise, Anne of the Indies, Belles on Their Toes, Les Miserables, Stars & Stripes Forever, Prince Valiant, Demetrius & the Gladiators, Princess of the Nile, Gambler from Natchez, White Feather, Seven Angry Men, Last Hunt, Ten Commandments, Tales of Terror, The Haunted Palace.

PAGETT, NICOLA: Actress. b. Cairo, Egypt, June 15, 1945. r.n. Nicola Scott. e. Royal Acad. of Dramatic Art. Appeared with Citizen's Rep. Theatre, Glasgow.
THEATER: Cornelia (debut, 1964, Worthing, U.K.); A Boston Story (London debut, 1968); A Midsummer Night's Dream; Widowers' Houses; The Misanthrope; A Voyage 'Round My Father; The Ride Across Lake Constance; Ghosts; The Seagull; Hamlet; The Marriage of Figaro; A Family and a Fortune; Gaslight; Yahoo; Old Times (L.A.).
PICTURES: Anne of the Thousand Days (1969); There's a Girl in My Soup; Operation Daybreak; Oliver's Story; Privates on Parade.
TELEVISION: Series: Upstairs, Downstairs (Elizabeth Bellamy); Movies: Frankenstein: The True Story; The Sweeney; Aren't We All; A Woman of Substance (mini-series); Anna Karenina.

PAIGE, JANIS: Actress (Star of Tomorrow, 1947). r.n. Donna Mae Jaden. b. Tacoma, WA, Sept. 16, 1923. Sang with Tacoma Opera Co. m.p. debut, 1944, Hollywood Canteen, N.Y. stage in 1951, and TV in 1956.
STAGE: Pajama Game, Remains to Be Seen, Alone Together.
PICTURES: Of Human Bondage, Two Gals and a Guy, Fugitive Lady, The Time the Place and the Girl, Two Guys from Milwaukee, Her Kind of Man, Cheyenne, Love and Learn, Wallflower, Winter Meeting, One Sunday Afternoon, Romance on High Seas, House Across the Street, Younger Brothers, Mr. Universe, Remains to be Seen, Please Don't Eat the Daisies, The Caretakers, Welcome to Hard Times.
TELEVISION: It's Always Jan (series), Roberta (1958 and 1969), Columbo, Banacek, Flamingo Road, St. Elsewhere, Baby Makes Five (series), Lanigan's Rabbi (series).

PAINE, CHARLES F.: Executive. b. Cushing, TX, Dec. 23, 1920. e. Stephen F. Austin U. Pres. Tercar Theatre Company; pres., NATO of Texas, 1972–73. NATO board member, 1973 to present; Motion Picture Pioneers member; Variety Club of Texas member.

PAKULA, ALAN J.: Producer, Director. b. New York, NY, April 7, 1928. e. Yale U., B.A., 1948. Worked in Leland Hayward's office; asst. administrator, Warner Bros. cartoon dept, Prod. apprentice, MGM, 1950; prod. asst., Para. 1951; prod. Para., 1955. Own prod. co., Pakula-Mulligan Prod. Stage prod. and m.p. dir. prod. 1988 received Eastman Award for Continued Excellence in M.P.
STAGE: Comes a Day, Laurette, There Must Be a Pony.
PICTURES: *Producer:* Fear Strikes Out, To Kill a Mockingbird, Love with the Proper Stranger, Baby the Rain Must Fall, Inside Daisy Clover, Up the Down Staircase, The Stalking Moon, The Sterile Cuckoo (dir. only), Klute (dir., co-prod.), Love and Pain and the Whole Damned Thing (prod. only), The Parallax View (prod., dir.), All the President's Men (dir.), Comes a Horseman (dir.), Starting Over (co.-prod., dir.). Roll-over (dir.); Sophie's Choice (s.p., dir., prod.); Dream Lover (co-prod.-dir.), Orphans (prod., dir.), See You in the Morning (s.p., prod., dir.), Presumed Innocent (dir.).
AWARDS: N.Y. Film Critics for best director, All the President's Men (1976); London Film Critics for best director, Klute (1971).

PALANCE, JACK: Actor. b. Lattimer, PA, Feb. 18, 1920. e. U. of North Carolina. Professional fighter; U.S. Air Corps. Broadway stage. Film debut: Panic in the Streets (1950).
STAGE: The Big Two, Temporary Island, The Vigil, Streetcar Named Desire, Darkness at Head.
PICTURES: Halls of Montezuma, Shane, Sudden Fear, Flight to Tangier, Man in the Attic, Sign of the Pagan, Silver Chalice, Kiss of Fire, Big Knife, I Died a Thousand Times, Attack!, Lonely Man, House of Numbers, Ten Seconds to Hell, Warriors Five, Barabbas, Contempt, Torture Garden, Kill a Dragon, They Came to Rob Las Vegas, The Desperadoes, Che, The Mercenary, Justine, Legion of the Damned, A Bullet for Rommel, The McMasters, Monte Walsh, Companeros, The Horsemen, The Professionals, Oklahoma Crude, Craze, The Four Deuces, The Diamond Mercenaries, Hawk the Slayer, Gor, Bagdad Cafe, Young Guns, Outlaw of Gor, Batman.
TELEVISION: Requiem for a Heavyweight, Dr. Jekyll and

Mr. Hyde, Dracula, Bronk (series), Ripley's Believe It or Not (series host).

PALCY, EUZHAN: Director. b. Martinique, 1957. e. Earned a degree in French lit., Sorbonne and a film degree from Vaugirard School in Paris. Began career working as TV writer and dir. in Martinique. Also made 2 children's records. In Paris worked as film editor, screenwriter and dir. of shorts. She received grant from French gov. to make 1st feature Sugar Cane Alley which cost $800,000 and won Silver Lion Prize at Venice Film Fest., 1983.
PICTURES: Sugar Cane Alley, A Dry White Season (also co-s.p.).

PALEY, WILLIAM S.: Executive. b. Chicago, IL, Sept. 28, 1901. e. U. of Pennsylvania. Took over operation Columbia Broadcasting System (now CBS, Inc.) as pres. 1928; chairman of the board from January, 1946 to April 1983, when named founder-chmn.; 1987, returned to chairmanship. built network to leading position and est. innovations in broadcasting. During war on leave to supervise OWI radio in Mediterranean area. Chief of radio of Psychological Warfare Division, SHAEF, 1944–45; Dep. Chief Info. Control Div. of U.S.G.C.C. 1945; Colonel, A.U.S. Deputy Chief Psychological Warfare Division, SHAEF, 1945; pres. & dir., William S. Paley Foundation, Inc.; partner, Whitcom Investment Co.; co-chmn., Intl. Herald Tribune; pres. & dir., Greenpark Foundation, Inc. Founder and Chairman of the Board of Trustees of the Museum of Broadcasting; trustee, emeritus, Columbia U.; trustee and chairman, emeritus, Museum of Modern Art. Trustee, North Shore University Hospital 1949–73, Co-Chairman of the Board, 1954–73. Decorations include the Legion of Merit, Medal for Merit. Legion of Honor, Croix de Guerre with Palm. Chairman of President's Materials Policy Comm., 1951–52, which issued report, Resources for Freedom.

PALIN, MICHAEL: Actor, Writer. b. Sheffield, Yorkshire, England, May 5, 1943. e. Oxford. Member of Monty Python's Flying Circus. On stage with troupe both in London and on Bdwy.
PICTURES: And Now for Something Completely Different, Monty Python and the Holy Grail, Jabberwocky, Life of Brian, Time Bandits, The Missionary (also co-prod., s.p.), Monty Python's The Meaning of Life (also music), A Private Function, Brazil, A Fish Called Wanda.
TELEVISION: Do Not Adjust Your Set, The Frost Report, Marty Feldman Comedy Machine, How To Irritate People, Pythons in Deutschland, Secrets, Ripping Yarns, etc.

PALMER, BETSY: Actress. b. East Chicago, IN, Nov. 1, 1926. e. DePaul U. Studied at Neighborhood Playhouse, HB Studio with Uta Hagen. On Broadway in The Grand Prize, Affair of Honor, Cactus Flower, Roar Like a Dove, Eccentricities of a Nightingale, Same Time Next Year and many regional prods.
PICTURES: The Long Gray Line, Queen Bee, The Other Life of Lynn Stuart, The Tin Star, The Last Angry Man, Mister Roberts, Friday the 13th, Friday the 13th, Part II.
TELEVISION: All major live shows such as Studio One, U.S. Steel Hour, Kraft Theatre. Panelist, I've Got a Secret (11 years), No. 96 (series), Candid Camera (host), Wifeline (host), As the World Turns. Movies: Isabel's Choice, Windmills of the Gods, Goddess of Love.

PALMER, GREGG: Actor. r.n. Palmer Lee. b. San Francisco, CA, Jan. 25, 1927; e. U. of Utah. U.S. Air Force, 1945–46; radio announcer, disc jockey; then to Hollywood; over 800 TV appearances.
PICTURES: Cimarron Kid, Battle at Apache Pass, Son of Ali Baba, Red Ball Express, Francis Goes to West Point, Sally and St. Anne, The Raiders, Back at the Front, Redhead From Wyoming, Column South, Veils of Bagdad, Golden Blade, The All American, Taza Son of Cochise, Magnificent Obsession, Playgirl, To Hell and Back, Creature Walks Among Us, Hilda Crane, Zombies of Mora Tau, Revolt of Fort Laramie, Rebel Set, Thundering Jets, Forty Pounds of Trouble, Night Hunt, The Undefeated, Chisum, Rio Lobo, Big Jake, Providenza (Italy), Ci Risiamo Vero Providenza (Italy, Spain). The Shootist.
TELEVISION: Guest appearances incl: Wagon Train, Loretta Young, Wyatt Earp, Have Gun Will Travel, Sea Hunt, Roaring 20's, Mannix, The High Chaparral, Cannon, Baretta, Gunsmoke, etc. Movies: Go West Young Girl, Hostage Heart, How the West Was Won, True Grit, Beggarman, Thief; The Man with Bogart's Face, The Blue and the Gray (mini-series).

PALMER, PATRICK: Producer. b. Los Angeles, CA, Dec. 28. Began career with 10-year apprenticeship at Mirisch Company, involved in making of West Side Story, Seven Days in May, The Fortune Cookie, etc. 1966, associated with Norman Jewison, serving as assoc. prod. on The Landlord, Fiddler on the Roof, Jesus Christ Superstar, Rollerball, etc. 1972, prod. with Jewison Billy Two Hats; exec. prod. on The Dogs of War.
PICTURES: Co-prod.: Best Friends, Iceman, A Soldier's Story, Agnes of God, Children of a Lesser God, Moonstruck.

PALTROW, BRUCE: Director, Producer, Writer. b. New York, NY, Nov. 26, 1943. e. Tulane U., B.F.A. m. actress Blythe Danner. Produced stage plays.
PICTURE: A Little Sex (co-prod., dir.).
TELEVISION: Shirts and Skins; You're Gonna Love It Here; Big City Boys; The White Shadow (creat. dir.); St. Elsewhere (exec. prod.-dir.), Tattinger's (exec. prod., dir., co-writer), Nick & Hillary (exec. prod.).

PAM, JERRY: Publicist. b. London, England, Oct. 17, 1926. e. Cambridge, London U. Reporter, Paris, London; freelance writing, Australia; 1950–53. To U.S. in 1953, on Hollywood Reporter, drama ed. Beverly Hills Citizen, 1953–54; publicist, Moulin Rouge, MGM studios; drama ed., Valley Times 1959–61; partner, Pam and Joseph pub. rel. counsellors; est. Jerry Pam & Associates, pub. rel., April 1965; formed Guttman & Pam, Ltd., 1971. Exec. prod., Highpoint, 1979. Prod., On the Film Scene (weekly series on Z Channel).

PAMPANINI, SILVANA: Actress. b. Rome, Italy, Sept. 25, 1925. e. Academy of St. Cecilia. Studied singing, several concert appearances. Elected Miss Italia of 1946–47; m.p. debut in Secret of Don Giovanni.
PICTURES: Second Ark, Twin Trouble, O.K. Nero, City Stands Trial, A Husband for Anna, Songs of Half a Century, Songs Songs Songs, Matrimony, Enchanting Enemy, A Day in District Court, Loves of Half a Century, Slave of Sin, Orient Express, Merry Squadron, Princess of the Canary Islands, Mademoiselle Gobette, Don Juan's Night of Love, Roman Tales.

PAN, HERMES: Dance director. b. Tennessee, 1910. In 1933 after successful musical theater career became asst. dance dir. on Fred Astaire's second film Flying Down to Rio. Thereafter was choreographer on all Astaire-Rogers films as well as creating water ballets for Esther Williams and ice dances for Sonja Henie. In 1938 won Academy Awards for dance direction Damsel in Distress. National Film Award, achievement in cinema, 1980; Joffrey Ballet Award, 1986.
PICTURES: The Gay Divorcee, Top Hat, Old Man Rhythm, In Person, I Dream Too Much, Follow the Fleet, Roberta, Swing Time, Shall We Dance, Damsel in Distress, Carefree, The Story of Vernon and Irene Castle, That Night in Rio, Moon Over Miami, Rise and Shine, Pin-up Girl, Blue Skies, The Shocking Miss Pilgrim, I Wonder Who's Kissing Her Now, The Barkleys of Broadway, Radio City Revels, Let's Dance, Three Little Words, Excuse My Dust, Texas Carnival, Lovely to Look At, Sombrero, Kiss Me Kate, Student Prince, Hit the Deck, Jupiter's Darling, Meet Me in Las Vegas, Silk Stockings, Porgy and Bess, Can-Can, Flower Drum Song, Cleopatra, My Fair Lady, Finian's Rainbow, Darling Lili, Lost Horizon.
TELEVISION: An Evening with Fred Astaire (Emmy Award, choreography), Astaire Time, Sounds of America, Star-times Academy Awards of Songs, Remember How Great, Frances Langford Show.

PANAMA, CHARLES A. (CHUCK): Publicist, b. Chicago, IL, Feb. 2, 1925. e. Northwestern U., Beloit Coll., U. of California at L.A. Publicist, Los Angeles Jr. Chamber of Commerce; So. Calif. sports ed., Los Angeles bureau, INS; publicist, 20th Century-Fox Studios; adv.-pub. dir., Arcola Pics.; opened L.A. office, John Springer Associates; v.p. Jerry Pam & Assoc.; Account exec., Rogers, Cowan & Brenner, Inc.; dir. m.p. div., Jim Mahoney & Assoc.; v.p. Guttman & Pam, Ltd.; asst. pub. dir., 20th-Fox TV.

PANAMA, NORMAN: Writer, Producer, Director. b. Wrote, co-prod. & dir., with Melvin Frank, White Christmas, Li'l Abner, Facts of Life, The Road to Hong Kong, Mr. Blandings Builds His Dream House. Recent works: Co-authored The Glass Bed (novel), and two plays: A Talent for Murder & The Bats of Portobello.
PICTURES: Road to Utopia, My Favorite Blonde, Happy Go Lucky, Star-Spangled Rhythm, Thank Your Lucky Stars, And the Angels Sing, Duffy's Tavern, Our Hearts Were Growing Up, Monsieur Beaucaire, It Had to Be You, Return of October, The Reformer and the Redhead, Strictly Dishonorable, Callaway Went Thataway, Above and Beyond, Knock on Wood, The Court Jester, Not With My Wife You Don't, How to Commit Marriage, Coffee, Tea, or Me. Wrote and directed: I Will, I Will...For Now. Directed, Barnaby and Me; Wrote Fade In—Fade Out, The Stewardesses, Li'l Abner, for NBC-TV. Mrs. Katz and Katz (TV pilot); Judgment Day, Cheek to Cheek, The Marathon, Too Much Johnson. Checkmate!, Donovan, How Come You Never See Dr. Jekyll and Mr. Hyde Together?

PANTAGES, CLAYTON G.: Executive. b. Hartford, CT, March 6, 1927. e. Trinity Coll. Served various executive posts for 11 years with 20th Century-Fox; gen. sales mgr. Magna Pictures; Pres., International Coproductions, Inc., S.P. Films, Pantheon Entertainment Ltd., Clayton's Classics.

PAPAS, IRENE: Actress. b. near Corinth, Greece, 1926. Entered dramatic school at 12. At 16 sang and danced in variety

shows. Film debut in 1951 Greek film, Lost Angels; 1958 Greek Popular theatre in Athens.
STAGE: The Idiot, Journey's End, The Merchant of Venice, Inherit the Wind, That Summer, That Fall, Iphigenia in Aulis.
PICTURES: Dead City, The Unfaithful, Atilla the Hun, Theodora, Whirlpool, Tribute to a Bad Man, The Guns of Navarone, Antigone (Best Actress Award, Salonika Film Fest.), Electra (Best Actress Award, Salonika Film Fest.), Zorba the Greek, The Brotherhood, Anne of a Thousand Days, Z, A Dream of Kings, A Ciascuno il Suo, The Odyssey, The Trojan Women, Moses, Mohammed: Messenger of God, Lion of the Desert, Into the Night, The Assisi Underground, Sweet Country, High Season, Island, Drums of Fire, Banquet, Zoe.
TELEVISION: Moses the Lawgiver.

PARE, MICHAEL: Actor. b. Brooklyn, NY, 1959. e. Culinary Inst. of America, Hyde Park, NY. Worked as chef, and model before being discovered by ABC talent agent. Debut as singer-actor in Eddie and the Cruisers (1983).
PICTURES: The Philadelphia Experiment, Under Cover (Aust.), Streets of Fire, The Women's Club, World Gone Wild, Moon 44, Eddie and the Cruisers: Eddie Lives.
TELEVISION: Series: The Greatest American Hero (1981–83), Houston Knights. Movies: Crazy Times.

PARISH, JAMES ROBERT: Film historian/marketing exec. b. Cambridge, MA e. U. of PA (BBA, Phi Beta Kappa); U. of PA Law School (LLB). Member of NY Bar. Founder Entertainment Copyright Research Co., Inc. 1968–69, film reporter, Motion Picture Daily, weekly Variety. 1969–70, entertainment publicist, Harold Rand & co (NY). Currently marketing consultant in direct marketing industry, contributor to arts sections of major national newspapers and entertainment trade papers, series editor of show business books and author of over 75 books on the entertainment industry including: Hollywood Songster, The Great Detective Pictures, The Great Cop Pictures, The Great Science Fiction Pictures II, Complete Actors TV Credits (1948–88). The Great Combat Pictures; Black Action Pictures From Hollywood; The Great Detective Pictures; The Great Western Pictures II: The Great Gangster Pictures II: The Great Spy Pictures II; Actors TV Credits; The Best of MGM; The Forties Gals; The Great American Movies Book; Hollywood Happiness; The Funsters; Hollywood on Hollywood; The Hollywood Beauties; Elvis!; The Great Science Fiction Pictures; The Child Stars; The Jeannette MacDonald Story; Great Movie Heroes; Liza!; The RKO Gals; Vincent Price Unmasked; The George Raft File; and The Emmy Awards.

PARK, ROBERT H.: Executive. b. Atlanta, GA, May 11, 1916. e. U. of Texas. Attorney for Jefferson Amusement Co.; now bd. chmn., Tercar Theatre Company.

PARKER, ALAN: Director, Writer. b. Islington, London, England, Feb. 14, 1944. Worked way up in advertising industry from mail room to top writer and director of nearly 500 TV commercials between 1969–78.
PICTURES: Melody (s.p., 1968); No Hard Feelings (dir., s.p.); Our Cissy (dir., s.p.); Footsteps (dir., s.p.); Bugsy Malone (dir., s.p.; 5 British Academy Awards, 1975); Midnight Express (2 Acad. Awards), Fame (2 Acad. Awards), Shoot the Moon, Pink Floyd—The Wall, Birdy, Angel Heart, Mississippi Burning, Come and See the Paradise (dir., s.p.).
TELEVISION: The Evacuees.

PARKER, ELEANOR: Actress. b. Cedarville, OH, June 26, 1922. In Cleveland play group; in summer stock Martha's Vineyard; at Pasadena Community Playhouse.
PICTURES: They Died With Their Boots On, Buses Roar, Mission to Moscow, Between Two Worlds, Very Thought of You, Crime By Night, Last Ride, Never Say Goodbye, Pride of the Marines, Of Human Bondage, Escape Me Never, Woman in White, Voice of the Turtle, Chain Lightning, Caged, Three Secrets, Valentino, Millionaire for Christy, Detective Story, Scaramouche, Above and Beyond, Escape from Fort Bravo, Naked Jungle, Valley of the Kings, Many Rivers to Cross, Interrupted Melody, Man with the Golden Arm, King and Four Queens, Lizzie, Seventh Sin, Home from the Hill, Return to Peyton Place, Madison Avenue, The Oscar, An American Dream, Warning Shot, The Eye of the Cat, The Sound of Music, Sunburn.
TELEVISION: Bracken's World, Vanished, Guess Who's Coming to Dinner (pilot), Murder She Wrote, Fantasy Island.

PARKER, FESS: Actor. b. Fort Worth, TX, Aug. 16, 1925. e. U. of Southern California. U.S. Navy, 1943–46; national co., Mr. Roberts, 1951; m.p. debut, Untamed Frontier, 1952.
PICTURES: No Room for the Groom, Springfield Rifle, Thunder Over the Plains, Island in the Sky, Kid from Left Field, Take Me to Town, Them, Battle Cry, Davy Crockett, King of the Wild Frontier, Davy Crockett and the River Pirates, Great Locomotive Chase, Westward Ho the Wagons, Old Yeller, The Light in the Forest, The Hangman, The Jayhawkers, Hell Is for Heroes, Smoky.
TELEVISION: Davy Crockett (series), Mr. Smith Goes to Washington (series), Daniel Boone (series), Jonathan Winters, Walt Disney presents, Ed Sullivan, Phyllis Diller, Joey Bishop, Dean Martin, Red Skelton, Glen Campbell.

PARKER, JAMESON: Actor. b. Baltimore, MD, Nov. 18, 1947. e. Beloit Coll. Professional stage debut in Washington Theatre Club production, Caligula. Acted with Arena Stage in DC; worked in dinner theatres and summer stock. Moved to N.Y., working in TV commercials and toured in play, Equus. Feature film debut in The Bell Jar (1979).
PICTURES: A Small Circle of Friends, White Dog, American Justice (also prod.), Prince of Darkness, The Crystal Eye.
TELEVISION: Series: Somerset, One Life to Live, Simon and Simon. Movies: Women at West Point, Anatomy of a Seduction, The Gathering, Part II, The Promise of Love, Callie and Son, A Caribbean Mystery, Who Is Julia?

PARKER, SUZY: Actress. r.n. Cecelia Parker. b. San Antonio, TX, Oct. 28, 1933. m. actor Bradford Dillman. e. schools in NY, FL. Began career at 17 as fashion model; becoming the highest paid fashion model and cover girl in U.S.; went to Paris under contract to fashion magazine; film debut as model in Funny Face (1957); signed by 20th-Fox prod. chief Buddy Adler for part opposite Cary Grant in Kiss Them for Me.
PICTURES: Kiss Them For Me, Ten North Frederick, The Best of Everything, Circle of Deception, The Interns.

PARKINS, BARBARA: Actress. b. Vancouver, Canada, May 22, 1943.
PICTURES: Valley of the Dolls, The Kremlin Letter, Puppet on a Chain, The Mephisto Waltz, Bear Island.
TELEVISION: Peyton Place (series). Movies: A Taste of Evil, Snatched, Law of the Land, Captains and the Kings, Young Joe, The Forgotten Kennedy, Testimony of Two Men, Ziegfield: The Man and His Women, The Critical List, To Catch a King, Calendar Girl Murders, Peyton Place: The Next Generation, The Manions of America, Jennie: Lady Randolph Churchill.

PARKS, BERT: Announcer, M.C. b. Atlanta, GA, Dec. 30, 1914. Announcer, then chief announcer in Atlanta radio station; announcer, network, N.Y., for Eddie Cantor; m.c. for Xavier Cugat's show; U.S. Army, W.W.II; radio shows include Break the Bank, Stop the Music, Double or Nothing. Announcer Miss America Pageant, 1956–79.
TELEVISION: Break the Bank, Stop the Music.

PARKS, GORDON: Director, Writer, Photographer, Composer, Poet, Photojournalist. b. Fort Scott, KS, Nov. 30, 1912. From the age of 15 worked as piano player, bus boy, dining car waiter and prof. basketball player in MN before taking up photog. in late 1930s. Awarded 1st Julius Rosenwald Fellowship in photog. 1942. Worked with Roy Stryker at Farm Security Admin., WWII Office of War Info. correspondent. Photo-journalist, Life Mag., 1949–68, editorial dir.: Essence Magazine 1970–73 (and founder). Film debut 1961 with doc. Flavio (dir. and writer), followed by Diary of a Harlem Family (doc.) (Emmy Award). Winner of numerous awards including NAACP's Spingarn Medal and Governor's Medal of Honor. Recipient of 19 honorary degrees in lit., fine arts, humane letters.
AUTHOR: The Learning Tree; A Choice of Weapons; A Poet and His Camera; Whispers of Intimate Things; In Love; Born Black, Moments Without Proper Names, Flavio, To Smile in Autumn, Shannon.
PICTURES: The Learning Tree, Shaft, Shaft's Big Score, Super Cops, Leadbelly.
TELEVISION: The Odyssey of Solomon Northrup.

PARKS, MICHAEL: Actor. b. April 4, 1938. Made m.p. debut in Wild Seed, 1964.
PICTURES: Bus Riley's Back in Town, The Bible, The Idol, The Happening, The Last Hard Men, Sidewinder One. ffolkes, Hard Country, Savannah Smiles, King of the City, The Return of Josey Wales, Spiker, Arizona Heat, Nightmare Beach, Prime Suspect.
TELEVISION: Along Came Bronson (series), numerous TV movies: Can Ellen Be Saved?, Savage Bees, Chase, Dangerous Affection, Gore Vidal's Billy the Kid.

PARRISH, ROBERT R.: Director, Producer. b. Columbus, GA, Jan. 4, 1916. Actor before joining RKO in 1933, first as assistant director, then film editor. With various companies since, including 20th Century-Fox, Universal, Columbia, United Artists, J. Arthur Rank, etc. Won Academy Award, best film editing, Body and Soul, 1947. U.S. Navy 1941–45; won documentary Academy Award, 1942 and 1943 for Battle of Midway and December 7th. Formed own independent production company, Trimark Productions, Inc., 1955. Autobiographies: Growing Up in Hollywood, 1976; Hollywood Doesn't Live Here Anymore.
PICTURES: City Lights, All Quiet on the Western Front, The Divine Lady, A Double Life, Caught, No Minor Vices, All the King's Men, Cry Danger (dir.), The Mob, San Francisco Story, Assignment–Paris, My Pal Gus, Shoot First, The

Purple Plain, Lucy Gallant, Fire Down Below, Saddle the Wind, The Wonderful Country, In the French Style, Up From the Beach, Casino Royale, The Bobo, Duffy, A Town Called Bastard, The Marseilles Contract, Flashman, Mississippi Blues (doc., co-dir. with Bertrand Tavernier).

PARSONS, ESTELLE: Actress. b. Marblehead, MA, Jan. 20, 1927. e. Connecticut Coll. for Women, Bachelor's degree in political science. Attended Boston U. Law Sch. Helped harvest crops in England with the Women's Land Army. Was active in politics; worked for the Committee for the Nation's Health in Wash. and the Republican Finance Committee in Boston. Was elected to public office in Marblehead, Mass. Joined NBC-TV's Today Show as prod. asst.; then writer, feature producer and commentator. Appeared in two Julius Monk revues, Jerry Herman's Nightcap and the Threepenny Opera. Has appeared with the Lincoln Center Repertory Theatre, Mahagonny.
STAGE: Happy Hunting; Whoop Up; Beg, Borrow or Steal; Mrs. Dally Has a Lover (Theater World Award), Next Time I'll Sing to You (Obie Award), In the Summer House (Obie Award), Ready When You Are, C.B. Malcolm, The Seven Descents of Myrtle, And Miss Reardon Drinks a Little, The Norman Conquests, Ladies of the Alamo, Miss Margarida's Way, Pirates of Penzance, The Unguided Missile.
PICTURES: Ladybug, Ladybug, Bonnie and Clyde (Acad. Award, supporting actress, 1967), Rachel, Rachel, Don't Drink the Water, Strangers, Watermelon Man, I Never Sang For My Father, I Walk the Line, Two People, For Pete's Sake.
TELEVISION: Backstairs at the White House, The Front Page, All in the Family, The Gun and the Pulpit, Open Admissions.

PARSONS, LINDSLEY: Executive Vice Pres., Film Finances, Inc. Pres., Completion Service Co., Hollywood. Toronto. b. Tacoma, WA, Sept. 12, 1915. e. U. of California at L.A. On ed. staff City News Service, L.A.: Alhambra Post-Advocate; Calexico Chronicle; Santa Rosa Press Democrat; Humboldt Times; San Marino News (ed. & pub.). Joined Monogram 1931 as pub. dir. in 1933 author s.p. Sagebrush Trails; then wrote orig. s.p. Westerns for Monogram, Republic, Grand Nat'l. In 1939 assoc. prod. Tough Kid; from 1940 prod. numerous westerns; prod. Wayne Morris & James Oliver Curwood series for Allied Artists; prod. Motion Pictures Int'l, 1956–72. Exec. v.p., dir., Film Finances, Inc.
PICTURES: Rocky Rhythm Inn, Casa Manana, Big Timber, Call of the Klondike, Sierra Passage, Yukon, Manhunt, Yellow Fin, Northwest Territory, Desert Pursuit, Torpedo Alley, Jack Slade, Loophole, Cry Vengeance, Finger Man, Return of Jack Slade, Come On, The Intruder, Cruel Tower, Dragon Wells Massacre, Portland Expose, Oregon Passage, Wolf Larsen, Crash Boat, The Purple Gang, Mara of the Wilderness, Good Times, The Big Cube.
TELEVISION: Gray Ghost (series); Files of Jeffrey Jones, The Whistler.

PARTON, DOLLY: Singer, Composer, Actress. b. Sevierville, TN, Jan. 19, 1946. Gained fame as country music singer, composer and radio and TV personality. Many awards for recordings. Co-partner with Sandy Gallin, Sandollar Prods.
PICTURES: Nine to Five, The Best Little Whorehouse in Texas, Rhinestone (also music), Steel Magnolias.
TELEVISION: Porter Wagoner Show, Cass Walker program, Bill Anderson Show, Wilbur Bros. Show, Kenny, Dolly & Willie: Something Inside So Strong. Movies: A Smoky Mountain Christmas. 1987: Dolly (series); A Tennessee Mountain Thanksgiving.

PARTRIDGE, DEREK: TV talk and magazine show host, Interviewer, Newscaster, Presenter, Narrator, Writer. b. London, England, 1935. Ent. journalism on the Daily Express. Ent. industry 1959 as documentary scriptwriter with Film Producers' Guild. 1976–78: Rhodesian TV: Chief news anchor, live magazine programme Frankly Partridge, quizmaster The Kwhizz Kids. 1979 (Miami): newscaster, daily What's Happening South Florida, and Focus (WKAT/ABC). 1980 (New York): To the Point, and Special Edition. 1981–82: TV (Los Angeles): Newscaster/writer/interviewer for Financial News Network. 1982: The Romance of Words. The Guinness Book of Records Specials (announcer). Video Aktuell (Hollywood celebrities for German TV). Financial Inquiry (anchor/interviewer). 1984: Election Coverage '84. The Story of a News Story (Emmy winner), Travel Time. Information Power (Emmy winner). 1986–88: Music programmes host (Gulf Air, Saudia, Royal Jordanian). Interviewer: TV's Bloopers & Practical Jokes. Health Line '87; American Life Styles; Star du Siècle (French TV); Sexuality—Today's Decisions. 1988: Law in America; World Access TV; Over 50. Corporate videos for: Bank of America, Transamerica, Hilton Hotels, Coca Cola, Mercedes Benz, Armand Hammer, Getty Oil, American Red Cross, Lincoln Mercury.

PASETTA, MARTY: Producer-Director. b. June 16, 1932. e. U. Santa Clara.
TELEVISION: AFI Salutes to Fred Astaire, John Huston, Lillian Gish, Alfred Hitchcock and Jimmy Stewart; Gene Kelly Special; Elvis Aloha From Hawaii; Oscar, Emmy and Grammy Award Shows; A Country Christmas (1978–81); The Monte Carlo Show; Texaco Star Theatre-Opening Night; Burnett Discovers Domingo; Disneyland's 30th Anniversary Celebration; 10 Years of Cerebral Palsy Telethon; A Night at the Moulin Rouge; Soap Opera Awards; An All-Star Celebration Honoring Martin Luther King; Disneyland's Summer Vacation Party; Disney's "Captain EO" Grand Opening; 15th Anniversary of Disney World; Beach Boys. . . 25 Years Together; Super Night At the Superbowl; 20th Anniversary of Caesars Palace; Paris by Night with George Burns; "I Call You Friend" Papal Spacebridge '87; Walt Disney World's Celebrity Circus; Las Vegas—An All-Star 75th Anniversary; Julio Iglesias—Sold Out; The Ice Capades with Kirk Cameron; American All-Star Tribute Honoring Elizabeth Taylor.

PASSER, IVAN: Director, Writer. b. Prague, Czechoslovakia, July 10, 1933. e. Film Faculty of Acad. of Musical Arts, Prague. 1961, asst. dir. to Milos Forman on Audition which led to scripting for Forman. 1969, moved to U.S., worked in NY as longshoreman while studying Eng. U.S. dir. debut: Born to Win, 1971.
PICTURES: Writer: Loves of a Blonde, Fireman's Ball. Director: A Boring Afternoon (1965), Intimate Lighting, Born to Win, Law and Disorder, Crime and Passion, The Silver Bears, Cutter and Bone, Creator, Haunted Summer.
TELEVISION: (U.S.) Faerie Tale Theatre.

PASTER, GARY M.: Executive. b. St. Louis, MO, July 4, 1943. e. U. of Missouri, B.A.; U. of California at L.A., U. of Southern California Graduate Sch. of Business. 1970, joined The Burbank Studios as asst. to the pres. and as treas. 1976 v.p.—admin. and chmn. of the exec. comm. September, 1977 pres. Board of Directors/Trustees: Permanent Charities Committee of Entertainment Industry, St. Joseph Medical Center Fdn. American Women in Radio & TV, William H. Parker L.A. Police Fdn. Member: Academy of Motion Picture Arts and Sciences, Los Angeles Film Dev. Council, Hollywood Radio and T.V. Society, Acad. of Television Arts and Sciences. Advisory bd., Kaufman Astoria Studios, N.Y.

PASTERNAK, JOE: Producer. b. Szilagysomlyo, Hungary, Sept. 19, 1901. 2nd asst. dir. Paramount 1923; asst. dir. Universal (Hollywood), 1926, then prod. mgr. Berlin; made pictures in Vienna and Budapest, returned to Hollywood 1937; assoc. prod. then prod. A Champion of Champion producers in Fame ratings. Autobiography: Easy the Hard Way, 1956.
PICTURES: Zwei Menschen, Unter Falscher Flagge, Grosse Schensucht, Unsichtbare Front, Fraulein Paprika, Gruss Und Gruss, Veronika, Scandal in Budapest, Csibi, Spring Parade, Katherine, Three Smart Girls, 100 Men and a Girl, Mad About Music, That Certain Age, Three Smart Girls Grow Up, Destry Rides Again, It's a Date, Nice Girl, It Started With Eve, Presenting Lily Mars, Thousands Cheer, Two Girls and a Sailor, Music for Millions, Thrill of a Romance, Anchors Aweigh, Her Highness and the Bellboy, Two Sisters from Boston, Holiday in Mexico, No Leave No Love, This Time for Keeps, Three Daring Daughters, On an Island With You, Date With Judy, In the Good Old Summertime, Big City, Unfinished Dance, Nancy Goes to Rio, Summer Stock, That Midnight Kiss, Toast of New Orleans, The Great Caruso, Rich, Young and Pretty, The Strip, Merry Widow, Skirts Ahoy!, Because You're Mine, Small Town Girl, Latin Lovers, Easy to Love, Flame and the Flesh, Student Prince, Athena, Hit the Deck, Love Me or Leave Me, Meet Me in Las Vegas, Opposite Sex, 10,000 Bedrooms, This Could Be the Night, Where the Boys Are, Jumbo, A Ticklish Affair, Girl Happy, Penelope, The Sweet Ride.

PATERSON, NEIL: Novelist, Screenwriter. b. Scotland, Dec. 15, 1916. e. Edinburgh U. War Service Lt. R.N.V.R. Early career as novelist. Awarded Atlantic Award in Literature, 1946. Dir. Grampian TV 1960–86. Member Chmn. of Production; dir., consultant: films of Scotland 1954–78. Gov., British Film Institute 1958–60. Gov., National Film School 1970–80. Gov., Pitlochry Fest. Theatre, 1966–76. Chmn., Literature Comm. Scottish Arts Council 1967–76. Member Arts Council Gt. Britain 1974–76.
NOVELS: The China Run, Behold Thy Daughter, And Delilah, Man on the Tight Rope.
PICTURES: Man on a Tight Rope, The Little Kidnappers, Woman for Joe, High Tide at Noon, The Shiralee, Innocent Sinners, Room at the Top (s.p. Acad. Award, 1960), The Spiral Road, The Golden Fool, The Forty Days of Musa Dagh, Keeper of My Heart.

PATINKIN, MANDY: Actor. b. Chicago, IL, Nov. 20, 1947. e. U. of Kansas, Juilliard Sch. (Drama Div.) (1972–74). In regional theatre before coming to New York where played with Shakespeare Festival Public Theater (Trelawny of the Wells, Hamlet, Rebel Women). Recording: Mandy Patinkin: Dress Casual, 1989.
THEATER: Savages, Shadow Box (Bdwy debut), Evita (Tony Award), Henry IV, Part I (Central Park), Sunday in the Park With George (Tony Award), The Knife, Follies in Concert, A Winter's Tale, Dress Casual (solo concert).

PICTURES: The Big Fix, French Postcards, The Last Embrace, Night of the Juggler, Ragtime, Daniel, Yentl, Maxie, The Princess Bride, The House on Carroll Street, Alien Nation, Dick Tracy, Impromtu.
TELEVISION: That Thing on ABC, That 2nd Thing on ABC, Charleston (movie), Taxi, Sparrow, Streets of Gold, Midnight Special.

PATRICK, C.L.: Theatre Executive. b. Honaker, VA., Dec. 6, 1918. Former pres. of Fuqua Industries which owned Martin Theatres and Gulf States Theatres. Prior to this was pres. and chairman of Martin Theatres. Presently chairman of board Carmike Cinemas, Inc. Member NATO exec. com.; v.p. Variety International; director, Will Rogers Institute; Motion Picture Pioneer of 1976; Recipient of: the Sherrill Corwin Award, 1984; Salah Hassanein Humanitarian Award, Show-East '88.

PATRICK, MICHAEL W.: Executive. b. Columbus, GA, May 17, 1950. e. Columbus Coll, B.S., 1972. Pres., Carmike Cinemas. 1989, assumed additional post of chief exec.
MEMBER: v.p., NATO; pres., Ga. Theatre Owners Assn.; exec. comm., Will Rogers Institute; Variety Intl.; Motion Picture Pioneers.

PATTON, WILL: Actor. b. Charleston, SC. e. NC School of the Arts, 1975.
THEATER: Tourists and Refugees #2 (La Mama E.T.C., Obie Award, Best Actor), Fool For Love (1982 Obie Award, Best Actor), Goose and Tomtom (Public Theatre), A Lie of the Mind.
PICTURES: Silkwood, After Hours, Desperately Seeking Susan, A Gathering of Old Men, Belizaire (the Cajun), No Way Out, Stars and Bars, Wildfire, The Lizard's Tale, Signs of Life, Everybody Wins, Jackal's Run, A Shock to the System.
TELEVISION: Kent State, Ryan's Hope, Search For Tomorrow.

PAUL, M. B.: Cameraman, Director. r.n. Morrison Bloomfield Paul. b. Montreal, Canada. Sept. 30, 1909. e. De Paul U. Newsreel, publicity picture service; partner, Seymour Studios, 1930–33; film test biz. own studio. Hollywood, 1933–35; prod. adv. films, asst. in N.Y. E.W. Hammons, 1945–47; Acad. Award, one-piece color translucent background system, 1950. Dir. of photography, optical effects, Daystar, United Artists, Outer Limits, 1963; designed, patented, Scenoramic process, 1965. Camera, Paradise Road. Features, Film project supervision A/V consult. Sceno 360 surround system development. Mem. AMPAS, Friars, SMPTE.

PAUL, STEVEN: Director, Actor. b. New York, NY, May 16, 1958.
THEATER: Actor: Happy Birthday Wanda June, Burning.
PICTURES: Slapstick, Falling in Love Again (prod., dir., s.p., actor); Never Too Young Too Die, Fate, Eternity (prod., dir., co-s.p.), Emanon (exec. prod., actor).
TELEVISION: Actor: A Visiting Angel, Whatever Happened to Dobie Gillis?

PAULEY, JANE: TV host and journalist. b. Indianapolis, IN, Oct. 31, 1950. m. Doonesbury creator Garry Trudeau. e. Indiana U. Involved in Indiana state politics before joining WISH-TV, Indianapolis, as reporter. Co-anchored midday news reports and anchored weekend news reports. Co-anchor of nightly news at WMAQ-TV, NBC station in Chicago. Joined Today show in October, 1976, as featured regular, prior to which had made guest appearances on that program. Now co-host Today Show.

PAVAN, MARISA: Actress, r.n. Marisa Pierangeli. b. Cagliari, Sardinia, Italy, June 19, 1932. m. actor Jean Pierre Aumont. e. Torquato Tasso Coll. Twin sister of late Pier Angeli, actress. Came to U.S. 1950; m.p. debut in What Price Glory (1952).
PICTURES: Down Three Dark Streets, Drum Beat, Rose Tattoo, Diane, Man in the Gray Flannel Suit, John Paul Jones, Solomon and Sheba, Midnight Story.

PAVLIK, JOHN M.: Executive. b. Melrose, IA, Dec. 3, 1939. e. U. of Minnesota, B.A., 1963. Reporter, Racine (WI) Journal-Times, San Bernardino (CA) Sun-Telegram, 1963–66; Writer, News Bureau, Pacific Telephone, Los Angeles, 1966–68; asst. dir. of public relations, Association of Motion Picture and Television Producers, 1968–72; dir. of public relations, 1972–78; v.p., 1978–79; exec. administrator, Academy of Motion Picture Arts and Sciences, 1979–82; exec. dir., M.P. & TV Fund, 1982–88; member, board of dir., Permanent Charities Comm. of the Entertainment Industries, 1979–84; member, bd. of dir., Hollywood Chamber of Commerce, 1979–85; v.p., Los Angeles Film Dev. Committee, 1977– 78, member, exec. council, 1974–85; special consultant, California Motion Picture Council, 1974–79.

PAVLOW, MURIEL: Actress. b. June 27, 1921. e. England, Switzerland. Stage debut in Dear Octopus, 1938; screen debut in Romance in Flanders (1937).
PICTURES: Quiet Wedding, Night Boat to Dublin, Shop at Sly Corner, It Started in Paradise, The Net (Project M7), Malta Story, Conflict of Wings (Fuss Over Feathers), Doctor in the House, Simon and Laura, Reach for the Sky, Eye Witness, Tiger in the Smoke, Doctor at Large, Rooney, Whirlpool, Meet Miss Marple.

PAY, WILLIAM: UK Manager Quigley Publishing Co., Inc. b. London, England. Joined London office Quigley Publications. Served in RAF, 1941–46; rejoined Quigley; dir. Burnup Service Ltd., 1951; London news ed., Quigley Pub., 1955. Dir., Quigley Pub. Ltd., 1961; appt. mgr. dir., 1963; mgr. dir., Burnup Company. Appt. Sec. British Kinematograph Sound & TV Society. Conference Co-ordinator biennial Intern. Film & TV Technology Conferences in U.K., 1975–87.

PAYNE, JOHN: Actor. b. Roanoke, VA, 1912. e. Mercersburg Acad., PA; Roanoke Coll. of Virginia; Columbia. On radio programs. Stage debut, 1973, Good News.
PICTURES: Dodsworth, Wings of the Navy, Indianapolis Speedway, Kid Nightingale, Stardust, Maryland, Great Profile, Tin Pan Alley, King of the Lumberjacks, Tear Gas Squad, Great American Broadcast, Sun Valley Serenade, Week-End in Havana, Remember the Day, To the Shores of Tripoli, Hello Frisco Hello, The Dolly Sisters, Sentimental Journey, Razor's Edge, Wake Up and Dream, Miracle on 34th Street, Larceny, Saxon Charm, El Paso, Crooked Way, Captain China, Eagle and Hawk, Passage West, Crosswinds, Blazing Forest, Caribbean, The Vanquished, Kansas City, Confidential, Raiders of the 7 Seas, 99 River Street, Rails into Laramie, Silver Lode, Hell's Island, Santa Fe Passage, Road to Denver, Tennessee's Partner, Hell's Island, Slightly Scarlet, Rebel in Town, The Boss, Bail Out at 43,000, Hidden Fear, The Gift of the Nile.
TELEVISION: The Restless Gun (series), Call of the West (series), The Philadelphia Story.

PAYNE, NORMAN: Artists' and writers' manager. b. London, England. Ent. entertainment ind., 1939. Early career music, then formed talent agency, J.P. Productions, 1945. Later bought by MCA, 1951. Became dir. MCA and head of light ent. for theatres and TV throughout Europe. On MCA terminating reformed agency. TV offices also in Germany, Australia.

PAYNTER, ROBERT: Cinematographer. b. London, England. e. Mercer Sch. First job in industry at 15 years as camera trainee with Government Film Dept.
PICTURES: Hannibal Brooks (debut, 1969), The Nightcomers, The Mechanic, Firepower, Superman, Superman II, Trading Places, An American Werewolf in London, The Final Conflict (co-cine.), Superman III, When the Whales Came.

PAYS, AMANDA: Actress. b. Berkshire, England, 1959. m. actor Corbin Bernsen. Began as a model. Studied French, art and pottery at Hammersmith Polytechnic. Acting debut: Cold Room (HBO).
PICTURES: The Kindred, Oxford Blues, Off Limits, Leviathan.
TELEVISION: A.D. (mini-series), Max Headroom (series), The Pretenders.

PAYSON, MARTIN D.: Executive. Practiced law privately before joining Warner Communications, Inc. as v.p. 1970. Later named exec. v.p.–gen. counsel. 1987, appt. to 3-member office of pres., WCI.

PEAKER, E. J.: Actress, Singer, Dancer. Edra Jeanne Peaker, b. Tulsa, OK, Feb. 22. e. U. of New Mexico, U. of Vienna, Austria. Stage debut Bye, Bye Birdie; film debut Hello, Dolly (1969). Films include All American Boy, Private Roads, The Four Deuces, Graduation Day, Fire in the Night.
TELEVISION: That's Life series, The Flying Nun, That Girl, Movie of the Week, Love American Style, Odd Couple, Police Woman, Rockford Files, Get Christie Love.

PEARCE, CHRISTOPHER: Producer. b. Dursley, Eng. Entered industry as gen. mgr. American Zoetrope. From 1982 to 1985 served as exec. in chg. of prod. for Cannon Films Inc. overseeing prod. on 150 films incl. That Championship Season, Runaway Train, Fool For Love and Barfly. In 1987 became sr. v.p. and chief operating officer Cannon Group. Since May, 1989 pres., and chief operating officer Cannon Pictures.
PICTURES: Prod. Coming Out of the Ice.

PEARCE, RICHARD: Director, Cinematographer. b. San Diego, CA. e. Yale U., degree in Eng. lit., 1965. New School for Social Research, M.A., political economics. Worked with Don Pennebaker on documentaries and with a Seattle-based owner of TV stations in the Pacific Northwest. Photographed Emile de Antonio's America Is Hard to See. In 1970 went to Chile where he dir., photographed and edited Campamento, an award-winning documentary.
PICTURES: As photographer: Woodstock; Marjoe; Interviews With My Lai Veterans; Hearts and Minds.
PICTURES: As director: Heartland; Threshold; Country; No Mercy, The Long Walk Home.
TELEVISION: The Gardener's Son; Siege; No Other Love; Sessions, Dead Man Out.

PECK, GREGORY: Actor, Producer. b. La Jolla, CA, April 5, 1916. e. U. of California; Neighborhood Playhouse Sch. of Dramatics. On dramatic stage (The Doctor's Dilemma, The Male Animal, Once in a Lifetime, The Play's the Thing, You Can't Take It With You, The Morning Star, The Willow and I, Sons and Soldiers, etc.); on screen 1944 in Days of Glory. Voted one of ten best Money-Making Stars Motion Picture Herald-Fame Poll, 1947, 1952. Co-prod. and starred in Big Country, for his company, Anthony Productions; prod. the Trial of the Catonsville Nine, The Dove (St. George Productions). Pres., Acad. M.P. Arts and Sciences, 1967–70. Founding mem., bd. mem and chmn. American Film Inst. Recipient, Jean Hersholt Humanitarian Award, 1986. AFI Life Achievement Award, 1989.

PICTURES: Days of Glory (debut, 1944), Keys of the Kingdom, Valley of Decision, Spellbound, Yearling, Duel in the Sun, Macomber Affair, Gentleman's Agreement, The Macomber Affair, The Paradine Case, Yellow Sky, 12 O'Clock High, The Great Sinner, The Gunfighter, Only the Valiant, David and Bathsheba, Captain Horatio Hornblower, The World in His Arms, The Snows of Kilimanjaro, Roman Holiday, Night People, Man With a Million, Purple Plains, Man in the Gray Flannel Suit, Moby Dick, Designing Woman, The Big Country, The Bravados, Pork Chop Hill (also prod.), On the Beach, Beloved Infidel, Guns of Navarone, Cape Fear (also prod.), To Kill a Mockingbird (Acad. Award, 1963), Captain Newman, M.D., Behold a Pale Horse (also prod.), Mirage, Arabesque, MacKenna's Gold, Stalking Moon, The Chairman, Marooned, I Walk the Line, Shootout, Billy Two Hats, The Omen, MacArthur (also prod.), The Boys from Brazil (also prod.), The Sea Wolves (also prod.), Amazing Grace and Chuck, Old Gringo.

TELEVISION: Mini-series: The Blue and the Gray, Movies: The Scarlet and the Black (also prod.). Specials: We the People 200: The Constitutional Gala.

PEERCE, LARRY: Director. b. Bronx, NY. Son of late singer Jan Peerce.

PICTURES: One Potato, Two Potato, The Incident, Goodbye Columbus, The Sporting Club, The Big TNT Show, A Separate Peace, Ash Wednesday, The Other Side of the Mountain, Two Minute Warning, The Other Side of the Mountain—Part II, The Bell Jar, Why Would I Lie?, Love Child, Hard to Hold, Wired.

TELEVISION: A Stranger Who Looks Like Me, Love Lives On, I Take These Men, The Fifth Missile, Prison for Children, Queenie, Elvis and Me, The Neon Ceiling.

PELLATT, JOHN: Production Executive. Abandoned school for theatre at age of 14. Became stage manager before serving in H.M. forces. Then became assistant director for Warner Bros., MGM, London Films, etc. Since 1955 worked as prod. manager/assoc. producer with British Lion, Columbia, Paramount, United Artists, Ivan Tors, American International. Also while assistant gen. prod. mgr. 20th Century Fox, associated with Inn of Sixth Happiness, Roots of Heaven, The Blue Angel, Sons and Lovers, Sink the Bismarck.

PICTURES: Noose, The Wooden Horse, Silent Dust, Lavender Hill Mob, Man in the White Suit, Ivanhoe, Innocents in Paris, Mogambo, Knights of the Round Table, A Kid for Two Farthings, Oh Rosalinda, The Twelve Days of Christmas, The Captain's Paradise, Zarak Khan, The Green Man, St. Trinians, Only Two Can Play, They're a Weird Mob, Age of Consent, Count Five and Die, Help, The Revolutionary, Wuthering Heights, Elephant Country, Who Slew Auntie Roo, Tower of Evil, The Diamond Mercenaries (Killer Force in U.S.), One Away. (South & S.W. Africa).

TELEVISION: Series for Incorporated Television Espionage. Worked in Europe, Middle and Far East, India, East and North Africa, Congo, Bahamas, Australia, Hollywood, Southern Africa, The Zoo Gang TV series, Born Free TV series (Kenya).

PENN, ARTHUR: Director. b. Philadelphia, PA, Sept. 27, 1922. e. Black Mountain Coll., Asheville, NC; U. of Perugia, U. of Florence in Italy. Began as TV dir. in 1953, twice winner of Sylvania Award. Dir. stage plays Two for the Seesaw, Miracle Worker (Tony Award), Toys in the Attic, All the Way Home, Golden Boy, Wait Until Dark, Sly Fox, Monday After the Miracle, Hunting Cockroaches. Entered m.p. as dir. of Left-Handed Gun in 1958.

PICTURES: The Miracle Worker, Mickey One, The Chase, Bonnie and Clyde, Alice's Restaurant, Little Big Man, Visions of Eight (co-dir.), Night Moves, The Missouri Breaks, Four Friends (also co-prod.), Target, Penn and Teller Get Killed (prod., dir.).

PENN, CHRISTOPHER: Actor. Brother of actor Sean Penn.

PICTURES: Rumble Fish, All the Right Moves, Footloose, The Wild Life, Pale Rider, Return From the River Kwai, Best of the Best.

PENN, SEAN: Actor. b. Burbank, CA, Aug. 17, 1960. Son of actor-director Leo Penn, actress Eileen Ryan. e. Santa Monica H.S. Served as apprentice for two years at Group Repertory Theatre, L.A. Acted in Earthworms, Heartland, The Girl on the Via Flaminia, etc. First prof appearance as guest star on TV's Barnaby Jones. On Bdwy. in Heartland, then Slab Boys. Also Hurlyburly (Westwood Playhouse, LA).

PICTURES: Taps (debut), Fast Times at Ridgemont High, Bad Boys, Crackers, Racing with the Moon, The Falcon and the Snowman, At Close Range, Shanghai Surprise, Colors, Judgment in Berlin, Casualties of War, We're No Angels, State of Grace.

TELEVISION: Movies: Concrete Cowboys, Hellinger's Law, The Killing of Randy Webster. Series: Barnaby Jones.

PENNEBAKER, D.A.: Director. b. Evanston, IL, 1926. r.n. Donn Alan Pennebaker. e. Yale U. Studied engineering, then set up own electronics firm. Worked in advertising before writing and directing experimental films. 1959 joined Richard Leacock and others in equipment-sharing film co-op, Filmakers. 1963 set up own co. Uses cinema verite approach, often shooting in 16mm and blowing up to 35mm.

PICTURES: Opening in Moscow (1959); Primary (co-dir.); Balloon (co-dir.); David; Jane; Mr. Pearson; Don't Look Back; Monterey Pop; Beyond the Law (co-photo, only); One P.M.; Sweet Toronto; Maidstone (co-photo only); From the Pole to the Equator (ed. only).

PEPLOE, CLARE: Writer, director. Sister of screenwriter Mark Peploe and wife of dir. Bernardo Bertolucci.

PICTURES: Couples and Robbers (s.p.); Zabriskie Point (asst. to Antonioni); 1900 (asst. to Bertolucci); High Season (dir., co-s.p.).

PEPPARD, GEORGE: Actor, b. Detroit, MI, Oct. 1, 1928. e. Dearborn H.S., Carnegie Tech., B.F.A., fine arts. U.S. Marine Corps. Legit. stage debut, Pittsburgh Playhouse, 1949. Worked as mason, construction laborer, fencing instructor, Braddock, PA. Signed by Sam Spiegel to appear in The Strange One (debut, 1957).

STAGE: Girls of Summer, The Pleasure of His Company; Papa: The Legendary Lives of Ernest Hemingway (one-man show).

PICTURES: Pork Chop Hill, Home from the Hill, The Subterraneans, Breakfast At Tiffany's, How the West Was Won, The Victors, The Carpetbaggers, The Third Day, Operation Crossbow, The Blue Max, Tobruk, Rough Night in Jericho, P.J., House of Cards, What's So Bad About Feeling Good, Pendulum, Cannon for Cordoba, The Executioner, One More Train to Rob, The Groundstar Conspiracy, Newman's Law, Damnation Alley, Five Days From Home (also prod., dir., s.p.), Your Ticket Is No Longer Valid, Battle Beyond the Stars, Race to the Yankee Zephyr, From Hell to Victory, Silence Like Glass.

TELEVISION: Little Moon of Alban, Suspicion, U.S. Steel Hour, Alfred Hitchcock Presents, Matinee Theatre, Alcoa-Goodyear Playhouse, Studio One, Hallmark Hall of Fame, Banacek (series), The Bravos, Doctors Hospital, Story of Dr. Sam Sheppard, Crisis in Mid-Air, Torn Between Two Lovers, The A Team (series), Man Against the Mob.

PEPPERCORN, CARL: Executive. b. New York, NY. e. NYU. Ent. film ind. FBO (forerunner of RKO), held var. sls. positions, home office and branches. Lt. Comm. US Navy, WW II; pres. Military Bank of Naples, sales mgr. N.Y. branch RKO; asst. to Eastern sales mgr., RKO; gen'l sales mgr.,. RKO Canada; pres. Dairy-maid Chocolate Co., Toronto; v.p. Fairweather Dept. Stores, Canada; chmn. bd. Andako Mining Co., Canada; v.p. & gen'l sales mgr. Continental Dist. Inc.; v.p. & gen'l sales mgr. Embassy Pictures, Inc.; exec. v.p. and gen'l sales mgr. Cinema V Inc, pres. & sls. mgr., U.M. Film Distributors and Peppercorn-Wormser Film Distributors; Diversified Film Representatives, Inc., Peppercorn Enterprises.

PERAKOS, SPERIE P.: Executive. b. New Britain, CT, Nov. 12, 1915. e. Cheshire Acad., Yale U., Harvard Law Sch. Student mgr., Stanley-Warner thtrs., 1939–40; Perakos Theatres 1940 to present; Capt., U.S.A. Intelligence with 35 inf. division. Fellow, Pierson Coll., Yale, 1946–present; Yale Alumni Bd., 1949 to present; Yale Alumni Film Bd. 1952 to present; member Alumni Council for Yale Drama Sch.; past pres. Yale Club of New Britain, Conn.; dir. of Films & Filmings Seminars, Pierson Coll., Yale; prod. Antigone, 1962; pres. Norma Film Prod., Inc., 1962 to present. Past pres. now chmn. Yale's Peabody Museum Associates and member of the University Council of the Peabody Museum. Pres., Perakos Theatres, Conn. Theatre Circuit, Inc.

PERENCHIO, ANDREW J.: Executive. b. Fresno, CA, Dec. 20, 1930. e. U. of California. Vice pres., Music Corp. of America, 1958–62; General Artists Corp., 1962–64; pres., owner, Chartwell Artists, Ltd., theatrical agency, Los Angeles, 1964; pres. & CEO, Tandem Productions, Inc., and TAT Communications Co., 1973–83, then became principal with Norman Lear in Embassy Communications. Held post of pres. & CEO of Embassy Pictures.

PERKINS, ANTHONY: Actor. b. New York, NY, Apr. 14, 1932. Son of late actor Osgood Perkins. e. Columbia U., Rollins Coll.

Broadway stage debut in Tea and Sympathy. Wrote s.p. Last of Sheila, 1973.
STAGE: Tea and Sympathy (Theatre World Award, 1955), Look Homeward Angel, Greenwillow, Harold, The Star-Spangled Girl, Steambath (also dir.), Equus, Romantic Comedy.
PICTURES: The Actress, Friendly Persuasion, The Lonely Man, Fear Strikes Out, The Tin Star, This Bitter Earth, Desire Under the Elms, This Angry Age, The Matchmaker, Green Mansions, On the Beach, Tall Story, Psycho, Goodbye Again, Phaedra, Five Miles to Midnight, The Trial, Two Are Guilty, The Fool Killer, The Adorable Idiot, Is Paris Burning, A Ravishing Idiot, The Champagne Murders, Pretty Poison, Catch 22, Someone Behind the Door, Ten Days' Wonder, WUSA, The Life and Times of Judge Roy Bean, Play It As It Lays, Lovin' Molly, Murder on the Orient Express, Mahogany, Remember My Name, Winter Kills, The Black Hole, ffolkes, Double Negative, Twice a Woman, Psycho II, Crimes of Passion, For the Term of His Natural Life, The Thrill of Genius, Psycho III (also dir.), Shadow of Death, Destroyer, Edge of Sanity, Lucky Stiff (dir.), Enid's Sleeping, Love at Large.
TELEVISION: Kraft Theatre, Studio One, U.S. Steel Hour, Armstrong Theatre. Movies: How Awful About Allan, Les Miserables, First You Cry, Sins of Dorian Gray, Napoleon and Josephine: A Love Story.

PERKINS, ELIZABETH: Actress. b. Queens, NY, 1961. Grew up in Vermont. After high school moved to Chicago to study at Goodman School of Drama. Two months after moving to NY in 1984, landed a role in the national touring co. of Brighton Beach Memoirs, later performing part on Broadway. Acted with Playwright's Horizon, NY Ensemble Theater and Shakespeare in the Park.
PICTURES: About Last Night...(1987), From the Hip, Big, Sweethearts Dance, Queens Logic, Enid is Sleeping..

PERKINS, JOHN HENRY ROWLAND II: Executive. b. July 10, 1934, Los Angeles, CA. e. U. of Southern California, UCLA. Joined William Morris Agency, 1959; exec. in TV dept. In January, 1975, co-founded Creative Artists Agency, of which is senior partner and first pres. Member Hollywood Radio & TV Society since 1964, and Academy of TV Arts & Sciences since 1962. Mem. bd. of dir. of HRTS and bd. of gov. Acad. of TV Arts and Sciences. Served on bds. of various charities. Intl. dir., world organization of wine.

PERKINS, MILLIE: Actress. b. 1939.
PICTURES: The Diary of Anne Frank, Wild in the Country, Wild in the Streets, Lady Cocoa, Table for Five, At Close Range, Jake Speed, Slam Dance, Wall Street, Two Moon Junction.
TELEVISION: Series: Knots Landing. Movies: A.D., The Thanksgiving Promise, Penalty Phase, Anatomy of an Illness, Shattered Vows, License to Kill, Strange Voices, Broken Angel.

PERLMAN, RHEA: Actress. b. Brooklyn, NY, March 31, 1948. e. Hunter Coll. m. actor-dir. Danny DeVito. Co-founder Colonnades Theatre Lab., NY and New Street prod. co with Danny De Vito.
TELEVISION: Special: Funny, You Don't Look 200, Two Daddies (voice). Series: Cheers (Emmy, supp actress, 1984, 85, and 86). Movies: I Want to Keep My Baby! Stalk the Wild Child, Having Babies II, Intimate Strangers, Mary Jane Harper Cried Last Night, Like Normal People, Drop-out Father, The Ratings Game, Dangerous Affection, A Family Again.
PICTURES: Love Child, My Little Pony, Enid is Sleeping.

PERLMAN, RON: Actor. b. New York, NY, April 13. While in high school, part of comedy team that played clubs. e. City U. of NY, U. of Minnesota, M.F.A. Joined Classic Stage Company, NY, for 2 years.
THEATER: NY: The Architect and the Emperor of Assyria (also toured Europe), American Heroes, The Resistable Rise of Arturo Ui, Tiebele and Her Demon, La Tragedie de Carmen.
PICTURES: Quest for Fire, The Ice Pirates, The Name of the Rose.
TELEVISION: Series: Beauty and the Beast.

PERMUT, DAVID A.: Producer. b. New York, NY. e. U. of California, 1972. 1974, pres., Diversified Artists Intl.; 1975, pres., Theatre Television Corp.; 1979, formed Permut Presentations, Inc., of which is pres. Production deals with Columbia Pictures (1979), Lorimar Productions (1981), Universal (1985), and United Artists (1986).
PICTURES: Give 'Em Hell Harry (prod.); Fighting Back (exec. prod.); Blind Date (prod.); Richard Pryor—Live in Concert (exec. prod.); Dragnet (prod.).
TELEVISION: Mistress (sprv. prod.); Love Leads the Way (exec. prod.).

PERLMUTTER, DAVID M.: Producer. b. Toronto, Canada, 1934. e. U. of Toronto. Pres., Quadrant Films Ltd.
PICTURES: The Neptune Factor, 1972; Sunday in the Country; It Seemed Like a Good Idea at the Time; Love at First Sight, Find the Lady; Blood and Guts, The Third Walker, Two Solitudes; Fast Company; Double Negative, Nothing Personal; Misdeal, Love.

PERREAU, GIGI: Actress. r.n. Ghislaine Perreau; b. Los Angeles, CA, Feb. 6, 1941. Prof. m.p. debut in Madame Curie 1943; many stage and TV guest appearances.
PICTURES: Dark Waters, Abigail, Dear Heart, Family Honeymoon, Roseanna McCoy, High Barbaree, Song of Love, Green Dolphin Street, Two Girls and a Sailor, Shadow on the Wall, My Foolish Heart, For Heaven's Sake, Never a Dull Moment, Reunion in Reno, Lady Pays Off, Weekend with Father, Has Anybody Seen My Gal, Bonzo Goes to College, There's Always Tomorrow, Man in the Gray Flannel Suit, Dance With Me Henry, Tammy Tell Me True, Journey to the Center of Time, Hell on Wheels.

PERRINE, VALERIE: Actress. b. Phoenix, AZ, Sept. 3 1943. e. U. of Arizona. Was showgirl in Las Vegas before discovered by agent Robert Walker who got her contract with Universal Pictures. Film debut in Slaughterhouse Five (1972).
PICTURES: The Last American Hero, Lenny (N.Y. Film Critics Award, best supp. actress, Acad. Award nom., Best Actress, Cannes Fest., Actress of the Year, United Motion Picture Assn.), W. C. Fields and Me, Mr. Billion, Superman, The Electric Horseman, Can't Stop the Music, Superman II, The Border, Water, Maid to Order, Bright Angel.
TELEVISION: When Your Lover Leaves, Malibu, The Couple Takes a Wife, Ziegfeld: The Man and His Women, Faerie Tale Theatre, Rodney Dangerfield, Special, Marion Rose White, Steambath, Una Casa a Roma. Series: Leo and Liz in Beverly Hills.

PERRY, ANTHONY: Producer. b. London, England, 1929. Ent. m.p. ind. 1948 with Two Cities story dept. asst. story ed., Rank Prods. Wrote orig. story and prod. asst. Simba. Prod., The Secret Place in 1957. Created and prod. TV series, Interpol Calling, 1959; founded Eyeline Films, prod. many Brit. prize-winning commercials. Sold Eyeline Films, 1963; wrote, dir. Emma, 1964–65, res. prod. Keep Films/Embassy Prods., London, 1966–67; prod. Dare I Weep, Dare I Mourn, for ABC-TV, and Fernandel TV series. Admin. Yellow Submarine, joined Trickfilm as man. dir. Chmn. Film & TV Copyrights, Ltd.
PICTURES: The Impersonator, Girl on Approval, The Party's Over.

PERRY, EARL: Circuit Executive. b. Aug. 11, 1921. e. Tulane U. Spent 4 yrs. as Air Force officer in World War II. Worked for Twentieth Century Fox for four years; then entered exhibition in 1951 as vice pres. and gen. mgr. of Pittman Theatres; in 1966, formed Ogden-Perry Theatres, and as pres., operates theatres in Louisiana, Mississippi, Tennessee, and Florida. Past President of NATO of Louisiana; Past Chief Barker of Variety Club Tent 45.

PERRY, FRANK: Executive, Director, Producer, Writer. b. 1930. Served as apprentice, Westport, CT Country Playhouse; spent nine years in theater as stage mgr., prod. mgr., and managing director. U.S. Army, 1952–54; director-observer, Actors Studio, 1955; also prod. for the Theatre Guild. Pres. & CEO Corsair Pictures.
PICTURES: Somersault, David and Lisa, Ladybug, Ladybug, The Swimmer, Last Summer, Trilogy, Diary of a Mad Housewife, Doc, Play It As It Lays, The Man on the Swing, Rancho Deluxe, Mommie Dearest (also co-s.p.), Monsignor, Hello Again (prod., dir.).
TELEVISION: Truman Capote's A Christmas Memory, Thanksgiving Visitors, JFK—A One Man Show, Skag (premiere), Dummy.

PERRY, SIMON: Producer, Writer. b. England. Ent. ind. 1974. Early career in stage and television production. Prod. mini-budget feature Knots; prod. dir. Eclipse. Served on bureau staff of Variety. Ran the National Film Development Fund for two years. In 1982 set up Umbrella Films to produce Another Time, Another Place, Loose Connections, Hotel Du Paradis, Nanon, White Mischief.

PERSCHY, MARIA: Actress. b. Eisenstadt, Austria, Sept. 23, 1940. e. Max Rheinhardt Seminar, Vienna. Widow of John Melson, writer. Started in 1958 with German film (Nasser Asphalt) and has appeared in over 50 European and U.S. features. Has also appeared on European TV. Recipient of Laurel Award in 1963.
PICTURES: Man's Favorite Sport, Squadron 633, Ride the High Wind, Murders in the Rue Morgue, Last Day of the War, The Desperate Ones, The Tall Woman, Witch Without a Broom, etc.
TELEVISION: General Hospital, Hawaii Five-O.

PERSKY, LESTER: Executive. b. New York, NY, July 6, 1927. e. Brooklyn Coll. Officer in U.S. Merchant Marine, 1946–48. Founder and pres. of own adv. agency, 1951–1964. Theatrical stage producer, 1966–69. Produced Fortune and Men's Eyes for MGM in 1971. In 1973 creative director and co-owner Persky Bright Org. (owner-financier of numerous motion pictures for private investment group). Films include Last Detail, Golden Voyage of Sinbad, For Pete's Sake, California Split, The Man Who Would Be King, The Front, Shampoo. Also Hard Times, Taxi Driver, Missouri Breaks, Funny Lady, Gator, Bound for Glory, Sinbad and the Eye of the Tiger. Lester Persky Productions, Inc.

PICTURES: Produced Equus, Hair, Yanks.

TELEVISION: Poor Little Rich Girl (mini-series; winner 3 Emmys, Golden Globe, best mini-series).

PERSOFF, NEHEMIAH: Actor. b. Jerusalem, Israel, Aug. 2, 1919. e. Hebrew Technical Inst., 1934–37. Actors Studio electrician, 1937–39; signal maint., N.Y. subway, 1939–41. L.A. Critics Award 1971 for Sholem-Sholem Alecheim, and The Dybbuk.

STAGE: Sundown Beach, Galileo, Richard III, King Lear, Peter Pan, Peer Gynt, Tiger At the Gates, Colombe, Flahooly, Montserrat, Only in America. Tour: Fiddler on the Roof, Man of La Mancha, Oliver, Death of a Salesman (Stratford, Ont.), Peter Pan (Capt. Hook).

PICTURES: Al Capone, Some Like It Hot, The Harder They Fall, The Badlanders, The Wrong Man, In Search of the Real Jesus, Men in War, This Angry Age, The Big Show, The Commancheros, Fate Is the Hunter, The Greatest Story Ever Told, The Wild Party, The Power, Mrs. Pollifax—Spy, Red Sky at Morning, Psychic Killer, Voyage of the Damned, Yentl, The Last Temptation of Christ, Testament, Twins, The Dispossessed.

TELEVISION: Philco-Goodyear Show, Kraft, Producers Showcase, Danger, You Are There, Untouchables, Route 66, Naked City, Wagon Train, Rawhide, Gunsmoke, Thriller, Hitchcock Thriller, Bus Stop, Five Fingers, Mr. Lucky, The Wild, Wild West, I Spy, Columbo, Barney Miller, Sadat, Adderly, The French Atlantic Affair, The Big Knife.

PERTWEE, JON: TV Performer. b. London, England, July 7, 1919. e. Sherborne, Royal Acad. of Dramatic Art. Early career, Arts League Traveling Theatre, 5 yrs. repertory; regularly on radio, TV, music hall, cabaret and circus.

PICTURES: Murder At the Windmill, Miss Pilgrim's Progress, Will Any Gentleman?, Gay Dog, It's A Wonderful Life, Mr. Drake's Duck, A Yank in Ermine, Ugly Duckling, Just Joe, Not a Hope in Hell, Nearly a Nasty Accident, Ladies Who Do, Carry on Cleo, I've Gotta Horse, Carry On Cowboy, Carry On Screaming, A Funny Thing Happened On the Way To The Forum, Up in the Air, The Hod, March of the Desert, One of our Dinosaurs Is Missing, The House that Dripped Blood, The Island of Young Tigers, The Boys in Blue.

TELEVISION: Own series, Sunday Night, London Palladium Compere Variety Show, Doctor Who series, Who Dunnit, Worzel Gummidge.

RADIO: Navy Lark.

STAGE: See You Inside, A Funny Thing Happened On The Way To The Forum, There's A Girl In My Soup, Oh Clarence, My Dear Gilbert, The Bedwinner, Don't Just Lie There, Say Something, Irene, Touch It Light, Dr. Who-The Ultimate Adventure.

PERTWEE, MICHAEL: Writer. b. April 24, 1916. e. Sherborne Sch., France. Early career, journalist; ent. m.p. ind. 1937. Co-author, co-presentation many BBC plays and serials; many appearances panel games.

PICTURES: Laughter in Paradise, On Monday Next, Top Secret, Happy Ever After, Now and Forever, Against the Wind, Interrupted Journey, The Naked Truth, Too Many Crooks, Bottoms Up, Make Mine Mink, It Started in Naples, In the Doghouse, Mouse on the Moon, Ladies Who Do, Finders Keepers, Strange Bedfellows, A Funny Thing Happened on the Way to the Forum, Salt and Pepper, One More Time, Don't Just Lie There Say Something, Digby the Biggest Dog in the World.

TELEVISION: Rainy Day, Strictly Personal, Grove Family, Man in a Moon, The Frightened Man, Yakity Yak (ATV 1956), The Old Campaigner, Terry Thomas series, B and B series, Never a Cross Word, Six of Rix, Men of Affairs.

STAGE: The Four Musketeers, Drury Lane, She's Done It Again, Don't Just Lie There Say Something, Birds of Paradise, A Bit Between the Teeth, Six of One, Ace In A Hole, Find the Lady, Do Not Disturb, Look No Hans!, Holiday Swap, King's Rhapsody (adapt.), You'll Do For Me.

PESCOW, DONNA: Actress. b. Brooklyn, NY, March 24, 1954. e. American Acad. of Dramatic Arts. Started career on summer tour in Ah Wilderness in 1975. Did bit in ABC daytime series, One Life to Live. Film debut in Saturday Night Fever (1977).

PICTURES: Saturday Night Fever, Jake Speed.

TELEVISION: Advice to the Lovelorn, The Day the Bubble Burst, Policewoman Centerfold, Obsessed with a Married Woman, Angie (series), Out of this World (series).

PETERS, BERNADETTE: Actress. r.n. Bernadette Lazzara. b. New York, NY, Feb. 28, 1948. e. Quintano Sch. for Young Professionals, NY. Professional debut at age 5 on TV's Horn & Hardart Children's Hour, followed by Juvenile Jury and Name That Tune. Stage debut with N.Y. City Center production of The Most Happy Fella (1959). Screen debut, Ace Eli and Rodger of the Skies (1973).

THEATER: Gypsy (1961), This is Google, Riverwind, The Penny Friend, Curly McDimple, Johnny No-Trump, George M!, Dames at Sea (Drama Desk Award), La Strada, W.C., On the Town (1971 revival), Tartuffe, Mack and Mabel, Sally and Marsha, Sunday in the Park With George, Song and Dance (Tony and Drama Desk Awards), Into the Woods.

PICTURES: Ace Eli and Roger of the Skies, The Longest Yard, W.C. Fields & Me, Vigilante Force, Silent Movie, The Jerk, Tulips, Pennies from Heaven, Heartbeeps, Annie, Slaves of New York, Pink Cadillac, Impromptu.

TELEVISION: All's Fair (series, 1976–77), The Martian Chronicles, They Said It with Music, The Starmakers, Lonely Man, House of Numbers, Ten Seconds to Hell, Warriors Five, Party at Annapolis, Rich, Thin and Beautiful (host), Faerie Tale Theatre, David, many specials.

PETERS, BROCK: Actor. r.n. Brock Fisher. b. Harlem, NY, July 2, 1927. e. CCNY U. of Chicago. Had numerous featured roles on and off Bdwy. in road and stock cos., nightclubs, TV. Toured with DePaur Infantry Chorus as bass soloist, 1947–50. Made m.p. debut, Carmen Jones (1955).

THEATER: Porgy and Bess (debut, 1943), Anna Lucasta, My Darlin' Aida, Mister Johnson, King of the Dark Chamber, Othello, Kwamina, The Great White Hope (tour), Lost in the Stars, Driving Miss Daisy (Natl. Co.).

PICTURES: Carmen Jones, Porgy and Bess, To Kill a Mockingbird, Heavens Above, The L-Shaped Room, The Pawnbroker, Major Dundee, P.J., The Daring Game, The Incident, Ace High, The MacMasters, Black Girl, Soylent Green, Slaughter's Big Rip-off, Lost in the Stars, Million Dollar Dixie Deliverance, Framed, Two-Minute Warning, From These Roots (short), Star Trek IV: The Voyage Home.

TELEVISION: Arthur Godfrey's Talent Scouts (debut, 1953), Series: The Young and the Restless, Eleventh Hour. Guest: It Takes a Thief, Mannix, Mod Squad, Mini-series: Seventh Avenue, Black Beauty, Roots: the Next Generation. Movies: Welcome Home, Johnny Bristol, SST: Death Flight, The Incredible Journey of Doctor Meg Laurel, The Adventures of Huckleberry Finn, Agatha Christie's Caribbean Mystery, To Heal a Nation, Broken Angel. Specials: Challenge of the Go Bots (voice), Living the Dream: A Tribute to Dr. Martin Luther King. Co-prod.: This Far By Faith (1975).

PETERS, JON: Producer. b. Van Nuys, CA, 1947. Started hair-styling business; built it into multimillion-dollar firm before turning film producer. Formed Jon Peters Organization. 1980, joined with Peter Guber and Neil Bogart to form The Boardwalk Co. (dissolved 1981). Later Guber-Peters-Barris Company.

PICTURES: A Star Is Born, The Eyes of Laura Mars, The Main Event, Die Laughing, Caddyshack, Co-prod./co-exec. prod. with Peter Guber: An American Werewolf in London (exec. prod.), Missing (exec. prod), Flashdance (exec. prod.), Six Weeks, D.C. Cab, Visionquest, Clue (exec. prod.), The Color Purple (exec. prod.), The Witches of Eastwick (prod.); Innerspace (exec. prod.), Who's That Girl (exec. prod.), Gorillas in the Mist (exec. prod.), Caddyshack II (prod.), Rain Man (exec. prod.), Batman (prod.), The Bonfires of the Vanities, Tango and Cash.

TELEVISION: Bay Coven (co-exec. prod.), Nightmare at Bitter Creek (exec. prod.).

PETERSEN, WILLIAM: Actor. b. Chicago, IL, 1953. Active in Chicago theatre; helped to found Ix, an ensemble acting group now called the Remains Theatre. Acted in Moby Dick, In the Belly of the Beast, A Streetcar Named Desire, etc. 1986, formed company with actor John Malkovich called High Horse Prods.

PICTURES: To Live and Die in L.A., Manhunter, Amazing Grace and Chuck.

TELEVISION: Long Gone (HBO movie), The Kennedys of Massachusetts.

PETERSEN, WOLFGANG: Director. b. Emden, Germany, Mar. 14, 1941. Career as asst. state director at Ernst Deutsch Theatre in Hamburg before starting to direct for television and later theatrical films.

PICTURES: Black and White Like Day, The Consequence, Das Boot (The Boat), The NeverEnding Story, Enemy Mine, The Plastic Nightmare (prod., dir., s.p.).

TELEVISION: Scenes of the Crime (series).

PETERSON, S. DEAN: Executive. b. Toronto, Canada, December 18, 1923. e. Victoria Coll., U. of Toronto. W.W.II service RCNVR; 1946 TV newsreel cameraman NBC; founded own prod. co. in 1947; incorporated Dordean Realty Limited to acquire new studios 1959; formed Peterson Production Limited in 1957 to make TV commercials and sponsored theatrical shorts; has intl. awards as prod., dir., dir. of photography; formed Studio City Limited in 1965 to produce TV series and features acquiring an additional studio complex and backlot in Kleinberg, Ontario; 1972 formed SDP Communications Ltd. to package M.P. and TV; 1970 incorporated Intermedia Financial Services Limited to provide specialized financing and consultation to companies in M.P. and TV industries.

Past-President Canadian Film and Television Assn., mbr. Variety Club, Tent 28; Canadian Society of Cinematographers; Directors Guild of America, Directors Guild of Canada, SMPTE.

PETERSON, PAUL: Actor. b. Glendale, CA, Sept. 23, 1945. e. Valley Coll. Original Disney Mouseketeer (TV). In the late 1960's turned to writing—beginning with a Marcus Welby script followed by paperback novels in 1970's. Also book about Disney empire, Walt, Mickey and Me, 1977.

PICTURES: Houseboat, This Could Be the Night.

TELEVISION: The Donna Reed Show (series), Playhouse 90, Lux Video Theatre, GE Theatre, The Virginian, Ford Theatre, Valentine's Day, Shindig.

PETERSON, RICHARD W.: Executive. b. Denver, CO, June 15, 1949. e. Col. Sch. of Broadcasting, Harper Coll. Joined Kennedy Theatres, Chicago, 1966. In 1968 went with Great States Theatres (now Plitt Theatres), Chicago. Was city mgr. of Crocker and Grove Theatres, Elgin, IL. In 1973 joined American Automated Theatres, Oklahoma City, as dir. of adv., pub. Promoted to dir. of U.S. theatre operations. Worked for American International Pictures, Dallas, TX. Then moved to Dal Art Film Exchange and B & B Theatres as general mgr.; 1987 took over 7 screens from McLendon and formed own co., Peterson Theatres, Inc.

PETRIE, DANIEL: Director. b. Glace Bay, Nova Scotia, Nov. 26, 1920. e. St. Francis Xavier U., Nova Scotia; Columbia U., MA, 1945; postgrad. Northwestern U. Broadway actor 1945–46. TV director from 1950.

PICTURES: The Bramble Bush, A Raisin in the Sun; Lifeguard, Buster and Billie; Spy With A Cold Nose; The Idol; Stolen Hours; The Betsy, Resurrection, Fort Apache, The Bronx, Six Pack, The Bay Boy, Square Dance, Rocket Gibralter; Cocoon: The Return (dir., co-story).

THEATRE: Shadow of My Enemy; Who'll Save The Plowboy?; Mornin' Sun; Monopoly, The Cherry Orchard, Volpone, A Lesson from Aloes.

TV FILMS: Eleanor and Franklin (Emmy, 1976), Sybil, Eleanor and Franklin: The White House Years (Emmy, 1977), Silent Night, Lonely Night, Harry Truman, Plain Speaking, The Dollmaker, The Execution of Raymond Graham, Half a Lifetime, My Name is Bill W. (also prod.).

PETROU, DAVID MICHAEL: Writer, Producer, Public Relations Executive. b. Washington, DC, Nov. 3, 1949. e. U. of Maryland, B.A.; Georgetown U., M.A. Publicity assoc., Psychiatric Institutes of America, Washington, DC, 1971; assoc. dir. of publicity & film liaison, Random House, 1974; guest lecturer, screen writing & film production, The American University Consortium, Washington, DC, spring, 1980; Woodrow Wilson Fellowship, 1971. Entered industry in 1975. Joined Salkind Organization in chg. of literary projects. Worked in numerous production capacities on Crossed Swords, Superman, Superman II. 1977, exec. in chg. of literary development, Salkind. Wrote Crossed Swords (1978) and The Making of Superman. Co-authored screenplay, Shoot to Kill. 1978–79, promotional dev. on Time after Time for Warner Bros.; 1980–83, dir., special projects Joseph Kennedy Foundation. Organized U.S. premiere of Superman II and The Empire Strikes Back; 1983–84, sr. editor for entertainment, Regardie's Magazine; 1984, organized Washington, DC premiere of Indiana Jones and the Temple of Doom; 1984–86, sr. exec., p.r. div., Abramson Associates; 1986–88, sr. v.p., Eisner, Held & Petrou, Inc., p.r. agency; 1988–present, pres. & chief operating officer, Eisner, Petrou & Associate Inc. Baltimore-Wash., p.r. marketing communications agency.

PEVERALL, JOHN: Producer. b. Islington, England. Started in entertainment industry in 1945 in mail room of J. Arthur Rank Prods. Promoted to asst. dir. Time out for military service in Royal Air Force Air-Sea Rescue Unit. Resumed career as asst. dir. and unit prod. mgr. on several films produced in Britain and throughout Europe. In 1969 became associated with newly-formed Cinema Center Films as prod. exec. in London. When firm suspended activities became freelance as asst. dir.

PICTURES: Conduct Unbecoming and The Man Who Fell to Earth (both assoc. prod.), The Deer Hunter (prod.).

PEVNEY, JOSEPH: Director, Actor. b. New York, NY, 1920. e. NYU. m. the late Mitzi Green, child star, actress, nightclub entertainer. Began career in vaudeville at 13 as jr. mem. song & dance team; later stage in Home of the Brave. US Army ETO W.W.II. Actor turned director.

STAGE: Counsellor at Law, Key Largo, Native Son; (dir.) Swan Song, Let Freedom Sing.

PICTURES: (acting) Nocturne, Outside The Wall, Body & Soul; Counsellor at Law (dir.), Key Largo, Native Son. Director: The Strange Door, Shakedown, Air Cadet, Lady from Texas, Meet Danny Wilson, Iron Man, Flesh and Fury, Just Across the Street, Because of You, Desert Legion, It Happens Every Thursday, Back to God's Country, Yankee Pasha, Playgirl, Three Ring Circus, Six Bridges to Cross, Foxfire, Female on the Beach, Away All Boats, Congo Crossing, Tammy and the Bachelor, The Midnight Man, Man of a Thousand Faces, Twilight for the Gods, Torpedo Run, Cash McCall, The Plunderers (also prod.), Crowded Sky, Portrait of a Mobster, Night of the Grizzly.

TELEVISION: Trapper John M.D., Contract for Life: The S.A.D.D. Story. Movies: Who is the Black Dahlia, My Darling Daughter's Anniversary, Mysterious Island of Beautiful Women.

PEYSER, JOHN: Producer, Director. b. New York, NY, Aug. 10, 1916. e. Colgate U., 1938. In TV ind. since 1939, with Psychological Warfare Div., ETO., W.W.II; pres. Peyser/Lance Productions, Woodland Hills, CA.

TELEVISION: Director: Hawaii Five-O, Mannix, Movin On, Swiss Family Robinson, Bronk, Combat, Untouchables, Rat Patrol, Honeymoon with a Stranger.

PICTURES: Spain, The Open Door; Kashmiri Run; Four Rode Out; Massacre Harbor.

PFEIFFER, MICHELLE: Actress. b. Santa Ana, CA, 1957. While attending jr. coll. and working as supermarket checkout clerk, began taking acting classes in L.A. At 20, signed as regular in short lived TV series Delta House.

PICTURES: Charlie Chan and The Curse of the Dragon (1980), Falling in Love Again, Hollywood Nights, Grease II, Scarface, Into the Night, Ladyhawke, Sweet Liberty, The Witches of Eastwick, Married to the Mob, Tequilla Sunrise, Dangerous Liaisons, The Fabulous Baker Boys.

TELEVISION: Delta House (series), B.A.D. Cats (series), Callie and Son, The Children Nobody Wanted, Splendor in the Grass, One Too Many, Natica Jackson.

PHILLIPS, D. JOHN: Motion Picture Theatre Consultant. b. New York, NY. Advertising and publicity mgr. Borden Co. Produce Sales Div., 1933–36; adv. & pub. mgr., Paul R. Dillon Co., Inc., 1936–41. Became field exploitation rep., United Artists Corp., 1941–42; Short Subjects & Paramount News adv. & pub. mgr. Paramount Pictures, 1942–47; exec. dir. Metropolitan Motion Pictures Theatres Assn., 1947–79, New York.

PHILLIPS, JULIA: Producer. b. Brooklyn, NY, April 7, 1944. e. Mt. Holyoke Coll. Production asst. at McCall's Magazine; later became textbook copywriter for Macmillan; story editor, Paramount; creative exec., First Artists Prods., NY. In 1970 with former husband, Michael Phillips and actor Tony Bill formed Bill/Phillips Productions to develop film projects.

PICTURES: Steelyard Blues, The Sting, Taxi Driver, The Big Bus, Close Encounters of the Third Kind, The Beat (co-prod.).

PHILLIPS, LESLIE: Actor, Producer. b. London, England, April 20, 1924. Early career as child actor. Ent. m.p. ind. 1935.

PICTURES: The Citadel (debut, 1938), Pool of London, Breaking the Sound Barrier, Train of Events, The Fake, The Limping Man, THe Gamma People, The Barretts of Wimpole Street, Brothers in Law, High Flight, Just My Luck, Les Girls, Smallest Show on Earth, Value for Money, I Was Monte's Double, The Angry Hills, Carry on Nurse, King Ferdinand of Naples, This Other Eden, The Navy Lark, Doctor in Love, Watch Your Stern, No Kidding, Week-End With Lulu, VIP, Carry on Constable, Inn for Trouble, Please Turn Over, Raising the Wind, In the Doghouse, Crooks Anonymous, Fast Lady, Father Came Too, Doctor in Clover, You Must Be Joking, Maroc 7, Some Will Some Won't, Doctor in Trouble, The Magnificent 7 & Deadly Sins, Not Now Darling, Don't Just Lie There, Spanish Fly, Not Now Comrade, Out of Africa, Empire of the Sun, Mountains of the Moon, Scandal.

TELEVISION: Our Man at St. Marks, Impasse, The Gong Game, Time and Motion Man, Reluctant Debutante, A Very Fine Line, The Suit, The Culture Vultures (series), Edward Woodward Show, Casanova 74 (series), Redundant—or the Wife's Revenge. TV film: You'll Never See Me Again, Mr. Palfrey of Westminister, Monte Carlo, Rumpole, Summers Lease.

PHILLIPS, LOU DIAMOND: Actor. b. Philippines, 1962. m. asst. dir of La Bamba, Julie Cypher. Raised in Arlington, TX. e. U. of Texas, Arlington (BFA. drama). Studied film technique with Adam Roarke, becoming asst. dir./instructor with the Film Actor's Lab, 1983–86. Regional theater includes: A Hatful of Rain, Whose Life Is It, Anyway?, P.S. Your Cat Is Dead, The Lady's Not for Burning, Doctor Faustus, Hamlet.

PICTURES: Angel Alley, Interface, Trespasses (also co-s.p.), Harley, La Bamba, Stand and Deliver, Young Guns, Dakota (also assoc. prod.), Disorganized Crime, Renegades, A Show of Force, Transit, Pentagram.

TELEVISION: Dallas, Miami Vice. Movie: Time Bomb.

PHILLIPS, MICHAEL: Producer b. Brooklyn, NY, Nov. 10, 1916. Mgr. & prof. pugilist (featherweight), 1930–36. Ent. m.p. ind. as secy to Ray Milland, 1937; apptd asst. dir., U.S. Army Special Service Div., 1942–45; script ed. & prod. activities, Eddie Bracken Radio Prod. until 1949 (orig. & s.p.) Double Cross; formed own prod. co. Demyrtha Prod., Inc. 1950.

PHILLIPS, MICHAEL: Producer. b. Brooklyn, NY, June 29, 1943. e. Dartmouth Coll., B.A., 1965. NYU, Law Sch. J.D., 1968. Securities analyst, NY 1968–70. Indep. m.p. prod. 1971. In 1970 formed prod. co. with former wife, Julia, and actor Tony Bill.
PICTURES: Steelyard Blues, The Sting, Taxi Driver, The Big Bus, Close Encounters of the Third Kind, Heartbeeps, Cannery Row, The Flamingo Kid, The Tender.

PHOENIX, RIVER: Actor. b. Madras, Oregon, August 23, 1971. Sisters Rainbow, Liberty and Summer and brother Leaf are also actors. Spent childhood traveling to Mexico, Puerto Rico, and Venezuela with parents who were then independent Christian missionaries with The Children of God. Returned to Florida at 7. First TV appearance, singing and playing guitar on Fantasy TV. Began acting career at 10 in Seven Brides for Seven Brothers on TV. Also plays guitar and records own original songs.
PICTURES: Explorers (debut, 1985), Stand By Me, Mosquito Coast, A Night in the Life of Jimmy Reardon, Little Nikita, Running on Empty (Acad. Award nom.), Indiana Jones and the Last Crusade, I Love You to Death.
TELEVISION: Hotel, It's Your Move, Family Ties. Movies: Celebrity, Robert Kennedy and His Times, Surviving: A Family in Crisis.

PIALAT, MAURICE: Director. b. Cunlhat, Puy de Dome, France, 1925. Worked as a painter and sometime actor before turning to film in 1952. Made a number of short films including L'Amour Existe (award winner Venice Film Fest., 1960) Worked in television before feature debut in 1967. Television: Janine (1961), Maitre Galip (1962), La Maison des Bois (1971).
PICTURES: L'Enfance Nue (1967, awarded Prix Jean Vigo); Nous Ne Viellirons pas Ensemble (1972), La Gueule Ouverte (1974); Passe Ton Bac D'Abord (1979); Loulou (1979); A Nos Amours (1983, Prix Louis Delluc); Police (1985); Under Satan's Sun (1987, winner Golden Palm, Cannes Festival).

PICCOLI, MICHEL: Actor. b. Paris, France, Dec. 27, 1925. r.n. Jacques Piccoli. Since his film debut in The Sorcerer in 1945 has had impressive career on the French stage and in films working for major French dirs. Renoir, Bunuel, Melville, Resnais, Clouzot, Godard as well as Hitchcock. Until 1957 was mgr. of Theatre Babylone in Paris. Formed prod. co. Films 66. Produced: Themroc (1972); La Faille; Les Enfants Gates.
PICTURES: The Sorcerer, Le Point du Jour; French Can Can; The Witches of Salem; Le Bal des Espiona; Gina; Le Doulos; Contempt; Diary of a Chambermaid; Lady L; La Guerre Est Finie; The Young Girls of Rochefort; Un Homme de Trop; Belle de Jour; La Chamade; Dillinger Is Dead; L'Invasion; The Milky Way; Topaz; The Things of Life; Ten Days' Wonder; The Discreet Charm of the Bourgeoisie; Themroc; Wedding in Blood; La Grande Bouffe; The Last Woman; Leonor; 7 Deaths by Prescription; The Weak Spot; F For Fairbanks; Mado; Todo Modo; Rene the Cane; Spoiled Children; Strauberg Is Here; The Fire's Share; Little Girl in Blue Velvet; The Savage State; The Sugar; The Bit Between the Teeth; La Divorcement; Leap into the Void; The Price for Survival; Atlantic City; The Prodigal Daughter; Beyond the Door; The Eyes, The Mouth; Passion; A Room in Town; Will the High Salaried Workers Please Raise Their Hands!!!; The General of the Dead Army; La Passante; The Prize of Peril; Adieu, Bonaparte; Dangerous Moves; Danger in the House; Long Live Life!; Success Is the Best Revenge; The Sailor 512; Departure, Return; Mon beau-frere a tue ma soeur; The Nonentity; The Prude; Bad Blood; Undiscovered Country; Blanc de Chine; Le Peuple Singe (narrator); The French Revolution, Milou in May.

PICERNI, PAUL: Actor. b. New York, NY, Dec. 1, 1922. e. Loyola U., Los Angeles. U.S. Air Force 1943–46; head of drama dept. Mt. St. Mary's Coll., 1949–50. TV credits include Untouchables (co-star).
TELEVISION: Philco Playhouse, Climax, Lux, Loretta Young Show, Desilu, Kojak, Mannix, Police Story, Lucy Special, Quincy, Alice, Trapper John, Vegas, Fall Guy, Capitol, Hardcastle and McCormick, Matt Houston, Simon and Simon.
PICTURES: Breakthrough, I Was a Communist for the FBI, Mara Maru, Desert Song, She's Back on Broadway, House of Wax, Shanghai Story, To Hell and Back, Miracle in the Rain, Bobby Ware Is Missing, Omar Khayyam, Brothers Rico, Young Philadelphians, The Young Marrieds, The Scalphunters, Airport, Kotch, Beyond the Posiedon Adventure, Dirty Dozen III.

PICKER, ARNOLD M.: Executive. b. New York, NY, Sept. 19, 1913. p. Celia and David V. Picker. e. City Coll. of New York, U. of London. Joined Columbia's foreign dept. in June, 1935. Asst. to foreign mgr.; then vice-pres. 1945, Columbia International Corp.; v.p. charge foreign dist., Oct., 1951; exec. v.p. UA, and in charge all distribution, June 1961; chmn. exec. com., 1967. Died Oct. 9, 1989.

PICKER, DAVID V.: Executive. b. New York, NY, May 14, 1931. e. Dartmouth Coll., B.A., 1953. Father Eugene Picker, exec. Loew's Theatres. Ent. industry in 1956 as adv. pub. & exploitation liaison with sls. dept., United Artists Corp.; exec. v.p. U.A. Records; asst. to Max Youngstein, v.p.; v.p. U.A.; first v.p. UA; pres. 1969 Resigned 1973 to form own production co. In 1976 joined Paramount Pictures as pres. of m.p. div.; v.p., Lorimar Productions; independent; 1987, pres. & COO, Columbia Pictures. Resigned.
PICTURES: Juggernaut, Lenny, Smile, Royal Flash, Won Ton Ton, The One and Only, Oliver's Story, Bloodline (prod.), The Jerk (prod.), Dead Men Don't Wear Plaid (prod.), The Man with Two Brains, Beat Street (prod.), The Appointments of Dennis Jennings (short, prod.), Stella (exec. prod.), The Normal Heart (prod.).

PICKER, EUGENE D.: Executive b. New York, NY, Nov. 17, 1903. p. David V. and Celia C. Picker. e. NYU and Sch. of Business. Started with father in Bronx theatres; joined Loew's Inc., 1920; in charge circuit operations, New York area, 1945; v.p. Loew's Theatres, Sept. 1954; member bd. of dir., 1956, exec. v.p. Sept. 1958; pres. Loew's Theatres, March 1959. Res. 1961 as pres. Loew's Theatres; joined U.A. as v.p., July 1961. Joined Trans-Lux Corp. as exec. v.p., Jan. 1967; pres. & chief oper. Officer of Entertainment Division of Trans-Lux Corp. to 1984 then confirmed as member bd. of directors; Exec. consultant motion picture industry Jan. 1, 1974 and Pres. E.D.P. Films Inc. as of June 1974 to 1982; pres. NATO, 1969–71, ch. bd., 1971–72, Bd. dir., Will Rogers Hospital, bd. ch. At present mem. bd. of dirs., Trans Lux Corp. and Foundation of Motion Picture Pioneers and Broadway Association.

PICKMAN, JEROME: Executive. b. New York, NY, Aug. 24, 1916. e. St. John's U.; Brooklyn Law Sch. of St. Lawrence U., LL.B. Reporter N.Y. newspapers, 1930–40; U.S. Army World War II; Ad-pub exec. 20th-Fox, 1945–46; Eagle-Lion Films, 1947; Paramount Pictures, 1949; v.p., dir., adv. & pub., Paramount, 1951; v.p. domestic gen. sls. mgr., Paramount 1960–62; sr. sls. exec. Columbia Pictures 1963–67; pres. Continental Motion Picture Div. of Walter Reade Org., 1967–70; pres., Levitt-Pickman Film Corp., 1971; sr. v.p., domestic distribution, Lorimar Productions, 1979–81; pres., Pickman Film Corp., Cineworld Enterprises Corp., 1982; pres. Scotti Bros. Pictures Distribution, 1986.

PIERCE, FREDERICK S.: Executive. b. New York, NY, April 8, 1933. e. Bernard Baruch Sch. of B.A., City Coll. of New York. Served with U.S. Combat Engineers in Korean War. Associated with Benj. Harrow & Son, CAP, before joining ABC in 1956. Served as analyst in TV research dep.; prom. to supvr. of audience measurements, 1957, named mgr. next year. In 1961 made dir. of research; 1962 dir. of research, sales dev. Named dir. of sales planning, sales devel. April, 1962; elec. v.p., Feb. 1964 and made nat. dir. of sales for TV. In 1968 named v.p., planning; March. 1970 named asst. to pres. In July 1972, named v.p, in chg. ABC TV planning and devel. and asst. to pres. ABC TV, March, 1973. Named sr. v.p., ABC TV, Jan., 1974. Elected pres., ABC Television Division, October, 1974. Pres. & chief operating off., ABC, Inc., 1983. Formed Frederick Pierce Co. and also Pierce/Silverman Co. with Fred Silverman, 1989.

PIERSON, FRANK: Producer, Director, Writer. b. Chappaqua, NY, May 12, 1925. e. Harvard U. Was correspondent for Time magazine before entering show business as story editor of TV series, Have Gun, Will Travel. Later served as both producer and director for show. Developed a number of properties for Screen Gems before writing theatrical screenplays.
PICTURES: Cat Ballou (co-s.p.), Cool Hand Luke (s.p.), The Anderson Tapes (s.p.), The Looking Glass War, (s.p., dir.), Dog Day Afternoon (s.p., Acad. Award, 1975), A Star Is Born (dir., s.p.), King of the Gypsies (dir., s.p.), In Country (co-s.p.), Presumed Innocent.
TELEVISION: Nicholas (series, prod.), Haywire (s.p.), The Neon Ceiling, Alfred Hitchcock Presents (1985).

PIGOTT-SMITH, TIM: Actor. b. Rugby, England, May 13, 1946. e. U. of Bristol, B.A. Acted with Bristol Old Vic, Royal Shakespeare Co. On stage in As You Like It, Major Barbara, Hamlet, School for Scandal, Sherlock Holmes (Bdwy debut, 1974), The Benefactors, Entertaining Strangers. Movie: Jury Duty.
PICTURES: Aces High (debut, 1975), Man in the Fog, Escape to Victory, Sweet William, Richard's Things, Clash of the Titans, Escape to Victory, Joseph Andrews, State of Emergency.
TELEVISION: Dr. Who (debut, 1970), Mini-series: Winston Churchill: The Wilderness Years, The Jewel in the Crown. Movies: Eustace and Hilda, The Lost Boys, I Remember Nelson. Henry IV, Day Christ Died, Hunchback of Notre Dame, Fame Is the Spur, Glittering Prizes, Dead Man's Folly, The Case of Sherlock Holmes (host); Double Helix, Hannah.

PIKE, JOHN S.: Executive. Joined Paramount Pictures as v.p., video programming; promoted to sr. v.p., video prog. 1984, named sr. v.p., current network programming; 1985, promoted to exec. v.p., Paramount Network TV. 1986, appt. pres., Paramount Network TV Division.

PILCHER, TONY: Producer. b. Boston, England, 1936. e. Shrewsbury Sch. Ent. m.p. industry 1960 with Anglo-Scottish Pictures. Became prod. exec. 1961, German rep. and exec. 1963. Joined AB-Pathe as German rep., TV and Advertising Films division 1964. TV prod., Heumann Ogilvy & Mather, Frankfurt, 1966; prod. Chambers and Partners; Guild TV; Wace Film, Signal Films, Rayant TV, Filmshop, Europartners 1967 to date.

PILE, SUSAN: Executive. First west coast editor of Interview magazine before entering entertainment industry as media buyer and acct. exec. on m.p. accts for Diener/Hauser/Bates. After 6 years left to become partner in Proper Exposure, specialized mktg. firm in m.p. field. Natl.mag. contact, Universal Pictures; unit publicist for Universal & Warner Bros. 1980, joined Paramount as dir., west coast adv. & pub. 1981, named v.p., west coast pub. & promo; 1985, sr. v.p., west coast publ, promo. & adv. Resigned 1988.

PINCHOT, BRONSON: Actor. b. New York, NY, May 20, 1959. e. Yale U. Grew up in Pasadena. Studied acting at Yale.
PICTURES: Risky Business (debut, 1983), Beverly Hills Cop, The Flamingo Kid, Hot Resort, After Hours, Second Sight.
TELEVISION: Series: Sara (1985), Perfect Strangers.

PINK, SIDNEY: Producer, Director, Writer. b. Pittsburgh, PA, Mar. 6, 1916. e. U. of Pittsburgh, B.S., 1934–37; U. of Southern California, law, 1940–41. Projectionist, mgr., booker, Warner Bros., PA, Fox West Coast, United Artists Theatres, Calif. Prod. budget mgr., Something to Sing About and Lost Horizon.
PICTURES: Bwana Devil, Angry Red Planet, Green-Eyed Elephant, Reptilicus, Journey to The Seventh Planet, Operation Camel, Valley of the Swords, Madigan's Millions.

PINSKER, ALLEN: Executive. b. New York, NY, Jan. 23, 1930. e. NYU. Mgr., Hempstead Theatre, 1950. In 1954 joined Island Theatre Circuit as booker-buyer; named head buyer 1958. In 1968 joined United Artists Eastern Theatres as film buyer; head buyer, 1969, v.p., 1970. Named v.p. United Artists Theatre Circuit, 1972. In 1973 named UAET exec. v.p., member bd., 1974. Appt. pres. & COO, UA Communications, Inc., theatre division, 1987. March, 1987, named pres. and CEO, United Artists Theatre Circuit, Inc. and exec. v.p., United Artists Communications, Inc.; 1988, became member, bd. dir. United Artists Comm. Inc.

PINTER, HAROLD: Writer, Director, Actor. b. London, England, Oct. 10, 1930. Began career as actor then turned to writing and direction. Plays include The Dumb Waiter, Slight Ache, The Room, The Birthday Party, The Caretaker, The Homecoming, The Collection, Landscape, Silence, Old Times, No Man's Land, The Hot House, Betrayal, One for the Road, Mountain Language.
PICTURES: The Caretaker, The Servant, The Pumpkin Eater, The Quiller Memorandum, Accident, The Go-Between, The Last Tycoon, The French Lieutenant's Woman, Betrayal, Turtle Diary, Reunion, The Handmaid's Tale, Comfort of Strangers.
TELEVISION: A Night Out, Night School, The Lover, Tea Party, The Basement, Heat of the Day.

PIROSH, ROBERT: Writer, Director, Producer. b. Baltimore, MD, April 1, 1910. S.p. credits include A Day at the Races, I Married a Witch, Rings on Her Fingers, Up in Arms, Battleground (solo orig. s.p. Academy Award winner), Hell Is for Heroes, A Gathering of Eagles, What's So Bad About Feeling Good, S.p.-dir. credits include Go for Broke, Washington Story, Valley of the Kings, The Girl Rush, Spring Reunion.
TELEVISION: (Wrote, prod. pilots) Laramie, Combat. (Writer) Hawaii Five-0, Ellery Queen, Mannix, Bonanza, Ironside, The Waltons, Barnaby Jones, The Bold Ones, etc.

PISANO, A. ROBERT: Executive. e. San Jose State U.; U. of California, Berkeley. Member, State Bar of CA, Board of Directors, American Corp. Counsel Assn., American Bar Assoc., L.A. County Bar Assoc. Joined O'Melveny & Myers as associate 1969; made partner 1976. 1979–82 headed its Paris office. In 1985 joined Paramount as exec. v.p. & gen. counsel.

PISCOPO, JOE: Actor, Comedian. b. Passaic, NJ, June 17, 1951. Stage appearances in regional and dinner theaters in South and Northeast. Worked as stand-up comic at the Improvisation and the Comic Strip clubs, NY 1976–80. Author: The Piscopo Tapes. Television debut as regular on Saturday Night Live, 1980–84.
PICTURES: American Tickler or the Winner of 10 Academy Awards (1976); Johnny Dangerously, Wise Guys.
TELEVISION: Saturday Night Live; Comic Relief (1986).

PISIER, MARIE-FRANCE: Actress. b. Indochina, 1944. First discovered by François Truffaut who cast her in Love at Twenty (1976). When film completed returned to school for degree in political science. Continued to work in films.
PICTURES: French Provincial, Trans-Europe Express, Stolen Kisses, Celine et Julie Vont en Bateau, Cousin Cousine, Souvenirs d'en France, Barocco, The Other Side of Midnight, Serail, Love on the Run, Les Apprentis Sourciers, The Bronte Sisters, French Postcards, La Banquiere, Chanel Solitaire, Der Zauberberg (The Magic Mountain), Ace of Aces, Hot Touch, The Prize of Peril, Der Stille Ocean, L'Ami de Vincent, The Abyss, Miss Right.
TELEVISION: (U.S.) French Atlantic Affair, Scruples.

PLACE, MARY KAY: Actress, Songwriter. b. Tulsa, OK, September, 1947. e. U. of Tulsa. Worked in production jobs and as Tim Conway's asst. for his TV show also as sect. for Norman Lear on Maude before starting to write for TV series (Mary Tyler Moore Show, Phyllis, Maude, M*A*S*H, etc.).
PICTURES: Bound For Glory (debut, 1976), More American Graffiti, New York, New York, Starting Over, Private Benjamin, Modern Problems, Waltz Across Texas, The Big Chill, Smooth Talk, A New Life.
TELEVISION: Guest: All in the Family and Mary Tyler Moore Show Series, Mary Hartman, Mary Hartman (Emmy, best comedy actress), The Tonight Show, Saturday Night Live (host), Fernwood 2-Night. Movies: The Girl Who Spelled Freedom, Act of Love, For Love or Money, Out on the Edge. Specials: John Denver Special, Martin Mull's History of White People in America I & II, Portrait of a White Marriage, 4 specials on religion, white crime, stress and politics.

PLATT, MILT: Executive. b. New York, NY. e. City Coll. of New York, RCA Inst., Ohio State U. U.S. Army 1942–46; div. mgr., RKO Radio Pictures until 1957; gen. sls. mgr. Continental Dist., 1957–65; vice-pres. & gen. sls. mgr. Sherpix, 1965; v.p. & gen. sls. mgr., Comet Film Distributors, Inc., 1965; v.p. & sls. mgr., Times Film Corp., 1968. Pres. Eagle Amusement Co., 1970. Appointed member of the Appeals Board of the MPA rating system, 1971; pres. of Pisces Group, Ltd., 1972; v.p. & gen. sls. mgr., International Co-productions, Inc., 1974. pres., Milton Platt Co., 1975. Member governing committee, IFIDA

PLEASENCE, DONALD: Actor. b. Worksop, England, Oct. 5, 1919. Repertory, first London appearance in Twelfth Night. RAF, WW II. Since London stage, N.Y. stage, ent. m.p, ind. 1953.
STAGE: Vicious Circle, Saint's Day, Hobson's Choice, The Rules of the Game, The Lark, Ebb Tide, The Caretaker, Poor Bitos, The Man in the Glass Booth, Wise Child (N.Y.); voted actor of the year, 1958.
PICTURES: Manuela, The Man in the Sky, Heart of a Child, Tale of Two Cities, Battle of the Sexes, The Shakedown, The Horsemasters, Spare the Rod, No Love for Johnnie, The Caretaker, The Great Escape, The Greatest Story Ever Told, Hallelujah Trail, Fantastic Voyage, Cul-de-Sac, You Only Live Twice, Matchless, 13, Will Penny, Arthur! Arthur, THX 1138, Soldier Blue, Outback, Jerusalem File, Pied Piper, Innocent Bystanders, Death Line, Wedding in White, The Rainbow Boys, The Black Windmill, Journey Into Fear, Escape to Witch Mountain, Hearts of the West, The Devil Within Her, The Last Tycoon, Passover Plot, Trial by Combat, The Eagle Has Landed, Goldenrod, Oh God!, Fear, the Uncanny, Telefon, Escape from New York, Halloween, Halloween II, Terror in the Aisles, Warrior Queen, Prince of Darkness, Hanna's War, The Commander, Halloween IV, Phantom of Death, Paganini Horror, Metropolitan Animals, Nosferatu in Venice, Ten Little Indians, River of Death, Edgar Allen Poe's Buried Alive, The Fall of the House of Usher, Halloween 5.
TELEVISION: Fate and Mr. Browne, Small Fish Are Sweet, The Silk Purse, A House of His Own, The Traitor, The Millionairess, The Cupboard Machinal, The Hatchet Man, The Bandstand, Ambrose, Thou Good and Faithful Servant, Call Me Daddy, Taste, The Fox Trot, Omnibus, Julius Caesar, Occupations, The Joke, The Cafeteria, Hindle Wakes, Master of the Game, Arch of Triumph, The Great Escape: The Untold Story, Scoop, Punishment Without Crime, The Room.

PLESHETTE, EUGENE: Executive. b. Brooklyn, NY, Jan. 7. e. City Coll. of New York, LaSalle U., Paramount Pict. Acting Sch. Stage actor; assoc. prod. and dir. three off-Broadway plays; treas. and house mgr. N.Y. Paramount; v.p. Reid-Singer Music; exec. mgr. Brooklyn Paramount thea., 1945; mgn. dir. 1953; v.p. in chg. of ABC Merchandising Inc., AB-PT, Inc. and American Broadcasting Co., 1962; exec. v.p., MSG-ABC Prods., Inc. 1965; exec. v.p. Don Reid TV Prod.; 1975, President, Pleshette Associates.

PLESHETTE, SUZANNE: Actress. b. New York, NY, Jan. 31, 1937. e. Performing Arts H.S., Finch Coll., Syracuse U. Broadway debut, Compulsion; m.p. debut Geisha Boy (1958).
STAGE: The Cold Wind and the Warm, The Golden Fleecing, The Miracle Worker, Compulsion, Two for the Seesaw, Special Occasions.
PICTURES: Rome Adventure, The Birds, 40 Pounds of Trouble, Wall of Noise, A Rage to Live, Youngblood Hawke, A Distant Trumpet, The Ugly Dachshund, Bullwhip Griffin, Fate

is the Hunter, Mr. Buddwing, Nevada Smith, Blackbeard's Ghost, The Power, If It's Tuesday This Must Be Belgium, Suppose They Gave a War and Nobody Came, Support Your Local Gunfighter, The Shaggy D.A., Oh, God! Book II.
TELEVISION: Series: The Bob Newhart Show (1972–78); Suzanne Pleshette Is Maggie Briggs; Bridges to Cross, Nightingales. Movies: Flesh and Blood; For Love or Money; Fantasies; If Things Were Different; Help-Wanted-Male; Dixie Changing Habits; Starmaker; One Cooks, The Other Doesn't; Legend of Valentino; Kojak The Belarus File; A Stranger Waits; Alone in the Neon Jungle.

PLESKOW, ERIC: Executive. b., Vienna, Austria, April 24, 1924. Served as film officer, U.S. War dept., 1946–48; entered industry in 1948 as asst. gen. mgr., Motion Picture Export Association, Germany; 1950–51, continental rep. for Sol Lesser Prods.; joined United Artists in 1951 as Far East Sales Mgr.; named mgr., S. Africa, 1952; mgr., Germany, 1953–58; exec. asst. to continental mgr., 1958–59; asst. continental mgr., 1959–60; continental mgr., 1960–62; v.p. in charge of foreign distribution, 1962; exec. v.p. & chief operating off., Jan. 1, 1973; pres. & chief exec. off., Oct. 1, 1973. Resigned in 1978 to become pres. and chief exec. officer of Orion Pictures Co.; 1982, became pres. & chief exec. off., Orion Pictures Corp.

PLIMPTON, MARTHA: Actress. b. New York, NY. Daughter of actors Shelley Plimpton and Keith Carradine. Acting debut in film workshop of Elizabeth Swados's musical Runaways. At 11 gained recognition as model in Richard Avedon's commercials for Calvin Klein jeans. Also on stage in The Hagadah.
PICTURES: Rollover (debut 1981 in bit role), The River Rat, Goonies, Mosquito Coast, Stars and Bars, Running on Empty, Another Women, Shy People, Parenthood, Silence Like Glass.

PLITT, HENRY G.: Executive. b. New York, NY, Nov. 26, 1918. e. Syracuse U., St. Lawrence U. Law Sch. War service, 6 yrs. (1st paratrooper from 101st Airbourne div. to land in Normandy); Paramount Pictures International Corp.; United Detroit Theatres; asst. gen. mgr., North Ohio Theatres Corp.; div. mgr., then v.p., Paramount Gulf Theatres, New Orleans; pres. gen. mgr. Paramount Gulf Theatres; pres., ABC Films, 1959–65; Pres. ABC Great States Inc., Great States Theas. 1966; v.p. Prairie Farmer publications, 1971, v.p., ABC Theatre Holdings, Inc.; 1974, purchased Northern Theatre Circuit from American Broadcasting Company, consisting of 127 theatres, naming these theatres Plitt Theatres, Inc., of which he is bd. chmn. 1978, purchased rest of ABC theatres from American Broadcasting Company consisting of 272 screens, and renamed them Plitt Theatres. Sold circuit interest in 1985. Presently bd. chmn., Showscan Film Corp. Received Raoul Wallenberg Hero in Our Time Award, 1989.

PLOWRIGHT, JOAN: C.B.E. Actress. b. Scunthrope, Brigg, Lincolnshire, Eng., Oct. 28, 1929. m. Lord Laurence Olivier. Trained for stage at Laban Art of Movement Studio, 1949–50; Old Vic Theatre Sch. 1950–52; with Michel St. Denis, Glen Byam Shaw and George Devine. London stage debut The Duenna, 1954. Broadway debut The Entertainer, 1958. Won Tony Award in 1961 for A Taste of Honey. With Bristol Old Vic Rep., Royal Court, National Theatre in numerous classics and contemporary plays.
RECENT THEATER: Saturday, Sunday, Monday; The Seagull; The Bed Before Yesterday; Filumena; Enjoy; Who's Afraid of Virginia Woolf; Cavell; The Cherry Orchard; The Way of the World; Mrs. Warren's Profession.
PICTURES: Moby Dick (1956), Time Without Pity, The Entertainer, Three Sisters, Equus, Richard Wagner, Brimstone and Treacle, Britannica Hospital, The Dressmaker, Drowning By Numbers, The Divider, Conquest of the South Pole, I Love You to Death.
TELEVISION: Odd Man In, Secret Agent, School for Scandal, The Diary of Anne Frank, Twelfth Night, Merchant of Venice, Daphne Laureola, Saturday, Sunday, Monday.

PLUMMER, AMANDA: Actress. b. New York, NY, March 23, 1957. e. Middlebury Coll. Daughter of Christopher Plummer and Tammy Grimes.
THEATER: Artichokes, A Month in the Country, A Taste of Honey, Agnes of God (Tony Award, featured actress, 1982), The Glass Menagerie, A Lie of the Mind, You Never Can Tell, Pygmalion, The Milk Train Doesn't Stop Here Anymore.
PICTURES: Cattle Annie and Little Britches, Daniel, The World According to Garp, The Hotel New Hampshire, Static, The Courtship, Made in Heaven, Drugstore Cowboy, Prisoners of Inertia, Joe Versus the Volcano, California Casanova.
TELEVISION: Movies: The Dollmaker, The Unforgivable Secret, Riders to the Sea, The Courtship. Special: Gryphon. Pilot: Truck One.

PLUMMER, CHRISTOPHER: Actor. b. Toronto, Canada, Dec. 13, 1927. Stage career started with English repertory group visiting Canada; toured U.S. in Nina, 1953; Bway debut in The Constant Wife, 1954; on road and in N.Y. with The Dark is Light Enough; American Shakespeare Festival at Stratford, CT, in Julius Caesar and The Tempest; Shakespeare Festival at Stratford, Ont., in Henry V, Twelfth Night, and Hamlet; on Bway in The Lark and Cyrano (musical, Tony Award, 1974), Othello, Macbeth.
TELEVISION: Oedipus Rex, Omnibus, After the Fall, The Moneychangers, Desperate Voyage, The Shadow Box, When the Circus Came to Town, Dial M for Murder, Little Gloria—Happy at Last, The Scarlet and the Black, The Thorn Birds, The Velveteen Rabbit, Crossings, A Hazard of Hearts.
PICTURES: Across the Everglades, Stage Struck, Inside Daisy Clover, The Sound of Music, Triple Cross, The Battle of Britain, The Royal Hunt of the Sun, Lock Up Your Daughters, The Pyx, The Return of the Pink Panther, Conduct Unbecoming, The Man Who Would Be King, International Velvet, The Silent Partner, Murder by Decree, Hanover Street, Somewhere in Time, Eyewitness, The Amateur, Dreamscape, Ordeal by Innocence, Lily in Love, The Boy in Blue, Dragnet, The Boss' Wife, Souvenir, Light Years (voice), Stage Fright, Nosferatu in Venice, I Love N.Y., Shadow Dancing, Mindfield.

PODELL, ALBERT N.: Executive. b. New York, NY, Feb. 25, 1937. e. Cornell U., U. of Chicago. Articles editor, Playboy magazine, 1959–61; dir. of photog., Argosy magazine, 1961–64; account exec. on 20th Century-Fox at Diener, Hauser, Greenthal, 1966–68; national advertising dir., Cinema Center Films, 1969; account supervisor on Columbia Pictures at Charles Schlaifer; creator & dir. of Annual Motion Picture Advertising Awards sponsored by Cinema Lodge, B'nai B'rith.

PODHORZER, MUNIO: Executive. b. Berlin, Germany, Sept. 18. e. Jahn-Realgymnasium, U. of Berlin Medical Sch. U.S. Army, 1943–47; pres. United Film Enterprises, Inc.; formerly secy.-treas. 86th St. Casino Theatre, N.Y.; former v.p. Atlantic Pictures Corp.; former pres. Casino Films, Inc.; former pres. Film Development Corp.; former rep. Export-Union of the German Film Ind.; former U.S. rep. Franco-London Film, Paris; former pres., Venus Productions Corp.; former U.S. rep. Atlas Int'l Film GmbH, Munich; former U.S. rep. Bavaria Ateller Gesellschaft U.S. past rep. Israfilm Ltd., Tel-Aviv; past rep. Tigon British Film Prod., London; past rep. Elias Querejeta, P.C., Madrid; past rep. Equiluz Films, Madrid, past rep. Airport Cine, Hawaii, Les Films Du Capricorne; Profilmes, Spain; Ligno, Spain; Films D'Alma, France; Intra Films, Italy. Member: Variety Club, Cinema Lodge, B'nai B'rith, Past Board of Governors IFIDA; past pres. CID Agents Assoc. Former gen. foreign sales mgr., theatrical division of National Telefilm Associates. Presently representing Atlas Film + AV, Germany; Barcino Films, S.A., Spain; Eagle Films Ltd., United Kingdom; Les Films Jacques Leitienne, France; Nero Films Classics U.S.A.; Schongerfilm Germany; Profilmes, S.A., Spain; KFM Films, Inc. U.S.A.; Compagnie France Film, Canada; Cia. Iberoamerican de TV, S.A. Spain; V.I.P. Ltd., Israel. Co-chmn., entertainment div., United Jewish Appeal, Federation of Jewish Philanthropies, 1981–83.

PODHORZER, NATHAN: Executive. b. Brody, Poland, Nov. 27, 1919. e. City Coll. of New York, Rutgers U., U. of Southern California. U.S. Army, 1942–46; documentary film prod., Israel, 1946–57; vice pres., secy., United Film Enterprises, Inc.

POE, STEPHEN: Executive. Began career as lawyer with Rutan & Tucker; continues active entertainment law practice, recently being indep. counsel for United Artists Pictures. 1976, joined 20th Century-Fox as prod. counsel; later v.p., business affairs. Turned to producing in 1982, first in association with Frank Mancuso Jr. Productions. 1987, joined CBS/Fox Video as sr. v.p. of acquisitions and programming.

POITIER, SIDNEY: Actor. b. Miami, FL, Feb. 24, 1924. m. actress Joanna Shimkus. e. Miami, FL. Appeared on stage with Amer. Negro Theatre in Days of Our Youth. Formed First Artists Prod. Co. Ltd., 1969, with Paul Newman and Barbra Streisand. Autobiography: This Life (1980).
STAGE: Strivers Road, You Can't Take It With You, Anna Lucasta (Bdwy debut, 1948), Lysistrata, Freight, A Raisin in the Sun.
PICTURES: No Way Out (debut 1950), Cry the Beloved Country, Red Ball Express, Go Man Go, Blackboard Jungle, Good-Bye My Lady, Edge of the City, Something of Value, Porgy and Bess, All the Young Men, Devil at Four O'Clock, A Raisin in the Sun, The Long Ships, Lilies of the Field (Acad. Award, 1963), Slender Thread, A Patch of Blue, Duel at Diablo, To Sir With Love, In the Heat of the Night, Guess Who's Coming to Dinner, The Lost Man, They Call Me Mister Tibbs, Brother John, For Love of Ivy, Buck and the Preacher (also dir.), A Warm December (dir., star), Uptown Saturday Night (dir., star), The Wilby Conspiracy, Let's Do It Again (dir., star), A Piece of the Action (dir., star), Stir Crazy (dir.), Hanky Panky (dir.), Fast Forward (dir.), Shoot To Kill, Little Nikita, Ghost Dad (dir.).

POLANSKI, ROMAN: Director, Writer. b. Paris, France, Aug. 18, 1933. Lived in Poland from age of three. Early career, art school in Cracow; Polish Natl. Film Acad., Lodz 1954–59.

Radio Actor 1945–47; on stage 1947–53; asst. dir., Kamera film prod. group 1959–61. Co-founder Cadre Films, 1964. On stage as actor in Amadeus (and dir., Warsaw), Metamorphosis (Paris, 1988). Acted in numerous Polish and intl. films (The Magic Christian, Blood of Dracula). Autobiography: Roman (1984).

PICTURES: Wrote and dir. shorts: Two Men in a Wardrobe, Le Gros et Le Maigre, Mammals. Features: Knife in the Water (Poland), Repulsion, Cul-De-Sac, Fearless Vampire Killers. Director: Rosemary's Baby, A Day at the Beach (prod. only), Macbeth (also prod.), What? (a.k.a. Che?), Chinatown. Director-writer: The Tenant (also actor), Tess, Pirates, Frantic.

POLIER, DAN A.: Executive. b. Atlanta, GA. e. Georgia Military Acad., U. of Illinois. Sports columnist, Charlotte (N.C.) News; sports editor, army wkly, Yank; entered m.p. industry adv. dept. 20th Century-Fox; head of booking dept. Fox West Coast Theatres; v.p. and director of film buying NTT Amusement Corp.; v.p. and co-director theatre operations, National General Corp. (formerly NTT); named v.p. in chg. of production, National General Productions, Inc., 1967. Joined Radnitz/Mattel Productions in 1972 as v.p. in chg. of distribution for Sounder; v.p. Mann Theatres Corp. of Calif., 1973. Rejoined Radnitz/Mattel Productions, 1975, as vice pres. in charge of marketing. Now pres., Knopf/Polier Representation.

POLL, MARTIN H.: Producer. b. New York, NY. e. Wharton Sch., U. of Pennsylvania. Pres. Gold Medal Studios.

PICTURES: prod. Love Is a Ball, Sylvia, The Lion in Winter, The Appointment, The Magic Garden of Stanley Sweetheart, The Man Who Loved Cat Dancing, Night Watch, Love and Death (exec. prod.); The Sailor who Fell From Grace with the Sea, Somebody Killed Her Husband, The Dain Curse, Nighthawks, A Town Called Alice, (Martin Poll presentation), Arthur the King, Gimme an F, Haunted Summer, Home Grown.

POLLACK, SYDNEY: Director, Producer. b. South Bend, IN, July 1, 1934. m. Claire Griswold. e. Neighborhood Playhouse. Assistant to Sanford Meisner at Neighborhood Playhouse. Appeared as actor on Bdwy in A Stone for Danny Fisher, The Dark is Light Enough. As TV actor: Playhouse 90 segments, Shotgun Slade, 15 Ben Caseys, A Cardinal Act of Mercy (won 5 Emmy nominations), The Game on Bob Hope-Chrysler Theatre (won Emmy for direction), Two is the Number. Dir. debut in 1960. Dir. play at UCLA, P.S. 193. Prepared the American version of The Leopard.

PICTURES: The Slender Thread (dir.), This Property is Condemned, The Scalphunters, Castle Keep, They Shoot Horses, Don't They?, Jeremiah Johnson, The Way We Were, The Yakuza, Three Days of the Condor, Bobby Deerfield, The Electric Horseman, Honeysuckle Rose (exec. prod. only), Absence of Malice (also prod.); Tootsie (also prod. and actor); Songwriter (prod. only); Out of Africa (also prod.), Bright Lights, Big City (prod. only), Scrooged (exec. prod.), The Fabulous Baker Boys (prod.), Presumed Innocent (prod.).

POLLARD, MICHAEL J.: Actor. b. Pacific, NJ, May 30, 1939. e. Actors Studio.

THEATER: Comes a Day, Loss of Roses, Enter Laughing, Bye Bye Birdie, Leda Had a Little Swan.

PICTURES: Hemingway's Adventures of a Young Man, The Stripper, Summer Magic, The Wild Angels, The Russians Are Coming, The Russians Are Coming, Caprice, Enter Laughing, Bonnie and Clyde, Jigsaw, Little Fauss and Big Halsey, Hannibal Brooks, Dirty Little Billy, The Legend of Frenchy King, Sunday in the Country, Between the Lines, Melvin and Howard, America, Heated Vengeance, The Patriot, The American Way (Riders of the Storm), Roxanne, Fast Food, Enid Is Sleeping.

TELEVISION: Guest: Alfred Hitchcock Presents (Anniversary Gift, 1959), Going My Way, Route 66, Here's Lucy, Mr. Novak, Honey West, I Spy, Dobie Gillis, Get Christie Love, Star Trek.

POLLEXFEN, JACK: Producer, Director, Writer. b. San Diego, CA, June 10, 1918. e. Los Angeles City Coll. Newspaperman, magazine writer, playwright: prod. for RKO, United Artists, Columbia, Allied Artists.

PICTURES: Son of Sinbad, At Swords Point, Secret of Convict Lake, Desert Hawk, Lady in the Iron Mask, Dragon's Gold, Problem Girls, Captive Women, Captain Kidd and the Slave Girl, Neanderthal Man, Captain John Smith and Pocahontas, Return to Treasure Island, Sword of Venus, 1000 Years from Now, Daughter of Dr. Jekyll, Monstrosity, Son of Dr. Jekyll, Mr. Big, Man from Planet X.

POLLOCK, DALE: Executive. b. Cleveland, OH, 1950. e. Brandeis U., B.A. anthropology, San Jose State U, M.A., mass communication. Began journalistic career in Santa Cruz in early '70s, serving as reporter and film critic for Daily Variety from 1977 to 1980. Then joined Los Angeles Times as film writer, winning paper's Award for Sustained Excellence in 1984. In 1985 left to take post with The Geffen Film Co. as executive in chg. creative development. Joined A&M Films as v.p. in chg. prod., Jan. 1986. Author: Skywalking (about George Lucas).

PICTURES: The Mighty Quinn (exec. prod.), Blaze (prod.).

POLLOCK, THOMAS: Executive. b. 1943. In 1971, after 3 years as business mgr. for American Film Institute's film marketing wing, formed law firm Pollock Bloom, and Dekom with young filmmakers such as George Lucas and Matthew Robbins as clients. Served as chmn. Filmex, 1973–81. 1986, named chmn. MCA's Universal motion picture group., also v.p., MCA, Inc.

POLONSKY, ABRAHAM: Director, Writer. b. New York, NY, Dec. 5, 1910. e. City Coll. of New York, B.A.; Columbia Law Sch. Taught at City Coll. 1932 until war. Wrote s.p. Golden Earrings, I Can Get it For You Wholesale. Wrote novels; The Enemy Sea, The Discoverers, The World Above, The Season of Fear, Zenia's Way. Wrote orig. story and s.p. Body and Soul; collab. s.p. and directed Force of Evil. Blacklisted from 1951–66; Odds Against Tomorrow (s.p.). Coll. s.p. Madigan 1968; dir. and s.p. Tell Them Willie Boy is Here, 1970; dir. Romance of a Horse Thief, 1971; Avalanche Express (s.p.); Monsignor, (s.p.) 1982.

PONTECORVO, GILLO: Director. b. Pisa, Italy, 1919. Younger brother of Prof. Bruno Pontecorvo, Harwell scientist who defected in 1950. Worked as asst. dir., directed documentary shorts before feature debut in 1957.

PICTURES: Die Windrose Giovanna; La Grande Strada Azzurra; Kapo; The Battle of Algiers; Queimada!; (Burn); Ogro.

PONTI, CARLO: Producer. b. Milan, Italy, Dec. 11, 1913. m. actress Sophia Loren. e. U. of Milan, 1934. Prod. first picture in Milan, Little Old World; prod. Lux Film Rome; prod. first of a series of famous Toto pictures, Toto Househunting.

PICTURES: A Dog's Life, The Knight Has Arrived, Musolino, The Outlaw, Romanticism, Sensuality, The White Slave, Europe 1951, Toto in Color, The Three Corsairs, Ulysses, The Woman of the River, An American of Rome, Attila, War and Peace, The Last Lover, The Black Orchid, That Kind of Woman, Marriage Italian Style, The Great Spy Mission, Happily Ever After, The Girl and the General, Sunflower, Best House in London, Lady Liberty, White Sister, What?, Andy Warhol's Frankenstein, The Passenger, The Cassandra Crossing, A Special Day, Saturday, Sunday, Monday.

TELEVISION: Mario Puzo's The Fortunate Pilgrim (exec. prod.).

POOLE, FRANK S.: Executive. b. London, England, 1913. e. Dulwich Coll., 1925–31. Ent. m.p. ind. 1931. Early career with Pathe Pictures, Twickenham Film Distributors, until joining 20th Century Fox as London branch office supervisor 1939. War service 1940–46. Rejoined Fox 1946–53; appt. Leed Branch mgr. 1954–59; supv. 1959–61; asst. sls. mgr., 1961 until joined Rank Film Distrib. as asst. sls. mgr. 1962. Appt. sls. mgr. July 1965, and to board as dir. of sls. Aug. 1965. Appt. gen. mgr. 1968; jnt. mng. dir. 1969; appt. mng. dir. July 1970; appt. dir. Rank Overseas Film Dist. Ltd., 1972; appt. co-chmn Fox-Rank Distributors Ltd., Dec. 1972; appt. vice-chairman Rank Film Distributors Ltd. 1977. 1975, elected to Committee of Cinema & TV Veterans. Oct., 1978, retired from Rank Organisation. Appt. chmn., Appeal Tribunal for the Film Industry. Appt. chmn., Grebelands Mgt. Committee & to exec. council of CTBF, 1979, assoc. Geoff Reeve & Associates. 1980, chmn. & mng. dir., Omandry Intl. Ltd.

PORTER, DON: Actor. b. Miami, OK, Sept. 24, 1912. e. Oregon Inst. of Tech. Wide theatre work; then m.p, roles. U.S. Army, 3 yrs.

TELEVISION: Co-star, Private Secretary, Ann Sothern Show, Gidget, Bionic Woman, Hawaii Five-O, Switch, Love Boat, Three's Company, The President's Mistress, The Murder That Wouldn't Die, The Last Song, Dallas; Old Money.

STAGE: The Best Man, Any Wednesday, Generation, Plaza Suite, The Price, How To Succeed in Business Without Really Trying, Harvey.

PICTURES: The Racket, The Savage, 711 Ocean Drive, Because You're Mine, Our Miss Brooks, Bachelor in Paradise, Youngblood Hawke, The Candidate, 40 Carats, Mame, White Line Fever.

POST, TED: Producer, Director. b. Brooklyn, NY, March 31, 1918. Dir. many stage plays; dir. CBS-TV Repertoire Thea.; Producer-dir., NBC-TV Coney Island of the Mind.

TELEVISION: Studio One, Ford Theatre, Playhouse of Stars, Fred Astaire Show, Gunsmoke, Rawhide, Twilight Zone, Wagon Train, Combat, Peyton Place, Alcoa, Defenders, Route 66, Baretta, and Columbo. Movies: Dr. Cook's Garden, Girls in One Office, Cagney & Lacey, Night Slaves, Five Desperate Women, Stagecoach, Yuma, The Bravos, Do Not Fold, Spindle or Mutilate. Mini-series: Rich Man, Poor Man II (episode 3).

PICTURES: The Peacemaker (1956), The Legend of Tom Dooley, Magnum Force, Hang 'em High, Beneath The Planet of the Apes, The Harrad Experiment, Good Guys Wear Black, Whiffs, Go Tell the Spartans, Nightkill.

POSTER, STEVEN: Cinematographer. e. L.A. Art Center Coll. Started as commercial cinematographer before moving into feature films. Member, American Society of Cinematographers.
PICTURES: Blood Beach, Dead and Buried, Spring Break, Strange Brew, Testament, The New Kids, The Heavenly Kid, Blue City, The Boy Who Could Fly, Aloha Summer, Someone to Watch Over Me, Big Top Pee-wee, Next of Kin, Opportunity Knocks.

POSTON, TOM: Actor. b. Columbus, OH, Oct. 17, 1927. Winner of Emmy for supporting work on Steve Allen Show (1959).
PICTURES: The City That Never Sleeps; Zotz; The Old Dark House; Cold Turkey; The Happy Hooker; Rabbit Test; Up the Academy; Carbon Copy.
TELEVISION: Movies: On the Rocks; We've Got Each Other; The Girl; The Gold Watch and Everything; Save the Dog! Series: Mork and Mindy, Fame, Newhart. Game Show: To Tell the Truth.

POTTER, DENNIS: Writer. b. Forest of Dean, Gloucester, Eng., May 17, 1935. e. New Coll., Oxford U.
THEATER: Vote, Vote, Vote for Nigel Barton (1968); Son of Man; Only Make Believe; Brimstone and Treacle; Sufficient Carbohydrate.
PICTURES: Pennies From Heaven; Gorky Park; Dreamchild, Track 29, Blackeyes (dir., s.p.).
TELEVISION: Series: Casanova; Mini-series: Pennies From Heaven; Blue Remembered Hills; Blade on the Feather, Rain on the Roof; Cream in My Coffee; Traitor; Paper Roses; The Singing Detective, Christabel (also exec. prod.). TELEPLAYS: The Confidence Courses; Stand Up Nigel Barton; Vote, Vote, Vote for Nigel Barton; Almost Cinderella; Son of Man; Lay Down Your Arms; Follow the Yellow Brick Road; Only Make Believe; Joe's Ark; Schmoedipus; Late Call; Double Dare; Where Adam Stood; Brimstone and Treacle.
NOVELS: The Glittering Coffin; The Changing Forest; Hide and Seek, Blackeyes.

POTTER, MADELEINE: Actress. b. Washington D.C. Daughter of diplomat, spent childhood traveling between Washington and Hong Kong and Tanzania. Stage debut at 15 in one-woman show as Sarah Bernhardt in Washington D.C.
THEATER: Lydie Breeze (NY debut), Plenty, Slab Boys, Coastal Disturbances, Hamlet (Folger Theater, Wash.), Richard III (NY Shakespeare Fest.), Abingdon Square, The Daughters of Dionysius, Metamorphosis.
PICTURES: The Bostonians (debut, 1984), Hello Again, The Suicide Club, Slaves of New York, Bloodhounds of Broadway.

POTTLE, HARRY: Production designer. b. London, England, 1925. e. Ealing Coll. of Arts. Fleet Air Arm, 1944–47. Ent. m.p. ind. 1947. Designed Blind Date, 1960. Human Jungle, Avengers (TV series). Art Director, You Only Live Twice, Chitty Chitty Bang Bang, The Adventurers. Production Designer, 39 Steps, Murder by Degree, Bear Island, Matarese Circle, Desert King.

POTTS, ANNIE: Actress. b. Nashville, TN, Oct. 28, 1952. e. Stephens Coll., MO, BFA. Amateur stage debut at 12 in Heidi. Then in summer stock; on road in Charley's Aunt, 1976. Serves as auxilliary bd. of MADD (Mothers Against Drunk Driving). Ambassador for Women for the Amer. Arthritis Fdn.
PICTURES: Corvette Summer, King of the Gypsies, Heartaches, Stick, Crimes of Passion, Ghostbusters, Pretty in Pink, Jumpin' Jack Flash, Pass the Ammo, Who's Harry Crumb?, Texasville.
TELEVISION: Movies: Flatbed Annie and Sweetie Pie, Cowboy, It Came Upon a Midnight Clear. Series: Goodtime Girls, Designing Women.

POUND, LESLIE: Executive. Entered industry in 1943 as reporter on British trade paper, Screen International. Following military service in India and Singapore returned to work for that publication until 1952 when joined Paramount pub. office in London on the The Greatest Show on Earth. Named dir. of adv./pub. in U.K. for Paramount. 1958, retained Para. position when Cinema Intl. Corp. was formed. 1977, joined Lew Grade in ITC Entertainment as worldwide dir. of pub./adv. 1982, intl. pub. chief for Embassy Pictures in Los Angeles. 1982, named Paramount Pictures v.p., intl. mktg. for motion picture div., N.Y. Now relocated in L.A. with mktg. div.

POWELL, CHARLES, M.: Executive. b. New York, NY, Feb. 17, 1934. e. NYU, B.S., journalism. Columbia Pictures national publicity mgr., national exploitation mgr., 1959–69. Paramount Pictures, national publicity coordinator, 1963–64. WNBC-Radio/TV, advertising/promotion mgr. 1965. Director adv., pub. for M. J. Frankovich 1969–71. Joined MGM as dir. adv. pub.-expl. in 1972; named div. v.p. & corp. v.p., 1974; Columbia Pictures, sr. v.p. marketing, 1975; Universal Pictures, sr. v.p., 1976–80. Powell & Young, m.p. consultants; exec. v.p. & dir., Color Systems Technology, Inc. Pres., CEO, Pegasus Entertainment, Inc. Board of Governors, Acad. of Motion Picture Arts & Sciences, since 1973. Current v.p. & member: Nat'l Acad. of Television Arts and Sciences. Founder & pres., Synagogue for the Performing Arts, L.A and Shofar Temple.

POWELL, JANE: Actress. r.n. Suzanne Burce. b. Portland, OR, Apr. 1, 1929. m. pub. relations exec. Dick Moore. Had own radio program over KOIN, Portland; singer on natl. networks; m.p. debut in Song of the Open Road, 1944, Star of Tomorrow, 1948. Autobiography: The Girl Next Door . . . and How She Grew (1988).
PICTURES: Holiday in Mexico, Three Daring Daughters, Luxury Liner, Date With Judy, Nancy Goes to Rio, Two Weeks With Love, Royal Wedding, Rich Young and Pretty, Small Town Girl, Three Sailors and a Girl, Seven Brides for Seven Brothers, Athena, Deep in My Heart, Hit the Deck, Girl Most Likely, The Enchanted Island.
STAGE: Irene (Broadway, 1974).
TELEVISION: Ruggles of Red Gap, Give My Regards to Broadway, Meet Me in St. Louis, Jane Powell Show, Loving (daytime drama), Growing Pains.

POWELL, MICHAEL: Producer, Director, Writer. b. Canterbury, Kent, England, Sept. 30, 1905. Collaborated for many years with the late Emeric Pressburger in making films.
PICTURES: Writer only: Caste, Park Lane, The Star Reporter, Hotel Splendide, The Fire Raisers, Night of the Party, Lazybones, The Phantom Light, The Man Behind the Mask, etc. Writer-Producer-Director: The Edge of the World, The Spy in Black, The Thief of Baghdad, 49th Parallel, One of Our Aircraft is Missing, The Life and Death of Colonel Blimp, A Canterbury Tale, I Know Where I'm Going, A Matter of Life and Death, Black Narcissus, The Red Shoes, The Small Back Room, Gone to Earth, The Elusive Pimpernel, The Tales of Hoffman, Ill Met by Moonlight, Peeping Tom, Honeymoon, The Queen's Guards, They're a Weird Mob, Sebastian (prod. only), Age of Consent, The Boy Turned Yellow, Return to the Edge of the World.

POWERS, MALA: Actress. r.n. Mary Ellen Powers. b. San Francisco, CA, Dec. 29, 1921. p. George and Dell Powers, latter, dramatic coach. e. Max Reinhardt Dramatic Sch., Hollywood, CA, UCLA. Pasadena Playhouse in For Keeps, 1946; Distant Isle; Actor's Lab, Hollywood; did considerable radio work. Writer, narrator Children's Story, Tell-Story and Dial A Story (1979). Author: Follow the Year (1984).
PICTURES: Outrage, Edge of Doom, Cyrano de Bergerac, Rose of Cimarron, City Beneath the Sea, City That Never Sleeps, Geraldine, Yellow Mountain, Rage at Dawn, Bengazi, Tammy and the Bachelor, Storm Rider, Flight of the Lost Balloon, Daddy's Gone-A-Hunting, Temple of the Ravens, Six Tickets to Hell.

POWERS, C. F. (MIKE) JR: Executive. b. San Francisco, CA, March 6, 1923. e. Park Coll., MO, Columbia U., N.Y., graduated U. of Oregon. Entered film business with P.R.C. in Portland, OR, 1947. Became Eagle Lion branch mgr. in Portland, 1950, and then United Artists. Moved to Seattle, WA as branch mgr. of 20th Century Fox, 1960. Was then western division mgr. for 20th Century Fox until 1967, then western division mgr. for Cinerama till 1973. Became exec. v.p., head film buyer for Robert L. Lippert Theatres, Transcontinental Theatres and Affiliated Theatres until 1978. Became western division mgr. for Filmways Pictures. President of Catholic Entertainment Guild of Northern Calif.; past Chief Barker of Variety Club Tent 32, San Francisco.

POWERS, STEFANIE: Actress. r.n. Stefania Federkiewicz. b. Hollywood, CA, Nov. 2, 1942. Theatrical m.p. debut in Among the Thorns, 1961. TV debut in The Girl from U.N.C.L.E. series.
PICTURES: Tammy Tell Me True, Experiment in Terror, The Interns, If a Man Answers, McClintock, Palm Springs Weekend, Fanatic, The New Interns, Die Die My Darling, Love Has Many Faces, The Young Sinner, Stagecoach, Warning Shot, The Boatnicks, Crescendo, The Magnificent 7 Ride, Herbie Rides Again, It Seemed Like a Good Idea at the Time, Escape to Athena, Invisible Stranger (a.k.a. The Astral Factor).
TELEVISION: Series: The Girl From U.N.C.L.E., Feather and Father, Gang, Hart to Hart. Mini-series: Washington: Behind Closed Doors. Movies: Five Desperate Women, Paper Man, Sweet, Sweet Rachel, Hardcase, No Place to Run, Shootout in a One-Dog Town, Skyway to Death, Sky Heist, Return to Earth, Family Secrets (also prod.), A Death in Canaan, Mistral's Daughter, Hollywood Wives, Deceptions, At Mother's Request, Beryl Markham: A Shadow on the Sun (also co-prod.), She Was Marked for Murder, Love and Betrayal.

PRATLEY, GERALD: Commentator, b. and e. London, Eng. Joined Canadian Broadcasting Corp., 1946; writer, narrator and producer of The Movie Scene and Music from the Films; asst. member British Film Academy, dir. Canadian Film Institute 1953; chairman Toronto and District Film Council

1956; co-dir. & founder A.G.E. Film Society, Toronto; contributor to U.S. and European film journals; film consult., Canadian Centennial Comm. Chmn., Canadian Film Awards; director, Stratford Film Festival; director, Ontario Film Institute, Toronto. Prof. of film, York U., U. of Toronto. Seneca Coll., McMaster U. Author: Cinema of John Frankenheimer; Otto Preminger; David Lean; John Huston, Torn Sprockets. Mem., classification board, Ontario Theatre branch. 1984, Mem. Advisory boards film depts., Humber College, Ryerson Polytechnical Institute; Mem. TV Ontario Adult Programming Order of Canada, 1984, Can. Picture Pioneers Assn. Cultural Executives, St. George's Society, Arts and Letters Club.

PRENTISS, PAULA: Actress, r.n. Paula Ragusa. b. San Antonio, TX, March 4, 1939. m. actor-director Richard Benjamin. e. Northwestern U., Bachelor degree in drama, 1959. On TV in He & She; on stage in As You Like It, Arf!
PICTURES: Where the Boys Are, The Honeymoon Machine, Bachelor in Paradise, Man's Favorite Sport, Catch 22, Move, The World of Henry Orient, In Harms Way, What's New Pussycat?, Scraping Bottom, Last of the Red Hot Lovers, The Parallax View, The Stepford Wives, The Black Marble, Buddy, Buddy, Saturday the 14th.

PRESLE, MICHELINE: Actress. r.n. Micheline Chassagne. b. Paris, France, Aug. 22, 1922. e. Raymond Rouleau Dram. Sch. m.p. debut in Je Chante; on stage in Colinette. Am. Stram Gram, Spectacle des Allies; to U.S., 1945.
PICTURES: Jeunes Filles en Detresse, L'Histoire de Rire, La Nuit Fantastique, Felicie Nanteuil, Seul Amour, Faibalas, Boule de Suif, Jeux Sont Faix, Diable au Corps, Under My Skin, American Guerilla in the Philippines, Adventures of Captain Fabian, Sins of Pompeii, House of Ricordi, Archipelago of Love, Thieves After Dark, Le Chien, At the Top of the Stairs, Fine Weather, But Storms Due Towards Evening, Confidences, Alouette, je te plumerai, I Want to Go Home.
TELEVISION: The Blood of Others.

PRESLEY, PRISCILLA: Actress. b. Brooklyn, NY, May 24, 1945. Raised in Connecticut. e. Wiesbaden, West Germany where met and married Elvis Presley (1967–73). Studied acting with Milton Katselas, dance at Steven Peck Theatre Art School and karate at Chuck Norris Karate School. Formed a business, Bis and Beau, marketing exclusive dress designs. Became TV spokesperson for beauty products.
PICTURES: The Naked Gun: From the Files of Police Squad! (debut, 1988).
TELEVISION: Series: Those Amazing Animals (host, 1980–81), Dallas. Movie: Elvis and Me (prod. only).

PRESSMAN, EDWARD R.: Producer. b. New York, NY. e. Fieldston Sch.; grad., Stanford U.; studied at London Sch. of Economics. Began career with film short, Girl, in collaboration with director Paul Williams in London. They formed Pressman-Williams Enterprises.
PICTURES: *Prod.:* Out of It, The Revolutionary, Dealing: or the Berkeley to Boston Forty Brick, Lost Bag Blues, Sisters, Badlands (exec. prod.), Phantom of the Paradise; Paradise Alley (exec. prod.); Old Boyfriends; Heartbeat (exec. prod.); The Hand; Conan the Barbarian (exec. prod.); Das Boot (exec. prod.); The Pirates of Penzance (exec. prod.); Crimewave (exec. prod.); Plenty; Half Moon Street (exec. prod.); True Stories (exec. prod.); Good Morning Babylon; Masters of the Universe (exec. prod.); Walker (exec. prod.); Wall Street; Cherry 2000; Paris By Night (exec. prod.); Talk Radio; Martians Go Home (exec. prod.), Blue Steel., Reversal of Fortune, To Sleep with Anger (exec. prod.), Waiting for the Light (exec. prod.).

PRESSMAN, LAWRENCE: Actor. b. Cynthiana, KY, July 10, 1939. e. Kentucky Northwestern U. On Bdwy. in Man in the Glass Booth, Play It Again, Sam, etc.
PICTURES: Man in the Glass Booth, The Crazy World of Julius Vrooder, Hellstrom Chronicle, Shaft, Making It, Walk Proud, Nine to Five, Some Kind of Hero, The Hanoi Hilton.
TELEVISION: Mulligan's Stew (series). Movies; Cannon, The Snoop Sisters, The Marcus-Nelson Murder, Winter Kill, The First 36 Hours of Dr. Durant, Rich Man, Poor Man, Man from Atlantis, The Trial of Lee Harvey Oswald, The Gathering, Like Mom, Like Me, Blind Ambition, Little Girl Lost, Breaking Point.

PRESSMAN, MICHAEL: Producer, Director. b. New York, NY, July 1, 1950. e. California Inst. of Arts. Comes from show business family; was actor in college.
PICTURES: Director: The Great Texas Dynamite Chase, The Bad News Bears Breaking Training, Boulevard Nights, Those Lips Those Eyes (also prod.), Some Kind of Hero, Doctor Detroit.
TELEVISION: Director: Like Mom, Like Me, The Imposter, The Christmas Gift, Final Jeopardy, Private Sessions, Secret Passions, And the Children Shall Lead, Sirens, Haunted by Her Past, To Heal a Nation, Shootdown, The Revenge of Al Capone, Incident at Dark River.

PREUSTER, CHRISTOPHER W.: Executive. b. Newark, NJ, Apr., 16, 1942. e. St. Peters Coll., Jersey City, 1960–64. Pub. acct. to many film cos. (UA, Fox, Universal), while with Peat Marwick Mitchell, 1964–67; joined Walter Reade Organization, 1968; named pres. 1984.

PREVIN, ANDRE: Composer, Conductor. b. Berlin, Germany, Apr. 6, 1929. Composed and conducted over 50 m.p. scores. Music director, Pittsburgh Symphony Orchestra, & conductor emeritus of London Symphony Orchestra. Music Director, Royal Philharmonic Orch., 1985–89. Guest conductor of most major symphony orchestras in U.S. and Europe.
PICTURES: Three Little Words, Cause for Alarm, It's Always Fair Weather, Bad Day at Black Rock, Invitation to the Dance, Catered Affair, Designing Woman, Silk Stockings, Gigi (Academy Award), Porgy and Bess (Academy Award), Subterraneans, Bells are Ringing, Pepe, Elmer Gantry, Four Horsemen of the Apocalypse, One Two Three, Two for the Seesaw, Long Day's Journey Into Night, Irma LaDouce (Academy Award), My Fair Lady (Academy Award), Goodbye Charlie, Inside Daisy Clover, Fortune Cookie, Thoroughly Modern Millie, Valley of the Dolls, Paint Your Wagon, The Music Lovers, Jesus Christ Superstar.

PRICE, FRANK: Executive. b. Decatur, IL, May 17, 1930. e. Michigan State U. following naval service. Joined CBS in N.Y. in 1951 as story editor and writer. Moved to Hollywood in 1953, serving as story editor first at Columbia and then NBC (Matinee Theatre). In 1958 joined Universal as an assoc. prod. and writer. In 1961 named exec. prod. of The Virginian TV series. Appt. exec. prod. of Ironside; later did It Takes a Thief and several World Premiere movies. In 1964 named v.p. of Universal TV; 1971, sr. v.p.; 1974, pres. Also v.p., MCA, Inc. In 1978 left to join Columbia as pres. of new company unit, Columbia Pictures Productions. In 1979 named chmn. & CEO of Columbia Pictures. In 1984 joined Universal: named chmn., motion picture group, pres. of Universal Pictures, and v.p. of MCA. In 1987 formed Price Entertainment Inc. as chmn. & CEO to produce movies and create TV shows for dist. through Columbia Pictures Entertainment.

PRICE, ROGER: Performer. b. Charleston, WV, Mar. 6, 1920. e. U. of Michigan, American Acad. of Art, Max Reinhardt Dramatic Workshop. Appeared at many nightclubs, many TV guest appearances; writing credits include the Don Knotts Show, Governor & J.J., Bob Hope, The Partners, The Bluffers. V.P. of Price, Stern, Sloan Publishers.
TELEVISION: Toast of the Town, Arthur Godfrey's Friends, Garry Moore Show, This Is Show Business, Jack Paar, Get Smart, Johnny Carson. creator of The Kallikaks (NBC); The Waltons, McMillan and Wife, Mike Douglas, Murder She Wrote, Ghost Chasers, Mama's Family, Superior Court, Get Smart Again.
PICTURES: Mame, Day of the Locust, The Strongest Man in the World, Mixed Company, At Long Last Love, Pete's Dragon, The Devil and Max Devlin, Love on the Run.

PRICE, VINCENT: Actor. b. St. Louis, MO, May 27, 1911. m. actress Coral Browne. e. Yale U., U. of London, Nuremberg U. Autobiography: I Know What I Like (1959).
PICTURES: The Song of Bernadette, Buffalo Bill, The Eve of St. Mark, Wilson, The Keys of the Kingdom, Laura, A Royal Scandal, Leave Her to Heaven, Dragonwyck, Shock, Long Night, Moss Rose, Three Musketeers, Rogues Regiment, The Web, The Bribe, Baron of Arizona, Champagne for Caesar, Bagdad, His Kind of Woman, Adventures of Captain Fabian, Las Vegas Story, House of Wax, Dangerous Mission, Mad Magician, Son of Sinbad, Serenade, While the City Sleeps, Mysterious House of Usher, Return of the Fly, The Bat, The Tingler, House on Haunted Hill, House of Usher, Pit and Pendulum, Tales of Terror, The Mask of the Red Death, War Gods of the Deep, Dr. Gold Foot and the Sex Machine, The House of 1,000 Dolls, More Dead Than Alive, The Oblong Box, Scream and Scream Again, Dr. Phibes, Dr. Phibes Rise Again!, Theatre of Blood, Madman, Scavenger Hunt, House of the Long Shadows, The Whales of August, Dead Heat, Backtrack, The Offspring.
TELEVISION: What's a Nice Girl Like You. . ., Batman, Time Express (series), Mystery! (host), many dramatic roles in 1950s and 60s as well as hosting E.S.P. and The Chevy Mystery Show and panelist on Pantomime Quiz (1950–52).

PRIES, RALPH W.: Executive. b. Atlanta, GA, August 31, 1919. Graduated Georgia Inst. of Technology. V.P., MEDIQ, Inc.; pres. MEDIQ/PRN Life Support Services, Inc.; past pres., Odgen Food Service Corp.; exec. comm. and bd., Firstrust Savings Bank and chmn. of audit comm.; Boards of St. Christopher's Hospital for Children, Moss Rehabilitation Hospital, United Hospital Corp., Philadelphia Heart Instit. Former intl pres., Variety Clubs Intl.; previously on bd. of Hahnemann U. and Hosp., chmn. of bd. Likoff Cardiovascular Instit., pres. Main Line Reform Temple, Wynnewood, PA.

PRIMUS, BARRY: Actor. b. New York, NY, Feb. 16, 1938. e. Bennington Coll., City Coll. of NY.
THEATER: The King and the Duke (debut, 1953); The

Nervous Set; Henry IV, Parts I and II; Creating the World; Teibele and the Demon, Lincoln Center Rep. (The Changling, After the Fall).
PICTURES: The Brotherhood (1969); Been Down So Long It Looks Like Up to Me; New York, New York; Avalanche; Autopsy; Night Games; The Rose; Heartland; Absence of Malice; The River; Down and Out in Beverly Hills; Jake Speed; Space Camp; The Stranger; Big Business; Cannibal Women in the Avocado Jungle of Death.
TELEVISION: Series: The Defenders; Cagney and Lacey. Movies: Washington Behind Closed Doors; Heart of Steel; Brotherly Love.

PRINCE: Singer, Actor. r.n. Rogers Nelson. b. Minneapolis, MN, 1960. Famous as rock star and recording artist before film debut in Purple Rain (1984).
PICTURES: Purple Rain, Under the Cherry Moon, Sign O' the Times (dir., actor, songs).

PRINCE, HAROLD: Director, Producer. b. New York, NY, Jan. 30, 1928. e. U. of Pennsylvania. Worked as stage mgr. for George Abbott on three shows, later co-produced, produced and/or directed the following: The Pajama Game (Tony Award), Damn Yankees (Tony Award), New Girl In Town, West Side Story, A Swim in the Sea, Fiorello! (Tony/Pulitzer), Tenderloin, Take Her, She's Mine, A Funny Thing Happened on the Way to the Forum (Tony Award), She Loves Me, The Matchmaker (revival), Fiddler On The Roof, Poor Bitos, Baker Street, Flora, The Red Menace, Superman, Cabaret (Tony Award), Zorba, Company, Follies, The Great God Brown, The Visit, Love for Love (the last three all revivals), A Little Night Music (Tony Award), Candide (Tony Award), Pacific Overtures, Side by Side by Sondheim, Some of My Best Friends, On the Twentieth Century, Evita (London, 1978, Bdwy. 1979, LA, Australia & Chicago, 1980; Vienna & Mexico City, 1981), Sweeney Todd (Bdwy., Tony Award 1979; London, 1980), Merrily We Roll Along, A Doll's Life, Play Memory, End of the World, Diamonds, Grind, Roza, Cabaret (revival), Phantom of the Opera (London, 1986; NY, 1988) (Tony Award), and also directed the operas Ashmadei, Silverlake, Sweeney Todd, Candide and Don Giovanni for N.Y. City Opera, Girl of Golden West for Chicago Lyric Opera Co. and San Francisco Opera; Willie Stark for Houston Grand Opera; Madame Butterfly for Chicago Lyric Opera and Turandot for Vienna State Opera and Faust for Metropolitan Opera.
MOVIES: Co-producer: The Pajama Game (1957), Damn Yankees. Director: Something for Everyone, A Little Night Music.
AUTHOR: Contradictions, Notes on Twenty-Six Years in the Theatre (Dodd, Mead & Co., New York, 1974).

PRINCE, WILLIAM: Actor. b. Nichols, NY, Jan. 26, 1913. With Maurice Evans, actor, 2 yrs., radio announcer. On N.Y. stage, Ah, Wilderness; m.p. debut in 1943. Many TV credits.
STAGE: Guest in the House, Across the Board on Tomorrow Morning, The Eve of St. Mark, John Loves Mary, As You Like It, I Am a Camera, Forward the Heart, Affair of Honor, Third Best Sport, The Highest Tree, Venus at Large, Strange Interlude, The Ballad of the Sad Cafe, Mercy Street.
PICTURES: Destination Tokyo, Cinderella Jones, The Very Thought of You, Roughly Speaking, Objective Burma, Pillow to Post, Lust for Gold, Cyrano de Bergerac, Secret of Treasure Mountain, Macabre, Sacco and Vanzetti, Dead Reckoning, The Heartbreak Kid, The Stepford Wives, Family Plot, Network, The Gauntlet, Rollercoaster, The Cat from Outer Space, The Promise, Bronco Billy, Love & Money, Kiss Me Goodbye, Movers and Shakers, Fever Pitch, Spies Like Us, Nuts, Vice Versa.
TELEVISION: War and Remembrance (mini-series).

PRINCIPAL, VICTORIA: Actress. b. Fukuoka, Japan, Jan 3, 1950. Went to New York to become model; studied acting privately with Jean Scott at Royal Acad. of Dramatic Art in London before moving to Hollywood. Film debut in The Life and Times of Judge Roy Bean (1972).
PICTURES: The Naked Ape, Earthquake, I Will, I Will . . . for Now, Vigilante Force.
TELEVISION: Fantasy Island (pilot), Love Story, Love, American Style, Greatest Heroes of the Bible, Dallas (series). Movies: The Night They Stole Miss Beautiful, The Pleasure Palace, Last Hours Before Morning, Not Just Another Affair, Mistress, Naked Lie.

PRINE, ANDREW: Actor. b. Jennings, FL, Feb. 14, 1936. e. U. of Miami. m. actress Heather Lowe. Mem. Actors Studio. On stage in Look Homeward, Angel, A Distant Bell. Ahmanson Theatre, LA: Long Day's Journey into Night, The Caine Mutiny. South Coast Rep.: Goodbye Freddy.
PICTURES: The Miracle Worker, Advance to the Rear, Company of Cowards, Bandolero!, The Devil's Brigade, This Savage Land, Generation, Chisum, Riding Tall, One Little Indian, The Centerfold Girls, Grizzly, The Town That Dreaded Sundown, Winds of Autumn, High Flying Lowe, The Evil, Amityville: The Possession, Playing with Fire, Eliminators, Chill Factor, The Big One.
TELEVISION: Series: The Wide Country, The Road West, W.E.B., Boone. Dallas. Movies: Split Second to an Epitaph, Along Came a Spider, Night Slaves, Wonder Woman, Law of the Land, Tail Gunner Joe, Last of the Mohicans, A Small Killing, Mind over Murder, M-Station Hawaii, Christmas Miracle in Caulfield, Young Abe Lincoln, U.S.A., Donner Pass: The Road to Survival, V: The Final Battle (mini-series).

PROSKY, ROBERT, Actor. b. Philadelphia, PA. Won TV amateur talent search contest, leading to scholarship with American Theatre Wing. 23-year veteran with Washington's Arena stage. Taught acting and appeared in over 150 plays including Death of a Salesman, Galileo, The Caucasian Chalk Circle, You Can't Take it With You. Broadway prods. include Moonchildren, A View from the Bridge, Pale Horse, Pale Rider, Arms and the Man, Glengarry Glen Ross, A Walk in the Woods, Heist.
PICTURES: Thief, Hanky Panky, Monsignor, The Lords of Discipline, Christine, The Keep, The Natural, Outrageous Fortune, Broadcast News, Big Shots, The Great Outdoors, Things Change, Gremlins II.
TELEVISION: World War III, The Ordeal of Bill Carny, Lou Grant, The Adams Chronicles, Old Dogs, Hill Street Blues (series), Into Thin Air, The Murder of Mary Phagan, Home Fires Burning, From the Dead of Night, A Walk in the Woods.

PROVINE, DOROTHY: Actress. b. Deadwood, SD, Jan. 20, 1937. e. U. of Washington.
TELEVISION: The Alaskans, The Roaring 20's.
PICTURES: The Bonnie Parker Story, It's A Mad, Mad, Mad World, Good Neighbor Sam, The Great Race, That Darn Cat, Who's Minding the Mint?, Never a Dull Moment.

PRYCE, JONATHAN: Actor. b. North Wales, 1947. e. Royal Acad. of Dramatic Art. Actor and artistic dir. of Liverpool Everyman Theatre Co. On London stage in Comedians, Taming of the Shrew, Antony and Cleopatra, Comedians, Hamlet, Macbeth, The Seagull, Uncle Vanya, Accidental Death of an Anarchist.
PICTURES: Voyage of the Damned, Breaking Glass, Loophole, Praying Mantis, The Ploughman's Lunch, Something Wicked This Way Comes, Brazil, Doctor and the Devils, Haunted Honeymoon, Man on Fire, Jumping Jack Flash, Consuming Passions, The Adventures of Baron Munchausen, The Rachel Papers.
TELEVISION: Comedians, Playthings, Partisans, For Tea on Sunday, Timon of Athens, Murder Is Easy, Daft as a Brush, Martin Luther, Heretic; The Caretaker, Glad Day, The Man From the PRU, Roger Doesn't Live Here Anymore.

PRYOR, RICHARD: Actor. b. Peoria, IL, Dec. 1, 1940. At age 7 played drums with professionals. Appearances on TV (Johnny Carson, Merv Griffin, Ed Sullivan) established him as standup comic. Wrote TV scripts for Lily Tomlin and Flip Wilson; co-author of film, Blazing Saddles. Several albums are best-selling hits.
PICTURES: Actor: Lady Sings the Blues, Bingo Long and the Travelin' All Stars, Silver Streak, Greased Lightning, Which Way Is Up?, Blue Collar, The Wiz, California Suite, Wholly Moses, In God We Trust, Stir Crazy, Bustin' Loose (star, co-prod.), Live on Sunset Strip (prod.), Some Kind of Hero, Richard Pryor: Here and Now (dir., s.p.), The Toy (also s.p., dir.), Brewster's Millions, Jo Jo Dancer Your Life Is Calling (also prod.-dir.-s.p.), Critical Condition, Moving, See No Evil, Hear No Evil, Harlem Nights.

PRYOR, THOMAS M.: Journalist. b. New York, NY, May 22, 1912. Joined NY Times, 1929; m.p. dept. 1931 as reporter, editor, asst. film critic; Hollywood bureau chief, corres., NY Times, 1951–59; editor, Daily Variety, 1959–88; 1988– Consultant to Variety & Daily Variety.

PTAK, JOHN: Agent. b. San Diego, CA. Graduated UCLA film department, 1968. Theatre mgr. and booker for Walter Reade Organization and Laemmle Theatres, 1966–1969. Admin. exec. at American Film Institute's Center for Advanced Studies, 1969–1971. Agent at the International Famous Agency (ICM), 1971–1975. Vice Pres., William Morris Agency, 1976 to present, representing motion picture and television talent. Responsible for the initial representation of such films as Jaws, The Sting, Taxi Driver, Close Encounters of the Third Kind, Coal Miner's Daughter, Airplane, National Lampoon's Vacation. Consultant for the National Endowment of the Arts.

PURCELL, PATRICK B.: Executive. b. Dublin, Ireland, Mar. 16, 1943. e. Fordham U., M.B.A., 1973. In pub. & acct., England, 1969–69; acct., Associated Hosp. Service, N.Y., 1968–70; joined Paramount Pictures, 1970; v.p., fin., 1980–83; exec. v.p. fin. & admin. 1983–.

PURDOM, EDMUND: Actor. b. Welwyn Garden City, England, Dec. 19, 1924. e. St. Ignatius Coll., London. Played leads, character roles for Northampton Rep. Co., Kettering Rep., two seasons at Stratford-On-Avon; London stage in Way Things Go, Malade Imaginaire, Romeo and Juliet, played in Caesar and Cleopatra, Antony and Cleopatra, London and N.Y.; TV and radio appearances N.Y., London.
PICTURES: Titanic, Julius Caesar, Student Prince, The

Egyptian, Athena, The Prodigal, King's Thief, Moment of Danger, Rasputin, The Comedy Man, The Beauty Jungle, Don't Open Till Christmas (also dir.), After the Fall of New York.
TELEVISION: Winds of War, Scarlet and the Black, Sophia Loren: Her Own Story.

PURL, LINDA: Actress. b. Greenwich, CT, Sept. 2, 1955. Moved to Japan at age 2. Appeared in Japanese theatre, TV. Back to US in 1971.
PICTURES: Jory; W.C. Fields & Me; Crazy Mama; Leo and Loree; The High Country; Visiting Hours; Vipers.
TELEVISION: Series: Beacon Hill, Young Pioneers, Happy Days, The Secret Storm, Matlock. Movies: Eleanor and Franklin; Little Ladies of the Night; Testimony of Two Men; A Last Cry for Help; Women at West Point; A Very Special Love; Like Normal People; The Flame is Love; The Night the City Screamed; The Adventures of Nellie Bly; The Last Days of Pompeii, The Manions of America, Sisterhood, Addicted to His Love, Spies, Lies and Naked Thighs.

PUTTNAM, DAVID, CBE: Hon. LL.D Bristol 1983; Hon. D. Litt, Leicester 1986. Producer. b. London, England 1941. e. Michenden Sch. In advertising before joining VPS/Goodtimes Prod. Co. Dir. of Britain's National Film Finance Corp. Also served on Cinema Films Council and governing council of the British Acad. of Film & Television Arts. Chevalier dans L'Ordre des Arts et des Lettres, 1986. Chmn. National Film and Television Sch., 1988. Trustee, Tate Gallery. Pres., Council for the Protection of Rural England; Fellow, Royal Soc. of Arts; Fellow, Royal Geographical Soc., appt. Chmn. & CEO, Columbia Pictures. Resigned 1987. Received Eastman 2nd Century Award, 1988. Sept., 1988 formed a joint venture for his Enigma Productions Ltd. with Warner Bros., Fujisankei Comm. Gp. of Japan, British Satellite Broadcasting & Country Nat West to prod. 6 films. Appt. chmn. ITEL intl. TV dist. agency, 1989.
PICTURES: Melody, The Pier Piper, That'll Be The Day, Stardust, Mahler, Bugsy Malone, The Duellists, Midnight Express; Foxes (co-prod.), Chariots of Fire, Local Hero, Cal, The Killing Fields. The Mission, Defence of the Realm. Co-produced documentaries: Swastika, James Dean—The First American Teenager, Double-Headed Eagle, Brother, Can You Spare a Dime?
TELEVISION: P'Tang Yang Kipperbang, Experience Preferred, Secrets, Those Glory Glory Days, Sharma and Beyond, Winter Flight.

PYKE, REX: Film-Television Producer, Director. Recent productions include Akenfield, Landscape, Eric Clapton's Rolling Hotel, Van Morrison in Ireland and Woodstock in Europe 1979.

Q

QUAID, DENNIS: Actor. b. Houston, TX Apr. 9, 1954. Brother of Randy Quaid. e. U. of Houston. Appeared in Houston stage productions before leaving for Hollywood. On N.Y. stage with his brother in True West, 1984. Performs with rock band The Electrics and wrote songs for films The Night the Lights Went Out in Georgia, Tough Enough, The Big Easy.
PICTURES: September 30, 1955 (debut, 1978). Crazy Mama, Our Winning Season, Seniors, Breaking Away, I Never Promised You a Rose Garden, Gorp, The Long Riders, All Night Long, Caveman, The Night the Lights Went Out in Georgia (also wrote songs), Tough Enough, Jaws 3-D, The Right Stuff, Dreamscape, Enemy Mine, The Big Easy (also composed and sang song), Innerspace, Suspect, D.O.A., Everyone's All- American, Great Balls of Fire, Lie Down With Lions, Postcards From the Edge, Come and See the Paradise, A 22 Cent Romance.
TELEVISION: Bill: On His Own, Johnny Belinda, Amateur Night at the Dixie Bar and Grill.

QUAID, RANDY: Actor. b. 1950. Discovered by Peter Bogdanovich while still jr. at Drama Dept. at U. of Houston and cast in his The Last Picture Show, 1971. Off-B'way debut: True West (1983).
PICTURES: What's Up, Doc?, Paper Moon, Lolly-Madonna XXX, The Last Detail, The Apprenticeship of Duddy Kravitz, Breakout, The Missouri Breaks, Bound for Glory, The Choirboys, Midnight Express, Foxes, The Long Riders, Heartbeeps, The Wild Life, The Slugger's Wife, Fool for Love, The Wraith, Sweet Country, Moving, No Man's Land, Bloodhounds of Broadway, Out Cold, Caddyshack II, Parents, Quick Change, Cold Dog Soup.
TELEVISION: Niagra, Raid on Coffeyville, To Race The Wind, Mad Messiah, Of Mice and Men, Inside the Third Reich, Cowboy, A Streetcar Named Desire, LBJ: The Early Years, Evil in Clear River.

QUIGLEY, MARTIN, JR.: Educator, Writer. b. Chicago, IL, Nov. 24, 1917. e. A.B. Georgetown U.; M.A., Ed. D, Columbia U. M.P. Herald, Oct. 1939; spcl. ed. rep., M.P. Herald & M.P. Daily, May, 1941; wartime work in U.S., England, Eire & Italy, Dec. 1941–Oct. 1945; assoc. ed., Quigley Pub., Oct. 1945; ed. M.P. Herald, July, 1949; also edit. dir. of all Quigley Pub., 1956; pres. Quigley Pub. Co., 1964; author, Great Gaels, 1944, Roman Notes, 1946, Magic Shadows—the Story of the Origin of Motion Pictures, 1948, Govt. Relations of Five Universities, 1975; Peace Without Hiroshima, 1990. Editor, New Screen Techniques, 1953; m.p. tech. section, Encyclopaedia Brit., 1956; co-author, Catholic Action in Practice, 1963. Co-author: Films in America, 1929–69, 1970. Pres., QWS, Inc., educational consultants, 1975–81. Adjunct professor of higher education, Baruch College Univ. City of New York 1977–. Village of Larchmont, N.Y., trustee, 1977–79; mayor, 1980–84. Board of managers, American Bible Society, 1984–; Religious Education Ass'n., treasurer, 1975–80 & chairperson, 1981–84; Laymen's Nat'l. Bible Association, chmn. education committee, 1983–; Will Rogers Institute, chmn. Health education committee, 1980–.

QUIGLEY, WILLIAM J.: Executive. b. New York, NY, July 6, 1951. e. Wesleyan U., B.A.; Columbia U., M.S., 1983. From 1973 to 1974 was advt. circulation mgr. for Quigley Publishing Co. Taught school in Kenya in 1974; returned to U.S. to join Grey Advt. as media planner. In 1975 joined Walter Reade Organization as asst. film buyer; promoted to head film buyer in 1977. Named v.p., 1982. In 1986 joined Vestron, Inc. as sr. v.p. to establish Vestron Pictures. Named pres., Vestron Pictures, 1987–89.
PICTURES: Exec. prod.: Steel Dawn, The Dead, Salome's Last Dance, The Unholy, Waxwork, Burning Secret, The Lair of the White Worm, Paint It Black, The Rainbow, Twister.

QUILLAN, EDDIE: Actor. b. Philadelphia, PA, March 31, 1907. p. Sarah Owen and Joseph Quillan, professionals; stage training playing in the Quillan act with his family. In 1926 discovered by Mack Sennett who signed him to long-term contract. Made 18 2-reel comedies. Then signed by Cecil B. De Mille for The Godless Girl. Starred in many pictures at Pathe and RKO-Pathe (incl.: Show Folks, Geraldine, Noisy Neighbors).
PICTURES: The Sophomore, Night Work, Big Money, A Little Bit of Everything, The Big Shot, Dark Mountain, This Is the Life, Moonlight and Cactus, Song of the Sarong, A Guy Could Change, Sensation Hunters, Sideshow, Mutiny on the Bounty (Screen Actors Guild Award), Grapes of Wrath, Broadway to Hollywood, Hollywood Party, London By Night, Big City, Kid Glove Killer, Brigadoon, Did You Hear the One About the Traveling Saleslady?, Angel in My Pocket, How to Frame a Figg.
TELEVISION: Series: Valentine's Day, Julia, Little House on the Prairie, Hell Town, Highway to Hell.

QUINLAN, KATHLEEN: Actress. b. Pasadena, CA, Nov. 19, 1954. Played small role in film, One Is a Lonely Number, while in high school. Also had small part in American Graffiti. Major role debut in Lifeguard (1976). Stage: Take in Marriage (NY Public Theatre), Uncommon Women and Others, Accent on Youth (Long Wharf, CT), Les Liaisons Dangereuses.
PICTURES: Airport '77, I Never Promised You a Rose Garden, The Promise, The Runner Stumbles, Sunday Lovers, Hanky Panky, Independence Day, Twilight Zone—The Movie, Warning Sign, The Last Winter, Wild Thing, Man Outside, Sunset, Clara's Heart.
TELEVISION: Movies: She's in the Army Now, When She Says No, Blackout, Can Ellen Be Saved: Children of the Night, Dreams Lost, Dreams Found; Trapped, The Operation.

QUINN, AIDAN: Actor. b. Chicago, IL, March 8, 1959. Moved back to Belfast with family while in high sch. Returned to Chicago at 19, worked as a tar roofer. Chicago stage: The Man in 605 (debut), Scheherazade, The Irish Hebrew Lesson, Hamlet.
THEATER: Fool for Love (off-Bdwy debut), A Lie of the Mind, A Streetcar Named Desire.
PICTURES: Reckless, Desperately Seeking Susan, The Mission, Stakeout, Crusoe, The Lemon Sisters, The Handmaid's Tale.
TELEVISION: All My Sons, An Early Frost, Perfect Witness.

QUINN, ANTHONY: Actor. b. Mexico, Apr. 21, 1915. Began on screen, 1936. Acad. Award, best supp. actor, Viva Zapata, 1952, and Lust for Life, 1956.
PICTURES: Guadalcanal Diary, Buffalo Bill, Irish Eyes Are Smiling, China Sky, Back to Bataan, Where Do We Go From Here?, Black Gold, Tycoon, The Brave Bulls, Mask of the Avenger, The Brigand, World in His Arms, Against All Flags, Ride Vaquero, City Beneath the Sea, Seminole, Blowing Wild, East of Sumatra, Long Wait, Magnificent Matador, Ulysses, Naked Street, Seven Cities of Gold, La Strada, Attila the Hun, Lust for Life, Wild Party, Man from Del Rio, Ride Back, Hunchback of Notre Dame, The River's Edge, Hot Spell, Black Orchid, Last Train From Gun Hill, Warlock, Heller With a Gun, Heller in Pink Tights, Savage Innocents, The Guns of Navarone, Barabbas, Requiem for a Heavyweight, Behold a Pale Horse, Zorba the Greek, High Wind in Jamaica, The Visit, Guns for San Sebastian, The Secret of

Santa Vittoria, A Dream of Kings, Flap, A Walk in the Spring Rain, R.P.M.*, Across 110th Street, Deaf Smith and Johnny Ears, The Don Is Dead, Mohammad, Messenger of God, The Greek Tycoon, Caravans, The Passage, Lion of the Desert, High Roll, Valentina, The Salamander, Treasure Island, A Man of Passion, Stradivarius, Regina, Revenge, Ghosts Can't Do It, The Actor.

TELEVISION: Much dramatic work in the early 1950s. Series: The City, American Playwrights Theater (host). Movies: Jesus of Nazareth, Treasure Island (Italian TV), Onassis: The Richest Man in the World, The Old Man and the Sea.

QUINN, STANLEY J., JR.: Producer, Director. b. Brooklyn, NY, Mar. 18, 1915; e. Princeton U., 1932–36. Radio writer for Edgar Bergen show; mgr., J. Walter Thompson radio dept. in Australia, 1941–43; war corresp., 1943–45; radio prod. J. Walter Thompson, 1946; prod., dir., Kraft TV Theatre, NBC, 1947–53; ABC, Oct. 1953; vice pres., J. Walter Thompson, June 1954; exec. prod. Lux Video Theatre, 1954; pres. Quinn, McKenney Prod.; v.p. head radio, TV dept., D.C.S.S.; prod., Grey Adv. for Revlon commercials. Dir. of Admin. MGM-TV Studios 1963–64; dir. Radio-TV Center U. of Conn. 1965–76. Commercial dir. Kraft Foods, 1964–72; Director, Radio/TV Div., CIMT, Univ. Conn., 1976–80. Freelance TV dir., 1980.

R

RABE, DAVID WILLIAM: Writer. b. Dubuque, IA, March 10, 1940. m. actress Jill Clayburgh. e. Loras Coll.

PLAYS: The Basic Training of Pavlo Hummel (Obie Award, 1971); Sticks and Bones (Tony Award, 1971); The Orphan; In the Boom Boom Room; Streamers; Hurlyburly.

PICTURES: I'm Dancing As Fast As I Can (exec. prod., s.p.); Streamers (s.p.), Casualties of War (s.p.). State of Grace (co-s.p.).

TELEVISION: Sticks and Bones.

RABINOVITZ, JASON: Executive. b. Boston, MA, e. Harvard Coll., B.A. where elected to Phi Beta Kappa. Following W.W.II service as military intelligence captain with paratroops, took M.B.A. at Harvard Business Sch., 1948. Started in industry in 1949 as asst. to secty.-treas., United Paramount Theatres. Asst. controller, ABC, 1953; adm. v.p., ABC-TV, 1956; joined MGM as asst. treas., 1957; named MGM-TV gen. mgr., director of business & financial affairs, 1958; treas. & chief financial officer, MGM, Inc., 1963; financial v.p. & chief financial officer, 1967. In 1971 named exec. v.p., Encyclopedia Brittanica Education Corp.; sr. v.p., American Film Theatre, 1974–75. Rejoined MGM as v.p./exec. asst. to the pres., 1976. Elected v.p. finance, 1979; promoted to sr. v.p., finance & corporate admin., MGM Film Co. & UA Prods. Resigned, 1984. Now film & TV consultant and indep. producer.

RACKMIL, MILTON R.: Executive. b. New York, NY. e. NYU. Certified Public Accountant prior to assoc. with Brunswick Record Co. 1929; co-founder Decca Records, 1934; pres. Decca Records, 1949; pres. and member of board of dir. Universal Pictures, 1952, after Decca bought controlling stock interest in Universal; pres. emeritus, Universal, 1973.

RADIN, PAUL: Producer. b. New York, NY, Sept. 15, 1913. e. NYU. After college went in adv. Became v.p. in chg. of m.p. div. of Buchanan & Co. During the war posted in Middle East as film chief for Office of War Information for that area. On return to U.S. assigned by Buchanan to ad campaign for Howard Hughes' The Outlaw. Turned to talent mgr., joining the Sam Jaffe Agency. Then joined Ashley-Famous Agency. Became exec. prod. for Yul Brynner's indep. prod. co. based in Switzerland, with whom made such films as The Journey, Once More with Feeling, Surprise Package.

PICTURES: Born Free, Living Free, Phase IV, The Blue Bird.

TELEVISION: The Incredible Journey of Dr. Meg Laurel, The Ordeal of Dr. Mudd, Crime of Innocence, Series: Born Free, The Wizard.

RADNITZ, ROBERT B.: Producer. b. Great Neck, NY, Aug. 9, 1924. e. U. of Virginia. Taught 2 years at U. of Virginia, then became reader for Harold Clurman; wrote several RKO This Is America scripts, then to Broadway where co-prod., The Frogs of Spring; prod. The Young and the Beautiful; to Hollywood working at United Artists, then as story consultant for 20th Century-Fox; prod. A Dog of Flanders (1960—first feature), first U.S. film to win Golden Lion Award at Venice Film Festival. Board of Directors, Producer Guild of America: v.p., last 3 years; first producer with retrospective at Museum of Modern Art. First producer honored by joint resolution of both houses of Congress, 1973. Sounder received four Academy Award nominations: best picture, best actor, best actress, best screenplay. Pres. Robert B. Radnitz Productions, Ltd. Vice pres., Producers Guild, 1982, 1984.

PICTURES: Misty, Island of the Blue Dolphins, And Now Miguel, My Side of the Mountain, The Little Ark, Sounder, Where the Lilies Bloom, Birch Interval, Sounder II, A Hero Ain't Nothin' But a Sandwich, Cross Creek (4 AA nominations).

TELEVISION: Mary White (Emmy for teleplay-nominated for best film) Christopher Award for TV special.

RAFELSON, BOB: Producer, Director, Writer. b. New York, NY, 1935. e. Dartmouth, B.A. (philosophy). Left NY in teens to ride in rodeos in AZ. Worked on cruise ship, then played drums and bass with jazz combos in Acapulco. 1953 won Frost Natl. Playwriting competition. Dir. his award-winning play at Hanover Experimental Theatre, N.H. After Army Service did program promotion for a radio station, was advisor for Shochiku Films, Japan, then hired by David Susskind to read scripts for Talent Assocs. Writer-assoc. prod., DuPont Show of the Month and Play of the Week (also script sprv.). Joined Screen Gems in California, developing program idea for Jackie Cooper, then head of TV prod. arm of Columbia. Later formed BBS Productions with Burt Schneider and Steve Blauner; their first film, Head (1968).

PICTURES: Prod.-Dir.-Co-s.p.: Head, Five Easy Pieces, The King of Marvin Gardens, Stay Hungry, The Postman Always Rings Twice (prod., dir.), Black Widow (dir.), Mountains of the Moon (dir., co-s.p.). Co-Prod. only: Easy Rider, The Last Picture Show, Drive, He Said.

TELEVISION: The Monkees (1966–68, creator, writer, dir., Emmy Award, 1967), Adapted 34 prods., Play of the Week.

RAFFERTY, FRANCES: Actress. b. Sioux City, IA, June 26, 1922; e. U. of California, premedical student UCLA. TV series, December Bride, Pete and Gladys.

PICTURES: Seven Sweethearts, Private Miss Jones, Girl Crazy, War Against Mrs. Hadley, Thousands Cheer, Dragon Seed, Honest Thief, Mrs. Parkington, Barbary Coast Gent, Hidden Eye, Abbott and Costello in Hollywood, Adventures of Don Coyote, Money Madness, Lady at Midnight, Old Fashioned Girl, Rodeo, Shanghai Story.

RAFFIN, DEBORAH: Actress. b. Los Angeles, CA, March 13, 1953. m. producer Michael Viner. Mother is actress Trudy Marshall. e. Valley Coll. Was active fashion model before turning to acting when discovered by Ted Witzer. Made m.p, debut in 40 Carats (1973). Publisher Dove Books On Tape. Head of Dove Films, prod. co.

PICTURES: The Dove, Once Is Not Enough, The Sentinel, Touched by Love, Death Wish 3.

TELEVISION: A Nightmare in Badham County, Willa, Haywire, Threesome, Sparkling Cyanide, James Clavell's Noble House, Windmills of the Gods (also co-prod.).

RAGLAND, ROBERT OLIVER: Composer. b. Chicago, IL, July 3, 1931. e. Northwestern U., American Conservatory of Music, Vienna Acad. of Music. Professional pianist at Chicago nightclubs. In U.S. Navy; on discharge joined Dorsey Bros. Orchestra as arranger. On sls. staff at NBC-TV, Chicago. 1970, moved to Hollywood to become composer for movies; has scored 43 feature films plus many TV movies and series segments. Has also written some 15 original songs.

PICTURES: The Touch of Melissa, The Yin and Yang of Mr. Go, The Thing with Two Heads, Project: Kill, Abby, Seven Alone, The Eyes of Dr. Chaney, Return to Macon County, The Daring Dobermans, Shark's Treasure, Grizzly, Pony Express Rider, Mansion of the Doomed, Mountain Family Robinson, Only Once in a Lifetime, Jaguar Lives, The Glove, Lovely But Deadly, "Q", The Day of the Assassin, A Time To Die, The Winged Serpent, Trial by Terror, The Guardian, Ten to Midnight, Dirty Rebel, Hysterical, Brainwaves, Where's Willie?, The Supernaturals, Nightstick, Messenger of Death.

TELEVISION: Photoplay's Stars of Tomorrow, Wonder Woman, Barnaby Jones, Streets of San Francisco, High Ice, The Girl on the Edge of Town, The Guardian, etc.

RAILSBACK, STEVE: Actor. b. Dallas, TX. Studied with Lee Strasberg. On stage in Orpheus Descending, This Property Is Condemned, Cherry Orchard, Skin of Our Teeth, etc.

PICTURES: The Visitors, Angela, The Stunt Man, Turkey Shoot, The Golden Seal, Deadly Games, Torchlight, Lifeforce, Distortions, Blue Monkey, The Wind, Deadly Intent, Nukie, Scenes From the Goldmine, Spearfield's Daughter.

TELEVISION: Helter Skelter, From Here to Eternity.

RAKOFF, ALVIN: Producer, Director. b. Toronto, Canada, 1937. e. U. of Toronto. Early career as journalist. Dir. in French & U.S. T.V. England, Canada. Emmy Award winner, 1968 for Call Me Daddy. Emmy Award, 1982 for A Voyage Around My Father. Pres., Directors Guild of Great Britain.

STAGE: Hamlet.

PICTURES: On Friday at 11, The Comedy Man, Crossplot, Hoffman, Say Hello to Yesterday, City on Fire, Death Ship, Dirty Tricks.

TELEVISION: The Caine Mutiny Court Martial, Requiem for a Heavyweight, Our Town, The Velvet Alley, A Town Has Turned to Dust, Jokers Justice, Call Me Back, Day Before Atlanta, Heart to Heart, The Seekers, Sweet War Man, The Move after Checkmate, The Stars in My Eyes, Call Me Daddy, Summer & Smoke, Don Quixote, Shadow of a

Gunman, The Impeachment of Andrew Johnson, Cheap in August, In Praise of Love, Nicest Man in the World, Dame of Sark, The Kitchen, Romeo and Juliet, Voyage Round My Father, Mr. Halpern and Mr. Johnson, The First Olympics—Athens 1896, Paradise Postponed.

RAKSIN, DAVID: Composer. b. Philadelphia, PA, Aug. 4, 1912. e. U. of Pennsylvania, studied music with Isadore Freed and Arnold Schoenberg. Composer for films, ballet, dramatic and musical comedy, stage, radio and TV, symphony orchestra and chamber ensembles. Arranger of music of Chaplin film, Modern Times; pres. Composers and Lyricists Guild of America, 1962–70; animated films include Madeline and The Unicorn in the Garden (UPA). Professor of Music and Urban Semester, U. of Southern California, and faculty, UCLA Sch. of Music. Coolidge Commission from the Library of Congress: Oedipus Memneitai (Oedipus Remembers) for bass/baritone, 6-part chorus and chamber orchestra premiered there under dir. of composer, Oct. 30, 1986.

PICTURES: Laura, Secret Life of Walter Mitty, Smoky, Force of Evil, Across the Wide Missouri, Carrie, Bad and the Beautiful, Apache, Suddenly, Big Combo, Jubal, Hilda Crane, Separate Tables, Al Capone, Night Tide, Too-Late Blues, Best of the Bolshoi (music for visual interludes), Two Weeks in Another Town, The Redeemer, Invitation to a Gunfighter, Sylvia, A Big Hand for the Little Lady, Will Penny, Glass Houses, What's the Matter with Helen?

TELEVISION: Wagon Train, Five Fingers, Journey, Life With Father, Tender is the Night, Father of the Bride, Ben Casey, Breaking Point, Prayer of the Ages, Report from America, Medical Center, The Olympics (CBC), The Day After.

RALSTON, RUDY: Producer. b. Prague, Czechoslovakia, Jan. 30, 1918. e. grad. eng., Realka U. Came to U.S. & joined Consolidated Lab.; exec. Republic Prod.; prod. Republic, 1950.

PICTURES: No Man's Woman, Double Jeopardy, Terror at Midnight, Hell's Crossroads, The Lawless Eighties, Last Stagecoach West, Man Who Died Twice.

RAMIS, HAROLD: Writer, Director, Actor. b. Chicago, IL, Nov. 21, 1944. e. Washington U., St. Louis. Assoc. ed. Playboy Mag. 1968–70; writer, Second City, Chicago 1970–73; National Lampoon Radio Show, Lampoon show 1974–75.

TELEVISION: Head writer and actor SCTV, 1976–78; prod., head writer Rodney Dangerfield Show 1982.

PICTURES: Co-writer: National Lampoon's Animal House, Meatballs, Caddyshack (also dir.), Stripes (also actor). National Lampoon's Vacation (dir only), Ghostbusters (also actor), Club Paradise (also dir.), Back to School (also exec. prod.), Armed and Dangerous (exec. prod.), Baby Boom (actor only), Caddyshack II (exec. prod. only), Stealing Home (actor only), Ghostbusters II (actor, co-s.p.), How to Get into College.

RAMPLING, CHARLOTTE: Actress. b. Sturmer, England, Feb. 5, 1946. e. Jeanne D'Arc Academie pour Jeune Filles, Versailles; St. Hilda's, Bushey, England. Ent. m.p. ind. 1966.

PICTURES: The Knack, Rotten to the Core, The Long Duel, Sequestro di Persona, Georgy Girl, The Damned, Three, The Vanishing Point, Ski Bum, Corky, Tis Pity She's a Whore, The Six Wives of Henry VIII, Asylum, The Night Porter, Giordano Bruno, Zardoz, Caravan to Vaccares, Yuppi Dui La Chair De L'orchidee, Farewell My Lovely, Foxtrot, Orca, The Mauve Taxi, Stardust Memories, Target: Harry, The Verdict, Viva La Vie, Angel Heart, Mascara, D.O.A., Max My Love, He Died with His Eyes Open, Paris By Night, The Riddle, Ocean Point, Helmut Newton: Frames from the Edge (doc.).

TELEVISION: Six More for BBC Series: The Superlative Seven, The Avengers. Movies: Sherlock Holmes in New York, Mystery of Cader Iscom, The Fantasists, What's in it for Henry, Zinotchka, Sherlock Holmes, Infidelities.

RAMSAY, PATRICK: b. Bristol, Eng., 1926. e. Marlborough Coll., Jesus Coll., Cambridge, M.A., History. Served with Royal Naval Volunteer Reserve (Fleet Air Arm) 1944–46. Joined BBC 1949 as a report writer in monitoring service. Became asst., appointments dept., 1953 and three years later rejoined BBC External Services as sr. admin. asst. In charge of news administration, radio and TV 1958 to 1963, helping develop the U.K. regional TV news network for BBC. 1963, appointed planning mgr. (projected arrangements), TV. 1966 asst. controller, programme services, television, then assistant controller, program planning, television, from December 1969. Controller, programme services, television, April 1972. Appointed controller, BBC-Scotland, May 1979.

RAND, HAROLD: Executive. b. New York, NY, Aug. 25, 1928. e. Long Island U., B.S., 1948–50; City Coll. of New York, 1945–46. U.S. Army 1946–48; ent. m.p. ind. 1950, pub. dept. 20th-Fox; variety of posts incl. writer, trade press, newspaper contacts; joined Walt Disney's Buena Vista pub. mgr., 1957; pub. mgr. Paramount Pictures, 1959; formed own pub. rel. firm, 1961; dir. of pub. Embassy Picture Corp. 1962; dir. of world pub. 20th Century Fox 1962; resigned 1963; dir. of adv. & pub., Landau Co., 1963; dir. world pub., Embassy Pictures, 1964; est. Harold Rand & Co., Inc., 1966, pres. of p.r. & mktg. firm. Appt. mktg., dir., Kaufman Astoria Studios, 1984; elected v.p., 1985.

RANDALL, STEPHEN F.: Executive. Held marketing posts with United Vintners and Clorox. Joined Columbia Pictures in 1978 as director of research; named v.p. in 1980 and sr. v.p. in 1982. 1983, joined Tri-Star Pictures as sr. v.p. of marketing; promoted to exec. v.p.; 1988 named sr. v.p. of prod., Tri-Star.

RANDALL, TONY: Actor. r.n. Leonard Rosenberg. b. Tulsa, OK, Feb. 26, 1920. e. Northwestern U. Prof. N.Y. debut as actor in Circle of Chalk; then in Candida and others; U.S. Army 1942–46; radio actor on many shows. Emmy Award for The Odd Couple, 1975.

STAGE: Corn is Green, Antony & Cleopatra, Caesar & Cleopatra, Inherit the Wind, Oh Men! Oh Women!, Oh Captain, The Sea Gull, The Master Builder, M. Butterfly.

PICTURES: Oh Men! Oh Women!, Will Success Spoil Rock Hunter, No Down Payment, The Mating Game, Pillow Talk, Adventures of Huckleberry Finn, Let's Make Love, Lover Come Back, Boys' Night Out, 7 Faces of Dr. Lao, Send Me No Flowers, Fluffy, The Alphabet Murders, Bang! You're Dead, Hello Down There, Everything You Always Wanted to Know About Sex*, Foolin' Around, Scavenger Hunt, The King of Comedy, That's Adequate, It Had to Be You.

TELEVISION: Series: One Man's Family, Mr. Peepers, The Odd Couple, The Tony Randall Show, Love Sidney. Guest: TV Playhouse, Max Liebman Spectaculars, Sid Caesar, Dinah Shore, Playhouse 90, Walt Disney World Celebrity Circus. Movies: Sunday Drive, Hitler's SS, Off Sides, Kate Bliss and Ticker Tape Kid, Save the Dog!, The Man in the Brown Suit, The Odd Couple One More Time.

RANSOHOFF, MARTIN: Executive. b. New Orleans, LA, 1927. e. Colgate U., 1949. Adv., Young & Rubicam, 1948–49; slsmn, writer, dir., Gravel Films, 1951; formed own co., Filmways, 1952; industrial films, commercials; formed Filmways TV Prods., Filmways, Inc., Filmways of Calif. chmn., bd. Filmways, Inc., resigned from Filmways in 1972 and formed own independent motion picture and television production company.

TELEVISION: Mister Ed, The Beverly Hillbillies, Petticoat Junction, Green Acres, The Addams Family.

PICTURES: The Americanization of Emily, The Sandpiper, Boys Night Out, The Loved One, The Wheeler Dealers, The Cincinnati Kid, See No Evil, Ten Rillington Place, King Lear, Topkapi, Fuzz, Castle Keep, Ice Station Zebra, Catch 22, Save The Tiger, The White Dawn, Silver Streak (exec. prod.), Nightwing, The Wanderers, Change of Seasons, American Pop, Hanky Panky, Class, The Jagged Edge, The Big Town (prod.), Switching Channels (prod.), Physical Evidence (prod.), Welcome Home.

RAPF, MATTHEW: Producer, Writer. b. New York, NY, Oct. 22, 1920. e. Dartmouth Coll., B.A., 1942; p. Harry Rapf, producer. U.S. Navy, W.W.II as Lt. (j.g.).

PICTURES: Adventures of Gallant Bess s.p., co-prod., assoc. prod., story, The Sellout; prod.: Desperate Search, Big Leaguer, Half a Hero.

TELEVISION: Loretta Young Show, Frontier, Great Gildersleeve, The Web, Jefferson Drum, Man From Blackhawk, Two Faces West, Ben Casey, Slattery's People, Iron Horse, Young Lawyers, Hardcase, Terror In the Sky, Shadow On the Land, Marcus-Nelson Murders, Kojak, Switch, Doctor's Hospital, Eischied, Oklahoma City Rolls, Gangster Chronicles.

RAPHAEL, FREDERIC: Writer. b. Chicago, IL, Aug. 14, 1931. e. Charterhouse, St. John's Coll., Cambridge. Novels: The Earlsdon Way, The Limits of Love, A Wild Surmise, The Graduate Wife, The Trouble With England, Lindmann, Orchestra and Beginners, Like Men Betrayed, Who Were You With Last Night? April, June and November, Richard's Things, California Time, The Glittering Prizes, Sleeps Six & Other Stories, Oxbridge Blues & Other Stories, Heaven & Earth, Think of England, After the War. Biographies: Somerset Maugham and His World, Byron. Translations: Poems of Catullus (with Kenneth McLeish), The Oresteia. Essays: Bookmarks, Cracks in the Ice. Ent. m.p. ind., 1956. Several plays for ATV, 1960–62.

PICTURES: Nothing But the Best (1964), Darling (Acad. Award, orig. s.p., 1965), Two for the Road, Far from the Madding Crowd, A Severed Head, Daisy Miller, The King's Whore.

TELEVISION: The Glittering Prizes (Royal TV Society Writer Award 1978), Rogue Male, School Play, Something's Wrong, Best of Friends, Richard's Things, Oxbridge Blues (ACE Award, best s.p.), After the War.

PLAYS: From the Greek (1979), An Early Life.

RAPHEL, DAVID: Executive. b. Boulogne-s/Seine, France, Jan. 9, 1925. e. university in France. Entered m.p. ind. as asst. to sales mgr. in France, 20th-Fox, 1950–51; asst. mgr. in Italy, 1951–54; mgr. in Holland, 1954–57; asst. to European mgr. in

Paris, 1957–59; European mgr. for TV activities in Paris, 1959–61; Continental mgr. in Paris, 1961–64, transferred to N.Y. as vice-pres. in chg. of international sales, 1964; named pres., 20th Century-Fox International, 1973. In Feb., 1975, also appointed sr. vice-pres., worldwide marketing, feature film division, for 20th-Fox, (L.A.). In Nov. 1976, joined ICM, appointed dir. general of ICM (Europe) headquartered in Paris. In 1979 elected pres. ICM (L.A.) 1980, formed Cambridge Film Group Ltd.

RAPPER, IRVING: Director. b. London, Eng., 1904. Stage prod. London: Five Star Final, assoc. Gilbert Miller, Grand Hotel. NY: The Animal Kingdom, The Firebird, The Late Christopher Bean.
PICTURES: Shining Victory, One Foot in Heaven, The Gay Sisters, The Adventures of Mark Twain, Rhapsody in Blue, The Corn Is Green, Deception, Now, Voyager, Voice of the Turtle, Anna Lucasta, The Glass Menagerie, Another Man's Poison, Forever Female, Bad For Each Other, The Brave One, Marjorie Morningstar, The Miracle, Joseph and His Brethren, Pontius Pilate, The Christine Jorgensen Story, Born Again, Justus.

RAPPOPORT, GERALD J.: Executive, Film Producer. b. New York, NY, 1925. e. NYU. U.S. Marine Corps. 1955–1958—pres., Major Artists Representatives Corp.; 1958–1960—director of Coast Sound Services, Hollywood; 1957 to present, pres., Sewan Music Publishers. 1960 to present, Pres. of International Film Exchange Ltd., N.Y., a subsidiary of Today Home Entertainment 1988.

RASHAD, PHYLICIA: Actress-singer. b. Houston, TX, June 19, 1948. m. sportscaster Ahmad Rashad. Sister of Debbie Allen. e. Howard U., B.F.A., magna cum laude, 1970. NY School of Ballet. Acted under maiden name of Phylicia Ayers-Allen. Recording, Josephine Superstar (1979).
THEATER: Ain't Supposed to Die a Natural Death, The Duplex, The Cherry Orchard, The Wiz, Weep Not For Me, Zooman and the Sign, In an Upstate Motel, Zora, Dreamgirls, Sons and Fathers of Sons, Puppetplay, A Raisin in the Sun, Into the Woods.
TELEVISION: Series: One Life to Live, The Cosby Show (People's Choice Award, NAACP Image Award, Emmy nom.). Movies: Uncle Tom's Cabin. Specials: Nell Carter-Never Too Old to Dream, Superstars and Their Moms, Our Kids and the Best of Everything, The Debbie Allen Special, etc.

RATHER, DAN: News Correspondent, Anchor. b. Wharton, TX, Oct. 31, 1931. e. Sam Houston State Coll., BA journalism. Instructor there for 1 year. Worked for UPI and Houston Chronicle. Joined radio staff KTRH, Houston. Joined CBS News in 1962 as chief of southwest bureau in Dallas. Transferred to overseas burs. (including chief of London Bureau 1965–66), then Vietnam before returning as White House corr. 1966. White House Correspondent, 1964 to 1974. Covered top news events, from Democratic and Republican national conventions to President Nixon's trip to Europe (1970) and to Peking and Moscow (1972). Anchored CBS Reports, 1974–75. Presently co-editor of 60 minutes (since 1975) and anchors Dan Rather Reporting on CBS Radio Network (since 1977). Winner of numerous awards, including 5 Emmys. Anchorman on CBS-TV Evening News, 1981–. Autobiography: The Camera Never Blinks: Adventures of a TV Journalist (co-author, 1977).

RAUCHER, HERMAN: Writer. b. Apr. 13, 1928. e. NYU. Author of novels—Summer of '42 and Ode to Billy Joe—adapted to films by him.
PICTURES: Sweet November, Hieronymus Merkin, Watermelon Man, Summer of '42, Class of '44, Ode to Billy Joe, The Other Side of Midnight.
TELEVISION: Studio One, Alcoa Hour, Goodyear Playhouse, Matinee Theatre, Remember When? (movie).

RAVELO, ROBERT F.: Executive. b. Santiago de Cuba, Oriente, Cuba, Aug. 30, 1947. Emigrated to U.S., 1961. e. U. of Connecticut, B.A. 1966–69, band leader and Latin percussionist. 1969–74, Winchester Intl. Marketing Dept. 1976–77, U.S. Air Force; capt., 1977–81. Entered industry in 1981 as prod. asst. to Robert Towne during filming of Personal Best. Now v.p./sls., v.p. production and operating officer, Arista Films, Inc.

RAVETCH, IRVING: Director, Scenarist, Producer. b. 1915. m. Harriet Frank.
PICTURES: The Long Hot Summer, The Sound and the Fury, Home from the Hill, The Dark at the Top of the Stairs, Hud, Hombre, The Reivers (also prod.), Conrack (co-s.p.), Norma Rae (co.-s.p.), Murphy's Romance (co-s.p.).

RAY, ALDO: Actor. r.n. Aldo DaRe. b. Pen Argyl, PA, Sept. 25, 1926. e. U. of California. U.S. Navy, June, 1944–May, 1946; constable. Crockett, Calif., Nov. 1950–Sept. 1951; m.p. debut in Saturday's Hero (1950). Star of Tomorrow, 1954. Stage debut: Stalag 17 (La Jolla Playhouse 1983). Member: SAG, AFTRA, American Legion.
PICTURES: The Marrying Kind, Pat and Mike, Let's Do It Again, Miss Sadie Thompson, Battle Cry, We're No Angels, Three Stripes in the Sun, Nightfall, Men in War, God's Little Acre, Four Desperate Men, Day They Robbed the Bank of England, Sylvia, What Did You Do in the War Daddy?, To Kill A Dragon, Dead Heat on a Merry-Go-Round, Welcome To Hard Times, The Power, My True Story, The Green Berets, The Violent Ones, Angel Unchained, And Hope To Die, Psychic Killer, Seven Alone, Evils of the Night, The Sicilian, Terminal Force, Drug Runners, Final Curtain, Crime of Crimes, Shooters.
TELEVISION: Desilu Playhouse, K.O. Kitty, The Virginian, Bonanza, Women in White, Promise Him Anything, Deadlock.

RAY, SATYAJIT: Director, Writer, Composer. b. India, May 2, 1921. Gained international acclaim for his Apu Trilogy in the 1950s.
PICTURES: Pather Panchali, The Unvanquished, The Music Room, The World of Apu, The Goddess, Kanchenjunga, The Adventures of Goopy and Bagha, The Adversary, Company Limited, Distant Thunder, The Middle Man, The Chess Player, The Elephant God, The Kingdom of Diamonds, The Home and the World, Ganashatru (Enemy of the People, dir., s.p., music).

RAYBURN, GENE: Performer, b. Christopher, IL, Dec. 22. e. Knox Coll., Galesburg, IL. NBC guide; with many radio stations in Baltimore, Philadelphia, N.Y.; U.S. Army Air Force, 1942–45, Rayburn and Finch, show, WNEW, NY., 1945–52; Gene Rayburn Show, NBC radio; TV shows: Many appearances as host-humorist on game shows, variety shows, drama shows. Summer stock: leads in comedies.
BROADWAY: Bye Bye Birdie, Come Blow Your Horn.
TELEVISION: Helluva Town, The Match Game, Love Boat, Fantasy Island, Tonight Show.

RAYE, MARTHA: Actress. b. Butte, MT, Aug. 27, 1916. p. Reed and Hooper, professionals. On stage: sang and did comedy with Paul Ash's orchestra; was in Earl Carroll's Sketch Book; Lew Brown's Calling All Stars. Appeared in night clubs.
PICTURES: Rhythm on the Range, The Big Broadcast of 1937, Hideway Girl, College Holiday, Waikiki Wedding, Mountain Music, Artists and Models, Double or Nothing, Pin Up Girl, Four Jills and a Jeep, Monsieur Verdoux, Pufnstuf, The Concorde—Airport '79.
TELEVISION: All Star Revue, Martha Raye Show, Alice, Gossip Columnist, Alice in Wonderland, Murder She Wrote.

RAYMOND, GENE: Actor, Director, Producer, Composer. r. n. Raymond Guion, b. New York, NY, Aug. 13, 1908. Began acting at age 5 in stock productions. Bdwy debut, The Piper, 1920. Air Force Reserve, W.W.II. Major, US Army Air Corps, 1942–45. Formed ind. prod. co., Masque Prod., 1949. Song composer. Vice-pres. Arthritis Found.; Past pres. Motion Pic. and TV Fund; Pres. LA Chapt., Air Force Assn.; trustee, Falcon Found; trustee SGA; Bd., Acad. TV Arts and Sciences; Mem. Players Club, NY Athletic Club, Army and Navy. Awarded Legion of Merit, USAF; Humanitarian Award, AF Assn.; Better World Award, VFW.
STAGE: Why Not?, The Potters, Cradle Snatchers, Take My Advice, Say When, Mirrors, Jones, Young Sinners, Shadow of My Enemy, 1957, National Co., The Best Man 1960, Write Me A Murder, Kiss Me Kate, Candida, Madly in Love.
PICTURES: Personal Maid, Ladies of the Big House, The Night of June 13th, Forgotten Commandments, If I Had A Million, Red Dust, Ex-Lady, Sadie McKee, Brief Moment, I am Suzanne, Flying Down to Rio, The Woman in Red, The House on 56th Street, Seven Keys to Baldpate, The Bride Walks Out, Hooray for Love, Zoo in Budapest, Behold My Wife, Mr. and Mrs. Smith, Smilin' Thru, The Locket, Sofia, Hit the Deck, Walking On Air, Coming Out Party, Life of the Party, She's Got Everything, Ann Carver's Profession, Transient Lady, The Best Man, I'd Rather Be Rich.
TELEVISION: Star-host, TV Fireside Theatre and TV Reader's Digest; Lux Video Theatre, Robert Montgomery Presents, Climax, Playhouse 90, Kraft Theatre, Red Skelton, U.S. Steel Hour, The Defenders, Outer Limits, Matinee Theater (actor, dir.), The Man From U.N.C.L.E.; Girl from U.N.C.L.E., Laredo, Ironsides, Julia, Judd For the Defense.

RAYMOND, PAULA: Actress. r.n. Paula Ramona Wright, b. San Francisco, CA., 1923 e. San Francisco Jr. Coll. 1942. Started career in little theatre groups, San Francisco; leading roles Ah! Wilderness, Peter Pan, other plays; model, Meade-Maddick Agency; TV appearance 1949.
PICTURES: Devil's Doorway, Inside Straight, Duchess of Idaho, Crisis, Grounds For Marriage, Tall Target, Texas Carnival, The Sellout, Bandits of Corsica, City That Never Sleeps, Beast from 20,000 Fathoms, King Richard & the Crusaders, Human Jungle, Gun That Won the West, The Flight That Disappeared, 5 Bloody Graves, Blood of Dracula's Castle.

RAYNOR, LYNN S.: Producer, Production Executive. b. 1940. Produced West Coast premiere of The Balcony by Genet,

The Crawling Arnold Review by Feiffer. Joined Television Enterprises, 1965; Commonwealth United, 1968 as business affairs exec. later production spvr. 1972 opened London branch of the Vidtronics Co. 1974, formed Paragon Entertainment. 1976, producer, PBS. 1977, producer, James Flocker Enterprises. 1979, exec. in charge of prod., Lawrance Schiller Prods. 1981, prod., Polygram Pictures; 1984, producer, Newland-Raynor Prods.; 1985, Columbia Pictures TV.
TELEVISION: Waiting for Godot; Camp Wilderness (synd. series); Marilyn, The Untold Story (movie); The Execution; The Pete Gray Story; The Kennedys of Massachusetts; Common Ground.
PICTURES: Ghosts That Still Walk, Alien Encounters, Fanny Hill, Dangerously.

REAGAN, RONALD: Actor, Politician. b. Tampico, IL, Feb. 6, 1911. e. high school, Eureka Coll. m. Nancy Davis. Lifeguard. Wrote weekly sports column for a Des Moines, IA newspaper; broadcast sporting events. Signed as actor by Warner Bros. in 1937. In W.W.II. 1942–45, capt., USAAF. Actor until 1966 on TV as well. Program supvr., General Electric Theatre, Death Valley Days. Gov., California, 1967–74. Businessman and rancher. Elected Pres. of U.S., 1980. Re-elected, 1984.
PICTURES: Love Is On the Air, Submarine D-1, Sergeant Murphy, Swing Your Lady, Accidents Will Happen, Cowboy from Brooklyn, Boy Meets Girl, Girls on Probation, Going Places, Dark Victory, Naughty but Nice, Hell's Kitchen, Kings Row, Juke Girl, Desperate Journey, This is the Army, The Killers, That Hagen Girl, Night Unto Night, Voice of the Turtle, John Loves Mary, Girl from Jones Beach, Hasty Heart, Louisa, Last Outpost, Bedtime for Bonzo, Storm Warning, Hong Kong, She's Working Her Way Through College, Winning Team, Tropic Zone, Law & Order, Prisoner of War, Cattle Queen of Montana, Tennessee's Partner, Hellcats of the Navy, The Killers.

REARDON, BARRY: Executive. Began industry career with Paramount Pictures; named v.p.; left to join General Cinema Theatres Corp. as sr. v.p. Now with Warner Bros. as pres. of domestic distribution co.

REASON, REX: Actor. b. Berlin, Germany, Nov. 30, 1928. e. Hoover H.S., Glendale, CA. Worked at various jobs; studied dramatics at Pasadena Playhouse.
PICTURES: Storm Over Tibet, Salome, Mission Over Korea, Taza Son of Cochise, This Island Earth, Smoke Signal, Lady Godiva, Kiss of Fire, Creature Walks Among Us, Raw Edge, Miracle of The Hills, The Rawhide Trail.

REASONER, HARRY: News correspondent. b. Dakota, IA. Apr. 17, 1923. e. Stanford U., U. of Minnesota. Beg. journalism career, reporter, Minneapolis Times 1941–43; U.S. Army, W.W.II. Ret. to Times, drama critic 1946–48. Author, book, Tell Me About Women, 1946; asst. dir. publicity, Northwest Airlines, 1948–50; newswriter, radio station WCCO. CBS affiliate. Minn., 1950–51; writer U.S. Information Agency Manila, 1951–54; news-dir., KEYD-TV (now KMSP-TV). Minn., 1954; Joined CBS News, N.Y., 1956–70; corresp. 60 Minutes 1968–70. ABC News 1970–78. Rejoined CBS 1978; co-editor, 60 Minutes.

REDDY, HELEN: Singer. b. Australia, Oct. 25, 1942. Parents were producer-writer-actor Max Reddy and actress Stella Lamond. e. in Australia. Began career at age four as singer and had appeared in hundreds of stage and radio roles with parents by age of 15. Came to New York in 1966, subsequently played nightclubs, appeared on TV. First single hit record: I Don't Know How To Love Him (Capitol). Grammy Award, 1973, as best female singer of year for I Am Woman. Other Gold singles: Delta Dawn, Leave Me Alone, Angle Baby. Gold Albums: Love Song for Jeffrey, Free & Easy, No Way to Treat a Lady, I Don't Know How To Love Him, Music, Music. Platinum albums: I Am Woman, Long Hard Climb, Helen Reddy's Greatest Hits. Most Played Artist by the music operators of America: American Music Award 1974; Los Angeles Times Woman of the Year (1975); No. 1 Female Vocalist in 1975 and 1976; Record World, Cash Box and Billboard; named one of the Most Exciting Women in the World by International Bachelor's Society, 1976. Heads prod. co. Helen Reddy, Inc..
PICTURES: Airport 1975 (debut), Pete's Dragon.
TELEVISION: David Frost Show, Flip Wilson Show, Mike Douglas Show, etc. The Helen Reddy Show (Summer, 1973), Permanent host of Midnight Special. Appearances on Tonight Show, Mac Davis Show. Hosted Merv Griffin Show, Sesame St.; Live in Australia (host, 1988); Tonight Show, Muppet Show.

REDFORD, ROBERT: Actor. b. Santa Monica, CA, Aug. 18, 1937. U. of Colorado, left to travel in Europe, 1957. Attended Pratt Inst. and American Acad. of Dramatic Arts. m. Lola Van Wagenen.
BROADWAY: Walk-on in Tall Story, also in The Highest Tree, Sunday in New York, Barefoot in the Park.
PICTURES: Warhunt, 1961; Situation Hopeless, But Not Serious, Inside Daisy Clover, The Chase, This Property Is Condemned, Barefoot in the Park, Tell Them Willie Boy is Here, Butch Cassidy and the Sundance Kid, Downhill Racer, The Crow Killer, The Hot Rock, The Candidate, Jeremiah Johnson, The Way We Were, The Sting, The Great Gatsby, The Great Waldo Pepper, Three Days of the Condor, All The President's Men, A Bridge Too Far, The Electric Horseman, Brubaker, The Natural, Out of Africa, Legal Eagles, Promised Land (co-exec. prod.), Some Girls (exec. prod.), *Director:* Ordinary People (AA), The Milagro Beanfield War (dir., co-prod.).
TELEVISION: The Iceman Cometh; In the Presence of Mine Enemies, Playhouse 90.

REDGRAVE, CORIN: Actor. b. London, England, July 16, 1939. e. Cambridge. Son of the late Sir Michael Redgrave. Brother of Vanessa and Lynn Redgrave. On stage with England Stage Co., plays including A Midsummer Night's Dream, Chips with Everything, Lady Windermere's Fan, Julius Caesar, Comedy of Errors, etc.
PICTURES: A Man for All Seasons, The Deadly Affair, Charge of the Light Brigade, The Magus, Oh What a Lovely War, When Eight Bells Toll, Serail, Excalibur, Eureka, etc.

REDGRAVE, LYNN: Actress. b. London, England, Mar. 8, 1943. Sister of Vanessa and Corin Redgrave. Youngest child of late Sir Michael Redgrave and Rachel Kempson. m. dir., actor, manager John Clark. Ent. m.p. and TV, 1962. Broadway debut Black Comedy.
THEATER: NY: My Fat Friend (1974), Mrs. Warren's Profession, Knock Knock, Misalliance, St. Joan, Twelfth Night (Amer. Shakespeare Fest), Sister Mary Ignatius Explains It All For You, Aren't We All?, Sweet Sue, Les Liaisons Dangereuses (Ahmanson, L.A.).
PICTURES: Tom Jones, Girl With Green Eyes, Georgy Girl, The Deadly Affair, Smashing Time, The Virgin Soldiers, The Last of the Mobile Hot-Shots, Viva la Muerta Tua, Every Little Crook and Nanny, Everything You Always Wanted to Know About Sex*, Don't Turn the Other Cheek, The National Health, The Happy Hooker, The Big Bus, Sunday Lovers, Home Front, Morgan Stewart's Coming Home, Midnight, Getting It Right.
TELEVISION: Pretty Polly, Ain't Afraid to Dance, The End of the Tunnel, I Am Osango, What's Wrong with Humpty Dumpty, Egg On the Face of the Tiger, Blank Pages, A Midsummer Night's Dream, Pygmalion, Turn of the Screw, William, Vienna 1900, Daft as a Brush, Not For Women Only, Co-host U.S. talkshow and A.M. America. Movies: Seduction of Miss Leona, Gauguin, Beggerman Thief, Centennial, Rehearsal for Murder, The Bad Seed, My Two Loves. Series: House Calls, Teachers Only, Chicken Soup, The Muppet Show, Walking on Air, Candid Camera Christmas Special, Woman Alone, Tales From the Hollywood Hills: The Old Reliable, Death of a Son.

REDGRAVE, VANESSA: O.B.E. Actress. b. London, England, Jan. 30, 1937. p. Sir Michael Redgrave and Rachel Kempson. Sister of Lynn and Corin Redgrave. Mother of actresses Joely and Natasha Richardson. Early career with Royal Shakespeare Company. Ent. m.p. 1958 in Behind the Mask.
STAGE: Daniel Deronda, Cato Street, The Threepenny Opera, Twelfth Night, As You Like It, Taming of the Shrew, Cymbeline, The Sea Gull, The Prime of Miss Jean Brodie, Antony & Cleopatra, Design for Living, Macbeth, Lady from the Sea, The Aspern Papers, Ghosts, Anthony and Cleopatra, Taming of the Shrew, Tomorrow Was War, A Touch of the Poet, Orpheus Descending, Madhouse in Goa.
PICTURES: Morgan, A Suitable Case for Treatment, A Man for All Seasons, Blow-up, Red and Blue, 1967 to Hollywood for Camelot, Charge of the Light Brigade, Isadora, Oh! What a Lovely War, The Seagull, A Quiet Place in the Country, Drop Out, Trojan Women, The Devils, La Vacanza, Mary Queen of Scots, Murder on the Orient-Express, Out of Season, Seven-per-cent Solution, Julia (Acad. Award, supp. actress), Agatha, Yanks, Bear Island, Wagner, The Bostonians, Steaming, Wetherby, Prick Up Your Ears, Consuming Passions, Comrades, The Children.
TELEVISION: A Farewell to Arms, Katherine Mansfield, Playing for Time (Emmy Award), My Body, My Child, Three Sovereigns for Sarah, Peter the Great, Second Serve, A Man For All Seasons.

REDSTONE, EDWARD S.: Exhib. b. Boston, MA, May 8, 1928. e. Colgate U., B.A., 1949; Harvard Grad. Sch. of Bus. Admin., M.B.A., 1952. v.p., treas., Northeast Drive-In Theatre Corp.; v.p., Theatre Owners of New England, 1962; chmn., advis. coms., mem. bd. dirs., TOA; gen. conven. chmn., joint convention TOA & NAC, 1962; pres. National Assn. of Concessionaires, 1963; chief barker. Variety Club of New England, 1963; pres., Theatre Owners of New England; gen. chmn., 35th annual reg. convention.

REDSTONE, SUMNER MURRAY: Theatre Executive, Lawyer; b. Boston, MA, May 27, 1923; s. Michael and Belle (Ostrovsky) R. e. Harvard, B.A., 1944, LLB., 1947. Served to 1st Lt. AUS, 1943–45. Admitted to MA Bar 1947; U.S. Ct. Appeals 1st Circuit 1948, 8th Circuit 1957, 9th Circuit 1948; D.C. 1951; U.S. Supreme Ct. 1952; law sec. U.S. Ct. Appeals for 9th

Circuit 1947–48; instr. U. San Francisco Law Sch. and Labor Management Sch., 1947; special asst. to U.S. Atty. General, 1948–51; partner firm Ford, Bergson, Adams, Borkland & Redstone, Washington, D.C. 1951–54; exec. v.p. Northeast Drive-In Theatre Corp., 1954–68; pres. Northeast Theatre Corp.; Chmn. bd., president & chief exec. officer, National Amusements, Inc; chmn. bd., Viacom International, Inc.; Asst. pres. Theatre Owners of America, 1960–63; pres. 1964–65; Bd chmn, National Assoc. of Theatre Owners, 1965–66; Member: Presidential Advisory Committee John F. Kennedy Center for the Performing Arts; chmn. Jimmy Fund, Boston 1960; met. div. Combined Jewish Philanthropies 1963; sponsor Boston Museum of Science; Trustee Children's Cancer Research Foundation; Art Lending Library; bd. dirs. Boston Arts Festival; v.p., exec. committee Will Rogers Memorial Fund; bd. overseers Dana Farber Cancer Institute; mem. corp. New England Medical Center; Motion Picture Pioneers; bd. mem. John F. Kennedy Library Foundation; 1984–85, 1985–86 State Crusade Chairman American Cancer Society; Board of Overseers Boston Museum of Fine Arts; Professor, Boston U. Law Sch. 1982–83, 1985–86.

AWARDS: Decorated Army Commendation medal. Named one of ten outstanding young men Greater Boston Chamber of Commerce 1958; William J. German Human Relations Award Entertainment and Communications Division American Jewish Committee, 1977; 1985 recipient, Boston U. Law Sch. Silver Shingle Award for Distinguished Public Service; Communicator of the Year B'nai B'rith Communications, Cinema Lodge 1980; named "Man of the Year," Entertainment Industries div., UJA-Federation, NY, 1988.

REED, OLIVER: Actor. b. Wimbledon, England, Feb. 13, 1938. Nephew of late British dir. Sir Carol Reed. Dropped out of school in teens and worked as a bouncer, a boxer, and a taxi driver before first break on BBC-TV series The Golden Spur. Film debut in The Rebel (1960).

PICTURES: The Rebel, His and Hers, Beat Girl, The Angry Silence, League of Gentlemen, Two Faces of Dr. Jekyll, Sword of Sherwood Forest, Bulldog Breed, Paranoic, No Love for Johnnie, Curse of the Werewolf, Pirates of Blood River, Curse of Captain Clegg, The Damned, The Party's Over, Scarlet Blade, Assassination Bureau, Shuttered Room, The System, Brigand of Kandahar, The Trap, I'll Never Forget What's His Name, Hannibal Brooks, The Jokers, Oliver, The Girl Getters, Women in Love, Take a Girl Like You, The Lady in the Car, Hunting Party, The Devils, Zero Population Growth, Sitting Target, Triple Echo, Fury Rides the Wind, Dirty Weekend, Revolver, Blue Blood, Three Musketeers, Death in Persepolis, Tommy, The Four Musketeers, Ten Little Indians, Royal Flash, Sell Out, Burnt Offerings, The Great Scout and Cathouse Thursday, The Prince and the Pauper, Assault on Paradise, Tomorrow Never Comes, The Big Sleep, The Class of Miss MacMichael, The Broad, Lion in the Desert, Dr. Heckle and Mr. Hype, Condorman, Venom, The Great Question, Deathbite, The Sting II, Masquerade, Second Chance, Two of a Kind, Christopher Columbus, Black Arrow, Heroine, Spasms, Gor, Captive, Castaway, Dragonard, Fair Trade, The Return of the Musketeers, Hold My Hand, I'm Dying; Fire With Fire; Rage to Kill; Skeleton Coast, Damnation Express, Captive Rage, The Adventures of Baron Munchausen, The Fall of the House of Usher, Saxman, Freedom or Death, Outlaws.

TELEVISION: The Lady and the Highwayman, Treasure Island.

REED, PAMELA: Actress. b. Tacoma, WA, 1953. Ran day-care center and worked with Head Start children before studying drama at U. of Washington. Worked on Trans-Alaska pipeline. Off-Broadway showcases. Television debut: series regular The Andros Targets, 1977. Off-Broadway debut: Curse of the Starving Class (1978).

THEATER: All's Well That Ends Well (Central Park), Getting Out, Fools, The November People (Broadway debut), Fen, Standing on My Knees, Elektra.

PICTURES: The Long Riders (1980), Melvin and Howard, Eyewitness, Young Doctors in Love, The Right Stuff, The Goodbye People, The Best of Times, Clan of the Cave Bear, Rachel River, Chattahoochee, Cadillac Man.

TELEVISION: Inmates—A Love Story; Until She Talks; I Want To Live; Heart of Steel; Scandal Sheet; Tanner '88; Hemingway, Caroline?

REES, ROGER: Actor. b. Aberystwyth, Wales, May 5, 1944. e. Camberwell Sch. of Art, Slade Sch. of Fine Art. Stage debut Hindle Wakes (Wimbledon, U.K., 1964). With Royal Shakespeare Co. from 1967. Starred in the title role The Adventures of Nicholas Nickleby (London and NY, 1980–81, Tony Award). Hapgood (London, L.A.). Assoc. dir. Bristol Old Vic Theatre Co., 1986–present. Playwright with Eric Elice of Double-Double and Elephant Manse.

PICTURES: Star 80 (debut, 1983), Keine Storung Bitte, Mountains of the Moon, Rosencrantz and Guildenstern Are Dead.

TELEVISION: Movies: A Christmas Carol, Place of Peace, Under Western Eyes, Bouquet of Barbed Wire, Saigon: The Year of the Cat. Imaginary Friends, The Adventures of Nicolas Nickleby, The Comedy of Errors, Macbeth, The Voysey Inheritance, The Ebony Tower, The Finding, Singles.

REEVE, CHRISTOPHER: Actor. b. New York, NY, Sept. 25, 1952. e. Cornell U., B.A.; graduate work at Julliard. Bdwy. debut with Katharine Hepburn in A Matter of Gravity. London debut: The Aspern Papers (1984).

THEATER: New York: A Matter of Gravity, Fifth of July, The Marriage of Figaro, My Life, The Winter's Tale. L.A.: Summer and Smoke. Williamstown: Mesmer, Richard Corey, Royal Family, The Seagull, The Greeks, Holiday, Camino Real.

PICTURES: Gray Lady Down, 1978, Superman, Somewhere in Time, Superman II, Deathtrap, Monsignore, Superman III, The Bostonians, The Aviator, Street Smart, Superman IV: The Quest for Peace, Switching Channels.

TELEVISION: (series), Anna Karenina, Love of Life, Faerie Tale Theatre, Enemies, The American Revolution, The Great Escape: The Untold Story.

REEVES, KEANU: Actor. b. Beirut, Lebanon, 1965. Lived in Australia and NY before family settled in Toronto. e. studied at Toronto's High School for the Performing Arts, then continued training at Second City Workshop. Made Coca-Cola commercial at 16. At 18 studied at Hedgerow Theatre in PA for summer. Professional debut on Hanging In, CBC local Toronto TV show. Toronto stage debut Wolf Boy.

PICTURES: Prodigal, Flying (Canadian films), River's Edge, The Night Before, Permanent Record, Prince of Pennsylvania, Bill and Ted's Excellent Adventure, Dangerous Liaisons, Parenthood, I Love You to Death, Aunt Julia and the Scriptwriter.

TELEVISION: Act of Vengeance, Under the Influence, I Wish I Were Eighteen Again, Babes in Toyland, Life Under Water.

REEVES, STEVE: Actor. b. Glasgow, MT, Jan. 21, 1926. Delivered newspapers. Mr. Pacific, Mr. America, Mr. World, Mr. Universe; ent. theatrical field, Kismet. Appeared The Vamp, Wish You Were Here.

PICTURES: Athena, Goliath and the Barbarians, Sword of Siracusa, Judos, David and Goliath, Hercules, Giant of Marathon, Last Days of Pompeii, Hercules Unchained, White Warrior, Morgan the Pirate, The Thief of Baghdad, The Trojan Horse, The Private Prince, A Long Ride From Hell.

REHME, ROBERT G.: Executive. b. Cincinnati, OH, May 5, 1935. e. U. of Cincinnati. 1953, mgr., RKO Theatres, Inc., Cincinnati; 1961, adv. mgr., Cincinnati Theatre Co.; 1966, dir. of field adv., United Artists Pictures; 1969, named dir. of pub. and field adv./promotion, Paramount Pictures; 1972, pres., BR Theatres and v.p., April Fools Films, gen. mgr. Tri-State Theatre Service; 1976, v.p. & gen. sls. mgr., New World Pictures; Feb. 1978, joined Avco Embassy Pictures as sr. v.p. & chief operating officer; Dec. 1978, named exec. v.p.; 1979, named pres., Avco Embassy Pictures, Inc,. 1981, joined Universal Pictures as pres. of distribution & marketing; 1982, named pres. of Universal Pictures; 1983, joined New World Pictures as co-chmn. & chief exec. officer. Elected pres., Academy Foundation, 1988.

REID, BERYL: O.B.E. Actress. b. Hereford, England, June 17, 1920. Career in radio before London stage debut in revue, After the Show, 1951. Also on stage in The Killing of Sister George (London, NY, Tony Award), Spring Awakening, Campiello, Born in the Gardens, etc.

PICTURES: The Belles of St. Trinian's, The Extra Day, Trial and Error, Two-Way Stretch. Inspector Clouseau, Star!, The Assassination Bureau, The Killing of Sister George, Entertaining Mr. Sloane, The Beast in the Cellar, Dr. Phibes Rides Again, Psychomania, Father Dear Father, No Sex Please We're British, Joseph Andrews, Carry on Emmanuelle, The Doctor and the Devils, Didn't You Kill My Brother?.

TELEVISION: Series: Educating Archie (BBC, 1952–56), Beryl Reid Says Good Evening, The Secret Diary of Adrian Mole. Movies: Tinker Tailor, Soldier, Spy, Smiley's People. Numerous specials.

REID, KATE: Actress. b. London, England, Nov. 4, 1930. Performed in stock in Canada and Bermuda. Joined Stratford Shakespeare Festival in Canada. On Bdwy. in Dylan, Cat on a Hot Tin Roof, Bosoms and Neglect, Death of a Salesman.

PICTURES: This Property Is Condemned, The Side Glances of a Pigeon Kicker, Andromeda Strain, A Delicate Balance, Equus, Highpoint, Death Ship, Double Negative, Plague, Circle of Two, Atlantic City, The Blood of Others, Heaven Help Us, Fire with Fire, Sweet Hearts Dance, Bye Bye Blues.

TELEVISION: Nellie McClung, Crossbar, Robbers, Rooftops and Witches, Death of a Salesman, Christmas Eve, Curse of the Corn People (pilot).

REILLY, CHARLES E., JR.: Communications Executive. b. Philadelphia, PA, Nov. 14, 1928. e. St. Joseph's Coll. Network liaison, TV Guide Magazine; asst. to the v.p. & dir., corporate relations, Young & Rubicam, 1964–66; executive dir., National Catholic Office for Radio, 1966–71; Secretary, Catholic

Communications Foundation (CCF) 1968–77; exec. v.p., Patrick Carr Associates 1971–73; corp. exec. Communispond Inc. of J. Walter Thompson Co., 1973–76; v.p., Speech Dynamics subsidiary, Ogilvy & Mather International, 1976–77; pres. & founder, In-Person Communications Inc. 1977–present. Also chmn., Executive Communications Group.

REILLY, CHARLES NELSON: Actor, Director. b. New York, NY, Jan. 13. 1931. e. U. of CT. On Broadway mostly in comedy roles before turning to TV and films. Recently directed stage plays.

THEATER: As actor: Bye Bye Birdie (debut); How to Succeed in Business, Hello Dolly!; Skyscraper; God's Favorite. Acted in 22 off-Bdwy plays. Founded musical comedy dept. HB Studios. Conceived and dir.: The Belle of Amherst, Paul Robeson, The Nerd (dir.). Resident dir.: Burt Reynolds' Jupiter Theatre.

PICTURES: A Face in the Crowd, Two Tickets to Paris, The Tiger Makes Out, Cannonball Run II, All Dogs Go to Heaven (voice).

TELEVISION: Guest host Tonight Show, Ghost and Mrs. Muir, Dean Martin Show, The Three Kings; game show host, Sweethearts.

REINAUER, RICHARD: Executive. b. Chicago, IL, April 28, 1926. e. U. of Illinois, grad. 1952. Prod., dir., freelance, 1952–59; bus. mgr., asst. prod., Showcase Theatre Evanston, 1952; prod., dir., NBC, Chicago, 1953–55; film dir., Kling Studios, 1956; asst. dir., Foote Cone & Belding, 1956–59; dir., radio, TV & m.p., American Medical Assoc., 1959–64; pres., Communications Counselors, 1963–64; exec. dir., TV Arts & Sciences Foundation, 1964; pres., Acad. of TV Arts & Sciences, Chicago Chapter, 1970–72. assoc. prod. & asst. dir. Wild Kingdom & asst. to pres., Don Meier Prods., 1965–present. Member–Illinois Nature Preserve Commission.

REINBERG, DEBORAH: Executive. Attorney in entertainment field for Manatt, Phelps, Rothenberg and Phillips before joining Elektra/Asylum Records as v.p., business affairs. July, 1984, joined Warner Bros. Inc. as dir. of music, business & legal affairs. 1985, promoted to newly created position of v.p., business affairs, music.

REINER, CARL: Performer, Director, Writer. b. New York, NY, March 20, 1923. Comedian on Bdwy, Call Me Mr., Inside U.S.A., Alive and Kicking; m.p. The Russians are Coming; on TV in Your Show of Shows, first Bob Hope Show, Caesar's Hour; Sid Caesar Invites You, 1958; prod.-writer, The Dick Van Dyke Show, CBS (Emmy Award-writing Comedy) 1961–62. Prod., The New Dick Van Dyke Show 1973; Heaven Help Us, 1975–76.

PICTURES: The Gazebo, writ. orig. s.p., The Thrill of It All, dir. co-author & co-prod. The Comic; Generation. A Performer: It's a Mad, Mad, Mad, Mad World; Happy Anniversary, Gidget Goes Hawaiian, The End. Enter Laughing (dir., co-s.p.); Dir: Where's Poppa, Oh, God!, The One and Only, The Jerk, Dead Men Don't Wear Plaid (s.p. & actor), The Man with Two Brains (dir, co-s.p.), All of Me (dir.), Summer Rental (dir.), Bert Rigby, You're a Fool (dir., s.p.).

RECORDINGS: Carl Reiner and Mel Brooks, The 2000 Year Old Man, The 2001 Year Old Man, 2013 Year Old Man.

AUTHOR: Broadway plays: Enter Laughing, Something Different.

REINER, ROB: Actor, Writer, Director. b. New York, NY, March 6, 1945. Son of actor/writer/director Carl Reiner. Worked as actor with regional theatres and improvisational comedy troupes. Wrote for the Smothers Brothers Comedy Hour. Breakthrough as actor came in 1971 when signed by Norman Lear for All in the Family on TV, playing Mike Stivic (Meathead). Directorial debut with This Is Spinal Tap, 1984.

PICTURES: Enter Laughing (actor only), Where's Poppa? (actor only), This is Spinal Tap (co-s.p., dir., act.); The Sure Thing (dir.), Stand By Me (dir.), The Princess Bride (dir.), Throw Momma from the Train (act. only), When Harry Met Sally (co-prod., dir.), Misery.

REINHARDT, GOTTFRIED: Producer, Writer. b. Berlin, Germany, 1911. p. Max Reinhardt, noted theatrical prod.; Else Reinhardt, actress; brother, Wolfgang Reinhardt, prod. e. Berlin. Began career at 19 as asst. to prod. Ernst Lubitsch, father's friend, with m.p. Design For Living; asst. to Walter Wanger; later to Bernard H. Hyman (Saratoga; San Francisco). Wrote orig. story, I Live My Life, The Great Waltz; collab. Bridal Suite; book for NY musicals, Rosalinda, Helen of Troy. U.S. Army service, Signal Corps. 1942–46.

PICTURES: Comrade X, Rage in Heaven, Two-Faced Woman, (co-prod.) Homecoming, Command Decision, The Great Sinner, The Red Badge of Courage, Invitation, Young Man With Ideas, (dir. 2 seq.) Story of Three Loves, Betrayed, Town Without Pity (prod.); Situation Hopeless, But Not Serious (prod.), Hitler: The Last Ten Days (prod., co. s.p.).

REINHOLD, JUDGE: Actor. b. Wilmington, DE, 1956. e. Mary Washington Coll., North Carolina Sch. of Arts. Acted in regional theatres including Burt Reynolds dinner theater in FL. before signed to TV contract at Paramount. Theatrical film debut in Running Scared, 1979.

PICTURES: Stripes, Thursday the Twelfth, Fast Times at Ridgemont High, Lords of Discipline, Gremlins, Beverly Hills Cop, Roadhouse, Head Office, Off Beat, Ruthless People, Beverly Hills Cop II, Vice Versa, A Soldier's Tale, Rosalie Goes Shopping, Enid is Sleeping, Daddy's Dyin'.

TELEVISION: Wonder Woman, Magnum P.I., The Survival of Dana, Brothers and Sisters, A Step Too Slow, The Willmar Eight, Booker, Promised a Miracle.

REISENBACH, SANFORD E.: Executive. e. NYU. Associated with Grey Advertising for 20 years; exec. v.p. and pres. of Grey's leisure/entertainment division in N.Y. In August, 1979, joined Warner Bros. as exec. v.p. in chg. of worldwide adv. & pub.; named pres., worldwide adv. & pub., 1985. Appt. exec. v.p. of marketing and planning, Warner Bros. Inc.

REISNER, ALLEN: Director. b. New York, NY.

PICTURES: The Day They Gave Babies Away; St. Louis Blues, All Mine to Give.

TELEVISION: : Movies: The Captain and the Kings; Mary Jane Harper Cried Last Night, Your Money or Your Wife; To Die in Paris; The Cliff; Skag; They're Playing Our Song; The Gentleman From Seventh Avenue; Escape of Pierre Mendes-France; Deliverance of Sister Cecelia; The Sound of Silence.

TV FILM SERIES: Murder She Wrote, Twilight Zone, Hardcastle & McCormick, Airwolf, The Mississippi, Hawaii Five-O, Blacke's Magic, Law and Harry McGraw.

LIVE TV SERIES: Playhouse 90, Studio One, Climax, United States Steel Hour, Suspense, Danger, etc.

REISNER, DEAN: Writer. Began career as director: Bill and Coo, 1947. Has collaborated on following screenplays, among others: Coogan's Bluff, Dirty Harry, Play Misty for Me, The Enforcer, Starman.

REISS, JEFFREY C.: Executive. b. Brooklyn, NY, April 14, 1942. e. Washington U., St. Louis, B.A., 1963. Consultant at NYU and Manhattanville Coll. and instructor at Brooklyn Coll. before entering industry. Agt. in literary dept. for General Artists Corp., 1966. Supervised development in N.Y. of Tandem Prods. for Norman Lear, 1968. Produced off-Bdwy. plays 1968–70. Dir. of progm. devel. for Cartridge TV, Inc. (mfg. of video-players-recorders) 1970–73. Joined ABC Entertainment as director of network feature films, 1973–75. Founder and pres., Showtime Entertainment (pay TV), 1976–80. Co-founder, pres., & CEO, Cable Health Network, 1981–83. in March, 1983, named vice chmn. & CEO, Cable Health Network. Chmn. & CEO, Reiss Media Enterprises, 1984; founder & CEO, Request Television (pay-per-view svc.), 1985.

REISS, STUART A.: Set decorator. b. Chicago, IL, July 15, 1921. e. L.A. High Sch., 1939. Property man, 20th-Fox, 1939–42; U.S. Army Air Corps, 1942–45; set decorator, 20th-Fox since 1945; 6 Acad. nom.; 2 Acad. Awards, Diary of Anne Frank, Fantastic Voyage.

PICTURES: Titanic, How to Marry a Millionaire, Hell and High Water, There's No Business Like Show Business, Soldier of Fortune, Seven Year Itch, Man in the Grey Flannel Suit, Teen Age Rebel, What a Way to Go, Doctor Doolittle, Fantastic Voyage, Oh God!, Swarm, Beyond the Poseidon Adventure, Carbon Copy, All the Marbles, The Man Who Loved Women, Micki and Maude, A Fine Mess.

REISZ, KAREL: Director. b. Czechoslovakia, 1926. m. actress Betsy Blair. e. Britain. Wrote, Technique of Film Editing for British Film Academy. Worked with British Film Institute and National Film Library, 1954.

PICTURES: Momma Don't Allow (co-dir. with Tony Richardson, 1957), Every Day Except Christmas (prod.), We Are the Lambeth Boys, Saturday Night & Sunday Morning, This Sporting Life (prod.), Night Must Fall, Morgan, Isadora, The Gambler, Dog Soldiers (U.S. Title: Who'll Stop the Rain) (1978), The French Lieutenant's Woman, (also co-prod.), Sweet Dreams, Everybody Wins.

TELEVISION: On the Road.

REITMAN, IVAN: Producer, Director. b. Czechoslovakia, Oct. 26, 1946. e. McMaster U. Moved to Canada, 1951. Produced Canadian TV show in 1970s with Dan Aykroyd as announcer.

THEATER: The National Lampoon Show (prod.), The Magic Show (co-prod.); Merlin (dir., prod.).

PICTURES: Columbus of Sex (aka My Secret Life, 1962), Foxy Lady, Cannibal Girls, They Came From Within (prod., aka Shivers), Death Weekend, The House By the Lake, Blackout, Animal House (prod.); Meatballs (prod.-dir.); Stripes (prod.-dir.); Heavy Metal (prod.); Spacehunter (exec. prod.); Ghostbusters (prod.-dir.); Legal Eagles (prod.-dir.), Big Shots (exec. prod.), Casual Sex? (exec. prod.); Feds (exec. prod.), Twins (prod., dir.), Ghostbusters II (prod., dir.).

TELEVISION: The Delta House.

RELPH, MICHAEL: Producer, Director, Writer, Designer. 1942 art dir. Ealing Studios then assoc. prod. to Michael Balcon on The Captive Heart, Frieda, Kind Hearts and Coronets, Saraband (also designed: nominated Oscar). 1948 appt.

producer and formed prod/dir. partnership Basil Dearden (until 1972). 1971–76 Governor Brit. Film Institute. Chairman B.F.I. Prod. Board. Chairman Film Prod. Assoc. of G.B., member Films Council.

PICTURES: (For Ealing) The Blue Lamp (Brit. Film Academy: Best Brit. Film 1950), I Believe in You, The Gentle Gunman, The Square Ring, The Rainbow Jacket, Out of the Clouds, The Ship That Died of Shame, Davy (for Brit. Lion), The Smallest Show on Earth. (for Rank) Violent Playground, Rockets Galore (Island Fling U.S.), Sapphire (Brit. Film Academy: Best Brit. Film 1959), 1960 Founder Dir. Allied Film Makers: Prod. The League of Gentlemen, Man in the Moon (co-author s.p.), Victim, Life For Ruth (Walk in the Shadow U.S.). Also produced: Secret Partner, All Night Long, The Mind Benders, A Place To Go (author s.p.), Woman of Straw (co-author s.p.), Masquerade (co-author s.p.), The Assassination Bureau (prod., s.p., designer), The Man Who Haunted Himself (prod., co-author s.p.). 1978, exec. in chg. prod., Kendon Films, Ltd. exec. prod., Scum, 1982, co-prod., An Unsuitable Job for a Woman. 1984, exec. prod.: Treasure Houses of Britain; TV series, prod., Heavenly Pursuits, 1985–86; Gospel According to Vic (U.S.).

RELPH, SIMON: Producer, Executive. b. London, Eng., April 13, 1940. Entered industry 1961. Chief executive officer, British Screen.

PICTURES: Reds (exec. prod.), The Return of the Soldier (co-prod.), Privates on Parade, The Ploughman's Lunch, Secret Places (co-prod.), Laughterhouse (exec. prod.), Wetherby, Comrades.

RELYEA, ROBERT E.: Producer, Executive. b. Santa Monica, CA, May 3, 1930. e. UCLA, B.S., 1952. In Army 1953–55. Entered industry in 1955 as assoc. prod. and 2nd unit dir. on The Great Escape; asst. dir. on The Magnificent Seven and West Side Story. Partnered with Steve McQueen was exec. prod. on Bullitt and The Reivers. 1979–82, exec. v.p. with Melvin Simon Prods. Served as exec. v.p. in chg. world wide prod., Keith Barish Prods. 1983–85. Served as sr. v.p. prod., Lorimar Prods. 1985–80. Named sr. v.p. features prod. management, Paramount Pictures Motion Picture Gp., 1989.

PICTURES: Exec. Prod.: Bullitt, The Reivers, Day of the Dolphin. Prod: Love at First Bite, My Bodyguard, Porkys.

REMBUSCH, TRUEMAN T.: Exhibitor. b. Shelbyville, IN, July 27, 1909. f. Frank J. Rembusch, pioneer exhibitor. Inventor & manufacturer Glass Mirror Screen. e. U. of Notre Dame Sch. of Commerce, 1928. m. Mary Agnes Finneran. Ent. m.p. ind., 1928, servicing sound equip., father's circuit; became mgr., 1932; elect. bd. of dir., Allied Theatre Owners of Ind., 1936–45, pres. 1945–51, 1952–53; dir. chmn. Allied TV Committee, 1945–50; pres. Allied States Assn., 1950–51; 1952, named by Allied as one of triumvirate heading COMPO; elected chmn. Joint Com. on Toll TV, 1954; Nov. 1953 named by Gov. of Indiana as dir. State Fair Board. Currently pres. Syndicate Thea., Inc., Franklin, Ind. member, In Notre Dame Club of Indianapolis (Man of Yr., 1950); BPOE, 4th Degree K of C, Meridian Hills Country Club, Marco Island Country Club. American Radio Relay League (amateur & commerce, licenses); OX5 Aviation Pioneers; awarded patent, recording 7 counting device, 1951; dir. Theatre Owners of Indiana; dir. to NATO; dir. NATO member ad hoc comm; 1972 chair., NATO Statistical Committee; presently chmn., trade practice comm.; 1976–NITE Award service to Independent Exhibition.

REMICK, LEE: Actress. b. Boston, MA, Dec. 14, 1935. e. Miss Hewitt's Sch., Barnard Coll. Started in summer stock; on tour in Jenny Kissed Me, The Seven Year Itch, Paint Your Wagon; first N.Y. stage appearance, Be Your Age; major TV shows incl. Studio 1, Playhouse 90, Armstrong Circle Theatre; m.p. debut in A Face in the Crowd (1956). 1988: became a full partner in (James) Garner/(Peter) Duchow Prods., forming Garner/Duchow/Remick Prods., Inc.

THEATER: Anyone Can Whistle, Wait Until Dark, Follies in Concert.

PICTURES: A Face in the Crowd (debut, 1956), The Long Hot Summer, Anatomy of a Murder, Wild River, Sanctuary, Experiment in Terror, The Days of Wine and Roses, The Wheeler Dealers, Baby the Rain Must Fall, Hallelujah Trail, Hard Contract, A Severed Head, Sometimes A Great Notion, A Delicate Balance, Hennessy, The Omen, Telefon, The Medusa Touch, The Europeans, The Competition, Tribute.

TELEVISION: The Tempest, And No One Could Save Her, The Blue Knight, Queen's Bench VII, Jennie: Lady Churchill, Eleanor Roosevelt: In Her Words; A Girl Named Sooner, Hustling, Breaking, Wheels, Torn Between Two Lovers, Ike: The War Years, Haywire, The Women's Room, The Letter, A Good Sport, The Gift of Love, Mistral's Daughter, Rearview Mirror, Toughlove, Of Pure Blood, Nutcracker: Money, Madness and Murder, Jesse, Bridge to Silence, Around the World in 80 Days, Dark Holiday.

REMSEN, BERT: Actor. b. Glen Cove, NY, Feb. 25, 1925. e. Ithaca Coll.

PICTURES: Pork Chop Hill, Kid Galahad, Moon Pilot, Brewster McCloud, Thieves Like us, Baby Blue Marine, McCabe and Mrs. Miller, Sweet Hostage, Nashville, The Awakening Land, California Split, Tarantulas, A Wedding, Buffalo Bill and the Indians, The Rose, Uncle Joe Shannon, Carny, Borderline, Second Hand Hearts, Joni, Inside Moves, Looking to Get Out, Sting II, Code of Silence, Stand Alone, Eye of the Tiger, South of Reno, Independence Day, Remote Control, Vietnam, Texas; Miss Firecracker.

TELEVISION: Who Is Julia?, The Awakening Land, Burning Rage, Crazy Times, Hobson's Choice, If Tomorrow Comes, Space, Love For Rent, Dallas (series), It's a Living, Mothers Against Drunk Driving, Little Ladies of the Night, Matlock, Jake and the Fatman, Memorial Day.

RESNAIS, ALAIN: Director. b. Cannes, France, June 3, 1922. Began career as asst. dir. to Nicole Vedres on compilation of film for Paris 1900. During '50s worked as asst. editor and editor; experimented with making his own 16mm films. Did series of shorts on various painters, culminating with documentary on Van Gogh, 1948, which he co-directed with Robert Hessens, with whom he later filmed Guernica. Co-directed The Statues Also Die, with Chris Marker.

PICTURES: Night and Fog, Hiroshima, Mon Amour, Last Year at Marienbad, Muriel, La Guerre Est Finie, Je t'Aime, Je t'Aime, Stavisky, Providence, Mon Oncle d'Amerique, Melo, I Want to Go Home.

RESNICK, JOEL H.: Executive. b. New York, NY. e. U. of Pennsylvania, B.A., 1958; New York Law Sch. 1961, admitted to N.Y. State Bar. In 1962 received Masters of Law degree in taxation. 1961–66 served as associate with New York law firm, Phillips, Nizer, Benjamin, Krim & Ballon. Was in-house counsel to United Artists Corp. 1967, joined UA as spec. asst. to the sr. v.p. & gen. mgr. 1970, moved to American Multi-Cinema, Inc., Kansas City, as asst. to pres. 1972, named v.p. in chg. development; 1976, promoted to v.p. in chg. film development. 1977, named exec. v.p. 1983, elected exec. v.p. & dir., AMC Entertainment. 1984, appt. to office of pres. as chmn. & CEO, film mktg. 1986, resigned to join Orion Pictures Distribution Corp. as pres. Has served as co-chmn. NATO trade practices comm. since 1979. In 1982 elected pres., NATO; 1984, became chmn. NATO bd.

RETTIG, TOM: Actor. b. Jackson Heights, NY, Dec. 10, 1941; on stage in Annie Get Your Gun. TV series: Lassie (1954–58).

PICTURES: Panic in the Streets, Two Weeks with Love, For Heaven's Sake, The Strip, Elopement, Gobs and Gals, Paula, Lady Wants Mink, 5000 Fingers of Dr. T., So Big, River of No Return, The Raid, The Egyptian, The Cobweb, Jackpot, The Last Wagon, At Gunpoint.

TELEVISION: Lassie, Studio One, Wagon Train, Mr. Novak, Matinee Theater, Lawman, U.S. Steel Hour, Burns and Allen Show, Peter Gunn, Death Valley Days, Allan Young Show, many others.

REVERE, ANNE: Actress. b. New York, NY, June 25, 1907. e. Wellesley Coll., B.A. m. Samuel Rosen, director. On stage, Stuart Walker Stock Co., 1928–29, Double Door, 1933–34. Children's Hour, 1934–37, org. & dir. Surry Theat., Maine, N.Y., 1936–39; Acad. Award best supporting role, National Velvet, 1945.

PICTURES: Double Door, Howards of Virginia, Men of Boys Town, Remember the Day, Star Spangled Rhythm, Song of Bernadette, National Velvet (Acad. Award, supp., 1945), Keys of the Kingdom, Sunday Dinner for a Soldier, Dragonwyck, Forever Amber, Body and Soul, Gentleman's Agreement, Place in the Sun, Great Missouri Raid, Tell Me That You Love Me Junie Moon, Birch Interval.

TELEVISION: Two for the Money, Search for Tomorrow, Sesame Street.

REVILL, CLIVE: Actor. r.n. Selsby. b. Wellington, New Zealand, Apr. 18, 1930. e. Rongotal Coll., Victoria U. Film debut 1965.

STAGE: Irma La Douce, The Mikado, Oliver, Marat/Sade, Jew of Malta, Sherry, Chichester Season, The Incomparable Max (N.Y.), Sherlock Holmes (N.Y.), Lolita (N.Y.), Pirates of Penzance (L.A.).

PICTURES: Bunny Lake Is Missing, Once Upon a Tractor, Modesty Blaise, A Fine Madness, Kaleidoscope, The Double Man, Fathom, Italian Secret Service, Nobody Runs Forever, Shoes of the Fisherman, Assassination Bureau, The Private Life of Sherlock Holmes, The Buttercup Chain, A Severed Head, Boulevard de Rhum, Avanti!, Flight to the Sun, The Legend of Hell House, The Little Prince, The Black Windmill, Ghost in the Noonday Sun, One of Our Dinosaurs Is Missing, Galileo, Matilda, Zorro, The Gay Blade, Rumpelstiltskin, The Emperor's New Clothes, Mack the Knife, CHUD II: Bud the Chud.

TELEVISION: Chicken Soup with Barley, Volpone, Bam, Pow, Zapp. Candida, Platonov, A Bit of Vision, Mill Hill, The Piano Player, Hopcroft in Europe, A Sprig of Broome, Ben Franklin in Paris, Pinocchio, The Great Houdini, Show Business Hall of Fame, Feather and Father, Winner Take All, The New Avengers, Licking Hitler, Columbo, Centennial, A Man Called Sloane, Nobody's Perfect, Marya, Moviola, Diary of Anne Frank, Mikado, The Sorcerer, Wizards & Warriors, George Washington, Murder She Wrote, Faerie Tale Theatre.

REY, FERNANDO: Actor. r.n. Fernando Casado Arambillet. b. La Coruña, Spain, Sept. 20, 1917. e. Madrid Sch. of Architecture. Left to fight in Spanish Civil War with father for 3 years. Dubbed dialogue of foreign films into Spanish before beginning acting career. Has made over 150 films since 1939. Made Knight of Arts and Letters, Cannes, 1986.
PICTURES: Tierra Sedienta, Don Quixote, The Mad Queen, Don Juan, Welcome Mr. Marshall, Viridiana, Chimes at Midnight, The Return of the Seven, The Phantom of Liberty, Tristana, The Adventurers, The French Connection, The Discreet Charm of the Bourgeoisie, Seven Beauties, French Connection II, That Obscure Object of Desire, Voyage of the Damned, The Assignment, Quintet, Monsignor, The Stranger, The Hit, Rustler's Rhapsody, Padre Nuestro, Saving Grace, The Enchanted Forest, Traffic Jam, Pasodoble, El Tunel, Hard to Be a God, Moon Over Parador, Diario de Invierno, Drums of Fire, Esmeralda Bay.
TELEVISION: A.D., Black Arrow, Jesus of Nazareth, Captain James Cook (Aust. TV).

REYNOLDS, BURT: Actor, Director. b. Waycross, GA, Feb. 11, 1936. m. actress Loni Anderson. Former Florida State U. football star. Professional football player with Baltimore Colts. TV and film stunt performer. Won fame as actor on TV in series: Riverboat. Founded the Burt Reynolds Dinner Theater in Jupiter, FL, 1979.
THEATER: Look We've Come Through (Bdwy debut, 1956), The Rainmaker.
PICTURES: Armored Command, Angel Baby, Operation CIA, Navajo Joe, Impasse, Shark, Sam Whiskey, 100 Rifles, Fade-In, Skullduggery, Everything You Wanted To Know About Sex, Fuzz, Deliverance, Shamus, White Lightning, The Man Who Loved Cat Dancing, The Longest Yard, W.W. & The Dixie Dancekings, At Long Last Love, Hustle, Lucky Lady, Gator (dir.-star), Silent Movie, Nickelodeon, Smokey & The Bandit, Semi-Tough, The End (dir-star), Hooper, Starting Over, Rough Cut, Smokey & The Bandit II, Cannonball Run, Paternity, Sharky's Machine (dir.-star), The Best Little Whorehouse in Texas, Best Friends, Stroker Ace, The Man Who Loved Women, Cannonball Run II, Stick (also dir.), City Heat, Heat, Malone, Rent a Cop, Switching Channels, Physical Evidence, All Dogs Go to Heaven (voice), Breaking In, Modern Love, Short Time.
TELEVISION: Host: The Story of Hollywood. Series: Riverboat, Gunsmoke, Hawk, Dan August, B.L. Stryker: The Dancer's Touch (also co-exec. prod.). Dir.: Alfred Hitchcock Presents (1985).

REYNOLDS, DEBBIE: Actress. r.n. Mary Frances Reynolds. b. El Paso, TX, April 1, 1932. Mother of actress Carrie Fisher. e. Burbank & John Burroughs H.S., Burbank, CA. With Burbank Youth Symphony during h.s.; beauty contest winner (Miss Burbank) 1948, signed by Warner Bros.; on stage in Personal Appearances, Blis-Hayden Theater, Star of Tomorrow, 1952. Autobiography: Debbie: My Life (1988).
PICTURES: The Daughter of Rosie O'Grady, Three Little Words, Two Weeks With Love, Mr. Imperium, Singing in the Rain, Skirts Ahoy, I Love Melvin, Give a Girl a Break, Affairs of Dobie Gillis, Susan Slept Here, Athena, Hit the Deck, Tender Trap, Catered Affair, Bundle of Joy, Tammy and the Bachelor, The Mating Game, Say One for Me, It Started with a Kiss, The Gazebo, The Rat Race, Pleasure of His Company, Second Time Around, How the West Was Won, Goodbye Charlie, The Unsinkable Molly Brown, The Singing Nun, Divorce, American Style, What's The Matter with Helen?, That's Entertainment!
TELEVISION: The Debbie Reynolds Show, Aloha Paradise (series), Sadie and Son, Jack Paar Is Alive and Well.
STAGE: Irene.

REYNOLDS, MARJORIE: Actress. b. Buhl, ID, Aug. 12, 1921. On screen as child 1923 & later (Scaramouche, Svengali, Revelation, etc.).
PICTURES: Murder in Greenwich Village (1937), College Humor, Holiday Inn, Star-Spangled Rhythm, Dixie, Ministry of Fear, Up in Mabel's Room, Three Is a Family, Duffy's Tavern, Bring on the Girls, Meet Me on Broadway, Heaven Only Knows, Bad Men of Tombstone, Great Jewel Robber, Rookie Fireman, Home Town Story, No Holds Barred, Models, Inc., Silent Witness.
TELEVISION: The Life of Riley (series).

REYNOLDS, SHELDON: Writer, Producer, Director. b. Philadelphia, PA, 1923. e. NYU. Radio-TV writer; programs include My Silent Partner, Robert Q. Lewis Show, We the People, Danger; writer, prod., dir. Foreign Intrigue film; TV: prod. dir. s.p. collab. story, Foreign Intrigue.

REYNOLDS, STUART: Producer. b. Chicago, IL, March 22, 1907. e. Chicago law schools. Adv. exec., Lord and Thomas, BBDO. General Mills; sales exec. Don Lee-Mutual; formed Stuart Reynolds Prod., TV films. Now motion picture & TV program consultant.
TELEVISION: General Electric Theatre, Cavalcade of America, Your Jeweler's Showcase, Wild Bill Hickok. Producer and worldwide distributor of educational/training films; Eye of the Beholder.

RHYS-DAVIES, JOHN: Actor. b. Salisbury, United Kingdom. Grew up in Wales and East Africa. Began acting at Truro School in Cornwall at 15. e. U. of East Angelia where he founded school's dramatic society. Worked as teacher before studying at Royal Academy of Dramatic Art, 1969. Appeared in 23 Shakespearean plays.
PICTURES: Sphinx, Raiders of the Lost Ark, Victor/Victoria, Sahara, Best Revenge, In the Shadow of Kilimanjaro, King Solomon's Mines, Firewalker, Indiana Jones and the Last Crusade, Young Toscanini, Dark Man.
TELEVISION: Mini-series: Shogun, James Clavell's Noble House, Riley, Ace of Spies, I, Claudius, War and Remembrance. Movies: The Little Match Girl, Sadat, Kim, The Naked Civil Servant, The Trial of the Incredible Hulk, Goddess of Love, The Gifted One, Great Expectations, Desperado. Pilot: Company.

RICH, DAVID LOWELL: Director. b. New York, NY, Aug. 31, 1920. Started career on live television in New York: Studio One, Playhouse, etc. 1950, left for Hollywood to work on TV series: Naked City, Route 66, etc.
PICTURES: Senior Prom, Hey Boy, Hey Girl, Have Rocket Will Travel, Madame X, The Plainsman, Rosie, A Lovely Way to Die, Eye of the Cat, Concorde—Airport '79, Chu Chu and the Philly Flash.
TELEVISION: Movies: See How They Run, Marcus Welby, M.D., The Mask of Sheba, The Sheriff, All My Darling Daughters, The Judge and Jake Wyler, Brock's Last Case, Crime Club, Satan's School for Girls, Sex Symbol, The Daughters of Joshua Cabe Return, You Lie So Deep My Love, Ransom for Alice, Telethon, Little Women, The Hearst and Davies Affair, His Mistress, Scandal Sheet, Infidelity.

RICH, JOHN: Producer, Director. b. Rockaway Beach, NY, e. U. of Michigan, B.A., Phi Beta Kappa, 1948; M.A. 1949; Sesquicentennial Award, 1967. bd. of dir., Screen Dir. Guild of America, 1954–1960; v.p. 1958–1960 Founder-Trustee, Producers-Directors Pension Plan, chmn. of bd. 1965, 1968, 1970; treasurer, Directors Guild of America, 1966–67; v.p. 1967–72.
TELEVISION: Academy Awards, The Dick Van Dyke Show, 1963; All in the Family, 1972 (director); All in the Family, 1973 (producer); Mr. Sunshine, Dear John, MacGyver (1985–present).
AWARDS: Directors Guild Award, Most Outstanding Directorial Achievement, 1971. Christopher award: Henry Fonda as Clarence Darrow, 1975. NAACP Image. Award, 1974; Golden Globe Awards, All in the Family, 1972–73.
PICTURES: Boeing-Boeing; The New Interns; Wives and Lovers; Roustabout; Easy Come, Easy Go.

RICH, LEE: Producer, Executive. b. Cleveland, OH, Dec. 10, 1926. e. Ohio U. Adv. exec.; resigned as sr. v.p., Benton & Bowles, to become producer for Mirisch-Rich TV, 1965 (Rat Patrol; Hey, Landlord). Resigned 1967 to join Leo Burnett Agency. Left to form Lorimar Productions in 1969 and served as pres. until 1986 when left to join MGM/UA Communications as chmn. & CEO. Resigned 1988; signed 3-year deal with Warner Bros. setting up Lee Rich Prods. there.
PICTURES: Producer: The Sporting Club, Executive Producer: The Man, The Choirboys, Who Is Killing the Great Chefs of Europe?, Marriage Is Alive and Well, The Big Red One, Seven Year Storm.
TELEVISION: Exec. Prod.: Series: The Waltons (1972–81, Emmy, 1973), Dallas, Knots Landing. Mini-series: The Blue Knight, Helter Skelter, Studs Lonigan. Movies: Do Not Fold, Spindle or Mutilate; The Homecoming: A Christmas Story, The Crooked Hearts, Pursuit, Don't Be Afraid of the Dark, A Dream for Christmas, Dying Room Only, Bad Ronald, The Stranger Within, The Blue Knight, Conspiracy of Terror, Eric, Returning Home, The Runaway Barge, Widow, Green Eyes, Killer on Board, Desperate Women, Long Journey Back, Mary and Joseph: A Story of Faith, Mr. Horn, Some Kind of Miracle, Young Love, First Love, A Man Called Intrepid, Flamingo Road, Marriage Is Alive and Well, A Perfect Match, Reward, Skag, Killjoy, A Matter of Life and Death, Our Family Business, Mother's Day on Walton's Mountain, This is Kate Bennett, Two of a Kind, A Wedding on Walton's Mountain, A Day of Thanks on Walton's Mountain, Secret of Midland Heights.
AWARDS: Honorary doctorate in communications, Ohio U., 1982; Distinguished Citizenship Award, Southwestern U. Sch. of Law, 1983; named Man of Year by Beverly Hills Lodge of B'nai B'rith, 1983. Has won 3 George Foster Peabody Awards, 4 Humanitas Awards, 2 Christopher Medals. Twice named Television Showman of the Year by Pub. Guild of Amer.

RICHARD, CLIFF: Singer, Actor. b. India, Oct. 14, 1940. Ent. show business 1958 in TV series Oh Boy. Other TV includes Sunday Night at the London Palladium, several Cliff Richard Shows; film debut in Serious Charge, 1959; star, play Aladdin, London Palladium Theatre, 1964–65. Top British Singer, 1960–71. Stageplays: Five Finger Exercise (1970),

The Potting Shed (1971). Twice rep. U.K. in Eurovision Song Contest. 3 BBC TV series plus doc. series. 34 silver discs, 13 gold discs for single record releases. Has made three videos. Starred in Time, rock musical, London 1986–87.
PICTURES: Expresso Bongo, The Young Ones, Summer Holiday, Wonderful Life, Voted top box-office Star of Grt. Britain, 1962–63, 1963–64. Finder's Keepers, Two a Penny, Take Me High.

RICHARDS, BEAH: Actress. b. Vicksburg, MS. e. Dillard U. On Bdwy. in The Miracle Worker, A Raisin in the Sun, etc.
PICTURES: Take a Giant Step, The Miracle Worker, Guess Who's Coming to Dinner, In the Heat of the Night, Hurry Sundown, Great White Hope, Mahogany, Homer and Eddie, Drugstore Cowboy.
TELEVISION: Series: Frank's Place (Emmy, 1988). Movies: Footsteps, Outrage, A Dream for Christmas, Just an Old Sweet Song, Ring of Passion, Roots II—The Next Generation, A Christmas Without Snow.

RICHARDS, DICK: Producer, Director, Writer. b. New York, NY, 1936. In U.S. Army as photo-journalist; worked for Life, Look, Time, Esquire, etc. as photographer. Won over 100 int'l. awards, for commercials and photographic art work.
PICTURES: The Culpepper Cattle Co. (prod., dir., s.p.), Rafferty and the Gold Dust Twins (dir.), Farewell, My Lovely (dir.), March or Die (prod., dir., s.p.), Tootsie (co-prod.); Death Valley (dir.); Man, Woman and Child (dir.), Heat (dir.).

RICHARDSON, JOELY: Actress. b. London, Eng., January 9, 1955. Daughter of actress Vanessa Redgrave and director Tony Richardson, sister of actress Natasha Richardson. e. Lycee, St. Paul's Girl's School, London; Pinellas Park H.S. (Florida), The Thacher Sch. (Ojai, CA), Royal Acad. of Dramatic Art. London stage debut: Steel Magnolias (1989).
PICTURES: Wetherby (debut, 1985 with mother), Drowning By Numbers.
TELEVISION: Body Contact, Behaving Badly.

RICHARDSON, MIRANDA: Actress. b. Lancashire, England, 1958. Studied acting at the drama program at Bristol. 1979, began acting on stage. Appeared in Moving, at the Queen's Theatre and continued in All My Sons, Who's Afraid of Virginia Woolf, The Life of Einstein in provincial theatres. Also A Lie of the Mind (London), The Changling, Mountain Language.
PICTURES: Dance with a Stranger (debut, 1985), The Innocent, Empire of the Sun, The Mad Monkey, Dr. Grassler.
TELEVISION: The Hard Word, Sorrel and Son, A Woman of Substance, Underworld, Death of the Heart, The Black Adder (series).

RICHARDSON, NATASHA: Actress. b. May 11, 1963. Daughter of actress Vanessa Redgrave and director Tony Richardson. e. Central Sch. of Speech and Drama. Appeared at the Leeds Playhouse in On the Razzle, Top Girls, Charley's Aunt. Performed A Midsummer Night's Dream and Hamlet with the Young Vic. In 1985 starred with mother in The Seagull (London), also starred in the musical High Society. Won London Theatre Critics Most Promising Newcomer award, 1986.
PICTURES: Every Picture Tells a Story (debut, 1984). Gothic, A Month in the Country, Patty Hearst, The Handmaid's Tale, The Comfort of Strangers.
TELEVISION: Ellis Island (mini-series), In a Secret State, The Copper Beeches (epis. of Sherlock Holmes), Ghosts, The Barringtons.

RICHARDSON, TONY: Director. b. Shipley, Yorks., Eng., June 5, 1928. Father of actresses Natasha and Joely Richardson. e. Wadham Coll., Oxford, where he dir. number prod. for O.U.D.S. Began career with BBC TV and directed such plays as Othello and The Gambler. In 1955 joined English Stage Co. as assoc. artistic dir. Started with Look Back in Anger, Member of the Wedding, 1958 at Shakespeare Memorial Theatre. 1960, N.Y. co-dir., A Taste of Honey. Recent stage work, dir., Seagull and St. Joan of the Stockyards, Threepenny Opera, I Claudius. Ent. m.p. ind. 1955 as co-dir. of short Mama Don't Allow. Through his Woodfall Films, dir. and produced the best of Britain's "Angry Young Man" films beginning with John Osborne's Look Back in Anger.
PICTURES: Look Back in Anger (1958, prod., dir.), The Entertainer (prod., dir.), Saturday Night and Sunday Morning (prod. only), Sanctuary, A Taste of Honey, Loneliness of the Long Distance Runner, Tom Jones (Acad. Award, 1963), The Loved One, Mademoiselle, The Sailor from Gibralter, Red and Blue, Charge of the Light Brigade, Laughter in the Dark, Hamlet, Ned Kelly, A Delicate Balance, Dead Cert, Joseph Andrews, The Border, The Hotel New Hampshire (also s.p.).
TELEVISION: Penalty Phase, A Death in Canaan, Beryl Markham: A Shadow on the Sun, Phantom of the Opera (mini-series).

RICHE, ALAN: Executive. e. U. of Arizona. Began career as music agent with GAC, later moving into its TV dept. Joined CMA 1969 as m.p. & literary agent. With Guber-Peters Co. as v.p., creative affairs. 1987, named sr. v.p. of prod. for De Laurentiis Entertainment Group. Resigned Dec. 1987.

RICHMAN, (PETER) MARK: Actor. b. Philadelphia, PA, April 16, 1927. Stage credits incl. End as a Man, Masquerade, Hatful of Rain, The Zoo Story, Blithe Spirit, 12 Angry Men, Babes in Toyland (1988).
PICTURES: Friendly Persuasion, Dark Intruder, Agent for H.A.R.M., For Singles Only, The Third Hand, Friday 13th Part VIII—Jason Takes Manahattan, Judgement Day.
TELEVISION: Series: Longstreet, Dynasty. Cain's Hundred. Movies: Dempsey, Blind Ambition, City Killer.

RICHMOND, TED: Producer. b. Norfolk, VA, June 10, 1912. e. Massachusetts Inst. of Technology. Ent. m.p. ind. as publicity dir., RKO Theats.; later mgr. Albany dist. Pub. dir. Fabian circuit, N.Y.: Paramount upper N.Y. state theats.; Grand Nat'l Pictures. Author Grand Nat'l series Trigger Pal, Six Gun Rhythm. Formed T. H. Richmond Prods., Inc., 1941. Formed Copa Prod. with Tyrone Power, 1954. Reactivated Copa Prod. Ltd., England, 1960.
PICTURES: Hit the Hay, The Milkman, Kansas Raiders, Shakedown, Smuggler's Island, Strange Door, Cimarron Kid, Bronco Buster, Has Anybody Seen My Gal, No Room for the Groom, Weekend with Father, The Mississippi Gambler, Desert Legion, Column South, Bonzo Goes to College, Forbidden, Walking My Baby Back Home, Francis Joins the Wacs, Bengal Brigade, Count Three and Pray, Nightfall, Abandon Ship, Solomon and Sheba, Charlemagne. Formed Ted Richmond Prod. Inc. for MGM release, 1959. Bachelor in Paradise, Advance to the Rear; Pancho Villa; Return of the 7; Red Sun; Producer, Papillon, The Fifth Musketeer.

RICHTER, W. D.: Writer, Director. b. New Britain, CT, Dec. 7, 1945. e. Dartmouth Coll, B.A.: U. of Southern California Film Sch., grad. study.
PICTURES: Writer: Slither, Peeper, Nickelodeon, Invasion of the Body Snatchers, Dracula, Brubaker, All Night Long, Adventures of Buckeroo Banzai (prod.-dir.), Big Trouble in Little China.

RICKERT, JOHN F.: Executive. b. Kansas City, MO, Oct. 29. e. U. of Southern California. Joined Universal Pictures in 1951; left in 1957 to start independent productions. From 1960 to 1968 handled indep. roadshow distribution (4-walling). In 1959 formed Cineworld Corporation, natl. dist. co., of which he is pres. In 1975–76 did tax shelter financing for 13 films. Currently involved in distribution, production packaging and intl. co-production as pres. of Coproducers Corp.

RIEGERT, PETER: Actor. b. New York, NY, Apr. 11, 1947. e. U. of Buffalo, B.A. Brief stints as 8th grade English teacher, social worker, and aide de camp to politician Bella Abzug 1970, before turned actor, off-off Bdwy. Appeared with improvisational comedy group War Babies. Debuted on Bdwy. in Dance with Me. Then as Chico Marx in Minnie's Boys, in Sexual Perversity in Chicago, Isn't it Romantic?, La Brea Tarpits, A Rosen By Any Other Name, The Nerd. First film in short, A Director Talks About His Film.
PICTURES: National Lampoon's Animal House, Americathon, Head Over Heels, National Lampoon Goes to the Movies, The City Girl, Local Hero, A Man in Love, Anne and Joey, The Big Carnival, The Stranger, Crossing Delancey, That's Adequate, The Passport, A Shock to the System.
TELEVISION: Concealed Enemies, Ellis Island, News at Eleven, The Hit List, W. Eugene Smith: Photography Made Difficult.

RIFKIN, HARMON "BUD": Theatre Executive. b. Springfield, MA, Apr. 1, 1942. e. Clark U., A.B., 1964; Boston Coll. Graduate Sch. of Business Admin., M.B.A., 1967. Worked for Rifkin Theatres while student; upon graduation continued in film and equipment purchasing and financial management for circuit. 1972, co-founded Cinema Centers Copr. & Theatre Management Services; pres. and C.E.O. of Hoyts Cinema Corp. with responsibility for new theatre dev. and gen. operations through 1988.
MEMBER: Exec. Comm. and v.p. of Natl. Assoc. of Theatre Owners. Past program chmn., v.p., pres. & chmn. of Theatre Owners of New England.

RIFKIN, JULIAN: Exhibitor. b. Boston, MA, May 26, 1915. e. Massachusetts Inst. of Technology. Member bd. of dir. Allied States Assoc.of M.P. Exhibitors, and Theatre Owners of America. Pres. Theatre Owners of New England 1961–63. Chairman bd. Theatre Owners of New England. 1964–65. Past pres. Allied Artists Corp. of New England. Pres., 1968–69, chmn. of bd. Nat'l Assoc. of Theatre Owners, 1970. Pres. Rifkin Theatres. Pres. Cinema Centers Corp. Chmn. NATO Code and Rating Comm., 1968–79. Received Sherrill C. Corwin Memorial Award, 1985. Senior consultant, Hoyts Cinema Corp.

RIGG, DIANA: C.B.E. (1987). Actress. b. Doncaster, England. July 20, 1938. With the Royal Shakespeare Co. at Aldwych Theatre, 1962–64. Ent. TV in The Avengers series, 1965. Ent. films 1967. Recent London stage: Follies.

PICTURES: The Assassination Bureau, On Her Majesty's Secret Service, Julius Caesar, The Hospital, Theatre of Blood, The Great Muppet Caper, A Little Night Music, Evil Under the Sun.
TELEVISION: Diana (series), In This House of Brede; Witness for the Prosecution; King Lear; Bleak House; A Hazard of Hearts, Mother Love; Mystery (host).

RINGWALD, MOLLY: Actress. b. Sacramento, CA, 1968. Daughter of jazz musician Bob Ringwald; began performing at age 4 with his Great Pacific Jazz Band at 6 and recorded album, Molly Sings. Professional debut at 5 in stage play, The Glass Harp. Appeared in TV's New Mickey Mouse Club, a West Coast stage production of Annie and in TV series, The Facts of Life, off-Bdwy debut: Lily Dale (1986).
PICTURES: Tempest (debut, 1982), Spacehunter: Adventures in the Forbidden Zone, Sixteen Candles, The Breakfast Club, Pretty in Pink, The Pick-Up Artist, For Keeps, King Lear, Fresh Horses, Loser Take All, Me and My Girl.
TELEVISION: Movies: Packin It In, P.K. and the Kid, Surviving.

RISI, DINO: Director. b. Italy, 1916. Studied medicine but left for film job as assistant on Mario Soldati's Giacomo L'Idealista. Interned in Switzerland in W.W.II. Returned home to make documentaries and short films before directing Vacanze col Gangster in 1952.
PICTURES: Sign of Venus, Poveri ma Bellis, Ill Sorpasso, Scent of a Woman, Sunday Lovers, Ghost of Love, Good King Dagobert (also s.p.), Madam at War (also s.p.).

RISSIEN, EDWARD L.: Executive. b. Des Moines, IA. e. Grinnell Coll., Stanford U., B.A., 1949. Army Air Force, W.W.II. Bdwy. stage, mgr., 1950–53; v.p., Mark Stevens. Prods., 1954–56; prod., v.p., Four Star, 1958–60; prog. exec., ABC-TV, 1960–62; v.p., Bing Crosby Prods., 1963–66; v.p., Filmways TV Prods.; assoc. producer, Columbia, 1968–69; indep. producer, 1970; prod., WB, 1971; exec. v.p., Playboy Prods., 1972–80; consultant & indep. prod., 1981–82; sr. consultant, cable, Playboy Prods., 1982–85; pres., Playboy Programs, 1985–present. Board of dirs.: Heritage Entertainment, Inc. 1985– present.
PICTURES: Snow Job (prod.); Castle Keep (prod. exec.); The Crazy World of Julius Vrooder (prod.); Saint Jack (exec. prod.).
TELEVISION: Movies: Exec. prod.: Minstrel Man; A Whale for the Killing; Ocean View Park; Big Bob Johnson; The Great Niagara; Third Girl from the Left; Summer Without Boys.

RISSNER, DANTON: Executive. b. New York, NY, March 27, 1940. Began as agent with Ashley Famous (later Intl. Famous), 1967–69. In 1969 joined Warner Bros. as v.p., chg. European prod.; 1970, moved to United Artists as v.p., chg. European prod. 1973, named v.p. in chg. East Coast & European prod. for UA; 1975, v.p. in chg. of world-wide prod. Resigned 1978; 1981, exec. v.p., 20th Century-Fox. 1984, joined UA as sr. v.p., motion pictures.
PICTURES: Prod.: Up the Academy, A Summer Story.
TELEVISION: Backfire (prod.).

RITCHIE, MICHAEL: Director. b. Waukesha, WI, Nov. 28, 1938. e. Harvard U. where he directed first production of Arthur Kopit's play, Oh Dad, Poor Dad, Mama's Hung You in the Closet and I'm Feeling So Sad. Professional career began as ass't. to Robert Saudek on Ford Foundation's Omnibus TV series. Later became assoc. prod. and then dir. on Saudek's Profiles in Courage series. Then had dir. assignments on top series (Man from U.N.C.L.E., Dr. Kildare, The Big Valley, Felony Squad).
PICTURES: Downhill Racer, Prime Cut, The Candidate, Smile (also prod., lyricist), The Bad News Bears, Semi-Tough, An Almost Perfect Affair (also co-s.p.), The Bad News Bears Go to Japan, The Island, Bette Midler's Divine Madness (also prod.), The Survivors, Fletch, Wildcats, The Golden Child, The Couch Trip, Fletch Lives, The Scout.
TELEVISION: Series: Profiles in Courage (also prod.), Man from U.N.C.L.E., Run for Your Life, Dr. Kildare, The Big Valley, Felony Squad, The Outsider (pilot), The Sound of Anger.

RITT, MARTIN: Director. b. New York, NY, March 2, 1920. e. Elon Coll., Burlington, KY. Started as actor with the Group Theatre in Golden Boy and Winged Victory. N.Y. stage; studied acting under Elia Kazan Acting teacher, Actors Studio 1951–56.
THEATER: As actor: Golden Boy (also asst. stage mgr.), Plant of the Sun, The Gentle People, The Flowering peach. *Director:* Mr. Peebles and Mr. Hooker, The Man, Set My People Free, The Man, Cry of the Peacock, A Memory of Two Mondays. A View from the Bridge, A Very Special Baby.
TELEVISION: Acted in 150 and dir. 100 TV dramas from 1948–51. Dir.: Danger, U.S. Steel Hour, Actors Studio Theatre.
PICTURES: Edge of the City (dir. debut, 1956), No Down Payment, The Long Hot Summer, The Black Orchid, The Sound and the Fury, Five Branded Women, Paris Blues, Adventures of a Young Man, Hud (also co-prod.), The Outrage, Spy Who Came in from the Cold (also prod.), Hombre (also prod.), The Brotherhood, The Molly Maguires (also prod.), The Great White Hope, Sounder, Pete 'n' Tillie, Conrack (also prod.), The Front (also prod.), Casey's Shadow, Norma Rae, Back Roads (also prod.), Cross Creek (also prod.), Murphy's Romance (also exec. prod.), Nuts, Stanley & Iris. *Actor:* Winged Victory (1944), End of the Game, The Slugger's Wife, Nuts.

RITTER, JOHN: Actor. b. Hollywood, CA, Sept. 17, 1948. Father was late Tex Ritter, country-western star. m. actress Nancy Morgan. Attended Hollywood H.S. Interest in acting began at U. of Southern California in 1968. Appeared with college cast at Edinburgh Festival; later with Eva Marie Saint in Desire Under the Elms. Gained fame as star of TV series, Three's Company.
PICTURES: Americathon, Hero at Large, Wholly Moses, They All Laughed, Real Men, Changes, Skin Deep.
TELEVISION: Movies: Leave Yesterday Behind, In Love with an Older Woman, Love Thy Neighbor, Letting Go, Unnatural Causes, The Last Fling, Prison for Children, Tricks of the Trade, My Brother's Wife. Series: Three's a Crowd, Hooperman, Have Faith (exec. prod.), Anything But Love (exec. prod.).

RIVE, KENNETH: Executive. b. London, England, July 26, 1919. Early career as actor, radio compere, theatrical agent. Served in Intell. Corps. during W.W.II. After demob. theatre sup. and gen. man. cinema co. promoted dir. 1947. Started in continental exhibition forming Gala Film Distrib. Ltd., 1950. Now dir., Pathe (UK) Ltd.; Pathe Releasing Ltd. (UK) Ltd.; Gala Film Distributors Ltd.
PICTURES: During One Night, The Boys, Devil Doll, Curse of Simba.

RIVERA, CHITA: Actress, Dancer. b. Washington, DC, Jan. 23, 1933. r.n. Concita del Rivero. m. dancer-director Anthony Mordente. Trained for stage at American School of Ballet.
THEATER: Call Me Madam (1952); Guys and Dolls; Can Can; Shoestring Revue; Seventh Heaven; Mr. Wonderful; Shinebone Alley; West Side Story; Bye Bye, Birdie; Bajour; Sondheim: A Musical Tribute; Chicago; Hey Look Me Over; Merlin; The Rink (Tony Award).
PICTURES: Sweet Charity (1969).
TELEVISION: The New Dick Van Dyke Show; Kennedy Center Tonight—Broadway to Washington!; Pippin; Toller Cranston's Strawberry Ice; TV Academy Hall of Fame, 1985.

RIVERA, GERALDO: TV Reporter. b. New York, NY, July 4, 1943. e. U. of Arizona, Brooklyn Law Sch., 1969, Columbia Sch. of Journalism. Started legal career 1st as clerk with Harlem Assertion of Rights Community Action for Legal Services 1968–70; chmn, One-to-One Foundation. Then practiced law. Then switched to journalism, making several TV documentaries on such subjects as institutions for retarded, drug addiction, migrant workers, etc. Joined WABC-TV, New York, in 1970. Winner 3 national and local Emmys, George Peabody Award, 2 Robert F. Kennedy Awards.
TELEVISION: Geraldo Rivera: Good Night America; Good Morning America (contributor); 20/20. Specials: The Mystery of Al Capone's Vault, American Vice: The Doping of a Nation; Innocence Lost: The Erosion of American Childhood; Sons of Scarface: The New Mafia; Murder: Live From Death Row, The Investigators (prods.), Devil Worship: Exposing Satan's Underground.

RIVERS, JOAN: Actress, Writer, Director. r.n. Joan Molinsky. b. New York, NY, June 8, 1933. e. Barnard Coll. (Phi Beta Kappa). Formerly fashion coordinator Bond clothing stores. Most of career on TV and in nightclubs; with Second City 1961–62; TV debut: Johnny Carson Show, 1965; nat'l syndicated columnist, Chicago Tribune 1973–76, Hadassah Woman of the Year, 1983; Jimmy Award for Best Comedian 1981; Chair. National Cystic Fibrosis Foundation. Author: Having a Baby Can Be a Scream (1974); Can We Talk? (1983); The Life and Hard Times of Heidi Abramowitz (1984). Broadway debut, Broadway Bound (1988).
PICTURES: The Swimmer (act.); Rabbit Test (act., dir., s.p.); Uncle Sam (act.); The Muppets Take Manhattan (act.).
TELEVISION: 1983–86 regular substitute guest host for Johnny Carson. 1986, hosted own TV talk show on Fox Network, The Late Show; Joan Rivers (morning talk show) 1989.

RIVKIN, ALLEN: Writer, Producer. b. Hayward, WI, Nov. 20, 1903. Newspaperman, novelist, playwright. Authored 85 s.p. including Farmer's Daughter, Battle Circus, Prisoner of War, Joe Smith American, Eternal Sea, Big Operator.
TELEVISION: Prod. Troubleshooters series, 1960 entertainment director: Democratic Nat'l Convention; author (with Laura Kerr) Hello, Hollywood; past pres. scr. br. and currently dir. pub. rel., consultant WGAW. Recipient of Morgan Cox and Valentine Davies Awards.

ROACH, HAL, JR.: President, owner Hal Roach Studios. Unit mgr. 20th Century-Fox, 1944–45; gen. mgr., Rainbow Prod., 1945–46. Member of Acad. of M.P. Arts & Sciences, M.P. Producers Assoc., Pres. Alliance of TV Film Producers; treas. & bd.

member and former pres. of Acad. of TV Arts & Sciences; pres. Rabco Corp., Hal Roach Prod., chmn. exec. officer, dir., F. I. Jacobs, Detroit; past chmn. bd., Mutual Broadcasting System, bd. member, Vitapix Corp.; gen. exec., TV Prod., Seven Arts Associated.

PICTURES: Block Heads, A Chump at Oxford, One Million B.C., Road Show, All American Co-ed, Calaboose, Prairie Chickens, Army training films, Physical Education & Military Training, Military Justice of Court Martials, Fighting Man series.

TELEVISION: Stu Erwin Show, Racket Squad, Public Defender, My Little Margie, Passport to Danger, Screen Directors Playhouse, Stories of John Nesbitt, Code 3, Charlie Farrell Show, Gale Storm Show, Blondie, Forest Ranger.

ROBARDS, JASON: Actor. b. Chicago, IL, July 26, 1922. Served in Navy during W.W.II. Studied acting at Acad. of Dramatic Arts. Began with Children's World Theatre (1947), radio parts, asst. stage mgr. on Stalag 17. First major break 1953 in play American Gothic. To Hollywood, 1958. Film debut: The Journey (1958).

THEATER: The Iceman Cometh, Long Day's Journey into Night, The Disenchanted, Toys in the Attic, Big Fish, Little Fish, A Thousand Clowns, After the Fall (Tony Award, 1959), But for Whom Charlie, Hughie, The Devils, We Bombed in New Haven, The Country Girl, A Moon for the Misbegotten, Long Day's Journey Into Night (Brooklyn Acad. of Music, 1975, Bdwy, 1988), A Touch of the Poet, O'Neill and Carlotta, You Can't Take It With You.

PICTURES: The Journey, By Love Possessed, Long Day's Journey Into Night, Tender Is the Night, Act One, A Thousand Clowns, Any Wednesday, Divorce: American Style, The St. Valentine's Day Massacre, The Night They Raided Minsky's, Hour of the Gun, The Loves of Isadora, Once Upon a Time in the West, Ballad of Cable Hogue, Fools, Johnny Got His Gun, Murders in the Rue Morgue, Pat Garrett and Billy the Kid, All the President's Men (Acad. Award, supp., 1977), Julia, Comes a Horseman, Hurricane, Raise the Titanic!, Caboblanco, Melvin and Howard, Something Wicked This Way Comes, Max Dugan Returns, Square Dance, Bright Lights, Big City; The Good Mother, Dream a Little Dream, Reunion, Parenthood, Black Rainbow, Quick Change.

TELEVISION: The Iceman Cometh, The Doll's House, For Whom the Bell Tolls, You Can't Take It WIth You, Hughie, Washington: Behind Closed Doors, The Day After, The Atlanta Child Murders, FDR: The Last Days, Sakharov, Johnny Bull, The Long Hot Summer, Laguna Heat, Norman Rockwell's Breaking Ties, Inherit the Wind, The Christmas Wife.

ROBARDS, SAM: Actor. b. New York, NY, December 16. m. actress Suzy Amis. Son of actors Jason Robards and Lauren Bacall. e. National Theater Institute and studied with Uta Hagen at H.B. Studios.

THEATER: Off-Bdwy: Album, Flux, Taking Steps, Moonchildren. Kennedy Center: Idiot's Delight and regional theater.

PICTURES: Tempest, Not Quite Paradise, Fandango, Bird, Bright Lights, Big City; Casualties of War.

TELEVISION: Series: Movin' Right Along (PBS), TV 101. Movies: Into Thin Air, Pancho Barnes. Special: Jacobo Timerman: Prisoner Without a Name, Cell Without a Number.

ROBBINS, MATTHEW: Writer, Director. e. U. of Southern California Sch. of Cinema. Wrote early scripts in collaboration with Hal Barwood, Robbins branching out into directing also with Corvette Summer in 1978.

PICTURES: Scripts, all with Barwood: The Sugarland Express, The Bingo Long Traveling All-Stars and Motor Kings, Corvette Summer (also dir.); Dragonslayer (also dir.), Warning Sign, Batteries Not Included (dir., co-s.p.).

ROBBINS, RICHARD: Composer. Studied piano and composition at New England Conservatory. Received Frank Hunting Beebe Fellowship to Austria where he studied musicology. Later became dir. of Mannes College of Music Preparatory School, N.Y. Has worked closely with James Ivory and Ismail Merchant. Also dir. doc. films Sweet Sounds, Street Musicians of Bombay.

PICTURES: The Europeans (supr. score), Jane Austen in Manhattan, Quartet, Heat and Dust, The Bostonians, A Room with a View, Maurice, Sweet Lorraine, My Little Girl, Slaves of New York.

TELEVISION: Love and Other Sorrows.

ROBBINS, TIM: Actor. b. West Covina, CA, Oct. 16, 1958. Son of Greenwich Village folksinger, worked as actor while in high school. e. NYU. Transferred to UCLA theatre prog. Studied French with actor George Bigot of the Theatre du Soleil. 1981 co-founder and artistic dir., The Actors Gang, in L.A.; dir. them in and co-author, Carnage: A Comedy (NY, 1989).

PICTURES: Fraternity Vacation (1984), No Small Affair, The Sure Thing, Wendell, Toy Soldiers, Top Gun, Howard the Duck, Five Corners, Bull Durham, Tapeheads, Miss Firecracker, Erik the Viking, Cadillac Man. Jacob's Ladder.

TELEVISION: Hardcastle and McCormick, St. Elsewhere, Hill St. Blues.

ROBERT, PATRICIA HARRISON: Executive. b. Atlanta, GA, March 31, 1939. e. Manhattanville Coll. of the Sacred Heart, Ecole Française (Paris), U. of Virginia Graduate Sch. Dir. of pub. & pub. relations, Gerald Rafshoon Advertising, 1965–69; drama critic, Atlanta Magazine, 1965–68; drama critic, feature writer, The Atlanta Constitution, 1968–69; asst. to publicity dir., The Walter Reade Organization, 1969–70; dir. of publicity—public relations, Radio City Music Hall, 1970. Became dir. of advertising—public relations, 1973; appt. v.p., 1976. Named east coast pub. dir., Universal Pictures, 1983. In 1984 appt. v.p., pub., Orion Pictures Dist. Corp.

ROBERTS, CURTIS: Producer. b. Dover, England. e. Cambridge U. Child actor. England, Germany; numerous pictures for Rank Org.; prod. England, on Broadway in Gertie, Island Visit; co-prod. on Broadway, Horses in Midstream, Golden Apple, Tonight or Never; tour and N.Y. The Journey, Bdwy. Now pres., CGC Films, Munich.

TELEVISION: Rendezvous, Deadly Species, Top Secret, The Ilona Massey Show, When In Rome, Ethan Frome, Black Chiffon, Illusion in Java (mini-series).

PICTURES: An Actress in Love, La Die, Hypocrite, Jet Over the Atlantic, The Vixen, Farewell Party, Polly's Return, Rain Before Seven, Halloween, Malaga, My Dear Children, Bus Stop, Eve Arden Show, Norma, The Lion's Consort, Whispers.

BOOKS: History of Summer Theatre; The History of Vaudeville; Other Side of the Coin, 1969; History of Music (Popular) 1900–70, 1970; History of English Music Halls, 1972; Latta, 1972; Then There Were Some, 1979; I Live to Love, 1985; Gabor the Merrier, 1988.

TOURS: Blithe Spirit, Showboat, Kiss Me Kate, Generation, The Camel Bell, Farewell Party, Twentieth Century, Great Sebastians, Goodbye Charlie, Time of the Cuckoo, Under Papa's Picture, Everybody's Gal, Divorce Me Darling, Gingerbread Lady, September Song, Same Time Next Year, Funny Girl, Pal Joey, South Pacific, It Girl; Fanny, Breaking Up the Act (pre-Bdwy.), Good, Good Friends, Together (pre-Bdwy, 1989–90).

ROBERTS, ERIC: Actor. b. Biloxi, MS, April 18, 1956. Father founded Actors and Writers Workshop in Atlanta, 1963. Brother of actress Julia Roberts. Began appearing in stage prods. at age 5. Studied in London at Royal Acad. of Dramatic Art, 1973–74. Returned to U.S. to study at American Acad. of Dramatic Arts. Stage debut in Rebel Women.

THEATER: Mass Appeal, The Glass Menagerie (Hartford Stage Co.), A Streetcar Named Desire, (Princeton's McCarter Theater), Alms for the Middle Class (Long Wharf), Burn This (Broadway).

PICTURES: King of the Gypsies (debut, 1978), Raggedy Man, Star 80, The Pope of Greenwich Village, The Coca Cola Kid, Runaway Train, Nobody's Fool, Rude Awakening, Options (cameo), Blood Red, Best of the Best, The Ambulance, Into Thin Air.

TELEVISION: Paul's Case, Miss Lonelyhearts, To Heal a Nation.

ROBERTS, JULIA: Actress. b. Smyrna, GA, 1967. Sister of actor Eric Roberts. Parents ran theater workshop in Atlanta.

PICTURES: Blood Red (debut, 1986 unreleased), Satisfaction, Mystic Pizza, Steel Magnolias.

TELEVISION: Movie: Baja Oklahoma.

ROBERTS, PERNELL: Actor. b. Waycross, GA, May 18, 1930. e. U. of Maryland. Left college to begin working with summer stock companies, joining Arena Stage in Washington, DC in 1950. In 1952 began appearing off-Bdwy. (where he won a Drama Desk Award for Macbeth, 1957); made Bdwy. debut in 1958 in Tonight in Samarkand. Film debut in Desire Under the Elms, 1958.

PICTURES: The Sheepman, Ride Lonesome, The Magic of Lassie.

TELEVISION: Series: Bonanza (1959–65), Vegas, Trapper John M.D. (1979–86). Movies: High Noon Part II: The Return of Will Kane, Desperado, Around the World in 80 Days, Perry Mason: The Case of the Sudden Death Payoff.

ROBERTS, STEPHEN: Executive. b. 1939. Started career at Columbia Pictures Industries in 1958; 1967, moved to intl. sls. div. of 20th Century-Fox. Named pres. of two Fox units: intl. theatres div. and licensing corp. In 1977 appt. pres. of Fox telecommunications div. and in 1979 chmn. of Fox Video (formerly Magnetic Video). In 1982 named pres. of new CBS-Fox Co., video cassette and disc firm.

ROBERTS, TONY: Actor. b. New York, NY, Oct. 22, 1939. e. Northwestern U. On Bdwy. in Play It Again Sam, Promises Promises, Barefoot in the Park, Absurd Person Singular, Sugar, Doubles. NY City Opera: Brigadoon, South Pacific.

PICTURES: Million Dollar Duck, The Star Spangled Girl, Play It Again Sam, Serpico, The Taking of Pelham One Two Three, Lovers Like Us, Annie Hall, Just Tell Me What You Want, Stardust Memories, A Midsummer Night's Sex Comedy, Amityville 3-D, Key Exchange, Hannah and Her Sisters, Radio Days, 18 Again.

TELEVISION: The Lindbergh Kidnapping Case, Girls in the Office, If Things Were Different, The Way They Were, A Question of Honor, A Different Affair, The Thorns (series).

ROBERTS, WILLIAM: Writer, Producer. b. Los Angeles, CA. e. U. of Southern California.
PICTURES: The Mating Game, The Magnificent Seven, Wonderful World of the Brothers Grimm, Come Fly With Me, The Devil's Brigade, The Bridge At Remagen, One More Train to Rob, Red Sun, The Last American Hero, Posse, Ten to Midnight.
TELEVISION: created Donna Reed Show.

ROBERTSON, CLIFF: Actor. b. La Jolla, CA, Sept. 9, 1925.
STAGE: Mr. Roberts, Late Love, The Lady and the Tiger, The Wisteria Tree, Orpheus Descending.
PICTURES: Picnic, Autumn Leaves, Battle of the Coral Sea, As the Sea Rages, Underworld, USA, The Big Show, Gidget, All in a Night's Work, The Interns, PT 109, The Best Man, 633 Squadron, Masquerade, The Honey Pot, The Devil's Brigade, Charly, (Academy Award, Best Actor, 1969), Too Late the Hero, The Great Northfield, Minnesota Raid, J. W. Coop (director, actor); Man On a Swing, Three Days of the Condor, Midway, Shoot, Dominique, Fraternity Row, Class, Brainstorm, Star 80, Shaker Run, Malone.
TELEVISION: Philco-Goodyear, Studio One, Robert Montgomery Presents; Man Without a Country; Washington: Behind Closed Doors; Dreams of Gold, Falcon Crest (series).

ROBERTSON, DALE: Executive, Actor, Producer (Star of Tomorrow, 1951). r.n. Dayle; b. Oklahoma City, OK, July 14, 1923. e. Oklahoma Military Coll. Prof. prizefighter; U.S. Army Sept. 1942–June 1945; Film debut in Fighting Man of the Plains (1949).
PICTURES: Caribou Trail, Two Flags West, Call Me Mister, Take Care of My Little Girl, Golden Girl, Lydia Bailey, Return of the Texan, Outcasts of Poker Flat, O. Henry's Full House, Farmer Takes a Wife, Gambler from Natchez, Sitting Bull, Son of Sinbad, Day of Fury, Law of the Lawless, Blood on the Arrow, The Walking Major, The Coast of Skeleton, The One-Eyed Soldier, The Last Ride of the Daltons, Dakota Incident, View from the Terrace, Fast and Sexy, Hell's Canyon.
TELEVISION: Series: Wells Fargo, The Iron Horse, Death Valley Days, J.J. Starbuck. Movies: Melvin Purvis, Kansas City Massacre.

ROBIN, DANY: Actress. b. Paris, France, 1927. Dancer since child. Played at the opera; acted on stage in Paris, then m.p.
PICTURES: Thirst of Men, Naughty Martine (L'Eventail); American Language debut in Act of Love, 1954. Holiday for Henrietta, Topaz, The Best House in London.

ROBINSON, BRUCE: Actor, Director, Writer. b. Kent, England, 1946. e. Central School of Speech and Drama. As actor appeared in 12 films but began writing novels and screenplays long before he gave up acting in 1975.
PICTURES: Actor: Romeo and Juliet (debut), The Story of Adele H. (last film as actor). The Killing Fields (s.p., Acad. Award nom.), Director-Writer: Withnail and I, How to Get Ahead in Advertising.

RODDAM, FRANC: Director. b. 1946, England. Studied at London Film Sch. Spent two years as adv. copywriter/prod. with Ogilvy, Benson, Mather before joining BBC as documentary filmmaker. Feature film debut, Quadrophenia.
PICTURES: The Lords of Discipline, Rain Forest, The Bride, Aria, War Party (co-exec. prod., dir.).
TELEVISION: The Family, Mini, Dummy, Aufwiedersehen Pet.

RODDENBERRY, GENE: Producer, Writer. b. El Paso, TX, Aug, 19, 1921. e. L.A. City Coll.; U. Miami; Columbia U.; U. Southern CA. Was airline pilot and L.A. Police Department sergeant. Freelance TV and m.p. writer 1953–62; Prod. TV and m.p. 1962–present.
PICTURES: Pretty Maids All in a Row (prod., s.p.). Star Trek—The Motion Picture, Star Trek V: The Final Frontier (exec. consultant).
TELEVISION: Star Trek (creator-prod.), Questor, The Lieutenant, Genesis 2; Star Trek: The Next Generation (exec. prod. and co-writer).

ROEG, NICOLAS: Director, Cameraman. b. London, England. Aug. 15, 1928. m. actress Theresa Russell. Entered film industry through cutting rooms of MGM's British Studios, dubbing French films into English. Moved into prod. as clapper boy and part of photographer Freddie Young's crew at Marylebone Studios London 1947. Next became camera operator (Trials of Oscar Wilde, The Sundowners). Had first experience as cameraman on TV series (Police Dog and Ghost Squad). Debut as director on Performance; co-directed with Donald Cammell. First solo dir. film, Walkabout.
PICTURES: *Cameraman:* The Miniver Story, The Trial of Oscar Wilde, The Sundowners, Lawrence of Arabia (co-c). *Director of Photography:* Jazz Boat, Information Received, The Great Van Robbery, The Caretaker, Dr. Crippen, Nothing But the Best, A Funny Thing Happened on the Way to the Forum, Masque of Red Death, Fahrenheit 451, Far from the Madding Crowd, The Girl Getters, Petulia. *Director-Cameraman:* Performance (co.-dir.), Walkabout, Don't Look Now, The Man Who Fell To Earth, Bad Timing, Eureka. *Director:* Insignificance, Castaway, Aria, Track 29, The Witches, The Dead Girls, Without You I'm Nothing (exec. prod.), Cold Heaven.
TELEVISION: Sweet Bird of Youth.

ROEVES, MAURICE: Actor, Director, Writer. b. Sunderland, England. Ent. industry, 1964. Played Macduff to Alec Guinness's Macbeth, London stage. Early films: Ulysses, Oh! What a Lovely War, Young Winston, The Eagle Has Landed, Who Dares Wins. Dir. many stage plays.
TELEVISION: In USA and UK incl.: Scobie (series), The Gambler, Allergy, Magnum P.I., Remington Steele, Escape to Victoria, Inside the Third Reich, Journal of Bridgitte Hitler, Tutti Fruitti, Unreported Incident, Bookie, North & South Part II.

ROGERS, CHARLES (BUDDY): Actor. b. Olathe, KS, Aug. 13, 1904. m. late silent screen star Mary Pickford. p. Maude & Bert Henry Rogers. e. U. of Kansas, and was trained for screen in Paramount Picture Sch. Appeared in Fascinating Youth and others. In armed services W.W.II. In 1945 named v.p. & treas. Comet Prods., Inc. Assoc. prod. Sleep My Love, 1950, pres. PRB, Inc., prod. radio, video shows.
PICTURES: Wings, My Best Girl, Get Your Man, Abie's Irish Rose, The Lawyer's Secret, Road to Reno, Working Girls, This Reckless Age, Best of Enemies. Fox: Take a Chance, Dance Band, Old Man Rhythm, One In a Million, Let's Make a Night of It, This Way Please, Golden Hoofs, Mexican Spitfire's Baby, Sing for Your Supper, Mexican Spitfire at Sea, Mexican Spitfire Sees a Ghost, Don't Trust Your Husband.

ROGERS, FRED: Television Host, Producer. b. Latrobe, PA, March 20, 1928. e. Rollins Coll., B.A., music composition; Pittsburgh Theol. Seminary, M. Div. 1962. In 1951 served as asst. prod. of NBC-TV's The Voice of Firestone and NBC-TV Opera Theatre. Later promoted to network floor dir., supervising Your Lucky Strike Hit Parade, Kate Smith Hour, etc. In Nov., 1953, joined WQED-TV in Pittsburgh, educational TV station, to handle programming. In 1954 started Children's Corner series, writing, producing and performing; it ran 7 years. In 1963 was ordained minister of Presbyterian Church, dedicated to working with children and families through TV. Same year introduced character of Mister Rogers on Canadian Bdctg. Corp. of 15-min. daily program. Ran for one year—was similar in content to present half-hour program, Mister Rogers' Neighborhood. In 1964 programs were incorporated into larger, half-hour format on ABC affiliate in Pittsburgh. In 1966, 100 programs acquired by Eastern Educational Network, broadcast in Pittsburgh, and seen for first time in other cities. Program now carried over 300 PBS stations. Author of numerous non-fiction books for children and albums released by Small World Enterprises.
AWARDS: George Foster Peabody, NET Special, Saturday Review TV, General Federation of Women's Club, Ralph Lowell, Gabriel, many honorary doctoral degrees from universities. Emmy, 1980, Outstanding Individual Achievement in Children's Programming; Abe Lincoln Distinguished Communications Recognition Award. Odyssey Award, 1981; Ohio State Award, 1983; Christopher Award, ACT Awards, 1984; Emmy, 1985. Friends of Children Award, 1986: Special Recognition Award—National Directors of Special Ed., 1986: Parents Choice Award, 1985, 1986: Distinguished Service Award—Spina Bifida Assoc.—1985. Action for Children's Television Hall of Fame Award, 1988; Ollie Award, 1987; Commissioners Award for PA Public TV, 1988; Parents Choice Award. 1987.

ROGERS, GINGER: Actress. r.n. Virginia Katherine McMath. b. Independence, MO, July 16, 1911. On stage in vaudeville, m.p. theat. presentations & musical comedy (Girl Crazy). Film debut 1930. Voted among ten best Money-Making Stars in M.P. Herald-Fame Poll 1935, '37.
PICTURES: Young Man of Manhattan (debut, 1930), Queen High, The Sap From Syracuse, Follow the Leader, Honor Among Lovers, The Tip Off, Suicide Fleet, Carnival Boat, The Tenderfoot, The 13th Guest, Hat Check Girl, You Said A Mouthful, 42nd Street, Broadway Bad, Gold Diggers of 1933, Professional Sweetheart, A Shriek in the Night, Don't Bet on Love, Sitting Pretty, Flying Down to Rio, The Gay Divorcee, Top Hat, Swing Time, The Story of Irene & Vernon Castle, Having Wonderful Time, Bachelor Mother, Tom Dick & Harry, Vivacious Lady, Stage Door, Primrose Path, Kitty Foyle (Acad. Award, 1940), Roxie Hart, The Major & the Minor, Once Upon a Honeymoon, Lady in the Dark, Tender Comrade, I'll be Seeing You, Week-End at the Waldorf, Heartbeat, Magnificent Doll, It Had to Be You, Barkeleys of Broadway, Perfect Strangers, Groom Wore Spurs, Storm Warning, We're Not Married, Dream Boat, Monkey Business, Forever Female, Black Widow, Twist of Fate, Tight Spot, First Traveling

Saleslady, Oh! Men, Oh! Women, Teenage Rebel, Harlow, The Confession.
TELEVISION: Perry Como Show, Pontiac, Pat Boone, Dinah Shore, Bob Hope, Ed Sullivan, Hollywood Palace, Chrysler, Steve Allen, Jack Benny, Cinderella.

ROGERS, HENRY C.: Chairman of the Executive Comm. b. Irvington, NJ, April 19, 1914. e. U. of Pennsylvania, 1934. Formed Rogers & Cowan, 1949, with Warren Cowan; 1969, bd. chmn., Rogers & Cowan, Inc.

ROGERS, KENNY: Singer, Actor, Songwriter. b. Crockett, TX, Aug. 21, 1938. Country and western singer. Member Bobby Doyle Trio, Christy Minstrels, 1966–67; The First Edition 1967–76. On screen in Six Pack (1982).
TELEVISION: Series: Rollin. Many specials and movies: Kenny Rogers as The Gambler, Coward of the County, The Gambler—The Adventure Continues, Wild Horses; Kenny Rogers as The Gambler—The Legend Continues. Special: Kenny, Dolly & Willie: Something Inside So Strong.

ROGERS, LAWRENCE H., II: Executive, b. Trenton, NJ, Sept. 6, 1921. e. Princeton U. 1942, U.S. Army, 1942–1946; WSAZ, Huntington, WV. Radio & TV, V.P. & gen. mgr., 1949–55; WSAZ, Inc., President, 1955–59; Taft Broadcasting Co., v.p., 1959–63; Taft Broadcasting Co., President, 1963–76. Vice Chairman, Hanna-Barbera Productions, L.A., CA, and Cinemobile Systems, Hollywood. Director: Cine Artists International, Hollywood; Cincinnati Financial Corp.; Inter-Ocean Insurance Co., Cinti.; Cardinal Fund, Ohio; Federal Reserve Bank of Cleveland, Cincinnati Branch; Theater Development Fund, New York; Greater Cincinnati Foundation; Rockford Coll., Rockford, IL.

ROGERS, MIMI: Actress. b. Coral Gables, FL, Jan. 27. m. actor Tom Cruise. Made film debut in Blue Skies Again.
PICTURES: Blue Skies Again, Gung Ho, Street Smart, Someone to Watch Over Me, The Mighty Quinn, Hider in the House, To Forget Palermo, The Desperate Hours.
TELEVISION: Series: The Rousters, Paper Dolls. Episodes: Magnum, P.I., Hart to Hart, Quincy, M.E., Hill Street Blues. Movies: Divorce Wars, Hear No Evil, You Ruined My Life.

ROGERS, PETER: Executive. b. Rochester, Eng., Feb. 20, 1916. e. Kings Sch., Rochester. Journalist and in theatre and BBC; joined G. W. H. Productions 1941 as script writer; with Gainsborough Studios; asst. scenario ed. to Muriel Box; assoc. prod.; personal asst. to Sydney Box 1949.
PICTURES: Dear Murderer, Holiday Camp, When the Bough Breaks, Here Come the Huggetts, Huggetts Abroad, Vote for Huggett, It's Not Cricket, Marry Me, Don't Ever Leave Me, Appointment with Venus (Island Rescue), The Clouded Yellow, The Dog and the Diamonds (Children's Film Found), Up to His Neck, You Know What Sailors Are, Cash on Delivery, To Dorothy A Son, Gay Dog, Circus Friends, Passionate Stranger, After the Ball, Time Lock, My Friend Charles, Chain of Events, Carry on Sergeant, Flying Scott, Cat Girl, Solitary Child, Carry On Teacher, Carry On Nurse, Carry On Constable, Please Turn Over, Watch Your Stern, The Tommy Steele Story, The Duke Wore Jeans, No Kidding, Carry On Regardless, Raising the Wind, Twice Around the Daffodils, Carry on Cruising, The Iron Maiden, Nurse on Wheels, Carry on Cabby, This Is My Street, Carry On Jack, Carry on Spying, Carry on Cleo, The Big Job, Carry on Cowboy, Carry on Screaming, Don't Lose Your Head, Follow that Camel, Carry on Doctor, Carry on Up the Khyber, Carry on Camping, Carry on Assault, Carry on Henry, Quest, Revenge, Carry on At Your Convenience, All Coppers Are. . ., Carry on Matron, Carry on Abroad, Bless This House, Carry on Girls, Carry on Dick, Carry on Behind, Carry on England, The Best of Carry On, Carry on Emmanuelle.
TELEVISION: Ivanhoe series, Carry on Laughing, Carry on Laughing (2), What a Carry on (2).

ROGERS, RODDY: Producer. b. Philadelphia, PA. e. St. George's Sch. R.I.; U. of Pennsylvania. Asst. acct. exec., Gray & Rogers Adv. Agency, Phila., 1946–48; stage mgr. and lighting coordinator at WFIL-TV, 1948; operations correlator, 1949; prod., dir., 1950; exec. prod. for WFIL-TV, 1951, prod. dir. Paul Whiteman TV Teen Club for ABC and Youth on the March, both on ABC-TV; dir. TV prod., WFIL-TV, 1953, mgr. radio, TV prod., Ward Wheelock Co., New York, 1954; prog. prod., radio-TV account supervisor N. W. Ayer & Son, 1955, N.Y.; chge. network sup. Ayer, N.Y. 1958; v.p., mgr. home office Ayer, 1959, pres. Agency Services Co.; pres. E. H. Rogers & Co., 1969.

ROGERS, ROY: Actor. r.n. Leonard Slye. b. Cincinnati, OH Nov. 5, 1911. m. actress-singer Dale Evans. Radio singer; many m.p. from 1937. Voted No. 1 Money-Making Western Star in M.P. Herald-Fame, 1943–54 inclusive; also voted one of ten best money-making stars in 1945, '46. Acting & prod. TV films, 1952 with wife, Dale Evans; one-hour spectaculars, Chevy Show, 1959–60; contracted for several TV specials and for nationwide appearances with Roy Rogers touring show in Canada & U.S., 1962; state fairs, rodeos since 1962; TV series. Happy Trails with Roy and Dale (cable). Star of 86 feature films and 104 TV episodes.
PICTURES: Under Western Stars, The Old Barn Dance, Billy the Kid Returns, Come On Rangers, Rough Riders, Round-Up, Frontier, Pony Express, Southward Ho!, In Old Caliente, Wall Street Cowboy, Heart of the Golden West, Sunset Serenade, Son of Paleface.

ROGERS, WAYNE: Actor. b. Birmingham, AL, April 7, 1933. e. Princeton U.
PICTURES: Odds Against Tomorrow, The Glory Guys, Chamber of Horrors, Cool Hand Luke, WUSA, Pocket Money, Once in Paris, Hot Touch, The Gig, The Killing Time.
TELEVISION: Series: Edge of Night, Housecalls, Stagecoach West, M*A*S*H, City of the Angels, High Risk (host). Movies: It Happened One Christmas, Making Babies II, The Top of the Hill, Chiefs, He's Fired She's Hired, The Lady from Yesterday, American Harvest, Drop-Out Mother, One Terrific Guy, Bluegrass, Passion and Paradise. Exec. prod.: Perfect Witness, Age-Old Friends.

ROGERS, WILL, JR.: Actor. b. New York, NY, Oct. 20, 1912. p. late Will Rogers, actor. e. Stanford U., 1935. Publisher, ed., Beverly Hills Citizen; for. corresp.; elected congressman from CA; U.S. Army, W.W.II; m.p. debut in Story of Will Rogers, since in Eddie Cantor Story, Boy From Oklahoma.

ROHMER, ERIC: Director. Writer. r.n. Jean Maurice Scherer. b. Nancy, France, April 4, 1920. Professor of literature. Film critic for La Gazette du Cinema and its successor Cahiers du Cinema which he edited, 1957–63. With Claude Chabrol wrote book on Alfred Hitchcock as a Catholic moralist, 1957. 1959 directorial debut, Le Signe du Lion. In 1962 began a series of 6 Moral Tales; from 1980 with The Aviator's Wife began another series of 7 films called Comedies and Proverbs. Staged Catherine de Heilbronn in Nanterre, 1979.
PICTURES: Short films: Presentation ou Charlotte et Son Steak (1951); Veronique et Son Cancre; Nadja a Paris; Place de L'etoile; Une Etudiante d'aujourd'hui; Fermiere a Montfaucon; Feature films: Le Signe du Lion; La Boulangere de Monceau; La Carriere Suzanne; My Night at Maude's; La Collectionneuse; Claire's Knee; Chloe in the Afternoon; The Marquise of O; Perceval; The Aviator's Wife; Le Beau Mariage; Pauline at the Beach; Full Moon in Paris; La Rayon Vert; Boyfriends and Girlfriends; Four Adventures of Reinette and Mirabelle; Conte de printemps.
TELEVISION: Carl Dreyer; Le Celluloid et le Marbre; Ville Nouvelle; Catherine de Heilbronn; between 1964–69 directed series of documentaries for French TV: Les Cabinets et Physique du XVIII siecle, Les Metamorphoses du Paysage Industriel; Perceval; Don Quichotte; Edgar Poe; Pascal; Louis Lumiere, etc.

ROIZMAN, OWEN: Cinematographer. b. Brooklyn, NY, Sept. 22, 1936.
PICTURES: The French Connection, The Gang That Couldn't Shoot Straight, Play It Again, Sam, The Heartbreak Kid, The Exorcist, The Taking of Pelham 1-2-3, The Stepford Wives, Independence, Three Days of the Condor, The Return of the Man Called Horse, Network, Straight Time, Sgt. Pepper's Lonely Hearts Club Band, The Electric Horseman, The Black Marble, True Confessions, Absence of Malice, Taps, Tootsie, Vision Quest, I Love You to Death.

ROLAND, GILBERT: Actor. r.n. Luis Alonso. b. Juarez, Mexico, Dec. 11, 1905. p. Father Francisco Alonso, a bullfighter in Spain. e. private schools in Mexico.
PICTURES: Captain Kidd, Pirates of Monterey, Dude Goes West, Malaya, We Were Strangers, Crisis, The Furies, The Torch, Bullfighter and Lady, Mark of Renegade, Ten Tall Men, My Six Convicts, Glory Alley, Miracle of Fatima, Apache War Smoke, Bad & the Beautiful, Thunder Bay, Diamond Queen, Beneath the 12-Mile Reef, French Line, Underwater, The Racers, That Lady, Treasure of Pancho Villa, Guns of the Timberland, The Wild Innocents, Eyes of Father Thomasino, The Big Circus, Samar, Cheyenne Autumn, The Reward, High Chaparral, Christian Licorice Store, Islands in the Stream, Caboblanco, Barbarosa.
TELEVISION: Bonanza, Alfred Hitchcock Presents, The FBI, Gunsmoke, The Fugitive, etc.

ROLLE, ESTHER: Actress. b. Pompano Beach, FL, Nov. 8. e. New School for Social Research. An original member of Negro Ensemble Co. in N.Y. Has appeared both off and on Bdwy (in The Blacks, Amen Corner, Blues for Mister Charlie, Don't Play Us Cheap, A Member of the Wedding) and in several TV series.
PICTURES: To Kill a Mockingbird, Nothing But a Man, The Learning Tree, Cleopatra Jones, P.K. and the Kid, The Mighty Quinn, Driving Miss Daisy.
TELEVISION: Guest roles in N.Y.P.D., Like It Is, The Winners. Regular on series: Maude, Good Times. Movies: I Know Why the Caged Bird Sings, Summer of My German Soldier (Emmy Award), A Raisin in the Sun, Age-Old Friends.

ROLLINS, HOWARD: Actor. b. Baltimore, MD, Oct. 17, 1950. e. Towson State Coll. NY stage in We Interrupt This Program, Traps, Streamers, The Mighty Gents, Medal of Honor Rag, G.R. Point.
PICTURES: Ragtime, The House of God, A Soldier's Story, Dear America: Letters Home From Vietnam (reader), On the Block.
TELEVISION: Series: Our Street (PBS 1969–73), All My Children, Moving Right Along, In the Heat of the Night. Mini-series: King, Roots: The Next Generation. Movies: My Old Man, Doctor's Story, He's Fired, She's Hired, The Boy King, The Children of Times Square. Johnie Mae Gibson: FBI. Specials: Eliza: Our Story.

ROLLINS, JACK: Producer. b. 1914. Co-founder of talent management firm Rollins, Joffe, Mora and Brezner Inc. handling careers of Woody Allen, Nichols and May, Robin Williams, Robert Klein, David Letterman, Dick Cavett, Billy Crystal.
PICTURES: Co-prod./exec.prod. with Charles Joffe: Take the Money and Run, Bananas, Everything You Always Wanted to Know About Sex..., Sleeper, Love and Death, The Front, Annie Hall, Interiors, Manhattan, Stardust Memories, Zelig, Broadway Danny Rose (also actor), The Purple Rose of Cairo, Hannah and Her Sisters, Radio Days, September, Another Woman, New York Stories (Oedipus Wrecks).
TELEVISION: Prod./exec. prod.: The Dick Cavett Show, Late Night With David Letterman.

ROMAN, LAWRENCE: Writer. b. Jersey City, NJ, May 30, 1921. e. UCLA, 1943. Author Bdwy plays: Under the Yum Yum Tree, P.S. I Love You, Alone Together. Wrote play, Buying Out, prod. in Buffalo, N.Y.; wrote play Crystal, Crystal Chandelier, (prod. in Stockbridge, Mass); Coulda, Woulda, Shoulda (prod. in Berlin, Germany).
PICTURES: (collab.) Drums Across the River, Vice Squad, (collab.) Naked Alibi, (collab.) One Desire, Man From Bitter Ridge, (s.p.) Kiss Before Dying, The Sharkfighters, (s.p.) Slaughter on Tenth Avenue, The Swinger, collab. s.p. Under the Yum Yum Tree, P.S. I Love You. s.p. Paper Lion, collab. Red Sun, orig. s.p. A Warm December; McQ, (orig. s.p.) The Mayflower Number; (orig. s.p.) Abracadabra (org. s.p.), Skeletons (orig. s.p.); Lovers Three (orig. s.p.).
TELEVISION: Movies: Omar Bradley, Anatomy of an Illness; Badge of the Assassin; Three Wishes for Jamie.

ROMAN, RUTH: Actress. b. Boston, MA, Dec. 23, 1924. p. professionals. e. Girls H.S., Boston; Bishop Lee Dramatic Sch. Started career with little theatre groups: New Eng. Repertory Co., Elizabeth Peabody Players. Screen debut in Universal serial, Queen of the Jungle, then minor roles; author stories, The Whip Son, The House of Seven Gables.
PICTURES: Good Sam, Belle Starr's Daughter, Whip Son, House of Seven Gables, The Window, Champion, Barricade, Beyond the Forest, Always Leave Them Laughing, Colt .45, Three Secrets, Dallas, Strangers on a Train, Tomorrow is Another Day, Invitation, Starlift, Mara Maru, Young Man With Ideas, Blowing Wild, Far Country, Shanghai Story, Tanganyika, Down Three Dark Streets, Joe Macbeth, Bottom of the Bottle, Great Day in the Morning, Rebel in Town, Bitter Victory, Look in Any Window, Miracle of the Cowards (Spanish prod.), Love Has Many Faces, The Killing Kind, Dead of Night, The Baby, Day of the Animals, Echoes.
TELEVISION: Naked City, Route 66, The Defenders, Breaking Point, Eleventh Hour, Producers Showcase, Dr. Kildare, The Long Hot Summer, Go Ask Alice (movie), Murder She Wrote.

ROMERO, CESAR: Actor. b. New York, NY, Feb. 15, 1907. e. Collegiate Sch., Riverdale Country Sch. In U.S. Coast Guard, W.W.II. In 1927 on N.Y. stage. Film debut: The Thin Man (1934).
PICTURES: British Agent, Show Them No Mercy, Metropolitan, Cardinal Richeleu, Love Before Breakfast, Wee Willie Winkie, Happy Landing, My Lucky Star, The Return of the Cisco Kid, The Little Princess, The Gay Caballero, Wintertime, Coney Island, Captain from Castile, Beautiful Blonde from Bashful Bend, Deep Waters, That Lady in Ermine, Diamond Jim Brady, Clive of India, Weekend in Havana, Springtime in the Rockies, Tales of Manhattan, Tall, Dark and Handsome, Once a Thief, The Jungle, Lost Continent, FBI Girl, Frontier Marshall, Happy Go Lovely, Scotland Yard Inspector, Prisoners of the Casbah, Shadow Man, The Americano, Vera Cruz, The Racers, Around the World in Eighty Days, Leather Saint, Ocean's 11, The Computer Wore Tennis Shoes, Madigan's Millions, Now You See Him, Now You Don't, The Spectre of Edgar Allan Poe, The Strongest Man in the World, Carioca Tiger, The Story of Father Kino, Lust in the Dust, Mortuary Academy, Simple Justice, Judgement Day.
TELEVISION: Falcon Crest (series), Passport to Danger.

ROMERO, GEORGE A.: Director, Writer. b. New York, NY, 1940.
PICTURES: Dir., s.p., cameraman: Night of the Living Dead; There's Always Vanilla; The Crazies; Jack's Wife (also ed.; Martin (also ed.); Dawn of the Dead; Knightriders (also s.p.); Creepshow (also co-ed.); Day of the Dead, Monkey Shines (dir., s.p.). Two Evil Eyes (The Facts in the Case of M.), Valdemar (dir., s.p.).
TELEVISION: Tales from the Dark Side (exec. prod., s.p.), It (dir.).

ROONEY, ANDREW A: Writer, Producer. b. Albany, NY, Jan. 14, 1920. e. Colgate U. Started career as writer for Arthur Godfrey then for Garry Moore, Sam Levenson, Victor Borge, wrote and produced documentaries, including Black History—Lost, Strayed or Stolen, An Essay on War, An Essay on Bridges, In Praise of New York City, Mr. Rooney Goes to Washington, etc. Regularly appears on 60 Minutes (CBS).

ROONEY, MICKEY: Actor. r.n. Joe Yule, Jr.; b. Brooklyn, NY, Sept. 23, 1920; son of Joe Yule & Nell Carter, vaudeville performers. U.S. Army, W.W.II. In vaudeville during early infancy with parents and others before m.p. debut and after; from age of 5 to 12 created screen version of Fontaine Fox newspaper comic character Mickey McGuire in series of short subjects of that title, also appeared in number of features (Not to be Trusted, Orchids and Ermine, The King, etc.). Adopting name of Mickey Rooney, ret. to vaudeville; resumed screen career 1932. Special Academy Award 1940 for Andy Hardy characterization; voted among first ten Money-Making Stars in M.P. Herald-Fame Poll. 1938–43. Broadway: Sugar Babies 1979. Autobiography: I.E. (1965). Honorary Academy Award, 1983.
PICTURES: As child: Information Kid, Fast Companions, My Pal the King, Beast of the City, The Big Cage, The Bowery, Broadway to Hollywood, The Big Chance, Manhattan Melodrama, A Midsummer Night's Dream, Reckless, Riff Raff, Little Lord Fauntleroy, Captains Courageous.
LATER FILMS: A Family Affair, Love Finds Andy Hardy, Babes in Arms, Strike Up the Band, Men of Boy's Town, Babes on Broadway, The Human Comedy, Girl Crazy, National Velvet, Words and Music, The Strip, Sound Off, Off Limits, All Ashore, Slight Case of Larcency, Drive a Crooked Road, Bridges at Toko-Ri, Atomic Kid, Twinkle in God's Eye, Bold and the Brave, Magnificent Roughnecks, The Last Mile, Big Operation, Private Lives of Adam and Eve, Platinum High School, King of the Roaring 20's, Breakfast at Tiffany's, It's a Mad, Mad, Mad, Mad World, Everything's Ducky. The Secret Invasion, The Extraordinary Seaman, The Comic, The Cockeyed Cowboys of Calico County, Skidoo, Pulp, Richard, B.J. Presents, That's Entertainment!, The Domino Principle, Pete's Dragon, The Black Stallion, Arabian Adventure, Erik the Viking.
TELEVISION: Playhouse 90, Pinocchio, Eddie, Somebody's Waiting, The Dick Powell Theater, Hey Mickey (series), Bill, Bill: On His Own, Bluegrass, Golden Girls.

ROONEY, PAT: Performer stage, nightclubs, pictures. Producer. e. Denver U., Santa Monica Coll., UCLA, Marquette U. Entertainer vaudeville, theatres, stage, TV and pictures. Captain U.S. Army Air Corps. during Korean War. Entertained troops Far East Commands. Producer, 1960, C.B.S. Films Inc., producing TV pilots and series. 1962, formed Pat Rooney Prods. with Del E. Webb, hotel and construction exec. 1963–68, producer for Jerry Buss Prods. %Paramount Pictures.
MAJOR PICTURES: Dime with a Halo, Danger Pass, Caged, Law of the Lawless, Requiem for a Gunfighter, Bounty Killer, Young Once, Hells Angels, Fools, Christmas Couple, Black Eye, Jan and Dean, Deadman's Curve.

ROOS, FRED: Producer. b. Santa Monica, CA, May 23, 1934. e. UCLA, B.A. Directed documentary films for Armed Forces Radio and Television Network. Worked briefly as agent for MCA and story editor for Robert Lippert Productions. Worked as casting dir. in 1960s and served as casting dir. on The Godfather, beginning longtime association with filmmakers Francis Coppola and George Lucas.
PICTURES: The Conversation; The Godfather Part II; Apocalypse Now; The Black Stallion; The Escape Artist (exec. prod.); The Black Stallion Returns; Hammett; One From the Heart; The Outsiders; Rumble Fish; The Cotton Club; One Magic Christmas; Seven Minutes in Heaven; Peggy Sue Got Married (special consultant); Barfly; Gardens of Stone (co-exec. prod.); Tucker: The Man and His Dream, New York Stories (Life Without Zoe), Wait Until Spring, Bandini.
TELEVISION: Series: The Outsiders (exec. prod.). Movie: Montana.

ROOT, WELLS: Writer. b. Buffalo, NY, March 21, 1900. e. Yale U. Drama ed., NY World; dramatic and film critic, Time mag.; fiction, articles, various magazines; many TV dramas, various programs.
PICTURES: I Cover the Waterfront, Tiger Shark, Bird of Paradise, Prisoner of Zenda, Magnificent Obsession, Texas Across the River.

ROSE, ALEX: Producer. r.n. Alexandra Rose. b. 1946. e. U. of WI, BS. Started in m.p. distribution with Medford Films. Later became asst. sls. mgr. for New World Pictures.
PICTURES: co-prod. with Tamara Asseyev: Drive-In, I Wanna Hold Your Hand, Big Wednesday, Norma Rae, Nothing in Common (solo prod.), Overboard (co-prod.), Quigley Down Under.

TELEVISION: Nothing in Common (co-exec. prod. with Garry Marshall), Pilots: Norma Rae, Just Us Kids.

ROSE, DAVID: Composer, Conductor. b. London, England, June 15, 1910. To U.S. 1914. Studied music, Chicago Coll. of Music. Pianist with Chicago orchestras; staff arranger for several radio stations; mus. dir., West Coast network; while in U.S. Army, comp. dir. of Winged Victory; songs include Holiday for Strings, Our Waltz.
PICTURES: Texas Carnival, Rich Young & Pretty, The Clown, Bright Road, Jupiter's Darling, Port Afrique.
TELEVISION: Musical dir., Red Skelton Show; composer-conductor, Bonanza. Little House on the Prairie, Highway to Heaven, Emmy, Fred Astaire special.

ROSE, JACK: Writer. b. Warsaw, Poland, Nov. 4, 1911. e. Ohio U. 1934, B.A. m. Audrey Mary Rose, writer, prod. Paramount Pictures, L.A.
PICTURES: Ladies Man, Sorrowful Jones, The Great Lover, It's A Great Feeling, Pale Face, My Favorite Brunette, Road to Rio, Daughter of Rosie O'Grady, Always Leave Them Laughing, On Moonlight Bay, Riding High, I'll See You in My Dreams, Room for One More, April in Paris, Trouble Along the Way, Living it Up, Seven Little Foys, Houseboat, Five Pennies, Beau James, It Started in Naples, Double Trouble, Papa's Delicate Condition, Who's Got the Action?, Who's Been Sleeping in My Bed?, A Touch of Class, The Duchess and the Dirtwater Fox, Lost and Found, The Great Muppet Caper.
TELEVISION: Academy Awards (1988, writer).

ROSE, REGINALD: Writer, b. New York, NY, Dec. 10, 1921. e. City Coll. of New York. Worked as clerk, publicist, Warner Bros.; adv. acct. exec., copy chief; U.S. Air Force, W.W.II; first TV play, Bus to Nowhere, 1951; since then numerous TV plays, Studio One, Playhouse 90. Creator of The Defenders, other programs.
PICTURES: Crime in the Streets, 12 Angry Men, Dino, Man of the West, The Man in the Net, Baxter, Somebody Killed Her Husband, The Wild Geese, The Sea Wolves, Whose Life Is It Anyway?, Wild Geese II, The Final Option.
TELEVISION: Dear Friends, Thunder on Sycamore Street, Tragedy in a Temporary Town, My Two Loves, The Rules of Marriage, Studs Lonigan, Escape from Sobibor.

ROSE, STEPHEN: Executive. Entered m.p. industry in 1964 with Columbia Pictures; named adv. dir. In 1970 joined Cinema V Distributing, Inc. as dir. of adv.; left in 1971 to take post at Cinemation Industries, where was named v.p. and bd. member. In 1975 joined Paramount Pictures as dir. of adv.; promoted to v.p./adv. In 1979 formed Barrich Prods. with Gordon Weaver. In Feb., 1982, rejoined Paramount as v.p., mktg; 1983, named v.p. of mktg. for Paramount; sr. v.p., mktg., 1983. Resigned in 1984 to form Barrich Marketing with Gordon Weaver.

ROSEN, ROBERT L.: Producer. b. Palm Springs, CA, Jan. 7, 1937. e. U. of Southern Calif.
PICTURES: The French Connection II; Black Sunday; Prophecy; Going Ape; The Challenge; Courage (also dir.); Porky's Revenge, World Gone Wild, Dead-Bang (exec. prod.). *Exec. in chg. of prod.:* Little Big Man, Le Mans, The Reivers, Rio Lobo, Big Jake, Scrooge.
TELEVISION: Gilligan's Island, Hawaii Five-O, Have Gun Will Travel.

ROSENBERG, FRANK P.: Producer, Writer. b. New York, NY, Nov. 22, 1913. e. Columbia U., NYU. Joined Columbia 1929; writer m.p. & radio; exploit, mgr., 1941; apptd. national dir. adv., publicity, exploitation, Columbia Pictures Feb. 1944. Pub. dir. M.P. Victory Loan, 1945; dir. pub. Columbia Pictures Studios, Hollywood, Jan. 1946. Resigned 1947 to enter production. Co-prod. Man Eater of Kumaon. Collab. adapt., assoc. prod. Where the Sidewalk Ends.
PICTURES: Secret of Convict Lake, Return of the Texan, The Farmer Takes a Wife, King of the Khyber Rifles, Illegal, Miracle in the Rain, Girl He Left Behind, One-Eyed Jacks, Critic's Choice, Madigan, exec. prod., The Steagle, prod. The Reincarnation of Peter Proud; sole adaptation, Gray Lady Down.
TELEVISION: Exec. prod. and prod. for Schlitz Playhouse programs during 1957–58; prod., The Troubleshooters; exec. prod., Arrest and Trial, 1963–64; exec. prod. Kraft Suspense Theatre, 1964–65; v.p. MCA Universal 1964; pres., Cutlass Prods., Inc.

ROSENBERG, GRANT E.: Executive. Started career in research dept., NBC; 1977, joined Paramount in research and later in development; 1984, v.p., dramatic dev.; then sr. v.p., dev., for TV group, Paramount. 1985, named sr. v.p., network TV for Walt Disney Pictures; 1988, named pres., Lee Rich Productions, TV div., and exec. prod. of Molloy TV series.

ROSENBERG, MARK: Executive. b. 1948. e. U. of Wisconsin. Started career in magazine publishing field in New York. Adv. exec. with Seiniger & Associates; agent in m.p. dept. of IFA (later became ICM). With literary agency of Adams, Ray, Rosenberg. In 1978 joined Warner Bros., as v.p., prod.; in 1980 promoted to snr. v.p. of prod.; 1983, pres., W B theatrical production division. 1986–89, partner with Sydney Pollack in Mirage Prods.
PICTURES: Bright Lights, Big City (co-prod.), Major League (exec. prod.), The Fabulous Baker Boys.

ROSENBERG, RICHARD K.: Executive. b. Paterson, NJ, Apr. 4, 1942. e. Indiana U. 1966–77 corp. & entertainment atty. for many major corps. & celebrities. 1974, produced Alice, Sweet Alice, debut film of Brooke Shields. Formed RKR Entertainment Group in 1977, with its subsidiaries, RKR Releasing, Inc., RKR Artists & RKR Prods.
PICTURES: Alice Sweet Alice, Hell's Angels Forever, Search for the Mother Lode, The Wild Duck.
PUBLICATIONS: Entertainment Industry Contracts, 1986.

ROSENBERG, RICK: Producer. b. Los Angeles, CA. e. Los Angeles City Coll., UCLA. Started career in mail room of Columbia Pictures, then asst. to prod. Jerry Bresler on Major Dundee and Love Has Many Faces. Asst. to Col. v.p., Arthur Kramer. Was assoc. prod. on The Reivers and in 1970 prod. first feature, Adam at Six A.M., with Bob Christiansen, with whom co-prod. all credits listed below.
PICTURES: Adam at Six A.M., Hide in Plain Sight.
TELEVISION: Features: Suddenly Single, The Glass House, A Brand New Life, The Man Who Could Talk to Kids, The Autobiography of Miss Jane Pittman, I Love You . . . Goodbye, Queen of the Stardust Ballroom, Born Innocent, A Death in Canaan, Strangers, Robert Kennedy and His Times, Kids Don't Tell, As Summers Die; Gore Vidal's Lincoln; Red Earth, White Earth, Heist.

ROSENBERG, STUART: Director, Producer. b. New York, NY, 1927. e. NYU. Emmy Award, 1962.
PICTURES: Murder, Inc., Cool Hand Luke, The April Fools, WUSA, Pocket Money, The Laughing Policeman, The Drowning Pool, Voyage Of The Damned, The Amityville Horror, Love and Bullets, Brubaker, The Pope of Greenwich Village, Home Grown.
TELEVISION: Numerous episodes of such series as The Untouchables, Naked City, The Defenders, Espionage, Chrysler Theatre, Twilight Zone, Alfred Hitchcock Theater.

ROSENFELT, FRANK E.: Executive. b. Peabody, MA, Nov. 15, 1921. e. Cornell U., B.S.; Cornell Law Sch., L.L.B. Served as atty. for RKO Radio Pictures, before joining MGM in 1955 as member of legal dept. Appt. secty. in 1966. Named v.p., gen. counsel in 1969 and pres. in 1973. In 1974 also named chief exec. officer. Bd. chmn. & chief exec. officer, MGM to 1981; now vice chmn., MGM/UA Communications Co. Member: Bd. of Governors, Academy of M.P. Arts & Sciences for 9 years.

ROSENFIELD, JONAS, JR.: Marketing Consultant. b. Dallas, TX, June 15, 1915. e. U. of Miami, A.B. In U.S. Navy, W.W.II. Warner Bros. advertising copy dept., adv. mgr. Walt Disney, Adv. copywriter Donahue & Coe. Advertising copy chief 20th Century-Fox. Pres. N.Y. Screen Publicists Guild. In July 1942, ex-officio member industry's War Activities Committee. In 1945 apptd. asst. adv. mgr., 20th Cent.-Fox; adv. mgr., 1949–51; dir. of pub. rel. for Italian Films Export 1952; v.p. chg. adv. prom., pub. IFE Releasing Corp., 1953–55; exec. asst. to Paul Lazarus; v.p., of Columbia Pictures, 1955; exec. in chg., avd., pub. expl., Columbia, 1958; v.p. in chg. adv. pub. expl. Columbia, 1960; elected v.p., Columbia Int'l Pictures Corp., 1962; elected gen. exec. officer, Columbia Pictures, 1962; v.p., worldwide advertising, publicity and promotion, 20th Century-Fox, 1963–77; film mktg. consultant, 1977–78; lecturer in mktg., U. of Southern California, 1978–79; v.p. in chg. of worldwide mktg., Melvin Simon Productions, 1979. In 1980 named sr. v.p.; 1981, joined Filmways Pictures as exec. v.p., worldwide adv./pub., promo. 1982, film mkt. consultant, lecturer adjunct, U.S.C. Sch. of Cinema & TV; 1983, exec. dir., American Film Mktg. Assn.; 1985 to present, pres. AFMA.

ROSENMAN, HOWARD: Producer. b. Brooklyn, NY. Asst. to Sir Michael Benthall on Bdwy. show; prod., Benton & Bowles Agency; ABC-TV; RSO Prods. Now independent prod., Howard Rosenman Prods.
PICTURES: Sparkle; The Main Event; Resurrection, The War at Home, Lost Angels, Gross Anatomy.
TELEVISION: Virginia Hill; The Bees.

ROSENMAN, LEONARD: Composer. b. New York, NY, Sept. 7, 1924. Winner of two Oscars: Barry Lyndon, Bound for Glory; and two Emmys: Sybil, Friendly Fire.
PICTURES: East of Eden, Cobweb, Rebel Without a Cause, Edge of the City, The Savage Eye, The Chapman Report, Fantastic Voyage, Hellfighters, Beneath the Planet of the Apes, Barry Lyndon, Birch Interval, Race With the Devil, Bound For Glory, A Man Called Horse, The Car, September 30, 1955, The Enemy of the People, The Lord of the Rings, Promises in the Dark, Prophecy, Hide in Plain Sight, The Jazz Singer, Making Love, Miss Lonely Hearts, Cross Creek, Heart of the Stag, Star Trek IV: The Voyage Home, Circles in a Forest.

TELEVISION: Sylvia, Friendly Fire, City in Fear, Murder in Texas, Vanished, The Wall, Miss Lonelyhearts, Celebrity, The Return of Marcus Welby MD, Heartsounds, First Steps, Promised a Miracle.

ROSENSTEIN, GERTRUDE: Director. b. New York, NY. e. Barnard Coll., B.A., Neighborhood Playhouse. exec. asst. to George Ballanchine & Lincoln Kirstein, N.Y.C. Ballet. Assoc. with Gian Carlo Menotti, Festival of Two Worlds, Spoleto, Italy.
TELEVISION: Assoc. dir., NBC Opera, Emmy Awards, Kennedy Memorial Mass; dir., Concentration. TV staff dir., NBC. Now freelance director, news programs, election coverage, commercials. Governor, NY Television Academy.

ROSENTHAL, BUD: Executive. b. Brooklyn, NY, Mar. 21, 1934. e. Brooklyn Coll., B.A., 1954, NYU. U.S. Army, 1954–56; college correspondent, N.Y. Times; ent. m.p. ind. as associate editor, Independent Film Journal, 1957. Joined Columbia Pictures publicity dept. as trade paper contact and news writer, 1959, newspaper and syndicate contact 1960; appointed national publicity mgr., Columbia Pictures Corp., 1962–67; asst. prod. Something For Everyone; pub. dir., Anderson Tapes, Such Good Friends; story ed. and casting dir., Sigma Prods., 1972–75; associate, prod., Broadway play, Full Circle, 1973, assoc. prod., Rosebud, 1974; dir. intl. press relations, The Bluebird, 1975; Warner Bros. project coordinator, Superman, 1977–79; Superman II, 1980–81; Superman III, 1982–83; Columbia Pictures intl. mktg. coordinator, Ghostbusters, 1984–85; Tri-Star intl. mktg. coordinator, Labyrinth, 1986–87; Warner Bros. worldwide mktg. coordinator, Batman, 1988–89.

ROSENTHAL, RICK: Director. b. New York, NY, June 15, 1949. Launched career as filmmaker-in-residence with New Hampshire TV Network. Moved to Los Angeles to study at American Film Institute where filmed Moonface, 1973. Theatrical feature debut: Halloween II, 1981.
PICTURES: Bad Boys, American Dreamer, Russkies, Distant Thunder.
TELEVISION: Fire on the Mountain, Code of Vengeance, Secrets of Midland Heights. Series: Life Goes On.

ROSENTHAL, ROBERT M.: Producer. b. New York, NY, Dec. 28, 1936. e. Lawrence Acad., MA, 1952–56. U. of Pennsylvania Wharton Sch., 1956–60. Pictorial Officer, Prod.-dir. for U.S. Army Signal Corp., 1960–62; Chief, U.S. Army Production Facilities, France, 1961–62. Production mgr., Gurney Productions Inc., 1963; comptroller, Jalor Productions Inc., 1964; pres. Rosenthal Productions Inc., 1964; prod. Lieut. Wolf, I Wonder Why, Been Down So Long It Looks Like Up To Me. Producer/atty.-at-law, Southwestern U. Sch. of Law, 1973–76. Pres., Bel Air Broadcasting Corp., 1984.

ROSENZWEIG, BARNEY: Executive. b. Los Angeles, CA, Dec. 23, 1937. e. U. of Southern California, 1959. Chmn. Weintraub Entertainment Group, TV division, 1988–.
TELEVISION: Assoc. prod.: Do Not Disturb, Prod.: Daniel Boone (series), Men of the Dragon, One of My Wives Is Missing, Charlie's Angels (series), Angel on My Shoulder, American Dream (pilot), John Steinbeck's East of Eden (mini-series). Exec. prod.: This Girl for Hire, Cagney and Lacey (series).
PICTURES: Morituri (assoc. prod.), Who Fears the Devil (prod.).

ROSI, FRANCESCO: Director. b. Naples, Italy, 1922. Apprenticed as asst. to Visconti and Antonioni; directed first feature La Sfida (The Challenge) in 1958.
PICTURES: Salvatore Giuiliano, Hands Over the City, More Than a Miracle, Just Another War, Lucky Luciano, The Mattei Affair, Eboli, Three Brothers, Chronicle of a Death Foretold, To Forget Palermo.

ROSS, DIANA: Singer, Actress. b. Detroit, MI, Mar. 26, 1944. Formed musical group at age 14 with two friends, Mary Wilson and Florence Ballard. In 1960 they auditioned for Berry Gordy, head of Motown Record Corp. and were hired to sing backgrounds on records for Motown acts. After completing high school, the trio was named the Supremes and went on tour with Motor Town Revue. Over period of 10 yrs. Supremes had 15 consecutive hit records and once had five consecutive records in no. one spot on charts. In 1969 Diana Ross went on her own, appearing on TV and in nightclubs.
PICTURES: Lady Sings the Blues (debut, 1973), Mahogany, The Wiz.
TELEVISION: Diana! (special; also exec. prod. & writer), Motown 25: Yesterday, Today, Forever; Motown Returns to the Apollo, Diana's World Tour.

ROSS, FRANK: Producer, Writer. b. Boston, MA, Aug. 12, 1904. e. Exeter, Princeton U. President, Frank Ross Inc. In 1939, asst. prod. Of Mice and Men, UA, Roach. In 1941, producer, The Devil and Miss Jones, RKO. Co-author of story and s.p. The More the Merrier. Spec. Acad. Award (1945) for prod. The House I Live In, short subject on tolerance.
PICTURES: The Lady Takes a Chance, Flame and the Arrow, The Lady Says No, The Robe, Demetrius and the Gladiators, Rain of Ranchipur, Kings Go Forth, Mr. Moses, Maurie (prod.), Where It's At.

ROSS, HERBERT: Director, b. New York, NY, May 13, 1927. m. Lee Radziwill. e. studied dance with Doris Humphrey, Helene Platove, Laird Leslie. Trained for stage Herbert Berghof, 1943–50. As Bdwy dancer in Follow the Girls, Bloomer Girl, Look Ma, I'm Dancing and with the American Ballet Theatre. Resident choreographer ABT 1959. Choreographer on Broadway for A Tree Grows in Brooklyn (1951), House of Flowers (also dir. musical numbers), The Gay Life (also dir. musical num.), I Can Get It For You Wholesale, Tovarich, Anyone Can Whistle, Do I Hear a Waltz, On a Clear Day You Can See Forever, The Apple Tree. Broadway dir.: Chapter Two. I Ought To Be in Pictures. Follies in Concert. Ent. m.p. ind. as choreographer for Carmen Jones, The Young Ones, Summer Holiday, Inside Daisy Clover, Dr. Doolittle, Funny Girl (also dir. musical numbers).
PICTURES: Goodbye Mr. Chips, The Owl and the Pussycat, Play It Again, Sam, The Last of Sheila (prod., dir.), T.R. Baskin, Funny Lady, The Sunshine Boys, The Seven-Per-Cent Solution (prod., dir.), The Turning Point (prod., dir.), The Goodbye Girl, California Suite, Nijinsky, Pennies from Heaven (prod., dir.), I Ought to Be in Pictures (co-prod., dir.), Max Dugan Returns (prod., dir.), Footloose, Protocol, The Secret of My Success (prod., dir.), Dancers, Steel Magnolias, Women on the Verge of a Nervous Breakdown.
TELEVISION: Choreographer: Series: Milton Berle Show (also prod., 1952–57), Martha Raye Show (also prod.), Bell Telephone Hour (also dir.), Specials: Wonderful Town (also dir.), Meet Me in St. Louis, Jerome Kern Special, Bea Lillie and Cyril Ritchard Show (also dir.), The Fantastiks (dir. only), The Fred Astaire Special (1963, dir.), Follies in Concert (dir.).

ROSS, KATHARINE: Actress. b. Los Angeles, CA, Jan. 29, 1943. m. actor Sam Elliott. e. Santa Rosa Coll. Joined the San Francisco Workshop, appeared in The Devil's Disciple, The Balcony. TV debut, 1962 in Sam Benedict segment.
TELEVISION: Doctors at Work, World Premiere, The Longest Hundred Miles, Ben Casey, The Bob Hope-Chrysler Theatre, The Virginian, Wagon Train, Kraft Mystery Theatre, the Lieutenant, The Road West, Secrets of a Mother and Daughter. Series: The Colbys.
PICTURES: Shenandoah, Mister Buddwing, The Singing Nun, Games, The Graduate (Acad. Award nom.; voted Most Promising Female Newcomer, Golden Globe Award), Hellfighters, Butch Cassidy and the Sundance Kid, Tell Them Willie Boy is Here, They Only Kill Their Masters, The Stepford Wives, Voyage of the Damned, The Betsy, The Swarm, The Legacy, The Final Countdown, Wrong Is Right, Red-Headed Stranger.

ROSS, KENNETH: Writer. b. London, Sept. 16, 1941. Entered m.p. industry 1970.
TELEVISION: The Roundelay, ATV Network, 1963. The Messenger, CBC Network, 1966.
THEATRE: The Raft, London, 1964. Under The Skin, Glasgow, 1968. Mr. Kilt & The Great I Am, London, 1970.
PICTURES: Screenplays: Brother Sun, Sister Moon, Slag, The Reckless Years (also orig. story). Abelard & Heloise, The Day of the Jackal (nom. for Writers' Guild, SFTA, and Golden Globe Awards), The Devil's Lieutenant, The Odessa File (nom. for Writers' Guild Award), Quest, (orig. story, s.p.), Black Sunday (Edgar Allen Poe Award, Mystery Writers of America, 1977), The Fourth War, Epiphany (orig. s.p.).

ROSS, STEVEN J.: Executive. b. Brooklyn, NY, Sept. 19, 1927. e. Paul Smith's Coll. 1948. Began career working for father-in-law's limousine rental service, expanding co. to include Kinney System parking lots. Merged the two businesses with an office cleaning and maintenance co. 1961 and his father-in-law's funeral parlor business, taking it public in 1962 under name of Kinney Service Corp. 1966 purchased National Cleaning Contractors and then Ashley Famous talent agency and Warner Bros.-Seven Arts in 1969. Pres., dir. Kinney Services Inc. 1966–72; chmn. bd., pres. and chief exec. officer Warner Communications Inc. 1972–present. Bd. dir., NY Convention and Visitors Bureau, NY State Alliance to Save Energy, mem. bd. sports medicine Lenox Hill Hosp.

ROSSELLINI, ISABELLA: Actress. b. Rome, Italy, June 18, 1952. Daughter of Ingrid Bergman and Roberto Rossellini. Came to America 1972. Worked as translator for Italian News Bureau. Taught Italian at New Sch. for Social Research. Worked 3 years on second unit assignments for journalist Gianni Mina and as NY corr. for Ital. TV series, The Other Sunday. Model for Vogue, Harper's Bazaar, Italian Elle.
PICTURES: A Matter of Time (debut 1976 with her mother), The Meadow, Il Papocchio, White Nights, Blue Velvet, Tough Guys Don't Dance, Siesta, Zelly and Me, Cousins, Adriana, Wild of Heart.

ROSSO, LEWIS, T.: Executive. b. Hoboken, NJ, Feb. 3, 1911. Ent. m.p. ind. 1930; prod. & mgt. for Consolidated Film Ind., 1930–44; Republic Prod., 1944–50; prod. mgr. Republic, 1950–55; asst. sec'y and asst. treas. Republic Pictures Corp., 1959;

exec. asst. to exec. prod. mgr., 20th Century-Fox Films, 1960; plant mgr., Samuel Goldwyn Studios, 1961–71; exec. admin. asst. plant mgr., The Burbank Studios, 1972–86.

ROSSOVICH, RICK: Actor. b. CA, August 28, 1957. e. Sacramento State (art history). Studied acting with coach Vincent Chase. After a succession of appearances of episodic TV in a bit part in Korean karate film and as a stand-in, made film debut in Lords of Discipline.
PICTURES: Losin It, Streets of Fire, The Morning After, The Terminator, Warning Signs, Top Gun, Roxanne, Paint It Black, Fast Forward, The Witching Hour, Spellbinder, Cognac.
TELEVISION: MacGruder and Loud (series). Movie: 14 Going On 30.

ROTH, BOBBY: Director.-Writer-Producer.
PICTURES: The Boss' Son; Circle of Power; Independence Day; Baja Oklahoma (dir., co-s.p.); Heartbreakers.
TELEVISION: Episodes of Miami Vice, The Insiders, Crime Story. Movies: Tonight's the Night, The Man Who Fell to Earth, Dead Solid Perfect (dir., co-s.p.), The Man Inside.

ROTH, JOE: Executive, Producer, Director. b. 1948. Began career working as prod. assistant on commercials and feature films in San Francisco. Also ran the lights for improv group Pitchel Players. Moved with them to Los Angeles, and produced their shows incl. the $250,000 film Tunnelvision. In 1987 co-founder independent film prod. co. Morgan Creek Productions. 1989 left to become chairman of newly-formed Fox Film Corp., the theatrical film unit of 20th Century Fox Film Corp. Also named head of News Corp. unit.
PICTURES: Producer: Tunnelvision, Cracking Up, Americathon, Our Winning Season, The Final Terror, The Stone Boy, Where the River Runs Black, Bachelor Party, Off Beat, Streets of Gold (dir. debut), Revenge of the Nerds II (dir.). Exec. prod.: Young Guns, Dead Ringers, Skin Deep, Major League, Renegades, Coupe de Ville (dir.), Enemies: A Love Story.

ROTH, PAUL A.: Executive. b. Asheville, NC, March 28, 1930. e. U. of North Carolina, A.B. political science, 1948–51; George Washington U. Law Sch., 1951–52. U.S. Army 1952–55. Dist. Mgr. Valley Enterprises, Inc. 1955–56. Vice Pres. Roth Enterprises, Inc. 1956–65. Pres. Roth Enterprises, Inc. 1965–present. President NATO of Virginia 1971–73. Chmn. bd. NATO of Virginia, 1973–75. Member National NATO Board, 1971–present. Exec. Comm. NATO of Metro-D.C. 1970–present. Variety Club Tent 11 Board Mem. 1959–65. President National NATO, 1973–75; chmn. National NATO bd. dir. 1975–77. Member Foundation Motion Picture Pioneers, 1973–present. Member & advisory committee, Will Rogers Hospital, 1973–present. Trustee American Film Institute, 1973–75. Pres., Valley Lanes, Inc., 1975–present. Director, Riggs Bank of Maryland, 1984–present. Director, Metro Mortgage Acceptance Corp., 1984–87. Vice-pres., CAPA, Ltd., 1976–present. Pres., Thrasher's Ocean Fries, Inc. 1987–present. Pres. Carolina Cinema Corp., 1980–present.

ROTH, RICHARD A.: Producer. b. Beverly Hills, CA, 1943. e. Stanford U. Law Sch. Worked for L.A. law firm before beginning film career as lawyer and literary agent for Ziegler-Ross Agency. In 1970 left to develop s.p. Summer of '42 with Herman Raucher.
PICTURES: Summer of '42, Our Time, The Adventures of Sherlock Holmes' Smarter Brother, Julia, Outland, In Country (co-prod.).

ROTHMAN, FRANK: Executive. b. Los Angeles, CA, Dec. 24, 1926. e. U. of Southern California, LL.B., 1951. Mem. Calif. Bar. Dept. city atty., Los Angeles, 1951–55; law firm, Wyman, Bautzer, Rothman, Kuchel & Silbert, Los Angeles, 1956–82; chmn. bd., MGM/UA Entertainment Co., 1982–86. Now partner in law firm.

ROTHMAN, THOMAS E: Executive. b. Baltimore, MD, Nov. 21, 1954. m. actress Jessica Harper. e. Brown U., B.A. 1976; Columbia Law Sch., J.D. 1980. Worked as law clerk with Second Circuit Court of Appeals 1981–82 before becoming partner in entertainment law firm, Frankfurt, Garbus, Klien & Selz 1982–87. In 1987 joined Columbia Pictures as exec. v.p. and asst. to pres., named exec. prod. v.p. Left in 1989 to join Samuel Goldwyn Co. as sr. v.p. and head of worldwide production.
PICTURES: Co-prod.: Down By Law, Candy Mountain.

ROTUNNO, GIUSEPPE: Cinematographer. b. Italy. Gained fame as leading cinematographer of Italian films working with Federico Fellini. Also worked for Lina Wertmuller and Luchino Visconti. Later worked in Hollywood.
PICTURES: Scandal in Sorrento, White Nights, Anna of Brooklyn, The Naked Maja, The Angel Wore Red, On the Beach, Rocco and His Brothers, The Best of Enemies, The Leopard, Yesterday, Today and Tomorrow, Anzio, The Secret of Santa Vittoria, Fellini's Roma, Casanova, Amarcord, Satyricon, Sunflower, Carnal Knowledge, Man of La Mancha, The Stranger, The Organizer, Juliet of the Spirits, Fellini's Roma, Amarcord, Casanova, Orchestra Rehearsal, City of Women, Love and Anarchy, All Screwed Up, The Bible, End of the World in Our Usual Bed in a Night Full of Rain, All That Jazz, City of Women, Popeye, Five Days One Summer, Rollover, And the Ship Sails On, American Dreamer, Desire, Nothing Left to Do But Cry, The Assassi, Underground, The Red Sonja, Julia and Julia, Rent-a-Cop, Haunted Summer, The Adventures of Baron Munchausen.
TELEVISION: The Scarlet and the Black.

ROUNDTREE, RICHARD: Actor. b. New Rochelle, NY, July 9, 1942. e. Southern Illinois U. Former model, Ebony Magazine Fashion Fair; joined workshop of Negro Ensemble Company, appeared in Kongi's Harvest, Man, Better Man, Mau Mau Room; played lead role in Philadelphia road company of The Great White Hope before film debut.
PICTURES: Shaft, Shaft's Big Score, Shaft in Africa, Charley One-Eye, Earthquake, Man Friday, Diamonds, Escape to Athena, An Eye for an Eye, The Winged Serpent, Inchon, City Heat, Opposing Force, Maniac Cop, Homer and Eddie, Angel III: The Final Chapter, The Party Line, Getting Even, American Cops, The Banker, Night Visitor, Rock House, Bad Jim, Lost Memories.
TELEVISION: Shaft (series, 1973), Firehouse (movie), Roots, A.D., The Fifth Missile, Outlaws.

ROURKE, MICKEY: Actor. b. Schenectady, NY, 1950. Moved to Miami as a boy. Fought as an amateur boxer 4 years in Miami. Studied acting with Sandra Seacat while working as a nightclub bouncer, a sidewalk pretzel vendor and other odd jobs. Moved to LA, 1978. Debut: TV movie City in Fear (1978).
PICTURES: Fade to Black, 1941, Heaven's Gate, Body Heat, Diner, Rumblefish, Eureka, The Pope of Greenwich Village, 9½ Weeks, Year of the Dragon, Angel Heart, Barfly, A Prayer for the Dying, Homeboy (and orig. story), Francesco, Johnny Handsome, Wild Orchid, The Desperate Hours.
TELEVISION: Rape and Marriage, The Rideout Case, Act of Love.

ROUSSELOT, PHILIPPE: Cinematographer. b. France. Worked as camera assistant to Nestor Almendros on My Night at Maud's, Claire's Knee, Love in the Afternoon.
PICTURES: The Guinea Pig Couple, Adom ou le sang d'Abel, For Clemence, Paradiso, Pauline et l'ordinateur, Peppermint Soda, Cocktail Molotov, A Girl From Lorraine, Diva (Cesar, National Society Film Critics, and Moscow Awards), The Jaws of the Wolf, The Moon in the Gutter, Thieves After Dark, The Emerald Forest, Therese, Hope and Glory, We're No Angels.

ROWAN, DANIELLE: Executive. Began career with Paramount Pictures 1980; asst. to pres. & gen. s.s. mgr. Canadian operations. 1984, transferred to N.Y. as asst. to sr. v.p., dist. 1985, appt. exec. administrator dist./mktg.

ROWE, ROY: Owner-operator, Rowe Amusement Co., Burgaw, NC. b. Burgaw, May 29, 1905. e. U. of North Carolina. Eng. instructor, private bus. coll., 1926–29; Publix Sch. for Mgrs., N.Y., 1930–31; mgr. theatres, Spartanburg, SC; Greensboro & Raleigh, NC; mgr., Warner Theatre, Pittsburgh, PA, 1931–34; city mgr. for Warner Theatres, Washington, PA, 1934–35; opened own theatres in NC 1935; member NC Senate, 1937, 1941, 1945, 1949, 1957, 1965; House of Rep., 1943; Major, Civil Air Patrol, W.W.II; pres. Carolina Aero Club, 1943–44; chmn. NC Aeornautics Comm., 1941–49; dir. Theatre Owners No. & So. Car. 1943–45; pres., Theatre Owners of S.C. & N.C. 1944–45; pres., Assn. of Governing Boards of State Universities, 1964. Owned and operated motel, Carolina Beach, NC, 1965–67., Rowe Insurance Agency, 1967–69. Mem. Exec. Bd., U. of N.C. Trustees, 1969. Principal Clerk, NC Senate 1969–75. Retired. Now watercolor artist and world traveller.

ROWLAND, ROY: Director. b. New York, NY, Dec. 31. e. U. of Southern California, law. Script clerk; asst. dir.; asst. to late W. S. Van Dyke on Tarzan pictures; dir. of shorts, "How to" Benchley series; Crime Does Not Pay series. Pete Smith Specialties.
PICTURES: Think First, Stranger in Town, Lost Angel, Our Vines Have Tender Grapes, Tenth Avenue Angel, Night patrol, Ski Soldier, Boys' Ranch, Romance of Rosy Ridge, Killer McCoy, Scene of the Crime, Outriders, Excuse My Dust, Two Weeks With Love, Bugles in Afternoon, 5000 Fingers of Dr. T. Affair with a Stranger, The Moonlighter, Witness to Murder, Rogue Cop, Many Rivers to Cross, Hit the Deck, Meet Me in Las Vegas, Slander, Somewhere I'll Find Him, Gun Glory, The Seven Hills of Rome, The Girl Hunters, Gunfighters of Casa Grande, They Called Him Gringo, Tiger of the Seven Seas, Thunder Over the Indian Ocean.

ROWLANDS, GENA: Actress. b. Cambria, WI, June 19, 1936. e. U. of Wisconsin. Came to New York to attend American Acad. of Dramatic Arts, where met and married John Cassavetes. Made Bdwy. debut as understudy and then succeeded to role of the Girl in The Seven Year Itch. Launched as star with part in The Middle of the Night, which she played 18 mos. Film debut in The High Cost of Living, 1958.

PICTURES: Lonely Are the Brave, The Spiral Road, A Child Is Waiting, Tony Rome, Faces, Minnie and Moskowitz, A Woman Under the Influence, Two Minute Warning, The Brink's Job, Gloria, Tempest, Love Streams, Light of Day, Another Woman.

TELEVISION: The Philco TV Playhouse, Studio One, Alfred Hitchcock Presents, Dr. Kildare, Bonanza, The Kraft Mystery Theatre, Columbo. Movies: Question of Love, Strangers: The Story of a Mother & Daughter, An Early Frost, The Betty Ford Story, Montana.

ROWLEY, JOHN H.: Executive. b. San Angelo, TX, Oct. 6, 1917. e. U. of Texas, 1935–39. Consultant, United Artists Theatre Circuit, Inc. Southwest Div.; past president, NATO of Texas; past Int'l Chief barker, Variety Clubs Int'l; past pres., TOA; pres., Variety Foundation of Texas.

ROZSA, MIKLOS: Composer. b. April 18, 1907, Budapest, Hungary. e. Leipzig Conservatory. Wrote great number of symphonic and chamber music works. Composed music for many m.p. In 1936, Knight Without Armor, Acad. Awards best music scoring Spellbound 1945; Double Life 1947; Ben-Hur, 1959. Pres., Screen Composers Assn. 1956. Cesar of French Academy for Providence, 1978.

PICTURES: Jungle Book, Thief of Bagdad, Double Idemnity, The Killers, Madame Bovary, The Lost Weekend, Spellbound, Asphalt Jungle, Quo Vadis, Ivanhoe, Julius Caesar, Story of Three Loves, Plymouth Adventure, Young Bess, Knights of the Round Table, A Time to Love and a Time to Die, The World the Flesh and the Devil, Ben Hur, Lust for Life, Something of Value, King of Kings, El Cid, Sodom and Gomorrah, The VIP's, The Power, The Green Berets, The Private Life of Sherlock Holmes, Sinbad's Golden Voyage, Providence, Secret Files of J. Edgar Hoover, Fedora, Last Embrace, Time After Time, Eye of the Needle, Dead Men Don't Wear Plaid.

RUBEN, JOSEPH: Director. b. Briarcliff, NY, 1951. e. U. of Michigan, majoring in theater and film; Brandeis U., B.A. Interest in film began in high sch. Bought a Super-8 camera and filmed his first movie, a teenage love story. First feature, The Sister-in-Law, a low budget feature which he wrote and dir. in 1975.

PICTURES: The Sister-in-Law (also s.p.), The Pom-Pom Girls (also s.p.), Joy Ride (also co-s.p.), Our Winning Season, Dreamscape, The Stepfather, True Believer.

TELEVISION: Breaking Away (pilot).

RUBIN, STANLEY: Producer, Writer. b. New York, NY, Oct. 8, 1917; ed. UCLA, 1933–37. Phi Beta Kappa. Writer—radio, magazines, pictures, 1937–41; U.S. Army Air Force, 1942–45; writer, prod., owner, Your Show Time, Story Theatre TV series; producer, RKO, 20th-Fox, U.I., MGM, Paramount, Rastar.

PICTURES: The Narrow Margin, My Pal Gus, Destination Gobi, River of No Return, Destry, Francis in the Navy, Behind the High Wall, Rawhide Years, The Girl Most Likely, Promise Her Anything, The President's Analyst, Revenge, White Hunter, Black Heart (co-prod.).

TELEVISION: G.E. Theatre, Ghost and Mrs. Muir, Bracken's World, The Man and the City, Executive Suite. Movies: Babe (co-prod.), And Your Name is Jonah, Don't Look Back: The Story of Satchel Page, Escape From Iran: The Canadian Caper (exec. prod.).

RUBINSTEIN, JOHN: Actor, Composer. b. Los Angeles, CA, December 8, 1946. Son of concert pianist Arthur Rubinstein and dancer-writer Aniela Rubinstein. e. UCLA.

THEATER: Pippin (NY debut, 1972); Picture (Mark Taper, LA); Children of a Lesser God (Tony Award, Drama Desk, L.A. Drama Critics Awards, 1980); Fools; The Caine Mutiny Court-Martial, M. Butterfly.

PICTURES: Journey to Shiloh (debut, 1966); Zachariah; In Search of Historic Jesus; The Trouble With Girls; Getting Straight; The Wild Pack; The Car; The Boys From Brazil; Daniel; Someone to Watch Over Me.

TELEVISION: The Virginian (1966); Ironside; Dragnet; Room 222; The Psychiatrist; The Mary Tyler Moore Show; Cannon; The Mod Squad, Nichols; Hawaii Five-O; Barnaby Jones; Policewoman; Barbary Coast; The Rookies; The Streets of San Francisco; Harry O; Vegas; The Class of '65; Movin' On; Stop the Presses; Wonder Woman; Lou Grant; Fantasy Island; The Quest; Quincy; Trapper John M.D. Movies: The Marriage Proposal; God Bless the Children; A Howling in the Woods; Something Evil; All Together Now; The Gift of the Maji; Roots: The Next Generations; Just Make Me an Offer; The French Atlantic Affair; Corey: For the People; Happily Ever After; Moviola; Skokie; The Mr. and Ms. Mysteries; Killjoy; Freedom to Speak; Someone's Killing the High Fashion Models; I Take These Men; M.A.D.D.: Mothers Against Drunk Driving; Liberace.

SCORES: FILMS: Paddy; Jeremiah Johnson; The Candidate; Kid Blue; The Killer Inside Me. TELEVISION: All Together Now; Emily, Emily; Stalk the Wild Child; Champions: A Love Story; To Race the Wind; The Ordeal of Patty Hearst; Amber Waves; Johnny Belinda; Secrets of a Mother and Daughter; Choices of the Heart; The Dollmaker; Family; The Fitzpatricks; The Mackenzies of Paradise Cove; The New Land: For Heaven's Sake; The Lazarus Syndrome.

RUBINSTEIN, RICHARD P.: Producer, Executive. b. New York, NY, June 15, 1947. e. American U. B.S. 1969, Columbia U. MBA 1971, Pres. Laurel Entertainment, Inc.

PICTURES: Martin (1977); Dawn Of The Dead; Knightriders; Creepshow; Day Of The Dead; Creepshow 2; Pet Sematary.

TELEVISION: exec. prod.: Series: Tales From the Darkside, Monsters.

RUDDY, ALBERT S.: Producer. b. Montreal, Canada, March 28, 1934. e. U. of Southern California, B.S. in design, Sch. of Architecture, 1956.

PICTURES: The Wild Seed (Pennebaker); prod., Little Fauss & Big Halsey; Making It; prod. The Godfather, 1974; The Longest Yard, Coonskin; Matilda; The Cannonball Run; Megaforce; Lassiter, Cannonball Run II, Farewell to the King, Paramedics, Speed Zone, Impulse.

RUDIE, EVELYN: Actress, Singer, Songwriter. r.n. Evelyn Rudie Bernauer, b. Hollywood, Calif. March 28. e. Hollywood H.S., U.C.L.A. At 19, after childstar career in TV and films, stage debut at Gallery Theatre in Hollywood as songwriter, musical dir., choreographer and star performer: Ostrogoths and King of the Schnorrers. Currently producer, artistic dir., Santa Monica Playhouse; founder of own repertoire co., among major productions: Author! Author!, Attorney at Love, Dreamplay, The Alchemist, The Fools, Red, Dear Gabby. Screen debut as child performer Daddy Longlegs. Received Emmy Nomination for first TV leading role, Eloise, Playhouse 90, 1956. Star in Hollywood's Walk of Fame.

PICTURES: The Wings of Eagles, Gift of Love, Bye Bye Birdie. Filmdom's Famous Fives critics award, 1958.

TV: Hostess with the Mostess, Playhouse 90, Dinah Shore, Red Skelton Show, George Gobel Show, Omnibus, Matinee Theatre, Hitchcock presents, Gale Storm Show, Jack Paar, Wagon Train, G.E. Theatre, 77 Sunset Strip, etc.

RUDIN, SCOTT: Executive. b. New York, NY, July 14, 1958. Began career as prod. asst. on Bdwy. for producers Kermit Bloomgarden, Robert Whitehead; then casting director. 1984, became producer for 20th Century Fox; named exec. v.p. prod.; 1986, appt. pres. prod., 20th-Fox. Resigned 1987.

TELEVISION: Little Gloria...Happy at Last (exec. prod.).

RUDOLPH, ALAN: Director, Writer. b. Los Angeles, CA, Dec., 1943. Son of Oscar Rudolph, TV director of '50s and '60s. Made his screen debut in his father's The Rocket Man (1954). Began in industry doing odd jobs in Hollywood studios. In 1969 accepted for Directors Guild assistant director's training program. Worked with Robert Altman on California Split and The Long Goodbye (asst. dir.) and co-writer on Buffalo Bill and the Indians.

PICTURES: Welcome to L.A. (debut as dir.), Remember My Name, Roadie, Endangered Species, Return Engagement, Songwriter, Choose Me, Trouble in Mind, Made in Heaven, The Moderns (dir., co-s.p.), Love at Large.

RUEHL, MERCEDES: Actress. b. Queens, NY. Raised in Silver Spring, MD. e. College of New Rochelle, B.A. English lit. Worked for years in regional theater, mostly in classics.

THEATER: Bdwy: I'm Not Rappaport; Off-Bdwy: American Notes, The Marriage of Bette and Boo (Obie Award), Coming of Age in Soho, Other People's Money.

PICTURES: The Warriors, Radio Days, Heartburn, The Secret of My Success, 84 Charing Cross Road, Big, Married to the Mob, Slaves of New York, Crazy People.

TELEVISION: Late Bloomer (pilot); Guest: Our Family Honor.

RUGOLO, PETE: Composer, Arranger. b. Sicily, Italy, Dec. 25, 1915. To U.S., 1919. e. San Francisco State Coll., Mills Coll., Oakland. Armed Forces, 1942–46; pianist, arr. for many orch. including Stan Kenton; m.p. and TV.

PICTURES: The Strip, Skirts Ahoy, Glory Alley, Latin Lovers, Easy to Love, Jack the Ripper, Foxtrot, Buddy, Buddy; Chu Chu and the Philly Falsh.

TELEVISION: Richard Diamond, The Thin Man, Thriller, more than 25 movies.

RULE, ELTON H.: Executive. b. Stockton, CA, 1917. e. Sacramento Coll. With Amer. Bdg. Cos., Inc., since 1952; gen. sls. mgr., KABC-TV, 1953–60; gen. mgr., 1961–68; pres., ABC TV Network 1968–70; group v.p. Am. Bdg. Cos. Inc., 1969–72; pres., ABC div. 1970–72; pres., chief operating officer, mem. exec. comm., Amer. Bdg. Cos., 1972–83; vice chmn., Amer. Bdg. Cos., Inc. & member exec. comm., 1983–84. Formed Rule/Starger Productions with Martin Starger. First pres. of reorganized Acad. of TV Arts & Sciences Foundation, 1989. Chmn. RP Cos.

RULE, JANICE: Actress. b. Cincinnati, OH, Aug. 15, 1931. e. Wheaton & Glenbard H.S., Glen Ellyn, IL. Dancer 4 yrs. in Chicago & New York nightclubs; stage experience in It's Great To Be Alive, as understudy of Bambi Lynn; in chorus of Miss Liberty; Broadway stage debut Picnic, 1953. Star of The Happiest Girl in the World. Screen debut, Goodbye My Fancy (1951).
PICTURES: Starlift, Holiday for Sinners, Rogue's March, Woman's Devotion, Gun for a Coward, Subterraneans, Invitation to a Gunfighter, The Chase, Welcome to Hard Times, The Ambushers, Kid Blue, 3 Women, Missing, The Swimmer, Rainy Day Friends.

RUSH, BARBARA: Actress. b. Denver, CO, Jan. 4. e. U. of California. First stage appearance at age of ten, Loberto Theatre, Santa Barbara, CA, in fantasy, Golden Ball; won acting award in coll. for characterization of Birdie (The Little Foxes); scholarship, Pasadena Playhouse Theatre Arts Coll.
STAGE: A Woman of Independent Means, 40 Carats, Same Time Next Year, Steel Magnolias.
PICTURES: The First Legion, Quebec, Molly, When Worlds Collide, Flaming Feather, Prince of Pirates, It Came From Outer Space, Taza Son of Cochise, Magnificent Obsession, Black Shield of Falworth, Captain Lightfoot, Kiss of Fire, World in My Corner, Bigger Than Life, Oh Men! Oh Women!, Harry Black and the Tiger, The Young Philadelphians, Bramble Bush, Strangers When We Meet, Come Blow Your Horn, Robin and the Seven Hoods, Hombre, Airport, The Man, Superdad, Can't Stop the Music, Summer Lovers.
TELEVISION: Flamingo Road, The Seekers, Suddenly Single, Eyes of Charles, Sand.

RUSH, HERMAN: Executive. b. Philadelphia, PA, June 20, 1929. e. Temple U., Headed Flamingo Telefilms, Inc. 1957–60; 1960–71, pres., television div. of Creative Mgt. Assoc. Pres., Herman Rush Assoc. Inc., 1971–77. In 1977–78 chmn bd., Rush-Flaherty Agency, Inc. In 1970 headed Marble Arch TV. In 1980 named pres., Columbia TV; 1984, named pres. of newly formed Columbia Pictures TV Group. In 1986, named chmn. of newly formed Coca-Cola Telecommunications, Inc. In 1988, chairman, Rush Entertainment Group.

RUSH, RICHARD: Director, Producer, Writer. b. New York, NY, 1930.
PICTURES: Director: Too Soon To Love (also prod., s.p.), Of Love and Desire (also prod., s.p.); A Man Called Dagger, Fickle Finger of Fate, Thunder Alley, Hell's Angels on Wheels, Psych-Out (also s.p.), Savage Seven, Getting Straight (also prod.), dir. prod. Freebie and the Bean (also prod.), The Stunt Man (also prod., s.p.; Acad. Award nom. for best dir., s.p.), Air America (s.p.).

RUSSELL, CHUCK: Director. Asst. dir. and line prod. on many low-budget films for Roger Corman and Sunn Classics, including Death Race 2000.
PICTURES: Dreamscape (co-s.p., line prod.); Back to School (prod.); Nightmare on Elm Street III (dir., co-s.p.); The Blob (dir., co-s.p.).

RUSSELL, JANE: Actress. b. Bemidji, MN, June 21, 1921. e. Max Reinhardt's Theatrical Workshop & Mme. Ouspenskaya. Photographer's model; m.p. debut in Outlaw, 1943.
PICTURES: Young Widow, Paleface, Montana Belle, His Kind of Woman, Double Dynamite, Macao, Son of Paleface, Las Vegas Story, Gentlemen Prefer Blondes, French Line, Underwater, Gentlemen Marry Brunettes, Foxfire, Tall Men, Hot Blood, Revolt of Mamie Stover, Fuzzy Pink Nightgown, Darker Than Amber, Born Losers, Fate Is The Hunter, Waco.
TELEVISION: Yellow Rose (series).

RUSSELL, JOHN: Actor. b. Los Angeles, CA, Jan. 3, 1921. e. U. of California. Served in U.S. Marine Corps. 1942–44, as 2nd Lt. m.p. debut in Frame-Up.
PICTURES: Story of Molly X, Gal Who Took the West, Slattery's Hurricane, Yellow Sky, Sitting Pretty, Forever Amber, Somewhere in the Night, Within These Walls, Don Juan Quilligan, Bell for Adano, Barefoot Mailman, Man in the Saddle, Hoodlum Empire, Oklahoma Annie, Fair Wind to Java, Sun Shines Bright, Jubilee Trail, Hell's Outpost, Last Command, Rio Bravo, Yellowstone Kelly, Fort Utah, Honky Tonk Man, Pale Rider, Under the Gun.
TELEVISION: Lawman (series), Alias Smith and Jones, Soldiers of Fortune.

RUSSELL, KEN: Director. b. Southampton, England, 1927. e. Walthamstow Art Sch. Early career as dancer, actor, stills photographer, TV documentary film-maker. Ent. TV ind. 1959. Made 33 documentaries for BBC-TV. Also made numerous pop videos.
PICTURES: Prokofiev, Elgar, Bartok, The Debussy films, Isadora Duncan, Song of Summer—Delius, Dance of the Seven Veils, French Dressing, Billion Dollar Brain, Women in Love, The Music Lovers, The Devils, The Boy Friend, Savage Messiah, Mahler, Tommy, Lisztomania, Valentino, Altered States, Crimes of Passion, Gothic, Aria (sequence), Salome's Last Dance (dir., s.p., actor), The Lair of the White Worm (prod., dir., s.p.), The Rainbow (prod., dir., co-s.p.).

RUSSELL, KURT: Actor. b. Springfield, MA, March 17, 1951. Son of former baseball player turned actor Bing Russell (deputy sheriff on Bonanza). At 12 got lead in The Travels of Jamie McPheeters (1963–64). Starred as child in many Disney shows and films. Professional baseball player 1971–73. Host, Kurt Russell Celebrity Shoot Out, 4-day hunting tournament.
PICTURES: The Absent-Minded Professor, Follow Me Boys, The Horse in the Grey Flannel Suit, Charley and the Angel, Superdad, Used Cars, Escape from New York, The Fox and The Hound (voice only), The Thing, Silkwood, Swing Shift, The Mean Season, The Best of Times, Big Trouble in Little China, Overboard, Tequila Sunrise, Winter People, Tango and Cash.
TELEVISION: Series: Travels of Jamie McPheeters, The New Land, The Quest. Movies: The Deadly Tower, Elvis, Amber Waves, Search for the Gods.

RUSSELL, THERESA: Actress. r.n. Theresa Paup. b. San Diego, CA, 1957. m. dir.-cinematographer Nicolas Roeg. e. Burbank H.S. Began modeling career at 12. Studied at Actors' Studio in Hollywood. Professional film debut in The Last Tycoon, 1977.
PICTURES: Straight Time, Bad Timing/A Sensual Obsession, Eureka, The Razor's Edge, Insignificance, Black Widow, Aria, Track 29, Physical Evidence, Impulse. Cold Heaven.
TELEVISION: Blind Ambition (mini-series).

RUTHERFORD, ANN: Actress. b. Toronto, Canada, 1924. Trained by mother (cousin of Richard Mansfield); with parents in stock as child; later on Los Angeles radio programs. Screen debut, 1935.
PICTURES: Gone With the Wind, Laramie Trail, Happy Land, Bermuda Mystery, Two O'Clock Courage, Bedside Manner, The Madonna's Secret, Murder in the Music Hall, Secret Life of Walter Mitty, Operation Haylift, Adventures of Don Juan, They Only Kill Their Masters.

RYAN, ARTHUR N.: Executive. Joined Paramount in N.Y. in 1967 as asst. treas; later made dir. of admin. and business affairs, exec. asst. to Robert Evans and asst. scty. In 1970 appt. v.p.-prod. adm. In 1975 named sr. v.p. handling all prod. operations for Paramount's m.p. and TV divisions. Named asst. to the chmn. & CEO 1976; chmn. & pres. Magicam, Inc.; chmn. Fortune General Corp.; chmn. Paramount Communications; co-chmn. of scholarship comm. of Academy of Motion Picture Arts and Sciences; trustee of Univ. Film Study Center in Boston. Joined Technicolor in August 1976 as pres., chief operating officer and director; vice chmn., 1983–85; chmn. & CEO, 1985 to date. Chmn. Technicolor Audio-Visual Systems International, Inc.; dir. Technicolor S.P.A.; dir. Technicolor, Film Intl.; and chmn. of exec. committee, Technicolor Graphics Services, Inc.; dir., Technicolor, Inc.; chmn., Technicolor Fotografica, S.A.; Chmn. Technicolor Film Intl. Service Company, Inc.; director and Deputy Chairman Technicolor Limited; chmn. & dir., The Vidtronics Company, Inc.; chmn. & CEO, Compact Video, Inc., 1984 to date; dir, Four Star Int'l., 1983 to date; dir., MacAndrews & Forbes, Inc. 1985 to date; Permanent charities committee of the Entertainment Industry; Hollywood Canteen Foundations. Vice-chmn. & dir., Calif. Inst. of Arts. Trustee: Motion Picture & Television Fund. In 1985 named chmn., Technicolor.

RYAN, MEG: Actress. b. Fairfield, CT, 1962. e. NYU. Supported herself while studying journalism by making commercials. Prof. debut on As the World Turns, 1983–85.
PICTURES: Rich and Famous (debut, 1981), Amityville 3-D, Top Gun, Armed and Dangerous, Innerspace, D.O.A., Promised Land, The Presidio, When Harry Met Sally, Joe Versus the Volcano.
TELEVISION: Wild Side (series).

RYAN, MITCHELL: Actor. b. Louisville, KY, Jan. 11, 1928. Entered acting following service in Navy during Korean War. Was New York stage actor working off-Bdwy. for Ted Mann and Joseph Papp; on Bdwy. in Wait Until Dark. Member of Arena Stage group in Washington.
PICTURES: Monte Walsh, The Hunting Party, My Old Man's Place, High Plains Drifter, The Friends of Eddie Coyle, ElectraGlide in Blue, Magnum Force, Labyrinth, Winter People.
TELEVISION: Series: Chase, Executive Suite, Having Babies, The Chisholms, Dark Shadows, High Performance, King Crossings; Movies: Angel City, The Five of Me, Death of a Centerfold—The Dorothy Stratten Story; Uncommon Valor; Medea, Kenny Rogers as the Gambler—The Adventure Continues, Robert Kennedy & His Times, Fatal Vision, Favorite Son, The Ryan White Story, Margaret Bourke-White.

RYDELL, MARK: Producer, Director, Actor. b. March 23, 1934. e. Juilliard Sch. of Music. Studied acting with Sanford Meisner of N.Y. Neighborhood Playhouse. Became member of Actors Studio. Was leading actor for six years on daytime CBS serial, As The World Turns. Made Broadway debut in

Seagulls over Sorrento and film bow in Crime in the Streets. Went to Hollywood as TV director (Ben Casey, I Spy, Gunsmoke, etc.). Theatrical feature debut: The Fox (1968). Partner with Sydney Pollack in Sanford Prods., film, TV prod. co.

PICTURES: Director: The Fox, The Reivers, The Cowboys (also prod.), Cinderella Liberty (also prod.), Harry and Walter Go To New York, The Rose, On Golden Pond, The River. Actor: The Long Goodbye, Punchline.

RYDER, WINONA: Actress. b. Winona, MN, 1971. Grew up in San Francisco. At 7, moved with family to Northern CA commune. At 13 discovered by talent scout during a performance at San Francisco's American Conservatory theatre where she was studying and given screen test.

PICTURES: Lucas, Square Dance, Beetlejuice, 1969, Heathers, Great Balls of Fire, Mermaid, Welcome Home, Roxy Carmichael.

S

SACKHEIM, WILLIAM B.: Producer, Writer. b. Gloversville, NY, Oct. 31, 1919. e. UCLA. Sr. v.p., Rastar Films. Joined Universal TV 1981 as creative consultant.

PICTURES: Smart Girls Don't Talk, One Last Fling, A Yank in Korea, Paula, Reunion in Reno, The Human Jungle, Border River, Chicago Syndicate, Art of Love, The In-Laws (co-prod.), The Competition, First Blood (co-s.p.), The Survivors (prod.), No Small Affair (prod.), The Hard Way (prod.).

TELEVISION: Gideon Oliver (series, exec. prod.), Almost Grown (exec. prod.).

SACKS, SAMUEL: Attorney, Agent. b. New York, NY, March 29, 1908. e. City Coll. of New York, St. John's Law Sch., LL.B., 1930. Admitted Calif. Bar, 1943; priv. prac., law, N.Y. 1931–42; attorney, William Morris Agency, Inc., Sept. 1942; head of west coast TV business affairs, 1948–75. bd. of dir., Alliance of Television Film Producers, 1956–60. L.A. Copyright Society Treasurer, Beverly Hills Bar Assn., Los Angeles Bar Assn., American Bar Assn.; Academy of TV Arts & Sciences; Hollywood Radio & TV Society. Pres. Adat Shalom Synagogue, 1967–69, chmn. of bd., 1969–71; pres., American Field Service West L.A. Chapter 1970–72, United Synagogue of America (Pacific Southwest region), v.p., 1974–88. Counsel, entertainment field, Simon & Sheridan, 1975–89, Los Angeles Citizens' Olympic Committee. Arbitrator for Screen Actors Guild, Assn. of Talent Agents and American Arbitration Assn. Chmn. Task Force Project Caring; board of dir., Jewish Family Service of L.A.; exec. comm., Congregational Cabinet University of Judaism, 1975 to date.

SAFER, MORLEY: News Correspondent. b. Toronto, Ont., 1931. e. U. of Western Ontario. Started as corresp. and prod. with Canadian Broadcasting Corp. Joined CBS News London Bureau 1964, chief of Saigon Bureau, 1965. Chief of CBS London bureau 1967–70. Joined 60 Minutes as co-editor in Dec., 1970.

SAFFLE, M. W. "BUD": Executive. b. Spokane, WA, June 29, 1923. e. U. of Washington. In service 1943–46. Started in m.p. business as booker, 1948. Entire career with Saffle Theatre Service as buyer-booker; named pres. in 1970. Also pres. of Grays Harbor Theatres, Inc., operating theatres in Aberdeen, WA. Also operates drive-in in Centralia, WA. On bd. of NATO of WA for 15 yrs; pres. of same for 2 terms and secty.-treas. 6 yrs. Elected to National NATO bd. in 1972. Founder of Variety Tent 46, serving as chief barker three times.

SAFIR, SIDNEY: Executive. b. Vienna, Austria, Feb. 2, 1923. e. London U. Ent. m.p. ind. 1940, Shipman & King Cinemas; RKO Radio Picture, 1941; salesman, British Lion, 1943; European sls. mgr., Lion Int'l, 1958; gen. sls. mgr. Lion Int'l, 1960; president, Lion Int'l Inc., 1965; man. dir. Lion Int'l Ltd. 1969; dir., British Lions Film Ltd., 1972. Formed Safir Films Ltd. with his son Lawrence, 1977.

SAGANSKY, JEFF: Executive. b. 1953. Joined CBS 1976 in bdcst. finance; 1977, NBC, assoc. in pgm. development.; 1977, mgr. film pgms.; 1978, dir. dramatic dev.; 1978, v.p., dev. David Gerber Co.; 1981, returned to NBC as series dev. v.p.; 1983, sr. v.p. series programming; 1985, joined Tri-Star Pictures as pres. of production; 1989 promoted to president of Tri-Star.

SAINT, EVA MARIE: Actress. b. Newark, NJ, July 4, 1924. e. Bowling Green State U., Ohio. Radio, TV actress; on Broadway in Trip to Bountiful; m.p. debut in On the Waterfront (Acad. Award, best supporting actress, 1954).

PICTURES: That Certain Feeling, Raintree County, Hatful of Rain, North by Northwest, Exodus, All Fall Down, Grand Prix, The Stalking Moon, Loving, Cancel My Reservation, Nothing in Common.

TELEVISION: Movies: Fatal Vision, The Last Days of Patton, A Year in the Life, Norman Rockwell's Breaking Ties, I'll Be Home for Christmas. Series: How the West Was Won, One Man's Family, Moonlighting.

ST. JACQUES, RAYMOND: Actor, Director. r.n. James Johnson. b. 1930. e. student, Yale U. Began career as actor, asst. dir. and fencing dir. for American Shakespeare Festival, Stratford, CT. Made prof. acting debut in off-Bdwy. play, High Name Today. Made m.p. debut, Black Like Me, 1964.

STAGE: The Blacks, Night Life, The Cool World, Seventh Heaven.

PICTURES: The Pawnbroker, The Comedians, The Heart is a Lonely Hunter, Mr. Moses, Madigan, Mister Buddwing, The Green Berets, Uptight, If He Hollers Let Him Go, Change of Mind, Cotton Comes to Harlem, Cool Breeze, Come Back Charleston Blue, Book of Numbers (also dir. debut), Lost in the Stars, Eyes of Laura Mars, The Evil That Men Do, The Wild Pair, They Live, Glory, Strange Turf.

TELEVISION: Dark Mansions, Roots, Sophisticated Gents, Search for the Gods. Series: Superior Court.

SAINT JAMES, SUSAN: Actress. b. Los Angeles, CA, Aug. 14, 1946. r.n. Susan Miller. e. Connecticut Coll. for Women. Was model for six years; then signed to contract by Universal Pictures.

TELEVISION: Series: The Name of the Game, McMillan & Wife, Kate and Allie. Movies: SOS Titanic, I Take These Men, Fame is the Name of the Game, Sex and the Single Parent, Night Cries. Specials: A Very Special Christmas Party.

PICTURES: What's So Bad About Feeling Good?, Jigsaw, P.J., Where Angels Go . . . Trouble Follows, Magic Carpet, Outlaw Blues, Love at First Bite, How to Beat the High Cost of Living, Carbon Copy.

ST. JOHN, JILL: Actress. r.n. Jill Oppenheim. b. Los Angeles, CA, Aug. 19, 1940. On radio series One Man's family. Television debut, A Christmas Carol, 1948. Theatrical film debut, Summer Love, 1957.

PICTURES: The Remarkable Mr. Pennypacker, Holiday for Lovers, The Roman Spring of Mrs. Stone, Tender Is the Night, Come Blow Your Horn, Who's Been Sleeping in My Bed?, Honeymoon Hotel, The Oscar, Banning, Tony Rome, Diamonds Are Forever.

TELEVISION: Fame Is the Name of the Game, Dupont Theatre, Fireside Theatre, Emerald Point NAS (series), Hart to Hart, Brenda Starr, Spy Killer, Telethon, Rooster, Around the World in 80 Days.

ST. JOHNS, RICHARD R.: Executive Producer. b. Los Angeles, CA, Jan. 20, 1929. Son of journalist Adela Rogers St. Johns. e. Stanford U., B.A., 1953; Stanford Law Sch., J.D., 1954. Joined law firm O'Melveny & Meyers 1954, specializing in entertainment law. 1963 became partner in law firm. 1968 became sr. v.p., Filmways, Inc., becoming president and chief operating office in 1969. 1972, formed Richard R. St. Johns and Associates, independent management and packaging firm. Formed Guinness Film Group in 1975, branching out into full-scale motion picture prod.

PICTURES: (exec. prod.): The Uncanny, Death Hunt, Matilda, The Silent Flute (Circle of Iron), Nightwing, The Wanderers, The Mountain Men, The Final Countdown, A Change of Seasons, Dead & Buried, Death Hunt, American Pop and Venom, Fire and Ice.

SAJAK, PAT: TV Host. b. Chicago, IL, 1946. e. Columbia Coll., Chicago. Broadcasting career began as newscaster for Chicago radio station. 1968 drafted into Army, where served 4 years as disc jockey for Armed Forces Radio in Saigon, Vietnam. Moved to Nashville, where continued radio career while also working as weatherman and host of public affairs prog. for local TV station. 1977 moved to LA to become nightly weatherman on KNBC. Took over as host of daytime edition of Wheel of Fortune and later the syndicated nighttime edition (4 Emmy nom.). 1989, The Pat Sajak Show.

PICTURE: Airplane II: The Sequel.

TELEVISION: Host: The Thanksgiving Day Parade, The Rose Parade.

SAKS, GENE: Director, Actor. b. New York, NY, Nov. 8, 1921. e. Cornell U. Attended dramatic workshop, New School for Social Research. Active in off-Broadway in 1948–49, forming cooperative theatre group at Cherry Lane Theatre. Joined Actor's Studio, followed by touring and stock. Also appeared in live TV dramas (Philco Playhouse, Producer's Showcase). Directed many Broadway plays before turning to film direction with Barefoot in the Park (1967).

BROADWAY: Director: Enter Laughing, Nobody Loves an Albatross, Generation, Half a Sixpence, Mame, A Mother's Kisses, Sheep on the Runway, How the Other Half Loves, Same Time Next Year, California Suite, I Love My Wife, Brighton Beach Memoirs, Biloxi Blues, The Odd Couple (1985), Broadway Bound, Rumors. Actor: Middle of the Night, Howie, The Tenth Man, A Shot in the Dark, A Thousand Clowns.

PICTURES: Director: Barefoot in the Park, The Odd Couple, Last of the Red Hot Lovers, Mame, Cactus Flower. Actor: A Thousand Clowns, Prisoner of Second Avenue, The

One and Only, Lovesick, The Goodbye People, Brighton Beach Memoirs.

SALANT, RICHARD S.: Executive. b. New York, NY, Apr. 14, 1914. e. Harvard Coll. A.B., 1931–35; Harvard Law Sch., 1935–38. Atty. Gen.'s Com. on Admin. Procedure, 1939–41; Office of Solicitor Gen., U.S. Dept. of Justice, 1941–43; U.S. Naval Res., 1943–46; assoc., Roseman, Goldmark, Colin & Kave, 1946–48; then partner, 1948–51; pres. CBS news div., 1961–64; v.p. special asst. to pres. CBS, Inc., 1951–61, 1964–66; pres., CBS news div., 1966; mem. bd. of dir., CBS, Inc. 1964–69; vice chmn., NBC bd., 1979–81; sr. adviser, 1981–83; pres. CEO, National News Council, 1983–84. Retired.

SALE, RICHARD: Writer, Director. b. New York, NY, Dec. 17, 1911. e. Washington & Lee, 1934. m. Irma Foster, designer. Author novels, over 400 published stories; honor roll Best Short Stories, 1935; ent. m.p. ind. with Paramount, 1944; member: WGAW, DGA: Acad. of M.P. Arts & Sciences, Authors League of Amer., BMI: pres. Voyager Films, Inc.; v.p. Libra Productions, Inc.
PICTURES: Strange Cargo, Rendezvous with Annie, Spoilers of the North, Campus Honeymoon, Lady at Midnight, Calendar Girl, Inside Story, Dude Goes West, Mother Is a Freshman, Father Was a Fullback, When Willie Comes Marching Home, Mr. Belvedere goes to College, Ticket to Tomahawk, I'll Get By, Driftwood, Meet Me After the Show, Half Angel, Let's Make It Legal, Girl Next Door, My Wife's Best Friend, Let's Do It Again, Torpedo Run, French Line, Suddenly, Women's World, Gentlemen Marry Brunettes, Abandon Ship, The Oscar, The White Buffalo, Assassination.

SALETRI, FRANK R.: Producer, Director, Writer. b. Chicago, IL, Jan. 20, 1928. Is criminal trial lawyer, member of Calif. bar. Heads FRSCO Prods., Ltd., m.p. prod.
PICTURES: Black Frankenstein—Blackenstein (s.p., prod.); Black the Ripper (s.p., dir.); The Return of the Ghost of the Son of the Bride of the House of Frankenstein, 1984 (s.p., dir.), The Skid Row Slasher, s.p., dir; The Secret of the Maltese Falcon, s.p., dir; Annually prod., s.p. & dir. for The Academy of Science Fiction, Horror and Fantasy Films. Annually prod., s.p. & dir. for The Annual Count Dracula Society Ann Radcliffe' Awards. (Both are documentaries).

SALKIND, ALEXANDER: Producer. b. Danzig/Gdansk, of Russian extraction. Grew up in Berlin where father, Miguel, produced films. Went to Cuba with father to assist him in film production. First solo venture a Buster Keaton comedy, 1945. Returned to Europe where made many pictures in Spain, Italy, France and Hungary.
PICTURES: Austerlitz, The Trial, The Light at the Edge of the World (exec. prod.), Kill! Kill! Kill! (with Ilya Salkind), Bluebeard, *Exec. prod.:* The Three Musketeers, The Four Musketeers, The Prince and the Pauper, Superman, Supergirl, Santa Claus: The Movie.

SALKIND, ILYA: Producer. b. Mexico City, 1948. e. U. of London. Grew up in many countries where father, Alexander, produced films. First film job as production runner on The Life of Cervantes for father. Was assoc. prod. on Light at the Edge of the World.
PICTURES: The Three Musketeers, The Four Musketeers, Superman, Superman II (exec. prod.); Supergirl (exec. prod.); Superman III (exec. prod.).
TELEVISION: Superboy (exec. prod.).

SALKOW, SIDNEY: Director, Writer. b. New York, NY, June 16, 1911. e. City Coll. of New York, B.A.; Harvard Law Sch. Stage dir. & prod. asst. number N.Y. dram. prods. (Dir. Bloodstream, Black Tower, etc.) and mgr. summer theatre. From 1933 variously dialogue dir., assoc. dir., writer & dir. numerous pictures Paramount, Universal, Republic, Columbia, etc.; dir. number of pictures in Lone Wolf series (for Columbia), Tillie the Toiler, Flight Lieutenant, etc. In armed service, W.W.II.
PICTURES: Millie's Daughter, Bulldog Drummond at Bay, Admiral Was a Lady, Fugitive Lady, Golden Hawk, Scarlet Angel, Pathfinder, Prince of Pirates, Jack McCall Desperado, Raiders of the 7 Seas, Sitting Bull, Robbers' Roost, Shadow of the Eagle, Las Vegas Shakedown, Toughest Man Alive, Chicago Confidential, Iron Sheriff, Great Sioux Massacre, Martin Eden.
TELEVISION: Created, prod. dir., This is Alice series for Desilu, Lassie, Fury, Wells Fargo series. Headed prod. for FF Prod. in Rome, 1967–71.

SALMI, ALBERT: Actor. b. Coney Island, NY, 1928. After serving in W.W.II, studied 1948–54 with Dramatic Workshop, American Theatre Wing, Actors Studio. Appeared in many off-Bdwy. plays and live TV prods. Bdwy. in Bus Stop, The Rainmaker and The Brothers Karamazov. Has appeared in over 20 feature films and over 200 TV shows.
PICTURES: The Lawman, Something Big, The Deserter, The Crazy World of Jules Vrooder, Empire of the Ants, Dragonslayer, Love Child, Hard to Hold, Breaking In, The Legend of Earl Durand.
TELEVISION: Gunsmoke, Barnaby Jones. Pilot: B Men. Movies: Dress Gray, Fatal Vision, Best Kept Secrets, Once an Eagle, 79 Park Avenue, Night Games, Jesse.

SALTER, HANS J.: Composer, Conductor. b. Vienna, Jan. 14, 1896. e. U. Acad. of Music, Vienna, Austria. Mus. dir.: Volksopera, Vienna; State Oper. Berlin; Metropole Theatre, Berlin; comp., cond., UFA, Berlin, 1929–33; European br., Universal, 1934–36; to U.S., Univ. 1938–47, 1950–52, wrote over 150 scores.
PICTURES: It Started With Eve, His Butler's Sister, Scarlet Street, Magnificent Doll, The Spoilers, Frenchie, Flesh and Fury, Golden Horde, The Sign of the Ram, Frightened City, Ghost of Frankenstein, Black Friday, House of Frankenstein, The Wolfman, Hold That Ghost, The Invisible Man Returns, the Mummy's Hand, Man-Eater of Kumaon, This Island Earth, Tomahawk, The Battle of Apache Pass, Please Believe Me, Apache Drums, Untamed Frontier, Lover Come Back, Thunder on the Hill, Bend of the River, Against All Flags, Black Shield of Falworth, Sign of the Pagan, Far Horizons, Man Without a Star, Wichita, Autumn Leaves, Red Sundown, Hold Back the Night, Rawhide Years, The Oklahoman, Three Brave Men, Pay the Devil, Law of the Trigger, Female Animal, Raw Wind in Eden, The Wild and the Innocent, Bat Masterson Story, Man in the Net, Come September, Follow That Dream, If a Man Answers, Bedtime Story, The Warlord, Beau Geste, Return of the Gunfighter.
TELEVISION: Wichita Town, Laramie, The Law and Mr. Jones, The Virginian, Wagon Train, Lost in Space, Maya.

SALTZMAN, HARRY: Producer. Lowndes Productions, Ltd. b. October, 1915. St. John, N.B., Canada. Ent. film ind. 1945. Chmn. bd., H.M. Tenment, Ltd., London.
PICTURES: The Iron Petticoat, Look Back in Anger, The Entertainer, Saturday Night, Sunday Morning, Ipcress File, Funeral in Berlin, Billion Dollar Brain, Battle of Britain, Nijinsky (exec. prod.). Also co-producer of 10 James Bond films.

SALZBURG, JOSEPH S.: Producer, Editor. b. New York, NY, July 27, 1917. Film librarian, then rose to v.p. in chg. of prod., Pictorial Films, 1935–42; civilian chief film ed. U.S. Army Signal Corps Photo Center, 1942–44; U.S. Army Air Forces, 1944–46; prod. mgr., Pictorial Films, 1946–50; prod. mgr. Associated Artists Prod., then M.P. for TV, 1950–51; org. m.p. prod. & edit. service for theatrical, non-theatrical & TV films 1951–56; prod. mgr., dir. of films oper., official Films. Oct. 1956–59; prod. sup. tech. dir. Lynn Romero Prod. features and TV; assoc. prod. Lynn Romero Prod. TV series, Counterthrust 1959–60; v.p., sec'y, B.L. Coleman Assoc., Inc. & Newspix, Inc. 1961; pres. National Production Assoc., Inc. 1960–1962, chief of production, UPI Newsfilm, 1963–66. Prod./account exec. Fred A. Niles Comm. Center, 1966. Appt. v.p., F.A. Niles Communications Centers Inc., N.Y., 1969. In 1979 appointed in addition exec. producer & gen. mgr., F. A. Niles Communication centers Inc., N.Y. studio. 1989, elected mem. bd. dir., Florida Motion Pictures & Television Assn., Palm Beach area chap.; 1989 teacher m.p. & TV prod. course at Palm Beach Comm. Coll.

SAMPSON, LEONARD E.: Exhibitor. b. New York, NY, Oct., 1918. e. City Coll. of New York, B.B.A., 1939. Entered m.p. industry as stagehand helper and usher, Skouras Park Plaza, Bronx 1932–36; asst. mgr. Gramercy Park, 1937–38; mgr., 5th Avenue Playhouse, 1939–41; mgr., Ascot Bronx, 1941–42. In Army 1942–46. On return entered into partnership with cousin Robert C. Spodick in Lincoln, a New Haven art house. Organized Nutmeg Theatres, operating 6 art and conventional theatres in CT, associated with Norman Bialek in Westport and Norwalk. Sold Nutmeg in 1968 to Robert Smerling (now Loews Theatres). Retains partnership with Spodick in New Haven's York Sq., Built Groton, CT, Cinemas I & II in 1970 and Norwich, CT, Cinema I & II, 1976 and acquired Village Cinemas I & II, Mystic, in association with Spodick and William Rosen. Operated as Gemini Theatre Circuit. Acquired Westerly Cinema I & II, 1982. Sold Gemini; Theatre Circuit to Hoyts Theatres, 1987.

SAMUELS, ABRAM: Executive. b. Allentown, PA, Sept. 15, 1920. e. Lehigh U. U.S. Army 1942–46; pres. Automatic Devices Co. 1946–76; named bd. chmn. in 1976.

SAMUELSON, DAVID W., F.R.P.S., F.B.K.S., B.S.C.: Executive. b. London, England, July 6, 1924. Son of early producer G. B. Samuelson. Joined ind. 1941 with British Movietone News. Later film cameraman, 1947. Left Movietone 1960 to join family company, Samuelson Film Service Ltd. Dir., Samuelson Group Plc, 1958–84. Past president British Kinematograph Sound & TV Soc., Chmn, British Board of Film Classification past chmn., London Intl. Film Sch. Author of Motion Picture Camera and Lighting Equipment, Motion Picture Camera Techniques, Motion Picture Camera Data, Samuelson Manual of Cinematography, Panaflex User's Manual and Cinematographers Computer Program. Currently consultant on technology film making, author, lecturer. Won Acad. Award for Engineering, 1980 and Acad. Award for Tech. Achievement, 1987.

SAMUELSON, PETER GEORGE WYLIE: Producer. b. London, England, October 16, 1951. e. Cambridge U., M.A., English literature. Early career as interpreter and production assistant. 1979–85, exec. v.p., Interscope Communications, Inc. Pres., Starlight Foundation. Director, Friends of British Academy 1986–88, pres., Film Associates, Inc. chmn., Samuelson Group, Inc. (USA).
PICTURES: Production Manager: Speed Merchants. (1973), High Velocity. One by One. Return of the Pink Panther, Sante Fe. Producer: A Man, A Woman and a Bank; Revenge of the Nerds; Turk 182 (exec. prod.).

SAMUELSON, SYDNEY, C.B.E., B.S.C., Hon. F.B.K.S., Executive. b. London, England, Dec. 7, 1925. Early career as cinema projectionist, 1939–42; Gaumont British News, 1942–43; Royal Air Force, 1943–47; asst. cameraman, cameraman, director/cameraman until 1960; founded Samuelson Film Service, 1955; now chmn. Samuelson Group plc; Trustee and chmn. board of management, British Acad. of Film and Television Arts (chmn. of Council 1973–76). Trustee and member of Exec. Council (Pres. 1983–86) Cinema and Television Benevolent Fund. Member of Executive, Cinema & Television Veterans (pres. 1980–81); assoc. member, American Society of Cinematographers. Hon. Tech. Adviser, Royal Naval Film Corp. Hon. member, Guild of British Camera Technicians (1986); Member, British Society of Cinematographers. (governor, 1969–79; 1st vice pres., 1976–77).

SANDA, DOMINIQUE: Actress. b. Paris, France, March 11, 1951. r.n. Dominique Varaigne. e. Saint Vincent de Paul, Paris. Was a popular model for women's magazines when cast by Robert Bresson as the tragic heroine in his Dostoyevsky adaptation Un Femme Douce (1968).
PICTURES: Un Femme Douce; First Love, The Conformist; The Garden of the Finzi-Continis; La Notte Dei Fiori; Sans Mobile Apparent; Impossible Object; The Mackintosh Man; Steppenwolf; Conversation Piece; 1900; L'Eredita Ferramonti; Damnation Alley; Beyond Good and Evil; The Song of Roland; Utopia; The Navire Night; Travels on the Sly; Caboblanco; A Room in Town; Dust of the Empire; The Way to Bresson; The Sailor 512; With All Hands, Il Decimo Clandestino, On a Moonlit Night, Warrior and Prisoners.
TELEVISION: The Sealed Train.

SANDERS, TERRY BARRETT: Producer, Director, Writer. b. New York, NY, Dec. 20, 1931. e. UCLA, 1951; Co-prod., photographed, A Time Out of War, 1954. Academy award best two-reel subject, and won first prize Venice Film Festival, etc.; co-wrote The Day Lincoln Was Shot, CBS-TV; s.p. The Naked and the Dead; prod. Crime and Punishment—USA., prod. War Hunt; prod. and dir. Portrait of Zubin Mehta for U.S.I.A. Assoc. dean, Film Sch., California Inst. of the Arts. Assoc. professor, UCLA. exec. v.p., American Film Foundation.
TELEVISION: Prod. dir.: Hollywood and the Stars, The Legend of Marilyn Monroe, National Geographic Society specials, The Kids from Fame, Film Bios Kennedy Center Honors; Slow Fires; Lillian Glsh: the Actor's Life for Me.

SANDRICH, JAY: Director. b. Los Angeles, CA, Feb. 24, 1932. e. UCLA.
PICTURES: Seems Like Old Times.
TELEVISION: The Lily Tomlin Show (DGA Award, 1975). Movies: The Crooked Hearts, What Are Best Friends For? Series: Mary Tyler Moore Show (1970–77; Emmy Awards 1971 & 1973); Soap (1977–78), Phyllis (pilot), Tony Randall Show (pilot), Bob Newhart Show (pilot), Benson (pilot); Golden Girls (pilot), Empty Nest (pilot), The Cosby Show (1985–89; Emmy Award 1985, 1986; DGA Award 1985).

SANDS, JULIEN: Actor. b. Yorkshire, Eng. 1958. e. Central School of Speech and Drama, London 1979. Formed small theater co. that played in schools and youth clubs. Professional debut in Derek Jarman's short, Broken English and one-line part in Privates on Parade. Then opposite Anthony Hopkins in British TV series A Married Man (1981).
PICTURES: The Killing Fields, Oxford Blues, After Darkness, Romance on the Orient Express, The Doctors and the Devils, A Room with a View, Harem, Gothic, Siesta, Vibes, Wherever You Are, Manika: the Girl Who Lived Twice, Warlock, Tennessee Waltz.
TELEVISION: The Room, Murder By Moonlight.

SANDS, TOMMY: Singer. b. Chicago, IL. e. Schools there and Greenwood, LA. Father, Benny Sands, concert pianist. Started career as guitar player, singer when 6, at KWKH station, Shreveport. One of pioneers of rock music. First manager was Col. Tom Parker. Acting debut: Kraft TV show The Singin' Idol; recording contract won him million record sales of Teen Age Crush.
PICTURES: Sing Boy Sing, Mardi Gras, Love in a Goldfish Bowl, Babes in Toyland, The Longest Day, Ensign Pulver, None But the Brave.

SANFORD, CHARLES: Musical Director. b. New York, NY, June 17, 1905. Has been conducting since age of 15; asst. cond. N.Y. Hippodrome; district musical supervisor, RKO; conducted various shows, assoc. cond. to Alexander Smallens, Porgy and Bess.
TELEVISION: Musical dir., Admiral Broadway Review, 1948; Your Show of Shows, 1950–54; Bob Hope, 1950–51; Elgin American Show, 1950; Beatrice Lillie Show, 1950–51; Max Liebman Presents, 1954–56; Producer's Showcase, 1957–58; Jerry Lewis, Patrice Munsel Shows; 1959–60 Max Liebman Specials, Phil Silvers, Sid Caesar Specials.

SANFORD, ISABEL: Actress. b. New York, NY, Aug. 29, 1917. e. Textile H.S., Evander Childs H.S. Began acting in elementary school and continued through high school. Joined American Negro Theatre in the 1930's (then The Star Players) which disbanded in W.W.II. Latter associated with YWCA project and off-Bdwy. plays. Bdwy. debut in The Amen Corner.
PICTURES: Guess Who's Coming to Dinner, Pendulum, Stand Up and Be Counted, The New Centurions, Love at First Bite.
TELEVISION: Series: The Carol Burnett Show, All in the Family, The Jeffersons, etc. Movie: The Great Man's Whiskers.

SANGSTER, JIMMY: Producer, Director, Screenwriter. b. England, Dec. 2, 1927. Ent. m.p. ind. 1943. Prod. man. for Break in the Circle, Men of Sherwood Forest, X the Unknown.
PICTURES: Man on the Beach, The Curse of Frankenstein, The Trollenberg Terror, The Georkel, The Blood of the Vampire, Dracula, Intent to Kill, The Revenge of Frankenstein, Jack the Ripper, The Mummy, The Brides of Dracula, The Man Who Could Cheat Death, The Siege of Sydney Street, The Criminal, The Hell Fire Club, See No Exit, 1960 prod. and scripted Taste of Fear for Hammer Films 1961. Prod. The Savage Guns; prod. s.p. Maniac, Nightmare, Devil Ship Pirates; prod. Hysteria, s.p., The Giants, Paranoiac; s.p. Brainstorm; prod., s.p. The Nanny, s.p. Deadlier Than the Male, The Bridge of Newgate Jail; s.p. Java Weed, s.p. The Anniversary; prod. s.p. Doubled in Diamonds, Hide and Seek, Foreign Exchange, Private I (prod.), s.p. The Killing Game, The Claw, Touchfeather, wrote, prod. dir. The Horror of Frankenstein; dir. Lust for a Vampire; co-wrote s.p. Gingerbread House, Murder by Month Club, A Taste of Evil, The Goldfish Bowl, s.p. prod., dir. Fear in the Night. Screenplay: The Fairytale Man, s.p. The Monstrous Defect, s.p. The Legacy, s.p., Phobia.
TELEVISION: Writer: Motive for Murder, The Assassins, I Can Destroy the Sun; exec. story consultant Screen Gems-NBC short story series, McCloud, Banacek, Cannon, Ironside, etc. 1977–78; prod. Young Dan'l Boone; wrote & produced pilot for CBS: Ebony Ivory and Jade; wrote pilot: Adventure; wrote pilot for Murder in Music City; The Concrete Cowboys; Once Upon a Spy (movie), No Place To Hide; writer/prod./dir., Ripley's Believe It or Not.

SANSOM, LESTER A.: Producer. b. Salt Lake City, UT. e. U. of Utah. Radio singer under name of Jack Allen, 1930; ent. m.p. ind. in editorial dept., Fox Film Corp., Dec. 1931; served in U.S. Navy as head of film library, Washington, DC, 1942–45; head of edit. dept. & post-prod., Allied Artists, from 1953; assoc. prod. Skabenga; prod., co-writer, Battle Flame; assoc. prod. Hell to Eternity, exec. prod. The Thin Red Line, prod. Crack in the World; prod. Bikini Paradise, Battle of the Bulge, Custer of the West, Co-prod., Krakatoa—East of Java; exec. prod. 12+1.

SAPERSTEIN, DAVID: Writer, Director. b. Brooklyn, NY, March 19, 1937. e. CCNY, Film Institute, Chemical Engineering. 1960–80 wrote, prod. and dir. documentary films, TV commercials. Also wrote lyrics and managed rhythm and blues and rock 'n roll groups. Author of novels: Cocoon, Killing Affair, Metamorphosis, Red Devil.
PICTURES: Cocoon (story), Killing Affair (dir., s.p.), Personal Choice (dir., s.p.), Fatal Reunion (s.p.), Queen of America (s.p.), Torch, Sara Deri, Hearts & Diamonds.
TELEVISION: The Vintage Years (pilot).

SAPERSTEIN, HENRY G.: Executive. b. Chicago, IL, June 2, 1918. e. U. of Chicago. Theatre owner, Chicago, 1943–45; pres. Television Personalities, Inc., 1955–67 Mister Magoo, Dick Tracy, TV shows, 1960–62; 1960–67 Glen Films, Inc.; prod., All-Star Golf, 1958–62; prod. Championship Bowling, 1958–60; prod. Ding Dong School, 1959–60; pres. owner, UPA Pictures, Inc. Prod.: Mr. Magoo, Dick Tracy cartoon series, Mr. Magoo's Christmas Carol, T.N.T. Show, Turnon, Tune In Drop Out. Pres. Screen Entertainment Co., Benedict Pictures Corp., United Prod. of America; pres. H. G. Saperstein & Associates. Producer: The Vaudeville Thing; Tchaikovsky Competition, Gerald McBoing Boing Show
PICTURES: Producer: Gay Purr-ee, What's Up Tiger Lily, T-A-M-I, Swan Lake, Hell in the Pacific, War of the Gargantuas, Invasion of the Astro Monsters.

SAPHIER, PETER: Executive. b. Los Angeles, CA, Aug. 5, 1940. e. Antioch Coll. Son of late James L. Saphier. Programmer, subscription TV, Santa Monica, CA 1964; prod. v.p., Universal, 1972–81; prod., Martin Bregman Prods.; sr. v.p., m.p. activities, Taft Entertainment Co., since 1984.

PICTURES: Scarface (co-prod.); Eddie Macon's Run (exec. prod.)
TELEVISION: The Four Seasons.

SARA, MIA: Actress. b. Brooklyn, NY, 1968. Started doing TV commercials; landed role in soap opera, All My Children. Theatrical m.p. debut, Legend (1986).
PICTURES: Ferris Bueller's Day Off, The Long Lost Friend, Apprentice to Murder, Imagination, Any Man's Death, Shadows in the Storm.
TELEVISION: Queenie. Big Time, Till We Meet Again.

SARAFIAN, RICHARD C.: Director. b. New York, NY. April 28, 1935. Studied medicine and law before entering film industry with director Robert Altman making industrial documentaries.
TELEVISION: Gunsmoke, Bonanza, Guns of Will Sonnet, I Spy Wild, Wild West; Maverick, Twilight Zone, Gangster Chronicles. Movies: Shadow on the Land, Disaster on the Coastline, Splendor in the Grass; A Killing Affair; Liberty; Golden Moment—An Olympic Love Story. As Actor: Foley Square (series).
PICTURES: Andy (debut, 1965), Run Wild, Run Free, Ballad of a Badman, Fragment of Fear, Man in the Wilderness, Vanishing Point, Lolly Madonna (XXX), The Man Who Loved Cat Dancing, The Next Man (also prod.), Sunburn, The Bear, Songwriter (actor only), Street Justice (also actor), Crisis 2050, Truk Lagoon.

SARANDON, CHRIS: Actor. b. Beckley, WV, July 24, 1942. e. U. of West Virginia. Mem. Catholic U.'s National Players touring U.S. in Shakespeare and Moliere. Acted with Washington, D.C. improvisational theater co. and Long Wharf. Bdwy debut, The Rothschilds. Then Two Gentlemen of Verona, Censored Scenes from King Kong, Marco Polo Sings a Solo, The Devil's Disciple, The Soldier's Tale, The Woods.
PICTURES: Dog Day Afternoon, Lipstick, The Sentinel, Cuba, The Osterman Weekend, Protocol, Fright Night, Collision Course, The Princess Bride, Child's Play, Slaves of New York, Forced March.
TELEVISION: Series: The Guilding Light. You Can't Go Home Again, The Day Christ Died, A Tale of Two Cities, This Child Is Mine, Broken Promises, Liberty, Mayflower Madam, Tailspin: Behind the Korean Airliner Tragedy.

SARANDON, SUSAN: Actress. b. New York, NY, Oct. 4, 1946. e. Catholic U. Came to New York to pursue acting, first signing with Ford Model Agency. Made film debut in Joe (1970). Also appeared on TV in A World Apart series. Co-produced film, The Last of the Cowboys.
THEATER: A Coupla White Chicks Sitting Around Talking, Extremities.
PICTURES: Lovin' Molly, The Front, The Great Waldo Pepper, The Rocky Horror Show, Dragonfly, Crash, The Great Smokey Roadblock, Walk Away Madden, The Other Side of Midnight, Pretty Baby, King of the Gypsies, Loving Couples, Atlantic City, Tempest, The Hunger, In Our Hands, The Buddy System, Compromising Positions, The Witches of Eastwick, Bull Durham, The January Man, Sweet Heart's Dance, Married to the Mob, A Dry White Season.
TELEVISION: Search For Tomorrow, Calucci's Dept., Who Am I This Time?, A.D., Mussolini and I, Women of Valor, He'll See You Now, F. Scott Fitzgerald & the Last of the Belles, Oxbridge Blues.

SARGENT ALVIN: Writer. Began career as writer for TV, then turned to theatrical films.
PICTURES: The Stalking Moon, Gambit, The Sterile Cuckoo, I Walk the Line, The Effect of Gamma Rays on Man-in-the-Moon Marigolds, Love and Pain (and the whole damn thing), Julia (Acad. Award, 1977), Bobby Deerfield, Straight Time, The Electric Horseman, Ordinary People (Acad. Award, 1980), Nuts (co-s.p.); Dominick and Eugene (co-s.p.).
TELEVISION: Footsteps, The Impatient Heart.

SARGENT, DICK: Actor. b. Carmel, CA, 1933. Veteran of over 140 TV shows, 17 feature films and four TV series.
PICTURES: Captain Newman, M.D., Operation Petticoat, Mardi Gras, Bernadine, Hardcore, Body Count, Teen Witch, Rock-a-Die-Baby.
TELEVISION: One Happy Family, Broadside, Bewitched.

SARGENT, JOSEPH: Director. r.n. Giuseppe Danielle Sargente. b. Jersey City, NJ, July 25, 1925. e. studied theatre, New Sch. for Social Research 1946–49.
PICTURES: One Spy Too Many, The Hell With Heroes, The Forbin Project, White Lightning, The Taking of Pelham One Two Three, MacArthur, Goldengirl, Coast to Coast, Nightmares, Jaws—The Revenge (also prod.).
TELEVISION: The Spy in the Green Hat, Mini-series: The Manions of America, James Mitchener's Space. Movies: The Sunshine Patriot, The Immortal (pilot), The Man, Tribes, The Marcus-Nelson Murders (Emmy award for tv movie that was pilot for Kojak series), Maybe I'll Come Home in the Spring (also Prod.), The Man Who Died Twice. The Night That Panicked America, Sunshine (also prod.), Friendly Persuasion, Amber Waves, Hustling, Freedom, Tomorrow's Child, Memorial Day. Terrible Joe Moran, Choices of the Heart (also prod.), Space, Love Is Never Silent, Passion Flower, Of Pure Blood, There Must Be a Pony, The Karen Carpenter Story, Day One, Incident at Lincoln Bluff, Caroline?

SARLUI, ED: Executive. b. Amsterdam, The Netherlands, Nov. 10, 1925. Owner, Peruvian Films, S.A.; pres., Radio Films of Peru, S.A.; pres. Bryant Films Educatoriana, S.A.; partner, United Producers de Colombia Ltd.; pres. Royal Film N.V.; pres., United Producers de Centroamerica, S.A.; pres. United Producers de Mexico, S.A.; pres., United Producers Int'l, Inc., Continental Motion Pictures, Inc. 1988, formed Cinema Corp. of America with Moshe Diamant and Elliott Kastner.
PICTURES: Exec. prod.: Full Moon in Blue Water, High Spirits, Teen Witch, Courage Mountain, Night Game.

SARNOFF, ROBERT W.: Executive. b. New York, NY, July 2, 1918. e. Harvard U., B.A., 1939; Columbia Law Sch. 1940. In office of Coordinator of Info., Wash., DC, Aug. 1941; the U.S. Navy, Mar. 1942; asst. to publisher, Gardner Cowles, Jr., 1945; mem. of staff Look Mag., 1946, with NBC, 1948–65; pres., Dec. 1955–58; chmn. bd., 1958; bd. of dir. RCA, 1957; chmn bd. chief exec. officer, NBC, 1958–65; pres. RCA, 1966; Chief Exec. Officer, 1968; bd. chmn., 1970–75. Mem., TV Pioneers, 1957; pres., 1952–53; International Radio & TV Society, Broadcasters Committee for Radio Free Europe. Am Home Products, Inc., dir., of Business Committee for the Arts.

SARNOFF, THOMAS W.: Executive. b. New York, NY, Feb. 23, 1927. e. Phillips Acad., Andover, MA, 1939–43, Princeton U., 1943–45, Stanford U. grad. 1948, B.S. in E.E.; Grad Sch. of Bus. Admin. 1948–49. Sgt., U.S. Army Signal Corps, 1945–46; prod. & sales, ABC-TV, Hollywood, 1949–50; prod. dept. MGM, 1951–52; asst. to dir. of finance and oper., NBC, 1952–54; dir. of prod. and bus. affairs, 1954–57; vice pres., prod. and bus. affairs, 1957–60; v.p. adm. west coast, 1960–62; v.p. west coast, 1962; exec. v.p. 1965–77; bd. of dir., NBC prods 1961–77; bd of dir. Hope Enterprises 1960–75; dir. NABCAT, Inc. 1967–75; dir. Valley County Cable TV, Inc. 1969–75; Pres. NBC Entertainment Corp. 1972–77; Pres. Sarnoff International Enterprises, Inc. 1977–81; pres., Sarnoff Entertainment Corp., 1981–; pres., Venturetainment Corp.; 1986–; Past pres. Research Foundation at St. Joseph Hospital of Burbank; past pres. Permanent Charities of the Entertainment Ind.; past ch. bd. of trustees, National Acad. of TV Arts and Sciences.

SARRAZIN, MICHAEL: Actor. r.n. Jacques Michel Andre Sarrazin. b. Quebec, Canada, May 22, 1940. Began acting at 17 on CBC TV; signed by Universal, 1965.
PICTURES: Gunfight in Abilene (debut), The Flim-Flam Man, The Sweet Ride, Journey to Shiloh, A Man Called Gannon, Eye of the Cat, In Search of Gregory, They Shoot Horses, Don't They?, The Pursuit of Happiness, Sometimes a Great Notion, Believe in Me, Harry in Your Pocket, For Pete's Sake, The Reincarnation of Peter Proud, Scaramouche, The Gumball Rally, Caravans, The Seduction, Fighting Back, Joshua Then and Now, Captive Hearts, Mascara, Keeping Track, Malarek: A Street Kid Who Made It.
TELEVISION: Chrysler Theatre, The Virginian, World Premiere. Movies: Beulah Land, Frankenstein: The True Story, Passion and Paradise.

SASSOWER, HARVEY L.: Advertising director. b. New York, NY, July 28, 1945. e. City Coll. of New York, B.A., advertising. 1968 asst. to adv. mg., United Artists. 1969, asst. to adv. dir., 20th Century-Fox, 1969, appointed adv. mgr. of ABC Pictures Corp., dir. of adv., ABC Pictures, 1970; pres., Universal Spectrum, Inc. (design & adv. studio). Art director; author.

SAUL, OSCAR: Writer. b. Brooklyn, NY, Dec. 26, 1912. e. Brooklyn Coll. 1932. Co-author play, Medicine Show; m.p. ed., U.S. Public Health Svce; numerous radio and TV plays.
PICTURES: collab. s.p., Once Upon a Time, Strange Affair; collab. story, Road House, Lady Gambles; s.p., Woman in Hiding, Secret of Convict Lake; adapt., Streetcar Named Desire; collab. s.p., Thunder on the Hill, Affair in Trinidad; prod., Let's Do It Again; collab. s.p. Helen Morgan Story; s.p. Joker Is Wild; collab. story Naked Maja; collab. s.p. Second Time Around, Major Dundee; s.p. The Silencers; collab. s.p. Man and Boy, The Amigos. Novel: The Dark Side of Love (NBC movie). 1984, adapted A Streetcar Named Desire (ABC-TV), many others.

SAUNDERS, WILLIAM: Executive. b. London, England, Jan. 4, 1923. e. left Upton House Central Sch. at 16 to help support family. Served in British Eighth Army, 1941–47. Entered industry in 1947 as salesman with 20th Century Fox Film Co. in London; sales mgr., Anglo-Amalgamated Film Co., London, 1951–61; with Motion Picture Producers Assoc. of Amer. as sales dir. in Lagos, Nigeria, dist. Amer. feature films to West African countries; joined 20th Century Fox TV Intl., Paris as v.p. European TV sales, 1962–64; 20th Century TV Intl., Los Angeles as sr. v.p., 1983; named exec. v.p. 1987 and president, 1988–present.

SAURA, CARLOS: Director. b. Huesca, Spain, January 4, 1932. e. educated as engineer. Worked as professional photographer from 1949. Studied at Instituto de Investigaciones y Experiencias Cinematograficos, Madrid, 1952–57 where he then taught from 1957–64 until being dismissed for political reasons. 1957–58 dir. shorts La tarde del domingo and Cuenca.
PICTURES: Director and s.p.: Los Golfos (The Urchins), Lament for a Bandit, La caza, Peppermint frappe, Stress es tres, tres; La Madriguera, The Garden of Delights, Ana and the Wolves, Cousin Angelica (jury prize, Cannes, 1974), Cria! (special jury prize, Cannes, 1976), Elisa Vide Mia, Los ojos vendados, Mama Cumple 100 Años, Hurry, Hurry (Golden Bear, Berlin Fest., 1981), Blood Wedding, Dulces Horas, Antonieta, Carmen, El Amor Brujo, El Durado, The Dark Night.

SAVAGE, DAVID: Executive Producer, Advertising Executive, b. New York, NY, March 17, 1929. e. Rochester Inst. of Technology. In research development & testing div., Eastman Kodak Co., 2 yrs.; adv. mgr. asst. nat'l sales mgr., Official Films; org., film dept. mgr. WCBS-TV; dir. of film procurement, CBS; mgr. of film procurement, NBC; mgr. planning, merchandising, Recorded Tape Dept., RCA Records; promo. mgr., special products mktg. RCA Records Div.; program and marketing chmn. RCA SelectaVision group; v.p., operations, Wunderman, Rilotto, & Kline, 1970; pres., Response Industries, Inc., (direct response adv. agency), 1973 which became affiliate of McCann Erickson, and was sr. v.p. of McCann Erickson Pres., Mattel Direct Marketing, 1982; v.p. and man. dir., Foote Cene Belding, subsid. Knipp-Taylor USA, 1985.

SAVAGE, FRED: Actor. b. Highland Park, IL, July 9, 1976. While in kindergarten auditioned for commercial at local community center. Didn't get the job but called back by same dir. for two more tests. Chosen for Pac-Man vitamin ad which led to 27 on-camera TV commercials and 36 voice-over radio spots.
PICTURES: The Boy Who Could Fly, The Princess Bride, Vice Versa, Little Monsters, The Wizard.
TELEVISION: Series: The Wonder Years. Movies: Convicted: A Mother's Story, Video Madness, Run Til You Fall. Special: Runaway Ralph. Guest: Morningstar/Eveningstar, The Twilight Zone.

SAVAGE, JOHN: Actor. b. Long Island, NY, Aug. 25, 1949. Studied at American Acad. of Dramatic Arts. In Manhattan organized Children's Theatre Group which performed in public housing. Has appeared in many plays both on and off Bdwy. Won Drama Circle Award for performance in One Flew Over the Cuckoo's Nest in Chicago and Los Angeles.
PICTURES: Bad Company, Steelyard Blues, All the Kind Strangers, The Deer Hunter, Hair, The Onion Field, Cattle Annie and Little Britches, Inside Moves, The Amateur, Brady's Escape, Maria's Lovers, Beauty and the Beast, Hotel Colonial, The Beat, Catacombs, War Shepherds, Caribe, Any Man's Death, Point of View, Do the Right Thing, Hunting.
STAGE: Fiddler on the Roof, Ari, Siamese Connections, The Hostage, American Buffalo.
TELEVISION: Gibbsville (series). Movies: Eric, Coming Out of the Ice, Silent Witness, The Nairobi Affair, Desperate, Date Rape (Afterschool Special).

SAVALAS, TELLY: Actor. r.n. Aristotle Savalas. b. Garden City, NY, Jan. 21, 1924. e. Columbia U., B.S. Joined Information Services of State Dept.; made exec. dir., then named sr. dir. of news, special events for ABC, where created Your Voice of America series. Acting career began with debut in Bring Home a Baby on Armstrong Circle Theatre TV.
PICTURES: Birdman of Alcatraz, Young Savages, Cape Fear, Man from the Diner's Club, Battle of the Bulge, Greatest Story Ever Told, Beau Geste, Dirty Dozen, Buona Sera, Mrs. Campbell, Crooks and Coronets, Kelly's Heroes, On Her Majesty's Secret Service, Killer Force, Lisa and the Devil, Capricorn One, Escape to Athena, Beyond the Poseidon Adventure, Cannonball Run II, The Secret of the Sahara, Faceless.
TELEVISION: Series: Kojak. Movies: Mongo's Back in Town, Visions, The Marcus-Nelson Murders, The Dirty Dozen: The Deadly Mission, Alice in Wonderland, The Cartier Affair, Return to the Titanic (host), The Dirty Dozen: The Fatal Mission.

SAWELSON, MEL: Executive b. Los Angeles, CA, Sept. 5, 1929. e. U. of Southern California, 1947–48; UCLA. 1948–49. Entered M.P. industry in 1947; mgr., Acme Film Laboratories, Inc., 1952; pres. Sports-TV; 1957–59, produced, Olympic Films, International Olympic Organization, 1956; produced, Big 10 Hilites, PCC Hilites, All American Game of the Week, 1957–59; 1st m.p. lab. exec. to install videotape, 1959; created Acme-chroma process of transferring color videotape to film; pres., Acme Film & Videotape Labs., 1967–71; v.p. Consolidated Film Industries, 1971, exec. v.p. 1972; pres., Glen Glenn Sound Co., 1972.

SAWYER, DIANE: News Correspondent, Anchor. b. Glasgow, KY, Dec. 22, 1945. m. director Mike Nichols. e. Wellesley Coll. Studied law before deciding on career in TV. Former Junior Miss winner and weather reporter on a Louisville TV station before arriving in Washington, 1970. Worked for Nixon Administration in press office from 1970–74; assisted Nixon in writing memoirs, 1975–78. Joined CBS News as reporter in Washington bureau in 1978; named correspondent in 1980. Served as CBS State Dept. correspondent 1980–81. Joined Charles Kuralt as co-anchor of the weekday editions of CBS Morning News in 1981; 1984–89 correspondent on 60 Minutes; 1989, signed by ABC News as co-anchor of Primetime Live news prog. with Sam Donaldson.

SAXON, JOHN: Actor. r.n. Carmine Orrico. b. Brooklyn, NY, Aug. 5, 1936. Model.
PICTURES: Running Wild (debut), The Unguarded Moment, Rock Pretty Baby, Summer Love, The Reluctant Debutante, This Happy Feeling, The Big Fisherman, The Restless Years, Cry Tough, Portrait in Black, The Unforgiven, Mr. Hobbs Takes a Vacation, The Plunderers, Posse from Hell, War Hunt, Nightmare, Evil Eye, For Singles Only, Joe Kidd, Enter The Dragon, Black Christmas, Strange Shadows in an Empty Room, The Electric Horseman, Wrong Is Right, The Big Score, Nightmare on Elm Street, Fever Pitch, Nightmare on Elm Street 3: Dream Warriors, Nightmare Beach, Death House (also dir.), My Mom's a Werewolf, Aftershock, Blood Salvage, Crossing the Line, Criminal Act.
TELEVISION: Series: The Bold Ones, Dynasty, Falcon Crest. Movies: The Doomsday Flight, Winchester 73, The Intruders, Planet Earth, Once an Eagle, 79 Park Avenue, Can Ellen Be Saved?, Golden Gate, The Immigrants, Raid on Entebbe.

SAYLES, JOHN: Writer, Director, Editor, Actor. b. Schnectady, NY, Sept. 28, 1950. e. Williams Coll., B.S. psychology, 1972. Wrote two novels: Pride of the Bimbos, 1975 and Union Dues, 1978; also The Anarchist's Convention, collection of short stories and, Thinking in Pictures: The Making of the Movie Matewan (1987). First screenplay: Piranha (1978). Wrote and directed plays off-Bdwy (New Hope for the Dead, Turnbuckle). Directed Bruce Springsteen music videos (Born in the U.S.A., I'm on Fire, Glory Days). Recipient of MacArthur Foundation Grant for genius.
PICTURES: Battle Beyond the Stars (s.p.), Lady in Red (s.p.), Return of the Secaucus Seven (s.p., dir., actor, editor), Alligator (s.p.), The Howling (co-s.p.), The Challenge (co-s.p.), Lianna (s.p., dir., editor), Baby, It's You (s.p., dir.), The Brother from Another Planet (s.p., dir., editor, actor), The Clan of the Cave Bear (s.p.), Wild Thing (s.p.), Hard Choices (actor only), Something Wild (actor only), Matewan (dir., s.p., actor), Eight Men Out (dir., s.p., actor), Breaking In (s.p. only).
TELEVISION: Enormous Changes at the Last Minute (co-s.p.), A Perfect Match, Unnatural Causes (actor, s.p.), Shannon's Deal (s.p.). Special: Mountain View (Alive From Off Center).

SCACCHI, GRETA: Actress. b. Milan, Italy. e. England and Australia.
PICTURES: Heat and Dust, Defense of the Realm, The Coca Cola Kid, A Man in Love, Good Morning, Babylon, White Mischief, Paura e Amore (Three Sisters), Woman in the Moon, Schoolmates, Presumed Innocent.
TELEVISION: Camille.

SCARDINO, DON: Actor. b. Canada. On Bdwy. in Godspell, King of Hearts, Johnny No Trump, As You Like It, etc.
PICTURES: The People Next Door, Homer, Squirm, Cruising, He Knows You're Alone.
TELEVISION: 27 Wagons Full of Cotton (dir.).

SCARWID, DIANA: Actress. b. Savannah, GA. Went to N.Y. after high school to attend American Acad. of Dramatic Arts, Pace U., 1975. Member of National Shakespeare Conservatory (Woodstock, NY) and worked in regional theatres before moving to Hollywood 1976. Motion picture debut in Pretty Baby, 1978.
PICTURES: Inside Moves, Honeysuckle Rose, Mommie Dearest, Rumble Fish, Strange Invaders, Silkwood, Extremities, The Ladies Club, Psycho III, Heat, Brenda Starr.
TELEVISION: Gibbsville (series), Studs Lonigan (mini-series), Movies: The Possessed, In the Glitter Palace, Forever, Battered, Desperate Lives, The Guyana Tragedy, Kingston Confidential, Thou Shalt Not Kill, A Bunny's Tale, After the Promise.

SCHAEFER, CARL: Media Consultant, Publicist, b. Cleveland, OH, Sept. 2. e. UCLA. Contr. to mag., including Vanity Fair, Hollywood Citizen-News, 1931–35; Warner Bros., 1935.; Huesped de Honor, Mexico, 1943; OSS W.W.II, 1944–45; Int'l Comt. AMPS, chmn. 1966–67; Italian Order of Merit, 1957; Chevalier de l'ordre de la Couronne, Belgium, 1963. Pres., Foreign Trade Assn. of Southern Calif., 1954; chmn. of bd., 1955; British-American C. of C., Dir., 1962; Chevalier French Legion d'Honneur, 1955; Comm. Hollywood Museum; dir., intl. relations, Warner Bros. Seven Arts Int'l Corp., 1960; formed own firm, Carl Schaefer Enterprises, 1971. Dir. pub. rel., British-American Chamber of Commerce, 1971; dir. pub. rel.

Iota Intl. Pictures, 1971; dir. pub. rel. Lyric Films Intl., 1971; bureau chief (Hollywood) Movie/TV Marketing, 1971; man. dir., Intl. Festival Advisory Council, 1971; dir. pub. rel. & adv. Francis Lederer Enterprises (Inc. American National Acad. of Performing Arts, and Canoga Mission Gallery) 1974; West Coast rep. Angelika Films of N.Y. 1974, Hwd. rep Korwitz/Geiger Products. 1975–; Hwd. corresp. Movie News, S'pore, & Femina, Hong Kong, 1974–; member Westn. Publications Assn. 1975–; field rep. Birch Records 1975; Hollywood rep Antena Magazine, Buenos Aires; dir pub rel Style Magazine. Coordinator Hollywood Reporter Annual Key Art Awards; coordinator Hollywood Reporter Annual Marketing Concept Awards; exec. comm. & historian ShoWest; Mem: National Panel of Consumer Arbitrators, 1985; Hollywood Corr., Gold Coast Times of Australia, 1986–87.

SCHAEFER, GEORGE: Producer, Director. b. Wallingford, CT, Dec. 16, 1920. e. Lafayette Coll., Yale Drama Sch. Bdwy. shows include The Linden Tree; Man and Superman; The Corn Is Green; The Heiress; Idiot's Delight; The Male Animal. Tovarich; Teahouse of the August Moon; Write Me a Murder; 1986, joined UCLA as chairman, Theatre, Film, TV.
PICTURES: Once Upon a Scoundrel; Generation; Doctors' Wives; Pendulum; Macbeth; An Enemy of the People.
TELEVISION: Hamlet; One Touch of Venus; The Corn Is Green; The Good Fairy; Born Yesterday; The Little Foxes; Little Moon of Alban; Harvey; Macbeth; The Magnificent Yankee; Kiss Me Kate; Pygmalion; F. Scott Fitzgerald; Blind Ambition; First You Cry; The People vs. Jean Harris; A Piano for Mrs. Cimino; The Deadly Game; Children in the Crossfire; Right of Way; Stone Pillow; Mrs. Delafield Wants to Marry; Laura Lansing Slept Here, Let Me Hear You Whisper.

SCHAFER, MARTIN: Executive. e. UCLA. Attorney-at-law. Served as producer on Modern Romance & The Awakening before joining Embassy Pictures as prod. exec. 1983; promoted to pres., prod. 1985, named exec. v.p., prod., for 20th Century Fox.
PICTURES: Co-prod.: The Mountain Men; The Awakening; Modern Romance.

SCHAFER, NATALIE: Actress. b. New York, NY, Nov. 5. e. Merrill Sch., Hamilton Inst.
BROADWAY: Lady in the Dark, Susan and God, The Doughgirls.
PICTURES: Marriage Is a Private Affair, Molly and Me, Dishonored Lady, The Time of Your Life, The Snake Pit, Caught, Anastasia, Oh Men! Oh Women!, Susan Slade, 40 Carats, The Day of the Locust, Beverly Hills Brats.
TELEVISION: I Love Lucy, Route 66, 77 Sunset Strip, Thriller, The Beverly Hillbillies, Gilligan's Island (series).

SCHAFFEL, ROBERT: Producer. b. Washington, DC, March 2, 1944. Partner with Jon Voight in Voight-Schaffel Prods. Now heads Robert Schaffel Prods.
PICTURES: Gordon's War; Sunnyside; Lookin' to Get Out; Table for Five, American Anthem, Distant Thunder, Jacknife.

SCHATZBERG, JERRY: Director. b. New York, NY, June 26, 1927. e. student U. of Miami, 1947–48. Early career in photography as asst. to Bill Helburn 1954–56. Freelance still photographer and TV commercials dir. 1956–69. Contrib. photographs to several mags. incl. Life.
PICTURES: Puzzle of a Downfall Child (1970), Panic in Needle Park, Scarecrow, Sweet Revenge (prod.-dir.), The Seduction of Joe Tynan, Honeysuckle Rose, Misunderstood, No Small Affair, Street Smart, Reunion.
TELEVISION: Clinton and Nadine.

SCHEIDER, ROY: Actor. b. Orange, NJ, Nov. 10, 1932. e. Franklin and Marshall Coll. where he won the Theresa Helburn Acting Award twice. First professional acting in N.Y. Shakespeare Festival 1961 prod. of Romeo and Juliet. Became member of Lincoln Center Repertory Co. and acted with Boston Arts Festival, American Shakespeare Festival, Arena Stage (Wash., DC) and American Repertory Co.
STAGE: Richard III, Stephen D, Sergeant Musgrave's Dance, The Alchemist, Betrayal.
PICTURES: Loving, Paper Lion, Stiletto, Star!, Puzzle of a Downfall Child, Klute, The French Connection, The Outside Man, The Seven Ups, The Inheritor, Sheila Levine, Jaws, Marathon Man, Sorcerer, Jaws II, Last Embrace, All That Jazz, Still of the Night, Blue Thunder, 2010, 52 Pick-up, The Men's Club, La Ciurma, Palisades Park, Listen to Me, Cohen and Tate, Night Game, The Crew, The Fourth Man.
TELEVISION: Hallmark Hall of Fame, Studio One, N.Y.P.D., Assignment Munich, Jacobo Timerman, Tiger Town, Portrait of the Soviet Union (host).

SCHELL, MARIA: Actress. b. Vienna, Austria, Jan. 5, 1926. Sister of Maximillian Schell. Made debut at 12 in Swiss film, The Gravel Pit. Subsequently appeared in many British and American films.
PICTURES: Angel with a Trumpet, So Little Time, The Magic Box, Angelika, The Heart of the Matter, The Rats, Napoleon, Gervaise, The Last Bridge, The Brothers Karamazov, The Hanging Tree, Rose Bernd, A Day Will Come, Cimarron, As the Sea Rages, The Mark, White Knights, End of Desire, I, Too Am Only a Woman, Devil By the Tail, The Odessa File, Voyage of the Damned, The Twist, Superman, 1919, Just a Gigalo.
TELEVISION: (U.S.): Christmas Lilies of the Field; Inside the Third Reich; Martian Chronicles; Samson and Delilah.

SCHELL, MAXIMILIAN: Actor, Director. b. Vienna, Dec. 8, 1930.
PICTURES: Children, Mother and the General, The Young Lions, Judgment at Nuremberg (Acad. Award), Five Finger Exercise, The Condemned of Altona, Return from the Ashes, The Deadly Affair, Counterpoint, The Desperate Ones, The Castle, Krakatoa East of Java, The Odessa File, First Love (dir., starred); The Man in the Glass Booth, End of the Game (dir., co-prod.), St. Ives, A Bridge Too Far, Cross of Iron, Julia, Players, The Black Hole, The Chosen, The Assisi Underground, Marlene (dir.), The Rose Garden, O'Keefe & Stieglitz (prod., dir., actor).
TELEVISION: Shows include: Playhouse 90, Judgment at Nuremberg, The Fifth Column, The Diary of Anne Frank, Turn The Key Deftly, Phantom of the Opera, Heidi, Peter the Great (mini-series).

SCHENCK, AUBREY: Producer. b. Brooklyn, NY, Aug. 26, 1908. e. Cornell U., NYU. With law firm of O'Brien, Driscoll & Raftery; buyer & attorney for Natl. Theatres, 1936; prod. for 20th Century-Fox 1945; exec. prod. Eagle Lion 1946; contract prod. Universal Internatl. 1948; Aubrey Schenck Productions, Inc.
PICTURES: Shock, Johnny Comes Flying Home, Strange Triangle, Repeat Performance, T-Men, Mickey, It's a Joke Son, Trapped, Port of New York, Wyoming Man, Undercover Girl, Fat Man, Target Unknown; formed own co. to prod. War Paint, Beachhead. Also: Yellow Tomahawk, Shield for Murder, Big House, U.S.A., Crime Against Joe, Emergency Hospital, Ghost Town, Broken Star, Rebels in Town, Pharaoh's Curse, Three Bad Sisters, Fort Yuma, Desert Sands, Quincannon, Frontier Scout, Black Sleep, Hot Cars, War Drums, Voodoo Island, Revolt at Fort Laramie, Tomahawk Trail, Untamed Youth, Girl in Black Stockings, Bop Girl Goes Calypso, Up Periscope, Violent Road, Reckless, Frankenstein 1970, Wild Harvest, Robinson Crusoe On Mars, Don't Worry, Ambush Bay, Kill a Dragon, Impasse, More Dead Than Alive, Barquero, Daughters of Satan.
TELEVISION: Miami Undercover, series.

SCHEPISI, FRED: Producer, Director, Writer. b. Melbourne, Australia, Dec. 26, 1939. Assessed student films at Melbourne's Swinburne Inst. of Tech., worked on gov. sponsored experimental Film Fund, Made TV commercials. Founded The Film House prod. co.
PICTURES: The Priest (dir.), The Devil's Playground (dir., prod., s.p.), The Chant of Jimmie Blacksmith (dir., prod., s.p.), Barbarosa (dir.), Iceman (dir.), Plenty (dir.), Roxanne (dir.), A Cry in the Dark (dir., co-s.p.), The Russia House (dir., co-prod.).

SCHERICK, EDGAR J: Executive, Producer. b. New York, NY, Oct. 16, 1924. e. Harvard U.; elected to Phi Beta Kappa. Asst. dir. of radio and TV; assoc. media dir. and dir. of sports special events, Dancer-Fitzgerald-Sample ad agency, NY during 1950s. Introduced Wide World of Sports on TV through his co., Sports Programs, Inc. Was v.p. in chg. of network programming at ABC-TV. Pres. of Palomar Pictures Int'l. Now independent producer.
PICTURES: For Love of Ivy, The Birthday Party, Take the Money and Run, They Shoot Horses, Don't They?, The Killing of Sister George, Ring of Bright Water, Jenny, Sleuth, The Heartbreak Kid, Law and Disorder, The Stepford Wives, I Never Promised You a Rose Garden, The Taking of Pelham One, Two, Three, The American Success Company, I'm Dancing As Fast As I Can, Shoot the Moon, White Dog, Reckless, Mrs. Soffel.
TELEVISION: The Man Who Wanted to Live Forever (1970); The Silence; Circle of Children; Raid on Entebbe; Panic in Echo Park; Zuma Beach; An American Christmas Carol; The Seduction of Miss Leona; Revenge of the Stepford Wives; Hitler's SS; The High Price of Passion; The Stepford Children; Unholy Matrimony; Little Gloria...Happy at Last; On Wings of Eagles; Hands of a Stranger; Home Fires; He Makes Me Feel Like Dancin' (Emmy and Acad. Awards, 1983); Stranger on My Land (exec. prod.); And the Band Played On; The Kennedys of Massachusetts; Satin's Touch (exec. prod.), Phantom of the Opera.

SCHIAVONE, JAMES: Executive. b. Niagara Falls, NY, Nov. 14, 1917. e. U. of Michigan. Started career as newspaperman; general manager WWJ-AM-FM-TV, Detroit, 1952–68; pres.-gen. mgr., KSAT-TV, San Antonio, TX, 1969–present.

SCHICK, ELLIOT: Executive. b. Brooklyn, NY, Dec. 24, 1924. e. Brooklyn Coll., B.A.; New School for Social Research, drama workshop, directing 1945–46. Author of book for Ballet Theatre, Manfred; book, The Administration of the Economic and Social Council. 1942–48, prod. & dir. radio shows for

WNYC, N.Y., composed and arranged music for radio and stage production; 1946–48; dialogue director, Republic Studios; 1948–50, prod. & dir. TV shows and commercials, Nova Productions; 1950–51, editor, United Nations Film Div.; 1951–53, editor, Candid Camera; 1953–55, asst. studio mgr., American Natl. Studios; 1955–56, prod. & dir. live and video tape shows for KCET.

PICTURES: Tora, Tora, Tora, 1969, asst. dir.; 1969–72, prod. mgr. for features: 3 in the Attic, Up in the Cellar, Bunny O'Hare, Honkers, Hickey and Boggs, Kansas City Bomber, White Lightning; 1973–77 spvr. prod. for AIP on Sugar Hill, Return to Macon County, Cooley High, Futureworld, Island of Dr. Moreau in 1977 joined EMI Films, Inc. as v.p. prod.; exec.-in-chg.-prod., Deer Hunter; produced The Earthling; Blue Skies Again (exec.-in-chg.-prod.); Fools Die (prod.); Fast Eddie (prod.); Marie (exec. prod.); Cherry-2000 (co-prod.), Masters of the Universe (co-prod.). Farewell to the King (exec. in chg. of prod.).

TELEVISION: prod., Private Benjamin (TV series), supvr. prod., Pippin (TV).

SCHIFRIN, LALO: Composer, b. Buenos Aires, Argentina, June 21, 1932. Father was conductor of Teatro Colon in B.A. for 30 years. Schifrin studied with Juan Carlos Paz in Arg. and later Paris Cons. Arranger for Xavier Cugat. Returned to homeland and wrote for stage, modern dance, TV. Became interested in jazz and joined Dizzie Gillespie's band in 1962 as pianist and composer. Settled in L.A. Pres. Young Musicians Fed. Music; dir. and conductor, Paris Philharmonic 1987.

PICTURES: The Cincinnati Kid, The Liquidator, Cool Hand Luke, The President's Analyst, The Fox, Kelly's Heroes, Hell's Chronicles, Dirty Harry, Magnum Force, Man on a Swing, The Four Musketeers, Voyage of the Damned, The Eagle Has Landed, Voyage of the Damned, Rollercoaster, Telefon, Nunzio, The Manitou, Boulevard Nights, The Concord—Airport '79, Love and Bullets, Serial, The Big Brawl, Brubaker, Escape to Athena, The Amityville Horror, The Nude Bomb, The Competition, When Time Ran Out, Caveman, Buddy, Buddy, The Seduction, A Stranger Is Watching, Amityville II: The Possession, The Sting II, The Osterman Weekend, Sudden Impact, The Mean Season, The New Kids, Doctor Detroit, Tank, The Silence at Bethany, Little Sweetheart, Berlin Blues (music and songs), Naked Tango, Return From the River Kwai.

TELEVISION: Mission Impossible (theme), Hollywood Wives, A.D., Private Sessions, Foster and Laurie, Starsky and Hutch, Earth Star Voyager, Princess Daisy, Falcon's Gold, Kung Fu: The Movie, Original Sin.

SCHILLER, FRED: Playwright, Screen & TV writer. Awarded: New York Literary Prize, for McCall magazine story Ten Men and a Prayer. Member of Dramatists' Guild. Formerly chief corres. European Newspaper Feature Services. Honored by the U. of Wyoming for literary achievements with a special Fred Schiller Collection for their library. Awarded Honorary Silver Cross by Austrian Govt., for literary achievements and for furthering cultural relations between Austria and U.S.

PICTURES FOR: MGM, Columbia, RKO, Republic and Henri Sokal Films, Paris.

TELEVISION: Wrote some 53 TV plays for all major networks. Adapted G.B. Shaw's play, The Inca of Perusalem, for an NBC special. Specials: Demandez Vicky! for Paris and Finder BitteMelden! for Austrian TV.

STAGE: Come On Up (U.S.), Anything Can Happen (London), Demandez Vicky (Paris), Finder Please Return (Athens, Madrid), Finder Bitte Melden (Berlin, Baden-Baden, and Vienna). Peter Sellars production at Kennedy Center, Come on Up (a Mae West revival), The Love Trap (Cambiya Playhouse).

SCHILLER, LAWRENCE J.: Producer, Director. b. New York, NY, Dec. 28, 1936. Photojournalist with Life Magazine & Saturday Evening Post, 1958–70; collaborated on numerous books including three by Norman Mailer: The Executioner's Song, Marilyn, and The Faith of Graffiti; Muhammad Ali with Wilfrid Sheed; Minamata with Eugene Smith.

PICTURES: The Man Who Skied Down Everest (editorial concept & direction); Lady Sings the Blues, Butch Cassidy & the Sundance Kid (conceived and executed special still montages & titles); The American Dreamer (prod., dir.).

TELEVISION: Hey, I'm Alive (prod., dir.); Producer: The Trial of Lee Harvey Oswald, The Winds of Kitty Hawk, Marilyn, The Untold Story, An Act of Love, Child Bride of Short Creek, The Executioner's Song (prod., dir.), Peter the Great, Margaret Bourke-White (prod., dir.).

SCHINE, G. DAVID: Executive. b. Gloversville, NY, Sept. 11, 1927. e. Harvard U., Pres., gen. mgr. Schine Hotels 1950–63. Film exhibitor until 1966 in New York, Ohio, Kentucky, Maryland, Delaware, and West Virginia. Exec. prod. of French Connection, 1971. Writer, prod., dir. of That's Action!, 1977. Chief Exec. officer of Schine Productions (production) and Epic Productions (distribution), Visual Sciences, Inc., High Resolution Sciences, Inc., and Studio Television Services, Inc.

SCHLAIFER, CHARLES: Executive. President, Charles Schlaifer and Company, Inc., advertising agency with offices in New York and Los Angeles. b. Omaha, NB. Reporter Daily News, World-Herald, (Omaha). In 1930 appt. adv. mgr. Paramount theatres, Omaha; then of Publix theats., Omaha; then of Tri-State circuit, Neb., Iowa; 1936–42 man. dir. United Artists Theats., San Francisco; advisor, nat'l adv., United Artists prod. In 1942 appt. adv. mgr. 20th Cent.-Fox; named asst. dir. adv., publicity, & exploitation, 1944; appt. v.p. & dir. of advertising, pub., exploitation and radio, 1945. Resigned 1949, to establish own adv. agency. Pres., Charles Schlaifer & Co., Inc. Chmn. advertising advisory council, MPAA; instructor at New School for Social Research, N.Y., on m.p.; revised m.p. adv. code; permanent chmn. first MPAA pub rel. com. Member; Nat'l Advisory Mental Health Council to U.S. Surgeon General; Founder and vice-chmn. bd. of gov., Nat'l Assn. of Mental Health. Lecturer, writer on adv. & mental health bd. of gov., Menninger Foundation; founder, co-chmn., Nat'l Mental Health Comm., secy., treas., Joint Comm. on Mental Illness & Health; expert witness Congress, govt. hearings creating National Institute of Mental Health in U.S. Public Health Service. Elected Hon. Fellow of the Amer. Psychiatric Assn., 1959; V. chmn., trustee in chg., Mental Health and Mental Retardation Facilities, NY State, 1964; secy., treas., Joint Commission Mental Health for Children; vice chmn. bd. Foundation for Child Mental Welfare, 1963. Mem. bd. trustees Research Found. 1966. Mem.: White House Conference on the Handicapped, 1952–65; elected honorary fellow, Post Graduate Psychiatric Institute, 1968. Hon. Doctor of Letters, John F. Kennedy Coll., Wahoo, Neb., 1969; Chmn. N.Y. State Health and Mental Hygiene Facilities Improvement Corp., 1970; Hon. Fellow—American Ortho Psychiatric Assoc., 1970; Hon. Fellow British Royal Society of Health. Wisdom Award Hon. Wisdom Mag., 1969; social conscience award Karen Horney Clinic, 1972. Chmn, NY State Facilities Dev. Corp., 1973–; Advisory Council to the National Institute of Mental Health to the Surgeon General of the U.S. 1976–.

SCHLANG, JOSEPH: Executive. b. New York, NY, Feb. 24, 1911, e. NYU. Owner and leader in N.Y. real estate, and exec. dir. of many enterprises. Pres. of International Opera Co. & Opera Presentations, Inc. Produced two weekly radio programs: Opera Stars of Tomorrow and 100 & More Ways to Improve N.Y.C. since April, 1973. Opera Presentations, Inc., a non-profit corp. distributes and exhibits opera, ballet and art films throughout America and the school system. Over 100 cultural films owned by Schlang are supplied to Opera Presentations free to use.

SCHLATTER, GEORGE: Producer, Director, Writer. b. Birmingham, AL, Dec. 31, 1932. m. former actress Jolene Brand. e. Pepperdine U. on football scholarship. First industry job was MCA agent in band and act dept. Then gen. mgr. and show producer Ciro's nightclub (where he met Dick Martin and Dan Rowan). Produced shows at Frontier Hotel and Silver Slipper, Las Vegas. Sang 2 seasons St. Louis Municipal Opera Co.

TELEVISION: Created Laugh-In, Real People (3 Emmys, 27 nominations). Specials with Goldie Hawn, Robin Williams, Shirley MacLaine, Doris Day, John Denver, Frank Sinatra, Jackie Gleason, Danny Thomas, Bob Hope, Milton Berle, Danny Kaye, George Burns, Dinah Shore, Lucille Ball, Goldie & Liza Together, Salute to Lady Liberty, Las Vegas 75th Anniversary, Speak Up America, Real Kids, Best of Times, Look At Us, Shape of Things, Magic or Miracle. Produced and wrote first 5 years of the Grammy Awards, TV series with Dinah Shore, Judy Garland, Bill Cosby, Robin Williams, Steve Lawrence. ABC American Comedy Awards (3 years), George Schlatter's Comedy Club, George Schlatter's Funny People, Beverly Hills 75th Anniversary, Humor and the Presidency and Frank, Liza & Sammy. . .The Ultimate.

SCHLESINGER, JOHN: Director, Producer. b. London, England, Feb. 16, 1926. e. Oxford U., BBC dir. 1958–60: Wrote and dir. Terminus for British Transport Films (Golden Lion, best doc., Venice); The Class. Some episodes The Valiant Years series. Appeared as actor in films: Sailor of the King (1953), Pursuit of the Graff Spee, Brothers in Law, The Divided Heart, The Last Man to Hang, Fifty Years of Action (DGA doc.). Assoc. dir., National Theatre, London 1973–.

PICTURES: A Kind of Loving (Golden Bear, Berlin 1961); Billy Liar; Darling (New York Film Critics Award); Far From the Madding Crowd. Midnight Cowboy (Best dir. and film, S.F.T.A. and Oscars' 1968); Sunday, Bloody Sunday (Best dir. and film, S.F.T.A.), Visions of Eight (sequence), The Day of the Locust, Marathon Man, Yanks, Honky Tonk Freeway, The Falcon and the Snowman (also co-prod.), The Believers (also co-prod.), Madame Sousatzka (dir., co-s.p.), Comfort of Strangers, Toy Soldiers.

TELEVISION: Separate Tables, An Englishman Abroad (BAFTA award).

OPERA: Les Contes d'Hoffmann (Royal Opera House 1981; SWET award); Der Rosenkavalier Un Ballo in Maschera (salzburg Fest., 1989).

THEATRE: No Why (RSC), 1964; Timon of Athens (RSC); Days in the Trees (RSC); I And Albert; Heartbreak House (NT); Julius Caesar (NT); True West (NT).

SCHLONDORFF, VOLKER: Director. b. Wiesbaden, Germany, March 31, 1939. Studied in France, acquiring degree in political science in Paris. Studied at French Intl. Film Sch. (IDHEC) before becoming asst. to Jean-Pierre Melville, Alain Resnais, and Louis Malle Debut film, Der Junge Torless (Young Torless), 1965.
PICTURES: A Degree of Murder; Michael Kohlhass; Baal, The Sudden Fortune of the Poor People of Kombach; Die Moral der Rugh Halbfass; A Free Woman; The Lost Honor of Katharine Blum; Le Coup de Grace; Valeska Gert; The Tin Drum; Circle of Deceit; Swann in Love, The Handmaid's Tale.
TELEVISION: Death of a Salesman; A Gathering of Old Men.

SCHLOSSBERG, JULIAN: Producer, Distributor, Director, Radio TV Host. b. New York, NY, Jan. 26, 1942. e. N.Y. Joined ABC-TV network 1964 as asst. acct. rep.; named act. rep. 1965; 1966, joined Walter Reade Organization as asst. v.p. chg. of TV; 1969, moved to WRO Theatre Div.; 1970, joined faculty of School of Visual Arts; 1971 named v.p. of WRO Theatres; 1976, joined Paramount Pictures as v.p. in charge of feature film acquisition. Since 1978 pres. & owner of Castle Hill Productions; 1974, prod. & moderated An Evening with Joseph E. Levine at Town Hall, N.Y.; 1974–1980, host of radio show Movie Talk on WMCA (N.Y.), WMEX (Boston), WICE (Providence); 1982–83 host of syndicated TV show, Julian Schlossbergs' Movie Talk; producers' rep. for Elia Kazan, Dustin Hoffman, Elaine May, George C. Scott.
PICTURES: Going Hollywood: The War Years, Hollywood Uncensored, Hollywood Ghost Stories, No Nukes, Going Hollywood: The 30's, 10 From Your Show of Shows, In the Spirit.
THEATRE: It Had To Be You, An Evening with Nichols and May, Rainbow Room, N.Y., 1983.
TELEVISION: Steve Allen's Golden Age of Comedy; All the Best, Steve Allen.

SCHLOSSER, HERBERT S.: Executive. b. Atlantic City, NJ, April 21, 1926. e. Princeton U., Yale Law Sch. Joined law firm of Phillips, Nizer, Benjamin, Krim & Ballon, 1954; attorney, California National Productions (subsidiary of National Broadcasting Company) 1957; v.p. & gen. mgr., 1960; director, talent & program administration, NBC television network, 1961; v.p., talent & program admin., 1962; v.p. programs, west coast, 1966–72; exec. v.p., NBC-TV, 1972; president, NBC Television Network, 1973, pres. & chief operating officer, NBC, April 1, 1974–76; Pres. & chief executive officer, 1977–78; exec. V.P. RCA 1978–85; sr. advisor, broadcasting & entertainment, Wertheim, Schroder & Co., 1986.

SCHLUSSELBERG, MARTIN: Film Executive. b. Sept. 1936. e. Yeshiva U. Booking clerk. UA. 1956; head booker, Citation Films, 1958; head booker, Desilu Dist., Co., 1961; head booker, and asst. to gen. sls. mgr., Medallion Pictures Corp., 1963; World Ent. Corp., 1966, Sales Mgr.; Crystal Pictures, 1978, sls. mgr., v.p.

SCHMIDT, WOLF: Producer, Distributor. b. Freiburg/Br., Germany, June 30, 1937. Came to U.S. 1962 as freelance journalist. Started producing in 1969, distributing independently since 1972. Now heads Kodiak Films.
PICTURES: Ski Fever (prod.), Stamping Ground (co-prod.), Young Hannah (exec. prod.), Things Fall Apart (prod.),The Passover Plot (prod.), Run For the Roses (co-prod.). Ghost Fever (exec. prod.); Defense Play (prod.); Riding the Edge (prod.), The Fourth War (prod.), The Crew (exec. prod.).

SCHMOELLER, DAVID: Writer, Director. b. Louisville, KY, Dec. 8, 1947. e. Universidad de Las Americas, 1967–69; studied film and theater under Luis Bunuel and Alejandro Jodorowsky, U. of Texas, B.A., M.A., 1969–74. Wrote and directed 7 short films while studying at U. of Texas; won 27 intl. awards. In Hollywood spent 6 months working as intern to Peter Hyams on film, Capricorn One. Now heads own co., The Schmoeller Corp.
PICTURES: Tourist Trap (debut as dir.); The Seduction (Dir., s.p.); Crawlspace (dir., s.p.). As writer only: The Day Time Ended, The Peeper, Last Chance Romance, Thrill Palace, Warriors of the Wind (Eng. adaptation), Ghost Town (story), Catacombs (dir.), Puppet Master (dir.).
TELEVISION: James at 15 (s.p.); Kid Flicks (cable; s.p., prod.).
NOVEL: The Seduction.

SCHNEER, CHARLES H.: Producer, b. Norfolk, VA, May 5, 1920. e. Columbia Coll. pres., Morningside Prods. Inc. & Pictures Corp.; 1956. Founded Andor Films 1974.
PICTURES: Prod. The 3 Worlds of Gulliver, The 7th Voyage of Sinbad, I Aim at the Stars, Face of a Fugitive, Good Day for a Hanging, Battle of the Coral Sea, Tarawa Beachhead, Mysterious Island, Jason and the Argonauts, First Men In The Moon, Half A Sixpence, Land Raiders, Valley of Gwangi, The Executioner, The Golden Voyage of Sinbad, Sinbad & The Eye of the Tiger, Clash of the Titans.

SCHNEIDER, DICK: Producer, Director. b. Cazadero, CA, Mar. 7. e. Coll. of the Pacific. U.S. Navy, W.W.II. Winner of 4 Emmys.
TELEVISION: Dough Re Mi, Wide Wide World, Colgate Comedy Hour, Beatrice Lilly & Jackie Gleason Comedy Hours, Henry Morgan Show, Kate Smith Show, Big Story, Treasury Men in Action, Doorway to Danger, Today Show, Home, Tonight Show, General Mills Circus; dir. coverage of political conventions; dir. NBC-TV coverage, Princess Margaret's wedding and Paris summit conference; dir. Eleanor Roosevelt Specials, 1959–60; Something Special 61, At This Very Moment, Inauguration, Gemini, Emmys, 1962, 1963, 1964; Papal Mass for all networks at Yankee Stadium, 1965–66; 1966–67 Tonight Show, Orange Bowl, Macy's Parade; Jr. Miss Pageant; 1967–70 College Queen, Emmy Award. Prod.; Macy's Parade, 1968–69 Orange Bowl Parade, 1968–69; Prod.-dir., NBC Expt. in TV, New Communication; prod., Big Sur; prod.-dir., Jr. Miss Pageant, 1968–69; dir. Dream House, ABC; dir. Who, What or Where, NBC; produced in 1970: Macy's Parade, Junior Miss, Orange Bowl Parade. 1971–79 Macy's Parade, Stars and Stripes; in 1972: Post Parade, Stars and Stripes 1973–75; Rose Parade 1974–81; Salute to Sir Lew; Jeopardy; NBC Star Salute, 1980; Emmy winner, 1980; Rose Parade, 1981-84; Star Salute, 1981; UCP Telethons, 1981-86. Macy's Parade, 1980–87; Diabetes Telethon, 1983; NBC Affiliate Convention, 1980–85; 1986, People's Choice, Jeopardy. 1984–87.

SCHNEIDER, JOHN: Actor. b. Mount Kisco, NY, Apr. 8, 1954. Active in drama club in high school in Atlanta. Worked as fashion model and played guitar singing own compositions in various Atlanta clubs. Active in local community theatre. Summer stock in New Hampshire.
PICTURES: Smokey and the Bandit, Million Dollar Dixie Deliverance, Eddie Macon's Run, Cocaine Wars, Speed Zone, Ministry of Vengeance.
TELEVISION: Dukes of Hazzard; John Schneider—Back Home. Movies: Dream House, Happy Endings, Stagecoach, Christmas Comes to Willow Creek, Outback Bound.

SCHNEIDER, JOHN, A.: Executive. b. Chicago, IL, Dec. 4, 1926. e. U. of Notre Dame, B.S. U.S.N.R., 1943–47, Exec. assignments with CBS-TV, in Chicago and New York 1950–58; VP, gen. mgr. WCAU-TV, Philadelphia 1958–64; WCBS-TV, New York 1964–65; pres. CBS-TV Network 1965–66; pres. CBS/Broadcast Group 1966–69, 1971–77; exec. VP CBS Inc. 1969–71, TV and MP consultant 1977–79; consultant WCI, 1979; pres., CEO Warner Amex Satellite Entertainment Corp., 1980.

SCHNEIER, FREDERICK: Executive. b. New York, NY, May 31, 1927; e. NYU, 1951, bus. admin.; NYU Grad. Sch., M.B.A., 1953. Dir. sls. planning, Mutual Broadcasting System, 1947–53; media research dir., RKO Teleradio, 1953–55; RKO Teleradio Advisory Comm., 1955–56; exec. staff RKO Teleradio & dir., marketing services, 1956–58; exec. vice-pres., Showcorporation, 1958–71; v.p. TV programming, RKO General, 1972–1973; v.p.; Hemdale Leisure Corporation, 1973–79; Viacom Enterprises v.p., feature films, 1979; sr. v.p., program acquisitions & motion pictures, 1980–83; sr. v.p., acquisitions, Showtime/The Movie Channel, 1983–85; sr. v.p. program acquisitions, program enterprises, 1985–87; now exec. v.p., programming.

SCHNUR, JEROME: Producer, Director. b. New York, NY, July 30, 1923. e. Carnegie Tech. Film prod. & dir. many indep. cos., 1939–43; prod., dir., training films, U.S. Air Force 1943–46; indep. film prod., Hollywood, 1946–50: on bd. of dir., Alson Prod., Inc. & Burwood Pictures Corp.; prod., dir., CBS-TV, N.Y., 1950–51; prod., dir., Goodson-Todson Prod., 1951–56; pres., Holiday Prod., indep. TV prod., 1956; Metropole Prod., indep. film prod., 1956; exec. prod. chg. creative prog. Frank Cooper Assoc., 1958; pres., Jerome Schnur Prods., Inc. Packager and Producer TV and Film. Recipient 1970–71 Peabody Award, 1970–71 Saturday Review Award, 1972 Emmy Citation; 1975 Ohio State Award.
TELEVISION: It's News to Me, Two for the Money, The Name's the Same, What's My Line, Beat the Clock, Robert Q. Lewis Show, Judge for Yourself, Holiday series, Fred Allen Show, Dotto, Make the Connection, Scene of the Crime, Who Pays, Shari Lewis Show, Bell Telephone Hour, U.S. Steel Spec., Private Eye—Private Eye, exec. prod., United Fund Simulcast This Is My Town; writer, dir., Mark of Cain, Chronicle, Tomorrow Was Yesterday; dir., L'Enfance du Christ; exec. prod., Supermarket Sweep; dir., Michelangelo's Pauline Chapel. dir., Jeptha's Daughter. St. Joan. TV ballet specials. Exec. Prod. Everybody's Talking; dir. Missions of San Antonio; Light in the Wilderness, and David Wept; Exec. prod. Politithon 1970—. Exec. prod. & dir., Threatened Paradise A Time To Live 1972; dir., Questions of Abraham Special Cantata; American Ballet Theatre Special; Luther. Exec. prod., Musical Chairs, Strategy, Dir., Joffrey ballet, PBS special; dir. Jerusalem Symphony, CBS spec.; 1977; dir. Song of Songs, dir., All Star-Jazz Show.

SCHOENFELD, LESTER: Executive. b. Brooklyn, NY, Dec. 6, 1916. e. City Coll. of New York, 1934–38. Asst. mgr., Randforce Amusement, 1936–38; mgr., Rugoff & Becker circuit, 1938–47; mgr., Golden & Ambassador Theatres, 1948; print & sales dept., Film Classics, 1948–50; chg. of theatrical, non-theatrical & TV dist., Brit. Info. Serv.; est. Lester A. Schoenfeld Films, 1958; Schoenfeld Films Distributing Corp., 1960.

SCHONFELD, NORMAN J.: Theater Executive, b. Newark, NJ, June 25, 1934. e. U. of Pennsylvania, B.A., 1955. Captain, U.S.A.F., 1957, sls. rep. Bache & Co. 1963, v.p. Tiger Films, Inc., 1966 founder and president, Wood Theater Group.

SCHORR, DANIEL: Television News Correspondent. b. New York, NY, Aug. 31, 1916. e. City Coll. of New York. Started with various news services and newspapers. Joined CBS in 1953 on special assignment; 1955, reopened CBS bureau in Moscow; 1958–60, roving assignment; 1960–1966, chief German Bureau; 1966–76, chief of Washington Bureau; 1979, Public Radio and TV; 1980, correspondent for Cable News Network.

SCHRADER, PAUL: Writer, Director. b. Grand Rapids, MI, July 22, 1946. m. actress Mary Beth Hurt. e. Calvin Coll. (theology & philosophy); Columbia U., UCLA, M.A., cinema. Served as film critic for L.A. Free Press and Cinema 1970–72. Former professor at Columbia U.

PICTURES: The Yakuza (co-s.p.), Taxi Driver (s.p.), Rolling Thunder (s.p.), Obsession (s.p.), Blue Collar (co-s.p., dir). Hardcore (s.p., dir.), Old Boyfriends (co-s.p., and exec. prod.), American Gigolo (s.p., dir.), Raging Bull (co-s.p.), Cat People (dir.), Mishima (co-s.p., dir.), Light of Day (dir., s.p.); The Mosquito Coast (s.p.), The Last Temptation of Christ (s.p.), Patty Hearst (dir.).

SCHRODER, RICKY: Actor. b. Staten Island, NY, April 3, 1970. Started modelling while only four months; did many TV commercials before theatrical film debut in The Champ, 1979, at age nine.

PICTURES: The Last Flight of Noah's Ark, The Earthling, Apt Pupil.

TELEVISION: Silver Spoon (series). Movies: Little Lord Fauntleroy, Two Kinds of Love, A Reason to Live, Too Young the Hero, Terror on Highway 91, Out on the Edge.

SCHROEDER, BARBET: Producer-Director. b. Teheran, Iran, April 26, 1941. e. Sorbonne (philosophy degree). Worked as a jazz tour operator in Europe, a photo-journalist in India and critic for Cahiers du Cinema and L'Air de Paris, 1958–63. 1963: asst. to Jean-Luc Godard on Les Carabiniers. 1964: formed own prod. co. Les Films du Losange. Prod. and acted in Rohmer's La Boulangere de Monceau. As actor only: Wait Until Spring, Bandini,

PICTURES AS PRODUCER: La Carriere de Suzanne (short); Mediterrannee; Paris Vu Par; The Collector; Tu Imagines Robinson; My Night at Maud's; Claire's Knee; Chloe in the Afternoon; Out One (co-prod.); The Mother and the Whore (co-prod.); Celine and Julie Go Boating; Flocons D'Or; The Marquise of O; Roulette Chinoise (co-prod.); The American Friend (co-prod.); Le Passe-Montagne; The Rites of Death; Perceval Le Gallois; Le Navire Night; Le Pont du Nord; Mauvaise Conduite.

PICTURES AS DIRECTOR: More (1969); Sing-Song (documentary); La Vallee; General Idi Amin Dada (doc.); Maitresse; Koko, The Talking Gorilla (doc.); Charles Bukowski (50 4-min. videos, 1982–84); Tricheurs; Barfly, Reversal of Fortune

SCHULBERG, BUDD WILSON: Writer. b. New York, NY, Mar. 27, 1914. son of B. P. Schulberg, prod. e. Dartmouth Coll. Publicist, Paramount Pictures, 1931; writer for screen from Armed services W.W.II. Syndicated newspaper columnist: The Schulberg Report.

THEATER: The Disenchanted (with Harvey Breit, 1958), What Makes Sammy Run? (bk. for musical).

PICTURES: A Star is Born (additional dial.), Nothing Sacred (add. dial.), Little Orphan Annie (co-s.p.), Winter Carnival (co-s.p. with F. Scott Fitzgerald), Weekend for Three (orig. and co-s.p.), City Without Men (co-story), Government Girl (adapt.), Original s.p.: On the Waterfront (Acad. Award, & Writers Guild Award, 1954), A Face in The Crowd, Wind Across the Everglades (co-s.p.), Joe Louis: For All Times (doc., Cine Golden Eagle Award, 1985).

BOOKS: Author, 3 best-selling novels including The Disenchanted. Harder They Fall; On the Waterfront, Face in the Crowd, Wind Across the Everglades. Everything That Moves, Moving Pictures: Memories of a Hollywood Prince; Non-fiction books; Writers in America, Swan Watch; Loser and Still Champion: Muhammad Ali

TELEVISION: What Makes Sammy Run?, Teleplay: A Question of Honor, A Table at Ciro's,

SCHULTZ, MICHAEL: Director, Producer. b. Milwaukee, WI, Nov. 10, 1938. e. U. of Wisconsin, Marquette U. Theatre includes Kongi's Harvest; Does a Tiger Wear a Necktie?; Operation Sidewinder, What the Winesellers Buy, The Cherry Orchard.

PICTURES: Director: Cooley High; Car Wash; Greased Lightning; Which Way Is Up?; Sgt. Pepper's Lonely Hearts Club Band; Scavenger Hunt; Carbon Copy; Bustin' Loose; The Last Dragon; Krush Groove, Disorderlies (prod., dir.).

TELEVISION: To Be Young, Gifted and Black; Ceremonies in Dark Old Men; Benny's Place; For Us The Living; The Jerk, Too; Fade Out—The Erosion of Black Images in the Media (documentary), Rock 'n' Roll Mom, Tarzan in Manhattan, Jury Duty.

SCHULMAN, JOHN A.: Executive. e. Yale U., 1968; law degree from Boalt Hall, U. of California, Berkeley, 1972. Founding partner in Beverly Hills law firm, Weissmann, Wolff, Bergman, Coleman & Schulman in 1981 after nine years with firm of Kaplan, Livingston, Goodwin, Berkowitz & Selvin. Joined Warner Bros. 1984 as v.p. & gen. counsel; 1989 appt. sr. v.p. and gen. counsel.

SCHUMACHER, JOEL: Writer, Director. b. New York, NY, 1939. Worked as design and display artist for Henri Bendel dept. store NY while attending Parson's Sch. of Design. As fashion designer opened own boutique, Paraphernalia. Joined Revlon as designer of clothing and packaging before entering m.p. indus. as costume designer on Interiors, Sleeper, The Last of Sheila, Blume in Love.

PICTURES: Writer: Car Wash, Sparkle, The Wiz. Director: The Incredible Shrinking Woman; D.C. Cab (also s.p.); St. Elmo's Fire (also s.p.), The Lost Boys, Cousins.

TELEVISION: Writer, Director: Virginia Hill; Amateur Night at the Dixie Bar & Grill; Music video Devil Inside for rock group INXS (dir.).

SCHUMAN, EDWARD L.: Executive. b. Lisbon, CT, Sept. 3, 1916. e. Wayne U., 1932–34; U. of Michigan, 1934–37. Mathematician, 1937–51, assistant actuary, Detroit City Employees Pension Fund. Pres., Studio Theatre Corp, Detroit, 1951 to 1975; pres., Studio 8 Theatre Corp., Detroit, 1953 to 1975; secy.-treas., Studio New Center Theatre Corp. of Detroit, 1975; v.p. and gen. mgr. Art Theatre Guild, 1954–60; v.p. Rugoff Theatres, N.Y., 1960–63. V.P. and bd. member, Walter Reade Organization 1963–75; exec. v.p. & partner, Quartet Films 1980–86. Associate producer Broadway plays, Same Time Next Year, The Comedians, Anna Christie, and Asinamali. Assoc. prod. of First Monday in October. Co-prod., Torch Song Trilogy in London.

SCHWAB, SHELLY: Executive. Station mgr., WAGA-TV, Atlanta; various sls. & mgr. posts with CBS. Joined MCA, 1978, becoming exec. v.p., MCA-TV. 1986, appt. pres., MCA TV Enterprises, 1989 appt. pres. MCA TV.

SCHWARTZ, BERNARD: Producer. Brought to Hollywood by the late Howard Hughes to watch his film interests; Schwartz teamed with atty. Greg Bautzer to package movie deals for clients. Re-cut number of Buster Keaton's silent movies into documentary anthologies (The Golden Age of Comedy, When Comedy Was King, etc.). Subsequently made TV series, One Step Beyond, followed by The Wackiest Ship in the Army, Miss Teen International specials, etc. Named pres. Joseph M. Schenck Enterprises, for which made Journey to the Center of the Earth, Eye of the Cat, A Cold Wind in August, I Passed for White, The Shattered Room, Trackdown. Presently partnered with Alan Silverman of Essaness Theatres.

PICTURES: Coal Miner's Daughter (prod.), Road Games (exec. prod.) Psycho II (exec. prod.), St. Elmo's Fire (co-exec. prod.).

TELEVISION: Elvis and Me (co-exec. prod.).

SCHWARTZ, LESLIE R.: Exhibitor. b. New York, NY, June 7, 1915; e. Lehigh U., 1937. Entered m.p. ind. with Century Theatres Construction Co., 1937–39; film buyer, Century Theatres, 1940–42; personnel exec. 1942–43; U.S. Army service, 1943–45; with Andrews, Inc., Century Theat. concessions, 1945–48; apptd. gen. theatre mgr. 1948; pres., 1955. Member: Pi Lambda Phi; North Shore Country Club; pres., Metropolitan Motion Picture Assn., 1960–62; pres., 1955–present.

SCHWARY, RONALD L.: Producer. b. Oregon, May 23, 1944. e. U. of Southern California.

PICTURES: Ordinary People; Absence of Malice; A Soldier's Story; Batteries Not Included, Havanna.

TELEVISION: Tour of Duty.

SCHWARZENEGGER, ARNOLD: Actor. b. Graz, Austria, July 30, 1947. m. NBC reporter Maria Shriver. e. U. Wisconsin, B.A. Titles: Three-time winner, Mr. Universe title, 7 times Mr. Olympia, also Mr. Europe, Mr. World and Jr. Mr. Europe. Special Olympics weightlifting Coach (1989), Prison Weightlifting Rehabilitation Prog. Awards: Sportsman of the Year (1977, Assn. Physical Fitness Ctrs.), Golden Globe (best newcomer, 1977), ShoWest '85 Intl. Star., ShoWest Career Achievement Award, NATO Male Star of Yr. (1987),

PICTURES: Hercules in New York (1969), The Long

Goodbye, The Villian, Stay Hungry, Pumping Iron, The Villain, Conan the Barbarian, Conan the Destroyer, The Terminator, Red Sonja, Commando, Raw Deal, Predator, Running Man, Red Heat, Twins, Total Recall.

TELEVISION: The Jayne Mansfield Story. A Very Special Christmas Party (host).

BOOKS: Arnold: The Education of a Bodybuilder; Arnold's Bodyshaping for Women; Arnold's Bodybuilding for Men; The Encyclopedia of Modern Bodybuilding.

SCHYGULLA, HANNA: Actress. b. Kattowitz, Germany, Dec. 25, 1943. Worked with Rainer Werner Fassbinder in Munich's Action Theater; a founder of the "anti-theatre" group.

PICTURES: Love Is Colder Than Death, Gods of the Plague, Rio Das Mortes, Beware of a Holy Whore, The Merchant of Four Seasons, The Bitter Tears of Petra Von Kant, House by the Sea, Jail Bait, Effi Briest, The Marriage of Maria Braun, Berlin Alexanderplatz, Lili Marleen, The Night of Varennes, Passion, A Labor of Love, A Love in Germany, The Future Is a Woman, Forever, Lulu; Miss Arizona, The Summer of Ms. Forbes.

TELEVISION: (U.S.): Peter the Great, Barnum, Casanova.

SCOFIELD, PAUL: Actor. b. Hurstpierpoint, England, Jan. 21, 1922. Gained greatest fame on London stage in much Shakespeare and modern plays, including Staircase and Desire Under the Elms, I'm Not Rappaport.

PICTURES: That Lady, Carve Her Name with Pride, The Train, A Man for All Seasons (Oscar, 1966), King Lear, Scorpio, A Delicate Balance, 1919, When the Whales Came, Henry V.

TELEVISION: (U.S.): Anna Karenina, The Attic: The Hiding of Anne Frank.

SCOLA, ETTORE: Director. b. Treviso, Italy, May 10, 1931. e. U. of Rome. Began career 1947 as journalist; 1950, wrote for radio shows. Then script writer 1954; debut as director, 1964. Has directed or co-directed 20 films, all of which he also scripted or co-wrote. Also has written 50 other scripts, mostly comedies, for other directors.

PICTURES: Let's Talk about Women, Economical Crisis, One Sketch, The Archdevil, Will Your Heroes Find Their Friends Who Disappeared so Mysteriously in Africa?, Inspector Pepe, Pizza Triangle, Excuse Me My Name Is Rocco Papaleo, The Greatest Evening of My Life, We All Loved Each Other so Much, Down and Dirty, Signore e Signori Buonanotte, A Special Day, Viva Italia, Chi Si Dice a Roma, The Terrace, Passion of Love, The Night of Varennes, Le Bal, Macaroni, The Family (also co-s.p.), Le Capitain Fracassa, Splendor (also s.p.), What Time is It? (also s.p.).

SCORSESE, MARTIN: Writer, Director, Editor. b. New York, NY, Nov. 17, 1942. Began career while film arts student at NYU, doing shorts What's A Nice Girl Like You Doing in a Place Like This? (dir., s.p.), It's Not Just You, Murray and The Big Shave.

PICTURES: Editor and asst. dir.: Woodstock, Medicine Ball Caravan, Elvis. Director: Who's That Knocking at My Door? (and assoc. prod.), Boxcar Bertha, Mean Streets (also co-s.p.), Alice Doesn't Live Here Anymore, Taxi Driver, New York, New York, The Last Waltz (also actor), Raging Bull, King of Comedy, After Hours, The Color of Money, The Last Temptation of Christ, New York Stories (Life Lessons), The Grifters (prod. only), Good Fellas, The Crew (exec. prod. only), Such Dreams I Have Dreamed (actor only).

TELEVISION: Amazing Stories.

SCOTT, GEORGE C.: Actor, Director. b. Wise, VA, Oct. 18, 1927. m. actress Trish VanDevere. Served 4 years Marine Corps. e. U. of Missouri, appeared in varsity productions, summer stock, Shakespeare.

THEATRE: Off-Broadway in Richard III, As You Like It, Children of Darkness, Merchant of Venice, Desire Under the Elms, Antony and Cleopatra; Broadway in Comes a Day, The Andersonville Trial, The Wall, The Little Foxes, Plaza Suite, Uncle Vanya, director All God's Chillun Got Wings, Death of a Salesman (dir., actor), Sly Fox, Present Laughter.

PICTURES: The Hanging Tree (debut, 1959), Anatomy of a Murder, The Hustler, List of Adrian Messenger, Dr. Strangelove, The Bible, Flim-Flam Man, Patton (Acad. Award), They Might Be Giants, The Last Run, Hospital, The New Centurions, Oklahoma Crude, The Day of the Dolphin, The Hindenburg, Islands in the Stream, Crossed Swords, Movie Movie, Hardcore, The Changeling, The Formula, Taps, Firestarter, The Exorcist: 1990.

Director-Actor, Rage; Director-Producer-Actor, The Savage Is Loose.

TELEVISION: Major TV playhouses including DuPont Show of the Month, Playhouse 90, Hallmark Hall of Fame, Kraft Theatre, Omnibus, Armstrong Theatre, Play of the Week, NBC Sunday Showcase, Dow Hour of Great Mysteries, Esso Theatre; East Side, West Side (series); The Crucible, Jane Eyre, The Price, Fear on Trial, Beauty and the Beast; The Andersonville Trial (dir.), A Christmas Carol, China Rose, Choices, The Last Days of Patton, The Murders in the Rue Morgue, Pals, The Ryan White Story. Mini-Series: Mussolini—The Untold Story, Mr. President (series).

SCOTT, GORDON: Actor. r.n. Gordon M. Werschkul. b. Portland, OR, Aug. 3, 1927. e. U. of Oregon. U.S. Army, 1944–47; then worked as fireman, cowboy, life guard; signed by Sol Lesser Prod. for role of Tarzan; debut in Tarzan's Hidden Jungle (1955); since in: Tarzan and the Lost Safari, Tarzan's Greatest Adventure, The Tramplers.

SCOTT, GORDON L. T.: Producer. b. Edinburgh, Scotland, January 3, 1920. e. George Watson's Boys Coll. Served H.M. Forces 1939–46. Ent. m.p. ind. 1946 as 3rd asst. dir. with Ealing Studios. 1948: 1st asst. dir. on Passport to Pimlico, Train of Events; joined Associated British 1949 and worked on The Dancing Years, The Franchise Affair, Laughter in Paradise, Angels One Five, Isn't Life Wonderful, Will Any Gentleman, Rob Roy; 1953 prod. man. The Weak and the Wicked, It's Great To Be Young, The Dam Busters; 1956 appt. production exec. asst.; prod. Look Back in Anger, Sands of the Desert, Petticoat Pirates, The Pot Carriers, The Punch & Judy Man, Crooks in Cloisters, Forbush and the Penguins, Voices, The Maids, Snow Children, Out of Season, Hedda, The Abbess. Left Associated British 1969. Currently free-lance. Recent Prods: Spectre Hanover Street, Friend or Foe, Tightrope to Terror, Lace, Haunters of the Deep, Out of the Darkness.

TELEVISION: (Prod): International Detective Series, The Avengers, Pathfinders, The Maids, Snow Children, A Man Called Intrepid, Undying Love, The Eye of the Yemanja.

SCOTT, J.C.: Executive. e. UCLA. Worked as prod. asst. on The Waltons and prod. coordinator for America at the Movies; two years at Intl. Creative Mgt. She joined Edward S. Feldman Co. at 20th-Fox as dir. of creative affairs; then v.p. of creative affairs for Marvin Worth Prods. Left to join Walt Disney Pictures 1983 as exec. asst. to Richard Berger, pres. 1984, promoted to v.p., m.p. prod. Assoc. prod.: The Sender.

SCOTT, MARTHA: Actress. b. Jamesport, September 22, 1916. e. U. of Michigan. In little theatres over U.S.; summer stock N.Y.; on radio with Orson Welles; Broadway debut Our Town (1938), film debut in Our Town, 1940 (Oscar nom.). Theater producer since 1968 with Henry Fonda and Alfred De Liagre at Kennedy Center and on Bdwy (Time of Your Life, First Monday in October).

PICTURES: Cheers for Miss Bishop, They Dare Not Love, One Foot in Heaven, In Old Oklahoma; Hi Diddle Diddle; So Well Remembered, When I Grow Up, Desperate Hours, Ben Hur, Ten Commandments, Airport 1975, Turning Point, Doin' Time on Planet Earth.

PLAYS INCLUDE: Soldier's Wife, Voice of the Turtle, The Number, Male Animal, Remarkable Mr. Pennypacker, Forty-Second Cousin.

TELEVISION: Beulah Land, Adam, Father Figure, Charleston, The Word, Murder She Wrote, Hotel, A Girl's Life (pilot). Movie: Daughters of the Street.

SCOTT, RIDLEY: Director, Producer. b. South Shields, Northumberland, Eng., 1939. Brother of director Tony Scott. e. Royal College of Art, London. Joined newly formed Film Sch. First film: Boy on Bicycle. Won design scholarship in NY. Returned to London and joined BBC as set designer (Z-Cars, The Informers series). Directed almost 3,000 commercials in 18 years.

PICTURES: The Duellists, Alien, Blade Runner, Legend, Someone to Watch Over Me (also exec. prod.), Black Rain.

SCOTT, TONY: Director. Began career in TV commercials, being partnered with his brother Ridley in prod. co. Winner of numerous Clios, Gold & Silver Lions, and other awards. Entered m.p. industry 1972, directing half-hr. film, One of the Missing, for British Film Inst. and Loving Memory, 1-hr. feature for Albert Finney.

PICTURES: The Hunger, Top Gun, Beverly Hills Cop II, Revenge.

SCOTT-THOMAS, KRISTIN: Actress. b. England. Lived in France since 18. e. Central School of Speech and Drama, London and Ecole Nationale des Arts et Technique de Theatre in Paris. Stage debut in La Lune Declinante Sur 4 Ou 5 Personnes Qui Danse. Other theater work in Paris.

PICTURES: Djamel Et Juliette, L'Agent Troube, La Meridienne, Under the Cherry Moon, A Handful of Dust, Force Majeure, Bille en tete.

TELEVISION: L'Ami D'Enfance de Maigret, Blockhaus, Chameleon/La Tricheuse (Aust.), Sentimental Journey (Germany), sSCOral's Daughter, The Tenth Man.

SCULLY, JOE: Talent Executive, Casting Director, Producer. b. Kearney, NJ, March 1, 1926. e. Goodman Memorial Theatre of the Art Inst. of Chicago, 1946. m. Penelope Gillette. Acted until 1951. CBS-TV, N.Y. Casting Dir., Danger You Are There, Omnibus, The Web, 1951–56. 1956–60, CBS-TV, Associate Prod., Studio One, Dupont Show of the Month, Playhouse 90. 1962–64, CBS Stations Div. KNXT, Producer, Repertoire Workshop. 1965–70 Casting Dir. 20th Century-Fox Films.

1978, Re-established Joe Scully-Casting, independent service to the industry. 1983, casting director, Walt Disney Pictures.

PICTURES: Hello Dolly, In Like Flint, Valley of the Dolls, Planet of the Apes, The Flim-Flam Man, Sounder, Lady Sings the Blues, Play It as It Lays, The Stone Killer, Parallax View, Lifeguard, Man in the Glass Booth, Middle Age Crazy, Death Wish II.

TELEVISION: Peyton Place, Room 222, Pilots: Julia, The Ghost & Mrs. Muir. 1970, Joe Scully Casting, Indep., The Bill Cosby Show, 1971: TV Feature, Thief, Missiles of October, Earth II; Series, Search, Bonanza, Nichols, Snoop Sisters, Columbo, Switch, McMillan & Wife, Tales of the Unexpected, Gone are the Days (Disney Channel, 1983).

SEAGROVE, JENNY: Actress. b. Kuala Lumpur. Stage debut 1979. Early TV: The Brack Report, The Woman in White, Diana. Recent stage: Jane Eyre.

PICTURES: Local Hero, Savage Islands, A Shocking Accident, Tattoo, The Sign of Four, Appointment With Death, A Chorus of Disapproval, The Guardian.

TELEVISION: A Woman of Substance, Hold The Dream, In Like Flynn, Killer, Lucy Walker, Magic Moments, Some Other Spring, The Betrothed.

SEALEY, PETER S.: Executive, b. Aug. 26, 1940. e. U. of Florida, B.S., economics; Yale U. Graduate Sch., master of industrial admin. Joined Coca-Cola Co.. 1969; named v.p., mgr. of mktg. planning dept., 1976–79. 1979–82, v.p. & mktg. dir. of The Wine Spectrum, Coca-Cola subsidiary. 1982, elected v.p. of Coca-Cola and named mgr. of corporate mktg. operations. 1986, named exec. v.p., Columbia Pictures Industries: then pres. of mktg. & dist., Columbia Pictures. 1987, named pres. & COO, Coca-Cola Telecommunications; Sept. 1988, appt. pres. worldwide marketing, Weintraub Entertainment Group.

SECOMBE, SIR HARRY, C.B.E.: Singer, Comedian, Actor. b. Swansea, Wales, Sept. 8, 1921. m.p. debut, Penny Points to Paradise, 1951; awarded, C.B.E., 1963. 1963–64: London stage starring in Pickwick. 1965: same role New York stage. 1967–68, The Four Musketeers; 1975, The Plumber's Progress.

PICTURES: Forces Sweetheart, Down Among the Z Men, Trilby, Davy, Jet Storm, Oliver, The Bed Sitting Room, Song of Norway, Rhubarb, Doctor in Trouble, The Magnificent Seven Deadly Sins, Sunstruck.

TELEVISION: Numerous appearances, incl. own series: Secombe and Friends, The Harry Secombe Show, Secombe with Music. Also special version, Pickwick. Presenter of Tyne Tees TV's Highway since 1983. Author of Twice Brightly, Goon for Lunch, Katy and the Nurgla, Welsh Fargo, Goon Abroad, The Harry Secombe Diet Book, Harry Secombe's Highway, The Highway Companion.

SEGAL, GEORGE: Actor. b. New York, NY, Feb. 13, 1934. m. Linda Rogoff. e. Columbia U., B.A., 1955. Worked as janitor, ticket-taker, soft-drink salesman, usher and under-study at N.Y.'s Circle in the Square theatre. Acting debut: Downtown Theatre's revival of Don Juan.

THEATER: The Iceman Cometh (1956 revival), Antony and Cleopatra N.Y. Shakespeare Festival, Leave It to Jane, The Premise (satiric improvisational revue), Rattle of a Simple Man, The Knack, Requiem for a Heavyweight.

Formed a nightclub singing act with Patricia Scott. Record album of ragtime songs and banjo music: The Yama, Yama Man. Dir. debut: Bucks County Playhouse prod. Scuba Duba.

TELEVISION: Death of a Salesman, Of Mice and Men, The Desperate Hours, The Cold Room, The Zany Adventures of Robin Hood, Not My Kid, Many Happy Returns, Take Five (series), Murphy's Law (series), Four Minute Mile.

PICTURES: The Young Doctors (1961), The Longest Day, Act One, The New Interns, Invitation to A Gunfighter, Ship of Fools, King Rat, The Lost Command, Who's Afraid of Virginia Woolf? (Acad. Award nom.), The Quiller Memorandum, The St. Valentine's Day Massacre, Bye Bye Braverman, No Way to Treat a Lady, The Southern Star, The Bridge at Remagen, The Girl Who Couldn't Say No, Loving, The Owl and the Pussycat, Where's Poppa?, Born to Win, Hot Rock, A Touch of Class, Blume in Love, The Terminal Man, California Split, The Black Bird, Russian Roulette, The Duchess and the Dirtwater Fox, Fun with Dick and Jane, Rollercoaster, Who Is Killing the Great Chefs of Europe?, Lost and Found, The Last Married Couple in America, Carbon Copy, Stick, All's Fair, Look Who's Talking, Run For Your Life.

SEGAL, MAURICE: Publicist. b. New York, NY, July 22, 1921. e. City Coll. of New York, 1937–41. Entered m.p. ind., adv. dept., 20th Fox, 1941–42; U.S. Army 1942–46; feature writer, pub. dept., 20th Fox, April, 1946; asst. to dir., adv., pub., Century Circuit, 1947; press book dept., Paramount, 1949; trade press rep. 1950; trade press rep. RKO Radio, Nov. 1952; res. to join Richard Condon-Kay Norton, publicists, May, 1953; adv., pub. dept., U-I. Sept. 1954; asst. pub. mgr., United Artists Apr. 1957. Hollywood pub.-exploit., coordinator, 1958; exec. in chg. of M.P. press dept., Universal City Studios, 1966; West Coast adv.-pub. dir., National Gen. Pictures, 1971; Pres., Maurice E. Segal Co., 1974; dir., West Coast operations, Charles Schlaifer & Co., 1976; v.p., Max Youngstein Enterprises, 1979; exec. v.p., Taft Intl. Pictures, 1980; pres. Maurice E. Segal Co., 1982.

SEIDELMAN, ARTHUR ALLAN: Director, Producer, Writer. b. New York, NY, October 11. e. Whittier Coll., B.A.; UCLA, M.A. Former staff member, Repertory Theatre of Lincoln Center and Phoenix Theatre, NY.

THEATER: The Beautiful People (dir., prod., L.A., 1960); The Awakening (dir., prod.); Director: Hamp, Ceremony of Innocence, The Justice Box, Billy, Vieux Carre, The World of My America, Awake and Sing; The Four Seasons, Inherit the Wind, as well as numerous regional prods. and national tours.

PICTURES: Children of Rage (1978, dir., s.p.); Echoes, The Caller, The Front Runner.

TELEVISION: Director: Ceremony of Innocence, Family, Magnum, P.I., Murder She Wrote, Hill Street Blues, Trapper John M.D., Paper Chase, Knots Landing, Bay City Blues. Movies: Which Mother is Mine? A Special Gift, Schoolboy Father, A Matter of Time, I Think I'm Having a Baby, Sin of Innocence, Kate's Secret, Poker Alice, The People Across the Lake, Addicted to His Love, A Friendship in Vienna, A Place at the Table, An Enemy Among Us, Glory Years, Strange Voices, False Witness, From Two Places (also co-prod.).

SEIDELMAN, SUSAN: Director. b. near Philadelphia, PA, Dec.11, 1952. e. Drexel Univ. B.A. Worked at a UHF television station in Phila., NYU film school M.F.A. Debut: 28-min. student film And You Act Like One Too. Then dir. Deficit (short, funded by AFI), and Yours Truly, Andrea G. Stern.

PICTURES: Smithereens (dir., prod., co-s.p.; 1st Amer. indep. feature accepted into competition at Cannes Film Fest., 1982); Desperately Seeking Susan; Making Mr. Right, Cookie, She-Devil.

SELBY, DAVID: Actor. b. Morganstown, WV. Feb. 5, 1941. e. U. of West Virginia. Acted in outdoor dramas in home state and did regional theatre elsewhere. Was ass't. instructor in lit. at Southern Illinois U.

PICTURES: Up the Sandbox, Super Cops, Lady in Blue, Night of Dark Shadows, Rich Kids, Rich and Famous.

TELEVISION: Series: Dark Shadows, Flamingo Road, Falcon Crest. Movies: Washington: Behind Closed Doors, Telethon, Family, King of the Olympics: The Lives and Loves of Avery Brundage.

SELF, WILLIAM: Producer. b. Dayton, OH, June 21, 1921. e. U. of Chicago, 1943. Prod.-dir., Schlitz Playhouse of Stars, 1952–56; prod., The Frank Sinatra Show, 1957; exec. prod., CBS-TV, The Twilight Zone, Hotel De Paree. 1960–61 exec. prod., 20th Century-Fox TV. Hong Kong, Adventures in Paradise, Bus Stop, Follow The Sun, Margie; v.p. in chg. of prod., 20th Century-Fox TV, 1962; exec. v.p., 1964. Pres., FOX TV 1969; v.p. 20th Century Fox Film Corp., 1969; pres. of William Self Productions, Inc., partner, FrankovicCPSelf Productions; 1975; vice-pres., programs, Hollywood CBS Television Network, 1976; 1977, v.p. motion pictures for television and miniseries, CBS Television Network; 1982, pres., CBS Theatrical Films. In 1985, pres., William Self Prods. in association with CBS Prods.

TELEVISION: The Tenth Man (exec. prod., prod.).

SELIG, ROBERT WILLIAM: Exhibitor. b. Cripple Creek, CO, Feb., 1910. e. U. of Denver, 1932, B.A.; doctorate, 1959. 1932 joined advertising sales div., 20th Century Fox, Denver. Founding mem. Theatre Owners of Amer. and NATO. Consultant, Pacific Theatres. Lifetime Trustee, U. of Denver. Member Kappa Sigma, Omicron Delta Kappa, Beta Gamma Sigma; Nat'l Methodist Church Foundation; Pres., Theatre Association of California and CEO NATO of CA; board of directors Los Angeles Chamber of Commerce; chmn. NATO/ShoWest Conventions. Received NATO Sherrill C. Corwin Award, 1989.

SELLECA, CONNIE: Actress. b. Bronx, NY, May 25, 1955.

TELEVISION: The Bermuda Depths (debut, 1978). Series: Flying High (1978–79), Beyond Westworld, The Greatest American Hero, Hotel. Pilots: Flying High, Captain America II, International Airport. Movies: She's Dressed to Kill, The Last Fling, Downpayment on Murder, Brotherhood of the Rose. Specials: The Celebrity Football Classic, Celebrity Challenge of the Sexes, Circus of the Stars.

SELLECK, TOM: Actor. b. Detroit, MI, Jan. 29, 1945. e. U. of Southern California.

PICTURES: Myra Breckenridge, Seven Minutes, Daughters of Satan, Terminal Island, Midway, The Washington Affair, Coma, High Road to China, Lassiter, Runaway, Three Men and a Baby, Her Alibi, An Innocent Man, Quigley Down Under.

TELEVISION: Series: Bracken's World, The Young and the Restless, The Rockford Files, Magnum, P.I. (Emmy, 1984), Movies: Countdown at the Superbowl, The Sacketts (miniseries), Gypsy Warriors, Boston and Kilbride, The Concrete

Cowboys, Divorce Wars—A Love Story, Returning Home, B.L. Stryker: The Dancer's Touch (exec. prod.), Shadow Riders .

SELLERS, ARLENE: Producer. b. Sept. 7, 1921. e. U. of CA at Berkeley, BA, LLB, JD. In partnership as attorneys in L.A. for 20 years with Alex Winitsky before they turned to financing and later production of films.
PICTURES: (co-prod. with Winitsky) End of the Game, The Seven-Per-Cent Solution, Cross of Iron, Night Calls, Silver Bears, Cuba, Blue Skies Again, Scandalous, Swing Shift, Bad Medicine.

SELTZER, DAVID: Writer, Director. b. Highland Park, IL, 1940. m. flutist Eugenia Zukerman. e. Northwestern U. School for Film and Television. Moved to NY where worked on TV game show I've Got a Secret. Made short My Trip to New York. 1966 moved to LA to write for David Wolper's Incredible World of Animals. Then dir. and prod. Wolper documentaries. Worked as ghostwriter on film Willy Wonka and the Chocolate Factory.
PICTURES: Writer: The Hellstrom Chronicle, One Is a Lonely Number, The Prophecy, The Omen, Damien: The Omen Part II; The Other Side of the Mountain, Six Weeks, Table for Five, Lucas (dir., s.p.), Punchline (dir., s.p.).
TELEVISION: National Geographic Specials (prod., dir., writer), William Holden in Unconquered Worlds (prod., dir., writer), The Underworld World of Jacques Cousteau. Movies: Writer: The Story of Eric, Green Eyes, My Father's House, Larry.

SELTZER, ROGER: Executive. b. Chicago, IL, Oct. 7, 1937. e. Indiana U., B.S., 1958; Harvard Graduate Sch. of Business, M.B.A., 1961. Joined ASI Market Research as v.p., 1964; named exec. v.p. 1974. Now v.p., market research, Universal Pictures.

SELTZER, WALTER: Executive. b. Philadelphia, PA, Nov. 7, 1914. e. U. of Pennsylvania. Publicity mgr. for Warner Bros. Theatres, Philadelphia; Fox West Coast Theatres; to Hollywood with MGM 1936–39; Columbia, 1940–41. Enlisted U.S. Marine Corp., 1941–44. Pub. dir., Hal Wallis, 1945–54; v.p. in chg. adv & pub., Hecht-Lancaster Orgn., Feb., 1954–55; assoc. prod., The Boss; partner, Glass-Seltzer, pub. rel. firm; v.p. & exec. prod, Pennebaker Production. 1982, v.p., M.P. & TV Fund. Pres., WSP Inc.
PICTURES: One-Eyed Jacks, Shake Hands With the Devil, Paris Blues, The Naked Edge, Man in the Middle, Wild Seed, War Lord, Beau Geste, Will Penny, Number One, Darker Than Amber, The Omega Man, Skyjacked, Soylent Green, The Cay, The Last Hard Men.

SEMEL, TERRY: Executive. b. New York, NY, Feb. 24, 1943. e. City Coll. of New York, M.B.A., 1967. Was with C.P.A. accounting firm, 1965–66. Entered ind. with Warner Bros. in 1966 as br. mgr., New York, Cleveland, Los Angeles. Domestic sls. mgr. for CBS—Cinema Center Films, 1971–73. In 1973 joined Buena Vista as v.p., gen. sls. mgr. In 1975 went to Warner Bros. as v.p., gen. sls. mgr. In 1978 named exec. v.p. and chief operating officer. Now pres., Warner Bros.

SEMPLE, LORENZO, JR.: Writer.
PICTURES: Fathom, Pretty Poison, Daddy's Gone A-Hunting (with Larry Cohen), The Sporting Club, The Marriage of a Young Stockbroker, Papillon (co-s.p.), Super Cops, The Parallex View (co-s.p.), The Drowning Pool (co-s.p.), Three Days of the Condor (co-s.p.), King Kong, Hurricane (and exec. prod.), Flash Gordon, Never Say Never Again, Sheena (co-s.p.).
TELEVISION: Series: Batman (1966). Movie: Rearview Mirror.

SEN, BACHOO: Producer, Distributor. Entered industry 1950 in India and 1958 in U.K. Director of English Film Co. Ltd., English Film Co. (Exports) Ltd. and English Film Co. (Productions) Ltd. Among 38 features produced: Her Private Hell, Loving Feeling, Love Is a Splendid Illusion, Tenderness, Adam and Nicole, The Intruders. In U.S., Nightmare Weekend. Chairman of Senemedici Inc. and All American Leisure Group Inc.

SENDREY, ALBERT: Music Composer, Arranger, Conductor. b. Chicago, IL, 1921. e. Trinity Coll. Music, London, U. of Southern California, Paris, & Leipzig Conservatories. Winner, Chi. Symphony Orch. prize for First Symphony, 1941; 1948, Reichhold Award Detroit Symph. Orch. for 2nd Symphony. Ohio Sesquicentenn. Award for Overture, Johnny Appleseed, 1953; French liberetto: One Act Opera: The Telltale Stones, 1964; arr., Mary Martin at Radio City Music Hall, 1965. Composer, arr., orch. for many plays, films and TV.
MEMBER: M.P. Academy, ASCAP, CLGA, ASMA, TV Academy.
BROADWAY: orch., arr.: Peter Pan, Ziegfeld Follies, New Faces, At the Grand, Pink Jungle, The Great Waltz, Turn to the Right.
PICTURES: Orch: The Yearling, Three Musketeers, Father's Little Dividend, Duchess of Idaho, Royal Wedding, Easy to Love, Great Caruso, American in Paris, Brigadoon, Athena, Finian's Rainbow, Guys and Dolls, Meet Me in Las Vegas, Opposite Sex, High Society, Raintree County, Let's Be Happy, Ride the High Country, Hallelujah Trail, The Hook, The Comancheros, Nevada Smith, The Oscar, Thoroughly Modern Millie, Hello Down There, Private Navy of Sgt. O'Farrell, Hard Times.
TELEVISION: comp. music: Laramie, Wagon Train, Ben Casey, Wolper Documentaries, Americans Abroad, J. F. Kennedy Anthology; Young Man from Boston, High Chaparral, (collab. with Harry Sukman), Bonanza (with D. Rose), The Monroes, Ken Murray's Hollywood, SWAT (collab. B. de Vorzon), Hard Times, (collab.), Napoleon and Josephine (orch.).

SENECA, JOE: Actor. Has been acting since 1973. In the 1950's was part of a satirical singing group, The Three Riffs performing at a New York club, Le Ruban Bleu. In the 1950s and '60s wrote songs. 1970–73 was a writer for Sesame Street.
THEATER: The Little Foxes (starring Elizabeth Taylor), Of Mice and Men (starring James Earl Jones), Sizwe Banzi Is Dead (Pittsburgh), Ma Rainey's Black Bottom (Yale Repertory and B'way).
PICTURES: Kramer vs. Kramer, The Verdict, Silverado, The Evil Men Do, Crossroads, School Daze, The Blob.
TELEVISION: The Wilma Rudolph Story, Terrible Joe Moran, Solomon Northrup's Odyssey, The House of Dies Drear, Dorothy and Son (Amazing Stories), A Gathering of Old Men.

SERNAS, JACQUES: Actor, Producer. b. Lithuania, July 30, 1925. Became naturalized French citizen, studying medicine in Paris. Was amateur boxer when heard Jean Gabin needed an acting boxer for The Mirror, in which he made professional debut as actor. Has appeared in over 80 films, made in recent years primarily in Italy, now his home.
PICTURES: Lost Youth, The Golden Salamander, Helen of Troy, Jump into Hell, The First Night, La Dolce Vita, 55 Days in Peking, F.B.I.: Operation Baalbeck (also prod.), Operation Gold in the Balearic Islands (also prod.), Super Fly TNT.
TELEVISION: The School of the Painters of Paris (prod. only), The 18th Century Seen Through Its Famous Painters (prod. only), The Red Triangle (Ital. series).

SERPE, RALPH B.: Producer. b. Portland, ME, Dec. 23, 1914. e. Columbia U. Ind. thea. agent, 1936. U.S. Army, Spec. Services, 1942. v.p., Scalera Films, 1946; v.p., Italian Films Export, 1948; U.S. rep., assoc. prod., exec. asst., Dino De Laurentiis, 1952.
PICTURES: War and Peace, Ulysses, The Tempest, Under Ten Flags, Yovanka, Barabbas, The Bible, Drum, The Brinks' Job.

SEVAREID, ERIC: News commentator. b. Velva, ND, Nov. 26, 1912. e. U. of Minnesota, Paris. Started career as reporter: Minneapolis Journal, Paris Herald Tribune, United Press; joined CBS radio news staff in Paris at outbreak of W.W.II; with CBS radio, TV since; nat. corres; retired 1977; Host Eric Sevareid's Chronicle, 1982.
BOOKS: author: Not So Wild a Dream, In One Ear, Small Sounds in the Night, This is Eric Sevareid.

SEVERINO, JOHN C.: Executive. b. New Haven, CT. e. U. of Connecticut. Joined ABC in 1965 as acct. exec. for WABC-TV; later served in various positions for ABC-TV Spot Sales in N.Y. and Chicago. In 1968 named sls. mgr., WLS-TV, Chicago; promoted to gen. sls. mgr., WXYZ-TV, Detroit, 1969. Returned to Chicago station in 1974 as v.p., gen. mgr. In 1974 named v.p., gen. mgr. of KABC-TV, Los Angeles. In 1981 named pres. of ABC Television.

SEWALL, BARBARA JEAN: Public Relations. b. CO, Jan. 6. e. Los Angeles City Coll., Mira Costa Coll, UCLA Pub. dir. & adv. mgr. Saks Fifth Ave., Beverly Hills Hollywood Athletic Club, owner-publicity agency representing actors and independent production cos.; RKO, Samuel Goldwyn Prods., MGM, Edward Small Prod., Warner Bros., 20th Century-Fox, Lowell Thomas, Cinerama, Wrather Television, VideoTravel Prods.

SEYMOUR, DAN: Actor. b. Chicago, IL, Feb. 22, 1915. Performer burlesque, nightclubs. Stage, screen and TV actor.
PLAYS: Rain, Amphitryon 38, Room Service, and others.
PICTURES: Casablanca, To Have and Have Not, Confidential Agent, Intrigue, Key Largo, Johnny Belinda, Rancho Notorious, Maru Maru, Glory Alley, Face to Face, The System, Second Chance, Big Heat, Human Desire, Moonfleet, Buster Keaton Story, Sad Sack, Watusi, Return of the Fly, Leader of the Pack, The Mummy, The Way We Were, Soft Touch, Escape from Witch Mountain, Rainbow Island.
TELEVISION: Casablanca (series), Restless Gun, Perry Mason, Untouchables, Holiday Inn, This Gun for Hire, 77 Sunset Strip, Hawaiian Eye, Get Smart, My Mother The Car, Batman, U.N.C.L.E., Beverly Hillbillies, Voyage to the Bottom of the Sea, My Favorite Martian, Don't Eat the Daisies, The

Bob Hope Show, Kojak, The Chase, Barbary Coast, Fantasy Island.

SEYMOUR, JANE: Actress. r.n. Joyce Frankenberg. b. Hillingdon, England, Feb. 15, 1951. Dancer with London Festival Ballet at 13. On Bdwy. in Amadeus (1980).
PICTURES: Oh! What a Lovely War (debut, 1968), Live and Let Die, The Only Way, Young Winston, Live and Let Die, Sinbad and the Eye of the Tiger, Battlestar Galactica, Oh, Heavenly Dog, Somewhere in Time, Lassiter, The Tunnel, The French Revolution.
TELEVISION: Series: The Onedin Line. Movies: Frankenstein: The True Story, Captains and the Kings, Benny and Barney: Las Vegas Undercover, Seventh Avenue, Killer on Board, The Four Feathers, The Awakening Land, Love's Dark Ride, Dallas Cowboys Cheerleaders, Our Mutual Friend, East of Eden, The Scarlet Pimpernal, Phantom of the Opera, The Haunting Passion, Dark Mirror, The Sun Also Rises, Obsessed with a Married Woman, Jamaica Inn, Crossings, War and Remembrance (mini-series), The Woman He Loved, Onassis: The Richest Man in the World, Jack the Ripper, Keys to Freedom.

SEYRIG, DELPHINE: Actress. b. Beirut, Lebanon, 1932. Formal dramatic training in Paris; later at Actors Studio, N.Y.
PICTURES: Pull My Daisy, Last Year in Marienbad, Muriel, La Musica, Accident, Mr. Freedom, Stolen Kisses, Daughters of Darkness, Peau d'Ane, The Discreet Charm of the Bourgeoisie, The Day of the Jackal, The Black Windmill, Aloise, Doll's House, Dear Michael, Le Dernier Cri, India Song, Faces of Love, Le Chemin Perdu, I Sent a Letter to My Love, Le Petit Pommier, Freak Orlando, Le Grain de Sable, Dorian Gray, Sur le Boulevard de la Presse a Scandale, The Golden Eighties, Letters Home, Johanne d'Arc of Mongolia.

SHABER, DAVID: Screenwriter. b. Cleveland, OH. e. Western Reserve U., Yale U., Taught at Allegheny Coll. in speech and drama dept. Contributor to Cosmopolitan, Life, Esquire; had several short stories in O'Henry prize collections. Also wrote dramas (Shake Hands with the Clown, The Youngest Shall Ask, etc.). First screenplay was Such Good Friends for Otto Preminger.
PICTURES: The Last Embrace, The Warriors, Those Lips, Those Eyes, Night Hawks, Rollover.

SHAGAN, STEVE: Writer. b. New York, NY. Oct. 25, 1927. Apprenticed in little theatres, film lab chores, stagehand jobs. Wrote, produced and directed film short, One Every Second; moved to Hollywood in 1959. Was IATSE man, working as grip, stagehand, electrician to support film writing. Was freelance advertising man and publicist; produced Tarzan TV show. In 1968 began writing and producing two-hour films for TV.
PICTURES: Save the Tiger (prod., s.p.-AA nomination—WGA award, best original s.p.), Hustle (s.p.), Voyage of the Damned (co.-s.p.-AA nomination), The Formula (s.p., prod.), Nightwing (co-s.p.), The Sicilian (s.p.).
TELEVISION: Writer-producer: River of Mystery, Spanish Portrait, Sole Survivor, A Step Out of Line, House on Garibaldi Street (s.p.).
BOOKS: Save the Tiger, City of Angels, The Formula, The Circle, The Discovery, Vendetta.

SHALIT, GENE: b. New York, NY, 1932. e. U. of Illinois. Started as freelance writer; joined NBC Radio Network, working on Monitor. Has been book and film critic, sports and general columnist. In January, 1973 replaced Joe Garagiola as featured regular on NBC Today Show.

SHANLEY, JOHN PATRICK: Writer. b. New York, NY, 1950. e. NYU.
THEATER: Danny and the Deep Blue Sea; Savage in Limbo; Dreamer Examines His Pillow; Italian-American Reconciliation (also dir.).
PICTURES: Five Corners; Moonstruck; The January Man; I Am Angry (short, 1987, dir., s.p.); Joe Versus the Volcano (dir., s.p.).

SHAPIRO, JACOB: Executive. b. Harbin, China, Aug. 26, 1928. e. Gakushuin U. (Peers' Sch.), Tokyo, Japan, B.A. Pol. Sci. Joined Columbia Pictures Intl., N.Y., 1961; Japan sales manager, 1961–65; Puerto Rico gen. mgr., 1965–68; appointed Japan and South Korea gen. mgr., Columbia, 1968; from 1970 became Columbia supv. for Philippines as well as gen. mgr. Japan and South Korea until Feb. 1981; from 1981 v.p. Far East and Australia, Twentieth Century Fox, Los Angeles.

SHAPIRO, KEN: Producer, Director, Writer, Actor. b. New Jersey, 1943. e. Bard Coll. Was child actor on tv and teacher in Brooklyn before opening "world's first video theatre" in East Village of Manhattan: Channel One, 90 mins. of TV lampoons and original material shown on TV monitors to live audience. Took 16 mm material on college dates with success, culminating in feature film: The Groove Tube, 1974.
PICTURE: Modern Problems (co-s.p., dir.).

SHAPIRO, ROBERT W.: Producer. b. Brooklyn, NY, March 1, 1938. e. U. of Southern CA., Joined William Morris Agency, Inc., 1958. dir. and head of motion picture dept., William Morris Agency (UK) Ltd., 1969; man. dir., 1970. 1974 vice president, head int'l. m.p. dept., William Morris, Inc. In March, 1977 joined Warner Bros. as exec. v.p. in chg. of worldwide production. 1981, named WB pres., theatrical production div. Resigned 1983 to produce films.
PICTURES: Pee-Wee's Big Adventure (prod.); Empire of the Sun (exec. prod.); Arthur 2 On the Rocks (prod.).

SHARAFF, IRENE: Costume Designer. b. 1910. Long career on stage and in films. Winner of Tony, two Donaldson Awards, five Academy Awards and 16 Oscar nominations. Has worked on more than 30 motion pictures.
PICTURES: Meet Me in St. Louis, Hello, Dolly, Guys and Dolls, Call Me Madam, Yolanda and the Thief, Brigadoon, Porgy and Bess, Flower Drum Song, The Best Years of Our Lives, The Taming of the Shrew, A Star is Born (1954), Mommie Dearest. Oscar winners include An American in Paris, The King and I, West Side Story, Cleopatra, Who's Afraid of Virginia Woolf?.

SHARE, MICHAEL: Executive. Began career with Paramount Pictures 1974 as booker in Indianapolis. 1975–76 appt. salesman; 1976–77 sls. mgr. in Philadelphia; 1977, Cincinnati branch mgr.; 1980, Chicago branch mgr. 1985, promoted to v.p., eastern div.

SHARIF, OMAR: Actor. r.n. Michel Shahoub. b. Alexandria, Egypt, April 10, 1932. e. Victoria Coll., Cairo.; pres. of College Dramatic Society. m. Faten Hamama. Starred in 21 Egyptian and two French films prior to Lawrence of Arabia. Left Egypt 1964. Champion contract bridge player. 1983 made rare stage appearance in The Sleeping Prince (Chistester, then West End).
PICTURES: Ciel d' enfer (1953, debut), The Mamluks, The Blazing Sun, Goha, Lawrence of Arabia, Ghengis Khan, The Fall of the Roman Empire, The Yellow Rolls-Royce, Behold a Pale Horse, Doctor Zhivago, Night of the Generals, More Than a Miracle, McKenna's Gold, Funny Girl, The Appointment, Mayerling, Che!, The Horsemen, The Burglars, The Tamarind Seed, The Mysterious Island of Captain Nemo, Juggernaut, Funny Lady, Crime and Passion, Ace Up My Sleeve, The Pink Panther Strikes Again, The Right to Love, Ashanti, Bloodline, The Baltimore Bullet, Oh, Heavenly Dog, Green Ice, Chanel Solitaire, Top Secret, The Possessed, Paradise Calling, The Blue Pyramids, Keys to Freedom, Novice, Mountains of the Moon, Michelangelo and Me, Drums of Fire, Le Guignol.
TELEVISION: S*H*E, Pleasure Palace, The Far Pavilions, Peter the Great, Harem, Anastasia, Grand Larceny, Omar Sharif Returns to Egypt, The Mysteries of the Pyramids Live (host).

SHARKEY, RAY: Actor. b. Red Hook, Brooklyn, NY, 1952. Began on TV, guesting in Kojak, Police Story, Barney Miller, etc. Also performed on stage in Los Angeles. Theatrical movie debut in Hot Tomorrows in 1976.
PICTURES: Trackdown, Stunts, Paradise Alley, Who'll Stop the Rain?, Heartbeat, Willie and Phil, The Idolmaker, Love and Money, Some Kind of Hero, No Mercy, Private Investigations, Act of Piracy, Scenes From the Class Struggle in Beverly Hills, Wired, Regina, The Neon Empire.
TELEVISION: Behind Enemy Lines, Wiseguy (series), The Revenge of Al Capone, 27 Wagons Full of Cotton.

SHARP, ALAN: Writer. b. Glasgow, Scotland. Writes western screenplays.
PICTURES: The Hired Hand, Ulzana's Raid, Billy Two Hats, Night Moves, The Osterman Weekend, Little Treasure (also dir.), Freeway, Cat Chaser (co-s.p.).
TELEVISION: Coming Out of the Ice.

SHARP, DON: Writer, director. b. Hobart, Tasmania, Australia, 1922. Early career as actor in Australia. Ent. m.p. ind. in England with Group Three as screenwriter, 1951. Began directing 1955 with doc. children's films, 2nd unit work and filmed TV series.
PICTURES: Kiss of the Vampire, It's All Happening, Devil Ship Pirates, Witchcraft, Those Magnificent Men in Their Flying Machines (2nd unit), Curse of the Fly, The Face of Fu Manchu, Rasputin—The Mad Monk, Our Man in Marrakesh, The Brides of Fu Manchu, Rocket to the Moon, Taste of Excitement, The Violent Enemy, Puppet on a Chain, Psychomania, Dark Places, Callan, Hennessy, The Four Feathers, The 39 Steps, Bear Island.
TELEVISION: Ghost Squad, The Champions, The Avengers, House of Horror, Q.E.D., A Woman of Substance, Tusitala, Hold the Dream, Tears in the Rain.

SHATNER, WILLIAM: Actor. b. Montreal, Quebec, Mar. 22, 1931. e. McGill U. Toured Canada in various stock, repertory companies. Bdwy. debut, Tamburlaine the Great, 1956.
PICTURES: The Brothers Karamazov, Judgment at Nuremberg, The Explosive Generation, The Intruder, The

Outrage, Big Hot Mama, Dead of Night, The Devil's Rain, Kingdom of the Spiders, Star Trek—The Motion Picture, The Kidnapping of the President, Star Trek II: The Wrath of Khan, Airplane II: The Sequel, Star Trek III: The Search for Spock, Star Trek IV: The Voyage Home, Star Trek V: The Final Frontier (also dir., orig. story).

TELEVISION: Star Trek (series), The Statesman, The Bastard, Disaster on the Coastline, The Baby Sitter, Andersonville, T.J. Hooker (series), Secrets of a Married Man, North Beach and Rawhide, Top Flight (host), Broken Angel, Voice of the Planet (mini-series), Rescue: 911 (host).

SHAVELSON, MELVILLE: Writer, Director. b. Brooklyn, NY, April 1, 1917. e. Cornell U., 1937, A.B. Radio writer: We The People, Bicycle Party, 1937, Bob Hope Show, 1938–43. Screen writer; apptd. prod., Warner Bros, 1951. Conceived for TV: Make Room for Daddy, My World and Welcome To It. Author: book, How To Make a Jewish Movie. Lualda, The Great Houdinis, The Eleventh Commandment, Ike. Pres., Writers Guild of America, West, 1969–71, 1979–81, 1985–87; Pres., Writers Guild Foundation 1978–88.

PICTURES: Princess & the Pirate, Wonder Man, Kid From Brooklyn, Sorrowful Jones, It's a Great Feeling, Daughter of Rosie O'Grady, Always Leave Them Laughing, Where There's Life, On Moonlight Bay, I'll See You in My Dreams, Room For One More, April in Paris, Trouble Along the Way, Living It Up, Seven Little Foys, Beau James, Houseboat, It Started in Naples, The Five Pennies, On the Double, The Pigeon That Took Rome, A New Kind of Love, Cast a Giant Shadow, Yours Mine and Ours, The War Between Men and Women, Mixed Company.

TV FEATURES: The Legend of Valentino, The Great Houdinis, Ike, The Other Woman, Deceptions; Academy Awards, 1988 (writer).

SHAVER, HELEN: Actress. b. St. Thomas, Ontario, Canada, Feb. 24, 1951. e. Banff Sch. of Fine Arts, Alberta. Worked on stage and screen in Canada before coming to Los Angeles 1978. Theatrical film debut Starship Invasions, 1977.

PICTURES: Christina; High-Ballin'; The Amityville Horror; In Praise of Older Women; Who Has Seen the Wind; Gas; The Osterman Weekend; Harry Tracy; Best Defense; Desert Hearts; The Color of Money; The Believers; The Land Before Time (voice), Bethune: The Making of a Hero, Walking After Midnight, Tree of Hands.

TELEVISION: Series: United States, Jessica Novak. Movies: Many Happy Returns, The Park is Mine, Countdown To Looking Glass, Between Two Brothers, Lovey: Circle of Children II, Ray Bradbury Theater III, No Blame, B.L. Stryker: The Dancer's Touch.

SHAWN, WALLACE: Playwright, Actor. b. New York, NY, Nov. 12, 1943. Son of former New Yorker editor and publisher William Shawn. e. Harvard; Oxford U. Taught English in India on a Fulbright scholarship 1956–66. English, Latin and drama teacher, NY 1968–70.

PLAYS: Our Late Night (1975, Obie Award); The Mandrake (translation); A Thought in Three Parts; Marie and Bruce; The Hotel Play; The Music Teacher; Ode to Napoleon Bonaparte; Aunt Dan and Lemon.

THEATER: Actor: The Mandrake (1977); The Master and Margerita; Chinchilla; The First Time; Ode to Napoleon Bonaparte.

PICTURES: All That Jazz (1979); Manhattan; Starting Over; Atlantic City; The First Time; Simon; A Little Sex; My Dinner With Andre (also s.p.); Deal of the Century; Lovesick; Strange Invaders; Saigon—Year of the Cat; Crackers; The Bostonians; Heaven Help Us; The Hotel New Hampshire; Micki and Maude; Head Office; The Bedroom Window; Prick Up Your Ears; Nice Girls Don't Explode; The Princess Bride; The Moderns; She's Out of Control; Scenes From the Class Struggle in Beverly Hills; We're No Angels.

SHAYE, ROBERT: Executive. b. Detroit, MI, Mar. 4, 1939. e. U. of Michigan, B.B.A.; Columbia U. Law. At 15 wrote, prod. dir. training film for father's supermarket staff. Later won first prize in Society of Cinematologists' Rosenthal Competition (best m.p. by American dir. under 25). Wrote, prod., dir., edited short films, trailers and TV commercials, including award-winning shorts, Image and On Fighting Witches (prod., dir.). Founded New Line Cinema 1967. Pres. & CEO, New Line Cinema.

PICTURES: Prod./exec. prod.: Stunts, XTRO, Alone in the Dark, The First Time, Polyester, Critters, Quiet Cool, My Demon Lover, A Nightmare on Elm Street (parts 1,2,3,4,5), The Hidden, Jack in the Box, Stranded, Critters 2, Hairspray, Heart Condition.

TELEVISION: A Nightmare on Elm Street-Freddy's Nightmare: the Series (exec. prod.).

SHAYNE, ROBERT: Actor. b. Yonkers, NY. On N.Y. stage, on screen 1943 in Shine on Harvest Moon.

PLAYS: Claudia, Night of January 16th, Both Your Houses, Yellow Jack, Whiteoaks, Without Love, etc.—70 in all

PICTURES: Mr. Skeffington, Christmas in Connecticut, Welcome Stranger, Neanderthal Man, North by Northwest, The Arrangement, Tora Tora Tora, Barefoot Executive, Million Dollar Duck—96 in all.

TELEVISION: Marcus Welby, M.D., Doris Day Show, S.W.A.T., Emergency, Superman series—350 segments in all.

SHEA, JOHN: Actor. b. Conway, NH, April 14, 1949. Raised in MA. e. Bates Coll., ME; Yale Drama School (1970), graduated as a director, 1973. Worked as asst. dir. Chelsea Westside Theater; taught part-time at Pratt Inst.

THEATER: Yentl (debut 1975, Off-Bdwy and Bdwy), Sorrows of Stephen, The Master and Margerita, Romeo and Juliet (Circle in the Sq.); With Manhattan Theatre Club: American Days (Drama Desk Award), The Dining Room (Obie Award); End of the World; The Normal Heart (London, 1987).

PICTURES: It's My Turn (debut, but scenes cut), Hussy, Missing, Windy City, Honeymoon, A New Life, Unsettled Land, Stealing Home.

TELEVISION: The Nativity, The Last Convertible, Kennedy, Hitler's SS: Portrait in Evil, Family Reunion, Coast to Coast (BBC), A Case of Deadly Force, The Impossible Spy, Baby M (Emmy Award), O Do You Know the Muffin Man, Small Sacrifices.

SHEAFF, DONALD J.: Executive. b. Oct. 23, 1925. e. U.of California at L.A., 1948; Pierce Coll., 1957. Served 4 yrs. during W.W.II in Navy Air Corps in South Pacific. 1946, joined Technicolor Motion Picture Div. in supervisory capacity; 1957, lab. supervisor, Lookout Mountain Air Force Station, handling Top Secret film for Air Force and Atomic Energy Commission. Est. and org. the installation of Vandenberg Air Force Base Lab. facilities, which Technicolor designed. 1961 joined Panacolor Corp., 1963; joined Pacific Title and Art Studio in charge of color control for special effects and titles. Returned to Technicolor Corp. 1966, app't. Plant Mgr. of Television Div., Oct. 1966, V.P. & Gen. Mgr. of the Television Div., July, 1973 appt v.p. & gen. mgr., Motion Picture Division; 1976; mgr., special visual effects, Universal City Studios. Member: SMPTE, Nat'l Academy of Television Arts & Sciences. Has conducted scientific seminars for SMPTE.

SHEARER, HARRY: Writer, Actor. b. Los Angeles, CA, Dec. 23, 1943. e. UCLA (pol. science); grad. work in urban gov., Harvard. At 7 appeared on The Jack Benny Show. Worked as freelance journalist for Newsweek, L.A. Times and publ. articles in New West, L.A. Magazine and Film Comment. Also taught h.s. Eng. and social studies and worked in CA State Legislature in Sacramento. Founding mem. The Credibility Gap, co-wrote, co-prod. and performed on comedy group's albums (A Great Gift Idea, The Bronze Age of Radio). Co-wrote, co-prod. Albert Brooks' album A Star is Bought. Host of Le Show, L.A. radio prog. Writer-cast mem. Saturday Night Live (1979–80 & 1984–85).

THEATER: Accomplice (Pasadena Playhouse).

PICTURES: Actor: Abbott and Costello Go to Mars (debut, as child, 1953); Cracking Up; Real Life (also co-s.p.); Animalympics; The Fish That Saved Pittsburgh, Serial; One-Trick Pony; The Right Stuff; This is Spinal Tap (also co-s.p.); Plain Clothes.

TELEVISION: Fernwood 2-Night (creative consultant). Specials: Likely Stories; It's Just TV; Paul Shaffer: Viva Shaf Vegas; Comedy Hour, Portrait of a White Marriage (dir., actor), The Magic of Live.

SHEEDY, ALLY: Actresss. r.n. Alexandra Sheedy. b. New York, NY, June 13, 1962. e. U. of Southern California. Daughter of literary agent Charlotte Sheedy. At age 12 wrote children's book, She Was Nice to Mice; later pieces in The New York Times, The Village Voice, Ms. Began acting in TV commercials at 15. Film debut in Bad Boys, 1983.

PICTURES: WarGames, Oxford Blues, The Breakfast Club, St. Elmo's Fire, Twice in a Lifetime, Blue City, Short Circuit, Maid to Order, Heart of Dixie, Rapid Fire, Fear.

TELEVISION: Episodes of Hill Street Blues. Movies: Homeroom, Splendor in the Grass, Best Little Girl in the World, Day the Loving Stopped, The Violation of Sarah McDavid, Deadly Lessons, We Are the Children.

SHEELER, MARK: Actor. r.n. Morris Sheeler. b. New York, NY, April 24, 1923. e. UCLA. Disc jockey 1942–48; aerial photographer. Air Corp. Photog. during war. Voices, animated cartoons, commercials. M.p. debut in Born Yesterday.

PLAYS: Hillbarn Thea., Calif.: Harvey, The Happy Time, Time of Your Life, Amphitryon 38, Send Me No Flowers, The Gazebo, 3 Men on a Horse, etc.

PICTURES: The High and the Mighty, Blood Alley, It Came From Beneath the Sea, Apache Warrior, Tank Battalion, P.O.W., Book of Israel, Why Must I Die?, Irma La Douce, The Raven, Elmer Gantry, How the West Was Won, Mary Poppins, Unsinkable Molly Brown, Sound of Music, After the Fox, See the Man Run, Capricorn I, Damien, Omen II, The Hand, Blue Thunder.

TELEVISION: Hitchcock Presents, Kraft Thea., Day in Court, Defenders, East Side, West Side, Dr. Kildare, The Fugitive, Mr. Ed, Jack Benny Show, Life of Riley, Man from

Uncle, Doctors & the Nurses, The Invaders, Batman, Here's Lucy, Dennis the Menace, Andy Griffith, Marcus Welby, Banachek, Moses the Lawgiver, All My Children, Kojak, Charlie's Angels, Police Woman, The Tonight Show, Mash, Fantasy Island, Photo Clinic (PBS), The C.C. Connection, Nero Wolfe, House Calls, China Smith, Highway Patrol, Three's Company, Ike: The War Years, Cagney and Lacey, Barnaby Jones, Mike Hammer, Trapper John, The D.A.'s Man, Mark of Zorro, Peoples Court, Sgt. Preston of the Yukon, Dragnet, Twilight Zone.

SHEEN, CHARLIE: Actor. b. Los Angeles, 1966. Son of Martin Sheen. Brother of actor Emilio Estevez. Made debut as extra in TV movie, The Execution of Private Slovik (starring father) and as extra in Apocalypse Now (also starring father).

PICTURES: Grizzly II—The Predator, The Red Dawn, Lucas, Platoon, Ferris Buehler's Day Off, The Wraith, Three for the Road, Wall Street, No Man's Land, Never on Tuesday, Eight Men Out, Johnny Utah, Young Guns, Beverly Hills Brats, Backtrack, Major League, Cadence, Men at Work, Courage Mountain, Navy Seals.

TELEVISION: Movies: Silence of the Heart, The Boys Next Door.

SHEEN, MARTIN: Actor. r.n. Ramon Estevez. b. Dayton, OH, Aug. 3, 1940. Father of actors Emilio Estevez and Charlie Sheen. Wrote play (as Ramon G. Estavez) Down the Morning Line (prod. Public Theatre, 1969). Emmy Award as dir., exec. prod. Babies Having Babies (1986).

THEATER: The Connection (debut, 1959 with the Living Theater), Women of Trachis, Many Loves, In the Jungle of Cities, Never Live Over a Pretzel Factory, The Subject Was Roses, The Wicked Crooks, Hamlet, Romeo and Juliet, Hello Goodbye, The Happiness Cage, Death of a Salesman (with George C. Scott), Julius Caesar.

PICTURES: The Subject Was Roses, The Incident, Catch 22, No Drums, No Bugles, Rage, Pickup on 101, Badlands, The Cassandra Crossing, The Little Girl Who Lives Down the Lane, Apocalypse Now, Eagle's Wing, The Final Countdown, Loophole, Gandhi, That Championship Season, Enigma, Man, Woman and Child, The Dead Zone, Firestarter, The Believers, A State of Emergency, Wall Street, Siesta, Walkway After Midnight, Personal Choice, Da (co-exec. prod., actor), Judgement in Berlin (exec. prod., actor), Beverly Hills Brats, Cadence (dir.), The Legend of Earl Durand.

TELEVISION: As the World Turns. Movies: Then Came Bronson, Mongo's Back in Town, Welcome Home, Johnny Bristol, That Certain Summer, Letters for Three Lovers, Pursuit, Catholics, Message to My Daughter, The Execution of Private Slovik, The California Kid, The Missiles of October, The Story of Pretty Boy Floyd, Sweet Hostage, The Guardian, The Last Survivors, Blind Ambition, The Long Road Home, (Emmy, 1981), In the Custody of Strangers, Choices of the Heart, Kennedy (mini-series), The Atlanta Child Murders, Consenting Adult, Shattered Spirits, News at Eleven, Out of the Darkness, Samaritan, Conspiracy: The Trial of the Chicago 8, No Means No (exec. prod. only), Nightbreaker (also exec. prod.).

SHEFFER, CRAIG: Actor. b. York, PA. e. East Stroudsberg Coll., PA. Started career in tv commercials; in soap opera, One Life to Live. On off-Bdwy. stage in Fresh Horses and on and off-Bdwy. in Torch Song Trilogy.

PICTURES: That Was Then . . . This Is Now, Fire with Fire, Voyage of the Rock Aliens, Split Decisions, Instant Karma (also exec. prod.), Nightbreed.

TELEVISION: Babycakes.

SHEFFIELD, JOHN: Actor. b. Pasadena, CA, April 11, 1931. e. UCLA. Stage debut at 7 in On Borrowed Time. Created screen role of Tarzan's son; in Tarzan pictures since.

PICTURES: Babes in Arms, Lucky Cisco Kid, Little Orvie, Bomba series, Million Dollar Baby, Knute Rockne, The Golden Idol, Lord of the Jungle, The Black Sheep, Roughly Speaking, Cisco Kid.

TELEVISION: series: Bantu the Zebra Boy.

SHEFTER, BERT: Composer, Conductor. b. Russia, May 15, 1904. e. Carnegie Inst. of Technology, Curtis Inst., Damrosch Inst. Member of piano team, Gould & Shefter, on radio & in theatres; org. own band; concert pianist; comp., cond. for many films and TV.

PICTURES: composer, conductor: Tall Texan, No Escape, Great Jesse James Raid, Sins of Jezebel, The Big Circus, The Fly, Lost World, Jack the Giant Killer, Monkey on My Back, Cattle King, Curse of the Fly, Last Man on Earth, Voyage to the Bottom of the Sea, The Bubble, Dog of Flanders.

TELEVISION: Written shows for Sunset Strip, Surfside, Hawaiian Eye, Maverick, Sugarfoot, Lawman, Bourbon St., Roaring 20's.

SHEINBERG, SIDNEY JAY: Executive. b. Corpus Christi, TX, Jan. 14, 1935. e. Columbia Coll., A.B. 1955; LL.B., 1958. Admitted to Calif. bar, 1958; assoc. in law U. of California Sch. of Law, Los Angeles, 1958–59; Joined MCA, Inc, 1959. Pres., TV div., 1971–74; exec. v.p., parent co., 1969–73. Named MCA pres. & chief oper. off., 1973.

SHELDON, DAVID: Director, Writer, Producer. b. New York, NY. e. Yale U. Sch. of Drama, M.F.A.; Principia Coll., B.A.; Actors Studio, directors unit. Directed N.Y. & L.A. companies of What the Butler Saw. Alley Oop, Jimmy Shine, From 1972–74 was exec. in chg. of dev. at American Intl. Pictures (now Orion Pictures) supervising various prod. & post-prod. aspects of such films as Dillinger, Sisters, Macon County Line, Reincarnation of Peter Proud, Slaughter, Dr. Phibes, Boxcar Bertha, Heavy Traffic. Mng. dir., The Gateway Playhouse in N.Y. where prod. & dir. over 50 plays and musicals.

PICTURES: Producer-Writer: Sheba, Baby, Grizzly, The Evil, Project: Kill. Producer: Just Before Dawn, Abby, Day of the Animals, The Manitou. Director: Bring Her Back Alive, Timelapse, Lovely But Deadly. Writer: The Predator.

SHELDON, JAMES: Director. r.n. Schleifer. b. New York, NY. Nov. 12. e. U. of North Carolina. Page boy, NBC; announcer-writer-dir., NBC Internat'l Div.; staff dir., ABC radio; staff prod. dir., Young & Rubicam; free lance prod. dir. of many programs live tape and film, N.Y. and Hollywood.

TELEVISION: prod., dir.: Mr. Peepers, Armstrong Circle Theatre, Robert Montgomery Presents, Schlitz Playhouse, West Point, Zane Grey Theatre, The Millionaire, Desilu Playhouse, Perry Mason, Twilight Zone, Route 66, Naked City, The Virginian, Alfred Hitchcock Presents, Fugitive, Espionage, Defenders, Nurses, Bing Crosby Show, Family Affair, Wonderful World of Disney, Man From UNCLE, Felony Squad, That Girl, Ironside, My World and Welcome To It, To Rome With Love, Owen Marshall, Room 222, Gidget Grows Up (movie), Apple's Way, Love American Style, McMillan and Wife, Sanford and Son, Ellery Queen, Rich Man, Poor Man II, Family, MASH, Switch, Loveboat, With This Ring (movie), Sheriff Lobo, Gossip Columnist (movie), Knots Landing, The Waltons, 240-Robert, Nurse, Dukes of Hazard, Todays F.B.I., McLain's Law, 7 Brides for 7 Brothers, Lottery, Partners in Crime, Jessie, Santa Barbara, Half Nelson, Stir Crazy, The Equalizer, Sledge Hammer.

SHELDON, SIDNEY: Writer, Producer, Novelist. b. Chicago, IL, Feb. 11, 1917. e. Northwestern U. Novels made into films include Other Side of Midnight, Bloodline, Naked Face. Awards: Oscar, Writers Guild, Tony, Edgar.

PICTURES: Bachelor and the Bobbysoxer, (Acad. Award, 1947), Easter Parade, Annie Get Your Gun, Dream Wife, Jumbo, Pardners, The Buster Keaton Story (s.p., prod., dir.), You're Never Too Young, Birds and the Bees, Three Guys Named Mike, Remains To Be Seen, Gambling Daughters, Dangerous Lady.

TELEVISION: Created Patty Duke Show; Created and produced I Dream of Jeannie, Nancy and created Hart to Hart. Novels made into mini-series: Rage of Angels, Master of the Game, Windmills of the Gods, If Tomorrow Comes.

NOVELS: The Naked Face, The Other Side of Midnight, A Stranger in the Mirror, Bloodline, Rage of Angels, Master of the Game, If Tomorrow Comes.

THEATER: Redhead (Tony Award, 1959).

SHELTON, RON: Writer, Director. b. Whittier, CA, Sept. 15, 1945. e. Westmont Coll., Santa Barbara, CA, 1967; U of Arizona, Tucson, AZ, 1974. For 5 years played second base for Baltimore Orioles farm team. Cleaned bars and dressed mannequins to support his art: painting and sculpture. A script he wrote, A Player to Be Named Later (which he later filmed himself as Bull Durham), attracted attention of dir. Roger Spottiswoode who directed his first two s.p.

PICTURES: Assoc. prod.: The Pursuit of D. B. Cooper. Writer-2nd unit dir.: Under Fire, The Best of Times; Dir.-writer: Bull Durham, Blaze.

SHENSON, WALTER: Producer. b. San Francisco, CA. e. Stanford U., Calif.; Ent. m.p. ind. 1941; studio exec., writing, prod., prom. shorts, trailers, Columbia; sup. publ., expl., London, Columbia European production, 1955.

PICTURES: prod.: The Mouse That Roared, A Matter of Who, The Mouse on the Moon, A Hard Day's Night, Help!, 30 is a Dangerous Age, Cynthia, Don't Raise the Bridge Lower the River, A Talent for Loving, Welcome to the Club (prod.-dir.), The Chicken Chronicles, Reuben, Reuben; Echo Park.

SHEPARD, SAM: Writer, Actor. r.n. Samuel Shepard Rogers. b. Fort Sheridan, IL, Nov. 5, 1943. Grew up in California, Montana and South Dakota. Worked as stable hand, sheep shearer, orange picker in CA, a car wrecker in MA and musician with rock group Holy Modal Roudners. Lived near San Francisco, where, in addition to writing, ran a drama workshop at the U. of California at Davis. Recipient of Brandeis U. Creative Arts Citation, 1976, and American Acad. of Arts and Letters Award, 1975.

PLAYS: Chicago Icarus' Mother, and Red Cross (triple bill—1966 Obie Award), La Turista (1967 Obie), Forensic and the Navigators, Melodrama Play, Tooth of Crime (1973 Obie), Back Dog Beast Bait, Operation Sidewinder, 4-H Club, The Unseen Hand, Mad Dog Blues, Shaved Splits, Rock Garden,

Curse of the Starving Class (1978 Obie), Buried Child (Pulitzer Prize, 1979, Obie), Fool For Love, A Lie of the Mind.

PICTURES: Actor: Days of Heaven, Renaldo and Clara, Resurrection, Raggedy Man, Frances, The Right Stuff, Country, Fool for Love, Crimes of the Heart, Baby Boom; Steel Magnolias, Hot Spot, Bright Angel, Defenseless.

SCREENPLAYS: Me and My Brother (with Robert Frank, 1967), Zabriskie Point (co-s.p.), Oh, Calcutta! (contributor), Renaldo and Clara (co-s.p.), Paris, Texas, Fool for Love, Far North (dir., s.p.).

TELEVISION: Fourteen Hundred Thousand Blue Bitch (BBC).

SHEPHERD, CYBILL: Actress, Singer. b. Memphis, TN, Feb. 18, 1950. e. Hunter Coll., NYU, U. of Southern California. Was fashion model before acting debut in 1971 (won Model of the Year title, 1968). Debut record album, Cybill Does It . . . To Cole Porter, 1974.

PICTURES: The Last Picture Show (debut), The Heartbreak Kid, Daisy Miller, At Long Last Love, Taxi Driver, Special Delivery, Silver Bears, The Return, Chances Are, Texasville.

TELEVISION: The Yellow Rose, Secrets of a Married Man, A Guide for the Married Woman, Seduced, The Lady Vanishes, The Long Hot Summer, Moonlighting (series).

SHEPHERD, RICHARD: Producer. b. Kansas City, MO, June 4, 1927. e. Stanford U. In U.S. Naval Reserve, 1944–45. Entered ent. field as exec. with MCA, 1948, functioning in radio, TV, and m.p. fields until 1956, with time out for U.S. Army, 1950–52. In 1956 became head of talent for Columbia Pictures. In 1962 joined CMA talent agency on its founding, becoming exec. v.p. in chg. of m.p. div. Left to join Warner Bros. in Aug., 1972, as exec. v.p. for prod. Resigned Oct. 1, 1974 to become indep. prod. In 1976 named MGM sr. vp. & worldwide head of theatrical prod.

PICTURES: Twelve Angry Men, The Hanging Tree, The Fugitive Kind, Breakfast at Tiffany's (prod.), Alex and the Gypsy, Robin and Marian, Volunteers, The Hunger.

SHER, LOUIS K.: Executive. b. Columbus, OH, Feb. 25, 1914. e. Ohio State U., 1933. Exec., Stone's Grills Co., 1934–37; owned & operated, Sher Vending Co., 1937–43. U.S. Army, 1943–46. V.p., Sons Bars & Grills, 1947–54; org. & pres. Art Theatre Guild, 1954; opened art theatres for first time in many cities, org. opera film series, film classic series and similar motion picture activities in many cities. Org., Film Festival at Antioch Coll., 1960; pioneer in fighting obscenity laws in Ohio; operates 10 theatres in midwest and western states. Co-producer of the musical broadway production Shenandoah and American Dance Machine. Produced film, Deathmask.

SHERAK, THOMAS: Executive. b. Brooklyn, NY June 22, 1945. e. New York Community Coll., mktg. degree. 1967–69, US Army, Specialist E5 Sgt.; 1970, began career in m.p. industry, Paramount Pictures sls. dept.; 1974, R/C Theatres, booking dept.; 1977, joined General Cinema Theatres as district film buyer; 1978, promoted to v.p., films; 1982, promoted to v.p. head film buyer; 1983, joined 20th Century Fox as pres., domestic dist. & mktg.; 1985, pres., domestic dist.; 1986, president, domestic dist. & marketing.

SHERMAN, GEORGE: Director. b. New York, NY. 1985: Formed Ronsher Productions with Cleo Ronson for feature and TV productions. Formed Shergari Corp. with F. H. Ricketson, Jr., and Ted R. Gamble made For the Love of Mike.

PICTURES: The Bandit of Sherwood Forest, Red Canyon, Yes Sir That's My Baby, Sword in the Desert, Comanche Territory, Sleeping City, Spy Hunt, Tomahawk, Target Unknown, Golden Horde, Steel Town, Raging Tide, Against All Flags, Battle at Apache Pass, The Lone Hand, Veils of Bagdad, War Arrow, Border River, Johnny Dark, Dawn at Socorro, Chief Crazy Horse, Count Three and Pray, Treasure of Pancho Villa, Comanche, Reprisal, Flying Fontaines, Enemy General. dir.: Panic Button, Wounds of Hunger, Jacquin Murieta, Smokey, Big Jake. wrote, prod., dir. Artie-Charley and Friend, indep. feature.

TELEVISION: Prod. and/or dir. for 20th Century-Fox, and NBC, CBS. 1978, prod., Little Mo (movie), Daniel Boone, Gentle Ben.

SHERMAN, RICHARD M.: Composer, Lyricist, Screenwriter. b. New York, NY, June 12, 1928. e. Bard Coll., B.A., 1949. Info. & Educ. Br., U.S. Army, 1953–55. Songwriter, composer, Walt Disney Prods 1960–71, then freelance. With partner-brother Robert has won 2 Acad. Awards (for song & score Mary Poppins, 1964), 9 Acad. Award nom., 2 Grammys, 14 gold and platinum albums, 1st Prize, Moscow Film Fest. (for Tom Sawyer) and a star on Hollywood Walk of Fame. Have written over 400 pub. and recorded songs. Also wrote score for Bdwy musical Over Here (1974) and songs for Disney Theme Parks.

SONGS: Things I Might Have Been, Tall Paul, Christmas in New Orleans, Mad Passionate Love, Midnight Oil, You're Sixteen, That Darn Cat, The Wonderful Thing About Tiggers, It's a Small World (after all), A Spoonful of Sugar, Supercalifragilistics, Feed the Birds, Age of Not Believing, When You're Love. Pineapple Princess, Let's Get Together, Maggie's Theme, Chim Chim Cheree (Acad. Award), Comedy Album: Smash Flops.

PICTURES: Nightmare, The Cruel Tower, Absent Minded Professor, The Parent Trap, Big Red, The Castaways, Moon Pilot, Bon Voyage, Legend of Lobo, Summer Magic, Miracle of the White Stallions, The Sword in the Stone, Merlin Jones, Mary Poppins (Acad. Award), Those Calloways, The Monkey's Uncle, That Darn Cat, Symposium of Popular Songs, Winnie the Pooh, Chitty Chitty Bang Bang, The Jungle Book, The Aristocats, Bedknobs & Broomsticks, Snoopy Come Home, Charlotte's Web, *Songs & S.P.:* Tom Sawyer, The Slipper and the Rose, The Magic of Lassie, Huckleberry Finn, Magic Journeys, Little Nemo.

TELEVISION: Wonderful World of Color, Bell Telephone Hour, Welcome to Pooh Corner, The Enchanted Musical Playhouse.

SHERMAN, ROBERT B.: Composer, Lyricist, Screenwriter. b. New York, NY, Dec. 19, 1925. e. Bard Coll., B.A., 1949. U.S. Army, W.W.II, 1943–45. Songwriter, 1952–60; pres., Music World Corp., 1958; songwriter, composer, Walt Disney, 1971, then freelance.

SONGS: Things I Might Have Been, Tall Paul, Christmas in New Orleans, Mad Passionate Love, Midnight Oil, You're Sixteen, That Darn Cat, The Wonderful Thing About Tiggers, It's a Small World (after all), A Spoonful of Sugar, Supercalifragilistics, Feed the Birds, Age of Not Believing, When You're Love. Pineapple Princess, Let's Get Together, Maggie's Theme, Chim Chim Cheree (Acad. Award), Comedy Album: Smash Flops.

PICTURES: Nightmare, The Cruel Tower, Absent Minded Professor, The Parent Trap, Big Red, The Castaways, Moon Pilot, Bon Voyage, Legend of Lobo, Summer Magic, Miracle of the White Stallions, The Sword in the Stone, Merlin Jones, Mary Poppins (Acad. Award), Those Calloways, The Monkey's Uncle, That Darn Cat, Symposium of Popular Songs, Winnie the Pooh, Chitty Chitty Bang Bang, The Jungle Book, The Aristocats, Bedknobs & Broomsticks, Snoopy Come Home, Charlotte's Web, *Songs & S.P.:* Tom Sawyer, The Slipper and the Rose, The Magic of Lassie, Huckleberry Finn, Magic Journeys, Little Nemo.

TELEVISION: Wonderful World of Color, Bell Telephone Hour, Welcome to Pooh Corner, The Enchanted Musical Playhouse.

SHERMAN, ROBERT M.: Executive. Entered ind. as agent for MCA; later joined Arthur P. Jacobs pub. rel. firm. Became acc't. exec. when Jacobs merged with Rogers & Cowan. In 1964 joined CMA; 1967 made v.p. in m.p. div., serving both in London and Hollywood. In 1972 formed own prod. co., Layton Prods., with first film, Scarecrow for WB. In 1973 prod. Night Moves, also for WB. In 1974 named v.p., prod., for 20th-Fox. Returned to independent prod.: The Missouri Breaks, Convoy, Oh God! You Devil, Deadly Friend.

SHERMAN, SAMUEL M.: Producer, Director, Writer. b. New York, NY. e. City Coll. of New York, B.A. Entered m.p. ind. as writer, cameraman, film ed., neg. & sound cutter; nat'l mag. ed., Westerns Magazine 1959; pres., Signature Films; prod., dir., TV pilot, The Three Mesquiteers, 1960; prod., Pulse Pounding Perils, 1961; helped create, ed., dir., Screen Thrills Illustrated; exec. prod., Screen Thrills; v.p., Golden Age Films, 1962; prod., Joe Franklin's Silent Screen, 1963; N.Y. rep., Victor Adamson Prods.; owns world rights; The Scarlet Letter; 1965; N.Y. rep., Tal prods., Hlywd.; adv. & pub. Hemisphere Pictures; ed., autobiog., Joe Bonomo; prod., writer, Chaplin's Art of Comedy, The Strongman; prod., Hollywood's Greatest Stuntman; story adapt., Fiend With the Electronic Brain. 1967, prod. Spanish version Chaplin Su Arte y Su Comedia; tech. consul., Hal Roach Studios, NBC, Music from the Land; 1968, N.Y. rep. East West Pict. of Hollywood. 1968, N.Y. rep., Al Adamson Prods. of Hollywood; Ed.-in-chief, bk., The Strongman. Pres., Independent-International Pictures Corp., pres., Producers Commercial Productions, Inc. Chmn. of Creditors' Committee, Allied Artists Television Corp.; president, Independent-International Entertainment, TV div. Independent-International Pictures Corp. Pres., Technovision Inc.; pres., Super Video, Inc.

PICTURES: assoc. prod.: Horror of the Blood Monsters, Blood of Ghastly Horror; prod., s.p.: Brain of Blood; prod. supervisor Dracula vs. Frankenstein; Exec. prod. Angels, Wild Women; The Naughty Stewardesses (prod., s.p.), Girls For Rent; TV special, Wild Wild World of Comedy; The Dynamite Brothers (exec. prod.); Blazing Stewardesses (prod., s.p.); Cinderella 2000 (exec. prod.); Team-Mates (also story); dir-s.p., Raiders of the Living Dead.

SHERMAN, VINCENT: Director. b. Vienna, GA, July 16, 1906. e. Oglethorpe U. B.A. Writer, actor, dialogue dir., then prod. dir.

PICTURES: Dir.: Return of Doctor X, Saturday's Children, Man Who Talked Too Much, Underground, Flight from Destiny, The Hard Way, All Through the Night, Old Acquaintances, In Our Time, Mr. Skeffington, Pillow to Post, Janie Gets Married, Nora Prentiss, The Unfaithful, Adventures of Don Juan, Somewhere in the City, Hasty Heart, Damned Don't Cry, Harriet Craig, Goodbye, My Fancy, Lone Star, Assignment—Paris; prod. dir.: Affair in Trinidad, The Young Philadelphians, The Naked Earth, Second Time Around, Ice Palace, Fever in the Blood, Garment Jungle.

TELEVISION: 35 episodes of Medical Center; Westside Medical; Baretta; Waltons; Doctors Hospital, Trapper John, Movies: The Last Hurrah; Women at West Point; The Yeagers (pilot), Bogey, The Dream Merchants, Trouble in High Timber Country, High Hopes—The Capra Years.

SHERRIN, NED: Producer, Director, Writer. b. Low Ham, Somerset, England, Feb. 18, 1931. Early career writing plays and musical plays. Prod., dir., ATV Birmingham, 1955–57; prod., Midlands Affairs, Paper Talk, etc. Joined BBC-TV 1957 and produced many TV talk programmes. Novels: (with Caryl Brahms) Cindy-Ella or I Gotta Shoe (also prod. as stage play), Rappell 1910, Benbow Was His Name.

TELEVISION: England: prod.: Ask Me Another, Henry Hall Show, Laugh Line, Parasol. Assoc. prod.: Tonight series. Little Beggars, 1962; prod., creator: That Was The Week That Was, 1962–63; prod., dir.: Benbow Was His Name (co-author), 1964; Take a Sapphire (co-author), The Long Garden Party, The Long Cocktail Party. ABC of Britain revue. Prod., dir.: thrice-weekly series Not So Much a Programme, More a Way of Life, 1964–65. Appearances inc. Your Witness, Quiz of The Week, Terra Firma, Who Said That, The Rather Reassuring Programme, Song by Song.

PICTURES: prod.: The Virgin Soldiers (with Leslie Gilliat), Every Home Should Have One, Up Pompeii, Girl Stroke Boy (co-author with Caryl Brahms), Up the Chastity Belt, Rentadick, The Garnet Saga, Up the Front, The National Health, The Cobblers of Umbridge (dir. with Ian Wilson).

SHERWOOD, MADELINE: Actress. b. Montreal, Canada, Nov. 13, 1922. e. Yale Drama Sch. Trained with Montreal Rep. and Actors Studio. Has dir. prods. at Actors Studio and regional theaters.

THEATER: The Crucible, Sweet Bird of Youth, Invitation to a March, The Garden of Sweets, Camelot, Hey You, Light Man!, Brecht on Brecht, Night of the Iguana, Arturo Ui, Do I Hear a Waltz?, Inadmissible Evidence, All Over, Older People, Getting Out, The Suicide.

PICTURES: Baby Doll, Cat on a Hot Tin Roof, Sweet Bird of Youth, Parrish, The 91st Day, Hurry Sundown, Pendulum, Until She Talks, Mr. Preble Gets Rid of His Wife, The Changeling, Resurrection, Wicked, Wicked, Teachers, An Unremarkable Life.

TELEVISION: The Flying Nun (series), Rich Man, Poor Man, Nobody's Child.

SHIELDS, BROOKE: Actress. b. New York, NY, May 31, 1965. e. Princeton U. Discovered at age 11 months by photographer Francesco Scavullo to pose in Ivory Soap ads. Later became Breck girl in commercials; appeared in Richard Avedon's Colgate ads for 3 yrs.

PICTURES: Alice Sweet Alice (Communion), Pretty Baby, Tilt, King of the Gypsies, Wanda Nevada, Just You and Me, Kid, The Blue Lagoon, Endless Love, Sahara, Brenda Starr, Speed Zone, The Actor, Backstreet Strays.

TELEVISION: The Prince of Central Park, After the Fall, Wet Gold, The Diamond Trap. and numerous specials.

SHIELDS, WILLIAM A.: Executive. b. New York, NY, 1946. e. El Camino Coll., California State Coll. Entered the motion picture industry in 1966 when he went to work for Pacific Theatres then MGM sales dept., L.A. and Denver, 1970; New World Pictures, Western Division mgr., 1972; branch mgr., 20th Century-Fox, Washington, 1973; New York district manager, 20th Century-Fox, 1973–75. Joined Mann Theatres Corporation of California as head booker in 1975. Gen. sls. mgr., Far West Films, 1977–79; joined Avco Embassy as Western div. mgr., promoted to asst. gen. sls. mgr., 1980; promoted to v.p.-gen. sls. mgr., January, 1981. In 1983 joined New World Pictures as exec. v.p., world-wide mktg. & acquisitions. Promoted to pres., worldwide sls. & mktg., 1985.

SHIFF, RICHARD: Executive. Joined Warner Bros. as sales analyst, 1977. In 1979 named dist, coordinator; 1980, asst. dir. sls. admin. 1982, promoted to post, dir. sls. admin. 1987, v.p., theatrical sls. operations.

SHIKATA, MASAO: Executive. b. Kyoto, Japan, Apr. 22, 1918. e. Naniwa Commercial Coll. Chmn., Sansha Electric Manufacturing Co. Ltd., Tokyo and Osaka, makers of power semiconductors & applied electronic equipment; pres. Japan Motion Picture Equipment Manufacturers & Suppliers Assoc.; v.p., Japan Machinery Design Center; v.p., Japan Optical Industry Assoc.; director, Federation of Japanese Film Industries Inc.

SHIMA, KOJI: Director. b. Japan. Entered m.p. ind. as actor, 1930; then asst. dir., director. Dir., Daiei M. P. Co. (now defunct). Presently indep. director.

PICTURES: Golden Demon, Phantom Horse.

SHINBACH, BRUCE D.: Executive. b. South Bend, IN, June, 1939. e. U. of Colorado, B.A., 1963; New York Inst. of Finance; Northwestern U., M.A., 1965. Stockbroker for Harris, Upham & Co., 1964, shopping center developer, Dixie Associates, 1966 to present. Pres., Monarch Theatres.

SHIRE, DAVID: Composer. b. Buffalo, NY, July 3, 1937. m. actress Didi Conn. e. Yale U., 1959, B.A. Composer of theater scores: The Sap of Life, Urban Blight, Starting Here, Starting Now; Baby, Closer Than Ever. Won Academy Award, best original song It Goes Like It Goes from Norma Rae, 1979; Acad. Award nom. I'll Never Say Good-bye from The Promise, 1979. Emmy noms. Raid on Entebbe, The Defection of Simas Kudirka, Do You Remember Love? Grammy Awards for Saturday Night Fever.

SONGS: No More Songs For Me, What About Today:, With You I'm Born Again, I'll Never Say Goodbye, It Goes Like It Goes.

PICTURES: One More Train to Rob, Summertree, Drive, He Said; Skin Game, To Find a Man, Class of '44, The Conversation, The Taking of Pelham 1-2-3, Farewell My Lovely, The Hindenberg, All the President's Men, The Big Bus, Harry and Walter Go to New York, Saturday Night Fever (adapt. & add. music), Straight Time, The Promise, Old Boyfriends, Norma Rae, Only When I Laugh, The Night the Lights Went Out in Georgia, Paternity, The World According to Garp, Max Dugan Returns, Oh God You Devil, 2010, Return to Oz, Short Circuit, 'night, Mother, Backfire, Vice Versa, Monkey Shines.

TELEVISION: Series themes: Sarge, McCloud, Lucas Tanner, Alice, Tales of the Unexpected. Movies: Priest Killer, McCloud, Harpy, Three Faces of Love, Keiller Tell Me Where It Hurts, Three for the Road, Amelia Earhart, Something for Joey, The Storyteller, Mayflower Madam, Echoes in the Darkness, Jesse, God Bless the Child, The Women of Brewster Place, I Know My First Name is Steven, The Kennedys of Massachusetts (mini-series), Backfire.

SHIRE, TALIA: Actress. b. New York, NY, April 25, 1946. Raised on road by her father, arranger-conductor Carmine Coppola, who toured with Broadway musicals. After 2 yrs. at Yale Sch. of Drama she moved to L.A. where appeared in many theatrical productions. Sister of Francis Ford Coppola.

PICTURES: The Dunwich Horror, Gas-s-s, The Christian Licorice Store, The Outside Man, The Godfather, The Godfather, Part II, Rocky, Old Boyfriends, Rocky II, Windows, Rocky III, Rocky IV, RAD, Never Say Never Again (prod.), Lionheart (co-prod.), New York Stories (Life Without Zoe), Bed and Breakfast.

TELEVISION: Rich Man, Poor Man, Kill Me If You Can, Foster and Laurie; Daddy I Don't Like It Like This.

SHIVAS, MARK: Producer, Director. TV credits incl: Presenter of Cinema. The Six Wives of Henry VIII, Casanova, The Edwardians, The Evacuees, The Glittering Prizes, Abide With Me, Rogue Male, 84 Charing Cross Road, The Three Hostages, She Fell Among Thieves, Professional Foul, Telford's Change, On Giant's Shoulders, & The Price, What If it's Raining?, The Story Teller. Now head of drama, BBC TV.

PICTURES: Producer: Richard's Things, Moonlighting, A Private Function. Exec. Prod.: Bad Blood; The Witches (prod.).

SHORE, DINAH: Singer. r.n. Frances Rose Shore. b. Winchester, TN, Mar. 1, 1917. e. Vanderbilt U., B.A., 1939. Became singer WNEW, N.Y., 1938; joined NBC as sustaining singer, 1938; started contract RCA-Victor, 1940; star Chamber Music Soc. of Lower Basin St. program, 1940; joined Eddie Cantor radio pgm., 1941; star own radio program, General Foods, 1943; entertained troops European Theatre of operations, 1944; radio program, Procter & Gamble. Star TV show, Chevrolet, 1951–61; Dinah Shore Specials, 1964–65. 1969: Dinah Shore Special, Like Hep. 1970–71: Dinah's Place (Emmy, 1973, 1974), Dinah! (Emmy, 1976), Death Car on the Freeway, A Conversation With Dinah (Cable 1989).

PICTURES: Thank Your Lucky Stars, Up in Arms, Belle of the Yukon, Follow the Boys, Make Mine Music, Till the Clouds Roll By, Fun and Fancy Free, Aaron Slick from Punkin Crick.

AWARDS: Awarded New Star of Radio Motion Picture Daily Poll and World Telegram-Scripps-Howard Poll, 1940; Best Popular Female Vocalist M.P. Daily Fame's Annual Poll Radio and TV 1941–61; Michael Award Best Female Vocalist, Radio and TV, 1950, 51, 52; Billboard Award; Favorite Female Vocalist in radio, 1949; Billboard Award Favorite Female Vocalist in records, 1947; Gallup Poll One of Most Admired Women in the World, 1958–61; 6 Emmy Awards 1954 to 59. Los Angeles Times Woman of the Year Award, 1957; TV-Radio Mirror mag. award, best female singer, radio, 1952, 53, 56, 57, 58; TV-Radio Mirror mag. award, TV's Best Musical Variety Show, 1956, 58, 59; Peabody TV Award, 1957; Fame's Critics' Poll, Best Female Vocalist, 1958, 63; Hollywood Foreign Press Assn's Golden Globe Award, 1959; Radio-TV Daily, Female Vocalist of the Year, 1949, 56.

SHORE, HOWARD: Composer, Musician. Began career as musical director for Saturday Night Live.
PICTURES: Scanners, Videodrome, The Brood, The Fly, After Hours, Heaven, Belizaire, The Cajun, Nadine, Moving, Big, Dead Ringers, The Lemon Sisters, An Innocent Man.
TELEVISION: Coca-Cola Presents Live: The Hard Rock.

SHORE, SIG: Producer. b. New York, NY. Served as navigator in Air Force, W.W.II. First job in films in pub. dept. at Warner Bros. Formed own ad agency on West Coast; then turned to TV production with The Errol Flynn Theatre. Engaged by David O. Selznick Films to dist. its films to TV outlets. Entered theatrical distribution, importing Hiroshima, Mon Amour, The 400 Blows, etc. In mid-50s became involved in cultural exchange program of US State Dept., importing and distributing Soviet films. Returned to TV production, turning out over 250 shows, including The Outdoor World for Shell Oil. Headed co. for Ivan Tors which made Flipper, Daktari, Gentle Ben series. In 1970 formed Plaza Pictures for theatrical dist.
PICTURES: Super Fly, Super Fly TNT, That's The Way of the World, Sudden Death. (s.p.-dir.).

SHORT, MARTIN: Actor, Comedian. b. Canada, 1951. e. McMaster U. Trained as social worker but instead performed on stage in Godspell as well as in revues and cabarets in Toronto, 1973–78 including a stint as a member of the Toronto unit of the Second City comedy troupe (1977–78). Best know for comic characters he created such as nerdy Ed Grimley and lounge lizard Jackie Rogers Jr. as well as impersonations of Katharine Hepburn and Jerry Lewis on Saturday Night Live (1985–86).
PICTURES: Three Amigos (debut, 1986); Innerspace; Cross My Heart; Three Fugitives; The Big Picture.
TELEVISION: Series: The Associates (1979); I'm a Big Girl Now; SCTV Network 90; Saturday Night Live; The Completely Mental Misadventures of Ed Grimley (cartoon series). Movies: All's Well That Ends Well; Really Weird Tales.

SHOWALTER, MAX: Actor, composer. s.n. Casey Adams. b. Caldwell, KS, June 2, 1917. e. Caldwell H.S.; Pasadena Playhouse. Composed background music for films: Vicki, Return of Jack Slade, Bdwy. Harrigan 'n Hart (composer).
BROADWAY: Knights of Song, Very Warm for May, My Sister Eileen, Showboat, John Loves Mary, Make Mine Manhattan, Lend an Ear, Hello Dolly!, The Grass Harp.
PICTURES: Always Leave Them Laughing, With a Song in My Heart, What Price Glory, My Wife's Best Friend, Niagara, Destination Gobi, Dangerous Crossing, Vicki, Night People, Naked Alibi, Never Say Goodbye, Bus Stop, Down Three Dark Streets, Designing Woman, Female Animal, Voice In the Mirror, The Naked and the Dead, It Happened to Jane, Elmer Gantry, Return to Peyton Place, Summer and Smoke, Music Man, Smog, Bon Voyage, My Six Loves, Lord Love a Duck, The Anderson Tapes, Move Over Darling, Sex and the Single Girl, Fate Is the Hunter, How to Murder Your Wife, The Moonshine War, Racing with the Moon, 10, Sixteen Candles.

SHUE, ELISABETH: Actress. b. 1963.
PICTURES: The Karate Kid, Adventures in Babysitting, Link, Cocktail.
TELEVISION: Call to Glory.

SHULER-DONNER, LAUREN: Producer. b. Cleveland, OH, June 23, 1949. e. Boston U. Began filmmaking career as ed. of educational films then story ed., creative affairs exec. and camera-woman in TV production, 1972; prod. TV movie: Amateur Night at the Dixie Bar and Grill.
PICTURES: Mr. Mom, Ladyhawke, St. Elmo's Fire, Pretty in Pink, Three Fugitives.

SHULL, RICHARD B.: Actor. b. Evanston, IL, Feb. 24, 1929. e. State U. of Iowa. B.A. drama, 1950., Kemper Mil. Sch. AA humanities, 1986. U.S. Army, 1953. 1953–56, exec. asst. prod. Gordon W. Pollock Prods.; 1954–56 stage mgr. Hyde Park Playhouse; other prod. jobs and freelance stage mgr. and dir. 1950–70. N.Y. stage debut in Wake Up, Darling (1956), also in Minnie's Boys. Film debut in The Anderson Tapes, 1971.
PICTURES: B.S. I Love You, Such Good Friends, Hail to the Chief, Slither, Sssss, Cockfighter, The Fortune, The Black Bird, Hearts of the West, The Big Bus, The Pack, Dreamer, Wholly Moses, Heartbeeps, Spring Break, Lovesick, Unfaithfully Yours, Splash, Garbo Talks.
TELEVISION: Your Hit Parade (1950), Holmes & Yoyo, Rockford Files, Good Times, Love American Style, Hart to Hart, Lou Grant, Movies: Ziegfeld: A Man and His Women, Studs Lonigan, Will There Really Be a Morning? The Boy Who Loved Trolls, Keeping the Faith, Seize the Day.

SHURPIN, SOL: Executive. b. New York, NY, Feb. 22, 1914. e. Pace Inst., 1936. Law stenog., 1932–33; Joe Hornstein, Inc., 1933–41; National Theatre Supply, 1941–48; purchased interest in Raytone Screen Corp., became v.p., 1948; pres., Raytone, 1952; pres., Technikote Corp., which succeeded Raytone Screen, 1956–present; sole owner, Technikote Corp., 1962.

SHUTT, BUFFY: Executive. Joined Paramount 1973 as sect. with N.Y. pub. staff; 1975, natl. mag. contact. 1978, named dir. of pub.; later exec. dir. of pub. Promoted 1980 to v.p., pub. & promo. Resigned to join Time-Life Films; as v.p. East coast prod; returned to Paramount in 1981 as sr. v.p. & asst. to pres. of Motion Picture Group. 1984, appt. exec. v.p.-mktg. for M.P. Group, Paramount. 1986, resigned. Formed Shutt-Jones Communications, marketing consultancy with Kathy Jones. 1989, appt. marketing pres., Columbia Pictures.

SIDARIS, ANDY: Producer, Director, Writer. b. Chicago, IL, Feb. 20, 1932. e. Southern Methodist U., B.A., radio-TV. Began television career in 1950 in Dallas, TX as a director at station WFAA-TV; now pres., The Sidaris Company. Won 8 Emmy Awards.
PICTURES: Dir., Stacey, The Racing Scene, M*A*S*H football sequences, Seven (prod.-dir.), Malibu Express (prod., dir., s.p.), Hard Ticket to Hawaii (dir., s.p.), Picasso Trigger (dir., s.p.), Savage Beach (dir., s.p.).
TELEVISION: Dir., The Racers/Mario Andretti/Joe Leonard/Al Unser, ABC's Championship Auto Racing, ABC's NCAA Game of the Week, 1968 Summer Olympics (Mexico City), 1972 Summer Olympics, 1976 Summer Olympics (Montreal), 1984 Summer Olympics (L.A.), 1964 Winter Olympics (Innsbruck), 1968 Winter Olympics (Grenoble), 1976 Winter Olympics (Innsbruck), 1980 Winter Olympics (Lake Placid), 1988 Winter Olympics (Calgary), Wide World of Sports, The Racers/Craig and Lee Breedlove, dir.: The Burt Reynolds Late Show, dir., Kojak episode, Nancy Drew, Dukes of Hazzard.

SIDNEY, GEORGE: Director, Producer. b. New York, NY, Oct. 4, 1916. Son of L. K. Sidney, veteran showman and v.p. MGM, and Hazel Mooney, actress. From 1932 at MGM as test, second unit and short subjects dir. Several Academy Awards for shorts, Our Gang Comedies, Pete Smith etc. In 1941 made feature dir., MGM. Pres., Director's Guild of America, 16 yrs; spec. presidential assignment to Atomic Energy Commission and U.S. Air Force; 1961–66, Pres., Hanna-Barbera Productions; Doctorate of Science Hanneman Medical University and Hospital. Mem. ASCAP. Pres., Directors, Inc., since 1969; v.p., Directors Foundation; v.p., D.W. Griffith Foundation; life mem., ACTT (England) and DGA.
PICTURES: dir., prod.: Free and Easy, Pacific Rendezvous, Pilot No. 5, Thousands Cheer, Bathing Beauty, Anchors Aweigh, Harvey Girls, Cass Timberlane, Three Musketeers, Red Danube, Key to the City, Annie Get Your Gun, Holiday in Mexico, Show Boat, Scaramouche, Young Bess, Kiss Me Kate, Jupiter's Darling, Eddie Duchin Story, Jeanne Eagels, Pal Joey, Who Was That Lady, Pepe, Bye Bye Birdie, A Ticklish Affair, Viva Las Vegas, Who Has Seen the Wind?, U.N. special; The Swinger, Half a Sixpence.

SIDNEY, SYLVIA: Actress. b. New York, NY, Aug. 8, 1910. r.n. Sophia Kosow. e. Theatre Guild Sch. On stage, then screen debut in Through Different Eyes (1929).
PLAYS: Nice Women, Crossroads, Bad Girl, The Gentle People, Auntie Mame, Joan of Lorraine, Angel Street, Enter Laughing, Vieux Carre.
PICTURES: City Streets, Ladies of the Big House, Confessions of a Co-Ed, An American Tragedy, Street Scene, The Miracle Man, Merrily We Go to Hell, Madame Butterfly, Pick-Up, Jennie Gerhardt, Good Dame, Thirty Day Princess, Behold My Wife, Accent on Youth, Mary Burns—Fugitive, Trail of the Lonesome Pine, Fury, A Woman Alone, You Only Live Once, Dead End, You and Me, One Third of a Nation, The Wagons Roll at Night, Blood on the Sun, Mr. Ace, Searching Wind, Love from a Stranger, Les Miserables, Violent Saturday, Behind the High Wall, Summer Wishes, Winter Dreams, I Never Promised You a Rose Garden, Damien-Omen II, Hammett, Beetlejuice, The Exorcist: 1990.
TELEVISION: Movies: Do Not Fold, Spindle or Mutilate, Death at Love House, Raid on Entebbe, The Gossip Columnist, FDR—The Last Year, The Shadow Box, A Small Killing, Come Along With Me, Having It All, Finnegan Begin Again, An Early Frost, Pals. Guest: thirtysomething.

SIEGEL, DON: Director. b. Chicago, IL, Oct. 26, 1912. e. Jesus Coll., Cambridge U., England. As actor appeared with the Royal Acad. of Dramatic Art, London, and Contemporary Theatre Group, Hollywood (1930). Cameo as actor: Edge of Eternity, The Killers, Coogan's Bluff, Play Misty for Me, Charley Varrick, Invasion of the Body Snatchers, Escape from Alcatraz, Into the Night. Joined Warner Bros. as asst. film librarian, 1934; became asst. cutter and head of insert dept. Organized montage dept.; wrote and dir. all montages. Second unit dir. for Michael Curtiz, Raoul Walsh, etc. 1940–45. Art dir.: Casablanca, Mission to Moscow. Directed many TV shows 1953–66.
PICTURES: dir.: Star in the Night and Hitler Lives (two Academy Awards for distinctive achievement for shorts, 1945). dir.: The Verdict, Night Unto Night, Big Steal, Duel at Silver Creek, No Time For Flowers, Count the Hours, China Venture, Riot in Cell Block 11, Private Hell 36, Annapolis Story, Invasion of the Body Snatchers, Baby Face Nelson,

Spanish Affair, The Gun Runners, The Lineup, Edge of Eternity (also prod.), Hound Dog Man, Flaming Star, Hell is for Heroes, The Killers, Madigan, Coogan's Bluff, Death of a Gunfighter, Two Mules for Sister Sara, The Beguiled, Dirty Harry; Play Misty for Me, (actor only), Charley Varrick, Black Windmill, The Shootist, Telefon, Escape from Alcatraz (also prod.), Rough Cut, Jinxed.
TELEVISION: Movies: The Killers, The Hanged Man, Stranger on the Run.

SIKKING, JAMES B.: Actor. b. Los Angeles, CA, March 5, 1934. e. UCLA, B.A. Theatre includes Waltz of the Toreadors, Plaza Suite, Damn Yankees, The Big Knife.
PICTURES: The Magnificent Seven; Von Ryan's Express; Chandler; The New Centurions; The Electric Horseman; Capricorn One; Ordinary People; Outland; The Star Chamber; Up the Creek; Star Trek III—The Search for Spock; Morons from Outer Space; Soul Man; Narrow Margin.
TELEVISION: Series: Turnabout; General Hospital; Hill Street Blues. Doogie Howser, M.D. Movies: The Jesse Owens Story; First Steps; The Golden Land; Ollie Hoopnoodles Haven of Bliss; Bay Coven; Leave Her to Heaven; Brotherhood of the Rose (mini-series), Too Good to be True, Around the World in 80 Days.

SILBERT, STEPHEN D.: Executive. b. Los Angeles, CA, Sept. 4, 1942. e. Claremont McKenna Coll., CA, B.A., Masters in Business Economics; Boalt Hall Sch. of Law, U. of California, Berkeley, J.D. Member: American Bar Assoc., State Bar of CA. Sr. partner, Wyman, Bautzer, Kuchel and Silbert; Sept. 1985–Oct. 1986, chmn. of exec. comm. of board of dir., MGM/UA Communications Co., and employed by Kirk Kerkorian; Oct. 1986–July 1988, pres. and COO, MGM/UA Communications; July 1988, became chmn. bd. and CEO, MGM/UA Communications Co. Resigned as of Jan. 1989. Joined Tracinda Corp.

SILLIPHANT, STIRLING: Executive, Writer. b. Detroit, MI, Jan. 16, 1918. e. U. of Southern California, B.A., 1938. On pub. staff, Walt Disney Productions, Burbank 1938–41; 1941–42, exploit. & pub., Hal Horne Org. for 20th Century-Fox in New York & other key cities, 1942–43, asst. to Spyros P. Skouras. U.S. Navy, W.W.II. Since 1946, 20th-Fox; in chg. special events and promotions, June 1949; appt. Eastern pub. mgr. 1951.
PICTURES: Prod., Joe Louis Story; co-prod., collab. s.p., 5 Against the House; screenwriter, producer, Naked City, Route 66, The Slender Thread, In the Heat of the Night; s.p., Marlowe; collab., s.p., The Liberation of L. B. Jones; s.p., A Walk in the Spring Rain; p., Shaft, Shaft in Africa, (s.p.). The New Centurions (s.p.), The Poseidon Adventure, (s.p.), The Towering Inferno (s.p.), The Killer Elite (co.-s.p.), The Enforcer (co.-s.p.), Telefon (co-s.p.), The Swarm, Circle of Iron (co-s.p.), When Time Ran Out, Over the Top (co-s.p.).
TELEVISION: Series: The Naked City, Route 66, Space, Golden Gate, Fly Away Home, (prod., s.p.), Mussolini—The Untold Story; Pearl, (exec. prod., writer), Salem's Lot (exec. prod.), Welcome to Paradise (exec. prod., s.p.), Travis McGee, The Three Kings (prod., s.p.), Brotherhood of the Rose (exec. prod.).

SILVA, HENRY: Actor. b. Puerto Rico, 1928.
PICTURES: Viva Zapata, Crowded Paradise, A Hatful of Rain, The Bravados, Green Mansions, Cinderfella, Ocean's Eleven, The Manchurian Candidate, Johnny Cool, The Return of Mr. Moto, The Reward, The Plainsman, The Hills Ran Red, Buck Rogers in the 25th Century, Thirst, Virus, Alligator, Sharkey's Machine, Wrong Is Right, Cannonball Run II, Lust in the Dust, Code of Silence, Alan Quartermain and the Lost City of Gold, Above the Law, Bulletproof, Fists of Steel, Trained to Kill.
TELEVISION: Contract on Cherry Street, Happy (series), Black Noon.

SILVER, JOAN MICKLIN: Writer, Director. b. Omaha, NB, May 24, 1935. m. producer Raphael Silver. Daughter is dir. Marisa Silver. e. Sarah Lawrence Coll. Began career as writer for educational films. Original s.p., Limbo, purchased by Universal Pictures. In 1972 Learning Corp. of Am. commissioned her to write and direct a 30-min. documentary, The Immigrant Experience. Also wrote and directed two children's films for same co. First feature was Hester Street, which she wrote and directed.
THEATER: Director: Album, Maybe I'm Doing It Wrong.
PICTURES: Hester Street (s.p., dir.); Bernice Bobs Her Hair (short, s.p.-dir., later shown on TV), Between the Lines (dir.); On the Yard (prod.), Head Over Heels (s.p., dir.; retitled Chilly Scenes of Winter), Crossing Delancey (dir.), Loverboy (dir.).
TELEVISION: Finnegan Begin Again (dir.), The Nightingale, Faerie Tale Theatre (s.p.).

SILVER, JOEL: Producer. e. NYU. Made first film, a short called Ten Pin Alley; moved to Los Angeles with job as asst. to Lawrence Gordon. Named pres., Lawrence Gordon Prods.; developed with Gordon and produced and marketed Hooper, The End, The Driver, The Warriors. At Universal Pictures as prod. v.p.; supervising Smokey and the Bandit II, Xanadu.
PICTURES: Co-Producer: 48 Hrs., Streets of Fire, Brewster's Millions. Producer: Weird Science, Commando, Jumpin' Jack Flash, Lethal Weapon, The Predator, Action Jackson, License to Drive, Die Hard, Road House, Lethal Weapon 2, Seven Year Storm, Hudson Hawk, Ford Fairlane.
TELEVISION: Tales from the Crypt (exec. prod. & prod.).

SILVER, LEON J.: Executive. b. Boston, MA, March 25, 1918. e. U. of Southern California, 1935–39. Independent prod. of short subjects, 1939; story analyst, Paramount, 1940, film writer, U.S. Army Pictorial Service, 1941–45; freelance writer, 1946; film writer. prod., U.S. Public Health Service, 1946–51, asst. chief, foreign film prod., U.S. Dept. of State, 1951–54; acting chief, domestic film prod., U.S. Information Agency, 1955. Division Chief, Worldwide Documentary Film & Television Product, U.S. Information Agency, Apr. 6, 1968, 1978 to 1980, sr. advisor IV, film production. Resigned, 1980. Now TV network writer-producer-novelist.

SILVER, MARISA: Director. b. New York, NY, April 23, 1960. Daughter of director Joan Micklin Silver and prod.-dir. Raphael Silver. e. Harvard U. where she directed short Dexter T. and edited doc. Light Coming Through: a Portrait of Maud Morgan.
PICTURES: Old Enough (prod. for $400,000) Permanent Record, Vital Signs.
TELEVISION: Co-dir.: A Community of Praise (an episode of PBS series Middletown, 1982).

SILVER, MILTON: Advertising executive. b. New York, NY. U.S. Army W.W.I. Co-ed. Who's Who on Screen and Little Movie Mirror books; co-author Broadway stage production, The Mystery Ship; dir. adv., exploit., Universal Pictures, trailer ed, adv. manager, National Screen Service; exec. asst. to dir. adv. pub. Republic Pictures; to Souvaine Selective Pictures as adv., pub. dir., 1951; adv. pub. dept. United Artists 1953. Freelance writer since 1960.

SILVER, RAPHAEL D.: Producer. b. Cleveland, OH, 1930. e. Harvard Coll. and Harvard Graduate Sch. of Business Adm. Is pres. of Midwestern Land Devel. Corp. and Hodgson Houses, Inc. In 1973 formed Midwest Film Productions to produce Hester Street, written and directed by his wife, Joan Micklin Silver. Also distributed film independently. Also produced Between the Lines, directed by wife. Directed On the Yard and a Walk on the Moon, Crossing Delancey (exec. prod.).

SILVER, RON: Actor. b. New York, NY, July 2, 1946. e. U. of Buffalo, St. John's U., Taiwan, M.A. Trained for stage at Herbert Berghof Studios and Actors Studio. N.Y. stage debut in Kasper and Public Insult, 1971. Film debut in Semi-Tough, 1977. TV debut in Rhoda, 1976.
THEATER: El Grande de Coca Cola, Lotta, More Than You Deserve, Angel City (Mark Taper, LA), Hurlyburly, Social Security, Hunting Cockroaches, Speed-the-Plow (Tony Award).
PICTURES: Tunnelvision, Welcome to L.A., Silent Rage, Best Friends, The Entity, Lovesick, Silkwood, Garbo Talks, Goodbye People, Eat and Run, Oh God! You Devil, Blue Steel, Enemies, A Love Story, Reversal of Fortune.
TELEVISION: Hill Street Blues, Stockard Channing Show (series), Mac Davis Show, Bakers Dozen, Dear Detective. Movies: Betrayal, Word of Honor, A Father's Revenge, Drive, He Said (Trying Times), Billionaire Boys Club, Fellow Traveler.

SILVERMAN, FRED: b. New York, NY, Sept., 1937. e. Syracuse U., Ohio State U., master's in TV and theatre arts. Joined WGN-TV, indep. sta. in Chicago. Came to N.Y. for exec. post at WPIX-TV, where stayed only six weeks CBS-TV hired him as dir. of daytime programs. Named v.p., programs 1970. In 1975 left CBS to become pres., ABC Entertainment. In 1978, named pres. and chief exec. officer of NBC. Now Pres., Fred Silverman Company, Los Angeles. Formed TV prod. co. Pierce/Silverman with Fred Pierce, 1989.
TELEVISION: Prod./exec. prod.: Series: Perry Mason Movies, Matlock, In the Heat of the Night, Jake and the Fatman, Father Dowling Mysteries, Braddock. One of the Boys, Jonathan Brandmeier specials, Loose Canon. Movies: The Astronaut, Family Flight, Man on a String, The Alpha Caper, Coffee, Tea, or Me; Outrage, The President's Plane is Missing, The FBI Story: The FBI vs. Alvin Karpis, The Last Hurrah, Young Joe: The Forgetten Kennedy, Kill Me If You Can, A Woman Called Moses, The Jesse Owens Story, First Steps, She Knows Too Much.

SILVERMAN, JIM: Executive. b. Des Moines, IA, June 26, 1950. e. U. of Hawaii, B.A., 1972; Taiwan National U., foreign language study, 1973. Exec. v.p. & co-founder, Commtron Corp., division of Bergen Brunswig Corp., 1975–83; pres. & founder, Continental Video, Inc., division of Cinema Group, Inc.
PICTURES: Prod.: Crack House.

SILVERMAN, RON: Producer, Writer. b. Los Angeles, CA, June 13, 1933. e. UCLA, 1951–53; U. of Arizona, 1953–55.

Reporter-reviewer, Daily Variety, 1957–61; asst. to prod.-dir. Mark Robson, Red Lion Films, 20th Century-Fox, 1961–62; assoc. prod., Daystar Productions, 1961; v.p., 1964; assoc. prod. Crackerby TV series, 1965. Prod. exec., Warner Bros. TV, 1966; prod. & exec. Ted Mann Prods., 1967.
PICTURES: Buster and Billie (prod. 1974), Lifeguard, Brubaker (prod.), Krull (prod.), Shoot to Kill (co-prod.).
TELEVISION: Wild Wild West (writer), 1967.

SILVERMAN, SYD: Executive. b. New York, NY, Jan 23, 1932. Grandson of Sime Silverman, founder of Variety in 1905. e. The Manlius Sch., 1946–50; Princeton U., 1950–54. Lt., U.S. Army, 1954–56. Publisher, Daily Variety and Weekly Variety.

SILVERSTEIN, ELLIOT: Director. b. Boston, MA, Aug. 3, 1927. e. Boston Coll., Yale U. Started career on television.
PICTURES: Cat Ballou, The Happening, A Man Called Horse, Deadly Honeymoon, The Car.
TELEVISION: Belle Sommers, Betrayed by Innocence, Night of Courage, Fight for Life.

SILVERSTEIN, MAURICE: Executive. b. Syracuse, NY, March 1, 1912. Booker, salesman, MGM domestic dep't; International Dep't, MGM; supervisor Southeast Asia Hdqts. Singapore, MGM, 1938–42; OWI chief, film distribution for Europe, hdqts. London, during W.W.II; asst. sales supervisor, Far East, MGM; regional director, Latin America, 1947; liaison exec. to handle independent productions MGM, 1956; vice-pres., MGM International, 1957; first vice-pres., 1958; pres., MGM International, 1963; vice-pres., parent company, Metro-Goldwyn-Mayer Inc. 1970; Silverstein Int'l Corp., pres.

SIMMONS, ANTHONY: Director, Writer. b. London, England. e. Grad. from the LSE with LL.B. Practiced briefly as a barrister before entering the industry as writer/director of documentaries, then commercials and feature films. Awards: Grand Prix (shorts), Venice, Grand Prix, Locarno; 2 Int. Emmys.
PICTURES: Sunday By the Sea, Bow Bells, Four in the Morning, The Optimists, Black Joy, Little Sweetheart.
TELEVISION: On Giant's Shoulders, Supergran and the Magic Ray, Day After the Fair, Inspector Morse.

SIMMONS, JEAN: Actress. b. London, England, Jan. 31, 1929. e. Aida Foster Sch., London. Screen debut 1944, at 14 in Give Us the Moon. Voted one of top ten British money-making stars in M.P. Herald-Fame Poll, 1950–51. London stage: A Little Night Music.
PICTURES: Mr. Emmanuel, Meet Sexton Blake, Kiss the Boys Goodbye, Sports Day, Caesar and Cleopatra, Way to the Stars, Great Expectations, Hungry Hill, Black Narcissus, The Women In the Hall, Blue Lagoon, Hamlet, (Venice Film Fest., Best Actress), Adam and Evelyne, Trio, So Long as the Fair, Cage of Gold, The Clouded Yellow, Androcles and the Lion (U.S. film debut), Angel Face, Young Bess, Affair with a Stranger, The Actress, The Robe, She Couldn't Say No, A Bullet Is Waiting, The Egyptian, Desiree, Footsteps in the Fog, Guys and Dolls, Hilda Crane, This Could Be the Night, Until They Sail, The Big Country, Home Before Dark, This Earth Is Mine, Spartacus, The Grass Is Greener, All the Way Home, Elmer Gantry, Divorce American Style, Rough Night in Jericho, The Happy Ending (Acad. Award nom.), Say Hello to Yesterday, Dominique, Going Undercover, The Dawning, Missionary Stew.
TELEVISION: Beggarman Thief, The Easter Promise, The Dain Curse, The Home Front, Golden Gate, Jacqueline Susann's, Valley of the Dolls 1981, A Small Killing, The Thorn Birds (Emmy award, supp., 1983), North & South Book II, Inherit the Wind, Great Expectations.

SIMMONS, JOHN: Producer, Director, Writer, Creative consultant. e. St. Clement Danes, U. of London, the Temple. Assoc. with many adv. doc. feature & TV films. Numerous International Festival awards, incl. Oscar nomin.; creative dir., Cinevista Ltd.; wrote, The Blue Bird, Loganberry Fair (lyrics, etc.), devised adv. campaigns, The Guns of Navarone, Summer Holiday; creative dir., John Simmons Creative Consultants Ltd. Join The Tea Set, Shell, Ovaltine, Waddington, Tide, Terylene, Marks & Spencer, Schweppes, Crown, Cleveland, Gold Camera Award (1st Place) for The Bosch Equation, U.S. Int. Ind. Film Festival, 1974. 1st Prize San Francisco Fest. 1975. Dev. & Dir. Cinema Ad. Awards, 1976. Corr. to Fin. Times, Variety, Campaign etc. Gold Camera Award 1977 for Stop Her, Silver Award, New York Fest. Consultant, Rank Advertising Awards (cinema) and commercial radio. Best radio commercial Award 1977. Award, Cannes 1978, A Clear Edge.

SIMMONS, MATTY: Producer. b. Oct. 3. As bd. chmn., National Lampoon, Inc. produced National Lampoon Radio Hour; National Lampoon Lemmings; National Lampoon Show. Resigned from National Lampoon Inc. 1989. Now heads Matty Simmons Productions.
PICTURES: National Lampoon's Animal House; National Lampoon's Vacation; National Lampoon Goes to the Movies; National Lampoon's Class Reunion; National Lampoon's European Vacation, National Lampoon's Family Dies, National Lampoon's Christmas Vacation (exec. prod.).
TELEVISION: National Lampoon's Disco Beavers, National Lampoon's Class of '86 (exec. prod.), Delta House.

SIMON, MELVIN: Executive. b. New York, NY, Oct. 21, 1926. e. City Coll.of New York, B.B.A., 1949; graduate work at Indiana U. Law Sch. Owns and operates, in partnership with two brothers, over 90 shopping centers in U.S. In 1978 formed Melvin Simon Productions, privately owned corp., to finance films. Dissolved Co. in 1983.
PICTURES: Exec. Prod.: Dominique, When a Stranger Calls, The Runner Stumbles, Scavenger Hunt, Cloud Dancer, The Stunt Man, My Bodyguard, Zorro—The Gay Blade, Chu Chu and the Philly Flash, Porky's, Porky's II—The Next Day, Uforia, Wolf Lake, Porky's Revenge.
MEMBER: Friars Club; N.Y. div.; 1978, v.p., Intl. Council of Shopping Centers; 1978, commerce and industry chmn. of muscular dystrophy; mem. bd., Indiana Repertory Theatre 1978, corporate sponsor: Indianapolis 500 Festival, Indianapolis Museum of Arts, Indianapolis Children's Museum; Indianapolis Zoological Society.

SIMON, NEIL: Playwright, Screenwriter, Producer. r.n. Marvin Neil Simon. b. Bronx, NY, July 4, 1927. e. NYU, U.S. Army Air Force, 1945–46. Wrote comedy for radio with brother, Danny, (Robert Q. Lewis Show and for Goodman Ace), also TV scripts for Sid Caesar, Red Buttons, Jackie Gleason, Phil Silvers, Garry Moore, Tallulah Bankhead Show. With Danny contributed to Bdwy revues Catch a Star (1955), and New Faces of 1956.
PLAYS: Come Blow Your Horn, Little Me, Barefoot in the Park, The Odd Couple, Sweet Charity, The Star Spangled Girl, Plaza Suite, Promises, Promises, The Last of the Red Hot Lovers, The Gingerbread Lady, The Prisoner of Second Avenue, The Sunshine Boys, The Good Doctor, God's Favorite, California Suite, Chapter Two, They're Playing Our Song, I Ought to Be in Pictures, Fools, Little Me (revised version), Brighton Beach Memoirs, Biloxi Blues, The Odd Couple (female version), Broadway Bound, Rumors. Adapted several of own plays to screen and wrote original s.p.s, The Out-of-Towners, and The Slugger's Wife.
PICTURES: After the Fox, Barefoot in the Park (also assoc. prod.), The Out-of-Towners, Plaza Suite, Last of the Red Hot Lovers, The Heartbreak Kid, The Prisoner of Second Avenue, The Sunshine Boys, Murder by Death, The Goodbye Girl, The Cheap Detective, California Suite, Seems Like Old Times, Only When I Laugh (also co-prod.), Chapter Two, I Ought to Be in Pictures (also co-prod.), Max Dugan Returns (also co-prod.), The Lonely Guy (adaptation), The Slugger's Wife, Brighton Beach Memoirs, Biloxi Blues (also co-prod.).
TELEVISION: The Trouble With People, A Quiet War, Plaza Suite.
AWARDS: Emmy Award: Sid Caesar Show (1957), The Phil Silvers Show (1959). Tony Award: The Odd Couple (1965), Biloxi Blues (1985). Special Tony Award, 1975. Writers Guild Screen Award: The Odd Couple (1969), The Out-of-Towners (1971).

SIMON, PAUL: Singer, Composer, Actor. b. Newark, NJ, Oct. 13, 1941. e. Queens Coll., BA; postgrad. Brooklyn Law Sch. Teamed with Art Garfunkel in 1964, writing and performing own songs; they parted in 1970. Reunited for concert in New York, 1982, which was televised on HBO. Songs: With Garfunkel: Mrs. Robinson (Grammy Award), The Boxer, Bridge Over Troubled Water (Grammy).
PICTURES: The Graduate (songs), Annie Hall (actor), One Trick Pony (s.p., act., comp.)
TELEVISION: The Paul Simon Special (Emmy), Home Box Office Presents Paul Simon, Graceland: The African Concert. Guest Seseme St.
ALBUMS: with Garfunkel: Wednesday Morning 3 a.m., Sounds of Silence, Parsley, Sage, Rosemary and Thyme, The Graduate (Grammy), Bookends, Bridge Over Troubled Waters (Grammy), Concert in the Park. Solo: Paul Simon, There Goes Rhymin' Simon, Live Rhymin', Still Crazy After All These Years (Grammy), Greatest Hits, One Trick Pony, Hearts and Bones, Graceland (Grammy).

SIMONE, SIMONE: Actress. b. April 23, 1914, Marseilles, France. Played in many films in Europe, among them Les Beaux Jours, and Lac aux Dames. On stage in Toi C'est Moi, and others.
PICTURES: Girl's Domitory, Ladies in Love, Seventh Heaven, Love and Kisses, Josette, Johnny Doesn't Live Here Any More, Silent Bell, Temptation, Harbor, Lost Women, La Ronde, Pit of Loneliness, Le Plaisir, Double Destin, The Extra Day.

SIMPSON, DON: Producer. b. Anchorage, AL, Oct. 29, 1945. e. U. of Oregon, Phi Beta Kappa, 1967. Began career in industry as acct. exec. with Jack Woodel Agency, San Francisco, where supervised mktg. of Warner Bros. films. Recruited by WB in 1971 as mktg. exec. specializing in youth market; oversaw Woodstock, Clockwork Orange, Billy Jack, etc. Co-writer on low-budget films, Aloha, Bobby and Rose and

Cannonball. Joined Paramount as prod. exec. 1975; promoted 1977 to v.p., prod. Named sr. v.p. of prod., 1980; pres. of worldwide prod., 1981. Formed Don Simpson/Jerry Bruckheimer Prods. 1983, entering into exclusive deal with Paramount to develop and produce for m.p. and TV divisions.
PICTURES: Co-writer: Aloha, Bobby and Rose, Cannonball. Producer: Flashdance, Thief of Hearts, Beverly Hills Cop, Top Gun, Beverly Hills Cop II, Daytona.

SIMPSON, GARRY: Producer, Director, Writer. e. Stanford U. Major shows with NBC-TV: Jimmy Durante Show, Armstrong Circle Theatre, Ed Wynn Show, Philco TV Playhouse, Ballet Theatre. Awards: Academy of TV Arts & Sci., Sylvania. Documentary film writer-producer awards: International Film & TV Festival, Chicago Film Festival, Broadcast Media Awards. Currently, independent prod.-dir.

SIMPSON, O.J.: Actor. b. San Francisco, CA, July 9, 1947. r.n. Orenthal James Simpson. e. U. of Southern California. Was star collegiate and professional football player and winner of Heisman Trophy. Began sportscasting 1969.
PICTURES: The Towering Inferno, The Klansman, Killer Force, Cassandra Crossing, Capricorn One, Firepower, Hambone & Hillie, The Naked Gun.
TELEVISION: Movies: Roots, A Killing Affair, Goldie and the Boxer (also exec. p.), Detour to Terror (exec. p.), Goldie and the Boxer Go to Hollywood (also prod.), Cocaine and Blue Eyes (also prod.), The Golden Moment—An Olympic Love Story, Student Exchange. Prod.: High Five (pilot), Superbowl Saturday Night.

SIMS, JOAN: Actress. b. London, England, May 9, 1930.
PICTURES: Dry Rot, Off the Record, No Time for Tears, Just My Luck, The Naked Truth, The Captain's Table, Passport to Shame, Emergency Ward 10, Most of the Carry On' films, Doctor in Love, Watch Your Stern, Twice Round the Daffodils, The Iron Maiden, Nurse on Wheels, Doctor in Clover, Doctor in Trouble, The Garnett Saga, Not Now Darling, Don't Just Lie There Say Something, Love Among the Ruins, One of Our Dinosaurs Is Missing, Till Death Us Do Part, The Way of the World, Deceptions.
TELEVISION: Love Among the Ruins, Born and Bred, Worzel Gummidge, Ladykillers, Crown Court, Cockles, Fairly Secret Army, Tickle on the Tum, Miss Marple: A Murder Is Announced, Hay Fever, In Loving Memory, Drummonds, Farrington of the F.O., Dr. Who.

SINATRA, FRANK: Actor, Singer. b. Hoboken, NJ, Dec. 12, 1915. Sportswriter; then singer on radio various N.Y. stations; joined Harry James orchestra, later Tommy Dorsey. On screen as a band vocalist in Las Vegas Nights, Ship Ahoy, Reveille with Beverly. Spec. Academy Award 1945 for acting in The House I Live In, short subject on tolerance. Received Jean Hersholt Humanitarian Award, 1971.
PICTURES: Higher and Higher, (acting debut, 1943), Step Lively, Anchors Aweigh, Words and Music, It Happened in Brooklyn, Till the Clouds Roll By, Miracle of the Bells, Kissing Bandit, Take Me Out to the Ball Game, On the Town, Double Dynamite, Meet Danny Wilson, From Here to Eternity (Acad. Award. best supporting actor, 1953), Suddenly, Young at Heart, Not as a Stranger, Guys and Dolls, Tender Trap, Man With the Golden Arm, Johnny Concho, High Society, Around The World in 80 Days, Pride and the Passion, The Joker is Wild, Pal Joey, Kings Go Forth, Some Came Running, A Hole in the Head, Never So Few, Ocean's 11, Devil at Four O'Clock, Sergeants 3, The Manchurian Candidate, Come Blow Your Horn, The List of Adrian Messenger, 4 for Texas, Robin and the Seven Hoods, None But the Brave (dir.), Von Ryan's Express, Marriage on the Rocks, Cast a Giant Shadow, Assault on a Queen, The Naked Runner, Tony Rome, The Detective, Lady in Cement, Dirty Dingus Magee, That's Entertainment!, The First Deadly Sin, (also exec. prod.), Who Framed Roger Rabbit (voice).
TELEVISION: The Frank Sinatra Show, numerous specials, etc. Won both an Emmy and a Peabody Award. 1977: Contract on Cherry Street (movie), Sinatra: Concert For the Americas, Magnum P.I.

SINCLAIR, ANDREW: Director, Writer. b. 1935. Early career as novelist and historian, playwright. Published over 20 books in U.K., U.S. Entered m.p. ind. 1968.
PICTURES: s.p.: Before Winter Comes, Adventures in the Skin Trade, The Voyage of the Beagle, You?; dir., s.p.: The Breaking of Bumbo, Under Milk Wood, 1971; prod. Malachi's Cove, 1973; Tuxedo Warrior, 1982; s.p.: The Representative, The Scarlet Letter; Martin Eden, Panic City.

SINCLAIR, MADGE: Actress. b. Kingston, Jamaica, April 28, 1938. e. Shortwood Women's College. Worked in Jamaica as a teacher and in the insurance business before moving to NY. Chairwoman, Madge Walters Sinclair Inc., women's wear manufacturer and distributor. Awards: NAACP Image Award, 1981 and 1983, best actress in dramatic series, Trapper John M.D.; Drama-Logue Critics Award, 1986, Boseman & Lena; Mother of the Year Award, 1984. Member: bd. of dir., Museum of African American Art, Gwen Bolden Foundation.
THEATER: Kumaliza (NYSF, debut, 1969); Iphigenia (NYSF, NY and with Young Vic, London); Mod Donna, Ti-Jean and His Brothers; Blood; Division Street (Mark Taper Forum); Boesman & Lena (LA Theatre Center); Tartuffe (L.A. Theatre Center); Trinity.
PICTURES: Conrack (debut, 1974); Cornbread, Earl & Me; Leadbelly: I Will, I Will...For Now; Convoy; Uncle Joe Shannon; Star Trek IV; Coming to America, One Point of View.
TELEVISION: Series: Grandpa Goes to Washington (1978–79); Trapper John M.D. (1980–86); O'Hara. Guest: Madigan, Medical Center, The Waltons; Joe Forester; Doctor's Hospital; Executive Suite; Medical Story; Serpico; The White Shadow; All in the Family; Mini-Series: Roots. Movies: I Love, You, Goodbye; One in a Million: The Ron LeFlore Story; The Autobiography of Miss Jane Pittman; I Know Why the Caged Bird Sings; High Ice; Jimmy B and Andre; Guyana Tragedy: The Story of Jim Jones; Victims; Look Away: The Emancipation of Mary Todd Lincoln, Divided We Stand.

SINDEN, DONALD: Actor. b. Plymouth, England, Oct. 9, 1923. Stage debut 1942 in fit-up shows; London stage includes There's a Girl in My Soup, The Relapse, Not Now Darling, King Lear, Othello, Present Laughter, Uncle Vanya, The School for Scandal, Two Into One, The Scarlet Pimpernel. Bdwy: London Assurance, Habeas Corpus. TV debut 1948; screen debut in 1953, Cruel Sea.
PICTURES: The Cruel Sea, Mogambo, A Day to Remember, You Know What Sailors Are, Doctor in the House, The Beachcomber, Mad About Men, An Alligator Named Daisy, Black Tent, Eyewitness, Tiger in the Smoke, Doctor at Large, Rockets Galore, The Captain's Table, Operation Bullshine, Your Money or Your Wife, The Siege of Sydney Street, Twice Around the Daffodils, Mix Me a Person, Decline and Fall, The Island at the Top of the World, That Lucky Touch.
TELEVISION: Bullet in the Ballet, Road to Rome, Dinner With the Family, Odd Man In, Love from Italy, The Frog, The Glove, The Mystery of Edwin Drood, The Happy Ones, The Comedy of Errors, The Wars of the Roses, The Red House, Blackmail, A Bachelor Gray, Our Man at St. Marks (3 series), The Wind in the Tall Paper Chimney, A Woman Above Reproach, Call My Bluff, Relatively Speaking, Father Dear Father, The 19th Hole, Seven Days in the Life of Andrew Pelham (serial), The Assyrian Rejuvenator, The Organization (serial), The Confederacy of Wives, Tell It to the Chancellor, The Rivals, Two's Company (4 series), All's Well That Ends Well, Never the Twain (8 series).

SINGER, LORI: Actress. b. Corpus Christi, TX, Nov. 6, 1962. Sister of actor Marc Singer and daughter of symphony conductor Jacques Singer. Concert cellist while in teens. Won starring role in TV series Fame (1981). Motion picture debut in Footloose (1984).
PICTURES: The Falcon and The Snowman, The Man with One Red Shoe, Trouble in Mind, Summer Heat, Made in U.S.A., Warlock.
TELEVISION: Born Beautiful.

SINGER, MARC: Actor. b. Vancouver, B.C., Canada, Jan. 29. Brother of actress Lori Singer. Son of symphony conductor Jacques Singer. Trained in summer stock and regional theatre.
PICTURES: Go Tell the Spartans, If You Could See What I Hear, The Beastmaster, Born to Race, A Man Called Sarge.
TELEVISION: Series: The Contender, Dallas. Movies: Roots: The Next Generation, 79 Park Avenue, Things in Their Season, Journey from Darkness, Something for Joey, Sergeant Matlovich vs. the U.S. Air Force, The Two Worlds of Jennie Logan, For Ladies Only, Her Life as a Man, "V" (movie and series), Dallas.

SINGER, ROBERT: Producer. b. Nyack, NY. e. NYU, B.S.
PICTURES: Independence Day; Cujo; The Howling; Restless.
TELEVISION: Lacy and the Mississippi Queen; Dog and Cat series; Night Stalker; 7 Wide World of Entertainment specials; The Children Nobody Wanted; Three Eyes; Sadat; V-The Final Battle (exec. prod.); V (series-exec. prod.), Midnight Caller (exec. prod.), Gambler (prod., dir.).

SINGLETON, PENNY: Actress. r.n. Dorothy McNulty. b. Philadelphia, PA, September 15, 1908. e. Columbia U. First Broadway success came as top comedienne in Good News., exec. pres. AGVA.
PICTURES: 28 films in Blondie series; Go West Young Lady, Footlight Glamor, Young Widow, The Best Man.
TELEVISION: The Jetsons (voice).

SIODMAK, CURT: Director, Writer. b. 1902. e. U. of Zurich. Engineer, newspaper reporter, writer in Berlin; novelist, including F.P.1 Does Not Answer, adapt. 1932 for Ufa. Originals and screenplays in France and England including France (Le Bal), Transatlantic Tunnel, GB.
PICTURES: In U.S. originals and screenplays, Her Jungle Love, Aloma of the South Sea; Invisible Woman; basis: Son of Dracula; s.p.: The Mantrap; (orig.) House of Frankenstein;

collab. orig. s.p.: Shady Lady; s.p.: Beast with Five Fingers; collab. s.p., story: Berlin Express; collab. s.p.: Tarzan's Magic Fountain, Four Days Leave; dir.: Bridge of the Gorilla; collab. s.p., dir.: The Magnetic Monster; s.p.: Riders to the Stars; story, s.p.: Creature with the Atom Brain; story: Earth vs. the Flying Saucers.

SIPES, DONALD: b. 1928. Executive. Attorney. Worked for talent agencies early in career; also for NBC and CBS networks as business affairs official. Joined MCA Inc. in 1975, becoming pres. of its Universal TV unit in 1978 and corporate v.p. in June, 1981. In November, 1981, named MGM Film Co. pres. and chief operating officer. 1983, named UA Corp. Chmn & CEO. In 1984, pres., Lorimar Dist. Group.

SKASE, CHRISTOPHER: Executive. b. Australia, 1946. Began career as reporter for Fairfax publication, Australian Financial Review. In 1970s set up investment company with about $20,000. Revived Australian TV Seven network in Melbourne and then in U.S. bought Hal Roach Studios and NY based prod.-dist. Robert Halmi which he merged into Qintex Entertainment. Qintex Entertainment produced TV mini-series Lonesome Dove.

SKELTON, RED: Actor, Comedian. r.n. Richard Skelton. b. Vincennes, IN, July 18, 1913. Joined medicine show at 10; later in show boat stock, minstrel shows, vaudeville, burlesque, circus. Screen debut 1939 in Having Wonderful Time. On radio from 1936. Red Skelton Show, TV, since 1950. Composer of music, writer of short stories and painter.
PICTURES: Flight Command, Lady Be Good, The People vs. Dr. Kildare, Whistling in the Dark, Whistling in Dixie, Ship Ahoy, Maisie Gets Her Man, Panama Hattie, Du Barry Was a Lady, Thousands Cheer, I Dood It, Whistling in Brooklyn, Bathing Beauty, Ziegfeld Follies, Fuller Brush Man, Southern Yankee, Neptune's Daughter, Yellow Cab Man, Three Little Words, Watch the Birdie, Excuse My Dust, Texas Carnival, Lovely to Look At, The Clown, Half a Hero, Great Diamond Robbery, Public Pigeon No. 1, Those Magnificent Men in Their Flying Machines.

SKERRITT, TOM: Actor. b. Detroit, MI, Aug. 25, 1933. e. Wayne State U., UCLA. Appeared in Italian movies 1972–76.
PICTURES: War Hunt, Those Calloways, One Man's Way, M*A*S*H, Fuzz, Wild Rovers, Big Bad Mama, Thieves Like Us, Harold and Maude, The Devil's Rain, The Turning Point, Ice Castles, Up in Smoke, Alien, Savage Harvest, Silence of the North, Fighting Back, A Dangerous Summer, The Dead Zone, Top Gun, Opposing Forces, Space Camp, Wisdom, Maid to Order, The Big Town, Poltergeist III, Steel Magnolias, Big Man on Campus, Honor Bound.
TELEVISION: Series: Ryan's Four, Cheers. Movies: The Bird Man, The Last Day, Maneaters Are Loose!, The Calendar Girl Murders, The Last Day, Miles to Go, Parent Trap II, A Touch of Scandal, Poker Alice, Moving Target, Nightmare at Bitter Creek, The Heist, Red King, White Knight.

SKIRBALL, WILLIAM N.: Exhibitor. b. Homestead, PA. Began career with Metro in Des Moines & Chicago; states rights distrib., Cleveland; assoc. with brother, Jack H. Skirball (of Skirball-Manning prod. team), educational films br. mgr.; also brother of Joseph Skirball, first nat'l franchise owner, Pittsburgh. Currently partner Skirball Bros. circuit (10 theatres, Ohio), hdqts., Cleveland, OH.

SKOLIMOWSKI, JERZY: Director. b. Poland, May 5, 1938. e. Warsaw U., State Superior Film Sch., Lodz, Poland. Scriptwriter for Wajda's Innocent Sorcerers Polanski's Knife in the Water and Lomnicki's Poslizg. Dir., designer, ed. and actor in Rysopis (1965). Author: Somewhere Close to Onself, Somebody Got Drowned.
PICTURES: Identification Marks—None, Walkover (also s.p., actor), The Barrier (also s.p.), The Departure, Hands Up (also s.p., actor), Dialogue, The Adventures of Gerard, The Deep End, King Queen Knave, Lady Frankenstein, The Shout (also co-s.p.), Circle of Deceit (act.), Moonlighting (also s.p., prod.); Success Is the Best Revenge, The Lightship, White Nights (actor), Big Shots (actor), Torrents of Spring (dir., s.p.), Before and After Death (dir., s.p.).

SKYE, IONE: Actress. b. Hollywood, CA 1971. r.n. Ione Skye Leitch. Daughter of folksinger Donovan (Leitch) and sister of actor Donovan Leitch. Fashion photo of her in magazine led to audition for film River's Edge.
PICTURES: River's Edge (debut, 1986 as Ione Skye Leitch), Stranded, A Night in the Life of Jimmy Reardon, Say Anything, The Rachel Papers.
TELEVISION: Napoleon and Josephine.

SLATER, CHRISTIAN: Actor. b. New York, Aug. 18, 1969. Mother is NY casting dir. Mary Jo Slater (now v.p. of talent MGM), father Los Angeles stage actor Michael Hawkins. Made prof. debut at 9 in The Music Man starring Dick Van Dyke in the natl. tour, then on Bdwy. Also on Bdwy in Macbeth, A Christmas Carol, David Copperfield and Merlin. Off-Bdwy in Landscape of the Body, Between Daylight and Boonville and Somewhere's Better. Also summer theatre.
PICTURES: The Invisible Boy, Twisted, The Legend of Billie Jean, The Name of the Rose, Tucker: the Man and His Dream, Gleaming the Cube, Heathers, Personal Choice, The Delinquents, Pump Up the Volume.
TELEVISION: Soap operas: One Life to Live, All My Children, Ryan's Hope. Movies: Pardon Me for Living, Tales from the Dark Side, The Haunted Mansion Mystery, Cry Wolf, Desperate For Love, Professional Man.

SLATER, DAPHNE: Actress. b. Bayswater, London, England, March 3, 1928. e. Haberdashers' Askes Sch.; Royal Acad. of Dramatic Art. Stage debut: The Rising Generation, 1945; plays include King Lear; m.p. debut in Courtneys of Curzon Street, 1947; TV debut for BBC in I Want to Be an Actor, 1946.
TELEVISION: Emma, Shout Aloud Salvation, All the Year Round, They Fly by Twilight, Pride and Prejudice, The Affair at Assino, Beau Brummell, Jane Eyre, Precious Bane, The Dark Is Light Enough, Mary Rose, Julius Caesar, Berkeley Square, Less Than Kind, The Burning Glass, Persuasion, The Winslow Boy, She Stoops to Conquer, Nothing to Pay, The Father, The Bald Prima Donna, The Big Breaker, The Cocktail Party, Photo Finish, The Seagull, Love Story, Emergency Ward 10, Jackanory, The First Freedom, Man of Our Times, The Jazz Age, Callan, The Piano Tuner, Happy Ever After, The Pretenders, Virtue, Elizabeth R, The Staff Room, Footprints in the Sand.

SLATER, HELEN: Actress. b. New York, NY, Dec. 19, 1963. Off-Bdwy: Responsible Parties, Almost Romance.
PICTURES: Supergirl, The Legend of Billie Jean, Ruthless People, The Secret of My Success, Sticky Fingers, Happy Together.
TELEVISION: Capital News.

SLATZER, ROBERT FRANKLIN: Writer, Director, Producer, Author; b. Marion, OH, April 4, 1927. e. Ohio State U., UCLA, 1947. Radio news commentator sportscaster, wrote radio serials; adv. dir., Brush-Moore Newspapers; feature writer, Scripps-Howard Newspapers; adv. exec., The Columbus Dispatch; syn. columnist, NY Journal-American; wrote guest columns for Walter Winchell and Dorothy Kilgallen; author of western short stories and novels; wrote, dir., prod. industrial films, docs., sports specials and commercials; 1949–51, writer for Grand National Studios Prods. Monogram Pictures, Republic Studios, Eagle-Lion Films; 1951, publicist, Hope Enterprises; pub. dir., Paramount Pictures; 1952, personal mgr. to Marilyn Monroe, Ken Maynard, James Craig, Gail Russell and other stars; 1953, story editor and assoc. prod., Joe Palooka Productions; 1953–54, staff writer Universal Studios, RKO Radio Pictures, MGM, Columbia and Paramount Studios; 1958, formed Robert F. Slatzer Productions; 1960, exec. in chg. of prod., Jaguar Pictures Corp.; 1963–65, pres., Slatzer Oil & Gas Co.; 1966–67, bd. dir., United Mining & Milling Corp.; 1967–70, wrote and dir. feature films; 1970–74, exec., Columbia Pictures Corp.; 1974, resumed producing and financing features and television films; 1976, honored as "Fellow", Mark Twain Inst.
PICTURES: White Gold, The Obsessed, Mike and the Heiress, Under Texas Skies, They Came To Kill, Trail of the Mounties, Jungle Goddess, Montana Desperado, Pride of the Blue, Green Grass of Wyoming, The Naked Jungle, Warpaint, Broken Lance, Elephant Walk, South of Death Valley, The Big Gusher, Arctic Flight, The Hellcats, Bigfoot, John Wayne's No Substitute for Victory', Joniko—Eskimo Boy, Operation North Slope, Don't Go West, Mulefeathers, The Unfinished, Single Room Furnished, Viva Zapata, Inchon.
TELEVISION: The Great Outdoors, Adventures of White Arrow, Let's Go Boating, The Joe Palooka Story, Amos & Andy, I Am the Law, Files of Jeffrey Jones, Fireside Theatre, The Unser Story, Year of Opportunity (Award winning spec.), The Big Ones, Ken Maynard's West, Where are They Now?, The Groovy Seven, The Untouchables, The Detectives, Wild Wild West, Wagon Train, Playhouse 90, Highway Patrol, David Frost Special, Today Show, ABC News, 20/20, Inside Edition, The Reporters, Current Affair, The Geraldo Show.
AUTHOR: (novels) Desert Empire, Rose of the Range, Rio, Rawhide Range, The Cowboy and the Heiress, Daphne, Campaign Girl, Scarlet, The Dance Studio Hucksters, Born to be Wild, Single Room Furnished, The West is Still Wild, Gusher, The Young Wildcats; (biographies) The Life and Curious Death of Marilyn Monroe, The Life and Legend of Ken Maynard, Who Killed Thelma Todd?, The Duke of Thieves, Bing Crosby—The Hollow Man, Duke: The Life and Times of John Wayne.

SLAVIN, GEORGE: Writer. b. Newark, NJ, May 2, 1916; e. Bucknell U., drama, Yale U.
PICTURES: story, co-s.p., Intrigue; co-story, Woman on Pier 18; co-s.p., The Nevadan, Mystery Submarine; co-story & s.p. Peggy, Red Mountain, City of Bad Men; co-story, Weekend with Father, Thunder Bay, Rocket Man; co-story, co-s.p., Smoke Signal, Uranium Boom; co-s.p., Desert Sands, The Halliday Brand, Son of Robin Hood.

SLOAN, JOHN R.: Producer. e. Merchiston Castle, Edinburg, 1932–39; asst. dir. and prod. man. Warners, London, Hollywood; 1939–46, Army Service.
PICTURES: Sea Devils, The End of the Affair, Port Afrique, Abandon Ship, The Safecracker, Beyond this Place, The Killers of Kilimanjaro, Johnny Nobody, The Reluctant Saint, The Running Man, The Last Command, To Sir With Love, Fragment of Fear, Dad's Army, Lord Jim, No Sex Please, We're British, The Odessa File, Force 10 From Navarone, The Children's Story.

SLOCOMBE, DOUGLAS: Cinematographer. b. England, Feb. 10, 1913. Former journalist. Filmed the invasion of Poland and Holland. Under contract to Ealing Studios 17 years.
PICTURES: Dead of Night, The Captive Heart, Hue and Cry, The Loves of Joanna Godden, It Always Rains on Sunday, Saraband for Dead Lovers, Kind Hearts and Coronets, Cage of Gold, The Lavender Hill Mob, Mandy, The Man in the White Suit, The Titfield Thunderbolt, Man in the Sky, Ludwig II, Lease on Life, The Smallest Show on Earth, Tread Softly, Stranger, Circus of Horrors, The Young Ones, The Mark, The L-Shaped Room, Freud, The Servant (BAFTA Award), Guns at Batashi, A High Wind in Jamaica, The Blue Max, Promise Her Anything, The Vampire Killers, Fathom, Robbery, Boom, The Lion in Winter, The Italian Job, The Music Lovers, Murphy's War, The Buttercup Chain, Travels With My Aunt (Acad. Award nom.), Jesus Christ Superstar, The Great Gatsby, Rollerball, Hedda, The Sailor Who Fell From Grace With the Sea, Nasty Habits, Julia, Close Encounters of the Third Kind, Caravans, Lost and Found, Nijinsky, Raiders of the Lost Ark, Never Say Never Again, The Pirates of Penzance, Water, Lady Jane, Indiana Jones and the Temple of Doom, Indiana Jones and the Last Crusade.
TELEVISION: Love Among the Ruins, The Corn Is Green.

SLOTE, A. R.: Bureau Chief in Pakistan for Quigley Publications. b. Bagasra, India, June 9, 1935. e. Pakistan National H.S., Muslim Sch. and Art. Coll., Karachi. Booker, Columbia Pictures Int. Corp. Asst. mgr., Plaza Cinema, Paradise Theatres, Ltd. Editor: Filmlife, 1959–64; Karachi correspondent for Weekly Chitrali, Pakistan Daily Observer, Dhaka, 1966–70. Editor, publisher: Pakistan Filmdom, 1966; Sind Film Directory, 1981; Platinum Jubilee Film Directory, 1987. Film Page Incharge, The Star Daily of Karachi since 1971.

SMAKWITZ, CHARLES A.: e. Syracuse U. Named by Warner Bros. as dist. mgr. Albany, Troy and Utica; named as zone mgr. Warner Bros., NY State Theatres. Made zone mgr. of Stanley Warner Theatres for NJ, and New York state theatres added to NJ Zone and made headquarters in Newark, NJ in 1955, transferred to NY home office as natl. dir. of public relations, publicity, advertising for Stanley Warner Corp. In the various areas was Mayor's Rehabilitation and Urban Development Com. of Albany, State Albany chmn. War Activities Committee, National Public Dir. Red Cross Fund Organized Albany V.C. Tent #9 and served as Chief Barker 3 years, 1949–1952, elected Natl. Rep. V.C. of America. Member NY State Program and Planning Committee, Pres. Heart Assn. of Albany County, NJ State chmn. Natl. Conf. of Christian and Jews 1955–62. Organized and pres. of Syr. U. of Greater N.Y. Served as v.p. of V.C. of N.Y. Assistant to Spyros R. Skoveas 1969–71, served as Intl.-Ambassador at large of V.C.; intl. consultant exhibition, production, promotion, real estate and public relations.

SMIGHT, JACK: Director. b. Minneapolis, MN, March 9, 1926. e. U. of MN, BA. Began as disc jockey then became TV dir. of One Man's Family (1953).
PICTURES: I'd Rather Be Rich, The Third Day, Harper, Kaleidoscope, The Secret War of Harry Frigg, No Way to Treat a Lady, Strategy of Terror, The Illustrated Man, The Travelling Executioner, Rabbit Run, Airport 1975, Midway, Damnation Alley, Fast Break, Loving Couples, Number One with a Bullet, The Favorite.
TELEVISION: Banacek, Columbo, Madigan. Movies: Eddie (Emmy, 1959), Roll of Thunder, Hear My Cry, Frankenstein—The True Story, Double Indemnity, Remembrance of Love, Linda, The Longest Night, The Screaming Woman.

SMITH, ALEXIS: Actress. b. Penticton, Can., June 8, 1921. m. actor Craig Stevens. e. Los Angeles City Coll. In summer stock British Columbia; star in coll. prod., Night of January 16th.
PICTURES: Smiling Ghost, Dive Bomber, Steel Against the Sky, Gentlemen Jim, Thank Your Luck Stars, Constant Nymph, Conflict, Adventures of Mark Twain, Rhapsody in Blue, Horn Blows at Midnight (Star of Tomorrow, 1943), One More Tomorrow, Night and Day, Of Human Bondage, Stallion Road, Two Mrs. Carrolls, Woman in White, Decision of Christopher Blake, Whiplash, South of St. Louis, Any Number Can Play, One Last Fling, Undercover Girl, Wyoming Hall, Montana, Here Comes the Groom, Cave of the Outlaws, Turning Point, Split Second, Sleeping Tiger, Eternal Sea, The Young Philadelphians, Once Is Not Enough, The Little Girl Who Lives Down the Lane, Casey's Shadow, Tough Guys.
BROADWAY: Follies (Tony Award), 1971, The Women, 1973, Summer Brave, 1975; Platinum, 1978.
TELEVISION: Movies: A Death in California, Dress Gray, Marcus Welby, M.D.-A Holiday Affair. Series: Hothouse.

SMITH, CHARLES MARTIN: Actor, Director. b. Oct. 30, 1953. e. California State U. Father is animation artist Frank Smith.
PICTURES: Actor: The Culpepper Cattle Company, Fuzz, The Spikes Gang, American Graffiti, More American Graffiti, Pat Garrett and Billy the Kid, Rafferty and the Gold Dust Twins, No Deposit No Return, The Buddy Holly Story, Herbie Goes Bananas, Never Cry Wolf, Starman, The Untouchables, Trick or Treat (dir.), The Experts, Boris & Natasha.
TELEVISION: Speed Buggy (voice), The Brady Bunch, Monte Nash, Baretta, Streets of San Francisco (dir.). Movies: Cotton Candy, Go Ask Alice, Law of the Land.

SMITH, DAVID R.: Archivist. b. Pasadena, CA, Oct. 13, 1940. e. Pasadena City Coll., A.A., 1960; U. of California, Berkeley, B.A. 1962, M.A. 1963. Writer of numerous historical articles. Worked as librarian at Library of Congress, 1963–65 and as reference librarian, UCLA 1965–70 before becoming archivist for The Walt Disney Co. 1970–present. Exec. dir., The Manuscript Society, 1980–; member, Society of American Archivists, Society of CA Archivists, Intl. Animated Film Society (ASIFA), American Assn. of State and Local History (AASLH). Received service award, ASIFA, and award of distinction, Manuscript Soc, 1983.

SMITH, HOWARD K.: News commentator. b. Ferriday, LA, May 12, 1914. e. Tulane U., 1936; Heidelberg U., Germany; Oxford U., Rhodes scholarship. United Press, London, 1939; United Press Bureau, Copenhagen; United Press, Berlin, 1940; joined CBS News, Berlin corr., 1941. Reported on occupied Europe from Switzerland to 1944; covered Nuremberg trials, 1946; ret. to U.S., moderator, commentator or reporter, CBS Reports, Face the Nation, Eyewitness to History, The Great Challenge, numerous news specials. Sunday night news analysis. CBS News Washington corr., 1957; chief corr. & mgr., Washington Bureau, 1961; joined, ABC News, Jan. 1962. News and comment, ABC news. Anchorman and commentator, ABC Evening News. Author: Last Train from Berlin, 1942, The State of Europe, 1949. Washington, D.C.—The Story of Our Nation's Capital, 1967.

SMITH, HY: Executive. b. New York, NY, June 3, 1934. e. Baruch Sch., City Coll. of New York, B.B.A. Joined Paramount Pictures 1967, foreign ad.-pub coordinator; 1969-joined United Artists as foreign ad.-pub mgr., named intl. ad.-pub dir., 1970; named v.p.; intl. adv.-pub. 1976; Appointed vice pres. worldwide advertising, publicity and promotion, 1978; 1981, named first v.p., adv./pub./promo; 1982, joined Rastar Films as v.p., intl. project director for Annie. 1983, joined United Intl. Pictures as sr. v.p., adv/pub, based in London. 1984, named sr. v.p., mktg.

SMITH, JACLYN: Actress. b. Houston, TX, Oct. 26, 1947. Started acting while in high school and studied drama and psychology at Trinity U. in San Antonio. Appeared in many commercials as model.
PICTURES: Bootleggers, The Adventures, Deja Vu.
TELEVISION: McCloud, Get Christy Love, The Rookies, World of Disney, Switch, Charlie's Angels (series). Movies: The Users, Nightkill, The Night They Saved Christmas, Sentimental Journey, Florence Nightingale, George Washington, Rage of Angels, Rage of Angels: The Story Continues, Windmills of the Gods, The Bourne Identity.

SMITH, JACQUELINE: Executive. b. Philadelphia, PA, May 24, 1933. e. Antioch Coll., 1954. m. William Dale Smith, novelist (pseudonym David Anthony). Actress, Bermudiana Theatre in Bermuda, The Antioch Theatre, OH and several little theatres in Washington, DC; with the Stanford U. Players. Did research and writing for RCA, worked as a nursery school teacher and directed Little Theatre groups in the West Coast area. 1957: wrote and produced over 100 weekly children's programs at KPIX, San Francisco. Promotion dir. at WPIX-TV, N.Y. Worked with CBS TV Network for over 5 yrs. as general prog. exec. and exec. prod. of CBS West Coast daytime programs. Dir. of special projects at Warner Bros. Television Dept. and exec. prod. of Warner Bros. animation div. 1969–73; v.p. daytime progs. ABC Entertainment, NY-1977–86. Pres. Pygmalion Prods.; 1989 appt. v.p. daytime progs., NBC Entertainment.

SMITH, JOSEPH P.: Executive. b. Brooklyn, NY. e. Columbia U. Started career Wall Street; joined RKO Radio Pictures, served in sales and managerial posts; exec. vice-pres., Lippert Productions, Hollywood; vice pres., Telepictures, Inc., formed and pres., Cinema-Vue Corp.; pres., Pathe Pictures, Inc., Pathe News, Inc.

SMITH, MAGGIE: C.B.E. Actress. b. Ilford, England, Dec. 28, 1934. Early career Oxford Playhouse. With the Old Vic 1959–60. Also with Stratford Ontario Shakespeare Fest. 1976–78, & 1980. Received C.B.E. 1970. Numerous TV appearances Britain, America.

THEATER: Twelfth Night (debut, 1952), New Faces of 1956 (NY debut, as comedienne), Share My Lettuce, The Stepmother, Rhinoceros, The Rehearsal, The Private Ear, The Public Eye, Mary, Mary, The Recruiting Officer, Othello, The Master Builder, Hay Fever, Much Ado About Nothing, Black Comedy, Miss Julie, Hedda Gabler, Private Lives (London & NY), Peter Pan, As You Like It, Macbeth, Night and Day, Virginia, Lettuce and Lovage.

PICTURES: Nowhere to Go, The Pumpkin Eater, The V.I.P.s, Young Cassidy, Othello, The Honey Pot, Hot Millions, The Prime of Miss Jean Brodie (Acad. Award), Oh What a Lovely War, Love and Pain, Travels with My Aunt, Murder by Death, Death on the Nile, California Suite (Acad. Award), Clash of the Titans, Quartet, Evil Under the Sun, Better Late Than Never, The Missionary, A Private Function, Lily in Love, A Room with a View, The Lonely Passion of Judith Hearne.

TELEVISION: Much Ado About Nothing, Man and Superman, On Approval, Home and Beauty, Bed Among the Lentils.

SMITH, MAURICE: Producer, Director, Writer. b. London, England, May 12, 1939. e. St. Ignatius Coll. Prior to entering m.p. industry, worked in bank in England, on newspaper in Canada, pool hustler, general contractor in Los Angeles, CA.

PICTURES: The Glory Stompers, Scream Free, Cycle Savages, Hard Trail, Diamond Stud, Love Swedish Style, November Children, How Come Nobody's On Our Side, Joys of Jezebel, Screwball Hotel, Grotesque (exec. prod.).

SMITH, ROGER: Actor, Producer. b. South Gate, CA, Dec. 18, 1932. m. actress-performer Ann Margret. e. U. of Arizona. Started career at age 7, one of the Meglin Kiddies, appearing at the Mayan Theater, Wilshire, Ebell. Sings, composes, American folk songs. Producer: Ann-Margret caberet and theater shows.

PICTURES: No Time to Be Young, Crash Landing, Operation Madball, Man of a Thousand Faces, Never Steal Anything Small, Auntie Mame, Rogues Gallery.

TELEVISION: The Horace Heidt Show, Ted Mack Original Amateur Hour, 77 Sunset Strip (series), writer, ABC-TV.

SMITH, WILLIAM: Actor. b. Columbia, MO, May 24, 1932. e. Syracuse, U., BA; UCLA, MA.

PICTURES: Darker Than Amber, C.C. and Company, The Losers, Run, Angel, Run, Blood and Guts, Seven, Fast Company, No Knife, Twilight's Last Gleaming, The Frisco Kid, Any Which Way You Can, Red Dawn, Moon in Scorpio, Maniac Cop, Emperor of the Bronx, Nam, B.O.R.N., Hell Comes to Frogtown, Terror in Beverly Hills, Hell on the Battleground, Forgotten Heroes, Instant Karma, Action U.S.A. Brothers in Arms. Deadly Breed, Empire of Ash, Emperor of the Bronx. Jungle Assault.

TELEVISION: Rich Man, Poor Man, Hawaii 5-0, The Jerk Too, The Rebels, Wild Times, Death Among Friends, Wildside.

SMITS, JIMMY: Actor. b. Brooklyn, NY, July 9, 1955. e. Brooklyn Coll., B.A.; Cornell U., M.F.A. Worked as community organizer before acting with NY Shakespeare Fest. Public Theater.

THEATER: Hamlet (NY Shakespeare Fest., 1983), Little Victories, Buck, The Ballad of Soapy Smith.

PICTURES: Running Scared (debut, 1986), The Believers, Old Gringo.

TELEVISION: Series: L.A. Law. Pilots: Miami Vice, Movies: Rockabye, The Highwayman, Dangerous Affection. Specials: The Other Side of the Border (narrator).

SMOLEN, DONALD E.: Executive. b. New York, NY, Aug. 10, 1923. e. NYU, 1943; Pratt Inst., 1947, Ecole Des Beaux Arts, 1949. Art dept. Fox, 1940–41; art dept. Kayton Spiero Advtg., 1942; illustrator designer, Gilbert Miller Studios 1946–49; free lance illustrator, designer, 1951–65 servicing such accounts as UA, Fox, Warner Bros., TWA, Ford Motors; dir. of adv., UA. Resigned 1974 to form own co., Donald E. Smolen and Associates, consultant for m.p. adv.; 1975 merged to form Smolen, Smith and Connolly, advertising and marketing consultants to m.p. industry. Created ad campaigns for All the Presidents' Men, Fiddler on the Roof, Rocky, Superman, Star Wars. 1987, joined newly formed distribution arm, Kings Road Entertainment.

SMOTHERS BROTHERS: Comedians, Singers.

SMOTHERS, DICK: b. New York, NY, Nov. 20, 1939. e. San Jose State College. Film debut: The Silver Bears (1978). On Bdwy in musical I Love My Wife (1978–79).

SMOTHERS, TOM: b. New York, NY, Feb. 2, 1937. e. San Jose State College. In films Get to Know Your Rabbit, The Silver Bears, Pandemonium. On Bdwy in musical I Love My Wife (1978–79).

Began career as coffeehouse folk singers with a bit of comic banter mixed in. After success at some of hipper West Coast clubs, appeared on Jack Paar's Tonight Show, The Jack Benny Show and as regulars on Steve Allen's show, 1961. 1962–65 had a series of popular albums. After starring in a situation comedy show, they hosted their own variety program which became progressively controversial as its topical humor began to cover the political and social turmoil of the 1960s until it was cancelled by CBS in 1969.

TELEVISION: The Steve Allen Show (1961), The Smothers Brothers Show (1965–66), The Smothers Brothers Comedy Hour (1967–69), The Smothers Brothers Show (1970, ABC), The Smothers Brothers Show (1975), Fitz and Bones, The Smothers Brothers Reunion (special, 1988), The Smothers Brothers Comedy Hour.

SNELL, PETER R. E.: Producer. b. Nov. 17, 1941. Entered industry 1967. Appt. head of prod. and man. dir. British Lion 1973. Joined Robert Stigwood group 1975. Returned to indep. prod., 1978; Hennessy. Appt. chief exec., Britannic Film & Television Ltd. 1985, purchased British Lion Film Prods., Ltd. from Thorn/EMI 1986–87. 1988: Chairman and chief executive British Lion.

PICTURES: Prod.: Winters Tale, Some May Live, A Month in the Country, Carnaby 68, Subterfuge, Julius Caesar, Goodbye Gemini, Anthony and Cleopatra, The Wicker Man, Hennessy, Bear Island, Motherlod, Lady Jane, Turtle Diary, A Prayer for the Dying.

TELEVISION: A Man For All Seasons (exec. prod.), Tears in the Rain, Treasure Island, Bumtwizzle.

SNODGRESS, CARRIE: Actress. b. Chicago, IL, Oct 27, 1945. e. Northern Illinois U. and M.A. degree from the Goodman Theatre. Plays include All Way Home, Oh What a Lovely War, Caesar and Cleopatra and Tartuffe (Sarah Siddons Award, 1966), The Price, Vanities, The Curse of the Starving Class.

PICTURES: Rabbit, Run, Diary of a Mad Housewife, The Fury, A Night in The Attic, Murphy's Law, Pale Rider, Blueberry Hill, The Chill Factor, Blue Suede Shoes, Nowhere to Run.

TELEVISION: World Premier (Silent Night, Lonely Night, The Whole World Is Watching), The Outsider, The Virginian, Judd for the Defense, Medical Center, Marcus Welby, M.D., The Dark Side, First Sight.

SNOW, MARK: Composer. b. Brooklyn, NY, 1946. e. Juilliard School of Music, 1968. As co-founder and member of New York Rock 'n' Roll Ensemble, appeared with the Boston Pops, at Carnegie Hall concerts and on the college circuit in the 1960s and 1970s.

PICTURES: Skateboard, Something Short of Paradise, High Risk, Jake Speed.

TELEVISION: Series: The Rookies, Starsky and Hutch, The Gemini Man, Family, The San Pedro Beach Bums, The Love Boat, The Next Step Beyond, Vega$, Hart to Hart, When the Whistle Blows, Dynasty, Falcon Crest, Strike Force, Cagney and Lacey, T.J. Hooker, The Family Tree, Lottery!, Double Trouble, Crazy Like a Fox, Hometown. Mini-series: Blood and Orchids. Movies: The Boy in the Plastic Bubble, Overboard, The Return of the Mod Squad, Angel City, Games Mother Never Taught You, John Steinbeck's Winter of Our Discontent, Packin' It In, I Married a Centerfold, Something About Amelia, Challenge of a Lifetime, California Girls, I Dream of Jeannie: Fifteen Years Later, Not My Kid, The Lady From Yesterday, Beverly Hills Cowgirl Blues, Acceptable Risks, News at Eleven, The Girl Who Spelled Freedom (Emmy nom.), Murder By the Book, A Hobo's Christmas, The Father Clements Story, Still Crazy Like a Fox, Cracked Up, Roman Holiday, Pals, Murder Ordained, Louis L'Amour's Down the Long Hills, The Saint, The Return of Ben Casey, Bluegrass, Alone in the Neon Jungle, Those She Left Behind. Specials: Day-to-Day Affairs, Vietnam War Story.

SNYDER, TOM: Newscaster, Show host. b. Milwaukee, WI, May 12, 1936. e. Marquette U. First job in news dept. of WRIT, Milwaukee. Subsequently with WSAV-TV, Savannah; WAII-TV, Atlanta; KTLA-TV, Los Angeles; and KYW-TV, Philadelphia, before moving to KNBC in L.A. in 1970 as anchorman for weeknight newscast. Named host of NBC-TV's Tomorrow program in Oct., 1973, and moved to NY in Dec., 1974, as anchorman of one-hour segment of NewsCenter 4. In Aug., 1975, inaugurated the NBC News Update, one-minute weeknight prime time news spot. Host for Tomorrow talk show, Tom Snyder Show (ABC Radio).

SNYDER, WILLIAM L.: Producer, Executive. b. Baltimore, MD, Feb. 14, 1920. e. The Johns Hopkins U., B.A., 1940. Lt. Comnder., U.S. Navy W.W.II, 1941–45. Established Rembrandt Films, N.Y., 1948 as importer and dist. of foreign films. Co-prod. White Mane (UA, dom.), winner Cannes Fest. Grand Prize, seven other intl awards, 1945. Prod. 13 Tom & Jerry Cartoons (MGM) and more than 100 Miss Nightingale, She, Little Lord Fauntleroy, The Secret Army (2 series). Popeye and Krazy Kat cartoons for U.S. TV plus number cartoons (Para.)., 1956. Won Acad. Award for cartoon Munro (Para.), 1961. Rec'd Acad. noms. for Self Defense for Cowards (1962), The Game (1963), How to Avoid Friendship (1964) and Nudnik (1965). Prod. cartoon feature Alice in Paris (Childhood Prods.), 1966. Prod. I a Woman II, 1968 (Chevron Picts.), and The Daughter (Chevron Picts.), 1970.

SOADY, WILLIAM C.: Executive. b. Oct. 7, 1943. Career with Universal Pictures started in 1970 when named Toronto branch mgr.; promoted to v.p. & gen. sls. mgr. of Universal Film (Canada) in 1971. Promoted to v.p. & gen. sls. mgr., Universal Pictures, 1981, in New York, relocating to L.A. in 1981. In 1983 named pres. of Universal Pictures Distribution, new domestic dist. div. of Universal; resigned Sept., 1988. Named exec. v.p. distribution, Tri-Star Pictures, 1989.

SOAMES, RICHARD: Executive. b. London, England, June 6, 1936. Joined Film Finances Ltd. 1972; Appt. director Film Finances Ltd., 1977: Appt. man. dir. 1979. Appt. pres. Film Finances Canada Ltd. 1982: Appt. pres., Film Finances Inc. Also formed Doric Prods, Inc.
PICTURES: The Boss's Wife, The Principal, Honey, I Shrunk the Kids, Tap.

SOBLE, RON: Actor. b. Chicago, IL, March 28, 1932. e. U. of Michigan. Served U.S. Army, 11th Airborne, in Japan. Studied acting in New York and was member of Jose Quintero's Circle in the Square Players. Acted in such plays as Romeo and Juliet, Murder in the Cathedral, The Petrified Forest; prod. assoc. on TV series Suspense and Danger, and appeared in 56 series. Co-star in The Monroes TV show.
PICTURES: Navajo Run, Al Capone, The Cincinnati Kid, Joe Kidd.

SOHMER, STEVE: Executive. b. 1942. 1977–82, v.p., adv./promo. CBS-TV. 1982, joined NBC as v.p. of adv./creative svcs. Promoted to exec. v.p., 1984. In 1985 joined Columbia Pictures as pres. & chief oper. officer. Resigned 1987 to heads Steve Sohmer Inc., creative boutique & advertising agency. 1989, named pres. and CEO Nelson Television. Author of novel Favorite Son.
PICTURES: Leonard Part 6 (exec. prod. for Bill Cosby).
TELEVISION: Favorite Son (exec. prod., s.p.).

SOKOLOW, DIANE: Executive. b. New York, NY. e. Temple U. m. Mel Sokolow. 1975, v.p., East Coast operations, for Lorimar; with Warner Bros. 1977–81; served as v.p. of East Coast production. Left to form The Sokolow Co. with husband, Mel, to produce films. 1982, returned to WB as v.p., East Coast prod. 1984, joined Motown Prods. as exec. v.p.; producer, MGM-UA 1986–87. Currently co-pres. Sokolow Co. with Mel Sokolow.
PICTURES: My Son's Brother (co-prod.).
TELEVISION: The Preppie Killing (exec. prod.), Mancuso (exec. prod., pilot).

SOLO, ROBERT H.: Producer. b. Waterbury, CT, Dec. 4, 1932. e. U. of Connecticut, BA. Early career as agent with Ashley-Famous; later production as exec. asst. to Jack Warner and Walter MacEwen at Warner Bros. In London prod. Scrooge for Cinema Center Films, 1970; 1971, named WB v.p., foreign production 1974, named exec. v.p., prod. at Burbank Studio. Now indep. prod.
PICTURES: The Devils (co-prod.), Invasion of the Body Snatchers; The Awakening; I, The Jury; Bad Boys; Colors; Above the Law (exec. prod.); Winter People.

SOLOMON, MICHAEL JAY: Executive. b. Jan. 20, 1938. e. Emerson, Boston; NYU. Evening Sch. of Commerce while working at first job with United Artists in 1956. Became student booker. Hired by Seymour Florin as booker for one year; returned to UA in intl. dept. January, 1960 went to Panama as asst. to mgr. of Central America. Transferred to Bogota after one yr.; made mgr. of UA in Peru and Bolivia. In 1964 joined MCA Latin American div., reorganizing office in Mexico and later opening office in Brazil. Made v.p., 1968, of MCA-TV. Supervised Latin American and Caribbean div., 1973 made head of feature film sales to tv stations internationally while still supervising MCA business in Latin America. Resigned 1977 to form Michael Jay Solomon Films International, Inc. & Solomon International TV Newsletter. In 1978 formed Telepictures Corp. to distribute films worldwide and enter production. Was chmn. & CEO. In 1986 merged with Lorimar to form Lorimar—Telepictures. Was member of 4-man office of the pres.
MEMBER: Vice-pres., N.Y. World TV Festival; bd. of dir., Intl. Council of NATAS; chmn., Intl. Comm. of NATPE; bd., AFMA; bd., U.S. Magazine.

SOLOMON, T. G.: Executive. b. Jan. 5, 1920. e. Louisiana State U., 1941. Past chmn. and past pres. of the National Association of Theatre Owners. Past chief barker, Variety Tent 45; past pres., Mississippi Theatre Owners; past pres., Texas Theatre Owners; chmn., Louisiana Film Commission; past pres., Louisiana Theatres Assn.

SOLT, ANDREW PETER: Writer. b. Budapest, Hungary, June 7, 1916; e. St. Stephen's Coll. Uncle of Andrew W. Solt.
PICTURES: They All Kissed the Bride, Without Reservations, Joan of Arc, Little Women, Jolson Story, In a Lonely Place, Thunder on the Hill, Lovely to Look At; orig. s.p. For the First Time (orig., s.p.).
TELEVISION: Hitchcock Presents, Ford Theatre, Douglas Fairbanks Presents, Wire Service, General Electric Theatre, BBC and Stuttgart TV.
STAGE: 1973, Geld In Der Tasche, produced by Theatre am Kurfurstendamm, West Berlin.

SOLT, ANDREW W.: Producer, Writer, Director. b. London, Eng. December 13, 1947; e. UCLA. Nephew of Andrew Peter Solt.
PICTURES: Imagine: John Lennon, This is Elvis, It Came From Hollywood.
TELEVISION: Honeymooners' Reunion, The Muppets. . .A Celebration of 30 Years, Cousteau: Mississippi, Happy Birthday Donald Duck, America Censored, Remembering Marilyn, Great Moments in Disney Animation, ET & Friends, Disney's DTV Monster Hits, Heroes of Rock 'n Roll, Bob Hope's Christmas Tours, Disney Goes To The Oscars, Cousteau: Oasis In Space Cousteau: Odyssey, The Rolling Stones, '89.

SOLTZ, CHARLENE E.: Executive. b. New London, CT. Director of press relations and public affairs for Motion Picture Association of America, Inc. and the Motion Picture Export Association of America, Inc.

SOMERS, SUZANNE: Actress. r.n. Suzanne Mahoney. b. San Bruno, CA, Oct. 16, 1946. e. Lone Mountain, San Francisco Coll. for Women. Pursued modeling career; worked as regular on Mantrap, syndicated talk show. Did summer stock and theatrical films. Author: Touch Me Again, Some People Live More Than Others. Biggest TV success in Three's Company series (1977–81).
PICTURES: Bullitt, Daddy's Gone A-Hunting, Fools, Magnum Force, American Graffiti, Yesterday's Hero, Nothing Personal.
TELEVISION: One Day at a Time, Lotsa Luck, The Rockford Files, Starsky & Hutch, The Rich Little Show, Battle of the Network Stars, Us Against the World, Love Boat, Three's Company (series), She's the Sheriff (series). Movies: Happily Ever After, It Happened at Lakewood Manor, Zuma Beach, Ants, Hollywood Wives, Disney's Totally Minnie.

SOMMER, ELKE: Actress. r.n. Elke Schletz. b. Germany, Nov. 5, 1940. To Britain 1956. Ent. films in Germany, 1958, and since made films in Germany and Italy incl. Friend of the Jaguar, Traveling Luxury, Heaven and Cupid, Ship of the Dead. 1960: made debut in British films.
PICTURES: Don't Bother to Knock, The Victors, The Prize, Love the Italian Way, A Shot in the Dark, The Art of Love, The Money Trap, The Oscar, Boy, Did I Get a Wrong Number, The Venetian Affair, Deadlier than the Male, Frontier Hellcat. Under contract to ABPC; The Corrupt Ones, The Wicked Dreams of Paula Schultz, They Came to Rob Las Vegas, The Wrecking Crew, Baron Blood, Zeppelin, Percy, Ten Little Indians, Lisa and the Devil, The Prisoner of Zenda, The Net, The Double McGuffin, Exit Sunset Blvd., The Man in Pyjamas, The Astral Factor, Lily in Love, Himmelsheim.
TELEVISION: Jenny's War, Peter the Great, Anastasia: The Mystery of Anya, Inside the Third Reich.

SOMMER, JOSEF: Actor. b. Greifswald, Germany, June 26, 1934. e. Carnegie-Mellon U. Studied at American Shakespeare Festival in Stratford, CT, 1962–64. US Army, 1958–60. NY stage debut in Othello, 1970. Film debut in Dirty Harry, 1971.
PICTURES: The Front, Close Encounters of the Third Kind, Oliver's Story, Hide in Plain Sight, Reds, Independence Day, Absence of Malice, Hanky Panky, Still of the Night, Rollover, Sophie's Choice (narrator), Silkwood, Iceman, D.A.R.Y.L., Witness, Target, The Rosary Murders, Chances Are, Dracula's Widow, Forced March, Bloodhounds of Broadway.
TELEVISION: Morning Becomes Electra, The Scarlet Letter, Saigon, Sparkling Cyanide, The Betty Ford Story, A Special Friendship, Hothouse (series), Bridge to Silence, The Bionic Showdown, The Six Million Dollar Man and the Bionic Woman, Dead Air.

SONDHEIM, STEPHEN: Composer, Writer. b. New York, NY, March 22, 1930. e. Williams Coll. Writer for Topper TV series, 1953. Wrote incidental music for The Girls of Summer (1956). Winner of 4 Grammy Awards: Cast Albums 1970, 1973, 1980 and song of the year 1975). Named visiting prof. of drama and musical theater, Oxford U. 1990.
THEATER: Lyrics only: West Side Story, Gypsy, Do I Hear a Waltz?. Music and lyrics: A Funny Thing Happened on the Way to the Forum, Anyone Can Whistle, Company (Tony Award, 1971), Follies (Tony, 1972), A Little Night Music (Tony, 1973), The Frogs (Yale Repertory), Candide (new lyrics for revival), Pacific Overtures, Sweeney Todd, (Tony, 1979), Merrily We Roll Along, Sunday in the Park with George (Pulitzer Prize, 1985), Into the Woods. (Tony, best score, 1988) Theater anthologies of his songs: Side By Side By Sondheim; Marry Me a Little.
PICTURES: West Side Story (lyrics), Gypsy (lyrics), A Funny Thing Happened on the Way to the Forum (music, lyrics), The Last of Sheila (s.p.), Stavisky (score), A Little Night Music (music, lyrics), Reds (score).

SORDI, ALBERTO: Actor. b. Rome, Italy, June 15, 1919. Won an Oliver Hardy sound-a-like contest at 13. Worked in Italian music halls before making film debut in 1938. Appeared in Fellini's early films. One of Italy's most popular film comedians, he has also had a successful career on TV with own series.

PICTURES: La Principessa Tarakanova (1938), I Vitelloni, The Sign of Venus, A Farewell to Arms, La Gran Guerra, The Best of Enemies, Tutti a Casa, Il Mafioso, Il Diavolo (To Bed or Not to Bed), Those Magnificent Men in Their Flying Machines, Le Streghe, Un Italiano in America, Viva Italia, Riusciranno i Nostri Eroi, Le Termoin, I Know That You Know That I Know (also dir.), A Taste of Life.

SORIANO, DALE: Publicist, b. Brooklyn, NY. Ent. m.p. ind. as a reelboy in projection room, later usher, sign painter, mgr., film booker stagehand (NBC-CBS-ABC). Orchestra leader, dir. of info. for various N.Y. depts., licenses, real estate, law, public events and firearms control board. Publicist for Americana festivals, various veteran orgs.: V.F.W., A.L., D.A.V., C.W.V. and Army & Navy Union and many philanthropic orgs. W.W.II served with 1st Marine Div. U.S.M.C. in S.W. Pacific thea. of opera. 1960–68 v.p. Publicists Assn., I.A.T.S.E. conducted many TV and vet columns for the Brooklyn Eagle and indep. newspapers. Show*Biz column 1st for the Brooklyn Daily Bulletin. Also stage, records, movies, radio and TV Editor. Pres. of Lighthouse Productions and pres. of Flatlands Chamber of Commerce; pres. National Council of Civic Assn. Member of Motion Picture Pioneers, National Publicists Association, American Newspaper Guild.

SORVINO, PAUL: Actor. b. New York, NY, 1939. Acted on Bdwy.; broke into films with Where's Poppa in 1970.

THEATER: Bajour, An American Millionaire, The Mating Dance, King Lear.

PICTURES: Day of the Dolphin, Made for Each Other, The Gambler, A Touch of Class, Oh, God, Bloodbrothers, Slow Dancing in the Big City, The Brink's Job, Lost and Found, Cruising, I, The Jury, That Championship Season, Off the Wall, Turk 182, The Stuff, Vasectomy, Dick Tracy, Good Fellas.

TELEVISION: Seventh Avenue, Tell Me Where It Hurts, Chiefs, Surviving, With Intent to Kill, The Oldest Rookie (series), Dummy.

SOTHERN, ANN: Actress. r.n. Harriet Lake. b. Valley City, ND, Jan. 22, 1919. e. Washington U. p. Annette Yde-Lake, opera singer. On stage, in m.p. since 1934. Star of 10 Maisie movies in series from 1939-47.

PICTURES: Let's Fall in Love, Melody in Spring, Kid Millions, Trade Winds, Hotel For Women, Maisie, Brother Orchid, Congo Maisie, Three Hearts for Julia, Swing Shift Maisie, Lady Be Good, Panama Hattie, Cry Havoc, Thousands Cheer, Maisie series, April Showers, Letter to Three Wives, Judge Steps Out, Words and Music, Nancy Goes to Rio, Blue Gardenia, Lady in a Cage, The Best Man, Sylvia, Chubasco, The Killing Kind, Golden Needles, Crazy Mama, The Manitou, The Little Dragons, The Whales of August (Acad. Award. nom).

TELEVISION: Private Secretary (series), Ann Sothern Show (series), My Mother The Car (voice of the car). Movies: The Great Man's Whiskers, Captain and the Kings, Letter to Three Wives.

SOUL, DAVID: Actor. r.n. David Solberg. b. Chicago, IL, Aug. 28, 1943. Attended several colleges but gave up studies to pursue a career in music. Made 25 singing appearances on The Merv Griffin Show where was spotted and given screen test. Signed contract with Screen Gems and given starring role in ABC-TV series, Here Come the Brides. Later Starsky and Hutch.

PICTURES: Johnny Got His Gun, Magnum Force, Dog Pound Shuffle, Appointment with Death, Hanoi Hilton, The Secret of the Sahara, Silent Hero, Friend to Friend. Captain Henkel.

TELEVISION: Guest Star: The Streets of San Francisco, Cannon, Medical Center, The Rookies, Ironside, Star Trek, McMillan and Wife, Dan August, Circle of Fear, Owen Marshall, Counselor at Law. Movies: A Country Christmas, Swan Song (also prod.), Homeward Bound, Rage, The Manions of America, World War III, Through Naked Eyes, The Disappearance of Flight 412, Intertect, Movin' On, Little Ladies of the Night, The Fifth Missile, Harry's Hong Kong, In the Line of Duty: The FBI Murders, Around the World in 80 Days, So Proudly We Hail. Series: Here Come the Brides, Starsky and Hutch, Casablanca, Yellow Rose, Bloody Friday, Unsub.

SPACEK, SISSY: Actress. r.n. Mary Elizabeth Spacek. b. Quitman, TX, Dec. 25, 1949. m. director Jack Fisk. Cousin of actor Rip Torn. Was photographic model; attended acting classes in New York under Lee Strasberg. Worked as set dir. on film Death Game (1974).

PICTURES: Prime Cut (debut), Ginger in the Morning, Badlands, Carrie, Welcome to L.A., 3 Women, Heart Beat, Coal Miner's Daughter (Acad. Award, 1980), Raggedy Man, Missing, The River, Marie, Violets Are Blue, 'night, Mother, Crimes of the Heart, The Long Walk Home, The Plastic Nightmare.

TELEVISION: Movies: The Girls of Huntington House, The Migrants, Katherine, Verna: USA Girl, and two episodes of The Waltons.

SPACEY, KEVIN: Actor. b. South Orange, NJ, 1960, raised in southern CA. e. L.A. Valley Coll., appearing in stage productions as well as stand-up comedy clubs, before attending Juilliard Sch. of Drama. Has appeared in numerous regional and repertory productions including the Kennedy Center (The Seagull), American National Theatre and Seattle Rep. Theatre, and with New York Shakespeare Fest.

THEATER: Henry IV Part I, The Robbers, Barbarians, Ghosts, Hurlyburly, Long Day's Journey into Night (with Jack Lemmon), Saved From Obscurity, National Anthems.

PICTURES: Heartburn (debut); Rocket Gibralter, Working Girl, See No Evil, Hear No Evil; Dad; A Show of Force.

TELEVISION: Long Day's Journey into Night, The Murder of Mary Phagan, Wiseguy (series).

SPADER, JAMES: Actor. b. Boston suburbs, MA, Feb. 7, 1960. e. Phillips Academy. Studied acting at Michael Chekhov Studio. Has worked as soda jerk, truck driver and stable boy between acting jobs.

PICTURES: Endless Love (debut, 1981); The New Kids; Tuff Turf; Pretty in Pink; Mannequin; Wall Street; Less Than Zero; Baby Boom; Jack's Back; Sex, Lies and Videotape (Cannes Fest., best actor award, 1989); The Rachel Papers; Bad Influence.

TELEVISION: The Family Tree (1983).

SPANO, VINCENT: Actor. b. New York, NY, Oct. 18, 1962. Stage debut at 14 in The Shadow Box (Long Wharf and Bdwy).

THEATER: Balm in Gilead.

PICTURES: Over the Edge, The Double McGuffin, Rumblefish, The Black Stallion Returns, Baby It's You, Alphabet City, Maria's Lovers, Creator, Good Morning Babylon, And God Created Woman, 1753: Venetian Red, High Frequency (aka Aquarium).

TELEVISION: Search for Tomorrow, The Gentleman Bandit, Senior Trip, Blood Ties.

SPEARS, JR., HAROLD T.: Executive. b. Atlanta, GA, June 21, 1929. e. U. of Georgia, 1951. With Floyd Theatres, Lakeland, FL, since 1953; now pres.

SPECKTOR, FREDERICK: Executive. b. Los Angeles, CA, April 24, 1933. e. U. of Southern California, UCLA. M.P. agent, Ashley Famous Agency, 1962–64; Artists Agency Corp., 1964–68; exec. M.P. dept., William Morris Agency, 1968–78; exec. Creative Artists Agency, 1978–present.

SPELLING, AARON: Executive. b. Dallas, TX, Apr. 22, 1928. Was actor/writer before becoming producer at Four Star in 1957. In 1967, formed Thomas/Spelling Productions to produce TV series and movies, including Mod Squad. In 1969, formed his own co., Aaron Spelling Productions. In 1972, partnered with Leonard Goldberg to produce The Rookies, Charlie's Angels, Fantasy Island, Starsky and Hutch, Hart to Hart, T.J. Hooker, and under own company banner, Love Boat, Vega$, Dynasty, Matt Houston, Hotel, The Colbys, Life with Lucy, Angels '88, HeartBeat and over 103 movies for television.

PICTURES: Mr. Mom (exec. prod.), Surrender, Three O'Clock High (exec. prod.), Satisfaction (co-prod.), Cross My Heart (co-exec. prod.).

RECENT TELEVISION: Exec. Prod.: The Three Kings, Nightingales, Day One (Emmy Award), The Love Boat: The Valentine Voyage.

SPENGLER, PIERRE: Producer. b. Paris, France, 1947. Went on stage at 15; returned to language studies at Alliance Française. Entered film industry as production runner and office boy. Teamed for first time with friend Ilya Salkind on The Light at the Edge of the World, produced by Alexander Salkind.

PICTURES: Bluebeard, The Three Musketeers, The Four Musketeers, Crossed Swords, Superman, Superman II, Superman III, Santa Claus: The Movie, The Return of the Musketeers.

SPENSER, JEREMY: Actor. b. Ceylon, 1937; e. Downshill Sch., Farnham, England. Ent. films 1947 in Anna Karenina.

PICTURES: It's Great To Be Young, The Prince and the Showgirl, Wonderful Things, Ferry to Hong Kong, Roman Spring of Mrs. Stone, Vengeance, King and Country, He Who Rides a Tiger.

SPEWACK, BELLA: Writer. b. Hungary, 1899. e. Washington Irving H.S., 1917. m. late Samuel Spewack, 1922; writer. Reporter N.Y. Call, N.Y. Mail, N.Y. World, N.Y. Evening World; feature writer, N.Y. Herald Tribune, N.Y. Times; nat'l pub. dir. Camp Fire Girls, then Girl Scouts; reporter under byline Bella Cohen for N.Y. World, and other newspapers 1922–26; author plays with husband include: Solitaire Man, Poppa, War Song, Clear All Wires, Spring Song, Boy Meets Girl, Leave It to Me, Kiss Me Kate, (Tony Award, 1949), My Three Angels, Festival. Member: Dramatists Guild; SWG; pres., N.Y. Girls Scholarship Fund.

PICTURES: Clear All Wires, Boy Meets Girl, Cat and the

Fiddle, Rendezvous, The Nuisance, Three Loves of Nancy, My Favorite Wife, When Ladies Meet, Weekend at the Waldorf, Move Over Darling, We're No Angels (based on play My Three Angels).

TELEVISION: Mr Broadway, Kiss Me Kate, My Three Angels, The Enchanted Nutcracker, Kiss Me Kate, BBC.

SPHEERIS, PENELOPE: Director. b. 1945. e. UCLA. Film Sch., MFA.

PICTURES: Real Life (prod. only); The Decline of Western Civilization (documentary); Suburbia; The Boys Next Door; Hollywood Vice Squad, Dudes, The Decline of Western Civilization—Part II: The Metal Years, Wedding Band (actress only).

TELEVISION: Saturday Night Live (prod. only).

SPIEGEL, LARRY: Producer, Writer, Director. b. Brooklyn, NY. e. Ohio U. With CBS-TV; Benton & Bowles; Wells, Rich, Green; BBDO. Now heads Appledown Films, Inc.

PICTURES: Hail (s.p.); Book of Numbers (s.p.); Death Game (prod.); Stunts (prod.); Spree (direc./s.p.); Phobia (prod.); Remo Williams: The Adventure Begins (prod.); Dove Against Death (prod.).

TELEVISION: Alexander (s.p., prod.); Incredible Indelible Magical Physical Mystery Trip (s.p.); Bear That Slept Through Christmas (s.p.); Never Fool With A Gypsy Ikon (s.p.); Mystery Trip Through Little Red's Head (s.p.); Planet of The Apes (animated) (s.p.); Jan Stephenson Golf Video (prod.); Remo Williams (pilot ABC; prod.).

SPIEGEL, TED: Publicist. b. New York, NY. e. NYU, B.S. 1948. Joined Columbia Pictures 1948 in adv. copy, exploitation, pub. depts.; foreign public rel., Columbia International 1956. Spec. adv., pub. rep., Kingsley Intl. Pictures, 1960; spec. asst. to pres. Kingsley Int'l Pictures, 1962; mgr. dir., theatre operations, The Landau Co., 1963; pub. exec., Embassy Pics. Corp., 1964; dir. pub., Avco Embassy Pictures, 1968. In 1976 joined A. Stirling Gold as dir. adv./pub. relations. In 1978 named acct. exec. for Solters & Roskin.

SPIELBERG, STEVEN: Director, Producer. b. Cincinnati, OH, Dec. 18, 1947. e. California State Coll. Made home movies as child; completed first film with story and actors at 12 yrs. old in Phoenix. At 13 won film contest for 40-min. war movie, Escape to Nowhere. At 16 made 140-min. film, Firelight. At California State Coll. made five films. First professional work, Amblin', 20 min. short which led to signing contract with Universal Pictures at age 20. Formed own co. Amblin Entertainment headquartered at Universal Studios. Received Irving Thalberg Memorial Award, 1987.

TELEVISION: Night Gallery, Duel, Savage, Something Evil, Steven Spielberg's Amazing Stories.

PICTURES: Ace Eli and Rodger of the Skies (story only); The Sugarland Express (also co-wrote story); Jaws; Close Encounters of The Third Kind (also s.p.); I Wanna Hold Your Hand (exec. prod. only); 1941; The Blues Brothers (actor only); Used Cars (exec. prod. only); Raiders of the Lost Ark; Continental Divide (exec. prod. only); E.T. The Extra-Terrestrial (also co-prod.); Poltergeist (prod., co-s.p. only); E.T.: The Extra-Terrestrial (dir.); Twilight Zone—The Movie (co-prod.—dir., one segment); Indiana Jones and the Temple of Doom (dir.); Gremlins (exec. prod. only).; Back to the Future (exec. prod. only); Goonies (story, exec. prod. only); Young Sherlock Holmes (exec. prod. only), The Color Purple (also co-prod.); The Money Pit (exec. prod. only); An American Tail (exec. prod. only); Innerspace (exec. prod. only); Empire of the Sun (also co-prod.); *Batteries Not Included (exec. prod. only), Who Framed Roger Rabbit? (exec. prod. only), The Land Before Time (exec. prod. only); Indiana Jones and the Last Crusade; Dad (exec. prod.), Joe Versus the Volcano (prod.), Always (dir.), Gremlins II (exec. prod.).

SPIKINGS, BARRY: Executive. b. Boston, England, Nov. 23, 1939. Ent. m.p. ind. 1973. Jnt. Man. Dir. British Lion Films Ltd., 1975. Appt. jnt. man. dir. EMI Films Ltd., 1977. 1979, appt. chmn. & chief exec., EMI Film & Theatre Corp.; chmn. & chief exec, EMI Films, Ltd., chmn. EMI Cinemas, Ltd.; chmn., Elstree Studios, Ltd. Chmn. EMI-TV Programs, Inc., 1980; appt. chmn. chief exec., EMI Films Group, Jan. 1982; June, 1985 Barry Spikings Productions Inc. (U.S.A.); June, 1985 became director Galactic Films Inc. (with Lord Anthony Rufus Issacs); Oct., 1986, acquired Embassy Home Entertainment from Coca Cola Co., renamed Nelson Entertainment Inc., appointed pres. and chief operating officer.

PICTURES: Co-prod.: Conduct Unbecoming, The Man Who Fell to Earth, The Deer Hunter. Exec. prod.: Convoy.

SPIRA, STEVEN S.: Executive. e. City Coll. of New York; Benjamin Cardozo Sch. of Law. Associated 10 years with N.Y. law firm, Monasch, Chazen & Stream. 1984, joined 20th Century Fox as sr. counsel; 1985, to Warner Bros. Now WB v.p., studio business affairs.

SPIRES, JOHN B.: Executive. b. New York, NY. e. NYU. Assistant manager Tribune Theatre, N.Y., 1934–36; Paramount Pictures lab., 1936–42; Capt. U.S. Army, 1942–46; Major U.S. Reserves, 1946–48; foreign rep., RKO, Europe, 1946; asst. foreign mgr., United World Films, 1947–48; in charge 16mm foreign oper., Universal 1949; asst. to European gen. mgr., Universal International, 1950; European gen. mgr., Continental Europe, Near East, Universal International, 1955; gen. mgr., foreign film sales, MCA-TV, 1958; dir., TV sls., 1964; named v.p. of MGM-TV, 1973; sr. v.p., MGM-TV, UK, Europe, MGM-TV, 1961; dir., Int'l TV sls., MGM-TV, 1978. Founded Phoenix Intl. TV Associates, 1980; pres., Phoenix Intl.

SPITZ, JAMES R.: Executive. b. Milwaukee, WI, Dec. 4, 1940. Began career in industry 1962 with Warner Bros., working way thru sls. dept. and holding various positions such as booker and office mgr. in New York, San Francisco, Salt Lake City, Seattle and Kansas City. Appt. branch mgr. of WB Seattle-Portland branch; then L.A. branch mgr. Worked at United Artists 1972–77, first as L.A. branch mgr. and then western div. mgr. Joined Avco Embassy as asst. gen. sls. mgr., 1979. In 1980 left to go to Columbia Pictures as v.p. & gen. sls. mgr. In 1981 promoted to pres. of Columbia Pictures' domestic distribution.

SPIVAK, LAWRENCE E.: TV-radio Producer. b. New York, NY, June 11, 1900. e. Harvard U. LL.D. (hon.) Wilberforce U.; Litt. D. (hon.) Suffolk U. L.H.D. (hon.) Tampa U. Began as bus. mgr., Antiques Mag., 1921–30; asst. to the pub., Hunting and Fishing, Nat. Sportsman mags., 1930–33; bus. mgr., American Mercury, 1934–39; pub., 1939–44; editor, pub., 1944–50; founder, 1941, pub. until 1954, of Ellery Queen's Mystery Mag., The Mag. of Fantasy and Science Fiction; Founder, American Mercury Library (Paperback Books) 1937; Mercury Mystery Books, Bookseller Mysteries, Jonathan Press Books; originator, producer, panel member, program, Meet the Press (radio 1945, TV 1947). Recipient two Peabody Awards. Winner of Emmy Award for outstanding achievement in Coverage of Special Events and Honor Award from U. of Missouri for Distinguished Service in Journalism. Published 1st series of Paperback Books in 1943 for Armed Services, which was forerunner of "The Armed Services Edition."

SPODICK, ROBERT C.: Exhibitor. b. New York, NY, Dec. 3, 1919. e. City Coll. of New York, 1940; ent. m.p. ind. as errand boy Skouras Park Plaza, Bronx 1932–33; reel boy, asst. mgr., Loew's Theatres; mgr., Little Carnegie and other art theatres; exploitation man, United Artists. Acquired Lincoln, New Haven art house in 1945 in partnership with cousin Leonard E. Sampson; developed Nutmeg Theatre circuit, which was sold in 1968 to Robert Smerling. Beginning in 1970, built Groton, CT., Cinemas I and II; Norwich Cinemas I and II, Village Cinemas I, II and III, Rosen, and Westerley Triple Cinemas in RI as Gemini Cinema Circuit in partnership with Sampson and William Rosen. Gemini sold to Interstate Theatres, 1986. With Sampson presently operates York Square Triple Cinemas in New Haven. Pres., Allied of CT, 1962–64; Pres. NATO of Conn. 1968–73. Past chmn. exec. comm., CT Ass'n of Theatre Owners, and active member.

SPOTTISWOODE, ROGER: Director. b. England. Film editor of TV commercials and documentaries before turning to direction.

PICTURES: *Editor:* Straw Dogs, The Getaway, Pat Garrett and Billy the Kid, Hard Times, The Gambler, Who'll Stop the Rain? (assoc. prod.), Baby (exec. prod.). *Director:* Terror Train; The Pursuit of D.B. Cooper; Under Fire; The Best of Times, Shoot to Kill; Turner & Hooch. Air America.

TELEVISION: The Renegades, The Last Innocent Man, Third Degree Burn. Special: Time Flies When You're Alive.

SPRADLIN, G.D.: Actor. b. Oklahoma. Started career as lawyer and active in local politics before turning to acting. Joined Oklahoma Repertory Theatre in 1964. Film debut in Will Penny (1968).

PICTURES: Monte Walsh, Tora! Tora! Tora!, The Hunting Party, The Godfather, Part II, North Dallas Forty, MacArthur, Wrong Is Right, The Formula, Apocalypse Now, The Lords of Discipline, Tank, One on One.

TELEVISION: Space, Nutcracker: Money, Madness, and Murder, Robert Kennedy and His Times, Resting Place, Dream West, Jayne Mansfield Story, War and Remembrance (mini-series).

SPRINGER, PAUL D.: Executive. e. Brooklyn Law Sch. Served as assoc. for N.Y. law firm, Johnson and Tannebaum. Later with legal dept. of Columbia Pictures. 1970, joined Paramount Pictures N.Y. legal dept. 1985, promoted to sr. v.p., chief resident counsel, 1987, promoted to sr. v.p., asst. general counsel responsible for all legal functions for Paramount's distribution and marketing depts. Mem., NY and California Bars.

SPRINGFIELD, RICK: Actor, Singer, Songwriter. b. Australia, Aug. 23, 1949.

PICTURES: Battlestar Galactica, Hard to Hold (act., addl. music).

TELEVISION: General Hospital, An Evening at the Improv, Countdown '81. Movie: Nick Knight.

SPRINGSTEEN, R. G.: Director. b. Tacoma, WA, Sept. 8, 1904. e. U. of Washington. With Universal Studios 1930; asst. dir. Fox; asst. dir. & dir. Republic.
PICTURES: Out of the Storm, Hellfire, Red Menace, Singing Guns, Honeychile, Toughest Man in Arizona, Gobs & Gals, Perilous Journey, Geraldine, I Cover the Underworld, Cross Channel, When Gangland Strikes, Come Next Spring, Track the Man Down, Secret Venture, Double Jeopardy, Johnny Reno, Red Tomahawk.

STACK, ROBERT: Actor. b. Los Angeles, CA, Jan. 13, 1919. e. U. of Southern California. In U.S. Armed Forces (Navy), W.W.II. Studied acting at Henry Duffy School of Theatre 6 mo. then signed a contract with Universal. National skeet champion at age 16. Autobiography: Straight Shooting.
PICTURES: First Love, When the Daltons Rode, Mortal Storm, Little Bit of Heaven, Nice Girl, Badlands of Dakota, To Be or Not To Be, Eagle Squadron, Men of Texas, Fighter Squadron, Date With Judy, Miss Tatlock's Millions, Mr. Music, Bullfighter and the Lady, My Outlaw Brother, Bwana Devil, War Paint, Conquest of Cochise, Sabre Jet, Iron Glove, High & the Mighty, House of Bamboo, Good Morning Miss Dove, Great Day in the Morning, Written on the Wind, John Paul Jones, Last Voyage, Killers of Kilimanjaro, The Caretakers, The Corrupt Ones, Story of a Woman, 1941, Airplane!, Uncommon Valor, Big Trouble, Plain Clothes, Caddyshack II, Dangerous Curves, Joe Versus the Volcano.
TELEVISION: Series: The Untouchables, Name of the Game, Most Wanted, Guest: Midas Valley (series), Strike Force, Playhouse 90 (Panic Button), Movies: They Knew What They Wanted, George Washington, Hollywood Wives, Unsolved Mysteries (host/narrator), Korea: The Forgotten War (host).

STAHL, AL: Executive. Syndicated newspaper cartoonist; asst. animator, Max Fleischer, gag ed. Terrytoons; U.S. Signal Corps; opened own studios, 1946; prod. first animated TV cartoon show; pres., Animated Prod., prod. live and animated commercials; member of bd. NTFC.

STALLONE, SYLVESTER: Actor, Writer, Director. b. New York, NY, July 6, 1946. After high school taught at American Coll. of Switzerland instructing children of career diplomats, young royalty, etc. Returned to U.S. in 1967 and studed drama U. of Miami, 1969. Came to New York to seek acting career, taking part-time jobs, including usher for Walter Reade Theatres. Then turned to writing, selling several TV scripts. Back to acting in Woody Allen's Bananas and with lead role in The Lords of Flatbush (1974). Formed White Eagle Enterprises.
PICTURES: Capone, Death Race 2000, Rocky (also s.p.), F.I.S.T. (actor, co.-s.p.), Paradise Alley (actor, s.p., dir). Rocky II (actor, s.p., dir.), Nighthawks, Victory, Rocky III (s.p.-dir.-actor); First Blood (co-s.p.-actor), Staying Alive (prod., dir., co-s.p.); Rhinestone (actor, co-s.p.); Rambo: First Blood Part II (actor, co-s.p.); Rocky IV (s.p.-dir.-actor); Cobra (s.p.-actor); Over the Top (actor, co-s.p.), Rambo III (co-s.p., actor), Lock Up, Tango and Cash, Rocky V (dir., s.p., actor).

STAMP, TERENCE: Actor. b. London, England, July 23, 1939. Stage experience including Alfie on Broadway. Recent stage: Dracula, The Lady from the Sea, Airborne Symphony.
PICTURES: Billy Budd (debut 1962, Acad. Award nom.), Term of Trial, The Collector (best actor award, Cannes, 1965), Modesty Blaise, Far from the Madding Crowd, Poor Cow, Blue, Tales of Mystery, Teorama, Spirits of the Dead, The Mind of Mr. Soames, A Season in Hell, Hu-Man, The Divine Creature, Strip-Tease, Superman, Meetings with Remarkable Men, The Thief of Baghdad, Together, Superman II, Monster Island, Death in the Vatican, The Hit, The Company of Wolves, Link, Legal Eagles, Under the Cherry Moon, The Sicilian, Wall Street, Young Guns, Alien Nation, Stranger in the House (also dir.).

STANDER, LIONEL: Actor. b. New York, NY, Jan. 11, 1908. e. coll. N.Y. stage, 1952. On TV in Hart to Hart.
PICTURES: Scoundrel, Page Miss Glory, Gay Deception, Music Goes 'Round, Mr. Deeds Goes to Town, A Star Is Born, Meet Nero Wolfe, Guadalcanal Diary, Big Show-Off, Specter of the Rose, In Old Sacramento, Kid from Brooklyn, Gentleman Joe Palooka, Pal Joey, Mad Wednesday, Call Northside 777, Unfaithfully Yours, Trouble Makers, Two Gals and a Guy, St. Benny the Dip, Cul de Sac, A Dandy in Aspic, The Gang That Couldn't Shoot Straight, Pulp, The Black Bird, The Cassandra Crossing, New York, New York, Matilda, 1941, Cookie, Wicked Stepmother.
TELEVISION: The Boys (pilot).

STANFILL, DENNIS C: Executive. b. Centerville, TN, April 1, 1927. e. Lawrenceburg H.S.; U.S. Naval Acad., B.S., 1949; Oxford U. (Rhodes scholar), M.A., 1953; U. of South Carolina, L.H.D. (hon.). Corporate finance specialist, Lehman Brothers 1959–65; v.p. finance, Times Mirror Company, Los Angeles, 1965–69; exec. v.p. finance, 20th Century-Fox Film Corp., 1969–71, pres., 1971, chmn. bd./chief exec. officer, 1971–81; pres., Stanfill, Doig & Co., venture capital firm, 1981–.

STANG, ARNOLD: Performer, b. Chelsea, MA, Sept. 28, 1927. Radio, 1935–50; on Bdwy, in five plays and in m.p. and short subjects; guest appearances on TV shows. Much voice-over cartoon work.
TELEVISION: Captain Video, Milton Berle, Danny Thomas, Perry Como, Ed Sullivan, Red Skelton, Frank Sinatra, Wagon Train, Top Cat, Jack Benny, Johnny Carson, December Bride, Playhouse 90, Batman, Bonanza, Bob Hope, Danny Kaye, Broadside, Jackie Gleason, Emergency, Feeling Good, Chico & the Man, Super Jaws & Catfish, Busting Loose, Flying High, Robert Klein Specials, Tales from the Dark Side.
PICTURES: So This is New York, Double for Della, Return of Marco Polo, Spirit of '76, Man with the Golden Arm, The Wonderful World of the Brothers Grimm, It's a Mad, Mad, Mad, Mad World, Pinocchio in Outer Space, Dondi, Alakazam the Great, Hello Down There, Skidoo, Walt Disney's Aristocats, Seven Days Leave, My Sister Eileen, Let's Go Steady, Raggedy Ann & Andy, Gang That Couldn't Shoot Straight, We Go Pogo, That's Life, Hercules in New York, They Got Me Covered. Starred in 36 shorts.

STANLEY, KIM: Actress. r.n. Patricia Reid. b. Tularosa, NM, Feb. 11, 1925. e. U. of New Mexico. Began stage acting in college and later in stock. Worked as model in NY while training with Elia Kazan and Lee Strasberg at Actors Studio. In late 1960s and 1970s taught drama, Coll. of Santa Fe, NM.
THEATER: The Dog, Beneath the Skin (NY debut, 1948), Him, Yes Is For a Very Young Man, Montserrat, The House of Bernarda Alba, The Chase, Picnic (NY Drama Critics Award, 1953), The Traveling Lady, The Great Dreamer, Bus Stop, A Clearing in the Woods, A Touch of the Poet, A Far Country, Natural Affection, The Three Sisters.
PICTURES: The Goddess, Seance on a Wet Afternoon (Acad. Award nom.), Frances, The Right Stuff.
TELEVISION: Clash by Night, The Travelling Lady, A Cardinal Mercy (Emmy, 1963), The Three Sisters, Cat on a Hot Tin Roof.

STANTON, HARRY DEAN: Actor. b. Kentucky, July 14, 1926. Acting debut at Pasadena Playhouse. Theatrical film debut in Tomahawk Trail, 1957.
PICTURES: The Proud Rebel, Pork Chop Hill, A Dog's Best Friend, Cool Hand Luke, Kelly's Heroes, Two-Lane Blacktop, Pat Garrett and Billy the Kid, Dillinger, Zandy's Bride, The Godfather Part II, Rancho Deluxe, Farewell, My Lovely, The Missouri Breaks, 92 in The Shade, Renaldo and Clara, Straight Time, The Rose, Wise Blood, Alien, Death Watch, The Black Marble, Private Benjamin, Escape from New York, One From the Heart, Young Doctors in Love, Tough Enough, Christine, Repo Man, Paris Texas, Uforia, Red Dawn, One Magic Christmas, Pretty in Pink, Fool for Love, The Bear, The Care Bears Movie, Slam Dance, Stars and Bars, Mr. North, The Last Temptation of Christ, Dream a Little Dream, Twister, Jackal's Run, Stranger in the House, Wild at Heart.
TELEVISION: I Want to Live, Flatbed Annie & Sweetiepie: Lady Truckers.

STANWYCK, BARBARA: Actress. r.n. Ruby Stevens; b. Brooklyn, NY, July 16, 1907. Film debut, Locked Door, 1929.
PICTURES: Ladies of Leisure, Night Nurse, So Big, Bitter Tea of General Yen, Brief Moment, Woman in Red, Annie Oakley, Plough and the Stars, Stella Dallas, Mad Miss Manton, Union Pacific, Golden Boy, Meet John Doe, Two Mrs. Carrolls, B.F.'s Daughter, Sorry, Wrong Number, Lady Gambles, East Side, West Side, Thelma Jordan, The Furies, No Man of Her Own, To Please a Lady, Man With a Cloak, Clash by Night, Jeopardy, All I Desire, Titanic, Blowing Wild, The Moonlighter, Executive Suite, Witness to Murder, Violent Men, Double Indemnity, Ball of Fire, Cattle Queen of Montana, Escape to Burma, There's Always Tomorrow, Maverick Queen, These Wilder Years, Crime of Passion, Trooper Hook, Forty Guns, Walk on the Wild Side, Roustabout, The Night Walker.
TELEVISION: Guest: Jack Benny, Ford, Zane Grey, Alcoa-Goodyear; The Big Valley (series, 1965–69), The Thorn Birds (Emmy award), The Colbys (series).

STAPLETON, JEAN: Actress. r.n. Jeanne Murray. b. New York, NY, e. Wadleigh H.S. Summer stock in NH, ME, MA, and PA. Broadway debut in In the Summer House (1953). President, Advisory bd., Women's Research and Education Instit. (Wash., D.C.); bd.: Eleanor Roosevelt Val-kill, Hyde Park; bd. Actors Fund of America, West Coast.
THEATER: Damn Yankees, Bells Are Ringing, Juno, Rhinoceros, Funny Girl, Arsenic and Old Lace (Bdwy and tour), The Mystery of Edwin Drood (natl. tour). and extensive regional work at the Totem Pole Playhouse, Fayettesville, PA, Pocono Playhouse, Mountain Home Pa; Peterborough Playhouse, N.H. and others. Operatic debut with Baltimore Opera Co. in Candide, then The Italian Lesson and Bon Appetit. Starred in San Jose Civic Light Opera Co.'s Sweeny Todd.
PICTURES: Damn Yankees, Bells Are Ringing, Something Wild, Up the Down Staircase, Cold Turkey, Klute, The Buddy System.

TELEVISION: All in the Family (3 Emmy Awards), Movies: Eleanor: First Lady of the World, You Can't Take It With you, Aunt Mary, Angel Dusted, A Matter of Sex, Dead Man's Folly, Grown-Ups (ACE nom.), Jack and the Beanstalk and Cinderella, (Faerie Tale Theatre), Something's Afoot, Let Me Hear You Whisper.

STAPLETON, MAUREEN: Actress. b. Troy, NY, June 21, 1925. Worked as a model and waitress while studying acting with Herbert Berghof in N.Y. in 1944 and became member of Actors Studio. Broadway debut, 1946, in The Playboy of the Western World. Became a star in 1951 in The Rose Tattoo. Film debut 1959 in Lonelyhearts.

THEATER: Anthony and Cleopatra, Detective Story, Bird Cage, The Rose Tattoo (Tony Award, 1951), The Emperor's Clothes, The Crucible, Richard III, The Seagull, 27 Wagons Full of Cotton, Orpheus Descending, The Cold Wind and the Warm, Toys in the Attic, The Glass Menagerie (1965 & 1975), Plaza Suite, Norman Is That You?, Gingerbread Lady (Tony Award, 1970), The Country Girl, Secret Affairs of Mildred Wild, The Gin Game, The Little Foxes.

PICTURES: The Fugitive Kind, A View from the Bridge, Bye Bye Birdie, Airport, Plaza Suite, Interiors, The Runner Stumbles, On the Right Track, Reds (Acad. Award, supp. 1981), Johnny Dangerously, Cocoon, The Money Pit, Made in Heaven, Heartburn, Sweet Lorraine, Nuts, Cocoon: The Return.

TELEVISION: Series: What Happened? (panelist, 1952); Movies: For Whom the Bell Tolls, Among the Paths to Eden (Emmy, 1968), Tell Me Where It Hurts, Queen of the Stardust Ballroom, Cat on a Hot Tin Roof, The Gathering, The Gathering Part II, Letters From Frank, The Electric Grandmother, Little Gloria—Happy at Last, Family Secrets, Sentimental Journey, Private Sessions, Liberace: Behind the Music.

STARGER, MARTIN: Executive. b. New York, NY, May 8, 1932. e. City Coll. of New York. Served in U.S. Army Signal Corp., where prod. training films. Joined BBDO, starting in TV prod. dept.; later made v.p. & assoc. dir. of TV. Joined ABC in April 1966, as v.p. of programs, ABC-TV, East Coast. In March, 1968, prom. to v.p. and natl prog. dir; in 1969 named v.p. in chg. progr. Named pres., ABC Entertainment, July 17, 1972. In June, 1975 formed Marstar Productions Inc., M.P. & TV production company of which he is pres. In March 1978 formed Marble Arch Productions, of which he is pres. Formed Rule/Starger Co. with Elton Rule, 1988.

PICTURES: Exec. prod.: Nashville, The Domino Principle, The Muppet Movie, Raise the Titanic, Saturn 3, The Great Muppet Caper, Hard Country, The Legend of the Lone Ranger, Sophie's Choice, Barbarosa, Mask.

TELEVISION: Escape from Sobibor, Earth Star Voyager, Marcus Welby, M.D.-A Holiday Affair.

STARK, RAY: Producer. e. Rutgers U. Began career after W.W.II as agent handling Red Ryder radio scripts, and later literary works for such writers as Costain, Marquand and Hecht. Publicity writer, Warner Bros. Joined Famous Artists Agency, where he represented such personalities as Marilyn Monroe, Kirk Douglas and Richard Burton; in 1957, resigned exec. position to form Seven Arts Prods. with Eliot Hyman, serving as exec. v.p. and head of production until July, 1966, when he left to take on personal production projects, including Reflections in a Golden Eye and Funny Girl. Founded Rastar Prods. and Ray Stark Prods. Received Irving Thalberg Award from Acad. of M.P. Arts and Sciences 1980.

PICTURES: The Sunshine Boys, Robin and Marian, Murder by Death, Casey's Shadow, The Cheap Detective, California Suite, The Electric Horseman, Chapter Two, Seems Like Old Times, Annie, The Slugger's Wife, Brighton Beach Memoirs, Biloxi Blues, Steel Magnolias, Revenge.

STARK, WILBUR: Producer, Director. b. New York, NY, Aug. 10, 1922. e. Columbia U. Started career as actor, Brooklyn Academy Players; slsm. & producer radio station WMCA-NY, 1942–46; for 18 yrs. producer-director of theatrical feature films and over 1500 live dramas and over 300 TV movies, including 81 for CBS as producer (directing over 30).

PICTURES: The Thing (exec. prod.); The Cat People, (exec. consultant); My Lover, My Son (prod., story); Vampire Circus (prod., story); The Love Box (prod., dir. s.p.); A Policeman's Lot (prod., dir); All I Want Is You, and You. . . (prod.); The Petrified Prince (prod., dir.), The Storyteller (exec. prod.), An Act of Reprisal (prod.).

TELEVISION: Producer: Newsstand Theatre, Rocky King, Detective; Modern Romances with Martha Scott; True Story, Col. Humphrey Flack, My Father Is a Detective, Brothers Branagan (prod.), The Object is . . . (prod.).

STARR, EVE: Columnist. b. Chicago, IL, May 1. e. Columbia U., Miami U., Julliard Sch. of Music. Radio-TV playwright, feature writer, actress. Hollywood foreign correspondent; m.p. writer, newspapers, mags.; m.p. columnist, Hollywood Citizen-News; Daily syndicated TV column, Inside TV—General Features Synd.; feature column, Tell It To Eve, International Newspapers; Traveling With Eve, Nat'l Syndicated Travel Column.

STARR, RINGO: O.B.E. Singer, Musician, Songwriter. r.n. Richard Starkey. b. Liverpool, England, July 7, 1949. Member of The Beatles. (Films: A Hard Day's Night, Help, Let It Be).

PICTURES ALONE: Actor: The Last Waltz, Sextette, The Kids Are Alright, Caveman, Give My Regards to Broad Street, Walking After Midnight.

TELEVISION: Actor: Princess Daisy, D.C. Beach Party—A Celebration.

STEEL, ANTHONY: Actor. b. London, Eng., May 21, 1920. e. private schools, south Ireland, Cambridge. Film debut in Saraband for Dead Lovers.

PICTURES: Portrait from Life, Christopher Columbus, Helter Skelter, Poet's Pub, The Blue Lamp, The Wooden Horse, Laughter in Paradise, The Mudlark, Where No Vultures Fly (Ivory Hunter), Another Man's Poison, Emergency Call, Something Money Can't Buy, The Planter's Wife (Outpost in Malaya), Malta Story, Master of Ballantrae, Albert, R.N. (Break to Freedom), West of Zanzibar, Sea Shall Not Have Them, Passage Home, Storm Over the Nile, Black Tent, Checkpoint, Valerie, A Question of Adultery, Harry Black, Honeymoon, The Switch, The Mirror Crack'd.

STEEL, DAWN: Executive. b. New York, NY, Aug. 19, 1946. m. producer Charles Roven. e. marketing student, Boston U. 1964–65, NYU 1966–67; sportswriter, Major League Baseball Digest NFL, NY 1968–69; 1968 joined Penthouse Magazine as secretary becoming ed. and dir. of merchandising 1969–74; Pres. O'Dawn! Inc. merchandising co. 1975–78. Joined Paramount Pictures 1978 as dir. of merchandising and licensing; promoted 1979 to v.p.; named v.p., production 1980; promoted to sr. v.p. 1983, named pres., prod. 1985 with involvement and responsibility for Flashdance, Footloose, Top Gun, Star Trek IV, Beverly Hills Cop II, The Untouchables, Fatal Attraction, The Accused. Joined Columbia Pictures 1987 as president, Columbia Pictures (first woman studio pres.).

MEMBER: Bd. trustees, Amer. Film Inst.; mem. Acad. of M.P. Arts and Sciences.

STEELE, TOMMY: Performer. r.n. Tommy Hicks. b. London, Dec. 17, 1936. Early career Merchant Navy. First TV and film appearances, 1956. Composed and sang title song for The Shiralee. stage musical: Singin' in the Rain, (London Palladium, 1983).

PICTURES: Kill Me Tomorrow, The Tommy Steele Story, The Duke Wore Jeans, Tommy the Toreador, Light Up the Sky, It's All Happening, The Happiest Millionaire, Half A Sixpence, Finian's Rainbow, Where's Jack?

TELEVISION: Tommy Steele Spectaculars, Richard Whittington Esquire (Rediffusion), Ed Sullivan Show, Gene Kelly Show, Perry Como Show, Twelfth Night, The Tommy Steele Hour, Tommy Steele in Search of Charlie Chaplin, Tommy Steele And A Show, Quincy's Quest.

STEENBURGEN, MARY: Actress. b. Newport, AZ, 1953. Studied at Neighborhood Playhouse.

PICTURES: Goin' South, Time after Time, Melvin and Howard (Acad. Award), Ragtime, A Midsummer Night's Sex Comedy, Cross Creek, One Magic Christmas, Dead of Winter, The Whales of August, End of the Line (also exec. prod.), Miss Firecracker, Parenthood.

TELEVISION: Tender Is the Night, Faerie Tale Theatre, The Attic: The Hiding of Anne Frank.

STEIGER, ROD: Actor. b. Westhampton, NY, Apr. 14, 1925. e. Westside H.S., Newark, NJ. Served in U.S. Navy, then employed in Civil Service; studied acting at N.Y. Theatre Wing Dramatic Workshop Actors' Studio; numerous TV plays; on Broadway in ANTA prod. of Night Music; m.p. debut in Teresa (1951).

PICTURES: On the Waterfront, The Big Knife, Oklahoma!, Court Martial of Billy Mitchell, Jubal, The Harder They Fall, Back from Eternity, Run of the Arrow, Unholy Wife, Al Capone, Seven Thieves, The Mark, Reprieve, 13 West Street, Hands Upon the City, The Time of Indifference, The Pawnbroker, In the Heat of the Night (Acad. Award), The Girl and the General, No Way to Treat a Lady, And There Came a Man, The Illustrated Man, Three Into Two Won't Go, Duck, You Sucker, Happy Birthday, Wanda June, Waterloo, The Lolly-Madonna War, Lucky Luciano, Hennessy, W. C. Fields and Me, F.I.S.T., The Amityville Horror, Lion of the Desert, Cattle Annie and Little Britches, The Chosen, The Naked Face, The Kindred, The January Man, Tennessee Waltz, That Summer of White Roses, A Question of Life, Men of Respect.

TELEVISION: Many appearances in 1950s live TV including Marty; Movies: Race to the Pole, Hollywood Wives, Jesus of Nazareth, Sword of Gideon, Desperado: Avalanche at Devil's Ridge, Passion and Paradise (mini-series).

STEINBERG, DAVID: Actor, Writer, Director. b. Winnipeg, Canada, Aug. 9, 1942. e. U. of Chicago; Hebrew Theological Coll. Member Second City troupe; comedian at comedy clubs: Mr. Kelly's Hungry i, Bitter End. Starred in London and Bdwy. stage prods. Bdwy. includes Little Murders; Carry Me Back to Morningside Heights.

PICTURES: Actor: The End, Something Short of Paradise, Willow. Director: Paternity, Going Berserk (also co.-s.p.).
TELEVISION: Music Scene (writer, co-host); Tonight Show (guest host); David Steinberg Summer Show; Second City: 25 Years in Revue. Director: Newhart episodes, The Popcorn Kid, Golden Girls, One Big Family, Faerie Tale Theatre, Richard Belzer Special, Baby on Board, Annie McGuire. and many commercials.

STEINBERG, HERB: b. New York, NY, July 3, 1921. e. City Coll. of New York, 1937–41. Capt. U.S. Army, 1942–46; pub. PRC, 1946, Eagle Lion, 1946–49, Paramount 1949; pub. mgr. 1951; expl. mgr., 1954; studio adv. & pub. dir., 1958; exec. chg. of spec. proj., press dept., Universal City Studio, 1963; v.p., Universal Studio Tours, 1971; 1974 v.p., MCA Recreation Services. Appt. to California Tourism Commission, 1984; consultant, MCA, Inc., 1987; bd. trustees, Motion Picture & TV Fund, 1987; Communications dir. Alliance of Motion Picture & Television Producers.

STEINMAN, MONTE: Executive. Joined Paramount Pictures 1980 as sr. financial analyst. Series of promotions followed, culminating in appt. as dir. of financial planning of Gulf + Western's Entertainment and Communications Group, in February, 1984. In 1985, named exec. dir., financial planning.

STELOFF, ARTHUR "SKIP": Executive. b. New York, NY, Aug. 10, 1925. Son of Ike Steloff, "Saratoga Ike", professional gambler. e. U.S. Naval Acad. Served in the Navy. Sold television and radio spot time for WWDC in Washington, D.C. 1951–52. Sold ZIV film library for Matty Fox 1952–56; Sales mgr. C&C TV 1956–58. Founded Heritage Entertainment Inc. 1966 originally as a radio syndication business, then as indep. film prod. and dist. company. Chairman and CEO of Heritage.
PICTURES: Exec. prod.: Without Warning; Mr. North, Manson: In His Own Words.

STEMBLER, JOHN H.: Executive. b. Miami, FL, Feb. 18, 1913. e. U. of Florida Law Sch., 1937. Asst. U.S. att., South. dist. of Fla., 1941; U.S. Air Force, 1941–45; pres. Georgia Theatre Co., 1957; named chmn., 1983; NATO member exec. comm. and past pres.; Major Gen. USAF (Ret); past bd. chmn., National Bank of Georgia.

STEMBLER, WILLIAM J.: Executive. b. Atlanta, GA, Nov. 29, 1946. e. Westminister Sch., 1964; U. of Florida, 1968; U. of Georgia Law Sch., 1971. 1st. lt. U.S. Army, 1971; capt., U.S. Army Reserve; resigned 1976. Enforcement atty., SEC, Atlanta office, 1972–73; joined Georgia Theatre Co., 1973; pres. 1983–86; joined United Artists Communications, Inc., 1986, as v.p.; Incorporated Value Cinemas opened 6 months later, 1988.
MEMBER: bd. of dir., Merchant Bank of Atlanta; bd. of dir., & v.p., NATO, 1983–present; mbr., NATO OF GA & past-pres., 1983–85.

STERLING, JAN: Actress. r.n. Jane Sterling Adriance. b. April 3, 1923. e. private tutors; Fay Compton Sch. of Dramatic Art, London. N.Y. stage debut: Bachelor Born.
STAGE: Panama Hattie, Present Laughter, John Loves Mary, Two Blind Mice, Front Page, Over 21, Born Yesterday, The November People.
PICTURES: Johnny Belinda (debut), Appointment with Danger, Mating Season, Union Station, Skipper Surprised His Wife, Big Carnival, Caged, Rhubarb, Flesh and Fury, Sky Full of Moon, Pony Express, The Vanquished, Split Second, Alaska Seas, High & the Mighty, Return From the Sea, Human Jungle, Women's Prison, Female on the Beach, Man with the Gun, 1984, The Harder They Fall, Love in a Goldfish Bowl, The Incident, The Minx.
TELEVISION: Series: You're in the Picture, (panelist, 1961), Made in America, The Guiding Light (1969–70), Movies: Backstairs at the White House; Dangerous Company; My Kidnapper, My Love.

STERLING, ROBERT: Actor. r.n. William Sterling Hart. b. Newcastle, PA, Nov. 13, 1917. e. U. of Pittsburgh. m. Anne Jeffreys, actress. Father of actress Tisha Sterling. Fountain pen salesman, day laborer, clerk, industrial branch credit mgr., clothing salesman on West Coast; served as pilot-instructor U.S. Army Corps. 3 yrs.
PICTURES: Blondie Meets the Boss, Only Angels Have Wings, Manhattan Heartbeat, Yesterday's Heroes, Gay Caballero, Penalty, I'll Wait for You, Get-Away, Ringside Maisie, Two-Faced Woman, Dr. Kildare's Victory, Johnny Eager, This Time for Keeps, Somewhere I'll Find You, Secret Heart, Roughshod, Bunco Squad, Sundowners, Show Boat, Column South.
TELEVISION: Series: Topper, Love That Jill, Ichabod and Me. Movie: Beggarman, Thief.

STERN, ALFRED E. F.: Public relations executive. b. Boston, MA, Aug. 4. e. Boston U. Reporter, editor, Lowell Sun, Quincy Patriot-Ledger, Dartmouth News; publicist, RKO Radio Pictures, 1946–54; publicity dir., 1955; West Coast publicity dir., NTA, 1958; own public relations org., Alfred E. F. Stern Co., Inc., 1960.

STERN, DANIEL: Actor. b. Bethesda, MD, Aug. 28, 1957.
PICTURES: Breaking Away, It's My Turn, One-Trick Pony, Stardust Memories, Diner, I'm Dancing As Fast As I Can, Blue Thunder, Get Crazy, The Boss' Wife, Hannah and Her Sisters, D.O.A., The Milagro Beanfield War, Leviathan, Little Monsters, Crazy Horse, Coupe de Ville.
TELEVISION: Samson and Delilah, Weekend War. Series: Hometown, The Wonder Years (narrator).

STERN, EDDIE: Film buyer. b. New York, NY, Jan. 13, 1917. e. Columbia Sch. of Journalism. Head film buyer and booker, specializing in art theatres, for Rugoff and Becker, N.Y.; Captain, USAF; joined Wometco Ent. in 1952 as asst. to film buyer; v.p. motion picture theatre film buying and booking, Wometco Enterprises, Inc. Retired from Wometco 1985. Now handling film buying and booking for Theatres of Nassau, Ltd.

STERN, EZRA E.: Attorney. b. New York, NY, Mar. 22, 1908. e. Southwestern U. 1930, LL.B. pres., Wilshire Bar Assn. Former legal counsel for So. Calif. Theatre Owners Assn. Member: Calif. State Bar; member, Int'l Variety Clubs; former chief barker, Variety Club So. Calif. Tent 25; pres., Variety Int'l Boys' Club; board of dir., Los Angeles Metropolitan Recreation & Youth Services Council; bd. of trustees, Welfare Planning Council, Los Angeles Region; former mem. Los Angeles Area Council, Boys' Club of America; pres., Variety International Boys' Club 1976–77 and 1979–80. Member bd., Will Rogers Inst., M.P. Pioneers. 1984, honored by Variety Boys and Girls Club as founder of youth recreational facility.

STERN, STEWART: Writer. b. New York, NY, Mar. 22, 1922. e. Ethical Culture Sch., 1927–40; U. of Iowa, 1940–43. Rifle Squad Leader, S/Sgt. 106th Inf. Div., 1943–45; actor, asst. stage mgr., The French Touch, B'way, 1945–46; dialogue dir. Eagle-Lion Studios, 1946–48. 1948 to date: screenwriter.
TELEVISION: (Plays) Crip, And Crown Thy Good, Thunder of Silence, Heart of Darkness, A Christmas to Remember, Sybil (Emmy, 1977).
PICTURES: Teresa, Benjy (orig. s.p.) Rebel Without a Cause, The Rack, The James Dean Story, The Outsider, The Ugly American, Rachel, Rachel, The Last Movie, Summer Wishes—Winter Dreams (orig. s.p.).

STERNHAGEN, FRANCES: Actress. b. Washington, DC, Jan. 13, 1930. e. Vassar Coll., drama dept.; Perry-Mansfield School of Theatre. Studied with Sanford Meisner at Neighborhood Playhouse, NY. Was teacher at Milton Acad. in MA. Acted with Arena Stage, Washington, DC, 1953–54.
THEATER: Thieves Carnival (off-Bdwy debut, 1955), The Skin of Our Teeth, The Carefree Tree, The Admirable Bashville, Ulysses in Night Town, Viva Madison Avenue!, Red Eye of Love, Misalliance, Great Day in the Morning, The Right Honorable Gentleman, The Displaced Person, The Cocktail Party, Cock-a-Doodle Dandy, Playboy of the Western World, The Sign in Sidney Brustein's Window, Enemeis, The Good Doctor (Tony Award, 1973), Equus, Angel, On Golden Pond, The Father, Grownups, Summer, You Can't Take It With You, Home Front, Driving Miss Daisy.
PICTURES: Up the Down Staircase (debut, 1967), The Tiger Makes Out, The Hospital, Two People, Fedora, Starting Over, Outland, Independence Day, Romantic Comedy, Bright Lights, Big City; Communion.
TELEVISION: Series: Love of Life, Doctors. Movies: Who Will Save Our Children?, Prototype, Under One Roof.

STEUER, ROBERT B.: Executive. b. New Orleans, LA, Nov. 18, 1937. e. U. of Illinois, & 1955–57; Tulane U., 1957–59, B.B.A. Booker-Southern D.I. circuit, New Orleans, 1959; assoc., prod., Poor White Trash; 1960; v.p. Cinema Dist. America, 1961; co-prod., Flesh Eaters, Common Law Wife, 1963; Flack Black Pussy Cat, 1966; partner, gen. mgr., radio station WTVF, Mobile, 1963; dir. special projects, American Intl. Pictures, 1967; so. div. sls. mgr., AIP, 1971; v.p. asst. gen. sls. mgr., AIP, 1974; partner, United Producers Organization, producing Screamers, 1977; v.p., sls., Ely Landau Org., 1979; v.p., gen. sls. mgr., Film Ventures Intl., 1981; exec. v.p. worldwide mktg., 1983; pres., FVI, 1986–89. 1987, exec. v.p. worldwide mktg. Film Ventures Intl; 1987–88 exec. prod. Operation: Take No Prisoners, Most Dangerous Women Alive, Mad Crush, Criminal Act. To date worldwide marketing and sales consultant to entertainment indust.

STEVENS, ANDREW: Actor. b. Memphis, TN, June 10, 1955. Son of actress Stella Stevens. e. Antioch U., L.A., B.A. (psychology). Studied acting with Strasberg, David Craig, Vincent Chase, and Pat Randall. Began balancing work between film, TV and stage. L.A. stage includes Journey's End, Billy Budd (also prod.), P.S. Your Cat is Dead, Bouncers (L.A. Drama Circle Critics Award), Also producer and writer.
PICTURES: Shampoo, Day of the Animals, Ten to Midnight, Massacre at Central High, Las Vegas Lady, Vigilante Force, The Boys in Company C, The Fury, Death Hunt, The Seduction, Scared Stiff, Tusks, Fine Gold, Deadly Innocents, Down the Drain, Eyewitness to Murder, The Ranch, A Man of Passion, The Terror Within, Blood Chase, Counterforce, Eyewitness to Murder.

TELEVISION: Adam-12, Apple's Way, The Quest, Police Story, Shazam, Murder She Wrote, Love Boat. Series: Oregon Trail, Code Red, Emerald Point N.A.S., Dallas. Mini-series: Hollywood Wives, Beggarman Thief, The Rebels, The Bastard, Once an Eagle. Movies: The Last Survivors, Werewolf of Woodstock, The Oregon Trail, Secrets, Topper (also prod.), Women at Westpoint, Code Red, Miracle on Ice, Journey's End, Forbidden Love.

STEVENS, CONNIE: Actress. r.n. Concetta Ann Ingolia. b. Brooklyn, NY, August 8, 1938. e. Sacred Heart Acad., Hollywood Professional Sch. Began career as winner of several talent contests in Hollywood; prof. debut, Hollywood Repertory Theatre's prod. Finian's Rainbow; recordings include: Kookie, Kookie, Lend Me Your Comb, 16 Reasons, What Did You Wanna Make Me Cry For, From Me to You, They're Jealous of Me, A Girl Never Knows.
PICTURES: Eighteen and Anxious, Young and Dangerous, Drag Strip Riot, Rock-a-Bye Baby, Parish, Susan Slade, Palm Springs Weekend, Never Too Late, The Grissom Gang, Sex Symbol, Grease 2, Tapeheads, Back to the Beach, Way Way Out.
TELEVISION: Call Her Mom, Scruples, Playmates, The Sex Symbol, Bring Me the Head of Dobie Gillis. Series: Hawaiian Eye, Wendy and Me, Starting from Scratch.

STEVENS, CRAIG: Actor. r.n. Gail Shekles. b. Liberty, MO, July 8, 1918. m. actress Alexis Smith. e. U. of Kansas. Played in coll. dramatics. On screen 1941 in Affectionately Yours.
PICTURES: Since You Went Away, The Doughgirls, Roughly Speaking, Too Young to Know, Humoresque, The Man I Love, That Way With Women, Night Unto Night, Love and Learn, Lady Takes a Sailor, Phone Call from a Stranger, French Line, Where the Sidewalk Ends, Duel on the Mississippi, The Name's Buchanan, Gunn, Limbo Line, The Snoop Sisters, "S.O.B."
TELEVISION: Lux Video Theatre, Four Star Playhouse, Loretta Young Show, Schlitz Playhouse, Dinah Shore, Ernie Ford Shows, Chevy Show, Summer on Ice, The Millionaire, The Bold Ones; Series: Peter Gunn (1958–61), Man of the World (ATV England); Mr. Broadway, Name of the Game, The Invisible Man, Rich Man, Poor Man (mini-series), Dallas; Movies: The Killer Bees; The Love Boat; The Cabot Connection; The Home Front; Supercarrier, Marcus Welby, M.D.—A Holiday Affair.
STAGE: Here's Love, King of Hearts, Plain and Fancy, Critics Choice, Mary Mary; Cactus Flower (natl. co.).

STEVENS, FISHER: b. Chicago, IL, Nov. 27, 1963. e. NYU.
THEATER: Off-Bdwy.: Torch Song Trilogy. Bdwy: Brighton Beach Memoirs.
PICTURES: The Burning, Baby, It's You; Brother From Another Planet, The Flamingo Kid, My Science Project, Short Circuit, The Boss's Wife.
TELEVISION: Columbo.

STEVENS, GEORGE, JR.: Director, Writer, Producer. b. Los Angeles, CA, Apr. 3, 1932. Son of late director George Stevens. e. Occidental Coll., 1949–53, B.A. 1st Lieut. U.S. Air Force; TV dir., Alfred Hitchcock Presents, Peter Gunn, 1957–61; prod. asst. Giant Productions, 1953–54; prod. asst. Mark VII, Ltd., 1956–57; dir. M.P. Service, U.S. Information Agency 1962–67; chmn., U.S. deleg. to Film Festivals at Cannes (1962, 1964), Venice (1962, 1963), Moscow (1963); Founding director, American Film Institute, 1967–79; co-chmn., American Film Institute, 1979 to present.
PICTURES: The Diary of Anne Frank (assoc. prod., dir.), 1957–59; The Greatest Story Ever Told, (assoc. prod., dir.), 1959–62; John F. Kennedy; Years of Lightning, Day of Drums (prod.). America at the Movies (Producer) (1976). George Stevens: A Filmmaker's Journey (dir.,writer, prod.) 1984; 1988 WGA Award for TV broadcast).
TELEVISION: The American Film Institute's Salute to James Cagney (Emmy Award) 1975; American Film Institute's Salutes (producer/writer, 1973–89); The Stars Salute America's Greatest Movies, (exec. prod., 1977); The Kennedy Center Honors, (prod./writer, 1978–88; Emmy Award 1983, 1985); America Entertains Vice Premier Deng, (prod./writer, 1978). Christmas in Washington, (exec. prod./s.p., 1982–88); The Murder of Mary Phagan (co-writer, prod., 1988; Emmy, Christopher and George Foster Peabody Awards).

STEVENS, K. T.: Actress, r.n. Gloria Wood. b. Hollywood, CA, 1919. e. U. of Southern California. Daughter of late director Sam Wood.
STAGE: You Can't Take It With You, The Man Who Came to Dinner, My Sister Eileen, Nine Girls, St. Joan, The Voice of the Turtle, The Tender Trap.
PICTURES: (debut) Peck's Bad Boy, The Great Man's Lady, Nine Girls, Address Unknown, Kitty Foyle, Harriet Craig, Vice Squad, Tumbleweed, Missile to the Moon, Bob and Ted and Carol and Alice, Pets, They're Playing With Fire.

STEVENS, LESLIE: Executive, Writer, Producer, Director. b. Washington, DC, Feb. 3, 1924. e. Westminister Sch., London, Yale Drama Sch., American Theatre Wing, N.Y. Sold first play, The Mechanical Rat at 15; wrote six plays for summer stock groups, 1941–42; U.S. Air Force, 1943; pres., exec. prod. Daystar Prods.
STAGE: Bullfight (off B'way) 1953–54; wrote, Broadway: Champagne Complex; The Lovers; The Marriage-Go-Round; The Pink Jungle, Joy Joy.
TELEVISION: For Playhouse 90: Invitation to a Gunfighter, Charley's Aunt, Rumors of Evening, The Violent Heart, Portrait of a Murderer, The Second Man; Kraft TV Theatre, Duel; Four Star Playhouse, Award, Producers Showcase, Bloomer Girl; created, prod., dir. Stoney Burke, (series), created, prod., dir. Outer Limits, pilot It Takes a Thief; exec. prod. series; prod.-writer pilot McCloud; exec. prod. series; exec. prod. Men From Shiloh series; exec. prod., writer-dir., Name of the Game, (Leslie Stevens Productions), prod.-writer, pilot of Search, exec. prod., series creator, series Movie of Today, Paperback Playhouse, Earthside Missile Base. Exec. prod., Invisible Man, 1975. Supervising prod. Gemini Man, (1976 pilot and series), Battlestar Galactica (co-prod., pilot), Buck Rogers (co-s.p., 1979), The Highwayman (sprv. prod.).
PICTURES: The Left-Handed Gun 1958 (s.p.). Private Property (co-prod., dir., s.p.); The Marriage-Go-Round (s.p.); Hero's Island (prod., dir., s.p.); Battlestar Galactica (co-prod.), Buck Rogers (writer, prod.), Three Kinds of Heat (dir., prod., s.p.).

STEVENS, MARK: Actor. r.n. Richard Stevens. b. Cleveland, OH, Dec. 13, 1922. e. privately; Beaux Arts and Sir George Williams Sch. of Fine Arts, Montreal. Had varied career before appearing on stage and radio in Canada; later joined station WAKB in Akron; then prod. mgr., WJW, Akron. Screen debut in Objective Burma. Formed Mark Stevens Prod., Mark Stevens Television Prod., 1955.
PICTURES: God Is My Co-Pilot, Pride of the Marines, From This Day Forward, The Dark Corner, I Wonder Who's Kissing Her Now, Between Midnight and Dawn, Katie Did It, Little Egypt, Reunion in Reno, Mutiny, Big Frame, Torpedo Alley, Jack Slade, Cry Vengeance, Timetable, September Storm, Fate Is the Hunter, Frozen Alive, Sunscorched.
TELEVISION: Series: Martin Kane; Big Town (also prod., s.p.); Murder She Wrote.

STEVENS, STELLA: Actress, (Director), b. Yazoo City, MS, Oct. 1, 1938. Mother of actor Andrew Stevens. e. Attended Memphis State U. Modeled in Memphis when she was discovered by talent scouts. Was briefly a term contract actress at 20th Century-Fox, later under exclusive contract to Paramount, then Columbia. Director: Just For a Laugh (A.F.I. film), The American Heroine (feature length doc.), The Ranch (feature comedy).
PICTURES: Say One For Me (debut), The Blue Angel, Li'l Abner, Man Trap, Girls! Girls!, Too Late Blues, The Nutty Professor, The Courtship of Eddie's Father, Advance to the Rear, Synanon, The Secret of My Success, The Silencers, Rage, Where Angels Go, Trouble Follows; How To Save A Marriage and Ruin Your Life, Sol Madrid, The Mad Room, The Ballad of Cable Hogue, A Town Called Hell, Slaughter, Stand Up & Be Counted, The Poseidon Adventure, Arnold, Cleopatra Jones and the Casino of Gold, Las Vegas Lady, Nickelodeon, The Manitou, Whacko, Chained Heat, The Longshot, Monster in the Closet, Down the Drain, Mom, The Ranch (dir.).
TELEVISION: Series: Flamingo Road. Guest: Bob Hope Bing Crosby Special, Frontier Circus, Johnny Ringo, Alfred Hitchcock, Love Boat, Highway to Heaven, Murder She Wrote, Martin Mull's White America, A Table at Ciros. Movies: In Borad Daylight, Climb and Angry Mountain, Linda, The Day The Earth Moved, Honky Tonk, New Original Wonder Woman (pilot), Kiss Me Kill Me, Wanted the Sundance Woman, Charlie Cobb (pilot), The Night They Took Miss Beautiful, Murder in Peyton Place, The Jordan Chance, Cruise into Terror, New Love Boat (pilot), Friendship, Secrets, and Lies, Hart to Hart (pilot), The French Atlantic Affair, The Pendragon Affair (Eddie Capra Mystery pilot), Make Me an Offer, Children of Divorce, Twirl, Amazons, Women of San Quentin, No Man's Land, A Masterpiece of Murder, Fatal Confessions (Father Dowling pilot), Man Against The Mob, The Old Dick.

STEVENSON, PARKER: Actor. b. Philadelphia, PA, June 4, 1953. e. Princeton U. Began professional acting career by starring in film, A Separate Peace, while high school senior, having attracted attention through work on TV commercials.
PICTURES: A Separate Peace (debut, 1972), Our Time, Lifeguard, Stroker Ace, Stitches.
TELEVISION: The Streets of San Francisco, Gunsmoke. Series: Hardy Boys Mysteries, Falcon Crest, Probe. Mini-Series: North & South Book II. Movie: Shooting Stars, This House Possessed, That Secret Sunday, Baywatch: Panic at Malibu Pier, The Cover Girl and the Cop.

STEWART, DOUGLAS DAY: Writer, Director.
PICTURES: Writer: The Blue Lagoon, An Officer and a Gentleman, Director-Writer: Thief of Hearts, Listen to Me.

TELEVISION: Boy in the Plastic Bubble, The Man Who Could Talk to Kids, Murder or Mercy.

STEWART, ELAINE: Actress. b. Montclair, NJ, May 31, 1929. Usher, cashier, m.p. theatre, Montclair; model, Conover Agcy., 1948; many TV shows; screen debut in Sailor Beware (1951); Star of Tomorrow, 1954.
PICTURES: Sky Full of Moon, The Bad and the Beautiful, Desperate Search, Code Two, Slight Case of Larceny, Young Bess, Take the High Ground, Brigadoon, Adventures of Hajji Baba, Tattered Dress, Rise and Fall of Legs Diamond, Most Dangerous Man Alive.

STEWART, JAMES: Actor. b. Indiana, PA, May 20, 1908. e. Mercersburg Acad.; Princeton U. With Falmouth Stock Co., Cape Cod; on N.Y. stage in Goodbye Again; stage mgr. for Camille with Jane Cowl (Boston). In films since 1935; joined U.S. Air Force 1942, commissioned Col. 1944. Retired as Brig. Gen. Voted one of top ten money-making stars, M.P. Herald-Fame poll, 1950, 52, 54, 57; No. 1 Money-Making Star, 1955. 1968, Screen Actors Guild Award. Mem.: Bd. of Trustees, Princeton U. Trustee, Claremont Coll.; exec. bd. of Los Angeles Council of Boy Scouts of America; bd. of dirs., Project Hope. Honorary Academy Award, 1984. Author: Jimmy Stewart and His Poems (1989).
STAGE: Spring in Autumn, All Good Americans, Yellow Jack, Journey at Night, Harvey.
PICTURES: Murder Man, Rose Marie, Wife vs. Secretary, Next Time We Love, Small Town Girl, Speed, Gorgeous Hussy, Born to Dance, Seventh Heaven, After the Thin Man, You Can't Take It With You, The Last Gangster, Navy Blue and Gold, Of Human Hearts, Vivacious Lady, Shopworn Angel, Made For Each Other, Ice Follies of 1939, Mr. Smith Goes to Washington, It's A Wonderful World, Destry Rides Again, Shop Around the Corner, Mortal Storm, No Time For Comedy, The Philadelphia Story (Acad. Award, 1940), Come Live With Me, Pot O'Gold, Ziegfeld Girl, It's a Wonderful Life, Magic Town, Call Northside 777, On Our Merry Way, Rope, You Gotta Stay Happy, Stratton Story, Malaya, Winchester '73, Broken Arrow, Harvey, Jackpot, No Highway in the Sky, Greatest Show on Earth, Carbine Williams, Bend of the River, Naked Spur, Thunder Bay, Glenn Miller Story, Far Country, Rear Window, Strategic Air Command, Man From Laramie, Man Who Knew Too Much, Spirit of St. Louis, Night Passage, Vertigo, Bell Book and Candle, Anatomy of a Murder, FBI Story, The Mountain Road, Two Rode Together, Man Who Shot Liberty Valance, Mr. Hobbs Takes a Vacation, How the West Was Won, Take Her, She's Mine, Cheyenne Autumn, Dear Brigitte, Shenandoah, The Rare Breed, Flight of the Phoenix, Firecreek, Bandolero, Cheyenne Social Club, Fool's Parade, That's Entertainment, The Shootist, Airport '77, The Magic of Lassie, The Big Sleep.
TELEVISION: Series: The Jimmy Stewart Show (1971–72), Hawkins, 1973–74; Movies: Hawkins on Murder, Right of Way, 1984.

STEWART, JAMES L.: Executive. e. U. of Southern California, B.A. in cinema-TV and M.B.A. in finance. Worked for two years in sales for CBS Radio Network—West Coast. Spent four years with MGM in promotion and marketing. With Walt Disney Prods. for 12 years, functioning in marketing, management and administrative activities; named v.p.-corp. relations & admin. asst. to pres. In 1978 joined in formation of Aurora Pictures, of which is exec. v.p., secty., & COO.
PICTURES: Exec. Prod.: Why Would I Lie?, The Secret of NIMH, Eddie and the Cruisers, Heart Like a Wheel, East of the Sun, West of the Moon, Maxie.

STEWART, KEN: Executive. First affiliated with Universal as asst. to head of trailers dept. Joined Paramount in 1981 as member of West Coast pub. dep.; later administrator, audio visual Services. 1984, appt. exec. dir. of creative services (New York).

STEWART, MARILYN: Marketing & Public Relations Executive. b. New York, NY. e. Hunter Coll. Entered ind. as scty. then asst. to MGM dir. of adv. Left to become prom.-pub. dir. for Verve/Folkways Records; duties also included ar and talent scouting. In 1966 joined 20th-Fox as radio/tv pub. coordinator. In 1969 went to Para. Pictures as mag. pub. coordinator; 1970 named worldwide dir. of pub. for Para., including creation of overall mkt. concepts, becoming 1st woman to be appt. to that position at major co. Campaigns included Love Story and The Godfather. In 1972 opened own consulting office specializing in m.p. marketing and p.r. Headquarters in N.Y.; repr. in L.A. Has represented The Lords of Flatbush, Bang the Drum Slowly, The Kids Are Alright, Autumn Sonata, The Tin Drum, A Cry in the Dark, Filmex, Michael Moriarty, Fred Schepisi, Volker Schlondorff, Lucasfilm.

STIGWOOD, ROBERT: Executive. b. Adelaide, Australia, April 16, 1934. e. Sacred Heart Coll. Began career as copywriter for Aust. ad agency; at 21 left home for England. Series of first jobs led to his opening a London theatrical agency. Began casting commercials for TV; prod. records for clients. Became first independent record producer in Great Britain. In mid '60s joined forces with Brian Epstein, mgr. of Beatles, to become co-mgr. of NEMS Enterprises. At Epstein's death formed own co., launching careers of such artists as Bee Gees, Cream, etc. Moved into theatre prod. in London: Hair, Jesus Christ Superstar, Pippin, Oh Calcutta!, Evita. Entered film prod. with Jesus Christ Superstar. Formed RSO Records in 1973.
PICTURES: Jesus Christ Superstar, Tommy, Saturday Night Fever, Grease, Sgt. Pepper's Lonely Hearts Club Band, Moment by Moment, Times Square (co.-prod.), The Fan, Gallipoli, Grease 2, Staying Alive.

STING: Musician, Actor. r.n. Gordon Matthew Sumner. b. Newcastle-Upon-Tyne, England, Oct. 2, 1951. e. Warwick U. A schoolteacher before helping form rock group, The Police as songwriter, singer and bass player. Broadway debut, Threepenny Opera, 1989.
PICTURES: Quadrophenia, Radio On, The Great Rock 'n' Roll Swindle, Brimstone and Treacle, The Bride, Dune, Plenty, Bring on the Night, Julia and Julia, Stormy Monday, The Adventures of Baron Munchausen, The Passion, Rosencrantz and Guilderstern Are Dead.

STOCKWELL, DEAN: Actor. b. Hollywood, CA, Mar. 5, 1935. p. Harry and Betty Veronica Stockwell. e. Long Island public schools and Martin Milmore, Boston. On stage in Theatre Guild prod. Innocent Voyage. Appeared on radio in Death Valley Days and Dr. Christian. Named in 1949 M.P. Herald-Fame Stars of Tomorrow poll; 1976 retired to Santa Monica as a licensed real estate broker but soon returned to acting.
PICTURES: Anchors Aweigh (debut), The Valley of Decision, Abbott and Costello in Hollywood, The Green Years, Home Sweet Homicide, The Mighty McGurk, The Arnelo Affair, The Romance of Rosy Ridge, Song of the Thin Man, Gentleman's Agreement, Deep Waters, Down to Sea in Ships, Boy with Green Hair, The Secret Garden, Happy Years, Kim, Stars in My Crown, Cattle Drive, Compulsion, Sons and Lovers, Long Day's Journey Into Night, Psych-out, The Dunwich Horror, Ecstasy, The Last Movie, The Loners, Another Day at the Races, Werewolf of Washington, Won Ton Ton The Dog Who Saved Hollywood, Win, Place, or Steal, Tracks, Wrong Is Right, To Kill a Stranger, Paris, Texas, Dune, To Live and Die in L.A., Blue Velvet, Beverly Hills Cop II, Gardens of Stone, The Blue Iguana, Tucker: The Man and His Dream, Time Guardian, Buying Time, Married to the Mob, Palais Royale, Backtrack, Jorge um Brasileiro, Papa Was a Preacher.
TELEVISION: Miami Vice, Hart to Hart, Simon and Simon, The A-Team, Series: Quantum Leap. Movies: The Failing of Raymond, The Gambler III: The Legend Continues.

STODDARD, BRANDON: Executive. b. Canaan, NY, March 31, 1937. e. Yale U., Columbia Law Sch. Was program ass't. at Batton, Barton, Durstine and Osborn before joining Grey Advertising, where was successively, program operations supvr., dir. daytime programming, v.p. in chg. of TV, radio programming. Joined ABC in 1970; named v.p. daytime programs for ABC Entertainment, 1972; v.p. children's programs, 1973. Named v.p., motion pictures for TV, 1974. In 1976 named v.p., dramatic programs and m.p. for TV. In June, 1979, named pres., ABC Motion Pictures. In 1985 appt. pres., ABC Entertainment. Resigned March, 1989 to head ABC Prods. unit to create and prod. series and movies for the network.

STOLBER, DEAN: Executive. b. Philadelphia, PA, Sept. 2, 1944. e. Harvard, A.B., 1966; NYU Sch. of Law, J.D., 1969. Acted on Broadway and in TV before starting career in law and business affairs in films. 1979, sr. v.p., business affairs, for United Artists Corp.; 1981 named exec. v.p.; 1982, sr. v.p., MGM/UA Entertainment Co.

STOLNITZ, ART: Executive. b. Rochester, NY, March 13, 1928. e. U. of Tennessee, LL.B., 1952. U.S. Navy Air Force. Legal dept., William Morris Agency, 1953, dir. business affairs, ZIV, 1959; dir. new program development, ZIV-United Artists, 1960; literary agent, MCA, 1961; dir. business affairs, Selmur Productions, Selmur Pictures, 1963; v.p. ABC Pictures, 1969; v.p. Metromedia Producers Corporation, 1970, executive v.p. Metromedia Producers Corporation; 1975 exec. v.p. and prod. Charles Fries Prods. 1976, prod. Edgar J. Scherick Productions; 1976–77 prod., Grizzly Adams (TV); 1977; v.p. business affairs, Warner Bros.-TV; 1980, sr. v.p., business affairs.

STOLOFF, VICTOR: Producer, Writer, Director, Editor. b. March 17, 1913. e. French Law U. Ac. Fines Arts. Prod. dir. writer of award winning documentaries (Warner Bros. release); Prod. dir. writer first U.S. film made in Italy, When in Rome; First U.S. film made in Egypt; Collaborator William Dieterle films; Contract writer, dir. to Sidney Buchman, Columbia, S.p.: Volcano, The Sinner, Shark Reef, Journey Around the World. Of Love and Desire (prod., s.p.); Intimacy (prod., dir.), The Washington Affair (prod., dir.), The 300 Year Weekend (dir., orig. s.p.).
TELEVISION: Ford Theatre, Lloyd Bridges series, National Velvet, High Adventure, with Lowell Thomas, Prod. on

location 22, Hawaii Five-O, Why? Director (orig. s.p.) Created Woman of Russia, first of TV series.

STOLTZ, ERIC: Actor. b. American Samoa, 1961. Family moved to California when he was 8. Spent 2 years at U. of Southern California in theatre arts; left to study with Stella Adler and later William Traylor and Peggy Feury. Stage work with an American rep. co. in Scotland in Tobacco Road, You're a Good Man Charlie Brown, Working. Off-Bdwy, The Widow Claire (1986). Broadway debut Our Town (1988, Tony nom. & Drama Desk nom.)

PICTURES: Fast Times at Ridgemont High, 1982. Lucky 13, Next of Kin, The Wild Life, Code Name: Emerald, Mask, Some Kind of Wonderful, Lionheart, Sister Sister, Haunted Summer, Manifesto, The Fly II, Say Anything (cameo), Memphis Belle.

TELEVISION: Many series appearances. Movies: A Killer in the Family, Paper Dolls, Thursday's Child, The Violation of Sara McDavid, The Seekers, Things Are Looking Up. Special: Our Town.

STONE, ANDREW L.: Producer, Director. b. California, July 16, 1902. e. U. of California. Ent. ind. 1918 at Universal San Francisco exch.; later author, prod., dir. series of pictures for Paramount; prod., dir. for Sono-Art; 1932–36. org. and oper. Race Night company; prod., dir., The Girl Said No, 1936; Stolen Heaven, Say It in French, The Great Victory Herbert, Magician Music, 1940. Dir. Stormy Weather; formed Andrew Stone Prods., 1943.

PICTURES: The Great Victor Herbert, Stormy Weather, Hi Diddle Diddle, Sensations of 1945, Bedside Manner, Bachelor's Daughter, Fun on a Weekend, Highway 301, Confidence Girl, Steel Trap, Blueprint for Murder, Night Holds Terror, Julie, Cry Terror, The Decks Ran Red, The Last Voyage, Ring of Fire, Password is Courage, Never Put It in Writing, Secret of My Success, Song of Norway, The Great Waltz.

STONE, BURTON J.: Executive. b. Feb. 16, 1928; e. Florida Southern Coll. Was film ed., Hollywood Film Co. 1951–53; serv. mgr., sales mgr. and gen. mgr., Consolidated Film Inds., 1953–61; nat'l sales mgr., Movielab, 1961–63; pres., Allservice Film Laboratories, 1963–; v.p. Technicolor, Inc., 1963–70. Pres., Precision Film Labs., 1972–78. Pres., Deluxe Laboratories, Inc., a wholly-owned subsidiary of 20th Century Fox, 1978–present.

MEMBER: Board of directors, Will Rogers Foundation and Motion Picture Pioneers; member Acad. of Motion Picture Arts & Sciences, American Society of Cinematographers; awarded fellowship in Society of Motion Picture & Television Engineers; pres., Association of Cinema & Video Laboratories; awarded fellowship in British Kinematograph, Sound & Television Society.

STONE, DEE WALLACE: Actress. r.n. Deanna Bowers. b. Kansas City, MO, Dec. 14, 1948. m. actor Christopher Stone. e. U. of Kansas, theater and education. Taught high school English. Came to NY to audition for Hal Prince and spent 2 years working in commercials and industrial shows. First break in Police Story episode.

PICTURES: The Hills Have Eyes, 10, The Howling, E.T. the Extra-Terrestrial, Jimmy the Kid, Cujo, King of the City, Critters, Secret Admirer, Shadow Play, The White Dragon.

TELEVISION: Chips, Series: Together We Stand, Lassie, Movies: The Sky's No Limit, Young Love, First Love, The Secret War of Jackie's Girls, Child Bride of Short Creek, The Five of Me, A Whale for the Killing, Skeezer, Wait Til Your Mother Gets Home, Happy, I Take These Men, Hostage Flight, Sin of Innocence, Addicted to His Love, Stranger on My Land. Terror in the Sky, The Christmas Visitor.

STONE, EZRA C.: Actor, Dir., Writer, Prod., Teacher, Lecturer, Farmer. b. New Bedford, MA, Dec. 2, 1917. e. American Acad. of Dramatic Arts, N.Y., 1934–35. Actor: National Junior Theatre, 1931; Broadway: Parade, Ah Wilderness, Oh Evening Star, Three Men on a Horse, Room Service, Brother Rat; created Henry Aldrich, What a Life, The Alchemist, She Stoops to Conquer; prod. asst. to George Abbott, 1935–40; created Henry Aldrich on radio's Aldrich Family, 1938; starred, Those Were the Days, This is the Army, USAAF, 1941–45; directed on Broadway: See My Lawyer, 1939, Reunion in New York, 1940.

STAGE: This Is the Army; January Thaw; At War with the Army; To Tell You the Truth; Me and Molly; Wake Up Darling; Make a Million; The Man That Corrupted Hadleyburg; The Pink Elephant; Dear Ruth; Come Blow Your Horn; God Bless Our Bank, Fallen Angels; Finishing Touches; Dracula—The Vampire King; Sweet Land (exec. prod., dir.); Centennial Celebration of Founding Newtown, PA (actor).

PICTURES: Did 300 documentary films for IBM. American Heart Assn., Chapman Coll., University of Judaism, Jewish Theological Seminary; dir. live action sequences for The Daydreamer; The Forty Million (prod., dir., co-narrator).

TELEVISION: Aldrich Family, Danny Thomas, Ed Wynn, Ezio Pinza, Martha Raye, Fred Allen, Herb Shriner, Life With Father, Sid Caesar, Joan Davis, dir. Joe and Mabel, prod., dir. Bachelor Father, Angel, The Hathaways, spec. Affairs of Antol, Shari Lewis, Bob Hope, My Living Doll, Munsters, Karen, Tammy, O.K. Crackerby, Please Don't Eat the Daisies; dir., writer Woody Allen pilot, Loredo, Pistols & Petticoats, Petticoat Junction, Phyllis Diller Show, Lost in Space, Tammy Grimes show, Julia, Flying Nun, Debbie Reynolds, The Jimmy Stewart Show, Lassie, Sandy Duncan Show, Tribute to the Lunts, Love American Style, Bob Newhart, Space Academy, Munster's Revenge, Quincy, ABC Circle Playhouse Project UFO, Actor, (PBS Paul Muni, biography film). Has over 25 intl. film awards; Grand Prize, Barcelona Int'l Film Festival.

AUTHOR: Coming Major, 1945, co-author; Deems Taylor; Liberte, Puccini Opera, 1951; contributor to: Variety, Magazine Digest, N.Y. Post; Equity Magazine, etc. Teacher: American Acad. Dramatic Arts, assoc. dir., American Theatre Wing; American Coll. Theatre Fest., Princeton, Yale, UCLA: pres./dir., David Library of Amer. Revolution.

STONE, MARIANNE: Actress. b. London, England. Studied Royal Acad. of Dramatic Art, West End debut in The Kingmaker, 1946.

TELEVISION: Maigret, Bootsie and Snudge, Jimmy Edwards Show, Wayne and Schuster Show, Roy Hudd Show, Harry Worth Show, Steptoe and Son, Informer, Love Story, Father Dear Father, Bless This House, The Man Outside, Crown Court, Public Eye, Miss Nightingale, She, Little Lord Fauntleroy, The Secret Army (2 series), Shillingbury Tale, The Bright Side (series), Tickets for the Titanic (series), The Balance of Nature, Always, Hammer House of Mystery & Suspense, The Nineteenth Hole.

PICTURES: Brighton Rock, Seven Days to Noon, The Clouded Yellow, Wrong Arm of the Law, Heavens Above, Stolen Hours, Nothing But the Best, Curse of the Mummy's Tomb, Hysteria, The Beauty Jungle, A Hard Day's Night, Rattle of a Simple Man, Echo of Diana, Act of Murder, Catch Us If You Can, You Must Be Joking, The Countess from Hong Kong, The Wrong Box, To Sir With Love, The Bliss of Mrs. Blossom, Here We Go Round the Mulberry Bush, Carry on Doctor, The Twisted Nerve, The Best House in London, Oh! What a Lovely War; The Raging Moon, There's a Girl in My Soup, All the Right Noises, Assault, Carry On at Your Convenience, All Coppers Are. . ., Carry on Girls, Penny Gold, The Vault of Horror, Percy's Progress, Confessions of a Window Cleaner, Carry on Dick, That Lucky Touch, Sarah, Carry on Behind, Confessions From a Holiday Camp, The Chiffy Kids, What's Up Superdoc?; The Class of Miss McMichael, The Human Factor, Dangerous Davies, Funny Money, Terry on the Fence, Carry on Laughing.

STONE, OLIVER: Director, Writer. b. New York, NY, Sept. 15, 1946. e. Yale U., NYU, B.F.A., 1971. Teacher in Cholon, Vietnam 1965–66. U.S. Infantry specialist 4th Class. 1967–68 in Vietnam (Purple Heart, Bronze Star with Oak Leaf Cluster honors).

PICTURES: Seizure (dir., s.p., 1974), Midnight Express (s.p. Acad. Award, s.p. adapt.), The Hand (dir., s.p., cameo), Conan the Barbarian (s.p.), Scarface (s.p.); 8 Million Ways to Die (s.p. only),Year of the Dragon (s.p.), Salvador (dir., co-s.p.), Platoon (dir., s.p., cameo; Acad. Award. dir., 1987 & DGA Award), Wall Street (dir., co-s.p.), Talk Radio (dir., co-s.p.), Born on the Fourth of July (dir., s.p.), Blue Steel (co-prod.), Reversal of Fortune (co-prod. only).

STONE, PETER H.: Writer. b. Los Angeles, CA, Feb. 27, 1930. Son of film prod. John Stone and screenwriter Hilda Hess Stone. e. Bard Col., B.A. 1951; Yale U, M.F.A., 1953.

THEATER: Kean, Skyscraper, 1776 (Tony and Drama Desk Awards, 1969), Two By Two, Sugar, Full Circle, Woman of the Year (Tony Award, 1981), My One and Only.

PICTURES: Charade, Father Goose (Acad. Award, 1964), Mirage, Arabesque, Secret War of Harry Frigg, Jigsaw, Sweet Charity, Skin Game, The Taking of Pelham One Two Three, 1776 (adapted own stage musical book to screen), Silver Bears, Who Is Killing the Great Chefs of Europe?, Why Would I Lie?, Nesting.

TELEVISION: Studio One, Brenner, Witness, Asphalt Jungle, The Defenders (Emmy, 1962). Androcles and the Lion, Adam's Rib (series), Ivan the Terrible.

STONEMAN, JAMES M.: Executive. b. Jan. 16, 1927. Pres., Interstate Theatres Corp., Boston. 1985, pres., Theatre Owners of New England. NATO bd.; Variety Club of New England & South Florida.

STORARO, VITTORIO: Cinematographer. b. Rome, Italy, 1940. Trained at Rome's Centro Sperimentale and began filming short films. His work as Bernardo Bertolucci's regular cameraman has won him an international reputation and award-winning work in Europe and America.

PICTURES: Giovinezza, Giovinezza (Youthful, Youthful, 1970); The Spider's Stratagem; The Conformist; 'Tis a Pity She's a Whore; Last Tango in Paris; Giordano Bruno; 1900; La Luna; Apocalypse Now (Acad. Award); Submission; Agatha; Reds (Acad. Award); One From the Heart; Wagner; Peter the Great; Ladyhawke; The Last Emperor (Acad. Award); Tucker: The Man and His Dream; New York Stories (Life Without Zoe), Dick Tracy.

STOREY, FREDERICK: Executive. b. Columbus, GA, Nov. 12, 1909. e. Georgia Tech. Adv. staff Atlanta Journal, 1933–38; adv. staff C. P. Clark Adv. Agcy., 1938; partner 1940; U.S. Navy, 1941–46; staff Georgia Theatre Co., 1946; v.p. 1947–52. Founded Storey Theatres Inc., Atlanta, GA; 1952, now bd. chmn. (formerly pres.) of Georgia State Theatres; dir. numerous theatre cos.; v.p. dir., Motion Picture Theatre Owners of Georgia, Dist. Alumnus award, Georgia Tech, 1979.

STORKE, WILLIAM F.: Producer. b. Rochester, NY. e. UCLA, B.A. 1948. In Navy in W.W.II. First position with NBC Hollywood guest relations staff, 1948. Moved to continuity acceptance dept. as comm. editor. Prom. to asst. mgr, comm. spvr. before joining NBC West Coast sales dept., 1953. Transferred to N.Y. as prog. acct. exec., 1955; named administrator, participating prog. sales, Nov., 1957. Named dir., participating program sales, 1959. Named dir., program adm., NBC-TV, Jan., 1964; in Feb. elected v.p., program adm. In 1967 named v.p., programs, East Coast; in 1968, appt. v.p., special programs, NBC-TV Network; 1979, pres., Claridge Group, Ltd.; exec. v.p. Entertainment Partners, Inc., N.Y., 1982–.
TELEVISION: Producer: Oliver Twist, To Catch A King, A Christmas Carol, The Last Days of Patton, A Special Friendship, The Ted Kennedy Jr. Story, Buck James (series, exec. prod.), Old Man and the Sea.

STORM, GALE: Actress. r.n. Josephine Cottle. b. Bloomington, TX, April 5, 1922. Won a "Gateway to Hollywood" talent contest while still in high school, in 1939. Made several minor films in the 1940s including several Roy Rogers westerns, before becoming popular TV comedienne on My Little Margie (1952–55). Also launched successful recording career. Autobiography: I Ain't Down Yet (1981).
PICTURES: Tom Brown's Schooldays (debut, 1939), Foreign Agent, Nearly Eighteen, The Right to Live, Sunbonnet Sue, It Happened on Fifth Avenue, Abandoned, Between Midnight and Dawn, Underworld Story, Curtain Call at Cactus Creek, Al Jennings of Oklahoma, Texas Rangers, Woman of the North Country.
TELEVISION: Series: My Little Margie, Oh Susanna.

STOSSEL, JOHN: News Correspondent. b. 1947. e. Princeton U. Started as producer-reporter with KGW-TV in Portland, OR. Joined WCBS-TV in New York as investigative reporter and consumer editor, winning 15 local Emmy Awards. In June, 1981 joined ABC-TV, appearing on Good Morning America and 20/20 as consumer editor. Also provides twice-weekly consumer reports on ABC Radio Information Network. Author: Shopping Smart (1982).

STOVER, WENDY: Executive. Joined Orion Pictures (then Filmways Pictures) 1977 as asst. in legal dept. Named dir. of admin., heading insurance and personnel depts. 1985, named v.p., admin. 1987, sr. v.p. in chg. admin. Also holds title of v.p., branch admin. for Orion Pictures Distribution Corp.

STRADLING, HARRY, JR.: Cinematographer. b. New York, NY, Jan. 7, 1925. Son of Harry Stradling, renowned cinematographer.
PICTURES: Welcome to Hard Times, Support Your Local Sheriff, The Mad Room, Something Big, Fools Parade, The Way We Were, Bite the Bullet, Skyjacked, Midway, The Big Bus, Born Again, Convoy, Go Tell the Spartans, Prophecy, Carney, S.O.B., Buddy, Buddy, The Pursuit of D.B. Cooper, Micki and Maude, Blind Date, Caddyshack II.
TELEVISION: George Washington (mini-series).

STRAIGHT, BEATRICE: Actress. b. Old Westbury, NY, Aug. 2, 1918. Trained in classics; won Tony award early in career for best actress in Arthur Miller's The Crucible. Many films and TV programs.
THEATER: King Lear, Twelfth Night, The Possessed, Land of Fame, Eastward in Eden, The Heiress (Bdwy. & on tour), The Crucible, Phedra, Everything in the Garden, Ghosts, All My Sons, and regional theater (Streetcar Named Desire, A Lion in Winter, Old Times).
PICTURES: Phone Call from a Stranger, Patterns, The Nun's Story, Garden Party, Network (Acad. Award, supp. actress), Bloodline, The Promise, The Formula, Endless Love, Poltergeist, Two of a Kind, Power.
TELEVISION: Beacon Hill (series), The Dain Curse, The Borrowers, Murder on Board, King's Crossing (series), The Princess and the Pea (Faerie Tale Theatre), Morning Star/Evening Star, Jack and Mike (series), Robert Kennedy and His Times, Under Siege, Run Till You Fall.

STRASBERG, SUSAN: Actress. b. New York, NY, May 22, 1938.; e. N.Y. Parents: late Lee Strasberg, stage dir. & dir. of Actors Studio, and Paula Miller, actress. Off-Bdwy stage debut in Maya; on TV in series, The Marriage and Toma, The Duchess and the Smugs, Romeo and Juliet. Starred on Bdwy in The Diary of Anne Frank, Time Remembered, Zeffirelli's Lady of the Camillias, Shadow of a Gunman. Author, Bittersweet. Acting Teacher, like father.
PICTURES: Picnic, Stage Struck, Scream of Fear, Adventures of a Young Man, The Trip, Psych-Out, The Name of the Game Is Kill, Kapo, High Bright Sun, Rollercoaster, The Manitou, In Praise of Older Women, The Delta Force, Prime Suspect, The Runnin Kind.
TELEVISION: Beggarman, Thief; The Immigrants; Toma; Frankenstein; Rona Jaffe's Mazes and Monsters; Murder She Wrote.

STRASSBERG, STEPHEN: Publicist. b. New York, NY. e. City Coll. of New York, B.S.S. Joined Loew's Inc., 1940; served in U.S. Army, WW II; publicist with Republic Pictures, 1946–49; asst. nat'l adv. dir., Film Classics, 1949–50; pub. dir., Eagle Lion Classics, 1950; publicist Lopert Films, Inc., 1951; dir. of adv., pub., Imperial Films, 1953; pub. dir., WABC, WABC-TV, N.Y., 1955; asst. dir., Press Information; ABC, 1957; dir. press info. ABC-TV Network, 1958; dir., News Information, ABC-TV Network, 1975.

STRATTON, JOHN: Actor. b. Clitheroe, England, 1925; e. Royal Grammar Sch., Clitheroe. Early career in repertory; m.p. and TV debut 1948.
TELEVISION: The First Mrs. Fraser, The Confidential Clerk, Adams Apple, You Know What People Are (series). Death of a Salesman, Quatermass in The Pit, The Wind and the Rain, The Secret Kingdom, Kipps, The Dobson Fund, The Problem of Mary Winshaw, A Perfect Woman, Climate of Fear, Thank You and Goodnight, What's In It for Walter, A Free Weekend, Workshop Limits, 24 Hour Call, 2 Cars, The Odd Man, It's Dark Outside, For the West, Man in Room 17, Julie's Gone, The Trouble Shooters, Turn out the Lights, Mr. Rose, The Black Doctor, Sir Arthur Conan Doyle, The Newcomers, Tickle Time, Letters from the Dead, Z Car, Wanted Single Gentleman, Softly Softly, Fall of the Goat, City '68, Artist in Crime, The First Lady, Print and Be Damned, The Expert, Resurrection (serial), Sherlock Holmes, Measure of Malice, The Elusive Pimpernel (serial), The Pallisers, Fall of the Eagles, Clayhanger, Trinity Tales, Witch of Pendle, When We Are Married, Just William, Backs to the Land, Forget Me Not, A Superstition, The Professionals, Mill on the Floss, The Good Companions, Great Expectations, The Forgotten Story, The Tales of Beatrix Potter, My Cousin Rachel, Dr. Who: Juliet Brajo.
PICTURES: Small Back Room, Seven Days to Noon, Appointment With Venus (Island Rescue), Happy Family, Cruel Sea, Long Arm, Man In the Sky, Seven Waves Away (Abandon Ship), The Challenge, Strangler's Web.

STRAUSS, PETER: Actor. b. Croton-on-Hudson, NY., Feb. 20, 1947. e. Northwestern U. Spotted at N.U. by talent agent and sent to Hollywood. Stage, at Mark Taper Theatre in Dance Next Door, The Dirty Man.
PICTURES: Hail, Hero! (debut, 1969), Soldier Blue, The Trail of the Catonsville Nine, The Last Tycoon, Spacehunter.
TELEVISION: Man Without a Country, Attack on Terror, The FBI Story; Young Joe: The Forgotten Kennedy, The Jericho Mile (Emmy Award), Angel on My Shoulder; Heart of Steel, Under Siege. Mini-Series: Rich Man, Poor Man, Masada, Kane & Abel, A Whale for the Killing, Tender Is The Night, Penalty Phase, The Proud Men, Brotherhood of the Rose, Peter Gunn.

STRAUSS, PETER E.: Executive. b. Oct. 7, 1940. e. Oberlin Coll., London Sch. of Economics, Columbia U. Sch. of Law, L.L.B., 1965. Vice pres., University Dormitory Dev. Co., 1965–68; v.p., Allart Cinema 16, 1968–69; v.p. prod., Allied Artists Pictures Corp., 1970; June 14, 1974 elected exec. v.p. Joined Rastar Films; left to become independent. Pres. of the Movie Group.
PICTURE: Best of the Best (prod.).

STREEP, MERYL: Actress. r.n. Mary Louise Streep. b. Bernardsville, NJ, April 22, 1949. e. Vassar. Acted for a season with traveling theater co. in VT. Awarded scholarship to Yale Drama School, 1972, where she was cast in 12–15 roles a year. NY stage debut: Trelawny of the Wells (1975) with New York Shakespeare Fest.
THEATER: Off-Broadway: 27 Wagons Full of Cotton, A Memory of Two Mondays, Secret Service, Henry V, (New York Shakespeare Fest.), Measure for Measure (NYSF), The Cherry Orchard, Happy End (Broadway debut, 1977), Taming of the Shrew (NYSF), Alice in Concert.
PICTURES: Julia, Manhattan, The Deer Hunter, The Seduction of Joe Tynan, Kramer vs. Kramer (Acad. Award, best supporting actress, 1979), The French Lieutenant's Woman, Still of the Night, Sophie's Choice (Acad. Award, 1982), Silkwood, Falling in Love, Plenty, Out of Africa, Heartburn, Ironweed, A Cry in the Dark, She-Devil, Postcards From the Edge.
TELEVISION: Holocaust, The Deadliest Season.

STREISAND, BARBRA: Singer, Actress. b. New York, April 24, 1942. e. Erasmus H.S., Brooklyn. Appeared in New York night clubs. NY stage debut: Another Evening with Harry Stoones (1961). On Broadway in I Can Get It For You Wholesale, Funny Girl.
PICTURES: Funny Girl (debut, Acad. Award, 1968), Hello

Dolly, On A Clear Day You Can See Forever, The Owl and the Pussycat, What's Up Doc?, Up the Sandbox, The Way We Were, For Pete's Sake, Funny Lady, A Star Is Born, (star, prod.), The Main Event (star, co-prod.), All Night Long, Yentl (prod., dir., co.s.p., star), Nuts (actress, prod., music).
TELEVISION: My Name is Barbra, Color Me Barbra, Bell of 14th Street, A Happening in Central Park, Barbra Streisand: One Voice.

STRICKLYN, RAY: Actor. b. Houston, TX, October 8, 1930. e. U. of Houston.
PLAYS: Broadway debut in Moss Hart's The Climate of Eden. Tour: Stalag 17, Confessions of a Nightingale. Off-B'way: The Grass Harp, Confessions of a Nightingale. Los Angeles: Confessions of a Nightingale, Vieux Carre, Compulsion and The Caretaker, Naomi. Court.
FILMS: The Proud and the Profane, Crime In the Streets, Somebody Up There Likes Me, The Catered Affair, The Last Wagon, Return of Dracula, 10 North Frederick, The Remarkable Mr. Pennypacker, The Big Fisherman, Young Jesse James, The Plunderers, The Lost World, Track of Thunder, Arizona Raiders, Dogpound Shuffle.
AWARDS: Theatre World Award; 2 Hollywood Foreign Press Golden Globe noms. (10 North Frederick and The Plunderers); Best Actor Awards 1984 & 86 for Vieux Carre and Confessions of a Nightingale (LA Drama Critics, LA. Weekly Award, Drama-Logue, Robby Award, AGLA Media Award, Oscar Wilde Award).

STRINGER, HOWARD: Executive. b. Cardiff, Wales. Feb. 19, 1942. e. Oxford U., B.A., M.A., modern history/international relations. Received Army Commendation Medal for meritorious achievement for service in Vietnam (1965–67). Joined CBS, 1965, at WCBS-TV, NY, rising from assoc. prod., prod. to exec. prod. of documentary broadcasts. Served as prod., dir. and writer of CBS Reports: The Palestinians (Overseas Press Club of America, Writers Guild Awards, 1974); The Rockefellers (Emmy Award, 1973). Won 9 Emmy Awards as exec. prod., prod., writer or dir: CBS Reports: The Boston Goes to China; CBS Reports: The Defense of the United States; CBS Evening News with Dan Rather: The Beirut Bombing; The Countdown Against Cancer; The Black Family. Exec. prod., CBS Reports; exec. prod., CBS Evening News with Dan Rather, 1981–84. Appointed exec. vice pres., CBS News Division, 1984; pres., CBS News, 1986; pres., CBS/Broadcast Group, 1988.

STRITCH, ELAINE: Actress. b. Detroit, MI, Feb. 2, 1926. e. studied acting with Erwin Piscator at the New Sch. for Social Research. Major career on stage. Bdwy debut 1946 in Loco.
THEATER: Made in Heaven, Angel in the Wings, Call Me Madam, Pal Joey, On Your Toes, Bus Stop, Goldilocks, Sail Away, Who's Afraid of Virginia Woolf?, Wonderful Town, Company. London: Gingerbread Lady, Small Craft Warnings.
PICTURES: The Scarlet Hour (debut, 1955), Three Violent People, A Farewell to Arms, The Perfect Furlough, Who Killed Teddy Bear?, Sidelong Glances of a Pigeon Kicker, The Spiral Staircase, Providence, September, Cocoon: The Return.
TELEVISION: Series: Growing Pains (1949), Pantomine Quiz (regular, 1953–55, 1958), My Sister Eileen, The Trials of O'Brien, Two's Company, Nobody's Perfect (also adapt.) The Ellen Burstyn Show. Specials: Company: the Making of the Album, Kennedy Center Tonight, Follies in Concert.

STROCK, HERBERT L.: Producer, Writer, Director, Film editor. b. Boston, MA, Jan. 13, 1918. e. U. of Southern California, A.B., M.A. in cinema. Prof. of cinema, U. of Southern California, 1941. Started career, publicity leg man, Jimmy Fidler, Hollywood columnist; editorial dept., MGM, 1941–47; pres., IM-PPRO, Inc., 1955–59; assoc. prod.-supv. film ed., U.A.; director: AIP, Warner Bros. independent, Phoenix Films. Pres., Herbert L. Strock Prods.
PICTURES: Storm Over Tibet, Magnetic Monster, Riders to the Stars, The Glass Wall. Director: Gog, Battle Taxi, Donovan's Brain, Rider on a Dead Horse, Devil's Messenger, Brother on the Run, One Hour of Hell, Witches Brew, Blood of Dracula, I Was a Teenage Frankenstein, The Crawling Hand; Soul Brothers Die Hard, Monstroids. Writer-film editor, Hurray for Betty Boop (cartoon). Sound Effects editor on Katy Caterpillar (cartoon feature). Editor: Night Screams. Post-prod. spvr.: King Kung Fu. Co-director: Deadly Presence. Editor: Summer Seductions: Dir., ed. Gramma's Gold.
TELEVISION: Highway Patrol, Harbor Command, Men of Annapolis, I Led Three Lives, The Veil, Dragnet, 77 Sunset Strip, Maverick, Cheyenne, Bronco, Sugarfoot, Colt 45, Science Fiction Thea., Seahunt, Corliss Archer, Bonanza, Hallmark Hall of Fame, The Small Miracle, Hans Brinker, The Inventing of America (specials); What Will We Say to a Hungry World (telethon), They Search for Survival (special), Flipper (series). Documentaries: Atlantis, Legends, UFO Journals, UFO Syndrome, Legend of the Lochness Monster, China-Mao to Now, El-Papa—Journey to Tibet. Editor: Peace Corps' Partnership in Health. L.A. Dept. of Water & Power: Water You Can Trust; Olympic Comm. Your Olympic Legacy—AAF.

STRODE, WOODY: Actor. r.n. Woodrow Strode. b. 1914. Before W.W.II at UCLA. With Kenny Washington was one of first black players to integrate collegiate football. For 9 years after W.W.II was a professional wrestler. Worked for John Ford, Cecil B. DeMille, Henry Hathaway.
PICTURES: The Lion Hunters, (debut, 1951), The Gambler From Natchez, The Ten Commandments, Tarzan's Fight for Life, Pork Chop Hill, The Last Voyage, Sergeant Rutldge, Spartacus, The Sins of Rachel Cade, Two Rode Together, The Man Who Shot Liberty Valance, Genghis Khan, 7 Women, The Professionals, Shalako, Che!, The Revengers, The Gatling Gun, Winterhawk, Loaded Guns, The Black Stallion Returns, Vigilante, The Cotton Club.
TELEVISION: Breakout, Key West, A Gathering of Old Men.

STROLLER, LOUIS A.: Producer. b. Brooklyn, NY, April 3, 1942. e. Nicholas Coll. of Business Admin., BBA, 1963. Entered film business in 1963 doing a variety of jobs in local NY studios, and TV commercials. Unit manager on The Producers. Moved to L.A. in 1970s. First asst. dir. Charley, Take the Money and Run, Lovers and Other Strangers, They Might Be Giants, Man on a Swing, 92 in the Shade. Prod. mgr.: Mortadella, Sisters, Sweet Revenge, The Eyes of Laura Mars, Telefon. Assoc. prod.: Badlands, Carrie. In 1978 met prod. Martin Bregman beginning an assoc. with The Seduction of Joe Tynan.
PICTURES: Exec. prod. or prod.: Simon, The Four Seasons, Venom, Eddie Macon's Run, Scarface, Sweet Liberty, Real Men, A New Life, Sea of Love.
TELEVISION: Half a Lifetime (exec. prod.).

STRONG, JOHN: Producer, Director, Writer, Actor. b. New York, NY, Dec. 3. e. U. of Miami, Cornell U., B.S., architectural engineering. Began acting in small role in film Duel in the Sun; on Bdwy in Annie Get Your Gun and understudy for James Dean in Immoralist. Appeared in many radio and TV serials, regular on Captain Video and the Video Ranger, later under contract as actor to Universal and Warner Bros. Member, Writers Guild America West, Directors Guild of America, Producers Guild of America, Dramatists Guild. Pres., Cinevent Corp.
PICTURES: Perilous Journey (exec. prod., writer), Eddie & the Cruisers (sprv. prod.), Heart Like a Wheel (sprv. prod.), For Your Eyes Only (s.p.), The Earthling (prod.), The Mountain Men (actor, prod.), Savage Streets (prod.), Steel Justice (prod.), Knights of the City (prod.), Garbage Pail Kids (sprv. prod.), Cop (sprv. prod.), Wild Thing (sprv. prod.), Summer Heat (sprv. prod.), Teen Wolf II (sprv. prod.), Atlantic Entertainment (sprv. prod.), Show of Force (prod., s.p.), Prime Directive (prod., s.p.), Sinapore Sling (prod., s.p.), Willie Sutton Story (prod.), Bandit Queen (prod.).
TELEVISION: The John Strong Show (host, exec. prod.), The Nurse (special, writer), McCloud (prod., writer), The Thrill of the Fall (prod.), Search (prod., writer, 2nd unit dir.), Outer Limits (exec. chg. prod.), Name of the Game (exec. chg. prod.), I Spy (writer), Love American Style (writer), All in the Family (writer), Changes (prod., dir., writer), Charlie's Angels (writer), Hawaii Five O' (writer).

STROUD, DON: Actor. b. Honolulu, Hawaii, Sept. 1, 1937.
PICTURES: Madigan, Games, What's So Bad About Feeling Good?, Coogan's Bluff, Bloody Mama, Explosion, Von Richtofen and Brown, Angel Unchained, Hat Full of Rain, Murf the Surf, Sudden Death, Slaughter, Tick Tick, Tick, Joe Kidd, Scalaway, The Killer Inside Me, The Choirboys, The House by the Lake, The Buddy Holly Story, The Amityville Horror, The Night the Lights Went Out in Georgia, Search and Destroy, Striking Back, Sweet Sixteen, Armed and Dangerous, Licence to Kill, Down the Drain.
TELEVISION: Mike Hammer (series). Movie: Two to Tango.

STRUTHERS, SALLY: Actress. b. Portland, OR, July 28, 1948.
PICTURES: The Phynx, Charlotte, Five Easy Pieces, The Getaway.
TELEVISION: Summer Bros. Smothers Show, Tim Conway Comedy Hour, Series: All in the Family, Gloria, 9 to 5. Movies: The Great Houdinis, Aloha Means Goodbye, Hey, I'm Alive, Intimate Strangers, And Your Name is Jonah, A Gun in the House, A Deadly Silence.

STUBBS, IMOGEN: Actress. b. Newcastle-upon-Tyne, 1961. Brought up in West London on sailing barge on the Thames. Grandmother was playwright Esther McCracken. e. Exeter Coll. at Oxford U. in English. Joined Oxford U. Dramatic Society appearing in revues and at Edinburgh Festival in play called Poison. Trained for stage at Royal Acad. of Dramatic Art. Prof. stage debut in Cabaret and The Boyfriend, in Ipswich. Acted with Royal Shakespeare Co. in The Two Noble Kinsmen, The Rover, Richard II.
PICTURES: A Summer Story, Nanou, Erik the Viking.
TELEVISION: The Browning Version, Deadline, The Rainbow, Fellow Traveller.

STULBERG, GORDON: Executive. b. Toronto, Canada, Dec. 17, 1923. e. U. of Toronto, B.A., Cornell Law Sch., LL.B. Was assoc. & member, Pacht, Ross, Warne & Bernhard; ent. m.p. ind. as exec. asst. to v.p., Columbia Pictures Corp., 1956–60; v.p. & chief studio admin. off., 1960–67; pres. of Cinema Center Films (div. of CBS) 1967–71; pres. 20th Century-Fox, Sept. 1971–75; 1980, named pres. & chief operating officer, PolyGram Pictures. Member of NY, Calif. bars, Chairman, American Interactive Media (Polygram subsidiary).

STURGES, JOHN ELIOT: Director. b. Oak Park, IL, Jan. 3, 1910. e. Marin Jr. Coll. asst. in blueprint dept., RKO-Radio Pictures, 1932; art dept; asst. film ed.; prod. asst., David O. Selznick; film ed.; Captain, Air Corps, W.W.II; directed, edited, 45 documentaries, training films.
PICTURES: The Man Who Dared, Shadowed, Alias Mr. Twilight, For the Love of Rusty, Keeper of the Bees, Best Man Wins, Sign of the Ram, The Walking Hills, The Capture, Mystery Street, Right Cross, The Magnificent Yankee, Kind Lady, The People vs. O'Hara, The Girl in White, Jeopardy, Fast Company, Escape from Fort Bravo, Bad Day at Black Rock, Gunfight at the O.K. Corral, The Old Man and the Sea, Last Train from Gun Hill, Never So Few, The Magnificent Seven, By Love Possessed, Sergeants Three, A Girl Named Tamiko, The Great Escape, The Satan Bug, Hallelujah Trail, Hour of the Gun, Ice Station Zebra, Marooned, Joe Kidd, McQ, The Eagle Has Landed.

STURGIS, NORMAN: Director, Actor, Writer. b. Dallas, TX, 1922. Prod., Your Navy Sings, Evanston; TV dir. Space X, Theaterama, Plays Anthology, The Viewers, TV commercials, educational films and newsfilms.
TELEVISION: The Web, Gunsmoke, Twilight Zone, Alcoa Goodyear Theatre, Bat Masterson, The Untouchables.
PICTURES: Solid Gold Cadillac, Bernardine, Mardi Gras, Compulsion.

STYNE, JULE: Composer, Producer. r.n. Jules Stein. b. London, Eng., Dec. 31, 1905. To U.S. as a child; guest piano soloist with Chicago Symph. Orch. at 8; played with many dance bands; gen. mus. dir. Granada & Marbro Theat., Chicago; vocal coach, arranger, conductor & comp. for several m.p. studios; entertainment consult.
SONGS: I've Heard That Song Before, It's Magic, I'll Walk Alone, It's Been a Long, Long Time; Let It Snow, 3 Coins in the Fountain (Acad. Award in collab. Sammy Cahn, 1954), Make Someone Happy, Just in Time, The Party's Over, Small World, Everything's Coming Up Roses, People.
STAGE: High Button Shoes, Gentlemen Prefer Blondes, Two on the Aisle, Hazel Flagg, Sugar, Peter Pan, Bells Are Ringing, Gypsy, Funny Girl, Hallelujah Baby (Tony Award), Bar Mitzvah Boy.
PICTURES: Scores: Kid from Brooklyn, It Happened in Brooklyn, Romance on the High Seas, It's a Great Feeling, West Point Story, Meet Me After the Show, Living It Up, My Sister Eileen. Films of musicals: Bells Are Ringing, Gypsy, Funny Girl.

SUBOTSKY, MILTON: Writer, Producer. b. New York, NY, Sept. 27, 1921. Early career studying engineering. Ent. m.p. ind. 1938. Wrote, dir. and edited doc. & educational films. Wrote and prod. live TV programs 1941, TV film series Junior Science 1954. TV series: Classic Fairy Tales.
PICTURES: Rock, Rock, Rock; Jamboree, The Last Mile, in U.S. In England: City of the Dead, It's Trad Dad, Just for Fun, Dr. Terror's House of Horrors, Dr. Who and The Daleks, Daleks' Invasion Earth 2150 A.D., The Skull, The Psychopath, The Deadly Bees, The Terrornauts, They Came From Beyond Space, Torture Garden, Danger Route, The Birthday Party, Thank You All Very Much (Brit. title: A Touch of Love), Scream and Scream Again, The Mind of Mr. Soames, The House That Dripped Blood, I Monster, What Became of Jack and Jill, Tales From the Crypt, Asylum, Vault of Horror, And Now the Screaming Starts, Madhouse, From Beyond the Grave, The Beast Must Die, The Land That Time Forgot, At The Earth's Core, The Uncanny, Dominique, The Martian Chronicles, The Monster Club, Cat's Eye, Maximum Overdrive.

SUGAR, JOSEPH M.: Executive. b. New York, NY, June 4, 1922. e. NYU. Started with Republic Pictures 1938; after service, U.S. Army Air Force, went to Eagle Lion which was taken over by United Artists; 1953, U.A., N.Y., metropolitan district mgr.; 1959, Magna Pictures Corp., v.p. sls.; 1962, 20th Century-Fox, v.p. domestic distribution; 1967, Warner-7 Arts, exec. v.p.; 1968, pres., Cinerama Rel. Corp.; 1974, formed Joe Sugar, Inc.; 1976, joined A.I.P. as exec. v.p. worldwide sls. & pres., A.I.P. Distribution Co.—A.I.P. later became Filmways; 1983, Embassy Pictures, exec. v.p. dist; 1986, Joe Sugar, Inc. when Embassy sold to Coca Cola. Member Cinema Lodge, B'nai B'rith; A.F.I.; Motion Picture Pioneers, Variety Club.

SUGAR, LARRY: Executive. b. Phoenix, AZ, May 26, 1945. m. Bonnie Sugar. e. Cheshire Acad., 1962; CSUN, B.A., 1967; U. of Southern Calif., J.D., 1971. Writer and co-author, Calif. Primary Reading Program, 1967–68. Joined Warner Bros. as dir., legal and corp. affairs, 1971–74; 20th Century Fox legal staff, 1974–77; co-owner with Bonnie Sugar, Serendipity Prods., 1977–81; named pres., intl., Lorimar Prods. 1981–84; exec. v.p., distribution, CBS 1984–85; exec. v.p. worldwide distribution, Weintraub Entertainment Group 1987–89; formed Sugar Entertainment, chmn., 1989–present.
PICTURES: Exec. prod.: Slapstick, Steel Dawn, Options, Damned River, No Cause for Alarm, The Best (pre-prod.).

SUGARMAN, BURT: Producer. b. Beverly Hills, CA, Jan. 4. e. U. of Southern California. Chmn. & CEO, Giant Group, Ltd., diversified co. traded on NYSE. Heads Barris Industries Inc.
PICTURES: Kiss Me Goodbye, Extremities, Children of a Lesser God, Crimes of the Heart.
TELEVISION: Midnight Special, Switched on Symphony, The Mancini Generation, Johnny Mann's Stand Up and Cheer, etc.

SUHOSKY, BOB: Publicist. b. Philadelphia, PA, Nov. 23, 1928. Marine Corps 1946–57; 20th Century Fox Television, publicist, 1959, publicity director, 1964–70; pres. Bob Suhosky Assoc., public relations, 1971–77. Chairman, Suhosky & Hardiman Public Relations, 1977 to date. Wrote s.p. for Lone Star Girls (theatrical film) and Code R (TV).

SULLIVAN, BARRY: Actor. r.n. Patrick Barry. b. New York, NY, Aug. 29, 1912. e. NYU, Temple U. Usher in theatre.; buyer for dept. stores; N.Y. stage: The Man Who Came to Dinner, Brother Rat, Idiot's Delight, The Land is Bright, Caine Mutiny Court Martial, etc.
PICTURES: Woman of the Town, Lady in the Dark, Rainbow Island, Two Years Before the Mast, And Now Tomorrow, Duffy's Tavern, Three Guys Named Mike, Cause for Alarm, Grounds for Marriage, Life of Her Own, Nancy Goes to Rio, Inside Straight, Payment on Demand, Mr. Imperium, No Questions Asked, Unknown Man, Skirts Ahoy, Bad & the Beautiful, Jeopardy, Cry of the Hunted, China Venture, Loophole, Her 12 Men, Miami Story, Playgirl, Queen Bee, Texas Lady, Maverick Queen, Strategic Air Command, Purple Gang, Seven Ways from Sundown, Light in the Piazza, War Lords of Outer Space, Stage to Thunder Rock, Buckskin, Tell Them Willie Boy Is Here, Earthquake, The Human Factor, Oh, God!, Caravans.
TELEVISION: Night Gallery, Series: Man Called X (1955–56); Harbourmaster, The Tall Man, The Immortal, Road West, Movies: Once an Eagle, Rich Man, Poor Man—Book II, Johnny Belinda, Yuma.

SULLIVAN, J. CHRISTOPHER: Actor. b. Greenville, TX, Sept. 15, 1932. e. Prairie View A & M U.; Sorbonne (Paris); U. of Texas., Ph.D. Stage debut in The Sign in Sidney Brustein's Window. Also appeared in Hatful of Rain, Anna Lucasta, Ceremonies in Dark Old Men, Dark of the Moon, Take a Giant Step, Therese. First black to teach at any predominantly white university in the south as an instructor of speech and communications at U. of Texas, Austin, 1964. Winner NAACP Image Award 1986; best theatre actor, Anna Lucasta.
PICTURES: Night Call Nurses, The Venetian Affair, The Lost Man, Body Heat, Black Starlet, The Black Gestapo, The Happy Ending, D.C. Cab, Critters II, Arthur 2 On the Rocks, Presidio, L.A. Bounty.
TELEVISION: The White Shadow, Jeffersons, Good Times, One Day at a Time, General Hospital, Serpico, Starsky & Hutch, Death Flight, McClain's Law, Growing Pains, Hill Street Blues, Superior Court. Movies: Elvis and Me, Roots Christmas: The Gift, The Judge, Give Me My Child.

SULLIVAN, REV. PATRICK J., S.J., S.T.D.: Provost, Graduate Center at Tarrytown, Fordham U. b. New York, NY, March 25, 1920. e. Regis H.S.: Georgetown U., A.B., 1943; Woodstock Coll., M.A., 1944; Fordham U., 1945–47; S.T.L. Weston Coll., 1947–51; S.T.D. Gregorian U. (Rome), 1952–54. Prof. of Theology, Woodstock Coll., 1954–57; Consultor, Pontifical Commission for Social Communications.

SUNSHINE, MORTON: Honorary Executive Vice President, Variety Clubs Intl. special consultant; International executive director, Variety Clubs International, 1975–86. b. Brooklyn, NY, Sept. 20, 1915. B.S. in S.S., 1935; LL.B., 1938; J.S.D., 1939. Admitted to N.Y. Bar 1939. Federal Bar 1941. Practicing attorney, 1941–44; Federal investigator with U.S.C.S.C. 1944–45; business mgr., Independent Theatre Owners Assn. 1945–46; exec. dir. since 1946; member COMPO tax & legis. com., 1950; sp. rep. Org. of M.P. Ind. of City of N.Y., 1952–55; exec. coord. Tony Awards Amer. Theatre Wing, 1958–60, Sophie Tucker Golden Jubilee; ind. trib. to Jimmy Durante; Al Jolson; Will Rogers; A. Montague; Herman Robbins; S. H. Fabian; Rodgers-Hammerstein; Eric Johnston; Diamond Jubilee, Stagehands, 1962. Danny Thomas; indus. pub. rel. consultant; (William Morris Agency, Movielab, etc.) exec. coord. IFIDA Intl Film Awards Dinners; pres. cabinet, Natl Assn. of Theatre Owners, exec. dir., Variety Club of N.Y.; consultant to American Film Institute, 1973–75; exec. dir., Motion Picture Pioneers, 1970–75; Editor-Publisher, Independent Film Journal, 1947–75; Founder & 1st Chief Barker, Variety Club of the Palm Beaches, 1987–88.

SUNSHINE, ROBERT HOWARD: Publisher. b. Brooklyn, NY, Jan. 17, 1946. e. U. of Rhode Island; Brooklyn Law Sch., 1971. Admitted to NY State Bar, 1971. President of Pubsun Corp., owner of The Film Journal. Publisher of The Film Journal. Exec. dir., Theatre Equipment Association, 1979–present; exec. dir., Variety, The Children's Charity of New York, 1975–present; secretary and exec. dir. Foundation of the Motion Picture Pioneers, 1975–present; exec. dir., Natl. Assoc. of Theatre Owners of NY State, 1985–present; Producer of Variety Telethon, 1985–present; coordinator and producer, Show East convention.

SURTEES, BRUCE: Cinematographer. Son of cinematographer Robert L. Surtees.
PICTURES: The Beguiled, Play Misty for Me, Dirty Harry, The Great Northfield Minnesota Raid, High Plains Drifter, Blume in Love, Joe Kidd, Lenny (A.A. nomination), Leadbelly, Night Moves, The Outlaw Josey Wales, The Shootist, Three Warriors, Sparkle, Movie, Movie; Dreamer, Big Wednesday, Escape from Alcatraz, Ladies and Gentlemen, the Fabulous Stains, White Dog, Firefox, Inchon, Honkytonk Man, Bad Boys, Risky Business, Sudden Impact, Tightrope, Beverly Hills Cop, Pale Rider, Psycho III, Out of Bounds, Ratboy, License to Drive, Men Don't Leave.

SUSCHITZKY, PETER: Cinematographer. Spent long time in Latin America as documentatory cinematographer. Later made commercials in France, England, and U.S. First feature It Happened Here, 1962.
PICTURES: A Midsummer Night's Dream, Lisztomania, Leo the Last, Privilege, Charlie Bubbles, Entertaining Mr. Sloane, That'll Be the Day, The Rocky Horror Picture Show, Valentino, The Empire Strikes Back, Krull, Falling in Love, In Extremis, Dead Ringers.
TELEVISION: A Touch of Love, All Creatures Great and Small.

SUTHERLAND, DONALD: Actor. b. St. John, New Brunswick, Canada, July 17, 1934. Father of actor Kiefer Sutherland. e. U. of Toronto, B.A., 1956. At 14 became a radio announcer and disc jockey. Worked in a mine in Finland. Theatre includes: The Male Animal (debut), The Tempest (Hart House Theatre, U. of Toronto), Two years at London Acad. of Music and Dramatic Art. Spent a year and a half with the Perth Repertory Theatre in Scotland, then repertory at Nottingham, Chesterfield, Bromley and Sheffield.
STAGE: London stage debut: August for the People. On a Clear Day You Can See Canterbury, The Shewing Up of Blanco Posnet, The Spoon River Anthology, Lolita (Bdwy debut 1981).
PICTURES: Castle of the Living Dead, The World Ten Times Over, Dr. Terror's House of Horrors, Die, Die My Darling, Fanatic, The Bedford Incident, Promise Her Anything, The Dirty Dozen, Billion Dollar Brain, Oedipus the King, Interlude, Joanna, The Split, Start the Revolution Without Me, The Act of the Heart, M*A*S*H*, Kelly's Heroes, Little Murders, Alex in Wonderland, Klute, Johnny Got His Gun, F.T.A., Steelyard Blues, Lady Ice, Alien Thunder, Don't Look Now, S*P*Y*S*, The Day of the Locust, Murder on the Bridge, Casanova, The Eagle Has Landed, 1900, The Disappearance, Blood Relatives, Kentucky Fried Movie, National Lampoon's Animal House, Invasion of the Body Snatchers, Murder by Decree, The Great Train Robbery, Bear Island, A Man, A Woman and a Bank, Nothing Personal, Ordinary People, Gas, Eye of the Needle, Max Dugan Returns, Threshold, Crackers, Ordeal by Innocence, Heaven Help Us, Revolution, Wolf at the Door, The Rosary Murders, Bethune: The Making of a Hero, The Trouble With Spies, Apprentice to Murder, Lost Angels, A Dry White Season, Lock Up.
TELEVISION: (British) Gore Vidal's Marching to the Sea, Albee's The Death of Bessie Smith, Hamlet at Elsinore, The Saint, The Avengers, Gideon's Way, The Champions, The Winter of Our Discontent, Give Me Your Answer True.

SUTHERLAND, KIEFER: Actor. b. London, England, 1967. Son of actor Donald Sutherland and actress Shirley Douglas. Moved to Toronto at 10. m. actress Camelia (Kath) Sutherland. Debut with L.A. Odyssey Theater at 9 in Throne of Straw. Worked in local Toronto theater workshops. Film debut The Bay Boy (1984) for which he won Canadian equivalent of Acad. Award. TV debut: Trapped in Silence, 1986.
PICTURES: The Bay Boy, At Close Range, Crazy Moon, Stand By Me, The Lost Boys, The Killing Time, Bright Lights, Big City, 1969, Promised Land, Young Guns, Renegades, Flashback, Chicago Joe and the Showgirl.
TELEVISION: Trapped in Silence.

SUTTON, JAMES T.: Executive. b. California, Sept. 13. e. Columbia U. Film inspector, U.S. government; overseas m.p. service, WW II; co-owner, gen. mgr., Hal Davis Studios; hd. TV commercial div., Allan Sandler Films; Academy Art Pictures; pres., chmn. of bd., exec. prod., Royal Russian Studios, Inc., western hemisphere div.; pres. exec. prod. Gold Lion Prods., Inc.; pres. exec. prod. James T. Sutton-John L. Carpenter Prods.; pres., exec. dir., Airax Corp.; pres. of Skyax (div. of Airax).

SUZMAN, JANET: Actress. b. Johannesburg, South Africa, Feb. 9, 1939. e. Kingsmead Coll., U. of Witwaterstrand. London stage debut in The Comedy of Errors. Recent stage: Another Time. Director: Othello for Market Theatre and Channel 4 (TV).
PICTURES: A Day in the Death of Joe Egg, Nicholas and Alexandra (Acad. Award nom. 1971), The Black Windmill, Nijinsky, Priest of Love, The Draughtsman's Contract, And the Ship Sails On, A Dry White Season, Nuns on the Run.
TELEVISION: The Three Sisters, Hedda Gabler, The House on Garibaldi Street (movie). The Zany Adventures of Robin Hood (movie), Macbeth, Mountbatten—Last Viceroy of India (series), The Singing Detective (series), Clayhanger (series), The Miser, Revolutionary Witness, Saint Joan, Twelfth Night. Dir.: Othello.

SVENSON, BO: Actor. b. Goteborg, Sweden, Feb. 13, 1941. e. U. of Meiji, 1960–63; UCLA, 1970–74. U.S. Marine Corps 1959–65. Immigrated to U.S., 1958. Was professional race car driver and professional hockey player. Third degree black belt in Judo. Far East heavyweight div. champion, 1961.
PICTURES: Maurie (1973), The Great Waldo Pepper, Part 2: Walking Tall, The Breaking Point, Special Delivery, Final Chapter—Walking Tall, Our Man in Mecca, Son of the Sheik, Snow Beast, Gold of the Amazon, North Dallas Forty, Virus, Thunder Warrior, Deadly Impact, Wizards of the Lost Kingdom, The Manhunt, The Delta Force, Choke Canyon, Heartbreak Ridge, War Bus 2, Silent Hero, Justice Done, The Train, Soda Cracker, Curse II: The Bite, Captain Henkel. Running Combat.
TELEVISION: Series: Here Come the Brides (1968–70); Walking Tall.

SWAIM, BOB: Director, Writer. b. Evanston, IL, Nov. 2, 1943. e. Calif. State U, B.A.; L'Ecole Nationale de la Cinematographie, Paris, BTS 1969. American director who has often worked in France. Began career making shorts: Le Journal de M Bonnafous, Self Portrait of a Pornographer, Vive les Jacques. Received Cesar award French Acad. M.P., 1982; Chevalier des Arts et des Lettres 1985.
PICTURES: La Nuit de Saint-Germain-des-Pres (1977); La Balance; Half Moon Street; Masquerade.

SWALLOW, NORMAN: Producer. b. Manchester, Eng., Feb. 17, 1921. e. Manchester Grammar Sch., Keble Coll., Oxford U. British Army 1941–46; BBC as writer-prod. of doc., 1946; wrote 3 doc. films, 1948; TV as doc. prod., 1950; prods. include American Looks at Britain, with Howard K. Smith for CBS, Wilfred Pickles at Home series; orig. Speaking Personally series with appearance of people like Bertrand Russell; co-prod. TV coverage of Britain's general election, 1951; ed. prod. BBC monthly prog. Special Inquiry, 1952–56; World is Ours, 1954–56; study tour Middle East, India, Pakistan, Ceylon, 1956–57; writer, prod. Line of Defense, I Was a Stranger; asst. head films for BBC, 1957; writer-prod., On Target, 1959; apptd. chief asst. (doc. & gen.), BBC-TV, 1960; asst. editor, Panorama, BBC-TV, 1961. Joined Denis Mitchell films, May 1963; writer, prod., Pomp and Pageantry, The Right to Health, A Wedding on Saturday; The End of a Street; exec. prod., Report from Britain; writer, prod., Youth, British, Football; co-prod. This England. prod. A Railwayman for Me; co-prod. Ten Days That Shook the World. The Long Bridge; prod., dir.: The Three Happiest Years; exec. prod. Omnibus series, 1968–70. Writer, prod., dir. To Leningrad With Love; exec. prod. Omnibus Series, 1968–72. Writer, co-prod. Eisenstein. BBC-TV Head of Arts Features 1972–74. Prod.-dir. series A Lasting Joy. Exec. Prod. Granada TV since 1974 of The Christians, This England, Clouds of Glory. Winner Desmond Davis Award (UK) 1977. Exec. prod. A Conductor At Work, A Pianist At Work. Prod., A Lot of Happiness (1982 Emmy Award). Freelance producer/director since 1985. The Last Day for BBC-TV, 1986.

SWAYZE, JOHN CAMERON: Reporter, Commercial spokesman. b. Wichita, KS, Apr. 4, 1906. e. U. of Kansas; Anderson-Milton Dramatic Sch. Reporter and ed., Kansas City, MO Journal-Post; news dept. KMBC, Kansas City; head of news, NBC western network, Hollywood; NBC radio news reports, N.Y.; covered political conv. TV 1948–52; began News Caravan on NBC in 1949–56; panel mem. Who Said That, 1949–51; Watch the World on NBC-TV, 1948–50; Sightseeing With The Swayzes (with family) NBC-TV, 1953; news program, ABC, 1957. Host: Circle Theatre, NBC, and panel member, To Tell the Truth, CBS. Voted best news commentator, M.P. Daily TV Poll, 1951–55.
MEMBER: Lambs Club; National Press Club, Washington, Greenwich, Conn., CC.

SWAYZE, PATRICK: Actor, Dancer. b. Houston, TX. Aug. 18, 1954. Son of Patsy Swayze choreographer (Urban Cowboy). Began as dancer appearing in Disney on Parade on tour as Prince Charming. Songwriter and singer with 6 bands. Studied dance at Harkness and Joffrey Ballet Schs. On Bdwy. as dancer in Goodtime Charley, Grease.
PICTURES: Skatetown USA (debut, 1979), The Outsiders,

Uncommon Valor, Red Dawn, Grandview USA (also choreographer), Youngblood, Dirty Dancing (co-wrote song and sings She's Like the Wind), Steel Dawn, Tiger Warsaw, Road House, Next of Kin, Ghost.
TELEVISION: North and South: Books I and II, The New Season, Pigs vs. Freaks, The Comeback Kid, The Return of the Rebels, The Renegades.

SWERLING, JO: Writer. b. Russia, Apr. 8, 1897. Newspaper & mag. writer; author vaude. sketches; co-author plays, The Kibitzer, Guys and Dolls (Tony Award, 1951).
PICTURES: s.p., The Kibitzer, Guys and Dolls (co-author, orig. play); Platinum Blonde, Washington Merry-Go-Round, Dirigible, Man's Castle; collab. s.p., Whole Town's Talking; s.p., No Greater Glory, Pennies from Heaven, Double Wedding, Made for Each Other; collab. s.p., The Westerner; s.p., Confirm or Deny, Blood and Sand; collab. s.p., Pride of the Yankees; story, Lady Takes a Chance; s.p., Crash Dive, Lifeboat, Leave Her to Heaven, Thunder in the East.
TELEVISION: collab. The Lord Don't Play Favorites, NBC.

SWERLING, JO, JR.: Executive, Producer. b. Los Angeles, CA, June 18, 1931. e. UCLA, 1948–51; California Maritime Acad., 1951–54. Son of writer Jo Swerling. Active duty US Navy 1954–56. Joined Revue Prods./Universal Television, 1957–81, as prod. coordinator, assoc. prod., prod., assoc. exec. prod., exec. prod., writer, director, actor; currently sr. v.p. and supervising prod., The Cannell Studios.
TELEVISION: Series: Kraft Suspense Theater (prod.), Run for Your Life (prod., writer, Emmy, nom.), The Rockford Files (prod., writer), Cool Million (prod.), Alias Smith & Jones (assoc. exec. prod.), Baretta (prod., Emmy nom.), City of Angels (exec. prod.), Toma (exec. prod.), Jigsaw (prod.). The Bold Ones (prod., writer). Lawyers (prod., writer). Mini-series: Captains and the Kings (prod., Emmy nom.), Aspen (prod.), The Last Convertible (exec. prod., dir.). Movies: Producer: This Is the West That Was, The Whole World Is Watching, The Invasion of Johnson County, The Outsider, Do You Take This Stranger, Burn the Town Down, The Three-Thousand Mile Chase, How to Steal an Airplane. Supervising prod. Stephen J. Cannell Productions: The Greatest American Hero, Quest, The A-Team, Hardcastle & McCormick, Riptide, The Last Precinct, Hunter, Stingray, Wiseguy, 21 Jump Street, J.J. Starbuck, Sonny Spoon, The Rousters, Unsub, Booker, Top of the Hill.

SWIFT, DAVID: Producer, Director, Writer. b. Minneapolis, MN, 1919. Served with 8th Air Force in England, W.W.II. Entered m.p. ind. in Walt Disney animation dept. After service, comedy writer for radio. Later, starting in 1949, TV drama writer for Philco Playhouse, Studio One, Kraft Theatre, Omnibus. Created Mr. Peepers, Jamie. Writer-dir. Playhouse 90, Rifleman, Wagon Train, Climax, others. First feature film Pollyana (writer-dir.).
PICTURES: The Parent Trap, The Interns, Love Is a Ball, Under the Yum Yum Tree; pr.-dir.-writer, Good Neighbor Sam, How to Succeed in Business Without Really Trying, Candleshoe, Foolin' Around (co-s.p.).

SWIFT, LELA: Director.
TELEVISION: Studio One, Suspense, The Web, Justice, DuPont Show of the Week, Purex Specials For Women, (Emmy Award) Dark Shadows, Norman Corwin Presents, ABC Late Night 90 min. Specials, ABC Daytime 90 min. Play Break. Won three Emmy awards for best director of day-time serial: Ryan's Hope (1977, 1979, 1980). Monitor award for best director of a daytime serial: Ryan's Hope, 1985.

SWINK, ROBERT E.: Film editor, Director. b. Rocky Ford, CO, June 3, 1918. Joined editorial dept., RKO Radio, 1936; appt. film ed., 1941. In U.S. Army Signal Corps, 1944–45; supv. editor, Fox studio. Edited numerous productions.
PICTURES: Detective Story, Carrie, Roman Holiday, Desperate House, Friendly Persuasion, The Big Country, The Diary of Anne Frank, The Young Doctors, The Children's Hour, The Best Man, The Collector, How To Steal A Million, Flim Flam Man, Funny Girl, The Liberation of L. B. Jones, The Cowboys, Skyjacked, Lady Ice, Papillion, Three the Hard Way, Rooster Cogburn, Midway, Islands in the Stream, Gray Lady Down, The Boys From Brazil, The In-Laws, Going in Style, The Sphinx, Welcome Home.

SWISS, FERN: Executive. Executive director-financial planning for Motion Picture Group of Paramount Pictures. Joined co. in 1979 as financial analyst and advance to controller-TV in 1983. Named to present post, 1984.

SWIT, LORETTA: Actress. b. Passaic, NJ, Nov. 4, 1937. Stage debut in Any Wednesday. Toured in Mame for year. Arrived in Hollywood in 1969 and began TV career. Theatrical film debut in Stand Up and Be Counted, 1972.
PICTURES: Freebie and the Bean, Race with the Devil, S.O.B., Beer.
TELEVISION: M*A*S*H, (Emmy Awards, 1980, 1982), Gunsmoke, Mannix, Hawaii Five-O, Mission: Impossible, The Doctors, Cade's County. Films: Hostage Heart, Shirts/Skin, Coffeeville, Valentine, Mirrors, Mirror, Friendships, Secrets and Lies, Cagney & Lacey, (pilot as Cagney), Games Mother Never Taught You, The Walls Came Tumbling Down, First Affair, The Execution, Dreams of Gold, 14 Going on 30, My Dad Can't Be Crazy, Can He?

SWOPE, HERBERT BAYARD, JR.: Director, Producer, Commentator. b. New York, NY. e. Horace Mann Sch., Princeton U. U.S. Navy, 1941–46; rejoined CBS-TV as remote unit dir., 1946 directing many "firsts" in sportscasting; winner, Variety Show Management Award for sports coverage & citation by Amer. TV Society, 1948; joined NBC as dir., 1949; prod. dir., 1951; Lights Out, The Clock, The Black Robe, dir., Robt. Montgomery Presents; winner, 1952 Sylvania. TV Award Outstanding Achievement in Dir. Technique; became exec. prod., NBC-TV in charge of Wide, Wide, World; directed Helen Hayes, Billie Burke, Boris Karloff & Peter Loree in Arsenic & Old Lace on live TV, Climax. Film prod., 20th Century-Fox, Hilda Crane, Three Brave Men, True Story of Jesse James, The Bravados, The Fiend who Walked the West; 1960–62; exec. prod. 20th-Fox TV; Many Loves of Dobie Gillis, Five Fingers; dir. co-prod. on Broadway, Step On A Crack, Fragile Fox, Fair Game for Lovers. 1970–72 exec. at N.Y. Off-Track Betting Corp. 1973–74; v.p., Walter Reade Organization, Inc.; 1975–76 producer-host, This Was TV, Growth of a Giant; 1976 to present commentator, Swope's Scope, (radio—WPBR-AM)); Critic (TV); Critic's Views; Column: Now and Then (Palm Beach Pictorial).

SYKES, ERIC, O.B.E.: Scriptwriter, Comedian. b. Oldham, England, 1924. Early career actor; ent. TV industry, 1948; wrote first three series, BBC's Educating Archie and radio, TV comedy series for Frankie Howerd, Max Bygraves, Harry Secombe. BBC panel show member. Longterm contract ATV, 1956; own BBC series, 1958–78, Sykes Versus TV, The Frankie Howard Show; Sykes and a Big, Big Show, 1971, 1978 19th Year BBC-TV series. Toured extensively in Big Bad Mouse. 1977 Summer Show Sykes. 1978 Tour of Sykes to Rhodesia, Australia, Canada, The Plank, Rhubarb. Toured one man show, 1982. Time and Time Again, 1983; Run for Your Wife (London, Canada).
PICTURES: Watch Your Stern, Invasion Quartet, Village of Daughters, Kill or Cure, Heavens Above, The Bargee, One Way Pendulum, Those Magnificent Men and Their Flying Machines, Rotten to the Core, The Liquidator, Spy With The Cold Nose. Dir. s.p. The Plank, Shalako, The Monte Carlo Rally, Theatre of Blood.
TELEVISION: Varying specials, remade The Plank, If You Go Down to the Woods Today, It's Your Move, Mr. H is Late, Rhubarb.

SYLBERT, ANTHEA: Executive. b. New York, NY, Oct. 6, 1939. e. Barnard Coll., B.A.; Parsons Sch. of Design, M.A. Early career in costume design with range of Bdwy. (The Real Thing), off-Bdwy. and m.p. credits (Rosemary's Baby, F.I.S.T., Shampoo, The Fortune, A New Leaf, The Heartbreak Kid. Two A.A. nominations for creative costume designs for Julia and Chinatown. Joined Warner Bros. in October, 1977, as v.p., special projects, acting as liaison between creative executives, production dept., and creative talent producing films for company. In October, 1978, named v.p., production (projects included One Trick Pony, Personal Best, etc.). In March, 1980 appointed v.p.—production, for United Artists, working on Stab, Jinx, etc. For Warner Bros.: Swing Shift, Protocol, Wildcats.

SYMS, SYLVIA: Actress. b. London, Dec. 3, 1934. e. Convent and Grammar Sch. Film debut, 1955, My Teenage Daughter.
PICTURES: No Time For Tears, Birthday Present, Woman In A Dressing Gown, Ice Cold in Alex, The Devil's Disciple, Moonraker, Bachelor of Hearts, No Trees in the Street, Ferry to Hong Kong, Expresso Bongo, Conspiracy of Hearts, The World of Suzie Wong, Flame in the Streets, Victim, Quare Fellow, Punch & Judy Man, The World Ten Times Over, East of Sudan, The Eliminator, Operation Crossbow, The Big Job, Hostile Witness, The Marauders, The White Cold, Danger Route, Run Wild, Run Free, The Desperados, The Tamarind Seed, Give Us This Day, There Goes the Bride, Absolute Beginners, A Chorus of Disapproval. Shirley Valentine.
TELEVISION: The Human Jungle (series), Something to Declare, The Saint (series), The Baron (series), Bat Out of Hell, Department in Terror, Friends and Romans, Strange Report, Half-hour Story, The Root of All Evil, The Bridesmaid, Clutterbuck, Movie Quiz, My Good Woman, Looks Familiar, Love and Marriage, The Truth About Verity, I'm Bob, He's Dickie, Blankety Blank, The Story of Nancy Astor, Give Us a Clue, Sykes, Crown Court, A Murder Is Announced, Murder at Lynch Cross, Rockcliffes Follies, Dr. Who, Countdown.

SZABO, ISTVAN: Director. b. Budapest, Hungary, Feb. 18, 1938. e. Academy of Theatre and Film Art, Budapest, 1961. Debut Koncert (short, diploma film) 1961.
PICTURES: Variations on a Theme (short), You (short), The Age of Daydreaming, Father, Piety (short), Love Film Budapest, Why I Love It (series of shorts), 25 Fireman's

Street, Premiere, Budapest Tales, City Map (short), Confidence (Silver Bear, Berlin Festival), The Green Bird, Mephisto (Best screenplay, Cannes Festival; Hungarian Film Critics Award; Academy Award, Best Foreign Film, 1982), Colonel Redl, Hanussen (dir., co-s.p.), Opera Europa, Tusztortenet (Stand Off) (actor only).

SZWARC, JEANNOT: Director. b. Paris, France, Nov. 21, 1939.
PICTURES: Extreme Close-Up; Bug; Jaws II; Somewhere in Time; Enigma; Santa Claus—The Movie; Supergirl, Honor Bound.
TELEVISION: Ironside; To Catch a Thief; Kojak; Columbo; Night Gallery; Crime Club; True Life Stories; Twilight Zone (1986). Movies: Night Terror, You'll Never See Me Again, The Small Miracle, Murders in the Rue Morgue.

T

TAFFNER DONALD L.: Executive. b. New York, NY. e. St. Johns U. William Morris Agency, 1950–59; Paramount Pictures. 1959–63; D. L. Taffner Ltd., 1963-present.
TELEVISION: Prod.: Three's Company, Too Close For Comfort.

TAKEI, GEORGE: Actor. b. Los Angeles, CA, April 20. e. U. of California, UCLA. Professional debut in Playhouse 90 production while training at Desilu Workshop in Hollywood. Gained fame as Sulu in Star Trek TV series. Co-author of novel, Mirror Friend, Mirror Foe.
PICTURES: Ice Palace, A Majority of One, Hell to Eternity, An American Dream, Walk, Don't Run, The Green Berets, Star Trek—The Motion Picture, Star Trek II: The Wrath of Khan, Star Trek III: The Search for Spock, Star Trek IV: The Voyage Home, Star Trek V: The FInal Frontier, Return From the River Kwai.
TELEVISION: Perry Mason, Alcoa Premiere, Mr. Novak, The Wackiest Ship in the Army, I Spy, Magnum PI, Trapper John M.D., Miami Vice, Murder She Wrote, McGyver.

TALBOT, LYLE: Actor. r.n. Lysle Hollywood. b. Pittsburgh, PA, Feb. 8, 1904. In Army Air Corps, W.W.II. First screen appearance in Vitaphone short; then in Love Is A Racket, 1932.
PICTURES: Up in Arms, Sensations of 1945, One Body Too Many, Dixie Jamboree, Gambler's Choice, Strange Impersonation, Vicious Circle, Mutineers, Sky Dragon, The Jackpot, Sea Tiger, Down Among the Sheltering Palms, Star of Texas, Capt. Kidd & the Slave Girl, Tobor the Great, Steel Cage, There's No Business Like Show Business, Jail Busters, Sudden Danger.
TELEVISION: Newhart (1987).
MEMBER: Masonic Lodge (Shriner), Lambs, Masquers, American Legion.

TAMBLYN, RUSS: Actor b. Los Angeles, CA, Dec. 30, 1935. e. No. Hollywood H.S. West Coast radio shows; on stage with little theatre group; song-and-dance act in Los Angeles clubs, veterans hospitals.
PICTURES: Boy with Green Hair, Reign of Terror, Samson and Delilah, Deadly Is the Female, Kid from Cleveland, Captain Carey, U.S.A., Father of the Bride, As Young As You Feel, Father's Little Dividend, Winning Team, Retreat Hell, Take the High Ground, Seven Brides for Seven Brothers, Many Rivers to Cross, Hit the Deck, Last Hunt, Fastest Gun Alive, Young Guns, Don't Go Near the Water, Peyton Place, High School Confidential, Tom Thumb, Cimarron, West Side Story, Wonderful World of the Brothers Grimm, The Haunting, Long Ships, Son of Gunfighter, The Last Movie, Aftershock, Commando Squad, Cyclone, Necromancer, B.O.R.N., Phantom Empire, Demon Sword.

TANDY, JESSICA: Actress. b. London, Eng., June 7, 1909. m. actor-writer-dir. Hume Cronyn. On London, N.Y. stage, 1928–42.
THEATRE: N.Y. stage. A Streetcar Named Desire (Tony Award, 1948), Hilda Crane, The Four Poster, Coward In Two Keys; The Way of the World, Eve and A Midsummer Night's Dream at Stratford Festival 1976, Canada; limited tours of Many Faces of Love 1974–76 and for CBC, Canada 1977; performed in The Gin Game, Long Wharf Thea., CT, Long Day's Journey Into Night, (Canada). The Gin Game, (Pulitzer Prize winning play, Tony Award, 1978), and toured with it in U.S., Toronto, London and U.S.S.R., 1979, and Long Day's Journey Into Night, Foxfire, (Stratford Festival 1980, Rose Cort, N.Y.); Foxfire, (Guthrie Theatre, Minneapolis 1981 and N.Y.); The Glass Menagerie, (N.Y.), Salonika, The Petition.
PICTURES: The Seventh Cross, Dragonwyck, The Green Years, Forever Amber, A Woman's Vengeance, September Affair, The Desert Fox, A Light In The Forest, Adventures of a Young Man, Butley, The Birds, Honky Tonk Freeway, Still of the Night, The World According to Garp, Best Friends, The Bostonians, Cocoon, Batteries Not Included, The House on Carroll Street, Cocoon: The Return, Driving Miss Daisy.
TELEVISION: Portrait of a Madonna (1948), The Marriage (summer comedy series with Hume Cronyn, 1954), The Fourposter, The Fallen Idol, Moon and the Sixpence, Tennessee Williams's Faces of Live, The Gin Game, Foxfire.

TANEN, NED: Executive. b. Los Angeles, CA, 1931. e. UCLA, law degree. Joined MCA, Inc. 1954; Appt. v.p. in 1968. Brought Uni Records, since absorbed by MCA Records, to best-seller status with such artists as Neil Diamond, Elton John, Olivia Newton-John. First became active in theatrical film prod. in 1972. In 1975 began overseeing feature prod. for Universal. In 1976 named pres. of Universal Theatrical Motion Pictures, established as div. of Universal City Studios. Left in 1982 to become independent producer. 1985, joined Paramount Pictures as pres. of Motion Picture Group. Resigned 1988 to continue as sr. advisor at Paramount.

TANKERSLEY, ROBERT K.: Executive. b. Decatur, IL, July 31, 1927. In U.S. Navy, 1945–46; Marine Corps, 1949–55. With Natl. Theatre Supply as salesman in Denver 13 yrs. 1959–87, pres. Western Service & Supply, Denver, theatre equip. co.; 1960–87, mgr., Tankersley Enterprises theatre equip. Also was CEO of Theatre Operators, Inc., Bozeman, Mont. Member: Theatre Equipment Assn. (past pres.), National NATO Presidents Advisory Council; Rocky Mt. Motion Picture Assn. (past pres.), SMPTE, Motion Picture Pioneers, past chief barker, Variety Club Tent #37. Colorado, Wyoming NATO (past pres.) chmn.-elect Exhibitors West.

TANNER, WINSTON R.: Exhibitor. b. Appomattox, VA, Feb. 10, 1905. e. U. of Richmond. Entered m.p. ind., 1939 as asst. to owner, mgr. Free State Victoria Theatres, Kenbridge, Va.; dir. partner Kendig-Tanner Theatres, 1942; bought partner's interest in 1957; operator Tanner Theatres 7 houses, in Va.; operates Winston R. Tanner booking-buying service.

TAPLIN, JONATHAN: Producer. b. Cleveland, OH, July 18, 1947. e. Princeton U.
PICTURES: Mean Streets, The Last Waltz, Carny (exec. prod.), Grandview U.S.A. (co-exec. prod.), Under Fire, Baby, My Science Project.
TELEVISION: Six episodes of Shelly Duvall's Faerie Tale Theatre.

TAPS, JONIE: Producer. Executive. Columbia Studio.
PICTURES: Jolson Story, Down to Earth, Thrill of Brazil. Produced: When You're Smiling, Sunny Side of Street, Sound Off, Rainbow Round My Shoulder, All Ashore, Cruisin' Down the River, Drive a Crooked Road, Three for the Show, Bring Your Smile Along, He Laughed Last, Shadow on the Window.
MEMBER: Friars Club, Hillcrest Country Club.

TARADASH, DANIEL: Writer, Director. b. Louisville, KY, Jan. 29, 1913. e. Harvard Coll., B.A., 1933; Harvard Law Sch., LL.B., 1936. Passed NY Bar, 1937; won nationwide playwriting contest, 1938; U.S. Army W.W.II. Pres. Screen Writers Branch, WGA, 1955–56; v.p., Writers Guild of America, West 1956–59; mem. Writers Guild Council, 1954–65; mem., bd. of govnrs. Motion Picture Acad. Arts & Sciences, 1964–74, v.p. 1968–70 and pres. 1970–73. Trustee, Producers-Writers Guild Pension plan 1960–73. chmn., 1965. Mem. Bd. of Trustees of American Film Institute 1967–69. WGA's Valentine Davies Award, 1971. Pres., Academy M.P. Arts & Sciences, 1970–73, mem. bd. trustees, Entertainment Hall of Fame Foundation. Mem., Public Media General Programs panel for the National Foundation for the Arts, Pres. Writers Guild of America, West, 1977–79. Natl. chmn., Writers Guild of America, 1979–81. WGA's Morgan Cox Award, 1988.
PICTURES: Collab. s.p. Golden Boy, A Little Bit of Heaven, Knock on Any Door; s.p.: Rancho Notorious, Don't Bother to Knock, From Here to Eternity (Acad. Award 1953); Desiree; Storm Center (dir., co-story, s.p.), Picnic, Bell Book and Candle The Saboteur Code Name—Morituri; Hawaii (co-s.p.); Castle Keep (co-s.p.). Doctors' Wives; The Other Side of Midnight (co-s.p.), Polonaise (s.p.).

TARNOFF, JOHN B.: Producer. b. New York, NY, Mar. 3, 1952. e. UCLA, motion pictures & TV, 1973–74; Amherst Coll., B.A., 1969–73. Named field exec. with Taylor-Laughlin Distribution (company arm of Billy Jack Enterprises) 1974; left in 1975 to be literary agent with Bart/Levy, Inc.; later with Michael Levy & Associates, Paul Kohner/Michael Levy Agency; Headed TV dept., Kohner/Levy, 1979. Joined MGM as production exec., 1979; v.p., development, 1979–80; sr. v.p. production & devel., 1981–82; exec. v.p., Kings Road Prods., 1983–84; v.p., prod., Orion Pictures Corp., 1985; exec. prod., Out of Bounds, Columbia Pictures, 1986; v.p., prod., De Laurentiis Entertainment Group, 1987. Head of production, DeLaurentiis Entertainment, Australia, 1987–.

TARSES, JAY: Producer, Writer, Actor. b. Baltimore, MD, July 3, 1939. e. U. of Washington, degree in theater. Wrote and acted with little-theater co. in Pittsburgh, drove a truck in NY for Allen Funt's Candid Camera and worked in advertising and promotion for Armstrong Cork Co. in Lancaster, PA where met Tom Patchett. Formed Patchett and Tarses, stand-up comedy team that played coffeehouse circuit in the late 1960s. Later twosome became TV writing team and joined writing staff of Carol Burnett Show winning Emmy in 1972.

TELEVISION: As actor: Series: Make Your Own Kind of Music, Open All Night, The Days and Nights of Molly Dodd. Specials: Arthur Godfrey's Portable Electric Medicine Show, The Duck Factory.

With Tom Patchett: The Bob Newhart Show (exec. prod., writer), The Tony Randell Show (creator, exec. prod., writer), We've Got Each Other (creator, exec. prod.), Mary (prod.), Open All Night (creator, prod., writer), Buffalo Bill (exec. prod., writer). Solo: The Days and Nights of Molly Dodd (creator, prod., writer), The "Slap" Maxwell Story (creator, prod., writer). Pilots: The Chopped Liver Brothers (exec. prod., writer), The Faculty (exec. prod., dir., writer).

PICTURES: Co-s.p. with Patchett: Up the Academy, The Great Muppet Caper, The Muppets Take Manhattan.

TARTIKOFF, BRANDON: Executive. b. New York, NY, Jan. 13, 1949. e. Yale U. Started TV career in 1971 in promo. dept. of ABC affiliates in New Haven, CT Joined promo. staff at ABC affiliate in Chicago. In 1976 went to New York, with ABC-TV as mgr., dramatic development; moved to NBC Entertainment in Sept., 1977, as dir., comedy programs. In 1978 appt. v.p., programs, West Coast, NBC Entertainment; 1980, named pres. of that division. Pres. NBC Entertainment since 1980. Also heads own prod. co., NBC Productions.

PICTURES: Square Dance, Satisfaction.

TASCO, RAI: Actor, Announcer. r.n. Ridgeway Tasco. b. Boston, MA, Aug. 12, 1917. e. Boston English High. 1935. U.S. Army, 1935–45. Grad., Cambridge Sch. of Radio & TV, New York, 1950. Appeared in most TV and radio dramatic shows, and stage plays, New York and Hollywood; Broadway stage & films; dramatic instructor.

TATUM, DONN B.: Executive. b. Los Angeles, CA, January 9, 1913. e. Stanford U., Oxford U. Director, retired chmn. & chief exec., Walt Disney Co. 1943, lawyer, RCA, NBC, and ABC. 1949, v.p., counsel, Dir. of Don Lee Companies. Gen. Mgr., KABC-TV, dir. of Television, Western Division ABC. 1956, prod. business mgr. for Walt Disney Productions; exec. v.p. Disneyland, v.p. TV sales; v.p. and adm. asst. to pres. and exec. comm.; exec. v.p.; president; chmn; now mem. bd. of Dir.; dir. of Western Digital Corp; dir. and chmn. John Tracy Clinic; dir. & v.p. Community Building Funds of So. Calif.; trustee of Calif. Institute of the Arts, the Salk Institute, the St. John's Hospital Foundation; overseer, Huntington Library.

TAVERNIER, BERTRAND: Director, Writer. b. Lyon, France, April 25, 1941. After 2 yrs. of law study, quit to become film critic for Cahiers du Cinema and Cinema 60. Asst. to dir. Jean-Pierre Melville on Leon Morin, Priest (1961), also worked as film publicist. Wrote film scripts and a book on the Western and a history of American cinema. Partner for 6 yrs. with Pierre Rissient in film promotion company, during which time he studied all aspects of film-making. 1963: directed episode of Les Baisers. Pres., Lumiere Inst., Lyon.

PICTURES: The Clockmaker, Let Joy Reign Supreme (dir., co-s.p.), The Judge and the Assassin, Spoiled Children, Deathwatch, A Week's Vacation, Clean Slate, Mississippi Blues (co-dir. with Robert Parusa), A Sunday in the Country, 'Round Midnight, Beatrice, Season of Fear, Life and Nothing But.

TELEVISION: Phillippe Soupault, October Country (co-dir. with Robert Parrish), Lyon, le regard interieur.

TAVIANI, PAOLO and VITTORIO: Directors, Writers. b. San Miniato, Pisa, Italy, (Paolo: Nov. 8, 1931; Vittorio: Sept. 20, 1929); e. Univ. of Pisa (Paolo: liberal arts; Vittorio: law). The two brothers always work in collaboration from script preparation through shooting and editing. 1950: With Valentino Orsini ran cine-club at Pisa. 1954: In collab. with Caesare Zavattini directed short about Nazi massacre at San Miniato. 1954–59: with Orsini made series of short documentaries (Curatorne e Montanara; Carlo Pisacane; Ville della Brianza; Lavatori della pietra; Pitori in cita; I Pazzi della domenica; Moravia, Cabunara). Worked as assistant to Rosellini, Luciano Emmer and Raymond Pellegrini. 1960: collaborated on an episode of Italy Is Not a Poor Country.

FEATURE FILMS (all by both): A Man to Burn (1962); Matrimonial Outlaws, The Subversives, Under the Sign of Scorpio, Saint Michael Had a Rooster, Allonsanfan, Padre Padrone (1977, Best Film and International Critics Prize, Cannes Festival); The Meadow, The Night of the Shooting Stars (1981–Best Director Award, Natl. Society of Film Critics and Special Jury Prize, Cannes); Kaos, Good Morning, Babylon.

TAYLOR, ANTHONY: Producer. b. Los Angeles, CA, Feb. 5, 1931. e. U. of Southern California. U.S.A.F. 1954–56; mem. Chicago Board of Trade, 1962–65; columnist, L.A. Herald Examiner, 1964–65; also mem. N.Y. Mercantile Exchange, Chicago Mercantile Exchange; partner Commodity Futures Co., Westwood, CA; 1966, produced feature Incubus; 1966, award for motion picture excellence, San Francisco Int'l Film Festival; 1967, award Incubus, Cork Int'l Film Festival, Ireland; 1968: prod. feature, Possession.

TAYLOR, DELORES: Actress, Writer. b. Winner, SD. e. U. of South Dakota, studying commercial art. m. Tom Laughlin. First TV experience was heading art dept. at RCA wholesale center in Milwaukee. Made feature film debut as actress in Billy Jack in 1971. Wrote s.p. with husband for that and the sequel, The Trial of Billy Jack, under pseudonym Teresa Christina.

PICTURES: Billy Jack, The Trial of Billy Jack.

TAYLOR, DON: Actor, Director. b. Freeport, PA, Dec. 13, 1920. e. Pennsylvania State U. Appeared in Army Air Corps' Winged Victory on stage & screen; author short stories, screenplays, one-act plays, TV shows.

PICTURES: Actor: Girl Crazy, Naked City, For the Love of Mary, Battleground, Father of the Bride, Father's Little Dividend, Submarine Command, Flying Leathernecks, Blue Veil, Japanese War Bride, Stalag 17, The Girls of Pleasure Island, Destination Gobi, Johnny Dark, I'll Cry Tomorrow, Bold and the Brave. Director: Jack of Diamonds, Five Man Army, Escape from The Planet of the Apes, Tom Sawyer, Echoes Of A Summer, The Great Scout and Cathouse Thursday, The Island of Dr. Moreau, Damien-Omen II, The Final Countdown.

TELEVISION: Director: He's Not Your Son, Circle of Children, Broken Promise, Red Flag, Drop Out Father, September Gun, My Wicked Wicked Ways, Secret Weapons, Going for the Gold, Classified Cove, Ghost of a Chance, The Diamond Trap.

TAYLOR, ELIZABETH: Actress. b. London, Eng., Feb. 27, 1932. e. Bryon House, London. When 3 years old danced before Princess Elizabeth, Margaret Rose. Came to U.S. on outbreak W.W.II. Author: Elizabeth Takes Off (1988).

PICTURES: There's One Born Every Minute (debut, 1942), Lassie Come Home, Jane Eyre, National Velvet, Life with Father, Cynthia, Courage of Lassie, Little Women, White Cliffs of Dover, Date With Judy, Conspirator, Big Hangover, Father of the Bride, Father's Little Dividend, Love Is Better Than Ever, A Place in the Sun, Ivanhoe, The Girl Who Had Everything, Rhapsody, Elephant Walk, Beau Brummell, Last Time I Saw Paris, Giant, Raintree Country, Suddenly, Last Summer, Butterfield 8, Cleopatra, The V.I.P.'s, The Night of the Iguana, Who's Afraid of Virginia Woolf, The Taming of the Shrew, The Sandpiper, Doctor Faustus, The Comedians, Reflections In A Golden Eye, Boom!, Secret Ceremony, The Only Game in Town, X, Y, and Zee, Hammersmith Is Out, Night Watch, Ash Wednesday, That's Entertainment!, The Driver's Seat, The Blue Bird, A Little Night Music, The Mirror Crack'd, Young Toscanini.

TELEVISION: Elizabeth Taylor in London (1963), Here's Lucy (1970 with Richard Burton), General Hospital (1981), All My Children (1983), America's All-Star Salute to Elizabeth Taylor. Movies: Divorce His, Divorce Hers, Victory at Entebbe, Repeat Performance, Between Friends, Malice in Wonderland, There Must Be a Pony, Poker Alice, North and South, Sweet Bird of Youth.

TAYLOR, MICHAEL: Executive. b. New York, NY, March 28. Joined United Artists in 1973 as trainee. Named asst. to v.p. in chg. of production, 1975. Appointed exec. in chg. of production in London, working in acquisition and production of such pictures as The Spy Who Loved Me, Valentino, The Pink Panther Strikes Again, etc. Left U.A. to form Taylor/Wigutow Productions in 1977. Produced Last Embrace, The Pursuit of D. B. Cooper. In 1982 joined Orion Pictures as exec. asst. to pres; made corporate v.p., 1984.

TAYLOR, RENEE: Actress, Writer. b. March 19, 1945. Wife of actor Joseph Bologna, with whom she collaborates in writing. Their Bdwy. plays include Lovers and Other Strangers.

PICTURES: Actress: The Last of the Red Hot Lovers, The Errand Boys, The Detective, The Producers, A New Leaf, Lovers and Other Strangers (also s.p.), Made for Each Other (also s.p.), Lovesick, It Had to Be You (also co-dir., co-s.p.), That's Adequate.

TELEVISION: Writer: Acts of Love and Other Comedies (Emmy), Paradise, Calucci's Department, The American Dream Machine, etc.

TAYLOR, ROD: Actor. b. Sydney, Australia, Jan. 11, 1930. e. East Sydney Fine Arts Coll. Started out as artist then turned to acting on stage. After co-starring in film Long John Silver, to Hollywood in 1954. Formed own company, Rodler, Inc., for TV-film production.

PICTURES: Top Gun, The Virgin Queen, Catered Affair, Giant, King of the Coral Sea, The Rack, World Without End, Hell on Frisco Bay, Raintree County, Separate Tables, Step Down to Terror, Ask Any Girl, The Time Machine, The V.I.P.'s, The Birds, Sunday in New York, Young Cassidy, Seven Seas to Calais, A Gathering of Eagles, 36 Hours, Fate is the Hunter, Do Not Disturb, The Glass Bottom Boat, Hotel, The Liquidator, Chuka (also prod.), Dark of the Sun, High Commissioner, The Hell with Heroes, Darker Than Amber, The Man Who Had Power Over Women, Zabriskie Point, The Train Robbers, Trader Horn, The Deadly Trackers, A Time To Die, On the Run.

TELEVISION: Movies: Powerkeg, Family Flight, Cry of the

Innocent, Jacqueline Bouvier Kennedy, Charles and Diana: A Royal Love Story. Series: Hong Kong (1960–63), Bearcats, Masquerade. Pilots: The Oregon Trail, Outlaws, Falcon Crest.

TAYLOR, RONNIE: Director of Photography. b. London, England, 1924. Ent. m.p. ind. 1941 at Gainsborough Studios.
PICTURES: Tommy, The Silent Flute, The Reef, Circle of Iron, Savage Harvest, Gandhi, High Road to China, The Hound of the Baskervilles, The Champions, Master of the Game (UK shoot), A Chorus Line, Foreign Body, Cry Freedom, Opera (Italy), The Experts, Sea of Love.

TAYLOR, JOHN RUSSELL: Writer, Critic. b. Dover, England, June 19, 1935. e. Cambridge U., B.A., 1956. Editor: Times Educational Supplement, London, 1959–60; film critic, The Times, London, 1962–73; art critic, 1978–; editor, Films and Filming, 1983–; prof., division of Cinema, USC, 1972–78. Member: London Film and TV Press Guild, London Critics Circle, NY Society of Cinematologists.
BOOKS: Joseph L. Mankiewicz: An Index; The Angry Theatre; Anatomy of a Television Play; Cinema Eye, Cinema Ear; Shakespeare: A Celebration (cont.); New English Dramatists 8 (ed. & intr.); The Hollywood Musical; The Second Wave: Hollywood Dramatists for the 70s; Masterworks of the British Cinema; Directors and Directions: Peter Shaffer; Hitch; Cukor's Hollywood; Impressionism; Strangers in Paradise; Ingrid Bergman; Alec Guinness: A Celebration; Vivien Leigh; Hollywood 1940s; Portraits of the British Cinema.

TAYLOR-YOUNG, LEIGH: Actress. b. Washington, DC, Jan. 25, 1945. e. Northwestern U. Off-Bdwy debut Catastrophe (1983). Also on stage with New Theatre for Now (L.A. 1984).
PICTURES: I Love You, Alice B. Toklas, The Big Bounce, The Adventurers, The Buttercup Chain, The Horseman, The Gang That Couldn't Shoot Straight, Soylent Green, Can't Stop the Music, Looker, Secret Admirer, Jagged Edge, For Better or For Worse, Accidents.
TELEVISION: Series: Peyton Place, The Devlin Connection, The Hamptons, Houston Knights. Movies: Marathon, Napoleon and Josephine: A Love Story, Perry Mason: The Case of the Sinister Spirit, Who Gets the Friends.

TEAGUE, LEWIS: Director. b. 1941. e. NYU.
PICTURES: Dirty O'Neil (co-dir.); Lady in Red (also editor); Alligator; Fighting Back; Cujo; Cat's Eye; Jewel of the Nile.
TELEVISION: Alfred Hitchcock Presents; Daredevils, Shannon's Deal.

TEITELBAUM, PEDRO: Executive. b. Porto Alegre, Rio Grande Do Sul, Brazil, Nov. 21, 1922. e. Colegio Uniao, Brazil, 1942, C.P.A.; Univ. of Porto Alegre, Brazil, 1945, economics & business admin. 1939; Columbia Pictures; 1943, Warner Brothers; 1958, Latin-American supervisor for Republic Pictures; 1957, producer, distributor, exhibitor in Brazil; 1968, area supervisor for United Artists; 1973, v.p. intl. sales; 1975, v.p. international sales & distribution; 1976, sr. v.p. and foreign manager. In Jan., 1977, joined CIC as sr. exec. v.p. Named pres., July, 1977.

TELLER, IRA Executive, b. New York, NY, July 3, 1940. e. City Coll. of New York, & 1957–61; NYU Graduate Sch. of Arts, 1961–62. Publicist, Pressbook Dept., 20th Century Fox., 1961–62; asst. to adv. mgr., Embassy Pictures Corp., 1962–63; asst. adv. mgr., Columbia Pictures Corp., 1963; adv. mgr., Columbia Pictures Corp., 1964, 1964–65; asst. to chmn. of bd., Diener, Hauser, Greenthal Agy., 1966; adv. mgr., 20th Century-Fox, 1966–67; 1967, adv. dir. 20th Cent.-Fox.; dir. of adv., Nat'l General Pictures Corp., 1969; eastern dir., adv.-pub., 1972; national dir., adv-pub., 1973; Bryanston Distributors, Inc. v.p. adv.-pub., 1974; Cine Artists Pictures Corp. v.p. adv-pub., 1975; Lorimar Productions, v.p., adv.-marketing, 1976–77. 1977-present, pres. Ira Teller and Company, Inc.

TEMPLE (BLACK), SHIRLEY JANE: Actress, Diplomat. b. Santa Monica, CA, April 23, 1928. In 1932 screen debut, Red Haired Alibi. In 1933 To the Last Man; then leading figure in Baby Burlesque series educational shorts until Stand Up and Cheer, 1934, which resulted in career as child and teen star. Voted one of ten best Money-Making Stars in Motion Picture Herald-Fame Poll, 1934–39. As an adult, turned her attention to government and international issues. Republican candidate for U.S. House of Representatives, 1967. Rep. to 24th General Assembly of U.N. (1969–70). Special asst. to chmn., President's Council on the Environment (1970–72). U.S. Ambassador to Ghana (1974–76). Chief of Protocol, White House (1976–77); member of U.S. delegation on African Refugee problems, Geneva, 1981; 1987 made 1st honorary U.S. Foreign Service Rep. for State Dept.; 1989, appt. Ambassador to Czechoslovakia. Autobiography: Child Star (1988).
PICTURES: Baby Takes a Bow, Bright Eyes, Now I'll Tell, Change of Heart, Little Miss Marker, Now and Forever, The Little Colonel, Our Little Girl, Curly Top, The Littlest Rebel, Captain January, Poor Little Rich Girl, Dimples, Stowaway, Wee Willie Winkle, Heidi, Rebecca of Sunnybrook Farm, Little Miss Broadway, Just Around the Corner, Little Princess, Susannah of the Mounties, The Blue Bird, Young People, Kathleen, Miss Annie Rooney. Since You Went Away, I'll Be Seeing You, Kiss and Tell, That Hagen Girl, Honeymoon, Fort Apache, Bachelor and the Bobby-Soxer, Mr. Belvedere Goes to College, Adventure in Baltimore, Story of Seabiscuit, Kiss for Corliss.
TELEVISION: Hostess, fairy tale series: Shirley Temple's Storybook; The Shirley Temple Show.

TENNANT, VICTORIA: Actress. b. London, England, Sept. 30, 1953. m. actor, writer Steve Martin. e. Central Sch. of Speech & Drama. Daughter of ballerina Irene Baronova and talent agent Cecil Tennant.
PICTURES: The Ragman's Daughter, The Speckled Band, The Killing, Strangers Kiss, Horror Planet, (Inseminoid), All of Me, Flowers in the Attic, Best Seller, Fool's Mate, The Handmaid's Tale.
TELEVISION: Winds of War, Dempsey, Chiefs, War and Remembrance, Claire Booth Luce, Voice of the Heart, Maigret.

TENNANT, WILLIAM: Executive. Partner in literary agency of Ziegler, Ross and Tennant. Turned to m.p. production with Cleopatra Jones for Warner Bros., following with writing and producing of sequel, Cleopatra and the Casino of Gold. In 1975 joined Columbia Pictures as v.p.-prod. headquartering at Burbank Studios. Named pres., Casablanca Filmworks; now pres., PolyGram Pictures m.p. division.
PICTURES: As exec. prod.: The Hollywood Knights, King of the Mountain, The Pursuit of D.B. Cooper (co-exec. prod.).
TELEVISION: Act of Will (U.K.).

TERRY, SIR JOHN: Film Consultant. b. London, England, 1913. e. Mill Hill Sch. Early career as solicitor. Entered m.p. ind. Film Producers Guild 1946–47; then legal dept. Rank Organisation until 1949; joined National Film Finance Corporation; its chief solicitor 1949–57; sec., 1956–57; man. dir., 1958–78.

TESICH, STEVE: Writer. b. Yugoslavia, 1941. e. Indiana U., Columbia U. Came to U.S. at age 14. While doing graduate work in Russian literature at Columbia left to begin writing. Taken up by American Place Theatre which did his play, The Carpenters, in 1970 and then six others.
PICTURES: Breaking Away, Four Friends, Eyewitness, The World According to Garp, Eleni, Love Business.

TESLER, BRIAN: C.B.E. Chairman, Managing Director, London Weekend Television Ltd. b. London, England, 1929. e. Chiswick Country School and Exeter College, Oxford. Ent. TV ind. as trainee prod., BBC. 1952–56 Prod. Light Entertainment, BBC TV. 1957–59 Prod. Light Entertainment, ATV. 1960–63 joined ABC Television as head of features and light ent. then programme controller and director of programmes. 1968 appt. dir. of programmes, Thames Television. appt. dep. chief executive LWT. 1976 appt. man. dir. LWT. 1976. Appt. mem. Working Party on Future of British Film Industry. 1977 appt. governor, National Film and Television School. 1979 appt. dir. ITN. 1980 Appt. chairman, ITCA Council (until 1982). 1980–85 dir. Channel 4. Mem. board of management, Services Kinema Corporation. Dir. Oracle Teletext Ltd. 1981 appt. chmn. ITCA Cable and Satellite Television Working Party Then chmn. Super Channel Steering Group. Dir. LWT Intl. 1982 appt. dep. chmn. and man. dir. LWT becoming chmn. and man. dir. 1984. 1986 appt. chmn. ITV Super Channel, governor BFI, chmn. The Music Channel (trading as Super Channel) and Network Programme Comm. 1986 awarded CBE.

TETZLAFF, TED: Director. b. Los Angeles, CA, June 3, 1903. Joined camera dept. Fox Studios, became first cameraman; dir., 1940; served in U.S. Air Corps as a Major, W.W.II.
PICTURES: cameraman: Enchanted Cottage, Notorious; dir.: World Premiere, Riffraff, Fighting Father Dunne, Window, Johnny Allegro, Dangerous Profession, Gambling House, White Tower, Under the Gun, Treasure of Lost Canyon, Terror on a Train, Son of Sinbad.

TEWKESBURY, JOAN: Writer, Director. b. Redlands, CA, April 8, 1936. e. U. of Southern California. Student American Sch. Dance 1947–54. Ostrich and understudy in Mary Martin's Peter Pan. Directed and choreographed Little Theatre prods. in L.A. area; taught dance and theory, American Sch. of Dance 1959–64; taught in theatre arts depts. of two universities: U. of Southern California, Immaculate Heart. Became script supvr. for Robert Altman on McCabe & Mrs. Miller. Off-Bdwy: Cowboy Jack Street (writer, dir.). Teacher in film dept. UCLA.
PICTURES: Thieves Like Us (co.-s.p.), Nashville, (s.p.), Old Boyfriends (dir.), Hampstead Center (doc. of Anna Freud, writer, dir.), Angel's Dance Card (dir., s.p.), A Night in Heaven (s.p.).
TELEVISION: The Acorn People (dir., s.p.), The Tenth Month (dir., s.p.), Alfred Hitchcock Presents (dir., s.p., 1986), Elysian Fields (pilot, writer, dir., exec. prod.), Almost Grown (dir.,), Cold Sassy Tree (dir., s.p.).

THACHER, RUSSELL: Producer, Writer. b. Hackensack, NJ, May 29. e. Bucknell U., NYU. Author of novels: The Captain, The

Tender Age, A Break in the Clouds. Editor Omnibook Magazine, 1946–58; Book of the Month Club, 1958–63. Exec, story editor, MGM, 1963–69. Exec. prod., MGM, 1969–72. Dir., creative affairs, Samuel Goldwyn Co., 1983–84.
PICTURES: Travels with My Aunt (assoc. prod.), Soylent Green, The Cay, Last Hard Men, The Golden Seal (assoc. prod.), Once Bitten (assoc. prod.).

THALHIMER, JR., MORTON G.: Former Theatre Executive. b. Richmond, VA, June 27, 1924. e. Dartmouth Coll., 1948, B.A.; U. of Virginia, 1959. Naval aviator in W.W.II. Joined Century Theatres as trainee 1948; Jamestown Amusement, 1949–50. Past pres. Neighborhood Theatre, Inc. 1967–86. Charter member of Theatre Owners of America; continuing member and v.p. of NATO, served on finance comm. and Trade Practice comm. bd. member and past president of NATO of VA, 1973–75. Mem. Variety Club Int'l., Tent 11; patron life member, Variety Club of Israel, Tent 51.

THAXTER, PHYLLIS: Actress. b. Portland, ME, Nov. 20, 1921. e. St. Genevieve Sch., Montreal. Screen debut in Thirty Seconds Over Tokyo (1944).
PICTURES: Weekend at the Waldorf, Bewitched, Tenth Avenue Angel, Sign of the Ram, Blood on the Moon, The Breaking Point, Fort Worth, Jim Thorpe—All American, Come Fill the Cup, She's Working Her Way Through College, Operation Secret, Springfield Rifle, Women's Prison, The World of Henry Orient, Superman.
TELEVISION: Wagon Train, Alfred Hitchcock, Twilight Zone, Purex Specials For Women, Playhouse 90, The Fugitive, Defenders, The Longest Night, Three Sovereigns for Sarah, etc.

THEODORAKIS, MIKIS: Composer. b. Greece, 1925.
PICTURES: Eva, Night Ambush, Shadow of the Cat, Phaedra, Five Miles to Midnight, Zorba the Greek, The Day the Fish Came Out, The Trojan Women, State of Siege, Serpico, Iphigenia.

THINNES, ROY: Actor. b. Chicago, IL, April 6, 1938.
PICTURES: Journey to the Far Side of the Sun, Charlie One-Eye, Airport 75, The Hindenburg, Rush Week.
TELEVISION: Series: General Hospital (1963–65), The Long Hot Summer, The Invaders, The Psychiatrist, Falcon Crest. Movies: The Other Man, God Bless the Children, Black Noon, The Horror at 37,000 Feet, The Norliss Tales, Satan's School for Girls, Death Race, The Manhunter, Secrets, Code Name: Diamond Head, Sizzle, The Return of the Mod Squad, Freedom, Dark Holiday, Mini-series: From Here to Eternity, Scruples.

THOMAS, DANNY: Actor. r.n. Amos Jacobs. b. Deerfield, MI, Jan. 6, 1914. Father of actress Marlo Thomas and producer Tony Thomas. Began career in teens as a "candy butcher" in burlesque theater. Nightclub entertainer; on radio and TV, films. Formed prod. partnership with Sheldon Leonard and later Aaron Spelling (co. prod.: Andy Griffith Show, Dick Van Dyke Show, Gomer Pyle, U.S.M.C. and The Mod Squad). Endowed St. Jude's Children's Hospital, Memphis, TN.
TELEVISION: Own TV show, Make Room for Daddy (retitled The Danny Thomas Show) 1953–64; NBC-TV specials 1964–66, Danny Thomas Show, 1967–68; Specials 1967 & 1970. Make Room for Grandaddy (series) 1970–71; The Practice, 1976–77. Movie: Side By Side.
PICTURES: Unfinished Dance, Big City, Call Me Mister, I'll See You in My Dreams, The Jazz Singer.

THOMAS, DOUGLAS: Executive. b. London, England, 1954. Managing director Rank Screen Advertising. President: Cinema Advertising Association. Member of Council Advertising Association, Advertising Standards Board of Finance, British Code of Advertising Practice Committee, vice pres. Screen Advertising World Association.

THOMAS, GERALD: Producer, Director. b. Hull, England, 1920. Entered m.p. industry 1946.
PICTURES: Tony Draws a Horse, Appointment With Venus, Venetian Bird, Sword and the Rose, A Day to Remember, Mad About Men, Doctor in the House, Above Us the Waves, A Novel Affair, After the Ball, Timelock, Vicious Circle, Chain of Events, Solitary Child, The Duke Wore Jeans, Carry on Sergeant, Carry on Nurse, Carry on Teacher, Please Turn Over, Carry on Constable, Watch Your Stern, No Kidding, Carry on Regardless, Raising The Wind, Twice Around the Daffodils, Carry on Cruising, The Iron Maiden, Nurse on Wheels, Call Me a Cab, Carry on Jack, Carry on Spying, Carry on Cleo, The Big Job, Carry On Cowboy, Carry on Screaming, Don't Lose Your Head, Follow That Camel, Carry on Doctor, Carry On Up The Khyber, Carry on Up the Jungle, Carry on Loving, Carry on Camping, Carry on Again, Doctor, Carry on, Henry, Carry on at Your Convenience, Carry on Matron, Carry on Abroad, Bless This House, Carry On Girls, Carry on Dick, Carry on Behind, Carry on England, That's Carry On, Carry on Emmanuelle, The Second Victory.
TELEVISION: Prod. and dir. Rob Roy, serial. Prod. Carry on Christmas. Prod., Carry on Laughing. Dir. Best of Carry On. Prod. Odd Man Out, (series). Dir., Carry on Laughing, Comedy Tonight (Canada), What a Carry On, Just for Laughs.

THOMAS, HARRY E.: Exhibitor. b. Monroe, LA, May 22, 1920. e. Louisiana State U., 1938–41. Psychological Branch of Army Air Force, 1942–46. Past pres., secy., and treas. of NATO of MS. Dir. of Design & Const. & Sec. Gulf State Theatres Inc. Retired 1978.

THOMAS, JEREMY: Producer. b. London, Eng., July 27, 1949. Son of dir. Ralph Thomas ("Doctor" comedies) and nephew of dir. Gerald Thomas ("Carry On . . ." comedies). Entered industry 1969. Worked as film ed. on Brother Can You Spare a Dime, 1974.
PICTURES: Mad Dog, The Shout, The Great Rock 'n' Roll Swindle (exec. prod.), Bad Timing: A Sensual Obsession, Eureka, Merry Christmas, Mr. Lawrence; The Hit, Insignificance, The Last Emperor (Acad. Award, 1987).

THOMAS, MARLO: Actress. b. Detroit, MI, Nov. 21, 1938. Father is Danny Thomas. m. Phil Donahue. Sister of TV producer Tony Thomas. e. U. of Southern California. Started career with small TV roles, summer stock. Appeared in London stage prod. of Barefoot in the Park. Debut in own TV series, That Girl, 1966. Most Promising Newcomer Awards from both Fame and Photoplay. Conceived book, record and TV special Free to Be You and Me (Emmy, 1974).
THEATER: Thieves, Social Security.
PICTURES: Jenny, Thieves, In the Spirit.
TELEVISION: Free To Be You and Me, Free to Be a Family (host, exec. prod.) Movies: The Lost Honor of Kathryn Beck (also exec. prod.), Consenting Adult, Nobody's Child, Leap of Faith (exec. prod.), Torn Apart (exec. prod.).

THOMAS, PHILIP MICHAEL: Actor. b. Columbus, OH, May 26, 1949. e. Oakwood Coll.
PICTURE: Black Fist.
TELEVISION: Miami Vice (series); This Man Stands Alone, Valentine, Toma, A Fight for Jenny (movie), Disney's Totally Minnie.

THOMAS, RALPH: Director. b. Hull, Yorkshire, England, Aug. 10, 1915. e. Tellisford Coll., Clifton and University Coll., London. Journalist in early career, entered m.p. ind. 1932 as film ed.; service with 9th Lancers, 1939–45; then film director.
PICTURES: prod.: The Clouded Yellow; Dir.: Appointment with Venus (Island Rescue), Day to Remember, Travellers' Joy, Venetian Bird, Once Upon a Dream, Doctor in the House, Mad about Men, Above Us the Waves, Doctor At Sea, Iron Petticoat, Checkpoint, Doctor at Large, Campbell's Kingdom, A Tale of Two Cities, The Wind Cannot Read, The 39 Steps, Upstairs and Downstairs, Conspiracy of Hearts, Doctors in Love, No Love for Johnnie, No, My Darling Daughter, A Pair of Briefs, The Wild & the Willing, Doctor in Distress, Hot Enough for June, The High Bright Sun, Agent 008½, Doctor in Clover, Deadlier Than the Male, Nobody Runs Forever, Some Girls Do, Doctor in Trouble, Percy, Quest, The Love Ban, Percy's Progress, A Nightingale Sang in Berkeley Square, Pop Pirates.

THOMAS, RICHARD: Actor. b. New York, NY, June 13, 1951. e. Columbia U. Made TV debut at age 7 and featured in several series.
PICTURES: Winning, Last Summer, Red Sky at Morning, The Todd Killings, Cactus in the Snow, You'll Like My Mother, September 30th, 1955, Battle Beyond the Stars.
TELEVISION: Medical Center, Marcus Welby, M.D., The F.B.I., The Waltons (series). Movies: The Fifth of July, The Master of Ballantrae, All Quiet on the Western Front, To Find My Son, Berlin Tunnel: 21, Hobson's Choice, Final Jeopardy, Glory, Glory, Go Toward the Light, The Silence.

THOMAS, ROBERT G. ("BOB"): Producer, Director. b. Glen Ridge, NJ, July 21, 1943. e. U. of Bridgeport, Fairleigh Dickinson U. Prod. educational radio programs, 1962, WPKN-FM. Asst. stage mgr. Meadowbrook Dinner Theatre, 1963; 1964 began career as TV cameraman for NY stations. Worked both full-time and freelance for major TV and video tape studios. 1968, started Bob Thomas Productions, producing business/sales films and TV commercials. Has 8 awards from natl. film festivals; nominated for 5 Emmys for TV series called The Jersey Side he produced for WOR-TV.
PICTURES: Shorts: Valley Forge with Bob Hope, New Jersey—200 Years. Road-Eo '77.
TELEVISION: The Jersey Side (talk/entertainment), Jersey People (weekly talk/entertainment prog), Movies '89 (synd. film preview series).

THOMAS, ROBERT J. ("BOB"): Columnist, Associated Press, Hollywood. b. San Diego, CA, Jan. 26, 1922. p. George H. Thomas, publicist. e. UCLA. Joined Associated Press staff, Los Angeles, 1943; corr. Fresno, 1944; Hollywood since 1944. Writer mag. articles; appearances, radio; orig. story Big Mike.
BOOKS: author: The Art of Animation, King Cohn, Thalberg, Selznick, Winchell, Secret Boss of California; The Heart of Hollywood; Howard, The Amazing Mr. Hughes; Weekend '33; Marlon, Portrait of the Rebel as an Artist; Walt

Disney, An American Original; Bud and Lou, The Abbott and Costello Story; The Road to Hollywood (with Bob Hope); The One and Only Bing, Joan Crawford; Golden Boy: The Secret Life of William Holden; Astaire: The Man, The Dancer; I Got Rhythm, The Ethel Merman Story; Liberace.

THOMOPOULOS, ANTHONY D.: Executive. b. Mt. Vernon, NY, Feb. 7, 1938. e. Georgetown U. Began career in broadcasting at NBC, 1959, starting as mailroom clerk and moving to radio division in prod. & admin. Shortly named to post in intl. division sales, involved with programming for stations and in dev. TV systems for other nations. Joined Four Star Entertainment Corp. as dir. of foreign sales, 1964; named v.p., 1965; exec. v.p., 1969. In 1970 joined RCA SelectaVision Div. as dir. of programming. In 1971 joined Tomorrow Entertainment as v.p. In 1973 joined ABC as v.p., prime-time programs in N.Y.; 1974, named v.p., prime-time TV creative operations, ABC Entertainment. In 1975 named v.p. of special programs, ABC Entertainment; 1976 made v.p., ABC-TV, assisting pres. Frederick S. Pierce in supervising all activities of the division. In Feb., 1978 named pres. of ABC Entertainment. In June 1983 promoted to pres., ABC Broadcast Group in chg. all TV & radio operations. 1986, pres. & COO, United Artists Corp. Resigned Sept., 1988. Independent prod. with Columbia, 1989.

THOMPSON, J. LEE: Writer, Director, Producer. b. England, 1914. On Brit. stage; writer of stage plays including: Murder Without Crime, Cousin Simon, Curious Dr. Robson (collab.) Thousands of Summers, Human Touch. Writer and m.p. director.
PICTURES: The Middle Watch (s.p.), For Them That Trespass (s.p.), Murder Without Crime (dir., s.p.), The Yellow Balloon, Weak and the Wicked. Director: As Long as They're Happy, For Better or Worse, An Alligator Named Daisy, Yield To The Night, The Good Companions (co-prod., dir.), Woman In The Dressing Gown, Ice Cold in Alex, No Trees in the Street, Tiger Bay, I Aim at the Stars, The Guns of Navarone, Taras Bulba, Cape Fear, Kings of the Sun, What A Way to Go, John Goldfarb, Please Come Home, Return From the Ashes, Eye of the Devil, MacKenna's Gold, Battle for the Planet of the Apes, Before Winter Comes, The Chairman, Country Dance, Conquest of the Planet of the Apes, Huckleberry Finn, The Reincarnation of Peter Proud, St. Ives, The White Buffalo, The Greek Tycoon, The Passage, Caboblanco, Happy Birthday To Me, The Ambassador, 10 to Midnight, The Evil That Men Do, King Solomon's Mines, Murphy's Law, Firewalker, Death Wish IV, Messenger of Death, Kinjite.
TELEVISION: A Great American Tragedy, The Blue Knight, Widow.

THOMPSON, JACK: Actor. r.n. John Payne. b. Sydney, Australia, Aug. 31, 1940. e. Queensland U. Joined drama workshop at school; first part was in TV soap opera as continuing character. 1988, appt. to bd. of Australian Film Finance Corp. Formed Pan Film Enterprises.
PICTURES: Outback, Wake in Fright, Libido, Petersen, A Sunday Too Far Away, Caddie, Mad Dog Coll, The Chant of Jimmie Blacksmith, Breaker Morant (Australian award), The Earthling, The Club, The Man From Snowy River, Bad Blood, Merry Christmas, Mr. Lawrence, Flesh and Blood.
TELEVISION: The Last Frontier, A Woman Called Golda, Waterfront, The Letter, Beryl Markham: A Shadow on the Sun, Paradise.

THOMPSON, LEA: Actress. b. Rochester, MN, 1962. Danced professionally since age of 14; won scholarship to Penn. Ballet Co., American Ballet Theatre, San Francisco Ballet. Gave up that career for acting. Motion picture debut in Jaws 3-D (1983).
PICTURES: All the Right Moves, Red Dawn, The Wild Life, Back to the Future, Yellow Pages, Space Camp, Howard the Duck, Some Kind of Wonderful, The Wizard of Loneliness, Casual Sex?, Going Undercover, Back to the Future II & III.
TELEVISION: Nightbreaker.

THOMPSON, MARSHALL: Actor. r.n. James Marshall Thompson; b. Peoria, IL, Nov. 27, 1926. e. Occidental Coll., L.A. In school dramatics; studied for clergy; wrote play Faith, prod. by Westwood Players; in Westwood Players as actor; m.p. debut in Reckless Age, 1944.
PICTURES: They Were Expendable, Gallant Bess, Valley of Decision, Homecoming, B.F.'s Daughter, Words and Music, Command Decision, Roseanna McCoy, Battleground, Dial 1119, Devil's Doorway, Mystery Street, Tall Target, Basketball Fix, My Six Convicts, Rose Bowl Story, The Caddy, Battle Taxi, Port of Hell, Cult of the Cobra, Crashout, To Hell and Back, Clarence, The Cross-eyed Lion, Around the World Under the Sea, The Turning Point, White Dog.
TELEVISION: Series: The World of Giants, Angel, Daktari, Mini-series: Centennial.

THOMPSON, SADA: Actress. b. Des Moines, IA, Sept. 27, 1929. e. Carnegie Inst. of Technology, Pittsburgh. First N.Y. stage appearance in Under Milkwood with Dylan Thomas. Bdwy. career has produced many awards topped by The Effects of Gamma Rays, for which she won Obie, Drama Desk, Variety Poll. Recent theater: Real Estate.
PICTURES: Desperate Characters.
TELEVISION: Sandburg's Lincoln, The Entertainer, Marco Polo, My Two Loves, Our Town, Princess Daisy, Fatal Confession: A Father Dowling Mystery, Home Fires Burning. Series: Family (Emmy Award, 1978).

THORPE, RICHARD: Director. b. Hutchinson, KS, Feb. 24, 1896. m. Belva Kay, prof. In vaudeville, stock & musical comedy, 1915–18. Now retired.
PICTURES: cast, Torchy Comedies, Three O'Clock in the Morning, Burn 'Em Up Barnes, Flame of Desire; dir. since 1933. dir., Night Must Fall, Ivanhoe, Double Wedding, Crowd Roars, Earl of Chicago, Huckleberry Finn, White Cargo, Two Girls and a Sailor, Sun Comes Up, Big Jack, Challenge to Lassie, Malaya, Black Hand, Three Little Words, Vengeance Valley, The Great Caruso, Unknown Man, It's a Big Country, Carbine Williams, Prisoner of Zenda, The Girl Who Had Everything, All the Brothers Were Valiant, Knights of the Round Table, Student Prince, Athena, Quentin Durward, The Prodigal, The Tartars, Honeymoon Machine, Horizontal Lieutenant, Follow The Boys, The Truth About Spring, That Funny Feeling, Scorpio Letters, Last Challenge.

THULIN, INGRID: Actress, Director. b. Solleftea, Sweden, Jan. 27, 1929. m. Harry Schein, founder and head of Sweden's Film Inst. Made acting debut at 15 at the Municipal Theatre in Norrkoping. Studied at Stockholm's Royal Dramatic Theatre. Worked with Malmo repertory. Appeared on Swedish stage in Gigi, Peer Gynt, Two for the Seesaw, Twelfth Night, Miss Julie. Has directed plays in Stockholm. N.Y. stage debut, 1967: Of Love Remembered.
PICTURES: For Ingmar Bergman: Wild Strawberries, Brink of Life (Best Actress Award, Cannes Film Festival), The Magician, Winter Light, The Silence, The Hour of the Wolf, The Ritual, Night Games, The Bathers, Adelaide, La Guerre Est Finie, The Four Horsemen of the Apocalypse, Return From Ashes, The Damned, Cries and Whispers, Moses, The Cassandra Crossing, Madame Kitty, After the Rehearsal, Rabbit Face. Dir. short film: Devotion.

THUNA, LEONORA: Writer, Producer. b. May 3, 1929. e. Hunter Coll., A.B., 1951. Playwright, The Natural Look (Broadway, 1967); Show Me Where the Good Times Are (1970); Let Me Hear You Smile (1973); Fugue (1987); and other plays and musicals off-Bdwy. and on tour.
TELEVISION: Family Secrets (movie; s.p., co-prod.); The Natural Look (s.p., prod., pilot); I Know Why the Caged Bird Sings (s.p.); Madam (movie). Wrote episodes of Family, Lou Grant, and In the Beginning and worked on Starting Fresh (prod.); Grandpa Goes to Washington (co-exec. prod.); Angie (exec. prod.); The Goodtime Girls (co-creator & supvr. prod.). Also writer for Broadway variety special for Entertainment Channel.
PICTURE: How to Beat the High Cost of Living (story).

THURMAN, UMA: Actress. b. 1970. Named after a Hindu deity. Raised in Woodstock, NY and Amherst, MA where father taught Asian studies. Father's work took family to India where they lived three years. e. Professional Children's School, NY. Worked as model while still in high school.
PICTURES: Kiss Daddy Good Night, Johnny Be Good, Dangerous Liaisons, The Adventures of Baron Munchausen.

TIERNEY, GENE: Actress. b. Brooklyn, NY, Nov. 20, 1920. e. St. Margaret's Sch., Brilmont, Switzerland; Miss Farmer's Sch., Farmington, CT. Autobiography: Self Portrait (1979).
PICTURES: Return of Frank James, Hudson's Bay, Tobacco Road, Belle Starr, Sundown, Shanghai Gesture, Son of Fury, Heaven Can Wait, Laura, Bell for Adano, Leave Her to Heaven, Dragonwyck, Razor's Edge, Ghost and Mrs. Muir, Iron Curtain, That Wonderful Urge, Whirlpool, Where the Sidewalk Ends, Night and the City, Mating Season, On the Riviera, Secret of Convict Lake, Way of a Gaucho, Close To My Heart, Plymouth Adventure, Never Let Me Go, Personal Affair, The Egyptian, Black Widow, Left Hand of God, Advise & Consent.
TELEVISION: The F.B.I., Daughter of the Mind, Scruples.

TIERNEY, LAWRENCE: Actor. b. Brooklyn, NY, Mar. 15, 1919. Brother of actor Scott Brady. e. Manhattan Coll. Track athlete (natl. championship Cross Country Team, N.Y. Athletic Club). On stage as actor. Screen debut 1943 in The Ghost Ship.
PICTURES: Government Girl, The Falcon Out West, Youth Runs Wild, Back to Bataan, Dillinger, Mama Loves Papa, Those Endearing Young Charms, Badman's Territory, Step By Step, San Quentin, Devil Thumbs a Ride, Born to Kill, Bodyguard, Kill or Be Killed, Best of the Bad Men, Shakedown, Greatest Show on Earth, Hoodlum, Bushwackers, Steel Cage, Female Jungle, Singing in the Dark, A Child Is Waiting, Custer of the West, Such Good Friends, Abduction, Bad, Kirlian, Witness, Arthur, Midnight, Gloria, Prizzi's Honor, Silver Bullet, Murphy's Law, Tough Guys Don't Dance, Offspring, The Horror Show.

TELEVISION: Terrible Joe Moran, Guest: Hill Street Blues, Star Trek: the Next Generation.

TIFFIN, PAMELA: Actress. r.n. Pamela Wonso. b. Oklahoma City, OK, Oct. 13, 1942. e. Hunter Coll., Columbia U., Loyola U, Rome Center. Studied acting with Stella Adler and Harold Clurman. Started modeling as a teenager. Film debut in Summer and Smoke (1961).
PICTURES: One Two Three, State Fair, Come Fly with Me, For Those Who Think Young, The Pleasure Seekers, The Hallelujah Trail, Harper, Paranoia, Kiss the Other Sheik, Viva Max, Deaf Smith and Johnny Ears, Evil Fingers.
PLAYS: Dinner at Eight, Uncle Vanya.

TILLY, MEG: Actress. b. California, 1960. Raised in Victoria, B.C., where began acting and dancing in community theatrical prods. while in high school. To New York at 16; appeared on TV in Hill Street Blues. Film debut was a few lines in Fame.
PICTURES: Tex (debut), Psycho II, One Dark Night, The Big Chill, Rest in Peace, Impulse, Agnes of God, Off Beat, Masquerade, Valmont, The Girl in a Swing, The Two Jakes.
Television: The Trouble With Grandpa, Camilla (Nightmare classics).

TINKER, GRANT A.: Executive. b. Stamford, CT., Jan. 11, 1926. e. Dartmouth Coll., 1947. Joined NBC radio prog. dept. 1949. In 1954 with McCann-Erickson ad agency, TV dept. In 1958, Benton & Bowles Ad Agency, TV dept. From 1961–66 with NBC, v.p., programs, West Coast; v.p. in chg. of programming, N.Y., 1966–67. Joined Universal Television as v.p., 1968–69; 20th-Fox, v.p., 1969–70. Became pres. MTM Enterprises, Inc. 1970. Named NBC bd. chmn. & CEO, 1981–86. Formed indep. prod. co. G.T.G. Entertainment, 1988.

TISCH, LAURENCE A.: Executive. b. Brooklyn, NY, March 5, 1923. e. NYU, 1941; U. of Pennsylvania Wharton Sch., 1942; Harvard Law Sch., 1946. Pres. Tisch Hotels, Inc., 1950–59; pres. Americana Hotel, Inc., Miami Beach, 1956–59; Chmn. of bd. and chief executive officer of Loews Corp since 1960. Also chmn. of bd. of CNA Financial Corp since 1947. Chief executive officer and chmn. of board, CBS since 1986.

TISCH, PRESTON ROBERT: Executive. b. Brooklyn, NY, April 29, 1926. e. Bucknell U., Lewisberg, PA, 1943–44; U. of Michigan, B.A., 1948. Pres. Loew's Corporation. Postmaster General of the U.S. 1986–1988. March, 1988 returned to Loews Corp. as president and co-chief executive. Elected member of bd. CBS Inc. Sept., 1988.

TISCH, STEVE: Producer. b. Lakewood, NJ, 1949. e. Tufts U. Son of Preston Tisch. Worked during school breaks for John Avildsen and Fred Weintraub. Signed upon graduation as exec. asst. to Peter Guber, then prod. head at Columbia Pictures. Entered producer ranks with Outlaw Blues, 1977, collaborating with Jon Avnet with whom formed Tisch/Avnet Prods. Alliance with Phoenix Entertainment 1988.
PICTURES: Coast to Coast, Risky Business, Deal of the Century, Soul Man, Big Business, Hot to Trot, Heart of Dixie.
TELEVISION: Homeward Bound, No Other Love, Prime Suspect, Something So Right, The Burning Bed (exec. prod.), Call to Glory (series), Silence of the Heart, In Love and War (sole prod.), Evil in Clear River, Dirty Dancing (series), Out on the Edge (exec. prod.).

TOBACK, JAMES: Writer, Producer, Director. b. New York, NY, 1944. e. Harvard U. Taught literature at City Coll. of New York; contributed articles and criticism to Harper's, Esquire, Commentary, etc. Wrote book Jim, on actor-athlete Jim Brown (1971). First screenplay, The Gambler, filmed in 1974.
PICTURES: Fingers (s.p., dir.); Love and Money (s.p., dir., prod.), Exposed (dir., prod., s.p.), The Pick-Up Artist (dir., s.p.), The Big Bang (dir., s.p.).

TODD, ANN: Actress. b. Hartford, England, 1909. e. Central Sch. of Speech Training & Dramatic Art. Wrote, prod. and dir. travel documentaries in the 1960s. Autobiography: The Eighth Veil, 1980.
BRITISH STAGE PLAYS: Service, When Ladies Meet, Man in Half-Moon Street, Peter Pan, Brit., Lottie Dundass. Ret. to theatre Feb., 1951 in stage version, Seventh Veil, So Evil My Love; Old Vic. Theatre, 1954–55: Doctor's Dilemma, Four Winds, Duel of Angels, One Woman's Story.
PICTURES: Keepers of Youth (debut, 1931), These Charming People, The Ghost Train, The Water Gypsies, The Return of Bulldog Drummund, Things to Come, Squeaker, Action for Slander, South Riding, Poison Pen, Danny Boy, Ships With Wings, Perfect Strangers, The Seventh Veil, Perfect Strangers, Gaiety George, Daybreak, So Evil My Love, Hollywood debut in Paradine Case. Passionate Friends, Madeleine, The Sound Barrier, Green Scarf, Time Without Pity, Taste of Fear, Son of Captain Blood, Ninety Degrees in The Shade, The Fiend, The Human Factor.
TELEVISION: Many appearances and TV films, New York, Hollywood, The Paradine Case, So Evil My Love. London incl.: Camille, The Vortex, The Door, Snows of Kilimanjaro, TV film, Hollywood. 1964: Prod., travelogue in Nepal, Love Story, Makes own Diary Documentaries and appears in them. Films for cinema and TV incl. Thunder in Heaven, Thunder of Gods, Thunder of Kings. Persian Fairy Tale. Free in the Sun, Thunder of Silence. The Last Target, Maelstrom (series), The McGuffon.

TODD, RICHARD: Actor. b. Dublin, Eire, June 11, 1919. e. Shrewsbury. In repertory, 1937; founder-member, Dundee Repertory Theatre, 1939; distinguished war service, 1939–46; Dundee Repertory, 1946–48; screen debut, 1948; For Them That Trespass, 1948. 1970 Founder-Director Triumph Theatre Productions. Published autobiography, 1986.
PICTURES: The Hasty Heart, Lightning Strikes Twice (U.S.), Robin Hood, The Venetian Bird, Sword and the Rose, Rob Roy, A Man Called Peter (U.S.), Virgin Queen (U.S.), The Bed, Dam Busters, D-Day the Sixth of June (U.S.), Marie Antoinette, Yangtse Incident, Chase a Crooked Shadow, The Naked Earth, Danger Within, The Long the Short and the Tall, The Hellions, Never Let Go, The Longest Day, The Boys, The Very Edge, exec. prod., star own prod. Don't Bother to Knock, Operation Crossbow, Coast of Skeletons, Asylum, The Big Sleep, House of the Long Shadows.
STAGE: 1966–67, An Ideal Husband; Dear Octopus. Co-founder, Triumph Theatre Prods., Ltd. plays since 1970: Roar Like a Dove, Grass Is Greener, The Marquise (U.S.). Sleuth, 1972–73 (England and Australia). Murder by Numbers, The Hollow Crown (with RSC), Equus. On Approval, Quadrille, This Happy Breed, The Business of Murder, 1981–86 (London).

TODMAN, HOWARD: Executive. b. New York, NY, Nov. 24, 1920. e. Hamilton Coll., 1941. Dir. business affairs, Goodson-Todman Productions; treas., Goodson-Todman Associates, inc.; v.p. & treas., Goodson-Todman Enterprises, Ltd.; Treasurer, Peak Prods., Inc.; Treas. Goodson-Todman Bcstg. Inc.; v.p. Price Productions, Inc.; v.p. Celebrity Productions, Inc.; chmn., N.Y. Cancer Crusade, radio & TV.

TOGNAZZI, UGO: Actor. b. Cremona, Italy, March 23, 1922. Graduate of law. Started entertainment career in 1945 as comic in music hall revues. Film career began in 1950 with Les Cadets de Gascogne. Has produced four films and a detective series for TV. Also acted on stage.
PICTURES: His Women (also dir.), The Fascist, Queen Bee (aka The Conjugal Bed), The Magnificent Cuckold, An American Wife, Question of Honor, Barbarella, Property Is No Longer a Theft, Blowout, Duck in Orange Sauce, Goodnight Ladies and Gentlemen, Bishop's Bedroom, Viva Italia!, La Cage aux Folles, La Cage II, Sunday Lovers, Tragedy of a Ridiculous Man, Amici, Miei, Atto 2, Claretta and Ben, La Cage aux Folles 3: The Wedding, Ultimo Momento, Traffic Jam, Torrents of Spring, A Question of Life, Drums of Fire.

TOKOFSKY, JERRY H.: Executive. b. New York, NY, Apr. 14, 1936. e. NYU, B.S., journalism, 1956; New York Law, 1959. Entered William Morris Agency while at NYU 1953, working in night club dept. to live TV. Moved to Beverly Hills office, 1959. Entered m.p. div. WMA, 1960. Joined Columbia Pictures, as prod. v.p., 1963–70. Joined Paramount Pictures 1970 as prod. v.p. To MGM as prod. v.p., 1971. Now producer & exec. v.p., Zupnik Enterprises, Inc.
PICTURES: Producer: Where's Poppa, Born to Win, Paternity, Dreamscape, Fear City, Wildfire, Glengarry Glen Ross.

TOM, C. Y.: Cinematographer, Distributor. b. Toy Shan, Kwangtung, China, Nov. 6, 1907. Graduated N.Y. Inst. of Photography, 1926. Photographed newsreels for The Great Wall Film Co. of Shanghai; in New York, 1926–29; in charge of production, Shanghai, 1929–32. Studied production techniques in Hollywood. Toured Europe, managing Chinese vaudeville, 1934–35. Studio mgr. and dir. photography for Chi Ming Motion Picture Co., 1935–41. President, Chinamerica Film Exchange and Chinamerica Film Studio, Hong Kong and Shanghai. Distributor, Monogram, Film Classics and Telenews, Hong Kong, Macao and China; asst. man. dir., Capitol Theatre, Hong Kong, 1948–59.

TOMBRAGEL, MAURICE: Writer.
PICTURES: Legion of Lost Flyers, Horror Island, Mutiny in the Arctic, Two Senoritas from Chicago, Lone Wolf in Mexico, Return of the Whistler, Prince of Thieves, The Creeper, Highway 13, Thunder in the Pines, Sky Liner, Arson Inc., Motor Patrol, Fort Bowie, Moon Pilot, s.p. Monkeys Go Home; v.p. Running Wild, Golden Circle Prods., 1973.
TELEVISION: Wild Bill Hickock, Stories of the Century, Annie Oakley, Soldiers of Fortune, Western Marshal, Wyatt Earp, Frontier Doctor, Texas Rangers, Sergeant Preston, Adventures of Jim Bowie, Bat Masterson, Walt Disney's Elfego Baca, Life of Johann Strauss, Escapade in Florence, Bristle Face. Series: John Slaughter, Gallegher, The Tenderfoot. For Disney, The Treasure of San Marco (2 parts), The Gentle Ben (series).

TOMLIN, LILY: Actress. r.n. Mary Jean Tomlin. b. Detroit, MI, Sept. 1, 1939. Wayne State U. (studied pre-med). Studied mime with Paul Curtis. Started inventing characters for comedy sketches in college, used them in cafe and night club dates in

Detroit. 1966 went to NY performing skits on coffee-house circuit and landing job on The Garry Moore Show. 1969, first appeared on Laugh-In, TV series, gaining national attention with such characters as telephone operator Ernestine and child Edith Ann.

THEATER: Appearing Nightly (Special Tony Award, 1977), The Search for Signs of Intelligent Life in the Universe (1986, on Bdwy and on tour).

TELEVISION: The Music Scene (host, 1969–70). Laugh-In, The Lily Tomlin Show (Emmys as writer and star, 1974), The Paul Simon Special (Emmy, as writer 1978), Lily—Sold Out (also exec. prod., 2 Emmys as prod. and star, 1981), The Muppets Go to the Movies, Lily for President? Live—and in Person, Funny, You Don't Look 200, Free to Be. . .a Family.

PICTURES: Nashville, (debut, 1975; NY Film Critics Award, supp. actress; Acad Award nom.), The Late Show, Moment by Moment, Nine to Five, The Incredible Shrinking Woman, All of Me, Lily Tomlin (doc. behind the scenes of The Search for Intelligent Life); Big Business.

RECORDS: This Is a Recording, And That's The Truth, Appearing Nightly (Grammy Award, 1971).

TOOMEY, REGIS: Actor. b. Pittsburgh, PA, Aug. 13, 1902. e. U. of Pittsburgh; Carnegie Inst. of Technology (drama). On N.Y. & London stage 5 yrs; film debut in Alibi, 1929.

PICTURES: Spellbound, Big Sleep, Her Sister's Secret, Guilty, High Tide, Magic Town, Bishop's Wife, Boy With Green Hair, Mighty Joe Young, Come to the Stable, Cry Danger, Tall Target, People Against O'Hara, Show Boat, My Six Convicts, Battle at Apache Pass, Just For You, My Pal Gus, Never Wave at a Wac, It Happens Every Thursday, High and the Mighty, Top Gun, Guys and Dolls, Great Day in the Morning, 3 for Jamie Down, Dakota Incident, Warlock, Guns of the Timberland, The Day of the Gun, The Last Sundown, Journey to the Bottom of the Sea, Man's Favorite Sport, Peter Gunn, Change of Habit, Run Shadow Run, The Carey Treatment.

TELEVISION: Four Star Theatre, December Bride, Hey Mulligan, Dodsworth, Richard Diamond (series), Shannon (series), Burke's Law (series), Petticoat Junction (series).

TOPOL: Actor. b. Israel, Sept. 9, 1935. r.n. Chaim Topol. On London's West End & Manchester in Fiddler on the Roof repeating role on screen; 1989 repeated role in U.S. tour.

PICTURES: Cast a Giant Shadow, Sallah, Before Winter Comes, Fiddler on the Roof, Follow Me, Galileo, Flash Gordon, For Your Eyes Only.

TELEVISION: House on Garibaldi Street, The Winds of War, Queenie, War and Remembrance.

TORME, MEL: Singer, Actor. b. Chicago, IL, Sept. 13, 1925. Singing debut at age of 4; won radio audition 1933; on radio; composed song Lament to Love; with Chico Marx's orchestra as drummer, arranger & vocalist 1942; served in U.S. Army, W.W.II; m.p. debut in Higher and Higher, 1943; org. vocal group Meltones; many recordings; night clubs, concerts.

PICTURES: Pardon My Rhythm, Good News, Let's Go Steady, Janie Gets Married, Junior Miss, Night and Day, Good News, Words and Music, Duchess of Idaho, The Big Operator, Girls Town, Walk Like a Dragon, The Patsy, A Man Called Adam, The Land of No Return, (Snowman), Daffy Duck's Quackbusters (voice).

TORN, RIP: Actor. r.n. Elmore Torn, Jr. b. Temple, TX, Feb. 6, 1931. e. Texas A & M U., U. of Texas. Served in army. Signed as understudy for lead in Cat on a Hot Tin Roof on Broadway.

THEATER: Orpheus Descending, Sweet Bird of Youth, Daughter of Silence, Macbeth, Desire Under the Elms, Strange Interlude, Blues For Mr. Charlie, The Kitchen, The Deer Park (Obie Award), The Beard, The Cuban Thing, Dream of a Blacklisted Actor, The Dance of Death.

PICTURES: Baby Doll, A Face in the Crowd, Time Limit, Pork Chop Hill, King of Kings, Hero's Island, Sweet Bird of Youth, Critics Choice, The Cincinnati Kid, One Spy Too Many, You're a Big Boy Now, Beach Red, Sol Madrid, Beyond the Law, Coming Apart, Tropic of Cancer, Payday, Crazy Joe, Birch Interval, Maidstone, The Man Who Fell to Earth, Nasty Habits, Coma, The Seduction of Joe Tynan, One Trick Pony, First Family, Heartland, The Beastmaster, Jinxed, Airplane II: The Sequel, Cross Creek, Misunderstood, Songwriter, Flashpoint, City Heat, Summer Rental, Beer, Extreme Prejudice, Nadine, The Telephone (dir.), Cold Feet, Hit List, Silence Like Glass, Death List, Blind Curve, The Hunt for Red October, Beautiful Dreamers.

TELEVISION: Betrayal, The President's Plane is Missing, The FBI vs. the Ku Klux Klan, Song of Myself, The Execution, When She Says No, The Atlanta Child Murders, J. Edgar Hoover, Sophia Loren—Her Story, Rape and Marriage—The Rideout Case, Blind Ambition, Montserrat, Laguna Heat, Steel Cowboy, Cat on a Hot Tin Roof, The King of Love, April Morning.

TOTTER, AUDREY: Actress. b. Joliet, IL, Dec. 20, 1923. In many stage plays. On radio 1939–44; film debut in Main Street, 1944.

PLAYS: Copperhead, Stage Door, Late Christopher Bean, My Sister Eileen.

PICTURES: Her Highness and the Bellboy, Dangerous Partners, Sailor Takes a Wife, Cockeyed Miracle, Lady in the Lake, High Wall, Beginning or the End, Unsuspected, Alias Nick Beal, Saxon Charm, Any Number Can Play, Tension, Set-Up, Under the Gun, Blue Veil, Sellout, F.B.I. Girl, Assignment-Paris, My Pal Gus, Woman They Almost Lynched, Cruisin' Down the River, Man in the Dark, Mission Over Korea, Champ for a Day, Massacre Canyon, Women's Prison, A Bullet for Joey, Vanishing American, The Carpetbaggers, Chubasco, The Apple Dumpling Gang Rides Again.

TELEVISION: Series: Cimarron City, Our Man Higgins, Medical Center (series 1972–76); Movies: The Great Cash Giveaway, City Killer, Murder, She Wrote.

TOWERS, CONSTANCE: Actress. b. Whitefish, MT, May 20, 1934. m. John Gavin, actor and former U.S. Ambassador to Mexico. e. Juilliard Sch. of Music. Stage work on Broadway and tour.

THEATER: King and I (1977–79 opp. Yul Brynner), Steel Magnolias (Chicago, 1989).

PICTURES: Horse Soldiers, Sergeant Rutledge, Fate Is the Hunter, Shock Corridor, Naked Kiss, The Spy, Sylvester, Fast Forward.

TELEVISION: Series: Love Is a Many Splendored Thing, VTV, Capitol. Mini-Series: On Wings of Eagles, Home Show, The Loner, Murder, She Wrote, STN, Hour Mag, MacGyver.

TOWERS, HARRY ALAN: Executive, Producer. b. London, England, 1920. Prod. and wrote: 1963: Sanders of the River; 1964: Code Seven Victim Five.

PICTURES: City of Fear, Mozambique, Coast of Skeletons, Sandy the Seal, 24 Hours to Kill, The Face of Fu Manchu, Ten Little Indians, Marrakesh, Circus of Fear, The Brides of Fu Manchu, Sumuru, Five Golden Dragons, The Vengeance of Fu Manchu, Jules Verne's Rocket to the Moon, House of a Thousand Dolls, The Face of Eve, Blood of Fu Manchu, 99 Women, Girl From Rio, Marquis de Sade's Justine, Castle of Fu Manchu, Venus in Furs, Philosophy in the Boudoir, Eugenie, Dorian Gray, Count Dracula, The Bloody Judge. Black Beauty, Night Hair Child, The Call of the Wild, Treasure Island, White Fang, Death in Persepolis, Ten Little Indians, End of Innocence, Black Cobra, Black Velvet-White Silk, Night of The High Tide, King Solomon's Treasure, Shape of Things to Come, Klondike Fever, Fanny Hill, Frank and I, Black Venus, Christmas, Black Arrow, Pompeii, Love Circles, Lightning—White Stallion, Gor, Outlaw of Gor, Dragonard, Skeleton Coast, Master of Dragonard Hill, Nam, Fire With Fire, Jekyll and Hyde, River of Death, Cobra Strike, The Howling IV—The Original Nightmare, Skeleton Coast, Edge of Sanity, Ten Little Indians, Platoon Leader, Captive Rage, American Ninja III: Blood Hunt, The Fall of the House of Usher, Edgar Allan Poe's Buried Alive, Phantom of the Opera, Oddball Hall, Terror of Manhattan.

TOWNE, ROBERT: Writer, Director, Producer. b. 1936. Was member of Warren Beatty's production staff on Bonnie and Clyde and contributed to that screenplay. Also uncredited, contrib. to Pacino-Brando garden scene in The Godfather, also script doctor on Marathon Man, The Missouri Breaks and others.

PICTURES: Villa Rides, The Tomb of Ligeia, The Last Detail, Chinatown, Shampoo (co-s.p.), The Yazuka (co.-s.p.), Personal Best (s.p., prod., dir.), Greystoke: The Legend of Tarzan, The Pick-Up Artist (actor), The Bedroom Windown (exec. prod.), Tequila Sunrise (dir., s.p.), The Two Jakes (s.p.).

TOWNSEND, CLAIRE: b. New York, NY, Feb. 20, 1952. e. Princeton U. Joined 20th Century-Fox in 1976; named west coast story editor & v.p, creative affairs. Left in 1978 to go to United Artists, where named v.p. of production, responsible for managing the acquisition, development and production of feature films. Now independent producer.

TOWNSEND, ROBERT: Producer, Director, Writer, Actor. b. Chicago, IL, Feb. 6, 1957. e. attended Illinois State U. and Hunter Coll. Planned baseball career before turning to acting. Veteran of Experimental Black Actors Guild and Second City. Film debut: Cooley High (1974). TV commercials; stand-up comedy at NY Improvisation; taped Evening at the Improv.

PICTURES: Actor: Willie and Phil, A Soldier's Story, Streets of Fire, American Flyers, Odd Jobs, Ratboy. Producer-Director-Actor-Writer: Hollywood Shuffle ($100,000 budget), Eddie Murphy Raw (dir.), Finding Maubee (actor).

TELEVISION; Another Page (PBS series), Robert Townsend and His Partners in Crime; Take No Prisoners: Robert Townsend and His Partners in Crime II (HBO).

TRAMBUKIS, WILLIAM J.: Executive. b. July 26, 1926. Began career as usher with Loew's in Providence, RI, 1941. Served 1943–46 with Navy Seabees. Recipient of Quigley Awards. Managed/supervised Loew's Theatres in several New England cities, Harrisburg, PA, Syracuse, Rochester, Buffalo, NY, Washington, DC, Richmond, Norfolk, VA, Toronto, Canada, Atlanta, GA. Appt. Loew's NorthEastern Division mgr. 1964, Loew's gen. mgr. 1975: v.p. in 1976; sr. v.p., 1985. Retired, 1987.

TRAVANTI, DANIEL J.: Actor. b. Kenosha, WI, March 7, 1940. e. U. of Wisconsin, Yale Sch. of Drama. Woodrow Wilson fellow, 1961. On stage in Twigs, Othello, I Never Sang for My Father.
PICTURE: St. Ives, Midnight Crossing, Millenium, Fellow Traveler.
TELEVISION: Hill Street Blues (series), A Case of Libel, Adam, Aurora, Murrow, Adam: His Song Continues, I Never Sang for My Father.

TRAVERS, BILL: Actor, Producer, Director. b. Newcastle-on-Tyne, England. Jan. 3, 1922. Actor in repertory co.; London stage in Cage Me a Peacock, Damask Cheek, Square Ring, I Captured the Castle; A Cook for Mr. General (Broadway); Royal Shakespeare Theatre Co., 1962. Abraham Cochrane, Peter Pan.
PICTURES: Square Ring, Romeo and Juliet, Geordie, Footsteps in the Fog, Bhowani Junction, Barretts of Wimpole Street, Smallest Show on Earth, Seventh Sin, Passionate Summer, Bridal Path, Gorgo, The Green Helmet, Two Living—One Dead, Born Free, Duel at Diablo, A Midsummer Night's Dream, Ring of Bright Water, Boulevard du Rhum, The Belstone Fox.
TELEVISION: A Cook for the General (Kraft), Episode, A Giant Is Born (U.S.), Espionage, Rawhide, CBS Voice of America (Rome), Lorna Doone, The Admirable Crichton. Producer/Director/Writer: The Lions Are Free, An Elephant Called Slowly, The Lion at Worlds End, Christian the Lion, Wild Dogs of Africa, Baboons of Gombe, The Hyena Story, Deathtrap, Lions of the Serengeti, River of Sand, Bloody Ivory, Sexual Encounters of the Floral Kind.

TRAVIS, J. MARK: Executive. b. Los Angeles, CA, , March 7, 1953. e. Yale. U. 1971, v.p., Sackheim Agency; 1973, pres., Entertainment 4; 1975, chmn., CEO, Theatre Television Corp.; 1977, pres., Special Event Entertainment; 1979, Columbia Pictures—Travis Productions; 1980, Lorimar Productions—Travis; 1983, pres. & CEO, Movie Music Co., Inc.
PICTURES: Give em Hell Harry (prod.); Stop the World I Want to Get Off (prod.), Richard Pryor Live in Concert (prod.); Fighting Back (exec. prod.).

TRAVOLTA, JOHN: Actor. b. Englewood, NJ, Feb. 18, 1954. Quit school at 16 to pursue theatre career; first stage role in Who Will Save the Plowboy? Did off-Bdwy prod. of Rain; next to Broadway in Grease. Toured with latter for 10 months. Also in Over Here on Bdwy. with Andrew Sisters for 10 months.
PICTURES: Carrie, Saturday Night Fever, Grease, Moment by Moment, Urban Cowboy, Blow Out, Staying Alive, Two of a Kind, Perfect, The Experts, The Tender, Look Who's Talking, Chains of Gold.
TELEVISION: Emergency, Owen Marshall, The Rookies, Medical Center, Welcome Back, Kotter (series), Movie: The Boy in the Plastic Bubble.

TREMAYNE, LES: Actor. b. London, England, Apr. 16, 1913. e. Northwestern U., Chicago Art Inst., Columbia U., UCLA. First professional appearance in British mp., 1916, with mother; stock, litte theatres, vaudeville, 1925–40; entered radio field, 1930; numerous shows on all networks. Blue ribbon award for best perf. of the month for A Man Called Peter; dir. Hollywood Rep. Theatre, 1957; pres. Hollywood Actors' Council, 1951–58; chmn. Actors Div. workshop com. Acad. TV Arts & Sciences; Mem.: The Workshop Comm. of the Hollywood M.P. & TV Museum Comm. One of 17 founding members, Pacific Pioneer Broadcasters; Life member, Actor's Fund; charter/founding mem. AFTRA, Chicago local. (delegate to most conventions since 1938). mem. Local, L.A, and Natl. AFTRA bds.
SHOWS: Woman in My House, Errand of Mercy, You Are There, One Man's Family, Heartbeat Theatre, The First Nighter (lead 7 yrs.); on Broadway in Heads or Tails, Detective Story.
TELEVISION: Lux Video Theatre, 20th Century-Fox Hour, Navy Log, One Man's Family, Meet Mille, The Millionaire, The Whistler, Truth or Consequences, NBC Matinee, The Girl, O'Henry series, Rin Tin Tin, Bachelor Father, The Texan, Adventures of Ellery Queen, Court of Last Resort, Rifleman, State Trooper, Rescue 8, June Allyson-Dupont Show, Wagon Train, M Squad, Hitchcock Presents, Mr. Ed., Perry Mason.
PICTURES: The Racket, Blue Veil, Francis Goes to West Point, It Grows on Trees, I Love Melvin, Under the Red Sea, Dream Wife, War of the Worlds, Susan Slept Here, Lieutenant Wore Skirts, Unguarded Moment, Everything But the Truth, Monolith Monsters, Perfect Furlough, North by Northwest, Say One for Me, The Gallant Hours, The Angry Red Planet, The Story of Ruth, The Fortune Cookie.

TREVOR, CLAIRE: Actress. b. New York, NY, 1910. e. American Acad. of Dramatic Arts; Columbia U. On Broadway in Party's Over, Whistling in the Dark, Big Two.
PICTURES: Life in the Raw, Last Trail, Mad Game, Jimmy and Sally, Stagecoach, Allegheny Uprising, Dark Command, Murder, My Sweet, Johnny Angel, Crack-Up, Bachelor's Daughters, Born to Kill, Raw Deal, Valley of the Giants, Babe Ruth, Velvet Touch, Key Largo (Acad. Award), Lucky Stiff, Best of the Bad Men, Border Line, Hoodlum, Empire, Hard, Fast and Beautiful, My Man and I, Stop, You're Killing Me, Stranger Wore a Gun, High and the Mighty, Man Without a Star, Luch Gallant, The Mountain, Marjorie Morningstar, Two Weeks in Another Town, The Stripper, How to Murder Your Wife, Capetown Affair, Kiss Me Goodbye.
TELEVISION: Dodsworth (Emmy Award). Ladies in Retirement, Alfred Hitchcock Presents, The Untouchables, Love Boat, Murder, She Wrote.

TREXLER, CHARLES B.: Exhibitor. b. Wadesboro, NC, Feb. 8, 1916. From 1937 to Nov. 1948 was practicing CPA except for 2 yrs. in U.S. Army in W.W.II. Joined Stewart & Everett Theatres in 1948 as controller. In March, 1953 named gen. mgr.; Jan. 1, 1954, exec. v.p., treas.; May, 1962 named pres.; Feb. 1, 1983, named bd. chmn. Former bd. chmn., NATO of North and South Carolina; v.p. & bd. mem., National NATO.

TRIKONIS, GUS: Director. b. New York, NY. Started career in chorus of West Side Story on Bdwy. Turned to direction, making low-budget weekenders (films shot in 12 days only on weekends).
PICTURES: Moonshine County Express, The Evil Touched by Love, Take This Job and Shove It.
TELEVISION: Dark Side of Terror, Dressed To Kill, The Last Convertible (final three hours), Dempsey, Elvis and the Beauty Queen, Flamingo Road, Malice in Wonderland, Twilight Zone (1986), Open Admissions.

TRINTIGNANT, JEAN-LOUIS: Actor. b. Aix-en-Provence, France, Dec. 11, 1930. m. Nadine Marquand, director. Theatre debut: 1951, To Each According to His Hunger. Then Mary Stuart, Macbeth (at the Comedie de Saint-Etienne). 1955 screen debut.
PICTURES: Si Tous Les Gars du Monde, La Loi des Rues, And God Created Woman, Club de Femmes, Les Liaisons Dangereuses, L'Ete Violent, Austerlitz, La Millieme Fenetre, Plein Feux sur L'Assasin, Coeur Battant, L'Atlantide, The Game of Truth, Horace 62, Les Sept Peches Capitaux (7 Capital Sins), Le Combat dans L'Ile, The Easy Life, Il Successo, Nutty, Naughty Chateau, Les Pas Perdus, La Bonne Occase, Mata-Hari, Meurtre a L'Italienne, La Longue Marche, Le 17eme Ciel, Un Jour a Paris, Is Paris Burning?, The Sleeping Car Murders, A Man and a Woman, Enigma, Safari Diamants, Trans-Europ-Express, Mon Amour, Mon Amour, Un Homme a Abattre, La Morte Ha Fatto L'Uovo, Les Biches, Grand Silence, Z, Ma Nuit Chez Maud (My Night at Maud's), The Conformist, The Crook, Without Apparent Motive, The Outside Man, The French Conspiracy, Simon the Swiss, Agression, Les Violons du Bal, The Sunday Woman, Under Fire, La Nuit de Varennes, Long Live Life!, Next Summer, Departure, Return, The Man With the Silver Eyes, Femme Je Personne, Confidentially Yours, A Man and a Woman: 20 Years Later, La Vallee Fantome; Rendezvous, Bunker Palace Hotel.

TROELL, JAN: Writer, Director, Cinematographer. b. Sweden, July 23, 1931. Was teacher before entering industry. In early 60s photographed Bo Widerberg's first film, The Pram. Became apprentice in TV; made m.p. debut as director in 1965 with Stay in the Marshland.
PICTURES: Here Is Your Life, Eeny, Meeny, Miny, Mo, The Emigrants, The New Land, Zandy's Bride, Hurricane, The Fairytale Country (dir., editor), The Flight of the Eagle.

TROSPER, GUY: Writer. b. Lander, WY. Started as reader, Samuel Goldwyn; then story ed.; screen writer since 1941.
PICTURES: Stratton Story (co-s.p.); Devil's Doorway, Inside Straight; Pride of St. Louis (story); Many Rivers to Cross (co-s.p.); The Americano, Girl He Left Behind, Jailhouse Rock, Darby's Rangers, One-Eyed Jacks (co-s.p.); Birdman of Alcatraz; The Spy Who Came in From the Cold (co-s.p.).

TRUMBULL, DOUGLAS: Cinematographer, Director, Writer. Inventor Showscan Film process. President, Berkshire Motion Picture.
PICTURES: Did special effects for Silent Running; 2001: A Space Odyssey; The Andromeda Strain; Close Encounters of the Third Kind; Blade Runner, Star Trek: The Motion Picture. Produced and directed Brainstorm, dir.: Silent Running.

TRYON, THOMAS: Actor. b. Hartford, CT, Jan. 14, 1926. e. Yale U. Served in U.S. Navy, W.W.II, studied at Art Students League; with Cape Playhouse, Dennis, MA, as set painter, asst. stage mgr., actor; prod. asst., CBS; then TV actor.
PLAYS INCLUDE: Wish You Were Here, Cyrano de Bergerac, Richard III.
PICTURES: m.p. debut in Scarlet Hour; since in Screaming Eagles, Three Violent People, Moon Pilot, Marines Let's Go, The Cardinal, The Glory Guys, The Other (exec. prod., s.p.), The Horsemen, Johnny Got His Gun (also prod.), Fedora (orig. story).
TELEVISION: Texas John Slaughter (series).
AUTHOR: The Other, Harvest Home, Lady, Crowned Heads.

TSUKASA, YOKO: Actress. b. Tottori, Japan, Aug. 20, 1934. e.

Kyoritsu Coll. joined Toho Studio 1954 after period as magazine cover girl.
PICTURES: Don't Die My Darling, Blue Beast, Eternity of Love, End of Summer, Three Treasures, Yojimbo (The Bodyguard), Women of Design.

TUCKER, MELVILLE: Executive. b. New York, NY, Mar. 4, 1916. e. Princeton U. Asst. purchasing agent Consolidated Laboratories, N.Y., 1934–36; sound effects & picture ed., Republic Productions, Inc. 1936–8; then asst. production mgr. & first asst. dir., 1938–42; served in U.S. Army 1942–46; asst. prod. Republic 1946; assoc. producer, 1947–52; prod., Universal 1952–54; prod. exec. v.p., Universal, 1955–70; production exec. U-I, 1954–71; prod.-Verdon Prods., 1971–present.
PICTURES: The Missourians, Thunder in God's Country, Rodeo King and the Senorita, Utah Wagon Train. U-I prod., 1953: Drums Across the River, Black Shield of Falworth; prod. A Warm December, Uptown Saturday Night, Let's Do It Again, A Piece of the Action, exec. prod.: Stir Crazy, Hanky Panky, Fast Forward.

TUCKER, MICHAEL: Actor. b. Baltimore, MD, Feb. 6, 1944. m. actress Jill Eikenberry. e. Carnegie Tech. Drama Sch. Worked in regional theater (Washington's Arena Stage) and with the New York Shakespeare Festival in Trelawney of the Wells, Comedy of Errors, Measure for Measure, The Merry Wives of Windsor. Also prod. revivel of El Grande de Coca Cola (1986).
THEATER: Also includes Moonchildren, Modigliani, The Goodbye People, The Rivals, Mother Courage, Waiting for Godot, Oh, What a Lovely War, I'm Not Rappaport (American Place Theatre).
PICTURES: A Night Full of Rain (1977), The Eyes of Laura Mars, An Unmarried Woman, Diner, The Goodbye People, The Purple Rose of Cairo, Radio Days, Tin Men, Checking Out.
TELEVISION: Hill Street Blues. Series: L.A. Law. Movies: Concealed Enemies, Vampire, Assault and Matrimony, Day One. Specials: Love, Sex. . .and Marriage, A Family Again.

TUCKERMAN, DAVID R.: Executive. b. Perth Amboy, NJ, Nov. 9, 1946. e. Monmouth Coll., Florida U., 1967–70; B.S.B.A. Entered industry with A.I.T. Theatres, 1967; gen. mgr., Music Makers Theatres, 1973; v.p., Leigh Group, MMT, head film buyer, 1976; sr. v.p., MMT, 1980; Loews Film Buyer, 1986.
MEMBER: SMPTE, Variety Int., MPBC, AFI.

TUGGLE, RICHARD: Director, Writer. b. Coral Gables, FL, Aug. 8, 1948. e. U. Virginia, B.A. 1970. Wrote screenplays before directorial debut with Tightrope, 1984.
PICTURES: Escape from Alcatraz (s.p.), Tightrope (dir., s.p.), Out of Bounds (dir.).

TULIPAN, IRA H.: Publicist. b. New York, NY. e. NYU, B.S., 1934. Entered m.p. ind. as theatre mgr., Boston, 1934; pub. dept. Warner Bros. home office, 1935–40; joined 20th Century-Fox 1942; U.S. Army service 1943–46; returned to Fox upon disch., feature writer, press book ed.; trade paper contact; newspaper contact; pub. mgr. 1955; ass't. dir. adv. pub. expl. Columbia Pictures. 1960; exec. adm. asst. to adv., publ., v.p., Columbia, 1963; dir. overseas prod. pub., 1966. Returned to U.S. in 1978 as eastern pub.-coordinator; 1984, pub. consultant, Universal Pictures.

TUNBERG, KARL: Writer. b. Spokane, WA, 1909. From 1937 collab. many Hollywood s.p.
PICTURES: You Can't Have Everything, My Lucky Star, Hold That Co-Ed, Down Argentine Way, Yank in the RAF, (co-s.p.) My Gal Sal, Orchestra Wives, Tall, Dark and Handsome (s.p. & story); Weekend in Havana (s.p. & story), I Was an Adventuress (s.p.), Lucky Jordan, (co-s.p.) Dixie, Standing Room Only, Bring on the Girls; (prod. & co-s.p.) Kitty; (prod.) You Gotta Stay Happy; (co-s.p.) Love That Brute, Night Into Morning, Law and the Lady, Because You're Mine, Scandal at Scourie, Valley of the Kings; s.p. Beau Brummell, Scarlet Coat, Seventh Sin, Ben Hur, s.p. Count Your Blessings; s.p. Libel, Taras Bulba; I Thank A Fool; The Seventh Dawn, Harlow (story); Where Were You When the Lights Went Out? (co-s.p.)

TUNE, TOMMY: Actor, Director, Choreographer, Dancer. b. Wichita Falls, TX, Feb. 28, 1939. Began professional career dancing in chorus of Bdwy. shows (Baker Street, A Joyful Noise, How Now Dow Jones, etc.). Signed by 20th-Fox and cast in Hello, Dolly! (1969).
PICTURE: The Boy Friend.
STAGE: Performer: Seesaw, My One and Only. Director and/or choreographer: The Club, Cloud 9, The Best Little Whorehouse in Texas, Nine. A Day in Hollywood/A Night in the Ukraine, Stepping Out, My One and Only.
TELEVISION: Dean Martin Presents the Golddiggers, numerous specials and Tony Award Shows.

TURMAN, LAWRENCE: Producer. b. Los Angeles, CA, Nov. 28, 1926. e. UCLA. In textile business 5 years, then joined Kurt Frings Agency; left in 1960 to form Millar-Turman Prods.
PICTURES: Prod. The Young Doctors, I Could Go on Singing, The Best Man. Formed own prod. co., Lawrence Turman, Inc., to make The Flim-Flam Man, The Graduate, Pretty Poison, The Drowning Pool, First Love, Heroes, Walk Proud, Caveman (co-prod.), The Thing, Second Thoughts (prod., dir., s.p.), Mass Appeal, The Mean Season, Short Circuit, Running Scared, Full Moon in Blue Water, Short Circuit 2, Gleaming the Cube.
TELEVISION: Co-prod. with David Foster: The Gift of Love, The Morning After, News at Eleven, Between Two Brothers, She Lives, Unwed Father. Co-exec. prod.: Jesse.

TURNER, CLIFFORD: Producer. b. Leeds, England, 1913. Ent. m.p. industry as cutting room asst. Gaumont British. Edited number early British pictures, before going to Hollywood in 1935. Subsequently edited for Warners, Columbia, Universal, Fox. Returned to England 1948 to edit The Small Back Room. Dir. and exec. prod. since 1950 in Hollywood and NY. Formed Boulevard Film Productions Ltd., Screen Biographies Intl. Inc., Television Enterprises Inc. Four Against the Bank of England. 1972: Utrillo, Rose of Cimarron, Mystery of the General Grant; La Cicatrice, The Valadon Story, Streets of Montmartre, The Murderess, Le Nain Rouge.

TURNER, FREDERICK: Executive. b. London, England. Ent. m.p. ind. 1946. Early career with Eagle-Lion before transferring to Rank Overseas Film Distributors, then Rank Film Distributors. Became financial controller and appt. managing director 1981. Currently responsible for Film Investments and Distribution, UK and Overseas, covering all media.

TURNER, KATHLEEN: Actress. b. Springfield, MO, June 19, 1954. e. U. of Maryland. Starred in NBC soap opera, The Doctors; on Bdwy. stage in Gemini. Starred in Camille (Long Wharf, CT, 1987). Film debut in Body Heat, 1981.
PICTURES: The Man With Two Brains, Romancing the Stone, Crimes of Passion, A Breed Apart, Prizzi's Honor, Jewel of the Nile, Peggy Sue Got Married, Switching Channels, Julia and Julia, Who Framed Roger Rabbit (voice), The Accidental Tourist, Dear America: Letters Home From Vietnam (reader), The War of the Roses, Hard Boiled.

TURNER, LANA: Actress. b. Wallace, ID, Feb. 8, 1921. Parents, Virgil Turner and Mildred Cowan.
PICTURES: They Won't Forget, Great Garrick, Adventures of Marco Polo, Love Finds Andy Hardy; Rich Man, Poor Girl; Dramatic School, Calling Dr. Kildare, These Glamour Girls, Dancing Coed. Two Girls on Broadway, We Who Are Young, Ziegfeld Girl, Dr. Jekyll and Mr. Hyde, Johnny Eager, Slightly Dangerous, Marriage Is a Private Affair, Keep Your Powder Dry, Week-End at the Waldorf, Postman Always Rings Twice, Green Dolphin Street, Cass Timberlane, Homecoming, Three Musketeers, Life of Her Own, Mr. Imperium, The Merry Widow, Bad & the Beautiful, Latin Lovers, Flame & the Flesh, Betrayed, The Prodigal, Sea Chase, Rains of Ranchipur, Diane, Lady and the Flyer, Imitation of Life, Portrait in Black, By Love Possessed, Bachelor in Paradise, Who's Got the Action?, Love Has Many Faces, Madame X, The Big Cube, Persecution, Bittersweet Love.
TELEVISION: The Survivors (series), Love Boat, Falcon Crest.

TURNER, ROBERT EDWARD (TED): Executive. b. Cincinnati, OH., Nov. 19, 1938. e. Brown U. Began career in Savannah in family's outdoor adv. business, selling space on billboards. Bought co. in 1963 and in 1970 entered broadcasting with purchase of a failing TV station in Atlanta which he turned into WTBS, a "superstation" which in 1985 reached 80% of U.S. homes equipped with cable. 1980, established CNN a 24-hr. cable news service. Purchased MGM. Co-owner two professional sports teams in Atlanta: Braves (baseball) and Hawks (basketball). Started Turner Network Television 1988.

TURNER, TINA: Singer, Actress. r.n. Annie Mae Bullock. b. Brownsville, TX, Nov. 26, 1939. Previously married to Ike Turner and appeared with him on road in Ike and Tina Turner Revue. Many hit records.
PICTURES: Gimme Shelter, Soul to Soul, Tommy, Sound of the City, Mad Max Beyond Thunderdrome.
TELEVISION: Tina—Live From Rio.

TURTURRO, JOHN: Actor. b. Brooklyn, NY, Feb. 28, 1957. e. SUNY/New Paltz; Yale Drama School, 1983. Worked in regional theater and off-Bdwy in Danny and the Deep Blue Sea (Obie Award, 1985), Men Without Dates, Tooth of the Crime, La Puta Viva, Chaos and Hard Times, The Bald Soprano, Of Mice and Men. Bdwy debut, Death of a Salesman (1984).
PICTURES: Raging Bull, Desperately Seeking Susan, Exterminator II, The Flamingo Kid, Gung Ho, Offbeat, Hannah and Her Sisters, To Live and Die in L.A., The Color of Money, Five Corners, The Sicilian, Do the Right Thing, Miller's Crossing, Men of Respect, Love Supreme.

TUSHINGHAM, RITA: Actress. b. Liverpool, England, March 14, 1940. m. director Ousama Rawi. Student at Liverpool Playhouse. M.p. debut 1961 in A Taste of Honey (1961).
THEATER: The Giveaway, Lorna and Ted, Mistress of

Novices, The Undiscovered Country, Mysteries.
PICTURES: The Leather Boys, A Place to Go, Girl With The Green Eyes, The Knack, Dr. Zhivago, The Trap, Smashing Time, Diamonds for Breakfast, The Guru, The Bedsitting Room, Straight on 'til Morning, Situation, Instant Coffee, The Human Factor, Rachel's Man, The Slum Boy, The Black Journal, Bread, Butter and Jam, Mysteries, Felix Krull, Lady Killers, The Spaghetti Thing, Seeing Red, The Housekeeper, Resurrected.
TELEVISION: (U.S.) Green Eyes.

TUTIN, DOROTHY: Actress. b. London, Eng., Apr. 8, 1930. e. St. Catherine's Sch. Bramley, Guildford (Surrey). Stage debut in The Thistle & the Rose, 1949.
PLAYS INCLUDE: Much Ado About Nothing, The Living Room, I Am a Camera, The Lark, Wild Duck, Juliet, Ophelia, Viola, Portia, Cressida, Rosalind, The Devils, Once More With Feeling, The Cherry Orchard, Victoria Regina-Portrait of a Queen, Old Times, Peter Pan, What Every Woman Knows, Month in the Country, Macbeth, Antony and Cleopatra, Undiscovered Country, Reflections, After the Lions, Ballerina, A Kind of Alaska, Are You Sitting Comfortably?, Chalk Garden, Brighton Beach Memoirs, Thursday's Ladies, The Browning Version.
PICTURES: Screen debut in The Importance of Being Earnest. Also: The Beggar's Opera, A Tale of Two Cities, Cromwell, Savage Messiah, The Shooting Party, Murder with Mirrors.
TELEVISION: Living Room, Victoria Regina, Invitation to a Voyage, Antigone, Colombe, Carrington V.C., The Hollow Crown, Scent of Fear, From Chekhov With Love, Anne Boleyn in The Six Wives of Henry VIII, Flotsam and Jetsam, Mother & Son, South Riding, Willow Cabins, Ghosts, Sister Dora, The Double Dealer, The Combination, La Ronde, Tales of the Unexpected, 10 Downing Street, Life After Death, King Lear, Landscape, The Father, The Demon Lover, Robin Hood.

TWAINE, MICHAEL: Actor, Director. b. New York, NY, Nov. 1, 1939. e. Ohio State U. Served U.S. Army. While studying with Lee Strasberg, worked as private detective, school teacher. Made stage debut City Center, 1956, in Mr. Roberts. Became village coffee house and club comedian 1968 to 1972.
PICTURES: Marriage Italian Style (voice only); American Soap, Blood Bath, F.I.S.T., Cheap Shots.
TELEVISION: The Silent Drum, Starsky & Hutch, Wonder Woman, Streets of San Francisco, Soap, Lou Grant, Diff'rent Strokes, Nurse, Stalk the Wild Child, The Courage and the Passion, Eischied, America's Most Wanted.

TWIGGY: Actress. Recording Artist. r.n. Leslie Hornby. b. London, England, Sept. 19, 1949. m. actor Michael Witney. At 17 regarded as world's leading high fashion model. Made m.p. debut in The Boy Friend, 1971. Starred in many London West End Shows, including Cinderella and Captain Beaky Presents. Star of Broadway and touring stage productions of Funny Face. 1983: on Broadway in musical, My One and Only.
TELEVISION: Hosted and starred in major American & British music shows including Twiggy (U.K.), Twiggy and Friends (U.K.), and Juke Box (U.S.); also in Pygmalion (England), Sun Child (Eng.), Young Charlie Chaplin. Movie: The Diamond Trap.
PICTURES: W, There Goes the Bride, The Blues Brothers, The Doctor and the Devils, Club Paradise, Madame Sousatzka, Istanbul.

TWYMAN, ALAN P.: Executive. b. Dayton, OH, May 30, 1934. e. U. of Cincinnati. Twyman Films, Inc. sales 1958, vice pres.-pres., 1975. NAVA board of directors, 1964–69; pres. 1970, chmn. of bd., 1972. In 1983 left to form own co., Alan Twyman Presents.

TYRRELL, SUSAN: Actress. b. San Francisco, CA, 1946. Made first prof. appearance with Art Carney in summer theatre tour prod. of Time Out for Ginger. Worked in off-Bdwy. prods. and as waitress in coffee house before attracting attention in Lincoln Center Repertory Co. prods. of A Cry of Players, The Time of Your Life, Camino Real.
THEATER: The Knack, Futz, Father's Day, A Coupla White Chicks Sitting Around Talking.
PICTURES: The Steagle (debut, 1971), Been Down So Long, It Looks Like Up to Me, Shoot Out, Fat City, Catch My Soul, Zandy's Bride, The Killer Inside Me, Islands in the Stream, Andy Warhol's Bad, I Never Promised You A Rose Garden, Another Man, Another Chance, September 30, 1955, Forbidden Zone, Subway Riders, Tales of Ordinary Madness, Loose Shoes, Fast-Walking, Liar's Moon, Fire and Ice, Night Warning, Angel, The Killers, Avenging Angel, Flesh and Blood, Tapeheads, The Underachievers, Big Top Pee-Wee Far From Home, Cry Baby.
TELEVISION: Open All Night (series), Windmills of the Gods, Lady of the House, Midnight Lace, Jealousy, Thompson's Last Run, Poker Alice, The Christmas Star, If Tomorrow Comes.

TYSON, CICELY: Actress. b. New York, NY, Dec. 19, 1933. e. NYU. Studied at Actor's Studio. Former secretary and model. Co-founder, Dance Theatre of Harlem.
THEATER: The Blacks, Moon on a Rainbow Shawl, Tiger Tiger Burning Bright, The Corn Is Green.
PICTURES: Twelve Angry Men, Odds Against Tomorrow, Last Angry Man, A Man Called Adam, The Comedians, The Heart Is a Lonely Hunter, Sounder, The Blue Bird, The River Niger, A Hero Ain't Nothin, But a Sandwich, The Concorde—Airport '79.
TELEVISION: East Side, West Side (series), The Autobiography of Miss Jane Pittman (Emmy Award), Roots, A Woman Called Moses, King, Just An Old Sweet Song, The Marva Collins Story, Benny's Place, Wilma, Playing with Fire, Acceptable Risks, Samaritan, The Women of Brewster Place, Without Borders (host).

U

UGGAMS, LESLIE: Singer. b. New York, NY, May 25, 1943. e. Professional Children's Sch., grad., 1960. Juilliard Sch. of Music. Beg. singing career age 5. TV debut as Ethel Waters' niece on Beulah. Also on Johnny Olsen's TV kids at age 7, Your Show of Shows as singer, 1953; Recording artist for Columbia Records, Atlantic, Motown Wrote The Leslie Uggams Beauty Book (1962).
STAGE: Hallelujah Baby (Tony Award, 1968), Her First Roman, Blues in the Night, Jerry's Girls, Anything Goes (natl. co. & Bdwy).
PICTURES: Two Weeks in Another Town, Poor Pretty Eddie, Black Girl, Heartbreak Motel, Skyjacked.
RADIO: Peter Lind Hayes-Mary Healy Show, Milton Berle, Arthur Godfrey, Star Time.
TELEVISION: Beulah (1949), Kids and Company, Milton Berle Show, Name That Tune, Jack Paar Show, Garry Moore, Series: Sing Along With Mitch, The Leslie Uggams Show (1969). Movies: Roots, Sizzle, Backstairs at the White House (mini-series), The Book of Lists (co-host). Fantasy (Emmy, 1983, host), I Love Men, Specials: 'S Wonderful, 'S Marvelous, 'S Gershwin, Sinatra and Friends. Placido Domingo Steppin' Out With the Ladies.

ULLMAN, TRACEY: Actress, Comedian, Singer. b. Hackbridge, England. m. British TV prod. Allan McKeown. e. won a performance sch. scholarship at 12. Attended the Italia Conti School for 4 years. Soon after appeared on British TV and onstage in Grease and The Rocky Horror Picture Show. Also performed in improvisational play Four in a Million (1981) at the Royal Court Theatre, London (London Theatre Critics Award). Recorded gold-selling album You Broke My Heart in Seventeen Places. Film debut, Plenty (1985). U.S. TV debut, The Tracey Ullman Show (debuted April, 1987).
PICTURES: Plenty, Give My Regards to Broad Street, Jumpin' Jack Flash, I Love You to Death.
TELEVISION: Three of a King (BBC series), They Don't Know (Music video).

ULLMANN, LIV: Actress. b. Japan of Norwegian parents, Dec. 16, 1939. Accompanied parents to Canada when W.W.II began and later returned to Norway. Was catapulted to fame in a succession of Swedish films directed by Ingmar Bergman. Author: Changing, (1977). Choices.
THEATER: (U.S.) A Doll's House, Anna Christie, I Remember Mama (musical), Ghosts.
PICTURES: The Wayward Girl (debut, 1959), Swedish: Persona (debut), Hour of the Wolf, Shame, The Passion of Anna, The Emigrants, Face to Face, Cries and Whispers; Scenes From a Marriage, The Serpent's Egg, Autumn Sonata, American: The Devil's Imposter (formerly Pope Joan), Lost Horizon, 40 Carats, The New Land, Zandy's Bride, The Abdication, Leonor, Richard's Things, A Bridge Too Far, The Wild Duck, Bay Boy, The Night Visitor, Gaby—A True Story. Italian: Moscow Adieu (Donatello Award, Best Actress, 1987); A Time of Indifference, La Amiga, The Rose Garden, Mindwalk.
TELEVISION: Lady From the Sea, Jacobo Timerman: Prisoner Without a Name, Cell Without a Number.

UNGER, ANTHONY B.: Executive, Producer. b. New York, NY, Oct. 19, 1940. e. Duke U., U. of Southern California. Prod. ass't Third Man, TV series, 1961. v.p. Unger Productions, Inc., 1964; v.p. Landau-Unger Co., Inc., 1965; v.p. Commonwealth United Entertainment in London, 1968; pres., Unger Prods. Inc., 1978–present.
PICTURES: assoc. prod.: The Desperate Ones. The Madwoman of Chaillot. The Battle of Neretva, The Magic Christian, Julius Caesar. The Devil's Widow. Don't Look Now; co-prod.: Force Ten From Navarone, The Unseen; Silent Rage.

UNGER, KURT: Producer. b. Berlin, Jan. 10, 1922. Entered ind. in 1939 in chg. m.p. entertainment British troops in Middle East.

Subsequently distributor for United Artists Corp. in Israel and Italy.
PICTURES: Judith, Best House in London, Puppet on a Chain, Pope Joan (The Devil's Imposter), Return From the River Kwai.

UNGER, STEPHEN A.: Executive. b. New York, NY, May 31, 1946. e. NYU, Grad. Film and Television Instit. Started as independent prod. and dist. of theatrical and TV films. In June, 1978, joined Universal Pictures Intl. Sales as foreign sls. mgr. Named v.p. Universal Theatrical Motion Pictures in 1979, responsible for licensing theatrical or TV features not handled by U.I.P. in territories outside U.S. & Canada and worldwide acquisitions. In 1980 joined CBS Theatrical Films as intl. v.p., sls.; 1982–88, pres., Unger Intl. Distributors, Inc.; 1988 joined Korn/Ferry Intl. as exec. v.p., worldwide entertainment div. Promoted to mng. dir., 1989.

URICH, ROBERT: Actor. b. Toronto, OH, Dec. 19, 1947. e. Florida State U., B.A., radio and TV communications; Michigan State U., M.A. Communications Mgmt. Appeared in university plays. Was sales account executive at WGN Radio, Chicago, before turning to stage acting (Ivanhoe Theatre, Chicago).
TELEVISION: The FBI, Gunsmoke, Kung Fu, Marcus Welby, MD, S.W.A.T., Bob & Carol & Ted & Alice, Soap, Tabitha, The Love Boat, Vega$, Spenser For Hire; Movies: Fighting Back, Bunco, When She Was Bad, Princess Daisy, Invitation to Hell, Mistral's Daughter, His Mistress, Scandal Sheet, Young Again, Spenser for Hire, Amerika, April Morning, The Comeback, She Knows Too Much, Murder By Night, Night Walk.
PICTURES: Magnum Force, Endangered Species, The Ice Pirates, Turk 182.

URMAN, MARK: Executive. b. New York, NY, Nov. 24, 1952. e. Union Coll., 1973; NYU, cinema, 1973–74. m. story analyst Deborah Davis. 1973, apprentice publicist, Universal Pictures; 1973–82, United Artists intl. dept. as assoc. publicist, sr. publicist and ultimately asst. to v.p. worldwide ad-pub.; 1982–84, dir., publicity and marketing, Triumph Films (Columbia/Gaumont); 1985–86, exec. dir. East Coast pub., Columbia Pictures; 1986–89, v.p. East Coast pub., Columbia Pictures. Joined Dennis Davidson Associates as v.p., 1989. Member: Motion Picture Assoc. Ratings Appeal Board; advisory comm., U.S. Film Festival.

URQUHART, ROBERT: Actor, Writer. b. Scotland, October 16, 1922. e. George Heriots, Edinburgh. Served in Merchant Navy 1938–45; stage debut, Park Theatre, Glasgow; screen debut: You're Only Young Twice, 1951.
PICTURES: Isn't Life Wonderful, The House Of The Arrow, Knights of the Round Table, Happy Ever After (Tonight's the Night), Golden Ivory, The Dark Avenger, You Can't Escape, Yangtse Incident, Curse of Frankenstein, Dunkirk, The Trouble with Eve, Danger Tomorrow, Foxhole in Cairo, Murder in Mind, The Bulldog Greed, 55 Days At Peking, The Break, Murder at the Gallup, The Syndicate, The Limbo Line, The Looking Glass War, Brotherly Love (Country Dance), Playing Away, Restless Natives, Sharma and Beyond, P'Tang Bang Clipper Bang, Kitchen Toto.
TELEVISION: Tamer Tamed, Infinite Shoeblack, Morning Departure, The Human Touch, The Iron Harp, Sleeping Clergyman, The Naked Lady, For Services Rendered, The Bright One, Jango, Murder Swamp, She Died Young, Plane Makers (series), Reporter, Inheritors (series); Mr. Goodall (series), The Nearly Man, The Button Man, Happy Returns, Endless-Aimless, Bleak House, The Queens Arms, Shostakovich.
AUTHOR: (Wrote TV) House of Lies, End of the Tether, Landfall, The Touch of a Dead Hand.

USLAN, MICHAEL E.: Producer, Writer. b. Bayonne, NJ, 1951. e. Indiana U., A.B., M.S., J.D. Wrote 12 books, including Dick Clark's 1st 25 Years of Rock 'n' Roll; 1976–80 atty. with United Artists; Produced with Benjamin Melniker: First National Trivia Quiz (prod., writer); Dinosaucers (series, exec. prod., creator, writer); Three Sovereigns for Sarah (exec. prod.); Television's Greatest Bits (prod., creator, writer).
PICTURES: Swamp Thing (prod.), The Return of the Swamp Thing, Batman (exec. prod.).

USTINOV, PETER: O.B.E. Actor, Writer, Director. b. London, Eng., Apr. 16, 1921. e. Westminster Sch. In Brit. Army, W.W.II. On Brit. stage from 1937. Screen debut 1941 in Brit. picture Mein Kampf, My Crimes, Commander, Order of British Empire 1975. Awards: 2 Acad. Awards, supp. actor; Golden Globe; 3 Emmy Awards; 1 Grammy; NY Critics Award and Donaldson, best foreign play (The Love of Four Colonels); British Critics Award (Romanoff and Juliet).
THEATER: Romanoff and Juliet, N.Y., London; and 17 other plays. Dir., acted, Photo Finish; wrote, Life In My Hands, The Unknown Soldier and His Wife, Half Way Up The Tree, King Lear, Beethoven's Tenth, etc.
PICTURES: *Actor:* The Goose Steps Out, One of Our Aircraft Is Missing, Let the People Sing, The Way Ahead, The True Glory, The Way Ahead (co-s.p.); School for Secrets (wrote, dir. & co-prod.), Vice Versa; Private Angelo (adapt., dir., co-prod.), Odette, Quo Vadis, Hotel Sahara, The Egyptian, Beau Brummell, We're No Angels, Lola Montez, The Spies, An Angel Flew over Brooklyn, The Sundowners, Spartacus; Romanoff and Juliet (prod., s.p., actor), Billy Budd (prod., dir., s.p., actor), Topkapi, John Goldfarb Please Come Home; Lady L., Blackbeard's Ghost (prod., dir.), The Comedians, Hot Millions, Viva Max. Hammersmith Is Out (dir., actor), Big Truck, Poor Clare, Logan's Run, Treasure of Matecumbe, One of Our Dinosaurs Is Missing, Le Taxi Mauve, The Last Remake of Beau Geste, Doppio Delitto, Death on the Nile, Charlie Chan and the Curse of the Dragon Queen, The Great Muppet Caper, Evil Under the Sun; Memed My Hawk (dir., prod., actor); Appointment with Death; Murder in Mesopotamia; The French Revolution, The Man Who Loved Hitchcock.
RECENT TV: The Well Tempered Bach, 13 at Dinner, Deadman's Folly, Peter Ustinov's Russia, World Challenge, Murder in Three Acts, The Secret Identity of Jack the Ripper (host), Around the World in 80 Days.

V

VACCARO, BRENDA: Actress. b. Brooklyn, NY, Nov. 18, 1939. e. Thomas Jefferson H.S., Dallas; studied two yrs. at Neighborhood Playhouse in N.Y. Was waitress and model before landing first Bdwy. role in Everybody Loves Opal. Toured in Tunnel of Love and returned to N.Y. for role in The Affair.
THEATER: The Affair, Children From Their Games, Cactus Flower (Tony Award, supp. actress, 1965), The Natural Look, How Now Dow Jones, The Goodbye People, Father's Day.
PICTURES: (debut) Midnight Cowboy, I Love My Wife, Summertree, Going Home, Once Is Not Enough, Airport '77, House by the Lake, Capricorn One, The First Deadly Sin, Zorro, the Gay Blade, Supergirl, Water, Cookie, Heart of Midnight, Ten Little Indians, The Masque of Red Death.
TELEVISION: The F.B.I., The Name of the Game, The Helen Reddy Show, The Shape of Things (special, Emmy, supp. actress, 1974). Series: Sara, Dear Detective, Paper Dolls. Movies: Sunshine, Deception, Julius and Ethel Rosenberg, Guyana Tragedy, Star Maker, Honor Thy Father, A Long Way Home, The Pride of Jesse Hallam.

VADIM, ROGER: Director, Writer. b. Paris, Jan. 26, 1928. r.n. Roger Vadim Plemiannikow.
PICTURES: Futures Vedettes (s.p.). Writer-Director: And God Created Woman, Heaven Fell That Night, Les Liaisons Dangereuses, Warrior's Rest, Vice and Virtue, La Ronde, The Game is Over. Director: Barbarella, Pretty Maids All in a Row, Don Juan, Night Games, A Faithful Woman, Hot Touch, And God Created Woman (1988).
TELEVISION: Beauty and the Beast (Faerie Tale Theatre).

VAJNA, ANDREW: Executive. b. Budapest, Hungary, Aug. 1, 1944. e. UCLA. Launched career with purchase of m.p. theaters in Far East. Founded Panasia Film Ltd. in Hong Kong. Exhibitor and dist. of feature films since 1970. Formed Carolco Service, Inc. (foreign sls. org.), with Mario Kassar 1976. Founder and Pres., American Film Mkt. Assn., 1982.
PICTURES: Exec. Prod.: The Silent Partner, The Changeling, Suzanne, The Amateur, Your Ticket Is No Longer Valid, Carbon Copy, First Blood, First Blood Part II, Angel Heart, Extreme Prejudice, Red Heat, Iron Eagle II, Deepstar Six, Johnny Handsome, Air America, Total Recall.

VALE, EUGENE: Writer. b. April 11, 1916. e. Zurich, Switzerland. m. Evelyn Wahl. Story and s.p., The Second Face, The Shattered Dream, 1954 SWG award nom., best written telefilm; The Dark Wave. 1957, m.p. academy award nominations.
PICTURES: A Global Affair, Francis of Assissi, The Bridge of San Luis Rey.
TELEVISION: Four Star Playhouse, Fireside Theatre, 20th Century Fox Hour, Schlitz Playhouse, Hollywood Opening Night, NBC, Crusader, Lux Video Theatre, Danger, CBS, Chevron Theatre, Douglas Fairbanks, Pepsi Cola Playhouse, Waterfront, Christophers, Cavalcade of America, Hallmark Hall of Fame.
AUTHOR: Technique of Screenplay Writing.

VALENTI, JACK J.: Executive. b. Sept. 5, 1921. e. U. of Houston, B.A., 1946; Harvard U., M.B.A., bus. admin., 1948. Air force pilot in European theatre, W.W.II; adv. and pub. rel. exec. in Houston; special asst. and advisor to Pres. Lyndon B. Johnson, 1963–66, elected pres., Motion Picture Association of America, MPEA and AMPTP, since June, 1966. Named Motion Picture Pioneer of the Year, 1988.

VALENTINE, KAREN: Actress. b. Sebastopol, CA, May 25, 1947.
PICTURES: Forever Young, Forever Free, Hot Lead and Cold Feet, The North Avenue Irregulars.
TELEVISION:Series: Room 222 (Emmy), Karen, My Friend Tony, Hollywood Squares, Laugh-In, The Bold Ones, Sonny and Cher, Mike Hammer, Murder, She Wrote. Movies: Gidget

Grows Up, The Daughters of Joshua Cabe, Coffee, Tea or Me?, The Girl Who Came Gift-Wrapped, The Love Boat, Having Babies, Murder at the World Series, Return to Fantasy Island, Go West, Young Girl, American 2100, Only the Pretty Girls Die, Muggable Mary, He's Fired, She's Hired; A Fighting Choice, Jane Doe, Skeezer, Money on the Side, Perfect People.

VALLI, ALIDA: Actress. r.n. Alida von Altenburger. b. Pola, Italy, May 31, 1921. e. M.P. Acad., Rome (dramatics); m. Oscar de Mejo, pianist-composer. In Italian m.p.; won Venice Film Festival Award in Piccolo Mondo Antico (Little Old World).
PICTURES: Vita Ricomincia, Giovanna; to U.S. 1947; U.S. m.p. debut in Paradine Case, 1947, Miracle of the Bells, The Third Man, Walk Softly Stranger, White Tower, Lovers of Toledo, Stranger's Hand, The Castilian, Ophelia, Spider's Stratagem, The Cassandra Crossing, Suspiria, 1900, Luna, Le Jupon Rouge, A Notre Regrettable epoux.

VALLONE, RAF: Actor. b. Turin, Italy, Feb. 17, 1916. e. U. of Turin. Newspaper writer; m.p. debut in Bitter Rice (1948).
PICTURES: Under the Olive Tree, Anna, Path of Hope, White Line, Rome 11 O'Clock, Strange Deception, Anita Garibaldi, Daughters of Destiny, Teresa Raquin, Riviera, The Secret Invasion. Two Women, El Cid, A View From the Bridge, Phaedra, Kiss The Girls and Make Them Die, The Desperate Ones, The Cardinal, The Italian Job, The Kremlin Letter, Summertime Killer, Rosebud, The Human Factor, The Other Side of Midnight, The Greek Tycoon, Lion of the Desert.
TELEVISION: Fame (Hallmark Hall of Fame), Honor Thy Father, Catholics, The Scarlet and the Black, Christopher Columbus, Goya.

VAN ARK, JOAN: Actress. b. New York, NY, June 16, 1943. m. NBC news reporter John Marshall. e. Yale U of Drama. Two early appearances on Dallas led to role in spin off Knots Landing on which she has starred 11 years. Began career in touring co. then on Broadway and in London in Barefoot in the Park. Also appeared on Bdwy with the APA-Phoenix Rep. Co. in the 1970s. As a runner has competed in 12 marathons. On TV also created voices for animated series Spiderwoman, Thundarr and Dingbat and the Creeps and special Cyrano de Bergerac.
THEATER: School for Wives, The Rules of the Game (Theatre World Award), L.A. Cyrano de Bergerac, Ring Around the Moon, Chemin de Fer, As You Like It (L.A. Drama Critics Award), Williamston Theatre Fest.: Night of the Iguana, The Legend of Oedipus; Off-Bdwy: Love Letters.
PICTURES: The Frogs.
TELEVISION: Series: Temperatures Rising, We've Got Each Other, Dallas, Knots Landing. Guest: The F.B.I., The Girl with Something Extra, Quark, Dallas, Quincy, Rockford Files, Rhoda. Co-host: Miss USA and Miss Universe Pageants, Battle of the Network Stars. Movies: A Testimony of Two Men, The Last Dinosaur, Big Rose, The Bionic Boy, The Judge and Jake Wyler, Red Flag—The Ultimate Game, Glitter, Shakedown on Sunset Strip, My First Love.

VANCE, LEIGH: Scriptwriter, Producer. b. Harrogate, England, March 18, 1922. e. Shrewsbury Coll. Early career; reporter, critic. Ent. TV 1951, then films, many TV scripts; 1961, won Edgar Allan Poe Award, 1969 brought to Hollywood by Paramount.
PICTURES: The Flesh Is Weak, Heart of a Child, Picadilly Third Stop, Women Shall Weep, The Shakedown, Eyes of Youth, The Frightened City, It's All Happening Dr. Crippen, Outcast, Walk Like A Man, Cross Plot, Tall Cool Girl, The Black Windmill.
TELEVISION: Mannix, Mission Impossible, many pilots and movies-of-the-week. The Avengers, The Saint, Cannon (exec. story consultant, 1973), Caribe (exec. story consultant), Bronk (prod.), Baretta (exec. prod.), Switch (exec. prod.), The Phoenix (prod.), Hart to Hart (prod.).

VAN CLEEF, LEE: Actor. b. Somerville, NJ, Jan. 9, 1925. e. Somerville H.S., 1942. Joined U.S. Navy, 1942; asst. mgr. in summer camp, public accountant; then joined little theatre group.
PICTURES: High Noon, Beast from 20,000 Fathoms, Vice Squad, The Nebraskan, Gypsy Colt, Arrow in the Dust, Yellow Tomahawk, Dawn at Socorro, Princess of the Nile, Ten Wanted Men, The Conqueror, Big Combo, Treasure of Ruby Hills, I Cover the Underworld, Road To Denver, Posse from Hell, The Man Who Shot Liberty Valance, A Man Alone, Vanishing American, Tribute to a Bad Man, For a Few Dollars More, The Good, the Bad and the Ugly, The Big Gundown, Death Rides a Horse, Day of Anger, Barquero, El Condor, The Magnificent Seven Ride, Return of Sabata, Escape from New York, Amred Response, Codename: Wild Geese, The Commander, Speed Zone.

VAN DEVERE, TRISH: Actress. b. Englewood Cliffs, NJ, March 9, 1945. e. Ohio Wesleyan U. Wife of actor George Scott. On Bdwy. in Sly Fox, Tricks of the Trade, etc.
PICTURES: Where's Poppa?, The Last Run, One Is a Lonely Number, The Day of the Dolphin, The Savage Is Loose, Fifty-Two Pickup, Movie, Movie, The Changeling, The Hearse, Findings, Messenger of Death.
TELEVISION: Mayflower—The Pilgrim's Adventure, All God's Children, Haunted.

VAN DOREN, MAMIE: Actress. r.n. Joan Lucille Olander. b. Rowena, SD, Feb. 6, 1933. e. Los Angeles H.S. Secy. law firm, L.A.; prof. debut as singer with Ted Fio Rita orch.
THEATRE: Appeared in many stock plays incl.: Once in a Lifetime, Boy Meets Girl, Come Back Little Sheba.
PICTURES: (m.p. debut) Forbidden; All American, Yankee Pasha, Francis Joins the Wacs, Ain't Misbehavin, Second Greatest Sex, Running Wild, Star in the Dust, Untamed Youth, Girl in Black Stockings, Teachers Pet, The Navy Vs. the Night Monsters.

VAN DYKE, DICK: Actor. b. West Plains, MO, Dec., 18, 1925. U.S.A.F., W.W.II. After discharged from service, opened advertising agency, Danville, IL; folded next year. Teamed with friend in nightclub act called Eric and Van, The Merry Mutes, and for 6 yrs. toured country doing a routine in which they pantomimed and lip-synched to records. 1953 hosted local TV show in Atlanta, then New Orleans. 1956 to NY as host of prime time cartoon show. Emmy Awards: Best actor in a series (1964, 1965); Best actor in a comedy series (1966); Star, best comedy-variety series (Van Dyke and Company, 1977), Best performer in children's prog. (The Wrong Way Kid, 1984).
THEATRE: The Girls Against the Boys, Bye Bye Birdie (Tony Award, 1961), The Music Man (revival).
PICTURES: Bye Bye Birdie, Mary Poppins, What a Way to Go, The Art of Love, Lieutenant Robinson Crusoe, Divorce American Style, What's New Fitzwilly?, Chitty Chitty Bang Bang, Some Kind of Nut, The Comic, Cold Turkey, The Runner Stumbles.
TELEVISION: The Merry Mute Show, The Music Shop, The Dick Van Dyke Show (series), CBS Cartoon Theater (host), The Chevy Showroom, The New Dick Van Dyke Show (series), The Carol Burnett Show, The Van Dyke Show (series, 1988–89). Movies: The Morning After, Drop-Out Father, Found Money, Ghost of a Chance.

VAN FLEET, JO: Actress. b. Oakland, CA, 1922. e. Coll. of the Pacific. Neighborhood Playhouse.
THEATRE: On Broadway in Winter's Tale, Whole World Over, Closing Door, King Lear, Flight into Egypt, Camino Real, Trip to Bountiful (Tony Award); Look Homeward Angel (Critics Award); The Glass Menagerie; The Alligators, Oh Dad, Poor Dad, Mama's Hung You in the Closet and I'm Feeling So Sad.
PICTURES: East of Eden (Academy Award, best supporting actress, 1955); I'll Cry Tomorrow (Look Award), Rose Tattoo, This Angry Age, King and Four Queens, Gunfight at the OK Corral; Wild River, Cool Hand Luke, I Love You, Alice B. Toklas, Gang Who Couldn't Shoot Straight, The Tenant.
TELEVISION: Cinderella, Bonanza, Mod Squad, Power, Paradise Lost, Seize the Day.

VANGELIS: Composer, Conductor. Full name: Vangelis Papathanassiou. b. Greece. Began composing as child, performing own compositions at 6. Left Greece for Paris by late 1960s. Composed and recorded his symphonic poem Faire que ton reve soit plus long que la nuit. and album Terra. Collaborated with filmmaker Frederic Rossif for whom composed La Cantique des Creatures. Moved to London then to Greece in 1989. Formed band Formynx in Greece; then Aphrodite's Child in Paris.
PICTURES: Chariots of Fire (Oscar), Antarctica, Missing, Blade Runner, The Bounty, Wonders of Life, Wild and Beautiful, Francesco.

VAN HEUSEN, JIMMY: Composer. r.n. Edward Chester Babcock. b. Syracuse, NY, Jan. 26, 1913. e. Syracuse U. Pianist with publishing houses; songs for many m.p. Academy Award for Swinging on a Star, High Hopes, All the Way, Call Me Irresponsible.
PICTURES: Road to Rio, Emperor Waltz, Connecticut Yankee, Mr. Music, Riding High, Road to Bali, Bells of St. Mary's. Little Boy Lost. Emmy for Love and Marriage; Songwriters Hall of Fame. Many scores for Bing Crosby pictures, including Going My Way.

VANOCUR, SANDER: News Commentator. b. Cleveland, OH, Jan. 8, 1928. e. Northwestern U. Began career as journalist in London; City staff, NY Times 1955–57. Joined NBC in 1957, hosting First Tuesday series. Resigned in 1971 to be correspondent of the National Public Affairs Center for PBC. In 1977 joined ABC News as v.p., special reporting units 1977–80. Chief overview corr. ABC news, 1980–81; sr. corr. 1981–present. Author: Business World.

VAN PALLANDT, NINA: Actress. b. Copenhagen, Denmark, July 15, 1932. e. U. of Southern California. Returned to Denmark where married Baron Frederik Van Pallandt with whom she had appeared as folk singer throughout Europe. Made 3 films

with him; went on world tour together. Now divorced. Has appeared in New York as singer.
PICTURES: The Long Goodbye, A Wedding, Assault on Agathon, Quintet, American Gigolo, Cloud Dancer, Cutter and Bone, Asi Como Habian Sido, Time Out, O.C. and Stiggs.
TELEVISION: The Sam Shepherd Murder Case.

VAN PATTEN, DICK: b. New York, NY, Dec. 9, 1928. Began career as child actor with Bdwy. debut at 7 yrs., playing son of Melvyn Douglas in Tapestry in Gray. Has worked since in stage, radio, TV, films.
PICTURES: Making It, Joe Kidd, Soylent Green, Dirty Little Billy, Westworld, Strongest Man in the World, Gus, Treasure of Matecumbe, Freaky Friday, High Anxiety, Spaceballs, The New Adventures of Pippi Longstocking.
TELEVISION: Guest: Arnie, The Rookies, Cannon, Banyon, The Little People, The Streets of San Francisco, When Things Were Rotten. Hotel, Growing Pains, Love Boat, Murder She Wrote. Series: I Remember Mama, The Partners, The New Dick Van Dyke Show, Eight is Enough. Movies and specials: Jay Leno's Family Comedy Hour, A Mouse, A Mystery and Me, 14 Going On 30, Eight is Enough Reunion, Going to the Chapel.
STAGE: The Lady Who Came to Stay, O Mistress Mine, On Borrowed Time, Ah, Wilderness, Watch on the Rhine, The Skin of Our Teeth, Kiss and Tell, Mister Roberts, Thieves.

VAN PATTEN, JOYCE: Actress. b. New York, NY, March 9, 1936. Sister of actor Dick Van Patten.
PICTURES: The Goddess, I Love You Alice B. Toklas, Mame, Something Big, Thumb Tripping, Mikey and Nicky, The Falcon and the Snowman, St. Elmo's Fire, Blind Date, Trust Me, Monkey Shines.
TELEVISION: Series: The Danny Kaye Show, The Good Guys, Mary Tyler Moore Variety Hour. Many specials and movies: Shadow of Fear, The Martian Chronicles, Eleanor First Lady of the World, Bus Stop, In Defense of Kids, Malice in Wonderland, Under the Influence, Sirens.

VAN PEBBLES, MARIO: Actor, Director, Producer, Writer. b. Mexico D.F., Mexico, Jan. 15, 1957. Father is filmmaker Melvin Van Pebbles. e. Columbia U., B.A. economics, 1980. Studied acting with Stella Adler 1983. Served as budget analyst for NY Mayor Ed Koch and later worked as an Elite model. Directed music videos for Kid Creole and the Coconuts, Nighttrain (dir., prod., cameo) and for film Identity Crisis. Appeared as child in father's film Sweet Sweetback's Baadasssss Song.
THEATER: Waltz of the Stork (Bdwy debut, 1984), Take Me Along, The Legend of Deadwood Dick.
PICTURES: The Cotton Club, Delivery Boys, Exterminator II, 3:15. Rappin', Heartbreak Ridge, Last Resort, Jaws: the Revenge, Hot Shot, Identity Crisis (also co-prod., s.p.). Also dir., prod., wrote and starred in short, Juliet.
TELEVISION: Series: Sonny Spoons. Guest: L.A. Law, One Life to Live, The Cosby Show. Movies: The Cable Car Murder, Sophisticated Gents, Children of the Night (Bronze Halo Award), The Facts of Life Down Under, The Child Saver. Specials: American Masters: A Glory of Ghosts (Emperor Jones, All God's Chillun), Third & Oak (CBS play). Director: Sonny Spoons, 21 Jump Street, Top of the Hill, Wise Guys, Booker.

VAN PEEBLES, MELVIN: Producer, Director, Writer, Composer. b. Chicago, IL, Aug. 21, 1932. Father of actor Mario Van Peebles. Was portrait painter in Mexico, cable car driver in San Francisco; journalist in Paris and (in 1970s) options trader on Wall Street. Dir. Funky Beat music video.
AUTHOR—BOOKS: The Big Heart, A Bear for the FBI, Le Chinois de XIV, La Permission (Story of a Three Day Pass) La Fete a Harlem, The True American, Sweet Sweetback's Baadasssss Song, Just an Old Sweet Song, Bold Money.
PICTURES: The Story of a Three-Day Pass (prod., dir., s.p.), Watermelon Man (dir.), Sweet Sweetback's Baadasssss Song (prod., dir., s.p., actor), Greased Lightning (co-s.p. only), Identity Crisis (prod., dir., actor).
STAGE: Bdwy: Author, prod., dir.: Waltz of the Stork (also actor). Off-Bdwy: Champeen, Waltz of the Stork.
TELEVISION: Author: Down Home, Just an Old Sweet Song, Sophisticated Gents (actor), The Day They Came to Arrest the Book (Emmy Award). Actor" Taking Care of Terrific, Sonny Spoons (series).
ALBUMS: Composer: Brer Soul, Watermelon Man, Sweet Sweetback's Baadasssss Song, As Serious as a Heart Attack, Don't Play Us Cheap, Ain't Suppose to Die a Natural Death, What the #*!% You Mean, I Can't Sing.

VAN PRAAG, WILLIAM: Executive, Producer, Director, Writer, Editor. Advertising Consultant. b. New York, NY, Sept. 13, 1924. e. CREI, Columbia U. U.S. Army, 1942. Paramount, 1945; Brandt Bros. Prods., 1946; NBC, 1947; v.p. Television Features, 1948. Devlpd. vidicon system in m.p. prod., 1949. Started, pres., Van Praag Prod. Inc. 1951. Formed Ernst-Van Praag, Inc. 1971, a communications and marketing counseling firm (N.Y., Brussels, Tokyo). Pres., International Film, TV and A-V Producers Assn, 1969, Creator of Van-O-Vision. Winner of commercial, short subject and feature theatrical awards. Author of Color Your Picture, Primer of Creative Editing, and Van Praag's Magic Eye. Past pres., Film Producer's Assn, mem. DGA, SAG, 771 IATSE, National Academy of TV Arts and Sciences, International Radio and TV Executive Society and Soc. of MP and TV Engineers.

VAN RIKFOORD, HAROLD C.: Producer. b. New York, NY, Jan. 1, 1935. e. Bryant H.S., grad., 1952; NYU. Errand boy, stage mgr., N.Y., 1954–57. Co-prod. two Broadway plays. Prod., The Long Ride Home, Rome, 1957; prod., short subject films; prod., Moment of Crisis, 1959; prod., television pilot films; exec. prod., Jonathan Shields Prod.

VAN THAL, DENNIS: Executive. b. London, June 4, 1909. e. University Coll. Early career musical dir.; war service, Royal Navy; entered m.p. industry 1946; casting dir. Pinewood Studios; dir., Myron Selznick Ltd.; joined dir. Alexander Korda as prod. exec., 1953; apptd. dir., Big Ben Films, 1955; joined Ealing Films, 1956; prod. assoc. Anastasia; assoc. prod. The Admirable Crichton, Barnacle Bill, The Scapegoat; mgr. dir. London Management, Ltd.

VARDA, AGNES: Photographer, Director, Writer. b. France, 1928. Started as still photographer for The Theatre National Populaire de Jean Vilar. Became a photo-journalist. In 1954 wrote and directed first film, La Pointe Courte. Afterwards made both documentaries and features.
PICTURES: Cleo from 5 to 7, Le Bonheur, Les Creatures, Lion's Love, One Sings, The Other Doesn't, Kung Fu Master! (prod., dir., s.p.); Jane B. par Agnes V. (dir., editor, s.p., actress).

VARSI, DIANE: Actress. b. San Francisco, CA, Feb. 1938.
PICTURES: Peyton Place, Ten North Frederick, From Hell to Texas, Compulsion, Sweet Love, Bitter, Wild in the Streets, Killers Three, Bloody Mama, Johnny Got His Gun, I Never Promised You a Rose Garden.
TELEVISION: The People (movie).

VAUGHN, ROBERT: Actor. b. New York, NY, Nov. 22, 1932. e. L.A. State coll., B.S. and M.A. Theatre Arts 1956; USC, Ph.D. Communications, 1970. Gained fame as Napoleon Solo in The Man From U.N.C.L.E. TV series. Author: Only Victims, 1972.
PICTURES: Hell's Crossroads, No Time to Be Young, Unwed Mother, Good Day for a Hanging, The Young Philadelphians, The City Jungle (Acad. Award nom.), The Magnificent Seven, The Big Show, The Caretakers, To Trap a Spy, The Spy With My Face, One Spy Too Many, The Venetian Affair, How to Steal the World, Bullitt, The Bridge at Remagen, The Mind of Mr. Soames, If It's Tuesday, This Must Be Belgium, Julius Caesar, The Statue, The Clay Pigeon, One of Our Spies Is Missing (TV, Great Britain), The Spy In the Green Hat (TV, Great Britain), The Towering Inferno, Starship Invasions, S.O.B., Superman III, The Delta Force, Black Moon Rising, Rampage, Fire With Fire, Skeleton Coast, B.U.D., River of Death, Captive Rage, Nobody's Perfect, Fair trade, Edgar Allan Poe's Buried Alive, That's Adequate, C.H.U.D. II. The Emissary, Transylvania Twist.
TELEVISION: Washington: Behind Closed Doors, The Blue and the Gray, Evergreen, International Airport, Murrow, Prince of Bel Air, Desperado, Full Circle Again, Ray Bradbury Theater III.

VEITCH, JOHN: Executive. b. New York, NY, June 22, 1925. Started production career as asst. director and moved through ranks as prod. mgr., assoc. prod., prod., second unit dir., and exec. prod. mgr. Appointed Columbia Pictures exec. asst. prod. mgr., 1961; became exec. prod. mgr., 1963. Named v.p. & exec. prod. mgr., 1966; promoted in 1977 to exec. v.p. & exec. prod. mgr. of world-wide productions. In 1979 named pres. of Columbia Pictures Productions. Resigned 1983 to be consultant and independent producer exclusively for Columbia.
PICTURES: Fast Forward, Suspect (exec. prod.).

VELAZCO, ROBERT E.: r.n. Emil Velazco, Jr. b. Dallas, TX, Jan 1, 1924. e. Columbia U., business admin., 1942–43. Started in film business with father, Emil Velazco, 1942. Following yrs. worked for Emil Velazco, Inc., NTA, Ross Gaffney, Inc. During this time worked on over 8,500 productions from 5 sec. to feature films. In charge of Velazco, Inc., Kansas City, MO, 1947–49. Owner and pres., Musifex Co., Inc., 1958. Opened Musifex Inc. Arlington, VA, 1972. Two films scored by Velazco nom. for Academy Award, 1978 and 1980. In 1983 expanded into video tape music editing and video mixing. Retired 1985. Sold co. to Frank A. Maniglia Sr.

VELDE, JAMES R.: Executive. b. Bloomington, IL, Nov. 1, 1913. e. Illinois Wesleyan U. Entered m.p. ind. as night shipper Paramount ex. Detroit, 1934; then city salesman, office mgr. until joining Army, 1943, rejoining same ex. upon dischge., 1946; to Paramount, Washington as Baltimore city salesman, same yr.; br. mgr. Selznick Rel. Org. Pittsburgh, 1948; salesman Eagle-Lion Classics, Pittsburgh, 1949; br. mgr.

ELC, Des Moines, 1949; br. mgr., ELC, Detroit, 1950; west coast dist. mgr., United Artists, April, 1951; Western div. mgr. UA, 1952; gen. sales mgr., 1956; v.p., 1958; dir., UA, 1968; sr. v.p., 1972. Retired, 1977. Worked with Ray Stark as advisor, 1978–83.

VENORA, DIANE: Actress. b. Hartford, CT, 1952. Member of Juilliard's Acting Company and the Ensemble Studio Theatre. Theater includes A Midsummer Night's Dream, the title role in Hamlet (New York Shakespeare Festival), Uncle Vanya (at La Mama), Messiah, Penguin Toquet, Tomorrow's Monday (Circle Rep). Largo Desolato, School for Scandal, Peer Gynt (Williamstown Fest.), The Winter's Tale (Pub. Theater).
PICTURES: All That Jazz, The Critical List, Wolfen, Terminal Choice, The Cotton Club, F/X, Ironweed, Bird, Reversal of Fortune.
TELEVISION: Mini-series: A.D. Movie: Cook and Peary: The Race to the Pole. Special: Getting There.

VERDON, GWEN: Actress, Dancer, Choreographer. b. Culver City, CA, Jan. 13, 1925. Married to late dir.-choreographer Bob Fosse. Studied dancing with her mother, E. Belcher, Carmelita Marrachi, and Jack Cole.
THEATER: Bonanza Bound! (1947), Magdalena (asst. choreographer to Jack Cole), Alive and Kicking (1950), Can-Can (Donaldson Award and Tony Awards), Damn Yankees (Tony Award), New Girl in Town (Tony Award), Redhead (Tony Award), Sweet Charity, Children! Children!, Milliken's Breakfast Show (Waldorf Astoria, 1973), Damn Yankees (revival Westbury, Long Island, 1974), Chicago, Dancin' (asst. choreographer, prod. sprv. road co.), Sing Happy (tribute to Kander and Ebb, 1978), Parade of Stars Playing the Palace (Actors' Fund benefit, 1983), Night of 100 Stars II (1985).
PICTURES: On the Riviera (debut, 1951), David and Bathsheba, Meet Me After the Show, The Merry Widow, The I Don't Care Girl, Farmer Takes a Wife, Damn Yankees, Cocoon, The Cotton Club, Nadine, Cocoon: The Return.
TELEVISION: M*A*S*H, Fame, All My Children, Magnum P.I., The Equalizer, All is Forgiven, Legs, The Jerk Too.

VEREEN, BEN: Singer, Dancer, Actor. b. Miami, FL, Oct. 10, 1946. e. High School of Performing Arts. On stage in Hair, Sweet Charity, Jesus Christ Superstar, Pippin (Tony), Grind.
PICTURES: Gasss, Funny Lady, All That Jazz, The Zoo Gang, Buy and Cell, Friend to Friend.
TELEVISION: Movies: Louis Armstrong—Chicago Style, Roots, Ellis Island, Jesse Owens Story, A.D., Ten Speed and Brown Shoe (series), J.J. Starbuck (series). Specials: Ben Vereen—His Roots, Uptown—A Tribute to the Apollo Theatre, Ellis Island, A. D.

VERHOEVEN, PAUL: Director. b. The Netherlands, 1940. e. U. of Leiden, Ph.D., (mathematics and physics) where he began making films.
PICTURES: Soldier of Orange (debut, 1979), Spetters, The Fourth Man, Flesh and Blood, Robocop, Total Recall.

VERNON, ANNE: Actress. r.n. Edith Antoinette Alexandrine Vignaud. b. Paris, Jan. 7, 1924. e. Ecole des Beaux Arts, Paris. Worked for French designer; screen debut in French films; toured with French theatre group; first starring role, Le Mannequin Assassine 1948. Wrote French cookbooks. Was subject of 1980 French TV film detailing her paintings, Les Peintres Enchanteurs.
PICTURES: Edouar et Caroline, Terror on a Train, Ainsi Finit La Nuit, A Warning to Wantons, Patto Col Diavolo, A Tale of Five Cities, Shakedown, Song of Paris, The Umbrellas of Cherbourg, General Della Rovere, La Rue L'Estrapade, Love Lottery.

VERNON, JOHN: Actor. b. Canada, 1936. e. Banff Sch. of Fine Arts, Royal Acad. of Dramatic Art.
PICTURES: Point Blank, Justine, Topaz, One More Train to Rob, Dirty Harry, Charlie Varrick, The Black Windmill, Fear Is the Key, Cat and Mouse, Brannigan, The Outlaw Josey Wales, Angela, A Special Day, National Lampoon's Animal House, Fantastica, Crunch, Herbie Goes Bananas, Chained Heat, Curtains, Savage Streets, Doin' Time, Ernest Goes to Camp, Blue Monkey, Nightstick, Deadly Stranger, Dixie Lanes, Killer Klowns From Outer Space, I'm Gonna Git Yu Sucka, Office Party, Blood of Others, Curtains, Double Exposure, Mob Story, Deadly Stranger.
TELEVISION: Movies: Trial Run, Escape, Cool Million, Hunter, The Questor Tapes, Mousey, The Virginia Hill Story, The Imposter, Swiss Family Robinson, The Barbary Coast, Matt Helm, Mary Jane Harper Cried Last Night, The Sacketts, The Blue and the Gray, Rat Tales. Pilot: B-Men.

VERONA, STEPHEN: Director, Producer, Writer. b. Illinois, Sept. 11, 1940. e. Sch. of Visual Arts. Directed and wrote some 300 commercials (over 50 award-winners) before turning to feature films in 1972, which he wrote as well. Also dir. award-winning short subjects (featuring Barbra Streisand, The Beatles, Simon and Garfunkle and The Lovin' Spoonful). Also prod., dir. of Angela Lansbury's Positive Moves video. Is an artist whose works have been exhibited at numerous CA and NY galleries.
PICTURES: The Rehearsal (short Acad. Award nom, 1972), The Lords of Flatbush (prod., co-dir., co-s.p.), Pipe Dreams (prod., dir., s.p.), Boardwalk (and co-s.p.), Talking Walls (dir., s.p.).
TELEVISION: Class of 1966 (prod. designer, ani. dir.); Diff'rent Strokes; The Music People; Sesame Street; Take a Giant Step; Double Exposure; Flatbush Avenue (pilot, prod., co-s.p.); War of the Worlds.

VETTER, RICHARD: Executive. b. San Diego, CA, Feb. 24, 1928. e. Pepperdine Coll., B.A., 1950; San Diego State Coll., M.A., 1953; UCLA, Ph.D., 1959. U.S. Navy: aerial phot., 1946–48, reserve instr., San Diego County Schools, 1951–54; asst. prof., audio-vis. commun., U.C.L.A., 1960–63. Inventor, co-dev., Dimension 150 Widescreen Process. 1957–63: formed D-150 Inc., 1963; exec. v.p. mem.: SMPTE, Technical & Scientific Awards Committee, AMPAS.

VICTOR, JAMES: Actor. r.n. Lincoln Rafael Peralta Diaz. b. Santiago, Dominican Republic, July 27, 1939. e. Haaren H.S., N.Y. Studied at Actors Studio West. On stage in Bullfight, Ceremony for an Assassinated Blackman, Latina, The Man in the Glass Booth, The M.C. (1985 Drama-Logue Critics, and Cesar best actor awards), I Gave You a Calendar (1983 Drama-Logue Critics Award), I Don't Have To Show You No Stinking Badges (1986 Drama-Logue Critics Award). 10 yr. mem. Actors branch AMPAS.
PICTURES: Fuzz, Rolling Thunder, Boulevard Nights, Defiance, Losin' It, Borderline; Stand and Deliver.
TELEVISION: Series: Viva Valdez, Condo, I Married Dora, Angelica Mi Vida. Many appearances on specials. Movies: Robert Kennedy and His Times, Twin Detectives, The Hound of Hell, Remington Steel; The Streets of L.A.; I, Desire; Second Serve, Hardball.
AWARDS: Cleo, 1975, for Mug Shot; L.A. Drama-Logue Critics Award, 1980, for Latina; Golden Eagle Award, 1981, for consistent outstanding performances in motion pictures.

VILLECHAIZE, HERVE: Actor. b. Paris, France, April 23, 1943. Sought career as artist, studying in Paris and then coming to New York to the Art Students League. Studied acting with Julie Bovasso. First film, The Guitar, shot in Spain. On Broadway in Elizabeth the First and Gloria and Esperenze. Also performed mime in N.Y. City Opera productions.
PICTURES: Hollywood Blvd. No. 2, Hot Tomorrow, The Man with the Golden Gun, Crazy Joe, The Gang That Couldn't Shoot Straight, Seizure, The One and Only, Forbidden Zone, Two Moon Junction.
TELEVISION: Fantasy Island (series).

VINCENT, JAN-MICHAEL: Actor. b. Denver, CO, July 15, 1944. e. Ventura City (CA) Coll. as art major. Joined National Guard. Discovered by agent Dick Clayton. Hired by Robert Conrad to appear in his film, Los Bandidos. Signed to 6-mo. contract by Universal, for which made Journey to Shiloh. Then did pilot TV movie for 20th-Fox based on Hardy Boys series of book. Originally called self Michael Vincent; changed after The Undefeated.
PICTURES: Los Bandidos, Journey to Shiloh, The Undefeated, Going Home, The Mechanic, The World's Greatest Athlete, Buster and Billie, Bite the Bullet, White Line Fever, Baby Blue Marine, Vigilante Force, Shadow of the Hawk, Damnation Alley, Big Wednesday, Hooper, Defiance, Hard Country, The Last Plane Out, Born in East L.A., Hit List, Deadly Embrace, Heartstone, Alienator.
TELEVISION: Lassie, Bonanza, The Banana Splits Adventure Hour, The Survivors (series), Airwolf (series). Movies: Tribes, The Catcher, Sandcastle, Six Against the Rock.

VINCENT, JR., FRANCIS T: Executive. b. Waterbury, CT, May 29, 1938. e. Williams Coll. B.A., 1960; Yale Law Sch. LL.B., 1963. Bar, CT 1963; NY, 1964; D.C. 1969. 1969–78, partner in law firm of Caplin & Drysdale, specializing in corporate banking and securities matters. 1978, assoc. dir. of, Division of Corporation Finance of Securities & Exchange Commission. Exec. v.p. of the Coca-Cola Company and pres. & CEO of its entertainment business sector. Also chmn. & CEO of Columbia Pictures Industries, Inc.; appt. pres. CEO, 1978. Mem. bd. of dir. of The Coca-Cola Bottling Co. of New York. 1987–June 1988. Rejoined law firm of Caplin & Drysdale, Washington, D.C., 1988. Trustee of Williams Coll. & The Hotchkiss Sch.

VINCENT, KATHARINE: Actress. r.n. Ella Vincenti. b. St. Louis, MO, May 28, 1918. e. Two years of high school, left in 1937 to go on the stage. m. the late Pandeno Descanto, producer.
THEATRE: Broadway shows include: Love or Bust, 1938; Could She Tell?, 1939; Banners of 1939; Czarina Smith, 1940. Numerous roadshow tours.
PICTURES: Peptipa's Waltz, 1942 (debut), Error in Her Ways, Stars and Stripes on Tour, 1943, Skin Deep, 1944, The Hungry, Voodoo Village, Welcome to Genoa, 1950, Unknown Betrayal, 1956, The Hooker, 1962 (Descanto films).
TELEVISION: The Untouchables, Moses, The Lawgiver, Dolce Far Niente (mini-series TVF Roma).

VINER, MICHAEL: Producer, Writer. b. 1945. m. actress Deborah Raffin. e. Harvard U., Georgetown U. Served as aide to Robert Kennedy; was legman for political columnist Jack Anderson. Settled in Hollywood, where worked for prod. Aaron Rosenberg, first as prod. asst. on three Frank Sinatra films; then asst. prod. on Joaquin Murietta. In music industry was record producer, manager, executive, eventually heading own division, at MGM. Debut as writer-producer in 1976 with TV special, Special of the Stars. Theatrical film debut as prod.-co-writer of Touched by Love, 1980. Television: Windmills of the Gods (exec. prod.).

VITALE, JOSEPH A.: Actor. b. New York, NY, Sept. 6, 1901. In 1924, on dramatic stage (Hold on to Your Hats, Page Miss Glory, All Editions, I'd Rather Be Right, Common Ground). Screen debut, 1943.
PICTURES: None But the Lonely Heart, Lady Luck, Road to Rio, Where There's Life, Connecticut Yankee, Illegal Entry, Red Hot and Blue, Paleface, Fancy Pants, My Friend Irma Goes West, Stop You're Killing Me, Stranger Wore a Gun, Square Jungle, Rumble On the Docks, Apache Rifles.
TELEVISION: Climax, Lineup, Bengal Lancers, Wagon Train, Schlitz Playhouse, Cimmaron City, Telephone Time, Wyatt Earp, Rawhide, Red Skelton, The Thin Man, M Squad, Dawson, Ben Casey, Empire, Hazel, Mr. Ed, To Rome With Love, Fisherman's Wharf (pilot).

VITTI, MONICA: Actress. r.n. Monica Luisa Ceciarelli. b. Italy, 1933.
PICTURES: L'Avventura, La Notte, L'Eclipse, Dragees du Poivre, The Nutty, Naughty Chateau, The Red Desert, Modesty Blaise, The Chastity Belt, Girl with a Pistol, The Pacifist, Duck in Orange Sauce, An Almost Perfect Affair, The Mystery of Oberwald, The Flirt, Secret Scandal (dir. debut).

VOIGHT, JON: Actor. b. Yonkers, NY. Dec. 29, 1938. e. Archbishop Stepinac H.S., White Plains, NY; Catholic U., B.F.A., 1960; studied acting at the Neighborhood Playhouse and in private classes with Stanford Meisner, four yrs. Off-Broadway in: A View From the Bridge (revival), 1964. Won the Theatre World Award for Broadway prod. That Summer, That Fall. Played Romeo, San Diego Shakespeare Festival.
TELEVISION: Public Broadcast Lab.'s The Dwarf, also Gunsmoke, Cimarron Strip.
PICTURES: Hour of the Gun, Fearless Frank, Midnight Cowboy (Acad. Award nom., best actor), Out of It, Catch 22, The Revolutionary, All American Boy, Deliverance, Conrack, The Odessa File, End of the Game, Coming Home, The Champ, Lookin' To Get Out (also co-s.p.), Table for Five, Runaway Train, Desert Bloom, Eternity.

VOLONTE, GIAN MARIA: Actor. b. Milan, April 9, 1933. e. Rome's National Acad. of Dramatic Art, 1957 graduate. Entered on professional theatrical career, playing Shakespeare and Racine, along with modern works, Sacco and Vanzetti and The Deputy. On TV in Chekov's Uncle Vanya and Dostoyevsky's The Idiot. First major film roles in Un Uomo da Bruciare, 1961 and Il Terrorista, 1963. Called self John Welles in credits for spaghetti westerns.
PICTURES: For a Fistful of Dollars, For a Few Dollars More, Investigation of a Citizen Above Suspicion, The Working Class Goes to Heaven, Wind from the East, Sacco and Vanzetti, L'Attenat, Slap the Monster on Page One, Just Another War, The Mattei Affair, Lucky Luciano, Eboli, The Death of Mario Ricci, Chronicle of a Death Foretold.

VON ROTHKIRCH, Dr. EDWARD: Producer. b. July 30, 1919. e. Friedrich Wilhelm U., Berlin; Rockhurst Coll., Midwestern Coll. Prod. asst., research, Pan American Prod., 1941; research Pacific Films, 1942; U.S. Air Force, 1942–44; asst. prod., Pan American Productions, 1945; analyst, Cambridge Prod., 1947; assoc. prod., Pentagon Films, 1949; assoc. prod., Reelestic Pictures, 1950; assoc. prod. Cambridge-Meran Prod. Co., 1951; assoc. exec. prod., Cambridge Prod., 1954; also v.-p. Continental Prod. Services; assoc. exec. prod. Trinity Hill Productions, produced Pan-American Highway 1954, The Keepers TV series, 1953–58, Famous Women of the Bible, 1955–58; To the Stars TV series, 1954–58; also sec.-treas. Crusader Records and v.p. Orbit Records. Member of many professional societies, director Intl. Association of Independent Producers, presently exec. prod., Galaxie Productions, and Encore Records also exec. editor, Intercontinental Media Services, Ltd.

VON SYDOW, MAX: Actor. b. Lund, Sweden, April 10, 1929. m. Keratin Olin, actress, 1951. Theatrical debut in a Cathedral Sch. of Lund prod. of The Nobel Prize. Served in the Swedish Quartermaster Corps two yrs. Studied at Royal Dramatic Theatre Sch. in Stockholm. Tour in municipal theatres. Has appeared on stage in Stockholm, London (The Tempest, 1988). Paris and Helsinki in Faust, The Legend and The Misanthrope. 1954 won Sweden's Royal Foundation Cultural Award.
PICTURES: Wild Strawberries, Brink of Life, The Magician, The Seventh Seal, The Virgin Spring, Through a Glass Darkly, Winter Light, Hawaii, The Greatest Story Ever Told, The Reward, Hour of the Wolf, Shame, The Kremlin Letter, The Passion of Anna, The Immigrants, Night Visitor, The Emigrants, The New Land, Three Days of The Condor, Voyage of the Damned, Exorcist II: The Heretic, March or Die, Flash Gordon, Victory, Conan The Barbarian, Never Say Never Again, Dreamscape, Dune, Code Name: Emerald, Hannah and Her Sisters, Duet for One, The Second Victory, Pelle the Conqueror, Katinka (dir.), The Exorcist 1990, Red King, White Knight, Dr. Grassler.
TELEVISION: Samson and Delilah, Christopher Columbus, Kojak: The Belarus File, Brotherhood of the Rose.

VONDERHAAR, RAYMOND T.: Executive. b. Rugby, N.D., Nov. 1, 1919. e. St. Cloud State. Spent entire career in exhibition. Pres., Allied Theatre Assn., 1963–64; pre., NATO North Central States, 1965–76; National NATO bd., 1965–84; also memb. exec. comm. 1965–84; NATO No. Central, chmn., 1976–84.

VON TROTTA, MARGARETHE: Director, Writer. b. Berlin, Germany, Feb. 21, 1942. m. dir. Volker Schlondorff. e. Studied German and Latin literature in Munich and Paris. Studied acting in Munich and began career as actress. First on stage then since 1969 on TV and in films by Fassbinder, Chabrol. 1970 began collaborating on Schlondorff's films as well as acting in them.
PICTURES: Actress: Schrage Vogel, Brandstifter, Gotter der Pest, Baal, Der amerikanische Soldat, Der plotzliche Reichtum der armen Leute von Kombach (also co-s.p.), Die Moral der Ruth Halbfass, Strohfeuer (also co-s.p.), Desaster, Ubernachtung in Tirol, etc.
PICTURES: Dir. and co-s.p.: The Lost Honor of Katharina Blum (co-dir. with husband), The Second Awakening of Christa Klages, Sisters, or the Balance of Happiness, Die bleierne Zeit, Heller Wahn (Sheer Madness), Rosa Luxemburg, Friends and Husbands, Paura e Amore (Three Sisters).

VON ZERNECK, FRANK: Producer. b. New York, NY, Nov. 3, 1940. e. Hofstra Coll., 1962. Has produced plays in New York, Los Angeles, and on national tour and over 45 films and mini-series. Founded (with Robert Greenwald) Moonlight Prods. Devised Portrait film genre for TV movies: Portrait of a Stripper, Portrait of a Mistress, Portrait of a Centerfold, etc.
TELEVISION: 21 Hours at Munich, Dress Gray, Miracle on Ice, Combat High, Queenie, In the Custody of Strangers, The First Time, Baby Sister, Policewoman Centerfold, Obsessive Love, Invitation to Hell, Romance on the Orient Express, Hostage Flight, The Tall Men, *Exec. prod.:* The Proud Men, Man Against the Mob, To Heal a Nation, Lady Mobster, Maybe Baby, Full Exposure: the Sex Tapes Scandal, Gore Vidal's Billy the Kid.
Past chmn. of California Theatre Council; former officer of League of Resident theatres; active member of League of New York Theatres & Producers; bd. of gov., Producers Guild of America, the Caucus for Producers, Writers, and Directors, Museum of Broadcasting.

VORHAUS, BERNARD: Director. b. 1898. In 1933, wrote and directed Money for Speed (UA-British). Has lectured on film.
PICTURES: 1934, The Ghost Camera, Crime on the Hill, Night Club Queen, Broken Melody, Blind Justice, Ten Minutes Alibi, Street Song, Last Journey, Twickenham, Dark World. Associate producer Broken Blossoms; director, Dusty Ermine, Twickenham; Cotton Queen, Rock Studios, Bury Me Dead, Winter Wonderland, The Spiritualist, So Young, So Bad, Pardon My French.

VUILLE, GEORGES-ALAIN: Producer. b. Lausanne, Switzerland, Oct. 28, 1948. Entered film industry at the age of 18 as an exhibitor in Switzerland. Pictures: Ashanti, Clair De Femme, The Favorite.

W

WADLEIGH, MICHAEL: Director. b. Akron, OH, Sept. 24, 1941. e. Ohio State U., B.S., B.A., M.A., Columbia Medical Sch. Directed Woodstock (1970), Wolfen (dir., co-s.p.), Out of Order, The Village at the End of the Universe (dir., s.p.).

WAGGONER, LYLE: Actor, b. Kansas City, KS, April 13, 1935. e. Washington U., St. Louis, Was salesman before becoming actor with road co. prod. of Li'l Abner. Formed own sales-promo co. to finance trip to CA for acting career in 1965. Did commercials, then signed by 20th-Fox for new-talent school.
TELEVISION: The Carol Burnett Show (series), It's Your Bet (host), The New Adventures of Wonder Woman (series).
PICTURES: Love Me Deadly, Journey to the Center of Time, Catalina Caper, Surf II, Murder Weapon.

WAGNER, JANE: Writer, Director. b. Morristown, TN, Feb. 2, 1935. e. attended Sch. of Visual Arts, NY. Worked as designer for Kimberly Clark and Fieldcrest. Bdwy. work as dir. and co-writer includes Appearing Nitely and The Search for

Signs of Intelligent Life in the Universe—both starring Lily Tomlin.
PICTURES: Moment by Moment (s.p., dir.); The Incredible Shrinking Woman (exec. prod., s.p.).
TELEVISION: Laugh-In (writer, 1970–73), Specials: J.T. (co-writer, Peabody Award), Lily (prod., s.p., Emmy & WGA Award), Lily Tomlin (prod., s.p., Emmy), People, Lily—Sold Out (exec. prod., s.p., Emmy), Lily for President? (exec. prod., s.p.).

WAGNER, LINDSAY: Actress. b. Los Angeles, CA, June 22, 1949. Appeared in school plays in Portland, OR; studied singing and worked professionally with rock group. In 1968 went to L.A. Signed to Universal contract in 1971.
PICTURES: Two People, Paper Chase, Second Wind, Nighthawks, Martin's Day.
TELEVISION: The F.B.I., Owen Marshall, Counselor at Law, Night Gallery, The Bold Ones, Marcus Welby, M.D., The Rockford Files, The Six Million Dollar Man, The Bionic Woman (series, Emmy, 1977), Jessie (series); A Peaceable Kingdom (series). Movies: Two Kinds of Love, Passions, Child's Cry, Convicted, This Child Is Mine, Young Again, Stranger in My Bed, The Return of the Six Million Dollar Man and the Bionic Woman, Scruples, Student Exchange, The Incredible Journey of Dr. Meg Laurel, Callie and Son, I Want to Live, Evil in Clear River, The Taking of Flight 847, Nightmare at Bitter Creek, Voice of the Heart, To Be the Best, From the Dead of Night, The Bionic Showdown: The Six-Million Dollar Man and the Bionic Woman.

WAGNER, RAYMOND JAMES: Producer. b. College Point, NY, Nov. 3, 1925. e. Middlebury Coll., Williams Coll. Joined Young & Rubicam, Inc., as radio-TV commercial head in Hollywood, 1950–59. Head of pilot development, Universal Studios, 1960–65. V.p. of production (features) for MGM, 1972–79. Presently independent producer.
PICTURES: Prod.: Petulia, Loving (exec. prod.), Code of Silence, Rent-a-Cop, Hero and the Terror, Turner and Hooch.

WAGNER, ROBERT: Actor. b. Detroit, MI, Feb. 10, 1930. e. Saint Monica's H.S. Film debut, Halls of Montezuma (1950).
PICTURES: The Frogmen, Let's Make It Legal, With A Song in My Heart, What Price Glory, Stars and Stripes Forever, The Silver Whip, Titanic, (Star of Tomorrow, 1953). Beneath the 12-Mile Reef, Prince Valiant, Broken Lance, White Feather, Kiss Before Dying, The Mountain, True Story of Jesse James, Stopover Tokyo, The Hunters, In Love and War, Say One for Me, Between Heaven and Hell, All the Fine Young Cannibals, Sail a Crooked Ship, The Longest Day, The War Lover, The Condemned of Altona, Harper, Banning, The Biggest Bundle of Them All, Don't Just Stand There, Winning, The Towering Inferno, Midway, The Concorde—Airport '79, Curse of the Pink Panther, I Am the Cheese.
TELEVISION: Series: It Takes A Thief, Switch, Hart to Hart. Movies: Pearl, Cat on a Hot Tin Roof, To Catch a King, There Must Be a Pony, Love Among Thieves, Windmills of the Gods, Indiscreet. Mini-series: Around the World in 80 Days.

WAHL, KEN: Actor. b. Chicago, IL, Feb. 14, 1960. No acting experience when cast in The Wanderers in 1978.
PICTURES: Fort Apache, The Bronx, Race for the Yankee Zephyr, Running Scared, Jinxed, The Soldier, Purple Hearts.
TELEVISION: The Dirty Dozen: The Next Mission, Double Dare, The Gladiator, Single Again. Series: Wiseguy.

WAITE, RALPH: Actor. b. White Plains, NY, June 22, 1929. e. Bucknell U., Yale U. Social worker, publicity director, assistant editor and minister before turning to acting. Appeared in many Bdwy. plays, including Hogan's Goat, The Watering Place, Trial of Lee Harvey Oswald, off-Bdwy. and regional theatres. Biggest success on TV in The Waltons. Is founder of the Los Angeles Actors Theatre. Wrote, produced, directed and acted in theatrical film, On the Nickel.
PICTURES: Five Easy Pieces, Lawman, The Grissom Gang, Dime Box, The Sporting Club.
TELEVISION: Series: The Waltons, The Mississippi. Movies: Red Alert, The Secret Life of John Chapman, Ohms, Angel City, A Good Start, Crime of Innocence; Red Earth, White Earth. Mini-series: Roots.

WAITE, RIC: Cinematographer. Photographed more than 40 movies-of-the-week for TV, 1979–83. First theatrical film, The Other Side of the Mountain, 1975.
PICTURES: Defiance, On the Nickel, The Long Riders, The Border, Tex, 48 Hrs., Class, Uncommon Valor, Footloose, Red Dawn, Volunteers, Summer Rental, Brewster's Millions, Cobra, Adventures in Babysitting, The Great Outdoors.
TELEVISION: Captains and the Kings (Emmy, 1977), Tail Gunner Joe, Huey P. Long, Revenge of the Stepford Wives, Baby Comes Homes.

WAITS, TOM: Singer, Composer, Actor. b. Pomona, CA, Dec. 7, 1949. Recorded numerous albums and received Acad. Award nom. for his song score of One from the Heart. Composed songs for On the Nickel, Streetwise, Paradise Alley, Wolfen. Has also starred in Chicago's Steppenwolf Theatre Co.'s Frank's Wild Years for which he wrote the music and Los Angeles Theatre Co.'s Demon Wine.
PICTURES: As actor: Paradise Alley (1978), Poetry in Motion, The Outsiders, Rumble Fish, The Cotton Club, Down by Law (also music), Ironweed, Big Time (also co-s.p., performer), Cold Feet, The Bearskin, On a Moonlit Night (music only), Queens Logic.

WAJDA, ANDRZEJ: Director, Writer. b. Suwalki, Poland, March 6, 1927. e. Fine Arts Academy, Krakow, Poland, 1945–48; High School of Cinematography, Lodz, Poland, 1950–52. 1940–43, worked as asst. in restoration of church paintings. 1942, joined Polish gov. in exile's A.K. (Home Army Resistance) against German occupation. 1950–52, directed shorts (While You Sleep; The Bad Boy, The Pottery of Ilzecka) as part of film school degree; 1954, asst. dir. to Aleksander Ford on 5 Boys from Barska Street. Work flourished under easing of political restraints in Poland during late 1950s. 1981, concentrated on theatrical projects in Poland and film prods. with non-Polish studios. 1983, gov. dissolved his Studio X film prod. group. 1984, gov. demanded Wajda's resignation as head of filmmakers' assoc. in order to continue org.'s existence. 1989, appt. artistic dir. of Teatr Powszechny, official Warsaw theater. Also leader of the Cultural Comm. of the Citizen's Committee.
PICTURES: Dir.-Writer: A Generation (debut, 1957); I Walk to the Sun; Kanal; Ashes and Diamonds; Lotna; Innocent Sorcerers; Samson; Lady Macbeth of Mtsensk; Warszawa (episode of Love at 20); Ashes; Gates to Paradise; Everything for Sale; Landscape After the Battle; The Wedding; Promised Land; The Shadow Line; Man of Marble; Without Anesthetic; Invitation to the Inside; The Orchestra Conductor; The Girls from Wilko; Man of Iron (Golden Palm Award, Cannes, 1981); Danton; A Love in Germany; Cronic of Love Affairs; The Possessed, Land of Promise.
TELEVISION: Poly-Poly; The Birch Wood; Pilate and the Others; The Dead Class; November Night; Crime and Punishment.

WALD, MALVIN: Writer, Producer. b. New York, NY, Aug. 8, 1917. e. Brooklyn Coll., B.A., J.D. Woodland U. Coll. of Law; grad. work Columbia U., NYU, U. of Southern CA. Newspaper reporter and editor, publicist, social worker, radio actor. Screenplays and original stories for Columbia, 20th-Fox, UA, MGM, WB; U.S. Air Force; tech. sgt., wrote 30 doc. films for film unit. Exec. prod., 20th Century Fox TV Doc. Unit, 1963–64 writer-prod. U.S.I.A., 1964–65; writer-prod., Ivan Tors Films, 1965–69; prof., U. of Southern California Sch. of Cinema, Television, 1983–85 bd. of dir.; Writer's Guild of America; 1986–89, Trustee, Writers Guild Foundation; Acad. of Motion Picture Arts and Sciences, co-author of book, Three Major Screenplays. Contributor to books, American Screenwriters, Close-Ups. Published s.p., Naked City. Consultant, Natl. Endowment for Humanities and Corp. for Public Broadcasting. Visiting professor, Southern Illinois Univ. Preselection judge, Focus writing awards. Media & prod. consultant, Apache Mountain Spirit (PBS); playwright, ANTA-West. Co-author, L.A. Press Club 40th Anniversary Show, 1987. Dramatists Guild.
PICTURES: The Naked City (Acad. Award nom., best story); Behind Locked Doors, The Dark Past, Ten Gentlemen from West Point, The Powers Girl, Two in a Taxi, Undercover Man, Outrage, On the Loose; (assoc. prod. and sec.-treas., Filmakers Pictures, Inc.); Battle Taxi, Man on Fire, Al Capone, Venus in Furs, In Search of Historic Jesus, Legend of Sleepy Hollow. Shorts: An Answer, Employees Only (Acad. Award nom., best sht. doc.), Boy Who Owned a Melephant (Venice Children's Film Fest. gold medal), Unarmed in Africa, The Policeman, James Weldon Johnson, Me an Alcoholic?, Problem Solving, Managerial Control.
TELEVISION: Many credits including Playhouse 90, Marilyn Monroe, Hollywood: The Golden Years, The Rafer Johnson Story, D-Day, Project: Man in Space, Tales of Hans Christian Andersen, John F. Kennedy, Biography of A Rookie, Alcoa-Goodyear Hour, Climax, Shirley Temple Storybook, Life of Riley, Peter Gunn, Perry Mason, Dobie Gillis, Combat, Moonport (U.S.I.A.; prod., writer), Daktari, (assoc. prod.) Primus, California Tomorrow, prod. Mod Squad, Untamed World, Around the World of Mike Todd, The Billie Jean King Show, Life and Times of Grizzly Adams, Mark Twain's America, Greatest Heroes of the Bible, Littlest Hobo., Rich Little's You Asked For It, Hugh Hefner's Bunny Memories.

WALD, RICHARD C.: Executive. b. New York, NY, 1931. e. Columbia Coll., Clare Coll. (Cambridge). Joined the New York Herald Tribune in 1951 as Columbia Coll. correspondent; religion editor, political reporter; foreign correspondent (London, Bonn), 1959–63; assoc. editor, 1963–65; mgn. editor from 1965 until paper ceased publication in 1966; Sunday editor, World Journal Tribune, 1966; mgn. editor, Washington Post, 1967; vice president, Whitney Communications Corp., 1967–68; joined National Broadcasting Company as vice president, NBC News, 1968; exec. v.p., 1972; president, NBC News, 1973; sr. v.p., ABC News, 1978.

WALDMAN, WALTER: Publicist. b. New York, NY. e. City Coll. of New York, Columbia U. Newspaper reporter; magazine writer; radio-television-film critic; radio news writer, Current Events, Triangle Publications; The Bronx Home News; Grolier Society; Netherlands Information Bureau, station WLIB; free-lance New York Times and New York Herald Tribune; writer, press book dept., 20th Century-Fox; copy writer, advertising dept., Republic Pictures; writer, Variety, Box Office Magazine; publicity writer, copy chief, publicity dept., Paramount Pictures; publicity copy chief, contact, MGM/United Artists Entertainment Co.

WALKEN, CHRISTOPHER: Actor. b. Astoria, NY, Mar. 31, 1943. Began career in off-Bdwy. musical, Best Foot Forward, starring Liza Minnelli. Continued in musicals until cast in original Bdwy. production of The Lion in Winter, winning Clarence Derwent Award for performance as King Philip. Switched to dramatic roles, winning Obie Award for title role in Kid Champion and Theater World Award for performance in N.Y. City Center revival of Rose Tattoo. Bdwy. appearance, Hurlyburly, Coriolanus (NY Shakespeare Fest.).
PICTURES: The Anderson Tapes (debut), Next Stop, Greenwich Village, Roseland, Santa Fe–1936, The Sentinel, Annie Hall, The Deer Hunter, Heaven's Gate, The Dogs of War, Pennies from Heaven, Brainstorm, The War Zone, A View to a Kill, At Close Range, Biloxi Blues, Deadline, The Milagro Beanfield War, Puss in Boots, Slaves of New York, Homeboy, Communion, Atuk, In From the Cold, King of New York, The Comfort of Strangers.

WALKER, CLINT: Actor. b. Hartford, IL, May 30, 1927. e. schools there. Joined Merchant Marine 1944, worked as sheet metal worker, carpenter, other jobs in Alton, IL; set out with wife and infant daughter for oil fields in TX; decided to try acting. Got screen test at Paramount Studios for Cecil B. De Mille; later landed contract to star in Cheyenne TV films at Warner.
PICTURES: Fort Dobbs, Yellowstone Kelly, None But the Brave, Pancho Villa, Maya, Night of the Grizzly, Gold of the Seven Saints, Send Me No Flowers, The Dirty Dozen, The Great Bank Robbery, Sam Whisky, More Dead Than Alive, The Legend of Grizzly Adams.
TELEVISION: Cheyenne (series), Hardcase, Killdozer, Bounty Man, Centennial, Scream of the Wolf, Yuma.

WALKER, E. CARDON: Executive. b. Rexburg, ID, Jan. 9, 1916. e. UCLA, B.A. 1938. Four years officer, U.S. Navy, Started with Walt Disney Productions 1938; camera, story, unit director short subjects, budget control. Headed, 1950, adv. & pub. 1956, v.p. in chg. of adv. & sales. 1960 member bd. of dir. & exec. comm. 1965 v.p., mkt. 1967 exec. v.p. operations 1968, exec. v.p. and chief operating officer; pres., 1971; Nov. 1976 pres. and chief executive officer; June, 1980, named bd. chmn. & chief executive officer; May, 1983, became chmn. of exec. committee, which position he retained until Sept. 1984. Remains a board member.

WALKER, KATHRYN: Actress. b. Philadelphia, PA, Jan. 9. m. singer-songwriter James Taylor. e. Wells Coll., Harvard. Studied acting at London Acad. of Music and Dramatic Art on Fulbright Fellowship. Stage roles include part in Private Lives with Elizabeth Taylor and Richard Burton, and Wild Honey with Ian McKellen.
PICTURES: Rich Kids, Slap Shot, Neighbors, D.A.R.Y.L., Dangerous Game.
TELEVISION: Series: Beacon Hill; Movies: Family Reunion, FDR: The Final Years, Special Bulletin, O Youth and Beauty, The Adams Chronicles (Emmy, 1978), The Murder of Mary Phagan.

WALKER, NANCY: Actress, Director. r.n. Anna Swoyer Barto. b. Philadelphia, PA, May 10, 1922. m. singer, vocal teacher David Craig. e. Bentley Sch., and Professional Children's Sch. As child toured Europe with her parents, The Barto and Mann vaudeville team. Pursued career as serious vocalist until George Abbott steered her toward comedy when she auditioned for Broadway prod., Best Foot Forward at 19 in 1941. Directed film, Can't Stop the Music, 1980.
STAGE: On the Town, Barefoot, Boy with Cheek, Look, Ma, I'm Dancin', Along Fifth Avenue Revue, A Month of Sundays, Pal Joey, Phoenix '55 Revue, Fallen Angels, Copper and Brass, Wonderful Town, Girls Against the Boys, Do Re Mi, The Cherry Orchard, The Cocktail Party, The Show Off, (with APA Phoenix), A Funny Thing Happened on the Way to the Forum (Ahmanson, L.A.), Sondheim: A Musical Tribute.
PICTURES: Best Foot Forward, Girl Crazy, Broadway Rhythm, Meet the People, Lucky Me, Stand Up and Be Counted, The World's Greatest Athlete, Forty Carats, Won Ton Ton, Murder by Death.
TELEVISION: Nearly every major TV show, plus series: Family Affair, McMillan & Wife, Rhoda, The Nancy Walker Show, Blansky's Beauties.

WALLACE, IRVING: Writer. b. Chicago, IL, March 19, 1916. e. Williams Inst., Berkeley, CA, 1935–36. For. correspondent in Japan & China, Liberty Mag., 1940; U.S. Army doing m.p. & photog.; covered France, Germany, Spain for Sat. Evening Post, Collier's, Reader's Digest, 1946, 1947, 1949, 1953.
AUTHOR: The Fabulous Originals, 1955; The Square Pegs; The Sins of Philip Fleming; The Fabulous Showman; The Chapman Report; The Twenty-Seventh Wife; The Prize; The Three Sirens; The Man; The Sunday Gentleman; The Plot; The Writing of One Novel; The Seven Minutes; The Nympho and Other Maniacs; The Word; The Fan Club; The People's Almanac; The R Document; The Book of Lists; The Tow; The Pigeon Project; The Second Lady; The Almighty, Significa; The Miracle; The Seventh Secret; The Celestial Bed; The Golden Room; The Guest of Honor.
PICTURES: story, collab. s.p., West Point Story; s.p., Meet Me at the Fair; collab. s.p. Desert Legion, Gun Fury; collab. story and s.p., Split Second; s.p., The Burning Hills, Bombers B-52; novel (basis for film), The Chapman Report, The Prize, The Seven Minutes, The Man; The Word.

WALLACE, JEAN: Actress. b. Chicago, IL, Oct. 12, 1930. As teenager signed by Paramount as contract player and studied at Actors Laboratory (method school) in Hollywood. Later, switched to 20th Century-Fox. In 1951 went to Argentina to star in first film, Native Son. Board of Directors Permanent Charities Committee and (Womens Auxiliary), Antans (The Womens Auxiliary of the American National Theater and Academy); hospitality chmn., Beverly Hills P.T.A. Member, So. Calif. Motion Picture Council and recipient of its Bronze Halo Award of Special Merit. Mbr., L.A.D.I.E.S; bd. of dir. of Screen Smart Set.
PICTURES: Storm Fear, The Big Combo, The Man on the Eiffel Tower, The Devil's Hairpin, Maracaibo, The Sword of Lancelot, Beach Red, No Blade of Grass.

WALLACE, MIKE: TV Commentator, Interviewer. b. Brookline, MA, May 9, 1918. e. U. of Michigan, 1939. Night Beat, WABD, N.Y., 1956; The Mike Wallace Interview, ABC, 1956–58; Newspaper col., Mike Wallace Asks, N.Y. Post, 1957–58; News Beat, WNTA-TV, 1959–61; The Mike Wallace Interview, WNTA-TV, 1959–61; Biography, 1962; correspondent, CBS News, 1963, CBS Radio; Personal Closeup, Mike Wallace at Large; Co-editor, 60 Minutes, CBS News.

WALLACH, ELI: Actor. b. Brooklyn, NY, Dec. 7, 1915. m. actress Anne Jackson. e. U. of Texas. Capt. in Medical Admin. Corps during W.W.II. After college acting, appeared in summer stock. Made Broadway debut in Skydrift, 1945, followed by Antony & Cleopatra, The Rose Tattoo, Major Barbara, Rhinoceros, Luv, Twice Around the Park, Cafe Crown. Charter member, Actors Studio in 1947.
PICTURES: Baby Doll (debut, 1957), The Magnificent Seven, Seven Thieves, The Misfits, The Victors, Hemingway's Adventures of A Young Man, How the West Was Won, Act One, Genghis Khan, The Moonspinners, Lord Jim, How to Steal a Million, The Good, the Bad and the Ugly, The Tiger Makes Out, Band of Gold, How to Save a Marriage and Ruin Your Life, A Lovely Way to Die, Ace High, The Brain, Zigzag, The People Next Door, Romance of a Horse Thief, Cinderella Liberty, Crazy Joe, Movie Movie, The Hunter, Sam's Son, Tough Guys, Nuts, The Two Jakes.
TELEVISION: Studio One, Philco Playhouse, Playhouse 90, A Poppy Is Also a Flower (Emmy Award). Movies: Anatomy of an Illness, Murder: By Reason of Insanity, Something in Common, Executioner's Song, Christopher Columbus, Embassy, The Impossible Spy.

WALLACH, GEORGE: Producer, Writer, Director. b. New York, NY, Sept. 25, 1918. e. NYU. Actor in theatre & radio 1938–45; U.S. Navy 1942–45; supvr. radio-TV Div. of Amer. Thea. Wing 1946–48; dir., WNEW, 1946–48; prod./div., Wendy Barrie Show, 1948–49; prod.-dir. for WNBC-WNBT, 1950; Dir., news, spec. events WNBT-WNBC, 1951–52; prod. mgr., NBC Film Div. since 1953; CBS-TV; formed George Wallach Prod., 1956; prod. dir. It Happened in Havana, appt. TV officer, U.S.I.A., 1957. Film-TV officer American Embassy, Bonn, Germany, 1961. Film-TV officer American Embassy; Tehran, Iran, 1965–66; MoPix Prod. Officer, JUSPAO, American Embassy, Saigon, 1966; prod.-dir.-wr., Greece Today, 1967–68. Exec. prod.-dir., George Wallach Productions, spec. doc., travel, and industrial films, chairman, Film-TV Dept., N.Y. Institute of Photography, 1968–75; Prof. film-TV-radio, Brooklyn Coll., 1975–80; Dir., special projects, Directors Guild of America 1978–88; presently international film consultant, China and Soviet Union.
PICTURES: NBC-producer: Inner Sanctum, The Falcon, His Honor Homer Bell, Watch the World; assoc. prod., prod. mgr., Bwana Devil; dir., Wanted, CBS-TV series.

WALSH, J.T.: Actor. Did not begin acting until age 30, when quit job in sales to join off-Broadway theater co.
THEATER: Glengarry Glen Ross, Rose, Last Licks, Richard III.
PICTURES: Tin Men, House of Games, Power, Hannah and Her Sisters, Tequila Sunrise, The Big Picture, Wired.
TELEVISION: Movies: On the Edge, Right to Kill, Little Gloria: Happy at Last, Today's FBI, Prisoner Without a Name, Cell Without a Number.

WALSH, M. EMMET: Actor. b. 1935. e. graduated coll. with degree in business admin.
PICTURES: Midnight Cowboy, Stiletto, Alice's Restaurant, End of the Road, The Traveling Executioner, Little Big Man, Cold Turkey, Loving, The Jerk, Straight Time, Ordinary People, Back Roads, Reds, Fast-Walking, The Escape Artist, Blade Runner, Silkwood, Blood Simple, The Pope of Greenwich Village, Missing in Action, The Best of Times, Wildcats, Critters, Raisin' Arizona, Red Scorpion, No Man's Land, The Milagro Beanfield War, Sunset, The Might Quinn, War Party, Clean and Sober, Catch Me If You Can, Sundown, Thunderground, Sandino.
TELEVISION: Series: The Sandy Duncan Show (1972), Dear Detective, UNSUB. Movies: East of Eden, High Noon Part II, Hellinger's Law, Night Partners, You Are the Jury, The Deliberate Stranger, Resting Place, Broken Vows, Murder Ordained, Brotherhood of the Rose, Narrow Margin.

WALSH, RICHARD F.: President Emeritus International Alliance Theatrical Stage Employees and M.P. Machine Operators. b. Brooklyn, NY, 1900. In 1917 became apprentice stage electrician; 1920 full member Local 4, Brooklyn stagehand union IATSE & MPMO. Stage electrician various theatres. In 1924 elected pres. Local 4. 1926 business agent: 1934 int'l vice-pres. IATSE & MPMO; Nov., 1941 named pres. by exec. board; elected pres. by convention June, 1942; re-elected International pres. by convention thereafter; v.p., AFL-CIO, 1956; ch. of bd., Will Rogers Hospital; pres., Union Label Dept, retired as IATSE president in 1974.

WALSTON, RAY: Actor, Director. b. New Orleans, LA, Nov. 2, 1918. Dir. of Bdwy. musical, Damn Yankees, 1974.
TELEVISION: You Are There, Producers Showcase, There Shall Be No Night, Studio One, Playhouse 90, My Favorite Martian (series), Oh Madeline (series), Fast Times at Ridgemont High (series), Crash Course, Amos, Red River, I Know My First Name is Steven.
PICTURES: South Pacific, Damn Yankees, Kiss Them For Me, Say One for Me, The Tall Story, The Apartment, Portrait In Black, Convicts Four, Wives and Lovers, Who's Minding the Store, Kiss Me Stupid, Caprice, Paint Your Wagon, The Sting, Silver Streak, Popeye, Fast Times at Ridgemont High, Johnny Dangerously, RAD, From the Hip, O.C. and the Stiggs, A Man of Passion, Blood Relations, Saturday the 14th Strikes Back, Paramedics, Ski Patrol, Blood Salvage.

WALTER, JESSICA: Actress. b. Brooklyn, NY, Jan. 31, 1944. m. actor Ron Leibman. e. H.S. of the Performing Arts. Studied at Bucks County Playhouse and Neighborhood Playhouse. Many TV performances plus lead in series, For the People. Broadway debut in Advise and Consent, 1961. Also, Photo Finish (Clarence Derwent Award), Night Life, A Severed Head, Rumors.
PICTURES: Lilith, The Group, Grand Prix, Bye Bye Braverman, Number One, Play Misty For Me, Going Ape, The Flamingo Kid, Tapeheads.
TELEVISION: Love of Life, Ironside, Amy Prentiss (Emmy, 1975), All That Glitters, Wheels, Bare Essence, Secret of Three Hungry Wives, She's Dressed to Kill, Scruples, The Execution, Aaron's Way.

WALTERS, BARBARA: Broadcast Journalist. b. Boston, MA, Sept. 25, 1931. m. Merv Adelson, TV prod. executive. Daughter of Latin Quarter nightclub impressario Lou Walters. e. Sarah Lawrence Coll. Began working in TV after graduation. Joined The Today Show in 1961 as writer-researcher, making occasional on-camera appearances. In 1963 became full-time on camera. In April, 1974, named permanent co-host. Also hosted own synd. prog., Not for Women Only. In 1976 joined ABC-TV Evening News; 20/20 (host, 1976–78), correspondent World News Tonight (1978); corresp. 20/20 (1981–84), Host of series of interview specials. Author: How to Talk with Practically Anybody About Practically Anything (1970). Recipient of numerous awards incl. Emmy, Media, Peabody. Named one of women most admired by American People in 1982 & 84 Gallup Polls.

WALTERS, JULIE: Actress. b. Birmingham, England, 1950. Trained for 2 years to be a nurse before studying drama at Manchester Polytechnic, followed by year at Granada's Stables Theatre. Joined Everyman Theatre, Liverpool. Also toured Dockland pubs with songs, dance and imitations.
THEATER: Breezeblock Park, Funny Perculiar, The Glad Hand, Talent (written by Victoria Wood, with whom she began comedy partnership), Good Fun, Educating Rita (1980), Macbeth, Having a Ball.
PICTURES: Educating Rita, She'll Be Wearing Pink Pyjamas, Car Trouble, Personal Services, Prick Up Your Ears, Buster, Mack the Knife, Killing Dad.
TELEVISION: Unfair Exchanges, Talent, Nearly a Happy Ending, Family Man, Happy Since I Met You, The Secret Diaries of Adrian Mole (series); Wood and Walters (series); Me—I'm Afraid of Virginia Woolf, Say Something Happened, Intensive Care, The Boys from the Black Stuff, Monologues, Victoria Wood as Seen on TV (series), The Birthday Party.

WALTON, FREDERICK R.: Director.
PICTURES: When a Stranger Calls; April Fool's Day.
TELEVISION: I Saw What You Did, Trapped (dir., co-s.p.).

WANAMAKER, SAM: Actor, Stage producer, Film director. b. Chicago, IL, June 14, 1919. e. Drake U. On Broadway stage as actor, producer, presenter.
THEATER: London West End stage: Winter Journey, The Big Knife, The Threepenny Opera, The Rainmaker; 1956, acting, producing London and Liverpool stage; 1959–60, acting at Stratford-on-Avon; 1961–62, acting on New York stage in The Far Country; prod. dir. Children From Their Games, (N.Y.); Rhinoceros (Washington, D.C.). Opera prods.: King Priam, Forza Del Destino; A Case of Libel (dir.), Founder and exec. dir.: Shakespeare Globe Trust. Dir. Sydney Opera House Opening, Bankside Festival (prod.), U.S. tour, Shakespeare's Globe, Aida, San Francisco Opera.
PICTURES: My Girl Tisa, Give Us This Day, Mr. Denning Drives North, The Secret, The Criminal, Taras Bulba, Man in the Middle, Those Magnificent Men in Their Flying Machines, The Spy Who Came in from the Cold, The Warning Shot, The Day the Fish Came Out, Voyage of the Damned; The Executioner (dir.), The Eliminator, The Chinese Visitor; Catlow; Sinbad and the Eye of the Tiger; Private Benjamin, The Competition, The Aviator, Irreconcilable Differences, Raw Deal, Superman IV, Baby Boom, Judgement in Berlin, Cognac.
TELEVISION: The Big Wheel, The White Death, A Young Lady of Property (dir.), The Defenders, Oedipus Rex, Russian Self Impressions. Man of World (series), Espionage, Outer Limits. Dir. several episodes The Defenders series, Arturo Ui, War and Peace, The Ferret, Heartsounds, The Berrengers, The Ghost Writer, Sadie and Son, Deceptions, The Law, Baby Boom (series).

WANG, WAYNE: Director. b. Hong Kong, 1949. m. actress Cora Miao. e. came to U.S. to study photography at College of Arts and Crafts, Oakland, CA. With a Master's Degree in film and television, returned to Hong Kong. Worked on TV comedy series. First dir. work, as asst. dir. for Chinese sequences of Golden Needle. First film A Man, A Woman and a Killer. Won grant from AFI and National Endowment of the Arts, used to finance Chan is Missing (1982) which cost $22,000.
PICTURES: Chan is Missing (dir., s.p., editor, prod.), Dim Sum: A Little Big of Heart, Slam Dance, Eat a Bowl of Tea, Life is Cheap (prod., dir.).

WARD, BURT: Actor, Executive. b. Los Angeles, CA, July 6, 1945. Pres. of Pinnacle Associates, Inc. and the World of Earlybird, a publicly traded holding co. and a children's social value education program, respectively.
TELEVISION: Batman (co-starred as Robin 1966–68).

WARD, DAVID S.: Writer, Director. b. Providence, RI, Oct. 24, 1945. e. U. of Southern California where attended film school. First script was Steelyard Blues produced at Warner Bros. in 1972 by producers Michael and Julia Phillips.
PICTURES: The Sting (Acad. Award, best orig. s.p.); Cannery Row (s.p., dir.); The Sting II (s.p.), The Milagro Beanfield War (co-s.p.), Major League (dir., s.p.).

WARD, FRED: Actor. b. San Diego, CA, 1943. Studied at Herbert Berghof Studio. On stage in The Glass Menagerie, One Flew over the Cuckoo's Nest.
PICTURES: No Available Witness, Tilt, Escape from Alcatraz, Southern Comfort, Timerider, The Right Stuff, Warriors of the Wasteland. Silkwood, Uncommon Valor, Swing Shift, Uforia, Secret Admirer, Remo Williams: The Adventure Begins, Saigon, Train of Dreams, Off Limits, Big Business, The Prince of Pennsylvania, Backtrack, Miami Blues, Tremors.
TELEVISION: Florida Straits, Belle Starr.

WARD, RACHEL: Actress. b. London, 1957. m. actor Bryan Brown. Top fashion and TV commercial model before becoming actress. Studied acting with Stella Adler and Robert Modica.
PICTURES: Night School, Three Blind Mice, Sharky's Machine, Dead Men Don't Wear Plaid, Against All Odds, The Final Terror, The Good Wife, Hotel Colonial, How to Get Ahead in Advertising.
TELEVISION: Mini-series: The Thorn Birds, Shadow of the Cobra (U.K.). Movies: Christmas Lillies of the Field. Fortress.

WARD, SARAH E.: Executive. b. Warrenton, VA, April 5, 1920. 1949–1962, office clerical positions with RKO, 20th Century-Fox, Todd AO Corp; v.p. sales mgr. for Europix Consolidated Corp., 1968; v.p.—sec'y for Europix International Ltd., 1971.

WARD, SIMON: Actor. b. Beckenham, England, Oct. 19, 1941. Ent. ind. 1964.
PICTURES: If, Frankenstein Must Be Destroyed, I Start Counting, Young Winston, Hitler—The Last Ten Days, The Three Musketeers, The Four Musketeers, Children of Rage, Deadly Strangers. All Creatures Great & Small, Aces High, The Battle Flag, Holocaust 2000, Zulu Dawn, Supergirl.
TELEVISION: Spoiled, Chips with Everything, The Corsi-

can Brothers, Dracula, The Last Giraffe, Around the World in 80 Days.

WARDEN, JACK: Actor. b. Newark, NJ, Sept. 18, 1920. With Margo Jones theatre in Dallas.
THEATRE: View from the Bridge, Very Special Baby.
PICTURES: From Here to Eternity, 12 Angry Men, Edge of the City, Bachelor Party, Escape from Zahrain, The Thin Red Line, Summertree, Who Is Harry Kellerman?, The Sporting Club, Welcome to the Club, Billy Two Hats, The Apprenticeship of Duddy Kravitz, Shampoo, All the President's Men, Heaven Can Wait, Death on the Nile, And Justice for All, Being There, The Great Muppet Caper, Carbon Copy, So Fine, The Verdict, Crackers, The Aviator, September, The Presidio, Everybody Wins.
TELEVISION: Philco Goodyear Producer's Showcase, Kraft. Movies: Raid on Entebbe, Robert Kennedy and His Times, Hobson's Choice, A. D., Crazy Like a Fox (series), Hoover vs. The Kennedys, The Three Kings, Dead Solid Perfect.

WARNER, DAVID: Actor. b. Manchester, England, July 29, 1941. e. Royal Acad. of Dramatic Art. Made London stage debut in Tony Richardson's version of A Midsummer Night's Dream (1962). Four seasons with Royal Shakespeare Co. Theater includes Afore Night Come, The Tempest, The Wars of the Roses, The Government Inspector, Twelfth Night, I, Claudius.
PICTURES: Tom Jones, Morgan, Work Is a Four Letter Word, The Bofors Gun, The Fixer, The Seagull, Michael Kohlhaas, The Ballard of Cable Hogue, Perfect Friday, Straw Dogs, A Doll's House, Tales from the Crypt, Providence, Cross of Iron, The Omen, Silver Bears, The 39 Steps (remake), The Concorde—Airport '79, Time After Time, The Island, Time Bandits, Tron, The Man With Two Brains, The Company of Wolves, Hansel and Gretel, Hanna's War, Mr. North, My Best Friend is a Vampire, Waxwork, Silent Night, Office Party, Pulse Pounders, Keys to Freedom, Star Trek V: The Final Frontier, Magdalene, S.P.O.O.K.S., Tripwire, Mortal Passions.
TELEVISION: Desperado, A Christmas Carol, Hitler's SS—Portrait in Evil, Holocaust, Marco Polo, Masada (Emmy, supp., 1981), SOS Titanic, Love's Labour's Lost.

WARNER, JACK JR.: Producer. b. San Francisco, CA, Mar. 27, 1916. p. Jack L. Warner, and Mrs. Albert S. Rogell. e. Beverly Hills H.S.; U. of Southern California, B.A. Entered Warner New York office studying distrib. and exhib. for 1½ years. Transferred to prod. dept. at West Coast studios, then to short subject dept. as assoc. prod. As reserve officer called to active duty in 1942 and served as combat photo unit officer in 164th Signal Photo Co. for one year. Transf. to Signal Corps Photographic Center, Astoria, NY, where participated in prod. Army Signal Corps training films. Was asst. to chief of training films prod. In 1944 assigned to Hq. First U.S. Army Group to assist in planning combat photography for invasion of Europe. Until cessation of hostilities was asst. chief Photo Branch Office of Chief Signal Officer in 12th Army Group and on fall of Germany was on staff of General Eisenhower in Frankfurt as asst. and acting photo officer, Office of the Chief Signal Officer, Theatre Service Forces European Theatre (TSFET). Released from active duty April 20, 1945. Commissioned Lt. Col. Signal Corps Reserve. In 1947 with Warner Bros. Pictures Distrib. Corp., making survey of exhib. and distrib. as related to prod.; liaison between Warner and Assoc. Brit. Pictures on The Hasty Heart, 1948–49; org. Jack M. Warner Prod., Inc., 1949; first film, The Man Who Cheated Himself, distrib. by 20th Cent.-Fox; prod. dept., Warner Bros., 1951; prod. exec. Warners 1953. In charge of TV film prod. for Warners 1955; exec. in charge of television comm. and ind. film dept., Warner Bros. 1956; v.p., Warner Bros. Pictures, Inc., Jan. 1958; Warner association terminated Jan. 1959. Reactivated indep. m.p. co. Jack M. Warner Prod. to prod. feature TV and industrial films; pres., Jack Warner Prods., Inc., prod. theatrical films, 1961; prod., dir., Brushfire; Commissioned Colonel, Signal Corps. U.S. Army Reserve, 1962; 1977–78: Prod.: TV series & films for theatrical and TV, Jack Warner Pdns; writer, 1979–81. Author: Bijou Dream (novel, 1982).1983-87: writer, projected TV series and theatrical films. Completing novel and screenplay.

WARNER, MALCOLM-JAMAL: Actor. b. Jersey City, NJ, Aug. 18, 1970. Raised in Los Angeles. Was 13 years old when signed to play Bill Cosby's son on The Cosby Show.
THEATER: Three Ways Home (off-Bdwy debut, 1988).
TELEVISION: The Cosby Show (series, since 1984); Movie: The Father Clements Story, Mother's Day.

WARREN, CHARLES MARQUIS: Director, Producer, Writer. b. Baltimore, MD, Dec. 16, 1917. e. McDonogh Sch. (MD), Baltimore City Coll. Commander U.S. Navy, W.W.II (Bronze Star, Purple Heart, 5 Battle Stars); then to Hollywood. Writer for screen, magazines; author of books.
BOOKS: Only the Valiant, Valley of the Shadow, Wilderness, Deadhead, History of American Dental Surgery.
PICTURES: Only the Valiant, Beyond Glory, Redhead and the Cowboy, Streets of Laredo, Springfield Rifle, Day of the Evil Gun, Little Big Horn, Hellgate, Pony Express, Arrowhead, Flight to Tangier, 7 Angry Men, Trooper Hook, Tension at Table Rock, Cattle Empire, Charro!, Down to the Sea, Time of the Furies, Copper Sky, Ride a Violent Mile, Blood Arrow, The Unknown Terror, Hunter, The Final Day, The Head of the Serpent.
TELEVISION: Creator of Gunsmoke, Rawhide, Gunslinger, and the Virginian series as well as prod.-dir.-writer.; exec. prod. on Iron Horse series.

WARREN, GENE: Executive. b. Denver, CO, Aug. 12, 1916. Pres. of Excelsior Prods., prod. co. specializing in special effects and animation. Has headed 2 other cos. of similar nature over past 20 years, functioning at various times as prod., dir., studio prod. head and writer. Producer-director of following shorts: The Tool Box, Suzy Snowflake, Santa and the Three Dwarfs, Land of the Midnight Sun and these documentaries/training films: Mariner I, Mariner III, Apollo, U.S. Navy titles.
Special effects on theatrical features incl: Black Sunday, McNamara's Band, Satan's School for Girls, My Name Is John, The Power, 7 Faces of Dr. Lao, Wonderful World of the Brothers Grimm, The Time Machine, Tom Thumb. TV series include: The Man from Atlantis, Land of the Lost, Star Trek, Outer Limits, Twilight Zone, Mission Impossible.

WARREN, JENNIFER: Actress, Producer. b. New York, NY, Aug. 12, 1941. e. U. of Wisconsin, Madison, B.A. Grad work at Wesleyan U. Studied acting with Uta Hagen at HB Studios. As part of AFI Women's Directing Workshop, directed Point of Departure, short film which received Cine Golden Eagle and Aspen Film Festival Awards. Formed Tiger Rose Productions, indep. film-TV prod. co., 1988. Exec. prod., You Don't Have to Die (Acad. Award, doc. short, 1989).
THEATER: Scuba Duba (off-Bdwy. debut, 1987); 6 RMS RIV VU; Harvey; P.S., Your Cat Is Dead; Bdwy: Saint Joan; Volpone; Henry V (Guthrie Theatre).
PICTURES: Night Moves (debut, 1975); Slapshot; Another Man, Another Chance; Ice Castles; Fatal Beauty.
TELEVISION: Kojak (1975) Series: The Smothers Brothers Comedy Hour (1967–69); Paper Dolls. Movies: Shark Kill; Steel Cowboy; First, You Cry; Champions: A Love Story; Angel City; Freedom; The Choice; The Intruder Within; Confessions of a Married Man; Celebrity; Amazons, Gambler, Full Exposure: The Sex Tape Scandal.

WARREN, LESLEY ANN: Actress. b. New York, NY, Aug. 16, 1946. Studied acting under Lee Strasberg. Big break came in Rodgers and Hammerstein's Cinderella on TV 1964; where seen by Disney scout. Broadway debut in 110 in the Shade (1963). Film debut in The Happiest Millionaire (1967).
PICTURES: The One and Only Genuine Original Family Band, Pickup on 101, Harry and Walter Go to New York, Victor/Victoria (Acad. Award nom.), A Night in Heaven, Songwriter, Choose Me, Race to the Yankee Zephyr, Clue, Burglar, Blood on the Moon, Cop, Two Too Many.
TELEVISION: Series: Mission: Impossible (1970–71), Mini-series: 79 Park Avenue, Beulah Land, Pearl, Evergreen. Movies: Seven in Darkness, Love, Hate, Love, The L Letters, The Legend of Valentino, Assignment Munich, Portrait of a Stripper, Portrait of a Showgirl, Betrayal, A Fight for Jenny, Apology, Baja Oklahoma, Family of Spies: the Walker Spy Ring. Specials: The Saga of Sonora, It's a Bird, It's a Plane, It's Superman, A Special Eddie Rabbit, The Dancing Princess, 27 Wagons Full of Cotton.

WARRICK, RUTH: Actress. b. St. Joseph, MO, June 29, 1916. Film debut in 1941: Citizen Kane.
PICTURES: Obliging Young Lady, The Corsican Brothers, Journey Into Fear, Forever and a Day, Perilous Holiday, Father of the Bride, The Iron Major, Secret Command, Mr. Winkle Goes to War, Guest in the House, China Sky, Song of the South, Driftwood, Daisy Kenyon, Arch of Triumph, The Great Dan Patch, Make Believe Ballroom, Three Husbands, Let's Dance, One Too Many, Roogie's Bump, The Great Bank Robbery, The Returning.
TELEVISION: Studio One, Robert Montgomery Presents, Lux Star Playhouse, Sometimes I Don't Love My Mother, Peyton Place—The Next Generation. Series: Peyton Place, All My Children.

WASHBURN, DERIC: Writer. b. Buffalo, NY. e. Harvard U., English lit. Has written number of plays, including The Love Nest and Ginger Anne.
PICTURES: Silent Running (co-s.p.), The Deer Hunter, The Border.

WASHINGTON, DENZEL: Actor. b. Mt. Vernon, NY, Dec. 28, 1954. e. Fordham U., B.A., journalism. Studied acting with American Conservatory Theatre, San Francisco.
THEATER: When the Chickens Come Home to Roost (Audelco Award); Coriolanus; Spell #7; The Mighty Gents; Ceremonies in Dark Old Men; A Soldier's Play; Checkmates.
PICTURES: Carbon Copy (1981), A Soldier's Story, Power, Cry Freedom, For Queen and Country, The Mighty Quinn, Glory, Heart Condition.
TELEVISION: Movies: Wilma, Flesh and Blood, License to Kill. Series: St. Elsewhere (1982–88).

WASSERMAN, DALE: Writer, Producer. b. Rhinelander, WI, Nov. 2, 1917. Stage: lighting designer, dir., prod.; dir. for. attractions, S. Hurok; began writing, 1954. Founding member & trustee of O'Neill Theatre Centre; artistic dir. Midwest Playwrights Laboratory; member, Acad. M.P. Arts & Sciences; awards include Emmy, Tony, Critics Circle (Broadway), Outer Circle; Writers Guild.
TELEVISION: The Fog, The Citadel, The Power and the Glory, Engineer of Death, The Lincoln Murder Case, I Don Quixote, Elisha and the Long Knives, and others.
PLAYS: Livin' the Life, 998, One Flew Over the Cuckoo's Nest, The Pencil of God, Man of La Mancha, Play With Fire, Shakespeare and the Indians, Mountain High, Western Star, Green.
PICTURES: Cleopatra, The Vikings, The Sea and the Shadow, Quick, Before It Melts, Mister Buddwing, A Walk with Love and Death, Man of La Mancha.

WASSERMAN, LEW: Executive. b. Cleveland, OH, March 15, 1913. National dir. advertising and publ. Music Corporation of Amer. 1936–38; v.p. 1938–39; v.p. motion picture div. 1940; Chairman of the bd., Chief Executive Officer, MCA, Inc., Universal City, CA. Received Jean Hersholt Humanitarian Award, 1973.

WASSON, CRAIG: Actor. b. Eugene, OR, March 15, 1954. On stage in Godspell, All God's Chillun Got Wings, Death of a Salesman, The Glass Menagerie. Also musician.
PICTURES: The Boys in Company C (also music), Go Tell the Spartans, The Outsider, Carny, Schizoid, Night at O'Rears, Ghost Story, Second Thoughts, Four Friends, Body Double, The Men's Club, Bum Rap, The Trackers.
TELEVISION: Phyllis, Baa Baa Black Sheep, Serpico, Movies: Skag, Why Me?, Thornwell, The Silence, Mrs. R's Daughter.

WATANABE, GEDDE: Actor. b. Ogden, UT, June 26. Trained for stage at American Conservatory Theatre, San Francisco. Appeared with N.Y. Shakespeare Fest. Shakespeare in the Park series and with Pan Asian Repertory Theatre, N.Y.
THEATER: Pacific Overtures (debut, as Tree Boy, Bdwy. and on tour, 1976); Oedipus the King; Bullet Headed Birds; Poor Little Lambs.
PICTURES: Sixteen Candles (debut, 1984); Volunteers; Gung Ho; Vamp; UHF, The Spring.
TELEVISION: Gung Ho (series).

WATERHOUSE, KEITH: Writer. b. Leeds, England, Feb. 6, 1929. Early career as journalist, novelist. Author of There is a Happy Land, Billy Liar, Jubb, The Bucket Shop. Ent. m.p. ind. 1960.
PICTURES: s.p. (with Willis Hall): Whistle Down The Wind, A Kind of Loving, Billy Liar, Man in the Middle, Pretty Polly, Lock Up Your Daughters, The Valiant, West Eleven.
TELEVISION: (series): Inside George Webley, Queenie's Castle, Budgie, Billy Liar, There is a Happy Land, Charters and Caldicott.

WATERS, JOHN: Director, Writer. b. Baltimore, MD, 1946. Renowned for elevating "bad taste" to outrageous high comedy. First short film Hag in a Black Leather Jacket (1964) shot in Baltimore, as are most of his films. Other shorts include Roman Candles, and Eat Your Makeup. Feature debut, Mondo Trasho.
PICTURES: Multiple Maniacs (dir., prod., editor, sound; film marked the debut of Waters' star Divine), Pink Flamingos, Desperate Living, Female Trouble, Polyester (filmed in "Odorama" complete with scratch and sniff cards, prod., dir., s.p.), Hairspray (dir., s.p., co-prod., actor), Cry Baby (dir., s.p.).

WATERSTON, SAM: Actor. b. Cambridge, MA, Nov. 15, 1940. e. Yale U. Spent jr. year at Sorbonne in Paris where was part of the Amer. Actors' Workshop run by American dir. John Berry. Broadway debut in Oh Dad, Poor Dad...(1963). Film debut, The Plastic Dome of Norma Jean (1965). TV debut Pound (Camera Three). Has worked in New York Shakespeare Festival prods. since As You Like It (1963).
THEATER: N.Y. Shakespeare Festival: As You Like It, Ergo, Henry IV (Part I & II), Cymbeline, Hamlet, Much Ado About Nothing, The Tempest. Off Bdwy: The Knack, La Turista, Waiting for Godot, The Three Sisters. Broadway: The Paisley Convertible, Halfway Up the Tree, Indian, Hay Fever, The Trial of Cantonsville Nine, A Meeting by the River, Much Ado About Nothing (Drama Desk and Obie Awards), A Doll's House, Lunch Hour, Benefactors, A Walk in the Woods.
PICTURES: Fitzwilly, Three, Generation, Mahoney's Estate, Who Killed Mary What's 'er Name?, Savages, The Great Gatsby, Journey Into Fear, Rancho Deluxe, Dandy, Capricorn One, Eagle's Wing, Sweet William, Coup de Foudre, Interiors, Hopscotch, Heaven's Gate, The Killing Fields, Warning Sign, Hannah and Her Sisters, Just Between Friends, A Certain Desire, The Devil's Paradise, September, Welcome Home, The French Revolution, The Teddy Bear Habit, Mindwalk.
TELEVISION: The Good Lieutenant, Much Ado About Nothing, The Glass Menagerie, Reflections of a Murder, Friendly Fire, Oppenheimer, O.E.D., In Defense of Kids, Games Mother Never Taught You, Dempsey, Finnegan Begin Again, Love Lives On, Steven Spielberg's Amazing Stories, The Fifth Missile, The Room Upstairs, Terrorist on Trial: The United States vs. Salim Ajami, Gore Vidal's Lincoln, The Nightmare Years (mini-series), Jane of Lantern Hill, The Shell Seekers.

WATKIN, DAVID: Director of Photography. b. Margate, Eng., March 23, 1925. Entered British documentary industry in Jan., 1948. With British Transport Films as asst. cameraman, 1950–55; as cameraman, 1955–61. Feature film debut The Knack beginning long creative relationship with director Richard Lester.
PICTURES: The Knack (1964); Help!; Marat/Sade; How I Won the War; Charge of the Light Brigade; Catch 22; The Devils; The Boyfriend; The Homecoming; A Delicate Balance; The Three Musketeers; The Four Musketeers; Jesus of Nazareth; Mahogany; To the Devil, a Daughter; Robin and Marian; Joseph Andrews; Cuba; Hanover Street; The Summer; Endless Love; Chariots of Fire; Return to Oz; Yentl; The Hotel New Hampshire; White Nights; Out of Africa (Acad. Award, 1985); Moonstruck; Sky Bandits; The Good Mother, Masquerade, Last Rites. Journey to the Center of the Earth, Memphis Belle.
TELEVISION: Murder By Moonlight.

WATKINS, GRATH: Actor. b. London, Aug. 8, 1922. e. University Coll. Sch. Served in Royal Air Force 1944–45. Entered films in 1945 with role in The Captive Heart.
PICTURES: Bedelia, Gaiety George, A Matter of Life and Death, The Hanging Judge, Goodbye Mr. Chips, Cromwell, The Rise and Fall of Michael Rimmer, Virgin Witch, Fright, Naughty, Twins of Evil, Mary, Queen of Scots, Steptoe and Son, Henry VIII, Cinderella, The Omen.
TELEVISION: People in Conflict (Canada).

WATTLES, JOSHUA S.: Executive. Now sr. v.p. and deputy gen. counsel also in chg. of music matters. for Paramount Pictures. Previously worked with Richard Zimbert, exec. v.p. Prior to joining Para. legal dept. in 1981 was atty. in office of gen. counsel at ASCAP. Member N.Y. and Calif. Bars.

WAX, MO.: Publisher and editor of Film Bulletin. b. Philadelphia, PA. e. Villanova U. Also pres., Audienscope, Inc., Entertainment research organization.

WAX, MORTON DENNIS: Public Relations Executive. b. New York, NY, March 13, 1932. e. Brooklyn Coll., 1952. President of Morton Dennis Wax & Assoc., Inc., p.r. and marketing firm servicing intl. creative marketplace, established 1956. Contrib. writer to Box Office Magazine, intl. editorial consultant, Film Journal. Recent articles: Creativity (Advertising Age), Rolling Stone's Marketing Through Music, Words & Music, Campaign Magazine, Songwriters Guild of America National Edition. As sect. of VPA, conceptualized intl. Monitor Award, an annual event, currently under auspices of ITS. Public relations counsel to London Intl. Advertising Awards. Member: The Public Relations Society of America, Natl. Acad. of TV Arts & Sciences, Natl. Acad. of Recording Arts & Sciences, Publishers Publicity Assoc., M.P. Bookers Club, Friars Club, English Speaking Union.

WAYLAND, LEN: Actor. b. California, Dec. 28. e. Junior Coll., Modesto, CA. Wrote, prod. weekly radio series 1939–41, KPAS, KTRB, Calif. Service, radar navigator, 1941–45; en. theatre, Tobacco Road, 1946; 1973, formed Len Wayland Prods. for prod. of theatrical pictures and TV series. In 1976–77: prod./dir.: Don't Let It Bother You. 1978, prod., dir., You're not there yet, for own co.
THEATRE: Played summer and winter stock 1947–49. Bdwy, Streetcar Named Desire, 1949, and tour; toured, Heaven Can Wait; My Name Is Legion; Love of Four Colonels, Stalag 17, A Time to Live (serial), prod., USA (off-Bdwy); A Man For All Seasons, Bdwy.
TELEVISION: First Love, 1955; Armstrong Circle Theatre, Justice, Sgt. Bilko, Kraft Theatre; Dr. Weaver, From These Roots. Profiles in Courage, Dr. Kildare, Gunsmoke, Slattery's People, Ben Casey, A Noise in the World, Love Is a Many Splendored Thing; Dragnet, Outsider; Ironside, Name of the Game, The Bold Ones, Daniel Boone, The Virginian, Project U.F.O., Sam (series), The Blue and the Gray.

WAYNE, DAVID: Actor, r.n. Wayne McKeekan; b. Traverse City, MI, Jan. 30, 1916. e. Western Michigan U., 1936; in marionette shows, 1937.
THEATRE: Finian's Rainbow (Tony Award, 1947), Mister Roberts, Teahouse of the August Moon (Tony Award, 1954).
PICTURES: Portrait of Jennie, Adam's Rib, Reformer and the Redhead, My Blue Heaven, Stella, M, Up Front, As Young As You Feel, With a Song in My Heart, Wait 'Til the Sun Shines, Nellie; Down Among the Sheltering Palms, The I Don't Care Girl, We're Not Married, O. Henry's Full House, Tonight We Sing, How to Marry a Millionaire, Hell and High Water, Tender Trap, The Three Faces of Eve, The Last Angry Man, The Big Gamble, The Andromeda Strain, The African Elephant (narrator), Huckleberry Finn, The Front Page, The

Apple Dumpling Gang, Lassie: A New Beginning, House Calls, Finders Keepers.
TELEVISION: Series: Norby (1955), The Adventures of Ellery Queen, Dallas, House Calls. Specials: The Ruggles of Red Gap, The Devil and Daniel Webster, Escape Clause (Twilight Zone), Movies: The FBI vs. Alvin Karpis, Benjamin Franklin, Statesman, Once an Eagle, Gift of Love, Black Beauty, Loose Change, American Christmas Carol.

WAYNE, JOEL: Executive. Began career with Grey Advertising; in 17 years won many awards (60 Clios, 25 N.Y. Art Director Club Awards, etc.). Was exec. v.p. & creative dir. of agency when left in 1979 to join Warner Bros. as v.p., creative adv. 1987, named sr. v.p., worldwide creative adv.

WAYNE, MICHAEL A.: Executive. r.n. Michael A. Morrison. b. Los Angeles, CA, Nov. 23, 1934. Son of late actor John Wayne. e. Loyola H.S.; Loyola U., B.B.A. Asst. dir., various companies, 1955–56; asst. dir., Revue Prods., 1956–57; pres. Batjac Prods, and Romina Prods., 1961; asst. to producer: China Doll, 1957; Escort West; The Alamo; prod., McClintock; co-prod., Cast Giant Shadow; prod. The Green Berets; exec. prod. Chisum; prod. Big Jake; prod. The Train Robbers; prod. Cahill, U.S. Marshall, exec. prod. McQ, Brannigan.

WAYNE, PATRICK: Actor. b. July 15, 1939. Son of late actor John Wayne. Made film debut at age 11 in Rio Grande with father.
PICTURES: The Searchers, The Alamo, The Comancheros, McClintock, The Bears and I, Big Jake, Sinbad and the Eye of the Tiger, The People Time Forgot, Rustler's Rhapsody, Young Guns, Her Alibi, Chill Factor.
TELEVISION: Last Hurrah, Sole Survivor, Yesterday's Child, Frank's Place.

WEAKLAND, KEVIN L.: Producer, Entertainer. b. Philadelphia, PA, Aug. 14, 1963. e. Holy Family Coll. 1977–82, entertainment consultant and actor; 1982–present, entertainment producer and financier as well as entertainer (singer-actor). Company: KLW International, Inc.
MEMBER: Association of Independent Video and Filmmakers; National Academy of Video Arts & Sciences; Mid-Atlantic Arts Consortium; National Music Publishers Assn.; New Jersey Associations of Media Artists.

WEAVER, DENNIS: Actor, Director. b. Joplin, MO, June 4, 1925. e. U. of Oklahoma, B.A., fine arts, 1948.
TELEVISION: Series: Chester, in Gunsmoke, 1955–64; title role, Kentucky Jones, 1964–65; Gentle Ben, 1967–69; McCloud, 1970–76; Stone (1979–80); Emerald Point NAS (1983–84); Buck James (1987–88). Movies: The Forgotten Man, Duel, The Rolling Man, The Great Man's Whiskers, Terror on the Beach, Intimate Strangers, Pearl, Centennial; Amber Waves, Dr. Mudd, Cocaine: One Man's Seduction, Go for the Gold, Bluffing It, Disaster at Silo 7, The Return of McCloud.
PICTURES: Duel at Diablo, Way Way Out, Gentle Giant, A Man Called Sledge, What's the Matter with Helen?, The Gallant Hours, Mission, Batangas, Walking After Midnight.

WEAVER, FRITZ: Actor. b. Pittsburgh, PA, Jan. 19, 1926. e. U. of Chicago. On stage in Chalk Garden, Miss Lonelyhearts, All American, Shot in the Dark, Baker Street, Child's Play (Tony), The Price, etc.
PICTURES: Fail Safe (debut, 1964), The Maltese Bippy, A Walk in the Spring Rain, Demon Seed, Marathon Man, Black Sunday, The Day of the Dolphin, The Guns of August, The Big Fix, Creepshow, Power.
TELEVISION: Movies: The Borgia Stick, Berlin Affair, Heat of Anger, The Snoop Sisters, Hunter, The Legend of Lizzie Borden, Captains Courageous, Holocaust, The Hearst and Davies Affair, A Death in California, I'll Take Manhattan, My Name is Bill W. Mini-Series: Dream West.

WEAVER, SIGOURNEY: Actress. r.n. Susan Weaver. b. New York, NY, Oct. 8, 1949. e. Stanford U., Yale U. Daughter of Sylvester "Pat" Weaver, former NBC pres. Mother, actress Elizabeth Inglis (one-time contract player for Warner Bros.). After college formed working partnership with fellow student Christopher Durang for off-Bdwy. improvisational productions. First professional appearance on stage in 1974 in The Constant Wife with Ingrid Bergman.
THEATER: Off-Bdwy: Titanic, Das Lusitania Songspiel; Gemini (by Yale class mate Albert Innaurato), Marco Polo Sings a Solo, Beyond Therapy, Hurlyburly (Broadway).
PICTURES: Madman (Israeli, debut, 1976), Alien, Eyewitness, The Year of Living Dangerously, Deal of the Century, Ghostbusters, One Woman or Two, Aliens, Half Moon Street, Gorillas in the Mist, Working Girl, Helmut Newton: Frames From the Edge (doc.), Ghostbusters II.
TELEVISION: The Best of Families, Somerset, The Sorrows of Gin.

WEAVER, SYLVESTER L., JR.: Executive. b. Los Angeles, CA, Dec. 21, 1908. e. Dartmouth Coll. CBS, Don Lee Network, 1932–35; Young & Rubicam adv. agency, 1935–38; adv. mgr., American Tobacco Co., 1938–47; v.p. Young & Rubicam, 1947–49; joined NBC as v.p., chg. TV, 1949; appt'd v.p. chg. NBC Radio & TV networks, 1952; vice-chmn. bd., NBC, Jan., 1953; pres., NBC, Dec., 1953; bd. chmn., Dec. 1955; As head of NBC during TV's formative years, Weaver is credited as the father of TV talk/service program, founding both Tonight and Today shows, also innovated the rotating multi-star anthology series, the Wide Wide World series and concept of TV "special." Own firm, 430 Park Avenue., N.Y., 1956; chmn. of bd. McCann-Erickson Corp. (Intl.), 1959; pres., Subscription TV, Inc. Comm. Consultant in Los Angeles, CA and President, Weaver Productions, Inc. On magazine series Television: Inside and Out (1981–82).
AWARDS: Emmy Trustees' and Governor's Award (1967) and Governor's Award (1983).

WEBB, CHLOE: Actress. b. New York, NY. e. Boston Conservatory of Music and Drama. On stage with Boston Shakespeare Co., Goodman Theatre in Chicago and Mark Taper Forum, L.A. In Forbidden Broadway (Off-Bdwy. and L.A.) impersonating Angela Lansbury, Mary Martin and Carol Channing.
PICTURES: Sid and Nancy (debut, 1986); The Belly of an Architect, Twins, Queens Logic.
TELEVISION: Remington Steele; China Beach (pilot), Movie: Who Am I This Time?

WEBB, ROBERT D.: Director. b. 1903.
PICTURES: assoc. prod., Lure of the Wilderness; dir., Glory Brigade, Proud Ones. Prod., dir.: Threshold of Space, Seven Cities of Gold, Beneath the 12 Mile Reef, White Feather, The Jackals, Capetown Affair, Love Me Tender, The Way to the Gold, Seven Women From Hell, The Agony and the Ecstasy (2nd unit), Capetown Affair, The Hawaiians.

WEBSTER, R.A.: Executive. b. Montreal, Canada, 1933. e. Bishop's Univ. (BA), Univ. of New Brunswick (BCL) and Univ. of London (LLM). Early career as barrister and solicitor. Ent. m.p. ind. 1961 as asst. company secretary, Associated British Picture Corp. 1966: booking dir., Associated British Cinemas; 1974: managing dir., Associated British Cinemas; 1979: chmn.-mgn. dir., Thorn EMI Cinemas; 1981: dir. of product acquisition, Thorn EMI Screen Entertainment; 1986: pres., theatre div., Cinema International Corp. BV (CIC).

WEDGEWORTH, ANN: Actress. b. Abilene, TX, Jan. 21, 1935. e. U. of Texas. On stage in Thieves, Blues for Mr. Charlie, Chapter Two, etc.
PICTURES: Handle with Care, Thieves, Bang the Drum Slowly, Scarecrow, Law and Disorder, Dragon Fly, The Birch Interval, No Small Affair, Sweet Dreams, The Men's Club, Made in Heaven, Far North, Miss Firecracker.
TELEVISION: The Edge of Night, Another World, Somerset, All That Glitters, Three's Company, Filthy Rich, Right to Kill?, A Stranger Waits.

WEILER, GERALD E.: Producer. b. Mannheim, Germany, May 8, 1928. e. Harvard, 1946–48; Columbia, B.S., 1949–51; New York U. Grad. Sch., 1951–53. Writer, WHN, N.Y. writer, sports ed., news ed., Telenews Prod., Inc., 1948–52; asst. to prod., Richard de Rochemont, Vavin, Inc., 1952; U.S. Army, 1953–55; v.p., Vavin Inc. 1955–73; President, Weiler Communications Inc. 1973. Winner, NY "Lotto" Lottery, 1988; retired 1989.

WEILL, CLAUDIA: Director. b. New York, NY 1947. e. Radcliffe, B.A., 1969. Teacher of acting, Cornish Institute, 1983; guest lecturer on film directing, NYU and Columbia U. Winner of Donatello Award, best director, 1979; Mademoiselle Woman of the Year, 1974; AFI Independent Filmmakers Grant, 1973. Worked as prod. asst. on doc. Revolution.
THEATER: An Evening for Merlin Finch (debut, 1975, Williamstown); Stillife; Found a Peanut; The Longest Walk.
PICTURES: Doc. shorts: This Is the Home of Mrs. Levant Grahame; Roaches' Serenade. Director: The Other Half of the Sky—A China Memoir; Girlfriends; It's My Turn.
TELEVISION: The 51st State; Sesame Street; Joyce at 34; The Great Love Experiment; thirtysomething (series).

WEINBLATT, MIKE: Television Executive. b. Perth Amboy, NJ, June 10, 1929. e. Syracuse U. Served in Army as counter-intelligence agent, mostly in Japan (1952–53). Joined NBC in 1957; has headed two major TV network functions—talent/program admin. & sls. Joined network business affairs dept. in 1958 as mgr., business affairs, facilities operations; rose to post of director, pricing & financial services before moving to sales in November, 1962, as mgr., participating program sales. Named v.p., eastern sales, NBC-TV, 1968. Named v.p., talent & program admin., October, 1968; promoted to v.p. sales, February, 1973. January, 1975 named sr. v.p., sales; later became exec. v.p. Appointed exec. v.p. & gen. mgr. of NBC TV network in August, 1977. 1983, joined Showtime/Movie Channel as pres. & chief oper. off. 1984, pres., Multi Media Entertainment.

WEINGROD, HERSCHEL: Writer, Producer. b. Milwaukee, WI, Oct. 30, 1947. e. U. of Wisconsin, 1965–69; London Film Sch., 1969–71.
PICTURES: Co-writer with Timothy Harris: Cheaper to Keep Her, Trading Places (BAFTA nom., best orig. s.p.; NAACP Image Award, best m.p., 1983), Brewster's Millions,

My Stepmother Is An Alien, Paint It Black, Twins (People's Choice Award, best comedy 1988).
TELEVISION: Street of Dreams (exec. prod.).

WEINSTEIN, HENRY T.: Executive Producer. b. New York, NY, July 12, 1924. e. City Coll. of New York, Carnegie Inst. of Technology. Dir. of: the Brattle Theatre, Theatre in the Round, Houston, Texas. Prod. for The Theatre Guild, N.Y. Producer, 20th Century-Fox, M.G.M. Exec. in chg. of prod. American Film Theatre, Skyfield Productions. Currently, v.p., creative affairs, Cannon Films.
PICTURES: Tender is the Night, Joy in the Morning, Cervantes, Madwoman of Chaillot, The Battle of Neretva, Magic Christian, A Delicate Balance, The Homecoming, The Iceman Cometh, Lost in the Stars, Butley, Luther, Rhinoceros, Galileo, The Man in the Glass Booth, In Celebration, Runaway Train, 52 Pick-Up, Texasville.
TELEVISION: Play of the Week series, prod.

WEINSTEIN, PAULA: Independent Producer. b. Nov. 19, 1945. e. Columbia U. Daughter of late prod. Hannah Weinstein. Partnered with Gareth Wigan in WW Productions at Warner Brothers. Started as theatrical agent with William Morris and International Creative Management. With Warner Brothers, 1976–78 as production v.p.: left to go to 20th Century-Fox in same capacity. Named Fox sr. v.p., worldwide prod. In 1980 appointed v.p., prod., the Ladd Company. 1981, joined United Artists as pres., motion picture div. In 1983, began own prod. company at Columbia Pictures, also serving as a consultant for Columbia. 1987, joined MGM as exec. consultant. Prod.: A Dry White Season, The Fabulous Baker Boys.

WEINTRAUB, FRED: Executive, Producer. b. Bronx, NY, April 27, 1928. e. U. of Pennsylvania Wharton Sch. of Business. Owner of The Bitter End Coffeehouse to 1971. Personal management, Campus Coffee House Entertainment Circuit; TV Production Hootenanny, Popendipity; syndicated TV show host: From The Bitter End; motion picture prod.; v.p., creative services, Warner Bros. 1969, exec. in chg. Woodstock; prod. motion pictures, Weintraub-Heller Productions, 1974.
PICTURES: Enter The Dragon, Rage, Black Belt Jones, Truck Turner, Golden Needles, Animal Stars, Hot Potato, The Ultimate Warrior, Dirty Knights Work, Those Cuckoo Crazy Animals, Crash, Outlaw Blues, The Pack, The Promise, Tom Horn, Battle Creek Brawl, Force Five, High Road to China, Out of Control, Gymkata, Princess Academy.
TELEVISION: My Father, My Son (prod.).

WEINTRAUB, JERRY: Producer. b. New York, NY, Sept. 26, 1937. m. former singer Jayne Morgan. Sole owner and chmn. of Management Three, representing entertainment personalities, including John Denver, John Davidson, Frank Sinatra, Neil Diamond, etc. Also involved with Intercontinental Broadcasting Systems, Inc. (cable programming) and Jerry Weintraub/Armand Hammer Prods. (production co.). 1985, named United Artists Corp. chmn. Resigned, 1986. 1987: formed Weintraub Entertainment Group.
PICTURES: Nashville, Oh, God!, Cruising, All Night Long, Diner, The Karate Kid, The Karate Kid Part II, The Karate Kid Part III.

WEINTRAUB, SY: Executive. b. New York, NY, 1923. e. U. of Missouri, B.A., journalism, 1947; graduate of American Theater Wing. Started career in 1949 forming with associates a TV syndication co., Flamingo Films, Inc., which merged with Associated Artists to form Motion Pictures for Television, Inc., largest syndicator at that time. He originated Superman and Grand Ol' Opry series for TV. In 1958 bought Sol Lesser Prods., owners of film rights for Tarzan, and began producing and distributing Tarzan films through Banner Productions, Inc. Also formerly chmn. of bd. of Panavision, Inc.; bd. mem. and pres. of National General Television Corp., and pres. of KMGM-TV in Minneapolis. In 1978 named chmn. of Columbia Pictures Industries' new Film Entertainment Group, also joining office of the chief executive of CPI.

WEIR, PETER: Director, Writer. b. Sydney, Australia, Aug. 8, 1944. e. attended Scots Coll. and Sydney U. Briefly worked selling real estate, traveled to Eng. 1965. Entered Australian TV industry as stagehand 1967 while prod. amateur revues. Dir. shorts: Count Vim's Last Exercise, The Life and Times of Reverend Buck Shotte, Homeside, Incredible Floridas, What Ever Happened to Green Valley ? 1967–73.
PICTURES: First prof. credit: director-writer of Michael, an episode of the feature, Three To Go (1970). Writer-Director: The Cars That Ate Paris (also s.p.), The Last Wave (also s.p.), The Plumber (also s.p.). Picnic at Hanging Rock, Gallipoli (also co-s.p.), The Year of Living Dangerously, Witness, The Mosquito Coast, Dead Poets Society, Green Card.

WEIS, DON: Writer, Director, Producer. b. Milwaukee, WI, May 13, 1922. e. U. of Southern California.
PICTURES: (dial. dir.) Body and Soul, The Red Pony, Champion, Home of the Brave, The Men; (dir.) Letter From a Soldier, sequence in It's a Big Country, Bannerline, Just This Once, You for Me, I Love Melvin, Remains To Be Seen, A Slight Case of Larceny, Half a Hero, Affairs of Dobie Gillis, Adventures of Haiji Baba, Ride the High Iron, Catch Me If You Can, Gene Krupa Story, Critic's Choice, Looking for Love, The King's Pirate, Repo.
TELEVISION: Dear Phoebe. Best TV director, 1956, 1958. Screen Dir. Guild, The Longest Hundred Miles, It Takes a Thief, Ironside, M*A*S*H., Happy Days, Planet of the Apes, Bronk, Petrocelli, The Magician, Mannix, Night Stalker, Barbary Coast, Courtship of Eddie's Father, Starsky & Hutch, Hawaii Five-O, Chips, Charlie's Angels, Love Boat, Fantasy Island.

WEIS, JACK: Producer, Director, Writer, Cinematographer, Film Editor. b. Tampa, FL, October 1, 1932. e. U. of Notre Dame, B.S.; U. of Chicago, M.S. Was in U.S. Air Force six yrs. Founded Associated Productions/Associated Advertising Productions, Inc. in New Orleans in Aug., 1967, and has been involved in over 120 films and approx. 1,500 commercials. Produced, directed and wrote original s.p.s. for several HEW youth rehabilitation pictures. Member: Cinematography Local 666, Chicago IATSE; Film Editor Local 780, IATSE, Chicago; Directors Guild of America; Writers Guild of America.
PICTURES: Quadroon (dir.), Storyville (prod., dir., s.p.), Damballa (prod., dir., s.p.); creature from Hony Island Swamp (prod.-dir., s.p.); Lehia (prod., dir., camera), You Never Gave Me Roses, (s.p., prod., dir.); The Perfect Circle (TV-s.p., prod., dir.); Crypt of Dark Secrets (prod., dir., s.p.); Mardi Gras Massacre, prod., dir., s.p., editor), Witches Bayou (prod., dir., s.p.).

WEISBERG, BRENDA: Writer. b. Rowne, Poland. Magazine writer, social service, public health, drama instructor. Married to the late Morris Meckler.
PICTURES: s.p., China Sky; s.p., When a Girl's Beautiful, Burning Cross, Port Said, Rusty series, Girl's School; collab. s.p., Isle of Samoa; collab. orig., Reunion in Reno, Alias Mr. Twilight, King of the Wild Horses, Little Tough Guy, s.p. Shadowed. Collaborator, Scarlet Claw, Ding Dong Williams, Babes On Swing Street, Weird Woman, The Mummy's Ghost, The Mad Ghoul, Keep 'Em Slugging, Mug Town, Tough As They Come, Mob Town, There's One Born Every Minute, Hit the Road, Sing Another Chorus, You're Not So Tough.
TELEVISION: Fireside Theatre, Philco Theatre, Matinee Theatre.
AUTHOR: U (short stories), Woman's Home Companion, Collier's. American Mercury (Mencken's) Plain Talk, Forum, Papa Was a Farmer (book).

WEISS, STEVEN ALAN: Executive. b. Glendale, CA, Oct. 19, 1944. e. Los Angeles City Coll., A.A., 1964; U. of Southern California, B.S., 1966; Northwestern U., B.S., 1967; LaSalle Extension U., J.D., 1970. U.S. Navy-San Diego, Great Lakes, Vallejo & Treasure Island, 1966–67; shipyard liaison officer, Pearl Harbor Naval Shipyard, U.S. Navy, 1970; gen. mgr., Adrian Weiss Prods., 1970–74; organized Weiss Global Enterprises with Adrian Weiss 1974 for production, acquisition & distribution of films. Purchased with Tom J. Corradine and Adrian Weiss from the Benedict E. Bogeaus Estate nine features, 1974. Secty./treas. of Film Investment Corp. & Weiss Global Enterprises. (Cos. own, control or have dist. rights to over 300 features, many TV series, documentaries, etc.)
MEMBER: Natl. Assn. of TV Program Executive Intl.; National Cable TV Assn.; American Film Institute.

WEISSMAN, MURRAY: Executive. b. New York, NY, Dec. 23. e. U. of Southern California. Promotion mgr., TV Guide, 1952; asst. publicity director, KABC-TV, 1953–60; asst. dir. of press info., CBS, 1960–66; mgr., TV press dept., Universal Studio, 1966–68; executive in charge of m.p. press dept., Universal Studios & asst. secy., Universal Pictures, 1968–76; marketing exec., Columbia Pictures, 1976–77; vice pres. of advertising & publicity, Lorimar Productions, 1977; vice pres., ICPR Public Relations Company, 1978–81; now principal, Weissman/Angellotti.

WEISSMAN, SEYMOUR J.: Executive, Producer, Director. Weissman Franz Productions. b. Brooklyn, NY, May 28, 1931. e. Kenyon Coll., Eng. Lit., A.B., 1953; U. of Southern California, cinema, 1955. Unity Films, 1954; Henry Strauss & Co., 1954; Dir. of motion pictures, White Sands Proving Grounds, N.M., 1954–55; M.P.O., 1955; Coleman Prod., 1956; prod. dir., Dynamic Films, Inc., 1958–59; prod., dir., Viston Assoc., 1959–64; dir., VPI Prods., 1966.

WEITZLER, LINDA: Executive. Began career in entertainment industry at ABC-TV, where worked 11 yrs. Joined Columbia Pictures 1981 as v.p. talent relations, working with publicity and promotion depts.; 1984, moved to Universal Pictures in similar capacity. 1987, appt. corporate p.r. dir. for corporate special projects.

WEITZNER, DAVID: Executive. b. New York, NY, Nov. 13, 1938. e. Michigan State U. Entered industry in 1960 as member Columbia Pictures adv. dep't; later with Donahue and Coe as ass't exec. and Loew's Theatres adv. dep't; later with

Embassy Pictures, adv. mgr.; dir. of adv. and exploitation for Palomar Pictures Corp.; v.p. in charge of adv., pub., and exploitation for ABC Pictures Corp.; v.p., entertainment/leisure div., Grey Advertising; v.p., worldwide adv., 20th Century Fox; exec. v.p. adv./pub./promo., Universal Pictures; exec. v.p., mktg. & dist., Embassy Pictures; 1985, joined 20th Century-Fox Films as pres. of mktg. 1987, pres., mktg., Weintraub Entertainment Group; 1988 joined MCA/Universal as pres. worldwide marketing, MCA Recreation Services.

WELCH, RAQUEL: Actress. r.n. Raquel Tejada. b. Chicago, IL, Sept. 5, 1940. Mother of actress Tahnee Welch. e. La Jolla H.S. Fashion and photographic modeling. Co-hostess, Hollywood Palace. Broadway debut, Woman of the Year, 1981.
PICTURES: Roustabout; A House Is Not a Home; Swinging Summer; Fantastic Voyage; Shoot Louder . . . I Don't Understand; One Million Years B.C.; Fathom; Bedazzled; The Biggest Bundle of Them All; The Queens; Bandolero; Lady in Cement; 100 Rifles; Flare Up; The Magic Christian; Myra Breckinridge; Hannie Caulder; Kansas City Bomber, Fuzz; The Last of Sheila, The Three Musketeers; The Four Musketeers; The Wild Party; Mother, Jugs and Speed; Crossed Swords; L'Animal.
TELEVISION: From Raquel With Love (also writer), Legend of Walks Far Woman; Right to Die; Scandal in a Small Town, Paradise.

WELD, TUESDAY: Actress. r.n. Susan Weld. b. New York, NY, Aug. 27, 1943. m. violinist Pinchas Zuckerman. e. Hollywood Professional Sch. Began modeling at 4 yrs. Film debut, Rock, Rock, Rock (1956).
PICTURES: Rally Round The Flag, Boys! The Five Pennies, The Private Lives of Adam and Eve, Return to Peyton Place, Wild in the Country, Bachelor Flat, Lord Love a Duck, Pretty Poison, I Walk the Line, A Safe Place, Play It As It Lays, Looking for Mr. Goodbar, Who'll Stop the Rain, Thief, Author! Author!, Once Upon a Time in America; Heartbreak Hotel.
TELEVISION: The Many Loves of Dobie Gillis (series, 1959–60). Movies: Mother and Daughter: The Loving War, Winter of Our Discontent, F. Scott Fitzgerald in Hollywood, Madame X, Seduced and Swindled, Something in Common, Circle of Violence, The Rainmaker.

WELK, LAWRENCE: Orchestra leader. b. Strasburg, ND, March 11, 1903. Played accordion community dances, church socials, etc. Started own group. Biggest Little Band in America. Played hotels, ballrooms, music became known as Champagne Music. Signed Aragon Ballroom, Pacific Ocean Park, CA, 1951, with weekly television show. Champagne Music Makers, ABC-TV, July 2, 1955; The Lawrence Welk Show, ABC; signed lifetime contract, Hollywood Palladium, July 1961. Recording: Calcutta, 1961; syndicated network show started 1971.

WELLER, PETER: Actor. b. Stevens Point, WI, June 24, 1947. Acting since 10 years old. e. North Texas State U. Studied at American Acad. of Dramatic Arts with Uta Hagen. Member, Actor's Studio.
PICTURES: Butch and Sundance: The Early Years, Just Tell Me What You Want, Shoot the Moon, Of Unknown Origin, Vera, Buckeroo Banzai, Firstborn, Robocop, Shakedown, Leviathan, A Killing Affair, The Tunnel, Cat Chaser, Roger Corman's Frankenstein Unbound, RoboCop II.
TELEVISION: Lou Grant, Exit 10. Movies: Two Kinds of Love, Kentucky Woman, The Silence, Apology.
STAGE: Sticks and Bones (moved up from understudy, Bdwy. debut), Summer Brave, Macbeth, The Wool-Gatherers, Rebel Women, Streamers, The Woods, Serenading Louie.

WELLS, FRANK G.: Executive. b. California, March 4, 1932. e. Pomona Coll., 1949–53; Oxford U., 1953–55; Rhodes Scholarship Jurisprudence. U.S. Army, Infantry first lieutenant, 1955–57; Stanford Law Sch. 1957–59. Joined Gang, Tyre & Brown (entertainment industry law firm) 1959; partner, 1962–69; mem., State Bar of Calif., American Bar Assoc., Los Angeles County Bar Assoc., vice chmn., Warner Bros. Inc.; 1985, pres. & COO, Walt Disney Prods., Inc.

WENDERS, WIM: Director. b. Dusseldorf, Germany, August 14, 1945. Studied film 1967–70 at Filmhochschule in Munich. Worked as film critic 1968–70 for Filmkritik and Die Suddeutsche Zeitung. In 1967 made first short films (Schauplatze) and three others before first feature, Summer in the City, in 1970.
PICTURES: Die Angst Des Tormanns Beim Elfmeter, The Scarlet Letter, Aus Der Familie Der Panzerechsen, Falsche Bewegung, Alice in the Cities, The Goalie's Anxiety at the Penalty Kick, Kings of the Road, The American Friend, Lightning Over Water, Hammett, The State of Things, Paris, Texas, Tokyo-Ga, Wings of Desire, All Night Long (as actor), Till the End of the World.

WENDKOS, PAUL: Director. b. Philadelphia, PA, Sept. 20, 1926.
PICTURES: The Burglar; Tarawa Beachhead; Gidget; Face of a Fugitive; Because They're Young; Angel Baby; Gidget Goes to Rome; Miles to Terror; Guns of the Magnificent Seven; Cannon for Cordova; The Mephisto Waltz; Special Delivery.
TELEVISION: Hawkins: Murder in the Slave Trade; Fear No Evil; The Brotherhood of the Bell; A Death of Innocence; The Underground Man; The Woman I Love; The Legend of Lizzie Borden; Honor Thy Father; The Death of Ritchie; 79 Park Avenue; Ordeal of Doctor Mudd; The Five of Me; The Search for Patty Hearst; A Woman Called Moses; A Cry for Love; Cocaine; One Man's Poison; Celebrity; Intimate Agony; Scorned and Swindled; The Execution; Picking Up the Pieces; The Bad Seed; Six Against the Rock; Rage of Angels: The Story Continues; Right to Die; The Taking of Flight 847, From the Dead of Night; The Great Escape II: The Untold Story (co-dir.), Cross of Fire.

WERNER, PETER: Producer, Director. b. New York, NY, Jan. 17, 1947. e. Dartmouth Coll.
PICTURES: In the Region of Ice, Don't Cry It's Only Thunder, No Man's Land.
TELEVISION: Producer: Battered, Barnburning, Learning in Focus. Director: Aunt Mary, Hard Knox, I Married a Centerfold, Women in Song, Sins of the Father. LBJ: The Early Years. Men (exec. prod., dir.).

WERTHEIMER, THOMAS: Executive. b. 1938. e. Princeton U., B.A. 1960; Columbia U., LLB, 1963. Vice pres. business affairs subs. ABC 1964–72; joined MCA Inc 1972. Vice-pres. Universal TV dir.; corp. v.p. 1974–83; exec. v.p. 1983–director and officer of subsidiaries. Member exec. committee.

WERTMULLER, LINA: Writer, Director. b. Rome, Aug. 14, 1928. m. sculptor-set designer Enrico Job. e. Acad. of Theatre, Rome, 1951. Began working in theatre in 1951; Prod.-dir. avant-garde plays in Italy 1951–52; mem. puppet troupe 1952–62; actress, stage mgr., set designer, publicity writer, for theater, radio & TV 1952–62. Began film career as asst. to Fellini on 8½ in 1962. Following year wrote and directed first film, The Lizards. Had big TV success with series called Gian Burasca and then returned to theatre for a time. 1988, named Special Commissioner of Centro Sperimentale di Cinematografia.
PICTURES: This Time, Let's Talk About Men, The Seduction of Mimi (Cannes Fest, best dir. award 1972), Love and Anarchy, All Screwed Up, Swept Away, Seven Beauties, A Night Full of Rain, Blood Feud, A Joke of Destiny, Sotto Sotto, Camorra, Summer Night, On a Moonlit Night (dir., s.p.), Saturday, Sunday, Monday.
TELEVISION: I1 Decimo Clandestino (Cannes Fest.).

WEST, ADAM: Actor. b. 1938. r.n. William West Anderson.
PICTURES: The Young Philadelphians; Geronimo; Soldier in the Rain; Robinson Crusoe on Mars; Mara of the Wilderness; Alexander the Great; Batman; The Girl Who Knew Too Much; Marriage of a Young Stockbroker; The Specialist; Hell River; Hooper; One Dark Night; Doin' Time on Planet Earth, Return Fire: Jungle Wolf II, Mad About You, John Travis: Solar Survivor, Night Raiders.
TELEVISION: Series: The Detectives; Batman; The Last Precinct; Movies: For the Love of It; I Take These Men; Nevada Smith; Poor Devil.

WEST, TIMOTHY: Actor. b. Yorkshire, England, Oct. 20, 1934. m. actress Prunella Scales. Ent. ind. 1960. Began acting 1956 after two years as recording engineer. Worked in regional repertory, London's West End and for Royal Shakespeare Company. Dec., 1979 appointed artistic controller of Old Vic. Has directed extensively in the theatre.
PICTURES: Twisted Nerve, The Looking Glass War, Nicholas and Alexandra, The Day of the Jackal, Hedda, Joseph Andrews, The Devil's Advocate, Agatha, The Thirty Nine Steps, Rough Cut, Oliver Twist, Cry Freedom, Consuming Passions.
TELEVISION: Edward VII, Hard Times, Crime and Punishment, Henry VIII, Churchill and the Generals, Brass, The Monocled Mutineer, The Good Doctor, Bodkin Adams, What the Butler Saw, Harry's Kingdom, The Train, When We Are Married, Breakthrough at Reykjavik, Strife, A Shadow on the Sun, The Contractor, Blore.

WESTCOTT, HELEN: Actress. r.n. Myrthas Helen Hickman. b. Hollywood, CA, 1929. e. Los Angeles Jr. Coll., 1946. In play The Drunkard, at 7, for 9 yrs.; many radio shows.
PICTURES: A Midsummer Night's Dream (as child), Adventures of Don Juan, Girl from Jones Beach, Mr. Belvedere Goes to College, Whirlpool, Dancing in the Dark, The Gunfighter, Three Came Home, Secret of Convict Lake, Phone Call from a Stranger, Return of Texan, With a Song in My Heart, Loan Shark, Abbott and Costello Meet Dr. J. & Mr. H., Charge at Feather River, Hot Blood, The Last Hurrah, I Love My Wife.

WESTON, JACK: Actor. b. Cleveland, OH, Aug. 21, 1924. Began career in 1934 in children's division of Cleveland Playhouse. In Army in W.W.II. Success came in Broadway hit, Season in

the Sun. Was frequent performer in top TV shows during 1950s. Film debut in Stage Struck in 1958.
PICTURES: Stage Struck, Please Don't East the Daisies, All in a Night's Work, The Honeymoon Machine, It's Only Money, Palm Springs Weekend, The Incredible Mr. Limpet, Mirage, The Cincinnati Kid, Wait Until Dark, The Thomas Crown Affair, The April Fools, Cactus Flower, A New Leaf, Fuzz, Marco, Gator, The Ritz, Cuba, The Four Seasons, The Longshot, RAD, Ishtar, Dirty Dancing, Short Circuit 2.
TELEVISION: Studio One, Philco Theatre, Kraft Playhouse, Rod Browning of the Rocket Rangers. Movies: If Tomorrow Comes, 79 Park Avenue, Deliver Us From Evil, I Love a Mystery.

WESTON, JAY: Producer. b. New York, NY, March 9, 1929. e. New York U. Operated own pub. agency before moving into film prod. In 1965 launched Weston Production; sold orig. s.p., The War Horses, to Embassy Pictures; acquired and marketed other properties. Became prod. story exec. for Palomar-ABC Pictures in 1967.
PICTURES: For Love of Ivy (co-prod.), Lady Sings the Blues (co-prod.), W.C. Fields and Me, Chu Chu and the Philly Flash, Night of the Juggler, Buddy, Buddy.
STAGE: Does a Tiger Wear a Necktie (co-prod.).
TELEVISION: Laguna Heat (exec. prod.).

WESTON, ROBERT R.: Executive. b. New York, NY. e. Peekskill Military Acad., Fordham U. Publicity dir., WFUV-FM, 3 yrs.; copy writer, Columbia Pictures, asst. acct. exec., Donahue & Coe, asst. adv. mgr., United Artists adv. dir., Embassy Pictures, v.p., asst. to exec. v.p.; v.p. asst. to pres., resigned to become independent film prod., 1971. Pres., Harold Robbins Int'l., film prod. co. Prod.: The Betsy, The Lonely Lady.

WEXLER, HASKELL: Cinematographer, Director. b. Chicago, 1926. Photographed educational and industrial films before features. Documentaries as cin. include: The Living City, The Savage Eye, T. for Tumbleweed, Stakeout on Dope Street, Brazil—A Report on Torture, Interviews With Mai Lai Veterans, Interview—Chile's President Allende, Introduction to the Enemy.
PICTURES: Studs Lonigan, Five Bold Women, The Hoodlum Priest, Angel Baby, A Face In the Rain, America, America, The Best Man, The Bus (also dir. prod.), The Loved One (also co-prod.), Who's Afraid of Virginia Woolf (Acad. Award, 1966), In the Heat of the Night, The Thomas Crown Affair, Medium Cool (also co-prod., dir., s.p.), Trial of Catonsville Nine, American Graffiti, One Flew Over the Cuckoo's Nest, Bound for Glory (Acad. Award, 1976), Days of Heaven (addit. photog.), Richard Pryor: Live on the Sunset Strip, No Nukes (also co-dir.), Second Hand Hearts, Lookin' to Get Out, Coming Home, The Man Who Loved Women, Matewan, Colors, Latino (dir., writer only), Three Fugitives, Blaze.
TELEVISION: The Kid From Nowhere.

WHALLEY-KILMER, JOANNE: Actress. b. Salford, England, 1964. m. actor Val Kilmer. Began stage career while in teens including season of Edward Bond plays at Royal Court Theatre (Olivier Award nom.) and The Three Sisters.
PICTURES: Pink Floyd-the Wall, Dance With a Stranger, No Surrender, The Good Father, To Kill a Priest, Willow, Scandal, Kill Me Again.
TELEVISION: The Singing Detective, A Kind of Loving, A Quiet Life, The Gentle Touch, Bergerac, Reilly, Edge of Darkness, A Christmas Carol (movie).

WHEATON, WIL: Actor. b. California. Began acting in commercials at age 7.
PICTURES: The Buddy System (debut, 1984); Hambone and Hillie; The Last Starfighter; The Farm; Stand by Me; The Curse.
TELEVISION: A Long Way Home (debut); The Shooting. Pilots: Long Time Gone, 13 Thirteenth Avenue; The Man Who Fell to Earth. Movies: The Defiant Ones. Series: Star Trek II: The Next Generation. Special: My Dad Can't Be Crazy, Can He?

WHEELER, LYLE: Art director. b. Woburn, MA, Feb. 12, 1905. e. U. of Southern California. Mag. illustrator, industrial designer before entering m.p. ind. as art dir. of Garden of Allah. In 1944 apptd. supervising art dir. 20th Century-Fox. Academy Award, in collab. art-direction black & white for Anna and the King of Siam; Gone With the Wind, color art dir., collab., The Robe, 1953. Love Is a Many-Splendored Thing, Daddy Longlegs, The Diary of Anne Frank (Acad. Award, 1959), Journey to the Center of the Earth, The Cardinal.
TELEVISION: Perfect Gentlemen, Flight to Holocaust.

WHITAKER, FOREST: Actor. b. Longview, TX, 1961. Raised in Los Angeles. e. studied voice at U. of Southern California, Music Conservatory. Former all-league defensive tackle. Stage credits include Swan, Romeo and Juliet, Hamlet, Ring Around the Moon, Craig's Wife, Whose Life Is It Anyway?, The Greeks, (all at Drama Studio London), Patchwork Shakespeare (CA Youth Theatre). Beggar's Opera, Jesus Christ Superstar.
PICTURES: Tag, Fast Times at Ridgemont High, Vision Quest, The Color of Money, Platoon, Stakeout, Good Morning Vietnam, Bird (best actor, Cannes Fest., 1988), Johnny Handsome, Downtown, Rage in Harlem.
TELEVISION: Guest: Amazing Stories, Hill Street Blues, Cagney and Lacey, Trapper John M.D., The Fall Guy, Different Strokes. Movies: Hands of a Stranger, North and South, Parts I & II, The Grand Baby.

WHITE, BETTY: Actress. b. Oak Park, IL, Jan. 17, 1924. m. late Allen Ludden. Began on radio in Blondie, The Great Gildersleeve, This Is Your F.B.I. Moved into TV with live local show, L.A.
TELEVISION: Panelist: Make the Connection (1955), Match Game P.M., Liar's Club, Life with Elisabeth (Emmy), The Betty White Show (1954–58), A Date With the Angels (1957–58), Tonight Show, Mary Tyler Moore Show (Emmy 1975, 1976), The Pet Set, Macy's Thanksgiving Parade (hostess for 10 yrs.), The Betty White Show, The Best Place To Be, The Gossip Columnist, The Carol Burnett Show, Just Men (host, Emmy, 1983), Mama's Family, Golden Girls (Emmy, 1986).

WHITE, JESSE: Actor. r.n. Jesse Weidenfeld. b. Buffalo, NY, Jan. 13, 1919. e. Akron, OH H.S. Did odd jobs, then salesman; radio, vaudeville, burlesque, nightclubs and little theatre work; Broadway stage debut in Moon is Down, 1942; other shows include Harvey, Born Yesterday, etc. Has appeared on numerous radio and TV shows, regular on Private Secretary, Danny Thomas, Ann Sothern Show. Best known as Maytag repairman on long-running commercial 1967–89.
PICTURES: Harvey, Death of a Salesman, Callaway Went Thataway, Million Dollar Mermaid, Witness to Murder, Forever Female, Not as a Stranger, Bad Seed, Back from Eternity, Designing Woman, Marjorie Morningstar, Legs Diamond, Fever in the Blood, Sail a Crooked Ship, It's Only Money, The Yellow Canary, It's a Mad, Mad, Mad, Mad World, Looking For Love, A House Is Not a Home, Bless the Beasts and Children, The Cat from Outer Space, The Monster in the Closet.

WHITE, LAWRENCE R.: Executive. b. 1926. e. Syracuse U. Began career as producer-director for the DuMont Television Network in 1948. Dir. of programming, Benton & Bowles, Inc., 1951; joined CBS TV network as v.p., daytime programming, 1959; dir. of program dev., CBS, 1963; joined NBC TV network in 1965 as v.p., daytime prog.; v.p. programs, east coast, 1969; v.p. programs, NBC-TV, 1972; ind. prod. affiliated with CPT, 1975. Resigned 1980 to become indep. prod.
TELEVISION: Exec. prod.: Goliath Awaits, The Blue and the Gray, The Master of Ballantrae, The First Olympics—Athens 1896, Twist of Fate (prod. & exec. prod.).

WHITE, LEONARD: Producer, Director, Actor. b. Sussex, Eng. TV dir., prod., CBC-TV (Canada), T.W.W. Ltd. T.T. TV & ABC-TV; Jupiter Thea., Inc.; Crest Theatre; Royal Alexandra Thea.; Toronto Thea., 1953–57. England, Playhouse, Oxford, Perth Repertory Thea., Hornchurch, Guilford Repertory Thea. Belgrade Thea., Coventry. Actor: U.S.A. debut in A Sleep of Prisoners, 1951–52; London West End. In the White Devil, He Who Gets Slapped, Macbeth, Still She Wished for Company, Point of Departure.
PICTURES: The Dark Man, The Large Rope, River Beat, Hunted, Martin Luther, Passage Home, Breakout, Circumstantial Evidence, At the Stroke of Nine, etc.
TELEVISION: All networks, G. Britain and CBC (Canada). Prod., ABC-TV, 1960–68. Series: Inside Story, Armchair Mystery Thea., Police Surgeon, The Avengers, Out of This World, Armchair Theatre. Prod., 1968–69; prod., Thames Television, 1969–70. Drama consultant CBC-TV Toronto, 1970–80 HTV (UK); 1980–87 STV (UK). 350 drama productions for ITV (UK) Network.

WHITE, PAUL: Executive, Producer, Director. b. New York, NY. e. Columbia U. N.Y. Times Wide World Pictures; man. ed., Nation-Wide News Service; ed./publisher of Key Magazine; home office exec. Paramount Pictures. Author, alone & in collab., books including I Find Treason. Served in U.S. Marine Corps as officer-in-chg. combat photography in the Pacific W.W.II, prod. & dir. wire recording from foxholes of first sound ever made of actual warfare sounds under battle fire in the Marshalls. Joined David O. Selznick as gen. mgr. European operations 1946; formed own co., Paul White Productions, Inc. 1948; pres., PSI-TV 1953. Joined Subscription TV 1958 as v.p. in chg. pgmg; pioneer Cablevision and Pay-TV; pres. MCI; created 11 audio-visual inventions; 1973 Paul White Enterprises (consultants). Clients: RCA; Impresario Hurok; Radix Intl. Corp.; Motivational Systems, Inc.; Liberty Mint. The Education Guild; Hi-Tech Industries, Inc.; Creative Holographics, U.K.; 1979 co-founder & chmn., Holoptics Network Intl. (N.Y./London) viz. Dimensional Imaging: Holography; Linear Optics; 3-D Film System; (co-inventor) pat pend anti-counterfeit ID labeling sys. with visible 3-D or animated tickets, labels, etc., invisibly encoded inside label, which portable mini computer can decode & display essential readout info re product, 1984 co-founder, bd. chmn. & CEO Holoptic 3D Systems, Inc. Optical inventions: The Holoptic

Converters enable standard 2D still and m.p. 35mm cameras and single projectors to shoot and show full color 3D images using polarized viewer glasses; an advanced 3D prototype syst. that eliminates the need for glasses or accessories. Currently dev. 3D TV syst.

PICTURES: Battle of the Marshalls, Saipan, Tinian, To the Shores of Iwo Jima, Song of Siam, Pearl of the Orient, Land of Fair Dinkum, Unusual Sports, Flying Doctor.

TELEVISION: Series Created and/or supervised incl.: Playhouse of Stars, China Smith, Play of The Week, Orient Express, prod. & dir. The Keys to Peace (Pope Paul's U.S. Visit); exec. prod. The Bolshoi Ballet; Bicentennial project; OP Sail 1976, The Tall Ships; Creative & technical svcs. for 3-D TV & multi-graphic applications.

WHITE, ROY B.: Executive, Exhibitor. b. Cincinnati, OH, July 30, 1926. e. U. of Cincinnati. Flight engineer, U.S. Air Force during W.W.II; worked in sales department of 20th Century-Fox, 1949–52; began in exhibition, 1952; past pres., Mid-States Theatres; pres., R. M. White Management, Inc.; past president, National Association of Theatre Owners, past Chairman of the Board, National Association of Theatre Owners: Board of Trustees—American Film Inst.; Board of Directors NATO of Ohio, v.p., Motion Picture Pioneers Foundation; Will Rogers Hospital, Nat'l. Endowment for Arts.

WHITELAW, BILLIE: Actress. b. Coventry, England, June 6, 1932. Acted on radio and television since childhood. Winner of the TV Actress of the Year and 1972, Guild Award, Best Actress, 1960. British Acad. Award 1969; U.S. National Society of Film Critics Award best supp. actress, 1968. Evening News, Best Film Actress, 1977; best actress Sony Radio Radio Award 1987.

STAGE: 3 years with National Theatre of Great Britain. England, My England (Revue). Progress to the Park, A Touch of the Poet, Othello, Trelawney of the Wells, After Haggerty, Not I, Alphabetical Order, Footfalls, Molly, The Greeks, Happy Days, Passion Play, Rockaby (also in N.Y. and Adelaide Festival), Tales from Hollywood, Who's Afraid of Virginia Woolf?

PICTURES: No Love for Johnnie, Mr. Topaze, Hell Is a City, Payroll, Charlies Bubbles, The Adding Machine, Twisted Nerve, Start the Revolution Without Me, Leo the Last, Eagle in a Cage, Gumshoe, Frenzy, Nightwatch, The Omen, The Water Babies, An Unsuitable Job for a Woman, Slayground, Shadey, The Chain, Maurice, The Dressmaker, Joyriders.

TELEVISION: Over 100 leading roles incl. No Trains to Lime Street, Lady of the Camelias, Resurrection, The Pity of it All, You and Me, A World of Time, Dr. Jekyll and Mr. Hyde, Poet Game, Sextet (8 plays for BBC), Wessex Tales, The Fifty Pound Note, Supernatural (2 plays), Three plays by Samuel Beckett, Eustace and Hilda, The Oresteia of Aeschylus, The Haunted Man, Private Schultz, Jamaica Inn, Rockaby, Camille, Imaginary Friends, The Secret Garden, The Picnic, A Tale of Two Cities, The Fifteen Streets, Three Beckett plays.

WHITEMORE, HUGH: Writer. b. England, 1936. Studied acting at Royal Acad. of Dramatic Art. Has since written for television, film, theatre.

THEATER: Stevie, Pack of Lies, Breaking the Code, The Best of Friends.

PICTURES: All Neat in Black Stockings, All Creatures Great and Small, Stevie, The Return of the Soldier, 84 Charing Cross Road, Pack of Lies.

TELEVISION: Cider With Rosie (Writers' Guild Award 1971), Elizabeth R (Emmy Award 1971), Country Matters (Writers' Guild Award 1972), Dummy (RAT–Prix Italia 1979), Rebecca, All For Love, A Dedicated Man, Down at the Hydro, A Bit of Singing and Dancing, Concealed Enemies (Emmy, Neil Simon Awards 1984), Pack of Lies.

WHITFIELD, RICHARD ALLEN: Producer, Executive. b. Goldsboro, NC, 1946. e. U. of North Carolina. Adv. writer-prod. for American Brands, PepsiCola, 1970–73; TV-film prod., industrial-educational, 1973–77; v.p., adv., Independents International Films, Inc., dist., 1978; v.p.-prod., Rick Friedberg & Associates, 1979; pres. Golden Image Motion Picture Corp., feature production, 1980.

PICTURES: K-GOD (exec. prod.), Used Cars (video segments prod.), Bones of Peking (prod.), Terror on Tour, To All a Goodnight.

WHITMAN, STUART: Actor. b. San Francisco, CA., Feb. 1, 1928. Army Corp. of Engineers (1945–1948), at Fort Lewis, WA; while in army, competed as light heavyweight boxer. Studied drama under G.I. Bill at Ben Bard Drama Sch. and L.A. City Coll., Performed in Heaven Can Wait and became member of Michael Chekhov Stage Society and Arthur Kennedy Group. Entered films in early 1950s. TV debut on 26 episodes Highway Patrol.

PICTURES: When Worlds Collide, The Day The Earth Stood Still, Rhapsody, Seven Men From Now, War Drums, Johnny Trouble, Darby's Rangers, Ten North Frederick, The Decks Ran Red, China Doll, The Sound and the Fury, These Thousand Hills, Hound Dog Man, The Story of Ruth, Murder, Inc., Francis of Assisi, The Fiercest Heart, The Mark (Acad. Award nom.), The Comancheros, Convicts 4, The Longest Day, The Day and the Hour (Fr./It.), Shock Treatment; Rio Conchos, Those Magnificent Men In Their Flying Machines, The Sands of the Kalahari, Signpost to Murder, An American Dream, The Last Escape; The Invincible Six; The Only Way Out Is Dead, Captain Apache (US/Sp.), The Man Who Wanted to Live Forever, Night Of The Lepus, Hostages; The Man Who Died Twice; Welcome To Arrow Beach/Tender Flesh, Call Him Mr. Shatter; Ransom; Crazy Mama, Las Vegas Lady; Tony Saitta/Tough Tony (It.), Strange Shadows In An Empty Room; Ruby; The White Buffalo; Death Trap/Eaten Alive; The Thoroughbreds; Maniac; Oil (It. as Red Adair), La Murjer de la Tierra Caliente (Sp./It.); Run For The Roses, Delta Fox; Guyana-Crime Of The Century, Key West Crossing, Jamaican Gold, Treasure Of The Amazon, John Travis: Solar Survivor, Deadly Reactor, Moving Target.

TELEVISION: Cimarron Strip (series 1967–68), The Crowd Pleaser (Alcoa-Goodyear), Highway Patrol, Dr. Christian, Hangman's Noose (Zane Grey), The Last Convertible, Stillwatch, Condominium, Once Upon a Texas Train, Hemingway.

WHITMORE, JAMES: Actor. r.n. James Allen Whitmore, Jr. b. White Plains, NY, Oct. 1, 1921. e. Yale U. In Yale Drama Sch. players; co-founder Yale radio station, 1942; U.S. Marine Corps, W.W.II; in USO, in American Wing Theatre school, in stock. Broadway debut in Command Decision, 1947; m.p. debut in Undercover Man (1949). Star of Tomorrow.

PICTURES: Battleground, Asphalt Jungle, Next Voice You Hear, Mrs. O'Malley and Mr. Malone, Outriders, Please Believe Me, Across the Wide Missouri, It's a Big Country, Because You're Mine, Above and Beyond, Girl Who Had Everything, All the Brothers Were Valiant, Kiss Me Kate, The Command, Them, Battle Cry, McConell Story, Last Frontier, Oklahoma, Face of Fire, Eddie Duchin Story, Who Was That Lady?, Black Like Me, Chuka, Water Hole No. 3, Nobody's Perfect, Planet of the Apes, Madigan, The Split, Guns of the Magnificent Seven, Chato's Land, Where the Red Fern Grows, Give 'em Hell, Harry, The Serpent's Egg, The First Deadly Sin, Nuts, Old Explorers.

TELEVISION: Series: The Law and Mr. Jones, Temperature's Rising, Movies/Mini-series: Celebrity, All My Sons, The Word, I Will Fight No More Forever, Rage, The Challenge, Mark I Love You, Favorite Son (mini-series), Glory, Glory.

WHITTELL, JAMES: Executive. b. Clatterbridge, England, 1943. Ent. ind. 1962 holding various management positions with Odeon Cinemas. 1969: operations exec. 1972: operations exec. Rank Motorway Service Areas. 1981: managing dir.: Rank Tuschinski, Netherlands. 1983: operations dir. Pizzerland Restaurants, UK. 1986 appt. managing dir., Odeon Cinemas UK.

WIARD, WILLIAM O.: Director.

PICTURE: Tom Horn.

TELEVISION: Scott Free; The Girl, The Gold Watch and Everything; Ski Lift to Death; This House Is Possessed; Fantasies; Help Wanted: Male; Deadly Lessons; Kicks.

WICKES, MARY: Actress. r.n. Mary Wickenhauser. b. St. Louis, MO, June 13, 1916. e. Washington U., Doctor of Arts (hon.), 1969.

THEATRE: (Bdwy) The Man Who Came to Dinner, Town House, Stage Door, Danton's Death. Stock includes: St. Louis Municipal Opera, Starlight Theatre, Houston Music Theatre.

PICTURES: The Man Who Came to Dinner, Now, Voyager, White Christmas, The Music Man, The Trouble With Angels, Where Angels Go Trouble Follows, Napoleon and Samantha, Snowball Express, Touched by Love.

TELEVISION: The Halls of Ivy, The Danny Thomas Show, Dennis the Menace, Bonino, Alfred Hitchcock Presents, Studio One, Playhouse 90, Fatal Confession: A Father Dowling Mystery.

WIDMARK, RICHARD: Actor. b. Sunrise, MN, Dec. 26, 1914. e. Lake Forest U. Instructor, 1938. On radio, then stage, films.

PICTURES: Kiss of Death, Cry of the City, Road House, Street With No Name, Yellow Sky, Down to the Sea in Ships, Slattery's Hurricane, Night and the City, Panic in the Streets, No Way Out, Halls of Montezuma, The Frogmen, Red Skies of Montana, Don't Bother to Knock, O. Henry's Full House, My Pal Gus, Destination Gobi, Pickup on South Street, Take the High Ground, Hell & High Water, Broken Lance, Prize of Gold, The Cobweb, Backlash, Last Wagon, Saint Joan, Warlock, Kingdom of Man, The Long Ships, Run for the Sun, The Alamo, Judgment at Nuremberg, How the West Was Won, The Way West, Madigan, Death of a Gunfighter, When The Legends Die, Murder on the Orient Express, Twilight's Last Gleaming, The Domino Principle, Rollercoaster, Coma, The Swarm, Hanky Panky, The Final Option, Against All Odds.

TELEVISION: Madigan (series). Movies: Vanished (mini-series), The Last Day, Benjamin Franklin, A Whale For the Killing, All God's Children, Blackout, A Gathering of Old Men, Once Upon a Texas Train, Cold Sassy Tree.

WIDOM, DIANE: Executive. Held marketing positions with Warner Bros., in New York, London, Burbank, for 10 years prior to joining 20th Century Fox in 1980 as West Coast pub. dir. 1982, named dir. of natl. mag. pub. & special photography. Promoted to natl. pub. dir. 1985, named v.p., pub., Fox m.p. div.

WIENER, JACK: Executive. b. Paris, France, June 8, 1926. Pub. rep., MGM, New Orleans, Jacksonville, FL, 1952–56; joined Columbia Pictures Int. Corp., 1956, continental publicity mgr., Columbia, Paris; v.p., Columbia Pics. Int'l. 1966; continental prod. exec., 1968; v.p. Columbia Pictures Corp., 1970. In 1972 became indep. prod., making Vampira, The Eagle Has Landed, Escape to Athena, Green Ice, F/X.

WIESEN, BERNARD: Producer, Director, Writer, Executive. b. New York, NY. e. City Coll. of New York, B.B.A.; Pasadena Playhouse Coll. of Theatre, master of theatre arts; dramatic workshop of New School.

PICTURES: Producer-Director: Fear No More. Asst. Dir. The King and I, The Left Hand of God, The Rains of Ranchipur, To Catch a Thief, The Trouble with Harry.

TELEVISION: Director: How to Marry A Millionaire, Valentine's Day. Assoc. Producer: Valentine's Day, Three on an Island, Cap'n Ahab, Sally and Sam. Assoc. Prod.: Daniel Boone. Producer/Director: Julia, Co-Producer-Director: The Jimmy Stewart Show. Prod. Exec.: Executive Suite (pilot). Exec. Paramount TV, director of current programming. Writer: Love 4 Love.

STAGE: First Monday in October (Bdwy.)—co. prod.

WIEST, DIANNE: Actress. b. Kansas City, MO, March 28, 1948. e. U. of Maryland. Studied ballet but abandoned it for theatre. Did regional theatre work (Yale Repertory, Arena Stage) and performed with N.Y. Shakespeare Festival. Film debut in I'm Dancing As Fast As I Can, 1982.

THEATER: Toured with Amer. Shakespeare Co.; Arena Stage (Heartbreak House, Our Town, The Dybbuk, Inherit the Wind). Public Theater (Ashes, Agamennon, Leave it to Beaver is Dead), Frankenstein (Bdwy), Othello, Beyond Therapy, Not About Heroes (dir., Williamstown Fest.)

PICTURES: It's My Turn, Independence Day, Footloose, Falling in Love, The Purple Rose of Cairo, Hannah and Her Sisters (Acad. Award), Radio Days, Lost Boys, September, Bright Lights, Big City; Cookie, Parenthood.

TELEVISION: Zalman or the Madness of God, Out of Our Father's House, The Wall, The Face of Rage.

WIGAN, GARETH: Executive. b. London, England, Dec. 2, 1931. e. Oxford. Agent, MCA London; 1957; John Redway & Associates, 1960; co-founder, agent Gregson & Wigan Ltd., 1961; co-founder, agent London Intl., 1968; independent prod., 1970; v.p., creative affairs, 20th Century Fox, 1975; v.p., prod., Fox, 1976; v.p., The Ladd Co., 1979–83. Company W.W. Prods. Currently exec. production consultant, Columbia Pictures.

PICTURES: Unman Wittering & Zigo; Running Scared; etc.

WIHTOL, ARN S.: Executive. b. Millville, NJ, Sept. 4, 1944. e. San Jose State. Exec. v.p., international sales, Pacific International Enterprises.

PICTURES: Production Exec. and Co-Writer: Mystery Mansion. Casting and Controller: Dream Chasers. Producer's assistant: Sacred Ground.

WILBY, JAMES: Actor. b. Rangoon, Burma, 1958. Lived a nomadic childhood moving from Burma to Ceylon, then Jamaica and finally England. e. Durham U. Trained at Royal Acad. of Dramatic Art where he played Shakespearean roles and landed a part in Oxford Film Foundation's Privileged (1982). West End stage debut Another Country. Also acted in regional theater. 1988: The Common Pursuit.

PICTURES: Dreamchild (debut, 1985); A Room with a View (walk-on); Maurice; A Handful of Dust; A Summer Story, Conspiracy.

TELEVISION: Sherlock Holmes; The Crooked Man; Dutch Girls.

WILCOX, CLAIRE: Actress. b. Toronto, Canada, 1955. Photographer's model, 3 yrs. of age; appeared on numerous national magazine covers; TV commercials; signed contract, Curtis Enterprises.

PICTURES: 40 Pounds of Trouble, Wives and Lovers.

TELEVISION: Harris Versus the World.

WILDE, ARTHUR L.: Publicist. b. San Francisco, CA, May 27. S.F. Daily News; Matson Lines; pub. dept., Warner Bros., 1936; dir. exploitation, CBS; pub. dir., Hal Wallis Prod.; pub. dept., Paramount; pub., Hecht-Hill-Lancaster; v.p., Arthur Jacobs, public rel.; Blowitz-Maskell Publicity Agency; pub. dir., C. V. Whitney Pictures; gen. v.p., 1958; owner, pub.-ad. agency, The Arthur L. Wilde Co., 1961–65; freelance publicist, 1965–66; pub. rel. consultant, Marineland of Florida, 1965; unit publicity dir., United Artists, National General, Paramount, 1966–69; free lance publicity, 1971; unit publicist, MGM, Paramount, United Artists, 1972–74; staff position; Features Publicity at Paramount Pictures, 1973. Freelance unit publicist again in 1976 at Universal, Paramount and Lorimar Productions. 1978–79, Columbia Pictures & Universal Studios; 1980, Marble Arch. Prods. & Northstar Intl. Pictures; 1981, studio pub. mgr., 20th Century-Fox; recently staff unit publicist for 20th-Fox; 1984–89, free lance unit publicist for feature films.

WILDER, BILLY: Producer, Director, Writer. r.n. Samuel Wilder. b. Austria, June 22, 1906. Newspaperman in Vienna and Berlin; then author screen story People on Sunday (debut, 1930) followed by 10 other German films. s.p.: Emil and the Detectives (in Museum of Modern Art), UFA. French films, wrote, dir., Mauvaise Graine, and wrote Adorable. To Hollywood 1934, Head Film Section, Psych. Warfare Div., U.S. Army, 1945, Am. Zone, Germany. American Film Institute Life Achievement Award 1987. Irving Thalberg Memorial Award 1988.

PICTURES: As co-writer: Music in the Air, Lottery Lover, Bluebeard's Eighth Wife, Midnight, Ninotchka, What a Life, Arise My Love, Ball of Fire, Hold Back the Dawn.

PICTURES: As director & co-writer: The Major and the Minor, Five Graves to Cairo, Double Indemnity, The Lost Weekend (Acad. Award, best dir., best co-s.p., 1945), The Emperor Waltz, A Foreign Affair, Sunset Boulevard (Acad. Award, best story and s.p., 1950); (collab. s.p., dir., prod) The Big Carnival (a.k.a. Ace in the Hole), Stalag 17, Sabrina, The Seven Year Itch, The Spirit of St. Louis, Love in the Afternoon, Witness for the Prosecution, Some Like It Hot, The Apartment (Acad. Award, dir. story, and s.p., best picture, 1960); One, Two, Three, Irma La Douce; (co-prod.) Kiss Me, Stupid, The Fortune Cookie, The Private Life of Sherlock Holmes, Avanti, The Front Page, Fedora, Buddy, Buddy.

WILDER, GENE: Actor, Director. r.n. Jerry Silberman. b. Milwaukee, WI, June 11, 1935. m. late actress Gilda Radner. e. U. of Iowa. Joined Bristol Old Vic company in England, became champion fencer; in NY, worked as chauffeur, fencing instructor, etc. before N.Y. off-Broadway debut in Roots.

BROADWAY: The Complaisant Lover, Mother Courage, Luv.

PICTURES: Bonnie and Clyde, The Producers, Start the Revolution Without Me, Quackser Fortune Has a Cousin in the Bronx, Willy Wonka and the Chocolate Factory, Everything You Always Wanted to Know About Sex*, Blazing Saddles, Rhinoceros, Young Frankenstein, The Little Prince, Adventures of Sherlock Holmes Smarter Brother (s.p., dir., actor), Silver Streak, The World's Greatest Lover (s.p., dir., actor), The Frisco Kid, Stir Crazy, Sunday Lovers, (dir., s.p., actor.), Hanky Panky, The Woman in Red (dir., s.p., act.), Haunted Honeymoon (dir., s.p., act.), See No Evil, Hear No Evil (also co-s.p.), Benito.

TELEVISION: The Trouble With People, Marlo Thomas Special (1973), Thursday's Game (movie).

WILDER, W. LEE: Producer, director. Brother of Billy Wilder. b. Austria. e. U. of Vienna. Awards: First prize 1950 Venice Film Festival musical documentary category.

PICTURES: The Vicious Circle, Shadows of Fire, The Pretender, Once A Thief, Three Steps North, Phantom from Space, Killers from Space, Snow Creature, Big Bluff, Manfish, Man Without a Body, Fright, Spy in the Sky, Bluebeard's Ten Honeymoons.

WILK, TED: Theatrical agent. b. Minneapolis, MN, Jan. 5, 1908. e. U. of Michigan, 1926–30. Publix Theatres, Duluth, MN, 1930; Warner Bros., Minneapolis, 1932–33; Film Daily, Hollywood, 1934–40; U.S. Army, 1941–46; Lou Irwin agency 1946–61; Ted Wilk Agency, since 1961.

WILLIAMS, BERT: Executive, Actor. b. Newark, NJ, April 12, 1922. e. U. of Southern California. Navy, 1942–45. Summer Stock, 1940–41; world's prof. diving champion, 1945–48; star diver, Larry Crosby, Buster Crabbe, Johnny Weismuller, Dutch Smith Shows, 1945–48; writer, asst. prod., Martin Mooney Prods., PRC, Goldwyn Studios; pres., Bert Prods., Bert Williams Motion Picture Producers and Distributors, Inc. Member, M.P. Academy of Fine Arts & TV Academy of Arts & Science.

THEATRE: roadshow plays include: Cat on a Hot Tin Roof, Hamlet, Run From The Hunter, Sugar and Spice, Hope Is a Thing Called Feathers, 69 Below, Tribute.

PICTURES: Actor, Angel Baby; The Nest of the Cuckoo Birds (also prod., dir.), Around the World Under the Sea; Deathwatch 28 (s.p.), Twenty Eight Watched (dir.), Adventure To Treasure Reef (prod., dir.), Knife Fighters (s.p.). Black Freedom; A Crime of Sex, The Masters (prod., dir.), Crazy Joe, Serpico, Lady Ice, The Klansman, Report to the Commissioner, Tracks, All the President's Men, From Noon Till Three, While Buffalo, Helter Skelter, Shark Bait (s.p.), The Big Bus, Wanda Nevada, Cuba Crossing, Sunnyside, Cuba, The Last Resort, The All Night Treasure Hunt. Tom Horn, Kill Castro, Midnight Madness, The All-American Hustler, 10 to Midnight, Police Academy 2, One More Werewolf Picture, Murphy's Law, Cobra, Assassinations, Penitentiary III, Messenger of Death, Death Under the Rock.

TELEVISION: Flipper, Sea Hunt, prod., Speargun, Gentle Ben, The Law (pilot) and Police Story (actor). Get Christy Love, General Hospital, Columbo, Brenner for the People, Mayday 40,000 Feet, Jigsaw John (Blue Knight episode), Police Woman, Chips, Mobil One, Street Killing, East of Eden, Rose for Emily, Brett Maverick, Today's F.B.I., The Judge. Fifth St. Gym (also prod., dir., s.p.; pilot) Guest: Mike Douglas Show, Johnny Carson Show, Tales on Dark Side, The Last Car, This Is the Life, Deadly Intentions, Tales on the Dark Side, The Last Car, Divorce Court, Man Who Broke 1000 Chains, Nightmare Classics (The Eye of the Panther).

WILLIAMS, BILL: Actor. r.n. William Katt. b. Brooklyn, NY, 1916. m. actress Barbara Hale. Father of actor William Katt. e. Pratt Inst., Brooklyn. In U.S. Army, W.W.II. Began as professional swimmer; later with Municipal Opera House, St. Louis; then on vaudeville tour, U.S. & England. Screen debut 1944 in Murder in the Blue Room.

PICTURES: Thirty Seconds Over Tokyo, Those Endearing Young Charms, Blue Blood, Great Missouri Raid, Operation Haylift, Cariboo Trail, Havana Rose, Rose of Cimarron, Son of Paleface, Bronco Buster, Pace That Thrills, Torpedo Alley, Racing Blood, Outlaw's Daughter, Apache Ambush, Hell's Horizon, Wiretapper, Broken Star, Dog's Best Friend, Buckskin, Tickle Me, Scandalous John.

TELEVISION: Series: Kit Carson (1952–54), Assignment Underwater.

WILLIAMS, BILLY DEE: Actor. b. New York, NY, April 6, 1937. e. National Acad. of Fine Arts and Design. Studied acting with Paul Mann and Sidney Poitier at actor's workshop in Harlem. Was child actor in the Firebrand of Florence with Lotte Lenya; Broadway adult debut in The Cool World in 1961.

STAGE: A Taste of Honey, Hallelujah, Baby, I Have a Dream, Fences.

PICTURES: The Last Angry Man (debut), The Out-of-Towners, The Final Comedown, Lady Sings the Blues, Hit! Mahogany, The Bingo Long Travelling All-Stars, The Empire Strikes Back, Nighthawks, Return of the Jedi, Marvin and Tige, Fear City, Number One with a Bullet, Deadly Illusion, Batman, The Pit and the Pendulum.

TELEVISION: Brian's Song, The Glass House, Christmas Lilies of the Field, Oceans of Fire, Chiefs, The Right of the People, Courage, Stranded, The Return of the Desperado, Scott Joplin, King of Ragtime and appearances on series: The F.B.I., The Interns, Mission Impossible, Mod Squad, Dynasty.

WILLIAMS, CARA: Comedienne. r.n. Bernice Kamiat. b. Brooklyn, NY, 1925. e. Hollywood Professional Sch. Ent. ind., 20th Century Fox, child actress.

PICTURES: Boomerang, Something For the Boys, Meet Me In Las Vegas, Never Steal Anything Small, The Defiant Ones, The Man from the Diners' Club, Doctors' Wives.

TELEVISION: Pete and Gladys, Alfred Hitchcock Presents, Desilu Playhouse, The Jackie Gleason Show, Henry Fonda Special, The Cara Williams Show.

WILLIAMS, CARL W.: Executive. b. Decatur, IL, March 9, 1927. e. Illinois State Normal U., B.S., 1949; UCLA, M.A., 1950. dir. adv. photo., Clark Equipment Co., 1951–54; film dir., WKAR-TV, E. Lansing, MI, 1954–56; Prod., dir., Capital Films, E. Lansing, MI, 1957; dir., A-V Laboratory, U.C.L.A., 1957–63; co-dev. Dimension 150 Widescreen process, 1957; formed D-150 Inc., 1963; Filbert Co., 1970, v.p., 1977; v.p., Cinema Equipment Sales of Calif., Inc., 1986.

MEMBER: MAMPAS, SMPTE, AFI.

WILLIAMS, CINDY: Actress. b. Van Nuys, CA., Aug. 22, 1947. e. Los Angeles City Coll. Appeared in high school and college plays; first prof. role in Roger Corman's film Gas. Made TV debut in Room 222 and had continuing role.

PICTURES: Gas, Beware the Blob, Drive, He Said, The Christian Licorice Store, Travels with My Aunt, American Graffiti, The Conversation, Mr. Ricco, The First Nudie Musical, More American Graffiti, Uforia, Big Man on Campus, Rude Awakening, 101.

TELEVISION: Episodes of The Funny Side, The Neighbors, Barefoot in the Park, My World and Welcome to It, Love, American Style, Nanny and the Professor, The Bobby Sherman Show—Getting Together; Series: Laverne and Shirley. Movies: The Migrants, Helped Wanted: Kids, Save the Dog, Tricks of the Trade.

WILLIAMS, DIAHN: Actress. b. Gainesville, FL, June 30. e. U. of Miami, B.A., psychology, speech; also attended U. of Florida, UCLA. m. Thomas J. McGrath, prod. & atty. Started as fashion model in New York, France, Germany. Top woman exec. as assoc. dir. of pub. rel. at Chesebrough-Ponds, 1971–72.

PICTURES: Chair de Poule, Another Nice Mess, Deadly Hero.

TELEVISION: Harry's Girls (series, 1963–64), Somerset (series, 1973–74) and guest-starred in many TV shows, including I Spy, Get Smart, Tarzan, Here Comes the Brides, Andy Griffith Show, G.E. Theatre, etc.

WILLIAMS, ELMO: Film editor. b. Oklahoma City, OK, Apr. 30, 1913. Film editor 1933–39, with British & Dominion Studio, England. Since then with RKO-Radio as film editor for numerous major productions; mgr., dir., 20th Century Fox Prod. Ltd. v.p., worldwide production, 20th Century-Fox Film 1971. President Ibex Films. Exec. v.p., Gaylord Prods., 1979; promoted to pres., worldwide prods.

PICTURES: High Noon, 1952 (Acad. Award, best film ed. collab.); Tall Texan (dir. film ed.); The Cowboy (prod. dir., ed.); 20,000 Leagues Under the Sea (ed.); Apache Kid (dir.); The Vikings (second unit dir., film ed.); The Big Gamble (dir. 2nd Unit DFZ prod.); The Longest Day (assoc. prod.), Tora! Tora! Tora! (prod.), Sidewinder One (ed.), Caravans (ed.), Exec. prod.: Those Magnificent Men in Their Flying Machines, The Blue Max, Zorba The Greek, Man, Woman and Child (prod.).

TELEVISION: co-prod. dir., Tales of the Vikings.

WILLIAMS, ESTHER: Actress. b. Los Angeles, CA, Aug. 8, 1923. e. U. of Southern California. Swimmer San Francisco World's Fair Aquacade; professional model. On screen 1942 in Andy Hardy Steps Out. Voted one of Top Ten Money-Making Stars in M.P. Herald-Fame poll, 1950.

PICTURES: A Guy Named Joe, Bathing Beauty, Thrill of a Romance, This Time for Keeps, Ziegfeld Follies, Hoodlum Saint, Easy to Wed, Fiesta, On an Island With You, Take Me Out to the Ball Game, Neptune's Daughter, Pagan Love Song, Duchess of Idaho, Texas Carnival, Skirts Ahoy!, Million Dollars Mermaid, Dangerous When Wet, Easy to Love, Jupiter's Darling, Unguarded Moment, the Big Show, The Magic Fountain (s.p.).

WILLIAMS, JO BETH: Actress. b. Houston, TX, 1953. m. director John Pasquin. e. Brown U. One of Glamour Magazine's top 10 college girls, 1969–70. Acted with rep. companies in Rhode Island, Philadelphia, Boston, Washington, DC, etc. Spent over two years in New York-based daytime serials, Somerset and The Guiding Light. Film debut in Kramer Vs. Kramer, 1979.

THEATER: Ladyhouse Blues (1979), A Coupla White Chicks Sitting Around Talking, Gardenia.

PICTURES: Stir Crazy, The Dogs of War, Poltergeist, Endangered Species, The Big Chill, American Dreamer, Teachers, Desert Bloom, Poltergeist II, Memories of Me, Welcome Home.

TELEVISION: Movies: Fun and Games, The Big Black Pill, Feasting with Panthers, Jabberwocky, The Day After, Adam, Kids Don't Tell, Adam: His Song Continues, Murder Ordained, Baby M, My Name is Bill W.

WILLIAMS, JOHN: Composer. b. New York, NY, Feb. 8, 1932. e. UCLA, Juilliard Sch. Worked as session musician in '50s; began career as film composer in late '50s. Considerable experience as musical director and conductor as well as composer. Since 1977 conductor of Boston Pops.

PICTURES: I Passed for White, Because They're Young, The Secret Ways, Bachelor Flat, Diamond Head, Gidget Goes to Rome, The Killers, None But the Brave, John Goldfarb Please Come Home, The Rare Breed, How To Steal A Million, The Plainsman, Not with My Wife You Don't, Penelope, A Guide for the Married Man, Fitzwilly, Valley of the Dolls, Daddy's Gone A-Hunting, Good-bye Mr. Chips (mus. supvr. & dir.), The Reivers, Fiddler on the Roof (musc. dir.). The Cowboys, Images, Pete 'n' Tillie, The Poseidon Adventure, Tom Sawyer (musc. supvr.), The Long Goodbye, The Man Who Loved Cat Dancing, The Paper Chase, Cinderella Liberty, Conrack, The Sugarland Express, Earthquake, The Towering Inferno, The Eiger Sanction, Jaws, Family Plot, The Missouri Breaks, Midway, Black Sunday, Star Wars, Close Encounters of the Third Kind, The Fury, Jaws II, Meteor, Quintet, Dracula, 1941, Close Encounters of the Third Kind (special edition), The Empire Strikes Back, Heartbeeps, Raiders of the Lost Ark; E.T.: The Extra-Terrestrial, Return of the Jedi, Monsignor, Indiana Jones and the Temple of Doom, The River, Space Camp, The Witches of Eastwick, The Accidental Tourist, Indiana Jones and the Last Crusade.

TELEVISION: Once Upon a Savage Night, Jane Eyre (Emmy Award), Sergeant Ryker, Heidi (Emmy Award), The Ewok Adventure, NBC News Theme, Amazing Stories.

WILLIAMS, OSCAR: Writer, Producer, Director. e. San Francisco State U., getting degree in film, TV. Was director's intern on The Great White Hope (directed by Martin Ritt) through the American Film Inst.

PICTURES: The Final Comedown (s.p., prod. dir.); Black Belt Jones (s.p., assoc. prod.) Five on the Black Hand Side (dir.), Truck Turner (s.p.), Hot Potato (s.p., dir.).

WILLIAMS, PAUL: Actor, Composer. b. Omaha, NE, Sept. 19, 1940. Began career at studios as set painter and stunt parachutist. Bit and character parts in commercials followed. Seen briefly in The Chase and The Loved One. Became song writer, collaborating briefly with Biff Rose and later with Roger Nichols, with whom wrote several best-sellers, including We've Only Just Begun, Rainy Days and Mondays, Just an Old-Fashioned Love Song, Evergreen (Acad. Award with Barbra Streisand, 1976).

PICTURES: As actor: Watermelon Man, Planet of the Apes, The Cheap Detective, Smokey and the Bandit (& II), The End, Stone Cold Dead, The Muppet Movie (and score), The Chill Factor. Scores: Cinderella Liberty, Phantom of the Paradise (also actor), Bugsy Malone, A Star Is Born (songs), Grease (title song), Agatha, One on One.
TELEVISION: Rooster, Night They Saved Christmas, Wild, Wild West Revisited, Flight to Holocaust.

WILLIAMS, PAUL: Director. First gained attention as director of film short, Girl, which won Golden Eagle award, made in collaboration with producer Edward R. Pressman, with whom he formed Pressman-Williams Enterprises which prod. Badlands, Phantom of the Paradise, etc.
PICTURES: Out of It, The Revolutionary, Dealing: or the Berkeley to Boston Forty Brick, Lost Bag Blues, Nunzio, Miss Right (also story).

WILLIAMS, RICHARD: Producer, Painter, Film animator. b. March, 1933, Toronto, Canada. Entered industry in 1955. Founded Richard Williams Animation Ltd. in 1962, having entered films by producing The Little Island (1st Prize, Venice Film Festival) in 1955. His company produces TV commercials for Eng., Amer., France and Germany, entertainment shorts and animated films. Designed animated feature titles for What's New Pussycat?, A Funny Thing Happened On The Way To The Forum, Casino Royale, etc. (20 feature titles in 6 years). 1969: Animated sequences: Charge of the Light Brigade (Woodfall). 1971: A Christmas Carol, animated TV special for ABC-TV. Who Framed Roger Rabbit (dir. of animation).
AWARDS: at Festivals at Venice, Edinburgh, Mannheim, Montreal, Trieste, Melbourne, West Germany, New York, Locarno, Vancouver, Philadelphia, Zagreb, Hollywood, Cork, Los Angeles. 1973: Won Academy Award, best cartoon. 1989, BAFTA Award for special effects and AMPAS Award, special effects, also Special Achievement Awards for work over 30 years, esp. Roger Rabbit by both BAFTA and AMPAS.

WILLIAMS, ROBIN: Actor, Comedian. b. Chicago, IL, July 21, 1952. e. Claremont Men's Coll. (CA), Coll. of Marin (CA) studying acting at latter. Continued studies at Juilliard with John Houseman in New York augmenting income as a street mime. As San Francisco club performer appeared at Holy City Zoo, Intersection, the Great American Music Hall and The Boardinghouse. In Los Angeles performed as stand-up comedian at Comedy Store, Improvisation, and The Ice House. First TV appearance on Laugh In, followed by The Great American Laugh Off. Guest on Happy Days as extraterrestrial named Mork from Ork.
TELEVISION: Series: The Richard Pryor Show (1977), Laugh-In (revival 1977–78), Mork and Mindy. Guest: America Tonight, Ninety Minutes Live, The Alan Hamel Show, E.T. & Friends, Faerie Tale Theatre, Free To Be. . .a Family. Movie: Seize the Day.
PICTURES: The Last Laugh, Popeye, The World According to Garp, The Survivors, Moscow on the Hudson, The Best of Times, Club Paradise, Good Morning Vietnam, Dear America: Letters Home From Vietnam (reader), The Adventures of Baron Munchausen, Dead Poet's Society, Cadillac Man.

WILLIAMS, ROGER: Pianist, Concert, film, TV Personality. b. Omaha, NB, Oct. 1, 1926. e. Drake U., Idaho State Coll. Hon. Ph.D. Midland and Wagner Colls. Served U.S. Navy W.W.II. Appeared as guest artist in number of films. Public debut on TV's Arthur Godfrey Talent Scouts and Chance of a Lifetime. Other TV appearances include Ed Sullivan, Hollywood Palace, Kraft Summer Series, Celanese Special. Tours in addition to U.S. and Australia. Concert Halls—Japan, Mexico, Union of South Africa. Recorded 75 Albums, Kapp (now MCA) Records, with sales over 15 million albums.

WILLIAMS, TREAT: Actor. r.n. Richard Williams. b. Rowayton, CT, 1952. e. Franklin and Marshall Coll. Landed role on Bdwy. in musical, Over There! also played leading role in Grease on Bdwy. Film debut in The Ritz (1976).
THEATER: Bus Stop (Equity Library Theatre), Once in a Lifetime, The Pirates of Penzance, Some Men Need Help.
PICTURES: Deadly Hero (debut, 1976), The Eagle Has Landed, Hair, 1941, Why Would I Lie?, The Pursuit of D. B. Cooper, Prince of the City, Once Upon a Time in America, Flashpoint, Smooth Talk, The Men's Club, Dead Heat, Sweet Lies, Heart of Dixie, Night of the Sharks, Russicum, Beyond the Ocean.
TELEVISION: Movies: Dempsey, A Streetcar Named Desire, J. Edgar Hoover, Echoes in the Darkness, Third Degree Burn, Desperados: the "Kiki" Camarera Story, Max and Helen: A Remarkable Love Story.

WILLIAMS-JONES, MICHAEL: Executive. b. England, June 3, 1947. Joined United Artists as trainee, 1967; territorial mgr., South Africa, 1969; territorial mgr., Brazil, 1971; territorial mgr., England, 1976; appt. v.p., continental European mgr., 1978; sr. v.p. foreign mgr., 1979; In 1982 joined United Intl. Pictures as sr. v.p. intl. sls., based in London. 1984, named pres. UIP motion picture group; 1986, named pres. & CEO.

WILLIAMSON, FRED: Actor, Director, Writer. b. Gary, IN, March 5, 1937. e. Northwestern U. Spent 10 yrs. playing pro football before turning to acting.
PICTURES: M*A*S*H, Tell Me That You Love Me, Junie Moon, The Legend of Nigger Charley, Hammer, Black Caesar, The Soul of Nigger Charley, Hell Up in Harlem, That Man Bolt, Crazy Joe, Three Tough Guys, Black Eye, Three the Hard Way, Boss Nigger, Darktown, Bucktown, No Way Back (also prod., dir. s.p.), Take a Hard Ride, Adios Amigo, Death Journey (also prod., dir.), Joshua, Blind Rage, Fist of Fear Touch of Death, 1990: The Bronx Warriors, One Down Two to Go (also prod. dir.), Vigilante, Warriors of the Wasteland, Deadly Impact, The Big Score (dir., actor), The Last Fight (dir., actor), Foxtrap (prod., dir., actor), Warrior of the Lost World, Deadly Intent, Delta Force, Commando, Taxi Killer (prod.), Hell's Heroes, Justice Done (dir., actor), Soda Cracker (prod., dir., actor).
TELEVISION: Julia (series), Police Story, Monday Night Football, Half Nelson.

WILLIAMSON, NICOL: Actor. b. England, Sept. 14, 1938. Has played many classical roles with Royal Shakespeare Co., including Macbeth, Malvolio, and Coriolanus. Starred on Broadway in Inadmissible Evidence; Rex (musical debut).
PICTURES: Six Sided Triangle, Inadmissible Evidence, The Bofors Gun, Laughter in the Dark, The Reckoning, Hamlet, The Jerusalem File, The Seven-Per-Cent Solution, The Goodbye Girl (cameo), The Cheap Detective, The Human Factor, Excalibur, Venom, I'm Dancing As Fast As I Can, Return to Oz, Black Widow, Apt Pupil.
TELEVISION: Passion Flower, Lord Mountbatten, The Word, Macbeth, Christopher Columbus.

WILLIAMSON, PATRICK: Executive. b. England, Oct. 1929. Joined Columbia Pictures London office 1944—career spanned advertising & publicity responsibilities until 1967 when appt. managing dir. Columbia Great Britain in 1971. Also man. dir. on formation of Columbia-Warner. Promoted to executive position in Columbia's home office, New York, April, 1973 and pres. of international operations Feb. 1974. Vice pres., Coca-Cola Export Corp., April, 1983; exec. v.p. Columbia Pictures Industries, 1985; director, CPI, 1985; exec. v.p., Coca-Cola Entertainment Business Sector, 1987; promoted to special asst. to pres. & CEO of Coca-Cola Entertainment Business Sector, July, 1987. Serves on boards of Tri-Star-Pictures, RCA/Columbia Home Video, RCA/Columbia Int'l. Video. 1987, named pres. Triumph Releasing Corp., a unit of Columbia Pictures Entertainment. Resigned to become consultant to Columbia, 1989.

WILLIS, BRUCE: Actor. b. Germany, March 19, 1955. Moved to New Jersey when he was 2. After graduating high school, worked at DuPont plant in neighboring town. First entertainment work was as harmonica player in band called Loose Goose. Formed Night Owl Promotions and attended Montclair State Coll., NJ where he acted in Cat on a Hot Tin Roof. NY stage debut: Heaven and Earth. Member of Barbara Contardi's First Amendment Comedy Theatre; supplemented acting work by doing Levi's 501 jeans commercials and as bartender in a N.Y. nightclub, Kamikaze.
THEATER: Fool for Love.
PICTURES: Blind Date, Sunset, Die Hard, In Country, That's Adequate, The Right to Remain Silent, Hudson Hawk.
TELEVISION: Hart to Hart, Miami Vice, Moonlighting (series).

WILLIS, GORDON: Cinematographer. Acted two summers in stock at Gloucester, MA, where also did stage settings and scenery. Photographer in Air Force; then cameraman, making documentaries. In TV did commercials and documentaries.
PICTURES: End of the Road, Loving, The Landlord, The People Next Door, Little Murders, Bad Company, Klute, Up the Sandbox, The Paper Chase, The Godfather, The Parallax View, The Godfather, Part II, The Downing Pool, All the President's Men, September 30, 1955, Annie Hall, Comes a Horseman, Interiors, Manhattan, Stardust Memories, Pennies from Heaven, A Midsummer Night's Sex Comedy, Perfect, Zelig, Broadway Danny Rose, The Purple Rose of Cairo, The Money Pit, The Pick-Up Artist, Bright Lights, Big City, Dolores. Director: Windows (1980; debut).
TELEVISION: The Lost Honor of Kathryn Beck.

WILLIS, (LORD) TED: Screenwriter, Dramatist. b. England, Jan. 13, 1918.
PICTURES: The Blue Lamp (orig. treatment), Good-Time, Trouble in Store, One Good Turn, Top of the Form, Up to His Neck, Woman in a Dressing Gown, The Young and the Guilty, Great to Be Young, No Trees in the Street, The Horsemasters, Flame in the Streets, Bitter Harvest, The Naked Sun, Mrs. Harris M.P., Spy on Ice, Mrs. Hams Goes to New York, Mrs. Harris Goes to Moscow, Mrs. Harris Goes to Monte Carlo, Mrs. Harris and the Tree of Idleness.
TELEVISION: Dixon of Dock Green, Big City, Look in Any Window, Strictly for the Sparrows, Scent of Fear, Inside Story, Hot Summer Night, Sergeant Cork, The Four Seasons of Rosie Carr, The Sullivan Brothers, Knock On Any Door, Virgin

of the Secret Service, Crime of Passion, Black Beauty, Hunter's Walk, Valley of the Kings, A Place for Animals, The Campbells in Canada, Racecourse, Minna, Anna and Luzieci, Vincent Vincent.

WILSON, ELIZABETH: Actress. b. Grand Rapids, MI, April 4, 1925. On Bdwy. in Picnic (debut, 1953), The Desk Set, The Tunnel of Love, Little Murders, Dark of the Moon, Sticks and Bones (Tony), Uncle Vanya, Morning's at Seven, Ah! Wilderness.
PICTURES: The Goddess, Little Murders, Day of the Dolphin, Man on the Swing, The Happy Hooker, The Prisoner of Second Avenue, Nine to Five, The Incredible Shrinking Woman, Grace Quigley, Where Are the Children?, The Believers.
TELEVISION: Doc (series), Million Dollar Infield, Miles to Go Before I Sleep, Sanctuary of Fear, Morning's at Seven, Nutcracker: Money, Madness and Murder, Conspiracy of Love.

WILSON, FLIP: Performer. r.n. Clerow Wilson. b. Newark, NJ, Dec. 8, 1933. Left school at 16 to join Air Force; played clubs in FL & Bahamas until 1965 when made guest appearance on NBC. The Flip Wilson Show debuted 1970–71 (Emmy, 1971), Charlie and Company (1985–86).
PICTURE: Uptown Saturday Night, Skatetown USA, The Fish That Saved Pittsburgh.

WILSON, HUGH: Producer, Director, Writer. b. Miami, FL, Aug. 21, 1943. Gained fame for creating, writing, producing and directing TV series, WKRP in Cincinnati, Frank's Place and The Famous Teddy Z. Feature film dir. debut with Police Academy (1984).
PICTURES: Stroker Ace (co-s.p.), Police Academy (dir. and co-s.p.), Rustler's Rhapsody (dir., s.p.), Burglar (dir., co.s.p.).

WILSON, RICHARD: Producer, Director. b. McKeesport, PA, Dec. 25, 1915. e. Denver U. Actor, announcer, Denver radio stations; radio actor, N.Y.; actor, asst. stage mgr., stage mgr., prod. asst. with Mercury Theatre, 1937–38; mgr., prod., summer theatres, 1939–40; assoc. with all Orson Welles films & radio shows to 1951; U.S. Air Force, 1942–45; assoc., prod., then prod., U-I.
PICTURES: assoc. prod., Lady from Shanghai, Macbeth, Ma and Pa Kettle on Vacation, Ma and Pa Kettle Go to Waikiki, Redhead from Wyoming; prod., Ma and Pa Kettle at Home, Golden Blade, Man with a Gun, Kettles in the Ozarks; The Big Boodle (dir.), Man with a Gun (dir., co-s.p.), Raw Wind in Eden (dir., co-s.p.), Al Capone (dir.), Invitation to a Gunfighter (dir., co-s.p.), Three in the Attic (prod.-dir.).

WILSON, SCOTT: Actor. b. Atlanta, GA, 1942. Was college athlete on basketball scholarship when injured and had to leave school. Moved to L.A. and enrolled in local acting class.
PICTURES: In the Heat of the Night (debut, 1967), In Cold Blood, The Grissom Gang, The Gypsy Moths, Castle Keep, In the Heat of the Night, The New Centurions, Lolly-Madonna XXX, The Great Gatsby, The Passover Plot, The Ninth Configuration, The Right Stuff, The Aviator, On the Line, A Year of the Quiet Sun, Blue City, Malone, The Exorcist: 1990.
TELEVISION: The Tracker. Movie: Jesse.

WINCER, SIMON: Director. b. Australia. Directed over 200 hours of dramatic programs for Australian TV, including Cash and Company, Tandarra, Ryan, Against the Wind, The Sullivans, etc. Exec. prod. of The Man from Snowy River, then the top-grossing theatrical film in Australia.
PICTURES: Snapshot, Harlequin, Phar Lap, D.A.R.Y.L., The Lighthorsemen (dir., co.-prod.), Quigley Down Under.
TELEVISION: The Last Frontier, Bluegrass, Lonesome Dove, The Girl Who Spelled Freedom.

WINCHELL, PAUL: Performer. b. New York, NY, 1924. e. Sch. of Industrial Arts. At 13 won first prize Major Bowes Radio Amateur Hour; signed by Ted Weems; created Jerry Mahoney when 17; Host of The Bigelow Show (1948–49), ventriloquist & star own Paul Winchell-Jerry Mahoney show (1950–54). Ringmaster Circus Time and panelist on Keep Talking. In The Treasure Chest (TV movie, 1975). Provides voices for numerous films (The Aristocats, Winnie the Pooh, The Fox and the Hound) and Saturday morning cartoons (Dastardly and Muttley, Goober and the Ghost Chasers). In the news in 1975 as inventor of an artificial heart.

WINDSOR, MARIE: Actress. r.n. Emily Marie Bertelsen. b. Maryvale, UT, Dec. 11, 1922. Winner of beauty contests, including Miss Utah. Worked as telephone girl, dancing teacher. Trained for acting by Maria Ouspenskaya. Won Look Mag. Award, best supporting actress, 1957.
PICTURES: Song of the Thin Man, Force of Evil, Dakota Lil, Little Big Horn, The Narrow Margin, The Eddie Cantor Story, The Bounty Hunter, Swamp Woman, The Killing, The Story of Mankind, Critics Choice, Mail Order Bride, Chamber of Horrors, Support Your Local Gunfighter, One More Train To Rob, Cahill, U.S. Marshall, The Outfit, Hearts of the West, Freaky Friday, Lovely But Deadly.
TELEVISION: Salem's Lot, J.O.E. and the Colonel, Manhunter, Wild Women.

WINELAND, FRED L.: Theatre Executive. b. Washington, DC, 1926. e. Southeastern U., 1957. Pres., Wineland Theatres, circuit which owns and operates two Maryland drive-ins, three Maryland indoor multi-cinemas and two Virginia multi-cinemas.

WINFIELD, PAUL: Actor. b. Los Angeles, CA, May 22, 1940. e. attended U. of Portland 1957–59, Stanford U., L.A. City Coll, and UCLA. Inducted in Black Filmmakers Hall of Fame.
THEATER: Regional work at Dallas Theatre Center (A Lesson From Aloes), Goodman Theatre (Enemy of the People), Stanford Repertory Theatre and Inner City Cultural Center, L.A.; At Lincoln Center in The Latent Heterosexual, and Richard III. Broadway: Checkmates.
PICTURES: The Lost Man, RPM, Brother John, Sounder, Trouble Man, Gordon's War, Conrack, Huckleberry Finn, Hustle, Damnation Alley, The Greatest, A Hero Ain't Nothin' But a Sandwich, High Velocity, Twilight's Last Gleaming, Carbon Copy, Star Trek II—The Wrath of Khan, White Dog, On the Run, Mike's Murder, The Terminator, Blue City, Death Before Dishonor, Big Shots, The Serpent and the Rainbow, Presumed Innocent.
TELEVISION: Series: Julia (1968–70), The Charmings, 227. Movies: The Horror at 37,000 Feet, It's Good to Be Alive, Green Eyes, King, Backstairs at the White House, Angel City, Key Tortuga, The Sophisticated Gents, Dreams Don't Die, Sister Sister, The Blue and the Gray, For Us the Living, Go Tell It on the Mountain, Under Siege, The Roy Campanella Story, Roots: The Next Generation (mini-series), Guilty of Innocence, Women of Brewster Place, Roots: The Gift.

WINFREY, OPRAH: TV Talk Show Hostess, Actress. b. Kosciusko, MS, 1954. e. Tennessee State U. Started as radio reporter then TV news reporter-anchor in Nashville. Moved to Baltimore in same capacity, later co-hosting successful morning talk show. Left for Chicago to host own show AM Chicago which became top-rated in only a month; expanded to national syndication in 1986. Formed own production co., Harpo Productions, Inc. in 1986 which assumed ownership and prod. of The Oprah Winfrey Show in 1988. Named Broadcaster of the Year by Intl. Radio and TV Soc., 1988. Purchased Chicago movie and TV production facility, 1988; renamed Harpo Studios. National Daytime Emmy Award, 1987, Outstanding Talk/Service Program Host. Theatrical film debut in The Color Purple (1985), Native Son, Throw Momma From the Train (cameo).
TELEVISION: Guest: Pee-wee's Playhouse Christmas Special. Movie: The Women of Brewster Place (actress, co-exec. prod.).

WINGER, DEBRA: Actress. b. Cleveland, OH, May 17, 1955. m. Timothy Hutton, actor. e. California State U. Served in Israeli Army. Began career in TV series Wonder Woman; also featured in TV film, Special Olympics. Feature film debut: Slumber Party, 1976.
PICTURES: Thank God, It's Friday, French Postcards, Urban Cowboy, Cannery Row, An Officer and a Gentleman, Mike's Murder, Terms of Endearment, Legal Eagles, Made in Heaven, Black Widow, Sundown, Betrayed, Everybody Wins, The Barber of Siberia, The Sheltering Sky.

WINITSKY, ALEX: Producer. b. New York, NY, Dec. 27, 1924. e. NYU, BS, LLB, JD. In partnership as attorneys in L.A. for 20 years with Arlene Sellers before they turned to financing and later production of films.
PICTURES: (co-prod. with Sellers) End of the Game, The Seven-Per-Cent Solution, Cross of Iron, Night Calls, Silver Bears, The Lady Vanishes, Breakthrough, Cuba, Blue Skies Again, Irreconcilable Differences, Scandalous, Swing Shift, Bad Medicine.
TELEVISION: Ford—The Man and the Machine.

WINKLER, HENRY: Actor. b. New York, NY, Oct. 30, 1945. e. Emerson Coll., Yale Sch. of Drama, MA. Appeared with Yale Repertory Co.; returned to N.Y. to work in radio. Did 30 TV commercials before starring in The Great American Dream Machine and Masquerade on TV. Formed Winkler/Daniel Prod. Co. with Ann Daniel.
PICTURES: The Lords of Flatbush (debut), Crazy Joe, Heroes, The One and Only, Night Shift, Memories of Me (dir.).
TELEVISION: The Mary Tyler Moore Show, The Bob Newhart Show, The Paul Sand Show, Rhoda, Happy Days (series), Laverne & Shirley, Ryans Four (series, exec. prod.), Mr. Sunshine (prod.), McGyver (prod.), A Life Apart (prod.). Specials: Henry Winkler Meets William Shakespeare, America Salutes Richard Rodgers, An American Christmas Carol, A Family Again (exec. prod.), Two Daddies (voice, exec. prod.). Movie: Katherine. Director: A Smoky Mountain Christmas, All the Kids Do It (actor and dir. and Emmy as exec. prod., 1985). Exec. prod.: Who Are the DeBolts—and Where Did They Get 19 Kids? Scandal Sheet, When Your Loves Leaves, Starflight, Second Start, Morning Glory (pilot).

WINKLER, IRWIN: Producer. b. New York, NY, May 28, 1931. e. NYU. Started in mailroom at William Morris Agency 1955–62. With Robert I. Chartoff formed production co., Chartoff-

Winkler Prods. All films co-produced with Chartoff until Revolution (1985). Then solo prod. Winkler Films.
PICTURES: Double Trouble, Point Blank, The Split, They Shoot Horses, Don't They?, The Strawberry Statement, Leo the Last, Believe in Me, The Gang That Couldn't Shoot Straight, The New Centurions, Up the Sandbox, The Mechanic, Busting, S*P*Y*S, The Gambler, Breakout, Rocky, Nickelodeon, New York, New York, Valentino, Comes a Horseman, Uncle Joe Shannon, Rocky II, Raging Bull, True Confessions, Rocky III, Author! Author!; The Right Stuff, Rocky IV, Revolution, 'Round Midnight, Betrayed, Music Box, Good Fellas, Rocky V.

WINNER, MICHAEL: Producer, Director, Writer. b. London, Eng., Oct. 30, 1935. e. Cambridge U. Ent. m.p. ind. as columnist, dir., Drummer Films.
TELEVISION: White Hunter series, Dick and the Duchess series.
PICTURES: orig. s.p., Man With A Gun; prod. dir., writ., Shoot to Kill, Swiss Holiday, Climb Up the Wall, Out of the Shadow, Some Like it Cool, Girls, Girls, Girls, It's Magic, Behave Yourself; formed, Scimitar Films; prod. dir., Haunted England, Play It Cool, The Cool Mikado; dir., West 11; co-prod., dir., The System; You Must Be Joking (dir., co-s.p.); The Jokers (co-prod., dir., s.p.); I'll Never Forget What's 'Is Name (prod., dir.); Hannibal Brooks (prod., dir.), The Nightcomers, Chato's Land; dir. The Mechanic, Scorpio, The Stone Killer (dir.), Death Wish, Won Ton Ton, The Dog That Saved Hollywood, The Sentinel, The Big Sleep; Firepower; Death Wish II; The Wicked Lady (also co-s.p.); Scream for Help (prod., dir.); Death Wish 3 (prod., dir.); Appointment with Death (prod., dir., s.p.), A Chorus of Disapproval (prod., dir., s.p.), Bullseye! (prod., dir.).

WINNINGHAM, MARE: Actress. b. CA, May 6, 1959. TV debut at age 16 as a singer on The Gong Show.
PICTURES: One-Trick Pony (1980); Threshold; St. Elmo's Fire; Nobody's Fool; Shy People; Miracle Mile, Turner and Hooch.
TELEVISION: Mini-series: The Thorn Birds, Studs Lonigan. Movies: Special Olympics, Amber Waves (Emmy Award), The Women's Room, Off the Minnesota Strip, A Few Days in Weasel Creek, Freedom, Missing Children: A Mother's Story. Helen Keller: The Miracle Continues, Single Bars, Single Women; Love Is Never Silent, Who is Julia, A Winner Never Quits, Eye on the Sparrow, God Bless the Child.

WINTERS, DEBORAH: Actress. b. Los Angeles, CA. e. Professional Children's Sch., New York; began studying acting at Stella Adler's with Pearl Pearson. at age 13 and Lee Strasberg at 16. Acting debut at age 5 in TV commercials. Casting dir.: Aloha Summer (asst.), Breakdancers From Mars (assoc. prod., casting dir.), Into the Spider's Web, The Hidden Jungle (assoc. prod., casting dir.).
PICTURES: Me, Natalie, Hail Hero!, The People Next Door, Kotch, Class of '44, Blue Sunshine, The Lamp, The Outing.
TELEVISION: Six Characters in Search of an Author, Matt Houston Medical Center. Movies: The People Next Door, The Winds of War, Crisis in Sun Valley, Gemini Man. Tarantulas: The Deadly Cargo, Little Girl Lost.

WINTERS, DAVID: Choreographer, Actor, Director. b. London, April 5, 1939. Acted in both Broadway and m.p. version of West Side Story (as A-rab). Directed and acted in number of TV shows. Choreography credits include films Viva Las Vegas, Billie, Send Me No Flowers, Tickle Me, Pajama Party, Girl Happy, The Swinger, Made in Paris, Easy Come, Easy Go, The Island of Doctor Moreau, Roller Boogie, A Star is Born, Blame It on the Night. Was choreographer for TV series Hullabaloo, Shindig, Donny and Marie Osmond, The Big Show, and Steve Allen Show, and TV specials starring Joey Heatherton, Nancy Sinatra, Diana Ross, Raquel Welch, Ann Margret, Lucille Ball. Pres., A.I.P. Distribution, A.I.P. Productions and A.I.P. Home Video.
THEATER: Of Love Remembered (Bdwy, dir.), Pajama Tops (prod.).
PICTURES: Racquet (dir., prod.), Welcome to My Nightmare (dir.), The Last Horror Film (prod., dir.), Fanatic (dir., prod.), Rage to Kill (dir., prod., s.p.), Mission Kill (dir.), Thrashin' (dir.), Space Mutiny (prod., dir.), Code Name Vengeance (prod., dir.), *Exec. prod.:* The Bounty Hunter, Future Force, Future Force II, Order of the Eagle, Time Burst, Deadly Reactor, Hell on the Battleground, Chase, Nightwars, Dead End City, Born Killer, Rapid Fire, Jungle Assault, Deadly Dancer, The Shooters, Lost Platoon, Operation Warzone, Aerobicide, Phoenix the Warrior, Mankillers, Deadly Prey, Invasion Force, Final Sanction.
TELEVISION: The Monkees (series, dir.), Where the Girls Are (dir.), Prod.: Leslie Uggams Special, The Spring Thing, Old Faithful, Go, Saga of Sonora, Hot Stuff, Story Theatre, Lucy in London; Exec. Prod.: Barbara McNair Show, Once Upon a Wheel (series), The Darin Invasion, The Lou Rawls Show, Bobby Sherman Special, Sonny and Cher Nitty Gritty Hour, 5th Dimension: Traveling Sunshine Show, Rolling on the River, Timex All-Star Swing Festival. Director-Producer: Ann-Margret From Hollywood With Love, Ann-Margret Show, The London Bridge Special, Racquel, Dr. Jekyll and Mr. Hyde, Diana Ross Show (world tour).

WINTERS, JERRY: Producer, Director. b. Waterbury, CT, Aug. 18, 1917. e. Antioch Coll., B.A., 1940. Photog., 1940–42; U.S. Air Force, 1942–46; photog., Hollywood, 1946–47; prod. assoc. Tonight on Broadway, CBS-TV, 1949; assc. prod., College Bowl, ABC-TV, 1950–51; in charge N.Y. film prod., Television Varieties, Inc., 1951–54; Production head Eldorado Int'l Pictures Corp., 1964–67; vice president, Edutornics Corp., 1968; pres. Giralda Pros., 1971.
PICTURES: prod., Renoir; prod.-dir., Herman Melville's Moby Dick, Speak to Me Child; prod; English version, The Loves of Liszt.

WINTERS, JONATHAN: Performer. b. Dayton, OH, Nov. 11, 1925. e. Kenyon Coll.; Dayton Art Inst., B.F.A. Disc jockey, Dayton and Columbus stations; night club comedian. Performed at Blue Angel, NY and on Bdwy. in John Murray Anderson's Almanac. Author: Mouse Breath, Conformity and Other Social Ills.
TELEVISION: And Here's the Show, Columbus—TV, NBC Comedy Hour, Jonathan Winters Show, Masquerade Party (panelist), 'Tis the Season to Be Smurphy (voice), Hot Dog, The Wacky World of Jonathan Winters, Mork and Mindy, The Smurfs (voice of Papa Smurf), The Completely Mental Misadventures of Ed Grimley (voices).
PICTURES: It's A Mad, Mad, Mad, Mad World; Oh, Dad, Poor Dad; The Loved One, The Russians Are Coming, the Russians Are Coming, Penelope, On the Lam, Viva Max, The Fish That Saved Pittsburgh, The Longshot, Midnight Oil, Moon Over Parador, The Teddy Bear Habit.

WINTERS, ROLAND: Actor. b. Boston, MA, Nov. 22, 1905. Appeared on stage and in stock, 1923–33; numerous radio programs, 1933–47. On screen in 13 Rue Madeleine, Return of October. Starred as Charlie Chan in pictures for Monogram.
PICTURES: West Point Story, Follow the Sun, Inside Straight, She's Working Her Way Through College, Jet Pilot, So Big, Loving.

WINTERS, SHELLEY: Actress. r.n. Shirley Schrift. b. St. Louis, MO, Aug. 18, 1922. e. Wayne U. Clerked in 5 & 10 cent store; in vaudeville; NY stage (Conquest, Night Before Christmas, Meet the People, Rosalinda, A Hatful of Rain, Girls of Summer, Minnie's Boys. One Night Stand of a Noisy Passenger. (Off-Bdwy). Autobiography, The Best of Times—The Worst of Times (1989).
PICTURES: Nine Girls (debut, 1943), Sailor's Holiday, Knickerbocker Holiday, Cover Girl, Double Life, Cry of the City, Larceny, Take one False Step, Johnny Stool Pigeon, Great Gatsby, South Sea Sinner, Winchester '73, Place in the Sun, Untamed Frontier, My Man and I, Tennessee Champ, Executive Suite, Saskatchewan, Playgirl, Mambo, Night of the Hunter, I Am a Camera, Big Knife, Treasure of Pancho Villa, I Died a Thousand Times, Cash on Delivery, Diary of Anne Frank (Acad. Award, supp., 1959), Young Savages, Lolita, Chapman Report, A House Is Not a Home, A Patch of Blue (Acad. Award, supp., 1965), Alfie, Enter Laughing, The Scalphunters, Wild in the Streets, Buena Sera Mrs. Campbell, The Mad Room, Bloody Mama, What's the Matter with Helen?, The Poseidon Adventure, Cleopatra Jones, Something to Hide, Blume in Love, Diamonds, Next Stop Greenwich Village, The Tenant, Pete's Dragon, City on Fire, "S.O.B.", Over the Brooklyn Bridge, Ellie, Witchfire (also assoc. prod.), Deja Vu, The Delta Force, The Order of Things, Purple People Eater, An Unremarkable Life.
TELEVISION: Two is the Number (Emmy, 1964), Big Rose, Alice in Wonderland, French Atlantic Affair, Death of Innocence, Adventures of Nick Carter, Elvis.

WINTMAN, MELVIN R.: Theatre Executive, b. Chelsea, MA. e. U. of Massachusetts, Northeastern U., J.D. Major, infantry, AUS, W.W.II. Attorney. Now consultant & dir., General Cinema Corp.; formerly exec. v.p., GCC and pres., GCC Theatres, Inc., Boston. Dir. Will Rogers Memorial Fund. Former pres. Theatre Owners of New England (1969–70); past dir. NATO (1969–70); treas., Nat'l Assoc. of Concessionaires (1960).

WISBERG, AUBREY: Writer, Producer, Director. b. London, Eng., Oct. 20, 1909. e. Columbia U. Newspaper writer, radio, TV dramatist U.S. Eng., Australia, radio diffusionist, Paris, France. Author novels Bushman at Large, Patrol Boat 999, This Is the Life; plays Virtue, Inc., Whiphand.
PICTURES: s.p., prod. The Man From Planet X, Captive Women, Sword of Venus, The Neanderthal Man, Capt. John Smith & Pocahontas, Problem Girls, Dragon's Gold, Capt. Kidd & the Slave Girl, Return to Treasure Island, Murder is My Beat, The Women of Pitcairn Island, Port Sinister, Submarine Raider, Counter Espionage, Escape in the Fog, U-Boat Prisoner, Power of the Whistler, Adventures of Rusty, After Midnight, The Wreck of the Hesperus, The Big Fix, Betrayal from the East. The Falcon's Adventure, Son of Sinbad, At Swords Point, Hit Parade, They Came to Blow Up

America, Bombers Moon, Rendezvous 24, The Lady in the Iron Mask, The Steel Lady, Treasure of Monte Cristo, Road to the Big House, The Burning Cross, St. Montana Mike, Casanova's Big Night, So Dark the Night, The Desert Hawk, s.p. Just Before Dawn, Out of the Depths, Target Minus Forty, Mission Mars, Ride the Wild Wind, Hercules in N.Y., Evil in the Blood.

WISDOM, NORMAN: Actor, Singer, Comedian. Musical and legit. b. London, Eng., Feb. 4, 1918. Many London West End stage shows including royal command performances. New York Broadway shows include Walking Happy and Not Now Darling. Two Broadway awards. Films include Trouble in Store, One Good Turn, Man of the Moment, Up in the World, Just My Luck, The Square Peg, There Was a Crooked Man, The Bulldog Breed, The Girl on the Boat, On the Beat, A Stitch in Time, The Early Bird, Press for Time, The Sandwich Man, What's Good for the Goose, and others mostly for the Rank Organisation and United Artists. In US: The Night They Raided Minsky's. TV musical: Androcles and the Lion.

WISE, ROBERT: Director, Producer. b. Winchester, IN, Sept. 10, 1914. e. Franklin Coll., Franklin, IN. Ent. m.p. ind. in cutting dept. RKO, 1933; sound cutter, asst. ed.; film ed., 1938; dir., 1943; to 20th Century-Fox, 1949; ass'n. Mirisch Co. independent prod. 1959; assn. MGM independent prod., 1962; assn. 20th Century Fox Independent Prod. 1963. Partner, Filmakers Group, The Tripar Group.

PICTURES: The Body Snatchers, Blood on the Moon, The Set Up, Day the Earth Stood Still, Captive City, So Big, Executive Suite, Helen of Troy, Tribute to a Bad Man, Somebody Up There Likes Me, Until They Sail, Run Silent Run Deep, I Want to Live, Odds Against Tomorrow, West Side Story, Two For the Seesaw, The Haunting, The Sound of Music, The Sand Pebbles, Star!, The Andromeda Strain, Two People, The Hindenburg, Audrey Rose, Star Trek, Wisdom (exec. prod. only), Rooftops (dir.).

WISEMAN, FREDERICK: Documentary filmmaker. b. Boston, MA, Jan. 1, 1930. e. Williams College, B.A., 1951; Yale Law Sch., L.L.B., 1954. Member: MA Bar. Private law practice, Paris, 1956–57. Lecturer-in-Law, Boston U. Law Sch., 1959–61; Russell Sage Fndn. Fellowship, Harvard U., 1961–62; research assoc., Brandeis U., dept. of sociology, 1966–69; visiting lecturer at numerous universities. Author: Psychiatry and Law: Use and Abuse of Psychiatry in a Murder Case (American Journal of Psychiatry, Oct. 1961). Co-author: Implementation (section of report of President's Comm. on Law Enforcement and Administration of Justice).

Award-winning prod., dir., editor, makes non-judgemental docs. that record the detailed daily lives of various institutions (a mental institution, the Army, a meat-packing plant, the police), and are distributed through his Zipporah Films.

PICTURES: Titicut Follies (1967); High School; Law and Order; Hospital; Basic Training; Essene; Juvenile Court; Primate; Welfare; Meat; Canal Zone; Sinai Field Mission; Manoeuvre; Model; Seraphia's Diary; The Store; Racetrack; Deaf, Blind, Multi-Handicapped; Adjustment and Work; Missile, Near Death, Central Park.

WISEMAN, JOSEPH: Actor. b. Montreal, Canada, May 15, 1918. Began acting in the thirties, including Bdwy. stage, radio, m.p. and later TV.

PICTURES: Viva Zapata, Les Miserables, The Silver Chalice, The Garment Jungle, Dr. No, Bye Bye Braverman, The Night They Raided Minsky's, The Valachi Papers, The Apprenticeship of Duddy Kravitz, The Betsy.

STAGE: King Lear, Golden Boy, The Diary of Anne Frank, Uncle Vanya, The Last Analysis, Enemies.

TELEVISION: Masada, QB VII, Rage of Angels, Seize the Day, Lady Mobster.

WITHERS, GOOGIE: Actress. b. Karachi, India, Mar. 12, 1917. Trained as a dancer under Italia Conti, Helena Lehmiski & Buddy Bradley; stage debut Victoria Palace in Windmill Man, 1929. Best Actress Award, Deep Blue Sea, 1954. Began screen career at 18. TV also. Theatrical tours Australia, Sun Award, Best Actress, 1974. Awarded officer of the Order of Australia (A.O.) 1980. U.S. ACE Cable award, best actress for Time After Time, 1988.

PICTURES: Traveler's Joy, Night and the City, White Corridors, Derby Day, Devil on Horseback, Safe Harbor, Nickel Queen.

STAGE: (Britain) Winter Journey, Deep Blue Sea, Hamlet, Much Ado About Nothing. (Australia) Plaza Suite, Relatively Speaking, Beckman Place, Woman in a Dressing Gown, The Constant Wife, First Four Hundred Years, Roar Like a Dove, The Cherry Orchard, An Ideal Husband. (London) Getting Married, Exit the King. (New York) The Complaisant Lover, Chichester Festival Theatre and Haymarket, London, in The Circle, The Kingfisher, Importance of Being Earnest, The Cherry Orchard, Dandy Dick, The Kingfisher (Australia and Middle East), Time and the Conways (Chichester), School for Scandal (London), Stardust (UK tour). 1986: The Chalk Garden, Hay Fever, Ring Round the Moon.

TELEVISION: Series, Within These Walls, Time After Time, Movies: Hotel Du Lac, Northanger Abbey, Ending Up.

WITHERS, JANE: Actress. b. Atlanta, GA, April 12, 1927. By 1934 attracted attention as child player on screen, after radio appearance in Los Angeles and experimental pictures parts, in 1934 in Fox production Bright Eyes, Ginger; thereafter to 1942 featured or starred in numerous 20th-Fox prod. Voted Money-Making Star M.P. Herald-Fame Poll, 1937, 1938. Starred as Josephine the Plumber in Comet commercials.

PICTURES: North Star, Johnny Doughboy, My Best Gal, Faces in the Fog, Dangerous Partners, Affairs of Geraldine, Danger Street, Giant, The Right Approach, Captain Newman, M.D.

WIZAN, JOE: Executive. b. Los Angeles, CA, Jan. 7, 1935. e. UCLA. Started in industry as agent for William Morris Agency. Left to form London Intl. Artists, Ltd. in association with Richard Gregson, Alan Ladd, Jr. and Mike Gruskoff. When firm dissolved joined Creative Management Associates as v.p. in chg. of creative services. In 1969 formed own indep. prod. co. 1981, named pres., CBS Theatrical Film Div. 1982, returned to 20th Century-Fox as independent producer. 1983, named pres., 20th-Fox Prods.; Resigned in 1984.

PICTURES: Jeremiah Johnson, Junior Bonner, Prime Cut, The Last American Hero, Audrey Rose, Voices, And Justice for All, Best Friends, Unfaithfully Yours, Two of a Kind, Tough Guys, Witching Hour, Split Decisions, Spellbinder (prod.), Short Time (exec. prod.).

WIZEMAN, JR., DONALD G.: Executive. b. Fort Smith, AK, Nov. 17, 1944. e. Old Dominion U. Formed Wizeman & Associates, Ltd. Advertising Agency and Artus Specialty Company in 1967; is pres. of both. In 1971 formed Filmakers, Ltd. which also heads.

PICTURES: Moonchild (exec. prod.), Come Out of the Bathroom Hannibal Fry (exec. prod.).

WOLF, EMANUEL, L.: Executive b. Brooklyn, NY, Mar. 27, 1927. e. Syracuse U., B.A., 1950; Maxwell Sch., Syracuse U., M.A. 1952; Maxwell Scholar in Public Admin.-Economics; Chi Eta Sigma (Econ. Hon.). 1952–55. Management consultant, exec. office of Secretary of Navy & Dept. of Interior, Wash., DC, 1956. National dir. of Program & Admin. of a Veterans Org. 1957–61. Pres. E. L. Wolf Associates, Washington, DC, 1961–Jan. 1965. Treasurer, Kalvex, Inc. Dec. 1962. Dir. Kalvex, Inc. March 1963. Dir. Allied Artists Pictures Corp., Jan. 1965. Pres. Kalvex, Inc. April 1966–present, pres. & chmn. of the Bd. Kalvex, Inc.; Chmn. of the Bd. Vitabath, Inc.; Chmn. of the Bd. Lexington Instruments; pres. & chairman of the bd. Pharmaceutical Savings Plan, Inc. Syracuse U. Corporate Advisory Board, American Committee for the Weizmann Institute of Science (Bd. of Directors). Pres. & chmn. of bd., Allied Artists Pictures Corp: January, 1976: pres., bd. chmn. & CEO Allied Artists Industries Inc., created by Merger of Allied Artists Pictures Corp., Kalvex Inc. and PSP, Inc. 1985, formed indep. prod. co., Emanuel L. Wolf Prods.; 1986–present, pres. & chmn. of bd., Today Home Entertainment.

WOLF, THOMAS HOWARD: TV news exec. b. New York, NY, April 22, 1916. e. Princeton U., B.A., magna cum laude, 1937. Time & Life Mag. 1937–39; 1937–39 NEA (Scripps-Howard) 1940–46; European mgr., NEA, 1942–46. War correspondent, ETO, MTO) NBC radio correspondent, Paris, 1944–45; co-owner, pres., Information Prod., Inc. founded 1951; co-owner, chmn. Butterfield & Wolf, Inc. founded 1955; prod. CBS series. Tomorrow, 1960; exec. prod., CBS daily live Calendar Show, 1961–62; sr. prod., ABC News Report, 1963; exec. prod., ABC Scope, 1964–66. v.p. dir. of TV Documentaries, 1966; v.p., dir. of TV Public Affairs, 1974; dir. TV Cultural Affairs, 1976.

WOLFSON, RICHARD: Executive. b. New York, NY, Jan. 7, 1923. e. Harvard Coll., Yale Law Sch., 1945–47, law sect'y to Justice Wiley Rutledge, U.S. Supreme Court. Law instructor at NYU Law Sch.; later received Guggenheim Fellowship; 1952, joined Wometco Ent. as counsel and asst. to pres.; named v.p. and dir. in 1959 and sr. v.p. in 1962; named exec. v.p. and general counsel in 1973; named chmn., exec. comm., 1976; co-author of Jurisdiction of the Supreme Court of the United States and author of articles in various legal publications. Retired from Wometco 1982; counsel, Valdes-Fanli, Cobb, Petrey and Bischoff. Miami, FL.

WOLPER, DAVID L.: Producer. b. New York, NY, Jan. 11, 1928. m. Gloria Diane Hill. e. Drake U., U. of Southern California. Treas., Flamingo Films, 1948; merged with Associated Artist to form M.P. for TV, Inc., acting as v.p. in chg. of West Coast oper., 1950; v.p. reactivated Flamingo Films, 1954; also pres. Harris-Wolper Pictures, Inc.; pres. Wolper Prod. 1958; pres. Dawn Prod.; v.p. Bd. Dir. Metromedia, 1965; pres. Wolper Pictures Ltd. 1967; ch. of bd. Wolper Prod., Inc., 1967; pres. Wolper Pictures, 1968; pres. Wolper Productions, 1970; pres. & ch. of bd. of dir. The Wolper Organization, Inc., 1971; consultant to Warner Bros. & Warner Communications. Pres., David L. Wolper Prods., Inc. 1977. Received Jean Hersholt

Humanitarian Award, 1985; Intl. Documentary Assn. Career Achievement Award, 1988.
TELEVISION: The Race For Space, 1958; Story of . . . series, Biography series, Hollywood and the Stars series, The Making of the President, 1960, 1964, 1968; Men in Crisis series, National Geographic Society Specials, 1965–68, 1971–75; The March of Time series, 1965–66; The Rise and Fall of the Third Reich, 1967–68; The Undersea World of Jacques Cousteau, 1967–68; Plimpton specials, 1970–72; Appointment With Destiny series, 1971–73; American Heritage specials, 1973–74; Primal Man specials, 1973–75; Get Christie Love series, 1974; Judgment specials, 1974; Chico and the Man series, 1974–; Smithsonian Specials, 1974–; Sandburg's Lincoln, 1974–76; Welcome Back, Kotter series, 1975–; I Will Fight No More, Forever, 1975; Collison Course, Victory at Entebbe, 1976; Roots, 1977; Roots: The Next Generation, 1978; Moviola, 1980; Agatha Christie: Murder Is Easy, 1981; The Man Who Saw Tomorrow (exec. prod.); Casablanca, 1982; The Thorn Birds, 1983; Opening & Closing Ceremonies, Olympic Games, 1984; North and South Book I, 1985; North and South, Book II, 1986; Liberty Weekend, 1986; Napoleon and Josephine, 1987, What Price Victory, Roots: The Gift.
PICTURES: Four Days in November, If It's Tuesday, This Must Be Belgium, Say Goodbye, 1971, Willie Wonka and the Chocolate Factory, Visions of Eight, Birds Do it, Bees Do It, Imagine: John Lennon.

WOODARD, ALFRE: Actress. b. Tulsa, OK, Nov. 8, 1953. e. Boston U., B.A. Soon after graduation landed role in Washington, D.C. Arena Stage theater in Horatio, and Saved.
THEATER: A Christmas Carol; Bugs, Guns; Leander Stillwell; For Colored Girls Who Have Considered Suicide/When the Rainbow Is Enuf; A Map of the World, A Winter's Tale, Two By South.
PICTURES: Health; Remember My Name; Cross Creek (Acad. Award nom.); Go Tell It on the Mountain; Extremities, Scrooged, Miss Firecracker, A State of Independence, Show of Force.
TELEVISION: Tucker's Witch; Hill Street Blues (Emmy supporting actress, 1984); Sara; Orleans, Movies: Palmerstown, USA; The Class of '65; Ambush Murders; Sophisticated Gents; Freedom Road; For Colored Girls Who Have Considered Suicide/When the Rainbow Is Enuf; Trial of the Moke; The Killing Ground; Sweet Revenge; L.A. Law (Emmy, guest star, 1987), St. Elsewhere, Words By Heart, Unnatural Causes; The Killing Floor; Mandela; The Child Saver.

WOODS, DONALD: Actor. b. 1906.
PICTURES: Sweet Adeline (1933), Watch on the Rhine, Roughly Speaking, 13 Ghosts, Kissin' Cousins, Moment to Moment, A Time to Sing.
STAGE: Two for the Seesaw, L.A., 1961; Rosmersholm, N.Y., 1962; One by One, N.Y., 1964; Soldier, You Can't Take It With You, Chicago, 1969; Twelfth Night, Assassination 1865; Chicago, 1969–71.
TELEVISION: G.E. Theatre, Wagon Train, Thrillers, Sunset Strip, Ben Casey, Laramie, The Rebel, The Law and Mr. Jones, The Roaring 20's, Wild Wild West, Bonanza. Series: Craig Kennedy Criminologist (1953), Tammy.

WOODS, JAMES: Actor. b. Vernal UT, Apr. 18, 1947. e. Massachusetts Inst. of Technology (appeared in 36 plays at M.I.T., Harvard and Theatre Co. of Boston). Left college to pursue acting career in New York; Broadway in Borstal Boy, Conduct Unbecoming (off-Bdwy, Obie Award), Saved, Trial of the Catonsville Nine, Moonchildren (Theatre World Award), Green Julia (off-Bdwy.), Finishing Touches, etc. Feature film debut in The Visitors (1971).
PICTURES: The Way We Were, Alex and the Gypsy, Distance, Night Moves, The Choirboys, The Onion Field, The Black Marble, Eyewitness, Fast Walking, Videodrome, Split Image, Against All Odds, Once Upon a Time in America, Cat's Eye, Joshua Then and Now, Salvador (Acad. Award nom., Independent Film Project Spirit Award), Best Seller, Cop (also co-prod.), The Boost, True Believer, Immediate Family, The Hard Way.
TELEVISION: Movies: All the Way Home, The Great American Tragedy, And the Name is Jonah, The Disappearance of Aimee, Raid on Entebbe, Billion Dollar Bubble, Badge of the Assassin. Movies: Promise (Emmy, Golden Globe, Golden Apple Awards), In Love and War, My Name is Bill W. (Emmy). Special: Crimes of Passion (host). Mini-series: Holocaust.

WOODWARD, EDWARD, O.B.E.: Actor, Singer. b. Croydon, England, June 1, 1930. e. Royal Acad. of Dramatic Art. As singer has recorded 11 LPs. 2 Gold Discs. Television Actor of the Year, 1969–70; also Sun Award, Best Actor, 1970, 71, 72.
THEATRE: 16 West End plays and musicals, including The Art of Living, The Little Doctor, A Rattle of a Simple Man, The High Bid, The Male of the Species. High Spirits, 1962 (Bdwy musical), The Best Laid Plans. Recent stage: On Approval, Richard III, The Assassin.
TELEVISION: Sword of Honour, Callan series. Over 300 TV plays latest: Bassplayer and Blonde, Saturday, Sunday, Monday, 1990 series, Nice Work, Rod of Iron, The Trial of Lady Chatterly, Wet Job—Callan Special, Churchill: The Wilderness Years, Blunt Instrument, Killer Contract, Uncle Tom's Cabin, The Equalizer (series), Codename: Kyril (movie). Hunted, The Man in the Brown Suit.
PICTURES: Where There's a Will (debut, 1955), Becket, File on the Golden Goose, Incense for the Damned, Murders in the Rue Morgue, Julius Caesar, The Listener, Young Winston, Sitting Target, Hunted, Charley One-Eye, Wicker Man, Callan, Stand Up Virgin Soldiers, Breaker Morant, The Appointment, Who Dares Wins, Forever Love, Merlin and the Sword, Champions, A Christmas Carol, King David.

WOODWARD, JOANNE: Actress. b. Thomasville, GA, Feb. 27, 1930. m. Paul Newman. e. Louisiana State U. Studied at Neighborhood Playhouse Dramatic Sch. and the Actors Studio. Appeared in many TV dramatic shows; on B'way in Picnic; m.p. debut in Count Three and Pray (1953).
THEATER: The Lovers, Baby Want a Kiss, The Glass Menagerie, (Williamstown, The Long Wharf).
PICTURES: Kiss Before Dying, Three Faces of Eve (Acad. Award 1957, best actress); Long Hot Summer, No Down Payment, Rally Round the Flag Boys, The Sound and the Fury, From the Terrace, Fugitive Kind, Paris Blues, The Stripper, A New Kind of Love, Signpost to Murder, A Big Hand for the Little Lady, A Fine Madness, Rachel, Rachel (Acad. Award nom.); Winning, WUSA, They Might Be Giants, The Effect of Gamma Rays on Man-in-the-Moon Marigolds, Summer Wishes, Winter Dreams, The Drowning Pool, The End, Harry and Son, The Glass Menagerie, Mr. and Mrs. Bridge.
TELEVISION: Broadway's Dreamers: The Legacy of The Group Theater (host, co-prod.). Movies: The Shadow Box, Crisis at Central High, Family (Thanksgiving special, dir.), Sybil, See How She Runs (Emmy, 1978), Passions, Do You Remember Love.

WOOLDRIDGE, SUSAN: Actress. b. London, England. Ent. ind. 1971.
THEATER incl.: Macbeth, School for Scandal, Merchant of Venice, The Cherry Orchard, Look Back in Anger, 'night Mother.
PICTURES: The Shout, Butley, Loyalties, Hope and Glory, How to Get Ahead in Advertising, Bye Bye Blues.
TELEVISION: The Naked Civil Servant, John McNab, The Racing Game, The Jewel in the Crown, The Last Place on Earth, Hay Fever, Time and the Conways, Dead Man's Folly, The Devil's Disciple, The Dark Room, Pastoralcare, The Small Assassin, A Fine Romance, Ticket to Ride, Changing Step.

WOOLF, SIR JOHN: Knighted 1975. Producer. b. England, 1913. e. Institut Montana, Switzerland. Awarded U.S. Bronze star for service in WWII. Asst. dir. Army Kinematography, War Office 1944–45; Founder and chmn. Romulus Films Ltd, since 1948. Man dir. since 1967; chmn. since 1982 of British & American Film Holdings Plc; dir. First Leisure Corp. Plc since 1982. Co-founder and exec. dir., Anglia TV Group PLC, 1958–83. Member: Cinematograph Films Council, 1969–79; bd. of gov., Services Sound & Vision Corp (formerly Services Kinema Corp.) 1974–83; exec. council and trustee, Cinema and Television Benevolent Fund; Freeman, City of London, 1982; FRSA 1978. Received special awards for contribution of British film indust. from Cinematograph Exhibitors Assoc. 1969. and Variety Club of GB, 1974.
PICTURES: Prod. by Romulus Gp.: The African Queen, Pandora and the Flying Dutchman, Moulin Rouge, Beat the Devil, I Am a Camera, Carrington VC, Story of Ester Costello, Room at the Top (Brit. Film Acad. Award, best film, 1958). Wrong Arm of the Law, The L-Shaped Room, Term of Trial, Life at the Top, Oliver! (Acad. Award, Golden Globe, best film 1969), Day of the Jackal, The Odessa File.
TELEVISION: Prod. for Anglia TV: 100 Tales of the Unexpected, Miss Morrison's Ghosts, The Kingfisher, Edwin, Love Song.

WOPAT, TOM: Actor. b. Lodi, WI, Sept. 9, 1951. e. U. of Wisconsin. Left school to travel for two years with rock group as lead singer and guitarist. Spent two summers at Barn Theater in MI. Came to New York; off-Bdwy. in A Bistro Car on the CNR. On Bdwy. in hit musical, I Love My Wife.
TELEVISION: The Dukes of Hazzard (series), Blue Skies (series), A Peaceable Kingdom. Movies: Christmas Comes to Willow Creek, Burning Rage.

WORKMAN, CHUCK: Director, Writer, Producer. b. Philadelphia, PA., June 5. e. Rutgers U., B.A.; Cornell U. Pres., International Documentary Assoc. 1987–88; Member: Directors Guild of America Special Projects Comm., DGA Directors Council, 1987; Bd. mem.: Santa Monica Arts Fdn. Lecturer, U. of Southern California. Pres. Calliope Films, Inc. Winner Clio Award, 1969, 1970. Acad. Award, 1986.
PLAYS: Bruno's Ghost (1981, writer, dir.), Diplomacy (writer, dir.), The Man Who Wore White Shoes (writer); Bloomers (writer).

PICTURES: Monday's Child (1967, editor); Traitors of San Angel (editor); The Money (dir., s.p.); Protocol (dir., media sequences); Stoogemania (dir., co-s.p.); Precious Images (Acad. Award, Best Live Action Short, 1986; Gold Hugo Award, Cannes Film Fest., N.Y. Film Fest.); Words (Best Short, Houston Fest., N.Y. Film Fest., 1988), Pieces of Silver.
DOCUMENTARIES: Writer, Producer, Director: The Making of the Deep; The Director and the Image (CINE Golden Eagle Award, 1980); The Game; The Best Show in Town (CINE Golden Eagle); And the Winner Is. . . , The Keeper of the Light.

WORTH, IRENE: Actress. b. Nebraska, June 23, 1916. e. UCLA. Formerly a teacher. Bdwy. debut in The Two Mrs. Carrolls, after which went to London where made her home. Appeared with Old Vic and Royal Shakespeare Co.; returned to U.S. to appear on Bdwy. in the Cocktail Party.
THEATER: Hotel Paradiso, Mary Stuart, The Potting Shed, Toys in the Attic, Tiny Alice (Tony Award, 1965), Sweet Bird of Youth (Tony Award, 1976), Cherry Orchard; Old Times, Happy Days; Coriolanus (NY Shakespeare Fest).
PICTURES: Orders to Kill (British AA, best actress), The Scapegoat, King Lear, Nicholas and Alexander, Rich Kids, Eyewitness, Deathtrap, Fast Forward.
TELEVISION:: The Lady from the Sea, The Duchess of Malfi, The Way of the World, Prince Orestes, Forbidden, The Big Knife, The Shell Seekers.

WORTH, MARVIN: Producer, Writer. b. Brooklyn, NY. Jazz promoter and manager before starting to write special material for Alan King, Buddy Hackett, Joey Bishop, Lenny Bruce.
PICTURES: *Writer:* Boys Night Out, Three on a Couch, Promise Her Anything. *Producer:* Where's Poppa?, Malcolm X, Lenny, Fire Sale, The Rose, Up the Academy, Soup for One, Unfaithfully Yours, Rhinestone, Falling in Love, Less Than Zero, Patty Hearst, Running Mates, See No Evil, Hear No Evil, Flashback.
THEATER: Lenny.
TELEVISION: Steve Allen Show, Jackie Gleason, Chevy Shows, Milton Berle Show, Colgate Comedy Hour, Martha Raye Show, Judy Garland Show, Get Smart.

WOWCHUK, HARRY N.: Actor, Writer, Photographer, Producer, Executive. b. Philadelphia, PA. Oct. 16, 1948. e. Santa Monica City Coll., UCLA, theater arts, 1970. Started film career as actor, stunt-driver-photographer. T.V. and commercial credits include: Warner Bros.; Columbia Records; R.C.A.; Playboy Magazine: TV Guide; Seal Test; Camel Cigarettes; Miller High Life; American Motors; Camera V; AW Rootbeer; Harold Robbins Productions. Former exec. v.p. International Cinema, in chg. of prod. and distribution; V.P. J. Newport Film Productions; pres., United West Productions.
PICTURES: The Lost Dutchman, Las Vegas Lady, This Is A Hijack, Tidal Wave, Tunnel Vision, Incredible 2-Headed Transplant, Jud, Bad Charleston Charlie, Some Call It Loving, Summer School Teachers, Five Minutes of Freedom, Pushing Up Daisies, Money-Marbles-Chalk, The Models, Love Swedish Style, Up-Down-Up, Sunday's Child, Soul Brothers, Freedom Riders, Perilous Journey, Claws of Death, Georgia Peaches.

WOWCHUK, NICHOLAS: Executive, Producer, Writer, Editor, Financier. b. Philadelphia, PA. e. St. Basil's Coll., UCLA. Founder-publisher: All-American Athlete Magazine; Sports and Health Digest; The Spectator. Former sports writer: Phila. Evening Public Ledger; Phila. Daily Record; Phila. Inquirer. Founder & bd. chmn.: Mutual Realty Investment Co.; Mutual Mortgage Co., Beverly Hills, CA. President: Mutual General Films, Bev. Hills, CA; Abbey Theatrical Films, N.Y.; Mutual Film Distribution Co.; Mutual Recording & Broadcasting Enterprises.
PICTURES: Exec. Prod.: Perilous Journey; Incredible 2-Headed Transplant; Pushing Up Daisies; Money-Marbles-Chalk; Five Minutes of Freedom; The Campaign; Claws of Death. Prod.: Scorpion's Web; Pursuit; Brave Men; Sea of Despair; The Hetman; Cossacks In Battle; The Straight White Line; Tilt, Rooster, To Live . . . You Gotta Win.

WRAY, FAY: Actress. b. Alberta, Canada, Sept. 10, 1907. m. Robert Riskin, writer. On stage in Pilgrimage Play, Hollywood, 1923; m.p. debut in Gasoline Love; thereafter in many m.p. for Paramount to 1930; then in films for various Hollywood and Brit. prod. Autobiography: On the Other Hand (1989).
PICTURES: Streets of Sin, The Wedding March, The Four Feathers, The Texan, Dirigible, Doctor X, The Most Dangerous Game, The Vampire Bat, The Mystery of the Wax Museum, King Kong, The Bowery, Madame Spy, The Affairs of Cellini, The Clairvoyant, They Met in a Taxi, Murder in Greenwich Village, The Jury's Secret, Adam Had Four Sons, Small Town Girl, Treasure of the Golden Condor, Queen Bee, Rock Pretty Baby, Tammy, Out of Time, The Cobweb, Summer Love.
TELEVISION: Pride of the Family (series), Gideon's Trumpet (movie).

WRIGHT, ROBERT C.: Executive. b. Rockville Center, NY. April 23, 1943. e. Coll. Holy Cross, B.A. history; 1965; U. of Virginia, LLB 1968. Mem. NY, VA, MA, NJ Bar. 1969, joined General Electric; lawyer in plastics div. Later moved into product & sls. management in plastics div. 1980, moved to Cox Cable as pres. Returned to GE 1983 heading small appliances div.; moved to GE Financial Services & GE Credit Corp. as pres., which posts he held when named head of NBC following purchase of NBC's parent RCA by GE. President and Chief Exec. Off., National Broadcasting Co. (NBC), as of September 1986.

WRIGHT, TERESA: Actress. b. New York, NY, Oct. 27, 1918. Ent. m.p. 1941, The Little Foxes, Goldwyn-RKO.
PICTURES: Pride of the Yankees, Mrs. Miniver (Acad. Award, supporting actress), Shadow of a Doubt, Casanova Brown, Best Years of Our Lives, Trouble with Women, Pursued, Imperfect Lady, Enchantment, The Capture, The Men, Something to Live For, California Conquest, Steel Trap, Count the Hours, The Actress, Track of the Cat, Hail Hero, The Happy Ending, Roseland, Somewhere in Time, The Good Mother.
STAGE: Tours: Mary, Mary, Tchin-Tchin, The Effect of Gamma Rays on Man-in-the-Moon Marigolds, Noel Coward in Two Keys, The Master Builder. Regional Theatre: Long Day's, Journey into Night, You Can't Take It With You, All The Way Home, Wings. New York: Life with Father, Dark at the Top of the Stairs, Mary, Mary, I Never Sang for My Father, Death of a Salesman, Ah, Wilderness!, Morning's at Seven (Broadway and London).
TELEVISION: The Margaret Bourke-White Story, The Miracle Worker, The Golden Honeymoon, Bill-on His Own, The Fig Tree.

WRIGHT, TONY: Actor. b. London, Dec. 10, 1925. Stage debut in repertory, South Africa; screen debut; Flanagan Boy, 1951.
PICTURES: A Toi De Jouer Callaghan, Plus De Whiskey, Pour Callaghan (France), Jumping for Joy, Jacqueline, Tiger in the Smoke, Seven Thunders, Broth of a Boy, Faces in the Dark, In the Wake of a Stranger, Journey to Nowhere, The Liquidator.
TELEVISION: Compact, Marriage Lines, No Hiding Place, The Saint, Mystery Theatre, Curtains for Sheila, Crossroads, Make Me A Widow, Wednesday's Train, Onedin Line, 6 Saints, Persuaders, The Jensen Code, Follow Me, Kidnapped.

WYATT, JANE: Actress. b. New York, NY, Aug. 10, 1913. e. Miss Chapin's Sch., Barnard Coll. m. Edgar B. Ward. Joined Apprentice Sch., Berkshire Playhouse, Stockbridge, Mass. Understudied in Tradewinds and The Vinegar Tree. Appeared in Give Me Yesterday and the Tadpole. In 1933 succeeded Margaret Sullavan in Dinner at Eight. New York stage, The Autumn Garden, 1951; other plays, The Bishop Misbehaves, Conquest, Eveninsong, The Mad Hopes.
PICTURES: Great Expectations, (1934), One More River, The Luckiest Girl in the World, Lost Horizon, Kisses for Breakfast, The Navy Comes Through, The Kansan, The Iron Road, None But the Lonely Heart, Boomerang, Gentlemen's Agreement, No Minor Vices, Bad Boy, Canadian Pacific, Pitfall, Task Force, Our Very Own, My Blue Heaven, Man Who Cheated Himself, Criminal Lawyer, Never Too Late, Treasure of Matecumbe.
TELEVISION: Father Knows Best (1954–59, winner 3 Emmy Awards), Bob Hope Chrysler Theater, The Virginian, Wagon Train, U.S. Steel Hour, Bell Telephone Hour, Hostess moderator, Confidential For Women, My Father My Mother. Guest star—Star Trek, Barefoot in the Park (pilot), The Ghost and Mrs. Muir, Here Come the Brides, Love American Style, Fantasy Island, Love Boat, Movies: Katherine, Tom Sawyer; Father Knows Best Reunion, A Love Affair, Amelia Earhart, Superdome, The Nativity, The Millionaire, Missing Children—A Mother's Story, Amityville: The Evil Escapes.

WYMAN, JANE: Actress. r.n. Sarah Jane Fulks. b. St. Joseph, MO, Jan. 4, 1914. In 1936: My Man Godfrey, Cain and Mabel, Smart Blonde. Voted one of top ten money-making stars in M.P. Herald-Fame poll, 1954.
PICTURES: Larceny, Inc., My Favorite Spy, Footlight Serenade, Princess O'Rourke, Doughgirls, Make Your Own Bed, Crime by Night, Lost Weekend, One More Tomorrow, Night and Day, The Yearling, Cheyenne, Magic Town; Johnny Belinda (Acad. award, best actress, 1948), Three Guys Named Mike, Here Comes the Groom, Blue Veil, Just for You, Story of Will Rogers, Let's Do It Again, So Big, Magnificent Obsession, Lucy Gallant, All That Heaven Allows, Miracle in the Rain, Pollyanna, Holiday for Lovers, Bon Voyage, How to Commit Marriage.
TELEVISION: Series: Jane Wyman Theater (1956–60), Fireside Theatre, Amanda Fallon, Falcon Crest. Movies: The Failing of Raymond, The Incredible Journey of Dr. Meg Laurel.

WYMAN, THOMAS H.: Executive. b. 1931. Joined CBS, Inc. in 1980 as pres. & chief exec. Then chmn until 1986. Prior career as chief exec. of Green Giant Co.; became v. chmn. to 1988, of Pillsbury Co. when it acquired Green Giant in 1979.

WYMORE, PATRICE: Actress. b. Miltonvale, KS, Dec. 17, 1926. p. James A. Wymore, oper. exhib. film delivery service throughout Kans.; ret. Widow of actor Errol Flynn. Began career as child performer, tent shows, county fairs, vaudeville; later, toured night clubs in middle west, own song & dance act; modelled, Chicago understudy Betty Bruce, Up in Central Park, played role Hollywood Bowl; then, N.Y. stage, Hold It! All For Love; radio & TV roles.
PICTURES: Screen debut: Tea for Two, 1950, then Rocky Mountain, I'll See You In My Dreams, Star-Lift, Big Trees, Man Behind the Gun, She's Working Her Way Through College, She's Back on Broadway, Chamber of Horrors.

WYNN, TRACY KEENAN: Writer. b. Hollywood, CA, Feb. 28, 1945. Fourth generation in show business; son of actor Keenan Wynn; grandson of Ed Wynn; great-grandson of Frank Keenan, Irish Shakespearean actor who made Bdwy. debut in 1880.
PICTURES: The Longest Yard, The Drowning Pool (co-s.p.), The Deep (co. s.p.).
TELEVISION: The Glass House, Tribes, The Autobiography of Miss Jane Pittman, Quest, Bloody Friday. Pilot: Mancuso.

WYNTER, DANA: Actress. b. London, England. June 8, 1930. e. Rhodes U. On stage in London; TV appearances include Robert Montgomery Show, Suspense, Studio One, U.S. Steel Hour.
PICTURES: Invasion of the Body Snatchers, View from Pompey's Head, D-Day, The Sixth of June, Something of Value, Fraulein, Shake Hands with the Devil, In Love and War, Sink the Bismarck, The List of Adrian Messenger, If He Hollers, Let Him Go, Airport.
TELEVISION: Playhouse 90, Dick Powell Show, Wagon Train, Virginian, Burkes Law, Bob Hope Presents, Alfred Hitchcock, Twelve O'Clock High, The Rogues, Ben Casey, FBI Story, My Three Sons, Wild Wild West, Movies: The Man Who Never Was, The Royal Romance of Charles and Diana, In the Line of Duty: The FBI Murders.

Y

YABLANS, FRANK: Executive. B. Brooklyn, NY, Aug. 27, 1935. Ent. m.p. ind. as Warner Bros. booker, 1957. Warner Bros. salesman in N.Y., Boston, Milwaukee, Chicago, 1957–59. Milwaukee br. mgr. Buena Vista, 1959–66. Midwest sales mgr., Sigma III, 1966. Eastern sales mgr., 1967, sales v.p. 1968. V.P. general sales mgr., Paramount Pic. Corp., 1969; v.p.-dist., April 1970; sr. v.p.-mkt., Oct., 1970; exec. v.p., April 1971; named pres. May, 1971. In Jan., 1975, became an indep. prod., his company called, Frank Yablans Presentations Inc. 1983, MGM/UA Entertainment Co. as bd. chmn. & chief oper. off. Held titles of bd. chmn. & chief exec. off. with both MGM and UA Corp when resigned, 1985. Same year teamed with PSO Delphi to form Northstar Entertainment Co.; 1986, non-exclusive deal with Empire Entertainment; 1988, non-exclusive 3-year deal with Columbia Pictures.
PICTURES: Silver Streak (exec. prod.), The Other Side of Midnight (prod.), The Fury (prod.), North Dallas Forty (prod.-co-s.p.), Mommie Dearest (prod.-co-s.p.); Monsignor (co.-prod), Star Chamber, Kidco, Buy and Cell (prod.), Lisa (prod.).

YABLANS, IRWIN: Executive. b. Brooklyn, NY, June 25, 1934. Began career in industry at WB in 1956 after two-yr. stint with U.S. Army in Germany. Held m.p. sales posts in Washington, DC, Albany, Detroit, Milwaukee and Portland. In 1962 joined Paramount as L.A. mgr.; in 1964 made western sales mgr. In 1972 entered production as assoc. prod. on Howard W. Koch's Badge 373. Pres. of Compass Int'l. Pictures. Exec. v.p., low budget films, Lorimar Productions. Resigned June, 1984. In 1985 named chmn., Orion Pictures Distributing Corp. 1988: named chmn. and CEO of newly formed Epic Pictures.
PICTURES: The Education of Sonny Carson (1974). Exec. prod.: Halloween, Roller Boogie (also story), Fade To Black (story), Seduction (prod.), Halloween II, Halloween III, The Season of the Witch, Parasite, Tank, Hell Night, Prison Arena, Why Me?

YATES, PETER: Producer, Director. b. Ewshoot, Eng., July 24, 1929. e. Royal Acad. of Dramatic Art. Ent. m.p. ind. as studio mgr. and dubbing asst. with De Lane Lea. Asst. dir.: The Entertainer, The Guns of Navarone, A Taste of Honey, The Roman Spring of Mrs. Stone. Stage: dir. The American Dream, The Death of Bessie Smith, Passing Game, Interpreters.
TELEVISION: Series: Danger Man (Secret Agent), The Saint.
PICTURES: Summer Holiday, One Way Pendulum, Robbery (also co-s.p.), Bullitt, John and Mary, Murphy's War, The Hot Rock, The Friends of Eddie Coyle, For Pete's Sake, Mother, Jugs and Speed (also prod.), The Deep, Breaking Away (dir., prod.), Eyewitness (dir., prod.), Krull, The Dresser (dir., prod.), Eleni, Suspect, The House on Carroll Street (prod., dir.), An Innocent Man.

YELLEN, LINDA: Producer, Director, Writer. b. New York, NY, July 13, 1949. e. Barnard Coll., B.A., 1969; Columbia U., M.F.A., 1972; Ph.D., 1974. Also lecturer Barnard Coll., Yale U., asst. professor, City U. of New York. Member, executive council, Directors Guild of America.
PICTURES: Looking Up (prod., dir., 1978); Prospera; Come Out, Come Out.
TELEVISION: Mayflower: The Pilgrims' Adventure (prod.); Playing for Time (prod., Emmy, Peabody, Christopher Awards, 1980); Hardhat and Legs (prod.); The Royal Romance of Charles and Diana (exec. prod., co-s.p.); Prisoner Without a Name, Cell Without a Number (prod., dir., co-s.p.; Peabody, Writers Guild Awards, 1985), Liberace: Behind the Music (exec. prod.), Sweet Bird of Youth (exec. prod.), Rebound (dir., co-s.p.).

YORDAN, PHILIP: Writer. b. Chicago, IL, 1913. e. U. of Illinois, B.A., Kent Coll. of Law, LL.D. Author, producer, playwright (Anna Lucasta). Began screen writing 1942 with collab. s.p. Syncopation.
PICTURES: Unknown Guest, Johnny Doesn't Live Here, When Strangers Marry, Dillinger (Acad. Award nom.), Whistle Stop, The Chase, Suspense; play & s.p. Anna Lucasta, House of Strangers; s.p. Edge of Doom; collab. s.p. Detective Story, (Acad. Award nom.) Mary Maru, s.p., Houdini, Blowing Wild; collab. s.p., Man Crazy, Naked Jungle; s.p., Johnny Guitar; story, Broken Lance (Acad. Award, 1954); adapt. Conquest of Space; collab. s.p. Man from Laramie, Last Frontier; prod. s.p. Harder They Fall, Men In War, No Down Payment, God's Little Acre; s.p. Bravados, Time Machine, The Day of the Outlaw, Studs Lonigan, King of Kings; collab., El Cid, 55 Days at Peking, Fall of the Roman Empire; prod., Crack in the World, Battle of the Bulge, Royal Hunt of the Sun, Brigham, Cataclysm, Night Train to Terror, Satan's Warriors, Cry Wilderness, Bloody Wednesday (prod., s.p.), The Unholy (co-s.p.), Dead Girls Don't Dance (prod., s.p.).

YORK, DICK: Actor. r.n. Richard Allen York. b. Fort Wayne, IN, Sept. 4, 1928. e. De Paul U. Drama Sch. Appeared on radio shows; then films; on Broadway in Tea and Sympathy, Bus Stop; TV appearances.
TELEVISION: Omnibus, Robert Montgomery Show, Mr. D.A., The Web, Wagon Train, Alfred Hitchcock, Twilight Zone, Route 66, Series: Going My Way, Bewitched.
PICTURES: Inherit the Wind, Cowboy, They Came to Cordura, My Sister Eileen, Three Stripes in the Sun.

YORK, MICHAEL: Actor. r.n. Michael York-Johnson. b. Fulmer, England, March 27, 1942. Early career with Oxford U. Dramatic Society and National Youth Theatre; later Dundee Repertory, National Theatre.
THEATER: Any Just Cause, Hamlet, Ring Round the Moon (Los Angeles), Cyrano de Bergerac Bdwy: Outcry, Bent, The Little Prince and the Aviator.
PICTURES: The Taming of the Shrew, Accident, Red and Blue, Smashing Time, Romeo and Juliet, The Strange Affair, The Guru, Alfred the Great, Justine, Something for Everyone, Zeppelin, La Poudre D'Escampette, Cabaret, England Made Me, Lost Horizon, The Three Musketeers, Murder on the Orient Express, The Four Musketeers, Conduct Unbecoming, Logan's Run, Seven Nights in Japan, The Last Remake of Beau Geste, The Island of Dr. Moreau, Fedora, The Riddle of the Sands (also assoc. prod.), The White Lions, Final Assignment, The Weather in the Streets, Success Is the Best Revenge, Dawn, Lethal Obsession (Der Joker), Midnight Cop, The Return of the Musketeers, Phantom of Death, The Secret of the Sahara, Killing Blue.
TELEVISION: The Forsyte Saga, Rebel in the Grave, Jesus of Nazareth, True Patriot, Much Ado About Nothing, Series: Knot's Landing, Dynasty. Movies: Great Expectations, A Man Called Intrepid, The Phantom of the Opera, The Master of Ballantrae, Space, For Those I Loved, The Far Country, Dark Mansions, Sword of Gideon, Four Minute Mile, The Lady and the Highwayman, The Heat of the Day, Till We Meet Again. Host: The Hunt for Stolen War Treasure.

YORK, SUSANNAH: Actress. b. London, England, Jan. 9, 1941. Ent. TV 1959. Ent. films in 1960. Wrote two books: In Search of Unicorns and Lark's Castle.
THEATER: A Cheap Bunch of Flowers, Wings of the Dove, Singular Life of Albert Nobbs, Man and Superman, Mrs. Warren's Profession, Peter Pan, The Maids, Private Lives, The Importance of Being Earnest, Hedda Gabler (New York), Agnes of God, The Human Voice. Produced The Big One, a variety show for peace, 1984. Penthesilea, Fatal Attraction, The Apple Cart, Private Treason, Lyric for a Tango, The Glass Menagerie.
PICTURES: Tunes of Glory, There Was a Crooked Man, Greengage Summer, Freud, Tom Jones, While the Tiger Sleeps, The Seventh Dawn, Scene Nun—Take One, Sands of Kalahari, Scruggs, Kaleidoscope, A Man for All Seasons, Sebastian, The Killing of Sister George, Oh What a Lovely War, The Battle of Britain, Lock Up Your Daughters, They

Shoot Horses Don't They? (Acad. Award nom.), Brotherly Love, Zee & Co., Happy Birthday Wanda June, Images, The Maids, Gold, Conduct Unbecoming, Heaven Save Us From Our Friends, Sky Riders, The Silent Partner, Superman, The Shout, Superman II, Falling in Love Again, Alice Loophole, The Awakening, Mio My Mio, Christmas Card, Prettykill, Bluebeard Bluebeard, A Summer Story, American Roulette, Falcon's Malteser, Just Ask For Diamond, Melancholia, A Handful of Time.

TELEVISION: The Crucible, The Rebel and the Soldier, The First Gentleman, The Richest Man in the World, Slaughter of St. Teresa's Day, Kiss On A Grass Green Pillow, Fallen Angels, Prince Regent, Second Chance, Betjeman's Briton, We'll Meet Again, Jane Eyre, A Christmas Carol, Star Quality, Macho, Return Journey, After the War, The Man From Pru, The Haunting of the New.

YORKIN, BUD: Producer, Director. r.n. Alan "Bud" Yorkin. b. Washington, PA, Feb. 22, 1926. e. Carnegie Tech., Columbia U. U.S. Navy, 1942–45; Began career in TV in NBC's engineering dept. Moved into prod., first as stage mgr., then assoc. dir. of Colgate Comedy Hour (Martin and Lewis) and dir. of Dinah Shore Show. Formed Tandem Productions with Norman Lear; 1974 formed own production co.

TELEVISION: Song at Twilight, Martin & Lewis Show, Abbott and Costello Show, Ritz Bros. Show, Spike Jones Show; writer, prod. dir.: Tony Martin Show, 1954–55; dir., George Gobel Show, 1954–55; prod. dir.: The Ernie Ford Show 1956–57; An Evening with Fred Astaire (1958, 3 Emmys), Another Evening with Fred Astaire (1959); owner. co-prod.: All In The Family; Sanford and Son; Maude; Good Times; What's Happening!!; Carter Country.

PICTURES: Come Blow Your Horn (dir., co-prod., adapt.), Never Too Late (dir); Divorce American Style (dir.); Inspector Clouseau (dir.); Start the Revolution Without Me (prod., dir.); Thief Who Came to Dinner (prod., dir.), The Night They Raided Minsky's (exec. prod.); Cold Turkey, (exec. prod.), Blade Runner (exec. prod.), Deal of the Century, (prod.), Twice in a Lifetime (prod., dir.), Arthur 2 on the Rocks (dir.), Love Hurts (co-prod., dir.).

YOSHISAKA, KIYOJI: Executive. b. Shanghai, China 1908. e. Thomas Hambury Coll., Shanghai. Ent. ind. 1930 RCA Victor of China, 1932 Victor Talking Machine, 1938 Manchuria Talking Machine, 1940 Victor of Japan. Left Photophone Div. of Victor in 1950 for Tokyo Theatre Supply 1950–58; 1959–63 Rhythm Friend Corp.; exec. dir.s Nichior 1964–66; became consultant Nihon Eiga Shizai 1966 and after name changed to Toshiba Photo Phone became mgr. trade. div. 1969 then dir. and gen. mgr. of trade div. in 1970. Retired.

YOUNG, ALAN: Actor. r.n. Angus Young; b. North Shield, Northumberland, England, Nov. 19, 1919. Cartoonist, acted first as monologist at 13 years in Canada; radio comedian 10 yrs. in Canada and U.S.; served in Canadian Navy as sub-lt. 1942–44; wrote, dir. and acted in comedy broadcasts.

PICTURES: Margie (debut, 1946), Chicken Every Sunday, Mr. Belvedere Goes to College, Aaron Slick from Punkin Crick, Androcles and the Lion, Gentlemen Marry Brunettes, Tom Thumb, Time Machine, The Cat from Outer Space.

TELEVISION: Series: The Alan Young Show (2 Emmys), Mr. Ed, Coming of Age.

YOUNG, BUDDY: Executive. b. New York, NY, June 15, 1935. e. City Coll. of New York. UA publicity dept. 1952; asst. pub. mgr., UA 1963; pub. dir. Fox, Oct. 1965; west coast coordinator of adv. and publicity UA. In 1975 joined Columbia Pictures as worldwide dir. of adv.-pub.-exp. In 1976 named MGM adv.-pub. co-ordinator. Joined Universal Pictures in 1976 as dir. of pub. & promo. promoted to v.p., of advertising, publicity and promotion; 1980, partner in m.p. consulting firm, Powell & Young; 1983, pres. & dir., Color Systems Technology, Inc.

YOUNG, BURT: Actor, Writer. b. New York, NY, April 30, 1940. Worked at variety of jobs (boxer, trucker, etc.) before turning to acting and joining Actor's Studio. Appeared in off-Bdwy. plays which led to Hollywood career.

PICTURES: Cinderella Liberty, The Gambler, The Killer Elite, Chinatown, Rocky, The Choirboys, Convoy, Uncle Joe Shannon (actor, s.p.), All the Marbles, Rocky III, Lookin' To Get Out, Amityville II: The Possession, Over the Brooklyn Bridge, Once Upon a Time in America, The Pope of Greenwich Village, Rocky IV, Back to School, Beverly Hills Brats, The Last Exit to Brooklyn, Medium Rare, Blood Red, Wait Until Spring, Bandini; Diving In, Trouble in the Night, Backstreet Strays, Bright Angels.

TELEVISION: M*A*S*H, Baretta. Movies: A Summer to Remember, Serpico, Hustling, Daddy I Don't Like It Like This (also s.p.), The Great Niagara, This Deadly Game, Murder Can Hurt You.

YOUNG, CARROLL: Writer. b. Cincinnati, OH. e. St. Xavier Coll. Publicist for Pathe Studios, Fox West Coast Theatres, RKO Studios, MGM, 1930–35; story ed. Sol Lesser Prod., Ernst Lubitsch Prod., 1936–40; asst. to exec. prod., RKO, 1941; U.S. Army Air Force, 1942–44.

PICTURES: story, collab. s.p. Tarzan Triumphs; story, Tarzan's Desert Mystery; story, s.p. Tarzan and Leopard Woman, Tarzan and Mermaids; s.p. many in Jungle Jim series, Hidden City, The Jungle; story, Lost Continent; collab. s.p. Tarzan and the She-Devil; story s.p. Cannibal Attack; collab. story & s.p. Apache Warrior; collab. s.p. She-Devil, The Deerslayer; collab. s.p. Machete.

YOUNG, FREDDIE: O.B.E. Cinematographer. b. England, 1902. r.n. Frederick Young. Entered British film industry in 1917. Gaumont Studio Shepherd's Bush, London as lab asst. First picture as chief cameraman, 1927 then chief cameraman to Herbert Wilcox British & Dominions Studios Elstree Herts. Army capt. Army Film prod. group directing training films 3 yrs. Invalided out. Signed with MGM British 15 yrs. Also credited as F.A. Young. Winner of three Academy Awards for work on epic films of David Lean: Lawrence of Arabia, Doctor Zhivago and Ryan's Daughter. BAFTA Fellowship 1972, Prix D'Honeur (Lawrence of Arabia) O.B.E. 1970. Emmy, (Macbeth).

PICTURES: Victory 1918, A Peep Behind the Scenes, The Speckled Band, Goodnight Vienna, The Loves of Robert Burns, The King of Paris, White Cargo (first British talkie), Rookery Nook, A Cuckoo in the Nest, Canaries Sometimes Sing, A Night Like This, Plunder, Thark, On Approval, Mischief, Return of the Rat, The Happy Ending, Yes, Mr. Brown; This'll Make You Whistle, That's a Good Girl, Nell Gwynne, Peg of Old Drury, The Little Damozel, Bitter Sweet, The Queen's Affair, Sport of Kings, A Warm Corner, The W Plan, Victoria the Great, Sixty Glorious Years, Goodbye Mr. Chips, Nurse Edith Cavell, The 49th Parallel, Contraband, Busman's Honeymoon, The Young Mr. Pitt, Caesar and Cleopatra, Escape, So Well Remembered, Edward, My Son; The Conspirator, The Winslow Boy, Calling Bulldog Drummond, Ivanhoe, Knights of the Round Table, Mogambo, Invitation to the Dance, Bhowani Junction, The Barretts of Wimpole Street, The Little Hut, Indiscreet, I Accuse, Inn of the Sixth Happiness, Solomon and Sheba, Betrayed, Island in the Sun, Treasure Island, Lust for Life, Macbeth, Greengage Summer, Lawrence of Arabia (Acad. Award, 1962), The Seventh Dawn, Lord Jim, The Deadly Affair, Rotten to the Core, Doctor Zhivago (Acad. Award, 1965), You Only Live Twice, The Battle of Britain, Ryan's Daughter (Acad. Award, 1970), Nicholas and Alexandra, Luther, The Tamarind Seed, Permission to Kill, The Blue Bird, Seven Nights in Japan, Stevie, Bloodline, Rough Cut, Richard's Things.

TELEVISION: Great Expectations, The Man in the Iron Mask, Macbeth (Emmy; 1960), Ike: The War Years, Arthur's Hollowed Ground (director).

YOUNG, IRWIN: Executive. b. New York, NY. e. Perkiomen Sch., Lehigh U., B.S., 1950. Pres., Du Art Film Laboratories, Inc.

YOUNG, LORETTA: Actress. r.n. Gretchen Young; b. Salt Lake City, UT, Jan. 6, 1913. e. Ramona Convent, Alhambra, CA, Immaculate Heart Coll. Hollywood. After small part in Naughty But Nice, lead in Laugh Clown, Laugh. Played in almost 100 films. Autobiography: The Things I Had to Learn (1962).

PICTURES: Laugh Clown Laugh (debut, 1928), Loose Ankles, The Squall. Kismet etc. I Like Your Nerve. The Devil to Pay. Platinum Blonde. The Hatchet Man. Big Business Girl. Life Beings. Zoo in Budapest. Man's Castle. The House of Rothschild. Midnight Mary. The Crusaders. Clive of India. Call of the Wild. Shanghai. Ramona. Ladies in Love. Wife, Doctor and Nurse. Second Honeymoon. Four Men and a Prayer. Suez. Kentucky. Three Blind Mice. The Story of Alexander Graham Bell. The Doctor Takes a Wife. He Stayed for Breakfast. Lady from Cheyenne. The Men in Her Life. A Night to Remember. China. Ladies Courageous. And Now Tomorrow. The Stranger. Along Came Jones. The Perfect Marriage. The Farmer's Daughter (Acad. Award, 1947), The Bishop's Wife. Rachel and the Stranger. Come to the Stable. Cause for Alarm. Half Angel. Paula. Because of You. It Happens Every Thursday.

TELEVISION: Loretta Young Show, (NBC-TV 1953–61); New Loretta Young Show (CBS-TV 1962); won Emmy Awards, 1954–56–59. Returned to TV, 1986; in movies: Christmas Eve (1986), Lady in a Corner.

YOUNG, ROBERT: Actor. b. Chicago, IL, Feb. 22, 1907. Star numerous pictures before and after sound; from 1932 in many productions, various Hollywood producers.

PICTURES: The Sin of Madelon Claudet (debut, 1931), Strange Interlude, The Kid From Spain, Hell Below, Tugboat Annie, Lazy River, The House of Rothchild, Spitfire, Whom the God's Destroy, Remember Last Night?, West Point of the Air, It's Love Again, Secret Agent, Stowaway, The Emperor's Candlesticks, I Met Him in Paris, The Bride Wore Red, Josette, Frou, Frou, Three Comrades, Rich Man, Poor Girl, Honolulu, Miracles For Sale, Maisie, Northwest Passage, The Mortal Storm, Florian, Western Union, The Trial of Mary Dugan, Lady Be Good, H.M. Pulham, Esq., Joe Smith American, Cairo, Journey for Margaret, Claudia, Sweet Rosie O'Grady, The Canterville Ghost, Secrets in the Dark, The

Enchanted Cottage, Those Endearing Young Charms, Claudia and David, Lady Luck, They Won't Believe Me, Crossfire, Sitting Pretty, Adventures in Baltimore, And Baby Makes Three, Bride for Sale, Second Woman, That Forsyte Woman, Goodbye My Fancy, Half-Breed, Secret of the Incas.
TELEVISION: Father Knows Best (series), Window on Main Street, Marcus Welby, M.D. (series); Movies: Mercy or Murder, Conspiracy of Love, Little Women, Marcus Welby, M.D.—A Holiday Affair.

YOUNG, ROBERT M.: Director. b. New York, NY, Nov. 22, 1924. e. Harvard.
PICTURES: Nothing But a Man; Short Eyes; Rich Kids; One-Trick Pony; The Ballad of Gregorio Cortez; Alambrista! (also s.p., cinematography), Extremities, Dominick and Eugene, Triumph of the Spirit.
TELEVISION: Sit-In; Angola—Journey to a War; The Inferno (a.k.a. Cortile Cascino, documentary; also prod., s.p. editor), Anatomy of a Hospital; Eskimo; Fight for Life (Emmy), Murder in Mississippi.

YOUNG, SEAN: Actress. b. Louisville, KY, Nov. 20, 1959. e. Interlochen Arts Acad., MI, studied dance. After graduating, moved to N.Y., worked as receptionist, model for 6 months and signed with ICM where mother Lee Guthrie worked in lit. dept. Shortly after signed for film debut in Jane Austen in Manhattan (1980).
PICTURES: Jane Austen in Manhattan, Stripes, Blade Runner, Young Doctors in Love, Dune, Baby, The Secret of the Lost Legend, No Way Out, Wall Street, The Boost, Cousins.
TELEVISION: Under the Biltmore Clock, Tender Is the Night, Blood and Orchids.

YOUNG, TERENCE: Director, Writer, b. Shanghai, China, June 20, 1915. e. Cambridge U. Served with Guards Armoured Div., W.W.II; ent. m.p. ind. 1936 at BIP Studios. Screenwriter turned director.
PICTURES: Writer: On the Night of the Fire, On Approval, Dangerous Moonlight, Theirs is the Glory; Director: Corridor of Mirrors, One Night With You, Woman Hater, They Were Not Divided, The Valley of the Eagles, Red Beret (Paratrooper), That Lady, Safari, Storm Over the Nile, Action of the Tiger, Serious Charge, Black Tights, Dr. No. From Russia With Love, Moll Flanders, Thunderball, Triple Cross, The Rover, Wait Until Dark, Mayerling, The Christmas Tree, The Red Sun, Grand Slam, The Valachi Papers, War Goddess, The Klansman, Jackpot, Bloodline, Inchon, The Jigsaw Man, Takeover.

YOUNGSTEIN, MAX E.: Executive. b. March 21, 1913. e. Fordham U. Member New York Bar. Motion picture consultant and indep. prod. Member, Producers Guild. Pres., Max E. Youngstein Enterprises. 1940–41, dir. adv. & pub., 20th Century Fox; later dir. studio special svcs.; asst. to pres. 1942–44, US Army Signal Corps. 1945, v.p. & gen. mgr., Stanley Kramer Prods. 1946–48, dir. adv. & pub., Eagle Lion Films; v.p. chg. adv. & pub. & prod. liaison. 1949–50, dir. adv. & pub., Paramount; mem. exec. comm. & v.p. & dir. dist. co. 1951–62, gen. v.p., partner, bd. mem., dir. adv. & pub., United Artists Corp. Formed UA Music Co. Pres., UA Records. 1977, consultant to Bart-Palevsky Prods. Advisor, Golden Harvest Films. Consultant, Rico-Lion. 1979, Shamrock Prods., Rank Film Distributors, Taft Bdcst. Co., Encore Prods., Bobrun Prods., Selkirk Films. 1980, named Chmn. & CEO, Taft Int'l. Pictures. 1984, Consultant, Orion, 20th Century-Fox. 1985–86, pres., Great American Pictures. Consultant, H&M Trust, Color Systems Technology, Mickey Rooney Film Prods., Peachtree Prods.
PICTURES: Young Billy Young, Best of Cinerama, Man in the Middle, Fail Safe, The Money Trap, The Dangerous Days of Kiowa Jones, Welcome to Hard Times.

YULIN, HARRIS: Actor. On Bdwy. in Watch on the Rhine, A Lesson from Aloes, etc.
PICTURES: End of the Road, Doc, The Midnight Man, Night Moves, Steel, Scarface, The Believers, Candy Mountain, Fatal Beauty, Bad Dreams, Judgement in Berlin, Another Woman, Ghostbusters II.
TELEVISION: The Thirteenth Day—The Story of Esther, When Every Day Was the Fourth of July, Missiles of October, Conspiracy: Trial of the Chicago Seven, Last Ride of the Dalton Gang, Robert Kennedy and His Times, Tailspin: Behind the Korean Airlines Tragedy.

Z

ZADORA, PIA: Singer, Actress. b. New York, NY, May 4. e. H.S. of Professional Arts. m. Meshulam Riklis. On Bdwy in Henry Sweet Henry. Singer in nightclubs, concerts, records, and has appeared on numerous talk and variety TV shows.
PICTURES: Santa Claus Conquers the Martians (debut, 1964), Butterfly, Fakeout, The Lonely Lady, Voyage of the Rock Aliens, Hairspray.
TELEVISION: Pajama Tops (cable). Specials: Star Spangled Celebration, ABC's 75th Anniversary—Las Vegas.

ZAENTZ, SAUL: Producer. b. Passaic, NJ.
PICTURES: One Flew Over the Cuckoo's Nest (Acad. Award), Three Warriors, The Lord of the Rings, Amadeus, The Mosquito Coast (exec. prod.), The Unbearable Lightness of Being.

ZAMPA, LUIGI: Director. b. Rome, Italy, 1905. Playwright, studied at Experimental Film Center, Rome, 1935–1938; script writer, Neo-realist director.
PICTURES: American on Vacation, To Live in Peace, Difficult Years, Angelina, The White Line, City on Trial, Two Gentlemen in a Carriage, His Last 12 Hours, We Women, Woman of Rome, Art of Getting Along, A Flower in His Mouth, Tigers in Lipstick, Portrait of a Lovely, Lucky Woman (TV, 1985).

ZAMPI, GIULIO: Associate producer. b. London, Eng., Sept. 29, 1923. p. Mario Zampi. e. Rome U. Ed. to Marcel Varnel, then to Mario Zampi; dir. of Anglofilm Ltd. Transocean Films Ltd.
PICTURES: Phantom Shot, Fatal Night, Shadow of the Past, Come Dance with Me, Third Time Lucky, Laughter in Paradise, Top Secret, I Have Chosen Love, Happy Ever After (Tonight's the Night), Now and Forever, The Naked Truth, Too Many Crooks, Bottoms Up, Five Golden Hours.

ZANUCK, RICHARD DARRYL: Executive, b. Los Angeles, CA, Dec 13, 1934. e. Stanford U. 1952–56. f. Darryl Zanuck. Story dept., 20th Century Fox, 1954; N.Y. pub. dept., 1955; asst. to prod., Island in the Sun, 1957; The Sun Also Rises, 1956; v.p. Darryl F. Zanuck Prod. 1958; prod. Compulsion, 1959, DFZ Prod., 20th Century Fox; prod., Sanctuary, 1961; prod., The Chapman Report, 1962; asst. to prod., The Longest Day, 1962; president's prod. rep., 20th Century Fox Studio, 1963; v.p. charge prod., 20th Fox; pres., 20th Fox TV exec. v.p. chge. prod., 20th Fox, 1967. 1968: Chmn. of Bd., Television div., 20th Century Fox, 1969: Pres., 20th Century Fox Film Corp. Joined Warner Bros., March 1971, as sr. exec. v.p.; Resigned July, 1972 to form Zanuck-Brown Production Company, Universal Pictures. Joined 20th Century-Fox, 1980–83. To Warner Bros., 1983. To MGM Entertainment, 1986. 1988, dissolved 16-year partnership with David Brown. Formed The Zanuck Company, Jan., 1989.
PICTURES: Sssssss, The Sugarland Express; Willie Dynamite; The Sting; The Black Windmill, The Girl from Petrovka; The Eiger Sanction; Jaws; MacArthur; Jaws 2; The Island; Neighbors; The Verdict; Cocoon; Target; Cocoon: The Return, Driving Miss Daisy.

ZANUSSI, KRZYSZTOF: b. Warsaw, Poland, 1939. e. Warsaw University, (physics); attended lectures on cinema at Polish Acad. of Science's Inst. of Arts. Made first film for Warsaw U. Amateur Film Club before enrolling as grad. student in philosophy at Cracow U., 1959. Grad. Lodz State Coll. of Film, 1966. Made several short films before feature debut with the Structure of Crystals, 1969. Head of one of 3 gov.-supported film units in Poland. Was active in Solidarity. Has since maintained ties with Polish film indust. while making films abroad.
PICTURES: Shorts: The Way to the Skies, Proba Cisnienia; The Death of a Provincial; Industry; Computers; Face to Face; Zaliczenie; Mountains at Dusk; The Role; Behind the Wall; Hypothesis. Features: The Structure of Crystals; Family Life; Illumination; The Catamount Killing; A Woman's Decision; Penderecki, Lutoslawski, Baird; Camouflage; Anatomy Lesson; House of Women (TV); Spiral; Ways in the Night; My Cracow; The Constant Factor; Contract; From a Far Country—Pope John Paul II; Temptation; Imperative; The Unapproachable (TV); Vatican Capitale; Bluebeard; The Year of the Quiet Sun; The Power of Evil; Wherever You Are (dir., s.p.); The Young Magician (co-prod. only), And the Violins Stopped Playing (exec. prod. only), Deep in the Heart (dir.).

ZEFFIRELLI, FRANCO: Director. b. Italy, Feb. 12, 1923. Was stage director before entering film industry. Set designer 1949–52 for Visconti plays (A Streetcar Named Desire, The Three Sisters). Director of operas.
PICTURES: The Taming of the Shrew, Romeo and Juliet, Brother Sun, Sister Moon, The Champ, Endless Love, La Traviata, Otello, Young Toscanini, Hamlet.
TELEVISION: Jesus of Nazareth.

ZELNICK, STRAUSS: Executive. b. Boston, MA, June 26, 1957. e. Wesleyan U. B.A., 1979 (Summa Cum Laude); Harvard Grad. School of Business Administration, M.B.A., 1983; Harvard Law School, J.D., 1983 (Cum Laude). 1983–86, v.p., international television sales, Columbia Pictures International Corp. 1988–89, pres. & chief operating officer, Vestron, Inc.; 1989 named pres. & chief operating officer, Fox Film Corp.

ZEMECKIS, ROBERT: Director, Writer. b. Chicago, IL, 1952. e. U. of Southern California Sch. of Cinema. At U.S.C. wrote, prod., dir. a 14-minute film, A Field of Honor, which won special jury award at Second Annual Student Film Awards sponsored by M.P. Academy of Arts & Sciences, plus 15 intl. honors. Has film editing background, having worked as cutter on TV commercials in Illinois. Also cut films at NBC News,

Chicago, as summer job. After schooling went to Universal to observe on set of TV series, McCloud. Wrote script for that series in collab. with Bob Gale. Turned to feature films, directing I Wanna Hold Your Hand and co-writing s.p. with Gale and co-writing 1941 with him.
PICTURES: Used Cars, Romancing the Stone, Back to the Future, Who Framed Roger Rabbit?, Back to the Future II & III.
TELEVISION: Tales From the Crypt (exec. prod., dir., All Through the House).

ZENS, WILL: Producer, Director. b. Milwaukee, WI, June 26, 1920. e. Marquette U., U. of Southern California, B.A., M.A. Wrote, produced and directed many TV shows. Formed Riviera Productions in 1960 to produce theatrical motion pictures.
TELEVISION: Punch & Trudy, Your Police, Aqua Lung Adventures.
PICTURES: Capture That Capsule, The Starfighters, To the Shores of Hell, Road to Nashville, Hell on Wheels, From Nashville with Music, Yankee Station, Help Me . . . I'm Possessed!, Hot Summer in Barefoot County, The Fix, Truckin' Man, The Satan Crossing (dir., s.p.), Residue of Honor (dir.).

ZETTERLING, MAI: Actress, Director. b. Sweden, May 24, 1925. e. Ordtuery Sch., Theater Sch. First m.p.: Sweden, Frenzy. Has made numerous stage and screen appearances since in Sweden. British screen debut, Frieda. Since 1969 directing plays & films in Sweden. Won Golden Lion at Venice in 1964 for The War Game.
PICTURES: Bad Lord Byron, Quartet, Portrait from Life, Romantic Age, Blackmailed, Hell is Sold Out, Desperate Moment, Knock on Wood, Dance Little Lady, Prize of Gold, Seven Waves Away (Abandon Ship), The Truth About Women, Jetstorm, Faces in the Dark, Piccadilly Third Stop, Offbeat, Only Two Can Play, The Main Attraction. 1965–66 wrote, dir. Loving Couples, Night Games. 1968: Dr. Glas, The Girls, The Rain Hat, We Have Many Names, The Witches.
TELEVISION: Idiot's Delight, Mayerling, Doll's House, Dance of Death, etc. dir, doc. for BBC and in Sweden. Wrote and dir. Scrubbers, Amorosa.

ZIDE, LARRY M: Executive. b. Flushing, NY, Oct. 16, 1954. 3rd generation in mp. industry. Started 1972 with American Intl. Pictures in sls. & adv.; 1973, named branch sls. mgr., Memphis. 1975, joined Dimension Pictures as print controller; 1978, formed Zica Films Co. serving m.p. industry. 1985, Zica merged with Filmtreat Intl. Corp; named pres., newly formed Filmtreat West Corp.

ZIDE, MICHAEL (MICKEY): Executive. b. Detroit, MI, May 31, 1932. Joined m.p. industry with American Intl. Pictures as print controller; 1962, promoted to asst. gen. sls. mgr. Named v.p., special projects, 1970; 1972, joined Academy Pictures as v.p. of prod. Later went with Zica Film Co.; 1985, named exec. v.p., Filmtreat West Corp.

ZIEFF, HOWARD: Director. b. Los Angeles, CA, 1943. Started as artist and photographer, working as newsreel photographer for L.A. TV station. Went to N.Y. to do still photography; became top photo artist in advertising. Turned to film direction with Slither in 1972.
PICTURES: Slither, Hearts of the West, House Calls, The Main Event, Private Benjamin, Unfaithfully Yours, The Dream Team.

ZIFKIN, WALTER: Executive. b. July 16, 1936. New York, NY. e. UCLA, A.B., 1958; U. of Southern California, LL.B., 1961. CBS legal dept., 1961–63; William Morris Agency 1963–present; exec. vice-pres.; 1989 also chief operating officer.

ZIMBALIST, EFREM, JR.: Actor. b. New York, NY, Nov. 30, 1923. Son of violinist Efrem Zimbalist and opera singer Alma Gluck. Father of actress Stephanie Zimbalist. e. Fay Sch., Southboro, MA; St. Paul's, Concord, NH; Yale. Studied drama, Neighborhood Playhouse. N.Y. Stage debut, The Rugged Path. Shows with American Repertory Theatre; Henry VIII, Androcles and the Lion, What Every Woman Knows, Yellow Jack, Appeared, Hedda Gabler. Co-prod., The Medium, The Telephone, The Consul, (Critics Award, Pulitzer Prize). Screen debut, House of Strangers (1949). Gave up acting after death of his wife and served as asst. to father, Curtis Inst. of Music for 4 years. Returned to acting, stock co., Hammonton, NJ, 1954.
TELEVISION: Philco, Goodyear Playhouse, U.S. Steel Hour. Series: Maverick, 77 Sunset Strip, The FBI. Movies: The Black Dahlia, Terror Out of the Sky, Scruples, The Gathering II, A Family Upside Down, Best Place to Be, A Family of Winners, Insight/Checkmate, Beyond Witch Mountain, Family in Blue, Baby Sister, Shooting Stars, You Are the Jury (host).
PICTURES: Bomber B-52, Band of Angels, The Deep Six, Violent Road, Girl on the Run, Too Much Too Soon, Home Before Dark, The Crowded Sky, A Fever in the Blood, By Love Possessed, Chapman Report, The Reward, Harlow (electronovision), Airport 1975, Elmira.

ZIMBALIST, STEPHANIE: Actress. b. New York, NY, Oct. 8, 1956. Daughter of actor Efrem Zimbalist Jr.
THEATER: The Cherry Orchard (Long Wharf, CT, 1984). Toured in My One and Only.
PICTURES: The Magic of Lassie, The Awakening.
TELEVISION: Series: Remington Steele (1982–87). Mini-series: Centennial. Movies: Yesterday's Child, In the Matter of Karen Ann Quinlan, The Gathering, The Long Journey Back, Forever, The Triangle Factory Fire Scandal, The Best Place to Be, The Baby Sitter, The Golden Moment-An Olympic Love Story, Elvis and the Beauty Queen, Tomorrow's Child, Love on the Run, A Letter to Three Wives, Celebration Family.

ZIMBERT, RICHARD: Executive. Member, California bar. Has been with Paramount Pictures in executive capacities since 1975. In 1985 named exec. v.p. of co.

ZINNEMANN, FRED: Director. b. Vienna, Austria, Apr. 29, 1907. e. Vienna U., law. Studied violin as a boy; after law, studied photographic technique, lighting & mechanics (Paris); asst. cameraman 1 yr. Paris; came to U.S. 1929; extra in m.p. All Quiet on the Western Front, 1930; asst. to Berthold Viertel, script clerk & asst. to Robert Flaherty, 1931; dir. Mexican documentary The Wave; short subjects dir., MGM, winning Academy Award for That Mothers Might Live, 1938; feature dir. 1941; winner of first Screen Directors' Award 1948 with The Search. 4 N.Y. Film Critics Awards; 2 Director's Guild Annual Awards; 4 Acad. Awards. Other awards: U.S. Congressional Life Achievement Award (1987), Gold Medal City of Vienna, Donatello Award (Italy), Order of Arts & Letters (France), Golden Thistle Award (Edinburgh, Scotland), etc.
PICTURES: The Seventh Cross, The Search, The Men, Teresa, High Noon (N.Y. Film Critics Award), Benjy, short for L.A. Orthopedic Hosp. (Acad. Award, best doc. short, 1951); Member of the Wedding; From Here to Eternity (Acad. Award, best dir., 1953, N.Y. Film Critics Award, Directors' Guild Award), Oklahoma, Hatful of Rain, Nun's Story (N.Y. Film Critics Award), Sundowners, Behold a Pale Horse, A Man for All Seasons, (Oscars, best picture & direction, Directors' Guild Award) Day of the Jackal, Julia, Five Days One Summer.

ZINNEMANN, TIM: Producer. b. Los Angeles, CA. e. Columbia U. Son of dir. Fred Zinnemann. Began career industry as film editor; then asst. dir. on 20 films. Production mgr. for 5 projects; assoc. prod. on The Cowboys and Smile. Produced Straight Time for Warners with Stanley Beck.
PICTURES: A Small Circle of Friends, The Long Riders, Tex, Impulse, Fandango, Crossroads, The Running Man, Pet Semetary (exec. prod.).
TELEVISION: The Jericho Mile (ABC).

ZITO, JOSEPH: Director. b. New York, NY, May 14, 1946. e. City Coll. of New York.
PICTURES: Abduction, The Prowler, Friday the 13th: The Final Chapter, Missing in Action, Invasion U.S.A., Red Scorpion.

ZOUARY, MAURICE H.: Executive. b. Brooklyn, NY, July 17, 1921. e. Sch. of Industrial Design & Art, 1937. Trans-Lux Theatres, 1941; U.S. Armed Forces, 1943; production, acct. exec. ad agencies; Bud Gamble Prod., 1948; TV dept., Edward S. Kellogg Agency, L.A.; formed Zouary TV-Film Prod., 1950; prod. supvr. Films for Industry, 1950–52; TV prod., Grey Adv. Agency, 1952–54; prod, new commercials div., Guild Films, 1955–56; prod. Dore Prod., 1956–57; reactivated Zouary TV Film Prod., 1957; formed Filmvideo Releasing Corp. film stock shot library, 1957. Prod.: Freedom (feature film); Prod. Kiddie Camera (TV series); Prod.: The Vaudevillains (TV special); Prod.: Dr. DeForest. In 1975 formed TV National Releasing Corp., supplier of TV programming. Wrote and produced two cassettes for Movietronics: Buster Keaton & The First Sound of Movies—The Case for Dr. Lee DeForest.

ZSIGMOND, VILMOS: Cinematographer. b. Czeged, Hungary, June 16, 1930. e. National Film Sch. Began career photographing Hungarian Revolution of 1956. Later escaped from Hungary with friend Laszlo Kovacs, also a cinematographer. Winner of several int'l and domestic awards as dir. of TV commercials through own co., Cinematic Directions (formed 1985).
PICTURES: The Time Travelers (1964), The Sadist, The Name of the Game is Kill, Futz, Picasso Summer, The Monitors, Red Sky at Morning, McCabe and Mrs. Miller, The Hired Hand, The Ski Bum, Images, Deliverance, Scarecrow, The Long Goodbye, Cinderella Liberty, Sugarland Express, The Girl From Petrovka, Obsession, Close Encounters of the Third Kind (Acad. Award, 1977), Winter Kills, The Deer Hunter, The Rose, The Last Waltz, Heaven's Gate, Blow Out, Jinxed, Table for Five, No Small Affair, The River, Real Genius, The Witches of Eastwick, Adventure at Eagle Island, The Two Jakes, Journey to Spirit Island.
TELEVISION: Flesh and Blood.

ZUCKER, DAVID: Producer, Director, Writer. b. Milwaukee, WI, Oct. 16, 1947. e. U. of Wisconsin, majoring in film. With brother, Jerry, and friend Jim Abrahams founded the Kentucky Fried Theatre in Madison in 1969, (moved theater to L.A. 1972) later wrote script for film of that name released in 1977. Trio followed this with Airplane, 1980, which they wrote and jointly directed while serving as executive producers.

PICTURES: Top Secret (co-dir., co-s.p., co-prod.); Ruthless People (co-dir.), The Naked Gun (exec. prod., dir., co-s.p.).

TELEVISION: Police Squad (series); Our Planet Tonight (special).

ZUCKER, JERRY: Producer, Director. Writer. b. Milwaukee, WI, Mar. 11, 1950. e. U. of Wisconsin, majoring in film. With brother, David, and friend Jim Abrahams founded the Kentucky Fried Theatre in Madison in 1969 and wrote script for film of that name released in 1977. Trio followed this with Airplane! in 1980 which they wrote and jointly directed and served as executive producers.

PICTURES: Rock 'n' Roll High School (2nd unit dir.), Top Secret (co-dir., co-s.p.); Ruthless People (co-dir.), The Naked Gun (exec. prod., co-s.p.), Ghost (dir.).

ZUGSMITH, ALBERT: Producer, Director, Writer. b. Atlantic City, NJ, April 24, 1910. e. U. of Virginia. Pres. Intercontinental Broadcasting Corp.; ed. publ. Atlantic City Daily World; v.p. Smith Davis Corp.; Chmn of bd., Continental Telecasting Corp., Television Corp. of America; assoc. ed. American Press; pres. World Printing Co.; exec. CBS; pres. American Pictures Corp.; pres. Famous Players Int'l Corp.

PICTURES: Written on the Wind, Man in the Shadow, Red Sundown, Star in the Dust, Tarnished Angels, The Incredible Shrinking Man, The Girl in the Kremlin, The Square Jungle, Female on the Beach, Touch of Evil, Captive Women, Sword of Venus, Port Sinister, Invasion U.S.A., Top Banana, Paris Model, Slaughter on Tenth Avenue, The Female Animal, High School Confidential, Night of the Quarter Moon, Beat Generation, The Big Operator, Girls Town, Violated!, Platinum High School, Private Lives of Adam and Eve, Dondi, College Confidential, Confessions of an Opium Eater, The Great Space Adventure, On Her Bed of Roses, Fanny Hill, The Rapist! author, Private Lives of Adam and Eve, The Beat Generation, How to Break Into the Movies, The Chinese Room, Street Girl, The President's Girl Friend, The Phantom Gunslinger, Sappho, Darling, Menage a Trois, Two Roses and a Goldenrod, The Friendly Neighbors, Why Me, God?, Tom Jones Rides Again, etc.

ZWICK, EDWARD: Writer, Producer, Director. b. Chicago, IL, Oct. 8, 1952. e. Harvard U., B.A., 1974; American Film Inst. Center for Advanced Film Studies, M.F.A., 1976. Editor and feature writer, The New Republic and Rolling Stone magazines, 1972–74. Author: Literature and Liberalism (1975). Formed Bedford Falls Production Co. with Special Bulletin collaborator Marshall Herskovitz.

PICTURES: About Last Night (dir., debut, 1986), Glory.

TELEVISION: Family (writer, then story editor, dir., prod., Humanitas Prize Award, 1980); Paper Dolls (dir.); Hang It All (dir.); Special Bulletin (writer, prod., dir.; Directors Guild, Writers Guild Awards, 2 Emmys, Humanitas Prize Award, 1983); thirtysomething (exec. prod. with Marshall Herskovitz), Dream Street (exec. prod.).

ZWICK, JOEL: Director. b. Brooklyn, NY, Jan. 11, 1942. e. Brooklyn Coll., B.A., M.A.

THEATER: Dance with Me.

PICTURE: Second Sight.

TELEVISION: Laverne and Shirley; Mork and Mindy; Angie (pilot); It's a Living; Bosom Buddies (pilot); Struck by Lightning (pilot); America 2100; Goodtime Girls; Hot W.A.C.S. (also exec. prod.); Little Darlings; Joanie Loves Chachi; Star of the Family (pilot); The New Odd Couple (and supv. prod.); Webster; Brothers (supv. prod.), Perfect Strangers (and pilot), Full House (and pilot), Family Matters (pilot), Adventures in Babysitting (pilot), Morning Glory (pilot).

ON MICROFILM
MOTION PICTURE
HERALD
MOTION PICTURE
DAILY

Services

Animation

CALIFORNIA

A I A PRODUCTIONS, INC., 15132 LaMaida St., Sherman Oaks, CA 91403; (818) 501-4406.
ADAMS PRODS., 961 Vernon Ave., Venice, CA 90291; (213) 465-6428; 396-3416.
DAVID ALLEN PRODS., 918 W. Oak St., Burbank, CA 91506; (818) 845-9270; 848-0303.
ANGEL ARTS DESIGN INC., 11729 King St., North Hollywood, CA 91607; (818) 763-8023.
APOGEE PRODUCTIONS, INC., 6842 Valjean Ave., Van Nuys, CA 91406; (818) 989-5757.
ARCCA ANIMATION, 279 S. Beverly Hills Dr., Suite 339, Beverly Hills, CA 90212; (213) 271-5928.
AVAILABLE LIGHT LTD., 3110 W. Burbank, Burbank, CA 91505-2313; (818) 842-2109.
BAER ANIMATION CO., 4729 Lankershim Blvd., North Hollywood, CA 91603; (818) 505-0447.
BASS/YAGER & ASSOCS., 7039 Sunset Blvd., Los Angeles, CA 90028; (213) 466-9701.
BOSUSTOW VIDEO, 3030 Pennsylvania Ave., Santa Monica, CA 90404; (213) 453-7973.
BRAVERMAN PRODS. INC., 1861 S. Bundy Dr., Los Angeles, CA 90025; (213) 826-6466.
THE BRUBAKER GROUP, 10560 Dolcedo Way, Los Angeles, CA 90077; (213) 472-4766.
CALICO LTD., 8843 Shirley Ave., Northridge, CA 91324; (818) 885-6663; 701-5862; FAX: (818) 772-1484.
CARTOON A WORLD, 2547 Glen Green, Hollywood, CA 90068; (213) 464-8093.
CELESTIAL MECHANIX INC., 612 Hampton Dr., Venice, CA 90291; (213) 392-8771.
BOB CLAMPETT PRODS. INC., 729 Seward St., Los Angeles, CA 90038; (213) 466-0264.
COAST PRODS., 1001 N. Poinsetta Pl., Los Angeles, CA 90046-6795; (213) 876-2021.
CRUSE & COMPANY, 7000 Romaine St., Hollywood, CA 90038; (213) 851-8814.
DIC ENTERPRISES, INC., 3601 W. Olive, Burbank, CA 91505; (818) 955-5400.
DIGITAL VISION ENTERTAINMENT, 7080 Hollywood Blvd., Los Angeles, CA 90028; (213) 462-3790.
DREAM QUEST INC., 2635 Park Center Dr., Simi Valley, CA 93065; (213) 558-4051.
DREAMLIGHT IMAGES INC., 932 N. La Brea Ave., Suite C, Hollywood, CA 90038; (213) 850-1996.
DUCK SOUP PRODUCTIONS, 1026 Montana Ave., Santa Monica, CA 90403; (213) 451-0771.
ENERGY PRODUCTIONS, 2690 Beachwood Dr., Los Angeles, CA 90068; (213) 462-3310.
FANTASY II FILM EFFECTS, 504 S. Varney, Burbank CA 91502; (818) 843-1413.
FILMFAIR, 10900 Ventura Blvd., Studio City, CA 91604; (818) 766-9441; 766-8770.
FINE ARTS PRODUCTIONS, INC., 3960 Laurel Canyon, Studio City, CA 91604; (818) 506-0928; (213) 874-8114.
FLINT PRODUCTIONS INC., 7758 Sunset Blvd., West Hollywood, CA 90046; (213) 851-1060.
FORMAT PRODUCTIONS INC., 4253 Reyes Dr., Tarzana, CA 91356; (818) 987-2390.
HANNA BARBERA, 3400 W. Cahuenga Blvd., Hollywood, CA 90068; (213) 851-5000.
INTERACTIVE PRODUCTION ASSOCIATES, 3310 Airport Ave., Santa Monica, CA 90405; (213) 390-9466; FAX: (213) 390-7525.
INTROVISION SYSTEMS INC., 1011 N. Fuller Ave., Hollywood, CA 90046; (213) 851-9262; FAX: (213) 851-1649.
JEAN-GUY JACQUE & COMPANY, 13214 Moorpark, Suite 303, Sherman Oaks, 91423; (818) 981-0596.
KURTZ & FRIENDS, 2312 W. Olive Ave., Burbank, CA 91506; (818) 841-8188.
KUSHNER-LOCKE, INC., 10850 Wilshire Blvd., 9th Fl., Los Angeles, CA 90024; (213) 470-0400.
WALTER LANTZ, 4444 Lakeside Dr., Suite 310, Burbank, CA 91505; (818) 569-3625.
WILLIAM LITTLEJOHN PRODS., INC., 23425 Malibu Colony Dr., Malibu, CA 90265; (213) 456-8620.
LUMENI PRODUCTIONS, 1727 N. Ivar Ave., Hollywood, CA 90028; (213) 462-2110; FAX: (213) 462-8250.
MAINSTREET IMAGERY, INC., 13105 Saticoy St., N. Hollywood, CA 91605; (818) 503-0931; FAX: (818) 982-9383.
MARKS COMMUNICATIONS INC., 5550 Wilshire Blvd., Suite 306, Los Angeles, CA 90036; (213) 937-3464; FAX: (213) 937-9659.
McKOWN & COMPANY, P.O. Box 25134, Los Angeles, CA 90025; (213) 479-1941.
FRITZ MILLER ANIMATION/GRAPHICS, 10806 Ventura Blvd., Suite 4, Studio City, CA 91604; (818) 985-6074.
NELVANA, 9000 Sunset Blvd., Suite 911, Los Angeles, CA 90069; (213) 278-8466; FAX: (213) 278-4872.
NEWMAN/FRANKS, 2956 Nicada Dr., Los Angeles, CA 90077; (213) 470-0140; 470-0145; FAX: (213) 470-2410.
OPTICAM, INC., 1653 18 St., Santa Monica, CA 90404; (213) 453-5451.
PLAYHOUSE PICTURES, 1401 N. La Brea Ave., Hollywood, CA 90028; (213) 851-2112.
QUARTET FILMS, INC., 12345 Ventura Blvd., #M, Studio City, CA 91604; (818) 509-0100.
RUBY-SPEARS PRODUCTIONS, 3330 Cahuenga Blvd., W., 2nd Fl., Los Angeles, 90068; (213) 874-5100.
SABAN PRODUCTIONS, 11724 Ventura Blvd., Suite A, Studio City, CA 91604; (818) 985-3805.
SINGLE FRAME FILMS, 437½ N. Genessee Ave., Los Angeles, CA 90036; (213) 655-2664.
SIR REEL PICTURES, 8036 Shady Glade Ave., North Hollywood, CA 91605; (818) 768-9778.
SOUND CONCEPTS INC., 3485 Meier St., Los Angeles, CA 90066; (213) 390-7406.
STOKES/KOHNE, 738 N. Cahuenga Blvd., Hollywood, CA 90038; (213) 469-8176; FAX: (213) 469-0377.
STUDIO PRODUCTION INC., 650 N. Bronson Ave., Suite 223, Hollywood, CA 90004; (213) 856-8048; FAX: (213) 461-4202.
ARNIE WONG TIGERFLY INC., 225 Santa Monica, CA 90401; (213) 458-4194.
RICK ZETTNER & ASSOCIATES, INC., 211 N. Victory Blvd., Burbank, CA 91502; (818) 848-7673; FAX: (818) 841-1917.

ORLANDO

WALT DISNEY/MGM STUDIOS, 1675 Buena Vista Blvd., Lake Buena Vista, FL 32830; (305) 828-1313.

NEW YORK

APA STUDIOS INC., 230 W. 10 St., New York, NY 10014; (212) 929-9436; 675-4894.
ABACUS PRODUCTIONS, 124 E. 24 St., New York, NY 10010; (212) 532-6677.
ALEXANDER, SAM, PRODUCTIONS INC., 311 W. 43 St., New York, NY 10036; (212) 765-5180.
ANI LIVE FILM SERVICE INC., 222 E. 46 St., New York, NY 10017; (212) 983-1918.
ANIMATED PRODUCTIONS, INC., 1600 Broadway, New York, NY 10019; (212) 265-2942.
ANIMOTION, 501 W. Fayette St., Syracuse, NY 13204; (315) 471-3533.
BASKT, EDWARD, 160 W. 96 St., New York, NY 10025; (212) 666-2579.
BEBELL LABS, 420 E. 55th St., Suite 6U, New York, NY 10022; (212) 486-6577.
BECKERMAN, HOWARD, ANIMATION, 25 W. 45 St., New York, NY 10036; (212) 869-0595.
BIGMAN PICTURES, 133 W. 19 St., New York, NY 10011; (212) 242-1411.
BLECHMAN, R.O., 2 W. 47 St., New York, NY 10036; (212) 869-1630.
BROADCAST ARTS, INC., 632 Broadway, 2nd floor, New York, NY 10012; (212) 254-5400.
BROADWAY VIDEO, 1619 Broadway, New York, NY 10019; (212) 265-7600.
ELINOR BUNIN PRODUCTIONS, INC., 30 E. 60 St., New York, NY 10022; (212) 688-0759.
BUZZCO ASSOCIATES, INC., 110 W. 40 St., New York, NY 10010; (212) 840-0411.
CAESAR VIDEO GRAPHICS, INC., 137 E. 25 St., New York, NY 10010; (212) 684-7672.
CELEFEX, 33 W. 67th St., New York, NY 10023; (212) 689-3300.
CHARLEX, 2. W. 45 St., New York, NY 10036; (212) 719-4600.
CHELSEA ANIMATION CO., 36 E. 23 St., New York, NY 10010; (212) 473-6446.
CLARK, IAN 229 E. 96 St., New York, NY 10028; (212) 289-0998.
COREY DESIGN STUDIO, 42 E. 23 St., New York, NY 10010; (212) 529-7238.
DARINO FILMS, 222 Park Ave. S., New York, NY 10003; (212) 228-4024.
DA SILVA INC., 311 E. 85 St., New York, NY 10028; (212) 535-5760.
DATA MOTION ARTS, INC., 231 E. 55 St., 6th Fl., New York, NY 10022; (212) 888-0400; (203) 327-3714.
DOROS ANIMATION STUDIO, INC., 156 Fifth Ave., New York, NY 10010; (212) 627-7220.
EDITEL, 222 E. 44 St., New York, NY 10017; (212) 867-4600.
F-STOP STUDIO, (Gary Becker Animation/Motion Graphics), Suite 901, 114 E. 32 St., New York, NY 10016; (212) 686-2292.
THE FANTASTIC ANIMATION MACHINE, INC., 12 E. 46 St., New York, NY 10017; (212) 697-2525.

FEIGENBAUM PRODUCTIONS, INC., 508 W. 57 St., New York, NY 10019; (212) 246-5099.
FILIGREE FILMS, INC., 155 Ave. of the Americas, 10th floor, New York, NY 10013; (212) 627-1770.
FILM PLANNING ASSOCIATES, INC., 44 W. 24 St., New York, NY 10010; (212) 989-0611.
FOCH, BILL, GRAPHICS, 25 W. 45 St., #203, New York, NY 10036; (212) 921-9414.
J. FREEMAN ASSOCIATES, 221 W. 57th St., New York, NY 10019; (212) 307-6936.
FRIEDMAN, HAROLD, CONSORTIUM, 420 Lexington Ave., New York, NY 10017; (212) 697-0858.
GATI, JOHN, FILM EFFECTS, INC., 154 W. 57 St., Suite 832, New York, NY 10019; (212) 582-9060.
R/GREENBERG ASSOC. INC., 350 W. 39 St., New York, NY 10018; (212) 239-6767; FAX: (212) 947-3769.
GROSSMAN BROS., 19 Crosby St., New York, NY 10013; (212) 925-1965.
HUBLEY STUDIO, 2575 Palisade Ave., Riverdale, NY 10463; (212) 543-5958.
ICE TEA PRODUCTIONS, 307 E. 37 St., New York, NY 10016; (212) 557-8185.
THE INK TANK, 2 W. 47 St., New York, NY 10036; (212) 869-1630.
JSL VIDEO SERVICES, 25 W. 45 St., New York, NY (212) 575-5082.
KCMP PRODUCTIONS, INC. 50 W. 40 St., New York, NY 10018; (212) 944-7766.
KIMMELMAN ANIMATION, 50 W. 40 St., New York, NY 10018; (212) 944-7766.
KURTZ & FRIENDS Block Film Group, 1 Union Sq. W., Suite 211, New York, NY 10003; (212) 989-3535.
K. LANDMAN INC., 156 Fifth Ave., Suite 302, New York, NY 10010; (212) 924-4254.
LIBERTY STUDIOS, INC., 238 E. 26 St., New York, NY 10010, (212) 532-1865.
LIEBMAN, JERRY, PRODUCTIONS, 76 Laight St., New York, NY 10013; (212) 431-3452.
LYONS, ROBERT, 258 17 St., Brooklyn, NY 11215; (718) 788-0335.
MAGNO SOUND & VIDEO, 729 Seventh Ave., New York, NY 10019; (212) 302-2505.
RB/MAVERICKS MOTION GRAPHICS, 35 W. 45 St., New York, NY 10036: (212) 382-2424.
METROPOLIS GRAPHICS, 28 E. 4 St., New York, NY 10003; (212) 677-0630.
MIMONDO PRODUCTIONS LTD., 15 W. 26 St., New York, NY 10010; (212) 686-9620.
MOTIONPICKER STUDIOS, INC., (Clay Animation), 416 Ocean Ave., Brooklyn, NY 11226; (718) 856-2763.
MUSICVISION, INC., 185 E. 85 St., New York, NY 10028; (212) 860-4420.
NEW YORK ANIMATION, 200 W. 79 St., New York, NY 10024; (212) 362-6992.
NOYES & LAYBOURNE ENTERPRISES, INC., 77 Hudson St., New York, NY 10013; (212) 406-7377.
OVATION FILMS INC., 15 W. 26 St., New York, NY 10010; (212) 686-4540.
PAN PRODUCTIONS, 223 Water St., Brooklyn, NY, 11201; (718) 237-1945.
PERPETUAL ANIMATION, INC., 245 Fifth Ave., New York, NY 10016; (212) 481-4120.
PLANET PICTURES, 66 E. 7 St., New York, NY 10003; (212) 477-1032.
POLESTAR FILM & ASSOC., 15 W. 26 St., New York, NY 10010; (212) 213-0806.
PRISM FILM & TAPE, 15 W. 38 St., New York, NY 10018; (212) 944-0420.
RANKIN/BASS PRODUCTIONS 1 E. 53 St., , New York, NY 10022; (212) 759-7721.
REMBRANDT FILMS, 59 E. 54 St., New York, NY 10022; (212) 758-1024.
SELWOOD, MAUREEN, FILMS, 627 West End Ave., New York, NY 10024; (212) 873-0288.
SHADOW LIGHT PRODUCTIONS, INC., 12 W. 27 St., New York, NY 10001; (212) 689-7511.
SPORN, MICHAEL, ANIMATION, 34 W. 38 St., New York, NY 10018; (212) 730-1314.
STREAMLINE FILM MANUFACTURING, 109 E. 29 St., New York, NY 10016; (212) 696-2616.
TELMATED MP, P.O. Box 176, Prince Station, New York, NY 10012; (212) 475-8050.
TELEZIGN, 460 W. 42 St., New York, NY 10036; (212) 279-2000.
VIDEART, INC., 39 W. 38 St., New York, NY 10018; (212) 840-2163.
VIDEO WORKS, 24 W. 40 St., New York, NY 10018; (212) 869-2500.
WALLACH, PETER, PRODUCTIONS, 419 Broome St,. New York, NY (212) 966-1970.
WOO ART INTERNATIONAL, 133 W. 19 St., New York, NY 10011; (212) 989-7870.
ZANDER, MARK, PRODUCTIONS, 118 E. 25 St., New York, NY 10010; (212) 477-3900.

Colorization by Computer

AMERICAN FILM TECHNOLOGIES, 12100 Wilshire Blvd., Los Angeles, CA 90025; (213) 826-4766.
COLOR SYSTEMS TECHNOLOGY, INC., 4553 Glencoe Ave., Marina Del Rey, CA 90292; (213) 822-6567.

Commercial Jingles

CALIFORNIA

ARTSONG MUSIC PRODUCTIONS, 4437 Finley Ave., Los Angeles, CA 90027; (213) 667-0726.
ASSOCIATED PRODUCTION MUSIC, 6255 Sunset Blvd., Suite 724, Hollywood, CA 90028; (213) 461-3211; FAX: (213) 461-9102.
AUSPEX RECORDS, P.O. Box 1740,, Studio City, CA 91604; (213) 877-1078; (818) 763-1955.
BERTUS PRODUCTIONS, 22723 Berdon St., Woodland Hills, CA 91367; (818) 883-1920.
BLUE DOLPHIN PRODUCTIONS, 650 N. Bronson Ave., Hollywood, CA 90004; (213) 467-7660.
MICHAEL BODDICKER, 13630 Ventura Blvd., Sherman Oaks, CA 91423; (818) 981-1136.
BULLETS—TOTAL MUSIC CO., 4520 Callada Place, Tarzana, CA 91356; (818)708-7359.
CALIFORNIA STAR PRODUCTIONS, 8843 Shirley Ave., Northridge, CA 91324; (818) 993-4584.
CANDLEWICK PRODUCTIONS, 1161 N. Highland Ave., Hollywood, CA 90038; (213) 462-7979.
CREATIVE SERVICES GROUP, 5739 Babbitt Ave., Encino, CA 91316; (818) 343-7005.
DANA PRODUCTIONS, 6249 Babcock Ave., North Hollywood, CA 91606; (213) 877-9246.
WILLIAM ERICSON AGENCY, 1024 Mission St., South Pasadena, CA 91030; (213) 461-4969; (818) 799-2404.
RICK FLEISHMAN MUSIC, 5739 Babbitt Ave., Encino, CA 91316; (818) 343-7005.
FULLER SOUND AV RECORDING, 1948 Riverside Dr., Los Angeles, CA 90039; (213) 660-4914.
GRAND STAFF MUSIC PRODUCTIONS, 5740 Tujunga Ave., N. Hollywood, CA 91601; (818) 760-2205.
HLC, 6528 Sunset Blvd., Hollywood, CA 90028; (213) 464-6333.
BRUCE HANIFAN PRODUCTIONS, 9023 Beverlywood St., Los Angeles, CA 90034; (213) 559-4522.
HARK'S SOUND STUDIO, 1041 N. Orange Dr., Hollywood, CA 90038; (213) 463-3288.
CRAIG HARRIS MUSIC, P.O. Box 110, North Hollywood, CA 91603; (818) 508-8000.
HOOK, LINE & SINGERS, 10700 Ventura Blvd., Suite E., North Hollywood, CA 91604; (818) 761-7773.
INTERLOK STUDIOS, 1522 Crossroads of the World, Hollywood, CA 90028; (213) 469-3986.
KAFKA MUSIC CO., P.O. Box 241724, Los Angeles, CA 90024; (213) 556-3723.
L.A./NY MUSIC CO., 9034 Sunset Blvd., Suite 101, Los Angeles, CA 90069; (213) 273-1667.
L.A. TRAX INC., 8033 N. Sunset Blvd., Suite 1010, Los Angeles, CA 90046; (213) 852-1980.
LUBINSKY MUSIC, BAHLER PRODUCTIONS, 1606 N. Highland Ave., Hollywood, CA 90028; (213) 464-1106; FAX: (213) 464-8793.
LEE MAGID INC, P.O. Box 532, Malibu, CA 90265; (213) 463- 5998.
EDDY MANSON PRODUCTIONS, INC., 7245 Hillside Ave., Suite 216, Los Angeles, CA 90046; (213) 874-9318.
McKOWN & COMPANY, P.O. Box 25134, Los Angeles, CA 90025; (213) 479-1941.
911 MUSIC, (213) 850-6911; 850-M911.
RICK NOWELS PRODUCTIONS, 7469 Melrose Ave., Suite 33, Hollywood, CA 90046; (213) 655-7990.
ONE NOTE PRODUCTIONS, 30014 Harvester Rd., Malibu, CA 90265; (213) 457-6670.
TED PERLMAN ARRANGEMENTS, 4519 Coldwater Canyon Ave., Suite 6, Studio City, CA 91607; (818) 762-2758.
PIECE OF CAKE, INC., 4425 Clybourn Ave., North Hollywood, CA 91602; (818) 763-2087.
RITZ & ASSOCIATES ADVERTISING, 636 N. Robertson Blvd., Los Angeles, CA 90069; (213) 652-9813.
RUSK SOUND STUDIO, 1556 N. La Brea Ave., Hollywood, CA 90028; (213) 462-6477.

SHADOE STEVENS PRODUCTIONS, 9100 Sunset Blvd., Suite 113, Los Angeles, CA 90069; (213) 274-1244.
SUNWEST RECORDING STUDIOS, 5533 Sunset Blvd., Los Angeles, CA 90028; (213) 465-1000.
TARTAGLIA MUSIC PRODUCTIONS, 3815 W. Olive Ave., Suite 102, Burbank, CA 91505; (818) 841-3585.
TRIANON RECORDING STUDIOS, 1435 South St., Long Beach, CA 90805; (213) 422-2095.
UNDERSCORE ASSOCIATES, 8306 Wilshire Blvd., Suite 355, Beverly Hills, CA 90211; (818) 845-4000.
WESTLAKE AUDIO, INC., 8447 Beverly Blvd., Los Angeles, CA 90048; (213) 654-2155.
WIRTH-HOWARD PRODUCTIONS, 5706 Ostin St., Woodland Hills, CA 91367; (818) 888-6198.
WORDS & MUSIC, 943 N. Cole, Hollywood, CA 90038; (213) 464-3070.
Y.L.S. PRODUCTIONS, P.O. Box 34, Los Alamitos, CA 90720; (213) 430-2890.

NEW YORK

JOHN ERIC, ALEXANDER MUSIC INC., 311 W. 43 St., Suite 202, New York, NY 10036; (212) 581-8560.
MUSIC MAKERS, INC., 57 W. 57 St., New York, NY 10019; (212) 644-5757.
SHELTON LEIGH PALMER & CO., 19 W. 36 St., New York, NY 10018; (212) 714-1710; 967-6210.

Completion Guarantees and Bonding

CALIFORNIA

A.I.G. ENTERTAINMENT RISKS, 3699 Wilshire Blvd, Los Angeles, CA 90010; (213) 480-3570.
ALEXANDER & ALEXANDER, 3550 Wilshire Blvd., Los Angeles, CA 90010; (213) 385-5211.
AMERICAN NATIONAL GENERAL AGENCIES, INC., 3801 Barham Blvd., Suite 320, Los Angeles, CA 90068-1007; (213) 850-5880; 661-5700; FAX: (213) 850-6138.
BAYLY, MARTIN & FAY INC., 3801 Barham Blvd., Suite 100, Los Angeles, CA 90068-1094; (213) 850-6060; 850-4118.
CINE GUARANTORS INC. (div. Taft Entertainment Co.), 3330 Cahuenga Blvd., Los Angeles, CA 90068; (213) 969-2800.
COHEN INSURANCE, 2121 Ave. of the Stars, Suite 1260, Los Angeles, CA 90067; (213) 277-6540; FAX: (213) 277-0214.
THE COMPLETION BOND COMPANY, INC., 2121 Ave. of the Stars, Suite 830, Century City, CA 90067-5001; (213) 553-8300; FAX: (213) 553-6610.
DE WITT/STERN OF CALIFORNIA, 11365 Ventura Blvd., Suite 113, Studio City, CA 91604; (818) 763-9365; FAX: (818) 762-2242.
DISC INSURANCE SERVICES, 3601 W. Olive Ave., 8th Floor, Burbank, CA 91505; (818) 955-6000.
ENTERTAINMENT COMPLETIONS, INC., 4217 Coldwater Canyon Ave., Studio City, CA 91604; (818) 760-8172.
FILM FINANCES INC., 9000 Sunset Blvd., Suite 808, Los Angeles, CA 90069; (213) 275-7323.
FIREMAN'S FUND INSURANCE CO., Entertainment Industry Div., 2121 Avenue of the Stars, Suite 750, Los Angeles, CA 90067; (213) 282-0160; FAX: (213) 785-9341.
GATEWAY FORWARDERS INTL., 3911 E. Floral Dr., Los Angeles, CA 90063; (213) 261-4833.
GELAND-NEWMAN-WASSERMAN, 11550 W. Olympic Blvd., Suite 404, Los Angeles, CA 90064; (213) 473-2522.
THE HART AGENCY, INC., 6404 Wilshire Blvd., Suite 525, Los Angeles, CA 90048; (213) 653-4634.
HOLLINGSWORTH INSURANCE, 1930 Wilshire Blvd., Los Angeles, CA 90057; (213) 484-2100.
PERCENTERPRISES COMPLETION SERVICES INC., 1801 Ave. of the Stars, #1106, Los Angeles, CA 90067; (213) 551-0371.
PERFORMANCE GUARANTEES INC., 1554 S. Sepulveda Blvd., #102, Los Angeles, CA 90025; (213) 478-3355.
ALBERT G. RUBEN & CO., INC., 2121 Ave. of the Stars, Suite 700, Los Angeles, CA 90067; (213) 551-1101; FAX: (213) 201-0847.
TRUMAN VAN DYKE CO., 6255 Sunset Blvd., Suite 1220, Hollywood, CA 90028; (213) 462-3300; FAX: (213) 462-4857.
WORLDWIDE COMPLETION SERVICES, INC., 9200 Sunset Blvd., #401, Los Angeles, CA 90069, (213) 276-4084; New York office: 888 Seventh Ave., 10106, (212) 489-7666. Services include payroll, cash flow projections, budget analysis, accounting, etc.

NEW YORK

BAYLY, MARTIN & FAY, INC., 10 E. 40th St., New York, NY 10016; (212) 683-8585.
R. A. BOYAR (div. Marsh & McLennon), 1221 Avenue of Americas, New York, NY 10020; (212) 997-7400.
BC BURNHAM & COMPANY, 130 William St., New York, NY 10038; 482 Hudson Terrace, Box 1096, Englewood Cliffs, NJ 07632; (212) 563-7000.
COHEN INSURANCE, 225 W. 34th St., New York, NY 10122; (212) 244-8075.
DE WITT STERN, GUTMANN CO., 420 Lexington Ave., New York, NY 10170; (212) 867-3550.
ENTERTAINMENT INSURANCE NETWORK, 15 W. 44th St., New York, NY 10036; (212) 840-2866.
D. R. REIFF & ASSOCIATES, 221 W. 57th St., New York, NY 10019; (212) 877-1099; 603-0231.
RICHMAR BROKERAGE, 310 Northern Blvd., Great Neck, NY 11021; (718) 895-7151; (516) 829-5200.
ALBERT G. RUBEN & CO., 48 W. 25 St., 12 Floor, New York, NY 10010; (212) 627-7400.

Consultants

CALIFORNIA

BLUE MOUNTAIN PRODUCTIONS INC., 1800 N. Highland Ave., #411, Hollywood, CA 90068; (213) 464-0871.
THE CORPORATE SEAL, 1310 N. Cherokee Ave., Los Angeles, CA 90028; (213) 464-8357.
CREATIVE ENTERPRISE INTL. INC., 6630 Sunset Blvd., Hollywood, CA 90028; (213) 466-1237.
CAROLE LIEBERMAN (Psychiatric Script Consultant), 247 S. Beverly Dr., Beverly Hills, CA 90212; (213) 456-2458.
M 2 RESEARCH, 1020 N. La Brea Ave., Los Angeles, CA 90038; (213) 464-7414.
MARSHALL/PLUMB RESEARCH ASSOCIATES (Legal research, script clearances), 4150 Riverside Dr., Suite 212, Burbank, CA 91505; (818) 848-7071.
MIRAMAR ENTERPRISES, P.O. Box 4621, N. Hollywood, CA 91607; (818) 784-4177.
MOTION PICTURE MARINE, 616 Venice Blvd., Marina Del Rey, CA 90291; (213) 822-1100.
2nd UNIT INC., 616 Venice Blvd., Venice, CA 90291; (213) 822-8648.

NEW YORK

BENNER MEDICAL PRODUCTIONS, INC., 446 E. 86 St., #6-D, New York, NY 10028; (212) 737-7402.
BOOZ, ALLEN & HAMILTON INC., 101 Park Ave., New York, NY 10178; (212) 697-1900.
BROADCAST BUSINESS CONSULTANTS, LTD., 41 E. 42 St., New York, NY 10017; (212) 687-3525.
CONSULTANTS FOR TALENT PAYMENT INC., 22 W. 27 St., New York, NY 10001; (212) 696-1100.
COOPER & CO., 28 W. 25 St., 12 Fl., New York, NY 10010-2705; (212) 243-3434.
DALE SYSTEM INC., 1101 Stewart Ave., Garden City, NY 11530; (516) 794-2800; 250 W. 57 St., New York, NY 10107; (212) 586-1320.
DE WITT MEDIA INC., 250 W. 57 St., New York, NY 10107; (212) 713-1890.
DELTA CONSULTANTS INC., 333 W. 52 St., #410, New York, NY 10019; (212) 245-2570.
FILM COUNSELORS, INC., 630 Ninth Ave., New York, NY 10019; (212) 315-3950.
GRAPHIC MEDIA COMMUNICATIONS, 12 W. 27 St., 12th floor, New York, NY 10001; (212) 696-0880.
IMAGE TECHNOLOGY, 10 E. 18 St., 3 Fl., New York, NY 10003-1904; (212) 463-0385.
KOLMOR VISIONS INT'L LTD., 286 Fifth Ave., New York, NY 10001; (212) 947-7517.
MEDIA RESOURCES ASSOCS., 420 E. 64 St., #W2H, New York, NY 10021; (212) 935-9040.
PRODUCTION MANAGEMENT ASSOCS., 333 W. 42 St., #2901, New York, NY 10036; (212) 594-6766.
REEVES COMMUNICATIONS CORP., 708 Third Ave., New York, NY 10017; (212) 573-8888; 573-8600.
ROSS-GAFFNEY, 21 W. 46 St., New York, NY 10036; (212) 719-2744.
SECOND LINE SEARCH, 330 W. 42 St., #2901, New York, NY 10036; (212) 594-5544.
SOUND ENTERPRISES, 305 E. 40 St., #18G, New York, NY 10016; (212) 986-2097.

Costumes & Uniforms

NEW YORK

AAA ACADEMY TUXEDOS, Broadway & 54th St., New York, NY 10019; (212) 765-1440.
ALLAN UNIFORM RENTAL SERVICE INC., 112 E. 23 St., New York, NY 10010; (212) 529-4655.
ANIMAL OUTFITS FOR PEOPLE CO., 2255 Broadway, New York, NY 10023; (212) 877-5085.
CHENKO STUDIO, 167 W. 46 St., New York, NY 10036; (212) 944-0215.
COSTUME ARMOUR INC., 2 Mill St., Cornwall-on-Hudson, NY 12520; (914) 534-9120.
COSTUME COSTUME, 330 W. 38 St., New York, NY 10018; (212) 564-9541.
THE COSTUME SHOP INC., 114 W. 26 St., New York, NY 10001; (212) 255-2345.
CREATIVE COSTUME CO., 330 W. 38 St., New York, NY 10018; (212) 564-5552.
DAVID'S OUTFITTERS, INC., 36 W. 20 St., New York, NY 10011; (212) 691-7388.
DOMSEY INTERNATIONAL SALES CORP., 734 Broadway, New York, NY 10003; (212) 505-5411; (718) 384-6000.
EAVES-BROOKS COSTUME CO., INC., 21-07 41st Ave., Long Island City, NY 11101; (718) 729-1010.
HOUSE OF COSTUMES LTD., 166 Jericho Turnpike, Mineola, NY 11501; (516) 294-0170.
IN COSTUME, 37 W. 20 St., New York, NY 10011; (212) 255-5502.
IZQUIERDO STUDIOS, 118 W. 22 St., New York, NY 10011; (212) 807-9757.
LAZAR, CATHY, COSTUMES & SOFT PROPS, 155 E. 23 St., New York, NY 10010; (212) 473-0363.
LILLIAN COSTUME CO. OF L.I. INC. 226 Jericho Turnpike, Mineola, NY 11501; (516) 746-6060.
ODDS RENTAL, 233 W. 42 St., #506, New York, NY 10036; (212) 575-5927.
RUBIE'S COSTUME CO., INC., 120-08 Jamaica Ave., Richmond Hill, Queens, NY 11418; (718) 846-1008.
UNIVERSAL COSTUME CO., INC., 535 Eighth Ave., New York, NY 10018; (212) 239-3222.

WEST COAST

ADELE'S OF HOLLYWOOD, 5034 Hollywood Blvd., Los Angeles, 90027; (213) 663-2231.
AMERICAN COSTUME CORP., 12980 Raymer St., North Hollywood, CA 91605; (818) 764-2239.
BERMANS COSTUME CO., 2019 Stradella Rd., Los Angeles, CA 90077; (213) 472-1844.
BUENA VISTA STUDIOS, 500 S. Buena Vista St., Burbank, CA 91521; (818) 560-0044.
THE BURBANK STUDIOS, 4000 Warner Blvd., Burbank, CA 91522; (818) 954-6000.
C. T. G. COSTUME SHOP, 3301 E. 14th St., Los Angeles, CA 90023; (213) 267-1230.
CALIFORNIA COSTUME/NORCOSTO, 5867 Lankershim Blvd., N. Hollywood, CA 91601; (818) 760-2911; (213) 461-6555.
CENTER THEATRE GROUP COSTUME SHOP, 3301 E. 14th St., Los Angeles, CA 90023; (213) 267-1230.
THE COSTUME PLACE, 7211 Santa Monica Blvd., Los Angeles, CA 90046; (213) 876-7979.
COSTUME RENTALS CO., 7007 Lankershim Blvd., North Hollywood, CA 91605; (818) 765-8877; FAX: (818) 503-1913.
ELIZABETH COURTNEY COSTUMES, 8636 Melrose Ave., Los Angeles, CA; (213) 657-4360.
DRESSED TO KILL, INC., 8762 Holloway Dr., W. Hollywood, CA 90069; (213) 652-4334.
E. C. 2 COSTUMES, 431 S. Fairfax Ave., Los Angeles, CA 90036; (213) 934-1131; 934-1138.
FANTASY COSTUMES, 4649½ San Fernando Rd., Glendale, CA 91204; (213) 245-7367.
FORMAL TOUCH ANTIQUE TUXEDO SERVICE, 842 N. Fairfax Ave., Los Angeles, CA 90046; (213) 658-5553.
HOLLYWOOD TOYS & COSTUMES, 6562 Hollywood Blvd., Hollywood, CA 90028; (213) 465-3119.
INTERNATIONAL COSTUME, 1269 Sartori Ave., Torrance, CA 90501; (213) 320-6392.
ELIZABETH LUCAS COLLECTION, 1021 Montana Ave., Santa Monica, CA 90403; (213) 451-4058.
PALACE COSTUME COMPANY, 835 N. Fairfax Ave., Los Angeles, CA 90046; (213) 651-5458.
SOMEWHERE IN TIME COSTUMES, 98 E. Colorado Blvd., Pasadena, CA 91105; (818) 792-7503.
THE STUDIO WARDROBE DEPT., P.O. Box 3158, Van Nuys, CA 91407; (818) 781-4267.
TUXEDO CENTER, 7360 Sunset Blvd., Los Angeles, 90046; (213) 874-4200.
URSULA'S COSTUMES INC., 9067 Venice Blvd., Los Angeles, CA 90034; (213) 559-8210.
VALLEY STUDIO, 150 W. Cypress Ave., Suite G, Burbank, CA 91502; (818) 843-1861.
WESTERN COSTUME CO., 5335 Melrose Ave., Hollywood, CA 90038; (213) 469-1451.
J. WIGGENS THEATRICAL WARDROBE, 11853 Kling, Suite 23, N. Hollywood, CA 91607; (818) 762-4819.

Cutting Rooms

LOS ANGELES

ASTROFILM SERVICE, 932 N. La Brea Ave., Los Angeles, CA 90038; (213) 851-1673.
CANNON SOUND STUDIOS, 640 S. San Vicente Blvd., Los Angeles, CA 90048; (213) 658-2012.
CREST NATIONAL FILM & VIDEOTAPE LABS, 1141 N. Seward St., Hollywood, CA 90038; (213) 466-0624; 462-6696; FAX: (213) 461-8901.
DELTA PRODUCTIONS, 3333 Glendale, Suite 3, Los Angeles, CA 90039; (213) 663-8754.
THE EDITING COMPANY, 8300 Beverly Blvd., Los Angeles, CA 90048; (213) 653-3570.
THE FILM PLACE, 1311 N. Highland Ave., Los Angeles, CA 90028; (213) 464-0116.
INDEPENDENT PRODUCERS STUDIO INC., 1741 N. Ivar Ave., Suite 109, Hollywood, CA 90028; (213) 461-6966.
JHD SOUND, 12156 Olympic Blvd., Los Angeles, CA 90064-1079; (213) 820-8802.
MOVIE TECH INC., 832 N. Seward St., Hollywood, CA 90038; (213) 467-8491; 467-5423; FAX: (213) 467-8471.
PRODUCTIONS WEST, 6311 Romaine, Suite 7319-25, Los Angeles, CA 90038; (213) 464-0169.
TRIO VISUAL, 4907 N. Lankershim Blvd., N. Hollywood, CA 91601; (818) 762-1182.
UNIVERSAL FACILITIES RENTAL DIV., 100 Universal City Plaza, Universal City, CA 91608; (818) 777-3000; 777-2731.
YAMAHA INTERNATIONAL CORP., P.O. Box 6600, Buena Park, CA 90622; (714) 522-9011.

NEW YORK

ANIMATED PRODS., INC., 1600 Broadway, New York, NY 10019; (212) 265-2942.
ANOMALY FILMS, 135 Hudson St., New York, NY 10013; (212) 925-1500.
ARCHIVE FILM PRODUCTIONS, 530 W. 25 St., New York, NY 10001; (212) 929-7543.
CAMERA MART, THE, 456 W. 55 St., New York, NY 10019; (212) 757-6977.
JOHN CARTER ASSOCS., INC., 300 W. 55 St., #10-V, New York, NY 10019; (212) 541-7006.
CINERGY COMMUNICATIONS CORP., 321 W. 44 St., 10036; (212) 582-2900.
CINEMA ARTS ASSOCS., INC., 333 W. 52 St., New York, NY 10019; (212) 246-2860.
CINETUDES FILM PRODS., 295 W. 4 St., New York, NY 10014; (212) 924-0400.
CUTTING EDGE ENTERPRISES, 630 Ninth Ave., 14th floor, New York, NY 10036; (212) 541-9664.
DARINO FILMS, 222 Park Ave. S, #2A, New York, NY 10003; (212) 228-4024.
EARTHRISE PRODUCTIONS, 1974 Broadway, #200, New York, NY 10023; (212) 724-3250.
EASY EDIT, 630 Ninth Ave., New York, NY 10036; (212) 541-9664.
THE EDITING MACHINE, INC., 630 Ninth Ave., New York, NY 10036; (212) 757-5420.
FILM/VIDEO ARTS INC., 817 Broadway, 2nd floor, New York, NY 10003-4797; (212) 673-9361.
KEM EDITING SYSTEMS, INC., 653 11 Ave., New York, NY 10024; (212) 765-2868.
KOPEL FILMS INC., 630 Ninth Ave., #910, New York, NY 10036; (212) 757-4742.
MAGNO SOUND & VIDEO, 729 Seventh Ave., New York, NY 10019; (212) 302-2505.
MAYSLES FILM INC., 250 W. 54 St., New York, NY 10019; (212) 582-6050.
THE MULTIVIDEO GROUP LTD., 50 E. 42 St., #1107, New York, NY 10017; (212) 986-1577; 972-1015.
NATIONAL BROADCASTING CO., 30 Rockefeller Plaza, #412, New York, NY 10112; (212) 664-4754.

PHANTASMAGORIA PRODS., 630 Ninth Ave., #801, New York, NY 10036; (212) 586-4890.
REFLECTIONS XXII M.P. CO., 263 W. 54 St., New York, NY 10019; (212) 247-5370.
ROBERT RICHTER PRODS., INC. 330 W. 42 St., New York, NY 10036; (212) 947-1395.
ROSS-GAFFNEY, INC., 21 W. 46 St., New York, NY 10036; (212) 719-2744.
TONY SILVER FILMS INC., 242 E. 58 St., New York, NY 10022; (212) 826-6336.
SOUND ONE CORP., 1619 Broadway, 8th floor, New York, NY 10019; (212) 765-4757.
TODD-AO STUDIOS EAST, 254, 259 W. 54 St., New York, NY 10019; (212) 265-6225.
UPTOWN EDIT, 21 W. 86 St., New York, NY 10024; (212) 580-2075.
VALKHN FILMS INC., 1600 Broadway, Suite 404, New York, NY 10019; (212) 586-1603.

Editing Equipment

LOS ANGELES

AMETHYST STUDIOS, 7000 Santa Monica Blvd., Hollywood, CA 90038; (213) 467-3700.
AMPEX CORP., 340 Parkside Dr., San Fernando, CA 91340; (818) 365-8627.
ASTROFILM SERVICE, 932 N. La Brea Ave., Los Angeles, CA 90038; (213) 851-1673.
BEXEL CORP., 801 S. Main St., Burbank, CA 91506; (818) 841-5051.
BIRNS & SAWYER, INC., 1026 N. Highland Ave., Hollywood, CA 90038; (213) 466-8211; FAX: (213) 466-7049.
CALIFORNIA COMMS. INC., 6900 Santa Monica Blvd., Los Angeles, CA 90038; (213) 466-8511.
CHENOWETH FILMS, 1860 E. N. Hills Dr., La Habra, CA 90631; (213) 691-1652.
CHRISTY'S, 135 N. Victory, Burbank, CA 91502; (818) 845-1755; (213) 849-1148.
CINE MAGIC & ASSOCIATES, 11121 Salt Lake Ave., Northridge, CA 91326; (818) 845-7651.
CINEDCO, 1125 Grand Central Ave., Glendale, CA 91201-2425, (818) 502-9100; FAX: (818) 502-0052.
CINEMA PRODUCTS CORP., 3211 S. La Cienega Blvd., Los Angeles, CA 90016-3112; (213) 836-7991.
CRAIG PRODUCTIONS, 6314 La Mirada Ave., Los Angeles, CA 90038; (213) 476-7146.
EAGLE EYE FILM COMPANY, 4019 Tujunga Ave., P.O. Box 1968, Studio City, CA 91604; (818) 506-6100.
EDIQUIP, 6820 Romaine St., Hollywood, CA 90038; (213) 467-3107.
ALAN GORDON ENTERPRISES, INC., 1430 Cahuenga Blvd., Hollywood, CA 90028; (213) 466-3561; (818) 985-5500; FAX: (213) 871-2193.
THE GRASS VALLEY GROUP INC., 21243 Ventura Blvd., #143, Woodland Hills, CA 91364; (818) 999-2303.
HOLLYWOOD FILM CO., 3294 E. 26th St., Los Angeles, CA 90023; (213) 462-3284.
J & R FILM CO., INC., 6820 Romaine St., Hollywood, CA 90038; (213) 467-3107.
JACOBSON, GARY, 1248 S. Fairfax, Malibu, CA 90019; (213) 937-6588.
KEM WEST INC., 5417 N. Cahuenga Blvd., Suite A, N. Hollywood, CA 91601; (213) 850-0200.
MAGNASYNC/MOVIELA CORP. P.O. Box 707, 5539 Riverton Ave., North Hollywood, CA 91601,; (818) 763-8441.
MARKET STREET SOUND, 73 Market St., Venice, CA 90291; (213) 396-5937; (818) 842-4441.
NEWMAN/FRANKS, 2956 Nicada Dr., Los Angeles, CA 90077; (213) 470-0140; 470-0145; FAX: (213) 470-2410.
PLASTIC REEL CORP. OF AMERICA, 8140 Webb Ave., North Hollywood, CA 91605; (818) 504-0400.
RBC ENTERPRISES, 1860 E. North Hills Dr., La Habra, CA 90631; (213) 691-1652.
GLENN ROLAND FILMS, 10711 Wellworth Ave., Los Angeles, CA 90024; (213) 475-0937.
RUBBER DUBBERS, INC., 626 Justin Ave., Glendale, CA 91201; (818) 241-5600.
SPECTRA SYSTEMS, INC., 2040 N. Lincoln St., Burbank, CA 91504; (818) 842-1111.
STEENBECK INC., 9554 Vasser Ave., Chatsworth, CA 91311; (818) 998-4033.
VIDEO SUPPORT SERVICES, 3473½ Cahuenga Blvd., W. Los Angeles, CA 90068; (213) 469-9000.

ORLANDO

THE POST GROUP, % Walt Disney/MGM Studios, Roy O. Disney Production Center, Lake Buena Vista, FL 32830; (407) 560-5600.

NEW YORK

BROADCAST EQUIPMENT SUPPLY CORP., Box 7460, Rego Park, Queens, NY 11374; (718) 843-6839.
THE CAMERA MART, INC., 456 W. 55 St., New York, NY 10019; (212) 757-6977.
CAMERA SERVICE CENTER INC., 625 W. 54 St., New York, NY 10019; (212) 757-0906.
CINERGY COMMUNICATIONS, CORP., 321 W. 44 St., New York, NY 10036; (212) 582-2900.
COMPREHENSIVE SERVICE AV INC., Box 881, New York, NY 10108; (212) 586-6161.
CUTTING EDGE, 630 Ninth Ave., New York, NY 10036; (212) 541-9664.
EASY EDIT, 630 Ninth Ave., New York, NY 10036; (212) 541-9664.
THE EDITING MACHINE, 630 Ninth Ave. #1000 New York, NY 10036; (212) 757-5420.
J & R FILM CO., INC., 636 Eleventh Ave., New York, NY 10036; (212) 247-0972.
KEM EDITING SYSTEMS, 315 W. 57 St., New York, NY 10019; (212) 582-7338.
LAUMIC CO., INC., 306 E. 39 St., New York, NY 10016; (212) 889-3300.
MPCS VIDEO INDUSTRIES INC., 514 W. 57 St., New York, NY 10019; (212) 586-3690; (800) 223-0622.
MAYSLES FILM, INC., 250 W. 54 St., New York, NY 10019; (212) 582-6050.
MONTAGE GROUP LTD., 1 W. 85 St., New York, NY 10024; (212) 362-0892.
MOTION PICTURES ENTERPRISES, INC. 430 W. 45 St., New York, NY 10036; (212) 245-0969.
NEUMADE, P.O. Box 5001, Norwalk, CT 06856; (203) 866-7600.
PLASTIC REEL CORP. OF AMERICA, Brisbin Ave., Lyndhurst, NJ 07071; (201) 933-5100; (212) 541-6464.
PREVIEW EQUIPMENT CO., 432 W. 45 St., New York, NY 10036; (212) 245-0969.
ROSS-GAFFNEY INC., 21 W. 46 St., 9th floor, New York, NY 10036; (212) 719-2744.
SPERA CORP., 511 W. 33 St., New York, NY 10001-1302; (212) 629-0009.
STUDIO FILM & TAPE INC., 630 Ninth Ave., New York, NY 10036; (212) 977-9330.

Editing Services

LOS ANGELES

ACE & EDIE 2, 722 N. Seward St., Los Angeles, CA 90038; (213) 462-2185; FAX: (213) 461-4993.
ADVENTURE FILM & TAPE, 1034 N. Seward St., Hollywood, CA 90038; (213) 460-4557.
ALTER IMAGE, 113 N. Naomi St., Burbank, CA 91505; (818) 842-5870.
ASTROFILM SERVICE, 932 N. La Brea Ave., Los Angeles, CA 90038; (213) 851-1673.
AVAILABLE LIGHT LTD., 3110 W. Burbank Blvd., Burbank, CA 91505; (818) 842-2109.
THE BURBANK STUDIOS, 4000 Warner Blvd., Burbank, CA 91522; (818) 954-6000.
CFI (CONSOLIDATED FILM INDUSTRIES), 959 Seward St., Hollywood, CA 90038; (213) 462-3161; 960-7444; FAX: (213) 460-4885.
CHRISTY'S EDITORIAL FILM SUPPLY, INC., 135 N. Victory Blvd., Burbank, CA 91502; (818) 845-1755; (213) 849-1148; FAX: (213) 849-2048.
THE CINEASTE GROUP, 812 N. Highland Ave., Hollywood, CA 90038; (213) 464-8158.
COMPACT VIDEO SERVICES, INC., 2813 W. Alameda Ave., Burbank, CA 91505; (818) 840-7000; (800) 423-2277.
CRAWFORD EDITORIAL, 2440 El Contento Dr., Hollywood, CA 90068; (213) 462-2818.
CROSS CUTS, 1330 N. Vine St., Hollywood, CA 90028; (213) 465-2292.
THE CULVER STUDIOS, 9336 W. Washington Blvd., Culver City, CA 90230; (213) 202-3396; 836-5537.
DELTA PRODUCTIONS, 3333 Glendale Blvd., Suite 3, Los Angeles, CA 90039; (213) 663-8754.
EAGLE EYE FILM CO., 4019 Tujunga Ave., P.O. Box 1968, Studio City, CA 91604; (818) 506-6100.
ECHO FILM SERVICES, INC., 4119 Burbank Blvd., Burbank, CA 91505; (818) 841-4114.

THE EDITING COMPANY, 8300 Beverly Blvd., Los Angeles, CA 90048; (213) 653-3570.
ELECTRONIC ARTS & TECHNOLOGY, 3655 Motor Ave., Los Angeles, CA 90034; (213) 836-2556.
FILM CORE, 849 N. Seward St., Hollywood, 90038; (213) 464-7303.
FILM PLACE, THE, 1311 N. Highland Ave., Los Angeles 90028; (213) 464-0116.
FILMSERVICE LABORATORIES, INC., 1019 N. Cole Ave., Suite 5, Los Angeles, CA 90038; (213) 464-5141.
525 POST PRODUCTION, 6425 Santa Monica Blvd., Hollywood, CA 90038; (213) 466-3348; FAX: (213) 467-1589.
FREUD & KLEPPEL INC., 6290 Sunset Blvd., #603, Los Angeles, CA 90028; (213) 469-1444.
HOLLYWOOD ASSOCIATES, INC., 359 E. Magnolia Blvd., Suite G, Burbank, CA 91502.
IMAGE TRANSFORM LAB., 4142 Lankershim Blvd., No. Hollywood, CA 91602; (818) 985-7566; (800) 423-2652.
INDEPENDENT PRODUCERS STUDIO INC., 1741 N. Ivar Ave., Suite 109, Hollywood, CA 90028; (213) 461-6966.
KEM WEST, 5417 N. Cahuenga Blvd., Suite A, North Hollywood, CA 91601; (213) 850-0200.
LASER EDIT, INC., 540 N. Hollywood Way, Burbank, CA 91505; (818) 842-0777.
LION'S GATE STUDIOS, 1861 S. Bundy Dr., Los Angeles, CA 90025; (213) 820-7751; FAX: (213) 315-2110.
MATHERS, JIM, FILM COMPANY, P.O. Box 1973, Studio City, CA 91604; (818) 762-2214.
MOFFIT, WILLIAM ASSOCS., 747 N. Lake Ave., #B, Pasadena, CA 91104; (818) 791-2559.
MOVIE TECH INC., 832 N. Seward St., Hollywood, CA 90038; (213) 467-8491; 467-5423; FAX: (213) 467-8471.
PARAMOUNT STUDIO GROUP, 5555 Melrose Ave., Hollywood 90038; (213) 468-5000.
POST PLUS INC., 6650 Santa Monica Blvd., 2nd floor, Hollywood, CA 90038; (213) 463-7108.
PRO VIDEO/CINETAPE, 801 N. La Brea Ave., Los Angeles, CA 90038; (213) 934-8836; 934-8840.
THE PRODUCTION GROUP, 1330 N. Vine St., Los Angeles, CA 90028; (213) 469-8111; FAX: (213) 462-0836.
RED CAR, 1040 N. Las Palmas Ave., Los Angeles, CA 90038; (213) 466-4467; FAX: (213) 466-4925.
REEL THING OF CALIFORNIA INC., 1253 N. Vine St., Suite 14, Hollywood, CA 90038; (213) 466-8588.
RENCHER'S EDITORIAL SERVICE, 738 Cahuenga Blvd., Hollywood, CA 90038; (213) 463-9836.
TELEVISION CENTER, 6311 Romaine St., Los Angeles, CA 90038; (213) 464-6638.
UNIVERSAL FACILITIES RENTAL DIVISION, 100 Universal City Plaza, Universal City 91608; (818) 777-3000; 777-2731.
WARNER HOLLYWOOD STUDIOS, 1041 N. Formosa Ave., W. Hollywood, CA 90046; (213) 850-2500.
WILDWOOD FILM SERVICE, 6855 Santa Monica Blvd., Suite 400, Los Angeles, CA 90038; (213) 462-6388.
WOLLIN PRODUCTION SERVICES, INC., 666 N. Robertson Blvd., Los Angeles, CA 90069; (213) 659-0175.

NEW YORK

A & R, INC., 214 E. 49 St., New York, NY 10017; (212) 371-3221.
ALSCHULER, JANE & CO., 1180 Ave. of the Americas, 10th Floor, New York, NY 10036; (212) 790-4813.
ANI-LIVE FILM SERVICE, INC., 45 W 45 St., New York, NY 10036; (212) 819-0700.
ANIMATED PRODS., INC., 1600 Broadway, 10019; (212) 265-2942.
ANOTHER DIRECTION, 231 E. 51 St., 10022; (212) 753-8250.
BACKSTREET EDIT, INC., 49 W. 27 St., New York, NY 10001; (212) 684-5001.
BENDER EDITORIAL SERVICE, INC., 27 E. 39 St., New York, NY 10016; (212) 867- 1515.
BERT'S PLACE, 141 E. 44 St., New York, NY 10017; (212) 682-5891.
B. CANARICK'S CO., LTD., 50 E. 42 St., New York, NY 10017; (212) 972-1015.
CHARLES, MICHAEL, EDITORIAL, 6 E. 45 St., New York, NY 10017; (212) 953-2490.
CHUNG GROUP, INC., 11 E. 47 St., 5th floor, New York, NY 10017; (212) 832-0530.
CINE METRIC, INC., 290 Madison Ave., New York, NY 10017; (212) 532-4140.
CINE TAPE, INC., 241 E. 51 St., New York, NY 10022; (212) 355-0070.
CRESCENT CUTTERS, INC., 304 E. 45 St., New York, NY 10017; (212) 687-2802.
CREW CUTS FILM & TAPE, INC., 9 E. 47 St., New York, NY 10017; (212) 371-4545.
A CUT ABOVE, EDITORIAL INC., 17 E. 45 St., New York, NY 10017; (212) 661-4949.
THE CUTTING EDGE/EDITORIAL, 420 Lexington Ave., New York, NY 10017; (212) 599-4233.
DJM FILMS, INC., 4 E. 46 St., New York, NY 10017; (212) 687-0404; 687-0111.
DEE, DAVID, 62 W. 45 St., New York, NY 10036; (212) 764-4700.
DELL, JEFF, ENTERPRISES, INC., 241 E. 51 St., New York, NY 10022; (212) 371-7915.
EDITING CONCEPTS, 214 E. 50 St., New York, NY 10022; (212) 980-3340.
THE EDITING HOUSE, INC., 250 E. 48 St., New York, NY 10017; (212) 688-8280.
THE EDITORS, 220 E. 48 St., New York, NY 10017; (212) 371-0862.
EDITORS CORNER, 415 E. 71 St., New York, NY 10021; (212) 535-8668.
EDITOR'S GAS, 16 E. 48 St., New York, NY 10017; (212) 832-6690.
EDITORS HIDEAWAY, INC., 219 E. 44 St., New York, NY 10022; (212) 661-3850.
EDITORS SCENE INC., 250 E. 48 St., New York, NY 10017; (212) 688-8280.
FILM BILLDERS, 10 E. 40 St., New York, NY 10016; (212) 683-4004.
FILM-RITE, INC., 1185 Ave. of the Americas, New York, NY 10036; (212) 575-6801.
FINAMORE, D.P., 619 W. 54 St., New York, NY 10019; (212) 582-5265.
FIRST CUT PRODUCTION, 16 W. 45 St., New York, NY 10036; (212) 869-8198.
FIRST EDITION/COMPOSITE FILMS, 5 E. 47 St., New York, NY 10017; (212) 838-3044.
FREDERIC FISCHER FILMS, 28 Verandah Pl., Brooklyn, NY 11201; (718) 852-2643.
GOLD, JAY, INC., 342 Madison Ave., #424, New York, NY 10173; (212) 681-7171.
GRENADIER PRODS., INC., 220 E. 23 St., New York, NY 10010; (212) 545-0388.
GROVE, ERIC, FILM, 32 W. 22 St., New York, NY 10010; (212) 242-7447.
HARVEY'S PLACE, 919 Third Ave., New York, NY 10022; (212) 688-5510.
HAYES, DENNIS, FILM EDITING, INC., 9 E. 40 St., New York, NY 10016; (213) 683-5080.
HORN/EISENBERG FILM & TAPE EDITING, 16 W. 46 St., New York, NY 10036; (212) 391-8166.
HOROWITZ, ROBERT, FILMS, 321 W. 44 St., New York, NY 10036; (212) 397-9380.
HUDSON, SCOTT, EDITORIAL, 25 W. 43 St., New York, NY 10036; (212) 840-3860.
JPC VISUALS, 11 E. 47 St., New York, NY 10017; (212) 223-0555.
ROBERT JUBIN LTD., 11 E. 47 St., New York, NY 10017; (212) 319-4747.
JUPITER EDITORIAL SERVICE, 201 E. 16 St., New York, NY 10003, (212) 460-5600.
KOPEL FILMS, INC., 630 Ninth Ave., New York, NY 10036; (212) 757-4742.
LFR EDITORIAL, INC., 20 E. 46 St., New York, NY 10017; (212) 682-5950.
LANDA, SAUL, INC., 35 W. 87 St., New York, NY 10024; (212) 877-5553; 764-4700.
MBC EDITORIAL INC., 241 E. 51 St., New York, NY 10022; (212) 371-7915.
MAGNO SOUND & VIDEO, 729 Seventh Ave., 10019; (212) 302-2505.
MESSINA EDITORIAL, INC., 18 E. 41 St., New York, NY 10017; (212) 481-3456.
MS EDITORIAL, INC. 200 W. 57 St., Suite 901, New York, NY 10019; (212) 333-7590.
MORTY'S FILM SERVICES, LTD., 10 E. 40 St., New York, NY 10016; (212) 696-5040.
OASIS FILM & TAPE EDITORIAL SERVICES, INC., 141 E. 44 St., New York, NY 10017; (212) 983-3131.
P.A.T. FILM SERVICES, 630 Ninth Ave., New York, NY 10036; (212) 247-0900.
PDR PRODUCTIONS, INC., 219 E. 44 St., New York, NY 10017; (212) 986-2020.
PALESTRINI FILM EDITING, INC., 575 Lexington Ave., New York, NY 10022; (212) 752-EDIT.
PELCO EDITORIAL INC., 757 Third Ave., New York, NY 10017; (212) 319-EDIT.
PHOTOSONIC EDITING, INC., 420 Lexington Ave., New York, NY 10017; (212) 599-4233.
PINEYRO, GLORIA, FILM SERVICES CORP., 19 W. 21 St., New York, NY 10010; (212) 627-0707.
POWER POST PRODUCTION, 25 W. 43 St., New York, NY 10036; (212) 840-3860.
REBELEDIT, 292 Madison Ave., 26th Floor, New York, NY 10017; (212) 686-8622.
REFLECTIONS XXII M.P. CO., 263 W. 54 St., New York, NY 10019; (212) 247-5370.

RICH ENTERPRISES CORP., 15 W. 26 St., New York, NY 10010; (212) 685-0040.
ROSEBUD PRODUCTIONS, INC., 141 E. 44 St., New York, NY 10017; (212) 972-8895.
ROSS-GAFFNEY, INC., 21 W. 46 St., New York, NY 10036; (212) 719-2744; 997-1464.
SG VIDEO, 16 W. 22 St., New York, NY 10010; (212) 691-1414.
SALAMANDRA IMAGES, INC., 6 E. 39 St., New York, NY 10016; (212) 779-0707.
SANDPIPER EDITORIAL SERVICE, 50 W. 40 St., New York, NY 10018; (212) 921-1570.
SELIGMAN, MAX, P.O. Box 710, Jackson Heights, NY 11372; (718) 803-0885.
SOLOMON, LAURENCE, FILM GROUP, 244 W. 49th St., Suite 400, New York, NY 10019; (212) 582-6246.
SPECTRUM ASSOCS. INC., 536 W. 29 St., New York, NY 10001, (212) 563-1680.
SPLICE IS NICE, 141 E. 44 St., New York, NY 10017; (212) 599-1711.
START MARK, 16 E. 52 St., New York, NY 10022; (212) 935-9160.
STONE-CUTTERS, 422 Madison Ave., New York, NY 10017; (212) 421-9404.
SYLIANOU, MICHEL, PRODUCTIONS, NC., 301 Madison Ave., New York, NY 10017; (212) 687-5708.
SYNCRO FILM SERVICES, INC., 72 W. 45 St., New York, NY 10036; (212) 719-2966.
TAKE 5 EDITORIAL SERVICES, INC., 681 Lexington Ave., New York, NY 10022; (212) 759-7404.
THE TAPE HOUSE EDITORIAL, 216 E. 45 St., New York, NY 10017; (212) 557-4949.
TAPESTRY PRODUCTIONS, LTD., 924 Broadway, 2nd floor, New York, NY 10010; (212) 677-6007.
THE TRAILER SHOP, INC., 21 W. 46 St., New York, NY 10036; (212) 944-0318.
TRAIMAN, HENRY, ASSOCIATES, 160 Madison Ave., New York, NY 10016; (212) 889-3400.
VALKHN FILMS INC., 1600 Broadway, Suite 406, New York, NY 10019; (212) 586-1603.
WACHTER, GARY, EDITORIAL, INC., 159 W. 53 St., New York, NY 10019; (212) 399-7770.
WARMFLASH PRODUCTIONS, INC., 630 Ninth Ave., New York, NY 10036; (212) 757-5969.
WESTBROOK FILM SERVICE INC., 118 E. 25 St., 8 Floor, New York, NY 10010; (212) 254-9563.
WILLIAMS, BILLY, EDITORIAL, 231 E. 51 St., New York, NY 10022; (212) 753-8250.
WORLD CINEVISION SERVICES, INC., 321 W. 44 St., New York, NY 10036; (212) 265-4587.

Film Processing Labs

ATLANTA

CINEFILM LABORATORY, 2156 Faulkner Rd., N.E., 30324; (404) 633-1448; (800) 633-1448.
SOUTHERN FILM LAB INC., 2050-H Chamblee Tucker Rd., Chamblee, GA 30341; (404) 458-0026.

BOSTON

CINE SERVICE LABORATORIES, INC., 1380 Soldiers Field Rd., Brighton, 02135; (617) 254-7882.
DU ART BOSTON/NEW ENGLAND, 650 Beacon St., 02215; (617) 267-8717; 969-0666.
FILM SERVICE LAB, 93 Harvey St., Cambridge, MA 02140; (617) 542-8501.
SPORTS FILM LAB, 361 W. Broadway, South Boston 02127; (617) 268-8388.

CHICAGO

ALLIED FILM & VIDEO SERVICES, 1322 W. Belmont Ave., 60657; (312) 348-0373.
ASTRO COLOR LAB, 61 W. Erie, 60610; (312) 280-5500.
CINEMA VIDEO CENTER, 211 E. Grand Ave., 60611; (312) 527-4050.
EASTMAN KODAK CO., 1331 Business Center Dr., Mt. Prospect 60056; (312) 635-5900.
FILMACK, 1327 S. Wabash, 60605; (312) 427-3395.
SPECTRUM MOTION PICTURE LAB, 399 Gundersen, Carol Stream, IL 60187; (312) 665-4242; (800) 345-6522.

COLUMBIA, SC

SOUTHEASTERN FILM COMPANY, 3604 Main St., 29203; (803) 252-3753.

COLUMBUS, OH

JOHN R. BENNETT, 2553 Cleveland Ave., 43211; (614) 267-7007.

DALLAS

ALLIED & WBS FILM & VIDEO SERVICES, 4 Dallas Communications Complex, #111, Irving 75039; (214) 869-0100.
SOUTHWEST FILM LABORATORY, INC., 3024 Fort Worth Ave., 75211; (214) 331-8347.

DAYTON, OH

VALDHERE INC., 3060 Valleywood Dr., Dayton, 45429; (513) 293-2191.

DETROIT

FILM CRAFT LAB., INC., 66 Sibley, 48201; (313) 962-2611.
MULTI-MEDIA INC., 7154 E. Nevada St., 48234; (313) 366- 5200.
PRODUCERS COLOR SERVICE, 2921 E. Grand Blvd., 48202; (313) 874-1112.
WILLIAMS SERVICE, 601 W. Fort, 48226; (313) 962-9070.

HOLLYWOOD-LOS ANGELES

ALPHA CINE LABORATORY INC., 5724 W. Third St., Suite 311, Los Angeles, 90036; (213) 934-6307.
ASHLAND FILM LAB., 747 N. Seward St., Hollywood 90038; (213) 462-3231.
AUDIO VISUAL HEADQUARTERS CORP., 361 N. Oak, Inglewood 90302; (213) 419-4040.
BROADCAST STANDARDS, INC., 2044 Cottner Ave., Los Angeles, 90025; (213) 312-9060.
CINESERVICE, INC., 6518½ Santa Monica Blvd., Los Angeles, 90038; (213) 463-3178.
CONRAD FILM DUPLICATING COMPANY, 6750 Santa Monica Blvd., Hollywood, 90038; (213) 463-5614.
CONSOLIDATED FILM INDUSTRIES, 959 N. Seward St., Hollywood, 90038; (213) 960-7444; FAX: (213) 460-4885.
CREST NATIONAL FILM & VIDEO LABS, 1141 N. Seward St., Hollywood, 90038; (213) 466-0624; 462-6696; FAX: (213) 461-8901.
DELUXE LABORATORIES, INC., 1377 N. Serrano Ave., Hollywood, 90027; (213) 462-6171; (800) 2DE-LUXE.
EASTMAN KODAK LABORATORY 1017 N. Las Palmas Ave., Los Angeles, 90038; (213) 465-7152; (800) 621-1234.
FILM TECHNOLOGY CO. INC., 6900 Santa Monica Blvd., Los Angeles, 90038; (213) 464-3456
FILMSERVICE & VIDEO LABS, INC., 1019 N. Cole Ave., Suite 5, Hollywood, 90038; (213) 464-5141.
FLORA COLOR, 1715 N. Mariposa, Hollywood, CA 90027; (213) 663-2291.
FOTO-KEM FOTO-TRONICS, FILM-VIDEO LAB, 2800 W. Olive Ave., Burbank, 91505; (818) 846-3101; FAX: (818) 841-2040.
FOTORAMA, 1507 N. Cahuenga Blvd., Los Angeles, 90028; (213) 469-1578.
GETTY FILM LAB, 7641 Densmore Ave., Van Nuys, CA 91406; (818) 997-7801.
HOLLYWOOD FILM & VIDEO INC., 6060 Sunset Blvd., Hollywood, 90028; (213) 464-2181; FAX: (213) 464-0893.
HOLMES, FRANK, LABORATORIES, 1947 First St., San Fernando, 91340; (818) 365-4501.
IMAGE TRANSFORM LABORATORY, 3611 N. San Fernando Rd., Burbank, 91505; (818) 841-3812.
MGM/UA LABS., INC. 10202 W. Washington Blvd., Culver City, 90230; (213) 558-5858.
METROCOLOR LAB, (div. of Lorimar Telepictures), 10202 W. Washington Blvd., Culver City, 90232-3783; (213) 280-5858; 280-8000.
MORCRAFT FILMS, 837 N. Cahuenga Blvd., Los Angeles, 90038; (213) 464-2009.
MULTI-LAB, 1633 Maria St., Burbank, 91504; (213) 465-9970.
NEWELL COLOR LAB, 221 N. Westmoreland Ave., Los Angeles, 90004; (213) 380-2980.
NEWSFILM LABORATORY, INC., 516 N. Larchmont Blvd., Hollywood, 90004; (213) 462-6814.
PACIFIC FILM LABORATORIES, 835 N. Seward, Los Angeles, 90038; (213) 461-9921.
PACIFIC TITLE & ART STUDIO, 6350 Santa Monica Blvd., Los Angeles, 90038; (213) 464-0121; 938-3711.
PEERLESS FILM PROCESSING CORP., 920 Allen Ave., Glendale, 91201; (818) 242-2181.
RGB COLOR LAB, 816 N. Highland Ave., Los Angeles, 90038; (213) 469-1959.
SINA'S CUSTOM LAB, 3136 Wilshire Blvd., Los Angeles, 90010; (213) 381-5161.

SUPER CINE, INC., 2214 W. Olive Ave., Burbank, 91506; (818) 843-8260.
TECHNICOLOR INC., (Professional Film Division), 4050 Lankershim Bl., North Hollywood, 91608; (818) 769-8500.
UNITED COLOR LAB. INC., 835 N. Seward, Hollywood, 90038; (213) 461-9921; 469-7291.
UNIVERSAL FACILITIES RENTAL DIVISION, 100 Universal City Plaza, Universal City, 91608; (818) 777-3000; 777-2731.
YALE LABS, 1509 N. Gordon St., Los Angeles, 90028; (213) 464-6181.

HOUSTON

THE PHOTOGRAPHIC LABORATORIES, 1926 W. Gray, 77019; (713) 527-9300.

MEMPHIS, TN

MOTION PICTURE LABORATORIES, INC., 781 S. Main St. 38101; (901) 774-4944; (800) 444-4675.

MIAMI, FL

CONTINENTAL FILM LABS, INC., 1998 Northeast 150 St., N. Miami, 33181; (305) 949-4252; (800) 327-8296.

MILWAUKEE, WI

CENTRAL FILM LABORATORY & PHOTO SUPPLY, 1003 North Third St., 53203; (414) 272-0606.

NEW ORLEANS

PAN AMERICAN FILMS, 822 N. Rampart St., 70116; (504) 522-5364.

NEW YORK CITY

A-1 REVERSE-O-LAB INC., 333 W. 39 St., 10018; (212) 239-9530.
ACCURATE FILM LABS, 45 W. 45 St., 10036; (212) 730-0555.
ACCUTREAT FILM, INC., 630 Ninth Ave., 10036; (212) 247-3415.
CINE MAGNETICS FILM & VIDEO, 50 W. 40 St., 10018; (212) 921-1299.
DELUXE GENERAL INC., 630 Ninth Ave., 10036; (212) 489-8800.
DU-ART FILM LABORATORIES, 245 W. 55 St., 10019; (212) 757-4580.
GUFFANTI FILM LABORATORIES INC., 630 Ninth Ave., 10036; (212) 265-5530.
HBO STUDIO PRODS., 120A E. 23 St., 10010; (212) 512-7800.
J & D LABS INC., 12 W. 21 St., 10010; (212) 691-5613.
JAN FILM LAB, INC., 302 W. 37 St., 10018; (212) 279-5438.
KIN-O-LUX, INC., 17 W. 45 St., 10036; (212) 869-5595.
LAB-LINK, INC., 115 W. 45 St., 10036; (212) 302-7373.
KEN LIEBERMAN LABORATORIES INC., 118 W. 22 St., 10011; (212) 633-0500.
MAGNO SOUND & VIDEO, 729 Seventh Ave., 10019; (212) 302-2505; FAX: (212) 819-1282.
MAGNO VISUALS, 115 W. 45 St., 10036; (212) 575-5162; 575-5159.
MILLENNIUM FILM WORK SHOP, 66 E. 4 St., 10003; (212) 673-0090.
MOVIELAB INC., 619 W. 54 St., 10019; (212) 586-0360.
PRECISION FILM & VIDEO LABS, 630 Ninth Ave., 10036; (212) 489-8800.
STUDIO FILM & VIDEO LABS INC., 321 W. 44 St. #512, 10036; (212) 582-5578.
STUDIO WEST LTD., 321 W. 44 St., #504, 10036; (212) 489-1190.
TVC LABS, INC., 311 W. 43 St., 10036; (212) 397-8600; Outside NY: (800) 225-6566.
TECHNICOLOR INC., 321 W. 44 St., 10036; (212) 582-7310.
VAN CHROMES CORP., 21 W. 46 St., 10036; (212) 302-5700.

OMAHA

CORNHUSKER FILM PROCESSING LAB, 1817 Vinton St., 68108; (402) 341-4290.

PITTSBURGH

WRS MOTION PICTURE LAB., 210 Semple St., 15213; (412) 687-3700.

PORTLAND OR

TEKNIFILM INC., 909 N.W. 19th, 97209; (503) 224-3835.

SALT LAKE CITY, UT

ALPHA CINE LAB. INC., 450 S. 900 St., #205, 84102; (801) 363-9465.

SAN FRANCISCO

DINER/ALLIED FILM & VIDEO, 620 Third St., 94107; (415) 777-1700.
HIGHLAND LABS., 840 Battery St., 94111; (415) 981-5010.
LUCASFILM LTD., P.O. Box 2009, San Rafael, CA 94912; (415) 662-1800.
MONACO LABORATORIES, INC., 234 Ninth St., 94103; (415) 864-5350.

SEATTLE, WA

ALPHA CINE LABORATORY, 1001 Lenora St., 98121; (206) 682-8230; (800) 426-7070.
FORDE MOTION PICTURE LABORATORY, 306 Fairview Ave. N., 98109; (206) 682-2510; (800) 682-2510.

SPRINGFIELD, MA

PENFIELD PRODUCTIONS LTD., 35 Springfield St., Agawarm 01001; (413) 786-4454.

TAMPA, FL

BEACON FILM LABORATORY, 8029 N. Nebraska Ave.; (813) 932-9636.

Film Preservation

ACCUTREAT FILMS, INC., 630 Ninth Ave., #1101, New York, NY 10036; (212) 247-3415.
AFD/PHOTOGRAD FILM COATING LAB, 1015 N. Cahuenga Blvd., Hollywood, CA 90038; (213) 469-8141.
BARTCO CO., 924 N. Formosa, Hollywood, CA 90046; (213) 851-5411.
BONDED SERVICES, 5260 Vineland Ave., N. Hollywood, CA 91601; (818) 761-4058; FAX: (818) 761-5939.
DELTA PRODUCTIONS, 3333 Glendale Blvd., Suite 3, Los Angeles, CA 90039; (213) 663-8754.
DURAFILM CO., 137 No. La Brea Ave., Hollywood, CA 90036; (213) 936-1156.
FILMLIFE INCORPORATED, Filmlife Bldg., 141 Moonachie Road, Moonachie, NJ 07074; (201) 440-8500.
FILMTREAT INTERNATIONAL CORP., 42-24 Orchard St., Long Island City, NY 11101; (718) 784-4040. Y. W. Mociuk, pres. (See display ad on P. 365.)
FILMTREAT WEST CORP., 12326 Montague Lane, Pacoima, CA 91331; (818) 506-3276.
HOLLYWOOD VAULTS, 742 N. Seward St., Los Angeles, CA 90038; (213) 461-6464; (805) 569-5336.
INTERNATIONAL CINE SERVICES, INC., 733 Salem St., Glendale, CA 91203; (818) 242-3839.
PEERLESS FILM PROCESSING CORPORATION, 42-24 Orchard St., Long Island City, NY 11101; (718) 784-4040. Y. M. Mociuk, pres.
PERMAFILM NORTH AMERICA CORP., 280 High St., Milford, CT 06460; (203) 877-7746.
PRODUCERS FILM CENTER, 948 N. Sycamore Ave., Los Angeles, CA 90038; (213) 851-1122.
TITRA FILM CALIFORNIA INC., 733 Salem St., Glendale, CA 91203; (818) 244-3663.
WESTERN FILM INDUSTRIES, 30941 W. Agoura Rd., Suite 302, Westlake Village, CA 91361; (818) 889-7350; FAX: (818) 707-3937.

Film Storage Vaults

ATLANTA

BENTON FILM FORWARDING CO., 168 Baker St., N.W.; (404) 577-2821.

FORT LEE, NJ

BONDED FILM STORAGE, service & storage: 550 Main St., Fort Lee, NJ 07024; (212) 557-6732; (201) 944-3700.
BONDED SERVICES, exec. offices: 2050 Center Ave., 07024; (201) 592-7868; (212) 695-2034 (NY).
FORT LEE FILM STORAGE & SERVICE, 504 Jane St., 07024; (201) 944-1030.

HOLLYWOOD-LOS ANGELES

(Hollywood studios have their own storage vaults)

AMERICAN ARCHIVES, INC., 11120 Weddington St., North Hollywood, 91601; (818) 506-STOR; (818) 506-6688.
ARCHIVES FOR ADVANCED MEDIA, 838 N. Seward St., Los Angeles, 90038; (213) 466-2454.
BEKINS RECORDS MANAGEMENT, 1025 N. Highland Ave., Hollywood, 90038; (213) 466-9271.
BELL & HOWELL RECORDS MANAGEMENT, 1025 N. Highland Ave., Los Angeles, 90038; (213) 466-9271.
BONDED SERVICES, 5260 Vineland Ave., North Hollywood, 91601; (818) 761-4058; FAX: (818) 761-5939.
BRAKEWATER TRANSPORT, INC., 8401 E. Slauson Ave., Pico Rivera, CA 90660; (213) 949-6639.
CONSOLIDATED FILM INDUSTRIES, 959 N. Seward St., Hollywood CA 90038; (213) 462-3161. (Stores only film which Consolidated Laboratory is handling.)
RAY HACKIE FILM SERVICE, 1738 Cordova St., Los Angeles, 90007; (213) 734-5418; (213) 737-6062.
HOLLYWOOD FILM CO., 5446 Carlton Way, Hollywood, 90027; (213) 462-1971; 462-3284; FAX: (213) 263-9665.
HOLLYWOOD VAULTS, INC., Vault: 742 N. Seward St., Hollywood 90038; Office: 1780 Prospect Ave., Santa Barbara, CA 93103; (805) 569-5336; FAX: (805) 569-1657.
INTERNATIONAL CINE SERVICES, INC., 733 Salem St., Glendale, 91203; (818) 242-3839.
TYLIE JONES/WEST, 3519 W. Pacific Ave., Burbank, 91505; (818) 955-7600, (818) 980-7300.
PACIFIC TITLE ARCHIVES, 4800 San Vicente Blvd., Los Angeles, 90019; (213) 938-3711; 561 Mateo St., Los Angeles, 90013; (213) 617-8650; 617-8405; FAX: (213) 938-6364; 10717 Vanowen St., N. Hollywood, 91605; (818) 760-4223.
PRODUCERS FILM CENTER, 948 N. Sycamore Ave., Hollywood, 90038; (213) 851-1122.
S.A. GLOBEL STUDIOS, 201 N. Occidental Blvd., Los Angeles, 90026; (213) 384-3331.
TAPE-FILM INDUSTRIES (TFI), 941 N. Highland Ave., Hollywood 90038; (213) 461-3361.
THEATRE TRANSIT, INC., 8401 E. Slauson Ave., Pico Rivera, 90660; (213) 949-6659.
THE VAULT WORKS, 7306 Coldwater Canyon Ave., North Hollywood 91605; (818) 764-0685.

NEW YORK CITY

ANI LIVE FILM SERVICE, INC., 222 E. 46 St., 10017; (212) 983-1918.
BEKINS RECORDS MANAGEMENT, 609 W. 51 St., 10019; (212) 489-7890.
BELL & HOWELL RECORDS MGT., 609 W. 51 St., 10019; (212) 489-7890; 225 Varick St.; New York, NY 10014; (212) 645-0868.
BONDED SERVICES, 250 W. 57 St., 10019; (212) 956-2212; 550 Main St., Ft. Lee, NJ; (212) 557-6733; (201) 944-3700.
PAT FILM SERVICES, INC., 630 Ninth Ave., 10036; (212) 247-0900.
RAPID FILM TECHNIQUE, INC., 37-02 27th St., Long Island City, 11101; (212) 786-4600.
TAPE-FILM INDUSTRIES, 619 W. 54 St., 10019; (212) 708-0500.

Financing Companies & Banking Services

J.E. ANDARY PRODUCTIONS & FINANCING, 7080 Hollywood Blvd. #114, Los Angeles, CA 90028; (213) 466-3379.
BANK OF AMERICA Entertainment Industries Division, 555 S. Flower St., Los Angeles, CA 90071; (213) 228-4096.
BANK OF BEVERLY HILLS, 9808 Wilshire Blvd., Suite 207, Beverly Hills, CA 90212; (213) 274-9240.
BANK OF CALIFORNIA Entertainment Division, 9401 Wilshire Blvd., Beverly Hills, CA 90212; (213) 273-7200; 205-3035; FAX: (213) 273-9030.
BANK OF NEW YORK, 530 Fifth Ave., New York, NY 10036; (212) 536-9109.
BANKERS TRUST, Media Division, 280 Park Ave., 15th floor, New York, NY 10017; (212) 850-3220.
CAMDEN ENTERTAINMENT FINANCE INC., 9454 Wilshire Blvd., #650, Beverly Hills, CA 90212; (213) 659-5317.
CHARTER FINANCIAL INC., One Rockefeller Plaza, New York, NY 10020; (212) 399-7777.
CHASE MANHATTAN BANK, N.A., Media & Communications Component, 1 Chase Manhattan Plaza, 5th floor, New York, NY 10081; (212) 552-2222; 552-4848.
CHEMICAL BANK Entertainment Industries Group, 277 Park Ave., New York, NY 10172; (212) 310-5624; 333 S. Grand Ave., Suite 2600, Los Angeles, CA 90071; (213) 5057; 253-5006.
CINEMA GROUP, 8758 Venice Blvd., Los Angeles, CA 90034; (213) 204-0102.
CINEREP SERVICES, 28 Avenue 28th, Marina Del Rey, CA 90291; (213) 305-1394.
CITICORP, USA, INC., 725 S. Figueroa St., Los Angeles, CA 90017; (213) 239-1400; 239-1800.
CITY NATIONAL BANK Entertainment Division, 400 N. Roxbury Dr., Suite 400, Beverly Hills, CA 90210; (213) 550-5696.
CONSTANT FINANCIAL SERVICES INC., 8749 Holloway Dr., Los Angeles, CA 90069; (213) 650-5227.
THE CROCKER BANK, Entertainment Industries Group, 10100 Santa Monica Blvd., Suite 420-A, Los Angeles, CA 90067; (213) 253-3300.
DnC AMERICA BANKING CORP., 600 Fifth Ave., 16th Floor, New York, NY 10020; (212) 315-6581.
EUROPEAN AMERICAN BANK, Entertainment Finance, 10 Hanover Sq., New York, NY 10015; (212) 437-2275.
FILM FINANCES, INC., 9000 Sunset Blvd., Suite 808, Los Angeles, CA 90069; (213) 275-7323; FAX: (213) 275-1706; TELEX: 183-205.
FIRST BANK NATIONAL ASSOCIATION, Entertainment Division, 444 S. Flower St., Suite 1730, Los Angeles, CA 90017; (213) 623-8267.
FIRST CHARTER BANK Entertainment Division, 265 N. Beverly Drive, Beverly Hills, CA 90210; (213) 275-2225.
FIRST INTERSTATE BANK OF CALIFORNIA, Entertainment Division, 9601 Wilshire Blvd., Beverly Hills, CA 90210; (213) 858-5585.
FIRST LOS ANGELES BANK Entertainment Division, 9595 Wilshire Blvd., Beverly Hills, CA 90212; (213) 557-1211.
FLEET CREDIT CORPORATION, 3990 Westerly Place, Suite 100, Newport Beach, CA 92660; (714) 955-2574.
GOLCHAN, FREDERIC PRODUCTIONS, 4000 Warner Blvd. Production One, Room 104A, Burbank, CA 91505; (818) 854-2418.
HERITAGE ENTERTAINMENT, INC., 11500 W. Olympic Blvd., Suite 300, Los Angeles, CA 90064; (213) 477-8100.
HILTON FINANCIAL GROUP, INC., 3500 W. Olive Ave., Suite 740, Burbank, CA 91505; (818) 953-4161.
IMPERIAL BANKING, Entertainment Banking, 9777 Wilshire Blvd., Beverly Hills, CA 90212; (213) 858-1430.
INDEPENDENT PRODUCTION RESOURCES, INC., (a unit of M.C.E.G. Inc.), 575 Fifth Ave., Suite 24C, New York, NY 10017; (212) 983-5799; FAX: (212) 867-1565.
THE LEWIS HORWITZ ORGANIZATION, 1840 Century Park East, Los Angeles, CA 90067; (213) 275-7171.
M.C.E.G. (Management Co. Entertainment Group Inc.), 11355 Olympic Blvd., #500, Los Angeles, CA 90064; (213) 208-8899; 575 Fifth Ave., #24-C, New York, NY 10017; (212) 983-5799.
MERCANTILE NATIONAL BANK, 1840 Century Park East, Los Angeles, CA 90067; (213) 277-2265.
METRO BANK Entertainment Division, 10900 Wilshire Blvd., 3rd floor, Los Angeles, CA 90024; (213) 824-5700.
MOTION PICTURES INVESTMENT CO., 430 S. Burnside Ave., Los Angeles, CA 90036; (213) 931-9241.
PHOENIX FINANCIAL GROUP, 630 Third Ave., New York, NY 10017; (212) 687-2121.
SECURITY PACIFIC MERCHANT BANK, 333 S. Hope St., H14-60, Los Angeles, CA 90071; (213) 345-5353; 345-5343.
SPECTRUM ENTERTAINMENT LTD., 8800 Sunset Blvd, Suite 302, Los Angeles, CA 90069; (213) 855-1412.
TOKAI BANK OF CALIFORNIA, 200 E. Colorado Blvd., Pasadena, CA 91105; (818) 570-6391.
TOUCHE ROSS, 2029 Century Park E., Suite 300, Los Angeles, CA 90067-2900; (213) 551-6700; FAX: (213) 284-9029.
UNION BANK, 9460 Wilshire Blvd., 1st Floor, Beverly Hills, CA 90213; (213) 550-6627; 550-6617; FAX: (213) 859-3813.
WALKER CORPORATE FINANCIAL CONSULTING, P.O. Box 93-543, Sunset Station, Hollywood, CA 90093.
WELLS FARGO BANK Entertainment Division, 9600 Santa Monica Blvd., Beverly Hills, CA 92010; (213) 550-2262; FAX: (213) 859-9958.
WESTERN SECURITY BANK, ENTERTAINMENT DIVISION, 4100 W. Alameda Ave., Toluca Lake, CA 91505; (818) 843-0707.

Lighting Equipment

CALIFORNIA

ACEY-DECY EQUIPMENT CO., 5420 Vineland Ave., N. Hollywood, CA 91601; (818) 766-9445; FAX: (818) 766-4758.
ADCO EQUIPMENT, INC., 605 Freeway at Rose Hill Rd., P.O. Box 2100, City of Industry, CA 91746; (213) 695-0748; (714) 670-0333.
AMERICAN NEONICS, INC., 5542 Satsuma Ave., North Hollywood, CA 91601; (818) 982-0316; (213) 875-1815; FAX: (818) 985-2364.
AMETRON RENTALS, 1200 N. Vine St., Hollywood, CA 90038; (213) 466-4321.

AUTOMATED STUDIO LIGHTING, 545 Rodier St., Glendale, CA 91201; (818) 500-1646.

BARDWELL & MC ALISTER INC., 2621 Empire Ave., Burbank, CA 91504; (213) 849-5533; (818) 843-6821.

BERC (BROADCAST EQUIPMENT RENTAL COMPANY), 4545 Chermak St., Burbank, CA 91505; (818) 841-3000; (213) 464-7655; FAX: (818) 841-7919.

BERLIN LIGHTING & GENERATORS, 9315 Burnet Ave., Sepulveda, CA 91343; (818) 341-5105.

BIFROST EFFECTS/LASERFX, 6733 Sale Ave., Canoga Park, CA 91307; (818) 704-0423.

BIRNS & SAWYER INC., 1026 N. Highland Ave., Hollywood, CA 90038; (213) 466-8211; FAX: (213) 466-7049.

BUENA VISTA STUDIOS, 500 S. Buena Vista St., Burbank, CA 91521; (818) 560-0044.

THE BURBANK STUDIOS, 4000 Warner Blvd., Burbank, CA 91522; (818) 954-6000.

CALIFORNIA VIDEO CENTER, 5432 W. 102 St., Los Angeles, CA 90045; (213) 216-5400; (213) 216-5400; FAX: (213) 216-5498.

CASTEX RENTALS, INC., 1044 N. Cole Ave., Los Angeles, CA 90038; (213) 462-1468.

CHINDIT EQUIPMENT CO., 717 S. Victory Blvd., Burbank, CA 91502; (818) 842-1817.

CINE VIDEO, 948 N. Cahuenga Blvd., Hollywood, CA 90038; (213) 464-6200.

CINELEASE INC., 2020 N. Lincoln St., Burbank, CA 91504; (818) 841-8282.

CINEVANS LOCATION EQUIPMENT, P.O. Box 2390, Toluca Lake Station, North Hollywood, CA 91602; (818) 846-5386.

CINEWORKS—CINERENTS, 1119 N. Hudson Ave., Los Angeles, CA 90038; (213) 464-0296.

COOL LIGHT COMPANY INC., 5723 Auckland Ave., North Hollywood, CA 91601; (818) 761-6116.

CUSTOM NEON, 2210 S. La Brea Ave., Los Angeles, CA 90016; (213) 937-NEON.

EXPENDABLE SUPPLY STORE, 7830 N. San Fernando Rd., Sun Valley, CA 91352; (818) 767-5065; (213) 875-2409; 1316 N. Western Ave., Hollywood, CA 90027; (213) 465-3191; FAX: (818) 768-2422.

EXPENDABLES PLUS (Div. of Cinelease Inc.), 140 S. Victory Blvd., Burbank, CA 91502; (818) 842-4800; FAX: (818) 954-9641.

FAX COMPANY, 1430 N. Cahuenga Blvd., Hollywood, CA 90028; (213) 466-3561; (818) 985-5500; FAX: (213) 871-2193.

FILMTRUCKS, INC., 1116 Gault St., N. Hollywood, CA 91605; (818) 764-9900; (213) 243-1500.

FIORENTINO IMERO ASSOCIATES, 7060 Hollywood Blvd., Suite 1000, Los Angeles, CA 90028; (213) 467-4020.

G-FORCE INTERNATIONAL ENTERTAINMENT CORP., 279 S. Beverly Dr., Suite 1038, Beverly Hills, CA 90212; (213) 271-0700.

GMT STUDIOS, 5751 Buckingham Pkway, Unit C, Culver City, CA 90230; (213) 649-3733.

ALAN GORDON ENTERPRISES, INC., 1430 N. Cahuenga Blvd, Hollywood, CA 90028; (213) 466-3561; (818) 985-5500; FAX: (213) 871-2193.

HARRAH'S THEATRE SERVICE & SUPPLY, 624B S. San Fernando Blvd., Burbank, CA 91502; (818) 842-5111; FAX: (818) 842-4141.

HARRIS, DENNY, INC., OF CALIFORNIA, 12166 W. Olympic Blvd., Los Angeles, CA 90064; (213) 826-6565.

HOFFMAN VIDEO SYSTEMS, 870 N. Vine St., Hollywood, CA 90038; (213) 465-6900.

HOLLYWOOD CENTER STUDIOS INC., 1040 N. Las Palmas Ave., Los Angeles, CA 90038; (213) 469-5000; FAX: (213) 871-8105.

HOLLYWOOD RENTAL COMPANY, INC., 7848 N. San Fernando Rd., Sun Valley, CA 91352; (818) 768-8018; (213) 849-1326; FAX: (818) 768-2422.

INTER VIDEO/TRITRONICS, INC., 733 N. Victory Blvd., Burbank, CA 91502; (818) 843-3633; 569-4000; FAX: (818) 843-6884.

J & L SERVICE, 10555 Victory Blvd., North Hollywood, CA 91606; (818) 508-7780.

JLW STUDIO RENTALS, 8033 Sunset Blvd., Suite 5010, Los Angeles, CA 90046; (818) 763-4965.

KEYLITE PSI, 333 S. Front St., Burbank, CA 91502; (818) 841-5483; FAX: (818) 843-9546.

L.A. MARQUEE INC., 12023 Ventura Blvd., Studio City, CA 91604; (818) 505-6572.

LASER MEDIA, INC., 2046 Armacost Ave., Los Angeles, CA 90025; (213) 820-3750; FAX: (213) 207-9630.

LEE AMERICA WEST INC., 3620 Valhalla Dr., Burbank, CA 91505; (818) 848-1111; FAX: (818) 848-1381.

LEE COLORTRAN, INC., 1015 Chestnut St., Burbank, CA 91506; (818) 843-1200; FAX: (818) 954-8520.

LEONETTI CINE RENTALS, 5609 Sunset Blvd., Los Angeles, CA 90028; (213) 469-2987; FAX: (213) 469-9223.

LEXUS LIGHTING, INC., 7562 San Fernando Rd., Sun Valley, CA 91352; (818) 768-4508.

LOWEY & CO., 2307 Castilian Dr., Hollywood, CA 90068; (213) 876-7808.

LTM CORP. OF AMERICA, 11646 Pendleton St., Sun Valley, CA 91352; (213) 460-6166.

MOLE-RICHARDSON CO., 937 N. Sycamore Ave., Hollywood, CA 90038; (213) 851-0111; FAX: (213) 851-5593.

NIGHTS OF NEON, 7337 Varna Ave., N. Hollywood, CA 91605; (818) 982-3592; FAX: (818) 503-1090.

NORCOSTCO, INC., 5867 Lankershim Blvd., N. Hollywood, CA 91601; (213) 461-6555; (818) 760-2911; FAX: (818) 980-4737.

ONE PASS FILM & VIDEO, One China Basin Bldg., San Francisco, CA 94107; (415) 777-5777.

THE PALADIN GROUP, INC., 7356 Santa Monica, Los Angeles, CA 90046; (213) 851-8222.

PALINKO'S STUDIO, 9901 Edmore Pl., Sun Valley, CA 91352; (818) 767-5925; 768-2013.

PROFESSIONAL DESIGN PRODUCTS, INC., 5123 Dahlia Dr., P.O. Box 41174, Los Angeles, CA 90041; (213) 257-2121; FAX: (213) 257-7520.

RALEIGH STUDIOS, 650 N. Bronson Ave., Los Angeles, CA 90004; (213) 466-3111; FAX: (213) 871-4428.

ROSCO LABORATORIES INC., 1135 N. Highland Ave., Hollywood, CA 90038; (213) 462-2233.

S.A. GLOBAL STUDIOS, 201 N. Occidental Blvd., Los Angeles, CA 90026; (213) 384-3331.

THE SHOTMAKER/LIGHTMAKER COMPANY, 28145 Avenue Crocker, Valencia, CA 91355; (805) 257-1444; (800) 426-6284; FAX: (805) 257-6197.

S.I.R. LIGHTING INC., 6048 Sunset Blvd., Hollywood, CA 90028; (213) 466-3417; 466-1314.

SPRINGBOARD STUDIOS, 12229 Montague St., Arleta, CA 91331; (818) 896-4321.

STRAND CENTURY LIGHTING, 18111 S. Santa Fe Ave., Rancho Dominguez, CA 90221; (213) 637-7500.

STUDIO SPECTRUM INC., 1056 N. Lake St., Burbank, CA 91502; (818) 843-1610.

SUNDANCE, 4211 Arch Dr., Suite 201, Studio City, CA 91604; (818) 985-9740.

SUPERSTAGE, 5724 Santa Monica Blvd., Hollywood, CA 90038; (213) 464-0296.

TM MOTION PICTURE EQUIPMENT RENTALS, 7365 Greenbush Ave., North Hollywood, CA 91605; (818) 764-7479.

TELEMEDIA PRODUCTIONS, 18321 Ventura Blvd., Suite 660, Tarzana, CA 91356; (818) 708-2005.

TRIANGLE SCENERY/DRAPERY/LIGHTING CO., 1215 Bates Ave., Los Angeles, CA 90029; (213) 662-8129.

ULTRAVISION INC., 7022 Sunset Blvd., Hollywood, CA 90028; (213) 871-2727.

UNITED TELEPRODUCTION SERVICES, 15055 Oxnard St., Van Nuys, CA 91411; (818) 997-0100.

UNIVERSAL FACILITIES RENTAL DIVISION, 100 Universal City Plaza, Universal City, CA 91608; (818) 777-3000; 777-2731.

UT PHOTO SERVICE, 3088 N. Clybourn Ave., Burbank, CA 91505; (213) 245-6631.

THE VALENCIA STUDIOS, 28343 Avenue Crocker, Valencia, CA 91355; (805) 257-1202; (800) STA-GEIT; FAX: (805) 257-1002.

VISUAL EYES PRODUCTIONS, 2401 Main St., Santa Monica, CA 90405; (213) 392-8300; FAX: (213) 392-7480.

THE WASHINGTON SOURCE FOR LIGHTING, INC., 8702 Old Ardmore Rd., Landover, MD 20785; (301) 341-7284.

WHITEHOUSE AUDIO VISUAL, 11511 W. Pico Blvd., Los Angeles, CA 90064; (213) 479-8313.

EAST COAST

BARBIZON ELECTRIC, 426 W. 55 St., New York, NY 10019; (212) 586-1620; 3 Draper St., Woburn, MA 01801; (617) 935-3920; 1125 N. 53 Court, West Palm Beach, FL 33407; (407) 844-5973; 6437G General Green Way, Alexandria, VA 22312; (703) 750-3900.

BIG APPLE CINE SERVICE, 51-02 21 St., Long Island City, NY 11101; (719) 361-5508.

BOKEN, INC., 513 W. 54 St., New York, NY 10019; (212) 581-5507.

THE CAMERA GROUP, 599 Eleventh Ave., 6th Floor, New York, NY 10036; (212) 254-3600.

THE CAMERA MART, 456 W. 55 St., New York, NY 10019; (212) 757-6977.

CAMERA SERVICE CENTER, 625 W. 54 St., New York, NY 10019 (213) 757-0906.

CECO INTERNATIONAL CORP., 440 W. 15 St., New York, NY 10011; (212) 206-8280.

CESTARE, THOMAS, INC., 188 Herricks Rd., Mineola, NY, 11501; (516) 742-5550.

CHELSEA FILM & VIDEO, INC., 1 W. 19 St., New York, NY 10011; (212) 243-8923.

ERIK LIGHTING INC., 4077 Park Ave., Bronx, NY 10457; (212) 901-3100; (800) 858-4450.

FEATURE SYSTEMS, INC., 512 W. 36 St., New York, NY 10018; (212) 736-0447.

FERCO, 707 Eleventh Ave., New York, NY 10019; (212) 245-4800.
FILMTRUCKS, INC., Pier 40 North River, New York, NY 10014; (212) 243-1500.
FIORENTINO, IMERO, ASSOCIATES, 44 W. 63 St., New York, NY 10023; (212) 246-0600.
GOBLIN MARKET FILM SERVICE, 52 St. Marks Pl., Staten Island, NY 10301; (718) 447-7157.
HOTLIGHTS, 133 W. 19 St., New York, NY 10011; (212) 645-5295.
LTM CORP. OF AMERICA, 437 W. 16 St., New York, NY 10011; (212) 243-9288.
LEE LIGHTING AMERICA, LTD., 534 W. 25 St., New York, NY 10001; (212) 691-1910.
LEGS/MANHATTAN, Pier 62, North River, New York, NY 10011; (212) 807-6644; 807-6645; FAX: (212) 645-8477.
LIBERTY LIGHTING LIMITED, 236 W. 27 St., #4A, New York, NY 10001; (212) 627-9455.
LIGHTING & PRODUCTION EQUIPMENT, INC., 1676 DeForrest Circle, Atlanta, GA 30318; (404) 352-0464.
LOCATION POWER & ILLUMINATION, 19½ Lafayette St., Saratoga Springs, NY 12866; (518) 583-3431.
LOWEL-LIGHT MANUFACTURING, 140 58 St., Brooklyn, NY 11220; (718) 921-0600.
MOVIE LITES LTD., 460 W. 24 St., New York, NY 10011: (212) 989-2318.
MOVIE MOBILE, INC., 30-15 Vernon Blvd., Astoria, NY 11102; (718) 545-7200.
PARIS FILMS PRODS., 31-00 47 Ave., Long Island City, NY 11101; (718) 482-7633.
PROCAMERA & LIGHTING RENTALS, INC., 511 W. 33 St., New York, NY 10001; (212) 695-1517.
PRODUCTION ARTS LIGHTING, INC., 636 Eleventh Ave., New York, NY 10036; (212) 489-0312; FAX: (212) 245-3723.
R.D. SPARKS LTD., 16 Jane St., New York, NY 10014; (212) 633-1969.
STARK LIGHTING, (914) 225-4855; (212) 674-2195.
STARLIGHT PRODUCTIONS, INC., 98 Union St., Brooklyn, NY 11231-1418; (718) 855-1304.
TELETECHNIQUES SALES AND RENTALS, 1 W. 19 St., New York, NY 10011; (212) 206-1475; 633-1868.
TEMMER LIGHTING, 1 W. 19 St., New York, NY 10011; (212) 206-1475; 633-1868.
TIMES SQUARE THEATRICAL & STUDIO SUPPLY CORP., 318 W. 47 St., New York, NY 10036; (212) 245-4155.
XENO-LIGHTS INC., 1 Hudson St., New York, NY 10013; (212) 766-0786.

Market Research

LOS ANGELES

ASI MARKET RESEARCH, INC., 2600 W. Olive Ave., Burbank, CA 91505; (818) 843-4400.
AMERICAN MARKETING ASSOCIATION, 5301 Laurel Canyon Blvd., Suite 250, North Hollywood, CA 91607; (818) 762-4669.
ARBITRON CO., 3333 Wilshire Blvd., Los Angeles, CA 90036; (213) 736-0700.
BLACK & HART ASSOCIATES, 9016 Wilshire Blvd., Suite 500, Beverly Hills, CA 90211-9960; (800) AIR-MAIL.
CASSIDY-WATSON ASSOCIATES (CWA), 1614 N. Argyle Ave., Hollywood, CA 90028; (213) 462-1739.
CRA INC., DR. IRVING S. WHITE, 908 Tiverton Ave., Los Angeles, CA 90024; (213) 824-1811.
DMR AUDIENCE PREVIEWS & SURVEYS, P.O. Box 69556, Los Angeles, CA 90069; (213) 271-7111.
EDWARDS, ROGER M., ENTERTAINMENT RESEARCH, 636 S. Dunsmuir Ave., Los Angeles, CA 90036; (213) 936-3800.
ENTERTAINMENT DATA, INC., 331 N. Maple Dr., Beverly Hills, CA 90210; (213) 271-2105; (800) NAT-GROSS; FAX: (213) 271-2256.
FREEMAN, ALLAN MARKETING & RESEARCH ASSOCIATES, 9696 Moorgate Rd., Beverly Hills, CA 90210; (213) 276-2140.
GERBER, ROBIN & ASSOCIATES, INC., 15910 Ventura Blvd., Suite 706, Encino, CA 91436; (818) 501-8881; (213) 274-6014.
GLOBAL MEDIA ASSOCIATES/USA, 22837 Ventura Blvd., Suite 302, Woodland Hills, CA 91367; (818) 888-1033; Telex: 9102504157.
GOLDBERG, MAX & ASSOCIATES, INC., 4289 Bakman Ave., Studio City, CA 91602; (818) 980-5879.
HERST ENTERTAINMENT RESOURCES, 231 N. Orchard Dr., Burbank, CA 91506; (818) 841-2595.
HILTON FINANCIAL GROUP, INC., 3500 W. Olive Ave., Suite 740, Burbank, CA 91505; (818) 953-4161.
HISPANIC ENTERTAINMENT SPECIALIST, 6381 Hollywood Blvd., Suite 410, Hollywood, CA 90028; (213) 466-9060.
IDC SERVICES INC., 2600 W. Olive Ave., Burbank, CA 91505; (818) 569-5100.
IMAGE ANALYSTS, 5462 Crenshaw Blvd., Los Angeles, CA 90043; (213) 399-2422.
IMMEDIATO, JEFFREY & ASSOCIATES, P.O. Box 5611, Long Beach, CA 90805; (213) 422-9295.
JOYCE COMMUNICATIONS, 953 N. Highland Ave., Los Angeles, CA 90038; (213) 467-2446.
KROWN/YOUNG & RUBICAM, (Entertainment Marketing Group), 9696 Culver Blvd., Suite 201, Culver City, CA 90232; (213) 202-8100.
LOWELL, SIGMUND, 11930 Montana Ave., Los Angeles, CA 90049; (213) 207-5947.
MANPEAL RESEARCH & CONSULTING, INC., 9624 Wendover Dr., Beverly Hills, CA 90210; (213) 278-8613.
McCANN-ERICKSON INC., 6420 Wilshire Blvd., Los Angeles, CA 90048; (213) 655-9420.
MICHAELS, HARMON, & ASSOCIATES, 16900 Parthenia, Suite 10, Sepulveda, CA 91343; (818) 702-8011.
MORRIS VIDEO, INC., 2730 Monterey St., Suite 105, Torrance, CA 90503; (213) 533-4800.
MOSES, CHARLES A., 3219 W. Alameda Ave., Burbank, CA 91505; (818) 848-0513.
A.C. NIELSEN COMPANY, 6255 Sunset Blvd., Suite 1006, Los Angeles, CA 90028; (213) 466-4391.
PENLAND PRODUCTIONS, INC., 303 N. Glenoaks Blvd., Suite 780, Burbank, CA 91502; (818) 840-9461.
PROFESSIONAL RESEARCH ASSOCIATES, P.O. Box 5447, Culver City, CA 90231; (213) 394-1650.
QWEST AUDIENCE RESEARCH & DEVELOPMENT, 574 Lillian Way, Los Angeles, CA 90004; (213) 465-2696.
RADIO TV REPORTS, 7033 Sunset Blvd., Suite 200, Los Angeles, CA 90028; (213) 466-6124.
THE RESEARCH DEPARTMENT, 18653 Ventura Blvd., Suite 351, Tarzana, CA 91365; (818) 342-5355.
RESEARCH FRONTIERS CORPORATION, 3524 Caribeth Dr., Encino, CA 91436-4101; (818) 783-1620.
RITZ & ASSOCIATES ADVERTISING, 636 N. Robertson Blvd., Los Angeles, CA 90069; (213) 652-9813.
SHULMAN RESEARCH, 672 S. Lafayette Park Place, Los Angeles, CA 90057; (213) 383-1281; FAX: (213) 383-1949.
SNOW, JANET & ASSOCIATES, 327 Reeves Dr., Beverly Hills, CA 90212; (213) 552-0082.
TISHKOFF & ASSOCIATES, INC., 3440 Motor Ave., Ground 71. Suite, Los Angeles, CA 90034; (213) 837-0792.
VACANTI/McMAHON COMMUNICATIONS, 2700 Cahuenga Blvd., Los Angeles, CA 90068; (213) 850-1990.
VIDEO MARKETING NEWSLETTER, 1680 Vine St., Suite 820, Hollywood, CA 90028; (213) 462-6350; FAX: (213) 467-0314.
VIDEO MONITORING SERVICES OF AMERICA, 3434 W. Sixth St., Los Angeles, CA 90020-2536; (213) 380-5011.
VIDEO VIEWS/CINEMA SURVEY, 6777 Hollywood Blvd., Suite 206, Los Angeles, CA 90028; (213) 469-9880.
WESTERN INTERNATIONAL RESEARCH, 8544 Sunset Blvd., Los Angeles, CA 90069; (213) 659-5711.
WORLD CLASS SPORTS AGENCY, 9171 Wilshire Blvd., Suite 404, Beverly Hills, CA 90210; (213) 278-2010.

NEW YORK

AGB TELEVISION RESEARCH, INC., 540 Madison Ave., New York, NY 10022; (212) 319-8800; FAX: (212) 319-8109.
CERTIFIED MARKETING SERVICES, INC. (CMS), Route 9, Kinderhook, NY 12106; (518) 758-6405. (National field coverage for in-theatre research/audience reaction cards and tabulation. Trailer monitoring and tracking programs.) William P. Smith, pres.; Joan Tooher, research dir.; Donna Card, mgr.
THE GALLUP ORGANIZATION, 53 Bank St., Princeton, NJ 08540; (609) 924-9600.
MARKET RESEARCH CORP. OF AMERICA, 4 Landmark Sq., Stamford, CT 06901; (203) 324-9600; 819 S. Wabash, Chicago, IL 60605; (312) 480-9600; 2215 Sanders Road, Northbrook, IL 60062; (312) 480-9600.
A. C. NIELSEN, CO., MEDIA RESEARCH, Nielsen Plaza, Northbrook, IL 60062, (312) 498-6300; 1290 Ave. of the Americas, New York, NY 10019, (212) 956-2500; 6255 Sunset Blvd., Los Angeles, CA 90028; (213) 466-4391.
OPINION RESEARCH CORP., P.O. Box 183, Princeton, NJ 08542-0183; (212) 489-7340; (609) 924-5900.
POLITZ, ALFRED, MEDIA STUDIES, 300 Park Ave. South, New York, NY 10010; (212) 982-7600.
ROPER ORGANIZATION, THE, 205 E. 42 St., New York, NY 10017; (212) 599-0700.
SINDLINGER & CO., INC., 405 Osborne St., Wallingford, PA 19086; (215) 565-0247.
STARCH INRA HOOPER, INC., 566 East Boston Post Rd., Mamaroneck, NY 10543; (914) 698-0800.

Merchandisers

DISNEY, WALT, PRODUCTIONS, (Character Merchandising Division), 500 Park Ave., New York, NY 10022; (212) 593-8900.

HARVEY PUBLICATIONS, INC., 250 W. 57th St., New York, NY 10107; (212) 582-2244.

LICENSING COMPANY OF AMERICA, 75 Rockefeller Plaza, New York, NY 10019; (212) 484-8807; 4000 Warner Blvd., Burbank, CA 91522; (818) 954-6640.

LUCASFILM LICENSING, P.O. Box 2009, San Rafael, CA 94912; (415) 662-1800.

Music, Music Libraries and Music Cutting

CALIFORNIA

ALSHIRE INTERNATIONAL, INC., 1015 Isabel St., P.O. Box 7107, Burbank, CA 91510; (213) 849-4671; (818) 843-6792; FAX: (818) 569-3718.

ANNELO/CEXTON PRODUCTION GROUP, 2740 S. Harbor Blvd., Suite D, Santa Ana, CA 92704; (714) 641-1074.

ASSOCIATED PRODUCTION MUSIC, 6255 Sunset Blvd., Suite 724, Hollywood, CA 90028; (213) 461-3211; FAX (213) 461-9102.

AUDIO ACHIEVEMENTS RECORDING STUDIO, 1327 Cabrillo Ave., Torrance, CA 90501; (213) 533-9531.

AUDIO POST, 3755 Cahuenga Blvd., West, Suite C, Studio City, CA 91604; (818) 761-5220.

BERTUS PRODUCTIONS, 22723 Berdon St., Woodland Hills, CA 91367; (818) 883-1920.

BLUEFIELD MUSIC DESIGN, 2147 Holly Dr., Los Angeles, CA 90068; (213) 463-SONG.

BUZZY'S RECORDING SERVICES, 6900 Melrose Ave., Los Angeles, CA 90038; (213) 931-1867; FAX: (213) 931-9681.

CANDLEWICK PRODUCTIONS, 1161 N. Highland Ave., Hollywood, CA 90038; (213) 462-7979.

CARBONE, JOEY, 5724 Third St., Suite 303, Los Angeles, CA 90036; (213) 462-3380.

CARMAN PRODUCTIONS INC., 15456 Cabrito Road, Van Nuys, CA 91406; (213) 873-7370; (818) 787-6436.

CEXTON RECORDS, 2740 S. Harbor Blvd., Suite D, Santa Ana, CA 92704; (714) 641-1074.

CLAY, TOM, PRODUCTIONS, 6515 Sunset Blvd., Suite 201A Hollywood, CA 90028; (213) 464-6566.

DEBOOGEDY MUSIC, 1521 Clark Ave., Burbank, CA 91506; (818) 845-3118; (818) 763-6443.

FIDELITY RECORDING STUDIO, 4412 Whitsett Ave., Studio City, CA 91604; (818) 508-3263.

FLEISHMAN, RICK, MUSIC, 5739 Babbitt Ave., Encino, CA 91316; (818) 343-7005.

FRONT ROW CENTER THEATRE MEMORABILIA, 8127 W. Third St., W. Hollywood, CA 90048; (213) 852-0149.

FULLER SOUND AV RECORDING, 1948 Riverside Dr., Los Angeles, CA 90039; (213) 660-4914.

HANIFAN, BRUCE, PRODUCTIONS, 9023 Beverlywood St., Los Angeles, CA 90034; (213) 559-4522.

INTERSOUND, INC., 8746 Sunset Blvd., Los Angeles, CA 90069; (213) 652-3741; Telex: 798563; Answbk: INTERSOUND INC.

MANSON, EDDY, PRODUCTIONS, INC., 7245 Hillside Ave., Suite 216, Los Angeles, CA 90046; (213) 874-9318.

MARGERY MUSIC CO., 7245 Hillside Ave., Suite 216, Los Angeles, CA 90038; (213) 874-9318.

MOVIE TECH INC., 832 N. Seward St., Hollywood, CA 90038; (213) 467-8491; (213) 467-5423; FAX: (213) 467-8471.

MUNCHKIN MUSIC, (Frank Zappa Catalog) P.O. Box 5265, N. Hollywood, CA 91616; (818) 764-0800; Telex: 880469; Answbk: ICAUD.

MUSICUM LAUDE, 2988 Avenel Terrace, Los Angeles, CA 90039; (213) 660-5444.

NAMRAC MUSIC, 15456 Cabrito Road, Van Nuys, CA 91406; (213) 873-7370.

NIDA MUSIC PUBLISHING CO., 4014 Murietta Ave., Sherman Oaks, CA 91423; (818) 981-5331.

OUTLAW SOUND, 1140 N. La Brea Ave., Los Angeles, CA 90038; (213) 462-1873; FAX: (213) 856-4311.

QUALITY SOUND, INC., 5625 Melrose Ave., Hollywood, CA 90038; (213) 467-7154.

RESEARCH VIDEO, 4900 Vineland Ave., N. Hollywood, CA 91601; (818) 509-0506; Telex: 298873; Answbk: USSM UR.

SELECTED SOUND RECORDED MUSIC LIBRARY, 6777 Hollywood Blvd., Suite 209, Hollywood, CA 90028; (213) 469-9910.

SINGING STORE U.S.A., 16851 Victory Blvd., Suite 10, Van Nuys, CA 91406; (818) 781-9098; FAX: (818) 781-8979.

SOUTHERN LIBRARY OF RECORDED MUSIC, 6777 Hollywood Blvd., Suite 209, Hollywood, CA 90028; (213) 469-9910.

STEVENS, KRIS, ENTERPRISES INC., 14241 Ventura Blvd., Suite 204, Sherman Oaks, CA 91423; (818) 981-8255; FAX: (818) 990-4350.

TOM THUMB MUSIC, Box 34485, Whitney Building, Los Angeles, CA 90034; (213) 836-4678.

TODD-AO/GLEN GLENN STUDIOS, 900 N. Seward St., Hollywood, CA 90038; (213) 469-7221.

WILLIAMS, MARY, MUSIC CLEARANCE CORPORATION, 6223 Selma Ave., Suite 211, Hollywood, CA 90028; (213) 462-6575; FAX: (213) 462-3433.

THE SAUL ZAENTA COMPANY FILM CENTER, 2600 Tenth St., Berkeley, CA 94710; (415) 549-2500; (800) 227-0466; FAX: (415) 486-2015.

ZAPPA, FRANK, MUSIC, P.O. Box 5265, N. Hollywood, CA 91616; (818) 764-0800.

NEW YORK

AJR MUSIC PRODUCTIONS, 302 W. 87th St., Suite 86, New York, NY 10024; (212) 724-5658.

ALEXANDER, JOHN ERIC, MUSIC, 311 W. 43rd St., New York, NY 10036; (212) 581-8560.

ALTAVISTA MUSIC, 77 Warren St., New York, NY 10007; (212) 349-8095.

ANTLAND PRODUCTIONS, INC., 231 E. 55th St., New York, NY 10022; (212) 355-1600, ext. 255.

AQUARIUS TRANSFER, 12 E. 46 St., New York, NY 10017; (212) 581-0123.

ARIES SOUND INTERNATIONAL, 245 E. 63 St., New York, NY 10021; (212) 838-4940.

AR-VEE SOUND SERVICES, 630 9th Ave., #400, New York, NY 10036; (212) 450-9588.

AUDIO DIRECTORS, INC., 325 W. 19 St., New York, NY 10011; (212) 924-5850.

AUDIO VISUAL ARTS, INC., 146 W. 57th St., New York, NY 10019; (212) 397-3771.

BLACK, ARNOLD, PRODUCTIONS, INC., 895 West End Ave., New York, NY 10025; (212) 865-5933.

BLACKSTONE, WENDY, MUSIC, INC., 59 W. 10th St., Suite 4E, New York, NY 10011; (212) 228-4091.

BRAUNSTEIN, ALAN, MUSIC INC., 400 West 43rd St., #14S, New York, NY 10036; (212) 736-0067.

BRUHA HA MUSIC PRODUCTIONS, 133 Greene St., New York, NY 10012; (212) 353-9468.

CHAPELL MUSIC LIBRARY, 810 Seventh Ave., New York, NY 10019; (212) 399-7373.

CORELLI-JACOBS/RECORDING/DE WOLFE MUSIC LIBRARY, 25 W. 45 St., New York, NY 10036; (212) 382-0220.

ELECTRO-NOVA PRODUCTIONS, 342 Madison Ave., New York, NY 10017; (212) 687-5838.

ELIAS ASSOCIATES 6 W. 20 St., New York, NY 10011; (212) 807-6151.

FILM SCORES BY JERRY MARKOE, 11 Fort George Hill 13c, New York, NY 10040; (212) 942-0004. Jerry Markoe, composer-conductor.

4-4 PRODUCTIONS, 320 W. 46th St., 6th Fl., New York, NY 10036; (212) 581-3970.

GERARDI, BOB, MUSIC, 160 W. 73rd St., New York, NY 10023; (212) 374-6436.

GOODMAN, TOMMY, ENTERPRISES, INC., 101 W. 57th St., #12H, New York, NY 10019; (212) 489-1641.

HARMONIC RANCH, (Audio for Video-Sound Effects-Composer Referral Service) 59 Franklin St., New York, NY 10013; (212) 966-3141.

HASTINGS SOUND EDITORIAL INC., 119 Rosedale Ave., Hastings-on-Hudson, NY 10706; (914) 478-0227.

HILL, JOHN, MUSIC, 116 E. 37th St., New York, NY 10016; (212) 683-2273.

HOFFMAN, PAUL, PRODUCTIONS, INC., 148 W. 23, Suite 4K, New York, NY 10011; (212) 255-2443.

HOROWITZ, DAVID, MUSIC ASSOCIATES, 301 Madison Ave., New York, NY 10017; (212) 661-6880.

IBERO-AMERICAN PRODUCTIONS, Background Music, Jingles, Film/Video/Radio; (212) 245-7826.

KAMEN AUDIO PRODUCTIONS, INC., 701 7th Ave., 6th Fl., New York, NY 10036; (212) 575-4660.

KARP, MICHAEL, MUSIC, INC., 260 W. 39 St., New York, NY 10018; (212) 840-3285.

KINGSLEY MUSIC, 201 W. 70th St., New York, NY 10023; (212) 787-4975.

LAVSKY, RICHARD, MUSIC HOUSE, INC., 16 E. 42 St., New York, NY 10017; (212) 697-9800.

LEVIN, LOUIS, MUSIC, 211 E. 53rd St., New York, NY 10022; (212) 223-0025.

LICHT, DAN, MUSIC, 112 E. 7th St., New York, NY 10009; (212) 475-2675.

LINO SOUND, Louis Lino: Original Music & Sound Design, 108 N. 6th St., Brooklyn, NY 11211; (718) 388-3314.
LOOK & COMPANY, 170 5th Ave., New York, NY 10010; (212) 627-3500.
MACROSE MUSIC, INC., Composer/Arranger-Fred Thaler, 353 W. 19th St., New York, NY 10011; (212) 206-1323.
MORROW, CHARLES, ASSOCIATES INC., 611 Broadway, #817, New York, NY 10012; (212) 529-4550.
MSP MUSIC, INC., 476 Broadway, New York, NY 10013; (212) 226-1030.
MUSEFFECTS, INC., 12 E. 46th St., New York, NY 10017; (212) 682-1860.
MUSIC FOR MEDIA, 269 W. 12th St., New York, NY 10014; (212) 807-7941.
MUSIC HOUSE INC., 16 E. 42 St., New York, NY 10017; (212) 697-9800.
THE MUSIC SOURCE, 12 E. 32nd St., New York, NY 10016; (212) 686-8687.
NEWFOUND MUSIC PRODUCTIONS, INC., 250 W. 27th St., Suite 5H, New York, NY 10001; (212) 691-9667.
NORTH FORTY PRODUCTIONS, INC., 252 E. 51st St., New York, NY 10022; (212) 751-8300.
NOT JUST JINGLES, 420 W. 45th St., New York, NY 10036; (212) 246-6468.
OMNIMUSIC, 52 Main St., Port Washington, New York, NY 11050; (516) 883-0121.
PATCO RESOURCES, 799 Broadway, New York, NY 10003; (212) 505-9490.
PERFECT SOUND, 1697 Broadway, Suite 1106, New York, NY 10019; (212) 315-5852.
PICTURE SCORES, INC., 42 W. 38 St., New York, NY 10018; (212) 869-5885.
PISCES MUSIC LTD., 12 E. 46 St., New York, NY 10017; (212) 682-1860.
PURE FORM, 248 W. 105 St.-2D, New York, NY 10025; (212) 749-2725.
RADIO BAND OF AMERICA, 1350 Avenue of the Americas, New York, NY 10019; (212) 687-4800.
RICE, TODD, 211 E. 58th St., New York, NY 10019; (212) 489-2321.
RIVELLINO MUSIC, Call for demo, Contact: Dennis Rivellino; (914) 769-5734.
ROSS-GAFFNEY, INC., 21 W. 46 St., New York, NY, 10036; (212) 719-2744.
SCORE PRODUCTIONS, INC., 254 E. 49 St., New York, NY 10017; (212) 751-2510.
SHELTON LEIGH PALMER & CO., 19 W. 36 St., New York, NY 10018; (212) 714-1710.
SOKOLOV, E., MUSIC, %Elec. Art, 228 E. 45th St., New York, NY 10017; (212) 503-6394.
SOUND PATROL, LTD., 6 E. 39 St., New York, NY 10016; (212) 213-6666.
SOUND SHOP, 321 W. 44 St., New York, NY 10036; (212) 757-5837.
SPLASH PRODUCTIONS INC., 123 W. 28th St., New York, NY 10001; (212) 695-3665.
STOCK ROCK, 421 Hudson St., #220, New York, NY 10014; (212) 989-7845.
SUNDAY PRODUCTIONS, INC., 888 8th Ave., New York, NY 10019; (212) 246-2000.
SUTCLIFFE MUSIC INC., 41 Fifth Ave., Suite 1D, New York, NY 10003; (212) 420-9292.
TNG/EARTHLING-BOB SAKAYAMA, 110 W. 86th St., New York, NY 10024; (212) 799-4181.
TRIPP, JIM, MUSIC, 146 W. 57th St., New York, NY 10019; (212) 397-3771.
ULFIK, RICK, PRODUCTIONS, 130 W. 42nd St., Suite 904, New York, NY 10036; (212) 704-0888.
VALENTINO, THOMAS J., INC, 151 W. 46 St., New York, NY 10036; (212) 391-1500.
WILBUR, SANDY, MUSIC, INC., 48 E. 43rd St., New York, NY 10017; (212) 949-1190.
WOLOSHIN, SID, INC., 95 Madison Ave., New York, NY 10016; (212) 684-7222.

MASSACHUSETTS

SOUND IN MOTION, P.O. Box 464, Brookline, MA 02147; (617) 734-6190; Phred Churchill, composer.

Properties and Scenery

LOS ANGELES

ANTIQUARIAN TRADERS WAREHOUSE, 4851 S. Alameda St., Los Angeles, CA 90058; (213) 627-2144.
ANTIQUE & CLASSIC CAR RENTALS, 611 W. Vernon Ave., Los Angeles, CA 90037; (213) 232-7211.
BAYBERRY CARRIAGE COMPANY, P.O. Box 4006, West Hills, CA 91308; (818) 992-8448.
BEVERLY HILLS FOUNTAIN CENTER, 7856 Santa Monica Blvd., Los Angeles, CA 90046; (213) 651-5252.
BREUNERS FURNITURE RENTAL, 14255 Ventura Blvd., Sherman Oaks, CA 91423; (818) 986-6500; 3281 Wilshire Blvd., Los Angeles, CA 90010; (818) 382-8262; 9020 Olympic Blvd., Beverly Hills, CA 90210; (213) 271-7242.
BRICK PRICE'S MOVIE MINIATURES (WONDERWORKS), 7231 Remmet Ave., #F, Canoga Park, CA 91303-1532; (818) 992-8811.
THE BRUBAKER GROUP, 10560 Dolcedo Way, Los Angeles, CA 90077; (213) 472-4766; 478-9588.
BUENA VISTA STUDIOS, 500 S. Buena Vista St., Burbank, CA 91521; (818) 560-0044.
THE BURBANK STUDIOS, 4000 Warner Blvd., Burbank, CA 91522; (818) 954-6000.
CAMERA READY CARS, 1577 Placentia, Newport Beach, CA 92663; (714) 645-4700.
CARTHAY SET SERVICES, 5176 Santa Monica Blvd., Los Angeles, CA 90029; (213) 469-7475.
CINEMAFLOAT, 1624 W. Ocean Front, Newport Beach, CA 92663; (714) 675-8888.
CAR CASTING, P.O. Box 931568, Hollywood, CA 90093; (213) 463-1714.
CLASSIC CAR SUPPLIERS, 1905 Sunset Plaza Dr., Los Angeles, CA 90069; (213) 657-7823.
CLASSIC LEASING COMPANY, 1100 Santa Monica Blvd., Santa Monica, CA 90401 (213) 393-9100.
CONTINENTAL SCENERY, 1022 N. La Brea Ave., Los Angeles, CA 90038; (213) 461-4139.
DOZAR CO., 2656 S. Western Ave., Los Angeles, CA 90018; (213) 732-6173; 732-8367; FAX: (213) 730-0157.
ELLIS MERCANTILE CO., 169 N. La Brea Ave., Los Angeles, CA 90036; (213) 933-7334.
EXPENDABLE SUPPLY STORE, 1316 N. Western Ave., Hollywood, CA 90027; (213) 465-3191; FAX: (818) 768-2422; 7830 N. San Fernando Rd., Sun Valley, CA 91352; (818) 767-5065; (213) 875-2409.
FILMTRIX, INC., 11054 Chandler Blvd., N. Hollywood, CA 91601; (818) 980-3700; FAX: (818) 980-3703.
FIORITTO, LARRY, SPECIAL EFFECTS SERVICES, 1067 E. Orange Grove, Burbank, CA 91501; (818) 954-9829.
GROSH, SCENIC STUDIOS, 4114 Sunset Blvd.; Los Angeles CA, 90029; (213) 662-1134.
HB VENDING MACHINES, 10623 Magnolia Blvd., North Hollywood, CA 91601; (818) 766-3400; 877-5841.
HAND PROP ROOM, INC., 5700 Venice Blvd., Los Angeles, CA 90019; (213) 931-1534; 938-2982.
HISTORY FOR HIRE, 11401 Chandler Blvd., North Hollywood, CA 91601; (818) 762-9937.
HOLLYWOOD CENTRAL PROPS, 525 W. Elk Ave., Glendale, CA 91204; (818) 240-4504.
HOLLYWOOD PICTURE VEHICLES, 7046 Darby Ave., Reseda, CA 91301; (818) 506-7562.
HORSELESS CARRIAGE CLUB OF AMERICA, 7210 Jordan Ave., Box D-76, Canoga Park, CA 91303; (818) 704-4253.
HOUSE OF PROPS, 1117 Gower St., Hollywood, CA 90038; (213) 463-3166.
IMAGE ENGINEERING, INC., 632 N. Victory Blvd., Burbank, CA 91502; (818) 846-5865; FAX: (818) 846-5127.
INDEPENDENT STUDIO SERVICES, 11907 Wicks St., Sun Valley, CA 91352; (818) 764-0840; 768-5711.
IWASAKI IMAGES, (food replicas), 19330 Van Ness Ave., Torrance, CA 90501; (213) 328-7121.
KREISS COLLECTION, 8619 Melrose Ave., Los Angeles, CA 90069-5010; (213) 656-1606.
LAZZARINI'S S/VFX, THE CREATURE SHOP, 2554 Lincoln Blvd., Suite 1067, Marina Del Rey, CA 90291; (818) 989-0220.
MGM/UA STUDIOS PROP DEPT., 10202 W. Washington Blvd., Culver City, CA 90230; (213) 558-5787.
MODERN PROPS, 4063 Redwood Ave., Los Angeles, CA 90066; (213) 306-1400; FAX: (213) 882-5992.
NIGHTS OF NEON, 7442 Varna Ave., N. Hollywood, CA 91605; (818) 982-3592; FAX: (818) 503-1090.
NORCOSTCO, INC., 5867 Lankershim Blvd., N. Hollywood, CA 91601; (213) 461-6555; (818) 760-2911; FAX: (818) 980-4737.
OMEGA CINEMA PROPS., 5857 Santa Monica, Blvd., Los Angeles, 90038; (213) 466-8201.
PROP CITY/LAIRD INT'L STUDIOS, 9336 W. Washington Blvd., Culver City, CA 90230; (213) 559-7022; 202-3350.
PROP MASTERS, INC., 420 S. First St., Burbank, CA 91502; (818) 846-3915; 846-3957; FAX: (818) 846-1278.
PROP SERVICES WEST INC., 915 N. Citrus Ave., Los Angeles, CA 90038; (213) 461-3371.

ROSCHU, 6514 Santa Monica Blvd., Los Angeles 90038; (213) 469-2749.
SARTINO, JACQUELINE, 953 N. Edinburgh Ave., Los Angeles, CA 90046; (213) 654-3326.
SCENERY WEST, 1126 N. Citrus Ave., Hollywood, CA 90038; (213) 467-7495.
SCENIC EXPRESS, 3025 Fletcher Dr., Los Angeles, CA 90065; (213) 254-4351.
R.J. SHOWTIME, 1011 Gower St., Hollywood, CA 90038; (213) 467-2127; FAX: (213) 467-4894.
SPECIAL EFFECTS UNLIMITED, 752 N. Cahuenga Blvd., Los Angeles, CA 90038; (213) 466-3361.
STUDIO PICTURE VEHICLES, 10901 Sherman Way, Sun Valley, CA 91352; (818) 765-1201; 781-4223.
THORNBIRD ARMS, 21626 Lassen St., Chatsworth, CA 91311; (818) 341-8227.
TRIANGLE SCENERY/DRAPERY/LIGHTING CO., 1215 Bates Ave., Los Angeles, CA 90029; (213) 662-8129.

NEW YORK

ATI MEDICAL STUDIO PRODUCTIONS, 532 Fifth Ave., Pelham, NY 10803; (914) 738-5777.
ADVERTISING IN MOVIES INC., Kaufman Astoria Studios, 34-12 36th St., Astoria, Queens, NY 11106; (718) 729-9288.
ALTMAN'S LUGGAGE, 135 Orchard St., New York, NY 10002; (212) 254-7275.
AMERICAN ARTISTS TAXICABS, 312 W. 48 St., New York, NY 10036; (212) 262-7012.
ANTIQUE & CLASSIC AUTOS, (Leonard Shiller), 811 Union St., Brooklyn, NY 11215; (718) 788-3400.
ARENSON OFFICE FURNISHING, 315 E. 62 St., New York, NY 10021; (212) 838-8880.
ARTS & CRAFTERS INC., 175 Johnson St., Brooklyn, NY 11201; (718) 875-8151.
BROOKLYN MODEL WORKS, 60 Washington Ave., Brooklyn, NY 11205; (718) 834-1944.
CAVE FURNITURE, 58 E. First St., New York, NY 10011; (212) 254-2882.
CENTRAL PROPERTIES, 514 W. 49 St., 2nd Floor, New York, NY 10019; (212) 265-7767.
CENTRE FIREARMS CO, INC., 10 W. 37 St., New York, NY 10018; (212) 244-4040.
CINEMA GALLERIES, 517 W. 35 St., New York, NY 10001; (212) 627-1222.
CINEMA WORLD PRODUCTS, INC., 2621 Palisade Ave., Riverdale, NY 10463; (212) 548-1928.
CLASSIC CARS BY TALLEYHO, 171 Madison Ave., New York, NY 10016; (914) 365-0452.
COOPER FILM CARS, 132 Perry, New York, NY 10014; (212) 929-3909.
DARROW'S FUN ANTIQUES, 309 E. 61 St., New York, NY 10021; (212) 838-0730.
EAST COAST FILM CARS, 757 Hicks St., Brooklyn, NY 11231; (718) 624-6050.
ECLECTIC/ENCORE PROPERTIES INC., 620 W. 26 St., 4th floor, New York, NY 10001; (212) 645-8880.
ENVIRION VISION, 3074 Whaleneck Dr., Merrick, NY 11566; (516) 378-2250.
FINKEL, LARRY, CENTURY SALES, 55 Spruce St., Cedarhurst, NY 11516; (516) 569-3099.
GALI KITCHEN RENTAL EQUIPMENT, INC., 404 E. 88 St., New York, NY 10028; (212) 289-5405.
GREAT AMERICAN SALVAGE CO., 34 Cooper Sq., New York, NY 10003; (212) 505-0070.
GEORGE J. KEMPLER CO., INC., 160 Fifth Ave., New York, NY 10010; (212) 989-1180.
HOLLAND PARADISE, 800 Sixth Ave., New York, NY 10001; (212) 684-3397.
KENMORE FURNITURE CO., 352 Park Avenue South, New York, NY 10010; (212) 683-1888.
KUTTNER PROP RENTALS INC., 56 W. 22 St., New York, NY 10010; (212) 242-7969.
THE LENS & REPRO EQUIPMENT CORP., 33 W. 17 St., New York, NY 10011; (212) 675-1900.
MERCURY NEON SIGN SHOP, 86 Hester St., New York, NY 10002; (212) 219-0542.
NICCOLINI ANTIQUES, 114 E. 25 St., New York, NY 10010; (212) 254-2900.
NORTHEAST AUTO CLASSICS, (718) 634-9206.
PICTURE CARS, EAST, 757 Hicks St., Brooklyn, NY 11231; (718) 852-2300.
THE PROP HOUSE, INC., 653 Eleventh Ave., New York, NY 10036; (212) 713-0760.
PROPS FOR TODAY, 121 W. 19 St., 3rd floor, New York, NY 10011; (212) 206-0330.
SAY IT IN NEON, INC., 430 Hudson St., New York, NY 10014; (212) 691-7977.
SCHOEPFER STUDIO, 138 W. 31 St., New York, NY 10001; (212) 736-6934.
THE SET DRESSING SHOP, 450 W. 31 St., New York, NY 10001; (212) 967-7794.
SHOWROOM OUTLET, 625/35 W. 55 St., New York, NY 10019; (212) 581-0470.
STARBUCK STUDIO, 162 W. 21 St., New York, NY 10011; (212) 807-7299.
VISUAL SERVICES, 40 W. 72 St., New York, NY 10023; (212) 580-9551.
WAVES (Antique radios), 32 E. 13 St., New York, NY 10003; (212) 989-9284.
WEAPONS SPECIALISTS, 61 Lexington Ave., New York, NY 10010; (212) 941-7696.

Raw Stock Manufacturers

AGFA CORPORATION, MOTION PICTURE PRODUCTS DIVISION. (Manufacturer, distributor 35mm color, black, white raw stock.) Executive offices: 100 Challenger Rd., Ridgefield Park, NJ 07660; (201) 440-2500 or (212) 971-0260.
BRANCHES:
San Francisco, 94080; 601 Gateway Blvd., Ste. 500, South San Francisco, CA; (415) 589-0700.
Los Angeles, 90067: 1801 Century Park East, Suite 110; (213) 552-9622.
EASTMAN KODAK CO., MOTION PICTURES AUDIOVISUAL PRODUCTS DIVISION. 343 State St., Rochester, NY; Tel.: (716) 724-4000. 1901 W. 22nd St., Oakbrook, IL 60521; Tel.: (312) 654-5300. 6700 Santa Monica Blvd., Hollywood, CA, 90038; Tel.: (213) 464-6131. 1133 Ave. of the Americas, New York, NY 10036; Tel.: (212) 930-8000.
FUJI PHOTO FILM U.S.A., INC., (distributor of Fuji Professional Motion Picture Film) Northeast Region Sales & Dist. Ctr., 800 Central Blvd., Carlstadt, NJ 07072; (201) 935-6022; Corp. headquarters: 555 Taxter Rd., Elmsford, NY 10523; (914) 789-8100; (800) 241-7695.
ILFORD, INC., W. 70 Century Rd., Paramus, NJ 07653; (201) 265-6000.
3M COMPANY (MINNESOTA MINING & MANUFACTURING CO.), Photo Color Systems Division, (Manufacturer and distributor of color 35mm film, C-41 process.) 3M Center, Bldg. 223-2SE-05, St. Paul, MN 55144; (800) 654-5007.
RESEARCH TECHNOLOGY, INC., 4700 Chase Ave., Lincolnwood, IL 60646; (312) 677-3000.

Rental Studios and Production Facilities

ATLANTA

LIGHTING & PRODUCTION EQUIPMENT, INC., 1676 DeFoor Circle; 30318; (404) 352-0464.

BOSTON

CHARLES RIVER STUDIOS, 1380 Soldiers Field Rd, Boston, MA 02135; (617) 783-3535.

CHICAGO

HARPO STUDIOS, 1058 W. Washington Blvd., Chicago, IL 60607; (312) 738-3456.

LOS ANGELES

ACTORS CENTER, 11969; Ventura Blvd., Studio City, CA 91604; (818) 505-9400.
AMERICAN INSTITUTE OF VIDEO, 20850 Dearborn St., Chatsworth, CA 91311; (818) 700-8987.
AMETHYST STUDIOS, 7000 Santa Monica Blvd., Hollywood, CA 90038; (213) 467-3700.
ANDERSON, TOM FILMWORKS, 6382 Hollywood Blvd., Suite 308, Los Angeles, CA 90028; (213) 464-0386.
BOWEN VIDEO FACILITIES & STAGE, 7826 Clybourn Ave., Sun Valley, CA 91352; (818) 504-0070.
BUENA VISTA STUDIOS, 500 S. Buena Vista St., Burbank, CA 91521; (818) 560-0044.

BURBANK PRODUCTION PLAZA, 801 S. Main St., Burbank, CA 91506; (818) 846-7677; 841-5051; FAX: (818) 841-1572.
BURBANK STUDIOS, THE, 4000 Warner Blvd., Burbank, CA 91522; (213) 954-2923.
CBS/MTM STUDIOS, 4024 N. Radford Ave., Studio City, CA 91604; (818) 760-5000.
CFI (CONSOLIDATED FILM INDUSTRIES), 959 Seward St., Hollywood, CA 90038; (213) 960-7444.
CARMEN PRODUCTIONS INC., 15456 Cabrito Rd., Van Nuys, CA 91406; (213) 873-7370; (818) 787-6436.
CARTHAY STUDIOS, INC., 5903-07 W. Pico Blvd., Los Angeles 90035; (213) 938-2101.
CHAPLIN STAGE, 1416 N. La Brea Ave., Hollywood, CA 90028; (213) 469-2411; 856-2682.
CINEWORKS-SUPERSTAGE, 1119 N. Hudson Ave., Los Angeles, CA 90038; (213) 464-0296.
COLUMBIA PICTURES INDUSTRIES, 4000 Warner Blvd., Columbia Plaza S., Burbank, 91505; (818) 954-6000.
THE COMPLEX, 2323 Corinth St., Los Angeles, CA 90064; (213) 477-1938.
CULVER CITY STUDIOS, INC., 9336 W. Washington, Culver City, CA 90230; (213) 202-3396; 836-5537.
DESIGN ARTS STUDIOS/THE STAGE, 1128 N. Las Palmas, Hollywood, CA 90038; (213) 464-9118.
THE WALT DISNEY STUDIOS, 500 S. Buena Vista St., Burbank, CA 91521; (818) 560-5151.
ERECTER SET, INC., 1150 S. La Brea Ave., Los Angeles, CA 90019; (213) 938-4762.
GMT STUDIOS, 5751 Buckingham Parkway, Unit C, Culver City, CA 90230; (213) 649-3733.
GLEN-WARREN PRODUCTIONS, LTD., 9911 W. Pico Blvd., PH M, Los Angeles, CA 90035; (213) 553-9233.
GLENDALE STUDIOS, 1239 S. Glendale Ave., Glendale, CA 91205; (818) 502-5300.
GROUP W. PRODUCTIONS, One Lakeside Plaza, 3801 Barham Blvd., Los Angeles, CA 90068; (213) 850-3800; FAX: (213) 850-3889.
HARK'S SOUND STUDIOS, 1041 N. Orange Dr., Hollywood, CA 90036; (213) 463-3288.
HOLLYWOOD CENTER STUDIOS, INC., 1040 N. Las Palmas Ave., Los Angeles, CA 90038; (213) 469-5000; FAX: (213) 871-8105.
INTER VIDEO/TRITRONICS, INC., 733 N. Victory Blvd., Burbank, CA 91502; (818) 843-3633; 569-4000; FAX: (818) 843-6884.
INTERSOUND, INC., 8746 Sunset Blvd., Los Angeles, CA 90069; (213) 652-3741.
JLW STUDIO RENTALS, 8033 Sunset Blvd., Suite 5010, Los Angeles, CA 90046; (714) 630-7733.
JOHNSON, RAY, STUDIOS, 5435 Denny St., N. Hollywood, CA 91601; (818) 508-7348.
KITAY, BEN, PRODUCTIONS, STAGES 10 & 15, 1015 N. Cahuenga Blvd., Stage 15, Hollywood, CA 90038; (213) 466-9015.
LORIMAR STUDIOS (div. Lorimar Telepictures), 10202 W. Washington Blvd., Culver City, CA 90232; (213) 280-8000.
MGM, 10000 W. Washington Blvd., Culver City, CA 90230; (213) 836-3000; 558-5000.
MELROSE STAGE, 4361 Melrose Ave., Los Angeles, CA 90029; (213) 660-8466.
MOLE-RICHARDSON CO., 937 N. Sycamore Ave., Los Angeles 90038; (213) 831-0111.
MORO-LANDIS/DUPUY, LTD., 10960 Ventura Blvd., Studio City, CA 91601; (213) 877-8070; (818) 761-9510.
PARAMOUNT STUDIO GROUP, DIV., 5555 Melrose Ave., Los Angeles, CA 90038; (213) 468-5000.
PEG STUDIOS (Patchett Entertainment Group), 8621 Hayden Place, Culver City, CA 90232; (213) 202-8997.
R & S STUDIOS/ ROSE & SALLMAN PRODUCTIONS, INC., 7336 Hinds Ave., N. Hollywood, CA 91605; (818) 503-8808.
RALEIGH STUDIOS, 650 N. Bronson Ave., Los Angeles, CA 90004; (213) 466-3111.
REN-MAR STUDIOS, 846 N. Cahuenga Blvd., Los Angeles, CA 90038; (213) 463-0808.
S.A. GLOBAL STUDIOS, 201 N. Occidental Blvd., Los Angeles, CA 90026; (213) 384-3331.
S.I.R. MUSIC FILM STUDIOS, INC., 6048 Sunset Blvd., Hollywood, CA 90028; (213) 466-3417; 466-1314.
SILVERLAKE ENTERTAINMENT CENTER, 2405 Glendale Blvd., Los Angeles, CA 90039; (213) 665-4187.
STAGE 15, 1015 N. Cahuenga Blvd., Hollywood, CA 90038; (213) 466-9015.
TELEVISION CENTER, 6311 Romaine St., Los Angeles, CA 90038; (213) 464-6638.
UNIVERSAL CITY STUDIOS, 100 Universal City Plaza, Universal City, 91608; (818) 777-3000; 777-2731.
THE VALENCIA STUDIOS, 28343 Ave. Crocker, Valencia, CA 91355; (800) 257-1202; (800) 782-4348; FAX: (805) 257-1002.
WESTHEIMER CO., 736 N. Seward St., Los Angeles, CA 90038; (213) 466-8271.
WHITEFIRE THEATRE, THE SOUNDSTAGE RENTAL, 13500 Ventura Blvd., Sherman Oaks, CA 91423; (818) 990-2324.

MIAMI

GREAT SOUTHERN STUDIOS, 15221 N.E. 21 Ave., N. Miami Beach, FL 33162; (305) 947-0430.
LIMELIGHT, 7355 N.W. 41st St., Miami, FL 33166; (305) 593- 6969.

NEW YORK

ACTION INSERT STUDIO, 14 E. 39 St., NY, NY 10016; (212) 684-4284.
ADVENTURE FILM STUDIOS, 40-13 104 St., Queens, NY 11368; (718) 478-2639.
APOLLO THEATRE TV CENTRE, 253 W. 125 St., NY, NY 10027; (212) 222-0992.
ATELIER FOURTH ST. STAGES, 295 W. 4 St., New York, NY 10014; (212) 243-3550.
BC STUDIO, 152 W. 25 St., New York, NY 10001; (212) 242-4065.
BOKEN SOUND STUDIO, 513 W. 54 St., New York, NY 10019; (212) 581-5507; 111 LeRoy St., New York, NY 10014; (212) 924-0438; 511 W. 55 St., New York, NY 10019; (212) 247-0170.
BREITROSE-SELTZER STAGES, INC., 383 W. 12 St., New York, NY 10014; (212) 807-0664.
BROADWAY STUDIOS, 25-09 Broadway, Astoria, New York, NY 11106; (718) 274-9121.
CAMERA MART STAGES, 460 W. 54 St., New York, NY 10019; (212) 757-6977.
CECO INTERNATIONAL CORP., 440 W. 15 St., New York, NY 10011; (212) 206-8280.
CESTARE STUDIOS, INC., 188 Henricks Rd., Mineola, NY 11501; (516) 742-5550.
CINE STUDIO, 241 W. 54 St., New York, NY 10019; (212) 581-1916.
COM/TECH, 770 Lexington Ave., New York, NY 10021; (212) 826-2935.
DE FILIPPO STUDIO, 215 E. 37 St., New York, NY 10016; (212) 986-5444.
EMPIRE STAGES OF NY, 50-20 25 St., Long Island, NY 11101; (718) 392-4747.
FARKAS FILMS, INC., 385 Third Ave., New York, NY 10016; (212) 679-8212.
GLOBUS STUDIOS, (212) 1008,
HBO STUDIO PRODS., 120 E. 23 St., 10010; (212) 512-7800.
HORVATH & ASSOCIATES STUDIOS LTD., 95 Charles St., New York, NY 10014; (212) 741-0300.
KAUFMAN ASTORIA STUDIOS, 34-12 36th St., Astoria, NY 11106; (718) 392-5600; FAX: (718) 706-7733.
LRP VIDEO, 3 Dag Hammarskjold Plaza, New York, NY 10017; (212) 759-0822.
MAGNO SOUND & VIDEO, 729 Seventh Ave., 10019; (212) 302-2505.
MIDTOWN STUDIO, 101 Fifth Ave., New York, NY 10003; (212) 633-8484; FAX: (212) 255-3930.
MODERN TELECOMMUNICATIONS/MTI, 885 Second Ave., New York, NY 10017; (212) 355-0510.
MOTHERS SOUND STAGE, 210 E. 5 St., New York, NY 10003; (212) 260-2050.
NATIONAL VIDEO CENTER/RECORDING STUDIOS, INC., 460 W. 42 St., New York, NY 10036; (212) 279-2000.
NEW YORK PRODUCTION CENTER, 222 E. 44th St., New York, NY 10017; (212) 868-4030.
THE 95TH STREET STUDIO, INC., 206 E. 95 St., New York, NY 10028; (212) 831-1946.
NORTH STAR VIDEO LTD., 581 Avenue of the Americas, New York, NY 10011; (212) 337-3200.
PHOENIX STAGES, 537 W. 59 St., New York, NY 10019; (212) 581-7670.
PRIMALUX VIDEO & FILM, 30 W. 26 St., New York, NY 10010; (212) 206-1402.
PRODUCTION CENTER, 221 W. 26 St., New York, NY 10001; (212) 675-2211.
REEVES COMMUNICATIONS, 708 Third Ave., New York, NY 10017; (212) 573-8600.
RIVERVIEW STUDIOS, 30-15 Vernon Blvd., Astoria, NY 11102; (718) 545-7200.
SHINBONE ALLEY STAGE, 680 Broadway, New York, NY 10012; (212) 420-8463.
SILVERCUP STUDIOS, 42-25 21st St., Long Island City, NY 11101; (718) 784-3390.
TELETECHNIQUES, INC., 1 W. 19 St., New York, NY 10011; (212) 206-1475; 633-1868.
3-G STAGE CORP., 236 W. 61 St., New York, NY 10023; (212) 247-3130.
UNITED FILM ENTERPRISES, INC., 26 W. Park Ave., Suite 107, Long Beach, NY 11561; (516)431-2687.
UNITEL VIDEO INC., 515 W. 57 St., New York, NY 10019; (212) 265-3600.

VCA TELETRONICS, CENTER STAGE, 503 W. 33 St., New York, NY 10001; (212) 736-7677; 736-7717.
VERITAS STUDIOS, 527 W. 45 St., New York, NY 10036; (212) 581-2050.
VIDEO PLANNING INC!, 325 W. 56 St., New York, NY 10019; (212) 582-5066.
WALLACH, PETER, PRODS., 419 Broome St., New York, NY 10013; (212) 966-1970.

ORLANDO

UNIVERSAL STUDIOS FLORIDA, 1000 Universal Studios Plaza, Orlando, FL 32819; (407) 363-8400.
WALT DISNEY/MGM STUDIOS, 3300 N. Bonnett Creek Rd., Lake Buena Vista, FL 32830-0200; (407) 560-5353; 560-6188.

TEMPE, AZ

WONDER BROTHERS, 2244 S. Industrial Park Ave., Tempe, AZ 85281; (602) 921-0139.

Screening Rooms

ATLANTA

CINEVISION CORP., 1771 Tully Circle, N.E., Atlanta 30329; (404) 321-6333.

BOSTON

BOSTON LIGHT & SOUND, 124 Brighton Ave., #134; Boston, MA 02134; (617) 787-3131.
E.M. LOEW ENTERPRISES, 75 Arlington, Boston, 02116; (617) 482-9200.
UNIVERSAL FILM EXCHANGE, 44 Winchester St., 02116; (617) 426-8760.

CHICAGO

CHICAGO INTERNATIONAL FILM FESTIVAL, 415 N. Dearborn, Chicago 60613; (312) 644-3400.
EXCELLENCE THEATRES CORPORATION, 230 W. Monroe St., Suite 2700, Chicago 60606; (312) 332-7465.

LOS ANGELES

ACADEMY LITTLE THEATER, 8949 Wilshire Blvd., 3rd Floor, Beverly Hills, 90211; (213) 278-8990; FAX: (213) 859-9619.
AIDIKOFF, CHARLES, SCREENING ROOM, 9255 W. Sunset Blvd., Suite 104, 90069; (213) 274-0866.
AMERICAN FILM INSTITUTE, 2021 N. Western Ave., Los Angeles, CA 90027; (213) 856-7600; FAX: (213) 467-4578.
BEVERLY HILLS SCREENING INC., 8949 Sunset Blvd., Suite 201, Beverly Hills, CA 90069; (213) 275-3088.
BURBANK STUDIOS, 4000 Warner Blvd., Burbank, CA 91522; (818) 954-6000.
CANNON SOUND STUDIOS, 640 S. San Vicente Blvd., Los Angeles, CA 90048; (213) 658-2012.
DAUGHERTY AUDIO/VIDEO DESIGN, 2172 Ridgemont, Los Angeles, CA 90046; (213) 650-5665; 718-5531.
DIRECTORS GUILD OF AMERICA, 7950 W. Sunset Blvd., Los Angeles 90046; (213) 656-1220; FAX: (213) 656-9076.
GOLDWYN,SAMUEL, THEATER, 8949 Wilshire Blvd., Beverly Hills, CA 90211; (213) 278-8990; FAX: (213) 859-9619.
HARRAH'S THEATRE SERVICE & SUPPLY, 624B S. San Fernando Blvd., Burbank, CA 91502; (818) 842-5111.
HOLLY-VINE SCREENING ROOM, 6253 Hollywood Blvd., Suite 1210, Los Angeles, CA 90028; (213) 462-3498.
HOLLYWOOD NEWSREEL SYNDICATE, INC., 1622 N. Gower St., Los Angeles, CA 90028; (213) 469-7307.
HOLLYWOOD SCREENING ROOM, 1800 N. Highland Ave., Suite 509, Hollywood 90028; (213) 466-1888.
L'IMAGE AUDIO/VISUAL CO., 10729 Devonshire St., Suite 143, Northridge, CA 91325; (818) 368-9584.
JDH SOUND, 12156 Olympic Blvd., Los Angeles, CA 90064; (213) 820-8802; FAX: (213) 207-0914.
LION'S GATE STUDIOS, 1861 S. Bundy Dr., Los Angeles, CA 90025; (213) 820-7751; FAX: (213) 315-2110.
MAINSTREET INAMGERY, 13105 Saticoy St., N. Hollywood, CA 91605; (818) 530-0931; FAX: (818) 982-9383.
PREVIEW HOUSE, 7655 Sunset Blvd., Los Angeles 90046; (213) 876-6600.
QUALITY SOUND, INC., 5625 Melrose Ave., Hollywood, CA 90038; (213) 467-7154.
RALEIGH STUDIOS, 650 N. Bronson Ave., Los Angeles, CA 90004; (213) 466-3111.
GLENN ROLAND FILMS, 10711 Wellworth Ave., Los Angeles, CA 90024; (213) 475-0937.
S.A. GLOBEL STUDIOS, 201 N. Occidental Blvd., Los Angeles, CA 90026; (213) 384-3331.
JOE SHORE'S SCREENING ROOM, 9118½ Sunset Blvd., Los Angeles 90069; (213) 274-4888.
SOUND WEST INC., 12166 Olympic Blvd., Los Angeles, CA 90064; (213) 826-6560.
VAN DE VEER PHOTO EFFECTS, 724 S. Victory Blvd., Burbank, CA 91502; (818) 841-2512.
WRITERS GUILD DOHENY PLAZA THEATER, 135 S. Doheny Dr. Beverly Hills, CA 90212; (213) 550-1000.

MILWAUKEE

MARCUS THEATRES, 212 W. Wisconsin Ave., 53203; (414) 272-6020.

MISSION, KS

DICKINSON OPERATING CO., 5913 Woodson Rd., Mission, KS 66202; (913) 432-2334.

NEW YORK

(All major producers-distributors have screening rooms at their home offices in New York for their own use. Most also have screening room facilities at their New York exchanges).
THE BROADWAY SCREENING ROOM, 1619 Broadway, 5th Floor, New York, NY 10019; (212) 307-0990.
CINE-METRIC THEATRE CORP., 290 Madison Ave., New York, NY 10017; (212) 532-4140.
MAGNO PREVIEW THEATRE, 1600 Broadway, New York, NY 10019; (212) 302- 2505.
MAGNO SOUND SCREENING ROOM, 729 Seventh Ave., New York, NY 10019; (212) 302-2505.
MOVIE MAKERS THEATRE, 311 W. 43 St., New York, NY 10036; (212) 397-9787; outside NY: (800) 225-6566.
NAVESYNC SOUND, 513 W. 54 St., New York, NY 10019; (212) 246-0100.
PRECISION FILM LABS' SCREENING THEATRE, 630 Ninth Ave., New York, NY, 10036; (212) 489-8800.
PREVIEW THEATRE, 1600 Broadway, New York, NY 10019; (212) 246-0865.
TECHNICOLOR, 321 W. 44 St., New York, NY 10036; (212) 582-7310.
TODD-AO STUDIOS EAST, 259 W. 54 St., New York, NY 10019; (212) 265-6225.

SAN FRANCISCO

THE EXPLORATORIUM, McBEAN THEATER, 3601 Lyon St., San Francisco, CA 94123; (415) 563-7337.
MOTION PICTURE SERVICE CO., 125 Hyde St., San Francisco, CA 94107; (415) 673-9162.
PACIFIC FILM ARCHIVE, 2625 Durant Ave., Berkeley, CA 94720; (415) 642-1412.
THE SAUL ZAENTZ CO. FILM CENTER, 2600 Tenth St., Berkeley, CA 94710; (415) 549-2500.

Sound and Recording Services

DETROIT

MOTION PICTURE SOUND INC., (MPS), 3026 E. Grand Blvd., Detroit, MI 48202; (313) 873-4655.

HOLLYWOOD

AUDIO EFFECTS COMPANY, 1600 N. Western Ave., Hollywood 90027; (213) 469-3692. (Complete recording services).
B & B SOUND STUDIOS, 3610 W. Magnolia Blvd., Burbank, CA 91505; (818) 848-4496.
BURBANK STUDIOS, THE, 4000 Warner Blvd., Burbank, CA 91522; (818) 954-6000.
BUZZY'S RECORDING SERVICES, 6900 Melrose Ave., Los Angeles, CA 90038; (213) 931-1867; FAX: (213) 931-9681.

CINESOUND, 915 N. Highland Ave., Hollywood, CA 90038; (213) 464-1155.
COMPACT VIDEO SERVICES, 2813 Alameda Ave., Burbank, CA 91505; (818) 840-7000; (800) 423-2277; FAX: (818) 846-5197.
CRYSTAL SOUND RECORDING, 1014 N. Vine St., Los Angeles, CA 90038; (213) 466-6452.
DOLBY LABORATORIES, INC., 1149 N. McCadden Pl., Los Angeles, CA 90038; (213) 464-4596.
EVERGREEN RECORDING STUDIOS, 4403 W. Magnolia Blvd., Burbank, CA 91505; (818) 841-6800.
FIDELITY RECORDING STUDIO, 4412 Whitsett Ave., Studio City, CA 91604; (818) 508-3263.
FIESTA SOUND & VIDEO, 1655 S. Compton Ave., Los Angeles, CA 90021; (213) 748-2057; 748-2665.
GLEN GLENN SOUND CO., 900 N. Seward St., Hollywood, CA 90038; (213) 469-7221.
GROUP IV RECORDING, 1541 Wilcox Ave., Los Angeles, CA 90028; (213) 466-6444.
HARK'S SOUND STUDIO, 1041 N. Orange Dr., Hollywood, CA 90038; (213) 463-3288.
INTERSOUND INC., 8746 Sunset Blvd., Los Angeles, CA 90069; (213) 652-3741.
LARRABEE SOUND, 8811 Santa Monica Blvd., W. Hollywood, CA 90069; (213) 657-6750.
LION'S SHARE RECORDING STUDIOS, 8255 Beverly Blvd., Los Angeles, CA 90048; (213) 658-5990.
MCA/ WHITNEY RECORDING, 1516 W. Glenoaks Blvd., Glenoaks, CA 91201; (818) 507-1041.
MUSIC GRINDERS STUDIOS, 7460 Melrose Ave., Los Angeles, CA 90046; (213) 655-2996.
NEW JACK SOUND RECORDERS, 1956 N. Cahuenga Blvd., Los Angeles, CA 90068; (213) 466-6141.
PARAMOUNT RECORDING STUDIOS, 6245 Santa Monica Blvd., Hollywood, CA 90038; (213) 461-3717.
PRODUCERS 1 & 2 RECORDING STUDIOS, 6035 Hollywood Blvd., Los Angeles, CA 90028; (213) 466-7766.
QUALITY SOUND, 5625 Melrose Ave., Los Angeles, CA 90038; (213) 467-7154.
REPUBLIC SOUND STUDIOS INC., 7060 Hollywood Blvd., Los Angeles, CA 90028; (213) 462-6897.
RYDER SOUND SERVICES, INC., 1611 Vine St., Hollywood, CA 90038; (213) 469-3511.
SANTA MONICA SOUND RECORDERS, 2114 Pico Blvd., Santa Monica, CA 90405; (213) 450-3193.
SCOTTSOUND, INC., 6110 Santa Monica Blvd., Los Angeles, CA 90038; (213) 462-6981.
SCREENMUSIC STUDIOS, 11700 Ventura Blvd., Studio City, CA 91604; (213) 887-0300; (818) 985-0900.
SKYLINE RECORDING, 1402 Old Topanga Canyon Rd., Topanga Park, CA 90290; (213) 455-2044.
SOUND CITY, INC., 15456 Cabrito Rd., Van Nuys, CA 91406; (213) 873-2842; (818) 787-3722.
SOUND IMAGE STUDIO, 6556 Wilkinson Ave., N. Hollywood, CA 91606-2320; (818) 762-8881.
SOUND SERVICES, INC., (SSI), 7155 Santa Monica Blvd., Los Angeles, CA 90046; (213) 874-9344.
SOUNDS UNLIMITED, P.O. Box 69C, West Hollywood, CA 90069; (213) 659-9578.
SOUNDCASTLE RECORDING STUDIO, 2840 Rowena Ave., Los Angeles, CA 90039; (213) 665-5201.
STUDIO M PRODUCTIONS UNLIMITED, 16027 Royal Oak Rd., Encino, CA 91436; (818) 906-8728.
SUNSET SOUND RECORDERS, 6850 Sunset Blvd., Hollywood, CA 90028.
SUNWEST RECORDING STUDIOS, 5533 Sunset Blvd., Hollywood, CA 90028; (213) 465-1000.
TRIANON RECORDING STUDIOS, 1435 South St., Long Beach, CA 90805; (213) 422-2095.
TODD-AO GLEN-GLEN STUDIOS, 1021 N. Seward St., Hollywood, CA 90038; (213) 463-1136; 463-1136.
UNIVERSAL CITY STUDIOS, 100 Universal City Plaza, Universal City, CA 91608; (213) 985-4321.
VALENTINE RECORDING STUDIOS, 5330 Laurel Canyon Blvd., N. Hollywood, CA 91607; (818) 769-1515.
WARNER HOLLYWOOD STUDIOS, 1041 N. Formosa, Los Angeles, CA 90046; (213) 850-2500.
WAVES SOUND RECORDERS, 1956 N. Cahuenga Blvd., Hollywood, CA 90048; (213) 466-6141; FAX: (213) 466-3751.
WESTLAKE STUDIOS, C.D. & E., 7265 Santa Monica Blvd., Los Angeles, CA 90046; (213) 851-9800; 655-0303.
WESTWORLD RECORDERS, 7118 Van Nuys Blvd., Van Nuys, CA 91405; (818) 782-8449.

NEW YORK

A & J RECORDING STUDIOS, INC., 225 W. 57 St., New York, NY 10019; (212) 247-4860.
AQUARIUS TRANSFER, 12 E. 46 St., New York, NY 10017; (212) 697-3636.
AR-VEE SOUND SERVICES, 630 Ninth Ave., #400, New York, NY 10036; (212) 459-9588.
THE AUDIO DEPARTMENT, 119 W. 57 St., New York, NY 10019; (212) 586-3503.
BEE VEE SOUND INC., 211 E. 43 St., #603, New York, NY 10017; (212) 949-9170.
BLANK TAPES, INC., RECORDING STUDIOS, 37 W. 20 St., New York, NY 10011; (212) 255-5313.
CP SOUND, 123 W. 18 St., New York, NY 10011; (212) 677-7700.
CINEQUIP, INC., 241 E. 51 St., New York, NY 10022; (212) 308-5100.
CORELLI-JACOBS RECORDING, 25 W. 45 St., New York, NY 10036; (212) 382-0220.
CREATIVE AUDIO RECORDING SERVICES, 19 W. 36 St., New York, NY 10018; (212) 714-0976.
CUE RECORDINGS, INC., 1156 Ave. of the Americas, New York, NY 10036; (212) 921-9221.
DB SOUND STUDIOS, INC., 25 W. 45 St., New York, NY 10036; (212) 764-6000.
DOLBY LABORATORIES INC., 1350 Ave. of the Americas, 28th Floor, New York, NY 10019-4703; (212) 645-1522.
DOWNTOWN TRANSFER, 167 Perry St., New York, NY 10014; (212) 255-8698.
EAST SIDE FILM & VIDEO CENTER, 216 E. 45 St., New York, NY 10017; (212) 867-0730.
ELECTRO-NOVA PRODUCTIONS, 342 Madison Ave., New York, NY 10017; (212) 687-5838.
EMPIRE SOUND, 18 W. 45 St., New York, NY 10036; (212) 302-2505.
HIT FACTORY, THE, INC., 237 W. 54 St., 10019; (212) 664-1000.
IBERO-AMERICAN PRODUCTIONS, 630 Ninth Ave., New York, NY 10036; (212) 245-7826.
MAGNO SOUND & VIDEO, 729 Seventh Ave., 10019; (212) 302-2505.
THE MIX PLACE, 663 Fifth Ave., New York, NY 10022; (212) 759-8311.
NATIONAL VIDEO CENTER RECORDING STUDIOS, 460 W. 42 St., New York, NY 10036; (212) 279-2000.
NAVESYNC SOUND, 513 W. 54 St., New York, NY 10019; (212) 246-0100.
NEW BREED STUDIOS, 251 W. 30 St., New York, NY 10001; (212) 714-9379.
PHOTO MAG. SOUND STUDIOS, 222 E. 44 St., New York, NY 10017; (212) 687-9030.
PRINCZKO PRODUCTIONS, 9 E. 38 St., New York, NY 10016; (212) 683-1300.
REGENT SOUND STUDIOS, 1619 Broadway, New York, NY 10019; (212) 245-2630.
ROSS-GAFFNEY, INC., 21 W. 46 St., New York, NY 10018; (212) 719-2744.
SCHWARTZ, HOWARD M., RECORDING, INC., 420 Lexington Ave., New York, NY 10017: (212) 687-4180.
SOUND ONE CORP., 1619 Broadway, New York, NY 10019; (212) 765-4757.
SOUND PATROL, LTD., 6 E. 39 St., New York, NY 10016; (212) 213-6666.
SOUND SHOP, THE, 321 W. 44 St., New York, NY 10036; (212) 757-5700.
TITRA SOUND CORP., 1600 Broadway, New York, NY 10019; (212) 757-7129.
TODD-AO STUDIOS EAST, 259 W. 54 St., New York, NY 10019; (212) 265-6225.
TRACK TRANSFERS, INC., 45 W. 45 St., New York, NY 10036; (212) 730-1635; 730-0555.
UNITED RECORDING, 681 Fifth Ave., New York, NY 10022; (212) 751-4660.
THOMAS J. VALENTINO, 151 W. 46 St., #803,New York, NY 10036; (212) 869-5210; (800) 223-6278.
VOICES, 16 E. 48 St., New York, NY 10017; (212) 935-9820.
WAREHOUSE RECORDING, 320 W. 46 St., New York, NY 10036; (212) 265-6060.

ORLANDO

WALT DISNEY/MGM STUDIOS, P.O. Box 10200, Lake Buena Vista, FL 32830-0200; (407) 560-7299.

SAN FRANCISCO

DOLBY LABORATORIES, INC. Head Office & U.S. Sales, 100 Potrero Ave., 94103; (415) 558-0200; Telex: 34409.
LUCASFILM LTD. (Sprocket Systs., Inc.,) P.O. Box 2009, San Rafael, CA 94912; (415) 662-1800; FAX: (415) 662-2460.

MUSIC ANNEX INC., 69 Green St., San Francisco, CA 94112; (415) 421-6622.
RUSSIAN HILL RECORDING, 1520 Pacific Ave., San Francisco, CA 94109; (415) 474-4520.
THE SAUL ZAENTZ FILM CENTER, 2600 Tenth St., Berkeley, CA 94710; (415) 549-2500.

Special Effects

HOLLYWOOD

ANDERSON, HOWARD A., CO., 1016 N. Cole Ave., Hollywood, CA 90038; (213) 463-2336.
APOGEE, INC., 6842 Valjean Ave., Van Nuys, CA 91406; (818) 989-5757.
ART F/X, 3575 Cahuenga Blvd., W., Suite 560, Los Angeles, CA 90068; (213) 876-9469.
BIFROST EFFECTS/ LASERFX, 6733 Sale Ave., Canoga Park, CA 91307; (818) 704-0423.
BUENA VISTA VISUAL EFFECTS GROUP, 500 S. Buena Vista St., Burbank, CA 91521; (818) 560-5284.
DIGITAL VISION ENTERTAINMENT, 7080 Hollywood, Suite 901, Los Angeles, CA 90028; (213) 462-3790.
DREAMLIGHT IMAGES, INC., 932 N. La Brea Ave., Suite C, Hollywood, CA 90038; (213) 850-1996; FAX: (213) 850-5318.
ENERGY PRODUCTIONS, 2690 Beachwood Dr., Hollywood, CA 90068; (213) 462-3310; FAX: (213) 871-2763.
FANTASY II FILM EFFECTS, 504 S. Varney St., Burbank, CA 91502; (818) 843-1413.
FILMTRIX, INC., 11054 Chandler Blvd., N. Hollywood, CA 91601; (818) 980-3700; FAX: (818) 980-3703.
JOHNSON, RAY, STUDIOS, 5435 Denny St., N. Hollywood, CA 91601; (818) 508-7348.
JOHNSON'S, STEVE X. FX., INC., 8010 Wheatland Ave., Unit J, Sun Valley, CA 91352; (818) 504-2177; FAX: (818) 504-2838.
LASER MEDIA, 2046 Armacost, Los Angeles, CA 90025; (213) 820-3750.
MERLIN S/FX CO., Raleigh Studios, 5300 Melrose Ave., Hollywood, CA 90038; (213) 871-4433; FAX: (213) 871-4428.
MODERN FILM EFFECTS, 6860 Lexington Ave., Los Angeles, CA 90038; (213) 460-4111.
PACIFIC TITLE & ART STUDIO, 6350 Santa Monica Blvd., Los Angeles 90038; (213) 464-0121; 938-3711.
SPECIAL EFFECTS UNLIMITED, 752 N. Cahuenga Blvd., Los Angeles, CA 90038; (213) 466-3361.
VAN DER VEER PHOTO EFFECTS, 724 S. Victory Blvd., Burbank, CA 91502; (818) 841-2512.
YOUNG, GENE EFFECTS, 517 W. Windsor St., Glendale, CA 91204; (818) 243-8593; 848-7471.

NEW YORK

APA, 230 W. 10 St., New York, NY 10014; (212) 929-9436; 675-4894.
ALFIE & ASSOCIATES, 222 E. 44 St., New York, NY 10017; (212) 983-2686.
AMERICAN FILM ANIMATION CORP., 151 W. 28 St., New York, NY 10001; (212) 563-5720.
ANIMUS FILMS, 2 W. 47 St., New York, NY 10036; (212) 391-8716.
BALSMEYER & EVERETT, 230 W. 17 St., New York, NY 10011; (212) 627-3430.
BROADCAST ARTS, INC., 632 Broadway, New York, NY 10012; (212) 254-5400.
BROOKLYN MODEL WORKS, 60 Washington Ave., Brooklyn, NY 11205: (718) 834-1944.
CACIOPPO PRODUCTION DESIGN INC., 708 Third Ave., New York, NY 10017; (212) 573-8753.
CHARLEX, 2 W. 45 St., New York, NY 10036; (212) 719-4600.
CIMMELLI INC., 120 N. Pascack Rd., Spring Valley, NY 10977; (914) 356-2232.
CLELAND STUDIO, INC., 122 Spring St., New York, NY 10012; (212) 431-9185.
D'ANDREA PRODUCTIONS INC., 25 W. 45 St., New York, NY 10036; (212) 764-9200.
DARINO, 222 Park Ave. South, #2A New York, NY 10003; (212) 228-4024.
DOM DE FILIPPO STUDIO, INC., 215 E. 37 St., New York, NY 10016; (212) 986-5444; 867-4220.
DENARO, SAL, AND PUPPETS, 174 DeGraw St., Brooklyn, NY 11231; (718) 875-1711.
DOROS ANIMATION STUDIO, INC., 156 Fifth Ave., Suite 1119, New York, NY 10010; (212) 627-7220.
EDITEL/NEW YORK, 222 E. 44 St., New York, NY 10017; (212) 867-4600.
EFEX SPECIALISTS, 35-39 37th St., Long Island City, NY 11101; (718) 937-2417.
EFX UNLIMITED, 321 W. 44 St., #401, New York, NY 10036; (212) 541-9220.
EUE/SCREEN GEM PRINTS, 222 E. 44 St., New York, NY 10017; (212) 867-4030.
THE FANTASTIC ANIMATION MACHINE, INC., 12 E. 46 St., New York, NY 10017; (212) 697-2525.
FILM OPTICALS, INC., 144 E. 44 St., New York, NY 10017; (212) 697-4744.
FRIEDMAN, HAROLD CONSORTIUM, 420 Lexington Ave., New York, NY 10017; (212) 697-0858.
GATI, JOHN, FILM EFFECTS, INC., 154 W. 57 St., Suite 832, New York, NY 10019; (212) 582-9060.
GEARY, MICHAEL, NEW YORK SPECIAL EFFECTS, Pier 60 N. River, New York, NY ; (212) 741-0218.
GIZMO SPECIAL EFFECTS, 111 W. 24 St., New York, NY 10011; (212) 242-1504.
GLOBUS BROTHERS STAGES, 44 W. 24 St., New York, NY 10010; (212) 243-1008.
R/GREENBERG ASSOCIATES, 350 W. 39 St., New York, NY 10018; (212) 239-6767.
HOLOGRAPHIC LASERLAND, 240 E. 26 St., New York, NY 10010; (212) 686-9397.
I.F. STUDIOS, INC., 15 W. 38 St., New York, NY 10018; (212) 819-1880.
KUNZ, PETER, CO., INC., RDl Box 223, High Falls, NY 12440; (914) 687-0400.
LEVY, DANIEL, 408 E. 13 St., New York, NY 10009; (212) 254-8964.
LIBERTY STUDIOS, INC. 238 E. 26 St., New York, NY 10010; (212) 532-1865.
MS25, 516 W. 25 St., New York, NY 10001; (212) 989-2100.
MALLIE, DALE, & COMPANY, INC., 40 Stevens Pl., Lawrence, NY 11559; (516) 239-8782.
MANTELL, PAUL, SPECIAL CREATIONS, 181 Hudson St., New York, NY 10013; (212) 645-8565.
MERCURY NEON, 86 Hester St., New York, NY 10002; (212) 219-0542.
NEW YORK SPECIAL EFFECTS, Pier 62, North River, New York, NY 10011; (212) 741-0218.
OPTICAL HOUSE, INC., 25 W. 45 St., New York, NY 10036; (212) 869-5840.
PROP EFFECTS & RIGGING, 713 Snediker Ave., Brooklyn, NY 11207; (718) 272-1613.
PUPPET PROJECTS, 97 Eagle St., Brooklyn, NY 11222; (800) 365-4485.
DEED ROSSITER SPECIAL EFFECTS, (914) 359-8884.
SMA VIDEO, INC., 84 Wooster St., New York, NY 10012; (212) 226-7474.
SPECIAL EFFECTS UNLIMITED, 18 Euclid Ave., Yonkers, NY; (914) 965-5625.
SPECIAL MAKE-UP EFFECTS STUDIO, 68 Colonial Ave., Dobbs Ferry, NY 10522; (914) 693-2752.
THEATER EFFECTS, INC., 52 Cottage St., Port Chester, NY 10573; (914) 937-9266.
TRILOGY, SUNFLOWER FILMS INC., 25 W. 45th St., New York, NY 10036; (212) 869-0123.
VILLANUEVA, 238 Troutman St., Brooklyn, NY 11237; (718) 366-2754.
WALLACH, PETER, PRODS., 419 Broome St., New York, NY 10013; (212) 966-1970.
WEISS, PETER, DESIGNS, 32 Union Sq. E., New York, NY 10003; (212) 477-2659.
WIZARDWORKS, 39-40 21st St., Long Island City, NY 11101; (718) 786-8383.
YURKIW LTD., 568 Broadway, New York, NY 10012; (212) 226-6338.
ZELLER INTERNATIONAL, (212) 627-7676; (607) 363-7792.

SAN FRANCISCO

MAGIC VISTA STUDIOS INC., 39 Dorman Ave., San Francisco, CA 94124; (415) 821-7979.

SAN RAFAEL

LUCASFILM, LTD., P.O. Box 2009, San Rafael, CA 94912; (415) 662-1800.

ORLANDO

WALT DISNEY/MGM STUDIOS, P.O. Box 10200, Lake Buena Vista, FL 32830; (407) 560-7299.

Stock-Shot Film Libraries

HOLLYWOOD-LOS ANGELES

ACADEMY OF MOTION PICTURE ARTS & SCIENCES LIBRARY, 8949 Wilshire Blvd., Beverly Hills, CA 90211; (213) 278-4313.
AFTER IMAGE INC., 6100 Wilshire Blvd., Suite 240, Los Angeles, 90048; (213) 480-1105.
AMERICAN FILM INSTITUTE LIBRARY, 2021 N. Western Ave., Los Angeles, 90027; (213) 856-7600; 856-7655.
TOM ANDERSON FILMWORKS, 6362 Hollywood Blvd., Suite 308, Los Angeles, 90028; (213) 464-0386.
ASSOCIATED MEDIA IMAGES, INC., 650 N. Bronson, Suite 300, Los Angeles, 90004; (213) 871-1340.
BUDGET FILMS, 4590 Santa Monica Blvd., Los Angeles, 90029; (213) 660- 0187.
BUENA VISTA STUDIOS, 500 S. Buena Vista St., Burbank, 91521; (818) 560-0044.
CAMEO FILM LIBRARY, 10620 Burbank Blvd., North Hollywood, 91601; (818) 980-8700.
CINEMAPHILE AMALGAMATED PICTURES, P.O. Box 8054, Universal City, 91608; (213) 939-9042.
DICK CLARK MEDIA ARCHIVES, INC., 3003 W. Olive Ave., Burbank, CA 91505; (818) 841-3003.
THE CLIP JOINT FOR FILM, 5304 Agnes Ave., North Hollywood, CA 91607; (818) 761-0545; 761-3228.
LARRY DORN ASSOCS., 5550 Wilshire Blvd., #303, Los Angeles, 90036; (213) 935-6266; FAX: (213) 935-9523.
DREAMLIGHT IMAGES, INC., 932 N. La Brea Ave., Suite C, Hollywood, 90038; (213) 850-1996; FAX: (213) 850-5318.
ENERGY PRODUCTIONS, 2690 Beachwood Dr., Los Angeles, 90068; (213) 462-3310; FAX: (213) 871-2763.
ENTERPRISES PRODUCTIONS, 5912 Ramirez Canyon, Malibu, 90265-4423; (213) 457-8081.
FILM BANK, 3306 W. Burbank Blvd., Burbank, 91505; (818) 841-9176.
FILM SEARCH, 9583 Alcott Ave., #201, Los Angeles, 90035; (213) 550-1947.
FISH FILMS INC., 4548 Van Noord Ave., Studio City, 91604-1013; (818) 905-1071.
JAMES FOSHER COLLECTION OF ARCHIVAL FOOTAGE, 953 N. Highland Ave., Los Angeles, 90038; (213) 461-0178.
G-FORCE INTERNATIONAL ENTERTAINMENT CORP., 279 S. Beverly Dr., Suite 1038, Beverly Hills, 90212; (213) 271-0700.
GREAT WAVES FILM LIBRARY, 483 Mariposa Dr., Ventura, 93001; (805) 653-2699.
SHERMAN GRINBERG FILM LIBRARIES, INC., 1040 N. McCadden Pl., Hollywood, CA 90038; (213) 464-7491; FAX: (213) 462-5352.
H.B. HALICKI PRODS., 17902 S. Vermont Ave., P.O. Box 2123, Gardena 90248; (213) 770-1744; 327-1744.
HERITAGE ENTERTAINMENT INC., 7920 Sunset Blvd., Suite 200, Los Angeles, 90046; (213) 850-5858.
HOLLYWOOD NEWSREEL SYNDICATE INC., 1622 N. Gower St., Hollywood, 90028; (213) 469-7307.
THE IMAGE BANK WEST, 4526 Wilshire Blvd., Los Angeles, 90010; (213) 930-0797.
INTERVIDEO, 733 N. Victory Blvd., Burbank 91502; (818) 843-3633; 569-4000; FAX: 843-6884.
CLAY LACY AVIATION INC., 7435 Valjean Ave., Van Nuys, 91406; (818) 989-2900.
MAC GILLIVRAY FREEMAN FILM & TAPE LIBRARY, P.O. Box 205, S. Laguna, 92677; (714) 494-1055; FAX: (714) 494-2079.
MAINSTREET IMAGERY, INC., 13105 Saticoy St., N. Hollywood, 91605; (818) 503-0931; FAX: (818) 982-9383.
PALISADES WILDLIFE LIBRARY, 1205 S. Ogden Dr., Los Angeles, 90019; (213) 931-6186.
PHOTO-CHUTING ENTERPRISES, 12619 S. Manor Dr., Hawthorne, 90250; (213) 678-0163.
PRODUCERS LIBRARY SERVICE, 1051 N. Cole Ave., Hollywood, 90038; (213) 465-0572.
PYRAMID FILM & VIDEO, 2801 Colorado Ave., Santa Monica, 90404; (213) 828-7577; FAX: (213) 453-9083.
RON SAWADE CINEMATOGRAPHY, 3724 Berry Dr., Studio City, 91604; (818) 769-1737.
THE STOCK HOUSE, 6922 Hollywood Blvd., Suite 621, Los Angeles, 90028; (213) 461-0061.
TURNER ENTERTAINMENT CO., 10100 Venice Blvd., Culver City, 90232; (213) 558-7300.
TWA MOVIE & TV PROMOTIONS, 5550 Wilshire Blvd., Suite 303, Los Angeles, 90036; (213) 935-6266; FAX: (213) 935-9523.
UNITED STATES AIR FORCE, Office of Public Affairs, Western Region, 11000 Wilshire Blvd., Suite 10114, Los Angeles, 90024; (213) 209-7525; 209-7522; FAX: (213) 437-9960.
UNITED STATES ARMY, Office of Public Affairs, 11000 Wilshire Blvd, Suite 10104, Los Angeles, 90024-3688; (213) 209-7621; FAX: (213) 473-8874.
UNIVERSAL CITY STUDIOS, 100 Universal City Plaza, Universal City, 91608; (818) 777-3000; FAX: 777-2731.
VIDEO TAPE LIBRARY LTD., 1509 N. Crescent Heights, Blvd. #2, Los Angeles, 90046; (213) 656-4330; FAX: (213) 656-8746.
WORLDWIDE ENTERTAINMENT CORP., 5912 Ramirez Canyon, Malibu, 90265; (213) 457-8081.

MIAMI

KESSER POST PRODUCTION, 21 SW 15 Rd., Miami, 33129; (305) 358-7900.

MIDWEST

BRITANNICA FILMS, 425 N. Michigan Ave., Chicago, IL 60611; (312) 347-7400, ext. 6512; (800) 554-9862.
FILM TAPE COMPANY, 210 E. Pearson, Chicago, IL 60611; (312) 649-0599; (800) 637-TAPE.
WHITE JANSSEN, INC., 604 Davis St., Evanston, IL 60201; (312) 328-2221.

NEW YORK

AMERICAN MUSEUM OF NATURAL HISTORY FILM ARCHIVES, Central Park West at 79 St., 10024; (212) 769- 5419.
ARCHIVE FILM PRODUCTIONS, INC., 530 W. 25 St., 10001; (212) 620-3955; FAX: (212) 645-2137.
CHERTOK ASSOCIATES, INC., 185 West End Ave., 10023; (212) 874-0797.
CINE SCAN (Newsreel Access Systems, Inc.), 150 E. 58th St., 10155; (800) 242-CINE.
COE FILM ASSOCIATES, INC., 65 E. 96 St., 10128; (212) 831-5355; FAX: (212) 645-0681.
THE FILM PRESERVE, P.O. Box 397, Mamaroneck, NY 10543-0397; (914) 381-2993.
FILM SEARCH, 232 Madison Ave., 10016, (212) 532-0600.
SHERMAN GRINBERG FILM LIBRARIES, INC., 630 Ninth Ave., NY 10036; (212) 765-5170; FAX: (212) 245-2339.
HALCYON DAYS PRODUCTIONS, 12 West End Ave., 10023; (212) 397-8785.
THE IMAGE BANK, 111 Fifth Ave., 10003; (212) 529-6700; FAX: (212) 529-8886.
IMAGEWAYS, INC. 440 W. 47 St., Suite 4G, 10036; (212) 265-1287.
JALBERT PRODUCTIONS, INC., 775 Park Ave., Huntington, NY 11743; (516) 351-5878.
KILLIAM SHOWS, INC., 6 E. 39 St., 10016; (212) 679-8230.
MOVIETONEWS, INC. FILM LIBRARY, (Subsidiary of 20th Century Fox), 460 W. 54 St., 10019; (212) 408-8450.
MUSEUM OF MODERN ART FILM LIBRARY, 11 W. 53 St., 10019; (212) 245-8900.
NBC NEWS ARCHIVES, 30 Rockefeller Plaza, 10112; (212) 664-3797.
NEWSREEL ACCESS SYSTEMS, INC., 150 E. 58 St., 10155; (800) 242-CINE.
PETRIFIED FILMS INC., 430 W. 14 St., 10014; (212) 242-5461.
PRELINGER ASSOC., INC., 430 W. 14 St., 10014; (212) 255- 8866.
THE PORT AUTHORITY OF NY & NJ, 1 World Trade Center, 10048; (212) 466-7646.
SECOND LINE SEARCH, 330 W. 42 St., Room 2901, 10036; (212) 594-5544.
RICK SPALLA VIDEO PRODUCTIONS, 301 W. 45 St., 10036; (212) 765-4646; 462-4710.
STREAMLINE FILM ARCHIVES, 109 E. 29 St., 10016; (212) 696-2616.
TIMESTEPS PRODUCTIONS, (201) 669-1930; (213) 462-6565.
WTN-WORLDWIDE TV NEWS CORP., 1995 Broadway, 10023; (212) 362-4440.

TUCSON, AZ

THE SOURCE STOCK FOOTAGE, 1709 S. 29 Place, Tucson, AZ 85710; (602) 298-4810.

Stop Watches

DUCOMMUN, M., CO., 48 Main St., Warwick, NY 10990; (914) 986-5757.
MARCEL WATCH CORP., 1115 Broadway, New York, NY 10010; (212) 620-8181.
SMITH TIME, P.O. Box 496, Ivy, VA 22945; (804) 977-7440.

Subtitles

CALIFORNIA

AND/OR, P.O. Box 445, Burbank, CA 91503; (818) 577-4142.
CAPTIONS, INC., 2479 Lanterman Terr., Los Angeles, CA 90039; (213) 665-4860.
CINETYP, INC., 843 Seward St., Hollywood, CA 90038; (213) 463-8569.
CREST NATIONAL FILM AND VIDEOTAPE LABS, 1141 N. Seward St., Hollywood, CA 90038; (213) 466-0624; 462-6696; FAX: (213) 461-8901.
FOREIGN LANGUAGE GRAPHICS, 4099 N. Mission Rd., Los Angeles, CA 90032; (213) 221-4992.
GLOBAL LANGUAGE SERVICES, 2027 Las Lunas, Pasadena, CA 91107; (818) 792-0862; 792-0576; FAX: (818) 792-8793.
GOOSI, 13273 Ventura Blvd., #212, Studio City, CA 91604; (818) 906-9946.
HEADLEY INTERNATIONAL PICTURES, 738 N. Cahuenga Blvd., #F, Los Angeles, CA 90038; (213) 969-9650.
HOMER AND ASSOCIATES, INC., Sunset Gower Studios, 1420 N. Beachwood Dr., Hollywood, CA 90028; (213) 462-4710.
INTERSOUND, INC., 8746 Sunset Blvd., Los Angeles, CA 90069; (213) 652-3741.
INTEX AUDIOVISUALS, 9021 Melrose Ave., Suite 205, Los Angeles, CA 90069; (213) 275-9571.
LINGUATHEQUE OF L.A., P.O. Box 44281, Van Nuys, CA 91412; (818) 894-2882.
MAINSTREET IMAGERY, INC., 13105 Saticoy St., N. Hollywood, CA 91605; (818) 503-0931.
P.F.M. DUBBING INTERNATIONAL, 8306 Wilshire Blvd., Suite 947, Beverly Hills, CA 90211; (213) 936-7577; FAX: (213) 936-1691.
PACIFIC TITLE & ART STUDIO, 6350 Santa Monica Blvd., Los Angeles, CA 90038; (213) 464-5451; 938-3711.
RENCHER'S EDITORIAL SERVICE, 738 Cahuenga Blvd., Hollywood, CA 90038; (213) 463-9836.
ROLAND FRENCH TRANSLATION SERVICES, 10711 Wellworth Ave., Los Angeles, CA 90024; (213) 475-4347.

NEW YORK

THE CAPTION CENTER, 231 E. 55 St., New York, NY 10022; (212) 223-4930.
DEVLIN VIDEO SERVICE, 1501 Broadway, Suite 408, New York, NY 10036; (212) 391-1313.
EISENMAN, HELEN, 630 Ninth Ave., Suite 909, New York, NY 10036; (212) 757-5969; 749-3655.
FRIEDMAN, SONYA, 853 Broadway, Suite 1501, New York, NY 10011; (212) 505-1990.
FIMA NOVECK PRODUCTIONS, 231 W. 44 St., 4th floor, New York, NY 10036; (212) 315-4220.
RENNERT BILINGUAL TRANSLATIONS, 2 W. 45 St., 5th floor, New York, NY 10036; (212) 819-1776.

Trailers

ATLANTA

CINEMA CONCEPTS THEATRE SERVICE, INC., 6720 Powers Ferry Rd., Atlanta, GA 30339; (404) 956-7460.

CHICAGO

FILMACK CORP., 1327 S. Wabash Ave., Chicago, IL 60605; (312) 427-3395.

KANSAS CITY, MO

NATIONAL SCREEN SERVICE GROUP, INC., 1800 Baltimore Ave., Kansas City, MO 64108; (816) 842-5893.
UNIVERSAL IMAGES, LTD., P.O. Box 9313, Kansas City, MO 64133; (816) 358-6166. (Produces advertising commercials, for showing on theatre screens, and special trailers, e.g., "No Smoking," "Intermission," etc.)

LOS ANGELES

ANDERSON, HOWARD A., CO., 1016 N. Cole Ave., Los Angeles, CA 90038; (213) 463-2336.
AVAILABLE LIGHT LTD., 3110 W. Burbank Blvd., CA 91505; (818) 842-2109.
BOSUSTOW VIDEO, 2207 Colby Ave., West Los Angeles, CA 90064; (213) 478-0821.
COMING ATTRACTIONS, 550 N. Brand Blvd., Suite 700, Glendale, CA 91203; (213) 465-4129.
THE CREATIVE PARTNERSHIP, INC., 7525 Fountain Ave., Hollywood, CA 90046; (213) 850-5551; FAX: (213) 850-0391.
CRUSE & CO., 7000 Romaine St., Hollywood, CA 90038; (213) 851-8814.
EMERALD LIGHT PICTURES, 2111 Woodland Way, Hollywood, CA 90068; (213) 876-9693.
B.D. FOX & FRIENDS, INC. ADVERTISING, 1111 Broadway, Santa Monica, CA 90401; (213) 394-7150; FAX: (213) 393-1569.
FERRO, PABLO & ASSOCIATES, 1756 N. Sierra Bonita Ave., Hollywood, CA 90046; (213) 850-6193.
GLASS/SCHOOR/BROOKMAN, 722 S. Citrus Ave., Los Angeles, CA 90036; (213) 930-2030; FAX: (213) 930-2031.
HOLLYWOOD NEWSREEL SYNDICATE INC., 1622 N. Gower St., Los Angeles, Ca 90028; (213) 469-7307.
HOMER & ASSOCIATES, INC., 1420 N. Beachwood Dr., Hollywood, CA 90028; (213) 462-4710.
INTEX AUDIO VISUALS, 9021 Melrose Ave., Suite 205, Los Angeles, CA 90069; (213) 275-9571; FAX: (213) 271-1319.
JKR PRODUCTIONS, INC., 12140 W. Olympic Blvd., Suite 21, Los Angeles, CA 90064; (213) 826-3666.
KALEIDOSCOPE FILMS INC., 844 N. Seward St., Hollywood, CA 90038; (213) 465-1151.
KEY WEST EDITING, 5701 Buckingham Pkwy., Suite C, Culver City, CA 90230; (213) 645-3348.
LAJON PRODUCTIONS, INC., 2907 W. Olive Ave., Burbank, CA 91505; (213) 841-1440.
LEE FILM DESIGN, 2293 El Contento, Hollywood, CA 90068; (213) 467-9317.
LUMENI PRODUCTIONS, 1727 N. Ivar Ave., Hollywood, CA 90028; (213) 462-2110.
MAINSTREET IMAGERY, INC., 13105 Saticoy St., N. Hollywood, CA 91605; (818) 503-0931; FAX: (818) 982-9383.
MARS PRODUCTION CORP., 4405 Riverside Dr., Suite 305, Burbank, CA 91505; (818) 841-0101.
MERCER TITLES & OPTICAL EFFECTS LTD., 106 W. Burbank Blvd., Burbank, CA 91502; (818) 840-8828.
MULTI-MEDIA WORKS, 7227 Beverly Blvd., Los Angeles, CA 90036; (213) 939-1185.
NATIONAL SCREEN SERVICE GROUP INC., 2001 S. La Cienega Blvd., Los Angeles, CA 90034; (213) 836-1505.
NEWMAN/FRANKS, 2956 Nicada Dr., Los Angeles, CA 90077; (213) 470-0140; 470-0145; FAX: (213) 470-2410.
RENCHER'S EDITORIAL SERVICE, 738 Cahuenga Blvd., Hollywood, CA 90038; (213) 463-9836.
RUBBER DUBBERS, INC., 626 Justin Ave., Glendale, CA 91201; (818) 241-5600.
RUXIM, JIM, 12140 W. Olympic Blvd., Suite 21, Los Angeles, CA 90064; (213) 826-3666.
SKYLIGHT PRODUCTIOS INC., 6815 W. Willoughby Ave., Suite 201, Los Angeles, CA 90038; (213) 464-4500; FAX: (213) 463-1884.
SOUND SERVICES INC., 7155 Santa Monica Blvd., Los Angeles, CA 90046; (213) 874-9344; (818) 986-3255.
SOUTH, LEONARD, PRODUCTIONS, 4883 Lankershim Blvd., N. Hollywood, CA 91601; (818) 760-8383.
STROCK, HERBERT L., PRODUCTIONS, 6500 Barton Ave., Los Angeles, CA 90038; (213) 461-1298.
UNIVERSAL FACILITIES RENTAL DIVISION, 100 Universal City Plaza, Universal City, CA 91608, (818) 777-3000; 777-2731.
VIDCOM ENTERTAINMENT, INC., P.O. Box 2926, Hollywood, CA 90078; (213) 301-8433.
VIDE-U PRODUCTIONS, 612 N. Sepulveda Blvd., Los Angeles, CA 90049; (213) 472-7023.

NEW YORK CITY

ALEXANDER, JOHN ERIC, MUSIC INC., 311 W. 43 St., Suite 202, New York, NY 10036; (212) 581-8560.
ALEXANDER, SAM, PRODUCTIONS INC., 311 W. 43rd St., New York, NY 10036: (212) 756-5180.
DARINO FILMS,222 Park Ave. South, New York, NY 10003, (212) 228-4024.
EAST END PRODUCTIONS, 513 W. 54 St., New York, NY 10019; (212) 489-1865.
GLASS/SCHOOR/BROOKMAN, 42 W. 38 St., New York, NY 10019; (212) 944-0140; FAX: (212) 947-869-1473.
R/GREENBERG ASSOCIATES INC., 350 W. 39 St., New York, NY 10018; (212) 239-6767.
NATIONAL SCREEN SERVICE, GROUP INC., 40 Rockwood Pl., Englewood, NJ 07631; (201) 871-7900.
QUARTERMOON PRODUCTIONS INC., 106 Lexington Ave., New York, NY 10016; (212) 725-5565.

Talent and Literary Agencies

HOLLYWOOD

(Telephone area code is 213, unless otherwise indicated.)

ABRAMS-RUBALOFF & LAWRENCE., INC., 8075 West 3rd, 90048; 935- 1700
AGENCY FOR PERFORMING ARTS, 9000 Sunset Blvd., 12th floor, 90069; 273-0744; FAX: (213) 275-9401.
AGENCY THE, 10351 Santa Monica Blvd., Suite 211, 90025; 271-4662.
AIMEE ENTERTAINMENT ASSOCIATION, 13743 Victory Blvd., Van Nuys, CA 91401; (818) 994-9354
ALL TALENT AGENCY, 2437 E. Washington Blvd., Pasadena, 91104; (818) 797-2422.
ALVARADO, CARLOS, AGENCY, 8820 Sunset Blvd., Suites A & B, 90069; 652-0272; 652-0245.
AMARAL TALENT AGENCY, 10000 Riverside Dr., Suite 3, Toluca Lake, 91602; (818) 980-1013
AMSEL, FRED & ASSOCIATES, INC., 6310 San Vicente Blvd., Suite 407, 90048; 939-1188.
ASSOCIATED TALENT INTL., 9744 Wilshire Blvd., Suite 312, Beverly Hills, 90212; 271-4662.
BAUBER BENEDEK AGENCY, 9255 Sunset blvd., Suite 716, 90069; 275-2421; FAX: (213) 275-6421.
BEAKEL & DeBORD TALENT AGENCY, 10637 Burbank Blvd., N. Hollywood, 91601; (818) 506-7615.
BLANCHARD, NINA ENTERPRISES INC., 7060 Hollywood Blvd., 90028; 462-7274
BLOOM, MICHAEL J., 9200 Sunset Blvd., Suite 710, 90069; 275-6800
CALDER AGENCY, 4150 Riverside Dr., Suite 204, Burbank, 91505; (818) 845-7434
CAMDEN ARTISTS, LTD., 2121 Ave. of the Stars, Suite 410, 90067; 566-2022; FAX: (213) 556-2861.
CARROLL, WILLIAM, AGENCY, 120 S. Victory, Suite 104, Burbank, 91502; (818) 848-9948.
CAVALERI & ASSOCIATES, 6605 Hollywood Blvd., Suite 220, 90028; 461-2940; FAX: (213) 469-1213.
CENTURY ARTISTS, LTD., 9744 Wilshire Blvd., Suite 308, Beverly Hills, 90212; 273-4366
CHARTER MANAGEMENT, 9000 Sunset Blvd., Suite 1112, 90069; 278-1690.
THE CHASIN AGENCY, 190 N. Canon Dr., Suite 201, Beverly Hills, CA 90212; 278-7505.
CINEMA TALENT AGENCY, 7906 Santa Monica Blvd., Suite 212, 90046; 656-1937.
COMMERCIALS UNLTD., INC., 7461 Beverly Blvd., Suite 400, 90036; 937-2220
CONTEMPORARY ARTISTS LTD., 132 Lasky Dr., Beverly Hills 90212; 278-8250; FAX: (213) 278-0415.
CORALIE JR. AGENCY, 4789 Vineland Ave., #100, N. Hollywood, CA 91602; (818) 766-9501.
CREATIVE ARTISTS AGENCY, 1888 Century Park E. #1400, 90067; 277-4545.
CUMBER, LIL, ATTRACTIONS AGENCY, 6515 Sunset Blvd., Suite 300 A, 90028; 469-1919; 294-8245.
CUNNINGHAM, ESCOTT, DIPENE & ASSOC. 261 S. Robertson, Beverly Hills, 90211; 855-1700; 855-1011.
DIAMOND ARTISTS AGENCY, LTD., 9200 Sunset Blvd., 90069; 278-8146
ENTERTAINMENT ENTERPRISES, 1680 Vine St., Suite 519, 90028; 462-6001; FAX: (213) 462-6003.
EXCLUSIVE ARTISTS AGENCY, 2501 W. Burbank Blvd., Suite 304, Burbank, CA 91505; (818) 846-0262.
FELBER, WM., 2126 Cahuenga Blvd., 90068; 466-7627
FILM ARTISTS ASSOCIATES, 7080 Hollywood Blvd., Suite 704, Los Angeles, CA 90028; 463-1010.
FRINGS, KURT, AGENCY, 119 S. Beverly Dr., Beverly Hills, 90212; 277-1103.
GARRICK, DALE, INTL. AGENCY, 8831 Sunset Blvd., #402, 90069; 657-2661.
GEDDES AGENCY, 8457 Melrose Pl., Suite 200, 90069; 651-2401.
GERSH AGENCY, THE, 222 N. Canon Dr., Beverly Hills, 90210; 274-6611
GOLD, HARRY & ASSOCIATES, 12725 Ventura Blvd., #E, Studio City, 91604; (818) 769-5003.
GREEN AGENCY, IVAN, 8383 Wilshire Blvd., Suite 1039, Beverly Hills, CA 90211; 277-1541
GROSSMAN & ASSOCIATES, 211 S. Beverly Dr., Suite 206, 90212; 550-8127
HAMILBURG AGENCY, 292 S. La Cienega, Suite 312, Beverly Hills, 90211; 657-1501
HECHT, BEVERLY, AGENCY, 8949 Sunset Blvd., 90069; 278-3544
HENDERSON/HOGAN AGENCY, 247 S. Beverly Dr., #102, Beverly Hills, CA 90210; 274-7815.
HUNT, GEORGE B., & ASSOCIATES, 121 Twin Palms Dr., Palm Springs, CA 92264; (619) 323-1126.
INT'L CREATIVE MANAGEMENT, 8899 Beverly Blvd., 90048; 550-4000; FAX: (213) 550-4108.
KELMAN/ARLETTA AGENCY, 7813 Sunset Blvd., 90046; 851-8822
KINGSLEY COLTON & ASSOCIATES, 16661 Ventura Blvd., Suite 400, Encino, CA 91436; (818) 788-6043.
KOHNER-PAUL, INC., 9169 Sunset Blvd., 90069; 550-1060; FAX: (213) 276-1083.
LANTZ OFFICE, 9255 Sunset Blvd., #505, 90069; 858-1144; FAX: (213) 858-0828.
LAZAR, IRVING PAUL, 120 El Camino Dr., Suite 206, Beverly Hills, 90212; 275-6153
LIGHT, ROBERT, AGENCY, 6404 Wilshire Blvd., Suite 800, 90048; 651-1777; FAX: (213) 651-4933.
LYONS, GRACE, MANAGEMENT, 8350 Melrose Ave., Suite 202, 90069; 655-5100.
McCARTT ORECK BARRETT, 10390 Santa Monica Blvd., #310, 90025; 553-2600
McHUGH AGENCY, JAMES, 8150 Beverly Blvd., 90048; 651-2770
McMILLIAN, HAZEL, AGENCY, 126 N. Doheny Dr., 90211; Beverly Hills, 276-9823; (714) 883-6800.
MEDIA ARTISTS GROUP, 6255 Sunset Blvd., 90028; 463-5610.
MISHKIN AGENCY, 2355 Benedict Canyon, Beverly Hills, CA 90210; 274-5261
MORRIS, WILLIAM, 151 El Camino Dr., Beverly Hills, 90212; 274-7451
MOSS, BURTON, AGENCY, 113 N. San Vicente Blvd., Suite 202, Beverly Hills, CA 90211; 655-1156.
PRESCOTT, GUY, 8920 Wonderland Ave., 90046; 656-1963
PRIVILEGE TALENT AGENCY, 8344 Beverly Blvd., 2nd Floor, 90048; 658-8781.
ROBINSON-WEINTRAUB, GROSS & ASSOCIATES, 8428 Melrose Place, 90069; 653-5802
SANDERS AGENCY, LTD., 721 N. La Brea Ave., #200, 90038; 938-9113.
SCHECTER, IRV, COMPANY, 9300 Wilshire Blvd., #410, Beverly Hills, CA 90212; 278-8070.
SCHWARTZ & ASSOC., DON, 8749 Sunset Blvd., 90069; 657-8910
SHAPIRA, DAVID, ASSOCIATES, INC., 15301 Ventura Blvd., Suite 345, Sherman Oaks, CA 91403; (818) 906-0322; FAX: (818) 783-2562.
SHERRELL AGENCY LEW, 7060 Hollywood Blvd., 90028; 461-9955
SMITH-FREEDMAN & ASSOCIATES, 121 N. San Vicente Blvd., Beverly Hills, 90211; 852-4777.
STE REPRESENTATION LTD., 9301 Wilshire Blvd., Beverly Hills, CA 90210; 550-3982; FAX: (213) 550-5991.
STONE/MANNERS AGENCY, 9113 Sunset Blvd., 90069; 275-9599.
SWANSON, H.N., 8523 Sunset Blvd., 90069; 652-5385.
TANNEN & ASSOC. HERB, 1800 N. Vine St., Suite 120, 90028; 466-6191; FAX: (213) 466-0863.
TOBIAS, HERB & ASSOCIATES, 1901 Ave. of the Stars, Suite 840, 90067; 277-6211.
TRIAD ARTISTS, 10100 Santa Monica Blvd., 16th floor, 90067; 556-2727.
TWENTIETH CENTURY ARTISTS, 3800 Barham Blvd., #303, 90068; 850-5516; FAX: (213) 850-1418.
WEBB, RUTH, ENTERPRISES, INC., 7500 De Vista Dr. 90069; 874-1700.
WRITERS & ARTISTS AGENCY, 11726 San Vicente Blvd., #300, 90049; 820-2240; FAX: (213) 207-3781.

NEW YORK

(Area telephone code is 212.)

ABRAMS ARTISTS & ASSOCIATES, INC., 420 Madison Ave., Suite 1400, 10017; 935-8980.
ACTORS GROUP AGENCY, THE, 157 W. 57 St., Suite 211, 10019; 245-2930.
AGENCY FOR PERFORMING ARTS, 888 Seventh Ave., 10106; 582-1500; FAX: (212) 245- 1647.
AMERICAN-INT'L TALENT 303 W. 42 St., 10036; 245-8888
ANDERSON, BEVERLY, 1472 Broadway, Ste. 806, 10036; 944-7773

ASSOCIATED ARTISTS MANAGEMENT, 311 W. 43rd St., #6806, 10036; 974-0044.
ASSOCIATED BOOKING CORP., 1995 Broadway, 10023; 874-2400
ASTOR, RICHARD, 1697 Broadway, 10019; 581-1970
BAUMAN, HILLER & ASSOCIATES, 250 W. 57 St., #803, 10019; 757-0098.
BRESLER, KELLY & ASSOCIATES, 111 W. 57 St., #1409, 10019; 265-1980; FAX: (212) 265-2671.
CASE, BERTHA, 42 W. 53 St., 10019; 581-6282.
COLEMAN-ROSENBERG AGCY., 210 E. 58 St., 10022; 838-0734
COOPER ASSOC., BILL, 224 W. 49 St., #411, 10019; 307-1100
CUNNINGHAM, ESCOTT, DIPENE & ASSOCIATES, 118 E. 25 St., 6 Fl., 10010; 477-1666.
DEACY, JANE, 181 Revolutionary Rd., Scarborough, 10510; (914) 941-1414.
DIAMOND ARTISTS, LTD., 119 W. 57 St., 10019; 247-3025
FLICK EAST-WEST TALENTS, INC., Carnegie Hall Studio 110, 881 7 Ave., 10019; 307-1850.
GAGE GROUP, THE, 1650 Broadway, #406,, 10019; 541-5250
GARRICK, DALE INTL. AGENCY, 117 W. 48 St., 10036; 246-8985.
GERSH AGENCY INC., THE, 130 W. 42 St., #1804, 10036; 997-1818.
HARTIG, MICHAEL, 114 E. 28 St., #203,, 10016; 684-0010
HENDERSON/HOGAN AGENCY, 200 W. 57 St., 10019; 765-5190
HUNT, DIANA, 44 W. 44 St., 10036; 391-4971
INT'L CREATIVE MANAGEMENT, 40 W. 57 St., 10019; 556-5600
JACOBSON/WILDER, INC., 419 Park Ave. S., 10016; 686-6100.
JAN J. AGENCY, 328 E. 61 St., 10021; 759-9775
JORDAN, JOE TALENT AGCY., 156 Fifth Ave., #711,, 10010; 463-8455
KENNEDY ARTISTS REP., 237 W. 11 St., 10014; 675-3944
KROLL LUCY, 390 West End Ave., 10024; 877-0627
LANTZ OFFICE, 888 Seventh Ave., 10106; 586-0200.
LARNER, LIONEL LTD., 130 W. 57 St., 10019; 246-3105
LEIGH ENTERPRISES, LTD., SANFORD, 440 E. 62 St., 10021; 752-4450
LEWIS ASSOC., LESTER, 110 W. 40 St., 10018; 921-8370
McDERMOTT, MARGE, 216 E. 39 St., 10016; 889-1583
MARTINELLI, JOHN ATTRACTIONS, 888 Eighth Ave., 10019; 586-0963
MORRIS AGENCY, WM., 1350 Ave. of the Americas, 10019; 586-5100
OPPENHEIM-CHRISTIE ASSOC., 13 E. 37 St., 10016; 213-4330
OSCARD,FIFI AGENCY, 19 W. 44 St., 10036; 764-1100
OSTERTAG, BARNA, 501 Fifth Ave., 10017; 697-6339
PREMIER TALENT ASSOC., 3 E. 54 St., 10003; 758-4900
RUBENSTEIN, BERNARD, 215 Park Ave. S., 10016; 460-9800
RYAN, CHARLES VERNON, 200 W. 57 St., 10019; 245-2225
SANDERS AGENCY, LTD., THE, 156 Fifth Ave., #222, 10010; 627-7726.
STE REPRESENTATION LTD., 888 Seventh Ave., #201, 10019; 246-1030.
SCHULLER TALENT, 276 Fifth Ave.,, 10001; 532-6005.
SILVER, MONTY, 200 W. 57 St., 10019; 765-4040
SMITH-FREEDMAN & ASSOCIATES, 850 Seventh Ave., 10019; 581-4490.
TALENT REPS., INC., 20 E. 53 St., 10022; 752-1835
TRIAD ARTISTS, 888 Seventh Ave., Suite 1602, 10106; 489-8100.
WATERS AGENCY, BOB, 1501 Broadway, #705, 10036; 302-8787
WOLTERS, HANNS, 10 W. 37 St., 10018; 714-0100
WRIGHT REPS., ANN, 136 E. 56 St., 10022; 832-0110
WRITERS & ARTISTS AGENCY, 70 W. 36 St., #501, 10018; 947-8765.

Advertising & Publicity Representatives

HOLLYWOOD-LOS ANGELES-BEVERLY HILLS

(Area code is 213 unless otherwise indicated.)

ABRAMS, BOB, AND ASSOCIATES, 2030 Prosser Ave., Los Angeles 90025; 475-7739.
BBDO, 10960 Wilshire Blvd., # 1600, Los Angeles, 90024; 479-3979.
BARLOR ASSOCIATES, 428 N. Palm Dr., BH 90210; 278-1998.
BENDER, GOLDMAN & HELPER, 11500 W. Olympic Blvd., Suite 655, Los Angeles, CA 90064; 473-4147; FAX: (213) 478-4727.
BRAVERMAN-MIRISCH, INC., 1517 Schuyler Rd., Beverly Hills, CA 90210; 274-5204.
BROCATO & KELMAN, INC., 8425 W. 3rd St., Los Angeles 90048; 653-9595; FAX: (213) 659-1765.
DICK BROOKS UNLIMITED, 3511 Beverly Ridge Dr., Sherman Oaks, CA 91403; 273-8477.
CLEIN, FELDMAN,WHITE, 8584 Melrose Ave., W. Hollywood 90069; 659-4141; FAX: (213) 659-3995.
DANCER-FITZGERALD-SAMPLE INC., 3501 Sepulveda, Torrace 90505; 214-6000.
D'ARCY, MASIUS, BENTON & BOWLES, 6500 Wilshire Blvd., Los Angeles 90048; 658-4500.
DENNIS DAVIDSON & ASSOCS. INC., 211 S. Beverly Dr., #200, BH 90212; 275-8505.
DELLA FEMINA TRAVISANO & PARTNERS, 5900 Wilshire Blvd., #1900, Los Angeles 90036; 937-8540.
DENTSU INC., 4751 Wilshire Blvd., #203, Los Angeles 90010, 939-3452.
DORN, LARRY, ASSOCS. INC., 5550 Wilshire Blvd., Suite 303, Los Angeles 90036; 935-6266; FAX: (213) 935-9523.
DOUGHERTY & ASSOCS. PUBLIC RELS., 139 S. Beverly Dr., Suite 311, Beverly Hills, 90212; 273-8177.
EDELMAN, DANIEL, INC., 10866 Wilshire Blvd, # 550, Los Angeles 90024; 475-1500.
GELFOND, GORDON AND ASSOCIATES, 11500 Olympic Blvd., Suite 377, Los Angeles, CA 90064; 478-3600; FAX: (213) 477-4825.
GUTTMAN & PAM LTD., 8500 Wilshire Blvd., Suite 801, Beverly Hills, 90211; 659-6888.
HANSON & SCHWAM, 9200 Sunset Blvd., Los Angeles 90069; 278-1255; FAX: 276-9253.
LEE & ASSOCIATES, 145 S. Fairfax Ave., Los Angeles 90036; 938-3300.
LEVINE, MICHAEL, PUB. REL. CO., 8730 Sunset Blvd., Los Angeles, CA 90069; (213) 659-6400.
LEWIS & ASSOCIATES, 3600 Wilshire Blvd., # 200, Los Angeles 90010; 739-1000.
LIBERMAN, FRANK, AND ASSOCIATES, 9021 Melrose Ave., Los Angeles 90069; 278-1993.
MAHONEY/WASSERMAN & ASSOCIATES, 117 N. Robertson Blvd., Los Angeles 90048; (213) 550-3922.
McKENZIE, KING & GORDON, 1680 N. Vine St., # 710, Hollywood 90028; (213) 466-3421.
MILLER, RENEE PUBLIC RELATIONS, P.O. Box 35237, Los Angeles, CA 90035; 273-5173; (213) 271-8714.
PMK INC., 8436 W. Third St., Suite 650, Los Angeles, 90048; 658-5800; FAX: (213) 658-1103.
PUBLICITY WEST, 2155 N. Ridgemont Dr., Los Angeles, 90046; 654-3816; (818) 954-1951.
ROGERS & COWAN, 10000 Santa Monica Blvd., Los Angeles, 90067; 201-8800; FAX: (213) 552-0412.
RUDER, FINN & ROTMAN, INC., 3345 Wilshire Blvd., #909, Los Angeles, CA 90010; (213) 385-5271.
SAATCHI & SAATCHI/DFS, 3501 Sepulveda Blvd., Torrence, 90505; 214-6000.
SOLTERS, ROSKIN, FRIEDMAN, INC., 5455, # 2200, Los Angeles, CA 90036; (213) 936-7900.
THOMPSON, J. WALTER CO., 10100 Santa Monica Blvd., Suite 1200, Los Angeles, 90067; 553-8383.

NEW YORK

(Area code is 212 unless otherwise indicated)

AYER, INC., N.W., Worldwide Plaza, 825 Eighth Ave., 10019-7498; 474-5000; FAX: (212) 474-5400.
BACKER, SPIELVOGEL, BATES, WORLDWIDE INC., 405 Lexington Ave., 8th Fl., 10174; 297-7000.
BATTEN, BARTON, DURSTINE & OSBORNE, INC., 1285 Ave. of the Americas, 10019; 459-5000.
BENDER, GOLDMAN & HELPER, 509 Madison Ave., #1400, 10022; 371-0798.
BILLINGS, M/S, PUBLICITY LTD, 250 W. 57 St., #2420, 10107; 581-4493.
CLEIN, FELDMAN, WHITE, 33 W. 54th St., 10019; 247-4100.
COMMUNICATIONS PLUS INC., 360 Park Ave. So., 10010; 686-9570.
DDB NEEDHAM WORLDWIDE INC., 437 Madison Ave., 10022; 415-2000.
D'ARCY, MASIUS, BENTON & BOWLES, 909 Third Ave., 10022; 758-6200.
DAVIS, AL, PUBLICITY, 6 E. 39 St., 10016; 725-0850.
DELLA FEMINA, TRAVISANO & PARTNERS, 625 Madison Ave., 10022; 421-7180.
EISEN, MAX, 234 W. 44 St., 10036; 391-1072.
FURST, RENEE, 303 E. 57 St., 10022; 758-8535.
GIFFORD/WALLACE, INC., 1211 Park Ave., 10128; 427-7600.
GOODMAN, FRANK, 1776 Broadway, 10019; 246-4180.
GREY ADVERTISING AGENCY, 777 Third Ave., 10017; 546-2000.
GREY ENTERTAINMENT & MEDIA, 777 Third Ave., 10022; 303-2400.
LYNN, BRUCE, PUBLICITY, 170 W. 23rd St., # 2 U, 10011; 691-7515.
McCANN-ERICKSON, INC., 250 Third, 10017; 697- 6000.

OGILVY & MATHER, 40 W. 57, 10019; 977-9400.
PMK (PICKWICK, MASLANSKY, KOENIGBERG) 1 Lincoln Plaza, 10023; 580-1700.
POST, MYRNA ASSOCIATES, 145 E. 49 St., 10022; 935-7122.
ROFFMAN, RICHARD H., ASSOCIATES, 697 West End Ave., 10025; 749-3647.
ROGERS & COWAN, INC., 122 E. 42 St., 10016; 490-8200.
RUDER, FINN & ROTMAN, INC., 301 E. 57 St. 10022; 593-6400.
SCHLAIFER & CO., INC., CHARLES, 150 E. 69 St., 10155; 879-4310.
SAATCHI & SAATCHI ADVERTISING, 375 Hudson St., 10014-3620; 463-2000.
SEIFERT-WHITE ASSOCIATES, 18 E. 53 St., 10022; 838-0888.
SOLTERS, ROSKIN, AND FREIDMAN, INC., 45 W. 34 St., 10001; 947-0515.
THOMPSON, J. WALTER, 466 Lexington Ave., 10017; 210-7000.
WAX, MORTON D. PUBLIC RELATIONS, 1560 Broadway, 10019; 302-5360.
WELLS, RICH, GREENE, 1740 Broadway, 10019; 468-7400.
WOLHANDER, JOE, ASSOCIATES, INC., 11 W. 30 St., Suite 10R, 10001; 947-6015.
YOUNG & RUBICAM INTERNATIONAL, 285 Madison Ave., 10017; 210-3000.

Federal Government Film & Media Services

EXECUTIVE DEPARTMENTS

DEPARTMENT OF AGRICULTURE

Video and Teleconference Division, 1614 South Bldg., USDA, Washington, DC 20250-1300; (202) 447-2592; Larry Quinn, chief of division.
Produces video, film, and teleconference presentations for use and distribution both inside and outside of the department.
(For information on obtaining USDA productions, see *National Archives and Records Administration,* below.)

DEPARTMENT OF COMMERCE

Audiovisual Section, Office of Public Affairs, 14th St., Rm. 5521, Washington, DC 20230; (202) 377-3263; Bob Amdur, section chief.
Productions of department (by individual bureaus) videos and films are contracted out; distribution is free of charge and handled by an outside company. Contact this number for more information.
International Trade Administration, Office of Service Industries, Information Industries Division, 14th St. and Constitution Ave. room 1114, Washington, DC 20230; (202) 377-4781; John Siegmund, International Trade Specialist.
Studies and reports statistics of the industry at home and abroad; the material gathered is published in department reports along with comparative information from other industries. Also concerned with promoting the industry abroad and overcoming trade barriers.
National Telecommunications and Information Administration, Main Commerce Bldg., Washington, DC 20230; (202) 377-1840; Janice Obuchowski, Asst. Secretary for Communications and Information.
Develops telecommunications policy for executive branch; conducts technical research on various aspects of telecommunications; makes and administers grants to noncommercial public telecommunications services for construction of facilities.

DEPARTMENT OF DEFENSE

Special Assistant (Audiovisual), Office of the Assistant Secretary of Defense (Public Affairs), the Pentagon, Room 2E789, Washington, DC, 20301; (202) 695-2936; Mr. Philip M. Strub, head of division; Captain Susan Hankey, USAF, deputy.
Acts on all requests for Department of Defense assistance from the film and television industries involved in entertainment productions and documentaries not dealing specifically with news.
Broadcast-Pictorial Branch, Office of the Assistant Secretary of Defense (Public Affairs), the Pentagon, Room 2E765, Washington, DC, 20301; (202) 695-0128; Lieutenant Colonel Steve Titunik, USA, branch chief.
Provides still photographs and motion media materials to non-government electronic and print news media, news documentary producers, non-entertainment oriented producers, educational institutions, and publishers.
Federal Audiovisual Contract Management Office, 601 N. Fairfax St. Alexandria, VA 22314-2007; (202) 274-4876; Florence Harley, Audiovisual management specialist.
Maintains lists of qualified film and video producers; contracts throughout the federal government will only be awarded to producers who appear on these lists.
MILITARY SERVICES
Secretary of the Air Force, Office of Public Affairs, Public Communications Branch, the Pentagon, Room 4A120, Washington, DC 20330-1000; (202) 697-2769; Lt. Col. Dennis J. Gauci, chief of branch.
Secretary of the Army, Media Relations Division, Army Public Affairs, the Pentagon, Room 2E641, Washington, DC 20310-1500, (202) 697-2564; Col. William L. Mulvey, chief of division.
Department of the Navy, Chief of Information, Audiovisual Entertainment, the Pentagon, Room 2E352, Washington, DC 20350-1200; (202) 697-0866; Robert Manning, director.
Headquarters, U.S. Marine Corps, Media Branch Public Affairs Division, Code PAM, Washington, DC 20380; (202) 694-1492; Lt. Col. Fred C. Peck, chief of branch.
(The above public affairs offices all have regional branches; contact the Washington addresses for more information.)

DEPARTMENT OF EDUCATION

Office of Public Affairs, Audiovisual Division, 400 Maryland Ave. SW, Rm. 2089, FOB #6, Washington, DC 20202; (202) 732-4559; Greg Grafson, Audiovisual officer.
Monitors all film, video, and audio materials generated by department contracts with, or grants to, companies or non-profit organizations. Distribution of these materials is through the National Audiovisual Center (see *National Archives and Records Administration,* below) or by special arrangements with producers.
Office of Special Education and Rehabilitation Services, 400 Maryland Ave. SW, Switzer Bldg., Rm. 4629, Washington, DC, 20202; (202) 732-1172; Harvey Liebergott , acting branch chief, captioning.
This division purchases already produced films and captions them for use by the hearing impaired; contact Mr. Liebergott for a catalogue of titles.

DEPARTMENT OF ENERGY

Office of Public Affairs, 1000 Independence Ave. SW, CP24, Washington, DC 20585; (202) 586-6250; Chett Gray, Public Information Specialist.
This department contracts film and video productions to a private company.

DEPARTMENT OF HEALTH AND HUMAN SERVICES

Office of Public Affairs, 200 Independence Ave. SW, room 634E, Washington, DC, 20201; (202) 245-1897; Jim Miller, Director of Communications.
Produces, distributes, and contracts out video and radio productions. Each of the five branches of HHS has its own public affairs and audivisual office, listed below.
Family Support Administration, 370 L'Enfant Promenade SW, 6th floor, Washington, DC 20447; (202) 252-4518; David Siegel, acting Associate Administrator of Public Affairs.
FSA contracts to produce videos outside of the department.
Health Care Financing Administration, 200 Independence Ave. SW, Rm. 314G, Washington, DC 20201; (202) 245-6726; Dennis Siebert, Director of Public Affairs.
Produces, distributes, and contracts out films and tapes.
Office of Human Development Services, 200 Independence Ave. SW, Rm. 348F, Washington, DC 20201; (202) 472-7257; Terri Lukach, Director of Public Affairs.
This division contracts to produce films and tapes outside of the department.
Social Security Administration, Office of Public Affairs, 4200 West High Rise, 6401 Security Blvd., Baltimore, MD 21235; (301) 965-1720; Gary Good,acting, Associate Commissioner.
Produces and distributes films and tapes.
U.S. Public Health Service (including *Alcohol, Drug Abuse, and Mental Health Administration, Centers for Disease Control, Food and Drug Administration, Health Resources and Services Administration, Indian Health Service, National Institutes of Health)* Office of Communications, 200 Independence Ave. SW, Rm. 717H, Washington, DC 20201; (202) 245-6867; James Brown, Director, News Division.
Produces, distributes, and contracts out films and tapes.

DEPARTMENT OF HOUSING AND URBAN DEVELOPMENT

Office of Public Affairs, HUD Bldg., 451 7th St. SW, Rm. 10132, Washington, DC 20410; (202) 755-6685; Sherrie Rollins, Director of Public Affairs.
This department occasionally contracts outside the government for video productions.

DEPARTMENT OF THE INTERIOR

Bureau of Mines,
Audiovisual Library, Cochransmill Road, P.O. Box 18070, Pittsburgh, PA 15236; (412) 892-6845; Evelyn Donnelly, librarian (for distribution and purchase of films and tapes).
Office of Public Information, Audiovisual Programs, 2401 E St. NW, Washington, DC 20241; (202) 634-1335; William Gage, Manager of Audiovisual Programs..
The bureau maintains a library of 16mm films, 3/4, and 1/2 inch videos depicting mining, metallurgical operations, and related manufacturing processes. One branch of the program, Mineral Resource Series, is composed of broad-based documentaries directed toward a general audience; the films are produced by independent producers and industrial concerns (they do not carry trademarks, trade names, or other direct advertising). The second branch, Technology Transfer Film Program, is produced by bureau research divisions and is directed toward industry and specialized educational programs. All films and tapes are loaned free of charge (except for return postage) to educational institutions, industries, training workers, engineering and scientific societies, and civic and business associations. Information and catalogues may be obtained from both of the above addresses.

DEPARTMENT OF JUSTICE

Audiovisual Services, 10th St. and Pennsylvania Ave., Rm. 1313, Washington, DC 20530; (202) 633-4694; Mathew White, supervisor.
Records department ceremonies and functions; no distribution.

DEPARTMENT OF LABOR

Audiovisual and Photographic Services Branch, Audiovisual Division, 200 Constitution Ave. NW, N6311, Washington, DC 20210; (202) 523-7820; Stan Hankin, chief of branch.

Produces 16mm, 35mm, and video productions and documents department ceremonies; contracts work outside the department as well.

DEPARTMENT OF STATE

International Communications and Information Policy, Department of State, Rm. 6317, Washington, DC 20520; (202) 647-5727; Sonia Landau, U.S. Coordinator and Director.

Develops, implements, and oversees international communication policy for the department; acts as a liaison for other federal agencies and the private sector in international communications issues.

Office of International Trade, Department of State, Rm. 3831, Washington, DC 20520; (202) 647-2325; Donald McConville, Director.

Concerned with commercial aspects of film industry, trade treaties, restrictions, quotas, copyrights, etc; call for information on specific questions.

Special Projects Staff, Office of Public Communications, Bureau of Public Affairs, Department of State, Rm. 4827A, Washington, DC 20520; (202) 647-8926; James Murray, Director of Staff.

Produces video documentaries on foreign policy topics; available for free educational and public distribution through the Washington office and a number of regional centers. Contact the above address for more information and a catalogue.

DEPARTMENT OF TRANSPORTATION

Office of Public Affairs, 400 7th St. SW, Rm. 10413, Washington, DC 20590; (202) 366-5580; Bill Mosley, Public Affairs officer.

Departmental productions contracted out, although individual agencies do produce films and tapes. Three of the ten agencies are listed below.

Federal Highway Administration, Audiovisual and Visual Aids, 400 7th St. SW, Rm. 4429, HMS24, Washington, DC 20590; (202) 366-9125; Norma Lesser, section chief.

Produces videos and films to transportation professionals; distribution is through National Audio Visual Center (see, National Archives and Records Administration, below).

National Highway and Traffic Safety Administration, Public Affairs, Audiovisual Section, 400 7th St. SW, Rm. 5232, Washington, DC 20590; (202) 366-9550; Tina Foley, Public Affairs Specialist.

Produces and distributes videos and films; also, contracts work outside of the department.

United States Coast Guard, Public Affairs, Audiovisual Branch, Commandante, CPI, 2100 2nd St. SW, Washington, DC 20593; (202) 267-0923; Wayne Paul, branch chief.

Oversees film and video production and distribution (collection also handled by the National Audiovisual Center, see below), and coordinates the work of the regional film liaison offices.

U.S. Coast Guard Hollywood Liaison, Public Affairs Liaison, Federal Bld., Suite 10125, 1100 Wilshire Blvd., Los Angeles, CA 90024-3612; (213) 209-7817; Cdr. John McElwaine, Hollywood Liaison.

DEPARTMENT OF TREASURY

Office of Public Affairs, 1500 Pennsylvania Ave. NW, Rm. 3442, Washington, DC 20220; (202) 566-8773; Desiree Tucker-Sorini, Deputy Asst. for P.A.

Productions are made by individual bureaus within the department (such as the Internal Revenue Service). Contact this address and phone number for more information.

EXECUTIVE AGENCIES

ENVIRONMENTAL PROTECTION AGENCY

Audiovisual Division, Office of Public Affairs, 401 M St. SW, A-107, Washington, DC 20460; (202) 382-2044; Michael Scott, Director.

Produces and distributes videos and films on the environment, pollution, conservation, and related subjects; contracts some productions outside of the agency. Some distribution through the National Audiovisual Center (see, National Archives and Records Administration, below); loans are mostly free of charge (videos are dubbed on to blank tapes mailed to the division).

FEDERAL COMMUNICATIONS COMMISSION

1919 M St. NW, Washington, DC 20554; (202) 632-6600; Alfred C. Sikes, Chairman.

Regulates interstate and foreign communications by television, radio, satellite, cable, wire, and microwave. Reviews applications for construction permits and licenses for such services. Selected divisions listed below; for further information, contact *Office of Public Affairs;* (202) 632-5050; Maureen Peratino, acting Director.

Engineering and Technology Bureau; (202) 632-7060; Thomas Stanley, chief engineer;

Advises FCC on all technical matters and assists in development of telecommunications policy. Reviews developments in telecommunication technology. Technical library open to the public.

Mass Media Bureau; (202) 632-6460; Alex Felker, chief.

Licenses, regulates, and develops audio and video services in traditional broadcasting, cable, and emerging systems including high definition television; processes applications for licensing of commercial and non-commercial television and radio broadcast equipment and facilities; handles renewals and changes of ownership; investigates public complaints.

Cable Television Branch; (202) 632-7480; Ronald Parver, chief.

Processes applications and notifications for licensing of cable television relay service stations; registers cable television systems; develops, administer, and enforces regulation of cable TV and CARS.

FEDERAL TRADE COMMISSION

6th St. and Pennsylvania Ave. NW, Washington, DC 20580; (202) 326-2180.

Administers statutes designed to promote fair competetion; institutes proceedings to prevent unfair or deceptive practices, combinations in restraint of trade, false advertising, and illegal price discrimination. Supervises associations of exporters under the Export Trade Act. (For specific bureaus or further information, contact the *Public Affairs Office* at the above address and phone number.)

LIBRARY OF CONGRESS

Audiovisual Section of the *Special Materials Cataloging Division, Processing Services Department,* Madison Bldg., Rm. 547, Washington, DC 20540; (202) 707-6758; Jeffery Heynen, chief of section.

Supervises the cataloging of motion pictures, videos, and sets of slides and transparencies, largely on the basis of information supplied by producers and media libraries.

Copyright Office, Madison Bldg., Rm. 403, Washington, DC 20540; (202) 707-8350; Ralph Oman, Register of Copyrights.

Registers films and videos for copyrights.

Copyright Cataloging Division, Rm. 513; (202) 707-8040; Raoul le Mat, acting chief of division.

Supervises the preparation of the semi-annual *Catalog of Copyright Entries: Motion Pictures and Film Strips* which is distributed by the Superintendent of Documents, Government Printing Office, Washington, DC 20402. This publication contains descriptive data for all theatrical and non-theatrical films and videos registered for copyright during each six-month period.

Motion Picture, Broadcast and Recorded Sound Division of the *Research Services Department,* Madison Bldg., Rm. 338, Washington, DC 20540; (202) 707-5840; Robert Saudek, chief of division.

Supervises the library's collection of more than 331,000 films and videos. The collection is an archive of copyright deposits plus some gift materials. It contains 35mm, 16mm, and 3/4 inch features and television programs, and some documentary, educational, scientific, religious, and industrial productions. The collection is chiefly American, but includes German, Italian, and Japanese films. The division has an entensive film and video preservation program and houses historically important films from the early days of the industry.

NATIONAL ARCHIVES AND RECORDS ADMINISTRATION

Motion Picture Sound and Video Branch, 7th St. & Pennslyvania Ave. NW, Washington, DC 20408; (202) 786-0041, 0042, 0043; William Murphy, chief of branch.

Houses one of the world's largest audiovisual archives, including more than 120,000 films and 13,000 videos; collection includes documentaries, newreels, combat films, and raw historical footage (government productions as well as gift collections from film corporations and television networks).

National Audiovisual Center, Customer Services Section, 8700 Edgeworth Dr., Capitol Heights, MD 20743-3701; (301) 763-1896; Kevin Flood, director.

Holds relatively current collection of over 8,500 U.S. government audiovisual productions for sale and rental (available in all formats). Distributes the collections of many government departments and agencies, in addition to those specifically noted above.

Presidential Libraries Central Office, 7th St. & Pennslyvania Ave. NW, Washington, DC 20408; (202) 523-3212; John Fawcett, Director.

The eight presidential libraries, located throughout the country, can be reached from this office. Each library has extensive audiovisual materials relevant to that administration; the collection begins with President Hoover.

NATIONAL ENDOWMENT FOR THE ARTS

Media Arts Program: Film/Radio/Television, 1100 Pennsylvania Ave. NW, Washington, DC 20506; (202) 682-5452; Brian O'Doherty, director.

Provides grants to individuals and non-profit organizations for film, video, and radio productions; supports arts programming for public television and radio.

NATIONAL ENDOWMENT FOR THE HUMANITIES

Humanities Projects in Media, 1100 Pennsylvania Ave. NW, Washington, DC 20506; (202) 786-0278; James Dougherty, director.

Provides grants for non-profit media projects aimed at advancing the use and understanding of the humanities.

SECURITIES AND EXCHANGE COMMISSION

Division of Corporation Finance, 450 5th St. NW, Washington, DC 20549.

Reviews financial statements and disclosures.

Radio, Television, and Telegraph, Rm. 3113; (202) 272-2683; H. Christopher Owings, Asst., Director.

Motion Pictures, Rm. 3134; (202) 272-3275; James Daly, Asst. Director.

(For further information concerning registration of security offerings and supervision of trading, contact *Public Affairs*, (202) 272-2650.

SMITHSONIAN INSTITUTION

Film Archives, Information Management Division, National Air and Space Museum, Washington, DC 20560; (202) 357-4721; Mark Taylor, Film Archivist.

Houses about 10,000 films and videos from Smithsonian, government, other museums, and industry collections.

Smithsonian World, 955 L'Enfant Plaza, Suite 7100, Washington, DC 20024; (202) 488-4500; Adrian Malone, Executive Producer.

One hour program series broadcast on public television stations.

Telecommunications Office, National Museum of American History, Rm. BB40, Washington, DC 20560; (202) 357-2984; Paul Johnson, Director.

Produces films and videos which are distributed for a fee through a private company. Contact this office for more information.

(Other museums and galleries have small archive collections; contact the *Office of Public Affairs* for more information, (202) 357-2627.)

U.S. INFORMATION AGENCY

Television and Film Service, 601 D St. NW, Rm. 5000, Washington, DC 20547; (202) 376-1127; Stephen E. Murphy, Director.

USIA produces and acquires about 200 film and television documentaries annually for information and cultural programs in 117 countries. In addition, close to 350 targeted, and 150 worldwide news clips are made for use on foreign television. These are seen abroad in commercial theatres, on television, in schools and community centers, and by clubs, universities, and other audiences. Television and Film Service also certifies the exemption of import duties if a film is educational.

U.S. INTERNATIONAL TRADE COMMISSION

Office of the Secretary, 500 E Street, Rm. 112, Washington, DC 20436; (202) 252-1000; Kenneth Mason, Secretary.

Conducts countervailing duty, anti-dumping, and patent and trademark infringement investigations; the commission is a fact-finding body which addresses business complaints, holds hearings, and makes recommendations to the Department of Commerce.

Film Distributors in Key Cities

ATLANTA

Buena Vista Distribution Co., 1190 W. Druid Hill Dr., Suite T-75, 30329; (404) 634-6525. Rod Rodriguez, Div. mgr.
Clark Film, Inc., 2200 Northlake Pkwy., Tucker, GA 30084; (404) 491-7766. Lewis Owens.
Double Helix Films, 846 Penn. Ave. #B, 30308; (404) 876-7008.
MGM/UA Distribution Co., 2600 Century Parkway, N.E., 30345; (404) 325-3470. Larry Terrell, SE reg. director.
New Line Cinema Corp., 4501 Circle 75 Parkway NW, 30339; (404) 952-0056.
New World Pictures, 2400 Herodian Way, Suite 222, Smyrna, 30080; (404) 951-8020. James Dixon, Mgr.
Orion Pictures Distribution Corp., 2970 Clairmont, #240; (404) 325-7155. Glenn Simonds.
Paramount Film Distributing Corp., 2600 Century Parkway, 30345; (404) 325-7674. M. V. McAfee.
Triumph Releasing Corp., 3100 Breckinridge Blvd., #135, Duluth, GA 30136; (404) 564-8521. Judith Marsh, managing dir.
Twentieth Century-Fox Film Corp., 2635 Century Parkway, N.E., 30345; (404) 321-1178. Larry Jameson, Branch Mgr.
Universal Film Exchange, 6060 McDonough Dr., Norcross GA 30093; (404) 448-8032. Curtis Fainn, Mgr.
Warner Bros., 2970 Clairmont Rd., 30329; (404) 325-0301. Barry Nelson, Branch Mgr.

BOSTON

Buena Vista Distribution Co., 990 Washington St., Dedham, MA, 02026; (617) 461-0870. John Molson, Branch Mgr.
Cine Research Assoc., 32 Fisher Avenue, Roxbury, 02161; (617) 442-9756.
Cinema Booking Service of New England, PO Box 827, Needham, 02191; (617) 986-2122.
Cinema Consultants Inc., PO Box 331, 02199; (617) 437-7050.
Lockwood & McKinnon, Film Corp., 20 Pickering St., Needham, MA 02192; (617) 449-7777.
MGM/UA Distribution Co., 100 Grandview Rd., Braintree, MA, 02184; (617) 849-0131. Joe Griffin, NE Reg. VP.
Natl. Film Service Operating Corp., 20 Freeport Way, Dorchester 02122; (617) 288-1600.
Orion Pictures Distribution Corp., 31 St. James Ave., 02116; (617) 542-0677. Beth Weiner, mgr.
Paramount Film Distributing Corp., Parking Way Bldg., 10 Granite St., Quincy, 02169-9134; (617) 773-3100. Joe Rathgab.
Triumph Releasing Corp., 20 Park Plaza, #905, 02116; (617) 426-8980. John Monahan, man. dir.
Universal Film Exchanges, Inc., 44 Winchester St., 02116; (617) 426-8760. Joan Corrado.
Warner Bros. Pictures Dist. Corp., 45 Braintree Hill, Office P/C 301, 02184; (617) 848-2550. Andrew Silverman, Branch Mgr.
Zipporah Films, 1 Richdale Ave. #4, Cambridge, 02140; (617) 576-3603.

CHARLOTTE

Carolina Booking Service, 230 S. Tryon St., 28202; (704) 377-9341.
Carolina Film Service Inc., 522 Penman St., 28203; (704) 333-2115.

CHICAGO

Beacon Films, 930 Pitner Ave., Evanston, IL 60202; (800) 323-5448.
Buena Vista Distribution Co. Inc. 9700 Higgins Rd., Suite 550, Rosemont, 60018; (312) 696-0900. Rick Rice, Div. mgr.
Triumph ReleasingCorp., 2800 River Rd., #230, Des Plaines, IL 60018; (312) 699-6800. Glenn Abrams, managing dir.
MGM/UA Distribution Co., 6133 River Rd., Suite 900, Rosemont, 60018; (312) 518-0500. Raymond Russo, Mid-West Reg. VP.
Orion Pictures Distribution Corp., 75 E. Wacker Dr., Suite 800, 60601; (312) 332-4755. Will Doebel, Div. mgr.
Paramount Film Distributing Co., 8750 W. Bryn Mawr Ave., 60631; (312) 380-4560. Bob Weiss.
Twentieth Century Fox Film Corp., 1100 Woodfield Rd., Schaumburg, IL, 60173; (312) 706-9240. Bert Livingston, Div. mgr.
Universal Film Exchanges, 425 N. Michigan Ave., 60611; (312) 822-0513. William Gehring, mgr.
Warner Bros. Dist. Corp., 1111 East Touhy Ave., Des Plaines, IL 60018; (312) 296-5070. Floyd Brethour, Div. mgr.

CINCINNATI

C. J. Ruff Film Distributing Co., 1601 Harrison Ave., Fairmont, 45214; (513) 921-8200.

CLEVELAND

Triumph Releasing Corp., 6000 Freedom Sq. Dr., #540, Independence, OH 44131; (216) 524-3880.

DALLAS

Buena Vista Distribution, 10300 N. Central Expressway, 75206; (214) 363-9494. Jim Nocella, Div. mgr.
Crump Distributors, Inc. 6545 Lange Circle, 75214; (214) 826-6331. Jim Crump.
MGM/UA Distribution Co., 6060 N. Central Expressway, Suite 258, 75206; (214) 692-0777. Jeffery Kaufman, SW Reg. Director.
Orion Pictures Distribution Corp., 7557 Rambler Rd., 75231; (214) 363-7600. Redmond Gautier, Div. mgr.
Paramount Film Distributing Corp., 12222 Merit Dr., Suite 840, 75251; (214) 387-4400. John Hersker, mgr.
Taurus Ent., 1900 S. Central Expressway, 75215; (214) 421-1900. Sara Murray, mgr.
Triumph Releasing Corp., 12770 Merit Dr., #702, 75251; (214) 770-4220. Kenneth Newbert, managing dir.
Twentieth Century Fox Film Corp., 12222 Merit Dr., 75251; (214) 233-4571. Richard King, Div. mgr.
Universal Film Exchanges, Inc., 7502 Greenville Ave., 75231; (214) 360-0022. Mark Gaines, br. mgr.
Warner Bros. Distributing Corp., 8144 Walnut Hill Lane 920, 75231; (214) 691-6101. J. R. Motley, Div. mgr.

DENVER

Crest Distributing Co., 1443 Larimer, 80202; (303) 571-5569.

DETROIT

DRD Distributors, 14380 Fenkell Ave., 48227; (313) 838-6006. Al Dezel, George Rossman.
Natl. Film Service Operating Corp., 6111 Concord, 48211; (313) 923-2150.
Orion Pictures Distribution Corp., 24700 Northwestern Hwy., Southfield, MI 48075; (313) 358-0733. Linda Victel, mgr.

HONOLULU, HI

Pacific Motion Picture Co. Ltd., 470 N. Nimitz Hwy., 96817; (808) 531-1117.

JACKSONVILLE, FL

Clark Film Releasing, 905 North St., 32211; (904) 721-2122. Harry Clark, pres. Belton Clark, gen. mgr.
United Film Distribution Co., 9333 Atlantic Blvd., 32225; (904) 725-4077. Richard Settoon, mgr.

KANSAS CITY, MO

Midwest Films, 3879 W. 95th St., Shawnee Mission, KS 66206; (913) 381-2058. Gene Irwin.
Orion Pictures Distribution Corp., 3101 Broadway, 64111; (816) 932-6500. Jack Klug, mgr.

LOS ANGELES

Atlantic Releasing Corp., 8255 Sunset Blvd., Suite 104, L.A. 90046; (213) 650-2500.
Azteca Films, Inc., 555 N. La Brea Ave., 90036; (213) 938-2413.
Seymour Borde Associates, 1800 N. Highland Ave., Hollywood, CA 90028; (213) 461-3936.
Buena Vista Dist. Co. Inc., 3800 W. Alameda Ave., Suite 358, Burbank, 91505; (818) 569-7300. Pat Pade, Div. mgr.
Cori Films International, 2049 Central Park E., #1200, 90067; (213) 557-0173.
Crest Film Distributors, 116 No. Robertson Blvd., 90052; (213) 652-8844. J. Persell.

Crown International Pictures, 8701 Wilshire Blvd., B.H. 90211; (213) 657-6700.
Empire Pictures, 1551 N. La Brea Ave., 90028; (213) 850-6110 or (818) 999-3800. Jim Rogers.
Hollywood International Film Corp. of America, 1044 S. Hill St., L.A. 90015; (213) 749-2067.
MGM/UA Distribution Co., 11111 Santa Monica Blvd., 90025; (213) 444-1600. Corky Lewin, L.A. Reg. VP.
Orion Pictures Distribution Corp., 1888 Century Park E., Suite 416, Century City, 90067; (213) 282-2828. Greg Potash, Div. mgr.
Paramount Film Dist. Corp. 15260 Ventura Blvd., Suite 1140, Sherman Oaks, 91403; (818) 789-2900. Robert Box, mgr.
Toho-Towa Co. Ltd., 2 Century Plaza, 2049 Century Park E., 90067; (213) 553-3191.
Triumph Releasing Corp., 8671 Wilshire Blvd., 6th Fl., Beverly Hills, CA 90211; (213) 657-6410. Roger Cels, managing dir.
Twentieth Century Fox Film Corp., 15250 Ventura Blvd., Sherman Oaks, CA 91403; (818) 995-7975. James Naify, Div. mgr.
Universal Film Exchange, 8901 Beverly Blvd., 90048; (213) 550-7461. Jack Finn, mgr.
Warner Bros. Pictures Distribution Corp., 15821 Ventura Blvd., #685, Encino, 91436; (818) 784-7494. Richard Hill, Div. mgr.

NEW ORLEANS

Clark Movie Distributing Co., 4904 Tartan Dr., Metairie, LA, 70010; (504) 733-3555.
Howco International Pictures, 3939 Airline Highway, Metairie; (504) 834-8511.

NEW YORK

American General Film Distribution Inc., 1600 Broadway, 10019; (212) 977-8670.
Bedford Entertainment, 101 W. 57th St., 10019; (212) 265-0680.
Buena Vista Distribution Co., 500 Park Ave., 10022; (212) 735-5421. Phil Fortune, Div. mgr.
Cinecom Intl. Films Inc., 1250 Broadway; (212) 239-8360.
Cinevista Releasing, 347 W. 39 St., 10018; (212) 947-4373.
Films Inc., 799 Broadway; (212) 475-5114.
Filmworld Distributors, Inc., 165 W. 46 St., 10036; (212) 757-0708.
First Run Features, 153 Waverly Place, 10011; (212) 243-0600.
Grange Communications, Inc., 45 W. 60 St., 10023; (212) 582-4261.
Gray City, Inc., 853 Broadway, 10001; (212) 473-3600.
Independent International Pictures Corp., 223 State Hwy. #18, East Brunswick, NJ 08816; (201) 249-8982.
Independent Feature Project, 1776 Broadway, 10019; (212) 245-1622.
Italtoons Corp., 32 W. 40 St., 10018; (212) 730-0280.
ITM Releasing Corp., 321 W. 44 St., 10036; (212) 582-6946.
MGM/UA Distribution Co., 1350 Ave. of the Americas, 10019; (212) 708-0393. Bob Burke, NY Reg. VP.
Marvin Films, Inc., 1560 Broadway, 10019; (212) 575-7753.
Miramax Films, 18 E. 48th St., #1601, 10017; (212) 888-2662.
Orion Pictures Distribution Corp., 9 W. 57 St., 10019; (212) 980-1117. Rob Lawinski, Div. mgr.
Paramount Film Distributing Corp., 15 Columbus Circle, 10023; (212) 373-8000. Pam Pritzker.
Promovision International Films, Ltd., 347 W. 39 St., 10018; (212) 947-4373.
Skouras Pictures, 380 Bleecker St.; (212) 645-3466.
Taurus Entertainment, 2545 Hempstead Turnpike, East Meadow, 11554; (516) 579-8400.
Third World Newsreel, 335 W. 38 St., 10018; (212) 947-9277.
Times Film Corp., 157 W. 57 St., 10019; (212) 757-6980.
Toho International, 1501 Broadway, 10036; (212) 391-9058.
Triumph Releasing Corp., 1700 Broadway, 10019; (212) 408-8205. Joseph Curtin, managing dir.
Twentieth Century Fox Film Corp., 1211 Ave. of the Americas, 3rd Fl., 10036; (212) 556-2490. Carl Bertolino, Div. mgr. Ronald Polon, NY Div. mgr.
Universal Film Exchange, 445 Park Ave., 10022; (212) 759-7500. Gary Rocco, mgr.
Warner Bros. Distributing Corporation, 75 Rockefeller Plaza, 14th floor, 10019; (212) 484-6203. Robert Miller, Div. mgr.

PHILADELPHIA

Triumph Releasing Corp., 1617 John F. Kennedy Blvd., #800, 19103; (215) 568-3889; Joe Saladino, managing dir.

PITTSBURGH

Paramount Film Distributing Corp., Fulton Bldg., 107 6th St., 15222; (412) 281-9270. Kay Grotto, mgr.

SAN FRANCISCO

Warner Bros. Pictures Distributing Corp., 150–4th St., 91403; (415) 543-8015. Mike Timko.

SEATTLE

MGM/UA Distribution Co., 225-108th Ave., N.E. Bellevue, WA 98004; (206) 453-1172. S. Amato, NW Sr. Sales mgr.
Northwest Diversified Entertainment, 2819 First, 98121; (206) 441-5380.
Seattle National Film Service, 900 Maynard S., (206) 682-6685.

WASHINGTON, DC

Key Theatre Ent., 1325½ Wisconsin Ave., N.W., 20007; (202) 965-4401. David Levy.
Orion Pictures Distribution Corp., 5205 Leesburg Pike, Suite 311, Falls Church, VA 22041; (703) 824-1600. Charles Vaden, Div. mgr.
Warner Bros. Dist. Corp., 1700 Rockville Pike, Rockville, MD 20852; (301) 230-1324. Daniel Chinich, Branch Mgr.

Distributors of 16mm Feature Films

Following is a listing of distributors having substantial selections of 16mm films for lease or rental. Additionally, some of the companies may have prints available for outright purchase. Inquiries for catalogs listing complete product should be made to the addresses given below.

BENCHMARK FILMS
145 Scarborough Road, Briarcliff Manor, NY 10510; (914) 762-3838.

BIOGRAPH ENTERTAINMENT
P.O. Box 190, Mamaroneck, NY 10543-0190; (914) 381-5570.

BLACKHAWK CATALOG
12636 Beatrice St., Los Angeles, CA 90066; (213) 306-4040.

BUDGET FILMS
4590 Santa Monica Blvd., Los Angeles, CA 90029; (213) 660-0187.

BUENA VISTA PICTURES DISTRIBUTION-NON-THEATRICAL
350 S. Buena Vista St., room 143 ROD, Burbank, CA 91521; (818) 560-7405.

CAPITOL ENTERTAINMENT
4818 Yuma St. NW, Washington, DC 20016; (202) 363-8800.

CAROUSEL FILMS
260 5th Ave., room 705, New York, NY 10001; (212) 683-1160.

CINECOM PICTURES
1250 Broadway, New York, NY 10001; (212) 239-8360.

CINEMA GUILD
1697 Broadway, New York, NY 10019; (212) 246-5522.

CIRCLE RELEASING
2445 M St., Suite 225, Washington, DC 20037; (202) 331-3838.

CLEM WILLIAMS
2240 Noblestown Rd., Pittsburgh, PA 15205; (412) 921-5810.

COLUMBIA CLASSICS
Columbia Pictures, The Burbank Studios, Burbank, CA 91505; (818) 954-4485.

CORINTH FILMS
34 Gansevoort St., New York, NY 10014; (212) 463-0305.

DIRECT CINEMA
P.O. Box 69799, Los Angeles, CA 90069; (213) 652-8000.

EM GEE FILM LIBRARY
6924 Canby Ave., Suite 103, Reseda, CA 91335; (818) 981-5506.

EURO-AMERICAN FILMS
4818 Yuma St. NW, Washington, DC 20016; (202) 363-8800.

FILM-MAKERS COOPERATIVE
175 Lexington Ave., New York, NY 10016; (212) 889-3820.

FILMS INCORPORATED
5547 N. Ravenswood Ave., Chicago, IL 60640; (312) 878-2600.

FIRST RUN/ICARUS
153 Waverly Place, New York, NY 10004; (212) 674-3375.

HURLOCK CINE-WORLD, INC.
Box 34619, Juneau, AK 99803; (907) 789-3995.

IFEX FILMS/INTERNATIONAL FILM EXCHANGE LTD.
201 W. 52 St., New York, NY 10019; (212) 582-4318.

INTERAMA
301 W. 53 St., Suite 19E, New York, NY 10019; (212) 977-4836.

IVY FILM
165 W. 46 St., New York, NY 10036; (212) 382-0111.

KINO INTERNATIONAL
333 W. 39 St., Suite 503, New York, NY 10018; (212) 629-6880.

KIT PARKER
1245 10th St., Monterey, CA 93940; (408) 649-5573.

MANBECK PICTURES CORP.
3621 Wakonda Dr., Des Moines, IA 50321; (515) 285-8345.

MODERN SOUND
1402 Howard St., Omaha, NE 68102; (402) 341-8476.

MUSEUM OF MODERN ART FILM LIBRARY
11 W. 53 St., New York, NY 10019; (212) 708-9433.

NEW LINE CINEMA
575 Eighth Ave., New York, NY 10018; (212) 239-8880.

NEW YORKER FILMS
16 W. 61 St., New York, NY 10023; (212) 247-6110.

PRESTIGE FILM CORPORATION
18 E. 48 St., Suite 1601, New York, NY 10017; (212) 888-2662.

PYRAMID FILMS
P.O. Box 1048, Santa Monica, CA 90406; (213) 828-7577.

REPUBLIC PICTURES CORPORATION
12636 Beatrice St., Los Angeles, CA 90066; (213) 306-4040.

SAMUEL GOLDWYN COMPANY
10203 Santa Monica Blvd., Los Angeles, CA 90067; (213) 552-2255.

SWANK MOTION PICTURES
201 S. Jefferson Ave., St. Louis, MO 63103; (314) 534-6300.

THIRD WORLD NEWSREEL
335 W. 38 St., New York, NY 10018; (212) 947-9277 (feature documentaries and short fiction).

TRANS-WORLD FILMS
332 S. Michigan Ave., Chicago, IL 60604; (312) 922-1530.

Corporate Histories of the Networks

Corporate Histories of the Networks

Capital Cities/ABC, Inc.

Like the other major U.S. television networks, ABC had its origins in radio. In the beginning Radio Corporation of America (RCA) owned two radio networks: the Blue and the Red. In 1941 the FCC decreed that the same company could not own two networks, so RCA incorporated the Blue under the name of American Broadcasting System and established it as an independent subsidiary with 116 stations. RCA then sold this network to Edward J. Noble, founder and chairman of the Life Savers Corporation, for $8 million. The name was changed to the American Broadcasting Company in 1944, at which time the network had 197 radio affiliates.

Television arrived for ABC in 1948 when, on April 19, ABC carried its first TV program: "On the Corner," with Henry Morgan, which was sponsored by the Admiral Radio Corp. Later in the year ABC scored two "firsts": the live broadcast of an opera (Verdi's "Otello") from the Metropolitan Opera House in New York and a TV documentary, "The Marshall Plan."

The next big step for ABC came in 1952 with its merger with United Paramount Theatres, the motion picture theatre circuit founded when Paramount Pictures was required under the Sherman Anti-Trust Act to separate its film production unit from its theatres. This merger was engineered by Leonard H. Goldenson, then the president of UPT. The new company was called American Broadcasting-Paramount Theatres, Inc.

During the 1950's ABC began operation at a profit although it had to struggle fiercely to acquire new affiliates. In 1954 ABC made a deal with Walt Disney to acquire a 35 per cent interest in Disneyland and all TV programs produced by Disney. The following year ABC signed an exclusive rights contract with Warner Bros. for TV programming.

The 1960's brought many changes to ABC beginning with the introduction of color programming for the fall season of 1962; this was expanded in 1966 to include full color broadcasting. In 1965 AB-PT's name was changed to American Broadcasting Companies, Inc. and the company's corporate headquarters were moved from West 66th Street in New York to 1330 Avenue of the Americas, where they remained until 1989.

High points in the decade of the '60s also included the introduction of the blockbuster theatrical movie to TV with spectacular rating results when "The Bridge on the River Kwai" was viewed (in 1966) by 60 million Americans.

In 1967 the ABC evening news was expanded from 15 minutes to a half hour, and Joey Bishop inaugurated ABC's late-night programming with his talk show.

An attempt to gain control of ABC by Howard Hughes was circumvented by Goldenson in 1968. Hughes said publicly that he abandoned his efforts to acquire the network because of the strong resistance of Goldenson; however, it was speculated elsewhere that he gave up because as new owner of ABC he would have had to attend a public hearing under the auspices of the FCC. The fanatically reclusive Hughes, it was assumed, would never have agreed to come out of seclusion for such an event.

The decade of the Seventies was an eventful one for ABC, too, not the least because in 1972 it was able to operate at a profit for the first time in ten years. Also in the 1976–77 season ABC moved for the first time into first place in the ratings race. It held the lead for the next two years and then dropped back into second place in 1979–80, a position it held until 1983–84 when it dropped to third position. It was unable to rise above that until 1987–88 when it displaced CBS in second place, primarily because of special sports programming, such as the World Series and the Superbowl. It remained second in 1988–89.

In 1976 Barbara Walters joined ABC, becoming the first anchorwoman in television history. Her almost $1 million a year salary caused lifted eyebrows among her fellow anchor persons, including Harry Reasoner and Howard K. Smith.

In 1977 the mini-series "Roots" appeared on ABC and became the all-time highest-rated program. This helped immensely in the ratings race, and credit must go in large part to Fred Silverman who two years before had joined the company as president of ABC international. He left in 1978 to go to NBC.

The decade of the Eighties was a turbulent one for the television industry as cable TV and home video began whittling away at their audiences. ABC was no exception. Halfway through the period—in 1985—ABC agreed to be purchased by Capital Cities Communications at a cost of $3.5 billion. 1986 saw formal completion of the takeover and the merged company's name was changed to Capital Cities/ABC, Inc.

With the departure of Goldenson, that year also brought other important changes in management. Daniel B. Burke replaced Frederick J. Pierce as president and chief operating officer. There were also sweeping reductions in personnel in the interests of economy and streamlining. (At least 1,000 employees were fired.)

Budget cuts notwithstanding Capital Cities/ABC chairman Thomas Murphy pledged ABC would not scrimp on programming. Instead the focus was to be on the network's non-programming expenses which accounted for about 30 per cent of the budget. One result was to cut out internally-generated research which was to be contracted for on an ad hoc basis as needed.

Capital Cities/ABC owns eight television stations and 21 radio stations and is a partner in ESPN, the highly successful cable TV sports channel and two other cable TV services—Arts & Entertainment and Lifetime. It also owns publishing operations which include nine daily newspapers, several weeklies and a variety of trade and consumer magazines.

Columbia Broadcasting System, Inc.

CBS first saw the light of day in 1927 as a radio network with 16 stations—United Independent Broadcasters, Inc.—founded by Arthur Judson, a concert tour manager. In need of money, Judson secured backing from Louis Sterling, president of the Columbia Phonograph Company, and changed the network name to Columbia Phonograph Broadcasting System. Later other investors were invited in, the most prominent of whom was William S. Paley, who, on September 26, 1928, at the age of 27, became president of the firm whose name was changed again. Now it was called the Columbia Broadcasting System.

Paley introduced many innovations to radio broadcasting, most significant of which was the signing of an agreement in 1931 with Paramount Pictures whereby film stars were heard on radio for the first time. This laid the groundwork for the CBS policy in television from the outset to feature shows built around stars (Ed Sullivan, Lucille Ball, Arthur Godfrey, Jack Benny, Burns & Allen, Garry Moore, etc.).

Actually CBS was in TV as early as 1931 when it began regularly scheduled TV programming over experimental station W2XAB in New York City. In 1941 CBS began weekly broadcast of black-and-white TV programming over WCBS-TV in New York. By 1948 it had 30 affiliated stations.

The decade of the 1950's brought many important advances. In 1951 CBS broadcast the first live coast-to-coast TV transmission between New York and San Francisco. In 1952 there came opening of Television City in Hollywood—the industry's first self-contained TV production facility. In 1956 "Playhouse 90" made its debut and set new high standards for drama originated on TV.

But the big event of the decade came along early—in 1951—with the debut of "I Love Lucy." The road to creating that phenomenal success was a rocky one. For one thing CBS did not want Desi Arnaz, and signed him only on the insistence of Lucille Ball. Second, the couple wanted to work before a live audience—a practice also anathema to the CBS powers-that-be. Ball and Arnaz persisted, and their efforts led to what is regarded as the invention of the situation-comedy format.

1951 was also the year that Bill Gordon designed the CBS Eye—destined to become one of the most famous logos in the world.

In the field of soap operas CBS was both leader and winner, virtually monopolizing that market from 1951 to 1956. In 1951 it introduced "Search for Tomorrow," which was to become the longest-running show ever in that genre. This was followed by "Love of Life" (1951) "The Guiding Light" (1952)—both overnight hits. "Guiding Light" was still on the air in 1988, as was the fourth soap CBS introduced, "As the World Turns" (1956).

In the late '50s and through the '60s and '70s CBS reigned as king of prime time ratings as tallied by the Nielsen Company. It had tied with NBC in 1969–70 and 1970–71 and ABC led in three seasons; but the rest of the time CBS was Number One. Thus it was quite a jolt to the company when in 1985–86 it slipped to second place and stayed there through the following season. Then came the worst blow of all: in 1987–88 CBS came in third for the first time in TV history.

CBS maintained its long-running lead with such successes as "Gunsmoke" (1957), "The Defenders" (1961), "The Beverly Hillbillies" (1962), "All in the Family" (1972) and "Dallas" (1978). Also helping was "60 Minutes," the news-oriented show, which in 1988 had remained in the Top Ten prime time shows for 11 consecutive seasons.

CBS began the turbulent Eighties with a new president, Thomas Wyman (replacing John D. Backe). Worst year for the company so far in that decade was surely 1985 when the company was sent reeling under three major assaults.

First, Gen. William C. Westmoreland filed a $120 million law suit, charging he had been libeled during a 1982 "CBS Reports" documentary. The subsequent trial ended 18 weeks after it began in New York Federal Court after the general heard some of his closest advisers during the Vietnam War testify they supported the CBS documentary contention in that he had deliberately underestimated the enemy troop strength on the field. Fearing he would lose, Westmoreland dropped the action before it could go to a jury.

Second, Senator Jesse Helms (Rep., N.C.) and his Fairness in Media committee launched an unfriendly takeover bid to "become Dan Rather's boss." (Rather had replaced Walter Cronkite as chief news anchor in 1981.)

Third, Atlanta broadcast entrepreneur Ted Turner made an unfriendly junk-bond bid for CBS. In a clever move the network bought up 21 per cent of its own stock for $956 million and thwarted the takeover. Turner went after MGM/UA instead.

Meanwhile Laurence A. Tisch, a former theatre chain executive, had become the major stockholder in CBS and in 1986 he instigated some sweeping changes in the interests of cost-cutting and efficiency. Some 700 jobs were eliminated at the CBS Broadcast Group. Tisch also removed Wyman as president, named himself chief executive officer and induced founder William Paley to return to active duty as acting chairman of the board.

In 1988, stung by CBS' worst prime time rating performance ever, Tisch shuffled executive ranks again, naming Howard Stringer, previously president of CBS News, as president of the Broadcasting Group. He replaced Gene F. Jankowski, who was named to the newly created position of chairman of the Broadcast Group. At the same time Tisch reported the CBS second-quarter income for 1988 rose 40 per cent to a new quarterly record. He attributed this to higher sales achieved despite a slow advertising market and to improvement of operating margin through reduction of costs and making operations more efficient. It was all, said Tisch, the beginning of "a new era" for CBS.

In the 1988–89 season, however, CBS was in third place again.

National Broadcasting Company

Television began for NBC in 1928, when on April 4, it acquired from the Federal Communications Commission a permit to operate an experimental station, W2XBS. Actual transmission from the Empire State Building did not begin, however, until October 30, 1931. Some eight years late the network began broadcasting on a regular basis, beginning with the opening of the New York World's Fair on April 30, 1939.

NBC, like the other networks, was an outgrowth of radio operations. Radio Corp. of America, General Electric and Westinghouse jointly launched a network in 1926 which had 31 stations; 25 in a network called Red and 6 in one called Blue. A year later it was forced to sell the Blue network to ABC (see history of that network), keeping for itself the one known as Red.

In 1930 RCA bought out its partners, GE and Westinghouse, and NBC became its wholly owned subsidiary.

NBC became a TV network on January 12, 1940, when two stations, WNBC-TV, New York, and WRGB-TV, Schenectady, New York, carried the first network programming. In June, 1941, the FCC granted NBC the first commercial TV license and a month later it had four advertisers signed up: Procter & Gamble, Lever Brothers, Sun Oil and Bulova.

After World War II NBC scored two big "firsts." On June 19, 1946, Gillette became the first advertiser to sponsor a TV network show, the Joe Louis-Billy Conn boxing match. That same year Bristol-Myers became the first sponsor of a network TV series, "Geographically Speaking."

NBC can also claim to be the first to introduce coast-to-coast network TV coverage. On September 4, 1951, when the U.S.-Japanese peace treaty was signed in San Francisco, its cameras were on hand.

In 1952 NBC pioneered early morning programming when it introduced "The Today Show."

NBC can also claim the first regularly scheduled network color series: "The Marriage," launched in 1954. That same year it achieved the first west-to-east TV transmission with the television of the Tournament of Roses Parade in color. At the start of the 1965–66 season it could declare it was the "only all-color network."

In 1968 NBC introduced new forms of TV programming with "The Name of the Game," a series that incorporated feature-film elements into a 90-minute show. This then spawned the "NBC Mystery Movie"—a series of programs composed of "Colombo," "Hec Ramsey", "McMillan and Wife," "McCloud," "Amy Prentiss," "McCoy," and "Quincy, M.E.".

In 1972 NBC broke new ground again when it introduced "The Tomorrow Show" shown from 1:00 a.m. to 2:00 a.m. This was a talk program and it demonstrated that in the wee small hours of the morning something more than re-runs and old movies could be shown. In 1974 another late-night show called "Weekend" was begun.

In 1976 NBC's telecast of "Gone with the Wind" drew the largest audience to that date for an entertainment program. In 1978 its "Holocaust" mini-series attracted 107 million viewers and won 21 major awards.

Such programs helped NBC in the ratings, but in 1976–77 it fell to third place, where it stayed until 1983–84. (Ironically 1976 was the year in which NBC celebrated its 50th anniversary in broadcasting with a four-hour, star-filled special.) In 1984–85 it edged up to second place, and the following year it was ranked Number One in prime-time viewing for the first time in the three decades of such tallying by Nielsen. (For the record NBC did tie for first place with CBS in 1969–70 and 1970–71.)

NBC held on solidly to its first place standing for 1986–87, 1987–88, and 1988–89.

Along with the other networks NBC moved into a period of turmoil during the decade of the Eighties, fighting off rising costs and competition from cable TV and home video. In 1986 General Electric Corporation purchased RCA (NBC's parent) for $6.28 billion; GE, it will be remembered, helped launch the radio network in 1926 which led to the development of NBC-TV. This brought personnel changes led by the replacement of Grant A. Tinker as NBC chief executive officer by Robert Wright, although Wright was not given Tinker's chairman title, that being taken by John F. Welch of GE. Instead Wright was named president as well as chief executive officer. Along with its competition NBC started cutting staff and budgets in 1986.

NBC owns television stations located in Chicago, Cleveland, Los Angeles, New York City and Washington, D.C. GE, the parent company, also owns TV station subsidiaries in Denver and Miami, which are operated under the aegis of NBC.

In 1987 NBC owned eight radio stations in various cities, but it is reconfiguring these operations and plans to sell some of them and also to acquire other stations in different cities.

In 1987 NBC released some interesting figures about costs of television production. It revealed the average prime time half-hour series program for the 1986–87 season cost about $500,000 for two showings; that the average hour program costs $1 million or more; and that a feature film made for TV runs to about $3 million.

Television Companies

* NETWORKS
* SET MANUFACTURERS
* MAJOR PRODUCERS

Companies

Capital Cities/ABC, Inc.

77 W. 66th St., New York, NY 10023; (212) 456-7777; 2040 Avenue of the Stars, Century City, CA 90067; (213) 557-7777.

CHM. OF BOARD & CHIEF EXECUTIVE OFFICER
Thomas S. Murphy
PRESIDENT & CHIEF OPERATING OFFICER
Daniel B. Burke
EXECUTIVE VICE PRESIDENT; CHAIRMAN & CHIEF EXECUTIVE OFFICER, FAIRCHILD PUBLICATIONS
John B. Fairchild
EXECUTIVE VICE PRESIDENT; PRESIDENT, ABC TELEVISION NETWORK GROUP
John B. Sias
SENIOR VICE PRESIDENT; CHIEF FINANCIAL OFFICER
Ronald J. Doerfler
SENIOR VICE PRESIDENT; PRESIDENT, BROADCAST GROUP
Michael P. Mallardi
SENIOR VICE-PRESIDENT; PRESIDENT, PUBLISHING GROUP
Phillip J. Meek
SENIOR VICE PRESIDENT & GENERAL COUNSEL
Stephen A. Weiswasser
VICE PRESIDENT & CONTROLLER
Allan J. Edelson
VICE PRESIDENT, INVESTOR RELATIONS
Joseph M. Fitzgerald
VICE PRESIDENT, HUMAN RESOURCES
John E. Frisoli
VICE PRESIDENT, TAXES
James M. Goldberg
VICE PRESIDENT, ADMINISTRATION
Robert T. Goldman
VICE PRESIDENT
Andrew E. Jackson
VICE PRESIDENT & ASSISTANT CONTROLLER
David S. Loewith
VICE PRESIDENT, CORPORATE COMMUNICATIONS
Patricia J. Matson
VICE PRESIDENT, LABOR RELATIONS
Jeffrey Ruthizer
VICE PRESIDENT, BROADCAST STANDARDS & PRACTICES
Alfred R. Schneider
VICE PRESIDENT & TREASURER
David J. Vondrak
SECRETARY
Philip R. Farnsworth
ASSISTANT TREASURER
Allen S. Bomes
VICE PRESIDENT & PRESIDENT CAPITAL CITIES/ABC RADIO DIVISION OF THE BROADCAST GROUP
James P. Arcasa
VICE PRESIDENT
Philip R. Bouth
VICE PRESIDENT & PRESIDENT ABC PUBLISHING
Robert G. Burton
VICE PRESIDENT & PRESIDENT CAPITAL CITIES/ABC VIDEO ENTERPRISES
Herbert A. Granath
VICE PRESIDENT & SENIOR VICE PRESIDENT FINANCE, ABC TELEVISION NETWORK GROUP
Ann Maynard Gray
VICE PRESIDENT & PRESIDENT CAPITAL CITIES/ABC OWNED TV STATIONS—WEST
Kenneth H. Johnson
VICE PRESIDENT & DIRECTOR OF ENGINEERING, CAPITAL CITIES/ABC BROADCAST GROUP
Robert O. Niles
VICE PRESIDENT & PRESIDENT CAPITAL CITIES/ABC OWNED TV STATIONS—EAST
Lawrence J. Pollock
BOARD OF DIRECTORS
Thomas S. Murphy (chmn. of the bd., CEO); Daniel B. Burke (pres., COO); Robert P. Bauman (chmn. of the bd., Smith Klein, Beecham p.l.c.); Warren E. Buffett (chmn. of the bd., CEO, Berkshire Hathaway Inc.); Frank T. Cary (former chmn. of the bd., IBM); John B. Fairchild (exec. v.p., chmn., CEO, Fairchild Publications); Leonard H. Goldenson (chmn., executive committee; retired chmn. of the bd., American Broadcasting Companies, Inc.); George P. Jenkins (consultant to W.R. Grace & Co.; retired chmn. of the bd., Metropolitan Life Insurance Company); Frank S. Jones (Ford Professor of Urban Affairs, Massachusetts Institute of Technology); Ann Dibble Jordan (former director of Social Service Dept., University of Chicago Medical School); Thomas M. Macioce (partner, Shea & Gold, Attorneys at Law; former chmn. of the bd., CEO, Allied Stores Corporation); John H. Muller Jr. (chmn., pres., CEO, General Housewares Corp.); John B. Sias (exec. v.p.; pres., ABC Television Network Group); William I. Spencer (retired pres., chief admin. officer, Citicorp and Citibank, N.A.); M. Cabell Woodward, Jr (vice chmn., CFO, ITT Corp.).

FINANCIAL (ALL CAPITAL CITIES/ABC, INC.)

SENIOR VICE PRESIDENT AND CHIEF FINANCIAL OFFICER
Ronald J. Doerfler
VICE PRESIDENT & TREASURER
David S. Vondrak
VICE PRESIDENT & COMPTROLLER
Allan J. Edelson
VICE PRESIDENT & ASSISTANT COMPTROLLER
David S. Loewith
VICE PRESIDENT, TAXES
James M. Goldberg
VICE PRESIDENT, TAX PLANNING & ADMINISTRATION
Andrew C. Govesnali
VICE PRESIDENT, INVESTOR RELATIONS
Joseph M. Fitzgerald

ADMINISTRATION

VICE-PRESIDENT, ADMINISTRATION, CAPITAL CITIES/ABC, INC.
Robert T. Goldman
VICE PRESIDENT OF REAL ESTATE AND CONSTRUCTION
Richard E. Hockman
VICE PRESIDENT, ADMINISTRATION, WEST COAST
Roger K. Lund

TECHNOLOGY & STRATEGIC PLANNING

SENIOR VICE PRESIDENT
Julius Barnathan

HUMAN RESOURCES

VICE PRESIDENT, HUMAN RESOURCES, CAPITAL CITIES/ABC, INC.
John E. Frisoli
VICE PRESIDENT, PERSONNEL, CAPITAL CITIES/ABC, INC.
Anita Hecht
VICE PRESIDENT, EMPLOYEE BENEFITS & HUMAN RESOURCE INFORMATION SYSTEMS
Thomas J. Gorey
VICE PRESIDENT, COMPENSATION & ORGANIZATION PLANNING
William Wilkinson
VICE PRESIDENT, PERSONNEL, WEST COAST
Anthony Sproule

OFFICE OF CORPORATE INITIATIVES

VICE PRESIDENT, OFFICE OF CORPORATE INITIATIVES
Charles Keller
VICE PRESIDENT, OFFICE OF COMMUNICATION
John E. (Jack) Harr

LEGAL

SENIOR VICE PRESIDENT AND GENERAL COUNSEL, CAPITAL CITIES/ABC, INC.
Stephen A. Weiswasser
VICE PRESIDENT, LAW & REGULATION
Samuel Antar
VICE PRESIDENT, CORPORATE LEGAL AFFAIRS
Griffith W. Foxley
VICE PRESIDENT, VIDEO ENTERPRISES & PUBLISHING
Larry M. Loeb
VICE PRESIDENT, LITIGATION
Jeffrey S. Rosen

VICE PRESIDENT, LEGAL & BUSINESS AFFAIRS BROADCASTING
Charles Stanford

BROADCAST STANDARDS & PRACTICES

VICE PRESIDENT, BROADCAST STANDARDS & PRACTICES
Alfred R. Schneider
VICE PRESIDENT, BROADCAST STANDARDS & PRACTICES, EAST COAST
Christine Hikawa
VICE PRESIDENT, BROADCAST STANDARDS & PRACTICES, WEST COAST
Brett A. White
VICE PRESIDENT, COMMERCIAL CLEARANCE, BROADCAST STANDARDS & PRACTICES, EAST COAST
Harvey Cary Dzodin

CORPORATE COMMUNICATIONS

VICE PRESIDENT, CORPORATE COMMUNICATIONS, ABC, INC.
Patricia J. Matson
VICE PRESIDENT, CORPORATE PROJECTS
Julie Hoover
DIRECTOR, CORPORATE
Veronica Pollard

ABC TELEVISION NETWORK GROUP

PRESIDENT
John B. Sias
PRESIDENT, ABC ENTERTAINMENT
Robert A. Iger
GROUP PRESIDENT, ABC NEWS AND SPORTS, AND PRESIDENT, ABC NEWS
Roone Arledge
PRESIDENT, ABC SPORTS
Dennis Swanson
PRESIDENT, ABC TELEVISION NETWORK
Mark Mandala
PRESIDENT, DAYTIME, CHILDREN'S & LATE NIGHT ENTERTAINMENT
Michael Brockman
SENIOR VICE PRESIDENT
James J. Allegro
EXECUTIVE VICE PRESIDENT, SALES
H. Weller Keever
EXECUTIVE VICE PRESIDENT, AFFILIATE RELATIONS
George M. Newi
SENIOR VICE PRESIDENT, FINANCE
Ann M. Gray
VICE PRESIDENT, OPERATIONS
Mark Roth
SENIOR VICE PRESIDENT, MARKETING & RESEARCH SERVICES
Alan Wurtzel
VICE PRESIDENT & EXECUTIVE PRODUCER, MORNING TELEVISION
Philip R. Bouth

AFFILIATE RELATIONS

SENIOR VICE PRESIDENT IN CHARGE OF AFFILIATE RELATIONS
George H. Newi
VICE PRESIDENT AND DIRECTOR OF AFFILIATE OPERATIONS
William (Buzz) Mathesius
VICE PRESIDENT & DIRECTOR OF STATION RELATIONS
Bryce Rathbone
VICE PRESIDENT, AFFILIATE FINANCIAL AFFAIRS
Arnold Marfoglia

NETWORK SALES

EXECUTIVE VICE PRESIDENT IN CHARGE OF SALES
H. Weller (Jake) Keever
SENIOR VICE PRESIDENT GENERAL SALES MANAGER
Marvin G. Goldsmith
SENIOR VICE PRESIDENT, NATIONAL SALES MANAGER
George M. Cain
VICE PRESIDENT, SALES MARKETING
Madeline Nagel
VICE PRESIDENT, PROMOTIONAL SALES
Harry H. Factor
VICE PRESIDENT & DIRECTOR OF SALES MARKETING
Keith Ritter
VICE PRESIDENT, DAYTIME SALES
John R. Shanley, Jr.
VICE PRESIDENT, DIRECTOR DAYTIME SALES
Paul Rittenberg
VICE PRESIDENT, SPORTS SALES
James Wasilko
VICE PRESIDENT AND DIRECTOR, SPORTS SALES
Robert Sedlachek
VICE PRESIDENT, NEWS AND EARLY MORNING SALES
Lawrence Fried
VICE PRESIDENT, DIRECTOR NEWS/EARLY MORNING SALES
Cynthia Ponce
VICE PRESIDENT, SALES DEVELOPMENT/CREATIVE SERVICES
Charles Gabelman
VICE PRESIDENT, SALES ADMINISTRATION
Charles C. Allen
VICE PRESIDENT, SPECIAL PROGRAM SALES
Robert Cagliero
VICE PRESIDENT, REVENUE, PLANNING & SALES ADMINISTRATION
Robert S. Wallen
VICE PRESIDENT, DIRECTOR OF REVENUE ANALYSIS
John Abbattista
VICE PRESIDENT, REGIONAL SALES
Edmond P. Ryan
VICE PRESIDENT AND DIRECTOR OF EASTERN SALES
James M. Casey
VICE PRESIDENT, DIRECTOR EASTERN DIVISION SALES
Raymond R. Warren
VICE PRESIDENT AND DIRECTOR, DAYTIME SALES
Paul Rittenberg
VICE PRESIDENT, PRIME TIME SALE PROPOSALS
Elaine Chin Ming

PUBLIC RELATIONS

VICE PRESIDENT, PUBLIC RELATIONS, CAPITAL CITIES/ABC TELEVISION NETWORK GROUP
Richard J. Connelly
EAST COAST VICE PRESIDENT, PROGRAM INFORMATION
Tom Mackin
DIRECTOR, NEWS INFORMATION
Elise Adde
DIRECTOR, MEDIA PHOTOGRAPHY
Peter Murray
DIRECTOR, COMMUNITY RELATIONS
Jane Paley
DIRECTOR, PROGRAM INFORMATION
David Horowitz
DIRECTOR, DAYTIME PROGRAM PUBLICITY
Regina DiMartino
MANAGER SPORTS INFORMATION
Robert Wheeler
DIRECTOR, PRESS RELATIONS
Janice Gretemeyer Adams
WEST COAST:
VICE PRESIDENT, PUBLIC RELATIONS
Bob Wright
DIRECTOR, PROGRAM PUBLICITY
Rosalind Jarrett
MANAGER, BUSINESS INFORMATION
Jim Brochu
DIRECTOR, BROADCAST PUBLICITY
Jerry Hellard

ABC ENTERTAINMENT

PRESIDENT
Robert A. Iger
EXECUTIVE VICE PRESIDENT, PRIME TIME DEVELOPMENT
Stuart Bloomberg
EXECUTIVE VICE PRESIDENT, PRIME TIME
Edward W. Harbert
VICE PRESIDENT, CASTING & TALENT RELATIONS
Donna L. Rosenstein
VICE PRESIDENT, MOTION PICTURES FOR TV & MINISERIES
Allen Sabinson
VICE PRESIDENT, COMEDY SERIES DEVELOPMENT
Kim Fleary
VICE PRESIDENT, DRAMATIC SERIES DEVELOPMENT
Gary Levine
VICE PRESIDENT, CURRENT SERIES PROGRAMS
John L. Barber
VICE PRESIDENT, PROGRAM PLANNING & SCHEDULING
George Keramidas
VICE PRESIDENT, MOTION PICTURE POST PRODUCTION
Andre de Szekeley
VICE PRESIDENT, PROGRAM ADMINISTRATION
Stephen K. Nenno
VICE PRESIDENT, SPECIAL PROGRAMS
John Hamlin

VICE PRESIDENT, MINI SERIES
Judd Parkin
VICE PRESIDENT, MARKETING
Mark C. Zakarin
VICE PRESIDENT, CREATIVE PICTURES, ON-AIR PROMOTION
Stuart L. Bower

BUSINESS AFFAIRS

SENIOR VICE PRESIDENT, BUSINESS AFFAIRS & CONTRACTS
Ronald V. Sunderland
VICE PRESIDENT, BUSINESS AFFAIRS, WEST COAST
Barry Gordon
VICE PRESIDENT, BUSINESS AFFAIRS & CONTRACTS, WEST COAST
Alan Kaplan
VICE PRESIDENT, BUSINESS AFFAIRS ADMINISTRATION, WEST COAST
Ronald Pratz
DIRECTOR, BUSINESS AFFAIRS
Pat Thompson
VICE PRESIDENT, CONTRACTS, EAST COAST
David L. Sherman
VICE PRESIDENT, BUSINESS AFFAIRS & CONTRACTS, EAST COAST
Donal L. Flynn
VICE PRESIDENT, BUSINESS AFFAIRS, EAST COAST
Anthony S. Farinacci

DAYTIME, CHILDREN'S & LATE NIGHT ENTERTAINMENT

PRESIDENT
Michael Brockman
VICE PRESIDENT, DAYTIME PROGRAMS
Jo Ann Emmerich
VICE PRESIDENT, DAYTIME PROGRAMS, EAST COAST
Mary Alice Dwyer-Dobbin
VICE PRESIDENT, CHILDREN'S PROGRAM SERES
Jeannette B. Trias
VICE PRESIDENT, FINANCE, ADMINISTRATION & OPERATIONS FOR DAYTIME CHILDREN'S & LATE NIGHT ENTERTAINMENT
Albert Rubin

ABC SPORTS, INC.

PRESIDENT, SPORTS
Dennis Swanson
SENIOR VICE PRESIDENT OF SPORTS PLANNING & ADMINISTRATION
Stephen J. Solomon
SENIOR VICE PRESIDENT, PRODUCTION
Dennis Lewin
EXECUTIVE PRODUCER OF ABC SPORTS
Geoff Mason
VICE PRESIDENT, PROGRAMMING
David Downs
VICE PRESIDENT OF ADMINISTRATION AND FINANCIAL CONTROLS
Robert H. Apter

BROADCAST GROUP

PRESIDENT
Michael P. Mallardi
PRESIDENT, BROADCAST OPERATIONS AND ENGINEERING
Robert R. Siegenthaler
PRESIDENT, ABC VIDEO ENTERPRISES
Herbert A. Granath
PRESIDENT, TELEVISION STATIONS, EAST
Lawrence J. Pollock
PRESIDENT, TELEVISION STATIONS, WEST
Kenneth M. Johnson
PRESIDENT, NATIONAL TELEVISION SALES
John B. Watkins
PRESIDENT, RADIO
James B. Arcara
PRESIDENT, RADIO STATIONS
Don B. Bouloukos
PRESIDENT, RADIO NETWORKS
Aaron M. Daniels

CAPITAL CITIES/ABC NATIONAL TELEVISION SALES

PRESIDENT
John B. Watkins
VICE PRESIDENT
Philip J. Sweenie
GENERAL SALES MANAGER, EASTERN SALES
Joseph Cohen

CAPITAL CITIES/ABC-OWNED TELEVISION STATIONS

PRESIDENT—EAST
Lawrence J. Pollock
PRESIDENT—WEST
Kenneth M. Johnson
PRESIDENT AND GENERAL MANAGER, WABC-TV, NEW YORK
Walter C. Liss
PRESIDENT AND GENERAL MANAGER, WLS-TV, CHICAGO
Joseph Ahern
PRESIDENT AND GENERAL MANAGER, WTVD, DURHAM-RALEIGH
G. Alan Nesbitt
PRESIDENT, GENERAL MANAGER, WPUI-TV, PHILADELPHIA, PA
Richard F. Spinner
PRESIDENT AND GENERAL MANAGER, KFSN-TV, FRESNO
Marc Edwards
PRESIDENT AND GENERAL MANAGER, KTRK-TV, HOUSTON
Paul L. Bures, Jr.
PRESIDENT AND GENERAL MANAGER, KABC-TV, LOS ANGELES
Terry Crofoot
PRESIDENT AND GENERAL MANAGER, KGO-TV, SAN FRANCISCO
James G. Topping

ABC VIDEO ENTERPRISES

PRESIDENT, ABC VIDEO ENTERPRISES
Herbert Granath
EXECUTIVE VICE PRESIDENT
Bruce Maggin
SENIOR VICE PRESIDENT, INTERNATIONAL & PROGRAM DEVELOPMENT
Phil Boyer
VICE PRESIDENT, OPERATIONS
Michael S. Dubester

ABC DISTRIBUTION CO.

PRESIDENT
John T. Healy
SENIOR VICE PRESIDENT
Archie C. Purvis
VICE PRESIDENT, PROGRAM ACQUISITIONS & DEVELOPMENT
Paul D. Coss
VICE PRESIDENT, FINANCE & ADMINISTRATION
Jeremiah G. Sullivan

ABC NEWS

PRESIDENT, ABC NEWS
Roone Arledge
SR. VICE PRESIDENT
Richard Wald
V.P. & EXECUTIVE PRODUCER, "CAPITAL TO CAPITAL"
Jeff Gralnick
EXECUTIVE PRODUCER, "20/20"
Victor Neufeld
VICE PRESIDENT & WASHINGTON BUREAU CHIEF
George Watson
VICE PRESIDENT, NEWS PRACTICES
Walter Porges
EXECUTIVE PRODUCER, "PRIME TIME LIVE"
Richard Kaplan
SENIOR VICE PRESIDENT, FINANCE
Irwin W. Weiner
VICE PRESIDENT & ASSISTANT TO THE PRESIDENT
Joanna E. Bistany
EXECUTIVE PRODUCER OF "WORLD NEWS TONIGHT WITH PETER JENNINGS"
Paul Friedman
SENIOR PRODUCER, WASHINGTON BUREAU, ABC NEWS "WORLD NEWS TONIGHT WITH PETER JENNINGS"
Herbert J. Dudnick
SENIOR PRODUCER "NIGHTLINE"
Deborah Leff
EXECUTIVE PRODUCER "BUSINESS WORLD"
Eleanor Prescott

SENIOR BROADCAST PRODUCER "WORLD NEWS TONIGHT WITH PETER JENNINGS"
Robert Roy
EXECUTIVE IN CHARGE OF LONG FORM PROGRAMMING & EXECUTIVE PRODUCER "THIS WEEK WITH DAVID BRINKLEY"
Dorrance Smith
EXECUTIVE PRODUCER
Phyllis McGrady

BROADCAST OPERATIONS AND ENGINEERING

PRESIDENT
Robert Siegenthaler
VICE PRESIDENT AND GENERAL MANAGER, BROADCAST OPERATIONS, EAST COAST
Joseph T. Di Giovanna
V.P., BROADCAST ENGINEERING
Max Berry
VICE PRESIDENT AND GENERAL MANAGER, BROADCAST OPERATIONS & ENGINEERING, WEST COAST
Jack Neitlich
VICE PRESIDENT, BROADCAST OPERATIONS & ENGINEERING WASHINGTON OPERATIONS
James Truelove
VICE PRESIDENT OF ADMINISTRATION, FINANCE & PLANNING
Neil MacLeod
VICE PRESIDENT, TELEVISION OPERATIONS
Preston Davis
VICE PRESIDENT & DIRECTOR, INTERNATIONAL PRODUCTION OPERATIONS
Jacques Lesgards

Buena Vista Television

(see the Walt Disney Company)

CBS Inc.

51 W. 52 St., New York, NY 10019; (212) 975-4321; 7800 Beverly Blvd., Los Angeles, CA 90036; (213) 852-2345.

BOARD OF DIRECTORS
William Paley, Roswell L. Gilpatric, Franklin A. Thomas, Henry B. Schact, Marietta Tree, Newton N. Minow, Harold Brown, James R. Houghton, James D. Wolfensohn, Michel Bergerac, Walter Cronkite, Laurence A. Tisch, Edson W. Spencer, Preston R. Tisch.
CHAIRMAN
William Paley
PRESIDENT & CHIEF EXECUTIVE OFFICER
Laurence A. Tisch
SENIOR VICE PRESIDENT
Jay Kriegel
SENIOR VICE PRESIDENT, OPERATIONS & ADMINISTRATION
Edward Grebow
PRESIDENT, CBS/BROADCAST GROUP
Howard Stringer

CBS ENTERTAINMENT (HOLLYWOOD)

PRESIDENT, CBS ENTERTAINMENT
Kim LeMasters
EXECUTIVE VICE PRESIDENT, PRIMETIME PROGRAMS
Barbara Corday
VICE PRESIDENT, BUSINESS AFFAIRS, WEST COAST
Layne Britton
VICE PRESIDENT, TALENT AND CASTING
Lisa Freisberger
VICE PRESIDENT, TALENT AND GUILD NEGOTIATIONS
Leola Gorius
VICE PRESIDENT, BUSINESS AFFAIRS, MUSIC OPERATIONS
Harry Heitzer
VICE PRESIDENT, BUSINESS AFFAIRS
William B. Klein
VICE PRESIDENT, BUSINESS AFFAIRS, LONG FORM CONTRACTS & ACQUISITIONS
Sid Lyons
VICE PRESIDENT, BUSINESS AFFAIRS, ADMINISTRATION
James F. McGowan
VICE PRESIDENT, MOTION PICTURES FOR TV, MINISERIES
Pat Faulstich
VICE PRESIDENT, CBS ENTERTAINMENT PRODUCTIONS
Norman Powell
VICE PRESIDENT, CHILDREN'S PROGRAMS AND DAYTIME SPECIALS
Judy Price
VICE PRESIDENT, ENTERTAINMENT AND INFORMATIONAL SPECIALS
Fred Rappoport
VICE PRESIDENT, PLANNING AND SCHEDULING
Peter F. Tortorici
VICE PRESIDENT, COMEDY PROGRAM DEVELOPMENT
Tim Flack
VICE PRESIDENT, CURRENT PROGRAMS
Madalene Horne
VICE PRESIDENT, DAYTIME PROGRAMS
Lucy Johnson
VICE PRESIDENT, DRAMATIC PROGRAM DEVELOPMENT
Jonathan Levin
VICE PRESIDENT, LATE NIGHT PROGRAMS
Rod Perth
DIRECTOR, LATE NIGHT PROGRAMS & FEATURE FILMS
Joe Bowen
DIRECTOR, MOTION PICTURES FOR TV
Robert Drummel
DIRECTOR, CASTING
Anthony Barnao
DIRECTOR, DAYTIME PROGRAMS
Barbara Hunter
DIRECTOR, CURRENT PROGRAMS & PLANNING
Carol Lem
DIRECTOR, DRAMATIC PROGRAM DEVELOPMENT
Marian Davis
DIRECTOR, MOTION PICTURES FOR TV
Adoley Odunton
DIRECTOR, CASTING
Margaret McSharry
SENIOR DIRECTOR, CASTING
Christopher Gorman
DIRECTOR, MINISERIES
Dighton Spooner
DIRECTOR, MOTION PICTURES FOR TV
Larry Strichman
SENIOR DIRECTOR, INFORMATIONAL & CONCEPT SPECIALS
Suzan Sosna
DIRECTOR, COMEDY SERIES DEVELOPMENT
Kelly Goode
DIRECTOR, MOTION PICTURES FOR TELEVISION
Sunta Izzicupo
SENIOR DIRECTOR, CBS ENTERTAINMENT PRODUCTIONS
Mary Mazur
DIRECTOR, DAYTIME PROGRAMS
Margot Wain

CBS ENTERTAINMENT (NEW YORK)

DIRECTOR, DAYTIME PROGRAMS, NEW YORK
Judy Jenkins
DIRECTOR CHILDREN'S PROGRAMS, NEW YORK
Carolyn Ceslik
DIRECTOR, DAYTIME CASTING, NEW YORK
Laura Marino
DIRECTOR, PRIMETIME CASTING, NEW YORK
Amy Introcaso

CBS/BROADCAST GROUP (NEW YORK)

PRESIDENT, CBS BROADCAST GROUP
Howard Stringer
SENIOR VICE PRESIDENT, COMMUNICATIONS
George F. Schweitzer
SENIOR VICE PRESIDENT, PLANNING & RESEARCH
David F. Poltrack
VICE PRESIDENT, FINANCE
Jay D. Gold
VICE PRESIDENT & ASSISTANT TO THE PRESIDENT
Beth Waxman Bressan
VICE PRESIDENT, VIDEO
Kenneth L. Ross
VICE PRESIDENT, MEDIA RELATIONS
Ann Morfogen
VICE PRESIDENT, CREATIVE SERVICES
Jerold Goldberg
VICE PRESIDENT, TELEVISION AUDIENCE MEASUREMENT, NATIONAL TELEVISION RESEARCH
Michael Eisenberg
VICE PRESIDENT, TELEVISION RESEARCH, NEW YORK
Charles Moschetto
ASSISTANT CONTROLLER, CBS TELEVISION NETWORK
Frank Tinghitella

VICE PRESIDENT, PROGRAM PRACTICES, NEW YORK
Matthew Margo

CBS/BROADCAST GROUP (HOLLYWOOD)

VICE PRESIDENT, PROGRAM PRACTICES, HOLLYWOOD
Carol A. Altieri
VICE PRESIDENT, ADVERTISING & PROMOTION (located in L.A.)
Michael Mischler
VICE PRESIDENT, PUBLICITY, WEST COAST
Susan Tick
VICE PRESIDENT, AFFILIATE ADVERTISING & PROMOTION
John Bradford Crum
VICE PRESIDENT, ON-AIR PROMOTION
Steve Jacobson
VICE PRESIDENT, TELEVISION RESEARCH, LOS ANGELES
Arnold Becker
VICE PRESIDENT, FINANCE (Hollywood)
Gary McCarthy

CBS OPERATIONS & ADMINISTRATION (New York)

VICE PRESIDENT, EAST COAST OPERATIONS
Christopher J. Cookson
VICE PRESIDENT, BROADCAST TRANSMISSION OPERATIONS
Dave White
VICE PRESIDENT, TELEVISION OPERATIONS
Charles Dages
VICE PRESIDENT AND GENERAL MANAGER, ENGINEERING & DEVELOPMENT
Joseph Flaherty
VICE PRESIDENT, DEVELOPMENT
Richard Streeter

CBS OPERATIONS & ADMINISTRATION (Hollywood)

VICE PRESIDENT, WEST COAST BROADCAST OPERATIONS
Charles Cappleman

CBS MARKETING DIVISION

PRESIDENT, CBS MARKETING DIVISION
Thomas F. Leahy
VICE PRESIDENT, ADMINISTRATION
Mary Lou Jennerjahn
SENIOR VICE PRESIDENT, SALES
Jerome Dominus
VICE PRESIDENT, SPORTS MARKETING & SALES
Hal Trencher
VICE PRESIDENT, NEWS MARKETING & SALES
Robert I. Silberberg
VICE PRESIDENT, SALES PLANNING & ADMINISTRATION
Dorothy Schwartz
VICE PRESIDENT, PROMOTION & MERCHANDISING
Paul LaRocca
VICE PRESIDENT, MARKETING SERVICES
Bruce Thomas
SENIOR VICE PRESIDENT & GENERAL MANAGER, CBS BROADCAST INTERNATIONAL
Donald D. Wear, Jr.
VICE PRESIDENT, SALES & MARKETING, CBS BROADCAST INTERNATIONAL
Rainer Siek
VICE PRESIDENT, PRODUCTION & ADMINISTRATION, CBS BROADCAST INTERNATIONAL
David P. Berman

CBS AFFILIATE RELATIONS DIVISION

PRESIDENT, CBS AFFILIATE RELATIONS DIVISION
Anthony C. Malara
VICE PRESIDENT & DIRECTOR, AFFILIATE RELATIONS
Scott Michels

CBS NEWS DIVISION

PRESIDENT
David Burke
VICE PRESIDENT, NEWS COVERAGE & OPERATIONS
Donald DeCesare
VICE PRESIDENT & ASSISTANT TO THE PRESIDENT
Joseph Peyronin
VICE PRESIDENT, NEWS SERVICES
John Frazee
VICE PRESIDENT, FINANCE & ADMINISTRATION
James M. McKenna
VICE PRESIDENT, ADMINISTRATION
Theodore C. Savaglio
VICE PRESIDENT, BUSINESS AFFAIRS
Robert E. McCarthy
VICE PRESIDENT, BUREAU CHIEF, CBS NEWS WASHINGTON
Barbara Cohen
VICE PRESIDENT, RADIO
Larry D. Cooper
DIRECTOR, EXECUTIVE PRODUCER, SPECIAL EVENTS
Lane Venardos

CBS TELEVISION STATIONS DIVISION

PRESIDENT, CBS TELEVISION STATIONS
Eric Ober
VICE PRESIDENT, FINANCE
Carl Wenhold
VICE PRESIDENT, PROGRAMMING
Eugene Lothery
VICE PRESIDENT, MARKETING SERVICES
Gordon Hughes
VICE PRESIDENT & GENERAL MANAGER, SALES & MARKETING
Philip S. Press

CBS SPORTS DIVISION

PRESIDENT
Neal H. Pilson
VICE PRESIDENT, PROGRAMMING
Jay B. Rosenstein
VICE PRESIDENT, OLYMPICS
Mark H. Harrington III
VICE PRESIDENT, PROGRAM ADMINISTRATION & OPERATIONS
James F. Harrington
VICE PRESIDENT, SPORTS PLANNING
Richard Pinkham
VICE PRESIDENT, SPORTS BUSINESS AFFAIRS AND COMPLIANCE
Noel B. Berman

CBS RADIO DIVISION

PRESIDENT
Nancy C. Widmann
VICE PRESIDENT, CBS OWNED AM STATIONS
Anna Mae Sokusky
VICE PRESIDENT, CBS OWNED FM STATIONS
George L. Sosson
VICE PRESIDENT, CBS RADIO NETWORKS
Robert P. Kipperman
VICE PRESIDENT, GENERAL MANAGER, CBS RADIO REPRESENTATIVES
Anthony C. Miraglia
VICE PRESIDENT, MEDIA PRACTICES
Elizabeth Hayter
VICE PRESIDENT & CONTROLLER
Michael H. O'Neal

Children's Television Workshop

1 Lincoln Plaza, New York, NY 10023; (212) 595-3456. (Educational Broadcasting.)

CHAIRMAN—CEO
Joan Ganz Cooney
PRESIDENT—COO
David V. B. Britt
SENIOR VICE PRESIDENT, CORPORATE AFFAIRS
Emily Swenson
VICE PRESIDENT AND EXECUTIVE PRODUCER
David D. Connell
VICE PRESIDENT, FINANCE
Kenneth J. Gruber
VICE PRESIDENT, COMMUNITY EDUCATION SERVICES
Evelyn P. Davis
VICE PRESIDENT, PUBLIC AFFAIRS
Fran Kaufman
VICE PRESIDENT, PRODUCTION
Franklin Getchell
VICE PRESIDENT AND PUBLISHER, MAGAZINE GROUP
Nina B. Link
VICE PRESIDENT AND TREASURER
Wayne W. Luteran
VICE PRESIDENT, INTERACTIVE TECHNOLOGY & SCHOOL SERVICES
Robert L. Madell
VICE PRESIDENT, RESEARCH
Keith W. Mielke

PRESIDENT, CTW PRODUCTS AND INTERNATIONAL TELEVISION
William F. Whaley

Columbia Pictures Television

(A unit of Columbia Pictures Entertainment, Inc.)
3400 Riverside Dr., Burbank, CA 91505; (818) 954-6000; 1438 North Gower St., Los Angeles, CA 90028; (213) 460-7200.

CHAIRMAN AND CHIEF EXECUTIVE OFFICER
Gary Lieberthal
PRESIDENT
Scott Siegler
PRESIDENT, SYNDICATION
Barry Thurston
EXECUTIVE VICE PRESIDENT, DRAMA
Steven H. Berman
EXECUTIVE VICE PRESIDENT, COMEDY
Frances C. McConnell
SENIOR VICE PRESIDENT, BUSINESS AFFAIRS
Jan E. Abrams
SENIOR VICE PRESIDENT, CURRENT PROGRAMS, COMEDY
Deborah Curtan
SENIOR VICE PRESIDENT, CORPORATE COMMUNICATIONS/PUBLICITY
Don DeMesquita
SENIOR VICE PRESIDENT, FILM PRODUCTION
Seymour Friedman
SENIOR VICE PRESIDENT
Andrew J. Kaplan
SENIOR VICE PRESIDENT, RESEARCH
David Mumford
SENIOR VICE PRESIDENT, MARKETING
Michael Zucker
VICE PRESIDENT, SYNDICATION OPERATIONS
Francine Beougher
VICE PRESIDENT, CURRENT PROGRAMS, COMEDY
Jeanie Bradley
VICE PRESIDENT, CURRENT PROGRAMS, COMEDY
Eduardo G. Cervantes
VICE PRESIDENT, TALENT & CASTING
Dennis Cornell
VICE PRESIDENT, SYNDICATION POST PRODUCTION
Lawrence (Lon) Feldman
VICE PRESIDENT, BUSINESS AFFAIRS
Richard Frankie
VICE PRESIDENT, POST-PRODUCTION
Christine J. Freidgen
VICE PRESIDENT, SYNDICATION, SOUTHEAST REGION
Susan Grant
VICE PRESIDENT, STUDIO OPERATIONS
David Holman
VICE PRESIDENT, TALENT & CASTING
Rick Jacobs
VICE PRESIDENT, BUSINESS AFFAIRS ADMINISTRATION
Stephanie Knauer
VICE PRESIDENT, TAPE PRODUCTION
Edward Lammi
VICE PRESIDENT, SYNDICATION, EASTERN REGION
Gary Lico
VICE PRESIDENT, SYNDICATION, WESTERN REGION
Terry Mackin
VICE PRESIDENT, COMEDY DEVELOPMENT
Steve Medelson
VICE PRESIDENT, SYNDICATION, MIDWEST REGION
John Rohrs
VICE PRESIDENT, RESEARCH
Doug Roth
VICE PRESIDENT, MOTION PICTURE SALES AND ACQUISITIONS
Leslie Z. Tobin
VICE PRESIDENT, DRAMA DEVELOPMENT
Jimmy Veres
VICE PRESIDENT, SYNDICATION, EASTERN REGION
Herbert O. Weiss
VICE PRESIDENT, BUSINESS AFFAIRS
Jeffrey Weiss

COLUMBIA PICTURES TELEVISION SYNDICATION

Studio Plaza, 3400 Riverside Drive, Burbank, CA 91505

CHAIRMAN AND CHIEF EXECUTIVE OFFICER
Gary Lieberthal
PRESIDENT, SYNDICATION
Barry Thurston
SENIOR VICE PRESIDENT, MARKETING
Michael Zucker
SENIOR VICE PRESIDENT, RESEARCH
David Mumford
VICE PRESIDENT, RESEARCH
Doug Roth
VICE PRESIDENT, MOTION PICTURE SALES AND ACQUISITIONS
Leslie Tobin
VICE PRESIDENT, SYNDICATION POST PRODUCTION
Lon Feldman
VICE PRESIDENT, DISTRIBUTION OPERATIONS
Francine Beougher
VICE PRESIDENT, WESTERN REGION
Terry Mackin
DIRECTOR, SPECIAL MARKETING
William L. Clark
DIRECTOR, SYNDICATION CONTRACTS
Elise Keen
DIRECTOR, MOTION PICTURE SYNDICATION
Eric Marx
DIRECTOR, PUBLICITY
Bill Coveny
DIRECTOR, ADVERTISING AND PROMOTION
Alan Daniels

BRANCH OFFICES:

New York: Columbia Pictures Television, 711 Fifth Avenue, New York, NY 10022; (212) 702-2920; (FAX) (212) 702-6239. Gary Lico, v.p., Eastern region; Herb Weiss, v.p., Eastern region.

Chicago: Columbia Pictures Television, 645 N. Michigan Avenue, Suite 634, Chicago, IL 60611; (312) 916-1230; FAX: (312) 916-0685. John Rohrs, Jr., v.p., Midwestern region; Stuart Walker, Account Executive, Midwestern region.

Atlanta: Columbia Pictures Television, One Atlantic Center, 1201 W. Peachtree St., #4820, Atlanta, GA 30309; (404) 892-2725; FAX: (404) 892-1063. Susan Grant, v.p., Southeastern region; Joe Kissack, account exec.; Brian Fleming, account exec.

Columbia Pictures International Television

(A unit of Columbia Pictures Entertainment, Inc.)
711 Fifth Ave., New York, NY 10022; (212) 751-4400.

PRESIDENT
Nicholas Bingham
SENIOR VICE PRESIDENT, INTERNATIONAL TELEVISION SALES
Michael Grindon
VICE PRESIDENT, WORLD-WIDE PAY TV
Dennis Wood
DIRECTOR, SALES ADMINISTRATION
Nancy Coleman
VICE PRESIDENT AND GENERAL MANAGER, LATIN/SOUTH AMERICA
Helios Alvarez
VICE PRESIDENT AND GENERAL MANAGER, JAPAN/KOREA
Toru Ohnuki
MANAGING DIRECTOR, AUSTRALIA/FAR EAST
Tony McMullen
DIRECTOR, CLIENT SERVICES (WEST COAST)
Susan West

INTERNATIONAL OFFICES

Argentina: Columbia Pictures of Argentina, Inc., Ayacucho 520, (1026) Buenos Aires, Argentina, Tel: 45-0261, Armando Cortez, gen. mgr.

Australia: Columbia Pictures Television Pty., Ltd., 45 Macquarie Street, Sydney, N.S.W. Australia 2000, Tel: 231-5985, Tony McMullen, Managing Director, Australia/Far East.

Brazil: Screen Gems-Columbia Pictures of Brazil, Inc., Rua Santa Isabel 160, 7 Andar, 01221 Sao Paolo, Brazil, Tel: 220-5200, Helios Alvarez, VP and General Manager—Latin/South America, Nelson Duarte, Latin America Operations Manager, Octavio De Silva, Sales Manager Brazil.

Canada: EPS Programming Services Ltd., Columbia Pictures Television Canada, 720 King Street West., Suite 600, Toronto, Ontario, M5V 2T3, Tel: 416-364-3894, David Jackson, President, EPS.

France: Columbia Pictures Television, 20 Rue Troyon, 75017 Paris, France, Tel: 4380-7000, Jacques Porteret, Program Sales Manager, Jeff Wright, Sales Representative, Patricia Ciolek, Sales Representative.

Italy: T.V. Overseas S.R.L., Via Sicilia N. 50, 00187 Rome, Italy, Tel: 445-4940, Jimmy Manca, Agent.

Japan: Japan International Enterprises, Inc., 4th floor, Yoneda Building, 17–20, Shimbashi 6-Chome, Minato-Ku, Tokyo Pref. 105, Japan, Tel: 431-1372, Toru Ohnuko, VP and General Manager, Japan/Korea.

Mexico: Columbia Pictures International Television, Darwin 68, Office 301, Mexico 5, D.F., Tel: 254-0899, Evencio Gomez, Dubbing/Traffic Controller.

Philippines: Columbia Pictures International Television, Room 307, President Lines Building, 1000 United Nations Avenue, Manila, Philippines, Tel: 521-1381, Conrad Javier, Sales Representative.

United Kingdom: Columbia Pictures International Television, 19/23 Wells Street, London W1P 3FP, England, Tel: 637-8444, Nicholas Bingham, President, CPIT, Jimmy Graham, Director of N. Europe/Middle East/Africa, Justin Hattfield, Sales Manager N. Europe/Middle East/Africa.

The Walt Disney Company

500 South Buena Vista Street, Burbank, California 91521; (818) 560-1000.

CHAIRMAN OF THE BOARD AND CHIEF EXECUTIVE OFFICER
Michael D. Eisner
PRESIDENT AND CHIEF OPERATING OFFICER
Frank G. Wells
VICE CHAIRMAN OF THE BOARD
Roy E. Disney
EXECUTIVE VICE PRESIDENT AND CHIEF FINANCIAL OFFICER
Gary L. Wilson
SENIOR VICE PRESIDENT—STRATEGIC PLANNING AND DEVELOPMENT
Lawrence P. Murphy
SENIOR VICE PRESIDENT—CORP. COMMUNICATIONS
Erwin D. Okun
SENIOR VICE PRESIDENT & GENERAL COUNSEL
Joe Shapiro
VICE PRESIDENT—TREASURER
John H. Forsgren
VICE PRESIDENT—CORPORATE PROJECTS
Arthur Levitt III
VICE PRESIDENT—PLANNING & CONTROL
Neil R. McCarthy
VICE PRESIDENT—COUNSEL AND ASSISTANT SECRETARY
Peter F. Nolan
VICE PRESIDENT—COUNSEL AND ASSISTANT SECRETARY
Joseph M. Santaniello
VICE PRESIDENT AND SECRETARY
Doris A. Smith
VICE PRESIDENT/CONTROLLER
Timothy V. Wolf

BUENA VISTA TELEVISION

(A division of The Walt Disney Company)
500 South Buena Vista St., Burbank, CA 91521; (818) 560-5151.

PRESIDENT
Robert Jacquemin
SENIOR VICE PRESIDENT—MARKETING
Carole Black
SENIOR VICE PRESIDENT—SALES
Mort Marcus
VICE PRESIDENT—CABLE SALES
Peter Affe
VICE PRESIDENT/GENERAL SALES MANAGER—WEST COAST
Rick Jacobson
VICE PRESIDENT—PRODUCTION
Mary Kellogg-Joslyn
VICE PRESIDENT—WESTERN REGIONAL MANAGER
Janice Marinelli-Mazza
VICE PRESIDENT—MEDIA STRATEGY
Michael Mellon
VICE PRESIDENT—CREATIVE SERVICES
Sal Sardo
VICE PRESIDENT—MARKETING
Catherine P. Schulte
VICE PRESIDENT/EASTERN REGIONAL MANAGER
Ken Solomon
VICE PRESIDENT—GENERAL MANAGER
Mark Zoradi

BUENA VISTA TELEVISION PRODUCTIONS

SENIOR VICE PRESIDENT
James S. Bennett
VICE PRESIDENT, PROGRAMMING
Mark A. (Bruno) Cohen
VICE PRESIDENT, PROGRAMMING
Mary Kellogg-Joslyn
VICE PRESIDENT, PROGRAMMING—EUROPE (London)
David L. Simon

WALT DISNEY PICTURES AND TELEVISION

EXECUTIVE VICE PRESIDENT—MOTION PICTURE & TELEVISION PRODUCTION
Marty Katz
SENIOR VICE PRESIDENT—FINANCE
Chris McGurk
VICE PRESIDENT & CONTROLLER
Eugne C. Brown
VICE PRESIDENT—INFORMATION SERVICES
John Covas
VICE PRESIDENT—STUDIO OPERATIONS
Ben Cowitt
VICE PRESIDENT—DOMESTIC & INTERNATIONAL—ANTI-PIRACY
Judy Denenholz
VICE PRESIDENT—PRODUCTION RESOURCES
Scott Dorman
VICE PRESIDENT—LABOR RELATIONS
Robert W. Johnson
VICE PRESIDENT—POST PRODUCTION
David McCann
VICE PRESIDENT—MUSIC
Chris Montan
VICE PRESIDENT—CASTING
Gretchen Rennell

WALT DISNEY TELEVISION

PRESIDENT OF NETWORK TELEVISION PRODUCTION
Garth Ancier
EXECUTIVE VICE PRESIDENT—ANIMATION
Gary Krisel
SENIOR VICE PRESIDENT—MAGICAL WORLD OF DISNEY
John Litvack
SENIOR VICE PRESIDENT—BUSINESS AND LEGAL AFFAIRS
John J. Reagan
VICE PRESIDENT—PRODUCTION
Mitch Ackerman
VICE PRESIDENT—BUSINESS AFFAIRS—WORLDWIDE HOME VIDEO & PAY/CABLE TV
Jere R. Hausfater
VICE PRESIDENT—LEGAL AFFAIRS
Lawrence Kaplan
VICE PRESIDENT—LEGAL COUNSEL
David Mayer
VICE PRESIDENT—SPECIALS
Pam McKissick
VICE PRESIDENT—ESTIMATING & AUDITING
Walter O'Neal
VICE PRESIDENT—DRAMA DEVELOPMENT
Ron Taylor
VICE PRESIDENT—COMEDY DEVELOPMENT
Dean Valentine
VICE PRESIDENT—TELEVISION ANIMATION
Michael Webster
VICE PRESIDENT—BUSINESS AFFAIRS
Kenneth D. Werner
VICE PRESIDENT—FINANCE NETWORK TV & BROADCASTING
Chris Winners
VICE PRESIDENT—BUSINESS AFFAIRS
Laurie Younger

Eastman Kodak Company

343 State St., Rochester, NY 14650; (716) 724-4000; 1901 W. 22nd St., Oakbrook, IL 60522-9004; (312) 218-5175; 6700 Santa Monica Blvd., Hollywood, CA 90038; (213) 464-6131; 1133 Ave. of the Americas, New York, NY 10036; (212) 930-8000; Williams Square, 5221 N. O'Connor Blvd., Irving, TX 75039-3798; (214) 506- 9700; 4 Con-

course Parkway, Suite 300, Atlanta, GA 30328; (404) 668-0500; 1122 Mapunapuna St., Honolulu, Hawaii 96817; (808) 833-1661. (Motion picture film offices & laboratories.)
CHAIRMAN OF THE BOARD & CHIEF EXECUTIVE OFFICER
Colby H. Chandler
PRESIDENT & EXECUTIVE OFFICER
Kay R. Whitmore
VICE CHAIRMAN & EXECUTIVE OFFICER
J. Phillip Samper
GROUP VICE PRESIDENT & GENERAL MANAGER, PHOTOGRAPHIC PRODUCTS GROUP
Wilbur J. Prezzano
VICE PRESIDENT & GENERAL MANAGER, MOTION PICTURE & AUDIOVISUAL PRODUCTS DIVISION
Joerg D. Agin
VICE PRESIDENT & MOTION PICTURE MARKETING MANAGER
Leonard F. Coleman

Fox Inc.

P.O. Box 900, Beverly Hills, CA 90213; (213) 277-2211. Fox Inc. is the parent company of Fox Broadcasting Co., Fox Television Stations Inc., Twentieth Century Fox Film Corporation.

CHAIRMAN AND CHIEF EXECUTIVE OFFICER
Barry Diller
PRESIDENT
Jonathan Dolgen
EXECUTIVE VICE PRESIDENT
Chase Carey
SENIOR VICE PRESIDENT, EMPLOYEE RELATIONS
Dean Ferris
SENIOR VICE PRESIDENT, GENERAL COUNSEL
David Handleman
SENIOR VICE PRESIDENT, FINANCE
Harvey Finkel
SENIOR VICE PRESIDENT, BANKING
John Meehan
SENIOR VICE PRESIDENT, BROADCAST OPERATIONS & ENGINEERING
Andrew Setos
DIRECTOR, CORPORATE COMMUNICATIONS
Dennis E. Petrosky
VICE PRESIDENT AND ASSISTANT TO THE CHAIRMAN
Beth Colloty
VICE PRESIDENT, LABOR RELATIONS
Pamela DiGiovanni
VICE PRESIDENT, LEGAL AFFAIRS
Daphne Gronich
VICE PRESIDENT, ASSISTANT GENERAL COUNSEL
Mary Anne Harrison
VICE PRESIDENT, COMPENSATION/BENEFITS
Lynn Franzoi

Fox Broadcasting Company

P.O. Box 900, Beverly Hills, CA 90213; (213) 277-2211; New York office: 40 W. 57 St., New York, NY 10019; (212) 977-5500. Chicago office: 625 N. Michigan Ave., Suite 401, Chicago, IL 60611; (312) 440-0012.

CHAIRMAN AND CHIEF EXECUTIVE OFFICER, FOX, INC.
Barry Diller
PRESIDENT AND CHIEF OPERATING OFFICER, FOX BROADCASTING COMPANY
Jamie Kellner
PRESIDENT, FOX BROADCASTING ENTERTAINMENT GROUP
Peter Cherin
EXECUTIVE VICE PRESIDENT, SERIES PROGRAMMING, FOX BROADCASTING COMPANY
Paul Stupin
SENIOR VICE PRESIDENT, FINANCE AND ADMINISTRATION
Tom Allen
SENIOR VICE PRESIDENT, PROGRAMMING & DEVELOPMENT, FOX BROADCASTING COMPANY
Robert Kenneally
SENIOR VICE PRESIDENT, PUBLICITY AND CORPORATE CREATIVE SERVICES
Brad Turell
VICE PRESIDENT, ON-AIR PROMOTION AND CREATIVE MARKETING
Bobb Bibb
VICE PRESIDENT, RESEARCH & MARKETING
Andy Fessel
VICE PRESIDENT, ON-AIR PROMOTION & SPECIAL PROJECTS
Lewis Goldstein
VICE PRESIDENT, DEVELOPMENT
Joe Davola
SENIOR VICE PRESIDENT, BUSINESS AFFAIRS, FOX BROADCASTING COMPANY
Ira Kurgan
VICE PRESIDENT, AFFILIATE RELATIONS—WESTERN REGION
David Ferrara
VICE PRESIDENT, WESTERN SALES
Deborah Myers
VICE PRESIDENT, SPECIAL PROGRAMMING
Michael Binkow
VICE PRESIDENT, LEGAL AFFAIRS
Eric Yeldell
VICE PRESIDENT, SALES & ADMINISTRATION
Susan Watcher

NEW YORK OFFICE
SENIOR VICE PRESIDENT, SALES
Jon Nesvig
VICE PRESIDENT, EASTERN SALES
David Cassaro
VICE PRESIDENT, AFFILIATE RELATIONS, EASTERN REGION
Gregory Gush

CHICAGO OFFICE
VICE PRESIDENT, AFFILIATE RELATIONS, CENTRAL REGION
Bob Mariano
VICE PRESIDENT, CENTRAL SALES
Jean Rossi

LOS ANGELES OFFICE
SENIOR VICE PRESIDENT, ADVERTISING & PROMOTION, FOX BROADCASTING COMPANY
Sandy Grushow
SENIOR VICE PRESIDENT, SERIES PROGRAMMING, FOX BROADCASTING COMPANY
Lillah McCarthy
SENIOR VICE PRESIDENT OF PRODUCTION, MOTION PICTURES FOR TELEVISION & MINI-SERIES
Wendy Riche
VICE PRESIDENT, AFFILIATE PROMOTION
Gary Berberet
VICE PRESIDENT, NATIONAL MEDIA
Pam Satterfield
VICE PRESIDENT, ON-AIR & BROADCAST OPERATIONS
Stephen Weinheimer
VICE PRESIDENT, BROADCAST STANDARDS AND PRACTICES
Don Bay
VICE PRESIDENT, BUSINESS AFFAIRS
Rich Vokulich
VICE PRESIDENT, CONTROLLER
Michelle Varon
VICE PRESIDENT, FILMS ACQUISITIONS
Suzanne Horenstein
VICE PRESIDENT, CURRENT PROGRAMMING
Michael Lansbury
VICE PRESIDENT, LONGFORM PROGRAMMING
Paul Nagle

Fox Television Stations Inc.

5746 Sunset Blvd., Los Angeles, CA 90028; (213) 856-1000.

CHAIRMAN AND CHIEF EXECUTIVE OFFICER, FOX INC.
Barry Diller
PRESIDENT AND CHIEF OPERATING OFFICER
Robert M. Kreek
VICE PRESIDENT, DEVELOPMENT
Stephen Chao
VICE PRESIDENT, LEGAL AFFAIRS
Gerald Friedman
VICE PRESIDENT, GENERAL MANAGER—FOX TAPE
Steve McPeek
VICE PRESIDENT, LABOR RELATIONS
Hugo Rossiter
VICE PRESIDENT, PROGRAMMING
Steve Leblang
VICE PRESIDENT AND CHIEF FINANCIAL OFFICER
Mitchell Stern
VICE PRESIDENT, FIRST RUN PROGRAMMING
Jake Tauber

FOX TELEVISION STATION GROUP

WNYW/New York—Channel 5, Carolyn Wall gen. mgr.; **KTTV/Los Angeles**—Channel 11, Robert Morse gen. mgr.; **WFLD/Chicago**—Channel 32, Cary Jones gen. mgr.; **WFXT/Boston**—Channel 25, Joseph Robinowitz gen. mgr.; **KDAF/Dallas**—Channel 33, Gayle Brammer gen. mgr.; **WTTG/Washington**—Channel 5, Betty Endicott gen. mgr.; **KRIV/Houston**—Channel 26, Jerry Marcus gen. mgr.

GTG Entertainment

(A partnership formed between the Gannett Co. and Grant A. Tinker.)

9336 W. Washington Blvd., Culver City, CA (213) 202-3250. Organized 1986. (Develops and produces television programs, both entertainment and reality-based.)

PRESIDENT
Grant A. Tinker
EXECUTIVE VICE PRESIDENT
Stuart P. Erwin, Jr.
SENIOR VICE PRESIDENT
Jay Sandrich
SENIOR VICE PRESIDENT
M.S. Rukeyser, Jr.
VICE PRESIDENT, BUSINESS AFFAIRS
Richard J. Katz
VICE PRESIDENT, ADMINISTRATION & PLANNING
Alan Sternfield
VICE PRESIDENT, PRODUCTION
Jack Clements
VICE PRESIDENT, PUBLIC RELATIONS
Robin McMillan
VICE PRESIDENT, TALENT & CASTING
Peter Golden
VICE PRESIDENT, TALENT & NETWORK BUSINESS AFFAIRS
Russell Schwartz
BRANCHES
GTG East/New York; GTG Marketing/New York

Great American Broadcasting

3400 Cahuenga Blvd., Los Angeles, CA 90068; (213) 851-8000 (Producer).

CHAIRMAN & CHIEF EXECUTIVE OFFICER
Charles S. Mechem, Jr.
SENIOR VICE PRESIDENT, CREATIVE
Joel Cohen

DIVISIONS INCLUDE:

Hanna-Barbera Productions, Inc., 3400 Cahuenga Blvd., Los Angeles, CA 90068; (213) 851-5000.

Ruby-Spears Enterprises, 3330 Cahuenga Blvd., Los Angeles, CA 90068; (213) 874-5100.

Hamilton Projects, 215 Lexington Ave., New York, NY 10016; (212) 684-4388.

Titus Productions, 211 E. 51 St., New York, NY 10022; (212) 752-6460.

Merv Griffin Enterprises

(A unit of Columbia Pictures Entertainment, Inc.)

1541 N. Vine St., Hollywood, CA 90028; (213) 461-4701. (Producers of game/talk shows, TV specials, motion pictures and films for television.)

CHAIRMAN
Merv Griffin
PRESIDENT
Robert J. Murphy
VICE PRESIDENT OF MOTION PICTURES AND FILMS FOR TELEVISION
Peter Barsocchini

International Creative Management, Inc.

40 W. 57 St., New York, NY 10019; (212) 556-5600. 8899 Beverly Blvd., Los Angeles, CA 90048; (213) 550-4000. (Representatives of performing and creative talent in the entertainment industry.) A subsidiary of Josephson International Inc.

PRESIDENT
Jeff Berg

Lorimar Television

(A Division of Warner Bros.).

10202 W. Washington Blvd., Culver City, CA 90232; (213) 280-8000.

CHAIRMAN AND CHIEF EXECUTIVE OFFICER
Merv Adelson
OFFICE OF THE PRESIDENT
Dick Robertson, David E. Salzman, Michael Jay Solomon
PRESIDENT
David Salzman

Creative Affairs

EXECUTIVE VICE PRESIDENT, CREATIVE AFFAIRS
Leslie Moonves
SENIOR VICE PRESIDENT, COMEDY DEVELOPMENT
Ellen Franklin
SENIOR VICE PRESIDENT, DRAMA DEVELOPMENT
Tony Jonas
VICE PRESIDENT, MOVIES & MINI-SERIES
Cindy Dunne
DIRECTOR, COMEDY DEVELOPMENT
Hank Cohen
DIRECTOR, MOVIES & MINI-SERIES
Joan Harrison

First-Run Development & Production

VICE PRESIDENT, FIRST-RUN TELEVISION
Jim Paratore
DIRECTOR, FIRST-RUN DEVELOPMENT
Hilary Estey
DIRECTOR, PRODUCTION
Jay Weinman

Business Affairs

EXECUTIVE VICE PRESIDENT, BUSINESS & FINANCIAL AFFAIRS
David Stanley
SENIOR VICE PRESIDENT, BUSINESS AFFAIRS
Julie Waxman
VICE PRESIDENT, BUSINESS AFFAIRS
Roni Mueller
VICE PRESIDENT, BUSINESS AFFAIRS
Bruce Rosenblum
VICE PRESIDENT, BUSINESS AFFAIRS
Nancy Reiss Tellem
DIRECTOR, BUSINESS AFFAIRS
Karen Cease
DIRECTOR, BUSINESS AFFAIRS
David Engel

Production

SENIOR VICE PRESIDENT, NETWORK PRODUCTION
Robert Rosenbaum
VICE PRESIDENT, NETWORK PRODUCTION
Andy Ackerman
VICE PRESIDENT, NETWORK PRODUCTION
Judith Zaylor
VICE PRESIDENT, TELEVISION MUSIC
Richard Berres
VICE PRESIDENT, NETWORK POST-PRODUCTION
Ted Rich

Current Programs

SENIOR VICE PRESIDENT, CURRENT PROGRAMS
March Kessler
VICE PRESIDENT, CURRENT PROGRAMS
Pat Ambrose
VICE PRESIDENT, CURRENT PROGRAMS
Adam Gold
VICE PRESIDENT, CURRENT PROGRAMS
Marcia Zwilling
VICE PRESIDENT, CURRENT PROGRAMS
David Zuckerman

Lorimar Productions

SENIOR VICE PRESIDENT, TALENT
Barbara Miller
SENIOR VICE PRESIDENT, PRODUCTION CONTROLLER
Mary Van Houten
VICE PRESIDENT, COST CONTROL/ESTIMATING
Bea Blondell

VICE PRESIDENT, LABOR RELATIONS
Jon Gilbert
VICE PRESIDENT, MUSIC
Richard Berres
DIRECTOR, MUSIC
Charlotte Lawrence
DIRECTOR, LABOR RELATIONS
Joan Birdt
DIRECTOR, CASTING
Jackie Briskey
DIRECTOR, CASTING
Alice Cassidy
DIRECTOR, CASTING
Melinda Gartzman
DIRECTOR, CASTING
Shawn Linahan
DIRECTOR, CASTING
Irene Mariano
DIRECTOR, CASTING
Megan Whitaker

Legal Affairs

SENIOR VICE PRESIDENT
Paul Stager
VICE PRESIDENT
Sarah Noddings
VICE PRESIDENT
Barbara Zuckerman
DIRECTOR
Marcy Lifton
DIRECTOR
Jay Gendron

Publicity, Promotion & Advertising

SENIOR VICE PRESIDENT, PUBLICITY, PROMOTION & ADVERTISING
Barry Stagg
VICE PRESIDENT, PUBLICITY
Sarah Goldstein

Studio Facilities

SENIOR VICE PRESIDENT
Arnold Shupack
VICE PRESIDENT
Barbara Francuz
DIRECTOR
Randy Harris

MCA TV

100 Universal Plaza, Universal City, CA 91608; (818) 777-1000; FAX: (818) 777-8221. (Distributor. A subsidiary of MCA, Inc. as is Universal Television, the production arm. See separate listing.)

CHAIRMAN, MCA TV GROUP
Al Rush
PRESIDENT, MCA TV
Shelly Schwab
SENIOR VICE PRESIDENT, DIRECTOR OF SALES, OFF-NET
Jim Kraus
SENIOR VICE PRESIDENT, DIRECTOR OF SALES, FIRST RUN
Bobbi Fisher
SENIOR VICE PRESIDENT, CREATIVE SERVICES
Mort Slakoff
SENIOR VICE PRESIDENT, PROGRAM DEVELOPMENT
Ken Arber
VICE PRESIDENT OF LEGAL & BUSINESS AFFAIRS
Sara Rutenberg
VICE PRESIDENT, DIRECTOR OF RESEARCH & DEVELOPMENT
Gerald Farrell
DIRECTOR OF LEGAL & BUSINESS AFFAIRS
David Pulido
VICE PRESIDENT, SYNDICATION SERVICES
Bill Vrbanic
VICE PRESIDENT, WESTERN AREA
Richard Nailling
WESTERN REGIONAL MANAGER
Bill Trotter
BRANCH OFFICES:
Eastern: 445 Park Ave., New York, NY 10022; (212) 759-7500; FAX: (212) 832-6864
SENIOR VICE PRESIDENT, ADVERTISER SALES
David Brenner
DIRECTOR OF ADVERTISER SALES
Jeff Manoff
VICE PRESIDENT, NORTHEAST AREA
Bob Raleigh
EASTERN SALES MANAGER
Steve Rosenberg
Southwest: 12740 Hillcrest Rd., Suite 115, Dallas, TX 75230; (214) 386-6400; FAX: (214) 386-5906.
VICE PRESIDENT, SOUTHWEST REGION
Tom Maples
MANAGER, SOUTHWEST REGION
Steve Hackett
Southeast: 600 W. Peachtree St., Suite 1480, Atlanta, GA 30308; (404) 875-1133; FAX: (404) 874-4096.
SOUTHEAST REGION MANAGERS
Albert L. Strada
Charlotte Sweet
Central-Midwest: 435 No. Michigan Ave., Suite 515, Chicago, IL 60611; (312) 337-1100; FAX: (312) 822-9703.
VICE PRESIDENT, MIDWEST AREA
Paul Hoffman
MANAGER, CENTRAL REGION
Chris Rovtar
ACCOUNT EXECUTIVE, CENTRAL DIVISION
Dan MacKimm
DIRECTOR OF ADVERTISER SALES, MIDWEST
Dan Zifkin

MGM/UA Communications Co.

10000 W. Washington Blvd., Culver City, CA 90232; (213) 280-6000. Consists of four operating groups (as of August 25, 1989): Metro-Goldwyn-Mayer Film Group, MGM/UA Distribution Co., MGM/UA Telecommunications, which includes MGM/UA Home Video, Inc. and MGM/UA Television Production Group.

CHAIRMAN OF THE BOARD, PRESIDENT & CHIEF EXECUTIVE OFFICER
Jeffrey C. Barbakow
CHAIRMAN OF THE EXECUTIVE COMMITTEE
Fred Benninger
SENIOR EXECUTIVE VICE PRESIDENT
Sidney H. Sapsowitz
EXECUTIVE VICE PRESIDENT
Kenin M. Spivak
SENIOR VICE PRESIDENT—FINANCE AND CHIEF FINANCIAL OFFICER
Thomas P. Carson
SENIOR VICE PRESIDENT
Trevor Fetter
SENIOR VICE PRESIDENT, CORPORATE GENERAL COUNSEL AND SECRETARY
William Allen Jones
SENIOR VICE PRESIDENT—LABOR RELATIONS
Benjamin B. Kahane
VICE PRESIDENT AND CONTROLLER
Kathleen A. Coughlan
VICE PRESIDENT AND TREASURER
Walter C. Hoffer
VICE PRESIDENT—STUDIO LEGAL AFFAIRS
Nancy Niederman
VICE PRESIDENT—MANAGEMENT INFORMATION SERVICES
John Sanders
VICE PRESIDENT—CORPORATE LEGAL AFFAIRS
Sally Suchil
VICE PRESIDENT—TAXES
Daniel J. Taylor
VICE PRESIDENT—CORPORATE AUDIT
David Terrasi
BOARD OF DIRECTORS
Fred Benninger, Terry Christensen, Willie D. Davis, Ann Getty, Edward A. Horrigan, Jr., Kirk Kerkorian, Arthur G. Linkletter, Frank Rothman, Sidney Sapsowitz, Walter M. Sharp, Stephen D. Silbert, Kenneth L. Trefftzs
EXECUTIVE COMMITTEE
Fred Benninger, Terry Christensen, Kirk Kerkorian, Frank Rothman, Sidney H. Sapsowitz, Walter H. Sharp, Stephen D. Silbert

MGM/UA TELEVISION PRODUCTION GROUP, INC.

CHAIRMAN OF THE BOARD AND CHIEF EXECUTIVE OFFICER
David Gerber

PRESIDENT
Lynn Loring
EXECUTIVE VICE PRESIDENT
Kenin M. Spivak
SENIOR VICE PRESIDENT—FINANCE
Thomas P. Carson
SENIOR VICE PRESIDENT, CORPORATE GENERAL COUNSEL AND SECRETARY
William A. Jones
SENIOR VICE PRESIDENT—LABOR RELATIONS
Benjamin B. Kahane
SENIOR VICE PRESIDENT—STUDIO LEGAL AFFAIRS
Nancy Niederman
SENIOR VICE PRESIDENT—BUSINESS AFFAIRS AND ADMINISTRATION
Mark Pedowitz
SENIOR VICE PRESIDENT—TELEVISION PRODUCTION
Christopher Seitz
VICE PRESIDENT—VIDEOTAPE OPERATIONS
Dee Baker
VICE PRESIDENT AND CONTROLLER
Kathleen Coughlan
VICE PRESIDENT—ADMINISTRATION
Leslie H. Frends
VICE PRESIDENT—NETWORK PRIMETIME SERIES PROGRAMMING
Susan Harbert
VICE PRESIDENT AND TREASURER
Walter C. Hoffer
VICE PRESIDENT—CURRENT PROGRAMMING
Ron Levinson
VICE PRESIDENT—FINANCIAL ADMINISTRATION
Thomas Malanga
VICE PRESIDENT—POST PRODUCTION
Bruce Pobjoy
VICE PRESIDENT—ADVERTISING, AND PUBLICITY
Kim Reed
VICE PRESIDENT—CREATIVE AFFAIRS
Jeff Ryder
VICE PRESIDENT—BUSINESS AFFAIRS
Lorna Shepherd
VICE PRESIDENT—TALENT CASTING
Mary Jo Slater
VICE PRESIDENT—TAXES
Daniel J. Taylor
VICE PRESIDENT—PRODUCTION
Ron Von Schimmelmann
BOARD OF DIRECTORS
Fred Benninger, David Gerber, Frank Rothman, Sidney H. Sapsowitz, Walter M. Sharp, Stephen D. Silbert
EXECUTIVE COMMITTEE
David Gerber, Sidney H. Sapsowitz, Stephen D. Silbert

MGM/UA TELECOMMUNICATIONS, INC.

CHAIRMAN OF THE BOARD
Sidney H. Sapsowitz
SENIOR EXECUTIVE VICE PRESIDENT
Randolph Blotky
EXECUTIVE VICE PRESIDENT—DOMESTIC TELEVISION DISTRIBUTION
Richard Cignarelli
EXECUTIVE VICE PRESIDENT—INTERNATIONAL TELEVISION DISTRIBUTION & WORLDWIDE PAY TELEVISION
Anthony J. Lynn
EXECUTIVE VICE PRESIDENT
Kenin M. Spivak
SENIOR VICE PRESIDENT—FINANCE
Thomas P. Carson
SENIOR VICE PRESIDENT, CORPORATE GENERAL COUNSEL AND SECRETARY
William A. Jones
SENIOR VICE PRESIDENT—STUDIO LEGAL AFFAIRS
Nancy Niederman
SENIOR VICE PRESIDENT—RESEARCH
Jack Smith
SENIOR VICE PRESIDENT—FINANCE AND ADMINISTRATION
Bernie Vanderfin
VICE PRESIDENT—PAY TELEVISION
Joseph Abrams
VICE PRESIDENT—EASTERN DIVISION
Charles Atkins
VICE PRESIDENT AND CONTROLLER
Kathleen Coughlan
PRESIDENT—BUSINESS AFFAIRS
Myron Dubow
VICE PRESIDENT—INTERNATIONAL TELEVISION DISTRIBUTION
Marion Edwards
VICE PRESIDENT—BUSINESS AFFAIRS
Rick Gire
VICE PRESIDENT AND TREASURER
Walter C. Hoffer
VICE PRESIDENT—MIDWESTERN DIVISION
Robert Horen
VICE PRESIDENT—BUSINESS AFFAIRS
William E. Josey
VICE PRESIDENT—FIRST RUN PRODUCTION
Mark Massari
VICE PRESIDENT—WESTERN DIVISION
Peter Preis
VICE PRESIDENT—SOUTHEASTERN DIVISION
Philip Smith
VICE PRESIDENT—TAXES
Daniel J. Taylor
VICE PRESIDENT—SALES—EUROPE
(Foreign TV syndication division)
James R. Wills
VICE PRESIDENT—TELEVISION SALES—CANADA
William F. Wineberg

MTM Enterprises, Inc.

4024 Radford Avenue, Studio City, CA 91604; (818) 760-5000. Organized 1970. (TV program production)

PRESIDENT
Arthur Price
SENIOR EXECUTIVE VICE PRESIDENT
Mel D. Blumenthal
PRESIDENT, TELEVISION
Peter Grad

Magno Sound & Video

729 Seventh Ave., New York, NY 10019; (212) 302-2505. (Full production services)

PRESIDENT
Ralph Friedman
VICE PRESIDENT
Robert Friedman
VICE PRESIDENT
David Friedman

National Broadcasting Co., Inc.

30 Rockefeller Plaza, New York, NY 10112; (212) 664-4444. Registered Telegraphic Address: NAT-BROCAST, NY; West Coast: 3000 W. Alameda Blvd., Burbank, CA 91523; (818) 840-4444.

CHAIRMAN OF THE BOARD, NBC, INC.
John F. Welch, Jr.
PRESIDENT AND CHIEF EXECUTIVE OFFICER
Robert C. Wright
EXECUTIVE VICE PRESIDENT
Alfred F. Barber
PRESIDENT, NBC ENTERTAINMENT
Brandon Tartikoff
PRESIDENT, NBC TELEVISION NETWORK
Pierson Mapes
PRESIDENT OPERATIONS AND TECHNICAL SERVICES
Michael Sherlock
PRESIDENT, NBC TELEVISION STATIONS
Albert Jerome
PRESIDENT, NBC NEWS
Michael Gartner
PRESIDENT, NBC SPORTS
Dick Ebersol
EXECUTIVE VICE PRESIDENT & SENIOR COUNSEL TO THE PRESIDENT
Corydon Dunham
EXECUTIVE VICE PRESIDENT PERSONNEL AND LABOR RELATIONS
Edward L. Scanlon
SENIOR VICE PRESIDENT CORPORATE COMMUNICATIONS
Betty Hudson

SENIOR VICE PRESIDENT BUSINESS AFFAIRS AND EXECUTIVE VICE PRESIDENT, NBC PRODUCTIONS & NBC TV NETWORK BUSINESS AFFAIRS
John Agoglia
EXECUTIVE VICE PRESIDENT
Arthur Watson

NBC Entertainment

PRESIDENT
Brandon Tartikoff
EXECUTIVE VICE PRESIDENT, PRIMETIME PROGRAMS
Warren Littlefield
VICE PRESIDENT, PROGRAM PRODUCTION
Perry Massey, Jr.
SENIOR VICE PRESIDENT, MOTION PICTURES FOR TV & MINI SERIES, NBC ENTERTAINMENT & NBC PRODUCTIONS
Anthony Masucci
SENIOR VICE PRESIDENT, NBC ENTERTAINMENT
John Miller
VICE PRESIDENT, NBC ENTERTAINMENT & NBC PRODUCTIONS
Susan Beckett
VICE PRESIDENT, MINI-SERIES
Ruth Slawson
SENIOR VICE PRESIDENT, EAST COAST, PROGRAM AND PROGRAM PLANNING
Lee Currlin
SENIOR VICE PRESIDENT, SERIES PROGRAMS
Perry Simon
VICE PRESIDENT, PROGRAMS, EAST COAST
David Wedeck
VICE PRESIDENT, COMEDY DEVELOPMENT
Leslie Laurie
VICE PRESIDENT, TALENT & CASTING
Lori Openden
VICE PRESIDENT, ON-AIR PROMOTION
John Luma
VICE PRESIDENT, CHILDREN'S AND FAMILY PROGRAMS
Phyllis Vinson
VICE PRESIDENT, SPECIALS AND VARIETY PROGRAMS
Richard Ludwin
VICE PRESIDENT, DAYTIME PROGRAMS
Jacqueline Smith
VICE PRESIDENT, FINANCE & ADMINISTRATION CONTROL, WEST COAST
Joseph Cicero
VICE PRESIDENT, DRAMA DEVELOPMENT
Dan Filie
VICE PRESIDENT, CURRENT COMEDY PROGRAMS
Ted Frank
VICE PRESIDENT DAYTIME DRAMA
Susan Lee
VICE PRESIDENT, CURRENT DRAMA PROGRAMS
Brian Pike
VICE PRESIDENT, FILM PRODUCTION
Charles Goldstein
VICE PRESIDENT, ENTERTAINMENT PRODUCTION & FINANCE
Timothy Quealy
VICE PRESIDENT, PROGRAM & MEDIA PLANNING
Paul Wang

NBC Cable & Business Development

PRESIDENT
Thomas Rogers
VICE PRESIDENT, BUSINESS DEVELOPMENT & PLANNING
Susan Greene
VICE PRESIDENT & GENERAL MANAGER
J. B. Holston
PRESIDENT CONSUMER NEWS & BUSINESS CHANNEL (CNBC)
Michael Eskridge
SENIOR VICE PRESIDENT, REGIONAL NEWS
Thomas Wolzien

NBC Network

PRESIDENT, NBC-TV NETWORK
Pierson Mapes
EXECUTIVE VICE PRESIDENT, NBC-TV NETWORK
Robert Blackmore
VICE PRESIDENT, PART PROGRAM SALES
Ron Dobson
SENIOR VICE PRESIDENT, NATIONAL SALES
Larry Hoffmer
VICE PRESIDENT, DAYTIME & SPECIALS SALES
Diane Seamans
VICE PRESIDENT, EASTERN SALES
Richard Plastine
VICE PRESIDENT, NETWORK MARKETING
Alan Cohen
VICE PRESIDENT, SPORTS SALES AND MARKETING
James Burnette
VICE PRESIDENT, OLYMPIC SALES AND MARKETING
Bert Zeldin
VICE PRESIDENT, WEST COAST AND SPECIAL PROGRAMS SALES
Carl Meyer
VICE PRESIDENT, PLANNING AND PRICING
William Caulfield
VICE PRESIDENT, CLIENT MARKETING
Ronald Kos
VICE PRESIDENT NETWORK SERVICES
Jean Dietz
VICE PRESIDENT NETWORK OPERATIONS
Richard Quackenboss
VICE PRESIDENT, PROGRAM STANDARDS & MARKETING POLICY
Alan Gierson
VICE PRESIDENT, RESEARCH
Robert Niles
VICE PRESIDENT, CENTRAL AND NATIONAL FIELD SALES
Richard Schade
VICE PRESIDENT, DETROIT SALES
John Spain Jr.
VICE PRESIDENT, AFFILIATE RELATIONS AND OPERATIONS
John Damiano
VICE PRESIDENT, AFFILIATE ADMINISTRATION & SERVICES
James Ritter
VICE PRESIDENT, AFFILIATE RELATIONS, OPERATIONS WITH AFFILIATE MARKETING
William Fouch
VICE PRESIDENT, AFFILIATE ADVERTISING AND PROMOTION SERVICES—ENTERTAINMENT DIVISION
Martha Stanville
VICE PRESIDENT, SPECIAL PROMOTION PROJECTS—ENTERTAINMENT DIVISION
Charles Stepner

Legal

EXECUTIVE VICE PRESIDENT AND GENERAL COUNSEL
Richard Cotton
VICE PRESIDENT, NBC LAW
Ellen S. Agress
VICE PRESIDENT, GOVERNMENT RELATIONS
Terence Mahony
VICE PRESIDENT, LAW, NEW YORK
Steve Stander
VICE PRESIDENT, LAW, WEST COAST
Don Zachary
VICE PRESIDENT, PROGRAM INFORMATION RESOURCES
Bettye Hoffman
VICE PRESIDENT NEWS MARKETING & NEW BUSINESS DEVELOPMENT
Theresa Byrne
DIRECTOR, NEWS OPERATIONS
Robert Keyes
MANAGING DIRECTOR, NEWS PRODUCTION & TECHNICAL SERVICES
Thomas Wolzien
VICE PRESIDENT, BROADCAST STANDARDS, EAST COAST, PROGRAM STANDARDS & COMMUNITY RELATIONS
Lois Weinman

News Division

PRESIDENT, NBC NEWS
Michael Gartner
SENIOR VICE PRESIDENT WASHINGTON
Timothy J. Russert
SENIOR VICE PRESIDENT NEWS
Thomas Ross
SENIOR VICE PRESIDENT
Joseph Angotti
VICE PRESIDENT, FINANCE AND ADMIN.
Natalie Parks Hunter

Operations & Technical Services

PRESIDENT, OPERATIONS & TECHNICAL SERVICES
Michael Sherlock
VICE PRESIDENT, ENGINEERING
Steve Bonica
VICE PRESIDENT, OPERATIONS AND TECHNICAL SERVICES, WEST COAST
Crawford McGill

VICE PRESIDENT, FACILITIES AND SERVICES, WEST COAST
(vacant)
VICE PRESIDENT, PRODUCTION OPERATIONS
Frank Accarrino
VICE PRESIDENT, OPERATIONS SYSTEMS SOFTWARE
Eric Koopmann
VICE PRESIDENT, SYSTEMS DEVELOPMENT
Rachele Lowenbraun
VICE PRESIDENT, MANAGEMENT INFORMATION SERVICES
Maurice Greenfield
VICE PRESIDENT, MANAGEMENT INFORMATION SERVICES, WEST COAST
Gerald Reeves
VICE PRESIDENT, FINANCE AND ADMINISTRATION, WEST COAST
John O'Neill, Jr.
VICE PRESIDENT, FACILITIES AND SERVICES
Anthony Pedalino
VICE PRESIDENT, BROADCAST OPERATIONS
Dave Baylor

Personnel & Labor Relations

EXECUTIVE VICE PRESIDENT, EMPLOYEE RELATIONS, NBC
Edward L. Scanlon
VICE PRESIDENT, EMPLOYEE RELATIONS, WEST COAST
Wayne Rickert
VICE PRESIDENT, LABOR RELATIONS, WEST COAST
Bernard Gehan

Corporate Communications

VICE PRESIDENT CORPORATE AND MEDIA RELATIONS
Elizabeth Hudson
VICE PRESIDENT CORPORATE INFORMATION, WEST COAST
Jay Rodriguez
VICE PRESIDENT, TALENT RELATIONS & MEDIA SERVICES, WEST COAST
Kathleen Tucci
VICE PRESIDENT, MEDIA RELATIONS, EAST COAST
Curtis Block
VICE PRESIDENT, MEDIA RELATIONS, WEST COAST
Sue Binford
VICE PRESIDENT, CORPORATE AFFAIRS
Victor Garvey
VICE PRESIDENT, ADVERTISING AND PROMOTION
John Miller
VICE PRESIDENT, ADVERTISING AND PROMOTION, EAST COAST
Tim Miller
VICE PRESIDENT, PRINT ADVERTISING
Jenness Brewer
VICE PRESIDENT, ON-AIR PROMOTION
John Luma
VICE PRESIDENT, AFFILIATE ADVERTISING AND PROMOTION SERVICES
Martha Stanville
VICE PRESIDENT, SPECIAL PROMOTION PROJECTS
Charles Stepner

Sports

PRESIDENT
Dick Ebersol
EXECUTIVE VICE PRESIDENT
Kenneth Schanzer
SENIOR VICE PRESIDENT, OLYMPICS
Randy Falco
VICE PRESIDENT PROGRAM PLANNING AND DEVELOPMENT
Jonathan Miller
VICE PRESIDENT SPORTS NEGOTIATIONS
Bertram Zeldin
VICE PRESIDENT, SPORTS NEGOTIATIONS
Jeff Cokin
VICE PRESIDENT OPERATIONS
Kenneth Aagaard

Television Business Affairs

EXECUTIVE VICE PRESIDENT, NBC-TV BUSINESS AFFAIRS
John Agoglia
VICE PRESIDENT, PROGRAM ACQUISITIONS
Joseph Bures
VICE PRESIDENT, BUSINESS AFFAIRS, PRIMETIME PROGRAMS
Gary Newman
VICE PRESIDENT, BUSINESS AFFAIRS
Leigh Brecheen
VICE PRESIDENT, PROGRAM AND TALENT CONTRACTS
Jay Goldberg
VICE PRESIDENT, STRATEGIC PLANNING
Barbara Watson

Television Stations

PRESIDENT, NBC TELEVISION STATIONS
Albert Jerome
VICE PRESIDENT FINANCE AND OPERATIONS
Robert Finnerty
VICE PRESIDENT TV OPERATIONS AND ENGINEERING
Duffy Sasser II
VICE PRESIDENT, SALES
Bud Hirsch
VICE PRESIDENT, SPOT SALES
James Zafiros
VICE PRESIDENT AND GENERAL MANAGER, WMAQ-TV
Robert Morse
VICE PRESIDENT AND GENERAL MANAGER, KNBC-TV
John Rohrbeck
VICE PRESIDENT AND GENERAL MANAGER, WKYC-TV
John Llewellyn
VICE PRESIDENT AND GENERAL MANAGER, WNBC-TV
Carl Carey
VICE PRESIDENT AND GENERAL MANAGER, WRC-TV
Allan Horlick
VICE PRESIDENT AND GENERAL MANAGER, WTVJ
Richard Lobo
PRESIDENT AND GENREAL MANAGER, KCNC
Roger Ogden

NBC Productions

PRESIDENT, NBC PRODS.
Brandon Tartikoff
EXECUTIVE VICE PRESIDENT, NBC PRODS.
John Agoglia
SENIOR VICE PRESIDENT, NBC PRODS.
Don Loughery
VICE PRESIDENT, PRODUCTION OPERATIONS
Gary Considine
VICE PRESIDENT, PRODUCTION, NBC PRODS.
William Phillips
VICE PRESIDENT, MEDIA PLANNING, NBC PRODS.
Gene Walsh
VICE PRESIDENT, CREATIVE AFFAIRS, NBC PRODS.
Brian Frong
VICE PRESIDENT, FINANCE, NBC PRODS.
Gerard Petry

New World Entertainment

1440 S. Sepulveda Blvd., Los Angeles, 90025; (213) 444-8100; Telex.: 661937 NWLSA; FAX: (213) 444-8101. (Producer and distributor.)

PRESIDENT AND CHIEF EXECUTIVE OFFICER
Edward B. Gradinger
PRESIDENT, NEW WORLD TELEVISION
Jon Feltheimer
EXECUTIVE VICE PRESIDENT
George Reeves
EXECUTIVE VICE PRESIDENT
Robert A. Stern
VICE PRESIDENT, ADMINISTRATION
James Walsh

NEW WORLD TELEVISION

SENIOR VICE PRESIDENT, CREATIVE AFFAIRS
Michael Levine
SENIOR VICE PRESIDENT, MOVIES & MINISERIES
Helen Verno
SENIOR VICE PRESIDENT, PRODUCTION
Lorin Salob
VICE PRESIDENT, PROGRAMS
Lea Stalmaster
VICE PRESIDENT, PRIMETIME SERIES
Eric Tannenbaum
VICE PRESIDENT, POST PRODUCTION
Larry Levin
VICE PRESIDENT, SPECIAL PROJECTS & MEDIA RELATIONS
Justin Pierce
DIRECTOR, MOVIES & MINISERIES
Stacy Smith-Ehrenhalt
DIRECTOR OF PRODUCTION & BUDGETS
Al d'Ossche

DIRECTOR, POST PRODUCTION
Sid Mandell
ASSOC. DIRECTOR, SERIES DEVELOPMENT
Helene Michaels

NEW WORLD BUSINESS & LEGAL AFFAIRS/FINANCE

VICE PRESIDENT, LEGAL AFFAIRS & NWE SECRETARY
James Zemelman
VICE PRESIDENT, BUSINESS AFFAIRS
Neil Shenker
VICE PRESIDENT, BUSINESS AFFAIRS
Honi Almond
VICE PRESIDENT, BUSINESS AFFAIRS
Sandra Stern
CONTROLLER
Barbara Frischer
PRODUCTION CONTROLLER
John Janisch
DIRECTOR, MUSIC BUSINESS AFFAIRS
Margaret Rogers

NEW WORLD MARKETING/PUBLICITY/ ADVERTISING/PROMOTION

VICE PRESIDENT, ADVERTISING
Gloria Lamont
VICE PRESIDENT, INTERNATIONAL PUBLICITY & PROMOTION
Jerry Zanitsch
DIRECTOR, ADVERTISING
Nanea Reeves
MANAGER, PUBLICITY & PROMOTION
Renee Madrigal

NEW WORLD INTERNATIONAL

PRESIDENT
Jim McNamara
MANAGING DIRECTOR
Ray Donahue
DIRECTOR, INTERNATIONAL SALES
Thea Diserio
DIRECTOR, INTERNATIONAL SERVICING
Esther Kho
DIRECTOR, CONTRACT ADMINISTRATION
Teresa Lee
DIRECTOR, INTERNATIONAL SALES
Christy Smith

NEW WORLD DOMESTIC DISTRIBUTION

PRESIDENT
Tony Brown
V.P., NATIONAL SALES MGR.
Joe Middelburg
V.P., DIVISIONAL SALES MGR.
Tony Fasola
V.P., DIVISIONAL SALES MGR.
Robert Greenstein
REGIONAL SALES MANAGER
Frank L. Browne
REGIONAL SALES MANAGER
Sandy Lang
DIRECTOR OF SALES SERVICE
Dorothy Hamilton
DIRECTOR, ANCILLARY & DOMESTIC SYNDICATION, POST PRODUCTION
Ronald Smith
DIRECTOR OF SERVICING
George Gale

MARVEL PRODUCTIONS

PRESIDENT & CHIEF EXECUTIVE OFFICER
Margaret Loesch
VICE PRESIDENT, PRODUCTION
James Graziano

LEARNING CORPORATION OF AMERICA

CHIEF EXECUTIVE OFFICER
Robert C. Peters
PRESIDENT
B. Donald Greene

FOUR STAR INTERNATIONAL

SENIOR VICE PRESIDENT
Lance Thompson

Orion Home Entertainment Corporation

711 Fifth Ave., New York, NY 10022; (212) 758-5100.

CHAIRMAN OF THE BOARD, CHIEF EXECUTIVE OFFICER
Lawrence B. Hilford
EXECUTIVE VICE PRESIDENT
William Bernstein
SENIOR VICE PRESIDENT, GENERAL COUNSEL AND SECRETARY
Leonard B. Pack
SENIOR VICE PRESIDENT FOR BUSINESS AFFAIRS
Robert A. Mirisch
SENIOR VICE PRESIDENT, CFO & TREASURER
Edwin L. Schwartz
VICE PRESIDENT FOR BUSINESS AFFAIRS
Kimberle A. Aronzon
VICE PRESIDENT, CHIEF ACCOUNTING OFFICER
Lawrence Bernstein
ASSISTANT SECRETARY
John W. Hester
ASSISTANT TREASURER
Richards T. Matthews

ORION TELEVISION, ENTERTAINMENT

(A division of Orion Pictures Corporation.)
1888 Century Park E., Los Angeles, CA 90067; (213) 282-0550.

CHAIRMAN AND CHIEF EXECTIVE OFFICER
Gary Nardino
PRESIDENT OF PRODUCTION
Gary A. Randall
PRESIDENT DOMESTIC TELEVISION DISTRIBUTION
J. Scott Towle
SENIOR VICE PRESIDENT DOMESTIC TELEVISION DISTRIBUTION
Thomas Cerio
SENIOR VICE PRESIDENT DOMESTIC TELEVISION DISTRIBUTION
Larry P. Hutchings
SENIOR VICE PRESIDENT, LEGAL AFFAIRS
Robert A. Mirisch
SENIOR VICE PRESIDENT, BUSINESS AFFAIRS, LEGAL AND FINANCE
Irwin Moss
SENIOR VICE PRESIDENT, PRODUCTION MANAGEMENT
Stanley Neufeld
SENIOR VICE PRESIDENT PRODUCTION, COMEDY
Richard A. Rosen
SENIOR VICE PRESIDENT PRODUCTION
Jeffrey Wachtel
VICE PRESIDENT, BUSINESS AFFAIRS
Douglass Bergmann
VICE PRESIDENT, POST PRODUCTION
Mick McAfee
VICE PRESIDENT, ADVERTISING, PUBLICITY & PROMOTION
Robert Oswaks
VICE PRESIDENT PRODUCTION, FIRST RUN SYNDICATION, DAYTIME & LATE NIGHT
Robert I. Sanitsky
VICE PRESIDENT AND CONTROLLER
Steven C. Smith
VICE PRESIDENT, LEGAL AFFAIRS
Debra Stasson

ORION TELEVISION SYNDICATION

(A Division of Orion Pictures Corporation) 1888 Century Park East, Los Angeles, CA 90067; (213) 282-0550. Branches: 400 Perimeter Center Terrace, Atlanta, GA 30346; 625 N. Michigan Ave., Chicago, IL 60611.

PRESIDENT
J. Scott Towle
SENIOR VICE PRESIDENT, NATIONAL SALES MANAGER
Thomas Cerio
SENIOR VICE PRESIDENT, SALES AND MARKETING
Larry P. Hutchings
SENIOR VICE PRESIDENT, BUSINESS AFFAIRS
Robert A. Mirisch
VICE PRESIDENT—CENTRAL DIVISION
Donald Frehe
VICE PRESIDENT ADMINISTRATION/LEGAL AFFAIRS, EAST COAST
Ralph E. Goldberg
VICE PRESIDENT—EASTERN DIVISION
Arthur Hasson
VICE PRESIDENT, OPERATIONS
Kathy Haynsworth

VICE PRESIDENT—WESTERN DIVISION
Stephen Mulderrig
VICE PRESIDENT ADVERTISING, PUBLICITY & PROMOTION
Robert Oswaks
VICE PRESIDENT—SOUTHERN DIVISION
Timothy Richard Overmyer
VICE PRESIDENT, RESEARCH
Richard Zimmer

Paramount Television Group

(A Division of Paramount Pictures Corporation) 5555 Melrose, Hollywood, CA 90038; (213) 468-5000. 15 Columbus Circle, New York, NY 10023; (212) 373-8000.

TELEVISION GROUP

PRESIDENT
Mel Harris
SENIOR VICE PRESIDENT, BUSINESS DEVELOPMENT
Alan Cole-Ford
VICE PRESIDENT, CONTROLLER
Mark Lebowitz
VICE PRESIDENT, OPERATIONS
Philip Murphy
VICE PRESIDENT, PLANNING
Jack Waterman

DOMESTIC TELEVISION DIVISION

PRESIDENT
Lucille Salhany
EXECUTIVE VICE PRESIDENT, SALES & MARKETING
Steven Goldman
EXECUTIVE VICE PRESIDENT, PROGRAMMING
Frank Kelly
EXECUTIVE VICE PRESIDENT, GENERAL SALES MANAGER
R. Gregory Meidel
SENIOR VICE PRESIDENT, ADVERTISING & PROMOTION
Meryl Cohen
SENIOR VICE PRESIDENT, BUSINESS AFFAIRS/FINANCE
Robert Sheehan
SENIOR VICE PRESIDENT, BUSINESS AFFAIRS
Vance Scott Van Petten
VICE PRESIDENT, LEGAL AFFAIRS
Thomas Fortuin
VICE PRESIDENT, OFF-NETWORK, FEATURES & CABLE SALES
Joel Berman
VICE PRESIDENT, ADMINISTRATION, SALES/CONTRACTS
Howard Green
VICE PRESIDENT, PROGRAMMING
Carlotte Koppe
VICE PRESIDENT, PRODUCTION
Clifford Lachman
VICE PRESIDENT, RESEARCH & SALES DEVELOPMENT
Jim Martz
VICE PRESIDENT, WESTERN REGIONAL MANAGER
Dick Montgomery
VICE PRESIDENT, CREATIVE AFFAIRS
Steven Nalevansky
VICE PRESIDENT, CENTRAL REGIONAL MANAGER
Gerald Noonan
VICE PRESIDENT, SOUTHERN REGIONAL MANAGER
Al Rothstein
VICE PRESIDENT, PRODUCTION
Jack Wartlieb
VICE PRESIDENT, EASTERN REGIONAL MANAGER
R. Edward Wilson

NETWORK TELEVISION DIVISION

PRESIDENT
John Pike
EXECUTIVE VICE PRESIDENT, BUSINESS AFFAIRS
Cecelia Andrews
EXECUTIVE VICE PRESIDENT, CREATIVE AFFAIRS
John Symes
SENIOR VICE PRESIDENT, LEGAL AFFAIRS
Howard Barton
SENIOR VICE PRESIDENT, DEVELOPMENT
Paul J. Heller
VICE PRESIDENT, FINANCE
Gerald Goldman
VICE PRESIDENT, BUSINESS AFFAIRS
Ronald Jacobson
VICE PRESIDENT, TALENT & CASTING
Helen Mossler
VICE PRESIDENT, PRODUCTION
Michael Schoenbrun

INTERNATIONAL TELEVISION DIVISION (Bermuda)

PRESIDENT
Bruce Gordon
VICE PRESIDENT, EUROPEAN SALES
Peter Cary
VICE PRESIDENT, OPERATIONS
Joseph Lucas
VICE PRESIDENT, FAR EAST SALES
George Mooratoff
VICE PRESIDENT, TV SALES, CANADA
Malcolm Orme
VICE PRESIDENT, LATIN AMERICA SALES
Ramon Perez

INTERNATIONAL SALES OFFICES

ENGLAND: Paramount TV Ltd., 23 Berkeley House, Hay Hill, London, W1X 8JB, England.
VICE PRESIDENT, EUROPEAN SALES
Peter Cary
AUSTRALIA: Paramount Pictures Pty., Ltd., Suite 3209, Australia Square, Box 4272 GPO, Sydney, 2001, N.S.W. Australia.
VICE PRESIDENT, FAR EAST SALES
George Mooratoff
CANADA: Paramount Pictures Corp. Ltd., 146 Bloor Street W., Toronto, Ontario M5S 1M4, Canada.
VICE PRESIDENT, TV SALES, CANADA
Malcolm Orme
LOS ANGELES:
VICE PRESIDENT, LATIN AMERICA
Ramon Perez

Public Broadcasting Service

DC Office: 1320 Braddock Place, Alexandria, VA 22314-1698; (703) 739-5000; New York Office: 1790 Broadway, New York, NY 10019-1412; (212) 708-3000; Los Angeles office: 4401 Sunset Blvd., Suite 335, Los Angeles, CA 90027; (213) 667-9289. (A private non-profit corporation providing national programming, distribution, and related services for public TV stations.)

CHAIRMAN, PBS BOARD OF DIRECTORS
Ted R. Capener
PRESIDENT & CHIEF EXECUTIVE OFFICER
Bruce L. Christensen
EXECUTIVE VICE PRESIDENT & CHIEF OPERATING OFFICER
Neil B. Mahrer
SENIOR VICE PRESIDENT, EDUCATION
Dee Brock
SENIOR VICE PRESIDENT, PROGRAM SUPPORT GROUP
Peter Downey
SENIOR VICE PRESIDENT, GENERAL COUNSEL & CORPORATE SECRETARY
Paula A. Jameson
SENIOR VICE PRESIDENT, BROADCAST OPERATIONS & ENGINEERING
Howard Miller
SENIOR VICE PRESIDENT, ADMINISTRATION & COMPUTER SERVICES & PERSONNEL
Eric L. Sass
SENIOR VICE PRESIDENT, DEVELOPMENT
Michael B. Soper
SENIOR VICE PRESIDENT, CHIEF FINANCIAL OFFICER & TREASURER
Beth Wolfe
SENIOR VICE PRESIDENT, NATIONAL PROGRAMMING & PROMOTION SERVICES
vacant
SENIOR VICE PRESIDENT, POLICY AND PLANNING
Michael E. Hobbs
VICE PRESIDENT, PROGRAM ADMINISTRATION
Lance W. Ozier
VICE PRESIDENT, DEPUTY GENERAL COUNSEL & ASSISTANT CORPORATE SECRETARY
Nancy Hendry
VICE PRESIDENT, SATELLITE TECHNOLOGY
Carlos Girod
VICE PRESIDENT, PROMOTION & ADVERTISING
Susan Fergenson Petroff

VICE PRESIDENT, NATIONAL PROGRAMMING & PROMOTION SERVICES
Daniel C. Agan
VICE PRESIDENT, PBS PROGRAMMING
Barry O. Chase

Quanta, Ltd.

P.O. Box 13, Springfield, VA 22150; (703) 451-3300. (British television and video production company specializing in interpreting and science and technology to general audiences.)

U.S. REPRESENTATIVE
W. G. WILLIAMS

Rank Cintel Inc.

(Marketing of telecine equipment) PO Box 710, 704 Executive Blvd., Valley Cottage, NY 10989-009, USA; (914) 268-8911; FAX: (914) 268-5939.

EXECUTIVE VICE PRESIDENT
Colin Brown

Rank Precision Industries

RANK CINTEL LTD.

(Manufacturer of telecine equipment for broadcast and film/tape transfer) Watton Road, Ware, Hertfordshire SC12 OAE. Tel. 0920 3939; Telex: 81415; FAX: 0920 60803.

GENERAL MANAGER
Jack R. Brittain

RANK TAYLOR HOBSON LTD.

(Manufacturer of precision measurement equipment, professional cine lenses.) P.O. Box 36, 1 New Star Road, Thurmaston Lane, Leicester LE3 7JQ. Tel: (Leicester) 763771; Telex: 3422338.

MANAGING DIRECTOR
Christopher Waldron

RANK PRECISION INDUSTRIES GmbH (West German Office)

(Marketing of telecine equipment and motion picture camera lenses) Postfach 4827, Kreuzberger Ring 6 6200 Wiesbaden, West Germany; Tel: 06121 700874; Telex: 04186175; FAX: 06121 702495.

GESCHAFTSFUHRER
H-U Rathgeber

RANK PRECISION INDUSTRIES S.p.A. (Italian Office)

(Marketing of telecine equipment and motion picture camera lenses) Via Vassallo 31, 20125 Milan, Italy; Tel: 392 688 9451; Telex: 330362; FAX: 392 607 0180.

DIRECTOR AND GENERAL MANAGER
A. Resasco

RANK PRECISION INDUSTRIES MARKETING Ges.m.b.H. (Austrian Office)

(Marketing of telecine equipment) Amalienstrasse 68, A-1130 Wien-Austria; Tel: 43 222 825571; FAX: 43 222 82557116.

GESCHAFTSFUHRER
Eric Pelz

RANK TAYLOR HOBSON K.K. (Japanese Office)

(Marketing of professional cine lenses) Kokudokan Buildings, 9-13, 4-chome, Chuo-Ku, Ginza, Tokyo 336, Japan; Tel: 813 545 1451; Telex: 7227684; FAX: 813 545 6522.

PRESIDENT
K. Fujimoto

International Division

STRAND LIGHTING, INC.

(Marketing of lighting and lighting control equipment) 18111 Santa Fe Ave., Rancho Dominquez, CA 90221; (213) 637-7500; FAX: (213) 632-5519; Telex: 200473.

PRESIDENT
Tom Sullivan

STRAND LIGHTING LTD. (U.K. Office)

(Manufacturer of lighting and lighting control equipment) Grant Way, Off Syon Lane, Isleworth, Middx: TW7 5QD. Tel: 01 560 3171; Telex: 27976; FAX: 01 568 2103.

MANAGING DIRECTOR
Oliver Hartreee

STRAND LIGHTING PTY. LTD. (Australian Office)

(Marketing of lighting and lighting control equipment) 264-270 Normanby Road, South Melbourne, Victoria 3205, Australia; Tel: 0106 3 646 4522; FAX: 0106 13 646 5020; Telex: 34732.

GENERAL MANAGER
I. Haddon

STRAND LIGHTING CANADA LIMITED (Canadian Office)

(Marketing of lighting and lighting control equipment) 6490 Viscount Road, Mississauga, Ont. L4V 1H3, Canada; (416) 677-7130; Telex: 06968646; FAX: 0101 416 677 6859.

PRESIDENT
Mrs. D. Appleton

STRAND LIGHTING FRANCE S.A. (French Office)

(Marketing of lighting and lighting control equipment) 26 Villa des Fleurs, 92400 Courbevoie, France; Tel: 010 331 478 86666; FAX: 010 331 433 37175; Telex: 214593.

GENERAL MANAGER
B. Bouchet

STRAND LIGHTING ASIA LIMITED (Hong Kong Office)

(Marketing of lighting and lighting control equipment) 802 Houston Centre, 63 Mody Road, Tsimshatsui East, Kowloon, Hong Kong; Tel: 010 852 3 685161; Telex: 449553; FAX: 010 852 3 694890.

MANAGING DIRECTOR
P. O'Donnel

STRAND LIGHTING S.p.A. (Italian Office)

(Marketing of lighting and lighting control equipment) 00137 Roma, 80 Via Cermenati, Italy; Tel: 010 396 6120241; FAX: 010 396 8171845.

MANAGING DIRECTOR
A. Rossi

STRAND LIGHTING GmbH (West German Office)

(Marketing of lighting and lighting control equipment) P.O. Box 4449, 3300 Braunschweig, West Germany; Tel: 010 49 5331 7951; Telex: 95641; FAX: 010 49 5331 78883.

GENERAL MANAGER
H.J. Fritz

Republic Pictures Corporation

12636 Beatrice St., Los Angeles, CA 90066-0930; (213) 306-4040; FAX: (213) 301-0221.

CHAIRMAN OF THE BOARD
Russell Goldsmith
PRESIDENT
Charles W. Larsen
SENIOR VICE PRESIDENT
Stephen P. Beeks
VICE PRESIDENT—ACQUISITIONS
Mel Layton
VICE PRESIDENT & CHIEF FINANCIAL OFFICER
David Kirchheimer
SENIOR VICE PRESIDENT, HOME VIDEO, SALES & MARKETING
Vallery Kountze
SENIOR VICE PRESIDENT, INTERNATIONAL SALES
Joe Levinsohn
EXECUTIVE VICE PRESIDENT
Laurie Levit
VICE PRESIDENT—MARKETING
Glenn Ross
VICE PRESIDENT—BUSINESS AFFAIRS & LEGAL
Richard Kurshner

CANADA: Kaleidoscope Entertainment, Inc./Randy Zalken, pres., 101 Duncan Mill Road, Suite 102, Don Mills, Ontario, M3B 1Z3.

UNITED KINGDOM & SELECTED PORTIONS OF WESTERN EUROPE: TV Programmes International, Ltd./Bernard Shaw, sales repr., 21 Cherry Garden Lane, Folkestone, Kent, England. Telephone: 303-76897, Telex: 966560 SHAW TV.

GREECE AND BALKANS: 46 King Constantine Ave./Panos Spyropoulos, sales repr., Athens, 516 Greece. Telephone: 7224-243/7234-896; Telex: 221880 APOL GR.

TURKEY: Umut Sanat Urunleri/Seher Karabol, sales repr., Istiklal Caddesi Lale Han No. 87/6, Beyoglu, Istanbul, Turkey. Telephone: 149-77-35/143-44-39, Telex: 23359 BOTX TR.

AUSTRIA: Post Box 192, Postamt 1140, Vienna, Austria, Mounir J. Chammas, sales rep.

Sony Corp. of America

One Sony Dr., Park Ridge, NJ 07656; (201) 930-1000. (Set manufacturer)

PRESIDENT, SONY CORP. OF AMERICA
Neil Vander Dussen
PRESIDENT, SONY COMMUNICATIONS PRODUCTS CO.
Richard Wheeler
PRESIDENT, SONY MAGNETIC PRODUCTS COMPANY
John Bermingham
PRESIDENT, SONY PERSONAL AUDIO PRODUCTS CO.
Marnix Van Gemert
PRESIDENT, SONY AUDIO COMPONENT SYSTEMS CO.
Martin Homlisch
PRESIDENT, SONY CONSUMER VIDEO PRODUCTS CO.
John Briesch (acting)
PRESIDENT, SONY CONSUMER DISPLAY PRODUCTS CO.
James Palumbo
PRESIDENT, SONY CONSUMER SALES CO.
Thomas Harvey
PRESIDENT, SONY CONSUMER PRODUCTS GROUP
John Briesch
PRESIDENT, SONY ADVANCED SYSTEMS CO.
William Connolly
PRESIDENT, SONY TECH. & ENGINEERING CO.
Harry Taxin
PRESIDENT, SONY VIDEO COMMUNICATIONS SYSTEMS CO.
Donald Haight
PRESIDENT, SONY PERIPHERAL SYSTEMS CO.
Mark Gray
PRESIDENT, SONY DIVERSIFIED BUSINESS CO.
Shinichi Takagi

Thomson Consumer Electronics, Inc.

P.O. Box 1976, Indianapolis, IN 46206; (317) 267-5000. (RCA/GE set manufacturer.)

PRESIDENT & CEO
Joseph Fogiano
SENIOR VICE PRESIDENT
D. Joseph Donahue
VICE PRESIDENT, MARKETING
Marin Holleran

Twentieth Television Corporation

P.O. Box 900, Beverly Hills, CA 90213; (213) 277-2211. A division of Fox Film Corp.

TELEVISION DIVISION

PRESIDENT, TWENTIETH CENTURY FOX TELEVISION DIVISION
Jonathan Dolgen

TELEVISION PRODUCTION

PRESIDENT, TELEVISION PRODUCTION
Harris L. Katleman
SENIOR VICE PRESIDENT, PRODUCTION AND FINANCE
Charles Goldstein
SENIOR VICE PRESIDENT, CREATIVE AFFAIRS
Stuart Sheslow
SENIOR VICE PRESIDENT, BUSINESS AFFAIRS
Larry Jones
VICE PRESIDENT, TELEVISION POST—PRODUCTION
Edward Nassour
VICE PRESIDENT, CREATIVE AFFAIRS
Stephen Gelber
VICE PRESIDENT, PRODUCTION MANAGEMENT
Bob Gros
VICE PRESIDENT, BUSINESS AFFAIRS
David Robinson
VICE PRESIDENT, BUSINESS AFFAIRS
Pamela Wisne
VICE PRESIDENT, TAPE PRODUCTION
Joel Hornstock
VICE PRESIDENT, LEGAL AFFAIRS
Walter Swanson

DOMESTIC SYNDICATION

PRESIDENT, DOMESTIC SYNDICATION
Michael J. Lambert
SENIOR VICE PRESIDENT, ADMINISTRATION AND OPERATIONS, TELEVISION OPERATIONS
Leonard J. Grossi
SENIOR VICE PRESIDENT, SALES, DEVELOPMENT AND FEATURE FILM PLANNING
Joseph Greene
SENIOR VICE PRESIDENT, SALES, EASTERN DIVISION
Daniel Greenblatt
SENIOR VICE PRESIDENT, SALES, WESTERN DIVISION
Anthony Bauer
VICE PRESIDENT, BUSINESS AFFAIRS
Benson H. Begun
SENIOR VICE PRESIDENT, CREATIVE SERVICES
Fred Bierman
VICE PRESIDENT, RESEARCH
Steve Leblang
VICE PRESIDENT, ADMINISTRATIVE AND STRATEGIC PLANNING
Jennifer Fate
VICE PRESIDENT, WESTERN DIVISION
John J. Campagnolo
SALES EXECUTIVE WESTERN DIVISION
Timothy Mudd
VICE PRESIDENT, MIDWEST SALES
Matthew F. Jacobson
VICE PRESIDENT, SOUTHEASTERN DIVISION
Michael Newsom
VICE PRESIDENT, SOUTHWESTERN DIVISION
Vic Zimmerman
DIRECTOR, DOMESTIC SALES AND CLEARANCES
Barbara Van Buskirk
DIRECTOR, CREATIVE SERVICES
J. Mathy Simon

INTERNATIONAL SYNDICATION

EXECUTIVE VICE PRESIDENT, INTERNATIONAL SYNDICATION
William Saunders

VICE PRESIDENT, AUSTRALIA AND FAR EAST TERRITORIES
Peter Broome
VICE PRESIDENT, LATIN AMERICA
Elie Wahba
VICE PRESIDENT, TELEVISION SALES—EUROPE
Malcolm Vaughan
SALES MANAGER, MEXICO
Gustavo Montaudon
SALES MANAGER, LONDON
Steve Cornish
SALES MANAGER, FRANCE
Gilles Meunier

VIDEO AND PAY TELEVISION

SENIOR VICE PRESIDENT, VIDEO AND PAY TELEVISION
Jim Griffiths
VICE PRESIDENT, PAY TV WORLDWIDE
Doug Lee
VICE PRESIDENT, WORLDWIDE NON-THEATRICAL SALES
Sam Weinstein

BRANCH OFFICES

- NEW YORK: 40 W. 57 St., New York, NY 10019; (212) 977-5500; Joseph Greene, sr. v.p., domestic syndication; Ted Baker, Northeastern division sls. mgr. Harry Mulford, v,p, natl. sls.
- CHICAGO: 35 E. Wacker Dr., Suite 1234, Chicago, Illinois 60601; (312) 372-1589; Dennis Juravic, central division v.p.
- DALLAS: 11551 Forest Central Dr., Suite 300, Dallas, Texas 75243; (214) 343-9252; Al Shore, southwestern division v.p.
- ATLANTA: 2200 Century Parkway, Suite 560, Atlanta, Georgia 30345; (404) 634-0011; Michael Newson, southeastern division v.p.
- LOS ANGELES: Box 900, Beverly Hills, California 90213; (213) 203-2841; Tony Bauer, western division v.p.

FOREIGN SALES OFFICES:

Twentieth Century-Fox France, Inc., 114 Rue la Boetie, 75008, Paris, France. Gilles Meunier, sales mgr.

Twentieth Century-Fox Film Company, Ltd., 31-32 Soho Square, London, W1V 6AP, England. Malcolm Vaughn, vice president, United Kingdom, Europe Middle/Near East and Africa. Stephen Cornish, sls. mgr.

Twentieth Century-Fox Film Corp. (Australia), P.O. Box Q301, Queen Victoria Building, Sydney 2000, Australia. Peter Broome, vice president, Australia Far East. Paul Herbert, sls. mgr.

Twentieth Century-Fox Far East, Inc., Fukide Building, 1-13 Toranomon 4, Chome Minato-Ku, Tokyo 105, Japan. Goro Uzaki tv sls. rep.

Fox Interamericana, S.A., Apartado 6-1023, Mexico, D.F. 06600 Gustavo Montaudon, sls. mgr.

Fox Film do Brazil, S.A.–TV Division, Rua Dr. Costa Jr. 230 C.E.P., 05002 São Paulo, Brazil. Elie Wahba, v.p., Latin America.

Universal Television

(A division of Universal City Studios Inc, a subsidiary of MCA Inc.)

Universal City Studios, Universal City, CA 91608; (213) 985-4321. (Producer of TV programs)

PRESIDENT, UNIVERSAL TELEVISION
Kerry McCluggage
EXECUTIVE VICE PRESIDENT, ADMINISTRATION
Ed Masket
EXECUTIVE VICE PRESIDENT IN CHARGE OF PRODUCTION
Earl Bellamy
EXECUTIVE VICE PRESIDENT, CREATIVE AFFAIRS
Richard Lindheim
VICE PRESIDENT, CURRENT PROGRAMMING
Garrett Hart
SENIOR VICE PRESIDENT, DRAMATIC & LONGFORM PROGRAMMING
Charmaine Balian
VICE PRESIDENT, PUBLICITY, PROMOTION AND ADVERTISING
Robert Crutchfield
VICE PRESIDENT, TELEVISION CASTING
Joan Sittenfield
SUPERVISING DIRECTOR, TV CASTING
Ron Stephenson
VICE PRESIDENT, COMEDY DEVELOPMENT
Brad Johnson
VICE PRESIDENT, BUSINESS AFFAIRS
Paul Miller
VICE PRESIDENT, BUSINESS AFFAIRS
Arnold Shane
VICE PRESIDENT, TALENT DEVELOPMENT & ACQUISITIONS
Pete Terranova
VICE PRESIDENT, TELEVISION PRODUCTION MANAGEMENT
Ralph Sariego

Univision Holdings, Inc.

330 Madison Ave., 26th floor, New York, NY 10017; (212) 983-8500; FAX: (212) 983-8595. (Producers of Spanish-language programming for television; has 450 satellite interconnected TV affiliates and 6 non-connected TV affiliates.)

PRESIDENT & CHIEF EXECUTIVE OFFICER
J. William Grimes
VICE PRESIDENT, BUSINESS AFFAIRS
Andy Goldman
SENIOR VICE PRESIDENT, BUSINESS DEVELOPMENT
Blaine Decker

Univision Network

767 Fifth Avenue, 12th Floor, New York, NY 10153; Tel: (212) 826-5200; FAX: (212) 755-5659.

PRESIDENT
Joaquin F. Blaya
SENIOR VICE PRESIDENT, MARKETING SERVICES
Emma J. Carrasco
VICE PRESIDENT, NETWORK SALES MANAGER
Raul Torano
VICE PRESIDENT, NETWORK SPOT SALES MANAGER
Peter Von Gal
VICE PRESIDENT, DIRECTOR OF MARKETING
Karen Anderson
VICE PRESIDENT, DIRECTOR OF RESEARCH
Doug Darfield
VICE PRESIDENT, DIRECTOR OF OPERATIONS
Tony Oquendo
VICE PRESIDENT, DIRECTOR OF PROGRAMMING
Rosita Peru
VICE PRESIDENT, DIRECTOR OF NEWS
Guillermo Martinez
VICE PRESIDENT, DIRECTOR OF SPECIAL EVENTS
Omar Marchant

UNIVISION REGIONAL SALES OFFICES

9200 Sunset Blvd., Suite 1130, Los Angeles, CA 90069; (213) 859-7200; FAX: (213) 859-7424; Philip Wilkinson, sales mgr.

2010 Main St., Suite 590, Irvine, CA 92714; (714) 474-8585; FAX: (714) 474-8385; Hilary Dubin, sales mgr.

One Magnificent Mile, Suite 1120, Chicago, IL 60611-4501; (312) 944-2199; FAX: (312) 944-3124; Brian Pussilano, sales mgr.

550 Biltmore Way, Suite 760, Coral Gables, FL 33134; (305) 444-0800; FAX: (305) 441-2798; Barry Kandel, sales mgr.

600 E. Las Colinas Blvd., Suite 348, Irving, TX 75039; (214) 869-0202; FAX: (214) 869-2635; Marty Dugan, sales mgr.

601 Montgomery St., Suite 2015, San Francisco, CA 94111; (415) 392-2006; FAX: (415) 392-2009; Cynthia Saucedo, sales mgr.

30700 Telegraph Rd., Suite 3640, Birmingham, MI 48010; (313) 540-5705; FAX: (313) 540-2419; Chris Roman, sales mgr.

Viacom Inc.
Viacom International Inc.

1211 Avenue of the Americas, New York, NY 10036; (212) 575-5175.

(Viacom International Inc. is a diversified entertainment and communications company with five principal operating segments: Viacom Cable, Viacom Networks, Viacom Entertainment, Viacom Broadcasting and Viacom Pictures.)

(Viacom Inc., the holding company parent of Viacom International Inc., is an approximately 83% subsidiary of National Amusements, Inc., a closely held corporation which owns and operates approximately 520 movie screens in 14 states and the United Kingdom.)

CORPORATE AND DIVISIONAL OFFICERS

CHAIRMAN OF THE BOARD
Summer M. Redstone
PRESIDENT AND CHIEF EXECUTIVE OFFICER
Frank J. Biondi, Jr.

SENIOR VICE PRESIDENT—CORPORATE RELATIONS
Raymond A. Boyce
SENIOR VICE PRESIDENT—CORPORATE DEVELOPMENT AND ADMINISTRATION; CHAIRMAN/VIACOM PICTURES
Neil S. Braun
CHAIRMAN AND CEO/SHOWTIME NETWORKS INC.
Winston H. (Tony) Cox
VICE PRESIDENT AND TREASURER
Thomas E. Dooley
CHAIRMAN AND CEO/MTV NETWORKS
Thomas E. Freston
SENIOR VICE PRESIDENT, PRESIDENT AND CEO/VIACOM CABLE
John W. Goddard
SENIOR VICE PRESIDENT
Edward D. Horowitz
SENIOR VICE PRESIDENT
Ira A. Korff
VICE PRESIDENT, CONTROLLER AND CHIEF ACCOUNTING OFFICER
Kevin C. Lavan
VICE PRESIDENT—HUMAN RESOURCES AND ADMINISTRATION
William A. Roskin
SENIOR VICE PRESIDENT, CHAIRMAN AND CEO/VIACOM BROADCASTING AND VIACOM ENTERTAINMENT
Henry S. Schleiff
SENIOR VICE PRESIDENT AND CHIEF FINANCIAL OFFICER
George S. Smith, Jr.
SENIOR VICE PRESIDENT, GENERAL COUNSEL AND SECRETARY
Mark M. Weinstein

FINANCE DEPARTMENT

SENIOR VICE PRESIDENT AND CHIEF FINANCIAL OFFICER
George S. Smith, Jr.
VICE PRESIDENT AND TREASURER
Thomas E. Dooley
VICE PRESIDENT—INTERNAL AUDIT
Susan Gordon
VICE PRESIDENT, CONTROLLER AND CHIEF ACCOUNTING OFFICER
Kevin C. Lavan
VICE PRESIDENT—MIS
Thomas Mellina
VICE PRESIDENT—TAX
Walter Saffer

LAW DEPARTMENT

SENIOR VICE PRESIDENT, GENERAL COUNSEL AND SECRETARY
Mark M. Weinstein
EXECUTIVE VICE PRESIDENT—GENERAL COUNSEL/NETWORKS GROUP
Gregory J. Ricca
VICE PRESIDENT—COUNSEL/ENTERTAINMENT
Katherine A. Hogan
VICE PRESIDENT—COUNSEL/CORPORATE
Nancy Rosenfeld
VICE PRESIDENT—COUNSEL/COMMUNICATIONS
Edward N. Schor

CORPORATE RELATIONS DEPARTMENT

SENIOR VICE PRESIDENT
Raymond A. Boyce

CORPORATE DEVELOPMENT AND ADMINISTRATION

SENIOR VICE PRESIDENT
Neil S. Braun
VICE PRESIDENT—HUMAN RESOURCES AND ADMINISTRATION
William A. Roskin
VICE PRESIDENT—PERSONNEL AND EMPLOYEE RELATIONS
Patricia A. Ross
VICE PRESIDENT—CORPORATE DEVELOPMENT
Leslie Schine
VICE PRESIDENT—FACILITIES MANAGEMENT
Kenneth Sullivan

VIACOM INTERNATIONAL INC.

DIRECTOR—CORPORATE RELATIONS
Hilary E. Condit
VICE PRESIDENT AND TREASURER
Thomas E. Dooley
VICE PRESIDENT—PERSONNEL AND EMPLOYEE RELATIONS
Patricia A. Ross
VICE PRESIDENT—COUNSEL/CORPORATE
Nancy Rosenfeld

Viacom Entertainment

CHAIRMAN AND CHIEF EXECUTIVE OFFICER
Henry S. Schleiff
EXECUTIVE VICE PRESIDENT, PRESIDENT/WEST COAST OPERATIONS
Gus Lucas
SENIOR VICE PRESIDENT AND CHIEF FINANCIAL OFFICER
Robert S. Tucci
VICE PRESIDENT—COUNSEL
Katherine A. Hogan
VICE PRESIDENT—PUBLIC RELATIONS
Betsy Vorce
DIRECTOR—HUMAN RESOURCES
Cecelia Holloway

VIACOM ENTERPRISES

PRESIDENT
Arthur Kananack
PRESIDENT—ACQUISITIONS AND FIRST RUN PROGRAMMING
Michael H. Gerber
PRESIDENT—DOMESTIC SYNDICATION
Joseph D. Zaleski
EXECUTIVE VICE PRESIDENT—MARKETING
Dennis Gillespie
EXECUTIVE VICE PRESIDENT—SALES
Paul Kalvin
EXECUTIVE VICE PRESIDENT—INTERNATIONAL
Raul Lefcovich
SENIOR VICE PRESIDENT—SALES, CENTRAL
Dennis Emerson
SENIOR VICE PRESIDENT—SALES, SOUTH
Frank Flanagan
SENIOR VICE PRESIDENT—DEVELOPMENT AND PRODUCTION
Toby Martin
SENIOR VICE PRESIDENT—ANCILLARY RIGHTS AND SPECIAL PROJECTS
Peter A. Newman
SENIOR VICE PRESIDENT—OPERATIONS
Eric Veale

VIACOM PRODUCTIONS

PRESIDENT
Thomas Tannenbaum
SENIOR VICE PRESIDENT—BUSINESS AFFAIRS
Roger Kirman
SENIOR VICE PRESIDENT—PRODUCTIONS
Mike Moder

VIACOM WORLD WIDE

PRESIDENT
Arthur Kananack
VICE PRESIDENT—BUSINESS DEVELOPMENT
David Archer
VICE PRESIDENT—BUSINESS DEVELOPMENT
Judy Pless

VIACOM ENTERTAINMENT—PRIMARY CONTACTS

VICE PRESIDENT—PUBLIC RELATIONS
Betsy Vorce
DIRECTOR—HUMAN RESOURCES
Cecelia Holloway
VICE PRESIDENT—COUNSEL/ENTERTAINMENT
Katherine A. Hogan

Viacom Broadcasting

CHAIRMAN AND CHIEF EXECUTIVE OFFICER
Henry S. Schleiff
SENIOR VICE PRESIDENT, PRESIDENT/TELEVISION DIVISION
Francis P. Brady
SENIOR VICE PRESIDENT, PRESIDENT/RADIO DIVISION
William R. Figenshu
SENIOR VICE PRESIDENT AND CHIEF FINANCIAL OFFICER
Michael Keslo
VICE PRESIDENT—PUBLIC RELATIONS
Betsy Vorce
VICE PRESIDENT—HUMAN RESOURCES
Harrison Slaton
VICE PRESIDENT—COUNSEL/COMMUNICATIONS
Edward N. Schor

Viacom Networks

SHOWTIME NETWORKS INC.

CHAIRMAN AND CHIEF EXECUTIVE OFFICER
Winston H. (Tony) Cox
PRESIDENT/VIACOM NETWORK ENTERPRISES
Ronald C. Bernard

PRESIDENT/SHOWTIME EVENT TELEVISION
Scott Kurnit
EXECUTIVE VICE PRESIDENT—MARKETING
Matthew Blank
EXECUTIVE VICE PRESIDENT—SALES, BUSINESS DEVELOPMENT AND AFFILIATE MARKETING
Jack Heim
EXECUTIVE VICE PRESIDENT—GENERAL COUNSEL
Gregory J. Ricca
EXECUTIVE VICE PRESIDENT, GENERAL MANAGER/ SHOWTIME SATELLITE NETWORKS INC.
Stephen Schulte
SENIOR VICE PRESIDENT AND CFO
Arthur G. Cooper
SENIOR VICE PRESIDENT—OPERATIONS
Scott Davis
SENIOR VICE PRESIDENT—CREATIVE SERVICES
Ann Foley-Plunkett
SENIOR VICE PRESIDENT—ORIGINAL PROGRAMS
Steve Hewitt
SENIOR VICE PRESIDENT—AFFILIATE MARKETING
Rick Howe
SENIOR VICE PRESIDENT—ORIGINAL PROGRAMS
Gary Keeper
SENIOR VICE PRESIDENT—CORPORATE AFFAIRS
McAdory Lipscomb, Jr.
SENIOR VICE PRESIDENT—PROGRAMS ACQUISITIONS AND PLANNING
James Miller
SENIOR VICE PRESIDENT—SPECIAL MARKETS AND BUSINESS DEVELOPMENT
Matthew Riklin
SENIOR VICE PRESIDENT—BUSINESS AFFAIRS
William Rogers
SENIOR VICE PRESIDENT—CONSUMER MARKETING
Nora Ryan
SENIOR VICE PRESIDENT—ADMINISTRATION
Dwight Tierney

SHOWTIME NETWORKS INC.—PRIMARY CONTACTS

DIRECTOR—CORPORATE AND INDUSTRY RELATIONS
Nancy R. Glauberman
SENIOR VICE PRESIDENT—ADMINISTRATION
Dwight Tierney
EXECUTIVE VICE PRESIDENT—GENERAL COUNSEL/ NETWORKS GROUP
Gregory J. Ricca

MTV NETWORKS

CHAIRMAN AND CHIEF EXECUTIVE OFFICER
Thomas E. Freston
EXECUTIVE VICE PRESIDENT—CORPORATE AFFAIRS AND COMMUNICATIONS
Marshall Cohen
EXECUTIVE VICE PRESIDENT—NEW BUSINESS DEVELOPMENT
Sara Levinson
EXECUTIVE VICE PRESIDENT—GENERAL COUNSEL
Gregory J. Ricca
SENIOR VICE PRESIDENT—OPERATIONS
Scott Davis
SENIOR VICE PRESIDENT—ADVERTISING SALES
Douglas Greenlaw
SENIOR VICE PRESIDENT AND CHIEF FINANCIAL OFFICER
James M. Shaw
SENIOR VICE PRESIDENT—ADMINISTRATION
Dwight Tierney
VICE PRESIDENT—HUMAN RESOURCES
John Mulvey

MTV: MUSIC TELEVISION

PRESIDENT
John D. Reardon
EXECUTIVE VICE PRESIDENT AND GENERAL MANAGER
Lee Masters
SENIOR VICE PRESIDENT—MARKETING AND PROMOTION
Robert Friedman
SENIOR VICE PRESIDENT—PROGRAMS AND DEVELOPMENT
Douglas Herzog
SENIOR VICE PRESIDENT—CREATIVE DIRECTOR
Judith McGrath
SENIOR VICE PRESIDENT—AFFILIATE SALES AND MARKETING
Mark Rosenthal
SENIOR VICE PRESIDENT—AFFILIATE SALES AND MARKETING
John Shaker

NICKELODEON/NICK AT NITE

PRESIDENT
Geraldine Laybourne
SENIOR VICE PRESIDENT—PROGRAMMING
Deborah Beece
SENIOR VICE PRESIDENT—MARKETING
Richard Cronin
SENIOR VICE PRESIDENT—PRODUCTION
Geoffrey Darby

VH-1/VIDEO HITS ONE

PRESIDENT
Edward A. Bennett
VICE PRESIDENT
Jeffrey Rowe
VICE PRESIDENT—MARKETING
Leslye Schaefer

MTV NETWORKS—PRIMARY CONTACTS

VICE PRESIDENT—CORPORATE COMMUNICATIONS FOR PRESS AND PUBLIC AFFAIRS
Barry D. Kluger
SENIOR VICE PRESIDENT—ADMINISTRATION
Dwight Tierney
EXECUTIVE VICE PRESIDENT—GENERAL COUNSEL/ NETWORKS GROUP
Gregory J. Ricca

Viacom Cable

PRESIDENT AND CHIEF EXECUTIVE OFFICER
John W. Goddard
SENIOR VICE PRESIDENT—OPERATIONS REGION II
Garrett J. Girvan
SENIOR VICE PRESIDENT—OPERATIONS REGION I
Kurt E. Jorgensen
VICE PRESIDENT—HUMAN RESOURCES
Bruce Gillman
CHIEF FINANCIAL OFFICER
John Kopchik

VIACOM CABLE—PRIMARY CONTACTS

DIRECTOR—PUBLIC RELATIONS
Peggy Keegan
VICE PRESIDENT—HUMAN RESOURCES
Bruce Gillman
VICE PRESIDENT—COUNSEL/COMMUNICATIONS
Edward N. Schor

Viacom Pictures

CHAIRMAN
Neil S. Braun
PRESIDENT AND CHIEF EXECUTIVE OFFICER
Frederick Schneier
VICE PRESIDENT
Barbara Title
BOARD OF DIRECTORS
CHAIRMAN OF THE BOARD
Sumner M. Redstone
PRESIDENT AND CHIEF EXECUTIVE OFFICER
Frank J. Biondi, Jr.
PARTNER, WINER AND ABRAMS
George S. Abrams
PARTNER, SHEARMAN AND STERLING
Philippe P. Dauman
CHIEF OPERATING OFFICER, NATIONAL AMUSEMENTS, INC.
Ira A. Korff
TREASURER, NATIONAL AMUSEMENTS, INC.
Jerome Magner
CHAIRMAN, LODESTAR GROUP
Kenneth H. Miller
DEAN, BOSTON UNIVERSITY SCHOOL OF LAW
William Schwartz

REGIONAL OFFICES

New York: Viacom International Inc. 1211 Avenue of the Americas, New York, NY 10036; (212) 575-5175.

Los Angeles: Viacom Enterprises, Viacom Productions, Viacom Entertainment Group, Viacom Pictures, 10 Universal City Plaza, Universal City, CA 91608; (818) 505-7500.

Atlanta: Viacom Enterprises, 400 Perimeter Center Terrace, Suite 982, Atlanta, GA 30346; (404) 399-5356.

Chicago: Viacom Enterprises, 10 South Riverside Plaza, Suite 316, Chicago, IL 60606; (312) 648-0632.

Dallas: Viacom Enterprises, 433 East Las Colinas Boulevard, Suite 1160, Irving, TX 75039; (214) 402-9164.

Pleasanton: Viacom Cablevision (Headquarters), 5924 Stoneridge Drive, P.O. Box 13, Pleasanton, CA 94566; (415) 463-0870.

New York: MTV Networks (Headquarters), 1775 Broadway, New York, NY 10019; (212) 713-6400. Showtime Networks Inc. (Headquarters), 1633 Broadway, New York, NY 10019; (212) 703-1600.

INTERNATIONAL OFFICES

London: Viacom International Limited, 40 Conduit Street, London, England WIR 9FB; 011-441-434-4483.
Sydney: Viacom International Pty. Limited, 16th Floor, St. Martin's Tower, 31 Market Street, Sydney, N.S.W. 2000, Australia; 011-612-261-5391.
São Paulo: Viacom Video Audio Communicacoes Ltda., Alameda Jau', 1742-11 Andar, Caixa Postal 51521, 01420, São Paulo, Brazil; 011-55-11-853-4633.
Tokyo: Viacom Japan, Inc., 4F, Mitsuwa Building, 7–2 Ginza 6–Chome, Chuo-Ku, Tokyo 104, Japan; 011-813-573-0551.
Canada: 45 Charles Street, East, Toronto 5, Ontario, Canada M4Y 1S2; (416) 925-3161.
Switzerland: Viacom SA, Chamerstrasse 18, 6300 Zug, Switzerland; 011-41-42-21-8122.

Warner Bros. Television

4000 Warner Blvd., Burbank CA 91522; (818) 954-6000; Telex: 4720389. 75 Rockefeller Plaza, New York, NY 10019; (212) 484-8000.

TELEVISION PROGRAMMING

PRESIDENT
Harvey Shephard
EXECUTIVE VICE PRESIDENT
Barry M. Meyer
VICE PRESIDENT, SPECIAL PROJECTS
Karen Cooper Minnides
SENIOR VICE PRESIDENT, BUSINESS AFFAIRS
Art Stolnitz
VICE PRESIDENT, SENIOR ADVERTISING, PUBLICITY & PROMOTION EXECUTIVE
Doug Duitsman
SENIOR VICE PRESIDENT, PRODUCTION
Gary Credle
VICE PRESIDENT, MOVIES FOR TELEVISION AND MINI-SERIES
Norman Stephens
VICE PRESIDENT, CURRENT PROGRAMMING
David Sacks
VICE PRESIDENT, MOVIES & MINISERIES
Gregg Maday
VICE PRESIDENT, COMEDY DEVELOPMENT
Scott Kaufer
VICE PRESIDENT, CREATIVE AFFAIRS/EAST COAST
Susan Dalismer
VICE PRESIDENT, TALENT
Marcia Ross
VICE PRESIDENTS, BUSINESS AFFAIRS
Beverly Nix, Joe Reilly, Art Horan
VICE PRESIDENT, LEGAL AFFAIRS
Milt Segal
VICE PRESIDENT, FILM & TAPE PRODUCTION
Steve Papazian
VICE PRESIDENT, POST PRODUCTION
Karen Pingitore
VICE PRESIDENT, PRODUCTION & OPERATIONS
Tom Treloggen
VICE PRESIDENT, STORY & VOCATIONAL ADMINISTRATION
Gus Blackmon
DIRECTOR, PUBLICITY, PROMOTION & ADVERTISING
Claire Lee
DIRECTOR, FINANCIAL ADMINISTRATION
Rosalee Jeffries
DIRECTOR, TV ESTIMATING
Mike McKnight
DIRECTOR, TALENT
John Levey
DIRECTOR, DRAMA DEVELOPMENT
Susan Horowitz
DIRECTOR, COMEDY DEVELOPMENT
Shelley Raskov
DIRECTOR, CURRENT PROGRAMMING
Debbie Langford

NETWORK FEATURES, PAY TV & ANIMATION (WARNER BROS. CARTOONS, INC.)

75 Rockefeller Plaza, New York, NY 10019; (212) 484-8000.

PRESIDENT & PRESIDENT, WARNER BROS. ANIMATION
Edward Bleier
VICE PRESIDENT, PAY TV SALES & ADMINISTRATION
Stanley Solson
VICE PRESIDENT, MARKETING
Eric Frankel
DIRECTOR, FINANCIAL AFFAIRS
J. T. Shadoan
DIRECTOR, CLIENT SERVICES, PAY TV & NETWORK
Margaret Jelcich
MANAGER, ADVERTISING, PUBLICITY & PROMOTION
Barry Marx
MANAGER, PAY-TV MARKETING
Jeffrey Bernstein

WARNER BROS. ANIMATION, INC.

4000 Warner Blvd., Burbank, CA 91522; (818) 954-3713.

VICE PRESIDENT, GENERAL MANAGER
Jean MacCurdy
VICE PRESIDENT, PRODUCTION & ADMINISTRATION
Kathleen Helppie

WARNER BROS. DOMESTIC TELEVISION DISTRIBUTION

4000 Warner Blvd., Burbank, CA 91522; (818) 954-6000, Telex: 4720389.

PRESIDENT
Dick Robertson

FIRST RUN DIVISION

SENIOR VICE PRESIDENT
Scott Carlin

Eastern Sales
VICE PRESIDENT/MANAGER
Mark Robbins
VICE PRESIDENT
Alicia Windroth
VICE PRESIDENT
Damian Riordan
VICE PRESIDENT
Richard Cartier
DIRECTOR
Andrew Weir
DIRECTOR
Eric Strong
ACCOUNT EXECUTIVE
Jillian Lines

Western Sales
VICE PRESIDENT/MANAGER
Jeff Hufford
VICE PRESIDENT
Mark O'Brien
DIRECTOR
Ed Wasserman
DIRECTOR
Jacqueline Hartley
DIRECTOR
William Hague
DIRECTOR
Mary Markarian

OFF-NETWORK DIVISION

SENIOR VICE PRESIDENT
Keith Samples

New York
VICE PRESIDENT
Rob Barnett
DIRECTOR
Mary Voll
DIRECTOR
Scott Weber

Chicago
VICE PRESIDENT
Steve Knowles
VICE PRESIDENT
John Louis
DIRECTOR
Chris Smith

Los Angeles
VICE PRESIDENT
Vince Messina

VICE PRESIDENT
Jim Burke
MANAGER
Jeff Brooks

Atlanta
VICE PRESIDENT
Bruce Genter

FEATURE FILM DIVISION

SENIOR VICE PRESIDENT
Bill Hart
SALES ADMINISTRATOR
Eleanor Liebs

MEDIA SALES DIVISION

SENIOR VICE PRESIDENT
Karl Kuechenmeister
VICE PRESIDENT/GENERAL SALES MANAGER
Jim Engleman

New York
VICE PRESIDENT
Marc Solomon
VICE PRESIDENT
Julie Kantrowitz

Chicago
VICE PRESIDENT
Jim Harder

Los Angeles
SENIOR VICE PRESIDENT
Leon Luxenberg

CREATIVE SERVICES

SENIOR VICE PRESIDENT
Jim Moloshok
VICE PRESIDENT, CREATIVE SERVICES
Yelena Lazovich
VICE PRESIDENT, STATION PROMOTION
Martin Iker
DIRECTOR, CREATIVE SERVICES
Cynthia Stanley
DIRECTOR, CREATIVE SERVICES
Joel Kaplan
DIRECTOR, ART SERVICES
Ronald Ascher

RESEARCH

SENIOR VICE PRESIDENT
Bruce Rosenblum
VICE PRESIDENT, SENIOR RESEARCH ADVISOR
Wayne Neiman
VICE PRESIDENT, RESEARCH
Leonard Bart
VICE PRESIDENT, OFF-NETWORK & CABLE
Robert Jennings
DIRECTOR, FIRST RUN
Jocelyn Chan

ADMINISTRATION

SENIOR VICE PRESIDENT
Leon Luxenberg
VICE PRESIDENT, FINANCE
Julio Proietto
VICE PRESIDENT/DIR. DOM. CONTRACTS
Dan McRae
DIRECTOR DOMESTIC DIST.
Chip Aycock

BRANCH OFFICES

Chicago: 645 N. Michigan Avenue, Chicago, Illinois 60611.

New York: 1350 Avenue of the Americas, New York, NY 10019.

New Orleans: 406 Chartres St. #2, New Orleans, LA 70130.

Atlanta: 109 Stonington Drive, Peach Tree City, GA 30269.

Ft. Mitchell, Kentucky: 3058 Brookwood Circle, Fort Mitchell, KY 41017.

BOOKING & SERVICES DEPARTMENT

New York: 630 Ninth Avenue, New York, NY 10036; (212) 484-8000.

TECHNICAL SERVICE DIRECTOR
Erwin Markisch
MANAGER, BOOKING SERVICES
Joe Kivlehan
MANAGER, PROGRAM INFORMATION
Louis B. Marino

BRANCH OFFICES:

Covington: Lowe Davis Rd., P.O. Box 999, Covington, LA 70434; (504) 892-2703.

VICE PRESIDENT, SOUTHEASTERN SALES DIRECTOR
Bill Seiler

Los Angeles: 143 Patricia Way, P.O. Box 2749, Grass Valley, CA 95945; (916) 272-5343.

Ft. Mitchell: 3058 Brookwood Circle, Ft. Mitchell, KY 41017; (606) 341-2585.

VICE PRESIDENT, MIDWESTERN SALES
John H. Louis

Chicago: 4000 Warner Blvd., Burbank, CA 91522; (818) 954-6097.

NORTH CENTRAL SALES DIRECTOR
John Laing

Pennsylvania: 50 Belmont Ave., Apt. 316, Bala Cynwyd, PA 19004; (215) 664-7307.

EASTERN SALES DIRECTOR
Gary Cozen

WARNER BROS. INTERNATIONAL TELEVISION DISTRIBUTION

4000 Warner Blvd., Burbank, CA 91511; (818) 954-6000; Telex: 4720389.

PRESIDENT
Michael Jay Solomon
SENIOR VICE PRESIDENT
Jeffrey Schlesinger
SENIOR VICE PRESIDENT, LONDON
Stuart Graber
VICE PRESIDENT, LONDON
Bryan Hambleton
VICE PRESIDENT, FRANCE
Michel Lecourt
VICE PRESIDENT, AUSTRALIA & FAR EAST
Greg Robertson
VICE PRESIDENT, LATIN AMERICA
Jorge Sanchez
MANAGING DIRECTOR, ITALY
Rosario Ponzio
SALES EXECUTIVE, AUSTRALIA & FAR EAST
Greg Robertson
SALES EXECUTIVE, SPAIN
Kevin Williams
SALES EXECUTIVE, SCANDINAVIA-BENELUX
David Peebler
SALES EXECUTIVE, EASTERN EUROPE
Donna Brett
VICE PRESIDENT, INTERNATIONAL TELEVISION BUSINESS AFFAIRS
Adina Savin
VICE PRESIDENT, INTERNATIONAL TELEVISION DISTRIBUTION
Bonnie Adamson
VICE PRESIDENT, INTERNATIONAL CONTRACT ADMINISTRATION
John Whitesall
VICE PRESIDENT, INTERNATIONAL SALES ADMINISTRATION
Tommie Van Benschoten
VICE PRESIDENT, INTERNATIONAL TELEVISION OPERATIONS
Annette Bouso
DIRECTOR, PROMOTION & PUBLICITY
Sharon Kneller
DIRECTOR, INTERNATIONAL MARKETING
Brenda Geffner
MANAGER, HOME VIDEO SALES
Lisa Gregorian

FOREIGN SALES OFFICES

EUROPE, MIDDLE EAST & AFRICA: 135/141 Wardour St., London W1V 4AP, England.

VICE PRESIDENT SALES & ADMINISTRATION
Bryan Hambleton

ASSISTANT DIRECTOR SALES & ADMINISTRATION
Gary Phillips
SALES REPRESENTATIVE
Kevin Williams

FRENCH SPEAKING TERRITORIES: 20 Rue Troyon, 75017 Paris, France.

VICE PRESIDENT, TELEVISION
Michel Lecourt

AUSTRALIA, NEW ZEALAND & SOUTHEAST ASIA: 154 Castlereagh St.—5th floor, Alfred Moss House, Sydney, N.S.W., 2000 Australia, Box 2661, G.P.O. Sydney, N.S.W., 2001 Australia.

SALES DIRECTOR
Matt Brown

JAPAN: P.O. Box 762, Tokyo Central, Japan.

TELEVISION SALES
Ken Sugizaki

LATIN AMERICA: Acapulco 37, Mexico 7 D.F., Mexico.

VICE PRESIDENT SALES
Jorge Sanchez

BRAZIL: Warner Bros. (South) Inc., Rua Senador Dantas, 19-10 Andar, Rio de Janeiro, Brazil.

BRAZIL TELEVISION SUPERVISOR
Louremberg do Nascimento

ARGENTINA: Tucuman 1938, Buenos Aires, Argentina.

TELEVISION MANAGER
Luis D'Alterio

CANADA: Warner Bros. Distributing, (Canada) Ltd., 70 Carlton St., Toronto, Ontario, Canada, M5B 1L7; (416) 922-5145.

William Morris Agency, Inc.

1350 Avenue of the Americas, New York, NY 10019; (212) 586-5100; FAX: (212) 246-3583. Beverly Hills Office: 151 El Camino, Beverly Hills, CA 90212; (213) 274-7451; FAX: (213) 859-4462. Nashville Office: 2325 Crestmoor Rd., Nashville, TN 37215; (615) 385-0310; FAX: (615) 297-6694. Overseas offices: London, Rome,* Sydney,* Munich.* (Representatives for artists and all creative talent in the entertainment and literary worlds.) *Corresponding offices.

CHAIRMAN
Lou Weiss (New York)
PRESIDENT & CHIEF EXECUTIVE OFFICER
Norman Brokaw
EXECUTIVE VICE PRESIDENTS
Roger Davis, Tony Fantozzi, Walt Zifkin (Chief Operating Officer), Larry Auerbach, Leonard Hirshan, Jerry Katzman, Owen Laster
VICE PRESIDENT, TREASURER
Larry Lewis (New York)

MOTION PICTURE DEPARTMENT

Beverly Hills—Department Head, Sue Mengers
John Burnham, Jim Crabbe, Ames Cushing, Dodie Gold, David Goldman, Elaine Goldsmith, Jean-Pierre Henreaux, Leonard Hirshan, Andy Howard, Toni Howard, Joan Hyler, Alan Iezman, Ron Mardigian, Mike Peretzian, John Ptak, Jeff Rose, Judy Scott-Fox, Risa Shapiro, Mike Simpson, Dan Strone, Beth Swofford, Bobbi Thompson, Peter Turner, Irene Webb, Fred Westheimer, Cary Woods, Carol Yumkas, Scott Zimmerman.
New York—Department Head, Steven Starr
Boaty Boatwright, Anne Carey, Peter Franklin, Myrna Jacoby, George Lane, Owen Laster, Phyllis Levy, Biff Liff, Gilbert Parker, Johnnie Planco, Ed Robbins, Katy Rothacker, Tina Russell, Esther Sherman.

TELEVISION DEPARTMENT

Worldwide Head, Jerry Katzman
Beverly Hills—Department Head, Robert Crestani
Jeff Alpern, Larry Auerbach, Arthur Axelman, Bruce Brown, Lee Cohen, Ruth Engelhardt, Steve Glick, Michael Gruber, Sam Haskell, Dick Howard, Mark Itkin, Sol Leon, Greg Lipstone, Gary Loder, Deborah Miller, Larry Noveck, Bonnie Owens, Gary Rado, Elizabeth Ramsland, Leonard Rosenberg, Hal Ross, Marc Schwartz, Chris Simonian, Kathy Smith, Toper Taylor, Mark Teitlebaum, Steve Weiss, Jeff Witjas.
New York—Department Head, Leo Bookman/Jim Griffin
Adam Berkowitz, James Dixon, Art Fuhrer, Henry Reisch, David Segal, Cara Stein.
DIRECTOR OF PUBLICITY
Florence Gaines

Zenith Electronics Corporation

1000 Milwaukee Ave., Glenview, IL 60025; (312) 391-8181.

(Consumer home entertainment products; electronic do-it-yourself kits, instruments, home study education materials; microcomputer systems, video display terminals, components, and cable and subscription TV and videotex products.)

PRESIDENT AND CHIEF EXECUTIVE OFFICER
Revone W. Kluckman
SENIOR VICE PRESIDENT AND GROUP EXECUTIVE, CONSUMER PRODUCTS
Robert B. Hansen
GENERAL MANAGER CATV/STV OPERATIONS
James Faust

Television Producers-Distributors

* PROGRAMS
* COMMERCIALS
* TELEVISION FILMS
* SHORTS

Producers and Distributors

A.B. Enterprises, Inc.

1560 Broadway, Suite 1101, New York, NY 10036; (212) 575-9494. Alexander Beck, president. (Distributes feature films, shorts and Westerns.)

ABC Distribution Co.

(A division of Capital Cities/ABC Video Enterprises)
825 Seventh Ave., New York, NY 10019; (212) 887-1725. Telex: 234337. FAX: (212) 887-1708; 2040 Avenue of the Stars, Century City, CA 90067; (213) 557-6600; Fax: (213) 557-7925; Telex: 673127. John T. Healy, president, ABC Distribution Company; Archie Purvis, senior vice president; Paul Coss, vice president, acquisitions & development; Marvinia Anderson, director, worldwide cable/cassette marketing; Armando Nunex, Jr., director, international TV sales.

- Series: Crosstown, Globe TV, Visions, Heroes, Eagle & the Bear, Great TV News Stories, Miller & Mueller, Moonlighting, Secrets & Mysteries.
- Mini-Series: Baby M, Amerika, Ike, Out on A Limb.
- Made-For-TV Movies: Lady-Killers, Acceptable Risks, Amazons, Best Kept Secrets, A Bunny's Tale, Embassy, The Hearst and Davies Affair, Infidelity, Jacqueline Bouvier Kennedy, The Jericho Mile; Long Time Gone, Love Lives On, The Midnight Hour, Million Dollar Hijack, My Mother's Secret Life, Triplecross, Who Will Love My Children?
- Features: Cabaret, The Day After, The Flamingo Kid, Hoodwinked, Impulse, Milk & Honey, National Lampoon's Class Reunion, Prizzi's Honor, Silkwood, SpaceCamp, Young Doctors in Love, etc.
- Sports.
- News Specials.
- Documentaries.
- Children's Programming.
- Academy Awards Special—International version.

ABC News/Weintraub Productions

11111 Santa Monica Blvd., Los Angeles, CA 90025; (213) 477-8900.

- The Eagle & The Bear, Heroes.

ABR Entertainment Company

32123 Lindero Canyon Rd., Suite 2067, Westlake Village, CA 91361; (818) 706-7727. (Producer and distributor) Alexander B. Rosen, chm. & CEO; Ed Hawkins, exec. v.p.; Celinda Glickman, v.p., operations.

A.L.S. Production Services

6381 Virginia Hills Dr., Salt Lake City, UT 84121; Alvin Simmons, pres. (Motion picture & television producer's services, equipment rentals, sales, lease and servicing. All facets of production equipment & services.)

APA Studios, Inc.

230 W. 10 St., New York, NY 10014; (212) 929-9436. Organized 1963. (Special effects motion picture firm working in commercials, features, industrials; stop-motion, 3-D Animation hi-speed, time-lapse, locals and graphics, total production). Lee Howard, pres.; David Rogers, art director; Robert Self, production mgr.

Academy Film Productions, Inc.

3918 W. Estes Ave., Lincolnwood, IL 60645; (708) 674-2122. Bernard Howard, pres. (Produce live and filmed or video-taped shows and commercials, slides, animation, slide films and industrial films).

Act III Entertainment of Tennessee, Inc.

631 Mainstream Drive, Nashville, TN 37228; (615) 244-1717. Steve A. Womack, exec. vice president and gen. manager. (Producer.)

Act III Television

1800 Century Park East, Suite 200, Los Angeles, CA 90067; (213) 553-3636. Norman Lear, chmn., CEO; Deborah Aal, pres., television. (A division of Act III Communications, Inc. which owns and operates 6 indep. TV stations as well as Santikos and Presidio theater circuits, publishes several magazines and produces TV and motion pictures.)

Alden Films

P.O. Box 449, Clarksburg, NJ 08510; (201) 462-3522. Paul Weinberg, pres. (Film and video distributors for Jewish Chautauqua Society, Natl. Council of Jewish Women, Eternal Light Film Library, Jewish Natl. Fund, Women's American ORT, Pioneer Women/Namaat, United Jewish Appeal, American Red Magen David, American Society for Technion, State of Israel, Jewish Theological Seminary of America, Yeshiva U. Museum.)

All American Television

304 E. 45 St., New York, NY 10017; (212) 818-1200. (Distributor) George Back, pres.; Joseph E. Kovacs, exec. v.p.; Joan Marcus, v.p. synd.; Conrad Roth, sr. v.p.; John Reisenbach, senior v.p., national advertising sales; Carl W. Menk, Jr., v.p., station sales and marketing; Todd C. Jackson, v.p., international sales.

Almi Television Productions

1900 Broadway, New York, NY 10023; (212) 769-6400. Martin Schildkraut, exec.

- Theatrical feature packages: Almi Film Festival (10); Children's Cinema Classics (65); Kung-Fu (13); She's A Lady (19); Hot Rocks (8); Thriller (18); Almi Passport (33); Great Comedy Volume I (32); Great Comedy—Volume II (15); ½ hour animated special: Kitten's Christmas.

Amblin Entertainment

100 Universal Plaza, Bungalow 477, Universal City, CA 91608; (818) 777-4600. Carole Kirschner, v.p., television production.

- Amazing Stories.
- Specials: China Odyssey: Steven Spielberg's Empire of the Sun; Making of Raiders of the Lost Ark.

American Adventure Productions, Inc.

314 C Mediterranean Ave., Aspen, CO 81611; (303) 920-3777. John Wilcox, pres.; Josiah Wilcox, secty. (Producers of adventure and wildlife documentaries)

Amrit Productions, Inc.

215 W. 90 St., Penthouse B, New York, NY 10024; (212) 877-3623. Tirlok Malik, pres.; Chander Malik, v.p. (Producer and arranger of production and co-production of films for TV and video; arranges casting for Indian actors; also distributes video films.)

Animated Productions, Inc.

1600 Broadway, New York, NY 10019; Columbus 5-2942. Al Stahl, pres.; Richard Stahl, v.p.; Shirlee Debrier, production dir.; Peter Puzzo, exec. dir. (Producers of programs, television commercials, cartoons and shorts, industrial films, specialists in animation, stop motion, and fotomation.) Fully-animated with punched tape—animation stand, precision Super 8 blow-up optical bench, Super 8 with opticals.)

Arlington Film Studios

120–37 101st Ave. No., Seminole, FL 34642. Organized 1962. (Produce all types sound and silent motion picture films.) Producer: Frank Ruzz.

The Arthur Company

100 Universal City Plaza, Universal City, CA 91608; (818) 505-1200. Arthur Annecharico, exec. prod.

- Adam-12 (syndication)
- Blood Money

Arztco Pictures, Inc.

15 E. 61 Street, New York, NY 10021; (212) 753-1050. Organized 1967. (Production of motion pictures, commercials, industrials, and video.) Tony Arzt, pres., prod./dir.

Tamara Asseyev Productions, Inc.

10 University City Plaza, 32nd Floor, Universal City, CA 91608; (818) 505-7566; FAX: (818) 505-7599. Tamara Asseyev, pres.; E.J. Oshins, v.p., development.

Associated Press Broadcast Services

1825 K Street, N.W., Suite 615, Washington, D.C. 20007; (202) 955-7243. Jim Williams, deputy director. (TV Direct, the first nonexclusive video news service available to all TV news operations, including Washington Direct, BeatChecks, and AP Videographs; APTV Wire, the AP's high-speed selectable wire for TV stations.)

Associated Television International

P.O. Box 4180, Hollywood, CA 90078; (650 N. Bronson St., Suite 300) (213) 871-1340. Organized 1979. John Campbell Collins, v.p. marketing; Rex Piano, v.p. development; David McKenzie, C.O.O. (Television syndication and distribution.)

Atlantic Television, Inc.

Operational Headquarters, sales and distribution office: 8255 Sunset Blvd., Los Angeles, CA 90046; (213) 650-2500. Jonathan M. Dana, pres., m.p. & TV; Patricia Furnare, v.p., worldwide operations.

Atlantis Films Limited

Cinevillage, 65 Heward Ave., Toronto, Ontario, Canada M4M 2T5; (416) 462-0246. Organized 1982. Michael MacMillan, pres; Seaton McLean, v.p.s; Peter Sussman, exec. prod. (Television and film production.)

Atlantis Releasing

65 Heward Ave., Toronto, Ontario, Canada M4M 2T5; (416) 462-0016. Organized 1983. Ted Riley, pres.; Jacqueline Scott, manager of sales; Karen Lawrie, distribution assistant. Affiliated with Atlantis Films Limited. (Markets, sells and distributes films to Canadian and international television and home video marketplace.)

Audio Productions

(A division of Reeves Teletape, Inc.) 227 E. 45 St., New York, NY 10017. (212) 573-8656. Peter J. Mooney, pres.; (Producers of Educational-Documentary and Industrial Films).

Aurora General Entertainment Corp.

5950 West Oakland Park Blvd., Fort Lauderdale, FL 33313 (305); 733-3500.

- War Chronicles, Judy Garland specials, The Littlest Angel, Raggedy Ann and Andy, feature film packages, James Michener Specials, Upstairs at Xenon, The Amazing World of Kreskin.

B

BBC Enterprises Limited

Head Office: Woodlands, 80 Wood Lane, London W12 0TT. Tel.: (01) 576-2000. James Arnold-Baker, Chief Executive, BBC Australia, Hugh Sheppard, Westfield Towers, 80 William St., Sydney; Tel: Sydney 35866411. USA Television Sales: Lionheart Television International Inc., 630 Fifth Ave., Suite 2220, New York, NY 10111; (212) 541-7342. Canada, Educational & Training Sales, Hilary Read, Cinevillage, 65 Heward., Suite 111, Toronto, Ontario M4M 2TS. (BBC Enterprises distributes all types of BBC TV programming, licenses BBC titles for merchandising including the BBC microcomputer, produces BBC Video, BBC Records and BBC Books and provides facilities for other broadcasters.)

BBC/Lionheart Television

630 Fifth Avenue, #2220, New York, NY 10111; (212) 541-7000. (Distribution.) Jack Mastos, president & CEO; Maq Jawed, CFO; Sylvia Delia, v.p. ancillaries; Candace Carlisle, v.p. PBS sales; Beth Cleartiel, dir. programming; Susan Rosenberg, director creative services.

Bob Banner Associates, Inc.

132 S. Rodeo Dr., Suite 402, Beverly Hills, CA 90212; (213) 274-0442. Bob Banner, pres.; J. William Hayes, first v.p.; Stephen Pouliot, v.p. (Production of television programs, motion pictures and theatrical productions.)

Barbre Productions, Inc.

Div. of Combined Communications Corporation, P.O. Box 5667, 1089 Bannock St., Denver, CO 80217, (303) 266-3601. Alvin G. Flanagan, pres.; Jon D. Ackelson, producer/director. (Producer, distributor of filmed shows, producer of film commercials and business films.)

- Prairie World of the Kit Fox (1); Valley of the Standing Rocks (1); Harry Jackson—A Man and His Art; The Troopers Are Coming; Rocky Mountain Conquest.

Robert Baron & Associates

63-33 98th Pl., Forest Hills, NY 11374; (212) 302-1515. Robert Baron, pres., prod.; John Whited, director; West Coast studio facilities, Helen Miles, mgr. & Prod.; Jules Brenner & Gayne Rascher, cameramen; Angie Ross, supervising editor. (Producers of TV commercials, industrials, sales promotion film & multi-media presentations; complete video tape facilities.)

Barris Industries Inc.

1990 S. Bundy Dr., Penthouse, Los Angeles, CA 90025; (213) 820-2100. Jeff Wald, pres. TV division.

- Syndication: All New Dating Game; The Gong Show; The Newlywed Game; Kenny Rogers Classic Weekend; The Kenny Rogers Show.

Barry & Enright Productions

1888 Century Park East, Suite 1100, Los Angeles, CA, 90067; (213) 556-1000. Organized 1975. Dan Enright, pres.; Don Enright, v.p., development; Les Alexander, v.p., development; Louis "Deke" Heyward, v.p., development; Mike Bevan, v.p., development, games shows; Chris Sohl, v.p. administration. (Produces network and syndicated programs, games, quizzes, sitcoms, movies-of-the-week, features.)

Ben Barry & Associates, Inc.

10246 Briarwood Dr., Los Angeles, CA 90077; (213) 274-1523. Ben Barry, pres.

- Feature films, including The Family, Honey Comb, Sabra, Action Man, Assassination, I Killed Rasputin, Peking Blonde, Singapore, Singapore, Johnny Banco, Black Sun, Restless Breed, Magnificent Matador, Sword of Monte Cristo, One Russian Summer, etc.
- Feature films, under House of Horrors heading, including The She Beast, Death Dream, Fangs of the Living Dead, The Night Evelyn Came Out of the Grave, Murder Clinic, Children Shouldn't Play with Dead Things, Blood Spattered Bride, Don't Look in the Basement, Nightmare Hotel, Kiss of the Tarantula, Invisible Terror, Zombies. Science fiction features: Star Pilot, Invaders from Mars, Fantastic Invasion from Planet Earth, No Survivors Please, Electronic Monster, Fabulous World of Jules Verne. New: A Swingin' Summer, Invaders From Mars, Restless Breed, Magnificent Matador, Blood on the Arrow. Samuel Fuller classics: Shock Corridor, Naked Kiss.

The Beagle Group

420 Madison Ave., New York, NY 10017; (212) 832-0300; FAX: 832-8039. Michael Bennahum, pres. & CEO; Dan Farrell, exec. vice president; Roseanne Leto, sr. v.p. program development; Joanna Gleason, vice president. (Television and film production company.)

The Behrens Company, Inc.

51 S.W. 9th St., Miami, FL 33130; (305) 371-6077. Robert A. Behrens, pres.; Elizabeth H. Behrens, secty.

Bergman-Harris Productions, Inc.

850 Seventh Ave., Suite 404, New York, NY 10019; (212) 757-7921. Organized 1980. David Bergman, pres.; Paul Harris v.p. (Television production.)

Best Film & Video Corporation

98 Cutter Mill Rd., Great Neck, NY 11021; (516) 487-4515. Roy Winnick, pres.; Ben Tenn, exec. v.p.; Harvey Urman, sls. mgr. (Cable, video, cassette and disc distribution and production).

Binder Entertainment, Inc.

1040 N. Las Palmas, Bldg. #16, Hollywood, CA 90038; (213) 871-8102. Organized 1988. Steve Binder, pres. (Television and film production. Formerly BRB Entertainment, Inc.)

- On the Television, Beach Boys' Endless Summer series, Wayne Newton Live, Highway 101 Drive Inn for Elvis Presley, Diana Ross at Wembley Hall, London, Dionne Warwick & Friends, Zoobilee Zoo.

Milton Blackstone/Associates

P.O. Box 1892, La Jolla, CA 92038; (619) 459-8255. Milton H. Blackstone, exec. prod. (Talent, promotion and special events direction, true-life commercials, pr. films.)

- Comedians' Golf Classic; Comedy Hall of Fame (special); Wonderful World of Water (special); Beach Ball; (Pro) Am Team Golf Championship; Mother Goose Parade (special); Jr. World Golf Championship (special); Defending Champion (series); Let There Be Balls (special); Golf Derby; Show Biz Salutes (series and specials); Sports City (in preparation) '76 Andy Williams Open (90 min.); Feature Film: Cockeyed Charley; New Series in Development; Hobo; Pilot; Something to Celebrate; Days of Pleasure—Nights of Despair.

Blair Entertainment

(A division of John Blair Communications, Inc.) 1290 Ave. of the Americas, New York, NY 10104; (212) 603-5990. Alan I. Berkowitz, exec. v.p. & gen. mgr.; Michael Weiser, sr. v.p. & gen. sales mgr.; Howard Levy, v.p. of advertising sales; Ken DuBow, Northeast reg. mgr.; Ronald Geagan, Southern div. mgr.; John Buckholtz, account exec.; Evelyn Chigrinsky, account exec.

- First Run: Divorce Court (52 week first-run series).
- Feature Films: Impact I Movie Package (20 features); The Hall of Fame Collection (8 made for TV).
- Specials: Motown Merry Christmas (1 hr.); Has Anybody Seen My Child? (1 hr.); World's Greatest Stuntman (2 hrs.); Goldeneye (2 hrs.).
- Frederick Forsyth Movies (6 shows).

Steven Bochco Productions

P.O. Box 900, Beverly Hills, CA 90213; (213) 277-2211.

- Doogie Howser, M.D.

Braverman Productions, Inc.

17336 Sunset Blvd., Suite 142, Pacific Palisades, CA 90272; (213) 826-6466. Charles Braverman, pres.; Greg Griffin, development. (Producers of feature films, TV specials, documentaries, commercials, titles and special montages, specialists in kinestasis animation.)

Bray Studios, Inc.

19 Ketchum St., Westport, CT 06880; (203) 226-3777. Paul Bray, Jr., pres. (Producers and distributors of films, film strips, slides and multi-media presentations on wide variety of subject matter; services for producers include animation art and photography as well as location crews and equipment.)

Brookfield Productions, Inc.

11600 Washington Pl., Suite #201, Los Angeles, CA 90066; (213) 390-9767. Organized 1978. Norman G. Brooks, pres.; Fern Field, dir. of development. (Television film production.)

Barry Brown Brillig Prod., Inc.

770 Amalfi Dr., Pacific Palisades, CA 90272; (213) 459-4455. Organized 1959; Barry Brown, pres. (Feature motion pictures, industrial films & TV commercials.)

Buena Vista TV

(A subsidiary of The Walt Disney Company) 350 S. Buena Vista St., Burbank, CA 91521; (818) 560-5168. Robert Jacquemin, sr. v.p.; Peter Affe, v.p., eastern div. mgr.; Jamie Bennett, v.p., production/programming; Larry Frankenbach, v.p., midwest div. mgr.; Rich Goldman, v.p., gen. sls. mgr., Mary Kellogg, v.p., production; Michael Mellon, v.p., research, David Morris, v.p., western div. mgr.; Peter Newgard, v.p., southern div. mgr.

Buena Vista International, Inc.

(A subsidiary of The Walt Disney Company) 350 S. Buena Vista St., Burbank, CA 91521; (818) 560-5168. John Elia, dir. distribution; Etienne de Villiers, pres.

Bill Burrud Productions, Inc.

15922 Pacific Coast Highway, #200, Huntington Harbour, CA 92649; (213) 592-3486. Organized 1954. Bill Burrud, chmn. of bd.; John Burrud, pres.; Bruce Stuart Greenberg, v.p., in charge of production; Bev Young, exec. asst. (Feature film and TV production of animal/wildlife/human adventure documentaries/world exploration.)

- Return to Tarawa, New! Animal World, True Adventure, World of the Sea.

C

CBS Entertainment Productions

7800 Beverly Blvd., Los Angeles, CA 90036; (213) 852-2345.

- The Pat Sajak Show (CBS).

CCW Productions, Inc.

8915 Yolanda Ave., Northridge, CA 91324; (818) 993-7816; Branches: CCW Productions, Inc., Valley Bank Plaza, 300 South Fourth St., Suite 1501, Las Vegas, NE 89101. Organized 1983. Robert M. Cawley, pres./CEO; Philip L. Cuppett, v.p./CFO; Rena L. Winters, v.p., production; Bob Corrigan, prod. coordinator. (Production of feature films, TV movies and television specials).

Camelot Entertainment Sales

1700 Broadway, New York, NY 10019; (212) 315-4000. Steve Hirsch, pres.; Marsha Diamond, v.p., research.

- Wheel of Fortune; Jeopardy!; The Oprah Winfrey Show; Oprah Specials.

Steve Campus Productions, Inc.

24 Depot Square, Tuckahoe, NY 10707; (914) 961-1900. Steve Campus, pres. (Producer of educational, industrial, medical, documentary films, and multi-media productions.)

Stephen J. Cannell Prods.

7083 Hollywood Blvd., Hollywood, CA 90028; (213) 465-5800.

- The A-Team (NBC); Hardcastle & McCormick (ABC); Hunter (NBC); Riptide (NBC); The Lost Precinct (NBC), Stingray (NBC); J.J. Starbuck (NBC); Wiseguy (CBS); 21 Jump Street (FBC); Sonny Spoon (NBC); Unsub (NBC); Booker (FBC); Top of the Hill (CBS).

George Carlson & Associates

2512 Second Ave., #306, Seattle, WA 98121; (206) 441-1466. George Carlson, producer. (Program producers.)

- The Traveler/Northwest Traveler series.

Carson Productions

9489 Dayton Way, Penthouse, Beverly Hills, CA 90210; (213) 273-3777.

- Amen (NBC).
- Late Night With David Letterman (NBC).
- The Tonight Show Starring Johnny Carson (NBC).

Carthay Sound Stage

5907 W. Pico Blvd., Los Angeles, CA (213); 938-2101. (Complete film videotape services & rental center.) Contact: Helen Miles.

Casablanca Productions

8544 Sunset Blvd., Los Angeles, CA 90069; (213) 659-2067. Organized 1974. Dennis Holt, chm./chief exec. officer; David Nelson, pres./director; Gary Geweniger, exec. producer/head of production; Allen Forman, exec. producer/head of sales; Penny Johnson, post-production sprv.; Stu Berg, director; Chrissa Vayos, office coordinator. (Television commercial production.)

Castle Hill Television

1414 Ave. of the Americas, New York, NY 10019; (212) 888-0800. (Distributor)

- Regal Gold (20 theatrical features); Sterling Collection (12 theatrical features; Made in Hollywood USA (27 classic films); Fright Night (16 horror features); Muscles, Monsters & Myths (7 classics); The Best of Steve Allen (2 one-hr. specials).

CEL Communications, Inc.

515 Madison Ave., New York, NY 10022; (212) 421-4030. Merton Y. Koplin, chm. (A&E); Charles D. Grinker, vice chm., creative director; Martin L. Waldman, CEO, pres. (Creators of The Video Encyclopedia of the Twentieth Century,™ a visual encyclopedia of America in the 20th Century on videotape and laserdisc)

- Series: Creativity with Bill Moyers (A&E); A Walk Thru the 20th Century with Bill Moyers (A&E); Dining in France, 13 half-hours hosted by Pierre Salinger (PBS); The Magic Years in Sports (ESPN).

Charisma Artists Corporation

9348 Civic Center Dr., Suite 101, Beverly Hills, CA 90210; (213) 281-5915. Organized 1985. Nick Edenetti, exec. producer; Larry West, production mgr., Kathryn Lemon, secretary/treas., Aric Edenetti, casting coordinator; Fernando Alverado, associate prod.; François Favre, corp. attorney. (Television and motion picture production.)

Cinar Films Inc.

1207 St. Andre, Montreal, Quebec, H2W 1T1, Canada; (514) 843-7070. Organized 1976. Micheline Charest, pres.; Ronald A. Weinberg, v.p.; William Litwack, dir. Branches in Montreal, Toronto. (Film/TV production, distribution and video post-production).

Cinecraft Productions, Inc.

2515 Franklin Blvd., Cleveland, OH 44113; (216) 781-2300. Neil McCormick, pres.; Maria Keckan, CEO; (Production facility and services for video and film, for broadcast and corporate.)

Cinema Shares International Television, Ltd.

450 Park Ave., New York, NY 10022; (212) 421-3161. Ellen Cantor, pres. (TV distribution.)

Cinetudes Film Productions, Ltd.

295 W. 4 St., New York, NY 10014; (212) 924-0400. Christine Jurzykowski, pres.; Gale Goldberg, exec. prod.; Anita Cinnamon, mktg. dir.; Alex Gartner, dir. of devel., prod. & acquisition. (Production of TV programs, motion pictures and theatrical productions.)

Cineworld Corporation

2670 N.E. 24 St., Pompano Beach, FL 33064; (305) 781-2627. John F. Rickert, pres.; Ildiko M. Rickert, secty./treas. (Distribution, production, international co-production, financing and packaging.)

City Film Productions, City Film Center, Inc.

64-12 65th Place, Middle Village, Queens, NY 11379-1624; (718) 456-5050; John R. Gregory, exec. prod. (Producers of 8 mm/16 mm/35 mm motion pictures, for the fields of business, industry, advertising, sales, science, religion, education, health, entertainment and TV. Creative, consultation and production facilities.)

Dick Clark Productions, Inc.

3003 W. Olive Ave., Burbank, CA 91505; (213) 841-3003. Dick Clark chm. & CEO; Francis La Maina pres., COO; Ken Ferguson, CFO; Martin Weisberg, secty.; Neil Sterns, senior v.p., creative affairs; Ellen Glick, v.p., creative affairs; Karen Clark, v.p.-admin.; Michael Tenzer, v.p. bus. affairs; Aviva Bergman, v.p. business affairs; Richard Levine, v.p., pgm. & sls.; Bryan Thompson, cont.; Barry Ademlan, v.p., TV dept.; Richard Al Clark, producer; Lisa Demberg, v.p., creative affairs; Larry Klein, producer; Al Schwartz, v.p. prods.; Bruce Sterten, v.p. game show develp.; Gene Weed, v.p., TV.

Claster Television Productions

9630 Deereco Rd., Timonium, MD 21093; (301) 561-5500. (Distributor) John Claster, pres.; Sally C. Bell, exec. v.p.; Janice Corter, sr. v.p. sls.; Terri Akman, prog. dir.; Peggy Powell, acct. exec.; Jeffrey Hughes, director of advertising and promotion.

Coast Special Effects

4907 N. Lankershim Blvd, North Hollywood, CA 91601; (818) 762-1182. Nancy Evelyn, v.p.; Ron Seawright, sr. prod.; Joe Rayner & Peter Kleinow, spec. effects directors. (Special effects for TV commercials and feature films.)

Columbia Pictures Television

(A unit of Columbia Pictures Entertainment, Inc.) Studio Plaza, 3400 Riverside Dr., Burbank, CA 91505; (818) 954-6000. (For officers see listing in Companies section). Syndication personnel: Gary Lieberthal, chairman and CEO; Barry Thurston, president, syndication; Michael Zucker, senior v.p., marketing; David Mumford, sr. v.p., research; Doug Roth, v.p., research; Leslie Tobin, v.p. motion picture sales & acquisitions; Lon Feldman, v.p., syndication post production; Francine Beougher, v.p., distribution operations; Terry Mackin, v.p., western region; William L. Clark, dir., special marketing; Elise Keen, dir., syndication contracts; Eric Marx, dir., motion picture syndication; Bill Coveny, dir., publicity; Alan Daniels, dir., advertising and promotion. **Branch Offices:** *NEW YORK:* Columbia Pictures Television, 711 Fifth Ave., New York, NY 10022; (212) 702-2920; FAX: (212) 702-6239; Gary Lico, v.p., eastern region; Herb Weiss, v.p., eastern region. *CHICAGO:* Columbia Pictures Television, 645 N. Michigan Avenue, Suite 634, Chicago, IL 60611; (312) 915-1230; FAX: (312) 915-0685; John Rohrs, Jr., v.p., midwestern region; Stuart Walker, account exec., midwestern region. *ATLANTA:* Columbia Pictures Television, One Atlantic Center, 1201 W. Peachtree Street, #4820, Atlanta, GA 30309; (404) 892-2725; FAX: (404) 892-1063; Susan Grant, v.p., southeastern region; Joe Kissack, account exec.; Brian Fleming, account exec.

- SYNDICATION FEATURE FILM PACKAGES: Columbia Classics (34 titles); Columbia Gems I (214 titles); Columbia Gems II (22 titles); Columbia Night at the Movies (ad hoc quarterly barter network); Columbia Showcase I (22 titles); Embassy II (20 titles); Embassy III (20 titles); Entertainer of the Year (15 titles); Prime 4 (3 titles); TV 20 (20 titles); TVM One (19 titles); Volume I (28 titles); Volume IV (15 titles); Volume V (26 titles); Volume VI (21 titles).
- SYNDICATION OFF-NETWORK COMEDY SERIES: Archie Bunker's Place (97 ½-hour episodes); Barney Miller (170 ½-hour episodes); Benson (158 ½-hour episodes); Carson's Comedy Classics (130 ½-hour episodes); Carter Country (44 ½-hour episodes); Diff'rent Strokes (189 ½-hour episodes); The Facts of Life (209 ½-hour episodes); Fish (35 ½-hour episodes); Good Times (133 ½-hour episodes); The Jeffersons (253 ½-hour episodes); Maude (141 ½-hour episodes); One Day at a Time (209 ½-hour episodes); Punky Brewster (88 ½-hour episodes); Sanford & Son (136 ½-hour episodes); Silver Spoons (116 ½-hour episodes); Soap (93 ½-hour episodes); Square Pegs (20 ½-hour episodes); That's My Mama (39 ½-hour episodes); The Three Stooges (190 ½-hour episodes); Who's the Boss? (120 ½-hour episodes); 227 (116 ½-hour episodes).
- SYNDICATION OFF-NETWORK DRAMA SERIES: Charlie's Angels (115 one-hour episodes); Fantasy Island (200 ½-hour episodes, 152 one-hour episodes); Hart to Hart (112 one-hour episodes); Police Story (105 ½-hour episodes); Police Woman (91 one-hour episodes); S.W.A.T. (37 one-hour episodes); Starsky and Hutch (92 one-hour episodes); T.J. Hooker (90 one-hour episodes).

Communication Arts Corporation

P.O. Box 144, Hollywood, CA 90078; (213) 274-8600. Organized 1972. Gilbert A. "Gil" Cabot, exec. v.p., program and talent development; Kaye Merrill, casting v.p.; Thomas G. Barfield, v.p., prod.; Terry DeLyle, opns. mgr.; Nancy K. Austin, prod. coordinator.

- Divisions: Gil Cabot Associates, Inc.; StoryBrokers, Inc.; JenStar Productions, Inc.; Sundi Records, Inc.; TOBAC Music Pubberies, Inc.; Tic Toc Bunny Productions, Inc; Sweet Breeze Productions, Inc.

Communication Commission of National Council of the Churches of Christ in the USA.

475 Riverside Dr., New York, NY 10115; (212) 870-2575. J. Martin Bailey, acting assistant general secretary for communication; David W. Pomeroy, director, media resources. (Information about network religious TV programs).

Condor Pictures, Inc.

1536 Viewsite Terrace, Hollywood, CA 90069; (213) 652-7447. Milton Simon, gen. mgr. (TV pilot films. Films made to order.)

Contempo Communications Inc.

250 W. 19 St., New York, NY 10011; (212) 633-2333. Joan F. Marshall, pres. (Theatrical, business, documentary, award-winning live shows, mixed-media, motion pictures, video sales mtgs.)

Coproducers Corporation

2670 N.E. 24 St., Pompano Beach, FL 33064; (305) 781-2627. John F. Rickert, pres.; Ildiko M. Rickert, secty./treas. (Distribution, production, international co-production, financing and packaging.)

Coral Pictures Corporation

6850 Coral Way, Miami FL 33155; (305) 661-8922. Marcel Granier, pres. & CEO; Luis Guillermo Gonzalez, vice pres.; Jose Manuel Pagani, exec. v.p. & general mgr.; Manolo Vidal, exec. v.p., international sales.

Corniche Productions, Ltd.

101 East Victoria, Santa Barbara, CA 93101; (805) 564-8790. Organized 1982. Robert C. Acosta, managing partner; Venita Vancaspel, partner; Ann Trimbach Acosta, exec. prod.; Elizabeth Scott, co. mgr. (Creates, develops, produces and markets TV product.)

Corradine, Tom J., & Associates

3518 W. Cahuenga Blvd., Suite 301, Hollywood, CA., 90068; (213) 851-5811. Branch office in New York. Tom Corradine, pres.; Mark Deemer, v.p.; Bob Morgan, head booker; Edward Reagan, v.p., marketing; Paul Lisy, v.p., video cassette dir. (Distribute filmed series, feature films. Western representative for Weiss Global Enterprises and Bloom Film Group. National reps for TV National Releasing Corp., Lippert Pictures, Inc., and Film Video Releasing Corp.)

- 700 feature films, 192 Westerns, 500 cartoons, 6 series.

William G. Cox Film Enterprises

9726 Edward Dr., Sun City, AZ 85351. William G. Cox, owner-producer. (Produce commercials, news clips informational & public relations films.)

Thomas Craven Film Corporation

5 W. 19 St., New York, NY 10011; (212) 463-7190; FAX: (212) 627-4761. Michael Craven, pres.; Ernest Barbieri, v.p.; Frynne Hamden, secty. (Producers of films and videotapes. Producers of educational, informational, training, fund-raising, documentary, public relations and television films and tapes for corporate, non-profit and governmental clients. Producers of commercials and public service announcements. Producers of international films and tapes, with extensive overseas production experience. Brochure and additional info available on request.)

- Representative Credits: Recruiting films for Peace Corps; training and promotion films for Volkswagen, Porsche, Peugeot and Audi; training and informational tapes and films for several United Nations agencies; television specials on David Lean; Dylan Thomas and Samuel Taylor Coleridge; numerous films and tapes for U.S. military and governmental agencies.

Creative Programming, Inc.

30 E. 60 St., New York, NY 10022; (212) 688-9100. Organized 1982. Peter Wild, exec. prod. (Television and home video production.)

Bing Crosby Productions, Inc.

610 South Ardmore, Los Angeles, CA 90005; (213) 487-7150. James C. Kennedy, pres.; Stanley G. Mouse, v.p.; John G. Boyette, v.p. & treas. (Motion pictures, television (film & tape) syndication.)

Crossover Programming Company

17336 Sunset Blvd., Suite 142, Pacific Palisades, CA 90272; (213) 826-6466. Charles Braverman, pres.; Greg Griffin, development. (Producers of pay television series, specials, variety shows. Specialists in kinestasis animation.)

Crystal Pictures, Inc.

1560 Broadway, New York, NY 10036; (212) 840-6181; FAX: (212) 840-6182. Joshua Tager, president; S. Tager, dir. of sls. (Distribute features, Westerns, packages & reissue TV series.) Telex: 620852

- 60 features; 200 short subjects; comedies (Charlie Chaplin & other old time comedies) (112); TV series (one hr. and ½ hrs.) (410).

D

DIC Enterprises, Inc.

3601 W. Olive, Burbank, CA 91505; (818) 955-5400. Organized 1982. Andy Heyard, pres.; Jeff Wernick, v.p.; Mel Woods, chief fin. off.; Gregory B. Payne, secty. (Television production company.)

- Live Action: Archie Live—Action Movie for TV, Something Else
- Animated Specials: The Real Ghostbusters Halloween Special, G.I. Joe.
- Animated Series: Alf Tales, Kissyfur, The Slimer Show, The Real Ghostbusters, Maxie's World, Super Mario Brothers Super Show, Captain Planet, Captain N: The Game Master, Camp Candy, The Karate Kid.

Depicto Films Corp.

504-A Aspen Lane, Wyckoff, NY 07481. J. R. von Maur, president. (Producers of filmed commercials and industrial motion pictures. Sales meeting and conventions, road shows.)

Devillier Donegan Enterprises

1608 New Hampshire Ave. NW, Washington, D.C. 20006; (202) 232-8200. Organized 1981. Ron Devillier, pres.; Brian Donegan, exec. v.p.; Frank Liebert, dir., domestic sales; Linda Ekizian, dir., international sales; Joan Lanigan, dir., acquisitions; John Esteban, business mgr. (Movie and television distributor to broadcast and cable domestically and worldwide. Exclusive distributor in North America for NHK Tokyo, Film Australia, Channel Four, Monty Python, London, ABC Australia, Television New Zealand, National Film Board of Canada.)

Vin Di Bona Productions

4151 Prospect Ave., Los Angeles, CA 90027; (213) 557-4151.

- Animal Crack-Ups (ABC).

Digital Vision Entertainment

7080 Hollywood Blvd., Suite 901, Los Angeles, CA 90028; (213) 462-3790; FAX: (213) 462-3792. Organized 1981. Geoffrey de Valois, executive producer. (Motion picture, television, computer animation, production and distribution.)

Directions International Inc.

12150 Olympic Blvd., Los Angeles, CA 90064; (213) 207-0097; FAX: (213) 207-0947. Richard Squire, president; James Damalas, exec. v.p. Branches in San Jose, Costa Rica, New York. (TV and film production, commercial production, broadcast promotion production, creative services, theatrical trailers.)

Walt Disney Productions

500 S. Buena Vista, Burbank, CA., 91521; (818) 840-1000; 500 Park Ave., New York, NY, 10022; (212) 593-8900. (For officers and personnel see listing under Television Companies.)

Dixie Entertainment Productions, Inc.

215 Long Beach Blvd., 2nd floor, Long Beach, CA 90802; (213) 491-0332. Irene Jacobs, pres.; S. Giovannoli, chm.; Gil Benzeevi, senior v.p., marketing; Rudy Gerren, v.p. (Full service television production house, 1", ¾", ½"; also producer and distributor of video and motion pictures.)

Dubie-Do Productions, Inc.

New York City (212) 765-4240 or 1 Laurie Dr., Englewood Cliffs, NJ 07632; (201) 568-4214. Richard S. Dubelman, pres. (TV and theatrical productions.)

Dunn Cal. Studios, Inc.

P.O. Box 388670, Chicago IL 60638; (312) 644-7600. Deborah Rezzardi, pres. (Producers of motion pictures, multi-screen presentations, TV commercials, slidefilms for sales, training, promotion, indoctrination.)

E

Eagle/Horowitz Productions, Ltd., Inc.

2230 Hillsboro Ave., Los Angeles, CA 90034; (213) 837-1773. Organized 1984. David J. Eagle, pres.; David Horowitz, v.p.; Nancy Weingrow Eagle, secty.; Suzanne Horowitz, treas. (Television and motion picture production.)

Ralph Edwards Productions

1717 N. Highland Ave., Hollywood, CA 90028. Ralph Edwards, owner. (Creator, packager, producer television shows.)

- The People's Court-syndication.
- This is Your Life-syndication.
- Truth or Consequences—syndication

Ralph Edwards/Stu Billett Productions

1717 N. Highland Ave., Hollywood, CA 90028. (Creator, packager, producer television shows.)

- Superior Court—syndication.
- Family Medical Center—syndication.

Empire Television

1551 N. LaBrea Ave., Los Angeles, CA 90028; (213) 850-6110. Telex: 4790597 EMPIREINC.

- Theatrical features: Ghoulies; The Dungeonmaster; Walking the Edge; Trancers; The Alchemist; Zone Troopers; Ghost Warrior; Re-Animator; Troll; Mutant Hunt.
- Heroes, Pirates, and Warriors: 14-picture adventure package.

Entertainment Productions, Inc.

2210 Wilshire Blvd., Room 744, Santa Monica, CA 90403; (213) 456-3143. Organized 1971. Edward Coe, pres. (Motion picture and television productions for worldwide markets, including home video, cable, theatrical, etc.)

F

Family Films/Concordia

3558 S. Jefferson Ave., St. Louis, MO 63118. Dave Henrichs, manager.

Doris Faye Productions

325 W. 45 St., New York, NY 10036; (212) 246-0430. Organized 1959; Doris Faye, pres. (TV and film packagers; specialists in "educating through comedy" programs; on/off camera talent, script writing, video home-viewing.)

Don Fedderson Productions

16255 Ventura Blvd., Suite 205, Encino, CA 91436; (818) 986-3118. Don Fedderson, chairman of the board.

- My Three Sons (network); Family Affair (network).

The Film Company

111 Barrow St., New York, NY 10014; (212) 620-5654. Peter Bergmann, Anthony Lidelicato, Ronald Saland. (Motion picture production.)

Film/Jamel Productions, Inc.

195 S. Beverly Dr., Suite 412, Beverly Hills, CA 90212; (213) 273-7773. Gil Cates, pres. (Producers theatre, films, TV.)

Filmack Studios

1327 S. Wabash Ave., Chicago, IL 60605; (312) 427-3395. Joseph R. Mack, pres.; Robert Mack, v.p. (Motion picture film producer for theatres, TV and industry, as well as filmstrips and slides for education.)

Filmation

(A division of Group W. Productions, a Westinghouse Broadcasting Co. subsidiary) 6464 Canoga Ave., Woodland Hills, CA 91367; (818) 712-4900. (Production of children's programming for TV and theatrical release; animation.) Lou Scheimer, pres.; Arthur Nadel, v.p., creative affairs; Joe Mazzuca, v.p., prod.; Alice Donenfeld, v.p., sls.; John Grusd, v.p., art direction, Majid Saee, v.p., MIS systems.

- Bravestarr, Ghostbusters, She-Ra: The Princess of Power.

Films Five, Inc.

42 Overlook Rd., Great Neck, NY 11020; (516) 487-5865. Walter Bergman, head of studio oper. (Producers of industrials, documentaries, commercials, live film, videotape & animation. Editorial department & massprint distribution on premises.)

Films of the Nations

P.O. Box 449, Clarksburg, NJ 08510; (201) 462-3522. Maureen Mitnick, admin. Consulate General of Finland. (Distributors of TV, industrial and educational free sponsored films.) Color and b/w.

Fima Noveck Productions

321 W. 44 St., New York, NY 10036. (212) 315-4220. Fima Noveck, pres. (Production and post-production; commercials; features; MTV.)

Format Productions

4253 Reyes Dr., Tarzana, CA 91356; (818) 987-2390. Herbert Klynn, pres.; Marvin L. Klynn, exec. v.p. Selma Klynn, v.p.; Ruth Page, secty./treas. (Animation films for TV commercials, TV programming, theatrical shorts, feature and industrial films.)

Four Star International, Inc.

1440 S. Sepulveda, Los Angeles, CA 90025. Lance Thompson, senior v.p.

- Series: Big Valley; Wanted Dead or Alive; Achievers (13½ hrs.).
- Movies: Star Two (15 new films); Star One (15 new films); No Restrictions (13 new films); Cisco Kid Features (13 features); Dick Tracy (8 features); 200 feature films.

44 Blue Productions

1755 E. Bayshore Dr. #7, Redwood City, CA 94063; (415) 364-4445. Organized 1984. Rasha Drachkovitch, Stephanie Noonan-Drachkovitch, co-owners. (Produces television programming.)

- Winning Women: Great Moments in Women's Sports.
- Great Moments in College Bowl History.
- Legends of College Basketball.
- Aspire Higher.

Fox/Lorber Associates, Inc.

432 Park Ave. S., Suite 705, New York, NY 10016; (212) 686-6777. Richard Lorber, pres; David M. Fox, C.E.O.; Patrick J. McDarrah, synd. sales co-ordinator.

- Specials: The Elvis Collection (Elvis '56, Aloha From Hawaii, '68 Comeback Special, One Night With You); Great Performers (Mel Brooks, Rich Little, Bette Midler, Pee-wee Herman, Gladys Knight); King . . . Montgomery to Memphis; Legacy of a Dream; Country.
- Series—Michelob Presents Night Music (60 min., weekly) First Run: The Dr. Fad Show.
- Specials: Overboard; King . . . Montgomery to Memphis, Legacy of a Dream, The Elvis Collection (includes Aloha from Hawaii, 68 Comeback Special, One Night with You); Great Performers (Mel Brooks, Rich Little, Bette Midler, Pee Wee Herman, Gladys Knight, etc.)
- Features: Bad Girls (8 feature films starring Joan Collins, Raquel Welch, Susannah York, Deborah Harry).

Sandy Frank Entertainment, Inc.

115 E. 57 St., Suite 1410, New York, NY 10022; (212) 759-9199. Sandy Frank, pres.

Woody Fraser Productions, Inc.

3500 W. Olive Ave., Suite 500, Burbank, CA 91505; (818) 953-7600. Woody Fraser, pres. (Television production.)

- Home Show.
- Incredible Sunday.
- Life's Most Embarrassing Moments.
- On Trial.

The Fremantle Corporation—New York
Talbot Television Ltd.—U.K.
Fremantle International Productions, Pty. Ltd. Australia

660 Madison Ave., New York, NY 10021; (212) 421-4530; Telex: 423459; FAX: (212) 207-8357. (Distributor.) Paul Talbot, pres.; Daivd Champtaloup, senior v.p.; Julie Zulueta-Corbo, dir., home-video and Latin American sls.; Josh Braun, v.p., operations; Dawn Skelton, promotion mgr.; Russell Becker, dir., Far Eastern sls.; Richard Becker, asst. dir., Far East sls. (Aust.); Tony Gruner, CEO, Talbot TV Ltd. (U.K.); Peter Baker, European sls. chief; Skip Braun, v.p., Fremantle of Canada; Randy Zalken, v.p., Fremantle of Canada; Marshall Kesten, dir. of finance, Fremantle of Canada.

Fries Distribution Company

(A subsidiary of Fries Entertainment, Inc.) 6922 Hollywood Blvd., Los Angeles, CA 90028; (213) 466-2266. Telex: 3781675; FDC Fax: (213) 466-9407. Regional offices: New York (212) 593-2220; Chicago (312) 751-3483. (Production and distribution of features and series for TV, cable & home video.)

- TV movie packages: Fries Frame I—27 made-for-TV movies including Adam, Bill, The Burning Bed, The Jayne Mansfield Story and the two-part Dempsey; Fries Frame 2—20 made-for-TV movies including Do You Remember Love, Toughlove, Bitter Harvest, Rosie: The Rosemary Clooney Story and the two-part Martian Chronicles; Fries Frame 3—25 made-for-TV movies including An Early Frost, the two-part Fatal Vision, Poison Ivy and the Wilma Rudolph Story; Fries Frame 4—23 made-for-TV movies including the two-part Inside the Third Reich, Blood Vows: The Story of a Mafia Wife, The Jericho Mile and Mafia Princess; Fries Frame 5—17 films including Flowers in the Attic, Murder Ordained: Parts I & II, LBJ: The Early Years: Parts I & II, and Bridge to Silence; Fries Dynamite—11 films including 4 world premiere theatricals: Viper, The Siege of Firebase Gloria, Deadly Intent and Edge of Darkness; Fries Family Theatre: The Mark Twain Collection—6 films based on Twain classics including The Adventures of Huckleberry Finn.

Allen Funt Productions

P.O. Box 827, Monterey, CA 93940; (213) 851-3394.

- Candid Camera: Eat! Eat! (CBS).
- Candid Camera on Wheels (CBS).

G

GGP/GGP Sports

400 Tamal Plaza, Corte Madera, CA 94925; (415) 924-7500; FAX: (415) 924-0264. David L. Peterson, pres.; Robert C. Horowitz, v.p.-gen. mgr.; Henry Schneidman, v.p., gen. sls. mgr.; Kathryn Gray, controller. (TV sales, syndication and production, post-production and sports marketing).

GN Communications, Ltd.

2600 W. Peterson, Chicago, IL 60659; (312) 465-0085; FAX: (312) 465-7218. Organized 1984. Steven N. Polydoris, president. (Distributes quality TV programs for television and publishes magazine Chicago Film & Video News.)

GTG Entertainment

9336 W. Washington Blvd., Culver City, CA 90230; (213) 202-3250. (For officers and personnel, see listing under Television Companies.)

- Baywatch (NBC).
- USA Today on TV.

Galaxie Productions, Inc.

P.O. Box 1933, Washington, DC 20013; (202) 775-1113. Edward Jasen, president; Dr. Edward von Rothkirch, exec. v.p. & exec. prod.; S. McCormick, secty.-treas.; Paul Malec, chief engineer (Produce & distribute films for non-theatrical motion pictures & television: commercials, travelogues, documentaries, language dubbing on film, complete sound stage for audio recording, custom recording on tape or disk. Fully equipped audio visual, motion picture, & VTR remote truck for sound motion picture, VTR, & still photography. Branch offices: %A. L. Weintraub, 5th floor, 2250 S.W. 3rd Ave., Miami, FL 33129 & C.P.O. Box 1711, Tokyo 100-91 Japan; %V. J. Pandhi, Suite 6G, 102–45 62nd Rd., Rego Park, NY 11375.

Gaylord Production Company

66 Music Square West, Nashville, TN 37203; (615) 327-0110. Jane Grams, v.p. & gen. mgr. (Producer of programming for all television markets, including network, first and second syndication, cable and home video.)

Gaynes Productions Ltd.

6918 Oporto Dr., Hollywood, CA 90068; (213) 874-6909; (818) 840-8300. Organized 1980. Lloyd H. Gaynes, pres.; Kirsten Tellerz, v.p.; productions: John Alexander, Ellen Brown, Janie Flowers. (Television productions.)

- The Mother-Daughter Pageant U.S.A. The Mother-Daughter International Pageant 1989.

Gilson International

9200 Sunset Blvd., Los Angeles, CA 90069.

- Series: Hill Street Blues, Remington Steele, St. Elsewhere, Newhart, White Shadow, WKRP in Cincinnati, Last Resort, MTM Variety Hour, Paris, Duck Factory, Betty White Show, Doc, Three for the Road, Tony Randall Show, We've Got Each Other, Phyllis, Mary, Popcorn Kid, Beverly Hills Buntz, Eisenhower & Lutz, Tattingers, Mary Tyler Moore project.
- Films: Boy Who Drank Too Much, Fighting Back, First You Cry, In Defense of Kids, Nowhere to Run, Something for Joey, Thornwell, Vampire, Critical List (4-hr. mini-series), Carly's Web, Independence, Riviera, Fresno (6-hr. mini-series).
- Sports: For the Honor of Their Country (13-part Olympic series), Time Capsule: The 1936 Berlin Olympic Games (special).

Glen Glenn Sound Co. (Todd-Ao Corp.)

900 N. Seward St., Hollywood, CA 90038; (213) 469-7221. Robert Knudson, pres.; Ron Ward, opns. (Complete film and video-tape sound recording services for feature motion pictures and television programs).

Glenar Studios

211 S. Rose, Burbank, CA, 91505; (213) 848-0408. Sid Glenar, owner. (Produces films, commercials & animation.)

Global American Television, Inc.

Shearer Rd., Colrain, MA 01340; (413) 625-9893; FAX: (413) 625-9004. Organized 1982. Pamela M. Roberts, and Edward Wierzbowski, officers. (Produces socially relevant and cultural programming. Specializes in co-productions with Gosteleradio (Soviet TV). Sold first ads to foreign companies on Soviet TV in May, 1987.)

Melvin L. Gold Enterprises

301 E. 48 St., New York, NY 10017; (212) 688-0897. Mel Gold, pres. (Consultant, producer and packager of live and film TV programs, industrial films, commercials, features.)

Samuel Goldwyn Television

10203 Santa Monica Blvd., Los Angeles, CA 90067; (213) 552-2255; FAX: (213) 284-8493. Dick Askin, pres., television distribution; Jeri Sacks, v.p. cable and ancillary sales. Branches: 200 W. 57 St., Suite 808, New York, NY 10010; (212) 315-3030. 3011 Castle Pines Dr., Atlanta, GA 30136; (404) 497-9787; 4189 Bloomington Ave., #201, Arlington Heights, IL; (312) 632-1552; FAX: (312) 632-0822.

Mark Goodson Productions

375 Park Ave., New York, NY 10152; (212) 751-0600. 5750 Wilshire Blvd., Los Angeles, CA 90036; (213) 965-6500. Mark Goodson, owner; Giraud Chester, exec. v.p., Alan R. Sandler, v.p., finance; Gil Fates, exec. prod.; Howard Felsher, Chester Feldman, Jonathan Goodson, Mimi O'Brien, producers; Paul Alter, Marc Breslow, directors.

- The Rebel (film); The Richard Boone Show, Branded (film); Beat the Clock; To Tell The Truth; What's My Line; Password; The Price Is Right; Match Game PM; Tattletales; I've Got A Secret (all tape); Family Feud; Card Sharks; Mind Readers; Password Plus; Child's Play; Body Language; Trivia Trap; Super Password, Classic Concentrations, Blockbusters, New Family Feud.

Goulding-Elliott-Greybar Productions, Inc.

420 Lexington Ave., New York, NY 10017; (212) 532-9014. Organized 1955. Ray Goulding pres./secty.; Bob Elliott, v.p./treas. (Production of radio and TV commercials and radio & TV programs.)

Granada Television International

400 Madison Ave., Suite 1511, New York, NY 10017; (212) 753-3030.

- First Among Equals; Game, Set and Match; Lost Empires; Floodtide; Death of the Heart; Man and Music; 7 Up, 28 Up; The Jewel in the Crown; The Return of Sherlock Holmes.

Sherry Grant Enterprises

17915 Ventura Blvd., Suite 208, Encino, CA 91316; (818) 705-2535.

Gray-Schwartz Enterprises, Inc.

Teleflix Division, P.O. Box 9239, Calabasas, CA 91372; (818) 702-9888. Marv Gray, pres.

The Great Entertainment Co. Inc.

2170 Broadway, Suite 2275, New York, NY 10024; (212) 787-6291. Organized 1987. Nancy B. Dixon, CEO & president; John T. Welch, COO & president. Branches: Atlanta, Los Angeles. (Syndication of television programming.)

Greatest Fights of the Century, Inc.

9 E. 40 St., New York, NY 10016; William D. Cayton, pres. (Produce and distribute fight films.)

- Big Fights of the Decades Series (formerly titled Greatest Fights of the Century) 500 quarter-hour programs from 1900 to 1988, featuring all the world champions, each in his greatest, and most memorable fight, including George Foreman, Joe Frazier, Muhammad Ali, Floyd Patterson, Rocky Marciano, Joe Louis, Jack Dempsey, Sugar Ray Robinson, Rocky Graziano, Archie Moore, Larry Holmes, Marvin Hagler, Boom Boom Mancini, 35 Mike Tyson fights (31 by KO), etc.

The Earl Greenburg Organization

8730 Sunset Blvd., Suite 290, Los Angeles, CA 90069; (213) 657-2225. Organized 1988. Earl Greenburg, pres.; Stephan Matsuo, senior v.p.; Marcia Lewis, v.p., development. (Produces television and motion pictures.)

Greystone Communications, Inc.

1239 S. Glendale Ave., Glendale, CA 91205; (818) 502-5562. Organized 1986. Craig A. Haffner, pres.; Steven Lewis, Donna E. Lusitana, exec. v.p.s (Television production company for network, first run, cable, home video.)

Merv Griffin Enterprises

1541 N. Vine St., Hollywood, CA 90028; (213) 460-2231. Merv Griffin, chm. and CEO; Robert J. Murphy, pres. and COO; Peter Barsocchini, v.p., motion pictures and films for television, Ray Sneath, v.p., game shows and variety. (Production company.)

- Jeopardy.
- Wheel of Fortune.

Group W Productions (Westinghouse Broadcasting Company)

One Lakeside Plaza, 3801 Barham Blvd., Los Angeles, CA 90068; (213) 850-3800; FAX: (213) 850-3889. Derk Zimmerman, pres. & CEO; Sam Cue, v.p. controller; Meryl Marshall, v.p. program affairs; Owen S. Simon, v.p. creative services; Kim Schlotman, v.p. research & marketing; David Jacquemin, western region mgr.; Donald P. Spagnolia, dir. of visual communications; Mary F. Fisher, dir. of promotional media; Linda Magee, assoc. dir. of development.

888 Seventh Ave., New York, NY 10106; (212) 307-3000; FAX: (212) 307-3184. Dan Cosgrove, sr. v.p./media sales; Richard Sheingold, sr. v.p., marketing/sales; Peter Gimber, v.p./Eastern region mgr.; Glen Burnside, v.p./media sales; Steve Parker, Eastern division mgr.; Elizabeth Silverstein; sr. account exec.; Rhonda Schulik, account exec.

Division Offices: Chicago: 142 East Ontario, Suite 1500, Chicago, IL 60611; (312) 454-6975; FAX: (312) 454-6989; Brock Kruzic, Central division mgr.; Patricia Brown, Midwest mgr., media sales. Atlanta: 1400 Lake Hearn Dr., Suite 306, Altanta, GA 30319; (404) 843-5520; FAX: (404) 843-5778; Jeff Hoops, Southeast division mgr.; Dallas: 222 West Las Colinas Blvd., #535, Irving, TX 75039; (214) 506-0777; FAX: (214) 506-0774; Rick Shae, Southwest region mgr.

Group W. Videoservices (formerly TVSC), 310 Parkway View Dr., Pittsburgh, PA 15205; (412) 747-4700; FAX: (412) 747-4726; J. Michael Hudson, v.p./gen. mgr.; William Wuerch, v.p./sales; Dick Dreyfuss, sales rep. Division Office: *Los Angeles:* 3801 Barham Blvd., Los Angeles, CA 90068; (213) 850-3877; FAX: (213) 850-3889; Catherline Malatesta, West Coast sales mgr.; Katherine Ratajczak, sales coordinator.

- LifeQuest (6 one-hour), Teenage Mutant Ninja Turtles (13 half-hours), Life's Most Embarrassing Moments (weekly half-hour), This Evening (half-hours); Missing/Reward (half-hour weekly), Desperate Passage (2-hour special).

Reg Grundy Productions, Inc.

9911 W. Pico Blvd., Suite 720, Los Angeles, CA 90035; (213) 557-3555. N.Y. rep.: McManus International, Inc., 425 E. 63 St., Apt E-5F, New York, NY 10021. Organized 1979. Reg Grundy, O.B.E., pres. and chm.; Robert Crystal, v.p.; Sue McIntosh, secty. and treas. (Produces TV programs for network and syndication. All day parts.)

- Sale of the Century (NBC).
- Scrabble (NBC).

Gutman, Leo A., Inc.

230 Park Ave., New York, NY; (212) 682-5652.

- Hennessey—96 half-hours (b & w), starring Jackie Cooper and a host of guest stars.

Guymark Studios, Inc.

3019 Dixwell Ave., Hamden, CT 06518. Anthony Guarino, Jr., pres.; Guy Guarino, v,p., chg. of photo; Mark Guarino, v.p., chg. of audio & video. (Producers facilities and technical services for sound film video animation, product photography. 1200 sq. ft. sound stage w/ cyclorama complete ¼" & 16 mm sound studios, all format still photography studio, 16 mm animation studio, slide to film transfer, film to video transfer, ¾" video editing, Time Code, digital video effects, character & graphics generator.)

H

H-R Productions, Inc.

159 W. 53 St., New York, NY 10019; (212) 541-8015. Herbert Rosen, president. (Producer of films, package shows.)

Handel Film Corporation

8730 Sunset Blvd., W. Hollywood, CA 90069; (213) 657-8990. Leo A. Handel, pres.; Peter Mertens, producer. (Produces filmed series.)

- Magic of the Atom (10); The Age of the Atom (color special); Sweden-Vikings Today Style (color special); (color special); Police Dog; 1-hr TV special (1972); Art in America (series 1983–10); Thailand 1983; Philippines 1984; Computer Series 1983–; Measuring Things (series 3) 1985; Singapore 1986; Puerto Rico, 1988; Fiber Optics, 1988.

Hanna-Barbera Productions, Inc.

(A division of Great American Broadcasting) 3400 Cahuenga Blvd., West Hollywood, CA 90068; (213) 851-5000. Joseph Barbera, pres.; William Hanna, sr. v.p.; Martyn S. Weinberg, exec. v.p. & chief operating officer; Richard Sigler, v.p. bus. affairs; Jean MacCurdy, v.p., children's programs; John Michaeli, v.p. communications; Ross Sutherland, v.p. dir., personnel & labor relations; Iwao Takamoto, v.p. creative design; Maurice Morton, v.p. & gen. mgr; Joseph Taritero, v.p., creative affairs; Sam Edwing, v.p., development; Paul DeKorte, v.p. music; Jayne Barbera, v.p., animation production.

- Animated Series: The Yogi Bear Show (synd.); Snorks (synd.); Fantastic Max (synd.); The Further Adventures of Superted (synd.). Smurfs (NBC); The Completely Mental Misadventures of Ed Grimley (CBS); A Pup Named Scooby-Doo (ABC).
- Animated Specials: A Yabba Dabba Doo Celebration! 50 Years of Hanna-Barbera (TNT); Hagar the Horrible (CBS); Mad Magazine (CBS).

Dean Hargrove Productions

100 Universal City Plaza, #507-3E, Universal City, CA 91608; (818) 777-8305. (Producer in assoc. with Fred Silverman Co. & Viacom Prods.)

- Jake and the Fatman.
- Perry Mason Movies (made for TV films).
- Matlock.

Larry Harmon Pictures Corp.

650 N. Bronson Ave., Hollywood, CA 90004 (213) 463-2331. Larry Harmon, pres.

Harmony Gold U.S.A.

7655 Sunset Blvd., Los Angeles, CA 90046; FAX: (213) 851-5599. (Producer-distributor) Frank Agrama, president & CEO; Jim Mitchell, sr. exec. v.p. & COO.

- Animated cartoon series: Captain Harlock (65 half-hr. episodes); Robotech (85 half-hr. episodes).
- Shaka Zulu (10 hour mini-series).
- Raggedy Ann & Andy (3 holiday specials).
- Family Animation Showcase (20 animated features).
- 2-Part Classics (six 2-part, 4-hour series).
- Harmony Golden I (mini-package of 5 first-run features).
- Animals of Africa (52 half-hrs.).
- The King of the Olympics (4-hr. mini-series).
- The Man Who Lived at the Ritz (4-hr. mini-series).
- Animation Adventure Theatre (3 animated features).
- Travelin' Gourmet (13 half hours).
- Around the World in 80 Days (6 hour mini-series).
- The Secret Identity of Jack the Ripper (live special event).
- Confessional (4-hour mini-series).
- Paris/Dakar: The Great Adventure (4-hour mini-series).

Harpo Productions

35 E. Wacker Dr., #1782, Chicago, IL 60601; (312) 580-1950.

- The Oprah Winfrey Show.
- Prime Time Oprah: Just Between Friends.

Harris-Tuchman Productions

4293 Sarah St., Burbank, CA 91505; (818) 841-4100. Fran Harris, pres. & creative dir. (Producers of sales, training and industrial films.)

Harriscope Corporation

10920 Wilshire Blvd., Suite 1420, Los Angeles, CA 90024; (213) 208-6118; FAX: (213) 208-6120. Burt I. Harris, pres.; Harvey Simpson, finance dir. (Distribution of filmed programs and TV broadcasting.)

- Jalopy Races From Hollywood (26); Main Event Wrestling (65); All Girl Wrestling (26); So This Is Hollywood (24).

Hartley Film Foundation Inc.

59 Cat Rock Rd., Cos Cob, CT 06807; (203) 869-1818. Elda Hartley, pres. (Producer of films and video tapes on philosophy, psychology, religion, and health.)

Helios Productions

4140 Warner Blvd., Suite 314, Burbank, CA 91505; (818) 845-6888. Organized 1983. Joseph Maurer, Bradley Wigor, partners. (Produces quality television entertainment.)

Henley, Arthur, Productions

234 Fifth Ave., New York, NY 10001; (718) 263-0136. Arthur Henley, president. (Production, writing consultation, live and film.)

- Make Up Your Mind.

Henson Productions

117 E. 69th St., New York, NY 10021; (212) 794-2400.

- The Story Teller.
- Mother Goose.
- The Ghost of Fafner Hall.
- Jim Henson's Muppet Babies.

ITC Entertainment Group

12711 Ventura Blvd., Studio City, CA 91604; FAX: (818) 505-8121.

Domestic Distribution: Richard Colbert, sr. exec. v.p.; L.D. Harrison, mgr., sls. & admin.; Henry Urick, v.p., mrkting; John Herrin, v.p., ancillary sls.; Charlie Keys, v.p., western sls.; James Ricks, Jr., sr. v.p., southeastern sls.; Mike Russo, v.p. eastern sls.; Tony Dwyer, v.p., midwestern sls.

International Distribution: James P. Marrinan, sr. exec. v.p. & gen. mgr. intl.; Valerie Bisson-Delcourt, dir., intl. sls. admin.; Armando Nuñez, exec. v.p., foreign sales; Doralea Rosenberg, gen. mgr., ITC of Canada; Josh Elbaum, v.p. intl. sls.

- Series: Tic Tac Dough (260 half-hours, color); Secrets & Mysteries (26 half-hours, color); Thunderbirds 2086 (24 half-hours, color); The Saint (114 hrs., 43 color); Return of The Saint (22, color); Edward The King (13 one-hours, color); When Havoc Struck (12 half-hours, color); The Protectors (52 half-hours); My Partner the Ghost (26 hours); Department S (28 hours); The Persuaders (22 hours); The Adventurer (26 half-hours); The Baron (26 hours); Man in a Suitcase (28 hours); The Prisoner (17 hours); Secret Agent (45 hours); Fury (114 half-hours); Space: 1999 (40 hours, color).
- Features: Entertainment Volume Eight (18 features in color, including "The Big Easy," "Billionaire Boys Club," "Young Doctors in Love"); Entertainment Volume Seven (16 features in color, including "High Road to China," "Lassiter," "The Boys in Company C"); Entertainment Volume Six (16 features in color, including "Amos," "Not My Kid," & "Malice in Wonderland"); Entertainment Volume Five (16 features in color, including "All of Me," "Halloween," & "Sophie's Choice"); Entertainment Volume Four (16 features in color, including "On Golden Pond," "The Great Muppet Caper," & "The Elephant Man"); Entertainment Volume Three (16 features in color including "All Quiet on the Western Front," & "The Jazz Singer"); Entertainment Volume Two (16 features in color, including "The Boys from Brazil," "Capricorn One," & "Movie, Movie"); Entertainment, Volume One (14 features in color, including "The Return of the Pink Panther," "The Eagle Has Landed," and "Great Expectations"); The Thrillers (43 made-for-television movies, color). SST: Super Space Theatre (13 science fiction films); Hammer House of Horror Double Feature (6 double features or 12 one-hr. features); Cinema 12 (12 features).
- Specials: Superlative Seven (musical-variety hour specials, color, starring Julie Andrews, Steve Lawrence, Eydie Gorme, Ethel Merman, etc.); The Very Special Seven (musical-variety hour specials, color, starring Julie Andrews, Peggy Lee, Dick Van Dyke, etc.)

Image Organization, Inc.

9000 Sunset Blvd., Suite 915, Los Angeles, CA 90069; (213) 278-8751. Pierre David, chairman and CEO; Lawrence Goebel, senior vice president; Mark A. Horowitz, vice president, international sales; James Botko, director of acquisitions; W. Lee Matis, director of marketing. (International distribution of motion pictures, home video and television.)

Imagine Films Entertainment Inc.

1925 Century Park East, Suite 2300, Los Angeles, CA 90067; (213) 277-1665. Brian Grazer, Ron Howard, partners; Robert A. Harris, pres., motion pictures and TV; Joyce Brotman, sr. v.p., television; Todd Bergesen, v.p., television; Adene Walters, v.p., controller; Terry Spazek, sr. v.p., physical production.

Independent-International Pictures Corp.

Executive Plaza, 223 Route 18, East Brunswick, NY 08816; (201) 249-8982. Samuel M. Sherman, pres.; Dan Q. Kennis, chmn.; Al Adamson, exec. v.p. (Television distributor and packager-producer of feature film packages, TV specials, TV series.)

- Feature packages: Scream Showcase: Beyond the Living, Demons of the Dead, Doctor Dracula, Exorcism at Midnight, In Search of Dracula, Man with the Synthetic Brain, Midnight, Ship of Zombies, Terror of Frankenstein, Vampire Men of the Lost Planet, Hand of Power, Night Fiend, Horror of the Werewolf, Voice from the Grave; Action Group: The Gun Riders, Mission to Death, The Fakers, Queen of Sheba, The Barbarians, Submarine Attack, Fighting Rats of Tobruk, Money; Drive In Theatre: The Murder Gang, Intrigue in the Orient, Blazing Stewardesses, The Naughty Stewardesses, Trapped in the Desert, The Smiling Maniacs, Syndicate Sadists.

Independent Network, Inc.

11150 Olympic Blvd., Suite 1100, West Los Angeles, CA 90064; (213) 479-6755; Telex: 662612 INITEL FV LSA; FAX: (213) 479-1582. Irv Holender, pres.; Irving D. Ross, Dir. of U.S. sls. (Distribution & syndication; producers of films.)

- 104 hours of G.L.O.W. (Gorgeous Ladies of Wrestling).

- 16 features—Movie Madness #1.
- 14 features—Ninja/Kung Fu Theatre.
- 10 new features.
- 26 Auto International episodes.
- The Adventures of Oliver Twist (animated 93 min.).
- Hayley Mills—Storybook series (13 half-hr. mixed animation).

Interlingual Television, K.K.

Mori Bldg. No. 7, 1-11, 3-chone Toranomom, Minato-Ku Tokyo, Japan. Tel.: 434-2506; Cable Interlingual Tokyo; Telex: J22862, Interlin, Tokyo. Largest independent distributor of Television films in the the Far East, with affiliate offices in Australia, USA, Europe. Sub-licenses in Japan and other countries over 4,000 half-hours of telecasting film of U.S., European and Australian origin.

- Adventures of Long John Silver; Space Angel Cartoons; Four Seasons of Japan; Speed and Action; Big Challenge; Golf Around the World; Wings to Adventure; Let's Travel; World's Great Adventures; Filopat and Pitafil; Popeye the Sailor; Funny Company; Joe & The Bees; New Avengers; Spunky & Tadpole; The Living Ocean; In the Kingdom of the Dolphin; Wild World of the East; The Lighthouse; Alburria—A Trip to Remember; Here Comes the Grump; Texas Jack and His Pals; Famous Fairytales; Wonderful World of Brother Buzz; Feature films (color, 27 titles); George; Color Classics—The Best of the Past.

International Film Bureau Inc.

332 S. Michigan Ave., Chicago, IL 60604; (312) 427-4545. Wesley Greene, pres. (Distributes live action, animated shorts, documentaries. Curriculum and general audience films for television.)

International Film Exchange, Ltd. (A Today Home Entertainment Company)

201 W. 52 St., New York, NY 10019; (212) 582-4318; Cable: IFEX-REP—New York; Telex: 420748. FAX: (212) 956-2257; 9200 Sunset Blvd., Los Angeles, CA 90069; (213) 278-6490; Telex: 4972966; FAX: (213) 278-7939. Gerald J. Rappoport, Emanuel L. Wolf, Richard Grisar, Beulah Rappoport, Joy Pereths, Stephanie Holm, Robert Newman, exec. officers. (International distributors and producers of theatrical, non-theatrical, educational and television films.)

J

JEF Films Inc.

Film House, 143 Hickory Hill Circle, Osterville, MA 03265; (508) 428-7198; FAX: (508) 428-7198. Organized 1973. Branches: Los Angeles, CA (Film Classic Exchange); Australia, New Zealand, England, France, Spain, Portugal, Greece, Canada, Fiji, Switzerland, Austria, West Germany, Italy, Monaco, Ireland, Denmark, Finland, Sweden, Norway, Belgium, Luxembourg, Algeria, Morocco, Tunisia. Owns: Film Classic Exchange, XTC Video, WHAM! Video!, VIP Video, JEF Video line, JEF Films International, PHD Video, The Stock Exchange (stock footage). Jeffrey H. Aikman, CEO; Elsie Aikman, v.p.; Jo-Anne Polak, sls. mgr.; Janie Barber, promotions mgr; (Produces and distributes in the following media: television (network and syndication), motion pictures, home video, pay per view, non-theatrical. Also stock footage library of 30,000 films.)

K

KLW International Inc.

P.O. Box 806, Marmora, NJ 08223; (609) 391-0872. Organized 1985. Kevin L. Weakland, chairman/pres.; George Weakland, vice pres.; Shannon Weakland, secretary; Helyn Weakland, treasurer; Michael Beaumont, general mgr.. (Entertainment production, financing, and consulting.)

Stacy Keach Productions

5216 Laurel Canyon Blvd., North Hollywood, CA 91607; (818) 905-9601. Stacy Keach, Sr., pres.; Mary Keach, v.p.; James Keach, secty. (Producer of films, commercials, public information films.)

- Properties: Living Proof; Back in Action; Approved Exercises for Senior Citizens; Approved Exercises for the Heart Patient.

M. A. Kempner, Inc.

2151 W. Hillsboro Blvd., #110, Deerfield Beach, FL 33442; (305) 360-7252; FAX: (305) 360-7534; WATS: (800) 327-4994. Marvin A. Kempner, pres.

Killiam Shows, Inc.

6 E. 39 St., New York, NY 10016; (212) 679-8230. Paul Killiam, pres.; John Rogers, v.p. (Produces and distributes programs about silent films stock footage.)

King Features Entertainment Inc.

235 E. 45 St., New York, NY 10017; (212) 682-5600. Telex: 7105812391. J. F. D'Angelo, chmn.; Bruce L. Paisner, pres.; William E. Miller, exec. v.p.; Leonard Soglio, v.p, domestic sls. mgr.; Samuel Gang, intl. sls. mgr.

King International Corporation

124 Lasky Dr., Beverly Hills, CA 90212; (213) 274-0333. Frank King, pres.; Herman King, v.p. (Produces TV series.)

- Maya.

King World Productions, Inc.

1700 Broadway, New York, NY 10010; (212) 315-4000. 150 El Camino Dr., Suite 305, Beverly Hills, CA 90212; (213) 858-1833. 980 N. Michigan Ave., Suite 1400, Chicago, IL 60611; (312) 337-6765. Roger M. King, bd. chm.; Steve Palley, COO; Michael G. King, pres.; Sid Cohen, sr. v.p., sls.; Jeffrey Epstein, chief financial officer; Av Westin, sr. v.p. reality-based programming; Fred Cohen, head intl. sales div.; E. V. DiMassa, Jr., v.p. programming & dev.; Jonathan Birkhann, v.p. legal & business affairs; Kevin Stein, v.p. dev., West Coast; Allyson Kossow, v.p., public relations.

- Properties: ½ hr. strips: Wheel of Fortune, Jeopardy!, Headline Chasers. Movie Packages: Classic Detectives (34); Epics (5); Spotlight 10 (10); Popcorn Theatre (15). Off-net: Topper, Guns of Will Sonnett, Branded. Specials: Drug Wars (1 hr.), Wards of the Street (1 hr.).
- Inside Edition.

Walter J. Klein Company, Ltd.

6311 Carmel Rd., Box 2087, Charlotte, NC 28211-2087; (704) 542-1403. Walter J. Klein, pres.; Richard A. Klein, v.p. sales; David Jordan, controller; Betsy Klein, print sales dir.; Roxanne Mason, distribution dir.; Terry Losardo, production dir.; David Sherwin, editorial dir.; Charles Shedd, Jonathan Quade, Salvatore Messina, directors; Brady Brandwood, editor; Elizabeth Norkum, Barbara Cade, distribution assts.; Denise Joseph, Sandra Newton, Betty Stephens, Mary Babcock, John Edwards, administration. (Production and free distribution of sponsored films for industry, TV, government, associations for 40 years. complete film facilities on 2-acre lot.)

Steve Krantz Productions

12711 Ventura Blvd. #408, Studio City, CA 91604; (818) 769-5614. Steve Krantz, president. (Television production.)

Sid & Marty Krofft Picture Corp.

1040 N. Las Palmas, Los Angeles, CA 90038; (213) 467-3125. Marty Krofft, pres., Sid Krofft, v.p.

- D.C. Follies (Synd.), Red Eye Express (CBS).

The Kushner-Locke Co.

10850 Wilshire Blvd., 9th floor, Los Angeles, CA 90024; (213) 470-0400. Peter Locke, Donald Kushner, principals.

- Divorce Court (Synd.), 1st & Ten (HBO); Relatively Speaking (Synd.), Sweet Bird of Youth (NBC movie); Your Mother Wears Combat Boots (NBC).

L

LBS Communications Inc.

875 Third Ave., New York, NY 10022; (212) 418-3000; 9220 Sunset Blvd., Suite 101A, Los Angeles, CA 90069; (213) 859-1055; 625 N. Michigan Ave., Suite 1200, Chicago, IL 60611 (312) 943-0707; 14275 Midway Rd., Suite 220, Dallas, TX 75244; (214) 233-5972. Henry Siegel, chmn. & pres.; John Storrier, corporate exec. v.p., dir.; Phil Howort, president, LBS Telecommunications; Jon Not-

tingham, president, LBS Distribution; Paul Siegel, president, LBS Entertainment; Michael Welden, president, TV Horizons; Ira Bernstein, executive v.p., TV Horizons; Tony Intelisano, executive v.p., marketing & research; Rand Stoll, executive v.p., LBS Telecommunications; John Mansfield, sr. v.p., Western Region; Louise Perillo, sr., v.p., personnel administration; Gary Wald, sr., v.p., general mgr., LBS International; Joanne Burns, v.p., research services; Joanne DeRicco, v.p., creative services; Lou Israel, v.p., Midwest Region; Bill Smither, v.p., Northwest Region.

- Series: Family Feud.
- Live Event Specials: Return to the Titantic, Exploring Psychic Powers, UFO Cover-Up . . . The Mystery of the Pyramids, Manhunt, Hunt for the Stolen War Treasures.
- Children: Police Academy; The Series (65 half hour episodes and 2-hr movie); The Real Ghostbusters (99 half hours); He-Man; Heathcliff (86 half hours); Mask (75 half hours); Inspector Gadget (86 half hours).
- Features/Packages: It Nearly Wasn't Christmas; Mussolini: The Untold Story; Hope Diamonds (11 Bob Hope feature films).
- Specials: Adventures in Space; The Billy Martin Celebrity Roast; Crimebeat; Smithsonian Treasures; Test Series.
- Series/Off-Network: What's Happening!! (131 half hours); Crazy Like a Fox (74); Gidget (80 episodes); Hardcastle & McCormick (67); Family (85); The Monkees (58 half hours).
- LBS Classics: Burns & Allen (239 half hours); Dennis the Menace (146 half hours); The Donna Reed Show (153 half hours); Eischied (12 hours); Father Knows Best (191 half hours); Flying Nun (82 half hours); Ghost Story (22 hours); Hazel (156 half hours); Jungle Jim (26 half hours); Wild Bill Hickok (113 half hours); Route 66 (116 half hours).
- Titles from Corporation for Entertainment and Learning (CEL): America: The Way We Were (1 3-hour); Kennedy: A Celebration of His Life and Times (1 3-hour); A Walk Through the 20th Century (19 1-hour); Creativity (17 1-hour).
- From International Creative Exchange (ICE): John Fitzgerald Kennedy (1 hour); Marilyn Monroe (half-hour); Almanac (377 shorts); Battle Line (39 half-hours); Biography (65 half-hours).

The Landsburg Co., Inc.

11811 W. Olympic Blvd., Los Angeles, CA 90064; (213) 478-7878. Alan Landsburg, chm. of bd.; Howard Lipstone, pres; Kay Hoffman, exec. v.p.; Lindy DeKoven, v.p., movies & mini-series; Jane Lipstone, v.p., pub.; Victor Paddock, v.p., business affairs; Thomas Igner, controller. (Producer for TV and theatrical films and TV film and tape series.)

Don Lane Pictures, Inc.

545 Eighth Ave., New York, NY 10018; (212) 268-0101; FAX: (212) 268-1686. Donald J. Lane, pres., producer/director; Thomas Lalicki, v.p., producer; Carol Laufer, prod. mgr. (Produces medical, agricultural and industrial film and video tape, worldwide.)

Herbert S. Laufman & Company

8140 Rideway, Skokie, IL 60076; (312) 675-4578. Herbert S. Laufman,. pres. (Producers and distributors of live & film programs.)

- It's Baby Time (52).

Robert Lawrence Enterprises

305 Madison Ave., Suite 1146, New York, NY 10165; (212) 996-2836. Robert L. Lawrence.

Leach Entertainment Features

875 Third Ave., 18th Floor, New York, NY 10022; (212) 759-8787.

- Fame, Fortune & Romance (Synd.); Runaway with the Rich and Famous (Synd.); Lifestyles of the Rich & Famous (Synd.); The Rich & Famous 1988 World's Best (Synd.).

Herbert Leonard Enterprises, Inc.

5300 Fulton Ave., Van Nuys, CA 91401; (818) 783-0457. Herbert B. Leonard, pres.; Walter Bernstein, v.p.; James P. Tierney, Esq., secty. (Producers of filmed series and feature films.)

- Herbert B. Leonard produced Rin Tin Tin (164); Naked City (138); Route 66 (116); Popi (U.A.); produced and directed Going Home (MGM); Ladies Man (series); Breaking Away (pilot).

Levinson Entertainment Ventures International, Inc.

650 North Bronson Ave., Suite 250, Los Angeles, CA 90004; (213) 460-4545. Organized 1982. Robert S. Levinson, pres.; Sandra S. Levinson, vice pres.; Jed Leland, Jr., director of dev.; Deborah Scott, prod. associate. (Video, television, and film development and production. Affiliated with Program Partners Corp., N.Y.; Edge Records, L.A. and Together Productions, L.A. on co-prods.)

Liberty Studios, Inc.

238 E. 26 Street, New York, NY 10010; (212) 532-1865. Organized 1961. Anthony Lover, pres., producer-director; David Bruce, George Apostol, directors. (Complete live action and special effects production, including motion control graphics, blue screen. Owns and operates fully equipped sound stages, editing/optical facilities, camera lighting, grip and sound equipment, equipment transfer trucks for sound stage as well as location shooting. Video production includes off-line room and on-line Beta.)

Jack Lieb Productions, Inc.

100 West #4 Erie St., Chicago, IL 60610. Warren H. Lieb, pres.; Charles Kite, editor; Toba J. Cohen, prod.-dir. (Audio-visual producers).

Lionheart Television International

1762 Westwood Blvd., Los Angeles, CA 90024; (213) 470-3939. (Distributor) Frank R. Miller, pres. & CEO; Tay Voye, exec. v.p.; David Friedman, sr. v.p. com. sls.; Ray Krafft, v.p. pub. TV sls.

Lorimar Television

10202 Washington Blvd., Culver City, CA 90230; (213) 280-8000.

- Network series: Dallas; Falcon Crest; Knots Landing; Perfect Strangers; The Hogan Family, Full House, Midnight Caller, Paradise.
- First-run syndication: Mama's Family; It's a Living; ThunderCats; Love Connection; The People's Court; SilverHawks; Superior Court; She's the Sheriff; Freddy's Nightmares, Fun House, Family Medical Center, Gumby, N.I.W.S. (New Information Weekly Service).
- Mini-series: Jack the Ripper.

Lott Video Productions

The Lott Bldg., P.O. Box 1107, Santa Monica, CA; (213) 397-4217. D. N. Lott, owner. (Producers of film commercials.)

M

MCA Television

445 Park Ave., New York, NY 10022; (212) 759-7500. West Coast: 100 Universal Plaza, Universal City, CA 91608; (818) 777-1000; FAX: (818) 777-8221. (For officers see listing under Companies)

- Series/First Run: Out Of This World (24/28, strip 100 episodes); Lassie (weekly barter half-hr.); My Secret Identity (24/28 half-hrs.); The Munsters Today (24/28 half-hrs.); Inside Report (half-hr.); Charles in Charge (126 half-hr. episodes).
- Series/Off-Network: One-hour: Simon & Simon (156); Black Sheep Squadron (35); Magnum (162); The Columbo/McCloud/McMillan Mystery Movies (124); Quincy (148); Buck Rogers (37 1-hr. or 25 1-hrs. & 6 two-hrs.); Kojak (118); The Rockford Files (125); BJ/Lobo Show (85 half-hrs. or 86 hrs.); The Incredible Hulk (85); Emergency! (136); The A Team (98); Five Star Mystery: Delvecchio/Ellery Queen/Mrs. Colombo/O'Hara (87); Best Sellers I & II (incl. Captains and the Kings, Once and Eagle, Wheels-63); Ironside (198); It Takes a Thief (65); Run For Your Life (85); Thriller (67); Barbetta (82); Alias Smith or Jones (43); The Six Million Dollar Man (108); The Bionic Woman (58).
- Series: Half-hours: Amen (110); Gimme a Break (137); That's Incredible (165); The Jack Benny Show (104); Kate and Allie (122); Leave It to Beaver (234); The Munsters (70); The Deputy (76); Mickey Spillane's Mike Hammer (78); Rod Serling's Night Gallery (97).
- Series: 90-min.: Banacek (16); The Bold Ones (98); The Name of the Game (76); The Deputy (76 half-hrs.); Men from Shiloh (23); Wagon Train (32).
- Features/Packages: Universal Pictures Debut Network (33 features); Universal Pictures Debut Network II (35 features); Universal Pictures Debut III (31 features); Film Fest I (22 TV films); Universal's Most Wanted List (15); The Hit List (36); Universal Network Movies (85—52 two-hr., 33 1½ hrs.); Battlestar Galactica (12 two-hr. movies or 24 one-hrs.); Champagne Movies 34 (34); Universal Pictures Exploitable 13 (12 features); Universal Pictures Prestige 13 (13); Ninety Minutes Movies (49 made-for-TV); Universal Grand 50 (48); Universal Marvelous Ten (10 TV movies); Universal Network Movies 85 (84—2 hr. and 90 min. TV movies); Comedy Festival I (26); Paramount Pre '48 (496); Paramount 100

Select (100); Universal 53 (50); Universal 123 (114, 92 color); Universal Color One Hundred (99); Abbott and Costello (29); Reserve (169); Diabolic Dozen (12); Dead End Kids Movies.

MCA Television International

100 Universal City Plaza, Universal City, CA 91608; (818) 777-4275; TWX: 67-7053; FAX: (818) 777-6276. Colin P. Davis, pres.; Peter Hughes, v.p. marketing; Albert Barbee, mgr., intl. product services; Katarina Pranz, mgr., intl. promotion. Sales Offices: Brazil: Rua Said Aiach, 305, São Paulo, Brazil; 884-0166, Wanderley Fucciolo, v.p.; Australia: Universal House, Poplst & Pelican St., Sydney, NSW, Australia 2000; 267-9844, Pat Cleary, v.p.; Japan: Maison Hirakawa Bldg., 2-5-2 Hirakawa-cho, Chiyoda-ku, Tokyo; 265-5726, Keinosuke Kuragaki, v.p.; Canada: 2450 Victoria Park Ave., Willowdale, Toronto, Ontario M2J 4A2, Canada; (416) 491-3000, Ron Suter, mgr. of sales; Lebanon: Mutran Atalah St., Chahman Bldg., Fassouh Achrafleh, P.O. Box 16-6342, Beirut; 1-338533, Kamal Sayegh, v.p.; France: 8 Rue La Boetie, Paris 75008, France; 4-625-9780, Roger Cordjohn, v.p., Hendrik van Daalen, v.p.; England: 1 Hamilton Mews, W1V 9FF, England; (01) 491-4666, Roger Cordjohn, v.p., Bernadette Vacher, sales exec.

(MCA TV International is a company involved in developing, producing and distributing television programming. The company's film library consists of over 300 world premieres and TV movies as well as 2,500 Universal features.)

- Series: Half-Hour: Adam-12 (174); Adam-12 (26 new), Alfred Hitchcock Presents (1 2-hr.; 78 half-hrs.); Amen (89); BJ/Lobo (88); Bustin' Loose (26); Charles in Charge (126); Coach (26); Coming of Age (15); The D.A. (15); Domestic Life (10); Don Adams Screen Test (13); Dragnet (98); Dragnet Today (26); Family Affair (138); Family Man (7); Fay (10); Fast Times (7); Foul-Ups, Bleeps & Blunders (28); Four Seasons (13); George Burns Comedy Week (13); Gimme a Break (134 half-hrs./1 1-hr.); Good Times Harry (1 1-hr./5-half-hrs.); Harper Valley (29); He's the Mayor (13); Holmes & Yoyo (13); House Calls (57); Knight and Daye (7); Lassie (24); Leo & Liz in Beverly Hills (8); Major Dad (13); Mr. Terrific (17); The Munsters Today (48); My Secret Identity (48); Night Gallery/ Sixth Sense (97); Nobody's Perfect (8); No Soap Radio (5); Operation Petticoat (32 half-hrs./1 2-hr.); Out of This World (72); Partners (20); Puttin' On the Hits (134 half-hrs./1 2-hr.); Puttin' on the Kids (14); Safari to Adventure (24); The Street (40); Sunshine (13 half-hrs./1 2-hr.); Tammy (25); Together We Stand (19); Turnabout (7).
- Series: Hour: A Year in the Life (22); Almost Grown (12 hr./1 2-hr.); Airwolf (78 hr./1 2-hr.); The A-Team (96 hr./4 2-hr.); Alfred Hitchcock Hour (93); Alias Smith & Jones (48 hr./2 90-min.); Aloha Paradise (7 hr./1 2-hr.); BJ & the Bear (42 hr./1 90-min/2 2-hr.); Blacke's Magic (12 hr./1 2-hr.); Black Sheep Squadron (35 hr./1 2-hr.); Baretta (82); Battlestar Galactica (34/12 2-hr.); Bionic Woman (58); The Bold Ones (100); Buck Rogers (29/4 2-hr); Chase (22 hr./1 90-min.); Chrysler Theatre (37); City of Angels (13); Cliffhangers (11 or 8 2-hrs.); Class of '85 (18); Codename Foxfire (7 hr./1 2-hr.); The Contender (4 hr./1 90-min.); Crisis (57); Dalton (2 hr./2 2-hr.); Darkroom (7); Delvecchio (20); Doctors' Hospital (13 hr./1 2-hr.); Don Knotts Hours (24); The Duke (4 hr./1 2-hr.); Eddie Capra Mysteries (11 hr./2 2-hrs.); Ellery Queen (22 hr./1 2-hr.); Emergency (136); The Equalizer (88); Family Holvak (10); Fitz & Bones (4 hr./1 2-hr.); Gangster Chronicles (11 hr./1 2-hr.); Gemini Man (11 hr./1 2-hr.); Get Christie Love (22); Griff (12 hr./1 2-hr.); Hard Copy (10 hr./1 90-min.); Hardy Boys/Nancy Drew (48); Hawaiian Heat (10 hr./1 2-hr.); Incredible Hulk (85); The Insiders (13); Invisible Man (12 hr./1 90-min.); Ironside (188 hr./7 2-hr.); It Takes a Thief (68); Jigsaw (8 hr./1 90-min.); Kate Loves a Mystery—Mrs. Columbo (14 hr.); Kingston: Confidential (15); Knight Rider (78 hr./6 2-hr.); Kojak (113 hr./3 2-hr/1 3-hr.); The Law (3 hr./1 150-min.); The Law and Harry McGraw (15 hr./1 2-hr.); Legmen (8); Little Women (6); Lobo (37 hr./1 2-hr.); Lucas Tanner (22); Magnum, P.I. (150 hr./8 2-hr.); Man and the City (15 hr./1 2-hr.); Marcus Welby, M.D. (170); Matt Lincoln (16 hr./1 90-min.); McNaughton's Daughter (3 hr./1 2-hr.); Men (13); Miami Vice (108 hr./3 2-hr.); Misfits of Science (15 hr./1 2-hr.); Mobil One (13 hr./1 90-min.); Murder, She Wrote (130 hr./1 2-hr./1 90-min.); Night Gallery (30 hr./15 half-hr.); Night Stalker (20); O'Hara, U.S. Treasury (22 hr./1 2-hr.); Oregon Trail (13); Otherworld (8); Outlaws (11 hr./1 2-hr.); Outsiders (28 hr./1 2-hr.); Owen Marshall (69 hr./1 2-hr.); Private Eye (11 hr./1 2-hr.); Probe (6 hr./1 2-hr.); Psychiatrist (6); Quantum Leap (22 hr./1 2-hr.); Quincy (143 hr./1 90-min.); Rich Man, Poor Man (30 hr./1 2-hr.); Road West (29); Rockford Files (120 hr./3 90-min.); Rosetti and Ryan (6 hr./1 2-hr.); Run for Your Life (85); Salute (12); Sara (12); Sarge (14); Scene of the Crime (5); S.F. International (8); Shannon (10); Shirley (14); Sierra (11 hr./1 90-min.); Simon & Simon (152 hr./2 2-hr.); The Six Million Dollar Man (96 hr./3 2-hr./3 90-min.); Sixth Sense (25); Stone (11); Street Hawk (12 hr./1 90-min.); Sugar Ray Leonard's Golden Gloves (26); Survivors/Paris 7000 (25); Switch (70 hr./1 90-min.); Sword of Justice (7 hr./3 2-hr.); Tales of the Gold Monkey (20 hr./1 2-hr.); Toma (22); Voyagers! (20); When the Whistle Blows (10); Whiz Kids (18).
- Series: 90 Minutes: Men from Shiloh (24); Name of the Game (78); The Virginian (225); Wagon Train (32).
- Mystery Movies: Amy Prentiss (1 90-min./2 2-hr.); Banacek (16); Columbo (27); Cool Million (4); Faraday & Co. (4); Heck Ramsey (3 90-min./7 2-hr.); Madigan (6); McCloud (19 90-min./8 1-hr./21 2-hr.); McCoy (4 2-hr./1 90-min.); McMillan & Wife (24 90-min./18 2-hr.); New Mystery Movies (14 2-hr.); Snoop Sisters (4); Tenafly (5).
- Children: Children's Theatre: Alice in Wonderland (81 min.); Puss in Boots (93 min.); The Red Shoes (79 min.); Wind in the Willows (75 min.). Bionic Six (86 half-hr.); Blinkins (3 half-hr.); Calvin & the Colonel (26 half-hr.); Donkey Kong/Donkey Kong Junior (16 half-hr.); Emergency + 4 (28 half-hr.); Woody Woodpecker & Friends (113 half-hr.).
- Mini-Series: A Year in the Life (3 2-hr.); Aspen (3 2-hr.); The Bastard (2 2-hr.); Beggarman Thief (2 2-hr.); Black Beauty (6 80-min.); Brave New World (2 2-hr.); Captains & the Kings (6 2-hr. or 10 80-min.); Centennial (10 2-hr./2 3-hr.); Condominium (2 2-hr.); Desperado: Western Movie Series (3 2-hr.); Evening in Byzantium (2 2-hr.); Gossip Columnist (2-hr.); Guts & Glory (4 1-hr.); Harvest Homes (1 2-hr. or 1 3-hr.); Immigrants (2 2-hr.); Last Convertible (3 2-hr.); Little Women (2 2-hr.); Loose Change (3 2-hr.); Masada (4 2-hr.); Once and Eagle (2 2-hr./5 1-hr.); Peter & Paul (2 2-hr.); The Rebels (2 2-hr.); Rhinemann Exchange (2 2-hr./1 1-hr.); The Seekers (2 2-hr.); Seventh Avenue (3 2-hr./6 1-hr.); Seventy-Nine Park Avenue (3 2-hr.); Testimony of Two Men (3 2-hr./6 1-hr.); Treasure Island (4-hr.); Twelfth Night (1 2-hr.); Wheels (5 2-hr.); Women in White (1 2-hr.; 2 1-hr.).
- Specials: E.T. and Friends (1-hr.); Ray Charles Concert (1-hr.); Hollywood: The Gift of Laughter (3 1-hr.); The Complete Beatles (1 1-hr); The Loretta Lynn Concert (1-hr.); Utopia Concert (1-hr.).
- Features/Packages: Over 2,500 Universal features including pre-'48 Paramount titles, movies-for-television (over 150 2-hr. and over 100 90-min. world premieres and TV movies).

M.C.E.G., Inc./Manson International

2400 Broadway Ave., Suite 100, Santa Monica, CA 90404; (213) 315-7800; FAX: (213) 315-7850; Telex: 188198 MCEG UT. John Alexander, v.p., international sales.

- Distributors of 300 plus feature films, documentaries and entertainment specials to the international theatrical, video, cable TV and broadcast TV markets.

MGM/UA Television Distribution

1350 Ave. of the Americas, New York, NY 10019; (212) 708-0300. (For officers and personnel see listing under Companies.)

MGS Services

A subsidiary of Viacom International Inc., 619 W. 54 St., New York, NY 10019; (212) 765-4500; FAX: (212) 586-3771; (212) 757-6094. Chicago, IL: 201 E. Erie St., 60611; (312) 337-3761; Los Angeles, CA: 10507 Burbank Blvd., N. Hollywood, CA 91601; (818) 508-5488.

MPO Videotronics, Inc.

2580 Turquoise Circle, Newbury Park, CA 91320; (805) 499-8513; FAX: (805) 499-8206; Mark Barker, West. Reg. Mgr. *New York:* 619 W. 54 St., New York, NY 10019; (212) 708-0550; FAX: (212) 977-9458; Jeff Greenberg, East Reg. Mgr. *Chicago:* 5999 New Wilke Rd., Suite 204, Rolling Meadows, IL 60008; (312) 806-6780; FAX: (312) 806-6873; Bill Bailey, M.W. Reg. Mgr. *Atlanta:* (404) 875-0015; FAX: (404) 642-0138; Skip Bulkley, S.E. Reg. Mgr. *Canada:* 85 Curlew Drive, Don Mills, ONT M3A 2P8; (416) 445-2538; FAX: (416) 445-4051.

MRC Films Inc.

71 W. 23 St., New York, NY 10010; (212) 989-1754. Lawrence Mollot, exec. producer. (Producer of corporate, documentary, television films and TV commercials.)

MTM

Studio Center, 4024 Radford Ave., Studio City CA 91604; (818) 760-5942. (For corporate officers see Television Companies section.)

- Capital News (ABC).
- FM (NBC).
- Newhart (CBS).

Madison Square Garden Network

2 Pennsylvania Plaza, New York, NY 10121; (212) 563-8000; FAX: (212) 563-3794. Robert Gutkowski, exec. v.p., MSG Communications Group; Martin Brooks, v.p., programming & network opera-

tions; Lee Berke, v.p., marketing; Doug Moss, v.p., advertising sales; Paul Schneider, dir., public relations; Pete Silverman, v.p., exec. producer.

- Live Events: New York Knickerbockers basketball; New York Rangers hockey; New York Yankees baseball; College football and basketball, pro wrestling, pro boxing, track and field, tennis.

Manley Productions, Inc.

111 W. 57 St., New York, NY 10019; (212) 541-7733. Janice Manley, pres.; Walter H. Manley, gen. mgr.; Pat Hart, sls. mgr.; Robert Pistella, asst. sales mgr.; Mary Kay McTague, controller. Cable: WALTMANLY; Telex: 421832; FAX: (212) 957-9006. (Producers and distributors.)

Marathon International Productions, Inc.

Box BJ, Amagansett, NY 11930; (516) 267-7770; FAX: (516) 267-7771. Konstantin Kalser, pres. and exec. producer. (Produce & distribute motion pictures and public information films.)

Marvel Productions Ltd.

1861 S. Bundy, Los Angeles, CA 90025; (213) 315-2130.

- Animated series: Dinoriders (Synd.), Jim Henson's Muppet Babies (CBS, in assn. with Jim Henson Prods.), Robocop (Synd.), Monster Bed (ABC), Rude Dog and the Dweebs (CBS).

Medallion TV Enterprises, Inc.

8831 Sunset Blvd., West Hollywood, CA 90069; (213) 652-8100. Telex: 910-490-1139. FAX: (213) 659-8512. John A. Ettlinger, production. (Producers and distributors of film programs for TV, commercials, packages of live programs, local and network.)

- Celebrity Billiards (30); Wrestling Stars of the 60s; High Road To Danger (39); Kingdom of the Sea (41); Wonders of the World (117); Star Route (26); Creeping Terror Package—Volumes I, II, III & IV, 20/20 Feature Package; Las Vegas Fight of the Week (26); The New Roller Derby (26 hrs.); Wrestling Spectacular (26 hrs.); Man Who Skied Down Mt. Everest (90 min. special); Dinah East (95 min. special); Something Else (39 half hrs.); Scrooge's Rock and Roll Christmas (1-hour special); Elm Street: The Making of a Nightmare (1-hour special); Action I-Action II (60 min. specials).

Milner-Fenwick, Inc.

2125 Greenspring Dr., Timonium, MD 21093; (301) 252-1700. David Milner, pres.; Richard Milner, v.p.; Michael Quitt, sales mgr., v.p. (Producers of medical, educational, training and documentary films and video-tapes—16mm, Super 8mm, ¾" and ½" video. Full motion picture services including sound recording, animation, live photography and editing.)

Mode 2 Productions

P.O. Box 8050, Pittsburgh, PA 15216; (412) 343-8700. Robert L. Stone, pres.; James M. Seng, v.p. (Producers of documentary and industrial sales and safety films and television commercials.)

Modern Sound Pictures, Inc.

1402 Howard St., Omaha, Nebraska, 68102; (402) 341-8476. Keith T. Smith, pres. (Distributor of over 200 feature films and 300 shorts.)

Modern Talking Picture Service, Inc.

General Offices: 5000 Park St., North, St. Petersburg, FL 33709; (813) 541-7571. (Distributor of free-loan sponsored films and videocassettes, and collateral materials.)

Divisions

Modern TV: Distributor of free-loan 16mm-sound and color motion pictures and videocassettes. TV NewsBridge produces and distributes VNRs to TV stations and cable systems. PR-NewsBridge produces and distributes PSA to TV stations and cable systems. TV spot newsclips and public service announcements for television stations.

Modern Video Programs: Distributor of programs and series for Cable Television Stations.

Modern Satellite Services: Distributor of programs and services.

Affiliations

Modern Telecommunications, Inc.

One Dag Hammarskjold Plaza, New York, NY 10017; (212) 355-0510. Robert Weisgerger, pres. (A post-production company specializing in videotape services).

Moffitt-Lee Productions

1438 N. Gower St., Suite 250, Hollywood, CA 90028; (213) 463-6646; FAX: (213) 467-2946. Organized 1978. John Moffitt, exec. prod.-dir.; Pat Tourk Lee, exec. prod.; Amy Kimelman, coord. prod.; Matt Neuman, prod., Not Necessarily the News; Vic Kaplan, prod. consultant; Nancy Kurshner, assoc. producer. (Television production.)

Motion Picture Service Co., Inc.

125 Hyde St., San Francisco, CA 94102; (415) 673-9162. Lino Kwong, operations mgr. (Theatre advertising, special trailers, animated film strips, optical sound services, color film lab, computer graphics.)

Motown Productions

345 N. Maple Dr., #235, Beverly Hills, CA 90210; (213) 281-2684.

- Motown on Showtime Series: Smokey Robinson.
- Rollergames (ABC).
- Small Sacrifices (ABC).

Movietonews, Inc. (20th Century-Fox Film Corp.)

460 W. 54 St., New York, NY 10019; (212) 556-2560; FAX: Fox Film Corp.: (212) 869-7840. (Stock film library, international newsreels.)

Multimedia Entertainment

75 Rockefeller Plaza, 22nd Floor, New York, NY 10019; (212) 484-7025; FAX: (212) 484-7998. Peter Lund, pres.; Thomas Shannon, v.p., syndication sales; Diane Sass, v.p., marketing & research; Steve Fadem, v.p., business affairs; Robert Teach, v.p., finance; Tom Robertson, v.p., special programs. (A division of Multimedia, Inc., a diversified media communications company, headquartered in Greenville, SC, which publishes 14 daily and 40 non-daily newspapers, owns and operated 4 network-affiliated TV stations and 7 radio stations, operates more than 100 cable franchises in 4 states and produces and syndicates Emmy Award-winning shows Donahue and Sally Jessy Raphael.) Division: Spectrum, (same address), Joseph Cifarelli, v.p.

- Donahue.
- Sally Jessy Raphael.
- Young People's Specials.
- An Appointment with Sherlock Holmes.
- The 23rd Annual Music City News Country Awards.

N

NBC International, Ltd.

30 Rockefeller Plaza, New York, NY 10112; (212) 664-4444. Robert C. Blackmore, exec. vice pres., NBC-TV; Mike Perez, v.p., intl. sls.; Eric J. Stanley, dir., intl. sls.

- Movies, mini-series, children's shows, comedy and drama series, sporting events, information programs, news programs, etc.

NBC News Video Archives

30 Rockefeller Plaza, New York, NY 10112; (212) 664-3797; FAX: (212) 957-8917.

- Complete archives of NBC News.

NBC Productions

330 Bob Hope Drive., Burbank, CA 91523; (818) 840-7500.

- A Brand New Life (aka Blended Family); American River; Blessed; Family Man; Generations; Hardball; Mancuso F.B.I., The Nerd, Repeat Performance; Saved by the Bell; Strange Bedfellows; Truck One.

Nelvana

32 Atlantic Ave., Toronto, Ontario, Canada M6K 1X8; (416) 588-5588; Michael Hirsch, chmn.; Patrick Loubert, pres.; Clive Smith, treas.; 9000 Sunset Blvd., Suite 911, Los Angeles, CA 90069; (213) 278-8466; Stanford Blum, exec. v.p. (Animation production.)

- Barbara Animated TV Series (HBO).
- Beetlejuice Animated TV Series (ABC).
- The Care Bear Family (ABC).

- T and T (Synd.).
- Animated Feature: Barbar: The Movie.

New Century Telecommunications

545 Madison Ave., New York, NY 10022; (212) 371-9750. (Producer and distributor) Robert B. Morin, pres.; David Skillman, v.p., sls.; Jack E. Dube, v.p. intl.; Gene Lavelle, v.p., opns.; Steven Orr, v.p. sls.

New World Television

1440 S. Sepulveda Blvd., Los Angeles, CA 90025; (213) 444-8100. (For officers and personnel see listing under companies.)

- Santa Barbara (NBC); Tour of Duty (CBS); The Wonder Years (ABC); The Robert Guillaume Show (ABC); Elvis: Good Rockin' Tonight (ABC); False Witness (NBC movie); Nick Knight (CBS movie); Mick & Frankie (ABC); Hardball (CBS movie).

Nostalgia Productions

1555 S. Cardiff, Los Angeles, CA 90035; (213) 277-5865. Carla Howard, pres.; Scott Ben-Yashar, dir. opns. (Producer of custom family documentaries—histories.)

Odyssey Filmakers

1001 N. Poinsettia Place, Hollywood, CA 90046; (213) 876-2021; 514 West End Ave., #2C, New York, NY 10024; (212) 877-3683; 151 N. Michigan Ave., Chicago, IL 60601; (312) 856-1448. Sherry Seckel, pres. & exec. prod.; Directors: Bob Abel, Charlie Diercks, Stasch Radwanski, Henry Winkler; Marjorie Perrelli, West Coast rep; Paul Zara, Midwest rep.; Frank Coppola, East Coast rep. (Producers of TV commercials.)

Odyssey Productions, Inc.

24 E. 51 St., New York, NY 10022; (212) 421-9595.

- Lowell Thomas Television series, High Adventure (color-11); World of Lowell Thomas (half-hour-41).

Lillian Okun Productions

307 E. 44 St., New York, NY 10017; (212) 661-3958, ext. 311N. (Live shows—children and teen-age, women's.)

Orbis Communications, Inc.

432 Park Avenue South, New York, NY 10016; (212) 685-6699; FAX: (212) 213-3598. Robert L. Turner, pres.; John C. Ranck, exec. vice pres., international program sales; Ethan J. Podell exec. vice pres., business affairs; Hilary Hendler, senior vice pres., station sales; Frank Buquicchio, senior vice pres., finance. BRANCH OFFICES: 8800 Sunset Blvd., Suite 501, Los Angeles, CA 90067; (213) 289-7100; FAX: (213) 652-2340. Neil Russell, senior vice pres., program acquisitions & dev.; 35 East Wacker Dr., Suite 1356, Chicago, IL 60601; (617) 346-6333; FAX: (312) 346-0042. (Distributes cash movie package Carolco I, barter package Orbis Showcase Network, game show Joker's Wild, video countdown show Smash Hits, sports information Other Side of Victory, series of Oto's Raising Good Kids in Bad Times.)

Orion Pictures Television, Inc.

711 Fifth Ave., New York, NY 10022; 1888 Century Park E., Los Angeles, CA 90067. (For officers see listing under Television Companies)

- Films: Orion III Film Package, including Back to School.
- Series: Cagney & Lacey.
- First Run: Hollywood Squares, High Rollers.

Outdoor News Network

3176 Pullman, Suite 105, Costa Mesa, CA 92626; (714) 556-0330. Organized 1983. Sean Foxen, pres.; Bill Rico, vice pres.; Sandy Rice, secty./treas. (Television show.)

Jim Owens Companies

1525 McGavock St., Nashville, TN 37203; (615) 256-7700. James W. Owens, pres.; Judy McCracken, secretary. (Program producers of music entertainment and information programs for television syndication and cable network release.)

Earl Owensby Studios

P.O. Box 184, Shelby, NC 28150; (704) 482-0611. Earl Owensby, pres.; Eugene J. Kimling, pres.; John White Heart, secretary/treasurer.

P

P.A.T. Film Services Inc.

630 Ninth Ave., New York, NY 10036; (212) 247-0900; FAX: (212) 265-7087. Ervin Rosenfeld, pres.; Charles Haydon, v.p. secretary; Andrew Cuomo, v.p.; Len Laxter, video mgr.; Michael Rosenfeld, producer. (Produces and distributes TV shows and commercials; ¾", VHS & Beta cassettes for distribution. Standards conversion and videotape editing.)

Pacific International Enterprises, Inc.

1133 S. Riverside, Suite #1, P.O. Box 1727, Medford, OR 97501; (503) 779-0990; FAX: (503) 779-8880. Arthur R. Dubs, pres.-prod.; Arn S. Wihtol, v.p. sales/acquisitions; Barbara J. Brown, secty.-treas.; Paul W. Blumer, media-pub. dir.; Andy Gough, controller/office mgr.

- Features: Vanishing Wilderness, Wonder of It All, Challenge To Be Free, American Wilderness, The Adventures of the Wilderness Family, Wilderness Family Part 2, Mountain Family Robinson, Across the Great Divide, Cold River, Great Adventure, Young and Free, The Fourth Wish, Sacred Ground, Windwalker, Mystery Mansion, The Dream Chasers.

Pakula Productions, Inc.

330 W. 58 St., Suite 5H, New York, NY 10019; (212) 664-0640. (Motion picture and TV production) Alan J. Pakula, pres.: Hannah C. Pakula, v.p.; Eric Weissmann, secty.

Palladium Entertainment, Inc.

444 Madison Ave., 26th floor, New York, NY 10022; (212) 355-7070; FAX: (212) 319-4829. Gary Dartnall, Nathaniel T. Kwit, Sr. (Producers & distributor of film series). Subsidiaries include Lassie Television, Inc. and Lone Ranger Television, Inc.

- Lassie; Lone Ranger; Lone Ranger Cartoon, Sgt. Preston; Skippy the Bush Kangaroo; Magic of Lassie; Lassie the New Beginning.
- America at the Movies; An American Christmas Carol; Antonio and the Mayor; Aunt Mary; Bushido Blade; Chu Chu and the Philly Flash; City in Fear; Coffee, Tea or Me; Crime Club; Crisis in Mid-Air; Cutter's Trail; Daddy, I Don't Like It Like This; Deadly Harvest; Death of Innocence; Dr. Max; Escape; Face of Fear; Family Rico; The Four Feathers; Goodbye Raggedy Ann; Graduation Day; Horror at 37,000 Feet; Hunter; I Want to Keep My Baby; Legend of Walks Far Woman; Migrants; Mongo's Back in Town; Mother and Daughter; My Bodyguard; Nightmare; On the Right Track; Orphan Train; Relentless; Revenge of the Stepford Wives; The Seduction of Miss Leona; Something Evil; Thaddeus Rose and Eddie; That Lucky Touch; Travis Logan, D.A.; Visions of Death; When She Was Bad; Zorro the Gay Blade.
- Additional movie titles: Beyond Reason, Blade in Hong Kong, Cease Fire, The Coca Cola Kid, Consenting Adult, The Empty Beach, The Gold & Glory (aka The Coolangatta Gold), Oliver Twist, The Pilot.
- Jackpot: Game show strip.

Paramount Television

15 Columbus Circle, New York, NY 10023; (212) 373-7000. 5555 Melrose St., Hollywood, CA 90038; (213) 468-5000. For officers and personnel see listing under Companies.

- Series: Brothers (116 half-hrs.); Webster (150 half-hrs.); Cheers (146+ half-hrs.); Family Ties (154+ half-hrs.); Taxi (114 half-hrs.); Happy Days (255 half-hrs.); The Complete Star Trek (127+ hrs.); Love American Style (224 half-hrs.); Mission: Impossible (171 hrs.); The Untouchables (114 hrs.); The Lucy Show (156 half-hrs.); Mannix (130 hrs.).
- Series/First Run: The Arsenio Hall Show (6 daily hrs.); War of the Worlds (24 hrs.); Friday the 13th: The Series (26 hrs.); Star Trek: The Next Generation (22 hrs.); Entertainment Tonight (5 daily half-hrs. plus weekend hr. plus two 1-hr. specials); Geraldo (5 daily hrs.); Hard Copy (5 daily half-hrs.); Joan River (5 daily hrs.).
- Features/Packages (titles in parentheses): Portfolio XIII (27); Portfolio XII (26); Portfolio XI (22); Special Edition III (55); Special Edition II (40); Special Edition I (50); Preview IV (18); Preview III (20); Preview II (16); Marquee III (18); Marquee II (17); The Untouchables (3).
- Mini-Series: Shogun (12-hr. mini-series formatted for six 2-hr. episodes and/or one 3-hr theatrical feature); Winds of War (10-hr. mini-series formatted for five 2-hr. episodes).

Tom Parker Motion Pictures

18653 Ventura Blvd., Tarzana, CA 91536; (818) 342-9115. Telex: 858964; FAX: (818) 347-6208. Tom Parker, dir. of prod. & sls. (Licensing agent and distributor for intl. theatrical, home video and TV.)

Pathe Pictures, Inc.

161 W. 54 St., New York, NY 10019; (212) 247-4767. Joseph P. Smith, pres.; Samuel A. Costello, v.p., secty. & treas.; James J. Harrington, v.p. & gen. counsel.; Joseph A. Volatile, dir. opns. (Producer of documentaries, educational films and children's programs.)

- Milestones of the Century (365); Men of Destiny (130); Pathe Educational Shorts (103); Showtime at the Apollo (13); Musical Parade of Stars (1100); Captain David Grief (39); Showtime (39); When the Music's Over (hr. musical variety special).

Premier Film, Video & Recording Corp.

3033 Locust St., St. Louis, MO 63103; (314) 531-3555. Wilson Dalzell, pres. (Producers of motion pictures, TV spots, strip films & carts, recording and record pressings and video productions, film to video transfer, etc.)

Prijatel Productions, Inc.

1612 Prosser Ave., Dayton, OH 45409; (513) 298-8134. (Producer and distributor) Donald F. Prijatel, pres.; Julie Smith Prijatal, v.p., adv. & pub. rel.

Prime T.V. Films, Inc.

509 Madison Ave., New York, NY 10022; (212) 421-2170. Elsa Jane Campbell, pres.; Eduardo La Madrid, treas.

- Features: March of the Wooden Soldiers, When Comedy Was King, Golden Age of Comedy, Lady Take a Chance, D'Jango (color, western), Day the Sky Exploded, Incredible Petrified World, Teenage Zombies, Ape Man, Corpse Vanishes, Limping Man, White Fire, Memory of Love, Orient Express, Stars Look Down, Spotlight Scandals, Nine East Side Kids: East Side Kids, Boys of the City, That Gang of Mine, Flying Wild, Bowery Blitzkrieg, Mr. Wise Guy, Let's Get Tough, Smark Alecks, Neath Brooklyn Bridge.
- Series: Charlie Chaplin Comedy Theatre (26 half-hrs.); The Goldbergs; Courageous Cat (130 episodes, color, 5½ mins.).

Procter & Gamble Productions

9200 Sunset Blvd., Suite 525, Los Angeles, CA 90069; (213) 278-8528; FAX: (213) 276-8773. Organized 1983. Jack A. Wishard, v.p.; John K. Potter, dir. of programs. (Television development.)

Program Syndication Services, Inc.

375 Hudson St., New York, NY 10014-3620; (212) 463-3900.

ProServ Television, Inc.

10935 Estate Lane, #100, Dallas, TX 75238; (214) 343-1400; FAX: (214) 343-2068. Bob Briner, pres.; Dennis Spencer, sr. v.p.; Herb Swan, v.p. of intl. sls. (Producers of live events, made-for-TV specials, weekly series, industrials, and home videocassettes.)

Q

Qintex Entertainment, Inc.

345 N. Maple Dr., Suite 210, Beverly Hills, CA 90210; (213) 281-2600. Branches: 720 Fifth Ave., New York, NY 10012. Organized 1971. David Evans, pres., COO; Jonathan D. Lloyd, exec. v.p., CFO; Steve Mills, sr. exec. v.p. programming. (Television syndication/film distribution company, first run sales and production.)

Quality Program Sales, Inc.

824 Rome Dr., Los Angeles, CA 90065; (213) 222-8803. Kyle C. Thomas, pres. (Distributes films for TV.)

Quanta, Ltd.

1100 17th St., N.W., Washington, D.C. 20036; (202) 775-0334. W.G. Williams, U.S. representative. (British television and video production company specializing in interpreting and science and technology to general audiences.)

R

Radio and Television Packagers, Inc.

9 E. 40 St., New York, NY 10016; (212) 532-1711. William Cayton, pres. (Producer and distributor of filmed series.)

- Jungle: (59 ¼-hr. programs); Cartoon Classics—The Amazing Gift, Beauty and the Beast, The Brave Duckling, The Ice Witch, The Enchanted Princess, The Fisherman and the Fish, Tale of the Northern Lights, Gunnar the Sailor, The Valiant Knight, The Magic Antelope, The Tiny Oxen, Omar and the Ogres, The Strange Circus, Wanda and the Wicked Princess, The Wild Swans, The Woodcutter's Wish, The Frog Princess, The Fire Bird, The Space Explorers, New Adventures of the Space Explorers, Mr. E. from Tau Ceti, The Underseas Explorers, Journey to the Beginning of Time (also available in episode form); Treasure Island Revisited; The Adventures of Mutt & Jeff and Bugoff; When Funnies Were Funny (42 full-color cartoons from the geniuses of early animation); Animations (32 language arts subjects).

Carl Ragsdale Associates, Ltd.

4725 Stillbrooke, Houston, TX 77035; (713) 729-6530. Carl V. Ragsdale, pres. (Producer of documentaries and industrial motion pictures, television commercials, and theater short subjects.)

- Branches: Suite 200, 2120 "L" St. NW, Wash., DC 20037; (202) 347-7095, Arthur Neuman, exec. prod. in charge; 12522 Argyle Dr., Los Alamitos, CA 90720; (213) 598-4201, Frank Coghlan, exec. prod. in charge.

Harry Rasky Productions, Inc.

(Production of feature films and TV specials.) CBC, P.O. Box 500, Terminal A, Toronto, Canada; (416) 975-6867; FAX: (416) 975-6887. (World-wide co-productions.)

Raymond International

11 Soho St., Suite 104, Toronto, Ont., Canada M5T 1Z6; (416) 340-0130; FAX: (416) 340-0130. Bruce Raymond, pres.; Donovan B. Raymond, gen. mgr.; Antony B. Armstrong, mgr. prod. services. (Producers and distributors)

Redlin Productions, Inc.

19116 Lanark, Reseda, CA; (213) 885-8462. William A. Redlin, pres.; Emil F. Redlin, secty., treas. (Producer live and film programs, features.)

Reeves Entertainment Group

708 Third Ave., New York, NY; (212) 599-3072; 3500 W. Olive Ave., Burbank, CA 91505; (818) 953-7600. Richard S. Reisberg, pres.; Jeff Lawenda, sr. v.p.; Michael Yudin, sr. v.p.

- The Home Show (ABC).
- Incredible Sunday.
- Life's Most Embarrassing Moments (Synd.).
- On Trial (in assn. with Woody Fraser Prods.)
- Kate & Allie (CBS).
- A Doc's Life.

Republic Pictures Corporation

12636 Beatrice St., Los Angeles, CA 90066-0930; (213) 306-4040. Telex/Twx: 910-343-7417. (For officers see listing under Companies.)

- Off Network series: Beauty & the Beast (56 hours, available 9/91); Bonanza (260 hours), Get Smart (138 half hours); High Chaparral (98 hours).
- Film Packages: Classic Television Series (48 different series); Color-Imaged Specials (18 by 8/92); The John Wayne Collection (16 features); Hollywood Stars (16 features); Hollywood 1-2-3 (89 features); Action-Packed Package (28 features); Animated Features (5 features); Christmas Features (4 features); Home of the Cowboys (22 features); Classic Comedy (13 features); Serial Movies (26 features); Cartoons (15).

Riviera Productions

31628 Saddletree Dr., Westlake Village, CA 91361; (818) 889-5778. F. W. Zens, exec. producer; Leif Rise, assoc. producer. (Produces filmed series, commercials, features.)

- Punch and Trudy (6); Teletunes (15); Aqua-Lung Adventures (13).

Richard H. Roffman Associates

697 West End Ave., New York, NY 10025; (212) 749-3647. Richard H. Roffman, pres.; Malvina Cohn, John Bowman, Don Lester, Leo Blau, v.p.s. (Producers and distributors of shows also do Public Relations and publicity and promotion for shows—also do casting for shows, etc.; also use guests and feature information on numerous cable TV and UHF-TV and AM-FM radio shows in N.Y. area.)

Jack Rourke Productions

Box 1705 Burbank, CA 91507. Jack Rourke, pres.; William Hagens, v.p.; Jim Rourke, v.p., productions; sales; Hank Edwards, v.p., promotion.

Ruby-Spears Enterprises, Inc.

(A division of Great American Broadcasting.) 3330 Cahuenga Blvd. West, Hollywood, CA 90068; (213) 874-5100. Joseph Ruby, bd. chm.; Kenneth Spears, pres.

- Series: Punky Brewster (NBC); Lazer Tag (NBC); The Chipmunks (NBC); The Puppy's Great Adventures (CBS); The Centurions (Synd.); Rambo (Syns.); Chuck Norris Karate Kommandos (Synd.); A Mouse, a Mystery and Me (Synd.); Dink, the Little Dinosaur (CBS); Police Academy—The Series (Synd.).

S

SFM Entertainment

1180 Ave. of the Americas, New York, NY 10036; (212) 790-4800.

- SFM Holiday Network (package of family feature films.) March of Time series, Zoobilee Zoo; The Hugga Bunch, The Indomitable Teddy Roosevelt, Crusade in the Pacific, The Care Bears Crusade in Europe.

Saban International Services

11724 Ventura Blvd., Studio City, CA 91604; (818) 985-3805. Stan Golden, president. (Producer & distributor.)

Saban Productions/Haim Saban/dba

11724 Ventura Blvd., Studio City, CA 91604; (818) 985-3805. Organized 1980. Haim Saban, owner. Branches in Paris and Tel-Aviv. (Producers of music, cartoons, game shows programming.)

- Off-Shore TV (Synd.); Couch Potatoes (Synd.); American Expose: Live with Jack Anderson—Terrorism USA! (Synd.); The Adventures of Tom Sawyer (HBO); Alf Tales (NBC); Barbie and the Rockers (Synd.); Camp Candy (NBC); 15 Boys ((HBO); Kidd Video—The Special (Synd.); Kissyfur (NBC); Maple Town (Synd., Nickelodeon); Noozles (Nick.); $Rewards (Synd.); Tales of Little Women (HBO).

Sandollar Productions, Inc.

8730 Sunset Blvd., Penthouse West, Los Angeles, CA 90069; (213) 659-5933. Organized 1985. (Develops and produces projects for motion pictures and television.) Sand Gallin and Dolly Parton, owners; Carol Baum and Howard Rosenman, exec. v.p., producers; Candace Farrell, head of Sandollar TV; Jonathan Shestack, development.

Schaefer/Karpf Productions

3500 W. Olive Ave., Suite 730, Toluca Lake, CA 91505; (818) 953-7770.

George Schlatter Productions

8321 Beverly Blvd., Los Angeles, CA 90048; (213) 655-1400. Organized 1964. George H. Schlatter, pres.; Jolene B. Schlatter, v.p.; Nathan Golden, secty./treas. (Produces television shows and motion pictures.)

Scotti/Vinnedge Television

6277 Selma Ave., Hollywood, CA 90028; (213) 466-1006. Tony Scotti and Syd Vinnedge, exec. producers.

Arnold Shapiro Productions

5800 Sunset Blvd., Los Angeles, CA 90028; (213) 460-5202. Organized 1981. Arnold Shapiro, pres. (Produces documentaries and reality programs.)

- Rescue: 911 (CBS), The Truth about Teachers (Synd.), The American Dream Contest (Synd.).

The Silverbach-Lazarus Group

9911 W. Pico Blvd., Penthouse M, Los Angeles, CA 90035; (213) 552-2660. (Distributor) Alan Silverbach, chm.; Herb Lazarus, pres.; Toby Rodgers, sr. v.p.

The Fred Silverman Company

12400 Wilshire Blvd., Los Angeles, CA 90025; (213) 826-6050. Organized 1981. Fred Silverman, pres.; Gigi Levangie, dir., creative affairs. (Produces television and motion picture entertainment.)

- Matlock (NBC series); Jake and the Fatman (CBS series); Perry Mason movies (NBC); In the Heat of the Night (NBC); Father Dowling Mysteries (ABC); Black Widowers (CBS series); Loose Cannon (CBS series); Pig Out (animation series on Fox).

Slesinger, Stephen, Inc.

1111 N. Westshore Blvd., Tampa, FL 33607; (813) 289-4486 or (813) 837-8773. Shirley A. Lasswell, pres. (Produces films.)

Southern Star Productions

7364 Melrose Ave., Los Angeles, CA 90046; (213) 655-2966. (Producer.)

- Animated series: The Berenstain Bears Show (CBS), CBS Storybreak (CBS), Teen Wolf (CBS).
- Animated Specials: Marvin (CBS).

Rick Spalla Video Productions

Subsidiaries: Hollywood Newsreel Syndicate, Inc., and Rick Spalla Production, Inc.

1622 North Gower St., Hollywood, CA 90028 (213); 469-7307; 301 W. 45 St., New York, NY 10036; (212) 765-4646. Organized 1957. Rick Spalla, pres.; Anthony J. Spalla, v.p.; Jeff Spalla, prod. supvr.; Mike Spalla, music dir.; Maralee Spalla, p.r. (Film and video tape production-producer and packager of TV programs, commercials and industrial films.)

- Syndicated TV shows: Portrait of a Star; Hollywood Backstage; High Road to Danger; Hollywood Guest Shot; Hobby Nobbing . . . with the Stars; Century of Fashion; The Open Road, Hollywood's Fantastic Artists' and Models' Ball; Hollywood Star Newsreel, Holiday on Wheels, Portrait: The New Breed; Century of Fashion . . . in Motion Pictures; The Great Getaway; Live two-hr. special: California State network hook-up. Miss California International Beauty Pageant (2 hours) (Annual Competition in April.); The Wild . . . Wild . . . World of Spirit; Kay Crawford's Pep Arts Training Series (14 hrs.).

Spectacor Films

1145 N. McCadden, Los Angeles, CA 90038; (213) 871-2777. Organized 1987. Michael Jaffe, pres.; David Newlon, v.p. & CFO; Marie Jansen, exec. v.p., motion pictures; Daniel Sladek, dir., creative & administrative affairs; Chris Sacani, mgr., TV production. (Television, feature films and series production and distribution. Parent company to other producers.)

Aaron Spelling Productions, Inc.

1401 N. Formosa, Hollywood, CA 90046; (213) 850-2413. Organized 1965. Aaron Spelling, chmn. of the bd., chief exec. officer; Jules Haimovitz, president & chief operating officer; E. Duke Vincent, pres. of the exec. comm.; Ronald Lightstone, exec. v.p.; John T. Brady, sr. v.p., & chief financial officer; Arthur Frankel, sr. v.p., business and legal affairs; Renate Kamer, v.p. & secty.; Alan Greisman, v.p., motion pictures; Barbara Rubin, v.p., business affairs; Tony Shepherd, v.p., talent; Marcia Basichis, vice pres., programming; Michael Halpern, v.p., East Coast development; Keith Nicol, v.p., special services; Pam Bottaro, dir. of dev., motion pictures; Howard Rosenstein, dir. of television development; Board of directors: Aaron Spelling, Jules Haimovitz, Douglas S. Cramer, E. Duke Vincent, Arthur H. Bilger, J. William Hayes. (Development and production of all forms of TV programming, as well as the production of feature films.)

- Series: The Colbys, Dynasty, Hotel.

Bob Stewart Productions

1717 N. Highland Ave., Suite #;807, Hollywood, CA 90028; (213) 461-3721. Organized 1964. Robert Stewart, pres. (Television production company.)

- Jackpot (USA).
- The New Chain Reaction (USA).

Sunbow Productions, Inc.

130 Fifth Ave., New York, NY 10011; (212) 337-6100. Organized 1978. (Television production.) Thomas L. Griffin, chairman; Joe Bacal, pres.; Jay Bacal, senior v.p.-creative dir.; Eve Silverman, senior v.p.-dev.; Carole Weitzman, v.p./prod. & business affairs; v.p.-dev.; Anne Newman, v.p.-dev.; C. J. Kettler, senior v.p. Sunbow Intl.; David Wollos, v.p. sales & operations.

- Animated series: Visionaries (Synd.), The Transformers (Synd.), Jem (Synd.).

Survival Anglia Ltd.

420 Lexington Ave., New York, NY 10017; (212) 867-6979 . John F. Ball, pres.; James T. de Kay, senior v.p.; Victor Simpkins, v.p., business affairs & corporate communications.

- *Properties:* Tales of the Unexpected (66 half-hrs., bizarre, mystery-suspense anthology with international stars); Tales of the Unexpected, Series Three (22 half-hrs.); World of Survival (21 half-hr. wildlife episodes hosted by John Forsythe); For a Better World (6 one-hr. wildlife/natural history adventures from around the world); Lions of Etosha (one-hr. special on lions filmed by cinematographer Des Bartlett); Warriors of the Gods (one-hr. special on Asian elephants by Dieter Plage).

Syndicast Services, Inc.

360 Madison Ave., New York, NY 10017; (212) 557-0055. (Distributor) Leonard V. Koch, pres.; Gerry Lepkanich, v.p. sls.; Terry Paolillo, v.p., opns.; William Madden, dir. sta. sls.

T

TFI (A division of MPO)

619 W. 54 St., New York, NY 10019; (212) 708-0500; FAX: (212) 977-9458; 941 N. Highland Avenue, Los Angeles, CA 90038; (213) 461-3361; 640 N. LaSalle St., Chicago, IL; (312) 951-6700. Charles A. Ahto, pres. (Duplication and distribution of TV commercials, film trailers, advertising and promotional materials; film and video tape. Complete storage facilities in NJ & Delaware. Post-production services; fulfillment services.)

TMS Entertainment, Inc.

3575 Cahuenga Blvd W., Suite 370, Los Angeles, CA 90068; (213) 850-5550. Organized 1983 in U.S., 1964 in Tokyo. Eiji Katayama, exec. v.p., CEO; Sander Schwartz, sr. v.p. Branches: Tokyo Movie Shinsa (TMS). (Creates and produces fully-animated TV shows and feature films.)

TV Art International Inc.

300 Central Park West, Suite 2G, New York, NY 10024; (212) 580-2152; FAX: (212) 724-3785. Organized 1987. Jorge De Gregorio, pres.; Graciela Abelin, vice president; Freda Wang, exec. secretary; Jorge De Gregorio, Graciela Abelin, Charles Luetke, board of directors. (Distribution of programs in U.S.A. and Latin America—branch: TV Art Argentina.)

D. L. Taffner/Limited

31 W. 56 St., New York, NY 10019; (212) 245-4680. Donald L. Taffner, pres.; John P. Fitzgerald, chief exec. officer; Rick Levy, pres., sales and marketing/syndication; Bob Peyton, exec. v.p.-man. dir., domestic syndication; Joe Ceslik, v.p., gen. sales mgr/syndication; Dennis E. Doty, sr. v.p.; David Dreilinger, v.p., business & legal affairs, Dennis Ellis, v.p., chief financial officer; Leon Memoli, v.p., development; Martha Strauss, v.p., intl. sales; Christina Thomas, v.p., sales and development. (Distributor).

- Comedy: Benny Hill (85 half hrs.); Thames Comedy Originals (156 half hrs.); After Benny (40 half hrs.); Robins Nest (48 half hrs.); Man About the House (39 half hrs.); George & Mildred (38 half hrs.); Keep it in the Family (31 half hrs.)
- Feature Films: Best of Benny (90 mins.).
- Mini-Series: Blood & Honor (5 hrs.).
- Series/First Run: Too Close for Comfort (104 weeks); Check It Out (52 weeks); Ted Knight Show (52 weeks).
- Documentaries: Hollywood (13 hrs.); World at War (36 hrs.); Destination America (9 hrs.).
- Series/Off Network: Three's Company (222 half hrs.); Too Close for Comfort (107 half hrs.); The Ropers (26 half hrs.); Three's A Crowd (22 half hrs.).
- Specials: Benny Hill Specials I (5 hrs.).
- Animation: Danger Mouse (50 half hrs.).

Tall Pony Productions, Inc.

300 Loma Metisse, Malibu, CA 90265; (213) 456-7495; FAX: (213) 456-7254. Organized 1980. Anthony Eaton, president. (Television production.)

TeleAmerica Entertainment Inc.

4308 Via Marina, Marina Del Rey, CA 90292; (213) 827-2272; FAX: (213) 827-9045. Organized 1986. Lawrence P. O'Daly, president. (Television series producer.)

Telecine Film Studios, Inc.

R2 Box 7A1, Winterset, IA 50273. Byron L. Friend, pres. (Producers of motion pictures, TV series, TV commercials, videotape.)

- Zoo Parade; Magic Ranch.

Telemated Motion Pictures

137 S.W. 54th St., Cape Coral, FL 33914. Saul Taffet, producer-director. (Producer of documentaries, commercials, industrial, corporate image, public relations, training, sales promotion, and educational films.)

Telemount Pictures, Inc.

P.O. Box 1106, Santa Monica, CA 90406. Henry B. Donovan, pres. and producer. (Producers of Cowboy G-Men film series.)

- 39 Westerns; 13 shorts.

TeleVentures

(A partnership of Tri-Star Pictures, Stephen J. Cannell Productions and Witt/Thomas Productions.)

1925 Century Park East, Suite 2140, Los Angeles, CA 90067; (213) 785-0111; FAX: (213) 203-0267; 100 W. 57th St., New York, NY 10019; (212) 541-6040. Organized 1986. Pat Kenney, pres. & CEO; Bill Kunkel, pres., domestic distributions; Jerry Leifer, dir. of contract administration; Douglas Friedman, v.p., advertising & promotion; Drew Hallmann, v.p. of research. (Television program distribution—U.S. and international.

Television Program Enterprises

875 Third Ave., New York, NY 10022; (212) 759-8787; FAX: (212) 838-4696. (Producer and distributor.) Philbin S. Flanagan, pres. & general mgr.; Mary Jane Hastings, v.p. operations.

Teleworld, Inc.

245 W. 55 St., New York, NY 10019; (212) 489-9310; FAX: (212) 262-9395. Robert Seldelman, pres.

Foreign Offices: United Kingdom: Dandelion, 49 St. Peter's St., London N1 8JP, England; 354-2472. Noel Cronin, sls. rep. Mid East: Transworld Television Corp., 81 Piccadilly, London, W1V 9HB, England; 499-7419. Issam Hamaoul, sls. rep. Spain: Apartdao 33009, Madrid-23, Spain; 637-5540. Antoniette Brughera Miranda, sls. rep. Australia: Telepix Pty. Ltd., 155 Alexander St., Crows Nest NSW, 2065 Australia; 439-7377. Robert Lapthorne, sls. rep.

- Mini-Series: Chiefs (6 hrs.); Kennedy (U.S. only; 7 hrs.); Mistral's Daughter (U.S. only; 8 hrs.); Civilization & The Jews (intl. only; 9 hrs.)
- Features/Packages: Spiderman (U.S. only—7 live-action features); Teleworld's Top 50 (chiller & action features).
- Series/First Run: Powerhouse (16 half-hrs.).
- Series: Star Maidens (U.S. only—13 half-hrs.); Castaway (U.S. only—13 half-hrs.).
- Specials: Dinosaur (intl. only; 1 hr.)

Bob Thomas Productions

60 E. 42 St., New York, NY 10165; (212) 221-3602. Robert G. Thomas, pres. (Motion picture and TV producer; program syndication & satellite services to reach 270 independent television stations.)

Titus Productions, Inc.

(A division of Great American Broadcasting)

211 E. 51 St., New York, NY 10022; (212) 752-6460. Herbert Brodkin, pres.; Robert Buzz Berger, v.p. (Producers of motion pictures, television series and specials.)

Herb Tobias and Associates, Inc.

1901 Ave. of the Stars, Suite 840, Century City, Los Angeles, CA 90067; 277-6211. (Talent Agency.)

Tower Productions

11541 Landale St., No. Hollywood, CA 91602. H. G. and Barbara J. Rhinelander, owners. (Live programs.)

- Space Patrol (live, plus 300 half-hr. and 200 15-min. kinescopes).

Trans World International

11755 Wilshire Blvd., Los Angeles, CA 90025; (213) 473-0411. (Television production.)

- Battle of the Network Stars (ABC), Breeders' Crown (ESPN), Sports Forum (MSG); Starshop (ESPN), Superstars (NBC), Veteran Superstars (NBC), Survival of the Fittest (NBC).

Transvue TV International Co.

A Division of Transvue Pictures Corp., 5131 Colbath Ave., Sherman Oaks, CA 91423; (818) 990-5600. Herbert B. Schlosberg, pres.; K. Galloway, secty.

Tribune Entertainment Company

(A subsidiary of Tribune Broadcasting Co., Inc.) 435 N. Michigan Ave., Suite 1800, Chicago, IL 60611; (312) 222-4484. Sheldon Cooper, pres.; Donald Hacker, exec. v.p.; David Sifford, exec. v.p., marketing & sales; Peter Marino, v.p., program development; George Paris, v.p., programming (West Coast); Greg Miller, dir. of programming; Melvyn Smith, v.p., programming; Joseph Antelo, v.p., exec. prod., At the Movies; Carol Forace, v.p., dir. of research & sales; Tanya Neimark, dir. creative svcs.; Allan I. Grafman, v.p., project dir.; Mike Adinamis, dir. broadcast operations/midwest sales & mktg.; Bob Cambridge, mgr. of special projects. National media sales and station clearances by Teletrib, 875 Third Ave., New York, NY 10022; (212) 450-9190.

- Series: Geraldo (1 hour, weekly); At the Movies (½ hour weekly movie review); U.S. Farm Report (weekly); Soul Train (weekly); Monsters (½ hour, first run); Dionne & Friends (weekly); The Joan Rivers Show (1 hour, weekly).
- Specials: On Trial: Lee Harvey Oswald (2 hrs. with host Geraldo Rivera); The Geraldo Rivera Specials (2 hrs.); Soul Train Music Awards (2 hrs.); Nadia (2 hrs.); Living the Dream: A Tribute of Dr. Martin Luther King Jr. and Black History Notes (in association with Tribune Central City Productions); Hollywood Christmas Parade; The Tournament of Rose Parade.
- Sports: Chicago Cubs Baseball television network.

Turn of the Century Fights, Inc.

9 E. 40 St., New York, 10016; (212) 532-1711. William D. Cayton, pres. (Produce and distribute fight films.)

- Knock-Out (now total of 600 subjects, from 1897 through 1988).
- The Legendary Champions (90-min. feature)

Turner Program Services

1050 Techwood Dr., N.W., Atlanta, GA 30318; (404) 827-2085. Henry A. Gillespie, chm.; Russ Barry, pres.; Bob Schuessler, v.p.-CNN-special projects; Sid Pike, v.p., intl.; Howard Karshan, v.p., Europe; John Walden, v.p., mktg.; Bob Rierson, dir. programming; Ken Christensen, dir. adv. promo.

Twentieth Television Corp., Distribution Division

P.O. Box 900, Beverly Hills, CA 90213; (213) 277-2211. (For officers and personel see listing in Television Companies.)

- Series: Circus (52); That's Hollywood (74).
- Series/First Run: A Current Affair (daily live half-hour magazine show).
- Series/Off-Network: Small Wonder (96 half-hours); Mr. Belveder (95 half-hours); Dynasty (198 hours); 9 to 5 (85 half-hours); Fall Guy (112 hours); Trapper John (151 hours); Batman (120 half-hours); Daniel Boone (120 hours); The Ghost and Mrs. Muir (50 half-hours); Circus (52 half-hours); That's Hollywood (74 half-hours); M*A*S*H (255 half-hours); Jackie Gleason Show (100 half-hours); Animal Express (130 half-hours); Miller's Court (52 half-hours); Expedition Danger (26 half-hours); Audubon WIldlife Theater (78 half-hours); Julia (86 half-hours); Lancer (51 hours); Land of the Giants (51 hours); Lost in Space (83 hours, 54 color); Nanny and the Professor (54 half hours); Room 222 (113 hours); Voyage to the Bottom of the Sea (hours; 78 color, 32 b&w); 12 O'Clock High (78 hours; 17 color, 61 b&w); Vegas (68 hours); The Ann Sothern Show (93 half-hours); Private Secretary (104 hours)); Movin' On (44 hours); The Monroes (26 hours); Judd for the Defense (50 hours); Bracken's World (41 hours); Incredible World of Adventure (31 half-hours); Peyton Place (247 half hours color & 267 half-hours, b&w); Green Hornet (26 half-hours); Adventures in Paradise (91 b&w); Broken Arrow (72 b&w); Dobie Gillis (147 b&w); The Untamed World (156 half-hours).
- Specials: Charles Dickens' Classics (8); Hollywood: The Gift of Laughter (3 hours); The Making of M*A*S*H (1); The President's Command Performance (2); Inside Russia (1); Future Shock (1); Time of Man (1); Assassins Among Us (1); The Cancer Confrontation (1); Sex, Teenage Style (1); Divorce, Kids in the Middle (1); The Undersea World of Jacques Cousteau (36); Jane Goodall and the World of Animal Behavior (4); Fox Movietone News (520 newsreels); Summer Solstice (1 hr.); Godonov—The World to Dance In (1 hr.); Blind Alley (1 hr.); Anatomy of a Crime (1); War to End all Wars (1).
- First Run Syndication: 9 to 5; Dream Girl USA; 100,000 Pyramid; Small Wonder; Dance Fever.
- Features/Packages: Century 5, 6, 7, 8, 9, 20, 22, 23 (total of 220 titles, 212 color and 8 b&w); Century 13 (26), Century 14 (20 titles, includes Aliens, Black Widow, Cocoon, The Fly, The Jewel of the Nile, The Name of the Rose); Fox Premiere Movies (9, barter incl.: Enemy Mine, The Name of the Rose, Project X); Fox Mini Series I (4 titles: Tender Is the Night, Jamaica Inn, Little Gloria, Evergreen); Fox Hollywood Threatre '89–90 (7 titles incl: Miracle on 34th Street, Almost You, Eating Raoul, Kidco); Big 36 (36 titles, 5 color, 29 b&w); Special 41 (41 titles, 26 color, 15 b&w); Fox IV, V & VI (102 color, 102 b&w); Fox Mystery Theatre (13, 90-min. specials); Plant of the Apes (5); Premiere I (20); Premiere II (22); Premiere III (20); Time Tunnel (5); Mark I (10); Mark II (16); Mark III (25); Premium Plus (28); MPC-20 (20); Carry On (11); Golden Century (49 b&w); Super 65 (48 color, 17 b&w).
- Domestic Late-Night Network: The New Avengers (26 hours).
- Domestic Miniseries: Sara Dane (8 hours); Wild Times (4 hours); Roughnecks (4 hours); The Far Pavilions (6 hours); Empire, Inc. (6 hours); Mussolini and I (4 hours); Spearfield's Daughter (6 hours)
- Domestic Cartoons: Groovie Goolies & Friends (104 half-hours); Crusader Rabbit (13 color hours, 260 4-minute color episodes, 195 4-minute b & w episodes); Doctor Doolittle (17 half-hours); Fantastic Voyage (17 half-hours); The Hardy Boys (17 half-hours); Journey to the Center of the Earth (17 half-hours); Return to the Planet of the Apes (13 half-hours).

U

UPA Productions of America

14101 Valleyheart Dr., Suite 200, Sherman Oaks, CA 91423; (818) 990-3800; FAX: (800) 990-4854. Henry G. Saperstein, pres.; (Distributes Mr. Magoo, Dick Tracy, Gerald McBoing-Boing color cartoons, family specials, and features, Godzilla, Rodan, sci-fi features etc. Produces animated commercials, theatrical films, industrial & TV programs.)

United Press International

1400 I St., NW, Washington, DC 20005; (202) 898-8000; FAX: (202) 842-3625. Dr. Earl Brian, chm.; Paul Steinle, pres.; Al Rossiter, Jr., exec. editor. (Distributes news, audio and information services.) Entertainment queries should be directed to UPI Features, (202) 898-8052.

Universal Television

A Division of Universal City Studios, Inc. Universal City, CA 91608, (213) 985-4321. (For officers see listing under companies.)

- 1989–90 season:
- ABC Mystery Movies: Columbo, BL Stryker, Kojak, Jaclyn Smith project (2 hour movies).
- Half Hour and Hour: Coach, Major Dad, Murder She Wrote, Quantum Leap.

V

Valiant International Pictures

4774 Melrose Ave., Hollywood, CA 90029; (213) 665-5257; FAX: (213) 665-6473. Harry Novak, pres.; Ivan Levitan, v.p.; Carmen Novak, secty./treas. (Distributor.)

Van Praag Productions, Inc.

135 E. 55 St., New York, NY 10022; (212) 838-2111. William Van Praag, exec. dir., Eugene Van Praag, Anita Palumbo, Ray Van Praag, staff directors.

Veritas Productions, Inc.

1 Laurie Dr., Englewood Cliffs, NJ 07632; (201) 568-4214 or New York City (212) 765-4240. Richard S. Dubelman, pres.; Joan D. Morley, asst. to pres. (TV and motion picture production)

Versatile Television Production, Inc.

324 Broadway, Cape Girardeau, MO 335-8816. TWX Cape Girardeau 968; Robert O. Hirsch, press.; Jerry Hollis, mgr. (Producers of animated, live action film and video tape commercials and industrial.)

Vestron Television

1010 Washington Blvd., P.O. Box 10382, Stamford, CT 06901; (203) 978-5400; FAX: (203) 978-5818. David Armstrong, v.p., sales; Bruce Casino, mgr, dir., Eastern sales; Charles Byrd, mgr. adminsitration; Karen Setten, account coordinator. West Coast office: 2029 Century Park East, Los Angeles, CA 90067; (213) 551-1723. Central office: 1128 White Lake Court, Fort Worth, TX 76103; (817) 654-2401; Timothy Lavender, acct. exec.

- Over 50 theatrical motion pictures, including Hot Tickets; First Images; Double Images; The Eyes of War (hosted by Robert Mitchum); Empire of Terror; Heroes, Pirates and Warriors; The Beach Boys: An American Band; Dirty Dancing: Live in Concert.

Viacom International Inc.

1211 Ave. of the Americas, New York, NY 10036; (212) 575-5175. (For officers and corporate personnel, see Television Companies.)

- First-Run Programs: Remote Control (39 half-hours); Superboy (52 half-hours); Super Mario Bros. Super Show (65 half-hours); This Morning's Business (daily half-hour); Trial by Jury (160 half hours).
- Series, Off-Network: The Cosby Show (144 half-hours); All in the Family (207 half-hrs.); Andy Griffith Show (249 half-hrs.); The Beverly Hillbillies (274 half-hrs.); The Bob Newhart Show (142 half-hrs.); Cannon (122 hours, 1 2-hour special); Clint Eastwood in Rawhide (144 half-hrs.); December Bride (154 half-hrs.); Dick Van Dyke Show (158 half-hrs.); Family Affair (138 half-hrs.); Gomer Pyle (150 half-hrs.); Gunsmoke (402 hours); Have Gun Will Travel (156 half-hrs.); Hawaii Five-O (200 hrs.); Hogan's Heroes (168 half-hrs.); The Honeymooners (107 half-hrs.); I Love Lucy (179 half-hrs.); Marshall Dillon (233 half-hrs.); The Mary Tyler Moore Show (168 half-hrs.); My Three Sons (160 half-hrs.) Our Miss Brooks (127 half-hrs.); Perry Mason (271 hrs); Petticoat Junction (148 half-hrs.); The Rookies (90 hrs.); Twentieth Century (52 half-hrs.); The Twilight Zone (136 half hrs., 18 hours); The Wild, Wild West (104 hrs.).

Vidistrib, Inc.

4209 Troost Ave., Studio City, CA 91604; Tel.: (818) 762-3535. John P. Ballinger, pres.; Rita Cross, v.p.-treas. (TV show sales & distribution syndication, barter, consultation).

W

WW Entertainment

(A division of World Northal Corporation) 205 E. 42 St., New York, NY 10017; (212) 661-3350; Telex: 4973939; FAX: (212) 808-5469. Tony Elmaleh, v.p., prod.; James R. Waltz, sr. v.p.; Zita Siegel, dir. sls. adm.; Bernice Farnan, administrator/sales & research.

- Feature Films—Martial Arts Feature Films: Black I (13 titles); Black Belt II (26 titles); Black Belt III (13 titles); Black Belt IV (29 titles); Black Belt V (13 titles); Action Flicks (7 titles); WW Entertainment I (16 titles).
- Series—The Best of Groucho (130 half-hrs.); Skyways (130 hrs.)
- Co-productions-BBC: 24 feature films.

Roger Wade Productions, Inc.

15 W. 44 St., New York, NY 10036; (212) 575-9111; FAX: (212) 764-4178. Carolyn J. Wade, pres. (Producers of motion pictures and videotape for industry, sound slide films, multi-media, slides.)

Warner Bros. Television

4000 Warner Blvd., Burbank, CA 91522; (818) 954-6000. (For officers and personnel, see listing under Companies.)

Series and specials available for domestic sales (all color unless otherwise indicated)

- Miniseries: Hollywood Wives (6 hrs.); "V" (10 hrs.); Bare Essence (4 hrs. or 4½ hrs.); The Thorn Birds (10 hrs.); Pearl (6 hrs.); Scruples (6 hrs.); Roots (12 hrs.); Roots: The Next Generation (14 hrs.)
- Series/Off Network: Head of the Class (half-hrs.); Growing Pains (half-hrs.); Night Court (half-hrs.); Scarecrow and Mrs. King (88 hours); Matt Houston (68 hours); Private Benjamin (39 half-hrs.); The Dukes of Hazzard (147 hrs.); Alice (202 half-hrs.); Welcome Back, Kotter (95 half-hrs.); Chico and the Man (88 half-hrs.); F-Troop (65 half-hrs., 31 color); Superman (104 half-hrs., 52 color); Batman/Superman/Aquaman (69 animated half-hrs.) Harry-O (44 hrs.); Wonder Woman (61 hrs); Kung Fu (62 hrs.); The Waltons (221 hrs.); The FBI (234 hrs.); Tarzan (57 hrs.); Maverick (124 hrs.)
- Specials: The Phenomenon of Roots (1 hr.); David L. Wolper Specials of the Seventies (30 one-hr. specials)
- Features/Packages: Volume 27 (18 features); TV4 (13 features); Volume 26 (24 features); TV3 (13 features); Volume 25 (24 features); TV2 (13 feature titles); Volume 24 (18 features); 13 Classic Thrillers II (13 features); TVI (13 features); Volume 23 (20 features); Volume 22 (38 features); Volume 21 (26 features); The FBI Story (4 features); Volume 20 (30 features); Volume 19 (29 features, 28 in color); Volume 18 (28 features, 25 in color); Volume 17 (23 features, 21 in color); Volume 16 (18 features, 16 in color); Volume 14-15 (13 features, 12 in color); Volume 13 (25 features, 17 in color); Volume 2-A (22 features, 13 in color); Volume 1-A (24 features, 17 in color); 13 Classic Thrillers (13 features); Tarzan Features (32 features, 9 in color); The Bowery Boys (48 features); Starlite 6 (26 features, 12 in color); Starlite 5 (28 features, 18 in color); Starlite 4 (30 features, 16 in color); Starlite 3 (30 features, 19 in color); Special Features (17 features).
- Cartoons: Bugs Bunny & Friends (100 cartoons); Porky Pig & Friends (156 cartoons)

INTERNATIONAL

- Cartoons: Bugs Bunny & Friends (100 cartoons); Bugs Bunny cartoons (234 cartoons); Looney Toons (190 cartoons, 78 color, 112 black-and-white)
- Features/Packages: International 33 (36); International 21 (51); International 21 (34); International 30 (66); International 29 (44); International 28 (7); International 27 (5); International 26 (11); International 25 (32); International 24 (80); International 23 (99); International 22 (135); International 21 (56); International 20 (3); International 19 (28); International 18 (26); International 17 (28); International 16 (92); International 15 (33); International 14 (36); International 13 (35); International 12 (36); International 11 (36); International 9 (1); International 5 (48); International 4 (127)
- Miniseries: Napoleon and Josephine: A Love Story (6 hrs.); Nutcracker: Money, Madness and Murder (6 hrs.); Dream West (7 hrs.); Crossings (6 hrs.); Dress Gray (4 hrs.); North and South—I (12 hrs.); North and South—II (12 hrs.); Hollywood Wives (6 hrs.); The Thorn Birds (10); "V" (10); Roots (12); Roots: The Next Generation (14); The Mystic Warrior (5); Bare Essence (4); Scruples (6); Pearl (6); The Phenomenon of Roots (1); The Awakening Land (7); Born to the Wind (4); Hanging by a Thread (4); Haywire (4); Moviola (6); Night the Bridge Fell Down (4); Pirate (4); Salem's Lot (4)
- One-Hour Series: O'Hara (6); Scarecrow and Mrs. King (88); Hotel; The Colbys (49); Spenser: For Hire; Shell Game (6); Shadow Chasers (12); Hollywood Beat (14); "V" (19); Matt Houston (68); The Dukes of Hazzard (147); Harry O (44); Kung Fu (62); Tarzan (57); I Had Three Wives (6); MacGruder & Loud (13); Eye to Eye (6); Double Dare (6); Finder of Lost Loves (23); Glitter (13); The Yellow Rose (22); The Mississippi (23); Bare Essence (11); The Alaskans (36); Banyon (15); Bourbon Street Beat (39); Bret Maverick (16); Bronco (68); California Fever (10); Casablanca (5); Cheyenne (107); Code R (13); The Dakotas (19); Delphi Bureau (8); Dial M for Murder (13); Drama (42); Enos (17); The F.B.I. (238); Fitzpatricks (13); Freebie and the Bean (9); Gallant Men (25); Hawaiian Eye (134); High Performance (4); Life on Earth (13); Maverick (124); The New Land (13); Nichols (24); Notorious Woman (7); Rafferty (13); Roaring 20's (45); Search (23); 77 Sunset Strip (205); The Streets of San Francisco (119); Sugarfoot (69); Superfriends (93); Challenge of Superfriends (16); Surfside Six (74); Time Express (4); The Tribal Eye (7); The Waltons (219); Wizards and Warriors (8); Wonder Woman (13); New Adventures of Wonder Woman (46); The Yeagers (4); Young Maverick (6)
- Half-Hour Series: Night Court; Growing Pains; Life with Lucy (13); My Sister, Sam; Head of the Class; Welcome Back, Kotter (95);

Love, Sidney (44); Porky Pig Show (26); Private Benjamin (39); Roadrunner Show (26); Superman (104); Tarzan, Lord of the Jungle (34); Alice (202); Rubik, the Amazing Cube (13); Off the Rack (7); A.E.S Hudson Street (5); Another Day (13); Aquaman (18); At Ease (14); Batman (17); New Adventures of Batman (16); B.C. Archaeology of Bible Lands (12); Bugs Bunny Show (78); Chicago Teddy Bears (13); Chico and the Man (88); Colt .45 (67); The Cowboys (12); Dorothy (4); The Dukes—Animated (20); Fat Albert and the Cosby Kids (60); Flo (29); F Troop (65); Goodnight, Beantown (8); Jimmy Stewart Show (24); Lassie's Rescue Rangers (17); Lawman (156); Little People, The Brian Keith Show (46); Marine Boy (78); Me and Maxx (10); Merrie Melodies Show (24); Mr. Roberts (30); New Adventures of Superman (34); No Time for Sergeants (34); Park Place (5); Shazam! (28); TV Funnies (16)

Weiss Global Enterprises

2055 S. Saviers Rd., Suite 12, Oxnard, CA 93033-3693; (805) 486-4495. Cable: WEISSPICT. Adrian Weiss, pres.; Steven A. Weiss, secty./treas.; Ethel L. Weiss, v.p.; Laurie Weiss, v.p.; Beverly S. Verman, opns. mgr.; Alex Gordon, information services.

- Features: Galaxy "15" (15 features including Cactus in the Snow, Ginger in the Morning, Lovers Like Us, Molly and Lawless John); Golden $howmanship "9" (9 features including Cattle Queen of Montana, Slightly Scarlett); Impact "120" (120 features prod. by Robert L. Lippert incl. Baron of Arizona, I Shot Jesse James, King Dinosaur, Sins of Jezebel); Bride & The Beast; Westerns: (60 action features starring Johnny Mack Brown, Harry Carey, Fred Kohler, Jr., Rex Lease, Buddy Roosevelt and Bob Steele); Vintage Flicks (24 features from the '30's and '40's).
- One-Hour Documentaries: The Brave Rifles (51 mins.), Our Time in Hell (51 mins.); Those Crazy Americans (54 mins.).
- Serials: Custer's Last Stand (15 episodes); The Black Coin (15 episodes); The Clutching Hand (15 episodes).
- Series, First-Run: The Stan Kann Show (52 half-hrs.); Kids Say the Darndest Things (600 episodes, 5 min. each).
- Series, Off-Network: Make Room For Daddy (161 half-hr. programs); Canine Comments (13 quarter-hr. short subject); I Married Joan (98 half-hr. sit-coms); The Bill Dana Show (42 half-hrs.); Craig Kennedy, Crimonologist (26 half-hr. mysteries); Good Morning World (26 half-hr. sit-coms); Thrill of Your Life (13 half-hrs.); My Little Margie (126 half-hrs.); Rocky Jones, Space Ranger (39 half-hrs.); Waterfront (78 half-hrs.); The Adventures of Jim Bowie (76 half-hours).
- Comedy Shorts: The Chuckle Heads (150 five-min. slapstick comedy shorts).
- Cartoons: Alice by Walt Disney (10 Alice Comedy cartoons); Krazy Kid Kartunes (4 six-min. cartoons); Nursery Rhymes (6 1½-min. cartoons).

Witt/Thomas Productions

846 N. Cahuenga Blvd., Hollywood, CA 90038; (213) 464-1333.

- Beauty and the Beast (CBS) (in assn. with Republic Pictures).

Witt/Thomas/Harris Productions

846 N. Cahuenga Blvd., Hollywood, CA 90038; (213) 464-1333. Stephen Kurzfeld, v.p. creative affairs.

- Empty Nest (NBC) (in assn. with Touchstone).
- The Golden Girls (NBC) (in assn. with Touchstone).

The Wizard Group, Inc.

8831 Sunset Blvd., Suite 300, Los Angeles, CA 90069; (213) 854-6310. Organized 1988. Richard Harrison, pres.; Michael Rann, v.p.; Francesca Harrison, v.p., production. (Feature-length TV production. Affiliated with Harmony Gold Inc.)

Worldvision Enterprises, Inc.

660 Madison Ave., New York, NY 10021; (212) 832-3838; FAX: (212) 980-5970; Telex: 62401 (WOR UW). John D. Ryan, pres. & chief exec. officer; Bert Cohen, exec. v.p. & COO; Lawrence Gottlieb, exec. v.p., finance & admin.; Burt Rosenburgh, exec. v.p. & g.m., Evergreen Programs, Inc.; Elliott Abrams, sr. v.p., acquisitions; Steve Blank, senior v.p., finance; Randy Hanson, senior v.p., domestic sales; Gary G. Montanus, senior v.p., marketing; Charles Quinones, sr. v.p., operations; Tom Devlin, v.p. & g.m., Worldvision Home Video, Inc.; Bill Baffi, v.p., eastern division mgr.; Mitch Black, v.p., operations; Jerry Kaufer, v.p., creative services; Philip Marella, v.p., legal & business affairs; Donald Micallef, v.p., research & development; Andrea Roth, v.p., office management & personnel; Rita Scarfone, v.p., advertising & promotion; Dan Willis, v.p., international sales admin.; Noreen McGrath, asst. v.p., dir. of national marketing; Phil Martzolf, account exec., eastern div.; Karen Davidson, account exec., advertiser sales; Robert Dudelson, account exec., advertiser sales; Doreen Muldoon, account exec., advertiser sales; Andy Samet, dir. of promotion; Alan Winnikoff, dir. of communications.

DOMESTIC DIVISIONS

CENTRAL: 625 N. Michigan Avenue, Chicago, IL 60611; (312) 642-2650; FAX: (312) 642-8687. Gary Butterfield, v.p., Central div. mgr.; Brian O'Sullivan, acct. exec., Central div.; Jim Kauss, acct. exec., Central div., Evergreen Programs, Inc.; Jim Smith, dir. Midwest advertiser sales; Ken Williams, Central div. mgr., Worldvision Home Video, Inc.

SOUTHERN: 400 Perimeter Center Terrace, Altanta, GA 30346; (404) 394-7444; FAX: (404) 396-8996. Karl Middelburg, Southern div. mgr.; Reggie Jester, acct. exec., Southern Division; Bruce Knox, Southern div. mgr., Worldvision Home Video, Inc.

WESTERN: 9465 Wilshire Blvd., Beverly Hills, CA 90212; (213) 273-7667; FAX: (213) 273-3645. Paul Danylik, v.p., Western div. mgr., Martin Weisman, acct. exec., Western div.; Ed O'Brien, account exec., Western div., Evergreen Programs, Inc.; Jennifer Charlton, Western div. mgr., Worldvision Home Video, Inc.

- First Run Late Fringe Variety: After Hours (half-hour).
- First Run Weekly Series: Better Your Home With *Better Homes and Gardens* (half-hour).
- First Run Animated Series: Hanna-Barbera's Superstars 10 (10 2-hour movies).
- First Run Live-Action: Sword of Honour (6-hour mini-series), Starring the Actors (13 half-hours); Shark's Paradise (2-hour movie); Return to Eden (22 hours and 6-hour mini-series), Starting from Scratch (half-hour series).
- Animated Series: The Yogi Bear Show (65 half-hours); Smurfs' Adventures (65 half-hour); Funtastic World of Hanna-Barbera (2-hour block of 4 half-hour segs.); The Jetsons (75 half-hours).
- Animated Holiday Special: Yogi's First Christmas (2-hour movie).
- Hour Series (Off-Network): Barnaby Jones (177); Ben Casey (153); Breaking Point (30); Combat (152); Don Lane Show (130); Fugitive (120); The Invaders (43); Little House on the Prairie (216.5); Love Boat (140); Love Boat II (115); Man from Atlantis (13); Mod Squad (124); Streets of San Francisco (119).
- Half-Hour Series: Adventures of Champion (26); Annie Oakley (80); Buffalo Bill, Jr. (40); Come Along (13); Dark Shadows (780); Dickens & Fenster (32); Doris Day Show (128); Douglas Fairbanks Presents (115); High Road (36); It Pays to Be Ignorant (39); Love Boat II (115 ½ or 1 hour); Mickey Rooney (17); Next Step Beyond (24); N.Y.P.D. (49); On the Mat (52); One Step Beyond (94); People's Choice (104); Range Rider (76); The Rebel (76); Starring the Actors (13); Starting From Scratch (24); Take My Word for It (130); That Girl (136); Throb (48); Wendy and Me (34).
- Mini-Series: Against the Wind (13 hours); Holocaust (10 hours); Return to Eden (6 hours).
- Features: Prime VIII (20 color features); Prime VII (25 color features); Prime VI (19); Prime V (26); Prime IV (26); Prime III (16); Prime II (16); Prime I (10).
- Children's Programs: Fun World of Hanna-Barbera (84 half-hrs.); H-B's World of Super Adventure (129 half-hrs.); Banana Splits (125 half-hrs.); Saturday at the Movies (6 specials); Top Cat (30 half-hrs.); Wait Till Your Father Gets Home (48); Josie & The Pussycats (16); Josie & the Pussycats in Outer Space (16); Harvey/Casper, (244 cartoons) The Jackson Five (23 half-hrs.); The Jerry Lewis Show (17 half-hrs.); King Kong (26 half-hrs.); Lancelot Link-Secret Chimp (17 half-hr.); Milton the Monster (78, 6–8 min.); Professor Kitzel (104 cartoons); The Reluctant Dragon & Mr. Toad (17 half-hrs.); Smokey the Bear (51, 6–8 min.); George of the Jungle (17 half-hrs.); Rambo (65 half-hrs.); Centurions (65 half-hrs.); Chuck Norris Karate Kommandos (5 half-hours; mini-series); Discovery (103 half-hour); Yogi's First Christmas (2 hour movie).
- Specials: Jack Nicklaus at the Home of Golf (3 hrs.); The Fabulous Sixties (10 1-hrs.); The Bay City Rollers (1 hr.); Echo 1 (17 1 hour); Herbie Mann/Roland Kirk (half-hr.); Is It Christ? (1 hr.); The Last Nazi (1 hour); Raphael (half-hr.); Roberta Flack/Donny Hathaway (half-hr.); The World of Miss World (1 hr.); The New Fangled Wandering Minstrel Show (1 hr.); The Musical Ambassadors, Kenny Rogers & The First Edition in New Zealand (1 hr.); Ron Luciano's Lighter Side of Sports (half-hr.); A Christmas Carol (animated half-hr.); An Evening with Irish Television (1 hr.); Russian Festival of Music and Dance (1 hr.); The Bobby Vinton Show (1 hr.); A Shark's Paradise (2 hours); Amahl & the Night Visitors (1 hr.); Children of the Gael (1 hr.); Irish Rovers Special (1 hr.); The Night the Animals Talked (half-hour); Sunshine Specials (eight 1-hr.); A Little Bit of Irish: Bing Crosby (1 hr.).

Worldvision International:

AUSTRALIA: Worldvision Enterprises of Australia Pty. Ltd., 5–13 Northcliff St., Milsons Point 2061, Sydney; Tel.: (61-2) 922-4722; FAX: (011-61-2) 92-8207. Telex: (790) 70474. Brian Rhys-Jones.

BRAZIL: Worldvision Filmes do Brasil Ltd., Rua Macedo Sobrinho 50, Botafogo, CEP 22271, Rio de Janeiro; Tel.: (55-21) 286-8992;

FAX: (011-55-21) 266-4737; Telex: (391) 2123321 (WFBR BR). Raymundo Rodrigues, mgr. dir., Brazil.

CANADA: Worldvision Enterprises of Canada, 1200 Bay St., Toronto M5R 2A5, Canada; Tel.: (416) 967-1200; FAX: (416) 967-0521; Telex: (369) 06524659 (WVISTVPROG TOR). Bruce Swanson, v.p. and gen. mgr.

ENGLAND: Worldvision Enterprises, U.K. Ltd., 54 Pont St., London, S.W. 1, England, Tel.: (44-1) 584-5357; FAX: (011-44-1) 581-3483. William Peck, mng. dir., England.

FRANCE: Worldvision Enterprises S.A.R.L., 28, rue Bayard 75008, Paris, France; Tel.: (33-1) 4273-3995; FAX: (011-33-1) 4070-9269; Telex: (842) 648218F (WORLFRA). Mary Jane Fourniel, mng. dir.

GERMANY: Worldvision GmbH, Postfach 906, 8 München 33, Germany; Street address: Fuerstenfelder Strasse B8000, München 2; Tel.: (49-89) 26-4091; FAX: (011-49-89) 26-4091. Telex: (841) 523420 (WVIS D). Mex Hartmann, mng. dir.

ITALY: Worldvision Enterprises, Inc., Adalia Anstalt, Via Del Corso, 22/Interno 10, 00186, Rome, Italy; Tel.: (39-6) 67-87-056; FAX: (011-39-6) 679-9242. Martin Michael Kiwe, v.p., European operations.

JAPAN: Worldvision Enterprises, Inc., Tsukiji Hamarikyu Bldg., 7th floor, 5-3-3, Tsukiji, Chou-ku, Tokyo 104, Japan; Tel.: (81-3) 545-3977; FAX: (011-81-3) 545-3964; Telex: (781) 2525077 (AMCAST J). Mie Horasawa, sls. rep., Japan and Korea.

LOS ANGELES: Worldvision Enterprises, Inc., 9465 Wilshire Blvd., Suite 628, Beverly Hills, CA 90212; (213) 273-7667; FAX: (213) 273-3645; Telex: 910-490-2610. Harrington Silva.

- New Product: Twin Peaks (1-hour series); Monsters (half-hour series); After Hours (half-hour series); Starting from Scratch (22 half-hours); Hanna-Barbera Animation (new product; U.S. Network, 1989–90 fall season); Dallas (26 hours); General Hospital (hours); One Life to Live (serial, hours); All My Children (serial, hours); *Taft Barish Theatricals:* "Ironweed," "The Running Man," "Light of Day," "Monster Squad," *Hanna-Barbera Animation:* Paddington Bear (13 half-hours, limited availability); Fantastic Max (13 half-hours, limited availability); Hanna-Barbera's 50th: A Yabba Dabba Doo Celebration (2-hour special, limited availability); Don Coyote (26 half-hours, limited availability); A Pup Named Scooby Doo (21 half-hours); Internal Affairs (4-hour mini-series); Unholy Matrimony (96-minute); Rock Odyssey (90-minute animated special); 1988/89 Presidential Inaugural Gala (2-hour special); Stones for Ibarra (2-hour movie); Stranger on My Land (2 hours); Streets of San Francisco (119 hours); A.F.I. Life Achievement Award/Gregory Peck (90 minutes); A Mouse, A Mystery and Me (half-hour special); Home Fires (4-hour mini-series).
- Returning Product: Hanna-Barbera's Superstars 10 (10 2-hour movies); Hands of a Stranger (4-hour mini-series); Highway to Heaven (hours); Angel in Green (2 hours); Kids Like These (2 hours); Little Troll Prince (1-hour special); The Last Frontier (4-hour mini-series); The Stepford Children (2 hours); The Day They Came to Arrest the Book (1-hour special); Stone Fox (2 hours); Shark's Paradise (2 hours); When the Bough Breaks (2 hours); Night of Courage (2 hours); Stranger in My Bed (2 hours); The High Price of Passion (2 hours); Sable (1-hour series); Throb (48 half-hours); You Again? (26 half-hours); The Love Boat (hours); On Wings of Eagles (5-hour mini-series); Doubletake (4-hour mini-series); Key to Rebecca (4-hour mini-series); Sam's Son (2-hours); A Deadly Business (2 hours); My Two Loves (2 hours); Welcome Home Bobby (2 hours); Smurfs (266 animated half-hours, available only in U.K., Ireland, Canada); The Jetsons (75 half-hours); Wildfire (13 animated half-hours); The Flintstones 25th Anniversary (1-hour animated special); The 13 Ghosts of Scooby Doo (13 animated half-hours); Mr. T (30 animated half-hours); The Flintstone Kids (34 animated half-hours); Alvin & the Chipmunks (54 animated half-hours); Yogi's Treasure Hunt (27 half-hours); Sky Commanders (13 half-hours); Snorks (36 half-hours, available only in U.K., Ireland, Canada); Roboforce (half-hour special).
- Special Presentation Programming: Remember Me (2 hrs.); Little House on the Prairie Three Special Presentations—Look Back to Yesterday (2 hrs.), Bless All the Dear Children (2 hrs.), The Last Farewell (2 hrs.); An Act of Love: The Patricia Neal Story (2 hrs.); Worldvision Dramatic Specials (10 one-hr. specials); Holocaust (9½ hrs.); Against the Wind (13 hrs.); The Ordeal of Patty Hearst (3 hrs.); The Trial of Lee Harvey Oswald (4 hrs.); The Last Nazi (90 min.); Reincarnation (2 hrs.); Little Mo (3 hrs.); Freedom Road (4 hrs.); Russian Festival of Music and Dance (1 hr.); Candid Camera Special (5 one-hrs.).
- Feature Films: More than 200 titles—Paragon Features: over 90 color features: Stars include Robert Preston, Patty Duke, Valerie Perrine, Dom DeLuise, Patricia Elliott, Gary Coleman, Mickey Rooney, George C. Scott, Henry Fonda, James Whitmore, Dennis Weaver, David Janssen, James Woods, Lee Majors, James Earl Jones, Ed Asner, Suzanne Pleshette, William Devane; Prestige Features: 21 features in color including: "I Will, I Will . . . For Now," "Night Watch," "A Touch of Class," "Hedda," "Baker's Hawk," "Black Market Baby," "Breakthrough," "Book of Numbers," "Fingers," "Cry For Me Billy," "Sweet Hostage," "Nasty Habits," and "Thieves"; Prestige II Features: 10 features including "A Killing Affair," "Bad Guys," "Dirt Bike Kid," " Vasectomy," "Wizards of the Lost Kingdom," and "Hurry Up or I'll Be 30." Selznick Classics; 22 films including "Intermezzo," "Duel in the Sun," "Notorious," "Spellbound," "Rebecca," "The Spiral Staircase," "Portrait of Jenny," "The Farmer's Daughter," "The Garden of Allah," "Bill of Divorcement," "Made For Each Other," and "The Wild Heart"; ABC Pictures; including "Cabaret," "They Shoot Horses, Don't They?," "Charly," "Take the Money and Run," "Straw Dogs," "For Love of Ivy," "Song of Norway," "The Killing of Sister George," and "Krakatoa, East of Java" (all in color).
- Children's Programming: Casper the Friendly Ghost; Milton the Monster; Jerry Lewis Show; Jackson 5; Lancelot Link. Hanna-Barbera/Ruby-Spears representing thousands of half-hours of animated programming including "The Flintstones," "Yogi Bear," "Centurions," "Puppy's New Adventures," etc.
- Holiday Specials: Little Troll Prince; A Mouse, A Mystery and Me; 'Tis the Season to Be Smurfy; The Cabbage Patch Kids' First Christmas; Smurfily Ever After (U.K., Ireland & Canada only); I Love the Chipmunks Valentine Special; Alvin & The Chipmunks Reunion (Easter); A Flintstone Christmas; Yogi's First Christmas; Casper's First Christmas; Christmas Comes to Pacland; Smurfs Christmas Special (U.K., Ireland, Canada only); My Smurfy Valentine (U.K., Ireland & Canada only); Smurfs' Springtime Special/Easter (U.K., Ireland & Canada only); The Gathering; The Gathering II; Casper Halloween Special; The Pumpkin Who Couldn't Smile; The Thanksgiving Visitor; The Thanksgiving That Almost Wasn't; The Great Santa Claus Caper; A Christmas Story; A Christmas Memory; A Christmas Carol; The Night the Animals Talked; Amahl and the Night Visitors; A Little Bit of Irish; Russian Festival of Music and Dance.
- Series: Return to Eden (22 1-hr.); Lucie Arnaz Show (6 half-hr.); Starring the Actors (13 half-hrs.); Little House on the Prairie (216 1 hr.); Eight is Enough (112 1-hr.); Kaz (22 1-hr.); Project UFO (26 fact-based action-adventure, 1-hr.); The Andros Targets (13 1-hr.); Spencer's Pilots (11 1-hr.); Man From Atlantis (20 hours); Married: The First Year (4 1-hr.); Pruitts of Southampton (30 half-hr. comedy); The Doris Day Show (128 half-hrs.); Hunter (13 1-hr.); Mod Squad (124 hr.); The Invaders (43 hrs.); The Fugitive (120 hrs.); The Next Step Beyond (24 half-hr.); Thunder (12 half-hrs.); Garrison's Gorillas (26 hrs.); Cowboy in Africa (26 hrs.) Ben Casey (153 one-hr., b/w); That Girl (136 half-hr.).

Worldwide Television News

1995 Broadway, New York, NY 10023; (212) 362-4440. Kenneth Coyte, pres.; William H. Dudar, bureau chief; Michael Harbert, rgl. exec. for corporate video sls; Scott Michaeloff, rgl. exec. for TV facilities sls. (Produces and distributes intl. news coverage; produces weekly news cassettes including 2 programs—Roving Report & Earthwatch; video news releases, corporate promotional videos, crewing & production services.)

FILM LIBRARY: 1995 Broadway, New York, NY 10036; (212) 362-4440. Vincent O'Reilly, library mgr.

Wright, Carter, Enterprises

6533 Hollywood Blvd., Hollywood, CA 90028; (213) 469-0944. Carter Wright, pres.; June Wright, talent coordinator. (Live and film shows, commercials).

Ziv International

1875 Century Park E., Suite 1610, Los Angeles, CA 90067; (213) 277-9064. Telex: 698619.

- Series: Angel (50), Animator's Film Library (60), Candy Candy (65), Captain Future (52), Captain Harlock (42), Captain Nemo (15), Fables of the Green Forest (52), Gumby (34), King Arthur, (44), Robot Festival, (130), Space Angel (52), Spunky & Tadpole (15), Villa Alegre (260), Man from Buttonwillow (52), Children of the World (13).
- Specials: Tom Jones Live in Vegas, Tony Bennett/Nancy Wilson, Crystal Gayle, Bal Du Moulin Rouge, Peter Cottontail, Silent Knight, Les Miserables.
- Feature length films: 300.
- Merchandising and licensing.

Programs

* NETWORK PRIMETIME SHOWS
* SYNDICATED
* MOVIES AND MINI-SERIES MADE FOR TELEVISION

1989–90 Prime Time Shows

Series titles are listed alphabetically by network, along with time slots, suppliers, production staff heads (executive producer: EP; executive supervising producer: ESP; supervising producer: SP; senior producer: Sr. P; producer: P; co-producer: CP; director: D), cast regulars and semi-regulars.

ABC-TV

Series Title	Day	Hr.	Mins.	Supplier	Production Principals	Cast Regulars & Semi-Regulars
ABC Saturday Mystery, The	Sat.	9:00	120	Universal TV	SEP: William Link	
B.L. Stryker				Blue Period Prods.-TWS Prods.-Universal TV	EP: Tom Selleck, Burt Reynolds, Chas. Floyd Johnson, Chris Abbott SP: Tom Donnelly P: Alan Barnette	Burt Reynolds, Ossie Davis, Kristi Swanson, Dana Kaminski, Michael O. Smith, Alfie Wise, Rita Moreno
Christine Cromwell				Universal TV	EP: Dick Wolf P: Lynn Guthrie, Michael Dugan CP: Robert Palm, Dan Sackheim	Jaclyn Smith, Celeste Holm, Ralph Bellamy
Columbo				Universal TV	EP: Richard Alan Simmons SP: Philip Saltzman CP: Peter Ware	Peter Falk
Kojak				Universal TV	EP: James McAdams SP: Stuart Cohen P: Marc Laub CP: Judith Stevens	Telly Savalas
ABC Sunday Night Movie, The	Sun.	9:00	120	Various		
Anything But Love	Wed.	9:00	30	Adam Prods.-20th Fox TV	EP: Robert Myman, Peter Noah SP: Janis Hirsch P: Peter Schindler CP: Bruce Rasmussen	Jamie Lee Curtis, Richard Lewis, Ann Magnuson, Joseph Maher, Richard Frank, Holly Fulger
Chicken Soup	Tue.	9:30	30	Carsey-Werner Co.	EP: Marcy Carsey, Tom Werner, Saul Turteltaub & Bernie Orenstein SP: Paul Perlove P: Faye Oshima D: Alan Rafkin	Jackie Mason, Lynn Redgrave, Rita Karin, Kathryn Erbe, Johnny Pinto, Alisan Porter
China Beach	Wed.	10:00	60	Sacret Inc. Prods.-Warner Bros. TV	EP: John Sacret Young SP: John Wells, Georgia Jeffries P: Mimi Leder CP: Geno Escareega, Fred Gerber	Dana Delany, Brian Wimmer, Michael Boatman, Marg Helgenberger, Concetta Tomei, Robert Picardo, Jeff Kober, Ned Vaughn, Nancy Giles
Doogie Howser, M.D.	Wed.	9:30	30	Steven Bochco Prods.	EP: Steven Bochco SP: Stephen Cragg P: Scott Goldstein, Phil Kellard, Tom Moore, Jill Gordon, Vic Rauseo, Linda Morris	Neil Patrick Harris, James B. Sikking, Belinda Montgomery, Lawrence Pressman, Max Casella, Mitchell Anderson, Kathryn Layng
Family Matters	Fri.	8:30	30	Miller/Boyett Prods.-Lorimar-Telepictures	EP: Thomas L. Miller, Robert L. Boyett, William Bickley & Michael Warren SP: Alan Eisenstock & Larry Mintz P: Robert Blair CP: Harriette Ames-Regan	JoMarie Payton-France, Reggie VelJohnson, Rosetta LeNoire, Darius McCray, Kellie Williams, Jamie Foxworth, Telma Hopkins, Joseph Loyal Wright, Julius Royal Wright
Free Spirit	Sun.	9:00	30	Columbia Pictures TV	EP: Richard Gurman, Phil Doran SP: Howard Meyers P: Mark Fink CP:Bob Rosenfarb, Jon Spector D: Art Dielhenn	Corinne Bohrer, Frank Luz, Edan Gross, Paul Scherrer, Alyson Hannigan
Full House	Fri.	8:00	30	Jeff Franklin Prods.-Miller/Boyett Prods.-Lorimar-Telepictures	EP: Jeff Franklin, Thomas L. Miller, Robert L. Boyett SP: Rob Dames P: Don Van Atta, Lenny Ripps, Marc Warren, Dennis Rinsler CP: Kim Weiskopf	John Stamos, Bob Saget, David Coulier, Candace Cameron, Jodie Sweetin, Mary Kate Olsen, Ashley Fuller Olsen, Lori Loughlin
Growing Pains	Wed.	8:00	30	Warner Bros. TV	EP: Michael Sullivan, Dan Guntzelman, Steve Marshall, David Kendall P: Henry Johnson, Tim O'Donnell	Alan Thicke, Joanna Kerns, Kirk Cameron, Tracey Gold, Jeremy Miller

Series Title	Day	Hr.	Mins.	Supplier	Production Principals	Cast Regulars & Semi-Regulars
Head of the Class	Wed.	8:30	30	Eustis Elias Prods.-Warner Bros. TV	EP: Richard Eustis, Michael Elias P: Alan Rosen, Frank Pace CP: Ray Jessel, Steve Kreinberg, Andy Guerdat, Jonathan Roberts	Howard Hesseman, Jeannette Arnette, William G. Schilling, Dan Frischman, Robin Givens, Khrystyne Haje, Tony O'Dell, Kimberly Russell, Brian Robbins, Daniel Schneider, Rain Pryor, Michael DeLorenzo, Lara Piper, De'Voreaux White
Homeroom	Sun.	8:30	30	Castle Rock Entertainment	EP: Gary Gilbert, Andrew Scheinman, Topper Carew P: Jan Siegelman, David Cohen, Roger Schulman, Trish Soodik D: Linda Day	Darryl Sivad, Penny Johnson, Bill Cobbs, Jahary Bennett, Trent Cameron, Billy Dee Williams
Just the Ten of Us	Fri.	9:30	30	GSM Prods.-Warner Bros. TV	EP: Michael Sullivan, Dan Guntzelman, Steve Marshall P: Rich Reinhart, Nick Lerose, Henry Johnson	Bill Kirchenbauer, Deborah Harmon, Heather Langenkamp, Brooke Theiss, Jamie Luner, JoAnn Willette, Matt Shakman, Heidi Zeigler
Life Goes On	Sun.	7:00	60	Toots Prods.-Warner Bros. TV	EP: Michael Braverman SP-D: Ron Rubin P: Phillips Wylly Sr.	Bill Smitrovich, Patti LuPone, Monique Lanier, Christopher Burke, Kellie Martin
Living Dolls	Sat.	8:30	30	Columbia Pictures TV-ELP Communications	EP: Ross Brown, Phyllis Glick P: Bob Colleary, Martha Williamson CP: Valri Bromfield D: John Sgueglia	Michael Learned, Leah Remini, Alison Elliot, Deborah Tucker, Halle Berry, David Moscow
MacGyver	Mon.	8:00	60	Henry Winkler/John Rich Prods.-Paramount Network TV	EP: Henry Winkler, John Rich, Stephen Downing SP: Michael Greenburg	Richard Dean Anderson, Dana Elcar
Mission: Impossible	Thu.	8:00	60	Jeffrey Hayes Prods.-Paramount Network TV	EP: Jeffrey Hayes SP: Frank Abatemarco P: Ted Roberts, Darryl Sheen	Peter Graves, Thaao Penghlis, Tony Hamilton, Phil Morris, Jane Badler
Mr. Belvedere	Sat.	8:00	30	Lazy B/FOB Prods.-20th Fox TV	EP: Frank Dungan & Jeff Stein, Liz Sage SP: Jeff Ferro, Ric Weiss P: Patricia Rickey CP: Geri Maddern D: Don Corvan	Christopher Hewett, Ilene Graff, Rob Stone, Tracy Wells, Brice Beckham, Bob Uecker
NFL Monday Night Football	Mon.	9:00	120	ABC Sports	EP: Geoffrey Mason P: Ken Wolfe D: Craig Janoff	Al Michaels, Frank Gifford, Dan Dierdorf, Lynn Swann
Perfect Strangers	Fri.	9:00	30	Miller/Boyett Prods.-Lorimar TV	EP: Thomas L. Miller, Robert L. Boyett, William Bickley & Michael Warren SP: Paula A. Roth P: James O'Keefe, Bob Griffard, Howard Adler, Alan Plotkin	Bronson Pinchot, Mark Linn-Baker, Melanie Wilson, Rebeca Arthur, Belita Moreno, Sam Anderson
Primetime Live	Thu.	10:00	60	ABC News	EP: Richard N. Kaplan Sr. P: Ira Rosen, Amy Sacks	Diane Sawyer, Sam Donaldson, Chris Wallace
Roseanne	Tue.	9:00	30	Carsey-Werner Co.	EP: Marcy Carsey, Tom Werner, Jeff Harris, Allan Katz SP: Danny Jacobson P: Al Lowenstein CP: Norma Safford Vela D: John Pasquin	Roseanne Barr, John Goodman, Laurie Metcalf, Lecy Goranson, Sara Gilbert, Michael Fishman, Natalie West
thirtysomething	Tue.	10:00	60	Bedford Falls Co.-MGM/UA TV	EP: Marshall Herskovitz, Edward Zwick SP: Scott Winant P: Richard Kramer CP: Ellen S. Pressman	Timothy Busfield, Polly Draper, Mel Harris, Peter Horton, Melanie Mayron, Ken Olin, Patricia Wettig
20/20	Fri.	10:00	60	ABC News	EP: Victor Neufeld Sr. P: Jeff Diamond D: Jerry Paul	Hugh Downs, Barbara Walters, Bob Brown, John Stossel, Tom Jarriel
Who's the Boss?	Tue.	8:00	30	Columbia/Embassy TV	EP: Martin Cohan, Blake Hunter, Karen Wengrod, Ken Cinnamon SP: Danny Kallis P: John Anderson, Joe Fisch, Asaad Kelada D: Asaad Kelada	Tony Danza, Judith Light, Alyssa Milano, Danny Pintauro, Katherine Helmond
Wonder Years, The	Tue.	8:30	30	Black/Marlens Co.-New World TV	EP: Bob Brush, Bob Stevens P: Ken Topolsky CP: Matthew Carlson	Fred Savage, Dan Lauria, Alley Mills, Jason Hervey, Olivia d'Abo, Danica McKellar, Josh Saviano, Daniel Stern
Young Riders, The	Thu.	9:00	60	Ogiens/Kane Co.-MGM/UA TV	EP: Michael Ogiens, Josh Kane, Jonas McCord SP: Ed Spielman, Dennis Cooper P: Harvey Frand	Ty Miller, Josh Brolin, Stephen Baldwin, Greg Rainwater, Yvonne Suhor, Anthony Zerbe, Melissa Leo, Brett Cullen

CBS-TV

Series Title	Day	Hr.	Mins.	Supplier	Production Principals	Cast Regulars & Semi-Regulars
CBS Sunday Movie	Sun.	9:00	120	Various		

Series Title	Day	Hr.	Mins.	Supplier	Production Principals	Cast Regulars & Semi-Regulars
Dallas	Fri.	9:00	60	Lorimar TV	EP: Leonard Katzman, Larry Hagman, Ken Horton SP: Howard Lakin P: Cliff Fenneman, Mitchell Wayne Katzman	Barbara Bel Geddes, Patrick Duffy, Larry Hagman, Howard Keel, George Kennedy, Ken Kercheval, Cathy Podewell, Charlene Tilton, Sheree J. Wilson, Kimberly Foster, Michael Wilding, Sasha Mitchell
Designing Women	Mon.	10:00	30	Bloodworth/Thomason Mozark Prods.-Columbia Pictures TV	EP: Harry Thomason, Linda Bloodworth Thomason SP: Pam Norris P: Tommy Thompson, Douglas Jackson CP: David Trainer	Delta Burke, Dixie Carter, Annie Potts, Jean Smart, Meshach Taylor
Falcon Crest	Fri.	10:00	60	Amanda/MF Prods.-Lorimar TV	EP: Jerry Thorpe, Michael Filerman, Joel Surnow P: Philip L. Parslow	Jane Wyman, David Selby, Gregory Harrison, Lorenzo Lamas, Kristian Alfonson, Margaret Ladd, Chao-Li Chi
Famous Teddy Z, The	Mon.	9:30	30	Hugh Wilson Prods.-Columbia Pictures TV	EP: Hugh Wilson SP: Richard Dubin	Jon Cryer, Alex Rocco, Milton Selzer, Erica Yohn, Jane Sibbett, Tom LaGrua, Josh Blake
48 Hours	Thu.	8:00	60	CBS News	EP: Andrew Heyward Sr. P: Catherine Lasiewicz, Steve Glauber, Al Briganti	Dan Rather, Bernard Goldberg
Island Son	Tue.	10:00	60	Maili Point Enterprises-Lorimar TV	EP: Nigel & Carol Evan McKeand, Richard Chamberlain, Martin Rabbett SP: Les Carter, Susan Sisko P: Christopher Chulack	Richard Chamberlain, Ray Bumatai, Timothy Carhart, Betty Carvalho, Clyde Kusatsu, William McNamara, Brynn Thayer
Jake and the Fatman	Wed.	9:00	60	Fred Silverman Co.-Dean Hargrove Prods.-Viacom Prods.	EP: Fred Silverman, Dean Hargrove, David Moessinger, Jeri Taylor, Bernie Kowalski P: Fred McKnight	William Conrad, Joe Penny, Alan Campbell
Knots Landing	Thu	10:00	60	Roundelay/MF Prods.-Lorimar TV	EP: David Jacobs, Michael Filerman, Lawrence Kasha P: Mary-Catherine Harold, Lynn Marie Latham, Bernard Lechowick	William Devane, Kevin Dobson, Michele Lee, Donna Mills, Ted Shackelford, Joan Van Ark, Nicollette Sheridan, Lynne Moody, Larry Riley, Tonya Crowe, Pat Petersen
Major Dad	Mon.	8:00	30	SBB Prods.-Spanish Trail Prods.-Universal	EP: Earl Pomerantz, Richard C. Okie, Gerald McRaney, John C. Stephens	Gerald McRaney, Shanna Reed, Matt Mulhern, Marlon Archey, Whitney Kershaw, Marisa Ryan, Nicole Dubuc, Chelsea Hertford
Murder, She Wrote	Sun	8:00	60	Universal TV	EP: Peter S. Fischer SP: Robert F. O'Neill P: Robert Van Scoyk, Robert E. Swanson	Angela Lansbury, William Windom, Ron Masak
Murphy Brown	Mon	9:00	30	Shukovsky/English Prods.-Warner Bros. TV	EP: Diane English, Joel Shukovsky P: Tom Seeley, Norm Gunzenhauser, Russ Woody, Gary Dontzig, Steven Peterman, Barnet Kellerman CP: Deborah Smith	Candice Bergen, Pat Croley, Faith Ford, Charles Kimbrough, Joe Regalbuto, Robert Pastorelli, Grant Shaud
Newhart	Mon	10:30	30	MTM Enterprises	EP: Mark Egan, Mark Solomon SP: Bob Bendetson P: Stephen C. Grossman	Bob Newhart, Mary Frann, Peter Scolari, Julia Duffy, Tom Poston, William Sanderson, Tony Papenfuss, John Voldstad
Paradise	Sat	8:00	60	Roundelay Prods.-Lorimar TV	EP: David Jacobs SP: James H. Brown CP: Robert Porter, Joel J. Feigenbaum	Lee Horsley, Jenny Beck, Matthew Newmark, Brian Lando, Michael Carter, Dehl Berti, Sigrid Thornton
Peaceable Kingdom	Wed	8:00	60	Columbia Pictures TV	EP: Mark Waxman, Michael Vittes, Karen Harris P: Michael Vittes CP: Park Perine	Lindsay Wagner, Tom Wopat, David Ackroyd, David Renen, Michael Manasseri, Melissa Clayton, Victor DiMattia, Conchata Ferrell
People Next Door, The	Mon	8:30	30	The Sunshines Inc.-Wes Craven Films-Lorimar TV	EP: Steven & Madeline Sunshine, Wes Craven, Bruce Johnson SP: Robert Tischler P: Mark Masuoka, Robert Tischler CP: Lee Aronsohn D: J. D. Lobue	Jeffrey Jones, Mary Gross, Jaclyn Bernstein, Chance Quinn, Leslie Jordan, Christine Pickles
Rescue 911	Tue	8:00	60	Arnold Shapiro Prods.-CBS Entertainment Prods.	EP: Arnold Shapiro SP: Jean O'Neill P: Nancy Platt Jacoby D: Chris Pechin	William Shatner
Saturday Night with Connie Chung	Sat	10:00	60	CBS News	EP: Andrew Lack SP: Maurice Murad D: Don Roy King	Connie Chung
60 Minutes	Sun	7:00	60	CBS News	EP: Don Hewitt Sr. P: Philip Scheffler D: Arthur Bloom	Mike Wallace, Morley Safer, Harry Reasoner, Ed Bradley, Meredith Vieira, Steve Kroft, Andy Rooney
Snoops	Fri	8:00	60	Timolove Prods.-Viacom Prods.-Solt/Egan Co.	EP: Tim Reid, Hal Sitowitz, Sam Egan SP: Jo & Tom Perry P: David Auerbach CP: Lee Shaldon	Tim Reid, Daphne Maxwell Reid, John Karlen, Troy Curvey Jr.
Top of the Hill	Thu	9:00	60	Stephen J. Cannell Prods.	EP: Stephen J. Cannell SP: Jo Swerling Jr. P: Henry Colman	William Katt, Dick O'Neill, Jordan Baker

Series Title	Day	Hr.	Mins.	Supplier	Production Principals	Cast Regulars & Semi-Regulars
Tour of Duty	Sat	9:00	60	Zev Braun Prods.-New World TV	EP: Zev Braun SP: Steven Philip Smith P: Vahan Moosekian, Jim Westman CP: Jerry Patrick Brown, Robert Bielak, Carol Mendelsohn	Terence Knox, Stephen Caffrey, Tony Becker, Stan Foster, Ramon Franco, Miguel A. Nunez Jr., Dan Gauthier, Kim Delaney
Wiseguy	Wed	10:00	60	Stephen J. Cannell Prods.	EP: Stephen J. Cannell, Les Sheldon SP: David A. Burke, Stephen Kronish, Jo Swerling Jr. P: Alfonse Ruggiero Jr., John Shulian CP: Clifton Campbell	Ken Wahl, Jonathan Banks, Jim Byrnes
Wolf	Tue	9:00	60	CBS Entertainment Prods.	EP: David Pekinpah, Rod Holcomb SP: Garner Simmons P: Ken Swor CP: Tom Del Ruth	Jack Scalia, Nicholas Surovy, Joseph Sirola, J.C. Brandy, Mimi Kuzyk

NBC-TV

Series Title	Day	Hr.	Mins.	Supplier	Production Principals	Cast Regulars & Semi-Regulars
A Different World	Thu	8:30	30	Carsey-Werner Co.-Bill Cosby	EP: Marcy Carsey, Tom Werner, Thad Mumford, Margie Peters SP: Susan Fales P: Joanne Curley Kerner, Debbie Allen CP: Cheryl Gard D: Debbie Allen	Dawn Lewis, Jasmine Guy, Kadeem Hardison, Charnele Brown, Cree Summer, Darryl Bell, Sinbad, Glynn Turman, Lou Myers
Alf	Mon	8:00	30	Alien Prods.	EP: Tom Patchett, Bernie Brillstein SP: Lisa A. Bannick P: Paul Fusco CP: Steve Hollander	Max Wright, Anne Schedeen, Andrea Elson, Benji Gregory, Alf, JM J. Bullock, Liz Sheridan, John LaMotta, J.R. and, Charles Nickerson
Amen	Sat	8:30	30	Carson Prods.	EP: Ed. Weinberger, Artie Julian, Eric Cohen SP-D: Shelley Jensen P: Marty Nadler CP: Bill Daley, Ken Johnston, Reuben Cannon	Sherman Hemsley, Clifton Davis, Anne Maria Horsford, Barbara Montgomery, Roz Ryan, Jester Hairston
Baywatch	Fri	8:00	60	GTG Entertainment	SEP: Robert Silberling EP: Douglas Schwarts, Michael Berk, Ernie Wallengren P: Gregory Bonann, Jill Donner, Bill Schwartz	David Hasselhoff, Parker Stevenson, Shawn Weatherly, Billy Warlock, Erika Eleniak, Peter Phelps, Monte Markham, Brandon Call
Cheers	Thu	9:00	30	Charles/Burrows/ Charles Prods.-Paramount Network TV	EP: Glen & Les Charles, James Burrows SP: Cheri Eichen, Bill Steinkellner, Phoef Sutton P: Tim Berry	Ted Danson, Rhea Perlman, George Wendt, John Ratzenberger, Woody Harrelson, Kelsey Grammer, Kirstie Alley, Roger Rees, Bebe Neuwirth
Cosby Show, The	Thu	8:00	30	Carsey-Werner Co.-Bill Cosby	EP: Marcy Carsey, Tom Werner, John Markus SP: Carmen Finestra, Gary Kott P: Terry Guarnieri	Bill Cosby, Phylicia Rashad, Lisa Bonet, Sabrina LeBeauf, Malcolm-Jamal Warner, Tempestt Bledsoe, Keshia Knight Pulliam, Geoffrey Owens, Joseph C. Phillips, Raven-Symone
Dear John	Thu	9:30	30	Ed. Weinberger Prods.-Paramount Network TV	EP: Hal Cooper, Ed. Weinberger, Rod Parker P: Bob Ellison, Mike Milligan, Jay Moriarty, Mark Reisman, Jeremy Stevens, Georg Sunga D: Hal Cooper	Judd Hirsch, Jane Carr, Jere Burns, Isabella Hofmann, Harry Groener, Billie Bird
Empty Nest	Sat	9:30	30	Witt/Thomas/Harris Prods.-Touchstone TV	EP: Paul Junger Witt, Tony Thomas, Susan Harris, Gary Jacobs SP: Arnie Kogen, David Tyron King P: Susan Beavers, Gilbert Junger D: Steve Zuckerman	Richard Mulligan, Kristy McNichol, Dinah Manoff, David Leisure, Park Overall
Golden Girls, The	Sat	9:00	30	Witt/Thomas/Harris Prods.-Touchstone TV	EP: Paul Junger Witt, Tony Thomas, Susan Harris, Marc Sotkin, Terry Hughes SP: Philip Lasker, Tom Whedon P: Gail Parent, Robert Bruce, Martin Weiss CP: Tracy Gamble, Richard Vaczy D: Terry Hughes	Bea Arthur, Betty White, Rue McClanahan, Estelle Getty
Hardball	Fri	9:00	60	Columbia Pictures TV-NBC Prods.	EP: Frank Lupo, John Ashley, David Hemmings	John Ashton, Richard Tyson
Hogan Family, The	Mon	8:30	30	Miller/Boyett Prods.-Lorimar TV	EP: Tom Miller, Bob Boyett SP: Chip & Doug Keyes, Judy Pioli P: Bob Keyes, Deborah Oppenheimer CD: Rich Correll	Sandy Duncan, Jason Bateman, Danny Ponce, Jeremy Licht, Josh Taylor, Edie McClurg

Series Title	Day	Hr.	Mins.	Supplier	Production Principals	Cast Regulars & Semi-Regulars
Hunter	Sat	10:00	60	Stephen J. Cannell Prods.	EP: Fred Dryer, Larry Kubik, Marvin Kupfer SP: Jo Swerling Jr., Paul Waigner, David Balkan P: Terry Nelson CP: Vic Schiro	Fred Dryer, Stepfanie Kramer, Charles Hallahan, Garrett Morris
In The Heat of the Night	Tue	9:00	60	Fred Silverman Co.-Jadda Prods.-MGM/UA TV	EP: Fred Silverman, Carroll O'Connor SP: Mark Rodgers, Ed DeBlasio P: Edward Ledding CP: Nancy Bond, Walton Dornisch	Carroll O'Connor, Howard Rollins, Alan Autry, Anne-Marie Johnson, David Hart, Geoffrey Thorne, Hugh O'Connor
L.A. Law	Thu	10:00	60	20th Fox TV	EP: David E. Kelley, Rick Wallace SP: William M. Finkelstein P: Elodie Keene, Michael M. Robin CP: Robert M. Breech	Harry Hamlin, Susan Dey, Jill Eikenberry, Corbin Bernsen, Michael Tucker, Michele Greene, Alan Rachins, Jimmy Smits, Susan Ruttan, Blair Underwood, Richard Dysart, Larry Drake
Magical World of Disney, The	Sun	7:00	60	Walt Disney TV		Michael D. Eisner
Brand New Life				NBC Prods.	EP: Chris Carter P: George Perkins, Eric Laneuville AP: Elissa Rashkin D: Eric Laneuville	Barbara Eden, Don Murray, Shawnee Smith, Bryon Thames, David Tom, Jennie Garth, Alison Sweeney
Parent Trap III				Walt Disney TV		Hayley Mills, Barry Bostwick, Creel Triplets
Mancuso FBI	Fri	10:00	60	Steve Sohmer Inc.-NBC Prods.	EP: Steve Sohmer, Jeff Bleckner SP: R. W. Goodwin P: Ken Solarz, Steve Bello	Robert Loggia, Lindsay Frost, Fredric Lehne, Randi Brazen, Charles Siebert
Matlock	Tue	8:00	60	Viacom Prods.	EP: Fred Silverman, Dean Hargrove, Joel Steiger SP: Jeff Peters P: Richard Collins, Joyce Burditt, Bill Kerr	Andy Griffith, Nancy Stafford, Julie Sommars, Don Knotts, Clarence Gilyard Jr.
Midnight Caller	Tue	10:00	60	December 3rd Prods.-Gangbuster Films-Lorimar TV	EP: Robert Singer SP: David Israel, Stephen Zito P: John F. Perry CP: Randy Zisk, John Schulian	Gary Cole, Wendy Kilbourne, Arthur Taxier, Dennis Dun
My Two Dads	Sun	8:30	30	Michael Jacobs Prod., Inc.-Columbia Pictures TV	EP: Michael Jacobs, Bob Myer SP: Chuck Lorre P: Mark Brull, Roger Garrett, David Steven Simon CP: Arlene Grayson Coor. P: Mark Greenberg	Paul Reiser, Greg Evigan, Staci Keanan, Florence Stanley, Vonni Ribisi, Amy Hathaway, Chad Allen
NBC Monday Night at the Movies	Mon	9:00	120	Various		
NBC Sunday Night at the Movies	Sun	9:00	120	Various		
Night Court	Wed	9:00	30	Starry Nights Prods.-Warner Bros. TV	EP: Gary Murphy, Larry Strawther SP: Nancy Steen, Neil Thompson P: Fred Rubin, Bob Underwood, Tim Steele	Harry Anderson, John Larroquette, Markie Post, Charles Robinson, Richard Moll, Marsha Warfield
Nutt House, The	Wed	9:30	30	Touchstone TV	EP: Mel Brooks, Alan Spencer P: Alan Mandel, Ronald E. Frazier	Cloris Leachman, Harvey Korman, Brian McNamara, Molly Hagan, Gregory Itzin, Mark Blankfield
Quantum Leap	Wed	10:00	60	Belisarius Prods.-Universal TV	EP: Donald P. Bellisario SP: Deborah Pratt, Paul Belous, Robert Wolterstorff P: Parker Wade CP: Paul Brown, Chris Ruppenthall, Jeff Gourson AP: David Bellisario	Scott Bakula, Dean Stockwell
Sister Kate	Sun	8:00	30	Lazy B/FOB Prods.-Mea Culpa Prods.-20th Fox TV	EP: Frank Dungan & Jeff Stein, Tony Sheehan P: Patricia Rickey D: Jeff Melman	Stephanie Beacham, Harley Cross, Hannah Cutrona, Jason Priestly, Erin Reed, Joel Robinson, Penina Segall, Alexaundra Simmons
227	Sat	8:00	30	Columbia Pictures TV	EP: Irma Kalish, John Boni P: Roxie Wenk Evans, Larry Spencer D: Gerren Keith	Marla Gibbs, Jackee Hal Williams, Alaina Reed-Hall, Paul Winfield, Regina King, Helen Martin, Curtis Baldwin, Barry Sobel
Unsolved Mysteries	Wed	8:00	60	Cosgrove/Meurer Prods.	EP: John Cosgrove, Terry Dunn Meurer SP: Chris Pye, Edward R. Horwitz	Robert Stack

Fox

Series Title	Day	Hr.	Mins.	Supplier	Production Principals	Cast Regulars & Semi-Regulars
Alien Nation	Mon	9:00	60	Johnson Prods.-Twentieth Century Fox	W/D & EP: Kenneth Johnson P: Arthur Seidel	Gary Graham, Eric Pierpoint, Michele Scarabelli, Lauren Woodland, Sean Six, Terri Treas
America's Most Wanted	Sun	8:00	30	STF Prods.	EP: Michael Linder D: Glenn Weiss	John Walsh
Beyond Tomorrow	Sat	9:30	30	B.I.C. Prods.	EP: Peter Abbott	Gary Cubberley, Jean Hill, Susan Hunt, Randy Meier, Richard Wiese
Booker	Sun	7:00	60	Stephen J. Cannell Prods.	EP: Eric Blakeney	Richard Grieco
Cops	Sat	8:00	30	Barbour/Langley Prods.-Fox Television Stations	EP: John Langley, Malcolm Barbour	
It's Garry Shandling's Show	Sun	10:30	30	Brillstein Company	EP: Bernie Brillstein, Brad Grey, Garry Shandling D: Alan Rafkin	Garry Shandling, Molly Cheek, Michael Tucci, Scott Nemes, Bernadette Birkett, Paul Willson
Married with Children	Sun	9:00	30	Columbia Pictures Television	EP: Ron Leavitt, Michael G. Moye	Ed O'Neill, Katey Segal, Christina Applegate, David Faustino, David Garrison, Amanda Bearse
Open House	Sun	9:30	30	UBU Prods.-Paramount	EP: Ruth Bennett, Susan Seeger	Mary Page Keller, Alison LaPlaca, Chris Lemmon, Ginger Orsi, Arleen Sorkin, Philip Charles Mackenzie, Jon Cypher, Ellen DeGeneres, Danny Gans, Ray Buktenica
The Reporters	Sat	8:30	60	STF Prods.	EP: Gerald Stone	Steven Dunleavy, Rafael Abramovitz, Krista Bradford, Jim Paymar, Steve Dunlop, Steve Wilson
Totally Hidden Video	Sun	8:30	30	Quantum Media	EP: Tom Lassally, Brian Bedol	Steve Skrovan
The Tracey Ullman Show	Sun	10:00	30	20th Century Fox Television	EP: James L. Brooks, Jerry Belson, Ken Estin, Heide Perlman D: Ted Bessell, Sam Simon	Tracey Ullman, Julie Kavner, Dan Castellaneta, Sam McMurray, Joseph Malone, Anna Levine
21 Jump Street	Mon	8:00	60	Steven J. Cannell Prods.	EP: Steve Beers	Johnny Depp, Holly Robinson, Dustin Nguyen, Peter DeLuise, Steven Williams, Sal Jenco, Richard Grieco

Syndicated Shows, 1989–90

Half-Hour Off-Network Shows

Title	No. of Episodes (Original/Repeat)	Distributor
9 to 5	85	20th Century Fox
Alice	202	Warner Bros.
All in the Family	207	Viacom
Andy Griffith	249	Viacom
Angie	37	Paramount
Archie's Place	97	Columbia
BJ/Lobo	86	MCA
Barney Miller	170	Columbia
Batman	120	20th Century Fox
Benson	158	Columbia
Best of Groucho	130	W.W. Entertainment
Beverly Hillbillies	274	Viacom
Bewitched	252	DFS
Bob Newhart	142	Viacom
Bosom Buddies	37	Paramount
Brady Bunch	117	DFS
Branded	48	King World
Car 54, Where Are You?	60	Republic
Carol Burnett	150	C.B. Distribution
Carson Classics	130	Columbia
Cheers	112	Paramount
The Cosby Show	150	Viacom
Dick Van Dyke	158	Viacom
Diff'rent Strokes	189	Columbia
Facts of Life	209	Columbia
Fame, Fortune & Romance	115	TPE
Family Affair	138	Viacom
Family Ties	98	Paramount
Fantasy Island	200	Columbia
Flying Nun	82	Columbia
Get Smart	138	Republic
Gidget	80	Lexington
Gilligan's Island	98	Turner Program Sales
Gimme a Break	85	MCA
Gomer Pyle	150	Viacom
Good Times	133	Columbia
Growing Pains	110	Warner Bros.
Guns of Will Sonnett	50	King World
Happy Days	255	Paramount
Here's Lucy	144	Warner Bros.
Hitchcock Presents	265	MCA
Hogan's Heroes	168	Viacom
Honeymooners	107	Viacom
I Dream of Jeannie	139	DFS
I Love Lucy	179	Viacom
I Married Joan	98	Weiss Global
Jeffersons	253	Columbia
Kate & Allie	96	MCA
Knight Rider	90	MCA
Laugh-In	130	Warner Bros.
Laverne & Shirley	178	DFS
Leave It To Beaver	234	Paramount
Life of Riley	120	New World
Life of Riley	146	New World
Life of Riley	26	New World

Title	No. of Episodes (Original/Repeat)	Distributor
Love Boat II	115	Worldvision
M*A*S*H	255	20th Century Fox
Make Room for Daddy	161	Weiss Global
Maude	141	Columbia
Mayberry, R.F.D.	78	Warner Bros.
McHale's Navy	130	Qintex
Monkees	58	Lexington
Mork & Mindy	95	DFS
Mr. Belvedere	110	20th Century Fox
My Favorite Martian	107	Warner Bros.
My Little Margie	126	Weiss Global
Newhart	134	MTM
Night Court	101	Warner Bros.
Night Gallery	97	MCA
Odd Couple	114	DFS
One Day at a Time	209	Columbia
Partridge Family	96	DFS
Soap	93	Columbia
Square Pegs	20	Columbia
Tales of the Texas Rangers	52	Columbia
Taxi	93	Paramount
That Girl	136	Worldvision
That's Incredible	165	MCA
That's My Mama	39	Columbia
The Ropers	26	Taffner
Three's Company	174	Taffner
Too Close for Comfort	122	Taffner
Topper	78	King World
Twilight Zone	94	MGM/UA
Twilight Zone	136	Viacom
We Love Lucy	26	Viacom
Webster	98	Paramount
What's Happening	131	Lexington
Who's the Boss?	120	Columbia
WKRP in Cincinnati	90	Victory
Wyatt Earp	130	Columbia

Hour Off-Network Shows

Title	No. of Episodes	Distributor
12 O'Clock High	78	20th Century Fox
A-Team	128	MCA
Airwolf	80	MCA
Avengers	83	Orion
BJ/Lobo	86	MCA
Barnaby Jones	177	Worldvision
Black Sheep Squadron	35	MCA
Blue Knight	23	Warner Bros.
Bonanza	268	Republic
Buck Rogers	37	MCA
CHiPS	138	MGM/UA
Cagney & Lacey	125	Orion
Cannon	124	Viacom
Charlie's Angels	115	Columbia
Crazy Like a Fox	37	Lexington
Dallas	161	Warner Bros.
Dukes of Hazzard	143	Warner Bros.
Dynasty	178	20th Century Fox
Eight Is Enough	112	Warner Bros.
Falcon Crest	157	Warner Bros.

Title	No. of Episodes (Original/Repeat)	Distributor
Fall Guy	111	20th Century Fox
Fantasy Island	130	Columbia
Gunsmoke	402	Viacom
Hardcastle and McCormick	67	Lexington
Hart to Hart	112	Columbia
Hawaii Five-0	200	Viacom
High Chapparal	98	Republic
Hill St. Blues	146	Victory
Hitchcock Hour	93	MCA
Hunter	107	Televentures
Incredible Hulk	85	MCA
Jacques Cousteau	36	Turner Program Sales
Knight Rider	90	MCA
Knots Landing	128	Warner Bros.
Kojak	118	MCA
Little House on the Prairie	216	Worldvision
Lost in Space	83	20th Century Fox
Love Boat I	140	Worldvision
Love Boat II	115	Worldvision
Magnum, P.I.	129	MCA
Mannix	130	Paramount
Matt Houston	68	Warner Bros.
Mission: Impossible	171	Paramount
Mystery Movies	124	MCA
Perry Mason	271	Viacom
Police Story	105	Columbia
Police Woman	91	Columbia
Remington Steele	94	MTM
St. Elsewhere	116	MTM
Star Trek	79	Paramount
Streets of San Francisco	119	Worldvision
T.J. Hooker	90	Columbia
That's Incredible	107	MCA
The Man from U.N.C.L.E.	132	Turner Program Sales
The Prisoner	17	ITC
Trapper John	132	20th Century Fox
Twilight Zone	18	Viacom
Vegas	68	20th Century Fox
Voyage to the Bottom of the Sea	110	20th Century Fox
Waltons	221	Warner Bros.
We Love Lucy	13	Viacom
Wonder Woman	61	Warner Bros.
Wonderful World of Disney	185	Buena Vista

Firstrun Half-Hour Strips

Title	No. of Episodes (Original/Repeat)	Distributor
3rd Degree	195	Warner Bros.
After Hours	130	Worldvision
Benny Hill	100	Taffner
Brothers	114	Paramount
Bumper Stumpers	260	MG/Perin
Business This Morning	260	Viacom
CNN Headline News	260	Turner Program Sales
Couch Potato	95/75	Group W
Crimewatch Tonight	185	Orion
Crook and Chase	260	Intermedia Mgmt.
Current Affair	260	20th Century Fox
Divorce Court	160	Blair Entertainment
Entertainment Tonight	260	Paramount

Title	No. of Episodes (Original/Repeat)	Distributor
Everyday with Joan Lunden	195	Michael Krauss Prods.
Family Feud	195	Lexington
First Business	260	Biz Net
Hard Copy	195	Paramount
Independent Network News: USA Tonight	260	INN News
Inside Edition	260	King World
Inside Report	260	MCA
It's A Living	120	Warner Bros.
Jackpot	175	Palladium
Jeopardy	195	King World
Leave It to Beaver	105	Qintex
Littlest Hobo	130	Silverbach/Lazarus
Lone Ranger	221	Palladium
Love Connection	170	Warner Bros.
Mama's Family	160	Warner Bros.
Morning Stretch	130	PSS
People's Court	195	Warner Bros.
P.M. Magazine	195	Group W
Small Wonder	96	20th Century Fox
Tales of the Unexpected	90	Orbis
Talkabout	195	Taffner
The Judge	160	Genesis Ent.
The Last Word	175	Turner Program Sales
Trial by Jury	160	Viacom
USA Today on TV	260	GTG
Wheel of Fortune	195	King World
Win, Lose or Draw	185	Buena Vista

Hour: Firstrun Strip

Title	No. of Episodes (Original/Repeat)	Distributor
Arsenio Hall	200	Paramount
Dr. Who	260	Lionheart (BBC)
Everyday with Joan Lunden	195	Michael Krauss Prods.
Geraldo	240	Paramount/Tribune Ent.
Joan Rivers	200	Paramount
Live with Regis and Kathie Lee	230	Buena Vista
Oprah Winfrey Show	240	King World
Phil Donahue	230	Multimedia
Sally Jessy Raphael	230	Multimedia

Half Hours: Firstrun Weekly

Title	No. of Episodes (Original/Repeat)	Distributor
9 to 5	26	20th Century Fox
America's Top 10	48/4	All American
At the Movies	48/4	Tribune Entertainment
Better Your Home with/BHG	26	Worldvision
Charles in Charge	26	MCA
College Madhouse	26	Warner Bros.
Computer Show	39/13	Victory
Crime Stopper 800	39/13	All American
Ebony/Jet Showcase	26	Carl Meyers
George and Mildred	38	Taffner
Gidget	44	Lexington
INN Magazine	52	INN News
In Sport	50/2	Select Media
Inside Video This Week	52	MG/Perin
It's a Living	25	Warner Bros.

Title	No. of Episodes (Original/Repeat)	Distributor
Jeopardy	52	King World
Keep It In the Family	31	Taffner
Lassie 4	26	MCA
Mama's Family	68	Warner Bros.
Man About the House	39	Taffner
Missing Reward	24	Group W
Monsters	26	Tribune Entertainment
Motorweek Illustrated	52	Orbis
Munsters (new)	24	MCA
Music City, USA	26	Multimedia
My Secret Identity	26	MCA
Out of This World	24	MCA
Punky Brewster	22	Columbia
Remote Control	39/13	Viacom
Runaway with/Rich and Famous	26	TPE
Secret World	24	Turner Program Services
Secrets and Mysteries	26	ITC
Siskel and Ebert	46/6	Buena Vista
Small Wonder	24	20th Century Fox
Superboy	26	Viacom
T&T	24	Qintex
Tales from the Darkside	26	Tribune Entertainment
That's My Mama	22	Columbia
The Making Of . . .	26	Muller Media
Twilight Zone	90	MGM/UA
War Chronicles	13	Orbis
Wheel of Fortune	52	King World
World Class Women	13	Select Media
Youth Quake	26	J.M. Ent.

Hours: Firstrun Weekly

Title	No. of Episodes (Original/Repeat)	Distributor
American Gladiators	26	Samuel Goldwyn
Blake's 7	52	Lionheart
Byron Allen	26	Genesis
Classic Country	91	Genesis Entertainment
Cop Talk—Behind the Shield	26	Tribune Entertainment
Entertainment This Week	51	Paramount
Fairie Tale Theater	26	Silverbach/Lazarus
Freddie's Nightmare	22	Warner Bros.
Friday the 13th	26	Paramount
G.L.O.W.	26	MG/Perin
Hee Haw	26	Gaylord
Jacques Cousteau	12	Turner Program Services
Lifestyles of the Rich and Famous	26	TPE
Michelob Presents Night Music	24	Fox/Lorber
National Geographic on Assignment	12	Turner Program Services
National Geographic Explorer	12	Turner Program Services
National Geographic Specials	96	Genesis Entertainment
Robin Hood	26	Samuel Goldwyn
Roller Games	13	Qintex
Showtime at the Apollo	26	Raymond Horn
Smithsonian Treasures	6	Lexington
Soul Train	40/12	Tribune Entertainment
Space 1999	40	ITC
Star Search	26	TPE
Star Trek: The Next Generation	26	Paramount
The Eyes of War	8	Vestron
Tuff Trax	52	Qintex

Title	No. of Episodes (Original/Repeat)	Distributor
USA Today on TV	52	GTG
War of the Worlds	24	Paramount
World at War	36	Taffner
Youth Quake	7	J.M. Entertainment

Children's Animated

Title	No. of Episodes (Original/Repeat)	Distributor
Alvin & the Chipmunks	65	Warner Bros.
Animated Classics	8	Taffner
Bullwinkle	98	DFS
C.O.P.S.	65	Claster
Care Bears	65	SFM
Chip 'n Dale's Rescue Rangers	65	Buena Vista
Dennis the Menace	65	DFS
Denver The Last Dinosaur	52	World Events
Duck Tales	95	Buena Vista
Dudley Do-Right	38	DFS
Felix the Cat	65	Columbia
Flintstones	166	DFS
Funtastic World-Hanna/Barbera		Worldvision
Gumby (new series)	65	Warner Bros.
Gumby (original)	130	Ziv Intl.
Heathcliff	86	Lexington
Inch High Private Eye	13	DFS
Jem	75	Claster
Jetsons	75	Worldvision
M.A.S.K.	75	Lexington
Maxie's World	70	Claster
Mighty Mouse & Friends	130	Viacom
Muppet Babies	65	Claster
My Little Pony and Friends	65	Claster
New Archies	13	Claster
Real Ghostbusters	99	Lexington
Rocky and Friends	78	DFS
Scooby Doo	110	DFS
Smurfs	130	Worldvision
Snorks	65	Worldvision
Space Kidettes	20	DFS
Super Mario Brothers	65	Viacom
Super Sunday	14	Claster
Superfriends	110	Lexington
Teenage Mutant Ninja Turtles	65	Group W
Tennessee Tuxedo	140	DFS
Thunderbirds	24	ITC
Thundersub	27	Lionheart (BBC)
Uncle Waldo	52	DFS
Valley of the Dinosaurs	16	DFS
Visionaries	13	Claster
Wheelie And The Chopper Bunch	13	DFS
Yogi Bear	65	Worldvision
Young Samson	20	DFS

Children's: Live Action

Title	No. of Episodes	Distributor
Cisco Kid	156	Blair Entertainment
Dr. Fad	26	Fox/Lorber
Fun House	170	Warner Bros.

Title	No. of Episodes (Original/Repeat)	Distributor
Littlest Hobo	96	Warner Bros.
Muppets	120	ITC
Peppermint Place	52	Electra Pictures
Super Sloppy Double Dare	130	Viacom
Superman	104	Warner Bros.
Young Universe	26	Behrens

Short-Length Animation

Title	No. of Episodes (Original/Repeat)	Distributor
Bugs Bunny/Porky Pig	256	Warner Bros.
Casper the Friendly Ghost	244	Worldvision
Felix the Cat	260	Columbia
Hercules	130	Columbia
New Three Stooges	156	Muller Media
Tom and Jerry	308	Turner Program Sales

1988–89 Motion Pictures Made for Television

Listed herewith are new films especially made for television and shown for the first time during the 1988–89 season from September to August. Key for credits: P is Producer; Exec. P: Executive Producer; Sprv. P: Supervising Producer; D: Director; W: Writer; M: Music by. Running time indicated includes commercials. Mini-series (made for television movies shown in three parts or more) are in the list at the end of this section.

AGATHA CHRISTIE'S "THE MAN IN THE BROWN SUIT"

Alan Shayne Prods. Inc. in association with Warner Bros. Television. Exec. P: Alan Shayne. Prod. supervisor: Norman Foster. D: Alan Grint. W: Carla Jean Wagner. Shown on CBS January 4, 1989. (2 hrs.)

Cast: Stephanie Zimbalist, Rue McClanahan, Tony Randall, Edward Woodward, Ken Howard, Nickolas Grace, Simon Dutton.

AMITYVILLE: THE EVIL ESCAPES

Steve White Prods. & Spectator. Exec. P: Steve White, Sandor Stern. P: Barry Bernardi. Co-P: John G. Jones. D-W: Sandor Stern, based on book by John G. Jones. M: Rick Conrad. Shown on NBC May 12, 1989. (2 hrs.)

Cast: Patty Duke, Jane Wyatt, Frederic Lehne, Lou Hancock, Brandy Gold, Geri Betzler, Aron Eisenberg, Norman Lloyd, Robert Alan Browne.

BABYCAKES

The Konigsberg/Sanitsky Co. Exec. P: Frank Konigsberg, Larry Sanitsky. P: Diana Kerew. D: Paul Schneider. W: Joyce Eliason, based on German film "Sugarbaby" by Percy Adlon. M: William Olvis. Shown on CBS February 14, 1989. (2 hrs.)

Cast: Ricki Lake, Craig Sheffer, Nada Despotovich, Paul Benedict, Betty Buckley, John Karlen.

BACKFIRE

ITC Production. P: Danton Rissner. Exec. in chg. of prod.: Dennis A. Brown D; Gilbert Cates. W: Larry Brand, Rebecca Reynolds, M: David Shire. Shown on Showtime June 18, 1989 (95 minutes).

Cast: Karen Allen, Keith Carradine, Jeff Fahey, Dean Paul Martin, Philip Sterling, Dinah Manoff.

BAYWATCH: PANIC AT MALIBU PIER

GTG Entertainment. Exec. P-W: Douglas Schwartz, Michael Berk. P: Robert Hargrove, Gregory J. Bonann. D: Richard Compton. M: Arthur Rubinstein. Shown on NBC April 23, 1989. (2 hrs.)

Cast: David Hasselhoff, Parker Stevenson, Shawn Weatherly, Billy Warlock, Erika Eleniak, Peter Phelps, Gina Hecht, Brandon Call, Monte Markham, Madchen Amick, Wendie Malick, Richard Jaeckel.

BIONIC SHOWDOWN: THE SIX-MILLION DOLLAR MAN & THE BIONIC WOMAN

Universal TV. Exec. P-W: Michael Sloan. P: Nigel Watts, Bernie Joyce. Co-P: Richard Anderson, Lee Majors. D: Alan J. Levi. Shown on NBC April 30, 1989. (2 hrs.)

Cast: Lee Majors, Lindsay Wagner, Richard Anderson, Martin E. Brooks, Sandra Bullock, Jeff Yagher, Geraint Wyn Davies, Robert Lansing, Lee Majors 2nd, Josef Sommer.

BREAKING POINT

An Avnet/Kerner Co. Production. P: Jon Avnet, Jordan Kerner. D: Peter Markle. W: Stanley Greenberg. Shown on TNT August 18, 1989. (2 hours.)

Cast: Corbin Bernsen, John Glover, Joanna Pacula.

BRIDESMAIDS

Motown Prods., Quintex Entertainment and Deaun Prods. Exec. P: Suzanne de Passe. Sprv. P: Carol A. Caruso. P: Jay Benson. D: Lila Garrett. W: Bett Eyre. M: Paul Chihara. Shown on CBS February 21, 1989. (2 hrs.)

Cast: Shelley Hack, Sela Ward, Stephanie Faracy, Jack Coleman, Audra Lindley, Brooke Adams, Hamilton Camp, James F. Dean, Randy Ser, Kathryn Kimler.

BRIDGE TO SILENCE

Fries Entertainment in assoc. with Briggle, Hennessy, Carrothers & Associates. Exec. P: Charles Fries. P: Stockton Briggle, Dennis Hennessy, Richard Carrothers. Exec. in chg. of P: S. Bryan Hickox. Assoc. P: Jack Allen. D: Karen Arthur. W: Louisa Burns-Bisogno. M: Fred Karlin. Shown on CBS April 9, 1989. (2 hrs.)

Cast: Lee Remick, Marlee Matlin, Michael O'Keefe, Candace Brecker, Allison Silva, Josef Sommer, Phyllis Frelich.

BROTHERHOOD OF THE ROSE

NBC Productions. Exec P: Sterling Silliphant. P & D: Marvin J. Chomsky. W: Gy Waldron, based on novel by David Morrell. M: Laurence Rosenthal. Shown on NBC January 22 and 23, 1989. (4 hrs.)

Cast: Robert Mitchum, Peter Strauss, David Morse, Connie Sellecca, James Sikking, M. Emmet Walsh.

THE CASE OF THE HILLSIDE STRANGLERS

Kenwood Prods. & Fries Entertainment. Exec. P: Charles Fries, Mike Rosenfeld. P: Carole Coates. D: Stephen Gethers. W: Gethers, based on Dacey O'Brien's novel, Two of a Kind: the Hillside Stranglers. Shown on NBC April 2, 1989. (2 hrs.)

Cast: Richard Crenna, Dennis Farina, Billy Zane, Tony Plana, James Tolkan, Karen Austin, Matthew Faison, Robert Harper, Mary Jackson.

CHAMPAGNE CHARLIE

Champagne Charlie Prods., Falcon Prods., S.A. & CTV TV Network Ltd. P: David Patterson, Thierry Caillen. Co-P: Ronald I. Cohen. D: Allen Eastman. W: Robert Geoffrion, Jacqueline Lefevre. Shown in syndication April 12 & 18, 1989. (4 hrs.)

Cast: Hugh Grant, Megan Gallagher, Megan Follows, Stephane Audran, Georges Decrieres, Jean-Claude Dauphin, Alexandra Stewart, Jean-Paul Muel, Vladek Sheybak, R.H. Thomson, Kenneth Welsh, Dennis Forest.

THE CHRISTMAS WIFE

Edie Landau Prod. Exec. P: Edie Landau. P: Patrick Whitley. D: David Jones. W-Assoc. P: Katherine Ann Jones, based on short story by Helen Norris. M: Max Harris. Shown on HBO December 12, 1988. (1½ hrs.)

Cast: Jason Robards, Julie Harris, Don Francks, James Eckhouse.

THE COMEBACK

CBS Entertainment Production. P: Ron Roth. D: Jerrold Freedman. W: Percy Granger, based on "Eye of the Beholder" by Seymour Epstein. M: Craig Safan. Shown on CBS January 8, 1989. (2 hrs.)

Cast: Robert Urich, Chynna Phillips, Mitchell Anderson, Brynn Thayer, Harvey Martin, Ronny Cox.

THE COVER GIRL & THE COP

Barry & Enright/Alexander Productions. Exec. P: Dan Enright. P: Les Alexander and Dan Enright. D: Neal Israel. W: Michael Norell. M: Sylvester Levay. Shown on NBC January 16, 1989. (2 hrs.)

Cast: Dinah Manoff, Julia Duffy, John Karlen, David Carradine, Parker Stevenson, Jonathan Frakes, Robert Picardo, Arthur Taxier, Tom Silardi, Whip Hubley, Blair Underwood, Danitra Vance.

CROSSING THE MOB

Bateman Co. Prod. in assoc. with Interscope Communications Inc. Exec. P: Ted Field, Kent Bateman. P: Phil Parslow. D: Steven Hilliard Stern. W: Lewis Colick, Alan Shapiro. Shown on NBC October 14, 1988. (2 hrs.)

Cast: Jason Bateman, Frank Stallone, Patti D'Arbanville, Maura Tierney, Michael Manasseri, Evan Mirard, William Gallo, Louis Giambalvo, Brent and Brandon Goldman, Tony Brafa, Robert Costanzo.

DADAH IS DEATH

Steve Krantz Prods./Roadshow Coote & Carroll and Samuel Goldwyn Television. Exec. P: Steve Krantz, Matt Carroll. P-D: Jerry London. Sprv. P: Moya Iceton. W: Bill Kerby. M: Fred Karlin. Shown on CBS October 30 & 31, 1988. (4 hrs.)

Cast: Julie Christie, Hugo Weaving, John Polson, Sarah Jessica Parker, Kerry Armstrong, Robin Ramsey, Victor Banerjee.

DANCE 'TIL DAWN

Konigsberg/Sanitsky Prods. Exec. P: Frank Konigsberg, Larry Sanitsky. P: Whitney Green. D: Paul Schneider. W: Andrew Guerdat, Steve Kreinberg. Shown on NBC October 23, 1988. (2 hrs.)

Cast: Christina Applegate, Tempestt Bledsoe, Brian Bloom, Cliff DeYoung, Mary Frann, Tracy Gold, Kelsey Grammer, Edie McClurg, Alyssa Milano, Matthew Perry, Alan Thicke, Chris Young, Molly Cheek, Graham Jarvis, Candy Azzara.

DANNY, THE CHAMPION OF THE WORLD

The Disney Channel, PBS Wonderworks, Thames TV, Portobello Prods. & Children's Film & TV Foundation. P: Eric Abraham. D: Gavin Millar. W: John Goldsmith, based on story by Roald Dahl. M: Stanley Myers. Shown on Disney Channel April 29, 1989. (2 hrs.)

Cast: Jeremy Irons, Samuel Irons, Cyril Cusack, Robbie Coltrane, Michael Hordern, Lionel Jeffries, Jean Marsh, Jimmy Nail, Ronald Pickup, John Woodvine, William Armstrong, Ceri Jackson, James Walker.

DARK HOLIDAY

Peter Nelson/Lou Antonio Prods., The Finnegan/Pinchuk Co. & Orion TV. Exec. P-D: Lou Antonio. Sprv. P: Pat & Bill Finnegan, Sheldon Pinchuk. P: Peter Nelson. W: Rose Leiman Golemberg, based on Gene LePere's novel "Never Pass This Way Again." M: Paul Chihara. Shown on NBC May 1, 1989. (2 hrs.)

Cast: Lee Remick, Norma Aleandro, Tony Goldwyn, Roy Thinnes, John Standing, Suzanne Wouk, Shanit Keter, Jim Antonio.

DAVID

Tough Boys Inc., Donald March Prods. in assoc. with ITC Entertainment. P: Donald March. D: John Erman. W: Stephanie Liss. M: Marvin Hamlisch. Shown on ABC October 25, 1988. (2 hrs.)

Cast: Bernadette Peters, John Glover, Dan Lauria, Matthew Lawrence, George Grizzard.

DAY ONE

Aaron Spelling Prods. in assoc. with Paragon Motion Pictures and David W. Rintels Prods. Exec. P: Aaron Spelling, E. Duke Vincent. W-P: David W. Rintels, based on book "Day One: Before Hiroshima" by Peter Wyden. D: Joseph Sargent. M: Mason Daring. Shown on CBS March 5, 1989. (3 hrs.)

Cast: Brian Dennehy, David Strathairn, Michael Tucker, Hume Cronyn, Richard Dysart, Hal Holbrook, Barnard Hughes, John McMartin, David Ogden Stiers, Anne Twomey, Lawrence Dane, Ron Frazier, Olek Krupa, Bernie McInerney, John Pielmeiser, Ken Pogue, Gary Reineke, Alan Scarfe, John Seitz, Tony Shalhoub, Ester Spitz, Ron White.

DEAD MAN OUT

Citadel Entertainment. Exec. P: David R. Ginsburg. P: Forrest Murray. D: Richard Pearce. W: Ron Hutchinson, story by J.D. Maria, Lorna Soroko. M: Cliff Eidelman. Shown on HBO March 12, 1989. (90 mins.)

Cast: Danny Glover, Ruben Blades, Tom Atkins, Larry Block, Sam Jackson, Maria Ricossa.

DEAD SOLID PERFECT

HBO Pictures in assoc. with David Merrick. Exec. P: Dan Jenkins. Etan Merrick. P: Bill Badalato. D: Bobby Roth. W: Dan Jenkins, Bobby Roth. M: Tangerine Dream. Shown on HBO December 18, 1988. (95 mins.)

Cast: Randy Quaid, Kathryn Harrold, Corinne Bohrer, Brett Cullen, Larry Riley, DeLane Matthews, Bibi Besch, John M. Jackson, Jack Warden.

DEADLINE: MADRID

Universal Television. Exec. P: Karen Harris. Sprv. P: Kevin Donnelly. P: Pamela de Maigret. D: John Patterson. W: Karen Harris. M: Larry Carlton. Shown on ABC September 1, 1988. (2 hrs.)

Cast: Brynn Thayer, Leigh Lawson, Joe Santos, J. Kenneth Campbell, Valerie Wildman, Marta Dubois, Miriam Colon, Charles Cioffi, Andrew Rubin, Neva Patterson.

A DEADLY SILENCE

Robert Greenwald Prods. Inc. Exec. P: Robert Greenwald, Jennifer Miller. P: Philip Kleinbart, Paul Lussier. Co-P: Robert Florio. Assoc. P: Scott U. Adam. D: John Patterson. W: Jennifer Miller, based on book by Dena Kleinman. M: Richard Gibbs. Shown on ABC April 16, 1989. (2 hrs.)

Cast: Mike Farrell, Bruce Weitz, Charles Haid, Richard Portnow, Wally Ward, Heather Fairfield, Sally Struthers, Julliet Sorcey, Philip Linton, Susan Barnes, David Schwimmer, Donna Mitchell, Jeff Corey, Irene Tedrow.

DESPERATE FOR LOVE

Vishudda Prods. in assoc. with Andrew Adelson Co. and Lorimar Telepictures. Exec. P: Andrew Adelson, Judith Paige Mitchell. P: Steve McGlothen. D: Michael Tuchner. W: Judith Paige Mitchell. M: Charles Bernstein. Shown on CBS January 17, 1989. (2 hrs.)

Cast: Christian Slater, Tammy Lauren, Brian Bloom, Veronica Cartwright, Scott Paulin, Arthur Rosenberg, Amy O'Neill, Lulee Fisher, Michael Flynn, Billy Vera.

THE DIAMOND TRAP

Jay Bernstein Prods. in assoc. with Columbia Pictures TV. Exec. P: Jay Bernstein. Sprv. Exec. P: Patrick Dromgoole, Johnny Goodman. P: Neil T. Maffeo. Co-P: Jeffrey Morton. D: Don Taylor. W: David Peckinpah. M: Ron Ramin. Shown on CBS November 20, 1988. (2 hrs.)

Cast: Howard Hesseman, Brooke Shields, Ed Marinaro, Twiggy, Darren McGavin, Dick O'Neill, Nicholas Pryor, Tony Steedman.

DISASTER AT SILO 7

Mark Carliner Prods. Exec. P: Mark Carliner. P: Julian Krainin. Co-P: Lynn H. Guthrie. D: Larry Elikann. W: Douglas Lloyd McIntosh, Mark Carliner. M: Mark Snow. Shown on ABC November 27, 1988. (2 hrs.)

Cast: Ray Baker, Peter Boyle, Patricia Charbonneau, Perry King, Michael O'Keefe, Joe Spano, Dennis Weaver, Joe Urla, Brent Jennings.

DOUBLE STANDARD

Louis Rudolph Prods., Fenton Entertainment Group & Fries Entertainment. Exec. P-D: Louis Rudolph. P: Robert Fenton, S. Bryan Hickox. W: Robert E. Thompson, based on James Whitfield Ellison's book. M: Patrick Williams. Shown on NBC October 17, 1988. (2 hrs.)

Cast: Robert Foxworth, Michele Greene, Christianne Hirt, James Kee, Pamela Bellwood, Mary Armstrong, Philippe Ayoub, Steven Bednarski.

DREAM BREAKERS

CBS Entertainment Prods. Sprv. P: Robert Silberling. P-D: Stuart Millar. Co-P: Ken Swor. W: Victor Levin, Stuart Millar. M: Glenn Paxton. Shown on CBS January 13, 1989. (2 hrs.)

Cast: Robert Loggia, Kyle MacLachlan, D.W. Moffett, Charles Cioffi, Laila Robins, John McIntire, Helen Lloyd Breed, Finn Carter, Hal Linden, Maureen Mueller, Alan Wilder, Randy Arney, Don Dean, Frank Rice, Tommy Vee, Will Zahrn.

EVERYBODY'S BABY: THE RESUE OF JESSICA MCCLURE

Dick Berg/Stonchenge Prods., The Campbell Soup Co. in assoc. with Interscope Prods. Inc. Exec. P: Ted Field, Dick Berg, Patricia Clifford, Co-Exec. P: John Kander III. P: Diana Kerew. D: Mel Damski. W: David Eyre Jr. M: Mark Snow. Shown on ABC May 21, 1989. (2 hrs.)

Cast: Beau Bridges, Patty Duke, Pat Hingle, Roxana Zal, Will Oldham, Whip Hubley, Robin Gammell, Walter Olkewicz, Rudy Ramos, Jack Rader, Guy Stockwell, Daryl Anderson, Mills Watson, Bo Foxworth, Robin Frates, Don Hood.

FATAL JUDGMENT

Jack Farren Prod. Exec. P: Jack Farren. P: Paul Pompian. D: Gilbert Cates. W: Gerald Green. M: Lee Holdridge. Shown on CBS October 18, 1988. (2 hrs.)

Cast: Patty Duke, Tom Conti, Joe Regalbuto, Jo Henderson, Dana Gladstone, Peter Crook, Richard Cummings Jr., Merrya Small, Mary Tanner, Jane Harnick, Crystal McKellar.

FINISH LINE

Guber-Peters Entertainment Prods. in assoc. with Phoenix Entertainment Group. Exec. P: Peter Guber, Jon Peters, Gerald W. Abrams. P: Stanley M. Brooks, William P. Owens. Co-P: David Zelon. D: John Nicolella. W: Norman Morrill. M: William Patrick Olvis. Shown on TNT January 19, 1989 (2 hrs.) .

Cast: James Brolin, Josh Brolin, Mariska Hargitay, Kristoff St. John, Christopher Keyes, Billy Vera, Stephen Lang, Grand Bush, Joe Jackson, James Ray, Owen Engelmann, Todd Gerimonte, Karen Saddington.

THE FORGOTTEN

Keach/Railsback Prods., Forgotten Ltd., Wilshire Court Prods., Jadran Films—Jagreb. Exec. P: Steve Railsback, Keith Carradine. Sprv. P: Denny Salvaryn. P: James Keach. Co-P: Boris Gregoric. D: James Keach. W: James Keach, Steve Railsback, Matthew Barr, Glenn Benest. M: Laurence Rosenthal. Shown on USA Network April 26, 1989. (2 hrs.)

Cast: Keith Carradine, Steve Railsback, Stacy Keach, Pepe Serna, Richard Lawson, Don Opper, Michael Champion, Mimi Maynard, Kai Wulff, William Lucking.

FROM THE DEAD OF THE NIGHT

Shadowplay Films/Phoenix Entertainment Group. Exec. P: Hans Proppe. Co-P: Jody B. Paonessa. D: Paul Wendkos. W: William Bleich, from novel "Walkers" by Gary Brandner. M: Gil Melle. Shown on NBC February 27 & 28, 1989. (4 hrs.)

Cast: Lindsay Wagner, Bruce Boxleitner, Robin Thomas, Diahann Carroll, Robert Prosky.

THE FULFILLMENT OF MARY GRAY

Les Caplin Prods./Indian Neck Ent. Exec. P: Howard Baldwin, Richard M. Cohen, Lee Caplin. P: Harry R. Sherman. D: Piers Haggard. W: Laird Koenig, based on novel "The Fulfillment" by La Vyrle Spencer. M: Gary Scott. Shown on CBS February 19, 1989. (2 hrs.)

Cast: Cheryl Ladd, Ted Levine, Lewis Smith.

FULL EXPOSURE: THE SEX TAPES SCANDAL

Von Zerneck/Sertner Films. Exec. P: Frank von Zerneck, Robert M. Sertner. Co-P: Stephen Zito, Gregory Prange. D: Noel Nosseck. W: Stephen Zito. M: Dana Kaproff. Shown on NBC February 5, 1989. (2 hrs.)

Cast: Lisa Hartman, Anthony Denison, Vanessa Williams, Peter Jurasik, Jennifer O'Neill, John Anderson, James Avery, Rene Enriquez, Alan Fudge, Walter Olkeiwicz, Judson Scott, Jennifer Warren, Bill Applebaum, Tom Everett, Johnny Haymer, Allan Wasserman, Mort Sertner.

GET SMART, AGAIN!

The Indie Prod. Co. in assoc. with Phoenix Entertainment Group Inc. Exec. P: Leonard B. Stern, Daniel Melnick. P: Burt Nodella. Sprv. P: Bruce J. Sallan. D: Gary Nelson. W: Leonard B. Stern, Mark Curtiss, Rod Ash. M: Peter Melnick. Shown on ABC February 26, 1989. (2 hrs.)

Cast: Don Adams, Barbara Feldon, Bernie Kopell, Dick Gautier, Robert Karvelas, King Moody, Harold Gould, Kenneth Mars, John deLancie, Steve Levitt.

THE GIFTED ONE

Richard Rothstein Prod., NBC Prods. Exec. P: Richard Rothstein. P: Ariel Levy. D: Stephen Herek. W: Richard Rothstein, Lisa James. M: J. Peter Robinson. Shown on NBC June 25, 1989. (2 hrs.)

Cast: Pete Kowanko, John Rhys-Davies, G.W. Bailey, Greeg Henry, Krystyne Haje, Wendy Phillips, Thomas Callaway, Brandon Call.

GLITZ

Robert Cooper Films Inc. and Lorimar Telepictures. Exec. P: Gary Adelson, Robert Cooper, David Ginsberg. P: Steve McGlothen. D: Sandor Stern. W: Alan Trustman, Steve Zito. M: Dana Kaproff. Shown on NBC October 21, 1988. (2 hrs.)

Cast: Jimmy Smits, Markie Post, John Diehl, Ken Foree, Robin Strasser, Kathleen Freeman, George Touliatos, Tasia Valenza.

GLORY DAYS

Shane Co. with Sibling Rivalries. Exec. P: Joan Conrad. P: Roger Bacon, Glenn D. Banner. D: Robert Conrad. W: Timothy Stack, Larry Williams, David J. Kinghorn. Story: Timothy Stack, Larry Williams. M: Robert Folk. Shown on CBS December 11, 1988. (2 hrs.)

Cast: Robert Conrad, Jennifer O'Neill, Shane Conrad, Stacy Edwards, Pamela Gidley, Russell Curry, Duane Davis, Timothy Erwin, Micah Grant, Brian Andrew Smith, David E. Thompkins, Ed O'Ross.

GLORY! GLORY!

Atlantis Films Limited and Orion Television in co-prod. with Stan Daniels Prods. and Greif-Dore Co. Exec. P: Bonny Dore, Leslie Greif. P: Stan Daniels, Seaton McLean, Sprv. P: Michael MacMillan. Co-P: Jonathan Goodwill. D: Lindsay Anderson. W: Stan Daniels. M: Christopher Dedrick. Shown on HBO February 19 & 20, 1989. (3¼ hrs.)

Cast: Ellen Green, Richard Thomas, Winston Rekert, Barry Mores, James Whitmore.

GO TOWARD THE LIGHT

Corapeake Prods. & The Polson Co. Exec. P: Beth Polson. P: Nick Lombardo. D: Mike Robe. W: Susan Nanus, Beth Polson. M: James Newton Howard. Shown on CBS November 1, 1988. (2 hrs.)

Cast: Linda Hamilton, Piper Laurie, Joshua Harris, Ned Beatty, Gary Bayer, Rosemary Dunsmore, Steve Eckholdt, Brian Bonsall, Mitchell Allen, Richard Thomas.

THE GODDESS OF LOVE

Phil Margo Enterprises Inc./New World TV in assoc. with Phoenix Entertainment Group. Exec. P: Phil Margo. Co-P: Ray Manzella. P: Don Segall. D: Jim Drake. W: Don Segall, Phil Margo. M: Mitch Margo, Dennis Dreith, A.S. Diamond. Shown on NBC November 20, 1988. (2 hrs.)

Cast: Vanna White, David Naughton, David Leisure, Amanda Bearse, Philip Baker Hall, Betsy Palmer, John Rhys-Davies, Ray O'Connor, Michael Goldfinger.

GOING TO THE CHAPEL

Furia Org. in assoc. with Finnegan-Pinchuk Co. Exec. P: Barry Oringer. P: Sheldon Pinchuk, Bill Finnegan, Pat Finnegan. D: Paul Lynch. W: Erik Tarloff. M: Charles Fox. Shown on NBC October 9, 1988. (2 hrs.)

Cast: Barbara Billingsley, Eileen Brennan, Joel Brooks, Michele Greene, Wendy Kilbourne, Cloris Leachman, Mark Linn-Baker, John Ratzenberger, Jennifer Savidge, Jane Sibbett, Michael Talbott, Scott Valentine, Dick Van Patten, Max Wright.

GOODBYE, MISS 4TH OF JULY

Finnegan/Pinchuk Prods., Walt Disney Co. Exec. P: Pat Finnegan, Bill Finnegan, Sheldon Pinchuk. P: Christopher Seiter, Josephine Lyons, Peter Miller. D: George Miller. W: Kathy McCormick. Based on the book "Miss 4th of July, Goodbye," by Christopher C. Janus. M: Mark Snow. Shown on Disney Channel December 3, 1988. (90 mins.)

Cast: Louis Gossett, Jr., Chris Sarandon, Roxana Zal, Chantal Contoury, Chynna Phillips, Mitchell Anderson, Conchata Ferrell, Ed Lauter, Kai Wulff.

GORE VIDAL'S BILLY THE KID

Von Zerneck-Sertner Productions. P: Frank von Zerneck, Robert M. Sertner. D: William A. Graham. W: Gore Vidal. M: Laurence Rosenthal. Shown on TNT May 10, 1989. (2 hrs.)

Cast: Val Kilmer, Duncan Regehr, Wilford Brimley, Michael Parks.

THE GREAT ESCAPE II: THE UNTOLD STORY

Michael Jaffe Films Ltd. in assoc. with Spectacor Films. Exec. P: Michael Jaffe. P: Jud Taylor. D: Paul Wendkos, Jud Taylor. W: Walter Halsey David. M: Johnny Mandel. Shown on NBC November 6 & 7, 1988. (4 hrs.)

Cast: Christopher Reeve, Judd Hirsch, Anthony Denison, Charles Haid, Ian McShane, Donald Pleasence, Michael Nader, Mijou Kovacs, Ronald Lacey.

GUTS & GLORY: THE RISE AND FALL OF OLIVER NORTH

Mike Robe Prods. Inc. in assoc. with Papazian-Hirsch Entertainment. Exec. P-D-W: Mike Robe. P: Robert Papazian, James G. Hirsch. Based on book by Ben Bradlee Jr. M: Arthur B. Rubinstein. Shown on CBS April 30 and May 2, 1989. (4 hrs.)

Cast: David Keith, Barnard Hughes, Annette O'Toole, Peter Boyle, Paul Dooley, Amy Stock-Poynton, Bryan Clark, Joe Dorsey, Terry O'Quinn, Miguel Ferrer, Madison Mason, Suzanne Snyder, Scott Kraft.

THE HAUNTING OF SARAH HARDY

USA Network. Exec. P-D: Jerry London. P-Prod Mgr.: Richard Rothschild. W: Thomas Baum. Shown on USA Network May 31, 1989. (2 hrs.)

Cast: Sela Ward, Morgan Fairchild, Michael Woods, Polly Bergen.

HIGHER GROUND

Green/Epstein Prod. in assoc. with Columbia Pictures Television. Exec. P: Jim Green, Allen Epstein. Co-Exec. P: John Denver. D: Robert Day. W: Michael Eric Stein. M: John Denver, Lee Holdridge. Shown on CBS September 4, 1988. (2 hrs.)

Cast: John Denver, Meg Wittner, David Renan, Brandon Marsh, John Rhys-Davies, Martin Kove, Richard Masur, Gordon Tootoosis.

THE HIJACKING OF THE ACHILLE LAURO

Tamara Asseyev Prods./Spectator Films/New World Television. Exec. P: Tamara Asseyev. Sprv. P: Sue Miliken. W-D: Robert Collins. M: Chris Boardman. Shown on NBC February 13, 1989. (2 hrs.)

Cast: Karl Malden, Lee Grant, Vera Miles, E.G. Marshall, Christina Spiegel.

HOME FIRES BURNING

Marian Rees Associates Inc. Exec. P: Marian Rees. P-D: Glenn Jordan. W: Robert Inman. M: Don Davis. Shown on CBS January 29, 1989. (2 hrs.)

Cast: Barnard Hughes, Sada Thompson, Robert J. Prosky, Bill Pullman, Elizabeth Berridge, Neil Patrick Harris.

I KNOW MY FIRST NAME IS STEVEN

Andrew Adelson Co. in assoc. with Lorimar Television. Exec. P: Andrew Adelson. P: Kim C. Friese. D: Larry Elikann. W: JP. Miller, Cynthia Whitcomb. Story: JP Miller, suggested by material by W.H. (Mike) Echols II. M: David Shire. Shown on NBC May 22 and 23, 1989. (4 hrs.)

Cast: Corin "Corky" Nemec, Arliss Howard, Cindy Pickett, John Ashton, Luke Edwards.

I'LL BE HOME FOR CHRISTMAS

NBC Prods. Exec. P: Michael Manheim. P-D: Marvin J. Chomsky. W: Blanche Hanalis. M: Jorge Callandrelli. Shown on NBC December 12, 1988. (2 hrs.)

Cast: Hal Holbrook, Eva Marie Saint, Nancy Travis, Peter Gallagher, Courteney Cox, Jason Oliver, David Moscow.

IN THE LINE OF DUTY: THE FBI MURDERS

Telcom Entertainment Inc. in assoc. with World International Network. Exec. P: Michael Lepiner, Kenneth Kaufman. P: David Kappes. Exec. in chg. of prod: Marjorie Kalins. D: Dick Lowry. W: Tracy Keenan Wynn. Shown on NBC November 27, 1988. (2 hrs.)

Cast: Michael Gross, Doug Sheehan, David Soul, Ronny Cox, Bruce Greenwood, Ronald G. Joseph, Teri Copley.

INDISCREET

Republic Pictures. Exec. P: Karen Mack. P: John Davis. Sprv. P: Jane Petteway. D: Richard Michaels. W: Walter Lockwood, Sally Robinson, based on play/screenplay by Norman Krasna. M: Arthur B. Rubinstein. Shown on CBS October 24, 1988. (2 hrs.)

Cast: Robert Wagner, Lesley-Anne Down, Maggie Henderson, Robert McBain, Jeni Barnett, Fanny Carby.

INTERNAL AFFAIRS

Titus Prods. Inc. a Great American Broadcasting Co. Exec. P: Herbert Brodkin, Robert Berger. P: Thomas De Wolfe. D: Michael Tuchner. W: William Bayer. M: Arthur B. Rubinstein. Shown on CBS November 6 & 7, 1988. (4 hrs.)

Cast: Richard Crenna, Kate Capshaw, Cliff Gorman, Dennis Boutsikaris, Danton Stone, Sam Coppola, Caroline Kava, James McDaniel, Ronald Hunter, John Capodice, Philip Bosco, Min Luong, David Leary, Paul Guilfoyle, Lee Richardson, Michael Fischetti, Aki Aleong.

INTRIGUE

Crew Neck Prods. & Linnea Prods. in assoc. with Columbia Pictures Television. Exec. P: John Scheinfeld, Jeff Melvoin. P: Nick Gillott. D: David Drury. W: Jeff Melvoin, Robert Collins. Story: Robert Collins. M: Basil Poledouris. Shown on CBS September 11, 1988. (2 hrs.)

Cast: Scott Glenn, Robert Loggia, William Atherton, Martin Shaw, Cherie Lunghi, Eleanor Bron, Paul Maxwell, William Roberts, Don Fellows, Blain Fairman, Philip O'Brien.

JACK THE RIPPER

Euston Films Prod., Thames Television in association with Hill-O'Connor Ent. and Lorimar. Exec. P: Lloyd Shirely, Robert O'Connor, Leonard Hill. P-D: David Wickes. W: Derek Marlowe, David Wickes. M: John Cameron. Shown on CBS October 21 & 23, 1988. (4 hrs.)

Cast: Michael Caine, Armand Assante, Ray McAnally, Lewis Collins, Ken Bones, Susan George, Jane Seymour.

JESSE

Turman-Foster Co./Jordan Prod. in assoc. with Republic Pictures. Exec. P: Lawrence Turman, David Foster. P-D: Glenn Jordan. W: James Lee Barrett. M: David Shire. Shown on CBS October 4, 1988. (2 hrs.)

Cast: Lee Remick, Kevin Conway, Scott Wilson, Richard Marcus, Priscilla Lopez, Leon Rippy, Albert Salmi, Macon McCalman, Richard Erdman, Stephen Jace, Richard Glover.

THE KAREN CARPENTER STORY

Weintraub Entertainment Prods. Exec. P: Richard Carpenter. P: Robert A. Papazian, Hal Galli. D: Joseph Sargent. W: Barry Morrow. M: Richard Carpenter. Shown on CBS January 1, 1989. (2 hrs.)

Cast: Cynthia Gibb, Mitchell Anderson, Louise Fletcher, Peter Michael Goetz.

KILLER INSTINCT

Millar-Bromberg Prods. & ITC Entertainment. P: Stuart Millar, Conrad Bromberg. D: Waris Hussein. W: Conrad Bromberg. M: Paul Chihara. Shown on NBC November 22, 1988. (2 hrs.)

Cast: Melissa Gilbert, Woody Harrelson, Lane Smith, Kevin Conroy, Fernando Lopez, Roy Brocksmith, Michael Kaufman, Janet MacLachlan, William Marshall, Marco Rodriguez, Garn Stephens, Nat Bernstein, Anne Betancourt, Barry Dennen, Peter Iancangelo, Robert Schuch, Lorrine Vozoff.

KISS SHOT

London Prods. in assoc, with Whoop Inc. Exec. P-D: Jerry London. P: Salli Newman, Mel A. Bishop. Assoc. P: Chad Cooperman, Abra Edelman. W: Carl Kleinschmit. M: Steve Dorff. Shown on CBS April 11, 1989. (2 hrs.)

Cast: Whoopi Goldberg, Dorian Harewood, Dennis Franz, Tasha Scott, David Marciano, Teddy Wilson.

THE LADY AND THE HIGHWAYMAN

Lord Grade Prod. in assoc. with Gainsborough Pictures. Exec. P: Laurie Johnson. P: Albert Fennell, John Hough. D: John Hough. W: Terence Feely, Peter Manley. M: Laurie Johnson. Shown on CBS January 22, 1989. (2 hrs.)

Cast: Emma Samms, Oliver Reed, Michael York, Hugh Grant, Claire Bloom, Lysette Anthony, Christopher Cazenove, Gordon Jackson, Gareth Hunt, Ian Bannen.

LADY MOBSTER

Von Zerneck-Samuels Prod. Exec. P: Frank von Zerneck, Stu Samuels. P: Robert M. Sertner. D: John Llewellyn Moxey. W: Stephen Zito. Story: Bill & Jo La Mond, Stephen Zito. Shown on ABC October 16, 1988. (2 hrs.)

Cast: Susan Lucci, Michael Nader, Roscoe Born, Thom Bray, Al Ruscio, Hy Anzell, Jon Cypher, Helaine Lembeck, Joseph Wiseman.

LADYKILLERS

Barry Weitz Films Inc. in assoc. with ABC Circle Films. Exec. P: Barry Weitz. P: Andrew Hill. D: Robert Lewis. W: Greg Dinallo. M: Mark Snow. Shown on ABC November 9, 1988. (2 hrs.)

Cast: Marilu Henner, Susan Blakely, Lesley-Anne Down, Thomas Calabro, William Lucking, Alexandra Borrie, Mark Carlton, David Correia, Gary Hudson, Michael Ensign, Del Zamora, Keith David, Lela Ivey.

LEAP OF FAITH

Hart, Thomas & Berlin Prods. Exec. P: Carole Hart, Kathie Berlin, Marlo Thomas. P: Ira Marvin. D: Stephen Gyllenhaal. W: Bruce Hart. M: Charles Gross. Shown on CBS October 6, 1988. (2 hrs.)

Cast: Anne Archer, Sam Neill, Frances Lee McCain, Norman Parker, Louis Giambalvo, James Hong, James Tolkan, Elizabeth Ruscio, C.C.H. Pounder, Michael Constanine, Tony Abatemarco, Sharon Mansano.

LIBERACE

Liberace Foundation for the Performing & Creative Arts with Dick Clark Prods. Inc. in assoc. with Republic Pictures. Exec. P: Joel R. Strote, Dick Clark. P: Preston Fischer. D: Billy Hale. W: Anthony and Nancy Lawrence. M: Gary William Friedman. Shown on ABC October 2, 1988. (2 hrs.)

Cast: Andrew Robinson, John Rubinstein, Maris Valainis, Deborah Goodrich, Carmen Argenziano, Louis Giambalvo, Kario Salem, Rue McClanahan.

LIBERACE: BEHIND THE MUSIC

Canadian International Studios. Exec. P: Linda Yellen, Nancy Bein. P: Murray Shostak. D: David Greene. W: Gavin Lambert. M: Hagood Hardy. Shown on CBS October 9, 1988. (2 hrs.)

Cast: Victor Garber, Saul Rubinek, Maureen Stapleton, Michael Wikes, Paul Hipp, George Touliatos.

THE LITTLEST VICTIMS

CBS Entertainment. Exec. P: Marian Brayton. P: Fern Field. Sprv. P: Anne Carlucci, Norman G. Brooks. Assoc. P: Ray McCullough. Exec. in chg. of P: Norman S. Powell. D: Peter Levin. W: Kenneth Cavander, story by Richard Lees. M: Joel Rosenbaum. Shown on CBS April 23, 1989. (2 hrs.)

Cast: Tim Matheson, Lewis Arlt, Mary-Joan Negro, Maryann Plunkett, Nan-Lynn Nelson, Harsh Nayyar, Novella Nelson, Graham Brown, William Cain, Larry Keith, Richard Venture.

LOOKING FOR MIRACLES

Sullivan Films. Exec. P: Kevin Sullivan, Trudy Grant. P-D: Kevin Sullivan. W: Sullivan, Stuart McLean, Based on book by A. E. Hotchner. M: John Weisman. Shown on The Disney Channel June 3, 1989. (2 hrs.)

Cast: Greg Spottiswood, Zachary Bennett, Patricia Phillips, Joe Flaherty, Patricia Gage, Noah Godfrey, Paul Haddad, Dean Hamilton, Hugh Thompson, Eric Fink, Elliot Hurst.

LOVE AND BETRAYAL

ITC Entertainment. P: Marcy Gross, Ann Weston. D: Richard Michaels. W: Laurian Leggett. M: Charles Bernstein. Shown on CBS April 16, 1989. (2 hrs.)

Cast: Stefanie Powers, David Birney, Fran Drescher.

MAGIC MOMENTS

Arena Films, Atlantic Video Ventures, Yorkshire Television. Exec. P: Keith Richardson, Jonathan Dana, John Goldstone. P: David Conroy. D: Lawrence Gordon Clarke. W: Terence Brady, Charlotte Bingham. Based on the novel by Nora Roberts. M: Alan Hawkshaw. Shown on Showtime March 19, 1989. (2 hrs.)

Cast: John Shea, Jenny Seagrove, Paul Freeman, Debora Weston, Sam Douglas, Tony Caunter, Shirley Cassedy.

A MAN FOR ALL SEASONS

Agememnon Films Prods. Exec. P: Peter Snell. P: Fraser Heston. D: Charlton Heston. W: Robert Bolt. M: Julia Downes. Shown on TNT December 7, 1988. (2½ hrs.)

Cast: Charlton Heston, Vanessa Redgrave, John Gielgud, Nicholas Amer, Milton Cadman, Martin Chamberlain, Jonathan Hackett, John Hudson, Richard Johnson, Roy Kinnear, Valrie Minifie, Geof Owen, Adrienne Thomas, Benjamin Whitrow, Brian Badcoe.

THE MAN WHO LIVED AT THE RITZ

Harmony Gold Prods., ReteEuropa Prods., Bill McCutchen Prods. Exec. P: Bill McCutchen. P: Serge Touboul, Evelyne Madec, Frank Agrama, Henri Spade, Riccardo Tozzi. D: Desmond Davis. W: Gordon Cotler. Based on the novel by A.E. Hotchner. M: Richard Rodney Bennett. Shown in syndication (N.Y.) November 28 & 29, 1988. (4 hrs.)

Cast: Perry King, Leslie Caron, Cherie Lunghi, David McCallum, David Robb, Patachou, Mylene Demongeot, Sophie Barjac, Joss Ackland.

MARCUS WELBY, M.D.—A HOLIDAY AFFAIR

Marstar Ltd. & Condor Prods. Exec. P: Martin Stargar. P: Howard Alston, Peter-Christian Futer. D-W: Steven Gethers. M: Georges Garvarents. Shown on NBC December 19, 1988. (2 hrs.)

Cast: Robert Young, Alexis Smith, Delphine Forest, Craig Stevens, Robert Hardy, Betsy Blair, Robert McLeod, Paul Maxwell, Pierre Leclercq, Pauline Larrieu, Anna Gaylor, Mary Martlew, Alain Klarer, Daniel Leger.

MARGARET BOURKE-WHITE

TNT Inc., Project VII and Central TV Enterprises. Exec. P: Robert Halmi Jr., Rupert Dilnott-Cooper. P-D: Lawrence Schiller. Line P: Paul L. Cameron. Co-P: Ron Colby. W: Marjorie David, based on Vicki Goldberg's biography. M: John Cacavas. Shown on TNT April 24, 1989. (2 hrs.)

Cast: Farrah Fawcett, Frederic Forrest, Mitchell Ryan, David Huddleston, Jay Patterson, Robert Stanton, Robert Katims, Robert James Kearney.

MAYBE BABY

Perry Lafferty Prods. in assoc. with Von Zerneck/Samuels Prods. Exec. P: Perry Lafferty, Frank von Zerneck, Stu Samuels. P: Robert M. Sertner. D: Tom Moore. W: Janet Kovalcik. Shown on NBC December 5, 1988. (2 hrs.)

Cast: Jane Curtin, Dabney Coleman, Julia Duffy, Florence Stanley, David Doyle, David Bowe, Peter Michael Goetz.

MICKEY SPILLANE'S MIKE HAMMER: MURDER TAKES ALL

Jay Bernstein Prod. in assoc., with Columbia Pictures Television. Exec. P: Jay Bernstein. P: Jeffrey Morton. D: John Nicolella. W: Mark Edwards Edens. M: Ron Ramin. Shown on CBS May 21, 1989. (2 hrs.)

Cast: Stacy Keach, Lynda Carter, Lindsay Bloom, Don Stroud, Jim Carrey, Stacy Galina, Lyle Alzado, Royce D. Applegate, John Calvin, Jessie Lawrence Ferguson, Kristen Jensen, Paul Lieber, Ed Winter, Michelle Phillips.

MIRACLE AT BEEKMAN'S PLACE

Em/BE Inc. Prod. Exec. P: Scoey Mitchelll. P: Donald R. Boyle. D: Bernard L. Kowalski. W: Donald R. Boyle, Scoey Mitchelll. M: Harry Middlebrooks, Chris Page. Shown on NBC December 26, 1988. (2 hrs.)

Cast: Scoey Mitchelll, Theresa Merritt, Robert Costanzo, Liz Torres, Brian Matthews, Jane Sibbett, Hector Mercado, Jane Alden.

MOTHER'S DAY

CBN Production Group. Exec. P: S. Harry Young. P-D: Susan Rohrer. W: Duke & B.W. Sandefur. M: Brent Havens. Shown on CBN May 13, 1989. (2 hrs.)

Cast: Malcolm-Jamal Warner, Jose Ferrer, Denise Nicholas, Bernie Casey, Melba Moore, Greg Salata, Amber Kain, Joe Lambie, Ellen Dolan.

MURDER BY MOONLIGHT

Tamara Asseyev Prods. London Weekend TV and Viacom Prods. Exec. P: Tamara Asseyev. Co-P: Ron Carr. D: Michael Lindsay-Hogg. W: Carla Jean Wagner. M: Trevor Jones. Shown on CBS May 9, 1989. (2 hrs.)

Cast: Brigitte Nielsen, Julian Sands, Jane Lapotaire, Gerald McRaney, Brian Cox, Alphonsia Emmanuel, Celia Imre, David Yip, Michael J. Shannon, Stuart Milligan, Stephen Jenn.

MURDER BY NIGHT

NEI Motion Picture Company. Exec. P: Peter Simpson. Sprv. P: Ray Sager. Co-P: David Roessell. Assoc. P: Dan Johnson. Exec. in chg. of Prod.: Ilana Frank. D: Paul Lynch. W: Alan B. McElroy. Shown on USA Network July 19, 1989. (2 hrs.)

Cast: Robert Urich, Kay Lenz, Michael Ironside, Jim Metzler, Sandra P. Grant, Geoffrey Bowes.

MURDERERS AMONG US: THE SIMON WIESENTHAL STORY

Robert Cooper Prod. from Citadel Entertainment for TVS Films in assoc. with HBO and Hungarian Television. Exec. P: Robert Cooper, Abby Mann, Graham Benson. P: John Kemeny, Robert Cooper. D: Brian Gibson. W: Abby Mann, Robin Vote, Ron Hutchinson. M: Bill Conti. Shown on HBO April 23, 1989. (3 hrs.)

Cast: Ben Kingsley, Renee Soutendijk, Craig T. Nelson, Louisa Haigh, Jack Shepherd, Anton Lesser, Henry Goodman, Frigyes Harsanyi.

MY FIRST LOVE

Avnet/Kerner Co. Exec. P: Jon Avnet, Jordan Kerner. P: Gail Mutrux. Co-P & W: Ed Kaplan. D: Gilbert Cates. M: Alf Clausen. Shown on ABC December 4, 1988. (2 hrs.)

Cast: Beatrice Arthur, Richard Kiley, Joan Van Ark, Anne Francis, Richard Herd, Barbara Barrie, Edith Fields, Kate Charleson, Julia Meade, Tom Fridley, Lewis Arquette.

MY NAME IS BILL W.

Garner/Duchow Prods. for Hallmark Hall of Fame. Exec. P: Peter K. Duchow, James Garner. P-D: Daniel Petrie. W: William G. Borchert. M: Larry Rosenthal. Shown on ABC April 30, 1989. (2 hrs.)

Cast: James Woods, JoBeth Williams, James Garner, Gary Sinise, George Coe, Robert Harper, Ray Reinhardt, Fritz Weaver.

NAKED LIE

Shadowplay Films Inc., Phoenix Entertainment Group. Exec. P: Victoria Principal, Hans Proppe. P: Stephanie Austin. D: Richard A. Colla. W: Timothy Wurtz, Glenn M. Benest, John Robert Bensink. M: Bob Alcivar. Shown on CBS February 26, 1989. (2 hrs.)

Cast: Victoria Principal, James Farentino, Glenn Withrow, Dakin Mathews, William Lucking, Vic Polizos.

NICK NIGHT

Cuppa Blood Prods. Exec. P: Barry Weitz, Roberta Becker. P: S. Michael Formica. D: Farhad Mann. W: James D. Parriott. Shown on CBS August 20, 1989 (2 hrs.)

Cast: Rick Springfield, John Kapelos, Robert Harper, Laura Johnson, Michael Nader.

NIGHTBREAKER

Symphony Pictures. Exec. P: Martin Sheen, Jeffrey Auderbach. Co-Exec. P & W: T.S. Cook, adapted in part from Howard Rosenberg's novel "Atomic Soldiers." P: William R. Greenblatt. D: Peter Markle. M: Peter Bernstein. Shown on TNT March 8, 1989. (2 hrs.)

Cast: Martin Sheen, Emilio Estevez, Lea Thompson, Melinda Dillon, Joe Pantoliano, Geoffrey Blake, Paul Eidin, James Marshall, Lance Slaughter.

OPEN ADMISSIONS

The Mount Co. and Viacom Prods. Exec. P: Stevie Phillips, Thom Mount. P: Stevie Phillips. Co-P: J. Boyce Harman Jr. D: Gus Trinkonis. W: Shirley Lauro. M: Charles Gross. Shown on CBS September 8, 1988. (2 hrs.)

Cast: Jane Alexander, Dennis Farina, Estelle Parsons, Michael Beach, Wandachristine, James O'Reilly, Pat Bowie, Kyra K. Kyles, Betty Yee, Lori Kathryn Holton, Louise Jenkins, Jace Alexander, Domenica Cameron Scorsese, Bob Breuler, Ebony Grisby, Marji Bank, Steven J. Craton, Alger Ellis, Leo Washington Jones III.

ORIGINAL SIN

Larry A. Thompson Organization/New World Television. Exec. P: Larry A. Thompson. P: Ian Sander. D: Ron Satloff. W: Philip S. Messina. M: Lalo Schifrin. Shown on NBC February 20, 1989. (2 hrs.)

Cast: Ann Jillian, Charlton Heston, Robert Desiderio, Lou Liberatore.

OUT OF THE SHADOWS

Showtime in association with Yorkshire Television. Atlantic Videoadventures Prod. Exec. P: David Cunliffe, Jonathan Dana, John Goldstone. Prod. Exec: Timothy J. Fee. P: Derek Bennett. D: Willi Patterson. W: Michael J. Bird, adapted from novel by Andrea Davidson. M: Dave Lawson. Shown on Showtime September 11, 1988. (105 mins.)

Cast: Charles Dance, Alexandra Paul, Michael J. Shannon, David De Keyser, Wanda Ventham, Gregory Karr, David Sumner, John Grillo, Petro Fyssoon, Yannis Kakleas.

OUT ON THE EDGE

Rick Dawn Enterprises in assoc. with The Steve Tisch Co. and King Phoenix Entertainment. Exec. P: Steve Tisch. Co-Exec. P: Mireille Soria. P: Stephanie Austin. Assoc. P: Diane Schroder. D: John Pasquin. W: Rene Balcer. Shown on CBS May 14, 1989. (2 hrs.)

Cast: Rick Schroder, Mary Kay Place, Richard Jenkins, Natalia Nogulich, Joseph Hacker, Dakin Matthews, De Voreaux White Kim Myers, Maya Lebenzon, Grand L. Bush, Andrew Divott, Jason Horst, Patricia Allison, Chance Michael Corbitt, Ron Canada, Victor Gardell.

OUTBACK BOUND

Andrew Gottlieb Prod. in coop. with CBS Entertainment Prods. Exec. P: Robert Silberling. P: Andrew Gottlieb. Line P: Antonia Barnard. Assoc. P & W: Elizabeth & Luciano Comici. D: John Llewelyn Moxey. M: Miles Goodman. Shown on CBS October 11, 1988. (2 hrs.)

Cast: Donna Mills, Andrew Clarke, John Meillon, Collette Mann, Robert Harper, Nina Foch, John Schneider, Joanna Lockwood, Beth Child, Frank Holden, Warren Owens.

THE OUTSIDE WOMAN

Green-Epstein Prods. Exec. P: Jim Green, Allen Epstein. P-D: Lou Antonio. Co-P: Leigh Murray. W: William Blinn. Shown on CBS February 12, 1989. (2 hrs.)

Cast: Sharon Gless, Scott Glenn, Max Gail, Kyle Secor, Ken Jenkins, Everett Madison.

PANCHO BARNES

Blue Andre Prods. in assoc. with Orion TV. Exec. P: Blue Andre. D: Richard T. Heffron. W: John Michael Hayes. Shown on CBS October 25, 1988. (3 hrs.)

Cast: Valerie Bertinelli, James Stephens, Sam Robards, Geoffrey Lewis, Ted Wass, Richard Young, Cynthia Harris.

PARENT TRAP III

Walt Disney Television. P: Henry Colman, Jill Donner. D: Mollie Miller. M: Joel McNeely. Shown on NBC April 9, 1989. (2 hrs.)

Cast: Hayley Mills, Barry Bostwick, Ray Baker, Patricia Richardson, Christopher Gartin, Jon Maynard Pennell, Joy Creel, Leanna Creel, Monica Creel.

PASSION AND PARADISE

Picturebase Intl. and Primedia Prods. in assoc. with Leonard Hill Films. Exec. P: Leonard Hill, W. Patterson Ferns, Peter Jeffries. P: Michael Custance, Ian McDougall. Co-P: Joel Fields. D: Harvey Hart. W: Andrew Laskos. M: Hagood Hardy. Shown on ABC February 19 & 21, 1989. (4 hrs.)

Cast: Armand Assante, Catherine Mary Stewart, Mariette Hartley, Kevin McCarthy, Michael Sarrazin, Andrew Ray, Linda Griffiths, Rod Steiger, Wayne Rogers.

THE PENTHOUSE

Greene-White Prods./Spectator Films. Exec. P: David Greene, Stephen White. Co-Exec. P: Jerry Reger. P: Harold Tichenor. D: David Greene. W: William Wood, Frank De Felitta, based on novel by Elleston Trevor. M: Peter Manning Robinson. Shown on ABC March 5, 1989. (2 hrs.)

Cast: Robin Givens, David Hewlett, Robert Guillaume, Donnelly Rhodes, Cedric Smith.

THE PEOPLE ACROSS THE LAKE

Bill McCutchen Prod. Exec. P: Bill McCutchen. P: Richard L. O'Connor. D: Arthur Allan Seidelman. W: Dalene Young. Story: Bill McCutchen, Dalene Young. M: Dana Kaproff. Shown on NBC October 3, 1988. (2 hrs.)

Cast: Valerie Harper, Gerald McRaney, Barry Corbin, Tammy Lauren, Daryl Anderson, Jeff Kizer, Dorothy Lyman.

PERRY MASON: THE CASE OF THE LETHAL LESSON

Fred Silverman Co., Dean Hargrove Prods. and Viacom. Exec. P: Fred Silverman, Dean Hargrove. Sprv. P: Joel Steiger, Robert Hamilton. P: Peter Katz. D: Christian Y. Nyby 2d. W: Robert Hamilton. M: Dick DeBenedictis. Shown on NBC February 12, 1989. (2 hrs.)

Cast: Raymond Burr, Barbara Hale, Alexandra Paul, William R. Moses, Brian Keith, Leslie Ackerman, Richard Allen, Brian Backer, John De Mita, Karen Kopins, John LaMotta, Charley Long, John Allen Nelson, Marlene Warfield.

PERRY MASON: THE CASE OF THE MUSICAL MURDER

The Fred Silverman Co., Dean Hargrove Prods., Viacom. Exec. P: Dean Hargrove, Fred Silverman. Sprv. P: Robert Hamilton. P: Peter Katz. Co-P: David Solomon. D: Christian I. Nyby II. W: George Eckstein. Based on characters created by Erle Stanley Gardner. M: Dick DeBenedictis. Shown on NBC April 9, 1989. (2 hrs.)

Cast: Raymond Burr, Barbara Hale, Alexandra Paul, William R. Moses, Debbie Reynolds, Jerry Orbach, Dwight Schultz, Mary Cadorette, Alexa Hamilton, James McEachin, Jim Metzler, Valerie Mahaffey.

PETER GUNN

The Blake Edwards Co. in assoc. with New World Television. Exec. P: Blake Edwards, Tony Adams. P: Tony Adams. D-W: Blake Edwards. M: Henry Mancini. Shown on ABC April 23, 1989. (2 hrs.)

Cast: Peter Strauss, Barbara Williams, Peter Jurasik, Jennifer Edwards, Debra Sandlund, Charlie Cioffi, David Rappaport, Leo Rosi, Tony Longo, Pearl Bailey.

QUIET VICTORY: THE CHARLIE WEDEMEYER STORY

The Landsbury Co. Exec. P: Alan Landsburg, Joan Barnett. P: Linda Otto. D: Roy Campanella II. W: Barry Morrow. M: Don Davis. Shown on CBS December 26, 1988. (2 hrs.)

Cast: Michael Nouri, Pam Dawber, Bess Meyer, Peter Berg, James Handy, Dan Lauria, Reginald VelJohnson, Noble Willingham, Michael Gross.

RED EARTH, WHITE EARTH

Chris/Rose Prods. and Entcorp Communications. Exec. P: Rick Rosenberg, Bob Christiansen. P: Murray Shostak. D: David Greene. W: Michael DeGuzman. M: Ralph Grierson. Shown on CBS January 24, 1989. (2 hrs.)

Cast: Genevieve Bujold, Timothy Daly, Ralph Waite, Richard Farnsworth, Alberta Watson, Billy Merasty.

THE REVENGE OF AL CAPONE

Unity Prods. Inc./River City Prods. Exec. P: John Levoff, Robert Lovenheim. P: Vicki Niemi-Gordon. D: Michael Pressman. W: Tracy Keenan Wynn. M: Craig Safan. Shown on NBC February 26, 1989. (2 hrs.)

Cast: Keith Carradine, Ray Sharkey, Debrah Farentino, Jayne Atkinson, Scott Paulin, Charles Haid.

THE ROAD RAIDERS

New East Entertainment Inc. Exec. P: Glen A. Larson. P: Charles F. Engel. Co-P: Scott Levitta, J.C. Larson. Assoc. P: Chris Larson. D: Richard Lang. W: Glen A. Larson, Mark Jones. M: Stu Phillips. Shown on CBS April 25, 1989. (2 hrs.)

Cast: Bruce Boxleitner, Susan Diol, Reed McCants, Noble Willingham, Leslie Jordan, Stephen Geoffreys, David Paul, Peter Paul, Mark Blankfield, Clyde Kusatsu, Tia Carrere, John Fujioka.

ROE VS. WADE

The Manheim Co. in assoc. with NBC Prods. Exec. P: Michael Manheim. Co-P & W: Alison Cross. P-D: Gregory Hoblit. M: Snuffy Walden. Shown on NBC May 15, 1989. (2 hrs.)

Cast: Holly Hunter, Amy Madigan, Dion Anderson, Kathy Bates, James Gammon, Micole Mercurio, Chris Mulkey, Terry O'Quinn, Annabella Price, Stephen Tobolowsky.

ROOTS: THE GIFT

David L. Wolper Prod. in assoc. with Warner Bros. Television. Exec. P: David L. Wolper, Bernard Sofronski. P: Mark M. Wolper. D: Kevin Hooks. W: D. M. Eyre Jr. M: Gerald Fried. Shown on ABC December 11, 1988. (2 hrs.)

Cast: Louis Gossett Jr., LeVar Burton, Avery Brooks, Kate Mulgrew, Shaun Cassidy, John McMartin, Jerry Hardin, Annabella Price, Fran Bennett, Tim Russ, Michael Learned.

RUN TILL YOU FALL

CBS Entertainment Prods. P: Marvin Minoff. D: Mike Farrell. W: Gary Garrett, Dan Wilcox. M: Tom Scott. Shown on CBS September 9, 1988. (90 mins.)

Cast: Jamie Farr, Fred Savage, Shelley Fabares, C.C.H. Pounder, Clyde Kusatsu, Beatrice Straight, Douglas Rowe, Ann Nelson, Robert Ellenstein, Betty Jinnette, Jeffrey Josephson, Amy Davis, Mark Haining.

THE RYAN WHITE STORY

The Landsburg Co. Exec. P: Alan Landsburg, Joan Barnett. P: Linda Otto. D: John Herzfeld. W: Phil Penningroth, John Herzfeld. M: Mike Post. Shown on ABC January 16, 1989. (2 hrs.)

Cast: Judith Light, Lukas Haas, Michael Bowen, Nikki Cox, George Dzundza, Valerie Landsburg, Sarah Jessica Parker, Mitchell Ryan, Peter Scolari, Grace Zabriskie, George C. Scott, Kathy Wagner, Casey Ellison, Clif Bemis, Mark Joy, Ryan White.

THE SECRET LIFE OF KATHY MC CORMICK

Tamara Asseyev Prods. Inc. in assoc. with New World Television and American First Run Studios. Exec. P: Tamara Asseyev. Co-Exec. P: Barry Weitz. Co-P: Barbara Eden, Gloria Goldsmith. D: Robert Lewis. W: Jim Brecher. Story: Gloria Goldsmith. M: Mark Snow. Shown on NBC October 7, 1988. (2 hrs.)

Cast: Barbara Eden, Josh Taylor, Judith-Marie Bergan, Judy Geeson, Jenny O'Hara, Robert Costanzo, Jennifer Savidge, Ernie Lively, Paul Kent, Dick O'Neill.

SECRET WITNESS

Just Greene Prods. in assoc. with CBS Entertainment. P: Vanessa Greene. D: Eric Laneuville. W: Alfred Sole, Paul Monette. M: Robert Drasnin. Shown on CBS September 9, 1988. (90 mins.)

Cast: David Rasche, Paul LeMat, Leaf Phoenix, Kellie Martin, Barry Corbin, Paddi Edwards, Deborah Wakeham.

SHE KNOWS TOO MUCH

The Finnegan/Pinchuk Co., The Fred Silverman Co., MGM/UA Television. Exec. P: Fred Silverman. P: Pat Finnegan, Bill Finnegan, Sheldon Pinchuk. D: Paul Lynch. W: Michael Norell. Shown on NBC January 29, 1989. (2 hrs.)

Cast: Meredith Baxter Birney, Robert Urich, Erik Estrada, John Bennett Perry.

SHE WAS MARKED FOR MURDER

Litke/Jack Grossbart Prods. Exec. P: Jack Grossbart. P: Elaine Rich. D: Chris Thomson. W: David Stenn. M: Nan Schwartz. Shown on NBC December 18, 1988. (2 hrs.)

Cast: Stefanie Powers, Lloyd Bridges, Hunt Block, Debrah Farentino, Polly Bergen.

SHANNON'S DEAL

Stan Rogow Prod. in assoc. with NBC Prods. Exec. P & P: Stan Rogow. Asst. P: Lauren B. Caplan. Exec. in chg. of P: William Phillips. D: Lewis Teague. W: John Sayles. M: Wynton Marsalis. Shown on NBC June 4, 1989. (2 hrs.)

Cast: Jamey Sheridan, Elizabeth Pena, Martin Ferrero, Jenny Lewis, Alberta Watson, Michael Bowen, Claudia Christian, Jesse Dizon, Miguel Ferrer, Stefan Gierasch, Ronald G. Joseph, Ely Pouget, Brian Smiar, Eddie Velez, Richard Edson.

SHOOTDOWN

Leonard Hills Films. Exec. P: Leonard Hill, Robert O'Connor. P-W: Judy Merl, Paul Eric Myers. Co-P: Joel Fields. Sprv. P: Ron Gilbert. D: Michael Pressman. M: Craig Safan. Shown on NBC November 28, 1988. (2 hrs.)

Cast: Angela Lansbury, George Coe, Kyle Secor, Molly Hagan, Jennifer Savidge, Diana Bellamy, Alan Fudge, Booth Colman, Richard McKenzie, John Cullum, Robin Curtis, Terri Hanauer, Haunani Minn, Paul Linke.

SHOOTER

UBU Prods. in assoc. with Paramount Network Television. Exec. P-W: Stephen Kline, David Hume Kennerly. Co-P: Charles Jennings. P: Barry Berg. D: Gary Nelson. M: Paul Chihara. Shown on NBC September 11, 1988. (2 hrs.)

Cast: Jeffrey Nordling, Alan Ruck, Noble Willingham, Carol Huston, Rosalind Chao, Kario Salem, Jeffery Allan Chandler, Cu-ba Nguyen, Helen Hunt, Adrian Paul, Grace Zabriskie, Nick Cassavetes.

SPIES, LIES & NAKED THIGHS

Robert Halmi Prods. Exec. P: Ed Self, Bill Brademan, P: Robert Halmi. D: James Frawley. W: Ed Self. M: Jack Elliot. Shown on CBS November 22, 1988. (2 hrs.)

Cast: Harry Anderson, Ed Begley Jr., Linda Purl, Wendy Crewson, Brent Carver, Maria Mayenset, Raymond Singer, Rene Assa, Ilrant Alianak.

A STONING IN FULHAM COUNTY

The Landsburg Co. Exec. P: Alan Landsburg, Joan Barnett. P: Jud Kinberg. D: Larry Elikann. W: Jud Kinberg, Jackson Gillis. Story: Jackson Gillis. M: Don Davis. Shown on NBC October 24, 1988. (2 hrs.)

Cast: Ken Olin, Ron Perlman, Jill Eikenberry, Maureen Mueller, Gregg Henry, Nicholas Pryor, Peter Michael Goetz, Max Tucker.

STREETS OF DREAMS

Bill Stratton/Myrtos Prod. in assoc. with Phoenix Entertainment Group. Exec. P: Gerald W. Abrams. P: Richard M. Ravin. D: William A. Graham. W: Bill Stratton. M: Laurence Rosenthal. Shown on CBS October 7, 1988. (2 hrs.)

Cast: Ben Masters, Morgan Fairchild, Diane Salinger, Michael Cavanaugh, Alan Autry, Gerald Hiken, Wendell Wellman, Danny Goldman, John Putch, Mike Moroff, Richard Green, David Marciano, Willie Gault, John Hillerman.

SWIMSUIT

Musifilm Prods. and American First Run Studios. Exec. P: Carla Singer, Max A. Kellery, Micheline H. Keller, Charles Hairston. P:

Michael Lloyd, Rod Amateau, Robert Lloyd Lewis. D: Chris Thomson. W: Robin Schiff. M: Lloyd, John D'Andrea. Shown on NBC February 19, 1989. (2 hrs.)

Cast: William Katt, Catherine Oxenberg, Nia Peeples, Cheryl A. Pollak, Tom Villard, Jack P. Wagner, Ally Walker, Billy Warlock, Cyd Charise, Brian Patrick, Paul Johanssen, Robert L. Benedetti.

TAILSPIN: BEHIND THE KOREAN AIRLINER TRAGEDY

A Darlow Smithson Production in association with HBO Showcase and Granada. Exec. P: Ray Fitzwalter, Leslie Woodhead. P: John Smithson. Assoc. P: Redmond Morris. D: David Darlow. W: Brian Phelan. M: David Ferguson. Shown on HBO August 20, 1989 (90 minutes.)

Cast: Michael Moriarty, Michael Murphy, Chris Sarandon, Harris Yulin, Gavan O'Herlihy, Ed O'Ross, Jay Patterson.

TAKE MY DAUGHTERS, PLEASE

Michael Filerman Prods., NBC Prods. Exec. P: Michael Filerman. P: Karen Moore. D: Larry Elikann. W: Lindsay Harrison. M: Nan Schwartz. Shown on NBC November 21, 1988. (2 hrs.)

Cast: Rue McClanahan, Kim Delaney, Deidre Hall, Stepfanie Kramer, Susan Ruttan, Charles Frank, Sam McMurray, Michael T. Weiss, Audra Lindley.

TARZAN IN MANHATTAN

American First Run Studios. Exec. P: Max A. Keller, Micheline H. Keller. P: Charles Hairston. D: Michael Schultz. W: Anna Sandor, William Gough. Based on the Tarzan stories by Edgar Rice Burroughs. M: Charles Fox. Shown on CBS April 15, 1989. (2 hrs.)

Cast: Joe Lara, Kim Crosby, Tony Curtis, Jimmy Media Taggert, Jan-Michael Vincent, Joe Seneca.

TEARS IN THE RAIN

British Lion in assoc. with Yorkshire Television Ltd., Atlantic Video Ventures. Exec. P: Keith Richardson, Jonathan Dana, John Goldstone. P: Peter Snell. D: Don Sharp. W: Freda Kelsall from novel by Pamela Wallace. M: Barrie Guard. Shown on Showtime December 17, 1988. (101 mins.)

Cast: Sharon Stone, Christopher Cazenove, Leigh Lawson, Paul Daneman, Anna Massey.

THE TENTH MAN

Rosemont Productions Ltd./William Self Prods. Exec. P: Norman Rosemont, William Self. P: David A. Rosemont, William Self. D: Jack Gold. W: Lee Langley from Graham Greene's novel. Shown on CBS December 4, 1988. (2 hrs.)

Cast: Anthony Hopkins, Kristin Scott Thomas, Derek Jacobi, Cyril Cusack.

TERROR ON HIGHWAY 91

Katy Film Prods. Inc. Sprv. P: Henry Colam. P: Dan Witt, Courtney Pledger. D: Jerry Jameson. W: Stuart Schoffman. M: Artis Kane. Shown on CBS January 3, 1989. (2 hrs.)

Cast: Ricky Schroder, George Dzundza, Matt Clark, Lara Flynn Boyle.

THIRD DEGREE BURN

HBO Pictures Presentation in assoc. with MTM Entertainment Inc. prod. in assoc. with Paramount Pictures. Exec. P: Marianne Moloney. P: Fredda Weiss. D: Roger Spottiswoode. W: Duncan Gibbins, Yale Udoff. M: Charles Gross. Shown on HBO May 28, 1989. (96 mins.)

Cast: Treat Williams, Virginia Madsen, Richard Masur, Michael Chapman, CCH Pounder, Robert Nadir, Mary Armstrong.

THOSE SHE LEFT BEHIND

NBC Prods. P: R.W. Goodwin. D: Waris Hussein. W: Michael O'Hara. M: Mark Snow. Shown on NBC March 6, 1989 (2 hrs.)

Cast: Gary Cole, Joanna Kerns, Mary Page Keller, George Coe, Colleen Dewhurst.

TOO GOOD TO BE TRUE

Newland-Raynor Prods. Exec. P: Milton T. Raynor. P: John Newland, Judith Parker. D: Christian I. Nyby. W: Timothy Bradshaw, based on Ames Williams' novel "Leave Her To Heaven." M: Michael Rubini. Shown on NBC November 14, 1988. (2 hrs.)

Cast: Loni Anderson, Patrick Duffy, Glynnis O'Connor, Julie Harris, Larry Drake, James B. Sikking, Neil Patrick Harris, Elizabeth Norment, Carl Franklin, Carmen Argenziano, Lorinne Vozoff, Daniel Baldwin.

TRAPPED

Cine Enterprises. Exec. P: Jon Epstein. P: Joe Bellotti, Robert Skodis. D: Fred Walton. W: Fred Walton, Steve Feke. Shown on USA June 14, 1989. (2 hrs.)

Cast: Kathleen Quinlan, Bruce Abbott.

THE TRAVELING MAN

Irvin kershner Films. Exec. P.-W: David Taylor. P: Thomas M. Hammel. D: Irvin Kershner. M: Miles Goodman. Shown on HBO June, 25, 1989 (2 hrs)

Cast: John Lithgow, Jonathan Silverman, Margaret Colin, John Glover, John M. Jackson, Chynna Phillips, Dawn Arnemann.

THE TRIAL OF THE INCREDIBLE HULK

Bixby-Brandon Prods. & New World TV. Exec. P: Bill Bixby, Gerald Di Pego. P: Hugh Spencer-Phillips, Robert Ewing. D: Bill Bixby. W: Gerald Di Pego. M: Lance Rubin. Shown on NBC May 7, 1989. (2 hrs.)

Cast: Bill Bixby, Lou Ferrigno, Mata Dubois, Nancy Everhard, Nicholas Hormann, Richard Cummings Jr., Joseph Mascolo, John Rhys-Davies, Rex Smith, Linda Darolow, John Novak, Dwight Koss.

TRICKS OF THE TRADE

Leonard Hill Films. Exec. P: Leonard Hill, Robert O'Connor. P: Ron Gilbert. D: Jack Bender. W: Noreen Stone. M: Walter Murphy. Shown on CBS December 6, 1988. (2 hrs.)

Cast: Cindy Williams, Markie Post, Scott Paulin, James Whitmore Jr., Chris Mulkey.

TROUBLE IN PARADISE

Harvey Matofsky Entertainment, Qintex Entertainment. Exec. P: Harvey Matofsky. Sprv. P: Lynn Barker. P: Robert Halmi. D: Di Drew. W: Robert Sherman, Ben Marshall. M: Chris Neal. Shown on CBS May 16, 1989. (2 hrs.)

Cast: Raquel Welch, Jack Thompson, Nicholas Hammond, John Gregg, Anthony Wong, Ralph Cotterill, Adrian Bown, James Condon.

TWIST OF FATE

Henry Plitt/Larry White Prod., HTV Ltd. Jadran Films, Columbia Pictures Television. Exec. P: Larry White, Henry Plitt. P: Larry White. D: Ian Sharp. W: Bill Bast, Paul Huson, Gy Waldron, based on novel "Pursuit" by Robert L. Fish. M: Laurence Rosenthal. Shown on NBC January 8 & 9 1989. (4 hrs.)

Cast: Ben Cross, Veronica Hamel, John Glover, Bruce Greenwood.

UNCONQUERED

Alexandra Film Prods. Inc. in coop. with Double Helix and Dick Lowry Prod. Inc. P-D: Dick Lowry. Sprv. P: Derek Kavanagh. W: Pat Conroy. M: Arthur B. Rubinstein. Shown on CBS January 15, 1989. (2½ hrs.)

Cast: Peter Coyote, Dermot Mulroney, Tess Harper, Jenny Robertson, Frank Whaley, Bob Gunton, Larry Riley, R. D. Call, Noble Willingham.

UNHOLY MATRIMONY

Edgar J. Scherick Associates Prod. in assoc. with Taft Entertainment Television. Exec. P: Edgar J. Scherick, Gary Hoffman. P: Michael Barnathan. D: Jerrold Freedman. W: John McGreevey, based on book by John Dillman. M: Michel Rubini. Shown on CBS October 3, 1988 (2 hrs.)

Cast: Patrick Duffy, Charles Durning, Michael O'Keefe, Lisa Blount, Jacqueline Brookes, Fred Thompson, Ron Canada, Michael C. Gwynne, Richard Cox, Julie Fulton, Alexandra Powers.

A VERY BRADY CHRISTMAS

Sherwood Schwartz Co. in assoc. with Paramount Network Television. Exec. P: Sherwood Schwartz. P: Lloyd J. Schwartz, Barry Berg. D: Peter Baldwin. W: Sherwood Schwartz, Lloyd J. Schwartz. M: Laurence Juber. Shown on CBS December 18, 1988. (2 hrs.)

Cast: Florence Henderson, Robert Reed, Ann B. Davis, Maureen McCormick, Eve Plumb, Jennifer Runyon, Barry Williams, Christopher Knight, Michael Lookingland, Jerry Hauser.

WHEN WE WERE YOUNG

A Richard & Esther Shapiro Entertainment Inc. Production. Exec. P-W: Richard Shapiro, Esther Shapiro. P: George Eckstein. Assoc. P: Maria Padilla. D: Daryl Duke. M: Peter Matz. Shown on NBC July 17, 1989 (2 hrs.)

Cast: Jace Alexander, Lindsay Frost, Cynthia Gibb, Jane Krakowski, Eriq La Salle, Grant Show, Charles Hunter Wash, Steven Weber, Ronny Cox.

WHERE THE HELL'S THAT GOLD?!!!

Willie Nelson Prods. Brigade Prods. Inc. with Konisberg/Sanitsky Prods. P-D-W: Burt Kennedy. M: Arthur Rubinstein. Shown on CBS November 13, 1988. (2 hrs.)

Cast: Willie Nelson, Jack Elam, Delta Burke, Gerald McRainey, Alfonso Arau, Gregory Sierra, Michael Wren.

WINNIE

All Girl Prods. in assoc. with NBC Prods. Exec. P: Michael Manheim. P: Andrea Baynes. D: John Korty. W: Joyce Eliason. M: W. G. Snuffy Walden, Bennett Salvay. Shown on NBC October 10, 1988. (2 hrs.)

Cast: Meredith Baxter Birney, David Morse, Barbara Barrie, Peggy McCay, Jenny O'Hara, Tabi Cooper, Lee Garlington, Kay Boyer, Angela Paton, Terri Hanauer, Jenny Sullivan.

THE WOMEN OF BREWSTER PLACE

Harpo Prods. in assoc. with Phoenix Entertainment. Exec. P: Carole Isenberg, Oprah Winfrey. P: Patricia K. Meyer, Reuben Cannon. D: Donna Deitch. W: Karen Hall, based on novel by Gloria Naylor. M: David Shire. Shown on ABC March 19 & 20, 1989. (4 hrs.)

Cast: Oprah Winfrey, Lonette McKee, Paula Kelly, Jackee, Robin Givens, Moses Gunn, Cicely Tyson, Barbara Montgomery, Mary Alice, Paul Winfield.

YOUR MOTHER WEARS COMBAT BOOTS

Kushner-Locke Prods. Exec. P: Peter Locke, Donald Kushner. P: Bill Novodor. D: Anson Williams. W: Susan Hunter. M: Jeff Barry, Barry Fasman. Shown on NBC March 27, 1989 (2 hrs.)

Cast: Barbara Eden, Hector Elizondo, Meagan Fay, David Kaufman, Richard McGregor, Conchata Ferrell, Maria O'Brien, Annabelle Gurwitch, A.J. Stephans.

1988–89 Mini-Series

Mini-series are movies made for television shown in three parts or more.

AROUND THE WORLD IN 80 DAYS

Harmony Gold Prods., Rete Europa Prod. in assoc. with Valente/ Baerwald Prods. Exec. P: Renee Valente, Paul Baerwald. P: Renee Valente. D: Buzz Kulik. W: John Gay, from novel by Jules Verne. M: Billy Goldenberg. Shown on NBC April 16, 17, 18, 1989 (6 hrs.)

Cast: Pierce Brosnan, Eric Idle, Julia Nickson, Peter Ustinov, Henry Gibson, John Hillerman, Jack Klugman, Christopher Lee, Patrick Macnee, Roddy McDowall, Darren McGavin, John Mills, Robert Morley, Stephen Nichols, Lee Remick, Arielle Dombasle, Gabrielle Ferzetti, Pernell Roberts, James B. Sikking, Jill St. John, Robert Wagner, Simon Ward, Rick Jason, Anna Massey.

A DANGEROUS LIFE

McElroy & McElroy Prod. in assoc. with FilmAccord. P: Hal McElroy. D: Robert Markowitz. W: David Williamson. M: Brian May. Shown on HBO November 27, 28 & 30 1988. (6 hrs.)

Cast: Gary Busey, Rebecca Gilling, Tessie Tomas, Ruben Rustia, Laurice Guillen, James Handy.

FAVORITE SON

NBC Prods. Exec. P-W: Steve Sohmer. P: Jonathan Bernstein. D: Jeff Bleckner. Shown on NBC October 30, October 31, November 1, 1988. (6 hrs.)

Cast: Robert Loggia, Linda Kozlowski, Harry Hamlin, Lance Guest, James Whitmore, John Mahoney.

GREAT EXPECTATIONS

Primetime for Disney Channel in assoc. with HTV Limited and Tesauro Television. Exec. P. for Primetime: Michael Clark. Exec. P. for Disney Channel: Carol Rubin. P: Greg Smith. D: Kevin Connor. W: John Goldsmith. Shown on Disney Channel July 9, 10, 11, 1989 (6 hrs.)

Cast: Anthony Calf, Jean Simmons, Anthony Hopkins, Ray McAnally, Kim Thomson, John Rhys-Davies.

LONESOME DOVE

Motown Prods., Pangaea and Qintex Entertainment. Exec. P: Suzanne de Passe, Bill Wittliff, Robert Halmi Jr. Sprv. P: Michael L. Wiesbarth. P: Dyson Lovell. D: Simon Wincer. W: Bill Wittliff. M: Basil Poledouris. Shown on CBS February 5–8. (16 hrs.)

Cast: Robert Duvall, Tommy Lee Jones, Danny Glover, Diane Lane, Robert Urich, Frederic Forest, D.B. Sweeney, Ricky Schroder, Anjelica Huston, Chris Cooper, Tim Scott, Glenne Headly, Barry Corbin, William Sanderson, Barry Tubb, Gavin O'Herlihy, Steve Buscemi, Frederic Coffin, Travis Swords, Kevin O'Morrison, Ron Weyand, Leon Singer, Lanny Flaherty, Pierre Epstein, David Carpenter, Helena Humann, Adam Faraizi, Bradley Gregg.

WAR AND REMEMBRANCE, PARTS 1–7

Dan Curtis Prod. Exec. P-D: Dan Curtis. P: Barbara Steele. Assoc. P: Branko Lustig. Exec. Prod. Man.: Michael O'Gallant. W: Earl W. Wallace, Dan Curtis, Herman Wouk based on novel by Wouk. M: Bob Cobert. Shown on ABC November 13, November 15, November 16, November 17, November 20, November 22, November 23, 1988. (approx. 18 hrs.)

Cast: Robert Mitchum, Jane Seymour, Hart Bochner, Victoria Tennant, Polly Bergen, David Dukes, Michael Woods, Sharon Stone, Robert Morley, Barry Bostwick, Sami Frey, Topol, John Rhys-Davies, Ian McShane, William Schallert, Bill Wallis, Jeremy Kemp, Steven Berkoff, Robert Hardy, Ralph Bellamy, John Gielgud, G.W. Bailey, J. Kenneth Campbell, John Dehner, Peter Graves, Howard Duff, Pat Hingle, G.D. Spradlin, Jack Ging, Mike Connors, Eddie Albert, Nina Foch, Hardy Kruger, William Prince.

WAR AND REMEMBRANCE, PARTS 8–12

Shown May 7, May 8, May 9, May 10, May 14, 1989. (11½ hrs.)

Television Stations

* CHANNEL ALLOCATIONS
* PERSONNEL

Television Stations

[A listing of television stations in the United States. All stations are authorized by and operate under the approval of the Federal Communications Commission, Washington, DC]

ALABAMA

Anniston

WJSU-TV (Channel 40) CBS

P.O. Box 40, Anniston, AL 36202 (205) 237-8651.

Bob Ford, gen. mgr.; Lisa Bedford, prog.-traf.; Boyce Holt, gen. sls. mgr.; John Murrell, chief eng.

Operation: 1969.

Birmingham

WBMG (Channel 42) CBS

Birmingham Television Company, Box 6146, Birmingham, AL 35209 (205) 252-9821.

Roy H. Park, pres.; Hoyle S. Broome, v.p. & gen. mgr.; Gary Audrich, natl. sls. mgr.; Steve Cloy, lcl. sls. mgr.; Al Crouch, news dir.; Erskine Brantley, traf. mgr.; Fred Vinson, chief eng.

Operation: 1965. TV homes in area: 541,000.

WBRC-TV (Channel 6) ABC

Taft Broadcasting Company, P.O. Box 6, Birmingham, AL 35201 (205) 322-6666.

Nick Bolton, gen. mgr.; Bob Fanning, gen. sales mgr.; Jerry Thorn, chief eng.; Telerep Agency, nat'l rep.

Operation: 1949; TV sets in area: 695,500.

WCAJ (Channel 68)

Celtic Media, Inc., 800 Lakeshore Dr., Sanford U., Birmingham, AL 35229 (205) 871-6801.

Kelley L. Akers, gen. mgr.; August A. Russell, chief eng.

Operation: 1986.

WTTO (Channel 21)

HR Bdcstg. Corp. of Birmingham, 2021 Golden Crest Dr., Birmingham, AL 35029 (205) 251-2100.

Gary Gardner, gen. mgr.; Robert Cleary, gen. sls. mgr.; Marilyn Greene, prog. dir.; Michel Wilk, promo. mgr.; Ross Howard, lcl. sls. mgr.

Operation: 1982.

WVTM-TV (Channel 13) NBC

WVTM-TV, Inc., P.O. Box 10502, Birmingham, AL 35202 (205) 933-2720.

Jeff Rosser, v.p. & gen. mgr.; Frank Landers, gen. sls. mgr.; Everett Holle, film buyer & prog. dir.; Robin Cooper, prom. mgr. rep: HRP

Operation: 1949; TV sets in area: 699,260.

Dothan

WDHN (Channel 18) ABC

Morris Network, Inc., P.O. Box 6237, Dothan, AL 36302 (205) 793-1818.

H. Dean Hinson, pres.; Aubrey Wood, gen. mgr.; Charles Scott, prom. dir.; Jerry Knowles, gen. sls. mgr.; Glenda Powers, prog. dir.; Dan Billings, chief eng.

WTVY (Channel 4) CBS

WTVY, Inc., P.O. Box 1089, Dothan, AL 36302; (205) 792-3195.

Charles Woods, owner-mgr.; Reginald Mitchell, prgm. dir.; Jerry Vann, news dir.; Joe Earl Holloway, prodn. mgr.; John Gause, sales mgr.; Carl Blackmon, nat'l sls. mgr.; Doug Dansby, chief eng.; regional rep., nat'l rep.: Seltel, Inc.

Operation: 1955; TV sets in area: 587,300.

Florence

WOWL-TV (Channel 15)

Television Muscle Shoals, Inc., 840 Cypress Mill Road, P.O. Box 2220, Florence, AL 35630 (205) 767-1515.

Dick Biddle, chm. of bd. & CEO; Rick Biddle, pres. & gen. mgr.; Lincoln Williams, operations mgr.; Earl Shoborg, natl. sls. mgr.; Sara Biddle, community relations dir.; Cindy Davis, news desk mgr.

Operation: 1957; TV homes in area: approx. 256,000.

WTRT (Channel 26)

Bridgeland Television, Inc., 4600 Jackson Hwy., Sheffield, AL 35660. (205) 381-2600.

Les W. White, pres.; Barry Ross, v.p.

Gadsden

WNAL-TV (Channel 44)

WNAL-TV, Inc., 2729 11th Ave. South, Birmingham, AL 35205 (205) 547-4444.

Anthony J. Fant, pres. & gen. mgr.; Robert D. Hill, Jr., v.p.; Kyla B. Fant, prom. mgr.; Mike Hathcock, chief eng.; natl. rep.: Seltel.

Operation: April, 1986.

Huntsville

WAAY-TV (Channel 31)

Rocket City Television, Inc., 1000 Monte Sano Blvd., S.E.; Huntsville, AL 35801 (205) 533-3131.

M.D. Smith IV, pres.; Dan Whitsett, vp. & sls. mgr.; Robert A. Gay, chief eng.

Operation: 1959.

WAFF-TV (Channel 48) NBC

American Valley Corp., Huntsville, AL 35801 (205) 533-4848.

Lee Brantley, v.p. & gen. mgr.; Robert Lane, opns. mgr.; Lamar Reid, gen. sls. mgr.; Rod Hughes, chief eng.; Bob Morford, news dir.

Operation: 1954.

WHNT-TV (Channel 19) CBS

The Times Alabama Broadcasting, Inc., 200 Holmes Ave., P.O. Box 19, Huntsville, AL 35804 (205) 533-1919.

Bob Browning, pres. & gen. mgr.; Bill Ambrose, v.p. & sls. mgr.; Dick Wright, v.p. & opns. mgr.; Don Roden, chief eng.; John Woodin, news dir.

Operation: 1963.

WZDX (Channel 54)

Community Svc. Broadcasting, Box 3889, Huntsville, AL 35810 (205) 859-9854.

Richard Wagschal, gen. mgr.; Randy Stone, lcl. sls. mgr.; Dennis Packard, chief eng.

Operation: April, 1985.

Mobile

WALA-TV (Channel 10) NBC

Knight-Ridder Bdcst., Inc., 210 Government St., Mobile, AL 36602, P.O. Box 1548 (205) 433-3754. TWX 810 741-2642. FAX-FFB.

Joe Cook, pres. & gen. mgr.; Becky Farrell, gen. sls. mgr.; John Reese, chief eng.; Dave Cochran, news dir.; Darrel Taylor, promo. mgr.; nat'l rep.: HRP

Operation: 1953; TV sets in area: 425,900.

WKRG-TV (Channel 5) CBS

WKRG-TV, Inc., 555 Broadcast Drive, Mobile, AL 36606 (205) 479-5555.

Toulmin Greer, bd. chm.; D.H. Long Jr., pres. & film buyer; Thomas W. Diamond, sr. v.p. & sta. mgr.; Don Koch, chief eng.; nat'l rep.: Katz Agency.

Operation: 1955; TV sets in area: 422,400.

WPMI (Channel 15) FOX

WPMI TV Co., Inc., 764 St. Michael St., Mobile, AL 36602 (205) 433-1500.

Ric Gorman, v.p. & gen. mgr.; David D'Antuono, gen. sls. mgr.; Cathy Gretencord, prog. dir.; Harold Johnson, chief eng.; nat'l rep.: Seltel.

Operation: 1982.

WMPV-TV (Channel 21)

Rei-Way Partnership, 120 Zeigler Circle East, Mobile, AL 36608 (205) 633-2100.

Doyle Brunson, pres.; John Marshall, gen. mgr.; Kathy Himes, natl. sls. mgr.; Bonnie Anderson, promo. mgr.; Rish Mashburn, chief eng.

Operation: Dec. 19, 1985.

Montgomery

WAKA-TV (Channel 8) CBS

Alabama Telecasters, Inc., 3020 East Blvd., Montgomery, AL 36117 (205) 279-8787.

Jack Long, gen. mgr.; Mark Smith, pgm. dir. & opns. mgr.; Johnny Wright, chief eng.; Bill Byrd, sta. mgr.

Operation: 1960.

WCOV-TV (Channel 20) FOX

Woods Communications Corp., One WCOV Ave., Montgomery, AL 36111 (205) 288-7020.

David Woods, pres. & gen. mgr.; Phil Witt, chief eng.; nat'l rep.: Seltel.

Operation: 1953; TV sets in area, 172,300.

WKAB-TV (Channel 32) ABC

Montgomery Alabama Channel 32, P.O. Box 3236, Montgomery, AL 36192 (205) 272-5331.

Nory LeBrun, COO; Louis Frey, pres.; Steve Michaud, gen. sls. mgr.; David Murphy, opns. mgr.; Dan Metzger, chief eng.; Nat'l rep., Petry TV.

Operation: March 24, 1962; TV households: 217,900.

WMCF-TV (Channel 45)

Word of God Fellowship, Inc., 6000 Monticello Dr., Montgomery, AL 36117 (205) 277-4545.

Marcus Lamb, pres.

WSFA-TV (Channel 12) NBC

Cosmos Broadcasting Corp., 10 E. Delano, P.O. Box 2566, Montgomery, AL 36105 (205) 281-2900.

James Sefert, pres.; Mel Stebbins, v.p. & gen. mgr.; Tom Morris, gen. sls. mgr.; Carl M. Stephens, prog. mgr.; Leslie Morris, prom. dir.; Charles Halsten, chief eng.; nat'l rep: HRP.

Operation: 1954; TV sets in area: 417,250.

Opelika

WSWS-TV (Channel 66)

Box 870, Opelika, AL 36801 (205) 749-6666.

Ronald Moore, gen. mgr.

Operation: May 16, 1982.

Tuscaloosa

WCFT-TV (Channel 33) CBS

Beam Communication Corp., 4000 37rd St., East, Tuscaloosa, AL 35404 (205) 553-1333

Frank Beam, pres.; W. Tommy Ray, v.p. & gen. mgr.; Ronnie Quarles, sls. mgr.; Kip Tyner, news dir.; nat'l rep.: Katz.

Operation: Oct. 29, 1965; TV households: 53,4000.

WDBB (Channel 17)

Channel 17 Associates, Ltd., 651 Beacon Pkwy., West, Birmingham, AL 35209; (205) 942-1717.

David R. Dubose, pres.; Charles Rountree, gen. mgr.; Eva Lopez, promo. mgr.; Paul Bankston, gen. sls. mgr.; John Batson, chief eng.

Operation: October, 1984.

ALASKA

Anchorage

KIMO (Channel 13) ABC

Alaska 13 Corp. dba Alaska TV Network, 2700 E. Tudor Rd., Anchorage, AK 99507; (907) 561-1313.

Duane L. Triplett, pres. & CEO; Thomas Tierney, sta. mgr.; Larry Hogue, dir. mktg. & sls.; Lance Hopkins, chief eng.; nat'l rep., Katz.

Operation: 1967.

KTBY (Channel 4) FOX

Totem Broadcasting Corp., 510 L St., Anchorage, AK 99501.

Robert C. Ely, sec.; Huntly Gordon, treas.

Operation: 1983.

KTUU-TV (Channel 2) NBC

P.O. Box 102880, Anchorage, AK 99501; (907) 257-0200.

Jessica Longston, pres.; Al Bramstedt, Jr., gen. mgr.; Nancy Johson, dir. mktg. & natl. sls. mgr.; Andrew McLeod, lcl. sls. mgr.; Nancy Johnson, dir. mktg.; Leeland Verschuesen, chief eng.; nat'l rep.: Blair.

Operation: 1953; TV sets in area: 116,820.

KTVA (Channel 11) CBS

Northern Television, Inc., Box 10-2200, Anchorage, AK 99510; 562-3456.

A. G. Hiebert, chm.; Ron Moore, pres., Anchorage Div.;

Bruce Sloan, v.p., progr. dir.; nat'l rep.: Art Moore, Inc.; regional rep.: Adam Young, Inc.
Operation: 1953; TV sets in area: 110,180.

Fairbanks

KATN-TV (Channel 2) ABC, NBC
Fairbanks TV, Inc., Box 74730, Fairbanks, AK 99707.
Duane L. Triplett, pres.; David L. Geesin, v.p., gen. mgr.; J.B. Krause, sta. mgr.; Mike Boslet, chief eng.; nat'l rep: Katz.
Operation: 1955; TV sets in area: 23,000.

KTVF (Channel 11) CBS
Northern Television, Inc., Box 950, Fairbanks, AK 99707 (907) 452-5121.
A. G. Hiebert, chm.; Henry Hove, pres.; nat'l rep., Art Moore, Inc.
Operation: 1955; TV sets in area: 27,000.

Juneau

KJUD (Channel 8) ABC, CBS, NBC
1107 West Eighth St., Suite 2, Juneau, AK 99801 (907) 586-3145.
Duane Triplett, pres.; John Kaknos, sta. mgr.; Charles Payne, chief eng.; Terence O'Malley, news dir.; nat'l rep.: Katz, Tacher.
Operation: 1956.

Sitka

KTNL (Channel 13) CBS
520 Lake St., Sitka, AK 99835. (907) 747-8488.
Dr. Dan Etulain, pres. & gen. mgr.; Nat Mandel, prog. dir.; Garth Kanen, chief eng.
Operation: 1966.

ARIZONA

Flagstaff

KNAZ-TV (Channel 2) NBC
Grand Canyon TV Co., Box 1843, Flagstaff, AZ 86002 (602) 526-2232.
Don Purnell, gen. mgr.; Ed Bouchard, chief engr.
Operation: 1970.

Kingman

KMOH-TV (Channel 6)
Grand Canyon TV Co., Inc. 2999 Airway, Kingman, AZ 86401 (602) 757-7676.
Don Purnell, gen. mgr.; Bill Olsen, gen. sls. mgr.; Dolores Perkins, prog. dir.; David Sparks, news dir.; Ed Bouchard, chief eng.
Operation: Feb. 22, 1988.

Nogales-Tucson

KMSB (Channel 11) FOX
Mountain States Broadcasting, 2445 N. Tucson Blvd., Tucson, AZ 85716; (602) 795-0311.
Randy Cantrell, v.p. & gen. mgr.; Harry West, film buyer; Allen R. Canfield, compt.; Doug Gervais, promo. mgr.; Roy Mitchell, chief eng.; nat'l rep.: Telerep.
Operation: February, 1967; TV households: 275,000.

Phoenix

KNXV-TV (Channel 15)
Scripps Howard Bdcstg. Co., 4625 S. 33 Pl., Phoenix, AZ 85040 (602) 243-4151.
Stuart Powell, gen. mgr.; Mike Norten, gen. sls. mgr.; Matt Cooperstein, prog. & promo. dir.; Don Thomas, opns. & eng. mgr.; nat'l rep.: Katz.
Operation: 1979.

KPAZ (Channel 21)
Trinity Broadcasting of Arizona, Inc., 3351 E. McDowell Rd., Phoenix, AZ 85008 (602) 273-1477.
Paul F. Crouch, pres.
Operation: December, 1969; TV households: 310,000.

KPHO-TV (Channel 5)
Broadcasting Division, Meredith Corporation, 4016 N. Black Canyon, Phoenix, AZ 85017 (602) 264-1000.
Richard Q. DeAngelis, v.p. & gen. mgr.; Don Pauly, gen. sls. mgr.; Chuck Alvey, sta. mgr.; Chris Sehring, nat'l sls. mgr.; Greg Brannan, pgm. & promo. mgr.
Operation: 1949; Total TV Homes: in survey area, 1,784,800; metro area, 790,500.

KTSP-TV (Channel 10) CBS
KTSP-Great American Television: Radio Co., Inc., 511 W. Adams St., Phoenix, AZ 85003; (602) 257-1234.
Ron Bergamo, v.p. & gen. mgr.; Gary Rockey, prog. mgr.; Karen Donner, bus. mgr.; Dave Howell, news dir.; Al Hillstrom, chief eng.; Sandi Yost, promo. mgr.; Nat'l rep.: HRP.
Operation: 1953; TV households in total survey area: 1,475,800.

KTVK (Channel 3) ABC
Arizona Television Company, 3435 North 16th St., P.O. Box 5068, Phoenix, AZ.
Delbert F. Lewis, pres. & gen. mgr.; Bill Lawrence, chief eng.; James G. Tuton, bus. mgr.; nat'l rep.: Edward Petry Co., Inc.
Operation: 1955; TV homes in area: 480,000.

KTVW (Channel 33)
Seven Hills TV Co., 3019 E. Southern Ave., Phoenix, AZ 85040. (602) 243-3333.
Jose C. Cancela, gen. mgr.; Barry Levisohn, ops. mgr.; Lawrence Beckman, chief eng.
Operation: 1979.

KUTP (Channel 45)
United Television, Inc., 4630 S. 33 St., Phoenix, AZ 85040 (602) 268-4500.
Jerry Braet, v.p. & gen. mgr.; Mike Durand, gen. sls. mgr.; Tom Foy, chief eng.; nat'l rep.: Petry.
Operation: December, 1985.

Phoenix-Mesa

KPNX-TV (Channel 12) NBC
KPNX Broadcasting Co., 1101 N. Central Ave., P.O. Box 711, Phoenix, AZ 85001; (602) 257-1212.
C. E. Cooney, pres., gen. mgr.; Bob Allingham, v.p., prog. dir.; Leon Anglin, v.p., eng.; nat'l rep., Blair Television.
Operation: 1954; TV sets in area: 795,300.

Prescott

KUSK (Channel 7)

3211 Tower Rd., Prescott, AZ 86301; (602) 778-6770.

William H. Sauro, pres.; Rich Howe, gen. mgr. & sls. mgr.; Patricia Gray, opns. mgr.; Thayne Higgins, chief eng.

Operation: 1982.

Tucson

KGUN-TV (Channel 9)

KGUN, Inc., Box 5707, Tucson, AZ 85703 (602) 792-9933.

Carl D. Jaquint, v.p. & gen. mgr.; Steve Ochoa, gen. sls. mgr.; Bruce Franzen, prog. dir.; Mary Zakrasek, promo. mgr.; Phil Aaland, chief eng.; nat'l rep: Katz.

Operation: 1956; TV sets in area: 238,970.

KOLD-TV (Channel 13) CBS

Knight-Ridder Bdcstg. Inc., Tucson, AZ 85705; (602) 624-2511.

Jay Watson, pres. & gen. mgr.; Wanda Myers, gen. sls. mgr.; Tom Foos, prog. dir. & film buyer; Phil Dunton, chief eng.; Gerald Jensen, news dir.; nat'l rep., HRP.

Operation: 1953; TV sets in area, 190,000.

KPOL (Channel 40)

2475 Jack Rabbit Ave., Tucson, AZ 85745; (602) 884-9001.

Julius Polan, pres.; David M. Reaban, v.p., gen. mgr. & film buyer; Frank C. Idaspe, v.p. & gen. sls. mgr.; David J. Polan, sta. mgr.; nat. rep.: Avery-Knodel.

Operation: December, 1984.

KVOA-TV (Channel 4) NBC

Channel 4-TV, Inc., P.O. Box 5188, 209 W. Elm, Tucson, AZ 85703 (602) 792-2270.

Jon F. Ruby, pres. & gen. mgr.; Jim Joslyn, exec. v.p.; Dave Kerrigan, v.p.-prod.; Brink Chipman, news dir.; Dave Hatfield, v.p.-prog.; Ralph Turk, v.p.-eng.; Renee Bear, controller, nat'l. rep., Petry.

Operation: 1953; TV sets in area: 274,500.

Yuma

KYEL-TV (Channel 13) NBC

Beam Broadcasters, Ltd., Box 592, Yuma, AZ 85364; (602) 782-5113.

Peter Rosella, v.p. & gen. mgr.; Boyce Holt, gen. sls. mgr.; Dick Sampson, chief eng.; nat'l rep.: Katz.

Operation: December 1963; TV households, 755,900.

KYMA (Channel 11) ABC

Yuma Bdcstg. Co., 1385 S. Pacific Ave., Yuma, AZ 85365 (602) 782-1111.

Clyde E. Pettit Jr., pres.; Edd Lockwood, gen. mgr.; nat'l rep.: Blair.

ARKANSAS

El Dorado

KTVE (Channel 10) NBC

KTVE, Inc., 2909 Kilpatrick Blvd., Monroe, LA 71201; (318) 323-1300.

Terry McKenna, pres.; George Singleton, v.p. & gen. mgr.; David Brown, gen. sls. mgr.; Mike Caruso, chief eng.; Jerry Mayer, news dir.; Tommy Walker, opns.

Operation: 1955.

Fayetteville-Springdale

KHOG (Channel 29) ABC

Sigma Broadcasting (An Arkansas partnership), P.O. Box 4150, Fort Smith, AR 72914 (501) 783-4040.

Robert Hernreich, partner; Cynthia Hernreich, partner; Darrel Cunningham, gen. mgr.; Cliff Walker, sta. mgr.; Ron Evans, local sls. mgr.; Marvin Macedo, chief eng.

Operation: December, 1977; TV households: 41,300.

Ft. Smith

KFSM-TV (Channel 5) NBC, ABC

Times Southwest Bdcstg. Co., 318 N. 13th St., Ft. Smith, AR 72901 (501) 783-3131.

Robert H. Eoff, pres. & gen. mgr.; Gene Graham, gen. sls. mgr.; Larry Duncan, chief eng.

Operation: 1956.

KHBS (Channel 40) ABC

Sigma Broadcasting (An Arkansas partnership), 2415 N. Albert Pike, Ft. Smith, AR 72914 (501) 783-4040.

Robert E. Hernreich, partner; Cynthia Hernreich, partner; Jarrell Cunningham, gen. mgr.; Jarrel Wyatt, gen. sls. mgr.; Tim Bass, prog. dir.; Don Vest, dir. of eng.-opns.

Operation: 1971.

KPOM-TV (Channel 24)

Box 4610, 4624 Kelley Highway, Ft. Smith, AR 72914 (501) 785-2400.

John McCutcheon, v.p.-gen. mgr.; Bill Oltman, news dir.; Ken Hansen, chief eng.; nat'l rep.: Telerep.

Operation: 1978.

Jonesboro

KAIT-TV (Channel 8) ABC

Cosmos Bdcstg. Co., P.O. Box 790, Jonesboro, AR 72403 (501) 931-8888.

Harold Culver, v.p. & gen. mgr.; Mike Rickwald, gen. sls. mgr.; Al Banks, lcl. sls. mgr.; nat'l rep., HRP.

Operation: July, 1963; TV households: 328,400.

Little Rock

KARK-TV (Channel 4) NBC

Morris Network, Inc., 201 W. Third, Little Rock, AR 72203 (501) 376-2481; TWX 910-722-7417.

Dean Hinson, pres. & gen. mgr.; Clyde Anderson, gen. sls. mgr.; Tom Bonner, exec. v.p. & prog. dir.; Susan Newkirk, prom. mgr.; ; nat'l rep., Katz.

Operation: 1954; TV sets in area: 546,310.

KLRT (Channel 16)

11711 West Markham, Little Rock, AR 72211 (501) 375-1616.

Stephen G. Scollard, v.p. & gen. mgr.; Joanne Canelli, gen. sls. mgr.; Calvin Dring, natl. sls. mgr.; Victoria Tennant, prog. dir.; Dan McFadden, promo. dir.; Miguel Copello, opns. mgr.; Brian Coombs, chief eng.; Yvonne Cornett, dir. fin. affairs.

Operation: June, 1983.

KTHV (Channel 11) CBS

Arkansas Television Co., 8th & Izard Sts., P.O. Box 269, Little Rock, AR 72203 (501) 376-1111.

Robert L. Brown, pres. & gen. mgr., KTHV, Channel 11; C. S. Berry, chm. of bd., ARK Television Co.; Marcus George,

pres. & treas., ARK Television Co.; Lonnie Gibbons, nat'l sales mgr.; Bob Hicks, prog. mgr.; nat'l rep: Seltel.
Operation: 1955; TV sets in area: 647,500.

Little Rock-Pine Bluff

KATV (Channel 7) ABC

Albritton Communications, Inc., 401 Main, Box 77, Little Rock, AR 72203 (501) 372-7777.

Dale Nicholson, pres. & gen. mgr.; Joe Delgrosso, gen. sls. mgr.; Richard Farrester, prog. dir.; James Roddey, prom. mgr.; Jim Pitcock, news dir.; nat'l rep.: Petry.

Operation: 1953; TV sets in area; 647,500.

Pine Bluff

KASN-TV (Channel 38) FOX

MMC Television Corp., 7123 I-30, Suite 54, Little Rock, AR 72209 (501) 562-3838.

Paula Bard Pruett, pres.; Ed Groves, v.p. & gen. mgr.; Lanny Kiest, gen. sls. mgr.; Carol Humphries-Smith, prog. dir.; Joy Scarbrougn, prom. mgr.; Richard Duncan, chief eng.; natl. rep.: Blair.

KVTN (Channel 25)

Agape Church, Inc., Box 22007, Pine Bluff, AR 72221 (501) 223-2525.

H.L. Caldwell, pres.; Randy Wright, gen. mgr.; Ed Gillies, prog. dir.; Patty Roberts, traff.; Michael Clay, chief eng.

Operation: December 1, 1988.

CALIFORNIA

Anaheim

KDOC-TV (Channel 56)

1730 Clementine St., Anaheim, CA 92802 (714) 999-5000.

Pat Boone, pres.; Calvin Brack, v.p. & gen. mgr.; Calvin Brack, dir. bus. affairs; Hoshang Moaddeli, prod. mgr.; Roger Knipp, chief eng.

Operation: 1982.

Arcata

KREQ (Channel 23) FOX

The Mad River Bdcstg. Co., Inc., 1485 L St., Arcata, CA 95521-5742 (707) 826-2323.

Lawrence Rogow, pres. & gen. mgr.; Charles Lohr, gen. sls. mgr. & prog. dir.; John Doyle, prod. mgr.; Lynn Mackay, prom. mgr.; Steve Keeva, news dir.; Don Wilson, dir. eng.; natl. rep.: Adam Young.

Operation: August, 1987.

Bakersfield

KBAK-TV (Channel 29) ABC

Burnham Broadcasting Co., Box 2929, Bakersfield, CA 93303 (805) 327-7955.

Wayne W. Lansche, pres. & gen. mgr.; Bob Banks, chief eng'.; nat'l rep.: Katz.

Operation: 1953; TV sets in area: 560,100.

KERO-TV (Channel 23) CBS

McGraw-Hill Bdctg. Co., Inc., 321 21 Street, Bakersfield, CA 93303 (805) 327-1441. P.O. Box 2367.

Ronald E. Mires, v.p. & gen. mgr.; Norman Hall, dir. of eng.; Walt Brown, news dir.

Operation: 1953; TV sets in area: 280,000.

KGET-TV (Channel 17) NBC

Ackerley Communications, Inc., P.O. Box 1700, Bakersfield, CA 93302 (805) 327-7511.

Raymond A. Watson, v.p. & gen. mgr.; Tom Randour, gen. sls. mgr.; Shirley Sanford, prog. dir.; Doug Caldwell, news dir.; Tom Ballew, chief eng.

Operation: 1959; TV sets in area: 147,000.

Chico

KCPM (Channel 24) NBC

Chico Broadcasting Co., Box 4406, Chico, CA 95927.

Melvin Querio, pres. & gen. mgr.; Don McFarlane, natl. sls. mgr.; Dave West, lcl. sls. mgr.; Donna O'Connor, prom. mgr.; Richard Gray, prod. mgr.; Chuck Moorman, chief eng.

Operation: September, 1985.

KHSL-TV (Channel 12) CBS

Golden Empire Broadcasting Co., Box 489, Chico, CA 95927 (916) 342-0141.

C. H. Kinsley, Jr., exec. v.p.; Dino Corbin, gen. mgr.; Bill Meyer, gen. sls. mgr.; Dan Carter, prod. mgr.; Russell B. Pope, dir. of eng.; Donna Schiague, chief eng. nat'l rep.: Seltel.

Operation: 1953; TV sets in area: 150,600.

Concord

KFCB (Channel 42)

First Century Bcstg., Inc. 5101 Port Chicago Hwy., Concord, CA 94520 (415) 676-8969.

Ronn Haus, pres.; Debra Fraser, prog. dir.-sls.; Gary Johnson, prod. mgr.; Linda Demars, traf. mgr.

Operation: June, 1983.

El Centro

KECY-TV (Channel 9) CBS

Pacific Media Corporation, 646 Main Street, El Centro, CA 92243; (619) 353-9990.

Peter G. Sieler, gen. mgr.; Deborah Weekes, prog. dir.; Kevin Hanefeld, news dir.; nat'l rep.: Seltel.

Operation: Dec. 1968; TV Households: 60,300.

Eureka

KIEM (Channel 3) NBC

Precht Communications, Inc., 5650 S. Broadway, Eureka, CA (707) 443-3123.

Robert Precht, pres.; Marcy Levine, v.p. & gen. mgr.; Donald King, opns. mgr.; Hank Ingham, gen. sls. mgr.; nat'l rep.: Katz.

Operation: 1953.

KVIQ (Channel 6) CBS

Miller Bdcstg. Co., 1800 Broadway, Eureka, CA 95501 (707) 443-3061.

Ronald W. Miller, pres.; Pattison J. Christensen, v.p.; Mike Fiest, chief eng.

Operation: 1958.

Fresno

KAIL (Channel 53)

Trans-America Broadcasting Corp., P.O. Box 5188, Fresno, CA 93755 (209) 299-9753.

Albert J. Williams, pres.; C.B. Reis, gen. mgr.; Clemencia Vangas, prog. dir. & film buyer; Lee Cowan, chief eng.

Operation: 1961.

KFSN-TV (Channel 30) ABC

Capital Cities/ABC Inc., 1777 G. St., Fresno, CA 93706. (209) 442-1170.

Mark Edwards, v.p. & gen. mgr.; Dudley Few, gen. sls. mgr.; Mark Arminio, lcl. sls. mgr.; Dave Converse, chief eng.; Fernando Granado, prog. dir.

Operation: 1956.

KJEO (Channel 47) CBS

Retlaw Broadcasting Co., Box 5455, Fresno, CA (209) 222-2411.

Joseph C. Drilling, pres.; Donald C. Drilling, v.p. & gen. mgr.; Mark Libby, gen. sls. mgr.; Kathleen Williams, natl. sls. mgr.; Larry Mayfileld, chief eng.; Patricia Houlihan, prog. mgr.; Andrew Mastoras, v.p.-finance; Patrice Coulter, traffic mgr.; Barry Decrane, promo. dir.; nat'l. rep.: Katz.

Operation: 1953; Sets in area: 577,300.

KMPH (Channel 26)

Pappas Telecasting, Inc., 5111 McKinley Ave., Visalia, CA 93727 (209) 733-2600.

Harry J. Pappas, pres. & gen. mgr.; Edward G. Aiken, v.p./TV; Michael Granados, sta. mgr.; Joseph Shaffer, v.p./prog.; Lise Markham, natl. sls. mgr.; Joel Cheatwood;, news dir.; Dale Kelly, chief eng.

Operation: October, 1971.

KMSG-TV (Channel 59)

Sanger Telecasters, Inc., 706 W. Hendon Ave., Fresno, CA 93650 (209) 435-5900.

Diane D. Cocola, pres.; James K. Zahn, gen. mgr. & prog. dir.; Gary M. Cocola, gen. sls. mgr.; Steve Weber, chief eng.

Operation: July 17, 1985.

KSEE (Channel 24) NBC

San Joaquin Communications Corp., 5035 East McKinley Ave., Fresno, CA 93727; (209) 454-2424.

Todd Holmes, v.p. & gen. mgr.; Bill Spellman, gen. sls. mgr.; Ken Preston, dir. eng.; Doug Stewart, promo. mgr.; Ken Coy, news dir.

Operation: 1953; TV sets in area: 405,100.

Hanford-Fresno

KFTV (Channel 21)

Spanish International Communications Corp., 3239 W. Ashlan Ave., Fresno, CA 93722.

August Ruiz, gen. mgr.; Mac McKenzie, chief eng.; nat'l rep.: Univision.

Operation: 1962.

Los Angeles

KABC-TV (Channel 7) ABC

Capital Cities ABC Inc., 4151 Prospect Ave., Hollywood, CA 90027 (213) 557-7777.

Terry Crofoot, pres. & gen. mgr.; John Riedl, gen. sls. mgr.; Robert Burris, creative svcs. dir.; Don Corsini, prog. dir.; Bruce Gordon, fin. dir.; Robert Billeci, dir. eng.; nat'l rep.: ABC Television Spot Sales, Inc.

Operation: 1949.

KCBS (Channel 2) CBS

CBS, Inc. 6121 Sunset Blvd., Los Angeles, CA 90028

Robert Hyland, v.p. & gen. mgr.; Steve Gigliotti, sls. dir.; Jay Strong, dir. prog.; Edward Spray, bdcst. dir.; Erik Sorenson, news dir.; Robert Davis, dir. tech. opns.; Elizabeth Vendely, dir. comms.

Operation: 1950; TV sets in area: 10,300,000.

KCOP (Channel 13)

KCOP Television Inc., a Chris Craft Industries, station, 915 N. La Brea Ave., Hollywood, CA 90038 (213) 851-1000.

Bill Frank, pres. & gen. mgr.; Rick Feldman, gen. sls. mgr.; Peter Mathes, nat'l sls. mgr.; Suzann Thomason & Jill Thomason, lcl. sls. mgrs.; Win Korabell, dir. of eng.; Jane Clark, bus. mgr.; Peter Schlesinger, dir. of prgm. opns.; Carol Myers Martz, prgm. mgr.; Gary Davis, dir. of creative svcs.

Operation: 1948; TV sets in area: 4,132,100.

KHJ-TV (Channel 9)

KHJ-TV (Division of Walt Disney Co.), 5515 Melrose Avenue, Hollywood, CA 90038 (213) 467-5459.

Chuck Velona, v.p. & gen. mgr., KHJ-TV; Hank Oyster, gen. sls. mgr.; Walt Baker, v.p. & prog. dir.; Dick Paradise, promo. dir.; Buck Evans, chief eng.; nat'l rep., Blair.

Operation: 1948; TV sets in area: 3,511,000.

KMEX-TV (Channel 34)

Spanish International Bcstg. Co., 5420 Melrose Ave., Los Angeles, CA 90038 (213) 466-8131.

Daniel Villanueva, gen. mgr.; Robert Porter, v.p., eng.; Louis Sweeney, v.p., nat'l sls.; Charles Barry, sls. mgr.; rep., Spanish International Network Sales Inc.

Operation: September, 1962; TV households: 1,500,000.

KNBC (Channel 4) NBC

National Broadcasting Co., Inc., 3000 W. Alameda Ave., Burbank, CA 91523 (818) 840-4444.

John Rohrbeck, v.p. & gen. mgr.; Pat Wallace, dir. bdcstg.; Jim Sterling, gen. sls. mgr.; Carole Cartwright, prog. dir.; Regina Miyamoto, mgr. press & pub.; Tom Capra, news dir.; Harry Burbidge, chief eng.; Rep: NBC Spot Sales.

Operation: Jan. 1949.

KTLA (Channel 5)

KTLA, Inc., 5800 Sunset Blvd., Hollywood, CA 90028 (213) 460-550.

Steve Bell, sr. v.p. & gen. mgr.; Michael Eigner, v.p. & sta. mgr.; Tom Arnost, gen. sls. mgr.; Jeff Wald, news dir.; Ira Goldstone, eng. dir.

Operation: 1947; TV sets in area: 4,138,000.

KTTV (Channel 11) FOX

5746 Sunset Blvd., Los Angeles, CA 90028 (213) 856-1000.

Greg Nathanson, v.p. & gen. mgr.; John McCormick, v.p. & gen. sls. mgr.; Lee Hoegee & Dejon Coffin, natl. sls. mgrs.; Andrea Stoltzman & Susan Wilcox, lcl. sls. mgrs.; Lorraine D'Itri, comm. opns. dir.; Peter Margin, promo. dir.; Augie Martinez, v.p. fin. & admin.; Bill McGowan, sta. mgr.

Operation: Jan. 1949.

KWHY-TV (Channel 22)

Harriscope of Los Angeles,Inc., 5545 Sunset Blvd., Los Angeles, CA 90028 (213) 466-5441.

Burt I. Harris, pres.; Burt I. Harris, Jr., v.p. & gen. mgr.; Mike Wagner, acct. exec.; John H. Nelson, acct. exec.; Eugene A. Harris, David J. Zulli, chief eng.

Operation: 1963.

Modesto

KCSO (Channel 19) Spanish language

Sainte Limited., P.O. Box 3689, Modesto, CA 95352 (209) 578-1900.

Chester Smith, Naomi L. Smith, gen. partners.

Monterey

KMST-TV (Channel 46)

Retlaw Broadcasting Co., P.O. Box 1938, Monterey, CA 93940 (408) 649-0460.

Joseph Drilling, pres.; Ben Tucker, exec. v.p.; Dick Drilling, v.p. & gen. mgr.; Tom Tucker, sls. mgr.; Kathy Nash, public affairs dir.; Mark Walker, prod. mgr.; Roy Dasher, chief eng.; Bob Stock, pro. dir.; Dave Colson, promo. mgr.; Michelle McCullouch, traffic mgr.

Operations: February, 1969. TV households: 184,800.

Oxnard

KADY (Channel 63)

KADY-TV, Riklis Broadcasting, 663 Maulhardt, Oxnard, CA 93030 (805) 983-0044.

John Huddy, pres.; Ed Branca, sta. mgr.-gen. sls.; Jack Kirby, dir. devel.; Bob Malcolm, bus. mgr.; Roger Terneuzen, dir. opns.; Erica Huddy, prog. mgr.

Operation: August, 1985.

Palm Springs

KESQ-TV (Channel 42, Cable 3) ABC

P.O. Box 4200, Palm Springs, CA 92263. Owned by EFG Broadcast Corp., Dallas, TX; (619) 328-8881.

Scott Vaughan, gen. mgr.; Bill Evans, lcl. sls. mgr.; Kirk Gregory, natl. sls. mgr.; nat'l rep.: Katz.

Operation: October 1968; TV households: 63,700.

KMIR-TV (Channel 36) NBC

Desert Empire TV Corp., P.O. Box 1506, Palm Springs, CA 92263 (619) 568-3636.

John Conte, pres. & gen. mgr.; Jan Pearce, chief exec.; Tina Stein, news dir.; rep.: Seltel.

Operation: Oct. 1968; TV households: 65,400.

Redding

KRCR TV (Channel 7) ABC

California-Oregon Broadcasting, Inc., 755 Auditorium Dr., Redding (Shasta Co.), CA 96001 (916) 243-7777.

Richard W. Green, v.p. & gen. mgr.; Doreeta Domke, operations mgr.; nat'l rep., Blair.

Riverside

KSLD (Channel 62)

Sunland Bdcstg. Co., 4522 Woodman Ave., Suite C-236, Sherman Oaks, CA 91423 (818) 906-8834.

Jack Hodin, pres.; Andrew Soto, v.p.

Operation: December, 1988.

Sacramento

KCMY (Channel 29)

Ponce-Nicasio Bdcstg., Ltd. 1029 K St., Suite 23, Sacramento, CA 95814 (916) 442-6414.

Carmen Briggs, pres. & gen. mgr.

KCRA-TV (Channel 3) NBC

Kelly Broadcasting Co., 3 Television Circle, Sacramento, CA 95814-0794 (916) 444-7300.

Robert E. Kelly, partner; Jon S. Kelly, partner; John Kueneke, gen. mgr.; nat'l rep.; Blair Television, Inc.

Operation: 1955; TV sets in area: 558,900.

KRBK-TV (Channel 31)

500 Media Pl., Sacramento, CA 95815 (916) 929-0300

Ted Koplar, pres.; Elliott Troshinsky, v.p. & gen. mgr.

Operation: 1974.

KTXL (Channel 40) FOX

Channel 40, Inc., 4655 Fruitridge Rd., Sacramento, CA 95820-5299 (916) 454-4422.

Renaissance Communications Corp. of New York City; Michael A. Fisher, v.p. & gen. mgr.; Rod Bacon, gen. sls. mgr.; Cal Bollwinkel, prog.-oper. mgr.; Audrey Farington, promo. mgr.; Bob Cook, news dir.

Operation: 1968.

KXTV (Channel 10) CBS

Belo Broadcasting Corp., 400 Broadway, Sacramento, CA 95818 (916) 441-2345.

Phillip Keller, pres. & gen. mgr.; Byron Elton, gen. sls. mgr.; Matt Chan, creative svcs. dir.; Gary Duncan, mktg./promo. mgr.; nat'l rep.: Tele-Rep.

Operation: 1955; TV sets in area: 931,800.

Salinas

KCBA (Channel 35)

Cypress Broadcasting Inc., Box 3560, Salinas, CA 93912; (408) 422-3500.

Barbara Etrick, v.p. & gen. mgr.; Karl Kauffman, chief, eng.; Mary Moore, prog. mgr.

Operation: November, 1981

KSBW-TV (Channel 8) NBC

Gillett of California, Inc., P.O. Box 81651, 238 John St. Salinas, CA 93912 (408) 758-8888. (Affiliated with KSBY-TV, San Luis Obispo, CA)

Jeffrey H. Lee, pres. & gen. mgr.; Cynthia Lindsay, gen. sls. mgr.; Teresa Burgess, prog. mgr.; Mike Kronley, news dir.; Willis Wells, chief eng.

Operation: 1953; TV homes in area: 212,700.

San Bernardino

KAGL (Channel 30)

Angelese Bdcstg. Network, 318 Mira Loma Ave., Glendale, CA 91204 (714) 381-1724.

Glen Chambers, pres. & gen. mgr.; Beverly Chambers, gen. sls. mgr.; Ronna Scott, prog. & news dir.; Clint Scott, film buyer; Lee McAliley, prog. mgr.; Terry Wood, chief eng.

Operation: March, 1985.

KSCI-TV (Channel 18)

KSCI, Inc., 12401 West Olympic Blvd., Los Angeles, CA 90064 (213) 478-1818.

Ray Beindorf, pres.; Rosemary Fincher Danon, gen. mgr.; Dorothy Marsh, sta. mgr.

Operation: June, 1977.

San Diego

KNSD-TV (Channel 39) NBC

Gillett Communications of San Diego, Inc., 8330 Engineer Rd., San Diego, CA 92111 (619) 279-3939.

Neil E. Derrough, pres. & gen. mgr.; Jay Belbey, controller; Joseph M. Collins, gen. sls. mgr.; Tom Wimberly, dir. of tech. svcs.; Don Shafer, news dir.; Ric Schwartz, prod. mgr.; Penny Martin, prog. mgr.

Operation: 1965.

KFMB-TV (Channel 8) CBS

Midwest Television, Inc., 7677 Engineer Road, San Diego, CA 92101 (714) 292-5362.

August C. Meyer, Jr., pres.; Robert L. Myers, vice-pres. & gen. mgr.; Bill Moylan, v.p., operations; John Weigand, chief eng.; nat'l rep.. Petry.

Operation: 1949, TV sets in area: 1,015,800.

KGTV (Channel 10) ABC

McGraw-Hill Broadcasting Co., P.O. Box 85347, San Diego, CA 92138 (619) 237-1010.

Edward J. Quinn, v.p. & gen. mgr.; Ron Jennings, dir. of eng.; Howard Oleff, dir. lcl. sls.-mktg.; Steve Weber, local sls. mgr.; Mark Wilcox, natl. sls. mgr.; Darrell Brown, gen. sls. mgr.; Judy Vance, dir. creative svcs.; Kelly McMackin, reg. sls. mgr.; Jack Villarrubia, dir., business affairs; Don Lundy, prog. dir.

Operation: 1953.

KTTY (Channel 69)

San Diego Television, Inc., P.O. Box 121569, San Diego, CA 92112 (619) 575-6969.

James M. Harmon, pres. & gen. mgr.; Joseph Alvarez, sr. v.p.; Andy Feldman, lcl. sls. mgr.; Gayle Garrett, natl. sls. mgr.; Richard Thiriot, prog. consult.; Judy Albrecht, promo. mgr.

Operation: October, 1984.

KUSI-TV (Channel 51)

7377 Convoy Ct., San Diego, CA 92111 (619) 571-5151.

William Rust, pres.; Michael McKinnin, gen. mgr.; William E. Moore, sta. mgr.; Bruce Stein, gen. sls. mgr.; nat'l rep.: Katz.

Operation: 1982.

XETV (Channel 6) FOX

Bay City Television, Inc., 8253 Ronson Road, Television Heights, San Diego, CA 92111 (619) 279-6666.

Martin M. Colby, v.p. & gen. mgr.; Robert C. Taylor, treas./bus. mgr.; Joan O'Laughlin, sta. mgr. and gen. sls. mgr.; Valerie Hoffman, prog. mgr., Bob Anderson, prod. mgr.; Philip Paluso, promo. mgr.; Felipe Fernandez, chief eng.; Julian Kaufman, consultant; nat'l rep.: Telerep.

Operation: 1953; TV sets in area: 582,450.

XEWT-TV (Channel 12) Spanish language

Televisora de Calimex, S.A., P.O. Box 12, Tijuana, Baja California, Mexico (706) 685-9201 and 685-9202.

Jose Marquez, gen. mgr.; Carlos H. Luna, prog. prom. mgr.; Roberto Espinoza, business mgr.

San Francisco

KBHK-TV (Channel 44)

UTV of San Francisco Inc., 420 Taylor St., San Francisco, CA 94102 (415) 885-3750.

Robert Qudeen, v.p. & gen. mgr.; Richard Jones, gen. sls. mgr.; Cheryl Cox, natl. sls. mgr.; Suzanne Guyette, news & p.a. mgr.; Ed Hippe, eng. mgr.; Jacques Geoffrion, prod. mgr.

Operation: January, 1968. TV households: 3,953,400.

KDTV (Channel 14) Spanish language

Univision Station Group, Inc., 2200 Palou Ave., San Francisco, CA 94124. An affiliate of Univision, Inc.

August Ruiz, gen. mgr.; Jorge Belon, prod. & programming dir.; Sharon Michelucci, bus. mgr.; Mac McKenzie, chief eng.

Operation: 1975.

KGO-TV (Channel 7) ABC

Capital Cities ABC, Inc., 900 Front St., San Francisco, CA 94111 (415) 954-7777.

Leonard Spagnoletti, gen. mgr.; Bob Young, gen. sls. mgr.; John Moczulski, prog. svcs. mgr.; Harry Fuller, news dir.; Rosemary Roach, rsch. dir.; Ed Johnson, chief eng. rep.: ABC-TV

Operation: 1949; TV homes in area: 2,143,900.

KOFY (Channel 20)

Pacific FM Inc., 2500 Marin St., San Francisco, CA 94124. (415) 821-2020.

James J. Gabbert, pres.; Michael P. Lincoln, gen. mgr.; Richard Blue, v.p.; Hal Capron, dir. sls.

Operation: 1980; TV households, 1,200,000.

KPIX (Channel 5) CBS

Group W (Westinghouse Broadcasting Co.), 855 Battery St., San Francisco, CA 94111 (415) 362-5550.

Carolyn Wean, v.p. & gen. mgr.; Kennen Williams, gen. sls. mgr.; Chris Westerkamo, lcl. sls. mgr.; Jim Lutton, prog. dir.; Peter Maroney, news dir.

Operation: 1948; TV households in area: 3,451,000.

KRON-TV (Channel 4) NBC

Chronicle Broadcasting Co., subsidiary of The Chronicle Publishing Company, 1001 Van Ness Avenue, San Francisco, CA (415) 441-4444.

F.A. Martin III, pres. and chief exec. officer of Chronicle Bdcst. Co.; Amy McCombs, pres. & gen. mgr.; Laura Hewins, v.p., fin. & admin.; Rich Cerussi gen. sls. mgr.; Herb Dudnick, news dir.; David Salinger, dir. prog. & audience devel.; nat'l rep.: Petry Television.

Operation: 1949; TV households in area: 2,143,990.

KTSF-TV (Channel 26)

Lincoln Broadcasting Co., 100 Valley Dr., Brisbane, CA 94005; (415) 468-2626.

Lillian L. Howell, owner; Brian Holton, gen. mgr.; Michael Sherman, sta. mgr.

KTVU (Channel 2)

KTVU, Inc. No. 2 Jack London Square, Oakland, CA 94623 (415) 834-1212.

Kevin O'Brien, v.p. & gen. mgr.; Brooke Spectorsky, sta. mgr.; Jeff Block, gen. sls. mgr.; Thomas Jermain, nat'l sales mgr.; Charles Stuart, lcl. sls. mgr.; Caroline Chang, prog. dir.; Bill Templeton, contr.; Micki Byrnes, mktg. dir.; Ray Jacobs, dir. of operations; Fred Zehnder, news dir.; Sterling Davis, chief eng.

Operation: 1958.

KWBB (Channel 38)

45 Franklin St., San Francisco, CA 94102 (415) 558-8268.

Huntly Gordon, pres. & gen. mgr. & gen. sls. mgr., news dir.;

John T. Anderson, prog. dir. & film buyer; Joe Shackleford, chief eng.; nat'l rep.: Adam Young.
Operation: 1986.

Sanger

KMSG-TV (Channel 59)

Sanger Telecasters, Inc., 706 W. Herndon Ave., Fresno, CA 93650 (209) 435-5900.

Gary M. Cocola, CEO; Diane D. Cocola, pres.; James K. Zahn, gen. mgr.; Steve Weber, chief eng.; Jose Elgorriaga, acct. exec.; Keith Allen, opns. mgr.; Jim Zahn, prog. dir.

Operation: July, 1985.

San Jose

KICU-TV (Channel 36)

Ralph C. Wilson Industries, Inc., 1585 Schallenberger Rd., San Jose, CA 95131. (408) 298-3636. Studio: same address and phone.

William Hirshey, pres.; John Davidson, v.p. & gen. mgr.; John DuBóis, gen. sls. mgr., Jim Kraenzel, chief eng.

Operation: 1967.

KNTV (Channel 11)

Landmark Communications, 645 Park Avenue, San Jose, CA 95110; (408) 286-1111.

Richard A. Fraim, v.p. & gen. mgr.; Stewart B. Park, sta. mgr.; Martin Edelman, gen. sls. mgr.; Tom Moo, news dir.; Lou Bell, engr. mgr.; Barbara Smith, contr.; nat'l rep.: HRP.

Operation: 1955.

KSTS (Channel 48)

Telemundo of Northern California, Inc., 2349 Bering Dr., San Jose, CA 95131 (408) 435-8848.

Paul Niedermeyer, gen. mgr.; Kenneth Elkin, cont.; Jose Cruz, gen. sls. mgr.; Frank Ogden, chief eng.

Operation: 1981.

San Luis Obispo

KSBY-TV (Channel 6)

KSBY, Inc., 467 Hill St., San Luis Obispo, CA 93401 (805) 541-6666.

D. R. Oswald, pres. & gen. mgr.; James Brodsky, dir. tech. opns.; Vivi Zigler, sta. mgr.; Don Ready, chief eng.; Madeline Palaszewski, creative svcs. dir.; Jim Prather, news dir.

Operation: 1953.

Santa Ana

KTBN-TV (Channel 40)

Trinity Broadcasting Network, P.O. Box A, Santa Ana, CA 92711 (714) 832-2950.

Paul F. Crouch, pres.; Cindy Tatum, prog. dir.; Ben Miller, v.p., eng.; Rich Bemillez, sls.

Operation: 1967.

Santa Barbara

KEYT (Channel 3) ABC

Smith Broadcasting of California, P.O. drawer X, Santa Barbara, CA 93102.

Sandra G. Benton, v.p. & gen. mgr.; Steve Lakey, promo. mgr.; Renee Foley, prog. supvr.; King Harris, news dir.; Charles Good, chief eng.; nat'l rep.: Seltel.

Operation: 1953; TV sets in area: 393,300.

Santa Maria

KCOY-TV (Channel 12) CBS

Stauffer Communications, Inc., 1211 W. McCoy Lane, Santa Maria, CA 93454 (805) 925-1200.

Charles Stauffer, gen. mgr.; Dave Fete, oper. mgr.; Ed Wilson, news dir.; Wendy Eisele, dir. mktg. & promo.; Dennis Bornhoft, chief eng. Rep.: Katz.

Operation: 1964; TV households: 193,000.

Santa Rosa

KFTY (Channel 50)

Sonoma Broadcasting, Inc., Box 1150, Santa Rosa, CA 95402 (707) 526-5050.

James D. Johnson, exec. v.p. & gen. mgr.; Paul Sacks, sls. mgr.; Joe Perez, v.p., engineering; Don Ross, news dir.

Operation: 1981.

Stockton/Sacramento

KOVR—TV (Channel 13)

Anchor Media, 1216 Arden Way, Sacramento, CA 95815 (916) 927-1313. Stockton News Bureau, 225 E. Miner Ave., Stockton, CA 95202 (209) 466-6981.

Michael Fiorile, v.p. & gen. mgr.; Dave Ulrickson, gen. mgr.; Robert Hess, chief eng.; Kurt Eichsteadt, prog. mgr.; nat'l rep: Katz Agency.

Operation: 1954; TV sets in area (Sacramento/Stockton Mkt.) 932,000.

KSCH-TV (Channel 58)

Pegasus Bdcstg. of Stockton-Sacramento California, Inc., Box 2258, Sacramento, CA 95741; 3033 Gold Canal Dr., Sacramento, CA 95670.

Harry Delaney, gen. mgr.; John Mansker, gen. sls. mgr.; Donna Reith, prog. dir.; Steve Haliwell, prom. mgr.; Bob Olson, chief eng.

Operation: April, 1986.

Vallejo

KPST-TV (Channel 66)

Pan Pacific Television, Inc., 475 El Camino Real, Suite 308, Millibrae, CA 94030 (415) 697-6682.

David Li, pres. & gen. mgr.; C.T. Tuan, gen. sls. mgr.; Sammy Yang, prog. dir.; Michael Tu, promo. mgr.; Jake Niehoff, chief eng.

Operation: Nov. 25, 1986.

COLORADO

Boulder

KTVJ (Channel 14)

Boulder Telecasting Corp., 3505 N. Ashland Ave., Chicago, IL 60657 (312) 975-0400.

Fred Eychaner, pres.; Barbara Richardson, gen. mgr.; Neal Sabin, prog. dir.

Operation: March, 1986.

Colorado Springs/Pueblo

KKTV (Channel 11) CBS

KKTV Inc., P.O. Box 2110, 80901; 3100 N. Nevada Ave., Colorado Springs, CO (719) 634-2844.

James Lucas, v.p./gen. mgr.; nat'l rep.: Katz, West.

Operation: 1952; TV households in area: 367,300; Total households in survey area: 375,200.

KOAA-TV (Channel 5) NBC

Sangre de Cristo Communications, Inc., 2200 7th Avenue, Pueblo, CO 81003 (303) 544-5782.

John O. Gilbert, pres. & gen. mgr.; Kenneth Renfrow, chief eng.; Jack Sinclair, prog. dir.; Flo Isringhausen, nat'l sls. mgr.; Andy Lyon, news dir.; Dori Walls, lcl. sls. mgr., Pueblo; Elaine Rife, lcl. sls. mgr., Cob Springs.

Operation: 1953; TV sets in area: 296,700.

KRDO-TV (Channel 13) ABC

Pikes Peak Broadcasting Co., P.O. Box 1457, Colorado Springs, CO 80901 (719) 632-1515.

Harry W. Hoth, Jr., pres.; Neil O. Klocksiem, gen. mgr.; Charles H. Upton, chief eng.

Operation: 1953; TV sets in area: 239,280.

KXRM-TV (Channel 21)

KXRM, Inc., 5050 Edison Ave., Colorado Springs, CO 80915.

Larry W. Douglas, pres., gen. mgr., prog. dir. & film buyer; Mr. Kim Carlson, gen. sls. mgr.; Donna Tyree, promo. mgr.; Marty Martin, chief eng.

Operation: December, 1984.

Denver

KCNC (Channel 4) NBC

General Electric Property Management Company of Colorado, Inc., 1044 Lincoln Street, P.O. Box 5012 T.A., Denver, CO 80217 (303) 861-4444.

Roger L. Ogden, pres./gen. mgr.; J.H. MacDermott, v.p./sta. mgr.; David Layne, mgr. opns.; Rick Wardell, gen. sls. mgr.; Marv Rockford, v.p./news dir.; Lon Lee, v.p./prm. mgr.; Tom Edwards, production mgr.; Mike Jackson, promotion mgr.

KDVR (Channel 31)

Centennial Bcstg. Corpl., 501 Wazee St., Denver, CO 80204; (303) 595-3131.

Terence J. Brown, v.p. & sta. mgr.; Peter McCampbell, gen. sls. mgr.; Phil Kane, promo. mgr.; Steve Coulam, dir. eng.; Stephanie A. Campbell, dir. prog.; P. Bradley Short, cont. & secty.; nat'l rep.: MMT.

Operation: August, 1983.

KMGH-TV (Channel 7) CBS

McGraw-Hill Co., Inc., 123 Speer Blvd., Denver, CO 80203 (303) 832-7777.

Edward T. Reilly, pres.; Al Seethaler, v.p. & gen. mgr.; Jim Birschbach, gen. sls. mgr.; Mary Carole McDonnell, dir. of prog.; Robert A. Chernet, dir. of adv. & promo.; Shirley Thompson, traffic mgr.; Mike Youngren, news dir.; Larry Pozzi, dir. of eng.

Operation: 1953.

KUSA (Channel 9) ABC

Gamnett Broadcasting., 1089 Bannock St., Denver, CO 80204 (303) 893-9000.

Joe Franzgrote, pres. & gen. mgr.; Judy Moleres, controller; Butch Montoya, news dir.; Colleen Brown, v.p. bus. affairs & sta. relations.

Operation: 1952; TV sets in area: 1,008,000.

KWGN (Channel 2)

WGN of Colorado, Inc., 6160 S. Wabash Way, Englewood, CO (303) 740-2222.

John Suder, v.p. & gen. mgr.; Charles Biondo, creative svcs. dir.; Tom Burton, sr. producer/director; Tarey Thornburg, film dir.; Kent Gratteau, chief eng.; Royce Nation, v.p., treas. & CFO.

Operation: 1952; TV sets in area: 1,004,850.

Durango

KREZ-TV (Channel 6) CBS, NBC

(Satellite of KREX-TV, Grand Junction, CO)

Withers Broadcasting Co. of Colorado, P.O. Box 2508, Durango, CO 81302 (303) 259-6666.

Thomas McGill, gen. mgr.

Operation: Nov., 1963.

Glenwood Springs

KREG-TV (Channel 3) CBS, NBC

P.O. Box 250, Carbondale, CO 81623 (303) 963-3333.

W. Russell Withers, Jr., licensee.

Grand Junction

KJCT-TV (Channel 8)

ABC, P.O. Box 3788, Grand Junction, CO 81502

Harry W. Hoth, pres.; Jan Hammer, sta. mgr.; Roger Hightower, chief eng.

Operation: 1979; TV households: 66,100

KREX-TV (Channel 5) CBS, NBC

Withers Bdcst. of Colorado, 345 Hillcrest Manor, Grand Junction, CO (303) 242-5000.

Thomas McGill, gen. mgr. nat'l rep.: Katz.

Operation: 1954; TV sets in area: 61,000 (ARB).

Montrose

KREY-TV (Channel 10) CBS, NBC

(Satellite of KREX-TV, Grand Junction, CO)

Withers Broadcasting Co. of Colorado, 614 N. 1st St., Montrose, CO 81401 (303) 249-9601.

Tom McGill, gen. mgr.; nat'l rep.: Katz.

Operation: 1956.

Pueblo

KPCS (Channel 32)

% Hanna, Inc., 790 Madison Ave., New York, NY 10023 (212) 517-3300.

Edward Hanna, pres. & gen. mgr.

Steamboat Springs

KSBS-TV (Channel 24)

Steamboat Bdcstg. Systems, Inc., Box 775048, Torian Plum Plaza, Steamboat Springs, CO 80477 (303) 879-3724.

Thomas M. Greer, pres. & prog. dir.; Mary Effinger, gen. sls. mgr.; Tom Pearson, chief eng.

Operation: May, 1988.

Sterling

KTVS (Channel 3) CBS

Stauffer Communications, Inc., 712 W. Main St., Sterling, CO 80751 (303) 522-5743.

John Stauffer, pres.; Gene L. Huston, sta. mgr.; Barbara Parenti, prog. dir.; nat'l rep.: Katz.

Operation: Dec. 1963.

CONNECTICUT

Bridgeport

WHAI-TV (Channel 43)

Bridgeways Communications Corp., 274 Riverside Ave., Westport, CT 06880 (203) 227-0537.

Michael K. Vlock, pres.; Bradley Siegal, gen. mgr.

Operation: October, 1987

Hartford

WFSB-TV (Channel 3)

Post-Newsweek Stations, Connecticut, Inc., 3 Constitution Plaza, Hartford, CT 06103-1892 (203) 728-3333.

Barry Barth, v.p. & gen. mgr.; Dick Ahles, v.p. news; Beth Horowitz, v.p. CRTV svcs.

Operation: 1957; TV sets in area: 1,327,800.

WHCT-TV (Channel 18)

Astroline Communications Co., 18 Garden St., Hartford, CT 06105 (203) 547-1818.

Richard P. Ramirez, gen. mgr.; P.J. Lewis, natl. sls. mgr.; Terry Planell, sta. mgr. & prog. dir.; Paul Rossi, dir. eng.; natl. rep.: ITS.

Operation: Aug. 4, 1954.

WTIC (Channel 61)

Arch Communications, Inc., One Corporate Center, Hartford, CT 06103; (203) 527-6161.

Arnold L. Chase, pres.; Edward T. Karlick, gen. mgr.; Robert Gluck, v.p. & gen. sls. mgr.; Jim Perry, chief eng.; nat'l rep.: Katz.

Operation: September, 1984.

New Britain

WVIT (Channel 30) NBC

1422 New Britain Ave., West Hartford, CT 06110 (203) (203) 521-3030.

Al Bova, v.p./gen. mgr.; Aaron Olander, gen. sls. mgr.

Operation: 1953; TV sets in area: 820,000.

New Haven-Hartford

WTNH-TV (Channel 8) ABC

Cook Inlet Communications, Corp., Box 1859, New Haven, CT 06508 (203) 784-8888.

Lewis Freifeld, pres. & gen. mgr.; Fran Tivald, gen. sls. mgr.; Larry Manne, prog. dir.; Cathy Gugerty, dir. creative svcs.;; Robert Feldman, news dir.; Bob Russo, chief eng.; nat'l rep.: Katz.

Operation: 1948; TV sets in area: 1,949,200.

New London

WTWS (Channel 26)

R&R Media Corp., 216 Broad St., New London, CT 06320; (203) 444-2626.

Richard R. Rangoon, pres.; Jim Kontoleon, gen. mgr., prog. dir., film buyer; Bruce Fox, lcl. sls. mgr.; Steven Ellis, chief eng.

Operation: March, 1985.

Waterbury

WTXX (Channel 20) IND

Channel 20 Enterprises, 414 Meadow St., Waterbury, CT 06702 (203) 575-2020.

Michael Finkelstein, gen. partner; Geoffrey Rose, v.p. & gen. mgr.; Nancy McCormick, prog. dir.; Charles Allen, chief eng.; nat'l rep.: MMT, Inc.

Operation: 1953: TV sets in area: 813,000.

DELAWARE

Wilmington

WTGI-TV (Channel 61)

Delaware Broadcasters Ltd., One Christina Plaza, 303 A St., Wilmington, DE 19801 (302) 654-6161.

Daniel G. Slape, pres. & gen. mgr.; Jack Kline, gen. sls. mgr.; Everett Pettiecord, prom. mgr.; Don Borowitcz, chief eng.

Operation: July, 1986.

DISTRICT OF COLUMBIA

Washington

WDCA-TV (Channel 20)

Channel 20 Inc., 5202 River Rd., Washington, DC 20016.

Richard Williams, v.p. & gen. mgr.; Helen Feinbloom, gen. sls. mgr.; Pedro Perez, dir. of eng.; rep.: Seltel.

Operation: April, 1966; TV households: 1,724,500.

WFTY (Channel 50)

WFTY, Inc., 12276 Wilkins Ave., Rockville, MD 20852 (301) 230-1550.

Andy Ockershausen, v.p. & gen. mgr.; Eddie Sacks, gen. sls. mgr.; Donn Fraser, bus. mgr.; Pat Myers, traffic mgr.; Jim Lang, chief eng.

Operation: 1981.

WJLA-TV (Channel 7) ABC

Allbritton Communications Co., 3007 Tilden St., N.W. Washington, DC 20008.

Michael Moore, pres. & CEO; John Long, exec. v.p. & gen. mgr.; Jane Cohen, v.p. opns.; Thursa C. Thomas, v.p. communications; Bob Reiehblum, news dir.; Bob Casazza, v.p. mktg.; Joe DelGrosso, sls. mgr.; John Toilefson, v.p. eng.; natl. rep.: Petry.

WRC-TV (Channel 4) NBC

National Broadcasting Co., 4001 Nebraska Ave., N.W., Washington, DC 20016 (202) 885-4000.

Allan Horlick, v.p. & gen. mgr.; Larry Spero, dir. sls.; Kathy McCampbell, dir. prog.; Bret Marcus, news dir.; Tom Mann, dir. eng.

Operation: June, 1947; TV households: 4,637,400.

WTTG (Channel 5) FOX

Fox TV Stations, Inc., 5151 Wisconsin Ave., N.W. Washington DC 20016 (202) 244-5151.

Betty Endicott, v.p. & gen. mgr.; Michael Wortsman, v.p. & gen. sls. mgr.; Gary Quinn, chief eng.; William Cunningham, v.p. & bus. mgr.; Lindy Spero, v.p. & creative srvcs. dir.; nat'l rep.: Telerep.

Operation: 1947; TV sets in area: 2,647,100.

WUSA-TV (Channel 9) CBS

A division of the Evening News Association, Inc., 4001 Brandywine St., NW, Washington, DC 20016 (202) 364-3900.

Henry K. Yaggi, III, pres. & gen. mgr.; Lawrence P. Herbster, v.p.-bus. aff.; Steve Cook, gen. sls. mgr.; Sandra Butler-Jones, v.p.-bdcst. opns.; Herb Schubarth, v.p.-Gannett eng.; nat'l rep.: Blair.

Operation: 1949; TV households in ADI area: 1,390,300.

FLORIDA
Cape Coral

WFTX (Channel 36) FOX

Wabash Valley Bdcstg., Inc., 621 Pine Island Rd., Cape Coral, FL 33991 (813) 574-3636.

Chris Duffy, pres.; Chris Andrews, gen. mgr.; Rod Hall, sls. mgr.; Merrily Huff, prog. dir.; Dick Enderwood, prom. mgr.; Jerry Blevins, chief eng.; natl. rep.: ITS.

Operation: October, 1985.

Clearwater

WCLF (Channel 22)

Christian Television Corp., Inc., 6922 142nd Ave., N., Largo, FL 34641 (813) 535-5622.

Robert D'Andrea, gen. mgr.; Carl Berger, chief eng.

Operation: 1979.

Clermont

WKCF (Channel 68)

Press Bdcstg. Co., 5125 Adamson St., Suite 650, Orlando, FL 32804 (407) 628-4043.

Robert E. McAllan, pres.; Carlo Anneke, dir. of TV; Skip Painton, gen. mgr.; Nelle Ayers, sta. mgr.; Mike Kerrigan, gen. sls. mgr.; Chuck Hathaway, prog. coord.; Nancy Grassbart, promo. mgr.; Joe Addalia, acting chief eng.; nat'l rep.: ITS.

Operation: December, 1988.

Cocoa

WTGL-TV (Channel 52)

Box 1852, 26 Forrest Ave., Cocoa, FL 32922 (305) 631-2730.

Robert D'Andrea, pres.; Ken Mieksell, gen. mgr.; Phil Grace, v.p.; Jim Goodling, treas.; Gene Polino, secty.; Ken Mikesell, opns. dir.; Bob Kennedy, prog. dir.; Bill Bryan, chief eng.

Operation: 1982.

Daytona Beach-Orlando

WESH-TV (Channel 2) NBC

WESH-TV Broadcasting, Inc., P.O. Box 1551, Daytona Beach, FL 32015; (904) 252-2222; P.O. Box 547697, Orlando, FL 32854 (407) 645-2222.

Nolan Quam, pres. & gen. mgr.; Kenneth Smith, sta. mgr.; Paul W. Sherno, mktg. & promo. dir.; Mike Gehring, v.p. & dir. sls.; nat'l rep.: Petry.

Operation: 1956; TV households: 2,100,000.

Fort Lauderdale

WSCV (Channel 51)

Telemundo Group, Inc., 4035 N. 29th Ave., Hollywood, FL 33022 (305) 947-0051.

Julio Rumbaut, pres.

Operation: 1980.

Fort Myers

WBBH-TV (Channel 20) NBC

Waterman Broadcasting Corp. of Florida, 3719 Central Ave., Fort Myers, FL 33901 (813) 939-2020.

Steven H. Pontius, v.p. & gen. mgr.; Robert Cleveland, chief eng.; Gerald W. Poppe, dir. fin.; Diane Gower, gen. sls. mgr.; Chere Avery, news dir./anchor.

Operation: December, 1968; TV households: 235,400.

WINK-TV (Channel 11) CBS

Fort Myers Broadcasting Co., 2824 Palm Beach Blvd., Fort Myers, FL 33902 (813) 334-1331.

Edward J. McBride, pres.; Robert F. Doty, v.p. & gen. mgr.; Jr.; Mike Dixon, gen. sls. mgr.; Clarence Mosley, dir. eng.; Jim Bennett, news dir.; Fred Greene, public affairs dir.; nat'l rep.: Blair Television.

Operation: 1954.

Fort Pierce

WTVX (Channel 34) CBS

WTVW, Inc., Box 3434, Ft. Pierce, FL 34954 (407) 464-3434.

Frank K. Spain, pres.; Lynwood N. Wright, gen. mgr.; Eric Reed, prog. dir.; Valerie Hinton, promo. dir.; Max Berryhill, chief, eng.; nat't rep.: Seltel.

Operation: April 5, 1966; TV households: 69,400.

Fort Walton Beach

WFGX (Channel 35)

Family Group Ltd. II, 105 Beach Dr., Fort Walton Beach, FL 32548 (904) 863-3235.

Henry A. Ash, pres.; Patrick J. McNanara, gen. mgr. & film buyer; Frank Smith, gen. sls. mgr.; Jacquelyn S. Steiger, prog. dir.; Larry Counts, promo. mgr.; Arthur Ellington, chief eng.

Operation: Apr. 7, 1987.

WPAN (Channel 53)

Ft. Walton Beach Broadcasting, 11 Tupelo Ave., S.E., Ft. Walton Beach, FL 32548; (904) 244-5353.

Elbert R. Davis, pres. & gen. mgr.; Hank Taylor, sta. mgr., prog. dir. & film buyer; Jim Riggs, gen. sls. mgr.; Patty Vogt, promo. mgr.; Jerry O'Laughlin, news dir.; Richard Gilbert, chief eng.; nat'l rep.: Adam Young.

Operation: February, 1984.

Gainesville

WCJB (Channel 20) ABC

Gainesville Television, Inc., P.O. Box WCJB, Gainesville, FL 32602 (904) 377-2020.

Carolyn Catlin, v.p. & gen. mgr.; Bruce Swearingen, gen. sls. mgr.; Karen Woolfstead, prog. dir.; Michael A. Sherrill, chief eng.

Operation: 1971.

Hollywood

WYHS (Channel 69)

Channel 69 of Hollywood, 3600 S. St., RD. 7, Miramar, FL 33023 (305) 963-6900.

Eddie L. Whitehead, pres. & gen. mgr.

Operation: Aug. 10, 1988.

Jacksonville

WAWS-TV (Channel 30)

Malrite of Jacksonville, Inc., 8675 Hogan Rd., Jacksonville, FL 33216 (904) 642-3030.

Lynn Fairbanks, sta. gen. mgr.; Dan Gasby, gen. sls. mgr.; Joe Gersh, nat'l sls. mgr.; Richard M. Sullivan, dir. of prog. & operations.; nat'l rep.: I.N.T.V.

Operation: 1981.

WJKS-TV (Channel 17) NBC

9117 Hogan Rd., Box 17000, Jacksonville, FL 32216 (904) 641-1700.

L. W. White, v.p. & gen. mgr.; David Ayotte, opns. mgr.; Kathryn Bacon, promo. mgr.; Michael Crew, news dir.; Gus Mithoff, bus. mgr.; Roy Tym, gen. sls. mgr.; Joyce Lueders, prgm. mgr.
Operation: Feb. 1966.

WJXT (Channel 4) CBS

WJXT, operated by the Post-Newsweek Stations, Florida Inc., P.O. Box 5270, 1851 Southampton Road, Jacksonville, FL 32207 (904) 399-4000.
Steve Wasserman, v.p. & gen. mgr.; Ann Pace, v.p. & prog. dir.; Christy Birong, dir. community affairs; Don Carmichael, v.p. & gen. sls. mgr.; Ken Kaminski, bdcst. opns. mgr.; Cindy Hass, op. mgr.; Jim Biggers, eng. mgr.; David Way, bus. mgr.; Bart Feder, news dir.; natl. rep.: Petry.
Operation: 1949; TV sets in area: 546,000.

WNFT (Channel 47)

North Florida 47, Inc., 2117 University Blvd., So., Jacksonville, FL 32216 (904) 725-4700.
Ray Davis, v.p. & gen. mgr.; Phil St. Laurent, promo.-opns. mgr.; Lynn Mortimer, gen. sls. mgr.; Dave Murphy, bus. mgr.; Leanza Cornett, news dir.; Karen Gorman, prog. dir.; Charles McHan, chief eng.
Operation: 1980.

WTLV (Channel 12) ABC

Television 12 of Jacksonville, Inc., Television P.O. Box TV-12, Jacksonville, FL 32231 (904) 354-1212.
Linda Rios Brook, pres. & gen. mgr.; Ken Bauder, gen. sls. mgr.; Charles Self, nat'l sls. mgr.; Paul Baldwin, news dir.; Jerry Nordsiek, chief eng.
Operation: 1957.

Lakeland

WTMV (Channel 32)

4332 S. Florida Ave., Lakeland, FL 33803 (813) 376-4224
Dan L. Johnson, gen. mgr.; Betty Jo Johnson, sta. mgr.; Robert Hughes, promo. mgr.; Bill Brister, chief eng.
Operation: Arpil, 1986.

Leesburg

WACX-TV (SuperChannel 55)

Sharp Communications, Inc., 4520 Parkbreeze Ct., Orlando, FL 32808 (407) 297-0155.
Claud Bowers, pres. & gen. mgr.; Randy Rivers, prog. dir.; Carol Gentry & Ann Borderick, office mgrs.; Gary Hawkins, chief eng.; Jo Arrington, traf. dir.; Clairece Kibler, sls. mgr.
Operation: 1982.

Melbourne

WAYK (Channel 26)

TV 56 Ltd., 6525 Babcock St., S.E., Palm Bay, FL 32909 (305) 725-0056.
William Varecha, pres. & film buyer; Lana Johnson, gen. sls. mgr.; Michelle Phillips, asst. prog. dir.; Debra Scott, prom. mgr.; Donna Skattum, news dir.; Steve Schrader, chief eng.
Operation: June, 1986.

WBSF (Channel 43)

Blackstar Communications, Inc., 4450 Enterprise Ct., Melbourne, FL 32935(305) 254-4343.
John Oxendine, pres.; Ed Parker, v.p. & gen. mgr.; Sandie Schroedel, prog. dir.; Ron Marshall, chief eng.
Operation: July, 1982.

Miami

WBFS (Channel 33)

Ch. 33, Inc., 16550 N.W. 52 Ave., Miami, FL 33014; (305) 621-3333.
Milt Grant, pres.; Jerry Carr, gen. mgr.; Roger Green, gen. sls. mgr.
Operation: December, 1984.

WCIX-TV (Channel 6) CBS

CBS Television Stations, 8900 NW 18th Terrace, Miami, FL; (305) 593-0606.
Allen Sheklan, v.p.-gen. mgr.; Joy Newman, v.p. & sls. mgr.; Lee Sussman, bus. mgr.; Bernie Wimmers, dir. eng.; nat'l rep.: CBS Spot Sales. Seltel.
Operation: Sept. 1967; TV households: 1,213,200.

WDZL (Channel 39)

39 Bcstg. Ltd., 2055 Lee St., Hollywood, FL 33020 (305) 925-3939.
Odyssey Partners, owner; Harvey Cohen, exec. v.p. & gen. mgr.; Cyrus Russell, gen. sls. mgr.; Henry Hirsch, promo. mgr.; Robert Castillo, chief eng.; nat'l. rep.: Katz.
Operation: October, 1982.

WHFT-TV (Channel 45)

Trinity Bdcstg. of Florida, 3324 Pembroke Rd., Pembroke, FL 33021; (305) 962-1700.
Paul F. Crouch, pres.; Charles Saffell, sta. mgr.; Michael S. Everett, chief eng.
Operation: 1975.

WLTV (Channel 23)

Spanish International Communications Corp., 2600 SW Third Ave., Miami, FL 33186 (305) 856-2323.
Jose C. Cancela, v.p. & gen. mgr.; Cristina Schwartz, nat'l sls. mgr.; Marisa Chaves, lcl. sls. mgr.; Efrain Rivera, dir. eng.
Operation: 1954.

WPLG (Channel 10) ABC

Post-Newsweek Stations of FL Inc., 3900 Biscayne Blvd., Miami, FL 33137 (305) 576-1010.
John G. Garwood, v.p. & gen. mgr.; Mike Dorsey, v.p. sls. & mktg.; Sharon Harrison, opns. mgr.; Sherry Burns, prog. dir.; Jeff Kurtz, natl. sls. mgr.; Don Hain, chief eng.
Operation: November 1961; TV households: 1,925,000.

WSVN (Channel 7) NBC

Sunbeam Television Corp., 1401 79th Street Causeway, Miami, FL 33141 (305) 751-6692.
Edmund N. Ansin, pres.; Robert W. Leider, v.p. & gen. mgr.; John Fenwick, sls. mgr.; Mark Mayo, contr.; Merlin Haynie, chief eng.; Vicky Gregorian, ops. mgr.; Stacey Marks, creative services mgr.; nat'l rep.: Harrington, Righter & Parsons, Inc. Southern: Clem & Lowrance.
Operation: 1956; TV Households: 1,156,700.

WTVJ (Channel 4) NBC

WTVJ-TV, Inc., 316 N. Miami Ave., Miami, FL 33128 (305) 379-4444.
Dick Lobo, gen. mgr.; Alan Thiel, bus. mgr.; Nancy Valenta, news dir.; Dick Wexo, gen. sls. mgr.; Barry Allentuck, nat'l. sls. mgr.; Judy Girard, dir. pgrm.; Linda Button, dir. adv./promo.; nat'l rep.: NBC Spot Sales.
Operation: 1949; TV homes in area: 1,259,900.

Naples

WEVU (Channel 26) ABC

Caloosa TV Corp., 3451 Bonita Bay Blvd., Bonita Springs, FL 33923 (813) 332-0076.

Ray Karpowicz, pres. & gen. mgr.; Larry Landaker, v.p., sta. mgr. & gen. sls. mgr.; John Buckey, promo. mgr.; David McKelvey, v.p. eng.; Sue Peters, prog. dir. & film buyer; nat'l rep.: Seltel.

Operation: 1974.

Ocala

WOGX (Channel 51)

Wabash Valley Bdcstg. Corp., Box 3985, Ocala, FL 32678 (904) 351-5551.

Mel Grossman, v.p. & gen. mgr.; Randy Keiser, pgm. dir.

Operation: January, 1983.

Orlando

WAYQ (Channel 26)

Beach Television Partners, 944 Sea Breeze Blvd., Daytona Beach, FL 32018 (904) 254-0812.

William Varecha, CEO, gen. mgr. & film buyer; Wayne Croasdell, gen. sls. mgr.; Michele Phillips, prog. dir.; Debra Scott, promo. mgr.; Donna Skattum, news dir.; Ron Fries, chief eng.

Operation: October, 1988.

WCPX-TV (Channel 6) CBS

First Media Corp., P.O. Box 606000, Orlando, FL 32860 (305) 291-6000.

Glenn Potter, pres.; Michael Schweitzer, v.p.-gen. mgr.; Jim Posey, gen. sls. mgr.; Everett Hughes, prog. mgr.; Robert Diehl, chief eng.; nat'l rep.: Katz.

Operation: 1954; TV homes in area: 1,087,500.

WFTV (Channel 9) ABC

WFTV, Inc., 639 W. Central, Orlando, FL 32802 (305) 841-9000.

Clifton L. Conley, v.p. & gen. mgr.; Lou Sopowitz, gen. sls. mgr.; Paul Warnock, chief eng.; Scott Post, contr.

WOFL-TV (Channel 35)

Meredith Corp., 35 Skyline Dr., Lake Mary, FL 32746.

Norris Reichel, v.p. & gen. mgr.; Martin Ross, gen. sls. mgr.; Tom Calato, natl. sls. mgr.; Sharon DeLuca, lcl. sls. mgr.; Jim Miotke, sls.-rsrch. dev. dir.; Mark Simonsen, reg. sls. mgr.; Kate McSweeny, prog. mgr.; nat'l rep.: MMT Sales.

Operation: 1979.

Palm Beach

WPTV (Channel 5) NBC

Scripps-Howard Bcastg. Co., P.O. Box 510, Palm Beach, FL 33480. Studio: 622 N. Flagler Drive, West Palm Beach, FL (305) 655-5455.

William J. Brooks, gen. mgr.; Jim Knight, asst. gen. mgr. & gen.sls. mgr.; Arvo O. Katajisto, ops. dir.; Ed Roos, chief eng.; nat'l rep.: Blair.

Operation: Aug. 1954. TV households: 1,152,800.

Panama City

WJHG-TV (Channel 7) NBC

WJHG-TV, P.O. Box 2349, Panama City, FL 32401 (904) 234-2125.

James H. Gray, Jr., pres.; J. Jerry Smithwick, v.p. & gen. mgr.; Roger Jones, sales mgr.; Jack Crusan, prod. mgr.; Scott Clark, chief eng.; nat'l rep.: Katz.

Operation: 1953; TV households: 293,700.

WMBB (Channel 13) ABC

Buford Television, Inc., Box 1340, Panama City, FL 32401 (904) 769-2313.

Bob Buford, pres.; David Jernigan, exec. v.p. & gen. mgr.; Patti Clements, prog. dir.; Steve Cook, creative svcs. mgr.; Wendell Nelson, chief eng.; Paula Lunsford, bus. mgr.; Judi Barnes, lcl. sls. mgr.; Tom Najjar, regl. sls. mgr.; Jerry Fisher, news dir.

Operation: October, 1973; TV households: 255,200.

Pensacola

WEAR-TV (Channel 3) ABC

Heritage Media Corp., Box 12278, Pensacola, FL 32581 (904) 455-7311.

David N. Walthall, pres.; Jack J. Robinette, pres., TV div.; M. J. Groothand, gen. mgr. & film buyer; Bob Shields, gen. sls. mgr.; Joe Smith, op. mgr.; Harry Babb, chief eng.; A. P. Neumann, news. dir.; Kathy Musial, promo. dir.

Operation: 1954; TV households: 483,400.

WJTC (Channel 44)

Channel 44, Ltd., 700 S. Palafox St., Pensacola, FL 32501; (904) 438-4444.

Robert J. Williamson, pres.

Operation: November, 1984.

St. Petersburg

WTOG (Channel 44)

Hubbard Broadcasting Inc., 365-105th Terrace, N.E. St. Petersburg, FL 33716 (813) 576-4444.

Stanley S. Hubbard, pres.; Edward G. Aiken, gen. mgr.; Alan B. Frank, gen. sls. mgr.; John Kays, chief eng.

Operation: 1968.

WTSP-TV (Channel 10) ABC

Great American TV & Radio Co., St. Petersburg, FL, P.O. Box 10,000, St. Petersburg, FL 33733 (813) 477-1010.

Vincent F. Barresi, v.p. & gen. mgr.; Paul Siracuse, gen. sls. mgr.; Larry E. Cazavan, prog. dir. & film buyer; Barbara Sobocinski, promo. mgr.; P.J. Ford, dir. eng.

Sarasota

WWSB (Channel 40) ABC

Southern Bdcst. Corp. of Sarasota, 5725 Lawton Dr., Sarasota, FL 34233 (813) 922-0777.

Douglas C. Barker, pres. & gen. mgr.; J. Manuel Calvo, exec. v.p. & asst. gen. mgr.; Linda Des Marais, v.p. & sta. mgr.; Stanley B. Cramley, v.p. sls.

Operation: 1971.

Tallahassee

WTWC (Channel 40) NBC

Holt-Robinson TV, Inc., 8440 Deerlake Rd., Tallahassee, FL 32312 (904) 893-4140.

Bob Robinson, pres.; Tom Maguire, exec. v.p. & gen. mgr.; Wayne Boyd, gen. sls. mgr.; Ed Shaper, dir. eng.; Gil Daspit, prog. dir.; nat'l rep.: Seltel.

Operation: April, 1983.

WTXL-TV (Channel 27) ABC

Tallahassee 27 Ltd. Partnership, 8927 Thomasville Rd., Tallahassee, FL 32312; (904) 898-3127.

Joseph D. Tydings, pres.; Carl V. Bruce, v.p.-gen. mgr.; Chris Aldridge, gen. sls. mgr. & dir. opns.

Operation: September, 1976.

Tampa

WBHS (Channel 50)

Silver King Bdcstg. of Tampa, Inc., 2505 118th Ave., N., St. Petersburg, FL 33716 (813) 684-5550.

W. James Goodman, v.p. & gen. mgr.; Jackson M. Cooper, prog. dir.; J. Allen McCarthy, chief eng.

Operation: Feb. 1, 1988.

WFLA (Channel 8) NBC

905 East Jackson St., P.O. Box 1410, Tampa, FL 33601 (813) 228-8888.

Robert T. Sutton, pres.; James G. Saunders, v.p. & gen. mgr.; Paul Catoe, gen. sls. mgr.; Doug Duperrault, prog. dir.; Ardell Hill, chief eng.

Operation: 1955; TV sets in area: 1,199,760.

WFTS (Channel 28)

Tampa Bay TV, Inc., 4501 E. Columbus Dr., Tampa, FL 33605; (813) 623-2828.

Jim Major, v.p. &gen. mgr.; Larry Jopek, gen. sls. mgr.; Joseph Logsdon, prog. dir.; Laura Barton, promo. mgr.; Lee Melvin, eng. mgr.; Marsha Hames, nat'l sls. mgr.; Lu Romero, prod. mgr.; Joy Petit, comm. aff. mgr.; Paul Wilson, bus. mgr.; nat'l rep.: Blair.

Operation: November, 1981.

WTVT (Channel 13) CBS

WTVT Holdings, Inc., 3213 West Kennedy Blvd., Box 31113, Tampa, FL 33631; Transmitter, Route 1, Box 767, Riverview, FL 33569 (813) 876-1313.

Clarence V. McKee, pres. & CEO; C. David Whitaker, v.p. & gen. mgr.; John Westerberg, gen. sls. mgr.; Carol Mountain, prod. mgr.; Dick A'Hearn, oper. mgr.; Bob Franklin, news dir.; Lowell Otto, chief eng.; nat'l rep.: Tele Rep.

Operation: 1955; TV sets in area: 1,131,400.

W. Palm Beach

WFLX (Channel 29)

4119 West Blue Heron Blvd., West Palm Beach, FL 33404 (305) 845-2929.

Murray J. Green, v.p. & gen. mgr.; John C. Chaffee, pres., TV div.; nat'l rep.: Petry.

Operation: 1982.

WPEC-TV (Channel 12) CBS

Fairfield Drive, P. O. Box 24612, West Palm Beach, FL 33416 (305) 844-1212.

Alex W. Dreyfoos, Jr., pres.; Allen Sternberg, prog. dir.; Robert H. Lawson Jr., v.p. sls.; Larry Henrichs, news dir.; George Denner, chief eng.

Operation: 1955.

GEORGIA

Albany

WALB-TV (Channel 10) NBC)

Gray Communications Systems, Inc., P.O. Box 3130, Albany, GA 31708-7601 (912) 883-0154.

James H. Gray, Jr., pres.; Connie Greene, secty.; Phillip R. Greene, v.p. & gen. mgr.; Barbara Jones, treas.; William N. Williams, chief eng.; nat'l rep.: Katz.

Operation: 1954.

WTSG (Channel 31) FOX

Newsouth Bdcstg. Inc., P.O. Box 4050, Albany, GA 31708 (912) 453-3100.

Robert I. Ratcliff, exec. v.p. & gen. mgr.; Carol Ayers, gen. sls. mgr.; R. Darby Ratcliff, prog. dir.; Tony Gainous, chief eng.

Operation: 1982.

Atlanta

WAGA-TV (Channel 5) CBS

Gillett Communications of Atlantica, Inc., Box 4207, Atlanta, GA 30302 (404) 875-5551.

Jack Sander, pres. & gen. mgr.; John Dolive, dir. bdcst. opns.; nat'l rep.: Gillett TV sales.

Operation: 1949.

WATL (Channel 36)

WATL-TV, One Monroe Place, Atlanta, GA 30324 (404) 881-3600.

David Henderson, pres.; John Serrao, v.p. & gen. mgr.; Gene McHugh, gen. sls. mgr.; Don Hess, prog. dir.; Doug Furce, prod. mgr.; John Pelham, chief eng.; nat'l rep.: Katz.

Operation: 1969.

WGNX-TV (Channel 46)

Tribune Broadcasting Co., 1810 Briarcliff Rd., P.O. Box 98097, Atlanta, GA 30359 (404) 325-4646.

Herman Ramsey, v.p. & gen. mgr.; Wayne Spracklin, gen. sls. mgr.; Lorrie Shilling, prog. mgr.

Operation: 1971.

WSB-TV (Channel 2) ABC

Cox Broadcasting Corporation, 1601 W. Peachtree Street, N.E., Atlanta, GA 30309 (404) 897-7000.

Andrew S. Fisher, v.p. & gen. mgr.; David Lippoff, news dir.; A. R. Van Cantfort, prgm. mgr.; Bruce Baker, sls. dir.; Herbert Gilbert, dir. eng.

Operation: 1948.

WTBS (Channel 17)

Superstation, Inc., 1050 Techwood Dr., N.W., Atlanta, GA 30318 (404) 892-1717.

R. E. Turner, chm.; Gerald Hagan, pres.; Robert Levi, exec. v.p.; William Merriam, exec. v.p. prod. & oper.; Jack Verner, chief eng.

Operation: 1967.

WVEU (Channel 69)

Broadcasting Corp. of Georgia, 2700 N.E. Expressway, Bldg. A, Phoenix Business Park, Atlanta, GA 30345 (404) 325-6929.

David J. Harris, pres.; Vance L. Eckersley, v.p. & gen. mgr.; Mann Reed, gen. sls. mgr. & sta. mgr.; Gary Kelly, chief eng.; Marti Chitwood, p.a. mgr.; Peter L. Mandell, promo. mgr.; Sheldon Moss, lcl. sls. mgr.; Mary F. McKee, prog. mgr.

Operation: 1981.

WXIA-TV (Channel 11) NBC

Pacific & Southern Broadcasting Co., Inc., 1611 W. Peachtree St., N.E., Atlanta, GA 30309 (404) 892-1611.

Harvey Mars, pres. & gen. mgr.; Jack Lease, v.p. opns.; Howard Kaufman, v.p. & gen. sls. mgr.; Wayne Freedman, nat'l sls. mgr.; Steve Smith, news dir.; Jerry Michel, dir. eng.; John Heinen, promo. mgr.
Operation: Sept., 1951; TV households: 1,568,400.

Augusta

WAGT-TV (Channel 26) NBC

P.O. Box 1526, Augusta, GA 30903 (404) 826-0026.
A. Hal Edwards, gen. mgr.; Lee Sheridan, sta. mgr.; James Halpin, gen. sls. mgr.; Al Van Dinteren, chief eng.
Operation: Dec. 24, 1968; TV households: 222,000.

WJBF (Channel 6) ABC

Pegasus Bdcst. of Augusta, Georgia, Inc., Box 1404, Augusta, GA 30903 (803) 722-6664.
Terry R. Sams, pres. & gen. mgr.; John R. Bennett, v.p.-opns. & sta. mgr.; Ray Erb, v.p.-sls. & gen. sls. mgr.; Marty Bosshart, nat'l sls. mgr.; Mary Miller, bus. mgr.; Art Cabot, v.p.-prog. & promo.; Gerald Levy, v.p.-community relations; William Doker, chief eng.; Jimmy Thomas, prod. mgr.; Peter Michenfelder, news dir.
Operation: 1953; TV sets in area: 608,000.

WRDW-TV (Channel 12)

Television Station Partners, Drawer 1212, Augusta, GA 30903.
Ralph E. Becker, pres.; William A. Service, v.p. & gen. mgr.; Mary Mixon, gen. sls. mgr.; Lee Davis, chief eng.; Steve Johnston, program mgr.
Operation: Feb. 1954; TV households: 678,600.

Columbus

WLTZ (Channel 38) NBC

Columbus TV, Inc., Box 12289, Columbus, GA 31995; (404) 561-3838.
J. Curtis Lewis, Jr., pres.; Bob Walton, v.p. & gen. mgr.; Tom Breazeale, gen. sls. mgr.; R.C. Bartlett, prog. dir.; Sandra Stouder, promo mgr.; Borden Black, news dir.; Bob Hook, chief eng.; nat'l rep.: Adam Young.
Operation: October, 1970.

WRBL-TV (Channel 3) CBS

Columbus Broadcasting Co., Inc., 1350 13th Ave., Columbus, GA 31994 (404) 322-3333.
Mark Prather, v.p. & gen. mgr.; Alice Upshaw, pgm. dir.; Teresa Baker, gen. sls. mgr.; Royce Hackett, chief eng.
Operation: 1953; TV sets in area: 1,524,600.

WTVM (Channel 9) ABC

WTVM, Inc., Box 1848, Columbus, GA 31902 (404) 324-4671.
Wayne Daugherty, pres. & gen. mgr.; W. Carroll Ward, prog. dir.; Richard Heath, sls. mgr.; Dick Byrd, news dir.; David Williams, chief eng.; nat'l rep.: Blair Television.
Operation: 1953; TV sets in area: 719,900.

WXTX (Channel 54)

Columbus Family TV, Inc., 6524 Buena Vista Rd., Box 12188, Columbus, GA 31907; (404) 561-5400.
Ed Groves, gen. mgr.; Reid Walls, gen. sls. mgr.; Denise Murray, prog. dir.; Joy Scarbrough, promo. mgr.; Cliff Curley, film buyer, April Henry, film dir.; Karen Krieger, news dir.; Rick Liverett, chief eng.
Operation: June, 1983.

Macon

WGXA (Channel 24) ABC

Russell Rowe Communications, Box 340, Macon, GA 31297 (912) 745-2424.
Don Elliot Heald, pres.; Ken Gerdes, v.p. & gen. mgr.; Frank Shurling, gen. sls. mgr.; Jim Baker, opns. mgr.; Kelly Causey, promo. mgr.; Ron Wildman, news dir.; Richard Blanton, chief eng.; nat'l rep.: Blair.
Operation: 1982.

WMAZ-TV (Channel 13) CBS

Multimedia Broadcasting Company, Box 5008, Macon, GA 31213 (912) 746-1313.
James T. Lynagh, pres.; Don McGouirk, v.p. & gen. mgr.; Gostin Freeney, gen. sls. mgr.; Sydney Thum, prog. dir,; Lacy Worrell, dir. of eng.; nat'l rep.: Katz.

WMGT Channel 41) NBC

Morris Network, Inc., Box 4328, Macon, GA (912) 745-4141.
Dean Hinson, pres.; Charles Morris, chmn.; L.A. Sturdivant, gen. mgr.; Joe Ryan, gen. sls. mgr.; Lisa Hill, prom. mgr.; Debbie Soria, prog. dir.; Keith Murphy, news dir.; Joe Sears, chief eng.; nat'l rep.: Seltel.
Operation: 1968.

Savannah

WJCL (Channel 22) ABC

Lewis Bcstg. Corp., 10001 Abercorn St., Extension, Savannah, GA 31406 (912) 925-0022.
J. Fred Pierce, exec. v.p. & gen. mgr.; Mary Poythress, pgm. dir.; Larry Walker, opns. dir.
Operation: 1970.

WSAV (Channel 3) NBC

WSAV-TV, P.O. Box 2429, 1430 East Victory Drive., Savannah, GA 31402 (912) 651-0300. Station is owned by News-Press & Gazette Co., St. Joseph, MO; David R. Bradley, Jr., pres.
Harvey Libow, gen. mgr.; Jim Davis, gen. sls. mgr.; Keith Young, news dir.; Cecil K. Daniel, Jr., prod. mgr.; Dave Stagnitto, opns. mgr.; Byron Strong, chief eng.; nat'l rep.: Petry.
Operation: 1956; TV sets in area: 206,500.

WTOC-TV (Channel 11) CBS

American Savannah Broadcasting Co., 516 Abercorn St., Savannah, GA 31401 (912) 234-1111.
Jess Mooney, v.p. & gen. mgr.; Bud Bradbury, prom. dir.; LaVaughn Thompson, chief eng.; nat'l rep.: Katz Agency Inc.
Operations: 1954; TV sets in area: 394,800.

Thomasville, GA-Tallahassee, FL

WCTV (Channel 6) CBS

John H. Phipps, P.O. Box 3048, Tallahassee, FL 32315 (904) 893-6666.
John E. Phipps, chm.; Dennis O. Boyle, pres.; Jim Caruthers, v.p. & gen. mgr.; Melvin Blank, opns. mgr.; nat'l rep.: Blair TV.
Operation: 1955; TV sets in area: 416,500.

Toccoa

WNEG-TV (Channel 32)

Stephens County Broadcasting Co., 100 Blvd., Box 907, Toccoa, GA 30577; (404) 886-0032.
Roy E. Gaines, pres. & gen. mgr.; David Austin, gen. sls.

mgr.; Connie Gaines, prog. dir. & film buyer; Tony Garrison, promo. mgr.; Cindy Wood, prod. mgr.
Operation: September, 1984.

Valdosta

WVGA (Channel 44) ABC

Morris Network, Inc., Box 1588, Valdosta, GA 31601 (912) 242-4444.
Dean Hinson, pres.; Aubrey Wood, gen. mgr.; Marvin L. Keene, gen. sls.-sta. mgr.; Janet Stump, prog.-traf.
Operation: 1980.

HAWAIIAN ISLANDS

Hilo, Hawaii

KGMD-TV (Channel 9) CBS

(Satellite of KGMB-TV, Honolulu)
Lee Enterprises, Inc., 58 Manaolana Pl., Hilo, HI 96720 (808) 935-6221
Lee Carlson, gen. mgr.; Morris Nimi, asst. chief eng.
Operation: 1955.

KHBC-TV (Channel 2)

Kona Hilo Bdcstg. Corp., Box 4250, Hilo, HI 96720 (808) 969-2000.
Bill Evans, pres.; Abe Lagadon, sta. mgr.; Gerri Shimada, prog. dir.; Matt Sanders, Eve Fuller, news dirs.; Charles Epperson, chief eng.
Operation: August, 1983.

KHVO (Channel 13) ABC

(Satellite of KHVH-TV, Honolulu)
Shamrock Bdcstg. Co., Nani Loa Surf Hotel, Hilo, HI 96720 (808) 935-8289.
Operation: May, 1960; TV sets in area.

Honolulu, Oahu

KBFD (Channel 32)

Allen Bdcstg. Corp., 1188 Bishop St., Honolulu, HI 96813 (808) 521-8066.
Kea Sung Chung, pres. & gen. mgr.; Jaeh Hoon Chung, prog. dir.; Alvin C.H. Chang, chief eng.; Sandi Towers, asst. to pres.
Operation: Mar. 7, 1986.

KFVE (Channel 5)

Kailkena Lani TV Corp., 315 Sand Island Rd., Honolulu, HI 96819 (808) 842-5555.
Lee Holmes, pres.; Don Metzger, gen. mgr.; Sharon Kanaley, natl. sls. mgr.; Bryan Holmes, prog. dir.; Debby McGraw, promo. mgr.; Hank Kaul, chief eng.; rep.: ITS.

KGMB TV (Channel 9) CBS

Lee Enterprises, Incorporated 1534 Kapiolani Blvd., Honolulu, HI 96814 P.O. Box 581, Honolulu, HI 96809 (808) 944-5200.
Lee Carlson, gen.. mgr.; Sharon Kanaley, nat'l & gen. sls. mgr.; Phil Arnone, prog. dir., James Manke, news dir.; nat'l rep.: Katz Agency.
Operation: 1952. TV households (State): 261,170.

KHAI (Channel 20)

Media Central, Inc., 735 Sheridan St., Honolulu, HI 96814 (808) 943-1169.
Dan T. Kawakami, gen. mgr.; J. Bautista, gen. sls. mgr.; Sam F. Sugano, prog. dir.; Glenn Tenean, chf. oper.
Operation: December, 1983.

KHNL-TV (Channel 13)

King Bdcstg. Co., 150-B Puuhale Road, Honolulu, HI 96819
Richard J. Blangiardi, gen. mgr.; Shirley Feliciano, bus. mgr.
Operation: July, 1962; TV homes: 320,000.

KHON-TV (Channel 2) Honolulu
KAII-TV (Channel 7) WAILUKU SATELLITE
KHAW-TV (Channel 11) HILO SATELLITE

KHON-TV, Inc. 1116 Auahi St., Honolulu HI 96814.
William S. Snyder, pres. & gen. mgr.; nat'l rep.: HRP
Operation: 1952; TV sets in area: 323,720.

KITV (Channel 4) ABC

Tak Communications, Inc., 1290 Ala Moana Blvd., Honolulu, HI 96814; 545-4444.
Jim Matthews, pres. & gen. mgr.; Bob Kato, chief eng.; Muneo Hamada, bus. mgr.; Wally Zimmerman, news dir.; Mike Ainsworth, prod. mgr.; Tracy Keliihoomalu, prog. dir.
Operation: 1954.

KMGT (Channel 26)

Mount Wilson FM Broadcasters, 970 N. Kalaheo Ave., Kailua-Honolulu, HI 96734 (808) 254-5826.
Saul Levin, pres.; Thomas White, gen. mgr.; Dave Tipton, gen. sls. mgr. Garrett Nakahodo, prog. dir.; Darryl Shiroma, news dir.; Scott Jossart, chief eng.; rep.: Mutual TeleSales
Operation: Dec. 23, 1982.

KWHE (Channel 14)

Le Sea Bdcstg. Corp., 1188 Bishop St., Honolulu, HI 96813 (808) 538-1414.
Steve Smurall, gen. mgr.; Boyd Lions, opns. mgr.; Keith Spencer, chief eng.

Wailuku, Maui

KAII-TV (Channel 7) NBC

(Satellite of KHON-TV, Honolulu) KHON-TV, Inc., 1170 Auahi St., Honolulu, HI 96814.
Personnel: same as KHON-TV, Honolulu.
Operation: Nov. 1958.

KGMV-TV (Channel 3) CBS

(Satellite of KGMB-TV; Honolulu, Heftel Broadcasting-Maui, Inc., P.O. Box 1574, Kahului, HI 96732.
Cecil Heftel, pres., treas. & gen. mgr.; Earl McDaniel, gen. mgr.; Thomas Yoshida, chief eng. & sta. mgr.
Operation: 1955.

KMAU (Channel 12) ABC

(Semi-satellite of separately-owned, KITV, Honolulu)
Maui Publishing Co., Ltd., Box 550, Wailuku, HI 96814.
Operation: Dec., 1955.

IDAHO

Boise

KBCI-TV (Channel 2) CBS

Eugene Television, Inc., 1007 Jefferson St., Boise, ID 83707 (208) 336-5222.
Donald E. Tykeson, pres.; Timothy J. Bever, gen. mgr. & film buyer; Mark Jollie, gen. sls. mgr.; Gary Rogers, chief eng.; rep.:

Katz Television, Art Moore & Associates, Inc. (Pacific Northwest).
Operation: 1953; TV sets in area: 212,000.

KTVB-TV (Channel 7) NBC
KTVB, Inc. 5407 Fairview Ave., P.O. Box 7 Boise, ID 83707 (208) 375-7277.
Steve Clifford, pres.; Robert E. Krueger, v.p. & gen. mgr.; Rod Gramer, news dir.; nat'l rep.: Blair.

Idaho Falls

KIDK-TV (Channel 3) CBS
Retlaw Bdcstg. Co., P.O. Box 2008, Idaho Falls, ID 83403; (208) 522-5100.
Gerry Cornwell, sta. & gen. sls. mgr. & natl. sls. mgr.; Kim Southwick, opns. dir.; Gary Smith, chief eng.; nat'l rep.: Katz.
Operation: 1953; TV sets in area: 107,900.

KIFI-TV (Channel 8)
The Post Company, P.O. Box 2148, Idaho Falls, ID 83401 (208) 523-1171.
Rickie Orchin Brady, gen. mgr.; Herman G. Haefele, sta. mgr.; Shang Beard, chief eng.; nat'l rep.: Seltel.
Operation: 1961.

Lewiston

KIVI (Channel 6) ABC
Sawtooth Communications, Inc., 1866 East Chisholm Dr., Nampa, ID 83651 (208) 336-0500.
Larry J. Chase, pres./gen.mgr.; Ken Ritchie, sls. mgr.; Susu Mahood, local sls. mgr.; Dan Smede, news dir.; Andy Suk, chief eng.; nat'l rep.: Seltel; regional rep.: Tacher.
Operation: 1974.

KLEW-TV (Channel 3) CBS
Retlaw Bdcstg. Co., 2626 17th St., Lewiston, ID 83501; (208) 746-2636.
Fred Fickenwirth, mgr.; Marlin Jackson, chief eng.; Gene Haagenson, news dir.; nat'l rep.: Katz.
Operation: 1955.

Nampa

KTRV (Channel 12)
679 Sixth St., Nampa, ID 83651 (208) 466-1200.
Rex L. McArthur, v.p./gen. mgr.; Diane Frisch, sta. mgr.; Francis Wilson, chief eng.; Jim Barto, bus. mgr.; nat'l rep.: Petry.
Operation: 1981.

Pocatello-Blackfoot

KPVI (Channel 6) ABC
Ambassador Media Corp., P.O. Box 667, Pocatello, ID 83204 (208) 233-6667.
Sen. William Armstrong, pres.; Brian Hogan, v.p. & gen. mgr.; Mike Tracy, gen. sls. mgr.; Tony Divesti, chief eng.; Greg Licht, news dir.; nat'l rep.: Blair.
Operation: 1974; TV households: 102,000.

Twin Falls

KMVT (Channel 11) CBS
KMVT Broadcasting, Inc., 1100 Blue Lakes Blvd., N., Twin Falls, ID 83301 (208) 733-1100.
Jim Underwood, pres.; Lee Wagner, gen. mgr.; George Brown, ops. mgr.; Dennis Lowe, chief eng.; nat'l rep.: Katz.
Operation: 1955; TV sets in area: 60,000.

ILLINOIS

Aurora

WEHS (Channel 60)
Silver King Bdcstg. of Illinois, Inc., 4255 Westbrook Dr., Aurora, IL 60504 (312) 851-5960.
Jim Flynn, pres.; Jeff McGrath, v.p. & gen. mgr.; George Drase & Mario Steranini, rgnl. sls. mgr.; Monica Nettles-Gary, prog. dir.; Sandra Marx, news prod.; Dana Beifus, chief eng.
Operation: April 20, 1982.

Bloomington

WYZZ (Channel 43)
Bloomington Comco, Inc., 2714 East Lincoln St., Bloomington, IL 61701 (309) 662-4373.
G.J. Robinson, pres.; Rod Whisenant, gen. mgr.; Bob Bolton, sls. mgr.; Ethel Esters, prog. mgr.; John Wamsley, chief eng.
Operation: 1982.

Champaign

WCIA (Channel 3) CBS
Midwest Television, Inc., 509 S. Neil St., Champaign, IL 61820 (217) 356-8333.
A. C. Meyer, Jr., pres.; Guy Main, exec. v.p.; Jack B. Everette, exec. v.p. & treas.; Gerald P. Johnson, sls. mgr.; Leonard Davis, nat'l sales mgr.; Ed Mathais, prod. mgr.; Sheila Hickman, prog. dir. & film buyer; nat'l rep.: Petry.
Operation: 1953; TV sets in area: 329,000.

WICD-TV (Channel 15) NBC
Plains Television Partnership, 250 Country Fair Dr., Champaign, IL 61821 (217) 351-8500.
Elmer Balaban, partner; Joe Norris, stn. mgr; Ginger Rush, nat'l sls. mgr. Ed Mason, local sales mgr.; David Boyer, chief eng.; Larry Waters, ops. mgr.; nat'l rep., Katz Television Continental.
Operation: 1959.

Chicago

WBBM-TV (Channel 2) CBS
CBS, Inc., 630 N. McClurg Court, Chicago, IL 60611 (312) 944-6000.
Rod Perth, sta. mgr.; Johnathan Rodgers, v.p. & gen. mgr.; Sam Stallworth, sls. dir.; Karen Miller, bcstg. dir.; Joan Zucker, dir. press reltns.
Operation: 1946; TV sets in area: 2,679,260.

WCFC (Channel 38)
Christian Communications of Chicagoland, Inc., 1 N. Wacker Dr., Chicago, IL 60606. (312) 977-3838.
Jerry K. Rose, pres.; Kevin L. San Hamel, gen. sls. mgr.; Philip E. Mowbray, dir. opns.; David Oseland, prog. dir.; Alan Bolds, prom. mgr.; Jim Tillery, chief eng.
Operation: 1976.

WCIU-TV (Channel 26)
Weigel Bdg. Co., Board of Trade, Chicago, IL 60604.
Howard Shapiro, pres. & gen. mgr.; Peter Zomaya, asst. gen. mgr. & sls. mgr.; Merri Houser, film dir.; Bernie Hoelting, chief

eng.; Ben Larson, Eng. news dir.; Don Aguirre, Span. news. dir.; Norman Shapiro, dir. bus. & lgl. affairs.
Operation: 1964.

WFLD-TV (Channel 32) Fox
Fox TV Stations, Inc., 205 N. Michigan Ave., Chicago, IL 60601.
Cary Jones, v.p. & gen. mgr.; Rich Engberg, v.p. & gen. sls. mgr.; Dwain Schoonover, eng. mgr.; nat'l rep: Petry.
Operation: Jan., 1966; TV households: 3,138,000.

WGN-TV (Channel 9)
WGN, Continental Broadcasting Company, 2501 W. Bradley Pl., Chicago, IL 60618 (312) 528-2311.
Dennis Fitzsimons, v.p./gen. mgr.; Peter Walker, gen. sls. mgr.; Pam Pearson, dir. creative svcs.; Paul Davis, news dir.; Charlotte O'Brien, dir. of community affairs; Jim Zerwekh, dir. prog.

WLS-TV (Channel 7) ABC
WLS Television, Inc., 190 N. State St., Chicago, IL 60601 (312) 750-7777.
Joe Ahern, pres. & gen. mgr.; Mark Grant, gen. sls. mgr.; Tim Bennett, prog. dir.; Tom Dolan, news dir.; nat'l rep.: ABC TV Spot Sales.
Operation: Oct., 1943; TV homes: 2,995,000.

WMAQ-TV (Channel 5) NBC
National Bdcstg. Co., Merchandise Mart, Chicago, IL 60654 (312) 861-5555.
Richard Morse, v.p. & gen. mgr.; Ken Hall, dir. sls.; Lisa Churchville, sls. mgr.; Jim Powell, dir. bdcst. opns. & eng.; Dave Mayber, sls. mgr.; David Finney, prog. dir.; Jim Powell, chief eng. nat'l rep.: NBC Spot Sales.
Operation: 1949; TV sets in area: 3,530,230

WSNS-TV (Channel 44)
Video 44, a Joint Venture, 430 W. Grant Pl., Chicago, IL 60614 (312) 929-1200.
Jose Francisco Lamas, gen. mgr.; Armando Triana, gen. sls. mgr.; John Dickinson, opns. mgr.; Marissa Quiles, prog. dir.; David Cordova, news dir.; Charles Breeding, chief eng.
Operation: April, 1970.

Decatur

WAND (Channel 17) ABC
(Serving Decatur, Springfield & Champaign)
WAND-Television, Inc. (subsidiary of Lin Broadcasting Corp., Inc.), 904 Southside Drive, Decatur, IL 62525 (217) 424-2500.
T. J. Vaughan, v.p. sta. mgr.; Larry Katt, v.p. sls.; Nat'l Rep.: Blair.
Operation: 1953; TV sets in area: 569,506.

WFHL (Channel 23)
Decatur Foursquare Broadcasting, 2510 Parkway Ct., Decatur, IL 62526; (217) 428-2323.
Tim Peterson, pres.; Mark Drestadt, gen. mgr.-prog. dir.; Rita Gray, sls. mgr.; Paul Osborne, news dir.; Greg Danaha, chief eng.
Operation: May, 1984.

Harrisburg

WSIL-TV (Channel 3) ABC Primary
21 W. Poplar St., Harrisburg. IL; 62946.
Mel Wheeler, pres.; Steve Wheeler, gen. mgr. & prog. dir.; Emory McCullough, gen. sls. mgr.; Pat Victoria, chief eng.
Operation: 1953.

Joliet/Chicago

WGBO-TV (Channel 66)
Grant Bcstg. Co., 875 N. Michigan Ave., Suite 3141, Chicago, IL 60611 (312) 751-6666.
Steve Freidheim, gen. mgr.; George Leh, prog. dir.; Chuck Jennings, chief eng.
Operation: 1981.

Marion

WTCT-TV (Channel 27)
Tri-State Christian TV, Rt. 37, Marion, IL 62959 (618) 997-9333.
Garth Coonce, pres. & gen. mgr.; Dan Vawser, prod. mgr.; Christina M. Coonce, prog. dir.; nat'l rep.: Spot Time Ltd.
Operation: 1981.

Moline

WQAD-TV (Channel 8) ABC
3003 Park 16 St., Moline, IL 61625 (309) 764-8888.
H. Oliver Gillespie, pres. & gen. mgr.; Tharon Honeycutt, contr.; Gene Smith, gen. sls. mgr.; Marcia Green, prog. mgr.; Joh Riches, news dir.; Rick Serre, chief eng.
Operation: 1963.

Mount Vernon

WCEE (Channel 13)
Sudbrink Broadcasting Corp. of Ill., 4110 Broadway, Mount Vernon, IL 62864 (618) 822-6900.
Vic Rumore, pres.; Karen Shute, sta. mgr.; Kent Hogshead, chief eng.
Operation: 1983.

Peoria

WEEK-TV (Channel 25) NBC
Eagle Broadcasting Corporation, 2907 Springfield Rd., E. Peoria, IL 61611 (309) 698-2525.
Dennis Upah, v.p. & gen. mgr.; Amy Blain, opns. & promo. mgr.; Ken Tofanelli, chief eng.; Phil Supple, news dir. nat'l rep.: Katz Agency.
Operation: 1953; TV sets in area: 475,000.

WHOI-TV (Channel 19) ABC
Forward of Illinois, Inc. 500 N. Stewart St., Creve Coeur, IL 61611 (309) 698-1919.
Charles E. Sherman, pres. & gen. mgr.; William Thorson, gen. sls. mgr.; David Allen, news dir.; Carl Wolfe, chief eng.; nat'l rep.: Blair.
Operation: Oct. 1953; TV households; 475,300.

WMBD (Channel 31) CBS
Midwest Television, Inc., 3131 N. University, Peoria, IL 61611 (309) 688-3131.
August C. Meyer, Jr., pres.; Guy F. Main, exec. v.p.: Gene Robinson, v.p. and gen. mgr.; Gene C. Robinson, stat. mgr.; Lloyd Peterson, op. mgr.; Paul Baumgartner, chief eng.; nat'l rep.; Petry
Operation: 1958; TV sets in area: 338,300.

Quincy

WGEM-TV (Channel 10) NBC

Quincy Broadcasting Co., 513 Hampshire, P.O. Box 80, Quincy, IL 62306 (217) 228-6600.

T. A. Oakley, pres.; Ralph M. Oakley, v.p. & gen. mgr.; Ben Stewart, natl. slsl. mgr.; Jim Martens, chief eng.; nat'l rep.: Blair.

Operation: 1953; TV sets in area: 372,400.

Rockford

WIFR-TV (Channel 23) CBS

WIFR Television, Inc., 2523 N. Meridian Rd., Rockford, IL 61101.

Jim Grimes, gen. mgr.; Arles Hendershott, news dir.; Keith Bland, sls. mgr.; Will Shears, chief eng.; Doug Warkenthien, prod. mgr.; Barb Schobinger, prog. dir.; Judy Lung, bus. mgr.

Operation: 1965.

WQRF-TV (Channel 39)

Family Group Ltd. IV, 401 S. Main St., Rockford, IL 61101 (815) 987-3950.

Robb Gray, Jr., v.p. & gen. mgr.; Kemp Nichol, gen. sls. mgr.; Paul Klick, promo. mgr.; Dean Turman, chief eng.

Operation: 1978.

WREX-TV (Channel 13) ABC

WREX-TV, West Auburn at Winnebago Rds., Rockford, IL 61103 (815) 968-1813.

Owner: M-L Media Partners Ltd. I. Martin Pompadur, pres.; Ray Chumley, gen. mgr.; Richard Harbison, gen. sls. mgr.; Jack Willard, bus. mgr.; Gerry Meinders, chief eng.; nat'l rep.: Petry.

Operation: September, 1953; TV households: 401,600.

WTVO (Channel 17) NBC

Young Bdcstg. Inc., 1917 N. Meridian Rd. & State, Rockford, IL 61105 (815) 963-5413.

Harold Froelich, v.p. & mgr.; Tom Anderson, gen. sales mgr.; Al Petzke, chief eng.; nat'l rep.: Adam Yound, Inc.

Operation: 1953; TV sets in area: 580,300.

Rock Island

WHBF-TV (Channel 4) CBS

Citadel Communications Co., Ltd., Telco Bldg., 231 18 St., Rock Island, IL 61201 (309) 786-5441.

Phillip J. Lombardo, pres.; Robert Hoffman, gen. mgr.; Al Uzzell, opns. dir.; Coy Bullard, chief eng.; nat'l rep.: Telerep

Operation: 1950; TV sets in area: 486,000.

Springfield

WICS (Channel 20) NBC

2680 East Cook St., Springfield, IL 62703 (217) 753-5620.

John DiMatteo, pres.; Mike Bock, v.p., dir. bdcst. opns.; John V. Connors, v.p. & gen. mgr.; Don Squires, gen. sls. mgr.; Virginia Rush, nat'l sls. mgr.; Jerrold Merritt, chief eng.; Gary Spears, prog. mgr.; Peter Holmes, creative svcs. dir.; H.K. Springer, comtr.; nat'l rep.: Katz Agency.

Operation: 1953: TV sets in area: 805,000.

WRSP (Channel 55)

Springfield Independent TV Co., 3440 Clearlake Ave., Springfield, IL 62702; (217) 523-8855.

Tom Mochel, gen. mgr.; Michael T. Burns, gen. sls. mgr.; Ken Myers, chief eng.; nat'l rep.: Indep. TV Sls.

Operation: June, 1979.

INDIANA

Angola

WINM (Channel 63)

Tri-State Bdcstg., Inc., 2901 N. Clinton St., Ft. Wayne, IN 46805 (219) 484-0630.

Paul C. Paino, pres.; Wayne Paradise, gen. mgr.; Jerry Clark, v.p. sls.; Roger Rhodes, v.p. prog. & film buyer; Margo France, promo. mgr.; Stephen Buyze, chief eng.

Operation: Mar. 10, 1983.

Bloomington

WCLJ (Channel 42)

Trinity Bdcstg. of Indiana, Inc., 2528 U.S. 31 South, Greenwood, IN 46143 (317) 535-5542.

Robert Higley, gen. mgr.

Operation: August, 1987.

WIIB (Channel 63)

Channel 63, Inc., Rt. 1, Box 516, Trafalgar, IN 46181 (317) 878-5407.

Mary Ann Renee, gen. mgr.; Dennis Wallace, chief eng.

Operation: Dec. 27, 1988.

Bloomington-Indianapolis

WTTV (Channel 4) Independent

WTTV, Inc., 3490 Bluff Road, Indianapolis, IN 46217 (217) 787-2211.

Fred Barber, v.p. & gen. mgr.; Will Davis, opns. mgr.; Clyde Dutton, gen. sls. mgr.; Bernie Souers, lcl. sls. mgr.; Thomas Weber, dir. eng.

Operation: 1949; TV sets in area; 2,500,000.

Elkhart-South Bend

WSJV (Channel 28) ABC

WSJV, Inc. (owner)—Subsidiary of Quincy Newspapers (Illinois) Inc., Box 1646, Elkhart, IN 46515 (219) 293-8616; South Bend (219) 674-5106.

Thomas A. Oakley, pres.; Don E. Fuller, v.p. & gen. mgr.; Jon Hart, gen. sls. mgr.; natl rep., Blair.

Operation: 1954; TV sets in ADI: 281,300.

Evansville

WEHT-TV (Channel 25) CBS

Gilmore Broadcasting Corp., P.O. Box 25, Evansville, IN 47701 (812) 424-9215.

James S. Gilmore, Jr., pres.; Douglas A. Padgett, gen. mgr.; Mike Riley, gen. sls. mgr.; Jenny Gager, div. contrl.; Mike Peckenpaugh, chief eng.; nat'l rep.: Katz.

Operation: 1953; TV sets in area: 290,600.

WEVV (Channel 44) Fox Affiliate

Ralph C. Wilson Industries, Inc., 629 Walnut St., Evansville, IN 47708; (812) 424-9201.

Michael Brooks, gen. mgr.; John Sandwell, gen. sls. mgr.; Alice Lovell, prog. dir.; Don Hollingsworth, chief eng.; nat'l rep.: MMT Sales.

Operation: November, 1983.

WFIE (Channel 14) NBC

WFIE, Inc., 1115 Mt. Auburn Rd., Evansville, IN 47712 (812) 426-1414.

Conrad L. Cagle, pres. & gen. mgr.; Shirley Kirk, prog. dir.; Maaion Paul, chief eng.

Operation: 1953; TV sets in area: 214,000.

WTVW (Channel 7) ABC

Woods Communications Group, Inc., 477 Carpenter St., P. O. Box 7, Evansville, IN 47701; (812) 422-1121.

Charles Woods, pres.; Ken Schreiber, gen. mgr.; Ken Hawkins, gen. sls. mgr.; Jan Euras, promo. mgr.; John Sterne, news dir.; John Schuta, chief eng.; nat'l rep.: Seltel.

Operation: 1956; TV sets in area: 247,480.

Fort Wayne

WANE-TV (Channel 15) CBS

Indiana Broadcasting Corp., 2915 W. State Blvd., Fort Wayne, IN 46808 (219) 424-1515.

Frank Moore, pres. & gen. mgr.; Randall Culbertson, fin. mgr.; Mark Meyer, prog. dir.; Herb Lyons, chief eng.; nat'l rep.: Petry.

Operation: 1954; TV sets in area: 253,000.

WFFT-TV (Channel 55)

Great Trails Bdcstg. Corp., 3707 Hillegas Rd., Ft. Wayne, IN 46808 (219) 424-5555.

Alexander Williams, pres.; Clark Davis, exec. v.p.; Jeff Evans, v.p. & gen. mgr.; Jim Glendening, nat'l sls. mgr.

Operation: December, 1977.

WKJG-TV (Channel 33) NBC

Thirty-Three, Inc., 2633 W. State Blvd., Ft. Wayne, IN 46808 (219) 422-7474.

Joseph R. Cloutier, pres. & treas.; Hilliard Gates, v.p. & gen. mgr.; William Kline, gen. sls. mgr.; Ed Schmidt, chief eng.; nat'l rep.: MMT.

Operation: 1953; TV sets in area: 280,000.

WPTA (Channel 21) ABC

WPTA-TV, Pulitzer Bdcstg. Co., 3401 Butler Road, Ft. Wayne, IN 46808 (219) 483-0584.

Edwin C. Metcalfe, v.p./gen. mgr.; Marvin Gottlieb, gen. sls mgr.; Barbara Wigham, sta. mgr. & dir. of prgm. & promo.; Bill MacDonald, sls. mgr.; Wayne Ludkey, news dir.; Ray Krueger, chief eng.; nat'l rep.: Blair Television.

Operation: 1956.

Gary

WPWR-TV (Channel 50)

Channel 50 TV Corp., 2151 N. Elston Ave., Chicago, IL 60614 (219) 276-5050.

Fred Eychaner, pres. & gen. mgr.; Mike Dunlop, v.p. & gen. sls. mgr.; Brent Stephenson, v.p. & sta. mgr.; Neal Sabin, prog. dir.; Bob Minor, chief eng.; natl. rep.: MMT.

Operation: September, 1967.

Indianapolis

WHMB-TV (Channel 40)

LeSea Bldg., Co., Box 12, South Bend, IN (317) 773-5050.

Lester Sumrall, pres.; Doug Garlinger, chief eng.; Wanda Linville, traffic mgr.

Operation: 1971.

WISH-TV (Channel 8) CBS

Indiana Broadcasting Corp., 1950 N. Meridian St., Indianapolis, IN 46202 (317) 923-8888.

Peter K. Orne, pres. & gen. mgr.; Scott Blumenthal, gen. sls. mgr.; Terry VanBibber, chief eng.; nat'l rep.: Petry.

Operation: 1954; TV sets in area: 1,950,000.

WRTV (Channel 6) ABC

McGraw-Hill Broadcasting Company, Inc., 1330 North Meridian St., Indianapolis, IN 46206 (317) 635-9788.

John Proffitt, v.p. & gen. mgr.; Sharon Chalfin, gen. sls. mgr.; Ken Ladage, prog. dir.; Sharon Malmstone, promo. dir.; Martin Siddall, bus. mgr.; MMT Sales, Inc.

Operations: 1949.

WTHR (Channel 13) NBC

Video Indiana, Inc., 1000 N. Meridian St., Indianapolis, IN 46204 (317) 639-2311.

Michael J. Corken, gen. mgr.; Linda Kirby, publ. affairs dir.; Robert Shire, gen. sls. mgr.; Tom Rose, prog. dir.; William Hineman, chief eng.; Bob Campbell, news dir.; Mark Dillon, bus. mgr.; nat'l rep.: John Blair & Co.

Operation: 1957; Ownership change: 1975. TV sets in area: 1,284,200.

WXIN (Channel 59)

Atlin Communications, Inc., 1440 N. Meridian St., Indianapolis, IN 46202; (317) 632-5900.

Joseph A. Young, v.p. & gen. mgr.; Raymond Hunt, gen. sls. mgr.; Michael McKinnon, chief eng.

Operation: February, 1984.

Lafayette

WLFI-TV (Channel 18)

WLFI-TV, Inc., 2605 Yeager Rd., West Lafayette, IN 47906; (Studio); P.O. Box 7018, Lafayette, IN 47906 (mailing). (317) 463-3516.

Robert A. Ford, gen. mgr.; Thomas C. Combs, sls. mgr.; Ken Fitzgerald, chief eng.; Nina Hart, prog. mgr.

Operation: May, 1953; TV households: 319,900.

Marion

WMCC (Channel 23)

Marion TV, Inc., 13044 E. 246th St., Noblesville, IN 46060 (317) 552-0804.

G.J. Robinson, pres.; Joe Mazza, gen. mgr.

Operation: Nov. 1, 1987.

Richmond

WKOI (Channel 43)

Trinity Broadcasting of Indiana, 1702 S. Ninth St., Richmond, IN 47374 (317) 935-2390.

Paul Crouch, pres.; Mary L. Laird, mgr.; Joe Hoyer, prod./dir.; Carl Dole, chief eng.

Operation: 1982.

South Bend

WHME-TV (Channel 46)

Lester Sumrall Evangelistic Assn. Inc., Box 12, South Bend, IN 46624 (219) 291-8200.

Lester Sumrall, pres.; Steve Sumrall, group v.p.; Peter Sumrall, v.p. & gen. mgr.

Operations: July, 1974.

WNDU-TV (Channel 16) NBC

Michiana Telecasting Corp., Box 1616, South Bend, IN 46634.

Bazil O'Hagan, pres. & gen. mgr.; Harry Kevorkian, v.p., educ. & admin.; Gregory Giczi, v.p., opns.; nat'l rep.; Adam Young, Inc.

Operation: 1955; TV homes in area: 270,000.

WSBT-TV (Channel 22) CBS

WSBT, Inc., 300 W. Jefferson Blvd., South Bend, IN 46601 (219) 233-3141.

James D. Freeman, pres. & gen. mgr.; Roland Adeszko, gen. sls. mgr.; N. J. Gassensmith, program dir. & film dir.; Robert Bell, chief eng.; nat'l rep.; Katz Agency.

Operation: 1952; Sets in area: 327,200.

Terre Haute

WBAK-TV (Channel 38) ABC

WBAK Television Co., P.O. Box 719, Terre Haute, IN 47808 (812) 238-1515.

Cy N. Bahakel, pres.; Hal Edwards, gen. mgr.; David Pierce, chief eng.; Barry Sinnock, prod. mgr.; nat'l rep.: Seltel.

Operation: 1973.

WTHI-TV (Channel 10) CBS

Wabash Valley Broadcasting Corp., 918 Ohio St., Terre Haute, IN 47808 (812) 232-9481.

David L. Bailey, v.p. & gen. mgr.; Phil Johnson, gen. sls. mgr.; Rod Garvin, dir. opns., prog.; nat'l rep. Katz Agency.

Operation: 1954; TV sets in area: 876,000.

WTWO (Channel 2) NBC

Illiana Telecasting Corp., P.O. Box 299, Terre Haute, IN 47808.

Mark Allen, exec. v.p. & gen. mgr.; Jerry Tiller, gen. sls. mgr.; Phylis Martindale, opns. mgr.; nat'l rep.: Blair.

Operations: Sept., 1965.

IOWA

Ames

WOI-TV (Channel 5) ABC

Iowa State Univ. Bdcstg. Corp., Ames, IA 50011 (515) 294-5555.

Bob Helmers, pres. & gen. mgr.; Ed Powers, chief eng.; Vicky Cordes, film dir.; nat'l rep.: Katz.

Operation: 1950; TV sets in area: 552,600.

Burlington

KJMH (Channel 26) FOX

Burlington Bdcstg. Co., Inc., 200 Jefferson St., Burlington, IA 52601 (319) 752-0026.

Steven S. Hoth, pres.; George Van Hagen, gen. & gen. sls. mgr.; Rochelle Kobrin, prog. dir. & film buyer; Essie Garrett, promo. mgr.; Victoria Lind, news dir.; Del Morris, chief eng.

Operation: Jan. 6, 1988.

Cedar Rapids

KCRG-TV (Channel 9) ABC

Cedar Rapids Television Co., 2nd Ave. at 5th St. S.E., Cedar Rapids, IA 52401 (319) 398-8422.

Joseph F. Hladky, III, pres.; Bob Allen, v.p. & gen. mgr.; Kevin LeRoux, gen. sls. mgr.; Bill Anderson, prog. & prod. dir.; Dave Marshall, promo. mgr.; Bruce Kruse, chief eng.; Paul Dicker, prog. dir.; James Laymon, treas. & bus. mgr.; nat'l rep.: Petry.

Operation: 1953; TV homes in area: 493,300.

KGAN-TV (Channel 2) CBS

KGAN-TV, Broadcast Park, Box 3131, Cedar Rapids, IA 52406 (319) 395-9060.

Richard Herbst, v.p. & gen. mgr.; Denise Noonan, natl. sls. mgr.; John Ganahl, opns. mgr.; Bob Burns, chief eng.; nat'l rep.: The Katz Agency, Inc.

Operation: 1953; TV sets in area: 373,800.

Davenport

KLBJ-TV (Channel 18)

937 East 53 St., Suite D, Davenport, IA 52807 (319) 386-1818.

Gary Brandt, pres. & gen. mgr.; Bridget Bowen, gen. sls. mgr.; Dan Olson, nat'l sls. mgr.; Kathleen DeBoeuf, controller; Don Bargmann, chief eng.; Sue Passe, prod. mgr.; Randy Belk, prog. mgr.; Penny Foy, traffic mgr.; nat'l rep.: Seltel.

Operation: July, 1985.

KWQC-TV (Channel 6) NBC

KWQC Broadcasting Co., 805 Brady St., Davenport, IA 52808 (319) 383-7000.

John Sloan, sta. mgr.; Mike Vandran, sls. mgr.; John Hegamen, chief eng.; Kenneth H. MacQueen, v.p.,; William Ryan, pres.; Joseph Lentz, sta. mgr.

Operation: 1949; TV sets in area: 670,200.

Des Moines

KCCI-TV (Channel 8) CBS

H & C Communications, Inc., P.O. Box 10305, Des Moines, IA 50306 (515) 247-8800.

Paul Fredericksen, pres. & gen. mgr.; Dave Porepp, gen. sls. mgr.; Paul Rhoades, v.p./news; John Pascuzzi, v.p., opns.; Robert Day, dir. prog.; Pam Kulik, dir. promo. & comm. affairs.

Operation: 1955; TV sets in area: 529,200.

KDSM-TV (Channel 17)

Duchossois Communications of Iowa, 4023 Fleur Dr., Des Moines, IA 50321 (515) 287-1717.

Rolland Johnson, pres.; Tommy Thompson, v.p. & gen. mgr.; Ted Stephens, gen. sls. mgr.; Jerry Johnson, prom. mgr.; Marty Morfeld, chief eng.

Operation: March, 1983.

WHO-TV (Channel 13) NBC

Palmer Communications, Inc., 1801 Grand Ave., Des Moines, IA 50308 (515) 242-3500.

Joseph Lentz, gen. mgr.; Tom Heston, gen. sls. mgr.; nat'l rep.: Blair.

Operation: 1954; households: 379,500.

Dubuque

KDUB-TV (Channel 40) ABC

Dubuque TV, One Dubuque Plaza, Dubuque, IA 52001; (319) 556-4040.

Thomas Bond, gen. ptnr.; Marshal Porter, gen. sls. mgr.; Dave Basinger, opns. mgr.; Gary Haverland, chief eng.

Operation: June, 1970.

Kirksville, MO-Ottumwa, IA

KTVO (Channel 3) ABC

P.O. Box 949, Highway 63 N, Kirksville, MO 63501; (816) 627-3333.

Jerry Heilman, gen. mgr.; Dan Havens, sls. mgr.; Keith Reynolds, chief eng.; Pam Small, dir. pub. info.; nat'l rep.: MMT.

Operation: 1955: TV sets in area: 146,600.

Mason City

KIMT-TV (CHANNEL 3) CBS

Spartan Radiocasting, Inc., Second & Pennsylvania, Mason City, IA 50401; 423-2540.

John Shine, gen. mgr.; Dick Aune, gen. sls. mgr.; Dave Presler, lcl. sls. mgr.; Dale Byre, chief eng.; nat'l rep.: Katz Agency.

Operations: 1954; TV sets in area: 449,000.

Ottumwa

KOIA-TV (Channel 15) FOX

Public Interest Bdcst. Group, Inc., 820 W. Second St., Ottumwa, IA 52501 (515) 684-5415.

Dirk Engstrom, gen. mgr.; Al Crounse, gen. sls. mgr. & prog. dir.; Phil Benjamin, chief eng.; rep.: Mutual TeleSales.

Operation: June 29, 1987.

Sioux City

KCAU-TV (Channel 9) ABC-TV

Citadel Communications, Ltd., 7th & Douglas Sts., Sioux City, IA 51101 (712) 277-2345.

Ray Cole, v.p. & gen. mgr.; Don Hale, natl. sls. mgr.; Gary Seaberg, lcl. sls. mgr.; J. D. Walls, dir. bdcst. opns. & prog. dir.; Ken Gullette, news dir.; Rollin Ball, tech. opns. dir.; natl. rep.; Katz.

Operation: 1953; TV homes in area: 169,500.

KMEG-TV (Channel 14) CBS

KMEG Television, Inc., Box 657, 7th & Floyd Blvd., Sioux City, IA 51105 (712) 277-3554.

Bruce McGorrill, pres.; Bruce Lewis, gen. mgr.; Gary Duffy, lcl. sls. mgr.; Lyle Johnson, chief eng.; Greg Funk, bus. mgr.

Operation: Sept., 1967; TV homes: 167,700.

KTIV (Channel 4) NBC

KTIV Television Co., 3135 Floyd Blvd., Sioux City, IA 51105; (712) 239-4100.

Jim Waterbury, pres.; Mike Smith, v.p. & gen. mgr.; Mary Bracken, v.p./programming; Dale Russell, v.p., eng.; Jack Baker, v.p. sls.; nat'l rep.: John Blair Co.

Operation: 1954; TV sets in area: 372,200.

Waterloo

KWWL-TV (Channel 7) NBC

American Black Hawk Broadcasting Co., E. 4th & Franklin, Waterloo, IA 50703 (319) 291-1200.

James Waterbury, pres. & gen. mgr.; nat'l rep., Blair.

Operation: 1953; TV sets in area: 412,700.

KANSAS

Colby

KLBY (Channel 4) ABC

999 S. Range, Colby, KS 67701; (913) 462-8644.

Bob Surber, gen. mgr.; Wayne Roberts, sta. mgr.; Josie Taylor, news dir.; Tom Cook, farm dir., R. K. Wellman, chief eng.

Operation: July, 1984.

Ensign

KBSD-TV (Channel 6) CBS

KBS, Inc., Box 12, Wichita, KS 67201.

Operation: 1957.

Garden City

KSNG-TV (Channel 11) NBC

(Satellite of KSNW-TV, Wichita, KS
Part of Kansas State Network)

Kansas State Network, Inc., South Highway 83, Garden City, KS 67846 (316) 276-2311. Rep.: Katz.

Stan Orth, sta. mgr.

Operation: Nov. 1958.

KUPK-TV (Channel 13) ABC

Satellite of KAKE-TV, Wichita, KS)

KAKE-TV, Box 10, Wichita, KS 67201.

Ron Collins, pres. & gen. mgr.; Bob Surber, sta. mgr.; Jan McDaniel, news dir.; Paul Hinderliter, chief eng.; Roxie Tucker, prog. dir.

Operation: Oct., 1964.

Goodland

KLOE-TV (Channel 10) ABC, CBS

Kays, Inc., Broadcast Plaza Box 569, Goodland, KS 67735 (913) 899-2321.

Kay Melia, gen. mgr.; nat'l rep.: Blair.

Operation: 1958.

Great Bend

KSNC (Channel 2) NBC

(Satellite of KSNW-TV, Wichita, KA)

Kansas State Network, Inc., P.O. Box 689, Great Bend, KS 67530 (316) 793-7868. Bill Ranker, gen. mgr.; Gary Gore, sls. mgr.; Tim McQuade, news. dir.; Jim Bowers, chief eng.

Operation: November, 1954.

Hays

KAYS-TV (Channel 7) CBS, ABC

(Satellite KLOE-TV Goodland, KS)

KAYS Inc., Box 817, Hays, KS, 67601.

Bernard Brown, sta. mgr.; Dannia Massier, chief engineer; Liz Boyer, prod. mgr.

Operation: Sept., 1958; TV households: 97,000.

Lawrence

KMCI (Channel 38)

Miller Bdcstg. Inc., 9191 Barton, Overland Park, KA 66214 (913) 594-2238.

Monte M. Miller, pres. & gen. mgr.; Doris J. Miller, promo. mgr.

Operation: February, 1988.

Pittsburg

KOAM-TV (Channel 7) CBS

KOAM, Limited Partnership, Owned by TA Associates, Boston, MA. P.O. Box 659, Pittsburg, KS 66762 (316) 231-0400.

Donald J. Hicks, gen. mgr.; natl. rep.: Seltel.

Operation: 1953.

Topeka

KSNT (Channel 27) NBC

SJL, Inc., P.O. Box 2700, Topeka, KS 66601 (913) 582-4000.

Perry E. Chester, v.p. & gen. mgr.; Herbert L. Brown, gen. sls. mgr.; Douglas M. Retherford, news dir.

Operation: 1967; TV households: 814,900.

KTKA-TV (Channel 49) ABC

Northeast Kansas Bdcst. Service, Inc., 101 S.E. Monroe, Topeka, KS 66603 (913) 234-4949.

Joseph Brechner, pres.; Dennis Czechanski, gen. mgr.; Sandi Wilber, gen. sls. mgr.; Kevin Goodman, prom. mgr.; Bob Totten, news dir.; Gary Krohe, chief eng.; nat'l rep.: Seltel.

Operation: June, 1983.

WIBW-TV (Channel 13) CBS

Stauffer Communications, Inc., Box 119, Topeka, KS 66601 (913) 272-3456.

John H. Stauffer, pres.; Jerry Holley, v.p., brdgt.; George Logan, gen. mgr.; Vince Frye, gen. sls. mgr.; Kent Cornish, opns. mgr./prog. dir.; nat'l rep.: Blair.

Operation: November, 1953; TV households: 514,800.

Wichita

KAKE-TV (Channel 10) ABC

KAKE-TV, 1500 North West St., Box 10, Wichita, KS (316) 943-4221.

Ron Collins, pres. & gen. mgr.; Dale Morrell, chief eng.; Jerry Watson, v.p. and gen. sales mgr.; Jan McDaniel, exec. news dir.; Don Golledge, prog.-oper. mgr.; Mark Chamberlin, mktg. dir.; Tom McBroom, compt.; nat'l rep.: Petry.

Operation: 1954.

KSAS-TV (Channel 24)

Channel 24 Ltd., 316 N. West St., Wichita, KA 67203 (316) 942-2424.

R. Alan Rudy, pres.; Dale R. Bennett, gen. mgr.; Dan Wall, gen. sls. mgr.; Tom Gdsis, prom. mgr.; Kelly Womack, prog. dir.; Mac MacShane, chief eng.; nat'l rep.: Seltel.

Operation: August, 1985.

KSNW-TV (Channel 3) NBC

(Satellites—KSNC-TV, Great Bend, KS, Ch. 2; KSNG-TV, Garden City, KS, Ch. 11; KSNK-TV, McCook, NB, Ch. 8)

Kansas State Network, Inc., P.O. Box 333; 833 North Main St., Wichita, KS 67201 (316) 265-3333.

Al Buch, gen. mgr.; Mike Hanrahan, gen. sls. mgr.; Gary Gore, lcl. sls. mgr.; Jonna Buch, creative svcs. dir.; Marc Luedtke, opns. mgr.; Paul Fanning, prod. mgr.; natl. rep.; Katz.

Operation: 1955; TV sets in area: 417,000.

Wichita-Hutchinson

KWCH-TV (Channel 12) CBS

KBS, Inc., 2815 E. 37th St., North, Box 12, Wichita, KS 67219; (316) 838-1212; Studio: 1800 N. Plum St., Hutchinson, KS (316) 665-5503; Mailing address: P.O. Box 12, Wichita, KS 67201.

Sandy DiPasquale, pres. & gen. mgr.; John Mileham, dir. comm. rel.; Jon Roe, news dir.; Steve Merren, gen. sls. mgr.; Jay Zacharias, chief eng.; Robert Wine, contr.

Operation: 1953; TV sets in area: 427,400.

KENTUCKY

Ashland

WTSF (Channel 61)

Tri-State Family Bcstg., Inc., 3100 Bath Ave., Ashland, KY 41101 (606) 329-2700.

Claude H. Messinger, gen. mgr. & chief exec. off.; Anne Bledsoe, prog. dir.; Virgil Adkins, chief eng.

Operation: April, 1983.

Beattyville

WLJC-TV (Channel 65)

North Route 11, Beattyville, KY 41311 (606) 464-3600.

Forest Drake, pres.; Jonathan Drake, gen. mgr. & chief eng.; Debra Green, sls. mgr.; Rachel Drake, prog. dir.; Bonnie West, office mgr.; John Stone, news dir.

Operation: 1982

Bowling Green

WBKO (Channel 13) ABC

Bluegrass Television, Inc., 2727 Russellville Rd., P.O. Box 13000, Bowling Green, KY 42102-9800.

Clyde Payne, v.p. & gen. mgr.; Neal Morrison, natl. sls. mgr.; Gene Prather, opns. mgr.; Dave Chumley, chief eng.; Mike Green, news dir.; nat'l rep.: Katz.

Operation: June, 1962; TV households: 265,600.

Campbellsville

WGRB (Channel 34)

Green River Bcstg., Inc., Box 400, Campbellsville, KY 42718 (502) 465-2223.

Mike Harding, gen. mgr.; Joe DeSpain, asst. mgr.; Anita Begley, bus. mgr.; Mike Graham, chief eng.; nat'l rep.: Spot Time Ltd.

Operation: April, 1983.

Danville

WDKY-TV (Channel 56) FOX

WDKY License Co., 434 Interstate Ave., Lexington, KY 40505 (606) 299-3856.

David Godbout, v.p., gen. mgr., prog. dir. & film buyer; John Maybin, gen. sls. mgr.; John Keel, prom. mgr.; Scott Wills, chief eng.; natl. rep.: MMT.

Operation: February, 1986.

Hazard

WYMT-TV (Channel 57) CBS

Kentucky Central TV, Inc., P.O. Box 1299, Hazard, KY 41701 (606) 436-4444, 436-2522.

Ralph W. Gabbard, exec. v.p.; Wayne M. Martin, sta. mgr.; E. Scott Mason, prom. mgr.; Jim Combs, chief eng.

Operations: Oct., 1969.

Lexington

WKYT-TV (Channel 27) CBS

Kentucky Central Television Inc., Box 5037, Lexington, KY 40555; Offices: 2851 Winchester Rd.; (606) 299-0411.

Hart Hagan, pres.; Ralph Gabbard, exec. v.p.; Theodore B. Holcomb, v.p. sls.; Jere Pigue, v.p. & sta. mgr.; Barbara Carden, prog. dir.

Operation: June 1967; TV households: 409,800.

WLEX (Channel 18) NBC

WLEX-TV, Inc., P.O. Box 1457, Russell Cave Road, Lexington, KY 40591 (606) 255-4404.

Harry C. Barfield, pres. & gen. mgr.; John G. Atchison, secty.; Joe Oliver, v.p. & gen. sls. dir.; Paul Fast, lcl. sls. mgr.; L. Neuzel, chief prog.; Al Scheer, v.p. & chief eng.; John Duvall, v.p. bdcst. opns.; nat'l rep.: Blair.

Operation: 1955; TV households in area: 585,000.

WLKT (Channel 62)

FBC, Inc., 124 New Circle Rd., N.E., Lexington, KY 40506 (606) 252-6200.

Arch S. Chapman, gen. mgr.; Steve Kesten, gen. sls. mgr.; Pamela Mitchell, prog. dir.; David Jones, promo. mgr.; Robert Kline, chief eng.; rep.: ITS.

Operation: Oct. 15, 1988.

WTVQ-TV (Channel 36) ABC

Shamrock Broadcasting Co., P.O. Box 5590 Lexington, KY 40555 (606) 233-3600.

Diane Sutter, v.p. & gen. mgr.; Craig Alexander, news dir.; Jerry Fox, prog. mgr.; Jerry W. Fox, sta. mgr.; John Lackey, chief eng.; Rep.: Katz TV.

Operation: 1968; TV households: 212,100.

Louisville

WAVE-TV (Channel 3) NBC basic

Cosmos Broadcasting Corp., P.O. Box 32970, Louisville, KY 40232; 725 S. Floyd Street, Louisville, KY 40203 (502) 585-2201.

Guy Hempel, v.p. & gen. mgr.; Steve Langford, gen. sls. mgr.; Nick Ulmer, nat'l sls. mgr.; Roger Roebuck, prgm. dir.; Bill Eschback, chief eng.; Ed Godfrey, news dir.; Mark Young, prom. dir.; nat'l rep.: MMT.

Operation: 1948; TV sets in area: 950,400.

WBNA (Channel 21)

Word Bdcstg. Network, Inc., 3701 Fern Valley Rd., Louisville, KY 40219 (502) 964-2121.

Robert W. Rodgers, pres. & gen. mgr.; Steve Rayburn, sta. mgr.; Carl Piccuito, sls. mgr.; Bryan Bailey, prog. dir.; Terrell Smith, chief eng.; rep.: ITS.

Operation: Apr. 2, 1986

WDRB-TV (Channel 41)

Independence Television Co., Independence Square, Louisville, KY 40203 (502) 584-6441.

Elmer F. Jaspan, pres. & gen. mgr.; Robert Hurtman, gen. sls. mgr.; Glen Cook, chief eng.

Operation: 1971.

WHAS-TV (Channel 11) CBS

Journal Bdcstg. of Kentucky, Inc., P.O. Box 1100, Louisville, KY 40201; (502) 582- 7840.

Neil Kuvin, pres. & gen. mgr., Doug Roberts, natl. sls. mgr.; Tom Bornhauser, gen. sls. mgr.; Richard Sweeney, prog. dir.; Bill Bratton, dir. eng.; nat'l rep., Harrington, Righter and Parsons, Inc.

Operation: 1950; TV sets in area: 912,000.

WLKY-TV (Channel 32) ABC

Pulitzer Broadcasting Co., 1918 Mellwood Ave., P.O. Box 6205, Louisville, KY 40206 (502) 893-3671.

Lyn P. Stoyer, v.p. & gen. mgr.; Jim Oetken, gen. sls. mgr.; Jack Shafer, prog. dir.; Andy Barton, news dir.; Paul Kelley, chief eng.; Lora Bradshaw, community affairs dir.

Operation: September, 1961; households: 610,900.

Madisonville

WLCN (Channel 19)

Life Anew Ministries, Inc., Box 1087, 721 Princeton Pike, Madisonville, KY 42431; (502) 821-5433.

John Stalls, pres.; John Price, v.p.

Operation: September, 1983.

Owensboro

WROZ (Channel 61)

Powers Communications, 1745 Old Hickory Blvd., Owensboro, KY 37027 (615) 373-4721.

Glen Powers, pres.

Operation: January, 1988.

Paducah

WPSD-TV (Channel 6) NBC

Paducah Newspapers, Inc., P.O. Box 1197, 100 Television Lane, Paducah, KY 42001 (502) 442-8214.

Fred Paxton, pres. & mgring dir.; John Williams, gen. mgr.; nat'l rep., Blair.

Operation: 1957; TV sets in area: 325,000.

LOUISIANA

Alexandria

KALB-TV (Channel 5) NBC

Lanford Telecasting Co., Inc., 605-11 Washington St., Alexandria, LA 71301 (318) 445-2456.

Robert E. Miller, v.p. & gen. mgr.; Lesly Golmon, asst. gen. mgr. & gen. sls. mgr.; Berton Chaudoir, nat'l & regl. sls. mgr.; Dowell Bushnell, sls. mgr.; Tom Webb, news dir.; Jimmy Fox, mgr. creative svcs.; nat'l rep.: The Katz Agency.

Operation: 1954; TV sets in area; 507,900.

KLAX-TV (Channel 31)

Pollack-Belz Communications Co., Inc., 1811 England Dr., Alexandria, LA 71303 (318) 473-0037.

Gary F. Halleland, gen. mgr.; Duane Dargis, gen. sls. mgr.; Darrel Jordan, chief eng.

Operation: 1982.

Baton Rouge

WAFB-TV (Channel 9) CBS

American Family Bdcstg., 844 Government St., Baton Rouge, LA 70821.

Ronald E. Winders, v.p. & gen. mgr.; David Ward, asst. gen. mgr.; Ed Lamy, prog. dir.; Ray Sullivan, gen. sls. mgr.; Andree Boyd, promo. dir.; Carlton Cremeens, news dir.; Steve Schneider, sports dir.; Bill Comeaux, chief eng.; Ronnie Melancon, prod. mgr.

Operation: 1953; TV sets in area: 460,000.

WBRZ (Channel 2) ABC

Louisiana Television Broadcasting Corp., P.O. Box 2906, Baton Rouge, LA 70821; (504) 387-2222.

Douglas L. Manship, pres.; Charles Manship, treas.; Richard Manship, secty. & gen. mgr.; Pat Cheramie, asst. gen. mgr.; Denise Akers, mktg. dir.; Barbara Bree Shab, prog. dir.; William R. Yordy, dir. eng.; Raymond Drago, prod. mgr.; Kim Kirkendoll, bus. mgr.; Gus Luckett, finance mgr.; Fred Reno, sls. dir.; James Daboval III, nat'l regnl., sls. mgr.; John Spain, news dir.; Jamie Politz, personnel dir.; nat'l rep.: Blair Television.

Operation: 1955; TV HH TSA; 775,900; TV HH 258,600.

WVLA (Channel 33) NBC

WVLA Television, Inc., P.O. Box 14685, Baton Rouge, LA 70808 (504) 766-3233.

Cyril E. Vetter, pres. & sta. mgr.; Bill Hathorn, gen. sls. mgr.

Operation: 1971.

Lafayette

KADN (Channel 15)

KADN Broadcasting, Inc., 1506 Eraste Landry Rd., Lafayette, LA 70506 (318) 237-1500.

Charles Chatelain, gen. mgr.; Eddie Blanchard, prog. dir.; Clark White, gen. sls. mgr.; Dave Pierce, sls. mgr.; Keith Towndsin, chief eng.; nat'l rep.: ITS.

Operation: 1980.

KATC (Channel 3) ABC

KATC Associates, Box 93133, Lafayette, LA 70509 (318) 235-3333.

Paul Cassidy, gen. mgr. & film buyer; Judi Henderson, prog. coord.; Karen Granata, promo. mgr.; Bill Rumsey, chief eng.; rep.: Katz.

Operation: 1962; TV households: 357,600.

KLFY-TV (Channel 10) CBS

Young Broadcasting of Louisiana, Box 90665, Lafayette, LA 70509 (318) 981-4823.

Ron Kwasnick, pres.; Joe Varholy, v.p. & gen. mgr.; Terry Dover, op. mgr.; Dave Hebert, chief eng.; nat'l rep.: Adam Young.

Operation: 1955; TV sets in area: 321,000.

Lake Charles

KPLC-TV (Channel 7) NBC

Cosmos Bcstg. Corp., 320 Division St., P.O. Box 1488, Lake Charles, LA 70602 (318) 439-9071.

Jim Serra, gen. sls. mgr.; Ron Blansett, chief eng.; Ron Loewen, v.p.-gen. mgr.; James Smith, news dir.; Jim Brandenburg, opns. dir.; Paula Dupuis, mktg. mgr.; Robin Daugereau, prog. co-ord.; Peter Hemphill, creative svcs. dir.

Operation: 1954; TV sets in area: 76,500.

KVHP (Channel 29)

KVHP-TV, Partners, 129 W. Prien Lake Rd., Lake Charles, LA 70601; (318) 474-1316.

Gary D. Hardesty, pres.; Ken Smith, gen. mgr.; Jeff Pryor, opns. mgr.; Cathy High, bus. mgr.; Bill Leber, news dir.; natl. rep.: ITS.

Operation: December, 1982.

Monroe

KARD (Channel 14) ABC

Woods Communications Group, Inc., 701 Parkwood Dr., West Monroe, LA 71291 (318) 323-1972.

Charles Woods, pres.; Gwen Kidd, gen. mgr.; Rodney Evans, chief eng.

Operation: August, 1967; TV households: 182,600.

KNOE-TV (Channel 8) CBS

Noe Enterprises Inc., 1400 Oliver Rd., P.O. Box 4067, Monroe, LA 71211 (318) 322-8155.

James A. Noe, Jr., pres. & gen. mgr.; Dick French, gen. mgr. & natl. sls. mgr.; Jack McCall, prog. dir.; Raymond Boyd, dir. of eng.; Lloyd Voorhees, mgr. regional/local sls. mgr.; Ansel Smith, ops. mgr.; rep.: Blair.

Operation: 1953; TV sets in area: 800,000.

KTVE (Channel 10) NBC

(A Gray Communications System Station)

KTVE, Inc., 400 West Main, El Dorado, AR 71730 (318) 323-1300; 2909 Kilpatrick Blvd., Monroe, LA.

Jim Gray, Jr., v.p. & gen. mgr.; Mike Caruso, chief eng.; David Brown, reg. sls. mgr.; Fran Rogers, nat'l sls. mgr.; Helen Johnson, prog. dir.; rep.: Katz.

Operation: 1955; TV sets in area: 298,200.

New Orleans

WDSU-TV (Channel 6) NBC

Cosmos Broadcasting Corp., 520 Royal St., New Orleans, LA 70130 (504) 527-0666.

Jim Keelor, v.p. & gen. mgr.; Tano Compagno, prod. dir.; Anne Coleman, sta.-pgm. dir.; Mike Kibbey, gen. sls. mgr.; Mary McCarthy, news dir.; Linda Nix, adv.-mktg. dir.; Steve Mohammed, bus. mgr.; Bill Laughlin, chief eng.; nat'l rep.: HRP.

WGNO-TV (Channel 26) IND

Tribune Broadcasting Co., 2800 World Trade Center, 2 Canal St., New Orleans, LA 70130; (504) 581-2600.

James Dowdle, pres.; Robert Gremillion, sta. mgr.; Randy Davis, chief eng.; sales rep.: Telerep.

Operation: 1967; TV households: 657,600.

WNOL-TV (Channel 38)

TVX of New Orleans, 1661 Canal St., New Orleans, LA 70112; (504) 525-3838.

John Trinder, pres.; Madelyn Mix Bonnot, v.p. & gen. mgr.; Cheryl Faust, gen. sls. mgr.; nat'l rep.: Seltel

Operation: March, 1984.

WVUE-TV (Channel 8) ABC

Burnham Bdcstg. Co., 1025 S. Jefferson Davis Pkwy., New Orleans, LA 70125 (504) 486-6161; TWX 810-951-6090.

Phil Nye, pres. & gen. mgr.; Ron Jones, gen. sls. mgr.; Greg Buisson, mktg. dir.; Kevin Brennan, news dir.; nat'l rep.: Petry.

Operation: 1959: TV sets in area: 2,000,000.

WWL-TV (Channel 4) CBS

Loyola University, 6363 St. Charles Ave., New Orleans, LA 70118.

J. Michael Early, v.p. & gen. mgr.-prog. dir.; Jerrold Whaley, gen. sls. mgr.; Everett Bonner, natl. sls. mgr.; Ms. Jimmie Phillips, lcl. sls. mgr.; Joe Duke, news dir.; Phil Johnson, asst. gen. mgr.; nat'l rep.: Katz TV.

Operation: September, 1957; TV households: 684,000.

Shreveport

KMSS-TV (Channel 33)

SWMM/Shreveport Corp., Box 30033, Shreveport, LA 71130 (318) 631-5677.

Arthur A. Lanham, gen. mgr.-v.p.; Susan K. Newman, gen. sls. mgr.; Douglas Ginn, prog. dir.; Richard Logan, chief eng.; Phyliss Phillips, bus. dir.

Operation: October, 1985.

KSLA-TV (Channel 12) CBS basic

Viacom Bdcst., Inc., P.O. Box 4812, Shreveport, LA 71134-1812 (318) 222-1212.

Allen Cartwright, v.p. & gen. mgr.; Bill Womble, promo. dir.; Jerry Black, lcl. sls. mgr.

Operation: 1954; TV sets in area: 743,000.

KTAL-TV (Channel 6) NBC

KTAL-TV, Inc., 3150 No. Market St., Shreveport, LA 71104 (318) 425-2422. Texas: 3227 Summerhill Rd., Texarkana; (214) 793-1133.

W. E. Hussman, pres.; H. Lee Bryant, v.p. for bdcst'.; Doug Yoder, nat'l sls. mgr.; Kenny Gardner, sta. mgr.; Jean Byrd, prog. dir.; George Tracy, dir. of eng.
Operation: 1953; TV sets in area: 490,900.

KTBS-TV (Channel 3) ABC
KTBS, Inc., 312 E. Kings Highway, Shreveport, LA 868-3644.
Edwin Wray, pres. & gen. mgr.; George D. Wray, Jr., v.p.; Charles W. Wray, bd. chm. & secy-treas.; Don Wiegel, promo. mgr.; Marvin L. Perry, Jr., prog. dir.; Dave Hendricks, chief eng.; nat'l rep.: Katz Agency.
Operation: 1955; TV sets in area: 745,200.

MAINE
Bangor

WABI-TV (Channel 5) CBS
Community Broadcasting Service, 36 Hildreth St., Bangor, ME 04401 (207) 947-8321.
George J. Gonyar, v.p. & gen. mgr.; Dale Carter, chief eng.; nat'l rep.: Blair.
Operation: 1953; TV sets in area: 140,000.

WLBZ-TV (Channel 2) NBC
WLBZ Television, Inc., Box 934, Mt. Hope Ave., Bangor, ME 04401 (207) 942-4822.
Fred Thompson, pres.; Bruce McGorrill, exec. v.p.; Margo Cobb, v.p./gen. mgr.; J. Hopkins, chief eng.; nat'l rep.: Katz Agency.
Operation: 1954; TV sets in area: 125,000.

WVII-TV (Channel 7) ABC
Bangor Communications, Inc., 371 Target Industrial Circle, Bangor, ME 04401 (207) 945-6457.
Barbara J. Cyr, exec. v.p. & gen. mgr.; Michele Slater, lcl./Canadian sls. mgr.; Gary Kasparek, prod. mgr.; Tim Gaier, news dir.; Judy Vardamis, prog. dir., nat'l sls. mgr.; rep.: Seltel.
Operation: 1965, TV households: 220,000.

Poland Spring

WMTW-TV (Channel 8)
WMTW-TV, a division of Harron Communications Corp., Inc., Auburn, ME 04210; (207) 782-1800. Sales dept., Portland; (207) 775-1800.
Paul Harron, pres.; Al Ritter, v.p. & gen. mgr.; Bernie Aiello, sta. mgr.; Richard Cushman, chief eng.; nat'l rep.; Petry.
Operation: 1954.

Portland

WCSH-TV (Channel 6) NBC
Maine Radio and TV Co., One Congress Square, Portland, ME 04101; (207) 772-0181.
Bruce McGorill, exec. v.p.; Lew Colby, v.p. & gen. mgr.; nat'l rep.: Katz Agency.
Operation: 1953; TV sets in area: 210,000.

WGME-TV (Channel 13) CBS
Guy Gannett Broadcasting Services, Northport Plaza, Portland, ME 04104 (207) 797-9330.
Jean Gannett Hawley, pres.; Robert L. Gilbertson, exec. v.p.; David King, v.p. & gen. mgr.; Fred Desjardins, chief eng.; Jerry Senger, treas. nat'l rep., Blair TV assoc.
Operation: 1954; TV sets in area: 288,000.

WPXT (Channel 51) FOX
Portland Bdcstg., Inc., 2320 Congress St., Portland, ME 04102.
Josh McGraw, v.p. & gen. mgr.; Tony Palminteri, gen. sls. mgr.; Jennifer Dennison, prog. dir.; Doreen Morgan, prom. mgr.; Mark Beck, chief eng.; natl. rep.: Seltel.
Operation: September, 1986.

Presque Isle

WAGM-TV (Channel 8)
NEPSK, Inc., P.O. Box 1149, Presque Isle, ME 04769 (207) 764-4461.
Thom Shelburne III, pres.; Norm Johnson, v.p. & gen. mgr.
Operation: 1956.

MARYLAND
Baltimore

WBAL-TV (Channel 11) CBS
The Hearst Corp., 3800 Hooper Ave., Baltimore, MD 21211 (301) 467-3000.
John C. Conomikes, v.p. & gen. mgr., Hearst Broadcasting Stations; Malcolm D. Potter, v.p. & gen. mgr., WBAL-TV; Jack Gilmore, v.p. sls.; Kristin Long, nat'l sls. mgr.; David Elmore, lcl. sls. mgr.; nat'l rep.: Blair.
Operation: March, 1948; TV households: 2,613,200.

WBFF (Channel 45)
Chesapeake TV Inc., 3500 Parkdale Ave., Baltimore, MD 21211 (301) 462-4500.
Julian S. Smith, bd. chm.; Robert Simmons, pres.; Bruce Lumpkin, gen. mgr. & gen. sls. mgr.; Kim Laxton, nat'l sls. mgr.; Robert Smith, prog. mgr.; Mike Schroeder, promo. mgr.; Dwight Weems, prod. mgr.; Sharon Christopher Wylie, public affairs mgr.; Dennis Winters, chief eng.
Operation: 1971.

WHSW-TV (Channel 24)
Silver King Bdcstg. of MD, Inc., 4820 Seton Dr., Baltimore, MD 21215 (301) 358-2400.
Ken Becker, v.p. & sta. mgr., Barbara Brown, sls. mgr.; Brad Foltyn, prog. dir.; Sue Gallion, traffic mgr.; Jim Vest, chief eng.
Operation: December, 1985.

WJZ-TV (Channel 13) ABC
Westinghouse Broadcasting Co., Inc., 3725 Malden Ave., Baltimore, MD 21211 (301) 466-0013.
Burt Staniar, pres. & CEO; Jonathan Klein, v.p.-gen. mgr.; Philip Arrington, creative svcs. mgr.; Michael Easterling, prog. mgr.; Dana Fitzgerald, gen. sls. mgr.; Robert Ross, chief eng.; Natalea Brown, news dir.; Robert Cucuruto, controller.
Operation: 1948; TV sets in area: 2,653,500.

WMAR-TV (Channel 2) NBC
WMAR, Inc., 6400 York Road, Baltimore, MD 21212 (301) 377-2222.
Arnold J. Kleiner, pres. & gen. mgr.; Joseph Bruno, v.p. eng.; Emily L. Barr, dir. bdcst. opns.; Gary Wordlaw, dir. news; Howard Zeiden, v.p. sls.
Operation: 1947; TV sets in area: 2,390,600.

WNUV-TV (Channel 54)
WNUV-TV 54, Druid Park Dr., Baltimore, MD 21215 (301) 462-5400.

Gary Marshall, pres. & gen. mgr.; Dale Snyder, prog. dir. & film buyer; Paul Garnet, chief eng.

Operation: July, 1982.

Hagerstown

WHAG-TV

Williams Communications, Inc., 13 East Washington Street, Hagerstown, MD 21740 (301) 797-4400.

Alexander Williams, pres.; Hugh J. Breslin III, v.p. & gen. mgr.; Chuck Noland, prog. dir.; rep.: Katz.

Operation: 1970.

WJAL (Channel 68)

Good Companion Bdcstg. Co., Box 219, 11 N. Carlisle St., Greencastle, PA 17225 (717) 597-4076.

Louise J. Castriota, v.p., gen. mgr. & prog. dir.; Jack Hogue, promo. mgr.; Jerry Foreman, chief eng.; rep.: Landin Media Sales.

Operation: May 5, 1987.

Salisbury

WBOC-TV (Channel 16) CBS

WBOC-TV, Inc., 17291 N. Salisbury Blvd., Salisbury, MD 21801; (301) 749-1111.

Thomas Draper, pres.; William Kenton, gen. mgr.; Carol Hess, prog. dir.; Robert Getz, gen. sls. mgr.; Sally Cannon, news dir.; Vincent Donovan, chief eng.; rep.: Katz

Operation: 1954; TV sets in area: 139,150.

WMDT (Channel 47) ABC, NBC

Delmarva Broadcast Svc. Genl. Partnership, P.O. Box 4009, Salisbury, MD 21801; (301) 742-4747.

Frank Pilgrim, gen. mgr.; Rich Dipilla, reg. & nat'l sls. mgr.; Susan Kelly, lcl. sls. mgr.; Clay Spurrier, chief eng.; Ray Carter, news dir.; nat'l rep.: Blair.

Operation: 1980.

MASSACHUSETTS

Adams-Pittsfield

WCDC (Channel 19) ABC

(Satellite of WTEN, Albany, NY)

Knight-Ridder Broadcasting, Inc. 341 Northern Blvd., Albany, NY 12204 (518) 436-4822.

Dow C. Smith, gen. mgr.; John Hirsch, gen. sls. mgr.; Robert Peterson, prog. dir.; James Holland, news dir.

Boston

WBZ TV (Channel 4) NBC

Westinghouse Broadcasting Co., Inc., 1170 Soldiers Field Road, Boston, MA 02134 (617) 787-7000.

John J. Spinola, v.p. & gen. mgr.; Tony Vinciquerra, gen. sls. mgr.; Stan Hopkins, news dir.; George St. Andre, dir. of eng.; Barry Schulman, prog. mgr.; Eric Goldstein, creative services dir.; Kim Harbin, pub. comm. dir.; Algar Cox, human resources mgr.; Bob Houghton, cont.; Bob Hayes, sls. svc. dir.; Bill Ferrick, commercial ops. mgr.

Operation: 1948; TV sets in area: 2,700,000.

WCVB-TV (Channel 5) ABC

The Hearst Corp., 5 TV Place, Needham, MA 02192.

S. James Coppersmith, v.p. & gen. mgr.; Deborah Sinay, v.p., gen. sls. mgr.; Paul La Camera, v.p. & sta. mgr.; Philip Balboni, v.p. news; Burt Peretsky, pub. rel. mgr.; Edward Aaronson, dir. promos.; Donna Latson-Gittens, v.p. comm. prog.

Operation: 1972.

WFXT-TV (Channel 25) Fox

Fox TV Stations, Inc., 100 Second Ave., Needham Heights, MA 02194 (617) 449-4200.

Joe R. Robinowitz, gen. mgr.; David D. Leahy, gen. sls. mgr.; Arthur Carr, natl. sls. mgr.; Peter Hennessey lcl. sls. mgr.; Richard D. Beach, prog. dir.; Gayton Masters, promo. mgr.; Dennis Correia, chief eng.

Operation: 1977.

WNEV-TV (Channel 7) CBS

New England TV Corp., 7 Bulfinch Pl., Government Center, Boston, MA 02114 (617) 725-0777.

Seymour Yanoff, pres.; Vic Lai, v.p.-admin. fin.; Mike Wach, v.p. sls.; Bruce Marson, v.p. prog.; Jennifer Gillespie, dir. p.r.; Jim Thistle, v.p. news; Jackie Comeau, v.p. rsch; Richard Weisberg, v.p.-mktg. & creative svcs.; Karl Renwanz, v.p.-eng.; nat'l rep.: Telerep.

Operation: June, 1948; homes in area: 2,034,200.

WQTV (Channel 68)

Monitor TV, Inc., 1660 Soldiers Field Rd., Boston, MA 02135 (617) 787-6868.

David E. Morse, pres. & gen. mgr.; Jonathan A. Hunt, exec. v.p. & CEO; William Spitzer, sta. mgr.; Ray York, lcl. sls. mgr.; James Dunford, promo. mgr.; David Folsom, chief eng.; nat'l rep.: ITS

Operation: January, 1979.

WSBK-TV (Channel 38)

WSBK-TV, Gillett Communications of Boston, 83 Leo Birmingham Pkwy, Brighton, MA 02135 (617) 783-3838.

Daniel J. Berkery, pres. & gen. mgr.; Stuart P. Tauber, asst. gen. mgr.; Victoria Kendall, creative svcs. dir.; Viorginia C. Jones, controller; John Anderson, dir. sls. devel.; Francis Comerford, natl. sls. mgr.; Thomas Warner, lcl. sls. mgr.; James McCarthy, chief eng.

Operation: 1964.

Boston-Cambridge

WLVI-TV (Channel 56)

Gannett Massachusetts Broadcasting, Ind., 75 Morrissey Bldg., Boston, MA 02125 (617) 265-5656.

Gerald R. Walsh, pres. & gen. mgr.; Bill Butler, prog. mgr.; Peter Schruth, gen. sls. mgr.; Denis Dowdle, natl. sls. mgr.; Bob McCaughey, lcl. sls. mgr.; Ron Becker, v.p. news & opns.; Mike Izor, cont.; Barbara Behtea, prod. mgr.; Natalie McIver, news & pub. affairs mgr.

Operation: 1953.

Lawrence

WMFP (Channel 62)

MFP, Inc., One Parker St., Lawrence, MA 01843 (617) 975-3053.

Avi Nelson, pres.

Operation: Oct. 16, 1987.

Marlborough

WHSH (Channel 66)

Silver King. Bcstg. of Mass., 111 Speen St., Framingham, MA 01701 (617) 350-6666.

Merrill Buchhalter, gen. mgr.; David O'Leary, prog. dir.; Charles Fitch, chief eng.
Operation: March, 1983.

Springfield-Holyoke

WGGB-TV (Channel 40) ABC

The WHYN Stations Corp., 1300 Liberty Street, Springfield, MA 01101 (413) 785-1911.
Clifford Lefkovich, gen. mgr.; Dick Wylie, natl sls. mgr.; Rep.: Katz Agency.
Operation: 1953; TV sets in area: 1,213,500.

WWLP (Channel 22) NBC

Adams TV of Springfield, Inc., Box 2210, Springfield, MA 01102-2210 (413) 786-2200.
William M. Pepin, pres., gen. mgr.; Constance O'Brien, bus. mgr.; E. Holland Low, v.p., nat'l sls.; Daniel T. Sullivan, Jr., v.p., lcl. sls. mgr.; Max Marek, chief eng.; nat'l rep.: Blair.
Operation: 1953; TV sets in area: 714,900.

Vineyard Haven

WCVX-TV (Channel 58)

29 Bassett Lane, Hyannis, MA 02601 (617) 775-4242.
Daniel Carney, gen. mgr.; Fred Lungo, pgm. dir.; Ben Emery, gen. sls. mgr.; Greg Bush, news dir.; Don Moore, chief eng.
Operation: July, 1985.

Worcester

WHLL-TV (Channel 27)

Central Mass. TV, Inc., 27 Parker Rd., Shewsbury, MA 01545.
Michael Volpe, gen. mgr.; Michael Nurse, gen. sls. mgr.; Jim Barnett, prod. mgr.; Cathy Lane, traffic mgr.; Lynne MacNamme, news dir.; Fran Vaccan, chief eng.
Operation: 1970; TV households: 2,037,700.

MICHIGAN

Alpena-Oscoda

WBKB-TV (Channel 11) CBS

Thunder Bay Broadcasting Co., 1390 Bagley St., Alpena, MI 49707 (517) 356-3434.
Stephen A. Marks, pres. & gen. mgr.; Daniel H. Springer, news dir.; Michael Campbell, prod. mgr.; Mark Nowak, chief eng.; Jodie Bryant, prog. dir.
Operation: 1975.

Ann Arbor

WIHT (Channel 31)

Blackstar Communications of Michigan, Inc., 3975 Varsity Dr., Ann Arbor, MI 48108 (313) 373-7900.
Christopher Webb, gen. mgr. & gen. sls. mgr.; Robert Thompson, chief eng.
Operation: 1981.

Battle Creek-Kalamazoo

WUHQ-TV (Channel 41) ABC

Channel 41, Inc., 5200 West Dickman Road, Battle Creek, MI 49016 (616) 968-9341.
John W. Lawrence, pres.; William J. Lawrence, Jr., bd. chmn.; Jerry Colvin, exec. v.p. & gen. mgr.; Phil Hartman, prog. & prom. mgr.; Michael J. Laemers, chief eng. & ops. mgr.; Denny Monroe, controller; Brett Bowers, film dir.
Operation: 1971; Receivers in area: 938,000.

Bay City-Saginaw

WNEM-TV (Channel 5) NBC

WNEM-Television; Broadcasting div./Meredith Corp.; Offices and studios, 107 N. Franklin, Saginaw, MI (517) 755-8191. Sales office & studio: G-3426 Miller Road, Flint, MI (313) 732-2050.
Paul Virciglio, v.p. & gen. mgr.; Bill Avery, prog. dir.; Paula Morrissey, gen. sls. mgr.; Greg Surma, chief eng.; Bruce Whiteaker, news dir.; nat'l rep.: MMT Sales, Inc.
Operation: 1954; TV households in area: 433,300.

Cadillac

WWTV (Channel 9) CBS

Wilson Communications, Inc. P.O. Box 627; Cadillac, MI 49601 (616) 775-3478.
Ralph C. Wilson, Jr., chmn.; William R. Hirshey, pres.; J.A. Skip Simms, v.p. & gen. mgr.; nat'l rep.: Blair.
Operation: Jan. 1, 1954; TV sets in area: 1,234,200.

Cheboygan

WPBN-TV & WTOM-TV NBC

WPBN-TV & WTOM-TV, Inc., Box 546, Traverse City, MI 49684 (616) 947-7770.
Frank L. Beam, pres.; Peter S. Good, v.p. & gen. mgr.; Chuck O'Connor, natl. sls. mgr.; Leon Bush, chief eng.; nat'l rep.: Katz.
Operation: 1959.

Detroit

WDIV-TV (Channel 4) NBC

Post-Newsweek Station, Michigan, Inc. 550 Lafayette Blvd., Detroit, MI 48231 (313) 222-0444.
Alan W. Frank, v.p. & gen. mgr.; Robert Warfield, v.p. news & dir. bdcst. opns.
Operation: 1947; TV sets in area; U.S. total survey area: 3,324,00, total coverage area (inc. Canada): 3,525,000.

WGPR-TV (Channel 62)

WGPR, Inc., 3140-6 E. Jefferson Ave., Detroit, MI 48207 (313) 259-8862.
George Mathews, pres. & gen. mgr.; James W. Panagos, v.p. & gen. sls. mgr.; Joe Spencer, prog. dir.; Ulysses W. Boykin, v.p. public affairs.
Operation: 1975.

WJBK-TV (Channel 2) CBS

Gillett Communications of Detroit, Inc., Box 2000, Southfield, MI 48037 (313) 557-2000.
Steven R. Antoniotti, pres. & gen. mgr.; Spencer Koch, sta. mgr. & v.p., sls.
Operation: 1948; TV sets in area: 2,034,000.

WKBD-TV (Channel 50) FOX

Cox Communications, P.O. Box 50, Southfield, MI 48037 (313) 444-8500.
Duane Kell, v.p. & gen. mgr.; Ellen Bramson, gen. sls. mgr.; Paul Prange, prog. mgr.; G. R. Fitzgerald, business mgr.; David Jerrell, dir. of opns.; Toby Cunningham, prod. mgr.
Operation: 1965.

WXON-TV (Channel 20)

27777 Franklin Rd., Suite 708, Detroit, MI 48034 (313) 355-2900.

Aben E. Johnson Jr., pres.; Doug Johnson, v.p., gen. mgr. & prog. dir.; A.J. Schweizer, opns., mgr.; Gary King, chief eng.; Melanie Churell, news dir.; nat'l rep.: MMT.

Operation: September, 1968.

WXYZ-TV (Channel 7) ABC

WXYZ, Inc., Broadcast House, 20777 W. Ten Mile Rd., Southfield, MI 48037-0789 (313) 827-7777.

Thomas C. Griesdorn, v.p. & gen. mgr.; Grace Gilchrist, gen. sls. mgr.; Robert Sliva, natl. sls. mgr.; Joseph Trondle, lcl. sls. mgr.; Mimmi Mathis, dir. prog. devel. & adv.; Marla Drutz, dir. prog. acq. & mktg.; Jan Qualtiere, bus. mgr.; Wallace Rodammer chief eng. natl. rep.: Katz.

Operation: 1948; TV sets in area: 1,823,423.

Detroit-Windsor (Canada)

CBET (Channel 9) CBC

Canadian Bdg. Corp., 825 Riverside Drive West, Windsor, Ont. N9A 5K9 (519) 254-2831.

Bruce Taylor, dir. of TV; Fred Stecher, mgr. TV opns.; R. Kryger, mgr., TV tech. svcs.; J. Molnar, communications.

Operation; 1954.

Escanaba

WJMN-TV (Channel 3) ABC

(Satellite of WFRV-TV, Green Bay, WI)

WFRV Inc., P.O. Box 19055, Green Bay, WI 54307.

Rep.: Telerep.

Operation: 1969.

Flint

WJRT-TV (Channel 12) ABC

SJL Corp. of Kansas, 2302 Lapeer Rd., Flint MI 48502 (313) 233-3130.

P. Thomas Bryson, pres. & gen. mgr.; nat'l rep.; HRP.

Operation: 1958; TV households in area: 1,156,700.

Grand Rapids

WOTV-TV (Channel 8) NBC basic

Lin Central Broadcasting Corp., 120 College Ave., P.O. Box B, Grand Rapids, MI 49502; (616) 456-8888.

Bob Groothand, pres. & gen. mgr.; Lil Clary-Welti, bus. mgr.; Jim Thomas, prom. mgr.; Donald P. Gallagher, chief eng.; Sue McDonnell, gen. sls. mgr.; nat'l rep.: Blair.

Operation: 1951; TV sets in area: 532,500.

WXMI-TV (Channel 17)

3117 Plaza Drive, N.E., Grand Rapids, MI 49505; (616) 364-8722.

Pat Mullen, v.p. & gen. mgr.; Richard J. Stawicki, opns. dir.; Judy Kenney, sls. dir.; Mark Krause, prog. mgr.; Bonnie Hunter, dir. of off.; Pam Swenk, prom. mgr.; Cheryl Adams, news; Dale Scholten, dir. of eng.; nat'l rep.: Petry.

Operation: March, 1982.

WZZM (Channel 13) ABC

Western Michigan Bdcstg. Corp., P.O. Box Z, 645 Three Mile Rd., N.W., Grand Rapids, MI 49501.

Jack Mazzie, v.p.-gen. mgr.; Michael Seagly, prog.-opns. mgr.; Buss Kunst, gen. sls. mgr; Tim Siegel, nat'l sls. mgr.; Dale Wolters, chief eng.

Kalamazoo

WWMT (Channel 3) CBS

Busse Bcstg., Corp., 590 W. Maple St., Kalamazoo, MI 49008 (616) 388-3333.

Larry Busse, pres. & gen. mgr.; Gil Brettner, sta. mgr.; Michael Brunette, gen. sls. mgr.; Phil Parsons, promo. mgr.; James Steffey, chief eng.; nat'l rep.: MMT

Operation: 1950; TV sets in area: 932,000.

Lansing

WLAJ-TV (Channel 53)

Chase TV Corp., 600 W. Cavanaugh, Rd., Lansing, MI 48910 (517) 393-1320.

R. Charles McLravy, pres.

Operation: January, 1988.

WLNS-TV (Channel 6) CBS

Young Bdcstg., Inc., 2820 E. Saginaw, Lansing, MI 48912 (517) 372-8282.

Ronald Kwasnick, pres.; Grant Santimore, gen. mgr.; Robert E. Sene, gen. sls. mgr.; Dennis R. Selenka, corp. controller; Carl Onken, chief eng.; nat'l rep.: Adam Young.

Operation: 1950; TV homes in area: 1,063,100.

WSYM-TV (Channel 47)

600 West St. Joseph St., Lansing, MI 48933 (517) 484-7747.

Pete Bannister, v.p. & gen. mgr.; Bill Shipley, opns. mgr.; Larry Estlack, chief eng.; rep.: MMT Sales.

Operation: December, 1982.

Lansing-Onondaga

WILX-TV (Channel 10) NBC

Adams TV of Lansing, Inc., P.O. Box 30380, Lansing, MI 48909 (517) 783-2621.

Bill Snider, pres. & gen. mgr.; Roger Brandt, lcl. sls. mgr.; Steve Danowski, gen. mgr.; Sandy Rushton, v.p. & natl. sls. mgr.; Pamela Bobzien, v.p., finance; Nancie Gee, prog. dir.; Dan Tambellini, news dir.; Ray Pernot, chief eng.; nat'l rep: Blair.

Operation: 1959.

Marquette

WLUC-TV (Channel 6) CBS, NBC

Federal Bdcstg. Co., P.O. Box 460, Marquette, MI 49855

James Kizer, gen. mgr.; Brad Vansluyters, gen. sls. mgr.; Kim Parker, prog. mgr.; Jack Truitt, chief eng.; Kim Parker, promo. mgr.; Ed Kearney, news dir.; Dale Hemmila, assign. mgr.; nat'l rep.: MMT.

Operation: 1956.

Saginaw-Bay City

WEYI-TV (Channel 25) CBS

WEYI, Inc., 2225 W. Willard Rd., Clio, MI 48420 (517) 755-0525.

Robert A. Epstein, v.p. & gen. mgr.; Bill Beckwith, natl. sls. mgr.; Lynda Peterson, lcl. & reg. sls. mgr.; Jon L. Bengtson, prog. dir.; Don Westherup, promo. mgr.; Mike Hamilton, news dir.

Operation: 1953.

Sault Ste. Marie

WGTQ (Channel 8) ABC

201 East Front St., Traverse City, MI 49684
Jerry K. Moore, v.p. & gen. mgr.
Operation: 1982

WWUP-TV (Channel 10) CBS

Wilson Communications, Inc., Box 627, Cadillac, MI 49601.
Personnel: See WWTV, Cadillac.
Operation: 1962.

Traverse City

WGTU (Channel 29) WGTQ (Channel 8) ABC

Adams Communication Corp., 201 E. Front St., Traverse City, MI 49684; (616) 922-2900.
Jerry K. Moore, v.p. & sta. mgr.; Nancy M. Sundstrom, prog. dir.
Operation: 1971.

WPBN-TV (Channel 7) NBC

WPBN-TV, Inc., P.O. Box 546, Traverse City, MI 49685-0546 (616) 947-7770.
Frank Beam, pres.; Peter S. Good, v.p. & gen. mgr.; Leon Bush, chief eng.
Operation: 1954.

MINNESOTA

Alexandria

KCCO-TV (Channel 7) CBS

KCCO Television, Inc., 720 Hawthorne St., Alexandria, MN 56308 (612) 763-5166.
Vern Muzik, sta. mgr.; John Ginther, sls. mgr.; Wayne Quernemoen, chief eng.; rep.: Seltel; Ramsland (MN)
Operation: 1958.

KSAX (Channel 42) ABC

KSAX-TV, Inc., 415 Fillmore Ave., Alexandria, MN 55308 (612) 763-5729.
Robert R. Regalbuto, pres.; Michael Burgess, sta. mgr.; Dave Taylor, news dir.; Rex Nielson, chief eng.; rep.: Petry.
Operation: Sept. 15, 1987.

Austin

KAAL-TV (Channel 6) ABC

MDM, Inc., P.O. Box 577, Austin, MN 55912 (507) 433-8836.
Clark Cipra, pres. & gen. mgr.; Janet Anderson, prog. dir.; Jerald Jones, v.p./eng.; Dennis Fisher, news dir.; Greg Grimley, prod. mgr.

Duluth-Superior (WI)

KBJR-TV (Channel 6) NBC

RJR Communications, Inc., KBJR Building, Duluth MN 55802 (218) 727-8484.
F. Robert Kalthoff, pres. & gen. mgr.; Steven Rich, prog. dir.; Steve Bolf, sls. mgr.; nat'l rep.: Katz Agency.
Operation: 1954; TV sets in area: 336,500.

KDLH-TV (Channel 3) CBS

Benedek Broadcasting of Minnesota, Inc., 425 West Superior St., Duluth, MN 55802 (218) 727-8911.
John LaForge, gen. mgr.; Steve Hasskamp, chief eng.; Stu Lunsford, dir. sls.; James Cuzzo, prog. dir.; nat'l rep.: MMT.
Operation: 1954; TV sets in area: 326,090.

WDIO-TV (Channel 10) ABC

Channel 10, Inc., 10 Observation Road, Duluth, MN 55811 (218) 727-6864.
Robert Regalbutor, pres. & gen. mgr.; George Couture, sta. mgr.; Dave Poirier, prog. mgr.; George W. Woody, chief eng.; Joel Anderson, news dir.; Lucy Reichert, promo. mgr.
Operation: 1966.

Hibbing

WIRT (Channel 13) ABC

Channel 10, Inc., 10 Observation Rd., Duluth, MN 55811 (218) 727-6864.
Satellite of WDIO-TV, Duluth.
Operation: 1967.

Mankato

KEYC-TV (Channel 12) CBS

United Communications, Corp., P.O. Box 128, Mankato, MN 56001 (507) 890-8128.
Howard J. Brown, pres.; Dennis Wahlstrom, v.p. & gen. mgr.; Eugene W. Schulte, v.p.-secty.-treas.
Operation: October, 1960; TV households: 202,200.

Minneapolis-St. Paul

KARE-TV (Channel 11)

8811 Olson Memorial Hwy., Minneapolis, MN 55427 (612) 546-1111.
Joseph H. Franzgrote, pres. & gen. mgr.; Elliot Bass, gen. sls. mgr.; Lou Morline, lcl. sls. mgr.; Michael Hanrahan, nat'l sls. mgr.; Steven Thaxton, promo. mgr.; Tom Kirby, news dir.; Hillis Aldrich, chief eng.; nat'l rep.: Blair.
Operation: 1965; TV homes in area: 1,766,100.

KITN (Channel 29)

7325 Aspen Lane N., Minneapolis, MN 55428 (612) 424-2929.
Gail L. Brekke, gen. mgr.; Marty Sokoler, gen. sls. mgr.; Dale Palecek, prog. mgr.; Mark Gray, promo. mgr.; Don Kirby, chief eng.; nat'l rep.: MMT.
Operation: October, 1982.

KMSP-TV (Channel 9)

United Television, Inc. 6975 York Ave. So., Minneapolis, MN 55435 (612) 926-9999.
Evan Thompson, pres.; Stuart Swartz, sta. mgr.; Roger Werner, gen. sls. mgr.; Joe Carney, op. mgr.; Penny Parrish, news dir.; Darold Arvidson, dir. of eng.; nat'l rep.: Katz.
Operation: 1955; TV sets in area: 1,838,700.

KSTP-TV (Channel 5) ABC

Hubbard Broadcasting, Inc., 3415 University Ave., Minneapolis, MN 55414 (612) 646-5555.
Robert Regalbuto, pres. & gen. mgr.; John Degan, sta. mgr.; Karl Gersheimer, dir. sls.; nat'l rep.: Petry Television, Inc.
Operation: 1948.

KTMA-TV (Channel 23)

KTMA Acquisition Corp., 2505 N.E. Kennedy St., Minneapolis, MN 55403 (612) 623-0200.
Donald O'Connor, pres. & gen. mgr.; Mary O'Neill, prom.

dir.; James Clark, gen. sls. mgr.; Carolyn Greene, natl. sls. mgr.; nat'l rep.: Seltel.
Operation: September, 1982.

WCCO-TV (Channel 4) CBS
90 South 11th St., Minneapolis, MN 55403 (612) 339-4444.
Ron Handberg, v.p. & gen. mgr.; Bob McGann, v.p. & sta. mgr.; Greg Keck, bus. mgr.; Reid Johnson, dir. news; Marv Danielski, dir. adv. & promo.; nat'l rep.: Telerep.
Operation: 1949; TV sets in area 1,199,800.

Redwood Falls

KRWF (Channel 43) ABC
KSAX-TV, Inc., 3415 University Ave., St. Paul, MN 55114 (612) 646-5555.
Robert R. Regalbuto, pres.; rep.: Petry.
Operation: Apr. 14, 1987.

Rochester

KTTC-TV (Channel 10) NBC
KTTC Television, Inc., 601 First Ave., S.W., Rochester, MN 55901.
John Leifheit, v.p. & gen. mgr.; John Wade, sls. mgr.; Ronald E. Gruber, op. mgr.; C. H. Sanders, chief eng.; nat'l rep.: Seltel.
Operation: July, 1953; TV households: 363,300.

Thief River Falls

KBRR (Channel 10) FOX
Red River Bdcstg. Group, 4015 9th Ave., S.W., Fargo, ND 58103 (701) 277-1515.
Myron Kunin, pres.; Jane Boler, gen. mgr.; Greg Baldwin, gen. sls. mgr.; Kent Lien, prog. dir. & film buyer; Gary Goodrich, opns. mgr. & promo. mgr.; Tim Anderson, chief eng.; rep.: ITS.
Operation: July, 1985.

Walker

KCCW-TV (Channel 12) CBS
KCCO Television, Inc., P.O. Box 1149, 720 Hawthorne St., Alexandria, MN 56308 (Satellite to KCCO).
Vern Muzik, sta. mgr.; Wayne Quernemoen, chief eng.; John Froyd, news dir.
Operation: 1964.

MISSISSIPPI

Biloxi-Gulfport-Pascagoula

WLOX-TV (Channel 13) ABC
WLOX Television, Inc., Box 4596, Biloxi, MS 39531 (601) 896-1313.
John Hash, pres.; Leon Long, v.p. & gen. mgr.; Don Moore, v.p. & opns. mgr.; rep.: Blair
Operation; 1962; TV households: 369,100.

Columbus

WCBI-TV (Channel 4) CBS
Columbus Television, Inc., owner, P.O. Box 271, Columbus, MS 39701 (601) 327-4444.
Frank Imes, gen. mgr.; Brett Smith, prod. mgr.; Bill Doss, chief eng.; Vallory Williamson, prog. dir.; nat'l rep.: Seltel.
Operation: 1956; TV sets in area: 237,200.

Greenville

WXVT (Channel 15) CBS
Big River Broadcasting Co., 3015 E. Reed Rd., Greenville, MS 38701. (601) 334-1500.
Marshall Noecker, pres.; Joe Macione, Jr., v.p. & gen. mgr.; Peter Sparks, chief eng.
Operation: 1980.

Greenwood

WABG-TV (Channel 6) ABC
Mississippi Telecasting Co., Inc., P.O. Box 1243, Greenville, MS 38701 (601) 332-0949.
Cy N. Bahakel, pres.; John Rogers, gen. mgr.; Glenn York, opns. mgr.; Janet Ferguson, off. mgr.; Mike Seiler, gen. sls. mgr.; Jeff Piselli, news dir.; Brad LeBrun, chief eng.; Gene Dent, prog. & promo. dir.
Operation: 1959; TV households: 336,700.

Gulfport

WXXV-TV (Channel 25)
Four-O of Gulfport, Inc., Hwy. 49, P.O. Box 2500, Gulfport, MS 39505; (601) 832-2525.
David C. Hopper, gen. mgr.; Terry Smith, cheif eng.
Operation: January, 1985.

Hattiesburg

WHLT (Channel 22)
Broadcasters of Mississippi, 990 Hardy St., Hattiesburg, MS 39401 (601) 545-2077.
John MacGregor, pres.; Ben R. Strickland, gen. mgr.; Doug Johnson, news dir.; Buck Joston, chief eng.; rep.: Petry.
Operation: Jan. 12, 1987.

Jackson

WAPT (Channel 16) ABC
Magnolia Broadcasting Corp., Box 10297, Jackson, MS 39209 (601) 922-1607.
Robert Price, pres.; Ben Strickland, gen. mgr.; Joe Root, opns. mgr.; Johnny Baily, dir. of eng.
Operation: 1970; TV household: 538,600.

WDBD (Channel 40)
Jackson Television, Ltd., P.O. Box 10888, Jackson, MS 39209 (601) 922-1234.
Sam McLeod, gen. mgr.
Operation: November, 1984.

WJTV (Channel 12) CBS
News Press & Gazette Co., P.O. Box 8887, Jackson, MS 39204 (601) 372-6511.
John MacGregor, pres.; William H. Dilday, Jr., exec. v.p. & gen. mgr.; Jim Stembridge, chief eng.; Phyllis Brooks, prog. dir.; Walter Saddler, news dir.; rep.: Petry.
Operation: 1954; TV sets in area: 434,600.

WLBT (Channel 3) NBC
TV-3, Inc., 715 South Jefferson, Jackson, MS 39205 (601) 948-3333.
Frank E. Melton, gen. mgr. & CEO; Brad Streit, sta. mgr.; Dan Modisett, gen. sls. mgr.; Floyd Kinard, chief eng.; Larry Keeler, prod. mgr.; nat'l rep.: Katz.
Operation: 1953; TV sets in area: 342,000.

Laurel-Hattiesburg

WDAM-TV (Channel 7)

Beam Communications Corp., P.O. Box 1978, Hattiesburg, MS 39401.

Frank L. Beam, pres.; Marvin Reuben, exec. v.p.; Cliff Brown, gen. mgr.; Bobby Smith, chief eng. and oper. mgr.; Diane Schilling, prog. mgr.; nat'l rep.: Katz.

Operation: 1956; TV set in area: 204,500.

Meridian

WLBM-TV (Channel 30) NBC

TV-3, Inc., 4608 Skyland Dr., Meridian, MS 39302-5840 (601) 485-3030.

Frank Melton, CEO & pres.; Pluria Marshall, Jr., v.p. & gen. mgr.; Alfred Martin, lcl. sls. mgr.; Don Spann, prod. & promo. mgr.; Danny Johnson, chief eng.; nat'l rep.: Adam Young.

Operation: October, 1982.

WTOK-TV (Channel 11) ABC

WTOK-TV, Inc., Southern Bldg., Box 2988, Meridian, MS 39402 (601) 693-1441.

Bruce R. Miller, gen. mgr.; Bob Holland, sta. mgr.; Tom Wall, gen. sls. mgr.

Operation: 1953; TV sets in area: 151,900.

WTZH (Channel 24) CBS

Meridian Bdcstg. Partnership, Box 5185, Meridian, MS 39301 (609) 693-2933.

H.A. LeBrun III, pres.; Mike Mitchell, gen. mgr. & gen. sls. mgr.; Dawn Walker, prog. dir. & promo. mgr.; C.A. Page, chief eng.

Operation: June, 1968; TV households: 76,300.

Natchez

WNTZ (Channel 48)

MSLA Bdcstg., Inc., Television Plaza, Beltline Hwy., Natchez, MS 39120 (601) 442-4800.

Donald B. Wilburn, gen. & gen. sls. mgr., film buyer; Mark McKay, prog. dir. & prom. mgr.; Gwen Belton, news dir.; Charles Fisher, chief eng.; natl. rep.: Mutual.

Operation: November, 1985.

Tupelo

WTVA (Channel 9) NBC

WTWV, Inc., Beech Springs Rd., Box 350, Tupelo, MS 38801 (601) 842-7620.

Frank K. Spain, pres.; Mark Ledbetter, exec. v.p. & gen. mgr.; Bob Leech, dir. nat'l sls; Charles Ed Bishop, prog. dir.; Wendell Robionson, chief eng.

Operation: 1957; TV sets in area: 433,900.

West Point

WVSB-TV (Channel 27) ABC

Venture Systems, Inc., Box 777, West Point, MS 39773 (601) 494-8327.

David C. Hopper, pres. & gen. mgr.; Kathy Poulin, gen. sls. mgr.; Lynda Mize, prom. mgr.; Chuck Govan, news dir.; Terry Smith, chief eng.; nat'l rep.: Avery-Knodel.

Operation: May, 1983.

MISSOURI

Cape Girardeau

KBSI (Channel 23) FOX

Cape Girardeau Family TV Ltd., 806 Enterprise, Cape Girardeau, MO 63701 (314) 334-1223.

Linda J. Lawton, gen. mgr.; Constance S. Yeargain, bus. mgr.; Mark Culbertson, prog. dir.; Bryan Uptain, prom. mgr.; David Birdsong, chief eng.; natl. rep.: Seltel.

Operation: September, 1983.

KFVS-TV (Channel 12) FOX

American Hirsch Broadcasting Co., Box 310 Broadway, Cape Girardeau, MO 63701 (314) 335-1212.

Joe Goleniowski, gen. mgr.; Jim Wareham, gen. sls. mgr.; Bishop Ellison, prog. dir.; John Glim, promo. mgr.; nat'l rep.: Katz Agency.

Operation: 1954.

Columbia

KMIZ-TV (Channel 17) ABC

Stauffer Communications, Inc., 501 Business Loop 70 East, Columbia, MO 65201 (314) 449-0917.

Carlos Fernandez, gen. mgr.; Jean Viox, sls. mgr.; Paul Orgel, news dir.; Brad Strohman, chief eng.; Tom Chapman, prog. dir.; Greg Crain, promo. dir.; nat'l rep.: Blair.

Operation: 1971.

KOMU-TV (Channel 8) NBC

The Curators of the University of Missouri, Highway 63, South, Columbia, MO 65201 (314) 442-1122.

Thomas R. Gray, gen. mgr.; Don Ruggles, sales mgr.; Robert Austin, dir. of prog.; James Moore, chief eng.; John Quarderer, dir. of news; nat'l rep.: Seltel.

Operation: 1953; TV sets in area: 505,200.

Hannibal-Quincy (IL)

KHQA-TV (Channel 7) CBS

Benedek Bcstg. 510 Main St., Quincy, IL 62301 (217) 222-6200.

K. James Yager, v.p. Genedek Bdcst.; Lowell Johnson, gen. mgr.; Tana Kenny,, nat'l sls. mgr.; rep.: Katz.

Operation: 1953; TV sets in area: 212,000.

Jefferson City

KRCG-TV (Channel 13) CBS

Box 659, Jefferson City, MO 65102 (314) 896-5144.

Owned by Price Communications, Inc.

Robert Price, pres.; John C. Denshane, v.p.-gen. mgr.; Duane Lammers, sls. mgr.; Cleon Crum, chief eng.; Lee Gordon, prgm. dir.; Roger Wellman, news dir.; nat'l rep.: Katz.

Joplin

KODE-TV (Channel 12) ABC

Gilmore Broadcasting Corp. (licensee), 1928 W. 13th St., Joplin, MO (417) 623-7260.

Bill Acker, gen. mgr.; Gary Hood, gen. sls. mgr.; Mark Current, creative svcs. mgr.; nat'l rep.: Blair.

Operation: 1954; TV sets in area: 440,900 TV households per May '81 ARB.

KSNF (Channel 16) NBC

Tri-State Bdcstg. Corp., P.O. Box 1393, Joplin, MO 64802 (417) 781-2345.

Bill Bengtson, v.p. & gen. mgr.; Bill Ward, gen. sls. mgr.; Mel Brooks, chief eng.; Mike Pound, promo. mgr.; Gary Sisco, prod. mgr.; Steve Russell, news dir.

Operation: September, 1967; TV households: 290,600.

Kansas City

KCTV (Channel 5) CBS

4500 Shawnee Mission Parkway, Fairway, KS 66205 (913) 677-5555.

John C. Rose, v.p. & gen. mgr.; Pat North, gen. sls. mgr.; Erv Parthe, prog. dir.; Patti DeWalt, mktg. mgr.; nat'l rep.: MMT Sales.

Operation: 1953.

KMBC-TV (Channel 9) ABC

Division—The Hearst Corp., 1049 Central, Kansas City, MO 64105 (816) 221-9999.

Paul Dinovitz, v.p. & gen. mgr.; Bill Lind, gen. sls. mgr.; Cheryl Craigie Parker, nat'l sls. mgr.; Robert Twibeli, lcl. sls. mgr.; Deb McDermott, prog. dir.; Gerald Golden, resident controller; Michael Sullivan, news dir.; Joe Todaro, creative svs. dir.

Operation: August, 1953; TV households; 2,098,000.

KSHB-TV (Channel 41)

Scripps-Howard Broadcasting, 4720 Oak St., Kansas City, MO 64112 (816) 753-4141.

Bob Wormington, gen. mgr.; Peter D. Brake, asst. gen. mgr. & film buyer; Harold DeGood, chief eng.

Operation: September, 1970; TV households: 1,225,400.

KYFC (Channel 50)

Kansas City Youth for Christ., Inc. 4715 Rainbow Blvd., Shawnee Mission, KS 66205 (913) 262-1700.

Ronnie Metsker, exec. dir.

Operation: 1978.

KZKC-TV (Channel 62)

Media Central, Inc., 2111 Blue Summit Dr., Kansas City, MO 64126 (816) 254-6262.

Steve Engles, gen. mgr.; Jim MacDonald, gen. sls. mgr.; Todd Powers, prog. dir.; John Mertz, promo. dir.; Greg Fugate, chief eng.; nat'l rep.: Seltel.

Operation: December, 1983.

WDAF-TV (Channel 4) NBC

Great American Broadcasting Company, Signal Hill, Kansas City, MO 64108 (816) 753-4567.

Gary Gardner gen. mgr.; Ed Fulginiti, prog. dir.; Andre Renaud, promo. mgr.; Joyce Reed, news dir.; Jack Winter, chief eng.; nat'l rep.: Telerep.

Operation: 1949; TV sets in area: 1,510,400.

Poplar Bluff

KPOB-TV (Channel 15) ABC

(Satellite of WSIL-TV, Harrisburg, IL)

Mel Wheeler, Inc., 1710 Westminster, Suite F, Denton, TX 76205; nat'l rep.: MMT.

Operation: 1961.

St. Joseph

KQTV (Channel 2) ABC

Elba Development Corp., 270 Commerce Dr., Rochester, NY 14623. (716) 359-3000.

George Loar, v.p. & gen. mgr.; Denise Dailey, gen. sls. mgr.; Dave Tillery, news dir.

Operation: 1953.

KTAS (Channel 16)

All-American TV, Box 403A, Route 1, St. Joseph, MO 64401 (816) 253-9884.

Sonny Arguinzoni, pres.; Terry Hickey, gen. mgr.; Eugene Seibel, chief eng.; rep.: Trinity.

Operation: Oct. 6, 1986.

St. Louis

KDNL-TV (Channel 30)

KDNL, Inc., 1215 Cole St., St. Louis, MO 63106 (314) 436-3030.

William L. Viands, Jr., v.p. & gen. mgr.; Gregory A. Zeiger, gen. sls. mgr.; Bob West, prog. dir.; Otis Thomas, news dir.; James Lowrey, chief eng.; nat'l rep.: MMT.

Operation: 1969.

KMOV-TV (Channel 4) CBS

Viacom Bdcstg., Inc. One Memorial Drive, St. Louis, MO 63102 (314) 621-4444.

Allan Cohen, v.p., gen. mgr.; Peggy Milner, bus. mgr.; Jim Rothschild, opns. dir.; Bob Grissom, gen. sls. mgr.; Al Holzer, news dir.; Wilbur Allmeyer, asst. chief eng.; natl. rep.: Telerep.

Operation: 1959; est. TV sets in area: 1,037,390.

KPLR (Channel 11)

Koplar Communications, Inc., 4935 Lindell Blvd., St. Louis, MO. 63108 (314) 367-7211.

Edward Koplar, pres.; Barry Baker, sr. v.p. & dir. bdcst. div.; Robert Fulstone, v.p. & gen. mgr.; Tim McKernan, dir. sls.; Daniel Neumann, v.p. admin.; James Wright, v.p., opns.; Denny Van Valkenburgh, gen. sls. mgr.; Howard Stevens, prog. mgr.; nat'l rep.: Petry.

Operation: 1959; TV sets in area: 1,067,500.

KSDK (Channel 5) NBC

Multimedia Broadcasting Co. Div. Multimedia Inc., 1000 Market St., St. Louis, MO 63101 (314) 421-5055.

W. L. Bolster, v.p. & gen. mgr.; Wm. J. Katsafanas, gen. sls. mgr.; Edward J. Piette, dir. bdgst. opns.; Richard Brase, dir. creative svcs.; Robert Drewel, lcl. sls. mgr.; Terry Doll, dir. pub. rels.; Ron Turner, news dir.

Operation: 1947; TV households in area: 1,000,000.

KTVI (Channel 2) ABC

Times Mirror Broadcasting, 5915 Berthold Ave., St. Louis, MO 63110 (314) 647-2222.

John McCrory, pres.; Carson W. Capps, v.p. & gen. mgr.; Marshall W. Galliers, v.p. & sta. mgr.; V. Noble Redmon Jr., chief eng.; nat'l rep.: Harrington, Righter, & Parsons.

Operation: 1953; TV sets in area: 1,498,000.

Springfield

KDEB-TV (Channel 27) FOX

Woods Communications Group, Inc., 3000 Cherry St., Springfield, MO 65802 (417) 862-2727.

Charles Woods, pres.; Deborah Corbett, gen. mgr.; Rick Lipps, film buyer; Mike Scott, gen. sls. mgr.; Nancy Bingaman, prog. dir.; Paul Katona, chief eng.; nat'l rep.: Seltel.

Operation: 1968.

KOLR-TV (Channel 10) CBS

Independent Broadcasting Co., P.O. Box 1716 S.S.S., Springfield, MO 65805 (417) 862-1010.

J.H. Cooper, pres.; Ellis Shook, v.p. & gen. mgr.; John O. Cooper, treas.; Howard Frost, chief eng.; Bill Ferrell, gen. sls. mgr.; Al Riggs, lcl. sls. mgr.; nat'l rep., Katz.

Operation: 1953; TV sets in area: 494,300.

KSPR (Channel 33)

Davis-Goldfarb Co., 1359 S. Louis St., Springfield, MO 65802 (417) 831-1333.

B.G. Goldfarb, acting gen. mgr.; Randy Cleland, gen. sls. mgr.; Leland Sanders, prog. dir.; Paula Ringer, opns. mgr.; Gayle Kirchner, promo. mgr.; Jon Kaplan, news dir.; Lou Moyer, chief eng.

Operation: January, 1983.

KYTV (Channel 3) NBC

KY-3, Inc., P.O. Box 3500, Springfield, MO 65808 (417) 868-3800.

Stanley M. Pederson, pres. & gen. mgr.; Franklin D. Schurz, Jr., pres., Schurz Comm., Inc.

Operation: 1953; TV sets in area: 459,600.

MONTANA

Billings

KTVQ (Channel 2) CBS

SJL of Monta Ltd. Partnership, 3203 3rd Ave. N., P.O. Box 2557, Billings, MT (406) 252-5611.

Kelly Sugai, gen. mgr., sls. mgr. & film buyer; Lee Lareva, opers. dir.; Duane Grants, prod. mgr.; Ron Jacobson, chief eng.; nat'l rep.: Blair.

Operation: 1953; TV sets in area: 105,350.

KULR-TV (Channel 8) NBC

KULR Corp., P.O. Box 23909, Billings, MT 59104.

Ron Olsen, pres. & gen. mgr.

Operation: 1958; TV households: 100,300.

Butte

KTVM (Channel 6) ABC, NBC

(Satellite of KECI-TV, Missoula, MT)

Eagle Communications Inc., 750 Dewey Blvd., Butte MT 59701.

Bob Precht, chm.; Ann Ragsdale, v.p. & gen. mgr.; Larry Sem, sta. mgr.; Billy Ward, chief eng.

KXLF-TV (Channel 4) CBS

KXLF Communications, Inc., 1003 S. Montana St., Butte, MT 59701 (406) 792-9111.

Ron Cass, pres., gen. mgr., & nat'l sls. mgr.; Marla Wilkin, sls. mgr.; John Mizelle, chief eng.

Operation: 1953; TV households: 65,600.

Glendive

KXGN-TV (Channel 5) CBS, NBC

Glendive Broadcasting Corp., Broadcast Bldg., 210 South Douglas, Glendive, MT 59330 (406) 365-3377.

Lewis W. Moore, pres.; Dan Frenzel, mgr.; Winnifred Norton, office mgr.

Operation: 1957.

Great Falls

KFBB-TV (Channel 5) ABC

KFBB Corp., P.O. Box 1139, Great Falls, MT 59403 (406) 543-4377.

Stan Whitman, pres.; Jack Fisher, sr. gen. mgr.; Ted Schroeder, ops./prog. mgr.; Jack May, lcl. sls. mgr.; Carol Funston, prog. dir.; Ms. Parker Sullivan, promo. mgr.; Dick Pompa, news dir.; Ron Schlosser, chief eng.; Dick Pompa, news dir.; nat'l rep.: Katz.

Operation: 1954; TV homes in area: 92,700.

KRTV (Channel 3) CBS

KRTV Communications, Inc., P.O. Box 1331, Great Falls, MT 59403.

Donald G. Bradley, pres. & gen. mgr.

Operation: 1958.

KTGF (Channel 16) NBC

Continental Television Network, Inc., 118 Sixth St., So., Great Falls, MT 59405 (406) 761-8816.

James M. Colla, pres. & gen. mgr.; Penny L. Adkins, corp. v.p. & prom. mgr.; Chuck Outland, gen. sls. mgr.; & prog. dir.; M. Thomas Beam, admin. asst.; Cheryl Cordeiro, compt.; natl. rep.: Seltel.

Operation: September, 1986.

Hardin

KOUS-TV (Channel 4) NBC

Big Horn Communications, Inc., P.O. Box 23309, Billings, MT 59102 (406) 652-4743.

Daniel W. Coon, pres.; Thom Curtis, gen. mgr.; Steve Bruggeman, contr.; Tracy Nelson, traffic mgr.; nat'l rep.: Seltel.

Operation: 1980.

Helena

KTVH-TV (Channel 12) NBC

KTVH, Inc., Box 6125, Helena, MT 59604 (406) 443-5050.

Bill Stebbins, lcl. sls. mgr.; Hal Peck, promo. mgr. & film buyer; rep.: Adam Young.

Operation: Jan., 1958; TV households; 91,200.

Kalispell

KCFW-TV (Channel 9) ABC, NBC

(Satellite of KECI-TV: Missoula, MT)

401 First Ave. E., P.O. Box 857, Kalispell, MT 59901.

Anne Ragsdale, v.p.-gen. mgr., Eagle Communications; Steve Fetueit, sta. mgr.; Mark Holston, news dir.; Mike Stocklin, sls. mgr.; Chris Neuhausen, chief eng.

Operation: June, 1968.

Miles City

KYUS-TV (Channel 3) ABC

KYUS-TV, Inc., Box 1074, Miles City, MT 59301 (406) 232-3540.

Daniel Coon, pres.; Dana L. Kehr, v.p. & gen. mgr.; J. R. Middleton, eng.

Operation: Sept., 1969.

Missoula

KECI-TV (Channel 13) ABC, NBC

Eagle Communications, 340 West Main, Missoula, MT (406) 721-2063.

Bob Precht, chmn.; Anne Ragsdale, v.p. & gen. mgr.; Jean Crepeau, prog. dir.; Sharikay Hettick, traffic dir.
TV households in area: 140,000 (ARB).

KPAX-TV (Channel 8) ABC, CBS
KPAX Communications, Inc., Box 4827, Missoula, MT 59801
Bill Sullivan, pres. gen. mgr. & natl. sls. mgr.; Bob Hermas, sls. mgr.; Mark Rapson, chief eng.
Operation: May, 1970.

NEBRASKA

Albion

KCAN-TV (Channel 8) ABC
Citadel Communications Co., Ltd., % KCAU-TV, Sioux City, IA 51101 (402) 495-4995.
Phillip J. Lombardo, pres.; Dan Ackerman, chief eng.
Operation: December, 1964.

Grand Island

KGIN-TV (Channel 11) CBS
Busse Bdcstg. Inc., Box 1069, Grand Island, NE 68801 (308) 382-6100.
Cal Coleman, sta. mgr.; Laura Parks, news mgr.; nat'l rep.: MMT.
Operation: Oct., 1961.

Hastings

KHAS-TV (Channel 5) NBC
Nebraska Television Corp., Highway 281, Box 578, Hastings, NE 68901 (402) 463-1321.
John T. Benson, gen. mgr.; Donald R. Seaton, v.p.; James D. Conway, secty.-treas.; Randy Nicholson, film dir.; nat'l rep.: Seltel.
Operation: 1956; TV sets in area: 169,000.

Hayes Center

KWNB-TV (Channel 6) ABC
(Satellite of KHGI-TV, Kearney, NE)
Same personnel as KHGI-TV; nat'l rep.: Katz.
Operation: 1956; TV sets in area; 52,000.

Kearney

KHGI-TV (Channel 13) ABC
Gordon Bcstg., Inc., Box 220, Kearney, NE 68847; (308) 743-2494. (Also operates KWNB-TV, Hayes Center, NE; KSNB-TV, Superior, NE.)
Robert D. Gordon, pres. & gen. mgr.; Larry Landaker, v.p. sls.; Ron Tillery, v.p. opns. & film buyer; Mary Beth Richmond, promo. mgr.; Jerry Fuehrer, chief eng.; nat'l rep.: Katz.
Operation: 1953; TV households in area 615,800.

Lincoln

KOLN-TV/KGIN-TV (Channel 10) CBS
KOLN, Inc., Box 30350, Lincoln, NE 68503 (402) 467-4321.
Frank Jonas, pres. & gen. mgr.; Richard Nelson, gen. sls. mgr.; Lyle Kaufman, opns. mgr. & chief eng.; Robert Flinn, creative svcs. & prog. dir.; John Denney, news dir.; Christine McPike, contr.; natl. rep. MMT.
Operation: 1953; TV sets in area: 371,000.

McCook-Oberlin

KSNK (Channel 8) NBC
(Satellite of KARD-TV, Wichita, KS)
Kansas State Network Inc., P.O. Box 238, Oberlin, KS 67749.
Al Buch, gen. mgr.; Gary Gore, sls. mgr.; Joan Smith, prog. dir.; rep.: Katz.
Operation: November, 1959.

North Platte

KNOP-TV (Channel 2) NBC
North Platte Television, Inc., Box 749, North Platte, NE 69101. (308) 532-2222.
Ulysses A. Carlini, gen. mgr.; Jodi Ritacca, news dir.; Chris Davies, chf. eng.
Operation: 1958.

Omaha

KETV (Channel 7) ABC
Channel 7, 27th & Douglas Sts., Omaha, NE 68131 (402) 345-7777.
John F. Carpenter, v.p. & gen. mgr.; Howard Shrier, sls. mgr.; Richard S. Spark, bus. mgr.; nat'l rep.: Blair TV.
Operation: 1957; TV sets in area: 578,100.

KMTV (Channel 3) CBS
Lee Enterprises, Inc., 10714 Mockingbird Dr., Omaha, NE 68131 (402) 592-3333.
Howard Kennedy, v.p. & gen. mgr., KMTV; Don Browers, prog. mgr.; Larry Steele, chief eng.; David Kuehn, gen. sls. mgr.; nat'l rep.: Katz.
Operation: 1949; TV sets in area: 415,000.

KPTM (Channel 42)
Pappas Telecasting of the Midlands, 4625 Farnam St., Omaha, NE 68132 (402) 558-4200.
Harry J. Pappas, pres. & gen. mgr.; Jim McKernan, sta. mgr.-gen. mktg. mgr.; Roger Moody, natl. mktg. mgr.; Jill Butler, retail mktg. mgr.; Bruce Binenfeld, promo. mgr.; Jace Anderson, prod. mgr.; Marilyn Rothe, film dir.; Kevin Drewes, chief eng.; Kathi Blahz, accts. supvr.; Dan Rutledge, agency mktg. mgr.; natl. rep.: Telerep.
Operation: April, 1986.

WOWT (Channel 6) CBS
3501 Farnam St., Omaha, NE 68131 (402) 346-6666.
James H. Smith, pres. & gen. mgr.; Don Grubaugh, v.p. & sls. mgr.; John Dixon, prog. dir.; Steve Murphy, news dir.; Judy Horan, dir. promo. & merch.; Bruce Lee, natl.-reg. sls. mgr.; nat'l rep.: Petry.
Operation: 1949; TV sets in area 573,900.

Scottsbluff

KDUH-TV (Channel 4) ABC
Duhamel Bcstg. Enterprises, 1523 1st Ave., Scottsbluff, NE 69341 (308) 632-3071.
William F. Duhamel, pres.; Steve Duffy, gen. mgr.; Wes Haugan, gen. sls. mgr.; Monte Loos, prog. dir., prom. mgr. & film buyer; Helene Duhamel, news dir.; Tom Robinson, chief eng.; nat'l rep.: Katz.
Operation: March, 1958.

KSTF (Channel 10) CBS

(Satellite of KGWN-TV, Cheyenne, WY.)

Stauffer Comm., Inc., 2923 E. Lincolnway, Cheyenne, WY (307) 634-7755.

Carl J. Occhipinti, gen. mgr.; Timothy H. Daniels, res. mgr.; Tony Schaeffer, chief eng.; nat'l rep.: Katz.

Operation: 1955.

Superior

KSNB-TV (Channel 4) ABC

(Satellite of KHGI-TV, Kearney, NE.)

Same personnel as KHGI-TV.; nat'l rep.: Katz.

Operation: October, 1965.

NEVADA

Henderson-Las Vegas

KVVU-TV (Channel 5)

KVVU Broadcasting Corp., 25 TV5 Drive, Henderson, NV 89014 (702) 435-5555.

Phil Jones, pres.; Rusty Durante, gen. mgr.; Bill Utton, gen. sls. mgr.; Jack Smith, dir. of eng.

Operation: Sept., 1967; TV households: 261,100.

Las Vegas

KLAS-TV (Channel 8) CBS

3228 Channel 8 Dr., P.O. Box 15047, Las Vegas, NV 89114 (702) 733-8850.

Lemuel Lewis, v.p./gen. mgr.; Andy Henderson, gen. sls. mgr.; Craig Spellerberg, promo. mgr; John Nelson, chief eng.; nat'l rep.: Katz Television.

Operation: 1953; TV sets in area: 213,000.

KRLR (Channel 21)

Dres Media, Inc., Box 26815, Las Vegas, NV 89126; (702) 382-2121.

Charlene Scott, pres.; Rick Scott, gen. mgr.; Wayne Gartley, sta. mgr.; Chris Hume, promo. mgr.; Steve Scott, chief eng.

Operation: July, 1984.

KTNV-TV (Channel 13) ABC

KTNV-TV, 3355 S. Valley View, Las Vegas, NV 89102 (702) 876-1313.

Jim Behling, v.p. & gen. mgr.; Gary Plumlee, gen. sls. mgr.; Tim Foster, nat'l sls. mgr.; Stormi Lloyd-Drake, prog. dir.; Ron Futrell, sports dir.; Michael Williams, production mgr.; Richard Urey, news dir.; Terry Ostlund, chief eng.; Peter Sensenbaugh, bus. mgr.-contr.; Curt Hall, promo. mgr.

Operation: 1956; TV households: TSA 682,600.

KVBC (Channel 3) NBC

Valley Broadcasting Co., Box 44169, Las Vegas, NV 89116 (702) 649-0500.

Rolla D. Cleaver, gen. mgr.; Buzz Floyd, prog. mgr.; nat'l rep.: Blair TV.

Operation: 1955.

Reno

KAME-TV (Channel 21)

Page Enterprises, P.O. Box 11129, Reno, NV 89510 (702) 786-2121.

Bill Andrews, pres. & gen.mgr.; Mike Andrews, sls. mgr.; B.J. Andrews, sta. mgr.; Donald Schrader, prog. dir.; Al Ruch, chief eng.; nat'l rep.: Seltel.

Operation: October, 1981.

KCRL-TV (Channel 4) NBC

Circle L. Inc., 1790 Vassar St., Reno, NV 89502 (702) 322-9145.

Edward Neuhoff, pres.; Jim Elliott, v.p. & gen. mgr.; John Firpo, news dir.; Norvel Seyler, chief eng.; rep.: MMT

Operation: 1962; TV households: 166,600.

KOLO-TV (Channel 8) ABC

Donrey of Nevada, Box 10,000, Reno, NV 89510 (702) 786-8880.

Fred Smith, pres.; James C. Herzig. gen. mgr.; Bob Thompson, gen. sales mgr.; John Csia, prog. mgr.; Earl Ling, promo. dir.; Robert Northam, chief eng. ; nat'l rep.: Blair.

Operation: 1953; TV sets in area: 234,000.

KREN-TV (Channel 27)

Sainte Limited, P.O. Box 4159, Modesto, CA 95352-4159 (209) 523-0777.

Chester Smith, gen. partner; Herbert G. Crenshaw, eng.

Operation: November, 1985.

KTVN (Channel 2) CBS

Sarkes Tarzian, Inc., 4925 Energy Way, Reno, NV 89502 (702) 786-2212.

Dennis Slewert, gen. mgr; John Richardson, sta. & gen. sls. mgr.; Al Richards, chief eng.; Matt James, news editor; rep.: Katz.

Operation: 1967; TV households: 161,000.

NEW HAMPSHIRE

Concord

WNHT (Channel 21)

The Flatley Co., Box 2100, Concord, NH 03301 (603) 225-2100.

Thomas J. Flatley, pres.; Ronald Polera, gen. mgr.; Bob Joyce, prog. dir.; R. Gregg Chadwick, chief eng.

Operation: April, 1984.

Derry

WNDS (Channel 50)

CTV of Derry, Inc., TV-50 Place, Derry, NH 03038 (603) 434-8850.

John L. Foley, gen. mgr.; Kent Ohlman, prod. & promo. mgr.; Brooke Willis, news dir.; Paul Hunter, chief eng.

Operation: September, 1983.

Manchester

WMUR-TV (Channel 9) ABC

WMUR, Inc., 50 Phillippe Cote St., Manchester, NH 03105 (603) 669-9999.

David Zamichow, gen. mgr.; Miles Resnick, news dir.; nat'l rep.; Seltel.

Operation: 1954; TV sets in area: 965,576.

Merrimack

WGOT (Channel 60)

Golden Triangle TV 60 Corp., Box 60, Merrimack, NH 03054 (603) 424-6060.

John Fergie, gen. mgr.; Neal P. Cortell, sta. & prog. mgr.; Steve Tamposi, cons. mgr.; Sally Tamposi, news & pub. affrs.; S. Joseph Hoffman, treas. & sls. & mktg. mgr.

Operation: 1987.

NEW JERSEY

Atlantic City

WWAC-TV (Channel 53)

Channel 53 Corp., 3600 Conshohocken Ave., Philadelphia, PA 19131 (215) 473-9060.

William S. Gross, owner.

Operation: February, 1988.

Vineland

WHSP (Channel 65)

Silver King Bdcstg. of Vineland, Inc., 4449 N. Delsea Dr., Newfield, NJ 08344 (609) 691-6565.

Carmen J. Colucci, gen. mgr.; Chris Hill, prog. & news dir.; Dan Merlo, chief eng.

Operation: July, 1981.

Wildwood

WMGM-TV (Channel 40) NBC

South Jersey Broadcasting Corp., 15 Shore Rd., Linwood, NJ 08221 (609) 927-4440.

Howard Green, pres.; Jane B. Stark, sta. mgr.; Chris Adams, prog. dir.; Kathy McNiff, prod. mgr.; Jeff Whitaker, news dir.

Operation: 1966; TV households: 400,000.

NEW MEXICO

Albuquerque

KGGM-TV (Channel 13) CBS

New Mexico Broadcasting Co., Inc., 1414 Coal Ave., S.W., Albuquerque, NM 87104 (505) 243-2285.

Andrew B. Hebenstreit, pres.; Irwin P. Starr, v.p. & gen. mgr.; William W. Andrews, creative svcs. dir.; Alan P. Deme, chief eng.

KGSW (Channel 14)

Mountain States Broadcasting/Providence Journal Broadcasting, Box 25200, Albuquerque, NM 87125 (505) 842-1414.

Erick B. Steffens, gen. mgr.; Jason Gould, gen. sls. mgr.; James Gonsey, tech. opns. mgr.; Michael Maulano, natl. sls. mgr.; nat'l rep.: Telerep.

Operation: 1981

KNAT (Channel 23)

Trinity Bcstg. of Arizonia, Inc., 1510 Coors Blvd., N.W., Albuquerque, NM 87105 (505) 836-1992.

Bob Brewer, v.p. & gen. mgr.; Dave Cavileer, gen. sls. mgr.; Sandie Zolman, prog. dir.; Bill Frost, chief eng.

Operation: 1975.

KOAT-TV (Channel 7) ABC

KOAT-TV, Inc., Box 25982, Albuquerque, NM 87125 (505) 884-7777.

C. Wayne Godsey, v.p. & gen. mgr.; Elvin Smith, asst. gen. mgr.; James Sharman, chief eng.; Mary Lynn Roper, news dir.; nat'l rep.: Blair.

Operation: 1953, TV homes in area: 276,000.

KOB-TV (Channel 4) NBC

Hubbard Broadcasting, Inc., Box 1351, 4 Broadcast Plaza, S.W., Albuquerque, NM 87103 (505) 243-4411.

Stanley S. Hubbard, pres.; Jerry Danziger, gen. mgr.; Dave Herman, sta. mgr.; Bob Evans, sls. mgr.; Sam Tikkanen, chief eng.; nat'l rep.: Edward Petry Co.

Operation: 1948; TV sets in area: 442,700.

Carlsbad

KVIO-TV (Channel 6) ABC

Marsh Media of El Paso, Box 12077, Texas American Bank Bldg., Amarillo, TX 79101 (806) 372-5555.

Richard Pearson, gen. mgr.; Jack Wilkinson, chief eng.

Operation: 1956; TV sets in area: 15,600.

Clovis

KVIH-TV (Channel 12) ABC

Marsh Media, Inc., One Broadcast Center, Amarillo, TX 79101 (806) 373-1787. Satellite of KVII-TV, Amarillo, TX.

James R. McCormick, pres. & gen. mgr.; John Patrick, gen. sls. mgr.; Mac Douglas, prog. dir. & film buyer; Steve Pritchett, news dir.; Bill Canady, chief eng.; natl. rep.: Katz.

Operation: December, 1957.

Farmington

KOBF (Channel 12) NBC

P.O. Box 1620, Farmington, NM 87499 (505) 326-1141.

Bettie Cleveland, gen. mgr.; Bill Hirshey, prod. mgr.; Dan Bibeau, chief eng.

Operation 1972.

Las Cruces

KASK (Channel 48) ABC, NBC

Bayport Communications of New Mexico, Inc., 900 First National Tower, Las Cruces, NM 88001 (505) 524-2103.

Logan D. Matthews, pres. & gen. mgr.; Albert F. Gabalis, gen. sls. mgr.; Christopher Jackson, opns. mgr.; Gary Worth, news dir.; Ralph Quiroz, chief eng.; nat'l rep.: Spot Time.

Operation: October, 1984.

Roswell

KBIM-TV (Channel 10) CBS

Caprock Telecasting, Inc., Box 910, Roswell, NM 88201 (505) 622-2120.

Marc Reischman, gen. mgr.; E. Sills, dir. eng.; Dave Brown, v.p., news; nat'l rep.: Katz.

Operation: 1966; TV homes: 113,300.

KOBR (Channel 8) NBC

Hubbard Bdcstg., Inc., 124 E. Fourth St., Roswell, NM 88201 (505) 625-8888.

Stanley S. Hubbard, pres.; Tim Spinder, sta. mgr.; Larry Oldrup, gen. sls. mgr.; John Purvis, news dir.; Dave Atkins, chief eng.; natl. rep.: Petry.

Operation: June, 1953.

Santa Fe

KCHF (Channel 11)

Son Broadcasting, Inc., Box 4338, Albuquerque, NM 87106 (505) 983-1111.

Belarmino R. Gonzales, pres. & gen. mgr.; Susan Stein, gen. sls. mgr.; Mary Kay Gonzales, opns. & promo. mgr.; Luther Kent, chief eng.

Operation: November, 1983.

KNMZ-TV (Channel 2)

Coronado Communications, Co., P.O. Box 580, Santa Fe, NM 87504 (505) 473-2002.

Carl F. Floyd, v.p., gen. mgr.; Eva Lopez, prog. dir.; Cassie Travaini, gen. sls. mgr.

Operation: October, 1983.

Silver City

KWNM-TV (Channel 10) ABC

Box 25982, Albuquerque, NM 87125 (505) 884-7777.
James H. Sharman, chief eng.; natl. rep.: Blair.

NEW YORK

Albany

WNYT (Channel 13) NBC

Viacom Broadcasting Corp., P.O. Box 4035, Albany, NY 12204 (518) 436-4791.

Donald D. Perry, v.p. & gen. mgr.; Richard Klein, chief eng.; James Moore, dir. prod.; Noelle Wall, dir. opns.; Stephen Baboulis, news dir.; Tom Raponi, gen. sls. mgr.; Karl Davis, nat'l sls. mgr.; Linda Cummings, traffic mgr.; Thomas Blau, bus. mgr.; Douglas Jones, dir. prog. & pub. aff.

Operation: 1954.

WRGB (Channel 6) CBS

WRGB Bdcstg., Inc., 1400 Balltown Rd., Schenectady, NY 12309; (518) 346-6666.

David Lynch, v.p. & gen. mgr.; Terry Walden, mgr. prog.; Beverly Wittner, mgr. pub. affairs; Gary Whitaker, news. dir.; William Brandt, mgr., prom.

Operation: 1947.

WTEN (Channel 10)

Knight-Ridder Broadcasting Company, Incorporated, 341 Northern Blvd., Albany, NY 12204 (518) 436-4822.

Don C. Smith, pres. & gen. mgr.; John Hirsh, gen. sls. mgr.; Bob Peterson, prog. mgr.; James Holland, news dir.

WXXA-TV (Channel 23)

Heritage Bdcstg. Group, P.O. Box 6423, Albany, NY 12206 (518) 438-8700.

Will Meyl, v.p. & gen. mgr.; David Boaz, gen. sls. mgr.; Sargent Cathrall, chief eng.; nat'l rep.: Petry.

Operation: July, 1982.

Binghamton

WBNG-TV (Channel 12) CBS

Gateway Communications, Inc., 50 Front Street, Binghamton, NY 13902 (607) 723-7311.

John S. Mucha, v.p. & gen. mgr.; Mark Prutisto, prog. mgr.; Joseph McNamara, gen. sls. mgr.; Ronald Shoemaker, chief eng.

WICZ-TV (Channel 40)

Stainless Broadcasting, Vestal Parkway East, Binghampton, NY 13902 (607) 770-4040.

Jesse Pevear, v.p. & gen. mgr.; G. Ricciardelli, tech. dir.; nat'l rep.: MMT.

WMGC-TV (Channel 34) ABC

Citadel Communications, Ltd., Box 813, Binghamton, NY 13902.

Philip J. Lombardo, mng. gen. partner, gen. mgr.; Brad Worthen, gen. sls. mgr.; Mary Ann Connerton, lcl. sls. mgr.; M. Susan Boncek, bus. mgr.; Darcy Thorton, news dir.; nat'l rep.: Katz.

Operation: 1962; TV households: 171,000.

Buffalo

WGRZ-TV (Channel 2) NBC

WGRZ-TV, Inc., 259 Delaware Ave., Buffalo, NY 14202 (716) 856-1414.

Raymond P. Maselli, pres. & gen. mgr.; David Milldream, v.p. sls. & progmg.; Tom Cochran, gen. sls. mgr.; April Harrington Conton, prom. mgr.; Gary Legters, opns. mgr.; David Baer, news dir.; Richard Westlund, chief eng.; Joe Lentini, dir. community reltns.; nat'l rep.: Katz.

Operation: August, 1954.

WIVB-TV (Channel 4) CBS

Buffalo Broadcasting Co., Inc., 2077 Elmwood Ave., Buffalo, NY 14207; (716) 874-4410.

Leslie G. Arries, Jr., pres.; John Hayes, sta. mgr.; Wilson Shepard, gen. sls. mgr.; Ralph Thompsom, dir. of eng. nat'l rep.: Harrington, Righter & Parsons, Inc.

Operation: 1948; TV households in area: 1,038,700; U.S. & Canada: 2,700,300.

WKBW-TV (Channel 7)

WKBW-TV, Queen City Bdcstg., Inc., 7 Broadcast Plaza, Buffalo, NY 14202.

Steve Kimatian, pres. & gen. mgr.; Clifford Fisher, v.p. & gen. sales mgr.; Sarah Norat-Phillips, prog. & p.a. dir.; Don Holland, chief engineer; rep.: Petry.

Operation: 1958.

WNYB-TV (Channel 49)

Niagara Frontier Bdcstg., 699 Hertel Ave., Buffalo, NY 14207 (716) 875-4919.

Paul A. Mooney, pres.; Bill Saltzgiver, gen. mgr.; Joe Cayton, prog. dir.; Rick Mortellaro, prom. mgr.; Mike Anger, chief eng.; natl. rep.; Seltel.

Operation: September, 1987.

WUTV (Channel 29) FOX

Citadel Communications Co., Ltd., 951 Whitehaven Rd., Grand Island, NY 14072 (716) 773-7531

Philip J. Lombardo, pres.; Frank B. Gregg, v.p. & gen. mgr.; Dennis Majewicz, chief eng.; Ken Kaszubowski, mgr. bdcst. opns.; Tony McMahon, gen. sls. mgr.; Lois M. Ringle, prog. dir.

Operation: December, 1970; TV households: 1,213,100.

Carthage-Watertown

WWNY-TV (Channel 7) CBS, NBC

United Communication Corp., 120 Arcade St., Watertown, NY 13601 (315) 788-3800.

Howard J. Brown, pres.; Eugene W. Schulte, v.p.; Kevin Mastellon, gen. mgr.; Ed Dempsey, sls. mgr.; Lois Dempster, prog. dir.; Don Rohr, chief eng.; nat'l rep.: Katz TV.

Operation: 1954; TV sets in area: 156,920.

Elmira

WENY-TV (Channel 36) ABC

WENY, Inc., P.O. Box 208, Elmira, NY 14902 (707) 739-3636.

Howard L. Green, exec. v.p.; Patrick M. Parish, gen. mgr.; Meade Murtland, sta. mgr.; Don Ryan, dir. of eng.

Operation: Nov., 1969.

WETM-TV (Channel 18) NBC

(Satellite of WSTM-TV, Syracuse, NY)

WETM-TV, Inc., Box 1207, Elmira, NY 14902 (607) 733-5518.

Robert N. Smith, pres.; John Wingate, v.p. & gen. mgr.; Larry Taylor, chief eng.

Operation: 1956; TV sets in area: 83,600.

Kingston

WTZA (Channel 62)

WTZA-TV Associates, Box 1609, 721 Broadway, Kingston, NY 12401 (914) 339-6200.

Edward P. Sawyer, CEO; Gene Collins, sta. mgr.; John Wolfe, gen. sls. mgr.; Brian Madden, news dir.; Harry Kaemmerer, chief eng.

Operation: Dec. 15, 1985.

New York City

WABC-TV (Channel 7) ABC

Capital Cities/ABC, Inc., 7 Lincoln Square, New York, NY 10023 (212) 887-7777.

Walter C. Liss, Jr., pres. & gen. mgr.; Tom Kane, gen. sls. mgr.; Art Moore, prog. dir.; Cliff Love, public svc. dir.; Richard R. Graham, dir. fin.; Rob Battles, dir. of creative services; James Baker, chief eng.

Operation: 1948; TV sets in area: 6,000,000.

WCBS-TV (Channel 2) CBS

CBS Television Stations, Division of Columbia Broadcasting System, Inc., 524 W. 57 St., New York, NY 10019 (212) 975-4321.

Neil E. Derrough, pres.; Roger Colloff, v.p. & gen. mgr.; Robert Fogarty, sls. dir.; Dolores Danska, dir. bcstg.; Bill Lacey, dir. bcst. admin.; Steve Wasserman, news dir.; Toni Johnson, opns. mgr.

Operation: 1941; TV sets in area: 6,000,000.

WNBC-TV (Channel 4) NBC

WNBC-TV, 30 Rockefeller Plaza, New York, NY 10112 (212) 664-4444.

Carl V. Bud Carey, v.p. & gen. mgr.; Karen Lee Copeland, prog. dir.; Lou Abitabilo, dir. sls.; Linda Lipman, dir. adv. & promo.; Dave Vacheron, mgr. bdcst. standards; Julian Phillips, mgr. community relns.

Operation: 1941; TV sets in area: 6,000,000.

WNYW-TV (Channel 5) FOX

Fox TV Stations, Inc., 205 E. 67 St., New York, NY 10021 (212) 535-1000.

Robert Kreek, pres.; Carolyn Wall, v.p. & gen. mgr.; Rudy Taylor, gen. sls. mgr.; Jon Findley, prog. dir.; Joe Berini, chief eng.; nat'l rep.: Petry.

Operation: 1944; TV households in area: 6,471,396.

WWOR-TV (Channel 9) Secaucus, NJ

9 Broadcast Plaza, Secaucus, NJ 07096 (201) 348-0009.

Michael Alexander, exec. v.p. & gen. mgr.; Thomas Ryan, v.p./gen. sls. mgr.; Farrell Meiser, v.p. prog.; Rick Miner, v.p. prod. & opns.; Cynthia Harrison, dir. comm. aff. & p.r.; Tom Petner, v.p. news.

WPIX (Channel 11)

WPIX Inc., 11 WPIX Plaza, New York, NY 10017; (212) 949-1100.

Leavitt J. Pope, pres.; David Polinger, sr. v.p. asst. to pres.; Gerald Mulderring, sr. v.p. sls.; John Corporon, sr. v.p. news; Pat Austin, sr. v.p., finance; Julie Nunnari, v.p. prog.; Paul Bisonette, v.p. creative svcs.; Liz Goldberg, v.p. opns.; Bob Murch, v.p., eng.; Fred Witte, contr.; Jane Perlman, v.p. rsrch.; Claudia Gasparini, v.p., human resources; Martin Appel, v.p. sports & pub. reltns.; Kathleen Shepherd, v.p. prod. & community affairs; Laurence Linehan, Gerard Puccio, John McGowan, v.p., sls.; Elaine Huryn, v.p., planning.

Operation: 1948; TV households in area: 6,878,000 (ARB).

New York-Newark (NJ)

WHSE-TV (Channel 68/60)

Silver King Bdcstg. of New Jersey, Inc., 390 W. Market St., Newark, NJ 07107.

Ella Connors, v.p. & sta. mgr.; Alvin Saltzman, chief eng.; William Roller, prog. mgr.

Operation: July, 1977.

WNJU-TV (Channel 47)

47 Industrial Ave., Newark, NJ 07608 (201) 288-5550.

Carlos Barba, pres. & gen. mgr.; Thomas Johansen, v.p. & sls. dir.; Julio Omana, sta. mgr.; George Kraus, v.p., sta. mgr. & chief eng.; Sylvia Pascual, prog. dir.

Operation: May, 1965; TV households: 2,300,000.

New York-Paterson (NJ)

WXTV (Channel 41)

Univision Station Group, Inc., 24 Meadowland Parkway, Secaucus, NJ 07094.

Emilio Nicolas, Jr., gen. mgr.; Eileen M. Holmes, gen. sls. mgr.; Osvaldo Onoz, prog. dir.; Alan Cohen, chief eng.; rep.: Univision.

Operation: 1968.

Plattsburgh-Burlington (VT)

WPTZ (Channel 5) NBC

Heritage Media Corp., Old Moffitt Rd., Plattsburgh, NY 12901 (518) 561-5555.

Carl Leahy, gen. mgr.; Bruce Grindle, gen. sls. mgr.; Stacie Tetreault, opns. dir.; Bruce Carlin, promo. mgr.; Thomas Bradshaw, chief eng.

Operation: 1956; TV homes in area: 252,600 (U.S.); 954,880 (Canada).

Poughkeepsie

WTBY (Channel 54)

Trinity Broadcasting of New York, Box 534, Fishkill, NY 12524 (914) 896-4610.

Paul Crouch, pres. & gen. mgr.; Stan Hollin, gen. sls. mgr.; Terry Hickey, prog. dir. & film buyer; Lindy Dressler, promo. mgr.; Dale Osborn, chief eng.

Operation: April, 1981.

Riverhead

WLIG (Channel 55)

WLIG-TV 55, Inc. 300 Crossways Park Drive, Woodbury, NY 11797 (516) 364-1500.

Michael C. Pascucci, pres.; Marvin R. Chauvin, v.p. & gen. mgr.; Tara Leporati, sls. mgr.; Bruce David Klein, prog. dir.

Operation: January, 1985.

Rochester

WHEC-TV (Channel 10) CBS

WHEC, Inc., 191 East Avenue, Rochester, NY 14604 (716) 546-5670.

Arnold Klinsky, v.p. & gen. mgr.; Alan Cartwright, sls. dir.; John Walsh, chief eng.; Steve Hammel, news dir.; nat'l rep.: Telerep.

Operation: 1953; TV sets in area, 453,500.

WOKR (Channel 13) ABC

WOKR Partners, 4225 W. Henrietta Rd., Rochester, NY 14623 (716) 334-8700.

Vincent T. DeLuca, pres./gen. mgr.; Donald J. Loy, prog. dir.-creative svcs.; Margaret Camera, controller; Clyde Parker, eng. mgr.; Kent Beckwith, gen. sls. mgr.; Jim Sanders, nat'l sls. mgr.; nat'l rep.: MMT.

Operation: 1962; TV households: 1,191,800.

WROC-TV (Channel 8) NBC

Television Station Partners, 201 Humboldt St., Rochester, NY 14610 (716) 288-8400.

Thomas F. Kenney, v.p. & gen. mgr.; Geoff Proud, nat'l sls. mgr.; Jeff Ulrich, prog. mgr.; David Nolan, news dir.; Margaret Myers, promo. supvr.; John Coon, chief eng.

Operation: 1949; TV sets in area: 479,000.

WUHF (Channel 31) FOX

Mairite TV of New York, Inc., 360 East Ave., Rochester, NY 14604 (716) 232-3700.

Milton Matitz, chm.; Rick Rambaldo, v.p. & gen. mgr.; nat'l rep.: Blair TV.

Operation: 1980.

Smithtown

WHSI-TV (Channel 67)

Silver King Bcstg. of New Jersey, Inc. 390 West Market St., Newark NJ 07107; (516) 582-6700.

Ella Connors, sta. mgr.; David Porrello, prog. mgr.; Alvin Saltzman, chief eng.

Operation: November, 1973.

Syracuse

WIXT-TV (Channel 9) ABC

WIXT-TV, Inc., 5904 Bridge St., East Syracuse, NY 13057 (315) 446-4780.

Steve Kronquest, v.p. & gen. mgr.; Angela Roach, nat'l sls. mgr.; John King, chief eng.

Operation: 1962.

WSTM-TV (Channel 3) NBC

WSTM-TV, Inc., 1030 James St., Syracuse, NY 13203 (315) 474-5000.

Ronald W. Philips, pres. & gen. mgr.; Russ Hamilton, gen. sls. mgr.; John Mangione, creative svcs. dir.

Operation: 1950; TV sets in area: 525,000.

WSYT (Channel 68) FOX

1000 James St., Syracuse, NY, 13203 (315) 472-6800.

Vincent Arminio, gen. mgr.; Robert Jordan, opns. mgr.; Rick Herrmann, prog.-promo. dir.; Bill Hoctor, chief eng.; natl. rep.: Katz.

Operation: February, 1986.

WTVH-TV (Channel 5) CBS basic

Meredith Corp., 980 James St., Syracuse, NY 13203 (315) 425-5555.

Cathy Creany, v.p. & gen. mgr.; Michael Collins, gen. sls. mgr.; Louis Dennig, prog. dir.; David Oetjen, promo. mgr.; Edward D. Lewis, dir. of eng.; nat'l rep.: MMT Sales Inc.

Operation: 1948 as WHEN-TV; TV sets in area: 480,000.

Utica

WKTV (Channel 2) NBC

Harron Communications Corp., P.O. Box 2, Utica, NY 13503 (315) 733-0404.

Shell Storrier, sr. v.p. & gen. mgr.; Paul Harron, Jr., pres.; Daniel German, program. dir. & promo. mgr. & film dir.; Marie Zumpano, traffic mgr.; Merv Ainsworth, chief eng.; nat'l rep.: Katz.

Operation: 1949; TV homes in area: 340,100.

WTUV (Channel 33) FOX

Mohawk Valley Bdcstg., Inc., Greenfield Ave., Rome, NY 13440 (315) 336-6954.

Kevin O'Kane, pres. & gen. mgr.; John Amado, gen. sls. mgr.; Rick Lewis, promo. mgr.; John Bunkfeldt, chief eng.; rep.: Mutual.

Operations: October, 1986.

WUTR (Channel 20) ABC

Roy H. Park Bcstg. of Utica-Rome Inc., P.O. Box 20, Utica, NY 13503 (315) 797-5220.

Roy H. Park, pres.; Paul Kennedy, gen. mgr.; rep.: Blair.

Operation: Feb., 1970.

Watertown

WFYF (Channel 50)

Moreland Broadcast Associates, Box 6250, Watertown, NY 13601.

David J. Alteri, gen. mgr.

Operation: January, 1988.

NORTH CAROLINA

Asheville

WHNS-TV (Channel 21)

Pappas Telecasting of the Carolinas, Studio: 21 Interstate Ct., Greenville, SC 29615 (803) 288-2100; Sales Office: 521 College St., Asheville, NC 28801 (704) 258-2100.

Harry J. Pappas, pres.; Joseph A. Shaffer, v.p.-gen. mgr.; Henry Boyce, prog. mgr.; Anthony R. Thompson, gen. mktg. mgr.; Jerry Garvin, chief eng.

Operation: 1964; TV sets in area: 625,000.

WLOS-TV (Channel 13) ABC

WLOS TV, Inc., Box 1300, Asheville, NC 28802 (704) 255-0013. 105 N. Spring St., P.O. Box 2666, Greenville, SC 29602 (803) 271-1313.

James Cowshaftor, v.p. & gen. mgr.; Cliff Pine, prog. mgr.; J. David Burrell, gen. sls. mgr.; Bill Walsh, bus. mgr.; nat'l rep.: HRP.

Operation: 1954; TV households in area: 1,569,400 TSA.

Belmont

WJZY (Channel 46)

Capitol Bdcstg. Co., Inc., Box 668400, Charlotte, NC 28266-8400.; 3501 Performance Rd., Charlotte, NC 28214 (704) 398-0046.

James Goodmon, pres.; Mark Conrad, v.p. & gen. mgr.; Thomas Schenk, gen. sls. mgr.; Janet Noll, lcl. sls. mgr.; Steve Pickle, prom. mgr.; Ed Merritt, chief eng.; natl. rep.: Seltel.
Operation: March, 1987.

Burlington

WRDG (Channel 16)

Box 16, Burlington, NC 27215 (919) 376-9868.
Jack Rehburg, pres.; Steve Rehburg, gen. mgr. & prom.-adv. mgr.
Operations: August, 1984.

Charlotte

WBTV (Channel 3) CBS

Jefferson Pilot Broadcasting Co., One Julian Price Place, Charlotte, NC 28208 (704) 374-3500.
Joseph M. Bryan, chm. bd.; James G. Babb, Jr., pres.; Cullie M. Tareton, sr. v.p. & gen. mgr.; William F. Foy, news and info. mgr.; Marion Meginnis, program oprs. mgr.; Jerry Pelletier, gen. sls. mgr.; Paul Cameron, sports dir.; Mrs. Tommi L. Jones, v.p./personnel; Joseph B. Young, v.p./research & planning; Bill Napier, Jr., dir. of eng.
Operation: 1949; TV sets in area; 1,150,540.

WCCB-TV (Channel 18)

WCCB-TV, Inc., 1 Television Place, Charlotte, NC 28205 (704) 372-1800.
Cy N. Bahakel, pres.; Steven Soldinger, gen. mgr.; William Riordan, gen sls mgr.; Howard Trivette, prog. dir.; Robert Phillips, chief eng.; nat'l rep.: Katz.
Operation: Dec., 1953.

WPCQ-TV (Channel 36)

Journal Bdcstg. of Charlotte, Inc., P.O. Box 18665, Charlotte, NC 28218 (704) 536-3636.
John Hayes, pres. & gen. mgr.; Tim Bloodworth, prog. dir.; Rick Anderson, chief eng.; Nick Magnini, gen. sls. mgr.
Operation: 1967; TV households: 2,165,200.

WSOC-TV (Channel 9) ABC

Carolina Broadcasting Company, P.O. Box 34665, Charlotte, NC 28234 (704) 335-4999.
Grey Stone, v.p., gen. mgr.; Jack Callaghan, sta. mgr.; Merritt Rose, gen. sls. mgr.; Martin Fenton, lcl. sls. mgr.; A. Bruce Chastine, contr.; Alan Batten, dir., adv./promo.; Richard Moore, news dir.; Merle Thomas, chief eng.; nat'l rep.: Telerep.
Operation: 1957; TV sets in area. 2,892,800.

Durham

WTVD (Channel 11) ABC

Capital Cities/ABC, Inc., Box 2009, 411 Liberty St., Durham, NC 27702 (919) 683-1111.
Alan Nesbitt, pres./gen. mgr.; Denis O'Connor, gen. sls. mgr.; Jon L. Miller, prog. mgr.; Chrystle Swain, dir. of community affairs.; Dave Davis, news dir.; William Higgs, bus. mgr.; Edward Wall, chief eng.
Operation: 1954; TV homes in area: 621,000 (ADI).

Durham-Raleigh

WPTF-TV (Channel 28) NBC

Durham Life Broadcasting Service, Inc., 29521, 3012 Highwoods Blvd., Raleigh, NC 27604 (919) 832-8311.
Felton P. Coley, pres.; Robert B. Butler, v.p. & gen. mgr.; Robert Wolfe, prog. dir.; Barbara Nicely, promo. mgr.; Kevin Kelly, news dir.; nat'l rep.: Blair.
Operation: November, 1968; TV households, 598,000.

Fayetteville

WFCT (Channel 62)

Fayetteville Cumberland Telecasters, Inc., Drawer 62, Lumber Bridge, Fayetteville, NC 28357 (919) 843-3884.
Ernie Whitmeyer, gen. mgr.; Glenn Yearby, sls. mgr.; Jenny Martin, prog. opns.; Don O'Banion, chief eng.; nat'l rep.: Adam Young.
Operation: March, 1985.

WKFT (Channel 40)

SJL of No. Carolina Associates, 230 Donaldson St., Fayetteville, NC 28301 (919) 323-4040.
Richard Armfield, gen. mgr.; Arlene Mabry, prog. dir.
Operation: 1981.

Goldsboro

WYED (Channel 17)

Box 1117, 622 S. Barbour St., Clayton, NC 27520 (919) 553-1700.
Bob Peretic, sta. & gen. sls. mgr.; prog. dir.; film buyer; Niel Sollod, promo. mgr. & news dir.; Sam Garfield, chief eng.
Operation: Apr. 11, 1988.

Greensboro

WFMY-TV (Channel 2) CBS

WFMY Television Corp., P.O. Box TV2, Greensboro, NC 27420 (919) 379-9639.
Henry E. Price, gen. mgr.; Jerry Policoff, natl. sls. mgr.; Delois Strickland, prog. dir.; Jim Collins, opns. mgr.; Roz Fields, promo. mgr.; Gary Curtis, news dir.
Operation: 1949; TV homes in area: 797,800.

WGGT (Channel 48)

Guilford Telecasters, Inc., 330 S. Greene St., Greensboro, NC 27401 (919) 274-4848.
Eugene Bohi, pres. & gen. mgr.; Norm Cissna, gen. sls. mgr.; Kenneth Gonzalez, dir.-prog., opns.; Cheryl Fulcher, promo. dir.; nat'l rep.: Petry.
Operation: May, 1981.

WLXI-TV (Channel 61)

Box TV-61, Greensboro, NC 27420 (919) 855-5610.
Gary S. Smithwick, pres.; Richard C. Snowden, gen. mgr.; Jeff Johnson, prog. dir.
Operation: January, 1983.

Greenville

WNCT-TV (Channel 9) CBS

Roy A. Park Broadcasting, Inc., P.O. Box 898, Greenville, NC 27834 (919) 756-3180.
Roy H. Park, bd. chm.; Mrs. Dorothy D. Park, secretary; K. B. Skinner, dir.; Randall Stair, v.p. & treas.; Wright M. Thomas, pres.; Edward J. Adams, v.p.-gen. mgr.; Luther Griffin, gen. sls. mgr.; Lori Ohr, prod. mgr.; Shirley Dale, prog. mgr.; Bertie Cartwright, chief eng.; nat'l rep.: Blair TV.
Operation: 1953; TV sets in area: 476,300.

Hickory

WHKY-TV (Channel 14)

The Long Family Partnership, Box 1059, Hickory, NC 28603 (704) 322-5115.

Thomas E. Long, gen. mgr.; Jeffrey B. Long, sta. mgr.; nat'l sls. mgr.; Jim Carr, sls. mgr.; Frank Jones, news dir.; JuJu Phillips, sports dir.; Lynne Critcher, traffic mgr.

Operation: 1968; TV households: 125,700.

High Point

WGHP-TV (Channel 8)

P.O. Box TV 8, Greensboro, NC 27420; (919) 841-8888.

David Boylan, v.p./gen. mgr.; Frank Terry, bus. mgr.; Quinn Koontz, gen. sls. mgr.; Jim Ogle, news dir.

Operation: October, 1963; TV households: 1,618,000.

Lexington

WEJC (Channel 20)

Koinonia Ministries, Inc., Rt. 1, Box 2020, Lexington, NC 27292 (704) 246-2020.

William P. Register, pres. & gen. mgr.

Operation: October, 1985.

New Bern

WCTI-TV (Channel 12) ABC

Diversified Communications, P.O. Box 2325, New Bern, NC 28561 (919) 637-2111.

William D. Webb, v.p. & gen. mgr.; Bill Knowles, sta. mgr. & news dir.; Frank Brady, gen. sls. mgr.; Carolyn Stevens, prog. dir.; Mike Barrett, chief eng.

Raleigh

WLFL-TV (Channel 22) FOX

TVX of Raleigh-Durham, Inc., 1205 Front St., Raleigh, NC 27609 (919) 821-2200.

Linda Cochran, v.p. & gen. mgr.; Kathy Bennett, natl. sls. mgr.; Jenny Zoeller, prog. dir.; Don Ingram, chief eng.; rep.: Seltel.

Operation: December, 1981.

WRAL-TV (Channel 5) CBS

Capitol Broadcasting Co., P.O. Box 12,000, Raleigh, NC 27605 (919) 821-8500.

James F. Goodmon, pres. & chief exec. off.; John M. Brennan, sr. v.p. & treas.; John L. Greene, sr. v.p.; Louise S. Stephenson, secty.; Paul Quinn, sta. mgr.; Wilbur Brann, chief eng.; nat'l rep.: Katz Television American.

Operation: 1956; TV sets in area: 950,000.

Rocky Mount

WFXB (Channel 47) FOX

Family Bdcstg. Enterprises, Box 4750, Rocky Mount, NC 27801 (919) 985-2447.

V. Bruce Whitehead, pres.; Robert J. Pelletier, gen. mgr.; G.C. Hughes, gen. sls. mgr.; Becky Johnson, prog. dir.; Dimitri Ferrell, film buyer; Jean Almand, promo. mgr.; Butch Pindell, news dir.; Bob Pelletier, chief eng.; rep.: Landin Media Sales.

Operation: Aug. 31, 1987.

Washington

WITN-TV (Channel 7) NBC

WITN-TV Inc., U.S. 17 South, Box Office 468, Washington, NC 27889 (919) 946-3131.

Howard W. Meagle, Jr., v.p./gen. mgr.; Bill Stanley, gen. sls. mgr.; Mike Riddle, opns. mgr.; Al Manning, eng.; Fran Williams, bus. mgr.; Chris McDaniel, news dir.; nat'l rep.: Katz.

Operation: Sept. 1955; TVHH: 724,000.

Wilmington

WECT-TV (Channel 6) NBC

Atlantic Telecasting Corp., 322 Shipyard Blvd., Wilmington, NC 28401 (919) 791-8070.

Dan D. Cameron, pres.; Wayne Jackson, sta. mgr.; Bill Elks, Oper. dir.; C. D. Martin, Jr., sls. mgr.; Paul A. Brissette, Jr., exec. v.p. & gen. mgr.; Mike Loizides, chief eng.; Ernie Whitmeyer, prod. dir.; nat'l rep.: Adam Young.

Operation: 1954; TV sets in area: 325,000.

WJKA (Channel 26) CBS

Wilmington Telecasters, Inc., 1926 Oleander Dr., Wilmington, NC 28403 (919) 343-8826.

Kathrine Everett, pres.; Ty Watts, gen. mgr.; Bob Watson, gen. sls. mgr.; Aileen LeBlanc, dir. prog.; promo., public affairs.; Rick Carroll, chief eng.; Gina Klinefelter, bus. mgr.; nat'l rep.: Seltel.

Operation: September, 1984.

WWAY (Channel 3) ABC

Adams TV of Wilmington, Box 2068, 615 N. Front St. Wilmington, NC 28401 (919) 762-8581.

Paul A. Brissette, pres.-vice-chm.; Joe Schlegel, v.p. sls.; C.D. Martin, pres.-gen. mgr.; George Allen, v.p. opns.; Elliot Hunter, v.p., eng.; nat'l rep.: Blair.

Operation: 1964; TV households: 437,750.

Winston-Salem

WNRW-TV (Channel 45)

Act III Bdcst. of Greensboro, 3500 Myer-Lee Dr., Winston-Salem, NC 27101 (919) 722-4545.

Bert Ellis, pres.; Donita Todd, v.p. & gen. mgr.; Joel Kaczmarek, gen. sls. mgr.; Peter Wickwire, prog. dir. & film buyer; nat'l rep.: MMT.

Operation: September, 1979.

WXII-TV (Channel 12) NBC

700 Coliseum Drive, P.O. Box 11847, Winston-Salem, NC 27116 (919) 721-9944.

Reynard A. Corley, v.p. & gen. mgr.; Jim Hart, mktg. dir.; David L. Summers, gen. sls. mgr.; Roger Bergson, news dir.; Phyllis Sheffield, prog. dir.; Henry Hunt, dir. of engineering; nat'l rep.: Katz Television.

Operation: 1953; households: 1,603,900 (TSA-May '83 ARB).

NORTH DAKOTA

Bismarck

KBMY (Channel 17) ABC

WDAY, Inc., 4007 State St., Bismarck, ND 58501 (710) 223-1700.

Charles Bohnet, exec. v.p.; Dewey Heggen, gen. mgr.; Chuck Peterson, gen. sls. mgr.; Susan J. Elder, prog. dir.; Bob

Prowse, prom. mgr.; Becky Jones, news dir.; Jerry Grimstad, chief eng.; natl. rep.: Katz.
Operation: March, 1985.

KFYR-TV (Channel 5) NBC
Meyer Broadcasting Co., Broadway at Fourth, Bismarck, ND 58501 (701) 255-5757.
Judith Johnson, pres.; Tom Barr, gen. mgr.; Jerry Hegel, gen. sls. mgr.; Jim Sande, prog. & opns. mgr.; Rich Beierle, dir. eng.; nat'l rep: Blair Television Associates.
Operation: 1953; TV homes in area: 144,000.

KXMB-TV (Channel 12) CBS
Reiten Television, Inc., 1811 N. 15th, Bismarck, ND 58501 (701) 223-9197.
John VonRueden, gen. mgr. & gen. sls. mgr.; Darrell Dorgan, news dir.; George McDonald, prod. mgr.; Rocky Hefty, chief eng.; nat'l rep.: Seltel.
Operation: 1955; TV sets in area: 55,000.

Devil's Lake-Grand Forks

WDAZ-TV (Channel 8) ABC
(Satellite of WDAY-TV, Fargo, ND)
WDAY Inc., 301 So. 8th St. N, Fargo, ND 58102 (701) 237-6500.
Robert Keer, gen. mgr.; Karen Dietz, promo. mgr.; rep.: Katz; Andy McDermott Ltd. (Canada).
Operation: 1967.

Dickinson

KQCD-TV (Channel 7) NBC
Meyer Broadcasting Co., Radar Base Road, Dickinson, ND 58601 (201) 225-6843.
Tim Anderson, mgr.; nat'l rep.: Blair TV
Operation: 1980.

KXMA-TV (Channel 2) CBS
Reiten Television, Inc., Drawer B, Dickinson, ND 58602 (701) 227-1400.
Charles Tibor, pres. & gen. mgr. & sls. mgr.; Duane Parlicek, promo. mgr.; Louis Tysver, chief eng.; nat'l rep.: Seltel.
Operation: 1956; TV sets in area: 52,000.

Fargo

KTHI-TV, (Channel 11) NBC
Spokane Television, Inc., Box 1878, Fargo, ND 58102 (701) 237-5211; Box 127, Grand Forks, ND 58201 (701) 772-3481.
John Hrubesky, v.p. & gen. mgr.; Greg Holder, gen. sls. mgr.; Dale Bosch, sta. mgr.; Carol Gillett, traffic mgr.; Roger Johnson, chief eng.

KVRR (Channel 15)
Red River Broadcast Corp., 4015 9th Ave., SW Fargo, ND 58103 (701) 277-0515.
Jane Boler, gen. mgr.; Greg Baldwin, sls. mgr.; Kent Lien, prog. dir. & film buyer; Gary Goodrich, dir. mktg.; Chuck Trautner, dir. eng.
Operation: February, 1983.

WDAY-TV (Channel 6) ABC
WDAY, Inc., 301 So. 8th St., Fargo, ND 58102 (701) 237-6500.
Charles Bohnet, exec. v.p.-gen. mgr.; Robert Prowse, promo. mgr.; Cole Carley, gen. sls mgr.; nat'l rep: Katz.
Operation: 1953; TV sets in area: 174,700.

Jamestown

KJRR (Channel 7) FOX
Red River Bdcst. Corp., 4015 9th Ave., S.W., Fargo, ND 58103 (701) 277-1515.
Myron Kunin, pres.; Jane Boler, gen. mgr.; Greg Baldwin, gen. sls. mgr.; Kent Lien, prog. dir.; Wayne Ramsey, promo. mgr.; Tim Anderson, chief eng.; rep.: ITS.
Operation: Sept. 1, 1988.

Minot

KMCY (Channel 14) ABC
WDAY, Inc., Box 2276, Minot, ND 58702 (701) 838-6614.
Staff: same as KBMY, Bismarck, except Jerry Grimstad, chief. eng. Natl. rep.: Katz.
Operation: June, 1985.

KMOT (Channel 10) NBC
Meyer Broadcasting Co., Box 1120, Minot, ND 58701 (701) 852-4101.
Judy Johnson, pres.; Wayne L. Sanders, sta. mgr.

KXMC-TV (Channel 13) CBS
KXMC TV, Inc., 3425 S. Broadway, Box 1686, Minot, ND, 58702 (701) 852-2104.
Chester Reiten, pres. & gen. mgr.; Henry Buechler, mgr.; Rod Romine, prog. dir.; Duane Aase, chief eng.; nat'l rep.: Seltel.
Operation: 1953; TV sets in area: 129,000.

Valley City-Fargo

KXJB-TV (Channel 4) CBS
North American Communication Corp., 4302 13th Ave. So. Fargo, ND 58103 (701) 282-0444.
Bruce Barnes, pres. & gen. mgr.; Paul Wickre, gen. sls. mgr.; Arvid Sonstelie, chief eng.; nat'l rep., Seltel.
Operation: 1954; TV sets in area: 214,000.

Williston

KUMV-TV (Channel 8)
Box 1287, Williston, ND 58801; Meyer Broadcasting Co., 602 Main St., Williston, ND 58802
William A. Ekberg, pres.; Cherie Olson Harms, sta. mgr.
Operation: 1957.

KXMD-TV (Channel 11) CBS
1219 Knoll, P.O. Box 790, Williston, ND 58801 (701) 572-2345.
Chester Reiten, pres.; Marilyn Karst, gen. & gen. sls. mgr.; Rodney Romine, prog. dir.; Wayne MacNamara, chief eng.; Seltel.
Operation: 1969

OHIO

Akron

WAKC-TV (Channel 23) ABC
Group One Bcstg., 853 Copley Rd., Akron, OH 44320 (216) 535-7831.
Roger G. Berk, pres. & gen. mgr.; Chip Fox, v.p. & gen. sls. mgr.; Wm. F. O'Neil, Jr., prog. dir.; Leo Zody, film ed.; Earl Miller, chief eng.; nat'l rep.: Spot Time.
Operation: 1953; TV sets in area: 340,000.

WBNX-TV (Channel 55)

Winston Bdcstg., Network, Inc., 2690 State Rd., Cuyahoga Falls, OH 44223 (216) 928-5711. Mailing address: P.O. Box 91660, Cleveland, OH 44101 (216) 273-5511.

Lou Spangler, pres. & gen. mgr.; Terry Schultz, gen. sls. mgr.; Anne Catherine Keith, sta. mgr. & prog. dir.; Margie Coger, prom. mgr.; Steven Nelson, chief eng.

Operation: December, 1985.

Canton

WDLI (Channel 17)

Trinity Bdcstg. Network, 6600 Atlantic Blvd., Louisville, OH 44641 (216) 875-5542.

Dale K. Osborn, sta. mgr. & chief eng.; Rebecca Osborn, prog. dir.

Operation: January, 1967.

WOAC (Channel 67)

Canton 67, 4867 Fulton Dr., NW, Canton, OH 44718 (216) 492-5267.

Donald Kent, pres.; Mike Larson, gen. mgr.; Phil Sherck, gen. sls. mgr.; Kevin Hoffman, prog. dir.; Scott Davis, news dir.; Lee Carpenter, chief eng.

Operation: September 1981.

Cincinnati

WCPO-TV (Channel 9) CBS

Scripps-Howard Broadcasting Co., 500 Central Ave., Cincinnati, OH 45202 (513) 721-9900.

Frank Gardner, gen. mgr., J.B. Chase, asst. gen. mgr. & gen. sls. mgr.; Rick Reeves, dir. of ops.; J.B. Chase, gen. sls. mgr.; Jeff Sales, nat'l sls. mgr.; Jack Calalan, news dir.; Hasker Nelson, dir. of community affairs; Ruth Ackerman, lcl. sls.

WIII (Channel 64)

5177 Fishwick Dr., Cincinnati, OH 45216; (513) 641-4400.

Stephen Kent, gen. mgr.; Dolores Rehn, bus. mgr.; David Schackmann, sls. mgr.; Ray Pelzel, chief eng.

Operation: 1980.

WKRC-TV (Channel 12) ABC

Taft Broadcasting Company, 1906 Highland Avenue, Cincinnati, OH 45219 (513) 651-1200.

Charles Mechem, bd. chm.; Terry Connelly, gen. mgr. & v.p.; Ann Bryant, prog. dir.; Craig Millar, gen. sls. mgr.; Leon Brown, chief eng.; Chuck Denendra, nat'l sls. mgr.; Bob Weinstein, lcl. sls. mgr.; Don North, news dir.; John Hill, film dir.

Operation: 1949; TV sets in area: 1,004,100.

WLWT (Channel 5) NBC

140 W. Ninth St., Cincinnati, OH 45202; (513) 352-5000.

Anthony H. Kiernan, v.p. & gen. mgr.; Cliff Abromats, news dir.; Diana Richardson, prog. dir.; Harry Schneider, controller; Florence Parker, dir. community svcs.; Jerry Blankenbeker, chief eng.; Mickey Fisher, traf. mgr.; Thomas Storey, film dir.; natl rep.: Katz Television.

Operation: 1948; households: 2,221,800 (TSA—May '83 ARB).

WXIX-TV (Channel 19) FOX

Malrite Communications Group, Inc., 10490 Taconic Terrace, Cincinnati, OH 45215 (513) 772-1919.

John Chaffee, pres.; Bill Jenkins, v.p. & gen. mgr.; Patrice Mohn, prog. dir.; Gracelyn Brown, prom. mgr.; Suzanne Kay, news dir.; Jim Parker, chief eng.; natl. rep.: Petry.

Operation: November, 1983.

Cleveland

WEWS (Channel 5) ABC

Scripps Howard Broadcasting Co., 3001 Euclid Ave., Cleveland, OH 44115 (216) 431-5555.

Richard J. Janssen, pres. & CEO; James H. Knight, v.p. & gen. mgr.; Jane Sherwin, gen. sls. mgr.; John Tamerlano, natl. sls. mgr.; Gary Stark, prog. dir.; Seth Alspaugh, creative svcs. dir.; John L. Ray, news dir.; rep. Blair-TV, Inc.

Operation: 1947; Total TV househods: 1,824,400.

WJW-TV (Channel 8) CBS

Gillett Communications of Ohio, Inc., 5800 S. Marginal Rd., Cleveland OH 44103 (216) 431-8888.

Virgil Dominic, pres.; Mike Renda, dir. sls.; Mike Renda, nat'l sls. mgr.; Louis Gattozzi, dir. opns.; Thomas Miller, dir. tech. svcs.; Joann Stern, dir. creative svcs.; Thomas Flavelle, controller; Phyllis Quail, news dir.

Operation: 1949.

WKYC-TV (Channel 3) NBC

National Broadcasting Co., 1403 East Sixth Street, Cleveland, OH 44114 (216) 344-3333.

John Llewellyn, v.p. & gen. mgr.; Dan Klintworth, adv. & promo. mgr.; David Boylan, dir. of sls.; Raymond Smith, dir., tech. ops.; Kathleen McNulty, bus. mgr.; Gregory R. Stehlin, prog. dir.; Ron Bilek, news dir.; nat'l rep.: NBC Spot Sales.

Operation: 1948; TV sets in area: 3,663,800.

WQHS (Channel 61)

Silver King Bdcstg. of Ohio, Inc., 2861 W. Ridgewood Dr., Parma, OH 44134 (216) 888-0061.

Gerald Kerwin, v.p. & sta. mgr.; Sharon Roman, prog. dir.; Teri James, traf. mgr.; Dave Smith, chief eng.

Operation: Mar. 3, 1981.

Columbus

WBNS-TV (Channel 10) CBS

Dispatch Printing Co., 770 Twin Rivers Drive, Columbus, OH 43216 (216) 460-3700.

Gene D'Angelo, pres. & gen. mgr.; Arnold Routson, v.p. sls.; William Orr, v.p., eng'.; John A. Haldi, vice pres., prgm.; Dale Laackman, prod. dir.; Gerald Cary, treas.; Larry Maisel, News dir.; Jay Scafone, dir. adv. & promo.; nat'l rep.:. Blair TV Inc.

Operation: 1949; TV sets in area: 557,400.

WCMH-TV (Channel 4) NBC

Outlet Broadcasting, 3165 Olentagny River Rd., Columbus, OH 43202 (614) 263-5441.

David E. Henderson, pres.; Gary Robinson, v.p. & gen. mgr.; Jeff Cash, gen. sls. mgr.; Bill Lanesey, natl. sls. mgr.; Robert Shaw, prog. dir.; Janna Petry, promo. mgr.; Ron Bilek, news dir.; Ralph Landon, chief eng.; Paul Ernst, prog. dir.; Lance Carwile, film dir.; natl. rep.: Katz.

Operation: 1949; TV homes in area: 1,494,000.

WSYX (Channel 6) ABC

Anchor Media, 1271 Dublin Road, Columbus, OH 43216 (614) 481-6666.

Jack Sander, pres.; Charles Wing, v.p. & gen. mgr.; Jim Conshafter, gen. sls. mgr.; Russ Reed, prog. mgr.; Kathy Ward, promo. dir.; Bill Seaman, chief eng.; nat'l rep.: MMT.

Operation: 1949; TV sets in area: 727,000.

WTTE (Channel 28)
WTTE Channel 28, Inc., 6130 Sunbury Rd., Box 280, Columbus, OH 43216; (614) 895-2800.
John T. Quigley, gen. mgr.; Steve Marks, gen. sls. mgr.; Oran D. Gough, opns. dir.; Joe Subich, chief eng.; nat'l rep.: Seltel.
Operation: June, 1984.

Dayton

WDTN (Channel 2) ABC
4595 South Dixie Ave., P.O. Box 741, Dayton, OH 45401.
Philip M. Stolz, exec. v.p. & gen. mgr.; Larry Ryan, gen. sls. mgr.; Kirk Szesney, promo. mgr.; Steve Fisher, sta. mgr.; O. Ted Lester, chief eng.; nat'l rep.: Blair.
Operation: 1949; TV homes in area: 1,029,500.

WHIO-TV (Channel 7) CBS
Miami Valley Broadcasting Corp., 1414 Wilmington Avenue, Dayton, OH 45401 (513) 259-2111.
Stanley G. Mouse, pres.; Neil Pugh, v.p. & gen. mgr.; Don Kemper, sta. mgr.; John Hayes, gen. sls. mgr.; John Hanley, cont.; Robert Wells, dir. of info. svcs.; John Clark, prog. dir.; Sim Kollinger, chief eng.; nat'l rep.: Tele-rep.
Operation: 1949; TV households in area: 497,000.

WKEF (Channel 22) ABC
KT Communications, 1731 Soldiers Home Road, Dayton, OH 45418 (513) 263-2662.
James Graham, gen. mgr. & prog. dir.; Doug Gealy, lcl. sls. mgr.; Darrell Hunter, chief eng. & prod. mgr.; Sandy Patton, promo dir.; Bruce Parker, news dir.; rep.: Katz.
Operation: 1964; TV households: 1,399,000.

WRGT-TV (Channel 45) FOX
Dayton Telecasting, Inc., 45 Broadcast Plaza, Dayton, OH 45408; (503) 263-4500.
U. Bertram Ellis, pres. & CEO; Bill Castleman, exec. v.p.; Dave Miller, v.p. & gen. mgr.; Ken Beedle, gen. sls. mgr.; Linda Triplett, opns. mgr.; nat'l rep.: MMT.
Operation: September, 1984.

Lima

WLIO-TV (Channel 35) NBC
Lima Communications Corporation, 1424 Rice Ave., Lima, Ohio 45802 (419) 228-8835.
James C. Dages, pres. & gen. mgr.; James Garling, prog. dir; Fred Vobbe, chief eng.; Bruce A. Opperman, sls. mgr.; nat'l rep.: The Katz Co.
Operation: 1952; TV sets in area: 464,300.

WTLW (Channel 44)
American Christian TV Services, Inc., 1844 Baty Rd., Lima, OH 45807; (419) 339-4444.
Gary Cooper, pres.; Robert Placie, sta. mgr.; Ron Mighell, v.p., dir.; Jeffrey G. Millslagle, prog. dir.; John Owens, prod. dir.; Robert Armistead, devel. dir.; Ray Tanner, chief eng.
Operation: June, 1982.

Lorain-Cleveland

WUAB (Channel 43)
Gaylord Broadcasting Co. of Ohio, 8443 Day Dr., Parma, OH 44129 (216) 845-6043.
James R. Terrell, pres.; Michael E. Schuch, v.p. & gen. mgr.; Rex Rickly, chief eng.; rep.: MMT.

Newark

WSFJ (Channel 51)
Christian Television of Ohio, Inc., 10077 Jacksontown Rd., Thornville, OH 43076 (614) 833-0771.
Betty J. Stanley, pres. & gen. mgr.; Charlotte Reichley, prog. dir.; nat'l rep.: Hugh Wallace.
Operation: 1980.

Sandusky

WGGN-TV (Channel 52)
Christian Faith Bcstg., Box 2397, Sandusky, OH 44870 (419) 684-5311.
Rusty Yost, gen. mgr.; Gene Asberry, chief eng.
Operation: December, 1982.

Shaker Heights

WOIO (Channel 19) FOX
Channel 19, Inc., 2720 Van Aken Blvd., Cleveland, OH 44120; (216) 561-1919.
Hubert Payne, pres.; Dennis Thatcher, v.p. & gen. mgr.; Dave Smith, gen. sls. mgr.; Steve Daniloff, natl. sls. mgr.; Jackie Krejcik, lcl. sls. mgr.; Richard Sullivan, dir. opns.; Craig Wright, promo. mgr.; James Somich, chief eng.; natl. rep.: Petry.
Operation: May, 1985.

Springfield

WTJC (Channel 26)
Miami Valley Christian Television Inc., Box 26, Dayton, OH 45401 (513) 323-0026.
Marvin D. Sparks, pres.; Deborah H. Back, sls. mgr.; John Elliott, chief eng.; Rev. Jeff Mohr, dir. outreach; Vic Costello, prod. dir.
Operation: 1980

Steubenville

WTOV-TV (Channel 9) ABC, NBC
Television Station Partners, Box 9999, Steubenville, OH 43952.
I. Martin Pompadur, CEO; Ziff Corp.; Ralph E. Becker, COO; Gary R. Bolton, v.p. & gen. mgr.; James McCreary, v.p., cont.; Tim McCoy, opns. mgr.

Toledo

WNWO-TV (Channel 24) ABC
Toledo Television Investors Ltd. Partnership, 300 S. Byrne Rd., Toledo, OH 43615 (419) 535-0024.
Brett Cornwell, v.p./gen. mgr.; Linda Blackburn, gen. sls. mgr.; Michael S. Przybylski, bus. mgr.; Harold W. Thompson, chief eng.; rep.: Petry.
Operation: 1966; TV households: 1,775,100.

WTOL (Channel 11) CBS
Cosmos Broadcasting Corp., P.O. Box 715, Toledo, OH 43695 (419) 248-1111.
S. Wheeler Rudd, v.p. & gen. mgr.; John Cottingham, gen. sls. mgr.; Rita Wissman, nat'l sls. mgr.; Rick Gevers, news dir.; Steve Israel, prog. dir.; Wayne Thing, prod. mgr.; Sharon Newson, pub. affairs dir.; Don Kennedy, bus. mgr.; Stu Hinze,, chief eng.; Nancy Gruhler, traffic mgr.; nat'l rep.: MMT Sales.
Operation: 1958; TV sets in area: 1,405,800.

WTVG-TV (Channel 13) NBC
4247 Dorr St., Toledo OH 43607 (419) 255-1313.
H. W. Ray, pres.; Andy Lee, v.p., mgr.; George Carlino. nat'l sls. mgr.; Marc Stover, lcl. sls. mgr.; nat'l rep.: Katz.
Operation: 1948; TV sets in area: 2,414,100.

WUPW (Channel 36) FOX
Toledo TV Ltd., Four SeaGate, Toledo, OH 43604 (419) 244-3600.
Larry Blum pres. & gen. mgr.; Dennis C. Katell, prog. dir., promo. mgr. & film buyer; Steven W. Punitieri, chief eng.; rep.: Blair.
Operation: Sept. 22, 1985.

Youngstown

WFMJ-TV (Channel 21) NBC
WFMJ-TV, Inc., 101 W. Boardman St., Youngstown, OH 44503 (216) 744-8611.
Betty H. Brown Jagnow, pres.; John A. Grdic, gen. mgr.; Homean Baxter, film dir.; Larry Oleson, chief eng.; nat'l rep., Blair TV.
Operation: 1953; TV households in area: 280,500.

WKBN-TV (Channel 27) CBS
WKBN Broadcasting Corp., 3930 Sunset Blvd., Youngstown, OH 44501 (216) 782-1144.
W. P. Williamson, Jr., bd. chm.; Doris Saloom, secty.; W. P. Williamson, III, pres. & gen. mgr.; J.D. Williamson, v.p. bdcst. opns.; Mike Seachman, opns. mgr.; W.F. Decker, sta. mgr.; C.R. Wade, sls. mgr.; nat'l rep.: Katz Agency.
Operation: 1953; TV sets in area: 514,000.

WYTV (Channel 33) ABC
WYTV, 3800 Shady Run Rd., Youngstown, OH 44502 (216) 783-2930.
A. Richard Benedek, pres.; Geoffrey Pearce, gen. mgr.; Joseph S. Dobosh, gen. sls. mgr.; Frank Marafiote, prog. dir.; Tony Mancino, promo. mgr.; Tom Mock, news dir.; Arthur W. Taylor, chief eng.

Zanesville

WHIZ-TV (Channel 18) NBC, ABC
Southeastern Ohio Television System, Downard Rd., Zanesville, OH 43701 (614) 453-0361.
Allan Land, group mgr.; Barbara Mitter, prog. dir.; Van Vanelli, gen. sls. mgr.; Elmer Hartmeyer, chief eng.; Franklin Young, film oper. mgr.; nat'l rep.: Katz.
Operation: 1953; TV sets in area: 250,000.

OKLAHOMA

Ada

KTEN (Channel 10) ABC, CBS, NBC
Eastern Oklahoma Television Co., Inc., P.O. Box 728, Ada, OK 74820 (405) 332-3311.
Tom Johnson, pres. & gen. mgr.; Bill Green, chief eng.; Dan Hoover, v.p. & prog. dir.; nat'l rep.: Katz.
Operation: 1954; TV sets in area: 178,310.

Ardmore

KXII-TV (Channel 12) CBS, NBC
K-12, Ltd., Box 1175, Sherman, TX 75090 (214) 892-8123.
M.N. Bostick, pres.; Richard R. Adams, gen. mgr.; Dennis Kite, chief eng.; Mike Leucke, prod. mgr.; nat'l rep.: Seltel.
Operation: 1956.

Bartlesville

KDOR (Channel 17)
All American TV, Inc., Box 1700, Talala, OK 74080 (918) 743-1700.
Sonny Arguinzoni, pres.; Terry Hickey, exec. dir.; Thomas Harrison, gen. mgr.; Leonard Wallace, chief eng.
Operation: February, 1984.

Lawton

KSWO-TV (Channel 7) ABC
KSWO Television Co., Inc., P.O. Box 708, Lawton, OK 73502 (405) 355-7000.
R. H. Drewry, pres.; Larry Patton, gen. mgr.; Jim Lockerd, chief eng.
Operation: 1953; TV sets in area: 225,000.

Oklahoma City

KAUT (Channel 43)
Heritage Media of Oklahoma, Box 14843, Oklahoma City, OK 73113; (405) 478-4300.
Harlan Reams, gen. mgr.; Julie Nelson, lcl. sls. mgr.; Curtis Grant, promo. mgr.; Dian Johnson, prog. mgr.; Jay Holmes, chief eng.
Operation: November, 1980.

KGMC (Channel 34)
Oklahoma City Bdcstg. Co., 1501 NE 85th, Oklahoma City, OK 73131 (405) 478-3434.
Ted Baze, gen. mgr.; Ken Belford, gen. sls. mgr.; Greg Miller, v.p & chief eng.; Judy Lisenby, prog. dir.; nat'l rep.: Katz.
Operation: 1979.

KOCO-TV (Channel 5) ABC
Gannett Broadcast Group, 1300 E. Britton Road, Oklahoma City, OK 73113.
Tom Kirby, pres. & gen. mgr.; Lou Morlino, v.p. & gen. sls. mgr.; Ted Newcomb, v.p. & chief eng.; Lynette Rodriguez, compt.; Mike Palmer, v.p., bdcst. op.
Operation: 1954; TV households: 834,600.

KOKH (Channel 25)
Busse Broadcasting Corp., 1228 E. Wilshire Blvd., Oklahoma City, OK 73111 (405) 843-2525.
James Harmeyer, pres. & gen. mgr.; Craig Bachman, gen. sls. mgr.; Patricia Wallace, prog. dir.; Laura Shepherd, crea. svcs. dir.; Ronnie Kaye, news dir.; D.K. Hart, chief eng.
Operation: 1979.

KSBI (Channel 52)
Locke Supply Co., Box 26128, 1300 SE 82nd St., Oklahoma City, OK 73126 (405) 631-7335.
Don J. Locke, pres.; Ronald Tudor, chief eng.
Operation: Sept. 19, 1988.

KTBO-TV (Channel 14)
Trinity Bcstg. of Oklahoma, 3705 NW 63rd St., Oklahoma City, OK 73116 (405) 848-1414.
Paul F. Crouch, pres.; Al Brown, gen. mgr.; John Gordon, chief eng.
Operation: March, 1981.

KTVY (Channel 14) NBC
Knight-Ridder Bdcstg. Inc., 500 East Britton Road, Oklahoma City, OK 73114 (405) 478-1212.

Robert F. Finke, pres. & gen. mgr.; Paul Wise, gen. sls. mgr.; Stuart Kellogg, news & mktg. dir.; Bob Ablah, chief eng.
Operation: 1949; TV sets in area: 613,500.

KWTV (Channel 9) CBS
Griffin Television, Inc. P.O. Box 14159, Oklahoma City, OK 73113 (405) 843-6641.
Duane Harm, pres. & gen. mgr.; Al Sandubrae, sta. mgr.; Russ Elkin, chief eng.; Rick Buchanan, mktg. man.; nat'l rep.: Telerep.
Operation: 1953; TV sets in area: 847,800.

Sayre

KVIJ-TV
(Satellite of KVII-TV, Amarillo, TX)
Marsh Media, Inc., One Broadcast Center, Amarillo, TX 79101 (806) 373-1787.
Rep.: Katz Television.
Operation: 1961.

Tulsa

KGCT-TV (Channel 41)
5807 S. Garnett St., Tulsa, OK 74145 (918) 252-9589.
Leonard Anderson, pres.; William Dan Harley, mgr. & gen. sls. mgr.; Peggy Marsh, office mgr.; C.E. Martin, chief eng.; nat'l rep.: Spot Time.
Operation: May, 1981.

KJRH-TV (Channel 2) NBC
Scripps-Howard Broadcasting Company, P.O. Box 2, Tulsa, OK 74101 (918) 743-2222.
Ben Hevel, gen. mgr.; William J. Donahue, asst. gen. mgr.; Tom Hauff, news dir.; Michael J. Vrabac, gen. sls. mgr.; Vic Turner, chief eng.; nat'l rep.; Blair Television.
Operation: 1954; TV sets in area: 460,300.

KOKI-TV (Channel 23)
Tulsa 23, 7422 E. 46 Place, Tulsa, OK 74135 (918) 663-6880.
James U. Lavenstein, pres. & gen. mgr.; Mark Cortner, gen. sls. mgr.; Eugene Wilkin, prog. dir. & film buyer; Ben Frizzell, creative svcs. mgr.; Robert G. Hardie, chief eng.; nat'l rep.: Katz.
Operation: November, 1980.

KOTV (Channel 6) CBS
KOTV, Inc., 320 S. Frankfort St., Tulsa, OK 74120 (918) 582-6666.
Lee Salzberger, pres. & gen. mgr.; Jan Wilson, prog. coord.; David Cassidy, news dir.; Nick Nicholson, gen. sls. mgr.; nat'l rep.: Telerep.
Operation: 1949

KTUL-TV (Channel 8) ABC
KTUL-TV, Inc., Box 8, Tulsa, OK 74101 (918) 446-3351.
Allen Feuer, pres. & gen. mgr.; Randy Pratt, v.p. & gen. mgr. Terry Wilson, prog. dir.; Charles Ray, prom. mgr.; Roman Hlohowskyj, chief eng.; nat'l rep.: Petry.
Operation: 1954; TV homes in area: 481,400.

KWHB (Channel 47)
Television Communications, Inc., Box 470047, Tulsa, OK 74147 (918) 250-9402.
Peter Sumrall, gen. mgr.; Jim Shaffer, gen. sls. mgr.; Steve Morgan, opns. mgr.; Gary Murphy, lcl. sls. mgr.; Darryl Ferguson, chief eng.
Operation: April, 1985.

OREGON

Bend

KTVZ (Channel 21) CBS, NBC
Resort Bdcstg. Co., Box 149, Bend, OR 97709 (503) 389-6511.
John Larkin, gen. mgr.; Duncan Laing, sls. mgr.; Teresa Bollard, ops. mgr.; nat'l rep.: Katz.
Operation: 1977.

Coos Bay

KCBY-TV (Channel 11) CBS
(Satellite of KVAL-TV, Eugene, OR)
Northwest Television, Inc., P.O. Box 1156, Coos Bay, OR 97420 (503) 269-1111.
Bruce Bennett, sta. mgr.; Tim Hershiser, chief eng.

Eugene

KEZI-TV (Channel 9) ABC
KEZI, Inc., P.O. Box 7009, Eugene, OR 97401 (503) 485-5611.
Carolyn S. Chambers, pres.; Bruce Liljegren, gen. mgr.; Dave Larson, asst. sta. mgr.; Beth Cookson, nat'l/reg. sls.; Bruce A. Barrett, gen. sls. mgr.; Joe Smelser, prod. mgr.; Dennis Hunt, chief eng.
Operation: 1960; TV households: 226,200.

KMTR-TV (Channel 16) NBC
KMTR, Inc., Box 7308, Eugene, OR 97401 (503) 746-1600.
Robert W. Davis, pres. & gen. mgr.; Cam Wilson, v.p. & gen. sls. mgr. Julie Strandlien, prog. dir.; Cambra Ward, promo. mgr.; Paul Riess, news dir.; Jerry Madsen, chief eng.; nat'l rep.; Seltel.
Operation: October, 1982.

KVAL-TV (Channel 13) Primary CBS
Northwest Television, Inc., Blanton Heights, P.O. Box 1313, Eugene, OR 97401 (503) 342-4961.
James W. Putney, v.p., gen. mgr.; John Doyle, news dir.; Dave Weinkauf, gen. sls. mgr.; Greg Raschio, lcl. sls. dir.; Paul Greene, prog. dir.; Jim Bowen, chief eng.; nat'l rep.: Katz Television, Inc.
Operation: 1954; TV households in area: 482,200.

Klamath Falls

KOTI-TV (Channel 2) NBC
California/Oregon Broadcasting Co., P.O. Box 2K, Klamath Falls, OR 97601 (503) 882-2222.
Patricia Smullin, pres.; Ed Zander, gen. mgr.; nat'l rep.: Blair; reg. rep.: Blair.
Operation: 1956.

Medford

KDRV (Channel 12)
Sunshine TV, Inc., 1090 Knutson Ave., Medford, OR 97504 (503) 773-1212.
John Hash, pres.; Keith Lollis, gen. mgr; Rick Carrara, chief eng.
Operation: February, 1984.

KOBI-TV (Channel 5) NBC

California Oregon Broadcasting Inc., P.O. Box 5M, Medford, OR 97501 (503) 779-5555.

William B. Smullin, founder; Patricia C. Smullin, pres.; Patricia D. Smullin, v.p., treas.; Carol Anne Smullin Brown, v.p.; Richard W. Green, v.p.; Ed Zander, gen. mgr.; Bill Kirk, chief eng.; nat'l rep.: Blair.

Operation: 1953.

KTVL-TV (Channel 10) CBS

Freedom Communications, Inc., Box 10, Medford, OR 97501 (503) 773-7373.

Ed Ivey, v.p. & gen. mgr.; Thomas Long, gen. sls. mgr.; Marvin Rhodes, prog. dir.; Mel Tynan, chief eng.

Operation: 1961; TV households: 127,800.

Portland

KATU (Channel 2) ABC

Fisher Broadcasting, Inc., 2153 N.E. Sandy Blvd., Portland, OR 97232 (503) 231-4222.

Sherwood V. Hinman, v.p. & gen. mgr.; Robert D. Kalstad, v.p. & sta. mgr.; Leland Petrik, prog. dir.; Robert Moore, chief eng.; Thomas Oberg, gen. sls. mgr.; Jim Rogers, nat'l sls. mgr.; rep.: Telerep.

Operation: 1962; TV households: 795,100.

KGW-TV (Channel 8) NBC

King Broadcasting Company, 1501 S. W. Jefferson St., Portland, OR 97201 (503) 226-5000.

Steve Clifford, pres. & CEO; Eric Bremmer, pres. bdcst.; Dennis Williamson, v.p. & gen. mgr.; Steve Newman, gen. sls. mgr.; Craig Smith, prog. dir.; Joe Fellhauer, promo. mgr.; Reagan Ramsey, news dir.; Lynn Kurth, chief eng.

Operation: 1956.

KOIN-TV (Channel 6) CBS

KOIN-TV, Inc., 222 S.W. Columbia St., Portland, OR 97201 (503) 464-0600.

R. M. Schafbuch, gen. mgr.; Steve Currie, bdcst. opr. mgr.; Brian Holmes, gen. sls. mgr.; Karen Lee Rice, promo. mgr.; Lee Wood, chief eng.; nat'l rep.: Harrington, Righter & Parsons.

Operation: 1953; TV sets in area: 1,148,500.

KPTV (Channel 12)

Oregon Television, Inc., P.O. Box 3401, Portland, OR 97208; 735 S. W. 20th Place, Portland, OR (503) 222-9921.

Marty Brantley, pres. & gen. mgr.; Connie Martin, gen. sls. mgr.; Gregg Shelby, nat'l sls. mgr.; Gordon White, prog. mgr. & film buyer; Barbara Deaton, promo. mgr.; Bob Nelson, chief eng.; rep.: Tele-Rep.

Operation: 1952; TV households: 785,700.

Roseburg

KPIC (Channel 4) CBS Primary

(Affiliate of KVAL-TV, Eugene, OR)

Southwest Oregon Television Broadcasting Corp., studio & office: 655 West Umpqua, Roseburg, OR 97470; (503) 672-4481.

Don Tykeson, pres.; Don Cithero, sta. mgr.; Jim Putney, gen. mgr.; nat'l rep.: Katz.

Operation: 1956.

Salem

KBSP (Channel 22)

Blackstar Communications of Oregon, Inc., 4923 Indian School Rd., N.E., Salem, OR 97305 (503) 390-6829.

Christopher Desmond, pres., gen. mgr.; Judy Koeney, prog. dir. & film buyer; Tim Mance, chief eng.

Operation: November, 1981.

PENNSYLVANIA

Allentown

WFMZ-TV (Channel 69)

Maranatha Broadcasting Co., Inc., E. Rock Rd., Allentown, PA 18103 (215) 797-4530.

Richard C. Dean, pres. & gen. mgr.; David G. Hinson, prog. dir.; Brad Rinehart, news dir.; Dean Dallmann, sls. mgr.; Kathy Craine, office mgr.; Barry Fisher, chief eng.

Operation: November, 1976.

Altoona

WATM (Channel 23) NBC

Evergreen Bdcstg. Corp., 211 Townsend, Birmingham, MI 48009 (814) 266-8088.

Robert N. Smith, pres.; Martin Ostrow, gen. & gen. sls. mgr.; Chris Taylor, prog. dir. & film buyer; Bob Andrade, chief eng.

Operation: 1974.

WTAJ-TV (Channel 10) CBS

A Gateway Station; 5000 Sixth Avenue, Altoona, PA 16603 (814) 944-2031.

Stephen W. Dant, gen. mgr.; Bob Eger, nat'l sls. mgr.; David Metz, prog. mgr.; Richard Kline, chief eng.

Operation: 1953.

Erie

WETG (Channel 66)

Gannon Univ. Bdcstb., Inc., University Square, Erie, PA 16541 (814) 871-7446.

Anthony J. Miceli, gen. mgr.; Larry A. Lewis, gen. sls. mgr.; Anne Marie Brault, prog. dir.; Jeff Honard, prod. mgr.; Dennis Spagnolo, chief eng.; rep.: Commercial.

Operation: Sept. 2, 1986.

WICU (Channel 12) NBC

Great Lakes Communications, Inc., 3514 State St. Erie, PA 16508 (814) 454-5201.

Priscilla Lamb Schwier, pres.; Clarence Paolella, gen. mgr. & film buyer; Mike Csop, chief eng.; nat'l rep.: Katz

Operation: 1949; TV sets in area: 274,000.

WJET-TV (Channel 24) ABC

JET Broadcasting Co., Inc., 8455 Peach St., Erie, PA 16509 (814) 864-4902.

Myron Jones, pres.; John Kanzius, exec. v.p./gen. mgr.; John Kanzius, prog. dir.; Steve Drexler, news dir.; nat'l rep.: Blair.

Operation: 1966; TV households: 160,500.

WSEE (Channel 35) CBS

Keystone Bdcstg. Co., 1220 Peach St., Erie, PA 16501 (814) 455-7575.

Jerry Montgomery, v.p. & gen. mgr.; William Podbielski, chief eng.; nat'l rep.: MMT.

Operation: 1954; U.H.F. sets in area 245,400.

Greensburg/Pittsburgh

WPCB-TV

Cornerstone TeleVision, Inc., Wall, PA, Greensburg, PA 15148 (412) 824-3930.

R. Russell Bixler, pres.; Oleen Eagle, gen. mgr.; David Skeba, prog. mgr.; Blake Richert, chief eng.

Operation: April, 1979.

Harrisburg

WHP-TV (Channel 21) CBS-TV

WWHP, Inc., P.O. Box 1507, Harrisburg, PA 17105 (717) 238-2100.

Tom Girocco, pres. & gen. mgr.; Chris Fickes, news dir.; Tom Miller, nat'l sls. mgr.; Maurice Gannaway, dir. eng.; nat'l rep.: Katz.

Operation: 1953; TV households in ADI: 550,600.

WHTM-TV (Channel 27) ABC

Box 5860, Harrisburg, PA 17110 (717) 236-2727.

Robert Smith, pres.; John Purcell, v.p. & gen. mgr.; Paul O'Dell, sta. mgr.; Mary Felder, prom. mgr.; Holly Stewart, news dir.; Donald Landis, chief eng.; Joseph Fry, contrl.; nat'l rep.: Harrington, Righter & Parsons.

Operation: June, 1953; TV sets in area: 538,000.

Johnstown

WPJT-TV (Channel 19)

WFAT, Inc., 108 Allenbill Dr., Johnstwon Industrial Park, Johnstown, PA 15904 (814) 266-1919.

S.F. Royster, gen. mgr.; Ron Pateher, sta. mgr., prog. dir. & lcl. sls. mgr.; Earl Garber, tech. eng.

Operation: 1953.

WJAC-TV (Channel 6) NBC

WJAC, Inc., Hickory Lane, Johnstown, PA 15905 (814) 255-7600.

James M. Edwards, Sr., pres.; Richard D. Schrott, v.p.; Jolene Courter, prog. dir.; Rob Abele, chief eng.; nat'l rep.: Harrington, Righter & Parsons.

Operation: 1949; TV sets in area, 1,372,860.

WWCP-TV (Channel 8) FOX

Evergreen Bdcstg. Corp., 1450 Scalp Ave., Johnstown, PA 15904 (814) 266-8088.

Marty Ostrow, v.p., gen. & gen. sls. mgr.; Christopher J. Taylor, dir. opns.; Robert Andrade, chief eng.; rep.: Katz.

Operation: Oct. 13, 1986.

Lancaster

WGAL-TV (Channel 8) NBC

WGAL Television, Inc., 1300 Columbia Ave., Lancaster, PA 17604 (717) 393-5851.

David R. Dodds, v.p. & gen. mgr.; Rigby Wilson, gen. sls. mgr.; John Feeser, lcl. sls. mgr.; Mike Tully, natl. sls. mgr.; Nelson Sears, prog. mgr.; Ed Wickenheiser, news dir.; nat'l rep.: Blair.

Operation: March, 1949; TV households: 1,267,900.

Lancaster/Lebanon

WLYH-TV (Channel 15)

P.O. Box 1283, Television Hill, Lebanon, PA 17042 (717) 273-4551.

Gateway Communications, Inc., Suite 237, One Bala Plaza, Bala Cynwyd, PA 19004 (215) 664-4400.

Robert W. Eolin, v.p. & gen. mgr.

Operation: May 2, 1957.

Philadelphia

WKYW-TV (Channel 3) NBC

Group W (Westinghouse Broadcasting Co.), Independence Mall East, Philadelphia, PA 19106 (215) 238-4700.

James B. Thompson, vice pres. & gen. mgr.; Bob Jones, prgm. mgr.; Brian O'Neill, creative svcs. dir.; Allen Murphy, gen. sls. mgr.; Glenn Romsos, chief eng.; nat'l rep.: TVAR.

Operation: 1941; TV sets in area: 2,275,000.

WCAU-TV (Channel 10) CBS

WCAU-TV, Inc., City Ave. & Monument Rd., Philadelphia PA 19131 (215) 668-5510.

Steve Cohen, vice-pres. & gen. mgr.; Gordon Hughes, v.p. & sta. mgr.; Paul Gluck, news dir.; Dan Sitarski, dir. of opns. & bdcstg.; Dave Harvey, dir. tech. opns.; Dave Kenworthy, dir. creative svcs.; Alan Eisenstein, dir. sls.; Neal Zoren, dir. p.r.; nat'l rep.: CBS Television National Sales.

Operation: 1948; TV sets in area: 2,373,100.

WGBS-TV (Channel 57)

Grant Bdcstg. of Phila., Inc., 420 N. 20th St., Philadelphia, PA 19130 (215) 563-5757.

Robert O'Connor, gen. mgr.; Carol Healey, sta. mgr.; Mark Cooper, promo dir.; Dick Quinto, chief eng.

Operation: October, 1985.

WPHL-TV (Channel 17)

WPHL-TV Inc., 5001 Wynnefield Ave., Philadelphia, PA 19131 (215) 878-1700.

Randall E. Smith, exec. v.p. & gen. mgr.; Steve Mosko, sta. mgr.; Karen Corbin, prog. & mktg. mgr.; Jan Dickler, dir. sls.; Eric Gordon, prod. mgr.; Dan Reese, promo. mgr.; Wanda Fletcher, opns. mgr.; Dorie Lenz, pub. aff. dir.; David Smith, chief eng.; Bruce Wietlisbach, v.p., finance & treas.

Operation: July, 1960; TV households: 3,407,700.

WPVI (Channel 6) ABC

Capital Cities/ABC, Inc., 4100 City Line Ave., Philadelphia, PA 19131 (215) 878-9700.

Richard Spinner, pres. & gen. mgr.; Art Moore, dir. sta. promo. & adv.; Irwin L. Ross, chief eng.

Operation: 1947; TV sets in area: 4,556,200.

WTXF-TV (Channel 29) FOX

TVX of Philadelphia, Inc., 330 Market St., Philadelphia, PA 19106 (215) 925-2929

James D. Boaz, gen. mgr.; Michael Conway, gen. sls. mgr.; LaRhe Vestal, prog. dir.; Denise Rolfe, promo. mgr.; Diane E. Krach, chief eng.; rep.: Seltel.

Operation: 1965; TV households: 3,037,000.

Pittsburgh

KDKA-TV (Channel 2) CBS

Westinghouse Broadcasting Co., Inc., 1 Gateway Center, Pittsburgh, PA 15222 (412) 392-2200.

Joe Berwanger, v.p. & gen. mgr.; Jayne Adair, prog. mgr.; Hal Whack, gen. sls. mgr.; Jerry Kalke, opns. mgr.; Lorraine Saebold, creative svcs.; Bruce Kaplan, mktg. mgr.

WPGH-TV (Channel 53)

Renaissance Communications Co., 750 Ivory Ave., Pittsburgh, PA 15214 (412) 931-5300.

Geoffrey S. Rose, gen. mgr.; Gary S. Cozen, sta. mgr.; Michael Karas, prog. dir.

Households (TV): 1,678,900.

WPTT-TV (Channel 22)

Commercial Radio Institute, Inc., 500 Seco Rd., Pittsburgh, PA 15230 (412) 856-9010.

Carolyn Smith, pres.; Bruce Lumpkin, gen. mgr.; Thomas J. Shannen, sta. mgr.; Dale A. Remy, gen. sls. mgr.; William Standon, natl. sls. mgr.; Robert Skiviat, lcl. sls. mgr.

Operation: 1978.

WPXI (Channel 11) NBC

WPXI Corp., 11 Television Hill, Pittsburgh, PA 15230 (412) 237-1100.

John A. Howell III, v.p. & gen. mgr.; Bruno M. Graziano, gen. sls. mgr.; Mark W. Barash, prog. dir.; Steve Riley, promo. mgr.; Dick Tuininga, news dir.; Linc-Reed Nickerson, chief eng.

Operation, 1957.

WTAE-TV (Channel 4) ABC

400 Ardmore Blvd., Pittsburgh, PA 15221 (412) 242-4300.

Jim Hefner, v.p. & gen. mgr.; Rick Henry, v.p. sls.; Viki Gedrys-Regan, dir. creative svcs.; Marty Faubell, dir. of eng.; David Crantz, dir. of p.r. & spec. projects; Joe Rovitto, news dir.; nat'l rep.: Katz Agency Inc.

Reading

WTVE (Channel 51)

Reading Broadcasting, Inc., 1729 N. 11th St., Reading, PA 19604 (215) 921-9181.

Jeffrey D. Miller, gen. mgr.; Robert Pritchard, chief eng.; Walt Bubbenmoyer, sls. mgr.; Joe Harmuth, prod. adm.; Daniel Bendetti, prod. mgr.

Operation: 1980.

Red Lion

WGCB-TV (Channel 49)

Red Lion Television Inc., Box 88, Red Lion, PA 17356 (717) 246-1681.

John H. Norris, pres.; Fred W. Wise, v.p.; John E. Stockstill, gen. mgr.; Sally Horne, prog. dir.; nat'l rep.: Spot Time.

Operation: 1979.

Scranton/Wilkes-Barre

WNEP-TV (Channel 16) ABC

The New York Times Co., Wilkes-Barre/Scranton Airport, Avoca, PA 18641 (717) 826-1616.

Elden A. Hale Jr., exec. v.p. & gen. mgr.; Warren A. Reed, gen. sls. mgr.; Bill Christian, exec. prog. prod.; rep.: Katz.

Operation: 1954; TV sets in area: 352,375.

WOLF-TV (Channel 38) FOX

Scranton TV Partners, Ltd., 916 Oak St., Scranton, PA 18508 (717) 347-9653.

Guyon Turner, CEO; Gilbert Hoban, gen. sls. mgr.; Peter Kilcollen, prog. & promo.; Dave Swartz, chief eng.; nat'l rep.: ITS.

Operation: June, 1985.

WYOU-TV (Channel 22) CBS

Diversified Communications, 415 Lackawanna Ave., Scranton, PA 18503 (717) 961-2222.

Garry Ritchie, v.p. & gen. mgr.; Harry McClintock, prog. dir.; Marilyn Jaffe, gen. sls. mgr.; nat'l rep.: Blair.

Operation: 1953; TV sets in area: 843,200.

Wilkes-Barre

WBRE-TV (Channel 28) NBC

Northeastern Television Investor, Ltd. Partnership, 62 S. Franklin St., Wilkes-Barre, PA 18773; (717) 823-2828.

Tom Rosing, gen. sls. mgr.; nat'l rep.: Petry.

Operation: 1953; TV sets in area: 939,300.

York

WPMT (Channel 43) FOX

Westport-York Ltd. Partnership, 2005 S. Queen St., York, PA 17403.

Jonathan Hayes, pres. & gen. mgr.; Michael Lape, v.p. & gen. mgr.; Jon Piana, gen. sls. mgr.; Cindy Hunt, prog. opns. & prom. mgr.; Jack Schuster, chief eng.; nat'l rep.: Petry.

Operation: December, 1986; TV sets in area: 850,000.

RHODE ISLAND

Providence

WJAR-TV (Channel 10) NBC

Outlet Communications, Inc., 111 Dorrance St., Providence, RI 02903 (401) 751-5700.

Bruce G. Sundlun, chm. and CEO; David E. Henderson, pres. & COO; John Sawhill, v.p. & gen. mgr.; Fred Weiss, chief eng.; Charles Compagnone, nat'l sls. mgr.; Linda Sullivan, nat'l sls. mgr.; nat'l rep.: Katz.

Operation: 1949; TV sets in area: 1,891,000.

WLNE (Channel 6) CBS

430 County St., New Bedford, MA 02741; (617) 992-6666.

Paul A. Karpowicz, v.p. & gen. mgr.; Paul Kilcullen, gen. sls. mgr.; Doreen Dawson-Wade, sls. mgr.; Truman B. Taylor, prog. mgr.; Bryn Hazell, news dir.; Philip B. Taylor, chief eng.; Robert B. Rieske, mgr. spec. projects.

Operation: 1963; TV households: 533,700.

WNAC-TV (Channel 64) FOX

Rhode Island Bdcstg., 33 Pine St., Rehoboth, MA 02769 (508) 252-9711.

Robert Price, pres.; Peter A. Leone, v.p.-gen. mgr.; John Fignar, gen. sls. mgr.; Keith Folz, prog. dir.; Bradley Morgan, chief eng.; rep.: MMT.

Operation: December, 1981.

WPRI-TV (Channel 12) ABC

Knight-Ridder Broadcasting, Inc., 25 Catamore Boulevard, East Providence, RI 02914 (401) 438-7200.

Robert E. Rice, pres. & gen. mgr.; Archie Goodbee, gen. sls. mgr.; Sandi Morvillo, nat'l sls. mgr.; Sally Dickson, lcl. sls. mgr.; Rita Neuschatz, bus. mgr.; Stephen Davis, opns. mgr.; David Gwizdowski, news dir.; Gracelyn Brown, mktg. mgr.; nat'l rep.: MMT Sales, Inc.

Operation: 1955; TV Households: 2,737,600 (ARB 5-81).

SOUTH CAROLINA
Anderson

WAXA (Channel 40)
Mark III Bcstg. Co., P.O. Box 40, Anderson, SC 29622. Mary Kupris, pres.
Operation: October, 1984.

Charleston

WCBD-TV (Channel 2) ABC
Charleston Television, Inc., P.O. Box 879, Charleston, SC 29402.
Joseph W. (Bill) Evans, III, v.p. & gen. mgr.; David Cummings, gen. sls. mgr.; Alicia Wertimer, lcl. sls. mgr.; Steve Gleason, prog. mgr.; Tom Rogers, promo. mgr.; Richard Fordham, prod. mgr.; Michael Sullivan, news dir.
Operation: 1954.

WCIV (Channel 4) NBC
First Charleston Corp., Highway 703, Mt. Pleasant, SC 29464 (803) 884-8513.
Stephen G. Brock, pres. & gen. mgr.; Deborah Tibbetts, news mgr.; Ken Adkins, sls. mgr.; Carl Shaw, chief eng.

WCSC-TV (Channel 5) CBS
WCSC, Inc. 485 East Bay St., P.O. Box 186, Charleston, SC 29402 (803) 723-8371.
Harold Crump, CEO of WCSC-TV; Dave Allen Petry, co-owner of WCSC; WCSC-TV; Larry Shrum, v.p. & sta. mgr.; Eddie Bolling, v.p. & nat'l/reg. sls. mgr.; Lovell Waugh, v.p. & lcl. sls. mgr.; Jack Becknell, v.p., dir. of eng.; Charlie Thompson, v.p. & dir. prog.; Miriam McManus, v.p., contr.; Bob Lorenzen, promo. mgr.; natl rep: Petry.
Operation: 1953; TV Households: 197,100.

WTAT-TV (Channel 24) FOX
Charleston Television Ltd., 4301 Arco Lane, Charleston, SC 29418 (803) 744-2424.
Bill White, gen. mgr.; Bill Littleton, prog. dir.; David Bird, chief eng.; natl. rep.: Blair.
Operation: September, 1985.

Columbia

WACH (Channel 57)
FCVS Communications, 1221 Sunset Blvd., W., Columbia, SC 29169 (803) 791-5757.
Walter K. Flynn, pres.; Murray Michaels, gen. mgr.; John Livoti, gen. sls. mgr.; Paul Gorman, opns. mgr.; Lynn Rada, promo. mgr.
Operation: September, 1981.

WIS-TV (Channel 10) NBC
1111 Bull St., P.O. Box 367, Columbia, SC 29202; (803) 799-1010.
Dixon C. Lovvorn, sr. v.p. & gen. mgr.; Scott Parks, news dir.; Diane K. Bagwell, prog./promo./mgr.; C. Joseph Tonsing, gen. sls. mgr.; John Augustine, chief eng.
Operation: 1953; TV sets in area: 853,400.

WLTX-TV (Channel 19) CBS
Lewis Bdcstg. Corp., P.O. Drawer M, Columbia, SC 29250 (803) 266-2629.
J. Curtis Lewis, Jr., pres.; Richard T. Laughridge, gen. mgr.; Gene Upright, prog. dir.; Richard Hall, news dir.; Bill Aull, chief eng.; nat'l rep.: Petry.
Operation: 1953; TV sets in area: 289,800.

WOLO-TV (Channel 25) ABC
Columbia TV Broadcasters Inc., Box 4217, Columbia, SC 29240 (803) 754-7525.
David Aiken, gen. mgr.; Linda Patterson, sls. mgr.; Reggie Hall, news dir.; Rick Sprott, chief eng.; rep.: Katz.
Operation: 1961; TV households in area: 273,000.

Florence

WBTW (Channel 13) CBS
Spartan Radiocasting Co., 3430 N. TV Road, Florence, SC 29501 (803) 662-1565.
Jack West, gen. mgr.; Louis Wall, gen. sls. mgr.; Jim Briggs, opns. mgr.; Jim Griffin, news dir.; natl. rep.: Katz.
Operation: 1954; TV households: 613,300.

WPDE-TV (Channel 15) ABC
Diversified Communications, Inc., Box F-15, Florence, SC 29501 (803) 665-1515.
Bill Christian, v.p. & gen. mgr.; Lynn Young, nat'l sls. mgr.; Mike Reed, gen. sls. mgr.; Charl Jackson, opns. mgr.; Joyce Jordan, bus. mgr.; Jimmy Gamble, chief eng.; nat'l rep.: Blair.
Operation: 1980.

Greenville

WYFF-TV (Channel 4) NBC
Pulitzer Broadcasting Co., 505 Rutherford St., Greenville, SC 29602.
Douglas A. Smith, sr. vice pres. & gen. mgr.; Bill Wheless, sta. mgr.; John Scott, sls. dir.; Fritzie Mumford, prog. dir.; Bob King, chief eng.; Penny Henderson, bus. mgr.; Andy Scott, promo. mgr.; nat'l rep.: Petry.
Operation: 1953; TV sets in area: 956,230.

Hardeeville

WTGS (Channel 28) FOX
Hilton Head TV, Inc., Box 718, Hardeeville, SC 29927 (803) 726-5244.
Peter W. McTigue, pres.; Robert H. Stark, gen. mgr.; Edward Youmans, sta. mgr. & chief eng.; Rob Sciabarasi, gen. sls. mgr.; Robert Keele, prog. dir.; David Flander, promo. mgr.; rep.: ITS.
Operation: Nov. 1, 1984.

Spartanburg

WSPA-TV (Channel 7) CBS
Spartan Radiocasting Co., Box 1717, Spartanburg, SC 29304 (803) 576-7777.
Walter J. Brown, CEO; K. Nick Evans, pres.; Anthony Twibell, gen. mgr.; Boyd Bunting, secty,-treas.; Jimmy Sanders, prgm./stn. mgr.; Fred Tuck, chief eng.; Tom Ahner, trans. engineer; Bill Shatten, promo. mgr.; Gary Powers, gen. sls. mgr.; Otis Pickett, lcl. sls. mgr.; Harvey Cox, news dir.; nat'l rep.: Blair.
Operation: 1956; TV sets in area: 2,300,000.

SOUTH DAKOTA
Aberdeen

KABY-TV (Channel 9) ABC
SDTV, Inc., North Highway 281, Box 1520, Aberdeen, SD 57401 (605) 225-9200.
Eric Davis, mgr.; Ken Walker, news dir.; Earl Miller, chief eng.
Operation: 1958.

Florence

KDLO-TV (Channel 3) CBS

(Satellite of KELO-TV, Sioux Falls, SD)

Midcontinent Broadcasting Co., % KELO-TV, Phillips Ave. & 13th St., Sioux Falls, SD 57102 (605) 336-1100.

Joe Floyd, pres.; N. L. Benston, v.p.; E. R. Ruben, secty.-treas.; Evans Nord, pres. & gen. mgr. of KELO; Joe H. Floyd. v.p.; nat'l rep.: Seltel.

Operation: 1955; TV sets in area: 375,500.

Lead

KHSD-TV (Channel 11) ABC

Duhamel Broadcasting Enterprises, Box 1760, Rapid City, S.D. 57709.

William F. Duhamel, pres. & gen. mgr.; Monte Loos, opns. dir.; Frank Ethrington, dir. of eng.; rep.; Katz.

Operation: November, 1966.

KIVV-TV (Channel 5) NBC

Heritage Media, Inc., Box 677, Rapid City, SD 57709 (605) 394-7777.

Gerry Fenske, pres. & gen. mgr.; Harvey Sachau, mgr. of eng.; Gerry Fenske, gen. sls. mgr.; Les Hofland, prod. mgr.; Robert Slocum, prog. dir.; Dan Schillinger, news dir.; rep.: Petry.

Operation: July, 1976.

Pierre

KPRY-TV (Channel 4) ABC

(Satellite of KSFY-TV, Sioux Falls)

300 N. Dakato Ave., Sioux Falls, SD 57102 (605) 336-1300.

Personnel: See KSFY-TV, Sioux Falls

Operation: 1976.

Rapid City

KEVN-TV (Channel 7) NBC

Heritage Media, Inc., Box 677, Rapid City, SD 57709 (605) 394-7777.

Gerry Fenske, pres. & gen. mgr.; Harvey Sachau, mgr. of eng.; Gerry Fenske, gen. sls. mgr.; Les Hofland, prod. mgr.; Robert Slocum, prog. dir.; Dan Schillinger, news dir.; rep.: Petry.

Operation: July, 1976.

KOTA-TV (Channel 3) ABC

KDUH Channel 4, KHSD Channel 11, KSGW Channel 12 (satellites).

Duhamel Broadcasting Enterprises, Duhamel Bldg., 6th & St. Joe Streets, P.O. Box 1760, Rapid City, SD 57709 (605) 342-2000.

William F. Duhamel, pres. & gen. mgr.; Monte Loos, opns. mgr.; Frank Ethrington, dir. of engineering; Lindell Peterson, farm dir.; nat'l rep: Katz.

Operation: 1955; TV sets in area: 80,200.

Reliance

KPLO-TV (Channel 6) CBS

(Satellite of KELO-TV, Sioux Falls, SD)

Midcontinent Broadcasting Co., %KELO-TV., Phillips Ave. & 13th St., Sioux Falls, SD 57102 (605) 336-1100.

Joe Floyd, pres.; N. L. Bentson, v.p.; E. R. Ruben, secty.-treas.; Evans A. Nord, pres. & gen. mgr. of KELO; Joe H. Floyd, v.p.; nat'l rep.: Seltel.

Operation: 1957; TV sets in area, 375,500.

Sioux Falls

KDLT-TV (Channel 5) NBC

Heritage Media, Inc., 3600 S. Westport Ave., Mitchell SD 57116; (605) 361-5555.

Steven M. Herman, pres. & gen. mgr.; Peggy Huss, gen. sls. mgr.; Nancy Weeden, prog. dir.; David Mays, promo. mgr.; Steve Snyder, news dir.; nat'l rep.: Petry.

Operation: 1983; TV households: 235,000.

KELO-TV (Channel 11) CBS

Midcontinent Broadcasting Co., Phillips at 13th, Sioux Falls, SD 57102 (605) 336-1100.

Joe Floyd, pres.; N. L. Bentson, v.p.; E. R. Ruben, secty.-treas.; Evans A. Nord, pres. & gen. mgr. of KELO; Joe H. Floyd, v.p.; Dale Larson, prog. dir.; Jack Townsend, sls. devel. dir.; Scott Burri, prod. mgr.; Cynthia Nord, promo mgr.; Jerry Lofgren, natl. sls. mgr., nat'l rep.: Seltel.

Operation: 1953; TV sets in area: 375,500.

KSFY-TV (Channel 13)

SDTV, Inc., 300 N. Dakota Ave., Sioux Falls, SD 57102.

Randy Cleland, gen. mgr.; Wayne Gudgel, dir. eng.; Steve Carter, prom. dir.; Marge Hokenstad, prog. dir.; Kenneth Walker, news dir.; sales rep.: Katz.

Operation: July, 1960; TV households: 309,300.

KTTW (Channel 17) FOX

Independent Communications, Inc., 2000 W. 42nd St., Sioux Falls, SD 57105 (605) 336-9149.

Charles Poppen, gen. mgr.; Robert Matson, gen. sls. mgr.; Darcy Hunsaker, prog. dir.

Operation: Nov. 1, 1986.

TENNESSEE

Chattanooga

WDEF-TV (Channel 12) CBS

Roy H. Park, Broadcasting of Tennessee, Inc., Broadcast Center, 3300 Broad St., Chattanooga, TN 37408 (615) 267-3392.

Roy H. Park, pres.; Mark Keown, v.p. & gen. mgr.; D. Michael Hood, gen. sls. mgr.; Doris A. Ellis, prog. dir.; William M. Christman, chief eng.; Michael J. Newberry, bus. mgr.; nat'l rep.: Blair Television.

Operation: 1954; TV sets in area: 300,000.

WDSI (Channel 61)

WDSI Limited Partnership, 2401 E. Main St., Chattanooga, TN 37404 (615) 697-0661.

Alan Barrows, gen. mgr.; Kevin Mirek, gen. sls. mgr.; Cheryal Morgan, prog. dir.; Rick Jordan, chief eng. & opns. mgr.

Operation: January, 1972.

WRCB-TV (Channel 3) NBC

WRCB-TV, Sarkes Tarzian, Inc. 900 Whitehall Road, Chattanooga, TN 37405 (615) 267-5412.

Tom Tolar, gen. mgr.; Lawson Fox, prog. dir.; Doug Short, sls. mgr.; Patti Duffy, promo, mgr.

Operation: 1956; TV sets in area: 571,800.

WTVC (Channel 9) ABC

WTVC, Inc., Box 1150, Chattanooga, TN 37401 (615) 266-4151.

F. Lewis Robertson, v.p., gen. mgr. & progr. mgr.; Dennis Brown, chief eng.; nat'l rep.: Petry.

Operation: 1958; TV homes in area: 466,100.

Crossville

WINT-TV (Channel 20)

Cumberland Communications Corp., Box 608, Crossville, TN 38555; (615) 484-8424.

John A. Cunningham, gen. mgr. & chief eng.; James P. Young, sls. mgr.; Rita L. Young, prog. mgr.; Helen L. Cunningham, office mgr.; Wilda Golob, news & pub. affairs dir.; Robin Cunningham, film dir.

Operation: October, 1976.

Greeneville

WETO (Channel 39) FOX

East Tennessee's Own, Inc., Box 1074, Greeneville, TN 37744.

Patrick R. Pickel, gen. sls. mgr.; Jay D. Austin, gen. mgr. & prog. dir.; Danny R. Greene, promo. mgr.; Dennis H. Wilson, chief eng.; natl. rep.: ITS.

Operation: November, 1985.

Jackson

WBBJ-TV (Channel 7) ABC

Jackson Telecasters Inc.; Box 2387, Muse Street, Jackson, TN 38301 (901) 424-4515.

Al Marra, gen. mgr.; John Maybin, gen. sls. mgr.; Rip Ward, chief eng.; nat'l rep.: Katz.

Operation: 1965; TV homes in area: 426,200.

WJWT (Channel 16) FOX

Goldeon Circle Broadcasting, Inc., Box 2048, Jackson, TN 38301; (901) 424-1600.

Marvin Palmquist, pres.; Wade Griffith, gen. mgr.; Ron Lowerly, gen. sls. mgr.; Barbara Henson, prog. dir.; Billy Knott, chief eng.

Operation: April, 1985.

Johnson City

WJHL-TV (Channel 11) CBS

Roy H. Park Broadcasting of the Tri-Cities, Inc., 338 East Main St., Johnson City, TN 37602 (615) 926-2151.

Roy H. Park, pres.; W. H. Lancaster, Jr., v.p. & gen. mgr.; Jack Dempsey, sls. mgr.; Al Gregory, prog. dir.; K. B. Skinner, treas.; Mrs. Dorothy Park, secy.; Carl E. Dickenson, chief eng.; nat'l rep.: Blair-TV.

Operation: 1953; TV sets in area: 1,023,400 (ARB).

Kingsport-Johnson City-Bristol

WKPT-TV (Channel 19) ABC

Holston Valley Broadcasting Corp., 222 Commerce, Kingsport, TN 37660. Mail: Box WKPT, Kingsport, TN 37662.

George DeVault, Jr., pres. & gen. mgr.; Ray Walker, v.p., sta. mgr. & gen. sls. mgr.; Harold T. Dougherty, v.p. eng.; rep.: Seltel.

Operation: 1969; TV homes in ADI: 287,600.

Knoxville

WATE-TV (Channel 6) ABC

Nationwide Communications Inc., 1306 Broadway, N.E. Knoxville, TN 37917 (615) 637-9666.

Steve Berger, pres.; Jim Mikels, gen. mgr.; Jim Abbott, sta. mgr.; Bob Williams, chief eng.; Rick McCue, gen. sls. mgr.; Steve Oglesby, promo. dir.; nat'l rep.: Blair.

Operation: 1953; TV sets in area: 420,500.

WBIR-TV (Channel 10) NBC

Multimedia Broadcasting Co., 1513 Hutchinson, Knoxville, TN 37901 (615) 637-1010.

James T. Lynagh, pres.; James M. Hart, v.p. & gen. mgr.; Robert E. Horton, chief eng.; nat'l rep.: The Katz Agency.

Operation: 1956; TV sets in area: 384,800.

Memphis

WHBQ-TV (Channel 13) ABC

RKO General Inc. (NY), 485 So. Highland Ave., P.O. Box 11407, Memphis, TN 38111 (901) 320-1313.

Alex Bonner, v.p. & gen. mgr.; Jack Bolton, v.p. & gen. sls. mgr.; Dick Kvale, nat'l sls. mgr.; Jimmie Mitchell, lcl. sls. mgr.; Robert Lewis, prog. dir.; Larry Caughlan, chief eng.; nat'l rep.: Harrington, Righter & Parsons.

Operation: 1953; TV households in area: 554,400.

WMC-TV (Channel 5) NBC

Scripps-Howard Broadcasting Co., 1960 Union Ave., Memphis, TN 38104 (901) 726-0555.

Ronald G. Klayman, Jr., v.p. & gen. mgr.; Edw. F. Greaney, Jr., asst gen. mgr. news & public affairs; Joe W. Cooper, asst. gen. mgr., sls.; Charlotte Moore English, asst. gen. mgr.-prog.; J. Philip Slavick, opns. mgr.; Mason Granger, news. dir.; Michael I. Schwartz, eng. mgr.; Robert B. Mize, creative svcs. mgr.; Oliva Holmes, prom. mgr.; William S. Fee, nat'l sls. mgr.; nat'l rep.: Blair-TV, Inc.

Operation: 1948; TV sets in area: 944,100.

WMKW-TV (Channel 30)

West Tennessee Broadcast Corp., Box 30030, Memphis, TN 38130 (901) 346-3030.

James C. Warner, v.p. & gen. mgr.; Trey Murphree, lcl. sls. mgr.; Denise G. Reber, dir. finance; Jean Anders, dir. promo.; Denise King, prog. asst.; Jim Mattson, dir. eng.

Operation: April, 1983.

WPTY-TV (Channel 24)

Chase Bdcstg. of Memphis, Inc., 2225 Union Ave., Memphis, TN 38104; (901) 278-2424.

Kent E. Lillie, v.p. & gen. mgr.; Steve Barry, nat'l sls. mgr.; Steve Pickell, chief eng.; nat'l rep.: Petry Television.

Operation: 1978.

WREG-TV (Channel 3) CBS

New York Times Broadcasting Service, Inc., 803 Channel 3 Drive, Memphis, TN 38103 (901) 525-1313.

Olin F. Morris, pres. & gen. mgr.; Carl Bauman, dir. adv. & promo.; nat'l rep.: The Katz Agency, Inc.

Operation: 1956; TV sets in area: 515,000.

Nashville

WCAY-TV (Channel 30)

M.T. Communications, Inc. (Central Tennessee Bdcstg.), 300 Peabody St., Nashville, TN 37210 (615) 256-3030.

Michael Thompson, pres.; James Warner, v.p. sta. opns.; Tom MacArthur, gen. mgr.; Dale Foshee, gen. sls. mgr.; Kristen Bailey, assoc. dir. opns.; Deborah Little, promo, dir.; Ray McInturff, chief eng.; Maggi Bowden, bus. mgr.; nat'l rep.: Seltel.

Operation: February, 1984.

WKRN-TV (Channel 2) ABC

441 Murfreesboro Rd., Nashville, TN 37210 (615) 248-7222.

Art Elliot, gen. mgr.; Gene Parker, chief eng.; Bill Lord, news dir.; nat'l rep.: HRP.
Operation: 1953; TV sets in area: 634,500.

WSMV-TV (Channel 4) NBC
WSMV-TV, Inc., P.O. Box 4, Nashville, TN 37202 (615) 749-2244.
Mike Kettenring, pres. & gen. mgr.; Dan Akens, sta. mgr.; Brenda Jordan, prog. coord.; David Byars, chief eng.; nat'l rep.: MMT Sales.
Operation: 1950; TV homes in area: 1,083,200.

WTVF-TV (Channel 5) CBS
Channel Five Television Co., 474 James Robertson Pkwy., Nashville, TN 37219 (615) 244-5000.
Thomas E. Ervin, pres. & gen. mgr.; Carrie Brooks, v.p., treas.; Chris Clark, v.p., news dir.; Mark Binda, prog. dir.
Operation: 1954; TV sets in area: 689,000.

WZTV (Channel 17)
Act III Bdcstg. of Nashville, 631 Mainstream Dr., Nashville, TN 37228 (615) 244-1717.
Gary Dreispul, gen. mgr.; Leesa Crawford, traf. mgr.; Boy Jay, gen. sls. mgr.; Gloria Coscarelli, lcl. sls. mgr.; Dale Howard, chief eng.
Operation: March, 1976.

TEXAS

Abilene

KRBC-TV (Channel 9) NBC
Abilene Radio & Television Co., 4510 S. 14th St., Abilene, TX 79605 (915) 692-4242; TWX: 910-897-5414.
Dale Ackers, pres. & gen. mgr.; Ken Knox, sta. mgr.; Jerry Shackelford, prog. mgr.; Bob Lloyd, chief eng.; nat'l rep.: Blair Television.
Operation: 1953; TV sets in area: 200,000.

KTAB-TV (Channel 32) CBS
Big Country Television Co., Box 5676, Abilene, TX 79608 (915) 695-2777.
Wayne Roy, gen. mgr. & sls. mgr.; Bryan Mundy, ops. mgr.; Jerry Marshall, lcl. sls. mgr.; Bob Bartlett, news dir.; Leland Ohlhausen, chief eng.; nat'l rep.: Katz Television.
Operation: 1979; sets in area: 185,900.

Abilene-Sweetwater

KTXS-TV (Channel 12) ABC
Abilene-Sweetwater Bdcstg. Co., 4420 N. Clack, Abilene, TX 79603 (915) 677-2281.
Clay Milstead, gen. mgr.; Monte Williams, chief eng.; rep.: Seltel.

Alvin

KHSH (Channel 67)
Silver King Bdcstg. of Houston, Inc., 2522 Highland Square Mall, Alvin TX 77511 (713) 331-8867.
Jodie Tribble, sta. mgr.; Ann M. Pen, prog. dir.; Ray Cisneros, chief eng.
Operation: Jan. 27, 1986.

Amarillo

KAMR-TV (Channel 4) NBC
Cannan Communications, Inc., P.O. Box 1224, Wichita Falls, TX 76307 (806) 383-3321.
Darrold A. Cannan, Jr., pres.; William M. Dunaway, v.p. & gen. mgr.; Larry Taylor, sls. mgr.; John Schnabel, bus. mgr.; Ken High, chief eng.; Stan Hooker, op. mgr.; Lynn Walker, news dir.
Operation: 1953

KCIT (Channel 14) FOX
1019 S. Fillmore, Amarillo, TX 79101 (806) 374-1414.
Ralph C. Wilson Jr., pres.; Fred M. Hutching, gen. mgr.; Bill Embry, gen. sls. mgr.; Bonnie M. Loe, prog. dir.; Anita Adair, prom. mgr.; Dick Stafford, chief eng.; natl. rep.: MMT.
Operation: October, 1982.

KFDA-TV (Channel 10) CBS
Panhandle Telecasting Co., P.O. Box 1400, Amarillo, TX 79189; (806) 383-2226.
R. H. Drewry, pres.; Mike Lee, gen. mgr.; Sharon Harlin, bus. mgr.; Walt Howard, news dir.; Tim Winn, chief eng.; Joy Sherrod, sls. mgr.
Operation: 1953; TV sets in area: 222,200.

KVII (Channel 7) ABC
Marsh Media, Inc., One Broadcast Center, Amarillo, TX 79101 (806) 373-1787.
James R. McCormick, pres. & gen. mgr.; John Patrick, gen. sls. mgr.; Mac Douglas, prog. dir. & film buyer; Steve Pritchett, news dir.; Bill Canady, chief eng.; nat'l rep.: Katz.
Operation: December, 1957.

Austin

KBVO (Channel 42)
Drawer 2728, Austin, TX 78768.
Steve Beard, gen. mgr.; Ray McEachern, sta. mgr.; Gain Vorsaw, prom. mgr.; nat'l rep.: Katz.
Operation: December, 1983.

KTBC-TV (Channel 7) CBS
The Times Mirror Co., Box 2223, Austin, TX 78767 (512) 476-7777.
Jack E. Harrison, v.p. & gen. mgr.; Charlie King, gen. sls. mgr.

KVUE (Channel 24) ABC
KVUE-TV, Inc. Box 9927, Austin TX 78766 (512) 459-6521.
Craig Dubow, v.p. & gen. mgr.; Michael J. Wenglar, v.p., eng.
Operation: 1971.

KXAN (Channel 36) NBC
Kingstip Communications, Inc., P.O. Box 490, Austin TX 78767 (512) 476-3636.
Jane Wallace, pres. & gen. mgr.; Lyle Banks, gen. sls. mgr.; George Csahanin, chief eng.
Operation: 1965.

Beaumont

KBMT-TV (Channel 12) ABC
Texas Telecasting, Inc., Box 1550, Beaumont, TX 77706 (713) 883-7512.
Michael D. McKinnon, pres.; Max A. Sklower, exec. v.p. &

gen. mgr.; Tom Michalk, gen. sls. mgr.; Austin Hodges, chief eng.; nat'l rep.: Blair Television.
Operation: 1961.

KFDM-TV (Channel 6) CBS
Freedom TV Sub, Inc., P.O. Box 7128, 2955 Interstate 10 East, Beaumont, TX 77706 (409) 892-6622.
Larry Beaulieu, v.p. & sta. mgr.; Richard Kihn, chief eng.; nat'l rep., Petry & Co.
Operation: 1955; TV sets in area: 241,000.

Brownsville

KVEO (Channel 23) NBC
394 N. Expressway, Brownsville, TX 78520 (512) 544-2323.
L. William Heyman, Jr., gen. mgr.; Brent Skinner, gen. sls. mgr.; Brad Levy, prog. dir.; Ignacio Cantu, dir. eng.; nat'l rep.: Seltel.
Operation: 1981.

Bryan

KBTX-TV (Channel 3) CBS
Brazos Broadcasting Co., 4141 E. 29th St., P.O. Drawer 3730, Bryan, TX 77805 (409) 846-7777.
Thomas G. Pears, pres.; Ulman McMullen, sta. mgr.; nat'l rep.: Seltel.
Operation: May, 1957; TV sets in area: 220,000.

Corpus Christi

KIII (Channel 3) ABC
Texas Television, Inc., 4750 S. Padre Island Dr., Corpus Christi, TX 78404.
Michael D. McKinnon, pres.; Max Sklower, gen. mgr.; Leonard Roper, bus. mgr., Billy Brotherton, sta. mgr.; rep.: Katz.
Operation: 1964; TV households: 318,900.

KORO (Channel 28)
Telecorpus, Inc., 102 N. Mesquite, Corpus Christi, TX 78401 (512) 883-2823.
Servando Caballero, gen. mgr.; Felipe Franco, chf. eng.
Operation: 1977.

KRIS-TV (Channel 6) NBC
Gulf Coast Broadcasting Co., Box 840, Corpus Christi, TX 78403 (512) 883-6511.
T. Frank Smith, pres. & gen. mgr.; Van Johnson, sr. v.p., sta. mgr.; Charlie Barte, sls. mgr.; Marvin Born, dir. of eng.; nat'l rep.: Petry.
Operation: 1956; TV sets in area: 116,780.

KZTV (Channel 10) CBS
K-Six Television, Inc., 301 Artesian, P.O. Box TV-10, Corpus Christi, TX; 78401.
Vann M. Kennedy, pres. & gen. mgr.; Eugene Looper, prog. dir.; Jim Bixler, comm. mgr.; Walter Furley, news dir.; Lester Waters, chief eng.
Operation: 1956.

Dallas-Fort Worth

KDAF-TV (Channel 33) FOX
Fox TV Stations, 8001 Carpenter Freeway, Dallas, TX 75247; (214) 634-8833.
Gayle Brammer, v.p. & gen. mgr.; Mark Salditch, prog. dir.; Craig Miller, promo. mgr.; Joe Maggio, chief eng.; nat'l rep.: Petry.
Operation: 1980.

KDFI-TV (Channel 27)
P.O. Box 561427, Dallas, TX 75356-1427; (214) 637-2727.
John McKay, pres.; Thoren Schroeck, v.p., sls.; Ed Murlatt, chief eng.
Operation: January, 1981.

KDFW-TV (Channel 4) CBS
KDFW-TV, Inc., 400 North Griffin St., Dallas, TX 75202 (214) 720-4444.
Bill Baker, v.p. & gen. mgr.; Tom Collier, gen. sls. mgr; Joe Bell, prog. dir.; Warren Farrar, chief eng.; rep.: Harrington, Righter & Parsons.
Operation: 1949; TV sets in area: 1,645,980.

KTXA (Channel 21)
TVX of Ft. Worth-Dallas, Inc., 1712 E. Randol Mill Rd., Arlington, TX 76012 (817) 265-2100. Owned by TVX Broadcast Group, Inc.
Dirk Brinkerhoff, v.p. & gen. mgr.; Mike Dunlop, gen. sls. mgr.; Linda Danna, lcl. sls. mgr.; Greg Pittman, natl. sls. mgr.; Rick Davey, prod.-promo. mgr.; Tammy Salinas, prog. mgr.; Sue Stuechell, bus. mgr.
Operation: 1981.

KXAS-TV (Channel 5) NBC
North Texas Broadcasting Corp., 3900 Barnett St., Ft. Worth, TX 76101 (817) 429-1550.
Frank O'Neill, pres. & gen. mgr.; Russ Thornton, dir., admin. & devel.; Patty Parker, gen. sls. mgr.; Bill Shock, eng. dir.
Operation: 1948.

KXTX-TV (Channel 39)
CBN Continental Bcstg., 3900 Harry Hines Blvd., Dallas, TX 75219 (214) 521-3900.
Ted Norman, v.p. & gen. mgr.; Perry Sook, gen. sls. mgr.; Mike Carter, sta. mgr.; Nelson Flanagan, promo. mgr.; Harold Nash, chief eng.; sales rep.: Adam Young, Inc.
Operation: February, 1968; TV households: 2,006,100.

WFAA-TV (Channel 8) ABC
A. H. Belo Corp. (parent organization of The Dallas Morning News and WFAA-TV), Communications Center, Dallas, TX 75202-4810 (214) 748-9631.
David T. Lane, pres. & gen. mgr.; Buff Parham, gen. sls. mgr.; Bob Robinson, opns. mgr.; Marty Haag, v.p. & exec. news dir.; Beaven Els, chief engr.; Michael Grant, exec. dir. prog. & promo; John Irvin, exec. dir. admin.; Pat Oswald, controller; nat'l rep.: Telerep.
Operation: 1949; TV sets in area: 1,647,700.

El Paso

KCIK (Channel 14) FOX
KCIK-TV, Inc., 3100 N. Stanton St., El Paso, TX 79902 (915) 533-1414.
Jack Mulderrig, chm.; Don Caparis, pres. & gen. mgr.; Eddie Valdez, gen. sls. mgr.; Larry Pepin, prog. dir.; Kerry Cooper, chief eng.; nat'l rep: ITS.
Operation: 1979; sets in area: 283,200.

KDBC-TV (Channel 4) CBS

El Paso Television Co., 2201 Wyoming Ave., El Paso, Texas 79903 (915) 532-6551.

Hugh V. Roche, gen. mgr.; David Hornack, sls. mgr.; Richard Morales, bus. mgr.; Diane Lozano, prog. dir.; Walter Ward, chief eng.; nat'l rep.: Seltel.

Operation: 1953; TV sets in area: 222,000.

KINT-TV (Channel 26)

Paso Del Norte Bcstg. Corp., 5426 N. Mesa Dr., El Paso, TX 79912 (916) 581-1126.

Richard A. Najera, bd. chm.; Mary S. Ponce, pres.; Steve Ginst,; Karl W. Moran, contr.; Jose Luis Torres, news dir.; Sylvia Martinez, traf.-prog. dir.; Alfredo Durand, chief eng.

Operation: January, 1984.

KTSM-TV (Channel 9) NBC

Tri-State Broadcasting Co., Inc., 801 N. Oregon St., El Paso, TX 79903 (915) 532-5421.

Karl O. Wyler, pres. & gen. mgr.; Jack Rye, exec. v.p. & progs.; John Phelan, v.p., sls.; W. T. McGill, v.p., eng'.; nat'l rep.: Blair.

Operation: 1953; TV households in area: 306,260.

KVIA-TV (Channel 13)

KVIA-TV Marsh Media—El Paso, 4140 Rio Bravo, El Paso, TX 79902.

Richard E. Pearson, gen. mgr.; Cathy Franco, prog. dir.; Dan Overstreet, gen. sls. mgr.; Jack Wilkinson, chief eng.; natl rep.: Katz Television.

Operation: 1956; TV sets in area: 169,720.

Fort Worth

KTVT (Channel 11)

Gaylord Broadcasting Co., 5322 Bridge St., Fort Worth, TX 76103 (817) 738-1951; Branch office: 10111 N. Central Expressway, Dallas, TX 75231.

Charles L. Edwards, v.p. & gen. mgr.; Harry J. Delanmey, sta. mgr.; nat'l rep.: Telerep.

Galveston

KTMD (Channel 48)

Telemundo of Galveston-Houston, Inc., 3903 Stony Brook, Houston, TX 77063 (713) 974-4848.

Mauricio Mendez, v.p. & gen. mgr.; Becky Diaz, gen. sls. mgr.; Anna Cardona, prog. dir., film buyer & promo. mgr.; Marcello Marini, news dir.; Blane Huhn, chief eng.; rep.: Telemundo TV Group.

Operation: Dec. 12, 1987.

Garland

KUVN (Channel 23)

Univision Station Group, Inc., 3720 Marquis Drive, Garland, TX 75042 (214) 272-0686.

Elizabeth R. Vaughan, pres.; Mike Carver, chief eng.

Operation: Sept. 25, 1986.

Harlingen

KGBT-TV (Channel 4) CBS

Draper Communications, Inc., P.O. Box 2567, Harlingen, TX 78551. (512) 421-4444.

Thomas H. Draper, pres.; Robert P. Getz, v.p. & gen. mgr. Michael Opauski, chief eng.; John S. Clark, gen. sls. mgr.; nat'l rep.: Katz.

Operation: 1953. TV sets in area: 177,500.

Houston

KHOU-TV (Channel 11) CBS

Gulf Television Corp., P.O. Box 11, Houston, TX 77001 (713) 526-1111.

Allen E. Howard, pres. & gen. mgr.; Craig Bland, gen. sls. mgr.; Hal Kemp, prog. mgr.; Andrew Klarer, prod. mgr.; Paula Walker, news dir.; nat'l rep.: Telerep.

Operation: March, 1953; TV households: 1,326,000.

KHTV (Channel 39)

KHTV, Gaylord Bdcstg. Co., 7700 Westpark Drive, 77063 P.O. Box 630129, Houston, TX 77263-0129; (713) 781-3939.

Ed Trimble, v.p. & gen. mgr.; John De Roche, gen. sls. mgr.; Bob Clark, prog. dir.; Trish Naber, prom. mgr.; John R. Schilberg, chief eng.; nat'l rep.: MMT.

Operation 1967.

KPRC-TV (Channel 2) NBC

H & C Communications, Inc., 8181 Southwest Freeway, Houston, TX 77074 (713) 771-4631.

William P. Hobby, bd. chmn.; James E. Crowther, pres. bdcst. group; Tom Reiff, pres. & gen. mgr. Ch. 2; Red Koch, v.p., prog.; Art Biggs, v.p. eng.; Paul Paolicelli, v.p. news; Dick Daggett, gen. sls. mgr.; Bruce Bryant, creative svcs. dir.; nat'l rep.: Petry.

Operation: 1949; TV sets in area: 1,409,530.

KRIV-TV (Channel 26) FOX

Fox TV Stations, Inc., P.O. Box 22810, 3935 Westheimer, Houston, TX 77227 (713) 626-2610..

M. Jerry Marcus, v.p. & gen. mgr.; Gayle Brammer, v.p. & gen. sls. mgr.; Roz Brown, prog. dir.; Mary Delaney, prom. mgr.; nat'l rep.: Katz.

Operation: August, 1971; TV households: 1,115,900.

KTRK-TV (Channel 13) ABC

Capital Cities Communications, Inc.; mailing address: P.O. Box 12, Houston, TX 77001; offices and studios: 3310 Bissonnet, Houston, TX (713) 666-0713; TWX: 910-881-1511; Transmitter: Alameda, TX.

Thomas S. Murphy, pres. & chmn.; Paul Bures, v.p. & gen. mgr.; Jim Masucci, oper. dir.; Charles Wolf, creative svcs. mgr.; Gerald Kennedy, prod. supvr.; Margaret Shilstone, prom. supvr.; Jim Topping, news dir.; J. L. Hamilton, chief studio eng.; Art Giddings, chief transmitter eng.; spot sales rep., Capital Cities/ABC.

Operation: 1954; TV homes in area: 1,457,400.

KTXH (Channel 20)

TVX of Houston, Inc., 8950 Kirby Drive, Houston, TX 77054 (713) 661-2020.

Julio Bermudez, v.p. & gen. mgr.; Scott Sanders, gen. sls. mgr.; Patty Duncan, prog. dir.; Robert Kobarg, promo. dir.; Jim Aldendorf, bus. mgr.; Thomas Daniels, chief eng.; nat'l rep.: Seltel.

Operation: November, 1982.

Irving

KHSX (Channel 49)

Silver King Bdcstg. of Dallas, 1957 E. Irving Blvd., Irving, TX 75060 (214) 579-4900.

Jim Flynn, pres.; Jo Edgell, v.p. & sta. mgr.; Tony Montes, prog. dir.; Carol Holler, bus. mgr.; Art Runyon, chief eng.
Operation: April, 1984.

Jacksonville

KETK-TV (Channel 56) NBC
Texas American Bdcstg. Ltd., 5656 N. Jackson St., Jacksonville, TX 75766 (214) 586-5644.
Phil Hurley, pres. & gen. mgr.; John Gaston, gen. sls. mgr.; Jean Pavelka, prog. dir.; Mike Stanford, opns. mgr.; Bece Cantu, prom. mgr.; Jon McCall, news dir.; Moe Strout, chief eng.; Ruby Somerford, compt.; natl. rep.: Blair.
Operation: February, 1987.

Kerrville

KRRT (Channel 35) FOX
TVX of San Antonio, 6218 N.W. Loop 410, San Antonio, TX 78238 (512) 684-0035.
Morrie P. Beitch, v.p. & gen. mgr.; Tom Hurley, gen. sls. mgr.; Tom Bumbera, prog. dir.; Andrea Frazier, prom. mgr.; Kevin Busselman, chief eng.; natl. rep.: Seltel.
Operation: November, 1985.

Laredo

KGNS-TV (Channel 8) NBC
Fabri Development Corp., Box 2829, Laredo, TX 78041 (512) 727-8888.
Michael Clark, gen. mgr.; T. Frank Smith IV, gen. sls. mgr.; Velia Herrera, prog. dir.; rep.: Katz.
Operation: 1956; TV sets in area: 23,000

KLDO (Channel 27) ABC
Panorama Broadcasting Co., 1600 Water St., Riverdrive Mall, Laredo, TX 78040; (512) 727-0027.
Elia Johnston, gen. mgr., film buyer, gen. sls. mgr. & prog. dir.; Cindy Rodriguez, promo. mgr.; Randy Kent, news dir.; Rene Gonzalez, chief eng.; nat'l rep.: Adam Young.
Operation: December, 1984.

KVTV (Channel 13) CBS
2600 Shea, Laredo, TX 78040; P.O. Box 203, Laredo, TX 78044.
Vann M. Kennedy, pres. & gen. mgr.; E.L. Roskelley, sta. mgr.; Debbie Shoup, news dir.; Joe Martinez, chief eng.; B.E. Madrigal, sls. coor.; sls. rep.: Seltel.
Operation: December, 1973.

Longview

KLMG-TV (Channel 51) CBS
KLMG-TV, Inc., 701 N. Access Rd., Box 5151, Longview, TX 75608.
Stan Deck, gen. mgr.; John Blake, sta. mgr.; John Landsdale, prog. dir.; Ted Deck, promo. mgr.; Vickie Lafollett, news dir.; Bob Jeudevine, dir. eng.; nat'l rep.: Seltel.
Operation: September, 1984.

Lubbock

KAMC-TV (Channel 28) ABC
McAlister TV Enterprises Inc., Box 2805, Lubbock, TX 79408 (806) 745-2828.
Bob Nash, pres. & gen. mgr.; Bill Maddox, sls. mgr.; Bill Enloe, chief eng.; A. C. Wimberly, prog. dir.
Operation: 1968; TV homes in area: 147,180.

KCBD-TV (Channel 11) NBC
Caprock Telecasting Co., Inc., Box 2190, Lubbock, TX 79408 (806) 744-1414.
Bill de Tournillon, gen. mgr.; Peggy Sullivan, prog. dir.; Sherrell Lambert, dir. of eng.; Craig Wells, sls. mgr.; nat'l rep.: Katz.
Operation: 1953: TV sets in area: 224,00.

KJTV (Channel 34)
Box 3757, Lubbock, TX, 79452 (806) 745-1134.
Ray Moran, pres.; Brad Moran, gen. mgr. & prog. dir.; Randy Roberts, gen. sls. mgr.; Guy Smith, chief eng.; nat'l rep.: Seltel.
Operation: January, 1982.

KLBK-TV (Channel 13) CBS
Charles Woods TV Corp., 7400 University Ave., Lubbock, TX 79423 (806) 745-2345.
Charles Woods, pres.; Rick Lipps, gen. mgr.; Jim Arnold, sls. mgr.; Chris Alexander, news dir.; Don King, chief eng.; nat'l rep.: Blair.
Operation: 1952; TV sets in area: 188,000.

Lufkin

KTRE-TV (Channel 9) ABC
Buford Television Inc. of Lufkin, Box 729, Lufkin, TX 75901 (409) 853-5873.
Errol R. Kapellusch, gen. mgr.; Duane Dargis, sls. mgr.; nat'l rep.: Katz.
Operation: 1955.

Midland

KMID-TV (Channel 2) ABC
Telepictures Broadcasting Corp., Inc., KMID-TV, Midland, TX 79711 (915) 563-2222.
John Foster, gen. mgr.; nat'l rep.: Katz.
Operation: 1953; TV sets in area: 166,7000.

Monahans

KTPX-TV (Channel 9) NBC
MSP Television of Midland-Odessa, Box 6699, Midland, TX 79701 (915) 563-4210.
Dan Robbins, gen. mgr.; Richard Howard, news dir.; Grady Woodward, dir. of eng.
Operation: 1958; TV homes in area: 173,800.

Odessa

KOSA-TV (Channel 7) CBS
Adams TV of Texas, Inc., 1211 N. Whitaker, Odessa, TX 79760 (915) 337-8301.
Ben Strickland, v.p., gen. mgr. & gen. sls. mgr.; Vic Ludington, lcl. sls. mgr.; Al Harris, chief eng.; Dan Scott, news. dir.; nat'l rep.: Blair.
Operation: 1956; TV homes in area: 119,500.

KPEJ (Channel 24)
Southwest Multi Media-Odessa-Midland, Box 11009, Odessa, TX 79763 (915) 337-2424.
Joseph Sugg, gen. mgr.; Jamie Beeghley, gen. sls. mgr.; Joel Jackson, lcl. sls. mgr.; LeighAnn Kalenic, prog. dir.; Sue McEwen, promo. mgr.; Glen Edwards, chief eng.; nat'l rep.: MMT.
Operation: June, 1986.

Port Arthur

KJAC-TV (Channel 4) NBC

Southeast Texas Television Corp., P.O. Box 3257, Port Arthur, TX 77643 (409) 985-5557.

Rush Evans, v.p.-gen. mgr.; Linda Bruno, comm. mgr.; Charles Ravell, chief eng.; nat'l rep.: MMT.

Operation: 1957; TV sets in area: 167,000.

San Angelo

KACB-TV (Channel 3) NBC

(Satellite of KRBC-TV, Abilene)

Abilene Radio & TV Co., 4510 14th St., P.O. Box 178, Abilene, TX 79604 (915) 692-4242.

Dale Ackers, pres.; Ken Knox, sta. & sls. mgr.; Jerry Shackelford, prog. dir.; Glen Welch, chief eng.; rep.: Blair TV.

Operation: 1962.

KIDY (Channel 6) FOX

406 S. Irving, San Angelo, TX 76903 (915) 658-2666.

Raymond Schindler, pres.; Jim Batson, gen. mgr.; Marshall Twombley, gen. sls. mgr.; John Talley, prog. dir.; Paris Schindler, film buyer; C.D. Roper, chief eng.

Operation: July, 1983.

KLST (Channel 8) CBS

Jewell Television, 2800 Armstrong, San Angelo, TX 76903 (915) 949-8000.

Phil Brassie, gen. mgr.; Lou Kordek, news dir.; Larry White, chief eng.; nat'l rep.: Katz.

Operation: July, 1953; sets in area: 88,200.

San Antonio

KABB (Channel 29)

Alamo Bdcstg. Corp., 520 N. Medina, San Antonio, TX 78207 (512) 299-1129.

Paris R. Schindler, pres. & film buyer; Bill Carter, sta. mgr.; Kevin Mirek, gen. sls. mgr.; Sam Bickel, prog. dir.; Scott Macaninch, promo. mgr.; Cindy Rucker, pub. affrs.; Dale Taylor, chief eng.; rep.: Telerep.

Operation: Dec. 17, 1987.

KENS-TV (Channel 5) CBS

5400 Fredericksburg Rd., San Antonio, TX 78229; P.O. Box TV5, 78299; (512) 366-5000.

Mike Conly, pres. & gen. mgr.; Jack Forehand, v.p.-sta. mgr.; Bob Rogers, v.p., news; Susan Korbel, dir. mktg.; Marcelino Rodriguez, dir., finance; Bob King, chief eng.; Mike Simpson, lcl. sls. mgr.; Jerry Policoff, natl. sls. mgr.; nat'l rep.: Blair.

Operation: 1950; TV sets in area: 1,112,600.

KMOL-TV (Channel 4) NBC

United TV, Inc., P.O. Box 2641, San Antonio, TX 78205 (512) 226-4251.

Robert P. Donohue, v.p., gen. mgr.; Kevin Donohue, gen. sls. mgr.; John Seabers, natl. sls. mgr.; Dennis Marshall, creative svcs. dir.; Gene Hansbauer, bus. mgr.; Phil Johnson, lcl. sls. mgr.; Jack Carroll, prog. dir.; Ron Harris, news dir.; Harold Friesenhahn, chief eng.; Ray Laube, prod. dir.; rep.: MMT.

Operation: 1949; TV homes: 555,000.

KSAT-TV (Channel 12) ABC

H&C Communications, Inc., Box 2478, San Antonio, TX 78298 (512) 228-1200.

James Schiavone, pres. & gen. mgr.; Rick Andrycha, prog. mgr.; Jack Dix, gen. sls. mgr.; rep.: Petry.

Operation: 1957; TV homes in area: 945,300.

KWEX-TV (Channel 41)

The Univision Station Group, Inc., 411 E. Durango Blvd., San Antonio, TX 78204; (512) 227-4141.

Heberto Gutierrez, gen. mgr.; Jon Yasuda, gen. sls. mgr.; Joe Nolasco, contr.; James R. Meek, dir. eng.

Temple-Waco

KCEN-TV (Channel 6) NBC

Channel 6, Inc., P.O. Box 6103, Temple, TX 76503 (817) 773-6868; Waco office, 4716 W. Waco Drive, Waco, TX 76710 (817) 776-6665; TWX 910-890-4870.

Anyse Sue Mayborn, pres.; Dan Lesmeister, v.p. & gen. mgr.; Ken Smith, chief eng.; nat'l rep.: Blair TV.

Operation: 1953; TV sets in area: 245,600.

Tyler-Longview

KLTV (Channel 7) ABC

Channel 7, Inc., Box 957, Tyler, TX 75710 (214) 597-5588.

TV-3, Inc., owners; Larry Harris, exec. v.p. & gen. mgr.; Butch Adair, chief eng.; Errol Kapellusch, prog. dir.; nat'l rep.: Katz Agency.

Operation: 1954; TV sets in area: 178,500.

Victoria

KAVU-TV (Channel 25) NBC

Community Bcstg. of Coastal Bend, Inc., Box 4929, Victoria, TX 77903 (512) 576-5288.

Newton M. Warzecha, gen. mgr.; Bob Hesse, gen. sls. mgr.; Izena Frankhouser, prog. dir.; Mike Sizemore, news dir.; Charles Smithey, tech. eng.; nat'l rep.: Katz.

Operation: July, 1982.

KVCT (Channel 19) ABC

Victoria Communications Corporation, P.O. Box 1879, Victoria, TX 77902.

William Murphy, pres.; Betty Grimsinger, gen. mgr. & gen. sls. mgr.; Doris Littles, prog. dir.; Brenda Simpson, news dir.

Operation: 1969.

Waco

KWKT (Channel 44) FOX

Southwest Multi Media of Waco, Inc., 8803 Woodway Dr., Waco, TX 76712 (817) 776-3844.

Mark J. Jollie, gen. mgr. & film buyer; Ron Cooke, gen. sls. mgr.; Mark McKay, prog. dir. & promo. mgr.; Mike DeClue, chief eng.; rep.: MMT.

Operation: March, 1988.

KWTX-TV (Channel 10) CBS

KWTX Broadcasting Company, 6700 American Plaza, Waco, TX 76712. Mail: P.O. Box 2636, Waco, TX 76702.

M. N. Bostick, chm.; Thomas G. Pears, pres.; Ray Deaver, v.p., gen. mgr.; Robert Levy, sec.-treas.; Lisa Oatman, natl.-regl. sls. mgr.; Ken Musgrave, chief eng.; Ralph Webb, prog. dir.; natl. rep.: Seltel.

Operation: 1955; TV sets in area: 245,600.

KXXV (Channel 25) ABC

Shamrock Bdcstg., Box 2522, Waco, TX 76702 (817) 754-2525.

Bob Good, gen. mgr.; Don Shores, gen. sls. mgr.; Jinx Dennix, prog. dir.; Don Marion, news dir.; Lou Strowger, chief eng.; natl. rep.: Katz.
Operation: January, 1985.

Weslaco

KRGV-TV (Channel 5) ABC
Mobile Video Tapes, Inc., 900 E. Expressway Avenue, Weslaco, TX 78596 (512) 968-5555.
Douglas L. Manship, pres.; Ray Alexander, gen. mgr.; Jim Cook, lcl. sls. mgr.; Tom Hagner, gen. sls. mgr.; Julian Adame, prgm. dir.; Rick Diaz, news dir.; nat'l rep.: Blair Television.
Operation: 1954; TV sets in area: 218,000.

Wichita Falls

KAUZ-TV (Channel 6) CBS
Adams TV of Wichita Falls, P.O. Box 2130, Wichita Falls, TX 76307.
Mark Cumming, v.p. & gen. mgr. & natl. sls. mgr.; Linda Hilden, prog. dir.; Leon Hoeffner, chief eng.; Sandy Berthelot, natl. sls. asst.; nat'l rep.: Blair Television.

KFDX-TV (Channel 3) NBC
Price Communications, Box 4000, Wichita Falls, TX 76308 (817) 692-4530.
Bob Price, chmn.; Dick Appleton, sr. v.p., TV; Jack Young, lcl.-rgnl. sls. mgr.; Jim Smith, dir. of eng.; Peggy Edgar, film ed.; nat'l rep.: Katz.
Operation: 1953; TV sets in area: 250,000.

KJTL (Channel 18) FOX
Wichita Falls TV, Ltd., Box 4865, Wichita Falls, TX 76308 (817) 691-1808.
Peter D'Acosta, v.p. & gen. mgr.; Karen Dickins, sls. mgr.; Ken Thomason, chief eng.; nat'l rep.: Seltel.
Operation: May, 1985.

UTAH

Cedar City

KCCZ (Channel 4)
Box 188, Brian Head, UT 84719 (801) 677-2088.
Michael G. Golden, pres. & gen. mgr.
Operation: September, 1985.

Ogden

KOOG-TV (Channel 30)
Ogden Television, Inc., 1309 16th St., Ogden, UT 84404 (801) 621-3030.
Curt Westphal, sta. mgr., prog. dir. & film buyer; Dale Bradshaw, promo. mgr.
Operation: October, 1985.

Salt Lake City

KSL-TV (Channel 5) CBS
KSL, Inc., Broadcast House, 5 Triad Center, Salt Lake City, UT 84110-1160 (801) 575-5555.
Jack Adamson, pres.; William R. Murdoch, v.p., gen. mgr.; Jim Monroe, mktg. dir.; J. Talmage Ball, chief eng.; J. Spencer Kinard, v.p./news dir.; David Manookin, dir. prog.; nat'l rep.: Petry
Operation: 1949; TV homes in area: 841,900.

KSTU (Channel 13)
Mountain West Television, 5020 W. Amelia Earhart Dr., Salt Lake City, UT 84116 (801) 532-1300.
Milt Jouflas, gen. mgr.; Christy Elswood, prog. dir.; Susan Adams, natl. sls. mgr.; Douglas Beck, lcl. sls. mgr.; Wayne Marion, bus. mgr.; natl. rep.: Telerep.
Operation: 1978.

KTVX (Channel 4) ABC
United TV, Inc., 1760 Fremont Dr., Salt Lake City, UT 84104.
Evan Thompson, pres.; David J. Woodcock, v.p. & gen. mgr.; Robert Galle, gen. sls. mgr.; Gordon Acker, prog. dir.; Victor Shapiro, promo. mgr.; Jim McDermaid, tech dir.
Operation: 1948; TV sets in area: 901,000.

KUTV (Channel 2) NBC
KUTV Inc., 2185 S. 3600 West, Salt Lake City, UT 84119 (801) 973-3000.
George C. Hatch, chm.; Jeffrey B. Hatch, pres. & gen. mgr.; Maria Smith, prog. dir. & buyer; nat'l rep.: Katz.
Operation: 1954; TV set in area: 771,200.

VERMONT

Burlington

WCAX-TV (Channel 3) CBS
Mt. Mansfield Television, Inc., P.O. Box 608, Joy Dr., So. Burlington, VT 05402 (802) 862-5761.
S. T. Martin, pres. & gen. mgr.; Peter R. Martin, exec. v.p. & prog. dir.; Ken Jarvis, gen. sls. mgr.; Stuart Hall, v.p. & prod. mgr.; Charles Liese, chief eng.; Judy Clark, film mgr.; Ken Greene, dir. prom.-pub. affairs; Dolores Drolette, v.p., cont. nat'l rep., HRP, NY.
Operation: 1954; TV sets in area: U.S. 1,168,000, Canada 1,328,000.

WVNY-TV (Channel 22) ABC
Citadel Communications Co., Ltd., 100 Market Square, Burlington, VT 05401 (802) 658-8022.
Philip J. Lombardo, pres./gen. mgr.; William Bradley, gen. mgr. v.p.; Tom Hansen, dir. bdct. opns.; Brad Worthen, gen. sls. mgr.; Richard Meyers, chief eng.
Operation: 1982.

Hartford-Hanover

WNNE-TV (Channel 31) NBC
WNNE-TV, Inc., Box 1310, White River Junction, VT 05001 (802) 295-3100.
Gary Elfstrom, v.p. & gen. mgr.; Courtney Galluzzo, gen. sls. mgr.; Mike Smith, prog. dir.; Ken Aldrich, chief eng.
Operation: 1978.

VIRGINIA

Bristol

WCYB-TV (Channel 5) NBC, ABC
Appalachian Broadcasting Corporation, 101 Lee St., Bristol, VA 24201 (703) 669-4161.
Robert H. Smith, Jr., exec. v.p. & gen. mgr.; Jack Shaver, v.p. sls. & asst. to gen. mgr.; Echel Edens, chief eng.; Charles Lineberger, prog. mgr.; Rick McVey, opns. mgr.; Sandhi Kozsuch, dir. prod./creative svcs.; Steve Hawkins, news dir.; nat'l rep.: Petry.
Operation: 1956; TV sets in area: 1,125,000.

Charlottesville

WVIR-TV (Channel 29) NBC

Virginia Broadcasting Corp., P.O. Box 769, Charlottesville, VA 22902 (804) 977-7082.

Bernard E. Waterman, Jr., pres.; Harold B. Wright, Jr., v.p. & gen. mgr.; Jim Fernald, gen. sls. mgr.

Operation: March, 1973; TV households: 82,000.

Hampton-Norfolk

WVEC-TV (Channel 13) ABC

1930 E. Pembroke Ave., Hampton, VA 23663; 613 Woodis Ave., Norfolk, VA 23510; (804) 625-1313.

J. William Beindorf, v.p. & gen. mgr.; Rick Keilty, gen. sls. mgr.; Meyer Davis, opns. & prog. mgr.; Cil Frazier, adv./promo. mgr.; Dick Cannon, chief eng.; nat'l rep.: Petry.

Operation: 1953; TV sets in area: 502,900.

Harrisonburg

WHSV-TV (Channel 3) ABC

Benedek Bcstg. Corp., P.O. Box TV 3, Highway 33 West, Harrisonburg, VA 22801 (703) 433-9191.

Robert Ganzer, gen. mgr.; Bob Bolyard, gen. sls. mgr.; Richard Hiett, chief eng.

Operation: 1953; TV households: 293,500.

Lynchburg

WSET-TV (Channel 13) ABC

WSET, Inc. 2320 Langhorne Rd., P.O. Box 11588, Lynchburg, VA 24506 (804) 528-1313.

David F. McAtee, pres. & gen. mgr.; Beve Lutz, business mgr., Barry Corswandt, gen. sls. mgr.; Douglas Daniel, chief eng.; nat'l rep.: Katz Agency.

Operation: 1953; TV households in area: 350,630.

Manassas

WTKK (Channel 66)

National Capital Christian Broadcasting, Inc., 9008 Center St., Manassas, VA 22110 (703) 369-3400.

Lester R. Raker, pres.; Phil DeLorme, chief eng.; Dawn Morales, traffic mgr.; Tom Fultz, sta. mgr.; Kevin Thomas, sls. mgr.

Operation: 1978.

Norfolk

WTKR-TV (Channel 3) CBS

WTKR-TV, Inc., 720 Boush St., Norfolk, VA 23510 (804) 446-1000.

Bill Peterson, pres. & gen. mgr.; Rufus DeVane, gen. sls. mgr.; Joe Perkins, prog. dir.; Julie McCollum, dir. of community affairs/personnel; Gene Gildow, dir. of eng..

Operation: 1950; TV sets in area: 485,900.

WTVZ (Channel 33)

TVX Broadcast Group of Virginia, Box 148, Norfolk, VA 23501 (804) 622-3333.

Charles McFadden, v.p. & gen. mgr.; Jeff Armstrong, natl. sls. mgr.

Operation: 1979.

Norfolk-Portsmouth-Newport News

WAVY-TV (Channel 10) NBC

WAVY Television, Inc. (Division of LIN Broadcasting Corporation), 300 Wavy St., Portsmouth, VA 23704 (804) 393-1010.

Doug Adams, pres.; Bill Logan, sta. mgr.; Jack Paris, gen. sls. mgr.; Ted Hand, chief eng.; nat'l rep: Blair Television.

Operation: 1957.

Portsmouth

WYAH-TV (Channel 27)

CBN-Continental Broadcasting Network, Box 1338, Portsmouth, VA 23704 (804) 393-2501.

Tim Robertson, pres.; Thomas Smith, v.p. & gen. mgr.; Ken Reichenbach, chief eng.; David Whitener, prog. mgr.; Larry Harris, prod. mgr.

Operation: 1961; TV homes in area: 535,000.

Richmond

WRLH-TV (Channel 35)

Act III Bdcstg. Inc., 1925 Westmoreland St., Richmond, VA 23230 (804) 358-3535.

Don Richards, v.p. & gen. mgr.; Dan Peltier, gen. sls. mgr.; Anne Driscoll, prog. dir.; Eldon Brown, chief eng.; natl. rep.: MMT.

Operation: February, 1982.

WTVR (Channel 6) CBS

Roy H. Park Broadcasting of Virginia, Inc., 3301 W. Broad St., P.O. Box 11064, Richmond, VA 23201 (804) 254-3600.

Richard Pegram, exec. v.p. & gen. mgr.; Wanda Lewis, v.p. sls.; James Cosby, lcl. sls. mgr.; Ken Miller, chief eng.; Charles Fishburne, news dir. Don LaCombe, prog. & opns. mgr.

Operation: 1948; TV sets in area: 665,900.

WWBT (Channel 12) NBC

Jefferson Pilot Broadcasting Company of Virginia, P.O. Box 12, 5710 Midlothian Pike, Richmond, VA 23201 (804) 233-5461.

Jim Babb, pres.; John H. Hutchinson, Jr., gen. mgr.; Ellen Shuler, gen. sales mgr.; Dave Frasier, bdcst. op. mgr.; John Shreves, prog. mgr.; nat'l rep.: Petry.

Operation: 1956; TV sets in area: 498,700.

Richmond-Petersburg

WXEX-TV (Channel 8) ABC

Nationwide Communications, Inc. 21 Buford Rd., Richmond, VA 23235 (804) 320-3201.

H. Joseph Lewin, gen. mgr.; Jack Porray, gen. sls. mgr.; Gene Walsh, prgm. dir.; nat'l rep.: Katz.

Operation: 1955.

Roanoke

WDBJ-TV (Channel 7) CBS

WDBJ Television, Inc. Mailing Address: P.O. Box 7, Roanoke, VA 24022; Street Address: 2001 Colonial Ave., S.W., Roanoke, VA 24015 (703) 344-7000.

C. H. McKeever, pres. & gen. mgr.; Kay Hall, prog. & promo. dir.; George Bassett, dir.–sls. mktg.; Carl Guffey, dir. of opns. & eng.; Barbara Nicely, promo. dir.; Al Dyson, chief eng.; nat'l rep.: Harrington, Righter & Parsons, Inc.

Operation: 1955; TV homes in area: 985,100.

WEFC (Channel 38)
612 Bullitt Ave., S.E., Roanoke, VA 24013.
C. Kenneth Wright, pres.; R.B. Stewart, Sr., gen. mgr.; E.T. Griffis, prog. dir.; Andrew Wright, chief eng.
Operation: November, 1984.

WSLS-TV (Channel 10) NBC
Roy H. Park Broadcasting of Roanoke, Inc., Church Ave. & Third Street, Roanoke, VA 24011 (703) 981-9110.
James J. DeSchepper, v.p./gen. mgr.; Pete Watkins, gen. sls. mgr.; Mike Berkey, chief eng.; nat'l rep.: Blair TV.
Operation: 1952; TV sets in area: 680,900.

WVFT (Channel 27)
Family Group Ltd., 2618 Colonial Ave., Roanoke, VA 24015 (703) 345-7227.
Ian N. Wheeler, pres.; Howard D. Trickey, gen. mgr.; Suzanne Montgomery, gen. sls. mgr.; Jerry M. McCook, chief eng.; natl. rep.: ITS.
Operation: November, 1985.

WASHINGTON

Bellingham

KVOS-TV (Channel 12) CBS
KVOS TV, Inc., 1151 Ellis St., Bellingham, WA 98225 (206) 671-1212.
Barry Ackerley, pres.; David Reid, v.p. & gen. mgr.; Margot Wilson, opns. mgr.; rep.: Seltel.
Operation: 1953; TV sets in area: 2,000,000.

Pasco

KEPR-TV (Channel 19) CBS
Retlaw Enterprises, Inc., P.O. Box 702, Yakima, WA 98907 (509) 452-9111.
Dale Hazen, v.p. & gen. mgr.; Steve Crow, sta. mgr.; Stu Seibel, prog. dir.; Rick Olsen, news dir.; Don Eckis, chief eng.; nat'l rep.: Seltel; northwest: Art Moore & Associates, Inc.
Operation: 1954; TV sets in area: 334,400.

Richland-Pasco-Kennewick

KNDU (Channel 25) NBC
(Associated with KNDO, Yakima, WA)
Columbia Empire Broadcasting Corp., 1608 S. 24th Ave., Yakima, WA 98901; 3312 Kennewick Ave., Kennewick, WA 99336.
Elliot Kleeman, gen. mgr. & film buyer; Jerry Rogers, sta. mrg. & sls. mgr.; Ron Rutherford, news, dir.; Ed Lyon, chief eng.; nat'l rep.: Seltel.
Operation: 1961.

KVEW (Channel 42) ABC
(A Satellite of KAPP, Yakima, WA)
Apple Valley Broadcasting, Inc., 601 N. Edison, Kennewick, WA 99336 (509) 735-8369.
H. Darrell Blue, v.p. & gen. mgr.; J. Marcus Wood, sta. mgr.; Neil Bennett, chief eng.; David Williams, prod. mgr.
Operation: 1970.

Seattle

KCPQ (Channel 13)
Kelly TV Co., Box 98828, 4400 Steilacoom Blvd. SW, Tacoma, WA 98499 (206) 582-8613.
Roger Ottenbach, gen. mgr.; Robert E. Kelly, prog. dir./owner; Jay Maxey, gen. sls. mgr.; Dan Jensen, sta. mgr.; Robert Galvin, prom. mgr.; Larry Brandt, chief eng.; nat'l rep.: Telerep.
Operation: 1954.

KING-TV (Channel 5) NBC
King Broadcasting Co., 333 Dexter Ave., Seattle, WA 98109 (206) 448-5555.
Steven C. Clifford, pres.; Eric S. Bremmer, pres.; bdcstng; Steve Welch, v.p., finance; Stan Mak, v.p. radio; Suzanne Sorknes, v.p., gen. cnsl.; Sturges Dorrance, v.p. & gen. mgr., King TV; Craig Smith, prog. dir.; Don Varyu, news dir.; Ellen Hansen, p.a. dir.; Barbara Kersey, mktg. & adv. dir.; Robert Glover, gen. sls. mgr.; Tyrone Mortensen, chief eng.; rep.: Blair.
Operation: 1948; TV sets in area: 941,600.

KIRO-TV (Channel 7) CBS
KIRO, Inc., Broadcast House, Third & Broad, Seattle, WA. 98121 (206) 624-7077.
Kenneth L. Hatch, pres.; Al F. Mladenich, sen. v.p.; Glenn C. Wright, v.p. & sta. mgr.; Michael Poth, local sls. mgr.; Charles Morris, eng. dir.; Nick Freeman, prog. dir.; nat'l rep.: Petry Television, Inc.
Operation: February, 1958; TV households: 976,800.

KOMO-TV (Channel 4) ABC
Fisher Broadcasting Inc., 100 Fourth Ave. N., Seattle WA 98109.
John F. Behnke, pres. & CEO, Fischer Bdcstg.; Jay W. Giesa, exec. v.p. for adm., & secty. Fisher; Patrick M. Scott, v.p. & gen. mgr., KOMO; Don Wilkinson, v.p. dir. eng., Fisher; Ed J. Lackner, v.p. corp. affairs, Fisher; nat'l rep.: Katz.
Operation: 1953; TV sets in area: 1,133,700.

KTZZ-TV (22 UHF STEREO)
United States Television Seattle, 945 Dexter Ave., N., Seattle, WA 98109-3515 (206) 282-2202.
Dan Lutgen, sta. mgr.; Shelley Olds, prog. mgr.; Gina Huggerty, bus. mgr.; Karl Paulsen, chief eng.; natl. rep.: ITS.
Operation: June, 1985.

Spokane

KAYU-TV (Channel 28) FOX
KAYU-TV Partners, Ltd., Box 8115, Spokane, WA 99203 (509) 448-2828.
Robert Hamacher, gen. mgr.; Lane Guin, gen. sls. mgr.; Tim Burrows, film buyer; Kelly Bundy, promo. mgr.; Ronald Valley, eng. dir.; nat'l rep.: Petry.
Operation: October, 1982.

KHQ-TV (Channel 6) NBC
KHQ, Inc., 4202 S. Regal, Spokane, WA 99223 (509) 448-6000.
John Reber, pres. & gen. mgr.; Robt. L. Busse, contr.; Michael Gee, v.p., gen. sls. mgr.; Bill Storms, lcl. sls. mgr.; Larry W. Gants, dir. prog. & promo.; Don Carmichael, opns. mgr.; William Isbel, chief eng.; nat'l rep.: Katz Agency.
Operation: 1952; TV sets in area: 528,800 ARB.

KREM-TV (Channel 2) CBS
King Broadcasting Co., S-4103 Regal St., Spokane, WA 99223 (509) 448-2000.
Donna Zapata, v.p. & gen. mgr.; John Rowland, sls. mgr.; Meg Antonius, prog. dir.; Boyd Lundren, chief eng.; nat'l rep.: Blair.
Operation: 1954; TV sets in area: 393,200.

KXLY-TV (Channel 4) ABC

KXLY-TV (Spokane Television, Inc.) W. 500 Boone Ave., Spokane, WA 99201 (509) 328-9084.

Elizabeth M. Burns, pres.; Stephen R. Herling, v.p. & gen. mgr.; Eileen McKinnon, prog. dir.; Brian Williams, opns. mgr.; Don Pope, chief. eng.; Teddie Gibbon, sls. mgr.; nat'l rep: HRP.

Operation: 1953; TV sets in area: 842,250.

Tacoma

KSTW (Channel 11)

Gaylord Bdg. Co., Box 11411, Tacoma, WA 98411 (206) 572-5789.

Edward L. Gaylord, chm.; Kevin T. Hale, v.p. & gen. mgr.; Donald M. Lacy, asst. gen. mgr.; Tom Shannon, prog. mgr.; Paul Crittenden, chief eng.; rep.: Telerep.

Operation: 1953; TV households: 1,038,500.

KTBW-TV (Channel 20)

Trinity Bcstg. of Washington, 1909 S. 341 Place Federal Way, Tacoma, WA 98003 (206) 927-7720.

Paul F. Crouch, pres.; Dick F. Engh, acting sta. mgr.; Keith Norbut, asst. chief eng.

Operation: March, 1984.

Vancouver/Portland (OR)

KPDX (Channel 49)

Columbia River TV, Inc., Vancouver, WA 98660 (206) 254-4949; 910 N.E. Union, Portland, OR 97232 (503) 239-4949.

Jack F. Matranga, pres.; Walt Adler, natl. sls. mgr.; Dennis Updegraff, prog.-opns. mgr.; Dennis Beauchamp, chief eng.

Operation: October, 1983.

Wenatchee

KCWT (Channel 27)

Bingham Communications Group, 32B North Mission St., Wenatchee WA 98801 (509) 662-5298.

Michael O. Barry, pres. & gen. mgr.; Robert Clarke, sta. mgr.; Tim Dietz, chief eng.

Operation: April, 1984.

Yakima

KAPP (Channel 35) ABC

Apple Valley Bcstg. Co., 1610 South 24th Ave., Yakima, WA 98902 (509) 453-0351.

Elizabeth Burns, pres., Darrell Blue, gen. mgr.; Ron Simmons, prog. dir.; Judy Ernesti, gen. sls. mgr.; Jim Sollers, promo. mgr.; Dave Ettl, news dir.; rep.: Harrington.

Operation: September, 1970; TV households: 148,700.

KIMA-TV (Channel 29) CBS

Retlaw Enterprises, Inc., P.O. Box 702, Yakima, WA 98907 (509) 575-0029. Affiliated stations: KEPR-TV, Pasco, WA; KLEW-TV, Lewiston, ID.

Joseph Drilling, pres.; Dale Hazen, v.p. & gen. mgr.; Stu Seibel, prog. dir.; Dow Lambert, chief eng.; rep.: Katz.

Operation: 1953; TV sets in area 768,900.

KNDO (Channel 23) NBC

(Operates associated station KNDU, Richland-Pasco-Kenewick, WA)

Columbia Empire Broadcasting Corp., 1608 S. 24th Ave., Box 10028, Yakima, WA 98909 (509) 248-2300.

Elliot R. Kleeman, gen. mgr.; natl. rep.: Seltel.

Operation: 1959.

WEST VIRGINIA

Bluefield

WVVA (Channel 6) NBC

WVVA Television, Inc., P.O. Box 1930, Bluefield, WV 24731 (304) 325-5487.

Thomas Oakley, pres.; Charles E. Webb, v.p., gen. mgr.; Todd Andrick, opns. mgr.; Daniel Kurtz, promo. mgr.; Kenneth Dick, chief eng.; nat'l rep.: Seltel.

Operation: 1955; TV sets in area: 635,700.

Charleston

WCHS-TV (Channel 8) CBS

Heritage Media, Inc., 1301 Piedmont Rd., Charleston, WV 25301 (304) 346-5358.

Dennis Adkins, gen. mgr.; Robert Knowles, gen. sls. mgr.; Jo Corey, prog. dir.; Michael Hooper, promo. mgr.; Tim Sharp, news dir.; Robert Roush, chief eng.; nat'l rep.: Petry.

Operation: 1954.

WVAH-TV (Channel 11)

W.V. Telecasting, Inc., 11 Broadcast Plaza, Hurricane, WV 25526 (304) 757-0011.

Bert Ellis, pres. & CEO; William Castleman, COO; Don Wilburn, gen. mgr.; George Panicza, chief eng.

Operation: September, 1982.

Clarksburg

WBOY-TV (Channel 12)

912 West Pike Street, Clarksburg, WV 26301 (304) 623-3311.

B. Imes, pres.; Stan Siegel, v.p. & gen. mgr.; Joe Wright, chief eng.; nat'l rep.: Seltel.

Operation: 1957.

WLYJ (Channel 46)

Christian Communication Center, 775 West Pike St., Clarksburg, WV 26301 (304) 623-5782.

Joseph Rose, pres.; Jack L. Kincaid, mgr.; Wayne Fast, chief eng.

Operation: February, 1981.

Huntington-Charleston

WOWK-TV (Channel 13) CBS

Television Center, 555 Fifth Ave., Huntingon, WV 25701 (304) 525-7661.

Leo M. MacCourtney, v.p. & gen. mgr.; Paul N. Dicker, prog. dir.; Mike Ferko, gen. sls. mgr.; Andy Footo, natl. sls. mgr.; Brian Peterson, news dir.; Bob Willis, mktg. dir.; Al Grossniklaus, chief eng.; sls. rep.: Blair TV.

Operation: October, 1955; TV households: 877,300.

WSAZ-TV (Channel 3) NBC

Lee Enterprises, Inc., 645 Fifth Avenue, Huntington, WV 25701 (304) 697-4780.

Richard Gottlieb, pres. & COO; Gary Schmedding, v.p., bdcst.; Don Ray, gen. mgr.; Chris Leister, nat'l sls. mgr.; Robert Harris, Charleston operations mgr.; George M. Curry, prog. dir.; Bill Cummings, news mgr.; Bob Dean, mgr. eng.

Operation: 1949; TV sets in area: 684,700.

Oak Hill

WOAY-TV (Channel 4) ABC, Primary

Thomas Broadcasting Co., Box 251, Oak Hill, WV 25901 (304) 469-3361.

Robert R. Thomas III, pres.; Curtis W. Butler, v.p. & gen. mgr.; Don Watkins, prod. mgr.; nat'l rep.: Katz.

Operation: 1954; TV sets in area: 377,820.

Parkersburg

WTAP (Channel 15) NBC

Benedek Broadcasting Inc., 123 W. 7th St., Parkersburg, WV 26101 (304) 485-4588.

Dan Olsen, gen. mgr.; Joyce Ancrile, prog. dir. & chief eng.; nat'l rep.: MMT.

Operation: 1953; TV households in area: 70,620.

Weston-Clarksburg

WDTV (Channel 5) CBS

Withers Broadcasting Co. of WV, P.O. Box 480, Bridgeport, WV 26330 (304) 842-3558.

W. Russell Withers, Jr., Pres.; Dusty Wayman, gen. mgr.; Nick Pelligrin, prog. dir. & traffic dir.; rep.: Avery-Knodel.

Operation: 1960; TV households, 798,200.

Wheeling

WTRF-TV (Channel 7) ABC, CBS

Adams TV of Wheeling, Inc., 96 16th St., Wheeling, WV 26003 (304) 232-7777.

James G. Squibb, Jr., pres. & gen. mgr.; Jim Davis, lcl. sls. mgr.; Pat Gaughan, promo. mgr.; Sandra Hamm, news dir.; Joe Dumas, chief eng.

Operation: 1953; TV sets in area: 523,000.

WISCONSIN

Appleton

WXGZ-TV (Channel 32) FOX

Appleton Midwestern TV Ltd., 3025 N. Marshall Rd., Appleton, WI 54915 (414) 731-3232.

Roy Smith, gen. mgr.; Jonie Pave, gen. sls. mgr.; John Kremer, prog. dir.; John Rysso, chief eng.

Operation: December, 1983.

Eau Claire

WEAU-TV (Channel 13) NBC

WEAU-TV, 1907 South Hastings Way, Eau Claire, WI 54701.

Alvin K. Leitl, pres. & gen. mgr.; Dick Dionne, opr. mgr.; Ron Wiedemeier, chief eng.; nat'l rep.: MMT.

Operation: 1953; TV households: 421,640.

WQOW-TV (Channel 18) ABC

(A satellite of WXOW-TV, LaCrosse, WI) TAK Communications, Inc., 2881 S. Hastings Way, Eau Claire, WI 54701 (715) 835-1881.

Ron Montezon, sta. mgr.; Bob Braun, lcl. sls. mgr.; Barb Bennett, prog. dir.; John Hardman, promo. dir.; Larry Wentz, news dir.; Dave White, chief eng.

Operation: 1980.

Green Bay

WBAY-TV (Channel 2) CBS

A division of Nationwide Communications Inc., 115 So. Jefferson St., Green Bay, WI 54301 (414) 432-3331.

Ted Kohl, gen. mgr.; Robert Krieghoff, gen. sls. mgr.; Richard Millhiser, prog. dir.; nat'l rep.: Katz.

Operation: 1953; TV sets in area: 707,700.

WFRV-TV (Channel 5) ABC

WFRV Inc., P.O. Box 19055, Green Bay, WI 54307 (414) 437-5411.

Robert B. Forrow, gen. mgr.; Mitch Lambert, gen. sls. mgr.; Alan Eaton, dir. opns. & prog.; Greg Buzzell, chief eng.; nat'l rep.: TeleRep.

Operation: 1955; TV households in area: 485,040.

WGBA (Channel 26) IND

Family Group Ltd., III, 1391 North Rd., P.O. Box 19099, Green Bay, WI 54307 (414) 494-2626.

James Tomlin, gen. mgr.; David Lent, bus. mgr.; Michael Schuster, gen. sls. mgr.; nat'l rep.: Blair.

Operation: 1980.

WLUK-TV (Channel 11) NBC

WLUK-TV, Inc., P.O. Box 19011, Green Bay, WI 54307 (414) 494-8711.

Bill Fyffe, gen. mgr.; Jay Sollar, gen. sls. mgr.; Paula Bruce, prog. dir.; Jim Steffey, chief eng.; nat'l rep.: HPR.

Operation: 1954.

Kenosha

WHKE (Channel 55)

Le Sea Bdcstg. Corp., 4300 43rd Ave., Kenosha, WI 53142 (414) 657-9453.

Lester Sumrall, pres.; Peter Sumrall, gen. mgr.; Jim Shaffer, gen. sls. mgr.; prog. dir. & film buyer; Dave Russel, promo. mgr. & news dir.; Doug Garlinger, chief eng.; rep.: Landin Media.

Operation: June 1, 1988.

LaCrosse

WKBT (Channel 8) CBS

Young Bdcstg. Inc., 141 So. 6th St., La Crosse WI 54601 (608) 782-4678.

Ronald J. Kwasnick, pres.; Thomas M. Best, v.p. & gen. mgr.; Art Fahey, gen. sls. mgr.; Dick Konrad, opns. mgr.; nat'l rep.: Adam Young.

Operation: 1954; TV homes: 379,460 (NSI).

WLAX (Channel 25)

Family Group Ltd. III, 1305 Interchange Place, La Crosse, WI 54603 (608) 781-0025.

Nancy Martinsen, gen. mgr.; Wes Mishaelsen, sls. mgr.; Barb Quillin, prog. dir.; Mark Borg, chief eng.; natl. rep.: Blair.

Operation: September, 1986

WXOW-TV (Channel 19) ABC

(S-2 Satellite, Eau Claire, WI, Channel 18)

TAK Communications, P.O. Box C-4019, LaCrosse, WI 54602 (507) 895-9969.

Sharad Tak, pres.; Tom Hartman, v.p.; Chuck Roth, gen mgr.; Barbara Bennett, prog. dir.; Suzanne Grethen, promo. mgr.; Bill Hel, news dir.; Dale Scherbring, chief eng.; rep.: Katz.

Operation: March, 1970; TV households: 154,200.

Madison

WISC-TV (Channel 3) CBS
7025 Raymond Road, Madison, WI 53719 (608) 271-4321.
Elizabeth Murphy Burns, pres.; Gary DeHaven, gen. mgr.; Donna Kirner, nat'l sls. mgr.; Chris Cain, chief eng.; nat'l rep.: HRP.
Operation: 1956; TV sets in area: 635,000.

WKOW-TV (Channel 27) ABC
TAK Communications, Inc., 5727 Tokay Blvd., Madison WI 53701 (608) 274-1234.
Thomas Hartman, pres.; Bob McCall, gen. mgr.; nat'l rep.: Katz Agency.
Operation: 1953; TV households in area: 214,800.

WMSN-TV (Channel 47) FOX
Channel 47 Ltd. Partnership, 7847 Big Sky Dr., Madison, WI 53719 (608) 833-0047.
Paula Bairo Pruett, pres.; William J. Schereck Jr., gen. mgr.; James C. Custer, gen. sls. mgr.; John Noonan, prog. dir. & film buyer; Andy Murphy, chief eng.; natl. rep.: MMT.
Operation: June, 1986.

WMTV (Channel 15) NBC
Adams TV of Madison, Inc., 615 Forward Dr., Madison, WI 53711 (608) 274-1515.
Vickie Street, pres. & gen. mgr.; Fred Sole, opns. mgr.
Operation: 1953; TV households in area: 266,500.

Milwaukee

WCGV-TV (Channel 24) FOX
HR Broadcasting Corp. of Milwaukee, Inc., 5445 N. 27th St., Milwaukee, WI 53209 (414) 527-2424.
Robert J. Furlong, gen. mgr. & film buyer; Mitch Nye, gen. sls. mgr.; Betty Hertz, prog. mgr.; Walter White, chief eng.; nat'l rep.: Katz.
Operation: 1980.

WISN-TV (Channel 12) ABC
WISN Division—The Hearst Corp., 759 No. 19 St., Milwaukee, WI 53233 (414) 342-8812.
Howard F. Ritchie, v.p. & gen. mgr.; John Stewart, gen. sls. mgr. & dir. bdcst. opns.; Laura Hargis, natl. sls. mgr.; Peter Monfre, lcl. sls. mgr.; Gary Seymour, prod. mgr.; Steve Olszyk, news dir.; Patrick J. Baldwin, creative svcs. dir.; Noel Enders, resident contr.
Operation: 1954; TV sets in area: 675,600.

WITI-TV (Channel 6) CBS
Gillett Communications of Milwaukee, Inc., 9001 North Green Bay Road, Milwaukee, WI 53217 (414) 355-6666.
Andrew P. Potos, pres. & gen. mgr.; Ray Engelhart, opns. dir.; Donald Roering, chief eng.
Operation: 1956; TV sets in area: 756,000.

WTMJ-TV (Channel 4) NBC
WTMJ Inc., 720 East Capitol Drive, Milwaukee, WI 53201 (414) 332-9611.
Steve Smith, pres.; Wayne Barnett, v.p. & gen. mgr.; Norb Ryan, gen. sls. mgr.; Mark Le Grand, lcl. sls. mgr.; Tom Mikkelsen, mgr. of eng.; Gerald McGrath, prgm. mgr.; Ed Hinshaw, ed. dir.; Tom Luljak, news dir.; Gerry Skowronski, film supvr.; Rod Synnes, comm. rel. dir.; Mike Stutz, news mgr.; Mark Strachota, natl. sls. mgr.; Dennis Majewski, prod. mgr.; Lia Alcalay Riger, prog. mgr.; Mary Alice Tierney, community aff. mgr.
Operation: 1947; TV households in area: 700,000.

WVTV (Channel 18)
Gaylord Broadcasting Co., P.O. Box 1818, Millwaukee, WI 53201 (414) 442-7050.
Harold E. Protter, v.p. & gen. mgr.; rep.: Petry.
Operation: 1966; TV homes: 694,400.

Rhinelander (Wausau)

WJFW-TV (Channel 12) NBC
Northland TV Inc., Box 858, Rhinelander, WI 54501 (715) 369-4700.
James Buckner, pres.; Maria Platteter, gen. mgr.; Bette Henning, lcl. sls. mgr.; Brian Henning, chief eng. rep.: Seltel.
Operation: 1966; TV homes in area: 230,000.

Wausau

WAOW-TV (Channel 9) ABC
(Outlet of The Wisc. TV Network)
Wisconsin TV Network Assn., 1908 Grand Ave., Wausau WI 54401 (715) 842-2251.
Laurin Jorstad, gen. mgr., prog. dir. & film buyer; Ron Montezon, nat'l sls. mgr.; Sharon Reyer, promo. mgr.; Russ Crass, chief eng.; rep.: Katz Television.
Operation: 1965; TV households: 170,310.

WSAW-TV (Channel 7) CBS
Adams TV of Wausau, 1114 Grand Ave., Wausau, WI 54401 (715) 845-4211.
John Dudley, pres., gen. mgr., prog. dir., film buyer & promo. mgr.; Chris Eigenberger, gen. sls. mgr.; Mark Zelich, v.p., news & spts.; Donald Cochart, v.p. opns.; Joe Kamenick, chief eng.; nat'l rep.: Blair.
Operation: 1954.

WYOMING

Casper

KFNB-TV (Channel 20) ABC, FOX
First National Bcstg., 7075 Salt Creek Hwy., Casper, WY 82601 (307) 237-2020.
A.J. Stanton, pres.; Pete Sieler, gen. mgr.; Charles Vick, chief eng.; nat'l rep.: Avery Knodel, Bob Hix Co.
Operation: October, 1984.

KGWC-TV (Channel 14) CBS
Stauffer Communications, Inc., Box 170, Casper, WY 82601 (307) 234-1111.
Alan Nicksic, gen. mgr.; Jeremy Patey, dir. prog.; Tim Swanson, sls. mgr.; Bob Spain, chief eng.
Operation: 1980.

KTWO-TV (Channel 2) NBC
KTWO Corp., 4200 E. Second Street, Casper, WY 82601 (307) 237-3711.
Stan Whitman, pres.; Michelle Ferguson, gen. mgr.; Bruce Cummings, lcl. sls. mgr.; Debbie McLemore, natl. sls. mgr.; Dave Borino, prog. dir.; Jane Barry, promo. mgr.; Susan Anderson, news dir.; Bob Davis, chief eng.; rep.: Blair.
Operation: 1957; TV homes in area: 109,200.

Cheyenne

KGWN-TV (Channel 5) CBS, ABC

Stauffer Communications, Inc., 2923 East Lincolnway, Cheyenne, WY; 82001 (307) 634-7755.

Gerald Holley, v.p.; Carl Occhipinti, gen. mgr.; Dusty Thein, gen. sls. mgr.; Barbara Parenti, prog. dir.; Tony Schaefer, dir. eng.; rep.: Katz.

Operation: 1954; TV sets in area: 501,900.

KLWY (Channel 1 27)

Heart of Wyoming TV, Inc., 7020 Salt Creek Rte., Box 5, Casper, WY 82601 (307) 237-2020.

Daniel Burke, pres.; Peter C. Sieler, gen. mgr.; nat'l rep.: Adam Young.

Operation: November, 1987.

Lander

KGWL-TV (Channel 5) CBS

Stauffer Communications, Inc., 340 N. Center, Casper, WY 82601 (307) 234-1111.

John H. Stauffer, pres.; Robert L. Calvert, gen. mgr.; Tim Swanson, gen. sls. mgr.; Jeremy Patey, opns. dir.; Craig Kennedy, news dir.; Bob Spain, eng.; nat'l rep.: Blair.

Operation: September, 1982.

Rawlins

KFNR (Channel 11) ABC, CBS

First National Bdcstg. Corp., Box 1, 7075 Salt Creek Rte., Casper, WY 82601 (307) 237-2020.

Peter Sieler, gen. mgr.; George Vavra, promo. mgr.; Charles D. Vick, chief eng.; natl. rep.: Adam Young, Box Hix Co.

Operation: April, 1986.

Riverton

KFNE-TV (Channel 10) ABC, CBS

First National Bdcst. Corp., Box 1, Casper, WY 82601 (307) 237-2020.

Peter G. Sieler, gen. mgr.

Operation: 1980; Households: 17,800.

Rock Springs

KGWR-TV (Channel 13) CBS

Stauffer Communications, Inc., Box 170 Rock Springs, WY 82601 (307) 234-1111.

John H. Stauffer, pres.; Robert L. Clavert, gen. mgr.; Tim Swanson, gen. sls. mgr.; Jeremy Patey, prog. dir.; Kim Sherwood, news dir.; Bob Spain, chief eng.; nat'l rep.: Blair.

Operation: 1977.

Sheridan

KSGW-TV (Channel 12) ABC

(A satellite of KOTA-TV, Rapid City, SD) Duhamel Broadcasting Enterprises, Box 1760, Rapid City, SD 57709.

Personnel: See KOTA-TV, Rapid City, SD

Operation: 1977.

Public Broadcasting Service Station Affiliates

Alabama
Birmingham .... WBIQ
Demopolis .... WIIQ
Dozier .... WDIQ
Florence .... WFIQ
Huntsville .... WHIQ
Louisville .... WGIQ
Mobile .... WEIQ
Montgomery .... WAIQ
Mount Cheaha State Park .... WCIQ

Alaska
Anchorage .... KAKM
Bethel .... KYUK-TV
Fairbanks .... KUAC-TV
Juneau .... KTOO-TV

Arizona
Phoenix .... KAET
Tucson .... KUAS-TV
Tucson .... KUAT

Arkansas
Arkadelphia .... KETG
Fayetteville .... KAFT
Jonesboro .... KTEJ
Little Rock .... KETS
Mountain View .... KEMV
Newark .... KLEP

California
Cotati .... KRCB-TV
Eureka .... KEET
Fresno .... KMTF
Huntington Beach .... KOCE-TV
Los Angeles .... KCET
Los Angeles .... KLCS
Redding .... KIXE
Sacramento .... KVIE
San Bernardino .... KVCR-TV
San Diego .... KPBS-TV
San Francisco .... KQED
San Francisco .... KQEC
San Jose .... KTEH
San Mateo .... KCSM-TV

Colorado
Broomfield .... KBDI-TV
Denver .... KRMA-TV
Pueblo .... KTSC

Connecticut
Bridgeport .... WEDW
Hartford .... WEDH
New Haven .... WEDY
Norwich .... WEDN

Delaware
Seaford .... WDPB
Wilmington .... WHYY-TV

District of Columbia
Washington .... WETA-TV
Washington .... WHMM

Florida
Ft. Myers .... WSFP-TV
Gainesville .... WUFT
Jacksonville .... WJCT
Miami .... WPBT
Miami .... WLRN-TV
Orlando .... WMFE-TV
Pensacola .... WSRE
Tallahassee .... WFSU-TV
Tampa .... WUSF-TV
Tampa/St. Petersburg .... WEDU
West Palm Beach .... WXEL-TV

Georgia
Athens .... WGTV
Atlanta .... WPBA
Chatsworth .... WCLP-TV
Cochran .... WDCO-TV
Columbus .... WJSP-TV
Dawson .... WACS-TV
Pelham .... WABW-TV
Savannah .... WVAN-TV
Waycross .... WXGA-TV
Wrens .... WCES-TV

Guam
Agana .... KGTF

Hawaii
Honolulu .... KHET
Wailuku .... KMEB-TV

Idaho
Boise .... KAID
Moscow .... KUID-TV
Pocatello .... KISU-TV

Illinois
Carbondale .... WSIU-TV
Chicago .... WTTW
Chicago .... WYCC
Jacksonville .... WJPT
Macomb .... WIUM-TV
Moline .... WQPT
Olney .... WUSI-TV
Peoria .... WTVP
Quincy .... WQEC
Urbana .... WILL-TV

Indiana
Bloomington .... WTIU
Evansville .... WNIN
Gary .... WYIN
Indianapolis .... WFYI
Muncie .... WIPB
South Bend .... WNIT
Vincennes .... WVUT

Iowa
Council Bluffs .... KBIN
Des Moines .... KDIN-TV
Fort Dodge .... KTIN
Iowa City .... KIIN-TV
Mason City .... KYIN
Red Oak .... KHIN
Sioux City .... KSIN
Waterloo .... KRIN

Kansas
Hays .... KOOD
Hutchinson .... KPTS
Topeka .... KTWU

Kentucky
Ashland .... WKAS
Bowling Green .... WKGB
Bowling Green .... WKYU-TV
Covington .... WCVN
Elizabethtown .... WKZT
Hazard .... WKHA
Lexington .... WKLE
Louisville .... WKPC-TV
Louisville .... WKMJ
Madisonville .... WKMA
Morehead .... WKMR
Murray .... WKMU
Owensboro .... WKOH
Owenton .... WKON
Paducah .... WKPD
Pikeville .... WKPI
Somerset .... WKSO

Louisana
Alexandria .... KLPA-TV
Baton Rouge .... WLPB-TV

Lafayette .... KLPB-TV
Lake Charles .... KLTL-TV
Monroe .... KLTM-TV
New Orleans .... WLAE-TV
New Orleans .... WYES-TV
Shreveport .... KLTS-TV

Maine
Augusta .... WCBB
Biddeford .... WMEA
Calais .... WMED-TV
Orono .... WMEB-TV
Presque Isle .... WMEM-TV

Maryland
Annapolis .... WMPT
Baltimore .... WMPB
Frederick .... WFPT
Hagerstown .... WWPB-TV
Oakland .... WGPT
Salisbury .... WCPB

Massachusetts
Boston .... WGBH-TV
Boston .... WGBX-TV
Brainerd .... KAWB
Springfield .... WGBY-TV

Michigan
Alpena .... WCML-TV
Bad Axe .... WUCX-TV
Cadillac .... WCMV
Detroit .... WTVS
East Lansing .... WKAR-TV
Flint .... WFUM
Grand Rapids .... WGVU-TV
Kalamazoo .... WGVK
Manistee .... WCMW
Marquette .... WNMU-TV
Mt. Pleasant .... WCMU-TV
University Center .... WUCM-TV

Minnesota
Appleton .... KWCM-TV
Austin .... KSMQ-TV
Bemidji .... KAWE
Duluth-Superior, WI .... WDSE-TV
Minneapolis-St. Paul .... KTCA-TV
St. Paul .... KTCI-TV

Mississippi
Biloxi .... WMAH
Booneville .... WMAE
Bude .... WMAU
Greenwood .... WMAO
Jackson .... WMAA
Meridian .... WMAW
Oxford .... WMAV
State College .... WMAB

Missouri
Joplin .... KOZJ
Kansas City .... KCPT
St. Louis .... KETC
Sedalia-Warrensburg .... KMOS-TV
Springfield .... KOZK

Montana
Bozeman .... KUSM

Nebraska
Alliance .... KTNE-TV
Bassett .... KMNE-TV
Hastings .... KHNE-TV
Lexington .... KLNE-TV
Lincoln .... KUON-TV
Merriman .... KRNE-TV
Norfolk .... KXNE-TV
North Platte .... KPNE-TV
Omaha .... KYNE-TV

Nevada
Las Vegas .... KLVX
Reno .... KNPB

New Hampshire
Durham .... WENH
Keene .... WEKW-TV
Littleton .... WLED-TV

New Jersey
Camden .... WNJS
Montclair .... WNJM
New Brunswick .... WNJB
Trenton .... WNJT

New Mexico
Albuquerque .... KAZQ
Albuquerque .... KNME-TV
Las Cruces .... KRWG
Portales .... KENW

New York
Albany .... WMHX
Binghamton .... WSKG
Buffalo .... WNED-TV
Buffalo .... WNEQ-TV
Garden City .... WLIW
New York .... WNYC-TV
New York .... WNYE-TV
New York .... WNET
Norwood .... WNPI-TV
Plattsburgh .... WCFE-TV
Rochester .... WXXI-TV
Schenectady .... WMHT
Syracuse .... WCNY-TV
Watertown .... WNPE-TV

North Carolina
Asheville .... WUNF-TV
Chapel Hill .... WUNC-TV
Charlotte .... WTVI
Columbia .... WUND-TV
Concord .... WUNG-TV
Greenville .... WUNK-TV
Jacksonville .... WUNM-TV
Linville .... WUNE-TV
Roanoke Rapids .... WUNP
Wilmington .... WUNJ-TV
Winston-Salem .... WUNL-TV

North Dakota
Bismarck .... KBME
Dickinson .... KDSE
Fargo-Moorhead, Minn. .... KFME
Grand Forks .... KGFE
Minot .... KSRE
Williston .... KWSE

Ohio
Akron .... WEAO
Alliance .... WNEO
Athens .... WOUB-TV
Cambridge .... WOUC-TV
Cincinnati .... WCET
Cleveland .... WVIZ-TV
Columbus .... WOSU-TV
Dayton .... WPTD
Lima-Bowling Green .... WBGU-TV
Oxford .... WPTO
Portsmouth .... WPBO-TV
Toledo .... WGTE-TV

Oklahoma
Cheyenne .... KWET
Claremore .... KXON-TV
Eufaula .... KOET
Oklahoma City .... KETA
Tulsa .... KOED-TV

Oregon
Bend .... KOAB-TV
Corvallis .... KOAC-TV
La Grande .... KTVR
Medford .... KSYS
Portland .... KOAP-TV

Pennsylvania
Bethlehem-Allentown .... WLVT-TV
Clearfield .... WPSX-TV
Erie .... WQLN
Harrisburg .... WITF-TV
Pittsburgh .... WQED

Pittsburgh .... WQEX
Scranton-Wilkes-Barre .... WVIA-TV

Puerto Rico
Caguas .... WUJA
Fajardo .... WMTJ
Mayaguez .... WIPM-TV
Ponce .... WQTO
San Juan .... WIPR-TV

Rhode Island
Providence .... WSBE-TV

Samoa
Pago Pago .... KVZK

South Carolina
Allendale .... WEBA-TV
Beaufort .... WJWJ-TV
Charleston .... WITV
Columbia .... WRLK-TV
Conway .... WHMC
Florence .... WJPM-TV
Greenville .... WNTV
Greenwood .... WNEH
Rock Hill .... WNSC-TV
Spartanburg .... WRET-TV
Sumter .... WRJA-TV

South Dakota
Aberdeen .... KDSD-TV
Brookings .... KESD-TV
Eagle Butte .... KPSD-TV
Lowry .... KQSD-TV
Martin .... KZSD-TV
Pierre .... KTSD-TV
Rapid City .... KBHE-TV
Vermillion .... KUSD-TV

Tennessee
Chattanooga .... WTCI
Cookeville .... WCTE
Lexington .... WLJT-TV
Memphis .... WKNO-TV
Nashville .... WDCN-TV
Sneedville .... WSJK-TV

Texas
Amarillo .... KACV-TV
Austin-San Antonio .... KLRN-TV
Austin .... KLRU-TV
Beaumont .... KITU
Belton .... KNCT
College Station .... KAMU-TV
Corpus Christi .... KEDT
Dallas .... KERA-TV
El Paso .... KCOS
Harlingen .... KLUJ
Harlingen .... KMBH
Houston .... KETH
Houston .... KUHT
Lubbock .... KTXT
Odessa .... KOCV-TV
San Antonio .... KLRN-TV

Utah
Ogden .... KULC
Provo .... KBYU-TV
Salt Lake City .... KUED

Vermont
Burlington .... WETK
Rutland .... WVER
St. Johnsbury .... WVTB
Windsor .... WVTA

Virginia
Fairfax .... WNVC
Goldvein .... WNVT
Marion .... WMSY-TV
Norfolk .... WHRO-TV
Norton .... WSBN-TV
Richmond .... WCVE-TV
Richmond .... WCVW
Roanoke .... WBRA-TV
Staunton .... WVPT

Virgin Islands
Charlotte Amalie .... WTJX-TV

Washington
Centralia .... KCKA
Pullman .... KWSU-TV
Richland .... KTNW
Seattle .... KCTS-TV
Spokane .... KSPS-TV
Tacoma .... KTPS
Yakima .... KYVE-TV

West Virginia
Grandview .... WSWP-TV
Huntington .... WPBY-TV
Morgantown .... WNPB-TV

Wisconsin
Green Bay .... WPNE
La Crosse .... WHLA
Madison .... WHA-TV
Menomonie-Colifax .... WHWC-TV
Milwaukee .... WMVS
Milwaukee .... WMVT
Park Falls .... WLEF-TV
Wausau .... WHRM-TV

Wyoming
Lander .... KCWC-TV

Cable Television

* **STATISTICS AND HISTORY**
* **MAJOR CABLE SYSTEM OPERATORS**
* **MAJOR PROGRAM SUPPLIERS**

Cable Television

STATISTICS

HISTORICAL DATES

FIRST OVER-THE-AIR TOLL-TV EXPERIMENTS: 1950, Skiatron system tested over WOR-TV in New York City. 1951, Telemeter system tested over KTLA-TV, Los Angeles; Zenith tested its system over its own experimental station in Chicago.

FEBRUARY 10, 1955: Federal Communications Commission started proceedings to determine whether it should authorize TV stations to transmit programs paid for on a subscription basis. Study involved 92 docket volumes reflecting the views of over 25,000 persons on legal, technical and policy questions.

MAY 23, 1957: FCC concluded it had authority to authorize use of TV broadcast frequencies for subscription operations if it found it were in the public interest to do so. Did not define whether this service should be classified as "broadcasting" or some other.

OCTOBER 17, 1957: FCC adopted its first report on the proceedings and declared it would consider applications to conduct trial pay-TV operations over TV stations provided certain conditions were met.

MARCH 24, 1959: FCC issued third report saying it was ready to consider any pay-TV application by a commercial TV station conforming with requirements, among which were limitation of three-year trial authorizations to markets where there were at least four commercial TV stations (including the pay-TV one), and one trial system allowed per market.

JUNE 22, 1960: Hartford Phonevision Co. (later RKO General Phonevision Co.), a licensee of WHCT (Channel 18), Hartford, CT, applied for authority to conduct a three-year trial subscription-TV operation. Application granted February 23, 1961. Operations began June 29, 1962, and concluded in January, 1969.

JULY 3, 1967: FCC's subscription TV committee submitted a fourth report proposing an over-the-air subscription TV service. Rules were designed to integrate subscription TV into the total TV system so good programming would continue to be available over regular TV stations.

DECEMBER 12, 1968: FCC formally established over-the-air subscription TV as a regular broadcast service.

1975: Home Box Office became the first in the television industry to use a satellite for regular transmission of programming.

1984: The FCC officially deregulated the cable industry, permitting pricing flexibility and enabling operators to raise charges for basic cable services by adding new channels while reducing service charges for premium channels.

1985: The Court of Appeals struck down the "must carry" rules which required cable operators to carry all local broadcast stations.

Statistics for 1988

In 1988 there were 25,000 communities being served by cable television with over 47 million subscribers. This represents 52.8 per cent of total U.S. TV households.

Cable systems have reached a total of 9,300 with another 300 franchises approved but not yet built. Texas has the most systems with 600 and California the most subscribers at 4.9 million.

Industry revenues in 1988 were estimated at about $14 billion.

The national average monthly subscriber rate for basic services rose to $14 in 1989, compared to $13 in 1988 and less than $8 in 1981.

Over 1,860 systems accept advertising on the local origination channels—excluding automated channels—with rates from $2 to $300 per 30-second spot. Most cable systems derive less than 5 per cent of their gross revenues from advertising.

Cable systems are required by law to offer a minimum 20-channel capacity, which is the average; however, many systems offer more.

Pay cable (Home Box Office, Showtime, etc.) now operates on about 7,400 systems, reaching 35 million subscribers in all 50 states.

Almost 32 per cent of all cable systems have ties with broadcast interests; over 20 per cent with program producers; and about 18 per cent with newspapers. Many systems have multiple cross-ownership ties.

Tele-Communications, Inc., based in Denver, is the nation's largest developer and operator of cable systems with 4 million subscribers. Basic monthly rate charged by that company is now $15.50, an increase of 7 per cent over 1988.

In an optimistic report by the U.S. Commerce Dept., issued early in 1989, it was predicted that the number of cable subscribers would jump 5 per cent in 1989, reaching 49 million which would be a household penetration rate of 54 per cent. The Dept. also forecast that cable firms would continue to raise rates and adjust program packages which, combined with increases in ad revenues, should boost the total intake some 14 per cent to $14.5 billion in 1989. Cable, it was said further, will have penetrated 60 per cent of American households by 1993, with total revenues growing at an 8 per cent average annual rate.

Cable System Operators

Adelphia Communications Corp.

Box 472, 5 West Third St., Cloudersport, PA 16915; (814) 274-9830.

PRESIDENT & CHIEF EXECUTIVE OFFICER
John J. Rigas

American Television & Communications Corp.

300 First Stamford Place, Stamford, CT 06902-6732; (203) 328-0600. (A subsidiary of Time Inc.)

CHAIRMAN OF THE BOARD & CHIEF EXECUTIVE OFFICER
Joseph J. Collins
PRESIDENT & CHIEF OPERATING OFFICER
James H. Doolittle
EXECUTIVE VICE PRESIDENTS
James P. Cottingham, John F. Gault, Kevin H. Rorke
SENIOR VICE PRESIDENTS
James A. Chiddix, Henry J. Gerken, Edward McCarthy, Richard J. Davies, David E. O'Hayre

Cablevision Systems Corporation

One Media Crossways, Woodbury, NY 11797; (516) 364-8450.

CHAIRMAN & CHIEF EXECUTIVE OFFICER
Charles F. Dolan
PRESIDENT & CHIEF OPERATING OFFICER
John Tatta
VICE CHAIRMEN
Francis Randolph, William Bell

Cardinal Communications, Inc.

1800 N Meridian St., Indianapolis, IN 46202; (317) 923-6358.

CHAIRMAN & CHIEF EXECUTIVE OFFICER
James F. Ackerman
PRESIDENT & CHIEF OPERATING OFFICER
Myron T. Pattison

Comcast Cable Communications, Inc.

1414 South Penn Square, Philadelphia, PA 19102-2480.

PRESIDENT
Robert B. Clasen

Continental Cablevision, Inc.

The Pilot House, Lewis Wharf, Boston, MA 02110; (617) 742-9500.

CHAIRMAN & CHIEF EXECUTIVE OFFICER
Amos B. Hostetter, Jr.
PRESIDENT & CHIEF OPERATING OFFICER
Timothy P. Neher
EXECUTIVE VICE PRESIDENTS—OPERATIONS
John P. Rakoske, Michael J. Ritter, Charles J. Younger
SENIOR VICE PRESIDENT, MARKETING
Frederick C. Livingston
SENIOR VICE PRESIDENT, PROGRAMMING
Robert A. Stengel
SENIOR VICE PRESIDENT & TREASURER
Nancy Hawthorne Agne
SENIOR VICE PRESIDENT, LEGAL CORPORATE COUNSEL
Robert J. Sachs
SENIOR VICE PRESIDENT & CORPORATE CONTROLLER
Richard A. Hoffstein

Cooke CableVision Inc.

Box 4200, Woodland Hills, CA 91365; (818) 713-3800.

DIRECTOR OF MARKETING
Dan Sweeney

Cox Cable Communications, Inc.

1400 Lake Hearn Dr., Atlanta, GA 30319; (404) 843-5000. (A subsidiary of Cox Enterprises.)

PRESIDENT
James O. Robbins
SENIOR VICE PRESIDENT FINANCE
Robert C. O'Leary
SENIOR VICE PRESIDENTS—OPERATIONS
Barry R. Elson, Wayne D. Knighton and Robert G. McRann
VICE PRESIDENT MARKETING & PROGRAMMING
Ajit M. Dalvi
VICE PRESIDENT, TECHNOLOGY
Alex B. Best
VICE PRESIDENT, PUBLIC AFFAIRS
David C. Andersen

Heritage Communications, Inc.

2195 Ingersoll Ave., Des Moines, IA 50312; (515) 246-1440. (Owned by Tele-Communications Inc.)

CORPORATE OFFICERS

CHAIRMAN
James M. Hoak, Jr.
PRESIDENT
James S. Cownie
EXECUTIVE VICE PRESIDENT/OPERATIONS
Rod Thole
EXECUTIVE VICE PRESIDENT/SECRETARY
Wayne Kern
EXECUTIVE VICE PRESIDENT/FINANCE
David Lundquist
SENIOR VICE PRESIDENT/ENGINEERING
Doug Truckenmiller
VICE PRESIDENT/OPERATIONS
Nile McDonald
VICE PRESIDENT/OPERATIONS
Kevin Rice
VICE PRESIDENT/MARKETING
Dale Parker
VICE PRESIDENT/DEVELOPMENT
David Oman
VICE PRESIDENT/CONTROLLER
Loran Schlitz

Jones Intercable, Inc.

9697 East Mineral Ave., Englewood, CO 80112; (303) 792-3111. (A unit of Jones International Ltd.)

CHAIRMAN & CHIEF EXECUTIVE OFFICER
Glenn R. Jones
PRESIDENT
Gregory Liptak

NewChannels Corp.

112 Northern Concourse, North Syracuse, NY 13212; (315) 455-5826. (A subsidiary of Newhouse Broadcasting Corp.)

PRESIDENT
Robert Miron
EXECUTIVE VICE PRESIDENT
Leo A. Calistri
SENIOR VICE PRESIDENT
Dan Cavallo

SENIOR VICE PRESIDENT—ENGINEERING
Joe Majczak
VICE PRESIDENTS
Donald E. Newhouse, Patrick McCall, Mary Cotter

Paragon Communications

4582 S. Ulster St. Pkwy, Suite 405, Denver, CO 80237; (303) 771-0079. (Owned by American Television & Communications and Houston Industries Inc.)

PRESIDENT
David R. Van Valkenburg

Post-Newsweek Cable

2621 East Camelback Rd., Suite 150, Phoenix, AZ 85016; (602) 468-1177. (A subsidiary of The Washington Post Co.)

PRESIDENT
Howard E. Wall

Prime Cable

One American Center, Suite 3000, 600 Congress Ave., Austin, TX 78701; (512) 476-7888.

CHIEF EXECUTIVE OFFICER & CHAIRMAN
Robert W. Hughes
PRESIDENT
Gregory Marchbanks
SENIOR VICE PRESIDENTS
C. Ronald Dorchester, Jerry Lindauer

Rogers Communications, Inc.

Box 249, Toronto M5K 1J5 Ontario, Canada; (416) 864-2373.

CHAIRMAN
John W. Graham
VICE CHAIRMAN & CHIEF EXECUTIVE OFFICER
Edward S. Rogers
PRESIDENT
Colin D. Watson

Sammons Communications, Inc.

Box 15216, Dallas, TX 75201; (214) 742-9828.

PRESIDENT
James H. Whitson
SENIOR VICE PRESIDENT/OPERATIONS
Mark S. Weber
SENIOR VICE PRESIDENT & GENERAL COUNSEL
John Washburn
VICE PRESIDENT—ENGINEERING
Henry Cicconi

Service Electric Cable TV, Inc.

201 West Centre St., Mahanoy City, PA 17948; (717) 773-2585.

PRESIDENT/DIRECTOR
John Walson
SECRETARY/DIRECTOR
Margaret Walson

Spectradyne (Hotels/Motels)

1501 N. Plano Road, Richardson, TX 75081; (214) 234-2721.

PRESIDENT
John M. Lewis
VICE PRESIDENT OF PROGRAMMING
Bill Coleman

Storer Communications, Inc.

Box 61-8000, Miami, FL 33161; (305) 899-1000.

PRESIDENT/CABLE COMMUNICATIONS DIVISION
Kenneth L. Bagwell
EXECUTIVE VICE PRESIDENT
William P. Whelan

TCA Cable TV

Box 130489, Tyler, TX 75713-0489; (214) 595-3701.

TeleCable Corp.

Box 2098, 740 Duke St., Norfolk, VA 23510; (804) 624-5000.

CHAIRMAN OF THE BOARD
Frank Batten
PRESIDENT
Richard D. Roberts
VICE PRESIDENTS
Gordon R. Herring, James S. Key, Nicholas E. Worth
VICE PRESIDENT & TREASURER
Alfred F. Ritter, Jr.

Tele-Communications, Inc.

Regency Plaza One, 4643 S. Ulster Street, Ste. 600, Denver, CO 80237; (303) 771-8200. Mailing: P.O. Box 5630 T.A., Denver, CO 80217.

CHAIRMAN
Bob Magness
PRESIDENT & CHIEF EXECUTIVE OFFICER
John C. Malone
SENIOR VICE PRESIDENT & TREASURER
Donne F. Fisher
SENIOR VICE PRESIDENT
John Sie
VICE PRESIDENT, ASSISTANT SECRETARY & GENERAL COUNSEL
John M. Draper
VICE PRESIDENT & CONTROLLER
Gary K. Bracken
VICE PRESIDENTS
Stewart D. Blair, Peter Barton, Bernard W. Schotters

Texas Community Antennas, Inc.

3027 S.E. Loop 323, Tyler, TX 75701; (214) 595-3701.

PRESIDENT
Robert Rogers
VICE PRESIDENTS
R. Don Cowan, Wayne McKinney

Times Mirror Cable Television, Inc.

2381 Morse Ave., Irvine, CA 92714; (714) 660-0500.

PRESIDENT & CHIEF EXECUTIVE OFFICER
Larry W. Wangberg
CHAIRMAN
Ralph J. Swett
EXECUTIVE VICE PRESIDENT/ENGINEERING
Gilbert L. Tash
SENIOR VICE PRESIDENT & TREASURER
James F. Guthrie
SENIOR VICE PRESIDENT/GROUP OPERATIONS
James H. Smith III
SENIOR VICE PRESIDENT/GROUP OPERATIONS
Kent D. Franke

United Artists Cablesystems Corp.

2930 East 3rd Ave., Denver, CO 80206; (303) 321-4242. (Owned by Tele-Communications & United Artists Entertainment.)

CHAIRMAN
Stewart Blair
PRESIDENT & CHIEF EXECUTIVE OFFICER
Marvin J. Jones
SENIOR VICE PRESIDENT
Arthur C. Belanger
VICE PRESIDENT & TREASURER
David Bub

UACC Midwest, Inc.

1430 Balltown Road, Schenectady, NY 12309; (518) 385-1229.

PRESIDENT
Paul F. Schonewolf
SENIOR VICE PRESIDENT
Arthur C. Belanger
ENGINEERING VICE PRESIDENT
P. Pappas

United Cable Television Corp.

Denver Technological Center, 4700 S. Syracuse Pkwy., Denver, CO 80237; (303) 779-5999. (Owned by Tele-Communications, Inc.

CHAIRMAN & CHIEF EXECUTIVE OFFICER
Gene W. Schneider
PRESIDENT & CHIEF OPERATING OFFICER
Fred A. Vierra

Viacom Cable

1211 Ave. of the Americas, New York, NY 10036; (212) 575-5175. P.O. Box 13, Pleasanton, CA 94566; (415) 463-0870. (A division of Viacom International.)

PRESIDENT
John W. Goddard

SENIOR VICE PRESIDENTS
Garrett Girvan, Kurt Jorgensen, John Kopchik

Vision Cable Communications, Inc.

270 Sylvan Ave., Englewood Cliffs, NJ 07632; (201) 894-5555. (A division of Newhouse Group, Inc.)

EXECUTIVE VICE PRESIDENT & GENERAL MANAGER
Joel Fleming
VICE PRESIDENT/OPERATIONS
V. Mitchell Roberts
VICE PRESIDENT/PROGRAMMING
Pamela T. Hammond
VICE PRESIDENT/ENGINEERING
Richard M. White

Warner Cable Communications, Inc.

400 Metro Place North, Dublin, OH 43017; (614) 792-7000. (A division of Warner Communications, Inc.)

PRESIDENT & CHIEF OPERATING OFFICER
James L. Gray
EXECUTIVE VICE PRESIDENT & CHIEF FINANCIAL OFFICER
Jack L. Messman

Western Communications, Inc.

Suite 225, 2855 Mitchell Dr., Box 4610, Walnut Creek, CA 94596; (415) 935-3055. (Owned by Chronicle Publishing Co.)

CHAIRMAN & CHIEF EXECUTIVE OFFICER
Edward M. Allen
PRESIDENT
Charles C. Thieriot
VICE PRESIDENTS
Carl L. Badger, Christopher J. Lammers
SECRETARY
W. Ronald Ingram

Cable and Pay TV Program Suppliers

Pay cable services and pay-per-view services are designated as such. All others are basic cable services.

American Movie Classics

Rainbow Program Enterprises, 150 Crossways Park West, Woodbury, NY 11797; (516) 364-2222. A Pay-TV system.

Arts & Entertainment Network (A&E)

555 Fifth Ave., New York, NY 10017. (212) 661-4500. (A joint venture of Hearst Corp., ABC and NBC)

PRESIDENT & CHIEF EXECUTIVE OFFICER
Nickolas Davatzes
SENIOR VICE PRESIDENT, PROGRAMMING & PRODUCTION
Andrew H. Orgel
SENIOR VICE PRESIDENT, SALES & MARKETING
Whitney Goit
SENIOR VICE PRESIDENT, CHIEF FINANCIAL & ADMINISTRATIVE OFFICER
Seymour H. Lesser

Black Entertainment Television (BET)

1232-31st St., N.W., Washington, D.C. 20007; (202) 337-5260.

PRESIDENT
Robert L. Johnson
VICE PRESIDENT OF ADVERTISING
Janis P. Thomas
VICE PRESIDENT OF NETWORK OPERATIONS
Jeff Lee
VICE PRESIDENT OF FINANCE
Antonia O. Duncan

Bravo

Rainbow Program Enterprises, 150 Crossways Park West, Woodbury, NY 11797; (516) 364-2222. A Pay-TV system.

PRESIDENT & CHIEF OPERATING OFFICER
John Janas
VICE PRESIDENT, PROGRAMMING
Jonathan D. Sehring

Cable News Network

Turner Broadcasting System, One CNN Center, P.O. Box 105366, Atlanta, GA 30348-5366; (404) 827-1500.

BOARD CHAIRMAN & PRESIDENT OF TBS
R. E. (Ted) Turner
CNN EXECUTIVE VICE PRESIDENT
Burt Reinhardt
CNN SENIOR VICE PRESIDENT
Ed Turner

Cable News Network Headline News

One CNN Center, P.O. Box 105366, Atlanta, GA 30348-5366; (404) 827-1500.

BOARD CHAIRMAN
R. E. (Ted) Turner
PRESIDENT
Burt Reinhardt
VICE PRESIDENT, HEADLINE NEWS
Paul R. Amos

Christian Broadcasting Network

CBN Center, Virginia Beach, VA 24363; (804) 424-7777.

FOUNDER AND CHIEF EXECUTIVE OFFICER
M.G. (Pat) Robertson

CNBC (Consumer News & Business Channel)

2200 Fletcher Ave., Ft. Lee, NJ 07024; (201) 585-2622. (A subsidiary of National Broadcasting Co.)

PRESIDENT
Michael Eskridge
PRESIDENT, NBC CABLE & BUSINESS DEVELOPMENT
Tom Rogers

C-SPAN Cable Satellite Public Affairs Network

Suite 412, 444 N. Capitol, St., N.W., Washington, DC 20001; (202) 737-3220.

CHAIRMAN AND CHIEF EXECUTIVE OFFICER
Brian P. Lamb
EXECUTIVE VICE PRESIDENT
Mike Michaelson
VICE PRESIDENT, BUSINESS AFFAIRS
Robert Kennedy
VICE PRESIDENT, PROGRAMMING & CORPORATE COMMUNICATIONS
Susan Swain
VICE PRESIDENT, NETWORK OPERATIONS
Brian Lockman
VICE PRESIDENT, CORPORATE COUNSEL
Bruce Collins

Cinemax

1271 Ave. of the Americas, New York, NY 10020; (212) 484-1000. A second pay-TV service created by Home Box Office, Inc. and designed to complement the foundation HBO service.

PRESIDENT AND CHIEF OPERATING OFFICER
Michael Fuchs
SENIOR VICE PRESIDENT, CINEMAX
Larry Carlson
SENIOR VICE PRESIDENT, CINEMAX PROGRAMMING
Lee deBoer
SENIOR VICE PRESIDENT, CINEMAX MARKETING & SALES
Dick Beahrs
VICE PRESIDENT, CORPORATE AFFAIRS
David Pritchard

Discovery Channel

8201 Corporate Dr., Landover, MD 20785; (301) 577-1999.

CHAIRMAN & CHIEF EXECUTIVE OFFICER
John S. Hendricks
PRESIDENT & CHIEF OPERATING OFFICER
Ruth L. Otte
SENIOR VICE PRESIDENTS
Greg Durig, Judith McHale
SENIOR VICE PRESIDENT, PROGRAMMING
Greg Moyer
SENIOR VICE PRESIDENT, ADVERTISING SALES
Kathy Clinton
SENIOR VICE PRESIDENT, PROGRAM ACQUISITIONS & DEVELOPMENT
Suzanne Hayes
SENIOR VICE PRESIDENT, AFFILIATE SALES
Sandra McGovern

The Disney Channel

3800 West Alameda, Burbank, CA 91505; (818) 564-7500. (A Pay-TV system and a subsidiary of The Walt Disney Company)

PRESIDENT
John F. Cooke

ESPN, Inc.

ESPN Plaza, Bristol, CT 06010, (203) 585-2000; and 355 Lexington Ave., New York, NY 10017, (212) 661-6040. (Entertainment & Sports Programming Network)

PRESIDENT & CHIEF EXECUTIVE OFFICER
J. William Grimes
EXECUTIVE VICE PRESIDENT & CHIEF OPERATING OFFICER
Allan B. Connall
SENIOR VICE PRESIDENT/INTERNATIONAL & LEGAL AFFAIRS
Andrew P. Brilliant
VICE PRESIDENT, ADVERTISING SALES
John S. Bonanni

Financial News Network

Corporate Office: 320 Park Ave., New York, NY 10022; (212) 891-7300. Studios: 1251 Ave. of Americas, New York, NY 10020; (212) 827-0071 and 6701 Center Dr. West, Los Angeles, CA 90045; (213) 670-1100.

CHIEF EXECUTIVE OFFICER OF INFOTECHNOLOGY & CHAIRMAN OF FNN
Earl W. Brian, M.D.
EXECUTIVE VICE PRESIDENT, INFOTECHNOLOGY
David L. Meister
PRESIDENT
Michael Wheeler
EXECUTIVE VICE PRESIDENT & GENERAL MANAGER, FNN: SCORE
Arnie Rosenthal
NATIONAL SALES MANAGER
Rick North
SENIOR VICE PRESIDENT, AFFILIATE RELATIONS
Gil Faccio
VICE PRESIDENT PRODUCTION
Keith Manasco

Home Box Office, Inc.

1100 Ave. of the Americas, New York, NY 10036; (212) 512-1000. (A Pay-TV system and a subsidiary of Time, Inc.)

CHAIRMAN AND CHIEF EXECUTIVE OFFICER
Michael J. Fuchs
PRESIDENT
Joseph J. Collins
SENIOR VICE PRESIDENT, MARKETING
John Billock
EXECUTIVE VICE PRESIDENT, AFFILIATE OPERATIONS
Peter Frame
VICE PRESIDENT, CORPORATE AFFAIRS
David Pritchard

Viewer's Choice

909 Third Ave., 21st floor, New York, NY 10022; (212) 486-6600. (A pay-per-view cable network.)

PRESIDENT & CHIEF EXECUTIVE OFFICER
James O. Heyworth
VICE PRESIDENT/FINANCE
William A. Futera
VICE PRESIDENT/AFFILIATE RELATIONS & MARKETING
J. Robert Bedell
VICE PRESIDENT/PROGRAMMING
James L. English

Home Shopping Networks I & II

1529 U.A. 19S, Clearwater, FL 34624; (813) 530-9455. (live, discount shop-at-home TV service).

CHAIRMAN & CHIEF EXECUTIVE OFFICER
Roy M. Speer
PRESIDENT & CHIEF OPERATING OFFICER
Lowell W. Paxton
SENIOR VICE PRESIDENT, CORPORATE DEVELOPMENT
Charles H. Bohart

The Learning Channel

1525 Wilson Blvd., Rosslyn, VA 22209; (703) 276-0881.

CHAIRMAN & CHIEF EXECUTIVE OFFICER
Harold E. Morse, Ph.D.
PRESIDENT
Robert J. Shuman

Lifetime

1211 Ave. of the Americas, New York, NY 10036; (212) 719-8950. (Hearst/ABC-Viacom Entertainment Services)

PRESIDENT & CHIEF EXECUTIVE OFFICER
Thomas F. Burchill
VICE PRESIDENT/PROGRAMS
Charles B. Gingold
VICE PRESIDENT/MARKETING
Laurence E. Rebich

MTV Networks, Inc.

75 Rockefeller Plaza, New York, NY 10019; (212) 484-8680. (Provides MTV-24 hr. a day music video channel; VH-1/Video Hits One; and Nickelodeon, Nick at Nite children's and young adults' programming service)

PRESIDENT & CHIEF EXECUTIVE OFFICER
David H. Horowitz
EXECUTIVE VICE PRESIDENT & CHIEF OPERATING OFFICER
Robert W. Pittman

The Nashville Network

Box 10210, Stamford, CT 06904; (203) 965-6000. (A service of Opryland USA, Inc. and Group W Satellite Communications.) Production Center address: 2806 Opryland Dr., Nashville, TN 37214; (614) 889-6840

GENERAL MANAGER
David Hall
SENIOR VICE PRESIDENT, SALES & MARKETING
Lloyd Werner

The Playboy Channel

Playboy Enterprises, Inc., 8560 Sunset Blvd., Los Angeles, CA 90069; (213) 659-4080. (A Pay-TV service distributed by Playboy Video Entertainment Group)

PRISM

225 City Line Ave., Bala Cynwyd, PA 19004; (215) 668-2210. (A Pay-TV network)

VICE PRESIDENT AND GENERAL MANAGER
Donald L. Heller
VICE PRESIDENT AND ASSISTANT GENERAL MANAGER
Sam Schroeder

Rainbow Program Enterprises

150 Crossways Park West, Woodbury, NY 11797; (516) 364-2222. (Bravo, American Movie Classics, Sports-

Channel New York, Sports Channel New England, Sports-Vision Chicago, PRISM of Philadelphia, SportsChannel Florida, Rainbow Home Video, Rainbow Network Communications, News 12 Long Island)

PRESIDENT
Marc Lustgarten

Request Television

Reiss Media Enterprises, Inc., 140 East 45th St., New York, NY 10017; (212) 984-5900. (A pay-per-view cable network)

CHAIRMAN & CHIEF EXECUTIVE OFFICER
Jeffrey C. Reiss
EXECUTIVE VICE PRESIDENT
Leonard Fertig
SENIOR VICE PRESIDENT & GENERAL COUNSEL
Bruce Karpas
VICE PRESIDENT, SALES, MARKETING & PROGRAMMING
Paul FitzPatrick

SelecTV of California, Inc.

4755 Alla Rd., Marina del Rey, CA 90291; (213) 827-4400. (WHT Pay-TV system)

PRESIDENT
Thomas C. Hunt
VICE PRESIDENT SALES & MARKETING
Ronald E. Ruppe

Showtime/The Movie Channel, Inc.

1633 Broadway, New York, NY 10019; (212) 708-1600. (A Pay-TV system)

CHAIRMAN AND CHIEF EXECUTIVE OFFICER
Winston H. (Tony) Cox
EXECUTIVE VICE PRESIDENT, MARKETING & CREATIVE SERVICES
Matthew Blank
EXECUTIVE VICE PRESIDENT, PROGRAMMING
Fred Schneier
EXECUTIVE VICE PRESIDENT, BUSINESS DEVELOPMENT & AFFILIATE MARKETING
Jack Heim
PRESIDENT, VIACOM NETWORK ENTERPRISES
Ron Bernard
CHIEF FINANCIAL OFFICER & SENIOR VICE PRESIDENT
Jerry Cooper
PRESIDENT, VIEWER'S CHOICE
Scott Kurnit
SENIOR VICE PRESIDENT, GENERAL COUNSEL, VIACOM NETWORKS GROUP
Greg Ricca
SENIOR VICE PRESIDENT, PROGRAM PLANNING
Jim Miller
EXECUTIVE VICE PRESIDENT & GENERAL MANAGER, VIAMCOM SATELLITE NETWORKS
Stephan Wm. Schulte
SENIOR VICE PRESIDENT, ADMINISTRATION
Dwight Tierney

Silent Network

6363 Sunset Blvd., Ste. 930-B, Hollywood, CA 90028; (213) 464-SIGN. Organized 1980. (Cable TV network for deaf and hearing-impaired audiences utilizing sign language, voice and open captions.)

CHAIRMAN/CEO
Sheldon I. Altfeld
PRESIDENT
William C. Tauber
AFFILIATIONS
National Academy of Cable Programming, National Association for the Deaf, Academy of Television Arts & Sciences

Telstar Channel

555 Madison Ave., 6th floor, New York, NY 10022; (212) 838-3377. 1900 Ave. of the Stars, Los Angeles, CA 90067; (213) 556-5650. (A Pay-TV system).

CHAIRMAN OF THE BOARD
Gerald A. Bartell
VICE CHAIRMAN & CHIEF EXECUTIVE OFFICER
Joseph A. Corazzi
VICE PRESIDENT & SECRETARY-TREASURER
Stan Irwin
EXECUTIVE VICE PRESIDENT
Carl A. Sambus
SENIOR VICE PRESIDENT, PROGRAMMING & MARKETING
Dr. Gerry D. Jordan

TNT (Turner Network Television)

Box 105366, One CNN Center, Atlanta, GA 30348-5366; (404) 827-1647.

PRESIDENT, TURNER BROADCASTING SYSTEM'S ENTERTAINMENT NETWORKS
Gerry Hogan
EXECUTIVE VICE PRESIDENT, TNT
Scott Sassa
VICE PRESIDENT PROGRAM DEVELOPMENT
Linda Berman
VICE PRESIDENT BUSINESS AFFAIRS
Neal Baseman
VICE PRESIDENT CREATIVE DIRECTOR
Lee Hunt

Tower Productions Inc.

175 Fifth Ave., Suite 1101, New York, NY 10010; (212) 941-0702. Organized 1983. (Produces programming for broadcast, cable, corporate and home video.)

PRESIDENT
Donald A. Roosa

Trinity Broadcasting Network

Box A, Santa Ana, CA 92711; (714) 832-2950.

PRESIDENT
Paul F. Crouch
CHIEF OF OPERATIONS
Phillip Crouch
DIRECTOR ENGINEERING
Ben Miller
DIRECTOR SATELLITE SERVICES
Stan Hollon

Univision

Univision Holdings, Inc., 330 Madison Ave., New York, NY 10017; (212) 983-8500.

MANAGER, CORPORATE OFFICE
William D. Stiles
SENIOR VICE PRESIDENT, DIRECTOR OF SALES & MARKETING
Browning Holcombe, Jr.
SENIOR VICE PRESIDENT, BUSINESS DEVELOPMENT
Blaine Decker
VICE PRESIDENT, PROGRAM DIRECTOR
Rosita Peru
VICE PRESIDENT, NEWS DIRECTOR
Guillermo Martinez

USA Network

1230 Ave. of the Americas, New York, NY 10020; (212) 408-9100

PRESIDENT & CHIEF EXECUTIVE OFFICER
Kay Koplowitz
EXECUTIVE VICE PRESIDENT & CHIEF OPERATING OFFICER
Kent Replogle

VICE PRESIDENT, FINANCE & ADMINISTRATION
Doug Hamilton
VICE PRESIDENT, RESEARCH
David Bender
VICE PRESIDENT, MARKETING
Andrew Besch
SENIOR VICE PRESIDENT, BUSINESS AFFAIRS, OPERATIONS AND GENERAL COUNSEL
Stephen Brenner
SENIOR VICE PRESIDENT, AFFILIATE RELATIONS
Gil Faccio
SENIOR VICE PRESIDENT, PROGRAMMING
David Kenin
SENIOR VICE PRESIDENT, AD SALES
John Silvestri

The Weather Channel

2600 Cumberland Parkway, Atlanta, GA 30039; (404) 434-6800.

PRESIDENT
Michael J. Eckert
VICE PRESIDENT, SPECIAL PROJECTS
Dana Michaelis
VICE PRESIDENT, ADVERTISING SALES
Don Ershaw
VICE PRESIDENT/AFFILIATE SALES & SERVICES
Rebecca Ruthuen

WGN-TV

United Video, Inc., 3801 S. Sheridan, Tulsa, OK 74145; (918) 665-6690.

EXECUTIVE VICE PRESIDENT
Roy Bliss
VICE PRESIDENT SALES & MARKETING
Jeff Treeman

WPIX (NEW YORK)

United Video, Inc., 3801 S. Sheridan, Tulsa, OK 74145; (918) 446-6690. New York "superstation"

EXECUTIVE VICE PRESIDENT
Roy Bliss
VICE PRESIDENT MARKETING & SALES
Jeff Treeman

WTBS

Turner Broadcasting System, 1050 Techwood Drive, N.W., Atlanta, GA 30318; (404) 827-1717. Atlanta "superstation"

CHAIRMAN/PRESIDENT
R.E. (Ted) Turner

WWOR (TV)

Eastern Microwave, Box 4872, 112 Northern Concourse, Syracuse, NY 13221 (315) 455-5955. New York "superstation"

GENERAL MANAGER
Art Perkins
NATIONAL MARKETING MANAGER
Gil Korta
SALES MANAGER
Ann Marie Russell

Trade Names of Basic Cable & Pay-TV Suppliers

(See company listings)

A&E (Arts & Entertainment Network)
American Movie Classics (Rainbow)
BET (Black Entertainment Network)
Bravo (Rainbow Programming Services)
CBN (Christian Broadcasting Network)
CNBC (NBC Inc.)
CNN (Cable News Network—Turner Broadcasting)
Cinemax (Cinemax—Time, Inc.)
C-SPAN (Cable Satellite Public Affairs Network)
The Disney Channel (Group W/Disney)
ESPN (Entertainment & Sports Programming Network—Getty Oil)
FNN (Financial News Network)
Headline News (Turner)
Home Box Office (Home Box Office—Time, Inc.)
Lifetime (Hearst/ABC/Viacom)
MTV (MTV Network)
The Movie Channel (Showtime/The Movie Channel)
Nashville Network (Group W Satellite Communications)
Nick at Nite (MTV Networks)
Nickelodeon (MTV Networks)
The Playboy Channel (Playboy Enterprises)
Request Television (Reiss Media Enterprises)
Showtime (Showtime/The Movie Channel)
Telstar (Telestar Channel)
TLC (The Learning Channel)
TNT (Turner Broadcasting System)
Univision (Spanish International Network)
USA Network (USA Cable Network)
Video Hits One (MTV Networks)
Viewer's Choice (ATC, Cox TeleCable, Continental, Newhouse)
The Weather Channel (The Weather Channel)
WGN-TV (United Video)
WHT (SelecTV of California)
WPIX (United Video)
WTBS (Turner)
WWOR (Eastern Microwave)

Advertising Agencies

* **STATION REPRESENTATIVES**

Advertising Agencies

A. D. ADAMS ADVERTISING, 9 E. 38 St., New York, NY 10016; (212) 685-9060.
A. D. ADAMS, pres.

ALLIED ADVERTISING AGENCY, INC., 830 Statler Office Bldg., Boston, MA 02116; (617) 482-4100.
HOWARD SHAMBAN, TV dir.; MARC F. SHAMBAN, TV time buyer.

ANDERSON DAVID & SEEDS, INC., Colonial Bldg., Clinton, NY 13323; (212) 853-6141.
JAY C. ANDERSON, pres.; MARK ANDERSON, acct. exec.

ARNOLD & COMPANY, INC., Park Square Bldg., Boston, MA 02116; (617) 357-1900.
GERARD GOLDEN, pres.; ARNOLD Z. ROSOFF, chairman & treasurer; LEN KARSAVOL, creative dir.; DENNIS LEE, copy chief; MARIE KACHINSKI, media dir.; STAVROS COSMOPULOS, exec. v.p., creative services; FRED SIEGEL, media; PHYLLIS MAYNARD, media; ANNE GOTZ, JOAN BENNETT, GINNY MEANEY, media.

N. W. AYER INCORPORATED, Worldwide Plaza, 825 Eighth Ave., New York, NY 10019-7498; (212) 474-5000; FAX: (212) 474-5400.
MARCELLA ROSEN, sr. v.p. & media dir.; DAVID LEHMKUHL, group media dir., planning; JANE TWYON, group media dir., planning; RICHARD WELSH, group media dir., network & negotiation; DIANE ZGONC, group media dir., planning; SUSAN BELL, mgr. spot buying.

BACKER SPIELVOGEL BATES WORLDWIDE INC., 405 Lexington Avenue, 8th floor, New York, NY 10174; (212) 297-7000; FAX: (212) 986-0270.
ROBERT E. JACOBY, chmn.; ROBERT A. BRUNS, pres.; WALTER E. REICHEL, sr. v.p.-exec. dir. media & programs dept.; JOEL M. SEGAL, sr. v.p.-dir. TV/radio div. Division of BACKER SPIELVOGEL BATES WORLDWIDE INC. (same address) with affiliates in Fort Lauderdale, Chicago, Minneapolis, San Francisco, Los Angeles, Canada, Mexico, Argentina, Brazil, Chile, Colombia, Ecuador, Peru, Venezuela, United Kingdom, Norway, Sweden, Denmark, West Germany, Austria, Netherlands, Belgium, France, Spain, Italy, Greece, South Africa, Malaysia, Thailand, Singapore, Hong Kong, Japan, Philippines, Australia, New Zealand.

BBDO CHICAGO, INC., 410 N. Michigan Ave., Chicago, IL 60611; (312) Delaware 7-7860.
ROGER MOHR, chmn. of the bd.; ERIC HARKNA, pres.; CHUCK SHELDON, exec. prod.

BEHRENDS, BODLE & PARSONS, INC., 7031 Albert Pick Rd., Ste. 200, Greensboro, NY 27409; (919) 668-7272.
RICHARD D. BEHRENDS, pres.; RICHARD FURMANSKI, v.p. & senior art dir.; ROBERT A. BODLE, JR., v.p. & exec. creative dir.; SYLVIA Y. PASSAVANT, secty.-treas.; JERRY BLACKWELDER, media dir.

HERBERT S. BENJAMIN ASSOCIATES, INC., 2736 Florida St., Baton Rouge, LA 70802; (504) 387-0611.
LEE HERZBERG, JR., chmn./pres.; MARGARET S. WEBB, exec. v.p.; PATTI HASSELL, treas.; JACKLYN ROBBINS, secty.; LENORE USHER, v.p., acct. exec.; GUS WALES, v.p./creative dir.; RICHARD J. BARRA, v.p.; mgr. Lafayette branch office; ELISE GANETT, asst. v.p., exec. admin.

WALTER F. BENNETT CO., 20 N. Wacker Dr., Chicago, IL 60606; (312) 372-1131.
FRED DIENERT, pres.; TED DIENERT, exec. v.p.; JAN KLUTS, media dir.-time buyer. Other offices: 1634 Spruce St., Philadelphia, PA 19103; (215) 545-2003; 16479 Dallas Pkwy., Dallas, TX 72348; (214) 380-1122.

RALPH BING ADVERTISING CO., 16109 Selva Dr., San Diego, CA 92128; (714) 487-7444.
RALPH BING, TV dir.

FRANK BLOCK ASSOC., The Chase, 10th floor, St. Louis, MO 63108; (314) 367-9600.
DAVID STOBLE, dir. mktg.

BOTSFORD, KETCHUM, INC., 55 Union St., San Francisco, CA 94111.
DENIS HITCHMOUGH, senior v.p., media; MORTY BARAN, dir. broadcast prod.; PATTY MORAN, v.p. mgr. broadcast business affairs.

BRAVERMAN-MIRISCH INC., 1517 Schuyler Rd., Beverly Hills, CA 90210; (213) 274-5204.
MILLICENT BRAVERMAN, pres.

BROWER, LOWE & HALL ADVERTISING, INC., 215 East Stone Ave., P.O. Box 3357, Greenville, SC; (803) 242-5350.
EDWARD E. BROWER, JR., pres.; CHARLOTTE L. BROWER, sec.-tres.; KENNETH HOWIE, assoc. creative dir.; JERRY WHERITY, assoc. creative dir.

BURLINGAME/GROSSMAN, INC., 6200 N. Hiawatha Ave., Chicago, IL 60646; (312) 777-0610.
S. J. BRICHTA, TV dir.

LEO BURNETT COMPANY, INC., 35 W. Wacker, Chicago, IL 60601; (312) 220-5959.
HALL (CAP) ADAMS, CEO; RICHARD (RICK) FIZDALE, pres.; JOHN (JACK) SMITH, vice chmn.; JOHN (JACK) KRAFT, vice chmn. & chief admin. officer; WILLIAM (BILL) LYNCH, CEO, Leo Burnett U.S.A.; ROB NOLAN, vice chmn., Leo Burnett U.S.A.; THEODORE (TED) BELL, pres., Leo Burnett U.S.A.; WILLIAM (BILL) BORIS, exec. v.p., Leo Burnett U.S.A.; JAMES (JIM) SHYMKUS, exec. v.p., Leo Burnett U.S.A.; PETER HUSTING, exec.v.p., Leo Burnett U.S.A.; HENRY (HANK) FEELEY, chmn. & CEO, Leo Burnett Intl.; MICHAEL CONRAD, pres., Leo Burnett Intl.; SERGIO SUAREZ-SOLIS, vice chmn., Leo Burnett Intl., KERRY RUBIE, regional man. dir., Leo Burnett Intl.; ALBERT WINNINGHOFF, man. dir., Noordervliet & Winninghoff/Leo Burnett.

HAROLD CABOT & CO., INC., One Constitution Plaza, Boston, MA 02129; (617) 242-6200.
WILLIAM H. MONAGHAN, pres.; PETER CROWELL, media dir.; LOUIS STAMOULIS, dir. radio-TV.

CALDWELL VAN RIPER/FORT WAYNE, 701 S. Clinton St., Fort Wayne, IN 46802; (219) 422-7495.
DENISE DOUVILLE, media director.

CAMPBELL-MITHUN-ESTY, 222 South Ninth St., Minneapolis, MN 55402; (612) 347-1000.
WILLIAM D. DUNLAP, CEO (Mpls.); JOE O'DONNELL, chmn. (New York); BILL STEIN, pres. (Chicago); DAVID WELCH, vice chmn. (Detroit); GENE ZASKE, chief financial officer (Mpls.); CHUCK ABRAMS, sr. v.p., dir. of media services, Chicago, IL (312) 266-5100; RIC PASCHKE, exec. v.p., management dir., media, Southfield, MI (313) 354-5400; EARL HERZOG, sr. v.p., media dir., Minneapolis, MN (612) 347-1000; TOM WINNER, sr. v.p., media dir., New York, NY (212) 692-6200; Orange, CA (714) 928-3789.
Canada: Windsor, Ontario (519) 255-7041; Toronto, Ontario (416) 484-9150.
Subsidiaries/Affiliates: Cash Plus, Inc., Minneapolis, MN (612) 347-6900; Communications Workshop, Minneapolis, MN (612) 347-1700; Corner on Design, Minneapolis, MN (612) 347-7979; Future Marketing, Inc., Minneapolis, MN (612) 347-7999; Promotion Works, Inc., Minneapolis, MN (612) 347-1490.

THE CRAMER-KRASSELT CO., 733 N. Van Buren St., Milwaukee, WI 53202; (414) 276-3500.
ROBERT L. CHRISTIANSEN, chmn. of bd. & treas.; TED WING, pres; C. ROSS LITTIG, vice chmn. of bd.; DONALD E. POM, media dir.-TV/radio; CAROL WALCZAK, buyer/planner; KATHY HARRISON, buyler/planner; CATHY POCHERT, bdcst. svs. mgr.

CRESWELL, MUNSELL, FULTZ & ZIRBEL, P.O. Box 2879, 4211 Signal Ridge Road NE, Cedar Rapids, IA 52406; (319) 395-6500.
F. BAKER, pres., CMF&Z Cedar Rapids; M. WHITE, exec. v.p.; G. ANDERSON, R. CLINE, S. CUSTER, W. FRITZ, J. MEEKS, C. SNETZLER, D. STADLEN, R. THOMPSON, I. WAY, sr. v.p.s. radio/TV producers; T. TAYLOR, v.p. exec. broadcast producer; B. MONTGOMERY, M. MURRAY, prod.
CRESWELL, MUNSELL, FULTZ & ZIRBEL, P.O. Box 4807, 600 East Court, Suite E, Des Moines, IA 50309; (515) 246-3500. W. FULTZ, pres., CMF&Z Des Moines; W. RITCHIE, exec. v.p.; T. STOFFER, sr. v.p. radio/TV producers; M. JORGENSEN, broadcast production mgr.; J. STARK, asst. producer.

D'ARCY MASIUS BENTON & BOWLES, INC., 909 Third Ave., New York, NY 10022; (212) 758-6200; TELEX: 310-680-1331; FAX: (212) 909-9442 & 909-9219.
New York: MICHAEL MOORE, sr. v.p., worldwide media dir. Bloomfield Hills: GEORGE M. ROGERS, JR., sr. v.p./dir. of media services; STEPHEN C. KOPCHA, deputy managing dir./chief cre-

ative officer. Chicago: JOSEPH P. ZELLER, sr. v.p./dir. of media & financial services; GARY J. HORTON, deputy managing dir./chief creative officer. Los Angeles: RON LAWRENCE, sr. v.p./media dir.; JOHN ARMISTEAD, deputy managing dir./exec. creative dir. New York: RICHARD HAMILTON, sr. v.p./dir. of media; RICHARD N. LEVENSON, deputy managing dir./chief creative officer. St. Louis: JAMES M. PORCARELLI, sr. v.p./dir. of media serives; CHARLES E. CLAGGETT, deputy managing dir./chief creative officer.

DDB NEEDHAM WORLDWIDE INC., 437 Madison Ave., New York, NY 10022; (212) 415-2000.
KEITH REINHARD, chmn. of the bd. & CEO; JOHN BERNBACH, pres. DDB Needham Worldwide Inc.,; ROBERT HUNTINGTON, vice chair & COO; ROBERT MACKALL and JACK MARIUCCI, co-exec. creative dirs.; PETER FALCONE, pres. NY; ALAN PANDOW, pres. DDB Needham West; DAVE PARK, pres. DDB Needham LA.

W. B. DONER & CO., 25900 Northwestern Highway, Southfield, MI 48075; (313) 354-9700.
W. B. DONER, chmn. of exec. comm.; MICHAEL SHAPIRA, pres., Detroit; H. B. LEVINE, sr. v.p.; secy./treas.; SEYMOUR (SKIP) ROBERTS, exec. v.p. gen. mgr. Detroit.
also: 2305 N. Charles Street, Baltimore, MD 21218; (301) 338-1600.
HERBERT D. FRIED, chmn./CEO; JAMES DALE, vice chmn.; WILLIAM E. HOOPER, pres., Baltimore; DAVE SACKEY, exec. v.p., gen. mgr., Baltimore.

DOREMUS & COMPANY (Subsidiary of Omnicom Group, Inc.), 120 Broadway, New York, NY 10271; (212) 964-0700.
CURTIS R. TROEGER, chmn.; W. DEAN GENGE, dir. of acct. services; JOHN M. GARRE, creative dir.; DAVID J. BROWN, media dir.; RICHARD H. TRUITT, pres./public relations.
Branch offices: Boston, Chicago, Frankfurt, London, Los Angeles, Tokyo.

EARLE PALMER BROWN & SPIRO, 100 S. Broad St., Philadelphia, PA 19102; (215) 923-5400.
HERB SMITH, exec. v.p., general mgr.

EISNER & ASSOCIATES, INC., 12 W. Madison St., Baltimore, MD 21201; (301) 685-3390.
H. W. EISNER, chmn.; STEVE EISNER, pres.; GEORGE NILES, v.p., media.

FAHLGREN & SWINK, 655 Metro Place S., Dublin, OH 43017; (614) 766-3500.
CHRIS CLEMENTS, sr. v.p. media & mktg. svcs.; WILLIAM KIGHT, vice chairman, president, Columbus.

FAHLGREN & SWINK, PARKERSBURG, Rosemar Rd. & Seminary Dr., Parkersburg, WV 26102; (304) 424-3591.
WILLIAM FARSON, treasurer; H. SMOOT FAHLGREN, chairman/chief exec. officer; JIM SWEARINGEN, chief operating officer.

FAIRFAX INC., ADVERTISING, 635 Madison Ave., New York, NY 10022; (212) 350-1800.
STANLEY I. FISHEL, dir. of television; ROBERT McQUADE, producer; RICHARD MIRENDA, art director; MIKE COHN, media dir.

FOOTE, CONE & BELDING COMMUNICATIONS, INC., 101 East Erie Street, Chicago, IL 60611-2987; (312) 751-7000.
NORMAN W. BROWN, chmn./CEO.
ADVERTISING OFFICES: FCB/EAST: New York, Philadelphia, Hamilton; FCB/CENTRAL: Chicago, Montreal, Toronto, Vancouver; FCB/WEST: San Francisco, Los Angeles, Orange County; PUBLICIS, FCB/EUROPE: Amsterdam, Ancona, Athens, Barcelona, Bologna, Brussels, Copenhagen, Düsseldorf, Eindhoven, Frankfurt, Gothenburg, Hamburg, Helsingborg, Istanbul, Lausanne, Lisbon, London, Madrid, Mälmo, Manchester, Milan, Münich, Nottingham, Oslo, Paris, Rome, Stockholm, Vienna, Zürich; FCB/LATIN AMERICA-PACIFIC-AFRICA: Adelaide, Auckland, Bangkok, Bogotá, Buenos Aires, Cali, Cape Town, Caracas, Durban, Guatemala City, Guayaquil, Hong Kong, Johannesburg, Kingston, Kuala Lumpur, Manila, Medellín, Melbourne, Mexico City, Perth, Port of Spain, Quito, Rio de Janeiro, San José, San Juan, San Pedro, Santo Domingo, São Paulo, Sydney, Tegucigalpa, Tokyo.

FOSTER & DAVIES, INC., Hanna Bldg., Cleveland, OH 44115; (216) 241-0711.

ALBERT FRANK-GUENTHER LAW, INC., 71 Broadway, New York, NY 10006; (212) 248-5200.
STEPHEN J. WITT, chmn.; JOHN F. COWELL III, pres.
Branch office: San Francisco.

GERBER ADVERTISING AGENCY, 209 S.W. Oak Ave., Portland, OR 97204; (503) 221-0100.
BETTY CHIMENTI, v.p. media dir.

GILLHAM ADVERTISING INC., Fourth Floor, 102 W. 500 So., Salt Lake City, UT 84101; (801) 328-0281.
RONALD W. GRIFFITHS, senior v.p.; WENDY SARIS, media dir.; TERESA WESEMANN, traffic mgr.

GREY ADVERTISING, INC., 777 Third Ave., New York, NY 10017; (212) 546-2000; Grey Los Angeles, 6100 Wilshire Blvd., Los Angeles, CA 90048; (213) 936-6060; Grey Orange County, 6400 W. Katella Ave., Ste. 200, Cypress, CA 90630-5208; (714) 372-6600; Grey San Francisco, 2 Embarcadero Ctr., San Francisco, CA 94111; (415) 421-1000.
EDWARD H. MEYER, pres. & chief exec. officer; ALEC GERSTER, exec. v.p., media and programming services.
Branch offices: Aarhus (Denmark), Amsterdam, Auckland, Bankok, Barbados, Barcelona, Bombay, Brussels, Buenos Aires, Caracas, Canberra, Copenhagen, Dusseldorf, Geneva, Goteborg, Halmstad, Hamilton, Helsinki, Hong Kong, Kuala Lumpur (Malaysia), Lima, London, Los Angeles, Madrid, Malmo, Melbourne, Mexico D. F., Milan, Montevideo, Montreal, New York, Oslo, Paris, Rotterdam, San Francisco, San Juan, San Paolo, Sandefjord, Santiago, Seoul, Singapore, Stockholm, Sydney, Taiwan, Tokyo, Toronto, Vancouver, Vienna, Wellington, Zurich.

GRISWOLD, INC., Landmark Office Towers, 101 Prospect Ave. West, Cleveland, OH 44115; (216) 696-3400.
PATRICK J. MORIN, pres. and CEO; NEAL B. DAVIS, exec. vice pres., dir. of client services; THOMAS PAPADIMOULIS, senior vice pres., creative dir.

HARRIS & LOVE, INC./ADVERTISING, 136 East So. Temple, Salt Lake City, UT 84111; (801) 532-7333.
DONALD G. WARE, pres.

HART-CONWAY CO., INC., 300 Triangle Bldg., Rochester, NY 14604; (716) 232-2930.
PETER B. WHITCOMBE, pres.; WILLIAM WESTERFELD, exec. v.p.

HENDERSON ADVERTISING, INC., 60 Pelham Pointe, Greenville, SC 29615; P.O. Box 2247, Greenville, SC 29602 (Mailing Address); (803) 271-6000.
RALPH W. CALLAHAN JR., chmn. & pres.; BILL REYNOLDS, sr. v.p. media dir.

HICKS AND GREIST, INC., 220 E. 42 St., New York, NY 10036; (212) 370-9600.
CHARLES V. SKOOG, JR., chmn.; D. EDWARD RICCHIUTO, pres.; S. PARKER, media dir.; DEMETRI KONTUPOULOS, TV prod. dir.

HOLLAND ADVERTISING, 252 Ludlow Ave., Cincinnati, OH 45220; (513) 221-1252
MARK S. HOLLAND, executive v.p.

HOUCK ADVERTISING, 1402 Grandin Rd., Roanoke, VA 24015; (703) 989-6655.
WILLIAM B. HOUCK, chmn.; WILLIAM B. HOUCK, JR., pres.; CYNTHIA G. CALDWELL, media buyer.

HUTCHINS/YOUNG & RUBICAM INC., 400 Midtown Tower; Rochester, NY 14604; (716) 546-6480.
JAMES N. MOREY, pres. & chief exec. officer; HARVEY J. BOZZI, JR., sr. v.p./management sprv.; DANIEL LYTLE, v.p./ management sprv.; DAVID S. CULVER, v.p./gen. mgr. public relations, div.; MARY ANN SAPOS, sr. v.p./ telephone directory div.; CHARLES RELLER, exec. v.p./gen. mgr.; SHARON KIRK, sr. v.p./creative dir.; ROBERT H. MAHARRY, sr. v.p./creative dir.

HENRY J. KAUFMAN & ASSOCIATES, INC., 2233 Wisconsin Ave., N.W., Washington, DC 20007; (202) 333-0700.
STUART E. KARU, chmn. & CEO; MICHAEL G. CARBERRY, pres. & COO; MARY D. YERRICK, sr. v.p., development; J. ROGER VILSACK, exec. v.p. creative svcs.; MERRICK MURDOCK, exec. prod.

KELLY, ZAHRNDT & KELLY INC., 10805 Sunset Office Dr., St. Louis, MO 63127.
ROBERT W. KELLY, dir.; WILLIAM A. WILSON, MARY HOPPER, CHARLES CROWE, DAVE ERICH, acct. execs.

KETCHUM COMMUNICATIONS, INC., Six PPG Place, Pittsburgh, PA 15222; (412) 456-3500.
Pittsburgh: WILLIAM H. GENGE, chmn.; GERALD J. VOROS, pres.; HERBERT D. GORDON, sr. v.p., media services; JUDITH HOFSCHER, v.p., media dir.; RICHARD SLEEMAN, v.p. & broadcast services mgr.
New York office: Ketchum New York. THOMAS MILLER, pres.; JIM McHUGH, v.p., dir. media network, res. (N.Y.).

KEYES MARTIN, 841 Mountain Ave., Springfield, NJ; (201) 376-7300. Specialist: ROBYN GREEN-TAYLOR, media director.

KRUPNICK & ASSOCIATES, INC., 135 N. Meramec, St. Louis, MO 63105; (314) 862-9393.
WILLIAM W. QUADE, TV production.

KUTTNER & KUTTNER, INC., 212 W. Superior St., Chicago, IL 60610; (312) 787-7940.

LEWIS, GILMAN & KYNETT, INC., 200 S. Broad St., Philadelphia, PA 19103; (215) 790-4100.
ROBERT G. WILDER, chmn. bd.; PETER J. KEENAN, sr. v.p., fin. & admin.; JACQUELINE PETERS LOWELL, sr. v.p., exec. creative dir.; BRIAN J. GAIL, EDWARD MAHLMAN, PHILLIP R. PEGG, A. THOMAS TEBBENS, JR., ROBERT W. SCHELL, sr. v.p.s, gp. mngmt. supvr.; JAMES N. CLARK, v.p., gp. creative dir.; MICHAEL J. DALY, sr. v.p., dir. media services; GERALD J. DiRUSSO, DUDLEY A. FITZPATRICK, GERARD F. STANKUS, v.p.s, gp. creative dir.; DONALD M. CASILLO, VIRGINIA S. HANFT, v.p., mngmt. supvr.; RICHARD G. WEBSTER, sr. v.p., mngmt. supvr.; EDWIN R. BATES, v.p. sr. art dir.; CHESTER D. HARRINGTON, JR., v.p. business dev.; WESLEY G. HOTCHKISS, v.p. assoc. creative dir.

LINTAS: CAMPBELL-EWALD CO., 30400 Van Dyke, Warren, MI; (313) 574- 3400.
RICHARD D. O'CONNOR, chmn.; PETER A. DOW, pres.; LOUIS M. SCHULTZ, exec. v.p., media dir.
Branch Offices: Atlanta, Chicago, Los Angeles, New York, San Francisco, Dallas, Washington, Miami, Pittsburgh.

THE W. E. LONG ADVERTISING AGENCY, 300 W. Washington St., Chicago, IL 60606; (312) 726-4606.
PAUL FRANK, gen. mgr. & creative dir.; THOMAS E. RADTKE, dir. mktg.; ANITA RAUH, media dir.

McCANN-ERICKSON, 750 Third Avenue, New York, NY 10017; (212) 697-6000.
JOEL SEGAL, exec. v.p., dir. of natl. brdcst.; DONNA WOLFE, sr. v.p., dir. of natl. brdcst. negotiations; JAN PATTISON, CINDY GURMANN and WILLIAM SHERMAN, v.p., group supvrs.; LINDA SILLER, ROSEMARIE OMBRES, NANCY SCHNEIDER, SUSAN RAMEAU, LAURA ISOLA, MARTI KAVALER and WILLIAM SELLERS, network negotiators.

EDWARD J. McELROY ADV., INC., 3600 Wilshire Blvd., Los Angeles, CA 90005; (213) 381-3045.
E. D. BROTSOS, pres. & acct. sup.; VICKI PANAGIOTIS, media dir.; LISA C. MOLLER, acct. exec./prod. mgr.

McKENZIE, KING & GORDON, Box 2570, Hollywood, CA 90078; (213) 466-3421. By appointment only.
MARIE McKENZIE, pres.; DON McKENZIE, creative dir., MARIE SELTZER, media dir.; KEVIN MCKENZIE, assoc. creative dir.

MELDRUM & FEWSMITH, INC., 1220 Huron Rd., Cleveland 15, OH; (216) 241-2141.
CHRIS PERRY, chmn./CEO & creative dir.; ROBERT IREDELL IV, president; ROBERT P. HUDDILSTON, exec. v.p., CFO; JEFFREY H. BRYDEN, exec. v.p.; BRUCE S. CHILDERS, exec. v.p.; CATHERINE V. VOITLEIN, v.p., broadcast services; CYNTHIA E. HOLUB, broadcast prod.; MICHAEL LERNER, broadcast prod.

NEEDHAM & GROHMANN, INC., 30 Rockefeller Plaza, New York, NY 10112; 245-6200.
HOWARD A. HEINSIUS, president; WILLIAM R. HOGAN, art dir.; PETER R. WELLS, ANTHONY R. WRIGHT, ANTHONY E. F. CORNWELL, v.p.'s.

NOWAK ASSOCIATES, INC., 117 Highbridge St., Fayetteville, NY 13066; (305) 637-9895.
TRUMAN T. NOWAK, pres.

OHLMEYER ADVERTISING, 9 W. 57 St., New York, NY 10019; (212) 418-6900.
DON OHLMEYER, chmn.; PHIL HOWERT, pres.; LEE PRATT, v.p., media dir.; DEAN HEITLER, v.p. mgr. supvsr.; PETER CHRISANTHUPOULUS, v.p. bdcst. supvr.

THE PITLUK GROUP, 45 N.E. Loop 410, San Antonio, TX 78216; (512) 366-3100.
LOUIS H. PITLUK, pres.; JACK N. PITLUK, JR., v.p.; HELEN THOMPSON, med. dir.; JOHN HOEMANN, creative dir.

ROCKLIN, IRVING & ASSOCIATES, 65 E. Wacker Place, Suite 2400, Chicago, IL 60601; (312) 726-2324.
ROBERT ROCKLIN, pres.; MARK ROCKLIN, v.p.; PATTY JO WONG, creative dir.; MIKE ARBINI, writer; ANNA JIRIES, acct. exec.; ROBERT TOUROUNJIAN, art dir.; JEAN CARMOSINO, comptroller; YVONNE DAUGHERTY, traffic mgr.

RUDER, FINN & ROTMAN, INC., 110 E. 59 St. New York, NY 10022; (212) 593-6400.
DAVID FINN, chmn. of bd.; KATHY BLOOMGARDEN, pres.; AMY BORDE, pres. NY; CHARLOTTE LIPTON, vice chairman, bdcst. communications dept.

RUMRILL-HOYT, INC., 60 Corporate Woods, Rochester, NY 14623; (716) 272-6100.
RICHARD D. THOMSON, chairman & CEO; NICK ORLOFF, pres./COO; DONNA FARRINGTON, mgr. radio/TV prod.; FRANK KOPEC, v.p., dir. of media services.

LOWE RUNKLE CO., 6801 N. Broadway, Oklahoma City, OK 73114 (405) 848-6800.
OSCAR HEUSER, pres. & CEO; MARK BAUSKE, dir. bdcst. prod.

SAATCHI & SAATCHI COMPTON, INC., 405 Lexington Ave., New York, NY 10174; (212) 661-0800.
O. MILTON GOSSETT, pres. & CEO; C. CAPUANO, v.p. art & TV commercial production; BRUCE COX, sr. v.p./dir. bdcst. programming. Branch offices: Los Angeles, CA; Southfield, MI.

SHOTWELL AND PARTNERS, INCORPORATED, 801 East Blvd., Charlotte, NC 28203; (704) 372-8880

SIMONS MICHELSON ZIEVE INC., 900 Wilshire Dr., Troy, MI 48084-1600; (313) 362-4242.
MORTON ZIEVE, JAMES A. MICHELSON, officers; JON KATZ, TV dept. dir.

SIANO-SPITZ & ASSOCIATES, 530 Oak St., Syracuse, NY; (315) 479- 5581.
MIKE SIANO, president; CHRIS SLATER, radio-TV dir.; WILLIAM BROWNING, acct. exec.

TATHAM-LAIRD & KUDNER, 980 N. Michigan Ave., Chicago, IL 60611; (312) 337-4400.
CHARLOTTE BEERS, chmn. & CEO; WILLIAM YOUNGCLAUS, pres. & COO; RALPH RYDHOLM, mgr. partner, chief creative officer; JOHN J. VALVERDE, sr. partner, chief financial officer; PHILLIP GERBER, sr. partner, media opns. dir.; WERNER WOLFF, mgr. broadcast business affairs.

J. WALTER THOMPSON COMPANY, 466 Lexington Ave., New York, NY 10017; (212) 210-7000; FAX: (212) 210-7066.
BURT MANNING, chmn., CEO; BILL THOMPSON, vice chmn., client operations; PETER SCHWEITZER, vice chmn., agency operations (telephone Detroit 313-568-3800; FAX 313-567-0965); MARY CHURCHILL, dir. corporate communications.

J. Walter Thompson USA Inc., (subsidiary of J. Walter Thompson Co.) offices: Atlanta, Chicago, Detroit, Los Angeles, New York, San Francisco, Washington, DC.

Service offices: Charlotte, Dallas, Denver, Houston, Indianapolis, Kansas City, Memphis, New Jersey, New Orleans, Oklahoma City, Omaha, Philadelphia, Phoenix, Rochester, Salt Lake City, St. Louis.

J. Walter Thompson Co. International Offices: Asia/Pacific: Australia, Brisbane, Melbourne, Stepney, Subiaco, Sydney; Hong Kong; India, Bangalore, Bombay, Calcutta, Madras, New Delhi; Indonesia, Jakarta; Japan, Osaka, Tokyo; Korea, Seoul; Malaysia, Kuala Lumpur; New Zealand, Auckland, Wellington; Pakistan, Karachi; Philippines, Manila; Singapore; South Africa, Cape Town, Johannesburg; Sri Lanka, Colombo; Taiwan, Taipei; Thailand, Bangkok.

Europe: Austria, Vienna; Belgium, Brussels; Denmark, Copenhagen; Finland, Helsinki; France, Paris; Germany, Dusseldorf, Frankfurt, Hamburg; Greece, Athens; Italy, Milan, Rome; Netherlands, Amsterdam; Norway, Oslo; Portugal, Lisbon; Spain, Barcelona, Madrid; Sweden, Stockholm; Switzerland, Zurich; Turkey, Istanbul, Izmir; United Kingdom, London, Manchester.

Latin America: Argentina, Buenos Aires; Brazil, Rio de Janiero, São Paulo; Chile, Santiago; Colombia, Bogota; Dominican Republic, Santo Domingo; Ecuador, Guayaquil, Quito; Guatemala, Guatemala City; Mexico, Mexico City; Panama, El Dorado; Paraguay, Asuncion; Peru, Lima; Puerto Rico, San Juan; Uruguay, Montevideo; Venezuela, Caracas.

North America: Canada, Montreal, Toronto, Vancouver.

TRACY-LOCKE ADVERTISING INC., Plaza of the Americas, South Tower, P.O. Box 50129, Dallas, TX 75250; (214) 742-3131.
MORRIS HITE, bd. chmn.; NORM CAMPBELL, pres.; BOB BELTON, v.p. bdcst prod.; LARRY SPIEGEL, sr. v.p. dir. media & research; WALT ATKINSON, v.p., media serv. dir.; CLAUDE CAYLOR, v.p., media dir.; JUDY MILLER, v.p., media buying director; GINA BURKS, dir. of network; CAROL CASTELLANO, dir. of spot.

VAN BRUNT & CO., ADVERTISING-MARKETING INC., 300 E. 42 St., New York, NY 10017; (212) 949-1300.
EDWIN VAN BRUNT, chmn. bd.; ALBERT VAN BRUNT, pres.; WILLIAM BUCKLEY, dir. of broadcast.

VICTOR VAN DER LINDE CO., INC., 381 Broadway, Westwood, NJ 07675; (201) 664-6830.
A. K. KINGSLEY, v.p.

MORTON DENNIS WAX AND ASSOCIATES, 1560 Broadway, New York, NY 10036; (212) 302-5360
MORTON DENNIS WAX, pres.; SANDRA WAX, v.p./gen. mgr.

WILLIS/CASE/HARWOOD, INC., 3411 Office Park Drive, Dayton, OH 45439; (513) 299-7394.
MICHAEL G. HEALY, pres.; RONDA L. McCALL, broadcast producer.

YOUNG & RUBICAM INC., 285 Madison Ave., New York, NY 10017-6486; (212) 210-3000. This listing includes all offices of Young & Rubicam, its wholly owned subsidiary, Burson-Marsteller, and HDM, a joint venture between Young & Rubicam, Dentsu Inc., and Eurocom.
ALEXANDER S. KROLL, chmn. & CEO; PETER A. GEORGESCU, pres. Y&R advertising; R. JOHN COOPER, exec. v.p., general counsel; ROGER P. CRATON, exec. v.p., CFO; JOSEPH E. DE DEO, pres. Y&R Europe; JAMES H. DOWLING, pres. & CEO, Burson-Marsteller; ROBY HARRINGTON, exec. v.p., Major Markets Group (Detroit and San Francisco), chmn. National Group; ARTHUR R. KLEIN, pres. & CEO Y&RNY, pres. Direct Marketing Group; JAMES McCOUBREY, pres. Y&R Canada, area dir./Africa, Australia, New Zealand and Canada; JOHN P. McGARRY, chmn. Y&RNY, chmn. Client Services worldwide; TIM POLLAK, pres. & CEO, HDM; ALAN J. SHELDON, sr. v.p., Business Affairs worldwide; LARRY E. SNODDON, pres., Burson-Marsteler/Europe; HAROLD BURSON, chmn. Burson-Marsteller; LESTER WUNDERMAN, chmn. Wunderman Worldwide.
USA offices: Los Angeles and San Francisco, CA; Cedar Rapids & Des Moines, IA; Chicago, IL; Miami and Coral Springs, FL; Atlanta, GA; Cincinnati, OH; Denver, CO; Detroit, MI; New York, NY; Rochester, NY; Pittsburgh, PA; Washington, D.C.
International Offices: AFRICA: Cape Town and Johannesburg, South Africa; Harare, Zimbabwe; Lusaka, Zambia. AUSTRALIA/NEW ZEALAND: Adelaide, Brisbane, Canberra, Melbourne, Perth, Australia; Auckland, New Zealand. CANADA: Toronto, Montreal, Ottawa and Vancouver, Canada. EUROPE: Amsterdam, Rotterdam and The Hague, The Netherlands; Athens, Greece; Barcelona and Madrid, Spain; Brussels, Belgium; Copenhagen, Denmark; Frankfurt, Dusseldorf and Hamburg, Germany; Geneva and Zurich, Switzerland; Gothenburg and Stockholm, Sweden; Helsinki and Turku, Finland; Lisbon, Portugal; London and Belfast, United Kingdom; Milan, Turin and Rome, Italy; Oslo, Norway; Paris, France; Vienna, Austria; Istanbul, Turkey; Budapest, Hungary. LATIN AMERICA: Bogota and Cali, Colombia; Buenos Aires, Argentina; Caracas, Venezuela; Mexico City, Mexico; San Juan, Puerto Rico; Santiago, Chile; Santo Domingo, Dominican Republic; Sao Paolo, Brazil. ASIA PACIFIC: Bangkok, Thailand; Beijing and Shanghai, People's Republic of China; Bombay, India; Hong Kong; Jakarta, Indonesia; Kuala Lumpur, Malaysia; Manila, Philippines; Seoul, Korea; Taipei, Taiwan; Tokyo, Japan. SOVIET UNION: Moscow, USSR.

Station Representatives

AVERY-KNODEL TELEVISION, 437 Madison Ave., New York, NY 10022; (212) 421-5600.
J. W. KNODEL, chmn.; ROBERT J. KIZER, pres.; F. ROBERT KALTHOFF, exec. v.p.
Branch Offices: Chicago 60601, 2600 Prudential Plaza; (312) 467-6111, F. ROBERT KALTHOFF; San Francisco 94104, 155 Montgomery St.; (415) 986-8082, JOSEPH FRIEDMAN; Los Angeles 90005, 633 S. Shatto Place; (213) 385-6394; Atlanta 30326, 3340 Peachtree Road, N.E.; (404) 233-4474, JAMES GOSSETT; Dallas 75219, 3626 N. Hall St., Suite 608; (214) 528-1741 WALLIS S. IVY; Detroit, 48084, DAVID BRANGAN; St. Louis 63102, 410 Mansion House Center; (314) 241-5051, FRED W. JOHNSON; Minneapolis, St. Paul: toll free exchange, 929-1300, Edna, MN 55435, 6700 France Ave., Suite 155, MAUREEN KVAM; Denver 80206, 280 Columbine Ave.; (303) 321-1086, BOB HIX; Portland 97204, 620 SW 5th Suite 907; (503) 223-5980, RON HILLBURY; Seattle 98109, P.O. Box 19417; (206) 624-9200, JACK DAVIES; Haddonfield 08033, 537 Mt. Vernon Avenue, TOM WOOD.

BLAIR TELEVISION, 1290 Ave. of the Americas, New York, NY 10104; (212) 603-5000.
HARRY B. SMART, vice chmn. emeritus; TIMOTHY M. McAULIFF, pres. & COO; JAMES R. KELLY, sr. v.p./dir. of client services; WILLIAM E. BREDA, JR., sr. v.p./gen. sls. mgr.; FLOYD J. GELINI, sr. v.p./dir. of regional sls.; SANFORD S. ACKERMAN, sr. v.p./ dir. of finance/planning/admin.; JOHN B. POOR, JR.; sr. v.p./dir. of support services; STEVEN A. MURPHY, v.p./dir. of sales anal. & planning.
Branch Offices: Chicago, Atlanta, Boston, Charlotte, Cleveland, Dallas, Denver, Detroit, Houston, Jacksonville, Los Angeles, Miami, Minneapolis, Philadelphia, St. Louis, San Francisco, Seattle, Tampa.

CBS TELEVISION STATIONS NATIONAL SPOT SALES, 51 W. 52 St., New York, NY 10019; (212) 975-3647.
PHILIP PRESS, v.p. & gen. mgr., sls. & marketing; JIM CLAYTON, dir. natl. spot sls.; CARL MILLER, dir. eastern sls.; MELINDA DUCHAK, dir., research; GORDON HUGHES, v.p. marketing svcs.
Branch offices: Atlanta, 11 Piedmont Center, (404) 261-2227, JUDI PILLOW, mgr.; Boston, 218 Newbury St., 3rd Fl., (617) 262-7337, MGR., TBA; Chicago, 630 N. McClurg Ct., (312) 951-3391, PHILIP C. WATERMAN, JR., mgr.; Dallas, 545 East John Carpenter Frwy, Irving, (214) 556-1245, SANDY DELAUNAY, mgr.; Detroit, 26877 Northwestern Hwy, Southfield, (313) 351-2170, TOM CAPALDI, mgr.; Los Angeles, 6121 Sunset Blvd., (213) 460-3010, JULIE BALLARD, mgr.; San Francisco, One Embarcadero Center, (415) 765-4155, FRANK WHEELER, mgr.; Washington DC, 1800 M Street, NW, (202) 457-4509, SONJA MILLINER, mgr.

CC/ABC NATIONAL TELEVISION SALES, 77 W. 66 St., New York, NY 10023-6298; (212) 456-7777.
JOHN B. WATKINS, pres.; PHILIP J. SWEENIE, v.p.; ED PEARSON, gen. sls. mgr.; MICHAEL COLLERAN, dir. sls.-East; LARRY PRICE, dir. sls.-West.
Branch Offices: Chicago 60601, 190 N. State St., (312) 899-4200, SCOTT THOMAS, sls. mgr.; Los Angeles 90067, 2020 Ave. of Stars; (213) 557-6241, MICHAEL JACK; San Francisco 94111, 900 Front St.; (415) 954-7810, FRANKLIN LOWE; Southfield, MI (Detroit) 48075, 3000 Town Center, (313) 355-4490., JOE KREDER; Dallas 75251, 12222 Merit Dr.; (214) 960-7981, MICHAEL IRVINE; Atlanta, 30305, 3060 Peachtree Rd. NW, (404) 266-1750, DEBBIE SHAY; Boston, 02116, One Exeter Plaza, (617) 262-8989, TED RYAN; Charlotte, 28211, 6526 Morrison Blvd., (704) 364-6767, GERALYN STYNES; Philadelphia, 19131, 4100 City Line Ave., (215) 879-3100, BERNIE PRAZENICA; St. Louis, 63102, 10 South Broadway, (314) 231-6050, JERRY LYLES.

GROUP W TELEVISION SALES, 90 Park Ave., New York, NY 10016; (212) 883-6100.
EDWARD GOODMAN, pres.; JOEL SEGALL, senior v.p. & gen. sls. mgr.; GREG SCHAEFER, v.p. NY sales mgr.; BOB KAPLAN, group sales mgr.; KENT ATHERTON, natl sales mgr.; JEFF OSBORNE, v.p., admin. sls. & mktg.; ANTHONY DeTHOMAS, controller; JOSEPH PICCIRILLO, dir. research.
Branch offices: Atlanta, GA 30328, #2 Concourse Parkway; (404) 885-5336, CRAIG KOPPMANN; Boston, MA 02134, 1170 Soldiers Field Rd.; (617) 787-7220, DAVID BIGGS; Chicago, IL 60611, 625 N. Michigan Ave., Suite 400; (312) 454-6910, STEPHANIE LEVINE; Dallas, TX 75251, 12221 Merit Drive, Suite 620; (214) 458-9767, JERRY DANFORD; Detroit (Birmingham), MI 48010, 31000 Telegraph Rd., Suite 200; (313) 647-8960, ROBERT E. NEWSHAM; Los Angeles, CA 90048, 6500 Wilshire Blvd., Suite 1150; (213) 655-3556, ALAN BUCKMAN; Philadelphia, PA 19106, Independence Mall East; (215) 238-4966, THOMAS HOLLINGSHEAD; San Francisco, CA 94111, 825 Battery St.; (415) 765-8793, CHUCK PREWITY; Baltimore, MD 21211; 3725 Malden Ave., (301) 466-0013; Pittsburgh, PA 15222, 1 Gateway Center; (412) 392-2200, PHIL JOHNSON.

KATZ COMMUNICATIONS, INC., One Dag Hammarskjold Plaza, New York, NY 10017; (212) 572-5500.
JAMES L. GREENWALD, chmn., pres., CEO, COO; MICHAEL I. PACKMAN, sr. v.p., chief finan. officer; LUCILLE F. LUONGO, v.p. corp. relations.
KATZ TELEVISION GROUP: PETER GOULAZIAN, pres.; PAUL D. ARNZEN, sr. v.p., dir./new business; DICK WEINSTEIN, v.p./planning & development; JOHN VON SOOSTEN, v.p., dir./ programming; GEORGE FELDMAN, v.p., dir., management services/TV sls. research; LEN GRAZIANO, v.p., regional operations, MARK SHOTTLAND, v.p./special sls. projects.
KATZ AMERICAN TELEVISION: JAMES BELOYIANIS, pres., MICHAEL HUGGER, v.p., gen. sls. mgr., Red, Stars & Eagles; IBRA MORALES, v.p., gen. sls. mgr., White & Blue; KEITH GREEN, v.p., natl. sls. mgr., White; KEN PERREN, v.p., natl. sls. mgr., Blue; JOHN SHANNON, v.p., natl. sls. mgr., Red; SWAIN WEINER, v.p., natl. sls. mgr., Eagles; RUSS WHITE, v.p., natl. sls. mgr., Stars and office mgr.; BOB SCUTARI, mgr., Red; FRANK QUAGLIARIELLO, mgr., White; JOHN ROSSI, mgr., Stars; JONATHON SMITH, mgr., Eagles; JAY ZEITCHIK, v.p., mgr., Blue; BILL CARROLL, v.p., dir., programming; CHICKIE BUCCO, v.p., dir., direct response advertising; LISA SCHOENBACK, v.p., dir., sls. research; DONNA MOREAU-CUPP, assoc. dir., natl. sls. development.
KATZ CONTINENTAL TELEVISION: THOMAS OLSON, pres.; JACK HIGGINS, v.p., gen. mgr.; ARDIE BIALEK, v.p., natl. sls. mgr., West; JERRY CIFARELLI, v.p., natl. sls. mgr., East; JAY FRIESEL, v.p., natl. sls. mgr., Southeast; BOB SWAN, v.p., natl. sls. mgr., East Central; JOHN WALL, v.p., natl. sls. mgr., West Central; MAURY WIND, v.p., natl. sls. mgr., South Central; CHRIS JORDAN, v.p., mgr., East; MARK RYAN, v.p., mgr., West; GREGG ROBINSON, mgr., South Central; MICHAEL SPIESMAN, v.p., mgr., South East; MARGARET TJEPKEMA, v.p., mgr., East Central; MITCHELL PRAVER, v.p., dir., programming; CHICKIE BUCCO, v.p., dir., direct response advertising; MICHAEL STEINBERG, v.p., dir., sls research.
KATZ HISPANIC TELEVISION SALES: JOHN CUDDIHY, dir.
KATZ INDEPENDENT TELEVISION: MARTY OZER, pres.; MICKEY COLEN, v.p., regional sls. mgr.; PAT GARVEY, v.p., natl. sls. mgr., Lancers; MICHAEL RAOUNAS, v.p., natl. sls. mgr., Sabers; STUART ZUCKERMAN, v.p., natl. sls. mgr., Swords; JOE WHITE, v.p., natl. mgr., Swords; ANDI POCH, v.p., dir., sports and special sls., BOB EINHORN, v.p., dir., sls. research; DONNA FEE, dir., marketing.

MMT SALES, INC., 150 E. 52 St., New York, NY 10022; (212) 391-8008.
GARRY SCOLLARD, chmn.; NEIL KENNEDY, exec. v.p.; JACK OKEN, pres.; ROGER GOLDHAMER, sr. v.p., dir. natl. sls.; TED VAN ERK, v.p. dir. sls.; ELAINE LINKER, v.p. dir. sls.; JON GLUCK, v.p. dir. prog.; AL CANNARELLA, v.p., dir. rsch.
Branch offices in Atlanta, Boston, Charlotte, Chicago, Cleveland, Dallas, Detroit, Los Angeles, Miami, Minneapolis, Philadelphia, St. Louis, San Francisco, Seattle.

ART MOORE INC., 220 W. Mercer, Seattle, WA 98119; (206) 282-3400.
GREG SMITH, EARLE BAKER, SANDY RUNNION, RICK STAEB, RUTH HALLETT. Branch: Portland, OR 97214, 516 S.E. Morrison; (503) 228-2451, DARRELL RUTTER, BRUCE WORKMAN, TEDDI JONES, LYNN THORSEN.

NBC SPOT TELEVISION SALES, NATIONAL BROADCASTING COMPANY, INC., 30 Rockefeller Plaza, New York, NY 10020 (212) 664-4444.
BUD HIRSCH, v.p., sls. & marketing; JIM ZAFIROS, v.p., spot sls.; JAY LINDEN, dir. spot sls; JOE FRISCHER, Eastern sls. mgr.

NATIONAL TIME SALES, 9 E. 41 St., New York, NY 10016; (212) 661-6550.
H. FRANKLIN, sales mgr.
Branch offices: Chicago, 60645, 3322 W. Peterson Ave.; (312) 478-5544, HOOPER JONES; Atlanta, 30309, 1819 Peachtree Rd. N.E.; (404) 355-7961, BERNARD OCHS; Dallas, 75202, 1407 Main St.; (214) 748-2172, JACK RILEY; San Francisco, 94133, 559 Pacific Ave.; SAM POSNER; Beverly Hills, 90028, 111 N. La Cienega Blvd.; CHUCK DWYER; San Jose, 95129, 4320 Stevens Creek Blvd.; (408) 249-5287, GENE BERNALD.

THE BERNARD I. OCHS CO., 805 Longleaf Dr., N.E., Atlanta, GA 30342 (404) 262-1200.
BARNEY OCHS; PAT CASTLEBERRY, sec.

PETRY TELEVISION, INC., 3 E. 54th St., New York, NY 10022; (212) 688-0200.
PETRY INC.: DAVID S. ALLEN, president; C.W. SCHELLENGER, sr. v.p., finance & administration; HARRY STECKER, exec. vice pres., dir. of client services; JOHN SCOGNAMILLO, vice pres., controller; TOM BELVISO, vice pres., sales administration, regional office; WILLIAM WIEHE, vice pres., The Petry Marketing Group; GEORGE DENNIS, v.p., director of manpower dev.; MARIE IMBESI- CHIECA, v.p., dir. of personnel.
PETRY TELEVISION: WILLIAM FAGAN, pres.; George Blinn, sr. v.p., gen. sls. manager; JERRY LINEHAN, v.p., director of sls.; STEVE EISENBERG, v.p., dir. of sls.; ROBERT MIGGINS, v.p., regional area (West Coast); GREG MOLOZNIK, v.p., regional area mgr. (Midwest); PAT McNEW, v.p., regional area mgr. (North); LAVERNE COLE, v.p., regional area mgr. (South); TEDDY S. REYNOLDS, v.p., Director of Research; NEIL HITZIG, national sales director, The Petry Marketing Group; RICHARD KURLANDER, v.p., director of programming; RONALD MARTZOLF, director of programming; KEVIN NUGENT, v.p., group sales mgr., FALCONS; BILL SHAW, v.p., group sls. mgr., HAWKS; ROB FRIEDMAN, v.p., group sls. mgr., ROADRUNNERS; RICHARD LARCADE, v.p., group sales mgr., RAVENS; DONALD O'TOOLE, v.p., group sales mgr., THUNDERBIRDS.
PETRY NATIONAL: MICHAEL T. MEMBRADO, pres.; JOHN I. HEISE, senior v.p., gen. sales mgr.; PAUL MORRISSEY, v.p., dir. of sales; ROBERT HEBENSTREIT, v.p., dir. of research; JACK FENTRESS, v.p., dir. of programming; RONALD MARTZOLF, dir. of programming; JOSEPH LYONS, v.p., group sales mgr, RED; CHUCK HANRAHAN, v.p., group sales mgr., WHITE; RICHARD STEIN, group sls. mgr., BLUE; BILL HAHN, group sales mgr, GREEN; NEIL HITZIG, national sales director, The Petry Marketing Group.
BRANCH OFFICES: CHICAGO: 410 Michigan Ave., Suite 1180, 60611; Greg Moloznick, v.p., regional area mgr. (Midwest); James Ottolin, v.p., group sls. mgr., RED; Stewart Strizak, group sls. mgr., BLUE; Kent Francis, dir. of agri-marketing; Bill Carney, v.p., group sls. mgr., CHARGERS; Lynn Evans, group mgr., MUSTANGS; Stu Lutz, v.p., grp. mgr., BRONCOS; LOS ANGELES: 8383 Wilshire Blvd., Suite 626, Beverly Hills, CA 90211; Robert Miggins, v.p., dir. of West Coast Operations; Jim Valice, group sls. mgr., RED; Eleanor Gottleib, group sls. mgr., BLUE; Jack Devine, v.p., group mgr., COMETS; Jim Baral, group mgr, METEORS; ATLANTA, 950 E. Paces Ferry Rd., Suite 2940, Atlanta, GA 30326, Val Napolitano, v.p., sales mgr.; Chris Teter, group sls. mgr.; BOSTON, 419 Boylston St., Boston, MA 02116; Diane Gosdanian, v.p., sls. mgr.; M.P. Kelleher, group mgr.; CHARLOTTE: Two Fairview Plaza, 5950 Fairview Rd., Suite 804, Charlotte, NC 28210; Stockton Holt, sls. mgr.; CLEVELAND: 1111 Superior Ave., Suite 7A, Cleveland, OH 44114, Roger Stepic; DALLAS: 3811 Turtle Creek Blvd., Suite 520, Dallas, TX 75219; Laverne Cole, v.p., regional area mgr. (South); Cliffe Hahne, mgr.; DENVER: 6025 South Quebec, Suite 250, Englewood, CO 80111; Tony Kirk, mgr.; DETROIT, 3221 W. Big Beaver Rd., Suite 102, Troy, MI 48084; Patrick McNew, v.p., regional area mgr., (North); Kevin Moylan, v.p. group mgr; Carol Charron, group mgr.; HOUSTON: 3000 Post Oak Blvd., Suite 1590, Houston, TX 77056; Chuck Sitta, mgr.; MINNEAPOLIS: 706 Second Ave. S., Minneapolis, MN 55402; Tom Vannelli, mgr.; PHILADELPHIA: Two Penn Center Plaza, Suite 406, Philadelphia, PA 19102; Dave Bell, v.p. mgr.; ST. LOUIS, Ten South Broadway, Suite 525, St. Louis, MO 63102; Bruce Farber; SAN FRANCISCO: 909 Montgomery St., Suite 402, San Francisco, CA 94133, Don Brownstein, v.p. mgr.; SEATTLE, 2001 6th Ave., 1600 Westin Bldg., Seattle, WA 98121; Marc F. Maehl, mgr.; TAMPA/ST. PETERSBURG: 9800 Fourth St. N., Suite 108, St. Petersburg, FL 33702; Judy Obernier, mgr.

RADIO-TELEVISION REPRESENTATIVES LIMITED, 10 Price St., Toronto, Ont. M4W 1Z4; (416) 962-3221. FAX: (416) 962-1162.
ROBERT H. QUINN, pres. & gen. mgr.; R.R. LUCAS, v.p./tv sls. mgr.
Branch offices: Calgary: 300 5th Ave., S.W. Suite 2050, Calgary, Alta. T2P 3C4; Mark Simpson (403) 269-3496, FAX: (403) 265-6523; Vancouver: 999 W. Broadway, Vancouver, B.C. V5Z 1K5; (604) 736-6634, FAX: (604) 736-8059; FRANK JOBES; Winnipeg: 305-326 Broadway Ave., Winnipeg, Man. R3C 0S5; (204) 943-9574, FAX: (204) 943-6016; HENRY BOSCHMAN.

SELTEL, INC., 575 Fifth Ave., New York, NY 10017; (212) 370-4100. TWX: 710-581-6768; FAX: (212) 983-3481; (212) 687-2430; (212) 687-2649.
RAYMOND J. JOHNS, pres. & COO; STEVE BOUTIS, SR., v.p, finance; DAVID SCHWARTZ, sr. v.p., domestic sls.; JAMES P. MURTAGH, sr. v.p./marketing; CARL MATHIS, v.p./gen. mgr.; DAN PARISI, v.p./natl. sls. mgr., Indy-Raiders Team; MICHAEL RIX, natl. sls. mgr., Indy-Rockets Team; ROSEMARIE FERRARA, natl. sls. mgr., Indy-Rangers Team; GENE THOMPSON, natl. sls. mgr., Indy-Rebels Team; JUDY KLEINBERGER, natl. sls. mgr., Affiliate-White Team; PETER PENNI, natl. sls. mgr., Affiliate-Red Team; JANEEN BJORK, v.p./dir. of programming; PAULA DOPSCH, dir. of research.
Chicago: 211 E. Ontario, Suite 700, Chicago, IL 60611; (312) 642-2450. TWX: 910-221-0241, 0242, 5195. FAX: (312) 642-1631.
Atlanta: 1819 Peachtree Rd., N.E., Suite 600, Atlanta, GA 30309-1819; (404) 355-7701. TWX: 810-751-3103. FAX: (404) 352-5537. DAN GRIFFIN, gen. mgr.
Boston: 545 Boylston St., 7th floor, Boston, MA 02116; (617) 236-8666. TWX: 710-321-0016. FAX: (617) 236-4927. PETER DURAN, gen. mgr.
Charlotte: 5821 Park Rd., Suite 112, Charlotte, NC 28209; (704) 554-7124. TWX: 810-621-7832. SUZY PLETTNER, gen. mgr.
Dallas: 3010 LBJ Freeway, Suite 1130, Dallas, TX 75234; (214) 484-4871.. TWX: 910-861-4210. FAX: (214) 484-7980. STEVE HENDERSON, gen. mgr.
Denver: 222 Milwaukee St., Suite 210, Denver, CO 80206; (303) 333-4845. Telex: 100-230-450296. FAX: (303) 321-1087. CHRIS MATTHEWS, gen. mgr.
Detroit: 26211 Central Park Blvd., Suite 202, Southfield, MI 48076-4107; (313) 354-3611. TWX: 810-224-4502. FAX: (313) 354-2405. JESS CHALKER, gen., mgr.
Houston: 4848 Loop Central Dr., Suite 710, Houston, TX 77081. (713) 660-8881. TWX: 910-881-0063. STEVE GELTMAN, gen. mgr.
Los Angeles: 5757 Wilshire Blvd., Suite #1, Los Angeles, CA 90036; (213) 930-2450. TWX: 910-321-4124. FAX: (213) 931-2561; (213) 931-0567. LaVADA HEATH, gen. mgr.; DAVE WARE, sls. mgr. Indy-Raiders; VICTORIA GOLD, sls. mgr. Indy-Rangers; JUDY GRAGG, sls. mgr. Affiliate Red; RALPH CLAUSSEN, sls. mgr. Affiliate White.
Miami: 6101 Blue Lagoon Dr., Suite 460, Miami, FL 33126; (305) 266-4066. TWX: 810-848-0197. ENID BLUESTONE, gen. mgr.
Minneapolis: 625 Second Ave. South, Suite 408, Minneapolis, MN 55402; (612) 338-7017. TWX: 910-576-3419. MIKE CLEARY, gen. mgr.
Philadelphia: 1411 Walnut St., Suite 1125, Philadelphia, PA 19103; (215) 563-5400. TWX: 710-670-1017. FAX: (215) 563-2974. RICKIE ELLIS, gen. mgr.
Portland: 1512 S.W. 18th Ave., Portland, OR 97201; (503) 226-2911. EASY LINK: 629-275-56+. FAX: (503) 226-6596. RICHARD GOHLMAN, gen. mgr.
St. Louis: St. Louis Place, 200 N. Broadway, Suite 1125, St. Louis, MO 63102; (314) 241-4193. TWX: 910-761-0400. FAX: (314) 241-9849. RICHARD J. QUIGLEY III, gen. mgr.
San Francisco: 50 Francisco St., San Francisco, CA 94133; (415) 391-8890. TWX: 910-372-7361. FAX: (415) 391-4252, JOSEPH PEDRI, gen. mgr.
Seattle: 701 Dexter Ave., North, Suite 216, Seattle, WA 98109; (206) 285-1913. EASY LINK: 627-625-31. FAX: (206) 281-4178. BOB TACHER, gen. mgr.

STAUFFER COMMUNICATIONS, INC., 100% owner of WIBW-TV, Box 119, Topeka, KA 66601; (913) 272-3456.
GEORGE LOGAN, TV gen. mgr.; VINCE FRYE, natl. sales mgr. (and gsm.) Represented nationally by Blair, New York, Chicago, Dallas, Detroit, Atlanta, San Francisco, Los Angeles, Seattle, Charlotte, Cleveland, Memphis, Portland, Boston, Jacksonville, Minneapolis, St. Louis, Philadelphia.

STORER TELEVISION SALES, INC., 800 Third Ave., New York, NY 10022; (212) 935-6000.
FRANCIS BARRON, pres.; PETER E. MURRAY, exec. v.p., sales; PETER STORER, JR., research director.
Branch Offices: Chicago: 410 No. Michigan Ave., (312) 329-1930; CHARLES LIEBER, v.p., Midwest sales; Detroit: Number Two Storer Place, (313) 557-0300; ELAINE CARPENTER, Det. sls. mgr.; Atlanta: Three Piedmont Ctr., (404) 233-9935; RICHARD GOLDSTEIN, Southern sls. mgr.; San Francisco: 150 Lombard Street, (415) 981-8860, SHAWN McGREEVY, v.p., S.F. sls.; Los Angeles, 6420 Wilshire Blvd., (213) 651-0841, JOSEPH MERTENS, v.p., West Coast sls.

TELEREP, INC., 875 Third Ave., New York, NY 10022; (212) 759-8787.
ALFRED M. MASINI, pres. & gen. mgr.; STEVEN HERSON, v.p., dir. opns.; LARRY GOLDBERG, v.p., gen. sls. mgr., COUGAR STNS.; THOMAS BELVISO, v.p., gen. sls. mgr., TIGER STNS.; THOMAS TILSON, v.p., gen. sls. mgr. JAGUAR STNS.; SUSAN ZILLER BRAZELL, v.p., sls., LION STNS.
Branches in Atlanta, Chicago, Detroit, Los Angeles, Minneapolis, St. Louis, San Francisco, Philadelphia, Boston, Dallas, Cleveland, Houston, Memphis, Miami, Charlotte, Seattle.

ADAM YOUNG, INC., 3 E. 54 St., New York, NY 10022; (212) 688-5100. TWX: 710-581-3696. FAX: (212) 758-5090.
ADAM YOUNG, chmn. of the bd.; VINCENT J. YOUNG, pres.; ARTHUR W. SCOTT JR., exec. v.p./gen'l sales mgr.; MARIANNE O'LEARY, mgr., research & programming services; JOHN J. SCOTT, v.p./marketing dir.
Branch Offices: ATLANTA: 2 Piedmont Center, Suite 506, Atlanta, GA 30305; (404) 261-8800. TWX: 810-751-0057. FAX: (404) 261-8800. TOM DURR, mgr.; BOSTON: MICHAEL KRONENFELD, account exec.; (212) 688-5100. FAX: (212) 758-5090. CHICAGO: 444 N. Michigan Ave., Suite 920, Chicago, IL 60611; (312) 744-1313. TWX: 910-221-1191. FAX: (312) 744-0196. LOIS HAME-

LIN, mgr.; DALLAS: 1701 N. Market St., Suite 205, Dallas, TX 75202; (214) 748-2660. TWX: 910-861-0089; SUSAN WAGNER, mgr.; DENVER: 449 Grape St., Denver, CO 80220 (303) 377-1400; BOB HIX, mgr.; DETROIT: 2855 Coolidge, Suite 222, Troy, MI 48084; (313) 649-3999. Easylink: 62872846. FAX: (313) 649-6455. ALLAN BAUR, mgr.; LOS ANGELES: 6100 Wilshire Blvd., Suite 320, Los Angeles, CA 90048; (213) 938-2081. TWX: 910-321-2897. FAX: (213) 938-1483. STEVEN A. BAXTER, sls. mgr.; MINNEAPOLIS: 630 Baker Bldg., Minneapolis, MN 55402; (612) 339-3397. Easylink: 62615840. FAX: (612) 339-7182. JAMES O. RAMSLAND, mgr.; PHILADELPHIA & PITTSBURGH: Contact DONALD O'KEEFE, account exec.; (212) 688-5100. FAX: (212) 758-5090; ST. LOUIS: Box 50269, St. Louis, MO 63105; (314) 991-5249. TWX: 910-761-1145; BRUCE SCHNEIDER, mgr.; SAN FRANCISCO: 155 Montgomery St., Ste. 406, San Francisco, CA 94104; (415) 986-5366. TWX: 910-372-6010. FAX: (415) 986-0224. CHRISTINE PYNE/ROBERT TRYCE, acct. execs.

Television Organizations

- NATIONAL GROUPS
- REGIONAL UNITS
- GUILDS AND UNIONS

Organizations

Academy of Television Arts and Sciences

3500 W. Olive Ave., Suite 700, Burbank, CA 91505; (818) 953-7575. (Formed in 1948 to advance the arts and sciences of television.) Awards Emmys for nighttime programming and publishes Emmy Magazine, Hank Rieger, editor.

PRESIDENT
Doug Duitsman
FIRST VICE PRESIDENT
Leo Chaloukian
SECOND VICE PRESIDENT
Jan Scott
VICE PRESIDENT, LOS ANGELES
Jay Strong
SECRETARY
Susan Simons
TREASURER
Stu Berg
IMMEDIATE PAST PRESIDENT
Richard H. Frank
EXECUTIVE DIRECTOR
James Loper
CHIEF FINANCIAL OFFICER
John Macker
AWARDS DIRECTOR
John Leverence
BOARD OF GOVERNORS
Dorothy Andre, Loreen J. Arbus, Linda S. Arett, Curt Behlmer, Stuart H. Berg, Fred W. Berger, Sandra Bettin, Harry C. Blake, Mel D. Blumenthal, Daniel R. Brewes, Robert A. Broder, Fred Brooks, Bruce Bryant, Dan A. Carin, Carole B. Cartwright, Clifford B. Chally, Fred A. Chuck, Robert Crutchfield, Marc Daniels, Pamela Dawson, Clifford Dektar, Ron Estes, Lance Moore Evans, Jon H. Feltheimer, Preston Fischer, Ian Fraser, Mike Gavin, John Gay, David Graham, Douglas H. Grindstaff, Robin B. Groth, Romain Johnston, Alfred E. Lehman, Sydney Z. Litwack, Anthony J. Magliocco, Jim Malinda, Michael D. Margulies, Barry Meyer, Arthur H. Nadel, Meryl O'Loughlin, Richard L. Rawlings, Phil Roman, Stuart M. Rosen, Alexander Singer, Jerry R. Smith, Morton Stevens, Don Tillman, Winifred White, Nancy B. Wiard, Donald L. Zachary

Actor's Equity Association (AAAA-AFL-CIO-CLC)

(Organized May 16, 1913; Membership, 38,000) 165 W. 46 St., New York, NY 10036, (212) 869-8530.

PRESIDENT
Colleen Dewhurst
FIRST VICE-PRESIDENT
Patrick Quinn
SECOND VICE-PRESIDENT
Mary Lou Westerfeld
THIRD VICE-PRESIDENT
Arne Gundersen
FOURTH VICE PRESIDENT
Werner Klemperer
TREASURER
Conrad Fowkes
RECORDING SECRETARY
Lynn Archer
EXECUTIVE SECRETARY
Alan Eisenberg
EXECUTIVE CONSULTANT
Willard Swire
COUNSEL
Cohn, Glickstein, Lurie
MIDWEST REGIONAL V.P.
Madeleine Fallon
WESTERN REGIONAL V.P.
Joseph Ruskin

Advertising Council, The

825 Third Ave., New York, NY 10022; (212) 758-0400.

CHAIRMAN
Ira C. Herbert
PRESIDENT
Ruth A. Wooden
SENIOR VICE PRESIDENT, MEDIA
Nancy P. Clott
SENIOR VICE PRESIDENT, FINANCIAL DEVELOPMENT
Jane K. Dean
SENIOR VICE PRESIDENT, CAMPAIGN ADMINISTRATION
Elenore Hangley
EDITOR, PUBLIC SERVICE ADVERTISING BULLETIN
Sara Stern
SENIOR VICE PRESIDENT OF PUBLIC AFFAIRS
Eva N. Kasten
BRANCH OFFICES
The Advertising Council, 1717 N. Highland Ave., Los Angeles, CA; The Advertising Council, 1930 Rhode Island Ave., N.W., Washington, DC 20036.

Advertising Research Foundation

3 E. 54 St., New York, NY 10022; (212) 751-5656.

CHAIRMAN
John C. Webber
VICE CHAIRMAN
David F. Poltrack
PRESIDENT
Michael J. Naples
SENIOR VICE PRESIDENT, DIRECTOR OF OPERATIONS
James H. Moore
SENIOR VICE PRESIDENT, MEDIA RESEARCH
Lawrence R. Stoddard
SECRETARY
Tod Johnson
GENERAL COUNSEL
Gilbert H. Weil

Alliance of Motion Picture and Television Producers

(Membership: Major studios, independent production companies, and film processing laboratories) 14144 Ventura Blvd., 3rd floor, Sherman Oaks, CA 91423; (818) 995-3600.

PRESIDENT
J. Nicholas Counter III
VICE PRESIDENT-LEGAL AFFAIRS
Carol A. Lombardini
VICE PRESIDENT-CONTRACT ADMINISTRATION
Paul A. Westefer
CHIEF FINANCIAL OFFICER
Kathy Grotticelli

American Advertising Federation

1400 K St., NW, Suite 1000, Washington, DC 20005; (202) 898-0089.

CHAIRMAN OF THE BOARD
David Bell
PRESIDENT
Howard H. Bell

American Association of Advertising Agencies

666 Third Ave., New York, NY 10017; (212) 682-2500.

CHAIRMAN OF THE BOARD
Glen W. Fortinberry, Ross Roy Group, Bloomfield Hills, MI
VICE CHAIRMAN
Keith Reinhard, DDB, Needham Worldwide, New York

SECRETARY-TREASURER
Leonard Pearlstein, Keye/Donna/Pearlstein, Los Angeles
PRESIDENT
John E. O'Toole, A.A.A.A., New York
WASHINGTON REPRESENTATIVE
Hal Shoup, Executive Vice President
WESTERN OFFICE REPRESENTATIVE
Robert P. Stephens, Vice President, Beverly Hills, CA
EXECUTIVE VICE PRESIDENT
Harry Paster
CHAIRMAN OF OPERATIONS
O. Burtch Drake
SENIOR VICE PRESIDENTS
Tony Gruber, Marilyn Bockman, Donald C. Lewis, Donald Ambuhl, Bernard Ryan, James C. Martucci Jr.
VICE PRESIDENT
Robert J. Finn

American Cinema Editors

(Organized November 28, 1950; Membership: 2500) 2410 Beverly Blvd., #1, Los Angeles, CA 90057; (213) 660-4425.

PRESIDENT
George Grenville
VICE PRESIDENT
Bernard Balmuth
SECRETARY
George Hively
TREASURER
Les Green
EXECUTIVE DIRECTOR
Ruth Oreck
BOARD OF DIRECTORS
Jeanene Ambler, Edward M. Abroms, Bob Bring, Byron "Buzz" Brandt, Doug Ibold, Frederic L. Knudtson, Millie Moore.

American Federation of Musicians (AFL-CIO)

(Organized October, 1896; Membership: 280,000) Suite 600, Paramount Bldg., 1501 Broadway, New York, NY 10036; (212) 869-1330; FAX:(212) 489-0871.

PRESIDENT
J. Martin Emerson, Suite 600, Paramount Bldg., 1501 Broadway, New York, NY 10036; (212) 869-1330.
VICE PRESIDENT
Mark Tully Massagli, 5020 Stacey Ave., Las Vegas, NV 89108.
CANADA VICE PRESIDENT
J. Alan Wood, 75 The Donway West, Suite 1010, Don Mills, Ont., Canada M3C 2E9.
SECRETARY-TREASURER
Kelly L. Castleberry II, Suite 600, Paramount Bldg.,1501 Broadway, New York, NY 10036.
EXECUTIVE BOARD
Eugene Frey, Bob D'Arcy, Richard Q. Totusek, Ray Hair, Steve Young.
PRESIDENT EMERITUS
Victor W. Fuentealba

American Federation of Television and Radio Artists (AAAA-AFL-CIO)

(Organized August, 1937; Membership 72,000) 260 Madison Ave., 7th Fl., New York, NY 10016; (212) 532-0800.

PRESIDENT
Reed Ferrell
FIRST VICE PRESIDENT
Jackson Beck
SECOND VICE PRESIDENT
Denny Delk
VICE PRESIDENTS
Marvin Kaplan, Lois Davis, Belva Davis, Bob Edwards, Jim Ferguson, Margie Ghigo, Mel Alpern.
TREASURER
Kenneth Roberts
RECORDING SECRETARY
Fred Anderson
NATIONAL EXECUTIVE DIRECTOR
John C. Hall Jr.
DIRECTOR, CENTRAL REGION
Herbert Neuer
DIRECTOR, WESTERN REGION
Donald S. Tayer
DIRECTOR, EASTERN REGION
Dan Mallinger
CONTROLLER
Bill Herman
NATIONAL REPRESENTATIVES
Walter Grinspan, Louis Santillana, Jr.

American Guild of Musical Artists (AFL-CIO), Branch of Associated Actors and Artistes of America

(Organized 1936; Membership 5,500) 1727 Broadway, New York, NY 10019-5214; (212) 265-3687; FAX: (212) 262-9088.

PRESIDENT
Nedda Casei
FIRST VICE PRESIDENT
Eileen Schauler
SECOND VICE PRESIDENT
Chester Ludgin
THIRD VICE PRESIDENT
Eugene Lawrence
FOURTH VICE PRESIDENT
Barbara Bystrom
FIFTH VICE PRESIDENT
Pamela Smith
TREASURER
Lawrence Davidson
RECORDING SECRETARY
Yolanda Antoine
NATIONAL EXECUTIVE SECRETARY
Gene Boucher
ASSOCIATE NATIONAL EXECUTIVE SECRETARY
Alan Olsen
ASSISTANTS TO THE EXECUTIVE SECRETARY
Thomas Jamerson, Alexander Dubé
COUNSEL
Becker, London, Kossow & Jaffe
DIRECTOR OF MEMBERSHIP
Annelise Kamada
FINANCIAL SECRETARY
Grace Pedro
DIRECTOR OF PUBLIC RELATIONS
Michael Rubino
CANADA: Graham Spicer, 260 Richmond St. E, Toronto, Ontario M5A 1P4, (416) 867-9156; CHICAGO: Barbara J. Hillman, Cornfield & Feldman, 343 S. Dearborn St., 13th Fl., Chicago, IL 60604, (312) 922-2800; LOS ANGELES: Dennis Moss, 12650 Riverside Dr., Suite 205, North Hollywood, CA 91607, (213) 877-0683; NEW ENGLAND: Robert M. Segal, 11 Beacon St., Boston, MA 02108, (617) 742-0208; NEW ORLEANS: Rosemary Le Boeuf, 619 N. Hennessy, New Orleans, LA, (504) 486-9410; NORTHWEST: Carolyn Carpp, 5051 148 Ave., NE, J201, Bellevue, WA 98007, (206) 881-7235; PHILADELPHIA: Mark P. Muller, Lafayette Bldg., 8th floor, 5th and Chestnut St., Philadelphia, PA 19106, (215) 925-8400; SAN FRANCISCO: Harry Polland, Donald Tayer, Ann Sebastian, 100 Bush St., Suite 1500, San Francisco, CA 94104, (415) 986-4060; TEXAS: Benny Hopper, 3915 Fairlakes Dr., Dallas, TX 75228, (214) 279-4720; WASHINGTON/BALTIMORE: Joshua J. Kaufman, 918 16th St., NW, Suite 503, Washington, DC 20006, (202) 466-3030.

American Guild of Variety Artists (AAAA-AFL-CIO)

(Organized July 14, 1939; Registered Membership: 78,000; Active Membership: 5,000) 184 Fifth Ave., New York, NY 10010; (212) 675-1003.

HONORARY PRESIDENT
George Burns
HONORARY FIRST VICE PRESIDENT
Rip Taylor
HONORARY SECOND VICE PRESIDENT
Johnny Miles
HONORARY THIRD VICE PRESIDENT
Gloria DeHaven

PRESIDENT
Rod McKuen
EXECUTIVE VICE PRESIDENT
Eileen Collins
SECRETARY & TREASURER
Frances Gaar
REGIONAL VICE PRESIDENTS
Leigh Catlett, Ron Chisholm, Doris George, Wayne Hermans, Elaine Jacovini-Gonella, Eddy Lane, Tina Marie, Angela Martin, Thomas Merriweather, Don Phillips, Susan Streater, Carol Toman-Paracat, Roie Ward.

American Humane Association

(Organized 1877) Hollywood office: 14144 Ventura Blvd., Sherman Oaks, CA 91423; (818) 501-0123; National Headquarters: 9725 E. Hampden, Denver, CO 80231; (303) 695-0811. (Liaison with the television and motion picture industry as supervisors of the use of animals in television and motion picture production.)

NATIONAL PRESIDENT
Donald Anthony
VICE PRESIDENT
Hortense Landau
TREASURER
Charles W. Ennis
DIRECTOR—L.A. REGIONAL OFFICE
Betty Denny Smith

American Society of Cinematographers, Inc.

(Organized 1919; Membership: 286) 1782 N. Orange Dr., Hollywood, CA 90028; (213) 876-5080.

PRESIDENT
Leonard South
FIRST VICE PRESIDENT
Victor Kemper
SECOND VICE PRESIDENT
Charles Wheeler
THIRD VICE PRESIDENT
Joseph Westheimer
SECRETARY
Alfred Keller
TREASURER
Harry Wolf
CHIEF EXECUTIVE OFFICER
Dan Ross

American Society of Composers, Authors and Publishers (ASCAP)

(Organized February 13, 1914; Membership: 30,400 Writers, 12,900 Publishers) One Lincoln Plaza, New York, NY 10023; (212) 595-3050; 6430 Sunset Blvd., Hollywood, CA 90028; (213) 466-7681.

PRESIDENT
Morton Gould
VICE PRESIDENTS
Sammy Cahn, Sid Herman
SECRETARY
Arthur Hamilton
TREASURER
Leon J. Brettler
ASSISTANT SECRETARY
Elie Siegmeister
ASSISTANT TREASURER
Arnold Broido
COUNSEL
Bernard Korman
MANAGING DIRECTOR
Gloria Messinger
WESTERN REGIONAL DIRECTOR
Todd Brabec, ASCAP, 6430 Sunset Blvd., Hollywood, CA 90028
SOUTHERN REGIONAL EXECUTIVE DIRECTOR
Connie Bradley, ASCAP, 2 Music Square W., Nashville, TN 37203

Asian Cinevision, Inc.

32 East Broadway, New York, NY; (212) 925-8685. (A not-for-profit organization dedicated to encouraging the creation and presentation of Asian and Asian American media arts. Current programs include film festival exhibitions; media services (information and referral); archive library; publications; production services; video documentation editing, duplication, transfer screening.)

Associated Actors and Artistes of America (AAAA-AFL-CIO)

(Organized July 18, 1919; Membership: 85,000) 165 W. 46 St., New York, NY 10036; (212) 869-0358.

PRESIDENT
Theodore Bikel
VICE PRESIDENTS
Ken Orsatti, Sanford I. Wolff, Jack Rechtzeit, Rod McKuen
TREASURER
Willard Swire
EXECUTIVE SECRETARY
John C. Hall, Jr.
AFFILIATES
Actors' Equity Association, American Federation of Television and Radio Artists, American Guild of Musical Artists, American Guild of Variety Artists, Asociacion Puertorrique/tna de Artistas y Tecnicos del Espectaculo, Hebrew Actors Union, Italian Actors Union, Screen Actors Guild, Screen Extras Guild.

Association of Independent Commercial Producers

P.O. Box 2007, San Francisco, CA 94126-2007; (415) 771-6268. Organized 1972. (Seeks to improve the dialogue and working relationship between clients and the commercial production industry.)

PRESIDENT
Ron Lakis (Starrion Productions)
VICE PRESIDENTS
John Arnold (Arnold & Associates)
Robert Gondell (Group One)
SECRETARY/TREASURER
Roy Diner (Diner & Allied Film & Video Services)
VICE PRESIDENT ASSOC.
Debora Robins (San Francisco Production Group)
Shirley Bossier (CineRent West)
BOARD OF DIRECTORS
Ron Lakis, Robert Gondell, Roy Diner, John Arnold, Debora Robins, Shirley Bossier
BRANCHES
National—New York; Chicago, Denver, Miami, Dallas, Seattle, Los Angeles, San Francisco; Affiliate in Anchorage.

Association of Independent Television Stations

1200 18th St., N.W., Suite 502, Washigton, DC 20036; (202) 887-1970; FAX (202) 887-0950.

CHAIRMAN
John A. Serrao
PRESIDENT
Preston R. Padden
SECRETARY
L. Martin Brantley
TREASURER
Randall E. Smith
VICE PRESIDENT, GOVERNMENT RELATIONS
James B. Hedlund
VICE PRESIDENT, MARKETING
Lana King
BOARD OF DIRECTORS
LeBon Abercrombie, Edward G. Aiken, L. Martin Brantley, John C. Chaffee, Al DeVaney, Bertram Ellis, Dennis Fitzsimmons, Robert J. Hamacher, Robert Kreek, Milton Maltz, Kevin O'Brien, Preston R. Padden, John A. Serrao, Randall E. Smith, John A. Trinder

Association of Independent Video and Filmmakers, Inc.

625 Broadway, New York, NY 10012; (212) 473-3400. (Membership: over 5,000 independent professionals, including producers, directors, writers and technicians in film and video; publishes The Independent Magazine.)

EXECUTIVE DIRECTOR
Lawrence Sapadin

Association of National Advertisers, Inc.

155 E. 44 St., New York, NY 10017; (212) 697-5950.

PRESIDENT
DeWitt F. Helm, Jr.
SENIOR VICE PRESIDENT, WASHINGTON, D.C.
Daniel L. Jaffe
VICE PRESIDENTS
Peter Eder, Clark Holt, Gregory Faust

Association of Talent Agents

(Organized April, 1937; Membership: 150) (Official organization of talent agents in Hollywood.) 9255 Sunset Blvd., Suite 318, Los Angeles, CA 90069; (213) 274-0628.

EXECUTIVE DIRECTOR
Chester L. Migden
FIRST VICE PRESIDENT
Roger Davis
VICE PRESIDENTS
Carter Gibson, Eric Klass, Sid Craig, Sandy Bresler, Sonjia Warren Brandon
SECRETARY-TREASURER
Nina Blanchard

Authors' Guild, Inc.

(Membership: 6,600) 234 W. 44 St., New York, NY 10036; (212) 398-0838.

PRESIDENT
Robert K. Massie
VICE PRESIDENT
Carolyn G. Heilbrun
SECRETARY
J. Anthony Lukas
TREASURER
Gerold Frank
EXECUTIVE DIRECTOR
Helen A. Stephenson

The Authors League of America, Inc.

(Membership: 15,000) Authors League, 234 W. 44. St., New York, NY 10036; (212) 391-9198.

PRESIDENT
Garson Kanin
VICE PRESIDENT
Robert Anderson
SECRETARY
Eve Merriam
TREASURER
Gerold Frank
ADMINISTRATOR
Peggy Randall

Banff Television Festival

P.O. Box 1020, Banff, Alberta, Canada, TOL 0C0; (403) 762-3060. TELEX: TV FEST BNF 03-822804; FAX: (403) 762-5357. (Honors excellence in world TV)

PRESIDENT
Carrie Hunter
VICE PRESIDENT, PROGRAMMING
Jerry Ezekiel
VICE PRESIDENT, FINANCE
Jim Bertram

BMI (Broadcast Music, Inc.)

320 W. 57 St., New York, NY 10019 (212) 586-2000; 230 Half Mile Rd., Red Bank, NJ (201) 758-0700; 8730 Sunset Blvd., Los Angeles, CA 90069 (213) 656-9109; 6767 Forest Lawn Dr., Hollywood, CA 90068 (213) 851-6440; 1111 Bayhill Dr., San Bruno, CA 94066 (415) 583-8355; 727 N. 1st St., St. Louis, MO 63102 (314) 621-3100; 10 Music Square E., Nashville, TN 37203 (615) 259-3625; 8500 S.W. 117th Rd., Suite 116, Miami, FL 33183 (305) 271-8220; 3701 Algonquin Rd., Two Crossroads, Suite 360, Rolling Meadows, IL 60008 (312) 870-8060; Royal Bank Center, suite 710, Hato Rey, PR 00917 (809) 754-6490; 1325 S. Dairy Ashford, Suite 260, Houston, TX 77077, (713) 558-3500; Shovel Shop Square 3A, North Easton, MA 02356 (508) 238-0174; Ponce de Leon Ave., Pan Am Bldg., Suite 905, Hato Rey, Puerto Rico 00917 (809) 754-6490.

BOARD CHAIRMAN
Joseph Carriere
PRESIDENT
Frances W. Preston
SENIOR VICE PRESIDENT, SPECIAL COUNSEL TO THE PRESIDENT
Theodora Zavin
VICE PRESIDENT, NASHVILLE
Roger Sovine
VICE PRESIDENT, CALIFORNIA
Ronald M. Anton
VICE PRESIDENT FINANCE & CHIEF FINANCIAL OFFICER
Jeff White
VICE PRESIDENT, CORPORATE RELATIONS
Robbin Ahrold
VICE PRESIDENT, INTERNATIONAL
Ekke Schnabel
VICE PRESIDENT, SYSTEMS & DATA PROCESSING
Richard Mack
VICE PRESIDENT, LICENSING
Lawrence P. Sweeney
VICE PRESIDENT, ADMINISTRATION
Alan H. Smith
VICE PRESIDENT, SECRETARY, AND GENERAL COUNSEL
Edward W. Chapin
CONTROLLER AND TREASURER
Thomas Curry

Broadcast Pioneers

320 W. 57 St., New York, NY 10019; (212) 586-2000.

PRESIDENT
Wallace Dunlap
VICE PRESIDENT
James Delmonico
VICE PRESIDENT
Jim Greenwald
EXECUTIVE DIRECTOR
Edward J. DeGray

Cable Television Information Center (CTIC)

P.O. Box 1205, Annandale, VA 22003; (703) 941-1770. Organized 1972. (Provides community governments and consumers with objective information about the cable industry.)

PRESIDENT
Harold E. Horn

Catholic Actors Guild of America

(Organized April, 1914; Membership: 550) 1501 Broadway, Suite 510, New York, NY 10036; (212) 398-1868.

PRESIDENT
William J. O'Malley
FIRST VICE PRESIDENT
Frederick O'Neal
SECOND VICE PRESIDENT
Hildegarde

TREASURER
Martin Kiffel
CHAIRMAN OF EXECUTIVE BOARD
Lisa Di Julio

Catholic Broadcasting Office

(See U.S. Catholic Conference.)

Clear Channel Broadcasting Service

1776 K St., N.W., Washington, DC 20006; (202) 429-7020.

PRESIDENT
Wayne Vriesman, WGN, Chicago
LEGAL COUNSEL
John L. Bartlett, Wiley Rein & Fielding, Washington, DC.

Communication Commission of National Council of Churches of Christ in the USA

475 Riverside Dr., Room 860, New York, NY 10115; (212) 870-2574; FAX: (212) 870-2152.

CHAIRPERSON
Beverly Chain
ASSISTANT GENERAL SECRETARY FOR COMMUNICATION, NCC
Vacant
EXECUTIVE DIRECTOR FOR BROADCASTING AND FILM
Vacant
DIRECTOR FOR MEDIA RESOURCES
David W. Pomeroy

Corporation for Public Broadcasting

1111 16th St., N.W. Washington, DC 20036; (202) 955-5100.

PRESIDENT & CHIEF EXECUTIVE OFFICER
Donald E. Ledwig
VICE PRESIDENT, STATION RELATIONS & TREASURER
Frederick L. DeMarco
VICE PRESIDENT, GOVERNMENT RELATIONS
Gerald Hogan
VICE PRESIDENT, PROGRAMMING
Eugene Katt
VICE PRESIDENT, GENERAL COUNSEL & SECRETARY
Paul E. Symczak
VICE PRESIDENT, CORPORATE COMMUNICATIONS
Rozanne Weissman

Directors Guild of America, Inc. (DGA)

National office: 7920 Sunset Blvd., Hollywood, CA 90046; (213) 656-1220. 110 W. 57 St., New York, NY 10019; (212) 581-0370. Chicago: 520 N. Michigan Ave., Suite 400, Chicago, IL 60611; (312) 644-5050.

PRESIDENT
Arthur Hiller
NATIONAL VICE PRESIDENT
Yael Woll
NATIONAL EXECUTIVE DIRECTOR
Glenn Gumpel
VICE PRESIDENTS
Jane Schimel, Gene Reynolds, Max Schindler, Arthur Hiller, Yael Woll, Burt Bluestein
SECRETARY/TREASURER
Sheldon Leonard
ASSISTANT SECRETARY/TREASURER
Marilyn Jacobs

The Dramatists Guild, Inc.

(Membership: 866 Active; 6,421 Associate; 407 Subscribing) 234 W. 44 St., New York, NY 10036; (212) 398-9366; FAX: (212) 869-8237.

PRESIDENT
Peter Stone
VICE PRESIDENT
Terrence McNally
SECRETARY
A. R. Gurney
TREASURER
Marsha Norman
EXECUTIVE DIRECTOR
David E. LeVine
COUNSEL
Cahill Gordon & Reindel

Electronic Industries Association

2001 Eye St., N.W., Washington, DC 20006; (202) 457-4900.

CHAIRMAN OF THE BOARD
William G. Little, Quam-Nicholas Company, Inc.
PRESIDENT
Peter F. McCloskey
TREASURER
C. Travis Marshall, Vice President, Motorola, Inc.
VICE PRESIDENT PUBLIC AFFAIRS
Mark V. Rosenker

Episcopal Actors Guild of America, Inc.

(Organized 1926; 750 members) 1 E. 29 St., New York, NY 10016; (212) 685-2927.

HONORARY PRESIDENTS PRESIDING BISHOP
The Right Rev. Edmond L. Browning
BISHOP OF NEW YORK
The Right Reverend Paul Moore, Jr., S.T.D.
RETIRED BISHOP OF NEW YORK
The Right Reverend Horace W. B. Donegan, D.D.
PRESIDENT EMERITUS
Ray Heatherton
PRESIDENT
Barnard Hughes
VICE PRESIDENTS
Rev. Norman J. Catir, Jr., Warden of the Guild, Joan Fontaine, Rex Harrison, Mike Mearian
RECORDING SECRETARY
Joan Warren
TREASURER
L. Herndon Werth
EXECUTIVE SECRETARY
Lon C. Clark
EXECUTIVE ASSISTANT
Michelle Trudeau

Federal Communications Commission

1919 M St., N.W., Washington, DC 20554, (202) 632-7000.

CHAIRMAN
Alfred C. Sikes
COMMISSIONERS
James H. Quello, Patricia Diaz Dennis
CHIEF, OFFICE OF PLANS AND POLICY
John Haring
CHAIRMAN, REVIEW BOARD
Joseph A. Marino
CHIEF JUDGE, OFFICE OF ADMINISTRATIVE LAW JUDGES
Thomas B. Fitzpatrick
GENERAL COUNSEL
Diane Killory
MANAGING DIRECTOR
Edward Minkel
CHIEF/MASS MEDIA BUREAU
Alex D. Felker
CHIEF, COMMON CARRIER BUREAU
Gerald Brock
CHIEF, FIELD OPERATIONS BUREAU
Richard M. Smith
ACTING CHIEF, OFFICE OF LEGISLATIVE AFFAIRS
Stevenson Kaminer
ACTING CHIEF, OFFICE OF PUBLIC AFFAIRS
Maureen Peratino

The Harry Fox Agency

205 E. 42 St., New York, NY 10017; (212) 370-5330. (Music Licensing Bureau)

PRESIDENT
Edward P. Murphy

Girls Friday of Show Business

(See Women in Show Business)

Institute of Electrical and Electronics Engineers, Inc.

345 E. 47 St., New York, NY 10017 (212) 705-7900.

PRESIDENT
Dr. Bruno O. Weinschel
PRESIDENT-ELECT
Henry L. Bachman
EXECUTIVE VICE PRESIDENT
Dr. Emerson W. Pugh
VICE PRESIDENT—EDUCATIONAL ACTIVITIES
Dr. Cyrill J. Tunis
VICE PRESIDENT—PROFESSIONAL ACTIVITIES
Carleton A. Bayless
VICE PRESIDENT—PUBLICATION ACTIVITIES
Charles H. House
VICE PRESIDENT—REGIONAL ACTIVITIES
Dennis Bodson
VICE PRESIDENT—TECHNICAL ACTIVITIES
Merlin G. Smith
SECRETARY/TREASURER
Dr. Michiyuko Uenohara
TREASURER
Edward J. Doyle
GENERAL MANAGER AND EXECUTIVE DIRECTOR
Eric Herz

International Alliance of Theatrical Stage Employes & Moving Picture Machine Operators of the U.S. and Canada (AFL-CIO)

(Organized nationally, July 17, 1893; internationally, October 1, 1902.) 1515 Broadway, Suite 601, New York, NY 10036; (212) 730-1770; FAX: (212) 921-7699.

INTERNATIONAL PRESIDENT
Alfred W. Ditolla
INTERNATIONAL PRESIDENTS EMERITUS
Walter F. Diehl
Richard F. Walsh
GENERAL SECRETARY-TREASURER
James J. Riley
FIRST VICE PRESIDENT
Frank A. Hobbs, Niles, IL
SECOND VICE PRESIDENT
John J. Nolan, Paramus, NJ
THIRD VICE PRESIDENT
J. E. Johnson, Karnack, TX
FOURTH VICE PRESIDENT
John J. Ryan, Burtonsville, MD
FIFTH VICE PRESIDENT
Edward C. Powell, San Rafael, CA
SIXTH VICE PRESIDENT
Michael W. Proscia, North Bergen, NJ
SEVENTH VICE PRESIDENT
Alan L. Cowley, West Hill, Ont.
EIGHTH VICE PRESIDENT
Nick Long, Burbank, CA
NINTH VICE PRESIDENT
Daniel J. Kerins, Chicago, IL
TENTH VICE PRESIDENT
Donald T. Rohrbach, Sherman Oaks, CA
ELEVENTH VICE PRESIDENT
Thomas C. Short, Cleveland, OH
INTERNATIONAL TRUSTEES
Michael J. Sullivan, Hartford, CT; Nels L. Hansen, Las Vegas, NV; Ada S. Philpot, San Francisco, CA.

The Alliance is comprised of approximately 900 local unions covering the United States, Canada and Hawaii. Following is a list of the New York, Chicago and Hollywood locals:

PRODUCTION

AFFILIATED PROPERTY CRAFTSMEN LOCAL 44 (IATSE-AFL-CIO), HOLLYWOOD

(Organized May 15, 1939) 6180 Laurel Canyon Blvd. #275, North Hollywood, CA 91605; (818) 769-2500.

ART DIRECTORS, LOCAL 876 (IATSE) HOLLYWOOD

(Chartered January 7, 1960) 14724 Ventura Blvd., Sherman Oaks, CA 91403; (818) 905-0599.

FIRST AID EMPLOYEES, LOCAL 767 (IATSE), LOS ANGELES

(Chartered Oct. 30, 1942) 2611 Taffrail Lane, Oxnard CA 93033; (818) 760-5341.

INTERNATIONAL PHOTOGRAPHERS OF THE MOTION PICTURE INDUSTRIES (Cameramen) IPMPI LOCAL 666, CHICAGO

(Chartered Jan. 1, 1929) Suite 1122, 327 S. La Salle St., Chicago, IL 60604; (312) 341-0966.

IPMPI, LOCAL 659 (IATSE), LOS ANGELES

(Organized 1928) 7715 Sunset Blvd., Suite 150, Hollywood, CA 90046; (213) 876-0160.

IPMPI, LOCAL 644 (IATSE), NEW YORK

(Organized Nov. 15, 1926) 505 Eighth Ave., 16 Floor, New York, NY 10018; (212) 244-2121.

INTERNATIONAL SOUND TECHNICIANS OF THE MOTION PICTURE BROADCAST AND AMUSEMENT INDUSTRIES, LOCAL 695 (IATSE-AFL), LOS ANGELES

(Organized Sept. 15, 1930) 1131 Ventura Blvd., Suite 201, Studio City, CA 91604; (818) 985-9204.

LABORATORY TECHNICIANS, LOCAL 780 (IATSE), CHICAGO

(Chartered Nov. 10, 1944) 327 S. La Salle St., Room 1717, Chicago, IL, 60604; (312) 922-7105.

LABORATORY TECHNICIANS, LOCAL 683 (IATSE-AFL-CIO), LOS ANGELES

(Organized Sept. 29, 1919) 2600 W. Victory Blvd., Burbank, CA 91505 (818) 955-9720.

LABORATORY TECHNICIANS, LOCAL 702 (IATSE-AFL), NEW YORK

(Organized September, 1937) Room 605, 165 W. 46 St., New York, NY 10036; (212) 869-5540.

MAKE-UP ARTISTS & HAIR STYLISTS, LOCAL 706 (IATSE), HOLLYWOOD

11519 Chandler Blvd., No. Hollywood, CA 91601; (818) 984-1700.

MAKE-UP ARTISTS AND HAIR STYLISTS, LOCAL 798 (IATSE), NEW YORK

(Chartered Feb. 18, 1949) 31 W. 21 St., New York, NY 10010; (212) 627-0660.

MOTION PICTURE COSTUMERS, LOCAL 705 (IATSE-AFL), HOLLYWOOD

(Chartered Nov. 1, 1937) 1427 N. La Brea Ave., Hollywood, CA 90028; (213) 851-0220.

MOTION PICTURE AND VIDEO EDITORS GUILD, LOCAL 776 (IATSE), LOS ANGELES

(Chartered Aug. 2, 1944) Secretary's address: 7715 Sunset Blvd., Hollywood, CA 90046; (213) 876-4770.

MOTION PICTURE FILM & VIDEO TAPE EDITORS, LOCAL 771 (IATSE), NEW YORK

(Chartered Aug. 18, 1943) 353 W. 48 St., New York, NY 10036; (212) 581-0771.

MOTION PICTURE SCRIPT SUPERVISORS AND PRODUCTION OFFICE COORDINATORS LOCAL 161

1697 Broadway, Suite 902, New York, NY 10019; (212) 956-5410.

MOTION PICTURE SET PAINTERS, LOCAL 729 (IATSE), HOLLYWOOD

(Chartered Aug. 1, 1953) 11365 Ventura Blvd., Suite 202, Studio City, CA 91604; (818) 784-3000.

MOTION PICTURE SCREEN CARTOONISTS, LOCAL 839 (IATSE), HOLLYWOOD

(Chartered Jan. 18, 1952) 4729 Lankershim Blvd., North Hollywood, CA 91602; (213) 766-7151.

MOTION PICTURE STUDIO ELECTRICAL TECHNICIANS, LOCAL 728 (IATSE), AND M.P.M.O. OF U.S. AND CANADA-AFL-CIO

(Chartered May 15, 1939) 14629 Nordhoff St., Panorama City, CA 91402; (818) 891-0728.

MOTION PICTURE CRAFTS SERVICE, LOCAL 727 (IATSE), HOLLYWOOD

(Organized May 15, 1939) 14629 Nordoff St., Panorama City, CA 91402; (818) 891-0717.

MOTION PICTURE STUDIO ART CRAFTSMEN, (Illustrators and Matte Artists) LOCAL 790 (IATSE), HOLLYWOOD

(Chartered April 17, 1945) 14724 Ventura Blvd., Penthouse Suite, Sherman Oaks, CA 91403; (213) 784-6555, Los Angeles, CA 90046; (213) 876-2010.

MOTION PICTURE STUDIO GRIPS, LOCAL 80 (IATSE), HOLLYWOOD

(Organized May 15, 1939) 6926 Melrose Ave., Los Angeles, CA 90038; (213) 931-1419.

MOTION PICTURE STUDIO TEACHERS AND WELFARE WORKERS, LOCAL 884 (IATSE) HOLLYWOOD

(Chartered September 1, 1960) 2540 Astral Dr., Los Angeles, CA 90146.

PUBLICISTS, LOCAL 818 (IATSE), HOLLYWOOD

(Chartered July 11, 1955) 14724 Ventura Blvd., PH Suite, Sherman Oaks, 91403-3501; (213) 278-1993.

RADIO AND TELEVISION SOUND EFFECTS, LOCAL 844 (IATSE), NEW YORK

(Chartered July 17, 1952), Box 637, Ansonia Station, New York, NY 10023. (212) 887-3920.

SCENIC & TITLE ARTISTS, LOCAL 816 (IATSE) LOS ANGELES

(Chartered March 31, 1949) 6180 Laurel Canyon Blvd., #275, No. Hollywood, CA 91606; (818) 769-0816.

SCRIPT SUPERVISORS, LOCAL 871 (IATSE), HOLLYWOOD

(Chartered January 1, 1958) 7061 B Hayenhurst, Van Nuys, CA 91906; (818) 782-7063.

SET DESIGNERS AND MODEL MAKERS, LOCAL 847 (IATSE), HOLLYWOOD

(Chartered Nov. 14, 1952) 14724 Ventura Blvd., Penthouse Suite, Sherman Oaks, CA 91403; (818) 784-6555. Los Angeles, CA 90046; (213) 876-2010.

STORY ANALYSTS, LOCAL 854 (IATSE), HOLLYWOOD

(Chartered Oct. 18, 1954) 14724 Ventura Blvd., Penthouse Suite, Sherman Oaks, CA 91403; (818) 784-6555.

MOTION PICTURE STUDIO MECHANICS, LOCAL 476 (IATSE), CHICAGO

(Chartered Feb. 2, 1931) Room 1743–45; 327 S. La Salle St., Chicago, IL 60604; (312) 922-5215.

STUDIO MECHANICS, LOCAL 52 (IATSE-AFL), NEW YORK

(Organized 1924) 326 W. 48 St., New York, NY 10036; (212) 399-0980.

TELEVISION BROADCASTING STUDIO EMPLOYEES, LOCAL 794 (IATSE), NEW YORK

(Chartered June 7, 1945) P.O. Box 154, Lenox Hill Sta., NY 10021.

DISTRIBUTION

FILM EXCHANGE EMPLOYEES, BACK ROOM, LOCAL B-46 (IATSE), CHICAGO

(Chartered May 1, 1937) 875 N. Michigan Ave., Chicago, IL 60611; (312) 787-0220.

FILM EXCHANGE EMPLOYEES, BACK ROOM, LOCAL B-61 (IATSE), LOS ANGELES

(Chartered May 1, 1937) 14724 Ventura Blvd., Penthouse Suite, Sherman Oaks, CA 91403; (213) 906-7977.

COMBINED FILM EXCHANGE EMPLOYEES, OFFICE, LOCAL F-45 (IATSE), CHICAGO

(Chartered Sept. 4, 1942) #G. R. Kuehnl, Apt. 1611, 5455 Sheridan Rd., Chicago, IL 60640.

In addition to the above, there are 34 locals of Back Room Employees and 29 locals of Front Office Employees in the other exchange cities.

MOTION PICTURE HOME OFFICE AND FILM EXCHANGE EMPLOYEES, LOCAL H-63 (IATSE), NEW YORK

(Chartered Mar. 19, 1945) 1515 Broadway, New York, NY 10036; (212) 730-1770.

AMUSEMENT AREA EMPLOYEES, LOCAL B-192 (IATSE) LOS ANGELES

(Chartered Oct. 1, 1965) 14724 Ventura Blvd., Penthouse Suite, Sherman Oaks, CA 91403; (213) 906-7977.

EXHIBITION EMPLOYEES, LOCAL 829 (IATSE), NEW YORK

(Chartered December 11, 1950) 150 E. 58 St., New York, NY 10022; (212) 752-4427.

PROJECTIONISTS LOCAL 110 (IATSE), CHICAGO

(Chartered Feb. 4, 1915) 875 N. Michigan Ave. Suite 4160, Chicago, IL 60611; (312) 787-0220.

PROJECTIONISTS LOCAL 150 (IATSE), LOS ANGELES

(Chartered July 16, 1908) 2600 W. Victory Blvd., Burbank, CA 91505–1616; (818) 842-8900.

PROJECTIONISTS LOCAL 306 (IATSE), NEW YORK

(Organized July, 1913) 229 W. 42 St., New York, NY 10036; (212) 764-6274.

STAGE EMPLOYEES, LOCAL 4 (IATSE), BROOKLYN

(Chartered April 8, 1888) 2917 Glenwood Rd., Brooklyn, NY 11210; (718) 252-8777.

STAGE EMPLOYEES, LOCAL 2 (IATSE), CHICAGO

(Chartered July 17, 1893) 222 W. Adams St., Room 818, Chicago, IL 60606; (312) 236-3457.

STAGE EMPLOYEES, LOCAL 33 (IATSE), LOS ANGELES

(Chartered Mar. 1, 1896) 1720 W. Magnolia Blvd., Burbank, CA 91506; (818) 841-9233.

STAGE EMPLOYEES, LOCAL 1 (IATSE), NEW YORK

(Chartered July 17, 1893) 320 W. 46 St., New York, NY 10036; (212) 333-2500.

THEATRE EMPLOYEES, LOCAL B-46 (IATSE), CHICAGO

(Chartered May 1, 1937) 875 N. Michigan Ave. Suite 4160, Chicago, IL 60611; (312) 787-0220.

THEATRE EMPLOYEES, LOCAL B-183 (IATSE), NEW YORK

(Chartered May 6, 1942) 319 W. 48th St., New York, NY 10036; (212) 586-9620.

THEATRICAL WARDROBE ATTENDANTS, LOCAL 769 (IATSE), CHICAGO

9115 S. Roberts Rd., Chicago, IL 60457.

THEATRICAL WARDROBE ATTENDANTS, LOCAL 768 (IATSE), LOS ANGELES

(Chartered Dec. 3, 1942) 14724 Ventura Blvd., Penthouse Suite D, Sherman Oaks, CA 91403-3501; (818) 789-8735.

THEATRICAL WARDROBE ATTENDANTS, LOCAL 764 (IATSE), NEW YORK

(Chartered Sept. 4, 1942) 1501 Broadway, Room 1313, New York, NY 10036; (212) 221-1717.

TREASURERS AND TICKET SELLERS & CASHIERS, LOCAL 750 (IATSE), CHICAGO

(Chartered Aug. 1, 1941) 446 N. Edgewood LaGrange Park, IL 60525; (312) 579-9381.

TREASURERS AND TICKET SELLERS, LOCAL 857 (IATSE), LOS ANGELES

(Chartered June 1, 1955) 6513 Hollywood Blvd., Room 216, Hollywood, CA 90028; (213) 464-2846.

TREASURERS AND TICKET SELLERS, LOCAL 751 (IATSE), NEW YORK

(Chartered Aug. 1, 1941) 257 W. 52 St., New York, NY 10019; (212) 315-0544.

Outside the three cities covered by the above listings, there are over 900 IATSE locals in the exhibition field.

International Brotherhood of Electrical Workers (AFL)

(Organized November 28, 1891; Membership over 1 million) 1125 15th St., N.W., Washington, DC 20005; (202) 833-7000.

INTERNATIONAL PRESIDENT
John J. Barry, 1125 15th St., N.W., Washington, DC 20005
INTERNATIONAL SECRETARY
Jack F. Moore, 1125 15th St., N.W., Washington, DC 20005
INTERNATIONAL TREASURER
Thomas Van Arsdale, 158-11 Harry Van Arsdale Jr. Ave., Flushing, NY 11365
DISTRICT OFFICES
Willowdale, Ontario: 45 Sheppard Ave. East, Suite 401; Ken Woods.
Braintree, MA: Batterymarch Park, Quincy, MA 02169, John E. Flynn
Albany, NY: 16 Computer Dr. West, Suite C, Donald J. Funk
Cincinnati, OH: 7710 Reading Rd., Suite 9, Paul J. Witte
Birmingham, AL: No. 2 Metroplex Dr., Suite 304, D. H. Waters
Lombard, IL; 2200 S. Main St., Ste. 303, James P. Conway.
Oklahoma, OK; 4400 Will Rogers Pkwy. #309, Orville A. Tate, Jr.
Idaho Falls, ID 83402: P.O. Box 51216, Jon Walters
Walnut Creek, CA: 150 N. Wiget Lane, Suite 100, S. R. McCann
Rosemont, IL: 10400 W. Higgins Rd., Suite 110, Edward P. McEntee
Springfield, MO: 300 So. Jefferson, Suite 300, Ray Edwards
Chattanooga, TN: Franklin Bldg., Suite 515, John A. Hightower

IBEW LOCAL 349 (FILM)

(Organized April 24, 1904) 1657 N.W. 17th Ave. Miami, FL 33125; (305) 325-1330.

BUSINESS MANAGER
Art Fernandez

IBEW LOCAL 40 (FILM)

(Organized March 5, 1923) 5643 Vineland Ave., No. Hollywood, CA 91601; (818) 762-4239.

BUSINESS MANAGER
Russell J. Bartley

International Radio and Television Society Inc.

420 Lexington Ave. Suite 531, New York, NY 10170; (212) 867-6650.

PRESIDENT
Betty Hudson
FIRST VICE PRESIDENT
James H. Rosenfield
VICE PRESIDENTS
Gerald M. Levin, Neal H. Pilson, Ralph M. Baruch, Robert H. Alter, Stephen H. Coltrin
SECRETARY
Jerome S. Boros
TREASURER
Donn H. O'Brien
EXECUTIVE DIRECTOR
Stephen B. Labunski

National Academy of Television Arts and Sciences, The

National Office: 111 W. 57 St., New York, NY 10019; (212) 586-8424. (Formed to advance the arts and sciences of television.) (Organized 1947) Awards Emmys for daytime, children's, religious, sports and news documentary programming.

CHAIRMAN OF THE BOARD
Robert Wussler
PRESIDENT
John Cannon
VICE CHAIRMAN
Michael Collyer
VICE PRESIDENT
Mike Duncan
SECRETARY
Alice Marshall
TREASURER
Isadore Miller

National Association of Broadcasters

1771 N St., N.W., Washington, DC 20036; (202) 429-5300. (Organized 1922 to foster and promote the development of the arts of aural and visual broadcasting in all its forms; to protect its members in every lawful and proper manner from injustices and unjust exactions; to do all things necessary and proper to encourage and promote customs and practices which will strengthen and maintain the broadcasting industry to the end that it may best serve the public.)

CHAIRMAN
L. Lowry Mays
PRESIDENT
Edward O. Fritts
TELEVISION BOARD OF DIRECTORS
Thomas Goodman (chmn.), Benjamin McKeel (vice-chmn.), John Behnke, Joseph Carriere, Gary R. Chapman, Joel Chaseman, Jerry P. Colvin, Michael J. Conley, Eugene S. Cowen, William F. Duhamel, Martin D. Franks, Robert D. Hynes, Jr., Judith Ekberg Johnson, Mauricio Mendez, Leavitt J. Pope, Harold Protter, Patricia C. Smullin, Cullie M. Tarleton, Ronald Townsend, Cyril E. Vetter, Anita L. Wallgren, Glenn C. Wright.

National Association of Public Television Stations

1350 Connecticut Ave., N.W., Suite 200, Washington, D.C. 20036; (202) 887-1700. Organized 1979. (Does research, planning and representation for member public television stations throughout the U.S.)

PRESIDENT
David J. Brugger
VICE PRESIDENT
Richard Grefé
BOARD OF TRUSTEES
Ronald C. Bornstein, David J. Brugger, Donald C. Carlyon, Henry J. Cauthen, Dr. Margaret Chisholm, J. Michael Collins, Robert H. Ellis, W. Wayne Godwin, Robert M. Greber, Hope S. Green, Dr. Teruo Ihara, R. Bruce MacGregor, William J. McCarter, George L. Miles, Jr., Richard O. Moore, Dr. Richard E. Ottinger, Arthur J. Singer, Dr. Albert C. Van Dusen, Viviane Warren, Mary Faye Way.

AFFILIATIONS
Works closely with Corp. for Public Broadcasting & Public Broadcasting Service (PBS) but is not "affiliated."

NATPE INTERNATIONAL (National Association of Television Program Executives)

10100 Santa Monica Blvd., Ste. 300, Los Angeles, CA 90067; (213)282-8801.

PRESIDENT
A. Philip Corvo
CHAIRMAN OF THE BOARD
Lon C. Lee, KCNC, Denver

National Cable Television Association

1724 Massachusetts Ave., N.W., Washington, DC 20036; (202) 775-3550. Organized 1951. (Trade association that lobbies for cable television interest.)

PRESIDENT
James P. Mooney
EXECUTIVE VICE PRESIDENT
Decker Anstrom
VICE PRESIDENT, SCIENCE & TECHNOLOGY
Wendell Bailey
VICE PRESIDENT, PROGRAMMING & MARKETING
Char Beales
VICE PRESIDENT, ADMINISTRATION
Phylis Eagle
VICE PRESIDENT, SPECIAL POLICY PROJECTS
Brenda Fox
VICE PRESIDENT, ASSOCIATION AFFAIRS
Jadz Janucik
DEPUTY VICE PRESIDENT, GOVERNMENT RELATIONS
Katherine Meier
VICE RPESIDENT, INDUSTRY COMMUNICATIONS
Louise Rauscher
VICE PRESIDENT, INDUSTRY AFFAIRS
Barbara York
VICE PRESIDENT, RESEARCH & POLICY ANALYSIS
Cynthia Brumfield
BOARD OF DIRECTORS
John W. Goddard (chairman); Jerry D. Lindauer (secretary); James S. Cownie (immediate past chm.); Daniel Aaron; Edward M. Allen; Kenneth L. Bagwell; Robert Miron (vice chairmen); James O. Robbins (treas.); James P. Mooney (president); Gregory Bryan Blow; David A. Bohmer; William J. Bresnan; Carolyn S. Chambers; Joseph Collins; Winston H. Cox; Jerry D. Craft; Boyce Booley; Frank M. Drendel; John D. Evans; Michael J. Fuchs; Alan Gerry; James L. Gray; J. William Grimes; David W. Hamilton; Amos ("Bud") B. Hostetter, Jr.; Marvin L. Jones; Kay Koplovitz; Philip B. Lind; John C. Malone; John J. Rigas; Richard D. Roberts; Clive Runnells; Gene W. Schneider; William B. Strange, Jr.; John Tatta; Charles C. Townsend, III; June E. Travis; R.E. "Ted" Turner; Larry W. Wangberg; Maggie Wilderotter; John ("Dubby") O. Wynne.
AFFILIATIONS
National Academy of Cable Programmming, National Cable Forum

National Federation of Local Cable Programmers

P.O.Box 27290, Washington, DC 20038-7290; (202) 829-7186.

MEMBERSHIP MANAGER
Reginald Carter

National Music Publishers' Association, Inc.

205 E. 42 St., New York, NY 10017; (212) 370-5330.

CHAIRMAN
Irwin Z. Robinson
PRESIDENT AND CEO
Edward P. Murphy

VICE PRESIDENTS
William Lowery, Ralph Peer II, Leon J. Brettler
TREASURER
Sidney B. Herman

New York Women in Film

274 Madison Ave., Suite 1603, New York, NY 10016; (212) 679-0870. Organized 1977. (A not-for-profit organization, for career professionals working in film, television and other programming media. NYWIF plays an important role in recognizing and encouraging the contributions of women to the field and promotes the highest standards of professionalism through sponsorship of educational programs and career development activities. Also serves the industry as a whole and its audience, the general public, with information and events open to all.)

PRESIDENT
Mirra Bank Brockman
VICE PRESIDENT
Sylvia Delia
SECRETARY
Nancy Stern
TREASURER
Deborah Del Prete
EXECUTIVE DIRECTOR
Phyllis Schwartz
BOARD OF DIRECTORS 1989/90:
Jane Altschuler, Lois Bianchi, Dina Boogaard, Beth Dembitzer, Jackie Frank, Lisa Jackson, Marjorie Kalins, Kimberly Myers, Reene Schisgal, Susan Seidelman, Susan Steinberg, Katherine Wenning
CHAPTERS
Los Angeles, San Francisco, Atlanta, Dallas, Boston, Chicago, Washington, D.C., Toronto and worldwide

Permanent Charities Committee of The Entertainment Industries

Samuel Goldwyn-Permanent Charities Building, 463 N. La Cienega Blvd., Los Angeles, CA 90048; (213) 652-4680. (A donor federation within the entertainment industries supporting community wide charities.)

CHAIRMAN OF THE BOARD
Daniel E. Slusser
PRESIDENT
Paul C. Masterson
FIRST VICE PRESIDENT
Gene Allen
SECOND VICE PRESIDENT
Lew Gallo
SECRETARY
William K. Howard
TREASURER
Robert S. Colbert, CPA
VICE PRESIDENT, ADMINISTRATION & FINANCE
Irwin J. Kaplan
VICE PRESIDENT, DEVELOPMENT
Lisa C. Paulsen

Producer-Writers Guild of America Pension Plan

1015 No. Hollywood Way, Burbank, CA 91505; (818) 846-1015.

CHAIRMAN
Stephen Koppekin
VICE CHAIRMAN
Scott Nostaja
SECRETARY
George Malko
VICE SECRETARY
Jean Butler

SESAC, INC.

(One of the world's foremost music licensing organizations. A special projects department handles scoring for motion pictures, slide films, syndicated TV series and agency produced commercials; programming for background music and premium albums.)

156 W. 56 St., New York, NY 10019; (212) 586-3450.

CHAIRMAN & PRESIDENT
A. H. Prager
EXECUTIVE VICE PRESIDENT
Vincent Candilora

Screen Actors Guild (AAAA-AFL-CIO)

(Organized July, 1933; Membership: 73,000) 7065 Hollywood Blvd., Hollywood, CA 90028; (213) 465-4600. Branches— New York: 1515 Broadway, 44th Floor, New York, NY 10036, (212) 944-1030. John T. McGuire; Chicago: 307 N. Michigan Ave., Herbert H. Neuer; Boston, 11 Beacon St., Ira Sills, 28690 Southfield Rd., Lathrop Village, MI 48076, Barbara Honner; Dallas: 6309 N. O'Connor Rd., Dallas, TX 75039, Kat Krone; San Francisco: 100 Bush St., San Francisco, CA 94104, Kim Roberts; Miami: 2299 Douglas Rd. #200, Miami, FL 33145, Melvin B. Karl.

PRESIDENT
Barry Gordon
PRESIDENT EMERITUS
Leon Ames
FIRST VICE PRESIDENT
Joseph Ruskin
SECOND VICE PRESIDENT
Maureen Donnelly
THIRD VICE PRESIDENT
Daryl Anderson
FOURTH VICE PRESIDENT
Jordan Derwin
FIFTH VICE PRESIDENT
Reed Farrell
SIXTH VICE PRESIDENT
Dan Caldwell
VICE PRESIDENTS
Bruce McLaughlin, Larry Keith, J. Carlton Adair, Daryl Anderson, Frank Aletter, Dan Ingram
RECORDING SECRETARY
Sumi Haru
TREASURER
Yale Summers

NATIONAL EXECUTIVE STAFF

NATIONAL EXECUTIVE DIRECTOR
Ken Orsatti
ASSOCIATE NATIONAL EXECUTIVE DIRECTOR
John McGuire
PUBLIC RELATIONS DIRECTOR
Mark Locher
COUNSEL
Leo Geffner
CONTROLLER
Gerald Wilson

Society of Motion Picture and Television Engineers

(Organized 1916; Membership: 9,500) 595 W. Hartsdale Ave., White Plains, NY 10607; (914) 761-1100; FAX: (914) 761-3115.

PRESIDENT
Maurice L. French
PAST PRESIDENT
M. Carlos Kennedy
EXECUTIVE VICE PRESIDENT
Blaine Baker
ENGINEERING VICE PRESIDENT
Stanley N. Baron
EDITORIAL VICE PRESIDENT
Frank J. Haney
FINANCIAL VICE PRESIDENT
Richard K. Schafer
CONFERENCE VICE PRESIDENT
L. John Spring, Jr.
SECTIONS VICE PRESIDENT
Irwin W. Young

SECRETARY/TREASURER
Bernard L. Dickens
EXECUTIVE DIRECTOR
Lynette Robinson

The Songwriters Guild of America

276 Fifth Ave., Suite 306, New York, NY 10001; (212) 686-6820; California Office: 6430 Sunset Blvd., Hollywood, CA 90028; (213) 462-1108. Nashville Office: 50 Music Square W., Nashville, TN 37203; (615) 329-1782.

PRESIDENT
George David Weiss
EXECUTIVE DIRECTOR
Lewis M. Bachman

Station Representatives Association, Inc.

230 Park Ave., New York, NY 10017; (212) 687-2484.

PRESIDENT
Steve Herson
VICE PRESIDENT/RADIO
Jerry Cregan
VICE PRESIDENT/TV
Peter Ryan
SECRETARY
Dave Kaufman
TREASURER
Tony Miraglia
MANAGING DIRECTOR
Jerry Feniger
ADMINISTRATIVE ASSISTANT
Audrey Tanzer
DIRECTORS
(Radio board) Eduardo Caballero, George Pine, Stu Olds, Jerry Cregan, Tom Turner, Tony Miraglia, Dave Kaufman. (TV board) Peter Ryan, Pete Goulazian, Steve Herson, Ed Goldman, Art Scott, Tim McAuliffe, Ray Johns.

Television Bureau of Advertising

477 Madison Ave., New York, NY 10022; (212) 486-1111. (Organized 1954.); 3060 Mercer University Dr., Suite 310, Atlanta, GA 30341; (404) 451-2727; 3625 N. Hall, Dallas, TX 75219; (214) 520-2240; 400 No. Michigan Ave., Suite 616, Chicago, IL 60611; (312) 527-3373; 3155 W. Big Beaver Rd., Suite 217, Troy, MI 48084; (313) 649-6688; 5900 Wilshire Blvd., Los Angeles, CA 90036; (213) 937-2826.

PRESIDENT
William G. Moll
CHAIRMAN OF THE BOARD
James G. Babb
VICE PRESIDENT, LOCAL SALES
Peter Ryan
TREASURER
David Allen
CHAIRMAN EX-OFFICIO
E. Blake Byrne
EXECUTIVE VICE PRESIDENT GENERAL MANAGER
Richard Severance
SENIOR VICE PRESIDENT RESEARCH & MARKETING
Harvey Spiegel
SENIOR VICE PRESIDENT, RESOURCE DEVELOPMENT
Beverly Keene
SENIOR VICE PRESIDENT NATIONAL SALES
James A. Joyella
VICE PRESIDENT, MARKETING
John Krubski
DIRECTOR, COMMUNICATIONS
George Hoover
SENIOR VICE PRESIDENT, EDUCATION AND TRAINING
Barbara Zeiger
SENIOR VICE PRESIDENT, DEVELOPMENT
Diane Healey Linen
VICE PRESIDENT CENTRAL DIVISION
Michael Smythe
VICE PRESIDENT, AUTOMOTIVE MARKETING
Richard O'Donnell
VICE PRESIDENT, PACIFIC
Arthur Trudeau
VICE PRESIDENT, FINANCE
Robert D. Brady

Theatre Authority, Inc.

(Organized May 21, 1934) 16 East 42nd St., Suite 202, New York, NY 10017-6907; (212) 682-4215.

PRESIDENT
Willard Swire
EXECUTIVE DIRECTOR
Helen Leahy
TREASURER
Joan Greenspan
COUNSEL
Fred Krones

United States Catholic Conference, Department of Communications, Office For Film & Broadcasting

Suite #1300, 1011 First Ave., New York, NY 10022; (212) 644-1880.

DIRECTOR, OFFICE OF FILM & BROADCASTING
Henry Herx

The Department of Communication of the U.S. Catholic Conference (the public policy agency of the Catholic Bishops of America) addresses the Church's apostolate in and through the print and electronic media. It provides advice and technical assistance on more than 100 radio and network television programs a year.

The Department also publishes a weekly guide to current films and television programs that appear in 100 plus papers of the Catholic Press in the United States. In this activity the Department reviews all current nationally-released 35mm films, and provides information about resources for film utilization and education (16mm films, books, magazines, festivals). The critical reviews are addressed to the moral, as well as the aesthetic, dimensions of motion pictures, and are the result of a consensus based on the reactions of the Department's professional staff and Board of Consultors. All films reviewed are also classified according to the Department's rating system. In addition, this weekly service carries information and evaluative studies on trends and issues pertinent to television, with an emphasis on educational material.

The Department also plays a liaison role for the USCC with the film and broadcasting industries, national media, and religious agencies and organizations. It is a member of OCIC and UNDA, the international Catholic organizations for film and broadcasting, respectively. Consultation and information services are also provided for the Pontifical Commission for Social Communications and the communication offices of national episcopal offices throughout the world.

With staff assistance, the episcopal members of the Communication Committee administer funds raised through the Catholic Communication Campaign, an annual collection. These funds are used to support a variety of media programs, projects, and studies in this country and the Third World.

United Nations—Information Products Division, Department of Public Information

United Nations, New York, NY 10017; (212) 963-6945.

DIRECTOR, INFORMATION PRODUCTS DIVISION
Georges Leclère

Women in Communications, Inc.

P.O. Box 14760, (2101 Wilson Blvd., #417,) Arlington, VA 22201; (703) 528-4200; FAX: (703) 528-4205. Organized 1909. (Promotes advancement of women in communications, protects First Amendment, promotes high professional standards and recognizes distinguished professional achievements.)

PRESIDENT
Karen Carnahan
PRESIDENT ELECT
Janice DeNezza
NATIONAL EXECUTIVE VICE PRESIDENT
Susan Lowell Butler
BRANCHES
Over 180 professional and campus chapters.

Women in Film

(Non-profit organization formed in 1973 by professional women in the motion picture and television industries; purpose is to serve as a support group and act as a clearing house and resource of information on qualified professional women in those industries) 6464 Sunset Blvd., #660, Los Angeles, CA; (213) 463-6040. Branches in New York, Washington, D.C. and Atlanta, GA

PRESIDENT EMERITUS—FOUNDER
Tichi Wilkerson Kassel

Women in Show Business

(A philanthropic organization composed of women in the entertainment industry dedicated to providing funds for reconstructive and restorative surgery for children) P.O. Box 2535, North Hollywood, CA 91610; (213) 271-3415.

PRESIDENT
Scherr Lillico
EXECUTIVE VICE PRESIDENT/WAYS & MEANS
Kathy Grant
FIRST VICE PRESIDENT/PROGRAM
Cynthia Smith
EXECUTIVE VICE PRESIDENT, PHILANTHROPY
Audrey Fredgant
SECOND VICE PRESIDENT/MEMBERSHIP
Karen Haptas
RECORDING SECRETARY
Veronica Nocero
CORRESPONDING SECRETARY
Judy Raykoff
TREASURER
J.J. Jackson

Writers Guild of America

NATIONAL CHAIRMAN
Edward Adler

WRITERS GUILD OF AMERICA, EAST, INC.

555 W. 57 Street, New York, NY 10019; (212) 245-6180.

PRESIDENT
Edward Adler
VICE PRESIDENT
Adrian J. Meppen
SECRETARY-TREASURER
Jane C. Bollinger
EXECUTIVE DIRECTOR
Mona Mangan

WRITERS GUILD OF AMERICA, WEST, INC.

8955 Beverly Blvd., West Hollywood, CA 90048; (213) 550-1000; FAX: (213) 550-8185.

PRESIDENT
George Kirgo
VICE PRESIDENT
Del Reisman
SECRETARY-TREASURER
Alfred Levitt
EXECUTIVE DIRECTOR
Brian Walton

State Associations of Broadcasters

ALABAMA BROADCASTERS ASSOCIATION
Ben K. McKinnon, exec. dir.
Box 43525, Birmingham 35243; (205) 942-4571.

ALASKA BROADCASTERS ASSOCIATION
Roy Robinson, pres.
Box 102424, Anchorage, 99510; (907) 258-2424.

ARIZONA BROADCASTERS ASSOCIATION
Ken Heady, exec. dir.
Box 654, Scottsdale 85252; (602) 991-1700.

ARKANSAS BROADCASTERS ASSOCIATION
Dale Nicholson, pres.; Pat Willcox, exec. dir.
2024 Arkansas Valley Drive, Suite 201, Little Rock 72212; (501) 227-7564.

CALIFORNIA BROADCASTERS ASSOCIATION
Victor J. Biondi, exec. dir.; Karmi A. Speece, exec. asst.
1127 11th St., Suite 730, Sacramento 95814; (916) 444-2237.

COLORADO BROADCASTERS ASSOCIATION
Cliff Dodge, exec. dir.; Judy Gaughan, admin. asst.
1660 Lincoln #2202, Denver 80264; (303) 894-0911.

CONNECTICUT BROADCASTERS ASSOCIATION
Paul K. Taff, exec. dir.
101 Tall Timbers La., Glastonbury 06033; (203) 633-5031.

FLORIDA ASSOCIATION OF BROADCASTERS, INC.
514 E. College, Tallahassee, 32301; (904) 681-6444.

GEORGIA ASSOCIATION OF BROADCASTERS, INC.
William G. Sanders, exec. dir.; Eve Moffa, asst. dir.
500 Sugar Mill Rd., Atlanta 30350; (404) 993-2200.

HAWAIIAN ASSOCIATION OF BROADCASTERS
Dick Schaller (KIKU-TV, Honolulu), pres.
Station KIKI-TV, 150 B Puhale Rd., Honolulu 96819; (808) 847-1178. %KNUI Radio, Box 35, Kahului 96732; (808) 877-5566.

IDAHO STATE BROADCASTERS ASSOCIATION
Connie Searles, exec. dir.; Gerry Cornwell (KIDK-TV Pocatello), pres.
Box 884, Boise 83701; (208) 345-3072.

ILLINOIS BROADCASTERS ASSOCIATION
Wally Gair, exec. dir.
2126 S. MacArthur Rd., Springfield 62704; (217) 753-2636.

INDIANA BROADCASTERS ASSOCIATION, INC.
Joyce Martello, exec. dir..
310 N. Alabama, Suite A, Indianapolis 46204; (317) 638-1332.

IOWA BROADCASTERS ASSOCIATION
William F. Sanders (KICD, Spencer), pres.; Nolan Quam (KCCI-TV, Des Moines), v.p.; Glenn Olson (KQWC, Webster City), treas.; Jack Shelley, exec. secty.
1230 Marston Ave., Ames 50010; (515) 232-1449.

KANSAS ASSOICATION OF BROADCASTERS
Harriet J. Lange, exec. dir.
818 Merchants Nat'l Bank Bldg., Topeka 66612; (913) 235-1307.

KENTUCKY BROADCASTERS ASSOCIATION
J.T. Whitlock, exec. dir. & treas.
Box 680, Lebanon 40033; (502) 692-3126.

LOUISIANA ASSOCIATION OF BROADCASTERS
Manuel Broussard, pres.; Hugh Hyman, exec. dir.
732 North Blvd., Suite C, Baton Rouge 70802; (504) 383-7486.

MAINE ASSOCIATION OF BROADCASTERS
Helen Dudman, pres.; Norman Johnson, pres.-elect; Norman G. Gallant, exec. dir.
Box PI, 385 Western Ave., Augusta 04330; (207) 623-3870.

MARYLAND-DISTRICT OF COLUMBIA-DELAWARE BROADCASTERS ASSOCIATION, INC.
Edward Wetter (WABS, Arlington, VA), pres.; Malcolm D. Potter (WBAL-TV, Baltimore), v.p.; C. Robert Taylor (WDEL/WSTW, Wilmington, Del.), secty.; Robert B. Cochrane, exec. dir.
Route 1-Box 559, St. Michaels, MD 21663; (301) 745-5155.

MASSACHUSETTS BROADCASTERS ASSOCIATION
Robert S. Mehrman, exec. dir.
250 Summer St., 4th Floor, Boston 02210; (617) 439-7636.

MICHIGAN ASSOCIATION OF BROADCASTERS
Charles D. Mefford, pres.; Karole White, exec. dir.
819 N. Washington Ave., Lansing 48906; (517) 484-7444..

MINNESOTA BROADCASTERS ASSOCIATION
Ned Goodwin (KBUN/KBHP, Bemidji) pres.; Ray Foslid, exec. dir.
3517 Raleigh Ave., So., St. Louis Park 55416; (612) 926-8123.

MISSISSIPPI BROADCASTERS ASSOCIATION
Robert Ward, pres.; Jackie Lett, exec. dir.
Box 4561, Jackson 39216; (601) 362-5444.

MISSOURI BROADCASTERS ASSOCIATION
Terry King, pres.; Ted Griffin, exec. v.p.
1800 Southwest Blvd., Jefferson City 65101; (314) 636-6692.

MISSOURI PUBLIC RADIO ASSOCIATION
% Arlen Diamond, pres.
KSMU, 901 S. National, Springfield 65804; (417) 836-5878.

MONTANA BROADCASTERS ASSOCIATION
Robert W. Hoene, exec. dir.; Dean Williams, pres.
Box 503, Helena 59624; (406) 442-3961.

NEBRASKA BROADCASTERS ASSOCIATION
Ed Schafer, pres.; Ken Fearnow (WOW, Omaha) chm., Larry Rice (KBRB, Ainsworth) vice chmn.; Larry Walkin (KRNU, Lincoln), secty.-treas.
7101 Mercy Rd., Suite 419, Omaha 68106; (402) 391-8236.

NEVADA BROADCASTERS ASSOCIATION
David T. Newman, pres.
P.O. Box 1928, Reno 89505.

NEW HAMPSHIRE ASSOCIATION OF BROADCASTERS
B. Allan Sprague, exec. dir.
Box 900, Manchester 03105; (603) 669-5144.

NEW JERSEY BROADCASTERS ASSOCIATION
Arnold Zucker, exec. dir.; Joe Knox Jr., pres.; Michael Levine, v.p.
NJBA, 31 Wine, St., Rutgers University, New Brunswick 08903; (201) 247-3337.

NEW MEXICO BROADCASTERS ASSOCIATION
Art Schreiber (KKOB-AM-FM, Albuerque), pres.; Paul Thorne (KGGM-TV), pres. elect; Dee Schelling, exec. dir.
790-9D Tramway Lane NE, Albuquerque 87122; (505) 299-6908.

NEW YORK STATE BROADCASTERS ASSOCIATION, INC.
Joseph A. Reilly, pres. & exec. dir.; Belinda Bouchard, admin. asst.
90 State St., Suite 530, Albany, 12207; (518) 434-6100.

NORTH CAROLINA ASSOCIATION OF BROADCASTERS
John Greene, pres.; Wade H. Hargrove, exec. dir.
Box 627, Raleigh 27602; (919) 821-7300.

NORTH DAKOTA BROADCASTERS ASSOCIATION
Dewey Heggen, pres.
Box 8116, Grand Forks 58202; (701) 777-2577.

OHIO ASSOCIATION OF BROADCASTERS, INC.
Dale V. Bring, exec. v.p.
100 E. Broad St., Suite 1206, Columbus 43215; (614) 228-4052.

OKLAHOMA ASSOCIATION OF BROADCASTERS
Richard Adams (KXII-TV, Ardmore), pres.; Linda Saunders, exec. dir.
4545 N. Lincoln, Oklahoma City 73105; (405) 528-2475.

OREGON ASSOCIATION OF BROADCASTERS
Sherwood "Skip" Hinman, pres.; Vern Mueller, exec. dir.
Box 20037, Portland 97220; (503) 257-3041.

PENNSYLVANIA ASSOCIATION OF BROADCASTERS
Richard Wyckoff, pres.; Robert Eolin, Jr., (WLYH-TV, Lancaster), chmn; Brian Danzis (WCMB/WMIX-FM, Harrisburg), vice chmn.
114 South St., Harrisburg 17101; (717) 233-3511.

RHODE ISLAND BROADCASTERS ASSOCIATION
John D. Sawhill, pres.; Roger E. Bouchard, exec. dir.
%WNRI Radio, 786 Diamond Hill Rd., Woonsocket 02895; (401) 769-0600.

ROCKY MOUNTAIN BROADCASTERS ASSOCIATION
Bernard J. Bustos, pres.; Henry Fletcher, exec. dir.
Box 220, Pocatello, Idaho 83204; (208) 233-5020.

SOUTH CAROLINA BROADCASTERS ASSOCIATION
William Saunders, pres.; Dr. Richard M. Uray, exec. mgr.
Univ. of South Carolina College of Journalism, Columbia 29208; (803) 777-6783.

SOUTH DAKOTA BROADCASTERS ASSOCIATION
John Goeman, pres.; Joe Copper, exec. dir.
1018 S. Lyndale, Sioux Falls 57105; (605) 334-2682.

TENNESSEE ASSOCIATION OF BROADCASTERS
Thomas R. King, exec. dir.; Dan Newberg, pres.
Box 40185, Nashville 37204; (615) 331-4535.

TEXAS ASSOCIATION OF BROADCASTERS
Ann Arnold, exec. dir.; Stephanie Glass, office mgr.
400 W. 15th St., Suite 305, Austin 78701; (512) 322-9944.

UTAH BROADCASTERS ASSOCIATION
James Burgoyne (KBLQ) pres.; Earl J. Glade Jr., exec. dir.
Box 401, Provo 84603; (801) 226-3094.

VERMONT ASSOCIATION OF BROADCASTERS
Mark Brady, pres.
%WFAD, Middlebury; (802) 388-2490.

VIRGINIA ASSOCIATION OF BROADCASTERS
Peter Easter, exec. dir.
620 Stagecoach Rd., Charlottesville 22901; (804) 977-3716.

VIRGINIA PUBLIC RADIO ASSOCIATION
Jim Miskimen, pres.; Jerry Glass, secty.-treas.
%WMRA Radio, Harrisonburg 22607; (703) 568-6221.

WASHINGTON STATE ASSOCIATION OF BROADCASTERS
Ron Hughes, pres.; Val Linburgh, secty.-treas.; Karmi Speece, exec. dir.
111 Third Ave., Suite 712, Seattle 98101; (206) 625-0714.

WEST VIRGINIA BROADCASTERS ASSOCIATION
Dale B. Miller (WAJR/WVAQ, Morgantown), pres.; Marilyn Fletcher, exec. dir.
2120 Weberwood Dr., South Charleston 25303; (304) 344-3798.

WISCONSIN BROADCASTERS ASSOCIATION
Gary DeHaven (WISC-TV, Madison), chmn. of board; John Laabs, pres.
44 E. Mifflin St., Suite 205, Madison 53703; (608) 255-2600.

WYOMING ASSOCIATION OF BROADCASTERS
Ray Lansing, exec. secty.-treas.
Box 1873, Cheyenne 82003; (307) 632-7622.

U.S. State and City Film Commissions

ALABAMA

Mark L. Stricklin, Alabama Film Office, 340 N. Hull St., Montgomery, AL 36130; (800) 633-5898; (205) 261-4195; FAX: (205) 265-5078.

ALASKA

Mary Pignalberi, Coordinator, Alaska Motion Picture & TV Production Services, Frontier Bldg., 3601 "C" St., Suite 722, Anchorage, AK 99503; (907) 563-2167; FAX: (907) 562-0048.

ARIZONA

William E. MacCallum, Director, Arizona Film Commission, 1700 W. Washington, 4th floor, Phoenix, AZ 85007; (602) 255-5011; (800) 528-8421; FAX: (602) 542-2146.

City of Phoenix

Luci Alvarado, Motion Picture Coordinating Office, City of Phoenix, Municipal Building, 251 W. Washington St., Phoenix, AZ 85003; (602) 262-4850; (602) 262-8737.

City of Scottsdale

Andrea J. Baumer, Movie Logistics Coordinator, 3939 Civic Center Plaza, Scottsdale, AZ 85251; (602) 994-2335; (602) 994-7809.

City of Tucson

Tom B. Hilderband, Executive Director, Tucson Film Office, P.O. Box 27210, Tucson, AZ 85726; (602) 791-4000; (602) 449-1000; FAX: (602) 791-4017.

ARKANSAS

Christy Johnson, Director, AR Motion Picture Development Office, #One Capitol Mall, Room 2C-200, Little Rock, AR 72201, (501) 682-7676; FAX: (501) 682-7691.

Northwest Arkansas Motion Picture Commission

Phillip Steele, P.O. Box 269, Springdale, AR 72765; (501) 756-2230.

CALIFORNIA

Lisa Rawlins, Director, California Film Commission, 6922 Hollywood Blvd., Suite 600, Hollywood, CA 90028; (213) 736-2465; FAX: (213) 736-3159.

City of Los Angeles

R. Dirk Beving, Los Angeles Motion Picture & TV Coordinating Office, 6922 Hollywood Blvd., Suite 600. Los Angeles, CA 90028; (213) 485-5324; FAX: (213) 237-1020.

Charles M. Weisenberg, Director, Motion Picture/TV Affairs Office, 6922 Hollywood Blvd., Suite 600, Hollywood, CA 90028; (213) 461-8614.

County of Los Angeles

James C. Thornton, Filming Permit Officer, 6922 Hollywood Blvd., Suite 600, Los Angeles, CA 90028; (213) 738-3456; FAX: (213) 463-0613.

City of Oakland

Carol McArthur, Mayor's Film Liaison, Oakland Film Office, 505 14th St., #644, Oakland, CA 94612; (415) 273-3109.

City of San Diego

Wally Schlotter, Vice President & Director, Greg Perry, Assistant Director, San Diego Motion Picture and Television Bureau, 110 W. C St., Suite 1600, San Diego, CA 92101; (619) 234-3456; FAX: (619) 234-0571.

City of San Francisco

Robin Eickman, San Francisco Motion Picture Coordinator, Office of the Mayor, City Hall, Room 200, San Francisco, CA 94102; (415) 554-6144; FAX: (415) 554-6160.

City of San Jose

Joe O'Kane, Executive Director, San Jose Film & Video Commission, 333 W. San Carlos St., Suite 1000, San Jose, CA 95110; (408) 295-9600; (800) 725-2543; FAX: (408) 295-3937.

City of San Mateo

John G. Steen, San Mateo Film Commission, 601 Gateway Blvd., Suite 970, South San Francisco, CA 94080; (415) 952-7600; (800) 288-4448; FAX: (415) 952-5236.

Sonoma County

Sheree Green, Director, Sonoma County Film/Video Commission, 10 Fourth St., Santa Rosa, CA 95401; (707) 575-1191.

COLORADO

Karol Smith, Director; Stephanie Two Eagles, Assistant Director; Tony Schweikle, Asst. Director; Colorado Motion Picture and Television Advisory Commission, 1313 Sherman St., Room 500, Denver, CO 80203; (303) 866-2778; FAX: (303) 866-2251.

Boulder County

Shelly Helmerick, Boulder County Film Commission, 2440 Pearl St., Boulder CO 80302; (303) 442-1044; (800) 444-0447.

CONNECTICUT

Tricia Hood, Coordinator, Connecticut Film Commission, 210 Washington St., Hartford, CT 06106; (203) 566-7947; (203) 566-8458; FAX: (203) 566-4693.

DELAWARE

Kathryn Wheeler, Director, Delaware Development Office; 99 Kings Highway, P.O. Box 1401, Dover, DE 19901; (800) 441-8846; (302) 736-4271.

DISTRICT OF COLUMBIA

Crystal Palmer, Director, Mayor's Office of Motion Picture/Television Development, 1111 E St. NW, Suite 700, Washington, D.C. 20004-2000; (202) 727-6600.

FLORIDA

Ben Harris, Bureau Chief, Motion Picture and Television Bureau, Florida Dept. of Commerce, 501 Collins Bldg., Tallahassee, FL 32399; (908) 487-1100; FAX: (904) 487-1407.

City of Fort Lauderdale

Barbara Zucker, Director, Motion Picture & TV Office, Broward Economic Development Board, One E. Broward Blvd., Suite 1604, Fort Lauderdale, FL 33301; (305) 524-3113.

City of Jacksonville

Dale Eldridge, Motion Picture and Television Liaison Office, 4th Floor, 220 E. Bay St., Jacksonville, FL 32202; (904) 630-1073.

Metro-Dade County

Richard Renick, director, Miami-Dade Film Commission, 73 W. Flagler St., Suite 1900, Miami, FL 33130; (305) 375-3456; FAX: (305) 375-5667.

City of Miami

Nora Swan, Miami Office of Film, Video & Recording, 300 Biscayne Blvd. Way, Suite 400, Miami, FL 33131; (305) 579-3366; (305) 868-1776.

Ocala/Marion County

Sue Sargent, Community Liaison, Ocala/Marion County Film Commission, Economic Development Council, 110 E. Silver Springs Blvd., Ocala, FL 32670; (904) 629-2757; FAX: (904) 629-1581.

City of Orlando

Cathy Savino, director, Orlando Film Office, 315 E. Robinson St., Suite 510, Orlando, FL 32801-1950; (407) 422-7159; FAX: (407) 843-9514.

GEORGIA

Norman Bielowicz, Director, Georgia Film & Videotape Office, 230 Peachtree St. N.W., Suite 650, Atlanta, GA 30303; (404) 656-3591; (404) 656-3544; FAX: (404) 656-3567.

HAWAII

Georgette T. Deemer, Manager, Hawaii Film Industry Branch, P.O. Box 2359, Honolulu, HI 96804; (808) 548-4535; (808) 548-3006; FAX: 548-2189.

IDAHO

Peg Hamende, Film Promotion Specialist, Idaho Film Bureau, 700 W. State St., 2nd floor, Boise, ID 83720; (208) 334-2470; (800) 942-8338; FAX: (208) 334-2631.

ILLINOIS

Suzy Kellett, Director, Illinois Film Office, State of Illinois Center, 100 W. Randolph, Suite 3-400, Chicago, IL 60601; (312) 917-3600; FAX: (312) 917-6732.

City of Chicago

Kathryn Darrell, Director, Chicago Office of Film & Entertainment, 174 W. Randolph, Chicago, IL 60601; (312) 744-6415.

INDIANA

Karen Galvin, Executive Director, Indiana Film Commission, Indiana Department of Commerce, 1 N. Capitol Ave., Suite 700, Indianapolis, IN 42602-2288; (317) 232-8829.

IOWA

Wendol Jarvis, Iowa Film Office, 200 E. Grand Ave., Suite A, Des Moines, IA 50309; (515) 281-8319; (515) 277-3328.

KANSAS

Jerry Jones, Coordinator, Kansas Film Commission, 400 W. 8th, 5th floor, Topeka, KS 66603; (913) 296-2009; FAX: (913) 296-5055.

KENTUCKY

Bert Harberson, Film Commissioner, Kentucky Film Office, Berry Hill Mansion, Louisville Rd., Frankfort, KY 40601; (502) 564-FILM; FAX: (502) 564-3256.

LOUISIANA

Tesa La Violette, Director, Louisiana Office of Film and Video, P.O. Box 94361, Baton Rouge, LA 70804; (504) 342-8150.

City of Kenner

Charles Ward, Chairman, 1801 Williams Blvd., Kenner, LA 70062; (504) 468-7227.

MAINE

Leah Girardin, Director, Maine Film Commission, 189 State St., Station 59, Augusta, ME 04333; (207) 289-5710.

MARYLAND

Jay Schlossberg-Cohen, Director, Maryland Film Commission, 217 Redwood St., 9th floor, Baltimore, MD 21202; (301) 333-6633.

MASSACHUSETTS

Mary Lou Crane, Director, Massachusetts Film Office, Transportation Bldg., 10 Park Plaza, Suite 2310, Boston, MA 02116; (617) 973-8800.

MICHIGAN

Darryl Beasley, Acting Director, Michigan Film Office, Michigan Plaza Bldg., 1200 Sixth St., 19th floor, Detroit, MI 48226; (313) 256-2000; (313) 379-0642.

MINNESOTA

Kelly Pratt, Executive Director, Minnesota Motion Picture & TV Board, 100 N. 6th St., Suite 880C, Minneapolis, MN 55403; (612) 332-6493.

MISSISSIPPI

Phil Cole, director; Maida Morgan, asst. dir., Mississippi State Film Office, P.O. Box 849, Jackson, MS 39205; (601) 359-3449.

City of Biloxi

Reba Capers, Biloxi Film Commission, P.O. Box 246, Biloxi, MS 39533; (601) 374-3190.

City of Columbus

Carolyn Denton, Columbus Film Commission, P.O. Box 789, Columbus, MS 39703; (601) 329-1191; (800) 327-2686.

City of Natchez

Jack Gebhardt, Natchez Film Commission, 311 Natchez Rd., Natchez, MS 39120; (601) 446-6345; (800) 647-6724.

MISSOURI

Gary J. Gonder, Manager, Missouri Film Commission, Harry S. Truman Bldg., Room 770, P.O. Box 118, Jefferson City, MO 65102; (314) 751-9050; 751-4241; FAX: (314) 751-5183.

MONTANA

Garry Wunderwald, Director, Montana Film Commission, 1424 Ninth Ave., Helena, MT 59620; (406) 444-2654; (800) 548-3390; FAX: (406) 444-2808.

City of Billings

Earl Rosell, Billings Montana Film Commission, 4200 Rimrock Rd., Billings, MT 59102; (406) 656-0645; (406) 656-4226.

City of Butte/Silver Bow

Marilyn Maney, Butte/Silver Bow Film & Video Commission, Office of the Chief Executive, Courthouse, Butte, MT 59701; (406) 723-8262; (406) 782-2111.

NEBRASKA

Janet K. Traub, Film Officer, P.O. Box 95143, Lincoln NE 68509, (402) 471-2593; (800) 426-6506; FAX: (402) 471-3778.

City of Lincoln

Doug Breisch, coordinator, Lincoln Film & TV Office, 129 N. 10th St., Room 11, Lincoln, NE 68508; (402) 471-7375; (402) 471-7432.

NEVADA

Bob Hirsch, Motion Picture & TV Division, Nevada Commission on Economic Development, McCarran Intl. Airport, Esplanade Level, Las Vegas, NV 89158; (702) 486-7150; (702) 851-0836.

NEW HAMPSHIRE

Ann Kennard, Director, New Hampshire Film and Television Bureau, Box 856, Concord, NH 03301; (603) 271-2598; FAX: (603) 271-2629.

NEW JERSEY

Joe Friedman, Motion Picture and Television Commission, 1 Gateway Center, Suite 510, Newark, NJ 07102; (201) 648-6279.

NEW MEXICO

Linda Taylor Hutchison, Director, New Mexico Film Commission, 1050 Old Pecos Trail, Santa Fe, NM 87501; (800) 545-9871 (toll-free); (505) 827-8580 (in-state).

City of Albuquerque

Gordon Sanders, Film Commissioner, Albuquerque Film Commission, Mayor's Office, 1 Civic Plaza N.W., Albuquerque, NM 87103; (505) 768-4512.

NEW YORK

Pepper O'Brien, Commissioner, New York State Governor's Office for Motion Picture & Television Development, 1515 Broadway, 32nd floor, New York, NY 10036; (212) 575-6570.

City of New York

Patricia Reed-Scott, Mayor's Office of Motion Pictures, TV & Theatre, 254 W. 54 St., 10019; (212) 489-6710; (212) 489-6714; FAX: (212) 581-6949.

Nassau County

Stephanie Carlino, Director, Nassau County Film Office, 1550 Franklin Ave., Mineola, NY 11501; (516) 535-4160; FAX: (516) 535-4229.

Suffolk County

Martin R. Cantor, Director, Suffolk County Motion Picture & TV Commission, H. Lee Dennison Bldg., Veterans Memorial Highway, Happauge, NY 11788; (516) 360-4800.

NORTH CAROLINA

William Arnold, Director, North Carolina Film Commission, 430 N. Salisbury St., Raleigh, NC 27611; (919) 733-9900; FAX: (919) 733-0110.

NORTH DAKOTA

Pamela Staehnke, Director, North Dakota Film Office, Liberty Memorial Bldg., State Capitol, Bismarck, ND 58505; (701) 224-2525; (800) 437-2077.

OHIO

Eve Lapolla, Manager, Ohio Film Bureau, 30 E. Broad St., 23rd Floor, Columbus, OH 43266; (614) 466-2284 or (800) 848-1300.

OKLAHOMA

Mary Nell Clark, Director, Oklahoma Film Office, 6601 Broadway Extension, Oklahoma City, OK 73116; (800) 443-OKLA; (405) 841-5135; Telex: 350352; FAX: (405) 841-5199.

OREGON

Marjie Lundell, Director, Oregon Film Office, Film & Video Division, Economic Development Dept., 595 Cottage St., N.E., Salem, OR 97310; (503) 373-1232; (800) 547-7842.

City of Portland

Janet Hazzard, Film & Video Coordinator, Portland Film & Video Office, 1220 S.W. Fifth Ave., Suite 303, Portland, OR 97204; (503) 248-4739; FAX: (505) 243-7306.

PENNSYLVANIA

T. William Hanson, Film Bureau, Forum Bldg., Suite 449, Harrisburg, PA 17120; (717) 783-FILM (3456).

City of Philadelphia

Janet Herrington, Director, Film Office, 120 Municipal Services Bldg., Philadelphia, PA 19102-1684; (215) 686-2668.

RHODE ISLAND

Amy Shapiro, Executive Director, Rhode Island Film Commission, Old State House, 150 Benefit St., Providence, RI 02903; (401) 277-3456; (401) 277-3468.

SOUTH CAROLINA

Isabel Hill, South Carolina Film Office, P.O. Box 927, Columbia, SC 29201; (803) 737-0400; (803) 734-1400.

SOUTH DAKOTA

Gary Keller, Video-Films Promotions Coordinator, Capital Lake Plaza, Pierre, SD 57501; (605) 773-3301; (800) 843-8000; FAX: (605) 773-3256.

TENNESSEE

Dancy L. Jones, Executive Director of the Film, Entertainment & Music Commission, Rachel Jackson Bldg., 320 Sixth Ave., N., 7th floor, Nashville, TN 37219; (615) 741-3456; (800) 251-8594; FAX: (615) 741-5829.

Memphis & Shelby County

Linn Sitler, Executive Director, Memphis-Shelby Co. Film/Tape/Music Commission, 157 Poplar, Suite 402, Memphis, TN 38103; (901) 576-4284.

TEXAS

Dana Shelton, Texas Film Music Office, P.O. Box 12728, Capitol Station, Austin, TX 78711; (512) 469-9111; FAX: (512) 320-9674.

City of El Paso

Bob Knight, El Paso Film Commission, One Civic Center Plaza, El Paso, TX 79901; (915) 534-0698; (800) 351-6024; FAX: (915) 532-2963.

City of Houston

Lisa D. Graziano, Director, Houston Film Commission, 3300 Main St., Houston, TX 77002; (713) 523-5050 or (800) 231-7799; Telex: 203274; FAX: (713) 524-5376.

City of Irving

Ed Spacek, Film Commissioner, Irving Film Commission, 1 Dallas Communications Complex LB119, Irving, TX 75039-3510; (214) 252-CINE; (800) 247-8464.

North Texas

Roger Burke, North Texas Film Commission, 6311 N. O'Connor Road, #N57-LB57, Irving, TX 75039; (214) 869-7657; FAX: (214) 869-7748.

UTAH

Leigh von der Esch, Director, Utah Film Commission, State Office Bldg., Suite 6220, Salt Lake City, UT 84114; (801) 538-3039; (800) 453-8824; FAX: (801) 538-3396.

City of Moab

Bette L. Stanton, Executive Director, Moab Film Commission, 59 S. Main St., 2nd Floor, Moab, UT 84532; (801) 259-6388.

Park City

Gregg Goodwin, Director, Park City Film Commission, Park City Chamber of Commerce, P.O. Box 1630, Park City, UT 84060; (800) 453-1360; FAX: (801) 649-4132.

Southwest Utah

M. Ramona Larsen, Southwest Utah Film Commission, 97 E. St. George Blvd., St. George, UT 84770; (801) 673-8824.

VERMONT

J. Gregory Gerdel, Vermont Film Bureau, Agency of Development and Community Affairs, 134 State St., Montpelier, VT 05602; (802) 828-3236; (802) 828-3230; FAX: (802) 828-2222.

VIRGINIA

Jarold Sole, Deputy Director, Virginia Film Office, 1000 Washington Bldg., Richmond, VA 23219; (804) 786-3791.

Fairfax County

Pat Archer, Film Office, 8300 Boone Blvd., Suite 450, Vienna, VA 22180; (703) 790-0600.

WASHINGTON STATE

Christine Lewis, Manager, Washington State Film & Video Office, 312 First Ave. N., Seattle, WA 98109; (206) 464-7148; (206) 464-7650; FAX: (206) 464-7222.

WEST VIRGINIA

Steve Fesenmaier, Film Services & Library Commission, Science and Cultural Center, Charleston, WV 25305; (304) 348-3976.

WISCONSIN

Milton A. Strauss, Film Office, Department of Development, 123 W. Washington Ave., P.O. Box 7970, Madison, WI 53707; (608) 267-FILM; FAX: (608) 267-2829.

WYOMING

Bill D. Lindstrom, Director, Wyoming Film Office, Wyoming Travel Commission, Interstate 25 at College Dr., Cheyenne, WY 82002; (800) 458-6657 or (307) 777-7777; FAX: (307) 777-6904.

City of Jackson Hole

Carol Bowers, Director/Liaison, Jackson Hole Film Commission, P.O. Box E, Jackson, WY 83001; (307) 733-3316; FAX: (307) 733-5585.

Lander Valley

Linda Van Fleet, Manager, Lander Film Commission, 160 N. First St., Lander, WY 82520; (307) 332-3892; (800) 433-0662.

PUERTO RICO

Luis Ramos, Executive Director, Puerto Rico Film Institute, P.O. Box 2350, San Juan, PR 00936; (809) 758-4747; 754-7110; FAX: (809) 764-1415.

VIRGIN ISLANDS

Winston DeLugo, Director; Eric Matthews, Asst. Dir., Film Promotion Office, P.O. Box 6400, St. Thomas VI 00801; (809) 774-8784; (809) 776-0140; Telex: 3470063.

The Television Press

* TRADE PUBLICATIONS
* NEWSPAPER LISTING

Trade Publications

Quigley Publishing Company

Publishers of Motion Picture Almanac (Annual), Television and Video Almanac (Annual). 159 W. 53 St., New York, NY 10019; (212) 247-3100; Cable: Quigpubco, New York; FAX: (212) 489-0871.

PRESIDENT AND PUBLISHER
Martin Quigley, Jr.
VICE PRESIDENT & MANAGING DIRECTOR
Robert McDonald
EDITOR-IN-CHIEF
Jane Klain

LONDON BUREAU
William Pay, Manager and London Editor; 15 Samuel Rd., Langdon Hills, Basildon, Essex, England. Tel.: 0268-417-055.

CANADIAN BUREAU
Patricia Thompson, Editor; 1430 Yonge St., Suite 214, Toronto, Ont. M4T 1Y6 Canada.

FOREIGN CORRESPONDENTS

CHILE: Alan Hootnick, Lo Arcaya 1963, Vitacura Chile; 56-2-220-0807; FAX: 56-2-215-1802.
EGYPT: Ahmed Sami, 4 El Ommara St., Apt. 13, Abbassia, Cairo; Tel: 2825915/2588166.
FRANCE: Vernice Klier-Moskowitz, 80 Ave. Charles de Gaulle, Neuilly Sur Seine 92200 France.
GREECE: Rena Velissariou, 8432, Kolokotroni Str., Agia Paraskevi, Attikis, Athens. (804) 153 42, Greece; Tel: 65 67 665.
HOLLAND: Paul Silvius, 467 W. Halfront, 1183 JD Amstelveen, Netherlands.
INDIA: B. D. Garga, 55 Anita, Mt. Pleasant Rd., Bombay 400006, India; Tel.: 8122019.
JAPAN: A. C. Pinder, Whaley-Eaton Service, Central P.O. Box 190, Tokyo, Japan.
PAKISTAN: A.R. Slote, P.O. Box 7426, Karachi, 1–3.
SCANDINAVIA: Inge Hanson, Inge Hanson Publicity, P.O. Box 7050, S-17107, Solna, Sweden. Tel. & FAX: 46-8-850980.
SWITZERLAND: Gabriella Broggi, Via E. Maraini 20B, 6900 Massagna, Switzerland; Tel.: (091) 5629 10.
VENEZUELA: Victoria M. Marshall, RWI, 8621 Beverly Blvd., Suite 210, Beverly Hills, CA 90211.

Motion Picture Almanac

(Annually) 159 W. 53 St., New York, NY 10019; (212) 247-3100; Cable: Quigpubco, New York; FAX: (212) 489-0871.

EDITOR
Jane Klain
BRITISH EDITOR
William Pay
CANADIAN EDITOR
Patricia Thompson

Television & Video Almanac

(Annually) 159 W. 53 St., New York, NY 10019; (212) 247-3100; Cable: Quigpubco, New York; FAX: (212) 489-0871.

EDITOR
Jane Klain
BRITISH EDITOR
William Pay
CANADIAN EDITOR
Patricia Thompson

Advertising Age

(Weekly) 740 Rush St., Chicago, IL 60611; (312) 649-5200; 220 E. 42 St., New York, NY 10017; (212) 210-0100.

CHAIRMAN
Mrs. G. D. Crain
CHAIRMAN, EXECUTIVE COMMITTEE
S. R. Bernstein
PUBLISHER
Louis F. Demarco
PRESIDENT & EDITOR-IN-CHIEF
Rance Crain

The American Cinematographer

(Monthly on the 1st—Semi-technical) Published by American Society of Cinematographers, Inc., 1782 N. Orange Dr., Hollywood, CA 90028; (213) 876-5080.

EDITOR
George Turner
ASSISTANT EDITOR
Jean Turner
ADVERTISING
Angie Gollmann
CIRCULATION MANAGER
Patty Armacost

Back Stage

(Weekly dealing with theatrical and nontheatrical films, television shows and commercials, cassettes, radio, and theater, published Friday), 330 W. 42 St., New York, NY 10036; (212) 947-0020; 5150 Wilshire Blvd., Los Angeles, CA 90036; (213) 936-5200; 100 E. Ohio St., Chicago, IL 60611; (312) 943-0051.

ADVERTISING DIRECTOR & PUBLISHER
Ira Eaker
ASSOCIATE PUBLISHER
Anthony Vagnoni
EDITOR
Richard Miller

Back Stage TV, Film & Tape Production Directory

(Annually, March), 330 W. 42 St., New York, NY 10036; (212) 947-0020.

EDITOR
Theresa Piti

Billboard

(Weekly dealing with records, music, entertainment artists, video hardware and software, etc., published Saturdays), 9107 Wilshire Blvd., Beverly Hills, CA 90210; (213) 273-7040; 1515 Broadway, New York, NY 10036, (212) 764-7300; 49 Music Square W., Nashville, TN 37203; (615) 321-4290; 806 15 St., N.W., Washington, D.C. 20005; (202) 783-3282.

PUBLISHER/EDITOR-IN-CHIEF
Sam Holdsworth
ASSOCIATE PUBLISHER/DIRECTOR OF RESEARCH
Marty Feely
MANAGING EDITOR
Ken Schlager

Broadcasting—The News Magazine of the Fifth Estate

(Weekly on Monday; also publishes Broadcasting Yearbook every March.) Washington Headquarters: 1705 DeSales St., N.W., 20036; (202) 659-2340; New York: 630 Third Ave., 10017; (212) 599-2830; Hollywood: 1680 N. Vine St., 90028; (213) 463-3148.

PRESIDENT AND PUBLISHER
Lawrence B. Taishoff
VICE PRESIDENT/OPERATIONS
David N. Whitcombe
VICE PRESIDENT/MANAGING EDITOR
Donald V. West
VICE PRESIDENT/SALES & MARKETING
Kenneth W. Taishoff

Celebrity Bulletin

(A chronicle of the day-to-day activities of celebrities in New York, Hollywood, London, Paris and Rome. Published daily.) 1780 Broadway, New York, NY 10019; (212) 757-7979.

PUBLISHER
Celebrity Service, Inc.

Celebrity Register

(A biographical index, published every two years) 1780 Broadway, Suite 300, New York, NY 10019; (212) 757-7979; 1 (800) FOR ÇELEBS.

PUBLISHER
Gale Research
EDITOR
Patsy Maharam

Celebrity Services Contact Book

(An entertainment industry directory, published annually by Celebrity Service International) 1780 Broadway, Suite 300, New York, NY 10019; (212) 757- 7979.

EDITOR
Patsy Maharam

Daily Variety

(Motion picture, television, homevideo, pay-TV, cable, radio, theatre, night clubs, daily) 5700 Wilshire Blvd., Suite 120, Los Angeles, CA 90036, (213) 857-6600.

EDITOR
Peter P. Pryor
ASSOCIATE PUBLISHER
Michael Silverman
MANAGING EDITOR
Richard Bozanich
MARKETING DIRECTOR
Pattikay Lee
PRODUCTION MANAGER
Bob Butler

Electronics

(Industry management magazine covering technology and business. Published monthly) VNU Business Publication Inc., Ten Holland Dr., Hasbrook Heights, NJ 07604; (201) 393-6000.

PUBLISHER
Jim Uhl
EDITOR-IN-CHIEF
J. Robert Lineback
EXECUTIVE EDITOR
Jeremy Young

Film Quarterly

(Quarterly; published Fall, Winter, Spring, and Summer. A critical journal of motion pictures and their related arts; successor to *The Quarterly of Film, Radio and Television* and *The Hollywood Quarterly.*) Editorial, Sales, and Advertising office: University of California Press, 2120 Berkeley Way, Berkeley, CA 94720; (415) 642-6333.

EDITOR
Ernest Callenbach
Published by University of California Press

Hollywood Creative Directory

(Who's what and where in motion picture and television production and development. Over 750 companies and 2,400 names listed, indexed and cross-referenced. Published every four months.) 451 Kelton Ave., Los Angeles, CA 90024; (213) 208-1961. Organized 1987.

PUBLISHER/OWNER
David Sterling

Hollywood Reporter, The

(Film, TV, entertainment daily) 6715 Sunset Blvd., Hollywood, 90028 CA; (213) 464-7411; and 1501 Broadway, New York, NY, 10036; (212) 354-1858.

PRESIDENT
Robert J. Dowling
PUBLISHER & EDITOR-IN-CHIEF
Tichi Wilkerson Kassel
EDITOR
Teri Ritzer
BUREAUS
NEW YORK: 1501 Broadway, New York, NY 10036; (212) 354-1858.
WASHINGTON D.C.: Rm. 1139, National Press Bldg., Washington DC, 20045; (202) 737-2828.
LONDON: 57 Duke St., London W.1.; 01-629/6765, 6766.

I.A.T.S.E. Official Bulletin

(Quarterly) 1515 Broadway, Suite 601, New York, NY 10036; (212) 730-1770.

EDITOR
James J. Riley

International Photographer

(Monthly, on the 5th) 7715 Sunset Blvd., Suite 300, Hollywood, CA 90046; (213) 876-0160.

PUBLISHER
International Photographer
EDITOR
George Toscas

International Motion Picture Almanac

(See Quigley Publications)

International Television and Video Almanac

(See Quigley Publication)

Journal of the Society of Motion Picture and Television Engineers

(Technical monthly) Editorial office: SMPTE Headquarters, 595 W. Hartsdale Ave., White Plains, NY 10607; (914) 761-1100.

EDITOR
Jeffrey B. Friedman
ADVERTISING MANAGER
Pat Nagy

Journal of the Syd Cassyd Archives Academy of Television Arts & Sciences

(Quarterly) 917 S. Tremaine, Hollywood 90019, CA; (213) 939-2345. Founded 1946.

EDITOR
Syd Cassyd

Journal of Syd Cassyd Archives: Hollywood Report

(Quarterly) 917 S. Tremaine Ave., Hollywood, 90019, CA; (213) 939-2345.

EDITOR
Syd Cassyd

Millimeter

(A monthly magazine covering the motion picture and television production industries.) Headquarters: 826

Broadway, New York, NY 10003; (212) 477-4700; Fax: (212) 228-5859; 501 Santa Monica Blvd., Suite 504, Santa Monica, CA 90401; (213) 393-9285; 6725 Sunset Blvd., Suite 402, Los Angeles, CA 90028; (213) 461-6622.

PUBLISHER
Sam Kintzer
EDITOR
Alison Johns

The Producer's Master-Guide

(Annual) 330 W. 42 St., 16 Floor, New York, NY 10036-6994; (212) 465-8889; FAX: (212) 465-8880. International reference guide for producers in the motion picture, television, commercials, cable and videotape industries in the U.S., Canada, the Caribbean Islands, Bermuda, the United Kingdom, New Zealand, and Australia.

PUBLISHER
Shmuel Bension

QV Publishing, Inc.

P.O. Box 2000, York, ME 03909. Organized 1982. (Provides information about cable/television sports, pay-per-view, and interactive services for the lodging market via newsletters, directories and other publications and seminars. Publishes Pay Per Views Magazine.)

PRESIDENT
Dantia Gould

Radio-Electronics

(Monthly dealing with technical aspects of electronics, including TV, radio, computers, and electronic service technicians, high-fidelity enthusiasts and experimenters) 500B Bicounty Blvd., Farmingdale, NY 11735; (516) 293-3000.

PUBLISHER
Larry Steckler
EDITORIAL DIRECTOR
Art Kleiman
MANAGING EDITOR
Brian Fenton

SMPTE Journal

(Technical monthly) 595 West Hartsdale Ave., White Plains, NY 10607; (914) 761-1100.

EDITOR
Jeffrey B. Friedman
ADVERTISING MANAGER
Janice Baio

TV Facts, Figures, Film & TV

A Division of C.C. Publishing (Magazine for syndicated programming and promotion). 19 W. 44 St., Suite 812, New York, NY 10036; (212) 302-2680.

PUBLISHER
Harvey Seslowsky
VICE PRESIDENT & EDITOR-IN-CHIEF
Miss Avra Fliegelman

Television Digest

(Published weekly by Warren Publishing. Television Digest with Consumer Electronics, TV & Cable Action Update, Annual Television & Cable Factbook, Annual Cable & Station Coverage Atlas, Satellite Week, Video Week, Biweekly Public Broadcasting Report, Monthly Early Warning Report, Communications Daily, Bi-weekly Space Commerce Bulletin, Weekly Common Carrier Week) 2115 Ward Court, N.W., Washington, DC 20037; (202) 872-9200.

EDITOR & PUBLISHER
Albert Warren
EDITORIAL DIRECTOR
David Lachenbruch
EXECUTIVE EDITOR
Dawson B. Nail
SENIOR EDITOR & ASSOCIATE PUBLISHER
Paul L. Warren

Television & Cable Factbook

(Published annually by Warren Publishing, Inc.) 2115 Ward Court, N.W., Washington, DC 20037; (202) 872-9200.

EDITOR & PUBLISHER
Albert Warren
MANAGING EDITOR
Michael C. Taliaferro
EDITORIAL DIRECTOR
Mary Appel

Television Index

40-29 27th St., Long Island City, NY 11101, (718) 937-3990.

EDITOR & PUBLISHER
Jonathan Miller

Television/Radio Age

(Bi-weekly trade magazine) 1270 Ave. of the Americas, New York, NY 10020; (212) 757-8400.

PUBLISHER
Sol J. Paul
EDITOR
Sol J. Paul
EXECUTIVE EDITOR
Alfred J. Jaffe
MANAGING EDITOR
Ed Rosenthal
ASSISTANT EDITORS
Bob Sobel, George Swisshelm, Jim Forkan
PRODUCTION DIRECTOR
Marvin Rabach
BRANCH OFFICES
6290 Sunset Blvd., Suite 315, Los Angeles, CA 90028; Keepers Lodge, Hatfield Park, Hatfield Herts, England, AL9 5P5; 716 S. Wayne St., Arlington, VA 22204.

Variety

(A Cahners Publication) (International entertainment business weekly, published Wednesdays) 475 Park Ave. S., New York, NY 10016; (212) 779-1100; FAX: (212) 779-0026; 5700 Wilshire Blvd., Suite #120, Los Angeles, CA 90036; (213) 857-6600; 1483 Chain Bridge Rd., McLean, VA 22101; (703) 448-0510; 625 North Michigan Ave., Chicago, IL 60611; (312) 337-4984; *Paris*: 33 Champs Elysees, 75008 France; Phone 40 74 0001; *Rome:* VARIETY, Lungotevere Flaminio 22, Rome 00196; 361-3103; *London:* 34/35 Newman St., W1P 3PD England, 637-3663; *Madrid:* Calle Lagasca, 104, 28006, Spain; Phone 276-4262; *Sydney, Australia:* 1-7 Albion Place, 2000, N.S.W. Phone: 61-3124; *Toronto:* 74 Albany Ave., Ont.; (416) 531-1600; *Scandinavia:* 43 Vimmelskaftet, Copenhagen, Denmark; Phone: 33 91 0040; *Munich:* Zittelstrasse, 4 Germany; Phone: 30-89130.

PUBLISHER
Syd Silverman
EDITOR
Roger Watkins
SALES
Martin Feldman

GREAT BRITAIN

Image Technology

(Technical monthly) Journal of the British Kinematograph, Sound and Television Society. 549 Victoria House, Vernon Place, London, WC1B 4DJ. Tel.: 01 242-8400.

Screen International

Published by King Publications Ltd. Weekly, covering news, reviews, comment and pictures of the film and television industries. 6-7 Great Chapel Street, London, W.1. Tel.: 01 43 5741.

PUBLISHER
Peter King
EDITOR
Peter Noble

FRANCE

Le Film Français

(Weekly French motion picture trade magazine) 103 Blvd. St. Michel Paris, France, 75005; U.S. office: 1144 Corondo Terrace, Los Angeles, CA 90026 (818) 990-3800; FAX: (818) 990-4854.

PUBLISHER
Denis Jacob
EDITOR
Pierre Rival
U.S. EDITOR
Patricia Saperstein

Newspapers in Principal Markets of the U.S.

Arranged alphabetically by states, this list gives the names and addresses of newspapers in cities and market areas of over 100,000 population which maintain regular motion picture and television departments.

Alabama

Birmingham, The News, 2200 N. 4th Ave., 35202.
Birmingham, Post-Herald, 2200 N. 4th Ave., 35202.
Huntsville, Times, 2317 Memorial Pkway., 35807.
Mobile, Mobile Press Register., 304 Government St., 36602.
Montgomery, Advertiser, 200 Washington Ave., 36104.

Arizona

Phoenix, Gazette, 120 E. Van Buren St., 85004.
Phoenix, Republic, 120 E. Van Buren St., 85004.
Tucson, Arizona Daily Star, 4850 S. Park Ave., 85726.

Arkansas

Little Rock, Democrat, Capitol Ave. & Scott, 72203.
Little Rock, Arkansas Gazette, 112 W. Third St., 72203.

California

Fresno, Bee, 1626 E St., 93706.
Glendale, News Press, 111 N. Isabel, 91209.
Long Beach, Press-Telegram, 604 Pine Ave., 90801.
Los Angeles, Daily News, P.O. Box 4200, 90042.
Los Angeles, Herald-Examiner, 1111 S. Broadway., 90054.
Los Angeles, Times, Times Mirror Sq., 90053.
Oakland, The Tribune, 401 13th St., 94612.
Pasadena, Star News, 525 E. Colorado St., 91109.
Riverside, Press-Enterprise Co., 3512 14th St., 92502.
Sacramento, Bee, 2100 Q St., 95813.
Sacramento, Sacramento Union Inc., 301 Capitol Mall, 95812.
San Bernardino, Sun, 399 "D" St., 92401.
San Diego, DBA Union-Tribune, 351 Camino de la Reina, 92108.
San Francisco, Chronicle, 901 Mission St., 94119.
San Francisco, The Examiner, 110 5th St., 94119.
San Jose, Mercury-News, 750 Ridder Park Dr., 95131.
San Pedro, News Pilot, 362 W. 7th St., 90733.
Santa Ana, Orange County Register, 625 N. Grand Ave., 92711.
Stockton, Stockton Daily Record, 530 E. Market St., 95202.
Torrance, South Bay Breeze, 5215 Torrance Blvd., 90503.
West Covina, Tribune-San Gabriel Valley, 1210 N. Azusa Canyon Rd., 91790.

Colorado

Denver, The Post, 650 15th St., 80202.
Denver, Rocky Mountain News, 400 W. Colfax Ave., 80204.

Connecticut

Bridgeport, Post, 410 State St., 06602.
Hartford, Courant, 285 Broad St., 06101.
New Haven, Register, 40 Sargent Dr., 06511.
Waterbury, American-Republican, Inc., 389 Meadow St., 06702.

Delaware

Wilmington, News-Journal Co., 831 Orange St., 19899.

District of Columbia

Washington, Post, 1515 "L" St., N.W., 20005.
Washington, Times, 3600 New York Ave., N.E., 20002.
Washington, USA Today, 1001 16th St. N.W., 20036.

Florida

Fort Lauderdale, News, 101 N. New River Drive E., 33301.
Fort Lauderdale, Sun Sentinel, 101 N. New River Drive E., 33301.
Jacksonville, Florida Times-Union, One Riverside Ave., 32201.
Miami, Herald, 1 Herald Plaza, 33101.
Miami, The News, 1 Herald Plaza, 33101.
Orlando, Sentinel, 633 N. Orange Ave., 32801.
St. Petersburg, Times, 1301 34th St. N., 33713.
Sarasota, Herald Tribune, 801 S. Tamiami Trail, 34236.
Tampa, Tribune, 202 S. Parker, 33606.

Georgia

Atlanta, Journal-Constitution, 72 Marietta St. N.W., 30303.
Columbus, Ledger-Enquirer Newspapers, 17 W. 12th St., 31902.
Macon, Telegraph & News, 120 Broadway, 31201.
Savannah, Savannah News-Press, 105-111 W. Bay St., 31402.

Hawaii

Honolulu, Advertiser, P.O. Box 3110, 96802.
Honolulu, Honolulu Star-Bulletin, Inc., P.O. Box 3080, 96802.
Honolulu, Hawaii Hochi, 917 Kokea St., 96817.

Illinois

Chicago, The Sun-Times, 401 N. Wabash, 60611.
Chicago, Tribune, 435 N. Michigan Ave., 60611.
Joliet, Herald News, 300 Caterpillar Dr., 60436.
Lansing, Daily Calumet & Pointer, 18127 William, 60438.
Moline, Daily Dispatch, 1720 5th Ave., 61265.
Peoria, Peoria Journal Star Inc., 201 S.W. Jefferson Ave., 61602.
Rock Island, Argus, 1724 4th Ave., 61202.
Rockford, Register-Star, 99 E. State St., 61105.
Waukegan, News-Sun, 100 W. Madison St., 60085.

Indiana

Evansville, Courier & Press, 201 N.W. 2nd St., 47701.
Fort Wayne, Journal-Gazette, 600 W. Main St., 46802.
Fort Wayne, News Sentinel, 600 W. Main St., 46802.
Gary, Post-Tribune, 1065 Broadway, 46402.
Hammond, Times, 417 Fayette St., 46320.
Indianapolis, Star & News, 307 N. Pennsylvania St., 46206.
South Bend, Tribune, 225 W. Colfax, 46626.

Iowa

Cedar Rapids, Gazette, 500 3rd Ave., S.E., 52401.
Davenport, Quad City Times, 124 E. 2nd St., 52808.
Des Moines, Register & Tribune, 715 Locust St., 50304.
Sioux City, Journal, 515 Pavonia St., 51101.
Waterloo, Courier, 501 Commercial St., 50704.

Kansas

Kansas City, Kansan, 901 N. 8th St., 66101.
Topeka, Capital-Journal, 616 Jefferson, 66607.
Wichita, The Eagle and Beacon, 825 E. Douglas St., 67201.

Kentucky

Lexington, Herald-Leader, Main & Midland, 40507.
Louisville, The Courier-Journal & Times, 525 W. Broadway, 40202.

Louisiana

Baton Rouge, Advocate, 525 Lafayette St., 70821.
New Orleans, The Times-Picayune, 3800 Howard Ave., 70140.
Shreveport, Journal-Times, 222 Lake St., 71102.

Maryland

Baltimore, Sun, 501 North, 21230.

Massachusetts

Boston, Christian Science Monitor, One Norway St., 02115.
Boston, Globe, 135 Morrissey Blvd., 02107.
Boston, Boston-Herald, 1 Herald Square, 02106.
New Bedford, Standard-Times, 555 Pleasant St., 02742.
Springfield, Republican, 1860 Main St., 01101.
Worcester, Worcester Telegram & Gazette, 20 Franklin St., 01601.

Michigan

Ann Arbor, News, 340 E. Huron St., 48106.
Detroit, Free Press, 321 W. Lafayette Blvd., 48231.
Detroit, News, 615 W. Lafayette Blvd., 48231.
Flint, The Journal, 200 E. 1st St., 48502.
Grand Rapids, The Press, 155 Michigan N.W., 49503.
Kalamazoo, Kalamazoo Gazette, 401 S. Burdick St., 49003.
Lansing, State Journal, 120 E. Lenawee St., 48919.
Muskegon, Chronicle, 981 Third St., 49443.
Royal Oak, Tribune, 4500 Delemere Blvd., 48073.
Saginaw, News, 203 S. Washington Ave., 48605.

Minnesota

Duluth, News-Tribune, 424 W. 1st., 55801.
Minneapolis, Star & Tribune, 425 Portland Ave., 55415.
St. Paul, Pioneer Press Dispatch, 345 Cedar St., 55101.

Mississippi

Biloxi-Gulfport, Sun-Herald, 1320 De Buys Rd., 39531.
Jackson, Clarion Ledger-News, 311 E. Pearl, 39201.

Missouri

Kansas City, Star Times, 1729 Grand Ave., 64108.
St. Louis, The Post-Dispatch, 900 N. Tucker Blvd., 63101.
Springfield, Springfield News & Leader, 651 Boonville, 65801.

Nebraska

Lincoln, Journal-Star, 926 "P" Street, 68501.
Omaha, World-Herald, 14th & Dodge, Sts., 68102.

Nevada

Las Vegas, Review-Journal, 1111 W. Bonanza, 89106.
Las Vegas, Sun, 121 S. Highland Ave., 89104.

New Hampshire

Manchester, Union Leader, 35 Amherst St., 03105.

New Jersey

Cherry Hill, Courier-Post, P.O. Box 5300, 08034.
Elizabeth, Journal, 295-299 N. Broad St., 07207.
Hackensack, The Record, 150 River St., 07601.
Jersey City, Journal, 30 Journal Square, 07306.
Neptune, Asbury Park Press, 3601 State Hwy. 66, 07753.
Newark, Newark Star Ledger, 1 Star Ledger Plaza, 07101.
Passaic-Clifton, Herald-News, 988 Main Ave., 07055.
Paterson, News, News Plaza & Straight St., 07509.
Trenton, Times, 500 Perry St., 08618.

New Mexico

Albuquerque, Journal, 7777 Jefferson N.E., 87109.
Albuquerque, Tribune, 7777 Jefferson N.E., 87109.

New York

Buffalo, The Evening News, 1 News Plaza, 14203.
Colonie, Times-Union, News-Plaza, 12211.
Melville, Newsday, 235 Pinelawn Rd., 11747.
New York City:
Brooklyn Daily, Inc., 129 Montague St., Brooklyn, 11201.
The Daily News, 220 E. 42 St., 10017.
The Post, 210 South St., 10002
The Times, 229 W. 43 St.,10036.
The Village Voice, 842 Broadway, 10003.
Wall Street Journal, 200 Liberty St., 10281.
Niagara Falls, Gazette, 310 Niagara St., 14302.
Rochester, Gannett News, 55 Exchange St., 14614.
Rochester, Times-Union, 55 Exchange St., 14614.
Syracuse, The Post-Standard, Clinton Square, 13202.
Utica, Observer-Dispatch, 221 Oriskany Plaza, 13503.
Yonkers, The Herald Statesman, 733 Yonkers Ave., 10704.

North Carolina

Charlotte, Observer, 600 S. Tryon St., 28201.
Durham, Durham Morning Herald, 115-19 Market St., 27702.
Raleigh, News & Observer, 215 S. McDowell St., 27601.
Winston-Salem, Journal, 418 N. Marshall, 27102.

North Dakota

Fargo, Forum, 101 5th St., 58102.

Ohio

Akron, The Beacon Journal, 44 E. Exchange St., 44309.
Canton, The Repository, 500 Market Ave., South, 44702.
Cincinnati, The Enquirer, 617 Vine St., 45201.
Cincinnati, Post, 617 Vine St., 45201.
Cleveland, The Plain Dealer, 1801 Superior Ave., 44114.
Columbus, The Dispatch, 34 S. Third St., 43216.
Dayton, News Journal-Herald, 45 S. Ludlow St., 45402.
Toledo, The Toledo Blade, 541 Superior St., 43604.
Youngstown, The Vindicator, 107 Vindicator Square, 44501.

Oklahoma

Oklahoma City, Daily Oklahoman, 500 N. Broadway, 73125.
Tulsa, The Tribune, 315 S. Boulder Ave., 74102.
Tulsa, The World, 315 S. Boulder Ave., 74102.

Oregon

Portland, The Oregonian, 1320 SW Broadway, 97201.

Pennslyvania

Allentown, The Morning Call, 101 N. 6th St., 18105.
Erie, The Times, 20 E. 12th St., 16501.
Philadelphia, The Inquirer, 400 N. Broad St., 19101.
Philadelphia, The News, 400 N. Broad St., 19101.
Pittsburgh, Post Gazette, 50 Blvd. of Allies, 15222.
Pittsburgh, Pittsburgh Press Co., 34 Blvd. of Allies, 15222.
Reading, The Eagle, 345 Penn St., 19601.
Scranton, Tribune, 338 N. Washington Ave., 18501.
Scranton, The Times, Penn & Spruce, 18501.

Rhode Island

Providence, The Journal-Bulletin, 75 Fountain St., 02902.

South Carolina

Columbia, The State-Record, P.O. Box 1333, 29202.

Tennessee

Chattanooga, The News-Free Press, 400 E. 11th St., 37401.
Knoxville, The Journal, 210 W. Church Ave., 37901.
Knoxville, The News-Sentinel, 208 W. Church Ave., 37901.
Memphis, Commercial Appeal, 495 Union Ave., 38103.
Nashville, The Banner, 1100 Broadway, 37203.
Nashville, The Tennessean, 1100 Broadway, 37203.

Texas

Abilene, Reporter News, 100 Cypress St., 79604.
Amarillo, The Globe News, 900 S. Harrison St., 79105.
Austin, American-Statesman, 166 E. Riverside Dr., 78704.
Beaumont, The Enterprise, 380 Walnut St., 77704.
Corpus Christi, The Caller-Times, 820 N. Broadway, 78401.
Dallas, The Morning News, Communications Center, 75222.
Dallas, The Times Herald, 1101 Pacific, 75202.
El Paso, Herald-Post, 401 Mills Ave., 79901.
El Paso, Times, 401 Mills Ave., 79901.
Fort Worth, The Star-Telegram, 400 W. 7th St., 76101.
Houston, The Chronicle, 801 Texas St., 77002.
Houston, The Post, 4747 Southwest Freeway, 77001.
Lubbock, The Avalanche-Journal, 710 Avenue "J", 79401.
San Antonio, The Express News, Avenue "E" & 3rd St., 78205.
San Antonio, The Light, 420 Broadway, 78205.

Waco, Tribune-Herald, 900 Franklin, 76703.
Wichita Falls, The Times, 1301 Lamar St., 76307.

Utah

Salt Lake City, Deseret News, 30 E. 1st St., South, 84110.
Salt Lake City, The Tribune, 143 S. Main St., 84101.

Virginia

Alexandria, Gazette, 717 N. St. Asaph St., 22313.
Arlington, Northern Va. Sun, 1227 N. Ivy St., 22201.
Newport News-Hampton, The Daily Press, 7505 Warwick Blvd., 23607.
Norfolk, Virginian-Pilot, 150 W. Brambleton Ave., 23501.
Richmond, Times-Dispatch, 333 E. Grace St., 23213.
Roanoke, Times-World, 201-09. W. Campbell Ave., 24011.

Washington

Seattle, The Post-Intelligencer, 101 Elliot Ave. West, 98119.
Seattle, The Times, Fairview Ave. N & John, 98111.
Seattle, Daily Journal of Commerce, 83 Columbia St., 98104.
Tacoma, The News-Tribune, 1950 S. State, 98405.

Wisconsin

Madison, Capital-Times, 1901 Fish Hatchery Rd., 53713.
Milwaukee, The Journal, 333 W. State St., 53201.
Milwaukee, Sentinel, 333 W. State St., 53201.

The Industry in Great Britain and Ireland

* INDUSTRY DEVELOPMENTS
* BRITISH ACADEMY OF FILM AND TELEVISION ARTS AWARDS (1988)
* PROGRAM CONTRACTORS
* SATELLITE CABLE BROADCASTERS
* PRODUCERS, DISTRIBUTORS & SERVICE COMPANIES AND PERSONNEL
* ORGANIZATIONS
* SERVICES
* BRITISH BASED EQUIPMENT/SERVICES

British Year in Review

WHILE THE RESTRUCTURING OF BRITISH broadcasting continued apace during 1989, the first take-off of the new era, Sky's Satellite Channel, has had a minimal impact on television viewers and the industry. At the same time, BSB (British Satellite Broadcasting) also had its own misfortunes and is unlikely to be launched until 1990. Both have proved highly expensive and speculative launches. Ironically, the setback experienced by the satellite companies could well put the cable business on its feet. To date, there has been a low penetration of cable in the UK but it is now attracting American investment and could well benefit from the new public awareness of the choice of television programs and make the selling of cable services easier.

But these developments are just part of the government's plans to transform British television into a free market leisure industry. Its proposals—Broadcasting in the '90s: Competition, Choice and Quality—include the following recommendations:

- A fifth terrestrial channel, to start in 1993, with different companies providing services at different times of day; a sixth channel to follow, if technically feasible.
- ITV to be replaced by a regionally-based Channel 3, obliged to provide high-quality national and international news and current affairs and regional programming; franchises for this and Channel 5 to be awarded by competitive tender.
- Channel 4's remit to be preserved but its advertising to be sold separately from that on Channel 3; options are canvassed for its future constitution on this basis.
- A new flexible regime for the development of multichannel local services through cable and microwave transmission (MVDS).
- Two further direct broadcasting by satellite (DBS) frequencies to be advertised by the IBA in 1989.
- The IBA and Cable Authority to be replaced by a new Independent Television Commission, to license and supervise all parts of a liberalized commercial television sector and to operate with a lighter touch.
- The BBC to remain the cornerstone of public service broadcasting, but to move towards the eventual replacement of the licence fee.
- The Broadcasting Standards Council to be given statutory authority to reinforce standards on taste and decency and the portrayal of sex and violence.

It is anticipated that the 'single biggest advantage' of the proposed changes will be to give the viewer and listener a greater choice and a greater say.

Quite the most contentious of these proposals has been the insistence on an auction for the next ITV franchises to the highest bidder. These franchises currently expire in 1991 and already companies are lining up possible mergers and takeovers for their battles for survival. Potential bidders have been told that they must reach a higher quality threshold which means that ITV companies with the necessary funds will have a better chance of winning back licences.

Only the BBC—operators of two national public networks—supported by an annual licence fee, or tax, on TV set users—is likely to emerge from the 'revolution,' more or less, in its present form. Moreover, because the government has been unable to find an alternative funding method, the licence fee will remain for the foreseeable future to cushion the BBC's policy of 'educating, informing and entertaining the viewers.'

On the commercial front, although a television program contact is no longer 'a licence to print money,' the majority are earning good profits with many divesting their interests into other areas, for example the European market where the unified market comes about in 1992. Another obvious development of this 'opening up' of commercial television has been the need not only to improve the quality and variety of programming but also the volume of independent production. Over 70 per cent of the programs shown on ITV are made by ITV companies themselves. The five major companies—Central, Granada, LWT, Thames and Yorkshire—take the prime responsibility for the provision of network programming for the rest of ITV. The BBC's programme budget, reaching £20 million a year by the summer of 1990, would be earmarked for the independent sector, with such production accounting for 600 hours of the BBC's output in 1991–2.

It has been estimated that the two satellite companies, SKY and BSB, have already spent over $1 billion acquiring the rights to American motion pictures.

The vast majority of overseas material on the networks here still originates in the USA. ITV's and Channel 4's quota of overseas material is 14 per cent of total programme output. This comprises theatrical motion pictures, TV films and series. Estimates of the prices paid by local contractors and the BBC for American shows are around $13,000 for half-hour episodes to between $50,000 to $3 million for a feature film. Important changes to the CEA's (Cinema Exhibitor's Association's) holdback of feature films from television have been agreed to following concern expressed by the BFTPA (British Film & Television Producers' Association). The new arrangement, supported by key film and television organizations in the UK, will, it is hoped offer a boost to production investment. Under the new system, any cinema film on budget not exceeding £4 million ($6.4 million) may be screened on television immediately after its theatrical release if those responsible for its marketing decide that this is appropriate. English-language films exceeding this budget may still be televised immediately if a new committee representing different interests in the industry agree—and the previous three-year holdback applying to other English-language cinema films is now reduced to two years.

With the previous holdback in operation, the BBC and commercial television companies were finding that if they financed films for the cinema it would usually entail a three-year delay before the same films could be televised. The new arrangement removes this brake on investment at a time when the film industry is becoming increasingly dependent on television.

In defence of its policy of maintaining the holdback of films on television, the CEA states: "At present the initial audience for a film in the cinema pays a very high proportion of the total revenues accruing to film production. Later, films are acquired for showing on television, which is a secondary market and which plays a far less important role in recouping the original production costs. Apart from other markets, such as video, there are at present two quite separate boxoffices for films, one derived from cinema and one, albeit much smaller, derived from television. Any further reduction in the cinema-going audience will have serious social implications. Fewer cinemas, particularly in suburban and smaller town situations, would seriously reduce the already very limited number of places of entertainment and leisure available to the cinema audiences who are the least likely members of society to stay at home to watch any form of television."

In the meantime, the proportion of households with video recorders has risen to 61 per cent which means that 12.7 million households now have them (an increase of one million in a period of 12 months).

Organizations such as Rank and the BBC maintain an active interest in the World Market. Rank's Film and TV Services Division more than doubled its sales and trading profit and £133 million ($212 million) was spent on acquisitions, principally in North America. The BBC's commercial division—BBC Enterprises—expect to double its turnover to £200 million ($320 million) by 1991 with a profit target of £25 million ($40 million).

Nevertheless, as the new stations, new owners and more channels emerge, some commentators warn that the freer market must not be restricted to a diet of news, 'soaps,' adventure series and advertizements. Already, the government has announced plans to penalize companies who resort to sex and violence to raise viewing figures. Companies bidding for the new franchises will have to deposit 'performance bonds' to ensure they keep their promises about screening quality programs.

It is a very necessary criterion, for the home viewing business remains a lucrative one with 97 per cent of the population having access to it in their homes; but they do need to be fed quality programmes.

—William Pay

Viewing Audiences 1988–1989

The average amount of viewing per head per week in 1988–89 was over 25 hours, of which BBC Television accounted for 49%. Over the course of a typical week nearly everybody (99%) who watches television views some BBC Television, the average for such BBC viewing being just under 13 hours a week.

The table below shows, in percent, the daily and weekly reach for the various channels, that is, the proportion of the population viewing that channel at all during the week. The average amount of viewing per week is given in hours and minutes together with the percentage share of total viewing.

	Reach (% of population aged 4+)		Viewing per head/ week (hrs:mins)	Share of viewing (%)
	Daily	Weekly		
BBC1	66.2	91.7	9:45	38
BBC2	35.3	79.6	2:42	11
Any or all BBC	69.8	92.4	12:27	49
ITV	63.0	90.2	10:39	42
C4/S4C	32.8	76.3	2:13	9
Any or all commercial	67.1	91.5	12:52	51
Any or all television	77.5	93.7	25:19	100

Source: BARB/AGB April 1988–March 1989

Average Audiences for a Selection of BBC Programmes, April 1988–March 1989

BBC1

Light Entertainment	
Royal Variety Performance	18,100,000
Bread	17,100,000
Only Fools and Horses	16,700,000
A Night of Comic Relief	15,900,000
'Allo 'Allo!	12,600,000
Steptoe & Son	11,700,000
Brush Strokes	11,500,000
25 Years of Top of the Pops	11,500,000
Last of the Summer Wine	10,500,000
Drama	
EastEnders	18,300,000
Neighbours	16,100,000
First Born	14,000,000
Bergerac	13,300,000
The Rainbow	10,700,000
Tumbledown	10,500,000
Casualty	10,300,000
Campion	8,100,000
Sport	
Grand National 1988	14,300,000
Sports Review of the Year	11,500,000
London Marathon 1988	11,000,000
Wimbledon: Women's Singles Final	9,700,000
Olympics Today	7,500,000

General Interest	
Antiques Roadshow	13,200,000
Supersense	11,700,000
Children in Need	11,500,000
Crimewatch UK	10,800,000
Holiday '89	10,600,000
Snap!	10,200,000
Hearts of Gold	9,700,000
News and Current Affairs	
Six O'Clock News	8,100,000
Nine O'Clock News	7,500,000
Panorama	4,800,000
One O'Clock News	4,700,000
Question Time	4,500,000
On the Record	1,800,000
Breakfast Time (peak audience)	1,400,000
Programmes for Children and the Family	
Jim'll Fix It	10,300,000
Chronicles of Narnia	10,200,000
Grange Hill	8,100,000
Tom's Midnight Garden	7,100,000
Blue Peter	6,300,000
The Country Boy	6,100,000
Brainstorm	6,100,000

Average Audiences for a Selection of BBC Programmes *(Continued)*

BBC2			
Wimbledon: Men's Singles Final	7,400,000	Christabel	5,600,000
Forty Minutes: Raging Belles	7,300,000	Naked Video	5,300,000
World Snooker Final (1988)	6,400,000	Chelsea Flower Show	5,300,000
French & Saunders Xmas Special	6,400,000	Paul Daniels' Magic Show	5,300,000
The Nature of Australia	6,200,000	Food & Drink	5,100,000

Audience Appreciation

Among programmes achieving a Reaction Index of 75 or above from the Listening Panel were:

85 Plus	*80 Plus*	*75 Plus*
The Nature of Australia	Talking Heads	Byline
Only Fools & Horses	King & Company	Christabel
Atlantic Realm	Bread	The Franchise Affair
Dennis O'Neill & Friends	Casualty	Heart of the Matter
	The Chronicles of Narnia	Watchdog
	The Mind Machine	Saturday Night Clive
	Out of the Doll's House	Moving Stories
	Reaching for the Skies	

Broadcasting Receiving Licences

Licences at 31 March	Total	Issued free for blind persons	Issued for payment: Radio only	Radio and TV combined: Monochrome	Radio and TV combined: Colour
1927	2,269,644	5,750	2,263,894		
1930	3,092,324	16,496	3,075,828		
1940	8,951,045	53,427	8,897,618		
1950	12,219,448	56,376	11,819,190	343,882	
1960	15,005,011	54,958	4,480,300	10,469,753	
1970	18,183,719	22,174	2,279,017	15,609,131	273,397
1980	18,284,865	—	—	5,383,125	12,901,740
1985	18,715,937	—	—	2,896,263	15,819,674
1987	18,953,161	—	—	2,414,496	16,538,665
1988	19,354,442	—	—	2,220,482	17,133,960
1989	19,395,963	—	—	1,926,805	17,469,158

In 1947 there were 14,560 combined radio and monochrome television licences; in 1968 there were 20,428 combined radio and colour television licences.
Radio-only licences and combined radio and television licences were abolished on 1 February 1971; from that date television-only licences have been issued.
Dealer's demonstration fees and accommodation and residential care licences have been excluded from the figures.

Licence Fees

	Radio	Television: Monochrome *(combined with radio)*	Television: Colour *(combined with radio)*
1 Nov 1922	10s	—	—
1 June 1946	£1.00s	£2.00	—
1 June 1954	£1.00s	£3.00	—
1 Aug 1957	£1.00s	£4.00*	—
1 Oct 1963	£1.00s	£4.00†	—
1 Aug 1965	£1.5s	£5.00	—
1 Jan 1968	£1.5s	£5.00	£10.00
1 Jan 1969	£1.5s	£6.00	£11.00
1 Feb 1971	‡		
1 July 1971	—	£7.00	£12.00
1 April 1975	—	£8.00	£18.00
29 July 1977	—	£9.00	£21.00
25 Nov 1978	—	£10.00	£25.00
24 Nov 1979	—	£12.00	£34.00
1 Dec 1981	—	£15.00	£46.00
1 April 1985	—	£18.00	£58.00
1 April 1988	—	£21.00	£62.50
1 April 1989	—	£22.00	£66.00

*Excise duty of £1 imposed, not received by BBC.
†Excise duty abolished, BBC given full amount.
‡Radio-only licence fee abolished.

Home Services and BBC Enterprises Group

The year ended 31 March 1989 was the first year during which the licence fee was pegged to annual increases in the retail price index to the previous September. Colour fees increased from £58 in 1987–88 to £62.50 and monochrome from £18 to £21. There was a continuing conversion of monochrome licences to colour and a small increase in the total number of licences taken out. The licence fee still compared very well with the rest of Europe, as Figure 1 on the next page shows.

Enterprises' contribution to the Group showed significant improvements over the previous year with sales up 11.8% and pre-interest profits virtually doubled at £10.4m. After interest, Enterprises reported a profit of £11.6m compared with £6.4m in 1987–88. Enterprises' results for the year were boosted by the acquisition of Redwood Publishing.

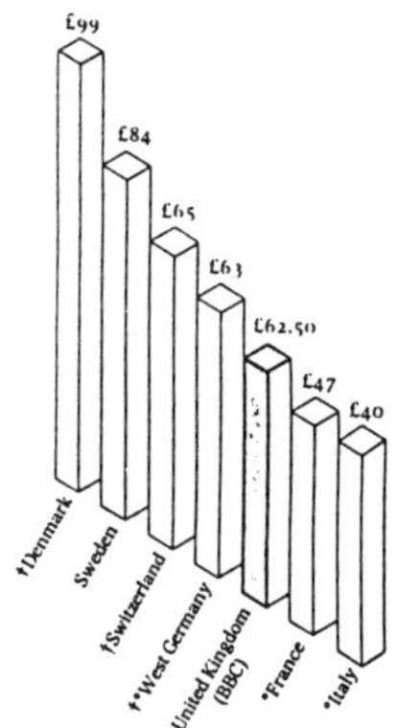

Independent Broadcasting—Key Figures
(years ending 31 March)

	1985	1986	1987	1988	1989
UKIB Services					
Television channels (terrestrial)	2	2	2	2	2
DBS TV channels (contract awarded)	—	—	—	3	3
DBS TV channels (contract pending)	—	—	—	—	2
ILR contractors on air	49	49	49	49	51
ITV programme contractors	16	16	16	16	16
Teletext: Television channels	2	2	2	2	2
DBS (draft contract offered)	—	—	—	3	3
ILR (contracts awarded)	—	—	2	2	2
Programme Hours Transmitted (per year)					
ITV (in average region)	5,443	5,473	5,568	6,046	7,111
TV-am	1,066	1,092	1,085	1,203	1,244
C4	3,595	3,914	4,138	5,332	6,072
Total	10,104	10,479	10,791	12,581	14,427
(per week ILR) (estimate for 1985)	6,450	6,580	7,860	7,900	9,500
Transmission					
IBA transmitters in operation (nos.)	1,344	1,536	1,754	1,888	1,945
UK coverage (%): ITV	99.1	99.2	99.3	99.4	99.4
Fourth Channel (C4 & SC4)	97.6	98.5	99.2	99.4	99.4
ILR (JICRAR Total Survey Areas)	86	86	89	90	91
Reliability (%): ITV	n/a	99.68	99.72	99.73	99.80
Fourth Channel (C4 & SC4)	n/a	99.81	99.84	99.78	99.78
ILR	n/a	99.98	99.98	99.98	99.97
Advertising Control (nos.)					
TV scripts submitted	15,614	16,576	16,096	15,721	14,276
Finished TV commercials viewed	6,317	6,658	6,566	6,806	6,851
Radio scripts submitted	8,608	8,875	10,790	11,221	10,960
Staff (average no.)					
IBA	1,480	1,438	1,411	1,407	1,340
Channel 4	230	246	267	303	329
*Finance (£m)**					
Net advertising revenue:					
ITV (including TV-am)	921	1,065	1,256	1,423	1,625
of which C4	75	113	155	213	256
of which S4C	2	2	3	4	4
ILR	66	65	73	94	116
IBA rentals: ITV (including BSB)	55	59	63	66	70.3
ILR	7.2	6.3	4.9	5.3	4.6
Fourth Channel subscription:	163	175	183	203	227
allocation: Channel 4	111	129	136	163	182
S4C	28	32	34	40	45
Exchequer levy	40	20	75	87	99

**IBA rentals* are in respect of IBA's costs for developing, operating and maintaining the transmission facilities for Independent Broadcasting and for programme and advertising control.
The Fourth Channel subscriptions are paid by the ITV programme contractors to the IBA to meet the operating costs of Channel 4, and the Welsh Fourth Channel (S4C). TV-am started paying towards the Fourth Channel on 1 April 1989 to fund the channel's new breakfast service.

The ITV Companies' Production

During the year, the ITV companies (excluding TV-am) and ITN produced or commissioned a weekly average of 212 hours of new programmes for transmission on the ITV channel. Of this total, an average of 45¼ hours per week came from the five largest companies and 15¾ hours from the other companies for network or part-network commission.

Independent Commissions

Transmissions on ITV of new commissions from independent producers during the year under review amounted to 452 hours wiith an additional 29 hours of independent material first shown on Channel 4. New and repeat transmissions of British independent commissions on Channel 4 amounted to 1,759 hours. In total, therefore, during the year 2,240 hours of independent commissions were transmitted by the two IBA channels.

Programme Transmissions on ITV*
(weekly average, year ending 2 April 1989)

	Duration (hrs:mins)	Percentage
News and news magazines	17:58	13.1
Current affairs, documentaries, and general factual material	19:55	14.6
Adult education**	1.53	1.4
Religion	2:18	1.7
Arts	0:58	0.7
Informative***	43:02	31.5
Plays, series and serials†	26:23	19.3
Feature films and TV movies†	17:13	12.6
Narrative	43.36	31.9
Entertainment	27:54	20.4
Sport	10:47	7.9
Children's programmes††	11:19	8.3
TOTAL All Programmes§	136:45	100%

*The amount a viewer could see in any part of a region, excluding TV-am transmission of 23 hours 55 minutes per week.
**Excluding local education and social action programming which is included within the factual material category.
***Informative material previously included pre-schools which is now included within the total for children's programmes.
†TV movies were previously included within the plays, series and serials category.
††This total comprises: Pre-school programming (2 hours 24 minutes); Drama and entertainment (8 hours 10 minutes); and Children's informative material (45 minutes).
§The opening routine of each day for a nominal one minute is not specified above but is included in the total.

Programme Transmissions on Channel 4
(weekly average, year ending 2 April 1989)

		Duration (hrs:mins)	Percentage
News		4:29	3.8
Factual material including documentaries and current affairs		22:01	18.8
Adult Education	6:16		
Open College	2:54		
ITV schools programmes	6:59		
Education		16:09	13.9
Religion		1:14	1.1
Arts		3:21	2.9
TOTAL Informative		47:14	40.5
Plays, series and serials*		11:41	10.0
Feature films and TV movies**		25:37	21.9
TOTAL Narrative		37:18	31.9
Entertainment		13:15	11.4
Sport		10:54	9.3
Children's programmes†		7:58	6.8
TOTAL All Programmes§		116:46	100

*TV movies were previously included within the plays, series and serials categories.
**Including Film on Four and Film on Four International which averaged 1:43 minutes per week.
†This total comprises: Pre-school programming (4 hours 38 minutes); Drama and entertainment (1 hour 25 minutes); and Children's informative material (1 hour 55 minutes).
§The opening routine of each day for a nominal one minute is not specified above but is included in the total.

New Production by ITV Companies for Local Interest
(year ending 1 January 1989)

ITV Company	Weekly Average (hrs:mins)	IBA Minimum Weekly Requirement 1988 (hrs:mins)
Anglia	7:53	7:30
Border	5:05	4:30
Central: Total	12:40	11:30*
West Midlands only	4:21	4:00
East Midlands only	4:21	4:00
Channel	4:45	4:00
Grampian	6:30	6:00
Granada	7:48	7:30
HTV West	7:20	7:00
HTV Wales	7:39	7:00
LWT	2:52	2:30
Scottish	9:20	9:00
Thames	5:54	5:30
TSW	7:49	7:00
TVS: Total	13:18	12:00*
South only	4:54	4:30
South East only	4:54	4:30
Tyne Tees: Total	8:38	8:30*
North only	0:50	1:00
South only	0:50	1:00
Ulster	7:04	6:00
Yorkshire: Total	7:51	7:30
West only	0:55	0:45
East only	0:55	0:45

*A minimum of 7½ hours per week to be provided for viewers in each part of the sub-area.

Complaints about Television Programmes

All programme complaints to the IBA, apart from those addressed specifically to the Chairman or Director General, are dealt with by a small administrative staff within Television Division and by staff in the regional offices. As necessary, particular programmes may be viewed by IBA staff, and complaints taken up by them direct with programme companies concerned.

Although viewers' compaints alone do not provide an accurate indication of the success or otherwise of the ITV and Channel 4 services, they do provide useful complementary information to structured research, and are always thoroughly investigated.

The following table lists the complaints received, by category, for the year under review. The total of 2,466 complaints compares with 2,141 received in 1987–88.

Summary of Complaints	ITV	%	Channel 4	%	Total ITV and Channel 4	%
Taste and decency	360	16.3	76	28.9	436	17.7
Language	81	3.7	6	2.3	87	3.5
Accuracy	55	2.5	13	4.9	68	2.8
Impartiality	120	5.5	54	20.5	174	7.0
Violence	125	5.7	22	8.4	147	6.0
Scheduling	584	26.5	38	14.4	622	25.2
Race/Religion	109	4.9	7	2.7	116	4.7
Misc.	769	34.9	47	17.9	816	33.1
Total	2203	100.0	263	100.0	2466	100.0

British Academy of Film and Television Arts (BAFTA) Awards (1988)

The Fellowship: Sir Alec Guinness

Film Production and Performance

The Michael Balcon Award for Outstanding British Contribution to Cinema: Charles Crichton

The Best Film: The Last Emperor, Jeremy Thomas/Bernardo Bertolucci

The Best Achievement in Direction: Louis Malle, Au Revoir Les Enfants

The Best Original Screenplay: Shawn Slovo, A World Apart

The Best Adapted Screenplay: Jean-Claude Carriere/Philip Kaufman, The Unbearable Lightness of Being

The Best Actress in a leading role: Maggie Smith, The Lonely Passion of Judith Hearne

The Best Actor in a leading role: John Cleese, A Fish Called Wanda

The Best Actress in a supporting role: Judi Dench, A Handful of Dust

The Best Actor in a supporting role: Michael Palin, A Fish Called Wanda

The Best Score for a Film: John Williams, Empire of the Sun

The Best Film Not in the English Language: Babette's Feast, Just Betzer/Bo Christensen/Gabriel Axel, (Denmark)

The Best Short Film: Defence Counsel Sedov, Eugene Tsymbal

Special Award: Leslie Hardcastle

Television Production and Performance

The Desmond Davis Award for Outstanding Creative Contribution to Television: Stuart Burge

The Best Single Drama: Tumbledown, Charles Wood/Richard Broke/Richard Eyre

The Best Drama Series/Serial: A Very British Coup, Alan Plater/Anne Skinner/Sally Hibbin/Mick Jackson

The Best Factual Series: Arena, Anthony Wall/Nigel Finch

The Best Light Entertainment Programme: An Audience with Victoria Wood, David G. Hillier

The Best Comedy Series: Only Fools and Horses, John Sullivan/Gareth Gwenlan/Tony Dow (Christmas Special)

The Best News or Outside Broadcast Coverage: The Production Team, Channel Four News

The Best Actress: Thora Hird, A Cream Cracker Under the Settee

The Best Actor: Ray McAnally, A Very British Coup

The Best Light Entertainment Performance: Victoria Wood, An Audience with Victoria Wood

The Best Original Television Music: Frank Ricotti, The Beiderbecke Connection

The Huw Wheldon Award: David Hinton, Bertolucci and the Last Emperor (The South Bank Show)

The Best Children's Programme (Documentary/Educational): Nicholas Whinnes, Going to School (Near and Far; Now and Then)

The Best Children's Programme (Entertainment/Drama): The Storyteller, Duncan Kenworthy

The Writer's Award: Alan Plater

The Richard Dimbleby Award: Ludovic Kennedy

The Foreign Television Programme Award: Tanner

1988 Television Award for Originality: Adrian Cowell

Film and Television Production and Performance

The Flaherty Documentary Award: Chris Oxley, Death on the Rock (This Week)

The Best Short Animated Film: Mark Baker, The Hill Farm

For Excellence in the Film Crafts of

Cinematography: Allen Daviau, Empire of the Sun

Editing: Michael Kahn/Peter E. Berger, Fatal Attraction

Sound: Charles L. Campbell/Lou Edeman/Colin Charles/Robert Knudson/Tony Dawe, Empire of the Sun

Production Design: Dean Tavoularis, Tucker: The Man and his Dream

Costume Design: James Acheson, The Last Emperor

Achievement in Special Effects: Richard Williams/Ken Ralston/George Gibbs/Edward Jones, Who Framed Roger Rabbit

Make Up Artist: Fabrizio Sforza, The Last Emperor

Special Award: Richard Williams for his excellent work on Who Framed Roger Rabbit

The BAFTA Scholarship awarded by The Post Office: Gillian Wilkinson

For Excellence in the Television Crafts of

Video Lighting: John Mason, The Chronicles of Narnia

Make Up: Shauna Harrison, Tumbledown

Film Cameraman: Andrew Dunn, Tumbledown

Costume Design: Ann Hollowood, The Storyteller

Graphics: Matt Forest, Wired

Film Sound: Christian Wangler/David Old/Peter Elliott, A Very British Coup

Film Editor: Don Fairservice, A Very British Coup

Sound Supervisor: Chris Holcombe/Mike Johnstone/Mike Robinson, The Nelson Mandela Concert

Video Cameraman: Rodney Taylor, Soldiering On and A Very Peculiar Practice

VTR Editor: The Editing Team, The Clothes Show

Design: Jim Clay, Christabel

The London Weekend Bursary is awarded to all Television Craft winners through the kind offices of LWT

Government Units and Program Contractors

HOME OFFICE
Queen Anne's Gate, London, SW1H 9AT. Tel: 01-213-3000.

The Secretary of State for the Home Department is empowered to licence persons or corporate bodies to operate broadcasting stations as laid down in the Wireless Telegraphy Act, 1949. The BBC is incorporated by Royal Charter and operates under this and a License and Agreement granted on the 2nd April 1981. The provisions of the Charter and the License Agreement run to 31st December 1996. The Independent Broadcasting Authority operates under the Broadcasting Act 1981 which extends the life of the Authority until 31st December 1996 and under a licence that runs to the same dates.

BRITISH BROADCASTING CORPORATION TELEVISION SERVICE
Television Centre, Wood Lane, London W.12. Tel: 01-743 8000.

Chairman of Governors: Marmaduke Hussey
Deputy Director General: John Birt
Managing Director, Television: Paul Fox
Controller BBC-1: Jonathan Powell
Controller BBC-2: Alan Yentob
Head of Presentation Department: (vacancy)
Community Programme Unit Editor: Tony Laryea
Head of Drama Group: Mark Shivas
Head of Light Entertainment Group: James Moir
Head of Sports Group and Events Group: Jonathan Martin
Head of Features and Documentary Group: Will Wyatt
Head of Science and Features: Mick Rhodes
Head of Music and Arts: Leslie Megahey
Head of School Broadcasting: Alan Rogers
Head of Religious Programmes: John Whale
Deputy Director News and Current Affairs: Ron Neil
Managing Editor News and Current Affairs: Ian Hargreaves
Editor News and Current Affairs Television: Tony Hall
Deputy Editor News and Current Affairs Television: Samir Shah
Head of Scenic Operations Television: W. O. Parkinson
Head of Costume Department: Mrs. J. Shardlow
Head of Television Make-up Department: Miss I. Mair
Head of Television Script Units: Miss S. Capon
BBC Enterprises Ltd. Chief Executive: J. Arnold-Baker
Head of Television Publicity: Keith Samuel
Controller Resource Operations, TV: Charles Paton
Assistant Controller, Resource Development Operations, Television: John Jarvie
Head of Engineering, Studio and Network TV: J. Hughes
General Manager International Relations: Malcolm Walker

INDEPENDENT BROADCASTING AUTHORITY
70 Brompton Road, London, SW3 1EY. Tel: 01-584 7011.

The Authority was created by Parliament in 1954 as the Independent Television Authority, to provide a comprehensive television service additional to that of the BBC. Under the terms of the Sound Broadcasting Act, 1972, the Authority was renamed the Independent Broadcasting Authority and its functions were extended to cover the provision of Independent Local Radio.

The Broadcasting Act 1980 provided for the setting up of the Channel Four Television Company as a subsidiary of the IBA; it started broadcasting in England, Scotland and Northern Ireland on November 2, 1982. A separate Welsh Fourth Channel Authority was also established by this Act; broadcasting on November 1, 1982. The Broadcasting Act 1981 has consolidated a number of Acts relating to the IBA.

The Authority selects and appoints the ITV & ILR programme companies; supervises the programmes provided by the contractors—and the Channel Four Television Company—and their scheduling; controls advertising, and builds, owns and operates transmitting stations. Fifteen ITV programme companies provide programmes in 14 regions of the United Kingdom (two companies operate in London). As a part of its review of the ITV system, the Authority, in December 1980, offered a contract to broadcast a new national breakfast-time television service, which started in February 1983, to TV-AM. In addition, changes were made to some ITV companies.

Some 46 Independent Local Radio stations now provide a programme service in areas of the United Kingdom (two companies operating in London).

Both ITV and ILR are financed mainly by the sale of advertising time.

The Members of the Authority are appointed by the Home Secretary and consist of a Chairman and Deputy Chairman and ten other members, of whom three make the interests of Scotland, Wales and Northern Ireland, respectively, their special care.

Chairman: The Rt. Hon. the Lord Thomson of Monifieth
Director General: John Whitney
Deputy Director General: Lady Littler
Director of Television: David Glencross
Director of Radio: Peter Baldwin
Director of Engineering: Dr. John Forrest
Director of Finance: Peter Rogers
Controller of Public Affairs: Colette Bowe
Controller of Advertising: Frank Willis
Deputy Director of Television: Miss Clare Mulholland
Head of Research: Barrie Gunter

INDEPENDENT BROADCASTING AUTHORITY GENERAL ADVISORY COUNCIL

Drawn from various walks of life, the Council is appointed to give the IBA impartial advice on the general pattern and content of ITV and Channel 4 programmes.
Chairman: Mrs. D. D. Jackson, A.C.I.S.

INDEPENDENT BROADCASTING AUTHORITY ADVERTISING ADVISORY COMMITTEE

The Committee, under the terms of the Broadcasting Act 1981, must be representative of organizations, authorities and persons concerned with standards of conduct of advertising including, in particular, the advertising of medical or surgical goods or services, and the public as consumers.
Chairman: Prof. A. L. Diamond

INDEPENDENT BROADCASTING AUTHORITY SCOTTISH COMMITTEE

Chairman: J. R. Purvis

INDEPENDENT BROADCASTING AUTHORITY NORTHERN IRELAND COMMITTEE

Chairman: Prof. J. F. Fulton

INDEPENDENT BROADCASTING AUTHORITY WELSH COMMITTEE

Chairman: G. R. Peregrine.

INDEPENDENT TELEVISION NEWS LTD.
ITN House, 48 Wells Street, London, W1P 4DE. Tel: 01-637 2424. Telex: 22101. FAX: 01-636 0349.

Chairman and Chief Executive: Sir David Nicholas

PROGRAM CONTRACTORS

(Appointed by the Independent Broadcasting Authority).

ANGLIA TELEVISION LTD.
Head office: Anglia House, Norwich, NR1 3JG. Tel: 0603 615151. Telex: 97424; FAX: 0603 631032. London Office: Brook House, Park Lane, London, W.1. Tel: 01408 2288. Telex: 25353. FAX: 01-493 2598.

EAST OF ENGLAND CONTRACTOR
DIRECTORS: P. W. Gibbings *(Chairman)*, P. C. Garner *(Director of Programmes)*, D. S. McCall, C.B.E. *(Chief Executive)*, Dr. Mary Archer, Timothy Colman, M. J. Hughes *(General Manager)*, Mrs. John Nutting, David Puttnam, C.B.E., P. G. Sharman, T. P. Wootton *(Group Marketing Director)*.
EXECUTIVES:
Religious Adviser: Canon I. J. Bailey
Chief Engineer: A. T. C. Barnett
Head of Press and Public Relations: V. B. H. Birtles
Production Controller: J. Bunyan
Head of Stills: D. Dawson
Controller, Regional & Network (Off-peak) Programmes: C. Ewing
Sales Controller: J. Hill
Head of Presentation: G. Jenkins
Programme Business Manager: D. S. Little
Controller of Network Programmes (Peak) & Managing Director, Anglia Television Films Ltd.: G. McDonald
Controller, Staff Relations: P. Meier
Administration Controller: R. J. Pinnock
Group Financial Controller/Company Secretary: G. M. Rae
Head of Drama: J. Rosenberg
Education Officer: P. Stibbons
Schedules Controller: I. Stuart
Station Engineer: P. J. Waldron
Programme Planning Controller: S. West

Controller, News Programmes: H. J. A. Wilson
Chief Accountant: R. Whitlam
International Television Enterprises Ltd:
Chief Executive: T. Buxton
Sales Director: A. Macbean

BORDER TELEVISION
The Television Centre, Carlisle, CA1 3NT, Cumbria. Tel: 0228 25101; London Office: 33 Margaret Street, London, W1N 7LA. Tel: 01-637 4363.

NORTHWEST ENGLAND—SOUTH SCOTLAND, NORTH NORTHUMBERLAND, AND ISLE OF MAN
DIRECTORS: The Earl of Lonsdale *(Chairman)*, James L. Graham *(Managing)*, P. Brownlow *(Financial Director)*, M. Bragg, J. R. Wills, P. Corlay, M. Sutherland, P. Corley *(Director of Programmes)*, Miss M. E. Burkett, O.B.E., B.A., F.M.A., J. I. M. Smail, O.B.E., M.C., T.D., D.L., J. C. Clucas, Dr. June Paterson-Brown, D. W. Trimble, M.A.
Secretary: P. Brownlow
Chief Engineer: R. Dale
Assistant Controller of Programmes (Planning): E. Hadwin
Editor: L. Howell

CENTRAL INDEPENDENT TELEVISION PLC
(Transmission Area—The Midlands. Period—All Week) *West Midlands:* Central House, Broad Street, Birmingham B1 2JP. Tel: 021 643 9898. *East Midlands:* TV Centre, Lenton Lane, Nottingham NG7 2NA. Tel: 0602 863322. *London:* 35/38 Portman Square, London W1H 9FH. Tel: 01-486 6688.

MIDLANDS CONTRACTOR
DIRECTORS: David Justham *(Chairman)*, Leslie Hill *(Managing Director)*, Andy Allan *(Director of Programmes)*, Cliff Baty *(Commercial Director)*, Richard Emery *(Director of Sales)*, Peter Gardner *(Director of Operations)*, Alan Pankhurst *(Director of Personnel and Industrial Relations)*, Marshall Stewart *(Director of Corporate Strategy)*, Sir Richard Bailey *(Chairman, West Regional Board)*, John Madocks, C.B.E., D.L. *(Chairman, East Regional Board)*, I R Maxwell, M.C., Jean Parker, Robert Phillis, Sir Leo Pliatzky, K.C.B., Murray Thomson.
OFFICERS:
Director of Legal Affairs: Colin Campbell
Director of Finance: Kevin Betts
Controller, Drama and Situation Comedy: Ted Childs
Controller, Features Group: Richard Creasey
Controller, Young People's Programmes: Lewis Rudd
Controller, Factual Programmes: Robert Southgate
Controller, Entertainment: Tony Wolfe
Controller, Programme Planning: Dawn Airey
Controller, Programme Department: Phillip Gilbert
Controller of Public Affairs: Keith Smith
Controller, Industrial Relations: Peter Gibson
Commissioning Executive, Comedy: Ray Butt
Commissioning Executive, Education and Religion: Philip Grosset
Commissioning Executive, Documentaries: Roger James
Commissioning Executive, Sport: Gary Newbon
Commissioning Executive, Current Affairs: Mike Townson
Programme Planning Consultant: John Terry
Head of Presentation and Promotion: Jim Stokoe
Head of News—West: Mike Warman
Head of News—East: Steve Clark
Managing Editor, Central News: Ted Trimmer
Editorial Manager, Central News: Laurie Upshon
Editor, Central News East: Chris Robertson
Editor, Central News West: Bill Campbell
General Manager—West: Peter Booth
General Manager—East: Peter Pearson
Head of Technical Resources and Engineering: Mike Snalam
Head of Production Operations: Phil Jordan
Head of Film and ENG: Sim Harris
Head of Information Services: Ian Grainger Clemson
Head of Company Promotion: Michael Taylor
Sales Controller: Nigel Emery
Head of Sales: David Sanders
Head of Marketing: Bill Harrison
Regional Sales Manager: Anna Kelly
Central Television Enterprises (CTE)
35-38 Portman, Square London W1A 2HZ. Tel: 01-486 6688
Managing Director: Philip Jones
Director, International Sales and Marketing: Bill Allan
General Manager and Director of Business Affairs: Rupert Dilnott-Cooper

CHANNEL FOUR TELEVISION
60 Charlotte Street, London, W1P 2AX. Tel: 01-631 4444. Telex 892355. FAX: 01-637 4872.

Chairman: Sir Richard Attenborough
Chief Executive: Michael Grade
Director of Programmes: Liz Forgan
Director of Finance: David Scott
Director of Acquiring and Sales: Colin Leverthal
Director and General Manager: Frank McGettigan

CHANNEL TELEVISION
CHANNEL ISLANDS. Serves the Bailiwicks of Jersey and Guernsey as well as several smaller islands. The Television Centre, St. Helier, Jersey, Channel Islands. Tel: 0534 73999. Telex: 4192265 CTV JY G. FAX: 0534 59446/24770. The Television Centre, St. George's Place, St. Peter Port, Guernsey, Channel Islands. Tel: 0481 23451/49250. FAX: 0481 710739.

DIRECTORS:
John Riley *(Chairman)*, John Henwood *(Managing Director)*, Michael Le Cocq *(Director of Sales & Marketing)*, Euan MacGregor *(Director of Finance)*, Geoffrey Dorey, Martine Kay-Mouat, David Le Marguand, John Rowe, Andrea Wonfor.
OFFICERS:
Chief Engineer: Andrew Hearne
Programme Controller: Michael Lucas
Publications Manager: Gordon de Ste. Croix
Guernsey Office Manager: Roger Bowns
Technical Facilities Manager: Roger Wilson
Head of Production: Bob Evans
Head of Programme Planning, Presentation & Promotion: Gillian Le Cornu

GRAMPIAN TELEVISION LTD.
Queen's Cross, Aberdeen, AB9 2XJ: Scotland. Tel: 0224-646464; Telex: 73151. FAX: 0224-635127 Albany House, 68 Albany Road, West Ferry, Dundee DD5 1NW. Tel: 0382-739363; FAX: 0382 480230; Advertising: 0382-739149. 6 Manor Place, Edinburgh EH3 7DD. Tel: 031-226-3926; FAX: 031-220-0305; Telex 728139. 23-25 Huntly Street, Inverness IV3 5PR. Tel: 0463-242624; FAX: 031-220-0305. Advertising 0463-242626; Telex 75655. 29 Glasshouse Street, London W1R 5RG. Tel: 01-439-3141; Telex: 267912; FAX: 01-439-1498.

NORTH SCOTLAND CONTRACTOR
NON-EXECUTIVE DIRECTORS:
Chairman: Sir Iain Tennant, K.T.
Deputy Chairman: Dr. Calum A. MacLeod, M.A., LL.B., LL.D.
Douglas F. Hardie, C.B.E., J.P. *(Chairman Designate)*, Fiona Lyall, M.B., Ch.B., D.P.H., Alistair Mair, M.B.E., B.Sc., Angus Stewart Macdonald, C.B.E., Sir George Sharp, O.B.E., J.P.
EXECUTIVE DIRECTORS:
Chief Executive: Donald H. Waters, C.A.
Director of Television: Robert Christie
Company Secretary: Graham Good, C.A.
Sales and Marketing Director: Neil R. Welling Dip M, MInst M
EXECUTIVES:
Regional Sales Manager: Denise Wilson
Head of Documentaries: Ted Brocklebank
Head of News and Current Affairs: Alistair Gracie
Sales Controller: Christopher Kidd MInst M
Publicity & Promotions Executive: Michael J. McLintock, M.A., D.I.P. C.A.M.
Programme Controller: George Mitchell
Production Services Executive: Eric M. Johnstone
Chief Engineer: Alec Ramsey
Sales Administration Manager: John R. Stacey

GRANADA TELEVISION LTD.
Granada TV Centre, Manchester 3. Tel: 061-832 7211. 36 Golden Square, London W.1. Tel: 01-734-8080. News Centre, Albert Dock, Liverpool L3 4BA; News Centre, White Cross, Lancaster LA1 4XQ; News Centre, Bridgegate House, Chester.

LANCASHIRE CONTRACTOR
DIRECTORS: D. E. Plowright *(Chairman)*, A. Bernstein *(Deputy Chairman)*, Prof. J. Ashworth, Lord Evans of Claughton, D. H. Harker, A. G. Brill, A. Quinn *(Managing Director)*, S. Towneley, M. Wall, A. Mutch *(Secretary)*, S. R. Morrison, V. Wallace
Granada International: Vivien Wallace (Chief Executive)

HTV GROUP PLC.
Culverhouse Cross, Cardiff CF5 6XJ. Tel: Cardiff 590590. HTV West Ltd., Television Centre, Bath Road, Bristol BS4 3HG. Tel: Bristol 778366. HTV Sales and Marketing Ltd., 99 Baker Street, London, W1-M 2AJ. Tel: 01-486 4311.

WALES AND WEST OF ENGLAND CONTRACTOR
Chairman, HTV Group PLC: Sir Melvyn
Chief Executive, HTV Group PLC: P. Dromgoole
Managing Director, West: R. S. Evans
Managing Director, Wales: M. H. Davies
Managing Director, Sales & Marketing: C. D. Romaine
Managing Director, Production Services: M. R. Towers
Research Executive: I. Platt
Secretary: G. S. Tovey, F.C.I.S., F.C.A.

LWT (London Weekend Television)
South Bank Television Centre, London SE1 9LT. Tel: 01-261 3434; FAX: 01-928 6941; Telex: 918123.

LONDON CONTRACTOR—Friday 5:15 p.m. to Monday 6:00 a.m.
Chairman and Managing Director: Brian Tesler, C.B.E.
Director of Programmes: Greg Dyke
Group Finance Director: Peter McNally

Sales Director: Ron Miller
Secretary: Judith T. Thomas
Director of Personnel and Administration: Roy van Gelder
Director of Production: Peter Cazaly
Director of Corporate Affairs: Barry Cox

RADIO TELEFIS EIREANN
Donnybrook Dublin 4, Ireland: Tel: (01) 693111. London Office: Ireland House, 150 New Bond Street, London, W1Y OHD Tel: 01-493 8921. NATIONAL NETWORK OF THE REPUBLIC OF IRELAND.

Chairman: James P. Culliton
Director-General: Vincent Finn
Asst. Director-General: R. K. Gahan
Asst. Director-General: J. P. Sorohan
Director of Television Programmes: Bob Collins
Director of Radio Programmes: Michael Carroll
Director of News: Weslay Boyd

SCOTTISH TELEVISION, Plc
Cowcaddens, Glasgow, G2 3PR Scotland. Tel: 041 332 9999; Telex 77388; 114 St. Martin's Lane, London, WC2N 4AZ. Tel: 836 1500; Telex 27622; The Gateway, Edinburgh EH7 4AH. Tel: 031 557 4554. Suite 306, Sunlight House, Quay Street, Manchester M33JY. Tel: 061-834 7621

CENTRAL SCOTLAND CONTRACTOR
DIRECTORS: Sir Campbell Fraser, LL.D., D.Univ. *(Chairman)*, William Brown, C.B.E. *(Managing Director and Deputy Chairman)**, Alan Chilton, *(Director of Sales)**, Don Kintoch, *(Director of Finance and Company Secretary)**, Gus Macdonald, *(Director of Programmes)**, Sir Kenneth Alexander, LL.D., D.Univ., Gavin Boyd, C.B.E., Rev. Robin D. Buchanan-Smith, Mrs. Dorothy Dunnett, Sir Charles Fraser, K.C.V.O., D.L., Mrs. Pauline Hyde, Gavin Laird.
*Members of the Executive Board.
EXECUTIVE BOARD:
Controller of Resources: Ken Blackie
Controller of Engineering: Shaun Clamp
Controller Education and Religion and Edinburgh Controller: Robert McPherson
Controller Personnel and Industrial Relations: George Neilson
Controller of Corporate Affairs: Simon Forrest

TELEVISION SOUTH PLC
Television Centre, Southampton SO9 5HZ. Tel: 0703 634211; FAX: 0703 834320; Telex: 477217. Television Centre, Maidstone ME14 5NZ. Tel: 0622 691111

SOUTH & SOUTH-EAST OF ENGLAND CONTRACTOR
DIRECTORS: Lord Boston of Faversham QC *(Chairman)*, James Gatward (Chief Executive), Anthony Brook FCA *(Managing Director, Television)*, John Fox *(Director of Sales and Marketing)*, Guy Libby, Mrs. Blanche Lucas, Baroness Sharples, Malcolm Truepenny JP *(Group Personnel Director)*, Alan Boyd *(Director of Programmes)*, Richard Adam *(Finance)*, Arthur Price, Mel Blumenthal, Etienne Mallet, Piere Lescure, John Elton

TELEVISION SOUTH WEST LTD.
Derry's Cross, Plymouth, Devon PL1 L25P. Tel: 0752 663322; Telex: 45566; FAX: (Groups 2 & 3) 0752 671970.

SOUTH WEST ENGLAND CONTRACTOR
DIRECTORS: Sir Brian Bailey, O.B.E. *(Chairman)*, Sir John Colfox, D.L. *(Vice Chairman)*, Harry Turner *(Managing Director)*, Paul Stewart Laing *(Director of Programmes)*, John Roberts, F.C.A., F.C.T., M.I.M.C. *(Financial Director)*, I. Stolliday, M.A. *(Director of Personnel and Company Secretary)*, David Jenkin, T.ENG (CEI) MITE *(Director of Engineering)*, David Sunderland *(Director of Presentation and Public Relations)*, Eloie Armes, A.M.B.I.M., Fred Hain, Lt. Cdr. Douglas Hale, R.N. (Ret'd), The Earl of Iddesleigh, David Johnstone, M.A., F.C.A., Gareth Keene, M.A., LL.B., John Peters, C.B.E., Norman Thompson, Bernard Webster, B.Sc.(ENG) C. ENG FIEE FIERE.
OFFICERS:
Head of Contracts and Rights: Richard Griffiths, LL.B.
Chief Accountant: Michael Boddy, F.C.M.A.
Head of News and Current Affairs: Richard Myers
Head of Features: Paul Stewart Laing
Head of Education and Religion: Tom Goodison
Head of Office Services: Wendy Bowes
Personnel & Training Manager: Karen Woodward
Industrial Relations and Training Manager: Eric Kennaugh
Director of Sales: Martin Bowley
Regional Sales Manager, Bristol: Derek Prosser
Regional Sales Manager, Plymouth: Rob Clilverd
Head of Programme Planning: Elizabeth Mahoney
Head of Press and Public Relations: Martin Morrall
Press Officer: Susan Rolling
Presentation Manager: Tony Smith
Deputy Head of Engineering: Brian Warner
Facilities Manager: Bob Bounsall
Operations Manager-Central Services: Peter Rodgers
Operations Manager-Production Facilities: Keith Lloyd

THAMES TELEVISION Plc
Thames Television House, 306-318 Euston Road, London NW1 3BB. Tel: 01-387 9494. Teddington Lock, Teddington, Middlesex TW11 9NT. Tel: 01-977 3252. Norfolk House, Smallbrook Queensway, Birmingham B5 4LF. Tel: 021-643 9151.

LONDON CONTRACTOR
DIRECTORS: Sir Ian Trethowan *(Chairman)*, Richard Dunn *(Managing Director)*, Mrs. Mary Baker, Lord Brabourne, David Elstein *(Director of Programmes)*, P. Hayman, H. Mourgue, Ben E. Marr, *(Company Secretary & Director of Personnel)*, J. T. Davey *(Deputy Chairman)*, Derek Hunt, *(Director of Finance)*, Jonathan Shier, *(Sales & Marketing)*, C. S. Wills, T. Gold Blyth.

THAMES TELEVISION INTERNATIONAL LTD.
(Wholly-owned subsidiary for programme sales)
149 Tottenham Court Road, London, W1P 9LL. Tel: 01-387 9494

Managing Director: M. Phillips

TV-am Plc
Breakfast Television Centre, Hawley Crescent, London NW1 8EF. Tel: 01-267-5483; FAX: 01-267 6513

DIRECTORS: Ian Irvine *(Chairman)*, Bruce Gyngell *(Managing Director)*, Tony Vickers *(Deputy Managing Director)*, Stratis Zographos *(Financial Director)*, Bill Ludford *(Director, News and Current Affairs)*, David Davidovitz *(Director of Operations)*, Edwina Coven, David Frost, Nigel Ryan, Richard Redmayne, Peter De Savart, *DIRECTORS: TV-am News:* Nigel Ryan *(Chairman)*, Bruce Gyngell, Tony Vickers, Stratis Zographos, Bill Ludford, Edwina Coven, David Frost, David Chipp, Kenneth Coyte, Anne Diamond.

TYNE TEES TELEVISION LTD.
Head Office: The Television Centre, City Road, Newcastle upon Tyne, NE1 2AL. Tel: 091-2610181; Middlesbrough Office: Corporation House, Corporation Road, Middlesbrough. Tel: 0642 219181; London Office: 15 Bloomsbury Square, London, WC1A 2LJ. Tel: 01-405 8474. York Office: Ground Floor, United House, Piccadilly. York, Y01 1PQ. Tel: 0904 610666.

NORTH EAST CONTRACTOR
DIRECTORS: D. W. Reay *(Managing)*, G. T. Davies, R. Eagle, D. S. Hellewell, I. R. Ritchie, Sir Ralph Carr-Ellison, T.D., R. H. Dickinson, M.A., D. C. Eccles, Viscount Ridley, T.D., G. Oliver Worsley, T.D., M.A., Prof. Laurence W. Martin, M.A., Ph.D., P. Nicholson, D.L., F.C.A., D. Stevenson, C.B.E., J. Wilkinson, B.A.Com., G. E. Ward Thomas, C.B.E., D.F.C.

ULSTER TELEVISION plc
Havelock House, Ormeau Road, Belfast BT7 1EB Tel: 0232 328122; Telex: 74654; FAX: 0232 246695; London Office: 6 York Street, London, W1H 1FA, Tel: 01-486-5211.

ITV CONTRACTOR FOR NORTHERN IRELAND
DIRECTORS: R. B. Henderson, C.B.E., M.A., F.R.T.S., DLitt, *(Chairman)*, J. D. Smyth, B.Sc., F.C.A. *(Managing)*, J. B. McGuckian B.Sc. (Econ.) *(Deputy Chairman)*, H. R. C. Catherwood *(Vice Chairman)*, Mrs. B. E. MacQuitty B.Sc. (Econ) *(Vice Chairman)*, P. C. J. Battle *(Sales)*, J. A. Creagh *(Assistant Managing)*, R. E. Benner, O.B.E., Lord Dunluce, F.R.S.A., Captain O. W. J. Henderson, O.B.E., D.L., F.B.I.M., G. C. Hutchinson; Lady McCollum, E. J. O'Driscoll.

S4C
Sophia Close, Cardiff CF19XY. Tel: (0222) 43421; Telex: 497146. PEDWAR G; FAX: 0222 41643

Chairman: John Howard Davies, C.B.E., D.L.
Members: Gwilym Peregrine, John Parry, Tom Jones, Eleri Wynne Jones
Chief Executive: Geraint Stanley Jones
Programme Controller: Euryn Ogwen Williams
Secretary and Head of Finance: Emyr Byron Hughes
Deputy Programme Controller: Deryk Williams
Chief Engineer: Rodger Fuse
Controller, Planning and Marketing: Christopher Grace
Head of Productions, North Wales: Dilwyn Jones
Head of Public Relations: Ann Beynon

YORKSHIRE TELEVISION LTD.
The Television Centre, Leeds, LS3 1JS. Tel: 0532 438283; Telex: 557232. Television House, 32 Bedford Row, London, WC1R 4HE. Tel: 01-242 1666. Charter Square, Sheffield, S1 4HS. Tel: 0742 23262. 185 Ferensway, Hull, HU1 3PH. Tel: 0482 24488. 88 Bailgate, Lincoln, LN1 3AR. Tel: 0522 30738. 8 Bullring Lane, Grimsby, South Humberside, DN31 1DY. Tel: 0472 57026. 1 Queen Street, Ripon HG4 1EG. Tel: 0765 701551. 8 Coppergate, York Y01 1NR. Tel: 0904 610066.

YORKSHIRE CONTRACTOR
DIRECTORS: Sir Derek Palmar *(Chairman)*, C. W. Leach; *(Managing Director)*, J. Fairley *(Director of Programmes)*, G. J. A. Hardy *(Commercial Director)*, T. Street *(Sales Director)*, F. S. K. Baron, M.A., Mrs. P. M. David, S. H. Hall, F.C.A., Sir

Gordon Linacre, C.B.E., A.F.C., D.F.M., N. G. W. Playne, V. Watson, M.A., I. R. Calvert *(Personnel Director)*, B. F. J. Harris *(Business Affairs Director)*, M. Burrell (alternate: A. del Tuf), Mrs. J. Jowitt, E. W. Wright *(General Manager)*.

EXECUTIVES:
Controller, Planning and Presentation: R. I. Bairstow
Controller of Corporate Affairs: G. Brownlee
Controller of Drama: K. Richardson
Controller of Entertainment: V. Lawrence
Controller, UK Regional Sales: D. Stevenson
Controller, Personnel and Staff Relations: M. Thornhill
Documentaries & Current Affairs: G. McKee
Contracts Manager: F. W. Cieslik
Company Secretary: R. J. Coyle
Head of Science & Features: D. M. Dallas
Head of Casting: A. M. Drury
Deputy Commercial Director: D. Bould
Head of Local Programmes & Sport: G. Ironside
Head of Education, Children's Programmes & Religion: C. Jelley
Chief Engineer: J. Q. Rogers
Head of Production Operations: W. P. Rogers
Head of Publicity: Mrs. S. E. Ryle
Head of Technical Operations: P. H. Smale
Head of Programme Administration: J. B. Smith

Satellite—Cable Broadcasters

ABERDEEN CABLE SERVICES
303 King Street, Aberdeen, AB2 3AP, Scotland. Tel: 0224 649444

THE ARTS CHANNEL
P.O. Box 7, Ebbw Vale, Gwent NP3 5YP. Tel: 496 306995.

BRIGHTSTAR
Visnews Ltd., Cumberland Avenue, London, NW10 7EH. Tel: 01-965 7733. Telex: 22678. FAX: 01-965 0620.

BRITISH CABLE SERVICES
Southern House, 1-4 Cambridge Terrace, Oxford 0X1 1UD. Tel: 0865 250110

BT VISION
Euston Tower, 286 Euston Road, London, NW1 3DG. Tel: 01-728 3798

BRITISH SATELLITE BROADCASTING (BSB)
The Marco Polo Building, 346 Queenstown Road, London, S.W.8.
Chairman: Sir Trevor Holdsworth
Chief Executive: A. J. Simonds-Gooding

CABLETEL COMMUNICATIONS
The Fieldway, Bristol Road, Greenford, Middx: UB6 8UN. Tel: 01-575 9000.

CABLEVISION
Central Hall Buildings, High Street, Wellingborough, Northants: NN8 4HT. Tel: 0933 222078

CLYDE CABLE VISION
40 Anderston Quay, Glasgow, G3 8DA, Scotland. Tel: 041 221 7040.

COVENTRY CABLE TELEVISION
Whitley Village, London Road, Coventry CV3 4HE. Tel: 0203 505345.

CNN INTERNATIONAL
25/28 Old Burlington Street, London, W1X 1LB. Tel: 01-434 9323.

THE CHILDREN'S CHANNEL
9-13 Grape Street, London, WC2H 8DR. Tel: 01-240 3422

CROYDON CABLE TV
Communications House, Blue Riband Estate, 5 Factory Lane, Croydon, Surrey CR9 3RA. Tel: 01 760 0222. FAX: 01-681 2340. Telex: 8814079.

EAST LONDON COMMUNICATIONS
ELT House, 2 Mill Harbour, London, E14 9TE. Tel: 01 538 4510

EUROSPORT
31-36 Foley Street, London, W1P 7LB. Tel: 01-636 4077.

THE LANDSCAPE CHANNEL
South Bank House, Black Prince Road, London, SE1. Tel: 01-587 1011.

THE LIFESTYLE CHANNEL
The Quadrangle, 180 Wardour Street, London, W1V 8AA. Tel: 01 439 1177.

PREMIERE
7 D'Arblay Street, London, W1A 2AD. Tel: 01-434 0611.

SCREENSPORT
The Quadrangle, 180 Wardour Street, London, W1V 4AE. Tel: 01-439 1177.

SKY TELEVISION PLC.
Centaur Business Park, Grant Way, Off Syon Lane, Isleworth, Middx. TW7 5QD. Tel: 01-782 3000. FAX: 01-782 3113.
Executive Chairman: Andrew Neil

SUPER CHANNEL
19-22 Rathbone Place, London, W1P 1DF. Tel: 01 631 5050.

SWINDON CABLE
Newcombe Drive, Hawksworth Estate, Swindon SN2 1TU. Tel: 0793 615601

TELEVISION BROADCASTING COMPANY
New Roman House, 10 East Road, London, N1. Tel: 01 251 1533.

WESTMINSTER CABLE CO.
87-89 Baker Street, London, W1M 1AJ. Tel: 01-935 6699

WINDSOR TELEVISION
The Keep, 21 Victoria Street, Windsor, SL4 1YE. Tel: 0753 856345

TV Program Material—Producers, Distributors and Service Companies

ABACUS PRODUCTIONS LTD.
731 Shelton Street, London, WC2. Tel: 01-240 1277; Cables: ABAFILMS LONDON.
Directors: John Mackey *(Chairman)*, Ron Trainer *(Managing)*, Betty J. Martin
Producers of TV and cinema commercials on both film and video. Matte process, stop motion, model animation, own studios, 2 stages, cove, 2 cutting rooms, Preview Theatre. Rostrum techniques, front projection screen.

ABC SPORTS
8 Carburton Street, London, W1P 7DT. Tel: 01-636 7366; Telex: 23625 ABC5PT G; FAX: 01-323 4986.

ADVISION LTD.
23 Gosfield Street, London, W1P 7HB. Tel: 01-580 5707; FAX: 01-631 1457.
Sound recording facilities: 3 studios, max. capacity 50 musicians. All studios have sound to picture facilities. Digital editing suite. Mobile recording studio for location work.

AEROFILMS
Gate Studios, Station Road, Boreham Wood, Herts., WD6 1EJ. Tel: 01-207 0666; FAX: 01-207 5433.

AIR-TIME PRODUCTIONS LTD.
50-Frith Street, London, W.1. Tel: 01-734 9304.
Director: Johnny Fielder

ALLIED VISION LTD.
360 Oxford Street, London, W1N 9HA. Tel: 01-409 1984.

ALPHA FILMS LTD.
Unit 1, McKay Trading Estate, Kensal Road, London, W10 5BX. Tel: 01-960 8211. Telex: 291877 Vision G.

JOHN ANDERSON HIRE
Court Lane, Iver, Bucks. Tel: Iver 653737 (production facilities).

ANDERSON BURR PARTNERSHIP LTD.
Greenman, Highmoor, Henley-on-Thames, Oxfordshire, RG9 5DH. Tel: 0491 641140; FAX: 0491 641080; Telex: 849467 FATHER G.

ANIMALS UNLIMITED
Careys Wood, Smallfield, Surrey. Tel: 034 284-2400.
(Animal agency.)

ANVIL FILM & RECORDING GROUP LTD.
Denham Studios, North Orbital Rd., Denham, Nr. Uxbridge, Middx. Tel: 0895 833522; Telex: 934704; FAX: 0895 833617.
Directors: R. W. Keen, K. Somerville, C. Eng. MIERE., Peter Gray
(Documentaries, etc.)

ANTELOPE FILMS LTD.
3 Fitzroy Square, London, W1P 5AH. Tel: 01-387 4454; Telex: 266205; FAX: 01-388 9935.

ARMADA PRODUCTIONS
86/88 Wardour Street, London, W1V 3LF. Tel: 01-734 6312.
Managing Director: J. D. Dooley

ATHOS FILM PRODUCTIONS LTD.
65 High Street, Hampton Hill, Middx., TW12 1NH. Tel: 01-783 0533. Telex: 28905 Ref. 325.
Directors: P. G. A. Bucknall, The Viscount Portman, D. B. Bucknall, R. Orr-Ewing
(Production, video and film, 35/16mm.)

ATLANTIC RELEASING BV
13-14 Golden Square, London, W1R 3AG. Tel: 01-494 3858; FAX: 01-437 0036; Telex: 24654 ATLANT G.

AUSTRALIAN BROADCASTING CORPORATION
54 Portland Place, London, W1N 4DY. Tel: 01-631 4456; Cables: Austcast, London; Telex: 263897 (News) 23494 (Admin.); FAX: 01-323 1125.
Bureau Chief (Europe): J. Highfield

AUSTRALIAN FILM COMMISSION
2nd Floor, Victory House, 99-101 Regent Street, London, W1. Tel: 01-734 9383; Telex: 28711 Ausfilm. G.

AUTOCUE LTD.
Autocue House, 265 Merton Road, London, SW18 5JS. Tel: 01-870 0104; Telex: 885039 Autocu G; FAX: 01-874 3726.
Contact: Mick Gould, Steve Powers
(Prompting facilities for film, TV and conferences; Aston Caption Charactor Generator Hire.)

BBC ENTERPRISES LTD.
Woodlands, 80 Wood Lane, London, W12 0TT. Tel: 01-743 5588 & 01-576 2000; Cables: Telecentre London; Telex: 934678 & 265781. Overseas Sales Offices: 80 William Street, Sydney, New South Wales 2011, Australia; Distributors for U.S.A.; Lionheart Television International; Lionheart Television: 630 Fifth Avenue, Suite 2220, New York, NY 10111, USA.
Director of Programme Sales: Keith Owen

BOULTON-HAWKER FILMS LTD.
Hadleigh, Ipswich, Suffolk, 1P7 5BG. Tel: 0473 82 2235.
Directors: K. P. Boulton, M. J. Boulton, N. H. L. Rea, D.A. Boulton.

BRENT WALKER FILM & THEATRE DIVISION
Knightsbridge House, 197, Knightsbridge, London, SW7 1RB. Tel: 01-225 1941. Telex: 23639.

BRIGHTSTAR
Visnews Ltd., Cumberland Avenue, London, NW10 7EH. Tel: 01-965 7733; Telex: 22678; FAX: 01-965 0620.

BRITISH DIRECT TELEVISION LTD.
3-4 Woking Business Park, Woking, Surrey, GU21 5JY. Tel: 04862 27676.
Directors: Lawrence R. Greetham, Simon D. Currey, Sue M. Greetham

BRITISH LION SCREEN ENTERTAINMENT
Pinewood Studios, Pinewood Road, Iver, Bucks., 5L0 0NH. Tel: 0753 651700; Telex: 847505; FAX: 0753 656391.
Chairman and Chief Executive: Peter R. E. Snell

BRITISH MOVIETONEWS LTD.
North Orbital Road, Denham, Uxbridge, Middx., UB9 5HQ. Tel: 0895 833071; FAX: 0895 834893.
Film Library: Barbara Heavens

BRITISH SCREEN
37-39 Oxford Street, London, W1R 1RE. Tel: 01-434 0291. Telex: 888694 BRISCR G. FAX: 01-434 9933.
Chief Executive: Simon Relph

BRITISH TRANSPORT FILMS
Lansdowne Vaults
Imperial Studios, Maxwell Road, Boreham Wood, Hertfordshire, WD6 1WE Tel: 01-207 4664.

BRYON PARKIN ASSOCIATES LTD.
37 Dover Street, London, W1X 3RA. Tel: 01-950 5151.

CABLE CONNECTIONS TELEVISION LTD.
201 Holland Park Avenue, London, W11 4UN. Tel: 01-603 4500; Telex: 8950117 AZITAP G; FAX: 01-603 1830.
(Music programs.)

CAMERA LOCATION SERVICES
16 St. James Close, St. John's Woking, Surrey. Tel: 04862 4645.
(Researchers, suppliers film and photographic locations.)

CANADIAN BROADCASTING CORPORATION
43-51 Great Titchfield Street, London, W1P 8DD. Tel: 01-580 0336; Telex: 23771.

CARLTON COMMUNICATIONS PLC.
15 St. George Street, London, W1R 9DE. Tel: 01-499 8050; FAX: 01-895 9575.
Chairman: Michael Green
Managing Director: Robert Phillis

CARLTON TELEVISION LTD.
St. John's Wood Studios, St. John's Wood Terrace, London, NW8 6PY. Tel: 01-722 9255; FAX: 01-483 4264.
Managing Director: Barry Johnstone

CASTLE COMMUNICATIONS
15-16 Northfields Prospect, Putney Bridge Road, London, SW18 1PE. Tel: 01-871 0470; FAX: 01-871 0470
Chairman: Terry Shand

CAVALIER FILMS LTD.
34 Deacon's Hill Road, Elstree, Herts. Tel: 01-953 1403.
Directors: D. T. Rogers, A. V. Kimber
(Specialized films, documentary, commercials.)

CBS BROADCAST
6 Albemarle Street, London, W.1.

CBS NEWS
100 Brompton Rd., London, S.W.3. Tel: 01-584 3366; Telex: 916 319; Cables: Colnews London.
(News, radio and TV coverage.)

CBS/FOX VIDEO
Perivale Industrial Park, Greenford, Middlesex, UB6 7RU. Tel: 01-997 2552; Telex: 8951742; FAX: 01-991 0251

CENTRAL FILMS
35-38 Portman Square, London, W1A 2HZ. Tel: 01-486 6688.
Managing Director: Ted Childs

CENTRAL OFFICE OF INFORMATION
Hercules Road, London, SE1 7DU. Tel: 01-928 2345.
Films and Television Division: *Director:* Charles Skinner
Radio Services: *Head:* Virginia Burdon

CHATSWORTH TELEVISION
97-99 Dean Street, London, W1V 5RA. Tel: 01-734 4302; Telex: 28604 Ref. 890; FAX: 01-437 3301.

ROGER CHERRILL LTD.
65-66 Dean Street, London, W1V 6PL. Tel: 01-437 6411; FAX: 01-437 6411.
(Post sync dialogue, dubbing and effects, film and TV production, post production.)

CHESS VALLEY FILMS LTD.
Film House, Little Chalfont, Bucks., HP7 9PY. Tel: 02-404 2222 and 2020.
Directors: Ronald E. Haddock, F.B.I.P.P., P. M. Trudi Drayton, Heather M. Davies, MBKSTS
(Production 35/16mm film broadcast and non-broadcast TV and allied services.)

CHRYSALIS VISUAL PROGRAMMING
12-13 Stratford Place, London, W1N 9AF. Tel: 01-408 2355; Telex: 21753.

CINE-LINGUAL SOUND STUDIOS LTD.
27-29 Berwick Street, London, W1V 3RF. Tel: 01-437 0136.
Directors: A. Anscombe, P. J. Anscombe, M. Anscombe, D. J. Old, D. J. Newman

CINEMA VERITY LTD.
The Mill House, Millers Way, 1A Shepherds Bush Road, London, W6 7NA. Tel: 01-749 8485; FAX: 01-743 5062.
Producer: Verity Lambert

CINESOUND EFFECTS LIBRARY LTD.
Imperial Studios, Maxwell Road, Elstree Way, Boreham Wood, Herts., WD6 IWE. Tel: 01-953 5837 and 5545, 1587, 4904.
(Sound effects.)

CINE VIDEO LTD.
7 Silver Road, White City Industrial Park, Wood Lane, London, W12 7SG. Tel: 01-743 3839; Telex: 915 282 CINEGP G; FAX: 01-749 3501.
(Broadcast television equipment hire.)

CINEVISTA LTD.
65 Corringway, London, W5 3HB. Tel: 01-998 2611.
Directors: John Simmons, Cecilia Simmons
(Entertainment and sponsored material.)

COLOUR VIDEO SERVICES LTD.
22-5 Portman Close, Baker Street, London, W1A 4BE. Tel: 01-486 2881; FAX: 01-486 4152.
Managing Director: David Chase
(Superscan tape-to-film transfer. 16mm or 35mm, cassette duplication, telecine, conference centre, equipment hire.)

COLUMBIA PICTURES TELEVISION
A Division of Columbia Pictures Corporation Ltd. St. Margaret's House, 19/23 Wells Street, London, W1P 3FP. Tel: 01-637 8444; Telex: 263392 COLP1C G; Cables: Columfilm, London.
President: Nicholas Bingham
(Production and distribution TV film series.)

CRANEZOOM LTD.
28 Saint Mary le Park Court, Albert Bridge Road, London, SW11 4PJ. Tel: 01-223 0034.

CROSSBOW FILMS LTD.
42 Connaught Square, London, W2 2HD. Tel: 01-724 6966; Telex: XBOW 21464.

CROWN TELEVISION PRODUCTIONS PLC.
Crown Television Centre, Church Road, Claygate, Esher, Surrey, KT10 0JP. Tel: 0372 69111. Telex: 8811232 GREENS G.

C.T.S. STUDIOS LTD.
Engineers Way, Wembley, Middlesex, HA9 0DR. Tel: 01-903 4611; Telex: 923400; FAX: 01-903 7130.
Contact: Adrian Kerridge

CTVC
Hillside Studios, Merry Hill Road, Bushey, Watford, WD2 1DR. Tel: 01-950 4426.
(Production and post production, film and video library hire facilities.)

CUCUMBER STUDIOS LTD.
19/21 Heddon Street, London, W1. Tel: 01-437 0109.

CYGNET LTD.
Bilton Centre, Coronation Road, High Wycombe, Bucks., HP12 3TA. Tel: 0494 450541; Telex: 83659 BIGGSC G.
Managing Director: D. N. Plunket

DEE & CO. LTD
46 Potters Lane, Barnet, Herts., EN5 5BE. Tel: 01-449 7533; Telex: 946240 CWEASY G Ref: 19028490

DE LANE LEA SOUND CENTRE
75 Dean Street, London, W.1. Tel: 01-439 1721.
(Sound recording, foreign version dubbing, editing facilities.)

DE WOLFE LTD.
80-88 Wardour Street, London, W1V 3LF. Tel: 01-439 8481.
Directors: James de Wolfe, Gordon Chambers, Warren de Wolfe
(Library recorded music, original scores, Angel Recording Studios Ltd.)

WALT DISNEY CO. LTD.
31-32 Soho Square, London, W1V 6AP. Tel: 01-734 8111; Telex: 21532; FAX 01-4398741.
Managing Director: Etienne de Villiers

DRAKE AUDIO VISUAL
89 St. Fagans Road, Fairwater, Cardiff CF5 3AE.
Managing Director: R. G. Drake
Marketing Director: H. Drake

DRUMMER FILMS LTD.
14 Haywood Close, Pinner, Middx., HA5 3LQ. Tel: 01-866 9466; FAX: 01-866 9466.
Managing Director: Martin M. Harris (Producer)

DUCK LANE FILM PRODUCTIONS LTD.
8 Duck Lane, London, W1V 1FL Tel: 01-439 3912; Telex: 25554.
Director: R. Andrews

EDUCATIONAL & TELEVISION FILMS LTD.
247a Upper Street, London, N1-1RU. Tel: 01-226 2298.
General Manager: Stanley Forman

ELECTRONIC PUBLISHING CO. LTD.
68-70 Wardour Street, London, W1V 3HP. Tel: 01-734 4609; Telex: Peclon 25554; FAX: 01-734 9471.

ELEPHANT VIDEO LTD.
15-17 Old Compton Street, London, W1V 5PJ. Tel: 01-437 9541; Cables: Eaglepix, London, W.1; Telex: 928152 GALAFI G.
Directors: Barry Jacobs, A. Jacobs

ENTERTAINMENT FILM PRODUCTIONS LTD.
27 Soho Square, London, W1V 5FL. Tel: 01-439 1606; FAX: 01-734 2483; Telex: 262428 ENT VIF.
Directors: Michael L. Green, Nigel Green, Trevor H. Green

ENTERTAINMENT IN VIDEO LTD.
27 Soho Square, London, W1V 5FL. Tel: 01-439 1979. Telex: 262428 ENTVIF. FAX: 734 2483.
Directors: Michael L. Green, Nigel Green, Trevor H. Green

EPA INTERNATIONAL PROGRAMMERS LTD.
P.O. Box 228, London, SW16 1BP. Tel: 01-677 7523.

EUREKA LOCATION MANAGEMENT
16 Broadwick St., London, W1V 1FH. Tel: 01-734 4100; FAX: 01-437 0086; Telex: 265 871, answerback MONREF G, quoting ref. 76:WJJ106; Electronic mail—Telecom gold.
Head of Operations: Ian Lloyd

EUSTON FILMS LTD.
365 Euston Road, London, NW1 3AR. Tel: 01-387 0911
Production Controller: Bill Launder

EWART TELEVISION
Wandworth Plain, London, SW18 1ET. Tel: 01-874 0131; Telex: 929509; FAX: 01-871 9737.
Managing Director: Keith Ewart
(Full studio and post production facility.)

EYELINE FILM AND VIDEO LTD.
77 Dean Street, London, W.1. Tel: 01-734 3391; Telex: 265351.
Directors: Harold Orton, Jacki Roblin, George H. Brown, Alfred Shaughnessy, Gordon Grimward
(Ent. advertising material.)

FALKMAN COMMUNICATIONS LTD.
33 Gresse Street, London, W1P 1PN. Tel: 01-636 1371; FAX: 01-631 1497.
Directors: B. Falk, L. Green, J. Finnis

FILM AND GENERAL PRODUCTIONS LTD.
10 Pembridge Place, London, W2 4XB. Tel: 01-221 1141.
Directors: Clive Parsons, Davina Belling, Richard Whatmore

FILMBOND SERVICES LTD.
Heston Industrial Estate, Aerodrome Way, Cranford Lane, Hounslow TW5 9QB. Tel: 01-897 7973; Telex: 21747.
Directors: A. Record, M. Woolley, A. Abeles, S. Shore, A. Loader, J. Reeves

FILMSCREEN INT. LTD.
Studio 3, 12 Neals Yard, Covent Garden, London, WC2H 9DP. Tel: 01-379 0733; Telex: 269445 SSINT G; FAX: 01-379 0117.

FLAMINGO FILM PRODUCTIONS
P.O. Box 130, Hove, East Sussex, BN3 6QU Tel: 0273 550088; Telex: 877050; FAX: 0273 540969.
Directors: R. Kruger, J. S. Kruger
(Producers of feature films, musical video films and television programming.)

MARK FORSTATER PRODUCTIONS LTD.
42a, Devonshire Close, Portland Place, London, W.1. Tel: 01-631 0611.

FOWLER-CHAPMAN COMPANY LTD.
28 Saint Mary le Park Court, Albert Bridge Road, London, SW11 4PJ. Tel: 01-223 0034.

FREMANTLE INTERNATIONAL, INC.
Greendon House, 7 c/d Bayham Street, London, NW1 0HE. Tel: 01-380 1189.
President: Paul Talbot
Chief Executive: Anthony Gruner
(TV film Distributors.)

FRIDAY PRODUCTIONS LTD.
83 Cadogan Lane, London, S.W.1. Tel: 01-235 1909

FRONTROOM PRODUCTIONS LTD.
779 Wardour Street, London, W1E 3TH. Tel: 01-734 4603.

GANNET FILMS LTD.
88 Gresham Road, Staines, Middx., TW18 2AE.
Directors: Bob Kellett, Anne Kellett

JAMES GARRETT & PARTNERS LTD.
25 Bruton Street, London, W1X 7DB. Tel: 499 6452. Telex: 261163. FAX: 409 1797.
Directors: J. L. M. P. Garrett *(Chmn.)*, M. Gilmour *(Managing)*, D. T. Cromwell *(Prod. Dir.)*, M. Garrett, F. Bloom
(Advertising film producers.)

GATEWAY AUDIOVISUAL/VIDEO
470-472 Green Lanes, Palmers Green, London, N13 5XF. Tel: 01-882 0177; Telex: 896462.
Director: G. L. Smart, A.R.P.S., M.B.K.S.
(Industrial, advertising, educational and training films.)

GENERAL SCREEN ENTERPRISES LTD.
Highbridge Estate, Oxford Road, Uxbridge, Middx., UB8 1LX. Tel: 0895 31931; Telex: 934883; FAX: 0895 35335.
Managing Director: Fred Chandler
Scriptwriter: Tony Church
(Main titles, trailers, commercials, opticals, special effects.)

G.H.W. PRODUCTIONS LTD.
52 Queen Anne Street, London, W1M 9LA. Tel: 01-935 1186.
Directors: Peter Rogers, Betty E. Box, O.B.E.; D. G. Truscott.

WILLIAM GILBERT ASSOCIATES LTD.
16 Brook Mews North, London, W2 3BW. Tel: 01-258 3620/1/2/3

GLINWOOD FILMS LTD.
Swann House, 52-53 Poland Street, London, W1V 3DF. Tel: 01-437 1181; FAX: 01-494 0634; Telex: 23788.

GLOBO INTERNATIONAL (LONDON) LTD.
14-15 Stratford Place, London, W1N 9AF. Tel: 01-409 1712.

BOB GODFREY FILMS LTD
55 Neal Street, London, W.C.2 Tel: 01-240 1793/1889.
(Animation for television and cinema. Commercials. 16/35 mm camera service.)

GOLDCREST FILMS AND TELEVISION LTD.
36-44 Brewer Street, London, W1R 3HP. Tel: 01-437 8696; Telex: 267458 Goldcr; FAX: 01-437 4448.

GOLDEN COMMUNICATIONS (OVERSEAS) LTD
47 Greek Street, London, W1V 5LQ. Tel: 01-439 1431.
Vice President (International Sales): David A. E. Shepperd

G.P.A. (FILMS) LTD.
22 Romily Street, London, W.1. Tel: 01-734 6994.
Director: Gerry Poulson

GRADE COMPANY
Embassy House, 3 Audley Square, London, W1Y 5DR. Tel: 01-409 1925; FAX: 01-408 2042.

GRANADA TELEVISION INTERNATIONAL LTD.
36 Golden Square, London, W1R 4AH Tel: 01-734 8080; Telex: 27937. 18 Rue Volney, 75002 Paris, France. Tel: (33 1) 42.61.79.10; Telex: 213008. 1221 Avenue of the Americas, Suite 3468, New York, NY 10020, U.S.A. Tel: (212) 869 8480; Telex: 62454 UW.
Chief Executive: Vivien Wallace
(Overseas distributors of TV programmes made by Granada.)

ELAINE GREENE LTD.
31, Newington Green, London, N16 9PU. Tel: 01-249 2971.
Directors: Elaine Greene, Ilsa Yardley, Timothy Webb
(Literary agency.)

GUILD HOME VIDEO LTD.
Crown House, 2 Church Street, Walton-on-Thames, Surrey, KT12 2QS. Tel: 01-546 3377; Telex: 269651; FAX: 01 546 4568.

HALLIFORD STUDIOS LTD
Manygate Lane, Shepperton, Middx., TW17 9EG. Tel: 0932 226341; FAX: 0932 246336.
Studio Manager: Allan d'Aguiar

HAMMER FILM PRODUCTIONS LTD.
Goldcrest Elstree Studios, Boreham, Herts. Tel: 01-953 1600.
Directors: Roy Skeggs, Timothy L. Kirby, Sir John Terry

HAMPDEN GURNEY STUDIOS, LTD.
39-41 Hanover Steps, St. Georges Fields, Albion Street, London, W2 2YG. Tel: 01-402 7543; FAX: 01-262 5736; Telex: 896559 GECOMS G.

STEWART HARDY FILMS LTD.
2-4 Wigton Gardens, Stanmore, Middx., HA7 18G. Tel: 01-204 4153.
Director: J. R. Williams
(Animation, diagram, cartoon films.)

HEMDALE HOLDINGS
21 Albion Street, London, W2 2AS. Tel: 01-724 1010; Telex: 25558.
Directors: J. Daly, A. D. Kerman, D. Gibson

HENSON INTERNATIONAL TELEVISION
2 Old Brewery Mews, Hampstead High Street, London, NW3 1PZ. Tel: 01-435 7121; Telex: 8955914 (Kermit G); FAX: 01-794 8150.

HISTORICA CONSULTANCY
8-9 The Incline, Coalport, Telford, Shrop., TF8 7HR. Tel: 0952 584043

GERARD HOLDSWORTH PRODUCTIONS LTD.
31 Palace Street, London, SW1E 5HW. Tel: 01-828 1671.

Directors: Mary V. Holdsworth, P. H. Filmer-Sankey, Don Kelly
(Documentaries, TV program material.)

IDEAL COMMUNICATIONS FILM & TV LTD.
26 Soho Square, London, W1V 5JF. Tel: 01-434 0011; FAX: 01-434 9625.

Managing Director: Kevin Christie

I.F.A. (SCOTLAND) LTD.
1 North Claremont Street, Glasgow, C3. Scotland. Tel: 041-332 3620.

INCA FILMS LTD.
76 Brewer Street, London, W1R 4HU. Tel: 01-437 3877.

Directors: Anne Balfour Fraser, Timothy Burrill, Brian Little, Eric Falk, Frances Cockburn
(Documentary, advertising and entertainment material.)

INDEPENDENT TELEVISION NEWS LTD.
ITN House, 48 Wells Street, London, W1P 4DE. Tel: 01-637 2424; Telex: 22101; FAX: 01-636 0349.

Chairman and Chief Executive: Sir David Nicholas
(Production facilities.)

INITIAL PICTURES & TV LTD.
22 Golden Square, London, W1R 3PA. Tel: 01-439 8994; FAX: 01-439 4726.

Directors: Eric Fellner, Scott Millaney, Malcolm Gerrie

INTERNATIONAL TELEVISION ENTERPRISES LTD.
27 Upper Brook Street, London, W1Y 1PD. Tel: 01-491 1441.

ISLAND PICTURES
22 St. Peter's Square, London, W.6. Tel: 01-741 1511.

ITC ENTERTAINMENT GROUP LTD.
24 Nutford Place, London, W.1. Tel: 01-262 3262; Telex: 261807.

Directors: J. Leider, C. Gorog, P. Shields, D. Cunliffe

ITEL
27 Upper Brook Street, London, W1Y 1PD. Tel: 01-491 1441; Telex: 25353; FAX: 01-493 2598.

ITN LTD.
ITN House, 48 Wells Street, London, W1P 4DE. Tel: 01-637 2424; Telex 22101; FAX: 01-636 0349.

Contact: Mike Jessey
(Studio, VTR and Conversion Facilities.)

ITV FILM PURCHASE GROUP
Knighton House, 56 Mortimer Street, London, W1N 8AN. Tel: 01-636 6866; Telex: 9419024.

IVS ENTERPRISES LTD.
54 Warwick Square, London, SW1V 2AJ. Tel: 01-834 6012; Telex: 27151; FAX: 01-630 6270.

BRIAN JACKSON FILMS LTD.
39-41 Hanover Steps, St. Georges Fields, Albion Street, London, W2 2YG. Tel: 01-402 7543 and 01-262 5736; FAX: 01-262 5736; Telex: 896559 GECOMS-G.

J & M ENTERTAINMENT
2 Dorset Square, London, NW1 6PU Tel: 01-723 6544. Telex: 298538 FILMIN G; FAX: 01-724 7541; Cables: Filming London NW1.

JARAS ENTERTAINMENTS LTD.
21 Cavendish Place, London, W1M 9DL. Tel: 01-580 5927.

CYRIL JENKINS PRODUCTIONS LTD.
7 Coniston Court, Carlton Drive, London, SW15 2BZ. Tel: 01-788 2733.

Directors: Cyril G. Jenkins, J. M. Jenkins
Entertainment, documentary and advertising material.)

KAVUR PRODUCTIONS LTD.
14 Lownes Square, London, SW1X 9HB. Tel: 01-235 4602; Telex: 21251 TICK G; FAX: 01-235 7718.

KRUGER LEISURE ORGANISATION (FILM, VIDEO & TV DISTRIBUTION)
P.O. Box 130, Hove, East Sussex, BN3 6QU. Tel: 0273 550088; Telex: 877050; FAX: 0273 540969.

Directors: J. S. Kruger, R. Kruger, H. R. Kruger

KIMPTON WALKER LTD.
47/49 Acre Lane, London, SW2 5TN. Tel: 01-737 3317; Telex: 27789; FAX: 01-274 4534.

(Theatre, film and television scenery.)

LIBERTY FILMS
4th Floor, The Forum, 74-80 Camden Street, London, NW1 0JL. Tel: 01-387 5733; FAX: 01-383 7111.

LE VIEN FILMS LTD.
15 Chesterfield Hill, London, W.1. Tel: 01-629 4545; Cables: Vienfilms London, W.1.

Executive Producer: Jack Le Vien
(TV films and features.)

LIBRA PRODUCTIONS LTD.
Marl Cottage, Mark Cross, Crowborough, Sussex. Tel: Rotherfield 2172/2746.

Directors: Kevin Scott (U.S.A.), Thomas Kyffin
(Producers of television programmes.)

LIMEHOUSE PRODUCTIONS LTD
The Trocadero, 19 Rupert Street, London, W1V 7FS. Tel: 01-287 3333; FAX: 01-287 1998.

Contact: Iain Bruce

LITTLE KING PRODUCTIONS LTD.
13-14 Bateman Street, London, W.1. Tel: 01-437 9611; FAX: 01-734 7143.

Contacts: Dr. Simon C. Nicholas, M.B., B. Chir., Simon Manley-Cooper
(Medical and industrial films for film & video.)

LONDON FILM PRODUCTIONS LTD
44a Floral Street, London WC2E 9DA. Tel: 01-379 3366; Telex: 896805.

LWTI Ltd.
Seymour Mews House, Seymour Mews, Wigmore Street, London, W1H 9PE. Tel: 01-935 9000; Telex: 22872 TV film G.

LORIMAR DISTRIBUTION LTD.
16 Berkeley Street, London, W.1. Tel: 01-493 1566.

Managing Director: Ray Lewis

LORIMAR-TELEPICTURES INTERNATIONAL LTD.
49 Berkeley Square, London, W1X 5DB. Tel: 01-409 1190; Telex: 25153 Lormar G; FAX: 01-629 2064 (2 or 3).

Managing Director: Stuart B. Graber

I.R. MAXWELL (FILM DISTRIBUTORS) LTD.
Headington Hill Hall, Oxford, OX3 0BW. Tel: 0865 64881; Telex: 83177.

McCANN INTERNATIONAL PROGRAMME MARKETING LTD.
88-94 Tottenham Court Road, London, W1P 9HE. Tel: 01-323 4641; Telex: 297957.

MAJESTIC FILMS INTERNATIONAL
Gloucester Mansions, Cambridge Circus, London, WC2H 8HD. Tel: 01-836 8630; FAX: 01-836 5819; Telex: 916746 MAJEST G.

Managing Director: Guy East

MARK I PRODUCTIONS LTD.
Lee International Studios, 128 Wembley Park Drive, Wembley, Middlesex, HA9 8JE. Tel: 01-902 1262.

MECCA INTERNATIONAL PRODUCTIONS LTD
14 Oxford Street, London, W1N 0HL. Tel: 01-637 9401.

MEDIA RELEASING DISTRIBUTORS LTD.
27 Soho Square, London, W.1. Tel: 01-437 2341; Telex: 943763 CROCOM G(MRD).

Directors: Trevor H. Green, J. Green

MEDUSA COMMUNICATIONS LTD.
Regal Chambers, 51 Bancroft, Hitchin, Herts., SG5 1LL. Tel: 0462 421818; FAX: 0462 420393.

Chairman: David Hodgins
Managing Director: Colin Simonds
Executive Director: Steve Rivers

THE MOVING PICTURE COMPANY
25 Noel Street, London, W.1. Tel: 01-434 3100. Telex: 27256; FAX: 437 3951

(Production Facilities.)

MUSIC BOX
19-21 Rathbone Place, London, W1P 1DF. Tel: 01-636 7888.

NBC NEWS WORLDWIDE INC.
8 Bedford Avenue London, WC1. Tel: 01-637 8655.

NATIONAL FILM AND TELEVISION SCHOOL
Beaconsfield Studios, Station Road, Beaconsfield, Bucks., HP9 1LG. Tel: 0494 671234; FAX: 0494 674042.

Director: Colin Young

NATIONAL SCREEN
Studios: 15 Wadsworth Road, Greenford, Middx., UB6 7JN. Tel: 01-998 2851; Telex: 934522. London Office: Wedge-

wood Mews, Greek Street London, W1V 5LE. Tel: 01-437 4851.

Directors: John Mahony, Norman Darkins, Brian McIlmail

NETWORK TELEVISION LTD.
47 Poland Street, London, W1V 3DF. Tel: 01-734 0496.

NEW CENTRAL FILM SERVICES LTD.
97-99 Dean Street, London, W.1. Tel.: 01-734 5827-8.

(Editing equipment hire, cutting rooms, production offices, cutting room supplies.)

NEW WORLD PICTURES (UK) LTD.
27 Soho Square, London, W1V 5FL. Tel: 01-434 0497; FAX: 01-434 0490.

NIXPARGO ANIMATIONS
Maidensgrove, Nr. Henley-on-Thames, Oxon., RG9 6EZ. Tel: 049 163-286.

Producers: Nicholas Spargo, Mary Spargo

NUMO PRODUCTIONS LTD.
3 Richmond Mews, London, W.1. Tel.: 01-439 4017.

NVC CABLE LTD.
32 Eccleston Square, London, SW1V 1PB. Tel: 01-834 2300; Telex: 893045 NVCG.

OPTICAL FILM EFFECTS LTD.
Pinewood Studios, Iver Heath, Bucks. 5L0 0NH. Tel: 0753 655486; Telex: 847505 G.

Directors: R. W. Field, R. A. Dimbleby

ORACLE TELETEXT
Craven House, 25-32 Marshall Street, London, W1V 1LL. Tel: 01-434 3121; Telex: 8813039; FAX: 01-437 8974.

Directors: Peter Paine, C.B.E., D.F.C. *(Chairman)*, Peter Bailey *(Managing Director)*, Chris O'Connor *(Financial Director)*, David Klein *(Editorial Director)*, Robbie Alexander *(Sales Director)*, Sir Brian Bailey O.B.E., James Gatward, Derek Hunt, Brian Tesler, C.B.E.
(Oracle provides the teletext service for ITV and Channel 4, and is jointly owned by the ITV contractors [except TV-am].)

OVERVIEW FILMS LTD.
113-117 Wardour Street, London, W1V 3TD. Tel: 01-439 7491; Telex: 21259 FILM G; FAX: 01-734 4970.

PALLADIUM INTERNATIONAL TELEVISION LTD.
6 Goodwins Court, St. Martin's Lane, London, WC2N 4LL. Tel: 01-836 0576; Telex: 267664; FAX: 01-836 4198.

DAVID PARADINE PRODUCTIONS LTD.
115-123 Bayham Street, London, NW1 0AG. Tel: 01-482 2898; Telex: 27613; FAX: 01-482 0871.

PARAMOUNT TELEVISION
23 Berkeley House, Hay Hill, London, W.1. Tel.: 01-629 1150.

Managing Director: Peter Cary
(TV film distributors.)

PARTNERS PRODUCTIONS LTD.
13 D'Arblay Street, London, W1V 3FP. Tel: 01-734 0671; FAX: 01-494 0197.

Directors: A. Brant, C. Shaw
Contact: Adrian Brant.

PEARL & DEAN LTD.
27 Sale Place, London, W2 1PT. Tel: 01-262 5000.

Managing Director: G. Brailey

PETROFILMS UK LTD
8 West Street, London W.C.2. Tel: 01-836 2112.

PHOENIX FILMS LTD.
Manor Road, Goring-On-Thames, RG8 9DP. Tel: 04-918 72365.

Directors: B. G. Hanson, M. E. Hanson
(Live-action, cartoon, stop motion.)

PIZAZZ PICTURESS
30 Berwick Street, London, W.1. Tel: 01-434 3581.

Producer: Pamela Dennis
Directors: Eric Goldberg, Mario Cavalli

PLATO FILMS LTD.
247A Upper Street, London, N1 1RU. Tel: 01-226 2298.

Managing Director: Stanley Forman

POLYGRAM FILMS (UK) Ltd.
(Polygram Music Video)
1, Rockley Road, London, W14 0DL. Tel: 01-743 3474; Telex: 298816.

(Producers, distributors, film and TV material, including music video programming).

POLYGRAM INTERNATIONAL
30 Berkeley Square, London, W1X 5HA. Tel: 01-493 8800; Telex: 263872.

POLYMUSE INTERNATIONAL TELEVISION
22 Cleveland Square, London, W2. Tel: 01-402 9066.

PORTMAN ENTERTAINMENT LTD.
Pinewood Studios, Pinewood Road, Iver Heath, Slough, Berks., SL0 0NH. Tel: 0753 630 366; FAX: 0753 630 332; Telex: 849516.

Directors: T. L. Donald *(Chrm.)*, Victor Glynn *(Int. Managing)*, Ian L. Donald *(Int. Managing)*, Ian R. Warren, John R. Sivers, A.C.A. *(Finance)*

PORTOBELLO PRODUCTIONS
42 Tavistock Road, London, W11 1AW. Tel: 01-221 2426; FAX: 01-221 5991.

Executive Prod./Dir.: Eric Abraham

POST OFFICE
Postal HQ, Film & Video Unit, 33 Grosvenor Place, London, SW1X 1PX.

PREMIER RELEASING LTD.
360 Oxford Street, London, W1N 9HA. Tel: 01-493 0440; FAX: 01-493 4286.

PRESTWICH HOLDINGS, PLC.
1 Euston Centre, London, NW1 3AJ. Tel: 01-388 5034; FAX: 01-388 5881.

RICHARD PRICE TELEVISION ASSOCIATES LTD
Seymour Mews House, Seymour Mews, London, W1H 9PE. Tel: 01-935 9000; FAX: 01-487 3975.

PRIMROSE FILM PRODUCTIONS LTD.
61 Regents Park Road, London, N.W.1. Tel: 01-722 7475 and 01-340 9627.

Directors: Louis Hagen, Anne Hagen
(Animation, live action, children's programmes.)

PRODUCTIONS ASSOCIATES (UK) LTD
The Stable Cottage, Pinewood Studios, Pinewood Road, Iver Heath, Bucks., SL0 0NH. Tel: 01-486 9921; FAX: 0753 656844.

PROSPECT STUDIOS LTD.
High Street, Barnes, London, SW13 9LE. Tel: 01-876 6284-5.

QUADRANT TELEVISION
Surrey House, Sutton, Surrey, 5M1 4QQ. Tel: 01-642 0924.

(Production and post-production facilities.)

QUIGLEY PUBLICATIONS
(Subsidiary of Quigley Publishing Co. Inc. of New York) 15 Samuel Road, Langdon Hills, Basildon, Essex SS16 6EZ. Tel: 0268 417055.

UK Manager: William Pay

RADIO LUXEMBOURG (LONDON) LTD.
38 Hertford Street, London, W1V 8BA. Tel: 01-493 5961.

Director of Sales and Marketing: Brian Mellor
(Representatives of European television production group Societé Internationale de Programmes Pour Telediffusion. British representatives of Radio Tele-Luxembourg.)

RANDOM FILM PRODUCTIONS LTD.
Unit 2, Cornwall Works, Cornwall Avenue, Finchley, London, N3 1LD. Tel: 01-349 9155.

Directors: F. G. Woosnam-Mills, M. R. Woosnam-Mills, M. P. Molloy
(Documentaries and educational.)

RANK ADVERTISING FILMS LTD.
127 Wardour Street, London, W.1. Tel: 01-439 9531; Telex: 262556; FAX: 01-439 2395.

Managing Director: Douglas Thomas
(Cinema and video contractors. Producers of industrial cinema and video films, TV cinema and video commercials.)

RANK FILM DISTRIBUTORS LTD.
127 Wardour Street, London, WIV 4AD. Tel: 01-437 9020. Telex: 262556.

Managing Director: F. P. Turner

RANK VIDEO SERVICES LTD.
Phoenix Park, Great West Road, Brentford, Middlesex, TW8 9PL; Tel: 01-568 4311. Telex: 22345; FAX: 01-847 4032.

Managing Director: Nicholas Watkins

RAVENSDALE FILM & TELEVISION LTD
34-35 Dean Street, London, W.1. Tel: 01-734 4686.

REALLY USEFUL GROUP PLC.
20 Greek Street, London, W1V 5LF. Tel: 01-734 2114; FAX: 01-734 6230; Telex: 8953151 USEFUL G.
Managing Director: John Whitney

REDIFFUSION FILMS LTD
P.O. Box 451, Buchanan House, 3 St. James's Square, London, SW1Y 4LS. Tel: 01-925 0550; Telex: 919673. Cables: Rediffuse; FAX: (Group 3) 01-839 7135.
Production Executive: Jelte Bonnevie

RKO PRODUCTIONS INTERNATIONAL
33 Dover Street, London, W1X 3RA; Tel: 01-629 4799.

THE ROBERT STIGWOOD GROUP LTD.
118/120 Wardour Street, London, W.1. Tel: 01-437 2512; Telex: 264267.

REX ROBERTS STUDIOS LTD.
22, Glasthule Road, Dun Laoghaire, Co. Dublin, Ireland. Tel: Dublin 808305.
(Adv. material.)

ROYAL SOCIETY FOR THE PROTECTION OF BIRDS (RSPB)
Film and Video Unit, The Lodge, Sandy, Beds., SG19 2DL. Tel: 0767 80551; Telex: 82469 RSPB; FAX: 0767 292365.
Head of Unit: Jeffery Boswall

SAGITTA PRODUCTIONS LTD.
%Pamela Gillis Management, 46 Sheldon Avenue, London, N6 4JR. Tel: 01-340 7868.
Managing Director: John Hawkesworth
(TV and film series.)

SAMUELSON GROUP PLC
Unit 27, 12 Taunton Road, Metropolitan Centre, Greenford, Middx., UB6 8UQ. Tel: 01-575 7300; FAX: 01-575 7088.
(Equipment supply)

SATELLITE TELEVISION PLC
31/36 Foley Street, London, W1P 7LB. Tel: 01-636 4077; Telex: 268395.

SEVEN SEAS FILMS LTD.
83 Duke Street, Grosvenor Square, London, W.1. Tel: 01-629 0788.
Directors: J. Rayfield, Brian Everett

SKY TELEVISION PLC.
Centaur Business Park, Grant Way, off Syon Lane, Isleworth, Middx., TW7 5QD. Tel: 01-782 3000; FAX: 01-782 3113.
Executive Chairman: Andrew Neil

SOUTHERN TELEVISION LTD
P.O. Box 15, 2-4 New Road, Southampton, SO9 7DF. Tel: 0703 28296/229666; Telex: 296149 LIMHSE G.
Managing Director: Frank Copplestone

SOVEREIGN PICTURES INC.
10 Greek Street, London, W1V 5LE. Tel: 01-494 1010; FAX: 01-494 3949.

SOVEXPORTFILM
60 Hillway, Highgate, London, N6 6DP. Tel: 01-340 86849.

SURVIVAL ANGLIA LTD.
Brook House, Park Lane, London, W.1. Tel: 01-408 2288.
Executive Director: M. A. Hay

SWIFT FILM PRODUCTIONS
1 Wool Road, Wimbledon, London, S.W.20. Tel: 01-946 2040.
Director: T. Peter Hadingham, M.B.K.S.
(Industrial, advertising and documentary & TV 16mm films, filmstrips, AV programmes.)

SWINDON CABLE LTD.
Newcome Drive, Hawksworth Estate, Swindon, SN2 1TU. Tel: 0793 615601.

TALBOT TELEVISION LTD.
Greendon House, 7C/D Bayham Street, London, NW1 0HE. Tel: 01-380 1189.
President: Paul Talbot
Chief Executive: Anthony Gruner
(TV film distributors.)

TELECINE
Video House, 48 Charlotte Street, London, W1P 1LX. Telex: 267283 TELCIN.

TELEVENTURES
5th Floor, 16 Hanover Square, London, W1R 0A. Tel: 01-491 3949.

TELEVISION INTERNATIONAL ENTERPRISES LIMITED
22 South Audley Street, London, W1Y 6ES. Tel: 01-499 9252.

TELEVISION REPORTERS INTERNATIONAL LTD.
Goldcrest Elstree Studios, Boreham Wood, Herts. Tel: 01-953 1600.
Directors: Robert S. Baker, Roger G. Moore, John Goodman

TELSO INTERNATIONAL
84-85 Buckingham Gate, London, SW1E 6PD. Tel: 01-976 7188; FAX: 01-976 7113.
Directors: Ann Siddell, Ann Harris

THAMES TELEVISION INTERNATIONAL LTD.
149 Tottenham Court Road, London, W1P 9LL. Tel: 01-387 9494.
Managing Director: M. Phillips

TITAN INTERNATIONAL PRODUCTIONS LTD
185A Newmarket Road, Norwich, Norfolk, NR4 6AP. Tel: 0603 51139.
Directors: P. Newbrook, E. Newbrook

TOWN AND COUNTRY PRODUCTIONS LTD
Parry's Lodge, Threapwood, Malpas, Cheshire, SY14 7AW. Tel: 0948 81 309.
Directors: J. C. A. Minoprio, C. P. Minoprio

TRANSATLANTIC FILMS
100 Blythe Road, London, W14 0HE.

TRANSWORLD INTERNATIONAL (UK) INC.
The Pier House, Strand on the Green, Chiswick, London, W4 3NN. Tel: 01-994 1444; FAX: 01-994 9606; Telex: 8955303 & 267486.

TRIANGLE FILM PRODUCTIONS LTD.
15 Oslo Court, Prince Albert Road, London, N.W.8 Tel: 01-722 5656; Cables: Triphilms London N.W.8; Telex: 885493 WINBNK.

TRIBUNE PRODUCTIONS LTD.
Goldcrest Elstree Studios, Boreham Wood, Herts. Tel: 01-953 1600.
Directors: Robert S. Baker, A. Baker, M. G. Baker, G. S. Barnett

TRICKFILM STUDIOS LTD.
13 Charlotte Mews, London, W.1. Tel: 01-580 0183.

TRILION VIDEO LTD.
36-44 Brewer Street, London, W.1. Tel: 01-439 4177.
Managing Director: Bill Hope

TRIUMPH FILMS INC.
10 Blomfield Villas, London, W.2. Tel: 01-286 1711.
Director: Peter Hanmer
(Producers of advertising film and shorts.)

TURNER INTERNATIONAL
25-58 Old Burlington Street, London, W1X 1LB. Tel: 01-434 4341.

TVI LTD.
142 Wardour Street, London, W1V 3AV. Tel: 01-434 2141; Telex: 268208; FAX: 439 3984.
Managing Director: Debbie Hills

TWICKENHAM FILM STUDIOS LTD.
St. Margarets, Twickenham, Middlesex, TW1 2AW. Tel: 01-892 4477.
Directors: G. Coen, G. Humphreys, M. Landserger, N. Daou
Secretary: A. Boys

TYBURN PRODUCTION LTD.
Pinewood Studios, Iver Heath, Bucks., SL0 0NH. Tel: 0753 651700; Telex: 847505; FAX: 0753 656844.
Directors: P. E. Rogers *(chairman)*, Kevin Francis, Gillian Garrow
Managing Director: Kevin Francis
Director of Research & Development: Gillian Garrow
Music Supervisor: Philip Markell
(Producers and distributors of TV and home video programming.)

UNICORN PICTURES LTD.
65 Corringway, London, W5 3HB. Tel: 01-998 2611.
Director: John Simmons
(Arts productions.)

UNITED INTERNATIONAL PICTURES
(A subsidiary of UNITED INTERNATIONAL PICTURES B.V., Postbus 9255, 1006 AG Amsterdam, The Netherlands) UIP House, 45 Beadon Road, Hammersmith, London, W6 0EG. Tel: 01-741-9041; Telex: 8956521; Telefax: 01-748-8990 (Distribution)

President & Chief Executive Officer: Michael Williams-Jones
Senior Vice Presidents: Ted McLean (Finance & Administration), Jean Prewitt (General Counsel), Hy Smith (Marketing)
Marketing/Sales Executives: Anne Bennett (VP publicity); Andrew Cripps (Sales Manager—South East Asia); Michael Macclesfield (VP sales—special markets); Michael Murphy (VP sales—Latin America); Howard Rochlin (VP sales); Tony Themistocleous (VP sales—Europe); Gina Wright (VP advertising)
Senior Executive/General Manager—Pay-TV Group: Joan Estes

UNITED VIDEO INTERNATIONAL
54 Warwick Square, London, SW1V 2AJ. Tel: 01-834 6012.

UNIVERSAL PICTURES LTD.
139 Picadilly, London, W1V 9FH. Tel: 01-629 7211.

VESTRON PICTURES (UK) LTD
69 New Oxford Street, London, W.1. Tel: 01-379 0221.

Managing Director: Michael Myers

VIRGIN VISION LTD.
328 Kensal Road, London, W10 5XJ. Tel: 01-968 8888; Telex: 892890 VIRGIN G. FAX; 01-968 8537.

Directors: Robert Devereux, Mike Watts, Stephan Navin, Julian Fortman, Peter Coles

VISUAL ENTERTAINMENTS LTD
51 South Audley Street, London, W1Y 6HB. Tel: 01-493 7428; FAX: 01-493 8552.

Directors: Benjamin Fisz, Maude Spector, Sue Carrington-Green

VIEWSPORT LTD
21 Cavendish Place, London, W1M 9DL. Tel: 01-580 5927.

Managing Director: Jarvis Astaire

VISNEWS LTD.
Cumberland Avenue, London, NW10 7EH. Tel: 01-965 7733; FAX: 01-965 0620.

Managing Director: Julian Kerr
General Manager: Barry MacDonald
NEWS DIVISION:
Head of News: Stephen Claypole
Manager, Facilities: Howard Barrow
(International production services supported by Worldwide Communications Network.)

VISUAL PROGRAMME SYSTEMS LTD.
77 Bedford Court Mansions, Bedford Avenue, London, WC1B 3AE.

VOICE OF LONDON LTD.
245 Old Marylebone Road, London, NW1 5RT. Tel: 01-402 8385.

Studio Manager: Miss Pat Smith
(Studio facilities.)

WARNER BROS. TELEVISION LTD.
Warner House, Pinewood Studios, Iver Heath, Bucks. Tel: Iver 654 545.

WATERLOO PRODUCTIONS
1 Lower James Street, London, W.1. Tel: 01-734 8311.

JOSEF WEINBERGER LTD.
12-14 Mortimer Street, London, W1N 8EL. Tel: 01-580 2827.

(Representing Telemusic Library, France.)

WEINTRAUB SCREEN ENTERTAINMENT
167-169 Wardour Street, London, W1V 3TA. Tel: 01-439 1790; FAX: 01-734 1509; Telex: 269919.

Executive Vice President, World Wide Distribution: Richard Milnes

RICHARD WILLIAMS ANIMATION LTD.
London Studio: 138 Royal College Street, London, NW1 0TA. Tel: 01-437 4455.

Director: Richard Williams

WORLD AUDIO VISUAL ENTERTAINMENT PLC
18 Great Marlborough Street, London, W1V 1AF. Tel: 01-439 9596; Telex: 264036 WAVE G.

WORLDMARK PRODUCTIONS LTD.
The Old Studio, 18 Middle Row, London, W10 5AT. Tel: 01-960 3251; Telex: 94018006 WLDM G; FAX: 01-960 6150.

Director: Drummond Challis

WORLD WIDE INTERNATIONAL TELEVISION
21-25 St. Anne's Court, London, W1V 3AW. Tel: 01-434 1121; Telex: 269 271; FAX: 01-734 0619.

Directors: Lord Willis, R. King, R. Townsend, Brian Redhead, C. Courtenay-Taylor, R. Marshall

WORLDWIDE TELEVISION NEWS
WTN House, 31-36 Foley Street, London, W1P 7LB. Tel: 01-323 3255; FAX: 01-580 1437; Telex: 23915; 1995 Broadway, New York, NY 10023, U.S.A. Tel: (212) 262-4440; Telex: 237853.

Equipment/facilities/services: Producers of sponsored programmes and video news release worldwide for television and industrial corporate sector. Film and video crews strategically located throughout the world to operate as first or second units to individual producers/directors. Worldwide communications network via regional bureaux in London, New York, Washington DC, Paris, Frankfurt, Rome, Johannesburg, Tel Aviv, Hong Kong, Tokyo and Sydney. Post productions facilities centres in London, New York and Frankfurt, with various format editing, standards conversion, satellite transmission/reception.
Marketing Services Manager: Lorrie Grabham Morgan

WYATT CATTANEO PRODUCTIONS LTD.
Charing Cross Rd., London, W.C.2. Tel: 01-379 6444.

SONNY ZAHL ASSOCIATES LTD.
57 Great Cumberland Place, London, W1H 7LJ. Tel: 01-724 3684 and 723 5699.

ZENITH PRODUCTIONS LTD
15 St. George Street, London, W1R 9DE. Tel: 01-499 8006; FAX: 01-895 9572; Telex: 23348 ZENITH.

Chief Executive: Charles Denton

ZOOM PRODUCTION COMPANY
102 Dean Street, London, W1V 5RA. Tel: 01-434 3895. Fax: 01-734 2751.

Services for TV Producers/Distributors

CAMERAS—ACCESSORIES FILM STOCK—TELE-CINE—VIDEO AND EDITING EQUIPMENT

ACMADE INTERNATIONAL
Oakside (Division of Oakside International Holdings Ltd.), Oxford Road, Uxbridge, Middlesex. Tel: Uxbridge 36313; Telex: 8954606.

ADVANCED VIDEO HIRE LTD.
51 The Cut, London, SE1 8LF. Tel: 01-928 1963.

AGFA (Motion Picture Division)
27 Great West Road, Brentford, Middlesex, TW8 9AX. Tel: 01-560 2131; FAX: 01-847 5803; Telex: 28154.

AMPEX GREAT BRITAIN LTD.
Acre Road, Reading, Berks. Tel: 0734 875200.

AMSTRAD plc
Brentwood House, 169 Kings Road, Brentwood, Essex, CM14 4EF. Tel: 0277 228888.

AUTOCUE LTD.
265 Merton Road, London, SW18 5JS. Tel: 01-870 0104; Telex: Autocue Telexir 885039 Autocu G.

F. W. O. BAUCH LTD.
49 Theobald Street, Boreham Wood, Herts., WD6 4RZ. Tel: 01-953 0091; Telex: 27502; FAX: 01-207 5970.

R. R. BEARD LTD.
f10 Trafalgar Avenue, London, SE15 6NR. Tel: 01-703 3136 and 9638.

BELL & HOWELL LTD.
Alperton House, Bridgewater Road, Wembley, Middlesex, HA0 1EG. Tel: 01-902 8812.

STUART BELL & PARTNERS LTD.
40 Frith Street, London, W1V 5TF. Tel: 01-439 2700.

BETTER SOUND LTD.
35 Endell Street, London, WC2. Tel: 01-836 0033.

CFS EQUIPMENT HIRE LTD.
10 Wadsworth Road, Perivale, Greenford, Middx., UB6 7JX. Tel: 01-998 2731; Telex: 24672.

CINESOUND INTERNATIONAL LTD.
Imperial Studios, Maxwell Road, Boreham Wood, Herts., LWD6 1WE. Tel: 01-953 5387.

CINETECHNIC LTD.
169 Oldfield Lane, Greenford, Middlesex. Tel: 01-578 1011; and 35 Briardale Gardens, London, NW3 7PN. Tel: 01-435 2289.

CINEVIDEO LTD.
7 Silver Road, White City Industrial Park, Wood Lane, London, W12 7SG. Tel: 01-743 3839; FAX: 01-749 3501; Telex: 915 282 CINEGP G.

DOLBY LABORATORIES INC.
346 Clapham Road, London, SW9 9AP. Tel: 01-720 1111; Telex: 919109; FAX: 01-720 4118.

JOE DUNTON CAMERAS LTD.
Wycombe Road, Wembley, Middlesex, HA0 1QN. Tel: 01-903 7933; Telex: 291843.

EDRIC AUDIO VISUAL LTD.
34-36 Oak End Way, Gerrard's Cross, Bucks. Tel: (02813) 84646/7/8.

ENGLISH ELECTRIC VALVE COMPANY LTD.
Waterhouse Lane, Chelmsford, Essex. Tel: 0245-493493; Telegrams: Enelectico, Chelmsford; Telex: 99103.

FRANSCOPE
Grove House, 551 London Road, Isleworth, Middx., TW7 4DS. Tel: 01-568 0131; Telex: 935054.

FUJI PHOTO FILM (UK) LTD.
Fuji Film House, 125 Finchley Road, London, NW3 6JH. Tel: 01-586 5900; Telex: 8812995.

HARKNESS SCREENS LTD.
Gate Studios, Station Road, Boreham Wood, Herts., WD6 1DQ. Tel: 01-953 3611; Cables: Screens, London; Telex: 8955602 PERLUX G; FAX: 01-207 3657.

HAYDEN LABORATORIES LTD.
Hayden House, Chiltem Hill, Chalfont St. Peter, Gerrards Cross, Bucks., SL9 9EW. Tel: 02-813 88447/89221.

HITACHI DENSHI (UK) LTD.
13-14 Garrick Ind. Centre, Irving Way, Hendon, London, NW9 6AZ. Tel. 01-202 4311.

INTERNATIONAL VIDEO CORPORATION
10 Portman Road, Reading, Berks., RG3 1JR. Tel: 0734 585421. Telex: 847579.

ITN LTD.
ITN House, 48 Wells Street, London, W1P 4DE. Tel: 01-637 2424; Telex: 22101; FAX: 01-636 0349.

KEM ELECTRONIC LTD
24 Vivian Avenue, Hendon Central, London, NW4 3XP. Tel: 01-202 0244; Telex: 28303.

K. G. M. VIDIAIDS LTD.
Clock Tower Road, Isleworth, Middx. Tel: 01-568 0151.

KODAK LTD. Motion Picture AV and Television Division
P.O. Box 66, Kodak House, Station Road, Hemel Hempstead, Herts., HP1 1JU. Tel: Hemel Hempstead (0442) 62331.

LEE COLORTRAN LTD.
Ladbroke Hall, Barlby Road, London, W10 5HH. Tel: 01-968 7000.

LEE ELECTRIC (LIGHTING) LTD.
Ladbroke Hall, 85 Barlby Road, London, W10 5HH. Tel: 01-960 2400; Telex: 924743. LEE LEC G; FAX: 01-960 2400.

LEE FILTERS LTD.
Central Way, Walworth Industrial Estate, Andover, Hants., SP10 5AN. Tel: 0264 66245; Telex: 477259.

LIMEHOUSE TELEVISION LTD.
The Trocadero, 19 Rupert Street, London, W1V 7FS. Tel: 01-287 3333; FAX: 01-287 1998.

Contact: A. Goddard

OB's Unit 11, The Gate Centre, Great West Road, Brentford, Middx., TW8 9DD. Tel: 01 569 8979; FAX: 01-568 0188.

Contact: K. Duckett.

LIPSNER-SMITH CO. LTD.
Unit 7, Longbridge Way, Cowley Mill Trading Estate, Uxbridge, UB8 2YG. Tel: Uxbridge 52191.

MARCONI COMMUNICATION SYSTEMS LTD.
Marconi House, Chelmsford, Essex, CM1 1PL. Tel: (0245) 353221.

ERNEST F. MOY LTD.
Unit 5, Brunswick Park Ind. Est., New Southgate, London, N11 1JF. Tel: 01-361 1211; Telegraphic Address: Movedor, London, N11.

NEILSON-HORDELL LTD.
Unit 11, Central Trading Estate, Staines, Middlesex, TW18 4UU. Tel: 0784 56456 and 54105.

PANASONIC BROADCAST EUROPE
Slough, Berks. Tel: 0753 692442.

PHOENIX VIDEO
Unit 4, Maple Cross Industrial Estate, Maple Cross, Nr. Rickmansworth. Herts., WD3 2AS. Tel: 0923 777782; FAX: 0923 772163.

PHOTOGRAPHIC ELECTRICAL CO. LTD.
71, Dean Street, London, W1V 6DE. Tel: 01-437 4633/4. Cables: Photoelect London; Telex: 25554.

PYE TELECOMMUNICATIONS LTD.
9 Priestley Way, Eldonwall Estate, Edgware Road, London, NW2 7AF. Tel: 01-452 6411. Head Office: St. Andrews Road, Cambridge. Tel: 0223 61222.

RADAMEC EPO LTD.
Bridge Road, Chertsey, Surrey, KT16 8LJ. Tel: 0932 561181; FAX: 0932 568775; Telex: 929945 RADEPOG.

RANK CINTEL
Watton Road, Ware, Herts. Tel: Ware 3939; Telex: 81415.
Managing Director: Chris Waldron.

RANK TAYLOR HOBSON LTD.
P.O. Box 36, 2 New Star Road, Leicester, LE4 7JQ. Tel: 0533 763-771; Telex: 342338; Cables: Metrology Lestr; FAX: 0533 740167.
Managing Director: Chris Waldron.

RECORDING & PRODUCTION SERVICES LTD.
10 Giltway, Giltbrook, Nottingham, NG16 2GN. Tel: 0602 384103.

PHILIP RIGBY & SONS LTD.
14 Creighton Avenue, Muswell Hill, London, N10 1NU. Tel: 01-883 3703.

RONFORD-BAKER
Braziers, Oxhey Lane, Watford, Herts., WD1 4RJ. Tel: 01-428 5941; FAX: 01-428 4743.

RONFORD LTD.
Lee International Film Studios, Studio Road, Shepperton, Middlesex, TW17 0QD. Tel: 0932-561423.

SAMUELSON GROUP PLC
Unit 27, 12 Taunton Road, Metropolitan Centre, Greenford, Middx., UB6 8UQ. Tel: 01-575 7300; FAX: 01-575 7088.

SET PARTNERS
13 D'Arblay Street, London, W1V 3FP. Tel: 01-734 1067; FAX: 01-494 0197.

SHURE ELECTRONICS LTD.
Eccleston Road, Maidstone, Kent, ME15 6AU. Tel: 0622 59881.

STRAND LIGHTING
P.O. Box 51, Great West Road, Brentford, Middlesex, TW8 9HR. Tel: 01-560 3171.

TECHNOVISION CAMERAS LTD.
Unit 4, St. Margaret's Business Centre, Drummond Place, Twickenham, Middlesex, TW1 1JN. Tel: 01-891 5961; Telex: 917408 TECNOV G; FAX: 01 744 1154.

3M UNITED KINGDOM PLC
3M House, P.O. Box 1, Bracknell, Berks., RG12 1JU. Tel: 0344 58571.

VARIAN TUT LTD.
P.O. Box 41, Coldhams Lane, Cambridge, CB1 3JU. Tel: 0223 245115; Telex: 81342. VARTUT G.; FAX: 0223 214632.

VIDEO TIME
22/24 Greek Street, London, W1V 5LG. Tel: 01-439 1211; Telex: 27256.

VIEWPLAN
1 Syon Gateway, Great West Road, Brentford, Middx., TW8 9DD. Tel: 01-847 5771.

W. VINTEN LTD.
Western Way, Bury St. Edmunds, Suffolk, IP33 3TB. Tel: 0284 75 2121; Telex: 81176 VINTEN G; FAX: 0284 706514.

WESTAR SALES & SERVICES LTD.
Unit 7, Cowley Mill Trading Estate, Longbridge Way, Uxbridge, Middx., UB8 2YG. Tel: 0895 34429; Telex: 8954169.

ZONAL LTD.
Holmethorpe Avenue, Redhill, Surrey, RH1 2NX. Tel: 0737 767171. FAX: 0737 767610.

MUSIC LIBRARIES-FACILITIES

ABBEY ROAD STUDIOS
3 Abbey Road, London NW8. Tel: 01-286 1161.

ACME FILM PRODUCTIONS LTD.
174 Wardour Street, London, W1V 3AB. Tel: 01-437 1572/1889.

BOOSEY & HAWKES MUSIC PUBLISHERS LIMITED
295 Regent Street, London, W1R 8JH. Tel: 01-580 2060; Telex: 8954613 Boosey G.

BOURNE MUSIC LTD.
34/36 Maddox Street, London, W1R 9PD. Tel: 01-493 6412 and 6583.

C.T.S. STUDIOS LTD.
Engineers Way, Wembley, Middlesex, HA9 0DR. Tel: 01-903 4611; Telex: 923400; FAX: 01-903 7130.

DE WOLFE LTD.
80-88 Wardour Street, London, W1V 3LF. Tel: 01-439 8481.

EMI MUSIC LTD.
30 Gloucester Place, London, W1A 1ES.

FILM BOOKING OFFICES, LTD.
(Film Library Ltd.)
174 Wardour Street, London, W1V 3AB. Tel: 01-437 1572.

ITN LTD.
ITN House, 48 Wells Street, London, W1P 4DE. Tel: 01-637 2424; Telex: 22101; FAX: 01-636 0349.

MOZART EDITION (GREAT BRITAIN) LTD.
5th Floor, Crown House, North Circular Road, London, NW10 7PN.

MUSIC SALES LTD.
8-9 Frith Street, London, W1V 5TZ. Tel: 01-434 0066.

PEER INTERNATIONAL LIBRARY LTD.
8 Denmark Street, London, WC2H 8LT. Tel: 01-836 4524.

POLYGRAM MUSIC VIDEO
1 Rockley Road, London, W14 DDL. Tel: 01-743 3474; Telex: 298816.

PORTLAND RECORDING STUDIOS LTD.
35 Portland Place, London, W1N 3AG. Tel: 01-637 2111/4.

SOUTHERN LIBRARY OF RECORDED MUSIC LTD.
8 Denmark Street, London, WC2H 8LT. Tel: 01-836 4524.

STUDIO FILM & VIDEO LABORATORIES LTD.
8-14 Meard Street, London, W1V 6DE. Tel: 01-437-0831.

VISNEWS LIMITED
Cumberland Avenue, London, NW10 7EH. Tel: 01-965 7733; Telex: 22678; Cables Visnews, London; FAX: 01-965 0620.

JOSEF WEINBERGER LTD.
12-14 Mortimer Street, London, W1N 8EL. Tel: 01-580 2827.
(Representing Telemusic Library, France.)

ZOMBA SCREEN MUSIC
11 Greek Street, London, W1V 5LE. Tel: 01-437 4266; Telex: 919884; FAX: 01-451 3900.

FILM LABORATORIES & VIDEO SERVICES

BUCKS MOTION PICTURE LABORATORIES LTD.
714 Banbury Avenue, Slough, Berks., SL1 4LH. Tel: 0753 76611; FAX: 0753 691762.
Contacts: Harry Rushton, Mike Bianchi

COLOUR FILM SERVICES LTD.
22-25 Portman Close, Baker Street, London, W1A 4BE. Tel: 01-486 2881; Telex: 24672; and 10 Wadsworth Road, Perivale, Greenford, Middx., UB6 7JX. Tel: 01-998 2731; Telex: 24672; FAX: 01-486 4152.

FILMATIC LABORATORIES LTD.
16 Colville Road, London, W11 2BS. Tel: 01-221 6081; Telex: 295046 FILMAT-G; FAX: 01-229 2718.
Chairman & Managing Director: D. L. Gibbs
Assistant Managing Director: I. Magowan

HALLIFORD STUDIOS
Manygate Lane, Shepperton, Middlesex. Tel: 0932 226341; FAX: 0932 246336.
Studio Manager: Allan d'Aguiar

KINGLY STUDIOS LTD.
17 Kingley Court, Kingley Street, London, W.1. Tel: Gerrard 6372.

METROCOLOR LONDON LTD.
22 Soho Square, London, W1V 5FL. Tel: 01-437-7811; Telex: 28463. 91/95 Gillespie Road, Highbury, London, N.5. Tel: 01-226 4422; Telex: 28463; FAX: 01-359 2353.
Managing Director: B. E. Compton

PORTLAND RECORDING STUDIOS LTD.
35 Portland Place, London, W1N 3AG. Tel: 01-637 2111/4.

RANK FILM LABORATORIES LTD.
Denham, Uxbridge, Middlesex, UB9 5HQ. Tel: Denham (0895) 832323; Telex: 934704; FAX: 0895 833617.

Managing Director: J. W. Downer
Sales Director: M. A. Levy

STUDIO FILM & VIDEO LABORATORIES LTD.
8-14 Meard Street, London, W1V 6DE. Tel: 01-437 0831.

TECHNICOLOR LTD.
P.O. Box 7, Bath Road, West Drayton, Middx., UB7 0DB. Tel: 01-759 5432; FAX: 01-897 2666.

TWICKENHAM FILM STUDIOS, LTD.
St. Margarets, Twickenham, Middlesex, TW1 2AW. Tel: 01-892 4477; Telex: 8814497 TWIKST G.

UNITED MOTION PICTURES (LONDON) LTD.
3 and 36/38 Fitzroy Square, London, W.1. Tel: 01-580 1171 and 01-388 1234.

WORLD WIDE SOUND
21-25, St. Anne's Court, London, W1V 3AW. Tel: 01-434 1121; Telex: 269271; FAX: 01-734 0619.

RECORDING STUDIOS

ADVISION SOUND STUDIOS
23 Gosfield Street, London, W1P 7HB. Tel: 01-580 5707; Telex: 28668; FAX: 01 631 1457.

AIR STUDIOS
214 Oxford Street, London, W.1. Tel: 01-637 2758.

EAMONN ANDREWS STUDIOS LTD.
The Television Club, 46/48, Harcourt Street, Dublin, Ireland. Tel: Dublin 758891.

ANVIL FILM & RECORDING GROUP LTD.
Denham Studios, North Orbital Road, Denham, Nr. Uxbridge, Middx., UB9 5HH. Tel: 0895 833522; Telex: 934704; FAX: 0895 833617.

AUDIO INTERNATIONAL RECORDING STUDIOS LTD.
18 Rodmarton Street, London, W1H 3FW. Tel: 01-486 6466.

CBS RECORDING STUDIOS
CBS Records, 31-37 Whitfield Street, London, W1P 5RE. Tel: 01-636 3434.

CINE-LINGUAL SOUND STUDIOS LTD
27-27 Berwick Street, London, W1V 3RF. Tel: 01-437 0136.

CINESOUND EFFECTS LIBRARY LTD.
Imperial Studios, Maxwell Road, Elstree Way, Boreham Wood, Herts., WD6 IWE. Tel: Elstree 5837 and 5545, 4904, 1587.

C.T.S. STUDIOS LTD.
Engineer's Way, Wembley, Middlesex, HA9 0DR. Tel: 01-903 4611; Telex: 923400; FAX: 01-903 7130.

DELTA SOUND SERVICES LTD.
Shepperton Studio Centre, Squires Bridge Road, Shepperton, Middx., TW17 0QD. Tel: Chertsey 62045/46.

ECO LTD.
The Exchange, Mount Stuart Square, Cardiff CF1 6EA, Wales. Tel: 0222-493321; FAX: 0222 471865; Telex: 94011989 (ECOL G).

GOLDCREST ELSTREE STUDIOS LTD.
Boreham Wood, Herts. Tel: 01-953 1600; Telegrams: Emifilms, Boreham Wood; Telex: 922436 EFILMS G; FAX: 01-207 0860.

MOTIVATION SOUND LTD,
(Voice-over Recording Studios)
35a Broadhurst Gardens, London, NW6 3QT. Tel: 01-624 7785.

NATIONAL SCREEN
15 Wadsworth Road, Greenford, Middlesex. Tel: 01-998-2851. 2. Wedgwood Mews, 12-13 Greek Street, London, W1V 5LE. Tel: 01-437 4851-6; Telex: 934522.

NEW CENTRAL FILM SERVICES LTD.
97-99 Dean Street, London W.1. Tel: 01-734 5827-8.

PORTLAND RECORDING STUDIOS LTD.
35 Portland Place, London, W1N 3AG. Tel: 01-637 2111.

RANK FILM LABORATORIES LTD.
Denham, Uxbridge, Middlesex, UB9 5HQ. Tel: Denham (0895) 832323; Telex: 934704; FAX: 0895 833617

Managing Director: J. W. Downer
Sales Director: M. A. Levy

SHEPPERTON STUDIO CENTRE
Studios Road, Shepperton, Middx., TW17 0QD. FAX: 0932 568989; Tel: 09325 62611; Telex: 929416 MOVIES G.

Contact: Paul Olliver

STUDIO FILM & VIDEO LABORATORIES LTD.
8-14 Meard Street, London, W1V 6DE. Tel: 01-437 0831.

UNITED MOTION PICTURES (LONDON) LTD.
Boston House, 36/38 Fitzroy Square, London, W.1. Tel: 01-580 1171.

W.F.S. (FILM FACILITIES) LTD.
153 Wardour Street, London, W1V 3TB. Tel: 01-437 5532.

WORLD WIDE SOUND
21-25 St. Anne's Court, London, W1V 3AW. Tel: 01-434 1121; FAX: 01-734 0619.

PRODUCTION SERVICES

AIRtv FACILITIES LTD.
Hawley Crescent, London, NW1 8NP. Tel: 01-485 4121.

AKA FILM SERVICES LTD.
60 Farringdon Road, London EC1R 3BP. Tel: 01-251 3885

GEOFF AXTEL ASSOCIATES LTD.
16a, Newman Street, London, W1P 3HD. Tel: 01-637 9321; FAX: 01-637 2850.

BARRY WESTWOOD PRODUCTIONS
231 West Street, Fareham, Hants., PO16 0HZ. Tel: 0329-285941.

CAMERA EFFECTS
8-11 Bateman Street, London W.1. Tel: 01-437 9377.

CENTRAL TELEVISION FACILITIES
Central House Broad Street, Birmingham, B1 2JP. Tel: 021 633 4227.

CHERRILL, ROGER LTD.
65-66 Dean Street, London, W1V 6PL. Tel: 01-437 7972. FAX: 01-437 6411.

CINEBUILD LTD.
1 Wheatsheaf Hall, Wheatsheaf Lane, London S.W.8. Tel: 01-582 8750. Telex: 943763 Crocom G Cinebuild.

CINEVIDEO LTD.
7 Silver Road, White City Industrial Park, Wood Lane, London, W12 7SG. Tel: 01-743 3839. Telex: 915 282 CINEGP G; FAX: 01-749 3501.

CLAPP, NIKKI
18 Cresswell Road, East Twickenham, Middx., TW1 2DZ. Tel: 01-891 0054.

Languages: Greek, Italian & French

COLOUR FILM SERVICES LTD.
22-25 Portman Close, Baker Street, London, W1A 4BE. Tel: 01-486 2881; Telex: 24672; FAX: 01-486 4152.

COMBINED PRINTS & PRODUCTION SERVICE LTD.
65-66 Dean Street, London, W1V 5HD. Tel: 01-437 7972; FAX: 01-437 6411.

COMPLETE VIDEO
3 Slingsby Place, London, WC2E 9AB. Tel: 01-379 7739.

CROW FILM & TV SERVICES LTD.
12 Wendell Road, London, W12 9RT. Tel: 01-749 6071; Telex: 931458 CROWTVG.

EDINBURGH FILM & TV STUDIOS
Nine Mile Burn, by Penicuik, Midlothian, EH 26 9LT, Scotland. Tel: Penicuik (0968) 72131.

EDIT ART POST PRODUCTION
86 Wardour Street, London, W1V 3LF. Tel: 01-734 8966.

EDIT 142
5th Floor, 142 Wardour Street, London W.1. Tel: 01-439 7934.

FILM PRODUCTION SERVICES
"Shortend," 82 Holywell Road, Studham, Nr. Dunstable, Beds. Tel: 0582 873107.

CHARLES H. FOX LTD.
22 Tavistock Street, Covent Garden, London WC2E 7PY. Tel. 01-240 3111.

GAZELLE FILM PRODUCTIONS LTD.
IPA House, Orange Street, Bristol, BS2 9HG. Tel: 421214/5.

GENERAL SCREEN ENTERPRIZES LTD.
97 Oxford Road, Uxbridge, Middlesex. Tel: 0895-31931. FAX: 0895 35335.

INFOVISION LTD.
Bradley Close, White Lion Street, London, N1 9PN. Tel: 01-837 0012; Telex: 299800 ACTION.

ISLAND FILMS/EDITING
22 St. Peter's Square, London, W6 9NW. Tel: 01-741 1511.

KAUFMAN, MIKE (POST PRODUCTIONS) LTD.
80-82 Wardour Street, London, W1V 3LF. Tel: 01-734 8335. Telex: 264864 Answerback MKPPLN G.

LIMEHOUSE TELEVISION LTD.
The Trocadero, 19 Rupert Street, London, W1V 7FS. Tel: 01-287 3333; FAX: 01-287 1998.

Contact: A. Goddard

LOUIS ELMAN + LEAH INTERNATIONAL PRODUCTIONS LTD.
Denham Studios, Denham, Nr. Uxbridge, Middlesex. Tel: 0895 833036 & 853522; Telex: 934704.

MAGPIE FILM PRODUCTIONS LTD.
22 Bodenham Road, Northfield, Birmingham, B31 5DP, West Midlands. Tel: 021-475 6666 & 021-471 1396.

MERCURY PRODUCTION OFFICES
Tel: 01-734 5000 (single offices or suites in Wardour Street, London).

METRO VIDEO
The Old Bacon Factory, 57-59 Great Suffolk Street, London, SE1 0BS. Tel: 01-929 2088.

MILLS, PETER FILM EDITING LTD.
75 Dean Street, London, W1V 5HA. Tel: 01-437 3003 & 01-439 1721.

MOLINARE
34 Fouberts Place, London, W1V 2BH. Tel: 01-439 2244; FAX: 01-734 6813; Telex: 299200 MOLI G.

NORWOOD STUDIOS LTD.
147 Victoria Road, Leeds, LS6 1DU. Tel: 0532-787539.

(For rushes—35mm and 16mm optical and mags.)

N S & H CREATIVE PARTNERSHIP
13 John Street, London, W.C.1. Tel: 01-405 2324.

ONE INCH VIDEO COMPANY
11/13 Neal's Yard, Covent Garden, London, WC2H 9LZ. Tel: 01-831 1900; FAX: 01-836 0914; Telex: 22125 VIDEO G.

PEERLESS CAMERA CO.
15 Neals Yard, London, WC2H 9DP. Tel: 01-836 3367.

PLATYPUS FILMS LTD.
9 Grape Street, London, WC2H 8DR. Tel: 01-240 0351.

PMPP FACILITIES
(Formerly Paul Miller Post Production)
69 Dean Street (Entrance Meard Street), London, W1V 5HB. Tel: 01-437 0979.

POST HOUSE (POST PRODUCTIONS) LTD.
12 D'Arblay Street, London, W1V 3FP. Tel: 01-439 1705/6/7.

PRATER AUDIO VISUAL LTD.
7A College Approach, Greenwich, London, SE10 9HY. Tel: 01-858 8939; FAX: 01-305 1537.

RANK VIDEO SERVICES LTD.
Phoenix Park, Great West Road, Brentford, Middlesex, TW8 9PL. Tel: 01-568 4311; Telex: 22345; FAX: 01-847 4032.

Managing Director: Nicholas Watkins

SAMUELSON GROUP PLC
Unit 27, 12 Taunton Road, Metropolitan Centre, Greenford, Middx., UB6 8UQ. Tel: 01-575 7300; FAX: 01-575 7088.

SET PARTNERS
13 D'Arblay Street, London, W1V 3FP. Tel: 01-734 1067; FAX: 01-494 0197.

SOLUS ENTERPRISES
35 Marshall Street, London, W1V 1LL. Tel: 01-734 0645 and 01-734 3384/5.

TABS
63 Stirling Court, Marshall Street, London W.1. Tel: 01-734 3356/7.

EC: Janet Easton
(Specialities: Technicians answering and booking service.)

TATTOOIST INTERNATIONAL LTD.
9 Lyme Steet, London N.W.1. Tel: 01-267 0242/3.

TELEVISUAL LTD.
58 Kew Road, Richmond, Surrey, TW9 2PQ. Tel: 01-940 1155.

THAMES TELEVISION PLC
306 Euston Road, London, NW1 3BB. Tel: 01-387 9494.

Contact: Peter Kew

VIDEO EUROPE
31 Ransome's Dock, Parkgate Road, Battersea, London, SW11 4NP. Tel: 01-585 0555.

VIDEO ROOM
155-157 Oxford Street, London, W1R 1TB. Tel: 01-434 0724.

VISNEWS LIMITED
Cumberland Avenue, London, NW10 7EH. Tel: 01-965 7733; Telex: 22678 Cables Visnews, London; FAX: 01-965 0620.

(International production services supported by World-wide Communications Network).

WSTV PRODUCTION LTD.
159-163 Great Portland Street, London, W1N 5FD. Tel: 01-580 5896.

(Video tape and TV production, TV cmml.)

WETFORD FILMS LTD.
Wetford Lodge, 163 Nightingale Lane, London S.W.12. Tel: 01-675 1333.

WOLFF PRODUCTIONS
6a Noel Street, London, W1V 3RB. Tel: 01-439 1838.

WOOD, PATRICK FILM SERVICES
13 South Road, Amersham, Bucks. Tel: 0494 724941.

WORLD WIDE INTERNATIONAL TELEVISION
21-25 St. Anne's Court, London, W1V 3AV. Tel: 01-434 1121; Telex: 269271; FAX: 01-734 0619.

TITLING—SPECIAL EFFECTS

CINE-SOUND EFFECTS LTD.
(Soundefex Ltd., Lansdowne Vaults Ltd.) Imperial Studios, Maxwell Road Boreham Wood, Herts. Tel: 01-953 5837 and 1587, 4904, 5545.

ELECTROCRAFT CONSULTANTS LTD.
Sales Office and Works: Liss Mill, Mill Road, Liss, Hants. Tel: Liss 89 3444.

FILMTEXT LTD.
37 Kew Road, Richmond Surrey, TW9 2NQ. Tel: 01-940 5034.

GENERAL SCREEN ENTERPRISES LTD.
97 Oxford Road, Uxbridge, Middx. Tel: 0895 31931; FAX: 0895 35335.

METROCOLOR LONDON LTD.
91/95 Gillespie Road, Highbury, London, N.5. Tel: 01-226 4422; Telex: 28463. Also, 22 Soho Square, London, W.1. Tel: 01-437 7811; Telex: 28463.

NATIONAL SCREEN
15 Wadsworth Road, Greenford, Middlesex, UB6 7JN. Tel: 01-998 2851. 2 Wedgwood Mews, Greek Street, London, W1V 5LE. Tel: 01-437 4851-6; Telex: 934522.

RANK FILM LABORATORIES LTD.
Denham Uxbridge, Middlesex, UB9 5HQ. Tel: Denham (0895) 832323; Telex: 832323; FAX: 0895 833617.

Managing Director: J. W. Downer
Sales Director: M. A. Levy

STUDIO FILM & VIDEO LABORATORIES LTD.
8-14 Meard Street London, W1V 6DE. Tel: 01-437 0831.

TECHNICOLOR LTD.
(Subsidiary of Technicolor Inc.) P.O. Box No. 7 Bath Road, West Drayton, Middlesex, UB7 0DB5. Tel: 01-759 5432; Telegraphic and Cable Address: Technicolor, West Drayton; Telex: 22344.

UNIVERSAL FILM LABORATORY LTD.
Braintree Road, Ruislip, Middlesex. Tel: 01-841 5101.

STUDIOS

BRAY STUDIOS
Windsor Road, Windsor, Berks. Tel: 0628 22111; FAX: 0628 770381.

(4 stages, total 23,600 sq. ft. All depts. theatre, workshops, bar and catering.)

BUSHEY
(Cygnet Ltd.)
Melbourne Road, Bushey, Herts. Tel: 01-950 1621.

Studio Manager: Philip Lee
2 Stages (66′×33′×15′ high with cycloroma backing; 30′×22′×12′ high with video gallery).

CARLTON TELEVISION LTD.
St. John's Wood Studios, St. John's Wood Terrace, London, NW8 6PY. Tel: 01-722 9255; FAX: 01-483 4264.

Managing Director: Barry Johnstone

CINEVIDEO LTD.
245 Old Marylebone Road, London, NW1 5QT. Tel: 01-402 8385.

CREATIVE FILM MAKERS LTD.
Pottery Lane House, Pottery Lane, Holland Park, London, W11 4LZ. Tel: 01-229 5131.

C.T.S. STUDIOS LTD.
Engineers Way, Wembley, Middlesex, HA9 ODR. Tel: 01-903 4611; Telex: 923400; FAX: 01-903 7130.

Contact: Adrian Kerridge

CTVC
Hillside Studios, Merry Hill Road, Bushey, Watford WD2 1DR. Tel: 01-950 4426.

GATEWAY AUDIO VISUAL/VIDEO
470-472 Green Lanes, London, NI3 5XF. Tel: 01-882 0177.

GOLDCREST ELSTREE STUDIOS LTD.
Boreham Wood, Herts. Tel: 01-953 1600; Telex: 922436 EFILMSG; FAX: 01-207 0860.

Managing Director: Andrew Mitchell
7 sound stages: (four 15,000 square feet, two 8,000 square feet, one 5,200 square feet.) 3 silent stages: (one 30,000 sq. ft., one 15,750 sq. ft., one 8,000 sq. ft.)
Theatres: Three viewing, one dubbing, one ADR and looping theatre. RCA sound. Complete Dolby installation in transfers, looping, re-recording and viewing for producing Dolby encoded optical sound tracks.

HALLIFORD FILM STUDIOS LTD.
Manygate Lane, Shepperton, Middlesex, TW17 9EG. Tel: 0932 226341; FAX: 0932 246336.

Studio Manager: Allan d'Aguiar
Two stages (60×60×40) totalling 6,000 sq. ft.

ITN LTD.
ITN House, 48 Wells Street, London, WIP 4DE. Tel: 01-637 2424; Telex: 22101; FAX: 01-636 0349.

Studio VTR and conversion facilities.
Contact: Mike Jessey

LEE INTERNATIONAL STUDIOS SHEPPERTON
Studios Road, Shepperton, Middlesex, TW17 0QD. Tel: 09325 62611; FAX: 0932 568989; Telex: 929416 MOVIES G.

Contact: Paul Olliver
12 sound stages
3 silent stages

LIMEHOUSE STUDIOS
The Trocadero, 19 Rupert Street, London, W1V 7FS. Tel: 01-287 3333; FAX: 01-287 1998.

Contact: A. Goddard

MORENO FILM STUDIOS
35 Broadhurst Gardens, London, N.W.6. Tel: Maida Vale 0645.

Directors: George Moreno (Managing), Fred Thompson

MTM ARDMORE STUDIOS LTD.
Herbert Road, Bray, Co. Wicklow, Ireland. Tel: Dublin 862971; Telex: 91504 PATT E1; FAX: Dublin 861894.

PINEWOOD STUDIOS
Iver Heath, Bucks., SL0 0NH. Tel: 0753 651700; Cables: Pinewood, Iver Heath, Telex: 847505 Pinew G, FAX: 0753 656844.

Managing Director: Cyril Howard
A. 165 ft.×110 ft.×35 ft. (with tank 40 ft.×30 ft.×8 ft.)
B. 110 ft.×81 ft.×34 ft.
C. 110 ft.×81 ft.×34 ft.
D. 165 ft.×110 ft.×35 ft. (with tank 40 ft.×30 ft.×8 ft.)
E. 165 ft.×110 ft.×35 ft. (with tank 40 ft.×30 ft.×8 ft.)
F. 100 ft.×75 ft.×35 ft. (with tank 20 ft.× 20 ft.×8 ft.)
G. 55 ft.×49 ft.×23 ft.
H. 90 ft.×37 ft.×28 ft.
J. 110 ft.×80 ft.×29 ft. 3 ins. (dual-purpose, film & TV).
K. 110 ft.×80 ft.×29 ft. 3 ins. (dual-purpose, film & TV).
L. 105 ft.×90 ft.×30 ft. (dual-purpose, film & TV).
M. 105 ft.×90 ft.×30 ft. (dual-purpose, film & TV). South Dock Stage (silent) 174′ × 96′ × 28′. North Dock Stage (silent) 125′ × 54′ × 27′. Special effects stage (silent)—89 ft. × 80 ft. × 20 ft. Small Process Stage—75 ft. × 32ft. 6 ins. × 17 ft. Large Process Stage—175 ft. × 28 ft. × 28 ft. 007 Stage—334′ × 136′ × 40′6″. (World's largest silent stage). 5 theatres for viewing, dubbing, and post-sync, effects. Any ratio, 16mm, 35mm, 70mm, viewing available, with sync separate sound. Up to 115 seats. Dubbing in multitrack, stereo, Dolby up to 6 tracks. 50 cutting rooms. Special effects: Matte stage. Vis 35mm. back projection. Fully equipped process projection dept. including front projection and 70m rear and foreground projection. Triple head process system. Models of all kinds including VistaVision Rear Projection and VistaVision Front Projection. Travelling Matte System comprising 70 ft. × 40 ft. Stewart Blue Screen and associated lighting ring. Stills: Stills studio. Dressing rooms. Production and Unit Offices: Many available. Exterior Lot: 72 acres with formal gardens, lake, woods, and concrete service roads. Multi-Purpose Catering Dept. Paddock tank 230 ft. wide narrowing to 110 ft. Backing 240 ft. 2 60 ft. Another tank 75 ft. × 225 ft. Both tanks contain approximately 800,000 gallons. Props available.

PROSPECT STUDIOS LTD.
High Street, Barnes, London, S.W.13. Tel: 876 6284/5.

TVi LTD
142 Wardour Street, London, W1V 3AV. Tel: 01-434 2141; Telex: 268208; FAX: 439 3984.

Managing Director: Debbie Hills
Videopost production facilities. VTR copying and standard conversion. Telecine, Studios.

TWICKENHAM
St. Margaret's, Twickenham, Middlesex, TW1 2AW. Tel: 01-892 4477; Telex: 8814497 TWIKST G.

Owned by Twickenham Film Studios, Ltd.
Stage One: 7,192 square feet. Stage Two: 2,000 square feet, Stage Three: 5,700 square feet.
RCA Sound. Re-Recording and dubbing theatres with 36 input 6 track stereo Rock & Roll (High speed 6 times).
Directors: G. Coen, G. Humphreys, M. Landsberger, N. Daou

W.F.S. (FILM FACILITIES) LTD.
153 Wardour Street, London, W1V 3TB. Tel: 01-437 5532.

WORLD WIDE SOUND
21-25 St. Anne's Court, London, W1V 3AW. Tel: 01-434 1121; FAX: 01-734 0619.

Director of Sound: R. King

NEWS FILM SERVICE

BRITISH MOVIETONEWS LTD.
North Orbital Road, Denham, Nr. Uxbridge, Middx. Tel: 0895 833071; FAX: 0895 834893.

Film Library: Barbara Heavens

CBS NEWS
100 Brompton Road, London S.W.3. Tel: 01-584 3366.

CCL NEWS & FEATURES
87 Charlotte Street, London, W1P 1LB. Tel: 01-631 5424; Telex: 266685 CCLLDN.

CHANNEL NINE AUSTRALIA INC.
(Television New Zealand News)
31-36 Foley Street, London, W1P 7LB. Tel: 01-636 0036; FAX: 01-636 9041.

INDEPENDENT TELEVISION NEWS LTD.
ITN House, 48 Wells Street, London, W1P 4DE. Tel: 01-637 2424; Telex: 22101; FAX: 01-636 0349.

NBC NEWS WORLDWIDE INC.
8 Bedford Avenue, London W.C.1. Tel: 01-637 8655.

VISNEWS LIMITED
Cumberland Avenue, London, NW10 7EH. Tel: 01-965 7733; Telex: 22678; Cables: Visnews London; FAX: 01-965 0620.

Managing Director: Julian Kerr
Head of News: Stephen Claypole

WORLDWIDE TELEVISION NEWS
WTN House, 31-36 Foley Street, London, W1P 7LB. Tel: 01-323 3255; Telex: 23915; FAX: 01-580 1437.
Marketing Services Manager: Lorrie Grabham Morgan

COSTUME SUPPLIERS

ANGELS
Morris Angel & Son Ltd.
119 Shaftesbury Avenue, London, WC2H 8AE. Tel: 01-836 5678; Telex: 24919 Angels G; FAX: 01-240 9527.
Managing Director: Tim Angel

BERMAN AND NATHANS LTD.
Head Office: 18 Irving Street, Leicester Square, London, WC2H 7AX. Tel: 01-839 1651.
Main Store: 40 Camden Street, London, NW1 0EN. Tel: 01-387 0999; Telex: Berman G 8952359; FAX: 01-383 5603.
Chief Executive: Noel J. Howard

TWENTIETH CENTURY COSTUMES
9 Dallington Street, London, EC1V 0BQ. Tel: 01-608 1966; FAX: 01-490 0155; Telex: 94013393 TWEN G.

LEADING ADVERTISING AGENCIES

ABBOTT, MEAD VICKERS/SMS LTD.
32 Aybrook Street, London, W1M 3JL. Tel: 01 486 0122.

ALLEN, BRADY AND MARSH LTD.
Lynton House, 7-12 Tavistock Square, London, WC1H 9SX. Tel: 01 388 1100.

TED BATES COMMUNICATIONS
Parkwood House, 33-34 Soho Square, London, W1A 1BD. Tel: 01 434 3111.

BBDO LTD.
6-10 Cambridge Terrace, Regents Park, London, NW1 4JA. Tel: 01 486 1277.

BOASE MASSIMI POLLITT PARTNERSHIP PLC
12 Bishops Bridge Road, London, W2 6AA. Tel: 01 258 3979.

LEO BURNETT LTD.
48 St. Martins Lane, London, WC2N 4EJ. Tel: 01 836 2424.

COLLETT DICKENSON PEARCE AND PARTNERS LTD.
110 Euston Road, London, NW1 2DQ. Tel: 01 388 2424.

D'ARCY MASIUS BENTON AND BOWLES
2 St James' Square, London, SW1Y 4SN. Tel: 01 839 3422.

DAVIDSON PEARCE LTD.
67 Brompton Road, London, SW3 1EF. Tel: 01 589 4595.

DFS DORLAND LTD.
121-141 Westbourne Terrace, London, W2 6JR. Tel: 262 5077.

FOOTE, CONE AND BELDING ADVERTISING LTD.
82 Baker Street, London, W1M 2AE. Tel: 01 935 4426.

GEERS GROSS ADVERTISING LTD.
110 St. Martins Lane, London, WC2N 4DY. Tel: 01 240 7100.

GOLD GREENLEES TROTT ADVERTISING LTD.
82 Dean Street, London, W1V 5AB. Tel: 01 437 0434.

GREY ADVERTISING LTD.
215-217 Great Portland Street, London, W1N 5HD. Tel: 01 636 3399.

KHBB-DOWNTON
82 Charing Cross Road, London, WC2H 0BA. Tel: 01 379 7350.

LOWE HOWARD-SPINK MARSCHALK
Bowater House, Knightsbridge, London, SW1. Tel: 01 584 5033.

McCANN-ERICKSON ADVERTISING LTD.
36 Howland Street, London, W1A 1AT. Tel: 01 580 6690.

McCORMICK-PUBLICIS LTD.
24 Nutford Place, London, W1H 5YN. Tel: 01 723 3484.

OGILVY AND MATHER LTD.
Brettenham House, Lancaster Place, London, WC2E 7EZ. Tel: 01 836 2466.

REEVES ROBERTSHAW NEEDHAM LTD.
5 Princes Gate, London SW7, 1QJ. Tel: 01 589 1445.

SAATCHI AND SAATCHI COMPTON LTD.
80 Charlotte St., London, W1A 1AQ. Tel: 01 636 5060.

SSC & B: LINTAS WORLDWIDE—LONDON
Lintas House, New Fetter Lane, London, EC4P 4EU. Tel: 01 822 8888.

J. WALTER THOMPSON LTD.
40 Berkeley Square, London, W1X 6AD. Tel: 01 629 9496.

WIGHT COLLINS RUTHERFORD SCOTT AND PARTNERS LTD. (WCRS)
41-44 Great Queen Street, London, WC2B 5AR. Tel: 01 242 2800.

YOUNG AND RUBICAM LTD.
Greater London House, Hampstead Road, London, NW1 7QP. Tel: 01 387 9366.

FINANCIAL SERVICES

BARCLAYS BANK PLC
The Media Section, Barclays Business Centre, 27 Soho Square, London, W1A 4WA. Tel: 01-439 6851; FAX: 01-434 9035.

BAYLY MARTIN & FAY INTERNATIONAL LTD.
Braintree House, Braintree Road, Ruislip, Middx., HA4 0YA. Tel: 01 841 4461; Telex: 935792 HOWINS G; FAX: 01 842 2124.

BRITISH & COMMONWEALTH MERCHANT BANK PLC
66 Cannon Street, London, EC4N 6AE. Tel: 01-248 0900; FAX: 01-248 0906; Telex: 884040 BCMB G.

BRITISH SCREEN LTD.
37-39 Oxford Street, London, W1R 1RE. Tel: 01-434 0291; Telex: 888694 BRISCR G; FAX: 01 434 9933.

COMPLETION BOND COMPANY INC.
Pinewood Studios, Iver Heath, Bucks., SL0 0NH. Tel: 0753 652433; Telex: 849003 CPLBND G; FAX: 0753 655697.

CONTRACTS INTERNATIONAL LTD.
13-14 Golden Square, London, W1R 3AG. Tel: 01-287 5800; FAX: 01-287 3779; Telex: 295835.

DISTANT HORIZON
4th Floor, 17 Great Cumberland Place, London, W1H 7LA. Tel: 01-724 3440; FAX: 010935 4402; Telex: 917354 PROTAC G.

FILM FINANCES LTD.
1/11 Hay Hill, Berkeley Square, London, W1X 7LF. Tel: 01-629 6557; Telex: 298060 FILFIN G; FAX: 01-491 7530.

FILM TRUSTEES LTD.
Swan House, 52 Poland Street, London, W1V 3DF. Tel: 01-439 8541; FAX: 01-495 3223; Telex: 23788.

GENERAL ENTERTAINMENT INVESTMENTS
65-67 Ledbury Road, London, W11 2AD. Tel: 01-221 3512; Telex: 28604; FAX: 0932 868989.

GUINNESS MAHON & CO. LTD.
32 St. Mary at Hill, London, EC3P 3AJ. Tel: 01-623 9333; FAX: 01-283 4811.

PARMEAD INSURANCE BROKERS LTD.
Lyon House, 160-166 Borough High Street, London, SE1 1JR. Tel: 01-467 8656; FAX: 01-295 1659.

PEAT MARWICK McLINTOCK
1 Puddle Dock, Blackfriars, London, EC4V 3PD. Tel: 01-236 8000.

PIERSON, BELDRING & PIERSON
City Tower, Level 15, 40 Basinghall Street, London, EC2V 5DE. Tel: 01-628 5091; Telex: 885119-8812941.

RUBEN SEDGWICK INSURANCE SERVICES
Pinewood Studios, Pinewood Road, Iver, Bucks., SL0 0NH. Tel: 011 44 753 654 555; Telex: 851 848708 SEDFOR G; FAX: 011-44-753 653 152

SARGENT-DISC LTD.
Pinewood Studios, Pinewood Road, Iver, Bucks. Tel: 0753 656631/655388; FAX: 0753 655881.

SPECTRUM ENTERTAINMENT GROUP PLC
The Pines, 11 Putney Hill, London, SW15 6BA. Tel: 01-780 2525; FAX: 01-780 1671; Telex: 261507.

TOUCHE ROSS
Hill House, 1 Little New Street, London, EC4A 3TR. Tel: 01-353 8011.

WASA FILM FINANCE CORPORATION LTD.
49 Park Lane, London, W1Y 4EQ. Tel: 01-491 2822; Telex: 264833 SAFIN G; FAX: 01-495 0338.

WILLIS WRIGHTSON LONDON LTD.
Willis Wrightson House, Wood Street, Surrey KT1 1UG. Tel: 01-860 6000; Telex: 929606; FAX: 01-943 4297.

PROFESSIONAL & TRADE ASSOCIATIONS

THE ADVERTISING ASSOCIATION
Abford House, 15 Wilton Road, London SW1V 1NJ. Tel: 01-828 2771; FAX: 01-931 0376.

The Advertising Association is the federated organisation representing the shared advertising interests of advertisers, agencies and the media. It is the central spokesman for the UK advertising business, at national and international levels, and as such maintains a continuing programme of research and information retrieval. It is responsible for the collection and dissemination of the UK statistics on advertising expenditure, and runs an annual programme of seminars and courses for people in the communications business.
Director General: Roger Underhill

THE ADVERTISING STANDARDS AUTHORITY
Brook House, 2-16 Torrington Place, London, WC1E 7HN. Tel: 01-580 5555 (9 lines); FAX: 01-631 3051 (Groups 2 & 3).

ASSOCIATION OF CINEMATOGRAPH, TELEVISION AND ALLIED TECHNICIANS
(Affiliated to Trades Union Congress and Labour Party). 111 Wardour Street, London W1V 4AY. Tel: 01-437 8506; FAX: 01-437 8268.

General Secretary: Alan Sapper
(The Association is the recognized Trade Union for film, television and radio technicians and negotiates salaries and working conditions. It also controls the A.C.T.T. Employment Bureau as an agency exclusively for film and TV technicians.)

ASSOCIATIONS OF INDEPENDENT PRODUCERS
17 Great Pulteney Street, London W1R 3DG. Tel: 01-434 0181; FAX: 01-437 0086.

Director: Jane Williams

ASSOCIATION OF PROFESSIONAL RECORDING STUDIOS LTD.
163A High Street, Rickmansworth, Herts., WD3 7AY. Tel: 0923 772907; FAX: 0923 773079.

Chief Executive: Philip Vaughan

ASSOCIATION OF PROFESSIONAL VIDEO DEALERS LTD.
P.O. Box 25, Godalming, Surrey, GU7 1PL. Tel: 04868 23429.
Director and Secretary: Charles Potter, M.B.E.

BRITISH ACADEMY OF FILM AND TELEVISION ARTS
195 Piccadilly, London, W1V 9LG. Tel: 01-734 0022.

President: H. R. H. The Princess Royal
Vice President: Sir Richard Attenborough, C.B.E.
Chairman: Johnny Goodman
Hon. Treasurer: Richard Price
Director: Tony Byrne.
The British Academy of Film and Television Arts exists in order to promote, improve and advance original and creative work amongst people engaged in film and television production.

BRITISH ACTORS' EQUITY ASSOCIATION
Incorporating the Variety Artistes Fed.) 8 Harley Street, London, W1N 2AB. Tel: 01-637 9311 and 636 6367; FAX: 01-580 0970.

President: Nigel Davenport
General Secretary: Peter Plouviez

BRITISH COUNCIL
Special Events Section, Film, Television and Video Department, 11 Portland Place, London, W1N 4EJ. Tel: 01-930 8466; Telex: 8952201 BRICON G; FAX: 01-839 6347.

Festivals Officers: Carole McFadden, Gill Henderson

BRITISH FILM DESIGNERS GUILD
26-28, Binney Street, London, W.1. Tel: 01-499 4336

Executive Consultant: John French

BRITISH FILM INSTITUTE
21-28 Stephen Street, London, W1P 1PL. Tel: 01-255 1444; Telex: 27624 BFILDNG; FAX: 01-436 7950.

Founded 1933. Principal object to encourage the development of the art of the film, to promote its use as a record of contemporary life and manners and to foster public appreciation and study of it from these points of view. The Institute has a similar role in relation to television. The Board of Governors is appointed by the Minister of the Arts, two are selected by a poll of the membership. The National Film Archive and the National Film Theatre are departments of the Institute which publishes Sight and Sound, a quarterly film magazine and the Monthly Film Bulletin, and provides services for education, film availability regions and production.
Chairman: Sir Richard Attenborough, C.B.E.
Director: Wilf Stevenson

BRITISH FILM & TELEVISION PRODUCERS ASSOCIATION LTD.
162-170 Wardour Street, London, W1V 4LA. Tel: 01-437 7700; FAX: 01-734 4564.

Chief Executive: Otto Plaschkes
Secretary: Andrew Patrick

BRITISH KINEMATOGRAPH SOUND AND TELEVISION SOCIETY
547-549 Victoria House, Vernon Place, London, WC1B 4AD. Tel: 01-242 8400; FAX: 01-405 3560.

Secretary: Ray Mobsby
Founded in 1931, the Society was incorporated in 1946 to service the industries of its title, encouraging technical and scientific progress. To further these aims, the Society disseminates to its Members information on technical developments within these industries, arranges technical lectures, international conferences, and demonstrations, and encourages the exchange of ideas. The broad nature of its purpose is made possible by the subscriptions of its Members and by its freedom from political or commercial bias. The *BKSTS Journal: Image Technology*, is published monthly and is sent free to all members.

BRITISH MUSIC INFORMATION CENTRE
10 Stratford Place, London, W1N 9AE. Tel: 01-499 8567.

(Reference library of works by 20th Century British composers.)

THE BRITISH RADIO AND ELECTRONIC EQUIPMENT MANUFACTURERS' ASSOCIATION
Landseer House, 19 Charing Cross Road, London, WC2H 0ES. Tel: 01-930 3206; Telex: 296215 BREMA G.

Director: O. P. Sutton, C.B.E.
Secretary: R. B. S. Purdy, O.B.E.

BRITISH SOCIETY OF CINEMATOGRAPHERS LTD.
Tree Tops, 11 Croft Road, Chalfont St. Peter, Gerrards Cross, Bucks., SL9 9AE. Tel: 0753 888052.

President: Tony Spratling, BSC.
Secretary and Treasurer: Frances Russell
(To promote and encourage the pursuit of the highest standards in the craft of motion picture photography.)

BRITISH VIDEOGRAM ASSOCIATION LTD
21-22 Poland Street, London, W1V 3DD. Tel: 01-437 5722; Telex: 295101; FAX: 01-437 0477.

Director General: Norman Abbott

BROADCASTING AND ENTERTAINMENT TRADES ALLIANCE
181-185 Wardour Street, London, W1V 3AA. Tel: 01-439 7585.

General Secretary: D. A. Hearn

CABLE AUTHORITY
Gillingham House, 38-44 Gillingham Street, London, SW1V 1HU. Tel: 01-821 6161; FAX: 01-821 5835.

CABLE TELEVISION ASSOCIATION
50 Frith Street, London, W1V 5TE. Tel: 01-437 0549/0983.
Director: Nicolas Melleash

CENTRAL CASTING LTD.
162-170 Wardour Street, London, W1V 3AT. Tel: 01-437 1881.

Directors: O. Beuselinck, J. Goodman, B. J. Kingham, I. Lewis, O. Plaschkes, J. A. Walton, B. T. Yeoman
Managing Director: B. T. Yeoman
(Licensed annually by the Dept. of Employment.)

CHILDREN'S FILM & TELEVISION FOUNDATION LTD.
Goldcrest Elstree Studios, Boreham Wood, Herts., WD6 1JG. Tel: 01-953 1600; FAX: 01-207 0860.

Administrator: S. T. Taylor, F.C.I.S.

CINEMA AND TELEVISION BENEVOLENT FUND
Royalty House, 72 Dean Street, London, W1V 6LT. Tel: 01-437 6567; FAX: 01-437 7186.

Executive Director: P. J. C. Ratcliffe, O.B.E.
Secretary: H. V. Hughes, F.C.A.
(The Fund gives relief by financial grants and allowances to needy members or ex-members of the film industry or independent TV,

and their widows; maintenance and education of orphans and generally to assist those in distress due to sickness, injury, unemployment or old age. Convalescence is available to assist in recovery after illness or operations at "Glebelands," Wokingham, Berks. Admission to Convalescent Home free upon application to the Secretary.)

COMPOSERS' GUILD OF GREAT BRITAIN
34 Hanway Street, London, W1P 9DE.

General Secretary: Miss Elizabeth Yeoman
(Objects: To further artistic and professional interests of its members.)

CONFEDERATION OF ENTERTAINMENT UNIONS
60-62 Clapham Road, London, SW9 0JJ.

President: Alan Sapper
Vice-President: P. Plouviez
Treasurer: P. Leech
Secretary: J. Morton
(Confederation of trades unions engaged in the entertainment industry.)

DIRECTORS GUILD OF GREAT BRITAIN
125 Tottenham Court Road, London, W1P 9HN. Tel: 01-387 7131; FAX: 01-387 1179.

Administrator: Suzan Dormer

ELECTRICAL ELECTRONIC TELECOMMUNICATION AND PLUMBING UNION
Hayes Court, West Common Road, Bromley, BR2 7AU. Tel: 01-462 7755; FAX: 01-462 4959.

(Representing electrical electronic lighting operatives engaged in production.)
General Secretary: Eric Hammond

ELECTRONIC ENGINEERING ASSOCIATION
Leicester House, 8 Leicester Street, London WC2H 7BN. Tel: 01-437 0678; Telex: 263536.

THE ENTERTAINMENT AGENTS' ASSOCIATION LTD.
04 Keyes House, Dolphin Square, London, SW1V 3NA. Tel: 01-834 0515.

President: Bunny Lewis
Secretary: Gordon Blackie
(Founded in 1927 as the Agents' Assoc. and name changed to present one in February, 1966. The Association comprises the principal agencies in all branches of the entertainment industry.)

FEDERATION AGAINST COPYRIGHT THEFT (FACT)
7 Victory Business Centre, Worton Road, Isleworth, Middlesex, TW7 6ER. Tel: 01-568 6646; Telex: 295007.

Director of Operations: R. Dixon

FILM ARTISTES' ASSOCIATION
F.A.A. House, 61 Marloes Road, London W.8. Tel: 01-937 4567.

General Secretary: Michael Reynel

GENERAL MUNICIPAL BOILERMAKERS & ALLIED TRADES UNION
Thorne House, Ruxley Ridge, Claygate, Esher, Surrey. Tel: 0372 62081; Telex: 27428.

General Secretary: John Edmonds

GUILD OF BRITISH CAMERA TECHNICIANS
5-11 Taunton Road, Metropolitan Centre, Greenford, Middx., UB6 8UQ. Tel: 01-578 9243.

Chairman. Lou Lavelly.

GUILD OF FILM PRODUCTION ACCOUNTANTS AND FINANCIAL ADMINISTRATORS (GFPA)
Twickenham Film Studios, St. Margaret's, Twickenham, Middx., TW1 2AW. Tel: 01-892 4477; Telex: 884497 TWIKST G; FAX: 01-891 0168.

President: Ron Swinburne
Hon. Secretary: Maurice Landsberger

GUILD OF FILM PRODUCTION EXECUTIVES
Pinewood Studios, Iver Heath, Bucks. Tel: 0753 651700.

President: Ian Lewis
(The Guild is an association of many of the more experienced production executives in the UK film industry.)

THE INCORPORATED SOCIETY OF BRITISH ADVERTISERS LTD.
44 Hertford Street, London W1Y 8AE. Tel: 01-499 7502.

(Objects: The protection and advancement of the advertising interests of all member companies.)
Director: K. N. Miles

INDEPENDENT PROGRAMME PRODUCERS' ASSOCIATION
50-51 Berwick Street, London, W1V 4RD. Tel: 01-439 7034; FAX: 01 494 2700.

INDEPENDENT TELEVISION ASSOCIATION (ITVA)
Knighton House, 56 Mortimer Street, London, W1N 8AN. Tel: 01-636 6866; Telex: 262988; FAX: 01-580 7892.

(The Association exists to represent and promote the interests of the programme companies appointed by the Independent Broadcasting Authority. The members are Anglia Television Ltd., Border Television p.l.c., Central Independent Television, p.l.c., Channel Television, Grampian Television p.l.c., Granada Television Ltd., HTV Ltd., London Weekend Television Ltd., Scottish Television p.l.c., TVS Television, TSW-Television South West Ltd., Thames Television Ltd., Tyne Tees Television Ltd., Ulster Television p.l.c., Yorkshire Television Ltd., TV-a.m. Ltd.)
Director: David Shaw

INSTITUTE OF PRACTITIONERS IN ADVERTISING
44 Belgrave Square, London, SW1X 8QS. Tel: 01-235 7020; FAX: 01-245 9904.

INTERNATIONAL ASSOCIATION OF BROADCASTING MANUFACTURERS
Triumph House, 1096 Uxbridge Road, Hayes, Middx., UB4 8QH. Tel: 01-573 8333; FAX: 01-848 8805.

Chairman: Tom McGann
Secretary: Claude Guillaume
Treasurer: Dan Anco
Administrator: Alan Hirst
Secretariat: Tony Owers
(*Objects:* The IABM was formed in 1976 with the purpose of fostering and co-ordinating the wide common interests of manufacturers of sound and television equipment and associated products worldwide.)

INTERNATIONAL VISUAL COMMUNICATIONS ASSOCIATION (IVCA)
Tel: 01-580 0962; FAX: 01-436 2606.

(*Objects:* IVCA is the professional association representing the interests and needs of the visual communications user or supplier. In particular, the association represents those organisations involved in the non-broadcast commissioned film, video and av market. The Association strives to advance the standing and recognition of the industry and its practitioners, and markets visual communications as a powerful tool for users.)
Executive Director: Stuart Appleton

MECHANICAL COPYRIGHT PROTECTION SOCIETY LTD.
Elgar House, 41 Streatham High Road, London, SW16 1ER. Tel: 01-769 4400; Cables and Telegrams: Mecolico, London S.W.16; Telex: 946792 MCPSG.

(*Objects:* The Society has the authority of some 33,000 music copyright owners in the U.K. and Commonwealth, the U.S.A., Germany, Italy and other countries to licence the use of their works for all forms of mechanical reproduction, including sound synchronisation in cinematograph, television and advertising films and records.)
Managing Director: R. W. Montgomery
Company Secretary and Financial Controller: K. R. D. Lowde
Commercial Operations Controller: G. J. Churchill

MOTION PICTURE EXPORT ASSOCIATION OF AMERICA INC.
162-170 Wardour Street, London, W1V 3AT. Tel: 01-437 2282; Telex: 262792 MPAAUK G; FAX: 01-439 1885.

Senior Vice-President: S. Frederick Gronich
Deputy Directors: Harlan G. Moen, Georg Eriksson

MUSICIANS' UNION
60-62, Clapham Road, London, SW9 0JJ. Cables: Amuse., London, S.W.9; Tel: 01-582 5566; Telex: 8814691; FAX: 01-582 9805.

General Secretary: John Morton

THE PERFORMING RIGHT SOCIETY LTD.
29-33 Berners Street, London, W1P 4AA. Tel: 01-580 5544; Telex: 892678 PRSLONG; FAX: 6314138.

Chief Executive: M. J. Freeguard, F.C.I.S.
Public Relations Manager: Miss Lesley Brat, B.A.
(Representing the composers and publishers of music.)

THE PERSONAL MANAGERS' ASSOCIATION LTD.
Angela Adler, Rivercroft, One Summer Road, East Molesey, Surrey, KT8 9LX.

(An association of the principal personal managers who represent stars, feature players, authors, writers, producers, directors and technicians.)
Secretary: Angela Adler

PHONOGRAPHIC PERFORMANCE LTD.
Ganton House, 14/22 Ganton Street, London, W1V 1LB. Tel: 01-437 0311.

(A company founded by the British recording industry to own and exercise the public performance and broadcasting rights in sound recordings in the U.K. and to issue licences for public performances and broadcasting.)

Chairman: J. A. Brooks
Managing Director: J. V. Love

THE RADIO, ELECTRICAL AND TELEVISION RETAILERS' ASSOCIATION (RETRA) LTD.
RETRA House, St. Johns' Terrace, 1 Ampthill Street, Bedford, MK42 9EY. Tel: 0234 269110; FAX: 0234 269609.

Chief Executive: J. Scott

THE RADIO INDUSTRY COUNCIL
Landseer House, 19 Charing Cross Road, London, WC2H 0ES. Tel: 01-930 3206; Telex: 296215 BREMAG.

Director: O. P. Sutton, C.B.E.
Secretary: R. B. S. Purdy, O.B.E.

RADIO SOCIETY OF GREAT BRITAIN
Lambda House, Cranborne Road, Potters Bar, Herts., EN6 3JE. Tel: 0707 59015.

Chief Executive/Secretary: David A. Evans

ROYAL TELEVISION SOCIETY
Tavistock House East, Tavistock Square, London, WC1H 9HR. Tel: 01-387 1970; FAX: 01-387 0358.

SCIENTIFIC FILM ASSOCIATION
℅British Universities Film and Video Council, 55 Greek Street, London, W1V 5LR. Tel: 01-734 3687.

Secretary: Murray Weston

SERVICES SOUND & VISION CORPORATION
Chalfont Grove, Narcot Lane, Gerrards Cross, Bucks., SL9 8TN. Tel: 02407 4461; Telex: 837254.

Managing Director: Alan H. Protheroe, M.B.B.
Director of Operations: John Bussell

Booking Manager: Renate Foster
Buying Manager: Anne Eva

SCREEN ADVERTISING WORLD ASSOCIATION LTD.
103A Oxford Street, London, W1R 1TF. Tel: 01-734 7621.

SOCIETY OF AUTHORS
84 Drayton Gardens, London, SW10 9SB. Tel: 01-373 6642.

(An independent trade union representing authors.)

SOCIETY OF AUTHORS BROADCASTING GROUP
84 Drayton Gardens, London, SW10 9SB. Tel: 01-363 6642.

(Representing film, TV and radio writers.)
(A subsidiary group within the Society of Authors.)

SOUND AND COMMUNICATIONS INDUSTRIES FEDERATION
4-B, High Street, Burnham, Slough, SL1 7JH. Tel: 0628 667633.

Chief Executive: Ken Walker, M.B.E.

VARIETY CLUB OF GT. BRITAIN (TENT NO. 36)
32 Welbeck, Street, London, W1M 7PG. Tel: 01-935 4466.

THE WRITERS GUILD OF GREAT BRITAIN
430 Edgware Road, London, W2 1EH. Tel: 01-723 8074.

(The Writers Guild of Great Britain is the Trades Union Council-affiliated union which is the recognised representative body for negotiating agreements for writers in film, television, and radio as well as in the field of theatre and of publishing. As well as negotiating industrial agreements, the Guild represents writers wherever their interests need to be represented.)

President: Bryan Forbes
Hon. Treasurer: Patrick Campbell
Gen. Sec.: Walter J. Jeffrey

Trade Publications

Broadcast

Published weekly by International Thomson Business Publishing, 100 Avenue Road, London, NW3 3TP. Tel: 01-935 6611.

EDITOR IN CHIEF AND PUBLISHER
Martin Jackson

Eyepiece

Journal of the Guild of British Camera Technicians, 5-11 Taunton Road, Metropolitan Centre, Greenford, Middx., UB6 8UQ. Tel: 01-578 9243.

EDITOR
Kevin Desmond
ADVTG. MANAGER
Ron Bowyer

Image Technology

(Technical monthly) Journal of the British Kinematograph, Sound and Television Society. 549 Victoria House, Vernon Place, London, WC1B 4DJ. Tel.: 01 242-8400.

EDITOR
John Gainsborough

Screen International

Published by King Publications Ltd. a subsidiary of Thomson Business Publications. Weekly, covering news, reviews, comment and pictures of the film and television industries. 6-7 Great Chapel Street, London, W1V 4BR. Tel.: 01-437 5741. FAX: 01-434 1898.

PUBLISHER
John Campbell
EDITOR-IN-CHIEF
Peter Noble

Televisual

Published monthly by the Centaur Group, St. Giles House, 50 Poland Street, London, W1V 4AX. Tel: 01 439 4222.

PUBLISHER
Philip Reevell
EDITOR
Mundy Ellis

The Television World Market

* MARKET ANALYSES
* STATIONS
* OUTLOOK
* PROGRAM SOURCES

The World Market

AFGHANISTAN

People's Radio & Television Afghanistan, Post Office Box 544, Kabul; 8 stations, 19,000 sets.

ALBANIA

Radiodiffusion TV Shqiptar, Tirana, government-owned experimental station, broadcasts sixteen hours weekly to some 210,000 sets, many of them located in public places so that segments of the populace not owning sets can view the programs.

ANGOLA

Television Popular de Angola, C.P. 2604, Luanda; 30,000 sets.

ARGENTINA

Population: 32 million.
Number of TV sets: Approximately 7.2 million.
System used: PAL-N since 1980.
Number of TV stations: Five stations in Buenos Aires, and 36 in the provinces with about 200 repeating stations or translators. There are 2 major cable outlets.
History of the industry and trends: Television had its debut in this country in 1951 with only one channel (7) in Buenos Aires. Since then, it has been joined by Channels 9, 11, and 13 (in 1960–61) all of which are state owned and operated; Channel 9 (under state control since 1974) was licensed back to Alejandro Romay in 1984. A fifth major station entered the market in 1988 when Channel 2 from near-by La Plata was privatized and re-equipped to reach the entire Buenos Aires area.

In 1988, Argentina suffered through 390% annual inflation, a $59 billion foreign debt, an investment drop of 14.5%, and a currency devaluation of 260%. This economic crisis had devastating effects on the television industry. During the summer, at the end of 1988 and the beginning of 1989, a shortage of hydroelectric power and constant power failures led the government to restrict broadcasting to 4 hours per day (the same restrictions applied to movie theaters); through spring 1989, airtime was still limited to five and then eight hours. Even within these time periods, almost a quarter of the potential audience was unable to view TV due to power cuts. Previously, the channels averaged 15 hours on air (with Channel 13 going around the clock) during which up to 180 minutes of commercials were broadcast; by the beginning of January 1989, that figure stood at 48 minutes. Millions of dollars more were lost when advertisers became reluctant to invest in new campaigns with such limited airtime. Discount rates were offered, but the networks were still forced to fill spot time with promos for their own shows and free political ads. State-run networks with big overheads were especially hard-hit, because the government debt meant that the treasury department was no longer able to cover their losses.

Distributors of foreign shows were pinched, because payments from the state stations or heavily-indebted Channel 2 were low or non-existent. A decline in the exchange rate exacerbated this situation. By mid-1989, many observers predicted an increase in local production of programs as a response to the lack of dollars. (Regardless of finances, local shows were the main hits of the 1988 season; "Miami Vice" and "Alf" were the only successful American products.)

With restricted broadcasts, news and public affairs programs were the most popular offerings. Dramas and sports programs were effectively edged out. (The TV drought brought unexpected business to the home-video industry whose business increased 150–180%.)

Another source of dire economic predictions for the television industry was a new law, pushed strongly by the Argentine Actors Guild, which required local dubbing for foreign shows. This measure was expected to provide much needed work for actors, yet greatly increase costs for distributors. Many distributors complained that they couldn't use Argentinian-dubbed product in the rest of Latin America where people were used to the more "neutral" Caribbean inflection (with most dubbing usually coming out of Mexico).

In contrast to the rest of the economic picture, cable television had a very good year. Argentine cable—the first in Latin America when it was introduced 6 years ago—had more than 350,000 households tuned in by early 1989. A 95% share of the market was split between CV in the interior of the country and VCC around Buenos Aires. (VCC also reached about 200,000 households in the interior via satellite.) In a country where a middle class earner rarely makes more than $700 a month, installation costs which start at $30 and monthly fees of $13 are quite high. Yet, sales have been brisk; one estimate put CV's monthly earnings at an average of $1.5 million.

One important topic in the 1988 political debate was the return of television to private hands. By mid 1989, the newly elected Peronist Carlos Mene pledged that all networks (except Channel 7, considered the official TV flagship) would return to private control. One stumbling block to the de-nationalization remained a law forbidding the cross-media ownership of public communication and advertising associations.

Principal Independent Distributors: (Suppliers and channels use these indies to take care of importing, printing, and sometimes dubbing) Telecinema Diprom, Ledafilms, Cintelba, Distelecine, Telefilms, Intertelefilms, Santa Clara, Crustel, Torneos y Competencias, Strazza Prods.

Principal Suppliers: (some of which deal directly with the channels) 20th Century Fox (represented by Ledafilms), Viacom (represented by MAC Films), Columbia, TB-Globo (represented by Dinter), Disney (represented by Genea), Transtel, RTVE Television Español (with agency in Chile), and sometimes Warner (out of Mexico), MCA (from São Paulo), Hal Roach (from Miami), and New World (out of Santiago).

Principal Broadcasters: Channel 7 ATC, Av. Córdova 323, 6th floor; Telex:22396 TVCOL AR. Channel 9 Libertad, Pasaje Gelly 3378; Telex: 22132 LIBER-AR. Channel 11, Pavón 2444; Telex: 22780 DICON. Channel 13 Proartel, San Juan 1170; Telex: ?1762 PATEL. La Plata's Channel 2, Cerrito 1266. Producing company: Estrellas, Río Bamba 280; ATA (Asociación de Teledifusoras Argentinas). Córdoba 323; Telex: 17253 ATA AR. Video Cable Communications (VCC), Cuba 2370, B.A.; Telex: 22909 VCCSA. Cablevisión: Bonpland 1773; Tel.: 771-3960, 774-7077, 774-6960.

AUSTRALIA

Population: 16,248,800.
Number of TV Sets: 5,105,200 with an average viewing time of 18 hours 11 minutes weekly for all age groups.
Networks: The Australian television industry, which first began broadcasting in 1956 and initiated color transmissions in the mid-1970s, consists of a mixture of government and private enterprise with three commercial networks: Network Ten, Australian Television Network (Seven) and Nine. In addition, there are two Public Broadcasting Networks: Australian Broadcasting Corporation and Special Broadcasting Service.
Trends: Controversy flared Down Under over content standards in commercial TV programming. After five years of intense study, the ABT (Australian Broadcasting Tribunal) wants a minimum of 50% of the 6 a.m.–midnight TV programming to be domestic product. By 1994, that percentage would rise to 60%. The Australian Content for Commercial Television Program Standard would give points to a program based on program format, length, and whether or not it has enough of an "Australian Look." The "Look" would be based on theme, perspective, language and character. Programs would be scored after they are televised . . . not before or during production. Industry groups have joined together in fighting ABT's dictum. The Screen Production Association of Australia, Actors Equity Association Australian Film Commission and Australian Screen Directors Guild, among others, fear that the new standards will work against industry efforts to sell Australian shows abroad and to create quality product. Low scores could result in less creative and adventuresome shows for the future.

The 1987/88 shakeup in commercial TV ownership saw the Australian Television Network (Network Seven) sold to Christopher Skase of Qintex/Universal Telecasters, Nine Network to Alan Bond (Bond Media) and Network Ten to Frank Lowy (Westfield Capital Corp./Northern Star Holdings). After thirteen months of investigation, the Australian Broadcasting Tribunal has found Alan Bond not to be a "fit and proper person" for holding a broadcasting license. The main complaint concerns Bond's $A400,000 payment to former Queensland premier Sir John Bjelke-Petersen and a threat he made to a competitor, the AMP Society. The tribunal also felt that attempts were made to mislead it in its inquiry. A long court case is expected.

The 1987 Broadcasting Amendment Act included a section which provides for Equalization Legislation. This policy allows rural areas, especially on the Eastern seaboard, to receive broadcasts from all three commercial networks, as well as the Australian Broadcasting Corporation and the Special Broadcast Service. The result, commonly called "Aggregation" occurs when the regional and commercial carriers combine or aggregate their licensing areas. This allows transmissions into two adjoining areas. Up to now, each regional carrier had a monopoly in its area.

Financing Incentives: The Australian Film Finances Corporation (FFC) was founded on July 12, 1988. The FFC provides funding for telemovies, miniseries, children's programming, documentaries and feature films. To qualify for government funds, a producer must: (1) secure 30% of his production costs from the private sector, (2) satisfy Australian content regulation, and (3) demonstrate market interest (usually by pre-sales to local and overseas broadcasters and distributors). Television mini-series assisted with funding include: Cassidy, All the Rivers Run II, and Flair. Children's programs include: Round the Twist, Cinderella's Secret, and The Greatest Time on Earth.

National Top Ten: The Comedy Company, Neighbors, National Nine News, A Country Practice, 60 Minutes, A Current Affair, The Cosby Show, Hey Hey It's Saturday, Beyond 2000, and Hey Dad.

AUSTRIA

Population: 7.6 million.

Number of TV Sets: 2,738,000.

Austria's only TV and radio network, the Austrian Broadcasting Corp (ORF), an independent public corporation, operates two TV channels FS 1, which broadcasts from 9 a.m. until midnight, and FS 2, which broadcasts from the afternoon to midnight.

Of Austria's 2,760,000 households, 95% have at least one TV set. On an average, ORF TV reaches approximately 72% of the country's 7,600,000 people daily with primetime viewership roughly 55% of the population. Additionally, in each of Austria's nine provinces, ORF has regional studios for local broadcasting of nine hours daily. Approximately 60% of ORF's review comes from radio and TV license fees, while 40% comes from radio and TV advertising.

A 35-member board of trustees, the Kuratorium, a 35-member committee of representatives from the radio and TV audience and a commission monitoring ORF compliance with the provisions of the Austrian broadcasting Act, is responsible for supervising ORF.

BAHRAIN

Bahrain TV, P.O. Box 1075, Manama, Bahrain, operates 1 channel and 1 relay for some 176,000 color sets.

BANGLADESH

Pilot station established in 1964 by government. Now includes originating station at Dacca with relay stations at Chittagong, Natore, Khulna, Sylhet, and Rangpur plus two under construction. Address Bangladesh TV, Television Bhaban, Rampura P.O. Box 456, Dacca. 450,000 sets.

BOLIVIA

Television broadcasting began here in 1969. The two networks are government-controlled. Channel 7 is national and the other is via eight university channels (Channel 13 in La Paz). Bolivia has about 450,000 TV sets. There is also a small cable operation, Channel 3. NTSC is the TV system, and there has been color since 1980. As no copyright laws exist in Bolivia, much product is pirated and many producers have stopped supplying product since there are no dollars available.

Empresa Nacional de Televisón Boliviana (Channel 7). Pres., Ricardo Ocampo, Ayacucho, 467, La Paz; Telex: 2312 TVBOL.

Dial (Channel 6). Pres., Javier Zuazo Chavez, v.p., Eduardo Quintanilla, Calle Batallón Colorados, Casilla 20574, La Paz; Telex: 2531BICSA.

Illimani de Communicaciones (Channel 9). Pres., Raul Garafulic Gutiérrez. Casilla 6122, La Paz; Telex: 3342.

Channel 13 (University Channel). Pres., Eduardo Barrientos. In operation since 1981. Av. 6 de agosto, Ed. Hoy.

Channel 3. Pay-TV channel, headed by Alvaro Valerama and Rolando Chiappe. Avds. Arce, Ed. Ilimani.

BRAZIL

Population: 141 million.

Number of TV sets: 24 million.

System Used: PAL-M (this PAL system of 525 lines is unique; it is compatible with NTSC, but not PAL or SECAM).

Number of TV Stations: 7.

History of the industry and trends: Television was introduced in 1951; by the late 1980s, the audience of roughly 100,000,000 made Brazil the highest selling and fastest growing market in Latin America.

Brazilian law requires that all owners of radio or TV stations be of Brazilian nationality. A further law stipulates that all foreign films shown on TV be dubbed, and that no station may transmit more than 22 half hours of foreign films for each 72 hours of weekly transmission time. Stations which transmit less than 12 hours per day have a corresponding lower quota. Seven sound studios, four in Rio de Janeiro and three in São Paulo take care of the dubbing of all American and some Italian, Argentine and Mexican films that come into the country.

Despite the country's severe economic problems in 1988–89, including 1000% inflation and a devaluation and price freeze in January 1989, Brazil's television industry seemed stronger than ever during the past year. Total ad revenue rose to $650 million; the lion's share of $420 million went to TV Globo. About 15% of the market went to the fast growing SBT, headed by popular TV host and political candidate Silvio Santos. Manchete and Bandeirantes tied for third place in earnings. The remaining revenues were split by a number of small independents. Globo continued to dominate the international sales market for series and features. Bandeirantes specialized in sports and live shows; the independents tended to concentrate their resources on equipment and personnel in order to become more competetive.

The country still did not have cable in 1988, but the first pay-TV station, Canal Plus, began 24 hour transmission of the all-sports ESPN network via satellite in April 1989. For the first month and a half any UHF viewer could pick up the programs. After this trial period, the signals were scrambled and interested viewers were invited to subscribe to the new station ($150 for residences, $1000 for apartment buildings, plus a $15 monthly fee). The programs come with simultaneous Portugese translation and the option of English language for those with stereo TV.

Principal Broadcasters and Organizations:

Rede Globo (Channel 4 in Rio). Brazil's huge media conglomerate, with interests in radio, TV, newspapers. Rua Lópes Quintas 303, Rio; Telex: 2121643 TVGB BR and 2122795 TVGB-BR.

Rede Manchete, Rue do Russell 804, Rio; Telex: 2133598 TVMT-BR and 2133597 TVMT-BR.

Rede Bandeirantes (Channel 13 in São Paulo), Rua Radiantes 13, Morumbi; Telex: 1153306 RTBA BR and 1181680 RTBA BR.

TV Record (Channel 7), Avda. Miruna 713, São Paulo; Telex: 1122245 RREC BR.

SBT (Channel 11), Rua Dona Santa Veloso 575, São Paulo; Telex: 1163892 SBT BR.

Funteve. Government agency for government-owned stations. Chain is composed of 17 stations, but they are not necessarily controlled by Funteve. Most important government-owned stations are TV E in Rio and TV Cultura in São Paulo. Rua Gomes Freire 474, Rio; Tel.: (021) 221-2227 PABX; Telex: (021) 22209, (021) 32541. Rua Seno Sbreghi 378, São Paulo; Tel.: (011) 263-9111; PABX (011) 65-6125 (programming); Telex: (011) 82055.

TV Gazeta, small but wealthy indie in São Paulo, Avenida Paulista 900, São Paulo; Tel.: (011) 287-4322 PABX; Telex: (011) 35914, (011) 39444.

TV Rio, New independent station in Rio. TV Rio is linked to another independent station owned by Athayde in the state of Goias, and exchanges programming with six stations throughout the country. Rua Miguel de Frias 57, Estacio, Rio de Janeiro; Tel.: (021) 293-0012 PABX; Telex: (021) 38183, (021) 38181.

BRUNEI

Established 1975 by governmental Radio TV Brunei, Bander Seri Begawan, Brunei. Two channels; 238,000 sets.

BULGARIA

Bulgarian Television, San Stefano Str 29, 1504 Sofia serves 2.6 million sets using 625-line Secam color.

BURMA

Burma Broadcasting Service, Prome Road, Kamayut Post Office, Rangoon. One station. 74,000 sets.

CAMBODIA (Kampuchea)

Radio Kampuchea Television, 28 Ave Preah Mohaksatryany Kossonak, Phnom Penh City, broadcasts daily on Channel 8 with relay to Bokor. Sets are estimated at 43,000.

CANADA

STATISTICS:

(as reported by Statistics Canada, a federal Government agency, except where otherwise noted)

Number of TV stations: 136—including 28 Canadian Broadcasting Corp.-owned stations and 35 privately-owned affiliates; and 28 CTV Television Network affiliate stations (Canadian Radio-Television and Telecommunications Commission).

Number of TV sets: In 1988, 95.1% of 9,244,000 households had at least one color TV set, compared to 72.3% in 1978; 32.6% of households had two or more color TV sets in 1988, a fivefold increase from a decade ago.

Cable TV/Cable Converters: In 1988, 69%—or 6,376,000 households out of 9,244,000—subscribed to cable TV services, a growth from 49.6% in 1978, a decade ago. Of these households, 3,783,000 have cable converters. The province of British Columbia, at 83.7%, has the largest proportion of cable subscribers.

Cable Companies: At August 1989 there were 797 cable companies and at July 1989, the Canadian Cable Television Association (CCTA) had 656 members, representing about 90% of all cable television subscribers in the country. The number of cable subscribers served by CCTA is 6,108,076. In 1987 the net profit before taxes of Canadian cable companies amounted to $C146.9 million.

Pay TV: In 1988, Pay TV in 10.5% of 9,244,000 households, a slight increase from 9.8% in 1986 (1987 figures not available), with the provinces of Ontario (14.6%) and British Columbia (12.8%) having the highest proportions.

TV Corporations: Canadian Broadcasting Corp., 1500 Bronson Ave., P.O. Box 8478, Ottawa, Ont. K1G 3J5; (613) 724-1200. English Networks: 1255 Bay St., P.O.Box 500, Stn. A, Toronto, Ont. M5W 1E6; (416) 975-3311. French Networks: 1400 est boul René Lévesque, P.O.Box 6000, Montréal, Qué. H3C 3A8; (514) 597-5970. CBC Enterprises/Les Entreprises Radio-Canada (English & French networks), Box 500, Stn. A, Toronto, Ont. M5W 1E6; (514) 975-3500. Channel 47 (A multilingual station serving 21 ethnic communities) 545 Lakeshore Blvd.W., Toronto, Ont. M5V 1A3. (416) 593-4747; Telex: 06-23643. City-TV, 299 Queen St. W., Toronto, Ont. M5V 2Z5; (416) 591-5757; Telex: 06-218283; FAX: (416) 591-7791. CTV Television Network Ltd., 42 Charles St. E., Toronto, Ont. M4Y 1T5 (416) 928-6000; Telex: Administration 06-22080/Sales Service: 06-22098; FAX: (416) 928-0907. Global Communications Limited (Global Television Network), 81 Barber Greene Rd., Don Mills, Ont. M3C 2A2, (416) 446-5311; FAX: (416) 446-5371.

Educational TV: Access Network (The Alberta Educational Communications Corporation) 16930 114 Ave., Edmonton, Alta. T5M 3S2; (403) 451-7272; FAX: (403) 451-7233; Telex: 037-3948; 295 Midpark Way S.E., Calgary, Alta. T2X 2A8; (403) 256-1100; Telex: 03-824867; FAX: (403) 256-6837. TVOntario (Province of Ontario educational network), 2180 Yonge St., Toronto, Ont. M4T 2T1; (416) 484-2600; Toll free: 1-800-268-8840; Telex: 06-23547; FAX: (416) 484-2725.

Pay TV: Allarcom Limited, 5325 104th St., Edmonton, Alta. T6H 5B8; (403) 436-1250. The Family Channel, 3 Mutual St., Toronto, Ont. M5B 2A7; (416) 867-8866 (National). First Choice Canadian Corporation, 98 Queen St. E., Toronto, Ont. M5C 1S6; (416) 364-9115; FAX: (416) 363-4709; TDD: (416) 364-2743 (covers eastern half of Canada from Ontario to Newfoundland). Newsworld, 1255 Bay St., 5th Floor, Toronto, Ont. M5W 1E6; (416) 975-2950; FAX: (416) 975-6080 (24-hour news & information network—basic cable). Superchannel/Alberta, 5324 Calgary Trail, Suite 200, Edmonton, Alta. T6H 4J8; (403) 437-7744 (covers western half of Canada from Manitoba to British Columbia). Télévision Quatre Saisons (Four Seasons Television Network Inc.), 405 Ogilvy, Montréal, Qué. H3N 1M4; (514) 271-3535 (French-language service in Québec). YTV Canada Incorporated, Administration: 525 Lakeshore Blvd. W., Toronto, Ont. M5V 1A3; (416) 534-1191; Production: 64 Jefferson Ave., Toronto, Ont. M6K 1Y4; (416) 340-1221 (National—children/teens/family).

Specialty Service: Cathay International Television, 494 W. 39th Ave., Vancouver, B.C. V5Y 2P7; (604) 321-5266; FAX: (604) 321-9625 (65 hours weekly of programming in Chinese, Hindi & Vietnamese). Chinavision Canada Corp. 160 Duncan Mills Rd., Don Mills, Ont. M3B 1Z5; (416) 391-3388; FAX: (416) 391-1322 (approx. 80 hours weekly of programming mainly in Cantonese, but also in Mandarin). MuchMusic Network, 299 Queen St. W., Toronto, Ont. M5V 2Z5; (416) 591-5757; Telex: 06-218283; FAX: (416) 591-7791 (National—basic cable). Telelatino Network Inc., 105 Carlton St., Toronto, Ont. M5B 1M2; (416) 591-6846 (approx. 90 hours weekly of Spanish & Italian programming). Vision TV: Canada's Faith Network, 315 Queen St. E., Toronto, Ont. M5A 1S7; (416) 366-9211 (Basic cable—multi-faith).

Industry Organizations: Canadian Cable Television Association, 360 Albert St., Suite 1010, Ottawa, Ont. K1R 7X7; (613) 232-2631. The Federation of Canadian Guilds and Unions in Film and Television, 65 Heward Ave., Toronto, Ont. M4M 2T5; (416) 462-1022.

—PATRICIA THOMPSON

CHILE

The television industry is expected to grow at an increasingly rapid pace, provided that the industry is allowed to expand as contemplated in pending legislation, and barring any political upheavals.

The explosion in TV advertising budgets is due to the GNP growth rate of almost 8% per year. This has financed increased consumer spending and hence a spectacular increase in the rate of TV set ownership. In 1970, only 19% of households had TV. In 1982, 78% had TV, by 1988 more than 85%, and ownership is expected to soon reach 95%.

The rate of TV set ownership is a barometer of Chilean society. In 1970, the economy was underdeveloped and low-tech. Illiteracy was four times higher than it is today. In 1970, 41% of children did not even finish grade 8, and only 8% finished high school. Today, more than one-third finish high school, six-year olds are now introduced to computers in the classroom and many grade schools are multilingual. Therefore this better-educated younger generation is more literate and worldly and naturally desires information and entertainment from TV.

The Structure of Chilean Television: As of mid-1989, the three national networks are: Television Nacional de Chile (state-owned); Universidad de Chile Television and Universidad Catolica de Chile Television. The Universidad Catolica de Valparaiso operates an autonomous channel in Valparaiso. There is also an affiliation of local channels in the northern cities called Telenorte. All regions of the country (including the Antarctic Zone and Easter Island) are served by at least one network.

The pending new Television Law would allow an unlimited number of VHF and UHF channels. There are several companies ready to begin operation once the new law becomes effective.

The networks transmit about 18 hours per day (in 1970, the networks transmitted only 6.5 hours per day). Transmissions in color became standard in April 1978.

Television Programming: Foreign-produced programming accounts for about 58% of daily transmission time. The most popular foreign programs are TV miniseries (at least one per week), specials such as the Oscars ceremony and Miss Universe pageant, and episode-series such as "Alf" and "Golden Girls." All foreign programming is dubbed into Spanish.

The Chilean-produced programming consists of news, sports, cultural-scientific, children's and "telenovelas" (prime-time "soaps" of about 75 minutes per day). There are also weekly variety shows on each of the networks featuring the most popular Latin American recording stars, human interest interviews and contests. General entertainment accounts for 50% of programming, followed by journalistic: 23%; cultural-educational: 14% and children's: 13%.

TVN has a second channel in Santiago dedicated exclusively to cultural programming.

Trends in Television Advertising: According to the annual survey done by Megatec S.A., the leading market research company in Chile, advertising revenue earned by the networks increased by over 7% in 1988. More than US$161 million in advtg. was purchased on the network "flagship" channels in Santiago. The percentage-share of revenue by network is as follows: U. Cat.: 46.5%, TVN: 46.2%, U. de Ch.: 6.2%, U. Cat. de V.: 1.1, in 1988; in 1987, 53.8%, 41.3%, 4.2%, and 0.7%, respectively. Total number of minutes sold on all Santiago channels in 1988: 177,300 minutes (485 mins. per day).

Percentage-share of time sold by network in 1988: U. Cat.: 32.2%; TVN: 34.2%; U. de Ch.: 23.1%; U. Cat. de V.: 10.5% = 100.0%.

The flagship channels of TVN & U. Cat. each invest about US$1 million in advertising in the print media to promote their programming.

According to the survey by Megatec, the ranking of the 10 most-advertised products on television is:

1) Political/Institutional (non-recurring); 2) Department Stores; 3) Soft Drinks; 4) Foods; 5) Lotteries; 6) Alcoholic Beverages; 7) Toys; 8) Cigarettes; 9) Banks; 10) Supermarkets.

The largest TV advertiser in 1988 was Lever Chile, followed by Nestlé Chile.

Cable TV: Since cable TV service began in Santiago in late 1987 with 4,200 homes connected, the coverage has tripled in one year, and will double again by 1990. Most new apartment buildings are equipped with cable, and many with satellite dishes. The four cable channels in Santiago are also successfully selling services to private homes. Their programming includes news, sports and specials not shown on network TV, as well as movies and business reports. There is one all-news channel.

Industry Organizations:

Networks: Television Nacional de Chile: Bellavista 0990, Providencia. Tel.: 77-4552; Telex: 241375 TVNCH-CL; Universidad Catolica de Chile Television: Ines Matte Urrejola 0848, Providencia. Tel.: 251-4000; Universidad de Chile Television: Ines Matte Urrejola 0825, Providencia. Tel.: 77-5994; FAX: 376675; Telex: 340492 TVUCH-CK; Universidad Catolica de Valparaiso Television: Guardia Vieja 12, Dp. 33, Providencia. Tel.: 231-8950; Telenorte: Condell 272, Santiago. Tel.: 225-6460; Telex: 341439 TVNOR CK.

Production Facilities: Chile Films: La Capitania 1200, Santiago. Tel.: 220-3086; FAX: 211-9826; Telex: 443099 FILMS CZ. Cristian Varela, gen. mgr.

Dubbing: Doblajes Internacionales: Av. Providencia 929, 6th Floor, Providencia. Tel.: 4-1763

Film & Television Commission of Chile: Lo Arcaya 1963, Vitacura (Santiago). Tel.: 220-3086; FAX: 215-1802; Telex: 341687 ALMAC CK. Alan Hootnick.

Regulatory Body: Consejo Nacional de Television: Moneda 1020, 4th Floor, Santiago. Tel.: 8-2306

Market Research: Megatec S.A.: Hernando de Aguirre 1070, Providencia (Santiago). Tel.: 231-5064 Fax: 231-5066 Paulette Ivovic, accts. mgr., Raul Vinuela, gen. mgr.

—ALAN HOOTNICK

CHINA (People's Republic)

Peking TV, opened in 1969, consists of three networks, one purely local and the other two broadcasting by microwave to the rest of the country. Color broadcasts began in 1973. Shanghai, China's largest city, has two channels on the air for about 9 hours daily with some 50% of the programs listed as entertainment, 20% movies, news or documentaries, and 20% sports or children's programs, in addition to educational and foreign language-instruction programs. Chinese officials blame the Cultural Revolution for the slow growth of TV and say that after the Gang of Four was ousted in the following decade TV stations were opened in all 29 of China's provinces and private set ownership rose to 120 million tuned to 70 stations and 130 relays. With some 7 million sets being added annually, China is producing 800 TV dramas a year. Twenty percent of all households now have TV sets and by 1990 this number will be doubled.

Following the 1984 ad barter agreement with CBS providing 60–70 hours of programming yearly, the biggest impact on Chinese audiences was the Walt Disney Company release of a 2-year cycle of films to be shown weekly under an agreement to share revenues from commercials.

In the past 5 years China has sold 10,000 hours of TV programs to 150 countries. China imports 100 TV programs annually, many of them older titles (mostly from MGM and Lorimar through Chinese-American middlemen).

CCTV began use of International Telecommunications Satellite Organization facilities to reach parts of China where reception is poor to nonexistent but only until they set up their own satellite service for which they are setting up 50 ground stations. Some 62% of the country is covered already as far as reception is concerned.

Some 93.3% of city homes have TV sets but the figure is only 11.5% for rural homes, due to poor reception. CCTV broadcasts 30hours weekly, programming news, instruction, cartoons, variety and drama. Audience estimated at 800 million.

China now manufactures some 8.2 million sets annually and it is estimated that the number of sets will soon reach 120 million, including sets open to the public audience. Total number of nationwide stations (including microwave relay stations) is over 40. Black-and-white sets sell for the equivalent of $370 and color sets for about $1,335 and there is a waiting list for the former. Domestic and imported films are broadcast from time to time, including American feature films occasionally.

Advertising on TV was introduced in 1979 and Coca-Cola, Kodak, Maxwell House Coffee and Toshiba are only some of the foreign products advertised on Chinese TV. CCTV ad rate is $7,500 per minute maximum.

Central Broadcasting Administration, Hsin Men, Peking, now offers nationwide TV commercials at rates ranging from about $625 for a 15-second spot to a full minute for $1,800.

CHINA (Taiwan)

Television began in 1962 by the Educational Television Station which later became the private China Television Service in 1971. There are now three networks: Taiwan Television Enterprise (1962), China Television Company (1969) and China Television Service. All three act as private corporations deriving revenues from commercials. These three stations have 24 transmitters with total broadcasts of about 265 hours weekly for some 5.9 million set owners (1.25 sets per family) who pay about $1.50 annually for a license. About 80% of the programs are domestic, with most of the imports from the U.S.A. Over half of the sets are color. Taiwan has two communication satellite stations. A new rule states that commercials must not exceed 15% total broadcast time. Movie theatre owners complain that the three imported feature films shown weekly on television hurt their box office.

All three networks broadcast in color, TTV and CTV 6 hours 25 minutes weekdays and 12 hours weekends and holidays while CTS broadcasts 10.15 hours weekdays, 15 hours on Saturday and 17 hours Sunday or holidays. News takes an average of 21%, public service over 10%, culture and education 20%, entertainment 48%. TTV has 10 transmitters, CTV 6, and CTS 8, plus an equal number of relay stations. Sets number 5,900,000. Of the 20.4 billion yuan spent for advertising 29.07% went to television.

New rules call for no commercials during programs of less than 30 minutes and all commercials to secure government approval. In the future, 80% of all programs must originate in Taiwan with entertainment programs taking up no more than 55% of broadcast time and 45% or more devoted to educational, cultural or news types.

With relay stations it is estimated that 100% of the island's population of 18 million receives TV reception. About 12% of programs are imports, mostly from America, and these are broadcast in the original English with Chinese captions, which has served to develop knowledge of the English language among the populace.

TV showings of full-length Chinese-language, feature films imported from Hong Kong were stopped following retaliatory action by local cinema interests but the government may step in later and permit such showings, except on Sundays and holidays when the theatres reap their largest harvest. Inquiries should be addressed: Ministry of Communications, Taipei, Taiwan, Republic of China, or to: China Radio/TV Assoc. 6-144 Hsin Shen (South) Rd., Section 1, Taipei, Taiwan, Republic of China.

CONGO

Radio-TV de Congo, B.P. 2241, Brazzaville. One station; 8,000 sets.

EGYPT

Television broadcasting in Egypt was launched on July 21, 1960 in black and white with color transmission beginning in 1979, beaming programs in the European Technical Transmission with an image of 825 Scansions known as Middle East SECAM.

The two main channels now cover large areas of the Middle East including Saudi Arabia, thus boosting advertising rates continuously.

Both channels transmit over 200 hours weekly, covering all spheres, and are hooked to international satellite for new updates and major world events. The capital, Cairo (with a population of 11 million), has one more local channel broadcasting over 28 hours weekly. Similar local channels started operating in 1989 to cover all major cities in Egypt.

The TV receivers in use are very close to 20 million, watched by double that number of viewers in a country where television is the major, and sometimes the sole, source of entertainment and information.

Television in Egypt is attached to the Ministry of Information, headed by Safwat El Sherif. Abdel Salam El Nady is now president of Egyptian TV.

—AHMED SAMI

ETHIOPIA

Ethiopia Television, Post Office Box 5544, Addis Ababa. Two stations; 48,000 sets.

FINLAND

Population: 4,926,000
Number of TV sets: 1.9 million
Number of TV Channels: 3

Finland has a three-channel television system that differs considerably from the other countries. There is at present in Finland one radio and television operation licence which has been granted to the Finnish Broadcasting Company, Oy Yleisradio Ab. The existence of MTV, Oy Mainow-TV-Reklam Ab, which is a private commercial TV company, is acknowledged in the same license.

Launched in Sept., 1986 semi-public Kolmoskanava (TV-3 Finland) owned by pubcaster YLE, commercial MTV and Nokia Industries, reaches 800,000 Finnish households (50%). Its programming balances foreign and domestic fare, news, documentaries, and feature films, series and soap operas. It now airs 7 hours a day—more on weekends.

In 1989 TV 4 was launched as a southern Finland over-the-air service picking up programming from Sweden's SVT and broadcasting to Swedish-speaking areas of Finland.

The basis for official relations between the companies were laid down in more detail in the basic agreement concluded in 1976. Television broadcasting in Finland is under parliamentary control. The Administrative Council of the Finnish Broadcasting Company appointed by Parliament is the highest organ exercising program policy. It has two functions. The Administrative Council exercises program policy control over both companies. In addition, as its name implies, it is the highest administrative organ in the Finnish Broadcasting Company.

MTV has its own corresponding administrative council.

As a bilingual country Finland also has programs in Swedish on all TV-channels.

Finland has had TV commercials on the air for 21 years, the longest span in Europe and in 1989 TV ads accounted for 20–25% of total ad revenue.

Some 19 hours per week—out of the total of 75—are sold by Oy Yleisradio Ab to MTV. MTV produces nearly 43% of its programs.

Helsinki TV, owned by Sanoma Publishing, a division of Finnish Eurocable, is a cable operator with a combination service of free and pay TV reaching 400,000 of Finland's cable households. In 1987 Sanoma set up Eurocable which owns Norway's Janco Cable, 31% of Ireland's Cork Communications and 10% of London's Westminster Cable.

The Finnish Broadcasting Company: Head Office, P.O. Box 10, SF-0241 Helsinki 24; Radio and TV Centre: Pasilankatu 39, SF-0240 Helsinki, Tel: 0-15001. TV 2 Television Center, Tohloppi, 33270 Tampere 27 (Telephone 445455), MTV, Ilmalantori 2 , SF-00240 Helsinki 24 (Telephone 15001); Kolmostelevisio Iy Ab-Channel Three Finland, Ilmalanakatu 2 C, SF-0240 Helsinki, Tel: 0-15001. FAX 0-1500677.

FRANCE

TV Households: 21,800,000
Networks: 4 private-held, 3 pubcasters.
Cable Penetration: less than 1%.

Regulatory Body: CSA (Conseil Supérieur de l'Audiovisuel), 56 rue Jacob, Paris 75006. Tel.: 42.61.83.18.

Privately-held Networks: *TF-1* 17, rue de l'Arrivée, 75737 Paris Cedex 15. Tel.: 42.75.12.34. FAX: 42.75.26.88. Telex: 250878. (Francis Bouygues, Robert Maxwell, others—50%, traded stock—50%). 99% penetration. Audience share: 39–45%.

La Cinq 19-21 rue Jean Goujon 75008 Paris; Tel.: 42 89 60 00; FAX: 42.89.38.95; Telex: 641635; Jerome Seydoux, president: Robert Hersant, vice pres.: Silvio Berlusconi. 68% penetration. Share: 12–14%.

Metropole-6 (Compagnie Luxembourgeoise de Telediffusion, Lyonnaise de Eaux, others) 16 Cours Albert ler, 75008 Paris; Tel.: 42 56 66 66 and 45 63 17 17; FAX: 45.63.78.52; Telex: 649781; president: Jean Drucker. 50% penetration. Share: 40%.

Canal Plus, 78, rue Olivier de Serres, 75015 Paris; Tel.: 45.33.74.74; FAX: 45.30.00.71; Telex: 201141 (pay-TV and unscrambled broadcast). (Havas, Compagnie Generale des Eaux, others). 2,200,000 subscribers, over-air penetration: 40%. Audience share: 4% André Rousselet, pres.

La Sept 35 quai Andre Citroen, 75015 Paris; Tel.: 40 59 77; FAX: 45.78.09.27; Telex: 204102; president: Georges Duby.

Public Broadcasters: *Antenne-2:* 22, avenue Montaigne, 75008 Paris. Phone: 42.99.42.42; FAX: 42.99.51.45; Telex: 642313; 60% revenues from ads, rest user tax. 99% penetration. Shares: 25–29%.

FR-3: 116, avenue du Président Kennedy, 75790 Paris Cedex 16. Tel.: 42.30.22.22; FAX: 46.47.92.94; Telex: 630720/615906; 15% ad revenues. 90%+ penetration. Share: 9–12%. (Shares based on Mediametrie, Monday–Sunday, highest and lowest scores since Jan.)

Networks: France's audiovisual landscape changed with the privitization of TF-1, controlled by Francis Bouygues and Robert Maxwell, and the addition of a fifth (La Cinq) and sixth channel (M-6). The end of the government monopoly in TV was begun in 1982 by Socialist President Francois Mitterand, and continued by the majority government of Prime Minister Jacques Chirac. The last five years have seen France go from three to seven national networks—two public, four private and one pay TV—and from strict state control to a comparatively wide diversity.

TF-1 still dominates the field, scoring ratings of 46% despite the success of the fourth channel (Canal-Plus, a pay-TV movie channel). Antenne 2, and the regional FR-3 are still state-operated, funded by the annual TV tax, and commercials. A new cultural channel, La Sept, began broadcasting in Spring, 1989. La Sept also has a vocation in funding TV and theatrical films. The originality of this station is that it programs European creations, cinemas, festivals, and spotlight events and auteurs.

Trends: This seems to be the year of increased regulation for French TV. On January 30, 1989 France's third broadcast regulatory board in eight years—the Conseil Superieur de Audiovisuel—took office, replacing its beleaguered predecessor, CNCL. With fewer members (9 instead of CNCL's 13) and greater power than either the Haute Autorite (1982–86), or the CNCL (1986–88), it is empowered to allocate radio, TV and satellite frequencies as well as cable channels. Moreover it names the head of State-owned TV's Antenne 2, FR3 and La Sept, Radio France and Telediffusion de France (TDF), and serves as watchdog on TV sex and violence, program quotas and political campaign fairness. In one of its first actions, the CSA voted to restrict TV channels from airing films rated off-limits to those 13 and younger and those rated restricted to viewers over 18 during prime time (before 10:30 P.M.).

Despite the European Community's decision to forego quotas on non-EC programming, the French government is preparing legislation to increase restrictions and quotas similar to that already in force for the public broadcasters, to the private channels limiting non-European shows (read American) to only 40% of airtime. Private network La-Cinq already had received punitive fines from the CNCL for taking more than one break during film broadcasts.

—VERNICE KLIER MOSKOWITZ

GHANA

Ghana Broadcasting Corporation, Broadcast House, Post Office Broad Box 1633, Accra. Five stations, 147,000 sets.

GREECE

Population: 9,500,000
Number of TV Sets: 1,570,300 Color; 1,285,750 B/W
Number of TV Stations: TV started operating here in 1966. There were two TV stations operating in Athens in the experimental stage at first—one by the National Radio and TV organization (ERT) and the other by the Information Service of the Army Forces (YENED). In 1983 both channels were merged under the Helliniki Radiophonia ke Tileorassi (ERT) as ERT 1 and ERT 2.

Both channels have operated in color since 1981. A third channel, ERT 3 stationed in Thessaloniki, started operating last year. There is also a relay station in Patras covering news only from Southern Greece.

Since October 1987 nine satellite channels—TV5, RAI UNO, RAI DUE, CNN, HORIZON, SAT 1, TVE 1, MTV, SKY—are downlinked with ERT in an experimental stage. They transmit (terresterially) unsubtitled foreign language programs but nevertheless they are hurting the home video business.

Since the government, yielding to strong public pressure, ended the state monopoly on radio broadcasting, opening it to the private sector in 1987, there have been several contenders hoping to privatize the television industry in Greece, the last member of the European Community to have state-controlled TV. After two attempts at private broadcasting—first in late 1988 by TV Plus Piraeus, the first commercial cable TV station in Greece, which was closed by court order in 1989, and a similar experiment in Thessaloniki—the Greek government in a surprise move in August 1989, agreed to allow commercial television by offering licenses to two newspaper publishing consortiums for two private channels expected to start up in autumn, 1989. The companies are Antenna, which operates Athens' most successful private radio station, and the other called Teletypes S.A.

TV Without Frontiers: At a ministers' meeting of the 12 countries in Luxemburg in the spring of 1989, members of the European Economic Community agreed to the establishment of a Directive concerning "Television without Frontiers" to be approved by the European Parliament. This directive would guarantee access of Television Channels within the EEC if program requirements were adhered to. If the European Parliament approves the text of this directive, it will be adopted within two years. It is doubtful, however, that this plan will be accepted because of the many differences among the respective countries.

Trends: ERT 1 transmits 12 hours of programming on weekdays and more on holidays; ERT 2, 8 hours programming daily and ERT 3, 5 hours. About 60% of the ERT 1 programming is comprised of news, education subjects, discussion panels, local films and local series and the rest by foreign films and series. On ERT 2 the ratio is 60% foreign (mostly American) and 40% local. ERT 3 programming covers news from Northern Greece and local films and serials previously put on the air by both the other channels. Although a great number of ad spots are sold daily by each of the Channels to several advertising agencies, there are no program interruptions for commercials on any channel.

Name and Addresses of Principal Broadcasters: ERT 1, 432 Messoguion Avenue, Aguia Paraskevi, Athens 153 42; ERT 2, Messoguion Avenue and Katechaki Str., Athens, 116 28; ERT 3, 2, Aguelaki Str., Thessaloniki 542 20

Agencies: There are several agencies acting on behalf of various foreign TV companies: Hellas Television International, 96 Academias Str. Athens. representing MGM, Screen Gems, Warner Bros., Sacis, RAI, Paramount, Rank, Titanus, Egyptian TV, Aussi TV, Spanish TV, Brazilian TV, World Vision, Rumulus, World Fair Communications and Thames TV; Apollon International Enterprises 46 King Constantinou Avenue, Athens representing Anthony Morris, Children TV Workshop, Embassy Telecommunications, Four Star Enterprise, Hanson International, John Pearson International, Lassis Television, London Films, Marvin Goofman Associates, Metromedia Productions, NBC International, Orion, P.S.O., Samuel Goldwyn, TriStar, Toho, Mexican TV, Strenghold Television etc. Yannis Triantafyllis, 9 Klisovis Str. Athens agent of ITC TV etc. Dennis Petropoulos agent of N,T,A, II Lycavitou Str. Athens, Constantinos Tricoupis II, Halkokondyli Str. Athens. Georguiades Electroniki s.a., 20 Lagoumitzi Callithea, Athens.

Local TV production: Both Channels ET 1 and ET 2 produce several films and series for local use and exportation to foreign TV stations. ET 1 is in addition subsidizing some Greek pictures which are shot as serials also. According to the provisions of the new law, an affiliated company of ERT 1 will be established to undertake local TV production.

Independent TV producers: Hellas TV Productions, 96 Academias Str., Athens, Manager Andreas Lappas. Dennis Petropoulos, II Licavitou Str. Athens. Panos Spyropoulos, 46 King Constantinou Avenue, Athens. Andromeda Dyas Epe, 47 Lemnou Str. Athens. Kinimatografiki Epe 4 Tim. Filimond Str. Athens. Basil Maros, 26 Democritou Str. Athens, N. Samaras 14 Strat. Syndesmou Str. Athens. TVEM, 52 Skoufa Str. Athens. Aris Triantafyllis 5-7 Kapodistriou Str. Athens, Astyr Film, Finos Film 53 Hiou Str. Athens, Georgiades Electroniki, 20 Lagoumitzi Str., Athens.

TV studios: Television Enterprises S.A. Head office 28, Kapodistriou Str. Athens. Manager Christos Elmatzoglou. ATA Studios head office Omerou 8 Str. Athens., Fin Films Spata Attikas, Sklavis Studio 59 Zoodochou Peyes Athens. Roussopoulos Bros. Studio. Cinemagic Studio, etc.

—RENA VELISSARIOU

GUAM (U.S. Possession)

Guam Television operates one station with two channels for 17 hours daily, servicing an estimated 15,000 sets in the hands of Americans and natives. Owner is Pacific Broadcasting Corp., Agana. Some color is broadcast. The Department of Education, Agana, operates Channel 12, some 14 hours daily.

GUINEA

Radio-Diffusion Guinienne, B.P. 391, Conraky. 11,500 sets.

HOLLAND

Population: 14,804,500
Number of TV Sets: 5,232,000
Number of TV Stations: 3
History: 1st station, N1, became operational October 2, 1951; 2nd station, N2, became operational October 2, 1964; 3rd station, Nederland 3 (a cultural and educational channel), became operational April 4, 1988; 1st color broadcast took place October 1, 1967. There are no privately owned stations.

Viewing Habits: The average time the Dutch spend watching TV is some two and a half hours daily. The young people still like to go to the cinemas.

Some 98% of the Dutch households have TV sets and of these some 76% have cable systems which generally broadcast 3 Dutch channels, 2 German, 2 Belgian, 2 English, 1 French plus the commercial stations of Sky and Super Channel. In addition, the Pay TV station FILMNET is operational. It has over 80,000 subscribers in Holland. Filmnet is operated by Esselte Pay TV, division of the Swedish Esselte Group. Their programs are distributed via the ECS-one Satellite and a subscription costs from Dfl. 22.75 to Dfl. 34.50 (for 24 hours a day) per month, depending on the number of features chosen (plus Dfl. 10. per month for the decoder). The address is: Esselte PayTV, PO Box 132, 3440 AC Woerden.

Advertising: There are no commercial stations.

Commercials are shown on the 3 Dutch channels in blocks, mostly before and following the newscasts. Programs are not interrupted by commercials.

Sky and Super Channels are only allowed on Dutch cable without Dutch subtitled programs, and publicity especially aimed at Dutch audiences is prohibited. It is rather unlikely that EEC rules will permit such restrictions in future.

The Ster, formed in 1965, administers sales and placement of ads on TV. Currently allowed to sell only 4.5% commercial time per day, which will expand to 7% soon, in 1989 the Ster generated 1182 million guilders ($591 million) to be divided among Dutch broadcasters. Broadcasters also receive a percentage of the TV tax (185 guilders or $92).

Broadcasters: There are 8 major broadcasting companies plus a number of minor ones (like TELEAC) which handle cultural and educational programs. The "8" are listed below.

NOS besides being a broadcaster is also the Central TV and Radio Organization.

The quality of Dutch programs is good and there are some excellent talkshows.

The NOS (Nederlandse Omroep Stichting) in Hilversum is the central TV and Radio Organization and there are 8 main subdivision stations: a Roman Catholic one: KRO, 2 political (left) ones: VARA and VPRO, 2 Protestant: NCRV and EO and 3 neutrals: AVRO, TROS and VERONICA. These three have the largest number of subscribers.

The 8 major companies are completely independent in their activities and buy a lot of product on the international market. There are also some minor TV organizations like TELEAC, which broadcast educational programs such as mathematical, languages and computer courses.

The yearly contribution for TV and Radio combined is Dfl. 158.

Radio and TV fall under the Ministry of Welfare, Social Health and Culture (WVC) which is particularly severe on the subject of "hidden" advertising.

As an average, feature films are shown 2–3 nights per week and also regularly in the afternoons. There is a window of 40 months, but it is possible to obtain exceptions to this rule. The decision lies with the Dutch Cinema Organization (NBB). Many American and English films are shown as well as TV series.

Prices of colour TV sets start at Dfl. 500. Price is obviously dependant on size of screens, remote control and Teletext.

Philips is the most important manufacturer in Holland. Import of Japan and German sets is also significant.

Trends: A number of contenders are vieing to establish the first Dutch-language commercial station in the Netherlands which looks to become a reality by the end of 1989. TV-10, from Channel 10 radio's Peter Jelgersma, the Rainbow Family Channel, a Christian TV service, Family Net service via satellite and RTV (which currently can be received with a satellite dish but wants access to cable systems) are all in the running. One of the most highly cabled nations in Europe, Holland requires every cable system to carry Netherlands channels 1, 2 and 3, but beyond that it is the local communities, and not the cable system operators, that decide which signals their systems carry.

Principal TV Broadcasters: AVRO, (neutral) P.O. Box 2, 1200 JA Hilversum; E.O., (Protestant), P.O. Box 565, 1200 AN Hilversum; KRO (Roman Catholic), P.O. Box 9000, 1201 DH Hilversum; NCRV, (Protestant), P.O. Box 121, 1200 JE Hilversum; NOS (central TV Organization), P.O. Box 444, 1200 JJ Hilversum; TROS, (neutral), P.O. Box 450, 1200 AL Hilversum; VARA (leftish), P.O. Box 175, 1200 AM Hilversum; VERONICA (neutral), P.O. Box 1234, 1200 BE Hilversum; VPRO, (leftish), P.O. Box 11, 1200 JC Hilversum; FILMNET, (movie channel subscription TV) Esselte Pay TV, P.O. Box 132, 3440 AC Woerden.

—PAUL SILVIUS

HONG KONG

Established 1957 by Rediffusion (HK) as closed circuit, converted to conventional TV in 1974. Asia Television (ATV) Central P.O Box 1414, Kowloon, Hong Kong. Additional outlets: Television Broadcast (HK-TVB), 77 Broadcast Drive, P.O. Box 70100, Kowloon, Hong Kong; and, Radio TV Hong Kong, Kowloon Central P.O. Box 200, Hong Kong (governmental unit acting as producer for above). Sets number 1,402,000.

In 1989 the government awarded the world's largest TV franchise—1.5 million potential customers—to a consortium of communications companies, known as Hong Kong Cable Communications. The service is expected to be on-line by 1991.

HUNGARY

Magyar Televizio, 1810 Budapest serves 3.4 million sets nationwide using 625-line Secam color, currently with two nationwide programs plus local station specials.

INDIA

Population: 800 million

A Brief History of Indian Television or Doordarshan as it is Known: Radio and Television in India are state-controlled. The first experimental TV center was set up in Delhi in 1959. Its growth was slow and cautious through the 1960s and 70s. However, in the mid 1970s India conducted an ambitious experiment, Satellite Instructional Television Experiment (SITE). The American Satellite ATS 6, was used to beam instructional programs on agriculture, health, hygiene, family welfare, science, education, etc. in 4 Indian languages, 4 hours daily for one year. About 2400 villages spread over 6 states were provided community viewing facilities.

In the 1980s the expansion of television has been phenomenal. Till 1983 television covered a mere 19% of the population. Within a year, with the setting up of 180 transmitters and networking them to Indian satellite INSAT-IB and microwave terresterial links, the coverage leaped to 70%. According to government plans the country will have 400 relay centers by 1990 covering 80% of the population.

At present the number of TV transmitters totals 265 (high power transmitters 51; low power transmitters 191; very low power transmitters 23). There are 18 full fledged TV stations with independent production facilities. These are located at Delhi, Bombay, Calcutta, Madras, Jalandhar, Lucknow, Trivandrum, Bangalore, Srinagar, Jaipur, Guwahati, Ahmedabad, Hyderabad, Cuttack, Gorakhpur, Nagpur, Rajkot, and Ranchi. Besides there are relay stations at Mussorie, Pune, Panaji, Asansol, Murshidabad, Kurseon, Kodaikanal, Amritsar, Kanpur, Chandigarh, Cochin. These stations transmit 4 to 5 hours daily. However National Programme from Delhi is telecast simultaneously through satellite by all the centers including those having their own production facilities. With a 7 hour daily schedule, the programs are generally aimed at creating a sense of unity in diversity. News and current affairs, development programs, communal harmony, arts, music, dance and folk lore are other themes which make up national programs.

There are well over 14 million TV sets in the country with an audience of nearly 80 million. About half the TV sets are concentrated in metropolitan towns but with LPTs now beaming out to cover half the country's population, the growth rate of TV sets is expected to rise dramatically.

Doordarshan commenced a commercial service in 1976 and from 1983 it started accepting sponsored programs which have brought into its coffers an ever increasing revenue. Last year it earned Rs.1360 million as against the previous year's Rs.980 million. Viewership surveys have revealed that feature films, Chitrahaar (composed of song sequences from feature films) and sponsored serials are some of the most popular programs all over the country. The prime viewing time is from 8–10:30 pm on weekdays and 9–12 noon on Sunday. But the Hindi feature film on Sunday evenings continues to be the most popular attraction.

Of late, Doordarshan has been sponsoring TV feature films. It also co-finances with the National Film Development Corporation, feature films by well-known filmmakers which have come to be known as parallel cinema. In addition it also purchases and telecasts "art" films which may otherwise remain on the shelf. This has given a fillip to low budget "art" filmmakers.

The power of television has been confirmed by two religious-themed programs. Nothing has been as popular as the two serials based on India's oldest epics—Ramayana and Mahabharata. Shown on prime time millions sat glued to their sets, wedding ceremonies and a ministerial swearing in were put off and advertisements in the papers read: "Car for sale. But call after Ramayana."

Cable TV: With the proliferation of color TVs and VCRs, the Cable Television (CATV) has become an industry in itself. Conservative estimates have it that there are 2,000 cable TV operators in Bombay alone. In all new buildings Cable TV is included as a part of the facility to the residents. For a monthly fee ranging between Rs.100–150 the CATV operators offer an assorted program of feature films in English-American, current domestic Hindi releases, Pakistani serials, and the latest from UK and America—series like Jewel in the Crown, Howard's Way, BBC and Channel 4 programs, Dallas, Dynasty, Colby's, Falcon Crest, etc. In addition all five-star hotels throughout the country have closed-circuit TV, some like the Taj Mahal Hotel in Bombay featuring 3 separate channels.

Systems: The television system in India is PAL standard color and VCRs use the VHS format.

—B.D. GARGA

INDONESIA

The government-owned RRI-TV, on the air since 1962 as the first developing nation to have complete TV coverage, in 1988 gave permission for one station, Rajawari Citra Televisi Indonesia, Jakarta, to carry commercials which had been banned since 1981. Since 1985 they have banned American or other imported TV shows on the grounds that the public preferred domestic fare, though the last showing of American TV fare indicated an average audience of 24 million viewers.

At present stations are operated on 2 channels in Jakarta, Bandung, Jogakarta, Semarang and Tjiribon, with some 203 relays. Broadcasting hours average above 40 hours weekly with some programs in color to sets estimated to number over 2 million. Programs are 50% entertainment, 25% educational, 25% public service, live 60% of the time, and 40% video-taped. With the departure of imported shows, the government will increase educational shows based on national culture. Indonesia is building 50 relays under its fourth 5-year plan since its 203 relays now reach only 27% of its population of 114 million. Inquiries to TV Republic Indonesia (TVRI), Yayasan Televisi, Senayan Jakarta. 10 stations; 4,950,000 sets.

IRAN

Islamic Republic of Iran Broadcasting, Post Office Box 98-200, Teheran. Sixteen stations, 2.2 million sets.

IRAQ

Iraq Broadcasting & Television, Broadcasting House, Salihiya, Baghdad. Six stations, 725,000 sets.

IRELAND

Population: 3,541,000
Number of TV Sets: 950,000
System Used: The national technical standard is a 625 line one, but programs are also broadcast on 405 lines in eastern and northwestern parts of the country.

Trends: Towards the end of 1988, Ireland's television system underwent some radical changes. Telefis Eireann, the service which began in 1962, was previously under the jurisdiction of the government Broadcasting Authority. The Minister for Post and Telegraphs was responsible for the autonomously-run agency. In November 1988, the Independent Radio and Television Commission was established to introduce commercial TV and radio and to issue franchises for broadcasting services. Many observers looked forward to an open and competitive broadcast environment under the new system. The commercial services were expected to be in operation by the end of 1989. There will be no license fees and advertising will be the sole source of revenue.

Another industry first being considered is the establishment of a Multi-Point Microwave Distribution System which would provide multi-channel choice to the entire country. At present, only main population centers have cable and satellite services. The proposed MMDS system would have 11 channels available by subscription.

ISRAEL

Israel television broadcasts daily in Arabic and Hebrew. Arabic programs start at 6:00 p.m. and continue to 8:00 p.m. Programs include documentaries, round-ups, news, films, variety shows, discussions, games, etc. These programs include, as well, weekly interviews with individuals of the Arab Israeli population who can convey regards to their relatives in neighboring countries, such as Egypt, Syria, Lebanon, Jordan, through this medium.

At 8:00 the Hebrew programs begin, offering the same variety of broadcast as the Arabic programs. Hebrew broadcasts continue up to 11:30 or midnight. The majority of Hebrew programs are subtitled in Arabic; and foreign language broadcasts, including films, are subtitled in both Hebrew and Arabic. Similarly, most of the Arabic programs have Hebrew subtitles.

Besides the above mentioned programs, television broadcasts every morning (except Saturday) educational programs beginning at 8:00 and continuing to 4:00. This is followed by children's programs which continue to 6:30 and include films, puzzles, games, cartoons, etc.

Currently Israel has one television channel. For the past 3 and a half years attempts have been made to launch a second channel but though test telecasts were made, transmittors only reach half the population and the new channel remains in a transitory state.

On the other hand the first three franchises for cable TV in Israel were granted by the Ministry of Communications in 1988 to Golden Channels & Co., CSS, ICS (the latter made up of American investors). Others have joined the budding cable industry and an Israeli Cable Television Association has been established. Operating as both a cable operator and programmer, the organization functions as a monopoly and has met opposition from former members. The four ICIA partners Golden Channels, Tevel, ICS and CSS, cover 649,000 households.

Organizations: Israel Broadcasting Authority, 14 Klausner St. Ramat Aviv 690011 Israel; Tel: 03 414155; Telex: 342325; Israel Broadcasting Authority Television Romema, P.O. Box 7139; Jerusalem 91905, Tel: 02 557111. Telex: 225301.

ITALY

Population: 57,400,000
Number of TV Households: 17,500,000
Average Viewership: 22,500,000 during primetime, midweek
Number of TV Channels: RAI Public Broadcasting, 3 channels; Private, 3 major networks, 3 medium-sized networks, 10 smaller networks and an estimated 400 local stations.

Trends: After 13 years of heated debate, and inaction, Italy's Parliament appears finally ready to promulgate a Broadcast Act that would bring some order and guidelines to an otherwise chaotic market controlled by two awesome powers, one public, one private.

The powers in question are RAI, the public broadcaster which has three channels (RAI-1, reaching 98% of the market and a 25–30% share; RAI-2, 91% range, 12–15% share; RAI-3, 65% coverage, 5–7% share) and the Silvio Berlusconi group, which controls the three principal private networks along with a number of other key media interests. The latter include Canale-5, which reaches 98% of the market and has a 22–25% share; Italia-1, 94% coverage, 11–14% share; and Rete 4, with 90% of the market and a 7–10% share.

In effect the RAI and Berlusconi camps have been a Duopoly with a lock on the Italian market. Now, with the anticipated Parliamentary bill, antitrust measures would be introduced which, nonetheless, would not dilute Berlusconi's power that much. Instead, they would prevent other groups with major media (e.g., newspaper) ownership from owning TV network interests.

Of more consequence to Berlusconi and his Fininvest company which owns the broadcasting interests, is a controversial proposal to guarantee that up to 50% of all advertising revenues earned by *all* broadcasters be poured back into RAI funding.

Also of negative impact on Fininvest is growing pressure, especially from the Communist political forces, to cut back sharply on the number of advertising spots allotted to its three networks. In practice, they operate relatively unfettered, not subject to the strict guidelines RAI must follow as a public broadcaster. Pressure is particularly intense on cutting back ad spots during the telecast of feature films (RAI allows only one break per film, while private TV can put 14–18% of its broadcast time into ads.)

Both Berlusconi and rival RAI face some revenue reduction from another proposed provision of the Act which would limit the amount of ad revenue earned from smaller networks that rely on them to supply programming and advertising services.

In terms of programming, the burgeoning of the private networks has resulted in a voracious appetite for feature films. While U.S. sales of series and soaps has declined over the past year, the slack has been taken up by feature film sales, which have always carried a far more premium pricetag than series or soaps.

In terms of administration, RAI is overseen by a Parliamentary commission which elects 10 of its 16 directors. RAI receives its operating authority from the Ministry of Post and Telecommunications; its finances are reviewed by the Ministry of Finance. It is funded by license fees and advertising, although latter is limited to 5% of all airtime.

IVORY COAST

TV Ivorienne, Television House, Latrille, BP 8883, Abidjan. Operates 11 stations. Sets estimated at 450,000.

JAPAN

Non-commercial TV broadcasting began in Tokyo Feb. 1, 1953, by the quasi-governmental Nippon Hoso Kyokai (NHK) followed seven months later by the first commercial TV broadcast of Nippon Television Network (NTV). Broadcast time for NHK, which began with only 866 set-owners paying a fee of Yen 200 monthly, was 4 hours a day compared to 6 hours by NTV, which was affiliated with the Yomiuri newspapers. By 1960 NHK possessed 60 stations and there were 47 commercial stations broadcasting, while the number of sets had increased to about 7 million, topping the 10 million mark two years later.

Although commercial networks as they are established in the U.S. are legally forbidden, there came about a nationwide grouping of commercial stations with the Tokyo stations acting as pivotal points and providing tieups and programs. Thus in 1959, 16 commercial stations formed Japan News Network which soon spread to other programming areas, with JOKR in Tokyo, followed by three other such groupings centering on NTV, Nippon Educational Television (renamed Asahi National Broadcasting in 1977), and the Fuji TV key stations in Tokyo. It was then apparent that several newspapers with national sales systems, through capital tieups, were virtually in control of the national commercial networks.

Educational broadcasts were begun by NHK in 1959, followed three weeks later by Nippon Educational Television, which later dropped the "educational" pretense and became a regular broadcaster, as TV Tokyo (JOTX) did later, when it was found impossible to operate a private educational TV station in Japan for financial reasons.

The Tokyo Metropolitan area, which comprises almost 30% of Japan's population of 122.4 million, is served by Channel 1 NHK general network station, Channel 3 NHK educational network station, Channels 4, 6, 8 and 10 operated by NTV, TBS, Fuji, TV Asahi commercial network stations, respectively, and semi-independent TV Tokyo (JOTX) on channel 12 and TVK (UHF) 42 in Yokohama.

NHK's general programming lists 16 regional stations throughout the nation, 54 local stations and numerous relay stations in the VHF range to bring general programming to 3,493 outlets (2,851 UHF outlets). NHK educational facilities comprise 9 regional stations, 39 local stations, 2,207 relay stations for a total of 3,417 outlets of which 2,778 are UHF, including use of mini-satellite relays. It must be emphasized that in most cases (but not all) the general and educational services make use of the same facilities.

There are 42 companies operating both radio and TV stations and 63 operating only TV stations. In the VHF sector some 48 companies operate 486 stations; in UHF 55 companies operate 5,841 stations, plus 9 SHF stations.

These four "networks" operate in the 8 key areas of Japan—Tokyo, Osaka, Nagoya, Fukuoka, Sapporo, Hiroshima, Sendai, and Hokkaido—which are 4 commercial-station areas (plus NHK). Other stations located in less populous areas use a cross network arrangement by which programs from plural key stations are received. There is Asahi National Broadcasting with 18 stations, Fuji Telecasting with 27, Tokyo Broadcasting System with 25, and Nippon Television with 29 stations. In addition several independent stations have ties and non-commercial NHK covers 30 million of Japan's 37 million households.

While NHK collects monthly fees from 32,133,475 registered sets, the Home Ministry estimates the total number is 62,495,000 (including households with more than one), of which 9,423,000 are black and white and 53,072,000 are color. Some 98.5% of registered households possess one or more color sets for which they are assessed a flat $7.73 a month versus $4.60 for black-and-white sets. Thus, it is no surprise that NHK is by far the wealthiest broadcasting corporation in the world with 16,000 employees, which it has promised to reduce to 15,000, and a 23-story headquarters in Tokyo.

With 29.8% of the national advertising budget, TV is the leading advertising medium with designated prime time from 7:00 to 11:00 p.m. and ad spot buying rates determined on the gross rating point though, with a seller's market, card rates are often disregarded. Top rate for a 60-second network shop is $48,000 and a 54-minute program for a month about $1.4 million; generally contracts are for 6 months but recently 3-month contracts became available, there being waiting lists for sponsors. Sporting events, especially baseball, in non-prime time bring top prices due to good results. Though rules call for not more than 18% of broadcast time be devoted to commercials, this rule is only loosely followed. In addition some stations persist in intensifying audio volume for favored commercials.

Although an agreement was once reached to restrict broadcasting hours to 16.5 a day to conserve energy, commercial stations are broadcasting past the midnight deadline practically 24 hours a day and even NHK now broadcasts past the deadline. While TV is undoubtedly the most influential medium for both young and old, various polls disagree when attempts are made to determine the average daily time a Japanese watches the tube. NHK says the average Japanese spends 2 hours 53 minutes daily (another poll says 3 hours 18 minutes) viewing TV. Nielsen gives the Tokyo viewing time as 8 hours 12 minutes daily, taking into consideration the viewing by each household member. Favorite shows have veered from soap operas to various kinds of emceed shows, especially quiz shows. Men prefer sports shows, including baseball, sumo wrestling, golf, and, recently, American-style football, though old-type samurai dramas are still popular with both sexes. The younger audience spends much time watching cartoons before graduating to teen-age singing shows, contests or quizzes. These imports, especially those from the U.S. tend to be grade B films or films made in America especially for TV. These are almost always dubbed into Japanese but a few are available in the original language on a different wavelength for the benefit of TV sets equipped with multiplex receivers.

Cable TV is still in its infancy, serving only hotels, high class apartment houses and some people with poor TV reception. The Motion Picture Producers Association contracted with CATV operators obligating them to pay $143 per showing of feature films, later to increase as CATV expands. Satellite dish reception began in 1987 when NHK, after previous satellite failure, finally opened a 24-hour service. Twelve CATV operators charge $540 for installation and monthly fees of $25. Thus far NHK's satellite subscribers number 645,000 with 65 percent representing joint reception in apartment buildings. Antenna and tuner for individuals runs $800 for individuals and joint reception $8,000. Japan Satellite Broadcasting, a private firm, says it will offer DBS service in 1990 when it puts its own satellite in orbit.

As for national advertising expenditures, Japanese TV took 29.8% of the total compared to 25.1% by newspapers. The TV share came to some $88.9 billion, up over last year. Food and beverage advertisers comprised 27% of the total followed by autos, 15.4%, cosmetics, 10.3%, pharmaceuticals, 8.5%, service-entertainment, 7.4%, and department stores, 7%.

A survey indicated imported feature films shown on TV cost more than domestic movies but are shown more often so tend to dominate the medium, so it must be assumed their frequency on TV reflects a response to demand, even taking into consideration the reluctance of Japanese movie studios to contribute to the prosperity of what they consider a dangerous competitor to their own industry.

As with the old TV programs purchased from abroad, Japanese buyers insist on rock bottom prices, the result being a formidable collection of full length feature films which, due to their age and caliber, are mostly trash. With few exceptions, they can only be characterized as mixed second- and third-rate. Despite that films are repeated year after year. Once dubbed into Japanese, some Japanese say, it does not make much difference if the film is good or not. Sellers abroad are advised when contracting to provide a special clause on re-runs without compensation.

"Sesame Street" returned to NHK after an absence of 7 years. NHK features very few late movies, specializing in a few movie classics and rare imported family dramas. The commercial stations now rarely feature imported TV shows on prime time, screening a few during daylight hours, and more during late night or very early morning hours when this comparatively cheap filler can be sued. "Alfred Hitchcock Presents" is used by Tokyo TV in prime time, while another network does the same for the "Colombo" series. Picked at random, sitcoms from abroad include: "A-Team," "Surfside 6," "Combat," "Hunter," "Star Trek," "Family Ties," "60 Minutes," "CBS Evening News," "That's Hollywood," "Mike Hammer," and "Twilight Zone." Since these are in both Japanese and English (via multiplex attachment) it would seem that their foreign audience was well served, but alas, 90 percent are shown from midnight on, with only 6% audience viewing.

NKH general stations average 19 hours daily, 37.3% devoted to news and commentaries, 21% to entertainment, 27% to culture, and 14% to education. Commercial stations average 23 hours with entertainment 40.6%, cultural 23.9%, news 16.4%, education 12.1%, sports 5.6% and announcements .6%. Of this broadcasting average, over 23 hours consisted of sponsored programs and 3 hr. of sustaining programs. Although broadcasters claimed that advertising commercials (including a daily average of 241 spot announcements) took only 6% of total broadcasting time of each station on the average, anyone with a stop watch knows that this is not true. Over 60% of Japanese polled indicated an opinion that there were far too many commercials, while 50% objected to the ads shown in conjunction with kiddies' programs and thought such programs should carry no ads.

NHK claims the average viewer watches TV on an average of 173 minutes daily, of which 49 minutes are devoted to NHK programs and with 124 minutes devoted to commercial stations, a slight decrease from the year before but these figures are ridiculed by commercial broadcasters.

Sponsors of a 30-minute prime time show pay about $10,000 on a Tokyo station with other spots going for $4,500 per sponsor.

Production cost for a one-hour program is only $90,000, about one-fifth of the cost in the U.S. Payments for authoring a 30-minute script is $500 at NHK and as low as $200 at commercial stations. However, writers with a national reputation get much more.

A study of 107 commercial TV stations reveals that although the UHF outlets located in the periphery of the large cities are doing only moderately well as regards operating profits, the older-established VHF stations, particularly those affiliated with networks and in Tokyo or Osaka, enjoyed a good year.

Japan exports very few TV programs of its own but it is the world's largest exporter of TV sets and in addition sells TV equipment, complete broadcasting studios and nationwide setups abroad.

While a critic would rate Japanese TV in general as somewhat below the not very high American standard, and take umbrage at the great percentage of time taken by commercials on all stations except those of NHK, the average Japanese is satisfied with it. Lately, the government tried steps to prevent further intensification by stations of audio volume for commercials and limited them to 18% of total program time.

Only 15% of viewers said they were satisfied fully with Japanese TV, says an NHK poll.

Quiz games have the highest average ratings followed by prime time cinema feature films. Then comes sports, samurai or home dramas, action dramas, kiddie and cartoon shows, musical, news, imported TV shows, and finally educational broadcasts.

The baseball craze is such that even high school championship games rate prime time coverage and get a huge audience.

There are no national cable TV systems but cable TV stations feed to 4.3 million households where TV reception is poor or nonexistent. In the cities, cable TV is piped to hotels (usually in English) and to some high-class apartment houses, and to a few private subscribers. In the suburbs some multi-storied housing complexes have their own cable TV. Very few dishes used for satellite reception now exist though the first private satellite broadcasting company promises it will be in full operation by 1990. Since 1985 NHK and private telecasters have had contracts to use Intelsat and a European satellite on a 24-hour basis but ordinarily they take only a few extra bits daily for inclusion on news broadcasts since they are not too interested in outside world news unless it affects Japan. In fact, this is also true as regards imported TV shows; they prefer their own, and imports are shown only on non-prime time and the late night hours.

The addresses of the commercial networks can be obtained from National Association of Commercial Broadcasters in Japan, Bungei Shunjusha Building, 3 Kioi-cho, Chiyoda-ku, Tokyo, All Japan TV Production Companies Assoc., Akasaka White House, 4-1-6 Akasaka, Minato-ku, Tokyo 107, or from Advertising Association of Broadcasters in Japan, 8-10 Nishi Ginza, Tokyo. For non-commercial TV information one should address Nippon Hoso Kyokai (NHK), 2-2-1 Jinnan, Shibuya-ku, Tokyo 150.

—A. C. PINDER

(Longtime correspondent for Quigley Publishing Company, A.C. Pindar died in 1989. Much of the above material was contributed by him before his death.)

JORDAN

Jordan Television Corporation, Post office Box 1041, Amman. 360,000 sets; 12 stations.

KENYA

Voice of Kenya TV, Broadcasting House, P.O. Box 30456, Nairobi. One channel, 275,000 sets.

LIBERIA

Liberia Broadcasting Corporation, Post Office Box 594, Monrovia. One station, 52,000 sets.

MADAGASCAR

Television Madagascar, P.O. Box 442, Tanarive, Madagascar, operates a single station and three relays. 97,000 sets.

MALAYSIA

TV Malaysia was established in 1963 and serves some 1,846,000 sets on an average of 6 hours daily, half of broadcasts are in color. Originating station is at Kuala Lumpur, serving three networks on the main peninsula. One network extends to Sabah, where there is also a secondary station at Kota Kinabalu, which operates a small network of its own, extending to

Sarawak. Inquiries to TV Malaysia (RIM), Broadcasting Dept., Kuala Lumpur 50614.

Malaysia opened its first commercial TV channel TV 3 in December, 1985.

MEXICO

Population: 86,988,000
Number of TV Sets: 15 million, estimated
System Used: NTSC
Number of TV Stations: 12 in Mexico City (7 over-air, 5 cable). Four of the over-air channels and all five cable are run by the privately owned Televisa, under government concession; the other three are run by the government. 29 independent stations around the country.

TV started in 1950.

Principal Broadcasters and Organizations:

Televisa (Channels 2, 4, 5, and 9): Chapultepec, 28, Mexico 06724, D.F. Prez, Emilio Azcárraga; vp, Alejandro Burillo; other top execs, Guillermo Cañedo, etc. Telex: 017-73154; FAX: 709-5920

Instituto Mexicana de Television (Imevisión): Government stations, Channel 7, 13, 22. Periférico sur 4121, Mexico 4141. Pres. is José Antonio Alvarez Lima; other execs are José Ramón Fernandez, Salvador Núñez Sánchez. Telex: 017-73878 TVGO; FAX: 203-1258.

Televisión de la República Mexicana: Government provincial educational network. Guanajuato 125, Col. Roma, Mexico 6.

Government Organizations

Dirección de Radio-Television-Cine: Headed by Oscar Levín Copell. Churubusco Studios. Mexico City. Telex: 1760298 CHURME.

Organización de la Televisión Iberoamericana (OTI): TV federation for most Latin American networks; headquartered in Mexico. Varsovia, 44 Mexico City 6. Secretary, Amaury Daumas; Aide, Dario de la Peña; Telex: 017-71140.

MICRONESIA

Micronesia Broadcasting Corp., Taga Hotel, Saipan, Mariana Islands, comprises two stations broadcasting 16 hours daily on a commercial basis.

MONGOLIA

This Communist bloc nation established Radio-TV Mongolia in 1970 and now consists of two stations with satellite connection with Soviet Russia. Located in Ulan Bator, broadcasting to 64,000 sets.

NEW CALEDONIA

Societé Nationale de Radio-TV, P.O. Box G3 Cedex, Noumea, broadcasts on 4 channels in color to an estimated 50,000 sets.

NEW ZEALAND

Population: 3,100,000
Number of TV Channels: 3
Number of TV Sets: 916,000
Number of VCRs: 405,625

Television came to New Zealand in the early 1960's as a State-owned and operated monopoly. Now deregulation has a foothold as the Broadcasting Corporation of New Zealand replaced itself with two state-owned operations: Television New Zealand and Radio New Zealand. Television New Zealand runs Networks One and Two. TV1 network which originates programs from the Avalon television complex in Lower Hutt (near Wellington), and the TV2 network which originates programs from the Auckland studios. TV1 transmits some 88 hours of programs a week, and TV2 about 71 hours. Five days are commercial. Sundays are non-commercial on each network. Fridays are non-commercial on TV1, and Saturdays non-commercial on TV2.

Locally made programs are estimated at about 3,000 hours annually, which includes drama, news and current affairs, light entertainment, religion, service programs and sports. The balance of program output is purchased from overseas, mainly from Britain (40–45%), the U.S. (48%) and Australia (10%). Use of satellite links permits same-day presentation of world news items and live telecasts, particularly of sports.

1989 will see Network Three, an independent, begin its broadcasting programming with heavy American product. An Australian, Kel Geddes, is Network Three's new president of network programming and has worked out deals with Disney and Touchstone.

Look for an increase in Australian/New Zealand co-productions as barriers to competition fall between the countries.

NIGERIA

Western Nigeria TV Service, Television House, Bompai Road, Kano. Ten stations, 4,486,500 sets.

NORTH KOREA

Experimental telecasting, using Russian equipment since 1960s, followed by establishment of a national network of 20 stations with regional stations and relays. Korean Central Broadcasting Committee, Television Section, Pyongyang, Democratic Peoples Republic of (North) Korea. Sets: 1,050,000.

OMAN

Oman Color TV, Ministry of Information & Culture, P.O. Box 600, Muscat, Oman. Three stations and 1 relay for 151,000 sets.

PAKISTAN

Population: 106 million plus 3.4 million Afghan refugees.

Number of TV Sets: There are 1,504,200 licensed television sets in the entire country. The number of unlicensed sets is said to be more than 40% of the above figure or over 600,000.

Number of TV Stations: Television came to Pakistan in 1964, when the first station of Lahore went on the air. There were hardly 500 sets then. In May, 1967, Pakistan Television Corporation Ltd., a public limited company was formed, all the shares of which are held by the Government of Pakistan, which now runs its five centres in Karachi, Lahore, Quetta, Peshawar and Islamabad. All produce and transmit colour programming, including foreign films for five to seven hours daily. There is, in addition to evening transmission, a regular morning telecast every day except Friday from 7 to 8:15 A.M.

Besides 5 full-fledged production centres, there are 28 transmitters, which cater to the needs of 89 million or 86.4% of the population, versus 56.25% million in 1979. The area under the umbrella of PTV signals has steadily risen from 8,029 sq. km. in 1964 to approximately 295,906 sq. km. in 1988. Transmission via satellite, which commenced in 1972, is now a regular feature and covers important international events, including sports, Haj, holy month of Ramadan, visits abroad of the heads of the State, UN special meetings, reports from various war fronts etc.

Color television came to Pakistan in 1976. To improve the standard and moral tone of TV commercials, the Corporation instituted Best Commercial Awards in 1969. The Corporation also instituted the annual Awards to acknowledge and honour excellence in various professions concerned with television. These Awards have been given every year since 1980. One more Award was introduced in 1988 by organizing a competition between all the five centres, in which viewers vote directly.

PTV exports a good number of its programs to other countries, particularly those where Pakistani and Indian nationals live in large quantity. Lahore, which produces programs in Arabic, exports documentary programs which are also shown in about 500 community centres all over the country.

Training Institute: A Central Training Institute was set up at Islamabad to train program producers and engineering personnel and is undergoing an expansion.

The PTV presents a number of imported programs including feature films every week. The biggest share, 16.39%, was given to foreign feature films and recorded sport events and the least transmission time, less than one percent, was given to domestic feature films during the first half of 1988. Total commercial broadcast time across the nation was 727 hours in 1987/88, as compared to 820 in 83/84. Pakistan manufactured 352,534 sets in 1988. Of these 203,284 were in black & white and remaining 149,250 were in color. The main sources of income for PTV are commercials and license fees of Rs.200 per year for domestic sets and Rs.400 per year for commercial sets. PTV's income from all sources reached a new height of Rs.800 million during the year 1988/89, because of the removal of a number of restrictions including appearance of women in commercials, musical programs for youth, exhibition of Pakistani feature films, etc.

There is no private broadcasting in Pakistan. Pakistan Broadcasting Corporation and Pakistan Television Corporation are owned by the Government of Pakistan.

Trends: Dramatic plays and musical programs are the most popular with viewers. Ever since the democratic, elected Government took office in late 1988, a change has come in programs, particularly in dramas, where a host of once unthinkable subjects, ranging from political prisoners to student violence and from ethnic prejudice to torture, are beginning to emerge on prime time. However, increased political content in plays is not liked by viewers. Pakistani features (once a month) are very popular with viewers, many of whom do not fail to see imported feature films, generally presented late night once a week. Direct telecast of sports, particularly cricket, is the most popular viewer fare.

Principal Broadcasters and Organizations: The Pakistan Television Corporation Ltd., Federal TV Complex, Constitution Avenue, P.O.Box No. 1221, ISLAMA-BAD. Cables: PAKTEEVEE. Telex: RP 5833. It has branches at Karachi, Lahore, Quetta, Peshawar.

—A. R. SLOTE

PHILIPPINES

Population: 60 million
Number of TV Sets: 38% of households have a TV (12% have a color set and 7% have a VCR)
Number of TV Stations: 5 main broadcast channels based in Manila (4 are privately owned); 2 cable systems (1 state-owned in Manila, 1 private in Batangas City)
Trends: Although broadcasts began in 1953, the industry in the Philippines is still at an early stage of development with only 38% of the households having a TV. Yet, viewing levels (5.6 hours per day) are quite high (e.g., in the U.K. and Italy levels average 5.2 and 5.4 hrs per day). Viewing patterns reflect particular characteristics of Filipino life: a large number of people per household and many home-based businesses translate into a noontime viewing rate of about 50% (compared with about 10% in the U.K.).

The main channels based in Manila reach the whole country through a series of replay stations; these stations usually broadcast programs one week after they are seen in the capital. At the start of 1989, ABS-CBN-2 began simultaneous broadcasts to the major cities through satellite links. Most programs are in the national language Filipino (sometimes called Tagalog); television has become a culturally unifying force in this diverse country of 54 ethnic groups and more than 100 languages or dialects. (About 30% of broadcasts are in English.)

The cable business is still small in the Philippines—fewer than 10,000 subscribers as of mid 1989. The state-owned system in Manila, started 10 years ago, has a general entertainment channel and the country's only Chinese language channel. The private system in Batangas City has 1 movie-based channel.

The programs on all four private broadcast channels are similar in content: variety shows and dramas during the day, movies and comedies at night. The state-owned channel ("People's Television" since the 1986 revolution) focuses on public information, talk shows, and sports. Most programs are locally produced; the top imports come from Japan and the U.S.

By Western standards, advertising expenditure is low: $148 million for all media in 1988. But that figure continues to grow; in 1985, the total ad budget was only $80 million.

POLAND

Population: 37.6 million
Number of TV Sets: about 9 million
System Used: SECAM
Number of TV Stations: 2 (supported mainly through a household license fee)

Poland has seven regional studios and 30% of the schedule is broadcast locally with the balance going out nationally. Most popular shows are news and current affairs, followed by features, documentaries, TV theatre, and music. (Theatrical feature films can be transmitted one year after original release.)

Foreign programs make up some 19% of the scheduling; they are acquired either through cash or barter deals. Advertising is permitted and foreign companies can buy time. There is no official censorship, but each station is responsible for what goes over the airways, both in programs and advertising.

Trends: The strong, and as yet untapped, demand for increased program options was illustrated by the growing number of illegal satellite dishes throughout Poland. This phenomenon, along with a booming business in illegal video cassettes, forced Polish Television (POLTEL) to improve its offerings in the past year. As a result, some of the most challenging recent films came from POLTEL.

Polish program options may also increase through a foreign-backed cable network tentatively slated to begin operation in Krakow and Warsaw by the mid 1990s. The partnership would be between PTT (the national telecommunications administration), POLTEL, the Economic Support Foundation, and a service trade co-op of private individuals (Pamit). Foreign capital would come through William Sinkunas of California and his partners. As of early 1989, the plan called for three services offering 19 channels (1) CNN's 24 hour news, Soviet programming, national, European and educational material, 24 hour sports; 2) documentaries, history, education, arts, and nature programs; 24 hour music and movies; 3) Rai Uno, Sky Channel, World Net, Superchannel, French TV and German language stations). Costs would range from $9–16 installation fee and a $5–8 monthly fee, depending on the kind of service ordered. Construction costs were estimated at $47 million for Warsaw and $26 million for Krakow. There were still a number of bureaucratic and technical problems to be ironed out before construction could begin.

PUERTO RICO

Population: 3,282,000
Number of TV Sets: About 750,000
System Used: NTSC
Number of TV Stations: 10 private stations
History of the Industry and Trends: Television started in 1954. By the late 1980s, most public places, such as restaurants and clubs, had television for their patrons; the medium is also available in local hotels upon request. Programming is in English and Spanish (e.g., the largest network has 30% of its programs in English, 10% of which have Spanish subtitles). Kinescope versions of top North American shows are broadcast.

Cable television is growing on the island. The largest operator is cable TV of Puerto Rico, owned by Harris Cable of Los Angeles since 1976. There are currently about 150,000 subscribers. Programming began with only HBO and Virgin Islands stations; there is now a variety of programs from the states and 21 channels in operation.

With TV revenues remaining the same as the 1987 figure of roughly $100 million, the big story in Puerto Rican TV in 1988 was the sale of the major networks. In November 1988, Telemundo (WKAQ, channel 2) fetched $160 million from Reliance Capital Group, an investor group organized by Cohen Cassara & Co. Telemundo has been a leader in the market for years, with a revenue share of 44% in mid 1988. Third-place Tele-Once (WLII-TV) and sister station WSUR in Ponce also changed hands.

One important industry development going into 1989 was a push for people meters in order to obtain more reliable ratings. The $8.8 million price tag over a 5 year period will be split between the stations ($6.8 million) and the ad agencies ($2 million). The operation will be handled by Arbitron.

Local production increased in 1988 led by WAPA-TV (channel 4). The second-place network upped its local product from 4 to 9-1/2 hours a day.

Principal Broadcasters:

WKAQ Telemundo (Channel 2), (now owned by Reliance) GPO Box W, San Juan 00936, Telex 3252774 TELEMUNDO.

WAPA-Televicentro (Channel 4), P.O. Box 2050, San Juan, PR 00936. Station now owned by Pegasus Broadcasting. Telex: 3450245 WAPA.

WSTE Super Siete (Channel 7), Owned by Malrite Communications Group. Small Wood, Parada 8, Old San Juan Station, San Juan PR 00902. FAX: 724-1348.

WKBM (Channel 11), Owned by Lorimar Telepictures Corp. Avda. Condado 657, Santurce, P.R. 00907. Telex 3859511.

WPRV (Channel 13), P.O. Box 31313, Rio Piedras, PR 00929. Broadcasting in English and Spanish. Telex 3252013.

WRWR (Channel 30), Owned by PLD Investments and Bay Broadcasting. Makes only feature films in Spanish. Contact in Miami: 5915 Ponce de Leon Blvd., Coral Gables, FL 33146. Univision affil. In P.R. (809) 724-3030.

WMTJ (Channel 40), Colegio Metropolitano, Universidad de Fajardo, Hato Rey, PR. Also Apartado CUM, Rio Piedras, PR 00928.

WVCO (Channel 44), P.O. Box 919, Quebradillas, PR 00792

Cable TV Puerto Rico, Eleanor Roosevelt Ave. 243, Hato Rey, 00919, P.O. Box 2296.

QATAR

Qatar TV Service (governmental), Ministry of Information, P.O. Box 1836 Doha, Qatar. Color since 1973. One station and relay; 122,000 sets.

SAMOA (AMERICAN)

Three TV stations serve some 42,000 sets on the American part of this Pacific island as well as a number of sets on the part administered by New Zealand. The station is also used daily for educational instructions to local schools. Address: Television of Samoa, Pago Pago. There are six channels.

SAUDI ARABIA

Established 1957, now 56 stations and 2 networks. General Directorate of TV, Ministry of Information, P.O. Box 570, Riyadh, Saudi Arabia; ARAMCO-TV, Box 96, Dhahran, Saudi Arabia. 4 million sets.

SIERRA LEONE

Sierra Leone TV Service, New England, Private Mail Bag, Freetown. One station, 32,000 sets.

SINGAPORE

TV Singapore went on the air in 1963 and now serves an estimated 750,000 sets on four channels in four languages. One channel broadcasts 66 hours weekly the others 40 hours; of this total about 146 hours weekly are in color. Inquiries to Radio-TV Singapore, P.O. Box 1902, Singapore 11. For the fourth consecutive year Singapore Broadcasting Corp. profits dropped-from U.S. $4.36 million to $720,000 most recently.

SOUTH AFRICA

South African Broadcasting Corp., P.O. Box 8606, Johannesburg 2000, started broadcasts in 1976 and now has over 80 stations with four services broadcasting 7 languages over 3 channels to over 3 million sets. From 1978 advertising was accepted.

Associated South West African Broadcasting, P.O. Box 321, Windhoek, Namibia, South West Africa, an autonomous statutory body, broadcasts 6 hours daily from Windhoek.

SOUTH KOREA

Commercial TV broadcasting began in 1956, but the station burned three years later and it was not until 1961 when the government established the Korea Broadcasting Service (KBS-TV) network. The commercial network of Tongyang Broadcasting Co. (TBC) began in 1964 and was followed by the commercial Munwha Broadcasting Co. (MBC) in 1969. The American Forces Korea Network (AFKN-TV) was also established to serve American troops, and now comprises 6 stations.

KBS, which is entirely government-owned and collects a montly fee from each household with a TV set, is somewhat unique since its takes commerical advertising, unlike most governmental networks. Political opponents of the regime are rarely mentioned on broadcasts; this one-sided coverage had led to a boycott by some of the public who refuse to pay fees. KBS also holds a controlling 70% interest in the only other commercial broadcaster, Munhwa Broadcasting Corp. which exists on advertising alone. Under the present regime, other stations were compelled by the government to merge with KBS, except for the Christian Broadcasting System which has been restricted since 1980 to broadcasting only religious programs. The government uses KBS profits from advertising revenues for education scholarships and expenses of newsmen traveling abroad.

KBS-TV has its key station in Seoul and 21 local stations, with other local stations, making a total of 33 TV stations, including those operated by MBC and the former TBC. Color broadcasting started in 1980. Almost 10 million sets are in operation, covering almost every household. If armed forces of USA are counted, the total stations number 33.

Korean broadcasts are limited to 6.5 hours of evening time and 4 hours mornings on weekdays, 11 hours on Saturday and 17 on Sunday. Monthly fees of about $1.00 are collected and advertisements are accepted.

On Saturdays and Sundays between 8 and 9 p.m. it is estimated that 60% or more of the population gathers before their sets to view commercial stations' soap operas, far beyond the average 30% viewing for most shows.

Both KBS and MBC carry some popular U.S. programming, but that field is dominated by the American Forces Korea Network, which primarily serves the large American military population stationed in the country since the Korean War. AFKN does not carry paid advertising.

In 1981 the Republic of Korea "consolidated" all news media and took over the private stations, so daily listings read: KBS-1 TV (7 cities), KBS-2 TV (2), KBS-3 TV-UHF (6), MBC-TV (6). Korean Broadcasting Advertisement Corporation handles all TV and radio advertising.

SPAIN

Population: 38.6 million
Number of TV Sets: 14,870,518

The first time Televisión Española—(now Radio-Televisión Española, RTVE)—transmitted on a regular basis was October 29, 1956, on a scan system of 625 lines at 25 frames per second. That program lasted three hours with a range of 70 kilometres, broadcasting for about 400 sets. The First Channel (VHF) was followed by a Second Channel (UHF) in 1967, complementary at first, but then somewhat competitive and with a clearer trend towards "culture." Channel 1 now covers all of Spain, including the Balearic and Canary Islands. Channel 2 reaches 80% of national territory. According to the Director of Television, Channel 2 has a ceiling of 85% of territory, since the investment costs double when the 70% level of coverage is reached.

RTVE is now an autonomous agency under the Ministry of Culture, Paseo de la Castellana 109, Madrid 16. All programs are controlled by a Censorship Board. Drama, films and episodes of series are classified according to ratings: "general" (no sign on the screen), "older than 14" (a small lozenge), "older than 18" (two small lozenges).

The production of programs is entirely financed by advertising and tie-in merchandising, since the government withdrew its annual subsidy. Both channels carry ad spots. Due to nocturnal habits of Spaniards, the costliest time comes around 10:30 p.m. The ad spots appear on the screen at regular half-hour or one hour intervals, till 7 p.m. Later the spots rhythm accelerates, mainly during feature films in spite of audience and film directors' protests.

Trends: After years of hints and promises, the Spanish government has finally made the prospect of private television a reality. By the beginning of 1990, three new national channels will have commenced operation—in addition to the State-owned RTVE network—along with four new public regional channels.

Under the government's Broadcasting Law, introduced in January of 1989, local TV broadcasting and cable TV will be permitted, as well as the introduction of 1,400 new radio stations.

Most significant, however, is the switchover to private broadcasting, the removal of the RTVE monopoly (although the state collects mandatory fees from the other networks for use of its relay stations, etc.) and the novelty of intense competition for the increasingly lucrative television advertising market.

Until now, RTVE held a broadcasting monopoly, still pulling approximately 91% of all TV advertising. Over the past ten years it has naturally resisted the introduction of private TV, which is estimated to pull 16–32% of all advertising revenues over the next two years. The bulk of this revenue will be at the expense of the national public channels TVE-1 and TVE-2.

Four regional channels have been in operation since 1984, but apart from Barcelona-based TV-3, the other channels have not yet had a significant impact on ad revenues. TV-3 is credited with a 7% share of those revenues.

The four new regional channels, subsidized by regional governments are Canal Sur, which began broadcasting in the Andalucia province in February, 1989; Canal 33 in Catalonia; TV Madrid in the nation's capital; and TV Valencia in the South.

Marking a landmark development, the first three 10-year commercial television broadcasting licenses were awarded in August, 1989 by the Spanish Government. Winning bidders were Antena 3, with an 18% ownership by Tisa (publisher of Lan Vanguardia) and 20% foreign backing; Canal Plus, whose backers include the French pay-TV giant of the same name (25%) and the Spanish media group Prisa, which publishes El Pais; and Tele 5 (Gestevision), which is 25%-owned by Italian broadcasting baron Silvio Berlusconi. Equivalent 25% stakes are held by the publishing group Anaya and the wealthy charitable organization for the blind, Once.

In all cases, government laws permit only a 25% maximum of non-Spanish capital; allow no single person or group to participate in more than one channel; and require that Spanish-originated programs be at least 45% of airtime. European Community members must have a minimum of 40% of all film transmissions, and license-holders must produce at least 15% of their own programming.

In terms of program buying power, the independent regional stations are expected to form a network, which will increase their buying and commercial power, while also increasing the potential revenues to programming suppliers, including the film majors.

Canal Sur is expected to link with ETB (Basque region), TV-3 (Catalonia) and TVG (Galicia) along with the in-progress Valencia and Madrid stations.

Although the competitive effects on RTVE are significant, the state operation still extracts a significant tithe by forcing stations to use its ground booster system. Companies obtaining license franchises must pay $27 million annually for use of the ground link, as well as $27 per hour of airtime. Based on a sliding scale, by 1993–94, each company would have to pay some $2.7 million monthly to the government, plus $329 per hour on the air. Since the advertising pie, while growing to an estimated $2.3 billion in 1988 to an expected $3.44 billiion in 1989, is still finite, it is expected that because of the high payments due the government, not all the new stations will prosper, at least in the initial years.

Regional TV Networks: also exist in the Basque provinces, Cataluña and Galicia. The Basque's Euskal Telebista (ETB) has two channels (one in Castilian, with Basque subtitles; one in Basque) headquartered in Durango and San Sebastian. In Cataluña with a 6 million population, Televisio de Catalunya (TV 3) is the most successful of the regional networks. Broadcasting from the outskirts of Barcelona, its programs are in the Catalan language without subtitles. TBG (Television de Galicia) is the newest network, and regional channels are anticipated in Valencia in 1989 and Andalucia by 1990.

Televisió de Catalunya (TV-3): started broadcasting 1984. Offices and studios in San Juan Despi, outside Barcelona. Director: Enric Canals.

Euskal Telebista (ETB): Basque regional TV, began broadcasting, 1983. Offices in Durango and San Sebastian. Director general: Josie Ortuondo.

Television de Galicia (TVG): Started 1985. Broadcasts from Santiago de Compostela. Director general: Abilio Bernaldo de Quiros.

SRI LANKA

Population: 16.1 million
Number of TV Sets: Approximately 880,000

The Independent Television Network (ITN) completed its first 10 years of operation on April 13th 1989. Although widely considered Sri Lanka's second television channel, ITN preceded the national television network, Rupavahini by a few years.

ITN began telecasts in time for the Sinhala and Tamil New Year, 13th April 1979, as the government made a surprise announcement that television was to be a New Year gift to the people of Sri Lanka. The signal was received by a limited number of viewers initially, while power breakdowns not only interrupted broadcasts but damaged sensitive equipment. In June, 1979, the government acquired the station. ITN is well known for providing viewers with a number of good, foreign programs. The majority of ITN productions are musical shows, merely radio with pictures. ITN provides programs from 6 to 10.30 P.M. daily, and its telecasts can be viewed by people within a range of 75 miles from Colombo.

ITN is likely to be converted into a joint stock company by the end of the year 1989. At present ITN holds the status of a Government-Owned Business Undertaking. The move to broadbase the ownership of ITN was initiated last year by its Competent Authority, Mr. Thevis Guruge. The proposal fell in line with the Government's desire to have government businesses either become fully-fledged corporations or revert to private ownership.

If ITN becomes a joint stock company involving both state and private share capital, Sri Lanka's first television station will benefit from the services of television professionals who are responsible for management and programming. ITN will also be the only television station in the South Asian region to enjoy private participation.

Rupavahini Corporation, the national TV network, was established by the Government of Sri Lanka with an outright gift from the government of Japan to build the studios and TV complex, equipment transmission station and to have its technicians trained by the Japanese, valued at Rs.350 million ($11,666,666). The Rupavahini network commenced its island-wide transmissions on the 5th January 1981. Japan has since given other gifts to construct another fully equipped Television studio and the United States provided helicopters from its Seventh fleet to airlift heavy equipment to the mountain-top transmission station. Rupavahini provides approximately nine hours of transmission daily, which include 2½ hours of local and imported educational telecasting in the morning. The regular television service commences at 5 P.M. on both networks and ends at 11 P.M.

Independent Television Network and Rupavahini are funded by income from sponsored tele-dramas and other commercial spot advertisings, with a percentage of revenue of television licensing, given them by the Government.

There are no private television networks in Sri Lanka. In contrast to India and Pakistan, Sri Lanka's film industry was weak and disjointed, and not entrenched enough to prevent television from becoming an instant success, having an influence few countries in the third world have.

While many call for a revamped TV system, including additional channels and stations one problem is having to cater to a multilingual audience using two television channels. The answer would be to isolate the areas and develop strategies to deal with them. Extra channels, whether private or government, would make the situation better. Sri Lankans have not yet learned to watch TV selectively.

Networks:

Rupavahini Corporation (National TV Network): Chairman: Kumar Abeyasinghe. Address: Torrington Square, Colombo 7, Sri Lanka. Tel: Chairman: 580131; Office General: 580123 to 580136.

Independent Television Network Ltd., Competent Authority: M.D.T.L. Guruge. Address. I.T.N. Studios, Wickremasinghepura, Kotte, Sri Lanka. Tel: 565491.

Sri Lanka Broadcasting Corporation: Torrington Square, Colombo 7, Sri Lanka. Chairman: M.D.T.L. Guruge. Tel: 596439 Office: 597491, 597500

TV Program Producers & Organizations: Telecine Ltd., 43 Hyde Park Corner, Colombo 2, Sri Lanka. Tel: 23909; Teleshan Ltd., 1st Fl, Vogue Bldg, 528 Galle Road, Colombo 3 T.P. 575436; Selacine, 2 Gregory's Avenue, Colombo 7 T.P. 596926.

Liaisoning and Promotion of Production of Television Films, Programs and sales of TV films, for Sri Lanka and Maldives Nepal and Burma:. Chandra S. Perera TV Producer, Director, Cinematographer, and Journalist representing N.B.C. TV News, National Broadcasting Co. of New York, W.T.N.-Worldwide Television News of London, Gamma Press Paris. Address: Telecinex, 437 Pethiyagoda, Kelaniya, Sri Lanka. Tel: 521885, Telex: 21918 Perimr Ce Atn: Chandra Perera; FAX: 547884 Unique Ce Atn: Chandra Perera.

—CHANDRA S. PERERA

SWITZERLAND

Population: 6 million

As of January, 1989, the Federal Post Office registered nearly 2.5 million households in which at least one TV set (mostly color) is operating. As most of the households own more than one set, the estimated number of TV-sets in operation is more than 5 million. The number of transmitters and boosters has increased from 1,330 (1988) to some 1350.

Number of TV Stations: Television was established in Switzerland in 1955. The first color broadcast was in 1970. There is a public broadcaster (Swiss Broadcast Corp.), which provides broadcasting in the languages German, French and Italian, maintaining the correspondent three independent broadcasters in the respective regions. As of January 1, 1989, there are 7 local stations, 6 of them broadcast only part time and test transmissions, 1 of them has a full time program.

Name and Address of the Principal Broadcaster: Swiss Broadcasting Corporation, Giacomettistr. 3, 3000 Berne 15.

Cable TV: is expanding steadily and is now the second highest in Europe. As of January 1989, there were over 2,000,000 subscribers; 68% of them are Swiss Germans, 64% French-language watchers, 54% Swiss Italians. This represents about 87% of all Swiss TV households.

Commercial TV was introduced on a limited basis on February 1, 1965. From November 1, 1985, 23 minutes weekly, only on workdays, were allowed; the cost per minute as of January 1, 1987, was 20,600 Swiss francs. On October 1, 1987, the cost of annual licenses was fixed at 184,80 Swiss francs for private sets. As of December, 1988, 97% of all Swiss households had color TV sets.

Swiss TV watcher's daily TV-sessions: on workdays, Swiss Italians dedicated an average 2 hours and 3 minutes a day to TV-watching, on Sundays an average of 2 hours and 31 minutes; French lingo watchers 2 hours on workdays and 2 hours and 43 minutes on Sundays; and Swiss-Germans 1 hour and 37 minutes on workdays and 2 hours and 25 minutes on Sundays.

Additionally, VCR owners are viewing videocassettes for 1 hour and 18 minutes on workdays and 2 hours and 26 minutes on weekends. An average of 86% of these cassettes are recorded from TV by themselves, only about 14% are rented cassettes. As for TV commercials, the government has decided in June 1989 to augment the daily advertising time from the actual 23 minutes to 28 minutes (on workdays only).

National channels (in German, French and Italian language) are tuned in only 46 minutes a day by Swiss Germans, who prefer foreign channels for the remaining 54 minutes; French lingo watchers tune in a national channel for an average 48 minutes a day and select foreign channels for 73 minutes; Swiss Italians watch national channels for 42 minutes a day (mainly the news) and switch to foreign channels for some 85 minutes of the TV-session.

—GABRIELLA BROGGI

TAHITI

Office of Radiodiff-Television Française, Papeete, operates four channels 34 hours weekly to serve the estimated 24,000 sets of this French possession. It is owned by the government and buys canned programs in Paris.

THAILAND

Thai Television Company (government-owned) opened its first station in 1955 and there are four stations (two using color) and 8 relays on a commercial basis. Stations are also operated under names of Bangkok Broadcasting & TV, Bangkok Entertainment Co. and Mass Communication Organization of Thailand, all located in Bangkok. Sets are estimated at 4 million, some color.

In 1980 a ban on broadcasts from 6:30 to 8:00 p.m., as a power-saving measure, allegedly improved "family relationships," so at present broadcasts are limited to 8 hours on weekdays, and 16 hours on weekends and holidays.

TURKEY

Turkish Radio Television Corp., P.O. Box 98, Kizilay-Ankara serves 5.8 million TV sets via 37 stations.

UNITED ARAB EMIRATES

Established 1969 by Thompson TV International and Abu Dhabi TV Service. In 1971 United Arab Emirates TV Service, P.O. Box 637, Abu Dhabi established separate facilities which now consist of three stations and three relays. Dubai Radio and Color TV, P.O. Box 1695, Kubai, now broadcasts on two channels from 1 station and 1 relay in Arabic, French and English. 147,000 sets.

U.S.S.R.

Population: 280 million
Number of TV Sets: 100 million
System Used: SECAM
Number of Television Stations: 1

History of the Industry and Trends: 1988 was a year of upheaval in the economic and program foundations of Soviet television. The giant government broadcasting agency, Gosteleradio, which beams 4 channels through 15 republics and into 100 million homes, is poised to establish a potentially self-supporting commercial arm, Sovteleexport. This plan is an effort to be more responsive to viewers and more competitive. All activities relating to buying and selling of programs, advertising, merchandising, home-video, the improvement of technical facilities, and coproduction will probably be run out of the new branch. There seems to be an especially keen interest in coproducing Western style entertainment programs, especially dramas and mini-series.

The tides of perestroika and glasnost also facilitated international hook-ups between Soviet viewers and their counterparts in other parts of the world. Ted Turner's broadcast of the Goodwill Games and the serial "Portrait of the Soviet Union" were extremely popular imports. Future international productions are slated with Fries Entertainment and England's Channel 4.

Another important consequence of Soviet political changes is the production of increasingly challenging social and historical documentaries. For example Marina Goldovskaya's "The Solovki Power," examining Gulag labor camps, would have been unthinkable a few years ago. The film played to SRO crowds in Moscow, was broadcast nationally, and went abroad to festivals. The newly organized Riga Video Center is an example of sponsorship for independent and avant garde works. RVC plans to function as an independent video supplier to television stations at home and abroad.

While the Soviet Union remains short of hard currency to purchase foreign television product, coproductions remain the best option to increase international exchange.

Soviet Television (USSR State Committee for Television and Broadcasting), TV Center, 12 Korolyov Street, Moscow, originating all TV programs direct and via satellite.

VENEZUELA

Market: The 1988 market and industry was stable and growing amidst its 18.7 million population. Television penetration reached 2.3 million on the NTSC broadcast system.

Eight national channels exist, with five of them located in the capital, Caracas, and three regionally located. The Caracas channels are Channels 2, 4, 5, 8 and 10. The government controls two channels, 5 and 8, broadcasting on one station. One cable station was established, Channel 12.

The government channels are re-orienting their extensive programming of U.S. production to favor domestic product following radical economic policy changes. The economic changes now make imported product much more expensive at the free-market pricing system.

Stations: Televisora Nacional—Channel 5 & 8, Apt. 3979, Caracas.

Corporacion Venezolana de Television [Venevision] Channel 4, Apt. 6674, Caracas; Av. La Salle, Cns Los Caobos. Tel: 782-4444, 781-1734, 781-9675.

R. Caracas TV [RCTV]—Channel 2, Apt. 2057, Caracas. Tel: 41.89.71, 239-9139, 72.00.85, 239-8518.

Televen—Channel 10. Channel 12 (cable), Edif.

Omnivision, Cl. Milan, L Reces. Tel: 21.01.26, 21.10.89, 256-5912.

—VICTORIA M. MARSHALL

VIETNAM

Since 1968 the Government Information Department of the Democratic Republic of Vietnam has operated one non-commercial station in Hanoi. Number of sets is about 2 million.

A second station was added in Saigon (now known as Ho Chi-Minh City) when South Vietnam was "liberated" and the divided country became one.

Hanoi has initiated use of a Russian satellite and 7 hours of color telecasts on weekdays and all day Saturday and Sunday, compared with the previous 4 hours a day in black and white.

WEST GERMANY

TV Households: Out of approximately 25.6 million German households, 26.5 million TV sets are registered with an estimated viewership of some 47.5 million.

Market and Trends: West Germany's two state-owned networks—ARD and ZDF—saw their long-held monopoly further eroded in the past year, as competition from the country's four privately owned national TV services soared.

Trends: With the opening of private, advertising-supported TV, West Germany has become the fastest-growing offshore market for U.S. television product (and feature films for TV).

In addition to the advantages of satellite-to-cable distribution enjoyed by Sat-1, RTL Plus, Tele 5 (which started operations in 1988) and Pro 7, the newcomers gained a further foothold by being allotted terrestrial frequencies, while cable potential continues to grow.

While ARD and ZDF remained flat in their revenues, Sat-1 and RTL Plus made spectacular gains in advertising gross revenues last year. Overall TV ad spending rose from 2.053 billion marks in 1987 to 2.344 billion marks in 1988, an increase of 14%.

These figures indicate that satellite-to-cable commercial services, while still not entirely in the black, are here to stay and pose a definite threat to the public broadcasters. While the private companies may reach a break-even situation in 1990, the public broadcasters can at least count on the fact that a fixed 60% of their income remains guaranteed in the form of monthly set fees.

Out of the 10 million homes passed by cable in West Germany, 4 million are actually hooked up to a service, up from a 30% penetration in 1987.

The Federal Office of Post and Communications in Bonn is responsible for the technical side of the TV medium, while the nation's 11 states, which under the constitution are allowed to formulate their own media policy, have supervisory TV and cable boards.

YEMEN (Arab Republic)

San'a Television, Ministry of Information, San'a, established in 1977, currently broadcasts on 3 channels to some 120,000 sets.

YEMEN (People's Republic)

Established in 1964, People's Democratic Republic of Yemen, P.O. Box 1264, Aden, broadcasts on 3 channels to an estimated 55,000 sets.

ZIMBABWE

Established in 1960 as Rhodesia TV, and now named Zimbabwe Broadcasting Corp., P.O. Box H.G. 200, Highlands, Harare, its 6 stations serve some 560,000 sets.

Home Video

Statistics & History

Freedom of choice—the control of one's own viewing habits—has been the major impact of home video on the leisure-time industry in America. Owners of videocassette recorders can view what they want when they want and are no longer subject to the programming schedules of the television networks and cable stations. The VCR owner is able to watch yesterday's motion pictures today (by renting or owning vintage Hollywood films, foreign features and television product, as well as films released theatrically as recently as six months ago) and today's television programming tomorrow—along with how-to tapes, music videos and home movies.

Time shifting, the ability of the viewer to tape a show for later viewing (as well as eliminating commercials—by editing them out or fast forwarding past them), is the most common usage of VCRs. One can watch one program while taping another, or tape with the tv set off and nobody home. One can select entertainment or instruction from the more than 50,000 prerecorded tapes now available from the more than 30,000 video specialty stores, supermarkets, hardware stores and libraries. There are more than 40 brands of VCRs with 150 models now available, offering electronic tuner-timers and such special effects as freeze-frame and forward-reverse picture scan as basic features and such extra options as wireless remote control, variable slow and fast motion, on-screen function display and full stereo sound. Home video has had a revolutionary effect on the entertainment habits of the nation.

Video History

1923: Though the patent for a video-camera-like device was filed in Germany one hundred years ago, the first practical product was devised by Vladimir Zworykin, a Russian/American immigrant in 1923.

1938: A primitive video disk was on sale at Selfridges of London.

Post World War II: With the development in the early 1930s of an electronic television signal and the audio tape recorder, and their coming into broadcast use in the mid-1940s, it was not long before experiments (by Ampex and RCA in the US, and BBC and Decca in Great Britain) in recording television shows and playing them back were made in earnest. Freeing directors to edit or re-shoot, and attempting to loosen the stranglehold live television broadcasting imposed on the medium, the first recorders were longitudinal machines that looked like audio recorders and used large reels of tape at high speeds.

Early 1955: BBC went on the air with its VERA (Vision Electronic Recording Apparatus) with a head gap of 20 microns and a tape speed of 200 inches per second. A reel about 5 feet in diameter was needed for taping a half-hour program.

April 1956: An American company, Ampex, produced the first working video recorders for broadcast use, using four (quad) recording heads on a rotating drum, and two-inch wide magnetic tape which was reusable. They were first used over the air at CBS's Hollywood studios in November, 1956. (A more portable system using narrower tape and a helical scan system had been patented in Germany in 1953, but the prototypes were far too expensive and difficult to use; a tape could be used only once, and each time it was used the machine had to be cleaned of tape particles.)

1967: A Japanese company, Sony, introduced the first transportable video system which used reel-to-reel tape and recorded in black and white only.

1970: Home video arrived when the first video cassette systems were produced, in the Philips Video Cassette Recorder or VCR. (Philips had also developed and licensed the compact audio cassette.) Sony introduced its ¾-inch U-Matic format intended for professional use in the film and television industries.

1972: Philips launched its N1500, the first video recorder with a tuner-timer, making domestic video recording a reality.

The simple video game, the first interactive use of the television, was introduced into viewing households, altering perception of the TV screen from one of passive reception of broadcast programs to participation.

Late 1975: Sony introduced the Betamax system, utilizing narrower 1½-inch tape (the narrower tape size resulted in lowered costs of recording and recorders). An optional timer was included to enable a viewer to tape even when he was not at home and offered the capability of recording one program while watching another. The cost was approximately $2,200 for a recorder with TV set. Blank tape cost $20.

1976: Cartrivision, V-Cord, and VHS (Video Home System) introduced systems incompatible with Betamax machines. The first two fell by the wayside while VHS (backed by Matsushita Electronics Corporation) emerged as the challenger to Sony's Betamax by making it possible to record up to 2 hours of broadcast material for the first time. Magnavox came out with a videodisc machine, strictly a playback system which used a disc similar in size and substance to a record album that is "read" by a laser beam. RCA manufactured a rival, incompatible videodisc system.

1977: The video software market was born when a small midwestern company called Magnetic Video Corporation licensed 50 feature-length films from 20th Century-Fox and released them for sale on Beta and VHS formats at retail prices of $49.95 to $79.95.

1983: Paramount Pictures paved the way for burgeoning cassette sales when it lowered the price of some of its strongest titles to $39.95 from $79.95. Other prerecorded cassette distributors soon followed suit.

Jan. 1984: United States Supreme Court, after lengthy consideration of a suit brought by MCA Inc. and Walt Disney Productions against Sony, ruled that home taping of broadcast programming is not a violation of copyright laws, in effect legitimizing what viewers were already doing.

1984: The FCC approved the start of Multi-Channel TV Sound Broadcasting, adding stereo sound to the home video experience.

May 1987: Super-VHS or S-VHS (with an expanded band width of up to 5.5 megahertz thus increasing the sharpness of picture image, and 400 lines of horizontal resolution as opposed to conventional VCR's 240) made its debut at the Consumer Electronics Show in Chicago.

Another innovation was the introduction of 5-inch CD Video singles at a $7–8 list price, that can hold up to 20 minutes of recorded music videos.

1988: The era of "personal video" was ushered in when Sony introduced the Video Walkman, a hand-held, ultra-compact combination of 8 millimeter VCR with a 3 inch flat-screen color television set. No larger than a VHS videocassette or paperback book, and weighing about 2½ lbs, the Video Walkman operates on AC, Battery or 12-volt. Matsushita Electronic Industrial Co. followed with its own 3-lb personal videocassette recorder-television which uses VHS-C tape instead of Sony's 8mm.

Sony also unveiled its Hi8, an 8mm camera-recorder and editing deck which produces an extra-high quality picture. It can play and record conventional 8mm tapes but recordings on Hi8 cannot be played on older 8mm equipment.

RCA/Columbia Pictures Home Video was the first home video manufacturer to release closed-captioned video cassettes for the hearing impaired.

Three feature films ("Julia and Julia," "Crack in the Mirror" and "Do It Up") as well as a made-for-television movie ("Innocent Victims") were shot using HDV, high definition video, then converted to 35mm using a tape-to-film transfer process which converts the tape's thirty pictures per second to twenty-four frames per second on film. Though unwieldy (HDV must be hooked up to a video tape recorder by means of cables) and with a lower ASA rating than film, this new technology is a step in breaking down the traditional barriers between film and video.

Trends: 1989

- In 1986 the media coined a new term, "couch potato," to describe those who enjoy staying at home and watching TV or a VCR as their pastime of choice. This trend is borne out in the fact that in 1988, while theatrical exhibition grossed $4.4 billion, the home video market (including the sale and rental of videocassettes) generated $3.5 billion according to a Cambridge Associates Survey. With the record-breaking sales of "E.T. The Extra-Terrestrial" (over 15 million tapes sold by the end of 1988 priced at $24.95 retail and $15 wholesale) returning more than $175 million to MCA followed by the success of "Cinderella" (over 7 million tapes sold by the end of 1988 at a list price of $29.95) the sell-through market came into its own in 1988.

During the 1988 holiday season from November 1 to mid-January, a record number of videocassettes were sold: 40 million units bringing in $740 million in sell-through sales (a 16% increase from the same period in 1987). According to a survey by Alexander & Associates cassette prices fell 62 cents in 1988 to an average of $18.69.

Despite the growth of sell-through, rentals continue to be the mainstay of the video industry, the source of 80% of retail sales in specialty stores.

- A continuing trend was the commercial sponsorship of videocassettes, with ads for Diet Pepsi prefacing the top-selling "Top Gun" videotape as the groundbreaker in early 1987. By the end of 1988 only 14 commercials have appeared on major video releases and some such as the Schweppes ad on the "A Fish Called Wanda" video attempted a witty spoof of such advertising to pacify any inate viewer hostility to the intrusion. Much more common, however, is tie-in sponsorship such as Walt Disney Home Video's partnership with Procter & Gamble and Coca-Cola utilizing sweepstakes, cross-promotional media buys, rebates and in store merchandising displays rather than commercials on the actual videocassette. Similar was Pepsi-Cola's tie-in with MCA Home Video's release of "E.T. The Extra-Terrestrial."

In an unusual joint cross-promotion, the U.S. Postal Service announced plans to market 4 commemorative dinosaur stamps on MCA Home Video's "The Land Before Time."

- On the legal front two restrictive laws threatened video retailers. The Child Protection & Obscenity Enforcement Act or Parental Leave Bill commonly called the Meese Bill which became effective November 19, 1988 makes possession with intent to distribute obscene matter a federal crime. The Act makes it illegal for a person to travel in interstate commerce or use facilities of interstate commerce "for the purpose of transporting" obscene matter. It also requires that anyone who "produces" (which includes copying) a video tape or record album cover containing a visual depiction of sexually explicit conduct, must keep records on every person appearing, showing their names and dates of birth, and must place a statement on each sexually explicit item, describing where these records are kept.

The Missouri Violence Law, House Bill 225, prohibits video retailers from renting "violent" videocassettes to minors and requires that "violent" programs and their promotional materials be kept in a separate part of the store designated off-limits to those under age. At the time the bill was to go into effect, August 28, 1989, the Video Software Dealers Assn. was preparing to file suit against the law. Similar bills are pending in Ohio and North Carolina.

On the other hand, video retailers practiced their own form of censorship in 1989 with Blockbuster Video, the nation's second largest video store chain and others deciding not to stock the video of Martin Scorsese's controversial film "The Last Temptation of Christ."

- Pay-per-transaction, a video tape leasing deal in which video stores pay about $8 per copy, rather than the standard purchase price of about $63 was a hotly debated topic in 1989. In exchange for the low leasing cost, stores would agree to split the rentals with the program supplier instead of the current system whereby the retailers keep all rental income. Orion Home Video concluded a year-long test of the P-P-T system but reached no decision on whether to continue it.

  A related development, was Alfredo Leone and Joel Snyder's invention of a system that counts how many times a video tape has been played. Licensed to Simplon Resources Ltd., the play-counting system would give studios, producers and distributors the data needed to potentially collect a royalty fee for each showing of a video. Playcount Co., an Australian company also has a video-play counter system that is backed by Capital Cities/ABC Video Enterprises.

- In 1989 Go-Video, manufacturer of the prototype VCR-2, a two-deck videocassette player with the ability to duplicate tapes, agreed to a cash settlement in its antitrust suit against 3 Japanese and Korean VCR manufacturers. Allaying MPAA fears that the machines would result in unauthorized duplication and copyright infringement, the company promised to add anticopying circuitry to the machines which would "read" a special coding on the tapes that copyright holders wished to protect. With a distribution agreement in place, the VCR-2 VCRs which enable a viewer to duplicate a recorded tape and to watch a tape while recording another, are anticipated to be in retail stores by Christmas, 1990.

- On the technological front, Rank Video Services America developed a videocassette that self destructs after a limited number of plays. Molded in green plastic to differentiate it from the usual black, the disposable tapes erase themselves and cannot be rerecorded on. MGM/UA announced plans to test-market the new videocassettes which would allow retail outlets to stock greater depth of copy of hit films as the cost to the retailer of disposable videos would be $30 instead of the average $60 per tape.

- Automation entered video retailing with the use of automated video rental machines. Fitting into a videostore window Automated Merchandise Concepts' Automated Movie Club, utilizes a computerized tape management system which enables unattended video rental and sales transactions on a 24-hour basis. Moreover, Bert Tenzer's Advanced Video Robotics Corp. hopes to replace video stores with videocassette-dispensing machines manned by an automated "Vidirobot 2001." Bringing the source of tapes closer to the consumer, the Vidirobot units would be placed in apartment lobbies, workplaces, convenience stores.

- Metaview Corp. introduced a combination VCR-personal computer-"artificial intelligence," the SmarTV system, which automatically tapes all shows a viewer might be interested in. It then plays back anything the viewer chooses from the list without the viewer touching any tape or the VCR itself. Another feature of SmarTV allows the viewer to zip past commercials at the rate of 1 second for every 30-second ad. Eventually it could be programmed to automatically delete all commercials at the viewer's request. With an initial sale price of $6,000, SmarTV is projected to sell for less than $1,000 in 2–3 years. A monthly service charge would be in the neighborhood of $5.
- Though many "A" videos were priced at $89.95, up from $79.95, they dropped in price to an average $29.95 after their first exposure on cable TV (usually in six months).

  Many sell-through videos, however, such as the record-breaking "E.T.: The Extra-Terrestrial" and "Cinderella" debuted at a list price of $24.95 and $29.95, respectively. In May, 1989 Paramount Home Video announced a "Sweet 15" promotion of top titles including "Beveraly Hills Cop," and 4 "Star Trek" movies at a $14.95 retail price (limited to a secondary sell-through window of a year or more after initial release.). HBO Video offered several packages of $14.99 videos. Disney followed with a drop in retail price to $12.99 for 44 non-theatrical animated features, eliminating the former $14.95 price point. Of the top-selling videos of 1988 the top seven all were priced at $29.95 or lower.

Facts and Statistics

- While the Japanese and Koreans dominate the hardware market of the video industry, American producers, distributors, and marketers and retailers fill the programming needs of the ever expanding industry.
- Estimates regarding the number of United States TV households that currently own a VCR vary from 61% (E.I.A.) to 67.3% (Aribritron Co.) (with Anchorage VCR penetration estimated at 84%; Fairbanks, 79%; Las Vegas, 74%; L.A., 72%; Chicago, 70%; and New York, 69%). An estimated 1 out of every 5 VCR households also owns a second VCR.
- Electronic Industries Association (E.I.A.) figures show that 12.8 million VCRs were sold in to dealers 1988, while 13.306 million were sold in 1987. The E.I.A. calculates that an estimated 135 million prerecorded videocassettes were sold to dealers in 1988 (up from 110 million in 1987).
- Estimated sales of prerecorded videocassettes increased in dollar sales to $2.97 billion and unit sales to 135 million in 1988 and were expected to rise again in 1989 to 145 million units worth $3.19 billion; blank videocassette sales rose to an estimated 297 million units sent to dealers.
- While table model and portable VCR sales declined, camcorder sales (increasing 25% annually since their introduction) rose in 1988 to 2.04 million up from 1.6 million in 1987.
- The top selling home video titles for 1988 were E.T.: The Extra-Terrestrial (MCA 15 million copies at $24.95); Cinderella (Disney 7.2 million at $29.95); 34-title Disney Holiday Promotion (4.1 million at $29.95 and $14.95); 20-titles Disney Summer promotion (2.5 million at $29.95 and $14.95), Good Morning, Vietnam (Disney 2.2 million at $29.95); Dirty Dancing (Vestron; 1.7 million at $89.95 and $29.99); Jane Fonda's Start-Up (WHV; 780,000 at $19.95); Three Men and a Baby (Touchstone; 535,000 at $89.95); Beverly Hills Cop II (Paramount; 500,000 at $89.95); Fatal Attraction (Paramount; 485,000 at $89.95) as reported by The Hollywood Reporter.

- Internationally, the video industry experienced considerable growth. A 1989 study by the London-based media research journal Screen Digest estimated that the total number of video households worldwide will be 187.32-million by the end of 1989, a global penetration of ⅓ of all television homes. Anticipated VCR sales will reach 38.7 million units (of which 14-million will be sold to homes already owning video equipment), an 8.7% increase over 1988. The estimated number of VCR homes in Japan is 24.1 million, a 79% penetration rate. The United Kingdom will have 13.3 million VCR households, 69.5% of homes with TVs.

  According to a survey by Paul Kagan & Associates, videocassette sales were up 26% in the top foreign markets in 1988 yielding $6.8 billion ($1.1 billion of which is returned to program producers.) The United Kingdom with $920 million in sales, Germany ($829 million), Japan ($751 million) and Canada ($480 million) continue to be the most profitable foreign territories.

- The major video distributors, which include the seven major movie studios and nine independent suppliers, earned $1.9 billion in wholesale revenue from the 427 titles they released on video in 1988 (a 60% increase in revenue and a 52% increase in number of titles released from 1987), according to a study conducted by Nelson Entertainment. Nearly 80% of those earnings came from ⅓ of the titles—those with the largest theatrical box office of $10 million or more.

  On the other hand, the average yield per tape of those 427 titles was $3.7 million wholesale, a 10% decline from per title income in 1987.

- The made-for-video industry grew in 1988 accounting for $730 million on sales of 40 million units in 1988, a 22% increase over 1987 sales figures according to the Fairfield Group.

  With an average production cost of between $40,000 and $100,000, a non-theatrical video priced to sell at less than $30 can easily break even with 6,000 sales. With exposure not only at video stores but in non-traditional outlets such as sporting goods shops and toy stores and in specialty catalogues, the made for video industry since its early hits "The Making of Michael Jackson's Thriller" and the Jane Fonda work-out tapes, is experiencing unabated growth.

- VCRs are owned by 80% of households earning $35,000 or more, 75% of two-income families, and 74% of households headed by executives according to the Roper Organization. Regionally, VCR ownership is highest in the West (65%), and Northeast (64%) with the Midwest (54%) and South (51%) following.

  The number of hours that VCR owners actually recorded declined since 1985. Then they recorded a median of 2½ hours of TV programs each week down to less than 1 hour and 20 minutes during an average week in 1988. Feature films and sports are still the most frequently recorded types of program. (Roper Org.).

- Six billion hours of prerecorded video were watched per year as compared to 221 billion hours of broadcast TV watched per year (Fairfield Group, 1988).
- An AGB research study from April, 1988 indicated that children under 18 spend an average of 50% more viewing time than adults watching prerecorded and home-recorded video tapes in VCR households. Those under 18 watch 3.4 hours per week while adults average 2.3 hours/week.
- In 1988 the average household used the VCR to time-shift an average of 2 hours, 22 minutes per week according to Nielsen Media Research. Its survey showed the highest time-shift usage was in February at 2 hours and 58 minutes and lowest in July at 1 hours, 50 minutes.
- In 1987 VCRs were used an average of 7 hours/week per household with 2.4 hours devoted to recording programs and 4.7 hours used playing prerecorded and home-recorded tapes. Some 49% of the 7 hours

per week of VCR usage were spent playing rented or purchased tapes, 17% playing home recorded material. Twenty-three % was spent recording when the television was off or tuned to another channel while 10% was spent recording the same program the viewer was watching. The AGB Television Research Study (released March, 1988) showed VCRs are more prevalent in pay-cable households (64%) than basic cable and non-cable homes (48% each). Of families with children under 18, 65% have VCRs while 48% of households without children do.

The same study found 40% of all home recordings are made in primetime, 31% in daytime. Sunday night has more recording (26%) than any other night, while Saturday is the preferred night for playback. (23%)

- In its annual membership survey, the American Video Association found that 52% of the 225 stores polled reported an increase in rental business in 1988 with even greater growth expected in 1989. 23% reported no change in business while 25% reported a drop in rentals.

Average rental price increased to $2.24 (up from $2.22 in 1987) and the average number of titles stocked increased in 1988 to 2,400 from 2,200.

Net sales were up 61%. About 90% of the video stores reported that they sell new, prerecorded tapes at an average rate of 19 per month and 94% said they sell 20 used tapes per month. 63 blank tapes were sold per month.

Of the stores questioned, 60% are computerized.

DEMOGRAPHICS OF CURRENT VIDEO TAPE RENTERS
As of February 1988

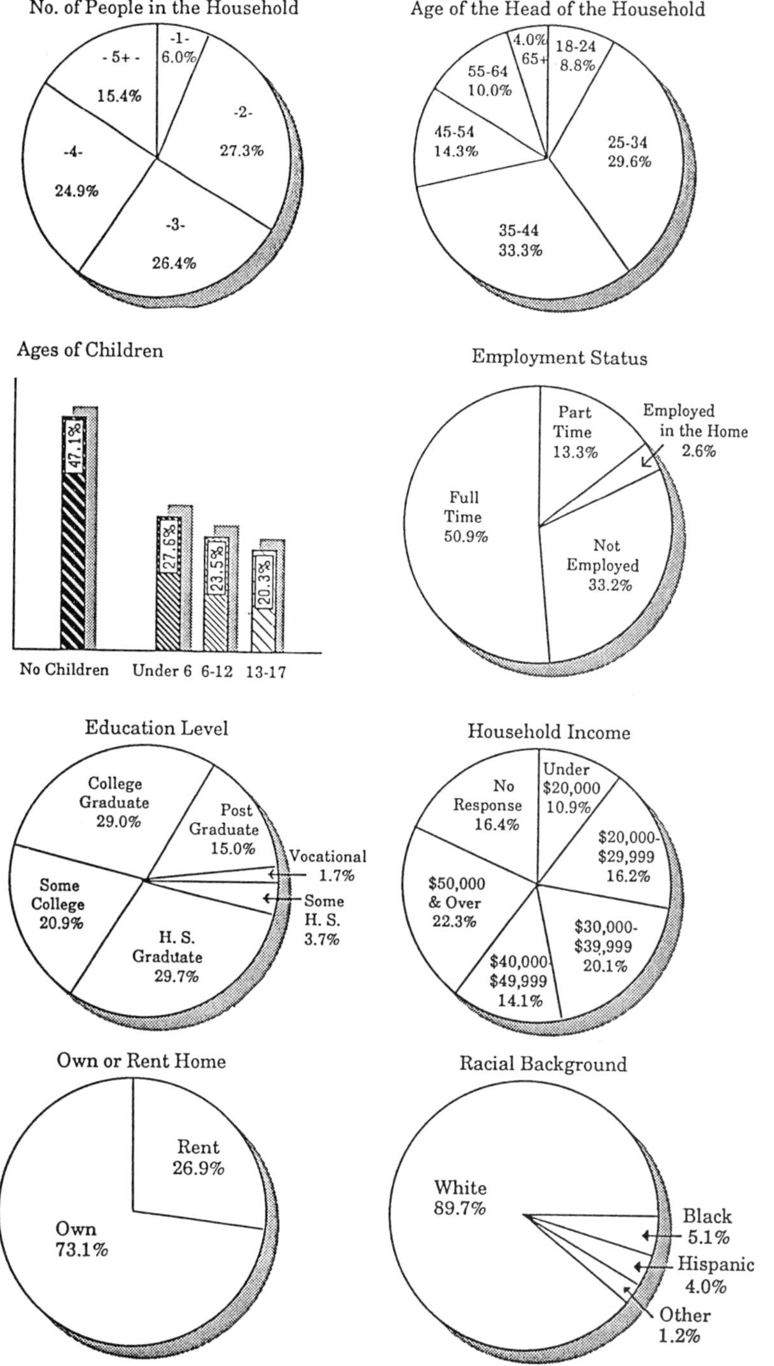

SOURCE: American Video Association

DEMOGRAPHICS OF PRE-RECORDED TAPE BUYERS

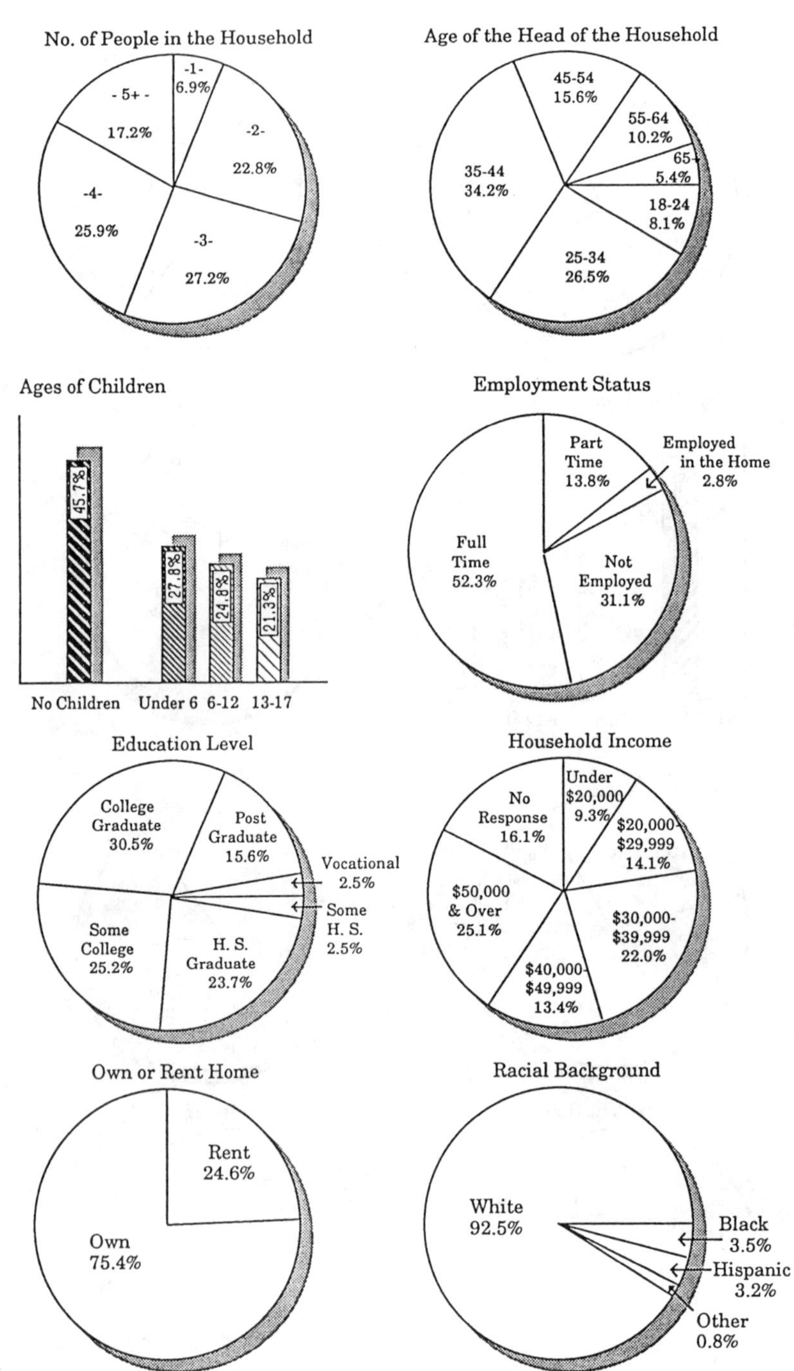

SOURCE: American Video Association

DEMOGRAPHIC CHARACTERISTICS
(As of February 1988)
Classified by VCR Owners and Non-Owners

No. of People in the Household		Owners	Non-Owners
	One	46.2%	53.8%
	Two	64.4%	35.6%
	Three	81.7%	18.3%
	Four	84.6%	15.4%
	Five	82.7%	17.3%

Ages of Children		Owners	Non-Owners
	No Children	64.2%	35.8%
	Under 6	80.6%	19.4%
	6 – 12	84.0%	16.0%
	13 – 17	84.5%	15.5%

Age of the Head of the Household		Owners	Non-Owners
	18 – 24	67.1%	32.9%
	25 – 34	80.6%	19.4%
	35 – 44	87.1%	12.9%
	45 – 54	74.6%	25.4%
	55 – 64	59.5%	40.5%
	65 & Over	39.6%	60.4%

Marital Status		Owners	Non-Owners
	Single	69.0%	31.0%
	Married	77.0%	23.0%
	Wid/Div/Sep	55.0%	45.0%

Own or Rent		Owners	Non-Owners
	Own	75.4%	24.6%
	Rent	65.6%	34.4%

Household Income		Owners	Non-Owners
	Under $20,000	49.0%	51.0%
	$20,000 – $29,999	70.9%	29.1%
	$30,000 – $39,999	79.4%	20.6%
	$40,000 – $49,999	87.8%	12.2%
	$50,000 & Over	89.0%	11.0%

Employment Status		Owners	Non-Owners
	Full-Time	83.4%	16.6%
	Part-Time	78.8%	21.2%
	Not Employed	60.4%	39.6%
	Emp. in the Home	69.6%	30.4%

Education Level		Owners	Non-Owners
	Some H.S. or less	45.6%	54.4%
	H.S. Graduate	70.1%	29.9%
	Some College	71.8%	28.2%
	College Graduate	80.0%	20.0%
	Post Graduate	80.2%	19.8%
	Vocational School	62.5%	37.5%

Racial Background		Owners	Non-Owners
	White	73.2%	26.8%
	Black	60.0%	40.0%
	Hispanic	84.6%	15.4%
	Oriental	57.1%	42.9%
	Other	66.7%	33.3%

SOURCE: American Video Association

VIDEOCASSETTE RECORDERS

	Total Sales to Dealers in Units (Thousands)	Total Factory Sales in Dollars (Millions)	Average Value (Dollars per Unit)
VIDEOCASSETTE RECORDERS (Table and Portable Only)			
1986	12,005	3,978	331
1987	11,702	3,442	294
1988	10,748	3,117	290
1989 (est.)	10,100	2,930	290
1990 (est.)	10,000	2,950	295
VIDEOCASSETTE RECORDERS WITH MTS (Built-In Stereo Capability) (Included in Table 9)			
1986	n/a	n/a	n/a
1987	n/a	n/a	n/a
1988	1,400	581	415
1989 (est.)	1,700	690	405
1990 (est.)	1,950	780	400
CAMCORDERS			
1986	1,169	1,280	1,095
1987	1,604	1,651	1,029
1988	2,044	1,985	971
1989 (est.)	2,500	2,350	940
1990 (est.)	2,800	2,520	900
TOTAL VIDEOCASSETTE RECORDERS (Sum of Tables 9 and 11)			
1986	13,174	5,258	399
1987	13,306	5,093	383
1988	12,792	5,102	399
1989 (est.)	12,600	5,280	419
1990 (est.)	12,800	5,470	427

n/a—not available

SOURCE: Electronic Industries Association

OTHER VIDEO PRODUCTS

	Total Sales to Dealers in Units (Thousands)	Total Factory Sales in Dollars (Millions)	Average Value (Dollars per Unit)
VIDEODISC PLAYERS*			
1986 (est.)	85	26	300
1987 (est.)	100	30	300
1988 (est.)	120	40	333
1989 (est.)	180	65	360
1990 (est.)	215	75	350

*Non-commercial.

	Total Sales to Dealers in Units (Thousands)	Total Factory Sales in Dollars (Millions)	Average Value (Dollars per Unit)
VIDEOCASSETTE PLAYERS			
1986 (est.)	150	26	175
1987 (est.)	160	26	165
1988 (est.)	170	30	175
1989 (est.)	190	33	175
1990 (est.)	205	36	175
HOME SATELLITE EARTH STATIONS			
1986 (est.)	375	750	2,000
1987 (est.)	250	625	2,500
1988 (est.)	275	655	2,380
1989 (est.)	275	550	2,000
1990 (est.)	300	570	1,900
BLANK VIDEOCASSETTES—Sales to Consumer Distribution			
1986	296,253	1,235	N/A
1987	273,830	1,006	N/A
1988*	296,947	936	N/A
1989* (est.)	305,000	1,000	N/A
1990* (est.)	315,000	1,025	N/A

*includes VHS, VHS-C, 8mm and Beta; prior to 1988, data includes VHS and Beta.
N/A—not applicable

	Total Sales to Dealers in Units (Thousands)	Total Factory Sales in Dollars (Millions)	Average Value (Dollars per Unit)
PRERECORDED VIDEOCASSETTES			
1986 (est.)	75,000	2,100	28
1987 (est.)	110,000	2,770	25
1988 (est.)	135,000	2,970	22
1989 (est.)	200,000	4,200	21
1990 (est.)	260,000	5,500	21

SOURCE: Electronic Industries Association

TOTAL FACTORY SALES OF
SOFTWARE PRODUCTS

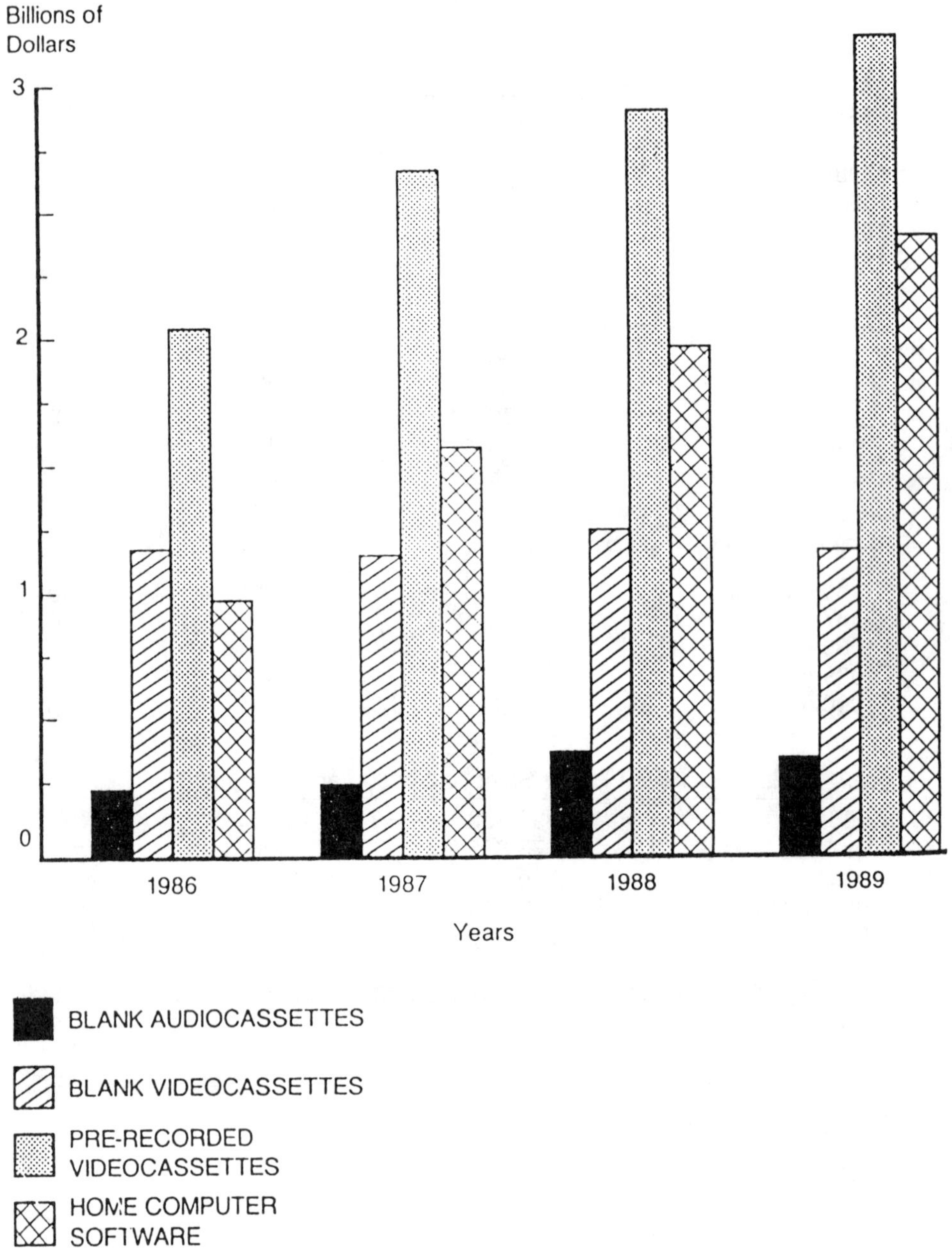

Billions of
Dollars

3

2

1

0

1986 1987 1988 1989

Years

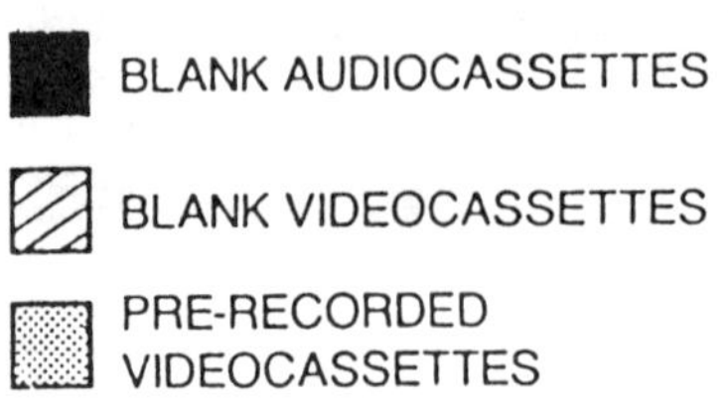

SOURCE: Electronic Industries Association

Home Video Companies

* **PRODUCTION COMPANIES**
* **WHOLESALE DISTRIBUTORS**

Home Video Companies

ABC Distribution Company

(A division of Capital Cities/ABC Video Enterprises, Inc.)

825 Seventh Ave., New York, NY 10019; (212) 887-1725. NY FAX: (212) 887-1708; CA FAX: (213) 557-7925. Organized 1986. (1979 under parent co.). (Licenses theatrical and television rights to movie exhibitors and television stations internationally. Licenses television and theatrical product to home video and cable distributors worldwide. Produces, co-produces and develops programming for domestic and international distribution.)

PRESIDENT
John T. Healy
SENIOR VICE PRESIDENT
Archie Purvis
DIRECTOR, CASSETTE/CABLE MARKETING
Marvinia Hunter
DIRECTOR, INT'L SALES
Armando Nunez, Jr.
DIRECTOR, THEATRICAL SALES
June Shelley
BRANCH
2040 Ave. of the Stars, Century City, CA 90067; (213) 557-6600; FAX: (213) 557-7925.
AFFILIATION
A division of Capital Cities/ABC Video Enterprises.

ABC Video Enterprises

2040 Ave. of the Stars, Los Angeles, CA 90067; (213) 557-6600; FAX: (213) 557-7925. Subsidiary of American Broadcasting Co., Inc.

PRESIDENT
Herb Granath
PRESIDENT, ABC DISTRIBUTION CO.
John T. Healy
SENIOR VICE PRESIDENT, ABC DISTRIBUTION CO.
Archie Purvis
VICE PRESIDENT, PROGRAM ACQUISITION & DEVELOPMENT
Paul D. Coss
DIRECTOR, WORLDWIDE CABLE/CASSETTE SALES
Marvinia Hunter

A.I.P. Home Video, Inc.

10726 McCune Ave., Los Angeles, CA 90034; (213) 559-8849; FAX: (213) 559-8849. (Affiliate of Action International Pictures Inc.)

PRESIDENT
Eric Parkinson

A & M Video

1416 N. La Brea Ave., Hollywood, CA 90028; (213) 469-2411.

V.P., BUSINESS DEVELOPMENT
Milton E. Olin, Jr.
DIRECTOR VIDEO SALES AND MARKETING
Steve Macon

A M Productions Home Video

46 S. De Lacey Ave., Suite 15, Pasadena, CA 91105; (818) 449-0683.

ANS International Video, Ltd.

396 Fifth Ave., New York, NY 10018; (212) 736-1007. Organized 1980. (Video/film production/post house.)

PRESIDENT
Apo Oguz
GENERAL MANAGER
Marilyn Cohen
PRODUCTION COORDINATOR
Meri Chermak
SALES
Edna Ozcan

ARC Video, Inc.

88 Lexington Ave., Suite 3-K, New York, NY 10016; (212) 725-5530. Organized 1976. (Produces performing arts TV programming—education/informational/performance-oriented.)

CO-DIRECTOR/TECHNICAL DIRECTOR
Jeff Bush
CO-DIRECTOR/ARTISTIC DIRECTOR
Celia Ipiotis

AV Designs

1233 Hermosa Ave., Suite 208, Hermosa Beach, CA 90254; (213) 379-5818. Organized 1984. (Producers of video, film and multi-image media for marketing, promotion, training and education.)

PRESIDENT
Genie Davis
VICE PRESIDENT
Don Davis
PRODUCTION COORDINATOR
Joy Gaston

AVS, Inc.

4660 Maryland Ave., Room #13, St. Louis, MO 63108; (314) 361-7072. (Consultants and producers of video and audio.)

PRESIDENT
Susan Meryl Greenberg

AW Industries

8415 Ardmore Rd., Landover, MD 20785; (301) 322-1000.

Academy Entertainment, Inc.

1 Pine Haven Shore Rd., Shelburne, VT 05482; (800) 972-0001.

PRESIDENT
Robert Baruc

Active Home Video

9300 West Pico Blvd., Los Angeles, CA 90035; (213) 274-8233; (800) 824-6109. Organized 1984. (Video production and distribution.)

PRESIDENT
Ron Levanson
VICE PRESIDENT, SALES
Rod Hurley
CREATIVE SERVICES DIRECTOR
Juanita Weber
SALES
Lisa Jamner
Alice de Buhr

Admit One Video Presentations

185 Frederick St., Toronto, Canada M5A 4L4; (416) 863-6836. ("B" movies, schlock horror, classics.)

PRESIDENT
Len Curtis
OPERATIONS
Joe Mancuso

Advanced American Communications, Inc.

5251 Genesta Ave., Encino, CA 91316; (213) 444-8100; FAX: (213) 444-8138. (Producer of educational/industrial film and video.)

Adventures in Cassettes

1401-B West River Rd., North, Minneapolis, MN 55411; (800) 328-0108. (Division of Metacom, Inc.)

MAIL ORDER MANAGER
Diane A. Goddard

Alameda County Office of Education

313 W. Winton Ave., Hayward, CA 94544-1198; (415) 887-0152 (ext 210).

All Seasons Entertainment

18121 Napa St., Northridge, CA 91325; (818) 886-8680; (800) 423-5599. Organized 1984. (Acquisition and distribution of feature films and programming to home video market.)

PRESIDENT
Fred Hirsch
VICE PRESIDENT
Kirk Benefiel
AFFILIATIONS
VSDA, IVPA

Lewis Allen Productions

1501 Broadway, Suite 1614, New York, NY 10036; (212) 768-4610. Organized 1983. (Film, television and theatrical production.)

PARTNER
Lewis Allen, President
ADMINISTRATIVE ASSOCIATE
Jane I. Roth

American Home Video Library

1457 Broadway, Suite 812, New York, NY 10036; (212) 869-2616.

American Humanist Association

Television Dept., P.O. Box 146, Amherst, NY 14226-0146; (716) 839-5085.

American Medical Television

535 N. Dearborn, Chicago, IL 60610; (312) 645-4420. (Original programming, production and distribution capabilities for broadcast, cable and satellite on healthcare and medical issues.)

American Red Cross

Production Center, 5816 Seminary Rd., Falls Church, VA 22041; (703) 379-8160. (Health, science and safety videos.)

American Sports Network, Inc.

P.O. Box 6100, Rosemead, CA 91770; (818) 572-4727. Organized 1976. (Sports production/video, television and cable.)

PRESIDENT
Louis Zwick

American Video Works

Box 333, Evanston, IL 60204; (312) 328-0400. Organized 1979. (Home video.)

CHIEF EXECUTIVE OFFICER
Graham Carlton
VICE PRESIDENT
Mike Rodgers

Amrit Productions Inc.

215 W. 90 St., PH-B, New York, NY 10024; (212) 877-3623. Organized 1982. (Produces and distributes film, video and how to tapes.)

PRODUCER/DIRECTOR/PRESIDENT
Tirlok Malik
DIRECTOR/VICE PRESIDENT
Chander Malik
BRANCHES
Amrit Productions Inc., C-28 Shiva Jee Park, New Delhi 11006, India

Amstar Productions

2020 Ave. of the Stars, Suite 240, Century City, CA 90067; (213) 556-1325.

PRESIDENT
R. J. Barich

Anovid Inc.

Box 180, Nesconset, NY 11767; (516) 724-4119. Organized 1980. (Film and video production company.)

PRESIDENT
E. Divona

Anti-Defamation League of B'Nai B'rith

823 United Nations Plaza, Audio-Visual Dept., New York, NY 10017; (212) 490-2525.

MARKETING DIRECTOR
Jay West
DIRECTOR OF TV & FILM
Steve Brody

Morris Anton Associates

301 W. 22 St., New York, NY 10011; (212) 989-2098.

PRESIDENT
Morris J. Anton

Anubis Productions International

P.O. Box 50859, Tucson AZ 85703; (602) 293-8088. Organized 1988. (Film and video production for broadcast and video distribution of documentaries, commercials and overseas assignments. Specializing in cultural, trade, travel, fine arts and dance.)

PRESIDENT
Gerald Harwood
VICE PRESIDENT
Sarajean Allen Harwood
AFFILIATIONS
Bastet Productions, Video Safaris International, Llamavision Productions.

Apex Productions, Inc.

3510 Shoreheights Dr., Malibu, CA 90265; (213) 459-8278. Organized 1985. (Produces feature films and video programs.)

PRESIDENT
Jim Silverman

Appalshop, Inc.

306 Madison St., Whitesburg, KY 41858; (606) 633-0108. Organized 1969. (Documents and presents history, culture and social issues of rural America.)

Apple Productions

215 W. 90 St., PH-B, New York, NY 10024; (212) 877-3623.

PRODUCER/DIRECTOR/VICE PRESIDENT
Tirlok Malik
DIRECTOR/VICE PRESIDENT
Chander Malik
BRANCHES
Amrit Productions Inc., C-28 Shiva Jee Park, New Delhi 11006, India

Arena Home Video, Inc.

211 Arizona Ave., Santa Monica, CA 90401; (213) 451-5510; (800) 468-1913; FAX: (213) 395-4058.

PRESIDENT
Arnie Lakeyn
VICE PRESIDENT
S. Leigh Savidge

Armenian Film Foundation

580 E. Thousand Oaks Blvd., Room 101, Thousand Oaks, CA 91360; (805) 495-0717. Organized 1979. (Produces and distributes films and videos of concerning Armenian heritage.)

CHAIRMAN
J. Michael Hapogian
VICE CHAIRMAN
Walter Karabian
TREASURER
Leo Garapedian
SECRETARY
Sharon Kalemkiarian
BOARD OF DIRECTORS
Mihran Agbabian, Mary Apick, Mona Asorian, Flora Dunaians, Glenn Farr, Levon Marashlian, Lilit, Marzbetuny

Arnold & Associates Production, Inc.

2159 Powell St., San Francisco, CA 94133; (415) 989-3490. Organized 1978. (Corporate image and marketing film and video production; TV commercials.)

PRESIDENT
John Arnold
VICE PRESIDENTS
Jim Morris
Jadine Wa

Artec Distributing, Inc.

One Pine Haven Shore Rd., Shelburne, VT 05482; (802) 985-9411, (800) 451-5160; FAX: (802) 985-3403. Organized 1970. (Full service videocassette and CD distributor, marketing to video specialty stores, supermarkets, mass merchants, etc. Artec Service Merchandising (ASM) provides full rack jobbing services.)

CHIEF EXECUTIVE OFFICER
Martin Gold
CHIEF FINANCE OFFICER
Howard Goldberg
SENIOR VICE PRESIDENT, MARKETING
Matt Brown
SENIOR VICE PRESIDENT, SALES
Ken Miller
CONTROLLER
Fred Ames
DIRECTOR OF SERVICE
David Borgendale
VICE PRESIDENT, MANAGEMENT INFORMATION SERVICES
Greg Casto
BRANCHES
Canton, MA; Middletown, CT; Pittsburgh, PA; W. Babylon, NY
AFFILIATIONS
VSDA, NAVD, NARM

Artists' Video Productions

32 Narrow Rocks Rd., Westport, CT 06880; (203) 226-0397. Organized 1986. (Produces and distributes videocassettes about artists.)

PARTNERS
William Schael
Joanna Foster

Artmusic, Inc.

330 W. 58 St., #11K, New York, NY 10019; (212) 265-8995. Organized 1980. (Presents and produces TV series/PBS video exhibitions and large scale music events.)

PRESIDENT
Wendy Chambers
SECRETARY
Tim Jensen
VICE PRESIDENT
Barbara Mayfield
BOARD OF DIRECTORS
Kelly Knauer, Andy Feigenbaum

artsAmerica, Inc.

12 Havemeyer Pl., Greenwich, CT 06830; (203) 869-4693; FAX: (203) 629-3748. Organized 1984. (Producer and distributor of videotapes and films about the visual arts. Publisher of artsAmerica Film Art, Film & Video Source Book.)

PRESIDENT
Bronwyn Dunne
DIRECTOR
Dorothy Tucker
BOARD OF ADVISORS
Philip Eliasoph, Ph.D., Mary Delahoyd, John Sharnik, Robert Sturgeon, Marilyn Boren

Asia Society

725 Park Ave., New York, NY 10021; (212) 288-6400; FAX: (212) 517-8315.

Atlantic Film

102 Harbor Rd., Kittery Point, ME 03905; (207) 439-3739. (Outdoor and educational videos.)

Atlantic Video Co. Inc.

725 S. Central Expressway, #C-3, Richardson, TX 75080; (214) 699-1014. Organized 1983. (Manufactures and distributes foreign films.)

PRESIDENT
Mohammed A. Molubhoy
VICE PRESIDENTS
Perwez M. Molubhoy
Salim M. Molubhoy
BOARD OF DIRECTORS
Mohammed A. Molubhoy, Perwez M. Molubhoy, Salim M. Molubhoy

Atlantis Productions, Inc.

1252 La Granada Dr., Thousand Oaks, CA 91362; (805) 495-2790. Organized 1952. (Produces documentary and educational films and videos.)

PRESIDENT
Dr. J. Michael Hagopian
VICE PRESIDENT
Becci Meadors
SECRETARY
Antoinette Hobden
BOARD OF DIRECTORS
Dr. J. Michael Hagopian, Becci Meadors, Antoinette Hobden

Aurora Educational Media, Inc.

74-10 35 Ave., Suite 607W, Jackson Heights, NY 11372; (718) 898-5327. Organized 1985. (Develops, produces and distributes dramatic and documentary film and video.)

PRESIDENT
Robert Spencer

Avant Communications, Partnership

370 Lexington Ave., Suite 1509; New York, NY 10016; (212) 759-3051.

C/O
Stan Ferbear

Avekta Productions Inc.

164 Madison Ave., 4th floor, New York, NY 10016; (212) 686-4550. Organized 1982. (Video production and computer animation.)

PRESIDENT
Maria Avgerakis
VICE PRESIDENT & CREATIVE DIRECTOR
George Avgerakis

Axon Video Corp.

1900 Broadway, New York, NY 10023; (212) 787-8228; FAX: (212) 769-9295. (Previously Access Video Corp.)

BFA Educational Media

468 Park Ave. S., New York, NY 10016; (212) 684-5910, (800) 221-1274. (Subsidiary of Phoenix Films Inc.)

PRESIDENT
H. Gelles
MARKETING AND SALES
Robert Dunlap

B.T. Supply, Inc., t/a Blank Tape Supply

1323-I Shepard Dr., P.O. Box 237, Sterling, VA 22170; (703) 450-6776; (800) 722-3300. Organized 1979. (Wholesale audio, video and computer products.)

PRESIDENT
Bob Vanjani
VICE PRESIDENT
Gayle Vanjani

Bandera Enterprises Inc.

Box 1107, Studio City, CA 91604; (818) 985-5050.

PRESIDENT
Don Flagg

Barr Films

12801 Schabarum Ave., Irwindale, CA 91706; (818) 338-7878. Organized 1957. (Produces informational, educational, motivational film and video for all markets.)

CEO & CFO
Allen Dohra
PRESIDENT
Donald Barr
EXECUTIVE VICE PRESIDENT
B. L. Earle
VICE PRESIDENT, PRODUCT DEVELOPMENT
George Holland
NATIONAL SALES MANAGER
Bob Gergen
BOARD OF DIRECTORS
Donald Barr (chairman), B. L. Earle, Allen Dohara

Basic Skills Video

P.O. Box 736, Conway, SC 29526; (803) 248-7160. Organized 1985. (Production, and duplication of special interest, how-to videos.)

OFFICERS
Dennis J. Allen
Frankie B. Allen

Bay Port Productions

4901 Morena Blvd., Suite #127, San Diego, CA 92117; (619) 581-6550. (Produces TV commercials, marketing and public relations videos.)

PRESIDENT & EXECUTIVE PRODUCER
Bill Polick
PRODUCTION MANAGER
Horace Barge III
ASSOCIATE PRODUCER
Amy Blum

Beacon Films, Inc.

(An Altschul Group Company.)

930 Pitner Ave., Evanston, IL 60202; (312) 328-6700. Organized 1978. (Distributor of curriculum-based and special interest AV programming to libraries, schools, and other educational organizations.)

PRESIDENT
Joseph Farragher
CHAIRMAN OF BOARD
Joel Altschul

Norman Beerger Productions

3217-A29, Arville St., Las Vegas, NV 89102-7612; (702) 876-2328. Organized 1984. (Produces and distributes wilderness home video programs.)

OWNER
Norman Beerger

Bellevue Home Entertainment

(A division of Astral Bellevue Pathé Inc.)

7215 Trans Canada Highway, Montreal, Quebec H4T 1A2; Canada; (514) 333-7555.

PRESIDENT
Sidney Greenberg
ASST. VICE PRESIDENT, FINANCE
Mark Pereira
MANAGER, OPERATIONS
Harry Kravitz
NATIONAL SALES MANAGER
Barry Brooker

Bellevue Home Entertainment

98 Orfus Rd., North York, Toronto, Ontario M6A 1C8, Canada; (416) 785-5580.

Bennett Marine Video

730 Washington St., Marina del Rey, CA 90292; (213) 821-3329; FAX: (213) 306-3162. Organized 1982. (Supplier and distributor of marine-oriented video, worldwide.)

PRESIDENT/OWNER
Michael S. Bennett
OPERATIONS MANAGER
Roderic P. Kavanagh

Bennu Productions, Inc.

165 Madison, Ave., New York, NY 10016; (212) 213-8511. Organized 1985. (Film and video production and distribution.)

PRESIDENT
Wayne J. Keeley
SENIOR VICE PRESIDENT
Kevin F. Cavaliere
VICE PRESIDENTS
Joanne Birkmann
Paul D. Sansone
BOARD OF DIRECTORS
Wayne J. Keeley, Kevin F. Cavaliere, Paul D. Sansone, Joanne Birkmann
AFFILIATIONS
NSSEA, AIVF, AFTRA, SIG, SAG, IFP

Best Film & Video

98 Cutter Hill Rd., Great Neck, NY 11021; (800) 527-2189; 20501 Ventura Blvd., Suite 375, Woodland Hills, CA 91364; (818) 999-2244.

PRESIDENT
Roy Winnick

The Blackhawk Catalog

12636 Beatrice Street, Los Angeles, CA 90066; (213) 306-4040.

VICE PRESIDENT
Philip J. Kromnick
OPERATIONS MANAGER/BUYER
Kimberly Baker

Michael Blackwood Productions, Inc.

251 W. 57 St., Suite 415, New York, NY 10019; (212) 247-4710; FAX: (212) 247-4713. (Produces and distributes documentaries on 20th-Century painters, sculptors, architects, choreographers and composers.)

PRESIDENT
Michael Blackwood

Les Blank's Flower Films and Video

10341 San Pablo Ave., El Cerrito, CA 94530; (415) 525-0942; FAX: (415) 525-1204. Organized 1967. (Seeks out and documents America's vanishing minority cultures, their music and traditions. Also produces music videos and independent films on such subjects as gap-toothed women, garlic and Werner Herzog.)

PRODUCER/DIRECTOR/CAMERA
Les Blank
DISTRIBUTION MANAGER
Toni Hanna
FOLKLORIST/2nd CAMERA—SOUND PRODUCTION MGR.
Christine Simon
EDITOR—SOUND
Maureen Gosling

Book-of-the-Month Club, Inc.

485 Lexington Ave., New York, NY 10017; (212) 867-4300.

DIRECTOR OF VIDEO DIVISION
George Spitzer

Bosustow Video

3030 Pennsylvania Ave., Santa Monica, CA 90404; (213) 453-7973. FAX: (213) 828-4053. Organized 1983. (Producers of award winning home videos, corporate videos, electronic press kits, point of sale videos, employee video newsletters, public relations videos, video white papers, training videos, and commercials. Distributors of television educational and home video product.)

PRESIDENT
Tee Bosustow
AFFILIATIONS
AMPTAS, ATVAS, IDA

Box Office Hits Inc.

10660 Westheimer, Houston, TX 77042; (713) 850-8500. Organized 1969. Wholesale distributor of used movies. Retail stores trading as National Video Superstores.)

PRESIDENT
Barry Lotz
VICE PRESIDENT, SALES
Linda Milligan
VICE PRESIDENT, RETAIL OPERATIONS
D. Craig Butler
AFFILIATIONS
Smash Hits Video Inc., Hollywood Hits Inc.

Breger Video, Inc.

915 Broadway, Room 1601, New York, NY 10010; (212) 254-3900. Organized 1983. (Produces cooking videos and PBS series "Madeleine Cooks" and "Pierre Franey's Cuisine Rapide.")

PRESIDENT/EXECUTIVE PRODUCER
Sue Breger
PRODUCER/DIRECTOR
Charles Pinsky
ASSOCIATE PRODUCER
Barbara Prisco

Brighton Video

(Division of Cortech Communications, Inc.
250 W. 57 St., Suite 2421, New York, NY 10019; (212) 315-2502; (800) 542-5554; FAX: (212) 582-0585. (Home-video program supplier.)

PRESIDENT
Gene Feldman
EXECUTIVE VICE PRESIDENT
Suzette Winter
OPERATIONS MANAGER
Hillary Schumer
NATIONAL SALES MANAGER
Priscilla Forance

Broadcast Quality Inc.

7800 S.W. 57th Ave., Suite 219, South Miami, FL 33142; (305) 665-5416.

VICE PRESIDENT
Diana Udel
PRODUCTION MANAGER
Steve Bradley
VICE PRESIDENT, ACQUISITIONS
Stephen Kabak

Broadman

127 Ninth Ave. N., Nashville, TN 37234; (615) 251-3697. (800) 251-3225, (800) 342-0021. (Tennessee).

Brooklyn College

Dept. of Television and Radio, 018 Whitehead Hall, Bedford Ave. H., Brooklyn, NY 11210; (718) 780-5555.

CHAIRMAN
Robert C. Williams

Budget Video Inc.

(d/b/a Hollywood Home Theatre)

1540 N. Highland Ave., Suite 110, Hollywood CA 90028; (213) 466-0121, (213) 466-0127. Organized 1979. (Dealer, distributor, retailer of video cassettes and laser discs.)

PRESIDENT
Larry S. Fine
VICE PRESIDENT
Stephen Stumbris

Buena Vista Home Video

500 S. Buena Vista, Burbank, CA 91521; (818) 560-1000. (Distributor of Walt Disney Home Video children's and family video.)

PRESIDENT, INTL. THEATRICAL DISTRIBUTION & WORLDWIDE VIDEO
William M. Mechanic
SENIOR VICE PRESIDENT
Richard B. Cohen
VICE PRESIDENT, BUSINESS AFFAIRS & ACQUISITIONS
Jere Hausfater

Bullfrog Films, Inc.

Oley, PA 19547; (215) 779-8226; (800) 543-FROG; FAX: (215) 370-1978. Organized 1973. (Distributes programs for personal self-reliance—how-to's on gardening, home improvements, energy-saving, etc.—and environmental responsibility.)

PRESIDENT
John Hoskyns-Abrahall
SECRETARY & TREASURER
Winifred Scherrer
CUSTOMER SERVICE MANAGER
Jennifer Daecher
BOARD OF DIRECTORS
John Hoskyns-Abrahall, Winifred Scherrer

Butterfly Video Productions

Box 184, High St., Antrim, NH 03440; (603) 588-2105. Organized 1986. (Produces and distributes how-to videos.)

PRODUCER
Sherry Smythe-Green

CBS/Fox Video

1211 Ave. of the Americas, New York, NY 10036; (212) 819-3200. (Subsidiary of CBS, Inc./20th-Century Fox)

PRESIDENT & CEO
George Krieger
PRESIDENT, INTERNATIONAL
Rafael Pastor
SENIOR VICE PRESIDENT, PROGRAMMING
Steven Poe
SENIOR VICE PRESIDENT, SALES
Sam Puleo
VICE PRESIDENT, PROGRAMMING
Jed Daly
PRESIDENT, NORTH AMERICA
Bob DeLellis
VICE PRESIDENT, MARKETING, NORTH AMERICA
Bruce Pfander
VICE PRESIDENT, REGION DIRECTOR, PACIFIC, CBS/FOX INTL.
Chris Windle
VICE PRESIDENT, INTL. PROGRAM ACQUISITION
Francesca Barra

CBS Video Club/CBS Video Library

1400 N. Fruitridge Ave., Terre Haute, IN 47811; (800) 457-0866. Executive offices at 51 W. 52nd St., New York, NY 10019; (212) 975-4875. (A unit of Columbia House, a division of CBS Records Inc.)

VICE PRESIDENT, CBS VIDEO CLUB
Brian Wood
VICE PRESIDENT, CBS VIDEO LIBRARY
Harry Elias

CBS Broadcast International

51 W. 52 St., New York, NY 10019; (212) 975-8585. (Subsidiary of CBS Broadcast Group, CBS Inc.)

CC Studios/Children's Circle

389 Newtown Turnpike, Weston, CT 06883; (203) 222-0002. Organized 1963. (Produces and markets home audio/video cassettes to consumers; adaptations of children's books.)

PRESIDENT & TREASURER
Morton Schindel
SECRETARY
Elisabeth Rommel
BOARD OF DIRECTORS
Morton Schindel, Elisabeth Rommel
AFFILIATIONS
Weston Woods; Georgetown Studios

Cable Films & Video

#7171 County Club Station, Kansas City, MO 64113; (913) 362-2804. Organized 1976. (300 classic films in all formats—PAL, SECAM, NTSC—for worldwide distribution; cable, TV and home video.)

PRESIDENT
Herb Miller
GENERAL MANAGER
Todd Randall
AFFILIATIONS
NCTA, NATPE, National Academy of TV Arts & Sciences, Mid-America Cable TV Association

Calypso Video, Inc.

2000 Bay Area Blvd., Suite 123, Houston, TX 77058-2001; (713) 480-3168.

PRESIDENT
C. Opfermann

Camp Home Video

8841 Wilbur Avenue, Northridge, CA 91324. (818) 349-2267; FAX: (818) 349-2464. Organized 1986. (Manufacturers, producers, distributors of horror/sci-fi home videos and theatricals.)

PRESIDENT
Salvatore Richichi
NATIONAL SALES MANAGER
Allen Yally

Steve Campus Productions, Inc.

24 Depot Square, Tuckahoe, NY 10707; (914) 961-1900; FAX: (914) 961-6733. Organized 1936. (Full service video production company—commercial, industrial, educational—satellite tele-conferencing; A/V design/production.)

PRESIDENT
Steve Campus
EXECUTIVE VICE PRESIDENT
Dennis Elliott

Camrac Studios

1775 Kuenzli St., Reno, NV 89502; (702) 323-0965. Organized 1979. (Independent studio/location production company that specializes in all film and video formats.

Productions include regional commercials, corporate presentations, and home entertainment.)
PRESIDENT
Shirley Mitchell
DIRECTOR/PRODUCER
Jim Mitchell
EDITOR
Larry Neroda
ACCOUNT REPRESENTATIVE & RESEARCH
Mitch Larson
AFFILIATIONS
Mitchell Productions (subsidiary), Mitchell Productions/Skyfire

Candlelight Studios

P.O. Box 627, Little River, CA 95456; (707) 937-5424. Organized 1981. (Provides fine art instruction for all ages on videotape.)
PRESIDENT
E. John Robinson

Cape Cod Writers' Conference

309 Green Dunes Dr., Box 111, West Hyannisport, MA 02672; (617) 775-4811. Organized 1963. (Promotes writing through video, audio, conferences, writer-in-the-schools, TV shows, books and the world.)
EXECUTIVE DIRECTOR
Marion Vuilleumier
PROGRAM DIRECTOR
Tom O'Connell
PRESIDENT
Katherine Fitzgerald
VICE PRESIDENT
Elinor Titus
SECRETARY & CLERK
Marian Logan
TREASURER
Olive St. Germaine
REGISTRAR
Jeannette Wilson
AFFILIATION
Cape Arts Workshops, Box 12, Cummaquid, MA 02637

Capezio Ballet Makers

33 W. 60 St., 8th floor, New York, NY 10023; (212) 247-7660.

Capital Communications

3807 Dickerson Rd., Nashville, TN 37207; (615) 868-2040. Organized 1965. (Provides programming for commercial, cable television, along with educational markets. Also provides home video programming.)
CHIEF EXECUTIVE OFFICER
Robert Springer
PRESIDENT
James Springer
SECRETARY—TREASURER
Nancy Springer
BOARD OF DIRECTORS
Robert Springer, James Springer, Nancy Springer
BRANCHES
Nashville, TN; Beverly Hills, CA

Capitol Home Video

4818 Yuma St., N.W., Washington D.C., 20016; (202) 363-8800; FAX: (202) 363-4680. Organized 1989.
PRESIDENT
Ted Goldberg
VICE PRESIDENT
Ronnie Goldberg

Capitol Records

1750 North Vine St., Tower-6, Hollywood, CA 90028. Organized 1940s. (Record label).
VICE PRESIDENT, MUSIC VIDEO
Mick Kleber
DIRECTOR, NATIONAL VIDEO PROMOTION
Michelle Peacock

Care Video Productions

1650 Crossings Parkway, Westlake, OH 44145; (216) 835-5872. Organized 1982. (Producer and distributor of medical education video.)
PRESIDENT
Priscilla L. (Pat) Lehman
VICE PRESIDENT
Darlene M. Hall
AFFILIATION
Distributor: Programming for 25 hospitals.

Catalina Video Distributing

6611 Santa Monica Blvd., Los Angeles, CA 90038; (213) 485-9105, (800) 421-3269.

Catholic Television Network/Bay Area Dioceses

324 Middlefield Rd., Menlo Park, CA 94025; (415) 326-7850.
CONTACT
Shirley Connolly

Celebrity Home Entertainment

6320 Canoga Ave., Penthouse Suite, Woodland Hills, CA 91365; (818) 715-1980. Organized 1987. (Video manufacturer, distributor, producer.)
CHAIRMAN
Noel C. Bloom
VICE PRESIDENT, ACQUISITIONS
Krickett Wertz
VICE PRESIDENT, BUSINESS/LEGAL AFFAIRS
Robert Norton
VICE PRESIDENT/SALES & MARKETING
Jack Talley

Central Sun Video Co.

P.O. Box 3135, Reston, VA 22091; (703) 444-2990; FAX: (202) 450-0468. Organized 1985. (Produces, acquires and distributes video folk and bluegrass, acoustic music.)
PRESIDENT & CEO
C. W. Weinberger, Jr.

Centre Films Inc.

1103 N. El Centro Ave., Hollywood, CA 90038; (213) 466-5123. Organized 1971. (Videotape production, stage and equipment rental.)
DIRECTOR/PRESIDENT
Winter D. Horton Jr.
SECRETARY/TREASURER
Carol Horton
PRODUCTION MANAGER
Steven Finkelstein

Century Home Video, Inc.

2672 S. La Cienega Blvd., Los Angeles, CA 90034; (213) 837-7000; (800) 323-0695; FAX: (213) 837-3066. (Distributor of Century Video Corp. library.)
CHAIRMAN
Lawrence Scheer

Champions on Film and Video

745 State Circle, Box 1941, Ann Arbor, MI 48106; (313) 761-5176; FAX: (313) 761-8711.

PRESIDENT
Donald N. Canham

Doris Chase Productions

222 W. 23 St., Suite #722, New York, NY 10011; (212) 243-3700. Organized 1972. (Produces for television, film and video art.)

AFFILIATIONS
Museum of Modern Art, Women Make Movies, Video Data Bank, Coronet Films, Jane Balfour Films Ltd.

Cherry Lane Video, Inc.

P.O. Box 430, Port Chester, NY 10573; (914) 937-8601; FAX: (914) 937-0614. (Producers: music instruction videos.)

EXECUTIVE VICE PRESIDENT
Lorain Levy

Christ for the Nations Inc.

P.O. Box 24910, Dallas TX 75224; (214) 376-1711.

DIRECTOR
Gene Steiner

Christophers

12 E. 48 St., New York, NY 10017; (212) 759-4050; FAX: (212) 838-5073.

DIRECTOR
Rev. John Catoir

Chronicle Videocassettes

2855 Mitchell Dr., Suite 225, Walnut Creek, CA 94598-1627; P.O. Box 4610, Walnut Creek, CA 94596; (415) 778-8117.

Churchill Films, Inc.

12210 Nebraska Ave., Los Angeles, CA 90025; (213) 207-6600. Organized 1961. (Educational producers and distributors—documentary, theatrical, television.)

PRESIDENT
George McQuilkin
VICE PRESIDENTS
Robert B. Churchill
Robert L. Glore
BOARD OF DIRECTORS
George McQuilkin, Robert B. Churchill, Robert L. Glore

Cinema Concepts, Inc.

2461 Berlin Turnpike, Newington, CT 06111; (203) 667-1251. Organized 1971. (Non-theatrical distribution of entertainment motion pictures in 16mm, VHS, U-Matic, to schools, libraries and home market. Mail-order plus two retail stores.)

PRESIDENT
Joel G. Jacobson
BRANCH
210 Main St., Old Saybrook, CT 06475; (203) 388-1481
AFFILIATIONS
Video Software Dealers Association (Joel Jacobson is a board director of CT chapter)

The Cinema Guild

1697 Broadway, Suite 802, New York, NY 10019; (212) 246-5522. Organized 1975. (Film and video distribution.)

PRESIDENT
Philip S. Hobel
VICE PRESIDENTS
Gary Crowdus
Mary-Ann Hobel

DISTRIBUTION MANAGER
Ted Hicks

Cinemagreats

15825 Rob Roy Dr., Oak Forest, IL 60452; (312) 687-7881.

Cinergy Entertainment

858 12th St., Suite 8, Santa Monica, CA 90403; (213) 396-7085. Organized 1988. (Distributor of "New Age" and children's videos.)

PRESIDENT
Adriana Shaw

Cinetel Productions

9701 Madison Ave., Knoxville, TN 37932; (615) 690-9950. Organized 1973. (Video production and post production. Programming, commercials, home video, training.)

CHIEF EXECUTIVE OFFICER
Ross K. Bagwell, Sr.
PRESIDENT
Ross K. Bagwell, Jr.
VICE PRESIDENT, DIRECTOR OF OPERATIONS
Patrick Leigh-Bell
VICE PRESIDENT, PRODUCTION COORDINATOR
Shirley Romine
VICE PRESIDENT, DIRECTOR OF ENGINEERING
Jerry Nantz
BOARD OF DIRECTORS
Ross K. Bagwell, Sr.; Ross K. Bagwell, Jr.; Sue B. Bagwell; Dee Haslam
AFFILIATION
A division of Bagwell Communications, Inc.

City Lights Home Video

8981 Sunset Blvd., #310, W. Hollywood, CA 90069; (213) 859-9702. Organized 1986.

PRESIDENT
Ronald L. Gilchrist
VICE PRESIDENT, INERNATIONAL SALES
Talaat Captan
VICE PRESIDENT, NATIONAL SALES
Robert Komisar
BOARD OF DIRECTORS
Ronald L Gilchrist, Richard Pepin, Joseph Merhi

City One Stop

2551 S. Alameda St., Los Angeles, CA 90058; (213) 234-3336; (800) 962-2009; FAX: (213) 234-4036. Subsidiary of Show Industries.

PRESIDENT
Lou Fogelman

Classic Family Entertainment

6649 Odessa Ave., Van Nuys, CA 91406; (818) 780-7100.

PRESIDENT
Sidney Niekerk

Coast Telecourses

11460 Warner Ave., Fountain Valley, CA 92708-2597; (714) 241-6109; FAX: (714) 241-6248. (Educational videos.)

Color Leasing, Inc.

330 Route 46, Fairfield, NJ 07006; (201) 575-1118, (212) 662-2655. Organized 1966.

PRESIDENT
Jack Berberian

Columbia Video Bible Series

P.O. Box 3122, Columbia, SC 29230; (803) 754-4100, ext. 131. (Provides quality Biblical teaching on video.)

DIRECTOR, COLUMBIA VIDEO BIBLE SERIES
Rick H. Byers

Comex Systems

The Mill Cottage, Mendham, NJ 07945; (201) 234-1616.

VICE PRESIDENT
Leo Prybylowski

Commtron Corp.

1501 50 St., Suite 300, West Des Moines, IA 50265; (515) 224-1784. Subsidiary of Bergen Brunswig Corp.

VICE PRESIDENT, SALES
John Farr

Communicorp, Inc.

220 S. Westmore Ave., Lombard, IL 60148; (708) 629-7070; FAX: (708) 629-7106. Organized 1983. (Video production of corporate, sports, healthcare and consumer videos.)

PRESIDENT
John F. Moran, Ph.D.
VICE PRESIDENT
Timothy Bukowski
PRODUCTION MANAGER
Andy Lock

Compuvid

815 N. Royal St., Alexandria, VA 22314; (703) 683-3234. (Computer and educational videos.)

Concord Video

(Admission of American Educational Computer, Inc.)
7506 N. Broadway Ext., Suite 505, Oklahoma City, OK 73116; (405) 840-6031. Organized 1984. (Manufacturer and distributor of children's educational videos and various other video categories.)

CEO
David Catlin
PRESIDENT
Clive Fox
BRANCHES
801 S. Main St., Burbank, CA 91506
AFFILIATIONS
Division of American Educational Computer, Inc., Affiliate of United Coupon Corp.

Concord Video

801 So. Main St., Burbank, CA 91506.

Concordia Publishing House

3558 S. Jefferson, St. Louis, MO 63118-3968; (314) 664-7000.

PRESIDENT & CEO
John W. Gerber

Congress Video Group, Inc.

1776 Broadway, Suite 1010, New York, NY 10019; (212) 581-4880. Organized 1983. (Publisher and distributor of videos on the sell-through mass merchandise home video market.)

PRESIDENT & COO
Robert Sigman
CHAIRMAN OF THE BOARD
Richard E. Burke
VICE CHAIRMAN OF THE BOARD
Lawrence Kieves
FINANCIAL CONTROLLING OFFICER
Thomas Schmitz
BOARD OF DIRECTORS
Howard Curd, Ronald Leeds, Jonathan Furer, Kirk C. Kirkorian, Tom E. Constance, Myron M. Blumenthal, Dr. Donald Shapiro
AFFILIATIONS
Congress Video Group, Inc., P.O. Box 12209, 4520 Beech St., Cincinnati, OH 45212; (513) 351-5577.

Connoisseur Video

8455 Beverly Blvd., #302, Los Angeles, CA 90048; (213) 653-8873. (Distributes classic and foreign film on video including such lines as Class Films Mundiales, East-West Classics, Germania Films, Hungarofilm, Intrafilm, Janus Films, Sprectrafilm, UGC and Western World films.)

PRESIDENT
Peter Marai

Corinth Films & Video

34 Gansevoort St., New York, NY 10014; (212) 463-0305. Organized 1977. (Film and video distribution.)

PRESIDENT
John M. Poole
EXECUTIVE VICE PRESIDENT
Peter J. Meyer
TECHNICAL DIRECTOR
Richard Evangelista
COMPTROLLER
Jane Gritau

Cornell University Audio Visual Center

8 Research Park, Ithaca, NY 14850; (607) 255-2091. Organized 1929. (Provides educational programs to Co-operative Extension agents, consumers, schools and other orgs.)

AFFILIATIONS
Consortium of University Film Centers, Educational Film Library Association

Coronet MTI Film & Video & Coronet Feature Video

108 Wilmot Rd., Deerfield, IL 60015; (312) 940-1260; (800) 621-2131; FAX: (312) 940-3600.

PRESIDENT
Wendell Shackelford

Covenant Video

3200 W. Foster Ave., Chicago, IL 60625; (312) 478-4676; (800) 621-1290. (Religious videos.)

MANAGER
Carol A. Nordstrom

Creative Programming, Inc.

30 E. 60 St., New York, NY 10022; (212) 688-9100. Organized 1982. (Television and home video production.)

EXECUTIVE PRODUCER
Peter Wild
DIRECTOR
Nancy Fisher

Creative Tax Planning Associates

349 Broadway, 2nd Floor, New York, NY 10013; (212) 966-4442.

OWNER
Howard Einbinder

Creative Visions Video

721 S. San Pedro St., Los Angeles, CA 90014; (213) 623-9254, (800) 421-8528. (Subsidiary of Image Laboratories, Inc.)

PRESIDENT
Robert Hoffman

Crocus Entertainment, Inc.

Twelve Oaks Center, 15500 Wayzata Blvd., #762, Wayzata, MN 55391; (612) 473-9002; FAX: (612) 473-0648. Organized 1986. (Manufacturer-supplier/wholesale distributor).

PRESIDENT, CEO
Henry T. Morrison, Jr.
SECRETARY & TREASURER
Cecil H. Bell
VICE PRESIDENT, SALES
Jay Douglas
CONTROLLER
James B. Haugen
BOARD OF DIRECTORS
Henry T. Morrison, Jr., Cecil H. Bell, Ford W. Bell
BRANCHES
Minneapolis
AFFILIATIONS
VSDA, RARM

Crown Video

(A division of Random House Home Video.)
225 Park Ave. S., New York, NY 10003; (212) 254-1600.

Crystallus Films, Inc.

11 Fayette St., Cambridge, MA 02139; (617) 492-6739. Organized 1979. (Produces and distributes films and television works of artistic and educational interest.)

PRESIDENT
Elliot Hoffman

A.S. Csaky Motion Picture and Video Productions

420 Legato Terrace, Silver Spring, MD 20901; (301) 681-3333 and 681-3390. Organized 1968. (Develops, produces and distributes motion picture and video productions and screenplays nationally and internationally.)

CHAIRMAN OF THE BOARD & PRESIDENT
A.S. Csaky
VICE PRESIDENT, PRODUCTION
Ramzi D. Seikaly
VICE PRESIDENT, SCREENPLAY DEVELOPMENT
Bud Fleischer
VICE PRESIDENT, TRAVEL MANAGEMENT
Albert Cambata
VICE PRESIDENT, PUBLIC RELATIONS
Cecilia Korda-Bros
VICE PRESIDENT, SALES & MARKETING
Catherine White
GRAPHICS DIRECTOR
John Franey
BRANCHES
Washington, DC, New York, NY, Hollywood, CA

Merce Cunningham Dance Foundation, Inc.

463 West St., New York, NY 10014; (212) 255-3130; FAX: (212) 633-2433. (Cultural and arts videos.)

Custom Films/Video, Inc.

11 Cob Dr., Westport, CT 06880; (203) 226-0300. Organized 1962. (Produces film and video.)

PRESIDENT
Lester S. Becker

Cycle Vision Tours, Inc.

1925 Bailey Hill Rd., Eugene, OR 97405; (503) 345-9635; (800) 624-4952. Organized 1983. (Production, marketing and distribution of the Videocycle series. Scenic video tapes for exercise bicycles.)

PRESIDENT
George L. Dixon, Jr., M.D.
VICE PRESIDENT
Margery M. Dixon
EXECUTIVE VICE PRESIDENT
Mark S. Lange
OPERATIONS
Martha D. Lange
BOARD OF DIRECTORS
George L. Dixon, Jr., M.D.; Margery M. Dixon; Mark S. Lange; Martha D. Lange

Czar Productions, Inc.

809 New Britain Ave., Hartford, CT 06106; (203) 953-0809.

PRESIDENT
Gene Czarnecki

Damon & Grace Corporation

Mind Fitness Company
9000 Sunset Blvd., Suite #601, Los Angeles, CA 90069; (213) 274-0211. Organized 1972. (Videos to better the quality of life for individuals through behavior modification.)

PRESIDENT
Grace A. Reinbold
VICE PRESIDENT
Jay Michaels

Dawn's Video

519 W. Foothill, Suite C, Rialto, CA 92376; (714) 874-1414. Organized 1980. (Video specialty store.)

OWNER
Gregory C. George
BRANCHES
2085 E. Highland Ave., San Bernardino, CA 92404; (714) 864-3113
9725 Sierra, Fontana, CA 92335; (714) 350-8833
267 E. 40th, San Bernardino, CA 92404; (714) 883-5737
1330 Massachusetts Ave., Riverside, CA 92507; (714) 784-1414

Daya, Inc.

6 Lookout La., Westport, CT 06880; (203) 226-1964. (Needlecraft, educational videos.)

Development Communications Incorporated

815 N. Royal St., Alexandria, VA 22314; (703) 638-3100; FAX: (703) 683-8444. Organized 1978. (Training tapes.)

PRESIDENT
Welby A. Smith, Jr.
VICE PRESIDENT
Lawrence M. Franks
SECRETARY-TREASURER
Elizabeth P. Smith
BOARD OF DIRECTORS
Welby A. Smith, Jr., Lawrence M. Franks, Elizabeth P. Smith
AFFILIATIONS
ITVA, Dept. of Defense QVPL, ADPA, ASTD, Washington Film Council

Diamond Entertainment

P.O. Box 2342, Stamford, CT 06901; (203) 327-2740. Organized 1988. (Video distributor.)

PRESIDENT
Gordon Bossin

Digital Touch Ltd.

303 W. 42 St., Suite 4034, New York, NY 10036; (212) 246-3811, ext. 683. Organized 1985. (Multi-media development and production.)

PRESIDENT
Jeffrey Selig
VICE PRESIDENT
Bruce E. Colfin
COUNSEL
Jeffrey E. Jacobson
BOARD OF DIRECTORS
Jeffrey Selig, Bruce E. Colfin, J. E. Jacobson
BRANCH
Boston
AFFILIATION
AES

Direct Cinema Limited, Inc.

P.O. Box 69799, Los Angeles, CA 90069; 291 S. La Cienega Blvd., PH, Beverly Hills, CA 90211; (213) 652-8000; FAX: (213) 652-2346. Organized 1974. (Specialized distributor of short videos and films, documentaries, independent features, animation.)

PRESIDENT
Mitchell W. Block
VICE PRESIDENTS
Joan Von Herrmann
Betsy A. McLane
COMPTROLLER
Sharon Levine

Discount Video Tapes, Inc.

P.O. Box 7122, Burbank, CA 91510; (818) 843-3366; FAX: (818) 843-3821. Organized 1979. (Specializing in rare and unusual pre-recorded videos. Retail and wholesale.)

PRESIDENT
Woody Wise

Walt Disney Educational Media Co.

500 S. Buena Vista St., Burbank, CA 91521; (818) 840-1000. (Division of Walt Disney Productions.)

MARKETING COORDINATOR
Linda Capuano

Disney Educational Productions

2600 W. Olive Ave., Tenth Floor, Burbank, CA 91505; Creative Dev.: (818) 972-3415. Marketing: (818) 972-3410. FAX: (818) 845-4570.

DIRECTOR OF MARKETING
James N. Gentry
DIRECTOR OF CREATIVE DEVELOPMENT
Sallie Zemlin-Kisor

Walt Disney Home Video

500 S. Buena Vista St., Burbank, CA 91521; (818) 840-1859.

PRESIDENT, INTERNATIONAL THEATRICAL DISTRIBUTION WORLDWIDE VIDEO
Bill Mechanic
SENIOR VICE PRESIDENT, BUENA VISTA HOME VIDEO
Richard Cohen
VICE PRESIDENT, MARKETING—DOMESTIC HOME VIDEO
Ann Daly
VICE PRESIDENT, SALES—DOMESTIC HOME VIDEO
Dick Longwell

Dixie Entertainment Productions Inc.

215 Long Beach Blvd., Box 2, Long Beach, CA 90802; (213) 491-0332. (Formerly See Hear Industries).

PRESIDENT
Raymond Jacobs

Dobovan Productions, Inc.

1575 S. Beretania St., #105, Honolulu, HI 96826; FAX: 943-0360.

PRESIDENT
John B. Dobovan

Documentary Educational Resources, Inc.

101 Morse St., Watertown, MA 02172; (617) 926-0491; FAX: (617) 926-9519. Organized 1971. (Produces and distributes 16mm films, videotapes and supplementary written materials to educational audiences.)

PRESIDENT
John K. Marshall
EXECUTIVE VICE PRESIDENT/SECRETARY AND TREASURER
Sue Marshall Cabezas
BOARD OF DIRECTORS
Peter B. Dow (chair), Timothy Asch, Sue Marshall Cabezas, Napoleon A. Chagnon, John K. Marshall, Judith Nierenberg, Mary Anne Wolff

Doko Communications

509 Madison Ave., Suite 1400, New York, NY 10022; (212) 686-6160. Organized 1985. (Video production and distribution.)

PRESIDENT
Reuven Dorot
BRANCH
Tel Aviv, Israel

Double Vision Video Productions

401 S St., Sacramento, CA 95814; (916) 448-8220. (Instructional videos.)

Dudkowski-Lynch Associates, Inc.

150 Shoreline Highway, Bldg. E, Mill Valley, CA 94941; (415) 332-5825. Organized 1974. (Video production and post-production.)

PRESIDENT
Ed Dudkowski
VICE PRESIDENT
Marijane Lynch

Eagle Productions Ltd.

7860 Mission Center Court, Suite 106, San Diego, CA 92108; (619) 297-8870.

East Texas Distributing

7171 Grand Blvd., Houston, TX 77504; (713) 748-2520, (800) 231-6648; 2732 W. McDowell, Phoenix, AZ 85009; (602) 233-3741, (800) 231-3218.

PRESIDENT
Ron Eisenberg
MARKETING & SALES
Jan Moore (Houston)
Janet Wheeler (Phoenix)

Eastin Phelan Corp.

P.O. Box 4528, Davenport, IA 52808; (319) 323-9735.

PRESIDENT
Robert Evans

Echo Film Productions

Box 4692, Aspen, CO 81612; (303) 925-5605. Organized 1968. (Sports films, environmental documentaries, adventure films, new age health and arts.)

OFFICERS
Wilk Wilkinson
Tulasi Wilkinson
Jama Wilkinson
AFFILIATIONS
AFI, 659

Educational Activities Video

(Division of Educational Activities, Inc.)
1937 Grand Ave., Baldwin, NY 11501; (516) 867-7878. Organized 1983. (Produces and distributes educational videotapes.)

PRESIDENT
Alfred S. Harris
VICE PRESIDENT
Richard E. Harris

Educational Development Corporation

10302 E. 55th Place, Tulsa, OK 74146; (918) 622-4522.

PRESIDENT
Randall W. White
VICE PRESIDENT, SCHOOL DIV.
C. Jan Tucker

Educational Video, Inc.

27601 Schoolcraft Rd., Suite C, Livonia, MI 48150; (313) 427-5980. Organized 1983. (Production and marketing of original pre-recorded videocassettes and custom productions.)

PRESIDENT
Robert Tollini
VICE PRESIDENTS
Pamela Bonk
Petra Pepellashi

Electronic University

P.O. Box 938, Pt. Reyes Station, CA 94956; (415) 663-9102. (Subsidiary of Electronic Educational Programs.)

PRESIDENT
Mark Watts

Emory Medical Television Network

1440 Clifton Rd., N.E., Atlanta, GA 30322; (404) 688-8736. (A subsidiary of Emory University School of Medicine.)

MARKETING & SALES
Julie S. Budnik

Encyclopedia Britannica Educational Corp.

310 S. Michigan Ave., Chicago, IL 60604; (800) 558-6968; (312) 321-6800.

Enter-Tel, Inc.

24400 Chagrin Blvd., Suite 301, Beachwood, OH 44122; (216) 831-6110.

CHAIRMAN
S. Michael Loveman

Entertainment Productions, Inc.

2210 Wilshire Blvd., Suite 744, Santa Monica, CA 90403; (213) 456-3143. Organized 1971. (Motion picture and television productions produced for worldwide markets, including home video, cable, theatrical, etc.)

PRESIDENT
Edward Coe

Environmental Video, Inc.

P.O. Box 577, Manhattan Beach, CA 90266; (213) 515-3302. Organized 1981. (Manufactures and produces pre-recorded videocassettes for the home video market.)

PRESIDENT
James R. Spencer

Episcopal Radio-TV Foundation, Inc.

3379 Peachtree Rd., N.E., Suite 230, Atlanta, GA 30326; (404) 233-5419

Equestrian Video Library

8841 Exposition Blvd., Culver City, CA 90232; (213) 202-1555. Subsidiary of Mercedes Maharis.

PRESIDENT
Mercedes Maharis
NATIONAL SALES DIRECTOR
Jim Renier

Ergo Media

P.O. Box 2037, Teaneck, NJ 07666; (201) 692-0404. Organized 1987. (Video publisher, manufacturer of pre-recorded videos of Jewish nature.)

PRESIDENT
Eric A. Goldman
SECRETARY-TREASURER
Susan Goldman
VICE PRESIDENT, MARKETING
Dan Rappoport
ASSOCIATE
Jane Zylberman

Evergreen Video Society

213 W. 35 St., New York, NY 10001; (212) 714-9860. Organized 1985. (Mail order videotape distribution.)

PRESIDENT
Steve Feltes
VICE PRESIDENT
Karen Chaikin
TREASURER
Roz Chaikin

Everything Video

P.O. Box 313, New Brunswick, NJ 08903; (201) 753-5826. Organized 1982. (Production of railroad videos and distribution of rare historical railroad video tapes.)

PRESIDENT
Norman Skolnick
VICE PRESIDENT
Murray Skolnick

Eye Contact, International

1435 Center St., Oakland, CA 94607; (415) 836-1180; FAX: (415) 835-1314. Organized 1982. (Provides multilingual production services in film and video.)

PRESIDENT
Carla Itzkowich
VICE PRESIDENT
Norma Armon

FFH Video

(Subsidiary of Films for the Humanities & Sciences.)
743 Alexander Rd., Princeton, NJ 08540; (609) 452-1128.

PRESIDENT
Harold Mantell

FJC-Intellimedia, Inc.

8332 Zenith Dr., Baldwinsville, NY 13027; (315) 622-1683.

PRESIDENT
Joseph Crisafulli
MARKETING AND SALES
D. LoSurdo

Facets Multimedia, Inc.

1517 W. Fullerton Ave., Chicago, IL 60614; (312) 281-9075; FAX: (312) 929-5437. Organized 1975. (Film exhibition—arts films—and video distribution.)

PRESIDENT
David Edelberg, M.D.
VICE PRESIDENT
Constance Qonleg
CO-DIRECTORS
Milos Stehlik
Nicole E. Dreiske

Fairview AudioVisuals

(A division of Health Cleveland Entertainment Inc.)
17909 Groveland Ave., Cleveland, OH 44111; (216) 476-7054. Organized 1974. (Produces and distributes educational videotapes for healthcare personnel and patients.)

CHIEF EXECUTIVE OFFICER
Jerold Federsen
SECRETARY/TREASURER
Dudley E. Lavely Jr.
ADMINISTRATIVE ASSISTANT
Lillian Zahara

Falcon West Media

596 W. 1200 North, Orem, UT 84057; (801) 225-4183.

PRESIDENT
Lorie Fowlke

Family Home Entertainment

15400 Sherman Way, P.O. Box 10124, Van Nuys, CA 91410-0124; (818) 908-0303; FAX: (818) 908-9514. (Children's video.)

SENIOR VICE PRESIDENT & GENERAL MANAGER
David A. Mount

Fanlight Productions

47 Halifax St., Boston, MA 02130; (617) 524-0980. Organized 1982. (Non-theatrical distributor of film and video programs dealing with health, mental health and family life issues.)

PRESIDENT (OWNER)
Ben Achtenberg
DISTRIBUTION MANAGER
Brenda Shanley
AFFILIATIONS
Plainsong Productions (film/video/AV production co. Also owned by Ben Achtenberg)

Ferde Grofe Films

3100 Airport Ave., Santa Monica, CA 90405; (213) 397-7524; (800) 854-0561, ext. 925. (Science and educational films.)

Festival Films

2841 Irving Ave. S., Minneapolis, MN 55408; (612) 870-4744. (Wholesale distributors).

PRESIDENT
Ronald A. Hall

Film Ideas, Inc.

3575 Commercial Ave., Northbrook, IL 60062; (708) 480-5760. Organized 1979. (Educational film and video distribution.)

PRESIDENT
Mike Collins
SECRETARY
Alice Collins

Films for the Humanities & Sciences

Box 2053, Princeton, NJ 08543; (609) 452-1128. Organized 1971. (Video distribution and production.)

PRESIDENT
Harold Mantell
VICE PRESIDENT, SALES AND MARKETING
Michael Mantell

Financial Video Resources

1365 N. Broadway, Walnut Creek, CA 94596; (415) 674-3574. Organized 1985. (Produces and distributes educational videotapes on financial subjects. Also distributes videotapes produced by Internal Revenue Service on income tax-related subjects.)

CEO
William P. Koch
CFO
Timothy Salisbury
GENERAL MANAGER
Susan Pace

First Movie Exchange of Colorado

3011 W. 74th Ave., Westminster, CO 80030; (303) 427-7788. Subsidiary of Wickman Ltd.

PRESIDENT
Dianne Lynn Wickman

First Run/Icarus Films, Inc.

200 Park Avenue South, #1319, New York, NY 10003; (212) 674-3375.

First Run Features

153 Waverly Place, NY 10014; (212) 243-0600; FAX: (212) 989-7649. Organized 1980. (Distributes film and video to theatrical, non-theatrical, cable, home video and foreign markets.)

PRESIDENT
Seymour Wishman

First Run Video

3620 Overland Ave., Los Angeles, CA 90034; (213) 838-2111. (Specialty label.)

VICE PRESIDENT, DIRECTOR OF SALES
Norman B. Smith

First Video Exchange

17503 S. Figueroa, Gardena, CA 90248; (213) 516-6422, (800) 247-2351. Organized 1981. (National movie exchange, stock rotation specialist for video movie dealers.)

PRESIDENT
Jeff Leyton

Focus International, Inc.

14 Oregon Dr., Huntington Station, NY 11746; (516) 549-5320; FAX: (516) 549-2066. Organized 1976. (Producers and distributors of film and video for sex education, research and therapy.)

PRESIDENT
Mark Schoen, Ph.D.

Forum Home Video

(See M.C.E.G. Home Entertainment/Forum Home Video)

Four Point Entertainment, Inc.

3575 Cahuenga Blvd. W., Suite 600, Los Angeles, CA 90068; (213) 850-1600. Organized 1984. (Television production, videocassette production.)

PRESIDENT
Ron Ziskin
CHAIRMAN
Shukri Ghalayini

Fox Hills Video

5730 Buckingham Parkway, Culver City, CA 90230; (213) 216-7900, (800) 421-4509. Organized 1986. (Distributes and produces programming for sell-through and rental markets.)

PRESIDENT
Jack Bernstein
VICE PRESIDENT, SALES
Michael Meyer
VICE PRESIDENT, MARKETING
Mark Gilule
VICE PRESIDENT, PUBLIC RELATIONS
Jim Gullo

Fox/Lorber Associates, Inc.

432 Park Ave. S., New York, NY 10016; (212) 686-6777. (Home video sales agent, international distributor and producer.)

PRESIDENT
Richard Lorber

Freewheelin' Films Ltd.

P.O. Box 599, Aspen, CO 81611; (303) 925-2640. (Sports and educational videos.)

DIRECTOR
Rodney Jacobs

Fries Home Video

(Division of Fries Entertainment, Inc.)
6922 Hollywood Blvd., Los Angeles, CA 90028; (213) 466-2266; (800) 248-1113; FAX: (213) 464-6082.

EXECUTIVE VICE PRESIDENT & COO
Len Levy
VICE PRESIDENT, SPECIAL MARKETS
Larry M. Klingman

Full Moon Video

9200 Sunset Blvd., Suite 530, Los Angeles, CA 90069; (213) 859-1040. Organized 1988. Division of Bandcompany. (Video producer.)

PRESIDENT
Charles Weinryt

G.G. Communications, Inc.

111 French Ave., Braintree, MA 02184; (617) 843-4860, (800) 525-3503.

PRESIDENT
Nicholas Russo

GME Piano Video

4150 Chestnut Ave., P.O. Box 7562, Long Beach, CA 90807; (213) 424-5177. Organized 1982. (Worldwide distribution of the piano video course Beginning Piano—An Adult Approach—15 cassettes, 3 books).

PRESIDENT AND TREASURER
Dr. Allen Giles
VICE PRESIDENT
Anne Diener Giles

GN Communications, Ltd.

2600 W. Peterson Ave., Chicago, IL 60659; (312) 465-0085; FAX: (312) 465-7218. Organized 1984. (Sells and produces special interest programming to the television and home market.)

PRESIDENT
Steven Polydoris

Galaxy Group

3790 Dunn Dr., Suite C., Los Angeles, CA 90034; (213) 204-3392.

Gateway Films Inc.

Box 540, 2030 Wentz Church Rd., Worcester, PA 19490; (215) 584-1893; FAX: (215) 584-4610. Organized 1972. (Motion picture production and distribution.)

PRESIDENT
A. Kenneth Curtis

Gaylord Production Company
Gaylord Syndicom

65 Music Square West, Nashville, TN 37203 (615) 327-0110. (Producer and syndicator of programming for all television markets including network, first and 2nd syndication, cable and home video.)

VP & GENERAL MANAGER
Jane Dowden Grams
AFFILIATIONS
Parent Company: Oklahoma Publishing. Affiliations: Gaylord Broadcasting (5 station group); The Nashville Network; Opryland/Opryland Hotel/Grand Ol' Opry, (3 radio stations) Texas Rangers

Genesis Project, Inc.

630 Fifth Ave., Suite 1510, New York, NY 10020; (212) 399-1020, (800) 336-4545. (Religious videos.)

PRESIDENT
Michael Manuel

Glenn Video Vistas

6924 Canby Ave., Suite 103, Reseda, CA 91335; (818) 981-5506. Organized 1980. (Sale of videotapes.)

OWNER/MANAGER
Murray Glass
AFFILIATION
Glenn Photo Supply

Global Video Distributors, Inc.

8181 N.W. 91 Terrace, Suite 7, Medley, FL 33166; (305) 887-1986; 887-2000; FAX: (305) 887-2000. Organized 1980. (Distribution of videocassettes.)

PRESIDENT
Angel Tamargo
TREASURER
Xiomara Tamargo

Global Village

454 Broome St., New York, NY 10013; (212) 966-7526.

Globe Three Inc.

Box 265, Room 4010, Middletown, OH 45042; (513) 422-4155. Organized 1985. (Educational videos geared to the arts and classics.)

PRESIDENT
Lois V. Schultz
SECRETARY/TREASURER
Sam Ashworth
VICE PRESIDENT
Jack Howard

Go-Video, Inc.

4141 North Scottsdale Rd., Suite 204, Scottsdale, AZ 85251; (602) 481-2900; FAX: (602) 481-2916. Organized 1984. (Video production and distributor of VCR 2.)

CHAIRMAN & CEO
R. Terren Dunlap
PRESIDENT
Eric J. Schedeler
VICE PRESIDENT, SECRETARY & TREASURER
Robert J. Brilon
BOARD OF DIRECTORS
R. Terren Dunlap, Merrill L. Ridgway, Richard L. Barrett, Eric J. Schedeler, Roy E. Dunlap
AFFILIATION
American Electronics Association

Golden Bay Video

20 Sunnyside Ave., Suite A 183, Mill Valley, CA 94941; (415) 381-2566. Organized 1982. (Video production.)

PRESIDENT
Vinton W. Medbury, Jr.

Golden Productions

249 Sunset Dr., Encinitas, CA 92024; (619) 942-2614. Organized 1983. (Education and training programs for mental health professionals.)

PRESIDENT
Dr. Kenneth M. Golden

Goodtimes/Kids Klassics Distribution Corp.

401 Fifth Ave., New York, NY 10016; (212) 889-0044.

PRESIDENT
Joseph Carey
SENIOR VICE PRESIDENT, THEATRICAL ACQUISITIONS
Jeff Baker

Gorgon Video

15825 Rob Roy Dr., Oak Forest, IL 60452; (312) 687-7881. (Horror videos.)

PRESIDENT
Nasser Zegar

Gospel Films, Inc.

P.O. Box 455, Muskegon, MI 49443; (616) 773-3361; (800) 253-0413 (outside Michigan); (800) 632-0139 (Michigan only); FAX: (616) 777-1847.

PRESIDENT
Rev. Billy Zeoli

Gospel Video

3790 Dunn Dr., Suite C, Los Angeles, CA 90034; (213) 204-3392.

Granada TV International

400 Madison Ave., Suite 1511, New York, NY 10017; (212) 753-3030.

DIRECTOR OF GTVI, NY
Leila Maw
SENIOR SALES EXECUTIVE
Merry Mullings
SALES ASSISTANT
Sally Millwood
BOARD OF DIRECTORS
Vivien Wallace (Chief Executive), David Plowright (managing director)
BRANCHES
36 Golden Square, London W1, England; 01-734-8080.
18 Rue Volney, Paris 75002, France; 4261 7910 (Director: Sara de St. Hubert)

Grass Roots Network, Inc.

300 Pacific Ave., Suite F, Aspen, CO 81611; (303) 925-8000.

EXECUTIVE DIRECTOR
Kevin D. Erdman

Gravity Sports Films, Inc.

100 Broadway, Jersey City, NJ 07306; (800) 346-4884; (201) 860-9633 in NJ. Organized 1982. (Video distribution of action-sports titles.)

PRESIDENT
Charles Mathieu
VICE PRESIDENT
Chris Hawkesworth
SECRETARY
Bruce Stafford
BOARD OF DIRECTORS
Charles Mathieu, Chris Hawkesworth, Bruce Stafford

Green Mountain Post Films

37 Ferry Rd., P.O. Box 229, Turners Falls, MA 01376; (413) 863-4754; 863-8248.

PRESIDENT
Daniel Keller

Grunko Films, Inc.

856 Coffeen Ave., Sheridan WY 82801; (307) 672-2487; (800) 638-7779; FAX: (307) 672-9294. Organized 1984. (Video production and distribution of wildlife, hunting, fishing, travel and children's videos.)

PRESIDENT
G. Wm. Grunkenmeyer
VICE PRESIDENT
Frank F. Johnson

HBO Video

1100 Ave. of the Americas, New York, NY 10019; (212) 977-8990.

PRESIDENT
Eric Kessler
SENIOR VICE PRESIDENT, MARKETING
Tracy Dolgin
SENIOR VICE PRESIDENT, PROGRAMMING
Henry McGee

HCP Research

20655 Sunrise Dr., Cupertino, CA 95104; (408) 727-1864.

PRESIDENT
H.C. Pellow
VICE PRESIDENT
M.R. Faix

HPG Home Video

400 South Houston, Suite 230, Dallas, TX 75202; (214) 741-5544; FAX: (214) 742-8423. Organized 1985. (Produces and markets special interest videos.)

PRESIDENT
Mickey Holden
DIRECTOR OF MARKETING
Karlene Lewis
AFFILIATIONS
VSDA, SIVA

Hands on Productions

633 Post St., Room 500, San Francisco, CA 94109; (415) 771-2055. Organized 1987. (Produces gay/lesbian interest videos.)

PRESIDENT
David Stuart

Hanna Barbera Video

3400 Cahuenga Blvd., Los Angeles, CA 90068-1376; (213) 851-5000; FAX: (213) 969-1201; 660 Madison Ave., New York, NY 10021; (212) 750-5366.

PRESIDENT
Joseph Barbera
SENIOR VICE PRESIDENT
William Hanna
VICE PRESIDENT & GENERAL MANAGER
Wendy Moss

Harmony Vision

116 N. Robertson Blvd., Suite 701, Los Angeles, CA 90048; (213) 652-8844. (Music and concert videos.)

PRESIDENT
Jerry Percell

Hartly Film Foundation, Inc.

Cat Rock Rd., Cos Cob, CT 06807; (203) 869-1818. Organized 1970. (Produces educational films.)

PRESIDENT
Elda Hartley
VICE PRESIDENT
Carol Grayson

Health Media of America, Inc.

11300 Sorrento Valley Rd., #250, San Diego, CA 92121; (619) 453-3887.

PRESIDENT
Robert H. Garrison, Jr.

Hearst Marine Books

105 Madison Ave., New York, NY 10016; (212) 889-3050. (Division of William Morrow, Inc.)

Henwood Cinema Video

Box 376, Jamison, PA 18929; (215) 788-7186. Organized 1976. (Television programming of motion pictures and videocassette programming of feature films.)

PRESIDENT
Alan Henwood, Jr.
SALES MANAGER
Mary Henwood
OFFICE MANAGER
Ron Hagen
ASSISTANT SALES MANAGER
Ann Miller

Hewlett-Packard

1819 Page Mill Rd., Palo Alto, CA 94304; (415) 857-2381. (How-to and educational videos.)

Hi-Tops Video

(See Media Home Entertainment).

Alfred Higgins Productions Inc.

9100 Sunset Blvd., Los Angeles, CA 90069; (213) 272-6500.

PRESIDENT
Alfred Higgins

High Gate Pictures

130 E. 59 St., New York, NY 10022; (212) 755-8600.

PRESIDENT
Steve Maier

Hollywood Home Theatre

1540 N. Highland Ave., #110, Hollywood, CA 90028; (213) 466-0121, (213) 466-0127.

PRESIDENT
Larry S. Fine

Hollywood International Film Corporation of America

1044 S. Hill St., Los Angeles, CA 90015; (213) 749-2067. Organized 1969. (Film production and distribution.)

PRESIDENT
Efrain Tobalina
VICE PRESIDENT
Maria-Pia Tobalina

Home and Industrial Distributors

300-1 Rte. 17S., Lodi, NJ 07644; (202) 777-4700, (800) 213-1586.

PRESIDENT
Alfred Goldberger

Home Vision

5547 N. Ravenswood, Chicago, IL 60640; (312) 878-2600, ext. 325. Organized 1985. (Source for fine and performing arts videos.)

EXECUTIVE SENIOR V.P., PUBLIC MEDIA, INC.
Gale Livengood

EXECUTIVE DIRECTOR OF HOME VISION
Christine Lundberg
NATIONAL SALES MANAGER
John Hillsman
CHAIRMAN OF PUBLIC MEDIA INC.
Charles Benton

Hot Licks Productions, Inc.

P.O. Box 337, Pound Ridge, NY 10576; (914) 763-8013. FAX: (914) 763-9453. Organized 1979. (Produces video and audio music instruction.)

PRESIDENT
Arlen Roth
VICE PRESIDENT
Deborah Roth
BOARD OF DIRECTORS
Arlen Roth, Deborah Roth
AFFILIATIONS
Labtek in U.K., Music Sales in Australia and New Zealand, Rumark Video in Canada.

Houghton Mifflin Company

One Beacon St. (executive offices); 2 Park St. (trade and reference divisions), Boston, MA 02108; (617) 725-5000. (Bird-watching and "Watching Birds with Roger Tory Peterson" video.)

Hyde Park Media

1314 Howard St., Suite 2, Chicago, IL 60626; (312) 274-3337.

PRESIDENT
A. E. De Bartolo

IFEX Films/International Film Exchange Ltd.

201 W. 52 St., New York, NY 10019; (212) 582-4318. Cable: IFEXREP-New York; Telex: 420748; Fax: (212) 956-2257; 9200 Sunset Blvd. PH 9, Los Angeles, CA 90069; (213) 278-6490; FAX: (213) 278-7939; TELEX; 4972966. Organized 1959. (Domestic and international distribution of feature films, documentaries, shorts and video programs.)

PRESIDENT
Gerald J. Rappoport
EXECUTIVE VICE PRESIDENT
Richard Grisar
SENIOR VICE PRESIDENT, INTERNATIONAL SALES
Joy Pereths
VICE PRESIDENT, BUSINESS AFFAIRS
Beulah Rappoport
VICE PRESIDENT, FOREIGN DISTRIBUTION
Stephanie Holm
VICE PRESIDENT, THEATRICAL DISTRIBUTION
Robert Newman

IRS Video

8335 Sunset Blvd., Suite 300, Los Angeles, CA 90069; (213) 650-8010. (Music videos.)

I.T.A. Publications

P.O. Box 281, Grand Blanc, MI 48439; (313) 655-6434. Organized 1974. (Produces, sells and distributes educational videos, training aids and publications.)

PRESIDENT
James S. Benko
EXECUTIVE SECRETARY
Siew-Hiang Benko
SALES MANAGER
Maureen Juno
EXECUTIVE DIRECTOR
Anne-Marie Curell
BOARD OF DIRECTORS
James S. Benko, Siew-Hiang Benko, Maureen Juno, Anne-Marie Curell, Nelson Curell, Michael Gould, Bruce A. Benko, Margaret Naessens
AFFILIATION
National Association of Deans

ITV Productions Ltd.

3941 Madison Ave., Culver City, CA 90232; (213) 559-7670; FAX: (213) 202-1409. Organized 1986. (Video-film production.)

PRESIDENT
David Shapiro
SECRETARY/TREASURER
Cid Hunter

IVCC

2035-39 S. 7th St., Philadelphia, PA 19148; (215) 271-1500; (800) 523-7676. Organized 1982. (Produces and distributes educational material on video tape.)

PRESIDENT
Stan Nicotera

Image Entertainment

6311 Romaine St., Hollywood, CA 90038; (213) 468-8867; FAX: (213) 468-9236. (Licensor and distributor of laser videodiscs.)

PRESIDENT
Martin Greenwald
SENIOR VICE PRESIDENT
Lee Kasper

Image Factory

29 W. Main, Bozeman, MT 59715; (406) 587-8918. Organized 1981. (Video production and film to video transfers.)

OWNER
Steve Flagg

Image Makers of Pittsford

6 Wood Gate, Pittsford, NY 14534; (716) 385-4567. Organized 1976. (Produces videotapes for industry, educational programs. The Practical Optics Division publishes the "Practical Optics" textbook and videotape program.)

PRESIDENT
Richard H. Roberts

Image Organization, Inc.

9000 Sunset Blvd., Suite 915, Los Angeles, CA 90069; (213) 278-8751. Organized 1987. (International distribution of motion pictures, home video and television.)

CHAIRMAN & CEO
Pierre David
SENIOR VICE PRESIDENT, OPERATIONS
Lawrence Goebel
SENIOR VICE PRESIDENT, INTERNATIONAL DISTRIBUTION
Mark A. Horowitz
VICE PRESIDENT, TELEVISION SALES
Marie-Claude Poulin
DIRECTOR OF MARKETING & POST PRODUCTION
Lee Matis
DIRECTOR OF ACQUISITIONS
Noel A. Zanitsch
CONTROLLER
Robert Hartsone
DIRECTOR OF INTERNATIONAL SERVICES
James D. Putt

BOARD OF DIRECTORS
Pierre David, Rene Malo, Michael Hirsh, Dimitri Villard, Robby Wald
BRANCHES
Los Angeles (head office), Paris, Montreal, Toronto
AFFILIATIONS
New Star Entertainment, Malofilm Group, Nelvana Entertainment, Pierre David Enterprises.

Images Video & Film Archive, Inc.

300 Phillips Park Rd., Mamaroneck, NY 10543; (914) 381-2994.

PRESIDENT
Robert A. Harris

Imperial Entertainment, Corp.

4640 Lankershim Blvd., 4th Floor, North Hollywood, CA 91602; (818) 762-0005; FAX: (818) 762-0006; TELEX: 4932651 VPDINTL. Organized 1987. (Film production, finance, distribution worldwide and video distribution, U.S.A.)

PRESIDENT
Sunil R. Shah
EXECUTIVE VICE PRESIDENT
Sundip R. Shah
VICE PRESIDENT, FINANCE & OPERATIONS
Juan C. Collas
VICE PRESIDENT OF SALES AND MARKETING
Brian Clendenen
EXECUTIVE VICE PRESIDENT, PRODUCTION
Ash R. Shah
VICE PRESIDENT, PRODUCTION
Eric Karson
VICE PRESIDENT, INTERNATIONAL
Chris Davis
BOARD OF DIRECTORS
Sunil R. Shah, Sundip R. Shah, Juan C. Collas
BRANCH
London: Bldg. No. 1, GEC Estate, East Lane, Wembley, Middlesex, HA9 7FF, England

Imperial Video Corp.

P.O. Box 475, Bethpage, NY 11714; (516) 935-5050, (800) 645-5060.

PRESIDENT
B. Rubinowitz

Important Records Distributors

187-07 Henderson Ave., Hollis, NY 11423; (718) 740-5700. (Relativity/Combat/In-Effect Records)

VICE PRESIDENT, MARKETING & SALES
Howard Gabriel

Increase Video

6914 Canby Ave., Suite 110, Reseda, CA 91335-4313; (818) 342-2880. FAX: (818) 342-4029.

PRESIDENT
Howard Silvers
DIRECTOR OF MARKETING
Len Chapman

Indiana University Audio-Visual Center

Field Services Division, Bloomington, IN 47405-5901; (812) 855-8087; FAX: (812) 855-8404. Organized 1940. (Audiovisual media marketing and distribution.)

EXECUTIVE DIRECTOR (AVC)
Thomas M. Schwen
DIVISION DIRECTOR
Chris Wagner
AFFILIATION
American Film & Video Assocation

Ingram Video, Inc.

1125 Heil Quaker Blvd., La Vergne, TN 37086-1986; (615) 361-5000; 793-5000; (800) 759-5000; FAX: (615) 399-3160; (615) 361-0236. (Subsidiary of Ingram Industries, Inc.)

PRESIDENT
John Taylor
SENIOR VICE PRESIDENT & GENERAL MANAGER
Ray Capp
VICE PRESIDENT, SALES
Steve Comm
VICE PRESIDENT, OPERATIONS & ADMINISTRATION
Buddy Pickler
VICE PRESIDENT, FINANCE
Jeff Bigach
VICE PRESIDENT, VIDEO PRODUCT
Bob Webb
DIRECTOR OF ADVERTISING & MARKETING
Michael Vassen

Innerquest Communications Corp.

6383 Rose La., Carpinteria, CA 93013; (805) 684-9977.

PRODUCER
Don L. Higley

Instant Replay Video Magazine

2951 S. Bayshore Dr., Miami, FL 33133; (305) 448-7088. Organized 1976. (Videotape magazine format about the video industry and TV Broadcasting. Sold on subscription basis. Available in ¾" and ½" Beta and VHS and 8 mm.)

PUBLISHER
Charles Azar

Instructional Video Cassette Corp.

2035 S. 7th St., Philadelphia, PA 19148; (215) 271-1500. (Produces and distributes special interest videocassette, PRO CHESS and PRO Blackjack).

PRESIDENT
Stan Nicotera

Intermedia Arts Minnesota

(formerly UC Video)
425 Ontario St., SE, Minneapolis, MN 55414; (612) 627-4444. (Non-profit media arts center producing, distributing and presenting social issue and contemporary interdisciplinary art and video.)

EXECUTIVE DIRECTOR
Tom Borrup

Inter-Global Communications

(div. Radio's Reliable Resources)
630 Park La., 2nd floor, Philadelphia, PA 19144-3713; (215) 849-3997. Organized 1962. (International film/tape program buying service for television stations and small dealers of home video.)

GENERAL MANAGER
F. O. Pease
OFFICE MANAGER
A. E. Pease
FOREIGN MANAGER
A. P. Taylor
BUYER
B. P. Weber
SALES MANAGER
J. K. Sperling
AFFILIATIONS
Inter-Global News div.

International Audio-Visual, Inc.

100 Northill Dr. #23, Brisbane, CA 94005; (415) 467-1032; 467-4663. (Chinese videos.)

PRESIDENT
S. S. Ling

International Film Foundation, Inc.

155 W. 72nd St., Suite 306, New York, NY 10023; (212) 580-1111. Organized 1945. (Produces and distributes educational films and videos.)

EXECUTIVE DIRECTOR
Dr. Sam Bryan
BOARD OF DIRECTORS
Richard Ford (president)

International Historic Films, Inc.

3533 South Archer Ave., Chicago, IL 60609; (312) 927-2900. Orders: P.O. Box 29035, Chicago, IL 60629. Organized 1976. (Distribution and production of military and political features and documentaries. Also distribution of Eastern European films. Provides stock footage to producers. Sales of films on videocassette through store and direct mail internationally. Videocassettes available on NTSC, PAL and SECAM videostandards.)

PRESIDENT
Peter Bernotas
MARKETING MANAGER
Frank Weinberg
AFFILIATION
Lithuanian Historical Society

International Home Video

431 N. Figueroa, Wilmington, CA 90744; (213) 513-1149. Organized 1983. (Manufactures and distributes prerecorded videocassettes.)

CHAIRMAN
Irving Katzef
PRESIDENT
Russell Greene
SECRETARY & TREASURER
Wayne Jones
BOARD OF DIRECTORS
Russell Greene, Irving Katzef
BRANCH
Video Latino, Country Video USA

International Marketing Services Inc.

2170 W. Broadway, Bldg. 522, Anaheim, CA 92804; (714) 891-6015.

VICE PRESIDENT
Jeff Scheirer

International Sailing Products

P.O. Box 355, Oyster Bay, NY 11771; (516) 922-5182, (800) 645-7676.

PRESIDENT
Steve Benjamin
VICE PRESIDENT
Paul Dickey

International Sunday School Lesson, Inc. (Bible Lessons International)

P.O. Box 1289, Marshall, TX 75671. Organized 1976. (Exegetical verse-by-verse Bible teaching using historical-grammatical hermeneutics.)

FOUNDER & HOST
Dr. Bob Utley

International Video Entertainment

15400 Sherman Way, Suite 500, Van Nuys, CA 91406; (818) 908-0303. FAX: (805) 908-0320. Organized 1986. (Home video producer and distributor.)

PRESIDENT & CHIEF OPERATING OFFICER
David Mount
CHIEF FINANCIAL OFFICER
Rodney Trovinger
VICE PRESIDENT, ADMINISTRATION
David Campbell
SENIOR VICE PRESIDENT, MANUFACTURING & DISTRIBUTION
Dave Mishra
SENIOR VICE PRESIDENT, PROGRAMMING
Ronna Wallace
AFFILIATIONS
(Subidiary of LIVE Entertainment, Inc.)

Ivy Video

165 W. 46 St., New York, NY 10036; (212) 382-0111. (Subsidiary of Ivy Entertainment, Inc.)

PRESIDENT
Sidney Tager
VICE PRESIDENT
Joshua Tager

JCI Video

5309 Derry Ave., Agoura Hills, CA 91301; (818) 889-9022; (800) 223-7479; FAX: (818) 889-0155. (Exercise video tapes.)

PRESIDENT
Jerome Bowie

JEF Films Inc.

Film House, 143 Hickory Hill Circle, Osterville, MA 02655; (508) 428-7198; FAX: (508) 428-7198. Organized 1973. (Production and distribution of films, TV shows [network and syndication] and video programs throughout the world.)

CHIEF EXECUTIVE OFFICER
Jeffrey H. Aikman
VICE PRESIDENT
Elsie Aikman
SALES MANAGER
Jo-Anne Polak
PROMOTION MANAGER
Janie Barber
BOARD OF DIRECTORS
Jeffrey H. Aikman, Elsie Aikman, Donald Aikman, Janie Barber, Jo-Anne Polak
BRANCHES
Film Classic Exchange, Los Angeles, CA
JEF Films Inc.—England, Canada, Australia, France, Spain, Portugal, Greece, Switzerland, Austria, Italy, Monaco, New Zealand, Norway, Denmark, Germany, Sweden, Hong Kong, Fiji, Ireland, Belgium, Luxembourg, Algeria, Morocco, Tunisia
AFFILIATIONS
Owner of Film Classic Exchange (founded 1916), VIP Video, XTC Video, WHAM! Video, JEF Video Line, JEF Films International, PHD Video, The Stock Exchange (stock footage).

JMJ Productions

P.O. Box 4449, Hollywood, FL 33083; (305) 652-3952. (Railroad related documentaries.)

PRESIDENT
Morry Farcus

J2 Communications, Inc.

10850 Wilshire Blvd., Suite 1000, Los Angeles, CA 90024; (213) 474-5252. Organized 1987. (Produces and distributes quality, original home videos in the sell-thru market.)

PRESIDENT & CEO
James P. Jimirro
VICE PRESIDENT & CFO
James Toll
VICE PRESIDENT OF SALES
Duncan Murray
VICE PRESIDENT, MARKETING
David Bowers
VICE PRESIDENT, PROGRAM DEVELOPMENT
Ellen Pittleman
VICE PRESIDENT, BUSINESS AFFAIRS
Scott Roth

J & R Film Co. Inc.

6820 Romaine, Hollywood, CA 90038; (213) 467-3107. Organized 1963. (Film and video post production.)

PRESIDENT
Joe Paskal
EXECUTIVE VICE PRESIDENT
Jim Reichow
VICE PRESIDENT, SALES
Ron Powell
BRANCHES
New York, Chicago, Denver

Jem Records

3619 Kennedy Rd., South Plainfield, NJ 07080; (201) 753-6100. (Distributes and manufactures records, tapes, compact discs, music video.)

PRESIDENT
Marty Scott
VICE PRESIDENT
Ed Grossi
TREASURER
Jeff Tenenbaum
BRANCHES
Grand Prairie TX; Reseda, CA

Journal Films, Inc.

930 Pitner Ave., Evanston, IL 60202; (312) 328-6700; (800) 323-5448. Organized 1955. (Distributor of educational videos and films for the school and library markets.)

PRESIDENT
Joe Farragher
CHAIRMAN
Joel Altschul
EXECUTIVE VICE PRESIDENT
Esther Altschul
VICE PRESIDENT
Bruce Colling
NATIONAL SALES MANAGER
John Kelly
AFFILIATION
An Altschul Group Company

Joyce Media, Inc.

32003 Crown Valley Rd., P.O. Box 57, Acton, CA 93510; (805) 269-1169; MODEM/FAX: (805) 269-2139. Organized 1971. (Produces and publishes videos.)

PRESIDENT
John Joyce
SECRETARY
M. Gayle Joyce
COMPTROLLER
Lois Knight

K-Video Productions

157 Wiltshire Rd., Claymont, DE 19703; (302) 798-2229. Organized 1980. (Educational tapes, corporate and private videos.)

PRESIDENT
John Kay
VICE PRESIDENT
Stan Kay
SECRETARY & TREASURER
Charmaine Imburgia
AFFILIATIONS
DBE, GWVCB, Delaware State Chamber of Commerce

KVC/Atlantic Home Video

7225 Woodland Dr., P.O. Box 68881, Indianapolis, IN 46268-0881; (317) 297-1888; (800) 582-2000; (800) 523-5851 (in IN).

PRESIDENT & CEO
Alan Saffron
EXECUTIVE VICE PRESIDENT
Mark Gilula
VICE PRESIDENT, SALES
Jeff Jacobs

Kalmbach Publishing Co.

21027 Crossroads Circle, P.O. Box 1612, Waukesha, WI 53187; (414) 796-8776; FAX: (414) 796-0126.

PRESIDENT
Walter J. Mundschau
MARKETING & SALES
Susan Poole

Keep the Faith Inc.

810 Belmont Ave., North Haledon, NJ 07508; (201) 423-5395, (800) 221-1564. (Catholic, family videos.)

Allan Keith Productions, Inc.

630 Ninth Ave., Suite 714, New York, NY 10036; (212) 246-0239. Organized 1961. (Produces and distributes educational subjects—film and video—speech, make up, sex equity, auto body repair, hairstyling, Yoga exercise and belly dance videos, etc.)

PRESIDENT
Allan Keith
VICE PRESIDENT
Michael Keith
SECRETARY
Laurie Schilling

Kennen Publishing Company

150 Shoreline Highway, Bldg. E., Mill Valley, CA 94941; (415) 332-5828. (How-to computer videos.)

PRESIDENT
Ed Dudkowski

Key Video

1211 Ave. of the Americas, New York, NY 10036; (212) 819-3200, (619) 459-0500. (Subsidiary of CBS/Fox Video.)

PRESIDENT
Herb Fischer
DIRECTOR OF PROD. MANAGEMENT
Joseph Annechino

Walter J. Klein Company, Ltd.

6311 Carmel Rd., Box 2087, Charlotte, NC 28247-2087; (704) 542-1403. Organized 1948. (Production and distribution of sponsored films and tapes.)

CHAIRMAN
Walter J. Klein
PRESIDENT
Richard A. Klein

VICE PRESIDENTS
Terry Losardo
David Jordan
SECRETARY
Elizabeth G. Klein
TREASURER
Betsy J. Klein
BOARD OF DIRECTORS
Walter J. Klein, Richard A Klein, Elizabeth G. Klein, Betsy J. Klein, Terry Losardo, David Jordan
BRANCH
Seven Devils, NC

Kultur International Films

121 Highway 36, West Long Branch, NJ 07764; (201) 229-2343; FAX: (201) 229-0066. Organized 1980. (Home video company dedicated solely to the performing arts with emphasis on ballet, opera, classical music, dance and performing artist profiles.)

PRESIDENT
Dennis M. Hedlund
VICE PRESIDENT
Pearl Lee
CHIEF FINANCIAL OFFICER
John Donahue
MANAGING DIRECTOR
Ron Davis
BUSINESS ADMINISTRATOR
Lynne Zecca
MARKETING DIRECTOR
Jim Wade
SALES MANAGER
Johanna Kelly
ACCOUNT REPRESENTATIVE
Diane Fay
ACQUISITIONS DIRECTOR
Ron Davis

Lawren Productions, Inc.

930 Pitner Ave., Evanston, IL 60202; (312) 328-6700. Organized 1961. (Distributes special education, child development, and attitude challenging AV programming to schools, colleges, hospitals and clinics.)

PRESIDENT
Joseph Farragher
CHAIRMAN OF BOARD
Joel Altschul
AFFILIATION
An Altschul Group Company

Learn Incorporated

113 Gaither Dr., Mt. Laurel, NJ 08054; (609) 234-6100. Organized 1968. (Publishes and markets "How to" video programs and audio programs with print materials.)

PRESIDENT
Bruce E. Corley
VICE PRESIDENT, FINANCE
Andrew S. Myers

Learning Corporation of America

1440 South Sepulveda Blvd., Suite 118, Los Angeles, CA 90025; (213) 444-8100; FAX: (213) 444-8130; 444-8101.

Legalvision, Inc.

℅Jacobson & Colfin, 150 Fifth Ave., Room 1103, New York, NY 10011, (212) 691-5630. Organized 1982. (Produces educational and instructional videotapes for attorneys and businesses.)

Leisure Enterprises Ltd.

P.O. Box 70677, New Orleans, LA 70172; (504) 561-0531; 561-8323; FAX: (504) 581-4752. Organized 1961. (Television productions, broadcast and home video.)

PRESIDENT
John Shoup
VICE PRESIDENT
John Beyer
SECRETARY
Cybil Curtis
TREASURER
Nick Kokoron
CHIEF FINANCIAL OFFICER
John Marsiglia
DIRECTOR OF MARKETING
Brian Heiden
CONTROLLER
Diana O'Rorke
BRANCHES
3509 18th St., Metairie, LA 70002
AFFILIATIONS
Great Chef Television Productions, Leisure Video Productions

Leisure Time Products/3M

(See 3M)

Liberty Entertainment Group, Inc.

1019 E. 53rd St., Davenport, IA 52807; (319) 386-0403. (Manufacturer and distributor of prerecorded video programming.)

PRESIDENT
Brad Tregloan
VICE PRESIDENT
Al Simmons
SECRETARY
Ed Moen

Life Video Gospel Association

1435 Central Ave., College Place, WA 99324; (509) 522-0784. Organized 1979. (Produces and distributes religious videotapes.)

PRESIDENT
Donald M Vories
TREASURER
Walter Anderson
SECRETARY
Jeanne Vories
BOARD OF DIRECTORS
Donald M. Vories, Walter Anderson, Jeanne Vories, Fred E. J. Harder, Vernon Shafer, Paul Turpel, D. K. Smith

Ligonier Ministries, Inc.

270 S. North Lake Blvd., Suite 1270, Altamonte Springs, FL 32701; (800) 435-4343; (407) 834-1633. (Adult Scripture/theological training materials).

VICE PRESIDENT, ADULT EDUCATION
Robert Ingram

Listening Library

One Park Ave., Old Greenwich, CT 06870; (203) 637-3616.

PRESIDENT
Timothy Ditlow

The Little Red Filmhouse

P.O. Box 691083, Los Angeles, CA 90069; (213) 653-0407. Organized 1975. (Produces and distributes film and video programming.)

PRESIDENT
Larry Klingman
VICE PRESIDENT
Anette Klingman

Llamavision Productions

P.O. Box 50859, Tucson, AZ 85703; (602) 293-8088. Organized 1984. (TV and video production from script to finished product. Producers of award-winning dance and international travel videos.)

PRESIDENT
Gerald D. Harwood, Ph.D.
VICE PRESIDENT
Sarajean A. Harwood
AFFILIATIONS
Anubis Productions, Bastet Productions and Video Safaris International

Lorimar Home Video

17942 Cowan Ave., Irvine, CA 92714; (714) 474-0355.

CHAIRMAN/CEO
Jerry Gottlieb
SENIOR VICE-PRESIDENT, FINANCE
Michael A. Piraino
SENIOR VICE-PRESIDENT
Neal S. Baseman

MAS Productions

18434 Bermuda St., Northridge, CA 91326; (818) 360-0371.

MCA Distributing Corp.

70 Universal City Plaza, 3rd Floor, Universal City, CA 91608; (818) 777-4000. (Distributor of prerecorded video cassettes and records.) A division of MCA/Universal.

PRESIDENT, MCA HOME VIDEO
Robert Blattner
EXECUTIVE VICE PRESIDENT
Tom Wertheimer
EXECUTIVE VICE PRESIDENT, DISTRIBUTION
John Burns
VICE PRESIDENT, VIDEO DISTRIBUTION
Bill Hickman
DIRECTOR OF NATIONAL VIDEO ACCOUNTS
Janis Durr
DIRECTOR OF SALES ADMINISTRATION
June Morishita
BRANCHES
REGIONAL VIDEO DIRECTOR (NORTHEAST)
Chet Furmanek
REGIONAL VIDEO DIRECTOR (SOUTHEAST)
Kip Puiia
REGIONAL VIDEO DIRECTOR (SOUTH)
Ron Gibson
REGIONAL VIDEO DIRECTOR (MIDWEST)
Dan Gant
REGIONAL VIDEO DIRECTOR (WEST)
Barbara Berger

M.C.E.G. Home Entertainment/Forum Home Video

2400 Broadway Ave., Suite 100, Santa Monica, CA 90404; (213) 315-7800; FAX: (213) 315-7850.

EXECUTIVE VICE PRESIDENT
Kathy Callahan

M.C.E.G./Virgin Home Entertainment

2400 Broadway, Santa Monica, CA 90404; (213) 315-7800.

PRESIDENT
Steve Bickel
EXECUTIVE VICE PRESIDENT
Kathy Callahan
VICE PRESIDENT, FINANCE AND ADMINISTRATION
Philip Midiri
VICE PRESIDENT, MARKETING
Margaret Cleave

MGM/UA Home Video, Inc.

Filmland, 10000 W. Washington Blvd., Culver City, CA 90232-2728; (213) 280-6000.

OFFICERS

PRESIDENT & CHIEF OPERATING OFFICER
Bernard "Bud" O'Shea
EXECUTIVE VICE PRESIDENT
Kenin M. Spivak
SENIOR VICE PRESIDENT—FINANCE
Thomas P. Carson
SENIOR VICE PRESIDENT—MARKETING & SALES
Herbert M. Fischer
SENIOR VICE PRESIDENT, CORPORATE GENERAL COUNSEL & SECRETARY
William Allen Jones
SENIOR VICE PRESIDENT—INTERNATIONAL
Patrick John Leone
SENIOR VICE PRESIDENT—STUDIO LEGAL AFFAIRS
Nancy Niederman
SENIOR VICE PRESIDENT, ACQUISITION, PROGRAMMING & DEVELOPMENT
John Ruscin
VICE PRESIDENT—SALES
David Bishop
VICE PRESIDENT & CONTROLLER
Kathleen Coughlan
VICE PRESIDENT—CREDIT & ADMINISTRATION
Sanford Friedman
VICE PRESIDENT—HOME VIDEO OPERATIONS
Adrian Gonzalez
VICE PRESIDENT & TREASURER
Walter C. Hoffer
VICE PRESIDENT—BUSINESS AFFAIRS
Ron Miele
VICE PRESIDENT—TAXES
Daniel J. Taylor
VICE PRESIDENT—MARKETING
Ralph Tribbey

MMI Video Incorporated

57 W. Grand Ave., #401, Chicago, IL 60610; (312) 644-2775. Organized 1983. (Produces and markets behavioral modification, self-help, and heatlh related videocassettes.)

PRESIDENT
Mitchell Morris

MPI Home Video

15825 Rob Roy Dr., Oak Forest, IL 60452; (312) 687-7881. (Production and distribution of programming for home video.)

PRESIDENT
Waleed B. Ali
VICE PRESIDENT
Malik B. Ali
MARKETING DIRECTORS
Jaffer Ali
Nasser Zegar
MARKETING DIRECTOR, WEST COAST
Peter Blachely
BOARD OF DIRECTORS
Waleed B. Ali, Malik B. Ali, Jeanean Othman

M.S. Distributing Co.

1050 Arthur Ave., Elk Grove, IL 60007; (312) 364-2888.

PRESIDENT
Tony Dalesandro
MARKETING & SALES
Rick Chrzan

M.S.V. Distributors

40 S. Carolina St., Baltimore, MD 21231; (301) 675-1400, (800) 992-7799, (800) 492-1443. (Subsidiary of Musical Sales.)

PRESIDENT
Michael J. Bereson
MARKETING & SALES
J. Anthony Ray

Macmillan Video

866 Third Ave., New York, NY 10022; (212) 702-3241, 702-2000. (Children's and educational videos.)

EXECUTIVE PRODUCER
James P. MacGuire

Magic Window

2901 W. Alameda Ave., Burbank, CA 91505; (818) 954-4950; 3500 W. Olive Ave., Burbank, CA 91505; (818) 953-7900. (A division of RCA/Columbia Home Video.) (Children's videos.)

Magna Systems, Inc.

W. Countyline 95, Barrington, IL 60010; (312) 382-6477. Organized 1978. (Produces and markets video learning programs.)

PRESIDENT
Wilbur S. Edwards
TREASURER
Jane H. Edwards
SECRETARY
Wilbur S. Edwards
BOARD OF DIRECTORS
Wilbur S. Edwards, Jane H. Edwards, Ashton S. Edwards, William J. Edwards II, Alisa English

Magnum Entertainment

9301 Wilshire Blvd., Room 602, Beverly Hills, CA 90210; (213) 278-9981. Organized 1984. (Manufactures prerecorded videocassettes for home use.)

PRESIDENT
Walter Gernert
EXECUTIVE VICE PRESIDENTS
Danny Kopels
Cheryl Gersch
AFFILIATIONS
VSDA, NAVD, NAD

Mercedes Maharis Productions

1025 Ocean Ave., Suite 201, Santa Monica, CA 90403; (213) 393-2180. (Horse-related educational and how-to videos.)

PRESIDENT
Mercedes Maharis

Major League Baseball Productions

(See The Phoenix Communications Group, Inc.)

Major Video Concepts, Inc.

7998 Georgetown Rd., Suite 100, P.O. Box 68000, Indianapolis, IN 46268; (317) 875-8000, (800) 365-0150; FAX: (312) 872-8067. (Subsidiary of Lacy Diversified Industries.)

PRESIDENT
Walter S. Wiseman

Maljack Productions, Inc.

15825 Rob Roy Dr., Oak Forest, IL 60452; (800) 323-0442. (Educational and documentary videos.)

The Market Place

4112 Marsh Ave., Rockford, IL 61111, (815) 877-1514. Organized 1985. (Videocassette distribution of inspirational programs to the home and church markets. Children's programs, music concert videos, financial planning seminar and a how-to fishing program.)

PRESIDENT
Max Anderson

Market W Productions, Inc.

3605 Earnscliff Place, Ste. 56, San Diego, CA 92111; (619) 576-1014. Organized 1984. (Home video, video production, scripting, marketing, distribution.)

PRESIDENT
Lois Winsen

Mass Media Video Ministries

2116 N. Charles St., Baltimore, MD 21218; (301) 727-3270; FAX: (301) 727-8192. Organized 1964. (A nationwide agency providing the educational and religious communities and other service organizations quality video programs.)

PRESIDENT
Clifford J. York
VICE PRESIDENT & TREASURER
Janice P. York
BOARD OF DIRECTORS
Clifford J. York, Janice P. York

Master Arts Video

15635 Saticoy St., Unit H, Van Nuys, CA 91406-3235; (818) 909-0233. Subsidiary of Multiple Development Corp. (Martial arts feature films.)

PRESIDENT
Joseph A. Pershes

MasterVision

969 Park Ave., Suite 8F, New York, NY 10028; (212) 879-0448. Organized 1980. (Special interest, cultural and educational videocassettes and discs in the arts, humanities, science, sports and how-to's.)

PRESIDENT
Richard Stadin

Mattingly Productions, Ltd.

10100 Main St., Fairfax, VA 22031; (703) 385-6625. Organized 1971. (Video production and training services.)

PRESIDENT
E. Grayson Mattingly
EXECUTIVE VICE PRESIDENT
Suzanne Fisher Mattingly
VICE PRESIDENT-EDITORIAL
Allan C. Fisher, Jr.
SECRETARY & TREASURER
William E. Mattingly
BOARD OF DIRECTORS
E. Grayson Mattingly, Suzanne Fisher Mattingly, Allan C. Fisher, Jr., William E. Mattingly

Cameron McKay Productions, Inc.

1011 N. Cole Ave., Hollywood, CA 90038; (213) 463-6073.

PRESIDENT
Cameron McKay

Medallion Productions

4909 Wyandotte, Kansas City, MO 64112; (816) 753-3358.

PRESIDENT
Rebecca B. Newman

Media Bus, Inc.

P.O. Box 718, Woodstock, NY 12498; (914) 679-7739.

PRESIDENT
Bart Friedman

Media Concepts, Inc.

559 49th St. S., St. Petersburg, FL 33707; (813) 321-2122. Organized 1974. (Video production and specialty house.)

PRESIDENT
Charles W.R. (Bob) Skidmore
VICE PRESIDENT
John P. Gallagher
GENERAL MANAGER
R. Edward Schmidt
MARKETING & SALES
Richard E. Smith (V.P., Pro Video)
John Gallagher
BRANCHES
Fort Myers, FL; Naples, FL

Media Home Entertainment, Inc.

5730 Buckingham Parkway, Culver City, CA 90230; (213) 216-7900, (800) 421-4509. Organized 1978. (Subsidiary of Heron Communications). (One of the largest independent home video companies—providing sports, fitness, and children's programming, as well as theatrically released films.) Hi-Tops Video is one of its brands.

PRESIDENT
Glenn Greene
SENIOR VICE PRESIDENT, MARKETING
Janice Whiffen
VICE PRESIDENT, FOREIGN SALES & ADMINISTRATION
Ted Rosenblatt
VICE PRESIDENT, PUBLIC RELATIONS
Barbara Hodgson

Mediacast T.V.

2350 E. Devon, Suite 250, Des Plaines, IL 60018; (312) 298-1300.

PRESIDENT
Tom Edinger

Meeting House Productions

Mennonite Church and Schuylkill Rds., Spring City, PA 19475; (215) 948-4800. (Family entertainment. Producers of American Video Magazine and original music tapes.)

Mercury Films

211 Arizona Ave., Santa Monica, CA 90401; (213) 451-5510. Organized 1986. (Pre-recorded videotape distribution.)

PRESIDENT
S. Leigh Savidge
VICE PRESIDENT
Arnie Lakeyn

Metacom Audio/Video Publishing Group

1401-B West River Rd. N., Minneapolis, MN 55411; (612) 588-2781. Organized 1970. (Manufactures and distributes—through direct mail—audio and video cassettes of subliminal self help and public domain movies, PD Films and special interest, old-time radio shows, kiddie product, languages.)

PRESIDENT
Dennis Levin
CHIEF EXECUTIVE OFFICER
Phillip T. Levin
VICE PRESIDENT OF FINANCE/CONTROLLER
David Benson

Metro Video Productions

36 Virginia Ave., Edgewater, MD 21037; (301) 261-7660. Organized 1981. (Video production and post production facility.)

PRESIDENT
Thomas Kreazburg
VICE PRESIDENT
Troy J. Jones
TREASURER
Dan Wolf

Metropolitan Museum of Art

Fifth Ave. and 82 St., New York, NY 10028; (212) 570-3806. (Art-related videos.)

Mill City Entertainment

Twelve Oaks Center, 15500 Wayzata Blvd., #762, Wayzata, MN 55391; (612) 473-7940; FAX: (612) 473-0648. Organized 1985. (Program supplier, home video corporation.)

PRESIDENT, CEO
Henry T. Morrison, Jr.
VICE PRESIDENTS
Ford Watson Bell
Cecil H. Bell
SECRETARY
Robert O. Mathson
BOARD OF DIRECTORS
Henry T. Morrison, Jr., Ford Watson Bell, Cecil H. Bell
BRANCH
Minneapolis

Million Dollar Video Corp.

5900 Wilshire Blvd., Suite 500, Los Angeles, Ca 90036; (213) 933-1616; (800) 444-8840; FAX: (213) 931-1999. Organized 1985. (Produces Spanish language home videocassettes and related materials, and distributes Mexican motion picture films in U.S.)

PRESIDENT
Miguel Kahan
CONTROLLER
Fred Rigaud
BOARD OF DIRECTORS
Miguel Kahan (chairman), Bruce C. Corwin, Irving Fuller, Esq., Allen Gilbert, Esq.
AFFILIATIONS
Metropolitan Theatres Corp, Los Angeles, and Productora Metropolitana, S.A. de C.V., Mexico City

Mindware Video Programming

P.O. Box 641, Kalaheo, HI 96741; (808) 332-9242. Organized 1976. (Produces stress reduction videos.)

PRESIDENT
Terry Kamen
AFFILIATION
Nebulae Productions

Mogul Communications, Inc.

452 S. Central Ave., Glendale, CA 91204; (818) 242-5892.

PRESIDENT
Joseph D. Dolan
VICE PRESIDENT
Phyllis Dolan

MANAGER
Judy V. Dundee (Slater)
BOARD OF DIRECTORS
Joseph D. Dolan, Phyllis Dolan
BRANCHES
All American Video, Mogul Video, Mogul Comm. Ltd., 35-37 Wardour St., London W1, England

Arthur Mokin Productions, Inc.

P.O. Box 1866, Santa Rosa, CA 95402; (707) 542-4868.

PRESIDENT
William Mokin

Monterey Home Video

5142 N. Clareton St., Suite 270, Agoura Hills, CA 91301; (818) 587-0047; FAX: (818) 597-0105.

PRINCIPAL
Scott Mansfield
SENIOR VICE PRESIDENT & CHIEF FINANCIAL OFFICER
Jere Rae-Mansfield

Morcraft Films Inc.

Box 65157, Los Angeles, CA 90065; 837 N. Cahuenga Blvd., Hollywood, CA 90038; (213) 464-2009. Organized 1976. (Restoring, re-releasing and printing old public domain films, cartoons and newsreels.)

PRESIDENT
Dermott W. Morgan

Morris Video

2730 Monterey, Suite #105, Monterey Business Park, Torrance, CA 90503; (213) 533-4800. Organized 1984. (Produces and distributes quality information and entertainment video.)

PRESIDENT
Dawn Morris
VICE PRESIDENT
George Morris, Ph.D.
DIRECTOR OF PUBLIC RELATIONS
Wendy Fulton
NATIONAL SALES MANAGER
Kandra Inga
NATIONAL SALES REP. MANAGER
Micki Smallman
BOARD OF DIRECTORS
Dawn Morris, George Morris, Ph.D., George Bott, David Van Horn.
BRANCH
663 The Village, Redondo Beach, CA 90277; (213) 374-4984.

Mossman Williams Productions

Box 7135, Kansas City, MO 64113; (816) 363-4352; (816) 921-3845.

PRESIDENT
Wade Williams

Motor Cycle Video/Power Sport Video

P.O. Drawer 30337, Las Vegas, NV 89030-1537; UPS: Suite 200, 1973 N. Nellis Blvd., Las Vegas, NV 89115; 24-hr. order #: (800) 628-2828, extension 916.

PRESIDENT
James W. Elbon, Jr.

Movie Buff Video

250 W. 95 St., New York, NY 10025; (212) 666-0331. (Subsidiary of Manhattan Movietime.)

MARKETING AND SALES
Bruce Goldstein

Movie Merchants, Inc.

3254 Youngfield St., Wheat Ridge, CO 80033; (303) 234-9282.

PRESIDENT
Shelley Gooch

Multi-Video Inc.

P.O. Box 35444, Charlotte, NC 28235; (704) 536-6928. ("Video Tape Repair" VHS Tape and repair supplies). (Educational and music videos.)

MultiVision of Denver

720 S. Colorado Blvd., Denver, CO 80222; (303) 691-2700.

PRESIDENT
William Peterson

Muppet Home Video

117 E. 69 St., New York, NY 10021; (212) 794-2400.

EXECUTIVE PRODUCER
Harriet Yassky

Museum of Modern Art of Latin America

1889 F St., N.W., Washington, DC 20006; (202) 789-6021.

MARKETING & SALES
Angel Hurtado

Music Media

5730 Buckingham Parkway, Culver City, CA 90230; (213) 216-7900, (800) 421-4509. Subsidiary of Media Home Entertainment.

VICE PRESIDENT, SALES
Alan Ostroff
VICE PRESIDENT, MARKETING
Jack Bernstein

NFL Films

330 Fellowship Rd., Mt. Laurel, NJ 08054; (609) 778-1600. Organized 1961. (Produces programming for the National Football League.) A subsidiary of the NFL.

PRESIDENT
Ed Sabol
EXECUTIVE VICE PRESIDENT
Steve Sabol
DIRECTOR OF VIDEO SALES
David Grassman

NSI Video

P.O. Box 895, Hermosa Beach, CA 90254; (213) 374-7476. Subsidiary of Native Son International. (Manufacturer and distributor of skateboard and other action sports videos.)

VICE PRESIDENT, DISTRIBUTION
Gerard Ravel

Naidoff Associates

65 Richard Rd., Ivyland, PA 18974; (215) 674-5410.

PRESIDENT
Bert Naidoff
MARKETING & SALES
Michael Smeyene

Narrative Video Network

1722 E. 57 St., Tulsa, OK 74105; (918) 742-6629. (Non-profit videocassette co. that distributes adapted versions of TV and film programming for the visually impaired.)

PRESIDENT
Jim Stovall

National Film Board of Canada

1251 Ave. of the Americas, 16th floor, New York, NY 10020; (212) 586-5131. (Film agency of Canada. Produces and distributes motion pictures.)

National Geographic Television

1145 17th St., N.W., Washington, D.C. 20036; (202) 857-7680; FAX: (202) 775-6590. Organized 1965.

VICE PRESIDENT, DIRECTOR OF TELEVISION
Tim Kelly
BOARD OF TRUSTEES
Gilbert M. Grosvenor (President and Chairman)
BRANCH
New York EXPLORER Office: 1251 Ave. of the Americas, Suite 1700, New York, NY 10020

National Golf Foundation

1150 South U.S. Highway One, Jupiter, FL 33477; (407) 744-6006. (Sports videos.)

National Hockey League

(See The Phoenix Communications Group, Inc.)

National Peregrine, Inc.

9229 Sunset Blvd., 9th Floor, Los Angeles, CA 90069; (213) 859-8250; FAX: (213) 274-6731. Organized 1965. (Film production and distribution to the world market.)

PRESIDENT
Hal Brown
CHIEF EXECUTIVE OFFICER
Neil Rosenstein
VICE PRESIDENT AND CHIEF FINANCIAL OFFICER
Larry Whitlock
BOARD OF DIRECTORS
Neil Rosenstein, Hal Brown, Aaron Grunfeld

Natural Reflections Video

P.O. Box 476, Coloma, CA 95667; (916) 621-1771. Organized 1980. (Broadcast productions—industrial, prime-time specials, home video productions—specializes in white water productions.)

PRESIDENT
Michael Dennis

Nebulae Productions

400 E. 85 St., New York, NY 10021; (212) 697-9800. Organized 1978. (Produces and distributes nature, relaxation and self-help video programs.)

PRESIDENT
Terry Kamen
VICE PRESIDENT
Roy Kamen

Sara Needham Gallery

The Mansion House, 11 Broadway, Apt. 25, Kingston, NY 12401; (914) 339-7832. Organized 1970. (Presents to the general public, knowledge of artist, writer, philosopher, Sara Needham, founder of Disabled Friends of Ulster County.)

CHIEF EXECUTIVE OFFICER
Sara Needham
BOARD OF DIRECTORS
Sara Needham, Henry Needham
BRANCHES
Woodstock, NY; Charleston, SC

Nelson Entertainment (North American Home Video Distribution)

(Subsidiary of Nelson Holdings International Ltd.)
335 North Maple Drive, Beverly Hills, CA 90210-3899; (213) 285-6150; FAX: (213) 285-6190.

CHAIRMAN OF THE BOARD AND CHIEF EXEC. OFFICER
F. Richard Northcott
PRESIDENT AND CHIEF OPERATING OFFICER
Barry P. Spikings
ACTING CHIEF FINANCIAL OFFICER
Ronald B. Cushey
SENIOR EXEC. VICE PRESIDENT AND CO-SECRETARY
Walter W.J. Olesiuk
SECRETARY
Nigel Sinclair
SENIOR VICE PRESIDENT, NELSON ENTERTAINMENT GROUP
Peter D. Graves
PRESIDENT AND CHIEF OPERATING OFFICER, NELSON ENTERTAINMENT AND EXEC. VICE PRESIDENT, NELSON HOLDINGS
Richard B. Childs
PRESIDENT AND CHIEF OPERATING OFFICER, NELSON ENTERTAINMENT INTL, AND EXEC. VICE PRESIDENT NELSON HOLDINGS
Ian R. Jessel
PRESIDENT OF PRODUCTION, NELSON FILMS AND SENIOR EXEC. VICE PRESIDENT NELSON GROUP
Richard M. Finkelstein
PRESIDENT & C.E.O., NELSON TELEVISION
Steve Sohmer
BOARD OF DIRECTORS
R. Richard Northcott, Barry P. Spikings, Malcolm P. Burke, Paul A. Carroll, Q.C., Timothy J.D. Hoare, Douglas E. McRae, Nigel Sinclair, K. Barry Sparks

New Age Video Inc.

1500 Broadway, New York, NY 10036; (212) 869-2616. (Educational, sports, music and dance videos.)

New & Unique Videos

2336 Sumac Dr., San Diego, CA 92105; (619) 282-6126; FAX: (619) 283-8264. Organized 1981. (Produces and distributes educational and entertainment videos for diverse audiences.)

PRESIDENT AND PRODUCER
Mark Schulze
VICE PRESIDENT AND CO-PRODUCER
Patricia Mooney
CREATIVE DIRECTOR
Glen Merritt
ASSOCIATE PRODUCER/DIRECTOR
Steve Languis
BRANCHES
San Diego
AFFILIATION
Crystal Pyramid Productions

New Breed Music & Video

1250 Maple View Drive, Pomona, CA 91766; (714) 627-1923.

PRESIDENT
Jesse Mac Lynum, Jr.

New Liberty Films

P.O. Box 25662, Shawnee Mission, KS 66225; (913) 451-2359. (Christian and issue-oriented videos.)

New Orleans Video Access Center

2010 Magazine St., New Orleans, LA 70130; (504) 524-8626. (Cultural/arts and educational videos.)

DIRECTOR
Karen Kern

New Star Video

260 S. Beverly Dr., Suite 200, Beverly Hills, CA 90212; (213) 205-0666. Organized 1987. (Pre-recorded videocassettes.)

PRESIDENT
Gary Hunt
SALES AND MARKETING MANAGER
Lynn Baldwin
NATIONAL ACCTS. MANAGER
Pierre Loubet
EASTERN REGIONAL SALES MANAGER
Karl Candello
SOUTHERN REGIONAL SALES MANAGER
Pat Flores
WESTERN REGIONAL SALES MANAGER
Pierre Loubet

New Video Center, Inc.

276 Third Ave., New York, NY 10003; (212) 473-6000.

VICE PRESIDENT, ACQUISITIONS
Mike Tollack

New World Video

1440 S. Sepulveda, Los Angeles, CA 90025; (213) 444-8100. Organized 1984. (Video distribution.)

VICE PRESIDENT & COMPTROLLER
Burton Messer
SENIOR VICE PRESIDENT, SALES AND MARKETING
David Pierce
EXECUTIVE DIRECTOR, CREATIVE SERVICES
Kim Yost
DIRECTOR, CREATIVE SERVICES
Susan Fields
DIRECTOR OF PROMOTION/MARKETING
Steve Okin

New York Times Productions

130 Fifth Ave., New York, NY 10011; (212) 645-3000. Organized 1978. (Produces programming for home video, network and syndication domestically and internationally.) A division of The New York Times Syndication Sales Corporation, an affiliate of The New York Times Company.

CHAIRMAN
Arthur Ochs Sulzberger
VICE CHAIRMAN
Sydney Gruson
PRESIDENT
Sam Summerlin
EXECUTIVE PRODUCER
Ted Harbert

Nightingale-Conant Corp.

7300 N. Lehigh Ave., Niles, IL 60648; (312) 467-0300. (Self-help and psychology videos.)

CUSTOMER CONTACT
Don Reaser

Nostalgia Merchant

5730 Buckingham Parkway, Culver City, CA 90230; (213) 216-7900, (800) 421-4509. (Subsidiary of Media Home Entertainment.)

VICE PRESIDENT, SALES
Alan K. Ostroff

Nova Video Art

10583 Felton Way, Cupertino, CA 95014; (408) 725-0708. Organized 1983. (Produces instructional dance videotapes—e.g., "Learn Classical Ballet and Enjoy It.")

OWNER/PRODUCER
Lilia Peloquin
MARKETING DIRECTOR
Mike Peloquin
GRAPHIC DESIGNER/NARRATOR
Katalin Maritza Balogh
AFFILIATIONS
Video Productions: Vertex Video Associates
Music: Silver Label Recording Co.

Ocean Video Inc.

#601, 4605 Lankershim Blvd., North Hollywood, CA 91602; (818) 506-3216. (Martial arts videos.)

VICE PRESIDENT
Aaron Yeung

On-Site Video

101 W. Main St., Bremen, OH 43107; (614) 569-4601. Organized 1982. (Video distribution.)

OWNER
Allen P. Brand

One Up Productions

1129A Folson St., San Francisco, CA 94103; (415) 558-8688; FAX: (415) 558-9814. Organized 1982. (Produces, markets and distributes videotapes for the home video market.)

PRESIDENT
Hamilton V. Bryan II
DIRECTOR OF MARKETING
David Wren
BRANCHES
Super Source Video (distributor of Super VHS prerecorded videotapes exclusively)

O'Neil and Jeffries Film Productions

3855 Lankershim Blvd., North Hollywood, CA 91604; (818) 760-6666. (Subsidiary of Jeffries Film Int'l.)

PRESIDENT
Hugh Jeffries

Optical Data Corp.

30 Technology Drive, Box 4919; Warren, NJ 07060; (201) 668-0022; (800) 524-2481; FAX: (201) 668-1322.

CORPORATE COMMUNICATIONS DIRECTOR
Pamela L. Herber

Optical Programming Associates

%Ira Roth, 11812 San Vicente Blvd., Suite 200, Los Angeles, CA 90049; (213) 207-4355. Organized 1980. (Produces interactive Laser discs.)

BUSINESS MANAGER
Ira Roth

Original Face Video

6116 Merced Ave., #165, Oakland, CA 94611; (415) 339-3126.

PRESIDENTS
Johanna Luther
Joseph Tieger

Orion Home Video

410 Park Ave., 7th Floor, New York, NY 10022; (212) 888-4500. Organized 1987. (Manufacturer of pre-recorded videocassettes.)

PRESIDENT & CHIEF OPERATING OFFICER
Leonard White
SENIOR VICE PRESIDENT, SALES
Eugene Silverman
SENIOR VICE PRESIDENT, ADMINISTRATION OPERATIONS
Gerald Sobczak
VICE PRESIDENT, PUBLIC AFFAIRS
Paul Wagner
VICE PRESIDENT, MARKETING
Susan Blodgett
VICE PRESIDENT, MERCHANDISING & BUSINESS DEVELOPMENT
Joseph Annechino
VICE PRESIDENT, CREDIT ADMINISTRATION
Robert Davie
BRANCHES
Livonia, MI; Toronto, Canada
AFFILIATION
Division of Orion Pictures Corp.

Ozman Inc.

496-A Hudson St., #K-17, New York, NY 10014; (212) 620-3832. Organized 1984. (Producer/distributor of educational and children's programs.)

PRESIDENT
Merav Ozeri
VICE PRESIDENT
Eytan Kaufman
BRANCH
Washington, D.C.
AFFILIATION
O-Tone Productions, Inc. (Music Productions)

Pacific Arts Video

50 N. LaCienega Blvd., Suite 210, Beverly Hills, CA 90211-2205; (213) 657-2233.

PRESIDENT
George Steele III

Pacific International Enterprises, Inc.

1133 S. Riverside, Suite #1, P.O. Box 1727, Medford, OR 97501; (503) 779-0990.

PRESIDENT/PRODUCER
Arthur R. Dubs
VICE PRESIDENT INTERNATIONAL SALES
Arn S. Withol
SECRETARY/TREASURER
Barbara J. Brown
MEDIA/PUBLICITY DIRECTOR
Paul W. Blumer
PROJECT DEVELOPMENT/ACQUISITIONS
George R. Elsom, Jr.
NATIONAL BOOKING MANAGER
Howard H. Lackey
OFFICE MANAGER
Andy Gough

Pacific Trade Group

94-527 Puahi St., Waipahu, HI 96782; (808) 671-6735. Organized 1977. (Publisher and distributor of books and video tapes.)

PRESIDENT & MANAGER
Peter W. Cannon
VICE PRESIDENT & SALES
Claudia L. Cannon
CONTROLLER
Donald Noguchi
BOARD OF DIRECTORS
Richard E. Pultz, Peter W. Cannon, Claudia L. Cannon

Palmer Video Corporation

1767 Morris Ave., Union, NJ 07083-3598; (201) 686-3030; FAX: (201) 686-2151. Organized 1981. (Franchisor—video stores.)

PRESIDENT & CEO
Peter Balner
VICE PRESIDENT
Peter Margaritondo
VICE PRESIDENT
Carl A. Pallini

Panic Distributing Co.

2999 Silver Dr., Columbus, OH 43224; (614) 267-1211.

Paperback Video, Inc.

1060 E. 800 S., Orem, UT 84058; (801) 226-0155. Organized 1986. (Video production.)

PRESIDENT
Linda H. Thomson

Paramount Home Video

5555 Melrose Ave., Los Angeles, CA 90038; (213) 468-5000.

PRESIDENT
Robert Klingensmith
EXECUTIVE VICE PRESIDENT, VIDEO DIVISION
Timothy Cloutt
VICE PRESIDENT, ADVERTISING
Hollace Brown
SR. VICE PRESIDENT, GENERAL MANAGER
Eric Doctorow
SENIOR VICE PRESIDENT, BUSINESS AFFAIRS & INTERNATIONAL
James Gianopulos
SENIOR VICE PRESIDENT, FINANCE & OPERATIONS
Jay Heifetz

Parent's Magazine

685 Third Ave., New York, NY 10017; (212) 878-8700. (Child development videos, new mother shape-up tape) Division of Gruner & Jahr, U.S.A. Publishing Inc.

PUBLISHER, SPECIAL PROJECTS
Frank Kelcz

Pat Film & Video Services Inc.

630 Ninth Ave., 5th floor, New York, NY 10036; (212) 247-0900. Organized 1964. (Production and distribution of television shows and commercials. Film to tape transfers, ½″ VHS-BETA and ¾″ duplication. 2″ and 1″ duplication. All standards conversions to and from all formats. Editing on and off-line.)

PRESIDENT
Ervin Rosenfeld
VICE PRESIDENT/SALES
Andrew Cuomo
GENERAL MANAGER
Peter Economos
PRODUCTION MANAGER
Mike Rosenfeld
VIDEO MANAGER
Leonard Laxer
ACCOUNTING
Bernard Weiner

Peak Performance Inc.

P.O. Box 2829, Duxbury, MA 02332; (617) 837-3398. (Sports and how-to videos.)

PRESIDENT
John Gillis

Perennial Education, Inc.

930 Pitner Ave., Evanston, IL 60202; (312) 328-6700. Organized 1966. (Distributor of sex education, family plan-

ning, reproductive health and social issues, AV programming to schools, planned parenthoods, health depts, libraries, hospitals, etc.)

PRESIDENT
Joseph Farragher
CHAIRMAN OF BOARD
Joel Altschul
AFFILIATIONS
An Altschul Group Company

Phipps and Company Productions

11375 E. 61st St., Suite 102, Broken Arrow, OK 74012. (Educational and sports videos.)

PRESIDENT
Terry L. Phipps

The Phoenix Communications Group, Inc.

1212 Ave. of the Americas, New York, NY 10036; (212) 921-8100; FAX: (212) 719-0614. (Operates Major League Baseball productions under license from Major League Baseball. Licensed by National Hockey League as official production company.)

CHAIRMAN
Joseph L. Podesta
PRESIDENT
James E. Holland
SENIOR VICE PRESIDENT, EXECUTIVE PRODUCER
Geoff Belinfante
SENIOR VICE PRESIDENT, SALES AND SYNDICATION
Terry Kassel

Phoenix Films Inc.

468 Park Ave. S., New York, NY 10016; (212) 684-5910; FAX: (212) 779-7493.

PRESIDENT
Heinz Gelles
MARKETING AND SALES
Robert Dunlap

Picture Start, Inc.

204 W. John St., Champaign, IL 61820; (217) 352-7353.

PRESIDENT
Ron Epple
MARKETING & SALES
Jeff Hellyer

Playhouse Video

1211 Ave. of the Americas, New York, NY 10036; (212) 819-3238. (Division of CBS/Fox Video.)

Plainsong Productions

47 Halifax St., Boston, MA 02130; (617) 524-0980. Organized 1980. (Full production and production services in film and video, both documentary and dramatic. Health care issues specialization.)

PRESIDENT & OWNER
Ben Achtenberg
AFFILIATION
Fanlight Productions (distribution co. also owned by Ben Achtenberg)

Plus A Video Ltd.

461 Goffler Rd., Wyckoff, NJ 07481; (201) 447-1501, (800) 524-0195.

PRESIDENT
Lee Friedman

Pola Productions, Inc.

18662 MacArthur Blvd., Room 200, Irvine, CA 92715; (714) 752-5700. Organized 1984. (Video production/distribution.)

CHAIRMAN
James Polakof
CHIEF EXECUTIVE OFFICER
Gloria J. Polakof
ASSOCIATE PRODUCER
Joan Cumming

Polo Trade Corp.

3821 Crescent St., Long Island City, NY 11101; (718) 482-7723.

MARKETING & SALES
Barbara Murphy

Polygram Music Video U.S.

810 Seventh Ave., New York, NY 10019; (212) 333-8559. Polygram Records, Inc.

SENIOR VICE PRESIDENT, MUSIC VIDEO
Len R. Epand

Potentials Unlimited, Inc.

4025 Broadmoor, S.E., Grand Rapids, MI 49508; (616) 940-2723. Organized 1979.

PRESIDENT
Gregg A. Banfill
VICE PRESIDENT
Stephanie L. Konicov
NATIONAL SALES MANAGER
Timothy J. Kelley
DISTRIBUTOR SALES MANAGER
Cheryl L. Moore
INTERNATIONAL SALES MANAGER
Michael L. Lankes
BOARD OF DIRECTORS
Barrie Konicov (chairman of the board)

Price Stern Sloan, Inc.

360 N. La Cienega, Los Angeles, CA 90048; (213) 657-6100.

DIRECTOR, VIDEO DIVISION
Claudia Sloan

Prince Leopard Film Productions, Inc.

307 E. 93 St., Suite 3E, New York, NY 10128; (212) 505-5508. Organized 1984. (Special interest home video tapes, programming and production.)

PRESIDENT
Sylvia Grodin
VICE PRESIDENT
Lenny Grodin
PRODUCTION COORDINATOR
Arietta Venizelos

Prism Entertainment Corporation

1888 Century Park E., Suite 1000, Los Angeles, CA 90067; (213) 277-3270. Organized 1983. (Home video and pre-recorded music, television syndication, film production.)

CHAIRMAN—DIRECTOR
Paul Levinson
PRESIDENT—DIRECTOR
Barry Collier
SENIOR VICE PRESIDENT
Earl Rosenstein

Producers International Corporation

3921 N. Meridian St., Indianapolis, IN 46208; (317) 924-5163. Organized 1968. (Business communications

producer. Carries "Jerry Yeagley's Fundamentals of Soccer" for the home video market.)
DIRECTOR OF MARKETING
Lori A. Feeney

Professional Research, Inc.

930 Pitner Ave., Evanston, IL 60202; (312) 328-6700. Organized 1965. (Produces and distributes health care and patient education AV programming to hospitals, clinics, HMO's, health depts., government agencies and private physicians.)
PRESIDENT
Joseph Farragher
CHAIRMAN OF BOARD
Joel Altschul
SALES MANAGER
Margaret Dugan
AFFILIATION
An Altschul Group Company

Progress Research, Inc

355 Grand Ave., Oakland, CA 94610; (415) 832-0305. (How-to, sports.)
PRESIDENT
Richard E. Johnson

Public Access Producers Association

2652 N. Winchell, Portland, OR 97217; (503) 289-2309.
DIRECTOR
R. S. Kolemaine

Public Production Group

900 Second St. N.E., Suite 4, Washington, D.C. 20002, (202) 898-1808; FAX: (202) 898-1811. (Educational and public interest videos.)
PRESIDENT
Sam Love

PyraVid International

P.O. Box 1510, San Anselmo, CA 94960; (415) 381-2567. (Distributes videos of the films of Robert Downey.)
PRESIDENT
L. Lee Buschel

Quadrus Media Ministry Inc.

128 Kishwaukee St., Rockford, IL 61104; (815) 987-3970. (Children's, music and dramatic videos.)
PRESIDENT
Joe Musser

Quality Video Service

P.O. Box 2622, Redmond, WA 98052; (206) 788-6840.
PRESIDENT
James P. Kehoe

Questar Video, Inc.

680 N. Lake Shore, Chicago, IL 60611; (312) 266-9400; FAX: (312) 266-9523. Organized 1986. (Produces and distributes high-quality non-theatrical videos: travel, history, and adventure.)
CHAIRMAN
Albert J. Nader
PRESIDENT
Jason J. Nader

RCA/Columbia Pictures Home Video

3500 West Olive Ave., Burbank, CA 91505; (818) 953-7900.
PRESIDENT
W. Patrick Campbell
EXECUTIVE VICE PRESIDENT & CHIEF FINANCIAL OFFICER
William Chardavoyne
EXECUTIVE VICE PRESIDENT
Chris Derring
EXECUTIVE VICE PRESIDENT
Gary Khammar
EXECUTIVE VICE PRESIDENT & COO
Paul Culberg
EXECUTIVE VICE PRESIDENT
James Tauber
VICE PRESIDENT, CONTROLLER
Mel Howard
EXECUTIVE VICE PRESIDENT WORLDWIDE OPERATIONS
Alan K. Pritchard
VICE PRESIDENT, SALES & MARKETING
Richard Pinson

RICON Enterprises

5863 Village Forest Court, Houston, TX 77092; (713) 683-0105. Organized 1983. (Production and distribution of videos about the space shuttle program and other NASA projects.)
OWNER
Richard C. Colton

RMI Media Productions, Inc.

2807 W. 47 St., Shawnee Mission, KS 62205; (913) 262-3974. (Instructional videos.)
PRESIDENT
David L. Little

Radio Vision International

7060 Hollywood Blvd., #525, Hollywood, CA 90028; (213) 469-5750. Organized 1982. (Distributor of music-based programming.)
PRESIDENT/CEO
Kevin Wall
CHIEF FINANCIAL OFFICER
Karl T. Wall
SENIOR VICE PRESIDENT, SALES
David Wyler
SENIOR VICE PRESIDENT, INTL. MARKETING
Lorenzo Camerana
SENIOR VICE PRESIDENT, BUSINESS AFFAIRS
Jay Shanker
INTERNATIONAL SALES
Melek Demir
ACQUISITIONS
Jeff Flower
BOARD OF DIRECTORS
Ed Simons, Harvey Goldsmith, Kevin Wall, Karl T. Wall
BRANCH
Radio Vision Int'l (UK), Avon House, 360 Oxford St., 4th Floor, London, W1N 9HA England; Tel: (01) 493-0439.

Radio Vision Video

7060 Hollywood Blvd., Suite 516, Hollywood, CA 90028; (213) 462-3690. Organized 1988. (Markets and distributes HIP vid clips and concerts.)
CHIEF EXECUTIVE OFFICER
Karl Wall
SENIOR V.P., SALES AND MARKETING
Kevin Johnston
BOARD OF DIRECTORS
Kevin Wall (chairman)
BRANCH
Avon House, 360 Oxford St., 4th floor, London W1N 9HA England
AFFILIATION
Radio Vision International

Raedon Productions

8707-D Lindley Ave., Suite 173, Northridge, CA 91325; (818) 349-9862; FAX: (818) 349-9869. Organized 1988. (Video producer-distributor.)

PRESIDENT
Dennis Donovan
EXECUTIVE VICE PRESIDENT
Ralie Rae Donovan
LEGAL AFFAIRS
Thomas Accinelli
AFFILIATION
Raedon Entertainment Group, Inc.

Random House, Inc.

201 E. 50 St., New York, NY 10022; (212) 751-2600. Organized 1955. (Publishing company.)

EXECUTIVE VICE PRESIDENT, HOME VIDEO
Gerald Harrison
CREATIVE DIRECTOR, HOME VIDEO
Sharon Lerner
MARKETING DIRECTOR
Robert Singer
VICE PRESIDENT, SALES
Edward Martin

Ravenswood Productions

25410 Dodge Ave., Suite J, Harbor City, CA 90710; (213) 549-5422.

PRESIDENT
James Sudalnik

Reader's Digest

Pleasantville, NY 10570; (914) 769-7000.

Reel Images

Box 137, Monroe, CT 06468; (800) 243-9289.

Reeves Corporate Services

708 Third Ave., 8th floor, New York, NY 10017; (212) 573-8570. Subsidiary of Communications Corp. (Film, video, meetings, multi-image presentations.)

PRESIDENT
Kevin P. Ward

Regency Home Video

9911 W. Pico Blvd., PH-M, Los Angeles, CA 90035; (213) 552-2431; FAX: (213) 552-9039. Organized 1986. (Produces, markets and distributes prerecorded videocassettes.)

CHAIRMAN
Alan Silverbach
PRESIDENT
Herb Lazarus
GENERAL MANAGER
Betty Jane Metz
BRANCHES
New York office—Toby Rogers
London office—George Blaug
AFFILIATION
Division of Silverbach-Lazarus Group.

Rego Irish Records and Tapes, Inc.—Rego Video

64 New Hyde Park Rd., Garden City, NY 11530; (516) 328-7800. Organized 1974. (Manufactures and distributes Irish recordings. Also manufactures and imports Irish videos.)

PRESIDENT
Patrick J. Noonan
VICE PRESIDENT
Margaret E. Noonan
MANAGER
Vincent Mitchell
AFFILIATION
Paddy Noonan Entertainments, Inc.

Rehabfilm

1123 Broadway, New York, NY 10010; (212) 741-5160. (Subsidiary of Rehabilitation Int'l., U.S.A.)

DIRECTOR OF MEDIA
John F. Moses

Rentrak Corporation

7227 NE 55th Avenue, Portland, OR 97218; (503) 284-7581; FAX: (503) 288-1563. Organized 1980. (Video distributor.)

PRESIDENT
Ron Berger
VICE PRESIDENT, OPERATIONS
Fergus O'Scannlain
VICE PRESIDENT, FINANCE & ADMINISTRATION, CFO
F. Kim Cox
BOARD OF DIRECTORS
Ron Berger, William LeVine, Jack Silverman, L. Barton Alexander, Lon Werner, Peter Dal Bianco, Stephen Roberts

Republic Pictures Home Video

12636 Beatrice St., Los Angeles, CA 90066; (213) 306-4040; FAX: (213) 301-0221. Organized 1952. (Film and video distribution.)

SENIOR VICE PRESIDENT
Vallery Kountze
VICE PRESIDENT, HOME VIDEO OPERATIONS
Phil Kromnick
VICE PRESIDENT & CFO
David Kirchheimer
VICE PRESIDENT, MARKETING
Glenn Ross
VICE PRESIDENT, SALES
Gary Jones
BOARD OF DIRECTORS
Russell Goldsmith (Chairman of the Board); Paul J. O'Brien (Secretary), Robert Magness, George Hatch, Bram Goldsmith, Tom Werner

Research Press

2612 N. Mattis, Box 3177, Champaign, IL 61821; (217) 352-3273. (Psychology and educational videos.)

PRESIDENT
Ann Wendel

Rhapsody Films Inc.

P.O. Box 179, New York, NY 10014; (212) 243-0152. Organized 1982. (Distributes jazz and blues films for all markets television, home video and non-theatrical.)

PRESIDENT
Bruce Ricker

Rhino Home Video

2225 Colorado Bl., Santa Monica, CA 90404, (213) 450-6323; (Horror feature films.)

PRESIDENT
Randi Freeman
MANAGING DIRECTOR
Arny Schor

Ed Rich Productions Inc.

1950 S. Ocean Dr., Hallandale, FL 33009; (305) 454-8068.

PRESIDENT
Ed Rich

Bob Richards/Chatham Films

P.O. Box 41158, Minneapolis, MN 55441-0158; (612) 339-8123. Organized 1980. (Distributes Bob Richards' films and videocassettes.)

PRESIDENT
S.H. Stenulson

Richman Brothers

6935 Airport Highway Lane, Pennsauken, NJ 08109; (609) 665-8085.

PRESIDENT
Jerry Richman
MARKETING & SALES
Charlene Engelbrecht

Riverside Distributing Co.

1208 W. Isabel St., Burbank, CA 91506; (818) 954-0880. Organized 1975. (Distributes video home movies and video accessories.)

PRESIDENT
Bernie Kirtin
VICE PRESIDENT
Saul Gerber
NATIONAL SALES MANAGER
Cliff Sawyer
WEST, REGIONAL MANAGER
Arnold Himmelstein
SECRETARY-TREASURER
Herb Bashkin
BOARD OF DIRECTORS
Saul Gerber, Cliff Sawyer, Bernie Kirtin, Herb Bashkin
BRANCHES
320 W. Madison St., Chicago IL 60606
AFFILIATIONS
Majestic Duplicating Service

Rizzoli Video

597 Fifth Ave., New York, NY 10017; (212) 223-0100. Organized 1985.

DIRECTOR
John Brancati

Robb Mavins Productions, Inc.

1210-240 Stradrook, Winnipeg, Manitoba R3B 0W5, Canada; (204) 477-6165. (Home video producer.)

Rocky Mountain Motion Pictures

P.O. Box 2850, Park City, UT 84060; (801) 649-1030. (Sports and travel videos.)

PRESIDENT
Dean Lyras

Rodale Press Inc.

33 E. Minor St., Emmaus, PA 18049; (215) 967-5171.

Henry Rosenberg & Assoc.

550 Sylvan Ave., Englewood Cliffs, NJ 07632; (201) 569-6560.

PRESIDENT
Henry Rosenberg

SBI Video

4901 Forbes Blvd., Lanham, MD 20706; (202) 459-8000, (800) 638-0243. (Division of Schwartz Bros. Inc.)

GENERAL MANAGER/VIDEO DIVISION
Patrick Lawrence
SALES MANAGER
Jake Lamb
BRANCHES
1165 Marlkress Rd., Cherry Hill, NJ 08003; (609) 424-2211. Richie Salvador, branch mgr.
1231 E. 26th St., Cleveland, OH 44114 (216) 696-2701. Harvey Korman, branch mgr.
1129 Bloomfield Ave., W. Caldwell, NJ 07006; (201) 882-2955. Andy Miele, branch mgr.

S.I. Video

14144 Ventura Blvd., Suite 200, Sherman Oaks, CA 91423; (818) 789-9955. Organized 1986. (Full service marketing and distribution for special interest videos.)

PRESIDENT
Claire Gruppo
VICE PRESIDENT, SALES
Roger Leonard

STS/Skehan Televideo Service Inc.

316 F St. N.E., Washington D.C., 20002; (202) 543-2323; (800) 426-9083; FAX: (202) 546-8199. Organized 1980. (Television field production company). Purchased CBI/Cirace Video International 1988.

PRESIDENT/TREASURER
Michael E. Skehan
VICE PRESIDENT
Patrick Skehan
SECRETARY
Andrea T. Skehan
CHIEF ENGINEER
Verdine O. (Butch) Palmer

SVS, Inc.

1700 Broadway, New York, NY 10019; (212) 757-4990; FAX: (212) 956-3792.

PRESIDENT
Michael Holzman
VICE PRESIDENT, BUSINESS AFFAIRS
Jeffrey Ringler
NATIONAL SALES MANAGER
Jeff Rabinovitz

San Francisco Rush Video

1554 Grove Street, San Francisco, CA 94117; (415) 921-8273. Organized 1983. (Video post-production, home video producers.)

OWNER-PRESIDENT
William Anthony Longen
VICE PRESIDENT
Stanton Schaffer

Saturn Productions, Inc.

1697 Broadway, New York, NY 10019; (212) 489-2460. Organized 1984. (Prerecorded videocassettes.) Parent company is Telefilm Inc.

PRESIDENT
Tom Ward

Schwartz Brothers, Inc.

4901 Forbes Blvd., Lanham, MD 20706; (301) 459-8000. Organized 1946. (Wholesale distributor of videocassettes, compact discs, records, blank tapes, prerecorded tapes, and accessories.)

PRESIDENT
James Schwartz
CHAIRMAN OF THE BOARD & EXECUTIVE VICE PRESIDENT
Stuart Schwartz

VICE PRESIDENT, FINANCE
Melvin C. Davis
VICE PRESIDENT, SALES
Jerome Jacobs
BOARD OF DIRECTORS
Milton Lyons, Joseph R. Cassidy, Howard Kolodny
BRANCHES
1165 Marlkress Rd., Cherry Hill, NJ 08003; (609) 424-2211 (Richard Salvador, vice president)
1129 Bloomfield Ave., W. Caldwell, NJ 07006; (201) 882-2955 (Andy Miele, branch manager)
1231 E. 26th St., Cleveland, OH 44114; (216) 696-2701 (Harvey Korman, branch manager)
3065 McCall Dr., Suite 4, Atlanta, GA 30340; (404) 986-0764 (Jim Maddix, branch manager)
AFFILIATIONS
National Association of Record Merchandisers
National Association of Video Distributors
Video Software Dealers Association
Country Music Association

Sea-TV

1619 Chapel St., New Haven, CT 06511; (203) 624-0470. Organized 1983. (Marketing and production of nautical video cassettes.)

PRESIDENT
Charles P. Croft
BOARD OF DIRECTORS
Herb Hild

Seen-By-Scene Productions

P.O. Box 1254, Orem, UT 84059; (801) 226-8209.

PRESIDENT
Cheryl L. Karr

Self Improvement Video, Inc.

Suite 283, 77 Ives St., Providence, RI 02906; (401) 246-0810; FAX: (401) 245-9060. Organized 1983. (Produces and markets home video programming.)

PRESIDENT
John R. Koenig
VICE PRESIDENT
Maria P. Koenig
BOARD OF DIRECTORS
John R. Koenig, Maria P. Koenig

Self Reliance Foundation

207 Montoya St., Santa Fe, NM 87501; (505) 984-0080.

PRESIDENT
Jeff Kline

Serendipity Communications

50 Briar Hollow, Suite 500, West Houston, TX 77027; (713) 622-3131; FAX: (713) 622-9414.

PRESIDENT
Fred R. Brison
DIRECTOR OF SALES
Mark Parthie

Shapiro Glickenhaus Home Video

12001 Ventura Place, 4th Floor, Studio City, CA 91604; (818) 766-8500.

SENIOR VICE PRESIDENT & GENERAL MANAGER
Peter Pidutti
DIRECTOR OF OPERATIONS
Andi Elliott

Sherwood Video Production Co.

676 N. St. Clair St., Suite 1880, Chicago, IL 60611; (312) 787-2723; FAX: (312) 787-2901. (Educational videos.)

PRESIDENT
Barry Torman

Shokus Video

P.O. Box 8434, Van Nuys, CA 91409; (818) 704-0400. Organized 1979. (Preservation of vintage TV films and kinescopes in the public domain.)

PRESIDENT
Stuart Shostak
AFFILIATIONS
AFTRA (since 1982), VSDA 1981–85

Sight and Sound Distributors

2055 Walton Rd., St. Louis, MO 63114; (314) 426-2388; (800) 325-9232.

DIRECTOR
Dan Thompson
BRANCHES
1144 Booth St., Kansas City, KS 66103; (913) 371-8152
2201 Brookwood Dr., Little Rock, AK 72202; (501) 664-1630

Single Concept Films

2 Terrain Dr., Rochester, NY 14618; (716) 442-9740. (Educational and medical videos.)

PRODUCER
Jack Ruda

Snoopy's Home Video Library

5730 Buckingham Parkway, Culver City, CA 90230; (213) 216-7900; (800) 421-4509. (Children's videos.) Subsidiary of Media Home Entertainment.

Society of Manufacturing Engineers

1 SME Dr., P.O. Box 930, Dearborn, MI 48121-0930; (313) 271-1500; (800) 535-8005; in MI (800) 533-9303.

PRESIDENT
Frank J. Riley, Jr.
MANAGER VIDEO COMMUNICATIONS
Timothy Savage

Softni-USA

11444 W. Olympic Blvd., 10th Floor, Los Angeles, CA 90064; (213) 312-9560; FAX: (213) 473-6052. (Video subtitling company which also sells software/hardware "System III" for subtitling video.)

PRESIDENT
Jose M. Salgado
SALES DIRECTOR
Eva M. Thompson
BRANCHES
Caracas, Venezuela; Madrid, Spain.

Sonoma Video Productions

553 Mendocino Ave., Santa Rosa, CA 95401; (707) 579-3902. (Full-service video production company. Instructional, educational, documentary, travel.)

GENERAL MANAGER
Ron Schilling

Sony Video Communications

(Division of Sony Corp. of America)
Sony Dr., Park Ridge, NJ 07656; (201) 930-1000.

CORPORATE PRESIDENT
Kenji Tamiya
PRESIDENT
Philip J. Stack

VICE PRESIDENT, SALES
Robert Mueller
NATIONAL SERVICE MANAGER
Philip Hart

Source Video Distributing Co., Inc.

1100 Hillsboro Rd., Franklin, TN 37064; (615) 790-5300; (800) 342-5014 (TN).

PRESIDENT
Lee Cowen
MARKETING & SALES
Fred W. Phister

South Gate Entertainment

7080 Hollywood Blvd., Los Angeles, CA 90028; (213) 962-8530. Organized 1989. (Video producer and distributor of "B" films.)

PRESIDENT
Yorem Pelman

Special Interest Video

553 Mendocino Ave., Santa Rosa, CA 95401 (707) 579-3936. Organized 1980. (Distribution of instructional and special interest video tapes.)

PRESIDENT
Michael Heumann
MARKETING VICE PRESIDENT
Christine Cannon
SECRETARY & TREASURER
Marcia Ludwig
AFFILIATION
VSDA

Spectacor Home Video

1145 N. McCadden Place, Los Angeles, CA 90038; (213) 871-2777. FAX: (213) 871-2763; East Coast headquarters: %Alfred Haber Marketing Inc., Palisades Park, NJ. (Specialty label featuring Spectacor Films telepictures and miniseries and Bolshoi Ballet series.)

PRESIDENT & GENERAL PARTNER, SPECTACOR FILMS
Michael Jaffe
PRESIDENT, WORLDWIDE DISTRIBUTION
Alfred Haber
VICE PRESIDENT & CHIEF FINANCIAL OFFICER
David Newlon
DIRECTOR OF CREATIVE & ADMINISTRATIVE AFFAIRS
Daniel J. Saldek

Spectrum Video

18121 Napa St., Northridge, CA 91325; (818) 886-8680, (800) 423-5599. (Acquisition and production of alternative non-theatrical, how-to programming for distribution to home video market place.)

PRESIDENT
Fred Hirsch
VICE PRESIDENT
Dwight Krizman
AFFILIATION
VSDA

Spinnaker Software Corp./Spinnaker Video

1 Kendall Square, Cambridge, MA 02139; (617) 494-1200. (800) 826-0706; FAX: (617) 494-1219. (Distributor of Video Ordnance Defense & Aerospace Technology series. Also distributes educational software.)

VICE PRESIDENT
Priscilla Seuss

Sports Films & Talents, Inc.

12755 State Highway 55, Minneapolis, MN 55441; (612) 540-5972. (Sports videos.)

Sports Performance Corporation

5816 Shakespeare Rd., Suite D., Columbia, SC 29223; (803) 735-0733. Organized 1981. (Golf and sports videos.)

PRESIDENT
D. Swing Meyer

Sports World Cinema

P.O. Box 17022, Salt Lake City, UT 84117; (801) 266-9300.

PRESIDENT
Gary B. Ewing

Sportsmen on Film

5038 N. Parkway Calabasas, #100, Calabasas, CA 91302. Organized 1984. (Produces video for hunters, shooters and outdoorsmen.)

PRESIDENT
Ken Wilson
VICE PRESIDENT
Greg Summitt
SECRETARY
Sandy Oliveira
BOARD OF DIRECTORS
Lorraine Wilson, (chairman)

Spotlight Video

12636 Beatrice St., Los Angeles, CA 90066; (213) 306-4040. (Subsidiary of Public Pictures Home Video Co.)

SENIOR VICE PRESIDENT
Nick Draklich

Star Classics Inc.

4301 Glenwood Rd., Brooklyn, NY 11210; (718) 434-1100. Organized 1985. (Produces and distributes video cassettes for the home entertainment market.)

PRESIDENT, C.E.O. & TREASURER
Martin Chopp
VICE PRESIDENT
Gerald Schwebel
SECRETARY
Manny Chopp
BOARD OF DIRECTORS
Martin Chopp (chairman); Gerald Schwebel, Manny Chopp

Star Video Entertainment, LP

550 Grand St., Jersey City, NJ 07302-4112; (201) 333-4600.

PRESIDENT
Bernard Herman

Stars To Go, Inc.

4751 Wilshire Blvd., Suite 140, Los Angeles, CA 90010; (213) 930-9300; FAX: (213) 933-0946. Organized 1984. (Video distribution and rack jobber.)

PRESIDENT & CEO
Jerry Welch
VICE PRESIDENT, SECRETARY & TREASURER
A. Duncan Longworth
CHAIRMAN OF THE BOARD
Fred Atchity, Jr.

CHIEF FINANCIAL OFFICER
A. Duncan Longworth
BOARD OF DIRECTORS
Fred Atchity, Jr., Jerry Welch, Herb Kohn, Jeff Chanin, Timothy Clark, Bernard F. Cohlan, Rodney L. Gray

Martha Stuart Communications, Inc.

Box 246, 2 Anthony St., Hillsdale, NY 12529; (518) 325-3900. (Educational and general interest videos.)

PRESIDENT
Martha Stuart
MARKETING & SALES
Victoria Simons

Summit Media Co.

27811 Hopkins Ave., Unit 1, Valencia, CA 91355; (805) 295-0675. Organized 1987. (Video production and distribution.)

PRESIDENT
William C. Hutten
VICE PRESIDENT
Tony Love

Sun Video

15 Donnybrook Dr., Demarest, NJ 07627; (201) 784-0662. Organized 1979. (Home videocassette production and distribution.)

CO-PRESIDENTS
Henry J. Stern
Serafim Karalexis
BOARD OF DIRECTORS
Henry J. Stern, Serafim Karalexis

Sunshine Communications

P.O. Box 1711, Tempe, AZ 85280; (602) 968-3217. Organized 1981. (Produces feature films, videocassettes and TV shows, audio cassettes and CDs.)

PRESIDENT
David Belskis
VICE PRESIDENT
Geri Caswell
SECRETARY
Michelle Caswell
MARKETING
Robert Levy
AFFILIATION
Member: American Film Institute

Supreme Video Works

15 E. 61 St., New York, NY 10021; (212) 753-1050. (Video production for corporate, documentary, TV, fashion, sales, promotion, music, performance videos.)

PRODUCER/DIRECTOR/DIRECTOR OF PHOTOGRAPHY
Tony Arzt

Surf Video Network, Inc.

825 Onstott Rd., Lompoc, CA 93436; (805) 733-1200. Organized 1980. (Produces and distributes surfing, skateboarding, windsurfing, BMX, snowboarding, skiing videos.)

PRESIDENT
Chris Darling
VICE PRESIDENT
David Natal

SyberVision Systems, Inc.

7133 Koll Center Parkway, Pleasanton, CA 94566; (415) 846-2244. Organized 1977. (Produces self-achievement and sports video and audio tapes.)

PRESIDENT
Michael Doepke
CO-FOUNDERS
Steven DeVore
Nasser Hamedani
VICE PRESIDENT, FINANCE
John Heinke
VICE PRESIDENT, OPERATIONS
Regan Jones
VICE PRESIDENT, PRODUCT DEVELOPMENT
Howard Jamison
AFFILIATIONS
Professional Ski Instructors of America, Direct Marketing Association, National Sporting Goods Association, International Tape/Disc Association, Video Software Dealers Association

Syndistar, Inc.

648 Hickory Ave., New Orleans, LA 70123; (504) 737-4486. Organized 1979. (Produces and distributes information films and video.)

PRESIDENT
Greg Fox
VICE PRESIDENT, SALES & MARKETING
Lynn Bourgeois
VICE PRESIDENT, OPERATIONS
Norman Landry
VICE PRESIDENT, PRODUCTION
Billie Rodrigue
AFFILIATIONS
ICIA, VSDA

TV Collector

P.O. Box 188, Needham, MA 02192; (508) 238-1179. (Old television programs and nostalgia; Memorabilia catalogs, published separately.)

PRESIDENTS
Stephen W. Albert
Diane L. Albert

TV Sports Scene, Inc.

(TVSS, Inc.)
5804 Ayrshire Blvd., Minneapolis, MN 55436; (612) 925-9661. Organized 1970. (TV program distribution, national and international.)

PRESIDENT & CHAIRMAN OF THE BOARD
Donald L. Herrick
VICE PRESIDENT
Robert C. Bruce
SECRETARY & TREASURER
Barbara Conley
BOARD OF DIRECTORS
Donald L. Herrick, Robert C. Bruce, Barbara Conley
AFFILIATIONS
Owner of U.S. Television Communications, Inc. (USTC)
Owner—Division Northwest Advertising & Marketing
Owner—Division MED TV
Owner—Division Consumer Products Division TV Sports Scene, Inc.

Tamarelle's International Films, Ltd.

1070 Marauder St., Suite G, Chico, CA 95926; (916) 895-3429; (800) 356-3577; in CA: (800) 334-0136; FAX: (916) 343-9144.

PRESIDENT
Claire Tamarelle

Teaching Films, Inc.

930 Pitner Ave., Evanston, IL 60202; (312) 328-6700; (800) 323-9084. (Distributor of educational films and videos for the professional medical and allied health markets.)

PRESIDENT
Joe Farragher

CHAIRMAN
Joel Altschul
EXECUTIVE VICE PRESIDENT
Esther Altschul
VICE PRESIDENT
Bruce Colling
MARKETING MANAGER
Beth Kon

Telecine Spanish Video

2151 Belmont Ave., New York, NY 10457; (212) 798-7028.

PRESIDENT
Peter Velez
MARKETING AND SALES
Ed Freeberg

Telefilm Co. Inc./Saturn Productions Inc.

1697 Broadway, Room 1102, New York, NY 10019; (212) 489-2460; FAX: (212) 397-0665. Organized 1981. (Theatrical, television, cable Saturn Productions pre-recorded videocassettes.)

PRESIDENT
Tom Ward

Telequest Inc.

14 Washington Road, Princeton Jct., NJ 08550; (609) 799-2105; FAX: (609) 799-4194. Organized 1977. (Film and video production for broadcast and industry.)

PRESIDENT
Richard Blofson
VICE PRESIDENT
Sam Russell
SECRETARY/TREASURER
Scott Nielsen

Telstar Inc.

Bob Miller, 1400 Energy Park Drive, Suite 24, St. Paul, MN 55108; (612) 644-4726. Organized 1968. (Produces and markets video training and instructional materials to industry, home and education.)

PRESIDENT
J.K. Wasley
VICE PRESIDENT
Bob Miller
BOARD OF DIRECTORS
J.K. Wasley, Bob Miller

Theta Mark Home Video, Inc.

1721 W. Plano Parkway, Plano, TX 75075; (214) 578-7651. Organized 1986. (Alternative video distributor/rack jobber)

PRESIDENT
Patrick J. Roper

Third Coast Productions

2929 Morton St., Fort Worth, TX 76107; (817) 877-0916; 334-0559; FAX: (817) 332-3288. Organized 1976. (Film and video tape producer specializing in underwater video and stills. Producers of "Scuba World," TV series.)

GENERAL MANAGER, PRODUCER
Perry W. Tong
MARKETING DIRECTOR
Jim Aden
ASSOCIATE PRODUCER
Keith Radons
CO-PRODUCER
Kyle Tong
CHIEF EDITOR, PRODUCER
Tharon Henderson

Thomson Productions, Inc.

1060 E. 800 S., Orem, UT 84058; (801) 226-0155; FAX: (801) 375-6880. Organized 1984. (Video distribution.)

PRESIDENT
Linda H. Thomson

3M Company/Leisure Time Products

3M Center, Building 223-3S-03, St. Paul, MN 55144; (612) 733-2665. (Sportsman's video collection.)

PROJECT MANAGER
Howard West
SALES SUPERVISOR
Tom Diehl
SENIOR MARKETING COORDINATOR
Carol Bystrzycki
EXECUTIVE PRODUCER
Barbara F. Slesinger

Time-Life Home Video

1271 Ave. of the Americas, New York, NY 10020; (212) 522-3534; (800) 255-8433. (Direct mail video membership club.)

PRESIDENT
Richard Schnabel
EXECUTIVE VICE PRESIDENT
Barr Potter

Today Home Entertainment

6464 Sunset Blvd., Suite 1100, Hollywood, CA 90028; (213) 461-0467; (800) 521-0107.

CHAIRMAN
Emanuel L. Wolfe
PRESIDENT
Adriana Shaw
DIRECTOR, SALES & MARKETING, VIDEO DIVISION
Michael Craft
DIRECTOR OF DEVELOPMENT
Dhani Lipsus

Touchstone Home Video

500 S. Buena Vista St., Burbank, CA 91521; (818) 840-6056. Subsidiary of Walt Disney.

DIRECTOR, NATIONAL SALES
Dick Longwell

Tournament Video Tapes

1615 W. Burbank Blvd., Burbank, CA 91506; (213) 843-0373. Division of Richard J. Soltys Productions. (Sports business videos.)

PRESIDENT
Richard J. Soltys

Tower Productions, Inc.

175 Fifth Ave., Suite 1101, New York, NY 10010; (212) 941-0702. Organized 1983. (Produces programming for broadcast, cable, corporate and home video.)

PRESIDENT
Donald A. Roosa

Trans World Video

3330 W. Cahuenga Blvd. #500, Los Angeles, CA 90068; (213) 969-2800; (800) 521-0107; FAX: (213) 969-8211. Organized 1983. (Production of feature films, sales of all media worldwide, domestic video distribution.)

CO-CHAIRMEN
Moshe Diamant
Eduard Sarlui

CHIEF EXECUTIVE OFFICER
Frank McKevitt
PRESIDENT
Don Rosenberg
AFFILIATION
TWE Group, Inc.

Tri-Coast Video, Inc.

134 Westgate Parkway, Dothan, AL 36303; (205) 677-1111.

PRESIDENT
C. A. Malugen

Troma, Inc.

733 Ninth Ave., 2nd floor, New York, NY 10019; (212) 757-4555. Organized 1974. (Produces and distributes high-concept, low budget films.)

PRESIDENT
Lloyd Kaufman
VICE PRESIDENT
Michael Herz
DIRECTOR OF THEATRICAL DISTRIBUTION
Carl Morano
DIRECTOR OF ANCILLARY SALES, WORLDWIDE
Jeffrey W. Sass
DIRECTOR OF INTERNATIONAL SALES
Robert Aft
DIRECTOR OF BUSINESS AFFAIRS
David Greenspan
DIRECTOR OF MARKETING
Steve Gaul

Trophy Video

2814 Hickory St., Yorktown Heights, NY 10598; (914) 245-1728. Organized 1985. (Hunting, fishing and adventure videos.)

OFFICERS
Don Todd
Virginia Todd

Trylon Video, Inc.

1370 Ave. of the Americas, New York, NY 10019; (212) 767-0500; (Video marketing company, keyed to distributing feature films and sell-through titles into the North American video distribution system.)

PRESIDENT & CHAIRMAN
Nicholas P. Santrizos
EXECUTIVE VICE PRESIDENT, MARKETING & SALES
Jay M. Press
VICE PRESIDENT, ADVERTISING & PROMOTION
Catherine McAdam
CHIEF FINANCIAL OFFICER
John Rago
BRANCH
Trylon Video, Inc., 19-23 Wells St., London, England WIP 3FP

Two Star Films Inc.

Box 495, St. James, NY 11780; (516) 584-7283. (Video documentaries.)

U.S.A. Homevideo

7920 Alabama Ave., Canoga Park, CA 91304-4991; (818) 888-3040, (800) 423-7455. (Subsidiary of International Video Entertainment.)

SENIOR VICE PRESIDENT & GENERAL MANAGER
Len Levy
NATIONAL SALES MANAGER
David Solomon

Understanding Personal Computers

P.O. Box 5849, Stanford, CA 94305; (415) 494-3737. (How-to videos.)

PRESIDENT
Colin Mick

Unicorn Video Inc.

20822 Dearborn St., Chatsworth, CA 91311; (818) 407-1333. Organized 1981. (Manufactures pre-recorded cassettes.)

PRESIDENT
Joanne Goldstein
VICE PRESIDENT
Edward Goldstein
SECRETARY & TREASURER
Anita Goldstein

Unisys Corp.

P.O. Box 2191, Princeton, NJ 08540; (201) 329-3899; (800) 222-0966. (Science and how-to videos.)

United Artists

(see MGM/UA Entertainment Group)

United Entertainment, Inc.

4111 S. Darlington St., Suite 600, Tulsa, OK 74135; (918) 622-6460. Organized 1983. (Distributes pre-recorded video.)

CHAIRMAN OF THE BOARD
Bill Blair
PRESIDENT
Robert Blair
BRANCH
3575 Cahuenga Blvd. W., Culver City, CA 90068

United Home Video

4111 S. Darlington, Suite 600, Tulsa, OK 74135; (918) 622-6460; (800) 331-4077. (How-to, general entertainment, religious, and science-fiction videos.)

PRESIDENT
Robert A. Blair

Universal

(see MCA Home Video)

Universal Home Video

919 N. Broad St., Philadelphia, PA 19123; (215) 232-1100. (Subsidiary of Universal Record Distributing Corp.)

PRESIDENT
Harold B. Lipsius
MARKETING & SALES
Tony Putnick
Lou Reeve

Upswing Artists Management, Ltd.

℅ Jacobson and Colfin, 150 Fifth Ave., Room 1103, New York, NY 10011; (213) 691-5630. Organized 1979. (Produces music video.)

PRESIDENT
Martin Steckler
VICE PRESIDENT
Bruce Colfin
BOARD OF DIRECTORS
Martin Steckler, Bruce E. Colfin
AFFILIATION
Performance Video

VC II Home Video

13402 Wyandotte Ave., North Hollywood, CA 91605; (800) 221-4274. Organized 1978. (Acquires program licensing for video distribution. Produces, manufactures and distributes [worldwide] theatrical, cable and video.)

CHIEF OPERATING OFFICER
Rudy Sutton
MARKETING DIRECTOR
Dave Stevens
ACQUISTIONS
Mike Fredrychs

V.I.E.W. Video Inc. (Video International Entertainment World)

34 E. 23 St., New York, NY 10010; (212) 674-5550. (Production, packaging, syndication, distribution, home video for programs in art, dance, jazz, opera, classical music, children's interactive, modern lifestyle.)

PRESIDENT
Bob Karcy
VICE PRESIDENT
Jack Arel
OPERATIONS
Maria Buerkli
SALES
Gerard Speno
BRANCH
28/30 Rue Mederic, 75017 Paris, France; (14) 267-1516

VIP Video

143 Hickory Hill Circle, Osterville, MA 02655; (508) 428-7198; FAX: (508) 428-7198. Subsidiary of JEF Films.

PRESIDENT
Jeffrey H. Aikman
MARKETING & SALES
Elsie Aikman

VPI/AC Video Inc.

381 Park Ave. South, Suite #1601, New York, NY 10016; (212) 685-5522.

PRESIDENT
Anna Canepa

Van Dam Productions

15 Van Dam St., New York, NY 10013; (212) 807-1877. Subsidiary of Teleculture, Inc.

PRESIDENT
Jordan Bock

Vanguard Video

6535 E. Skelley, Dr., Tulsa, OK 74145; (918) 622-6460; (800) 331-4077. Subsidiary of VCI.

PRESIDENT
Bill Blair

Vencompass, Inc.

824 Peach St., 3rd floor, Erie, PA 16501; (814) 453-7704. Organized 1983. (Produces educational corporate videos.)

PRESIDENT/CHAIRMAN OF THE BOARD
Pamela J. Venable
SECRETARY
Atty. John Leemhuis
TREASURER
John Petersen
BOARD OF DIRECTORS
Thomas L. Venable

Vestron Video

1010 Washington Blvd., P.O. Box 10382, Stamford, CT 06901; (203) 978-5400; 2029 Century Park East, Suite 200, Los Angeles, CA 90067; (213) 551-1723.

PRESIDENT & CHAIRMAN, VESTRON, INC.
Austin O. Furst
PRESIDENT, VESTRON VIDEO
Jon Peisinger
SENIOR VICE PRESIDENT, MARKETING, SALES AND DISTRIBUTION
Al Reuben
VICE PRESIDENT, SALES
Michael Karaffa
VICE PRESIDENT, SPECIAL MARKETS
Dan Markim
DIRECTOR, NON-THEATRICAL PROGRAMMING
Jeffrey Peisch
NATIONAL MARKETING DIRECTOR
William Perrault
VICE PRESIDENT/GENERAL MANAGER-VESTRON VIDEO ESPAÑOL
Edwin Friendly

VidAmerica

231 E. 55 St., New York, NY 10022; (212) 355-1600; P.O.P. Hotline: (800) 843-1994; FAX: (212) 355-4363.

EXECUTIVE VICE PRESIDENT
Gary Needle

Vid-Dimension, Inc.

4221 W. Sierra Madre, #109, Fresno, CA 93722; (209) 276-6000; (800) 233-0089 (U.S.); (800) 336-1005 (CA); FAX: (209) 276-6003. Organized 1985. (Manufactures and distributes prerecorded educational, religious and entertainment videos in Spanish—subtitled, dubbed.)

PRESIDENT
Abe G. Osuna
SECRETARY
Leo Lobato Kelly
BOARD OF DIRECTORS
Abe G. Osuna, Leo Lobato Kelly

Video Action

237 Ogden Ave., Jersey City, NJ 07307; (201) 792-3833. (Body building videos.)

OWNER
Bob Brennan

Video Action

708 W. First St., Los Angeles, CA 90012; (213) 687-8262. Organized 1981. (Video production and distribution.)

OWNER
Gregg S. Yokoyama

Video Aided Instruction, Inc.

182 Village Rd., East Hills, NY 11577; (516) 621-6176; FAX: (516) 484-8785. Organized 1983. (Produces instructional, educational videocassettes.)

PRESIDENT
Peter Lanzer
VICE PRESIDENT
Mona Lanzer
BOARD OF DIRECTORS
Peter Lanzer, Mona Lanzer

Video Album Ltd.

P.O. Box 24683, 4936 Maple Rd., Edina, MN 55424; (612) 925-9804; FAX: (612) 927-4578. Organized 1975. (Produces educational videos including How to Play the Piano videos.)

OFFICERS
Yakov Gelfand
Thelma Hunter
BOARD OF DIRECTORS
Ruth K. Noack, Charlene Witherell, Maren Mahowald M.D.

Video Artists International, Inc.

2112 Broadway, Suite 415, (P.O. Box 153, Ansonia Sta., 10023) New York, NY 10023; (212) 799-7798; FAX: (212) 799-7768. Organized 1983. (Manufactures home videocassettes.)

PRESIDENT
Ernest J. Gilbert
VICE PRESIDENT, NATIONAL SALES & MARKETING
Duncan Hutchinson
PRODUCT MANAGER
Robert J. Quintana
SALES & PUBLICITY
Allan Altman
ACCOUNTS RECEIVABLE/PAYABLE
Harold Gable
CUSTOMER SERVICE REP.
Ariel Prizont

Video Cassette Marketing Corp.

137 Eucalyptus, El Segundo, CA 90245; (213) 322-1140.

PRESIDENT
James Spencer

Video City Productions & Distributors

4266 Broadway, Oakland, CA 94611; (415) 428-0202. Organized 1983. (Manufactures and distributes pre-recorded VHS and Beta film product.)

MARKETING DIRECTOR
Bob Brown
OTHER COMPANY OWNED LABELS:
Combat Video, Art House Video, Chop 'Em Ups Video, World Aviation Video, Black Action Video.

The Video Connection

3123 Sylvania Ave., Toledo, OH 43613; (800) 365-0449.

PRESIDENT
John Day

Video Dimensions

530 W. 23 St., New York, NY 10011; (212) 929-6135.

Video Dynamics

Box 9550, Jackson, MS 39206; (601) 957-2722, (800) 647-2284. (Children's, educational, religious, and special interest.)

PRESIDENT
Pat Robinson
MARKETING & SALES
Steve Robinson

Video Gems

P.O. Box 38188, Los Angeles, CA 90038; (213) 398-3332. Organized 1979. (Manufacturer and distributor of pre-recorded videocassettes.)

PRESIDENT
Mary L. Greiner

Video International Publishers, Inc.

118 6th St. S., Great Falls, MT 59405; (406) 727-7133. Organized 1980. (Production and distribution of corporate communication, educational and how-to video programming.)

PRESIDENT
James M. Colla
VICE PRESIDENT
Penny L. Adkins
SECRETARY/TREASURER
Penny L. Adkins

Video Knowledge Inc.

29 Bramble Lane, Melville, NY 11747; (516) 367-4250.

PRESIDENT
Sally Dubrowsky
VICE PRESIDENT
Ed Dubrowsky
BOARD OF DIRECTOR
Geoffrey S. Dubrowsky

Video Latino

409 N. Figueroa, Wilmington, CA 90744; (213) 549-4490. (Spanish language general interest videos.)

PRESIDENT
Russell C. Greene

Video Learning Library

7201 Haven Ave., Suite E, Alta Loma, CA 91701; (714) 941-2822. Organized 1989. (Distributor of how-to and special interest videotapes.)

PRESIDENT
James R. Spencer

Video Library of Arts

716 S. Main, Broken Arrow, OK 74012; (918) 251-0466. Division of Ken Meyer Productions.

PRESIDENT
Ken Meyer

Video Marketing and Distributing Inc.

4301 Hwy. 7, St. Louis Park, MN 55416; (612) 920-8400.

PRESIDENT
Mark Saliterman

The Video Naturals Company

2590 Glen Green, Suite #6, Los Angeles, CA 90068; (213) 469-0019. Organized 1982. (Produces and distributes "mood videos" such as "Video Fireplace" and "Ocean Waves" for the home video market.)

PRESIDENT/OWNER
Steve Siporin
AFFILIATIONS
Distributors: Videotakes (1-800-526-7002)

Video One Video Inc.

1600 124 Ave. N.E. Suite E., Bellevue, WA 98005; (206) 454-5992.

VICE PRESIDENT, SALES
Jim Koch

Video Paradise, Inc.

115 W. Main St., Westboro, MA 01581; (617) 366-8890.

PRESIDENT
Donald Rogers

Video Presentations, Inc.

2326 Sixth Ave., Suite 230, Seattle, WA 98121; (206) 728-9241. Organized 1979. (Video off-line editing, production and duplication services in prof. BETACAM, ¾" U-matic and S-VHS.)

PRESIDENT
H. V. Wright
VICE PRESIDENT
Nancy L. Wright

Video Products Distributors, Inc.

2428 Glendale Lane, Sacramento, CA 95825; (916) 971-9111 or 971-1809; FAX: (916) 481-4736.

PRESIDENT
Tim Shannahan
BRANCHES
2350 E. Artesia, Long Beach, CA 90805
4551 Brickell Privado, Ontario, CA 91761

Video Properties, Inc.

33 E. 68 St., New York, NY 10021; (212) 570-1200.

PRESIDENT
John A. Friede

Video RX

7115 N. Austin, Niles, IL 60648; (312) 647-8400. (Video distributor.)

OWNERS
Marvin Steinberg
Burt Steinberg
OPERATIONS MANAGER
Marc Barnett

Video Reel, Inc.

16633 Ventura Blvd. #600, Encino, CA 91436-1861. Organized 1983. (Produces and duplicates how-to sports videos.)

PRESIDENT
Robert Mann
VICE PRESIDENT
Robert Mann
TREASURER
Robert Mann
SECRETARY
Robert Mann
BOARD OF DIRECTORS
Robert S. Mann, Bonnie L. Krolop
AFFILIATIONS
Recording Association of America, International Tape and Disc Assn.

Video Releasing Co. of Hawaii

1313 Kalakaua Ave., Honolulu, HI 96826; (808) 946-1000. Organized 1985. (Wholesale distribution of videocassette programs.)

DIRECTOR OF SALES
Judy Bottalico

Video Research

297 Newbury St., Boston, MA 02116; (617) 262-8934. Organized 1983. (Home video product development.)

PRESIDENT
David Burke
EXECUTIVE VICE PRESIDENT
Fred Surr
VICE PRESIDENT, FINANCE
Jane Lytle-Manns
VICE PRESIDENT, MARKETING
Bitsy McKay
BOARD OF DIRECTORS
David Burke, Fred Surr, Lila Hexner, Barry Unger, Judy Obermayer

Video Resources New York Inc.

220 W. 71 St., #91, New York, NY 10023; (213) 724-7055. Organized 1980. (Video and film production; stock footage, film restoration, film and TV library of history books, home video distributor of nostalgia films and early TV shows. Large collection of commercials from the 1940s through early 1970s. Also ½" and ¾" editing and dubbing.)

PRESIDENT, DIRECTOR, EDITOR, HISTORIAN, EXEC. PRODUCER
Ira H. Gallen
CO-PRODUCER, WRITER
John A. Gallagher
VIDEO TECHNICAL ADVISOR
Vic Tannenberg
CAMERA (D.P.)
Bill Coleman, Marc Hirschfeld

Video-Sig

1030 East Duane Ave., Suite C, Sunnyvale, CA 94086; (408) 730-9291; FAX: (408) 730-2107. Organized 1987. (Video publishers of primarily independent productions.)

FOUNDER
Richard Petersen
PROJECT COORDINATOR AND DIRECTOR OF SALES
Julie Hutton
ACQUISITIONS & PUBLICATIONS COORDINATOR
Anne Olson
PRODUCER AND VIDEOGRAPHER
Bruce Kent

Video Sports Productions

1704 Sweeney, Las Vegas, NV 89104; (702) 384-7514. (Golf and other sports videos.)

PRESIDENT
C. A. Montana

Video Tech

19346 Third N.W., Seattle, WA 98177; (206) 546-5401.

PRESIDENT
Eugene Ekblad

Video Ticket

11811 W. Olympic Blvd., Los Angeles, CA 90064; (213) 478-8499.

PRESIDENT
Peter Bieler

Video Travel, Inc.

153 W. Fourth St., Williamsport, PA 17701; (717) 326-6525. (Sports, how-to and travel videos.)

PRESIDENT
Larry Seaman

Video Treasures

1767 Morris Ave., Union, NJ 07083; (201) 964-5604. (Budget videocassette label.) Subsidiary of Handleman Co.

PRESIDENT
Peter Hyman
EXECUTIVE VICE PRESIDENT & CHIEF OPERATING OFFICER
George Port

Video Trend, Inc.

1011 E. Touhy Ave., Suite 500, Des Plaines, IL 60018; (312) 635-7100. Organized 1979. (Distributor of pre-recorded video.)

SENIOR VICE PRESIDENT
Robert Tollini
VICE PRESIDENTS
David Long (Detroit)
John Gallagher (Tampa)
Jim Weiss (Seattle)
Robert Stuben Rauch (Chicago)
SALES DEVELOPMENT & TRAINING
Robert Johnson
BRANCHES
Detroit, Chicago, Tampa, Seattle, Salt Lake City, Sacramento, San Francisco

Video Visa Inc.

12901 Coral Tree Place, Los Angeles, CA 90066; (213) 827-7222; FAX: (213) 828-1738.

PRODUCTION MANAGER
Marco Bracamontes

Video Yesteryear

Box C, Sandy Hook, CT 06482; FAX: (203) 797-0819. Organized 1978.

PRESIDENT
Jon Sonneborn

Videoactive Company (a Delaware Corp.)

29169 W. Heathercliff, #216, Malibu, CA 90265; (213) 457-1144. Organized 1982. (Producer and distributor of film and video tape programs: How-to, entertainment, advertising and promotional, and public relations. Also motion picture, full feature scripts and budget prep service.)

PRESIDENT
Bill Myers
VICE PRESIDENT, TECHNICAL
Bill Darst
VICE PRESIDENT, OPERATIONS
Linda Shockley
VICE PRESIDENT, TAPE DUPLICATION
Rock Walton
VICE PRESIDENT, PRODUCTION
Josh Golden
BOARD OF DIRECTORS
Bill Myers (chairman)
BRANCHES
Florida, London, Switzerland

Videocassette Marketing Corporation

137 Eucalyptus Dr., El Segundo, CA 90245; (213) 515-3302, (800) 332-1140. Organized 1984. (Distributes children's, how-to, non-theatrical, environmental and subliminal pre-recorded videocassettes to video stores and consumers.)

PRESIDENT
James Spencer
GENERAL MANAGER
Cindy E. Greisdorf

Videocom

502 Sprague St., Dedham, MA 02026; (617) 329-4080; FAX: (617) 329-8534; TELEX: 4430135 VIDEOCOM. Organized 1967. (Commercial and industrial production, satellite uplink and distribution, multi-format duplication, videoconferencing, post production.)

PRESIDENT
Dan Swartz
GENERAL MANAGER
Frank Cavallo
VICE PRESIDENT/DUPLICATION MANAGER
Harvey Hecker
EXECUTIVE PRODUCER/DIRECTOR
Andy Abrams
OPERATIONS MANAGER/SATELLITE
Bob Hanson
CONTROLLER
Allen MacDonald
CHIEF ENGINEER
Johnny Parker
TRAFFIC
Michele Mailhot

Videocraft Classics

1790 Broadway, New York, NY 10019; (212) 246-9849. (Produces and distributes educational videos.)

PRESIDENT
Lee Kraft
VICE PRESIDENT
Marc Weinstein

Videodisc Publishing Inc.

381 Park Ave. S., #1601, New York, NY 10016; (212) 685-5522.

PRESIDENT
Gene Fairly

Videofashion

1 W. 37 St., 5th floor, New York, NY 10018; (212) 869-4666. Telex: 225707. Vidmo UR. FAX: 869-8208. Organized 1976. (World's first "videomagazine." Internationally focused, magazine-format, fashion and lifestyle programs, available for worldwide distribution on videocassette, cable and broadcast. 40 ½-hour programs are produced each year in 4 program lines: Videofashion Monthly (12/year); Videofashion News (12/year) Videofashion Men (4/year); Videofashion Specials (24 available).

CHAIRMAN & PRESIDENT
Nicholas H. Charney
INTERNATIONAL MARKETING
Marlene B. McGinnis
MANAGING EDITOR
Anne V. Adami

Videograph

2833 25th St., San Francisco, CA 94110; (415) 282-6001. (English and Spanish health and educational videos.)

PRESIDENT
Jim Locker

Videolearning Systems, Inc.

354 W. Lancaster Ave., Haverford, PA 19041; (215) 896-6600.

PRESIDENT
Homer H. Hewitt, III

Videoplan, Inc.

13620 S. Crenshaw Blvd., Gardena, CA 90249; (213) 532-9024.

PRESIDENT
Peter Jacobs

Videosmith Inc.

2006 Chancellor St., Philadelphia, PA 19103; (215) 665-3690. Organized 1974. (Video/film production and post production, computer animation.)

PRESIDENT
Steve Smith
VICE PRESIDENT
Steve O'Driscoll

TREASURER/SECRETARY
Martha Smith
BRANCHES
3 Independence Way, Princeton, NJ 08540

Videotakes, Inc.

187 Route 71, Manasquan, NJ 08736; (201) 528-5000; (800) 526-7002. Organized 1982. (Marketing of non-feature film videocassettes.)

PRESIDENT
Joe Kennedy, 150 First Ave., Manasquan, NJ 08736

Vidmark, Inc.

2901 Ocean Park Blvd., Suite 123, Santa Monica, CA 90405-2906; (213) 399-8877, (800) 424-7070, (CA); (800) 351-7070; FAX: (213) 399-3828.

CHAIRMAN, CEO
Mark Amin
SENIOR VICE PRESIDENT
Barry Barnholtz
VICE PRESIDENT, MARKETING AND SALES
Sam Pirnazar
VICE PRESIDENT, INTERNATIONAL
Penny Karlin

Vision Media

625 Broadway, #902, New York, NY 10012; (212) 529-6880. Organized 1984. (Consulting, production and development services, specializing in original programming for home video.)

PRESIDENT/EXECUTIVE PRODUCER
Paul Tandlies

Vision Productions, Ltd.

311 E. 6th St., #2, Moscow, ID 83843; (208) 883-0105. Organized 1979. (Video production and marketing.)

PRESIDENT
John A. L. Francis
VICE PRESIDENT
E. A. Francis

Vista Home Video

1350 Ave. of the Americas, New York, NY 10019; (212) 582-0500.

PRESIDENT
Nick Santrizos

Vistar International Productions

3790 Dunn Dr., Suite C, Los Angeles, CA 90043; (213) 204-3392.

WEA, Corp. (Warner/Elektra/Atlantic Corp.)

111 N. Hollywood Way, Burbank, CA 91505; (818) 843-6311. (Subsidiary of Warner Communications, Inc.)

PRESIDENT
Henry Droz
MARKETING & SALES
George Rossi

WRI Education

World Research Incorporated, Campus Studies Institute, 968 Emerald St., Suite 6700, P.O. Box 9359, San Diego, CA 92109; (619) 456-5278.

PRESIDENT
Daniel T. Loeffler

Ken Walz Productions Inc.

219 E. 60 St., 4th floor, New York, NY 10022; (212) 826-6010. Organized 1972. (Produces television programs, music videos, home videos, commercials, corporate films and motion pictures.)

PRESIDENT
Ken Walz

Warner Home Video Inc.

3903 W. Olive Ave., Burbank, CA 91522; (818) 954-6000. Organized 1979. (Brings the motion picture and entertainment-media productions of Warner Bros. Inc. to the prerecorded home video marketplace.) A subsidiary of Warner Bros. Inc., a Warner Communications company.

PRESIDENT
Warren N. Lieberfarb
EXECUTIVE VICE PRESIDENT/GENERAL MANAGER, INTERNATIONAL
Edward J. Byrnes
VICE PRESIDENT WORLDWIDE PLANNING & OPERATIONS
James F. Cardwell
VICE PRESIDENT/MARKETING
Barbara O'Sullivan
VICE PRESIDENT, U.S. SALES
John Quinn
VICE PRESIDENT, PLANNING & OPERATIONS, NORTH AMERICA
Jaime Ovadia
VICE PRESIDENT, WORLDWIDE VIDEO ACQUISITION
Elyse Eisenberg
DIRECTOR PUBLIC RELATIONS, EDITORIAL & PROGRAMMING SERVICES
Michael Finnegan
DIRECTOR OF PRODUCTION
Lewis Ostrover

Wax Works/Video Works National Distributor

325 E. 3rd St., Owensboro, KY 42301;, (800) 626-1918. Organized 1979. (Video distributor of all national major lines. Also audio distributor.)

PRESIDENT
Terry Woodward
SALES MANAGER
Kirk Kirkpatrick
CREDIT MANAGER
Bill Burton
BUYER
Noel Clayton
BRANCH
4011 Winchester Rd., Memphis, TN 38118; (800) 331-0993, (901) 366-4088

Weiss Global Enterprises

2055 Saviers Rd., Suite 12, Oxnard, CA 93033-3693; Mailing address: P.O. Box 20360, Oxnard, CA 93034-0360; (805) 486-4495; FAX: (805) 487-3330. Cable: WEISSPICT. Organized 1974. (Distributes television and motion picture programming.)

PRESIDENT
Adrian Weiss
SECRETARY & TREASURER
Steven A. Weiss
VICE PRESIDENTS
Ethel L. Weiss
Laurie Weiss
OPERATIONS MANAGER
Beverly S. Verman
INFORMATION SERVICES
Alex Gordon
REPRESENTATIVES
Richard S. Ellman, 200 North Robertson, Suite 336, Beverly Hills, CA 90211; (213) 276-9420.
Marv Gray, P.O. Box 9239, Calabasas, CA 91302; (818) 702-9888
E. Melvin Pinsel, 10243 Pine Dr., Boynton Beach, FL 33437; (407) 734-7257.

Hank Profenius, 3207 W. Friendly Ave., Greensboro, NC 27408; (919) 292-1434
Robert Weisberg, 145 E. 92 St., Suite PH A, New York, NY 10128.
Foreign: Howard Karshan, 25 Old Burlington St., London W1X 1LB, (01) 434-4341

West Glen Communications

1430 Broadway, New York, NY 10018; (212) 921-2800; FAX: (212) 944-9055.

PRESIDENT
Stanley S. Zeitlin
EXECUTIVE VICE PRESIDENT
Vincent Capuzzi
SENIOR V.P. TELEVISION PRODUCTION
John Summerlin
SENIOR V.P. TELEVISION DISTRIBUTION
Annette Minkalis
V.P. THEATRICAL DISTRIBUTION
Sy Perry

Westcom Productions Inc.

1925 Bailey Hill Rd., Eugene, OR 97405; (503) 683-2236; (800) 950-4952. Organized 1984. (Complete video production, post production, duplication and marketing services.)

PRESIDENT
Bruce O'Neil
VICE PRESIDENT, OPERATION
John Wray
VICE PRESIDENT, MARKETING
Mark Lange
BUSINESS DEVELOPMENT
Jack Loe

Western Film & Video, Inc.

30941 W. Agoura Rd., Building 302/304, Westlake Village, CA 91361; (818) 889-7350. FAX: (818) 707-3937. Organized 1974. (Motion picture laboratory and complete video-tape facility. Productions, duplication, editing, film to tape transfers and standards conversions.)

PRESIDENT & CHIEF EXECUTIVE OFFICER
Gary R. Guenot
LAB MANAGER
Glenn Whitten
SECRETARY & TREASURER
Jim Guenot
BRANCH
Video Magic (mail-order software)
AFFILIATION
Part of the Westlake Media Center

Western Publishing Company, Inc.

1220 Mound Ave., Racine, WI 53404; (414) 633-2431. Subsidiary of Western Publishing Group, Inc. (How-to, children's, educational.)

PRESIDENT
Bill Nahikian
VICE PRESIDENT, SALES
James O'Donnell
NATIONAL SALES MANAGER-VIDEO DISTRIBUTION
Robert Komisar

Weston Woods Studios, Inc.

389 Newtown Turnpike, Weston, CT 06883; (203) 226-3355. Organized 1956. (Producers and distributors of film and video adaptations of children's picture books.)

PRESIDENT & TREASURER
Morton Schindel
DIRECTOR OF MARKETING
Blanche Stout
VICE PRESIDENT & SECRETARY
Elisabeth Rommel
BOARD OF DIRECTORS
Morton Schindel, Elisabeth Rommel, Cathy S. Knowles

White Janssen, Inc.

604 Davis St., Evanston, IL 60201; (312) 328-2221. Organized 1983. (Home video development company.)

OWNERS
Stefaan Janssen
Matthew White
AFFILIATIONS
Member: VSDA; Center for New Television; AIFV

Wild Wing Productions

7240 Valjean Ave., Van Nuys, CA 91406; (818) 994-4955; FAX: (818) 994-8405. Organized 1984. (Creates and produces documentary films and original home video programming in how-to, general entertainment, children's, and educational categories. Acquires special interest programming for home video distribution and TV syndication.)

PRESIDENT & CHIEF EXECUTIVE OFFICER
Drew Michaels
VICE PRESIDENT, MARKETING & PROMOTION
Andrew Rapaport
VICE PRESIDENT, ADMINISTRATIVE OPERATIONS
Kathryn Grossman
BOARD OF DIRECTORS
Drew Michaels, Chairman of the Board, Chief Executive Officer, President; John Smart, Director; Warren R. Kaufman, Director; Kathryn G. Grossman, Secretary.
AFFILIATIONS
Video Software Dealers Association; Special Interest Video Association

Wilderness Video

P.O. Box 2175, Redondo Beach, CA 90278; (213) 973-7544. Organized 1982. (Produces wilderness videos of national parks—Glacier, Yosemite, Yellowstone, Grand Canyon, Bryce/Zion, Big Sur.)

OWNER
R. W. Glusic

Wade Williams Productions

5500 Ward Parkway, Kansas City, MO 64113; (816) 523-2699. Organized 1980. (Production and distribution of science fiction motion pictures and home videos.)

PRESIDENT
Wade Williams
VICE PRESIDENT
Brian Mossman
SECRETARY
Ben Mossman

Win Records and Video, Inc.

76-05 51st Avenue, Elmhurst, NY 11373; (800) 221-1220, (800) 851-2525 (NY state). Organized 1955. (Wholesale distribution of home entertainment products: video software [full line]; records: tapes; CD's; and specially selected accessories.)

PRESIDENT
Sam Weiss
VICE PRESIDENT
George Weiss

Windward Video

P.O. Box 613, Paia, Maui, HI 96779; (808) 579-9313. (Film and video production—educational, corporate, and documentary.)

PRESIDENT
Jerry Rochford

Wishing Well Distributing Co.

P.O. Box 529, Graton, CA 95444; (707) 823-9355. Organized 1978. (Markets and sells over 2000 videos—educational, documentary, entertainment.)

PRESIDENT
Debra Giusti
GENERAL MANAGER
Larry Needlman
SALES MANAGER
Sue Lancaster

Wizard Video Inc.

1551 N. La Brea Ave., Los Angeles, CA 90028; (213) 850-6563.

Wombat Productions

(Division of Cortech Communications, Inc.)

250 W. 57 St., Suite 2421, New York, NY 10019; (212) 315-2502; FAX: (212) 582-0585. Organized 1970. (Produces television specials and entertainment documentaries.)

PRESIDENT
Gene Feldman
EXECUTIVE VICE PRESIDENT
Suzette Winter
VICE PRESIDENT, MARKETING
Stephen Janson

Women Make Movies, Inc.

225 Lafayette St., Room 212, New York, NY 10012; (212) 925-0606. Organized 1972. (Facilitates the production, exhibition and distribution of media by and about women.)

PRESIDENT
Joanne Sandler
VICE PRESIDENT
Linda Young
TREASURER
Tani Takagi
SECRETARY
Beni Matias
BOARD OF DIRECTORS
Barbara Abrash, Kathy Acey, Ariel Dougherty, Susan Horowitz, Joi Huckaby, Barrie Pribyl, Kathe Sandler, Raquel Rivera, Barbara Scheulen, Iris Morales, Marina Gonzalez.
AFFILIATIONS
AIVF, NAMAC, Media Alliance

Wood Knapp & Company, Inc.

5900 Wilshire Blvd., Los Angeles, CA 90036; (213) 965-3500. (Video production and distribution.)

PRESIDENT
Betsy Wood Knapp
VICE PRESIDENT, FINANCE/BUSINESS AFFAIRS
John Hunter
SENIOR VICE PRESIDENT, SALES & MARKETING
Mark Giula
BOARD OF DIRECTORS
Betsy Wood Knapp, Cleon T. Knapp (pres. & CEO, Knapp Communications Corp.), H. Stephen Cranston, Esq. (RMA Consulting).
BRANCHES
Wood Knapp Productions, 5900 Wilshire Blvd., Los Angeles, CA 90036; Wood Knapp Video, 140 E. 45 St., New York, NY 10017 (regional sales offices in Dallas, TX; Seattle, WA; Milwaukee, WI.
AFFILIATION
Knapp Communications Corp.

Woodenboat Publications, Inc.

Naskeag Rd., Brooklin, ME 04616; (207) 359-4651. (Wooden boat construction and repair; sailors' knots and splices.)

PRESIDENT
Jonathan Wilson

World Vision Home Video, Inc.

660 Madison Ave., 3rd floor, New York, NY 10021; (212) 832-3838. Organized 1980. (Domestic home video distribution, marketing and sales.)

VICE PRESIDENT & GENERAL MANAGER
Tom Devlin
ADMINISTRATIVE ASSISTANT
Mimi Wunderlich
MANAGER, SALES ADMINISTRATION
Robert Denney
MANAGER, OPERATIONS
Rich Vahi
AFFILIATION
Worldvision Enterprises

Worldwide Tape Distributors

223 Keats Dr., Sicklerville, NJ 08081; (609) 228-0205.

PRESIDENT
Ted Klempner

Xenon Home Video

211 Arizona Ave., Suite 25, Santa Monica, CA 90401; (213) 451-5510. (800) 468-1913; FAX: (213) 392-4058. Organized 1986. (Manufacturer of Black action and general video programming.)

PRESIDENT
S. Leigh Savidge
VICE PRESIDENT
Arnie Lakeyn
AFFILIATION
VSDA

Xerox Information Resources Group

P.O. Box 1600; Stamford, CT 06904-1288; (203) 625-5634. (Subsidiary of Xerox Corp.)

PRESIDENT
William J. Senter

ZBS Industries

701 Beta Dr., Cleveland, OH 44143; (800) 321-8774. Organized 1979. (Distributes pre-recorded video.)

PRESIDENT
Larry Beyer
VICE PRESIDENT
Earl Stein
SECRETARY/TREASURER
Jay Schultz
BOARD OF DIRECTORS
Larry Beyer, Earl Stein, Jay Schultz

Major Video Retailers

Aardvark Video

811 W. 11th St., Coffeyville, KS 67337; (316) 251-6165.

OWNER
Tim Kilpatrick

Academy Video

18122 Brookhurst St., #B, Fountain Valley, CA 92708; (714) 964-1691. (Video independent.)

OWNER
Don Rubin

Acorn Sports, Inc.

5816 Shakespeare Rd., Suite D, Columbia, SC 29204; (803) 735-0733. (Golf videos.)

PRESIDENT
D. Swing Meyer

Alice In Videoland Ltd.

738 Ulster Ave., P.O. Box 2000-H, Kingston, NY 12401; (914) 338-5288. Organized 1983. (Video sales/rentals—televisions, stereo. Related products' sales.)

PRESIDENT
Paula DeCesare

BRANCHES
Kingston, NY; Pleasant Valley, NY; Saugerties, NY; Phoenicia, NY; Great Barrington, MA

All American Video-Los Osos

2190 9 Street, Los Osos, CA 93402; (805) 528-2820. (Franchise.)

PRESIDENT
Keith Lilley

All-In-One-Video

2806 N. Highway 441-27, Fruitland, FL 32731; (904) 326-3633. (Video chain.)

PRESIDENT
Sharen Gonzalez

Alternative Video

604 Davis St., Evanston, IL 60201; (312) 328-2221. Organized 1983. (Direct marketing of special interest home video programs.)

OWNER
Division of White Janssen, Inc.

AFFILIATIONS
Member: VSDA; Center for New Television; AIFV

American Box Office Video Inc.

40 E. Main St., Hopkinton, MA 01748; (617) 435-5174, (617) 435-4270. Organized 1984. (4 video stores, video rack jobbers.)

PRESIDENT
Rachel Dworkin

BUYER
Steve Dworkin

CLERK
Mellissa Dworkin

BRANCHES
Milford, MA; Westboro, MA; Clinton, MA; Hudson, MA.

AFFILIATES
Somerville, Fitchburg, Framingham

American Drug Stores

1818 Swift Dr., Oak Brook, IL 60521; (312) 572-5000. Drug, Chain (650 stores. including Osco Drug and Svon Drug.)

CONSUMER ELECTRONICS BUYER
James H. Seifert

Applause Video

2622 S. 156 Circle, Omaha, NE 68130; (402) 330-1000; FAX: (402) 330-5679. Organized 1983. (Video chain with 60 stores.)

OWNER-CHAIRMAN
Allan Caplan

At the Movies

110 1H-35 North, #380, Round Rock, TX 78681; (512) 255-6021. Independent video.

Audio Visuals of Tampa, Inc.

4333 W. Kennedy Blvd., Box 10099, Tampa, FL 33609; (813) 876-8718. Independent audio/visual.

PRESIDENT
Murray Segal

Baker & Taylor Video

8140 Lehigh Ave., Morton Grove, IL 60053; (312) 965-8060.

Barnes & Noble Inc.

122 Fifth Ave., New York, NY 10003; (212) 206-8800. Bookstore—independent chain.

DIRECTOR OF MARKETING
Barry Denenberg

SOFTWARE BUYER
Susan Barkan

Bee Gee Records & Tapes, Inc.

10 Northway Lane N., Latham, NY 12110; (518) 785-1122. Video chain (11).

PURCHASING
Mike Raikowski

Norman Beerger Productions, Inc.

3217-A29, Arville St., Las Vegas, NV 89102-7612; (702) 876-2328. Organized 1984. (Produces and distributes wilderness home video programs.)

OWNER
Norman Beerger

Beverly Hills Videocentre, Inc.

145 S. Beverly Drive, Beverly Hills, CA 90212; (213) 550-1092. Organized 1980. (Sale and rental of pre-recorded videocassettes.)

PRESIDENT
Emil Reisman

SECRETARY
Jane Hamilton

BOARD OF DIRECTORS
Emil Reisman

BRANCH
West Hollywood, CA 90046

The Blackhawk Catalog

12626 Beatrice St., Los Angeles, CA 90066; (213) 306-4040.

VICE PRESIDENT
Philip J. Kromnick
OPERATIONS COORDINATOR
Kimberly Baker

Les Blank's Flower Films and Video

10341 San Pablo Ave., El Cerrrio, CA 94530; (415) 525-0942. Organized 1967. (Seeks out and documents America's vanishing minority cultures, their music and traditions.)

PRODUCER/DIRECTOR/CAMERA
Les Blank
DISTRIBUTION MANAGER
Toni Hanna
FOLKLORIST/2nd CAMERA
Christine Simon
EDITOR—SOUND
Maureen Gosling, Chris Simon

Blockbuster Entertainment Corporation

901 E. Las Olas Blvd., Ft. Lauderdale, FL 33301; (305) 524-8200; FAX: (305) 462-4139. Organized 1985. (Retail rental and sale of prerecorded video cassettes.)

CHAIRMAN, C.E.O.
H. Wayne Huizenga
PRESIDENT, C.O.O.
Luigi Salvaneschi
SENIOR VICE PRESIDENT/CHIEF FINANCIAL OFFICER
Steven R. Berrard
SENIOR VICE PRESIDENT/CHIEF MARKETING OFFICER
Thomas A. Gruber
SENIOR VICE PRESIDENT
James F. Ellis
SENIOR VICE PRESIDENT, PROGRAMMING, COMMUNICATIONS DEV.
J. Ronald Castell
CORPORATE CONTROLLER
Cary N. Vollintine
GENERAL COUNSEL & CORPORATE SECRETARY
Thomas W. Carton Jr.
VICE PRESIDENT, REAL ESTATE
Philip C. deMena
VICE PRESIDENT, FRANCHISE OPERATIONS
Douglas M. Kinney
VICE PRESIDENT, NATIONAL DEVELOPMENT
Robert A. Guerin
VICE PRESIDENT
Charles H. Martin
CORPORATE TREASURER
Joseph J. Burke
BOARD OF DIRECTORS
H. Wayne Huizenga (chairman), Donald F. Flynn, A. Clinton Allen III, John W. Croghan, Luigi Salvaneschi, Steven R. Berrard, Carl F. Barger, Gene W. Schneider
SUBSIDIARIES
Blockbuster Holding Corporation, Blockbuster Videos Inc., Video Library Inc., Major Video Corp., Chartbuster Entertainment Corporation Limited (U.K.)

Bradford Video

394 S. Main St., Bradford, MA 01830; (617) 372-3160. Independent video.

OWNER
David Court

Bridgeport Video

742 W. 31st St., Chicago, IL 60616; (312) 326-1467. Independent video.

Britannica Training & Development

310 South Michigan Avenue, Britannica Centre, Chicago, IL 60604; (312) 347-7900; (800) 554-9862; FAX: (312) 347-7903.

Broadway Video

168 S. Lake St., Forest Lake, MN 55025; (612) 464-8231. Organized 1982. (Videotape sales and rental.)

MANAGER/OWNER
Thomas M. Houle
OWNER
Stuart J. Houle
BRANCHES
Broadway Video, Rack Jobbing, Video Store of Spring Lake Park

Brookshire Brothers Inc.

P.O. Box 1688, Lufkin, TX 75901; (409) 634-8155. Video chain (50).

PRESIDENT
R. A. Brookshire
SOFTWARE & HARDWARE BUYER
Joe Ben Gann

Budget Video Inc.

(D/B/A Hollywood Home Theatre)
1540 N. Highland Ave., Suite 110, Hollywood, CA 90028; (213) 446-0121, (213) 466-0127. Organized 1979. (Dealer, distributor, retailer of video cassettes and laser discs.)

PRESIDENT
Larry S. Fine
VICE PRESIDENT
Stephen Stumbris

Canadian Tire Corp. Ltd.

P.O. Box 770, Station K, Toronto, Ont., Canada M4P 2V8; (416) 480-3000. Mass merchant. Chain (400 stores).

SOFTWARE BUYER
Patti Mills-Roy

Captain Video

1326 Broad St., Central Falls, RI 02863; (401) 724-1297. Video, independent.

PRESIDENT
Fred Kilsey
VICE PRESIDENT & TREASURER
Mark Feinstein

Carousel Music & Video

121 Winter Haven Mall, Winter Haven, FL 33880; (813) 294-8346; 293-0372. (Complete audio and video store.)

OWNERS
Gary E. Stewart
Ron Edmonds

Christopher's Video West, Inc.

8 S. 101st St., Rt. 59, Naperville, IL 60540; (312) 369-8993. Video independent.

PRESIDENT
P. A. Christopher
SECRETARY & TREASURER
S. L. Christopher

Cinema Concepts, Inc.

2461 Berlin Turnpike, Newington, CT 06111; (203) 667-1251. Organized 1971. (Non-theatrical distribution of entertainment motion pictures in 16mm, VHS, to school, libraries and home market. Mail-order plus two retail stores.)

PRESIDENT
Joel G. Jacobson

BRANCH
Porter Plaza, Main St., Old Saybrook, CT 06475.
AFFILIATION
Video Software Dealers Association (Joel Jacobson is a board director of CT chapter)

City Lights Video, Inc.

82 Front St. S., Issaquah, Washington, 98027; (206) 392-6700. Organized 1983. (Sales and rental of video software.)

PRESIDENT
Alan Ligda
AFFILIATIONS
VSDA (National and Washington State)

The Copps Corp.

2828 Wayne St., Stevens Point, WI 54481; (715) 344-5900. (Food and non-food distribution.)

CHAIRMAN
Michael Copps
PRESIDENT
Tim Copps
EXEC. VICE PRESIDENT, WHOLESALE DISTRIBUTION
Fred Copps
VICE PRESIDENT, MERCHANDISING
Don Copps
VICE PRESIDENT, PUBLIC AFFAIRS
Tom Copps
EXEC. VICE PRESIDENT, RETAIL OPERATIONS
Darrell Scherwinski
VICE PRESIDENT, FINANCE
Tom Sievwright

B. Dalton Bookseller

7505 Metro Blvd., Minneapolis, MN 55435; (612) 893-7000. (Subsidiary of Dayton Hudson.) Bookstore, chain.

SOFTWARE BUYER
Lesli Casciaro

Dawn's Video

519 W. Foothill, Suite C, Rialto, CA 92376; (714) 874-1414. Organized 1980. (Video specialty store.)

OWNER
Gregory C. George
BRANCHES
2085 E. Highland Ave., San Bernardino, CA 92404; (714) 864-3113
9725 Sierra, Fontana, CA 92335; (714) 350-8833
267 E. 40th, San Bernardino, CA 92404; (714) 883-5737
1330 Massachusetts Ave., Riverside, CA 92507; (714) 784-1414

Discount Video Tapes, Inc.

P.O. Box 7122, Burbank, CA 91510; (818) 843-3366; FAX: (818) 843-3821. Organized 1979. (Specializing in rare and unusual pre-recorded videos. Retail and wholesale.)

PRESIDENT
Woody Wise

Dodd Camera & Video

27179 Chagrin Blvd., Woodmere, OH 44122; (216) 292-2825. (Subsidiary of The Dodd Co.) Electronics, video chain (10 stores).

PRESIDENT
Richard L. Greiner, Sr.
MANAGER & SOFTWARE BUYER
Don Carter
VICE PRESIDENT & HARDWARE BUYER
Rick Greiner
GENERAL MANAGER
Don Carter

Doubleday Book and Record Clubs, Inc.

245 Park Ave., New York, NY 10167; (212) 984-7309. Mail order.

VICE PRESIDENT
Bernard Schwartz

Downtown Video

3110 W. Peterson, Chicago, IL 60659; (312) 338-1600. (Subsidiary of Downtown Records Inc.) Video chain (6 stores).

PRESIDENT
Howard Rosen
DIRECTOR & SOFTWARE BUYER
Ronald W. Kehr
HARDWARE BUYER
Ron Fischell

Erol's Inc.

6621 Electronic Dr., Springfield, VA 22151; (703) 451-8812. (Video chain with 165 locations.)

PRESIDENT & CHIEF OPERATING OFFICER
Carl Bellini
VICE PRESIDENT, OPERATIONS
Troy Cooper
VICE PRESIDENT, MERCHANDISING & MARKETING
Robert J. Morick

Everybody's Records Tapes & Video

5279 N. Lombard, Portland, OR 97203; (503) 286-9841. Organized 1971. (Home entertainment software.)

PRESIDENT
Tom Keenan
AFFILIATION
VSDA, NARM

Fairfield Video Partner I

1244 Stratfield Rd., Fairfield, CT 06430; (203) 371-4220. (Acquired 26-store Video World chain.)

CHAIRMAN
Stephen Wilson
PRESIDENT
Samuel MacArthur

Family Video

740 Mt. View Dr., Rapid City, SD 57702; (605) 348-7572. Video independent.

PRESIDENTS & BUYERS
Richard Ireland
Christine Ireland

The Federated Group

2161 Hutton, Carrollton, TX 75006; (214) 243-5700. (65 stores).

AUDIO/VIDEO BUYER
Armand Phillipi

Flower Films & Video

(see Les Blank's Flower Films & Video.)

French & Spanish Book Corp./The Dictionary Store

115 Fifth Ave., New York, NY 10003; (212) 673-7400. Bookstore, independent.

PRESIDENT
Emanuel Molho

G&A Stores, Inc. /d/b/a Curtis Mathes

15 E. Southridge Rd., Marshalltown, Iowa 50158; (515) 752-5541. Organized 1984. (Sells TVs, VCRs, video cameras, and movie rental.)

PRESIDENT & TREASURER
Glenn Stalzer
VICE PRESIDENT & SECRETARY
Ann Stalzer

Greenleaf Video, Inc.

3230 Nebraska Ave., Santa Monica, CA 90404; (213) 829-7675. Organized 1984. (Sells informational videos to schools, libraries and consumers.)

PRESIDENT
Barbara K. Greenleaf
SECRETARY
Jon W. Greenleaf

Grolier Book Clubs

Sherman Turnpike, Danbury, CT 06816. (Subsidiary of Times Mirror Co.) Book club.

EDITORIAL DIRECTOR
Grace Mishkin

Hearst Marine Books

105 Madison Ave., New York, NY 10016; (212) 889-3050; FAX: (212) 799-0965. (Division of William Morrow, Inc.) Catalog sales.

Home Film Festival

305 Linden St., Scranton, PA 18503; (717) 342-2185; (800) 258-3456. (Rents and sells hard-to-find videos, both foreign and domestic.)

PRESIDENT
Dan Jury
SOFTWARE BUYER
Linda Goodrich

Home Movies, Inc.

1016 Juan Tabo N.E., Albuquerque, NM 87112; (505) 292-8578. Organized 1983. (Video sales and rentals.)

CHIEF EXECUTIVE OFFICER & PRESIDENT
Troy D. Richards
VICE PRESIDENT
Kent Richards
BRANCHES
Home Movies II, 1115 San Mateo S.E., Albuquerque, NM 87108
Home Movies LTD., 7120 Wyoming Blvd., Albuquerque, NM 87109
Home Movies, Downtown, 505½ Fifth St., downtown Albuquerque, NM.

Home Theater Video

1504-A Wyoming N.E., Albuquerque, NM 87112; (505) 293-5784. Video independent.

PROPRIETOR
William R. Leonards

Home Video Network, Inc.

Route 93, Conyngham, PA 18219; (717) 788-5211. Video, drugstores, independent.

PRESIDENT
Walter Haentjens, Jr.
HARDWARE & SOFTWARE BUYERS
Joseph Bayzick
Rick Haentjens

IFEX Films/International Film Exchange Ltd.

201 W. 52 St., New York, NY 10019; (212) 582-4318. Cable: IFEXREP-New York. Telex: 420748; FAX: (212) 956-2257. Also 9200 Sunset Blvd., PH 9, Los Angeles, CA 90069; (213) 278-7939. FAX: (213) 278-7939; TELEX: 4972966. Organized 1959. (Domestic and international distribution of feature films, documentaries, shorts & video programs.)

PRESIDENT
Gerald J. Rappoport
EXECUTIVE VICE PRESIDENT
Richard Grisar
SENIOR VICE PRESIDENT, INTERNATIONAL SALES
Joy Pereths
VICE PRESIDENT, BUSINESS AFFAIRS
Beulah Rappoport
VICE PRESIDENT, FOREIGN DISTRIBUTION
Stephanie Holm
VICE PRESIDENT, THEATRICAL DISTRIBUTION
Robert Newman

International Sailing Products

P.O. Box 355, Oyster Bay, NY 11771; (516) 922-5182, (800) 645-7676; FAX: (516) 922-5178. Catalog, franchise (3 stores).

PRESIDENT
Steve Benjamin
VICE PRESIDENT
Betsy Madden

International Video

9576 Quivira Rd., Lenexa, KS 66215; (913) 492-2311. Organized 1983. (Retail video software.)

OWNER
Michael Rupani

Interstate Group

100 Western Maryland Parkway, Hagerstown, MD 21740; (301) 733-1378. (Video chain.)

VIDEO BUYER
Dan Greenwald
AUDIO BUYER
Gerri Kardosz

Kaleidoscope Home Video

700 E. Maple, Centerville, Iowa 52544; (515) 437-1674. Organized 1984. (Home video rental and sales.)

OWNERS
Russell K. Davis
Donna S. Davis
BRANCH
Video "Show" Room, Ottumwa, IA; (515) 682-8231

King's Video Center

1325 W. Warner, Santa Ana, CA 92704; (714) 662-2898. Organized 1982. (Retail video hardware and software, sales and rental.)

Leading Edge Video

2325 Harrison Avenue, Butte, MT 59701

BUYER
Robert C. Wilson

Listening Library

One Park Ave., Old Greenwich, CT 06870; (203) 637-3616.

PRESIDENT
Timothy Ditlow

Long Drug Stores

141 N. Civic Dr., Walnut Creek, CA 94596; (415) 937-1170; FAX: (415) 944-6657. Drugstores, chain (192 stores).

MERCHANDISE MANAGER
Barry Rennetz

MAS Productions

18434 Bermuda St., Northridge, CA 91326; (818) 360-0371. Mail order.

CUSTOMER CONTACT
Richard Stark

MSI Video

5020 Sunnyside Ave., Suite 112, Beltsville, MD 20705; (301) 474-2220. Organized 1981. (National mail order sales of videocassettes.)

PRESIDENT
Lee Masser

Mail Box Music

P.O. Box 341, Rye, NY 10580; (914) 937-8601. (Mail order.)

PRESIDENT
Lorain Levy

Major Video

7998 Georgetown Rd., Indianapolis, IN 42268; (317) 875-8000.

Manzi Video Sales, Inc.

261 Halstead Ave., Harrison, NY 10528; (914) 835-5005. (d/b/a The Video Connection #130.) Video franchise.

PRESIDENT & BUYER
Michael S. Manzi

Meredith Corp. Better Homes & Gardens Book Club

750 Third Ave., New York, NY 10017; (212) 551-7040. Mail order.

CUSTOMER CONTACT
Jane Hamada

Montgomery Video Inc.

18268 Village Mart Dr., Olney, MD 20832; (301) 774-2014. Video chain (5 stores.)

PRESIDENT & BUYER
Lou Kaufman

Morris Video

2730 Monterey, Suite #105, Monterey Business Park, Torrance, CA 90503; (213) 533-4800. Organized 1984. (Produces and distributes quality information and entertainment video. Mail order.)

PRESIDENT
Dawn Morris
VICE PRESIDENT
George Morris, Ph.D.
DIRECTOR OF PUBLIC RELATIONS
Wendy Fulton
NATIONAL SALES MANAGER
Kandra Inga
NATIONAL SALES REP. MANAGER
Micki Smallman
BOARD OF DIRECTORS
Dawn Morris, George Morris, Ph.D., George Bott, David Van Horn.
BRANCH
663 The Village, Redondo Beach, CA 90277; (213) 374-4984.

The Movie Exchange

Box 61, Audubon, PA 19407; (215) 265-0150. Organized 1983. (Video sale and rental, 200 locations.)

PRESIDENT
Shellie Tibbitts
CHAIRMAN OF BOARD
Lamont R. Tibbitts
DIRECTOR, STORE OPERATIONS
Glenn Gasser
DIRECTOR, FIELD OPERATIONS
Brian K. Ward
DIRECTOR, COMPUTER OPERATIONS
Mike Balik
COMPTROLLER
John Tritsch
BOARD OF DIRECTORS
Peter Morse, Peter Dale, Shellie Tibbitts, Lamont Tibbitts
AFFILIATION
VSDA

The Movie Merchants

3254 Youngfield St., Wheat Ridge, CO 80033; (303) 234-9282. Organized 1980. (Video retailer.)

PRESIDENT & TREASURER
Shelley Gooch
VICE PRESIDENT & SECRETARY
Patrick Gooch
BOARD OF DIRECTORS
William Rahmig, Ramon Morton
BRANCH
7562 S. University, Littleton, CO 80122
AFFILIATIONS
VSDA, Wheat Ridge Chamber of Commerce

Movies Tonite

935 E. Broad St., Columbus, OH 43205; (614) 253-0193. Video independent.

PRESIDENT
John Sandefur
VICE PRESIDENT, SOFTWARE BUYER
Debra Harrington
VICE PRESIDENT, HARDWARE BUYER
Jane Sandefur

Movies Unlimited

7421 Manchester, St. Louis, MO 63143; (314) 781-4111. (Subsidiary of Video Information Corp.) Video chain (4 stores).

PRESIDENT
Kevin R. Toal

Movies Unlimited

6736 Castor Ave., Philadelphia, PA 19149; (215) 722-8298. Retail stores, mail order.

GENERAL MANAGER
Mr. Weiss

Music Plus

2551 S. Alameda St., Los Angeles, CA 90058; (213) 234-3336. (Subsidiary of Show Industries d/b/a Music Plus.) Audio and video chain (60 stores).

PRESIDENT
Lou Fogelman
SOFTWARE BUYER
Mitch Perliss

Musical Sales Company

40 S. Caroline St., Baltimore, MD 21231; (301) 675-1400. (One-stop record, tape, CD, video [pre-recorded], and related accessories.)

PRESIDENT
Milton I. Bereson
VICE PRESIDENT
Molly E. Bereson

Nantucket Video Inc.

30 Main St., Nantucket, MA 02554; (617) 228-6870. Video independent.

PRESIDENT & BUYER
Gene Mahon

New Breed Music

1250 Maple View Drive, Pomona, CA 91766; (714) 627-1923. Independent video.

PRESIDENT
Jesse Mac Lynum, Jr.

Nightingale-Conant Corp.

7300 N. Lehigh Ave., Niles, IL 60648; (312) 647-0300; FAX: (312) 647-7145. Catalog sales.

CUSTOMER CONTACT
Don Reaser

Palmer Video Corporation

1767 Morris Ave., Union, NJ 07083-3598; (201) 686-3030. Organized 1981. (Franchisor, owner, operator video stores.)

PRESIDENT
Peter Balner
VICE PRESIDENT
Peter Margaritondo
VICE PRESIDENT
Carl A. Pallini

Paradise Video, Inc.

1063 Lower Main St., Suite C-109, Wailuku, Maui, HI 96793; (808) 244-9790. Organized 1981.

PRESIDENT
Calvin H. Inouye
VICE PRESIDENT
Jeffrey K. Yamanishi
SECRETARY & TREASURER
Alfred Cantorna
BRANCHES
250 Alamaha St., Kahului, Maui, HI 96732
7 Aewa Pl., Pukalani, Maui, HI 96768
1295 South Kihei Rd., Kihei, Maui, HI 96753
AFFILIATIONS
VSDA, AVA (American Video Association)

Pathmark

301 Blaire Rd., Woodbridge, NJ 07095; (201) 499-3000. Supermarket chain. Rental only.

CUSTOMER CONTACT
Gordon Keil

Public Access Producers Association

2652 N. Winchell, Portland, OR 97217; (503) 289-2309. Video, direct mail, independent.

DIRECTOR & SOFTWARE BUYER
R. S. Kolemaine

Publishers Central Bureau

225 Park Ave. S., New York, NY 10003; (212) 254-1600; FAX: (212) 254-7531. Catalog, mail order. Independent video.

DIRECTOR OF VIDEO
Judy Harper

Pueblo Home Video, Inc.

1302 N. Elizabeth, Pueblo, CO 81003; (303) 546-3555. Video, independent.

PRESIDENT & BUYER
Warren E. Lombard
VICE PRESIDENT & BUYER
Carol Lombard

Quality Life Publishing, Inc.

P.O. Box 800, Boulder, CO 80306; (303) 440-9109. (Direct mail catalog distributor of instructional and documentary videos to the home VCR owner.)

PRESIDENT
Robin Sutherland

RKO Warner Video, Inc.

250 W. 49th St., New York, NY 10019; (212) 315-8400; FAX: (212) 307-6428.

PRESIDENT
Steve Berns
VICE PRESIDENT, OPERATIONS
Kenneth Molnar
VICE PRESIDENT, PURCHASING
Jeff Levy
DIRECTOR OF CONSTRUCTION
Paul Smilowitz
CONTROLLER
Neal Goldner

Rare Bird Video, Inc.

482 Broome St., New York, NY 10013; (212) 334-8150. Video chain (3 stores).

PRESIDENT
Jack Morris
SOFTWARE & HARDWARE BUYERS
Jack Morris
Wayne Quackenbush

Record & Video Warehouse

3110 W. Peterson, Chicago, IL 60659; (312) 338-1600. (Subsidiary of Record & Video Warehouse Inc.) Video, chain (6 stores).

PRESIDENT
Howard Rosen
SOFTWARE BUYER & DIRECTOR
Ronald W. Kehr
HARDWARE BUYER
Ron Fischell

Red Fox Video

110 W. Main St., Lyrens, PA 17048; (717) 453-7165.

Rehabfilm

1123 Broadway, New York, NY 10010; (212) 741-5160. Non-profit, private organization. (Subsidairy of Rehabilitation Int'l, U.S.A.)

DIRECTOR OF MEDIA
John F. Moses

Rite Aid Corp.

Trindle Rd. and Railroad Ave., Shiremanstown, PA 17091; (717) 761-2633. Drug chain (1053 stores).

DIRECTOR
Jerry Cardinale
VIDEO BUYER
Sue Schuck

Rizzoli Video

597 Fifth Ave., New York, NY 10017; (212) 223-0100. Organized 1985. Bookstore chain.

DIRECTOR
John Brancati

Schnuck Markets, Inc.

12921 Enterprise Way, Bridgeton, MO 63044; (314) 344-9600. Food markets, chain.

PRESIDENT
Craig D. Schnuck
BUYER
Pamela J. Wissore

Sears and Roebuck, Co.

Sears Tower, Dept. 40-15, Chicago, IL 60684; (312) 875-8306; FAX: (312) 875-8351. Department store, chain (825 stores).

MARKETING COMMUNICATIONS MANAGER
Mike Mangan

Sound Warehouse

10911 Petal St., Dallas, TX 75238; (214) 343-4700. Video chain (100 stores).

SOFTWARE BUYER
Robert Kallish

Stansbury Stereo and Video Center

6330 Frankford Ave., Baltimore, MD 21206; (301) 488-9600. Electronics, independent video.

PRESIDENT
Jim Disney
VICE PRESIDENT & SOFTWARE BUYER
Dale Bennett
HARDWARE BUYERS
Jim Disney and Dale Bennett

Stars To Go, Inc.

4751 Wilshire Blvd., Suite #140, Los Angeles, CA 90010; (213) 930-9300; FAX: (213) 933-0946. Organized 1984. (Rents feature films on prerecorded videocassettes through its Stars To Go Video Centers located in convenience stores.)

CHAIRMAN OF THE BOARD
Fred J. Atchity, Jr.
PRESIDENT & CEO
Jerry R. Welch
VICE PRESIDENT, FINANCE, CFO
Richard D. Vermeer
VICE PRESIDENT, CORP. CONTROLLER
A. Duncan Longworth
VICE PRESIDENT, CUSTOMER SALES & SERVICE
Ronald W. Dunagan
VICE PRESIDENT, MOVIE MANAGEMENT
Peer Ghent
BOARD OF DIRECTORS
Fred J. Atchity, Jr. (chairman), Jerry R. Welch (director)

Sunset Software

2265 Westwood Blvd., #140, Los Angeles, CA 90064; (213) 474-2446 (not for orders). (Producer and direct mail marketer of R-rated video tapes.)

PRESIDENT & SOFTWARE BUYER
Will Swan

TV Collector

P.O. Box 188, Needham, MA 02192; (508) 238-1179. Organized 1976. (TV nostalgia magazine/tape trading marketplace.)

PUBLISHER
Stephen W. Albert
EDITOR
Diane L. Albert

Tele-Video Enterprises, Inc.

813 W. Main St., Suite 22, Battle Ground, WA 98604; (206) 687-7239 (d/b/a Video City USA) Independent.

PRESIDENT & BUYER
Curt Siebold

Tower Video

MTS. Inc., 2500 Delmonte, Building C, P.O. Box 919001, West Sacramento, CA 95691; (916) 373-2500.

James Townsend Enterprises

8460 F. Tyco Rd., Vienna, VA 22182; (703) 883-0106; FAX: (703) 821-1853. Organized 1977. (Video rental chain.)

PRESIDENT
James Townsend
VICE PRESIDENT
Phil Townsend
BRANCHES
Capitol Video, 514 8th Street S.E., Washington D.C. 20003
Capitol Video, 201 Massachusetts Ave., N.E. Washington D.C. 20003
Door to Door Video, 514 8th Street S.E., Washington, D.C. 20003.
AFFILIATIONS
VSDA, AVA

Toys "R" Us

395 W. Passaic St., Rochelle Park, NJ 07662; (201) 845-5033. Chain (199 stores). Children's programs.

Transworld Video Inc.

18100 W. Dixie Highway, North Miami Beach, FL 33160; (305) 944-0298. (Subsidiary of Video Connection of America.) National procurement office for Video Connection franchise stores.

NATIONAL SALES MANAGER
Peter Barry

United Video, Inc.

500 Church St. N., Concord, NC 28025; (704) 788-2012. Organized 1981.

PRESIDENT & TREASURER
Wayne Ball
VICE PRESIDENT & SECRETARY
Sharon Ball

Universal Video

2935 Pat Booker Rd. #138; Universal City, TX 78148-2748; (512) 659-7131. Independent.

PRESIDENT
Alice H. Lo

University of Southern California

Davidson Conference Center, University Park, Los Angeles, CA 90089-0871; (213) 743-5219; FAX: (213) 749-3689. Independent.

EXECUTIVE DIRECTOR
Philip J. Rapa

Video 1

8611 W. 95th St., Hickory Hills, IL 60457; (312) 598-1000. 8065 W. 95th St., Hickory Hills, IL 60457; (312) 598-0001; 8082 W. 111th St., Palos Hills, IL 60465; (312) 974-1000. Independent (3 stores).

PRESIDENT
Carole Bartolini
SOFTWARE & HARDWARE BUYER
Dave Able

Video Age, Inc.

4820 Excelsior Blvd., Suite 112, Minneapolis, MN 55416; (612) 927-7484. Mail order, telephone sales.

PRESIDENT
William J. Hudlow

Video Biz

113 S. Third St., Richmond, VA 23219; (804) 788-1902. Video chain (7 stores). (Subsidiary of Video Products, Inc.)

PRESIDENT & HARDWARE BUYER
Scott Moffett
SOFTWARE BUYERS
Scott Moffett
Sharon Krohn

Video Biz—North Shore, Inc.

50 Maplewood Ave., Gloucester, MA 01930; (617) 283-3721. Video, franchise.

PRESIDENT & BUYER
Sarah S. Wall

Video Boulevard, Inc.

241 Haverford Ave., Narberth, PA 19072; (215) 664-4136. Organized 1981. (Video rentals and sales.)

PRESIDENT
Steven J. Freid

Video Center Stores

802 S. Solano, Las Cruces, NM 88001; (505) 523-8907. (Subsidiary of Pata Corp.) Video, chain (6 stores).

PRESIDENT & SOFTWARE BUYER
Pat Kilpatrick

Video Centre

P.O. Box 1982, Winter Park, FL 32790; (305) 628-3070. Video, independent.

CHIEF EXECUTIVE OFFICER
Philip Lashinsky

Video Channel Inc.

20103-2 Saticoy St., Room 2, Winnetka, CA 91306; (818) 993-8273. Organized 1984. (Video tape sales and rentals.)

PRESIDENT & BUYER
Jeff S. Dickel

The Video Circuit

11525 S.W. Pacific Hwy., Portland, OR 97223; (503) 246-8851. Video chain (2 stores). (Subsidiary of Video Futures, Inc.)

PRESIDENT & BUYER
Leo A. Jerman

Video City Stores, Inc.

4266 Broadway, Oakland, CA 94611; (415) 428-0202. Organized 1983. Video chain—8 stores.

CHAIRMAN OF THE BOARD
Bob Brown
VICE PRESIDENT
Steve Fallzone
OTHER COMPANY OWNED LABELS:
Combat Video, Art House Video, Chop 'Em Ups Video, World Aviation Video, Black Action Video

Video Connection

3123 Sylvania Ave., Toledo, OH 43613; (419) 472-7727. Video specialty, chain (76 locations).

PRESIDENT
John Day

Video Connection of America, Inc.

18100 W. Dixie Highway, North Miami Beach, FL 33160; (305) 944-0298. National headquarters for 200 franchised video stores.

PRESIDENT
Bert Tenzer
DIRECTOR OF FRANCHISE SALES
John Barry

Video Corner

553 49th St. S., St. Petersburg, FL 33707; (813) 321-2122; FAX (813) 321-2272. Video, chain (3 stores).

PRESIDENT & HARDWARE BUYER
Bob Skidmore
VICE PRESIDENT
John P. Gallagher
VICE PRESIDENT, PRO VIDEO
Richard E. Smith
GENERAL MANAGER & HARDWARE & SOFTWARE BUYER
R. Edward Schmidt

Video Cove

4747 E. Elliot Rd., Suite 27, Phoenix, AZ 85044; (602) 893-9609. Video, independent.

PRESIDENT & BUYER
Bob Mulvihill

Video Crossroads

5448 Beach Blvd., Buena Park, CA 90621; (714) 521-3870. Video, franchise.

PRESIDENT
Ralph Zink
SOFTWARE & HARDWARE BUYER
Corinne Zink

Video Experience

401 I St., Suite B., Arcata, CA 95521; (707) 826-1105. Video, independent.

PRESIDENT & BUYER
Doug Simas

Video Flicks

141 Caldwell Blvd., Nampa, ID 83651; (208) 465-5773. Video, independent.

PRESIDENT & BUYER
Dale R. Durbin

Video Galore

4456 Lake St., Lake Charles, LA 70605; (318) 474-9791. Video, franchise.

OWNER & SOFTWARE BUYER
Michael K. O'Carroll

Video General/American Video Tape Library

5809 S. Broadway, Suite B, Littleton, CO 80121; (303) 798-3389. Organized 1978. (Tape rental and selling by mail and retail.)

MANAGERS
Mardell Peterson
Sandra Cornish
BOARD OF DIRECTORS
Mardell Peterson, Sandra Cornish
AFFILIATION
United Independent Video Dealers Association

Video Joe

1203 Eastridge Dr., Slidell, LA 70458; (504) 646-2482. Video, independent.

OWNER & BUYER
Joe B. Howard
BUYER
Rusty Howard

The Video Library

4184 Woodruff Ave., Lakewood, CA 90713; (213) 420-8383. Organized 1982. (Rentals and sales of video tapes and VCRs.)

PRESIDENT
Steve Cantril
SECRETARY & TREASURER
Debbie Cantril
BOARD OF DIRECTORS
Richard Burdick, Kathleen Burdick

Video Marts

7827 S. Redwood Rd., West Jordan, UT 84088; (801) 565-0064. Video chain (12 stores)

PRESIDENT
Clyde Roper

Video One

5055 Town North Dr., Shreveport, LA 71107; (318) 221-5837. Organized 1981. (Video software.)

OWNERS
Mary L. West
Samuel E. West
PURCHASING AGENT
Samuel L. West

Video Palace

4537 Duke St., Alexandria, VA 22304; (703) 823-5466. Video, independent.

PRESIDENT & BUYER
Rick Brooks
VICE PRESIDENT & BUYER
Doc Brooks

Video Paradise Inc.

115 W. Main St., Westboro, MA 01581; (617) 366-8890.

PRESIDENT
Donald Rogers

Video Playback

137 Route 516, Old Bridge, NJ 08857; (201) 254-5874. Video, independent chain (5 stores).

PRESIDENT & HARDWARE BUYER
Myron S. Kozak
SOFTWARE BUYER
Mary T. Kozak

Video & Plus Superstores, Inc.

Box 8350, Albuquerque, NM 87198; (505) 298-7705. Video, chain (3 stores).

PRESIDENT & SOFTWARE & HARDWARE BUYER
Lynne Landers

Video Product, Inc. T/A Video Biz

4736 N. Southside Plaza, Richmond, VA 23224; P.O. Box 24285; (804) 233-9703. Organized 1980. (Retail video.)

PRESIDENT & TREASURER
Scott Moffett
VICE PRESIDENT
Tabetha Moffett
SECRETARY
Deborah J. Moffett
BOARD OF DIRECTORS
Scott Moffett, Deborah Moffett, Tabetha Moffett, Robert Moffett
BRANCHES
Richmond, VA—4 locations; Colonial Heights, VA; Roanoke, VA; Salem VA—1 location
AFFILIATIONS
Video Biz, Inc., VSDA

Video Replay

1668 Merriman Rd., Akron, OH 44313; (216) 836-9773. Video, chain (3 stores).

PRESIDENT & HARDWARE BUYER
J. Dwight Taylor
SOFTWARE BUYER
Jane Friedhoff

Video Shack, Inc.

1608 Broadway, New York, NY 10019; (212) 581-6260. Video, independent (14 stores).

Video Show

(See JBC Video Vesting)

Video Specialties Company

153 Town and Country, Houston, TX 77024; (713) 465-0702. Organized 1972. (Sale and rental of videocassettes.)

PRESIDENT
John F. Dinwoodie
VICE PRESIDENT
Ann C. Dinwoodie
BUYER
David C. Dinwoodie

Video Station

513 McDowell, St., Asheville, NC 28803; (704) 258-1145. Video, electronics, independent.

PRESIDENT
Mariano Raigo
SECRETARY/TREASURER & BUYER
Robin Raigo

Video Station

3689 Sheridan Dr., Amherst, NY 14226; (716) 835-2577. Video chain (500 stores). (Subsidiary of Rob-Mer Corp.)

PRESIDENT & HARDWARE BUYER
R. A. Lozinak
SOFTWARE BUYER & MANAGER
M. Lozinak

Video Station

240 E. 1300 South, Orem, UT 84058; (801) 226-6626. Organized 1981. (Video rental, duplication, and production.)

OWNER
Mark Greer
MANAGER
Eve Greer
BRANCHES
346 W. 100 South, Orem, UT 84058; 1476 N. Freedom Blvd., Provo, UT 84058.

The Video Station

494A Main St., Woburn, MA 01801; (617) 933-1445. Organized 1980. (Consumer electronics, video retailing.)

PRESIDENT
Joseph V. Elia
VICE PRESIDENT
Jeanne M. Elia
BOARD OF DIRECTORS
Joseph V. Elia, Jeanne M. Elia, Vincent I. Melendy

Video Station, Inc.

374 Springfield Ave., Summit, NJ 07901; (201) 273-0024. Organized 1980. (Sales and rental of videocassettes, recorders, TVs, record-a-calls, radios, CDs; video production studio, ½″ and ¾″ video editing studio.)

PRESIDENT
Roger Cooper
VICE PRESIDENT
Sandi Cooper
BOARD OF DIRECTORS
Roger Cooper, Sandi Cooper

Video Stop

810 W. 21st St., Clovis, NM 88101; (505) 763-4553. (Subsidiary of Let Us Entertain You.) Video, chain (5 stores).

PRESIDENT
B. Lyons
MANAGER & BUYER
V. Starkey

The Video Store

4770 Duke Dr., Suite 300, Cincinnati, OH 45040; (513) 398-9700. (Video chain by parent company Vestron Inc. Bought NY based New Video chain in 1988.)

PRESIDENT, VESTRON VIDEO
Jon Peisinger
PRESIDENT, THE VIDEO STORE
John Eastburn
MANAGERS, NEW VIDEO
Steve Savage, Mark Pollack

Video Take #1

432 Paxon Ave., Trenton, NJ 08690-1915; (609) 587-2882. Video, independent.

PARTNERS
James Carlucci, Jr., Janet D. Carlucci

Video Today Inc.

63 E. 8th, Holland, MI 49423; (616) 392-2877. Organized 1981. (Video sales, rental and mail order.) Chain (4 stores).

PRESIDENT
Al Wagenaar
BRANCHES
977 Butternut, Holland, MI; (616) 399-2092
9505 School St., Jenison, MI; (616) 457-3150
755 Michigan, Holland, MI; (616) 392-6210
AFFILIATIONS
VSDA, SBA of Michigan

Video Trend

12900 Richfield St., Livonia, MI 48105; (313) 591-0200. (A Chas. Levy Co.,)

Video USA

13 W. Broadway, Derry, NH 03038; (603) 432-3236. Video.

PRESIDENT & HARDWARE BUYER
Donald Phelps
VICE PRESIDENT & SOFTWARE BUYER
Hollie Dustin

Video Vantage Inc.

1005 S. Gaylord St., Denver, CO 80209; (303) 777-0710. Organized 1983. (Supplies the Washington Park neighborhoods with their video needs.)

PRESIDENT
Hugh M. Boyd
VICE PRESIDENT
William Boyd
SECRETARY & TREASURER
Karen P. Taylor
AFFILIATIONS
Denver Chamber of Commerce, Video Software Dealers Association

Video Ventures, Inc.

262 W. Cottage Ave., Sandy, UT 84070-1431; (801) 255-0505. Video, 65 branches in drug and food chains.

PRESIDENT
Jerry Burke

Video Village

P.O. Box 38 (449 E. I-30), Rockwall, TX 75087; (214) 722-2222. Organized 1981. (VCR and television sales, movie rentals, disc sales.)

BRANCHES
3512 Highway 66, Rowlett, TX 75088
8602-R Highway 66, Rowlett, TX 75088
900 W. Rusk, Rockwall, TX 75087

Video Village/The Video House

P.O. Box 2595, Canyon Country, CA 91351; (805) 252-3048. Video, chain (4 stores).

PRESIDENT & HARDWARE BUYER
David M. Smith
OPERATION MANAGER & SOFTWARE BUYER
Maureen Brown

Video Worx

3011 W. 74th Ave., Westminster, CO 80030; (303) 427-1237. Video, independent.

PRESIDENT & BUYER
Don Wickman

Video Yesteryear

Box C, Sandy Hook, CT 06482. Organized 1978. Independent, mail order.

PRESIDENT & MARKETING & SALES
Jon Sonneborn

Video's To Go

9348½ Corbin Ave., Northridge, CA 91324; (818) 701-1115. Video, independent.

PRESIDENT & BUYER
Michael A. Meehan

Video-Forum

96 Broad St., Guilford, CT 06437; (203) 453-9794. (Subsidiary of Jeffrey Norton Publishers, Inc.) Catalog sales.

VICE PRESIDENT
Janis M. Yates

Videon, Inc.

6443 Fairview, Boise, ID 83704; (208) 375-8899. Video, chain (3 stores).

PRESIDENT
Brent Estep
MARKETING DIRECTOR & SOFTWARE BUYER
Jeff Troup
HARDWARE BUYER
Russ Riley

Waldenbooks

201 High Ridge Rd., Stamford, CT 06904; (203) 356-7500. (Subsidiary of K Mart Corp.) Bookstore, chain (900 stores).

PRESIDENT
Harry Hoffman
EXECUTIVE VICE PRESIDENT, MARKETING & NEW BUSINESS
Bonnie Predd

West Coast

9990 Global Rd., Philadelphia, PA 19115; (215) 677-1000.

Ric Webb's Video City

2610 W. Nob Hill Blvd., Yakima, WA 98902; (509) 452-4200. Video, independent.

PRESIDENT
Ric Webb
MANAGER
Garry Dressen
BUYER
Shawn Dressen

Wegmans Food Markets Inc.

1500 Brooks Ave., P.O. Box 844, Rochester, NY 14692; (716) 328-2550. Food stores, chain (37 stores).

ASSISTANT DIRECTOR, GENERAL MERCHANDISING
Kevin Kamholtz

Wherehouse Entertainment, Inc.

19701 Hamilton Ave., Torrance, CA 90502-1311; (213) 538-2314. (Video chain with over 200 stores in California and western U.S. Retailer of pre-recorded music, video movies, blank video and audiotape, personal and home computer software.)

Wilson's Video

213 E. Dakota, Pierre, SD 57501; (605) 224-0530. Video, independent.

PRESIDENT
Roger R. Wilson

Equipment Manufacturers

* VIDEO MONITORS
* VIDEOCASSETTE RECORDERS
* VIDEOTAPE

Video Monitors

Advanced Technology Division

(Subsidiary of ATD, Inc.)
6431 Independence Ave, Woodland Hills, CA 91367; (818) 999-1393.

CORP. PRESIDENT
Kenneth K. Kaylor
TECHNICAL DATA COORDINATOR
Arlene M. Kliewer
NATIONAL SERVICE MANAGER
Charlie Shade

Asaca/Shibasoku Corp. of America

12509 Beatrice St., Los Angeles, CA 90066; (213) 827-7144, (800) 423-6347, Fax (213) 306-1382.

CORPORATE PRESIDENT
T. Shigezaki
VICE PRESIDENT
Bruce Cope
OPERATIONS MANAGER
Sumio Ohya

Ball Electronic Systems Division

(Subsidiary of Ball Corp.)
P.O. Box 589, 9300 W. 108 Circle, Broomfield, CO 80020-0589; (303) 457-5260.

CORPORATE PRESIDENT
Richard Ringeon
PRESIDENT
H. Robert Gill
VICE PRESIDENT, MARKETING
H. Jurgen Mammitzch
NATIONAL SALES MANAGER
Richard Scarle

Burle Industries, Inc.

Security Products Division, 1000 New Holland Ave., Lancaster, PA 17601-5688; (717) 295-6000.

EXECUTIVE V.P., SECURITY PRODUCTS DIV.
C. L. Rintz
VICE PRESIDENT, MARKETING, SECURITY PRODUCTS DIV.
G. S. Brody

CCTV Corp.

315 Hudson St., New York, NY 10013; (212) 989-4433; (800) 221-2240; (800) GBC-CCTV.

CORPORATE PRESIDENT
Stephen Lefkowitz

Cetec Gauss

(Division of Cetec Corp.)
9130 Glenoaks Blvd., Sun Valley, CA 91352; (213) 875-1900. FAX: (818) 767-4479. Telex 194989.

CORPORATE PRESIDENT
Robert A. Nelson
PRESIDENT
James R. Williams

Cohu, Inc.

5755 Kearny Villa Rd., PO Box 85623, San Diego, CA 92138-5623; (619) 277-6700. Organized 1957. CCTV system equipment—manufacturer and distributor.

PRESIDENT & CHIEF EXECUTIVE OFFICER
James W. Barnes
VICE PRESIDENT, FINANCE
Charles A. Schwan
BOARD OF DIRECTORS
William S. Ivans, William N. Jenkins, Jack M. Keeney, Charles L. Blake, James W. Barnes, Gene E. Leary, Raymond C. Sebold, Frank W. Davis.
AFFILIATIONS
Cohu, Inc., Electronics Division; Delta Design Inc.; BMS, Inc.; FRL, Inc.

Cohu, Inc. Electronics Division

5755 Kearny Villa Rd., P.O. Box 85623, San Diego, CA 92138-5623; (619) 277-6700.

PRESIDENT & GENERAL MANAGER
James R. Brown
MARKETING MANAGER
John R. Foster
ENGINEERING MANAGER
William W. Steger
MANUFACTURING MANAGER
Gerald C. Samuel
QUALITY ASSURANCE MANAGER
Clyde Rainwater

Conrac Corporation, A Mark IV Industries Company

1724 S. Mountain Ave., Duarte, CA 91010; (818) 303-0095. Organized 1947. (Manufacturer and marketer of precision video display monitors for the broadcast, computer graphics, medical imaging, and process control industries.)

PRESIDENT
Vincent J. Hewitt
OPERATIONS MANAGER
Michael Taranto
MANAGER OF ENGINEERING
Monte Voigt
Q.A. MANAGER
Rey Roque
CONTROLLER
Vincent J. Hewitt (acting)
PERSONNEL ADMINISTRATOR
Jana Lewis
DIRECTOR OF SALES—BROADCAST
William A. Ems
DIRECTOR, MARKETING AND SALES
Gusti L. Ives
PRODUCT MARKETING MGR., COMPUTER PRODUCTS
Art Garcia
PRODUCT MARKETING MANAGER BROADCAST, MEDICAL
John McClimont
BOARD OF DIRECTORS (Mark IV Industries)
Sal H. Alfiero, Clement R. Arrison, Joseph G. Donohoo, Gerald S. Lippes, Esq; Herbert Roth, Jr.

Electrohome Limited

809 Wellington St., N., Kitchener, Ont., Canada N2G 4J6; (519) 744-7111.

CHAIRMAN, PRESIDENT & CHIEF EXECUTIVE OFFICER
J. A. Pollock
VICE PRESIDENT, FINANCE
J. G. Gingerich
VICE PRESIDENT, MOTORS
K. G. Hansen
VICE PRESIDENT, ELECTROHOME LIMITED, & PRESIDENT, C A P COMMUNICATIONS LIMITED
W. D. McGregor

SECRETARY/TREASURER
R. A. Bolden
VICE PRESIDENT, ELECTRONICS
W. M. Nobbs
DIRECTOR HUMAN RESOURCES
J. R. Boehmer

Hitachi Denshi America

(Division of Hitachi Denshi)
175 Crossways Park W., Woodbury, NY 11797; (516) 921-7200.

CORPORATION PRESIDENT
J. Tosaka
GENERAL MANAGER
M. Matsuhashi
VICE PRESIDENT, SALES
Bernard V. Munzelle

Ikegami Electronics (U.S.A.), Inc.

37 Brook Ave., Maywood, NJ 07607; (201) 368-9171. Organized 1964. (Manufactures and markets professional TV cameras and monitors.)

PRESIDENT
N. Nishi
SENIOR VICE PRESIDENT
S. La Conte
VICE PRESIDENT (DISPLAY MONITOR DIVISION)
Y. Sato
DIRECTOR, SALES & MARKETING
H. Winch
COMMUNICATIONS MANAGER
R. Estony

BRANCHES

Northeast: 37 Brook Avenue, Maywood, NJ 07607; (201) 368-9171. John Chow, regional sales manager.

Southeast: 5100 N.W. 33rd Ave., Suite 152, Ft. Lauderdale, FL 33309. John Webb, regional sales manager.

Midwest: 747 Church Rd., Units C4 & C5, Elmhurst, IL 60126; (312) 834-9774. Jerry Brinacombe, regional sales manager.

West Coast: 23105 Kashiwa Ct., Torrance, CA 90505; (213) 534-0050. Kelly Nelson, regional sales.

Southwest: Three Dallas Communications Complex, 6311 N. O'Connor Rd., Suite 100, Lock Box 100, Irving, TX 75039-3510; (214) 869-2363. Michael Mackin, sales mgr.

Hawaii: Ward Industrial Center, 1020 Auahi St., Bldg. 7, Bay 3A, Honolulu, HI 96814; (808) 946-5955. Kuniko Yamashiro, office administrator.

Networks and Canada: 37 Brook Ave., Maywood, NJ 07607; (201) 368-9171. Gordon Tubbs, regional sales manager.

Image Amplification Inc.

P.O. Box 699, 30 Chapin Rd., Pine Brook, NJ 07058; (201) 882-0584. Telex: 130236.

V.P. MARKETING & SALES
A. C. Ginsburg

JVC/Professional Products Company

(Division of US JVC Corp.)
41 Slater Dr., Elmwood Park, NJ 07407; (201) 794-3900.

PRESIDENT
Shinzo Nakao
GENERAL MANAGER
Tom McCarthy

Javelin Electronics, Inc.

19831 Magellan Dr., Torrance, CA 90502; (213) 327-7440, (800) 421-2716. Telex 19-444860 JAVELIN TRNC.

PRESIDENT
Donald T. Heckel
SALES OPERATIONS MANAGER
Michael M. Burton
NATIONAL SALES MANAGER
Russ Mayworm

Lectrotech, Inc.

5810 N. Western Ave., Chicago, IL 60659; (312) 769-6262.

PRESIDENT
William Grossman
VICE PRESIDENT
Barry Grossman

Lenco, Inc.

Electronics Division, 300 N. Maryland St., Jackson, MO 63755; (314) 243-3147. TWX 910-760-1382. FAX: (314) 243-7122.

PRESIDENT
Jerry Ford
GENERAL MANAGER
Paul Gerlach
DIRECTOR, MARKETING
Don Ford
NATIONAL SALES MANAGER
Von Haney
NATIONAL SERVICE MANAGER
Dave Aufdenberg

Matsushita Electric of Canada Ltd.

5770 Ambler Dr., Mississauga, Ont., L4W 2T3 Canada; (416) 624-5010.

CORPORATE PRESIDENT
A. Higashi
MANAGER, AUDIO VIDEO SYSTEMS GROUP
A. M. Evans
MANAGER, INDUSTRIAL VIDEO SYSTEMS DEPARTMENT
J. McDonald
MANAGER, CLOSED CIRCUIT TELEVISION DEPT.
Mary Lepage
MANAGER, PROFESSIONAL AUDIO-VIDEO DEPT.
Fred Nanos
NATIONAL PARTS MANAGER
S. Wan
NATIONAL SERVICE MANAGER
A. Gillespie

Mitsubishi Electronics of America, Inc.

(Division of Mitsubishi Electric.)
991 Knox St., Torrance, CA 90502; (213) 515-3993.

PRESIDENT
Takeshi Sakurai
NATIONAL SALES MANAGER
Don Arrons

NEC Home Electronics (USA) Inc.

(Video Products Division.)
1225 Michael Dr., Wood Dale, IL 60191-1094; (312) 860-9500.

PRESIDENT
Yuzi Ohashi
SENIOR VICE PRESIDENTS
Akira Sugiyama
Stanley Gray
VICE PRESIDENT, SALES
C. K. McCusker
DIRECTOR MARKETING
Bob Hana
DIRECTOR, MERCHANDISING & PRODUCT PLANNING
Brian Williams
SALES, VICE PRESIDENT
K. McCusker
SENIOR VICE PRESIDENT, OEM
A. Sugiyama
SENIOR VICE PRESIDENT, MANUFACTURING
N. Maeda

Panasonic Broadcast Systems Company

(Subsidiary of Matsushita Electric Corp. of America.)
One Panasonic Way, Secaucus, NJ 07094; (201) 348-7000.

PRESIDENT
Stan Basara

Pioneer Video Inc.

200 W. Grand Ave., Montvale, NJ 07645, (201) 573-1122.

PRESIDENT
Ken Kai
DIRECTOR, SPECIAL MARKETS
Brew Merrill

Quantel-Link Systems Group

Pear Tree Lane, Newbury, Berkshire, Eng., RG 13 2LT; Tel.: 0635-521303; FAX: 0635-49207; TELEX: 846091 Q LINK G

CHIEF EXECUTIVE
Stephen Christie
GENERAL MANAGER
Malcolm Brock

Quasar Company

(Division of Matsushita Electric Corp. of America)
1325 Pratt Blvd., Elk Grove Village, IL 60007; (312) 228-6366. Organized 1974. (Marketer of broad line of consumer electronics products.)

PRESIDENT
Mike Nakamura

RCA, New Products Division

(See Burle Industries, Inc.)

Sharp Electronics Corporation

P.O. Box 650, Sharp Plaza, Mahwah, NJ 07430; (201) 529-8200. Organized 1962 (in USA), 1912 (worldwide). (Manufacturer of quality electronics products for home, office, industrial and broadcast use.)

CHAIRMAN OF THE BOARD & DIRECTOR
Mr. T. Mitsuda
PRESIDENT & DIRECTOR
Mr. S. Hirooka
EXECUTIVE VICE PRESIDENT & DIRECTOR, CONSUMER
Mr. C. Daigneault
EXECUTIVE VICE PRESIDENT & DIRECTOR, ADMINISTRATION
Mr. K. Okuda
EXECUTIVE VICE PRESIDENT & DIRECTOR, INDUSTRIAL
Mr. T. Tajima
SENIOR EXECUTIVE VICE PRESIDENT
Mr. S. Okamato
BOARD OF DIRECTORS
Mr. T. Mitsuda, Mr. S. Hirooka, Mr. S. Okamoto, Mr. C. Daigneault, Mr. K. Okuda
BRANCHES
Atlanta, GA; Chicago, IL; Los Angeles, CA
AFFILIATION
Wholly owned subsidiary of Sharp Corporation, Osaka, Japan.

Sony Video Communications

(Division of Sony Corp. of America.)
Sony Dr., Park Ridge, NJ 07656; (201) 930-1000.

CORPORATE PRESIDENT
Kenji Tamiya
PRESIDENT
Philip J. Stack
VICE PRESIDENT, SALES
Robert Mueller
NATIONAL SERVICE MANAGER
Philip Hart

Tektronix, Inc.

P.O. Box 500, Beaverton, OR 97077; (503) 627-7111. TWX 910-467-8708.

CORPORATE PRESIDENT
Dave Friedley
GENERAL MANAGER
Dan Castles
MARKETING MANAGER
Steve Kerman
SALES MANAGER
Austin Basso

Toshiba America, Inc.

Corporate Headquarters: 375 Park Ave., Suite 1705, New York, NY 10152; (212) 308-2040; FAX: (212) 838-1179.

CHAIRMAN OF THE BOARD
Tadao Taguchi

Toshiba America Consumer Products, Inc.

82 Totowa Rd., Wayne, NJ 07470; (201) 628-8000. FAX: (201) 628-1875.

PRESIDENT
Kenichico Hiyama
VICE PRESIDENT, NATIONAL SERVICE
John Newman

Videotek, Inc.

243 Shoemaker Rd., Pottstown, PA 14964; (215) 327-2292. TWX 710-653-0125; FAX: (215) 327-9295.

CORPORATION PRESIDENT
Philip G. Steyaert
VICE PRESIDENT, NATIONAL SALES MANAGER
Peter H. Choi
NATIONAL SERVICE MANAGER
Rick Hollowbush

Videocassette Recorders

Ampex Corp. Recording Systems Division

401 Broadway, M.S. 3A-11, Redwood City, CA 94063; (415) 367- 2011; Telex: 348464; FAX: (415) 367-2761.

CORPORATE PRESIDENT
Max O. Mitchell
VICE PRESIDENT & GENERAL MANAGER, MARKETING SALES & SERVICE
Douglas M. Rowan
VICE PRESIDENT & GENERAL MANAGER, RECORDING SYSTEMS DIV.
Ronald J. Ritchie
DIRECTOR, U.S. SALES & SERVICE
James Carro

Curtis Mathes

P.O. Box 2096, Athens, TX 75751; (800) 527-7646; (214) 675-2292.

Hitachi Denshi America

(Division of Hitachi Denshi)

175 Crossways Park W., Woodbury, NY 11797, (516) 921-7200.

CORPORATION PRESIDENT
J. Tosaka
GENERAL MANAGER
M. Matsuhashi
VICE PRESIDENT, SALES
Bernard V. Munzelle

Ikegami Electronics (U.S.A.), Inc.

37 Brook Ave., Maywood, NJ 07607; (201) 368-9171. Organized 1964. (Manufactures and markets professional TV cameras and monitors.)

PRESIDENT
N. Nishi
SENIOR VICE PRESIDENT
S. La Conte
VICE PRESIDENT (DISPLAY MONITOR DIVISION)
Y. Sato
DIRECTOR, SALES & MARKETING
H. Winch
COMMUNICATIONS MANAGER
R. Estony

BRANCHES

Northeast: 37 Brook Ave., Maywood, NJ 07607; (201) 368- 9171. John Chow, regional sales manager.

Southeast: 5100 N.W. 33rd Ave., Suite 152, Ft. Lauderdale, FL 33309; John Webb, regional sales manager.

Midwest: 747 Church Rd., Units C4 & C5, Elmhurst, IL 60126; (312) 834-9774. Jerry Brinacombe, regional sales manager.

West Coast: 23105 Kashiwa Court, Torrance, CA 90505; (213) 534-0050. Kelly Nelson, regional sales.

Southwest: Three Dallas Communications Complex, 6311 North O'Connor Rd., Suite 100, Lock Box 100, Irving, TX 75039-3510; (214) 869-2363. Michael Mackin, sales manager.

Hawaii: Ward Industrial Center, 1020 Auahi St., Bldg. 7 Bay 3A, Honolulu, HI 96814; (808) 946-5955. Kuniko Yamashiro, office administrator.

Networks and Canada: 37 Brook Ave., Maywood, NJ 07607; (201) 368-9171. Gordon Tubbs, regional sales manager.

Instant Replay

2951 S. Bayshore Dr., Miami, FL 33133; (305) 448-7088. Organized 1976. (Manufactures specialized VCRs: RGB output, multistandard, built in caption decoder. VHS Hi Fi Multistd, Standards converters.)

PRESIDENT
Charles Azar
VICE PRESIDENT
Petra Azar

JVC Professional Products Company

(Division of U.S. JVC Corp.)

41 Slater Dr., Elmwood Park, NJ 07407; (201) 794-3900.

PRESIDENT
Shinzo Nakao
GENERAL MANAGER
Tom McCarthy

NEC Home Electronics (USA) Inc.

Video Products Division

1255 Michael Dr., Wood Dale, IL 60191-1094; (312) 860-9500.

PRESIDENT
Yuzi Ohashi
SENIOR VICE PRESIDENTS
Akira Sugiyama
Stan Gray
DIRECTOR, MARKETING
Robert Hana
DIRECTORS
Bob Hana
Brian Williams
SALES VICE PRESIDENT
C. K. McCusker
SENIOR VICE PRESIDENT, OEM
A. Sugiyama
SENIOR VICE PRESIDENT, MANUFACTURING
N. Maeda

Panasonic (Consumer Video Div.)

(Subsidiary of Matsushita Electric Corp. of America)

One Panasonic Way, Secaucus, NJ 07094; (201) 348-7000.

CORPORATE PRESIDENT
A. Imura
PRESIDENT
Stan Basara

Quasar Co.

(Division of Matsushita Electric Corp. of America)

1325 Pratt Blvd., Elk Grove Village, IL 60007; (312) 451-1200. Organized 1974. (Marketer of broad line of consumer electronics products.)

PRESIDENT
Mike Nakamura

Sanyo Fisher (USA) Corp.

21350 Lassen St., Chatsworth, CA 91311; (818) 998-7322.

CORPORATE PRESIDENT
M. Arata
EXECUTIVE VICE PRESIDENT, SALES & MARKETING
A. Takano

Sanyo Fisher (USA) Service Corp.

1200 W. Artesia Blvd., Compton, CA 90220; (213) 537-5830

CORPORATE PRESIDENT
K. Tominaga
SENIOR VICE PRESIDENT
D. La Benda
VICE PRESIDENT
J. L. Balbin

Sony Video Communications

(Division of Sony Corp. of America.)
Sony Dr., Park Ridge, NJ 07656; (201) 930-1000.

CORPORATE PRESIDENT
Kenji Tamiya
PRESIDENT
Philip J. Stack
VICE PRESIDENT, SALES
Robert Mueller
NATIONAL SERVICE MANAGER
Philip Hart

Toshiba America Consumer Products, Inc.

82 Totowa Rd., Wayne, NJ 07470; (201) 628-8000. FAX: (201) 628-1875.

PRESIDENT
Kenichico Hiyama
VICE PRESIDENT NATIONAL SERVICE
John Newman

Zenith Electronics Corporation

1000 Milwaukee Ave., Glenview, IL 60025-2493; (312) 391-7000. (Color television, video cassette recorders, camcorders, accessories, cable television decoders, teletext products, personal computers, high-resolution monitors, peripherals, high technology components and subsystems.)

CHAIRMAN & PRESIDENT
Jerry K. Pearlman
VICE PRESIDENT, FINANCE
Kell Benson
VICE PRESIDENT, GENERAL COUNSEL
John Borst
VICE PRESIDENT, HUMAN RESOURCES & PUBLIC AFFAIRS
Michael J. Kaplan
STAFF VICE PRESIDENT, TREASURER
Willard McNitt
DIRECTOR, CORPORATE PUBLIC RELATIONS AND COMMUNICATIONS
John I. Taylor

CONSUMER PRODUCTS GROUP
PRESIDENT, CONSUMER PRODS. GP.
Robert B. Hansen

Consumer Electronics
PRESIDENT, ZENITH SALES CO.
Gerald M. McCarthy
CONTROLLER
Robert Fisher
VICE PRESIDENT, MARKETING
Bruce A. Huber
VICE PRESIDENT, MANUFACTURING
H. Vincent Kamler, Jr.
VICE PRESIDENT, ENGINEERING
Peter C. Skerlos
VICE PRESIDENT, PURCHASING
James A. Stark
PRESIDENT, ZENITH CABLE PRODUCTS
James L. Faust

CRT Division
PRESIDENT
Martin Lerner

COMPUTER GROUP
PRESIDENT COMPUTER GROUP
Carl A. Michelotti
VICE PRESIDENT, OPERATIONS
Leo Kunkel
VICE PRESIDENT, FINANCE
David Kirkpatrick

Zenith Data Systems
PRESIDENT
John P. Frank
VICE PRESIDENT, FEDERAL SYSTEMS
Thomas Buchsbaum
VICE PRESIDENT, MARKETING
Andrew Czernek
VICE PRESIDENT, ENGINEERING
Michael Hakeem
SENIOR VICE PRESIDENT, SALES
Arthur Lambert

Heath Company
PRESIDENT
William E. Johnson

COMPONENTS GROUP
PRESIDENT, COMPONENTS GROUP
Otto M. Genutis
VICE PRESIDENT, MAGNETICS
Joseph Simone
VICE PRESIDENT, VIDEO DISPLAYS
Michael S. Tamkin

Videotape

Agfa Corporation

(Magnetic Tape Products)
100 Challenger Rd., Ridgefield Park, NJ 07660; (201) 440-2500.

CORPORATE PRESIDENT
Helge Wehmeir
VICE PRESIDENT & GENERAL MANAGER
Maria A. Curry
NATIONAL SALES MANAGER
Andrew Da Puzzo
NATIONAL MARKETING MANAGER, MAGNETIC TAPE PRODUCTS
Chris Emery
NATIONAL TECHNICAL MANAGER
John Matarazzo
MARKETING COMMUNICATIONS MANAGER
Teri Sosa
CONTROLLER
Kathi Smyth

Ampex Recording Media Corporation

401 Broadway, M.S. 22-02, Redwood City, CA 94063; (415) 367-3809; Telex 345363.

CHAIRMAN OF THE BOARD
Max Mitchell
PRESIDENT
Thomas J. Wheeler
VICE PRESIDENT, SALES & CUSTOMER SERVICE (U.S.A)
Richard Antonio

Fuji Photo Film USA, Inc., Magnetic Products Division

555 Taxter Rd., Elmsford, NY 10523; (914) 789-8100; Telex: ITT 423298.

CORPORATE PRESIDENT
Osamu Inoue
GENERAL MANAGER
Stan Bauer

JVC Professional Products Company

(Division of U.S. JVC Corp.)
41 Slater Dr., Elmwood Park, NJ 07407; (201) 794-3900.

PRESIDENT
Shinzo Nakao
GENERAL MANAGER
Tom McCarthy

Magnetic Media Video Corp.

500 Eastern Parkway, Farmingdale, NY 11735; (516) 293-1010, Telex 14-3223.

VICE PRESIDENT, GENERAL MANAGER
John Cristiano
VICE PRESIDENT, SALES MANAGER
Paul Mastroianni

Matsushita Electric of Canada Ltd.

5770 Ambler Dr., Mississauga, Ont., L4W 2T3 Canada; (416) 624-5010.

CORPORATE PRESIDENT
A. Higashi
MANAGER, AUDIO-VIDEO SYSTEMS GROUP
A. M. Evans
MANAGER, INDUSTRIAL VIDEO SYSTEMS DEPT.
J. McDonald
MANAGER, CLOSED CIRCUIT TELEVISION DEPT.
Mary Lepage
MANAGER, PROFESSIONAL AUDIO VIDEO DEPT.
Fred Nanos
NATIONAL PARTS MANAGER
S. Wan
NATIONAL SERVICE MANAGER
A. Gillespie

Maxell Corp. of America

22-08 Route 208, Fair Lawn, NJ 07410; (201) 794-5900; FAX: (201) 796-8790.

CORPORATE PRESIDENT
H. Matsumoto
VICE PRESIDENT
Ted Ozawa
GENERAL MANAGER
James J. Ringwood

Maxima Magnetics, Inc.

300 Bonair Ave., Hatboro, PA 19040; (215) 443-0700, (800) 3 MAXIMA. Organized 1982. (Sells blank video and audio tape to professional users.)

PRESIDENT
William R. Goss
EXECUTIVE VICE PRESIDENT
Susan R. Goss
VICE PRESIDENT, SALES AND MARKETING
Carol M. Moore
BOARD OF DIRECTORS
W.R. Goss, president; S.R. Goss, secretary/treasurer.

Panasonic Industrial Co.

(Subsidiary of Matsushita Electric Corp. of America)
One Panasonic Way, Secaucus, NJ 07094; (201) 348-7000.

CORPORATE PRESIDENT
A. Imura

Sony Video Communications

(Division of Sony Corp. of America)
Sony Drive, Park Ridge, NJ 07656; (201) 930-1000.

CORPORATE PRESIDENT
Kenji Tamiya
PRESIDENT
Philip J. Stack
VICE PRESIDENT, SALES
Robert Mueller
NATIONAL SERVICE MANAGER
Philip Hart

Sunkyong International, Inc.

30 Congress Dr., Moonachie, NJ 07074; (201) 440-5006, Telex WU 642177.

VICE PRESIDENT, MARKETING
George T. Saddler

TDK Electronics Corp.

12 Harbor Park Dr., Port Washington, NY 11050; (516) 625-0100, Telex 144535.

CORPORATION PRESIDENT
Takashi Tsujii
VICE PRESIDENT, SALES & MARKETING
Koyo Yokoi

Thor Electronics Corp.

321 Pennsylvania Ave., Linden, NJ 07036; (201) 486-3300. Telex 138968 THORLIND

CORPORATE PRESIDENT
Angelo Crudele
GENERAL MANAGER
Roy Gettis
MARKETING & SALES
D. Delane
NATIONAL PARTS MANAGER
Frank Destefano

3M/Consumer Video & Audio Products Division

223-5S-01, 3M Center, St. Paul, MN 55125; (612) 733-1387. (Manufactures and sells blank audio and video cassettes, floppy disks, systems care products and accessories.)

DIVISION VICE PRESIDENT
David Powell
MARKETING DIRECTOR
Robert F. Burnett
MARKETING OPERATIONS MANAGER
Robert Y. Kline

Video Consumer and Trade Publications

Quigley Publishing Company

Publishers of Motion Picture Almanac (Annual), Television and Video Almanac (Annual). 159 W. 53 St., New York, NY 10019; (212) 247-3100. Cable: Quigpubco, New York; FAX: (212) 489-0871.

PRESIDENT & PUBLISHER
Martin Quigley, Jr.
EDITOR
Jane Klain
VICE PRESIDENT & EXECUTIVE DIRECTOR
Robert McDonald

LONDON BUREAU

William Pay, Manager and London Editor; 15 Samuel Road, Langdon Hills, Basildon, Essex, England; 0268-417-055.

CANADIAN BUREAU

Patricia Thompson, Editor; 1430 Yonge St., Suite 214, Toronto, Ontario M4T 1Y6 Canada; (416) 922-5772.

FOREIGN CORRESPONDENTS

CHILE: Alan Hootnick, Lo Arcaya 1963, Vitacura, Chile; 56-2-200-0807; FAX: 56-2-215-1802.
EGYPT: Ahmed Sami, 4 El Ommara St., Apt. 13, Abbassia, Cairo; Tel.: 2825915/2588166.
FRANCE: Vernice Klier-Moskowitz, 80 Ave. Charles de Gaulle, Neuilly Sur Seine 92200 France.
GREECE: Rena Velissariou, 8432, Kolokotroni Str., Agia Paraskevi, Attikis, Athens. (804). 153 42, Greece; Tel.: 65 67 665.
HOLLAND: Paul Silvius, 467 West Halfront, 1183 JD Amstelveen, Netherlands.
INDIA: B. R. Garga, 55 Anita, Mt. Pleasant Rd., Bombay 4 00006, India; Tel.: 8122019.
JAPAN: A. C. Pinder, Whaley-Eaton, Service, Central P.O. Box 190, Tokyo, Japan.
PAKISTAN: A. R. Slote, P.O. Box 7426, Karachi 1-3.
SRI LANKA: Chandra Perera, 437 Pethiygoda, Kelanuja, Sri Lanka, Ceylon.
SCANDINAVIA: Inge Hanson, Inge Hanson Publicity, P.O. Box 7050, S-17107, Solna, Sweden; Tel. & FAX: 46-8-850 980.
SWITZERLAND: Gabriella Broggi, Via E. Maraini 20 B, 6900 Massagnas, Switzerland; Tel.: (091) 562910.
VENEZUELA: Victoria M. Marshall, RWI 8621 Beverly Blvd., Suite 210, Beverly Hills, CA 90211.

Motion Picture Almanac

(Annually) 159 W. 53 St., New York, NY 10019; (212) 247-3100; Cable: Quigpubco, New York; FAX: (212) 489-0871.

EDITOR
Jane Klain
BRITISH EDITOR
William Pay
CANADIAN EDITOR
Patricia Thompson

Television & Video Almanac

(Annually) 159 W. 53 St., New York, NY 10019; (212) 247-3100; Cable: Quigpubco, New York; FAX: (212) 489-0871.

EDITOR
Jane Klain
BRITISH EDITOR
William Pay
CANADIAN EDITOR
Patricia Thompson

artsAmerica, Inc.

12 Havemeyer Pl., Greenwich, CT 06830; (203) 869-4693. Organized 1984. (Publisher of artsAmerica Fine Art Film & Video Source Book; Distributor of videocassettes about the visual arts; producer of documentaries about the visual arts.)

PRESIDENT
Browyn Dunne
DIRECTOR
Dorothy Tucker

Back Stage

(See Television Press Section)

Back Stage Television, Film, Tape & Production Directory

(See Television Press Section)

Billboard

(See Television Press Section)

Classic Images

Box 809, Muscatine, IA 52671; (319) 263-2331.

Coming Attractions

(Published monthly by Star Video Entertainment LP and distributed to 2000 video stores.)
550 Grand St., Jersey City, NJ 07302; (201) 333-4600.

PUBLISHER
Carla Edwards

Daily Variety

(See Television Press Section)

Electronic Media

(Weekly publication covering the broadcast TV industry including radio, cable and video.) Crain Communications Inc., 740 N. Rush St., Chicago, IL 60611, (312) 649-5293.

Entertainment Business Media

1700 E. Dyer Rd., Suite 250, Santa Ana, CA 92715; (714) 250-8060. Organized 1979. (Publishes entertainment business and video magazines). Department of HBJ Publications, division of Harcourt Brace, Jovanovich, Inc.

PUBLISHER
David Rowe
PUBLISHER
Tom Adams

Film & Video Magazine

(A monthly international film and video production magazine.) Organized 1983. 8170 Beverly Blvd., #208, Los Angeles, CA 90048; (213) 653-8053.

PUBLISHER/PRESIDENT
David Swartz
SECRETARY/ASSOCIATE PUBLISHER/MANAGING EDITOR
Paula Swartz
VICE PRESIDENT/DIRECTOR OF ADVERTISING
Steven Rich

Hollywood Reporter, The

(See Television Press Section)

Home Video Publisher

(Weekly, analyzing home video publishing opportunities for special interest programming and feature film.) Knowledge Industry Publications, Inc., 701 Westchester Ave., White Plains, NY 10604; (914) 328-9157.

MANAGING EDITOR
Betsy Niesyn

Home Viewer

11 N. Second St., Philadelphia, PA 19106; (215) 629-1588.

In Motion Film & Video Production Magazine

(Film and video production trade magazine published 12 times a year.) 421 Fourth St., Annapolis, MD 21403; (301) 269-0605.

EDITOR & PUBLISHER
Steve Lehuray

Instant Replay Video Magazine

2951 S. Bayshore Dr., Miami, FL 33133; (305) 448-7088. Organized 1976. (Videotape magazine format about the video industry and TV Broadcasting. Sold on subscription basis. Available in 3/4″ and 1/2″ Beta and VHS and 8 mm.)

PUBLISHER
Charles Azar

Millimeter

(Published monthly. Motion picture and TV production industry magazine.) 826 Broadway, New York, NY 10003; (212) 477-4700.

Photo Business

(Photographic trade publication.) Organized 1956. Published by Billboard Publications, Inc., 1515 Broadway, New York, NY 10036; (212) 536-5193.

EDITOR & ASSOCIATE PUBLISHER
Willard Clark
ASSOCIATE PUBLISHER, MARKETING & SALES
Doris Burke
MANAGING EDITOR
Richard Brandes
PRODUCTION MANAGER
Phyllis Hall

The Producer's Masterguide

(See Television Press Section)

Rockamerica Magazine

(Monthly magazine dealing with the music industry.) 27 E. 21 St., New York, NY 10010; (212) 475-5791.

Show Business

1501 Broadway, Suite 2900, New York, NY 10036. Organized 1941. (Trade paper.)

OWNER
Leo Shull

Tape/Disc Business

(Monthly news publication). Published by Knowledge Industry Publications, Inc., 701 Westchester Ave., White Plains, NY 10604; (914) 328-9157.

EXECUTIVE EDITOR
Leslie Grey

Television Digest

(See Television Press Section)

TWICE (This Week in Consumer Electronics)

902 Broadway, New York, NY 10010; (212) 447-2200. Organized 1986. (Weekly news magazine.)

PUBLISHER
Marsha Grand
PRESIDENT
Richard Ekstract
EDITORIAL DIRECTOR
Robert Gerson
VIDEO EDITOR
Seth Goldstein

Variety

(See Television Press Section)

Video

(Monthly consumer magazine covering hardware, video technology and its impact on lifestyles, and programming.) Published by Reese Communications, 460 W. 34 St., 20th floor, New York, NY 10001; (212) 947-6500. Organized 1978.

PRESIDENT & MANAGING DIRECTOR
Jay Rosenfield
PUBLISHER
Debra Halpert
EDITOR
Art Lewis

Video Business

(Published 4 times per year by parent company International Thomson Retail Press. A business-to-business magazine for video dealers.) 345 Park Ave. S., 6th floor, New York, NY 10010; (212) 686-7744. Organized 1981.

PUBLISHER
Bill O'Brien
EDITOR
Bruce Apar
PRESIDENT & CHIEF EXECUTIVE OFFICER
Arthur Anderman
VICE PRESIDENT/CORP. EDITORIAL DIRECTOR
Howard Roth
EASTERN ADVERTISING
Stacey Kelley
WESTERN ADVERTISING
Mitchell Wallis

Video Insider

(Weekly news magazine for the video industry.) 223 Conestoga Rd., Wayne, PA 19087; (215) 688-7030.

The Video Register and Teleconferencing Resources Directory

(Annual. Directory listing organizations using video—manufacturers, dealers, program distributors, consultants/

producers, production facilities.) Published by Knowledge Industry Publications, Inc., 701 Westchester Ave., White Plains, NY 10604; (914) 328-9157.

Video Review Magazine

(Monthly. Home video consumer magazine.) Published by Viare Publishing, 902 Broadway, New York, NY 10010; (212) 477-2200.

The Video Source Book

(A listing of more than 50,000 programs available on video tape from more than 1200 sources.) The National Video Clearinghouse, Inc., 100 Lafayette Dr., Syosset, NY 11791; (516) 364-3686.

Video Store Magazine

(Monthly. Provides information to video retailers nationally on new releases, trends in the industry, industry statistics and promotional ideas.) 1700 E. Dyer Rd., #250, Santa Ana, CA 92705; (714) 250-8060. Organized 1979.

PRESIDENT OF PUBLICATIONS
Richard Moeller
GROUP PUBLISHER
Eileen Paulin
PUBLISHER
David Allen Shaw
EDITOR
Frank Moldstad
NATIONAL ADVERTISING SALES MANAGER
Colette Kreins
BRANCH
545 Fifth Ave., New York, NY 10017; (212) 503-2949.

Video Systems Magazine

9221 Quivira Rd., Overland Park, KS 66215; (913) 888-4664. Organized 1975. (Magazine for video professionals, serving the corporate/industrial video marketplace.)

SENIOR MANAGING EDITOR
Tom Cook
EDITOR
Ned Soseman
EDITORIAL DIRECTOR
Jerry Whitaker
PUBLISHER
Duane Hefner
GROUP VICE PRESIDENT
Cameron Bishop
TECHNICAL EDITOR
Rick Lehtinen
AD PRODUCTION MANAGER
Pat Eisenman
AFFILIATIONS
Member: American Business Press; Business Publications Audit of Circulation; Acoustical Society of America; International Television Assn; Professional Film and Video Equipment Association.

Video Tape and Disc Guide to Home Entertainment

(Updated reference guide containing titles and descriptive information about 10,000 available videocassettes and discs for the consumer market.) Published by National Video Clearinghouse, Inc., 100 Lafayette Dr., Syosset, NY 11791; (516) 364-3686.

Video Trade News

(Monthly—for manufacturers and dealers who sell professional video equipment.) Published by C.S. Tepfer Publishing Co. Inc., P.O. Box 597, Ridgefield, CT 06877; (203) 438-7224.

Video Vision Magazine

9241 S.W. 12th St., Miami, FL 33174; (305) 262-1505. Organized 1984. (Nationally circulated bilingual video magazine for the Hispanic market.)

PRESIDENT
Lomberto Perez
VICE PRESIDENT
Cary M. Perez

Video Week

(Weekly. Newsletter covering the business of program sales and distribution for videocassettes, disc, pay TV and news media.) Published by Warren Publishing, Inc. 2115 Ward Court N.W., Washington, DC 20037; (202) 872-9200.

Videography Magazine

(Monthly. Professional video production trade magazine.) Organized 1976. 2 Park Ave., (Suite 1820). New York, NY 10016; (212) 779-1919.

PUBLISHER
John Rice
EDITOR
Brian McKernan

Vidmar Communications

1680 Vine St., Suite 820, Hollywood, CA 90028; (213) 462-6350. Publishes following video-related publications:

VIDEO DIRECT RESPONSE
(Offers 64 case studies plus analysis of mail order, video clubs, catalog operations selling videocassettes.)
VIDEO MARKETING NEWSLETTER
(24 issues a year. News and analysis of home video business.)
VIDEO MARKETING SURVEYS & FORECASTS
(12 issues a year. Comprehensive market statistics annually for new electronic media. Graphs, charts, analysis.)
VIDEO TECHNOLOGY NEWSLETTER
(24 issues a year. Covers new media: HDTV, pay per view, advanced displays, production, fiber optics.)
VIDEONEWS INTERNATIONAL
(Monthly. Newsletter covering market for Video programming worldwide.)

Video Trade Organizations

American Film and Video Association

(Formerly Educational Film Library Association)

(Organized in 1943 as a non-profit membership organization to serve as a national clearinghouse for information about 16mm films. Now also serves as a source of information on video, and other nonprint media as well, including their production, distribution and use in education, the arts, science, industry, religion. Sponsor of the American Film and Video Festival and publisher of Sightlines Magazine and AFVA Evaluation.) 920 Barnsdale Rd., Suite 152, La Grange Park, IL 60525; (312) 482-4000.

EXECUTIVE DIRECTOR
Ron MacIntyre
FESTIVAL DIRECTOR
Kathryn Lamont
BOARD OF DIRECTORS
Mark Ritchie (pres.), Sharon Chaplock (past pres.), Beverly Teach (pres.-elect), Anthony Marshalek (treas.), June McWatt (secretary), Linda Artel, Roberto Esteves, Maria Johns, Olga Knight, Nora McMartin, Christine McDonald, Paul Neeb, Karen Sayer.

American Video Association

2885 N. Nevada #140, Chandler, AZ 85225; (602) 892-8553; (800) 528-7400; FAX: (602) 926-8358. Organized 1980. (National retailer owned and operated co-op. Provides buying, merchandising, and informational services to independent video dealers. Sponsors annual convention. Publishes bi-weekly newsletter and price references.)

CHAIRMAN
Tom Daugherty
PRESIDENT
John Power
VICE PRESIDENT, PURCHASING
Monty Crandon
VICE PRESIDENT, SPECIAL SERVICES
Mary Bonacci
SECRETARY/TREASURER
Jerry Ulibarri

Association of Independent Video and Filmmakers

625 Broadway, 9th floor, New York, NY 10012; (212) 473-3400; Cable: 226078 Aegisur. (Provides advocacy and professional services for the independent media community.)

EXECUTIVE DIRECTOR
Lawrence Sapadin
MEMBERSHIP/PROGRAMMING DIRECTOR
Ethan Young
FESTIVAL BUREAU DIRECTOR
Kathryn Bowser
BUSINESS MANAGER/AUDIO DIRECTOR
Morton Marks
EDITOR
Martha Gever
MANAGING EDITOR
Pat Thomson
BOARD OF DIRECTORS
Reggie Life (chmn.), Robert Richter (president), Loni Ding (vice president), Wendy Lidell (secretary), Skip Blumberg (treasurer), Robert Aaronson, Adrianne Benton, Christine Choy, Barton Weiss, Dai Sil Kim-Gibson, Lourdes Portillo, Deborah Shaffer

Association of Visual Communicators, Inc.

7044 North Figueroa, Suite 103, Los Angeles, CA 90041; (213) 340-1540. Organized 1957. (Promotes and encourages excellence in the informational audio-visual industry.)

EXECUTIVE DIRECTOR
Kathleen Foster
NATIONAL PRESIDENT
Glenn Otto

Electronic Industries Associtaion

(see Television Organizations)

International Communications Industries Association (ICIA)

3150 Spring St., Fairfax, VA 22031; (703) 273-7200. Organized 1939. (A trade association of the communications technologies industry dedicated to expanding and improving communications methods through the effective use of all types of media. As communications technologies become increasingly advanced and more widely used, ICIA members strive to help the world use these technologies more efficiently and cost-effectively.)

CHAIRMAN OF THE BOARD
Thomas Roberts
PRESIDENT
Edward Goodman Jr.
PRESIDENT-ELECT
John Culp
VICE PRESIDENT
Rosie Bogo
SECRETARY-TREASURER
Don Blumberg
EXECUTIVE VICE PRESIDENT
Kenton H. Pattie

International Tape/Disc Association

505 Eighth Ave., New York, NY 10018; (212) 643-0620. Organized 1970.

CHAIRMAN OF THE BOARD
J. Philip Stack
PRESIDENT
Alfred Markim
SENIOR VICE PRESIDENT
Maria A. Curry
VICE PRESIDENT
R. Patrick Leonard, Jr.
EUROPEAN VICE PRESIDENT
Andrew Bourne
TREASURER
Larry Finley
EXECUTIVE VICE PRESIDENT
Henry Brief
BOARD OF DIRECTORS
Officers are the following: Frank Day, Howard Schwartz, James Fiedler, R. Stanton Bauer, Michael Upton, James MacKay, Donald Winquist, James Ringwood, Bud O'Shea, Reg Childs, Steve Yuhas, Roel Buis, Larry Bennett, Tony Gelardi, Keizo Ito, Daniel Grynberg, Tom Wheeler, John Clarke, Robert Burnett.

International Teleproduction Society, Inc.

990 Ave. of the Americas, Suite 21E, New York, NY 10018; (212) 629-3266. (Not-for-profit international trade association. Promotes and furthers excellence in the use of video as a medium of communication; provides a source of information and education regarding video production and a forum for exchange of ideas. Establishes one unified voice which addresses common goals.)

EXECUTIVE DIRECTOR
Janet Luhrs
BOARD OF DIRECTORS
Tom Angell (president); Sam Holtz, executive vice president; Ron Herman, vice president; Dick Millais, vice president; Lou Di Giusto, secretary; Robert Henderson, treasurer; Walter Hamilton, Steve Carlisle, Jim Harmon, Scott Kane, Stan Kronquest, Dan McGuire, board members.
CHAPTERS
New York, Mid-Atlantic, Michigan, Chicago, Southern California, Northern California, Toronto

International Television Association

6311 N. O'Connor Rd., LB51, Irving, TX 75039; (214) 869-1112. Organized 1973. (Furthers the development of the professional video communicator; has 90 chapters in USA and 10 affiliates in foreign countries.)

PRESIDENT
Joseph Maiella
PRESIDENT ELECT
Beverly Hare
VICE PRESIDENT
David W. Thompson
EXECUTIVE DIRECTOR
Fred Wehrli
CHAIRMAN OF THE BOARD
Tim Donovan

National Association of Video Distributors

1255 23rd St. NW, Suite 850, Washington DC 20037; (202) 452-8100; FAX: (202) 833-3636. Organized 1983. (Promotes and enhances the video distribution industry.)

PRESIDENT
Walt Wiseman
VICE PRESIDENT
August (Gus) Umlauf
SECRETARY-TREASURER
Bill Burton
BOARD OF DIRECTORS
Tony Dalesandro, Dalton McArthur, David Bronstad
DIRECTOR, MEMBER SERVICES
Mark T. Engle

National Federation of Local Cable Programmers

P.O. Box 27290, Washington, DC 20038-7290; (202) 829-7189.

EXECUTIVE DIRECTOR
vacant

New York Women in Film

(see Television Organizations)

Video Dealers Association, Inc.

211 E. 43rd St., Suite 1306, New York, NY 10017; (212) 972-3315; FAX: (212) 687-4730. (Provides services for video rental stores.)

PRESIDENT
Arthur Lieberman

Video Software Dealers Association

3 Eves Drive, Suite 307, Marlton, NJ 08053; (609) 596-8500; FAX: (609) 596-3268. Organized 1982. (International trade association for the home video industry representing more than 4,000 companies engaged in retail sales, wholesale distribution and manufacture of home video software and related products.)

PRESIDENT 1988–90
Lou Berg
EXECUTIVE VICE PRESIDENT
Pam Horovitz
VICE PRESIDENT
Carol Pough
TREASURER
David Ballstad
SECRETARY
Gary Messenger

Video Services

* ANIMATION
* AUDIO MIXING & SWEETENING
* CLEANING & EVALUATION OF TAPES
* DUPLICATION
* EDITING & POST PRODUCTION
* EQUIPMENT—SALES & RENTAL
* EQUIPMENT REPAIR
* MOBILE UNITS
* PRODUCTION FACILITIES
* SCREENING ROOMS
* TRANSFERS—FILM TO TAPE
* TRANSFERS—TAPE TO FILM

Videotape Animation

LOS ANGELES

ACTION VIDEO, INC., 6616 Lexington Ave., Los Angeles, CA 90038; (213) 461-3611; FAX: 460-4023.
AMERICAN VIDEO FACTORY, 4150 Glencoe Ave., Marina Del Rey, CA 90292; (213) 823-8622, (800) 367-8433.
AUDIO-VIDEO CRAFT, INC., 6753 Santa Monica Blvd., Los Angeles, CA 90038; (213) 655-3511.
BERC, BROADCAST EQUIPMENT RENTAL COMPANY, 4545 Chermak St., Burbank, CA 91505; (818) 841-3000, (213) 464-7655; FAX: (818) 841-7919.
BOSUSTOW VIDEO, 3030 Pennsylvania Ave., Santa Monica, CA 90404-4112; (213) 453-7973; FAX: (213) 828-4053.
CALIFORNIA COMMUNICATIONS, INC., 6900 Santa Monica Blvd., Los Angeles, CA 90038; (213) 466-8511.
CALIFORNIA VIDEO CENTER, 15303 Ventura Blvd., Sherman Oaks, CA 91403; (818) 789-5000.
COTTON CANDY/EYE ON VIDEO, 224 N. Juanita Ave., Los Angeles, CA 90004; (213) 382-4048.
DEVONSHIRE AUDIO/VIDEO STUDIOS, 10729 Magnolia Blvd., N. Hollywood, CA 91601; (818) 985-1945.
GORDON, ALAN, ENTERPRISES, INC., 1430 Cahuenga Blvd., Hollywood, CA 90028; (213) 466-3561; (818) 985-5500.
HAMM, GENE, & ASSOCIATES, 6547 DeLongpre Ave., Los Angeles, CA 90028; (213) 465-2289.
HORIZONTAL EDITING STUDIOS, 2625 W. Olive Ave., Burbank, CA 91505; (818) 841-6750.
IMAGE WEST, 11846 Ventura Blvd., Studio City, CA 91604; (818) 506-5577.
INTER VIDEO/TRITRONICS, INC., 733 N. Victory Blvd., Burbank, CA 91502; (818) 843-3633; (818) 569-4000; FAX: (818) 843-6884.
JP VIDEO SERVICE BETA CAM PRODUCTIONS, 9538 W. Pico Blvd., Los Angeles, CA 90035; (213) 859-9903; 271-1209.
MILLER, FRITZ, ANIMATION/GRAPHICS, 10806 Ventura Blvd., Suite 11, Studio City, CA 91604; (818) 985-6074.
MISKIN, LEE, ANIMATION, 1463 Tamarind Ave., Hollywood, CA 90028; (213) 461-5977.
MULTI-MEDIA WORKS, 7227 Beverly Blvd., Los Angeles, CA 90036; (213) 939-1185.
NEWMAN/FRANKS, 2956 Nicada Dr., Los Angeles, CA 90077; (213) 470-0140; 470-0145; FAX: (213) 470-2410.
PACIFIC TITLE & ART STUDIO, 6350 Santa Monica, Hollywood, CA 90038; (213) 464-0121.
PACIFIC VIDEO, 809 N. Cahuenga Blvd., Los Angeles, CA 90038; (213) 462-6266.
PAINT BOX PLUS, 6464 Sunset Blvd., Suite 1000, Hollywood, CA 90028; (213) 856-8530; FAX: (213) 466-4802.
THE POST GROUP, 6335 Homewood Ave., Los Angeles, CA 90028; (213) 462-2300.
SABAN PRODUCTIONS, INC., 11724 Ventura Blvd., Studio City, CA 91604; (818) 985-3805.
SCHULMAN VIDEO CENTER, 861 Seward St., Hollywood, CA 90038; (213) 465-8110.
STUDIO ANIMATICS, 1950 Sawtelle Blvd., Suite 265, Los Angeles, CA 90025; (213) 933-0646; 478-7230.
STUDIO PRODUCTION, INC., 650 N. Bronson Ave., Suite 223, Hollywood, CA 90004; (213) 856-8048; FAX: (213) 461-4202.
SUNBREAK PRODUCTIONS, 256 S. La Cienega Blvd., Beverly Hills, CA 90211; (213) 659-2324.
TELEMEDIA PRODUCTIONS, 18321 Ventura Blvd., Suite 660, Tarzana, CA 91356.
VARITEL VIDEO, 3575 Cahuenga Blvd. W., Los Angeles, CA 90068; (213) 850-1165; FAX: (213) 850-6151.
VID-U PRODUCTIONS, 612 N. Sepulveda Blvd., Los Angeles, CA 90049; (213) 472-7023.
VIDEO IMAGE, 4121 Redwood Ave., Suite 215, Los Angeles, CA 90066; (213) 822-8872.

NEW YORK

ANIMATED VIDEO, 1600 Broadway, New York, NY 10019; (212) 265-2942.
BROADWAY VIDEO, 1619 Broadway, New York, NY 10019; (212) 265-7600; 713-0540.
C&C VISUAL, 225 W. 44 St., New York, NY 10036; (212) 869-4900.
CHARLEX, 2 W. 45 St., New York, NY 10036; (212) 719-4600.
COMP ART PLUS, 12 W. 27 St., New York, NY 10001; (212) 689-8670.
COM/TECH, 770 Lexington Ave., New York, NY 10021; (212) 826-2935.
CREATIVE WAYS, INC., 305 E. 46 St., New York, NY 10017; (212) 935-0145.
DARINO, 222 Park Ave. South, #2A, New York, NY 10003; (212) 228-4024.
DEVLIN VIDEO SERVICE, 1501 Broadway, New York, NY 10036; (212) 391-1313.
DI COMO & AGOSTINELLI PRODUCTIONS, INC., 225 E. 43 St., New York, NY 10017; (212) 697-7771.
DIGIMATION, INC., 10 E. 40th St., New York, NY 10016; (212) 213-6098.
DOROS ANIMATION STUDIO, INC., 156 Fifth Ave., Suite 1119, New York, NY 10010; (212) 627-7220.
EDITEL, 222 E. 44 St., New York, NY 10017; (212) 867-4600.
FAMA II PRODUCTIONS, 2750 Richmond Terrace, Staten Island, NY 10303; (718) 273-1780.
THE FANTASTIC ANIMATION MACHINE, INC., 12 E. 46 St., New York, NY 10017; (212) 697-2525.
JSL VIDEO SERVICES, 25 W. 45 St., New York, NY 10036; (212) 575-5082.
MTI TV CITY, 1443 Park Ave., New York, NY 10029; (212) 722-1818.
MAGNO SOUND & VIDEO, 729 Seventh Ave., New York, NY 10019; (212) 302-2505.
MODERN TELECOMMUNICATIONS INC., 1 Dag Hammarskjold Plaza, Level C, New York, NY 10017; (212) 722-1818.
NAPOLEON VIDEOGRAPHICS, 460 W. 42nd St., New York, NY 10036; (212) 279-2000.
NORTHEAST VIDEO, INC., 420 Lexington Ave., New York, NY 10017; (212) 661-8830.
R/GREENBERG ASSOCIATES, INC., 350 W. 39 St., New York, NY 10018; (212) 239-6767. FAX: (212) 947-3769.
RVI/RUTT VIDEO, 137 E. 25 St., New York, NY 10010; (212) 685-4000.
STARGATE PRODUCTIONS, INC., 231 W. 55th St., New York, NY 10022; (212) 333-3636.
SYNAPSE TELECOMMUNICATIONS, INC., 304 E. 45th St., New York, NY 10017; (212) 370-9191.
SYNESTHETICS, INC., 58 Walker St., New York, NY 10013; (212) 431-4112.
TELETECHNIQUES, INC., 1 W. 19th St., New York, NY 10011; (212) 206-1475; 633-1868.
TODAY VIDEO, 45 W. 45th St., New York, NY 10036; (212) 391-1020.
UNITEL VISUAL DYNAMICS, 515 W. 57 St., New York, NY 10019; (212) 265-3600; FAX: (212) 765-5801.
VCA/TELETRONICS, 231 E. 55 St., New York, NY 10022; (212) 355-1600.
VIDEO WORKS, 24 W. 40 St., New York, NY 10018; (212) 869-2500.
VISUAL CREATIONS, INC., 305 E. 46 St., New York, NY 10017; (212) 935-0145.
WINDSOR VIDEO, 8 W. 38th St., New York, NY 10018; (212) 944-9090.

SAN FRANCISCO

ONE PASS FILM & VIDEO, One China Basin Bldg., San Francisco, CA 94107; (415) 777-5777.

Video Audio Mixing & Sweetening

LOS ANGELES

ALTAVIDEO, 3501 Cahuenga Blvd. W., Los Angeles, CA 90068; (213) 876-8008.
AMERICAN INSTITUTE OF VIDEO, 20850 Dearborn St., Chatsworth, CA 91311; (818) 700-8987.
AMERICAN VIDEO FACTORY, 4150 Glencoe Ave., Marina Del Rey, CA 90292; (213) 823-8622; (800) 367-8433.
AMETHYST STUDIOS, 7000 Santa Monica Blvd., Hollywood, CA 90038; (213) 467-3700.
AUDIO ACHIEVEMENTS RECORDING STUDIO, 1327 Cabrillo Ave., Torrance, CA 90501; (213) 533-9531.
AUDIO ARTS PUBLISHING CO., 5617 Melrose Ave., Los Angeles, CA 90038; (213) 461-3507.
AUDIO POST, 3755 Cahuenga Blvd. W., Suite C, Studio City, CA 91604; (818) 761-5220.
AUDIO RENTS INC., 7237 Santa Monica Blvd., Hollywood, CA 90046; (213) 874-1000; 265-4400.
AUDIO-VIDEO CRAFT INC., 6753 Santa Monica Blvd., Los Angeles, CA 90038; (213) 655-3511.
AUDIO VISUAL HEADQUARTERS CORP., 361 N. Oak St., Inglewood, CA 90302; (213) 419-4040.
BCS BROADCAST STORE, INC., 4525 Valerio St., Burbank, CA 91505; (818) 845-7000.
BLUE DOLPHIN STUDIO, 650 N. Bronson Ave., Hollywood, CA 90004; (213) 467-7660.
BURBANK STUDIOS, 4000 Warner Blvd., Burbank, CA 91522; (818) 954-6000.
BUZZY'S RECORDING SERVICES, 6900 Melrose Ave., Los Angeles, CA 90038; (213) 931-1867; FAX: (213) 931-9681.
CFI, 959 Seward St., Hollywood, CA 90038; (213) 462-3161.
CALIFORNIA COMMUNICATIONS INC., 6900 Santa Monica Blvd., Los Angeles, CA 90038; (213) 466-8511.
CALIFORNIA RECORDING & VIDEO, 5203 Sunset Blvd., Los Angeles, CA 90027; (213) 666-1244.
CANDLEWICK PRODUCTIONS, 1161 N. Highland Blvd., Hollywood, CA 90038; (213) 462-7979.
CARMAN PRODUCTIONS, INC., 15456 Cabrito Rd., Van Nuys, CA 91406; (213) 873-7370; (818) 787-6436.
COMPACT VIDEO SERVICES, INC., 2813 W. Alameda Ave., Burbank, CA 91505; (818) 840-7000.
THE COMPLEX, 2323 Corinth St., Los Angeles, CA 90064; (213) 477-1938.
CONSOLIDATED FILM INDUSTRIES, 959 Seward St., Los Angeles, CA 90038; (213) 462-3161.
CREST NATIONAL FILM & VIDEOTAPE LABS, 1141 N. Seward St., Los Angeles, CA 90038; (213) 466-0624; 462-6696; FAX: (213) 461-8901.
CRYSTAL SOUND RECORDING, 1014 N. Vine St., Los Angeles, CA 90038; (213) 466-6452.
DSR PRODUCTIONS, 607 N. Avenue 64, Los Angeles, CA 90042; (213) 258-6741.
DEVONSHIRE AUDIO/VIDEO STUDIOS, 10729 Magnolia Blvd., North Hollywood, CA 91601; (818) 985-1945.
DIGITAL SOUND RECORDING, 607 N. Ave. 64, Los Angeles, CA 90042; (213) 258-6741.
DIGGY, 1521 Clark Ave., Burbank, CA 91506; (818) 763-6443.
EYE ON VIDEO, 224 N. Juanita Ave., Los Angeles, CA 90004; (213) 382-4048.
FIDELITY RECORDING STUDIO, 4412 Whitsett Ave., Studio City, CA 91604; (818) 508-3263.
FOX TAPE, 5746 Sunset Blvd., Los Angeles, CA 90028; (213) 856-1000.
GOOCH, DON R., (dba Aural Design), 11100 Landale St., North Hollywood, CA 91602; (818) 769-6233.
GRACE & WILD STUDIOS, 3501 Cahuenga Blvd. West, Los Angeles, CA 90068; (213) 876-8008; FAX: (213) 876-0460.
GROUP IV RECORDING, 1541 N. Wilcox Ave., Los Angeles, CA 90028; (213) 466-6444.
GROUP W CABLE VIDEO PRODUCTION CENTER, 2939 Nebraska Ave., Santa Monica, CA 90404; (213) 829-2676; 829-5111.
HARMONEY HOUSE, 1915 W. Glenoaks Blvd., Suite 200, Glendale, CA 91201; (818) 500-0100.
HARMONY GOLD USA, INC., 8831 Sunset Blvd., Suite 300, Los Angeles, CA 90069; (213) 652-8720.
HARRIS, CRAIG (sound composer), P.O. Box 110, N. Hollywood, CA 91603; (818) 508-8000.
HIT CITY, 6146 W. Pico Blvd., Los Angeles, CA 90035; (213) 852-0186.
HOLLYWOOD NATIONAL STUDIOS, 6605 Eleanor Ave., Los Angeles, CA 90038; (213) 467-6272.
HOLLYWOOD NEWSREEL SYNDICATE INC., 1622 N. Gower St., Los Angeles, CA 90028; (213) 469-7307.
HOLLYWOOD SOUND SYSTEMS, 7237 Santa Monica Blvd., West Hollywood, CA 90046; (213) 466-2416.
HOMER & ASSOCIATES, INC., Sunset Gower Studios, 1420 N. Beachwood Dr., Hollywood, CA 90028; (213) 462-4710.
HORIZONTAL EDITING STUDIOS, 2625 W. Olive Ave., Burbank, CA 91505; (818) 841-6750.
INSTITUTE OF AUDIO/VIDEO ENGINEERING, 1831 Hyperion Ave., Hollywood, CA 90027; (213) 666-3003.
INTERLOK STUDIOS, 1522 Crossroads of the World, Hollywood, CA 90028; (213) 469-3986.
INTERMIX, INC., 2505 S. Robertson Blvd., Los Angeles, CA 90034; (213) 870-2121.
INTERSOUND, INC., 8746 Sunset Blvd., Los Angeles, CA 90069; (213) 652-3741.
INTEX AUDIOVISUALS, 9021 Melrose Ave., Suite 205, Los Angeles, CA 90069; (213) 275-9571; FAX: (213) 271-1319.
KEY WEST EDITING, 5701 Buckingham Parkway, Suite C, Culver City, CA 90230; (213) 645-3348.
L.A. STUDIOS INC., 3453 Cahuenga Blvd. W., Burbank, CA 91505; (818) 841-1440; FAX: (818) 841-4659.
LAJON PRODUCTIONS INC. 2907 W. Olive Ave., Burbank, CA 91505; (818) 841-1440.
LION SHARE RECORDING STUDIOS, 8255 Beverly Blvd., Los Angeles, CA 90048; (213) 658-5990.
M.F.I. VIDEO CENTER, 1905 Grace Ave., Hollywood, CA 90068; (213) 851-0373.
MASTER DIGITAL INC., 1749 14th St., Santa Monica, CA 90404; (213) 452-1511.
MEDIA MASTERS PRODUCTIONS, 1800 S. Robertson Blvd., Suite 306, Beverly Hills, CA 90035, (213) 451-8823.
MERIDIAN, P.O. Box 1941, Hollywood, CA 90028; (213) 874-4367.
METAVISION, 347 S. Ogden Dr., Suite 220, Los Angeles, CA 90036; (213) 936-8281.
MODERN VIDEOFILM, 7165 Sunset Blvd., Hollywood, CA 90046; (213) 851-8070; FAX: (213) 851-0704.
MUSIC LAB INC., 1831 Hyperion Ave., Hollywood, CA 90027; (213) 666-3003.
NEWMAN/FRANKS, 2956 Nicada Dr., Los Angeles, CA 90077; (213) 470-0140; 470-0145; FAX: (213) 470-2410.
ONE PASS FILM & VIDEO, One China Basin Building, San Francisco, CA 94107; (415) 777-5777.
PACIFIC VIDEO, 809 N. Cahuenga Blvd., Los Angeles, CA 90038; (213) 462-6266; FAX: (213) 464-3233.
PARAMOUNT RECORDING STUDIOS, 6245 Santa Monica Blvd., Hollywood, CA 90038; (212) 461-3717.
POSITIVE MEDIA, 5422 A. Fair Ave., North Hollywood, CA 91601; (818) 461-0092.
THE POST GROUP, 6335 Homewood Ave., Los Angeles, CA 90028; (213) 462-2300.
POST LOGIC, 6363 Sunset Blvd., Suite 830, Hollywood, CA 90028; (213) 461-7887.
POWERHOUSE AUDIO/VIDEO, 19347 Londelius St., Northridge, CA 91324; (818) 993-4778.
PRO VIDEO/CINETAPE, 801 N. La Brea Ave., Los Angeles, CA 90038; (213) 934-8836.
PRECISION FOLEY & ADR., 6353 Homewood Ave., Hollywood, CA 90028; (213) 462-8235.
PREMORE INC., 5130 Klump Ave., North Hollywood, CA 91601; (818) 506-7714.
RANK VIDEO, 970 W. 190 St., Suite 900, Torrance, CA 90502; (213) 515-6499.
RENCHER'S EDITORIAL SERVICE, 738 Cahuenga Blvd., Hollywood, CA 90038; (213) 463-9836.
ROCK SOLID PRODUCTIONS, 801 S. Main St., Burbank, CA 91506; (818) 841-8220.
ROLAND, GLENN, FILMS, 10711 Wellworth Ave., Los Angeles, CA 90024; (213) 475-0937.
RUBBER DUBBERS, INC., 626 Justin Ave., Glendale, CA 91201; (818) 241-5600.
RUSK SOUND STUDIO, 1556 N. La Brea Ave., Hollywood, CA 90028; (213) 462-6477.
RYDER SOUND SERVICES, INC., 1611 N. Vine St., Los Angeles, CA 90038; (213) 469-3511.
SAR PRODUCTIONS, 22801 Ventura Blvd., Suite 211, Woodland Hills, CA 91364; (818) 884-5646.
SALTY DOG RECORDING STUDIO, 14511 Delano St., Van Nuys, CA 91411; (818) 994-9973.

SCHULMAN VIDEO CENTER, 861 Seward St., Hollywood, CA 90038; (213) 465-8110.
SCOTTSOUND INC., 6110 Santa Monica Blvd., Los Angeles, CA 90038; (213) 462-6981.
SIERRA VIDEO, 11320 Chandler Blvd., N. Hollywood, CA 91601; (818) 506-4984; 579-7045.
SKYLAND SOUND, INC., 4740 Kraft Ave., Studio City, CA 91602; (818) 763-1951.
SOUND CHAMBER, 27 S. El Molino Ave., Pasadena, Ca 91101; (818) 449-8133.
SOUND IMAGE STUDIOS INC., 6556 Wilkinson Ave., North Hollywood, CA 91606; (818) 762-8881.
SOUND MASTER AUDIO/VIDEO, 10747 Magnolia Blvd., North Hollywood, CA 91601; (213) 650-8000.
SOUND SERVICES INC. (S.S.I.), 7155 Santa Monica Blvd., Los Angeles, CA 90046; (213) 874-9344; (818) 986-3255.
THE SOUND SURGEON, 10530 Burbank Blvd., N. Hollywood, CA 91601; (818) 763-6443.
SPALLA, RICK VIDEO PRODUCTIONS, 1622 N. Gower St., Hollywood, CA 90028; (213) 469-7307.
SPLIT REEL RECORDING, 870 N. Vine St., Suite B, Hollywood, CA 90038; (213) 466-3817.
STEVENS, KRIS ENTERPRISES INC., 14241 Ventura Blvd., Suite 204, Sherman Oaks, CA 91423; (818) 981-8255.
STEVENS, SHADOE, INC., 9100 Sunset Blvd., Suite 215, Los Angeles, CA 90069; (213) 274-1244.
SUNSET POST INC., 1813 Victory Blvd., Glendale, CA 91201; (818) 956-7912; FAX: (818) 545-7586.
SUNSET SOUND FACTORY, 6357 Selma Ave., Hollywood, CA 90028; (213) 467-2500.
SUNWEST STUDIOS, 5533 Sunset Blvd., Hollywood, CA 90028; (213) 465-1000.
SYNC, INC., 931 N. Gardner St., W. Hollywood, CA 90046; (213) 851-6624.
TAJ SOUNDWORKS, 8207 W. Third St., Los Angeles, CA 90048; (213) 655-2775.
TAV SOUND INC., 6200 W. 3rd St., Los Angeles, CA 90038; (213) 937-2460.
TODD-AO GLEN GLENN STUDIOS, 900 N. Seward St., Hollywood, CA 90038; (213) 469-7221.
TRACK RECORD, 5102 Vineland Ave., N. Hollywood, CA 91601; (818) 761-0511.
UNITED VIDEO INDUSTRIES INC., 5533 Sunset Blvd., Hollywood, CA 90028; (213) 465-1000.
USA PRODUCTIONS, 1645 Vine St., Suite 350, Hollywood, CA 90028; (213) 465-6320.
VIDCOM ENTERTAINMENT, INC., P.O. Box 2926, Hollywood, CA 90078; (213) 301-8433.
VIDEO ADVENTURES, 1015 Cahuenga Blvd., Hollywood, CA 90038; (213) 461-3288.
VIDEO CIRCUIT STUDIOS, 11440 Chandler Blvd., Studio 1400, N. Hollywood, CA 91601; (818) 506-5493.
THE VIDEO TAPE CO., 10545 Burbank Blvd., North Hollywood, CA 91601; (818) 985-1666.
VIDEO TECHNOLOGY & SERVICES, 500 N. Ventu Park Rd., Newbury Park, CA 91320; (818) 888-3040; (805) 499-5827.
VIDE-U PRODUCTIONS, 612 N. Sepulveda Blvd., Los Angeles, CA 90049; (213) 472-7023.
VILLAGE POST, 1616 Butler Ave., Los Angeles, CA 90025; (213) 478-8227; FAX: (213) 478-2414.
THE VILLAGE RECORDING STUDIOS, 1616 Butler Ave., West Los Angeles, CA 90025; (213) 478-8227.
VISUAL EYES PRODUCTIONS, 2401 Main St., Santa Monica, CA 90405; (213) 392-8300; FAX: (213) 392-7480.
VITELLO & ASSOCIATES, 1612 W. Olive, Suite 203, Burbank, CA 91506; (818) 848-5919.
VOICE OVER L.A. INC., 1717 N. Highland Ave., Suite 620, Hollywood, CA 90028; (213) 463-8652.
WAVES SOUND RECORDERS, 1956 N. Cahuenga Blvd., Hollywood, CA 90068; (213) 466-6141; FAX: (213) 466-3751.
WESTLAKE STUDIOS, 7265 Santa Monica Blvd., Los Angeles, CA 90046; (213) 851-9800; 655-0303.
WESTLAKE STUDIOS A & B, 8447 Beverly Blvd., Los Angeles, CA 90048; (213) 654-2155.
WILLIAM SOUND SERVICE, 1343 N. Highland Ave., Los Angeles, CA 90028; (213) 461-5321.

NEW YORK

AQUARIUS TRANSFORMATION, 12 E. 46 St., New York, NY 10017; (212) 697-3636.
BROADWAY VIDEO, 1619 Broadway, New York, NY 10019; (212) 265-7600; 713-0540.
EDITEL, NEW YORK, 222 E. 44 St., New York, NY 10017; (212) 867-4600.
HOME BASE, 147 W. 24 St., New York, NY 10011; (212) 691-7674.
MAGNO SOUND & VIDEO, 729 Seventh Ave., New York, 10019; (212) 302-2505.
MARKLE, WILLIAM, ASSOCIATES INC., 630 Ninth Ave., Suite 1409, New York, NY 10036; (212) 246-8642.
MEGA MEDIA CENTER, 727 Eleventh Ave., New York, NY 10019; (212) 265-8500.
MODERN TELECOMMUNICATIONS, 1 Dag Hammarskjold Plaza, New York, NY 10017; (212) 355-0510.
NEP PRODUCTIONS, 56 W. 45 St., New York, NY 10036; (212) 382-1100.
NATIONAL RECORDING STUDIOS, 460 W. 42 St., New York, NY 10036; (212) 279-2000.
NEW BREED STUDIOS, 251 W. 30 St., Suite 7RW, New York, NY 10001; (212) 714-9379.
SCHWARTZ, HOWARD M., RECORDING, INC., 420 Lexington Ave., New York, NY 10017; (212) 687-4180.
SOUND SHOP, 321 W. 44 St., New York, NY 10036; (212) 757-7500.
SPALLA, RICK, VIDEO PRODUCTIONS, 301 W. 45 St., New York, NY 10036; (212) 765-4646.
SYNC SOUND INC., 450 W. 56 St., New York, NY 10019; (212) 246-5580.
SYNESTHETICS, INC., 58 Walker St., New York, NY 10013; (212) 431-4112.
VCA/TELETRONICS, 231 E. 55 St., New York, NY 10022; (212) 355-1600.

Videotape Cleaning & Evaluation

LOS ANGELES

CALIFORNIA VIDEO CENTER, 5432 W. 102 St., Los Angeles, CA 90045; (213) 216-5400; FAX: (213) 216-5498.

CREATIVE VIDEO SERVICES, 500 Ventu Park Rd., Newbury Park, CA 91320; (818) 888-3040.

THE EDITING COMPANY, 8308 Beverly Blvd., Los Angeles, CA 90048; (213) 653-3570.

FILM ARTISTS ASSOCIATES, 470 S. San Vicente Blvd., Suite 104, Los Angeles, CA 90048; (213) 651-1700.

FILM PROCESSING CORP., 3602 S. Crenshaw Blvd., Los Angeles, CA 90016; (213) 737-8273.

GRACE & WILD STUDIOS HOLLYWOOD, 3501 Cahuenga Blvd. West, Los Angeles, CA 90068; (213) 876-8008; FAX: (213) 876-0460.

IMAGE TRANSFORM INC., 4142 Lankershim Blvd., North Hollywood, CA 91602; (818) 985-7566.

INTER VIDEO, 733 N. Victory Blvd., Burbank, CA 91502; (818) 843-3633; 843-2288.

MAJESTIC DUPLICATING & VIDEO SERVICE, 1208 W. Isabel St., Burbank, CA 91506; (213) 849-1535; (818) 843-1806.

MODERN VIDEOFILM, 7165 Sunset Blvd., Hollywood, CA 90046; (213) 851-8070; FAX: (213) 851-0704.

SOUND MASTER AUDIO/VIDEO, 10747 Magnolia Blvd., North Hollywood, CA 91601; (213) 650-8000.

STUDIO FILM & TAPE INC. 6674 Santa Monica Blvd., Los Angeles, CA 90038; (213) 466-8101; (800) 824-3130.

THE VIDEO TAPE CO., 10545 Burbank Blvd., North Hollywood, CA 91601; (818) 985-1666.

NEW YORK

BROADWAY VIDEO, 1619 Broadway, New York, NY 10019; (212) 265-7600; 713-0540.

EDITEL NEW YORK, 222 E. 44 St., New York, NY 10017; (212) 867-4600.

MTI TV CITY, 1443 Park Ave., New York, NY 10029; (212) 722-1818.

MAGNO SOUND & VIDEO, 729 Seventh Ave., New York, NY 10019; (212) 302-2505; FAX: (212) 819-1282.

MODERN TELECOMMUNICATIONS, 1 Dag Hammarskjold Plaza, New York, NY 10017; (212) 355-0510.

P.A.T. FILM SERVICES, 630 Ninth Ave., New York, NY 10036; (212) 247-0900.

ROSENBERG, WARREN, VIDEO SERVICE INC., 308 E. 79 St., Suite 17A, New York, NY 10021; (212) 744-1111.

VCA/TELETRONICS, 231 E. 55 St., New York, NY 10022; (212) 355-1600.

VIDEO RESOURCES NEW YORK INC., 220 W. 71st, New York, NY 10023; (212) 724-7055.

Videotape Duplication Service

LOS ANGELES

A.M.E. INC., 1133 N. Hollywood Way, Burbank, CA 91505; (818) 841-7440.
AT&T RECORDING, 501 N. Larchmont Blvd., Los Angeles, CA 90004; (213) 466-7756.
ABBEY TAPE DUPLICATORS INC., 9525 Vassar Ave., Chatsworth, CA 91311; (818) 882-5210.
ABERDEEN VIDEO, 3349 Cahuenga Blvd. W., Suite 1A, Los Angeles, CA 90068; (213) 874-3050.
ADVANCED VIDEO INC., 6753 Santa Monica Blvd., Los Angeles, CA 90038; (213) 469-0707.
ADVANCED VIDEO TECHNOLOGIES, INC., 9562 Topanga Canyon Blvd., Chatsworth, CA 91311; (213) 463-4220; (818) 718-1270.
ALPHA STUDIOS VIDEO INC., 4720 W. Magnolia Blvd., Burbank, CA 91505; (818) 760-2825.
ALTAVIDEO, 3501 Cahuenga Blvd. W., Los Angeles, CA 90068; (213) 876-8008.
AMERICAN VIDEO FACTORY, 4150 Glencoe Ave., Marina Del Rey, CA 90292; (213) 823-8622; (800) 367-8433.
AMERICAN VIDEOGRAM, INC., 12020 W. Pico Blvd., Los Angeles, CA 90064; (213) 477-1535; 477-1536.
AMETRON RENTALS, 1200 N. Vine St., Hollywood, CA 90038; (213) 466-4321.
ANDERSON, HOWARD A. & COMPANY, 1016 N. Cole Ave., Los Angeles, CA 90038; (213) 463-2336.
APOLLO VIDEO FACILITY, 1503 Cahuenga Blvd., Hollywood, CA 90028, (213) 464-7871.
AUDIO ARTS PUBLISHING CO., 5617 Melrose Ave., Los Angeles, CA 90038; (213) 461-3507.
AUDIO GRAPHIC FILMS AND VIDEO, 6509 De Longpre Ave., Hollywood, CA 90028, (213) 462-6596; (213) 467-1234.
AUDIO PLUS VIDEO INTERNATIONAL INC., 1438 N. Gower St., Hollywood, CA 90028; (213) 856-0152.
AUDIO-VIDEO CRAFT INC., 6753 Santa Monica Blvd., Los Angeles, CA 90038; (213) 655-3511.
AUDIO VISUAL HEADQUARTERS CORP., 361 N. Oak St., Inglewood, CA 90302; (213) 419-4040.
BEVERLY HILLS VIDEOCENTRE, 145 S. Beverly Dr., Beverly Hills, CA 90212; (213) 550-1092.
BOSUSTOW VIDEO, 3030 Pennsylvania Ave., Santa Monica, CA 90404; (213) 453-7973.
BROADCAST STANDARDS, INC., 2044 Cotner Ave., Los Angeles, CA 90025; (213) 312-9060; FAX: (213) 479-5771.
BURBANK PRODUCTION PLAZA, 801 S. Main St., Burbank, CA 91506; (818) 846-7677; 958-8842.
CAL VISTA INTERNATIONAL LTD., 6649 Odessa Ave., Van Nuys, CA 91406; (818) 780-9000; 780-7100; FAX: (818) 997-3064.
CALIFORNIA VIDEO CENTER, 5432 W. 102 St., Los Angeles, CA 90045; (213) 216-5400; FAX: (213) 216-5498.
CENTURY SOUTHWEST PRODUCTIONS, 2939 Nebraska Ave., Santa Monica, CA 90404; (213) 859-5111; 829-7624.
CINEMA GROUP ENTERTAINMENT, 1875 Century Park East, Los Angeles, CA 90067; (213) 785-3100; (800) 821-3427.
CLOCKWORK WINDOW DUBS., 6438 Nancy St., Los Angeles, CA 90045; (213) 215-0114.
COAST FILM LAB CO., 837 N. Cahuenga Blvd., Los Angeles, CA 90038; (213) 464-7293.
COMPACT VIDEO SERVICES INC., 2813 W. Alameda Ave., Burbank, CA 91505; (818) 840-7000.
COMPLETE POST, INC., 6087 Sunset Blvd., Hollywood, CA 90028; (213) 467-1244.
COMPOSITE IMAGE SYSTEMS, 815 N. Cahuenga Blvd., Hollywood, CA 90038; (213) 461-5734.
THE COMPLEX, 2323 Corinth St., Los Angeles, CA 90064; (213) 477-1938.
COMTEL, 2201 N. Hollywood Way, Burbank, CA 91505; (213) 849-6701; (818) 846-0770; 3152 E. La Palma, Suite D, Anaheim, CA 92806; (714) 630-4470; 7524 Clairmont Mesa Blvd., San Diego, CA 92111; (619) 292-1090.
CONSOLIDATED FILM INDUSTRIES, 959 Seward St., Los Angeles, CA 90038; (213) 960-7500; 462-3161.
THE CREATIVE PARTNERSHIP, INC., 7525 Fountain Ave., Hollywood, CA 90046; (213) 850-5551; FAX: (213) 850-0391.
CREATIVE SOUND CORPORATION, 6290 Sunset Blvd., Suite 1026, Hollywood, CA 90028; (213) 871-1010; 871-0806.
CREST NATIONAL FILM & VIDEOTAPE LABS, 1000 N. Highland Ave., Los Angeles, CA 90038; (213) 466-0624.
CUSTOM DUPLICATION INC., 3404 Century Blvd., Inglewood, CA 90303; (213) 776-4810.
DSR PRODUCTIONS, 607 64 Ave., Los Angeles, CA 90042; (213) 258-6741.
DELUXE LABORATORIES, INC., 1377 N. Serrano Ave., Hollywood, CA 90027; (213) 462-6171; (800) 233-5893.
DEVONSHIRE SOUND STUDIOS, 10729 Magnolia Blvd., North Hollywood, CA 91601; (818) 985-1945.
DUBS, INC., 6360 DeLongpre Ave., Hollywood, CA 90028; (213) 461-3726; FAX: (213) 466-7406.
DUPLITAPE, 15016 Ventura Blvd., Suite 1, Sherman Oaks, CA 91403; (818) 501-7370.
EDITEL LOS ANGELES, 729 N. Highland Ave., Hollywood, CA 90038; (213) 931-1821.
THE EDITING COMPANY, 8308 Beverly Blvd., Los Angeles, CA 90048; (213) 653-3570.
EMC PRODUCTIONS, 6855 Santa Monica Blvd., Suite 308, Hollywood, CA 90038; (213) 463-3282.
ENVIRONMENTAL VIDEO INC., P.O. Box 577, Manhattan Beach, CA 90266; (213) 546-4581.
FILM TECHNOLOGY CO., 6900 Santa Monica Blvd., Hollywood, CA 90038; (213) 464-3456.
FILMCORE PRINT AND TAPE, 901 N. Seward St., Los Angeles, CA 90038; (213) 464-7303; 464-8600.
FOTO-KEM/FOTO TRONICS FILM-VIDEO LAB, 2800 W. Olive Ave., Burbank, CA 91505; (818) 846-3101; FAX: (818) 841-2040.
FOX TAPE, 5746 Sunset Blvd., Los Angeles, CA 90028; (213) 856-1000.
G & B VIDEO LAB, 255 E. Colorado Blvd., Pasadena, CA 91101; (818) 440-1909
GLEN-WARREN PRODUCTION, LTD., 9911 W. Pico Blvd., Los Angeles, CA 90035; (213) 553-9233.
GLOBAL VISION CORPORATION, 3255 Cahuenga Blvd., Hollywood, CA 90068; (213) 851-1190.
GOLDEN WEST VIDEOTAPE, 5800 Sunset Blvd., Los Angeles, CA 90028; (213) 460-8989.
GRACE & WILD STUDIOS HOLLYWOOD, 3501 Cahuenga Blvd. W., Los Angeles, CA 90068; (213) 876-8008; FAX: (213) 876-0460.
H.C.V., 3034 Glendale Blvd., Los Angeles, CA 90039; (213) 662-1112.
HOLLYWOOD NEWSREEL SYNDICATE INC., 1622 N. Gower St., Los Angeles, CA 90028; (213) 469-7307.
HORIZONTAL EDITING STUDIOS, 2625 W. Olive Ave., Burbank, CA 91505; (818) 841-6750.
IMAGE TRANSFORM INC., 4142 Lankershim Blvd., North Hollywood, CA 91602; (818) 985-7566; (800) 423-2652.
IMAGE TRANSFORM LABORATORY, 3611 N. San Fernando Rd., Burbank, CA 91505; (818) 841-3812.
IMAGE WEST, 11846 Ventura Blvd., Studio City, CA 91604; (818) 506-5577.
IMMEDIATO, JEFFREY, & ASSOCIATES, P.O. Box 5611, Long Beach, CA 90805; (213) 422-9295.
INSTANT REPLAY COMMUNICATIONS CO., 11122 W. Washington Blvd., Culver City, CA 90232; (213) 870-1231; 5520 Westlawn Ave., Los Angeles, CA; (213) 870-9435.
INTER VIDEO/TRITRONICS, INC., 733 N. Victory Blvd., Burbank, CA 91502; (818) 843-3633, 569-4000.
INTERNATIONAL VIDEO CONVERSIONS, 815 N. Cahuenga Blvd., Hollywood, CA 90038; (213) 463-7884.
INTERNATIONAL VIDEO ENTERTAINMENT, INC., 500 N. Ventu Park Rd., P.O. Box 2520, Newbury Park, CA 91320; (805) 499-5827; FAX: (805) 498-3852.
INTERSOUND, 8746 Sunset Blvd., Los Angeles, CA 90069; (213) 652-3741.
J.P. VIDEO SERVICES, 9538 W. Pico Blvd., Los Angeles, CA 90035; (213) 271-1209, 859-9903.
JONES, TYLIE/WEST, 3519 W. Pacific Ave., Burbank, CA 91505; (818) 955-7600.
KWHY-TV, CHANNEL 22, 5545 Sunset Blvd., Los Angeles, CA 90028; (213) 466-5441.
KAPPA VIDEO, 801 S. Main St., Burbank, CA 91506; (818) 843-3400; 843-8099.
LP PRODUCTIONS, 223 Strand St., Suite K, Santa Monica, CA 90405; (213) 399-1101; (714) 857-1310.
LEVIN, KARL M., 20959 Elkwood St., Los Angeles, CA 91304; (818) 882-7262.
LIMELIGHT VIDEO WEST, 6464 Sunset Blvd., Hollywood, CA 90028; (213) 856-8530; (800) 634-5024.
LION SHARE RECORDING STUDIOS, 8255 Beverly Blvd., Los Angeles, CA 90048; (213) 658-5990.
LIONEL TELEVISION PRODUCTIONS, 417 Colorado Ave., Santa Monica, CA 90401; (213) 394-9697.

MFI VIDEO CENTER, 1905 Grace Ave., Hollywood, CA 90068; (213) 851-0373.
MGS SERVICES, 10507 Burbank Blvd., North Hollywood, CA 91601; (818) 508-5488; FAX: (818) 508-5493.
MACROVISION, 10201 Torre Ave., Suite 330, Cupertino, CA 95014; (408) 252-9600.
MAJESTIC DUPLICATION & VIDEO SERVICE, 1208 W. Isabel St., Burbank, CA 91506; (213) 849-1535; (818) 843-1806.
MANSFIELD STUDIOS, 1041 N. Mansfield Ave., Hollywood, CA 90038; (213) 461-9457; 461-3393.
MASTER DIGITAL INC., 1749 14th St., Santa Monica, CA 90404; (213) 452-1511.
McINTIRE-HOFFMAN, INC., (Jamar Productions), 11969 Ventura Blvd., Studio City, CA 91604; (818) 762-2077.
McKAY, CAMERON PRODUCTIONS, 6311 Romaine,, Los Angeles, CA 90038; (213) 463-6073.
MEDIA HOME ENTERTAINMENT INC., 5730 Buckingham Pkway, Culver City, CA 90230; (213) 216-7900; FAX: (213) 216-9305.
MEDIATECH WEST, 1640 N. Gower St., Hollywood, CA 90028; (213) 466-6442.
MIDTOWN VIDEO, 8489 W. Third St., Suite 1065, Los Angeles, CA 90048; (213) 651-2420.
MODERN VIDEOFILM, 7165 Sunset Blvd., Hollywood, CA 90046; (213) 851-8070.
MORRIS VIDEO INC., 2730 Monterey St., Suite 105, Torrance, CA 90503; (213) 533-4800.
MUSIC LAB INC., 1831 Hyperion Ave., Hollywood, CA 90027; (213) 666-3003.
NEWMAN/FRANKS, 2956 Nicarda Dr., Los Angeles, CA 90077; (213) 470-0140; 470-0145.
ORION ENTERPRISES, INC., 1015 N. Cahuenga Blvd., Los Angeles, CA 90038; (213) 461-3844; FAX: (213) 461-2958.
PACIFIC VIDEO LAB. INC., 5224 Santa Monica Blvd., Los Angeles, CA 90029; (213) 661-1144.
PAL VIDEO, 19061 Tina Pl., Tarzana, CA 91356; (818) 344-1603.
POSITIVE MEDIA, 5422 A Fair Ave., North Hollywood, CA 91601; (818) 761-5192.
THE POST GROUP, 6335 Homewood Ave., Los Angeles, CA 90028; (213) 462-2300.
POST PLUS INCORPORATED, 6650 Santa Monica Blvd., Hollywood, CA 90038; (213) 463-7108.
PROFESSIONAL ARTISTS GROUP, 845 N. Highland Ave., Hollywood, CA 90038; (213) 871-2222.
PROJECT ONE, 6669 Sunset Blvd., Hollywood, CA 90028; (213) 464-2285.
QUIK VIDEO COPIES, 11394 Ventura Blvd., Studio City, CA 91604; (818) 509-9316.
R. PRODUCTIONS & VIDEO EVENTS, 1741 N. Ivar, Suite 210, Hollywood, CA 90028; (213) 465-4197.
RANK VIDEO, 500 N. Ventu Park Rd., Newbury Park, CA 91320; (805) 499-5827; 970 W. 190 St., Suite 900, Torrance, CA 90502; (213) 515-6499.
RAZ VIDEO PRODUCTIONS, 1828 E. Walnut St., Pasadena, CA 91107; (818) 449-1175.
RED CAR EDITING, 1040 N. Las Palmas Ave., Los Angeles, CA 90038; (213) 466-4467; FAX: (213) 466-4925.
REEL TIME DUPLICATORS, INC., 801 S. Main St., Burbank, CA 91506; (818) 849-1823.
RENCHER'S JOY EDITORIAL SERVICE, 738 Cahuenga Blvd., Hollywood, CA 90038; (213) 463-9836.
ROLLING VIDEO, 18730 Oxnard, Tarzana, CA 91356; (818) 993-6912.
RUSK SOUND STUDIO, 1556 N. La Brea Ave., Hollywood, CA 90028; (213) 462-6477.
SCHULMAN VIDEO CENTER, 861 Seward St., Hollywood, CA 90038; (213) 465-8110.
SCREENMUSIC, 11700 Ventura Blvd., Studio City, CA 91604; (213) 877-0300; (818) 985-0900.
SELL PICTURES INC., 9701 Wilshire Blvd., Beverly Hills, CA 90212; (213) 874-5402.
SIERRA VIDEO (Diversified Video Industries, Inc.), 11320 Chandler, N. Hollywood, CA 91601; (818) 506-4984; 579-7045.
SKYLIGHT PRODUCTIONS INC., 6815 W. Willoughby, Suite 201, Los Angeles, CA 90038; (213) 464-4500; FAX: (213) 463-1884.
SOUND MASTER AUDIO/VIDEO, 10747 Magnolia Blvd., North Hollywood, CA 91601; (213) 650-8000.
SOUND SERVICES, INC. (S.S.I.), 7155 Santa Monica Blvd., Los Angeles, CA 90046; (213) 874-9344.
SOUTHLAND VIDEO, 3255 Cahuenga Blvd., Hollywood, CA 90068; (213) 851-1190.
SPALLA, RICK VIDEO PRODUCTIONS, 1622 N. Gower, Los Angeles, CA 90028; (213) 469-7307.
STAGE FRIGHT PRODUCTIONS, 8817 Amboy Ave., Sun Valley, CA 91352; (818) 768-3333.
STEVENS, KRIS ENTERPRISES INC., 14241 Ventura Blvd., Suite 204, Sherman Oaks, CA 91423; (818) 981-8255; FAX: (818) 990-4350.
SUNSET POST INC., 1813 Victory Blvd., Glendale, CA 91201; (818) 956-7912; FAX: (818) 545-7586.
SUNSHINE COMMUNICATIONS, 565 N. Gower St., Hollywood, CA 90004; (213) 464-6652.
SUPERCINE INC., 2214 W. Olive Ave., Burbank, CA 91506; (818) 843-8260.
TAPE-FILM INDUSTRIES (TFI), 941 N. Highland Ave., Hollywood, CA 90038; (213) 461-3361.
TELE VIDICS, 2223 E. 223rd St., Long Beach, CA 90810; (213) 830-5296.
TELEPRINT OF LOS ANGELES, 3779 Cahuenga Blvd., West, Studio City, CA 91604; (818) 760-3191.
TRANS-AMERICAN VIDEO INC., 1541 N. Vine St., Los Angeles, CA 90028; (213) 466-2141.
TRANSWORLD VIDEO LAB INC., 1811 W. Magnolia Blvd., Burbank, CA 91506; (818) 841-2416.
UCL VIDEO, 823 N. Seward St., Los Angeles, CA 90038; (213) 469-7291.
UDELL, BILL PRODUCTIONS, 6006 Vantage Ave., North Hollywood, CA 91606; (818) 985-6866.
UNITED AMERICAN VIDEO CORP., 279 S. Beverly Dr., P.O. Box 1031, Beverly Hills, CA 90212; (213) 859-1958; (800) 345-6782.
UNITED COLOR LAB, INC., 835 N. Seward St., Hollywood, CA 90038; (213) 461-9921; 469-7291.
UNITEL VIDEO, 5555 Melrose Ave., Studio G, Los Angeles, CA 90038; (213) 468-4606.
VCI DUPLICATION, 915 Hollywood Way, Burbank, CA 91505; (818) 650-8550.
V.M.G. INC, 16042 Ventura Blvd., Suite 206, Encino, CA 91426; (818) 905-5311.
VIDEO ADVENTURES INC., 1015 Cahuenga Blvd., Hollywood, CA 90038; (213) 461-3288.
VIDEO CIRCUIT STUDIOS, 11440 Chandler Blvd., Studio 1400, N. Hollywood, CA 91601; (818) 506-5493.
VIDEO CRAFTSMEN INC., 6311 Romaine St., Los Angeles, CA 90038; (213) 464-4351.
VIDEO-IT INC., 5000 Overland Ave., Suite 6, Culver City, CA 90232; (213) 280-0505; (818) VID-EOIT.
THE VIDEO TAPE CO., 10545 Burbank Blvd., North Hollywood, CA 91601; (818) 985-1666; 753-3051; FAX: (818) 985-0614.
VIDEO TAPE TRANSFER LABS, 450 S. Central Ave., Glendale, CA 91204; (818) 956-1669.
VIDEO TRANSITIONS, 910 N. Citrus Ave., Hollywood, CA 90038; (213) 465-3333; FAX: (213) 4631VTI.
VIDEO VISION, 9100 Sunset Blvd., Suite 350, Los Angeles, CA 90069; (213) 278-4875.
VIDEO WEST, 805 Larrabee St., W. Hollywood, CA 90069; (213) 659-5762
VID-FILM SERVICES, 1631 Gardena Ave., Glendale, CA 91204; (818) 500-9090; (213) 650-8550; FAX: (818) 500-4099.
VIDE-U PRODUCTIONS, 612 N. Sepulveda Blvd., Los Angeles, CA 90049; (213) 472-7023.
WEISBARTH, JACOB & ASSOC. INC., 9903 Santa Monica Blvd., Suite 256, Beverly Hills, CA 90212; (213) 277-9616.
WESTERN FILM INDUSTRIES, 30941 W. Agoura Rd., Suite 302, Westlake Village, CA 91361; (818) 889-7350; FAX: (818) 707-3937.
WILDER BROTHERS VIDEO, 10327 Santa Monica Blvd., Los Angeles, CA 90025; (213) 557-3500.
WOLD COMMUNICATIONS, 3415 S. Sepulveda Blvd., Suite 500, Los Angeles, CA 90034; (212) 390-5455; 6290 Sunset Blvd., Suite 1600, Hollywood, CA 90028; (213) 960-2250.

NEW YORK

A N S INTERNATIONAL VIDEO LTD., 396 Fifth Ave., New York, NY 10018; (212) 736-1007.
AVPS CORP., 31 W. 60 St., New York, NY 10023-7901; (212) 765-5060.
ACE AUDIO VISUAL CO., 13 E. 31 St., New York, NY 10016; (212) 685-3344; 33-49 55th St., Woodside, NY; (718) 458-3800.
ALL STAR FILM TO VIDEO, 251 W. 30 St., New York, NY 10001; (212) 594-2778.
AMERICAN VIDEO—CHANNELS INC., 321 W. 44 St., New York, NY 10036; (212) 765-6324.
ANIMATED VIDEO, INC., 1600 Broadway, New York, NY 10019; (212) 265-2942.
AQUARIUS TRANSFER, 12 E. 46 St., New York, NY 10017; (212) 697-3636.
BOGAZICI VIDEO LTD., 460 Seventh Ave., New York, NY 10001; (212) 563-9022.
BOMBAY BROADCASTING NETWORK, 1697 Broadway, Suite 304, New York, NY 10019; (212) 977-7700.
BROADWAY VIDEO, 1619 Broadway, New York, NY 10019; (212) 265-7600; 713-0540.
BROWN, TONY PRODUCTIONS, 721 Eleventh Ave., New York, NY 10019; (212) 247-4545.
C & C VISUAL, 225 W. 44 St., New York, NY 10036; (212) 869-4900.

CALAMAR PRODUCTIONS, 38 Greene St., New York, NY 10013; (212) 334-4952.
CHROMAVISION, 119 W. 22nd St., New York, NY 10011; (212) 463-8997.
CINE MAGNETICS FILM & VIDEO LABORATORIES, 50 W. 40 St., New York, NY 10018; (212) 542-0700.
DEVLIN VIDEO SERVICE, 1501 Broadway, Suite 408, New York, NY 10036; (212) 391-1313.
DU ART VIDEO, 245 W. 55 St., New York, NY 10019; (212) 757-3681.
EMC, 10 E. 39 St., New York, NY 10016; (212) 689-1259.
EDITEL, NEW YORK, 222 E. 44 St., New York, NY 10017; (212) 867-4600.
EDITING CONCEPTS PRINTS, INC., 216 E. 45 St., New York, NY 10017; (212) 557-4949.
FAMA II PRODUCTIONS, 2750 Richmond Terrace, Staten Island, NY 10303; (718) 273-1780.
FIRST TAKE PRODUCTIONS, 250 W. 78 St., New York, NY 10024; (212) 496-7405.
FOTO-VIDEO TRANSFER CENTER, 1 Times Square, New York, NY 10036; (212) 302-1866.
GHA FILM & TAPE, 1170 Broadway, New York, NY 10001; (212) 683-6304.
GLOBE VIDEO SERVICES, INC., 286 Fifth Ave., New York, NY 10001; (212) 695-6868.
HBO STUDIO PRODUCTIONS, 120-A E. 23 St., New York, NY 10010; (212) 512-7800.
HALLENDAL ENTERPRIZES, 15 W. 28 St., New York, NY 10010; (212) 481-1568.
INTERNATIONAL DUPLICATION CENTRE, INC., 321 W. 44 St., Suite 908, New York, NY 10036; (212) 581-3940; FAX: (212) 581-3979.
INTERNATIONAL PRODUCTION CENTER, 514 W. 57 St., New York, NY 10019; (212) 582-6530.
INTERNATIONAL VIDEO SERVICES, 1501 Broadway, New York, NY 10036; (212) 730-1411.
JSL VIDEO SERVICES, INC., 25 W. 45 St., New York, NY 10036; (212) JSL-5082.
JVL VIDEO DUPLICATION CENTER, 504 E. 74 St., New York, NY 10028; (212) 737-7477.
JONES, TYLIE, EAST, 248 E. 48 St., New York, NY 10017; (212) 753-9015.
LRP VIDEO, 3 Dag Hammarskjold Plaza, New York, NY 10017; (212) 759-0822.
LANDY VISION, INC., 400 E. 83 St., New York, NY 10028; (212) 734-1402.
MPCS VIDEO INDUSTRIES, 514 W. 57 St., New York, NY 10019; (212) 586-3690.
MTI TV CITY, 1443 Park Ave., New York, NY 10029; (212) 722-1818.
MAGNO SOUND & VIDEO, 729 Seventh Ave., New York, NY 10019; (212) 302-2505.
MEDIATECH EAST, 216 W. 18th St., New York, NY 10011; (212) 463-8300.
MODERN TELECOMMUNICATIONS INC., 1 Dag Hammarskjold Plaza, Level C, New York, NY 10017; (212) 355-0510.
MOONLIGHT VIDEO COMMUNICATIONS, INC., 1600 Broadway, 7th Floor, New York, NY 10019; (212) 245-6630.
MOVIE LAB VIDEO, INC., 619 W. 54 St., New York, NY 10019; (212) 586-0360; 956-3900.
NATIONAL VIDEO CENTER, 460 W. 42 St., New York, NY 10036; (212) 279-2000.
NATIONAL VIDEO INDUSTRIES, INC., 15 W. 17 St., New York, NY 10011; (212) 691-1300.
OCCASIONAL VIDEO, 534 E. 84 St., New York, NY 10028; (212) 737-3058.
P.A.T. FILM SERVICES, 630 Ninth Ave., New York, NY 10036; (212) 247-0900.
PDR PRODUCTIONS, INC., 219 E. 44 St., New York, NY 10017; (212) 986-2020.
PELCO PRINTS, INC., 757 Third Ave., New York, NY 10017; (212) 319-3348.
PICSONIC PRODUCTIONS CORP., 25 W. 45 St., New York, NY 10036; (212) 575-1910.
RAFIK, 814 Broadway, New York, NY 10001; (212) 475-7884.
REILLY VIDEO COMMUNICATIONS, 508 W. 26th St., New York, NY 10001; (212) 924-4880.
ROSENBERG, WARREN, VIDEO SERVICES, INC., 308 E. 79 St., New York, NY 10021; (212) 744-1111.
ROSS-LEVINE, 594 Broadway, New York, NY 10003; (212) 925-2020.
SPALLA, RICK, VIDEO PRODUCTIONS, 301 W. 45 St., New York, NY 10036; (212) 765-4646.
TFI, TAPE-FILM INDUSTRIES, 619 W. 54 St., New York, NY 10019, (212) 708-0500. Branches: L.A., 640 N. La Salle St., Chicago, IL 60610; (312) 957-6700.
TABCO FILM & VIDEO SERVICES, 850 Seventh Ave., New York, NY 10019; (212) 315-3880.
TELETECHNIQUES, 1 W. 19 St., New York, NY 10011; (212) 206-1475; 633-1868.
IIIDB VIDEO SPECIALISTS, INC., 121 E. 24 St., New York, NY 10010; (212) 677-6856.
TODAY VIDEO, INC., 45 W. 45 St., New York, NY 10036; (212) 391-1020.
UNITEL VIDEO, 515 W. 57 St., New York, NY 10019; (212) 265-3600; FAX: (212) 765-5801.
VCA TELETRONICS, 231 E. 55 St., New York, NY 10022; (212) 355-1600.
VIDEO CASSETTE TRANSFERS, 1501 Broadway, Suite 406, New York, NY 10036; (212) 575-8433.
VIDEO CENTRAL INC., 225 W. 36 St., New York, NY 10018; (212) 947-6960.
VIDEO DUB, INC., 423 W. 55 St., New York, NY 10019; (212) 757-3300.
VIDEO PLANNING INC., 250 W. 57 St., New York, NY 10019; (212) 582-5066.
VIDEO PORTFOLIOS, 142 W. 24 St., New York, NY 10011; (212) 989-3858.
VIDEO RESOURCES NEW YORK, INC., 220 W. 71 St., New York, NY 10023; (212) 724-7055.
VIDEO TRANSFERS INC., 1501 Broadway, Suite 406, New York, NY 10036; (212) 575-8433.
VIDEOLAB, 149 Fifth Ave., New York, NY 10010; (212) 979-7500; FAX: (212) 477-5132.
VIDEOROOM, 1487 Third Ave., New York, NY 10028; (212) 879-5333.
VIDEOWORKS, 24 W. 40 St., New York, NY 10018; (212) 869-2500.
VIDLO VIDEO, 40 E. 21 St., New York, NY 10010; (212) 475-4140.
WAVE VIDEO SERVICES, 2 E. 37 St., New York, NY 10016; (212) 685-8331.
WINDSOR VIDEO, 8 W. 38 St., New York, NY 10018; (212) 944-9090.
WINKLER VIDEO DUPLICATION, 248 E. 48 St., New York, NY 10017-1598; (212) 753-9300; 5801 Westside Ave., No. Bergen, NJ 07047; (201) 861-6500.

CALIFORNIA

ADVANCE RECORDING PRODUCTS, 7190 Clairemont Mesa Blvd., San Diego, CA 92111; (619) 277-2540.
CAL IMAGE, 3034 Gold Canal Dr., #B, Rancho Cordova, CA 95670; (916) 638-8383.
CARROL FILM & VIDEO, INC., 3535 Ross Ave., Bldg. II, Suite 205, San Jose, Ca 91524; (408) 978-2784.
INTERFACE PRODUCTIONS, 1534 Vallejo St., San Francisco, CA 94109; (415) 673-5946.
TELEVISION ASSOCIATES, INC., 2410 Charleston Rd., Mountain View, CA; (415) 967-6040.
WEST COAST DUPLICATING, INC., 330 Townsend St., San Francisco, CA 94107; (415) 543-2810.

CONNECTICUT

E.C.A. STUDIO, 149 Dudley Rd., Wilton, CT 06897; (203) 762-3380; 221 W. 57 St., New York, NY 10019; (212) 333-5656.
IMAGE PRODUCTIONS INC., 50 Water St., South Norwalk, CT 06854; (203) 853-3486.

ILLINOIS

AV CENTER, 5153 N. Lincoln Ave., Chicago, IL 60625; (312) 275-7098.
CINEMA VIDEO CENTER, INC., 211 E. Grand Ave., Chicago, IL 60611; (312) 644-1650.
MEDIATECH INC., 110 W. Hubbard St., Chicago, IL 60610; (312) 828-1146.
POLYCOM TELEPRODUCTIONS, 142 E. Ontario, Chicago, IL 60611; (312) 337-6000.
TFI (Tape Film Industries), 640 N. LaSalle St., #275, Chicago, IL 60610; (312) 951-6700.

MICHIGAN

PREMIERE VIDEO, INC., 35687 Industrial Rd., Livonia, MI 48150; (313) 464-4650.
PRODUCERS COLOR SERVICE INC., 24242 Northwestern Highway, Southfield, MI 48075; (313) 352-5353; (800) 727-8700.

PENNSYLVANIA

CENTER CITY VIDEO INC., 1503 Walnut St., Philadelphia, PA 19102; (215) 568-4134.
FILMMAKERS OF PHILADELPHIA, 725 N. 24 St., Philadelphia, PA 19130; (215) 763-3400.

INSTANT REPLAY, 2839 Tyson Ave., Philadelphia, PA 19149; (215) 624-2666.
LAIRD PRODUCTIONS, INC., 2153 Market St., Camp Hill, PA 17011; (717) 737-1556.
MEDIA CONCEPTS, 331 N. Broad St., Philadelphia, PA 19107; (215) 923-2545.
WRS MOTION PICTURE & VIDEO LAB, 210 Semple St., Pittsburgh, PA 15213; (412) 687-3700.

WASHINGTON

TELEMATION PRODUCTIONS, INC., 1200 Stewart St., Seattle, WA 98101; (206) 623-5934.
VIDEO PRESENTATIONS, 2326 Sixth Ave., Room 230, Seattle, WA 98121; (206) 728-9241.

CANADA

ASHLAND VIDEO CORP., 65 Heward Ave., #108, Toronto M4M 2T5; (416) 466-3214; 466-3522.
BELLEVUE PATHE QUEBEC VIDEO DUPLICATION CENTER, 5588 Cote de Liesse, Montreal, Que., H4P 1A9; (514) 737-2777.
CARLTON PRODUCTIONS INC., 1500 Merivale Rd., Nepean K2E 625; (613) 224-1313.
INSIGHT PRODUCTIONS, LTD., 1249 Howe St., Vancouver V6Z lR3, (604) 688-1257.
MANTA VIDEO LABS, 311 Adelaide St. E., Toronto, Ont., M5A IN2; (416) 863-9316.
PATHÉ VIDEO INC., 720 King St. W., Toronto, Ont., M5V 2T3;, (416) 364-6720.

Videotape Editing & Post Production Facilities and Services

CALIFORNIA

—A—

AGV ENTERPRISES, 6290 Sunset Blvd., Los Angeles, CA 90028; (213) 463-3301.

A.M.E. Inc., 1133 N. Hollywood Way, Burbank, CA 91505; (818) 841-7440.

AARON & LE DUC VIDEO PRODUCTION, 2002 21 St., Suite A, Santa Monica, CA 90404; (213) 450-8275.

ABERDEEN VIDEO, 3349 Cahuenga Blvd. West, Suite 1A, Los Angeles, CA 90068; (213) 874-3050.

ACTION VIDEO, 6616 Lexington Ave., Hollywood, CA 90038; (213) 461-3611; FAX: (213) 460-4033.

ADVANCED VIDEO, 6753 Santa Monica Blvd., Hollywood, CA 90038; (213) 469-0707.

ADVENTIST MEDIA PRODUCTIONS, 1100 Rancho Conejo Blvd., Newbury Park, CA 91320; (805) 373-7771; 373-7777.

ADVENTURES IN FILM & TAPE, 1034 N. Seward, Hollywood, CA 90038; (213) 460-4557.

ALL SEASONS ENTERTAINMENT, 18121 Napa St., Northridge, CA 91325; (818) 886-8680; (800) 423-5599.

ALPHA CINE LABORATORY, INC., 5724 W. Third St., Suite 311, Los Angeles, CA 90036; (213) 934-7793; FAX: (213) 934-6307.

ALPHA STUDIOS VIDEO INC., 4720 W. Magnolia Blvd., Burbank, CA 91505; (818) 760-2825.

ALTER IMAGE, 113 N. Naomi St., Burbank, CA 91505; (818) 842-5870.

AME, INC., 1133 N. Hollywood Way, Burbank, CA 91505; (818) 841-7440; FAX: (818) 842-8409.

AMERICAN INSTITUTE OF VIDEO, 20850 Dearborn St., Chatsworth, CA 91311; (818) 700-8987.

AMERICAN VIDEO FACTORY, 4150 Glencoe Ave., Marina Del Rey, CA 90292; (213) 823-8622; (800) 367-8433.

AMERICAN VIDEOGRAM INC., 12020 W. Pico Blvd., Los Angeles, CA 90064-1504; (213) 477-1535; 477-1536.

ANDERSON, HOWARD A., COMPANY, 100 Universal City Plaza, 504-3, Universal City, CA 91608; (818) 777-2402.

ANDERSON VIDEO, 3501 Cahuenga Blvd. W., Los Angeles, CA 90068; (213) 876-8008.

AQUARIUS THEATRE, 6230 Sunset Blvd., Hollywood, CA 90028; (213) 460-6700.

APOLLO VIDEO FACILITY, 1503 Cahuenga Blvd., Hollywood, CA 90028; (213) 464-7871.

APPLEGATE ENTERTAINMENT, 15229 Fonthill Ave., Lawndale, CA 90260; (213) 676-3262.

AUDIO ARTS PUBLISHING CO., 5617 Melrose Ave., Los Angeles, CA 90038; (213) 461-3507.

AUDIO GRAPHIC FILMS AND VIDEO, 6509 De Longpre Ave., Hollywood, CA 90028; (213) 462-6596; (213) 467-1234.

—B—

BERC, 4545 Chermak St., Burbank, CA 91505; (818) 841-3000; (213) 464-7655; FAX: (818) 841-7919.

BOSUSTOW VIDEO, 3030 Pennsylvania Ave., Santa Monica, CA 90404; (213) 453-7973.

BOULEVARD VIDEO PRODUCTIONS, 15016 Ventura Blvd., Suite 1, Sherman Oaks, CA 91403; (818) 501-7369.

BOWEN VIDEO FACILITIES & STAGE, 7826 Clybourn Ave., Sun Valley, CA 91352; (818) 504-0070.

BROADCAST STANDARDS, INC., 2044 Cotner Ave., Los Angeles, CA 90025; (213) 312-9060.

—C—

C&C VISUAL WEST LTD., 6464 Sunset Blvd., Hollywood, CA 90028; (213) 466-2369.

CCR VIDEO CORPORATION, 6410 Santa Monica Blvd., Los Angeles, CA 90038; (213) 464-7151.

CALIFORNIA COMMUNICATIONS INC., 6900 Santa Monica Blvd., Los Angeles, CA 90038; (213) 466-8511.

CALIFORNIA VIDEO CENTER, 5432 W. 102 St., Los Angeles, CA 90045; (213) 216-5400; FAX: (213) 216-5498.

CENTURY SOUTHWEST PRODUCTIONS, 2939 Nebraska Ave., Santa Monica, CA 90404; (213) 829-5111; 829-7624.

CHOICE TELEVISION, 800 S. Date Ave., Alhambra, CA 91803; (818) 576-2906; 289-7719.

CINETYP INC., 843 Seward St., Hollywood, CA 90038; (213) 463-8569.

CLARASOL PRODUCTION CO., 1028 La Brea Ave., Hollywood, CA 90038; (213) 462-7212; 464-0180.

CLOCKWORK WINDOW DUBS, 6483 Nancy St., Los Angeles, CA 90045; (213) 215-0114.

COMPACT VIDEO SERVICES INC., 2813 W. Alameda Ave., Burbank, CA 91505; (818) 840-7000.

COMPLETE POST INC., 6087 Sunset Blvd., Hollywood, CA 90028; (213) 467-1244.

THE COMPLEX, 2323 Corinth St., Los Angeles, CA 90064; (213) 477-1938.

COMPOSITE IMAGE SYSTEMS, 815 N. Cahuenga Blvd., Hollywood, CA 90038; (213) 461-5734.

CONSOLIDATED FILM INDUSTRIES, 959 Seward St., Los Angeles, CA 90038; (213) 462-3161.

THE CREATIVE PARTNERSHIP, 7526 Fountain Ave., Hollywood, CA 90046; (213) 850-5551; FAX: (213) 850-0391.

CREST NATIONAL FILM & VIDEOTAPE LABS, 1000 N. Highland Ave., Hollywood, CA 90038; (213) 466-0624; FAX: (213) 461-8901.

CROSS CUTS, 1330 N. Vine St., Hollywood, CA 90028; (213) 465-2292.

—D—

DSR PRODUCTIONS, 607 N. 64th Ave., Los Angeles, CA 90042; (213) 258-6741.

DELTA PRODUCTIONS, 3333 Glendale Blvd., Suite 3, Los Angeles, CA 90039; (213) 663-8754.

DEVONSHIRE AUDIO/VIDEO STUDIOS, 10729 Magnolia Blvd., North Hollywood, CA 91601; (818) 985-1945.

—E—

ECHO FILM SERVICES INC., 4119 Burbank Blvd., Burbank, CA 91505; (818) 841-4114.

EDIT POINT, P.O. Box 55760, Valencia, CA 91355; (818) 799-5611; (805) 254-2108.

EDITEL-LOS ANGELES, 729 N. Highland Ave., Hollywood, CA 90038; (213) 931-1821.

THE EDITING COMPANY, 8300 Beverly Blvd., Los Angeles, CA 90048; (213) 653-3570.

EFX SYSTEMS, 919 N. Victory Blvd., Burbank, CA 91502; (818) 843-4762; (213) 460-4474.

ELECTRONIC ARTS & TECHNOLOGY, 3655 Motor Ave., Los Angeles, CA 90034; (213) 836-2556.

ELFMAN, RICHARD, PRODUCTIONS, 723 Ocean Front Walk, Venice, CA 90291; (213) 399-9118.

ENCORE VIDEO INC., 6344 Fountain Ave., Hollywood, CA 90028; (213) 466-7663.

EYE ON STUDIO, 224 N. Juanita Ave., Los Angeles, CA 90004; (213) 465-7777.

EYE SQUARE VIDEO INC., 1749 14th St., Santa Monica, CA 90404; (213) 452-9076.

—F—

FBC PRODUCTION SERVICES, 12401 W. Olympic Blvd., Los Angeles, CA 90064; (213) 826-5264.

FACE BROADCAST PRODUCTIONS, 115 N. Hollywood Way, Suite 102, Burbank, CA 91505; (818) 842-9081.

FALCON COMMUNICATIONS, 800 S. Date Ave., Alhambra, CA 91803; (818) 576-2906.

FIDELITY RECORDING STUDIO, 4412 Whitsett Ave., Studio City, CA 91604; (818) 508-3263.

FILM CORE PRINT & TAPE, 849 N. Seward St., Los Angeles, CA 90038; (213) 464-7303.

THE FILM PLACE, 1311 N. Highland Ave., Los Angeles, CA 90028; (213) 464-0116.

FILMLAND CORPORATE CENTER, 10000 Washington Blvd., Culver City, CA 90232; (213) 558-0071.

FILMSERVICE LABORATORIES, INC., 1019 N. Cole Ave., Suite 5, Los Angeles, CA 90038; (213) 464-5141.

FRAME BY FRAME, 729 Seward St., Suite 115, Los Angeles, CA 90038; (213) 469-8264; 463-0145.

FREUND & KLEPPEL INC., 6290 Sunset Blvd., Suite 603, Los Angeles, CA 90028; (213) 469-1444.

—G—

GLEN-WARREN PRODUCTIONS, LTD., 9911 W. Pico Blvd., Penthouse M, Los Angeles, CA 90035; (213) 553-9233.

GLOBAL ENTERTAINMENT NETWORK, INC., 1832 N. Gower St., Hollywood, CA 90028; (213) 461-2534.
GRACE & WILD STUDIOS HOLLYWOOD, 3501 Cahuenga Blvd. West., Los Angeles, CA 90068; (213) 876-8008; FAX: (213) 876-0460.
GROUP W CABLE VIDEO PRODUCTION CENTER, 2939 Nebraska Ave., Santa Monica, CA 90404; (213) 829-2676.
GROUP W PRODUCTIONS, One Lakeside Pl., 3801 Barham Blvd., Los Angeles, CA 90068; (213) 850-3800; FAX: (213) 850-3889.

—H—

H.C.V., 3034 Glendale Blvd., Los Angeles, CA 90039; (213) 662-1112.
HEALTH TELEVISION CORP., PRODUCTION GROUP INC., 6605 Eleanor Ave., Hollywood, CA 90038; (213) 463-1713.
HIDEAWAY PRODUCTIONS, 16820 Solana Lane, Canyon Country, CA 91351; (805) 252-4508.
HOLLYWOOD NATIONAL STUDIOS, 6605 Eleanor Ave., Santa Fe Springs, CA 90038; (213) 467-6272.
HOLLYWOOD NEWSREEL SYNDICATE INC., 1622 N. Gower St., Los Angeles, CA 90028; (213) 469-7307.
HOLLYWOOD PACIFIC STUDIOS, 6290 Sunset Blvd., Hollywood, CA 90028; (213) 463-8118.
HOLLYWOOD VAULTS, 742 N. Seward St., Los Angeles, CA 90038; (213) 461-6464; (805) 569-5336.
HOMER & ASSOCIATES, INC., Sunset Gower Studios, 1420 N. Beachwood Dr., Hollywood, CA 90028; (213) 462-4710.
HORIZONTAL EDITING STUDIOS, 2625 W. Olive Ave., Burbank, CA 91505; (818) 841-6750.

—I—

IPS/INDEPENDENT PRODUCERS, 1741 N. Ivar Ave., Suite 109, Hollywood, CA 90028; (213) 461-6966.
IMAGE PRODUCTIONS, 1812 W. Victory Blvd., Burbank, CA 91506; (818) 846-2047.
IMAGE TRANSFORM INC., 4142 Lankershim Blvd., North Hollywood, CA 91602; (818) 985-7566.
IMMEDIATO, JEFFREY & ASSOCIATES, P.O. Box 5611, Long Beach, CA 90805; (213) 422-9295.
IN SYNC VIDEO, 9034 Sunset Blvd., Suite 112, W. Hollywood, CA 90069; (213) 276-0133.
INDEPENDENT PRODUCERS STUDIO, INC., 1604 Vista Del Mar Ave., Hollywood, CA 90028; (213) 461-6966.
INNOVATION UNLIMITED, 4444 Via Marina, Penthouse-81, Marina Del Rey, CA 90291; (213) 823-4251.
INSTANT REPLAY COMMUNICATIONS CO., 11122 W. Washington Blvd., Culver City, CA 90232; (213) 870-9435.
INSTITUTE OF AUDIO/VIDEO ENGINEERING, 1831 Hyperion Ave., Hollywood, CA 90027; (213) 666-2380.
INTER VIDEO/TRITRONICS, 733 N. Victory Blvd., Burbank, CA 91502; (818) 843-3633; 569-4000; FAX: (818) 843-6884.
INTERMIX INC., 2505 S. Robertson Blvd., Los Angeles, CA 90034; (213) 870-2121.
INTERSOUND, INC., 8746 Sunset Blvd., Los Angeles, CA 90069; (213) 652-3741.

—J—

JKR PRODUCTIONS, INC., 12140 W. Olympic Blvd., Suite 21, Los Angeles, CA 90064; (213) 826-3666.
J.P. VIDEO SERVICES, 9538 W. Pico Blvd., Los Angeles, CA 90035; (213) 271-1209; 859-9903.
JAMAR PRODUCTIONS, 11969 Ventura Blvd., Studio City, CA 91604; (818) 762-2077.
TYLIE JONES/WEST, 3519 W. Pacific Ave., Burbank, CA 91505; (818) 955-7600.

—K—

KTEH VIDEOSERVICES, 100 Skyport Dr., San Jose, CA 95115; (408) 998-5554.
KAPPA VIDEO, 801 S. Main St., Burbank, CA 91506; (818) 843-3400; 843-8099.
KEY WEST EDITING, 5701 Buckingham Parkway, #C, Culver City, CA 90230; (213) 645-3348.
KLASKY/CSUPO, 729 Seward St., Suite 101, Hollywood, CA 90038; (213) 463-0145.
KRAMER, JERRY & ASSOCIATES, 8640 W. Third St., Suite 11, Los Angeles, CA 90048; (213) 278-2947.
KUTT, DANIEL, 921 10th St., Santa Monica, CA 90403; (213) 394-6008.

—L—

LP PRODUCTIONS, 223 Strand St., Suite K, Santa Monica, CA 90405; (213) 399-1101; (714) 857-1310.
LAJON PRODUCTIONS INC., 2907 W. Olive Ave., Burbank, CA 91505; (818) 841-1440.
LASER EDIT INC., 540 N. Hollywood Way, Burbank, CA 91505; (818) 842-0777.
LEVIN, KARL M., 20959 Elkwood St., Canoga Park, CA 91304; (818) 882-7262.
LIONEL TELEVISION PRODUCTIONS, 3329 Brookside Dr., Malibu, CA 90265; (213) 456-5809.
LUCASFILM LTD., P.O. Box 2009, San Raphael, CA 94912; (415) 662-1800.

—M—

M.A.T.E. VIDEOTAPE, 1653 18th St., Suite 3, Santa Monica, CA 90404; (213) 828-8807.
M.F.I. VIDEO CENTER, 1905 Grace Ave., Hollywood, CA 90068; (213) 851-0373.
MACPHERSON'S FILM CONTINUITY SERVICE, 13371 Gladstone Ave., Sylmar, CA 91342; (818) 367-4769.
MACROVISION, 10201 Torre Ave., Suite 330, Cupertino, CA 95014, (408) 252-9600.
MADAHORNE VIDEO, 3818 W. Magnolia Blvd., Burbank, CA 91505; (818) 841-2685.
MASTER DIGITAL INC., 1749 14th St., Santa Monica, CA 90404; (213) 452-1511.
McINTIRE HOFFMAN INC., (Jamar Productions), 11969 Ventura Blvd., Studio City, CA 91604; (818) 762-2077.
MEDIA MASTERS PRODUCTIONS, 1800 S. Robertson Blvd., Suite 306, Beverly Hills, CA 90035; (213) 451-8823.
MEGA PRODUCTIONS INC., 1714 N. Wilton Pl., Hollywood, CA 90028; (213) 462-6342.
MERIDIAN, P.O. Box 1941, Hollywood, CA 90028; (213) 874-4367.
METAVISION, 347 S. Ogden Dr., Suite 200, Los Angeles, CA 90036; (213) 936-8281.
METROPOLITAN ENTERTAINMENT, 11946 Ash Dale Lane, Studio City, CA 91604; (213) 657-9265.
METROTAPE, (division of Metromedia), 5746 Sunset Blvd., Los Angeles, CA 90028; (213) 856-1356.
MIDTOWN VIDEO, 8489 W. Third St., Suite 1065, Los Angeles, CA 90048; (213) 651-2420.
MOBILEFAX, 710 N. Seward St., Hollywood, CA 90038, (213) 467-4000.
MODERN TALKING PICTURE SERVICE INC., 6735 San Fernando Rd., Glendale, CA 91201; (818) 240-0519; (813) 541-7571; FAX: (813) 544-4624.
MODERN VIDEOFILM, 7165 Sunset Blvd., Hollywood, CA 90046; (213) 851-8070; FAX: (213) 851-0704.
MUSIC LAB INC., 1831 Hyperion Ave., Hollywood, CA 90027; (213) 666-3003.

—N—

NATARNO'S, JAN, VIDEOTAPE EDITING, 6132 DeLongpre Ave., Hollywood, CA 90028; (213) 462-5511.
NATIONAL TELEVISION NEWS INC., 213A, 23480 Park Sorrento, Calabasas Park, CA 91302; (818) 883-6121.
NEWMAN/FRANKS, 2956 Nicada Dr., Los Angeles, CA 90077; (213) 470-0140; 470-0145.

—O—

ONE PASS FILM & VIDEO, One China Basin Building, San Francisco, CA 94107; (415) 777-5777.
ORION ENTERPRISES, INC., 1015 N. Cahuenga Blvd., Los Angeles, CA 90038; (213) 461-3844; FAX: (213) 461-2958.

—P—

PRC OF AMERICA (PLASTIC REEL CORPORATION), 8140 Webb Ave., N. Hollywood, CA 91605; (818) 504-0400.
PACIFIC VIDEO, INC., 809 N. Cahuenga Blvd., Los Angeles, CA 90038; (213) 462-6266; FAX: (213) 464-3233.
PAINT BOX PLUS, 6464 Sunset Blvd., Suite 1000, Hollywood, CA 90028; (213) 856-8530; FAX: (213) 466-4802.
POLYCOM DIGITAL POST, 2911 W. Olive, Burbank, CA 91504; (818) 845-1917.
POSITIVE MEDIA, 5422A Fair Ave., North Hollywood, CA 91601; (213) 461-0092.
THE POST GROUP, 6335 Homewood, Los Angeles, CA 90028; (213) 462-2300.
POST PLUS INC., 6650 Santa Monica Blvd., 2nd Floor, Hollywood, CA 90038; (213) 463-7108.
POST-PRODUCTION SYSTEMS, 2433 28th St., Suite H, Santa Monica, CA 90405; (213) 450-5094.
POST TIME EDITORIAL INC., 1777 N. Vine St., Suite 303, Los Angeles, CA 90028; (213) 462-6968.
POST 2, 115 N. Pacific Ave., Suite B, Glendale, CA 91202; (818) 242-7642.
PRECISION FOLEY & ADR, 6353 Homewood Ave., Hollywood, CA 90028; (213) 462-8235.
PREMORE INC., 5130 Klump Ave., North Hollywood, CA 91601; (818) 506-7714.
PRO VIDEO & CINETAPE, 801 N. La Brea Ave., Los Angeles, CA 90038; (213) 934-8836; 934-8840.

PRODUCERS ASSOCIATES, 7243 Santa Monica Blvd., W. Hollywood, CA 90046; (213) 851-4123.
PROFESSIONAL ARTISTS GROUP, 845 N. Highland Ave., Hollywood, CA 90038; (213) 871-2222.

—R—

R. PRODUCTIONS & VIDEO EVENTS, 1741 N. Ivar, Suite 210, Hollywood, CA 90028; (213) 465-4197.
R & S STUDIOS/ROSE & SALLMAN PRODUCTIONS INC., 7336 Hinds Ave., N. Hollywood, CA 91605; (818) 503-8808.
RANK VIDEO, 500 N. Ventu Park Rd., Newbury Park, CA 91320; 970 W. 190th St., Suite 900, Torrance, CA 90502; (213) 515-6499.
RAZ VIDEO PRODUCTIONS, 1828 E. Walnut St., Pasadena, CA 91107; (818) 449-1175.
RED CAR EDITING, 1040 N. Las Palmas, Los Angeles, CA 90038; (213) 466-4467; FAX: (213) 466-4925.
REEL MAGIC, 11684 Ventura Blvd., Suite 325, Studio City, CA 91604; (818) 762-5670.
THE REEL THING OF CALIFORNIA, INC., 1253 N. Vine St., Suite 14, Hollywood, CA 90038; (213) 466-8588.
RENCHER'S EDITORIAL SERVICE, 738 Cahuenga Blvd., Hollywood, CA 90038; (213) 463-9836.
ROCK SOLID PRODUCTIONS, 801 S. Main St., Burbank, CA 91506; (818) 841-8220.
ROLAND, GLENN FILMS, 10711 Wellworth Ave., Los Angeles, CA 90024; (213) 475-0937.
ROSS, NEIL, 261 S. Robertson Blvd., Beverly Hills, CA 90211; (213) 855-1700.
RUBBER DUBBERS, INC., 626 Justin Ave., Glendale Ave., CA 91201; (818) 241-5600.
RUSSIAN HILL RECORDING, 1520 Pacific Ave., San Francisco, CA 94109; (415) 474-4520.
RUXIN, JIM, 12140 Olympic Blvd., Suite 21, Los Angeles, CA 90064; (213) 826-3666.

—S—

SADLER, SIM, PRODUCTIONS, 1680 N. Vine St., Suite 920, Hollywood, CA 90028; (213) 739-4801.
SAR PRODUCTIONS, 22801 Ventura Blvd., Suite 211, Woodland Hills, CA 91364; (818) 884-5646.
SCHULMAN VIDEO CENTER, 861 Seward St., Hollywood, CA 90038; (213) 465-8110.
SCOTTSOUND INC., 6110 Santa Monica Blvd., Los Angeles, CA 90038; (213) 462-6981.
SCREENMUSIC, 11700 Ventura Blvd., Studio City, CA 91604; (213) 877-0300; (818) 985-0900.
SHORELINE PROFESSIONAL VIDEO SYSTEMS, 1622 N. Highland Ave., Hollywood, CA 90028; (213) 461-9800.
SIERRA VIDEO, 11320 Chandler, N. Hollywood, CA 91601; (818) 506-4984; 579-7045.
SILVERLAKE ENTERTAINMENT CENTER, 2405 Glendale Blvd., Los Angeles, CA 90039; (213) 665-4187.
SKYLIGHT PRODUCTION INC., 6815 W. Willoughby, Suite 201, Los Angeles, CA 90038; (213) 464-4500; FAX: (213) 463-1884.
SKYLINE PRODUCTIONS, 6309 Eleanor Ave., Hollywood, CA 90038; (213) 856-0033.
SOUND IMAGE STUDIOS, INC., 6556 Wilkinson Ave., N. Hollywood, CA 91606; (818) 762-8881.
SOUND MASTER, 10747 Magnolia Blvd., North Hollywood, CA 91601; (213) 650-8000.
SOUTH, LEONARD, PRODUCTIONS, 4883 Lankershim Blvd., N. Hollywood, CA 91601; (818) 760-8383.
SPALLA, RICK VIDEO PRODUCTIONS, 1622 N. Gower, Los Angeles, CA 90028; (213) 469-7307.
SPECTRA IMAGE INC., 540 N. Hollywood Way, Burbank, CA 91505; (818) 842-1111.
SPRINGBOARD STUDIOS, 12229 Montague St., Arleta, CA 91331; (818) 896-4321.
SQUARE WHEEL PRODUCTIONS/THE CONSULTANCY, P.O. Box 675, Van Nuys, CA 91408-0675; (818) 508-0332.
STAGE FRIGHT PRODUCTIONS, 8817 Amboy Ave., Sun Valley, CA 91352; (818) 768-3333.
STARFAX, 654 Hawthorne St., Glendale, CA 91204; (818) 244-3600.
STARLIGHT EDITING SERVICES, 5250 Strohm, North Hollywood, CA 91601; (818) 769-3874.
STEVENS, SHADOE, INC., 9100 Sunset Blvd., Suite 215, Los Angeles, CA 90069; (213) 274-1244.
SUNSET POST INC., 1813 Victory Blvd., Glendale, CA 91201; (818) 956-7912; FAX: (818) 545-7586.
SUNSHINE COMMUNICATIONS, 565 N. Gower St., Hollywood, CA 90004; (213) 464-6652.
SUNWEST RECORDING STUDIOS, 5533 Sunset Blvd., Hollywood, CA 90028; (213) 465-1000.
SUPERIOR VIDEO SERVICES, 13423 Saticoy St., North Hollywood, CA 91605; (818) 786-7060.
SYNC INC., 931 N. Gardner St., West Hollywood, CA 90046; (213) 851-6624.

—T—

TAJ SOUNDWORKS, 8207 W. 3rd St., Los Angeles, CA 90048; (213) 655-2775.
TAV/AME, INC., 1541 N. Vine St., Los Angeles, CA 90028; (213) 466-2141; FAX: (213) 464-4636.
TAURO PRODUCTIONS, 5019 York Blvd., Highland Park, CA 90042; (213) 258-2379.
TELEMEDIA PRODUCTIONS, 18321 Ventura Blvd., Suite 660, Tarzana, CA 91356; (818) 708-2005.
TELE VIDICS, 2223 E. 223rd St., Long Beach, CA 90810, (213) 830-5296.
TELEPRINT OF LOS ANGELES, 3779 Cahuenga West, Studio City, CA 91604; (818) 760-3191.
TODD-AO/GLEN GLENN STUDIOS, 900 N. Seward St., Hollywood, CA 90038; (213) 469-7221.
TOP VIDEO SERVICES INC., 10153 Riverside Dr., Suite 1B, Toluca Lake, CA 91602; (818) 763-1295.
TRANS-AMERICAN VIDEO INC., 1541 N. Vine St., Los Angeles, CA 90028; (213) 466-2141.
2M PRODUCTIONS, 11220 Moorpark, Suite 66, N. Hollywood, CA 91602; (818) 766-9832.

—U—

UCL VIDEO, 823 N. Seward St., Los Angeles, CA 90038; (213) 469-7291.
UDELL, BILL, PRODUCTIONS, 6006 Vantage Ave., North Hollywood, CA 91606; (818) 985-6866.
UNITEL VIDEO, 5555 Melrose Ave., Studio G, Los Angeles, CA 90038; (213) 468-4606.
UNIVERSAL FACILITIES (RENTAL DIVISION), 100 Universal City Plaza, Universal City, CA 91608; (818) 777-3000; 777-2731.
USA PRODUCTIONS, 1645 Vine St., Suite 350, Hollywood, CA 90028; (213) 465-6320.

—V—

VRA TELEPLAY PICTURES, P.O. Box 8471, Universal Plaza Station, North Hollywood, CA 91608; (213) 462-1099; FAX: (818) 795-8436.
VTR SERVICE COMPANY, 3169 Barbara Ct., Suite D, Hollywood, CA 90068; (213) 851-9700.
VALLEY PRODUCTION CENTER, 6633 Van Nuys Blvd., Van Nuys, CA 91405-4689; (818) 988-6601.
VALLEY VIDEO, 4209 W. Burbank Blvd., Burbank, CA 91505; (818) 841-2387.
VANTAGE POINT PRODUCTIONS, 228 Santa Monica Blvd., Suite 6, Santa Monica, CA 90401; (213) 394-5534; 394-3836; FAX: (213) 458-6324.
VARITEL VIDEO, 3575 Cahuenga Blvd. West, Los Angeles, CA 90068; (213) 850-1165; FAX: (213) 850-6151.
VECTOR PRODUCTIONS INC., P.O. Box 7000-645, Redondo Beach, CA 90277; (213) 757-0520, (213) 316-6031.
VENTURA COUNTY CABLEVISION, 30901 Agoura Rd., Westlake Village, CA 91361; (818) 889-0282.
VIA VISION PRODUCTIONS, 5919 Franklin Ave., Los Angeles, CA 90028; (213) 851-9607.
VIDCOM POST, 2600 W. Olive Ave., Suite 100, Burbank, CA 91505; (818) 841-1199; FAX: (818) 841-2350.
VIDCOM PRODUCTION FACILITY, 2426 Townsgate Rd., Suite K, Westlake Village, CA 91361; (818) 991-1974.
VIDEO ADVENTURES INC., 1015 Cahuenga Blvd., Hollywood, CA 90038; (213) 461-3288.
VIDEOASIS, 317 S. Verdugo Rd., Glendale, CA 91205; (818) 507-1037.
VIDEO CIRCUIT STUDIOS, 11440 Chandler Blvd., Studio 1400, N. Hollywood, CA 91601; (818) 506-5493.
VIDEO CRAFTSMEN INC., 6311 Romaine St., Los Angeles, CA 90038; (213) 464-4351.
VIDEO EVENTS INC., 6410 Santa Monica Blvd., Los Angeles, CA 90038; (213) 465-4197.
VIDEO HOUSE, 201 N. Hollywood Way, Suite 202, Burbank, CA 91505; (818) 954-9559.
VIDEO SUPPORT SERVICES INC., 3473½ Cahuenga Blvd. W., Los Angeles, CA 90068; (213) 469-9000.
THE VIDEO TAPE CO., 10545 Burbank Blvd., North Hollywood, CA 91601; (818) 985-1666; 753-3051; FAX: (818) 985-0614.
VIDEO TECHNOLOGY & SERVICES, 500 N. Ventu Park Rd., Newbury Park, CA 91320; (818) 888-3040.
VIDEO TRANSITIONS INC., 910 N. Citrus Ave., Los Angeles, CA 90038; (213) 465-3333; FAX: (213) 463-1VT1.
VIDEOWERKS, 1316 Third St., Suite 102, Santa Monica, CA 90401; (213) 393-8754.
VIDEO WEST, 805 Larrabbee St., W. Hollywood, CA 90069; (213) 659-5762.
VIDEO-IT INC., 5000 Overland Ave., Suite 6, Culver City, CA 90232; (818) VID-EOIT; (213) 280-0505.
VIDE-U PRODUCTIONS, 612 N. Sepulveda Blvd., Los Angeles, CA 90049; (213) 472-7023.

VISUAL EYES PRODUCTIONS, 2401 Main St., Santa Monica, CA 90405; (213) 392-8300; FAX: (213) 392-7480.
VITELLO & ASSOCIATES, 1612 W. Olive, Suite 203, Santa Monica, CA 91506; (818) 848-5919.

—W—

WEISBARTH, JACOB & ASSOC. INC., 9903 Santa Monica Blvd., Suite 256, Beverly Hills, CA 90212; (213) 277-9616.
WEST PRODUCTIONS, INC., 444 Irving Dr., Burbank, CA 91504; (818) 841-4500.
WESTERN FILM INDUSTRIES, 30941 W. Agoura Rd., Suite 302, Westlake Village, CA 91361; (818) 889-7350; FAX: (818) 707-3937.
WEXLER VIDEO, INC., 800 N. Victory Blvd., Burbank, CA 91502; (818) 846-9381.
WILDER BROTHERS VIDEO, 10327 Santa Monica Blvd., Los Angeles, CA 90025; (213) 557-3500.
WILDWOOD FILM SERVICE, 6855 Santa Monica Blvd., Suite 400, Los Angeles, CA 90038; (213) 462-6388.
WINTERS, GLENN, PRODUCTIONS, INC., P.O. Box 920, Montrose, CA 91020; (818) 790-4201.
WOLLIN PRODUCTION SERVICES INC., 666 N. Robertson Blvd., Los Angeles, CA 90069; (213) 659-0175.

NEW YORK

A.D.M. VIDEO PRODUCTIONS, 40 Seaview Blvd., Pt. Washington, NY 11050; (516) 484-6900.
A N S INTERNATIONAL VIDEO LTD., 396 Fifth Ave., New York, NY 10018; (212) 736-1007.
A.S.P. POST PRODUCTIONS, 630 Ninth Ave., Suite 405, New York, NY 10036; (212) 757-1711.
ALBA/EDITORIAL, 200 E. 94 St., New York, NY 10128; (212) 967-7345.
ALL CHANNELS VIDEO, INC., 630 Ninth Ave., New York, NY 10036; (212) 247-3428.
ALL-MOBILE VIDEO, 630 Ninth Ave., New York, NY 10036; (212) 757-8919.
AMERICAN TV VIDEO, 248 E. 48 St., New York, NY 10017; (212) 688-6222.
AQUARIUS TRANSFERMATION, 12 E. 46 St., New York, NY 10017; (212) 697-3636.
ARANESS COMMUNICATIONS, 244 W. 49 St., Suite 400, New York, NY 10019; (212) 582-6246.
ARTEL VIDEO, INC., 1600 Broadway, New York, NY 10019; (212) 315-5665.
BNS VIDEO SERVICES, INC. (division of Broadcast News Service, Inc.), GPO 2360, Pier 62, W. 23 St., New York, NY 10011; (213) 466-0234, (212) 223-0909.
BETELGEUSE PRODUCTIONS, 44 E. 32 St., New York, NY 10016; (212) 213-1333.
BOMBAY BROADCASTING NETWORK, 1697 Broadway, New York, NY 10019; (212) 977-7700.
BROADWAY VIDEO, 1619 Broadway, New York, NY 10019, (212) 265-7600.
BURTON, PHILIP, PRODUCTIONS, 1623 Third Ave., 33KW, New York, NY 10128; (212) 410-9203.
C & C VISUAL, 225 W. 44 St., New York, NY 10036; (212) 869-4900.
CAESAR VIDEO GRAPHICS, INC., 137 E. 25 St., New York, NY 10010; (212) 684-7673.
CAROB VIDEO, 250 W. 57 St., New York, NY 10107; (212) 957-9525.
CENTERLIGHT TELEVISION, 245 W. 19 St., New York, NY 10011; (212) 929-4745.
CHARLEX, INC., 2 W. 45 St., New York, NY 10036; (212) 719-4600.
CHROMAVISION, 119 W. 22 St., New York, NY 10011; (212) 463-8997.
CINERGY COMMUNICATIONS CORP., 321 W. 44 St., New York, NY 10036; (212) 582-2900.
CINETAPE, INC., 241 E. 51 St., New York, NY 10022; (212) 355-0070.
CINE-VID POST PRODUCTION, INC., 25 W. 45 St., New York, NY 10036; (212) 704-4000.
COMMUNICATIONS PLUS VIDEO, 360 Park Ave. South, New York, NY 10010; (212) 686-9570.
COM/TECH, INC., 770 Lexington Ave., New York, NY 10021; (212) 826-2935.
A CUT ABOVE/VIDEO, 17 E. 45 St., New York, NY 10017; (212) 661-4949.
THE CUTTING EDGE/EDITORIAL, 420 Lexington Ave., New York, NY 10017; (212) 599-4233.
DC VIDEO, 270 Lafayette St., New York, NY 10012; (212) 431-1646.
DJM FILMS INC., 4 E. 46 St., New York, NY 10017; (212) 687-0404.
DEVLIN VIDEO SERVICE, 1501 Broadway, Suite 408, New York, NY 10036; (212) 391-1313; FAX: (212) 391-2744.
EDITEL NEW YORK, 222 E. 44 St., New York, NY 10017; (212) 867-4600.
EDITING CONCEPTS, 214 E. 50 St., New York, NY 10022; (212) 980-3340.
EDITORS GAS VIDEO, INC., 16 E. 48 St., New York, NY 10017; (212) 832-6690.
ELECTRIC FILM, 87 Lafayette St., New York, NY 10013; (212) 925-3429.
ELECTRONIC CUTTING ROOM, INC., 1650 Broadway, New York, NY 10019; (212) 541-9441.
EMPIRE VIDEO, 216 E. 45 St., New York, NY 10017; (212) 687-2060.
EVEN TIME LTD., 62 W. 45 St., New York, NY 10036; (212) 764-4700.
FAMA II PRODUCTIONS INC., 2750 Richmond Terrace, Staten Island, NY 10303; (718) 273-1780.
FRAME ACCURATE, INC., 601 W. 50 St., New York, NY 10019; (212) 399-9877.
FRAME:RUNNER, INC., 1995 Broadway, Suite 1100, New York, NY 10023; (212) 874-1730.
GHA FILM & TAPE, 1170 Broadway, New York, NY 10001; (212) 683-6304.
GLOBE VIDEO SERVICES, INC., 286 Fifth Ave., New York, NY 10001; (212) 695-6868.
GROUND CONTROL VIDEO, 49 W. 27 St., Suite 903, New York, NY 10001; (212) 683-5455.
HORN/EISENBERG FILM & TAPE EDITING, 16 W. 46 St., New York, NY 10036; (212) 391-8166.
IPC, 514 W. 57 St., New York, NY 10019; (212) 582-6530.
IMAGE MIX, INC., 305 E. 46 St., New York, NY 10017; (212) 752-3010.
INTERNATIONAL PRODUCTION CENTER, 514 W. 57 St., New York, NY 10019; (212) 582-6530.
INTERNATIONAL VIDEO SERVICES, 1501 Broadway, Suite 1300, New York, NY 10036; (212) 730-1411.
JPC VIDEO INC., 11 E. 47 St., 4th floor, New York, NY 10017; (212) 223-0555.
JSL VIDEO SERVICES, INC., 25 W. 45th St., New York, NY 10036; (212) JSL-5082.
KTV CONSULTANTS, INC., 226 E. 54 St., New York, NY 10022; (212) 223-0520.
KALEIDOSCOPE PRODUCTIONS, 601 W. 50 St., New York, NY 10019; (212) 489-7150.
KOPEL FILMS, 630 Ninth Ave., New York, NY 10036; (212) 757-4742.
L & D FILM/VIDEO, 630 Ninth Ave., New York, NY 10036; (212) 315-0410.
LM COMMUNICATIONS CORP., 60 Hamilton Terr., New York, NY 10031; (212) 283-2509.
LRP VIDEO, 3 Dag Hammarskjold Plaza, New York, NY 10017; (212) 759-0822.
MAGNO SOUND & VIDEO, 729 Seventh Ave., New York, NY 10019; (212) 302-2505; FAX: (212) 819-1282.
MANHATTAN TRANSFER/EDIT, 545 Fifth Ave., New York, NY 10017; (212) 687-4000.
MANHATTAN VIDEO PRODUCTIONS, 12 W. 27 St., New York, NY 10001; (212) 683-6565.
MARKLE, WILLIAM, ASSOCIATES, 630 Ninth Ave., Suite 1409, New York, NY 10036; (212) 246-8642.
MATRIX VIDEO, 727 Eleventh Ave., New York, NY 10019; (212) 265-8500.
MEDIA CONTACT, INC., 206 E. 38 St., New York, NY; (212) 370-3983; 370-3959.
MEGA MEDIA CENTER, 727 Seventh Ave., New York, NY 10019; (212) 265-8500.
MODERN TELECOMMUNICATIONS, 1 Dag Hammarskjold Plaza, New York, NY 10017; (212) 355-0510.
MOVIELAB VIDEO, INC., 619 W. 54 St., New York, NY 10019; (212) 956-3900.
MULTI-VIDEO GROUP LTD., 50 E. 42 St., New York, NY 10017; (212) 986-1577.
MYRVIK, RON, PRODUCTIONS, 34 E. 29 St., New York, NY 10016; (212) 685-0726.
NEP PRODUCTIONS, INC., 56 W. 45 St., New York, NY 10036; (212) 382-1100.
NATIONAL VIDEO CENTER, 460 W. 42 St., New York, NY 10036; (212) 279-2000.
NATIONAL VIDEO INDUSTRIES, 15 W. 17 St., New York, NY 10011; (212) 691-1300.
NEXUS PRODUCTIONS, INC., 10 E. 40 St., New York, NY 10016; (212) 679-2180.
NORTH STAR VIDEO LTD., 581 Avenue of the Americas, New York, NY 10011; (212) 337-3200.
NORTHEAST VIDEO, INC., 420 Lexington Ave., New York, NY 10017; (212) 661-8830.
OCCASIONAL VIDEO, 534 E. 84 St., New York, NY 10028, (212) 737-3058.
OTTERSON TV, INC., 251 W. 30 St., 14 W, New York, NY 10001; (212) 695-7417.
P.A.T. FILM SERVICES, 630 Ninth Ave., New York, NY 10036; (212) 247-0900.
PHANTASMAGORIA PRODUCTIONS, INC., 630 Ninth Ave., New York, NY 10036; (212) 586-4890.

PICSONIC PRODUCTIONS, 25 W. 45 St., New York, NY 10036; (212) 575-1910.
PICTURE PERFECT PRODUCTIONS, 630 Ninth Ave., New York, NY 10036; (212) 582-6043.
POST EXPRESSIONS, 5 E. 47 St., New York, NY 10017; (212) 838-3044.
POST PERFECT, 220 E. 42 St., New York, NY 10017; (212) 972-3400.
PRIMA LUX VIDEO, 30 W. 26 St., New York, NY 10010, (212) 206-1402.
PRINCZKO PRODUCTIONS, 9 E. 38 St., New York, NY 10016; (212) 683-1300.
R.G. VIDEO, 21 W. 46 St., New York, NY 10036; (212) 997-1464; FAX: (212) 827-0726.
RVI/RUTT VIDEO INC., 137 E. 25 St., New York, NY 10010; (212) 685-4000.
REBO STUDIO, 530 W. 25 St., New York, NY 10001; (212) 989-9466; FAX: (212) 627-9083.
REEVES TELETAPE, 708 Third Ave., New York, NY 10017; (212) 573-8600.
ROSENBERG, WARREN, VIDEO SERVICES, 308 E. 79 St., New York, NY 10021; (212) 744-1111.
ROSS-GAFFNEY, 21 W. 46 St., New York, NY 10036; (212) 719-2744.
SAGA PRODUCTIONS, INC., 16 W. 19 St., New York, NY 10011; (212) 645-9600.
SALAMANDRA IMAGES, INC., 6 E. 39 St., New York, NY 10016; (212) 779-0707.
SHADOW LIGHT PRODUCTIONS, INC., 12 W. 27 St., New York, NY 10001; (212) 689-7511.
SPLICE IS NICE, 141 E. 44 St., New York, NY 10017; (212) 599-1711.
SYNESTHETICS INC., 58 Walker St., New York, NY 10013; (212) 431-4112.
TFI, TAPE-FILM INDUSTRIES, 619 W. 54 St., New York, NY 10019; (212) 708-0500.
TV-R/MASTER COLOR TRANSFER, INC., 333 W. 52 St., New York, NY 10019; (212) 541-4030.
TVC VIDEO, 225 E. 43 St., New York, NY 10017; (212) 599-1616.
TAKE THREE EDITORIAL INC., 141 E. 44 St., New York, NY 10017; (212) 687-3344.
THE TAPE HOUSE EDITORIAL CO., 216 E. 45 St., New York, NY 10017; (212) 557-4949.
TAPESTRY PRODUCTIONS, LTD., 924 Broadway, New York, NY 10010; (212) 677-6007.
TEATOWN VIDEO INC., 165 W. 46 St., New York, NY 10036; (212) 302-0722.
TELETECHNIQUES, INC., 1 W. 19 St., New York, NY 10011; (212) 206-1475; 633-1868.
TELSTAR EDITING, INC., 29 W. 38 St., New York, NY 10018; (212) 730-1000.
TODAY VIDEO, INC., 45 W. 45 St., New York, NY 10036; (212) 391-1020.
TRAIMAN, HENRY, ASSOCIATES, INC., 160 Madison Ave., New York, NY 10016; (212) 889-3400.
TRANSCOM MEDIA, 902 Broadway, New York, NY 10010; (212) 529-1000.
TULCHIN STUDIOS, 240 E. 45 St., New York, NY 10017, (212) 986-8270.
UNITEL, 515 W. 57 St., New York, NY 10019; (212) 265-3600.
VCA/TELETRONICS, 231 E. 55 St., New York, NY 10022, (212) 355-1600.
VALKAN FILMS, INC., 1600 Broadway, Suite 404, New York, NY 10019; (212) 586-1603.
VIDEO CASSETTE TRANSFERS, 1501 Broadway, New York, NY 10036; (212) 575-8433.
VIDEO CENTRAL, INC., 225 W. 36 St., New York, NY 10018; (212) 947-6960.
VIDEO MEDIA PRODUCTIONS, 1276 Holiday Park Dr., Wantagh, NY 11793; (516) 783-5450.
VIDEO PLANNING INC., 250 W. 57 St., New York, NY 10019; (212) 582-5066.
VIDEO PORTFOLIOS, 142 W. 24 St., New York, NY 10011, (212) 989-3858.
VIDEO RESOURCES NEW YORK, INC., 220 W. 71st St., New York, NY 10023; (212) 724-7055.
VIDEO TEAM, INC., 522 W. 36 St., New York, NY 10018; (212) 629-8010.
VIDEO TRANSFERS, 1501 Broadway, Suite 406, New York, NY 10036; (212) 575-8433.
VIDEOGENIX OF NY, INC., 503-11 Broadway, New York, NY 10012; (212) 925-0445.
VIDEOWORKS, INC., 24 W. 40 St., New York, NY 10018; (212) 869-2500; FAX: (212) 764-4947.
VIDLO VIDEO, 40 E. 21 St., New York, NY 10010; (212) 475-4140.
VISNEWS INTERNATIONAL (U.S.A.), 630 Fifth Ave., New York, NY 10111; (212) 698-4500.
WINDSOR TOTAL VIDEO, 8 W. 38th St., New York, NY 10018; (212) 944-9090.

CONNECTICUT

E.C.A. STUDIO, 149 Dudley Rd., Wilton, CT 06897; (203) 762-3380; 221 W. 57 St., New York, NY 10019; (212) 333-5656.
ENCORE TELEPRODUCTIONS CORP., 600 Main St., Monroe, CT 06468; (203) 268-7487.
IMAGE PRODUCTIONS INC., 50 Water St., South Norwalk, CT 06854; (203) 853-3486.

PENNSYLVANIA

CENTER CITY VIDEO, INC., 1503 Walnut St., Philadelphia, PA 19102; (215) 568-4134.
FILMMAKERS OF PHILADELPHIA, 725 N. 24 St., Philadelphia, PA 19130; (215) 763-3400.
STEWART, E. J., 525 Mildred Ave., Primos, PA 19018; (215) 626-6500.
VIDEOSMITH, INC., 2006 Chancellor St., Philadelphia, PA 19103; (215) 665-3690.

WASHINGTON, DC

CAPITOL VIDEO COMMUNICATIONS, INC., 2121 Wisconsin Ave., N.W., Washington, DC 20007; (202) 965-7800.
VOX-CAM ASSOCIATES, 813 Silver Springs Ave., Silver Spring, MD 20910; (301) 589-5377.

CANADA

MANTA VIDEO LABS, 311 Adelaide St. E., Toronto, Ont., M5A 1N2; (416) 863-9316.
PACIFIC FILM LABORATORIES, 916 Davie St., Vancouver, B.C., V62 1B8; (604) 734-7727.
PATHÉ SOUND & POST PRODUCTION CENTRE, 121 St. Patrick St., Toronto, Ont. M5T 1V3; (416) 598-2521.

Video Equipment—Sales, Rental and Repair

The following companies offer video equipment sales, rental and repairs except: * indicates sales and rentals only; ** indicates repairs only.

WEST COAST

AGV ENTERPRISES, 6290 Sunset Blvd., Los Angeles, CA 90028; (213) 463-3301.

***ADVANCED CRAFT INC.,** 6753 Santa Monica Blvd., Los Angeles, CA 90038; (213) 655-3511.

AMERICAN VIDEO FACTORY, 4150 Glencoe Ave., Marina Del Rey, CA 90292; (213) 823-8622.

***AMERICAN VIDEOGRAM INC.,** 12020 W. Pico Blvd., Los Angeles, CA 90064-1504; (213) 477-1535; 477-1536.

AMETRON RENTALS, 1200 N. Vine St., Los Angeles, CA 90038; (213) 466-4321.

****AMPAC VIDEO,** 3637 Cahuenga Blvd. W., Hollywood, CA 90068; (213) 851-7200.

***AQUASTAR SYSTEMS,** 3960 Laurel Canyon Blvd., #406, Studio City, CA 91604; (818) 880-5639; (800) 227-5606.

****ATLAS VIDEO,** 8113 State S Gt., Los Angeles, CA; (213) 569-1393.

****AUDIO ARTS PUBLISHING CO.,** 5617 Melrose Ave., Los Angeles, CA 90038; (213) 461-3507.

AUDIO GRAPHIC FILMS AND VIDEO, 6509 De Longpre Ave., Hollywood, CA 90028; (213) 462-6596, (213) 467-1234.

***AUDIO SERVICES CORPORATION,** 10639 Riverside Dr., N. Hollywood, CA 91602; (818) 980-9891; (800) 228-4429; FAX: (818) 980-9911.

AUDIO VISUAL HEADQUARTERS CORP., 361 N. Oak St., Inglewood, CA 90302; (213) 419-4040.

***AUTOGRAPHICS,** 6335 Homewood Ave., Hollywood, CA 90028; (213) 464-2244.

***BCS BROADCAST STORE, INC.** 4525 Valerio St., Burbank, CA 91505; (818) 845-7000.

BERC (BROADCAST EQUIPMENT RENTAL COMPANY), 4545 Chermak St., Burbank, CA 91505; (818) 841-3000, (213) 464-7655; FAX: (818) 841-7919.

BACKGROUND ENGINEERS INC., 1213 Flower St., Glendale, CA 91201; (818) 500-0454.

***BETACAM SPECIALISTS,** 317 S. Lamer St., Burbank, CA 91506; (818) 845-6480; FAX: (818) 848-0955.

****BEVERLY HILLS VIDEOCENTER,** 187 S. Beverly Dr., Beverly Hills, CA 90212; (213) 550-1092.

***BEXEL CORPORATION,** 801 S. Main St., Burbank, CA 91506; (818) 841-5051.

***BOSUSTOW VIDEO,** 3030 Pennsylvania Ave., Santa Monica, CA 90404; (213) 453-7973.

***BOWEN VIDEO FACILITIES & STAGE,** 7826 Clybourn Ave., Sun Valley, CA 91352; (818) 504-0070.

BROADCAST REMOTE, 415 S. Flower, Burbank, CA 91502; (818) 841-0919.

****BURBANK PRODUCTION PLAZA,** 801 S. Main St., Burbank, CA 91506; (818) 846-7677.

CCR VIDEO CORPORATION, 6410 Santa Monica Blvd., Los Angeles, CA 90038; (213) 464-7151.

***CALIFORNIA COMMUNICATIONS INC.,** 6900 Santa Monica Blvd., Los Angeles, CA 90038; (213) 466-8511.

***CALIFORNIA VIDEO CENTER,** 5432 W. 102 St., Los Angeles, CA 90045; (213) 216-5400; FAX: (213) 216-5498.

CINE VIDEO, 948 N. Cahuenga Blvd., Hollywood, CA 90038; (213) 464-6200.

CINEMA PRODUCTS CORPORATION, 3211 S. La Cienega Blvd., Los Angeles, CA 90016-3112; (213) 836-7991; 478-0711.

COMPREHENSIVE SERVICE CORPORATION, P.O. Box 38339; Los Angeles, CA 90038; (213) 462-0969.

***COMTEL,** 7524 Clairmont Mesa Blvd., San Diego, CA 92111; (619) 292-1090; 3152 E. La Palma, Suite D, Anaheim, CA 92806; (714) 630-4470.

CONTINENTAL CAMERA RENTALS, 7240 Valjean Ave., Van Nuys, CA 91406; (818) 989-5222; FAX: (818) 994-8405.

THE CREATIVE PARTNERSHIP, 7525 Fountain Ave., Hollywood, CA 90046; (213) 850-5551; FAX: (213) 850-0391.

DAVIS, WALT ENTERPRISES, INC., 931 N. Cole Ave., Hollywood, CA 90038; (213) 461-0700; FAX: (213) 461-0946.

EDIT POINT, P.O. Box 55760, Valencia, CA 91355; (818) 799-5611; (805) 254-2108.

ELECTRONIC SERVICE CENTER, 1141 Westminister, Suite 4, Alhambra, CA 91803; (818) 282-8684; 282-8719.

ELFMAN, RICHARD, PRODUCTIONS, 723 Ocean Front Walk, Venice, CA 90291; (213) 399-9118.

EYE ON STUDIO, 224 N. Juanita Ave., Los Angeles, CA 90004; (213) 465-7777.

EYE SQUARE VIDEO INC., 1749 14th St., Santa Monica, CA 90404; (213) 452-9076.

FACE BROADCAST PRODUCTIONS, 115 N. Hollywood Way, Suite 102, Burbank, CA 91505; (818) 842-9081.

GORDON, ALAN ENTERPRISES INC., 5362 Cahuenga Blvd., Beverly Hills, CA; (818) 985-5500; (213) 466-3561.

***GREENE, COWE & CO.,** 3083 N. Lima St., Burbank, CA 91504; (818) 841-7821.

***HARRISON, STAN,** 39039 Willowvale Rd., Palmdale, CA 93551; (818) 569-4528.

HOFFMAN VIDEO SYSTEMS, 870 N. Vine St., Hollywood, CA 90038; (213) 465-6900.

****HUCHINGSON MARTIN,** 3169 Barbara Court, Suite A, Los Angeles, CA 90068; (213) 876-4001.

****IMMEDIATO, JEFFREY & ASSOCIATES,** P.O. Box 5611, Long Beach, CA 90805; (213) 422-9295.

INTER VIDEO/TRITRONICS, INC., 733 N. Victory Blvd., Burbank, CA 91502; (818) 843-3633; 569-4000; FAX: (818) 843-6884.

KAPPA VIDEO, 801 S. Main St., Burbank, CA 91506; (818) 843-3400; 843-8099.

****KEM FILM/VIDEO SYSTEMS,** 662 N. Van Ness Ave., Suite 303, Los Angeles, CA 90004; (213) 467-1547.

****LIONEL TELEVISION PRODUCTIONS,** 3329 Brookside Dr., Malibu, CA 90265; (213) 456-5809.

MAGNASYNC MOVIOLA, 5539 Riverton Ave., North Hollywood, CA 91601; (818) 763-8441; FAX: (818) 505-9261.

***MAJESTIC DUPLICATING & VIDEO SERVICE,** 1208 W. Isabel St., Burbank, CA 91506; (213) 849-1535; (818) 843-1806.

***MIDTOWN VIDEO,** 8489 W. Third St., Suite 1065, Los Angeles, CA 90048; (213) 651-2420.

MILES & COMPANY, 1418 Dodson Ave., San Pedro, CA 90732; (213) 548-0462.

ONE PASS FILM & VIDEO, One China Basin Building, San Francisco, CA 94107; (415) 777-5777.

***P.D.S. VIDEO PRODUCTIONS,** 1102 W. Chestnut St., Burbank, CA 91506; (818) 841-4711.

***PROFESSIONAL ARTISTS GROUP,** 845 N. Highland Ave., Los Angeles, CA 90038; (213) 871-2222.

PROVIDEO, 10635 Van Owen St., Burbank, CA 91505; (818) 762-9671.

RANK CINTEL, INC., 13340 Saticoy, Unit F, North Hollywood, CA 91605; (818) 765-7265; FAX: (818) 765-3315.

***RAZ VIDEO PRODUCTIONS,** 1828 E. Walnut St., Pasadena, CA 91107; (818) 449-1175.

***RENTACAM,** 15016 Ventura Blvd., Suite 1, Sherman Oaks, CA 91403; (818) 501-7368.

SAWYER CAMERA VIDEO SERVICE, 1208 W. Isabel St., Burbank, CA 91506; (818) 843-1781; (213) 849-1535.

SCHULMAN VIDEO CENTER, 861 Seward St., Hollywood, CA 90038; (213) 465-8110.

SHORELINE PROFESSIONAL VIDEO SYSTEMS, 1622 N. Highland Ave., Hollywood, CA 90028; (213) 461-9800; FAX: (213) 461-1450.

****SPECTRA IMAGE INC.,** 540 N. Hollywood Way, Burbank, CA 91505; (818) 842-1111.

***SPRINGBOARD STUDIOS,** 12229 Montague St., Arleta, CA 91331; (818) 896-4321.

STARFAX, 654 Hawthorne St., Glendale, CA 91204; (818) 244-3600; FAX: (818) 244-3600.

STARLIGHT EDITING SERVICES, 5250 Strohm Ave., N. Hollywood, CA 91601; (818) 769-3874.

STATE OF THE ART AUDIO VISUAL EQUIPMENT, 23520 Telo Ave., Suite 10, Torrance, CA 90505; (213) 530-8711.

STEENBECK INC., 9554 Vassar Ave., Chatsworth, CA 91311; (818) 998-4033.

***STUDIO & REMOTE VIDEO,** 10650 Magnolia Blvd., North Hollywood, CA 91601; (818) 508-6010.

STUDIO SPECTRUM INC., 1056 N. Lake St., Burbank, CA 91502; (818) 843-1610; FAX: (818) 843-1145.

***TELEMEDIA PRODUCTIONS,** 18321 Ventura Blvd., Suite 660, Tarzana, CA 91356; (818) 708-2005.

***TIME LOGIC SYSTEMS,** 5555 Melrose Ave., Studio G, Hollywood, CA 90038; (213) 468-4608.

TOP VIDEO SERVICES, INC., 10153 Riverside Dr., Suite 1B, Toluca Lake, CA 91602; (818) 763-1295.

***UNITED TELEPRODUCTION SERVICES,** 15055 Oxnard St., Van Nuys, CA 91411; (818) 997-0100.

U.T. PHOTO SERVICE INC., 3088 N. Clybourn Ave., Burbank, CA 91505; (213) 245-6631.

VCC TELEVISION PRODUCTION SERVICES (Ventura Country Cablevision), 30901 Agoura Rd., Westlake Village, CA 91361; (818) 889-7370.
**VCR DOCTOR, 12471 Washington Blvd., Los Angeles, CA 90066; (213) 301-3222.
VTR SERVICE AND SALES, 3169 Barbara Ct., Suite D, Hollywood, CA 90068; (213) 851-9700.
VECTOR ENGINEERING, P.O. Box 7000-645, Redondo Beach, CA 90277; (213) 757-0520; (213) 316-6031.
**VIDEO CIRCUIT STUDIOS, 11440 Chandler Blvd., Studio 1400, N. Hollywood, CA 91601; (818) 506-5493.
*VIDEO EQUIPMENT RENTALS, 450 S. Central Ave., Glendale, CA 91204; (818) 956-0212.
*VIDEO IMAGE, 4121 Redwood Ave., Suite 215, Los Angeles, CA 90066; (213) 822-8872.
VIDEO-IT INC., 1016 N. Sycamore Ave., Hollywood, CA 90038; (213) 876-4055; (213) VID-EOIT.
*VIDEO POOL, 1832 N. Gower St., Hollywood, CA 90028; (213) 461-7665; (818) 798-4336.
VIDEO SUPPORT SERVICES INC., 3473½ Cahuenga Blvd. W., Los Angeles, CA 90068; (213) 469-9000.
VIDEOTAPE PRODUCTS INC., 320 N. Madison Ave., Los Angeles, CA 90004; (213) 664-1144; (800) 422-2444; FAX: (213) 661-2177.
*VISUAL EYES PRODUCTIONS, 2401 Main St., Santa Monica, CA 90405; (213) 392-8300; FAX: (213) 392-7480.
WESTERN FILM INDUSTRIES, 30941 W. Agoura Rd., Suite 302, Westlake Village, CA 91360; (818) 889-7350.
WEXLER VIDEO INC., 800 N. Victory Blvd., Burbank, CA 91502; (818) 846-9381.
WHIDBEY VIDEO, 12257 Riverside Dr., N. Hollywood, CA 91607; (818) 766-9855.
Z & A SERVICE, 9707 W. Washington Blvd., Culver City, CA 90232; (213) 836-3194.

NEW YORK

*ANS LABS, 396 Fifth Ave., New York, NY 10018; (212) 736-1007.
*ARC VIDEO EQUIPMENT, 511 W. 33 St., New York, NY 10001; (212) 629-0009.
*A/T SCHARFF, 599 Eleventh Ave., New York, NY 10036; (212) 582-4400.
*A.V. ELECTRONICS INTL. INC., 237 Centre St., New York, NY 10013; (212) 941-7015.
*ACE AUDIO-VISUAL, 13 E. 31 St., New York, NY 10010; (212) 685-3344; 33-49 55th St., Woodside, NY 11377; (718) 458-3800.
**ADVISORY TV & RADIO LABS, 175 Seventh Ave., New York, NY 10011; (212) 243-0786.
*ALBI, DOM, ASSOCIATES, INC., 121 W. 27 St., New York, NY 10001; (212) 727-2256.
**ALL CITY ELECTRONICS SERVICE INC., 1 E. 36 St., New York, NY 10016; (212) 689-7180.
*ALL-MOBILE VIDEO, INC., 630 Ninth Ave., New York, NY 10036; (212) 757-8919.
AMERICAN VIDEO INC., 717 Lexington Ave., New York, NY 10022; (212) 888-0888.
**AMERICAN VIDEO SERVICE DEPT., 516 Amsterdam Ave., New York, NY 10024; (212) 724-4870.
APEX VIDEO TV REPAIR, 1235 First Ave., New York, NY 10021; (212) 517-4300.
*AUDIO SERVICES CORPORATION, 326 W. 48 St., New York, NY 10036; (212) 977-5151.
AUDIOVISIONS, 1319 Second Ave., New York, NY 10021; (212) 988-5756.
AUTHORIZED FACTORY SERVICE CO., 902 Broadway, New York, NY 10010; (212) 598-4822.
*BLACK & HISPANIC IMAGES, INC., 11-45 47 Avenue, Suite 201, Long Island City, NY 11101; (718) 729-3232.
*BROADCAST VIDEO RENTALS, LTD., 333 W. 52 St., New York, NY 10019; (212) 541-5390.
BROADWAY VIDEO, 1619 Broadway, New York, NY 10019; (212) 265-7600; 713-0540.
CTL ELECTRONICS INC., 116 W. Broadway, New York, NY 10013; (212) 233-0754.
*THE CAMERA GROUP OF NEW YORK, INC., 599 Eleventh Ave., 6th Floor, New York, NY 10036; (212) 254-3600.
*THE CAMERA MART, 456 W. 55 St., New York, NY 10019; (212) 757-6977.
CAMERA SERVICE CENTER, INC., 625 W. 54 St., New York, NY 10019; (212) 757-0906.
*CINE MAGNETICS VIDEO, 50 W. 40 St., New York 10018; (212) 542-0700.
*CINERGY COMMUNICATIONS CORP., 321 W. 44 St., New York, NY 10036; (212) 582-2900.
*CITICAM VIDEO SERVICES, 630 Ninth Ave., Suite 910, New York, NY 10036; (212) 315-4855.
*COMPREHENSIVE SERVICE A-V INC., Box 881, New York, NY 10108; (212) 586-6161.
**E C ELECTRONICS, 254 W. 51 St., New York, NY 10019; (212) 586-6156.
FAMA II PRODUCTIONS, 2750 Richmond Terr., Staten Island, NY 10303; (718) 273-1780.
*FERCO VIDEO, 601 W. 50 St., New York, NY 10019; (212) 245-4800.
*FIRST RUN VIDEO INC., 1390 Third Ave., New York, NY 10021; (212) 772-3838.
*FOX TELEVISION OF AMERICA, INC., 333 W. 52 St., Suite 702, New York, NY 10019; (212) 246-4300.
*G & R VIDEO, 522 W. 36 St., New York, NY 10018; (212) 564-7260.
**GENERAL VIDEO, 34 E. 29 St., New York, NY 10016; (212) 725-7260.
*INTERCONTINENTAL TELEVIDEO INC., 29 W. 38 St., New York, NY 10018; (212) 719-0202.
*JEMS SOUND LTD., 785 Lexington Ave., New York, NY 10021; (212) 838-4716.
*K V L AUDIO VISUALS INC., 529 W. 46 St., New York, NY 10036; (212) 581-8050.
L & D FILM/VIDEO, 630 Ninth Ave., New York, NY 10036; (212) 315-0410.
*LAUMIC CO., 306 E. 39 St., New York, NY 10016; (212) 889-3300.
*LEONARD RADIO, 55 W. 44 St., New York, NY 10036; (212) 840-2025.
*LONGWOOD VIDEO, 32 W. 22 St., New York, NY 10010; (212) 741-3733.
**LUNAR VIDEO LTD., 138 E. 26 St., New York, NY 10010; (212) 686-4802.
*MPCS VIDEO INDUSTRIES, 514 W. 57 St., New York, NY 10019; (212) 586-3690; FAX: (212) 586-5282.
*MANHATTAN VIDEO PRODUCTIONS, 12 W. 27 St., New York, NY 10001; (212) 683-6565.
MARTIN AUDIO-VIDEO CORP., 423 W. 55 St., New York, NY 10019; (212) 541-5900.
MAYA VIDEO PRODS. INC., 172 Madison Ave., New York, NY 10001; (212) 532-6206.
MEDIA CONTACT, INC., 206 E. 38 St., New York, NY 10016; (212) 370-3959.
*MILLER L. MATTHEW, ASSOCIATES, LTD., 48 W. 21 St., New York, NY 10010; (212) 741-8011.
*MODERN TELECOMMUNICATIONS, INC., 1 Dag Hammarskjold Plaza, New York, NY 10017; (212) 355-0510.
*NATIONAL TELE-RENT INC., 150-09 12th Rd., Whitestone, NY 11357; (212) 829-1600.
*NEW YORK VIDEO, 717 Lexington Ave., New York, NY 10022; (212) 755-4640.
*NORTHEAST ELECTRONIC & VIDEO STORES, 420 Lexington Ave., New York, NY 10017; (212) 972-1799.
*OLDEN CAMERA VIDEO & COMPUTER STORE, 1265 Broadway, New York, NY 10001; (212) 725-1234.
*OMNI VIDEO SERVICES, LTD., 511 W. 33 St., New York, NY 10001; (212) 629-4303.
*REEVES A/V SYSTEMS INC., 227 E. 45 St., New York, NY 10017; (212) 573-8652; FAX: (212) 986-3591.
RELIANCE AUDIO-VISUAL CORP., 623 W. 51 St., New York, NY 10019; (212) 586-5000.
*RODNEY'S VIDEO WAREHOUSE, 109 Mamaroneck Ave., White Plains, NY; (914) 946-9696.
SELECT AUDIO VISUAL INC., 902 Broadway, New York, NY 10010; (212) 598-9800.
SONOCRAFT CORP., 360 W. 31st St., New York, NY 10001; (212) 760-9300.
*SOUND & VISION INC., 83 Leonard St., New York, NY 10012; (212) 219-3007.
SOUNDVIEW AV CO., 347 W. 39 St., New York, NY 10018; (212) 594-0183.
*SPATARO, CHARLIE, A. V. WORKSHOP, 333 W. 52 St., New York, NY 10019; (212) 397-5020.
*STREET VISIONS REMOTE INC., 34 Gansevoort St., New York, NY 10014; (212) 242-4324.
TECHNETRON ELECTRONICS INC., 43 E. 29 St., New York, NY 10016; (212) 725-8778; 725-8779.
TECHNISPHERE, 29 E. 19 St., New York, NY 10003; (212) 777-5100.
TELE-CASSETTE SERVICES, INC. 3315 Sycamore La., Yorktown Heights, NY 10598; (914) 245-5005.
*TELESTAR VIDEO, 206 E. 29 St., New York, NY 10016; (212) 689-1040.
*TELETECHNIQUES, INC., 1 W. 19 St., New York, NY 10011; (212) 206-1475; 663-1868.
**TELEVIDEO ELECTRONIC CORP., 233 W. 77 St., New York, NY 10024; (212) 874-7722.
*TEMMER LIGHTING, 1 W. 19 St., New York, NY 10011; (212) 206-1475; 633-1868.
**TRIBORO TELEVISION SERVICE, 1626 First Ave., New York, NY 10028; (212) 249-0327.
VI-AUD, SALES & SERVICE, 300 W. 43 St., New York, NY 10036; (212) 245-7966.

VICOM COMMUNICATIONS, 248 E. 33 St., New York, NY 10016; (212) 685-5232.

VIDEO CENTRAL, INC. 225 W. 36 St., New York, NY 10018; (212) 947-6960.

VIDEO INSTALLATIONS PLUS INC., 360 S. Broadway, Yonkers, NY 10705; (914) 968-3636.

***VIDEO OVERSEAS INC.,** 249 W. 23 St., New York, NY 10011; (212) 645-0797.

***VIDEO POWER USA INC.,** 511 W. 54 St., New York, NY 10019; (212) 315-0810.

***VIDEO RENTALS INC.,** 100 Oak St., Norwood, NJ 07648; (201) 768-3181; (800) 255-2874.

VIDEO 35, 425 Riverside Dr., #10B, New York, NY 10025; (212) 864-1408.

VIDEO SERVICE CENTER, 225 W. 36 St., New York, NY 10018; (212) 947-6960.

****VIDEO WORLD,** 138 W. Houston, New York, NY 10012; (212) 673-2435.

VISUAL WORD SYSTEMS INC., 17 E. 45 St., New York, NY 10017; (212) 661-3366.

WILLOUGHBYS, 110 W. 32 St., New York, NY 10001; (212) 564-1600.

WINDSOR VIDEO, 8 W. 38 St., New York, NY 10018; (212) 944-9090.

YK VIDEO, 432 Park Ave. S., New York, NY 10037; (212) 686-8515.

Video Mobile Units

LOS ANGELES

ABC TELEVISION CENTER, 4151 Prospect Ave., Los Angeles, CA 90027; (213) 557-7777.

ALL SEASONS ENTERTAINMENT, 18121 Napa St., Northridge, CA 91325; (818) 886-8680; (800) 423-5599.

AMERICAN VIDEO FACTORY, 4150 Glencoe Ave., Marina Del Rey, CA 90292; (213) 823-8622; (800) 367-8433.

AMERICAN VIDEOGRAM INC., 12020 W. Pico Blvd., Los Angeles, CA 90064; (213) 477-1535, 477-1536.

AQUASTAR SYSTEMS, 3960 Laurel Canyon Blvd., #406, Studio City, CA 91604; (818) 880-5639; (800) 227-5600.

AUTOGRAPHICS, 6335 Homewood Ave., Hollywood, CA 90028; (213) 464-2244.

BERC (BROADCAST EQUIPMENT RENTAL COMPANY), 4545 Chermak St., Burbank, CA 91505; (818) 841-3000; (213) 464-7655; FAX: (818) 841-7919.

BETACAM SPECIALISTS, 3719 Riverside Dr., Suite 9137, Burbank, CA 91505; (818) 845-6480.

BEXEL CORPORATION, 801 S. Main St., Burbank, CA 91506; (818) 841-5051.

BOWEN VIDEO FACILITIES & STAGE, 7826 Clybourn Ave., Sun Valley, CA 91352; (818) 504-0070.

BROADCAST REMOTE, 415 S. Flower, Burbank, CA 91502; (818) 841-0919.

BRYAN WORLD PRODUCTIONS, P.O. Box 74033, Los Angeles, CA 90004; (213) 856-9256.

CCR VIDEO CORPORATION, 6410 Santa Monica Blvd., Los Angeles, CA 90038; (213) 464-7151.

COLOR-VUE VIDEO ASSIST INC., 1800 S. Victory Blvd., Bldg. A, Burbank, CA 91201; (818) 244-7774.

DSR PRODUCTIONS, 607 N. 64 Ave., Los Angeles, CA 90042; (213) 258-6741.

DIVERSIFIED VIDEO INDUSTRIES, INC., 4216 N. Maxon Rd., El Monte, CA 91732.

EDIT POINT, P.O. Box 55760, Valencia, CA 91355; (818) 799-5611; (805) 254-2108.

EYE ON VIDEO, 224 N. Juanita Ave., Los Angeles, CA 90004; (213) 382-4048.

EYE SQUARE VIDEO INC., 1749 14th St., Santa Monica, CA 90404; (213) 452-9076.

HOLLYWOOD NATIONAL STUDIOS, 6605 Eleanor Ave., Los Angeles, CA 90038; (213) 467-6272.

HOLLYWOOD NEWSREEL SYNDICATE, INC., 1622 N. Gower St., Los Angeles, CA 90028; (213) 469-7307.

HUTCHINGSON MARTIN, 3169 Barbara Court, Suite A, Los Angeles, CA 90068; (213) 876-4001.

IMMEDIATO, JEFFREY, & ASSOCIATES, P.O. Box 5611, Long Beach, CA 90805; (213) 422-9295.

INTER VIDEO/TRITRONICS, INC., 733 N. Victory Blvd., Burbank, CA 91502; (818) 569-4000; 843-3633; FAX: (818) 843-6884.

INTERMIX INC., 2505 S. Robertson Blvd., Los Angeles, CA 90034; (213) 870-2121.

JP VIDEO SERVICES, (BETA CAM PRODUCTIONS), 9538 W. Pico Blvd., Los Angeles, CA 90035; (213) 271-1209; 859-9903.

KCOP TELEVISION INC., 915 N. La Brea Ave., Los Angeles, CA 90038; (213) 851-1000; 850-2229.

KNBC, 3000 W. Alameda St., Burbank, CA 91523; (818) 840-4444.

KTEH VIDEOSERVICES, 100 Skyport Dr., San Jose, CA 95115; (408) 998-5554.

LASER EDIT, INC., 540 N. Hollywood Way, Burbank, CA 91505; (818) 842-0777.

LEVIN, KARL M., 20959 Elkwood St., Canoga Park, CA 91304; (818) 882-7262.

M.F.I. VIDEO CENTER, 1905 Grace Ave., Hollywood, CA 90068; (213) 851-0373.

MEDIA MASTERS PRODUCTIONS, 1800 S. Robertson Blvd., Suite 306, Beverly Hills, CA 90035; (213) 451-8823.

MILES & CO., 1418 Dodson Ave., San Pedro, CA 90732; (213) 548-0462.

MOBILE IMAGE, 2944 W. Mountain Pine Dr., La Crescenta, CA 91214; (213) 873-5203, (818) 248-6905.

ONE PASS MOBILE SERVICES, 729 N. Highland Ave., Hollywood, CA 90038; (213) 937-4095.

P.D.S. VIDEO PRODUCTIONS, 1102 W. Chestnut St., Burbank, CA 91506; (818) 841-4711.

POSITIVE MEDIA, 5422A Fair Ave., North Hollywood, CA 91601; (818) 461-0092.

ROLAND, GLENN, FILMS, 10711 Wellworth Ave., Los Angeles, CA 90024; (213) 475-0937.

SCHULMAN VIDEO CENTER, 861 Seward St., Hollywood, CA 90038; (213) 465-8110.

SIERRA VIDEO, 11320 Chandler, N. Hollywood, CA 91601; (818) 506-4984; 579-7045.

SKYLINE PRODUCTIONS, 6309 Eleanor Ave., Hollywood, CA 90038; (213) 856-0033.

SOUND MASTER AUDIO/VISUAL, 10747 Magnolia Blvd., North Hollywood, CA 91601; (213) 650-8000.

SPALLA, RICK VIDEO PRODUCTIONS, 1622 N. Gower St., Los Angeles, CA 90028; (213) 469-7307.

STARFAX, INC., 654 Hawthorne St., Glendale, CA 91204; (818) 244-3600; FAX: (818) 244-0599.

SUNRISE CANYON VIDEO, P.O. Box 10968, Burbank, CA 91510; (818) 845-7473.

TBA PRODUCTION GROUP, 1925 Park East, Suite 260; Los Angeles, CA 90067; (213) 551-0898.

TELE VIDICS, 2223 E. 223 St., Long Beach, CA 90810; (213) 830-5296.

TOP VIDEO SERVICES, INC., 10153 Riverside Dr., Suite 1B, Toluca Lake, CA 91602; (818) 763-1295.

UNITED TELEPRODUCTION SERVICES, 15055 Oxnard St., Van Nuys, CA 91411; (818) 997-0100.

UNITEL VIDEO, 5555 Melrose Ave. Studio G, Los Angeles, CA 90038; (213) 468-4606.

VTE TELEVISION, 21041 Western Blvd., Torrance, CA 90501; (213) 328-1353; FAX: (213) 659-5710.

VALLEY PRODUCTION CENTER, 6633 Van Nuys Blvd., Van Nuys, CA 91405; (818) 988-6601.

VENTURA COUNTY CABLEVISION, 30901 Agoura Rd., Westlake Village, CA 91361; (818) 889-7370.

VIDCOM, 2426 Townsgate Rd., Suite K, Westlake Village, CA 91361; (818) 991-1974.

VIDEO ADVENTURES INC., 1015 Cahuenga Blvd., Hollywood, CA 90038; (213) 461-3288.

VIDEO CIRCUIT STUDIOS, 11440 Chandler Blvd., Studio 1400, N. Hollywood, CA 91601; (818) 506-5493.

VIDEO WEST, 805 Larrabee St., West Hollywood, CA 90069; (213) 659-5762.

VIDEOROOM, 1487 Third Ave., New York, NY 10028; (212) 879-5333.

VIDE-U PRODUCTIONS, 612 N. Sepulveda Blvd., Los Angeles, CA 90049; (213) 472-7023.

WHIDBEY VIDEO, 12257 Riverside Dr., N. Hollywood, CA 91607; (818) 766-9855.

NEW YORK

A.D.M. VIDEO PRODUCTIONS, 40 Seaview Blvd., Port Washington, NY 11050; (516) 484-6900.

ALL MOBILE VIDEO, 630 Ninth Ave., New York, NY 10036, (212) 757-8919.

CECO INTERNATIONAL CORP., 440 W. 15 St., New York, NY 10011; (212) 206-8280.

DEVLIN VIDEO SERVICE, 1501 Broadway, Suite 408, New York, NY 10036; (212) 391-1313.

FAMA II PRODUCTIONS, 2750 Richmond Terrace, Staten Island, NY 10303; (718) 273-1780.

FEATURE SYSTEMS, 512 W. 36 St., New York, NY 10018; (212) 736-0477.

FLYING TIGER COMMUNICATIONS, INC., 155 W. 18 St., New York, NY 10011; (212) 929-1156.

LEE PRODUCTIONS, INC., 12 W. 27 St., New York, NY 10001; (212) 213-4110.

L & D FILM/VIDEO, 630 Ninth Ave., New York, NY 10036; (212) 315-0410.

MTI TELEVISION CITY, 1443 Park Ave., New York, NY 10029; (212) 722-1818.

MAGNO SOUND & VIDEO, 729 Seventh Ave., New York, NY 10019; (212) 302-2505; FAX: (212) 819-1282.

MEGA MEDIA CENTER, 727 Eleventh Ave., New York, NY 10019; (212) 265-8500.

MODERN TELECOMMUNICATIONS, 1 Dag Hammarskjold Plaza, New York, NY 10017; (212) 355-0510.

NEP PRODUCTIONS, INC., 56 W. 45 St., New York, NY 10036; (212) 382-1100.

OMNI VIDEO SERVICES, LTD., 511 W. 33 St., New York, NY 10001; (212) 629-4303.

REBO STUDIO, 530 W. 25 St., New York, NY 10001; (212) 989-9466; FAX: (212) 627-9083.

TODAY VIDEO, 45 W. 45 St., New York, NY 10036; (212) 391-1020.

UNITEL VIDEO, 515 W. 57 St., New York, NY 10019; (212) 265-3600.

VIDEO PLANNING INC., 250 W. 57 St., New York, NY 10019; (212) 582-5066.

Video Production Facilities

LOS ANGELES

ABC TELEVISION CENTER, 4151 Prospect Ave., Los Angeles, CA 90027; (213) 557-7777; 557-5707.

ABERDEEN VIDEO, 3349 Cahuenga Blvd., Los Angeles, CA 90068; (213) 874-3050.

ACTION VIDEO, 6616 Lexington Ave., Hollywood, CA 90038; (213) 461-3611.

ACTORS CENTER, 11969 Ventura Blvd., Studio City, CA 91604; (818) 505-9400.

ALPHA STUDIOS, 4720 W. Magnolia Blvd., Burbank, CA 91505; (818) 760-2825.

AMERICAN VIDEO FACTORY, 4150 Glencoe Ave., Marina Del Rey, CA 90292; (213) 823-8622; 367-8433.

AMERICAN VIDEOGRAM INC., 12020 W. Pico Blvd., Los Angeles, CA 90064; (213) 477-1535; 477-1536.

ANDERSON, HOWARD A., & CO., 1016 N. Cole Ave., Los Angeles, CA 90038; (213) 463-2336.

APOLLO PRODUCTION FACILITY, 1503 Cahuenga Blvd., Hollywood, CA 90028; (213) 464-7871.

ATLANTIC/KUSHNER-LOCKE, 10880 Wilshire Blvd., Suite 2404, Westwood, CA 90024; (213) 470-0400.

AUDIO ARTS PUBLISHING CO., 5617 Melrose Ave., Los Angeles, CA 90038; (213) 461-3507.

AUDIO-VIDEO CRAFT INC., 6753 Santa Monica Blvd., Los Angeles, CA 90038; (213) 655-3511.

BCS BROADCAST STORE, INC., 4525 Valerio St., Burbank, CA 91505; (818) 845-7000.

BERC (BROADCAST EQUIPMENT RENTAL COMPANY), 4545 Chermak St., Burbank, CA 91505; (818) 841-3000; (213) 464-7655; FAX: (818) 841-7919.

BAKER-NISBET INC., 451 N. La Cienega Blvd., Suite 12, Los Angeles, CA 90048; (213) 657-5687.

BETACAM SPECIALISTS, 317 S. Lamer St., Burbank, CA 91506; (818) 845-6480.

BOSUSTOW VIDEO, 3030 Pennsylvania Ave., Santa Monica, CA 90404-4112; (212) 453-7973; FAX: (213) 828-4053.

BOWEN VIDEO FACILITIES & STAGE, 7826 Clybourn Ave., Sun Valley, CA 91352; (818) 504-0070.

BURBANK PRODUCTION PLAZA, 801 S. Main St., Burbank, CA 91506 (818) 846-7677; 841-5051; FAX: (818) 841-1572.

CALIFORNIA VIDEO CENTER, 15303 Ventura Blvd., Sherman Oaks, CA 91403; (818) 789-5000.

CENTRE FILMS INC., 1103 N. El Centro Ave., Los Angeles, CA 90038; (213) 466-5123.

CENTURY SOUTHWEST PRODUCTIONS, 2939 Nebraska Ave., Santa Monica, CA 90404; (213) 829-5111; 829-7624.

CHELSEA VIDEO STUDIOS, 6534 Sunset Blvd., Hollywood, CA 90028; (213) 464-5360.

CHOICE TELEVISION, 800 S. Date Ave., Alhambra, CA 91803; (818) 576-2906; 289-7719.

CINETYP, INC., 843 Seward St., Hollywood, CA 90038; (213) 463-8569.

CLARASOL PRODUCTION CO., 1028 N. La Brea Ave., Hollywood, CA 90038; (212) 462-7210; 464-0180.

COMPACT VIDEO SERVICES INC., 2813 W. Alameda Ave., Burbank, CA 91505; (818) 840-7000; (800) 423-2277.

COMPLETE POST INC., 6087 Sunset Blvd., Hollywood, CA 90028; (213) 467-1244.

THE COMPLEX, 2323 Corinth St., Los Angeles, CA 90064; (213) 477-1938.

CONSOLIDATED FILM INDUSTRIES, 959 Seward St., Los Angeles, CA 90038; (213) 462-3161; 960-7500.

CREATIVE SOUND CORP., 6290 Sunset Blvd., #1020, Hollywood, CA 90028; (213) 871-1010.

DSR PRODUCTIONS, 607 N. 64 Ave., Los Angeles, CA 90042; (213) 258-6741.

DEVONSHIRE SOUND STUDIOS, 10729 Magnolia Blvd., N. Hollywood, CA 91601; (818) 985-1945.

DUBS, INC., 6360 DeLongpre Ave., Hollywood, CA 90028; (213) 461-3726.

EYE ON VIDEO, 224 N. Juanita Ave., Los Angeles, CA 90004; (213) 382-4048.

EYE SQUARE VIDEO INC., 1749 14th St., Santa Monica, CA 90404; (213) 452-9076.

FIESTA SOUND & VIDEO, 1655 S. Compton Ave., Los Angeles, CA 90021; (213) 748-2057; 748-2665.

FOX TAPE, 5746 Sunset Blvd., Los Angeles, CA 90028; (213) 856- 1000.

GLENDALE STUDIOS, 1239 S. Glendale Ave., Glendale, CA 91205; (818) 502-5300.

GLOBAL ENTERTAINMENT NETWORK, INC., 1832 N. Gower St., Hollywood, CA; (213) 461-2534.

GOLDEN WEST VIDEOTAPE, 5800 Sunset Blvd., Los Angeles, CA 90028; (213) 460-8989.

GREENE, CROW & CO., 3083 N. Lima St., Los Angeles, CA 91504; (818) 841-7821.

GROUP W PRODUCTIONS, 3801 Barham Blvd., Los Angeles, CA 90068; (213) 850-3800.

HOLLYWOOD NATIONAL STUDIOS, 6605 Eleanor Ave., Los Angeles, CA 90038; (213) 467-6272.

HOLLYWOOD NEWSREEL SYNDICATE, INC., 1622 N. Gower St., Los Angeles, CA 90028; (213) 469-7307.

HOLLYWOOD PACIFIC STUDIOS, 62900 Sunset Blvd., Hollywood, CA 90028; (213) 463-8118.

IMAGE TRANSFORM INC., 4142 Lankershim Blvd., North Hollywood, CA 91602 (818) 985-7566.

IMAGE WEST, 11846 Ventura Blvd., Studio City, CA 91604; (818) 506-5577.

IMMEDIATO, JEFFREY & ASSOCIATES, P.O. Box 5611, Long Beach, CA 90805; (213) 422-9295.

INTER VIDEO/TRITRONICS INC., 733 N. Victory Blvd., Burbank, CA 91502; (818) 569-4000, 843-3633; FAX: (818) 843-6884.

INTERMIX INC., 2505 S. Robertson Blvd., Los Angeles, CA 90034; (213) 870-2121.

J.P. VIDEO SERVICES, 9538 W. Pico Blvd., Los Angeles, CA 90035; (213) 271-1209; 859-9903.

JAMAR PRODUCTIONS, 11969 Ventura Blvd., Studio City, CA 91604; (818) 762-2077.

KCET, 4401 Sunset Blvd., Los Angeles, CA 90027; (213) 666-6500.

KCOP TELEVISION INC., 915 N. La Brea Ave., Los Angeles, CA 90038; (213) 851-1000; 850-2229.

KWHY-TV, CHANNEL 22, 5545 Sunset Blvd., Los Angeles, CA 90028; (213) 466-5441.

KAPPA VIDEO, 801 S. Main St., Burbank, CA 91506; (818) 843-3400; 843-8099.

KEY WEST EDITING, 5701 Buckingham Pkwy., Suite C, Culver City, CA 90230; (213) 645-3348.

LMI PRODUCTIONS, %Lee Magid, Inc., P.O. Box 532, Malibu, CA 90265; (213) 463-7210.

LA BREA STUDIOS, 1028 N. La Brea Ave., Hollywood, CA 90038; (213) 462-7210.

LEVIN, KARL M., 20959 Elkwood St., Los Angeles, CA 91304; (818) 882-7262.

LIGHT-HOUSE PRODUCTIONS, 427 Linnie Canal, Venice, CA 90291; (213) 827-1537.

LIONEL TELEVISION PRODUCTIONS, 3329 Brookside Dr., Malibu, CA 90265; (213) 456-5809.

LOS ANGELES NEWS NETWORK, 1730 Camino Palmero, Suite 206, Los Angeles, CA 90046; (213) 850-5411.

MARSH INTERNATIONAL FILMS, 629 N. La Brea Ave., Los Angeles, CA 90036; (213) 936-7181.

MAXIMILLIAN TELEVISION & VIDEO, 411 W. 7th St., Los Angeles, CA 90014; (213) 624-8688.

McINTIRE-HOFFMAN, INC., 11969 Ventura Blvd., Studio City, CA 91604; (818) 762-2077.

MEDIA MASTERS PRODUCTIONS, 1800 S. Robertson Blvd., Suite 306, Beverly Hills, CA 90035; (213) 451-8823.

MEGA PRODUCTIONS INC., 1714 N. Wilton Pl., Hollywood, CA 90028; (213) 462-6342.

MIDTOWN VIDEO, 8489 W. Third St., Suite 1065, Los Angeles, CA 90048; (213) 651-2420.

MILES & COMPANY, 1418 Dodson Ave., San Pedro, CA 90732; (213) 548-0462.

MORRIS VIDEO INC., 2730 Monterey St., Suite 105, Torrance, CA 90503; (213) 533-4800.

NEWMAN/FRANKS, 2956 Nicada Dr., Los Angeles, CA 90077; (213) 470-0140; 470-0145; FAX: (213) 470-2410.

ONE PASS FILM & VIDEO, One China Basin Bldg., San Francisco, CA 94107; (415) 777-5777.

P.D.S. VIDEO PRODUCTIONS, 1102 W. Chestnut St., Burbank, CA 91506; (818) 841-4711.

PARALLAX PRODUCTIONS, P.O. Box 2413, Beverly Hills, CA 90213; (213) 840-4513.

POSITIVE MEDIA, 5422A Fair Ave., North Hollywood, CA 91601; (818) 761-5192.

THE POST PLACE, 12401 W. Olympic Blvd., Los Angeles, CA 90064; (213) 820-2900.

PREMORE INC., 5130 Klump Ave., N. Hollywood, CA 91601; (818) 506-7714.

THE PRODUCTION GROUP, 1330 N. Vine St., Hollywood, CA 90028; (213) 469-8111; FAX: (213) 462-0836.
PROFESSIONAL ARTISTS GROUP, 845 N. Highland Ave., Hollywood, CA 90038; (213) 871-2222.
PROFESSIONAL MEDIA SERVICE, 18301 Pammey Lane, Huntington Beach, CA 92648; (714) 964-0542.
REN-MAR STUDIOS, 846 N. Cahuenga Blvd., Los Angeles, CA 90038; (213) 463-0808.
S.A. GLOBAL STUDIOS, 201 N. Occidental Blvd., Los Angeles, CA 90026; (213) 384-3331.
SCHULMAN VIDEO CENTER, 861 Seward St., Hollywood, CA 90036; (213) 465-8110.
SOUND MASTER AUDIO/VIDEO, 10747 Magnolia Blvd., N. Hollywood, CA 91601; (213) 650-8000.
SOUTHLAND VIDEO, 3255 Cahuenga Blvd., Los Angeles, CA 90068; (213) 851-1190.
SPALLA, RICK, PRODUCTIONS, 1622 N. Gower St., Los Angeles, CA 90028; (213) 469-7307.
SPRINGBOARD STUDIOS, 12229 Montague St., Arleta, CA 91331; (818) 896-4321.
STUDIO & REMOTE VIDEO, 10650 Magnolia Blvd., North Hollywood, CA 91601; (818) 508-6010.
STUDIO PRODUCTIONS INC., 650 N. Bronson Ave., Suite 223, Hollywood, CA 90004; (213) 856-8048.
SUNRISE CANYON VIDEO, P.O. Box 10968, Burbank, CA 91510; (818) 845-7473.
SUPERCOLOSSAL PICTURES CORP., 3413 Cahuenga Blvd. W., Los Angeles, CA 90068; (213) 222-5550.
TAV/AME, INC., 1541 N. Vine St., Los Angeles, CA 90028; (213) 466-2141; FAX: (213) 464-4636.
TBA PRODUCTION GROUP, 1925 Century Park East, Suite 260, Los Angeles, CA 90067; (213) 551-0898.
TAPE-FILM INDUSTRIES (TFI), 941 N. Highland Ave., Hollywood, CA 90038; (213) 461-3361.
TELEVISION MATRIX, 1438 N. Gower St., Hollywood, CA 90028; (213) 465-9616.
TOP VIDEO SERVICES, INC., 10153 Riverside Dr., Suite 1B, Toluca Lake, CA 91602; (818) 763-1295.
TRANS-AMERICAN VIDEO INC., 1541 N. Vine St., Los Angeles, CA 90028; (213) 466-2141.
TRANSWORLD FILM CORP., 1520 S. Beverly Glen Blvd., Suite 304, Los Angeles, CA 90024; (213) 277-4250.
UNITEL VIDEO, 5555 Melrose Ave., Studio G, Los Angeles, CA 90038; (213) 468-4606.
THE VALENCIA STUDIOS, 28343 Avenue Crocker, Valencia, CA 91355; (800) STA-GEIT; (805) 257-1202; FAX: (805) 257-1002.
VALLEY PRODUCTION CENTER, 6633 Van Nuys Blvd., Van Nuys, CA 91405; (818) 988-6601.
VARITEL VIDEO, 3575 Cahuenga Blvd. W., Los Angeles, CA 90068; (213) 850-1165.
VIA VISION PRODUCTIONS, 5919 Franklin Ave., Los Angeles, CA 90028; (213) 460-4864.
VIDCOM ENTERTAINMENT, INC., P.O. Box 2926, Hollywood, CA 90078; (213) 301-8433.
VIDE-U PRODUCTIONS, 612 N. Sepulveda Blvd., Los Angeles, CA 90049; (213) 472-7023.
VIDEO ADVENTURES INC., 1015 Cahuenga Blvd., Hollywood, CA 90038; (213) 461-3288.
VIDEO CIRCUIT STUDIOS, 11440 Chandler Blvd., Studio 1400, N. Hollywood, CA 91601; (818) 506-5493.
VIDEO HOUSE, 201 N. Hollywood Way, Suite 202, Burbank, CA 91505; (818) 954-9559.
VIDEO IMAGE, 4121 Redwood Ave., Suite 215, Los Angeles, CA 90066, (213) 822-8872.
VIDEO TECHNICS, 1052B N. 5th St., San Jose, CA; (408) 275-1066; 1833 Evergreen St., San Mateo, CA 94402; (415) 343-8040.
VIDEO WEST, 805 Larrabee St., West Hollywood, CA 90069; (213) 659-5762.
VIDEO-IT INC., 5000 Overland Ave., Suite 6, Culver City, CA 90232; (213) 280-0505; (818) VID-EOIT.
VIDEO-PAC SYSTEMS LTD., 800 N. Seward St., Hollywood, CA 90038; (213) 469-7244.
VIDEOWERKS, INC., 1316 Third St., Suite 102, Santa Monica, CA 90401; (213) 393-8754.
WEXLER VIDEO INC., Burbank Production Plaza, 801 S. Main St., Burbank, CA 91506; (818) 846-9381.
WILDER BROTHERS VIDEO, 10327 Santa Monica Blvd., Los Angeles, CA 90025; (213) 557-3500.
WINTERS PRODUCTIONS, Box 920, Montrose, CA 91020; (818) 790-4201.

NEW YORK

ADM VIDEO PRODUCTIONS INC., 40 Seaview Blvd., Port Washington, NY 11050; (516) 484-6900.
ANS INTERNATIONAL VIDEO LTD., 396 Fifth Ave., New York, NY 10018; (212) 736-1007.
BETEGEUSE PRODUCTIONS, INC., 44 E. 32 St., New York, NY 10016; (212) 213-1333.
BROADWAY STUDIOS, 25-09 Broadway, Astoria, NY 11106; (718) 274-9121.
BROADWAY VIDEO, 1619 Broadway, New York, NY 10019; (212) 265-7600; 713-0540.
CALAMAR PRODUCTIONS, 38 Greene St., New York, NY 10012; (212) 334-4952.
CAMERA MART STAGES, INC., 456 W. 54 St., New York, NY 10019; (212) 757-6977.
CHARLEX, INC., 2 W. 45 St., New York, NY 10036; (212) 719-4600.
CHROMAVISION, 119 W. 22 St., New York, NY 10011; (212) 463-8997.
CINE-VID POST PRODUCTION, INC., 25 W. 45 St., New York, NY 10036; (212) 704-4000.
CREATIVE WAYS, 305 E. 46 St., New York, NY 10017; (212) 935-0145.
DEVLIN VIDEO SERVICE, 1501 Broadway, New York, NY 10036; (212) 391-1313; FAX: (212) 391-2744.
EMPIRE STAGES OF NY, 50-20 St., Long Island City, NY 11101; (718) 392-4747.
EQUITABLE PRODUCTION GROUP, 787 Seventh Ave., New York, NY 10019; (212) 554-1389.
FAMA II PRODUCTIONS, 2750 Richmond Terrace, Staten Island, NY 10303; (718) 273-1780.
FUTURE VIDEO PRODUCTIONS, 251 W. 30 St., New York, NY 10001; (212) 594-2778.
GLEN-WARREN PRODUCTIONS LTD., 551 Fifth Ave., #414, New York, NY 10017; (212) 883-0090.
HBO STUDIO PRODUCTIONS, 120A E. 23 St., New York, NY 10010; (212) 512-7800.
INTERNATIONAL PRODUCTION CENTER, 514 W. 57 St., New York, NY 10019; (212) 582-6530.
JPC VIDEO INC., 11 E. 47 St., #400, New York, NY 10017; (212) 223-0555; 755-4028.
KAUFMAN-ASTORIA STUDIOS, 34-12 36th St., Astoria, NY 11106; (718) 392-5600.
KOLMOR VISIONS INT'L LTD., 286 Fifth Ave., New York, NY 10001; (212) 947-7517.
LRP VIDEO, 3 Dag Hammarskjold Plaza, New York, NY 10017; (212) 759-0822.
LEE PRODUCTIONS, INC., 12 W. 27 St., New York, NY 10001; (212) 213-4110.
MPCS VIDEO INDUSTRIES, 514 W. 57 St., New York, NY 10019; (212) 586-3690.
MTI TV CITY, 1443 Park Ave., New York, NY 10029; (212) 722-1818.
MAGNO SOUND & VIDEO, 729 Seventh Ave., New York, NY 10019; (212) 302-2505.
MANHATTAN VIDEO PRODUCTIONS, INC., 12 W. 27 St., New York, NY 10001; (212) 683-6565.
MEGA MEDIA CENTER, 727 Eleventh Avenue, New York, NY 10019; (212) 265-8500.
MODERN TELECOMMUNICATIONS INC., 1 Dag Hammarskjold Plaza, Level C, New York, NY 10017; (212) 355-0510.
MOTHERS SOUND STAGES, 210 E. 5 St., New York, NY 10003; (212) 529-5097; 260-2050.
NBC TELESALES, 30 Rockefeller Plaza, New York, NY 10112; (212) 664-4754.
NATIONAL VIDEO CENTER/RECORDING STUDIOS, INC., 460 W. 42 St., New York, NY 10036; (212) 279-2000.
NATIONAL VIDEO INDUSTRIES, INC., 15 W. 17 St., New York, NY 10011; (212) 691-1300.
NORTHEAST VIDEO, 420 Lexington Ave., New York, NY 10017; (212) 661-8830.
NORTHSTAR VIDEO LTD., 423 E. 90 St., New York, NY 10028; (212) 996-9666.
PRIMA LUX VIDEO, 30 W. 26 St., New York, NY 10010; (212) 206-1402.
PROFESSIONAL COMMUNICATION SERVICES, 1776 Broadway, New York, NY 10019; (212) 247-7965.
REBO STUDIO, 530 W. 25 St., New York, NY 10001; (212) 989-9466; FAX: (212) 627-9083.
SILVER CUP STUDIOS, 42-25 21st St., Long Island City, NY 11101; (718) 784-3390.
SPALLA, RICK VIDEO PRODUCTIONS, 301 W. 45 St., New York, NY 10036; (212) 765-4646.
TELETECHNIQUES, 1 W. 19 St., New York, NY 10011; (212) 633-1868; 206-1475.
TELESTAR VIDEO, 206 E. 29 St., New York, NY 10016; (212) 689-1040.
TIMES SQUARE STUDIOS, 1481 Broadway, New York, NY 10036; (212) 704-9700.
TODAY VIDEO, 45 W. 45 St., New York, NY 10036; (212) 391-1020; FAX: (212) 768-1302.
TULCHIN STUDIOS, 240 E. 45 St., New York, NY 10017; (212) 986-8270.

UNITEL VIDEO, 515 W. 57 St., New York, NY 10019; (212) 265-3600.
VCA/TELETRONICS CENTER STAGE, 231 E. 55 St., New York, NY 10022; (212) 355-1600; 503 W. 33 St., New York, NY 10001; (212) 736-7717.
VIDEO PLANNING INC., 250 W. 57 St., New York, NY 10019; (212) 582-5066.
VIDEO PORTFOLIOS, 142 W. 24 St., New York, NY 10011; (212) 989-3858.
VIDEOWORKS, 24 W. 40 St., New York, NY 10018; (212) 869-2500.
VIDLO VIDEO, 40 E. 21 St., New York, NY 10010; (212) 475-4140.
WNET, 356 W. 58 St., New York, NY 10019; (212) 560-2068.
WINDSOR VIDEO, 8 W. 38 St., New York, NY 10017; (212) 944-9090.

NEW JERSEY

CENTENNIAL STUDIO, 140 Centennial Ave., Pisctaway, NJ 08854; (201) 457-8880.
COLOR LEASING STUDIO, 330 Rt. 46, Fairfield, NJ 07006; (201) 575-1118; (212) 662-2655.
PRESS BROADCASTING, P.O. Box 830, Press Plaza, Asbury Park, NJ 07712; (201) 774-7700.
SUBURBAN VIDEO PRODUCTIONS, 381 Lord St., Avenel, NJ 07001; (201) 750-0950.
VIDEOCENTER OF NJ INC., 228 Park Ave. E., Rutherford, NJ 07073; (201) 935-0900.

Video Screening Rooms

LOS ANGELES

ALTAVIDEO, 3501 Cahuenga Blvd. W., Los Angeles, CA 90068; (213) 876-8008.

AMERICAN VIDEO FACTORY, 4150 Glencoe Ave., Marina Del Rey, CA 90292; (213) 823-8622; (800) 367-8433.

AMPAC VIDEO, 3637 Cahuenga Blvd., Hollywood, CA 90068; (213) 851-7200.

AUDIO ARTS PUBLISHING CO., 5617 Melrose Ave., Los Angeles, CA 90038; (213) 461-3507.

AUDIO-VIDEO CRAFT INC., 6753 Santa Monica Blvd., Los Angeles, CA 90038; (213) 655-3511.

AUDIO VISUAL HEADQUARTERS CORP., 361 N. Oak St., Inglewood, CA 90302; (213) 419-4040.

BERC (BROADCAST EQUIPMENT RENTAL CO.), 4545 Chermak St., Burbank, CA 91505; (818) 841-3000, (213) 464-7655.

BOSUSTOW VIDEO, 2207 Colby Ave., West Los Angeles, CA 90064; (213) 478-0821.

CHELSEA VIDEO STUDIOS, 6534 Sunset Blvd., Hollywood, CA 90028; (213) 464-5360.

CHOICE TELEVISION, 800 S. Date Ave., Alhambra, CA 91803; (818) 576-2906; (213) 589-0553.

THE CREATIVE PARTNERSHIP, 7526 Fountain Ave., Hollywood, CA 90046; (213) 850-5551.

DAUGHERTY AUDIO/VISUAL DESIGN, 2172 Ridgemont, Los Angeles, CA 90046; (213) 650-5665; 718-5531.

DSR PRODUCTIONS, 607 N. Ave. 64, Los Angeles, CA 90042; (213) 258-6741.

THE EDITING COMPANY, 8300 Beverly Blvd., Los Angeles, CA 90048; (213) 653-3570.

ENGEL, RAY, PRODUCTIONS, 1730 Camino Palmero, Suite 206, Los Angeles, CA 90046; (213) 850-5411.

FOTO-KEM INDUSTRIES, 2800 W. Olive St., Burbank, CA 91505; (818) 846-3101.

GLOBAL VISION CORPORATION, 3255 Cahuenga Blvd., Hollywood, CA 90068; (213) 851-1190.

GRACE & WILD STUDIOS, HOLLYWOOD, 3501 Cahuenga Blvd. W., Los Angeles, CA 90068; (213) 876-8008; FAX: (213) 876-0460.

HARRAH'S THEATRE SERVICE & SUPPLY, 624B S. San Fernando Blvd., Burbank, CA 91502; (818) 842-5111; FAX: (818) 842-4141.

HORIZONTAL EDITING STUDIOS, 2625 W. Olive Ave., Burbank, CA 91505; (818) 841-6750.

IMAGE TRANSFORM, 4142 Lankershim Blvd., North Hollywood, CA 91602; (818) 985-7566.

IMAGE WEST, 11846 Ventura Blvd., Studio City, CA 91604; (818) 506-5577.

IMMEDIATO, JEFFREY, & ASSOCIATES, P.O. Box 5611, Long Beach, CA 90805; (213) 422-9295.

INDEPENDENT PRODUCERS STUDIO INC., 1604 Vista Del Mar Ave., Hollywood, CA 90028; (213) 461-6966.

INSTANT REPLAY COMMUNICATIONS CO., 11122 W. Washington Blvd., Hollywood, CA 90232; (213) 870-9435.

INTER VIDEO/TRITRONICS, 733 N. Victory Blvd., Burbank, CA 91502; (818) 569-4000; 843-3633; FAX: (818) 843-6884.

INTERMIX INC., 2505 S. Robertson, Los Angeles, CA 90034; (213) 870-2121.

J.P. VIDEO SERVICES, 9538 W. Pico Blvd., Los Angeles, CA 90035 (213) 271-1209; 859-9903.

KWHY-TV, CHANNEL 22, 5545 Sunset Blvd., Los Angeles, CA 90028; (213) 466-5441.

LEVIN, KARL M., 20959 Elkwood St., Canoga Park, CA 91304; (818) 882-7262.

MARKET STREET SCREENING ROOM, 73 Market St., Venice, CA 90291; (213) 396-5937.

MEDIA MASTERS PRODUCTIONS, 1800 S. Robertson Blvd., Suite 306, Beverly Hills, CA 90035; (213) 451-8823.

NEWMAN/FRANKS, 2956 Nicada Dr., Los Angeles, CA 90077. (213) 470-0140; 470-0145.

PACIFIC VIDEO, 809 N. Cahuenga Blvd., Los Angeles, CA 90038; (213) 462-6266.

POSITIVE MEDIA, 5422A Fair Ave., North Hollywood, CA 91601; (213) 461-0092.

THE POST GROUP, 6335 Homewood Ave., Los Angeles, CA 90028; (213) 462-2300.

POST PLUS INCORPORATED, 6650 Santa Monica Blvd., 2nd floor, Hollywood, CA 90038; (213) 463-7108.

RUBBER DUBBERS, INC., 626 Justin Ave., Glendale, CA 91201; (818) 241-5600.

S.A. GLOBAL STUDIOS, 201 N. Occidental Blvd., Los Angeles, CA 90026; (213) 384-3331.

SOUND MASTER AUDIO/VIDEO, 10747 Magnolia Blvd., North Hollywood, CA 91601; (213) 650-8000.

SOUTHLAND VIDEO, 3255 Cahuenga Blvd., Hollywood, CA 90068; (213) 851-1190.

STARLIGHT EDITING SERVICES, 5250 Strohm, North Hollywood, CA 91601; (818) 769-3874.

UCL VIDEO, 823 N. Seward St., Hollywood, CA 90038; (213) 469-7291.

UNITEL VIDEO, 5555 Melrose Ave., Studio G, Los Angeles, CA 90038; (213) 468-4606.

VALLEY VIDEO, 4209 W. Burbank Blvd., Burbank, CA 91505; (818) 841-2387.

VARITEL VIDEO, 3575 Cahuenga Blvd. W., Los Angeles, CA 90068; (213) 850-1165; FAX: (213) 850-6151.

VIDEO ADVENTURES INC., 1015 Cahuenga Blvd., Hollywood, CA 90038; (213) 461-3288.

VIDEO CIRCUIT STUDIOS, 11440 Chandler Blvd., Studio 1400, N. Hollywood, CA; 91601; (818) 506-5493.

VIDEO CRAFTSMEN INC., 6311 Romaine St., Los Angeles, CA 90038; (213) 464-4351.

THE VIDEO HOUSE, 201 N. Hollywood Way, Suite 202, Burbank, CA 91505; (818) 954-9559.

VIDEO-IT INC., 1016 N. Sycamore Ave., Hollywood, CA 90038; (213) 876-4055; (213) VID-EOIT.

THE VIDEO TAPE CO., 10545 Burbank Blvd., North Hollywood, CA 91601; (818) 985-1666.

VIDE-U PRODUCTIONS, 612 N. Sepulveda Blvd., Los Angeles, CA 90049; (213) 472-7023.

THE WILD SIDE THEATRE, 10945 Camarillo St., N. Hollywood, CA 91602; (818) 506-8838.

WILDER BROTHERS VIDEO, 10327 Santa Monica Blvd., Los Angeles, CA 90025; (213) 557-3500.

NEW YORK

ALL MOBILE VIDEO INC., 630 Ninth Ave., New York, NY 10036; (212) 757-8919.

DEVLIN VIDEO SERVICE, 1501 Broadway, Suite 408, New York, NY 10036; (212) 391-1313.

DU ART VIDEO, 245 W. 55 St., New York, NY 10019; (212) 757-3681.

LRP VIDEO, 3 Dag Hammarskjold Plaza, New York, NY 10017; (212) 759-0822.

MPCS VIDEO INDUSTRIES, 514 W. 57 St., New York, NY 10019; (212) 586-3690.

MAGNO SOUND & VIDEO, 729 Seventh Ave., New York, NY 10019; (212) 302-2505.

MODERN TELECOMMUNICATIONS INC., 1 Dag Hammarskjold Plaza, Level C, New York, NY 10017; (212) 355-0510.

MOVIE MAKERS THEATRE, 311 W. 43 St., New York, NY 10036; (212) 397-9787; outside NY: (800) 225-6566.

MOVIELAB THEATRE SERVICE, 619 W. 54 St., New York, NY 10019; (212) 586-0360.

NATIONAL VIDEO INDUSTRIES INC., 15 W. 17 St., New York, NY 10011; (212) 691-1300.

P.A.T. FILM SERVICES, 630 Ninth Ave., New York, NY 10036; (212) 247-0900.

TFI, TAPE-FILM INDUSTRIES, 619 W. 54 St., New York, NY 10019; (212) 708-0500.

TELETECHNIQUES, INC., 1 West 19 St., New York, NY 10011; (212) 206-1475; 633-1868.

VCA/TELETRONICS, 231 E. 55 St., New York, NY 10022; (212) 355-1600.

VIDEO CENTRAL, 225 W. 36 St., New York, NY 10018; (212) 847-6960.

WINDSOR VIDEO, 8 W. 38 St., New York, NY 10018; (212) 944-9090.

Videotape Transfer, Film to Tape

LOS ANGELES

A.M.E. INC., 1133 N. Hollywood Way, Burbank, CA 91505; (818) 841-7740; FAX: (818) 842-8409.

ACTION VIDEO, INC., 6616 Lexington Ave., Los Angeles, CA 90038; (213) 461-3611; FAX: (213) 460-4023.

ADVANCED VIDEO, 6753 Santa Monica, CA 90038; (213) 469-0707.

ALPHA CINE LABORATORY, INC., 5724 W. Third St., Suite 311, Los Angeles, CA 90036; (213) 934-7793; FAX: (213) 934-6307.

ALTAVIDEO, 3501 Cahuenga Blvd. W., Los Angeles, CA 90068; (213) 876-8008.

AMERICAN VIDEO FACTORY, 4150 Glencoe Ave., Marina Del Rey, CA 90292; (213) 823-8622; (800) 367-8433.

ANDERSON, HOWARD A., CO., 1016 N. Cole Ave., Los Angeles, CA 90038; (213) 463-2336.

APOLLO VIDEO FACILITY, 1503 Cahuenga Blvd., Hollywood, CA 90028; (213) 464-7871.

ASHFIELD FILM LAB, 747 N. Seward St., Hollywood, CA 90038; (213) 462-3231.

AUDIO ARTS PUBLISHING, CO., 5617 Melrose Ave., Los Angeles, CA 90038; (213) 461-3507.

AUDIO GRAPHICS FILMS AND VIDEO, 6509 De Longpre Ave., Hollywood, CA 90028; (213) 462-6596, (213) 467-1234.

AUDIO-VIDEO CRAFT INC., 6753 Santa Monica Blvd., Los Angeles, CA 90038; (213) 655-3511.

BCS BROADCAST STORE, INC., 4525 Valerio St., Burbank, CA 91505; (818) 845-7000.

BABYLON POST, 901 N. Seward St., Hollywood, CA 90038; (213) 460-4088.

BEVERLY HILLS VIDEOCENTRE, 145 S. Beverly Dr., Beverly Hills, CA 90212; (213) 550-1092; 8205 Santa Monica Blvd., W. Hollywood, CA 90046; (213) 656-4477.

BONDED SERVICES, 5260 Vineland Ave., North Hollywood, CA 91601; (818) 761-4058.

BOULEVARD VIDEO PRODUCTIONS, 15016 Ventura Blvd., Suite 1, Sherman Oaks, CA 91403; (818) 501-7369.

BROADCAST STANDARDS, INC., 2044 Cotner Ave., Los Angeles, CA 90025; (213) 312-9060; FAX: (213) 479-5771.

BUDGET VIDEO, 1540 N. Highland Ave., Suite 110, Los Angeles, CA 90028; (213) 466-2431; 466-0121.

CFI (CONSOLIDATED FILM INDUSTRIES), 959 Seward St., Hollywood, CA 90038; (213) 960-7444; FAX: (213) 460-4885.

CAL VISTA INTERNATIONAL INC., 6649 Odessa Ave., Van Nuys, CA 91406; (818) 780-9000.

CALIFORNIA COMMUNICATIONS INC., 6900 Santa Monica Blvd., Los Angeles, CA 90038; (213) 466-8511.

CHELSEA VIDEO STUDIOS, 6534 Sunset Blvd., Hollywood, CA 90028; (213) 464-5360.

COMPACT VIDEO SERVICES INC., 2813 W. Alameda Ave., Burbank, CA 91505; (818) 840-7000.

COMPLETE POST INC., 6087 Sunset Blvd., Hollywood, CA 90028; (213) 467-1244

COMPOSITE IMAGE SYSTEMS, 815 N. Cahuenga Blvd., Hollywood, CA 90038; (213) 461-5734; FAX: (213) 467-2324.

CONRAD FILM DUPLICATING CO., 6750 Santa Monica Blvd., Hollywood, CA 90038; (213) 463-5614.

CONSOLIDATED FILM INDUSTRIES, 959 Seward St., Los Angeles, CA 90038; (213) 462-3161.

CREST NATIONAL FILM & VIDEOTAPE LABS, 1141 N. Seward St., Los Angeles, CA 90038; (213) 466-0624; 462-6696; FAX: (213) 461-8901.

DELUXE LABORATORIES, INC., 1377 N. Serrano Ave., Hollywood, CA 90027; (213) 462-6171.

DEVONSHIRE AUDIO/VIDEO STUDIOS, 10729 Magnolia Blvd., N. Hollywood, CA 91601; (818) 985-1945.

DUPLITAPE, 15016 Ventura Blvd., Suite 1, Sherman Oaks, CA 91403; (818) 501-7370.

EDITEL-LOS ANGELES, 729 N. Highland Ave., Hollywood, CA 90038; (213) 931-1821.

THE EDITING COMPANY, 8300 Beverly Blvd., Los Angeles, CA 90048; (213) 653-3570.

ENCORE VIDEO INC., 6344 Fountain Ave., Hollywood, CA 90028; (213) 466-7663; FAX: (213) 467-5539.

EYE ON VIDEO, 224 N. Juanita Ave., Los Angeles, CA 90004; (213) 382-4048.

FILM & THEATRE SOCIETY, 1730 Camino, #206, Los Angeles, CA 90004; (213) 850-5411.

FILM TECHNOLOGY CO. INC., 6900 Santa Monica Blvd., Los Angeles, CA 90038; (213) 464-3456.

525 POST PRODUCTION, 6424 Santa Monica Blvd., Hollywood, CA 90038; (213) 466-3348; FAX: (213) 467-1589.

FOTO-KEM/FOTOTRONICS FILM-VIDEO LAB., 2800 W. Olive Ave., Burbank, CA 91505; (818) 846-3101; FAX: (818) 841-2040.

G & B VIDEO LAB, 255 E. Colorado Blvd., Pasadena, CA 91101; (818) 440-1909.

GLEN-WARREN PRODUCTIONS, LTD., 9911 W. Pico Blvd., Los Angeles, CA 90035; (213) 553-9233.

GLOBE TELEVISION, 1954 Cotner Ave., Los Angeles, CA 90025; (213) 479-8081.

GRACE & WILD STUDIOS HOLLYWOOD, 3501 Cahuenga Blvd. W., Los Angeles, CA 90068; (213) 876-8008; FAX: (213) 876-0460.

H.C.V., 3034 Glendale Blvd., Los Angeles, CA 90039; (213) 662-1112.

HOLLYWOOD NEWSREEL SYNDICATE INC., 1622 N. Gower St., Los Angeles, CA 90028; (213) 469-7307.

IMAGE TRANSFORM INC., 4142 Lankershim Blvd., North Hollywood, CA 91602; (818) 985-7566.

IMAGE TRANSFORM LABORATORY, 3611 N. San Fernando Rd., Burbank, CA 91505; (818) 841-3812.

INDEPENDENT PRODUCERS STUDIO INC., 1604 Vista Del Mar Ave., Hollywood, CA 90028; (213) 461-6966.

INTER VIDEO/TRITRONICS INC., 733 N. Victory Blvd., Burbank, CA 91502; (818) 843-2288; 569-4000; FAX: (818) 843-6884.

INTERSOUND, INC., 8746 Sunset Blvd., Los Angeles, CA 90069; (213) 652-3741.

IPS/INDEPENDENT PRODUCERS STUDIO INC., 1741 N. Ivar Ave., Suite 109, Hollywood, CA 90028; (213) 461-6966.

INTERNATIONAL VIDEO CONVERSIONS, 815 N. Cahuenga Blvd., Hollywood, CA 90038; (213) 463-7884.

JDH SOUND, 12156 W. Olympic Blvd., Los Angeles, CA 90064-1079; (213) 820-8802; FAX: (213) 207-0914.

JP VIDEO SERVICE, 9538 W. Pico Blvd., Los Angeles, CA 90035; (213) 859-9903; (213) 271-1209.

KWHY-TV, CHANNEL 22, 5545 Sunset Blvd., Los Angeles, CA 90028; (213) 466-5441.

LP PRODUCTION, 223 Strand St., Suite K, Santa Monica, CA 90405; (213) 399-1101; (714) 857-1310.

LAJON PRODUCTIONS, INC., 2907 W. Olive Ave., Burbank, CA 91505; (818) 841-1440.

M.F.I. VIDEO CENTER, 1905 Grace Ave., Hollywood, CA 90068; (213) 851-0373.

MAJESTIC DUPLICATING & VIDEO SERVICE, 1208 W. Isabel St., Burbank, CA 91506; (213) 849-1535; (818) 843-1806.

MAXIMILLIAN TELEVISION & VIDEO, 411 W. Seventh St., Los Angeles, CA 90014; (213) 624-8688.

McINTIRE-HOFFMAN INC., 11969 Ventura Blvd., Studio City, CA 91604; (818) 762-2077.

MEDIA MASTERS PRODUCTIONS, 1800 S. Robertson Blvd., Suite 306; Beverly Hills, CA 90035; (213) 451-8823.

MOBILE TRANSFERS, INC. 5417 N. Cahuenga Blvd., Suite A, N. Hollywood, CA 91601; (213) 466-2044.

MODERN TALKING PICTURE SERVICE INC., 6735 San Fernando Rd., Glendale, CA 91201; (818) 240-0519; (813) 541-7571; FAX: (813) 544-4624.

MODERN VIDEOFILM, 7165 Sunset Blvd., Hollywood, CA 90046; (213) 851-8070; FAX: (213) 851-0704.

MUSIC LAB INC., 1831 Hyperion Ave., Hollywood, CA 90027; (213) 666-3003.

ONE PASS FILM & VIDEO, One China Basin Building, San Francisco, CA 94107; (415) 777-5777.

PACIFIC TITLE & ART STUDIO, 6350 Santa Monica Blvd., Hollywood, CA 90038; (213) 464-0121.

PACIFIC VIDEO, 809 N. Cahuenga Blvd., Los Angeles, CA 90038; (213) 462-6266; (213) 464-3233.

PAL VIDEO, 19061 Tina Pl., Tarzana, CA 91356; (818) 344-1603.

THE POST GROUP, 6335 Homewood, Los Angeles, CA 90028; (213) 462-2300.

PRO VIDEO/CINETAPE, 801 N. La Brea Ave., Los Angeles, CA 90038; (213) 934-8836.

R. PRODUCTIONS & VIDEO EVENTS, 1741 N. Ivar, Suite 210, Hollywood, CA 90028; (213) 465-4197.

RALEIGH STUDIOS, 650 N. Bronson Ave., Los Angeles, CA 90004; (213) 466-3111; (213) 871-4428.

RANK VIDEO, 500 N. Ventu Rd., Newbury Park, CA 91320; (805) 499-5827; 970 W. 190 St., Suite 900, Torrance, CA 90502; (213) 515-6499.

RENCHER'S EDITORIAL SERVICE, 738 Cahuenga Blvd., Hollywood, CA 90038; (213) 463-9836.

RUBBER DUBBERS INC., 626 Justin Ave., Glendale, CA 91201; (818) 241-5600.
RUSK SOUND STUDIO, 1556 N. La Brea Ave., Hollywood, CA 90028; (213) 462-6477.
RUSSIAN HILL RECORDING, 1520 Pacific Ave., San Francisco, CA 94109; (415) 474-4520.
RUXTON LTD., 611 N. Orchard Dr., Burbank, CA 91506; (818) 845-3724.
SIERRA VIDEO, 11320 Chandler Blvd., N. Hollywood, CA 91601; (818) 506-4984; 579-7045.
SKYLINE PRODUCTIONS, 6309 Eleanor Ave., Hollywood, CA 90038; (213) 856-0033.
SOUND SERVICES INC. (S.S.I.), 7155 Santa Monica Blvd., Los Angeles, CA 90046; (213) 874-9344; 986-3255.
SOUND WEST, INC., 12166 Olympic Blvd., Los Angeles, CA 90064; (213) 826-6560.
SPALLA, RICK, VIDEO PRODUCTIONS, 1622 N. Gower St., Los Angeles, CA 90028; (213) 469-7307.
SPRINGBOARD STUDIOS, 12229 Montague St., Los Angeles, CA 91331; (818) 896-4321.
STARFAX, 654 Hawthorne St., Glendale, CA 91204; (818) 244-3600; FAX: (818) 244-0599.
STUDIO TELEVISION SERVICE, 7550 W. Sunset Blvd., Los Angeles, CA 90046; (213) 460-4400.
SUPERCINE INC., 2214 W. Olive Ave., Burbank, CA 91506; (818) 843-8260.
TAV/AME INC., 1541 N. Vine St., Los Angeles, CA 90028; (213) 466-2141; FAX: (213) 464-4636.
TAV SOUND INC., 6200 W. Third St., Los Angeles, CA 90038; (213) 937-2460.
TELEPRINT OF LOS ANGELES, 3779 Cahuenga Blvd. W., Studio City, CA 91604; (818) 760-3191.
TODD-AO/GLEN GLENN STUDIOS, 900 N. Seward St., Hollywood, CA 90038; (213) 469-7221.
TRANS-AMERICAN VIDEO INC., 1541 N. Vine St., Los Angeles, CA 90028; (213) 466-2141.
TRANSWORLD VIDEO LAB INC., 1811 W. Magnolia Blvd., Burbank, CA 91506; (818) 841-2416.
U C L VIDEO, 823 N. Seward St., Los Angeles, CA 90038; (213) 469-7291.
U P A PRODUCTIONS OF AMERICA, 1875 Century Park E., Suite 2140, Los Angeles, CA 90067; (213) 556-3800.
UNITED COLOR LAB, INC., 823 N. Seward St., Hollywood, CA 90038; (213) 461-9921.
UNITEL VIDEO, 5555 Melrose Ave., Studio G, Los Angeles, CA 90038; (213) 468-4606.
USA PRODUCTIONS, 1645 Vine St., Suite 350, Hollywood, CA 90028; (213) 465-6320.
V C I SERVICES (VID-FILM SERVICES), 1631 Gardena, Glendale, CA 91204; (818) 500-9090; (213) 650-8550; FAX: (818) 500-4099.
VALLEY VIDEO, 4209 W. Burbank Blvd., Burbank, CA 91505; (818) 841-2387.
VIDEO ADVENTURES INC., 1015 Cahuenga Blvd., Hollywood, CA 90038; (213) 461-3288.
VIDEO CIRCUIT STUDIOS, 11440 Chandler Blvd., Studio 1400, N. Hollywood, CA 91601; (818) 506-5493.
VIDEO CRAFTSMEN INC., 6311 Romaine St., Los Angeles, CA 90038; (213) 464-4351.
VIDEO EVENTS INC., 1741 N. Ivar, Suite 210, Hollywood, CA 90028; (213) 465-4197.
VIDEO IMAGE, 4121 Redwood Ave., Suite 215, Los Angeles, CA 90066; (213) 822-8872.
THE VIDEO TAPE CO., 10545 Burbank Blvd., North Hollywood, CA 91601; (818) 985-1666; 753-3051; FAX: (818) 985-0614.
VIDEO TECHNOLOGY & SERVICES, 500 N. Ventu Park Rd., Newbury Park, CA 91320; (818) 888-3040; (805) 499-5827.
VIDEO VIEW, 1617 N. El Centro Ave., Hollywood, CA 90038; (213) 463-4179.
VIDE-U PRODUCTIONS, 612 N. Sepulveda Blvd., Los Angeles, CA 90049; (213) 472-7023.
WESTERN FILM INDUSTRIES, 30941 W. Agoura Rd., Suite 302, Westlake Village, CA 91361; (818) 889-7350; FAX: (818) 707-3937.
WILDER BROTHERS VIDEO, 10327 Santa Monica Blvd., Los Angeles, CA 90025; (213) 557-3500.
WILLIAM SOUND SERVICE, INC., 1343 N. Highland Ave., Los Angeles, CA 90028; (213) 461-5321.
WORLD COMMUNICATIONS, 10880 Wilshire Blvd., Suite 2204, Los Angeles, CA 90024; (213) 474-3500.
YALE LABS, 1509 N. Gordon, Los Angeles, CA 90028, (213) 464-6181.

NEW YORK

A & D FILM/VIDEO, INC., 630 Ninth Ave., New York, NY 10036; (212) 315-0410.
ANS INTERNATIONAL VIDEO LTD., 396 Fifth Ave., New York, NY 10018; (212) 736-1007.
ACE AUDIO VISUAL CO., 13 E. 31 St., New York, NY 10016; (212) 685-3344.
ALL CHANELS VIDEO, INC. 630 Ninth Ave., New York, NY 10036; (212) 247-3428.
ALL MOBILE VIDEO, 630 Ninth Ave., New York, NY 10036; (212) 757-8919.
ALL STAR FILM TO VIDEO, 251 W. 30 St., #6RW, New York, NY 10001; (212) 594-2778.
AMERICAN TV VIDEO, 248 E. 48 St., New York, NY 10017; (212) 688-6222.
AMERICAN VIDEO CHANNELS, INC., 321 W. 44 St., New York, NY 10036; (212) 765-6324.
APPLE VIDEO SERVICES INC., 1697 Broadway, New York, NY 10019; (212) 586-2999.
AQUARIUS TRANSFERMATION, 12 E. 46 St., New York, NY 10017; (212) 697-3636.
AUDIO PLUS VIDEO INTERNATIONAL, INC., 240 Pegasus Ave., Northvale, NJ 07647; (201) 767-3800; FAX: (201) 767-4568.
BOGAZICI VIDEO LTD., 460 Seventh Ave., New York, NY 10001; (212) 563-9022.
CINE MAGNETICS FILM & VIDEO LABORATORIES, 650 Halstand Ave., Mamaroneck, NY; (914) 698-3434; 50 W. 40 St., New York, NY 10018; (212) 542-0700.
DEVLIN VIDEO SERVICE, 1501 Broadway, Suite 408, New York, NY 10036; (212) 391-1313; FAX: (212) 391-2744.
DU ART FILM LABS, 245 W. 55 St., New York, NY 10019; (212) 757-4580.
EDITEL—NEW YORK, 222 E. 44 St., New York, NY 10017; (212) 867-4600.
86TH ST. PHOTO, 1525 Third Ave., New York, NY 10028; (212) 737-2265.
FAMA II PRODUCTIONS, 2750 Richmond Terrace, Staten Island, NY 10303; (718) 273-1780.
FOTO-VIDEO TRANSFER CENTER, 1 Times Square, New York, NY 10036; (212) 302-1866.
FRAME:RUNNER, 1995 Broadway, Suite 1100, New York, NY 10023; (212) 874-1730.
FUTURE VIDEO PRODUCTIONS, 251 W. 30 St., New York, NY 10001; (212) 594-2777; 594-2778.
HBO STUDIO PRODUCTIONS, 120A E. 23 St., New York, NY 10010; (212) 512-7800.
IMAGE MIX, INC., 305 E. 46 St., New York, NY 10017; (212) 752-3010.
INTERNATIONAL VIDEO MARKET, 926 Second Ave., New York, NY 10022; (212) 826-1996.
INTERNATIONAL VIDEO SERVICES, 1501 Broadway, New York, NY 10036; (212) 730-1411.
JSL VIDEO SERVICES, INC., 25 W. 45 St., New York, NY 10036; (212) JSL-5082.
LRP VIDEO, 3 Dag Hammerskjold Plaza, New York, NY 10017; (212) 759-0822.
LANDMARK VIDEO INC., 350 Fifth Ave., New York, NY 10001; (212) 947-8637.
LANDYVISION, 400 E. 83 St., Suite 4A, New York, NY 10028; (212) 734-1402.
LASER VIDEO INC., 384 Bleecker St., New York, NY 10014; (212) 947-8637.
MGS SERVICES, 619 W. 54 St., New York, NY 10019; (212) 765-4500.
MPCS VIDEO INDUSTRIES, 514 W. 57 St., New York, NY 10019; (212) 586-3690.
MAGNO SOUND & VIDEO, 729 Seventh Ave., New York, NY 10019; (212) 302-2505; FAX: (212) 819-1282.
MANHATTAN TRANSFER/EDIT, 545 Fifth Ave., New York, NY 10017; (212) 687-4000.
MODERN TELECOMMUNICATIONS INC., 1443 Park Ave., New York, NY 10029; (212) 722-1818; 1 Dag Hammarskjold Plaza, New York, NY 10017; (212) 355-0510.
MOVIELAB VIDEO INC., 619 W. 54 St., New York, NY 10019; (212) 956-3900.
MULTI-VIDEO GROUP LTD., 50 E. 42 St., New York, NY 10017; (212) 986-1577.
NATIONAL VIDEO CENTER/RECORDING STUDIOS, INC., 460 W. 42 St., New York, NY 10036; (212) 279-2000.
PICSONIC PRODUCTIONS CORP., 25 W. 45 St., New York, NY 10036; (212) 575-1910.
R.G. VIDEO, 21 E. 46 St., New York, NY 10036; (212) 719-2744.
REEVES TELETAPE, 708 Third Ave., New York, NY 10017; (212) 573-8888; 1697 Broadway, New York, NY 10019; (212) 307-4880.
REGENT SOUND STUDIOS INC., 1619 Broadway, New York, NY 10019; (212) 245-2630.
ROSENBERG, WARREN, VIDEO SERVICES, 308 E. 79 St., New York, NY 10021; (212) 744-1111.
ROSS GAFFNEY VIDEO, 21 W. 46 St., New York, NY 10036; (212) 997-1464.
S/T VIDEOCASSETTE DUPLICATION CORP., 500 Willowtree Rd., Leonia, NJ; (212) 239-4653.

SOUND ONE CORP., 1619 Broadway, New York, NY 10019; (212) 765-4757.
SPALLA, RICK, PRODUCTIONS, 301 W. 45 St., New York, NY 10036; (212) 765-4646.
SPECTRUM LIGHT PRODUCTIONS, 928 Broadway, Room 702, New York, NY 10010; (212) 477-0346.
SYNAPSE TELECOMMUNICATIONS, INC., 304 E. 45 St., New York, NY 10017; (212) 370-9191.
TFI (TAPE FILM INDUSTRIES), 619 W. 54 St., New York, NY 10019; (212) 708-0500.
TVC VIDEO, 225 E. 43 St., New York, NY 10017; (212) 599-1616.
THE TAPE HOUSE EDITORIAL CO., 216 E. 45 St., New York, NY 10017; (212) 557-4949.
TV-R/MASTER COLOR TRANSFER, INC., 333 W. 52 St., New York, NY 10019; (212) 541-4030.
TODAY VIDEO, 45 W. 45 St., New York, NY 10036; (212) 391-1020.
UNITEL VIDEO, 515 W. 57 St., New York, NY 10019; (212) 265-3600.
VCA/TELETRONICS, 231 E. 55 St., New York, NY 10022; (212) 355-1600.
VIDEO CASSETTE TRANSFERS, 1501 Broadway, Suite 406, New York, NY 10036; (212) 575-8433.
VIDEO CENTRAL INC., 225 W. 36 St., New York, NY 10018; (212) 947-6960.
VIDEO CONNECTION, 2244 Broadway, New York, NY 10024; (212) 724-2727.
VIDEO DUB, INC., 423 W. 55 St., New York, NY 10019; (212) 757-3300.
VIDEO FEX, 321 W. 44 St., New York, NY 10036; (212) 541-9220.
VIDEO MEDIA PRODUCTIONS, 149-33 88th St., Howard Beach, NY; (718) 845-3709.
VIDEO PLANNING INC., 250 W. 57 St., New York, NY 10019; (212) 582-5066.
VIDEO RESOURCES NEW YORK, INC., 220 W. 71 St., New York, NY 10023; (212) 724-7055.
VIDEO STOP, 367 Third Ave., New York, NY 10016; (212) 685-6199.
VIDEO TRANSFERS INC., 1501 Broadway, Room 406, New York, NY 10036; (212) 575-8433.
VIDEOROOM, 1487 Third Ave., New York NY 10028; (212) 879-5333.
VIDEOWORKS, 24 W. 40 St., New York, NY 10018; (212) 869-2500.
WINDSOR VIDEO, 8 W. 38 St., New York, NY 10018; (212) 944-9090.

CANADA

BELLEVUE PATHÉ QUEBEC VIDEO DUPLICATION CENTER, 5588 Cote de Liesse, Montreal, Que., H4P 1A9; (514) 737-2777.
MANTA VIDEO LABS, 311 Adelaide St. E, Toronto, Ont., M5A IN2; (412) 863-9316.
PATHÉ SOUND & POST PRODUCTION CENTRE, 1212 St. Patrick St., Toronto, Ont.; (416) 598-2521.

Videotape Transfer, Tape to Film

LOS ANGELES

AMERICAN VIDEO FACTORY, 4150 Glencoe Ave., Marina Del Rey, CA 90292; (213) 823-8622.
APOLLO VIDEO FACILITY, 1503 Cahuenga Blvd., Hollywood, CA 90028; (213) 464-7871.
AUDIO GRAPHIC FILMS AND VIDEO, 6509 De Longpre Ave., Hollywood, CA 90028; (213) 462-6596, (213) 467-1234.
BEVERLY HILLS VIDEOCENTRE, 8205 Santa Monica Blvd., W. Hollywood, CA 90046; (213) 656-4477.
BROADCAST STANDARDS, INC., 2044 Cotner Ave., Los Angeles, CA 90025; (213) 312-9060; FAX: (213) 479-5771.
COMPACT VIDEO SERVICES INC., 2813 W. Alameda Ave., Burbank, CA 91505; (818) 840-7000.
CONSOLIDATED FILM INDUSTRIES, 959 Seward St., Los Angeles, CA 90038; (213) 462-3161.
CREATIVE VIDEO SERVICES, 500 Ventu Park Rd., Newbury Park, CA 91320; (818) 888-3040.
CREST NATIONAL FILM & VIDEOTAPE LABS, 1141 N. Seward St., Los Angeles, CA 90038; (213) 462-0624; 462-6696; FAX: (213) 461-8901.
DEVONSHIRE SOUND STUDIOS, 10729 Magnolia Blvd., N. Hollywood, CA 91601; (818) 985-1945.
THE EDITING COMPANY, 8300 Beverly Blvd., Los Angeles, CA 90048; (213) 653-3570.
ENCORE VIDEO, INC., 6344 Fountain Ave., Hollywood, CA 90028; (213) 466-7663.
IMAGE TRANSFORM INC., 4142 Lankershim Blvd., North Hollywood, CA 91602; (818) 985-7566.
IMAGE TRANSFORM LABORATORY, 3611 N. San Fernando Rd., Burbank, CA 91505; (818) 841-3812.
INTER VIDEO/TRITONICS INC., 733 N. Victory Blvd., Burbank, CA 91502; (818) 843-3633; 569-4000; FAX: (818) 843-6884.
INTERNATIONAL VIDEO CONVERSIONS, 815 N. Cahuenga Blvd., Hollywood, CA 90038; (213) 463-7884.
KWHY-TV, CHANNEL 22, 5545 Sunset Blvd., Los Angeles, CA 90028; (213) 466-5441.
MEDIA MASTERS PRODUCTIONS, 1800 S. Robertson Blvd., Suite 306, Beverly Hills, CA 90035; (213) 451-8823.
MODERN TALKING PICTURE SERVICE, INC., 6735 San Fernando Rd., Glendale, CA 91201; (818) 240-0519; (813) 541-7571; FAX: (813) 544-4624.
MODERN VIDEOFILM, 7165 Sunset Blvd., Hollywood, CA 90046; (213) 851-8070.
ONE PASS FILM & VIDEO, One China Basin Bldg., San Francisco, CA 94107; (415) 777-5777.
RVS—TAPE TO FILM TRANSFER SERVICES, 2408 W. Olive Ave., Burbank, CA 91506; (818) 954-8621.
RENCHER'S EDITORIAL SERVICE, 738 Cahuenga Blvd., Hollywood, CA 90038; (213) 463-9836.
RINGER VIDEO SERVICES, 2408 W. Olive Ave., Burbank, CA 91506; (818) 954-8621.
ROUZER STUDIO, 451 N. Mansfield, Los Angeles, CA 90036-2621; (213) 935-6124.
SOUND SERVICES INC., 7155 Santa Monica Blvd., Los Angeles, CA 90038; (213) 874-9344.
SPALLA, RICK, PRODUCTIONS, 1622 N. Gower St., Los Angeles, CA 90028; (213) 469-7307.
SPLIT REEL RECORDING, 870 N. Vine St., Suite B, Hollywood, CA 90038; (213) 466-3817.
TAV SOUND INC., 6200 W. Third St., Los Angeles, CA 90038; (213) 937-2460.
TAPE-FILM INDUSTRIES, 941 N. Highland Ave., Hollywood, CA 90038; (213) 461-3361.
TELEPRINT OF LOS ANGELES, 3779 Cahuenga Blvd. W., Studio City, CA 91604; (818) 760-3191.
TODD-AO/GLEN GLENN STUDIOS, 900 N. Seward St., Hollywood, CA 90038; (213) 469-7221.
USA PRODUCTIONS, 1645 Vine St., Suite 350, Hollywood, CA 90028; (213) 465-6320.
VECTOR PRODUCTIONS INC., P.O. Box 7000-645, Redondo Beach, CA 90277; (213) 757-0520, (213) 316-6031.
VIDEO CIRCUIT STUDIOS, 8103 Orion Ave., Van Nuys, CA 91406; (818) 785-6220.
VIDEO VIEW, 1617 N. El Centro Ave., Hollywood, CA 90028; (213) 463-4179.
WEISBARTH, JACOB & ASSOCIATES, INC., 9903 Santa Monica Blvd., Suite 256, Beverly Hills, CA 90212; (213) 277-9616.
WESTERN FILM INDUSTRIES, 30941 W. Agoura Rd., Suite 302, Westlake Village, CA 91360; (818) 889-7350.

NEW YORK

A & D FILM/VIDEO, 630 Ninth Ave., New York, NY 15036; (212) 315-0410.
AVPS CORP., 31 W. 60 St., New York, NY 10023; (212) 765-5060.
CINELAB CORP., 1600 Broadway #1008, New York, NY 10019; (212) 315-0600.
DEVLIN VIDEOSERVICE, INC., 1501 Broadway, Suite 408, New York, NY 10036; (212) 391-1313; FAX: (212) 391-2744.
DU ART FILM LABS INC., 245 W. 55 St., New York, NY 10019; (212) 757-4580; FAX: (212) 333-7647.
EDITEL NEW YORK, 222 E. 44 St., New York, NY 10017; (212) 867-4600.
MPCS VIDEO INDUSTRIES, INC., 514 W. 57 St., New York, NY 10019; (212) 586-3690; (800) 223-0622.
MTI TV CITY, 1443 Park Ave., New York, NY 10029; (212) 722-1818.
MAGNO SOUND & VIDEO, 729 Seventh Ave., New York, NY 10019; (212) 302-2505.
MAYFAIR RECORDING STUDIO INC., 701 Seventh Ave., New York, NY 10036; (212) 719-2810.
MODERN TELECOMMUNICATIONS INC., 885 Second Ave., New York, NY 10017; (212) 355-0510.
MOONLIGHT VIDEO COMMUNICATIONS, INC. 1600 Broadway, New York, NY 10019; (212) 245-6630.
NATIONAL FILM CENTER, 232 E. 46 St., New York, NY 10017; (212) 279-2000.
PICSONIC PRODUCTIONS CORP., 25 W. 45 St., #703; New York, NY 10036; (212) 575-1910.
POSITIVE TRANSFER LTD., 545 Fifth Ave., New York, NY 10017; (212) 888-2722.
SPALLA, RICK VIDEO PRODUCTIONS, 301 W. 45 St., New York, NY 10036; (212) 765-4646.
TFI, 619 W. 54 St., New York, NY 10019; (212) 708-0500.
TV-R INC., 333 W. 52 St., New York, NY 10019; (212) 541-4030.
VIDEO PRODUCTION INC., 333 W. 52 St., New York, NY 10019; (212) 581-7312.
VIDEO TRANSCRIPTS INC., 509 Madison Ave., New York, NY 10022; (212) 752-3131.
VIDEOROOM, 1487 Third Ave., New York, NY 10028; (212) 879-5333.
WARREN ROSENBERG VIDEO SERVICES, 308 E. 79 St., New York, NY 10021; (212) 744-1111.
WINDSOR VIDEO, 8W 38 St., New York, NY 10018; (212) 944-9090.

The Home Video World Market

* PRINCIPAL VIDEO DISTRIBUTORS

The Home Video World Market

ARGENTINA

Population: 32 million.
Number of VCRs: Estimated between 800,000 and 1 million in 1988.
Format Share: About 78% VHS, 22% Beta.
TV System: PAL N.
TV Distributors: AVH, Gati-Video, LK-TEL, Video Espagna, Legal Video, Transeuropa Video Entertainment, Transmundo Homevideo and some 20 smaller ones.
Number of Retail Video Outlets or Video Clubs: About 2,400.
Sell-In Price to Retailer: $60–$80.
Best Seller: About 3,000 units.
Hardware: $1,800–$2,000 for a VCR.
Product: A total of 323 films were released on video in 1988 (including national product), a 7% decrease from 1987 (348 videos) which was a 10% decrease from 1986.
Videodisks: Negligible.
Subtitles: Argentines prefer electronically subtitled films to dubbed versions. Subtitling is done locally.
Average video rental price: $1 overnight.
Industry: The extraordinary expansion in Argentina's home video industry in 1986 experienced a shakeout in 1987 as the market became saturated with product and the numerous videoclubs shuttered. Of the more than 100 videocassette traders operating in 1986, only 50 distributors remained by the end of 1988. Estimates of the number of VCRs in the country vary widely from 800,000 to 1 million because of the large number smuggled into the country.

During 1987 almost 70 legal actions were taken throughout Argentina against video piracy resulting in an estimate that while pirated copies accounted for 40–45% of all tapes previously, the figure is currently down to about 35%.

Videoclubs have set up an association to represent their interests, the Argentine Federation of Video Clubs (FAVIC).

High governmental taxes have also slowed the industry's previous rapid growth. A 100% levy on foreign goods including videocassette recorders, plus an import tax has actually raised the price of a VCR to about $2,000.

Trends: After a marked falling off of the video industry in 1987, videocassette rentals experienced a surprising surge in 1988 as a result of an electricity shortage and energy crisis which caused drastic cuts in TV broadcasting hours. With almost daily power cuts and electricity blackouts cancelling movie showings and restricting TV broadcasting to 4 hours a day, viewers voraciously sought out video tapes as their entertainment. The increase in videocassette rentals during this energy crisis is estimated from 50 to 100%. VCR sales are estimated to have increased 15–100%. While the average overnight rental charge per cassette has stayed at $1, with weekend rentals $2, the extraordinary demand has caused talk of an imminent doubling of prices.

Although most videocassettes in Argentina are subtitled, the proposed new Law 23.316, a compulsory dubbing law supported by the Actors' Guild, would mandate that all foreign-language videos be locally dubbed into Spanish by local actors. This has met with strong opposition from video distributors.

AUSTRALIA

Population: 16 million.
VCR penetration: One of the highest levels in the world, estimated at around 62% and as high as 90% in the vast rural regions. (This is up from 58% in 1987.)
Video rental revenue: $A600 million in 1988.
Video sell-through revenue: $A50 million.
Price of prerecorded videos: $A109.
Number of retail outlets: 2,800.
Ratio of VHS to Beta VCRs: 90% to 10%, with many new titles only being released in VHS format.
Statistics: A 1989 survey of video viewership and ownership conducted by AGB McNair for Television Bureau of Advertising revealed: 1) just under 2 out of every 3 Australians between the ages of 18 and 40 have a VCR and watch an average of 6 hours of video programming per week. (The Video Industry Distributors Association places VCR penetration at 62%). 2) Ten percent of VCR owners (or 5.6 of the population) have 2 VCRs. 3) The ratio of VCR owners who watch home recordings of TV programs to those who watch prerecorded tapes is 55% to 70%. 4) The growth in VCR ownership did not put a dent in TV viewership in a country where 95% watches commercial TV at some time and on an average watches about 20 hours per week.
Trends: Despite the increase in VCR penetration, the video industry on a whole is experiencing a plateauing in growth. Nevertheless, homevideo was responsible for 60% of the $A1-billion revenue generated by the entire film industry at the retail level in 1988, although only 25% of those returns reach the producers and most were paid to U.S. studios. In entertainment dollars, the video industry still grosses more than twice the revenue derived from cinema boxoffice ($A224 million in 1988) and equals the record industry. An Australian Film Commission report concluded that problems of depth of and breadth of copy left the consumer unsatisfied. Since less than half of the VCR owners in the country rent videos on a regular basis, the Video Industry Distributors Association (VIDA) representing the top 9 companies, has proposed a campaign to win larger viewership and enhance the industry's public image. While the main objectives of its lobbying efforts include fighting heavy censorship, parallel imports and the imminent prospect of pay TV (expected to become a reality by 1992), the VIDA has also proposed self-regulation in video advertising, the presentation of Video Awards chosen by public ballot, charity fundraising by the video industry to benefit the Starlight Foundation, and the introduction of generic advertising to promote the habit of video viewing.

In May, 1989, new censorship regulations went into effect governing the packaging, labelling and the advertising of films and videos. Designed to make the consumer aware of content at the point of entry or sale, the law requires standardized display of censorship ratings, and explanation in a 20 mm thick band across the tape and its box as well as the notice "Sexual content may offend" or "Violence and language may offend," along with the classification symbol and age identification. This information must also appear on all video advertising including posters and trailers.

Video piracy declined by about 5% in 1988 to 15%, still representing a loss of $A20 million to the industry. This decline is attributed to stiffer penalties and fines ranging from a maximum of $A10,000 per offense for an individual ($A50,000 for a company) to $50,000 in Federal court ($A250,000 for companies.)

AUSTRIA

VCR Penetration: 40% of Austria's households.
Number of Retail Stores: 700 (rentals account for 90% of market).
Industry Rental Income: 280–300 million shillings ($21.5–$23 million) in 1988.
Average Sell-Through Price: 1800 schillings ($140).
Average Video Rental Price: 35 schillings ($2.70).
Product: Action films top the rental list.
Format: VHS recorders predominate.
Trends: With VCR penetration estimated at 40% in 1989, but only 30% of VCR owners entering video shops, according to a recent survey, industry analysts predict a trend toward consolidation in Austria's video industry. Since 1981 when the first video shops opened in Austria, 700 video outlets have sprung up with many undercapitalized and owners lacking in expertise. Despite the high turnover rate in these shops, the annual revenue from video rentals and sales—280–300 million schillings ($21.5–23 million)—equals the rental turnover of film distribution in Austria. Also forecast in the survey is a price consolidation since daily rental prices vary from 10–60 schillings (75¢–$4.60). Because of a substantial drop in prices from 2,000 schillings to 800 with some selling for 300, sell-through is on the rise.

Some video shops stock 6,000 titles with action, fantasy, crime and adventure films the most popular. Hardcore pornography earns about 15% of revenues. However, while youth-protection laws ban the sale of porno to young people, there is no age limit set on entering video shops. The Austrian Parliament has appointed a committee to set guidelines preventing distribution of video "nasties" or violent slasher films.

A recent bill in parliament called for the federal government to start a study of violence and pornography in video software, a major concern in Austria. Currently federal laws differ from state laws, and state laws vary state to state. Youths may enter video stores but must show identity cards, meeting the *local* age limits.

The Austrian government imposed a levy of 3 schillings per tape hour in 1982 to offset losses from home taping and has collected 50,000,000 schillings ($5,000,000 to date) paid by the dealers. 51% of the blank tape tax goes into a special fund for cultural and social purposes (old age pension, health insurance, aid to film schools and producers).

BELGIUM

Population: 9.75 million.
VCR penetration: 28% of the 3,118,000 Belgian homes with TV in 1988.
Average video tape rental price: BFr 150 ($4).
VCR prices: BFr 14,900 ($387).
Video retail outlet revenues: in 1988 BFr2.5–3 million ($65–78 million).

The video industry in Belgium faces stiff competition from the highly-developed cable systems which carry a choice 20 TV channels in some areas. Coupled with the enormous 33% government VAT (value added tax) on VCRs the number of VCRs in Belgium only increased from 740,000 to about 873,040 in 1988.

Video clubs are the primary form of video rental here with club membership cards issued to clients. When first introduced in 1983, these clubs which currently stock about 2,650 different titles, charged BFr 3,000 ($78), but after a brief discontinuation of the membership fees, fees currently range from none to BFr 500 ($13). About 90% of the video clubs also rent out VCRs.

A recent statistical survey revealed that while the video club membership was once 90% male, today's share is 60% male, 40% female resulting in greater demand for romantic dramas. The age group 25–45 accounts for 60% of the homevideo rental market in Belgium while those under 25 share 25% of the market.

BRAZIL

Population (1988): 144,000,000.

Inflation (March 1989): 30% per month up from 18% per month in 1988.

Exchange rate (Feb. 23, 1988): $1 = 94,80 cruzados.

TV sets: 40,000,000.

Viewers reached: 130,000,000.

VCRs: 3 million.

Total revenues in 1987: $60,000,000 (official), $20–25,000,000 (pirated).

Retail Outlets: 5,000 of which only 2,000 are regular buyers from legitimate distributors. Therefore, about 3,000 handle old or unauthorized videos.

Average wholesale price per copy: $40.

Average rental per day: $0.90.

Top 10 videos 1988: 1) E.T.—The Extra Terrestrial (13,000 copies, CIC/Universal); 2) Carnival 88 (8,100, Globo Video); 3) The Untouchables (6,900 CIC/Par); 4) Fatal Attraction (6,500, CIC/Par); 5) Beverly Hills Cop 2 (5,800, CIC/Par); 6) Super Xuxa Contra o Baixo Astral (5,600, Globo Video—Brazilian); 7) Robocop (5,400, Globo Video/Orion); 8) Angel Heart (5,000, Transvideo/TriStar); 9) The Terminator (5,000, Globo Video/Orion); 10) Lethal Weapon (4,900, Warner Home Video). Dumbo (Abril Video/Disney), released in December 1988, sold 3,000 tapes in only three weeks.

Product: 1,180 new titles released in 1988 up from 1,000 in 1987.

Principal markets: São Paulo, Rio Grande do Sul, Rio de Janeiro.

Home video distribution was the fastest growing segment of Brazil's entertainment industry in 1987, despite the inhibiting factors of government regulation and piracy. Resolution 136 of Concine, Brazil's film and Video regulatory agency imposed a 25% quota for Brazilian product in number of titles and tapes in every distributor's catalog and mandated that all mastering and duplicating work be performed in local labs. It defined legal tapes as only those carrying a seal issued by Embrafilme after proof of copyright ownership and local lab work. Nearly 500 dealers have joined Abevc, one of several retailer organizations to remove illegal product from their shelves.

Although technically there are 120 home video distributors registered by Concine, only half of them are operational and only 30–35% operate at significant levels.

In the past two years there has been a 400% rise in the number of VCRs (up to 3 million) in Brazil. Sony, Mitsubishi, Philco, Sanyo, Sharp, CCE and Gradiente all assemble 12 different types of VCRs here and the retail price has dropped from $1,200 in 1986 to an average of $880 in 1988 (in stores, compared to $350 on the black market). Preference, however is for smuggled Panasonic and JVC models available for $550.

90% of the market is in VHS format and Brazilian system is the unique PAL-M (PAL 525 lines) however, conversion from NTSC can be easily done for $50. All tapes are manufactured in NTSC system.

Approximately 3,200 titles (6 million tapes) are available and rental is dominant. Wholesale price (for stores) is $40 and 24-hour rental average $1. Rental stores (5,000) have overtaken videoclubs (in which tapes were exchanged among members). Due to high taxes (15% tax on industrial products plus 17% tax on "circulation of goods.") piracy is exceptionally high. However, because of strict regulation, piracy has declined from an 80% level to 65%. An organization of pirates called "Pool" has circumvented the new law by printing new films over sealed tapes containing legitmate films already having the seal of control on their boxes.

Organizations

Concine: (Film/hv regulatory agency); Head: Roberto Farias, Rua da Imprensa, 16, Rio de Janeiro.

UBV: (Copyright owners assn.); Head: Roberto Mendes, Rua Mexico, 31, Rio de Janeiro.

ABEVC: (Retailers assn.); Head: Irapuã Valverde, Avenida Reboucas, 1206 cj 4, São Paulo.

CANADA

VCRs: In 1988, 52.0% of 9,244,000 households had a VCR, up from 45.2% in 1987, and 34.4% in 1986 (as reported by Statistics Canada, a federal Government agency).

Market: The current Canadian market compared to percentage of the U.S.: VCR population is estimated at 9% of the U.S. market; cassette sell-through volume of $C60,900,000, less than 1%; cassette rentals generate around $C802,400,000, about 7%. Monthly renters represent 81% of all VCR households, compared to 83% in the U.S. 1989 cassette rentals are estimated at about $1 billion, and almost $100 million in videotape purchases. 95% of the English market in Canada is serviced by two companies, Bellevue Home Entertainment Inc. and Video One Canada Ltd.

Retail: There are around 5,000 retail video stores across Canada, and 250 are members of the Video Dealers Association of Canada, which reports that the number of stores has remained static since 1985.

Trade Association: Video Dealers Association of Canada, 1 Eva Rd., Etobicoke, Ont. M9C 4Z5 (416) 620-6793; Executive Director: Don Braden

Data compiled by A.C. Nielsen of Canada:

Films are the most frequently recorded programs.

More than 50% of the usage occurs while the TV set is off, and the same percentage eliminates commercials while recording.

More than 20% of households watch more TV since purchase of a VCR.

Nearly 75% of households sampled cited recording of programs that would otherwise be missed as the chief reason for use.

—PATRICIA THOMPSON

CHINA (PEOPLE'S REPUBLIC)

Population: Approximately 1.07 billion.

Number of VCRs: Although there are no official statistics on the number of VCRs in China, it is estimated there are a total of 300,000, with Beijing and Shanghai accounting for 100,000 each.

VCR price: In Beijing the cost of a video machine is over $900.

Number of Video titles: From late 1986 through 1988 China Film's Beijing Video Co. released over 200 titles (of which over 45% is domestic programming). There were an estimated 100 million customers.

From the early 1980s videocassettes were smuggled into China mostly from Hong Kong, including many porno videos. Therefore in 1989, in order to stop unauthorized importation of videos and eliminate the spread of illegal video screening centers, the government gave sole responsibility for video distribution in China to China Film, the state's main film production and distribution organization. China Film established a video network and built video screening rooms into their existing theaters where audiences pay 3¢ for a video show. Many businesses own VCRs which they use to show free video programs to their employees.

CHINA (TAIWAN)

Population: 20 million.

Number of VCRs: 1 million.

Taiwan has over 10,000 rental outlets (about 3,000 are unlicensed). Average rental price is $2 per cassette with no time limit. The sell-through price is about $32 but the market is tiny as most prefer to watch videos at MTVs, 24-hour private videotheques, where one can rent a video and watch it with a group of friends. Despite a crackdown in the 1980s piracy still accounts for 20% of the video market.

CHILE

By the end of 1987 the number of VCRs in Chile is estimated at 150,000, and a substantial number of VCPs (videocassette players) were imported and sold at a lower price in Beta format.

Video industry gained legal status in 1986 and as of January 1, 1987 law No. 18,443 established penalties for piracy protecting legitimate videocassette distributors which at that time numbered only three; Video Chile, CCN Video and Videoman. Piracy is currently estimated to be 45%. By the end of 1987 import duties on VCRs were slashed by 40% encouraging sales.

EGYPT

Number of production companies for recording and distributing tapes: 209 in 1989—down from 217 in 1988.

Number of fully registered video clubs selling and renting video tapes: 19,980 in 1989 an increase from 19,800 in 1988. In addition, more than 2000 small shops and magazines also sell and rent video tapes to viewers.

Number of VCR owners: Near 8 million and expected to grow since it has become easier to buy a VCR on credit and watching films at home avoids the inconveniences of going out to cinemas—transportation and lack of parking areas, etc.

The Censorship Dept., which is headed by Mrs. Naiema Hamdy, and connected to the Ministry of Culture, is in charge of viewing, rating and granting the approval on general release to all and any local and/or foreign production on tapes.

Now in Egypt there is available a wireless video sender manufactured in Japan that can transmit from any VCR set to any number of TV sets within a range of 300 meters.

General: There's no doubt that video is spreading rapidly in Egypt and is beginning to have a serious effect on theatrical film business. The Indian public enjoys watching films in its own homes at inexpensive prices with all members of the family on hand and the ability to invite friends and neighbors if they wish. Going to a movie theatre is annoying to them for many reasons, including crowded streets, the cost of transportation, and the lack of parking areas.

—AHMED SAMI

FRANCE

French video has always had difficulty finding its market because of heavy taxes, piracy, restrictive windowing and basic disorganization. Video clubs have almost the same one year wait for a theatrical film as does television's Canal Plus. The same is true for American and other foreign films concerning the channels La 5 and M-6.

According to the CSEA (Chambre Syndicale de l'Edition Audio, tel.: 42.25.33.04), a total of 5.6 million VHS recorders were sold by 1989. Over 50 million blank cassettes were sold in 1988 and 16 million pre-recorded cassettes were sold in 1988 of which 2 million were destined to go to the some 2000 video clubs (down from 4000 in 1987) in France.

Producers hope that the VAT on both blank and pre-recorded video cassettes will be slashed from 28% in 1988 (33% in 1987) to 18.6% and eventually to 7% in the coming years.

The big change has been in the sale of pre-recorded cassettes which now have 54% of the market compared to the 15% in 1987. Much of this is due to slashed prices—285 FFS ($49) to 155 FFS ($27), the availability of the pre-recorded cassette in supermarkets and department store outlets, and the increased choice of over 8000 films. The stimulation in sales of pre-recorded cassettes seems to have helped the video rental market rather than hinder it as expected.

Video rentals plunged from 344 million francs in 1987 to 277 million francs last year, a 24% revenue loss. Among the many reasons for this is that the rental price has remained the same (between 25 and 35 FFS—that is, $4 to $6 a film), while first run theatrical viewing has become competitive with reduced prices on special days and hours and the reduced price cinema cards (valid for 4–6 films) available in most cinemas.

Trends: The European Economic Community's executive branch has levied a provisional tax on Korean and Japanese imports which undercut European prices, skimming off 30% of the market in 1987. Aside from the anti-dumping measures, Europe hardly presents a common front in regard to recorder prices which are 40% higher in France than in the United Kingdom.

—VERNICE KLIER-MOSKOWITZ

GREAT BRITAIN

Video hardware sales and the rental of video software continue to break records in the UK market. The proportion of households with video recorders has risen to 61%, which means that 12.7 million households now have VCRs (an increase of one million in a period of 12 months). Weekly tape rentals are 7.2 million and the average rental price per tape has increased from £1.36 ($2.17) to £1.42 ($2.27) thus producing the highest-ever value of weekly rentals £10.2 million ($16.32 million). Moreover, comparison of the volume of tape rentals in the same weeks of 1986, 1987, 1988 and 1989 reveals a remarkably consistent pattern, with peaks at such holiday periods as Easter, Summer school holidays and the period before Christmas. The selling price of features on tape is generally between £7–£10 ($11–$16). It has been estimated that rentals, including sell-through, will generate some $1 billion annually.

Leading distributors include Warner Home Video, CIC, RCA/Columbia, CBS/FOX, Buena Vista and MGM/UA. Others are Amaray, BBC Video, Braveworld, Castle Communications, GMH Entertainments, Guild Home Video, Medusa Communications, MSD Holdings, Nelson Entertainment, Odhams, Parkfield, Pendulum Communications, Pathe Video, Pickwick Video, Scores, Sony Video, Thames Video, Tredegar, Video Box Office and Virgin Vision.

As with the theatrical market, most of the product screened at home hails from America. According to the British Videogram Association (BVA), there are some 5,000 specialist libraries plus an additional 35,000 'racking' outlets with home video as a sideline. In addition, there are 5,000 outlets servicing the sell-through trade.

Having moved away from its early reputation for violent and sleazy product and as further evidence of the establishment of the video business as a reputable one, the BVA has introduced a scheme whereby sales of particularly successful titles distributed by its members, be recognized by the introduction of awards in both the rental and sell-through categories. Sales levels for the achievement of the awards are £1 million ($1.6 million) in the case of rental titles and £500,000 ($785,000) for sell-through titles. Top rental titles were Vestron's 'Buster,' Buena Vista's 'Good Morning Vietnam' and three from CIC, 'Coming to America,' 'Crocodile Dundee II' and 'Fatal Attraction.' Three sell-through titles earned awards: 'Dirty Dancing' (Vestron), 'U2: Rattle & Hum' (CIC) and 'Callanetics' (CIC).

BBC (British Broadcasting Corporation) Video is part of the Corporation's newly-formed Home Entertainment Department and dominates the sell-through market with a catalogue of comedy, sports, children's and documentary releases. "Watch With Mother" became the biggest and fastest-selling video with sales approaching 200,000. With the product supply dominated by the American 'majors,' another significant development has been a move on the part of the video companies to enter theatrical distribution. On the other hand, the Rank Organisation, with a view to the world market, continues to expand its international video interests. Recently, the group acquired Olympia Record Industries based in New York.

Serious opposition from cable, Pay-TV and Satellite broadcasting, has yet to hit the home video market. So, for a few more years, expansion will continue. After then, the test will be—who has the quality product?

—WILLIAM PAY

GREECE

Number of VCRs: 700,000.

Number of Video Distributors: 30.

Number of Rental (Retail) Video Shops: 2,500.

Average Rental Price Per Tape: $1.25–$2 the rental per tape to the consumer.

Sell-Through Price to Consumer: About $50 per tape unit.

Total Video Industry Revenues: $130 million.

Average Time Between Theatrical Release and Release on Video: Six months.

Video Systems: PAL and SECAM.

Piracy: Piracy is viewed as a large problem in this country. It is estimated that video piracy is up to 35%, less in Athens than in other regional places. Illegal videocassette copies are made on a duplicator from an authentic videocassette or from theatrical prints. The quality, is consequently very poor, with the exception of those made from masters smuggled in from Lebanon and/or Cyprus. The illegal copy of a videocassette is considered an act of forgery and is punished with a fine and imprisonment of 8–18 months. It is expected that this term is to be extended to reach ten years by a recently proposed Law. However, if the sentence is less than 20 months, the culprit can buy his way out at the rate of drachmas 400 per day ($2.35).

Six home video companies are grouped in the Greek Anti-Piracy Association (EPPAVE): The AudioVisual Enterprises, Home Video Hellas, MTC Video, VideoSonic, Spentzos Video, and Nea Kinissi Video. They have imported Polaroid stickers from United States to identify their videocassettes.

Video Decline: A retail video shop was considered a very profitable enterprise two years ago and resulted in an explosion of their number to more than 3000 all over the country. However, many of them were forced to shut down as the business was shared and the anti-piracy raids were more frequent. To be profitable the number of existing ones (2500) must be cut down by half. There was also a decline in the home video business in 1989, attributed to many reasons, one being the domestic production. As the motion picture production diminished, many local producers turned to video film production. Though their films and serials are low grade they are competing strongly against foreign product since their annual production reaches 300 films or more.

Other factors contributing to the home video trade's decline in 1989 are the political situation, Government elections, and the satellite Channels.

Hardware and Software Dealers: There are many dealers selling hardware and software equipment in Athens, operating or acting as agents of Akai, Asa, Blaupunkt, Grundig, Hitachi, Lowe, Panasonic, Magnasonic, Philips, Siemens, Telefunken, Salora, etc.

Producers, Wholesalers, Agents: There are more than one hundred videocassette producers in Greece, but it is expected that only the important ones will survive after the video boom subsides. Some of the most important ones are: Home Video Hellas S.A., 275, Messoguion Str., Athens 162 31; Audiovisual Enterprises, 7 Sochou Str., Athens 115 25; Key Video, 16-18 Skalidi Str., Athens 115-25; Nea Kinissi Video, 13 Gravias Str., Athens 106 78; Video Elit, 41-43 Kifissias Str. 151 23; Spentzos Films Video, 49 Themistocleous Str., Athens 106 85; Liberty Video, 292 Messoguion Str., Athens, 155 62; Mediterranean Trading Company (MTC), 5 Aristotelous Str., Callithea Athens 175 71; EMGEE Home Video, 70 Homerou Str., Nea Smyrni Athens 171 21; VideoSonic I Evrydamantos Str. Athens 117 43; CBS Enterprises, 311 Messoguion Str., Athens 152 31; Georguiadis Electroniki, 20 Lagoumutzi Str., Athens 176 71; Festival Home Video, 3 George Str. Athens 106 77; Hellas World Video, 442 Acharnon Str., Athens 111 43; International Video Business, 29 Mavromateon Str., Athens 104 34; Kino Video, Messoguion 230 Athens 151 61; Pap Video, 47 Didotou Str. Athens 106 80; AudioVideo Magnetics, Vassileos Constantinou & Kifissias Str., Athens 152 33; Home Video Center, 96 Academias Str., Athens 106 77; Libero Video, 10-12 Gravias Str., Athens 106; Master Home Video, 96 Academias Str., Athens 106 77, etc.

—RENA VELISSARIOU

HOLLAND

Population: 14,804,500.

Number of VCRs: 2,400,000 up from 2 million in 1987. This means that some 35% of Dutch families own VCRs.

Number of Distributors: some 40 of which only 22 are active. The most important are Esselte-CIC (Paramount, Universal), Warner Home Video (WB and UA), RCA-Columbia, CBS-Fox, RCV (Orion), CNR (MGM) Cannon (Cannon and Touchstone).

Number of Rental Shops: around 800 (down from 1000 in 1987).

Average Rental Price Per Tape: from Dfl. 5.50 per day. Estimated number of rentals per year: 33 million (down from 39 million in 1987).

Video Tape Sales: A growing market (1988: Dfl. 25 million up from Dfl. 11 million in 1987) at this moment mainly dealing in B-pictures, soft pornography and documentaries.

Price Per Tape: A-titles: Dfl. 29.95–39.95; B-titles: Dfl. 19.95.

Total Video Revenue for the Industry: Dfl. 205 million generated by some 3,000 titles.

Window: 6 months from first theatrical release.

Video Systems: 89% VHS. The purchase price of a VHS recorder starts at some Dfl. 800.

Philips, Blaupunkt and Gründig (West Germany), Sharp, Japanese video recorders (Sony, Akai, Hitachi), practically all VHS systems, are sold here.

Top Ten Videos of 1988: 1) Crocodile Dundee; 2) Top Gun; 3) The Golden Child; 4) The Living Daylights; 5) Platoon; 6) Police Academy IV; 7) Flodder (Dutch); 8) Over the Top; 9) Beverly Hills Cop II; 10) Dirty Dancing.

Piracy: Still important, but slowly going down. Now estimated at some Dfl. 45 million per year. In 1988 18,897 illegal video tapes were seized. The Dutch government has still not passed new legislation which would enable more severe punishment for copyright infringement. VIDEO VEILIG (Video Safe) is the venture which is constantly alert on infringement. Members are the NVPI (Video distributors), Stemra-Buma (Mechanical Copyright Organization), NBB (Filmdistributors, Exhibitors and Producers Organization), NOS (Television Organization) and the MPAA.

Trends: Though Video in general experienced a slight slump in 1988, the outlook for the branch is rather good. The sale of video titles shows an important increase over 1987 and is likely to keep growing as more and more interesting titles appear on the Dutch market. Video is obviously hurting the cinema trade. For a family of 4 it is obviously much cheaper to rent a film for Dfl. 5.50 than to go to a cinema which would cost Dfl. 45.

Purchase of a recorder is relatively high by those with a good income, mostly by those living in the west of the Netherlands (the most prosperous provinces), those who look often to TV, and by members of the most important TV organizations: A.V.R.O, T.R.O.S. and V.O.O. 70% of the owners of a recorder rent a print of pictures for instance with video companies. There are many stores in many cities and villages. TV programs are often copied (recorded) by 86% of the owners of a recorder.

Trade Associations: Producers & Importers: Nederlandse Vereniging van Producenten en Importeurs van Beeld en Geluidsdragers (NVPI), Albertus Perkstraat 36, 1217 NT Hilversum. Rental Shops: Nederlandse Video Detaillisten Organisatie (NVDO) Twijnstraat 46, 3511 ZL Utrecht.

—PAUL SILVIUS

INDIA

With the expansion of TV networks throughout the country an increasing number of VCRs have made their appearance in Indian homes. Although no precise figures are available, a rough estimate puts the total number of VCRs in the country at around 3 million. There are well over 100,000 video libraries renting out cassettes, with an almost equal number of video parlours. Videophiles borrow about 300,000 cassettes a month for home viewing from the libraries at a rental of Rs. 10–15 per cassette. The annual turnover of the industry is estimated to be Rs. 700 crores (1 crore = 10 million), a good part of which is claimed by video pirates who are believed to control almost 85 percent of the market.

Widespread video piracy has undoubtedly affected the film industry's export earnings. Through the film industry's concerted efforts the government has now passed a law against video piracy. Any person who exhibits or permits the exhibition of a video film in any place without proper certification is liable for imprisonment for a period of three years and a fine which may extend to Rs. 100,000. Taking advantage of the stringent laws film producers are now selling the video rights of their films for both domestic and overseas markets.

Home viewing rights (domestic) are made over for Rs.2 million for an 'A' grade movie and Rs.1 million for 'B' grade. These days long before a film is shot and edited, there is a fierce tussle for the home viewing rights. Four companies—Gold, Bombino, Magnum and Shemaroo have established a hold over the market and between them they buy up the rights for almost 80 percent of the movies which hit the Hindi screen. More than 40,000 prints of a new Hindi film are pushed into the market in the short space of 8 days after the movie's theatrical release and the figure is likely to double by the end of the year.

Pre-recorded cassettes cost around Rs.110 per tape. The Garware company in Bombay has the largest duplicating plant in the country, with a capacity of recording 18,000 video cassettes per day. Other units are located in northern India (Delhi, Rajasthan) and eastern and southern India.

Meanwhile the Indian video industry has created its own software. In the lead is Nari Hira, whose Hiba Video has turned out nearly 20 video movies. He has provided opportunities to young new talent and rescued old fading stars. The films cost around Rs.1 to 2 million to produce and nearly a third of the cost is offset by the advertisers. The subjects range from mystery, romance to thrillers.

A new trend in software is the video magazine in English and other major Indian languages. Currently there are at least 7 in the field. These comprise live variety shows, song and dance sequences from films, interviews with celebrities etc. One of India's most widely read fortnightly's, *India Today*, brings out its video magazine *Newstrack* which specializes in politics and current affairs.

—B. D. GARGA

ISRAEL

VCR Penetration: 33⅓% of the more than 4 million-person Jewish population (which was polled for VCR statistics in 1988.)

Number of VCRs: more than 400,000.

Total Video Revenue: Video distribution companies in Israel keep figures secret. However, the estimated gross to the video distribution companies in 1988 was $12–15 million.

Cost of Prerecorded Videocassettes: $55–$90 depending on the distribution company, with most costing an average $75. No private individual may buy a prerecorded videocassette with Hebrew subtitles because they are strictly for rent and may be sold only to video rental libraries.

Video Rental Libraries: 270 throughout the country which have over 100,000 subscribers who pay a deposit plus $2–$4 rental charge per tape, depending on whether the subscriber pays for 60 or only 20 cassettes in advance under a "package deal" system.

Owners of video libraries in turn have to buy an entire package of 12–15 titles from the major distributors all for the same price before being allowed to buy additional copies of top titles. A package typically costs about $900 for 12 films.

Top Video Companies: United King Golan Globus Video (has 34.7% share of video market), Channel 1, Cinema Empire Ltd., Forum Film Video, Seven Stars Video, which also own their own duplication studios.

Trends: A 1988 survey revealed that 42% of the adult (over 18) Jewish population, which equals more than 1 million, regularly watch prerecorded video tapes at home, 51% of those watch up to 6 films per month and 27% watch more than 12 films per month. In contrast, only 31% of this population goes to cinema theaters and 2/3 of those go twice a month at most. The same poll showed a growth in the number of video viewers and a decline in cinema-goers. Preference is for dramas and suspense films (30.7%) then action films and Westerns (15.7%), family films (13.1%), TV mini-series (11.8%), science fiction (5.6%) and musicals (3.7%).

Rampant piracy is the main problem in the video industry here. Apartment buildings are illegally wired for closed circuit TV. Pirate cable networks throughout Israel are thought to number 800 reaching 500,000 homes. Pirates are often the first to get product. For example, pirates were running "War and Remembrance" on cable simultaneously with its release on video and prior to airdate on the government-owned TV station. In 1988 many industry members joined with the MPEAA, investing nearly $1 million to hire private detectives to eradicate pirate cable networks. However, their efforts have met with indifference with law enforcement agencies, costing the video industry an estimated $2 million in losses per month.

ITALY

Population: 57,399,000.

VCR Penetration: Increased from 2.1 million at the end of 1987 to 3.3 million at the end of 1988. About 15% of the 20 million Italian TV households also have VCRs, up from only 300,000 VCRs in Italy in 1985.

Video Industry Revenue: $153.8 million not including porno tapes, up from $97 million in 1987. U.S. films distributed by the majors still earn most of the video revenue and eight of the bestselling videos were from the U.S. Hardcore porno tapes account for an estimated 40% of overall video trade.

Sell-Through Income: $18 million or 13% of the legitimate market. Tapes of top recent films sell for about $22 while non-feature or older titles go for $12–20. Italians traditionally don't like to rent. About 75% own their own home and very few rent TV or video hardware.

Retail Outlets: The number of videocassette outlets has grown from 4–5,000 in 1987 to 6–6,500 in 1988. This figure does not include secondary outlets such as bookstores, camera shops and record stores which would boost the total number to 10,000.

Top Video Rentals in 1988: (1) Sleeping Beauty (Walt Disney), (2) E.T. (RCA/Columbia), (3) The Last Emperor (RCA/Columbia), (4) Hamburger Hill (Domovideo) (5) Fatal Attraction (RCA/Columbia), (6) The Untouchables (RCA/Columbia), (7) Dirty Dancing (Domovideo), (8) Predator (Panarecord), (9) Robocop (RCA/Columbia), (10) Children of a Lesser God (RCA/Columbia).

Top Video Sell-Through Cassettes: The Sword in the Stone (Walt Disney), The Name of the Rose (Domovideo), The Key (Domovideo), Disney Masterpieces (Walt Disney), From Disney with Love (Walt Disney), Blade Runner (Warner Home Video), Once Upon a Time There Was a Mouse (Walt Disney), Tom & Jerry (Panarecord), The Pink Panther (Panarecord), Labyrinth (Domovideo).

Trends: A blow was struck against video retail outlets when Italy's highest court, the Constitutional Court, handed down a ruling that upheld and clarified a law forbidding the circulation of obscene material and imposing a maximum 3-year prison term on violators. Distributor earnings on hardcore porno tape sales to rental stores is estimated between $20–40 million a year. The rental outlets in turn earn an estimated 40–50% of their income from the rental of these porno tapes. Without the revenue from the porno rentals it is feared they will have less funds to spend on stocking mainstream titles. Moreover, the court's ruling specifically does not include newsstands which are free to stock porno videos.

Italy's top film producers-distributors Mario and Vittorio Cecchi Gori and the publishing house Rizzoli-Corriere della Sere formed a new major video label Vivivdeo in late 1988. Also entering the video market is Mondadori, Italy's largest publishing house and rival to Rizzoli. Both new companies expect to extend their sell-through markets through their bookselling channels—door-to-door sales agents, and direct-mail order book clubs. Additionally, the Video Electronics Club, a co-venture between Vincent Romagnoli's Acqua Marcia Co. and entrepreneur Roberto Cornona, offers book-club style video membership club for viewers seeking to build a library of high-quality video classics.

Despite the efforts of the newly-formed Anti-Piracy Federation, set up in 1988 by Univideo, the Italian Motion Picture Assn. and the Italian Society of Authors and Editors, and stiff laws which mandate a three-year prison term for people convicted of selling illicit tapes, it is estimated that video piracy accounts for a share of the video market nearly equal to that of legitimate distributors.

JAPAN

The Latin word video, to see, has been adopted for use in our modern world as a term which covers a rather large field in the electronics sector including videocassette recorders (VCRs) or video tape recorders (VTRs), and the compact disks (CDs) using laser beam technology. The Japanese, who are the most skillful people in the world in adapting ideas and improving on them, are the world leaders in video manufacturing. At present they make 90% of the world VCRs or VTRs produced, have close to 90% of the most lucrative American market, and perhaps 99% of the Japanese market, which includes 38.5 million households.

At present, nearly two-thirds of all Japanese households own VCRs. Local use of blank tape soared 10% in 1988.

At present, American production of videocassette recorders is negligible, as is production of CD systems, thus leaving 90 percent of sales to Japanese makers and the remainder mostly to South Korean or European makers. The report that Tandy Corp. (USA) had developed a new type of erasable CD system caught the Japanese by surprise and they were very skeptical that it could be done by the American company at the low price of $500 as claimed. Last year Japanese VTR production was down 12.2 percent (27.5 million units) to $20.159 billion of which $8 billion worth was exported (down 30.9 percent) while imports increased 288.6 percent to $90 million due mostly to cheap imports from South Korea. VTR production reached its peak in 1986 at 33,879,000 units, 27,689,000 of which were exported, decreasing to 30,544,000 of which 22,801,000 were exported.

Video has an important relationship with television as well as with the movie industry in the past decade in two ways: from legal sales of cassettes or solid discs of movies, and the adverse factor, illegal pirating of copyrighted material or sale to the public, which hurts both producers and exhibitors and is rampant in many countries.

Consumer use in Japan is considerable as one can see from these figures: the 40 video software-related industries in the past year reported total revenues of approximately $153 billion. Sales of videocassettes were $252.8 million, while rentals soared 47% over the previous year's revenues to $93.3 million.

Foreign feature films are most popular with sales of yen 32,096 million (up 47.2 percent) and overshadow Japanese movies (Yen 12,180 million, up 17.9 percent), followed by Japanese music and soft porn movies on tapes or disks. Videocassette rental indicated a slight preference for foreign films with yen 7,656 million (up 40.2 percent) compared to yen 7,225 (up 37.9 percent) for domestic feature films.

Part of sales of compact disks are due to the opening up in 1985 of a number of one-man-operated video theatres usually with seats for around 100 customers willing to pay from $4 to $10. These may have contributed to the admissions figure for regular movie-goers dropping from over 160 million to about 144 million, but the fault is really that of VTRs or CDs shown in 53 percent of Japanese homes.

Although film attendance in Japan has dropped, there have been diatribes by cinema importers, distributors, producers and exhibitors complaining of lost revenues due to black market or legal cassettes or compact discs. The Motion Picture Assoc. of America has set up teams to patrol video rental stores to warn them to refrain from sales of pirated tapes or discs of American films. Since there are over 8,000 regulated shops and an estimated 4,000–7,000 not regulated and selling pirated tapes, this is quite a task. What action has been taken by the authorities was limited to piracies of domestic Japanese software. At present 50% of tapes sold are pirated, resulting in losses of up to $1 billion to copyright holders. The Ministry of Education has submitted an amendment to the present copyright law which imposes a penalty on "display of pirated cassettes," including heavier fines and prison sentences (usually suspended).

While Japan has flooded the world with video exports, the public's use has been nowhere near the enthusiasm engendered in America, and to a lesser extent, Europe. The answer to this lies in the Japanese character and customs. It is true that increasing numbers of Japanese have been resorting to setting a timer to tape TV shows they are liable to miss and want to view later, and there are smaller numbers who tape the shows to send to family members working outside Japan and wish to keep up with what goes on in their homeland.

Going to the movies in Japan is either a habit or compulsion for youngsters, a "ceremony" for others and a chance to get out of the home. In general, the average Japanese would hesitate to pay out a goodly sum to purchase a cassette or solid disc for showing at home for his family, though admittedly the male members of the household might invest in soft pornography. A Japanese home is not meant for entertaining outsiders so there is no question of inviting neighbors or friends to a viewing. Entertaining is done outside the home and in no way consists of running a VTR for outsiders.

Of course, one cannot say with certainty that in the future these customs may not change and there may be a revolution in the use of VTRs or CDs such as took place in America or Europe. Thus, if there is blame to be handed out regarding competition with movies it still goes to TV.

What then will be done by the cinema industry, especially the exhibitors, if there is an explosive spread of video theatres in the future? Will they fight them or come to some sort of compromise, or even join them? Thus far there appears to be no opposition to them but that could change if box office profits fall and they begin to hurt the movie theatres or any other branch of the industry. Since they normally use imported features, producers and importers from abroad seem not worried.

Japan is foremost in the world in production and export of video tape recorders (VTRs) which now have a diffusion rate in households in the world's major market countries reaching 30% (compared to 40% in Japan's urban areas and 31% nationwide), a phenomenon which took only 20 years since introduction of black-and-white in 1964 by Sony and development of a color model in 1966, followed by introduction of its Betamax in 1975 for home use.

Here again is the example of how the Japanese lifted the technological know how and research of foreign companies such as RCA and Zenith in America, and Philips of Holland, estimated at costing as much as a billion dollars, and developed them to the advantage of Japanese business in the case of the CDs. The history of VTRs shows the same trends.

What Philips and the Japanese companies are working on now includes an erasable disc, a further improvement—which may control the future.

Both Matsushita and Hitachi have begun production of VTRs in America and expect to increase production 5 times within 3 years. The appreciated yen means lower production costs in the USA and defuses American criticisms of the Japanese trade surplus as well as the American charges of dumping. Sony is making VTRs in France. CDs for use in automobiles have now reached over 114,000 units and the trend is accelerating, and is expected to reach 300,000 this year.

In the past year video software industries rose from 38 to 50 with billings rising to yen 130 billion.

When any discussion of VTRs is made, it is necessary to mention the battle between Sony's Betamax system and the rival VHS systems which are incompatible in that the cassettes are not interchangeable on the other equipment. That battle has resulted in defeat by Sony with only an estimated 12% of the market with 88% for VHS (Video Home System) developed by Victor of Japan.

Sony replied to this by introducing the 8mm single-unit video system, whose recording time is 120 minutes, which VTR makers are already copying. It was also Sony who, when the large American companies decided against putting CDs in production because of the huge capital outlay despite the fact that they had paid for research, went into CD production, along with, on a much smaller scale, Philips of Holland.

In 1970 Sony discovered that Philips of Holland, as well as RCA and Zenith, both American, had spent hundreds of millions of dollars on research and development of a laser diode disc to record, and spent four years unsuccessfully trying to develop a system. In 1978 Philips, after the American companies had written off videodiscs as risky because of the expense, came to them with their technological data in order to prevent a second Betamax-VHS video tape problem by producing two incompatible competing systems.

This move was regarded by some as foolish since Sony then picked the ball up and carried it from there, in 1982 producing their first CD system with picture for $800. Other firms followed and now Japan has gone on to dominate not only the American market but also a lion's share of the world market to such an extent that the average person thinks it was Sony and not Philips who invented it. Sony still dominates the US market for CDs with Matsushita Electronics second. Philips has a good piece of the European market, and a very small bit of the Japanese market with Zenith dropping out before production, while RCA only produces some esoteric disk systems for the US government. A third American company MCA sold its factories to Pioneer Electronics of Japan. Apparently few American companies are interested in trying to buck the Japanese.

A random sampling by the Video Software Promotion Council indicated 27.9% of Japanese households used VTRs daily, 32% once in 2–3 days, and 25.4% once a week. Over 50% of units used were rental cassettes or discs, with 64.1% of foreign origin.

The Economic Planning Agency say 53 percent of Japan's 38.5 million households now have VTRs or CDs and diffusion in the Tokyo and Osaka regions is at a 40% rate and in rural districts 31%, terming it "the video revolution in Japan."

Toho-Towa established Towa Video to deal exclusively in cassette sales, contracting for Cannon's Over the Top series, joining Nikkatsu Video Films, Shochiku CBS/Fox Video, Toei Video, Herald Enterprises, Shochiku-Fuji, et al.

—A. C. PINDER

(Long-time correspondent A. C. Pinder died in 1989. Much of the material above was contributed by him prior to his death.)

NEW ZEALAND

Population: 3,500,000.
VCR households: 1,073,000 in 1988.
VCR penetration: 55%, up from 50% in 1987 and 30% in 1986.
Number of video titles: 8,000.
Value of market: NZ$30 million.
Retail dealers: 691 (up from 400 in 1987).
Retail value of market: NZ$150 million.
Rental cost: Overnight rental NZ$5.50 and NZ$7 for top titles, NZ$2 for catalog specials.

New Zealand home video has experienced continued growth in 1988. Contributing factors are the limited viewing choice offered by the monopolistic 2-channel TV broadcasting and the isolation of the rural population.

Responding to pressure from public interest groups and the video industry itself, a 1987 Video Recordings Act set up two rating authorities (the industry-based Labelling Body and the government-appointed Video Recording Authority) to determine video censorship and penalties for breaching the new regulations. All tapes released must be labeled with a colored rating sticker indicating content. A green label indicates G for general viewing; yellow is PG, PG-13 and PG-16 and red stickers indicate R, videotapes restricted to those 18 and over. The penalty for making, copying, selling, renting or exhibiting indecent videos is up to 3 months in jail for a fine of up to NZ$3,000 for individuals and NZ$10,000 for companies.

The chief film censor remains responsible for any videos intended for public performance. Some distributors have complained that videos banned from home viewing by the Video Recordings Labeling Body have been approved by the film censor for restricted public screenings, thus undercutting their business.

Playcount, an Australian system which counts the number of times a video has been played, made its debut in New Zealand in 1989. Backed by Capital Cities/ABC of the U.S., the Playcount system in New Zealand is used to record the number of transactions not the number of times a video is viewed and then log this information via computer to a central network using specially designed programs. Thus distributors and dealers can quickly access information on volume, stock control, sales trends and viewing use of titles. Under a sharing system, Playcount titles go to dealers with a NZ$15–20 handling charge instead of the usual wholesale price of up to NZ$140. Dealers also pay a NZ$24 per month fee to Playcount.

Principal organizations: Video Association, 246a Hobson St., Auckland. Tel.: (09) 389 421. Chief Censor of Films, 1 Fairway Dr., P.O. Box 46-009, Lower Hutt. Tel.: (04) 673 242.

PAKISTAN

Number of VCRs: There are approximately 1,200,000 VCRs in the country. Of these, about 700,000 are in households, a figure that increases day by day. A license fee of Rs.200 and Rs.400 (for domestic and commercial use respectively) is levied by the Government. The custom duty on the import of VCRs is Rs.3,000 per piece.

Number of Video Distributors: It runs into thousands, but the biggest ones are about a dozen—mostly in Karachi, the largest city of Pakistan.

Number of Rental Video Shops: There are two kinds of shops—one deals only in sales, the other rents them out. The number of the latter is around 70,000 (about 35,000 are in Karachi alone).

Average rental price per tape: Between Rs.5 and Rs.10 for 24 hours. In certain localities there is a monthly subscription system—between Rs.100 and Rs.150. Libraries in posh localities like Clifton, Defence Society, PECH Society etc. have introduced a 'home delivery system' on a subscription of Rs.200 to Rs.300 per month. Subscribers have only to dial and place their orders.

Price per tape: This is flexible according to the currency value and international market. The present price of a blank cassette is between Rs.110 and Rs.120 (imported). Recorded ones (slightly lower grade) are also available at the same rate. Sales of video tapes run over a million every month, as mostly they are used for copying foreign (mainly Indian) films smuggled-in from various countries and released simultaneously throughout the country.

Total video revenue for the industry: As video is an illegal business in the country, the figures of its revenue are not available with anybody. However, it runs in hundreds of millions of rupees every year.

Window: Almost simultaneously—in some cases video is released even before the theatrical release of Pakistani and Indian films.

Top ten videos of the year: All the top ten video honours go to Indian movies every year, as they are very popular and common with viewers. Films of Indian superstar Amitabh Bachchan are the most popular and generally they are among the top ten. His latest release is "Toofan" (Storm) which has created a new video sales record. Needless to say, costwise, it is also the number one for the year 1989.

The piracy problem: Video is said to be the villain of the Pakistan film trade. For those who cannot afford to buy a machine, there are hundreds of tea shops and video houses (in flats), each with a TV set and a VCR/VCP. They show the latest films, frequently pirated versions that become available the same day and in some cases even before the release of a new film in regular theatres.

The video outlets are the death of big cinema houses, which once were the key centers for popular entertainment. Moviegoers used to queue for tickets hours before show times—three shows a day, the parking lot was full and Urdu films ran six months to a year. Today, the theatres are barely a third occupied most of the time, the parking lots are empty and few films are shown more than three to four weeks. Thirty-one of Karachi's 96 cinemas have closed during the last ten years and many others are falling into disrepair. Belated efforts to beat the video challenge have not succeeded, mainly because the Government has levied a license fee of Rs.200 for a domestic VCR/VCP and Rs.400 for a "commercial" one. Definition of commercial is not mentioned.

For the moment, the film makers and exhibitors are at a loss as to how to stop piracy and make the film business a profitable one.

Trends: Like cinemagoers, video viewers also love to see action and thrills on the small screen, because generally the Censor Board permits little violence and vulgarity in 35mm films and there is no censorship of video films, as their trade is not legal.

Video Distributors: (Karachi) AA Video, 101, Rainbow Centre, Saddar; Sabah Video, 117, Rainbow Centre, Saddar; Rio Video Centre, Rainbow Centre, Saddar; Sabah International, 136, Rainbow Centre, Saddar; Time Video, Rainbow Centre, Saddar; Shalimar Recording Co. Ltd. 1st floor, Muhammadi House, Chundrigar Road; Gaylords Video, Rainbow Centre, Saddar; King Video, Rainbow Centre, Saddar; Al-Malik Trivideo, Rainbow Centre, Saddar; Look Video Co., Rainbow Centre, Saddar; Lucky Videos, Rainbow Centre, Saddar; Mister Video, Rainbow Centre, Saddar; Leo Video, Rainbow Centre, Saddar; KRC Videos, Rainbow Centre, Saddar; S.Z. Video Service, Rainbow Centre, Saddar; Mars Video, Rainbow Centre, Saddar; Victor Video Centre, Rainbow Centre, Saddar; All Seasons Enterprise, Rainbow Centre, Saddar; Devis Video, Rainbow Centre, Saddar; Unique Video, Rainbow Centre, Saddar; Silver Video Service, Rainbow Centre, Saddar; Noble Video, Rainbow Centre, Saddar; VIP Videos, Rainbow Centre, Saddar; Sony Videos, Rainbow Centre, Saddar; Fox Videos, Rainbow Centre, Saddar; Aamir's Videos, Rainbow Centre, Saddar; KARACHI.

—A. R. SLOTE

SCANDINAVIA

Denmark: Number of households: 2.2 million; VCRs sold in 1988: 95,000; total VCRs: 555,000; household penetration: 26%.

Finland: Number of households: 2.1 million; VCRs sold in 1988: 175,000; total VCRs: 830,000; household penetration: 41%.

Norway: Number of households: 1.6 million; VCRs sold in 1988: 100,000; total VCRs: 650,000; household penetration: 41%.

Sweden: Number of households: 3.5 million; VCRs sold in 1988: 300,000; total VCRs: 1,500,000; household penetration: 44%.

Total: Number of households: 9.4 million; VCRs sold in 1988: 670,000; total VCRs: 3,535,000; household penetration: 38%.

Taxes: The Swedish government has a tax on every VCR sold which is 600 SEK (about $92). There is also a tax on blank videocassettes of 15 SEK ($2.30). Another tax on videos goes to the Swedish Film Institute, to support Swedish film production. These taxes (or fees) are 60 SEK, about $9.20 on every pre-recorded cassette for rental. There is also a tax (fee) of 25 SEK ($3.85) on sell-through-cassettes.

Rental price: an average $8 for new releases and low as $1.50 for older releases.

Sell-through price: an average 198 SEK ($30) for new releases, but can go down as low as $15.

Blank cassette prices: average $12 for a Standard E180. Some shops have special offers for about $8 and in some cases there are lower prices, but that is for Far East-produced cassettes.

—INGE HANSON

(SOUTH) KOREA, REPUBLIC OF

Population: 42 million.

VCR penetration: estimated 20% in 1988.

Total video revenues: $50 million for the legal homevideo industry while the thriving piracy underground takes in 2 to 2½ times as much.

Number of titles available: Total of 3–4000 with about 130 new titles released every month.

Cost of VCR: approximately $400 (down from $700).

Trends: Although the government of the Republic of Korea in 1987 signed an agreement to honor U.S. copyrights and to join one of the international copyright treaties, it has failed to prosecute violators despite promises to do so. Therefore, South Korea remains one of the most flagrant havens for video piracy. Although the pirated tapes are of bad quality, they still account for 2 to 2½ times the revenue earned by the legitimate video industry.

SPAIN

Population: 38.6 million.

VCR penetration: 25% of available TV households.

Number of VCRs: approximately 4 million in 1988 (almost all in VHS with only 8% in the Beta format).

Sell-through price: $50–70. However, many new collections are now sold at an average price of $25.

Blank videocassette tapes: Price has dropped to about $6 per tape.

Trends: Although still accounting for only 4% of the total video revenues, sell-through is expanding in Spain. Following the lead of Warner Bros. and Disney's success in retailing video titles at competitive prices through larger stores, industry majors CBS/Fox and CIC/RCA have begun selling cassettes directly to the public with A-titles labeled "collectables" and retailing at about $25.

All the major American distributors are in the Spanish market and American videos dominate about 80% of the market. Virtually all home video films are released in Spanish-dubbed versions and feature films dominate the market with a small percentage for pornography and music videos.

A major impediment to video growth is piracy estimated in 1988 to be 35–40% nationwide and in some areas up to 90%. The local Anti-Piracy Federation, back by the MPEA spent $700,000 to combat piracy in Spain. Another problem is "community video" where blocks of apartment houses are wired and a master VCR shows 4–5 rented videos daily throughout the building. The legal status of community video organizations which number 700 to an audience of 1.5 million, has yet to be defined.

SRI LANKA

Number of VCRs: 361,000 sets in 148,930 households.
Number of video distributors: 32 in Colombo & 13 regional.
Number of rental video shops: 4,280 nationally.
Average rental price per tape: Rs.15– (45 cents) p.day.
Video tape sales: 1,500,000 per year App.
Price per video tape (prerecorded): Rs.250– ($7.50) to Rs.700– ($22).
Total video revenue for the industry: Rs.40 million ($1,176,470).
Window: Sri Lankan films (Sinhala or Tamil) which are normally released as a theatrical film, are released on video two years from the date of first exhibition in the theatres. All foreign Video films are available simultaneously or within weeks of their first release in theatres.
Top ten videos of the year (Sri Lanka in Sinhala): 1) Dimuthu Muthu, 2) Rata Giya Attho, 3) Yasoravaya, 4) Kopi Kade, 5) Nirupamala, 6) Gam Peraliya, 7) Amba Yakluvo, 8) Sudu Paraviyo, 9) Charu Latha, 10) Irata Handana Mal

Sri Lanka has now earned a name as a new operational centre in an international film piracy syndicate. One can find any big movie film on video tape almost within a week of its release in the U.S. or in Europe or elsewhere. Though the government occasionally assures film makers that it will pass laws to prevent pirated video films from entering and being exhibited here in Sri Lanka, there are still no signs of change.

The government plans to introduce tough new laws to crack down on video shops renting or exhibiting obscene films carrying "X" rating. According to Minister of State for Information, Mr. A.J. Ranasinghe, legislation would be designed to bring the booming video business under complete control of the Censors and a licensing scheme for Video Parlours will be introduced. Attorney-General of Sri Lanka had ruled that Video cassettes did not come under the category of films and had to be brought under the Public Performances Board, which oversees all video parlours and is responsible for supervision, licensing and all matters connected with the sale, rental and exhibition of video cassettes.

Ceylon Theatres Ltd, the country's largest cinema operators, is feeling the crunch of Video competition and with other problems, such as Video Mini cinemas, may consider closing some of its cinemas.

—CHANDRA S. PERERA

SWITZERLAND

In Switzerland in 1988, there were some 500 (down from 750 in 1987) videoshops which mostly work on a rental basis, while the outright sale of videocassettes is mainly done by the major distributors and by mail order. As Switzerland is trilingual, the turnover of videocassettes is divided: 60% German, 26% French and 6% Italian; only 6% are spoken in English. By genre, 58% of the hired or sold movies on cassettes are action dramas or thrillers (2–3% horror), 28% are family programs and 14% erotic films. Among the evergreens is the whole Disney family catalogue. Still selling and renting at a steady clip are film musicals.

According to statistics of the Swiss Videogram Association, by the end of 1989, in nearly 840,000 VCR households there are about 1.2 VCRs operating per household; this corresponds to a VCR penetration of 47%.

Trend is that small retailers diminish while the retail distribution is more and more assumed by supermarkets and department stores. 1988 Video tape sales, which are rising while rentals decrease, were 536,000, at an average price of 30 to 50 Swiss francs a piece. The average rental prices per tape varies from Sfrs. 5 to 8. The industry last year totaled 103,000,000 Swiss francs (retail) and 44,000,000 Sfr. (wholesale). Video retailers offered 1,179 full length pictures, newly released on video; normally the window between theatrical release and release on video is about 6 months. The better a picture does at the boxoffice, the longer it will be blocked for the video market.

So far piracy has been sued on basis of the copyright law only, which has been proved to be inefficient. A 1988 revision of this law will be sharpened again in 1989 or 1990. One chamber of the Swiss Parliament has voted in May 1989 for a clause which will prohibit so called "Brutalos" (violent TV-movies) and porno cassettes. An 80% of the Swiss Video Distributors have furthermore signed an agreement for self control and published for the first time a list of 50 x-marked Brutalos and hard core cassettes which will vanish from the shelves of the Video Shops.

Almost 100% of the recorders sold are the Japanese type Video Home System (VHS). The European device, Video 2000, a co-production of Philips and Grundig, has completely vanished, as well as Sony's Beta-System.

Governmental subsidy: January 1, 1986, the Federal Department of Culture, Federal Bureau of Cultural Promotion decided to extend subsidies on video productions, too, i.e. this authority grants contributions not only for national film productions but also for VHS- and U-matic video films which have artistic qualities.

Government Departments: Bundesamt fuer Kulturpflege, Sektion Film, Thunstrasse 20, 3000 Berne 6.

Associations: Schweizerischer Video-Verband, Schwarztorstrasse 7, P.O. Box 2485, 3001 Berne.

—GABRIELLA BROGGI

USSR

Population: 280 million.
Number of VCRs: 670,000 households or .8% of the 85 million households with TVs by the end of 1988 according to a survey by the Motion Picture Association of America.
Video rental outlets: all state run.
Number of video titles available: 900 foreign and domestic.
Average sell-through price: 85 roubles ($144).
Average video rental price: 2 roubles ($3.40).
Trends: Demand for both VCRs and video product runs high in the USSR where there is a serious shortage of titles in the video clubs, video libraries and video shops and long lines at the small public video projection rooms. Therefore, the ground breaking agreement between RCA/Columbia Worldwide Video and Videofilm Goskino (the unofficial Soviet theatrical and media company) for Russian distribution rights to 65–100 RCA/Columbia theatrical titles, has met with great enthusiasm on both sides. Described as a licensing deal with the USSR paying a straight fee for distribution rights for the titles—an advance against royalties in hard currency—in exchange for the right to choose product from a select list of recent and classic Columbia, Tri-Star and Orion titles.
Video trade organizations include: VNITIK (All-Union Institute Theory and History of Cinema); NIKFI (Research Institute for Film Equipment & Technology); VGIK (All-Union Institute of Cinematography) and LIKI (Leningrad Institute of Film Engineers).

VENEZUELA

Population: 18.7 million in 1988, with a calculated 2.3 million color TV penetration.

VCR market: The Venezuelan VCR market started about 1976, culminating in a 400,000 unit market with its rapid four year growth. There has been a small, fluctuating growth since then by 40–60,000 units. The 1988 home VCR market constituted roughly 400,000 units, 67% BETA and 33% VHS.

VCR market penetration: 20%.

The 1989 market is stagnant due to radical changes in national economic policy, converting from a highly subsidized economy to a free-market system.

Annual home VCR sales: estimated at 420,000 units, 62% BETA and 38% VHS, judging from 1st quarter activity. The increased percentage of the VHS market is partially due to 1982 residual problems of Sony's BETA operations and consequent stock deficiencies. Panasonic asserted a successful marketing promotions campaign and increased VHS market presence. The VCR market penetration may only augment to 21%, however.

Retail video outlets: 430 in 1988, declining to about 400 by mid-1989. Many video retail outlets are expected to go out of business during these expensive, more competitive times.

Video title releases: One hundred-twenty titles are released each month by the 12 video distributors, maintaining the previous year's marketing output. Total 1988 title releases were 10,000, with an estimate of 11,500 for 1989.

Price per tape: Wholesale blank videotape pricing was $5.30 during 1988, selling for $7.60 in 1989. Pre-recorded wholesale pricing is categorized in two genres, legal and pirate selling prices. The legal 1988 wholesale price was $12, marked up to between $19 and $32 for retail sales. A 50%–55% price increase is now evident in Caracas, the principal market center. Legal 1989 wholesale videos sell for $19 competing with a $12 pirated copy. Retail video copies are expected to increase to as much as $54 in 1989, but there is not any realistic viability of sustained sales at that price.

The consumer video industry started in 1976, with Sony Corporation instrumental in the establishment of this dominant BETA market.

The video release window after national theatrical premiere ranges from simultaneous to six months to one year.

The most preferred video product themes are first, action/adventure coupled with cartoons. The following themes constitute the majority of the film and video market: terror/horror, comedy and drama.

Video revenue: Total legal and estimated pirated revenue was $9 million for 720,000 units in 1988. Estimated video industry revenue is $11.5 million for 700,000 units in 1989.

Regulatory conditions: There were extensive import regulations and prohibitions in 1988. In 1989, however, there are no formal prohibitions and only import tax regulations of 60–80% for finished products, and 20–60% for raw materials.

No official censorship exists, but stated government "recommendations" against thematic content including or associated with 'drugs' is followed with foreboding precaution.

Piracy: The 90% piracy level in 1982 was successfully reduced after the MPAA legal suit and subsequent judicial confiscation of 24,000 pirated video tapes. Unfortunately, piracy has started to regain a substantial percentage of the market. Second generation copies sold in small retail outlets are emerging as the pirated booty, differing from earlier piracy by commercially authorized merchants. Pirated video market share was 15% in 1986, increased up to 21% in 1988, and expected to be 30% of market activity in 1989.

Leading distributors: There are 12 essential distributors [See Motion Picture Almanac distributors]. Principal video distributors are Blancic Video; Videos de Venezuela; Videovision; Videorama; and Rodven.

Conversion: Bolivares/U.S.$ exchange rate = Bs37/$1., 1988 average.

—VICTORIA M. MARSHALL

WEST GERMANY

Household VCR Penetration: 40% of 26,000,000 households (up from 34% in 1987; from 29% in 1986; 44% predicted by the end of 1989).

Rentals and sales volume: 530 million marks in 1988 ($300 million) up from 420,000,000 marks ($250,000,000) in 1987.

VCR Sales: A record 2.4 million wholesale sales in 1988 (up from the previous record of 2,150,000 in 1987); 97% of the country's VCRs utilize VHS format. Betamax and Video 2000 share the remaining 3%.

Blank Cassette Sales: 80 million sold at retail level in 1988 up from 70 million in 1987 (63 million in 1986).

Prerecorded Videocassettes: 2.4 million were sold at the wholesale level in 1988.

Video Premieres: Out of the 1,175 films released on videocassette in 1987, features without previous theatrical release soared to 808 last year from 316 in 1986.

Piracy: Despite better detection and stricter legislation with stiffer penalties, loss to the trade is still an estimated 300 million marks ($170 million) annually.

More than 45,000 illegal vidcassettes of features were confiscated in 1988. The GVU (Western German Association Against Copyright Theft) obtained 378 convictions, while the courts fined culprits a total of 400,000 marks ($230,000).

Retail Outlets: The number of video shops and sell-through outlets (including dept. stores) went through a period of consolidation falling from a total 7,800 in 1987 to 7,100 in 1988 with actual video shops numbering 5,100. Sell-through is also handled by mail order houses, department stores and supermarkets.

Value-added tax: 14% on video rentals and sales, while theaters only pay 7%.

Trends: Several factors combined to bring a downward trend or at least a plateauing to the West German video industry in 1988: competition from the country's growing commercial TV and cable services, and video suppliers' high-priced policy. Also dealers' cash-flow crunch resulted in a drop in depth of copy which frustrated customers and in turn discouraged trips to the video store. More than 10 million of West Germany's 26 million households received commercial TV and cable in 1988 up from only 4 million in 1987. Major video distributors either held to last year's high prices to dealers or hiked the cost of top-title pre-recorded videocassettes from a low of 70.95 marks ($38) to this year's high of 249 marks ($134). This creates a vicious circle for the video outlet which in turn reduces rental fees to increase volume and turnover but actually leaves the dealer less cash to buy top in-demand product, thus resulting in a lack of copy depth.

Demographic studies reveal that VCR purchasers are primarily from upper social classes and that they avoid video shops because of the negative image in West Germany. Only 40% of VCR owners rent video cassettes and of those only 19% on a regular basis. Currently most shops also carry porno titles and are not allowed to admit minors or post advertising in their windows by government decree. Recently the IVD, the West German video dealers' association, urged dealers to convert to family-style shops which means that any section vending hardcore titles has to be entirely separate and have a separate outside entrance.

Direct-to-video films have flooded the West German video market, the share of video premieres rising from 37.3% in 1985 to almost double, 71.8% during the first half of 1988. Most, however, do not do a substantial business.

The major video distributors in West Germany are: CBS/Fox; C.I.C. Video; Constantin Video; Euro Video; RCA/Columbia Pictures Video; Taurus Video; VCL/Virgin Communications; Vestron Video; Video Medien Pool; VPS Entertainment, Warner Home Video.

Principal Video Distributors in the World Market

ARGENTINA

ALL VIDEO, Riobamba 434, (1025) Buenos Aires. Tel: 953-6554, 953-3507.
ARGENTINA VIDEO HOME SA (AVH), Viamonte 2146, Piso 7, (1356) Buenos Aires. Tel: 48-8275/9800. Tlx: 21821 AVH AR.
KROMOS, Avda Callao 420, 1° Piso, (1022) Buenos Aires. Tel: 40-5157, 49-0371.
LEDA FILMS VIDEO HOME, Paseo Colón 221, 2° Piso, (1399) Buenos Aires. Tel: 331-3075/7; FAX: 331-3078.
LEGAL VIDEO, CBS-FOX, Tucuman 2235, (1051) Buenos Aires. Tel: 48- 3465/5305. Tlx: 23555 VIOMAN AR.
LUCIAN FILMS SA, Lavalle 1905, (1051), Buenos Aires. Tel: 46-2150.
PARIS VIDEO HOME, Lavalle 1763, (1048) Buenos Aires. Tel: 40-0902.
PLUS VIDEO SA, Lavalle 1880, (1051) Buenos Aires. Tel: 45-8570. Tlx: 18319 COTEL AR.
RADIOCOM SRI, Conesa 1003, (1426) Buenos Aires. Tel: 552-2580, 552-2608.
RENACIMENTO VIDEO COMMUNICACIONES SA, Mt de Alvear 624, 2° Piso 7, (1058) Buenos Aires. Tel: 312-0707.
SOCIEDAD de VIDEO INDEPENDIENTE (SVI),Corrientes 2470, 2° Piso 9, (1046) Buenos Aires. Tel: 47-1593.
TAURO VIDEO SA, Ayacucho 490, Piso 2, (1026) Buenos Aires. Tel: 953-3784. Tlx: 24835/24836 SEDEM AR.
TELECINEMA VIDEO HOME, Sanchez de Bustamante 886, 2° Piso, (1173) Buenos Aires. Tel: 88-5482, 86-4295. Tlx: 22778 TELEC AR.
TRANSEUROPA VIDEO ENTERTAINMENT, Ayacucho 586, (1026) Buenos Aires. Tel: 46-0558, 49-2219, 49-5037. Tlx: 17387 TRAFI AR.
TRANSMUNDO HOME VIDEO SA, Lavalle 1979, (1051) Buenos Aires. Tel: 40-4338/3862. Tlx: 25962 TRAFI AR.
VESTAL VIDEO SRL, Tucumán 2133, 7° Piso, (1050) Buenos Aires. Tel: 953-5573/6.
VIDEOCLAUEN, Lavalle 1924, (1051) Buenos Aires. Tel: 40-4399/ 45-8448.
VIDEO ESPAÑA SAN LUIS, Lavalle 1625, 7° Piso, (1048) Buenos Aires. Tel: 49-7382, 49-4280. Tlx: 22751 SUDAM AR.
VIDEO LASER PRODUCCIONES, Lavalle 1994, (1051) Buenos Aires. Tel: 49-0607.
VIDEOMAN INTERNACIONAL, Tucuman 2235, (1051) Buenos Aires. Tel: 48-3465/5305. Tlx: 23555 VIOMAN AR.

AUSTRALIA

New South Wales

ABC ENTERPRISES, 28 Atchison St., Crows Nest, NSW 2065. Tel: (02) 430 3999. Tlx: AA 177143. FAX: (02) 430 3888.
ALLIED VIDEO MERCHANTS, 179 Harris St., Pyrmont, NSW 2009, Tel: (02) 660 8999. Tlx: AA 123976.
CBS-FOX VIDEO (SOUTH PACIFIC), 407 Pacific Highway, North Sydney, NSW 2060. Tel: (02) 436 2911. FAX: (02) 439 5560.
CIC-TAFT VIDEO, 2/4 Skyline Place, Frenchs Forest, NSW 2086. Tel: (02) 975 1066. FAX: (02) 975 1115.
COMMUNICATIONS AND ENTERTAINMENT LTD, 185 Elizabeth St, Sydney, NSW 2000. Tel: (02) 268 9000. Tlx: 72900.
FILMPAC, 2nd Floor, 51 Walker St., North Sydney, NSW 2060. Tel: (02) 922 4188. Tlx: AA 25641. FAX: (02) 922 1262.
PALACE, 53–55 Liverpool St., Sydney, NSW 2000. Tel: (02) 267 2533. Tlx: 177413.
RCA-COLUMBIA-HOYTS VIDEO PTY LTD, 9th floor, 221-223 Miller St. North Sydney, NSW 2060. Tel: (02) 957 4186. FAX: (02) 922 3788.
ROADSHOW HOME VIDEO, 49 Market St, Sydney, NSW 2000. Tel: (02) 267 3522. Tlx: AA24161. Fax: (02) 264 2913.
VESTRON VIDEO INTERNATIONAL, Clemenger Building, 5th flr, 120 Pacific Hwy, St Leonards, 2065 NSW. Tel: (02) 436 4988. Tlx: AA 72047. FAX: (02) 436 4347.
VIDEO RAY PTY LTD., 4 Waters Rd., Neutral Bay, NSW 2089. Tel: (02) 908 4422.
WARNER HOME VIDEO, 1st flr, 15-19 Parraweena St, Cremorne, NSW 2090. Tel: (02) 908 3088. Tlx: AA74409 WEAWHV. FAX: 989 8494.

Victoria

CBS-FOX VIDEO (SOUTH PACIFIC), Suite 8, 322-332 St Kilda Rd, St Kilda VIC 3182. Tel: (03) 534 0937. Tlx: 33540 VIC/TAS.
CIC-TAFT VIDEO, 66 Albert Rd., Melbourne, VIC 3004. Tel: (03) 696 1711.
COMMUNICATIONS AND ENTERTAINMENT LTD., 162 Burnley St., Richmond, VIC 3121. Tel: (03) 429 6755. FAX: (03) 427 0797.
PALACE HOME VIDEO, 1051A High St, Armadale, VIC 3143. Tel: (03) 20 6911/20 8694.
RCA-COLUMBIA PICTURES-HOYTS HOME VIDEO, 424 St Kilda Rd, Melbourne, VIC 3004. Tel: (03) 267 6566. Tlx: 31437.
ROADSHOW HOME VIDEO, 206 Bourke St, Melbourne, or PO Box 1498N, VIC 3000. Tel: (03) 667 6555. Tlx: AA32502.
WARNER HOME VIDEO, 529 King St, Melbourne, VIC 3000. Tel: (03) 329 7922. Tlx: 38689.

Queensland

CBS-FOX (SOUTH PACIFIC), Suite 2, 10 Benson St, Toowong, QLD 4066. Tel: (07) 870 7877.
CIC-TAFT VIDEO, 4/470 Upper Roma St, Brisbane, QLD 4000. Tel: (07) 345 7255.
COMMUNICATIONS AND ENTERTAINMENT LTD, 22 Mayneview St, Suite 3, Milton, QLD 4064. Tel: (07) 369 9177.
PALACE HOME VIDEO, 418 Adelaide St, Brisbane, QLD 4000. Tel: (07) 831 0033.
RCA-COLUMBIA PICTURES-HOYTS VIDEO PTY LTD, 10 Benson St., Toowong, QLD 4066. Tel: (07) 870 3400.
WARNER HOME VIDEO, 476 Milton Rd, Auchenflower, QLD 4066. Tel: (07) 371 9100.

South Australia

CBS-FOX VIDEO (SOUTH PACIFIC), 17–21 Hackney Rd., Hackney, SA 5069. Tel: (08) 42 4580.
CIC TAFT VIDEO, 94 Rundle St., Kent Town, SA 5067. Tel: (08) 6367.
COMMUNICATIONS AND ENTERTAINMENT LTD., Bldg 25, 113 Tapleys Hill Rd., Hendon, SA 5014. Tel: (08) 243 1133. FAX: (08) 268 7259.
PALACE ENTERTAINMENT, 13 Byron Pl, Adelaide, SA 5000. Tel: (08) 231 2530. FAX: (08) 231 0813.
RCE-COLUMBIA PICTURES-HOYTS VIDEO, 7 Greenhill Rd., Wayville, SA 5034. Tel: (08) 272 8044. FAX: (08) 272 6582.
ROADSHOW HOME VIDEO, 27 Rundle St., Kent Town, SA 5067. Tel: (08) 362-7640.

Western Australia

CBS-FOX VIDEO (SOUTH PACIFIC), 26 Coghlan Rd., Subiaco, WA 6008. Tel: (09) 382 2777.
CIC-TAFT VIDEO, 15 Oxford Cl., Leederville, WA 6007. tel: (09) 382 3655.
COMMUNICATIONS AND ENTERTAINMENT LTD, 292 Rokeby Rd, Subiaco, WA 6008. Tel: (09) 382 2533.
PALACE ENTERTAINMENT, 123 Claisebrook St., E. Perth, WA 6000. Tel: (09) 328 2277. TAX: (09) 328 7972.
RCA-COLUMBIA PICTURES-HOYTS VIDEO PTY LTD, 22 Thorogood St, Victoria Pk, WA 6100. Tel: (09) 361 8666.
ROADSHOW HOME VIDEO, 6/59 East Parade, East Perth, WA 6000. Tel: (09) 221 3535.
WARNER HOME VIDEO, 185 Stirling St, Perth, WA 6000. Tel: (09) 328 999.

AUSTRIA

AUSTRIA VIDEOFILM VETRIEB, Wiener Neustädterstrasse 10, 2540 Bad Vöslau. Tel: 02252-74 61, 84 61 58, 84 67 24. FAX: 02252-84 11 98.
AUSTRO VIDEO, Zraunig GmbH, Ortsstrasse 18, 2331 Vösendorf. Tel: 69 25 86.
PAUKER GmbH, Ortsstrasse 18, 2331 Vösendorf. Tel: 69 25 89, 69 25 93.
IMPULS VIDEOCASSETTEN & HANDELSGNES mbH, Feldgasse 14, 1080 Wien. Tel: 0222-48 65 07.
MAGNA TON- UND BILDTRÄGER VERTRIEB GmbH, Propst-Peitl-Strasse 54, 2103 Langenzersdorf. Tel: 02244-26 53.
POLYGRAM GmbH, Edelsinnstrasse 4, 1120 Wien. Tel: 0222-83 15 24/112.
RAINBOW VIDEOCASSETTEN VETRIEB GmbH, Südrandstrasse/ Wagner Schönkirchgasse, A-1232 Wien. Tel: 0222-67 76 29. FAX: 0222-67 76 32.
VIDEOVERTRIEB GmbH, Webgasse 43, A-1060 Wien. Tel: 0222-59 79 795. FAX: 0222-59 75 64 633.
WARNER BROS GmbH, Zieglergasse 10, A-1070 Wien. Tel: 0222-96 36 72/13, 93 46 74. FAX: 0222-93 94 62.

BELGIUM

ALL VIDEO, Groenstraat 29, B-3588 Hechtel-Eksel. Tel: (011) 73 59 89
ANANDA CENTRE, Rue César de Paepe 5, B-6210, Ransart. Tel: (071) 34 28 70.
BATENS & DE MUNCK/BDM, Nijverheidslaan 161, B-9170 Waasmunster. Tel: (052) 46 01 02.
BELGIAN PRODUCTION VIDEO (BPV), Rue du College 5, B-6000 Charleroi. Tel: (071) 32 27 33.

BILL INTERNATIONAL, St Katelijnestraat 45, B-2800 Mechelen. Tel: (015) 20 40 80
BLEUMERS, Boomgaardstraat 66, B-2600 Berchem. Tel: (03) 230 94 53
CANNON, Ave Eugene Plasky 157, B-1040 Brussels. Tel: (02) 735 81 68. Tlx: 20814
CBS/FOX, Stephaniaplaats 20, 1050 Brussels. Tel: (02) 513 84 45. Tlx: 22642
CNR VIDEO BELGIUM, De Limburg Stirumlaan 132, B-1810 Wemmel. Tel: (02) 460 07 07. Tlx: 62455
DGD, Rue Isaac 2a, B-6000 Charleroi. Tel: (071) 32 44 64.
EDITIONS CENTRE VIDEO (ECV), Rue Gendebein 4, B-6070, Chatelineau. Tel: (071) 38 37 15.
ELECTRIC VIDEO, Frans Halsvest 24, B-2800 Mechelen. Tel: (015) 21 10 95.
ESSELTE CIC, Tollaan 95, B-1940 Sint Stevens Woluwe. Tel: (02) 720 97 20. Tlx: 20311
EUROPEAN VIDEO ASSOCIATION/EVA, Quinten Matsijslei 36/1, B-2018 Antwerp. Tel: (03) 231 04 33
EXCELVIDEO, de Keyserlei 15, B-2000 Antwerp. Tel: (03) 231 78 00, Tlx: 33141. FAX: (03) 232 11 52.
GNP, Passage International 2, B-1000 Brussels. Tel: (02) 218 42 66.
HVP, Rue Issac 14, B-6000 Charleroi. Tel: (071) 31 80 13.
HORIZON, Koningsstraat 312, B-1210 Brussels. Tel: (02) 217 96 30. FAX: (071) 51 94 10.
INTER VIDEO WORLD (IVW), Rue de Taillis Pré 86, B-6070 Chatelineau. Tel: (071) 39 53 20.
LEVI, Rue Hawis 25, B-4622 Ayeneux. Tel: (041) 77 25 95.
LUMINA COMMUNICATIONS, Zandvoorstraat 8, B-2800 Mechelen. Tel: (015) 20 37 35.
MÉDIATHÈQUE DE LA COMMUNAUTÉ FRANÇAISE DE BELGIQUE, Place Eugène Flagey, 18, B-1050 Brussels. Tel: (02) 640 38 15.
RCA/COLUMBIA PICTURES VIDEO, Opperstraat 38, B-1050 Brussels. Tel: (02) 513 86 82. Tlx: 26124. FAX: (02) 513 95 92.
SDA, Kasteelstraat 48, B-2540 Hove. Tel: (03) 455 50 74.
SUPERCLUB NV, Boomsesteenweg 56/1, B-2630 Aartselaar. Tel: (03) 870 17 11. Tlx: 71102. SUCLUB. FAX: (03) 887 40 25.
SUPER PRODUCTION VIDEO BELGIUM (SPVB), %Belga, Koningsstraat 241, B-1210, Brussels. Tel: (02) 218 72 80.
TRANSUNIVERSAL VIDEO, Handelskaai 18, B-8500 Kortrik.
VDS, Koningsstraat 195, B-1210 Brussels. Tel: (02) 217 18 70; (02) 217 19 33.
VESTRON VIDEO BELGIUM, Opperstraat 38, B-1050 Brussels. Tel: (02) 513 18 14. FAX: (02) 514 19 75.
VIDEO HOME ENTERTAINMENT (VHE), Lange Kouterstraat 14A, B-9200 Wetteren. Tel: (091) 69 67 03.
VIDEO PARTNERS, Meir 49, B-200 Antwerp. Tel: (03) 322 62 22, (03) 225 05 10. Tlx: 72820 T BUSAN B CODE 1033, FAX: (03) 322 14 20.
VIDEO PLAY, Quai de Flandres 7, 6000 Charleroi. Tel: (071) 33 07 01.
VRP SPRL, Rue de la Régence 6, 6000 Charleroi. Tel: (071) 31 80 13. Tlx: 51725
WARNER HOME VIDEO SA, Blvd Lambermont 440, B-1030 Brussels. Tel: (02) 242 58 94. FAX: (02) 245 17 09.

BRAZIL

AB VIDEO, Rua Traipu 260, São Paulo. Tel: 825 5599. Tlx: 21014.
ABRIL VIDEO, Rue Corope 186, São Paulo. Tel: 288 8242.
AMERICA VIDEO, Ave Pacaembu 1702, São Paulo. Tel: 864 9111. Tlx: 83505.
ARGOVIDEO, Rua Vitoria 158, São Paulo. Tel: 222 7988. Tlx: 35560.
CBV VIDEO, Rua do Acre 47/1101, Rio de Janeiro. Tel: 233 3484. Tlx: 34807.
CIC VIDEO, Rua Fradique Coutinho, 352 São Paulo. Tel: 282 3699.
COLORTEL, Rue Mena Barreto 165, Rio de Janeiro. Tel: 286 3522.
DIF, Rua Paraiso, 694, Sao Paulo-SP 04103. Tel: 2899655; Tlx: (011) 21083 EEPR BR
EVEREST VIDEO, Rua Mairinque 267, Vila Mariana, São Paulo. Tel: 549 8388. FAX: 549 1569.
GLOBO VIDEO, Rua Assuncão 443, Rio de Janeiro. Tel: 286 6482. Tlx: 3558.
HIPERVIDEO, Praça Floriano 51/22°, Rio de Janeiro. Tel: 533 3711.
HOLLYWOOD CLASSICS, Ave Santo Amaro 3784, São Paulo. Tel: 530 0720.
JOTA HOME VIDEO, Ave Marechal Camara 160/1422, Rio de Janeiro. Tel: 262-6659. Tlx: 38111.
JZ TV & CINEMA, Av Brig Faria Lima 1857/10°, São Paulo. Tel: 212-6533. Tlx: 22888 XPSP BR.
LK-TEL/RCA-COLUMBIA, Rua Rosa e Silva 163, São Paulo. Tel: 826 2144. Tlx: 30478.
LOOK VIDEO, Ave. dos Imares, 776, São Paulo. Tel: 240 8366. Tlx: 22289.
LORIMAR HOME VIDEO, Rua Conde de Bonfim 1337, Rio de Janeiro. Tel: 288 8142. Tlx: 30255.
F J LUCAS VIDEO, Ave São Jose 1588, São Paulo. Tel: 220 5622.
MACHINE VIDEO, Rua Bueno Andrade 467, São Paulo. Tel: 278 5408.
MANCHETE VIDEO, Rua do Russell 804, Rio de Janeiro. Tel: 285-0033.
MUNDIAL, Al dos Guaramonis 1124, São Paulo. Tel: 542 6677.
NETWORK/VTI, Rua General Bruce 55, Rio de Janeiro. Tel: 580 4258. Tlx: 23018.
OFFICE VIDEO, Rua Tabapũa 479, São Paulo. Tel: 881 9158.
OLYMPUS VIDEO, Rua Correia de Oliveira 15, São Paulo. Tel: 542 2616.
OMNI VIDEO, Ave Brig Faria Lima 1570, São Paulo. Tel: 212 5766.
ONYX VIDEO, Rua do Triunfo 134, São Paulo. Tel: 221 1340, 223 9142.
PHOENIX HOME VIDEO, Rua Stella 515, Villa Marlana, São Paulo. Tel: 572-9113. Tlx: 33476.
PODEROSA FILMES, Rua Bento Sabino dos Reis 26, São Paulo. Tel: 910 9099.
POLEVIDEO, Rua Pedroso Alvarenga 1203, São Paulo. Tel: 883 5747.
SKYLIGHT, Rua Marques de Olinda 69, Rio de Janeiro. Tel: 551 4997. Tlx: 23633.
TAIPAN VIDEO, Rua Cardeal Arcoverde 2987, São Paulo. Tel: 813 1366.
TAKE-TWO, Ave NS de Copacabana 605/1210, Rio de Janeiro. Tel: 255 6884. Tlx: 21791. FAX: 235 2081.
TEC HOME VIDEO, Rua Stella 515, São Paulo. Tel: 887 9730.
TOP TAPE VIDEO, Rue Alice 97, Laranjeiras, Rio de Janeiro. Tel: 205-5552. Tlx: 23923.
TRANS VIDEO/VIDEO MAX, Rua Estados Unidos 297, São Paulo. Tel: 887 5488. Tlx: 24062.
UNIVIDEO, Rua Tabapuã 594. São Paulo. Tel: 282 0945.
VIC VIDEO, Rua Ministro de Godoi 595, São Paulo. Tel: 262 3521.
VIDEOBAN, Rua dos Pinheiros 20/7°, São Paulo. Tel: 282 0945.
VIDEO CASSETE DO BRASIL, Rua Prof Artur Ramos 241, Jardim Paulistano, São Paulo. Tel: 210 4877.
VIDEO TAPES DO BRASIL, Ave Brig Luiz Antonio 1404, São Paulo. Tel: 575 4595.
WARNER HOME VIDEO, Rua Estados Unidos 840, Jardim Paulista, São Paulo. Tel: 280 9522.

BULGARIA

VIDEO BULGARE, Levsky St. 7, 1000 Sofia. Tel: (2) 857722. Tlx: 22652 KOMKUL.

CANADA

Direct Distributors

Bellevue Home Entertainment Inc. (a division of Astral Bellevue Pathé Inc.), Head Office: 7215 route Trans-canadienne, Montréal, Qué. H4T 1A2; (514) 333-7555. Branches: 96 Orfus Rd., North York, Ont. M6A 1C9; (416) 785-5580; (800) 263-2974; FAX: (416) 785-1219; 7215 route Trans-canadienne, Montréal, Qué. H4T 1A2; (514) 333-7555; (800) 361-3320; FAX: (514) 333-7309; 1420 Kootenay St., Vancouver, B.C. V5K 4R1; (604) 324-4343; (800) 663-4559; FAX: (604) 299-8494; 15043A-118th Ave., Edmonton, Alta. T5V 1H9, (403) 453-3007; (800) 252-7907; FAX: (403) 462-8026; 6143 - 4th St. S.E., Unit 9, Calgary, Alta. T2H 2H9; (403) 258-2131; (800) 352-8296; (800) 661-1545; FAX: (403) 253-3455; 100—1294 Border St., Winnipeg, Man. R3H 0M7; (204) 694-4421; (800) 665-8012; FAX: (204) 694-7177; 100 Ilsley Ave., Unit T, Dartmouth, N.S. B3B 1L3; (902) 465-4448; (800) 565-1778 (Newfoundland only); (800) 585-1681 (N.S./N.B./P.E.I.); FAX: (902) 469-7934.
Video One Canada Ltd., Head Office: Unit 101, Bldg. B, 93 Skyway Ave., Etobicoke, Ont. M9W 6C7, (416) 674-0192; FAX: (416) 674-8725. Branches: 105 - 2250 Boundary Rd., Burnaby, B.C. V5M 3Z3; (604) 437-4473; (800) 242-0648; FAX: (604) 432-6926; B-18 - 6020 2nd St. S.E., Calgary, Alta. T2H 2L8; (403) 258-3880; (800) 352-8245; FAX: (403) 252-3176; 11616 - 149th. St., Edmonton, Alta. T5M 3R3; (403) 451-9060; (800) 661-9635; FAX: (403) 452-1763; 515 - 45th. St. W., Saskatoon, Sask. S7L 5Z9; (306) 933-4930; FAX: (306) 933-4139; Unit 12, 1832 King Edward, Winnipeg, Man. R2R 0N1; (204) 694-6007; FAX: (204) 694-0928; 1110 Dearness Dr., Unit 12 London, Ont. N6E 1N9; (519) 685-1502; (800) 265-6054; FAX: (519) 668-2059; 1 Mobile Dr., Toronto, Ont. M4A 1H5; (416) 751-9600; (800) 387-4535; 2285 St. Laurent Blvd., Bldg. A, Units 11 & 13 Ottawa, Ont. K1G 4Z4; (613) 744-5102; FAX: (613) 521-8385; 520 Edinburgh Dr., Moncton, N.B. E1E 4C6; (506) 857-2917; FAX: (506) 857-1700; Unit 40—10 Morris Dr., Dartmouth, N.S. B3B 1K8; (902) 469-0661; FAX: (902) 468-2260; 20 Hallet Cr., Unit 102 St. John's, Nfld. A1B 4C5; (709) 739-5924; FAX: (709) 739-9532; Video Globe 1 (V-1) Inc., 341 Isabey, Ville St.-Laurent, Qué. H4T 1Y2; (514) 738-6665; (800) 361-7151; FAX: (514) 738-3923.

Wholesalers

Bellevue Home Entertainment (a division of Astral Bellevue Pathé Inc.), 7215 route Trans-Canadienne, Montréal, Qué. H4T 1A2; (514) 333-7555; (800) 361-3320. Showrooms/branch offices in Vancouver, Edmonton, Calgary, Winnipeg, Toronto, Montréal, Dartmouth.
BVA Video Ltd. (a division of Astral Bellevue Pathé Inc.), 175 Montpellier Blvd., Montréal, Qué. H4N 2G5; (514) 748-0669.
R.O.W. Entertainment, 255 Shields Ct., Markham, Ont. L3R 8V2; (416) 475-3550.
The Shannock Corp., 4222 Manor St., Burnaby, B.C. V5G 1B2; (604) 433-3331; FAX: (604) 433-4815; 70th Ave.S.E., Calgary, Alta. T2H 2J6; (403) 253-2113; FAX: (403) 255-3359; #23-156 Duncan Mill Rd., Don Mills, Ont. M3B 3N2; (416) 445-3906; 109 Ilsley Ave., Unit 15, Dartmouth, N.S. B3B 1S8.

Distribution

Alliance Releasing, Home Video Division, 355 Place Royale, Montréal, Qué. H2Y 2V3; (514) 844-3132; FAX: (514) 284-2340.
Astral Video (a Division of Astral Bellevue Pathé Inc.), 720 King St.W., Suite 600, Toronto, Ont. M5V 2T3; (416) 364-3894; Branch: 175 boul Montpellier, Montréal, Qué. H4N 2G5; (514) 748-6541; Telex: 05826734; FAX: (514) 748-1348.
France Film Company/Compagnie France Film, 505 Sherbrooke St.E., Suite 2401, Montréal, Qué. H2L 4N3; (514) 844-0680.
Homestar Communications Inc., 840 Yonge St., Toronto, Ont. M4W 2H1; (416) 920-5746; FAX: (416) 922-7806.
Intercanadian Video Sales (ICVS) (a division of Astral Bellevue Pathé), 720 King St. W., Suite 606, Toronto, Ont. M5V 2T3; (416) 362-3538; Branch: 175 Montpellier Blvd., Montréal, Qué. H4N 2G5; (514) 748-6541; Telex: 05826734; FAX: (514) 748-1348.
Malofilm Video Inc., 1207 rue St-André, 4e étage, Montréal, Qué. H2L 3S8; (514) 844-4555; FAX: (514) 844-1471; Telex: 055-61301.
Norstar Entertainment Inc., 86 Bloor St. W., 5th Fl., Toronto, Ont. M5S 1M5; (416) 961-6278; Telex: 06219870; FAX: (416) 961-5608.
North American Releasing Inc., 808 Nelson St., Suite 2204, Vancouver, B.C. V6Z 2H2; (604) 681-2165; Telex: 04-352823 Ambleside VCR; FAX: (604) 681-5538.
Videoville Showtime Inc., 4610 Côte Vertu, Ville St.-Laurent, Qué. H4S 1C7; (514) 336-0038; FAX: (514) 745-4274; Telex: 0524692 ATT: VIDEOVILLE.

CHINA

CCTV INTERNATIONAL TELEVISION SERVICE CORP., 2 Fuxingmenwai St., Beijing. Tel: (01) 862502. Tlx: 22235 CCTV CN.
CHINA RECORDS CORP., 2 Fuxingmenwai, Beijing. Tel: (01) 862625. Tlx: 222309. CKC CN.

DENMARK

ABCOLLECTION, Apt. S, Reventlowsgade 30, DK-1651, Copenhagen V. Tel: (01) 313144. Tlx: 16449 ABCOLDK.
ÅRHUS FILMVAERKSTED, Carl Blochsgade 28, DK-800 Århus C. Tel: 6-139871, 6-196555.
BREIENS FORLAG, Pile Alle 5F, DK-2000 Copenhagen F. Tel: 1-245181. FAX: 1-247881.
DAN-INA OG FOLKEFILMEN, Trekronergade 147B, DK-2500 Valby. Tel: 1-166166.
DANSK FILMINDUSTRI A/S, PO Box 229, Telegade 1, DK-2630 Tåstrup. Tel: 2-998555. FAX: 2-994777.
DANSK VIDEO SYNDIKAT A/S, Ryesgade 10, DK-8000 Århus C. Tel: 6-137922.
DANVIDEO, Frederikssundsvej 276, DK-2700 Brønshøj. Tel: 1-801122.
DØVEFILM-VIDEO, Bryggervangen 13, DK-2100 Copenhagen Ø. Tel: 1-201055.
EGMONT FILM A/S, Dortheavej 71, DK-2400 Copenhagen NV. Tel: 1-192000. Tlx: 22226. FAX: 1-882230. man dir: Steen Leise-Hansen; sls dirs: Preben Jørgensen, Søren Therkildsen; pr man: Elisabeth Rønn.
ERHVERVENES FILMCENTER, Thoravej 24, DK-2400 Copenhagen NV. Tel: 1-191144.
ESSELTE VIDEO A/S, Kobmagergade 19, 1150 Copenhagen K. Tel: (1) 320202. Tlx: 21136.
SAGA VIDEO OG/KORT FILM A/S, Fimaktiesel Skabct, Groennegade 27, 1107 Copenhagen 12. Tel: (01) 125758, (01) 142266.
FILMCOM A/S, Allegade 23, DK-2000, Frederiksberg. Tel: (01) 881811. Tlx: 27272 FILMCO DK.
FACILITY HOUSE, Østerbrogade 78, DK-2100 Copenhagen Ø. Tel: 1-430920, 1-430923.
FLERFILM DISTRIBUTION, Jægersborggade 56, DK-2200 Copenhagen N. Tel: 1-813370.
INDUSTRY-0G HANDELSSTYRELSEN, Tagensvej 135, DK-2200 Copenhagen N. Tel: 1-851066.
IRISH LYDBAND A/S, Handvaerkerbyen 7, 2670 Greve Strand. Tel: (02) 902700. FAX: (2) 900053.
KOMMUNEFILM, Vestbuen 143, DK-2750 Ballerup. Tel: 2-656262.
KÆRNE FILM ApS, Livjægergade 17, DK-2100 Copenhagen Ø. Tel: 1-264200, 3-683048.
MDC VIDEO A/S, Brabrandhus, Hovedgaden 54, DK-8220 Brabrand. Tel: 6-262444.
METRONOME VIDEO/WARNER HOME VIDEO, 16 Sondermarksvej DK-2500, Copenhagen/Valby. Tel: (1) 467755. Tlx: 19497 Unique DK.
NORDISK FILM VIDEO A/S, Axeltorv 7, DK-1609 Copenhagen V. Tel: 1-147606. Tlx: 15286. FAX: 1-325130. man dir: Kim Engell.
PILOT FILM, Produktionsvej 23 D, DK-2600 Glostrup. Tel: 2-844500.
POLYGRAM VIDEO, Emdrupvei 115A, 2400 Copenhagen NV. Tel: (01) 692522. Tlx: 19202.
REGINA FILM, Bregnegårdsvej 7, DK-2920 Charlottenlund. Tel: 1-629640.
RIVERSIDE PIX, Wilders Plads 19, DK-1403 Copenhagen K. Tel: 1-572727. Tlx: 21293. FAX: 1-572753.
SONET/DANSK FILM, Dortheavej 39, DK-2400 Copenhagen NV. Tel: 1-198590.
SONET VIDEO ApS, Store Kongensgade 40 C, DK-1264 Copenhagen K. Tel: 1-134211.
SPOT FILM ApS, Sankt Knudsvej 15, DK-1903 Frederiksberg C. Tel: 1-231700.
THE TAPE HOUSE EDITORIAL CO A/S, Store Kongensgade 66, DK-1264 Copenhagen K. Tel: 1-321330. FAX: 1-321571.
TOFT & FISCHER A/S, Lunikvej 5-7, DK-2670 Greve. Tel: 2-905510.
VIDEO INTERNATIONAL, L, 16 Gasvaerksvej, DK-1656, Copenhagen V. Tel: (01) 229999. Tlx: 22922 Video DK.

FINLAND

ARBITRAGE LTD, Sf-65280 Vasa 28. Tel: 61213622. Tlx: 74129 ARBIT SF.
BEST SELLER FILM AND VIDEO, Itaportti 4C, 02210 Espoo 21. Tel: 036266.
EGMONT FILM, Postipuunti 2, SF-02600, Espoo. Tel: 0-515077. Tlx: 122341. FAX: 0-513105.
OY MANDAG AB, Sarkiniementiie 5, SF-00210 Helsinki. Tel: 0-673351. Tlx: 122144.
OXFORD VIDEO FINLAND OY, Uudenmaankaty 7 A6, SF 00120, Helsinki 12. Tel: 0-603683, 603853.
SKT GROUP INC, Itaportti 4C, SF-02210 Espoo 21. Tel: 036266.
STARVIDEO OY, Karnaistenkatu 43, SF-08100 Lohja 10. Tel: 1223676.
VIDEOFORM FINLAND OY, Laiturik 10, SF-08100 Lohja 10. Tel: 1222189. Tlx: 1458 VIDEO SF.
VIDEOGRAMM OY, Laiturik 10, SF-08100 Lohja 10. Tel: 1222012. Tlx: 1458 VIDEO SF.

FRANCE

ADES VIDEO, 54 rue Saint-Lazare, 75009 Paris. Tel: 48 74 85 30. Tlx: 280422.
ALPHA VIDEO, 126 rue La Boétie, 75008 Paris. Tel: 45 63 44 11/45 63 55 53. Tlx: 641486.
CARRERE VIDEO, 27 rue de Surène, 75008 Paris. Tel: 42 68 13 00. Tlx: 641591.
CBS FOX, 8 Rue Bellini, 75116 Paris. Tel: 47-27-00-73.
CIC 3M FRANCE VIDEO, blvd de l'Oise, 95006 Cergy Pontoise Cedex, 15 rue de la Faisander, 75116 Paris. Tel: 704 62 65. Tlx: 615082.
CINEMA VIDEO CONSEIL, 18-20 av Edouard Herriot, 92350 Le Plessis Robinson. Tel: 40 94 13 13.
CINE COLLECTION, Edition CINE COLLECTION et JUNIOR COLLECTION, Chez Compagnie Internationale de Communication, 73 av Champs Elysees, 75008 Paris. Tel: 42 89 05 26.
COLMAX, 46 rue de la Comete, 92600 Asniere. Tel: 47 90 65 70.
CONCORDE, 276 rue des Pyrénées. 75020 Paris. Tel: 47 97 33 74. Tlx: 212052.
DELTA VIDEO DIFFUSION, 116 ave Champs-Elysées, 75008 Paris. Tel: 45 63 17 27. Tlx: 641605.
DOUNIA VIDEO, 116 blvd de Belleville, 75020 Paris. Tel: 47 97 47 92. Tlx: 212650.
ECHO, 53 rue de Paris, 92100 Boulogne. Tel: 46 04 88 66.
FILM OFFICE, 25 rue de Berry, 75008 Paris. Tel: 42 56 42 46.
FILMS 44 VIDEO, 1 rue de Bourbon Le Château, 75006 Paris. Tel: 43 25 89 14. Tlx: 270700.
FIP, 1 rue Lord Byron, 75008 Paris. Tel: 42 25 15 58.
G.C.R., 1 rue des Princes, 92100 Boulogne. Tel: 46 04 39 43.
INSEP, 11 av du Tremblay, 75012 Paris.
LAURA VIDEO, 64 bv Voltaire, 75011 Paris. Tel: 43 55 88 05.
MPM, 14 rue de Berry, 75008 Paris. Tel: 43 59 16 95.
POLYGRAM SA, 53 ave du President Franklin D. Roosevelt, 75008 Paris. Tel: 42 25 70 40. Tlx: 642589.
PROSERPINE, 25 rue de Madrid, 75008 Paris. Tel: 42 93 57 00.
RENE CHATEAU VIDEO, 72 rue Lauriston, 75116 Paris. Tel: 47 27 99 68. Tlx: 649932 F.
SUPER PRODUCTION VIDEO, 19 rue de Berri, 75008 Paris. Tel: 45 62 65 54. Tlx: 643067.
UGC VIDEO, 24 ave Charles de Gaulle, F-92522 Neuilly-sur-Seine. Tel: 46 37 11 11. Tlx: 614487.
VESTRON, 72 rue Rambuteau, 75001 Paris. Tel: 40 26 30 04.
VIDEO MARC DORCEL, 6 rue Bargue, 75015 Paris. Tel: 45 67 93 20. Tlx: 201838.
VIDEO MARKETING (IFM), 18 rue d'Armenonville, 92200 Neuilly-sur-Seine. Tel: 47 45 47 16. Tlx: 615262.
VIDEO 72, 45 rue de Ponthieu, 75008 Paris. Tel: 43 59 44 57. Tlx: 660312.
VIDEO PRESTIGE, 78 ave des Champs-Elysées, 75008 Paris. Tel: 43 59 59 90.
VIP VIDEO CLUB INTERNATIONAL, 44 rue du Colisée. 75008 Paris. Tel: 45 62 55 09. Tlx: 290441.
WALT DISNEY DISTRIBUTION, 44 Champs-Elysées, 75008 Paris. Tel: 43 59 17 80. Tlx: 640062.
WARNER HOME VIDEO, 32 blvd Henri IV, 75004 Paris. Tel: 48 04 97 04.

GREECE

AUDIOVISUAL ENTERPRISES (MGM, UA, Warner, Disney), 7 Sohou St, Athens 115 25. Tel: 6710263. Tlx: 223282.
C.A.S. CINE VIDEO, 29 Mavromateon St, Athens 104 34. Tel: 8214135 & 8213964.

CBS/FOX VIDEO, 311 Mesogion St, Chalandri, Athens 152 31. Tel: 6725234.
DALLAS HOME VIDEO, 7 An, Zini St, Athens 117 41. Tel: 9222902 & 9025622.
EM-ES VIDEO, 96 Academias St, Athens 106 77. Tel: 3623606 & 9226898.
EMGEE HOME VIDEO (BBC Video, Thames Video), 70 Omirou St, Nea Smyrni, Athens. 171 2i. Tel: 9353930.
HELLAS KOSMOS VIDEO, 442 Akadimias. St, Athens 10677. Tel: 3620533. Tlx: 215083.
HOME VIDEO HELLAS, 275 Messoguion Ave., Athens 152 31. Tel: 6473170 & 6712079. Tlx: 225537.
JOY VIDEO—VIDEO ELLT (ABC Video, Lorimar-Telepictures), 41-43 Kifislas Ave, 15123 Paradisos Amarousiou, Athens. Tel: 6833970-5. Tlx: 216686.
KEY VIDEO (GEORGE KATAYANNIS & CO.), 16-18 Skalidi St, Athens 115 25. Tel: 6708455 & 6717297.
KINO VIDEO, 138 Oifissias St, Maroussi, Athens 151 25. Tel: 8061454 & 8061213.
LEON FILM VIDEO, 96 Academias St, Athens 106 77. Tel: 3644320.
MASTER HOME VIDEO, 96 Academias St, Athens 106 77. Tel: 3607334 & 3632154.
MEDUSA VIDEO, SYMBOL VIDEO, FLY VIDEO, 198 Kifisias Ave, Neo Psyhiko, Athens 11525. Tel: 6726346/6716560/6473627. Tlx: 224312.
MR VIDEO S.A., 22 Ferron St, Athens 104 34. Tel: 8231163 & 8231111.
MTC VIDEO (Cannon), 8 Aristotelous St, Callithea, Athens 176 71. Tel: 9234032.
NEA KINISSI VIDEO & NEA KINIMATOGRAPHIA VIDEO, 9-13 Gravias St, 10878 Athens. Tel: 3628454 & 3608940. 91-81 Akadimias St, 10677 Athens. Tel: 3621162.
OLYMPIC VIDEO, 9-13 Gravias St, Athens 106 78. Tel: 3602932 & 3638700.
PANORAMA, 28 Meteoron & Filolaou St, Athens 116 31. Tel: 7513145 & 7513636.
PLUS VIDEO, 57 Vas Sofias Ave, Athens 11521. Tel: 7225058. Tlx: 225767.
SPENTZOS FILMS VIDEO, 9-13 Gravias St, Athens 106 78. Tel: 3620956.
SYMBOL VIDEO SA, Democratias & Kapodistriou Sts. 2, New Psyhiko, 154 51 Athens. Tel: 6716560/6716560. Tlx: 224312 FLY.
TV HOME VIDEO, 31 Arcadias St, Athens 115 26. Tel: 7713036.
TELEVISION ENTERPRISES SA, 28 Kapodistriou St, Athens 10682. Tel: 3626423. Tlx: 218712.
VENUS VIDEO, 23-25 Themistocleous St, Athens 106 77. Tel: 3609006.
VIDEO ACROPOLIS, 7 Klisovis St, Athens 106 71. Tel: 3611752 & 3611791.
VIDEO ELT, 41-43 Kifissias St, Maroussi, Athens 151 23. Tel: 6833970-5.
VIDEO MOVIES, 6 Dyivoynioyou St, Athens 117 41. Tel: 7503553 & 9233688.
VIDEOSONIC, 1 Evridamantos and Lagoumitzi St, Athens 11745. Tel: 9225350. Tlx: 223858.

GREAT BRITAIN

A & M SOUND PICTURES, 136-140 New Kings Rd., London SW6 4LZ. Tel: 01-736 3311. Tlx: 916342 ALMOSS G.
AMARAY INTERNATIONAL,Oak House, Oak End Way, Gerrards Cross, Bucks.
ANGLO AMERICAN FILM DISTRIBUTORS/VIDEO MEDIA LTD, 70 Wardour St., London W1. Tlx: 291565 AA FILM.
APEX VIDEO, 3 Standard Rd, Park Royal Ind. Est., London NW10 6EX. Tel: 01-965 5354. Tlx: 914382
ARIEL FILMS & VIDEO DISTRIBUTORS, 3 High St., Christchurch, Dorset DH23 1AB. Tel: 0202 479868. Tlx: 41594.
ATLANTIS VIDEO PRODUCTIONS LTD, Atlantis House, 60 Wapping High St., London E1 9LX. Tel: 01-481 3333. Tlx: 893970 ATLANT G.
AVATAR COMMUNICATIONS, Imperial Studios, Imperial Rd., London SW6 2AG. Tlx: 8950127.
BBC VIDEO, Woodlands, 80 Wood Lane, London W12 0TT. Tel: 01-576 2000; Head of Marketing: Tony Greenwood.
BORDEAUX FILMS INTERNATIONAL LTD, 3rd flr, 92 Wardour St., London W1. Tel: 01-434 3459. Tlx: 21879/25267 BOROFILMS LONDON W1.
BRENT WALKER VIDEO, Knightsbridge House, 197 Knightsbridge, London SW7 1RB. Tel: 01-225 1941. Tlx: 23639.
CANNON VIDEO, 30631 Golden Sq., London W1A 4DX. Tel: 01-437 9234.
CAREYVISION, Unit 4, Whitworth Rd. Ind. Est., Pin Green, Stevenage SG1 4QS. Tel: 0438 350660. Tlx: 825422 POURRI G.
CBS/FOX VIDEO, Perrivale Ind. Est., Greenford, Middx. UB6 7RU. Tel: 01-997 2552. Tlx: 268763.
CHANNEL 5 DISTRIBUTION LTD, 1 Rockley Rd., London W14 0DL. Tel: 01-743 3473. Tlx: 298816.
CHRYSALIS, 12 Strafford Pl., London W1N 9AF. Tel: 01-408 2355. Tlx: 21753.
CIC VIDEO, 4th flr, Glenthorne House, 5-17 Hammersmith Gr., London W6 0ND. Tel: 01-846 9433. Tlx: 268763.
CINEPLEX, Unit 4, The Whitworth Road Industrial Estate, Whitworth Road, Stevenage SG1 4QS. Tel: 01 965 5555. FAX: 01 961 8454; Managing dir.: Steve Mandy; Marketing dir: Phil Crace.
CITY VISION PIC, Unit 1 McKay Trad. Est., Kensal Rd., London W10 5BX. Tel: 01-960 8211. Tlx: 291877 VISION G.
DERANN FILM SERVICES LTD, 99 High St., Dudley, W. Midlands. Tel: 0384 233191. Tlx: 335893 DERANN.
ELECTRIC VIDEO, 41 Paddington St., London W1M 3RN. Tel: 01-935 7288. Tlx: 24583.
EMBASSY HOME ENTERTAINMENT, Sloane Sq. House, Holbein Pl., Sloane Sq., London SW1 8NS. Tel: 01-730 3455. Tlx: 895 0483.
ENTERTAINMENT AND VIDEO DISTRIBUTORS LTD, 27 Soho Sq., London W1. Tel: 01-439 1979. Tlx: 262428 ENTVIF.
FILMCENTRE OVERSEAS CORP, 113-117 Wardour St., London W1. Tel: 01-439 7491.
FILMTOWN VIDEO, 36 Soho Sq., London W1V 5DG. Tel: 01-434 9729. Tlx: 297648.
FUTURE VISION LTD, Unit 10, Brunswick Ind. Pk., Waterfall Rd., New Southgate N11 1JL. Tel: 01-368 1276.
GMH ENTERTAINMENTS, 22 Manasty Road, Orton, Southgate, Peterborough.
GO VIDEO LTD, PO Box 4BT, 35-37 Wardour St., London W1A 4BT. Tel: 01-734 7195/6. Tlx: 922488.
GRANADA VIDEO, 36 Golden Sq., London W1R 4AH. Tel: 01-734 8080. Tlx: 27937.
GTO FILMS & VIDEO INTERNATIONAL, 27A Queens' Ter., St John's Wood, London NW8. Tel: 01-580 7576. Tlx: 267811 MUSIC IQ.
GUILD HOME VIDEO, Crown House, 2 Church St., Walton-on-Thames, Surrey KT12 2QS. Tel: 0932 228899. Tlx: 269651.
HENDRING LTD., 20^ Eccleston St., London SW1W 9LT; Tel: 01-730 8691. FAX: 01-823 4934. Director: Christopher Stylianou; Production: Simon Saunders; Sales: Trevor Drane; Press/promotions: Stephanie Downs.
HERON HOME ENTERTAINMENT, Unit 4, Brunswick Ind. Pk., Brunswick Pk. Rd., New Southgate, London N11 1JL. Tel: 01-368 1226. Tlx: 897654.
IMPACT, 44 Gt Marlborough St., London W1V 1DB. Tel: 01-734 6813. Tlx: 264660 OVIDEO G.
INTERMOVIE, Agra House, 964 North Circular Rd., London NW2 7JR. Tel: 01-450 5477/78/79. Tlx: 928706.
ISLAND VISUAL ARTS, 334-336 King St., London W6 0RA. Tel: 01-846 9566. Tlx: 934541.
KINGS FEATURES ENTERTAINMENTS INC, 18 Hanover Sq., London W1R 9HG. Tel: 01-491 3382. Tlx: 266570 KINGSN G.
LONGMAN VIDEO, Longman House, Burnt Mill, Harlow, Essex CM20 2JE. Tel: 0279 26721.
MEDUSA COMMUNICATIONS, 109 Regal House, 51 Bancroft, Hitchin, Herts SG5 1LL. Tel: 0462 53612. Tlx: 826552.
MGM/UA HOME VIDEO, Hammer House, 113-117 Wardour St., London W1V 3TD. Tel: 01-439 9932. Tlx: 28527.
MISSING IN ACTION, Handle House, 1 Derby St., London W1Y 7HD. Tel: 10-493 9637. Tlx: 892756 HANDLE G.
NELSON ENTERTAINMENT, 8 Queen St., London W1X 7PM.
NEW REALM ENTERTAINMENTS LTD, Townsend House, 22-25 Dean St., London W1V 5AL. Tel: 01-437 9143/786 5818. Tlx: 892604 NRDLON G NUREALMPIC.
NEW WORLD VIDEO, 27 Soho Sq., London W1V 5FL. Tel: 01-434 0497. Tlx: 27950 ref: 2794. Fax: 01 434 0490; Managing director: Martin Goldthorpe.
NICKELODEON PICTURES LTD, 74 Queensway, 2nd flr, London W2. Tlx: 265905 HALEPI G.
ODYSSEY VIDEO, 44 Gt Marlborough St., London W1V 1DB. Tel: 01-439 2244. Tlx: 264660 OVIDEO.
PALACE VIDEO, 16-17 Wardour Mews, London W1V 3DG. Tel: 01-734 7060. Tlx: 263900 PALACE G.
PALAN ENTERTAINMENT CORPORATION, 1 Euston Centre, London NW1 3JG. Tel: 01-388 5034. Tlx: 268710 PALAN G.
PENDULUM COMMUNICATIONS LTD., Market House, Market Square, Bromley, Kent BR1 1NA. Tel: 01-460 5749. FAX: 01-460 5749. Chief executive: Brian Norris.
PICTURE MUSIC INTERNATIONAL, 20 Manchester Sq., London W1A 1ES. Tel: 01-486 4488. Tlx: 22643. FAX: 01-935 3852.
PICKWICK VIDEO LTD., The Hyde Industrial Estate, The Hyde, London, NW9 6JU.
POLYGRAM VIDEO, 1 Rockley Rd., London W14 0DL. Tel: 01-743 3474. Tlx: 298816. FAX: 01-743 2074.
(PVG) PALACE VIRGIN & GOLD DISTRIBUTION, 69 Flempton Rd., London E10 7NL. Tel: 01-539 5566. Tlx: 894793 S GOLD.
QUADRANT VIDEO, 37a High St., Carshalton, Surrey SM3 3BB. Tel: 01-669 1114. Tlx: 269556.
RCA/COLUMBIA PICTURES VIDEO (UK), Metropolis House, 22 Percy St., London W1P 9FF. Tel: 01-636 8373. Tlx: 23876.
SELECT VIDEO, PO Box 111, Gt Ducie St., Manchester M60 3BL. Tel: 061-834 4842. Tlx: 668609.
S GOLD AND SONS (RECORDS LTD), 69 Flempton Rd., Leyton, London E10 7 NL. Tel: 01-539 3600. Tlx: 894793.
SONY VIDEO SOFTWARE EUROPE, 41-42 Berners St., London W1P 3AA. Tel: 01-631 4000. FAX: 01 631 4665; Managing director: Bruce Wilkinson; Sales & Marketing mgr.: Peter Johnson.
SPAN PICTURES LTD., 1-2 John Princes Street, London, W.1. Tel: 01-491 4997.
STABLECANE, Unit 10, Brunswick Ind. Pk., Waterfall Rd., New Southgate London N11 1JL. Tel: 01-368 1276. Tlx: 269023 PREST G.
THAMES VIDEO, 149 Tottenham Court Rd., London W1P 9LL. Tel: 01-387 9494. Tlx: 25286. FAX: 01-388 6073; Head of Thames Video Intl.: Peter Sames.

TREDEGAR WHOLESALE VIDEO CENTRE, The House, 21 Greycaine Road, North Watford, WD2 4QT. Tel: 0923 226936.
VESTRON VIDEO (UK), 69 New Oxford St., London WC1 1DG.
VIDEO BOX OFFICE, 22 Manasty Road, Orton Southgate, Peterborough PE2 0UP. Tel: 0733 233464; Directors: G. Hopkins, I. Muspratt, Ms. D. Gardner, R. Parker.
VIDEO COLLECTION UNIT, 10 Brunswick Ind. Pk., Waterfall Rd., New Southgate N11 1JL. Tel: 01-368 1276.
VIDEO GEMS (A.M.T. Ltd), 3 Standard Rd., Park Royal Ind. Est., London NW10 6EX. Tel: 01-961 5646. Tlx: 914382 MSDLON G.
VIDEO INSTANT, 9 Sentinel House, Sentinel Sq., Brent St., Hendon, London N1 2EN. Tel: 01-202 9879.
VIDEO PROGRAMME DISTRIBUTORS LTD, Bldg 1, GEC Est, East Lane, Wembley, Middx. HA9 7FF. Tel: 01-904 0921. Tlx: 295369 VIDPRO G.
VIRGIN VISION VIDEO, 328 Kensal Rd., London W10 5XJ. Tel: 01-968 8888. Tlx: 892890.
WARNER HOME VIDEO, 135 Wardour St., London, W1V 4AP.
WIERNERWORLD LTD, 90 Old Church Lane, Stanmore, Middx. HA7 2RR. Tel: 01-954 8777. Tlx: 923753 MONREF or 946240 CWEASY.
WEEKEND VIDEO, Seymour Mews House, Seymour Mews, Wigmore St., London W1H 9PE. Tel: 01-935 9000. Tlx: 228726 FVFILM G.

HOLLAND

ARPA VIDEO, Molenkade 57A, 1115 AC Duivendrecht. Tel: 020-955503. FAX: 020-956625.
BESTVIDEO, Stadhoudersskade 165, 2983 CT Ridderkerk. Tel: 01804-17469. FAX: 01804-16285.
BOUDISQUE, De Ruytferkade 41-43, 1012 AA Amsterdam. Tel: 020-260311. Tlx: 12589.
BROOKLYN VIDEO, Postbus 109, 3620 AC Breukelen. Tel: 03462-65343.
CANNON VIDEO, De Lairessestraat 111-115, 1075 HH Amsterdam. Tel: 020-5751 751. Tlx: 15267. FAX: 020-6622085.
CBS/FOX VIDEO, Herenweg 115, 2105 MG Heemstede. Tel: 023-233211. Tlx: 41051. FAX: 023-292169.
CNR VIDEO, Flevolaan 62g, 1382 JZ Weesp. Tel: 02940. Tlx: 18669 cnr. nl. FAX: 2940-19063.
COR KOPPIES VIDEO, Postbus 5242, Amsterdam. Tel: 020-767841. Tlx: 18287. FAX: 020-714968.
ESSELTE CIC VIDEO BV, Ampereweg 13, 3442 AB Woerden. Tel: 03480-22254. Tlx: Esvd 76124. FAX: 03480-10576.
HAFBO BV, Postbus 424, 3740 AK Baarn. Tel: 02154-13213.
HDN, Filmamentlaan 2, 5632 AB Eindhoven. Tel: 040-421480.
KING MOVIE PRODUCTIONS BV, Koninginneweg 93, 1211 AN Hilversum. Tel: 035-16457. Tlx: 73324.
MANHATANN INTERNATIONAL VIDEO, Cardanuslaan 34, 6865 HK Doorwerth. Tel: 085-333383. Tlx: 75019 VIMAR.
MOVIES SELECT VIDEO BV, Haarlemmersdijk 163, 1013 KH Amsterdam. Tel: 020-238630. Tlx: 11223 MOVIE NL. FAX: 020-239489.
RCA/COLUMBIA PICTURES VIDEO BV, Vreelandseweg 42b, 1216 CH Hilversum. Tel: 035-13246. Tlx: 73534. FAX: 035-288997.
RCV 2001 NEDERLAND, Energieweg 45a, 2382 NC Zoeterwoude. Tel: 071-899373. Tlx: 39495. FAX: 071-891302.
SCALA AGENTUREN, Contactweg 28, 1014 AN Amsterdam. Tel: 020-828900. FAX: 020-828943.
SPRINGBOARD VIDEO, Havikstraat 55a, 3514 TM Utrecht. Tel: 030-719174. Tlx: 76242 S VID.
VESTRON BENELUX, Catharijnesingel 55, 3511 GD Utrecht. Tel: 030-316844. Tlx: 70276. FAX: 030-316926.
VIDEO EXCLUSIEF, Dulkaathof 3, 5551 VM Valkenswaard. Tel: 04902-43866. FAX: 04902-43137.
VIDEO NETWORK, Houtweg 32, 1251 CT Laren (NH). Tel: 02153-12917. Tlx: 43110. FAX: 02153-14155.
VIDEOSCREEN, Postbus 195, 3400 AD IJsselstein. Tel: 03408-89048. FAX: 03408-86206.
VISUALS INTERNATIONAL, Jan van Beierenstraat 123, 1211 HS Hilversum. Tel: 035-16457. Tlx: 73324. FAX: 035-284794.
VSR NEDERLAND, Postbus 7330, 1007 JH Amsterdam. Tel: 02977-43949. FAX: 02977-43708.
WARNER HOME VIDEO NETHERLANDS, De Boellaan 16, 1083 HJ Amsterdam. Tel: 020-464766. Tlx: 10685. FAX: 020-449001.
WINDMILL, Luikerweg 14A, Valkenswaard. Tel: 04902-44119.

HONG KONG

COMMUNICATIONS AND ENTERTAINMENT INTL, 8th flr, Printing Ho, 6 Duddell St Central.
FOTOMAX, 8th Floor, Shui On Centre, 6-8 Harbour Rd. Tel: 5 8616852. Tlx: 82750 SOG HX.
KPS VIDEO EXPRESS, 233-235 Ocean Galleries, Harbour City, Kowloon. Tel: 3 7397633.
ROBERT CHUA PRODUCTION HOUSE CO LTD., RCP-TV Studios, 1 Suffolk Rd., Kowloon Tong Kowloon.
TELEVISION BROADCASTS LTD., 77 Broadcast Dr., Kowloon.

INDIA

AMIT ELECTRONICS, 3 Velders St, Mount Rd, Madras 600 002. Tel: 849879/848130.
ARF VIDEO, Natraj Studio, 194 Andheri Kurla Rd, Bombay 400 069. Tel: 6360845/6141189.
BOMBINO VIDEO PVT LTD, 7/8 Udyog Nagar, 7 Shilay Industrial Estate, Goregoan (W), SV Rd, Bombay 400 062. Tel: 2046233/2048625/694554/692151.
DOSHI VIDEO, 417 Mint Street, Madras 79.
EAGLE VIDEO, 55, Ezra Street, Calcutta 1.
EMPEROR VIDEO, 3, Chittaranjan Avenue, Calcutta 72.
ESQUIRE VIDEO, unit 1A & 1B, Gr fl, Rehmat Manzil 75 Veer, Nariman Rd, Churchgate, Bombay 400 020. Tel: 230811/234226.
GARWARE PLASTICS & POLYESTER LTD., 50A, Swami Nityanand Marg, Western Express Highway, Vile Parle(E) Bombay 57.
GOLD VIDEO SHOP NO. 42, 291 Palika Bazar, New Delhi 1.
HIBA VIDEO, Vijaya Villas, 3rd floor, Warden Rd, Bombay 400 026. Tel: 8224807.
IMAGE VIDEO PVT LTD, Atlanta, 17th flr, Nariman Point, Bombay 400 021. Tel: 223747/223777.
INDUS VIDEO, 5, Marble Arch, Central Avenue, Santa Cruz (W) Bombay 54.
INFOCOM, 230 B Acharya, J C Bose Rd, Calcutta 700 020. Tel: 435107. Tlx: 021-7381 RONG IN.
KAZEM BUNARIS, 7 Shaly Industrial Estate, 8 Udyog Nagar, S V Rd, Goregaon, Bombay 400 062. Tel: 694554/692151.
MAGNEM VIDEO, 68 Hill Rd, Natraj Shopping Centre, Bandra, Bombay 400 050. Tel: 6427274/6429377.
MANORANJAN ELECTRONICS NO. 8, 1st Floor-1st Main St, Gandhinager, Bangalore 9.
M G VIDEO ELECTRIC (P) LTD, M G House, Plot no 22, Santacruz Electronic Export Processing Zone, Andheri (E), Bombay 400 096. Tel: 6301851/6327246.
MODERN ELECTRONICS, 22 Seva Sadan, D.J. Rd, Vile Parle (W) Bombay 56.
MULTI VIDEO PVT LTD, 341 Lajpatrai Market, New Delhi. Tel: 230079.
NAMDHARI ELECTRICALS, 1668 Bhagirath Palace, Chandni Chowk, Old Delhi 110 006.
NAVINA INVESTMENT CO, 3/33 Tardeo AC Mkt, Tardeo, Bombay 400 034.
NFDC (NATIONAL FILM DEVELOPMENT CORPORATION), D block, 5th flr, Shivsagar Estate, Dr Annie Besant Rd, Worli Bombay 400 018. Tel: 4929096/4922393. Tlx: 011-73489 NFDC IN.
ORSON VIDEO (P) LTD, Unit 46 and 47, Santacruz Electronic Export Processing Zone, Andheri (E), Bombay 400 096. Tel: 6329808/6321526/6323128.
OSCAR TRADING CO PVT LTD, 309 Arun Chambers, Tardeo Rd, Bombay 400 034. Tel: 4947602/4941735.
PANAMAX MARKETING PVT LTD., 602 B Block 'A' Poonam Chambers, Shivsagar Estate, Worli, Bombay 18.
PENTACON CONSULTANTS P LTD., 532 Sandhurst Bridge, Bombay 400 007.
RADHKA VIDEO, 58/64 Hari Chambers, S B Rd, Fort, Bombay 400 001. Tel: 2862339/2863319.
RAJSHREE ELECTRONICS, G-6 Kailash Colony, New Delhi 48.
R.B.L. VIDEO DISTRIBUTORS, Sewawala Bldg, Byculla Bombay.
RUBY FILMS, Turner Road, Bandra, Bombay 50.
SAGAR VIDEO INTERNATIONAL (PREM SAGAR), Nataraj Studio, 194 Andheri Kurla Rd, Bombay 400 069. Tel: 6360845/6141189.
SHEMAROO VIDEO P LTD., 3, Om Chambers, Kemp's Corner, Bombay 36.
SPECTRA VIDEO PVT LTD, 78 SDF III, Santacruz Electronic Export Processing Zone, Andheri (E), Bombay 400 096. Tel: 6300528/6301472.
SUN VIDEO (LIMELITE), 31 Kailash Darshan, Kennedy Bridge, Bombay 400 007. Tel: 356966/385597/388170. Tlx: 1175476 GOLD INDT.
SURYA BHARTI, Trisandhya A, 97 Dada Saheb Phalke Rd, Dadar, Bombay 400 014. Tel: 447261/447938.
TEISCO VIDEO VISION, 9/10/11 Amar Industrial Estate, Andheri Kurla Rd, Sakinaka, Bombay 400 072. Tel: 8220889/8121833. FAX: 5123602/5123315/5123022.
TELEVIDEO ELECTRONIC, Trisandhya A, Dada Saheb Phalke Rd, Dadar, Bombay 400 014. Tel: 447261/448036.
VARIETY VIDEO PRODUCTION, B-51 Connaught Place, New Delhi.
VGP VIDEO VISION OF INDIA, Unit 51, 2nd SDF bldg, Santacruz Electronic Export, Andheri (E), Bombay 400 096.
VIDEO KING (INDIA) PVT LTD, 1009 Dalamal Tower, Nariman Point, Bombay 400 021. Tel: 231187/226139. Tlx: 011-3668 HHGE-IN.
VIDEO MASTER, 39/40 Ratnajyot Industrial Estate, Irla Lane, Vile Parle (E), Bombay 400 056. Tel: 6360061/6362136.

ITALY

AVELCA VIDEO RECORD SpA, Via Lumière 6, 20093 Cologno Monzese. Tel: 25 47 22.
C B S DISCHI SpA, Via Amedei 9, 20123 Milan. Tel: 85 36.
C G D VIDEOSUONO SpA, Via MF Quintiliano 40, 20138 Milan. Tel: 50 84.
CINEHOLLYWOOD EDUCATIONALVIDEO SRL, Via Reguzzoni 15, 20125 Milan. Tel: 643 90 42.
DE LAURENTIIS RICORDI VIDEO SpA, Via Berchet 2, 20121 Milan. Tel: 88 81.
DELTA VIDEO SRL, Corso Buenos Aires 10, 20124 Milan. Tel: 20 99 53.

DOMOVIDEO SpA, Palazzo Perseo, Via Paracelso 12, 20041 Agrate Brianza. Tel: (039) 63 44 41.
DUPLI VIDEO CENTER SRL, Via Oslavia 17, 20134 Milan. Tel: 215 25 88.
DURIUM SpA, Via Lampedusa 11/a, 20141 Milan. Tel: 843 99 48.
EMI ITALIANA SpA, Via Bergamo 315, 21042 Caronno Pertusella Va. Tel: 965 07 01.
FUTURAMA SRL, Via Enrico Fermi 4, 20090 Noverasco di Opera. Tel: 524 97 60.
GENERAL VIDEO SAS, Via Panziera 28, 50047 Prato Fl. Tel: (0574) 63 10 13.
MARGY SRL, Via Orti 2, 20122 Milan. Tel: 551 75 45.
NUOVA FONIT CETRA SpA, Via Meda 45, 20141 Milan. Tel: 843 25 51.
PANARECORD SpA, Corso Venezia 40, 20121 Milan. Tel: 749 11 01.
POLYGRAM DISCHI SpA, Via Carlo Tenca 2, 20124 Milan. Tel: 679 61.
RCA COLUMBIA PICTURES VIDEO SpA, Via di S Alessandro 7, 00131 Rome. Tel: 436 61.
SAMPAOLO AUDIOVISIVI SRL, Via Portuense 746, 00148 Rome. Tel: 685 00 51.
VIDEOBOX SRL, Via Linati 7, 20128 Milan. Tel: 257 16 88.
VIDEO ELECTRONICS CLUB, Via della Nocetta 75, 00164 Rome. Tel: 626 11 59/60, 653 00 58.
VIDEOGRAM ITALIA SpA, Via Turati 29, 20121 Milan. Tel: 655 49 67/8.
VIRGIN DISCHI SRL, Via Belluno 4, 20132 Milan. Tel: 259 39 41/4.
VIVIDEO, Corso Garibaldi 86, 20121 Milan. Tel: 62 82 67 52.
WEA ITALIANA SpA, Via Milano 16, Redecesio, 20090 Segrate. Tel: 216 81.

JAPAN

BANDAI CO LTD, Ohashi Bldg, 2-3-13 Shinjuku, Shinjuku-ku, Tokyo 160. Tel: (03) 226-7531.
CBS/SONY GROUP INC, K-S Bldg. 3F, 2-4-1 Ichigaya-sadohara-cho, Shinjuku-ku, Tokyo 162. Tel: (03) 266-5041. Tlx: J34913 SVISONY. FAX: 03 235 8135.
CHANNEL COMMUNICATIONS, INC, Osakaya Bldg. 5F, 3-1-9 Mita, Minato-Ku, Tokyo 108. Tel: (03) 798-3304, (03) 798-3335, (03)798-3342. Tlx: 2423783 CHCOMMJ. FAX: 03 798 5072.
COMSTOCK LTD, Omotemachi Bldg. 806, 4-8-19 Akasaka, Minato-ku, Tokyo 107. Tel: (03) 403-0140. Tlx: J34864 COMSTOCK. FAX: 03 403 0343.
DISC CENTER CO LTD, PO Box 874, Osaka 530-91. Tel: (06) 323-6350. Tlx: J64488. FAX: 06 323 0249.
FUJI TELEVISION NETWORK INC, 7 Kawada-cho, Ichigaya, Shinjukuku, Tokyo 162. Tel: (03) 353-1111. Tlx: 358 8031 FCI; FAX: 03 353 3716.
GAGA COMMUNICATIONS INC, Kanda Bldg, 2-7-17 Hamamatsu-cho, Minato-ku, Tokyo 105. Tel: (03) 431-6121. Tlx: J34104 GAGA. FAX 03 431 6677.
JVC, 8-14, Nihonbashi-Honcho 4-chome, Chuo-ku, Tokyo 103. Tel: (03) 241-2035. Tlx: 2223240 JVCVHD J. FAX: 03 245 1538.
MITSUBISHI CORP, 6-3 Marunouchi, 2-chome, Chiyoda-ku, Tokyo 100. Tel: (03) 210-7374.
MODERN PROGRAMS INC, 501 Akasaka New Plaza, Minato-ku, Tokyo 107. Tel: (03) 585-4604. Tlx: J23415 MODPRO.
MT LIGHT CO, 703 Doeru Ichibankan, 10-11, Kikukawa 2-chome, Sumida-ku, Tokyo 130. Tel: (03) 635-8282. Tlx: J32837 MOUNTL. FAX: 03 635 6983.
NEW SELECT CO LTD, Nakamura Bldg, 5-9-13 Ginza, Chuo-ku, Tokyo 104. Tel: (03) 573-7571. Tlx: J29965 NW SELECT. FAX: 03 572 0139.
NIHON VICTOR CO LTD, 4-8-14 Nihonbashi-honcho, Chuo-ku, Tokyo 103. Tel: (03) 241-7811. Tlx: J26222. FAX: (03) 245 1402.
NIKKATSU, Hibiya Park Bldg 8-1, Yurakucho 1-chome, Chiyoda-ku, Tokyo 100. Tel: (03) 214-2182. Tlx: 26627 NIKKATSU, FAX: 03 214 2531.
NIKKATSU VIDEO FILMS, 2-16-2 Higashi-Azabu, Minato-ku, Tokyo 106. Tel: 505-2411. FAX: (03) 505 3036.
NIPPON COLUMBIA CO LTD, 4-14-14 Akasaka, Minato-ku, Tokyo 107. Tel: 584-8111. Tlx: J22591. FAX: (03) 586 1859.
NIPPON TELEVISION NETWORK CORP, 12 Niban-cho, Chiyoda-ku, Tokyo 102. Tel: (03) 265-2111. Tel: J24566.
PACK-IN VIDEO CO LTD, 1-7-1 Shinbashi, Minato-ku, Tokyo 105. Tel: (03) 572-6455.
PONY INC, 4-3-31 Kudan-kita, Chiyoda-ku, Tokyo 102. Tel: (03) 265-4164. Tlx: 0232408. FAX: (03) 265 4190.
SEIYU LTD, Sunshine 60 Bldg 1-1, Itigashi-Ikebukuro 3-chome, Toshima-ku, Tokyo 170. Tel: (03) 989-4566. Tlx: 02722444 SEIYUM J. FAX: 03 989 4319.
TDK CORE CO LTD, 1-9-6 Hatchobori, Chuo-ku, Tokyo 104. Tel: 505-1131. FAX: (03) 555 1033.
TELECAS JAPAN CO LTD, 214 Azabu Heights, 1-5-10 Roppongi, Minatoku, Tokyo. Tel: (03) 583-2900. Tlx: J23693.
TOEI VIDEO CO LTD, 15-10, 3-chome, Ginza, Chuo-ku, Tokyo 104. Tel: (03) 545-4511. Tlx: 2524541. FAX: (03) 545 5929.
TOHO TOWA CO LTD, Playguide Bldg, 2-6-4 Ginza, Chuo-ku, Tokyo 104. Tel: (03) 562-0111. Tlx: 981485. FAX: 03 561 3395.
TOKUMO COMMUNICATIONS CO LTD, No 1 Hibiya Bldg, 1-18-21 Shinbashi, Minato-ku, Tokyo 105. Tel: 591-9161.
TOKYO BROADCASTING SYSTEM INC, 5-3-6 Akasaka, Tokyo 107. Tel: (03) 584-3111. Tlx: J24883. FAX: (03) 555 1424.
TOKYO CHANNEL 12 LTD, 4-4-7 Shibakoen, Minato-ku, Tokyo. Tel: (03) 432-1212.
TOSHIBA-EMI LTD, 2-2-17 Akasaka, Minato-ku, Tokyo 107. Tel: 587-9111. Tlx:2422112TOE TOKJ. FAX: (03) 586 9253.
VAP CO LTD, NTV Yonbancho Annex, 4th fl, 5-6 Yonban-cho, Chiyoda-ku, Tokyo 102. Tel: (03) 234-5711. Tlx: J29410. FAX: (03) 234 5295.
VESTRON INTERNATIONAL GROUP, No 12 Mori Bldg, 1-17-3 Toranomon, Minato-ku, Tokyo 105. Tel: (03) 581-9505. Tlx: J34310 ESPER.
VICTOR MUSICA INDUSTRIES INC, 4-26-18 Jungumae, Shibuya-ku, Tokyo 150. Tel: (03) 405-5151. Tlx: 2424293 VICREC J. FAX: (03) 408 1761.
VIDEO FILMS INC, Komeido Bldg, 3-9 Yoesuya, Shinjuku-ku, Tokyo. Tel: (03) 357-65745. Tlx: J2324084. Videofj.
WORLD FILM & TELEVISION CORP, Ginza-8-10 Bldg, 6th flr, 8-10-8 Ginza, Chuo-ku, Tokyo. Tel: (03) 571-8047/9. Tlx: J25640 WORLDTYO.

NEW ZEALAND

CANNON SCREEN ENTERTAINMENT (NZ LTD), Private Bag, Newmarket, Auckland. Tel: 09 398 416. Tlx: NZ21341.
CBS FOX VIDEO, PO Box 37720 Parnell, Auckland. Tel: 09 31 513. Tlx: NZ21490.
CEL COMMUNICATIONS AND ENTERTAINMENT, 16 Liverpool St, Auckland. Tel: 09 389 706.
CIC TAFT VIDEO (NZ LTD), PO Box 3097, Auckland. Tel: 09 444 1824. Tlx: NZ60849.
KERRIDGE ODEON AMALGAMATED VIDEO SERVICES, PO Box 422, Auckland. Tel: 09 32 206.
RCA COLUMBIA PICTURES, HOYTS VIDEO, PO Box 68490, Newton, Auckland. Tel: 09 790 661. Tlx: NZ2208.
SHOWCASE VIDEO, PO Box 78115 Grey Lynn, Auckland. Tel: 09 762 750.
VIDEOCORP INTERNATIONAL, PO Box 39476, Auckland West. Tel: 09 389 899. Tlx: NZVideoNZ60191.
VIDEO WHOLESALERS, 25a East St, Newton, Auckland. Tel: 09 395 496.
WARNER HOME VIDEO, PO Box 2195, Auckland. Tel: 09 792 964. Tlx: NZ2839.

NORWAY

A/S CCV, PO Box 36, Alnabro, N-0614 Oslo 6. Tel: 2-647770. FAX: 2-642122. Contact: Amund Myklebust.
EGMONT FILM A/S, PO Box 95, Solbråveien 43, N-1371 Asker. Tel: 2-786121. FAX: 2-786175. Contact: Stig Worren, Roald Dye.
ESSELTE VIDEO, PO Box 148 Økern, N-0509 Oslo 5. Tel: 2-649290. FAX: 2-651733. Contact: Jimmy Joccumsen.
HOLLYWOOD VIDEO A/S, Baneviksgaten 7, N-4000 Stavanger. Tel: 4-53405. Tlx: 73129. FAX: 2-527398. Contact: Geir Helge Mæland.
JUNO MEDIA A/S, PO Box 18, N-1312 Slependen. Tel: 2-848900. FAX: 2-848577. Contact: Jan Feldborg.
MAYCO A/S, PO Box 22 Kjelsås, N-0411 Oslo 4. Tel.: 2-230581. FAX: 2-183746. Contact: May-Britt Iversen.
THE NORDIC FILM GROUP, Nedre Vollgaten 9, N-0158 Oslo 1. Tel: 2-414325. Tlx: 72767. FAX: 2-414325.
NOVIO A/S, Nes terrasse 45, N-1360 Nesbur. Tel: 2-849160. FAX: 2-980342. Contact: Michael Simonsen.
VCM NORWAY A/S, Kristian Augustsgaten 11, PO Box 6858 St, Olavs Plass, N-0130 Oslo 1. Tel: 2-200684. Tlx: 78163. FAX: 2-203154. Contact: Mikael Ostberg.
WARNER HOME VIDEO, Heigdehaugsveien 31, PO Box 7053 Homansbyen, N-0306 Oslo 3. Tel: 2-431800. Tlx: 78356. FAX: 2-554683. Contact: Dagfinn Thune.

PORTUGAL

DIGER VIDEO, Rua Almirante Barroso 9, 2° esq, 1000 Lisbon. Tel: (1) 52 70 39, 54 91 90. Tlx: 60225.
DEVA FILMES VIDEO, Av Duque de Loulé 75, 8° drt, 1000 Lisbon. Tel: (1) 57 36 98.
DOPERFILME, Rue Luciano Cordeiro 113, 1°, 1199 Lisbon Codex. Tel: (1) 56 10 41.
ECOVIDEO, Av da Liberdade 563, PO Box 62, 3701 São João da Madeira. Tel: (56) 28 45 54/6. Tlx: 27390 JOPINES.
EDIVIDEO, Rua Manuel Fereira de Andrade 6, B, 1500 Lisbon. Tel: (1) 74 03 81, 74 03 87, 74 06 64, 78 31 58. Tlx: 14495 EDISOMP.
FILMITALUS VIDEO, Rue Alexandre Herculano 2, 4° drt, 1200 Lisbon. Tel: (1) 54 79 88.
GANASH FILMS, Rua Rosa Damasceno 3, 1° F, 1900 Lisbon. Tel: (1) 53 57 07.
ITAD VIDEO, Rua Manual Joaquim dos Reis 38, B, Sobralinho, 2615 Alverca. Tel: (2) 50 16 27.
IMAVIDEO, Rua Marquês da Fronteira 117, 1°, 1000 Lisbon. Tel: (1) 65 75 41.
KODAK PORTUGUESA/WARNER HOME VIDEO. Edicficio Kodak, Apartado 12, 2796 Linda-A-Velha. Tel: (4) 19 50 68.
LEGAL VIDEO, Rua Rodrigues Sampaio 146, 1° drt, 1100 Lisbon. Tel: (1) 54 79 42/3.

MVM VIDEO. Rua Adelaide Cabeta 5, E, 1500 Lisbon. Tel: (1) 714 20 18. Tlx: 43471 TINNER.
MUNDIAL VIDEO, Rua S. José 203, 1° esq 1200 Lisbon. Tel: (1) 53 86 53, 57 08 60.
PUBLIVIDEO, Av. Duque de Loulé 77, 6 esq, 1000 Lisbon. Tel: (1) 65 69 32, 68 00 81.
RADIOTEVISÃO COMERCIAL (RTC), Av Fontes Pereira de Melo 17, 3°, 1000 Lisbon. Tel: (1) 54 83 35. Tlx: 64630 RTC.
SM VIDEO, Rua Actor Taborda 55, r/c, esq, 1000 Lisbon. Tel: (1) 52 22 44.
VCL COMMUNICATIONS, Rua Rosa Damasceno 3, 1° F, 1900 Lisbon. Tel: (1) 53 57 07.
VIDEO COMMERCIAL, Av Infante Santo 38, 7° F, 1300 Lisbon. Tel: (1) 67 76 34.
VIDEOTRÓNICA, Rua Rodrigues Sampaio 146, 1° drt, 1100 Lisbon. Tel: (1) 54 79 42/3.
VISTA VIDEO, Rua António Pedro 68, 1° drt, 1000 Lisbon. Tel: (1) 52 63 31.

SINGAPORE

AMARJIT PICTURES, 1 North Bridge Rd., 09-06 High St. Centre, Singapore 0617. Tel: 3371054. Tlx: 24275.
BURNEO FILM ORGANISATION SDN BHD, 3rd flr, Pawagam BFO Dalit, Jalan Bukit Merah (Bukit Merah Town Centre), Singapore 0315. Tel: 2739066. Tlx: 51020.
CATHAY ORGANISATION PTE LTD, 11 Dhoby Ghaut, 05-00 Cathay Bldg., Singapore 0922. Tel: 3378181. Tlx: 21124.
CEL VIDEO (S) PTE LTD, 14-07, 190 Middle Rd., Singapore 0718. Tel: 3361800.
SHAW & SHAW PTE LTD, 13th & 14th flrs, Shaw Centre, 1 Scotts Rd., Singapore 0922. Tel: 2532077. Tlx: 23957.
VIDEOVAN ENTERPRISES (S) PTE LTD, 04-10 Beach Centre, Beach Rd., Singapore 0718. Tel: 3398870.
VISIONEX PRODUCTION PTE LTD, 08-19/20, 101 A Upper Cross St., Singapore 0106. Tel: 5343288.

SPAIN

AL FILMS INTERNACIONAL, General Ampudia 3, Oficina 513, 28008 Madrid. Tel: (91) 418 47 84.
AVO, Leiva 17, 08014 Barcelona. Tel: (93) 431 52 65.
ANDROMEDA FILMS SA, Bertrán 47, 08023 Barcelona. Tel: (93) 418 47 78. Contact: Luis Lopez.
CB FILMS, Diagonal 407, Principal, 08008 Barcelona. Tel: (93) 217 93 54.
CBS/FOX VIDEO ESPAÑOLA SA, P°de la Castellana 141, 28046 Madrid. Tel: (91) 459 07 63.
CIC-RCA/COLUMBIA PICTURES VIDEO, Avenida de los Madroños 27, 28043 Madrid. Tel: (91) 200 80 40, (93) 254 98 05.
CYB VIDEO, Rafael Casanovas 104, 08620 Sant Vicenc dels Morts, Barcelona. Tel: (93) 656 33 61.
CONTINENTAL, Maria de Molina 26, 27006 Madrid. Tel: (91) 261 77 77.
CROWN FILMS HOME VIDEO, Palafox 21, 28010 Madrid. Tel: (91) 445 31 12, 445 38 00.
CYDIS VIDEO (IZARO CANNON), Doce de Octubre 28, 28001 Madrid. Tel: (91) 274 90 08.
DISTER VIDEO E FILM, Nuñez de Balboa 42, 28001 Madrid. Tel: (91) 435 66 85, 435 70 51. FAX: (91) 431 77 36.
EMPIRE DISTRIBUCIONES, Montera 38, 28006 Madrid. Tel: (91) 401 18 47.
FILMAYER VIDEO SA, Matires De Alcala 4, 28015 Madrid. Tel: (91) 248 92 05.
FILMS 4, Palafox 21, 28010 Madrid. Tel: (91) 445 31 12, 445 38 00.
FIVE VIDEO, Cespe 111, 08013 Barcelona. Tel: (93) 232 80 52, 232 85 13.
HIT VIDEO, Balmes 87, 08007 Barcelona.
IMAGE FILMS CORPORATION, Llansa 22, 08015 Barcelona.
INTERNATIONAL MASTER FILMS, General Ampudia 3, Oficina 513, 28003 Madrid. Tel: (91) 418 47 84.
INTERNATIONAL VIDEO SYSTEMS (IVS), Olite 37, 31004 Pamplona. Tel: 948 24 10 45, 24 26 39.
INTERVIDEO, Jarama 19m 28002 Madrid. Tel: (91) 458 21 62/6.
IVE DISTRIBUTORS SA, Ave Hospital Militar 52, 08023 Barcelona. Tel: (93) 219 25 00. FAX: (93) 210 55 53.
IVEX FILMS, Mariano Cubi 4, 08001 Barcelona. Tel: (93) 218 34 00.
JET FILMS, Victor Chauam 19, Oviedo. Tel: 985 22 29 72.
KALENDER VIDEO SA, Pintor Juan Gris 5, 28020 Madrid. Tel: (91) 455 44 77. FAX: 456 72 97.
LAUREN FILMS, VICEO HOGAR,, Balnes 87, pral., 08007 Barcelona. Tel: (93) 254 58 61.
LAX VIDEO SA, Jarama 19, 28002 Madrid. Tel: (91) 458 21 62.
OLIMPY, Ave Jijona 57, 03010 Alicante. Tel: (96) 525 04 11. FAX: (96) 525 41 46.
PREMIERE HOME VIDEO, Sánchez Pacheco 16, Bajos, 28002 Madrid. Tel: (91) 415 40 00.
RMS, Ave José Antonio 13, 24001 Leon. Tel: 943 23 66 11/2, 24 91 15.
RECORD VISION, Corcega 372, 08037 Barcelona. Tel: (93) 207 35 56.
STANDARD, Paisaje Buria 11, 08025 Barcelona. Tel: (93) 256 09 85.
TRAVELLING VIDEO, Isla de Sapian 75, 28035 Madrid. Tel: (91) 216 42 65, 723 06 94.
VTF, Rafael Calvo 42, 28010 Madrid. Tel: (91) 410 22 49, 410 23 49.
VICITECOR, Osa Mayor 50, Aravaca, 28023 Madrid. Tel: (91) 207 18 40/1.
VIDEOJOVEN, Castellana 52, 28046 Madrid. Tel: (91) 413 66 61.
VIDEOMAN INTERNACIONAL, Doce de Octubre 28, 28009 Madrid. Tel: (91) 274 90 08.
VISION FILMS VIDEO, Enrique Granados 44, pral, 08008 Barcelona. Tel: (93) 254 00 07. FAX: (93) 254 37 04.
WARNER HOME VIDEO, Alfonso Rodriguez Santamari.. ., 28002 Madrid. Tel: (91) 250 99 05.
WEEKEND VIDEO, Velazquez 12, 28001 Madrid. Tel: (91) 431 42 46. FAX: (91) 435 59 94.

SRI LANKA

LAGODAN (PTE) LTD, 302 Havelock Road, Colombo 5, Sri Lanka. Tel: 587508.
MARATHON VIDEO, 154 Deens Road, Colombo 10, Sri Lanka. Tel: 92578.
MOVIELAND, 89 1/8 538 Galle Road, Colombo 3, Sri Lanka. Tel: 574414.
PREMASIRI MULTI SHOP, 19 Liberty Plaza, Colombo 3, Sri Lanka.
MATHU VIDEO HOME, 163 New Chetty Street, Colombo 13, Sri Lanka.
THE VIDEO SHOP, 163 Galle Road, Colombo 4, Sri Lanka. Tel: 501955.
VIDEO MOVIE CENTRE, 69 Bankshall Street, Colombo 11. Sri Lanka.
TELE CINE LTD, 43 Hyde Park Corner, Colombo 2, Sri Lanka. Tel: 23909.
CINETRA, 437 Pethiyagoda, Kelaniya, Sri Lanka. Tlx: 21918 PERIMR CE.
CEYLON THEATRES LTD, 8 Sir Sittampalam Gardiner Mw, Colombo 2, Sri Lanka.

SWEDEN

BOX COLLECTION, PO Box 2043, S-421 02 Vastra Frolunda. Tel: (31) 498500.
CD-DISTRIBUTION, Långebergsgatan 26 B, S-421 32 Vastra Frolunda. Tel: (31) 680580.
EGMONT FILM AB, Svetsarvagen 2, PO Box 507, S-183 25 Taby. Tel: (76) 210050. FAX: (76) 212046. man dir: Mats Caneman.
ESSELTE VIDEO AB, Hornsgatan 166, PO Box 9006, S-102 71 Stockholm. Tel: (8) 7722500. FAX: (8) 845980.
GEBE FILM VIDEO AB, Artillerigatan 48, S-114 45 Stockholm. Tel: (8) 638520.
MDC VIDEO AB, PO Box 22003, S-500 03 Borås. Tel: (33) 118100.
MEDIA TRANSFER INTERNATIONAL AB, Franzengatan 6, PO Box 30115, S-104 25 Stockholm. Tel: (8) 520620. FAX: (8) 537305.
MELODY LINE HOLM & OLSSON, PO Box 31181, S-400 32 Goteborg. Tel: (31) 128120.
NORDIC FILM GROUP AB, Sjalbodgatan 10, S-211 35 Malmo. man dir: Thommy Andersson. Tel: (8) 241199. FAX: (8) 201515.
NORDISK FILM TV-DISTRIBUTION AB, Regeringsgatan 66 B8, S-103 89 Stockholm SV. Tel: (8) 241199. FAX: (8) 201515. man dir: Carl Goran Andersson.
POLYGRAM AB, PO Box 20510, S-161 20 Bromma. Tel: (8) 7647350.
PRISMA FILM & VIDEO AB, Birger Svenssons Väg 40, S-432 00 Varberg. Tel: (340) 89065.
SANDREW FILM & TEATER AB, Floragatan 4, PO Box 5612, S-114 86 Stockholm. Tel: (8) 234700. FAX: (8) 103850.
SONET VIDEO AB, Tappvägen 24, PO Box 20105, S-161 20 Bromma. Tel: (8) 7647700. FAX: (8) 299091.
SVENSKA WALTHERS VIDEO, PO Box 42137, S-126 12 Stockholm. Tel: (8) 7442010.
TOWER VISION FILM AB, St Pedersgatan 13, S-252 37 Helsingborg. Tel: (42) 129994.
VCM SWEDEN AB, PO Box 229, S-131 02 Nacka. Tel: (8) 7183320.
VESTRON VIDEO SWEDEN AB, Nytorpsvägen 28, S-183 53 Täby. Tel: (8) 7921480.
VIDEOTRADE AB, PO Box 2144, S-103 14 Stockholm. Tel: (8) 235080. FAX: (8) 219373.
VIRGIN VIDEO SWEDEN AB, PO Box 14084, S-161 14 Bromma. Tel: (8) 806340.
WARNER HOME VIDEO SWEDEN AB, Hornsbruksgatan 19, 3 tr, SI-117 34 Stockholm. Tel: (8) 581250.
WENDROS AB, PO Box 5100, S-141 05 Huddinge. Tel: (8) 7740425. FAX: (8) 7798316.

SWITZERLAND

CONDOR PRODUCTIONS AG, Restelbergstr 107, 8044 Zürich. Tel: 01-361 96 12. Tlx: 817032 COPRO. FAX: 01-361 95 75.
DISTRIBUTION INTERCONTINENTALE DE FILMS SA, Steinstrasse 21, 8036 Zürich. Tel: 462-01 12. Tlx: 813322 COFI CH.
FERNSEHEN DRS, Fernsehstrasse 1-4, Postfach, 8052 Zürich. Tel: 01-305 66 11. Tlx: 56756 (1267151).
HOME MOVIES AG, Römerstr 37, 8400 Winterthur. Tel: 052-27 47 21. Tlx: 896110. *Labels*: Highlight Video, VPS Video, New Vision, Starlight, Pacific Video, Mike Hunter Video, Inter Media Video, Splendid-Video, Skyline-Video, Noris-Buchboxen.

INTER MEDIA VIDEO, 5 Avenue Léon-Gaud, 1206 Geneva.
INSTITUT VIDEO LANGUES, 54 rue du Stand, 1204 Genève. Tel: 022-21 13 73. Tlx: 421504.
LIBRAPRIM SA, 210 Route de Jussy, 1243 Presinge. Tel: 022-59 18 47. Tlx: 421 372 (FLAG).
MEGAHERZ, Weststr 77, 800 3 Zürich. Tel: 01-462 86 80.
PARVIDEO SA, 7 Ave Léon-Gaud, 1206 Genève. Tel: 022-47 12 18. Tlx: 23654 PARK CH. FAX: 022-47 16 40.
POLIVIDEO SA, Via Stradonino 1, 6595 Riazzino-Locarno. Tel: 092-64 01 11. Tlx: 846 352 POVI CH.
RAINBOW VIDEO AG, Schönmattstr. 4, 4153 Reinach. *Labels*: CIC, Taurus, Constantin, Atlas, VCL, IHV/AVP.
SABZ-FILMVERLEIH, Postfach 54, Monbijoustr 61, 3000 Bern 23. Tel: 031-45 56 69.
SONOR SA, 15 rue des Savoises, 1211 Genève 11. Tel: 022-21 77 11. Tlx: 427666.
STARTRONIC, Ave du Grey 3, 1004 Lausanne. Tel: 021-36 36 63. Tlx: 25905
STELLA VIDEO AG, Postfach 322, Münchhaldenstr 10, 8034 Zürich. Tel: 01-55 55 80. Tlx: 816823. FAX: 01-55 54 85. *Labels*: Stella Video, Cannon Screen, Entertainment, Vestron, Ascot, Elite, Sky Movie, Praesens Video, ARS Viva Edition, VMP.
TELIMAGE SA, 18 ter Petit-Chêne, 1003 Lausanne. Tel: 021-20-25 68. Tlx: 455827 FVP. FAX: 021-23 62 09.
UNICEF—FONDS DES NATIONS UNIES POUR L'ENFANCE, Palais des Nations, 1211 Genève. Tel: 022-98 58 50. Tlx: 27908A UNF CH. Cables: UNICEF GENEVE.
VIDEOPHON AG, Bahnhofplaza, 6340 Baar. *Labels*: RCA/Columbia, Poly Gram Video, EuroVideo, MGM/UA, Electric Blue, Select Video, CBS/Fox, Mondial Video, Walt Disney, Touchstone/Buena Vista Home Video.
VIDE-O-TRONIC, Neue Winterthurerstr. 15, 8305 Dietlikon. *Labels*: CBS/Fox, Medusa Home Video, VSR International.
WARNER BROS. INC., Seestr. 19, 8702 Zollikon. *Labels*: Warner Home Video, United Artists.
R C WITSCHI TELEFILM, Himmelistr 6, Postfach 1602, 8700 Küsnacht. Tel: 01-910 17 09. Tlx: 829021. FAX: 01-730 74 97.

TAIWAN

HAI YANG VIDEO FILM CO, 12 Lane 166, Nung An St, Taipei. Tel: (02) 502-1355.
HSIN CH'UAN MOVIE CO LTD, 2/F, 85 Wuchang St, Sec 2, Taipei. Tel: (02) 314-3658.
HSUEH HO FILM CO LTD, Room 608, 6/F, 205 Tunhua North Rd, Taipei. Tel: (02) 716-2385.
HUA CH'I FILM CO LTD, 7/F, 2 Pateh Rd, Sec 3, Taipei. Tel: (02) 721-0607.
KUO LIEN FILM CO LTD, 2/F, 133 Fuhsing S Rd, Sec 2, Taipei. Tel: (02) 707-0504.
MEDIA CO LTD, 7/F, 317 Sungchiang Rd, Taipei. Tel: (02) 502-0277.
NAN CH'I FILM CO LTD, 12 Lane 22, Sung Puo St, Panchiao City, Taipei County. Tel: (02) 251-6546.
NIEN TAI FILM CO LTD, 3/F, 46 Pateh Rd, Sec 1, Taipei. Tel: (02) 397-1122.
SAN TIEN FILM CO LTD, 6-2/F, 281 Anho Rd, Taipei. Tel: (02) 707-3241.
SAN YI CO LTD, 6/F, 116 Hanchung St, Taipei. Tel: (02) 371-5191.
TAH CH'I FILM CO LTD, 2-2/F, 127 Keelung Rd, Sec 1, Taipei. Tel: (02) 764-5193.
TIEN YUN FILMS LTD, 1 Alley 62, Tachih St, Taipei. Tel: (02) 502-8082.
YUNG TSEN MOVIE CO LTD, 2/F, 168 Hsinyi Rd, Sec 4, Taipei. Tel: (02) 705-0708.

WEST GERMANY (FEDERAL REPUBLIC)

ALEXANDRA-VERLAG GmbH, Dachauerstr 37, 8000 Munich 2. Tel: (089) 297194. Tlx: 529096.
ALL-VIDEO VERTRIEBS GmbH, Industriestr 49, 4044 Kaarst 1. Tel: (02101) 604042. Tlx: 8518065.
ALL VIDEO PROGRAMM VERTRIEBSGESELLSCHAFT GmbH, Lazarettstr 19, 4300 Essen 1. Tel: (0201) 202866/69. Tlx: 8579531.
ARCADE VIDEO (DEUTSCHLAND) GmbH, Buckower, Chaussee 60-68, 1000 Berlin 48. Tel: (030) 7215042.
ARIOLA-EURODISC GmbH, Carl Bertelsmann-Str 161, Postfach 3306, 4830 Gütersloh 1. Tel: (05241) 805151. Tlx: 933787
ASCOT VIDEO, Frankenstr 143, 4300 Essen 1. Tel: (0201) 207866. FAX: (0201) 238911.
ATELIER-FILM & VIDEO VERLEIH GmbH, Rat-Kaffl-Str 6, 8011 Aschheim. Tel: (089) 907925/7. Tlx: 523975 loco d.
ATLAS FILM & AV GmbH & CO KG, Verleih und Vertrieb, Ludgeristr 14-16, 4100 Duisburg 1. Tel: (0203) 308280. Tlx: 8551128.
AV-FILM GmbH, Max-Planck-Str 38, 8056 Neufahrn. Tel: (08165) 5536.
BEATE UHSE-VIDEO, Gutenbergstr 12, Postfach 2955, 2390 Flensburg. Tel: (0461) 809206. Tlx: 17461307. FAX: (0461) 98613.
BENRA FILMVERLEIH KG/VIDEO, Raschigstr 100, 6700 Ludwigshafen/Rh. Tel: (0621) 552088/89.
REINHARD BERG FILMPRODUKTION, Körnerstr 5, 6200 Wiesbaden. Tel: (06121) 305919.
BRUCKMANN VERLAG MUNCHEN, Nymphenburger Str 86, Postfach 27, 8000 Munich 20. Tel: (089) 1257308. Tlx: 523739. FAX: (089) 12572232.
CALIG VERLAG GmbH, Schuhstr 4, Postfach 1047, 3200 Hildesheim. Tel: (05121) 169225.
CANNON SCREEN ENTERTAINMENT, Frankfurter Ring 115, 8000 Munich 40. Tel: (089) 35090266. Tlx: 5213397.
CBS/FOX VIDEO (GERMANY) GmbH, Am Forsthaus, Gravenbruch 7, 6078 Neu-Isenburg 2. Tel: 06102-5552. Tlx: 4185555. FAX: (06102) 5550.
CD-FILM, Lützowstr 20, 4100 Duisburg 1. Tel: (0203) 355164, 356623.
CHRONOS FILMVERLEIH GmbH, Schopenhauerstr 50, 1000 Berlin 38. Tel: (030) 8033051/52. Tlx: 181511.
CIC VIDEO GmbH, Frankfurter Str 74, 6236 Eschborn/Ts. Tel: (06196) 46054/8. Tlx: 418193.
COMPACT VIDEO, Fasanenweg 4, 8027 Neuried. Tel: (089) 7553272.
CON MEDIEN UND VERTRIEBS GmbH, Postfach 106545, Westerdeich 38, 2800 Bremen. Tel: (0421) 540012/3. Tlx: 246971 CON D.
CONSTANTIN VIDEO GmbH, Kaiserstr 39, 8000 Munich 40. Tel: (089) 38609382.
DATAKONTEXT VERLAG GmbH, Postfach 400253, 5000 Köln 40. Tel: (0221) 486503, 02234-78913.
EKSTASE-VIDEO, Postfach 2171, 4322 Sprockhövel 2.
ELECTRONIC CENTER GmbH, ECG TV-Studio, Adalbertstr 44-48, 6000 Frankfurt/Main 90. Tel: (069) 770611. Tlx: 412980.
EMI ELECTROLA GmbH, Maarweg 149, 5000 Köln 30. Tel: (0221) 4902/0. Tlx: 8881290.
ERF VERLAG VIDEO, Berliner Ring 62, Postfach 1444, 6330 Wetzlar. Tel: (06441) 5050.
ERNST KLETT VERLAG, Rotebühlstr 77, Postfach 809, 7000 Stuttgart 1. Tel: (0711) 6672/0. Tlx: 722225.
EUROVIDEO BILDPROGRAMM GmbH, Oskar-Messter-Str 15, 8045 Ismaning. Tel: (089) 960920. Tlx: 5215946.
GBM VERIAG BILDUNG UND MEDIEN GmbH,Schwedenstr 10, 8137 Berg 2/Starnberger See. Tel: (08151) 51156.
GEISELGASTEIG VIDEO GmbH, Grünwalderstr 14, 8000 Munich 71. Tel: (089) 799210. Tlx: 529418 fsped d.
GLOBAL FILM & VIDEO GmbH, Nederlingerstr 21, 8000 Munich 19. Tel: (089) 151063. Tlx: 5215019.
GLORIA VIDEO GmbH, Gutenbergstr 23-25, 6800 Mannheim 1. Tel: (0621) 371055. Tlx: 462906.
GOVI VIDEO, Gluckstr 67, 2000 Hamburg 76. Tel: (040) 291739. Tlx: 211992.
IITIS FILMVERLEIH GmbH, Schollstr 2, 8035 Gauting. Tel: (089) 8505468.
IVH INTERNATIONAL HOME VIDEO VERTRIEBS GmbH, Lazarettstr 19, 4300 Essen 1. Tel: (0201) 233551. Tlx: 8579685.
IMV INTERNATIONAL MEDIEN VERTRIEB, Oskar-Messter-Str 15, 8045 Ismaning. Tel: (089) 96123/7. Tlx: 5215946.
INSTITUT FÜR VIDEO INFORMATIONS SYSTEME VIS GmbH, Lakronstr 59, 4000 Düsseldorf 12. Tel: (0211) 283031.
INTER-PATHÉ GmbH & CO KG, Bolongarostr 141, 6230 Frankfurt/Main 80. Tel: (069) 304043/315680. Tlx: 411981.
ITALVIDEO GIACINTO SOLI IMPORT-EXPORT, Video und Tonträger, Schwalbenweg 3, 7258 Heimsheim. Tel. (07033) 31411, 31461. Tlx: 783374.
JAHRESZEITEN TV UND VIDEO PRODUKTION GmbH, Possmoorweg 5, 2000 Hamburg 60. Tel: (040) 2717/0. Tlx: 213214.
JAPAN HOME VIDEO TATSUNOKO FILM PRODUCTION GmbH, Heinrich-Berbalk-Str 56, 6000 Frankfurt/Main 56. Tel: (069) 5083540. Tlx: 4189533.
KLASING & CO GmbH, Delius Klasing Verlag, Siekerwass 21, 4800 Bielefeld 1. Tel: (0521) 5590. Tlx: 932934.
KV KOMPLETT-VIDEO, Flemingstr 15, 8000 Munich 81. Tel: (089) 928020. Tlx: 5216059.
LANGENSCHEIDT KG, Neusser Str 3, 8000 Munich 40. Tel: (089) 36096/0. Tlx: 5215379.
MARKT & TECHNIK VERLAG AKTIENGESELLSCHAFT, Hans-Pinsel-Str 2, 8013 Haar. Tel: (089) 4613/0. Tlx: 522052.
MARKETING FILM BOCHUM GmbH, Viktoriastr 23-25, 4630 Bochum T. Tel: (0234) 60745. Tlx: 825786.
MEDIENVILM VIDEO MAGAZIN GmbH, Alt Seulberg 73, Postfach 1360 6382 Friedrichsdorf/Ts. Tel: (06172) 72055/56. Tlx: 410884.
MERKUR FILM AGENCY GmbH, Krünerstr 65, 8000 Munich 70. Tel: (089) 7693424. Tlx: 5216092.
MIKE HUNTER VIDEO GmbH, Hohe Pforte 4-6, 5000 Köln 1. Tel: (0221) 210041/43. Tlx: 888900. FAX: (0221) 241356.
NB FILM & VIDEO ENTERTAINMENT GmbH & CO KG, Postfach 2120, 4150 Krefeld 1. Tel: (02151) 801122. Tlx: 8531121.
NEUE ATLAS MEDIEN PRODUCKTIONS-UND VERTRIEBS GmbH & CO KG, Ludgeristr 14-16, 4100 Duisburg 1. Tel: (0203) 3080. Tlx: 8551128.
OTTO MAIER VERLAG GmbH, Postfach 1860, 7980 Ravensburg. Tel: (0751) 861. Tlx: 732921.
PÄDAGOGISCHER VERLAG SCHWANN-BAGEL GmbH, Am Wehrhahn 100, Postfach 7640, 4000 Düsseldorf 1. Tel: (0211) 360301. Tlx: 8581345.
PIONEER-MELCHERS GmbH, Hansaallee 191, Postfach 110942, 4000 Düsseldorf 11. Tel: (0211) 5953/0. Tlx: 8587326.
POLYBAND GESELLSCHAFT F BILD-U TONTRÄGER GmbH & CO BETRIEBS KG, Am Moosfeld 37, 8000 Munich 82. Tel: (089) 420030. Tlx: 522636. FAX: (089) 4200342.
POLYGRAM VIDEO GmbH, Postfach 132266, Harvestehuder Weg 1-4, 2000 Hamburg 13. Tel: (040) 44181483/4.

RCA/COLUMBIA PICTURES VIDEO, Schatzbogen 50-52. 8000 Munich 62. Tel: (089) 4209010. FAX: (089) 42090122.
SELECT VIDEO GmbH, Raiffeisenstr 13, 7024 Filderstadt 4. Tel: (0711) 7700716. Tlx: 7255154.
SKYLINE VIDEO, Belgradstr 61, 8000 Munich 40. Tel: (089) 3007021. FAX: (089) 303915. Contact: Hans-Joachim Müller.
SPRINGER-VERLAG GmbH & CO KG, Heidelberger Platz 3, 1000 Berlin 33. Tel: (030) 8207/1. Tlx: 183319.
STARLIGHT-FILM PRODUKTIONS-UND VERTRIEBS GmbH, Steinring 45, 4630 Bochum 1. Tel: (0234) 3330402. Tlx: 825351. FAX:)0234) 311617.
SUNRISE VIDEO GmbH, Lorsbacher Str 1, 6238 Hofheim/Ts. Tel: (06192) 28901.
TAURUS-FILM VIDEO GmbH, Betastr 1, 8043 Unterföhring. Tel: (089) 95088311. Tlx: 523222/30. FAX: (089) 9506161.
TELEWISEEN GmbH, Plannmüllerweg 17a, 6100 Darmstadt. Tel: (06151) 76299.
TOPAZ CLASSIC MEDIENPROGRAMM GESELLSCHAFT, Pfisterstr 5, 8000 Munich 2. Tel: (089) 222122, 2283630. Tlx: 5218565.
UFA-VIDEO GmbH, Steinhauser Str 1-3, Postfach 800149, 8000 Munich 80. Tel: (089) 4136347. Tlx: 523487.
USI RHENANIA-FACHVERLAG GmbH, Possmoorweg 1, 2000 Hamburg 60. Tel: (040) 27172234. Tlx: 213214.
UVG, UNTERHALTUNGS-UND VIDEO VERKAUFS GmbH, Alt Seulberg 73, Postfach 1360, 6382 Friedrichsdorf/Ts. Tel: (06172) 72055/56. Tlx: 410884.
VCL, COMMUNICATIONS GmbH, Martin-Kollar-Str 1, 8000 Munich 82. Tel: (089) 42008/0. Tlx: 5212360 vcld. FAX: (089) 423404.
VERKAUF EXCLUSIVE ÜBER ALL VIDEO PROGRAMM VERTRIEBSGESELLSCHAFT, Lazarettstr 19, 4300 Essen 1. Tel: (020) 202866/69.
VERLAG DAS FREIE BUCH GmbH, Buch und Zeitlungsverlag, Tulbeckstr 4, 8000 Munich 2. Tel: (089) 5024834.
VERLAG E S MITTIER & SOHN GmbH, Steintorwall 17, Postfach 2352, 4900 Herford. Tel: (05221) 50001. Tlx: 934801.
VERTRIEBSGESELLSCHAFT RCA/COLUMBIA PICTURES VIDEO GmbH & CO KG, Osterstr 116, 2000 Hamburg 20. Tel: (040) 4902/1. Tlx: 2164193. Fax: (040) 2304.
VESTRON VIDEO GmbH, Am Moosfeld 85, 8000 Munich 82. Tel: (089) 429677. Tlx: 5218088 SSP D.
VGS VERLAGSGESELLSCHAFT, Breite Str 118/120, Postfach 180269, 5000 Köln 1. Tel: (0221) 219641.
VIA VIDEO GESELLSCHAFT FÜR VIDEO-WERBUNG UND VERTRIEB mbH, Eidigweg 23, Postfach 1173, 2077 Trittau. Tel: (04154) 81880. Tlx: 2189453.
VIDEAL VERTRIEB VON AUDIOVISUELLEN PRODUKTEN GmbH, Alsterkampt 17, 2000 Hamburg 13. Tel: (040) 4101027. Tlx: 2164167.
VIDEO-FILM LEASING GmbH (VFL), Obertorstr 38, 6490 Schlüchtern 1. Tel: (06661) 3001/3. Tlx: 49566.
VMP VIDEO MEDIEN POOL PRODUKTIONS-UND VERTRIEBS GmbH, Frankfurter Ring 115, 8000 Munich 40. Tel: (089) 3509040. FAX: (089) 35094101.
VMV VESTISCHER MEDIEN VERLAG, Scheideweg 120, 4390 Gladbeck. Tel: (02043) 64774.
VPS VIDEO PROGRAMM SERVICE GmbH, Saarstr 7, 8000 Munich 40. Tel: (089) 386010. Tlx: 5212767.
VTB VIDEO + TONBILD GmbH, Audiovisuelle Medien im Kollektiv, Spohrstr 26, 6000 Frankfurt/Main 1. Tel: (069) 5974016.
VTD VIDEO TONTRÄGER DR DRESSLER GmbH, Gollierstr 5, 8000. Munich 2. Tel: (089) 5026344. Tlx: 5214499.
WARA FILM UND TON GmbH & CO KG, Wittekindstr 15, 5000 Köln 41. Tel: (0221) 445007.
WARNER HOME VIDEO GmbH, Eine Warner Communications Gesellschaft, Arndtstr 16, 2000 Hamburg 76. Tel: (040) 22805/0. Tlx: 214881.

YUGOSLAVIA

CENTAR FILM, Berisa Kidriča 71, 11000 Belgrade. Tel: 011-341-281.
FILMOTEKA 16, Savska 9, 41000 Zagreb. Tel: 041-444 425.
JADRAN FILM, Oporovečka 12, 41041 Zagreb. Tel: 041-251-2222. Tlx: 21460.
MAKEDONIJA FILM, Nikola Vapcarov 7, 91000 Skopje. Tel: 091-234-535.
UNION FILM, Orfelimova 57, 11000 Belgrade. Tel: 011-556-857.